AGING in AMERICA

AGING in AMERICA

**Fourth Edition
2020**

Edited by Robert L. Scardamalia

Lanham • Boulder • New York • London

Published by Bernan Press
An imprint of The Rowman & Littlefield Publishing Group, Inc.
4501 Forbes Boulevard, Suite 200, Lanham, Maryland 20706
www.rowman.com
800-462-6420

6 Tinworth Street, London SE11 5AL, United Kingdom

ISBN: 978-1-64143-429-4
E-ISBN: 978-1-64143-430-0

Contents

Preface ix

Introduction xi
Volume Organization xi

Understanding the American Community Survey xiii
Some Key Facts about the ACS xiii
New Opportunities xiii
New Challenges xiv
Data Collection versus Data Reporting xv
The ACS Sample xv
Geography xv
Data Comparability xvi
Subjects Covered xvii
Availability of ACS Estimates xvii

Using the ACS xix
Differences between the ACS and the Decennial Census xix
Residence Rules xix
Reference Periods xx
Period Estimates xxi
Deciding Which ACS Estimate to Use xxiii
Margin of Error xxv

Accessing ACS Data Online xxvii

More ACS Resources xxix
Background and Overview Information xxix
Guidance on Data Products and Using the Data xxx

Part A — Population Summary 1
Selected State Rankings 6
Table A-1. States 7
Table A-2. Counties 8
Table A-3. Cities 20
Table A-4. Metropolitan/Micropolitan Areas 29
Table A-5. 116th Congressional Districts 36

Part B — Age Structure 43
Table B-1. States 48
Table B-2. Counties 49
Table B-3. Cities 60
Table B-4. Metropolitan/Micropolitan Statistical Areas 68
Table B-5. 116th Congressional Districts 75

Part C — Race and Ethnicity 83
Table C-1. States 89
Table C-2. Counties 90
Table C-3. Cities 102
Table C-4. Metropolitan/Micropolitan Statistical Areas 111
Table C-5. 116th Congressional Districts 118

Part D — Household Relationship 125
Table D-1. States 130
Table D-2. Counties 131
Table D-3. Cities 143
Table D-4. Metropolitan/Micropolitan Statistical Areas 152
Table D-5. 116th Congressional Districts 160

Part E — Educational Attainment and Veteran Status 167
Table E-1. States 172
Table E-2. Counties 173
Table E-3. Cities 185
Table E-4. Metropolitan/Micropolitan Statistical Areas 194
Table E-5. 116th Congressional Districts 201

Part F — Employment and Labor Force Status 209
Table F-1. States 214
Table F-2. Counties 215
Table F-3. Cities 226
Table F-4. Metropolitan/Micropolitan Statistical Areas 234
Table F-5. 116th Congressional Districts 241

Part G — Income and Poverty 249
Table G-1. States 255
Table G-2. Counties 256
Table G-3. Cities 268
Table G-4. Metropolitan/Micropolitan Statistical Areas 277
Table G-5. 116th Congressional Districts 284

Part H — Disability Status and Type 291
Table H-1. States. 297
Table H-2. Counties 298
Table H-3. Cities 310
Table H-4. Metropolitan/Micropolitan Statistical Areas 319
Table H-5. 116th Congressional Districts. 326

Part I — Health Insurance 333
Table I-1. States. 338
Table I-2. Counties 339
Table I-3. Cities 351
Table I-4. Metropolitan/Micropolitan Statistical Areas 360
Table I-5. 116th Congressional Districts 367

Part J — Housing Summary 375
Table J-1. States. 381
Table J-2. Counties 382
Table J-3. Cities 394
Table J-4. Metropolitan/Micropolitan Statistical Areas 403
Table J-5. 116th Congressional Districts 411

Appendixes 419
Appendix A. Core Based Statistical Areas (Metropolitan and Micropolitan),
   Metropolitan Divisions, and Components (as defined August 2017) 421
Appendix B. Cities by County 438

Index 465

Preface

The 2010 and 2020 censuses are different from any census in recent memory. All American households answered a simple questionnaire with about ten questions. No longer did some people get the "long form" which included dozens of detailed questions about employment, education, income, previous residence, housing characteristics, and more. The data gleaned from these important questions have long been used by federal, state, and local governments to evaluate their populations and program needs; by large and small businesses and nonprofit organizations for a variety of planning and location purposes; and by academic researchers to study trends in social and economic conditions. However, the cost, timeliness, and quality of the traditional long form data made it necessary to develop a new data collection strategy for gathering economic and demographic characteristics of the nation.

The "long form" was been replaced by the American Community Survey (ACS) in 2005. Under development since 1995, the ACS is an ongoing survey of the American people that ushered in a new era in social and economic data analysis. The census "long form" provided detailed estimates of social and economic characteristics every ten years. The ACS collects this same information on a rolling basis. It takes 5 years of ACS responses to accumulate a sample almost as large as the census "long form" collected at a single point in time. But data users now have the ability to study these characteristics and trends throughout the decade – annually for some areas.

Because the ACS is a sample survey, large numbers of sample cases are needed before reliable estimates can be made for small populations. Each year's sample is large enough to produce estimates for the nation, all the states, most metropolitan areas, and many counties and cities. The tables in this volume include single year estimates for 2018 (the most current year available) for the United States, all states and Congressional Districts, as well as, metropolitan and micropolitan areas, counties, and cities of 65,000 or more population.

The richness of the ACS data can be accessed in varying degrees. Much more subject matter detail is available for large geographic areas partly because reliable estimates for large areas can be produced with smaller samples, and partly because more data must be suppressed for the smaller areas to protect the confidentiality of the respondents.

This book is designed to include a sampling of key information about the older population but also help users understand the survey data and resources to access more detailed data available from the Census Bureau and the ACS. The ten subject area tables in this book include 130 data items for each geographic area. This is a small sampling of the detailed data available.

One of the most notable differences between the census "long form" and the ACS is the time frame of the estimates. We are accustomed to the census data that give us specific information every ten years, a snapshot of the country on April 1. The ACS multi-year estimates are different as the Census Bureau surveys nearly 300,000 households every month. The data in this book are from the ACS 1-year 2018 estimates which are produced from the 12 calendar months of survey data collection. The estimates reported here represent an "average" population profile over the 12 months of 2018. The sample cases are spread evenly throughout the year rather than the "point in time" decennial census estimates reported as of April 1.

To help in the understanding of these estimates, we have included a measure of population change for each geographic area. These are from the 2010 census and the 2018 estimates, showing the estimated population growth or decline in each geographic area. Each table shows population characteristics as estimated for 2018. It should be remembered that the decennial census and the Census Bureau's Population Estimates Program provide the official population counts that underlie the ACS sample. If an area experienced unusually large population growth or decline, we should understand that these short-term population impacts may not be reflected in the ACS period estimates. Changes due to a city annexing a large tract of land, many people moving into a new development, or many people leaving the area because of a plant closing may be hidden in the short-term.

With the ACS, there is always a trade-off between data currency and data reliability. More current 1-year estimates come from smaller samples and therefore have larger margins of error. Estimates from the 5-year data are based on five times the sample size and have smaller margins of error – but of course, they do not reflect the most current period. The first edition of Aging in American relied on the Census Bureau's 3-year (2010–2012) estimates because of the larger sample size and smaller margins of error inherent in the longer period estimates. Due to the elimination of the 3-year data series, the second edition (2014), third edition (2016) and current volume (2018) report the results of the 1-year data. Users may want to compare data between the four editions but should use caution as there will be more sample variability in the 2014, 2016 and 2018 data and small differences may not be meaningful. Users will also notice that there are a number of geographic areas where the estimates not reported due to the Census Bureau's data disclosure rules.

Finally, it is always critical to remember that all estimates are subject to sampling error. On the Census Bureau's website, every ACS estimate is accompanied by its margin of error. In the interests of space and simplicity, this book does not include the margins of error, but all users are encouraged to consult the Census Bureau's website and to understand some basics: small differences are very likely to represent no difference at all; do not draw conclusions from small numbers; use these numbers as a starting point to explore the wealth of information from the ACS.

Introduction

The American Community Survey (ACS) has ushered in the most substantial change in the decennial census in more than 60 years. Beginning with pilot testing in 1995, the survey was implemented nationwide in 2005. It replaced the decennial census long form in 2010, providing more current data throughout the decade by collecting long-form-type information annually rather than only once every 10 years. The ACS provides annual data for states, metropolitan areas, and large cities and counties over 65,000 in population and combines multiple years of survey responses to produce data for all communities, regardless of size. Very small communities (under 65,000 population) and statistical areas like census tracts and zip code tabulation areas require 5 years of survey responses to yield characteristic estimates.

The ACS gathers demographic, social, economic, housing and financial information about the nation's people and communities on a continuous basis. The ACS is an ongoing survey conducted by the U.S. Census Bureau in every county, American Indian and Alaska Native Area, and Hawaiian Home Land in the United States. The ACS is also conducted as the Puerto Rico Community Survey in every municipality in Puerto Rico. As the largest survey in the United States, it is the only source of small-area data on a wide range of important social and economic characteristics for all communities in the country.

Information about the ACS are available on the Census Bureau's website. The ACS main page is https://www.census.gov/programs-surveys/acs.html. Data from the ACS is available from American FactFinder at http://factfinder.census.gov.

A vast amount of information is collected in the ACS. This publication includes a small subset of data reflecting the older population in America and is assembled in various tables by subject and geographic type.

VOLUME ORGANIZATION

The data tables in this book pertain to the older population, generally those 60 years of age and over and include a selection of population and housing characteristics from the ACS in twelve subject areas:

- Population summary
- Age structure

- Race and ethnicity
- Household relationships and living arrangements
- Educational attainment and veterans status
- Employment and labor force status
- Income and poverty status
- Disability status
- Health Insurance Coverage
- Housing summary

The 1-year estimates from the American Community Survey provide data for all areas of 65,000 population or more. Each subject area includes data for the United States, the 50 states and the District of Columbia and the following:

- 800+ counties, listed alphabetically within state,
- 500+ metropolitan and micropolitan statistical areas, listed alphabetically,
- 550+ cities, listed alphabetically within state,
- All 435 Congressional districts, listed numerically by state and the District of Columbia delegate district.

In addition, each part is preceded by highlights, maps and/or summary tables that show how areas diverge from the national norm, as well as the differences among areas. These research aids are invaluable for helping people understand what the census data tell us about who we are, what we do, and where we live.

In the following sections, information about the ACS and how to use the data is included, much of it excerpted from the wealth of information available on the Census Bureau's website. Especially helpful are the instructions, definitions, and guidelines on using the data in the section on "Guidance for Data Users." Readers are encouraged to explore the Census Bureau's website to expand on the information contained here and to keep up to date with this constantly changing dataset.

Robert Scardamalia is President of RLS Demographics, Inc. a firm providing data and analysis to private organizations, government agencies, and not-for-profits, especially in the areas of aging services, demographic analysis and forecasting, and business development. He is an adjunct professor in the Sociology Department of the State University of New York at Albany. Prior to forming RLS Demographics, he was Chief Demographer of New York State and directed the Center for Research and Information Analysis in the New York Department of Economic Development. He also directed the New York State Data Center for more than 20 years. Mr. Scardamalia has served on the Board of the Association of Public Data Users and is a past President. He has chaired the national State Data Center Steering Committee and served on numerous Census Bureau committees. He holds a Master of Arts in Demography from Georgetown University and Bachelor of Arts in Sociology from Penn State University.

Understanding the American Community Survey

Every 10 years since 1790, as required by the U.S. Constitution, Congress has authorized funds to conduct a national census of the U.S. population. From 1960 through 2000, censuses have consisted of:

- a "short form," which included basic questions about age, sex, race, Hispanic origin (since 1980), household relationship, and owner/renter status, and

- a "long form" used for a sample of approximately one of every six households that included not only the basic short-form questions but also detailed questions about socioeconomic and housing characteristics.

Beginning with the 2010 census, the American Community Survey (ACS) replaced the decennial census long form by collecting long-form-type information annually rather than only once every 10 years, providing more current data throughout the decade. The 2010 Census counted the population to support the constitutional mandate—to provide population counts needed to apportion the seats in the U.S. House of Representatives. The ACS data now provide, for the first time, a regular stream of updated information for states and local areas, revolutionizing the way we use data to understand our communities. It produces social, housing, and economic characteristics for demographic groups, even for geographic areas as small as census tracts and block groups.

SOME KEY FACTS ABOUT THE ACS:

- The ACS annually provides the same kind of detailed information previously available only every 10 years from the census. The ACS is conducted under the authority of Title 13, United States Code, Sections 141 and 193.

- All answers are confidential. Any Census Bureau employee who violates that confidentiality is subject to a jail term, a fine, or both.

- The Census Bureau may use the information it collects only for statistical purposes.

- Addresses are selected at random from the Master Address File to represent similar households in the area. Approximately 290,000 addresses are selected each month and the survey is conducted by mail, telephone, and personal visit. Response to this survey is required by federal statute Section 221 of Title 13.

- Approximately 2.7 percent of U.S. households are surveyed each year. A sample of group quarters (nursing homes, college dormitories, etc.) is included in the ACS as well.

- While the ACS sample size approximates the traditional long-form census sample, it is a smaller sample resulting in somewhat larger margins of error.

The traditional long-form census taken once a decade provided the socio-economic portrait of the nation and communities but that portrait was fixed in time for 10 years. Data from the ACS provides a regular update to that portrait which is used for a variety of purposes that include: monitoring the well-being of America's older population, children and families, tracking trends in disability, analyzing the growth in the number of grandparents responsible for their grandchildren, determining the economic well-being of the elderly and working-poor families, or tracking social, economic, and demographic changes in the general U.S. population.

The ACS provides critical information for communities on a current basis, when they need it most. But the ACS is still a relatively new data collection instrument and a different measure of the characteristics of the population and households. Researchers are still working to understand the differences from the traditional census data so it is good to be cautious in the interpretation of differences between areas and across time. Small differences may not be meaningful. On the other hand, the ACS provides annual estimates and the frequency of updates and currency of the data far outweighs waiting 10 years for new results.

NEW OPPORTUNITIES

The main benefits of the ACS are timeliness and access to annual data for states, local areas, and small population subgroups. The ACS will deliver useful, relevant data, similar to data from previous census long forms, but updated every year rather than every 10 years. The ACS provides comparable information across and within states for program evaluation and use in funding formulas.

- ACS information is often used to determine the placement of new schools, senior residential services, hospitals, and highways.

- ACS data provides information for tracking the well-being of children, families, and the elderly allowing service providers to better target populations in need.

- The data will improve the distribution of aid through federal, state, and local governments. More than $1.5 trillion in federal program funds are distributed each year based, in whole or in part, on census and ACS data[1].

- The data are used by community programs, such as those for the elderly, libraries, hospitals, banks, and other organizations.

- The data are used by transportation planners to evaluate peak volumes of traffic in order to reduce congestion, plan for parking, and develop plans for carpooling and flexible work schedules.

- Corporations, small businesses, and individuals use these data to develop business plans, to set strategies for expansion or starting a business, and to determine trends in their service areas to meet current and future needs.

- Small towns and rural communities have much to gain from the ACS. Lacking the staff and resources to conduct their own research, many local communities have relied on decennial census information that became increasingly outdated throughout the decade, or used local administrative records that are not comparable with information collected in neighboring areas.

- The ACS also provides tools for those who want to conduct their own research. The ACS includes a Public Use Microdata Sample (PUMS) file each year that enables researchers to create custom universes and tabulations from individual ACS records that have been stripped of personally identifiable information.

- Because the ACS data collection occurs every month, the Census Bureau uses professional, highly trained, permanent interviewers which have improved the accuracy of ACS data compared with those from the decennial census long-form sample. This strategy has effectively reduced the number of refusals to complete the ACS questionnaire and allows interviewers to obtain more complete information than decennial census interviewers.

---

[1] Reamer, Andrew, "Counting for Dollars 2020: The Role of the Decennial Census in the Geographic Distribution of Federal Funds", GW Institute of Public Policy, The George Washington University, Washington, DC. 2019. https://gwipp.gwu.edu/counting-dollars-2020-role-decennial-census-geographic-distribution-federal-funds#Latest%20 Release

NEW CHALLENGES

The main challenges for ACS data users are understanding and using multi-year estimates and the relatively large margins of error associated with ACS data for smaller geographic areas and subgroups of the population.

- ACS data will be produced every year, but the sample size of the ACS is smaller than that of the Census 2000 long form sample. In addition, as the nation's population grows, the sampling rate will continue to decline unless additional funding in provided. Data users need to pay more attention to the margin of error.

- Data users have access to 5-year estimates of ACS data. The sample size based on 5-year period estimates of ACS data is still smaller than the long-form sample in the decennial census, resulting in larger margins of error in the ACS 5-year estimates.

- Prior to the current 2014 data release, the ACS produced 1-year, 3-year, and 5-year estimates so areas of 65,000 population or more received three separate estimates of the same characteristic every year. For example, a large city would receive 1-year, 3-year and 5-year estimates of the number of persons 65 and over in poverty. Data users had to decide which datasets were appropriate for their needs.

- As of 2014, the Census Bureau eliminated all 3-year estimates products as a cost saving measure. Areas of 65,000 or more will still receive annual estimates but all other areas below 65,000 will only receive estimates based on five years of data collection. Large areas of 65,000 or more will now only have two separate estimates rather than three. The historical 3-year data is still available. Data in this volume is based on the 1-year 2018 estimates.

- Data users will need to be aware of the implications of multi-year estimates, particularly in analyzing employment and income data that will span a full year or even a 5-year period.

- Multi-year estimates, especially the 5-year estimates will not reflect short-term changes in the population or economy of an area. The recent recession is a good example because the 5-year ACS estimates span both the fall into recession and the resulting growth coming out.

The ACS includes several questions that are very similar to those collected in other federal surveys—especially the Current Population Survey (CPS), the American Housing Survey, and the Survey of Income and Program Participation. In some cases, there are clear guidelines about which data to use. For example, the CPS is the official source of income and poverty data. It includes detailed questions on these topics and should be used in reporting national trends in these subject areas. The Census Bureau recommends that ACS information on income and poverty be used to supplement CPS data for areas below the state level and for population subgroups (such as age, sex, race, Hispanic origin, type of household) at the state level. For an explanation of various income and poverty data sources, see the Census Bureau's guidelines at: https://www.census.gov/topics/income-poverty/poverty/guidance.html.

For states, generally the Census Bureau recommends using the ACS, though the CPS is still valuable as a source for examining historical state income and poverty trends.

DATA COLLECTION VERSUS DATA REPORTING

Results from the ACS are reported each year which is a major advantage over the traditional long-form data from the decennial census. But unlike the release of data only once every 10 years in the decennial census, the annual release of data from the ACS can be quite confusing. The ACS sample size is such that the reliability of the data is greatly affected by the length of the data collection period and the size of geographic reporting areas. In survey sampling, it is well understood that larger samples yield more reliable estimates with smaller margins of error. In order to produce reliable estimates from the ACS, it is necessary to collect the data over differing periods of time in order to provide estimates for all areas, including small areas like census tracts.

Each set of period estimates is released each year, generally between September and December, and reflect data collection ending in the previous calendar year. Thus, the collection year 2018 1-year estimates for areas of 65,000 or more were released in September of 2019 while the 2014–2018 5-year estimates followed with a December 2019 release.

THE ACS SAMPLE

The ACS is sent each month to a sample of roughly 290,000 addresses in the United States and Puerto Rico, or about 3.5 million a year, resulting in more than 2.3 million final interviews. The sample represents all housing units and group quarters in the United States and Puerto Rico. (Group quarters include places such as college dormitories, prisons, military barracks, and nursing homes.) The addresses are selected from the Census Bureau's Master Address File (MAF), which is also the basis for the decennial census.

The annual ACS sample is smaller than that of the Census 2000 long-form sample, which included about 18 million housing units. As a result, the ACS needs to combine population or housing data from multiple years to produce reliable numbers for small counties, neighborhoods, and other local areas. To provide information for communities each year, the ACS will provide 1- and 5-year estimates.

The ACS sample is not spread evenly across all areas but includes a larger proportion of addresses in sparsely populated rural communities and American Indian reservations and a lower proportion in densely populated areas. Over a 5-year period, the ACS will sample more than 17 million addresses and complete interviews for about 11 million. This sample is sufficient to produce estimates for small geographic areas, such as neighborhoods and sparsely-populated rural counties though the estimates will have larger margins of error than the census long-form data. In a 5-year period no address will be selected for the ACS more than once, and many addresses will never be selected for the survey. It's important to remember that the sample is address based so while a given address will not be in sample again for at least five years, it is possible that individuals who move or have a second home could be surveyed more than once.

GEOGRAPHY

The ACS data are tabulated for a variety of geographic areas ranging in size from broad geographic regions (Northeast, Midwest, South, and West) to cities, towns, neighborhoods, and census block groups. Before December 2008, the ACS data were only available for geographic areas with at least 65,000 people, including regions, divisions, states, the District of Columbia, Puerto Rico, congressional districts, Public Use Microdata Areas

Data Product	Population Threshold	Years of Data Release							
		2012	2013	2014	2015	2016	2017	2018	2019
		Years of Data Collection							
1-year Estimates	65,000+	2011	2012	2013	2014	2015	2016	2017	2018
5-year Estimates	All Areas	2007–2011	2008–2012	2009–2013	2010–2014	2011–2015	2012–2016	2013–2017	2014–2018

(PUMAs)—census-constructed geographic areas, each with approximately a population of 100,000—and many large counties, metropolitan areas, cities, school districts, and American Indian areas. Starting in December 2008, 3-year estimates became available for all areas with at least 20,000 residents, and in 2010, 5-year estimates for geographic areas down to the block group level became available. One-, three-, and five-year estimates—three sets of numbers—were available and were refreshed every year up until the 2014 data release. Less populous areas receive only 5-year estimates. The vast majority of areas receive only 5-year estimates.

The data tables in this book contain data from the 1-year 2018 estimates. These tables are based on the 2010 tabulation geography for political and statistical areas, the same definitions as the 2010 Census. The metropolitan and micropolitan area definitions are based on the 2013 revisions by the U.S. Office of Management and Budget. Changes in area boundaries can occur as a result of annexation, new incorporation or disincorporation of cities, towns, and places. For multi-year estimates, the Census Bureau reports the data based on the most current geographic boundaries incorporating any changes occurring in the multi-year period.

DATA COMPARABILITY

Since the ACS data are collected continuously, they are not always comparable with data collected from the decennial census. For example, both surveys ask about employment status during the week prior to the survey. However, data from the decennial census are typically collected between March and July with a reference date of April 1st, whereas data from the ACS are collected nearly every day and reflect employment throughout the year. Other factors that may also have an impact on the data include seasonal variation in population and minor differences in question wording and question order.

While the categories of income by source are comparable with the decennial long-form data, the monthly collection of ACS data results in a significant difference in concept. In the decennial census, income refers to the previous calendar year whereas the ACS it refers to the previous 12-month period. Most people have a better understanding of what their calendar year income is, especially since the census is taken around tax time. With the ACS, individuals have to report income for a different period each month. A response to the survey in October of the year will report income from October of the previous year through September of the current year. This may require respondents to actually compute their 12-month income.

In 2006, the ACS began including samples of the population living in group quarters (e.g., jails, college dormitories, and nursing homes) for the first time. As a result, the ACS data from 2005 may not be comparable with 2006 data in areas with group quarters populations. This is especially true for estimates of young adults and the elderly, who are more likely than other groups to be living in group quarters facilities.

One of the most important uses of the ACS estimates is to make comparisons between estimates – over time or across areas. Several key types of comparisons are of general interest to users:

- Comparisons of estimates from different geographic areas within the same time period (e.g., comparing the proportion of seniors below the poverty level in two counties).

- Comparisons of estimates for the same geographic area across time periods (e.g., comparing the proportion of people below the poverty level in a metropolitan area for 2017 and 2018).

- Comparisons of ACS estimates with the corresponding estimates from past decennial census samples (e.g., comparing the proportion of people below the poverty level in a county in 2018 compared to 2010 ACS data and 2000 decennial data).

A number of conditions must be met when comparing survey estimates.

- When comparing data for different geographic areas, always use the same period estimates. When comparing data for an area which only has 5-year estimates to an area with 1- and 5-year estimates, it is important to compare only the 5-year estimates.

- When comparing over time for the same geographic area, again, only compare like-year period estimates. For example, it is not appropriate to compare a 1-year estimate for 2018 to a 5-year estimate for 2014–2018.

Of primary importance is that the comparison takes into account the sampling error associated with each estimate, thus determining whether the observed differences between estimates are statistically significant. Statistical significance means that there is statistical evidence that a true difference exists within the full population, and that the observed difference is unlikely to have occurred by chance due to sampling. A method for determining statistical significance when making comparisons, as well as considerations associated with the various types of comparisons, can be found in *Understanding and Using American Community Survey Data: What All Data Users*

Need to Know, July 2018 https://www.census.gov/programs-surveys/acs/guidance/handbooks/general.html.

- The statistical properties of survey samples like the ACS are dependent upon independence of samples. In the ACS multi-year period estimates, the estimates are based on the sampled households for each year. That means that when comparing estimates for the period 2013–2017 to 2014–2018, four fifths of the sample cases are the same households – those surveyed in 2014 through 2017. The only different (independent) households are those sampled in 2013 and 2018. When comparisons over time are made, it is best to compare non-overlapping samples. That is, compare estimates for 2009–2013 to the period 2014–2018 because both periods contain independent household samples.

Finally, the decennial census and the ACS have different residency rules. In the decennial census, population in tabulated by their "usual place of residence" typically where they spend six months or more of the year. This is subject to some seasonal variation due to persons with dual residences. In the ACS, there is a 2-month residency rule. That is, if the respondent has been in the sampled housing unit for 2 months or expects to be resident there for 2 months they are captured in the survey. This can have an impact on communities with highly seasonal populations and college communities.

SUBJECTS COVERED

The topics covered by the ACS focus on demographic, social, economic, and housing characteristics. These topics are virtually the same as those covered by the 2000 census long-form sample data.

Demographic Characteristics
Age, Sex, Hispanic Origin, Race, and Relationship to Householder (e.g., spouse)

Social Characteristics
Marital Status and Marital History; Fertility; Grandparents as Caregivers; Ancestry Place of Birth; Citizenship and Year of Entry; Language Spoken at Home; Educational Attainment and School Enrollment; Residence One Year Ago; Veteran Status, Period of Military Service, and VA Service-Connected Disability Rating; and Disability

Economic Characteristics
Income, Food Stamps Benefit, Labor Force Status, Industry, Occupation, Class of Worker, Place of Work and Journey to Work, Work Status Last Year, Vehicles Available, and Health Insurance Coverage

Housing Characteristics
Year Structure Built, Units in Structure, Year Moved Into Unit, Rooms, Bedrooms, Kitchen Facilities, Plumbing Facilities, House Heating Fuel, Telephone Service Available, and Farm Residence

Financial Characteristics
Tenure (Owner/Renter), Housing Value, Rent, and Selected Monthly Owner Costs

AVAILABILITY OF ACS ESTIMATES

The ACS went into full nationwide implementation in 2005 and began reporting results in 2006. From 2000 through 2004, while still in testing, the sample included between 740,000 and 900,000 addresses annually. In 2005, the ACS shifted from a demonstration program to the full sample size and design. It became the largest household survey in the United States, with an annual sample size of about 3 million addresses. Beginning with 2005, the ACS single-year estimates are available for geographic areas with a population of 65,000 or more. Three-year period estimates for areas of 20,000 or more were first released for the 2005–2007 time period and there are annual 3-year estimates through the 2011–2013 period. The 3-year estimates were discontinued for budgetary reasons. 5-year estimates for all areas were first released in 2010 and are available for every subsequent year with 2018 being the most current as of this writing. The ACS will continue to accumulate samples over 5-year intervals to produce estimates for smaller geographic areas, including census tracts and block groups.

Annually, the ACS produces updated, single-year estimates of demographic, housing, social, and economic characteristics for all states, as well as for larger counties, cities, metropolitan and urban areas, and congressional districts. Geographic areas must have a minimum population of 65,000 to qualify for estimates based on a single year's sample. Every congressional district meets this threshold and therefore new single year estimates are released each year for every congressional district. Some school districts, townships, and American Indian and Alaska Native areas also meet this population threshold.

For most geographic areas—including three-quarters of all counties, most school districts, and most cities, towns, and American Indian reservations—only 5-year estimates are available because of their population size. Because some federal grant programs allocate funds directly to these areas, Congress can use the 5-year estimates to evaluate needs at the relevant geographic level, compare characteristics between areas within and among states, and analyze how various formulas distribute funds. The vast majority of areas will receive only 5-year estimates. In partnership with the states, the Census Bureau created *Public Use Microdata Areas (PUMAs)*, which are special, non-overlapping areas within a state, each with a population of about 100,000. These areas will have annual 1-year estimates.

Definitions of these geographic areas are at: https://www.census.gov/programs-surveys/acs/geography-acs/concepts-definitions.html.

Using the ACS

DIFFERENCES BETWEEN THE ACS AND THE DECENNIAL CENSUS

While the main function of the decennial census is to provide *counts* of people for the purpose of congressional apportionment and legislative redistricting, the primary purpose of the ACS is to measure the changing social and economic *characteristics* of the U.S. population. As a result, the ACS does not provide official counts of the population though users of the data will report the estimate results as though they were counts. In non-decennial census years, the Census Bureau's Population Estimates Program continues to be the official source for annual population totals, by age, race, Hispanic origin, and sex. The ACS sample estimates are controlled to match the decennial census and the Census Bureau's annual population estimates by selected age, sex, race, and Hispanic origin categories. For more information about population estimates, visit the Census Bureau's website at http://www.census.gov/programs-surveys/popest.html.

There are many similarities between the methods used in the traditional decennial census sample and the ACS but there are also a number of differences in collection method and concepts. Response to both the ACS and decennial census is required by law, a factor that helps improve overall response. Both the ACS and the decennial census sample data are based on information from a sample of the population. The data from the Census 2000 sample of about one-sixth of the population were collected using a "long-form" questionnaire, whose content was the model for the ACS. The sample for the ACS is somewhat smaller, approximately 1 in 7 households, resulting in larger margins of error.

While some differences exist in the specific Census 2000 long-form question wording and that of the ACS, most questions are identical or nearly identical. Differences in the design and implementation of the two surveys are noted below with references provided to a series of evaluation studies that assess the degree to which these differences are likely to impact the estimates. The ACS produces period estimates (covering one or five years of data collection) so these estimates do not measure characteristics for the same time frame as the decennial census estimates, which are interpreted to be a snapshot as of April 1 of the census year.

Some data items were collected by both the ACS and the Census 2000 long form with slightly different definitions or reference periods that could affect the comparability of the estimates for these items. One example is annual costs for a mobile home. Census 2000 included installment loan costs in the total annual costs but the ACS does not. In this example, the ACS could be expected to yield smaller estimates than Census 2000.

While some differences were a part of the census and survey design objectives, other differences observed between ACS and census results were not by design, but due to nonsampling error—differences related to how well the surveys were conducted. The ACS and the census experience different levels and types of coverage error, different levels and treatment of housing unit and questionnaire item nonresponse, and different instances of measurement and processing error. Both Census 2000 and the ACS had similar high levels of survey coverage and low levels of unit nonresponse. Higher levels of unit nonresponse were found in the nonresponse follow-up stage of Census 2000 while lower levels of item nonresponse were found in the ACS due to a permanent staff of trained interviewers.

Census Bureau analysts have compared sample estimates from Census 2000 with 1-year ACS estimates based on data collected in 2000 and 3-year ACS estimates based on data collected in 1999–2001 in selected pilot counties. In general, ACS estimates were found to be quite similar to those produced from decennial census data.

Detailed information about the ACS methodology can be found at: *Understanding and Using American Community Survey Data: What All Data Users Need to Know, July 2018* https://www.census.gov/programs-surveys/acs/guidance/handbooks/general.html.

RESIDENCE RULES

The fundamentally different purposes of the ACS and the census, and their timing, led to important differences in the choice of data collection methods. For example, residence rules for a census or survey determine the sample unit's occupancy status and household membership at the time of collection. Defining the rules in a dissimilar way can affect those two very important estimates. The 2010 census residence rules, which determined where people should be counted, were based on the principle of "usual residence" on April 1, 2010, in keeping with the focus of the census on the requirements of congressional apportionment and state redistricting. To accomplish this, the decennial census attempts to restrict and determine a principal place of residence on one specific date for everyone enumerated. The ACS residence rules are based on a "current residence" concept since data are collected continuously throughout the entire year with responses provided relative to the continuously changing survey interview dates. Under this concept, anyone who is living or staying at an address for two months or more is considered a resident of that address. This method is consistent with the goal of the ACS to produce estimates that reflect annual averages of the characteristics of all areas.

Residence rules determine which individuals are considered to be residents of a particular housing unit or group quarters. While many people have definite ties to a single housing unit or group quarters, some people may stay in different places for significant periods of time over the course of the year. For example, "snow birds" can maintain residences in different states and do not live in any one location for the entire year. In the decennial census, it is their residence on April 1, or their interpretation of their "usual place of residence", that is the basis for their location. College students are another example. Students are enumerated at the college in the decennial census but may be counted at home in the ACS if sampled during their summer break. Differences in treatment of these populations in the census and ACS can lead to differences in estimates of the characteristics of some areas.

For the past several censuses, decennial census residence rules were designed to produce an accurate count of the population as of Census Day, April 1, while the ACS residence rules were designed to collect representative information to produce annual average estimates of the characteristics of all types of areas. The residence rules governing the census enumerations of people in group quarters depend on the type of group quarter and, where permitted, whether people claim a "usual residence" elsewhere. The ACS applies a straight de facto residence rule to every type of group quarter. Everyone living or staying in a group quarter on the day it is visited by an ACS interviewer is eligible to be sampled and interviewed for the survey.

Further information on residence rules can be found in Chapter 6 of the Design and Methodology report at: http://www.census.gov/programs-surveys/acs/methodology/design-and-methodology.html.

The differences in the ACS and census data, as a consequence of the different residence rules, are most likely minimal for most areas and most characteristics. However, for certain segments of the population the usual and current residence concepts could result in different residence decisions. The older population is one of those segments as many retired and active seniors maintain dual residences. Appreciable differences may occur in areas where large proportions of the total population spend several months of the year in what would not be considered their residence under decennial census rules. In particular, data for areas that include large beach, lake, or mountain vacation areas may differ appreciably between the census and the ACS if populations live there for more than 2 months. In addition, college students are to be counted at the location of the college rather than their parent's home. However, during summer months, college students can meet the 2 month residency rule for the ACS and be counted along with their parents rather than at the college.

REFERENCE PERIODS

Estimates produced by the ACS are not measuring exactly what decennial samples had been measuring. The ACS yearly samples, spread over 12 months, collect information that is anchored to the day on which the sampled unit was interviewed, whether it is the day that a mail questionnaire is completed or the day that an interview is conducted by telephone or personal visit. Individual questions with time references such as "last week" or "the last 12 months" all begin the reference period as of this interview date. Even the information on types and amounts of income refers to the 12 months prior to the day the question is answered. ACS interviews are conducted just about every day of the year, and all of the estimates that the survey releases are considered to be averages for a specific time period. The 1-year estimates reflect the full calendar year while the 5-year estimates reflect the full 60-month period.

Most decennial census sample estimates are anchored in this same way to the reference date of April 1. The most obvious difference between the ACS and the census is the overall time frame in which they are conducted. The census enumeration time period is less than half the time period used to collect data for each single-year ACS estimate. But a more important difference is that the distribution of census enumeration dates are highly clustered in March and April (when most census mail returns were received) with additional, smaller clusters seen in May and June (when nonresponse follow-up activities took place).

This means that the data from the decennial census, intended to reflect the characteristics of the population and housing on April 1, tend to describe the characteristics in the March through June time period (with an overrepresentation of March/April). The ACS data describe the characteristics nearly every day over the full calendar year. For employment and income estimates, the decennial census referred to the prior calendar year for all respondents, while the ACS asks about the 12 months preceding the interview.

Those who are interested in more information about differences in reference periods should refer to the Census Bureau's guidance on comparisons that contrasts for each question the specific reference periods used in Census 2000 with those used in the ACS: https://www.census.gov/programs-surveys/acs/guidance/comparing-acs-data.html. Individual tables can be compared with the Table Comparison Spreadsheet, downloadable from this site.

Some specific differences in reference periods between the ACS and the decennial census are described below. Users should consider the potential impact these different reference periods could have on distributions when comparing ACS estimates with Census 2000. As we get further and further away from use of the 2000 data, and compare current ACS data to prior years ACS data, these differences will become less important.

Income Data

To estimate annual income, the Census 2000 long-form sample used the calendar year prior to Census Day as the reference period, and the ACS uses the 12 months prior to the interview date as the reference period. Thus, while Census 2000 collected income information for calendar year 1999, the ACS collects income information for the 12 months preceding the interview date. The responses are a mixture of 12 reference periods ranging from, in the case of the 2016 ACS single-year estimates, the full calendar year 2015 through November 2016. The ACS income responses for each of these reference periods are individually inflation-adjusted to represent dollar values for the ACS collection year. Further inflation adjustments are made to the 5-year estimates to reflect dollar values of the final year of the estimate. It's important to note that the rotating reference period for income can result in misreporting. The calendar year reference period of the decennial census coincides with an individual's annual salary and is also collected around tax time. Respondents will have a good idea of what their annual salary is. In the ACS, the respondent has to calculate their income for the previous 12 months, a figure which can vary considerably throughout the year.

School Enrollment

The school enrollment question on the ACS asks if a person had "at any time in the last 3 months attended a school or college." A consistent 3-month reference period is used for all interviews. In contrast, Census 2000 asked if a person had "at any time since February 1 attended a school or college." Since Census 2000 data were collected from mid-March to late-August, the reference period could have been as short as about 6 weeks or as long as 7 months.

Utility Costs

The reference periods for two utility cost questions—gas and electricity—differ between Census 2000 and the ACS. The census asked for annual costs, while the ACS asks for the utility costs in the previous month.

PERIOD ESTIMATES

The ACS produces period estimates of socioeconomic and housing characteristics. It is designed to provide estimates that describe the average characteristics of an area over a specific time period. In the case of ACS single-year estimates, the period is the calendar year (e.g., the 2018 ACS covers January through December 2018). In the case of ACS multiyear estimates, the period covers 5 calendar years (e.g., the 2014–2018 ACS 5-year estimates cover January 2014 through December 2018). The ACS multiyear estimates are similar in many ways to the ACS single-year estimates, but they encompass a longer time period.

The differences in time periods between single-year and multiyear ACS estimates affect decisions about which set of estimates should be used for a particular analysis. While one may think of these estimates as representing average characteristics over a single calendar year or multiple calendar years, it must be remembered that the 1-year estimates are not calculated as an average of 12 monthly values and the multiyear estimates are not calculated as the average of 60 monthly values, nor are the multiyear estimates calculated as the average of the five single-year estimates. Rather, the ACS collects survey information continuously nearly every day of the year and then aggregates the results over a specific time period—1 year or 5 years. The data collection is spread evenly across the entire period represented so as not to over-represent any particular month or year within the period.

Because ACS estimates provide information about the characteristics of the population and housing for areas over an entire time frame, ACS single-year and multiyear estimates contrast with "point-in-time" estimates, such as those from the decennial census long-form samples or monthly employment estimates from the Current Population Survey (CPS), which are designed to measure characteristics as of a certain date or narrow time period. For example, Census 2000 was designed to measure the characteristics of the population and housing in the United States based upon data collected around April 1, 2000, and thus its data reflect a narrower time frame than ACS data. The monthly CPS collects data for an even narrower time frame, the week containing the 12th of each month.

Most areas have consistent population characteristics throughout the calendar year, and their period estimates may not look much different from estimates that would be obtained from a "point-in-time" survey design. However, some areas may experience changes in the estimated characteristics of the population, depending on when in the calendar year the measurement occurred. For these areas, the ACS period estimates (even for a single-year) may noticeably differ from "point-in-time" estimates. The impact will be more noticeable in smaller areas where changes such as a factory closing can have a large impact on population characteristics, and in areas with a large natural event such as Hurricane Katrina's impact on the New Orleans area.

This logic can be extended to better interpret 5-year estimates where the periods involved are much longer. If, over the full period of time there have been major or consistent changes in certain population or housing characteristics for an area, a period estimate for that area could differ markedly from estimates based on a "point-in-time" survey. For example, the 5-year estimates for 2014–2018 will be affected by the volatility in the economy and the housing market during those years that may affect some areas more than others. The longer period may mask shorter term fluctuations such as the improved economic climate or downturns from trade imbalances. Comparing these to estimates for the 2007–2011 period would be problematic because that 5-year period includes years prior to the recession and years of economic rebound.

The tables in this book were prepared from the 1-year 2018 survey results. In general, areas will largely recovered from the recession while others still struggle and haven't returned to previous levels of growth.

The important thing to keep in mind is that ACS single-year estimates describe the population and characteristics of an area for the full year, not for any specific day or period within the year. The ACS multiyear estimates describe the population and characteristics of an area for the full 5-year period, not for any specific day, period, or year within the multiyear time period.

Single-year estimates provide more current information

Single-year estimates provide more current information about areas that have changing population and/or housing characteristics because they are based on the most current data—survey responses from the past calendar year. In contrast, multiyear estimates provide less current information because they are based on both survey responses from the previous year and responses that are up to 5 years old. As noted earlier, for many areas with minimal change taking place, using the "less current" sample used to produce the multiyear estimates may not have a substantial influence on the estimates. However, in areas experiencing major changes over a given time period, the multiyear estimates may be quite different from the single-year estimates for any of the individual years. Single-year and multiyear estimates are not expected to be the same because they are based on data from two different time periods. This will be true even if the ACS single year is the midyear of the ACS multiyear period (e.g., 2016 single year, 2014–2018 multiyear).

Multiyear estimates are based on larger sample sizes and are therefore more reliable

The 5-year estimates are based on five times as many sample cases as the 1-year estimates. For some characteristics this increased sample is needed for the estimates to be reliable enough for use in certain applications. For other characteristics the increased sample may not be necessary.

Multiyear estimates are the only type of estimates available for geographic areas with populations of less than 65,000. Users may think that they only need to use multiyear estimates when they are working with small areas, but this isn't the case. Estimates for large geographic areas benefit from the increased sample, resulting in more precise estimates of population and housing characteristics, especially for subpopulations within those areas. In addition, users may determine that they want to use single-year estimates, despite their reduced reliability, as building blocks to produce estimates for meaningful higher levels of geography. These aggregations will similarly benefit from the increased sample sizes and gain reliability.

Currency	Reliability
1-year estimates provide information based on the most current year	Sample sizes producing estimates may be small and impact statistical reliability
3-year estimates provide information based on the last year and the 2 years before that	3-year estimates are based on 3 times as many sample cases as 1-year estimates
5-year estimates provide information based on the last year and the 4 years before that	5-year estimates are based on 5 times as many sample cases as 1-year estimates

DECIDING WHICH ACS ESTIMATE TO USE

Three primary uses of ACS estimates are:

- to understand the characteristics of the population of an area for local planning needs,
- to make comparisons across areas, and
- to assess change over time in an area.

Local planning could include making local decisions such as where to place schools or hospitals, determining the need for senior services or transportation, and carrying out other infrastructure analysis. In the past, decennial census sample data provided the most comprehensive information. However, the currency of those data suffered through the intercensal period, and the ability to assess change over time was limited. ACS estimates greatly improve the currency of data for understanding the characteristics of housing and population and enhance the ability to assess change over time. At the same time, small differences between ACS estimates can lead to misinterpretation due to larger margins of error.

Several key factors can help users decide whether to use single-year or multiyear ACS estimates for areas where both are available:

- intended use of the estimates
- required precision, or reliability, of the estimates
- currency of the estimates

All of these factors, along with an understanding of the differences between single-year and multiyear ACS estimates, should be taken into consideration when deciding which set of estimates to use.

For users analyzing estimates for areas of different size and for different time periods, it is important to recognize that the only option is to use the 5-year ACS estimates. When comparing areas of different size it is critical that users only make comparisons between similar period estimates. Even if the study area has 1-year estimates, it is not appropriate to compare the 1-year estimate to a 5-year estimate from a different area.

The key trade-off to be made in deciding whether to use single-year or multiyear estimates is between currency and reliability. In general, the single-year estimates are preferred, as they will be more relevant to the current conditions. However, the user must take into account the level of uncertainty present in the single-year estimates, which may be large for small subpopulation groups and rare characteristics. While single-year estimates offer more current estimates, they also have higher sampling variability. One measure, the coefficient of variation (CV) can help you determine the fitness for use of a single-year estimate in order to assess if you should opt instead to use the multiyear estimate. The CV is calculated as the ratio of the standard error of the estimate to the estimate, times 100. A single-year estimate with a small CV is usually preferable to a multiyear estimate as it is more up to date. However, multiyear estimates are an alternative option when a single-year estimate has an unacceptably high CV. Single-year estimates for small subpopulations (e.g., grandparents 65 and over who are responsible for grandchildren) will typically have larger CVs. In general, multiyear estimates are preferable to single-year estimates when looking at estimates for small subpopulations.

For the complete discussion on deciding which estimates to use and on calculating the CV, see: *Understanding and Using American Community Survey Data: What All Data Users Need to Know, July 2018* https://www.census.gov/programs-surveys/acs/guidance/handbooks/general.html.

Often users want to compare the characteristics of one area to those of another area. These comparisons can be in the form of rankings or of specific pairs of comparisons. Whenever you want to make a comparison between two different geographic areas you need to take the type of estimate into account. It is important that comparisons be made within the same estimate type. That is, 1-year estimates should only be compared with other 1-year estimates, 3-year estimates should only be compared with other 3-year estimates, and 5-year estimates should only be compared with other 5-year estimates.

You certainly can compare characteristics for areas with populations of 30,000 to areas with populations of 100,000 but you should use the data set that they have in common. In this example you could use the 3- or the 5-year estimates because they are available for areas of 30,000 and areas of 100,000. You should NOT compare the single year estimate for the area of 100,000 to the 3-year estimate for the area of 30,000. This book includes only the 1-year estimates for 2016 so comparisons across geographic areas will be appropriate.

Users are encouraged to make comparisons between sequential single-year estimates. In American FactFinder (AFF), comparison profiles are available beginning with the 2007 single-year data. These profiles identify statistically significant differences between each year from 2007 through the most recently released year.

Caution is needed when using multiyear estimates for estimating year-to-year change in a particular characteristic. This is because roughly four-fifths of the respondents in a 5-year estimate overlap with the respondents in the next year's 5-year estimate period. When comparing 5-year estimates from 2011–2015 with those from 2012–2016, the differences in overlapping multiyear estimates are driven by differences in the non-overlapping years (i.e. 2011 and 2016). A more appropriate comparison of change over time would be comparing the 2007–2011 5-year estimate to the 2012–2016 5-year estimate because they include responses from totally independent samples. Comparison of overlapping periods should be made with caution.

Users who are interested in comparing overlapping multiyear period estimates should refer to Chapter 3 of: *Understanding and Using American Community Survey Data: What All Data Users Need to Know, July 2018* https://www.census.gov/programs-surveys/acs/guidance/handbooks/general.html.

Multiyear estimates are likely to confuse some data users, in part because of their statistical properties, and in part because this is a new product from the Census Bureau. The ACS will provide all states and communities that have at least 65,000 residents with single-year estimates of demographic, housing, social, and economic characteristics—a boon to government agencies that need to budget and plan for public services like transportation, medical care, and schools. For geographic areas with smaller populations, the ACS samples too few households to provide reliable single-year estimates. For these communities, several years of data will be pooled together to create reliable 5-year estimates.

Single-year and 5-year estimates from the ACS are all "period" estimates that represent data collected over a period of time as opposed to "point-in-time" estimates, such as the decennial census. While a single-year estimate includes information collected over a 12-month period, a 5-year estimate includes data collected over a 60-month period. Therefore, ACS estimates based on data collected from 2014–2018 should not be called "2016" or "2018" estimates. Multiyear estimates should be labeled to indicate clearly the full period of time (e.g., "The poverty rate for persons 65 and over in 2014–2018 was x.x percent"). The primary advantage of using multiyear estimates is the increased statistical reliability of the data for less populated areas and small population subgroups.

Multiyear estimates should, in general, be used when single-year estimates have large CVs or when the precision of the estimates is more important than the currency of the data. Multiyear estimates should also be used when analyzing data for smaller geographies and smaller population subgroups in larger geographies. Multiyear estimates are also of value when examining change over non-overlapping time periods and for smoothing data trends over time.

Single-year estimates should, in general, be used for larger geographies and populations when currency is more important than the precision of the estimates. Single-year estimates should be used to examine year-to-year change for estimates with small CVs. Given the availability of a single-year estimate, calculating the CV provides useful information to determine if the single-year estimate should be used. For areas believed to be experiencing rapid changes in a characteristic, single-year estimates should generally be used rather than multiyear estimates as long as the CV for the single-year estimate is reasonable for the specific usage.

Local area variations may occur due to rapidly occurring changes. Multiyear estimates will tend to be insensitive to such changes when they first occur. Single-year estimates, if associated with sufficiently small CVs, can be very valuable in identifying and studying such phenomena.

Data users also need to use caution in looking at trends involving income or other measures that are adjusted for inflation, such as rental costs, home values, and energy costs. Note that inflation adjustment is based on a national-level consumer price index: it does not adjust for differences in costs of living across different geographic areas.

For information on the adjustment of single-year and multiyear ACS estimates for dollar-denominated data, uses should see Chapter 10 in:

Understanding and Using American Community Survey Data: What All Data Users Need to Know, July 2018 https://www.census.gov/programs-surveys/acs/guidance/handbooks/general.html.

MARGIN OF ERROR

All data that are based on samples, such as the ACS and the census long-form samples, include a range of uncertainty. Two broad types of error can occur: sampling error and nonsampling error. Nonsampling errors can result from mistakes in how the data are reported or coded, problems in the sampling frame or survey questionnaires, or problems related to nonresponse or interviewer bias. The Census Bureau tries to minimize nonsampling errors by using trained interviewers and by carefully reviewing the survey's sampling methods, data processing techniques, and questionnaire design.

Chapter 11 of the *ACS General Handbook* includes a more detailed description of different types of non-sampling errors in the ACS and other measures of ACS quality:

Understanding and Using American Community Survey Data: What All Data Users Need to Know, July 2018 https://www.census.gov/programs-surveys/acs/guidance/handbooks/general.html.

Sampling error occurs when data are based on a sample of a population rather than the full population. Sampling error is easier to measure than nonsampling error and can be used to assess the statistical reliability of survey data. For any given area, the larger the sample and the more months included in the data, the greater the confidence in the estimate. The Census Bureau reports the 90-percent confidence interval on all ACS estimates produced since 2005. Beginning with the release of the 2006 ACS data, *margins of error (MOE)* are now provided for every ACS estimate. Ninety percent confidence intervals define a range expected to contain the *true* value of an estimate with a level of confidence of 90 percent. Margins of error are easily converted into these confidence ranges. By adding and subtracting the margin of error

from the point estimate, we can calculate the 90-percent confidence interval for an estimate. Therefore, we can be 90 percent confident that the true number falls between the lower-bound interval and the upper-bound interval.

The margin of error around an estimate is important because it helps one draw conclusions about the data. Small differences between two estimates may not be statistically significant if the confidence intervals of those estimates overlap. However, the Census Bureau cautions data users not to rely on overlapping confidence intervals as a test for statistical significance, because this method will not always produce accurate results.

Detailed information about sampling error and instructions for calculating confidence intervals and margins of error are included in Chapter 7 of the *ACS General Handbook*:

Understanding and Using American Community Survey Data: What All Data Users Need to Know, July 2018 https://www.census.gov/programs-surveys/acs/guidance/handbooks/general.html.

In some cases, data users will need to construct custom ACS estimates by combining data across multiple geographic areas or population subgroups or it may be necessary to derive a new percentage, proportion, or ratio from published ACS data. In such cases, additional calculations are needed to produce confidence intervals and margins of error for the derived estimates. Chapter 8 of the *ACS General Handbook* also provides detailed instructions on how to make these calculations. Note that these error measures do not tell us about the magnitude of nonsampling errors.

Some advanced data users will also want to construct custom ACS estimates from the Census Bureau's Public Use Microdata Samples (PUMS). There are separate instructions for conducting significance tests for PUMS estimates, available on the Census Bureau's American FactFinder (AFF) website at: http://www2.census.gov/programs-surveys/acs/tech_docs/accuracy/ACS_Accuracy_of_Data_2018.pdf.

Accessing ACS Data Online

The Census Bureau's long standing data dissemination system, American FactFinder, has been retired. In the Spring of 2019 the Census Bureau launched https://data.census.gov and ran concurrently with American FactFinder as Census tested the new system and users were introduced to a new way of accessing Census data. There were no new data releases in American FactFinder after June 2019. The new platform is the primary way to access data from the 2018 and previous releases of the American Community survey, as well as the upcoming results of the 2020 Decennial Census.

While the data content of sources such as the American Community Survey hasn't changed from the old American FactFinder system to data.census.gov, the structure of some basic products and the access interface is very different.

Basic information on using the functions and features of data.census.gov can be found from the main page at https://data.census.gov/cedsci. Users will find the answers to a number of common questions about the transition away from American FactFinder and how to get started with data.census.gov under the "Questions?" heading. "Release Notes" will keep users informed of coming releases, enhancements and bug fixes. Tutorials, recorded webinars and user feedback to the Census Bureau can be found under "Stay Connected." The main page also provides quick links to sample "Data Profiles," "Maps and Visualizations" and "Industry and NAICS Codes". These and other main page links help users get started finding the data they need.

Some of the various ACS data products are described below.

- **Data Profiles.** The *data profiles* are good place to start for novice and experienced data users. *Data profiles* provide four separate fact sheets on the social, economic, demographic, and housing characteristics for different geographic areas. These profiles contain the most frequently requested data and summarize the data for single geographic areas with both counts and percentages.

- **Narrative Profiles.** *Narrative profiles* are short, analytic reports derived from the ACS 5-year estimates. Each Narrative Profile covers 15 different topic areas and provides text and bar charts to display highlights

of selected social, economic, housing and demographic estimates for a selected geographic area.

- **Ranking Tables.** *Ranking tables* provide state rankings of estimates across 86 key variable but are only available for 1-year estimates.

- **Subject tables.** These are similar to *data profiles* but are specific to a more detailed characteristic or topic (e.g., employment, education, and income). *Subject tables* provide pre-tabulated numbers and percentages for a wide variety of topics, often available separately by age (60 and over and 65 and over), gender, or race/ethnicity.

- **Selected population profiles.** The most detailed race/ethnic data are available through the *selected population profiles*, which provide summary tables separately for more than 400 detailed race, ethnic, tribal, ancestry, and country of birth groups.

- **Geographic Comparison Tables.** The *comparison tables* show data side-by-side from multiple years, indicating where there is a statistically significant difference between the two sets of estimates. Comparison profiles are only available for 1-year estimates.

- **Detailed tables.** The *detailed tables* are the best source for advanced data users or those who want access to the most comprehensive ACS tables. The tables in this book were developed through this option. For more advanced users, *detailed tables* are also available for download through the ACS *Summary File*: https://www.census.gov/programs-surveys/acs/data/summary-file.html.

- **Thematic Maps.** The pre-defined *thematic maps* provide graphic displays of the data available for various tables and geographies. Different shades of color are used to display variations in the data across geographic areas. Data users can also highlight areas with statistically different values from a selected state, county, or metropolitan area of interest. User created maps can be generated within data.census.gov by first selecting the required level of geography (census tracts for example), selecting the data variable and then producing a thematic map. Maps can then be downloaded as PDF files or captured via screenshots.

- **Summary File Data.** More experienced data users and those who need large numbers of either tabular or geographic data and access the ACS summary files through the Census Bureau's FTP site. Summary Files are sets of comma-delimited text files that contain all of the detailed tables for the ACS. The files are structured as sets of tables or sets of geographic areas. These can also be structured by state which allows downloading of all geographic areas (counties, sub-county areas, census tracts for example) for an entire state.

- **Public Use Microdata Sample files.** Those with expertise in using SAS, SPSS, or STATA may also be interested in the *Public Use Microdata Sample (PUMS) files*, which contain a sample of individual records of people and households that responded to the survey (stripped of all identifying information). The PUMS files permit analysis of specific population groups and custom variables that are not available through the summary tables in data.census.gov. For example, PUMS data users can look at the proportion of persons 60 to 69 with a disability by whether they own or rent their home or employment status and occupation of the 55 to 69 population. This flexibility is not provided by the pre-tabulated summary tables provided in data.census.gov. Data users can also combine multiple years of PUMS data to produce data for relatively small population subgroups (e.g., female physicians over age 55). More information about the PUMS is available at https://www.census.gov/programs-surveys/acs/data/pums.html.

For readers who were used to data from the traditional decennial census long-form, it is important to note that there are many conceptual and data collection differences in the ACS. The following is a summary of some of these differences which are described more fully in the chapter Using the ACS.

The ACS data are complex and cover a broad range of topics and geographic areas. The nature of multi-year period estimates and resulting sampling variability make it more difficult for many people to fully understand the interpretation and use the ACS data. The key points are summarized below.

- Use caution in comparing ACS data with data from the decennial census or other sources. Every survey uses different methods, which could affect the comparability of the numbers. Some characteristics in the ACS, such as income, reflect a different reference period from the traditional long-form census.

- The ACS was designed to provide estimates of the characteristics of the population, not to provide counts of the population in different geographic areas or population subgroups. However, counts of the population are often what is required by grant applications and researchers and is primarily what is provided in this publication.

- Be careful in drawing conclusions about small differences between two estimates because they may not be statistically different. Statistical testing should always be considered based on the sensitivity of conclusions to differences in the data results.

- Data users need to be careful not to interpret annual fluctuations in the data as long-term trends. Again, statistical testing is necessary to determine if annual fluctuations are real or merely a result of the sample.

- Use caution in comparing data from 2006 and later surveys with data from the 2005 survey. Unlike earlier survey, the 2006 and later ACS surveys include samples of the population living in group quarters (e.g., college dorms and nursing homes), so the data may not be comparable, especially for young adults and the elderly, who are more likely than other age groups to be living in group quarters facilities.

- The questionnaire series to define disability changed in 2008 making it impossible to compare disability status for periods before that date.

- Data users should not interpret or refer to multi-year period estimates as estimates of the middle year or last year in the series. For example, a 2010–2014 estimate is not a "2012 average."

- Data users should always be consistent in comparing similar period estimates over time or between geographic areas. Compare 1-year to 1-year, 3-year to 3-year and 5-year to 5-year estimates. Since geographic areas of different population size have different period estimates available, always compare make comparisons using the same period estimate. Do not compare a 1-year estimate for a large population size are to a 5-year estimate for a small area or census tract.

- Due to reductions in funding authorization for data products, the Census Bureau has eliminated the 3-year ACS estimates. The last set of 3-year estimates covered the period 2011–2013.

- Data users should *not* rely on overlapping confidence intervals as a test for statistical significance because this method will not always provide an accurate result.

More ACS Resources

There is a wealth of information about the ACS on the Web with new information available on a regular basis. Each year, the ACS data release represents a new stage in the process. Consequently, many new documents are required to explain the survey, year-to-year changes, and how to use it. These resources cover many of the topics discussed in this book, but in greater detail.

The best place to start is the Census Bureau's ACS main page: http://www.census.gov/programs-surveys/acs

BACKGROUND AND OVERVIEW INFORMATION

The American Community Survey home page provides an overview of the links and materials that are available online, including numerous reference documents.

The site map corresponds to the menu headings on the ACS main page and provides much more detail than the "drop-down" categories displayed.

About the Survey provides background and general information about the importance of the ACS, how sampled households are selected, response options, privacy protections and questionnaire information. It also includes information about how any individual household is selected for the survey.
http://www.census.gov/programs-surveys/acs/about.html

Data provides information about data updates and new releases. Links to data tables and tools are provided, as well as, other options for accessing data such as the Census Bureau's API source for developers.
http://www.census.gov/programs-surveys/acs/data.html

Guidance for Data Users provides detailed information that helps users understand the geographic coverage of the survey data, the subjects include, how and when to use the multi-year estimates and handbooks for users of various types.
http://www.census.gov/programs-surveys/acs/guidance.html

Geography and the ACS describes geographic concepts and definitions. This is where users will find information on the geographic areas with published data and if there have been geographic boundary changes to be aware of.
http://www.census.gov/programs-surveys/acs/geography-acs.html

Technical Documentation is critical for users who need to understand the details of the data that's available, research and detailed documentation for the various data file products.
http://www.census.gov/programs-surveys/acs/technical-documentation.html

Methodology provides the most detailed information about the survey sample size, response rates and data quality.
http://www.census.gov/programs-surveys/acs/methodology.html

Library is a link to volumes of research and papers describing aspects of survey methodology, research, and analytical reports categorized by year.
http://www.census.gov/programs-surveys/acs/library.html

Accuracy of the Data (2018)
Provides a basic understanding of the sample design, estimation methodology, and accuracy of the ACS data.
http://www2.census.gov/programs-surveys/acs/tech_docs/accuracy/ACS_Accuracy_of_Data_2018.pdf

ACS Sample Size
Provides sample size information for each state for each year of the ACS. The initial sample size, coverage measures and response rates are provided for individual states and the nation. Sample sizes for all published geographic entities starting with the 2007 ACS are available in the B98 series of detailed tables on American FactFinder.
http://www.census.gov/acs/www/methodology/sample-size-and-data-quality/

ACS Quality Measures
Multi-Year Estimate Study Quality Measures Definitions:

Includes information about the steps taken by the Census Bureau to improve the accuracy of ACS data. Four

indicators of survey quality are described and measures are provided at the national and state level.
https://www.census.gov/programs-surveys/acs/data/data-via-ftp/multiyear-estimates-study.html

GUIDANCE ON DATA PRODUCTS AND USING THE DATA

How to Use the Data:
Includes links to many documents and materials that explain the ACS data products.
http://www.census.gov/programs-surveys/acs/guidance.html

Comparing ACS Data to other sources:
Guidance on comparing the ACS data products to other years of ACS data and to Census 2000 long-form data.
https://www.census.gov/programs-surveys/acs/guidance/comparing-acs-data.html

When to Use 1-year, 3-year, or 5-year Estimates
The availability of multiple characteristic estimates for a given geographic area for different period estimates can be confusing for users of ACS data. Guidance on comparing across geographies and time periods.
https://www.census.gov/programs-surveys/acs/guidance/estimates.html

Information on Using Different Sources of Data for Income and Poverty:
Highlights the sources that should be used for data on income and poverty, focusing on comparing the ACS and the Current Population Survey (CPS).
http://www.census.gov/hhes/www/poverty/about/data-sources/description.html

Poverty: 2017 and 2018. American Community Survey Brief on poverty.
https://www.census.gov/library/publications/2019/acs/acsbr18-02.html

Public Use Microdata Sample (PUMS):
Provides guidance on accessing ACS microdata.
https://www.census.gov/programs-surveys/acs/technical-documentation/pums.html

Other Data Resources:

- Data.Census.Gov is the new data dissemination platform replacing American FactFinder (see for more information)

- American FactFinder Help (online help, census data information, glossary, and tutorial). AFF will be retired in the Spring of 2020 and is no longer updated with current data. http://factfinder.census.gov/help/en/index.htm#

- Guide to the Data Products (Web page) https://www.census.gov/acs/www/data/data-tables-and-tools/index.php

- *A Compass for Understanding and Using American Community Survey Data: What General Data Users Need to Know* provides a complete overview: https://www.census.gov/library/publications/2008/acs/general.html

- Other Compass handbooks are available for the business community, media, Congress and many other user groups at: https://www.census.gov/programs-surveys/acs/guidance/handbooks.html

- *Using the American Community Survey: Benefits and Challenges*, edited by Constance F. Citro and Graham Kalton (The National Academies Press, 2007). An excellent overview of the ACS, complete with several chapters of useful information for data users. The book is available for purchase and is also available to read online at no charge. http://www.nap.edu/catalog/11901/using-the-american-community-survey-benefits-and-challenges

PART A
POPULATION SUMMARY

POPULATION SUMMARY

In 1950 at the early stage of the Baby Boom genera-tion, the nation's population stood at 179,323,000. More than 30 percent of the population was under the age of 15 while less than 10 percent was age 65 or older. The median age in 1950 was 29.5 years. By 2018, less than 19 percent of the population was under the age of 15 and 16.0 percent was 65 or older with a median age of 38.2 years. Based on the Census Bureau's latest projections, by 2030 when the youngest of the Baby Boom genera-tion passes the age of 65, fully one out of every five resi-dents (20.6 percent) will be over the age of 65 while less than 18 percent are under 15 years of age resulting in a median age of 40.1 years. This remarkable growth in the older age population will take a pause holding at around 22 percent as the "Baby Bust" generation ages over 65. The Millennials, a larger birth cohort than the Baby Boomers, will again push the growth in the older population approaching 24 percent by 2060.

While the aging of the Baby Boom generation cap-tures a lot of national attention, it's important to note that change is not uniform across the country. As the geographic level of analysis gets smaller, the variation across our communities grows with some areas following national trends while others outpace or lag the nation. Analyzing population change is like telling a story of our communities. It's important to look at population change over time, the varying demographic composition of our communities, and how each compares to other areas. The text and tables in this volume are intended to provide the basic demographic portrait of the nation's older popula-tion at the state, county, city, metropolitan area, and Con-gressional district levels and allow planners, researchers, and interested individuals to tell their own stories.

The tables in this book are from the Census Bureau's 2018 American Community Survey for geographic areas of at least 65,000 population. The one exception is Table A which presents a population summary and includes the population change from the 2010 Census. *It is important to note that the April 1, 2010 Census figures reported here represent various revisions to the originally published Census counts. These populations are labeled "April 1, 2010 Census Population Estimates Base".* Most of these revisions represent the correction of small geographic misallocations. When this book is published, the Census Bureau will be busy tabulating the results of the 2020 Decennial Census.

POPULATION CHANGE

As we near the end of the decade, the nation's popula-tion has grown by over 18.4 million people, or 4.7 percent from the 2010 Census and totals 327.2 million people. California remains in the largest state with a population of 39.6 million, followed by Texas, Florida, New York and Pennsylvania as the remaining top five states. In 2014, Florida passed New York as the third largest state in the nation. More than a third (37.2 percent) of the nation's total population lives in these five largest states and they have about the same proportion (36.6 percent) of the population age 65 years or more. The smallest five states (Wyoming, Vermont, the District of Columbia, Alaska and North Dakota) total 3.4 million in population, just one percent of the nation's total. Their share of the 65 and over population is just over one percent.

The District of Columbia grew the fastest between 2010 and 2018 at 16.7 percent followed by Utah (14.4 percent), Texas (14.1 percent) and both Colorado and Florida at 13.3 percent. Ten states and the District of Columbia grew by more than 10 percent. Texas also experienced the larg-est absolute gain in population at 3.6 million while the District of Columbia increased by 100,700 people. Con-necticut, Illinois and West Virginia are the only states to show a population loss between 2010 and the 2018 esti-mates with Illinois declining by more than 90,000, West Virginia by more than 47,000 and Connecticut dropping by only 1,500. New York, Pennsylvania, Maine, Mis-sissippi, Rhode Island, and Vermont were the slowest growth states, each increasing by less than 1 percent.

One third of the nation's population (106.6 million peo-ple) lives in cities of over 65,000 population. New York City remains the largest city with a population of 8.4 mil-lion followed by Los Angeles with 4.0 million, Chicago with 2.7 million and Houston with 2.3 million residents. The data presented here is limited to 568 cities of 65,000 or more in population. The smallest cities in this group are East Orange City, New Jersey and Lorain City, Ohio with populations of 64,469 and 64,031 respectively. Of the 20 fastest growing cities, only Irvine City, CA is in the top

Percent of Persons 65 Years and Over Who are Living Alone

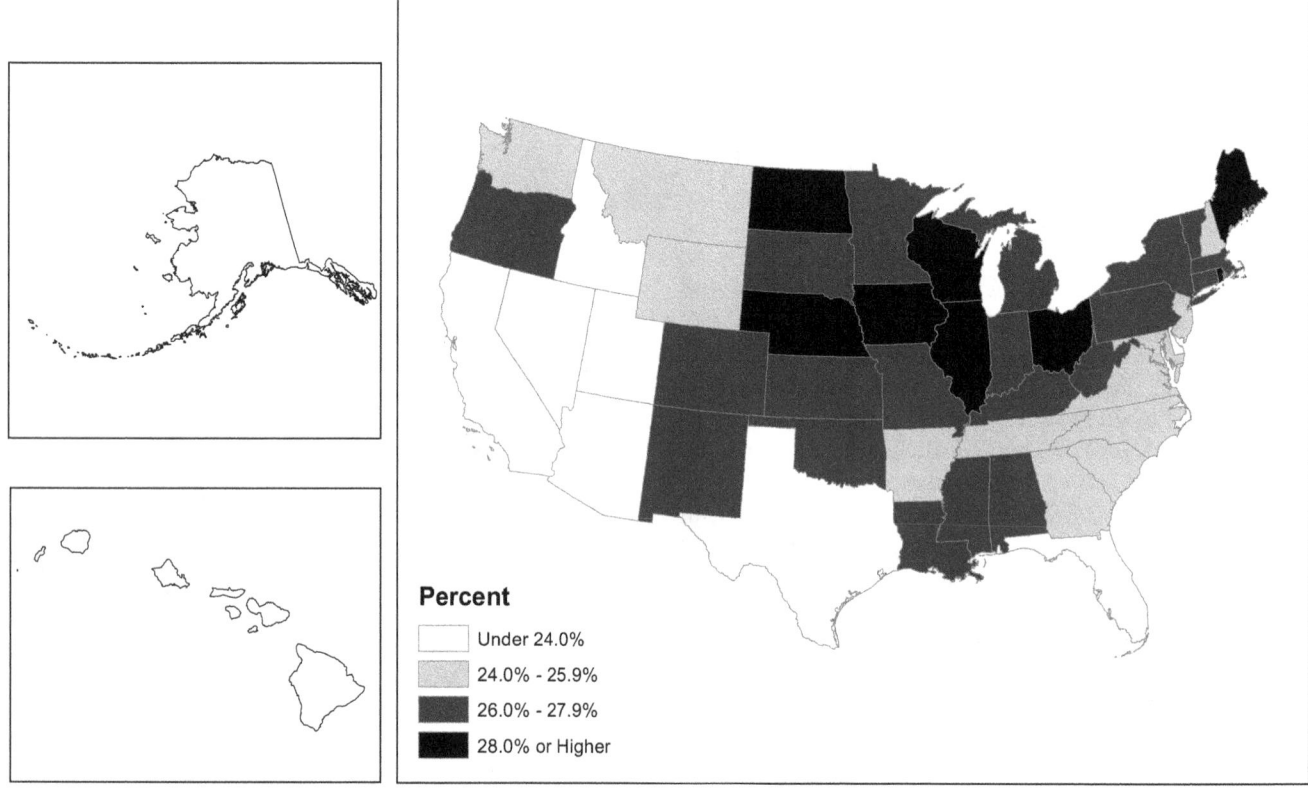

Percent

- Under 24.0%
- 24.0% - 25.9%
- 26.0% - 27.9%
- 28.0% or Higher

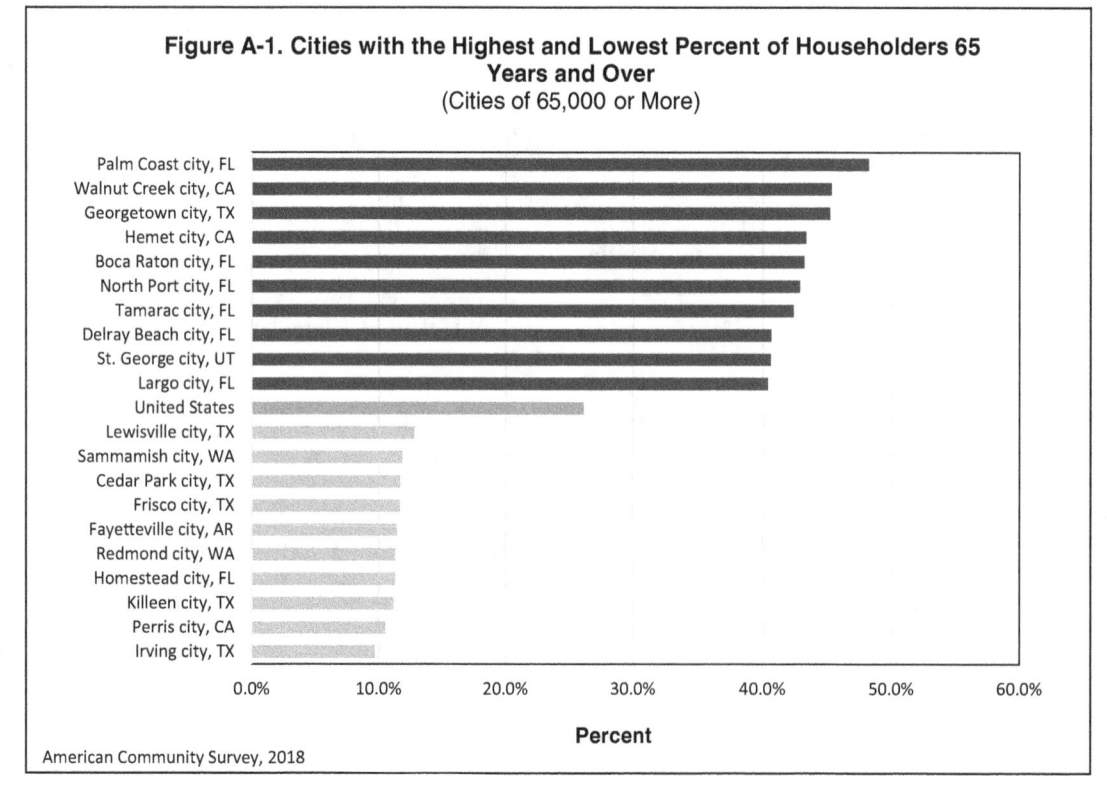

Figure A-1. Cities with the Highest and Lowest Percent of Householders 65 Years and Over
(Cities of 65,000 or More)

American Community Survey, 2018

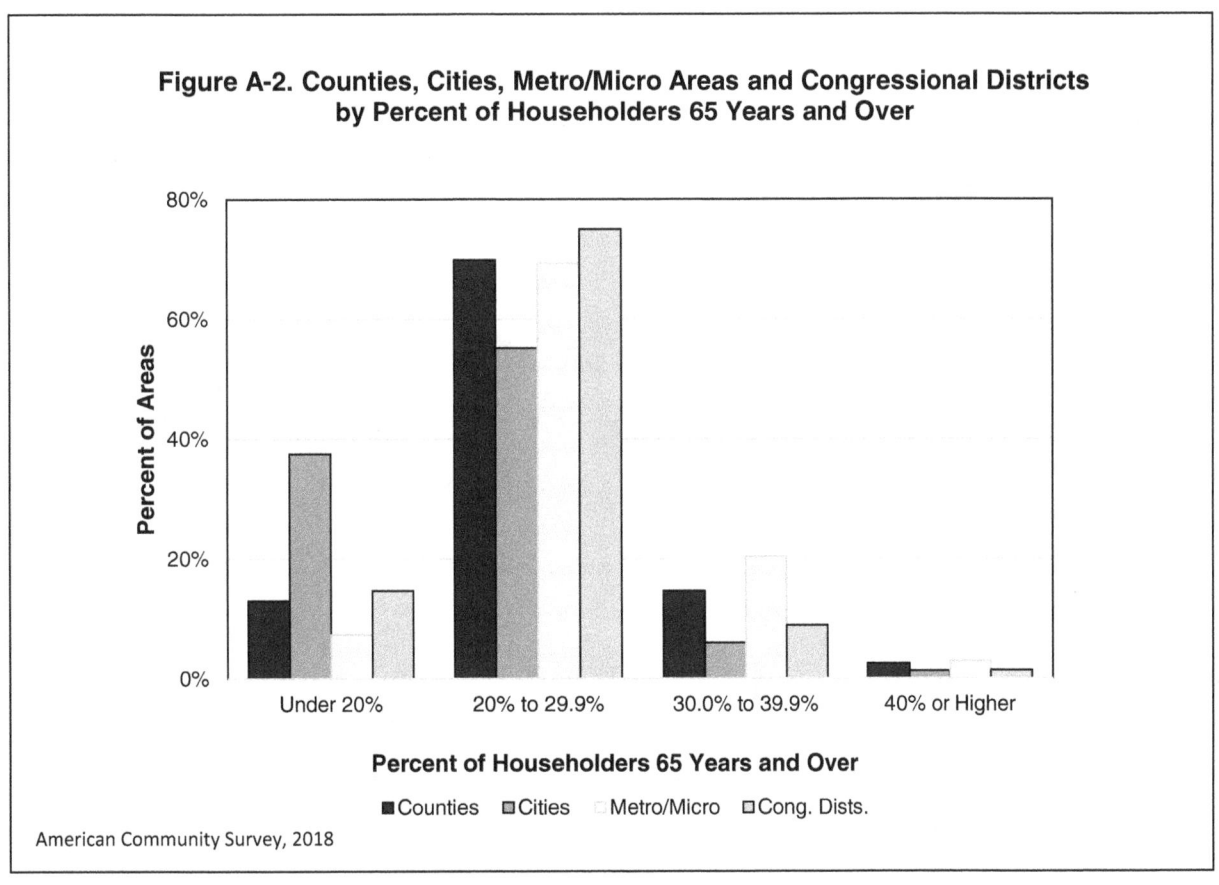

Figure A-2. Counties, Cities, Metro/Micro Areas and Congressional Districts by Percent of Householders 65 Years and Over

American Community Survey, 2018

100 of population size. The city of Frisco, TX shows the fastest rate of growth of any city at 60.6 percent. Georgetown City, TX had the next fastest rate of growth at 56.2 percent but it is the 472nd largest city. Ten cities have populations of over 1 million and 36 are over 500,000. There are 256 cities with populations between 65,000 and 100,000. California has the most cities over 65,000 with 137 while Alaska, Delaware, Hawaii, and Maine have only one each. Vermont and Wyoming have none.

The 512 Metropolitan and Micropolitan Statistical Areas over 65,000 shown here total 292.8 million in population or 89.5 percent of the U.S. total. The New York-Northern New Jersey-Long Island metro area is the largest at 20.0 million followed by Los Angeles-Long Beach-Anaheim at 13.3 million. Fifty three metropolitan areas have more than 1 million population while twice that number have populations of 500,000 or more. While the New York-Northern New Jersey-Long Island area is the largest, its growth rate ranked only 299th. The Villages, FL metropolitan area was the fastest growing at a rate of 37.8 percent but with 128,754 residents, it is the 318th largest area. The Pine Bluff, Arkansas metropolitan area, the 411th largest area, declined by 10.0 percent while the Roanoke Rapids, North Carolina micropolitan area declined by 8.5 percent. There were 143 metropolitan

and micropolitan areas that saw population declines between 2010 and 2018. The New York-Newark-Jersey City metro area has over 3.1 million residents over the age of 65 but the Hinesville, Georgia metropolitan area has only 6,690.

Nationwide, excluding the District of Columbia, the average population of the 435 congressional districts is 752,109. California has the largest congressional delegation with 53 seats while Alaska, Delaware, Montana, North Dakota, South Dakota, Vermont and Wyoming all have 1 seat each. Wyoming has the smallest population per representative at 577,737 while Montana's single representative represents more than 1 million residents. Eighty-four congressional districts are estimated to have lost population between the 2010 Census count and the 2018 American Community Survey estimates. Congressional District 22 in Texas had the fastest growth rate at 33.9 percent and 111 other districts grew by more than 10 percent. Congressional District 3 in West Virginia had the fastest decline in population at 6.6 percent while District 2 in Mississippi had the largest absolute decline at 46,065. Congressional District 11 in Florida has the largest population over the age of 65 at 281,669 while District 7 in Arizona is the smallest at 60,596.

Selected State Rankings

State	Total Population 2018	Population Rank	Percent Change 2010 to 2018	Percent Change Rank	Total Households 2018	Households Rank	Total Population 65 And Over	Population 65 and Over Rank
Alabama	4,887,871	24	2.3%	36	1,855,184	24	829,663	23
Alaska	737,438	48	3.8%	27	254,551	50	88,000	50
Arizona	7,171,646	14	12.2%	8	2,614,298	15	1,259,103	13
Arkansas	3,013,825	33	3.4%	29	1,156,347	31	507,676	31
California	39,557,045	1	6.2%	20	13,072,122	1	5,667,337	1
Colorado	5,695,564	21	13.2%	5	2,176,757	22	807,855	24
Connecticut	3,572,665	29	-0.0%	49	1,378,091	29	613,147	29
Delaware	967,171	45	7.7%	16	367,671	45	180,756	45
District of Columbia	702,455	49	16.7%	1	287,476	48	85,626	51
Florida	21,299,325	3	13.3%	4	7,809,358	3	4,358,784	2
Georgia	10,519,475	8	8.6%	14	3,803,012	10	1,456,428	10
Hawaii	1,420,491	40	4.4%	26	455,309	42	261,467	41
Idaho	1,754,208	39	11.9%	10	640,270	39	279,441	39
Illinois	12,741,080	6	-0.7%	50	4,864,864	6	1,990,548	7
Indiana	6,691,878	17	3.2%	30	2,599,169	17	1,051,146	17
Iowa	3,156,145	31	3.6%	28	1,267,873	30	537,818	30
Kansas	2,911,510	35	2.0%	38	1,133,408	32	462,191	34
Kentucky	4,468,402	26	3.0%	32	1,732,713	26	731,392	26
Louisiana	4,659,978	25	2.8%	33	1,737,220	25	720,610	27
Maine	1,338,404	42	0.8%	45	570,307	40	276,069	40
Maryland	6,042,718	19	4.7%	25	2,215,935	20	931,041	20
Massachusetts	6,902,149	15	5.4%	23	2,624,294	14	1,137,541	15
Michigan	9,995,915	10	1.1%	42	3,957,466	9	1,720,453	8
Minnesota	5,611,179	22	5.8%	21	2,194,452	21	888,634	22
Mississippi	2,986,530	34	0.6%	46	1,108,630	34	474,423	33
Missouri	6,126,452	18	2.3%	35	2,434,806	18	1,035,074	18
Montana	1,062,305	43	7.4%	17	431,421	43	200,239	43
Nebraska	1,929,268	37	5.6%	22	765,490	37	303,998	38
Nevada	3,034,392	32	12.4%	7	1,129,810	33	475,120	32
New Hampshire	1,356,458	41	3.0%	31	531,212	41	245,156	42
New Jersey	8,908,520	11	1.3%	40	3,249,567	11	1,438,289	11
New Mexico	2,095,428	36	1.8%	39	794,093	36	368,480	35
New York	19,542,209	4	0.8%	43	7,367,015	4	3,212,065	4
North Carolina	10,383,620	9	8.9%	13	4,011,462	8	1,688,574	9
North Dakota	760,077	47	13.0%	6	319,355	47	116,433	48
Ohio	11,689,442	7	1.3%	41	4,685,447	7	1,996,163	6
Oklahoma	3,943,079	28	5.1%	24	1,485,310	28	619,601	28
Oregon	4,190,713	27	9.4%	12	1,639,970	27	739,611	25
Pennsylvania	12,807,060	5	0.8%	44	5,070,931	5	2,332,369	5
Rhode Island	1,057,315	44	0.4%	47	406,573	44	182,645	44
South Carolina	5,084,127	23	9.9%	11	1,927,991	23	899,754	21
South Dakota	882,235	46	8.4%	15	345,449	46	146,358	46
Tennessee	6,770,010	16	6.7%	18	2,603,140	16	1,104,797	16
Texas	28,701,845	2	14.1%	3	9,776,083	2	3,599,599	3
Utah	3,161,105	30	14.4%	2	998,891	35	351,297	37
Vermont	626,299	50	0.1%	48	261,373	49	123,875	47
Virginia	8,517,685	12	6.5%	19	3,175,524	12	1,318,225	12
Washington	7,535,591	13	12.1%	9	2,895,575	13	1,163,987	14
West Virginia	1,805,832	38	-2.5%	51	734,703	38	361,216	36
Wisconsin	5,813,568	20	2.2%	37	2,371,960	19	986,483	19
Wyoming	577,737	51	2.5%	34	230,252	51	96,557	49

Table A-1: States - Summary Population Characteristics

	April 1, 2010 Census Population Estimates Base	2018 ACS Population	2010-2018 Population Change	2010-2018 Percent Change	Total Households	2018 ACS			
						Population 65 and Over	Population 85 and Over	Householders 65 and Over	Persons 65 and Over Living Alone
United States	308,758,105	327,167,439	18,409,334	6.0%	121,520,180	52,423,114	6,303,848	31,842,901	13,421,396
Alabama.................	4,780,138	4,887,871	107,733	2.3%	1,855,184	829,663	85,242	523,973	215,966
Alaska....................	710,249	737,438	27,189	3.8%	254,551	88,000	7,370	53,173	20,618
Arizona..................	6,392,288	7,171,646	779,358	12.2%	2,614,298	1,259,103	132,739	754,387	295,472
Arkansas................	2,916,028	3,013,825	97,797	3.4%	1,156,347	507,676	56,169	314,838	129,177
California...............	37,254,523	39,557,045	2,302,522	6.2%	13,072,122	5,667,337	729,580	3,197,217	1,249,751
Colorado	5,029,316	5,695,564	666,248	13.2%	2,176,757	807,855	87,406	499,802	211,903
Connecticut............	3,574,147	3,572,665	-1,482	-0.0%	1,378,091	613,147	87,696	374,793	168,018
Delaware................	897,934	967,171	69,237	7.7%	367,671	180,756	18,604	107,758	40,163
District of Columbia	601,766	702,455	100,689	16.7%	287,476	85,626	10,901	58,898	33,166
Florida...................	18,804,580	21,299,325	2,494,745	13.3%	7,809,358	4,358,784	561,000	2,522,233	1,026,882
Georgia	9,688,709	10,519,475	830,766	8.6%	3,803,012	1,456,428	142,800	886,919	364,633
Hawaii...................	1,360,307	1,420,491	60,184	4.4%	455,309	261,467	40,073	143,128	48,941
Idaho.....................	1,567,657	1,754,208	186,551	11.9%	640,270	279,441	29,703	168,614	66,304
Illinois..................	12,831,572	12,741,080	-90,492	-0.7%	4,864,864	1,990,548	259,568	1,242,040	558,371
Indiana..................	6,484,061	6,691,878	207,817	3.2%	2,599,169	1,051,146	126,577	659,809	289,121
Iowa......................	3,046,872	3,156,145	109,273	3.6%	1,267,873	537,818	75,616	338,159	154,589
Kansas	2,853,126	2,911,510	58,384	2.0%	1,133,408	462,191	63,786	287,156	128,282
Kentucky	4,339,333	4,468,402	129,069	3.0%	1,732,713	731,392	78,648	458,020	191,416
Louisiana	4,533,485	4,659,978	126,493	2.8%	1,737,220	720,610	73,844	446,979	190,943
Maine.....................	1,328,369	1,338,404	10,035	0.8%	570,307	276,069	34,849	175,923	78,602
Maryland................	5,773,798	6,042,718	268,920	4.7%	2,215,935	931,041	108,515	558,175	235,815
Massachusetts........	6,547,790	6,902,149	354,359	5.4%	2,624,294	1,137,541	153,729	700,037	315,036
Michigan................	9,884,117	9,995,915	111,798	1.1%	3,957,466	1,720,453	204,293	1,093,561	479,452
Minnesota.............	5,303,925	5,611,179	307,254	5.8%	2,194,452	888,634	115,373	552,433	244,096
Mississippi.............	2,968,118	2,986,530	18,412	0.6%	1,108,630	474,423	46,360	303,363	127,945
Missouri.................	5,988,952	6,126,452	137,500	2.3%	2,434,806	1,035,074	124,805	651,569	282,802
Montana................	989,409	1,062,305	72,896	7.4%	431,421	200,239	20,753	123,306	52,059
Nebraska...............	1,826,305	1,929,268	102,963	5.6%	765,490	303,998	41,952	194,541	90,667
Nevada..................	2,700,679	3,034,392	333,713	12.4%	1,129,810	475,120	44,280	279,933	113,980
New Hampshire.......	1,316,464	1,356,458	39,994	3.0%	531,212	245,156	30,824	145,788	60,736
New Jersey	8,791,962	8,908,520	116,558	1.3%	3,249,567	1,438,289	195,758	867,467	360,379
New Mexico	2,059,180	2,095,428	36,248	1.8%	794,093	368,480	40,735	228,095	97,771
New York...............	19,378,124	19,542,209	164,085	0.8%	7,367,015	3,212,065	432,629	1,972,352	891,304
North Carolina........	9,535,736	10,383,620	847,884	8.9%	4,011,462	1,688,574	179,067	1,044,996	436,730
North Dakota..........	672,576	760,077	87,501	13.0%	319,355	116,433	18,439	73,062	35,028
Ohio......................	11,536,757	11,689,442	152,685	1.3%	4,685,447	1,996,163	248,285	1,261,472	563,134
Oklahoma...............	3,751,583	3,943,079	191,496	5.1%	1,485,310	619,601	72,583	389,886	166,592
Oregon..................	3,831,075	4,190,713	359,638	9.4%	1,639,970	739,611	81,382	461,267	194,825
Pennsylvania..........	12,702,873	12,807,060	104,187	0.8%	5,070,931	2,332,369	313,640	1,458,606	650,681
Rhode Island..........	1,052,957	1,057,315	4,358	0.4%	406,573	182,645	26,459	113,963	54,937
South Carolina	4,625,381	5,084,127	458,746	9.9%	1,927,991	899,754	84,772	552,651	222,484
South Dakota	814,198	882,235	68,037	8.4%	345,449	146,358	21,761	91,545	38,909
Tennessee.............	6,346,286	6,770,010	423,724	6.7%	2,603,140	1,104,797	113,462	681,024	280,975
Texas....................	25,146,114	28,701,845	3,555,731	14.1%	9,776,083	3,599,599	382,935	2,107,858	818,397
Utah......................	2,763,891	3,161,105	397,214	14.4%	998,891	351,297	35,263	210,551	72,310
Vermont	625,744	626,299	555	0.1%	261,373	123,875	13,149	78,032	33,924
Virginia..................	8,001,055	8,517,685	516,630	6.5%	3,175,524	1,318,225	148,186	801,030	340,359
Washington............	6,724,540	7,535,591	811,051	12.1%	2,895,575	1,163,987	128,056	713,855	296,294
West Virginia..........	1,853,001	1,805,832	-47,169	-2.5%	734,703	361,216	40,219	231,585	100,039
Wisconsin	5,687,282	5,813,568	126,286	2.2%	2,371,960	986,483	124,755	625,177	276,652
Wyoming	563,773	577,737	13,964	2.5%	230,252	96,557	9,258	61,902	24,766

Table A-2: Counties - Summary Population Characteristics

	April 1, 2010 Census Population Estimates Base	2018 ACS Population	2010-2018 Population Change	2010-2018 Percent Change	Total Households	2018 ACS			
						Population 65 and Over	Population 85 and Over	Householders 65 and Over	Persons 65 and Over Living Alone
Alabama									
Baldwin County	182,264	218,022	35,758	19.6%	83,501	44,443	3,827	27,136	9,612
Calhoun County	118,594	114,277	-4,317	-3.6%	44,264	20,515	1,761	13,456	5,454
Cullman County	80,406	83,442	3,036	3.8%	30,323	15,541	855	9,912	4,379
DeKalb County	71,116	71,385	269	0.4%	26,462	12,261	1,542	8,140	3,351
Elmore County	79,293	81,887	2,594	3.3%	30,155	12,299	985	7,794	3,097
Etowah County	104,427	102,501	-1,926	-1.8%	38,625	19,632	2,194	12,152	5,154
Houston County	101,554	104,722	3,168	3.1%	38,861	18,790	1,854	11,982	5,131
Jefferson County	658,506	659,300	794	0.1%	255,940	104,700	11,594	67,575	28,235
Lauderdale County	92,709	92,387	-322	-0.3%	38,670	18,419	2,162	11,532	3,992
Lee County	140,300	163,941	23,641	16.9%	59,336	19,887	1,776	11,705	4,127
Limestone County	82,782	96,174	13,392	16.2%	32,333	15,095	1,796	9,407	3,608
Madison County	334,811	366,519	31,708	9.5%	152,723	55,665	5,334	36,105	15,047
Marshall County	93,019	96,109	3,090	3.3%	36,022	16,487	1,756	10,016	4,097
Mobile County	413,145	413,757	612	0.1%	158,627	66,558	6,972	43,522	18,530
Montgomery County	229,378	225,763	-3,615	-1.6%	87,553	34,276	3,875	22,480	10,029
Morgan County	119,486	119,089	-397	-0.3%	45,851	20,464	2,547	13,592	5,724
St. Clair County	83,345	88,690	5,345	6.4%	30,765	14,760	1,336	8,954	3,641
Shelby County	195,313	215,707	20,394	10.4%	80,944	33,295	3,025	20,757	8,159
Talladega County	82,283	79,828	-2,455	-3.0%	31,219	14,422	1,273	9,142	3,624
Tuscaloosa County	194,668	208,911	14,243	7.3%	74,053	27,472	2,537	16,785	6,353
Walker County	67,023	63,711	-3,312	-4.9%	24,870	12,061	1,159	7,671	3,158
Alaska									
Anchorage Municipality	291,829	291,538	-291	-0.1%	105,285	32,809	3,056	19,776	7,174
Fairbanks North Star Borough	97,585	98,971	1,386	1.4%	36,378	10,213	866	6,987	na
Matanuska-Susitna Borough	88,992	107,610	18,618	20.9%	32,198	13,051	1,291	7,032	2,595
Arizona									
Apache County	71,517	71,818	301	0.4%	21,936	10,932	1,303	6,942	2,776
Cochise County	131,357	126,770	-4,587	-3.5%	49,751	28,402	3,174	19,349	8,609
Coconino County	134,431	142,854	8,423	6.3%	47,275	17,813	1,440	10,903	3,597
Maricopa County	3,817,359	4,410,824	593,465	15.5%	1,582,464	669,199	77,143	391,504	156,842
Mohave County	200,182	209,550	9,368	4.7%	90,270	63,794	5,643	39,594	13,697
Navajo County	107,488	110,445	2,957	2.8%	34,285	20,162	2,184	12,780	5,147
Pima County	980,263	1,039,073	58,810	6.0%	402,323	205,547	21,309	126,887	50,885
Pinal County	375,768	447,138	71,370	19.0%	147,936	90,825	6,164	51,749	15,801
Yavapai County	211,014	231,993	20,979	9.9%	100,836	73,656	7,371	47,659	21,886
Yuma County	195,750	212,128	16,378	8.4%	74,532	39,979	3,154	22,994	6,851
Arkansas									
Benton County	221,351	272,608	51,257	23.2%	100,128	36,290	4,673	22,134	8,367
Craighead County	96,443	108,558	12,115	12.6%	42,631	15,167	1,102	9,754	4,044
Faulkner County	113,242	124,806	11,564	10.2%	43,701	15,720	1,549	9,348	3,292
Garland County	96,000	99,154	3,154	3.3%	40,407	22,991	2,956	14,925	5,562
Jefferson County	77,456	68,114	-9,342	-12.1%	25,689	11,671	1,715	7,901	3,360
Lonoke County	68,355	73,657	5,302	7.8%	28,132	9,757	963	5,827	2,201
Pulaski County	382,786	392,680	9,894	2.6%	157,678	61,104	7,487	37,415	16,387
Saline County	107,130	121,421	14,291	13.3%	43,496	21,793	2,148	12,627	4,005
Sebastian County	125,761	127,753	1,992	1.6%	51,739	20,168	2,045	13,267	6,024
Washington County	203,046	236,961	33,915	16.7%	90,001	26,922	3,243	16,807	5,565
White County	77,078	78,727	1,649	2.1%	29,577	12,307	1,307	8,138	na
California									
Alameda County	1,510,258	1,666,753	156,495	10.4%	575,410	230,510	27,564	129,181	54,151
Butte County	220,002	231,256	11,254	5.1%	88,636	42,820	4,441	25,859	9,972
Contra Costa County	1,049,204	1,150,215	101,011	9.6%	396,133	181,267	20,195	102,492	41,905
El Dorado County	181,058	190,678	9,620	5.3%	72,774	40,427	4,453	24,149	8,550
Fresno County	930,496	994,400	63,904	6.9%	309,519	121,540	17,185	72,341	30,520
Humboldt County	134,611	136,373	1,762	1.3%	55,773	24,296	2,817	16,123	7,063
Imperial County	174,524	181,827	7,303	4.2%	41,764	23,512	2,645	10,251	2,865
Kern County	839,619	896,764	57,145	6.8%	273,167	98,076	10,676	57,042	22,536
Kings County	152,982	151,366	-1,616	-1.1%	43,727	15,413	1,412	9,949	3,217
Lake County	64,664	64,382	-282	-0.4%	26,774	14,856	1,161	9,808	5,701
Los Angeles County	9,818,672	10,105,518	286,846	2.9%	3,313,908	1,375,959	192,748	750,779	294,537
Madera County	150,841	157,672	6,831	4.5%	44,484	22,099	2,668	11,632	4,137
Marin County	252,423	259,666	7,243	2.9%	104,954	58,213	6,346	37,113	15,671
Mendocino County	87,850	87,606	-244	-0.3%	33,794	19,072	1,475	12,167	5,777
Merced County	255,796	274,765	18,969	7.4%	79,487	30,748	3,475	18,366	7,595
Monterey County	415,061	435,594	20,533	4.9%	126,299	59,491	8,363	34,561	13,076
Napa County	136,578	139,417	2,839	2.1%	47,315	26,805	2,708	15,144	6,024
Nevada County	98,745	99,696	951	1.0%	41,447	27,746	3,152	16,239	6,016
Orange County	3,010,274	3,185,968	175,694	5.8%	1,040,394	471,226	65,417	259,739	100,102
Placer County	348,503	393,149	44,646	12.8%	144,691	76,749	9,123	46,330	19,182
Riverside County	2,189,765	2,450,758	260,993	11.9%	728,103	353,025	42,890	189,868	70,780
Sacramento County	1,418,735	1,540,975	122,240	8.6%	543,560	217,444	27,506	127,146	55,080
San Bernardino County	2,035,201	2,171,603	136,402	6.7%	638,647	251,168	25,753	136,143	48,360
San Diego County	3,095,349	3,343,364	248,015	8.0%	1,130,911	469,821	59,080	268,419	103,117
San Francisco County	805,184	883,305	78,121	9.7%	362,827	138,128	22,842	83,021	38,978
San Joaquin County	685,306	752,660	67,354	9.8%	231,917	95,844	10,931	51,357	19,028
San Luis Obispo County	269,597	284,010	14,413	5.3%	106,198	57,594	6,503	35,948	13,760

Table A-2: Counties - Summary Population Characteristics—*Continued*

	April 1, 2010 Census Population Estimates Base	2018 ACS Population	2010-2018 Population Change	2010-2018 Percent Change	Total Households	2018 ACS			
						Population 65 and Over	Population 85 and Over	Householders 65 and Over	Persons 65 and Over Living Alone
California—Cont.									
San Mateo County	718,518	769,545	51,027	7.1%	259,654	124,038	18,768	68,731	26,423
Santa Barbara County	423,947	446,527	22,580	5.3%	146,224	68,402	9,638	41,277	15,513
Santa Clara County	1,781,672	1,937,570	155,898	8.8%	645,108	261,252	37,517	138,818	47,377
Santa Cruz County	262,356	274,255	11,899	4.5%	94,994	45,349	3,835	27,799	10,508
Shasta County	177,221	180,040	2,819	1.6%	68,198	37,027	3,952	22,428	8,578
Solano County	413,298	446,610	33,312	8.1%	152,291	70,597	8,811	38,327	13,376
Sonoma County	483,868	499,942	16,074	3.3%	187,434	98,030	11,980	62,227	27,178
Stanislaus County	514,451	549,815	35,364	6.9%	175,171	72,507	8,557	41,197	14,471
Sutter County	94,756	96,807	2,051	2.2%	31,989	14,863	2,269	8,546	3,369
Tulare County	442,181	465,861	23,680	5.4%	139,197	52,622	6,294	29,774	11,998
Ventura County	823,393	850,967	27,574	3.3%	271,980	132,219	18,528	76,222	28,150
Yolo County	200,855	220,408	19,553	9.7%	74,428	27,177	3,545	15,948	6,040
Yuba County	72,146	78,041	5,895	8.2%	26,191	9,383	1,029	6,622	na
Colorado									
Adams County	441,698	511,868	70,170	15.9%	168,361	53,109	4,739	31,537	13,766
Arapahoe County	572,130	651,215	79,085	13.8%	242,141	85,009	9,712	52,237	22,345
Boulder County	294,561	326,078	31,517	10.7%	128,295	46,033	5,866	29,132	12,649
Broomfield County	55,856	69,267	13,411	24.0%	28,530	9,618	809	5,908	na
Denver County	599,815	716,492	116,677	19.5%	310,324	83,996	9,433	56,532	30,911
Douglas County	285,465	342,776	57,311	20.1%	125,035	39,922	3,749	24,015	8,298
El Paso County	622,250	713,856	91,606	14.7%	260,851	91,397	10,794	54,936	22,077
Jefferson County	534,829	580,233	45,404	8.5%	233,272	95,519	11,847	60,542	25,138
Larimer County	299,615	350,518	50,903	17.0%	139,382	55,002	5,527	33,694	12,513
Mesa County	146,717	153,207	6,490	4.4%	61,848	28,801	3,950	18,280	9,204
Pueblo County	159,063	167,529	8,466	5.3%	64,954	30,832	3,900	19,899	9,123
Weld County	252,847	314,305	61,458	24.3%	107,929	38,223	4,080	22,416	7,708
Connecticut									
Fairfield County	916,864	943,823	26,959	2.9%	345,634	149,824	21,890	92,257	39,760
Hartford County	894,033	892,697	-1,336	-0.1%	348,049	152,674	22,534	93,454	44,334
Litchfield County	189,925	181,111	-8,814	-4.6%	73,598	37,897	4,360	23,504	10,819
Middlesex County	165,676	162,682	-2,994	-1.8%	66,983	32,442	4,339	19,247	9,048
New Haven County	862,456	857,620	-4,836	-0.6%	335,539	148,789	22,610	90,805	40,417
New London County	274,068	266,784	-7,284	-2.7%	108,098	48,314	6,115	29,852	13,218
Tolland County	152,744	150,921	-1,823	-1.2%	55,619	24,281	3,147	14,669	6,403
Windham County	118,381	117,027	-1,354	-1.1%	44,571	18,926	2,701	11,005	4,019
Delaware									
Kent County	162,349	178,550	16,201	10.0%	67,841	29,812	2,980	17,737	6,654
New Castle County	538,479	559,335	20,856	3.9%	206,351	87,093	10,165	52,290	20,903
Sussex County	197,106	229,286	32,180	16.3%	93,479	63,851	5,459	37,731	12,606
Florida									
Alachua County	247,337	269,956	22,619	9.1%	97,782	37,727	4,765	22,273	10,191
Bay County	168,852	185,287	16,435	9.7%	73,856	30,927	3,293	19,306	8,137
Brevard County	543,372	596,849	53,477	9.8%	226,363	141,268	20,627	84,167	35,729
Broward County	1,748,146	1,951,260	203,114	11.6%	694,980	324,525	40,544	186,926	81,792
Charlotte County	159,964	184,998	25,034	15.6%	74,975	74,321	10,912	42,134	15,924
Citrus County	141,229	147,929	6,700	4.7%	62,293	53,832	6,810	33,165	14,744
Clay County	190,865	216,072	25,207	13.2%	75,958	34,752	2,576	19,867	7,567
Collier County	321,521	378,488	56,967	17.7%	144,172	122,463	18,268	68,705	24,323
Columbia County	67,526	70,503	2,977	4.4%	25,678	12,978	1,628	7,568	3,295
Duval County	864,267	950,181	85,914	9.9%	367,238	133,599	14,134	82,536	37,797
Escambia County	297,620	315,534	17,914	6.0%	118,820	52,996	6,102	33,082	13,893
Flagler County	95,703	112,067	16,364	17.1%	41,274	35,344	4,904	19,787	5,894
Hernando County	172,777	190,865	18,088	10.5%	76,163	52,643	6,749	32,130	11,544
Highlands County	98,786	105,424	6,638	6.7%	40,573	37,245	6,627	21,675	8,079
Hillsborough County	1,229,178	1,436,888	207,710	16.9%	540,142	205,808	24,244	120,806	51,156
Indian River County	138,028	157,413	19,385	14.0%	57,636	51,384	7,118	27,705	10,861
Lake County	297,052	356,495	59,443	20.0%	136,366	95,124	9,082	55,463	18,898
Lee County	618,754	754,610	135,856	22.0%	281,222	216,260	27,692	121,190	45,200
Leon County	275,484	292,502	17,018	6.2%	113,390	38,914	3,694	24,514	10,333
Manatee County	322,879	394,855	71,976	22.3%	150,814	107,787	13,799	64,211	25,655
Marion County	331,299	359,977	28,678	8.7%	143,441	104,024	12,155	62,379	23,454
Martin County	146,852	160,912	14,060	9.6%	63,070	50,419	8,115	30,294	13,320
Miami-Dade County	2,498,013	2,761,581	263,568	10.6%	895,801	447,968	68,933	223,196	84,484
Monroe County	73,090	75,027	1,937	2.7%	31,362	16,972	846	9,842	3,543
Nassau County	73,310	85,832	12,522	17.1%	32,624	18,787	1,159	10,932	3,679
Okaloosa County	180,825	207,269	26,444	14.6%	79,570	34,105	2,628	20,687	8,589
Orange County	1,145,954	1,380,645	234,691	20.5%	458,157	164,884	18,844	86,430	33,703
Osceola County	268,683	367,990	99,307	37.0%	102,705	48,427	4,802	22,387	7,267
Palm Beach County	1,320,135	1,485,941	165,806	12.6%	552,286	354,838	60,936	213,876	100,477
Pasco County	464,703	539,630	74,927	16.1%	205,128	122,134	13,520	72,140	31,336
Pinellas County	916,804	975,280	58,476	6.4%	405,892	241,848	35,047	150,207	73,628
Polk County	602,098	708,009	105,911	17.6%	241,171	143,426	14,993	84,267	31,331
Putnam County	74,368	74,163	-205	-0.3%	27,927	17,314	717	10,815	4,305
St. Johns County	190,034	254,261	64,227	33.8%	90,109	51,740	4,574	30,553	11,345
St. Lucie County	277,255	321,128	43,873	15.8%	118,768	77,208	7,694	44,264	15,447

Table A-2: Counties - Summary Population Characteristics—*Continued*

	April 1, 2010 Census Population Estimates Base	2018 ACS Population	2010-2018 Population Change	2010-2018 Percent Change	Total Households	2018 ACS			
						Population 65 and Over	Population 85 and Over	Householders 65 and Over	Persons 65 and Over Living Alone
Florida—Cont.									
Santa Rosa County	151,371	179,349	27,978	18.5%	63,891	28,416	2,114	15,555	3,677
Sarasota County	379,435	426,718	47,283	12.5%	183,721	157,066	22,673	95,330	37,125
Seminole County	422,713	467,832	45,119	10.7%	179,274	72,734	8,492	42,666	16,020
Sumter County	93,420	128,754	35,334	37.8%	62,854	73,154	4,848	44,756	16,140
Volusia County	494,596	547,538	52,942	10.7%	218,423	133,744	21,000	78,826	33,216
Walton County	55,043	71,375	16,332	29.7%	28,770	14,517	502	8,972	4,178
Georgia									
Barrow County	69,355	80,809	11,454	16.5%	27,525	10,243	1,006	6,000	2,150
Bartow County	100,128	106,408	6,280	6.3%	35,506	14,651	1,569	7,726	2,247
Bibb County	155,795	153,095	-2,700	-1.7%	57,905	23,974	2,802	15,152	7,294
Bulloch County	70,246	77,296	7,050	10.0%	27,097	8,545	963	5,700	na
Carroll County	110,580	118,121	7,541	6.8%	41,197	16,788	1,261	9,980	4,150
Catoosa County	63,937	67,420	3,483	5.4%	24,722	12,069	799	7,493	na
Chatham County	265,126	289,195	24,069	9.1%	107,921	44,131	4,738	27,712	11,855
Cherokee County	214,372	254,149	39,777	18.6%	89,974	36,209	2,256	20,674	6,165
Clarke County	116,697	127,330	10,633	9.1%	49,698	15,023	1,745	9,394	3,978
Clayton County	259,580	289,615	30,035	11.6%	96,286	26,880	1,689	15,984	6,321
Cobb County	688,071	756,865	68,794	10.0%	283,094	92,828	9,353	54,626	20,436
Columbia County	124,041	154,291	30,250	24.4%	47,167	21,329	2,175	11,988	4,695
Coweta County	127,353	145,864	18,511	14.5%	52,114	20,747	1,544	12,305	3,859
DeKalb County	691,971	756,558	64,587	9.3%	287,001	93,989	11,708	57,625	27,132
Dougherty County	94,562	91,243	-3,319	-3.5%	33,717	13,899	1,987	8,530	3,996
Douglas County	132,305	145,331	13,026	9.8%	49,534	17,286	1,530	9,366	3,032
Fayette County	106,564	113,459	6,895	6.5%	39,366	20,284	2,027	12,900	4,880
Floyd County	96,314	97,927	1,613	1.7%	34,672	16,533	1,843	10,194	4,360
Forsyth County	175,511	236,612	61,101	34.8%	81,353	28,398	1,598	15,347	4,415
Fulton County	920,441	1,050,114	129,673	14.1%	417,157	122,675	13,278	80,507	39,891
Glynn County	79,625	85,219	5,594	7.0%	34,634	16,955	2,011	10,819	3,898
Gwinnett County	805,326	927,781	122,455	15.2%	297,658	93,705	9,315	48,689	15,518
Hall County	179,726	202,148	22,422	12.5%	64,990	30,078	3,197	16,870	5,465
Henry County	203,830	230,220	26,390	12.9%	75,926	26,256	3,449	14,756	5,278
Houston County	139,914	155,469	15,555	11.1%	58,155	18,359	2,032	10,875	4,533
Jackson County	60,457	70,422	9,965	16.5%	23,640	10,244	1,201	5,719	na
Lowndes County	109,248	116,321	7,073	6.5%	41,734	14,530	1,583	9,605	4,298
Muscogee County	190,573	194,160	3,587	1.9%	72,862	26,086	3,698	17,648	8,554
Newton County	99,984	109,541	9,557	9.6%	38,436	14,379	1,294	8,151	1,906
Paulding County	142,379	164,044	21,665	15.2%	53,630	16,871	1,305	9,480	na
Richmond County	200,569	201,554	985	0.5%	70,534	28,148	2,777	19,335	9,979
Rockdale County	85,176	90,594	5,418	6.4%	31,460	12,806	1,088	7,593	3,039
Spalding County	64,098	66,100	2,002	3.1%	25,659	12,014	1,269	7,333	2,235
Troup County	67,039	70,034	2,995	4.5%	25,417	10,065	1,056	6,585	na
Walker County	68,749	69,410	661	1.0%	26,895	13,093	1,227	8,551	3,747
Walton County	83,767	93,503	9,736	11.6%	32,624	14,070	1,388	8,386	2,775
Whitfield County	102,593	104,062	1,469	1.4%	36,658	14,588	1,644	9,248	4,833
Hawaii									
Hawaii County	185,076	200,983	15,907	8.6%	71,565	42,643	4,237	25,848	10,755
Honolulu County	953,206	980,080	26,874	2.8%	308,208	173,612	30,273	91,320	29,882
Kauai County	67,095	72,133	5,038	7.5%	22,685	14,709	1,606	9,017	3,286
Maui County	154,840	167,218	12,378	8.0%	52,794	30,492	3,954	16,935	5,010
Idaho									
Ada County	392,371	469,966	77,595	19.8%	178,712	67,476	6,646	40,387	16,768
Bannock County	82,842	87,138	4,296	5.2%	30,635	12,344	1,616	7,726	3,210
Bonneville County	104,294	116,854	12,560	12.0%	40,224	15,046	2,395	9,539	3,734
Canyon County	188,922	223,499	34,577	18.3%	74,520	31,930	3,481	19,229	7,398
Kootenai County	138,466	161,505	23,039	16.6%	64,955	30,553	2,611	19,738	8,150
Twin Falls County	77,230	86,081	8,851	11.5%	32,041	12,925	1,207	7,820	2,852
Illinois									
Adams County	67,097	65,691	-1,406	-2.1%	26,397	13,297	1,867	8,147	na
Champaign County	201,081	209,983	8,902	4.4%	84,290	26,318	3,662	16,434	8,095
Cook County	5,195,026	5,180,493	-14,533	-0.3%	1,981,796	757,941	100,113	480,363	227,994
DeKalb County	105,160	104,143	-1,017	-1.0%	38,849	13,305	1,540	8,121	3,782
DuPage County	916,771	928,589	11,818	1.3%	345,714	143,761	18,214	85,766	34,430
Kane County	515,378	534,216	18,838	3.7%	183,633	73,081	7,571	43,059	18,071
Kankakee County	113,450	110,024	-3,426	-3.0%	40,642	18,344	2,763	10,631	4,926
Kendall County	114,803	127,915	13,112	11.4%	40,716	13,493	1,875	8,356	2,855
Lake County	703,396	700,832	-2,564	-0.4%	246,620	99,801	12,788	60,453	25,265
LaSalle County	113,915	109,430	-4,485	-3.9%	44,714	20,841	2,540	13,647	6,124
McHenry County	308,827	308,570	-257	-0.1%	114,544	44,617	5,179	26,901	11,267
McLean County	169,577	172,828	3,251	1.9%	65,998	22,728	3,397	14,126	6,144
Macon County	110,775	104,712	-6,063	-5.5%	44,562	21,167	2,441	13,096	5,826
Madison County	269,334	264,461	-4,873	-1.8%	108,977	45,758	5,391	29,762	12,485
Peoria County	186,496	180,621	-5,875	-3.2%	71,506	30,201	4,560	17,416	8,169
Rock Island County	147,546	143,477	-4,069	-2.8%	61,009	26,909	3,289	17,298	7,955
St. Clair County	270,062	261,059	-9,003	-3.3%	104,803	40,953	4,693	26,546	12,876
Sangamon County	197,465	195,348	-2,117	-1.1%	83,006	34,683	4,453	22,318	10,858
Tazewell County	135,392	132,328	-3,064	-2.3%	54,123	25,258	4,480	15,919	6,996
Vermilion County	81,625	76,806	-4,819	-5.9%	30,166	15,156	2,197	9,996	5,249

Table A-2: Counties - Summary Population Characteristics—*Continued*

	April 1, 2010 Census Population Estimates Base	2018 ACS Population	2010-2018 Population Change	2010-2018 Percent Change	Total Households	2018 ACS			
						Population 65 and Over	Population 85 and Over	Householders 65 and Over	Persons 65 and Over Living Alone
Illinois—Cont.									
Will County	677,560	692,310	14,750	2.2%	231,647	90,429	11,009	51,204	17,595
Williamson County	66,365	67,056	691	1.0%	27,815	12,562	1,224	8,284	na
Winnebago County	295,264	284,081	-11,183	-3.8%	114,337	49,568	6,226	31,273	13,216
Indiana									
Allen County	355,335	375,351	20,016	5.6%	147,638	54,528	6,099	35,683	16,914
Bartholomew County	76,786	82,753	5,967	7.8%	31,891	13,549	1,156	8,957	4,323
Boone County	56,638	66,999	10,361	18.3%	24,808	8,752	1,472	5,352	na
Clark County	110,228	117,360	7,132	6.5%	45,905	18,361	1,289	11,810	5,066
Delaware County	117,664	114,772	-2,892	-2.5%	45,311	19,931	3,185	12,849	5,641
Elkhart County	197,559	205,560	8,001	4.0%	73,660	29,730	4,138	17,003	6,355
Floyd County	74,579	77,781	3,202	4.3%	30,300	12,434	1,684	6,881	2,537
Grant County	70,063	65,936	-4,127	-5.9%	26,923	12,533	1,571	8,420	na
Hamilton County	274,569	330,086	55,517	20.2%	122,876	41,308	4,946	24,184	9,452
Hancock County	70,043	76,351	6,308	9.0%	29,605	12,948	1,174	8,585	na
Hendricks County	145,414	167,009	21,595	14.9%	60,368	22,917	1,884	12,843	4,845
Howard County	82,752	82,366	-386	-0.5%	35,139	15,917	2,363	10,516	3,644
Johnson County	139,857	156,225	16,368	11.7%	57,504	22,720	2,029	13,691	5,086
Kosciusko County	77,354	79,344	1,990	2.6%	30,798	13,068	1,548	8,548	3,801
Lake County	496,095	484,411	-11,684	-2.4%	186,769	79,924	10,516	52,044	24,579
LaPorte County	111,463	110,007	-1,456	-1.3%	43,122	19,676	1,943	13,199	6,152
Madison County	131,639	129,641	-1,998	-1.5%	50,426	23,638	2,891	14,595	5,819
Marion County	903,389	954,670	51,281	5.7%	373,634	120,092	14,097	76,295	36,797
Monroe County	137,959	146,917	8,958	6.5%	57,102	19,046	3,224	12,536	5,773
Morgan County	68,943	70,116	1,173	1.7%	25,968	11,732	1,462	7,099	2,659
Porter County	164,302	169,594	5,292	3.2%	66,144	27,395	3,079	16,756	6,665
St. Joseph County	266,925	270,771	3,846	1.4%	107,730	43,160	6,631	27,801	14,058
Tippecanoe County	172,803	193,048	20,245	11.7%	70,446	22,392	3,177	13,694	6,224
Vanderburgh County	179,703	180,974	1,271	0.7%	75,058	30,123	4,504	18,773	8,248
Vigo County	107,848	107,386	-462	-0.4%	43,262	17,118	2,089	9,677	3,816
Wayne County	68,996	65,936	-3,060	-4.4%	28,338	12,445	1,847	8,133	3,681
Iowa									
Black Hawk County	131,090	132,408	1,318	1.0%	53,386	21,218	2,505	13,831	6,115
Dallas County	66,138	90,180	24,042	36.4%	35,492	10,686	1,646	6,967	na
Dubuque County	93,643	96,854	3,211	3.4%	38,501	17,441	2,671	10,313	4,465
Johnson County	130,882	151,260	20,378	15.6%	60,868	17,571	2,093	10,996	4,064
Linn County	211,238	225,909	14,671	6.9%	91,747	36,397	4,681	23,528	11,042
Polk County	430,632	487,204	56,572	13.1%	189,546	63,048	7,258	39,485	18,050
Pottawattamie County	93,149	93,533	384	0.4%	36,635	16,444	2,085	10,494	4,685
Scott County	165,223	173,283	8,060	4.9%	66,905	27,591	3,144	16,858	8,334
Story County	89,542	98,105	8,563	9.6%	37,290	11,562	1,405	7,369	na
Woodbury County	102,175	102,539	364	0.4%	39,253	15,799	2,010	10,023	4,575
Kansas									
Butler County	65,884	66,765	881	1.3%	24,692	10,133	1,161	6,401	na
Douglas County	110,826	121,436	10,610	9.6%	48,907	15,300	2,395	9,782	4,452
Johnson County	544,181	597,555	53,374	9.8%	231,184	86,524	11,116	52,962	20,209
Leavenworth County	76,211	81,352	5,141	6.7%	26,654	12,165	1,671	7,105	3,110
Riley County	71,132	73,703	2,571	3.6%	26,617	7,035	1,030	4,379	na
Sedgwick County	498,358	513,607	15,249	3.1%	198,024	74,308	9,743	47,194	23,001
Shawnee County	177,934	177,499	-435	-0.2%	72,788	32,776	3,615	20,366	9,224
Wyandotte County	157,525	165,324	7,799	5.0%	60,708	20,344	1,605	12,679	5,388
Kentucky									
Boone County	118,815	131,533	12,718	10.7%	47,684	17,363	1,398	10,925	3,794
Bullitt County	74,308	81,069	6,761	9.1%	29,789	13,098	876	7,742	2,607
Campbell County	90,338	93,152	2,814	3.1%	36,992	14,825	1,829	9,207	4,900
Christian County	73,938	71,671	-2,267	-3.1%	26,114	8,870	1,220	5,652	na
Daviess County	96,643	101,104	4,461	4.6%	39,590	17,052	1,861	11,193	4,809
Fayette County	295,867	323,780	27,913	9.4%	131,067	42,959	4,478	26,964	12,739
Hardin County	105,538	110,356	4,818	4.6%	41,625	15,845	1,620	9,928	3,674
Jefferson County	741,075	770,517	29,442	4.0%	311,263	124,421	15,879	79,978	35,159
Kenton County	159,723	166,051	6,328	4.0%	64,611	24,028	2,487	14,963	6,637
McCracken County	65,561	65,346	-215	-0.3%	27,650	13,390	2,654	8,624	4,256
Madison County	82,913	92,368	9,455	11.4%	33,396	12,719	1,463	7,772	3,137
Oldham County	60,354	66,470	6,116	10.1%	21,237	8,651	648	4,507	1,410
Warren County	113,766	131,264	17,498	15.4%	48,843	17,362	1,651	10,751	4,827
Louisiana									
Ascension Parish	107,215	124,672	17,457	16.3%	45,102	14,179	1,529	8,396	2,996
Bossier Parish	117,027	127,185	10,158	8.7%	50,099	17,634	2,125	11,700	5,454
Caddo Parish	254,921	242,922	-11,999	-4.7%	94,778	41,620	5,211	26,450	11,429
Calcasieu Parish	192,773	203,112	10,339	5.4%	78,351	30,465	3,451	20,476	9,197
East Baton Rouge Parish	440,169	440,956	787	0.2%	163,274	62,577	6,571	38,674	15,677
Iberia Parish	73,094	70,941	-2,153	-2.9%	25,386	10,381	826	7,137	na
Jefferson Parish	432,573	434,051	1,478	0.3%	167,596	74,241	8,064	45,851	19,321
Lafayette Parish	221,724	242,782	21,058	9.5%	94,002	31,864	3,394	19,755	7,935
Lafourche Parish	96,662	98,115	1,453	1.5%	35,838	15,537	1,818	9,583	4,021
Livingston Parish	128,015	139,567	11,552	9.0%	49,084	18,939	1,584	9,735	3,783

Table A-2: Counties - Summary Population Characteristics—*Continued*

	April 1, 2010 Census Population Estimates Base	2018 ACS Population	2010-2018 Population Change	2010-2018 Percent Change	Total Households	2018 ACS			
						Population 65 and Over	Population 85 and Over	Householders 65 and Over	Persons 65 and Over Living Alone
Louisiana—Cont.									
Orleans Parish	343,828	391,006	47,178	13.7%	155,104	57,532	5,890	35,584	19,880
Ouachita Parish	153,731	154,475	744	0.5%	55,599	22,852	2,196	13,610	6,025
Rapides Parish	131,609	130,562	-1,047	-0.8%	48,915	21,274	2,054	13,287	6,388
St. Landry Parish	83,384	82,764	-620	-0.7%	29,965	13,167	1,402	8,223	3,947
St. Tammany Parish	233,754	258,111	24,357	10.4%	93,589	43,644	4,636	26,871	10,396
Tangipahoa Parish	121,107	133,777	12,670	10.5%	47,401	19,087	1,316	11,765	5,214
Terrebonne Parish	111,522	111,021	-501	-0.4%	37,911	16,642	1,436	10,103	3,665
Maine									
Androscoggin County	107,710	107,679	-31	-0.0%	44,897	19,292	2,055	12,277	6,291
Aroostook County	71,873	67,111	-4,762	-6.6%	29,931	16,193	2,822	10,076	5,199
Cumberland County	281,676	293,557	11,881	4.2%	123,485	53,973	6,638	34,701	15,645
Kennebec County	122,154	122,083	-71	-0.1%	54,299	24,870	3,578	16,362	7,734
Penobscot County	153,932	151,096	-2,836	-1.8%	61,765	27,761	3,630	17,420	8,188
York County	197,140	206,229	9,089	4.6%	88,416	42,314	4,575	27,343	11,673
Maryland									
Allegany County	75,047	70,975	-4,072	-5.4%	27,190	14,147	1,132	9,052	4,440
Anne Arundel County	537,631	576,031	38,400	7.1%	212,687	84,811	9,261	51,838	19,183
Baltimore County	805,229	828,431	23,202	2.9%	313,259	142,542	20,360	86,617	39,553
Calvert County	88,739	92,003	3,264	3.7%	32,145	13,475	1,555	7,043	2,557
Carroll County	167,142	168,429	1,287	0.8%	60,371	27,509	3,370	16,008	6,055
Cecil County	101,102	102,826	1,724	1.7%	36,620	16,204	1,894	9,943	3,330
Charles County	146,565	161,503	14,938	10.2%	56,947	19,917	2,322	10,869	3,262
Frederick County	233,391	255,648	22,257	9.5%	95,903	36,820	4,629	22,623	9,756
Harford County	244,826	253,956	9,130	3.7%	94,802	42,005	4,790	25,045	10,205
Howard County	287,123	323,196	36,073	12.6%	116,903	44,739	3,608	25,500	9,519
Montgomery County	971,964	1,052,567	80,603	8.3%	368,334	163,645	21,765	91,392	36,432
Prince George's County	863,349	909,308	45,959	5.3%	315,759	120,625	11,940	70,471	29,302
St. Mary's County	105,143	112,664	7,521	7.2%	41,239	15,006	1,132	9,007	4,065
Washington County	147,430	150,926	3,496	2.4%	56,306	26,066	2,751	15,971	6,763
Wicomico County	98,733	103,195	4,462	4.5%	38,084	16,246	1,751	10,517	4,445
Massachusetts									
Barnstable County	215,875	213,413	-2,462	-1.1%	86,671	65,453	7,670	39,226	15,767
Berkshire County	131,275	126,348	-4,927	-3.8%	55,212	29,239	3,829	18,271	8,300
Bristol County	548,254	564,022	15,768	2.9%	215,132	94,856	13,241	59,402	26,444
Essex County	743,081	790,638	47,557	6.4%	295,481	134,878	20,793	80,745	35,088
Franklin County	71,377	70,963	-414	-0.6%	30,391	15,424	2,182	9,784	4,462
Hampden County	463,625	470,406	6,781	1.5%	178,678	78,765	12,063	49,293	22,834
Hampshire County	158,056	161,355	3,299	2.1%	58,902	27,968	3,080	17,362	7,868
Middlesex County	1,503,123	1,614,714	111,591	7.4%	612,224	246,060	33,994	152,626	68,232
Norfolk County	670,907	705,388	34,481	5.1%	267,880	118,958	18,516	73,338	32,378
Plymouth County	494,937	518,132	23,195	4.7%	189,304	93,606	10,661	56,023	23,538
Suffolk County	722,190	807,252	85,062	11.8%	315,049	96,952	11,683	62,805	33,250
Worcester County	798,383	830,839	32,456	4.1%	308,831	129,842	15,596	77,110	35,000
Michigan									
Allegan County	111,407	117,327	5,920	5.3%	43,992	19,808	1,994	11,325	3,767
Bay County	107,773	103,923	-3,850	-3.6%	44,469	20,857	3,051	13,107	5,689
Berrien County	156,811	154,141	-2,670	-1.7%	64,783	30,468	4,686	19,901	8,338
Calhoun County	136,148	134,487	-1,661	-1.2%	53,914	24,047	3,723	15,477	6,857
Clinton County	75,367	79,332	3,965	5.3%	29,783	13,620	1,015	8,604	3,479
Eaton County	107,763	109,826	2,063	1.9%	44,879	20,280	1,910	12,391	4,894
Genesee County	425,789	406,892	-18,897	-4.4%	169,469	71,160	7,505	47,441	20,834
Grand Traverse County	86,981	92,573	5,592	6.4%	36,782	18,378	2,684	11,527	4,675
Ingham County	280,891	292,735	11,844	4.2%	112,170	39,816	5,759	25,597	11,794
Isabella County	70,313	70,562	249	0.4%	25,367	9,094	990	5,749	2,673
Jackson County	160,245	158,823	-1,422	-0.9%	62,598	28,547	3,269	17,558	8,067
Kalamazoo County	250,327	264,820	14,543	5.8%	104,234	39,828	4,425	25,026	12,175
Kent County	602,628	653,786	51,158	8.5%	244,046	89,751	10,779	56,530	25,688
Lapeer County	88,318	88,028	-290	-0.3%	33,560	15,967	1,369	10,168	4,128
Lenawee County	99,892	98,266	-1,626	-1.6%	38,388	18,092	2,130	11,422	4,978
Livingston County	180,961	191,224	10,263	5.7%	72,676	33,118	2,895	20,572	7,114
Macomb County	841,039	874,759	33,720	4.0%	347,508	149,007	18,692	93,956	43,609
Marquette County	67,071	66,516	-555	-0.8%	26,328	12,824	1,500	8,026	3,669
Midland County	83,626	83,209	-417	-0.5%	34,091	15,539	2,269	9,892	4,387
Monroe County	152,024	150,439	-1,585	-1.0%	61,586	27,543	3,738	18,137	7,605
Muskegon County	172,194	173,588	1,394	0.8%	67,196	29,441	3,263	18,617	7,321
Oakland County	1,202,384	1,259,201	56,817	4.7%	503,645	211,586	27,438	133,560	60,599
Ottawa County	263,795	290,494	26,699	10.1%	103,438	43,416	5,329	26,813	10,201
Saginaw County	200,169	190,800	-9,369	-4.7%	78,740	36,766	5,153	23,894	10,526
St. Clair County	163,049	159,337	-3,712	-2.3%	65,751	30,013	2,807	18,670	7,417
Shiawassee County	70,663	68,192	-2,471	-3.5%	28,218	12,597	1,419	7,895	3,344
Van Buren County	76,264	75,448	-816	-1.1%	28,607	14,089	1,373	8,273	3,068
Washtenaw County	345,104	370,963	25,859	7.5%	143,072	51,775	5,935	32,797	13,390
Wayne County	1,820,539	1,753,893	-66,646	-3.7%	687,546	270,261	33,176	179,772	88,429

Table A-2: Counties - Summary Population Characteristics—*Continued*

	April 1, 2010 Census Population Estimates Base	2018 ACS Population	2010-2018 Population Change	2010-2018 Percent Change	Total Households	2018 ACS			
						Population 65 and Over	Population 85 and Over	Householders 65 and Over	Persons 65 and Over Living Alone
Minnesota									
Anoka County	330,858	353,813	22,955	6.9%	128,140	49,826	4,354	29,075	11,204
Blue Earth County	64,013	67,427	3,414	5.3%	26,362	9,447	1,589	5,618	na
Carver County	91,086	103,551	12,465	13.7%	36,925	12,680	514	7,658	3,153
Dakota County	398,583	425,423	26,840	6.7%	162,496	59,233	6,412	36,874	16,115
Hennepin County	1,152,385	1,259,428	107,043	9.3%	508,964	176,860	23,877	111,929	53,436
Olmsted County	144,260	156,277	12,017	8.3%	63,462	24,295	3,483	14,876	6,564
Ramsey County	508,639	550,210	41,571	8.2%	209,287	79,420	11,530	51,150	25,734
Rice County	64,142	66,523	2,381	3.7%	23,358	10,297	1,714	6,671	3,179
St. Louis County	200,231	199,754	-477	-0.2%	84,370	38,593	5,692	24,853	12,070
Scott County	129,912	147,381	17,469	13.4%	50,040	16,292	1,999	8,759	2,670
Sherburne County	88,492	96,036	7,544	8.5%	32,033	10,593	1,360	6,298	2,515
Stearns County	150,642	159,256	8,614	5.7%	58,510	23,995	3,498	14,462	6,228
Washington County	238,114	259,201	21,087	8.9%	96,387	38,724	4,175	23,743	9,748
Wright County	124,697	136,349	11,652	9.3%	48,863	17,122	1,400	10,471	3,880
Mississippi									
DeSoto County	161,267	182,001	20,734	12.9%	63,075	22,973	2,171	13,892	5,750
Forrest County	74,928	75,036	108	0.1%	27,248	10,366	1,195	6,425	3,141
Harrison County	187,105	206,650	19,545	10.4%	82,375	30,988	2,845	19,440	7,412
Hinds County	245,365	237,085	-8,280	-3.4%	85,483	33,279	3,850	19,645	8,127
Jackson County	139,668	143,277	3,609	2.6%	51,659	22,736	815	14,177	5,236
Jones County	67,769	68,461	692	1.0%	25,098	11,875	1,375	7,485	2,735
Lauderdale County	80,267	75,317	-4,950	-6.2%	29,993	12,938	1,753	8,416	na
Lee County	82,910	85,202	2,292	2.8%	32,527	12,097	1,115	7,784	na
Madison County	95,203	105,630	10,427	11.0%	40,229	13,758	1,736	8,409	na
Rankin County	142,054	153,902	11,848	8.3%	55,483	23,460	2,160	14,879	6,560
Missouri									
Boone County	162,645	180,005	17,360	10.7%	72,217	21,937	3,032	14,295	6,664
Buchanan County	89,190	88,571	-619	-0.7%	33,621	15,014	2,038	9,946	3,832
Cape Girardeau County	75,673	78,753	3,080	4.1%	28,675	12,949	1,914	7,618	3,262
Cass County	99,505	104,954	5,449	5.5%	40,197	17,994	1,949	11,620	4,757
Christian County	77,417	86,983	9,566	12.4%	31,421	13,424	1,891	8,121	na
Clay County	221,943	246,365	24,422	11.0%	91,901	34,841	3,298	20,702	8,732
Cole County	75,975	76,796	821	1.1%	29,593	12,974	1,053	8,385	na
Franklin County	101,495	103,670	2,175	2.1%	40,387	17,948	2,201	11,011	4,566
Greene County	275,178	291,923	16,745	6.1%	128,691	48,313	5,816	32,556	16,571
Jackson County	674,134	700,307	26,173	3.9%	288,752	104,740	13,748	66,109	28,926
Jasper County	117,391	120,636	3,245	2.8%	47,846	18,699	2,312	13,326	6,502
Jefferson County	218,708	224,347	5,639	2.6%	85,892	33,824	3,014	20,859	8,424
Platte County	89,325	102,985	13,660	15.3%	40,086	15,028	1,337	8,509	2,786
St. Charles County	360,494	399,182	38,688	10.7%	149,951	59,689	6,712	37,374	14,926
St. Francois County	65,367	66,692	1,325	2.0%	25,670	11,343	1,561	7,061	na
St. Louis County	998,986	996,945	-2,041	-0.2%	408,117	180,521	24,454	115,361	48,700
Montana									
Cascade County	81,323	81,643	320	0.4%	35,558	15,005	1,940	9,377	4,494
Flathead County	90,927	102,106	11,179	12.3%	38,372	19,958	1,403	11,891	4,845
Gallatin County	89,513	111,876	22,363	25.0%	44,423	14,428	1,108	8,441	3,005
Lewis and Clark County	63,395	68,700	5,305	8.4%	27,842	12,668	1,813	7,748	3,558
Missoula County	109,296	118,791	9,495	8.7%	50,401	18,257	1,528	11,491	4,892
Yellowstone County	147,982	160,137	12,155	8.2%	66,805	27,163	3,942	17,535	7,808
Nebraska									
Douglas County	517,114	566,880	49,766	9.6%	220,858	73,861	9,740	48,243	23,783
Lancaster County	285,407	317,272	31,865	11.2%	125,917	43,830	5,149	28,792	13,191
Sarpy County	158,835	184,459	25,624	16.1%	66,273	22,169	2,881	13,859	5,604
Nevada									
Clark County	1,951,271	2,231,647	280,376	14.4%	808,605	328,690	31,017	187,797	74,898
Washoe County	421,425	465,735	44,310	10.5%	185,709	76,172	7,186	47,863	20,510
New Hampshire									
Cheshire County	77,122	76,493	-629	-0.8%	30,208	15,095	1,244	9,178	4,566
Grafton County	89,137	89,786	649	0.7%	35,394	18,635	2,226	11,656	4,721
Hillsborough County	400,699	415,247	14,548	3.6%	161,649	64,850	8,636	38,337	16,386
Merrimack County	146,457	151,132	4,675	3.2%	58,521	28,423	3,875	16,924	7,849
Rockingham County	295,211	309,176	13,965	4.7%	119,467	55,401	6,797	31,923	12,361
Strafford County	123,149	130,090	6,941	5.6%	48,393	19,182	2,464	11,506	4,624
New Jersey									
Atlantic County	274,521	265,429	-9,092	-3.3%	96,981	47,558	5,068	28,355	10,649
Bergen County	905,143	936,692	31,549	3.5%	339,953	160,999	26,056	94,096	38,637
Burlington County	448,730	445,384	-3,346	-0.7%	166,698	75,275	9,730	46,078	18,824
Camden County	513,719	507,078	-6,641	-1.3%	188,840	79,240	9,136	50,199	22,044
Cape May County	97,261	92,560	-4,701	-4.8%	39,208	24,068	2,635	14,880	6,081
Cumberland County	156,633	150,972	-5,661	-3.6%	50,034	23,222	2,317	14,558	6,796
Essex County	783,885	799,767	15,882	2.0%	289,921	108,532	15,642	64,811	28,179
Gloucester County	288,570	291,408	2,838	1.0%	101,414	46,579	6,059	27,052	10,958
Hudson County	634,245	676,061	41,816	6.6%	263,924	79,918	10,725	49,125	22,531
Hunterdon County	127,357	124,714	-2,643	-2.1%	47,733	23,280	2,922	13,988	5,202

Table A-2: Counties - Summary Population Characteristics—*Continued*

	April 1, 2010 Census Population Estimates Base	2018 ACS Population	2010-2018 Population Change	2010-2018 Percent Change	Total Households	2018 ACS Population 65 and Over	2018 ACS Population 85 and Over	2018 ACS Householders 65 and Over	2018 ACS Persons 65 and Over Living Alone
New Jersey—Cont.									
Mercer County	367,511	369,811	2,300	0.6%	132,980	56,001	7,193	35,066	15,731
Middlesex County	809,924	829,685	19,761	2.4%	285,480	124,138	18,158	70,241	27,367
Monmouth County	630,374	621,354	-9,020	-1.4%	236,327	109,200	14,565	69,245	29,281
Morris County	492,314	494,228	1,914	0.4%	181,738	84,314	12,437	48,046	17,767
Ocean County	576,546	601,651	25,105	4.4%	228,622	136,278	18,547	90,433	40,288
Passaic County	501,609	503,310	1,701	0.3%	169,521	73,211	9,257	41,317	15,262
Salem County	66,066	62,607	-3,459	-5.2%	23,952	11,735	1,431	7,083	2,685
Somerset County	323,433	331,164	7,731	2.4%	118,729	51,619	7,227	29,312	10,326
Sussex County	148,909	140,799	-8,110	-5.4%	53,749	23,676	1,947	14,851	5,179
Union County	536,567	558,067	21,500	4.0%	192,021	80,253	11,851	46,489	20,708
Warren County	108,645	105,779	-2,866	-2.6%	41,742	19,193	2,855	12,242	5,884
New Mexico									
Bernalillo County	662,487	678,701	16,214	2.4%	270,655	111,216	13,687	69,183	31,982
Chaves County	65,648	64,689	-959	-1.5%	22,616	10,830	1,559	6,568	2,938
Doña Ana County	209,202	217,522	8,320	4.0%	80,409	34,786	3,125	20,682	8,365
Lea County	64,727	69,611	4,884	7.5%	23,215	7,856	924	4,873	2,272
McKinley County	71,485	72,290	805	1.1%	21,449	9,281	1,514	5,709	1,782
Otero County	63,832	66,781	2,949	4.6%	23,747	10,722	829	6,635	na
Sandoval County	131,620	145,179	13,559	10.3%	53,996	25,763	2,094	15,111	4,376
San Juan County	130,045	125,043	-5,002	-3.8%	43,707	19,101	2,223	12,097	4,203
Santa Fe County	144,227	150,056	5,829	4.0%	62,707	36,568	2,730	22,869	9,366
Valencia County	76,582	76,456	-126	-0.2%	28,379	13,675	1,754	8,607	3,522
New York									
Albany County	304,208	307,117	2,909	1.0%	126,578	52,316	7,050	32,402	15,501
Bronx County	1,384,603	1,432,132	47,529	3.4%	507,370	183,165	21,188	115,624	60,592
Broome County	200,675	191,659	-9,016	-4.5%	75,539	36,793	6,334	23,184	10,636
Cattaraugus County	80,343	76,840	-3,503	-4.4%	32,079	14,641	1,524	9,120	3,804
Cayuga County	80,017	77,145	-2,872	-3.6%	30,083	14,322	1,676	8,949	4,196
Chautauqua County	134,907	127,939	-6,968	-5.2%	53,429	25,587	3,908	15,814	7,314
Chemung County	88,849	84,254	-4,595	-5.2%	34,325	16,613	1,905	10,247	4,715
Clinton County	82,131	80,695	-1,436	-1.7%	31,392	13,523	1,498	8,126	3,601
Dutchess County	297,462	293,718	-3,744	-1.3%	108,071	51,573	6,488	31,844	13,753
Erie County	919,129	919,719	590	0.1%	390,341	165,216	23,971	108,411	53,168
Jefferson County	116,234	111,755	-4,479	-3.9%	44,657	15,458	1,648	9,611	4,396
Kings County	2,504,717	2,582,830	78,113	3.1%	969,317	358,797	45,796	222,026	100,985
Livingston County	65,207	63,227	-1,980	-3.0%	23,746	11,117	1,016	6,572	2,653
Madison County	73,451	70,795	-2,656	-3.6%	26,127	13,087	1,389	7,634	3,220
Monroe County	744,399	742,474	-1,925	-0.3%	301,668	128,110	17,686	81,774	39,327
Nassau County	1,339,885	1,358,343	18,458	1.4%	447,123	241,330	39,183	137,207	50,657
New York County	1,586,360	1,628,701	42,341	2.7%	752,258	268,834	39,609	183,754	109,291
Niagara County	216,485	210,433	-6,052	-2.8%	89,765	39,813	5,800	26,063	12,378
Oneida County	234,869	229,577	-5,292	-2.3%	88,871	42,555	6,889	25,518	11,025
Onondaga County	467,064	461,809	-5,255	-1.1%	185,046	78,867	12,018	50,806	23,554
Ontario County	108,090	109,864	1,774	1.6%	44,079	21,645	2,645	13,724	6,414
Orange County	372,829	381,951	9,122	2.4%	128,259	53,391	7,057	31,943	13,210
Oswego County	122,105	117,898	-4,207	-3.4%	46,270	19,449	1,709	12,220	5,785
Putnam County	99,650	98,892	-758	-0.8%	35,425	17,094	1,596	9,588	3,384
Queens County	2,230,578	2,278,906	48,328	2.2%	788,110	357,630	45,173	199,825	81,145
Rensselaer County	159,433	159,442	9	0.0%	64,614	26,557	3,732	17,102	6,789
Richmond County	468,730	476,179	7,449	1.6%	167,441	77,054	8,601	45,957	18,686
Rockland County	311,694	325,695	14,001	4.5%	99,502	51,109	7,876	29,598	10,741
St. Lawrence County	111,940	108,047	-3,893	-3.5%	41,680	18,468	2,550	12,077	6,062
Saratoga County	219,593	230,163	10,570	4.8%	94,156	40,850	4,076	25,959	11,024
Schenectady County	154,751	155,350	599	0.4%	55,262	26,852	4,314	16,415	6,963
Steuben County	98,990	95,796	-3,194	-3.2%	40,578	18,663	2,160	11,538	5,442
Suffolk County	1,493,147	1,481,093	-12,054	-0.8%	496,784	250,082	31,103	144,184	53,877
Sullivan County	77,504	75,498	-2,006	-2.6%	28,900	14,198	1,117	8,582	4,034
Tompkins County	101,580	102,793	1,213	1.2%	40,250	14,209	2,039	9,079	3,639
Ulster County	182,512	178,599	-3,913	-2.1%	69,154	35,125	4,398	21,616	9,360
Warren County	65,698	64,265	-1,433	-2.2%	28,007	14,361	2,261	9,284	4,234
Wayne County	93,754	90,064	-3,690	-3.9%	35,927	17,292	2,110	10,643	4,441
Westchester County	949,220	967,612	18,392	1.9%	352,498	165,337	26,582	102,529	46,808
North Carolina									
Alamance County	151,160	166,436	15,276	10.1%	64,700	28,381	3,361	17,636	8,875
Brunswick County	107,429	136,744	29,315	27.3%	56,752	43,663	2,703	25,219	7,422
Buncombe County	238,331	259,103	20,772	8.7%	108,411	51,821	7,511	32,253	14,656
Burke County	90,832	90,382	-450	-0.5%	36,157	18,047	1,702	10,686	4,290
Cabarrus County	178,087	211,342	33,255	18.7%	73,751	28,208	3,071	16,169	6,219
Caldwell County	83,060	82,029	-1,031	-1.2%	31,544	16,043	2,011	9,499	3,580
Carteret County	66,463	69,524	3,061	4.6%	28,720	17,455	1,613	11,038	4,469
Catawba County	154,753	158,652	3,899	2.5%	62,861	28,020	3,006	18,289	7,161
Chatham County	63,481	73,139	9,658	15.2%	28,343	17,876	2,840	10,611	3,887
Cleveland County	98,032	97,645	-387	-0.4%	34,574	18,097	2,074	10,539	3,984
Craven County	103,503	102,912	-591	-0.6%	40,412	19,588	1,630	12,794	5,671
Cumberland County	319,433	332,330	12,897	4.0%	127,911	40,158	3,700	25,938	12,455
Davidson County	162,841	166,614	3,773	2.3%	68,761	30,038	2,636	18,381	7,940
Durham County	269,999	316,739	46,740	17.3%	127,527	41,915	4,202	25,415	9,744

Table A-2: Counties - Summary Population Characteristics—*Continued*

	April 1, 2010 Census Population Estimates Base	2018 ACS Population	2010-2018 Population Change	2010-2018 Percent Change	Total Households	2018 ACS			
						Population 65 and Over	Population 85 and Over	Householders 65 and Over	Persons 65 and Over Living Alone
North Carolina—Cont.									
Forsyth County	350,649	379,099	28,450	8.1%	150,437	60,385	7,111	39,419	19,214
Franklin County	60,553	67,560	7,007	11.6%	26,380	11,633	950	6,965	2,144
Gaston County	206,094	222,846	16,752	8.1%	84,999	35,389	3,645	22,081	9,400
Guilford County	488,421	533,670	45,249	9.3%	209,842	80,474	10,598	50,210	20,794
Harnett County	114,681	134,214	19,533	17.0%	46,015	17,041	1,380	9,992	4,051
Henderson County	106,713	116,748	10,035	9.4%	49,514	30,339	3,661	18,920	7,263
Iredell County	159,451	178,435	18,984	11.9%	68,328	27,867	2,547	16,967	6,149
Johnston County	168,877	202,675	33,798	20.0%	70,001	27,396	3,135	15,581	7,509
Lincoln County	77,985	83,770	5,785	7.4%	34,233	14,281	1,364	8,680	2,614
Mecklenburg County	919,668	1,093,901	174,233	18.9%	418,135	122,591	12,802	72,989	31,309
Moore County	88,242	98,682	10,440	11.8%	40,756	23,584	3,053	14,474	5,748
Nash County	95,829	94,016	-1,813	-1.9%	37,767	17,446	1,855	12,037	5,295
New Hanover County	202,683	232,274	29,591	14.6%	98,151	41,479	4,952	26,105	12,130
Onslow County	177,799	197,683	19,884	11.2%	66,834	18,036	1,610	10,186	3,775
Orange County	133,702	146,027	12,325	9.2%	53,959	20,753	972	12,791	5,218
Pitt County	168,167	179,914	11,747	7.0%	69,288	23,540	2,309	14,472	6,075
Randolph County	141,823	143,351	1,528	1.1%	54,783	25,207	2,452	15,535	6,120
Robeson County	134,229	131,831	-2,398	-1.8%	46,026	19,861	2,330	12,744	4,876
Rockingham County	93,641	90,690	-2,951	-3.2%	37,476	18,633	2,390	12,727	5,672
Rowan County	138,532	141,262	2,730	2.0%	53,806	24,596	2,601	15,670	6,468
Rutherford County	67,816	66,826	-990	-1.5%	26,305	14,058	1,281	9,054	3,216
Surry County	73,743	71,948	-1,795	-2.4%	29,230	15,066	1,964	9,879	4,348
Union County	201,334	235,908	34,574	17.2%	77,696	29,790	2,920	16,342	5,562
Wake County	901,058	1,092,305	191,247	21.2%	408,473	126,840	12,571	75,259	29,554
Wayne County	122,673	123,248	575	0.5%	49,019	20,507	1,988	13,389	5,179
Wilkes County	69,310	68,557	-753	-1.1%	30,123	14,695	1,297	10,532	5,099
Wilson County	81,218	81,455	237	0.3%	31,817	14,804	1,501	9,989	5,993
North Dakota									
Burleigh County	81,308	95,273	13,965	17.2%	40,736	15,157	2,661	9,661	na
Cass County	149,778	181,516	31,738	21.2%	74,343	21,599	3,206	13,333	6,179
Grand Forks County	66,864	70,770	3,906	5.8%	30,916	8,863	1,175	5,666	2,511
Ward County	61,675	67,744	6,069	9.8%	27,887	8,462	1,424	5,402	na
Ohio									
Allen County	106,315	102,663	-3,652	-3.4%	41,204	17,930	1,931	11,540	5,465
Ashtabula County	101,490	97,493	-3,997	-3.9%	35,445	18,569	2,281	11,704	5,038
Athens County	64,764	65,818	1,054	1.6%	22,533	8,637	1,103	5,581	2,990
Belmont County	70,405	67,505	-2,900	-4.1%	24,742	14,350	2,069	8,880	na
Butler County	368,135	382,378	14,243	3.9%	143,040	56,272	6,490	34,810	14,443
Clark County	138,341	134,585	-3,756	-2.7%	55,327	25,957	3,849	17,429	8,162
Clermont County	197,365	205,466	8,101	4.1%	77,920	32,976	3,187	20,408	8,747
Columbiana County	107,852	102,665	-5,187	-4.8%	41,884	21,175	2,147	12,925	5,398
Cuyahoga County	1,280,115	1,243,857	-36,258	-2.8%	542,122	226,137	31,808	150,843	77,143
Delaware County	174,172	204,826	30,654	17.6%	70,501	27,578	2,905	16,459	6,256
Erie County	77,066	74,615	-2,451	-3.2%	31,675	16,157	2,718	10,135	4,879
Fairfield County	146,182	155,782	9,600	6.6%	55,934	24,675	2,170	15,127	6,127
Franklin County	1,163,532	1,310,300	146,768	12.6%	519,468	157,541	18,180	100,883	42,998
Geauga County	93,409	94,031	622	0.7%	35,387	19,507	2,027	11,976	3,880
Greene County	161,576	167,995	6,419	4.0%	66,053	29,059	2,286	18,525	6,977
Hamilton County	802,372	816,684	14,312	1.8%	344,562	125,017	16,897	81,102	40,485
Hancock County	74,789	75,930	1,141	1.5%	31,606	12,829	1,977	8,173	3,795
Jefferson County	69,711	65,767	-3,944	-5.7%	27,292	14,457	1,518	9,203	4,176
Lake County	230,050	230,514	464	0.2%	96,577	46,347	5,847	28,890	11,172
Licking County	166,482	175,769	9,287	5.6%	62,237	28,733	3,520	16,952	6,466
Lorain County	301,371	309,461	8,090	2.7%	121,344	56,905	7,094	35,685	15,579
Lucas County	441,815	429,899	-11,916	-2.7%	178,289	70,209	8,461	43,704	19,954
Mahoning County	238,788	229,642	-9,146	-3.8%	97,365	48,140	8,163	30,605	15,360
Marion County	66,501	65,256	-1,245	-1.9%	24,205	11,407	1,689	6,905	3,058
Medina County	172,333	179,146	6,813	4.0%	70,609	32,074	3,000	19,624	7,080
Miami County	102,501	106,222	3,721	3.6%	41,148	20,536	1,822	11,957	5,568
Montgomery County	535,191	532,331	-2,860	-0.5%	224,225	95,644	13,646	62,017	29,250
Muskingum County	86,086	86,183	97	0.1%	34,471	15,189	1,424	10,134	4,282
Portage County	161,425	162,927	1,502	0.9%	60,801	27,185	2,762	16,186	7,286
Richland County	124,474	121,099	-3,375	-2.7%	48,105	23,735	3,751	15,028	6,416
Ross County	78,078	76,931	-1,147	-1.5%	29,779	13,356	692	8,430	3,311
Scioto County	79,493	75,502	-3,991	-5.0%	28,719	13,526	1,671	8,572	3,771
Stark County	375,590	371,574	-4,016	-1.1%	152,210	72,062	9,795	45,960	20,150
Summit County	541,778	541,918	140	0.0%	226,243	97,467	13,065	61,595	27,418
Trumbull County	210,325	198,627	-11,698	-5.6%	83,303	43,149	6,266	27,428	12,411
Tuscarawas County	92,587	92,176	-411	-0.4%	36,740	18,027	2,252	11,470	6,010
Warren County	212,820	232,173	19,353	9.1%	83,540	33,380	4,439	19,136	6,734
Wayne County	114,516	115,967	1,451	1.3%	43,908	20,264	2,366	12,744	4,994
Wood County	125,489	130,696	5,207	4.1%	50,694	20,051	2,790	12,245	4,627
Oklahoma									
Canadian County	115,540	144,447	28,907	25.0%	45,344	18,831	2,714	10,317	3,979
Cleveland County	256,009	281,669	25,660	10.0%	110,775	37,308	3,826	24,398	10,468
Comanche County	124,098	120,422	-3,676	-3.0%	42,489	15,223	1,873	9,851	4,408

Table A-2: Counties - Summary Population Characteristics—*Continued*

	April 1, 2010 Census Population Estimates Base	2018 ACS Population	2010-2018 Population Change	2010-2018 Percent Change	Total Households	2018 ACS Population 65 and Over	Population 85 and Over	Householders 65 and Over	Persons 65 and Over Living Alone
Oklahoma—Cont.									
Creek County	69,971	71,604	1,633	2.3%	26,957	12,424	1,760	8,005	3,094
Muskogee County	70,988	68,362	-2,626	-3.7%	26,566	11,320	1,478	7,165	3,270
Oklahoma County	718,377	792,582	74,205	10.3%	302,645	108,277	13,902	69,935	32,734
Payne County	77,350	82,040	4,690	6.1%	30,734	10,980	1,341	7,462	na
Pottawatomie County	69,443	72,679	3,236	4.7%	26,714	11,821	1,805	7,298	3,168
Rogers County	86,918	91,984	5,066	5.8%	35,254	14,987	1,574	8,552	3,209
Tulsa County	603,437	648,360	44,923	7.4%	250,492	93,319	10,975	59,066	26,408
Wagoner County	73,082	80,110	7,028	9.6%	30,186	12,971	959	8,077	2,818
Oregon									
Benton County	85,582	92,101	6,519	7.6%	35,520	14,843	1,412	8,774	3,076
Clackamas County	375,996	416,075	40,079	10.7%	158,749	74,649	8,426	45,626	18,687
Deschutes County	157,730	191,996	34,266	21.7%	79,950	38,748	4,754	25,139	9,571
Douglas County	107,684	110,283	2,599	2.4%	45,647	27,924	2,281	17,844	6,466
Jackson County	203,205	219,564	16,359	8.1%	89,787	48,689	6,082	29,411	12,533
Josephine County	82,718	87,393	4,675	5.7%	37,059	22,863	1,924	14,454	5,873
Klamath County	66,380	67,653	1,273	1.9%	26,798	14,610	1,581	8,846	4,298
Lane County	351,704	379,611	27,907	7.9%	156,072	73,700	7,578	46,536	19,758
Linn County	116,676	127,335	10,659	9.1%	48,464	24,586	3,069	15,144	6,168
Marion County	315,343	346,868	31,525	10.0%	119,511	53,475	6,568	31,849	13,476
Multnomah County	735,148	811,880	76,732	10.4%	330,223	108,862	11,642	70,367	35,880
Polk County	75,407	85,234	9,827	13.0%	31,218	15,300	1,566	9,211	2,905
Umatilla County	75,885	77,516	1,631	2.1%	26,048	11,922	1,245	7,442	3,282
Washington County	529,860	597,695	67,835	12.8%	225,955	80,377	9,604	49,424	20,411
Yamhill County	99,209	107,002	7,793	7.9%	37,235	17,824	2,161	11,361	4,927
Pennsylvania									
Adams County	101,424	102,811	1,387	1.4%	39,570	20,634	2,289	12,529	5,474
Allegheny County	1,223,323	1,218,452	-4,871	-0.4%	543,369	229,919	33,833	153,284	77,933
Armstrong County	68,944	65,263	-3,681	-5.3%	27,332	14,277	1,881	9,246	4,007
Beaver County	170,549	164,742	-5,807	-3.4%	73,059	35,619	4,737	23,418	10,870
Berks County	411,556	420,152	8,596	2.1%	157,006	72,315	10,860	43,204	18,558
Blair County	127,116	122,492	-4,624	-3.6%	51,096	25,493	3,145	16,090	7,234
Bucks County	625,266	628,195	2,929	0.5%	239,962	117,060	13,463	69,401	27,335
Butler County	183,856	187,888	4,032	2.2%	77,764	34,949	5,618	22,151	9,946
Cambria County	143,681	131,730	-11,951	-8.3%	56,483	29,664	4,365	19,834	8,569
Carbon County	65,252	64,227	-1,025	-1.6%	25,177	13,384	1,781	8,006	na
Centre County	154,001	162,805	8,804	5.7%	58,514	22,815	2,676	13,802	5,739
Chester County	499,133	522,046	22,913	4.6%	192,746	85,168	10,541	51,086	19,136
Clearfield County	81,616	79,388	-2,228	-2.7%	31,992	16,267	2,117	10,186	4,770
Columbia County	67,303	65,456	-1,847	-2.7%	26,655	12,712	2,114	7,962	4,318
Crawford County	88,750	85,063	-3,687	-4.2%	34,386	17,556	1,692	11,241	4,362
Cumberland County	235,405	251,423	16,018	6.8%	102,243	46,768	6,140	29,114	12,417
Dauphin County	268,123	277,097	8,974	3.3%	112,559	46,818	6,384	29,930	13,590
Delaware County	558,759	564,751	5,992	1.1%	207,499	92,451	14,624	55,867	26,081
Erie County	280,584	272,061	-8,523	-3.0%	109,797	48,926	7,068	31,393	13,702
Fayette County	136,595	130,441	-6,154	-4.5%	56,085	27,692	3,922	17,735	7,941
Franklin County	149,619	154,835	5,216	3.5%	59,834	29,943	3,936	18,693	6,813
Indiana County	88,889	84,501	-4,388	-4.9%	33,098	16,623	2,405	10,360	3,923
Lackawanna County	214,439	210,793	-3,646	-1.7%	88,268	41,876	6,370	26,916	12,504
Lancaster County	519,446	543,557	24,111	4.6%	202,490	98,751	12,133	57,454	21,281
Lawrence County	91,140	86,184	-4,956	-5.4%	37,497	18,978	1,872	11,822	4,880
Lebanon County	133,577	141,314	7,737	5.8%	54,522	27,709	4,149	17,563	7,191
Lehigh County	349,676	368,100	18,424	5.3%	138,586	62,294	10,260	36,901	15,722
Luzerne County	320,895	317,646	-3,249	-1.0%	128,301	63,359	8,590	39,885	19,130
Lycoming County	116,114	113,664	-2,450	-2.1%	44,585	21,901	2,301	13,364	5,576
Mercer County	116,668	110,683	-5,985	-5.1%	46,809	23,990	4,010	15,513	7,672
Monroe County	169,832	169,507	-325	-0.2%	55,109	28,128	2,571	15,553	5,815
Montgomery County	799,872	828,604	28,732	3.6%	313,336	147,157	21,958	87,931	37,567
Northampton County	297,694	304,807	7,113	2.4%	114,996	57,663	8,268	35,162	14,731
Northumberland County	94,483	91,083	-3,400	-3.6%	38,816	19,647	3,214	12,466	5,824
Philadelphia County	1,526,009	1,584,138	58,129	3.8%	608,233	215,755	26,170	144,301	76,821
Schuylkill County	148,291	142,067	-6,224	-4.2%	58,458	28,879	4,148	18,720	8,378
Somerset County	77,737	73,952	-3,785	-4.9%	28,796	16,525	1,976	9,473	3,910
Washington County	207,841	207,346	-495	-0.2%	85,835	42,146	4,395	26,622	11,921
Westmoreland County	365,194	350,611	-14,583	-4.0%	150,368	79,436	10,770	50,820	22,379
York County	435,008	448,273	13,265	3.0%	173,958	78,138	9,692	47,981	20,912
Rhode Island									
Kent County	166,113	163,861	-2,252	-1.4%	69,115	30,919	4,434	20,449	10,858
Newport County	83,141	82,542	-599	-0.7%	34,316	18,639	1,798	12,166	5,134
Providence County	626,762	636,084	9,322	1.5%	237,038	97,383	15,326	60,005	31,119
Washington County	127,094	126,179	-915	-0.7%	47,680	26,155	3,220	15,603	5,244
South Carolina									
Aiken County	160,114	169,401	9,287	5.8%	68,609	32,745	3,900	20,602	8,732
Anderson County	186,943	200,482	13,539	7.2%	78,500	35,930	3,018	23,011	10,589
Beaufort County	162,231	188,715	26,484	16.3%	74,679	51,535	4,276	29,332	8,553
Berkeley County	178,316	221,091	42,775	24.0%	78,168	30,809	2,548	17,710	6,832
Charleston County	350,150	405,905	55,755	15.9%	160,457	66,098	8,256	42,527	17,839

Table A-2: Counties - Summary Population Characteristics—*Continued*

	April 1, 2010 Census Population Estimates Base	2018 ACS Population	2010-2018 Population Change	2010-2018 Percent Change	Total Households	2018 ACS			
						Population 65 and Over	Population 85 and Over	Householders 65 and Over	Persons 65 and Over Living Alone
South Carolina—Cont.									
Darlington County	68,609	66,802	-1,807	-2.6%	25,308	12,640	1,053	8,433	4,158
Dorchester County	136,173	160,647	24,474	18.0%	55,799	22,439	1,983	12,874	4,614
Florence County	136,962	138,159	1,197	0.9%	50,518	23,398	1,984	13,974	5,359
Greenville County	451,184	514,213	63,029	14.0%	192,556	80,987	8,754	49,062	18,921
Greenwood County	69,711	70,741	1,030	1.5%	27,962	12,995	1,704	8,028	3,005
Horry County	269,126	344,147	75,021	27.9%	131,180	83,231	5,951	48,521	18,350
Kershaw County	61,592	65,592	4,000	6.5%	24,756	11,928	1,393	7,450	2,677
Lancaster County	76,653	95,380	18,727	24.4%	35,710	19,635	1,629	11,175	4,181
Laurens County	66,535	66,994	459	0.7%	25,423	12,626	497	7,397	na
Lexington County	262,429	295,032	32,603	12.4%	115,566	46,772	4,925	30,215	12,825
Oconee County	74,275	78,374	4,099	5.5%	31,612	18,633	1,482	11,515	na
Orangeburg County	92,509	86,934	-5,575	-6.0%	33,561	16,866	1,553	11,251	5,081
Pickens County	119,373	124,937	5,564	4.7%	48,185	20,689	1,799	13,758	6,471
Richland County	384,450	414,525	30,126	7.8%	152,227	52,878	5,606	33,419	14,577
Spartanburg County	284,317	313,888	29,571	10.4%	116,018	50,178	4,542	30,293	11,017
Sumter County	107,490	106,512	-978	-0.9%	40,396	17,568	1,872	10,897	4,324
York County	226,046	274,118	48,072	21.3%	100,623	39,364	2,894	22,448	9,225
South Dakota									
Minnehaha County	169,474	192,876	23,402	13.8%	76,630	25,354	3,762	16,459	7,937
Pennington County	100,957	111,729	10,772	10.7%	44,794	20,474	2,828	13,001	4,684
Tennessee									
Anderson County	75,089	76,482	1,393	1.9%	29,505	15,305	1,490	8,995	3,487
Blount County	123,098	131,349	8,251	6.7%	51,446	27,168	2,520	15,806	4,821
Bradley County	98,930	106,727	7,797	7.9%	39,104	18,022	2,214	11,158	4,615
Davidson County	626,560	692,587	66,027	10.5%	283,445	84,450	9,949	55,686	25,896
Greene County	68,825	69,087	262	0.4%	27,316	14,809	1,160	8,422	2,778
Hamilton County	336,486	364,286	27,800	8.3%	146,057	63,597	7,878	38,869	16,371
Knox County	432,269	465,289	33,020	7.6%	185,416	73,277	7,891	46,281	19,047
Madison County	98,301	97,605	-696	-0.7%	39,223	16,581	2,230	10,420	4,685
Maury County	80,932	94,340	13,408	16.6%	34,361	14,739	1,344	9,199	3,801
Montgomery County	172,363	205,950	33,587	19.5%	72,973	18,581	2,308	11,008	4,377
Putnam County	72,349	78,843	6,494	9.0%	33,388	13,201	1,759	7,759	3,093
Robertson County	66,332	71,012	4,680	7.1%	26,375	10,130	604	5,876	1,864
Rutherford County	262,582	324,890	62,308	23.7%	115,376	33,545	2,634	19,666	7,702
Sevier County	89,719	97,892	8,173	9.1%	36,861	19,160	1,991	11,040	2,946
Shelby County	927,682	935,764	8,082	0.9%	352,648	127,036	14,963	81,716	38,040
Sullivan County	156,800	157,668	868	0.6%	64,504	34,801	3,729	23,310	10,675
Sumner County	160,634	187,149	26,515	16.5%	68,439	29,379	3,459	18,119	6,939
Washington County	123,058	128,607	5,549	4.5%	54,433	23,505	2,967	14,279	6,203
Williamson County	183,265	231,729	48,464	26.4%	80,601	30,783	1,986	17,284	5,384
Wilson County	114,073	140,625	26,552	23.3%	52,489	22,498	1,761	13,424	4,645
Texas									
Angelina County	86,771	87,092	321	0.4%	29,898	13,896	1,972	7,583	3,358
Bastrop County	74,202	86,976	12,774	17.2%	25,334	12,308	596	6,748	1,887
Bell County	310,159	355,642	45,483	14.7%	123,188	38,659	3,064	23,244	8,548
Bexar County	1,714,772	1,986,049	271,277	15.8%	644,193	240,452	25,750	137,915	53,147
Bowie County	92,564	94,324	1,760	1.9%	35,228	15,312	1,410	9,487	4,769
Brazoria County	313,123	370,200	57,077	18.2%	120,802	43,656	3,623	24,397	9,527
Brazos County	194,861	226,758	31,897	16.4%	81,030	20,996	1,309	13,213	5,129
Cameron County	406,215	423,908	17,693	4.4%	124,812	58,006	8,300	33,403	10,765
Collin County	782,220	1,005,146	222,926	28.5%	344,824	110,445	10,644	57,562	20,614
Comal County	108,485	148,373	39,888	36.8%	53,182	26,442	3,363	14,429	4,106
Coryell County	75,474	74,808	-666	-0.9%	21,491	7,299	550	4,773	2,100
Dallas County	2,366,683	2,637,772	271,089	11.5%	937,438	283,182	31,424	166,769	69,011
Denton County	662,554	859,064	196,510	29.7%	297,899	87,138	8,514	46,502	17,100
Ector County	137,136	162,124	24,988	18.2%	54,326	15,171	1,261	9,917	4,518
Ellis County	149,604	179,436	29,832	19.9%	58,633	22,760	2,147	13,075	4,657
El Paso County	800,653	840,758	40,105	5.0%	270,160	103,054	12,670	61,672	24,607
Fort Bend County	584,690	787,858	203,168	34.7%	245,410	87,280	7,629	43,524	13,035
Galveston County	291,307	337,890	46,583	16.0%	121,976	48,735	4,419	30,752	13,654
Grayson County	120,875	133,991	13,116	10.9%	48,963	23,606	2,521	14,802	5,589
Gregg County	121,745	123,707	1,962	1.6%	45,513	18,974	2,827	11,452	4,719
Guadalupe County	131,534	163,694	32,160	24.4%	54,789	22,092	1,829	12,067	4,297
Harris County	4,093,188	4,698,619	605,431	14.8%	1,600,357	494,414	49,533	285,358	107,889
Harrison County	65,644	66,726	1,082	1.6%	22,928	10,877	1,144	6,821	na
Hays County	157,099	222,631	65,532	41.7%	75,164	24,844	1,943	13,714	4,308
Henderson County	78,534	82,299	3,765	4.8%	30,843	18,119	1,561	10,841	4,276
Hidalgo County	774,768	865,939	91,171	11.8%	237,323	96,015	10,542	56,271	19,029
Hunt County	86,162	96,493	10,331	12.0%	34,132	14,784	1,003	9,007	3,939
Jefferson County	252,271	255,001	2,724	1.1%	90,383	36,578	5,126	21,966	10,353
Johnson County	150,940	171,361	20,421	13.5%	59,180	23,673	1,534	13,050	4,399
Kaufman County	103,363	128,622	25,259	24.4%	39,049	15,025	1,622	8,730	2,968
Liberty County	75,641	86,323	10,682	14.1%	27,468	10,882	603	7,206	3,267
Lubbock County	278,918	307,412	28,494	10.2%	115,686	37,599	4,398	23,330	8,771
McLennan County	234,899	254,607	19,708	8.4%	92,158	36,582	4,459	22,514	8,925

Table A-2: Counties - Summary Population Characteristics—*Continued*

	April 1, 2010 Census Population Estimates Base	2018 ACS Population	2010-2018 Population Change	2010-2018 Percent Change	Total Households	2018 ACS			
						Population 65 and Over	Population 85 and Over	Householders 65 and Over	Persons 65 and Over Living Alone
Texas—Cont.									
Midland County	136,872	172,578	35,706	26.1%	57,636	18,200	2,333	12,129	6,212
Montgomery County	455,750	590,925	135,175	29.7%	202,797	78,414	5,611	45,322	17,109
Nacogdoches County	64,524	65,711	1,187	1.8%	23,442	9,550	867	6,068	na
Nueces County	340,223	362,265	22,042	6.5%	129,987	52,731	5,881	31,260	12,066
Orange County	81,837	83,572	1,735	2.1%	30,047	13,333	1,730	8,095	2,838
Parker County	116,957	138,371	21,414	18.3%	46,238	21,356	1,950	11,869	4,581
Potter County	121,078	119,648	-1,430	-1.2%	45,550	13,638	1,748	9,383	5,293
Randall County	120,720	136,271	15,551	12.9%	49,457	20,619	2,606	12,575	4,997
Rockwall County	78,330	100,657	22,327	28.5%	34,590	12,282	1,234	6,727	1,989
San Patricio County	64,802	66,893	2,091	3.2%	22,202	10,035	843	5,873	2,281
Smith County	209,725	230,221	20,496	9.8%	77,330	37,588	3,171	22,791	8,247
Tarrant County	1,810,655	2,084,931	274,276	15.1%	722,473	235,476	27,000	141,809	54,937
Taylor County	131,508	137,640	6,132	4.7%	49,811	19,400	2,620	11,722	4,961
Tom Green County	110,228	118,189	7,961	7.2%	43,301	17,887	2,322	11,584	4,570
Travis County	1,024,462	1,248,743	224,281	21.9%	486,548	123,434	13,640	73,603	29,353
Victoria County	86,793	92,035	5,242	6.0%	31,918	14,935	1,811	9,159	4,053
Walker County	67,861	72,480	4,619	6.8%	22,693	9,226	1,013	5,524	na
Webb County	250,304	275,910	25,606	10.2%	75,300	26,003	2,596	15,185	5,836
Wichita County	131,665	132,064	399	0.3%	46,757	19,162	2,351	12,421	5,224
Williamson County	422,501	566,719	144,218	34.1%	185,345	68,659	7,312	35,790	13,583
Wise County	59,100	68,305	9,205	15.6%	22,864	10,070	1,096	5,198	1,772
Utah									
Cache County	112,656	127,068	14,412	12.8%	39,224	11,531	1,174	7,056	2,907
Davis County	306,492	351,713	45,221	14.8%	104,462	35,673	3,139	20,403	5,302
Salt Lake County	1,029,590	1,152,633	123,043	12.0%	381,831	125,461	12,282	76,120	28,672
Tooele County	58,218	69,907	11,689	20.1%	20,411	6,359	669	3,537	na
Utah County	516,639	622,213	105,574	20.4%	171,117	48,066	4,479	28,053	7,971
Washington County	138,115	171,700	33,585	24.3%	59,863	37,295	4,525	22,266	6,770
Weber County	231,223	256,359	25,136	10.9%	85,615	29,562	3,266	18,545	6,388
Vermont									
Chittenden County	156,540	164,572	8,032	5.1%	66,095	26,108	3,083	16,604	6,982
Virginia									
Albemarle County	98,988	108,718	9,730	9.8%	41,956	20,964	2,866	12,912	5,067
Arlington County	207,687	237,521	29,834	14.4%	109,940	24,837	3,274	16,853	8,565
Augusta County	73,753	75,457	1,704	2.3%	29,783	16,099	1,927	10,715	4,034
Bedford County	74,936	78,747	3,811	5.1%	31,271	16,691	1,760	9,191	na
Chesterfield County	316,239	348,556	32,317	10.2%	126,748	52,026	4,358	31,844	11,770
Fairfax County	1,081,667	1,150,795	69,128	6.4%	396,628	154,639	16,063	85,588	30,876
Fauquier County	65,236	70,675	5,439	8.3%	25,134	11,933	896	6,873	2,631
Frederick County	78,283	88,355	10,072	12.9%	31,551	15,161	1,733	8,763	3,319
Hanover County	99,850	107,239	7,389	7.4%	39,929	18,887	2,297	10,935	3,836
Henrico County	306,810	329,261	22,451	7.3%	129,408	51,563	7,576	32,004	15,552
James City County	67,385	76,397	9,012	13.4%	29,849	19,525	2,065	11,180	3,544
Loudoun County	312,348	406,850	94,502	30.3%	133,417	37,721	3,868	19,719	7,346
Montgomery County	94,422	98,985	4,563	4.8%	34,585	12,143	1,606	7,323	3,293
Prince William County	401,997	468,011	66,014	16.4%	143,861	46,514	3,331	23,805	8,610
Roanoke County	92,462	94,073	1,611	1.7%	38,061	19,691	2,084	12,225	5,044
Rockingham County	76,321	81,244	4,923	6.5%	31,462	15,209	1,955	9,382	3,858
Spotsylvania County	122,449	134,238	11,789	9.6%	45,223	19,210	1,388	10,491	2,972
Stafford County	128,984	149,960	20,976	16.3%	48,418	15,406	742	7,863	2,238
York County	65,239	67,846	2,607	4.0%	24,996	11,536	1,571	6,668	3,489
Washington									
Benton County	175,169	201,877	26,708	15.2%	71,921	30,082	3,690	18,215	7,215
Chelan County	72,460	77,036	4,576	6.3%	31,587	14,418	1,582	8,663	3,547
Clallam County	71,404	76,737	5,333	7.5%	33,265	22,161	3,101	14,164	5,916
Clark County	425,360	481,857	56,497	13.3%	178,980	74,468	7,158	45,341	18,294
Cowlitz County	102,408	108,987	6,579	6.4%	43,279	20,856	2,494	13,407	5,218
Franklin County	78,163	94,347	16,184	20.7%	27,067	9,167	670	4,766	1,628
Grant County	89,124	97,331	8,207	9.2%	30,806	14,081	1,325	7,992	2,803
Grays Harbor County	72,798	73,901	1,103	1.5%	27,674	16,312	1,549	8,920	3,591
Island County	78,508	84,460	5,952	7.6%	34,572	20,803	1,834	12,750	4,860
King County	1,931,292	2,233,163	301,871	15.6%	897,476	294,891	38,126	180,631	81,110
Kitsap County	251,143	269,805	18,662	7.4%	105,411	47,748	3,225	30,033	12,170
Lewis County	75,457	79,604	4,147	5.5%	30,327	16,580	1,642	10,886	5,171
Mason County	60,692	65,507	4,815	7.9%	25,864	14,862	1,592	8,846	3,634
Pierce County	795,217	891,299	96,082	12.1%	328,519	123,257	13,351	75,373	31,432
Skagit County	116,893	128,206	11,313	9.7%	48,474	26,616	2,992	15,788	5,800
Snohomish County	713,296	814,901	101,605	14.2%	300,215	109,883	12,031	65,481	25,604
Spokane County	471,229	514,631	43,402	9.2%	206,191	83,502	8,547	52,471	24,384
Thurston County	252,260	286,419	34,159	13.5%	110,713	49,236	5,381	29,900	12,354
Whatcom County	201,146	225,685	24,539	12.2%	87,080	39,347	4,604	24,312	9,138
Yakima County	243,240	251,446	8,206	3.4%	83,320	34,329	3,726	21,499	8,569

Table A-2: Counties - Summary Population Characteristics—*Continued*

	April 1, 2010 Census Population Estimates Base	2018 ACS Population	2010-2018 Population Change	2010-2018 Percent Change	Total Households	2018 ACS			
						Population 65 and Over	Population 85 and Over	Householders 65 and Over	Persons 65 and Over Living Alone
West Virginia									
Berkeley County	104,172	117,123	12,951	12.4%	45,800	17,561	1,433	11,073	4,619
Cabell County	96,297	93,224	-3,073	-3.2%	38,024	16,984	1,698	10,637	4,866
Harrison County	69,108	67,554	-1,554	-2.2%	26,878	13,272	1,854	8,381	4,364
Kanawha County	193,051	180,454	-12,597	-6.5%	78,482	37,659	4,694	24,807	11,698
Monongalia County	96,190	106,420	10,230	10.6%	40,603	13,176	1,697	8,232	3,390
Raleigh County	78,865	74,254	-4,611	-5.8%	31,169	15,492	1,245	10,449	na
Wood County	86,953	84,203	-2,750	-3.2%	36,064	17,190	1,597	11,237	5,485
Wisconsin									
Brown County	248,007	263,378	15,371	6.2%	104,470	39,372	4,135	24,964	11,818
Dane County	488,067	542,364	54,297	11.1%	226,350	74,937	9,041	47,609	20,070
Dodge County	88,759	87,847	-912	-1.0%	35,221	15,571	2,621	9,515	3,774
Eau Claire County	98,879	104,534	5,655	5.7%	40,421	16,689	1,830	10,408	4,624
Fond du Lac County	101,627	103,066	1,439	1.4%	41,009	19,012	2,970	11,716	4,751
Jefferson County	83,683	85,129	1,446	1.7%	33,180	14,645	1,281	9,124	3,273
Kenosha County	166,424	169,290	2,866	1.7%	62,950	23,669	3,201	14,984	6,933
La Crosse County	114,638	118,230	3,592	3.1%	47,924	19,122	2,817	12,015	5,467
Manitowoc County	81,442	79,074	-2,368	-2.9%	35,259	15,941	2,333	10,386	4,827
Marathon County	134,061	135,428	1,367	1.0%	56,245	23,770	3,026	15,425	7,023
Milwaukee County	947,736	948,201	465	0.0%	384,281	128,936	19,165	84,663	44,192
Outagamie County	176,691	187,365	10,674	6.0%	74,603	27,576	3,097	17,486	7,157
Ozaukee County	86,395	89,147	2,752	3.2%	36,261	17,689	1,834	11,685	5,089
Portage County	70,021	70,942	921	1.3%	29,193	11,666	1,428	7,783	3,917
Racine County	195,428	196,584	1,156	0.6%	76,808	32,401	3,701	20,635	9,781
Rock County	160,335	163,129	2,794	1.7%	64,632	27,151	3,224	17,695	7,819
St. Croix County	84,347	89,694	5,347	6.3%	34,422	12,492	1,280	7,760	3,079
Sheboygan County	115,510	115,456	-54	-0.0%	46,308	20,696	2,692	13,487	6,451
Walworth County	102,228	103,718	1,490	1.5%	40,864	18,146	2,440	11,193	4,915
Washington County	131,885	135,693	3,808	2.9%	55,488	24,354	2,397	14,198	4,997
Waukesha County	389,938	403,072	13,134	3.4%	158,368	75,079	9,988	46,371	18,904
Winnebago County	166,996	171,020	4,024	2.4%	71,332	27,997	4,386	18,183	9,228
Wood County	74,749	73,055	-1,694	-2.3%	32,274	14,940	1,891	9,953	4,637
Wyoming									
Laramie County	91,885	98,976	7,091	7.7%	39,678	16,163	1,792	11,096	5,110
Natrona County	75,448	79,115	3,667	4.9%	32,240	11,900	1,687	7,880	na

Table A-3: Cities - Summary Population Characteristics

	April 1, 2010 Census Population Estimates Base	2018 ACS Population	2010-2018 Population Change	2010-2018 Percent Change	Total Households	2018 ACS			
						Population 65 and Over	Population 85 and Over	Householders 65 and Over	Persons 65 and Over Living Alone
Alabama									
Auburn city	53,453	65,737	12,284	23.0%	23,305	5,252	351	3,078	na
Birmingham city	212,003	209,294	-2,709	-1.3%	87,831	32,361	3,618	22,749	10,937
Dothan city	65,774	67,814	2,040	3.1%	26,031	13,304	1,609	8,443	3,876
Hoover city	80,621	85,115	4,494	5.6%	31,770	15,152	1,651	8,841	2,727
Huntsville city	180,416	199,808	19,392	10.7%	84,848	33,334	3,619	21,385	9,109
Mobile city	194,664	189,570	-5,094	-2.6%	79,748	33,153	4,344	21,750	11,116
Montgomery city	205,501	198,218	-7,283	-3.5%	77,024	27,928	3,437	18,587	8,562
Tuscaloosa city	90,373	101,111	10,738	11.9%	36,759	12,475	1,333	7,840	3,494
Alaska									
Anchorage municipality	291,829	291,538	-291	-0.1%	105,285	32,809	3,056	19,776	7,174
Arizona									
Avondale city	76,132	85,828	9,696	12.7%	27,840	7,662	528	4,308	1,441
Buckeye city	50,861	74,378	23,517	46.2%	21,069	12,006	343	5,705	na
Chandler city	236,187	257,153	20,966	8.9%	91,969	30,221	2,192	16,709	6,146
Flagstaff city	66,023	73,955	7,932	12.0%	24,569	6,692	306	4,178	na
Glendale city	226,099	250,705	24,606	10.9%	83,873	32,779	2,903	18,642	8,430
Goodyear city	65,254	82,837	17,583	26.9%	26,405	14,839	493	7,258	1,192
Mesa city	440,084	508,979	68,895	15.7%	185,509	83,582	9,417	48,772	19,098
Peoria city	154,090	172,272	18,182	11.8%	63,218	31,097	4,167	18,656	7,751
Phoenix city	1,446,914	1,660,272	213,358	14.7%	574,645	178,699	19,934	107,117	49,064
Scottsdale city	217,464	255,315	37,851	17.4%	117,024	58,368	8,821	36,272	15,512
Surprise city	117,501	138,144	20,643	17.6%	49,936	30,777	2,215	18,125	6,171
Tempe city	161,777	192,354	30,577	18.9%	74,266	20,178	2,395	13,034	5,235
Tucson city	526,635	545,987	19,352	3.7%	209,383	80,806	9,359	52,276	25,202
Yuma city	90,717	97,917	7,200	7.9%	35,548	15,465	1,308	9,186	2,744
Arkansas									
Conway city	58,871	66,421	7,550	12.8%	23,009	8,099	1,085	4,447	na
Fayetteville city	73,573	86,765	13,192	17.9%	36,882	6,564	1,175	4,201	na
Fort Smith city	86,269	87,851	1,582	1.8%	35,442	12,359	1,517	8,043	na
Jonesboro city	67,291	76,990	9,699	14.4%	29,492	8,745	865	5,818	na
Little Rock city	193,490	197,868	4,378	2.3%	81,517	27,950	3,959	17,594	8,782
North Little Rock city	62,368	66,126	3,758	6.0%	28,402	11,141	1,405	7,135	3,148
Rogers city	56,021	67,615	11,594	20.7%	24,440	6,577	798	4,044	1,391
Springdale city	70,808	81,641	10,833	15.3%	27,283	8,428	1,940	4,978	na
California									
Alameda city	73,812	78,322	4,510	6.1%	30,724	13,565	1,425	8,447	4,387
Alhambra city	83,118	84,650	1,532	1.8%	30,556	14,890	3,187	7,285	2,430
Anaheim city	336,443	352,018	15,575	4.6%	101,547	41,460	4,796	20,945	8,752
Antioch city	102,745	111,535	8,790	8.6%	34,518	14,372	1,452	6,874	2,417
Bakersfield city	348,255	383,601	35,346	10.1%	121,615	40,509	5,503	22,204	8,687
Baldwin Park city	75,397	75,806	409	0.5%	18,224	7,962	615	3,214	789
Bellflower city	76,610	77,132	522	0.7%	24,333	7,840	841	3,817	1,783
Berkeley city	112,494	121,654	9,160	8.1%	43,806	16,662	1,511	11,462	5,540
Buena Park city	80,619	82,435	1,816	2.3%	23,171	9,949	1,121	4,904	1,203
Burbank city	103,358	103,687	329	0.3%	43,060	15,541	2,557	10,096	6,376
Camarillo city	65,154	69,112	3,958	6.1%	25,137	14,347	2,373	9,179	na
Carlsbad city	105,329	115,897	10,568	10.0%	44,950	22,329	4,101	13,084	4,176
Carson city	91,714	91,899	185	0.2%	23,896	13,747	1,684	6,971	2,139
Chico city	86,807	94,787	7,980	9.2%	37,100	12,616	1,616	8,570	4,733
Chino city	78,078	91,589	13,511	17.3%	25,509	12,106	1,020	5,716	1,785
Chino Hills city	74,799	83,438	8,639	11.5%	24,015	7,838	821	3,550	1,278
Chula Vista city	243,923	271,653	27,730	11.4%	78,112	31,145	4,246	14,910	5,257
Citrus Heights city	83,274	87,916	4,642	5.6%	33,390	14,503	2,113	9,539	5,166
Clovis city	95,835	112,019	16,184	16.9%	38,223	15,491	1,825	9,531	4,288
Compton city	96,411	96,616	205	0.2%	24,489	9,116	1,670	4,758	1,930
Concord city	122,168	129,681	7,513	6.1%	49,444	20,253	2,188	11,688	5,754
Corona city	152,511	168,826	16,315	10.7%	43,987	16,276	1,342	7,160	2,258
Costa Mesa city	110,078	113,610	3,532	3.2%	40,295	13,097	2,507	8,335	4,106
Daly City city	101,132	107,016	5,884	5.8%	32,792	18,142	3,278	8,444	3,124
Davis city	65,639	69,288	3,649	5.6%	24,796	7,506	954	4,645	1,831
Downey city	111,775	112,262	487	0.4%	34,820	15,694	1,866	7,277	1,847
El Cajon city	99,513	103,229	3,716	3.7%	33,153	12,503	2,138	5,999	2,267
Elk Grove city	153,010	172,891	19,881	13.0%	53,620	23,605	3,032	12,035	3,965
El Monte city	113,507	115,602	2,095	1.8%	30,469	15,384	2,034	6,620	2,108
Escondido city	143,972	152,232	8,260	5.7%	51,439	21,512	3,109	12,019	5,240
Fairfield city	105,425	116,885	11,460	10.9%	38,964	15,227	2,380	8,335	3,022
Folsom city	72,196	79,015	6,819	9.4%	26,845	9,530	916	5,660	2,214
Fontana city	196,472	213,736	17,264	8.8%	54,788	16,851	1,413	7,231	2,273
Fremont city	214,072	237,815	23,743	11.1%	78,243	30,434	4,244	13,788	4,012
Fresno city	497,102	530,073	32,971	6.6%	171,209	60,638	8,155	36,313	17,075
Fullerton city	135,237	139,629	4,392	3.2%	45,180	18,229	2,894	10,226	3,787
Garden Grove city	170,956	172,652	1,696	1.0%	44,696	21,707	3,310	9,679	2,808
Glendale city	191,687	201,374	9,687	5.1%	73,675	35,731	5,373	18,215	8,140
Hawthorne city	84,293	86,970	2,677	3.2%	29,174	8,587	1,121	4,888	2,092
Hayward city	144,332	159,618	15,286	10.6%	48,865	20,792	2,537	10,293	3,653

Table A-3: Cities - Summary Population Characteristics—*Continued*

	April 1, 2010 Census Population Estimates Base	2018 ACS Population	2010-2018 Population Change	2010-2018 Percent Change	Total Households	2018 ACS			
						Population 65 and Over	Population 85 and Over	Householders 65 and Over	Persons 65 and Over Living Alone
California—Cont.									
Hemet city	78,627	85,291	6,664	8.5%	28,544	21,434	2,879	12,375	5,383
Hesperia city	90,117	95,267	5,150	5.7%	27,703	11,938	1,059	6,818	2,096
Huntington Beach city	191,037	200,658	9,621	5.0%	76,622	33,121	4,100	20,467	8,700
Indio city	79,138	91,235	12,097	15.3%	40,637	19,395	909	12,417	na
Inglewood city	109,672	109,427	-245	-0.2%	35,518	12,357	1,631	7,918	3,978
Irvine city	212,043	282,584	70,541	33.3%	100,150	29,682	3,386	17,345	6,592
Jurupa Valley city	94,989	108,400	13,411	14.1%	23,872	12,830	1,936	5,476	1,845
Laguna Niguel city	62,985	66,265	3,280	5.2%	25,471	11,267	1,456	6,905	2,966
Lake Elsinore city	53,312	68,187	14,875	27.9%	17,996	7,588	460	2,749	844
Lake Forest city	77,448	85,619	8,171	10.6%	30,760	12,928	1,197	7,709	2,672
Lakewood city	80,060	80,132	72	0.1%	25,993	9,585	1,232	5,200	1,876
Lancaster city	156,642	159,038	2,396	1.5%	46,309	15,937	1,612	8,875	3,402
Livermore city	81,414	90,258	8,844	10.9%	30,587	12,311	1,372	7,192	2,799
Lodi City	62,134	66,995	4,861	7.8%	23,951	10,112	1,610	6,230	2,916
Long Beach city	462,211	467,353	5,142	1.1%	173,432	52,953	7,063	31,067	13,234
Los Angeles city	3,792,820	3,990,469	197,649	5.2%	1,382,293	512,427	69,755	288,751	126,305
Lynwood city	69,766	70,492	726	1.0%	15,979	5,786	502	2,608	617
Madera city	61,416	65,711	4,295	7.0%	18,028	6,546	1,042	2,850	1,639
Manteca city	67,286	81,593	14,307	21.3%	27,051	11,318	1,067	7,040	2,162
Menifee city	77,496	92,602	15,106	19.5%	28,647	16,906	2,446	9,799	3,539
Merced city	78,957	83,311	4,354	5.5%	26,075	9,912	1,237	6,613	3,112
Milpitas city	66,820	80,424	13,604	20.4%	23,161	9,268	1,279	4,392	1,103
Mission Viejo city	93,112	95,196	2,084	2.2%	33,011	19,372	2,972	10,393	3,447
Modesto city	203,119	215,032	11,913	5.9%	70,756	27,056	3,614	15,223	5,647
Moreno Valley city	193,305	209,051	15,746	8.1%	47,952	17,054	1,507	6,958	1,541
Mountain View city	73,997	83,377	9,380	12.7%	33,400	9,074	1,724	5,756	na
Murrieta city	103,680	114,982	11,302	10.9%	32,391	13,702	3,025	7,282	2,562
Napa city	77,097	79,261	2,164	2.8%	28,245	14,605	1,657	8,742	4,425
Newport Beach city	85,222	85,315	93	0.1%	38,302	20,241	3,323	11,992	5,274
Norwalk city	105,549	105,125	-424	-0.4%	26,842	14,543	1,763	6,801	1,890
Oakland city	390,792	429,114	38,322	9.8%	165,590	58,105	6,015	37,316	18,993
Oceanside city	167,382	176,090	8,708	5.2%	60,537	30,065	3,197	18,880	7,604
Ontario city	163,925	181,119	17,194	10.5%	50,569	16,575	1,517	8,310	2,449
Orange city	136,432	139,502	3,070	2.3%	42,927	16,644	2,084	9,020	3,755
Oxnard city	197,964	209,886	11,922	6.0%	51,883	20,331	2,936	9,102	2,224
Palmdale city	152,751	156,661	3,910	2.6%	45,320	17,379	1,567	8,879	3,304
Palo Alto city	64,395	66,655	2,260	3.5%	26,518	13,105	2,138	7,856	3,587
Pasadena city	137,120	141,374	4,254	3.1%	53,901	23,746	3,945	14,655	6,900
Perris city	68,565	79,139	10,574	15.4%	17,206	4,609	195	1,811	na
Pittsburg city	63,259	72,443	9,184	14.5%	20,823	7,026	469	3,108	1,152
Pleasanton city	70,282	82,377	12,095	17.2%	27,955	12,434	1,226	7,142	3,281
Pomona city	149,030	152,348	3,318	2.2%	39,422	16,981	2,303	8,556	2,826
Rancho Cordova city	64,805	74,590	9,785	15.1%	27,879	11,997	1,182	7,093	2,476
Rancho Cucamonga city	165,380	177,742	12,362	7.5%	56,354	22,373	1,906	10,869	3,138
Redding city	89,861	91,777	1,916	2.1%	35,476	16,724	2,509	10,065	4,197
Redlands city	68,675	71,595	2,920	4.3%	25,917	11,760	1,814	7,484	2,821
Redondo Beach city	66,924	67,396	472	0.7%	26,720	9,059	823	5,749	na
Redwood City city	76,822	86,186	9,364	12.2%	29,498	12,463	1,920	7,272	3,297
Rialto city	99,112	103,446	4,334	4.4%	25,485	12,792	917	5,957	1,856
Richmond city	103,262	110,175	6,913	6.7%	36,057	15,060	2,071	8,175	2,882
Riverside city	304,033	330,080	26,047	8.6%	87,341	34,595	4,539	17,387	5,556
Rocklin city	57,131	67,231	10,100	17.7%	21,206	7,716	614	5,072	2,297
Roseville city	119,156	139,110	19,954	16.7%	51,727	23,575	3,378	14,164	6,655
Sacramento city	466,390	508,517	42,127	9.0%	182,677	67,610	9,057	40,628	19,703
Salinas city	150,615	156,275	5,660	3.8%	39,881	14,422	2,235	8,116	3,091
San Bernardino city	209,662	215,929	6,267	3.0%	58,972	19,532	2,081	10,266	4,669
San Buenaventura (Ventura) city	107,236	111,120	3,884	3.6%	42,744	19,458	2,611	12,031	5,268
San Clemente city	63,478	64,850	1,372	2.2%	23,213	11,744	1,363	6,396	2,499
San Diego city	1,301,949	1,425,999	124,050	9.5%	513,698	189,049	22,311	110,754	43,177
San Francisco city	805,184	883,305	78,121	9.7%	362,827	138,128	22,842	83,021	38,978
San Jose city	952,060	1,030,119	78,059	8.2%	327,848	134,053	16,959	68,180	22,933
San Leandro city	84,967	89,683	4,716	5.6%	30,749	13,412	2,522	7,415	3,272
San Marcos city	83,642	96,834	13,192	15.8%	30,118	11,646	2,000	6,903	3,555
San Mateo city	97,207	105,016	7,809	8.0%	38,951	17,795	3,331	10,492	4,781
San Ramon city	71,423	75,832	4,409	6.2%	26,474	8,324	824	4,157	1,917
Santa Ana city	324,778	332,727	7,949	2.4%	78,786	32,306	4,647	14,538	4,209
Santa Barbara city	88,380	91,330	2,950	3.3%	35,647	16,640	2,680	10,865	4,564
Santa Clara city	116,497	129,489	12,992	11.2%	45,173	16,419	1,910	8,261	2,728
Santa Clarita city	204,142	210,085	5,943	2.9%	67,509	26,584	3,000	16,083	6,324
Santa Cruz city	59,943	64,729	4,786	8.0%	21,707	8,428	578	5,094	1,840
Santa Maria city	99,595	107,424	7,829	7.9%	26,336	9,578	1,228	5,010	1,512
Santa Monica city	89,742	91,417	1,675	1.9%	44,495	15,695	3,694	11,136	7,179
Santa Rosa city	175,082	177,587	2,505	1.4%	65,587	30,999	3,862	20,307	9,567
Simi Valley city	124,243	125,844	1,601	1.3%	43,069	21,662	2,578	13,520	6,111
South Gate city	94,412	94,439	27	0.0%	23,691	8,900	799	4,131	1,037
South San Francisco city	63,660	67,736	4,076	6.4%	20,774	12,530	1,507	6,432	2,324
Stockton city	291,731	311,189	19,458	6.7%	95,557	38,174	3,663	19,714	7,437

Table A-3: Cities - Summary Population Characteristics—*Continued*

	April 1, 2010 Census Population Estimates Base	2018 ACS Population	2010-2018 Population Change	2010-2018 Percent Change	Total Households	2018 ACS			
						Population 65 and Over	Population 85 and Over	Householders 65 and Over	Persons 65 and Over Living Alone
California—Cont.									
Sunnyvale city	140,060	153,175	13,115	9.4%	56,537	18,443	3,260	9,604	3,281
Temecula city	100,020	114,749	14,729	14.7%	32,859	11,656	1,437	6,337	2,028
Thousand Oaks city	126,481	127,720	1,239	1.0%	44,092	23,503	4,450	13,526	4,439
Torrance city	145,173	145,181	8	0.0%	54,991	25,953	4,978	15,257	6,737
Tracy city	83,406	91,803	8,397	10.1%	25,793	8,242	838	4,163	1,240
Turlock city	68,621	73,490	4,869	7.1%	24,140	9,643	824	5,417	2,182
Tustin city	75,317	79,787	4,470	5.9%	24,407	7,753	1,319	4,036	1,540
Union City city	69,533	74,568	5,035	7.2%	19,990	11,691	1,875	5,253	1,012
Upland city	73,718	77,002	3,284	4.5%	26,244	11,522	1,368	6,867	2,494
Vacaville city	92,422	100,147	7,725	8.4%	32,503	14,831	2,065	8,159	3,072
Vallejo city	115,897	121,915	6,018	5.2%	41,730	19,775	1,810	10,423	3,314
Victorville city	115,899	122,305	6,406	5.5%	31,624	9,823	894	6,064	2,029
Visalia city	124,520	133,783	9,263	7.4%	42,729	15,897	1,886	9,818	4,630
Vista city	93,349	101,227	7,878	8.4%	30,581	9,944	1,248	5,624	2,151
Walnut Creek city	64,165	69,814	5,649	8.8%	31,675	22,223	3,624	14,353	7,466
West Covina city	106,108	106,314	206	0.2%	30,333	17,625	2,483	7,546	1,724
Westminster city	89,613	90,931	1,318	1.5%	27,019	17,651	1,689	7,501	1,884
Whittier city	85,313	86,060	747	0.9%	27,672	12,745	2,309	6,420	2,795
Yorba Linda city	64,169	67,804	3,635	5.7%	23,217	14,150	1,621	8,002	2,388
Yuba City city	65,634	66,988	1,354	2.1%	22,524	11,004	1,787	6,382	2,737
Colorado									
Arvada city	106,722	120,127	13,405	12.6%	50,322	22,525	2,750	14,039	5,875
Aurora city	324,675	373,487	48,812	15.0%	133,217	44,196	4,236	26,953	12,047
Boulder city	97,640	107,355	9,715	9.9%	43,328	12,347	1,741	7,982	4,066
Broomfield city	55,856	69,267	13,411	24.0%	28,530	9,618	809	5,908	na
Centennial city	100,635	110,822	10,187	10.1%	38,549	15,966	1,384	9,508	3,454
Colorado Springs city	417,433	472,666	55,233	13.2%	181,745	62,658	7,639	37,885	16,666
Denver city	599,815	716,492	116,677	19.5%	310,324	83,996	9,433	56,532	30,911
Fort Collins city	144,855	167,823	22,968	15.9%	65,688	18,011	1,870	11,496	5,249
Greeley city	92,945	107,345	14,400	15.5%	37,835	11,608	1,873	7,087	3,140
Lakewood city	142,626	156,779	14,153	9.9%	65,918	26,670	3,461	16,911	8,598
Longmont city	86,310	95,986	9,676	11.2%	37,327	15,837	2,267	9,656	4,129
Loveland city	66,890	77,444	10,554	15.8%	30,853	13,838	2,168	8,409	3,217
Pueblo city	106,544	111,751	5,207	4.9%	45,374	20,979	2,691	13,875	6,787
Thornton city	118,784	139,430	20,646	17.4%	46,374	12,822	859	7,800	3,698
Westminster city	106,144	113,473	7,329	6.9%	46,002	15,348	1,653	9,916	4,257
Connecticut									
Bridgeport city	144,239	144,898	659	0.5%	51,014	16,277	2,223	10,346	6,162
Danbury city	80,907	84,731	3,824	4.7%	28,748	10,095	1,675	6,133	2,440
Hartford city	124,770	122,591	-2,179	-1.7%	46,072	14,074	1,744	8,831	4,547
New Britain city	73,202	72,440	-762	-1.0%	27,440	8,674	1,203	5,621	3,410
New Haven city	129,884	130,407	523	0.4%	50,312	12,044	1,344	7,968	3,837
Norwalk city	85,623	89,049	3,426	4.0%	35,333	15,974	1,867	10,872	4,879
Stamford city	122,633	129,770	7,137	5.8%	50,847	21,124	3,267	12,629	5,860
Waterbury city	110,329	108,086	-2,243	-2.0%	42,894	13,430	2,067	9,041	4,827
Delaware									
Wilmington city	70,835	70,653	-182	-0.3%	29,609	8,346	765	5,866	3,569
District of Columbia									
Washington city	601,766	702,455	100,689	16.7%	287,476	85,626	10,901	58,898	33,166
Florida									
Boca Raton city	84,409	99,241	14,832	17.6%	41,943	29,765	3,712	18,122	8,650
Boynton Beach city	68,213	78,038	9,825	14.4%	29,184	17,876	3,049	10,430	5,528
Cape Coral city	154,314	189,342	35,028	22.7%	69,803	48,088	5,878	27,070	7,739
Clearwater city	109,019	116,484	7,465	6.8%	48,704	26,465	5,030	17,120	9,342
Coral Springs city	122,091	133,493	11,402	9.3%	42,371	16,430	1,431	8,449	2,346
Daytona Beach city	61,575	68,862	7,287	11.8%	28,467	14,612	2,145	8,605	3,838
Deerfield Beach city	75,021	80,854	5,833	7.8%	33,801	19,397	3,092	12,200	6,183
Delray Beach city	60,623	69,356	8,733	14.4%	28,772	17,509	2,742	11,705	5,678
Deltona city	85,117	91,946	6,829	8.0%	29,694	14,669	2,052	7,276	1,920
Fort Lauderdale city	165,763	182,611	16,848	10.2%	75,144	33,299	3,378	19,813	8,105
Fort Myers city	62,316	82,260	19,944	32.0%	30,937	19,920	2,790	10,903	5,532
Gainesville city	124,266	133,851	9,585	7.7%	45,354	13,503	2,021	8,012	3,999
Hialeah city	224,687	238,950	14,263	6.3%	72,672	45,558	9,602	21,708	8,130
Hollywood city	140,711	154,813	14,102	10.0%	56,930	25,257	3,036	14,285	5,891
Homestead city	60,752	70,469	9,717	16.0%	18,811	6,275	376	2,122	na
Jacksonville city	821,764	903,896	82,132	10.0%	345,865	124,132	12,958	76,032	34,666
Kissimmee city	59,600	73,596	13,996	23.5%	21,606	8,919	479	4,052	na
Lakeland city	97,309	110,494	13,185	13.5%	41,884	21,578	2,804	13,155	6,697
Largo city	79,358	85,008	5,650	7.1%	36,611	23,439	3,636	14,786	7,952
Lauderhill city	66,939	72,081	5,142	7.7%	22,398	9,529	1,325	6,441	3,234
Melbourne city	76,247	82,823	6,576	8.6%	30,349	16,184	3,149	10,170	5,591
Miami city	399,530	470,911	71,381	17.9%	182,631	83,023	13,566	45,095	21,728
Miami Beach city	87,739	91,715	3,976	4.5%	45,523	15,396	1,879	10,710	6,652
Miami Gardens city	107,162	113,085	5,923	5.5%	30,797	16,456	1,984	9,742	2,756
Miramar city	121,958	140,827	18,869	15.5%	38,080	14,169	1,323	5,109	1,367

Table A-3: Cities - Summary Population Characteristics—*Continued*

	April 1, 2010 Census Population Estimates Base	2018 ACS Population	2010-2018 Population Change	2010-2018 Percent Change	Total Households	2018 ACS			
						Population 65 and Over	Population 85 and Over	Householders 65 and Over	Persons 65 and Over Living Alone
Florida—Cont.									
North Port city	57,333	68,637	11,304	19.7%	25,687	20,819	1,540	11,014	2,674
Orlando city	238,813	285,705	46,892	19.6%	114,176	31,154	4,028	18,900	10,941
Palm Bay city	104,008	114,190	10,182	9.8%	39,676	26,330	3,952	15,364	6,165
Palm Coast city	75,205	87,617	12,412	16.5%	30,752	26,538	4,120	14,828	4,426
Pembroke Pines city	154,898	172,387	17,489	11.3%	56,934	32,384	3,664	18,567	8,417
Plantation city	84,880	94,291	9,411	11.1%	33,472	15,365	1,542	8,418	3,337
Pompano Beach city	99,844	111,930	12,086	12.1%	41,116	22,487	4,222	13,352	6,648
Port St. Lucie city	164,194	195,251	31,057	18.9%	68,178	41,126	3,738	21,897	6,494
St. Petersburg city	245,176	265,100	19,924	8.1%	105,616	46,994	6,131	28,351	13,907
Sunrise city	84,305	95,461	11,156	13.2%	35,105	19,088	2,485	11,102	5,567
Tallahassee city	181,211	193,550	12,339	6.8%	75,260	19,192	1,607	11,880	5,302
Tamarac city	60,245	66,043	5,798	9.6%	27,707	17,415	3,652	11,743	5,900
Tampa city	336,154	392,905	56,751	16.9%	154,047	49,295	7,349	31,364	15,665
Weston city	65,419	71,224	5,805	8.9%	20,315	6,986	784	3,280	na
West Palm Beach city	100,666	111,389	10,723	10.7%	41,161	21,917	4,463	12,879	6,973
Georgia									
Albany city	77,431	71,646	-5,785	-7.5%	27,077	10,050	1,797	6,242	3,724
Alpharetta city	57,383	66,263	8,880	15.5%	24,595	6,465	508	3,743	na
Athens-Clarke County unified govt (bal)	115,441	126,000	10,559	9.1%	49,119	14,783	1,697	9,273	3,923
Atlanta city	426,821	498,073	71,252	16.7%	211,819	55,303	6,820	40,686	24,975
Augusta-Richmond County consolidated govt (bal)	195,847	196,138	291	0.1%	68,803	27,566	2,777	18,909	9,768
Columbus city	190,573	194,160	3,587	1.9%	72,862	26,086	3,698	17,648	8,554
Johns Creek city	76,640	84,292	7,652	10.0%	26,971	9,449	1,207	4,176	1,438
Macon-Bibb County	155,795	153,095	-2,700	-1.7%	57,905	23,974	2,802	15,152	7,294
Roswell city	88,332	94,648	6,316	7.2%	35,856	12,887	1,150	7,520	na
Sandy Springs city	93,820	108,798	14,978	16.0%	47,746	15,300	2,300	9,541	4,551
Savannah city	137,002	145,852	8,850	6.5%	51,118	20,502	2,683	13,243	6,531
South Fulton city	85,569	97,266	11,697	13.7%	33,793	12,390	851	7,700	na
Warner Robins city	69,066	75,413	6,347	9.2%	29,566	8,035	885	5,478	na
Hawaii									
Urban Honolulu CDP	337,721	347,403	9,682	2.9%	125,103	70,415	12,809	40,268	16,713
Iowa									
Boise City city	209,389	228,807	19,418	9.3%	97,101	35,173	4,968	22,584	11,616
Meridian city	76,959	106,794	29,835	38.8%	35,855	10,340	818	5,859	na
Nampa city	81,843	96,245	14,402	17.6%	34,289	14,790	1,793	9,508	4,551
Illinois									
Aurora city	197,914	206,389	8,475	4.3%	65,784	18,483	2,391	11,020	4,822
Bloomington city	76,701	77,955	1,254	1.6%	31,450	10,513	1,528	6,317	na
Champaign city	81,272	88,033	6,761	8.3%	34,532	9,849	1,441	5,774	2,644
Chicago city	2,695,624	2,705,988	10,364	0.4%	1,077,886	349,712	41,608	229,844	118,369
Decatur city	76,131	71,860	-4,271	-5.6%	31,132	14,883	1,964	9,140	4,172
Elgin city	108,147	110,893	2,746	2.5%	38,244	14,015	1,048	7,342	3,117
Evanston city	74,483	74,110	-373	-0.5%	27,517	11,686	2,090	7,379	3,401
Joliet city	147,435	149,356	1,921	1.3%	46,775	13,782	1,635	8,394	3,602
Naperville city	142,154	147,823	5,669	4.0%	51,766	17,180	2,023	9,457	3,307
Peoria city	115,108	115,720	612	0.5%	45,533	17,711	3,128	10,274	5,213
Rockford city	153,283	147,676	-5,607	-3.7%	60,696	26,571	4,614	16,750	7,852
Springfield city	116,998	114,512	-2,486	-2.1%	49,689	19,787	2,912	12,893	6,906
Waukegan city	89,072	82,934	-6,138	-6.9%	28,317	7,664	677	4,818	2,134
Indiana									
Bloomington city	80,314	86,522	6,208	7.7%	32,414	8,292	1,688	5,687	na
Carmel city	79,189	95,767	16,578	20.9%	36,421	13,218	1,266	7,603	2,970
Evansville city	120,075	117,967	-2,108	-1.8%	50,976	18,304	3,345	11,731	5,653
Fishers city	77,325	93,790	16,465	21.3%	33,921	9,511	1,646	5,320	na
Fort Wayne city	253,739	264,170	10,431	4.1%	105,457	36,436	4,131	24,810	12,519
Gary city	80,315	69,602	-10,713	-13.3%	28,086	14,138	1,804	9,418	4,085
Hammond city	80,824	75,806	-5,018	-6.2%	27,967	10,389	1,318	7,138	3,655
Indianapolis city (bal)	820,436	864,131	43,695	5.3%	339,536	107,601	12,206	68,504	33,054
Lafayette city	68,862	72,393	3,531	5.1%	30,803	9,962	1,574	6,077	3,243
Muncie city	70,210	70,178	-32	-0.0%	27,203	10,151	1,668	6,857	na
Noblesville city	52,217	66,358	14,141	27.1%	24,239	7,000	998	4,276	2191
South Bend city	101,241	103,869	2,628	2.6%	40,315	13,616	2,164	9,506	5,122
Iowa									
Ames city	59,037	67,155	8,118	13.8%	25,470	6,589	943	4,147	na
Ankeny city	45,612	65,282	19,670	43.1%	25,445	8,003	758	5,142	na
Cedar Rapids city	126,430	133,169	6,739	5.3%	54,234	19,911	2,770	12,836	6,295
Davenport city	99,693	102,080	2,387	2.4%	38,994	15,308	1,981	9,367	4,808
Des Moines city	204,183	216,993	12,810	6.3%	83,972	25,436	3,711	16,685	8,635
Iowa City city	67,946	76,291	8,345	12.3%	31,833	8,238	1,373	5,255	na
Sioux City city	82,693	82,762	69	0.1%	31,318	11,623	1,380	7,283	3,496
Waterloo city	68,408	67,797	-611	-0.9%	29,104	11,975	1,804	8,154	3,976
West Des Moines city	56,706	67,127	10,421	18.4%	29,398	9,890	669	6,358	na

Table A-3: Cities - Summary Population Characteristics—*Continued*

	April 1, 2010 Census Population Estimates Base	2018 ACS Population	2010-2018 Population Change	2010-2018 Percent Change	Total Households	2018 ACS			
						Population 65 and Over	Population 85 and Over	Householders 65 and Over	Persons 65 and Over Living Alone
Kansas									
Kansas City city	145,785	154,361	8,576	5.9%	56,587	18,604	1,375	11,709	4,936
Lawrence city	87,757	97,293	9,536	10.9%	40,407	11,877	1,983	7,647	3,737
Olathe city	125,900	139,588	13,688	10.9%	48,543	14,007	1,575	8,432	2,732
Overland Park city	173,329	192,525	19,196	11.1%	79,571	30,952	4,455	19,297	8,384
Shawnee city	62,207	65,844	3,637	5.8%	23,817	8,386	689	4,535	na
Topeka city	127,631	125,908	-1,723	-1.3%	54,697	24,157	2,818	15,459	7,880
Wichita city	382,423	389,259	6,836	1.8%	154,512	57,099	7,662	36,646	18,563
Kentucky									
Bowling Green city	59,031	68,393	9,362	15.9%	25,223	8,230	1,015	5,035	3,296
Lexington-Fayette urban county	295,867	323,780	27,913	9.4%	131,067	42,959	4,478	26,964	12,739
Louisville/Jefferson County metro govt (bal)	595,386	620,149	24,763	4.2%	247,339	95,385	11,914	61,682	26,628
Louisiana									
Baton Rouge city	229,422	221,606	-7,816	-3.4%	85,723	33,975	4,597	21,311	8,632
Bossier City city	61,769	68,222	6,453	10.4%	27,128	10,242	1,430	6,459	3,138
Kenner city	66,685	66,656	-29	-0.0%	26,412	12,066	1,077	7,446	3,095
Lafayette city	121,667	126,149	4,482	3.7%	51,596	17,812	2,221	11,790	4,796
Lake Charles city	72,264	77,999	5,735	7.9%	32,981	11,414	1,313	8,012	na
New Orleans city	343,828	391,006	47,178	13.7%	155,104	57,532	5,890	35,584	19,880
Shreveport city	200,405	189,149	-11,256	-5.6%	74,650	32,183	3,787	19,851	8,643
Maine									
Portland city	66,193	66,420	227	0.3%	31,193	8,562	1,649	5,449	3,038
Maryland									
Baltimore city	620,862	602,495	-18,367	-3.0%	237,204	84,069	10,141	57,264	31,440
Frederick city	65,287	72,152	6,865	10.5%	28,558	9,659	1,181	5,710	2,820
Gaithersburg city	59,903	68,294	8,391	14.0%	25,404	8,959	1,147	4,865	2,020
Rockville city	61,255	68,252	6,997	11.4%	25,870	11,479	1,353	7,175	3,556
Massachusetts									
Boston city	617,786	695,926	78,140	12.6%	274,674	82,414	9,956	53,784	28,168
Brockton city	93,767	95,781	2,014	2.1%	31,852	13,279	1,863	7,542	3,845
Cambridge city	105,176	118,967	13,791	13.1%	46,383	12,219	1,021	8,519	4,688
Fall River city	88,857	89,662	805	0.9%	38,136	15,004	2,277	9,771	5,323
Framingham city	68,325	73,123	4,798	7.0%	28,470	12,701	1,595	6,830	2,447
Lawrence city	76,348	80,370	4,022	5.3%	25,992	7,031	1,080	4,387	2,203
Lowell city	106,528	111,666	5,138	4.8%	37,902	11,141	1,513	6,108	2,944
Lynn city	90,333	94,655	4,322	4.8%	31,429	11,568	1,473	7,139	3,578
New Bedford city	95,068	95,323	255	0.3%	37,910	12,825	2,541	8,184	4,737
Newton city	85,114	88,911	3,797	4.5%	31,221	17,849	2,239	10,928	4,254
Quincy city	92,262	94,590	2,328	2.5%	40,199	14,548	2,299	9,181	5,293
Somerville city	75,651	81,568	5,917	7.8%	33,113	6,289	727	4,390	2,547
Springfield city	153,173	155,029	1,856	1.2%	57,078	20,632	2,397	12,418	5,896
Worcester city	181,009	185,883	4,874	2.7%	71,688	24,763	3,097	14,900	8,382
Michigan									
Ann Arbor city	113,973	121,885	7,912	6.9%	46,385	13,110	2,028	8,275	3,428
Dearborn city	98,148	94,325	-3,823	-3.9%	31,061	11,814	1,583	7,367	3,530
Detroit city	713,885	672,681	-41,204	-5.8%	266,333	94,159	11,844	66,285	35,214
Farmington Hills city	79,722	81,103	1,381	1.7%	33,415	16,863	2,243	10,120	4,745
Flint city	102,230	95,932	-6,298	-6.2%	42,468	13,127	1,572	9,182	4,448
Grand Rapids city	188,031	200,230	12,199	6.5%	75,472	24,842	3,365	16,875	9,960
Kalamazoo city	74,261	76,557	2,296	3.1%	27,863	8,048	992	5,457	3,201
Lansing city	114,253	117,388	3,135	2.7%	48,631	15,125	2,340	9,985	4,957
Livonia city	96,857	93,970	-2,887	-3.0%	36,806	15,917	2,018	10,322	5,209
Rochester Hills city	70,985	74,700	3,715	5.2%	28,325	12,650	2,226	8,254	3,726
Southfield city	71,717	73,141	1,424	2.0%	31,489	16,791	2,443	11,169	6,092
Sterling Heights city	129,675	132,967	3,292	2.5%	49,032	22,357	3,247	13,015	5,047
Troy city	80,972	84,259	3,287	4.1%	30,729	13,874	1,178	7,644	2,704
Warren city	134,056	134,583	527	0.4%	55,156	22,710	3,508	14,523	7,237
Westland city	84,153	81,714	-2,439	-2.9%	35,991	13,696	1,598	10,074	6,135
Wyoming city	72,117	75,812	3,695	5.1%	27,438	9,427	927	5,251	2,350
Minnesota									
Blaine city	57,179	65,215	8,036	14.1%	22,718	7,580	372	4,267	na
Bloomington city	82,893	85,574	2,681	3.2%	36,011	17,745	2,640	12,145	5,802
Brooklyn Park city	75,776	80,614	4,838	6.4%	27,830	9,903	860	5,098	1,337
Duluth city	86,266	85,884	-382	-0.4%	36,198	15,453	2,743	9,899	5,002
Eagan city	64,150	66,539	2,389	3.7%	25,376	8,292	964	4,453	na
Lakeville city	55,999	65,871	9,872	17.6%	22,156	6,462	354	3,787	na
Maple Grove city	61,548	71,812	10,264	16.7%	29,047	11,137	916	6,625	na
Minneapolis city	382,603	425,395	42,792	11.2%	175,233	46,030	5,044	29,348	15,416
Plymouth city	70,589	79,437	8,848	12.5%	31,874	11,197	756	6,872	3,394
Rochester city	106,801	116,957	10,156	9.5%	49,361	18,037	2,964	11,259	5,543
St. Cloud city	65,926	68,928	3,002	4.6%	25,189	7,967	874	4,876	na
St. Paul city	285,067	307,701	22,634	7.9%	115,858	33,259	4,328	21,422	12,130
Woodbury city	61,965	71,299	9,334	15.1%	26,388	9,948	729	5,952	na

Table A-3: Cities - Summary Population Characteristics—*Continued*

	April 1, 2010 Census Population Estimates Base	2018 ACS Population	2010-2018 Population Change	2010-2018 Percent Change	Total Households	2018 ACS			
						Population 65 and Over	Population 85 and Over	Householders 65 and Over	Persons 65 and Over Living Alone
Mississippi									
Gulfport city	67,786	71,865	4,079	6.0%	29,899	8,711	774	5,550	2,366
Jackson city	173,590	164,720	-8,870	-5.1%	59,306	21,926	2,788	13,245	5,819
Missouri									
Columbia city	109,044	123,182	14,138	13.0%	49,437	13,439	2,292	9,132	na
Independence city	116,800	116,939	139	0.1%	48,237	19,652	3,301	12,015	4,830
Kansas City city	459,937	491,809	31,872	6.9%	207,377	64,994	8,447	41,780	21,023
Lee's Summit city	91,366	98,919	7,553	8.3%	37,758	17,122	2,328	10,450	3,976
O'Fallon city	79,493	88,464	8,971	11.3%	29,948	9,542	1,261	5,962	na
St. Charles city	66,140	70,770	4,630	7.0%	29,672	11,844	1,571	7,341	3,789
St. Joseph city	76,786	75,437	-1,349	-1.8%	28,314	12,953	1,772	8,757	3,487
St. Louis city	319,275	302,838	-16,437	-5.1%	144,295	41,739	5,489	29,792	18,195
Springfield city	159,453	168,113	8,660	5.4%	79,220	29,553	4,055	21,055	12,268
Montana									
Billings city	104,294	109,544	5,250	5.0%	47,494	19,207	3,198	12,848	6,409
Missoula city	66,828	74,427	7,599	11.4%	32,279	9,530	1,053	6,564	3,449
Nebraska									
Lincoln city	258,602	287,399	28,797	11.1%	114,870	37,864	4,612	25,353	12,151
Omaha city	450,238	468,267	18,029	4.0%	184,831	63,828	8,813	41,787	21,056
Nevada									
Henderson city	257,073	310,374	53,301	20.7%	120,678	58,693	6,318	34,479	13,869
Las Vegas city	584,509	644,664	60,155	10.3%	234,592	98,087	11,400	57,088	23,631
North Las Vegas city	216,670	245,949	29,279	13.5%	78,774	26,177	1,350	14,796	4,470
Reno city	225,411	250,989	25,578	11.3%	106,970	39,780	3,661	26,259	13,933
Sparks city	91,066	104,254	13,188	14.5%	39,015	17,884	1,901	10,698	3,809
New Hampshire									
Manchester city	109,549	112,529	2,980	2.7%	44,286	14,217	3,060	8,273	3,797
Nashua city	86,478	89,257	2,779	3.2%	38,520	15,416	2,369	9,562	4,731
New Jersey									
Bayonne city	63,015	65,082	2,067	3.3%	23,743	9,655	1,694	6,109	3,304
Camden city	77,043	73,968	-3,075	-4.0%	23,804	7,251	749	4,766	na
Clifton city	84,117	85,272	1,155	1.4%	30,647	13,745	2,596	7,380	3,060
East Orange city	64,169	64,469	300	0.5%	22,080	8,455	1,455	5,494	2,876
Elizabeth city	124,972	128,882	3,910	3.1%	40,118	12,726	1,141	7,324	3,228
Jersey City city	247,639	265,560	17,921	7.2%	102,353	28,326	3,056	17,688	7,645
Newark city	277,107	282,102	4,995	1.8%	101,689	28,004	3,490	17,220	8,475
Passaic city	69,811	69,945	134	0.2%	19,761	6,869	754	3,874	2,020
Paterson city	146,181	145,626	-555	-0.4%	48,926	15,988	1,488	10,224	3,764
Trenton city	84,964	83,973	-991	-1.2%	28,900	9,590	1,445	7,207	4,017
Union City city	66,439	68,521	2,082	3.1%	23,889	7,209	855	4,774	2,551
New Mexico									
Albuquerque city	546,191	560,234	14,043	2.6%	228,491	88,411	11,461	55,046	27,055
Las Cruces city	97,728	102,929	5,201	5.3%	43,143	17,718	1,800	10,769	4,871
Rio Rancho city	87,375	98,016	10,641	12.2%	36,868	16,598	1,584	9,930	3,043
Santa Fe city	80,878	84,605	3,727	4.6%	35,764	20,191	1,690	13,618	6,245
New York									
Albany city	97,841	97,273	-568	-0.6%	42,379	13,367	2,262	8,897	4,778
Buffalo city	261,372	256,322	-5,050	-1.9%	109,446	31,965	4,067	21,624	10,787
Mount Vernon city	67,303	67,606	303	0.5%	25,910	9,454	2,366	6,096	3,297
New Rochelle city	77,098	78,747	1,649	2.1%	26,873	12,330	2,339	7,613	3,404
New York city	8,174,988	8,398,748	223,760	2.7%	3,184,496	1,245,480	160,367	767,186	370,699
Rochester city	210,684	206,290	-4,394	-2.1%	84,868	23,423	2,559	16,006	9,190
Schenectady city	66,157	65,570	-587	-0.9%	24,267	9,319	1,483	6,127	3,166
Syracuse city	145,206	142,740	-2,466	-1.7%	53,949	16,283	2,449	10,721	6,340
Yonkers city	196,018	199,646	3,628	1.9%	79,178	34,169	4,617	21,929	11,510
North Carolina									
Asheville city	83,433	92,460	9,027	10.8%	40,968	18,090	2,600	11,818	6,190
Charlotte city	735,692	872,506	136,814	18.6%	335,918	94,775	9,140	56,551	24,278
Concord city	79,317	94,134	14,817	18.7%	33,523	13,020	1,618	7,679	3,046
Durham city	229,878	274,497	44,619	19.4%	112,342	33,485	3,160	20,298	7,841
Fayetteville city	200,565	209,465	8,900	4.4%	81,665	25,524	3,022	16,511	8,019
Gastonia city	71,722	77,021	5,299	7.4%	30,725	11,614	1,294	7,309	3,529
Greensboro city	268,924	294,726	25,802	9.6%	119,838	41,052	5,334	26,459	12,862
Greenville city	84,722	93,136	8,414	9.9%	36,501	8,620	1,099	5,662	3,411
High Point city	104,514	114,322	9,808	9.4%	43,169	16,646	2,245	10,080	4,073
Jacksonville city	70,169	72,895	2,726	3.9%	21,735	4,168	417	2,941	na
Raleigh city	404,073	470,509	66,436	16.4%	188,941	53,212	6,774	33,431	16,203
Wilmington city	106,454	122,610	16,156	15.2%	52,998	20,984	3,362	14,175	7,717
Winston-Salem city	229,634	246,334	16,700	7.3%	97,226	34,058	3,928	23,621	12,541
North Dakota									
Bismarck city	61,301	71,843	10,542	17.2%	32,629	12,354	2,520	7,969	na
Fargo city	105,610	125,040	19,430	18.4%	53,850	15,034	2,494	9,594	4,993

Table A-3: Cities - Summary Population Characteristics—*Continued*

	April 1, 2010 Census Population Estimates Base	2018 ACS Population	2010-2018 Population Change	2010-2018 Percent Change	Total Households	2018 ACS			
						Population 65 and Over	Population 85 and Over	Householders 65 and Over	Persons 65 and Over Living Alone
Ohio									
Akron city	199,135	198,025	-1,110	-0.6%	85,973	29,763	4,592	19,483	8,969
Canton city	73,043	70,469	-2,574	-3.5%	29,652	10,844	1,657	7,625	4,080
Cincinnati city	296,893	302,615	5,722	1.9%	138,767	37,749	5,773	26,344	16,370
Cleveland city	396,629	383,781	-12,848	-3.2%	173,025	54,735	6,768	38,722	22,818
Columbus city	789,011	895,877	106,866	13.5%	366,034	96,145	8,860	63,167	28,374
Dayton city	141,995	140,638	-1,357	-1.0%	60,096	19,434	2,482	13,731	7,507
Lorain city	64,099	64,031	-68	-0.1%	25,568	10,416	1,534	7,035	4,003
Parma city	81,589	78,746	-2,843	-3.5%	33,329	13,933	1,709	8,792	4,175
Toledo city	287,319	274,973	-12,346	-4.3%	116,849	38,614	4,942	25,440	13,432
Youngstown city	66,952	64,958	-1,994	-3.0%	27,783	11,549	2,122	7,822	4,633
Oklahoma									
Broken Arrow city	98,838	110,123	11,285	11.4%	39,101	16,499	1,764	9,346	2,993
Edmond city	81,149	93,118	11,969	14.7%	33,474	14,446	1,599	8,679	2,979
Lawton city	96,867	92,860	-4,007	-4.1%	33,335	11,580	1,545	7,754	3,675
Norman city	110,925	123,469	12,544	11.3%	49,674	14,300	1,309	9,153	4,098
Oklahoma City city	580,247	649,410	69,163	11.9%	245,772	83,034	11,388	54,178	26,133
Tulsa city	392,010	401,112	9,102	2.3%	163,083	58,975	7,695	38,643	18,959
Oregon									
Beaverton city	89,732	98,951	9,219	10.3%	38,762	10,763	1,172	7,603	na
Bend city	76,651	97,590	20,939	27.3%	41,160	16,399	2,596	11,110	5,607
Eugene city	156,428	171,259	14,831	9.5%	73,458	26,127	2,702	18,122	9,999
Gresham city	105,639	110,165	4,526	4.3%	40,253	14,900	1,742	9,363	4,811
Hillsboro city	92,274	108,382	16,108	17.5%	40,812	12,511	1,776	7,778	4,032
Medford city	74,943	82,348	7,405	9.9%	33,388	14,797	2,655	9,036	4,108
Portland city	583,792	652,573	68,781	11.8%	273,607	87,129	8,752	57,005	29,486
Salem city	154,909	173,420	18,511	11.9%	64,191	25,603	2,336	15,873	7,531
Pennsylvania									
Allentown city	118,097	121,429	3,332	2.8%	42,538	15,056	2,573	8,331	3,599
Bethlehem city	74,951	75,979	1,028	1.4%	29,635	13,253	2,295	7,903	4,283
Erie city	101,747	96,459	-5,288	-5.2%	40,446	15,551	2,415	10,444	5,770
Philadelphia city	1,526,009	1,584,138	58,129	3.8%	608,233	215,755	26,170	144,301	76,821
Pittsburgh city	305,376	301,038	-4,338	-1.4%	141,881	47,074	6,448	32,982	19,868
Reading city	88,016	88,508	492	0.6%	28,755	9,166	1,491	5,978	3,175
Scranton city	76,087	77,186	1,099	1.4%	30,273	12,796	1,832	7,941	3,960
Rhode Island									
Cranston city	80,559	81,282	723	0.9%	31,993	12,235	2,433	7,654	3,968
Pawtucket city	71,139	71,842	703	1.0%	29,051	10,085	1,475	6,774	3,168
Providence city	177,844	179,335	1,491	0.8%	60,883	20,992	3,101	13,328	7,735
Warwick city	82,674	80,842	-1,832	-2.2%	35,628	16,150	1,999	11,091	6,222
South Carolina									
Charleston city	120,574	141,088	20,514	17.0%	57,915	20,302	2,601	13,963	7,397
Columbia city	130,432	133,610	3,178	2.4%	46,888	13,045	1,639	8,917	na
Greenville city	59,149	68,543	9,394	15.9%	29,962	9,822	1,219	6,599	na
North Charleston city	97,559	119,214	21,655	22.2%	44,405	12,345	1,237	7,496	3,200
Rock Hill city	66,547	74,308	7,761	11.7%	26,768	10,431	932	5,845	2,608
South Dakota									
Rapid City city	68,461	75,448	6,987	10.2%	30,364	13,426	2,197	8,957	3,954
Sioux Falls city	153,972	181,906	27,934	18.1%	71,068	21,555	3,230	14,186	7,054
Tennessee									
Chattanooga city	170,309	180,551	10,242	6.0%	76,021	30,493	4,049	20,047	10,757
Clarksville city	132,897	156,800	23,903	18.0%	56,546	12,759	1,826	7,492	2,929
Franklin city	62,569	80,920	18,351	29.3%	30,291	9,787	741	6,006	na
Jackson city	66,847	66,900	53	0.1%	26,267	9,735	1,596	6,510	3,790
Johnson City city	63,380	68,245	4,865	7.7%	30,507	11,050	1,464	6,827	3,697
Knoxville city	178,310	187,514	9,204	5.2%	81,925	24,179	2,726	16,442	8,646
Memphis city	651,885	650,632	-1,253	-0.2%	252,517	84,936	10,310	56,780	30,006
Murfreesboro city	109,073	141,336	32,263	29.6%	53,894	13,966	938	8,601	4,062
Nashville-Davidson metropolitan govt (bal)	603,427	665,498	62,071	10.3%	272,826	79,913	9,426	52,740	24,562
Texas									
Abilene city	117,512	125,456	7,944	6.8%	42,752	15,739	2,481	9,709	4,501
Allen city	84,275	103,378	19,103	22.7%	35,783	10,585	1,029	5,183	na
Amarillo city	190,666	200,880	10,214	5.4%	77,403	26,413	3,745	17,074	8,797
Arlington city	365,337	398,122	32,785	9.0%	135,867	43,458	4,413	25,203	9,332
Austin city	802,078	964,243	162,165	20.2%	390,395	90,262	10,784	53,957	23,406
Baytown city	71,635	77,962	6,327	8.8%	27,351	9,933	1,055	5,868	1,851
Beaumont city	117,278	118,425	1,147	1.0%	44,288	17,801	2,342	10,825	4,666
Brownsville city	174,748	183,389	8,641	4.9%	51,334	21,346	3,676	11,430	3,512
Bryan city	76,226	85,447	9,221	12.1%	29,701	8,500	642	5,852	2,770
Carrollton city	119,176	136,869	17,693	14.8%	49,232	17,131	2,013	9,519	3,369
Cedar Park city	55,117	75,553	20,436	37.1%	24,767	6,330	1,139	2,886	1,063
College Station city	94,221	116,218	21,997	23.3%	41,868	9,026	505	5,365	na
Conroe city	65,259	87,656	22,397	34.3%	33,852	11,254	1,419	7,856	3,746
Corpus Christi city	305,226	326,566	21,340	7.0%	116,456	46,865	5,129	27,629	10,405
Dallas city	1,197,653	1,345,076	147,423	12.3%	521,198	143,795	18,090	88,938	40,264
Denton city	116,371	138,553	22,182	19.1%	48,769	15,406	1,928	8,968	3,953

Table A-3: Cities - Summary Population Characteristics—*Continued*

	April 1, 2010 Census Population Estimates Base	2018 ACS Population	2010-2018 Population Change	2010-2018 Percent Change	Total Households	2018 ACS			
						Population 65 and Over	Population 85 and Over	Householders 65 and Over	Persons 65 and Over Living Alone
Texas—Cont.									
Edinburg city	82,020	98,671	16,651	20.3%	28,003	8,887	731	4,650	na
El Paso city	648,254	682,686	34,432	5.3%	227,506	88,348	11,564	53,524	22,453
Fort Worth city	744,852	898,919	154,067	20.7%	308,188	87,550	11,248	55,700	24,078
Frisco city	117,170	188,153	70,983	60.6%	63,562	16,308	1,489	7,405	3,552
Garland city	226,910	242,402	15,492	6.8%	74,489	30,081	2,105	16,237	5,878
Georgetown city	47,483	74,176	26,693	56.2%	28,062	21,166	2,949	12,684	4,704
Grand Prairie city	175,468	194,600	19,132	10.9%	62,349	18,456	1,849	10,128	3,402
Harlingen city	64,912	65,434	522	0.8%	21,504	10,730	1,590	6,270	2,030
Houston city	2,093,615	2,326,090	232,475	11.1%	849,105	245,819	30,713	151,420	66,470
Irving city	216,285	242,228	25,943	12.0%	85,295	15,469	1,809	8,277	3,335
Killeen city	127,696	149,102	21,406	16.8%	52,186	9,599	254	5,812	2,400
Laredo city	235,809	259,512	23,703	10.1%	71,160	24,746	2,572	14,292	5,288
League City city	83,563	106,188	22,625	27.1%	37,234	11,875	1,457	6,742	3,233
Lewisville city	95,458	106,205	10,747	11.3%	38,738	9,316	1,320	4,946	2,286
Longview city	80,423	81,424	1,001	1.2%	30,554	12,495	2,392	7,341	3,233
Lubbock city	229,632	255,885	26,253	11.4%	97,457	31,448	4,085	19,833	7,743
McAllen city	131,559	143,429	11,870	9.0%	43,937	16,970	1,381	10,160	3,300
McKinney city	131,160	191,666	60,506	46.1%	63,889	21,449	1,624	10,076	3,296
Mansfield city	56,415	74,786	18,371	32.6%	22,719	6,527	795	3,653	1,251
Mesquite city	139,593	142,874	3,281	2.4%	47,591	13,735	1,688	8,820	3,996
Midland city	111,190	142,339	31,149	28.0%	47,827	14,260	1,860	9,382	4,796
Mission city	77,690	84,829	7,139	9.2%	24,385	11,570	1,525	6,720	2,463
Missouri City city	66,531	72,978	6,447	9.7%	24,522	10,387	720	5,928	na
New Braunfels city	57,677	85,566	27,889	48.4%	29,781	12,468	2,042	6,933	2,442
North Richland Hills city	63,338	70,839	7,501	11.8%	26,130	11,137	1,608	7,090	2,451
Odessa city	99,876	122,440	22,564	22.6%	42,819	11,607	1,020	8,100	na
Pasadena city	149,307	153,212	3,905	2.6%	46,703	14,155	1,077	8,322	3,230
Pearland city	93,128	124,321	31,193	33.5%	42,409	16,904	496	9,174	3,062
Pharr city	70,467	79,704	9,237	13.1%	20,861	8,434	621	5,023	2,209
Plano city	259,857	287,765	27,908	10.7%	102,778	38,026	4,995	22,495	8,735
Richardson city	99,251	120,954	21,703	21.9%	43,922	16,518	1,374	9,703	4,103
Round Rock city	100,010	128,490	28,480	28.5%	40,854	12,314	856	5,623	2,662
Rowlett city	56,242	66,686	10,444	18.6%	null	6,081	253	na	na
San Angelo city	93,221	101,824	8,603	9.2%	37,432	15,191	1,899	9,991	4,096
San Antonio city	1,326,768	1,532,212	205,444	15.5%	509,964	189,691	22,324	112,450	45,891
Sugar Land city	107,850	118,614	10,764	10.0%	39,378	20,641	2,000	10,314	3,557
Temple city	66,078	76,251	10,173	15.4%	28,805	13,207	1,547	7,481	2,689
Tyler city	96,887	105,727	8,840	9.1%	35,597	15,053	1,830	9,055	3,739
Victoria city	62,624	67,020	4,396	7.0%	23,878	11,152	1,439	6,962	3,251
Waco city	124,831	138,180	13,349	10.7%	48,032	15,289	2,167	9,383	3,960
Wichita Falls city	104,682	104,568	-114	-0.1%	35,436	13,863	1,891	9,028	4,084
Utah									
Layton city	67,500	77,306	9,806	14.5%	24,599	7,728	400	4,281	na
Lehi city	47,776	66,029	18,253	38.2%	18,203	5,188	99	2,816	na
Ogden city	82,838	87,305	4,467	5.4%	30,698	9,300	884	6,379	3,208
Orem city	88,328	97,512	9,184	10.4%	29,020	9,224	1,073	4,933	1,361
Provo city	112,487	116,713	4,226	3.8%	32,912	7,145	1,153	4,560	1,540
St. George city	72,759	87,178	14,419	19.8%	31,911	21,045	3,132	12,957	3,941
Salt Lake City city	186,443	200,576	14,133	7.6%	80,714	20,951	1,873	14,311	7,618
Sandy city	89,977	96,901	6,924	7.7%	33,349	15,514	1,343	9,341	3,178
South Jordan city	50,473	74,155	23,682	46.9%	21,252	6,593	496	4,058	na
West Jordan city	103,601	116,047	12,446	12.0%	32,895	9,078	318	4,550	986
West Valley City city	129,491	136,420	6,929	5.4%	38,898	12,467	1,102	6,852	2,208
Virginia									
Alexandria city	140,008	160,530	20,522	14.7%	71,740	19,595	3,016	13,624	8,223
Chesapeake city	222,306	242,634	20,328	9.1%	86,122	32,045	3,151	18,389	6,689
Hampton city	137,384	134,313	-3,071	-2.2%	54,800	20,695	2,824	12,573	5,975
Lynchburg city	75,533	82,126	6,593	8.7%	28,500	11,906	1,685	7,727	4,120
Newport News city	180,994	178,626	-2,368	-1.3%	71,291	23,417	1,991	15,446	7,873
Norfolk city	242,827	244,076	1,249	0.5%	89,338	27,271	3,921	18,377	8,938
Portsmouth city	95,527	94,632	-895	-0.9%	34,578	13,934	1,543	9,668	5,355
Richmond city	204,327	228,783	24,456	12.0%	91,359	30,213	4,933	21,348	12,716
Roanoke city	96,912	99,920	3,008	3.1%	41,353	16,905	3,051	11,021	5,326
Suffolk city	84,572	91,185	6,613	7.8%	34,890	13,145	1,289	8,257	4,180
Virginia Beach city	437,903	450,189	12,286	2.8%	172,183	63,851	7,798	40,323	16,693
Washington									
Auburn city	70,164	82,782	12,618	18.0%	32,041	11,488	1,035	7,522	3,261
Bellevue city	127,885	147,595	19,710	15.4%	58,465	21,314	3,729	12,440	4,814
Bellingham city	81,252	90,660	9,408	11.6%	36,744	13,246	1,365	8,672	3,808
Everett city	103,070	111,263	8,193	7.9%	43,260	13,948	1,848	8,600	4,548
Federal Way city	89,300	97,037	7,737	8.7%	35,640	12,240	1,221	7,679	3,465
Kennewick city	73,995	82,950	8,955	12.1%	29,292	11,355	1,206	6,553	2,563
Kent city	118,614	129,613	10,999	9.3%	44,303	16,365	2,424	9,298	3,984
Kirkland city	80,585	89,557	8,972	11.1%	35,325	9,444	730	6,343	2,681
Marysville city	60,007	69,765	9,758	16.3%	26,254	9,044	998	6,205	2,854
Pasco city	62,160	71,727	9,567	15.4%	20,988	6,928	328	3,832	1,322

Table A-3: Cities - Summary Population Characteristics—*Continued*

	April 1, 2010 Census Population Estimates Base	2018 ACS Population	2010-2018 Population Change	2010-2018 Percent Change	Total Households	2018 ACS			
						Population 65 and Over	Population 85 and Over	Householders 65 and Over	Persons 65 and Over Living Alone
Washington—Cont.									
Redmond city	54,511	67,680	13,169	24.2%	26,496	5,413	817	2,993	1,420
Renton city	91,903	102,152	10,249	11.2%	39,951	12,707	2,185	7,514	3,057
Sammamish city	57,445	65,726	8,281	14.4%	21,839	4,685	165	2,577	na
Seattle city	608,666	744,949	136,283	22.4%	338,002	97,253	11,724	61,825	32,411
Spokane city	209,455	219,197	9,742	4.7%	92,562	34,424	4,217	21,816	10,698
Spokane Valley city	89,743	99,703	9,960	11.1%	39,724	15,046	1,413	10,574	5,790
Tacoma city	198,243	216,271	18,028	9.1%	85,676	29,721	3,519	18,254	9,363
Vancouver city	167,185	183,017	15,832	9.5%	73,966	30,271	3,275	19,345	9,936
Yakima city	91,276	93,874	2,598	2.8%	34,526	15,981	2,163	10,440	5,698
Wisconsin									
Appleton city	72,673	74,345	1,672	2.3%	29,864	11,161	1,593	6,963	2,900
Eau Claire city	66,230	68,256	2,026	3.1%	27,185	10,401	1,294	6,794	na
Green Bay city	103,911	104,880	969	0.9%	41,272	13,967	1,991	8,978	4,918
Kenosha city	99,323	100,151	828	0.8%	37,135	12,652	1,793	8,044	4,001
Madison city	233,163	258,034	24,871	10.7%	111,663	32,290	4,369	21,198	10,259
Milwaukee city	594,511	592,002	-2,509	-0.4%	231,041	64,261	8,414	42,162	21,542
Oshkosh city	66,205	66,737	532	0.8%	26,703	9,063	1,885	6,107	3,580
Racine city	78,848	77,434	-1,414	-1.8%	30,158	9,194	852	6,171	na
Waukesha city	71,222	72,549	1,327	1.9%	29,955	10,600	1,730	6,698	2,887

Table A-4: Metropolitan/Micropolitan Areas - Summary Population Characteristics

	April 1, 2010 Census Population Estimates Base	2018 ACS Population	2010-2018 Population Change	2010-2018 Percent Change	Total Households	2018 ACS			
						Population 65 and Over	Population 85 and Over	Householders 65 and Over	Persons 65 and Over Living Alone
Aberdeen, WA Micro Area	72,798	73,901	1,103	1.5%	27,674	16,312	1,549	8,920	3,591
Abilene, TX Metro Area	165,246	174,006	8,760	5.3%	61,527	25,654	3,166	15,770	6,419
Adrian, MI Micro Area	99,892	98,266	-1,626	-1.6%	38,388	18,092	2,130	11,422	4,978
Akron, OH Metro Area	703,203	704,845	1,642	0.2%	287,044	124,652	15,827	77,781	34,704
Alamogordo, NM Micro Area	63,832	66,781	2,949	4.6%	23,747	10,722	829	6,635	na
Albany, GA Metro Area	157,493	151,158	-6,335	-4.0%	56,348	23,201	2,575	14,219	6,232
Albany, OR Metro Area	116,676	127,335	10,659	9.1%	48,464	24,586	3,069	15,144	6,168
Albany-Schenectady-Troy, NY Metro Area	870,714	883,169	12,455	1.4%	353,746	153,463	19,966	95,951	41,864
Albertville, AL Micro Area	93,019	96,109	3,090	3.3%	36,022	16,487	1,756	10,016	4,097
Albuquerque, NM Metro Area	887,064	916,791	29,727	3.4%	358,493	153,593	17,822	94,579	40,665
Alexandria, LA Metro Area	153,918	153,044	-874	-0.6%	55,127	24,740	2,442	15,380	7,019
Allentown-Bethlehem-Easton, PA-NJ Metro Area	821,267	842,913	21,646	2.6%	320,501	152,534	23,164	92,311	39,548
Altoona, PA Metro Area	127,116	122,492	-4,624	-3.6%	51,096	25,493	3,145	16,090	7,234
Amarillo, TX Metro Area	251,937	268,356	16,419	6.5%	98,518	36,617	4,851	23,028	10,726
Ames, IA Metro Area	89,542	98,105	8,563	9.6%	37,290	11,562	1,405	7,369	na
Anchorage, AK Metro Area	380,821	399,148	18,327	4.8%	137,483	45,860	4,347	26,808	9,769
Ann Arbor, MI Metro Area	345,104	370963	25,859	7.5%	143,072	51775	5935	32,797	13,390
Anniston-Oxford-Jacksonville, AL Metro Area	118,594	114,277	-4,317	-3.6%	44,264	20,515	1,761	13,456	5,454
Appleton, WI Metro Area	225,664	237,524	11,860	5.3%	94,810	34,977	3,829	22,073	9,020
Asheville, NC Metro Area	424,859	459,585	34,726	8.2%	191,889	102,665	13,766	64,037	27,912
Ashtabula, OH Micro Area	101,490	97,493	-3,997	-3.9%	35,445	18,569	2,281	11,704	5,038
Athens, OH Micro Area	64,764	65,818	1,054	1.6%	22,533	8,637	1,103	5,581	2,990
Athens, TX Micro Area	78,534	82,299	3,765	4.8%	30,843	18,119	1,561	10,841	4,276
Athens-Clarke County, GA Metro Area	192,564	211,802	19,238	10.0%	79,945	28,378	2,930	17,820	7,472
Atlanta-Sandy Springs-Roswell, GA Metro Area	5,286,750	5,950,828	664,078	12.6%	2,137,280	731,877	70,693	432,497	168,876
Atlantic City-Hammonton, NJ Metro Area	274,521	265,429	-9,092	-3.3%	96,981	47,558	5,068	28,355	10,649
Auburn, NY Micro Area	80,017	77,145	-2,872	-3.6%	30,083	14,322	1,676	8,949	4,196
Auburn-Opelika, AL Metro Area	140,300	163,941	23,641	16.9%	59,336	19,887	1,776	11,705	4,127
Augusta-Richmond County, GA-SC Metro Area	564,873	605,903	41,030	7.3%	214,107	95,845	10,304	60,753	27,554
Augusta-Waterville, ME Micro Area	122,154	122,083	-71	-0.1%	54,299	24,870	3,578	16,362	7,734
Austin-Round Rock, TX Metro Area	1,716,321	2,168,316	451,995	26.3%	786,341	235,122	24,255	133,162	50,530
Bakersfield, CA Metro Area	839,619	896,764	57,145	6.8%	273,167	98,076	10,676	57,042	22,536
Baltimore-Columbia-Towson, MD Metro Area	2,710,602	2,802,789	92,187	3.4%	1,054,226	434,964	52,193	267,577	117,470
Bangor, ME Metro Area	153,932	151,096	-2,836	-1.8%	61,765	27,761	3,630	17,420	8,188
Barnstable Town, MA Metro Area	215,875	213,413	-2,462	-1.1%	86,671	65,453	7,670	39,226	15,767
Baton Rouge, LA Metro Area	802,504	831,310	28,806	3.6%	301,509	118,179	11,026	70,045	27,305
Battle Creek, MI Metro Area	136,148	134,487	-1,661	-1.2%	53,914	24,047	3,723	15,477	6,857
Bay City, MI Metro Area	107,773	103,923	-3,850	-3.6%	44,469	20,857	3,051	13,107	5,689
Beaumont-Port Arthur, TX Metro Area	403,194	410,233	7,039	1.7%	145,130	62,177	8,262	37,296	16,047
Beaver Dam, WI Micro Area	88,759	87,847	-912	-1.0%	35,221	15,571	2,621	9,515	3,774
Beckley, WV Metro Area	124,914	117,272	-7,642	-6.1%	48,632	24,654	2,224	16,440	7,632
Bellingham, WA Metro Area	201,146	225,685	24,539	12.2%	87,080	39,347	4,604	24,312	9,138
Bend-Redmond, OR Metro Area	157,730	191,996	34,266	21.7%	79,950	38,748	4,754	25,139	9,571
Billings, MT Metro Area	158,944	171,894	12,950	8.1%	71,787	30,187	4,381	19,232	8,422
Binghamton, NY Metro Area	251,724	240,219	-11,505	-4.6%	95,740	46,627	7,461	29,458	13,005
Birmingham-Hoover, AL Metro Area	1,128,058	1,151,801	23,743	2.1%	435,832	186,874	19,644	118,093	48,240
Bismarck, ND Metro Area	114,779	132,317	17,538	15.3%	56,382	21,151	3,363	13,014	5,943
Blacksburg-Christiansburg-Radford, VA Metro Area	178,254	181,926	3,672	2.1%	68,412	30,061	3,630	18,506	8,427
Bloomington, IL Metro Area	186,135	190,884	4,749	2.6%	73,580	25,570	3,638	16,015	6,971
Bloomington, IN Metro Area	159,536	167,762	8,226	5.2%	65,571	22,954	3,708	14,936	7,123
Bloomsburg-Berwick, PA Metro Area	85,561	83,696	-1,865	-2.2%	34,470	16,556	2,821	10,275	5,456
Bluefield, WV-VA Micro Area	107,333	99,986	-7,347	-6.8%	42,744	22,137	1,665	14,834	6,314
Boise City, ID Metro Area	616,566	732,257	115,691	18.8%	268,289	108,418	11,133	65,182	26,054
Boston-Cambridge-Newton, MA-NH Metro Area	4,552,598	4,875,390	322,792	7.1%	1,847,798	765,037	104,908	468,966	209,471
Boulder, CO Metro Area	294,561	326,078	31,517	10.7%	128,295	46,033	5,866	29,132	12,649
Bowling Green, KY Metro Area	158,608	177,183	18,575	11.7%	67,424	25,680	2,728	15,939	7,373
Bozeman, MT Micro Area	89,513	111,876	22,363	25.0%	44,423	14,428	1,108	8,441	3,005
Brainerd, MN Micro Area	91,077	94,408	3,331	3.7%	40,501	22,062	2,140	13,607	5,184
Branson, MO Micro Area	83,885	87,601	3,716	4.4%	36,201	22,374	2,592	14,109	5,319
Bremerton-Silverdale, WA Metro Area	251,143	269,805	18,662	7.4%	105,411	47,748	3,225	30,033	12,170
Bridgeport-Stamford-Norwalk, CT Metro Area	916,864	943,823	26,959	2.9%	345,634	149,824	21,890	92,257	39,760
Brownsville-Harlingen, TX Metro Area	406,215	423,908	17,693	4.4%	124,812	58,006	8,300	33,403	10,765
Brunswick, GA Metro Area	112,371	116,864	4,493	4.0%	47,266	23,933	2,528	15,458	5,731
Buffalo-Cheektowaga-Niagara Falls, NY Metro Area	1,135,614	1,130,152	-5,462	-0.5%	480,106	205,029	29,771	134,474	65,546
Burlington, NC Metro Area	151,160	166,436	15,276	10.1%	64,700	28,381	3,361	17,636	8,875
Burlington-South Burlington, VT Metro Area	211,262	220,612	9,350	4.4%	87,329	35,826	4,284	22,055	9,404
California-Lexington Park, MD Metro Area	105,143	112,664	7,521	7.2%	41,239	15,006	1,132	9,007	4,065
Canton-Massillon, OH Metro Area	404,425	398,655	-5,770	-1.4%	163,626	77,782	10,317	49,338	21,506
Cape Coral-Fort Myers, FL Metro Area	618,754	754,610	135,856	22.0%	281,222	216,260	27,692	121,190	45,200
Cape Girardeau, MO-IL Metro Area	96,274	93,647	-2,627	-2.7%	34,368	15,988	2,503	9,720	4,267
Carbondale-Marion, IL Metro Area	126,574	124,475	-2,099	-1.7%	51,205	21,552	2,626	14,043	6,642
Carson City, NV Metro Area	55,274	55,414	140	0.3%	23,099	11,198	1,987	7,131	3,828
Casper, WY Metro Area	75,448	79,115	3,667	4.9%	32,240	11,900	1,687	7,880	na
Cedar Rapids, IA Metro Area	257,943	272,295	14,352	5.6%	109,191	45,634	5,685	28,796	13,247
Centralia, WA Micro Area	75,457	79,604	4,147	5.5%	30,327	16,580	1,642	10,886	5,171
Chambersburg-Waynesboro, PA Metro Area	149,619	154,835	5,216	3.5%	59,834	29,943	3,936	18,693	6,813
Champaign-Urbana, IL Metro Area	231,887	237,356	5,469	2.4%	96,449	32,097	4,572	20,067	9,770

Table A-4: Metropolitan/Micropolitan Areas - Summary Population Characteristics—*Continued*

	April 1, 2010 Census Population Estimates Base	2018 ACS Population	2010-2018 Population Change	2010-2018 Percent Change	Total Households	2018 ACS			
						Population 65 and Over	Population 85 and Over	Householders 65 and Over	Persons 65 and Over Living Alone
Charleston, WV Metro Area	227,060	211,285	-15,775	-6.9%	90,728	43,439	5,213	28,326	13,028
Charleston-North Charleston, SC Metro Area	664,639	787,643	123,004	18.5%	294,424	119,346	12,787	73,111	29,285
Charlotte-Concord-Gastonia, NC-SC Metro Area	2,216,997	2,569,213	352,216	15.9%	960,297	347,776	34,079	206,470	82,823
Charlottesville, VA Metro Area	218,701	231,565	12,864	5.9%	88,765	42,770	5,044	25,656	10,038
Chattanooga, TN-GA Metro Area	528,150	558,703	30,553	5.8%	221,133	100,228	11,287	62,125	25,867
Cheyenne, WY Metro Area	91,885	98,976	7,091	7.7%	39,678	16,163	1,792	11,096	5,110
Chicago-Naperville-Elgin, IL-IN-WI Metro Area	9,461,539	9,497,790	36,251	0.4%	3,538,101	1,383,405	176,383	858,556	383,698
Chico, CA Metro Area	220,002	231,256	11,254	5.1%	88,636	42,820	4,441	25,859	9,972
Chillicothe, OH Micro Area	78,078	76,931	-1,147	-1.5%	29,779	13,356	692	8,430	3,311
Cincinnati, OH-KY-IN Metro Area	2,114,659	2,189,442	74,783	3.5%	862,535	331,435	39,799	208,494	93,076
Claremont-Lebanon, NH-VT Micro Area	218,478	217,215	-1,263	-0.6%	90,652	47,095	5,114	29,867	12,102
Clarksburg, WV Micro Area	94,197	89,718	-4,479	-4.8%	35,992	18,274	2,442	11,562	5,738
Clarksville, TN-KY Metro Area	260,630	290,745	30,115	11.6%	104,502	29,943	3,609	18,117	7,111
Clearlake, CA Micro Area	64,664	64,382	-282	-0.4%	26,774	14,856	1,161	9,808	5,701
Cleveland, TN Metro Area	115,754	124,748	8,994	7.8%	46,778	21,700	2,434	13,167	5,361
Cleveland-Elyria, OH Metro Area	2,077,278	2,057,009	-20,269	-1.0%	866,039	380,970	49,776	247,018	114,854
Coeur d'Alene, ID Metro Area	138,466	161,505	23,039	16.6%	64,955	30,553	2,611	19,738	8,150
College Station-Bryan, TX Metro Area	228,668	265,024	36,356	15.9%	94,615	28,145	2,009	17,983	7,216
Colorado Springs, CO Metro Area	645,609	738,939	93,330	14.5%	271,694	97,633	11,241	58,991	23,895
Columbia, MO Metro Area	162,645	180,005	17,360	10.7%	72,217	21,937	3,032	14,295	6,664
Columbia, SC Metro Area	767,476	833,165	65,689	8.6%	315,092	123,451	13,307	78,101	32,837
Columbus, GA-AL Metro Area	295,523	307,149	11,626	3.9%	114,607	43,364	5,229	28,711	12,912
Columbus, IN Metro Area	76,786	82,753	5,967	7.8%	31,891	13,549	1,156	8,957	4,323
Columbus, OH Metro Area	1,902,007	2,106,541	204,534	10.8%	801,805	278,962	30,795	173,268	71,380
Concord, NH Micro Area	146,457	151,132	4,675	3.2%	58,521	28,423	3,875	16,924	7,849
Cookeville, TN Micro Area	106,061	111,825	5,764	5.4%	46,184	19,533	2,257	11,946	5,010
Coos Bay, OR Micro Area	63,054	64,389	1,335	2.1%	27,889	17,313	1,773	10,783	4,928
Corning, NY Micro Area	98,990	95,796	-3,194	-3.2%	40,578	18,663	2,160	11,538	5,442
Corpus Christi, TX Metro Area	428,183	452,927	24,744	5.8%	161,693	68,560	7,274	40,269	15,058
Corvallis, OR Metro Area	85,582	92,101	6,519	7.6%	35,520	14,843	1,412	8,774	3,076
Crestview-Fort Walton Beach-Destin, FL Metro Area	235,868	278,644	42,776	18.1%	108,340	48,622	3,130	29,659	12,767
Cullman, AL Micro Area	80,406	83,442	3,036	3.8%	30,323	15,541	855	9,912	4,379
Cumberland, MD-WV Metro Area	103,245	97,915	-5,330	-5.2%	37,893	20,248	2,022	12,799	6,010
Dallas-Fort Worth-Arlington, TX Metro Area	6,426,222	7,540,371	1,114,149	17.3%	2,623,878	853,501	89,898	490,522	189,578
Dalton, GA Metro Area	142,221	143,983	1,762	1.2%	51,023	20,266	2,297	12,910	6,805
Danville, IL Metro Area	81,625	76,806	-4,819	-5.9%	30,166	15,156	2,197	9,996	5,249
Danville, VA Micro Area	106,550	101,642	-4,908	-4.6%	43,260	22,402	2,496	14,421	5,771
Daphne-Fairhope-Foley, AL Metro Area	182,264	218,022	35,758	19.6%	83,501	44,443	3,827	27,136	9,612
Davenport-Moline-Rock Island, IA-IL Metro Area	379,688	380,106	418	0.1%	153,865	68,233	8,139	42,545	20,591
Dayton, OH Metro Area	799,268	806,548	7,280	0.9%	331,426	145,239	17,754	92,499	41,795
Decatur, AL Metro Area	153,825	152,046	-1,779	-1.2%	57,863	26,514	3,091	17,149	7,301
Decatur, IL Metro Area	110,775	104,712	-6,063	-5.5%	44,562	21,167	2,441	13,096	5,826
Deltona-Daytona Beach-Ormond Beach, FL Metro Area	590,299	659,605	69,306	11.7%	259,697	169,088	25,904	98,613	39,110
Denver-Aurora-Lakewood, CO Metro Area	2,543,602	2,932,415	388,813	15.3%	1,131,410	377,709	40,874	237,112	104,784
Des Moines-West Des Moines, IA Metro Area	569,632	655,409	85,777	15.1%	255,055	86,724	10,335	54,699	25,183
Detroit-Warren-Dearborn, MI Metro Area	4,296,290	4,326,442	30,152	0.7%	1,710,686	709,952	86,377	456,698	211,296
Dothan, AL Metro Area	145,641	148,245	2,604	1.8%	55,431	27,910	2,869	18,008	7,741
Dover, DE Metro Area	162,349	178,550	16,201	10.0%	67,841	29,812	2,980	17,737	6,654
DuBois, PA Micro Area	81,616	79,388	-2,228	-2.7%	31,992	16,267	2,117	10,186	4,770
Dubuque, IA Metro Area	93,643	96,854	3,211	3.4%	38,501	17,441	2,671	10,313	4,465
Duluth, MN-WI Metro Area	279,776	278,799	-977	-0.3%	117,226	52,704	7,332	33,939	15,931
Dunn, NC Micro Area	114,681	134,214	19,533	17.0%	46,015	17,041	1,380	9,992	4,051
Durham-Chapel Hill, NC Metro Area	506,660	575,412	68,752	13.6%	225,699	88,160	8,727	53,500	20,840
East Stroudsburg, PA Metro Area	169,832	169,507	-325	-0.2%	55,109	28,128	2,571	15,553	5,815
Eau Claire, WI Metro Area	161,385	168,669	7,284	4.5%	66,796	28,261	3,465	17,510	7,796
El Centro, CA Metro Area	174,524	181,827	7,303	4.2%	41,764	23,512	2,645	10,251	2,865
Elizabeth City, NC Micro Area	64,094	66,815	2,721	4.2%	26,417	13,025	1,497	8,400	3,062
Elizabethtown-Fort Knox, KY Metro Area	148,340	152,459	4,119	2.8%	57,098	22,144	1,953	13,754	5,169
Elkhart-Goshen, IN Metro Area	197,559	205,560	8,001	4.0%	73,660	29,730	4,138	17,003	6,355
Elmira, NY Metro Area	88,849	84,254	-4,595	-5.2%	34,325	16,613	1,905	10,247	4,715
El Paso, TX Metro Area	804,129	844,723	40,594	5.0%	271,122	103,468	12,670	61,959	24,789
Enid, OK Metro Area	60,580	60,913	333	0.5%	22,998	9,839	1,600	6,272	na
Erie, PA Metro Area	280,584	272,061	-8,523	-3.0%	109,797	48,926	7,068	31,393	13,702
Eugene, OR Metro Area	351,704	379,611	27,907	7.9%	156,072	73,700	7,578	46,536	19,758
Eureka-Arcata-Fortuna, CA Micro Area	134,611	136,373	1,762	1.3%	55,773	24,296	2,817	16,123	7,063
Evansville, IN-KY Metro Area	311,548	314,672	3,124	1.0%	128,680	53,702	7,233	32,167	13,516
Fairbanks, AK Metro Area	97,585	98,971	1,386	1.4%	36,378	10,213	866	6,987	na
Fargo, ND-MN Metro Area	208,777	245,471	36,694	17.6%	99,306	30,080	4,694	19,059	8,966
Faribault-Northfield, MN Micro Area	64,142	66,523	2,381	3.7%	23,358	10,297	1,714	6,671	3,179
Farmington, MO Micro Area	65,367	66,692	1,325	2.0%	25,670	11,343	1,561	7,061	na
Farmington, NM Metro Area	130,045	125,043	-5,002	-3.8%	43,707	19,101	2,223	12,097	4,203
Fayetteville, NC Metro Area	366,323	387,094	20,771	5.7%	146,760	45,402	4,304	29,362	14,067
Fayetteville-Springdale-Rogers, AR-MO Metro Area	463,202	553,795	90,593	19.6%	205,278	70,560	9,194	42,779	15,430
Findlay, OH Micro Area	74,789	75,930	1,141	1.5%	31,606	12,829	1,977	8,173	3,795
Flagstaff, AZ Metro Area	134,431	142,854	8,423	6.3%	47,275	17,813	1,440	10,903	3,597
Flint, MI Metro Area	425,789	406,892	-18,897	-4.4%	169,469	71,160	7,505	47,441	20,834

Table A-4: Metropolitan/Micropolitan Areas - Summary Population Characteristics—*Continued*

	April 1, 2010 Census Population Estimates Base	2018 ACS Population	2010-2018 Population Change	2010-2018 Percent Change	Total Households	2018 ACS			
						Population 65 and Over	Population 85 and Over	Householders 65 and Over	Persons 65 and Over Living Alone
Florence, SC Metro Area	205,571	204,961	-610	-0.3%	75,826	36,038	3,037	22,407	9,517
Florence-Muscle Shoals, AL Metro Area	147,137	147,149	12	0.0%	59,932	29,490	3,505	18,903	6,963
Fond du Lac, WI Metro Area	101,627	103,066	1,439	1.4%	41,009	19,012	2,970	11,716	4,751
Forest City, NC Micro Area	67,816	66,826	-990	-1.5%	26,305	14,058	1,281	9,054	3,216
Fort Collins, CO Metro Area	299,615	350,518	50,903	17.0%	139,382	55,002	5,527	33,694	12,513
Fort Payne, AL Micro Area	71,116	71,385	269	0.4%	26,462	12,261	1,542	8,140	3,351
Fort Smith, AR-OK Metro Area	280,532	282,318	1,786	0.6%	108,790	47,832	4,169	30,619	13,551
Fort Wayne, IN Metro Area	416,262	437,631	21,369	5.1%	172,311	65,841	7,914	42,222	19,391
Frankfort, KY Micro Area	70,730	73,478	2,748	3.9%	29,980	12,641	1,079	8,330	3,567
Fresno, CA Metro Area	930,496	994,400	63,904	6.9%	309,519	121,540	17,185	72,341	30,520
Gadsden, AL Metro Area	104,427	102,501	-1,926	-1.8%	38,625	19,632	2,194	12,152	5,154
Gainesville, FL Metro Area	264,278	288,711	24,433	9.2%	105,161	41,611	5,133	24,269	10,811
Gainesville, GA Metro Area	179,726	202,148	22,422	12.5%	64,990	30,078	3,197	16,870	5,465
Gallup, NM Micro Area	71,485	72,290	805	1.1%	21,449	9,281	1,514	5,709	1,782
Gettysburg, PA Metro Area	101,424	102,811	1,387	1.4%	39,570	20,634	2,289	12,529	5,474
Glens Falls, NY Metro Area	128,941	125,462	-3,479	-2.7%	51,996	26,079	3,888	16,847	7,400
Glenwood Springs, CO Micro Area	73,538	78,170	4,632	6.3%	26,357	11,593	531	5,314	2,596
Goldsboro, NC Metro Area	122,673	123,248	575	0.5%	49,019	20,507	1,988	13,389	5,179
Grand Forks, ND-MN Metro Area	98,464	102,299	3,835	3.9%	43,081	14,881	2,139	9,459	4,604
Grand Island, NE Metro Area	81,850	85,104	3,254	4.0%	32,687	14,224	2,284	8,741	na
Grand Junction, CO Metro Area	146,717	153,207	6,490	4.4%	61,848	28,801	3,950	18,280	9,204
Grand Rapids-Wyoming, MI Metro Area	988,940	1,069,405	80,465	8.1%	397,199	155,825	18,951	97,417	41,280
Grants Pass, OR Metro Area	82,718	87,393	4,675	5.7%	37,059	22,863	1,924	14,454	5,873
Great Falls, MT Metro Area	81,323	81,643	320	0.4%	35,558	15,005	1,940	9,377	4,494
Greeley, CO Metro Area	252,847	314,305	61,458	24.3%	107,929	38,223	4,080	22,416	7,708
Green Bay, WI Metro Area	306,241	321,591	15,350	5.0%	129,113	51,178	5,074	32,733	15,278
Greeneville, TN Micro Area	68,825	69,087	262	0.4%	27,316	14,809	1,160	8,422	2,778
Greenfield Town, MA Micro Area	71,377	70,963	-414	-0.6%	30,391	15,424	2,182	9,784	4,462
Greensboro-High Point, NC Metro Area	723,885	767,711	43,826	6.1%	302,101	124,314	15,440	78,472	32,586
Greenville, NC Metro Area	168,167	179,914	11,747	7.0%	69,288	23,540	2,309	14,472	6,075
Greenville-Anderson-Mauldin, SC Metro Area	824,035	906,626	82,591	10.0%	344,664	150,232	14,068	93,228	38,625
Greenwood, SC Micro Area	95,110	95,654	544	0.6%	37,799	17,587	2,162	10,883	4,027
Gulfport-Biloxi-Pascagoula, MS Metro Area	370,787	397,261	26,474	7.1%	155,026	63,278	4,220	39,804	14,964
Hagerstown-Martinsburg, MD-WV Metro Area	251,602	268,049	16,447	6.5%	102,106	43,627	4,184	27,044	11,382
Hammond, LA Metro Area	121,107	133,777	12,670	10.5%	47,401	19,087	1,316	11,765	5,214
Hanford-Corcoran, CA Metro Area	152,982	151,366	-1,616	-1.1%	43,727	15,413	1,412	9,949	3,217
Harrisburg-Carlisle, PA Metro Area	549,468	574,659	25,191	4.6%	233,591	102,158	13,096	64,145	27,879
Harrisonburg, VA Metro Area	125,221	135,277	10,056	8.0%	47,987	19,885	2,458	12,547	5,761
Hartford-West Hartford-East Hartford, CT Metro Area	1,212,453	1,206,300	-6,153	-0.5%	470,651	209,397	30,020	127,370	59,785
Hattiesburg, MS Metro Area	142,845	149,119	6,274	4.4%	54,084	20,861	2,590	13,122	5,882
Helena, MT Micro Area	74,798	78,791	3,993	5.3%	32,096	15,484	2,058	9,420	4,198
Hermiston-Pendleton, OR Micro Area	87,062	88,920	1,858	2.1%	29,590	13,062	1,415	8,178	3,619
Hickory-Lenoir-Morganton, NC Metro Area	365,830	368,416	2,586	0.7%	145,158	69,501	7,594	43,086	17,026
Hilo, HI Micro Area	185,076	200,983	15,907	8.6%	71,565	42,643	4,237	25,848	10,755
Hilton Head Island-Bluffton-Beaufort, SC Metro Area	187,010	217,686	30,676	16.4%	84,041	56,307	4,386	32,829	9,822
Hinesville, GA Metro Area	77,919	80,008	2,089	2.7%	31,296	6,690	461	4,212	na
Hobbs, NM Micro Area	64,727	69,611	4,884	7.5%	23,215	7,856	924	4,873	2,272
Holland, MI Micro Area	111,407	117,327	5,920	5.3%	43,992	19,808	1,994	11,325	3,767
Homosassa Springs, FL Metro Area	141,229	147,929	6,700	4.7%	62,293	53,832	6,810	33,165	14,744
Hot Springs, AR Metro Area	96,000	99,154	3,154	3.3%	40,407	22,991	2,956	14,925	5,562
Houma-Thibodaux, LA Metro Area	208,184	209,136	952	0.5%	73,749	32,179	3,254	19,686	7,686
Houston-The Woodlands-Sugar Land, TX Metro Area	5,920,487	6,997,384	1,076,897	18.2%	2,359,266	780,719	73,053	446,713	167,941
Huntington-Ashland, WV-KY-OH Metro Area	364,884	352,823	-12,061	-3.3%	136,769	67,808	7,793	41,113	17,565
Huntsville, AL Metro Area	417,593	462,693	45,100	10.8%	185,056	70,760	7,130	45,512	18,655
Huntsville, TX Micro Area	82,536	84,993	2,457	3.0%	27,735	13,320	1,690	7,993	na
Hutchinson, KS Micro Area	64,511	62,342	-2,169	-3.4%	25,256	12,432	1,781	7,982	4,054
Idaho Falls, ID Metro Area	133,329	149,051	15,722	11.8%	50,354	19,032	2,877	11,776	4,418
Indiana, PA Micro Area	88,889	84,501	-4,388	-4.9%	33,098	16,623	2,405	10,360	3,923
Indianapolis-Carmel-Anderson, IN Metro Area	1,888,085	2,048,428	160,343	8.5%	783,345	281,078	31,421	173,440	74,734
Iowa City, IA Metro Area	152,586	173,401	20,815	13.6%	69,686	21,826	2,920	13,552	5,097
Ithaca, NY Metro Area	101,580	102,793	1,213	1.2%	40,250	14,229	2,039	9,079	3,639
Jackson, MI Metro Area	160,245	158,823	-1,422	-0.9%	62,598	28,547	3,269	17,558	8,067
Jackson, MS Metro Area	567,632	583,080	15,448	2.7%	210,166	84,081	9,044	52,662	22,558
Jackson, TN Metro Area	130,022	129,209	-813	-0.6%	50,548	22,308	3,178	13,726	5,885
Jacksonville, FL Metro Area	1,345,591	1,534,701	189,110	14.1%	575,423	242,793	22,734	146,371	61,705
Jacksonville, NC Metro Area	177,799	197,683	19,884	11.2%	66,834	18,036	1,610	10,186	3,775
Jamestown-Dunkirk-Fredonia, NY Micro Area	134,907	127,939	-6,968	-5.2%	53,429	25,587	3,908	15,814	7,314
Janesville-Beloit, WI Metro Area	160,335	163,129	2,794	1.7%	64,632	27,151	3,224	17,695	7,819
Jefferson, GA Micro Area	60,457	70,422	9,965	16.5%	23,640	10,244	1,201	5,719	na
Jefferson City, MO Metro Area	149,797	150,243	446	0.3%	57,053	24,869	2,369	15,935	7,090
Johnson City, TN Metro Area	198,757	203,921	5,164	2.6%	85,430	39,791	4,951	23,772	10,138
Johnstown, PA Metro Area	143,681	131,730	-11,951	-8.3%	56,483	29,664	4,365	19,834	8,569
Jonesboro, AR Metro Area	121,020	132,532	11,512	9.5%	52,335	19,799	1,827	12,583	4,811
Joplin, MO Metro Area	175,509	178,902	3,393	1.9%	71,145	29,091	3,511	19,793	9,082
Kahului-Wailuku-Lahaina, HI Metro Area	154,930	167,295	12,365	8.0%	52,851	30,503	3,957	16,943	5,018
Kalamazoo-Portage, MI Metro Area	326,591	340,318	13,727	4.2%	132,841	53,917	5,798	33,299	15,243
Kalispell, MT Micro Area	90,927	102,106	11,179	12.3%	38,372	19,958	1,403	11,891	4,845

Table A-4: Metropolitan/Micropolitan Areas - Summary Population Characteristics—*Continued*

	April 1, 2010 Census Population Estimates Base	2018 ACS Population	2010-2018 Population Change	2010-2018 Percent Change	Total Households	2018 ACS			
						Population 65 and Over	Population 85 and Over	Householders 65 and Over	Persons 65 and Over Living Alone
Kankakee, IL Metro Area	113,450	110,024	-3,426	-3.0%	40,642	18,344	2,763	10,631	4,926
Kansas City, MO-KS Metro Area	2,009,341	2,142,419	133,078	6.6%	835,092	318,298	37,831	195,894	79,916
Kapaa, HI Micro Area	67,095	72,133	5,038	7.5%	22,685	14,709	1,606	9,017	3,286
Keene, NH Micro Area	77,122	76,493	-629	-0.8%	30,208	15,095	1,244	9,178	4,566
Kennewick-Richland, WA Metro Area	253,332	296,224	42,892	16.9%	98,988	39,249	4,360	22,981	8,843
Key West, FL Micro Area	73,090	75,027	1,937	2.7%	31,362	16,972	846	9,842	3,543
Killeen-Temple, TX Metro Area	405,313	451,681	46,368	11.4%	152,160	50,702	4,089	30,645	11,897
Kingsport-Bristol-Bristol, TN-VA Metro Area	309,502	306,562	-2,940	-0.9%	125,768	68,076	7,573	43,634	19,437
Kingston, NY Metro Area	182,512	178,599	-3,913	-2.1%	69,154	35,125	4,398	21,616	9,360
Klamath Falls, OR Micro Area	66,380	67,653	1,273	1.9%	26,798	14,610	1,581	8,846	4,298
Knoxville, TN Metro Area	837,677	882,598	44,921	5.4%	344,657	161,951	16,006	99,845	39,144
Kokomo, IN Metro Area	82,752	82,366	-386	-0.5%	35,139	15,917	2,363	10,516	3,644
La Crosse-Onalaska, WI-MN Metro Area	133,660	136,808	3,148	2.4%	56,157	23,140	3,632	14,525	6,414
Lafayette, LA Metro Area	466,736	489,364	22,628	4.8%	184,357	69,960	8,209	44,567	17,592
Lafayette-West Lafayette, IN Metro Area	201,794	222,676	20,882	10.3%	81,884	27,515	3,774	17,007	7,890
LaGrange, GA Micro Area	67,039	70,034	2,995	4.5%	25,417	10,065	1,056	6,585	na
Lake Charles, LA Metro Area	199,641	209,548	9,907	5.0%	80,385	31,237	3,489	20,957	9,230
Lake City, FL Micro Area	67,526	70,503	2,977	4.4%	25,678	12,978	1,628	7,568	3,295
Lake Havasu City-Kingman, AZ Metro Area	200,182	209,550	9,368	4.7%	90,270	63,794	5,643	39,594	13,697
Lakeland-Winter Haven, FL Metro Area	602,098	708,009	105,911	17.6%	241,171	143,426	14,993	84,267	31,331
Lancaster, PA Metro Area	519,446	543,557	24,111	4.6%	202,490	98,751	12,133	57,454	21,281
Lansing-East Lansing, MI Metro Area	464,021	481,893	17,872	3.9%	186,832	73,716	8,684	46,592	20,167
Laredo, TX Metro Area	250,304	275,910	25,606	10.2%	75,300	26,003	2,596	15,185	5,836
Las Cruces, NM Metro Area	209,202	217,522	8,320	4.0%	80,409	34,786	3,125	20,682	8,365
Las Vegas-Henderson-Paradise, NV Metro Area	1,951,271	2,231,647	280,376	14.4%	808,605	328,690	31,017	187,797	74,898
Laurel, MS Micro Area	84,834	81,762	-3,072	-3.6%	31,092	14,812	1,683	9,654	3,340
Lawrence, KS Metro Area	110,826	121,436	10,610	9.6%	48,907	15,300	2,395	9,782	4,452
Lawton, OK Metro Area	130,288	125,696	-4,592	-3.5%	44,611	16,238	1,942	10,434	4,613
Lebanon, PA Metro Area	133,577	141,314	7,737	5.8%	54,522	27,709	4,149	17,563	7,191
Lewiston, ID-WA Metro Area	60,893	63,018	2,125	3.5%	25,267	14,866	1,819	8,946	3,804
Lewiston-Auburn, ME Metro Area	107,710	107,679	-31	-0.0%	44,897	19,292	2,055	12,277	6,291
Lexington-Fayette, KY Metro Area	472,103	516,697	44,594	9.4%	204,420	72,676	7,530	44,993	19,558
Lima, OH Metro Area	106,315	102,663	-3,652	-3.4%	41,204	17,930	1,931	11,540	5,465
Lincoln, NE Metro Area	302,157	333,964	31,807	10.5%	132,621	46,767	5,421	30,654	13,970
Little Rock-North Little Rock-Conway, AR Metro Area	699,796	741,357	41,561	5.9%	284,383	114,827	12,519	69,133	27,007
Logan, UT-ID Metro Area	125,442	141,476	16,034	12.8%	43,423	13,682	1,248	8,243	3,126
London, KY Micro Area	126,370	128,214	1,844	1.5%	45,501	20,529	2,254	12,308	4,556
Longview, TX Metro Area	214,367	219,417	5,050	2.4%	76,416	35,679	4,134	21,507	8,414
Longview, WA Metro Area	102,408	108,987	6,579	6.4%	43,279	20,856	2,494	13,407	5,218
Los Angeles-Long Beach-Anaheim, CA Metro Area	12,828,946	13,291,486	462,540	3.6%	4,354,302	1,847,185	258,165	1,010,518	394,639
Louisville/Jefferson County, KY-IN Metro Area	1,235,691	1,296,815	61,124	4.9%	507,467	208,062	23,396	129,880	54,318
Lubbock, TX Metro Area	290,889	319,995	29,106	10.0%	120,125	39,904	4,573	24,925	9,552
Lufkin, TX Micro Area	86,771	87,092	321	0.4%	29,898	13,896	1,972	7,583	3,358
Lumberton, NC Micro Area	134,229	131,831	-2,398	-1.8%	46,026	19,861	2,330	12,744	4,876
Lynchburg, VA Metro Area	252,659	265,405	12,746	5.0%	103,276	50,205	6,320	31,368	14,131
Macon-Bibb County, GA Metro Area	232,287	226,680	-5,607	-2.4%	84,705	36,946	3,693	23,565	11,390
Madera, CA Metro Area	150,841	157,672	6,831	4.5%	44,484	22,099	2,668	11,632	4,137
Madison, WI Metro Area	605,449	660422	54,973	9.1%	275,594	96572	11507	61,984	26,847
Manchester-Nashua, NH Metro Area	400,699	415,247	14,548	3.6%	161,649	64,850	8,636	38,337	16,386
Manhattan, KS Metro Area	92,740	97,980	5,240	5.7%	35,912	10,584	1,179	6,689	3,227
Manitowoc, WI Micro Area	81,442	79,074	-2,368	-2.9%	35,259	15,941	2,333	10,386	4,817
Mankato-North Mankato, MN Metro Area	96,742	101,647	4,905	5.1%	39,263	14,938	2,250	9,313	3,962
Mansfield, OH Metro Area	124,474	121,099	-3,375	-2.7%	48,105	23,735	3,751	15,028	6,416
Marinette, WI-MI Micro Area	65,778	63,417	-2,361	-3.6%	29,110	15,235	2,039	9,494	4,374
Marion, IN Micro Area	70,063	65,936	-4,127	-5.9%	26,923	12,533	1,571	8,420	na
Marion, OH Micro Area	66,501	65,256	-1,245	-1.9%	24,205	11,407	1,689	6,905	3,058
Marquette, MI Micro Area	67,071	66,516	-555	-0.8%	26,328	12,824	1,500	8,026	3,669
Marshall, TX Micro Area	65,644	66,726	1,082	1.6%	22,928	10,877	1,144	6,821	na
Martinsville, VA Micro Area	67,996	64,947	-3,049	-4.5%	26,919	15,169	1,937	9,267	4,136
McAllen-Edinburg-Mission, TX Metro Area	774,768	865,939	91,171	11.8%	237,323	96,015	10,542	56,271	19,029
Meadville, PA Micro Area	88,750	85,063	-3,687	-4.2%	34,386	17,556	1,692	11,241	4,362
Medford, OR Metro Area	203,205	219,564	16,359	8.1%	89,787	48,689	6,082	29,411	12,533
Memphis, TN-MS-AR Metro Area	1,324,829	1,350,064	25,235	1.9%	504,141	188,539	20,369	120,430	53,721
Merced, CA Metro Area	255,796	274,765	18,969	7.4%	79,487	30,748	3,475	18,366	7,595
Meridian, MS Micro Area	107,445	104,181	-3,264	-3.0%	39,914	18,383	1,976	12,145	4,997
Miami-Fort Lauderdale-West Palm Beach, FL Metro Area	5,566,294	6,198,782	632,488	11.4%	2,143,067	1,127,331	170,413	623,998	266,753
Michigan City-La Porte, IN Metro Area	111,463	110,007	-1,456	-1.3%	43,122	19,676	1,943	13,199	6,152
Midland, MI Metro Area	83,626	83,209	-417	-0.5%	34,091	15,539	2,269	9,892	4,387
Midland, TX Metro Area	141,671	177,218	35,547	25.1%	59,179	19,160	2,333	12,836	6,687
Milwaukee-Waukesha-West Allis, WI Metro Area	1,555,954	1,576,113	20,159	1.3%	634,398	246,058	33,384	156,917	73,182
Minneapolis-St. Paul-Bloomington, MN-WI Metro Area	3,348,862	3,629,190	280,328	8.4%	1,386,468	507,293	61,141	313,964	138,995
Minot, ND Micro Area	69,537	75,668	6,131	8.8%	31,548	10,568	1,515	6,758	na
Missoula, MT Metro Area	109,296	118,791	9,495	8.7%	50,401	18,257	1,528	11,491	4,892
Mobile, AL Metro Area	413,145	413,757	612	0.1%	158,627	66,558	6,972	43,522	18,530
Modesto, CA Metro Area	514,451	549,815	35,364	6.9%	175,171	72,507	8,557	41,197	14,471
Monroe, LA Metro Area	176,505	176,805	300	0.2%	64,791	27,617	2,395	16,717	7,513
Monroe, MI Metro Area	152,024	150,439	-1,585	-1.0%	61,586	27,543	3,738	18,137	7,605
Montgomery, AL Metro Area	374,541	373,401	-1,140	-0.3%	142,728	57,249	6,199	37,384	15,729

Table A-4: Metropolitan/Micropolitan Areas - Summary Population Characteristics—*Continued*

	April 1, 2010 Census Population Estimates Base	2018 ACS Population	2010-2018 Population Change	2010-2018 Percent Change	Total Households	2018 ACS			
						Population 65 and Over	Population 85 and Over	Householders 65 and Over	Persons 65 and Over Living Alone
Morehead City, NC Micro Area	66,463	69,524	3,061	4.6%	28,720	17,455	1,613	11,038	4,469
Morgantown, WV Metro Area	129,710	140,259	10,549	8.1%	53,173	19,954	2,245	12,186	4,565
Morristown, TN Metro Area	114,199	118,581	4,382	3.8%	43,772	22,245	1,698	13,095	4,694
Moses Lake, WA Micro Area	89,124	97,331	8,207	9.2%	30,806	14,081	1,325	7,992	2,803
Mount Airy, NC Micro Area	73,743	71,948	-1,795	-2.4%	29,230	15,066	1,964	9,879	4,348
Mount Pleasant, MI Micro Area	70,313	70,562	249	0.4%	25,367	9,094	990	5,749	2,673
Mount Vernon-Anacortes, WA Metro Area	116,893	128,206	11,313	9.7%	48,474	26,616	2,992	15,788	5,800
Muncie, IN Metro Area	117,664	114,772	-2,892	-2.5%	45,311	19,931	3,185	12,849	5,641
Muskegon, MI Metro Area	172,194	173,588	1,394	0.8%	67,196	29,441	3,263	18,617	7,321
Muskogee, OK Micro Area	70,988	68,362	-2,626	-3.7%	26,566	11,320	1,478	7,165	3,270
Myrtle Beach-Conway-North Myrtle Beach, SC-NC Metro Area	376,555	480,891	104,336	27.7%	187,932	126,894	8,654	73,740	25,772
Nacogdoches, TX Micro Area	64,524	65,711	1,187	1.8%	23,442	9,550	867	6,068	na
Napa, CA Metro Area	136,578	139,417	2,839	2.1%	47,315	26,805	2,708	15,144	6,024
Naples-Immokalee-Marco Island, FL Metro Area	321,521	378,488	56,967	17.7%	144,172	122,463	18,268	68,705	24,323
Nashville-Davidson--Murfreesboro--Franklin, TN Metro Area	1,670,876	1,932,099	261,223	15.6%	730,709	256,271	23,901	157,468	63,492
New Bern, NC Metro Area	126,813	123,433	-3,380	-2.7%	49,527	25,525	2,149	16,581	7,214
New Castle, PA Micro Area	91,140	86,184	-4,956	-5.4%	37,497	18,978	1,872	11,822	4,880
New Haven-Milford, CT Metro Area	862,456	857,620	-4,836	-0.6%	335,539	148,789	22,610	90,805	40,417
New Orleans-Metairie, LA Metro Area	1,189,889	1,270,399	80,510	6.8%	482,442	201,182	20,857	123,478	54,655
New Philadelphia-Dover, OH Micro Area	92,587	92,176	-411	-0.4%	36,740	18,027	2,252	11,470	6,010
New York-Newark-Jersey City, NY-NJ-PA Metro Area	19,566,527	19,979,477	412,950	2.1%	7,282,923	3,143,409	430,919	1,893,325	826,350
Niles-Benton Harbor, MI Metro Area	156,811	154,141	-2,670	-1.7%	64,783	30,468	4,686	19,901	8,338
North Port-Sarasota-Bradenton, FL Metro Area	702,314	821,573	119,259	17.0%	334,535	264,853	36,472	159,541	62,780
North Wilkesboro, NC Micro Area	69,310	68,557	-753	-1.1%	30,123	14,695	1,297	10,532	5,099
Norwich-New London, CT Metro Area	274,068	266,784	-7,284	-2.7%	108,098	48,314	6,115	29,852	13,218
Oak Harbor, WA Micro Area	78,508	84,460	5,952	7.6%	34,572	20,803	1,834	12,750	4,860
Ocala, FL Metro Area	331,299	359,977	28,678	8.7%	143,441	104,024	12,155	62,379	23,454
Ocean City, NJ Metro Area	97,261	92,560	-4,701	-4.8%	39,208	24,068	2,635	14,880	6,081
Odessa, TX Metro Area	137,136	162,124	24,988	18.2%	54,326	15,171	1,261	9,917	4,518
Ogden-Clearfield, UT Metro Area	597,162	676,948	79,786	13.4%	211,332	74,241	7,439	44,316	13,412
Ogdensburg-Massena, NY Micro Area	111,940	108,047	-3,893	-3.5%	41,680	18,468	2,550	12,077	6,062
Oklahoma City, OK Metro Area	1,252,990	1,396,445	143,455	11.4%	522,039	193,989	22,571	123,243	54,609
Olean, NY Micro Area	80,343	76,840	-3,503	-4.4%	32,079	14,641	1,524	9,120	3,804
Olympia-Tumwater, WA Metro Area	252,260	286,419	34,159	13.5%	110,713	49,236	5,381	29,900	12,354
Omaha-Council Bluffs, NE-IA Metro Area	865,347	941,924	76,577	8.8%	362,764	130,302	16,979	83,376	38,067
Opelousas, LA Micro Area	83,384	82,764	-620	-0.7%	29,965	13,167	1,402	8,223	3,947
Orangeburg, SC Micro Area	92,509	86,934	-5,575	-6.0%	33,561	16,866	1,553	11,251	5,081
Orlando-Kissimmee-Sanford, FL Metro Area	2,134,402	2,572,962	438,560	20.5%	876,502	381,169	41,220	206,946	75,888
Oshkosh-Neenah, WI Metro Area	166,996	171,020	4,024	2.4%	71,332	27,997	4,386	18,183	9,228
Ottawa-Peru, IL Micro Area	154,901	147,853	-7,048	-4.6%	60,404	29,385	3,512	19,294	8,714
Owensboro, KY Metro Area	114,748	119,691	4,943	4.3%	46,687	20,637	2,279	13,373	5,483
Owosso, MI Micro Area	70,663	68,192	-2,471	-3.5%	28,218	12,597	1,419	7,895	3,344
Oxnard-Thousand Oaks-Ventura, CA Metro Area	823,393	850,967	27,574	3.3%	271,980	132,219	18,528	76,222	28,150
Paducah, KY-IL Micro Area	98,757	98,658	-99	-0.1%	39,679	19,943	3,337	12,805	5,884
Palatka, FL Micro Area	74,368	74,163	-205	-0.3%	27,927	17,314	717	10,815	4,305
Palm Bay-Melbourne-Titusville, FL Metro Area	543,372	596,849	53,477	9.8%	226,363	141,268	20,627	84,167	35,729
Panama City, FL Metro Area	184,713	202,977	18,264	9.9%	80,447	34,734	3,737	21,480	8,873
Parkersburg-Vienna, WV Metro Area	92,668	92,499	-169	-0.2%	38,995	18,568	1,749	12,125	5,737
Pensacola-Ferry Pass-Brent, FL Metro Area	448,991	494,883	45,892	10.2%	182,711	81,412	8,216	48,637	17,570
Peoria, IL Metro Area	379,182	368,683	-10,499	-2.8%	147,607	66,223	10,889	40,156	18,211
Philadelphia-Camden-Wilmington, PA-NJ-DE-MD Metro Area	5,965,705	6,096,372	130,667	2.2%	2,285,651	973,717	125,171	601,231	265,684
Phoenix-Mesa-Scottsdale, AZ Metro Area	4,193,127	4,857,962	664,835	15.9%	1,730,400	760,024	83,307	443,253	172,643
Pine Bluff, AR Metro Area	100,290	90,306	-9,984	-10.0%	32,467	15,329	2,136	9,953	4,160
Pinehurst-Southern Pines, NC Micro Area	88,242	98,682	10,440	11.8%	40,756	23,584	3,053	14,474	5,748
Pittsburgh, PA Metro Area	2,356,302	2,324,743	-31,559	-1.3%	1,013,812	464,038	65,156	303,276	144,997
Pittsfield, MA Metro Area	131,275	126,348	-4,927	-3.8%	55,212	29,239	3,829	18,271	8,300
Plattsburgh, NY Micro Area	82,131	80,695	-1,436	-1.7%	31,392	13,523	1,498	8,126	3,601
Pocatello, ID Metro Area	82,842	87,138	4,296	5.2%	30,635	12,344	1,616	7,726	3,210
Port Angeles, WA Micro Area	71,404	76,737	5,333	7.5%	33,265	22,161	3,101	14,164	5,916
Portland-South Portland, ME Metro Area	514,104	535,420	21,316	4.1%	228,248	104,289	12,472	67,209	29,399
Portland-Vancouver-Hillsboro, OR-WA Metro Area	2,225,996	2,478,996	253,000	11.4%	954,947	368,880	39,815	229,907	100,781
Port St. Lucie, FL Metro Area	424,107	482,040	57,933	13.7%	181,838	127,627	15,809	74,558	28,767
Portsmouth, OH Micro Area	79,493	75,502	-3,991	-5.0%	28,719	13,526	1,671	8,572	3,771
Pottsville, PA Micro Area	148,291	142,067	-6,224	-4.2%	58,458	28,879	4,148	18,720	8,378
Prescott, AZ Metro Area	211,014	231,993	20,979	9.9%	100,836	73,656	7,371	47,659	21,886
Providence-Warwick, RI-MA Metro Area	1,601,211	1,621,337	20,126	1.3%	621,705	277,501	39,700	173,365	81,381
Provo-Orem, UT Metro Area	526,885	632,705	105,820	20.1%	174,426	49,393	4,791	28,931	8,407
Pueblo, CO Metro Area	159,063	167,529	8,466	5.3%	64,954	30,832	3,900	19,899	9,123
Punta Gorda, FL Metro Area	159,964	184,998	25,034	15.6%	74,975	74,321	10,912	42,134	15,924
Quincy, IL-MO Micro Area	77,306	76,007	-1,299	-1.7%	30,277	14,888	2,212	9,049	4,072
Racine, WI Metro Area	195,428	196584	1,156	0.6%	76,808	32401	3701	20,635	9,781
Raleigh, NC Metro Area	1,130,488	1,362,540	232,052	20.5%	504,854	165,869	16,656	97,805	39,207
Rapid City, SD Metro Area	134,618	147,316	12,698	9.4%	58,509	26,254	3,476	16,401	6,187
Reading, PA Metro Area	411,556	420,152	8,596	2.1%	157,006	72,315	10,860	43,204	18,558
Redding, CA Metro Area	177,221	180,040	2,819	1.6%	68,198	37,027	3,952	22,428	8,578
Reno, NV Metro Area	425,439	471,265	45,826	10.8%	187,724	77,448	7,232	48,709	20,896
Richmond, IN Micro Area	68,996	65,936	-3,060	-4.4%	28,338	12,445	1,847	8,133	3,681

Table A-4: Metropolitan/Micropolitan Areas - Summary Population Characteristics—*Continued*

	April 1, 2010 Census Population Estimates Base	2018 ACS Population	2010-2018 Population Change	2010-2018 Percent Change	Total Households	2018 ACS Population 65 and Over	Population 85 and Over	Householders 65 and Over	Persons 65 and Over Living Alone
Richmond, VA Metro Area	1,208,089	1,303,621	95,532	7.9%	497,416	203,199	24,290	129,450	57,557
Richmond-Berea, KY Micro Area	99,969	108,961	8,992	9.0%	39,908	15,896	1,813	9,739	3,810
Riverside-San Bernardino-Ontario, CA Metro Area	4,224,966	4,622,361	397,395	9.4%	1,366,750	604,193	68,643	326,011	119,140
Roanoke, VA Metro Area	308,669	314,515	5,846	1.9%	126,687	64,438	8,073	38,848	16,680
Roanoke Rapids, NC Micro Area	76,733	70,250	-6,483	-8.4%	27,118	14,619	1,214	9,350	3,615
Rochester, MN Metro Area	206,882	219,802	12,920	6.2%	88,644	36,635	5,070	22,103	9,148
Rochester, NY Metro Area	1,079,697	1,071,082	-8,615	-0.8%	430,682	190,436	24,713	120,189	55,762
Rockford, IL Metro Area	349,431	337,658	-11,773	-3.4%	133,049	57,622	7,081	36,083	14,858
Rocky Mount, NC Metro Area	152,375	146,021	-6,354	-4.2%	58,844	27,750	2,580	19,318	8,448
Rome, GA Metro Area	96,314	97,927	1,613	1.7%	34,672	16,533	1,843	10,194	4,360
Roseburg, OR Micro Area	107,684	110,283	2,599	2.4%	45,647	27,924	2,281	17,844	6,466
Roswell, NM Micro Area	65,648	64,689	-959	-1.5%	22,616	10,830	1,559	6,568	2,938
Russellville, AR Micro Area	83,939	85,535	1,596	1.9%	29,267	13,431	1,651	7,873	3,171
Sacramento--Roseville--Arden-Arcade, CA Metro Area	2,149,151	2,345,210	196,059	9.1%	835,453	361,797	44,627	213,573	88,852
Saginaw, MI Metro Area	200,169	190,800	-9,369	-4.7%	78,740	36,766	5,153	23,894	10,526
St. Cloud, MN Metro Area	189,093	199,801	10,708	5.7%	74,937	29,710	4,276	18,046	7,930
St. George, UT Metro Area	138,115	171,700	33,585	24.3%	59,863	37,295	4,525	22,266	6,770
St. Joseph, MO-KS Metro Area	127,327	126,991	-336	-0.3%	46,816	21,361	2,930	13,619	5,645
St. Louis, MO-IL Metro Area	2,787,752	2804724	16,972	0.6%	1,137,478	463355	57901	297,140	129,833
Salem, OH Micro Area	107,852	102,665	-5,187	-4.8%	41,884	21,175	2,147	12,925	5,398
Salem, OR Metro Area	390,750	432,102	41,352	10.6%	150,729	68,775	8,134	41,060	16,381
Salinas, CA Metro Area	415,061	435,594	20,533	4.9%	126,299	59,491	8,363	34,561	13,076
Salisbury, MD-DE Metro Area	373,760	409,979	36,219	9.7%	161,305	98,792	8,876	59,544	21,853
Salt Lake City, UT Metro Area	1,087,808	1,222,540	134,732	12.4%	402,242	131,820	12,951	79,657	30,094
San Angelo, TX Metro Area	111,825	119,310	7,485	6.7%	43,938	18,297	2,438	11,834	4,648
San Antonio-New Braunfels, TX Metro Area	2,142,521	2,518,036	375,515	17.5%	823,888	328,673	36,204	187,397	69,133
San Diego-Carlsbad, CA Metro Area	3,095,349	3,343,364	248,015	8.0%	1,130,911	469,821	59,080	268,419	103,117
Sandusky, OH Micro Area	77,066	74,615	-2,451	-3.2%	31,675	16,157	2,718	10,135	4,879
San Francisco-Oakland-Hayward, CA Metro Area	4,335,587	4,729,484	393,897	9.1%	1,698,978	732,156	95,715	420,538	177,128
San Jose-Sunnyvale-Santa Clara, CA Metro Area	1,836,937	1,999,107	162,170	8.8%	663,870	269,192	38,328	143,608	48,695
San Luis Obispo-Paso Robles-Arroyo Grande, CA Metro Area	269,597	284,010	14,413	5.3%	106,198	57,594	6,503	35,948	13,760
Santa Cruz-Watsonville, CA Metro Area	262,356	274,255	11,899	4.5%	94,994	45,343	3,835	27,799	10,508
Santa Fe, NM Metro Area	144,227	150,056	5,829	4.0%	62,707	36,568	2,730	22,869	9,366
Santa Maria-Santa Barbara, CA Metro Area	423,947	446,527	22,580	5.3%	146,224	68,402	9,638	41,277	15,513
Santa Rosa, CA Metro Area	483,868	499,942	16,074	3.3%	187,434	98,030	11,980	62,227	27,178
Savannah, GA Metro Area	347,598	389,494	41,896	12.1%	142,909	55,207	5,596	34,075	13,981
Scranton--Wilkes-Barre--Hazleton, PA Metro Area	563,617	555,485	-8,132	-1.4%	227,731	110,941	15,650	70,268	33,119
Searcy, AR Micro Area	77,078	78,727	1,649	2.1%	29,577	12,307	1,307	8,138	na
Seattle-Tacoma-Bellevue, WA Metro Area	3,439,805	3,939,363	499,558	14.5%	1,526,210	528,031	63,508	321,485	138,146
Sebastian-Vero Beach, FL Metro Area	138,028	157,413	19,385	14.0%	57,636	51,384	7,118	27,705	10,861
Sebring, FL Metro Area	98,786	105,424	6,638	6.7%	40,573	37,245	6,627	21,675	8,079
Seneca, SC Micro Area	74,275	78,374	4,099	5.5%	31,612	18,633	1,482	11,515	na
Sevierville, TN Micro Area	89,719	97,892	8,173	9.1%	36,861	19,160	1,991	11,040	2,946
Shawnee, OK Micro Area	69,443	72,679	3,236	4.7%	26,714	11,821	1,805	7,298	3,168
Sheboygan, WI Metro Area	115,510	115,456	-54	-0.0%	46,308	20,696	2,692	13,487	6,451
Shelby, NC Micro Area	98,032	97,645	-387	-0.4%	34,574	18,097	2,074	10,539	3,984
Shelton, WA Micro Area	60,692	65,507	4,815	7.9%	25,864	14,862	1,592	8,846	3,634
Sherman-Denison, TX Metro Area	120,875	133,991	13,116	10.9%	48,963	23,606	2,521	14,802	5,589
Show Low, AZ Micro Area	107,488	110,445	2,957	2.8%	34,285	20,162	2,184	12,780	5,147
Shreveport-Bossier City, LA Metro Area	439,811	436,341	-3,470	-0.8%	171,540	72,054	8,532	45,920	18,961
Sierra Vista-Douglas, AZ Metro Area	131,357	126,770	-4,587	-3.5%	49,751	28,402	3,174	19,349	8,609
Sioux City, IA-NE-SD Metro Area	168,563	169,354	791	0.5%	65,930	26,366	3,727	16,332	7,058
Sioux Falls, SD Metro Area	228,262	266,100	37,838	16.6%	102,650	35,625	5,617	23,261	10,771
Somerset, PA Micro Area	77,737	73,952	-3,785	-4.9%	28,796	16,525	1,976	9,473	3,910
South Bend-Mishawaka, IN-MI Metro Area	319,213	322,424	3,211	1.0%	128,578	53,620	7,468	34,462	16,650
Spartanburg, SC Metro Area	313,289	341,298	28,009	8.9%	127,652	56,123	5,027	33,815	12,200
Spokane-Spokane Valley, WA Metro Area	527,753	573,527	45,774	8.7%	229,018	97,107	9,664	60,852	27,419
Springfield, IL Metro Area	210,170	207,676	-2,494	-1.2%	88,301	37,197	4,507	24,003	11,368
Springfield, MA Metro Area	621,981	631,761	10,080	1.6%	237,580	106,733	15,143	66,655	30,702
Springfield, MO Metro Area	436,709	468,126	31,417	7.2%	192,513	77,783	8,731	50,083	23,024
Springfield, OH Metro Area	138,341	134,585	-3,756	-2.7%	55,327	25,957	3,849	17,429	8,162
State College, PA Metro Area	154,001	162,805	8,804	5.7%	58,514	22,815	2,676	13,802	5,739
Statesboro, GA Micro Area	70,246	77,296	7,050	10.0%	27,097	8,545	963	5,700	na
Staunton-Waynesboro, VA Metro Area	118,496	123,007	4,511	3.8%	50,045	25,695	3,451	17,316	7,914
Stevens Point, WI Micro Area	70,021	70,942	921	1.3%	29,193	11,666	1,428	7,783	3,917
Stillwater, OK Micro Area	77,350	82,040	4,690	6.1%	30,734	10,980	1,341	7,462	na
Stockton-Lodi, CA Metro Area	685,306	752,660	67,354	9.8%	231,917	95,844	10,931	51,357	19,028
Sumter, SC Metro Area	107,490	106,512	-978	-0.9%	40,396	17,568	1,872	10,897	4,324
Sunbury, PA Micro Area	94,483	91,083	-3,400	-3.6%	38,816	19,647	3,214	12,466	5,824
Syracuse, NY Metro Area	662,620	650,502	-12,118	-1.8%	257,443	111,403	15,116	70,660	32,559
Talladega-Sylacauga, AL Micro Area	94,041	92,812	-1,229	-1.3%	35,349	17,371	1,583	10,347	3,925
Tallahassee, FL Metro Area	368,770	387,455	18,685	5.1%	146,351	55,474	5,527	35,295	14,570
Tampa-St. Petersburg-Clearwater, FL Metro Area	2,783,462	3,142,663	359,201	12.9%	1,227,325	622,433	79,560	375,283	167,664
Terre Haute, IN Metro Area	172,417	168,679	-3,738	-2.2%	67,747	28,382	3,442	16,800	6,687
Texarkana, TX-AR Metro Area	149,194	151,675	2,481	1.7%	56,610	25,009	2,138	15,677	7,881
The Villages, FL Metro Area	93,420	128,754	35,334	37.8%	62,854	73,154	4,848	44,756	16,140
Toledo, OH Metro Area	610,002	602,871	-7,131	-1.2%	245,652	97,880	12,053	60,641	26,784

Table A-4: Metropolitan/Micropolitan Areas - Summary Population Characteristics—*Continued*

	April 1, 2010 Census Population Estimates Base	2018 ACS Population	2010-2018 Population Change	2010-2018 Percent Change	Total Households	2018 ACS			
						Population 65 and Over	Population 85 and Over	Householders 65 and Over	Persons 65 and Over Living Alone
Topeka, KS Metro Area	233,867	232,594	-1,273	-0.5%	95,364	43,494	5,015	27,465	12,534
Torrington, CT Micro Area	189,925	181,111	-8,814	-4.6%	73,598	37,897	4,360	23,504	10,819
Traverse City, MI Micro Area	143,365	149,914	6,549	4.6%	58,740	33,278	4,352	19,878	7,697
Trenton, NJ Metro Area	367,511	369,811	2,300	0.6%	132,980	56,001	7,193	35,066	15,731
Truckee-Grass Valley, CA Micro Area	98,745	99,696	951	1.0%	41,447	27,746	3,152	16,239	6,016
Tucson, AZ Metro Area	980,263	1,039,073	58,810	6.0%	402,323	205,547	21,309	126,887	50,885
Tullahoma-Manchester, TN Micro Area	100,209	104,410	4,201	4.2%	40,656	19,964	2,201	12,013	5,371
Tulsa, OK Metro Area	937,532	993,928	56,396	6.0%	381,588	153,263	17,401	96,079	40,447
Tupelo, MS Micro Area	136,268	140,552	4,284	3.1%	50,535	20,507	2,115	12,167	4,180
Tuscaloosa, AL Metro Area	230,176	244,895	14,719	6.4%	87,597	34,392	3,236	21,717	8,830
Twin Falls, ID Micro Area	99,596	109,264	9,668	9.7%	40,130	15,967	1,613	9,741	3,632
Tyler, TX Metro Area	209,725	230,221	20,496	9.8%	77,330	37,588	3,171	22,791	8,247
Ukiah, CA Micro Area	87,850	87,606	-244	-0.3%	33,794	19,072	1,475	12,167	5,777
Urban Honolulu, HI Metro Area	953,206	980,080	26,874	2.8%	308,208	173,612	30,273	91,320	29,882
Utica-Rome, NY Metro Area	299,330	291,410	-7,920	-2.6%	112,800	55,405	8,640	33,811	14,838
Valdosta, GA Metro Area	139,660	145,577	5,917	4.2%	53,680	19,469	1,976	13,374	6,429
Vallejo-Fairfield, CA Metro Area	413,298	446,610	33,312	8.1%	152,291	70,597	8,811	38,327	13,376
Victoria, TX Metro Area	94,003	99,047	5,044	5.4%	34,730	16,458	1,999	10,278	4,563
Vineland-Bridgeton, NJ Metro Area	156,633	150,972	-5,661	-3.6%	50,034	23,222	2,317	14,558	6,796
Virginia Beach-Norfolk-Newport News, VA-NC Metro Area	1,676,823	1,729,114	52,291	3.1%	654,475	253,198	28,095	157,793	68,313
Visalia-Porterville, CA Metro Area	442,181	465,861	23,680	5.4%	139,197	52,622	6,294	29,774	11,998
Waco, TX Metro Area	252,766	270,566	17,800	7.0%	97,387	40,035	4,855	24,632	9,992
Walla Walla, WA Metro Area	62,859	65,611	2,752	4.4%	23,893	12,576	2,054	8,217	3,157
Warner Robins, GA Metro Area	179,604	193,729	14,125	7.9%	71,511	23,986	2,708	14,460	6,153
Warsaw, IN Micro Area	77,354	79,344	1,990	2.6%	30,798	13,068	1,548	8,548	3,801
Washington-Arlington-Alexandria, DC-VA-MD-WV Metro Area	5,636,363	6,251,240	614,877	10.9%	2,234,559	812,991	90,747	470,638	195,598
Waterloo-Cedar Falls, IA Metro Area	167,819	169,659	1,840	1.1%	68,384	28,653	3,493	18,517	8,090
Watertown-Fort Atkinson, WI Micro Area	83,683	85,129	1,446	1.7%	33,180	14,645	1,281	9,124	3,273
Watertown-Fort Drum, NY Metro Area	116,234	111,755	-4,479	-3.9%	44,657	15,458	1,648	9,611	4,396
Wausau, WI Metro Area	134,061	135,428	1,367	1.0%	56,245	23,770	3,026	15,425	7,023
Weirton-Steubenville, WV-OH Metro Area	124,450	120,228	-4,222	-3.4%	51,680	27,429	3,025	17,348	7,373
Wenatchee, WA Metro Area	110,887	119,943	9,056	8.2%	47,855	21,663	2,374	13,101	5,300
Wheeling, WV-OH Metro Area	147,960	140,045	-7,915	-5.3%	52,435	30,430	4,514	19,242	8,695
Whitewater-Elkhorn, WI Micro Area	102,228	103,718	1,490	1.5%	40,864	18,146	2,440	11,193	4,915
Wichita, KS Metro Area	630,923	645,031	14,108	2.2%	248,799	96,970	13,150	61,430	29,559
Wichita Falls, TX Metro Area	151,474	151,306	-168	-0.1%	54,429	23,264	2,750	14,948	6,319
Williamsport, PA Metro Area	116,114	113,664	-2,450	-2.1%	44,585	21,901	2,301	13,364	5,576
Wilmington, NC Metro Area	254,881	294,436	39,555	15.5%	120,886	52,496	6,253	32,231	14,403
Wilson, NC Micro Area	81,218	81,455	237	0.3%	31,817	14,804	1,501	9,989	5,993
Winchester, VA-WV Metro Area	128,475	141,848	13,373	10.4%	53,715	25,141	2,662	15,331	6,539
Winston-Salem, NC Metro Area	640,537	671,456	30,919	4.8%	270,772	116,408	13,096	74,764	34,662
Wisconsin Rapids-Marshfield, WI Micro Area	74,749	73,055	-1,694	-2.3%	32,274	14,940	1,891	9,953	4,637
Wooster, OH Micro Area	114,516	115,967	1,451	1.3%	43,908	20,264	2,366	12,744	4,994
Worcester, MA-CT Metro Area	916,764	947,866	31,102	3.4%	353,402	148,768	18,297	88,115	39,019
Yakima, WA Metro Area	243,240	251,446	8,206	3.4%	83,320	34,329	3,726	21,499	8,569
York-Hanover, PA Metro Area	435,008	448,273	13,265	3.0%	173,958	78,138	9,692	47,981	20,912
Youngstown-Warren-Boardman, OH-PA Metro Area	565,781	538,952	-26,829	-4.7%	227,477	115,279	18,439	73,546	35,443
Yuba City, CA Metro Area	166,902	174,848	7,946	4.8%	58,180	24,246	3,298	15,168	5,923
Yuma, AZ Metro Area	195,750	212,128	16,378	8.4%	74,532	39,979	3,154	22,994	6,851
Zanesville, OH Micro Area	86,086	86183	97	0.1%	34,471	15189	1424	10,134	4,282

Table A-5: 116th Congressional Districts - Summary Population Characteristics

	April 1, 2010 Census Population	2018 ACS Population	2010-2018 Population Change	2010-2018 Percent Change	Total Households	2018 ACS			
						Population 65 and Over	Population 85 and Over	Householders 65 and Over	Persons 65 and Over Living Alone
Alabama									
Congressional District 1	682,820	715,346	32,526	4.8%	272,626	127,083	12,627	81,162	32,810
Congressional District 2	682,820	678,122	-4,698	-0.7%	254,315	115,362	12,723	71,219	30,421
Congressional District 3	682,819	708,409	25,590	3.7%	264,595	119,519	10,181	73,987	29,360
Congressional District 4	682,819	686,297	3,478	0.5%	256,963	128,143	13,332	80,677	33,431
Congressional District 5	682,819	725,634	42,815	6.3%	290,207	119,725	12,667	76,457	30,078
Congressional District 6	682,819	713,595	30,776	4.5%	266,268	119,052	12,536	71,378	26,778
Congressional District 7	682,820	660,468	-22,352	-3.3%	250,210	100,779	11,176	69,093	33,088
Alaska									
Congressional District (at Large)	710,231	737,438	27,207	3.8%	254,551	88,000	7,370	53,173	20,618
Arizona									
Congressional District 1	710,224	770,392	60,168	8.5%	260,716	148,829	11,646	88,103	29,627
Congressional District 2	710,224	724,747	14,523	2.0%	299,328	157,202	18,404	100,367	43,157
Congressional District 3	710,224	798,359	88,135	12.4%	248,402	99,419	7,571	56,126	18,719
Congressional District 4	710,224	809,426	99,202	14.0%	324,737	224,318	20,480	138,453	52,872
Congressional District 5	710,224	841,344	131,120	18.5%	294,051	141,143	15,881	78,549	28,130
Congressional District 6	710,224	783,621	73,397	10.3%	324,886	149,354	17,340	91,030	38,369
Congressional District 7	710,224	854,749	144,525	20.3%	250,303	60,596	5,174	34,788	15,413
Congressional District 8	710,225	794,820	84,595	11.9%	294,239	183,219	23,125	105,814	39,877
Congressional District 9	710,224	794,188	83,964	11.8%	317,636	95,023	13,118	61,157	29,308
Arkansas									
Congressional District 1	728,765	724,622	-4,143	-0.6%	282,730	131,155	13,711	82,565	34,698
Congressional District 2	729,192	765,124	35,932	4.9%	294,135	121,838	14,284	74,690	30,402
Congressional District 3	728,959	819,235	90,276	12.4%	309,456	118,046	13,378	72,354	28,204
Congressional District 4	729,002	704,844	-24,158	-3.3%	270,026	136,637	14,796	85,229	35,873
California									
Congressional District 1	702,905	711,282	8,377	1.2%	279,836	155,882	16,073	94,923	38,497
Congressional District 2	702,905	722,370	19,465	2.8%	284,468	153,503	16,421	97,850	41,538
Congressional District 3	702,906	748,104	45,198	6.4%	250,729	107,218	13,330	63,179	24,044
Congressional District 4	702,906	754,525	51,619	7.3%	283,468	159,881	18,546	94,872	35,429
Congressional District 5	702,905	730,955	28,050	4.0%	263,687	130,207	14,483	78,373	34,156
Congressional District 6	702,905	777,985	75,080	10.7%	275,253	95,748	13,045	57,744	27,829
Congressional District 7	702,904	753,640	50,736	7.2%	267,550	120,191	14,795	68,407	26,747
Congressional District 8	702,905	717,107	14,202	2.0%	232,969	96,973	10,476	59,501	22,831
Congressional District 9	702,904	775,148	72,244	10.3%	239,810	103,224	11,330	53,666	20,276
Congressional District 10	702,905	761,485	58,580	8.3%	240,621	98,883	11,294	55,821	19,096
Congressional District 11	702,906	762,290	59,384	8.4%	269,243	127,281	15,084	74,681	31,584
Congressional District 12	702,905	764,043	61,138	8.7%	327,144	116,214	19,400	73,326	36,566
Congressional District 13	702,906	764,304	61,398	8.7%	288,611	108,061	12,426	68,697	34,268
Congressional District 14	702,905	759,415	56,510	8.0%	251,995	125,644	19,325	66,263	24,138
Congressional District 15	702,904	789,174	86,270	12.3%	251,826	106,877	12,930	54,142	18,654
Congressional District 16	702,904	749,967	47,063	6.7%	214,157	78,134	9,790	44,971	19,112
Congressional District 17	702,904	777,468	74,564	10.6%	260,959	96,078	13,023	45,945	14,373
Congressional District 18	702,906	750,295	47,389	6.7%	270,798	116,195	19,265	68,719	25,153
Congressional District 19	702,904	763,028	60,124	8.6%	233,952	102,973	11,658	52,503	18,026
Congressional District 20	702,906	739,352	36,446	5.2%	225,394	103,980	12,582	62,080	22,828
Congressional District 21	702,904	713,625	10,721	1.5%	190,073	64,614	7,331	37,272	12,602
Congressional District 22	702,905	771,095	68,190	9.7%	247,092	99,343	13,776	59,525	25,496
Congressional District 23	702,904	747,852	44,948	6.4%	247,855	98,579	11,477	57,426	23,730
Congressional District 24	702,904	738,707	35,803	5.1%	256,673	127,463	16,220	78,074	29,617
Congressional District 25	702,904	716,257	13,353	1.9%	222,661	93,789	8,800	53,821	19,932
Congressional District 26	702,905	728,927	26,022	3.7%	229,606	111,657	16,413	63,532	22,536
Congressional District 27	702,905	705,509	2,604	0.4%	239,888	127,057	20,949	65,770	20,989
Congressional District 28	702,904	709,450	6,546	0.9%	297,507	110,736	15,679	63,110	30,753
Congressional District 29	702,905	707,741	4,836	0.7%	207,024	82,368	8,910	42,712	16,328
Congressional District 30	702,904	766,513	63,609	9.0%	275,934	119,121	17,881	65,645	27,570
Congressional District 31	702,905	751,527	48,622	6.9%	222,791	88,386	9,201	46,483	16,284
Congressional District 32	702,905	716,199	13,294	1.9%	195,295	96,564	11,504	46,866	14,212
Congressional District 33	702,904	704,818	1,914	0.3%	288,478	132,040	21,452	82,134	33,632
Congressional District 34	702,904	748,812	45,908	6.5%	260,836	93,848	14,830	51,037	23,120
Congressional District 35	702,905	769,589	66,684	9.5%	201,610	74,498	7,379	35,525	11,255
Congressional District 36	702,905	752,138	49,233	7.0%	289,261	171,562	21,007	104,360	44,539
Congressional District 37	702,904	738,174	35,270	5.0%	274,939	92,876	13,847	59,276	30,462
Congressional District 38	702,905	716,331	13,426	1.9%	204,009	107,550	16,426	54,481	16,993
Congressional District 39	702,905	726,541	23,636	3.4%	222,659	111,862	14,340	57,416	17,267
Congressional District 40	702,904	716,470	13,566	1.9%	183,200	67,423	8,087	30,304	8,392
Congressional District 41	702,904	775,626	72,722	10.3%	188,128	73,535	8,830	33,386	9,838
Congressional District 42	702,906	826,801	123,895	17.6%	223,844	99,510	11,886	47,603	14,736
Congressional District 43	702,904	753,696	50,792	7.2%	245,576	92,544	12,257	51,696	21,489
Congressional District 44	702,904	725,177	22,273	3.2%	190,906	75,324	9,704	39,168	14,298
Congressional District 45	702,906	797,608	94,702	13.5%	281,020	122,823	17,525	71,030	27,647
Congressional District 46	702,906	735,139	32,233	4.6%	191,713	74,590	10,252	35,379	13,187
Congressional District 47	702,905	710,853	7,948	1.1%	249,015	91,255	12,125	51,252	20,426
Congressional District 48	702,906	719,486	16,580	2.4%	266,926	127,774	18,592	73,657	31,299
Congressional District 49	702,906	731,513	28,607	4.1%	254,413	122,829	15,853	73,126	27,296
Congressional District 50	702,905	751,551	48,646	6.9%	245,440	112,208	14,500	62,707	25,039

Table A-5: 116th Congressional Districts - Summary Population Characteristics—*Continued*

	April 1, 2010 Census Population	2018 ACS Population	2010-2018 Population Change	2010-2018 Percent Change	Total Households	2018 ACS Population 65 and Over	Population 85 and Over	Householders 65 and Over	Persons 65 and Over Living Alone
California—Cont.									
Congressional District 51	702,906	747,510	44,604	6.3%	201,521	88,372	11,343	45,161	14,974
Congressional District 52	702,904	767,172	64,268	9.1%	289,177	112,620	13,389	65,678	25,723
Congressional District 53	702,904	796,701	93,797	13.3%	274,582	99,470	12,539	56,942	22,945
Colorado									
Congressional District 1	718,457	841,497	123,040	17.1%	360,309	100,994	11,436	66,607	34,666
Congressional District 2	718,457	812,357	93,900	13.1%	318,851	122,089	11,611	75,019	27,968
Congressional District 3	718,457	753,595	35,138	4.9%	291,169	140,186	13,669	85,549	36,496
Congressional District 4	718,456	836,061	117,605	16.4%	305,869	116,803	12,948	70,674	26,860
Congressional District 5	718,457	815,466	97,009	13.5%	302,267	115,313	12,793	69,981	27,813
Congressional District 6	718,456	835,273	116,817	16.3%	298,909	101,182	10,852	62,030	26,090
Congressional District 7	718,456	801,315	82,859	11.5%	299,383	111,288	14,097	69,942	32,010
Connecticut									
Congressional District 1	714,820	715,049	229	0.0%	279,563	124,852	18,416	76,484	35,675
Congressional District 2	714,819	699,657	-15,162	-2.1%	273,946	126,055	17,204	76,003	31,998
Congressional District 3	714,819	712,272	-2,547	-0.4%	281,432	124,880	17,490	76,259	34,267
Congressional District 4	714,819	739,090	24,271	3.4%	269,293	115,192	17,460	70,411	30,569
Congressional District 5	714,820	706,597	-8,223	-1.2%	273,857	122,168	17,126	75,636	35,509
Delaware									
Congressional District (at Large)	897,934	967,171	69,237	7.7%	367,671	180,756	18,604	107,758	40,163
District of Columbia									
Delegate District (at Large)	601,723	702,455	100,732	16.7%	287,476	85,626	10,901	58,898	33,166
Florida									
Congressional District 1	696,345	784,532	88,187	12.7%	295,098	132,405	11,534	79,682	30,724
Congressional District 2	696,345	733,749	37,404	5.4%	278,484	148,454	15,245	91,997	36,026
Congressional District 3	696,345	758,275	61,930	8.9%	273,236	128,208	13,141	75,812	31,929
Congressional District 4	696,345	819,177	122,832	17.6%	314,432	137,230	14,047	82,281	34,687
Congressional District 5	696,345	738,862	42,517	6.1%	272,454	98,265	8,976	62,413	28,211
Congressional District 6	696,345	781,896	85,551	12.3%	307,602	200,306	28,871	116,759	45,607
Congressional District 7	696,345	786,041	89,696	12.9%	294,369	114,061	13,944	67,126	28,594
Congressional District 8	696,344	768,139	71,795	10.3%	288,761	195,565	28,313	113,656	46,960
Congressional District 9	696,344	902,812	206,468	29.7%	281,177	145,575	16,615	75,299	26,432
Congressional District 10	696,345	839,504	143,159	20.6%	270,167	97,785	9,800	50,722	17,519
Congressional District 11	696,344	789,849	93,505	13.4%	331,750	281,669	29,226	172,181	64,593
Congressional District 12	696,345	792,410	96,065	13.8%	312,209	193,965	23,063	117,538	53,482
Congressional District 13	696,345	735,935	39,590	5.7%	303,069	171,584	25,694	105,500	51,698
Congressional District 14	696,345	782,973	86,628	12.4%	307,827	104,514	12,969	61,564	28,355
Congressional District 15	696,345	808,723	112,378	16.1%	285,074	132,949	12,649	76,150	26,597
Congressional District 16	696,345	852,096	155,751	22.4%	331,394	226,843	31,418	137,379	57,194
Congressional District 17	696,345	789,236	92,891	13.3%	301,158	255,782	34,052	147,229	53,640
Congressional District 18	696,344	780,772	84,428	12.1%	301,578	201,423	26,048	119,666	48,742
Congressional District 19	696,345	836,359	140,014	20.1%	325,244	264,638	38,239	149,957	57,532
Congressional District 20	696,344	809,153	112,809	16.2%	247,772	108,899	15,921	59,499	26,631
Congressional District 21	696,345	785,042	88,697	12.7%	296,189	201,501	37,306	121,552	58,197
Congressional District 22	696,345	753,363	57,018	8.2%	308,398	165,568	23,499	101,164	47,102
Congressional District 23	696,345	756,447	60,102	8.6%	274,559	137,835	16,575	80,170	34,647
Congressional District 24	696,345	784,469	88,124	12.7%	251,800	107,971	13,870	58,706	23,427
Congressional District 25	696,345	775,326	78,981	11.3%	241,423	147,636	23,395	70,493	22,667
Congressional District 26	696,345	790,373	94,028	13.5%	229,243	117,449	13,117	53,165	14,239
Congressional District 27	696,345	763,812	67,467	9.7%	284,927	140,704	23,473	74,573	31,450
Georgia									
Congressional District 1	691,974	744,385	52,411	7.6%	278,248	109,215	10,157	68,406	26,966
Congressional District 2	691,976	665,539	-26,437	-3.8%	246,910	105,503	12,200	67,752	30,970
Congressional District 3	691,974	740,700	48,726	7.0%	268,358	114,866	11,321	70,993	27,865
Congressional District 4	691,976	785,104	93,128	13.5%	270,528	95,657	8,691	54,297	20,336
Congressional District 5	691,974	793,039	101,063	14.6%	319,839	86,695	9,939	61,350	33,249
Congressional District 6	691,975	754,299	62,324	9.0%	287,599	98,851	10,944	56,858	21,965
Congressional District 7	691,975	803,976	112,001	16.2%	265,599	84,707	7,947	44,166	14,344
Congressional District 8	691,974	714,720	22,744	3.3%	262,218	109,323	11,071	68,232	30,614
Congressional District 9	691,975	765,320	73,345	10.6%	281,627	142,766	12,327	85,846	31,736
Congressional District 10	691,976	767,352	75,376	10.9%	267,759	110,981	10,006	66,509	24,905
Congressional District 11	691,975	781,313	89,338	12.9%	291,526	102,184	10,449	60,558	22,406
Congressional District 12	691,975	723,334	31,359	4.5%	247,424	102,894	10,249	65,340	30,167
Congressional District 13	691,976	757,521	65,545	9.5%	258,975	85,526	7,060	49,732	18,982
Congressional District 14	691,974	722,873	30,899	4.5%	256,402	107,260	10,439	66,880	30,128
Hawaii									
Congressional District 1	680,496	709,286	28,790	4.2%	231,296	132,970	24,283	70,265	23,963
Congressional District 2	679,805	711,205	31,400	4.6%	224,013	128,497	15,790	72,863	24,978
Idaho									
Congressional District 1	784,132	912,950	128,818	16.4%	332,386	155,498	14,256	92,785	35,204
Congressional District 2	783,450	841,258	57,808	7.4%	307,884	123,943	15,447	75,829	31,100

Table A-5: 116th Congressional Districts - Summary Population Characteristics—*Continued*

	April 1, 2010 Census Population	2018 ACS Population	2010-2018 Population Change	2010-2018 Percent Change	Total Households	2018 ACS			
						Population 65 and Over	Population 85 and Over	Householders 65 and Over	Persons 65 and Over Living Alone
Illinois									
Congressional District 1	712,813	706,550	-6,263	-0.9%	269,599	112,861	14,825	75,535	35,518
Congressional District 2	712,813	694,459	-18,354	-2.6%	257,381	111,159	15,506	70,616	33,676
Congressional District 3	712,813	704,050	-8,763	-1.2%	246,239	108,168	14,512	65,535	27,839
Congressional District 4	712,813	702,062	-10,751	-1.5%	233,844	71,791	7,138	41,750	17,864
Congressional District 5	712,813	743,699	30,886	4.3%	304,941	95,746	13,653	59,359	28,231
Congressional District 6	712,813	730,345	17,532	2.5%	270,115	119,204	13,197	69,318	25,669
Congressional District 7	712,812	707,513	-5,299	-0.7%	301,839	96,514	8,967	68,489	37,922
Congressional District 8	712,812	707,268	-5,544	-0.8%	250,552	97,618	11,427	56,235	23,191
Congressional District 9	712,813	721,481	8,668	1.2%	290,016	126,337	21,276	79,138	39,068
Congressional District 10	712,813	711,265	-1,548	-0.2%	251,936	109,894	16,786	66,510	28,296
Congressional District 11	712,813	722,584	9,771	1.4%	249,169	90,133	10,903	52,546	20,482
Congressional District 12	712,813	687,072	-25,741	-3.6%	277,817	117,968	14,238	76,976	36,030
Congressional District 13	712,813	704,211	-8,602	-1.2%	286,809	111,496	16,142	70,188	32,835
Congressional District 14	712,813	742,235	29,422	4.1%	262,859	102,747	11,627	62,076	25,363
Congressional District 15	712,813	691,196	-21,617	-3.0%	276,514	133,930	17,685	85,584	38,006
Congressional District 16	712,813	684,888	-27,925	-3.9%	274,557	124,590	15,289	78,940	33,798
Congressional District 17	712,813	679,926	-32,887	-4.6%	280,917	126,888	16,821	80,793	38,376
Congressional District 18	712,813	700,276	-12,537	-1.8%	279,760	133,504	19,576	82,452	36,207
Indiana									
Congressional District 1	720,422	714,756	-5,666	-0.8%	276,543	118,463	14,430	76,616	35,055
Congressional District 2	720,423	723,483	3,060	0.4%	276,707	118,817	16,719	73,760	32,787
Congressional District 3	720,423	747,060	26,637	3.7%	288,583	115,773	13,571	73,190	32,568
Congressional District 4	720,422	768,025	47,603	6.6%	292,185	118,000	13,555	73,454	29,711
Congressional District 5	720,423	784,462	64,039	8.9%	306,483	116,399	14,306	70,733	29,434
Congressional District 6	720,422	719,771	-651	-0.1%	286,401	127,419	14,369	82,018	36,475
Congressional District 7	720,423	760,466	40,043	5.6%	292,119	92,272	10,647	59,136	28,539
Congressional District 8	720,422	718,591	-1,831	-0.3%	287,940	124,660	15,650	76,786	33,205
Congressional District 9	720,422	755,264	34,842	4.8%	292,208	119,343	13,330	74,116	31,347
Iowa									
Congressional District 1	761,548	773,628	12,080	1.6%	311,514	139,220	19,498	86,615	38,939
Congressional District 2	761,624	783,983	22,359	2.9%	313,626	134,426	18,478	85,169	40,599
Congressional District 3	761,612	843,598	81,986	10.8%	330,429	123,357	15,503	77,565	35,054
Congressional District 4	761,571	754,936	-6,635	-0.9%	312,304	140,815	22,137	88,810	39,997
Kansas									
Congressional District 1	713,278	698,323	-14,955	-2.1%	273,007	115,910	17,640	71,833	34,179
Congressional District 2	713,272	713,845	573	0.1%	282,985	123,084	17,516	76,380	33,800
Congressional District 3	713,287	775,243	61,956	8.7%	296,249	108,784	12,806	66,710	25,766
Congressional District 4	713,281	724,099	10,818	1.5%	281,167	114,413	15,824	72,233	34,537
Kentucky									
Congressional District 1	723,178	721,124	-2,054	-0.3%	282,020	133,233	15,093	82,414	33,900
Congressional District 2	723,137	769,850	46,713	6.5%	290,818	124,068	12,640	76,196	31,765
Congressional District 3	723,171	749,110	25,939	3.6%	302,502	120,473	15,541	77,540	34,480
Congressional District 4	723,450	754,387	30,937	4.3%	284,807	116,906	11,993	72,855	30,265
Congressional District 5	723,228	695,105	-28,123	-3.9%	266,607	121,959	12,116	77,515	30,571
Congressional District 6	723,203	778,826	55,623	7.7%	305,959	114,753	11,265	71,500	30,435
Louisiana									
Congressional District 1	755,445	806,638	51,193	6.8%	300,739	130,195	13,608	80,976	34,011
Congressional District 2	755,538	794,121	38,583	5.1%	296,535	115,542	10,444	71,183	34,055
Congressional District 3	755,596	783,545	27,949	3.7%	297,581	115,222	13,458	74,293	30,533
Congressional District 4	755,605	747,314	-8,291	-1.1%	286,839	122,592	12,945	78,294	34,782
Congressional District 5	755,581	738,249	-17,332	-2.3%	262,611	121,256	10,916	74,058	32,148
Congressional District 6	755,607	790,111	34,504	4.6%	292,915	115,803	12,473	68,175	25,414
Maine									
Congressional District 1	664,180	685,535	21,355	3.2%	295,578	138,926	17,583	89,874	39,638
Congressional District 2	664,181	652,869	-11,312	-1.7%	274,729	137,143	17,266	86,049	38,964
Maryland									
Congressional District 1	722,650	741,621	18,971	2.6%	277,758	138,984	15,117	83,966	31,070
Congressional District 2	723,447	768,511	45,064	6.2%	286,945	109,606	12,292	67,147	30,280
Congressional District 3	720,094	754,636	34,542	4.8%	288,000	115,494	17,034	71,063	32,657
Congressional District 4	720,065	760,398	40,333	5.6%	271,766	103,193	10,289	62,375	25,252
Congressional District 5	720,472	757,621	37,149	5.2%	262,835	105,734	10,486	59,391	23,277
Congressional District 6	728,448	758,943	30,495	4.2%	273,544	118,748	13,265	68,014	27,065
Congressional District 7	716,862	716,136	-726	-0.1%	270,505	113,001	13,973	70,691	33,812
Congressional District 8	721,514	784,852	63,338	8.8%	284,582	126,281	16,059	75,528	32,402
Massachusetts									
Congressional District 1	727,515	736,481	8,966	1.2%	288,420	132,153	18,278	82,753	38,197
Congressional District 2	727,514	745,347	17,833	2.5%	280,279	121,700	15,002	73,141	33,665
Congressional District 3	727,514	771,096	43,582	6.0%	279,358	105,527	14,523	63,762	28,010
Congressional District 4	727,514	766,019	38,505	5.3%	279,926	127,736	16,587	78,013	32,034
Congressional District 5	727,515	775,135	47,620	6.5%	300,644	125,377	16,865	78,114	35,884
Congressional District 6	727,515	780,524	53,009	7.3%	294,705	146,196	22,927	87,798	37,328
Congressional District 7	727,514	820,086	92,572	12.7%	308,906	89,349	10,668	56,604	29,085
Congressional District 8	727,514	764,891	37,377	5.1%	301,338	124,671	18,546	77,368	38,042
Congressional District 9	727,514	742,570	15,056	2.1%	290,718	164,832	20,333	102,484	42,791

Table A-5: 116th Congressional Districts - Summary Population Characteristics—*Continued*

	April 1, 2010 Census Population	2018 ACS Population	2010-2018 Population Change	2010-2018 Percent Change	Total Households	2018 ACS			
						Population 65 and Over	Population 85 and Over	Householders 65 and Over	Persons 65 and Over Living Alone
Michigan									
Congressional District 1	705,974	699,220	-6,754	-1.0%	293,025	163,475	18,537	101,550	41,132
Congressional District 2	705,975	743,361	37,386	5.3%	277,873	119,587	14,105	74,092	30,466
Congressional District 3	705,974	749,975	44,001	6.2%	283,940	112,791	14,020	71,288	30,005
Congressional District 4	705,974	704,592	-1,382	-0.2%	279,730	137,477	14,967	85,844	35,342
Congressional District 5	705,975	671,115	-34,860	-4.9%	283,846	124,550	14,616	82,413	36,970
Congressional District 6	705,974	721,736	15,762	2.2%	285,178	124,855	14,089	77,966	32,826
Congressional District 7	705,974	706,811	837	0.1%	279,677	130,623	14,811	81,726	34,477
Congressional District 8	705,975	749,011	43,036	6.1%	281,718	112,636	13,102	70,961	28,574
Congressional District 9	705,975	715,259	9,284	1.3%	298,288	119,353	16,889	77,949	37,440
Congressional District 10	705,974	722,722	16,748	2.4%	286,251	132,553	13,560	82,431	34,678
Congressional District 11	705,974	733,920	27,946	4.0%	287,025	123,503	14,436	74,520	32,471
Congressional District 12	705,974	709,832	3,858	0.5%	277,461	103,976	13,059	68,141	31,525
Congressional District 13	705,974	663,867	-42,107	-6.0%	266,256	97,265	12,140	66,480	34,977
Congressional District 14	705,974	704,494	-1,480	-0.2%	277,198	117,809	15,962	78,200	38,569
Minnesota									
Congressional District 1	662,991	678,418	15,427	2.3%	272,152	117,573	18,318	73,571	32,448
Congressional District 2	662,991	714,141	51,150	7.7%	264,954	99,093	11,325	60,310	24,950
Congressional District 3	662,990	723,994	61,004	9.2%	282,744	114,683	12,476	70,971	30,983
Congressional District 4	662,990	717,766	54,776	8.3%	271,654	104,637	13,752	66,731	32,277
Congressional District 5	662,991	718,802	55,811	8.4%	297,469	91,072	14,244	59,080	31,148
Congressional District 6	662,993	722,715	59,722	9.0%	257,420	94,077	9,306	55,451	20,670
Congressional District 7	662,988	663,069	81	0.0%	269,318	130,239	19,328	80,697	35,841
Congressional District 8	662,991	672,274	9,283	1.4%	278,741	137,260	16,624	85,622	35,779
Mississippi									
Congressional District 1	741,837	769,595	27,758	3.7%	281,673	121,547	11,824	76,815	33,065
Congressional District 2	741,862	695,797	-46,065	-6.2%	252,354	106,751	10,200	70,855	30,362
Congressional District 3	741,822	746,155	4,333	0.6%	281,354	122,887	13,669	76,840	31,948
Congressional District 4	741,776	774,983	33,207	4.5%	293,249	123,238	10,667	78,853	32,570
Missouri									
Congressional District 1	748,616	728,365	-20,251	-2.7%	321,228	106,576	14,661	73,344	38,441
Congressional District 2	748,616	760,689	12,073	1.6%	301,587	143,830	19,329	89,159	34,885
Congressional District 3	748,615	793,405	44,790	6.0%	302,574	128,004	12,931	78,130	30,530
Congressional District 4	748,616	770,500	21,884	2.9%	294,174	130,398	15,166	80,682	33,520
Congressional District 5	748,616	771,847	23,231	3.1%	319,116	119,698	15,839	75,846	34,111
Congressional District 6	748,616	780,002	31,386	4.2%	290,010	128,534	15,523	77,515	32,266
Congressional District 7	748,616	783,672	35,056	4.7%	319,781	138,312	16,590	89,835	41,046
Congressional District 8	748,616	737,972	-10,644	-1.4%	286,336	139,722	14,766	87,058	38,003
Montana									
Congressional District (at Large)	989,415	1,062,305	72,890	7.4%	431,421	200,239	20,753	123,306	52,059
Nebraska									
Congressional District 1	608,780	653,684	44,904	7.4%	258,151	99,097	13,573	63,478	28,088
Congressional District 2	608,781	673,005	64,224	10.5%	259,585	86,041	11,159	55,623	26,743
Congressional District 3	608,780	602,579	-6,201	-1.0%	247,754	118,860	17,220	75,440	35,836
Nevada									
Congressional District 1	675,138	685,427	10,289	1.5%	255,618	99,661	8,538	60,446	28,880
Congressional District 2	675,138	729,771	54,633	8.1%	289,415	126,080	11,982	79,157	33,605
Congressional District 3	675,138	846,761	171,623	25.4%	316,876	133,739	14,256	74,823	28,471
Congressional District 4	675,137	772,433	97,296	14.4%	267,901	115,640	9,504	65,507	23,024
New Hampshire									
Congressional District 1	658,233	686,820	28,587	4.3%	267,830	120,363	16,237	70,323	28,109
Congressional District 2	658,237	669,638	11,401	1.7%	263,382	124,793	14,587	75,465	32,627
New Jersey									
Congressional District 1	732,658	731,297	-1,361	-0.2%	268,996	113,725	13,348	71,071	30,856
Congressional District 2	732,658	703,117	-29,541	-4.0%	261,689	136,834	14,963	82,565	32,828
Congressional District 3	732,658	742,905	10,247	1.4%	282,262	142,831	18,902	91,189	38,466
Congressional District 4	732,657	748,858	16,201	2.2%	278,958	147,151	21,470	94,196	42,351
Congressional District 5	732,707	730,707	-1,951	-0.3%	263,762	131,230	19,802	77,517	29,951
Congressional District 6	732,657	730,114	-2,543	-0.3%	248,676	105,000	13,022	59,850	22,428
Congressional District 7	732,658	730,778	-1,880	-0.3%	262,845	120,534	17,568	69,109	26,845
Congressional District 8	732,658	764,837	32,179	4.4%	287,023	82,392	9,908	49,058	22,704
Congressional District 9	732,658	765,382	32,724	4.5%	273,966	110,980	15,791	65,187	28,091
Congressional District 10	732,658	759,704	27,046	3.7%	275,644	98,861	14,125	59,944	27,399
Congressional District 11	732,658	744,805	12,147	1.7%	272,269	132,036	20,066	75,106	27,490
Congressional District 12	732,658	756,016	23,358	3.2%	273,477	116,715	16,793	72,675	30,970
New Mexico									
Congressional District 1	686,393	697,064	10,671	1.6%	278,769	117,458	14,195	72,184	33,086
Congressional District 2	686,393	700,113	13,720	2.0%	256,162	122,410	14,129	76,332	33,928
Congressional District 3	686,393	698,251	11,858	1.7%	259,162	128,612	12,411	79,579	30,757
New York									
Congressional District 1	717,707	718,726	1,019	0.1%	250,870	129,004	15,291	76,483	29,700
Congressional District 2	717,708	709,605	-8,103	-1.1%	226,611	108,985	15,811	62,257	23,093
Congressional District 3	717,707	707,576	-10,131	-1.4%	247,880	146,620	23,439	82,562	29,337

Table A-5: 116th Congressional Districts - Summary Population Characteristics—*Continued*

	April 1, 2010 Census Population	2018 ACS Population	2010-2018 Population Change	2010-2018 Percent Change	Total Households	2018 ACS			
						Population 65 and Over	Population 85 and Over	Householders 65 and Over	Persons 65 and Over Living Alone
New York—Cont.									
Congressional District 4	717,708	729,582	11,874	1.7%	237,243	125,392	19,043	72,166	28,137
Congressional District 5	717,708	757,972	40,264	5.6%	229,294	110,647	12,282	58,232	20,832
Congressional District 6	717,707	734,183	16,476	2.3%	271,901	130,286	17,036	72,457	29,186
Congressional District 7	717,707	720,811	3,103	0.4%	256,906	84,981	9,801	52,238	24,134
Congressional District 8	717,708	791,211	73,503	10.2%	303,604	118,829	16,737	75,998	35,183
Congressional District 9	717,708	730,957	13,249	1.8%	285,134	110,059	13,506	68,265	29,892
Congressional District 10	717,707	711,678	-6,029	-0.8%	307,017	114,159	16,857	78,025	46,229
Congressional District 11	717,708	732,886	15,178	2.1%	263,966	123,577	15,038	73,411	32,349
Congressional District 12	717,707	698,928	-18,779	-2.6%	356,778	110,208	16,717	75,496	44,639
Congressional District 13	717,707	795,633	77,926	10.9%	294,395	101,638	12,590	63,218	33,335
Congressional District 14	717,708	706,440	-11,268	-1.6%	244,262	94,455	11,791	53,283	24,323
Congressional District 15	717,708	743,959	26,251	3.7%	259,910	80,341	7,598	54,658	28,531
Congressional District 16	717,707	732,981	15,274	2.1%	272,787	127,802	20,835	80,291	41,108
Congressional District 17	717,708	741,445	23,737	3.3%	248,008	124,138	19,321	74,563	29,609
Congressional District 18	717,707	722,226	4,519	0.6%	251,264	110,816	13,092	66,493	27,507
Congressional District 19	717,708	700,310	-17,398	-2.4%	271,736	144,119	17,548	87,516	37,100
Congressional District 20	717,708	722,529	4,821	0.7%	289,470	123,308	17,760	77,086	35,153
Congressional District 21	717,707	701,112	-16,595	-2.3%	278,649	125,887	14,768	79,962	35,974
Congressional District 22	717,708	697,372	-20,336	-2.8%	271,702	130,497	18,748	80,325	35,058
Congressional District 23	717,707	693,764	-23,943	-3.3%	279,327	130,512	16,529	81,195	35,993
Congressional District 24	717,707	701,664	-16,043	-2.2%	279,952	122,161	16,996	78,035	35,965
Congressional District 25	717,707	718,565	858	0.1%	291,950	123,290	17,225	78,730	38,255
Congressional District 26	717,707	707,190	-10,517	-1.5%	306,927	123,251	18,663	82,533	42,214
Congressional District 27	717,707	712,904	-4,803	-0.7%	289,472	137,103	17,607	86,874	38,468
North Carolina									
Congressional District 1	733,499	761,087	27,588	3.8%	294,568	126,081	12,496	80,889	36,186
Congressional District 2	733,499	858,938	125,439	17.1%	305,705	117,604	9,813	70,276	26,882
Congressional District 3	733,498	756,375	22,877	3.1%	293,837	132,134	11,897	82,624	33,864
Congressional District 4	733,499	871,589	138,090	18.8%	341,534	102,109	10,351	61,533	26,192
Congressional District 5	733,499	762,960	29,461	4.0%	307,844	138,964	16,560	91,378	41,896
Congressional District 6	733,498	772,716	39,218	5.3%	300,648	136,131	16,340	85,518	36,166
Congressional District 7	733,499	809,820	76,321	10.4%	319,287	160,657	16,005	98,199	39,841
Congressional District 8	733,499	797,935	64,436	8.8%	298,551	119,587	12,484	73,908	30,630
Congressional District 9	733,498	792,434	58,936	8.0%	285,092	122,555	12,566	74,337	31,223
Congressional District 10	733,499	762,919	29,420	4.0%	301,589	140,903	15,453	88,807	35,816
Congressional District 11	733,499	768,166	34,667	4.7%	314,271	173,932	20,981	105,969	43,058
Congressional District 12	733,498	880,550	147,052	20.0%	337,331	87,139	8,849	51,532	22,158
Congressional District 13	733,499	788,131	54,632	7.4%	311,205	130,778	15,272	80,026	32,818
North Dakota									
Congressional District (at Large)	672,591	760,077	87,486	13.0%	319,355	116,433	18,439	73,062	35,028
Ohio									
Congressional District 1	721,032	740,979	19,947	2.8%	294,505	111,917	14,260	70,419	31,894
Congressional District 2	721,031	734,712	13,681	1.9%	298,409	119,527	13,954	75,635	35,594
Congressional District 3	721,031	812,264	91,233	12.7%	316,961	84,005	8,584	57,111	27,025
Congressional District 4	721,032	707,219	-13,813	-1.9%	277,353	123,452	14,126	76,480	32,583
Congressional District 5	721,031	717,088	-3,943	-0.5%	289,660	130,512	17,198	80,319	33,822
Congressional District 6	721,032	694,694	-26,338	-3.7%	275,828	139,032	16,928	86,624	39,080
Congressional District 7	721,031	734,091	13,060	1.8%	285,123	135,066	16,926	83,646	35,589
Congressional District 8	721,032	731,637	10,605	1.5%	282,277	123,430	14,326	77,530	34,003
Congressional District 9	721,032	716,235	-4,797	-0.7%	303,955	112,349	13,958	73,334	37,126
Congressional District 10	721,032	725,301	4,269	0.6%	300,596	128,971	16,397	83,276	37,546
Congressional District 11	721,032	678,001	-43,031	-6.0%	304,410	119,878	17,666	81,847	43,807
Congressional District 12	721,031	789,634	68,603	9.5%	293,383	123,476	15,152	74,441	29,572
Congressional District 13	721,031	707,603	-13,428	-1.9%	298,600	132,490	18,563	85,480	41,382
Congressional District 14	721,032	720,551	-481	-0.1%	286,240	145,548	18,054	90,210	36,726
Congressional District 15	721,031	759,569	38,538	5.3%	290,228	120,773	13,376	74,245	29,785
Congressional District 16	721,031	719,864	-1,167	-0.2%	287,919	145,737	18,817	90,875	37,600
Oklahoma									
Congressional District 1	750,270	803,029	52,759	7.0%	310,290	120,002	13,713	75,187	32,836
Congressional District 2	750,270	747,632	-2,638	-0.4%	284,540	141,541	15,150	89,104	36,532
Congressional District 3	750,270	778,026	27,756	3.7%	280,204	125,904	15,780	77,764	31,503
Congressional District 4	750,270	791,927	41,657	5.6%	296,883	118,261	12,812	74,601	31,832
Congressional District 5	750,271	822,465	72,194	9.6%	313,393	113,893	15,128	73,230	33,889
Oregon									
Congressional District 1	766,216	858,910	92,694	12.1%	330,630	127,814	14,543	80,171	33,778
Congressional District 2	766,215	831,343	65,128	8.5%	332,236	173,438	20,256	107,493	44,744
Congressional District 3	766,215	841,456	75,241	9.8%	331,954	114,251	11,814	72,156	35,150
Congressional District 4	766,214	814,998	48,784	6.4%	331,882	173,359	16,917	108,647	43,646
Congressional District 5	766,214	844,006	77,792	10.2%	313,268	150,749	17,852	92,800	37,507
Pennsylvania									
Congressional District 1	705,688	713,685	7,997	1.1%	271,426	131,951	15,560	77,257	30,157
Congressional District 2	705,688	727,380	21,692	3.1%	256,540	97,633	10,784	60,881	30,171
Congressional District 3	705,688	736,340	30,652	4.3%	305,996	101,895	13,481	73,242	41,640
Congressional District 4	705,687	727,449	21,762	3.1%	277,740	129,655	19,389	78,776	34,301

Table A-5: 116th Congressional Districts - Summary Population Characteristics—*Continued*

	April 1, 2010 Census Population	2018 ACS Population	2010-2018 Population Change	2010-2018 Percent Change	Total Households	2018 ACS Population 65 and Over	Population 85 and Over	Householders 65 and Over	Persons 65 and Over Living Alone
Pennsylvania—Cont.									
Congressional District 5	705,688	718,076	12,388	1.8%	265,508	115,180	17,687	69,999	32,915
Congressional District 6	705,688	734,876	29,188	4.1%	269,735	117,746	15,906	70,325	27,838
Congressional District 7	705,688	731,168	25,480	3.6%	272,827	130,877	19,717	77,971	32,527
Congressional District 8	705,688	696,956	-8,732	-1.2%	273,634	136,309	18,422	83,465	37,322
Congressional District 9	705,688	702,489	-3,199	-0.5%	278,703	140,541	19,643	87,790	38,508
Congressional District 10	705,687	734,849	29,162	4.1%	292,987	126,901	17,388	79,383	36,557
Congressional District 11	705,688	737,394	31,706	4.5%	279,475	135,491	15,908	80,041	30,165
Congressional District 12	705,688	701,192	-4,496	-0.6%	273,471	134,560	17,042	82,658	34,439
Congressional District 13	705,687	692,835	-12,852	-1.8%	278,224	143,768	17,580	89,664	37,341
Congressional District 14	705,688	684,084	-21,604	-3.1%	288,288	146,513	18,777	93,691	41,638
Congressional District 15	705,687	680,927	-24,760	-3.5%	278,784	141,099	19,090	89,604	37,884
Congressional District 16	705,688	686,525	-19,163	-2.7%	284,137	134,058	18,398	85,638	38,110
Congressional District 17	705,687	717,264	11,577	1.6%	308,678	139,791	20,872	91,494	42,722
Congressional District 18	705,688	683,571	-22,117	-3.1%	314,778	128,401	17,996	86,727	46,446
Rhode Island									
Congressional District 1	526,283	532,590	6,307	1.2%	204,598	92,707	13,064	58,051	28,512
Congressional District 2	526,284	524,725	-1,559	-0.3%	201,975	89,938	13,395	55,912	26,425
South Carolina									
Congressional District 1	660,766	809,610	148,844	22.5%	309,161	147,364	14,812	88,046	31,670
Congressional District 2	660,766	717,231	56,465	8.5%	278,823	116,090	12,653	74,110	31,054
Congressional District 3	660,767	697,467	36,700	5.6%	269,147	130,586	11,585	81,613	34,800
Congressional District 4	660,766	736,750	75,984	11.5%	276,650	117,625	12,169	71,349	27,402
Congressional District 5	660,766	731,341	70,575	10.7%	272,378	123,080	11,088	74,188	29,032
Congressional District 6	660,766	659,483	-1,283	-0.2%	244,616	104,369	10,454	65,991	29,596
Congressional District 7	660,767	732,245	71,478	10.8%	277,216	160,640	12,011	97,354	38,930
South Dakota									
Congressional District (at Large)	814,180	882,235	68,055	8.4%	345,449	146,358	21,761	91,545	38,909
Tennessee									
Congressional District 1	705,123	720,358	15,235	2.2%	288,541	148,230	15,833	90,439	35,456
Congressional District 2	705,123	753,229	48,106	6.8%	296,678	135,135	13,062	82,510	31,656
Congressional District 3	705,122	736,889	31,767	4.5%	288,674	137,889	14,792	85,020	35,627
Congressional District 4	705,123	798,482	93,359	13.2%	292,287	118,257	10,682	71,779	28,789
Congressional District 5	705,123	777,696	72,573	10.3%	313,581	97,098	10,924	63,177	29,023
Congressional District 6	705,123	784,725	79,602	11.3%	301,799	138,856	12,916	84,448	33,459
Congressional District 7	705,123	786,523	81,400	11.5%	283,079	116,325	10,557	69,748	27,851
Congressional District 8	705,122	699,385	-5,737	-0.8%	264,635	124,434	14,369	74,087	27,353
Congressional District 9	705,123	712,723	7,600	1.1%	273,886	88,573	10,327	59,816	31,761
Texas									
Congressional District 1	698,488	725,555	27,067	3.9%	250,860	120,273	13,206	72,798	29,243
Congressional District 2	698,488	803,041	104,553	15.0%	286,897	95,769	8,613	54,196	19,037
Congressional District 3	698,488	899,784	201,296	28.8%	313,568	101,408	10,181	53,124	19,801
Congressional District 4	698,488	759,648	61,160	8.8%	272,905	126,918	11,951	78,259	31,922
Congressional District 5	698,488	749,808	51,320	7.3%	259,085	103,839	12,340	62,596	25,075
Congressional District 6	698,498	804,816	106,318	15.2%	272,878	93,745	9,843	53,825	20,072
Congressional District 7	698,488	775,198	76,710	11.0%	286,616	84,625	11,714	48,644	20,671
Congressional District 8	698,488	871,420	172,932	24.8%	294,523	120,514	10,437	69,143	26,182
Congressional District 9	698,488	786,925	88,437	12.7%	264,287	80,357	8,947	44,663	17,377
Congressional District 10	698,487	896,798	198,311	28.4%	312,919	115,433	12,912	65,686	24,481
Congressional District 11	698,488	782,337	83,849	12.0%	279,550	123,087	13,223	78,507	33,675
Congressional District 12	698,488	812,102	113,614	16.3%	295,792	105,145	13,987	64,573	27,953
Congressional District 13	698,488	711,672	13,184	1.9%	255,984	108,808	12,974	66,844	28,267
Congressional District 14	698,472	763,380	64,908	9.3%	266,981	106,186	11,692	64,687	28,573
Congressional District 15	698,488	795,511	97,023	13.9%	226,062	85,941	8,113	49,383	17,064
Congressional District 16	698,488	733,764	35,276	5.1%	241,212	91,704	11,872	54,922	22,789
Congressional District 17	698,487	793,513	95,026	13.6%	287,547	98,336	9,395	60,429	24,450
Congressional District 18	698,488	801,885	103,397	14.8%	274,598	76,522	6,268	48,394	20,094
Congressional District 19	698,487	731,759	33,272	4.8%	259,000	100,356	12,454	61,282	25,153
Congressional District 20	698,488	846,337	147,849	21.2%	257,032	93,978	10,309	54,396	20,613
Congressional District 21	698,488	818,281	119,793	17.2%	326,090	131,351	15,849	78,403	28,469
Congressional District 22	698,504	935,386	236,882	33.9%	301,036	104,393	8,944	53,978	17,493
Congressional District 23	698,488	794,879	96,391	13.8%	243,042	105,863	9,894	61,757	22,295
Congressional District 24	698,488	817,147	118,659	17.0%	318,936	91,697	9,516	53,834	20,928
Congressional District 25	698,478	786,976	88,498	12.7%	279,481	115,659	10,595	67,419	25,183
Congressional District 26	698,488	894,192	195,704	28.0%	299,529	90,210	8,275	47,608	16,225
Congressional District 27	698,487	739,719	41,232	5.9%	259,967	118,955	13,632	72,287	27,616
Congressional District 28	698,488	768,719	70,231	10.1%	218,960	89,807	11,026	51,475	18,121
Congressional District 29	698,488	765,435	66,947	9.6%	226,787	64,441	4,622	34,966	11,403
Congressional District 30	698,487	804,679	106,192	15.2%	270,339	86,687	9,766	51,624	20,749
Congressional District 31	698,487	883,347	184,860	26.5%	296,458	106,381	10,376	58,418	22,038
Congressional District 32	698,488	769,852	71,364	10.2%	292,242	95,901	10,419	54,836	21,863
Congressional District 33	698,488	777,745	79,257	11.3%	231,388	68,640	6,045	41,573	17,010
Congressional District 34	698,487	727,688	29,201	4.2%	213,973	101,984	13,582	58,605	20,992
Congressional District 35	698,488	818,369	119,881	17.2%	280,171	83,304	9,166	47,397	19,286
Congressional District 36	698,488	754,178	55,690	8.0%	259,388	111,382	10,797	67,327	26,234

Table A-5: 116th Congressional Districts - Summary Population Characteristics—*Continued*

	April 1, 2010 Census Population	2018 ACS Population	2010-2018 Population Change	2010-2018 Percent Change	Total Households	2018 ACS			
						Population 65 and Over	Population 85 and Over	Householders 65 and Over	Persons 65 and Over Living Alone
Utah									
Congressional District 1	690,971	776,910	85,939	12.4%	244,538	82,802	8,227	49,505	16,263
Congressional District 2	690,971	779,772	88,801	12.9%	264,379	104,260	10,977	63,114	23,713
Congressional District 3	690,972	773,622	82,650	12.0%	234,958	85,042	8,610	50,425	14,104
Congressional District 4	690,971	830,801	139,830	20.2%	255,016	79,193	7,449	47,507	18,230
Vermont									
Congressional District (at Large)	625,741	626,299	558	0.1%	261,373	123,875	13,149	78,032	33,924
Virginia									
Congressional District 1	727,366	813,878	86,512	11.9%	282,681	123,912	11,055	71,096	24,043
Congressional District 2	708,087	743,410	35,323	5.0%	279,178	112,245	14,337	70,186	30,678
Congressional District 3	746,645	744,804	-1,841	-0.2%	290,156	100,426	11,560	65,980	33,415
Congressional District 4	727,366	747,291	19,925	2.7%	283,821	115,128	13,086	73,062	34,190
Congressional District 5	727,365	739,410	12,045	1.7%	290,897	150,340	17,180	92,839	38,840
Congressional District 6	727,366	755,437	28,071	3.9%	290,904	141,158	17,516	88,775	38,969
Congressional District 7	727,366	812,385	85,019	11.7%	296,940	128,234	13,592	77,751	30,299
Congressional District 8	727,366	795,467	68,101	9.4%	324,141	96,724	12,418	61,139	29,598
Congressional District 9	727,366	704,831	-22,535	-3.1%	283,318	145,820	16,901	91,160	40,764
Congressional District 10	727,365	862,308	134,943	18.6%	285,017	108,403	10,804	58,139	20,220
Congressional District 11	727,366	798,464	71,098	9.8%	268,471	95,835	9,737	50,903	19,343
Washington									
Congressional District 1	672,444	768,363	95,919	14.3%	281,173	101,663	10,330	59,798	21,754
Congressional District 2	672,454	755,546	83,092	12.4%	294,886	125,330	13,704	76,941	30,558
Congressional District 3	672,448	743,322	70,874	10.5%	283,318	128,758	12,302	80,415	32,366
Congressional District 4	672,456	735,031	62,575	9.3%	247,728	103,987	10,744	63,042	24,521
Congressional District 5	672,455	725,964	53,509	8.0%	287,768	125,841	13,433	79,411	34,816
Congressional District 6	672,448	731,742	59,294	8.8%	293,137	147,594	14,005	90,782	37,280
Congressional District 7	672,457	799,589	127,132	18.9%	362,118	114,120	14,641	71,815	35,183
Congressional District 8	672,463	754,721	82,258	12.2%	280,830	102,853	10,286	63,049	24,529
Congressional District 9	672,460	765,285	92,825	13.8%	286,616	103,032	15,070	60,457	26,620
Congressional District 10	672,455	756,028	83,573	12.4%	278,001	110,809	13,541	68,145	28,667
West Virginia									
Congressional District 1	615,991	606,136	-9,855	-1.6%	244,052	120,219	14,120	75,979	33,557
Congressional District 2	620,862	624,120	3,258	0.5%	251,791	120,355	12,985	76,898	32,019
Congressional District 3	616,141	575,576	-40,565	-6.6%	238,860	120,642	13,114	78,708	34,463
Wisconsin									
Congressional District 1	710,874	717,716	6,842	1.0%	279,217	118,576	14,128	74,558	33,558
Congressional District 2	710,874	768,067	57,193	8.0%	319,184	115,716	14,792	73,821	31,484
Congressional District 3	710,873	724,568	13,695	1.9%	292,708	129,906	16,324	82,297	36,382
Congressional District 4	710,873	710,573	-300	-0.0%	281,405	86,994	12,267	56,464	28,735
Congressional District 5	710,873	731,341	20,468	2.9%	297,562	132,502	18,038	83,076	35,974
Congressional District 6	710,873	714,886	4,013	0.6%	294,811	132,131	18,362	85,253	39,395
Congressional District 7	710,873	710,420	-453	-0.1%	305,764	144,611	16,961	91,109	37,943
Congressional District 8	710,873	735,997	25,124	3.5%	301,309	126,047	13,883	78,599	33,181
Wyoming									
Congressional District (at Large)	563,626	577,737	14,111	2.5%	230,252	96,557	9,258	61,902	24,766

PART B

AGE STRUCTURE

AGE STRUCTURE

Based on the 2018 American Community Survey, 16.0 percent of the national population is age 65 years old or over while 1.9 percent was age 85 and over. This is a slight but growing change from the 2010 Census results where the 65 and over population was 13.0 percent and the 85 and over percent was 1.8 percent of the total. Though these are relatively small changes in the proportion of the older population, it indicates the coming growth in this segment as the oldest of the Baby Boom generation (age 72 in 2018) has passed this threshold and the numbers will continue to grow quickly. The youngest Boomers were just passing age 54 in 2018.

There are 52.4 million people in the United States over the age of 65 and 6.3 million of them are over the age of 85.

The proportion of the population that is over 65 is higher than the national average in 30 states while 26 states have a higher proportion of the 85 and over population. One might suspect that Florida would lead the nation with the largest proportion of population over 65 but Maine is slightly higher at 20.6 percent. Hawaii has the highest proportion of population over age 85 at 2.8 percent. States with older populations aren't all retirement destinations. Among the states with the highest percentage of population 65 and over, most are a result of the existing age structure rather than being a retirement destination as is the case in Maine, Pennsylvania, Vermont and West Virginia. The states with the lowest proportion of population 65 and over include Utah, Alaska, the District of Columbia and Texas where all are less than 13 percent. The younger population in Texas likely reflects its high in-migration status rather than attraction as a retirement destination.

Percent of the Population 65 Years and Over

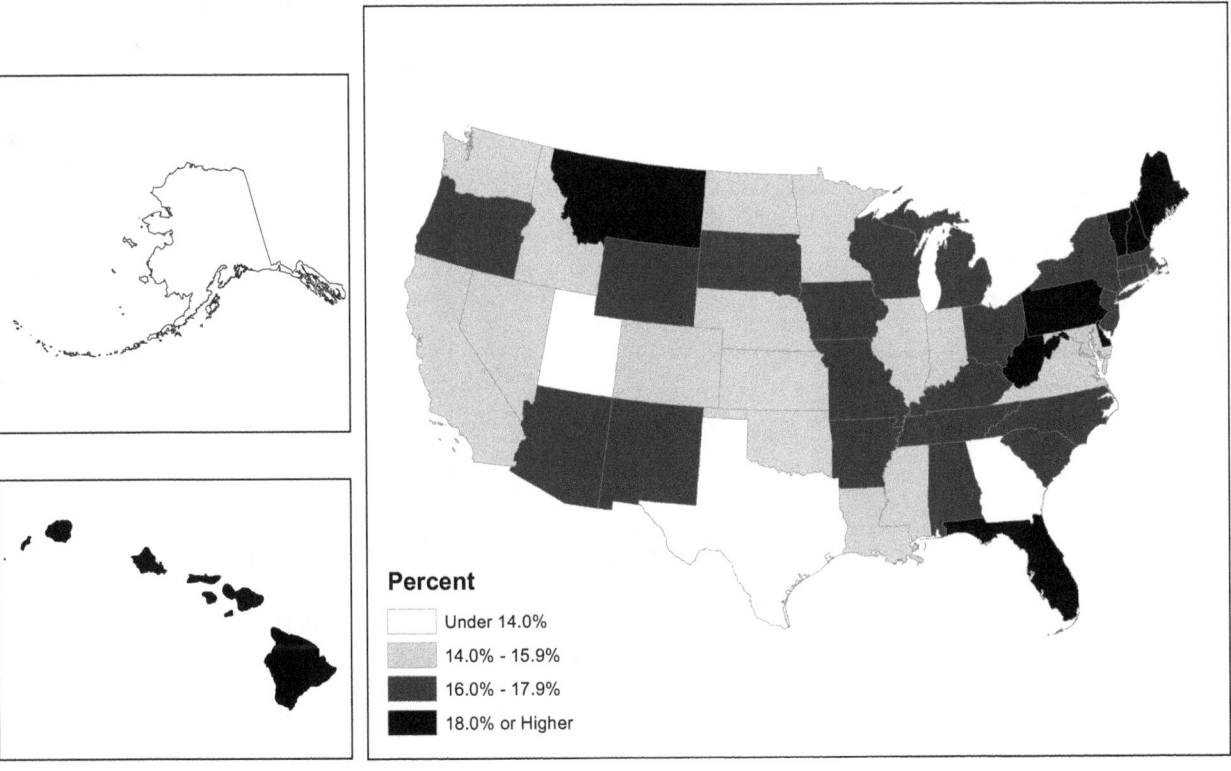

Percent
- Under 14.0%
- 14.0% - 15.9%
- 16.0% - 17.9%
- 18.0% or Higher

65 Years and Over – Top 10		65 Years and Over – Bottom 10	
Maine	20.6%	Washington	15.4%
Florida	20.5%	Maryland	15.4%
West Virginia	20.0%	North Dakota	15.3%
Vermont	19.8%	California	14.3%
Montana	18.8%	Colorado	14.2%
Delaware	18.7%	Georgia	13.8%
Hawaii	18.4%	Texas	12.5%
Pennsylvania	18.2%	District of Columbia	12.2%
New Hampshire	18.1%	Alaska	11.9%
South Carolina	17.7%	Utah	11.1%

Five of the states in the 65 and over top 10 are also among the 85 and over top 10. Florida, Hawaii, Maine, New Hampshire and Pennsylvania join the list. But six of the states in the 65 and over bottom 10 are also in the 85 and over bottom 10.

85 Years and Over – Top 10		85 Years and Over – Bottom 10	
Hawaii	2.8%	Wyoming	1.6%
Florida	2.6%	Louisiana	1.6%
Maine	2.6%	Mississippi	1.6%
Rhode Island	2.5%	District of Columbia	1.6%
South Dakota	2.5%	Colorado	1.5%
Connecticut	2.5%	Nevada	1.5%
Pennsylvania	2.4%	Georgia	1.4%
North Dakota	2.4%	Texas	1.3%
Iowa	2.4%	Utah	1.1%
New Hampshire	2.3%	Alaska	1.0%

Los Angeles County, California (1.4 million) and Cook County, Illinois (758,000) have the largest number of people age 65 and over but rank 645th and 556th, respectively, of the 814 counties in terms of the percent of their total population. Toole County, Utah has the fewest number of persons 65 and over at just 6,359 but Utah County, Utah has the lowest percentage at 7.7 percent. The ten counties with the largest 65 and over population account for 10.9 percent of the nation's 52.4 million population or a total of 5.8 million people. The smallest ten counties have only 80,500 people over age 65 and represent only 0.15 percent of the total. More than 426 counties have a larger proportion of their population over the age of 65 than the national average of 16.0 percent.

While cities make up more than one-third of the total population, they contain only 29.4 percent of the 65 and over population, indicating that a relatively larger proportion of the population live outside of the densest urban centers. Moreover, more than 3.4 million (6.5 percent of all 65 and over) people age 65 and over live in the top 10 cities. About the same proportion (6.9 percent) of the 85 and over population lives in the top 10 cities. Only 53,700 people 65 and over live in the bottom 10 cities and, like counties, account for only 0.85 percent of the total. New York City, Los Angeles and Chicago have the largest populations over age 65 but all rank low in terms of their percent of total 65 and over population. New York ranks 196th while Los Angeles and Chicago rank 325th and 320th, respectively. Jacksonville City, North Carolina has the smallest population 65 and over at 4,168. Of the 568 cities reported here, 185 are above the national percentage of 65 and over.

Nearly nine out of every ten people age 65 and over lives in a metropolitan or micropolitan area. This is almost 47 million people or 87.1 percent of the nation's 52.4 million

	Top 20 Areas - Percent 85 and Over							
Rank	Counties		Cities		Metropolitan/Micropolitan Areas		Congressional Districts	
1	Highlands County, FL	6.3%	Tamarac city, FL	5.5%	Sebring, FL Metro Area	6.3%	Congressional District 21 , FL	4.8%
2	Charlotte County, FL	5.9%	Walnut Creek city, CA	5.2%	Punta Gorda, FL Metro Area	5.9%	Congressional District 19 , FL	4.6%
3	Sarasota County, FL	5.3%	Palm Coast city, FL	4.7%	Naples-Immokalee-Marco Island, FL Metro Area	4.8%	Congressional District 17 , FL	4.3%
4	Martin County, FL	5.0%	Clearwater city, FL	4.3%	Homosassa Springs, FL Metro Area	4.6%	Congressional District 11 , FL	3.7%
5	Collier County, FL	4.8%	Largo city, FL	4.3%	Sebastian-Vero Beach, FL Metro Area	4.5%	Congressional District 6 , FL	3.7%
6	Citrus County, FL	4.6%	Santa Monica city, CA	4.0%	North Port-Sarasota-Bradenton, FL Metro Area	4.4%	Congressional District 16 , FL	3.7%
7	Indian River County, FL	4.5%	Hialeah city, FL	4.0%	Port Angeles, WA Micro Area	4.0%	Congressional District 8 , FL	3.7%
8	Flagler County, FL	4.4%	West Palm Beach city, FL	4.0%	Deltona-Daytona Beach-Ormond Beach, FL Metro Area	3.9%	Congressional District 13 , FL	3.5%
9	Aroostook County, ME	4.2%	Georgetown city, TX	4.0%	The Villages, FL Metro Area	3.8%	Congressional District 1 , HI	3.4%
10	Palm Beach County, FL	4.1%	Delray Beach city, FL	4.0%	Cape Coral-Fort Myers, FL Metro Area	3.7%	Congressional District 18 , FL	3.3%
11	McCracken County, KY	4.1%	Boynton Beach city, FL	3.9%	Sandusky, OH Micro Area	3.6%	Congressional District 3 , NY	3.3%
12	Clallam County, WA	4.0%	Newport Beach city, CA	3.9%	Barnstable Town, MA Metro Area	3.6%	Congressional District 22 , FL	3.1%
13	Chatham County, NC	3.9%	Deerfield Beach city, FL	3.8%	Carson City, NV Metro Area	3.6%	Congressional District 27 , FL	3.1%
14	Volusia County, FL	3.8%	Melbourne city, FL	3.8%	Sunbury, PA Micro Area	3.5%	Congressional District 33 , CA	3.0%
15	Sumter County, FL	3.8%	Pompano Beach city, FL	3.8%	Palm Bay-Melbourne-Titusville, FL Metro Area	3.5%	Congressional District 25 , FL	3.0%
16	Lee County, FL	3.7%	Alhambra city, CA	3.8%	Youngstown-Warren-Boardman, OH-PA Metro Area	3.4%	Congressional District 27 , CA	3.0%
17	Erie County, Ohio	3.6%	Boca Raton city, FL	3.7%	Paducah, KY-IL Micro Area	3.4%	Congressional District 9 , IL	2.9%
18	Mercer County, PA	3.6%	Urban Honolulu CDP, HI	3.7%	Ocala, FL Metro Area	3.4%	Congressional District 6 , MA	2.9%
19	Barnstable County, MA	3.6%	St. George city, UT	3.6%	Bloomsburg-Berwick, PA Metro Area	3.4%	Congressional District 4 , IA	2.9%
20	Pinellas County, FL	3.6%	Carlsbad city, CA	3.5%	Johnstown, PA Metro Area	3.3%	Congressional District 7 , MN	2.9%

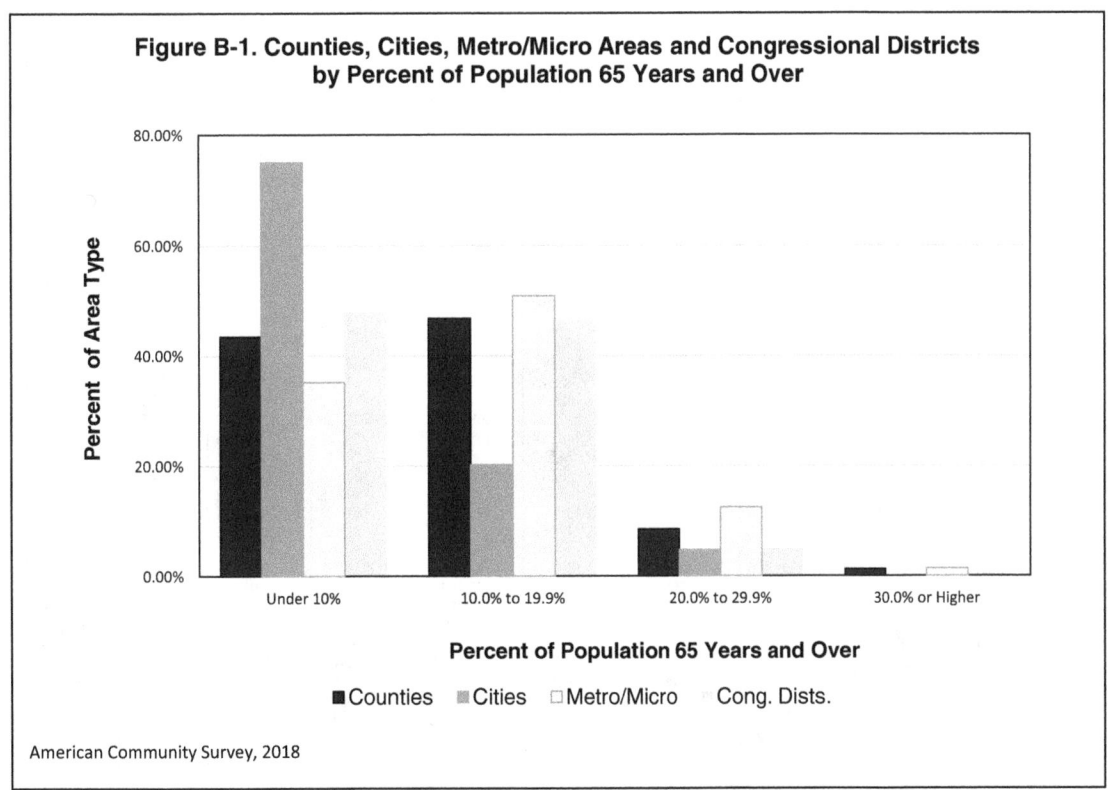

Figure B-1. Counties, Cities, Metro/Micro Areas and Congressional Districts by Percent of Population 65 Years and Over

American Community Survey, 2018

population age 65 and over. A slightly higher proportion, 87.8 percent of the nation's 85 and over population lives in metropolitan and micropolitan areas numbering 5.5 million. As with the city populations, the New York, Los Angeles, Chicago and Miami metropolitan areas have the largest 65 and over populations, all numbering more than 1 million. Just these four areas account for 14.3 percent of the national total or 7.5 million people. The Hinesville, Georgia metropolitan area has the lowest number of people 65 and over at 6,690 which is 8.4 percent of the Hinesville total population.

Congressional District 11 in Florida has the largest number of persons 65 and over at 281,669. That district also has the largest proportion of its total population over the age of 65 at 35.7 percent, more than one out of every three people in the District. However, the district includes the City of Tampa and surrounding area which ranks 53rd in total size of the 65 and over population but only 343rd in its proportion of the total. More than 2.2 million people 65 and over reside in the 10 congressional districts with the largest older population while 717,000 reside in the 10 districts with the smallest population. Congressional District 7 serving the south-central portion of the City of Phoenix, Arizona has the fewest residents age 65 and over at 60,600 and the lowest percentage of population 65 and over at 7.1 percent.

Table B-1: States - Older Population by Age

	Total Population	60 to 61 Years	62 to 64 Years	65 to 66 Years	67 to 69 Years	70 to 74 Years	75 to 79 Years	80 to 84 Years	85 Years and Over	65 Years and Over
United States	327,167,439	8,604,726	12,058,095	7,252,810	9,854,478	13,464,025	9,378,512	6,169,441	6,303,848	52,423,114
Alabama.................................	4,887,871	137,847	181,625	113,919	155,926	223,551	152,542	98,483	85,242	829,663
Alaska....................................	737,438	20,287	25,725	17,076	20,251	22,303	12,674	8,326	7,370	88,000
Arizona...................................	7,171,646	180,194	256,132	162,659	228,592	336,705	246,493	151,915	132,739	1,259,103
Arkansas................................	3,013,825	81,411	106,485	65,434	96,922	134,452	97,211	57,488	56,169	507,676
California...............................	39,557,045	972,712	1,323,664	794,567	1,062,088	1,429,806	975,951	675,345	729,580	5,667,337
Colorado................................	5,695,564	148,591	200,412	123,351	160,817	218,250	132,153	85,878	87,406	807,855
Connecticut............................	3,572,665	105,680	146,943	78,139	108,918	156,003	112,448	69,943	87,696	613,147
Delaware................................	967,171	26,537	41,002	24,560	35,335	48,000	36,377	17,880	18,604	180,756
District of Columbia	702,455	13,894	19,259	11,735	14,102	22,996	16,161	9,731	10,901	85,626
Florida...................................	21,299,325	588,625	818,239	530,273	760,940	1,113,021	836,522	557,028	561,000	4,358,784
Georgia..................................	10,519,475	261,531	352,733	205,941	291,113	399,894	259,680	157,000	142,800	1,456,428
Hawaii....................................	1,420,491	39,611	54,260	35,928	48,645	64,799	41,413	30,609	40,073	261,467
Idaho.....................................	1,754,208	38,604	64,781	42,148	54,376	71,873	52,724	28,617	29,703	279,441
Illinois...................................	12,741,080	344,960	469,291	272,714	369,458	501,157	355,876	231,775	259,568	1,990,548
Indiana...................................	6,691,878	175,177	251,501	149,994	199,966	263,739	189,014	121,856	126,577	1,051,146
Iowa......................................	3,156,145	82,249	123,548	74,532	96,291	128,510	94,950	67,919	75,616	537,818
Kansas...................................	2,911,510	75,505	108,253	68,311	88,962	106,777	78,558	55,797	63,786	462,191
Kentucky................................	4,468,402	122,220	173,091	103,387	141,123	190,955	127,372	89,907	78,648	731,392
Louisiana................................	4,659,978	122,935	176,317	107,947	143,954	182,996	128,374	83,495	73,844	720,610
Maine.....................................	1,338,404	44,191	64,062	42,259	50,139	71,555	45,849	31,418	34,849	276,069
Maryland.................................	6,042,718	159,416	234,463	130,637	172,469	243,336	169,159	106,925	108,515	931,041
Massachusetts.........................	6,902,149	182,547	268,028	156,304	209,456	290,786	196,148	131,118	153,729	1,137,541
Michigan.................................	9,995,915	290,344	410,619	244,861	326,213	438,112	307,120	199,854	204,293	1,720,453
Minnesota...............................	5,611,179	145,946	209,381	126,743	169,295	214,448	156,062	106,713	115,373	888,634
Mississippi..............................	2,986,530	82,684	109,966	66,545	89,022	128,789	89,936	53,771	46,360	474,423
Missouri.................................	6,126,452	164,046	249,247	137,018	188,729	270,876	189,386	124,260	124,805	1,035,074
Montana.................................	1,062,305	33,041	46,691	28,002	40,696	52,357	37,014	21,417	20,753	200,239
Nebraska................................	1,929,268	48,632	70,479	44,312	57,200	71,341	50,933	38,260	41,952	303,998
Nevada...................................	3,034,392	72,456	113,931	64,274	94,155	133,567	86,017	52,827	44,280	475,120
New Hampshire........................	1,356,458	45,326	56,180	35,113	47,291	64,195	42,049	25,684	30,824	245,156
New Jersey	8,908,520	247,350	336,633	194,947	255,146	362,260	259,900	170,278	195,758	1,438,289
New Mexico.............................	2,095,428	58,228	77,945	51,190	71,213	98,806	63,948	42,588	40,735	368,480
New York................................	19,542,209	537,733	730,660	423,264	575,485	812,846	573,314	394,527	432,629	3,212,065
North Carolina.........................	10,383,620	267,499	397,426	232,450	325,391	456,155	307,710	187,801	179,067	1,688,574
North Dakota...........................	760,077	20,382	25,405	17,786	19,942	26,319	18,784	15,163	18,439	116,433
Ohio......................................	11,689,442	334,099	462,417	282,751	375,229	494,381	363,833	231,684	248,285	1,996,163
Oklahoma...............................	3,943,079	99,520	138,478	82,746	116,647	162,446	109,524	75,655	72,583	619,601
Oregon...................................	4,190,713	110,799	165,770	107,756	151,856	187,984	128,833	81,800	81,382	739,611
Pennsylvania...........................	12,807,060	365,233	529,549	319,589	419,282	572,288	416,388	291,182	313,640	2,332,369
Rhode Island...........................	1,057,315	33,404	41,943	25,528	30,902	46,841	31,082	21,833	26,459	182,645
South Carolina	5,084,127	136,864	191,657	122,697	180,110	250,255	163,462	98,458	84,772	899,754
South Dakota...........................	882,235	22,722	36,227	22,888	26,029	36,105	23,706	15,869	21,761	146,358
Tennessee...............................	6,770,010	179,315	266,398	154,535	212,129	291,896	202,763	130,012	113,462	1,104,797
Texas.....................................	28,701,845	648,814	890,612	524,653	706,613	943,028	627,484	414,886	382,935	3,599,599
Utah......................................	3,161,105	59,719	88,133	51,249	69,437	91,520	59,154	44,674	35,263	351,297
Vermont..................................	626,299	19,275	29,759	18,940	24,188	32,627	21,829	13,142	13,149	123,875
Virginia...................................	8,517,685	220,159	308,866	186,031	259,114	334,357	235,977	154,560	148,186	1,318,225
Washington..............................	7,535,591	193,204	279,229	171,417	224,795	314,569	202,049	123,101	128,056	1,163,987
West Virginia...........................	1,805,832	53,149	78,053	51,063	76,611	87,616	64,656	41,051	40,219	361,216
Wisconsin................................	5,813,568	172,398	232,857	139,262	189,441	242,969	170,480	119,576	124,755	986,483
Wyoming	577,737	17,661	23,770	13,385	22,474	23,608	17,470	10,362	9,258	96,557

Table B-2: Counties - Older Population by Age

	Total Population	60 to 61 Years	62 to 64 Years	65 to 66 Years	67 to 69 Years	70 to 74 Years	75 to 79 Years	80 to 84 Years	85 Years and Over	65 Years and Over
Alabama										
Baldwin County	218,022	5,841	9,233	5,340	7,249	14,563	9,100	4,364	3,827	44,443
Calhoun County	114,277	3,407	4,448	2,960	3,764	5,516	4,733	1,781	1,761	20,515
Cullman County	83,442	3,235	2,888	1,779	2,596	4,741	2,765	2,805	855	15,541
DeKalb County	71,385	1,978	2,943	1,042	2,927	3,408	1,907	1,435	1,542	12,261
Elmore County	81,887	2,231	3,030	1,126	2,629	3,795	2,308	1,456	985	12,299
Etowah County	102,501	3,112	4,765	2,934	3,565	5,020	4,150	1,769	2,194	19,632
Houston County	104,722	2,852	4,168	2,333	3,739	4,955	3,734	2,175	1,854	18,790
Jefferson County	659,300	18,625	26,863	16,080	21,233	24,663	18,057	13,073	11,594	104,700
Lauderdale County	92,387	2,115	3,598	2,673	3,019	4,668	3,029	2,868	2,162	18,419
Lee County	163,941	4,017	5,258	3,591	3,963	5,781	2,302	2,474	1,776	19,887
Limestone County	96,174	3,011	2,527	2,694	2,250	4,122	2,098	2,135	1,796	15,095
Madison County	366,519	9,727	10,998	7,512	9,394	15,412	10,142	7,871	5,334	55,665
Marshall County	96,109	2,842	3,442	2,563	2,556	4,225	3,470	1,917	1,756	16,487
Mobile County	413,757	12,203	13,855	10,357	11,798	17,218	12,798	7,415	6,972	66,558
Montgomery County	225,763	6,259	7,282	5,435	6,478	8,541	5,422	4,525	3,875	34,276
Morgan County	119,089	3,233	5,288	2,678	3,150	6,222	2,858	3,009	2,547	20,464
St. Clair County	88,690	1,623	3,965	1,869	3,068	4,090	3,376	1,021	1,336	14,760
Shelby County	215,707	6,864	6,939	4,503	7,437	8,412	6,232	3,686	3,025	33,295
Talladega County	79,828	2,389	3,668	1,470	3,061	4,226	2,482	1,910	1,273	14,422
Tuscaloosa County	208,911	4,746	7,214	3,565	5,745	7,501	5,411	2,713	2,537	27,472
Walker County	63,711	1,347	1,856	974	2,138	4,030	2,725	1,035	1,159	12,061
Alaska										
Anchorage Municipality	291,538	8,209	7,674	6,022	7,382	8,388	3,892	4,069	3,056	32,809
Fairbanks North Star Borough	98,971	2,224	3,191	1,994	3,356	1,996	1,133	868	866	10,213
Matanuska-Susitna Borough	107,610	3,168	3,819	2,519	2,392	3,868	2,144	837	1,291	13,051
Arizona										
Apache County	71,818	1,804	2,534	1,722	2,216	2,528	1,951	1,212	1,303	10,932
Cochise County	126,770	4,462	5,808	3,639	4,969	7,522	6,003	3,095	3,174	28,402
Coconino County	142,854	2,742	5,143	2,453	3,757	4,951	3,627	1,585	1,440	17,813
Maricopa County	4,410,824	103,066	145,928	86,165	121,655	180,309	125,584	78,343	77,143	669,199
Mohave County	209,550	6,191	12,583	9,025	10,774	17,333	13,867	7,152	5,643	63,794
Navajo County	110,445	4,037	3,401	2,380	4,097	5,649	3,918	1,934	2,184	20,162
Pima County	1,039,073	27,714	38,184	27,449	37,670	52,154	41,296	25,669	21,309	205,547
Pinal County	447,138	11,010	16,799	11,543	16,301	27,162	18,482	11,173	6,164	90,825
Yavapai County	231,993	8,026	13,459	10,573	14,342	18,916	13,981	8,473	7,371	73,656
Yuma County	212,128	5,447	5,844	3,498	6,540	9,660	9,338	7,789	3,154	39,979
Arkansas										
Benton County	272,608	6,737	8,082	4,643	8,200	7,438	7,426	3,910	4,673	36,290
Craighead County	108,558	2,536	3,419	1,701	2,888	4,271	3,365	1,840	1,102	15,167
Faulkner County	124,806	2,987	4,092	2,844	2,904	4,167	3,033	1,223	1,549	15,720
Garland County	99,154	3,688	5,072	2,145	5,404	5,138	3,709	3,639	2,956	22,991
Jefferson County	68,114	2,356	2,949	1,362	2,941	2,679	1,508	1,466	1,715	11,671
Lonoke County	73,657	2,069	2,271	1,454	2,009	2,368	1,973	990	963	9,757
Pulaski County	392,680	9,013	14,761	8,604	12,325	16,236	10,061	6,391	7,487	61,104
Saline County	121,421	2,806	3,770	2,181	4,924	5,645	4,430	2,465	2,148	21,793
Sebastian County	127,753	3,003	3,888	2,769	3,532	5,696	3,802	2,324	2,045	20,168
Washington County	236,961	6,379	6,011	4,475	5,113	6,376	4,851	2,864	3,243	26,922
White County	78,727	2,254	2,083	1,317	2,412	3,326	1,901	2,044	1,307	12,307
California										
Alameda County	1,666,753	39,609	56,250	32,304	45,595	58,843	38,789	27,415	27,564	230,510
Butte County	231,256	6,272	9,528	6,963	7,986	10,320	8,903	4,207	4,441	42,820
Contra Costa County	1,150,215	30,997	41,638	22,826	35,591	47,941	32,092	22,622	20,195	181,267
El Dorado County	190,678	6,663	10,648	6,187	8,555	10,686	6,861	3,685	4,453	40,427
Fresno County	994,400	21,434	26,987	17,493	21,706	31,803	17,929	15,424	17,185	121,540
Humboldt County	136,373	4,426	6,565	2,745	5,423	7,059	3,664	2,588	2,817	24,296
Imperial County	181,827	4,268	4,128	3,923	4,169	5,267	4,116	3,392	2,645	23,512
Kern County	896,764	17,795	27,331	16,341	18,516	24,449	15,794	12,300	10,676	98,076
Kings County	151,366	1,902	3,636	2,361	2,124	4,266	2,466	2,784	1,412	15,413
Lake County	64,382	2,233	3,090	2,904	3,531	3,345	2,856	1,059	1,161	14,856
Los Angeles County	10,105,518	247,438	326,394	189,011	261,502	334,698	232,662	165,338	192,748	1,375,959
Madera County	157,672	3,106	4,949	2,850	3,373	7,290	2,937	2,981	2,668	22,099
Marin County	259,666	8,091	12,161	7,574	11,251	14,871	11,099	7,072	6,346	58,213
Mendocino County	87,606	2,270	4,626	3,524	3,052	5,744	2,860	2,417	1,475	19,072
Merced County	274,765	5,396	7,463	3,454	5,555	8,507	6,579	3,178	3,475	30,748
Monterey County	435,594	8,547	15,325	9,989	9,666	14,738	8,903	7,832	8,363	59,491
Napa County	139,417	4,062	5,221	3,160	5,438	7,258	5,005	3,236	2,708	26,805
Nevada County	99,696	3,531	5,307	3,658	5,826	8,009	4,169	2,932	3,152	27,746
Orange County	3,185,968	88,044	100,232	61,203	81,077	124,254	80,776	58,499	65,417	471,226
Placer County	393,149	10,590	15,783	9,824	14,059	19,433	14,102	10,208	9,123	76,749
Riverside County	2,450,758	52,168	77,671	45,088	67,528	88,063	67,972	41,484	42,890	353,025
Sacramento County	1,540,975	38,082	55,051	30,913	39,497	57,822	36,056	25,650	27,506	217,444
San Bernardino County	2,171,603	52,100	62,727	37,940	50,395	65,019	44,272	27,789	25,753	251,168
San Diego County	3,343,364	78,949	112,534	66,686	87,669	117,946	80,677	57,763	59,080	469,821
San Francisco County	883,305	23,977	29,161	20,385	23,356	32,881	21,482	17,182	22,842	138,128
San Joaquin County	752,660	16,613	25,856	14,654	17,730	24,340	18,037	10,152	10,931	95,844
San Luis Obispo County	284,010	7,581	12,502	7,683	11,316	16,424	9,250	6,418	6,503	57,594
San Mateo County	769,545	19,595	28,501	17,367	23,585	28,942	21,766	13,610	18,768	124,038
Santa Barbara County	446,527	10,347	14,553	8,705	12,099	16,779	12,760	8,421	9,638	68,402
Santa Clara County	1,937,570	44,989	63,349	37,705	45,408	62,533	45,446	32,643	37,517	261,252

Table B-2: Counties - Older Population by Age—*Continued*

	Total Population	60 to 61 Years	62 to 64 Years	65 to 66 Years	67 to 69 Years	70 to 74 Years	75 to 79 Years	80 to 84 Years	85 Years and Over	65 Years and Over
California—Cont.										
Santa Cruz County	274,255	7,085	11,441	8,196	9,637	11,620	7,120	4,941	3,835	45,349
Shasta County	180,040	5,361	8,430	4,575	6,453	10,453	6,499	5,095	3,952	37,027
Solano County	446,610	14,409	16,124	10,010	14,383	18,357	12,340	6,696	8,811	70,597
Sonoma County	499,942	15,657	20,698	14,196	20,476	25,550	16,420	9,408	11,980	98,030
Stanislaus County	549,815	11,222	17,348	13,107	13,084	16,946	13,055	7,758	8,557	72,507
Sutter County	96,807	2,800	3,674	2,011	2,396	3,340	3,193	1,654	2,269	14,863
Tulare County	465,861	10,084	13,983	7,206	9,235	14,594	8,854	6,439	6,294	52,622
Ventura County	850,967	22,436	28,401	20,144	24,575	31,341	21,965	15,666	18,528	132,219
Yolo County	220,408	4,624	6,454	4,076	5,025	6,663	4,310	3,558	3,545	27,177
Yuba County	78,041	2,092	3,515	1,125	2,378	2,293	1,501	1,057	1,029	9,383
Colorado										
Adams County	511,868	9,857	14,585	7,886	10,706	14,735	8,045	6,998	4,739	53,109
Arapahoe County	651,215	16,096	22,348	12,752	18,564	22,531	12,815	8,635	9,712	85,009
Boulder County	326,078	9,273	12,610	7,384	9,213	12,149	7,100	4,321	5,866	46,033
Broomfield County	69,267	1,051	2,080	1,958	1,574	2,192	1,722	1,363	809	9,618
Denver County	716,492	14,356	19,981	11,334	18,315	22,196	13,959	8,759	9,433	83,996
Douglas County	342,776	9,028	10,555	6,002	8,812	11,070	6,405	3,884	3,749	39,922
El Paso County	713,856	16,672	22,817	14,697	17,865	24,399	13,959	9,683	10,794	91,397
Jefferson County	580,233	19,001	22,606	14,211	17,113	27,118	15,263	9,967	11,847	95,519
Larimer County	350,518	9,695	12,582	9,317	9,436	15,502	10,225	4,995	5,527	55,002
Mesa County	153,207	4,003	6,053	3,427	4,908	8,190	4,253	4,073	3,950	28,801
Pueblo County	167,529	4,435	7,511	3,934	5,503	8,475	5,066	3,954	3,900	30,832
Weld County	314,305	7,982	11,606	6,167	8,184	9,700	6,439	3,653	4,080	38,223
Connecticut										
Fairfield County	943,823	25,819	37,762	18,648	24,723	38,652	27,938	17,973	21,890	149,824
Hartford County	892,697	24,412	34,794	19,164	26,470	38,948	27,912	17,646	22,534	152,674
Litchfield County	181,111	7,202	9,255	5,070	7,707	9,548	7,068	4,144	4,360	37,897
Middlesex County	162,682	5,840	7,964	4,122	6,302	8,088	5,483	4,108	4,339	32,442
New Haven County	857,620	26,473	34,295	17,779	28,172	37,199	27,022	16,007	22,610	148,789
New London County	266,784	8,362	11,577	7,250	7,733	12,368	9,005	5,843	6,115	48,314
Tolland County	150,921	3,638	6,360	3,430	4,430	6,220	4,565	2,489	3,147	24,281
Windham County	117,027	3,934	4,936	2,676	3,381	4,980	3,455	1,733	2,701	18,926
Delaware										
Kent County	178,550	4,291	6,512	4,135	5,205	7,998	5,537	3,957	2,980	29,812
New Castle County	559,335	14,633	21,335	12,310	16,269	22,482	17,893	7,974	10,165	87,093
Sussex County	229,286	7,613	13,155	8,115	13,861	17,520	12,947	5,949	5,459	63,851
Florida										
Alachua County	269,956	5,442	8,325	6,006	7,838	8,826	6,974	3,318	4,765	37,727
Bay County	185,287	5,901	7,930	3,303	6,167	8,701	5,881	3,582	3,293	30,927
Brevard County	596,849	21,484	28,664	17,680	26,935	31,680	26,236	18,110	20,627	141,268
Broward County	1,951,260	56,051	70,655	41,468	58,995	80,671	61,632	41,215	40,544	324,525
Charlotte County	184,998	6,692	10,865	8,139	13,307	17,892	13,351	10,720	10,912	74,321
Citrus County	147,929	5,256	9,191	6,985	9,420	13,054	10,321	7,242	6,810	53,832
Clay County	216,072	4,819	8,270	6,879	6,228	9,501	6,619	2,949	2,576	34,752
Collier County	378,488	9,879	16,905	13,380	17,410	29,421	26,458	17,526	18,268	122,463
Columbia County	70,503	1,903	3,228	1,250	2,464	3,719	2,610	1,307	1,628	12,978
Duval County	950,181	22,297	33,172	20,484	27,231	34,170	22,626	14,954	14,134	133,599
Escambia County	315,534	9,068	12,637	6,059	11,099	13,663	8,840	7,233	6,102	52,996
Flagler County	112,067	2,918	4,965	3,403	5,757	9,955	7,028	4,297	4,904	35,344
Hernando County	190,865	5,287	9,857	6,072	7,967	14,000	11,623	6,232	6,749	52,643
Highlands County	105,424	3,470	4,491	4,692	4,999	7,697	8,134	5,096	6,627	37,245
Hillsborough County	1,436,888	34,652	47,310	30,901	38,225	53,549	34,605	24,284	24,244	205,808
Indian River County	157,413	6,173	9,941	6,448	7,438	13,374	10,603	6,403	7,118	51,384
Lake County	356,495	11,526	14,198	10,522	14,357	26,491	22,044	12,628	9,082	95,124
Lee County	754,610	21,371	31,154	23,153	36,332	59,155	42,168	27,760	27,692	216,260
Leon County	292,502	7,162	9,663	6,510	7,808	9,900	7,285	3,717	3,694	38,914
Manatee County	394,855	10,088	19,293	11,016	18,940	28,158	22,438	13,436	13,799	107,787
Marion County	359,977	8,819	16,205	9,565	18,238	27,931	23,858	12,277	12,155	104,024
Martin County	160,912	5,050	7,360	4,481	6,781	13,152	10,305	7,585	8,115	50,419
Miami-Dade County	2,761,581	69,031	90,284	53,274	79,295	107,581	78,295	60,590	68,933	447,968
Monroe County	75,027	2,372	3,428	2,675	3,969	4,218	3,183	2,081	846	16,972
Nassau County	85,832	2,392	3,787	2,836	2,725	6,010	3,512	2,545	1,159	18,787
Okaloosa County	207,269	5,561	6,630	4,809	6,094	9,818	5,921	4,835	2,628	34,105
Orange County	1,380,645	34,755	40,616	24,925	33,111	42,060	27,215	18,729	18,844	164,884
Osceola County	367,990	10,626	9,987	5,924	12,717	11,435	8,867	4,682	4,802	48,427
Palm Beach County	1,485,941	39,769	56,368	34,491	49,249	88,221	73,448	48,493	60,936	354,838
Pasco County	539,630	14,647	20,775	15,906	20,653	30,824	25,702	15,529	13,520	122,134
Pinellas County	975,280	33,776	45,704	30,194	40,748	59,145	43,240	33,474	35,047	241,848
Polk County	708,009	18,239	24,036	16,988	23,866	40,292	30,432	16,855	14,993	143,426
Putnam County	74,163	2,668	2,667	2,227	2,441	5,935	3,921	2,073	717	17,314
St. Johns County	254,261	6,599	11,426	7,333	9,224	15,031	9,776	5,802	4,574	51,740
St. Lucie County	321,128	8,990	11,480	9,041	13,618	20,028	15,282	11,545	7,694	77,208
Santa Rosa County	179,349	6,674	7,527	3,703	5,431	8,235	6,008	2,925	2,114	28,416
Sarasota County	426,718	11,479	21,354	16,471	24,211	38,653	31,030	24,028	22,673	157,066
Seminole County	467,832	14,149	16,199	9,165	13,160	20,497	12,303	9,117	8,492	72,734
Sumter County	128,754	3,574	8,130	6,172	14,892	21,081	17,945	8,216	4,848	73,154
Volusia County	547,538	17,772	23,290	18,733	24,257	32,151	22,105	15,498	21,000	133,744
Walton County	71,375	2,017	3,387	2,312	2,994	3,864	3,081	1,764	502	14,517

Table B-2: Counties - Older Population by Age—*Continued*

	Total Population	60 to 61 Years	62 to 64 Years	65 to 66 Years	67 to 69 Years	70 to 74 Years	75 to 79 Years	80 to 84 Years	85 Years and Over	65 Years and Over
Georgia										
Barrow County	80,809	1,625	2,358	1,649	1,901	3,107	1,661	919	1,006	10,243
Bartow County	106,408	3,119	4,228	1,503	3,276	4,813	2,251	1,239	1,569	14,651
Bibb County	153,095	3,278	6,765	3,683	4,720	5,867	3,647	3,255	2,802	23,974
Bulloch County	77,296	1,513	2,902	986	2,166	2,022	1,254	1,154	963	8,545
Carroll County	118,121	2,940	3,869	1,841	3,815	4,609	2,798	2,464	1,261	16,788
Catoosa County	67,420	1,868	2,422	1,429	2,430	3,214	2,133	2,064	799	12,069
Chatham County	289,195	7,792	8,855	7,213	7,128	12,070	7,626	5,356	4,738	44,131
Cherokee County	254,149	5,309	9,073	4,963	6,665	11,783	6,653	3,889	2,256	36,209
Clarke County	127,330	1,951	3,660	2,476	2,629	4,162	2,500	1,511	1,745	15,023
Clayton County	289,615	6,299	7,936	4,202	7,240	6,678	5,104	1,967	1,689	26,880
Cobb County	756,865	17,154	24,480	13,871	17,957	26,903	14,312	10,432	9,353	92,828
Columbia County	154,291	4,443	4,425	2,948	4,251	6,935	2,558	2,462	2,175	21,329
Coweta County	145,864	3,848	5,420	3,206	4,488	5,587	4,161	1,761	1,544	20,747
DeKalb County	756,558	17,885	26,111	14,317	21,629	24,283	14,131	7,921	11,708	93,989
Dougherty County	91,243	2,669	2,568	1,698	2,800	3,783	1,876	1,755	1,987	13,899
Douglas County	145,331	3,426	4,407	2,716	3,158	5,272	3,117	1,493	1,530	17,286
Fayette County	113,459	3,063	4,590	1,943	3,681	7,061	4,397	1,175	2,027	20,284
Floyd County	97,927	1,905	4,442	2,121	2,755	4,282	3,578	1,954	1,843	16,533
Forsyth County	236,612	5,745	5,632	3,825	5,776	8,275	5,057	3,867	1,598	28,398
Fulton County	1,050,114	23,685	32,902	16,491	24,934	31,412	22,457	14,103	13,278	122,675
Glynn County	85,219	2,578	3,257	2,514	3,344	4,619	2,967	1,500	2,011	16,955
Gwinnett County	927,781	22,584	27,063	13,689	20,423	26,453	15,582	8,243	9,315	93,705
Hall County	202,148	5,237	6,008	3,150	4,860	9,494	5,546	3,831	3,197	30,078
Henry County	230,220	5,906	6,842	4,867	5,319	6,613	3,624	2,384	3,449	26,256
Houston County	155,469	4,220	4,534	2,610	3,039	5,606	3,277	1,795	2,032	18,359
Jackson County	70,422	1,480	2,255	1,515	1,876	2,588	2,168	896	1,201	10,244
Lowndes County	116,321	2,638	3,243	1,327	3,598	3,726	2,883	1,413	1,583	14,530
Muscogee County	194,160	6,604	5,329	3,925	4,813	6,396	4,086	3,168	3,698	26,086
Newton County	109,541	2,958	3,428	1,458	3,154	4,364	2,813	1,296	1,294	14,379
Paulding County	164,044	3,973	3,899	3,767	2,948	3,787	3,432	1,632	1,305	16,871
Richmond County	201,554	5,225	8,973	3,680	5,512	8,165	4,533	3,481	2,777	28,148
Rockdale County	90,594	2,668	3,522	1,918	2,453	3,677	2,175	1,495	1,088	12,806
Spalding County	66,100	1,281	2,311	1,909	2,267	2,974	2,209	1,386	1,269	12,014
Troup County	70,034	1,175	3,532	1,952	1,722	2,335	2,007	993	1,056	10,065
Walker County	69,410	2,226	2,538	1,288	3,125	2,912	3,019	1,522	1,227	13,093
Walton County	93,503	2,022	2,713	1,660	2,437	4,048	3,144	1,393	1,388	14,070
Whitfield County	104,062	2,142	3,324	1,606	3,311	3,897	2,530	1,600	1,644	14,588
Hawaii										
Hawaii County	200,983	6,789	9,414	5,133	10,205	12,065	7,260	3,743	4,237	42,643
Honolulu County	980,080	25,824	33,817	23,534	30,159	40,717	26,642	22,287	30,273	173,612
Kauai County	72,133	2,790	3,476	2,263	2,520	4,103	2,552	1,665	1,606	14,709
Maui County	167,218	4,199	7,553	4,998	5,753	7,914	4,959	2,914	3,954	30,492
Idaho										
Ada County	469,966	9,608	16,577	8,730	14,592	18,335	12,418	6,755	6,646	67,476
Bannock County	87,138	2,372	2,214	2,091	2,733	2,536	1,957	1,411	1,616	12,344
Bonneville County	116,854	2,445	3,490	2,445	2,605	3,857	2,600	1,144	2,395	15,046
Canyon County	223,499	4,239	7,405	5,358	5,506	8,258	6,463	2,864	3,481	31,930
Kootenai County	161,505	2,834	7,364	4,211	6,080	7,852	6,241	3,558	2,611	30,553
Twin Falls County	86,081	2,407	3,033	1,368	1,819	4,108	2,823	1,600	1,207	12,925
Illinois										
Adams County	65,691	1,762	2,265	1,504	2,005	3,399	3,378	1,144	1,867	13,297
Champaign County	209,983	4,595	7,743	3,337	4,940	7,392	4,085	2,902	3,662	26,318
Cook County	5,180,493	130,469	182,898	103,559	139,324	189,645	136,400	88,900	100,113	757,941
DeKalb County	104,143	2,279	3,366	1,642	2,420	3,715	2,545	1,443	1,540	13,305
DuPage County	928,589	27,672	36,325	21,925	25,325	37,979	24,145	16,173	18,214	143,761
Kane County	534,216	13,206	16,673	10,037	16,860	17,713	12,808	8,092	7,571	73,081
Kankakee County	110,024	2,622	4,660	2,696	2,872	4,752	3,009	2,252	2,763	18,344
Kendall County	127,915	2,659	3,534	1,185	2,929	3,743	2,750	1,011	1,875	13,493
Lake County	700,832	18,909	26,005	15,055	17,279	26,976	17,048	10,655	12,788	99,801
LaSalle County	109,430	2,793	4,601	2,961	3,769	4,912	3,723	2,936	2,540	20,841
McHenry County	308,570	9,452	11,024	6,675	9,326	11,716	7,121	4,600	5,179	44,617
McLean County	172,828	2,941	6,702	4,196	3,963	5,084	3,440	2,648	3,397	22,728
Macon County	104,712	3,984	4,703	2,151	4,395	5,135	3,983	3,062	2,441	21,167
Madison County	264,461	7,741	10,114	6,123	8,489	10,947	9,212	5,596	5,391	45,758
Peoria County	180,621	4,486	8,210	4,417	5,205	7,828	4,479	3,712	4,560	30,201
Rock Island County	143,477	3,354	5,889	3,918	4,880	6,041	5,250	3,531	3,289	26,909
St. Clair County	261,059	8,000	11,109	5,428	8,912	9,357	8,429	4,134	4,693	40,953
Sangamon County	195,348	4,984	9,018	6,049	6,228	8,097	5,947	3,909	4,453	34,683
Tazewell County	132,328	4,082	5,586	2,278	5,297	6,525	3,887	2,791	4,480	25,258
Vermilion County	76,806	1,893	2,646	2,354	2,682	3,244	2,783	1,896	2,197	15,156
Will County	692,310	19,859	22,107	13,150	18,435	23,429	15,679	8,727	11,009	90,429
Williamson County	67,056	2,322	3,400	2,024	2,226	2,984	3,016	1,088	1,224	12,562
Winnebago County	284,081	9,493	11,364	5,886	8,882	13,702	9,157	5,715	6,226	49,568
Indiana										
Allen County	375,351	9,029	12,093	7,947	10,841	13,677	9,676	6,288	6,099	54,528
Bartholomew County	82,753	1,945	2,654	2,482	2,242	2,865	2,712	2,092	1,156	13,549
Boone County	66,999	2,280	2,191	1,271	1,488	2,454	1,444	623	1,472	8,752
Clark County	117,360	3,944	4,520	2,544	3,591	5,299	3,762	1,876	1,289	18,361

Table B-2: Counties - Older Population by Age—*Continued*

	Total Population	60 to 61 Years	62 to 64 Years	65 to 66 Years	67 to 69 Years	70 to 74 Years	75 to 79 Years	80 to 84 Years	85 Years and Over	65 Years and Over
Indiana—Cont.										
Delaware County	114,772	2,229	4,352	2,941	2,615	5,449	3,220	2,521	3,185	19,931
Elkhart County	205,560	4,862	6,901	4,454	5,348	6,962	5,014	3,814	4,138	29,730
Floyd County	77,781	1,877	3,202	1,652	2,530	3,367	1,441	1,760	1,684	12,434
Grant County	65,936	1,631	2,873	1,401	2,504	2,753	2,548	1,756	1,571	12,533
Hamilton County	330,086	6,660	10,596	6,217	8,192	10,411	7,499	4,043	4,946	41,308
Hancock County	76,351	2,283	1,795	1,666	2,266	4,173	2,182	1,487	1,174	12,948
Hendricks County	167,009	4,893	6,101	2,562	5,085	6,141	3,175	4,070	1,884	22,917
Howard County	82,366	2,202	3,044	1,681	2,792	4,541	3,117	1,423	2,363	15,917
Johnson County	156,225	4,291	4,550	3,568	5,151	4,726	4,633	2,613	2,029	22,720
Kosciusko County	79,344	2,058	3,791	1,313	2,535	3,844	2,638	1,190	1,548	13,068
Lake County	484,411	12,849	20,776	11,948	15,143	19,016	13,589	9,712	10,516	79,924
LaPorte County	110,007	2,782	4,302	2,655	3,878	5,409	3,931	1,860	1,943	19,676
Madison County	129,641	2,698	6,092	3,184	4,070	6,443	4,863	2,187	2,891	23,638
Marion County	954,670	23,353	30,227	19,410	22,654	29,187	20,285	14,459	14,097	120,092
Monroe County	146,917	4,441	3,684	2,344	3,768	5,245	2,428	2,037	3,224	19,046
Morgan County	70,116	1,774	2,776	1,255	2,383	3,543	2,232	857	1,462	11,732
Porter County	169,594	4,730	7,080	4,167	4,404	7,845	5,168	2,732	3,079	27,395
St. Joseph County	270,771	7,934	9,965	7,933	7,444	9,430	7,172	4,550	6,631	43,160
Tippecanoe County	193,048	4,002	4,983	3,632	4,056	5,544	4,291	1,692	3,177	22,392
Vanderburgh County	180,974	5,297	7,773	4,103	6,184	6,921	4,996	3,415	4,504	30,123
Vigo County	107,386	2,600	3,936	2,344	2,884	4,544	3,087	2,170	2,089	17,118
Wayne County	65,936	1,750	2,853	1,878	2,254	2,718	2,048	1,700	1,847	12,445
Iowa										
Black Hawk County	132,408	2,707	5,440	3,507	3,494	5,030	4,613	2,069	2,505	21,218
Dallas County	90,180	1,332	1,959	1,503	2,657	2,146	1,741	993	1,646	10,686
Dubuque County	96,854	2,384	4,035	2,171	3,282	4,065	3,139	2,113	2,671	17,441
Johnson County	151,260	2,707	5,365	2,322	4,276	3,947	2,728	2,205	2,093	17,571
Linn County	225,909	5,373	7,216	5,255	5,917	9,491	5,687	5,366	4,681	36,397
Polk County	487,204	8,779	16,094	9,387	12,725	15,511	11,385	6,782	7,258	63,048
Pottawattamie County	93,533	2,446	4,254	2,047	2,943	4,547	3,369	1,453	2,085	16,444
Scott County	173,283	4,820	6,731	4,513	5,369	6,074	4,623	3,868	3,144	27,591
Story County	98,105	1,842	2,036	2,214	1,930	2,387	2,399	1,227	1,405	11,562
Woodbury County	102,539	2,867	3,951	2,103	3,231	3,722	2,158	2,575	2,010	15,799
Kansas										
Butler County	66,765	1,806	3,031	1,617	1,918	2,072	1,791	1,574	1,161	10,133
Douglas County	121,436	1,992	3,546	3,221	2,745	2,932	2,134	1,873	2,395	15,300
Johnson County	597,555	14,934	21,764	14,536	17,251	20,849	13,950	8,822	11,116	86,524
Leavenworth County	81,352	1,965	3,131	1,169	2,657	3,332	2,017	1,319	1,671	12,165
Riley County	73,703	1,698	1,457	699	1,691	1,741	1,406	468	1,030	7,035
Sedgwick County	513,607	13,810	17,892	10,450	14,621	18,851	11,802	8,841	9,743	74,308
Shawnee County	177,499	4,798	7,968	5,047	7,862	6,426	5,705	4,121	3,615	32,776
Wyandotte County	165,324	3,552	5,174	4,333	3,520	4,469	3,699	2,718	1,605	20,344
Kentucky										
Boone County	131,533	3,190	4,077	2,166	3,630	4,982	2,776	2,411	1,398	17,363
Bullitt County	81,069	1,759	3,521	1,812	2,197	4,207	2,258	1,748	876	13,098
Campbell County	93,152	3,465	3,050	1,837	3,136	3,704	2,786	1,533	1,829	14,825
Christian County	71,671	1,678	2,005	812	2,041	2,077	1,801	919	1,220	8,870
Daviess County	101,104	3,110	3,640	1,783	3,378	4,640	3,290	2,100	1,861	17,052
Fayette County	323,780	6,908	11,374	6,670	8,675	10,170	8,238	4,728	4,478	42,959
Hardin County	110,356	3,765	3,515	2,053	3,662	3,625	2,662	2,223	1,620	15,845
Jefferson County	770,517	22,185	29,031	18,142	25,407	29,533	19,784	15,676	15,879	124,421
Kenton County	166,051	4,061	6,215	4,053	4,685	6,167	4,069	2,567	2,487	24,028
McCracken County	65,346	1,599	3,178	1,377	2,128	3,500	2,082	1,649	2,654	13,390
Madison County	92,368	2,102	2,880	1,764	2,696	3,290	2,033	1,473	1,463	12,719
Oldham County	66,470	2,067	2,163	1,415	1,794	2,241	1,722	831	648	8,651
Warren County	131,264	2,958	3,579	2,994	3,043	4,711	3,193	1,770	1,651	17,362
Louisiana										
Ascension Parish	124,672	2,911	4,250	1,995	3,559	3,982	1,234	1,880	1,529	14,179
Bossier Parish	127,185	2,565	4,588	2,624	3,803	4,171	2,547	2,364	2,125	17,634
Caddo Parish	242,922	7,017	8,976	5,788	9,878	8,373	7,013	5,357	5,211	41,620
Calcasieu Parish	203,112	4,989	9,179	4,169	5,615	8,596	5,434	3,200	3,451	30,465
East Baton Rouge Parish	440,956	10,306	16,364	10,128	11,843	15,936	10,629	7,470	6,571	62,577
Iberia Parish	70,941	2,337	2,523	1,882	1,682	2,782	2,066	1,143	826	10,381
Jefferson Parish	434,051	13,643	16,758	10,971	14,583	18,114	13,487	9,022	8,064	74,241
Lafayette Parish	242,782	5,198	7,956	5,511	6,977	6,999	5,610	3,373	3,394	31,864
Lafourche Parish	98,115	3,080	4,280	3,065	2,703	2,660	3,619	1,672	1,818	15,537
Livingston Parish	139,567	4,316	4,857	2,842	3,656	4,860	4,617	1,380	1,584	18,939
Orleans Parish	391,006	9,091	15,461	8,722	12,744	14,350	9,594	6,232	5,890	57,532
Ouachita Parish	154,475	5,254	5,339	2,444	3,757	7,219	4,883	2,353	2,196	22,852
Rapides Parish	130,562	3,028	5,223	2,538	3,819	6,168	3,648	3,047	2,054	21,274
St. Landry Parish	82,764	2,407	3,111	1,715	3,096	2,999	2,599	1,356	1,402	13,167
St. Tammany Parish	258,111	7,731	9,693	6,264	8,567	11,870	7,334	4,973	4,636	43,644
Tangipahoa Parish	133,777	3,640	4,141	2,425	4,699	4,882	3,217	2,548	1,316	19,087
Terrebonne Parish	111,021	2,635	3,759	1,993	4,196	4,301	3,233	1,483	1,436	16,642
Maine										
Androscoggin County	107,679	3,310	4,085	3,605	3,697	4,071	3,842	2,022	2,055	19,292
Aroostook County	67,111	2,281	3,896	2,201	2,916	4,128	2,410	1,716	2,822	16,193
Cumberland County	293,557	7,169	13,423	9,093	9,764	13,175	9,314	5,989	6,638	53,973

Table B-2: Counties - Older Population by Age—*Continued*

	Total Population	60 to 61 Years	62 to 64 Years	65 to 66 Years	67 to 69 Years	70 to 74 Years	75 to 79 Years	80 to 84 Years	85 Years and Over	65 Years and Over
Maine—Cont.										
Kennebec County	122,083	3,703	6,262	3,402	4,271	6,954	4,444	2,221	3,578	24,870
Penobscot County	151,096	5,134	6,121	3,891	4,460	7,854	4,956	2,970	3,630	27,761
York County	206,229	7,627	9,748	6,327	8,013	10,805	6,839	5,755	4,575	42,314
Maryland										
Allegany County	70,975	1,609	2,628	1,538	2,301	3,820	3,257	2,099	1,132	14,147
Anne Arundel County	576,031	15,034	21,260	10,947	13,825	25,543	17,029	8,206	9,261	84,811
Baltimore County	828,431	22,670	34,346	18,808	26,903	33,903	25,831	16,737	20,360	142,542
Calvert County	92,003	2,446	3,685	2,216	2,001	4,130	2,275	1,298	1,555	13,475
Carroll County	168,429	4,461	7,653	3,395	5,443	7,076	4,412	3,813	3,370	27,509
Cecil County	102,826	3,121	5,662	1,729	3,596	4,930	2,619	1,436	1,894	16,204
Charles County	161,503	5,019	6,025	2,828	4,846	4,532	3,507	1,882	2,322	19,917
Frederick County	255,648	6,340	10,782	6,002	5,912	10,102	7,250	2,925	4,629	36,820
Harford County	253,956	7,926	10,070	5,757	6,748	12,409	7,569	4,732	4,790	42,005
Howard County	323,196	7,166	11,975	6,487	7,311	14,257	8,439	4,637	3,608	44,739
Montgomery County	1,052,567	26,342	39,029	24,593	30,384	37,954	29,025	19,924	21,765	163,645
Prince George's County	909,308	20,608	32,417	18,879	25,153	31,673	19,541	13,439	11,940	120,625
St. Mary's County	112,664	3,076	3,696	2,138	2,442	4,116	3,321	1,857	1,132	15,006
Washington County	150,926	5,648	5,493	3,516	4,363	6,733	4,748	3,955	2,751	26,066
Wicomico County	103,195	2,718	3,095	1,867	3,537	3,871	3,032	2,188	1,751	16,246
Massachusetts										
Barnstable County	213,413	7,053	11,621	8,744	11,203	17,375	12,431	8,030	7,670	65,453
Berkshire County	126,348	3,004	7,615	3,935	5,234	7,449	5,491	3,301	3,829	29,239
Bristol County	564,022	15,830	23,993	11,862	17,672	25,715	15,879	10,487	13,241	94,856
Essex County	790,638	20,753	31,344	17,369	26,121	34,112	21,004	15,479	20,793	134,878
Franklin County	70,963	2,717	4,630	2,228	2,894	4,546	1,938	1,636	2,182	15,424
Hampden County	470,406	12,782	18,036	10,888	14,569	19,367	14,351	7,527	12,063	78,765
Hampshire County	161,355	4,080	6,058	3,612	6,216	7,521	4,311	3,228	3,080	27,968
Middlesex County	1,614,714	40,955	57,786	34,627	42,004	62,498	42,851	30,086	33,994	246,060
Norfolk County	705,388	19,212	27,288	16,596	21,222	28,365	20,714	13,545	18,516	118,958
Plymouth County	518,132	15,265	22,282	13,146	16,861	26,038	16,879	10,021	10,661	93,606
Suffolk County	807,252	18,106	21,618	14,766	19,068	22,675	17,879	10,881	11,683	96,952
Worcester County	830,839	21,721	34,244	17,818	25,429	33,252	21,523	16,224	15,596	129,842
Michigan										
Allegan County	117,327	2,084	4,822	2,785	3,851	5,388	3,772	2,018	1,994	19,808
Bay County	103,923	4,126	4,933	2,670	3,836	5,315	3,985	2,000	3,051	20,857
Berrien County	154,141	5,067	7,289	4,211	5,816	7,299	4,712	3,744	4,686	30,468
Calhoun County	134,487	5,030	4,898	3,756	3,799	5,977	4,008	2,784	3,723	24,047
Clinton County	79,332	2,002	3,646	2,420	2,306	3,575	2,900	1,404	1,015	13,620
Eaton County	109,826	3,765	5,176	2,464	4,871	4,864	3,802	2,369	1,910	20,280
Genesee County	406,892	13,555	15,648	10,260	14,276	16,601	12,941	9,577	7,505	71,160
Grand Traverse County	92,573	2,653	4,217	2,899	3,406	4,863	3,143	1,383	2,684	18,378
Ingham County	292,735	7,126	10,560	5,471	9,090	9,877	5,817	3,802	5,759	39,816
Isabella County	70,562	1,377	2,644	1,090	1,936	2,362	1,615	1,101	990	9,094
Jackson County	158,823	4,824	6,195	4,555	4,950	7,432	5,281	3,060	3,269	28,547
Kalamazoo County	264,870	6,377	9,398	5,409	6,802	11,463	7,564	4,165	4,425	39,828
Kent County	653,786	16,729	22,697	13,476	16,655	23,118	14,939	10,784	10,779	89,751
Lapeer County	88,028	3,256	4,235	2,652	3,128	4,191	3,030	1,597	1,369	15,967
Lenawee County	98,266	3,148	4,324	3,097	3,905	3,877	3,323	1,760	2,130	18,092
Livingston County	191,224	5,891	9,237	5,564	6,749	8,233	5,961	3,716	2,895	33,118
Macomb County	874,759	26,573	34,837	19,993	26,486	38,576	26,496	18,764	18,692	149,007
Marquette County	66,516	1,932	2,990	1,813	2,454	3,250	2,459	1,348	1,500	12,824
Midland County	83,209	2,652	3,521	2,209	2,845	3,616	3,024	1,576	2,269	15,539
Monroe County	150,439	4,296	6,092	3,561	5,553	6,957	4,858	2,876	3,738	27,543
Muskegon County	173,588	4,990	7,194	4,455	5,276	7,858	5,118	3,471	3,263	29,441
Oakland County	1,259,201	37,979	51,239	30,255	40,501	54,051	37,163	22,178	27,438	211,586
Ottawa County	290,494	5,395	10,717	6,063	8,859	9,652	8,377	5,136	5,329	43,416
Saginaw County	190,800	4,744	8,110	4,754	6,284	9,836	6,121	4,618	5,153	36,766
St. Clair County	159,337	4,598	8,072	4,829	5,024	7,989	6,231	3,133	2,807	30,013
Shiawassee County	68,192	2,150	2,887	1,789	2,450	3,277	2,151	1,511	1,419	12,597
Van Buren County	75,448	1,554	3,622	2,095	3,278	3,124	2,526	1,693	1,373	14,089
Washtenaw County	370,963	8,595	11,824	7,277	10,152	14,221	9,179	5,011	5,935	51,775
Wayne County	1,753,893	48,383	68,280	38,702	51,728	67,765	44,672	34,218	33,176	270,261
Minnesota										
Anoka County	353,813	9,372	13,293	7,371	10,081	13,241	9,826	4,953	4,354	49,826
Blue Earth County	67,427	1,252	1,684	1,086	1,665	2,442	1,616	1,049	1,589	9,447
Carver County	103,551	2,368	3,152	1,830	2,955	2,920	2,745	1,716	514	12,680
Dakota County	425,423	12,121	13,352	9,028	12,041	14,309	10,588	6,855	6,412	59,233
Hennepin County	1,259,428	30,935	43,951	27,851	35,311	40,533	29,982	19,306	23,877	176,860
Olmsted County	156,277	4,095	4,463	2,972	4,053	6,174	4,974	2,639	3,483	24,295
Ramsey County	550,210	14,230	18,573	11,088	15,641	19,402	12,100	9,659	11,530	79,420
Rice County	66,523	1,273	2,775	1,641	1,805	2,424	1,791	922	1,714	10,297
St. Louis County	199,754	6,497	8,888	6,055	7,463	8,820	5,821	4,742	5,692	38,593
Scott County	147,381	2,590	4,793	2,249	3,803	3,803	2,846	1,592	1,999	16,292
Sherburne County	96,036	1,622	2,777	1,436	1,999	3,205	1,632	961	1,360	10,593
Stearns County	159,256	3,712	5,459	2,837	4,289	6,223	4,719	2,429	3,498	23,995
Washington County	259,201	6,046	9,555	5,718	8,402	9,269	6,300	4,860	4,175	38,724
Wright County	136,349	2,397	4,608	2,795	2,811	4,609	3,497	2,010	1,400	17,122

Table B-2: Counties - Older Population by Age—*Continued*

	Total Population	60 to 61 Years	62 to 64 Years	65 to 66 Years	67 to 69 Years	70 to 74 Years	75 to 79 Years	80 to 84 Years	85 Years and Over	65 Years and Over
Mississippi										
DeSoto County	182,001	4,968	6,669	3,697	3,904	6,192	3,757	3,252	2,171	22,973
Forrest County	75,036	1,952	2,735	1,389	2,261	2,692	1,687	1,142	1,195	10,366
Harrison County	206,650	5,586	5,803	4,694	5,216	8,742	6,312	3,179	2,845	30,988
Hinds County	237,085	5,964	8,849	5,625	6,255	8,021	5,918	3,610	3,850	33,279
Jackson County	143,277	5,298	4,576	2,666	3,858	7,054	4,528	3,815	815	22,736
Jones County	68,461	2,505	3,052	2,039	1,793	3,321	2,555	792	1,375	11,875
Lauderdale County	75,317	2,114	2,187	1,728	2,512	3,086	2,734	1,125	1,753	12,938
Lee County	85,202	2,269	3,551	1,097	2,323	3,480	1,922	2,160	1,115	12,097
Madison County	105,630	2,528	4,149	2,111	2,064	4,656	1,709	1,482	1,736	13,758
Rankin County	153,902	4,010	4,589	3,238	5,283	5,951	4,287	2,541	2,160	23,460
Missouri										
Boone County	180,005	4,259	6,012	3,995	4,449	4,755	3,069	2,637	3,032	21,937
Buchanan County	88,571	2,316	4,075	2,176	2,802	4,090	2,581	1,327	2,038	15,014
Cape Girardeau County	78,753	2,303	2,599	2,382	1,604	3,068	2,066	1,915	1,914	12,949
Cass County	104,954	2,884	4,437	1,811	3,564	4,978	3,094	2,598	1,949	17,994
Christian County	86,983	2,948	3,220	2,142	3,062	2,790	1,946	1,593	1,891	13,424
Clay County	246,365	5,776	9,260	3,863	8,232	9,056	5,848	4,544	3,298	34,841
Cole County	76,796	2,386	2,277	1,337	2,939	3,641	2,775	1,229	1,053	12,974
Franklin County	103,670	2,824	4,494	2,827	3,006	4,485	3,339	2,090	2,201	17,948
Greene County	291,923	6,982	9,804	4,777	9,688	12,502	10,553	4,977	5,816	48,313
Jackson County	700,307	18,735	25,804	14,265	18,633	28,060	18,659	11,375	13,748	104,740
Jasper County	120,636	2,320	3,438	2,261	3,007	5,365	3,249	2,505	2,312	18,699
Jefferson County	224,347	5,687	10,959	4,099	7,795	8,925	6,601	3,390	3,014	33,824
Platte County	102,985	2,749	3,419	1,706	3,217	4,386	3,131	1,251	1,337	15,028
St. Charles County	399,182	9,073	18,124	8,646	9,910	16,556	10,101	7,764	6,712	59,689
St. Francois County	66,692	1,474	2,085	1,165	977	4,441	2,069	1,130	1,561	11,343
St. Louis County	996,945	29,820	41,249	25,803	32,963	42,953	31,697	22,651	24,454	180,521
Montana										
Cascade County	81,643	2,108	4,256	1,917	2,881	3,603	2,789	1,875	1,940	15,005
Flathead County	102,106	3,376	5,264	3,055	4,057	5,500	3,771	2,172	1,403	19,958
Gallatin County	111,876	3,204	3,598	1,836	3,082	4,326	3,227	849	1,108	14,428
Lewis and Clark County	68,700	2,162	2,921	1,767	2,930	3,297	2,011	850	1,813	12,668
Missoula County	118,791	3,045	4,281	2,056	4,202	5,055	3,799	1,617	1,528	18,257
Yellowstone County	160,137	5,171	5,816	3,244	6,115	6,298	4,284	3,280	3,942	27,163
Nebraska										
Douglas County	566,880	13,266	18,297	11,233	14,070	19,287	10,671	8,860	9,740	73,861
Lancaster County	317,272	6,916	10,852	7,141	8,860	10,714	6,885	5,081	5,149	43,830
Sarpy County	184,459	4,585	4,863	3,103	4,085	6,210	3,283	2,607	2,881	22,169
Nevada										
Clark County	2,231,647	50,888	76,232	42,811	65,694	92,964	60,877	35,327	31,017	328,690
Washoe County	465,735	12,086	21,068	11,051	16,138	21,141	12,227	8,429	7,186	76,172
New Hampshire										
Cheshire County	76,493	2,512	3,896	1,829	3,465	3,700	2,854	2,003	1,244	15,095
Grafton County	89,786	3,129	3,418	2,919	2,889	5,198	3,348	2,055	2,226	18,635
Hillsborough County	415,247	13,605	15,991	9,152	12,730	16,346	11,127	6,859	8,636	64,850
Merrimack County	151,132	5,731	5,757	4,772	5,266	6,964	4,757	2,789	3,875	28,423
Rockingham County	309,176	10,071	13,720	8,276	10,905	14,592	9,322	5,509	6,797	55,401
Strafford County	130,090	4,100	4,439	2,683	3,984	4,666	3,209	2,176	2,464	19,182
New Jersey										
Atlantic County	265,429	7,441	10,594	5,641	7,375	14,340	9,805	5,329	5,068	47,558
Bergen County	936,692	25,779	35,062	21,205	25,386	40,901	27,091	20,360	26,056	160,999
Burlington County	445,384	12,931	18,258	10,432	13,197	19,305	12,819	9,792	9,730	75,275
Camden County	507,078	14,481	18,586	9,920	15,956	20,262	14,540	9,426	9,136	79,240
Cape May County	92,560	3,499	4,706	2,621	4,529	6,435	4,966	2,882	2,635	24,068
Cumberland County	150,972	3,978	4,762	3,568	4,450	5,663	4,103	3,121	2,317	23,222
Essex County	799,767	17,109	30,424	15,224	19,033	27,685	18,743	12,205	15,642	108,532
Gloucester County	291,408	10,489	9,967	7,375	8,084	12,164	7,481	5,416	6,059	46,579
Hudson County	676,061	15,006	21,637	10,730	15,159	19,718	14,364	9,222	10,725	79,918
Hunterdon County	124,714	4,331	4,499	3,021	5,299	5,809	3,851	2,378	2,922	23,280
Mercer County	369,811	10,956	12,075	8,928	10,697	12,990	8,786	7,407	7,193	56,001
Middlesex County	829,685	21,852	28,858	18,274	23,311	29,447	20,170	14,778	18,158	124,138
Monmouth County	621,354	19,999	26,113	15,290	19,514	27,920	20,266	11,645	14,565	109,200
Morris County	494,228	14,258	20,687	10,242	14,467	21,611	16,433	9,124	12,437	84,314
Ocean County	601,651	17,180	24,589	14,146	21,424	36,454	28,236	17,471	18,547	136,278
Passaic County	503,310	12,881	17,688	10,197	13,965	17,109	13,314	9,369	9,257	73,211
Salem County	62,607	2,273	2,653	1,770	2,226	2,763	2,762	783	1,431	11,735
Somerset County	331,164	9,211	15,218	8,282	8,735	11,521	8,759	7,095	7,227	51,619
Sussex County	140,799	5,532	6,393	3,960	5,372	5,281	4,296	2,820	1,947	23,676
Union County	558,067	14,315	19,206	11,157	14,253	19,766	15,006	8,220	11,851	80,253
Warren County	105,779	3,849	4,658	2,964	2,714	5,116	4,109	1,435	2,855	19,193
New Mexico										
Bernalillo County	678,701	18,660	23,225	14,870	20,785	31,030	18,053	12,791	13,687	111,216
Chaves County	64,689	2,222	2,265	813	2,494	2,598	1,706	1,660	1,559	10,830
Doña Ana County	217,522	3,749	8,076	4,712	6,095	9,044	6,520	5,290	3,125	34,786
Lea County	69,611	2,509	1,263	1,749	1,443	1,578	1,542	620	924	7,856
McKinley County	72,290	2,843	2,552	1,140	1,185	2,668	1,290	1,484	1,514	9,281
Otero County	66,781	1,250	3,125	1,013	3,034	2,459	2,484	903	829	10,722
Sandoval County	145,179	4,004	5,622	4,542	4,985	6,762	5,071	2,309	2,094	25,763

Table B-2: Counties - Older Population by Age—*Continued*

	Total Population	60 to 61 Years	62 to 64 Years	65 to 66 Years	67 to 69 Years	70 to 74 Years	75 to 79 Years	80 to 84 Years	85 Years and Over	65 Years and Over
New Mexico—Cont.										
San Juan County	125,043	3,425	4,098	2,754	4,236	4,240	3,592	2,056	2,223	19,101
Santa Fe County	150,056	4,211	7,769	5,176	7,463	10,798	6,858	3,543	2,730	36,568
Valencia County	76,456	2,626	3,402	2,544	2,046	3,654	2,204	1,473	1,754	13,675
New York										
Albany County	307,117	7,586	12,695	7,859	9,727	12,419	8,733	6,528	7,050	52,316
Bronx County	1,432,132	30,460	44,548	23,536	31,874	46,561	33,127	26,879	21,188	183,165
Broome County	191,659	6,957	7,166	4,050	6,012	9,555	6,395	4,447	6,334	36,793
Cattaraugus County	76,840	2,066	3,833	1,800	2,796	3,853	3,302	1,366	1,524	14,641
Cayuga County	77,145	2,224	3,153	2,052	2,611	3,575	1,870	2,538	1,676	14,322
Chautauqua County	127,939	4,056	5,424	3,768	4,380	6,120	4,837	2,574	3,908	25,587
Chemung County	84,254	2,401	3,166	2,591	3,203	3,725	3,208	1,981	1,905	16,613
Clinton County	80,695	3,459	2,897	1,983	2,556	3,326	2,212	1,948	1,498	13,523
Dutchess County	293,718	8,941	12,985	7,157	9,290	12,770	9,191	6,677	6,488	51,573
Erie County	919,719	27,089	37,539	21,069	28,563	42,123	29,333	20,157	23,971	165,216
Jefferson County	111,755	2,578	3,805	1,956	3,575	3,534	2,824	1,921	1,648	15,458
Kings County	2,582,830	58,332	82,689	48,376	66,900	88,781	65,210	43,734	45,796	358,797
Livingston County	63,227	1,744	3,127	1,599	1,566	3,297	2,019	1,620	1,016	11,117
Madison County	70,795	2,412	3,352	1,630	3,566	2,528	2,870	1,104	1,389	13,087
Monroe County	742,474	22,337	32,246	16,741	23,283	32,820	23,475	14,105	17,686	128,110
Nassau County	1,358,343	42,632	51,811	31,881	40,357	60,725	41,309	27,875	39,183	241,330
New York County	1,628,701	39,058	52,399	34,360	46,576	65,414	49,549	33,326	39,609	268,834
Niagara County	210,433	8,589	10,507	5,404	7,405	10,225	6,390	4,589	5,800	39,813
Oneida County	229,577	7,452	9,667	6,458	6,655	9,952	7,108	5,493	6,889	42,555
Onondaga County	461,809	13,754	19,236	10,691	14,041	19,833	13,316	8,968	12,018	78,867
Ontario County	109,864	3,888	4,635	3,251	4,047	5,380	3,802	2,520	2,645	21,645
Orange County	381,951	8,626	15,260	7,854	10,589	13,470	8,084	6,337	7,057	53,391
Oswego County	117,898	3,579	3,911	2,911	3,799	4,989	3,262	2,779	1,709	19,449
Putnam County	98,892	3,329	4,662	2,502	3,684	4,248	3,614	1,450	1,596	17,094
Queens County	2,278,906	64,157	77,516	48,118	63,080	90,377	64,901	45,981	45,173	357,630
Rensselaer County	159,442	3,863	7,240	3,560	5,669	6,778	4,248	2,570	3,732	26,557
Richmond County	476,179	12,626	21,031	10,875	15,816	19,292	14,287	8,183	8,601	77,054
Rockland County	325,695	7,081	12,577	6,676	9,611	11,666	7,409	7,871	7,876	51,109
St. Lawrence County	108,047	3,285	3,942	2,277	3,189	5,265	2,806	2,381	2,550	18,468
Saratoga County	230,163	6,477	7,757	4,951	8,197	11,518	7,360	4,748	4,076	40,850
Schenectady County	155,350	4,494	6,775	2,811	4,968	7,057	3,932	3,770	4,314	26,852
Steuben County	95,796	3,316	3,957	2,969	3,666	4,175	3,521	2,172	2,160	18,663
Suffolk County	1,481,093	43,300	57,497	29,265	43,034	68,169	47,481	31,030	31,103	250,082
Sullivan County	75,498	1,556	3,655	1,542	2,990	3,838	3,068	1,643	1,117	14,198
Tompkins County	102,793	2,308	4,931	2,097	2,046	4,443	2,144	1,440	2,039	14,209
Ulster County	178,599	7,267	7,028	4,761	6,472	9,173	6,732	3,589	4,398	35,125
Warren County	64,265	2,188	4,088	2,684	2,657	3,166	2,032	1,561	2,261	14,361
Wayne County	90,064	3,014	3,913	1,733	3,175	3,175	3,356	1,896	2,110	17,292
Westchester County	967,612	27,661	35,319	19,795	27,198	41,340	30,306	20,116	26,582	165,337
North Carolina										
Alamance County	166,436	4,544	5,997	4,339	5,630	6,118	4,441	4,492	3,361	28,381
Brunswick County	136,744	4,312	9,866	6,206	10,063	13,113	8,555	3,023	2,703	43,663
Buncombe County	259,103	6,817	12,007	7,429	9,055	13,885	9,715	4,226	7,511	51,821
Burke County	90,382	2,742	4,374	1,999	3,213	4,829	4,502	1,802	1,702	18,047
Cabarrus County	211,342	3,903	6,404	2,311	5,878	8,696	5,306	2,946	3,071	28,208
Caldwell County	82,029	2,629	3,184	2,289	2,834	4,440	2,668	1,801	2,011	16,043
Carteret County	69,524	1,976	3,786	2,203	3,119	5,448	3,513	1,559	1,613	17,455
Catawba County	158,652	4,285	6,682	3,593	4,627	8,679	4,381	3,734	3,006	28,020
Chatham County	73,139	2,154	3,205	1,515	3,745	5,022	3,194	1,560	2,840	17,876
Cleveland County	97,645	3,740	4,344	2,897	4,010	3,677	2,816	2,623	2,074	18,097
Craven County	102,912	2,694	4,524	2,247	3,099	5,693	4,036	2,883	1,630	19,588
Cumberland County	332,330	7,207	9,681	5,904	7,061	10,625	8,808	4,060	3,700	40,158
Davidson County	166,614	4,783	8,066	3,780	5,592	8,637	5,432	3,961	2,636	30,038
Durham County	316,739	7,078	10,891	6,428	8,708	10,444	7,491	4,642	4,202	41,915
Forsyth County	379,099	9,594	13,486	8,221	11,937	15,596	9,632	7,888	7,111	60,385
Franklin County	67,560	1,823	2,633	1,710	2,838	3,168	2,531	436	950	11,633
Gaston County	222,846	5,297	8,738	5,739	5,739	6,071	9,595	5,669	4,670	3,645	35,389
Guilford County	533,670	13,627	19,824	10,455	16,642	20,522	13,366	8,891	10,598	80,474
Harnett County	134,214	2,707	3,972	2,100	3,283	4,796	3,595	1,887	1,380	17,041
Henderson County	116,748	3,717	4,560	3,048	5,423	8,391	6,186	3,630	3,661	30,339
Iredell County	178,435	3,922	6,782	4,069	5,320	7,352	4,798	3,781	2,547	27,867
Johnston County	202,675	3,645	7,699	3,845	5,333	8,084	4,014	2,985	3,135	27,396
Lincoln County	83,770	2,353	3,012	2,765	2,787	3,351	2,987	1,027	1,364	14,281
Mecklenburg County	1,093,901	24,104	32,796	19,008	24,527	32,605	20,274	13,375	12,802	122,591
Moore County	98,682	2,437	5,100	3,283	3,222	6,186	5,811	2,029	3,053	23,584
Nash County	94,016	3,986	3,334	2,124	3,660	4,882	3,282	1,643	1,855	17,446
New Hanover County	232,274	4,703	9,587	5,804	7,711	11,511	7,154	4,347	4,952	41,479
Onslow County	197,683	3,169	3,706	2,750	3,081	4,596	3,443	2,556	1,610	18,036
Orange County	146,027	2,818	5,611	2,918	5,170	5,489	4,377	1,827	972	20,753
Pitt County	179,914	4,043	6,763	4,186	3,625	6,564	3,510	3,346	2,309	23,540
Randolph County	143,351	3,247	6,082	4,008	4,840	5,904	4,583	3,420	2,452	25,207
Robeson County	131,831	3,309	5,846	2,630	4,048	5,689	3,687	1,477	2,330	19,861
Rockingham County	90,690	2,514	4,865	2,181	3,542	5,028	3,569	1,923	2,390	18,633
Rowan County	141,262	2,724	5,624	3,995	4,601	5,830	5,317	2,252	2,601	24,596
Rutherford County	66,826	2,997	3,252	1,979	2,996	3,216	2,679	1,907	1,281	14,058

Table B-2: Counties - Older Population by Age—*Continued*

	Total Population	60 to 61 Years	62 to 64 Years	65 to 66 Years	67 to 69 Years	70 to 74 Years	75 to 79 Years	80 to 84 Years	85 Years and Over	65 Years and Over
North Carolina—Cont.										
Surry County	71,948	2,207	3,071	2,535	2,566	3,243	3,032	1,726	1,964	15,066
Union County	235,908	4,491	7,610	3,936	5,966	8,232	6,476	2,260	2,920	29,790
Wake County	1,092,305	23,387	32,636	16,512	26,919	36,436	22,027	12,375	12,571	126,840
Wayne County	123,248	4,921	5,065	2,343	3,507	6,328	3,457	2,884	1,988	20,507
Wilkes County	68,557	1,387	4,527	2,020	2,955	3,415	2,682	2,326	1,297	14,695
Wilson County	81,455	3,359	2,587	2,817	3,280	2,778	2,165	2,263	1,501	14,804
North Dakota										
Burleigh County	95,273	2,407	2,966	2,873	2,873	2,694	2,064	1,992	2,661	15,157
Cass County	181,516	4,851	6,017	3,169	3,322	5,836	2,655	3,411	3,206	21,599
Grand Forks County	70,770	1,889	2,079	1,157	1,807	2,106	1,644	974	1,175	8,863
Ward County	67,744	1,251	1,960	1,502	1,151	1,909	1,752	724	1,424	8,462
Ohio										
Allen County	102,663	3,241	4,156	2,073	3,010	4,988	3,095	2,833	1,931	17,930
Ashtabula County	97,493	3,118	4,814	2,990	3,311	4,539	3,478	1,970	2,281	18,569
Athens County	65,818	1,155	2,353	1,689	1,776	1,806	1,465	798	1,103	8,637
Belmont County	67,505	2,651	3,087	2,085	2,546	3,689	2,297	1,664	2,069	14,350
Butler County	382,378	10,205	14,476	9,601	9,201	14,513	10,724	5,743	6,490	56,272
Clark County	134,585	3,533	5,748	3,067	5,165	6,653	4,466	2,757	3,849	25,957
Clermont County	205,466	6,382	8,066	4,688	6,269	9,077	5,725	4,030	3,187	32,976
Columbiana County	102,665	3,595	4,391	2,695	4,661	5,024	4,218	2,430	2,147	21,175
Cuyahoga County	1,243,857	37,808	51,383	32,524	41,754	51,271	42,422	26,358	31,808	226,137
Delaware County	204,826	5,742	6,652	3,800	6,274	6,863	4,179	3,557	2,905	27,578
Erie County	74,615	2,586	2,587	1,865	2,639	4,648	2,730	1,557	2,718	16,157
Fairfield County	155,782	4,431	5,291	3,674	4,290	6,726	4,303	3,512	2,170	24,675
Franklin County	1,310,300	31,361	42,317	23,758	31,405	40,304	25,851	18,043	18,180	157,541
Geauga County	94,031	3,373	3,800	2,853	3,210	5,030	3,862	2,525	2,027	19,507
Greene County	167,995	5,114	6,160	4,423	5,458	7,142	5,168	4,582	2,286	29,059
Hamilton County	816,684	21,248	30,304	17,617	23,099	31,188	21,506	14,710	16,897	125,017
Hancock County	75,930	1,995	2,703	1,647	2,380	3,193	1,736	1,896	1,977	12,829
Jefferson County	65,767	1,604	3,764	2,233	2,548	3,430	2,905	1,823	1,518	14,457
Lake County	230,514	8,125	10,486	7,748	6,627	12,055	7,659	6,411	5,847	46,347
Licking County	175,769	5,439	6,105	4,263	4,460	8,055	5,046	3,389	3,520	28,733
Lorain County	309,461	8,692	13,988	7,921	11,312	14,013	9,690	6,875	7,094	56,905
Lucas County	429,899	12,561	15,854	10,502	16,024	14,906	10,899	9,417	8,461	70,209
Mahoning County	229,642	7,193	11,768	6,010	9,742	10,754	8,768	4,703	8,163	48,140
Marion County	65,256	2,115	2,369	1,516	2,486	2,751	1,862	1,103	1,689	11,407
Medina County	179,146	4,217	7,141	4,507	5,441	8,974	6,495	3,657	3,000	32,074
Miami County	106,222	2,050	5,233	2,768	3,739	5,079	5,158	1,970	1,822	20,536
Montgomery County	532,331	15,207	19,605	11,660	17,407	24,754	17,514	10,663	13,646	95,644
Muskingum County	86,183	3,369	3,361	2,391	2,998	3,278	3,255	1,843	1,424	15,189
Portage County	162,927	4,528	6,503	3,148	6,287	7,067	5,256	2,665	2,762	27,185
Richland County	121,099	2,979	4,665	2,743	4,095	5,776	4,262	3,108	3,751	23,735
Ross County	76,931	2,083	3,399	1,401	2,693	3,569	3,794	1,207	692	13,356
Scioto County	75,502	2,323	2,799	2,034	2,689	2,879	2,759	1,494	1,671	13,526
Stark County	371,574	10,446	15,172	9,483	13,335	17,757	13,718	7,974	9,795	72,062
Summit County	541,918	15,688	24,202	12,987	19,425	24,121	18,169	9,700	13,065	97,467
Trumbull County	198,627	6,326	8,488	6,174	7,886	10,660	7,493	4,670	6,266	43,149
Tuscarawas County	92,176	2,141	4,583	1,987	3,642	4,423	3,639	2,084	2,252	18,027
Warren County	232,173	4,639	7,654	3,929	7,029	9,192	4,796	3,995	4,439	33,380
Wayne County	115,967	3,321	5,024	2,655	4,004	4,742	4,723	1,774	2,366	20,264
Wood County	130,696	3,920	4,741	4,257	3,519	3,952	3,416	2,117	2,790	20,051
Oklahoma										
Canadian County	144,447	3,249	4,899	2,191	3,531	5,837	3,191	1,367	2,714	18,831
Cleveland County	281,669	5,738	7,878	5,196	6,238	11,289	7,246	3,513	3,826	37,308
Comanche County	120,422	3,700	3,467	1,793	3,200	3,949	2,479	1,929	1,873	15,223
Creek County	71,604	1,647	2,886	1,420	2,085	3,790	2,122	1,247	1,760	12,424
Muskogee County	68,362	1,653	2,336	1,214	2,280	2,762	1,936	1,650	1,478	11,320
Oklahoma County	792,582	18,568	24,983	14,841	21,438	28,033	17,847	12,216	13,902	108,277
Payne County	82,040	2,360	1,481	1,794	1,716	3,044	1,489	1,596	1,341	10,980
Pottawatomie County	72,679	2,482	2,667	1,466	2,165	3,512	1,618	1,255	1,805	11,821
Rogers County	91,984	2,075	3,577	1,554	2,754	4,624	2,706	1,017	1,574	14,987
Tulsa County	648,360	16,320	21,461	13,392	18,984	23,300	15,714	10,954	10,975	93,319
Wagoner County	80,110	2,151	3,171	2,052	2,269	3,690	2,554	1,447	959	12,971
Oregon										
Benton County	92,101	2,097	2,866	3,011	2,105	3,956	2,701	1,658	1,412	14,843
Clackamas County	416,051	12,914	16,100	10,876	14,947	19,675	11,283	9,442	8,426	74,649
Deschutes County	191,996	4,622	10,310	5,615	8,487	10,154	6,011	3,727	4,754	38,748
Douglas County	110,283	3,505	5,494	4,149	6,380	5,706	5,264	4,144	2,281	27,924
Jackson County	219,564	6,533	9,908	6,352	9,845	12,840	9,183	4,387	6,082	48,689
Josephine County	87,393	3,204	3,925	3,215	3,589	6,498	4,232	3,405	1,924	22,863
Klamath County	67,653	2,826	2,693	1,990	2,924	4,060	2,157	1,898	1,581	14,610
Lane County	379,611	11,174	15,163	11,352	15,099	18,580	12,664	8,427	7,578	73,700
Linn County	127,335	2,504	4,989	3,508	5,015	6,110	3,812	3,072	3,069	24,586
Marion County	346,868	8,440	14,769	8,100	10,933	12,034	9,067	6,773	6,568	53,475
Multnomah County	811,880	16,936	25,978	18,532	22,016	27,873	17,552	11,247	11,642	108,862
Polk County	85,234	1,628	3,171	1,527	3,640	3,732	2,616	2,219	1,566	15,300
Umatilla County	77,516	2,890	1,891	1,493	2,544	2,965	2,481	1,194	1,245	11,922
Washington County	597,695	13,865	20,627	10,476	18,532	20,112	14,557	7,096	9,604	80,377
Yamhill County	107,002	3,186	4,054	2,512	3,441	4,608	3,803	1,299	2,161	17,824

Table B-2: Counties - Older Population by Age—*Continued*

	Total Population	60 to 61 Years	62 to 64 Years	65 to 66 Years	67 to 69 Years	70 to 74 Years	75 to 79 Years	80 to 84 Years	85 Years and Over	65 Years and Over
Pennsylvania										
Adams County	102,811	2,833	4,638	2,210	4,104	5,526	3,515	2,990	2,289	20,634
Allegheny County	1,218,452	37,900	52,843	34,209	39,630	53,510	40,676	28,061	33,833	229,919
Armstrong County	65,263	2,429	2,922	1,893	2,314	3,746	2,617	1,826	1,881	14,277
Beaver County	164,742	4,993	7,026	5,176	7,414	7,184	6,245	4,863	4,737	35,619
Berks County	420,152	11,167	15,374	10,129	12,347	18,387	12,000	8,592	10,860	72,315
Blair County	122,492	3,739	4,465	3,446	4,437	6,277	4,903	3,285	3,145	25,493
Bucks County	628,195	17,997	27,044	17,141	19,332	30,224	22,355	14,545	13,463	117,060
Butler County	187,888	6,654	9,651	5,020	6,883	7,866	5,529	4,033	5,618	34,949
Cambria County	131,730	4,633	6,201	4,037	5,352	6,850	5,489	3,571	4,365	29,664
Carbon County	64,227	2,788	2,591	2,218	1,910	3,710	1,817	1,948	1,781	13,384
Centre County	162,805	3,423	5,246	2,969	3,944	6,022	4,386	2,818	2,676	22,815
Chester County	522,046	13,326	22,423	12,707	14,898	22,017	15,302	9,703	10,541	85,168
Clearfield County	79,388	2,422	3,030	2,743	2,522	3,689	3,285	1,911	2,117	16,267
Columbia County	65,456	2,036	2,729	1,798	2,687	2,779	1,574	1,760	2,114	12,712
Crawford County	85,063	2,589	4,020	2,685	2,724	4,979	3,321	2,155	1,692	17,556
Cumberland County	251,423	6,075	10,155	6,091	8,936	11,479	8,612	5,510	6,140	46,768
Dauphin County	277,097	7,220	11,986	6,509	9,370	11,098	7,084	6,373	6,384	46,818
Delaware County	564,751	15,201	21,278	11,976	17,229	22,354	14,224	12,044	14,624	92,451
Erie County	272,061	6,707	11,444	6,796	8,501	12,718	7,871	5,972	7,068	48,926
Fayette County	130,441	4,113	6,430	3,877	4,962	6,779	4,839	3,313	3,922	27,692
Franklin County	154,835	4,643	5,786	3,643	6,233	6,637	6,262	3,232	3,936	29,943
Indiana County	84,501	2,404	3,652	1,922	2,825	4,472	2,835	2,164	2,405	16,623
Lackawanna County	210,793	8,098	8,315	4,777	6,711	11,651	7,260	5,107	6,370	41,876
Lancaster County	543,557	13,348	20,945	11,007	19,426	22,835	18,873	14,477	12,133	98,751
Lawrence County	86,184	3,556	3,827	2,584	3,126	4,734	4,210	2,452	1,872	18,978
Lebanon County	141,314	3,995	6,070	3,042	5,583	6,541	4,445	3,949	4,149	27,709
Lehigh County	368,100	9,235	14,195	9,322	10,762	14,840	9,597	7,513	10,260	62,294
Luzerne County	317,646	9,783	13,117	8,426	10,480	16,391	10,855	8,617	8,590	63,359
Lycoming County	113,664	3,541	5,097	3,492	3,654	5,066	4,325	3,063	2,301	21,901
Mercer County	110,683	3,465	4,952	3,533	3,172	6,485	4,293	2,497	4,010	23,990
Monroe County	169,507	6,307	8,859	4,437	5,671	6,886	5,008	3,555	2,571	28,128
Montgomery County	828,604	21,909	33,314	22,171	24,999	33,512	26,061	18,456	21,958	147,157
Northampton County	304,807	7,617	11,591	7,780	9,413	14,513	11,013	6,676	8,268	57,663
Northumberland County	91,083	3,223	3,665	2,541	3,803	4,574	3,036	2,479	3,214	19,647
Philadelphia County	1,584,138	39,076	52,672	29,002	40,775	54,218	38,731	26,859	26,170	215,755
Schuylkill County	142,067	3,978	6,357	3,476	5,858	6,909	4,563	3,925	4,148	28,879
Somerset County	73,952	2,728	3,384	2,119	3,162	3,782	3,382	2,104	1,976	16,525
Washington County	207,346	6,333	9,805	4,634	8,310	11,206	7,981	5,620	4,395	42,146
Westmoreland County	350,611	11,369	18,090	10,464	14,369	19,241	14,598	9,994	10,770	79,436
York County	448,273	11,949	20,436	9,712	15,833	19,806	14,252	8,843	9,692	78,138
Rhode Island										
Kent County	163,861	6,138	7,575	3,840	5,002	8,866	5,230	3,547	4,434	30,919
Newport County	82,542	2,522	4,281	2,322	3,301	5,102	3,529	2,587	1,798	18,639
Providence County	636,084	19,493	22,390	14,019	15,758	24,243	15,501	12,536	15,326	97,383
Washington County	126,179	3,603	6,001	3,581	5,496	6,535	5,174	2,149	3,220	26,155
South Carolina										
Aiken County	169,401	4,566	6,637	4,649	5,983	8,940	6,138	3,135	3,900	32,745
Anderson County	200,482	4,650	7,837	5,832	6,882	8,717	6,641	4,840	3,018	35,930
Beaufort County	188,715	3,775	8,369	5,386	8,749	16,186	11,016	5,922	4,276	51,535
Berkeley County	221,091	6,153	7,444	4,290	6,357	9,148	5,705	2,761	2,548	30,809
Charleston County	405,905	8,896	14,302	8,757	12,971	19,462	10,760	5,892	8,256	66,098
Darlington County	66,802	1,649	4,080	2,399	2,526	2,859	2,320	1,483	1,053	12,640
Dorchester County	160,647	4,443	4,554	3,246	3,987	6,916	3,896	2,411	1,983	22,439
Florence County	138,159	3,866	4,892	3,107	5,648	5,556	4,060	3,043	1,984	23,398
Greenville County	514,213	14,417	17,978	11,085	16,730	20,591	13,933	9,894	8,754	80,987
Greenwood County	70,741	2,065	2,192	1,114	2,380	3,397	2,773	1,627	1,704	12,995
Horry County	344,147	11,210	17,078	11,010	18,272	26,073	15,081	6,844	5,951	83,231
Kershaw County	65,592	1,532	2,922	1,310	3,421	2,685	1,438	1,681	1,393	11,928
Lancaster County	95,380	2,664	3,264	2,263	4,027	5,654	4,330	1,732	1,629	19,635
Laurens County	66,994	1,366	3,119	1,572	2,876	3,416	2,957	1,308	497	12,626
Lexington County	295,032	8,726	11,243	6,435	9,623	12,697	7,791	5,301	4,925	46,772
Oconee County	78,374	2,575	3,583	2,163	4,100	5,099	3,617	2,172	1,482	18,633
Orangeburg County	86,934	2,667	3,271	1,966	4,166	3,931	4,191	1,059	1,553	16,866
Pickens County	124,937	3,839	3,267	3,028	4,015	4,770	4,043	3,034	1,799	20,689
Richland County	414,576	8,692	13,875	7,918	9,716	15,560	8,190	5,888	5,606	52,878
Spartanburg County	313,888	9,400	10,587	7,006	9,912	13,007	10,377	5,334	4,542	50,178
Sumter County	106,512	2,216	4,009	2,895	3,072	4,301	3,281	2,147	1,872	17,568
York County	274,118	7,339	8,286	5,812	7,948	10,990	6,439	5,281	2,894	39,364
South Dakota										
Minnehaha County	192,876	5,047	6,427	4,139	4,741	6,848	4,003	1,861	3,762	25,354
Pennington County	111,729	2,888	6,063	3,350	3,314	5,832	2,690	2,460	2,828	20,474
Tennessee										
Anderson County	76,482	2,264	3,514	2,119	2,969	3,703	2,202	2,822	1,490	15,305
Blount County	131,349	4,147	5,407	3,379	5,335	7,271	5,330	3,333	2,520	27,168
Bradley County	106,727	2,073	4,031	3,057	2,976	4,475	2,855	2,445	2,214	18,022
Davidson County	692,587	14,302	21,252	11,996	17,839	21,357	14,165	9,144	9,949	84,450
Greene County	69,087	2,903	3,004	1,305	2,683	4,586	3,539	1,536	1,160	14,809
Hamilton County	364,286	9,277	15,782	8,588	9,577	18,903	11,402	7,249	7,878	63,597

Table B-2: Counties - Older Population by Age—*Continued*

	Total Population	60 to 61 Years	62 to 64 Years	65 to 66 Years	67 to 69 Years	70 to 74 Years	75 to 79 Years	80 to 84 Years	85 Years and Over	65 Years and Over
Tennessee—Cont.										
Knox County	465,289	11,686	15,864	9,515	14,275	19,684	13,167	8,745	7,891	73,277
Madison County	97,605	3,133	4,168	2,800	3,346	3,718	2,345	2,142	2,230	16,581
Maury County	94,340	2,923	3,051	2,157	2,882	3,732	2,909	1,715	1,344	14,739
Montgomery County	205,950	4,098	5,461	2,983	3,613	3,877	3,104	2,696	2,308	18,581
Putnam County	78,843	2,733	2,799	1,553	2,434	3,337	2,751	1,367	1,759	13,201
Robertson County	71,012	2,023	2,779	1,620	1,366	3,296	2,061	1,183	604	10,130
Rutherford County	324,890	8,023	7,931	4,997	6,808	9,552	5,805	3,749	2,634	33,545
Sevier County	97,892	2,938	3,451	3,129	3,059	5,644	3,342	1,995	1,991	19,160
Shelby County	935,764	25,700	38,387	18,328	26,827	33,283	22,922	10,713	14,963	127,036
Sullivan County	157,668	4,794	8,186	4,412	6,655	8,617	6,703	4,685	3,729	34,801
Sumner County	187,149	4,614	7,130	4,889	4,539	8,151	5,667	2,674	3,459	29,379
Washington County	128,607	3,320	5,070	3,460	4,134	6,016	3,960	2,968	2,967	23,505
Williamson County	231,729	5,720	7,337	4,759	5,982	8,489	5,462	4,105	1,986	30,783
Wilson County	140,625	4,496	4,837	3,900	4,979	5,199	4,194	2,465	1,761	22,498
Texas										
Angelina County	87,092	1,752	3,544	2,176	2,203	3,445	2,575	1,525	1,972	13,896
Bastrop County	86,976	3,397	3,711	2,428	2,107	3,610	1,971	1,596	596	12,308
Bell County	355,642	6,328	9,174	4,828	7,832	10,517	7,890	4,528	3,064	38,659
Bexar County	1,986,049	43,503	57,014	31,431	49,876	62,795	42,614	27,986	25,750	240,452
Bowie County	94,324	2,903	3,355	2,112	2,572	4,217	3,087	1,914	1,410	15,312
Brazoria County	370,200	7,754	11,167	7,193	9,045	11,686	7,176	4,933	3,623	43,656
Brazos County	226,758	2,665	5,148	2,917	4,558	5,330	4,508	2,374	1,309	20,996
Cameron County	423,908	7,250	10,084	6,252	10,411	15,698	10,067	7,278	8,300	58,006
Collin County	1,005,146	19,466	29,836	14,712	24,594	30,805	18,950	10,740	10,644	110,445
Comal County	148,373	5,221	6,973	3,146	5,723	7,902	3,808	2,500	3,363	26,442
Coryell County	74,808	1,257	1,886	577	1,478	2,336	1,256	1,102	550	7,299
Dallas County	2,637,772	61,182	76,154	45,423	55,174	72,582	49,139	29,440	31,424	283,182
Denton County	859,064	18,060	23,632	11,359	18,253	26,523	13,884	8,603	8,514	87,138
Ector County	162,124	3,833	4,542	1,002	2,744	5,328	2,064	2,772	1,261	15,171
Ellis County	179,436	3,870	5,082	3,551	5,443	4,648	4,627	2,344	2,147	22,760
El Paso County	840,758	17,078	25,974	13,875	19,731	24,868	19,194	12,716	12,670	103,054
Fort Bend County	787,858	16,169	27,278	15,120	18,206	24,587	13,974	7,764	7,629	87,280
Galveston County	337,890	8,635	10,044	7,399	10,119	13,692	7,216	5,890	4,419	48,735
Grayson County	133,991	3,234	4,525	2,334	4,313	7,378	4,323	2,737	2,521	23,606
Gregg County	123,707	3,363	4,179	3,040	2,969	4,939	2,158	3,041	2,827	18,974
Guadalupe County	163,694	3,538	5,266	3,988	3,898	6,021	3,824	2,532	1,829	22,092
Harris County	4,698,619	107,021	138,887	83,407	96,904	128,863	83,375	52,332	49,533	494,414
Harrison County	66,726	1,442	3,288	2,375	2,340	2,014	1,696	1,308	1,144	10,877
Hays County	222,631	4,525	5,740	4,134	4,854	6,978	4,458	2,477	1,943	24,844
Henderson County	82,299	2,860	4,060	2,454	3,452	4,343	4,141	2,168	1,561	18,119
Hidalgo County	865,939	13,681	21,022	12,013	18,865	22,625	17,757	14,213	10,542	96,015
Hunt County	96,493	2,616	4,677	1,808	2,476	4,472	3,109	1,916	1,003	14,784
Jefferson County	255,001	6,696	9,508	4,504	5,827	9,837	7,374	3,910	5,126	36,578
Johnson County	171,361	3,468	5,325	3,690	4,359	6,218	5,370	2,502	1,534	23,673
Kaufman County	128,622	2,861	5,389	2,125	2,495	4,549	2,045	2,189	1,622	15,025
Liberty County	86,323	2,285	3,018	1,716	2,341	3,007	2,130	1,085	603	10,882
Lubbock County	307,412	8,148	8,996	5,254	8,042	8,180	6,843	4,882	4,398	37,599
McLennan County	254,607	5,164	9,165	5,470	6,967	8,878	6,225	4,583	4,459	36,582
Midland County	172,578	3,927	5,274	2,537	4,202	3,657	2,801	2,670	2,333	18,200
Montgomery County	590,925	14,378	16,635	12,664	17,941	18,687	13,837	9,674	5,611	78,414
Nacogdoches County	65,711	1,979	1,269	1,272	1,473	2,959	2,042	937	867	9,550
Nueces County	362,265	9,748	12,517	7,926	11,419	12,395	9,212	5,898	5,881	52,731
Orange County	83,572	2,770	3,370	1,847	2,362	3,409	2,148	1,837	1,730	13,333
Parker County	138,371	3,156	5,329	2,887	3,624	6,532	4,188	2,175	1,950	21,356
Potter County	119,648	2,924	3,272	2,160	2,574	3,091	2,330	1,735	1,748	13,638
Randall County	136,271	3,867	4,561	2,164	4,656	5,141	3,106	2,946	2,606	20,619
Rockwall County	100,657	1,630	3,217	1,550	2,693	3,381	1,804	1,620	1,234	12,282
San Patricio County	66,893	1,546	2,204	1,245	2,562	2,244	2,018	1,123	843	10,035
Smith County	230,221	6,473	8,043	4,981	7,232	9,483	8,194	4,527	3,171	37,588
Tarrant County	2,084,931	50,156	63,557	36,895	45,168	62,127	37,722	26,564	27,000	235,476
Taylor County	137,640	3,305	4,796	2,225	3,329	4,398	4,104	2,724	2,620	19,400
Tom Green County	118,189	2,555	4,086	2,601	3,928	4,464	2,734	1,838	2,322	17,887
Travis County	1,248,743	26,280	33,687	22,594	25,414	31,935	17,953	11,898	13,640	123,434
Victoria County	92,035	1,725	3,986	1,983	3,171	3,216	2,838	1,916	1,811	14,935
Walker County	72,480	1,764	2,505	1,623	1,261	3,002	1,035	1,292	1,013	9,226
Webb County	275,910	3,625	6,010	2,801	5,207	6,810	5,592	2,997	2,596	26,003
Wichita County	132,064	2,686	4,811	2,847	3,286	4,678	3,638	2,362	2,351	19,162
Williamson County	566,719	10,283	17,417	9,691	12,803	20,583	9,894	8,376	7,312	68,659
Wise County	68,305	1,557	3,244	1,142	2,265	2,769	1,581	1,217	1,096	10,070
Utah										
Cache County	127,068	2,069	2,845	1,913	2,219	2,561	2,153	1,511	1,174	11,531
Davis County	351,713	6,016	10,407	5,612	8,246	7,943	5,118	5,615	3,139	35,673
Salt Lake County	1,152,633	22,672	33,289	18,268	24,071	34,409	21,099	15,332	12,282	125,461
Tooele County	69,907	2,190	2,132	1,234	1,514	1,086	1,048	808	669	6,359
Utah County	622,213	7,123	12,838	6,142	8,890	13,747	8,654	6,154	4,479	48,066
Washington County	171,700	3,765	5,359	4,369	6,901	9,582	6,903	5,015	4,525	37,295
Weber County	256,359	5,434	7,595	5,452	5,330	7,444	4,409	3,661	3,266	29,562
Vermont										
Chittenden County	164,572	4,277	6,585	4,765	4,126	6,937	4,546	2,651	3,083	26,108

Table B-2: Counties - Older Population by Age—*Continued*

	Total Population	60 to 61 Years	62 to 64 Years	65 to 66 Years	67 to 69 Years	70 to 74 Years	75 to 79 Years	80 to 84 Years	85 Years and Over	65 Years and Over
Virginia										
Albemarle County	108,718	3,575	3,691	2,970	3,484	5,184	4,171	2,289	2,866	20,964
Arlington County	237,521	4,873	7,338	3,565	5,515	5,795	4,012	2,676	3,274	24,837
Augusta County	75,457	2,987	3,249	2,046	3,134	4,062	2,655	2,275	1,927	16,099
Bedford County	78,747	2,704	4,038	2,078	4,004	3,838	2,404	2,607	1,760	16,691
Chesterfield County	348,556	7,506	14,959	8,933	10,261	14,216	8,890	5,368	4,358	52,026
Fairfax County	1,150,795	29,715	38,296	24,523	30,732	38,826	26,752	17,743	16,063	154,639
Fauquier County	70,675	1,888	2,833	2,190	2,286	2,381	2,321	1,859	896	11,933
Frederick County	88,355	2,712	3,398	1,908	3,148	3,748	2,936	1,688	1,733	15,161
Hanover County	107,239	3,186	4,358	2,464	3,771	4,750	3,587	2,018	2,297	18,887
Henrico County	329,261	7,704	13,044	7,725	9,037	13,468	7,044	6,713	7,576	51,563
James City County	76,397	2,429	3,488	1,390	3,374	6,176	3,811	2,709	2,065	19,525
Loudoun County	406,850	9,139	9,877	6,256	7,811	8,862	7,288	3,636	3,868	37,721
Montgomery County	98,985	1,462	3,309	1,476	2,462	3,297	2,117	1,185	1,606	12,143
Prince William County	468,011	8,089	13,526	6,141	9,616	13,428	8,962	5,036	3,331	46,514
Roanoke County	94,073	3,051	3,167	2,161	3,356	5,367	4,556	2,167	2,084	19,691
Rockingham County	81,244	2,768	3,623	1,440	2,485	4,438	2,772	2,119	1,955	15,209
Spotsylvania County	134,238	2,287	5,571	2,967	4,315	4,740	3,757	2,043	1,388	19,210
Stafford County	149,960	3,311	4,149	3,078	3,826	3,485	2,418	1,857	742	15,406
York County	67,846	2,148	1,813	1,790	2,618	2,689	1,166	1,702	1,571	11,536
Washington										
Benton County	201,877	4,787	7,221	4,596	4,994	8,599	4,977	3,226	3,690	30,082
Chelan County	77,036	2,087	2,738	2,359	1,917	4,039	2,647	1,874	1,582	14,418
Clallam County	76,737	2,317	4,062	3,477	3,838	5,583	4,040	2,122	3,101	22,161
Clark County	481,857	11,829	18,239	11,341	14,286	20,874	12,271	8,538	7,158	74,468
Cowlitz County	108,987	2,956	5,284	3,146	4,389	5,114	3,345	2,368	2,494	20,856
Franklin County	94,347	1,629	2,659	1,141	1,307	3,243	1,802	1,004	670	9,167
Grant County	97,331	1,312	4,016	2,570	2,199	3,975	2,724	1,288	1,325	14,081
Grays Harbor County	73,901	2,785	3,074	2,191	3,543	4,356	3,466	1,207	1,549	16,312
Island County	84,460	2,650	3,998	2,879	2,932	6,862	3,585	2,711	1,834	20,803
King County	2,233,163	53,035	72,844	43,577	57,737	76,113	47,291	32,047	38,126	294,891
Kitsap County	269,805	7,159	11,337	6,713	9,795	13,750	9,399	4,866	3,225	47,748
Lewis County	79,604	2,757	3,966	1,431	3,763	4,698	3,118	1,928	1,642	16,580
Mason County	65,507	1,964	2,733	2,168	2,584	4,593	2,665	1,260	1,592	14,862
Pierce County	891,299	21,275	32,355	19,375	25,639	30,603	22,633	11,656	13,351	123,257
Skagit County	128,206	3,888	5,392	3,632	5,085	7,059	4,303	3,545	2,992	26,616
Snohomish County	814,901	23,358	29,137	17,202	22,155	29,533	19,202	9,760	12,031	109,883
Spokane County	514,631	12,145	18,287	9,287	15,343	25,918	15,167	9,240	8,547	83,502
Thurston County	286,419	8,248	11,206	7,942	9,796	13,679	7,529	4,909	5,381	49,236
Whatcom County	225,685	5,753	9,003	5,159	7,971	11,061	6,736	3,816	4,604	39,347
Yakima County	251,446	5,327	8,249	4,884	6,801	8,723	5,582	4,613	3,726	34,329
West Virginia										
Berkeley County	117,123	2,814	5,176	2,458	3,994	5,248	2,661	1,767	1,433	17,561
Cabell County	93,224	2,636	3,078	2,227	2,872	4,718	3,357	2,112	1,698	16,984
Harrison County	67,554	2,296	3,613	1,707	2,815	3,050	2,339	1,507	1,854	13,272
Kanawha County	180,454	4,085	9,202	5,832	8,258	7,935	6,832	4,108	4,694	37,659
Monongalia County	106,420	2,587	3,416	1,199	2,777	3,917	2,188	1,398	1,697	13,176
Raleigh County	74,254	2,257	3,558	2,837	3,270	3,270	2,939	1,931	1,245	15,492
Wood County	84,203	2,235	2,845	1,720	3,159	5,002	3,851	1,861	1,597	17,190
Wisconsin										
Brown County	263,378	7,238	9,198	5,797	7,649	9,592	7,604	4,595	4,135	39,372
Dane County	542,364	13,697	16,356	10,747	15,638	19,095	11,786	8,630	9,041	74,937
Dodge County	87,847	3,438	3,297	2,267	3,128	3,237	2,619	1,699	2,621	15,571
Eau Claire County	104,534	2,185	3,558	2,529	3,523	3,714	2,972	2,121	1,830	16,689
Fond du Lac County	103,066	3,406	4,209	2,097	4,259	4,499	3,332	1,855	2,970	19,012
Jefferson County	85,129	3,101	2,704	2,054	3,035	3,763	2,754	1,758	1,281	14,645
Kenosha County	169,290	4,906	5,850	3,579	4,771	5,784	3,690	2,644	3,201	23,669
La Crosse County	118,230	3,078	4,691	2,525	3,444	4,776	3,411	2,149	2,817	19,122
Manitowoc County	79,074	2,619	3,818	2,028	3,499	3,360	2,814	1,907	2,333	15,941
Marathon County	135,428	3,719	5,302	3,316	4,097	6,033	3,772	3,526	3,026	23,770
Milwaukee County	948,201	25,529	34,559	18,852	25,265	30,393	20,811	14,450	19,165	128,936
Outagamie County	187,365	5,321	6,175	3,434	5,701	6,682	4,679	3,983	3,097	27,576
Ozaukee County	89,147	3,782	3,906	2,221	3,939	3,963	3,515	2,217	1,834	17,689
Portage County	70,942	1,625	2,794	1,569	2,321	2,936	2,093	1,319	1,428	11,666
Racine County	196,584	6,975	7,395	4,724	6,152	8,049	5,638	4,137	3,701	32,401
Rock County	163,129	4,553	5,876	3,766	5,469	6,581	3,745	4,366	3,224	27,151
St. Croix County	89,694	2,294	2,840	1,830	2,767	3,135	2,220	1,260	1,280	12,492
Sheboygan County	115,456	3,303	4,485	3,911	3,538	4,517	3,276	2,762	2,692	20,696
Walworth County	103,718	2,236	4,559	2,563	3,963	4,235	2,932	2,013	2,440	18,146
Washington County	135,693	4,063	6,284	2,830	4,641	6,458	4,408	3,620	2,397	24,354
Waukesha County	403,072	12,897	19,429	11,022	12,373	19,343	12,903	9,450	9,988	75,079
Winnebago County	171,020	4,362	5,966	3,800	5,301	6,697	4,751	3,062	4,386	27,997
Wood County	73,055	1,905	3,375	2,648	2,182	3,345	3,134	1,740	1,891	14,940
Wyoming										
Laramie County	98,976	2,921	4,251	2,800	3,593	3,359	3,349	1,270	1,792	16,163
Natrona County	79,115	1,741	3,319	1,434	3,201	2,546	1,551	1,481	1,687	11,900

Table B-3: Cities - Older Population by Age

	Total Population	60 to 61 Years	62 to 64 Years	65 to 66 Years	67 to 69 Years	70 to 74 Years	75 to 79 Years	80 to 84 Years	85 Years and Over	65 Years and Over
Alabama										
Auburn city	65,737	1,187	2,187	1,260	1,267	1,139	635	600	351	5,252
Birmingham city	209,294	7,070	8,211	4,304	7,703	7,414	5,603	3,719	3,618	32,361
Dothan city	67,814	1,739	2,706	1,698	2,511	3,359	2,524	1,603	1,609	13,304
Hoover city	85,115	2,061	2,576	2,467	2,818	4,248	2,110	1,858	1,651	15,152
Huntsville city	199,808	3,747	5,115	4,480	4,819	9,238	6,156	5,022	3,619	33,334
Mobile city	189,570	5,530	5,836	5,031	5,728	8,154	5,938	3,958	4,344	33,153
Montgomery city	198,218	4,987	6,405	4,366	5,539	6,786	4,138	3,662	3,437	27,928
Tuscaloosa city	101,111	2,552	3,337	2,500	1,809	2,941	2,859	1,033	1,333	12,475
Alaska										
Anchorage municipality	291,538	8,209	7,674	6,022	7,382	8,388	3,892	4,069	3,056	32,809
Arizona										
Avondale city	85,828	1,859	2,043	1,135	1,887	2,176	1,387	549	528	7,662
Buckeye city	74,378	1,248	2,379	1,614	3,844	4,325	1,628	252	343	12,006
Chandler city	257,153	6,257	7,529	4,927	7,348	7,224	5,361	3,169	2,192	30,221
Flagstaff city	73,955	749	1,623	934	1,227	2,365	1,356	504	306	6,692
Glendale city	250,705	5,647	9,426	4,644	6,604	10,296	5,265	3,067	2,903	32,779
Goodyear city	82,837	1,875	2,996	2,490	2,914	5,341	2,547	1,054	493	14,839
Mesa city	508,979	12,118	15,598	10,222	14,349	23,625	16,516	9,453	9,417	83,582
Peoria city	172,272	5,339	6,985	3,995	5,484	8,436	5,544	3,471	4,167	31,097
Phoenix city	1,660,272	35,142	49,231	27,241	33,501	46,829	30,837	20,357	19,934	178,699
Scottsdale city	255,315	7,980	11,281	6,339	9,038	14,628	11,446	8,096	8,821	58,368
Surprise city	138,144	2,512	4,529	3,011	4,452	9,384	7,970	3,745	2,215	30,777
Tempe city	192,354	4,052	4,900	3,527	4,437	4,383	3,215	2,221	2,395	20,178
Tucson city	545,987	13,149	16,558	12,198	17,557	18,608	13,135	9,949	9,359	80,806
Yuma city	97,917	2,497	3,060	1,395	1,823	3,155	3,759	4,025	1,308	15,465
Arkansas										
Conway city	66,421	1,234	1,717	2,151	1,221	2,059	1,128	455	1,085	8,099
Fayetteville city	86,765	2,713	2,790	1,301	645	1,619	786	1,038	1,175	6,564
Fort Smith city	87,851	1,762	2,513	2,108	2,114	3,468	2,040	1,112	1,517	12,359
Jonesboro city	76,990	1,965	1,769	604	1,777	2,265	2,058	1,176	865	8,745
Little Rock city	197,868	4,415	7,668	3,902	6,632	6,252	3,807	3,398	3,959	27,950
North Little Rock city	66,126	1,524	1,923	1,862	1,843	3,446	1,535	1,050	1,405	11,141
Rogers city	67,615	1,669	2,079	852	1,776	1,039	1,603	509	798	6,577
Springdale city	81,641	1,773	1,895	920	1,669	1,325	1,755	819	1,940	8,428
California										
Alameda city	78,322	2,605	2,867	1,691	2,920	3,777	2,032	1,720	1,425	13,565
Alhambra city	84,650	1,031	3,171	1,963	2,538	3,306	2,149	1,747	3,187	14,890
Anaheim city	352,018	8,218	9,444	5,744	9,166	10,009	6,384	5,361	4,796	41,460
Antioch city	111,535	3,137	3,220	1,615	2,864	3,244	2,997	2,200	1,452	14,372
Bakersfield city	383,601	8,519	11,229	6,151	8,858	8,452	6,632	4,913	5,503	40,509
Baldwin Park city	75,806	1,945	2,821	887	1,648	2,503	1,493	816	615	7,962
Bellflower city	77,132	1,405	2,703	1,119	1,896	1,824	1,467	693	841	7,840
Berkeley city	121,654	2,609	3,431	2,701	3,210	5,062	2,550	1,628	1,511	16,662
Buena Park city	82,435	2,405	2,266	1,592	2,457	1,971	1,652	1,156	1,121	9,949
Burbank city	103,687	2,611	3,306	1,767	2,040	3,362	3,847	1,968	2,557	15,541
Camarillo city	69,112	1,432	1,987	1,391	2,164	3,220	2,948	2,251	2,373	14,347
Carlsbad city	115,897	4,820	3,671	2,478	3,593	5,147	4,485	2,525	4,101	22,329
Carson city	91,899	3,210	2,516	1,736	3,062	3,560	2,380	1,325	1,684	13,747
Chico city	94,787	1,769	2,821	2,674	1,692	3,049	2,484	1,101	1,616	12,616
Chino city	91,589	1,989	2,931	3,167	2,498	2,070	1,890	1,461	1,020	12,106
Chino Hills city	83,438	2,749	3,126	1,293	1,602	1,751	1,626	745	821	7,838
Chula Vista city	271,653	5,931	8,373	4,089	5,870	8,104	5,105	3,731	4,246	31,145
Citrus Heights city	87,916	2,033	4,143	1,767	3,056	3,690	2,326	1,551	2,113	14,503
Clovis city	112,019	2,063	3,098	2,871	3,116	4,035	1,966	1,678	1,825	15,491
Compton city	96,616	2,240	1,651	1,066	1,626	2,425	1,352	977	1,670	9,116
Concord city	129,681	4,367	5,121	2,708	3,444	6,025	2,767	3,121	2,188	20,253
Corona city	168,826	2,493	4,373	1,923	3,529	3,858	3,747	1,877	1,342	16,276
Costa Mesa city	113,610	2,331	3,320	1,417	2,011	3,981	2,059	1,122	2,507	13,097
Daly City city	107,016	2,405	4,161	1,552	4,395	3,466	3,316	2,135	3,278	18,142
Davis city	69,288	1,110	1,918	1,106	1,345	1,522	1,241	1,338	954	7,506
Downey city	112,262	1,901	3,790	2,028	4,139	4,237	2,151	1,273	1,866	15,694
El Cajon city	103,229	2,373	3,233	1,662	2,447	2,659	1,566	2,031	2,138	12,503
Elk Grove city	172,891	4,601	6,057	4,048	3,943	6,269	3,843	2,470	3,032	23,605
El Monte city	115,602	2,738	3,512	2,408	2,729	3,387	2,637	2,189	2,034	15,384
Escondido city	152,232	3,840	4,762	3,125	4,186	5,120	3,102	2,870	3,109	21,512
Fairfield city	116,885	3,106	3,110	2,411	2,658	3,686	2,374	1,718	2,380	15,227
Folsom city	79,015	1,733	3,325	1,216	1,821	2,709	1,587	1,281	916	9,530
Fontana city	213,736	3,490	4,094	3,283	2,943	5,078	2,429	1,705	1,413	16,851
Fremont city	237,815	5,410	7,896	3,898	6,170	6,479	5,629	4,014	4,244	30,434
Fresno city	530,073	10,113	13,912	8,416	11,465	15,414	9,285	7,903	8,155	60,638
Fullerton city	139,629	3,301	5,216	1,844	2,907	5,480	2,170	2,934	2,894	18,229
Garden Grove city	172,652	6,736	6,433	4,047	3,209	4,590	3,670	2,881	3,310	21,707
Glendale city	201,374	5,828	7,600	4,272	6,278	7,685	6,251	5,872	5,373	35,731
Hawthorne city	86,970	1,454	3,514	1,005	1,769	2,216	1,281	1,195	1,121	8,587
Hayward city	159,618	3,650	5,611	3,527	3,578	5,488	3,602	2,060	2,537	20,792
Hemet city	85,291	2,135	2,724	2,896	4,963	5,018	3,548	2,130	2,879	21,434
Hesperia city	95,267	2,804	3,237	1,211	2,067	3,355	2,871	1,375	1,059	11,938
Huntington Beach city	200,658	5,610	6,523	4,322	5,970	9,241	6,482	3,006	4,100	33,121

Table B-3: Cities - Older Population by Age—*Continued*

	Total Population	60 to 61 Years	62 to 64 Years	65 to 66 Years	67 to 69 Years	70 to 74 Years	75 to 79 Years	80 to 84 Years	85 Years and Over	65 Years and Over
California—Cont.										
Indio city	91,235	1,751	4,168	2,106	5,810	4,756	3,911	1,903	909	19,395
Inglewood city	109,427	2,671	2,791	2,631	2,529	2,574	2,170	822	1,631	12,357
Irvine city	282,584	6,464	5,881	4,762	5,531	7,375	5,301	3,327	3,386	29,682
Jurupa Valley city	108,400	2,232	3,690	2,231	2,562	3,340	2,077	684	1,936	12,830
Laguna Niguel city	66,265	3,262	3,154	1,036	2,516	3,210	2,057	992	1,456	11,267
Lake Elsinore city	68,187	778	905	1,235	1,478	1,318	1,240	1,857	460	7,588
Lake Forest city	85,619	2,364	2,360	1,261	3,614	4,211	1,997	648	1,197	12,928
Lakewood city	80,132	2,102	2,985	1,534	1,598	2,173	1,669	1,379	1,232	9,585
Lancaster city	159,038	3,637	4,291	2,180	3,110	3,975	3,630	1,430	1,612	15,937
Livermore city	90,258	2,613	3,222	1,681	2,252	3,273	2,772	961	1,372	12,311
Lodi City	66,995	1,646	2,963	1,593	1,857	2,166	1,786	1,100	1,610	10,112
Long Beach city	467,353	12,403	17,024	7,095	12,609	12,719	8,481	4,986	7,063	52,953
Los Angeles city	3,990,469	92,478	120,611	71,289	98,890	125,431	85,828	61,234	69,755	512,427
Lynwood city	70,492	2,186	2,041	1,221	1,184	833	1,369	677	502	5,786
Madera city	65,711	1,090	1,441	829	668	2,153	819	1,035	1,042	6,546
Manteca city	81,593	2,033	3,119	1,453	1,752	3,192	2,242	1,612	1,067	11,318
Menifee city	92,602	3,053	3,010	2,048	3,112	3,250	3,758	2,292	2,446	16,906
Merced city	83,311	1,760	1,655	1,344	1,543	2,699	2,047	1,042	1,237	9,912
Milpitas city	80,424	1,978	3,407	1,162	1,526	2,603	1,565	1,133	1,279	9,268
Mission Viejo city	95,196	3,535	3,535	2,277	3,771	4,636	3,468	2,248	2,972	19,372
Modesto city	215,032	4,456	6,793	5,440	4,602	5,722	4,938	2,740	3,614	27,056
Moreno Valley city	209,051	2,839	4,753	3,313	3,557	4,329	3,081	1,267	1,507	17,054
Mountain View city	83,377	1,890	1,796	1,354	1,387	2,218	1,329	1,062	1,724	9,074
Murrieta city	114,982	1,632	2,455	2,002	1,662	2,397	2,879	1,737	3,025	13,702
Napa city	79,261	2,004	3,433	1,910	3,648	3,233	2,253	1,904	1,657	14,605
Newport Beach city	85,315	3,159	2,942	1,861	3,038	6,434	3,170	2,415	3,323	20,241
Norwalk city	105,125	2,333	3,276	2,633	2,553	2,766	3,025	1,803	1,763	14,543
Oakland city	429,114	9,529	12,866	8,674	11,493	14,964	9,356	7,603	6,015	58,105
Oceanside city	176,090	4,426	5,540	4,018	4,965	8,521	5,934	3,430	3,197	30,065
Ontario city	181,119	3,004	4,493	3,300	3,295	3,688	3,169	1,606	1,517	16,575
Orange city	139,502	4,127	5,148	2,160	2,760	4,826	2,610	2,204	2,084	16,644
Oxnard city	209,886	4,307	6,203	3,903	3,849	3,453	3,937	2,253	2,936	20,331
Palmdale city	156,661	4,606	4,305	2,247	4,163	4,418	3,112	1,872	1,567	17,379
Palo Alto city	66,655	2,312	2,323	1,563	1,633	2,474	2,929	2,368	2,138	13,105
Pasadena city	141,374	3,925	3,738	2,773	3,880	5,292	4,119	3,737	3,945	23,746
Perris city	79,139	1,079	2,168	1,108	1,233	1,137	691	245	195	4,609
Pittsburg city	72,443	1,720	2,549	1,245	1,363	1,490	1,081	1,378	469	7,026
Pleasanton city	82,377	2,181	2,551	1,543	2,027	3,639	2,251	1,748	1,226	12,434
Pomona city	152,348	3,887	3,775	2,392	3,420	3,555	2,507	2,804	2,303	16,981
Rancho Cordova city	74,590	1,387	3,179	983	2,379	3,439	2,085	1,929	1,182	11,997
Rancho Cucamonga city	177,742	3,375	6,756	4,256	4,615	5,244	3,753	2,599	1,906	22,373
Redding city	91,777	2,412	3,303	1,607	3,064	4,733	2,486	2,325	2,509	16,724
Redlands city	71,595	3,193	2,424	1,963	2,638	2,338	2,564	443	1,814	11,760
Redondo Beach city	67,396	1,735	1,876	1,487	1,367	3,007	1,435	940	823	9,059
Redwood City city	86,186	2,450	1,875	2,684	2,174	3,131	1,644	910	1,920	12,463
Rialto city	103,446	2,471	3,292	1,835	2,514	3,602	2,073	1,851	917	12,792
Richmond city	110,175	2,719	3,803	2,184	3,815	3,775	2,069	1,146	2,071	15,060
Riverside city	330,080	6,508	8,884	4,254	6,641	9,271	5,666	4,224	4,539	34,595
Rocklin city	67,231	1,276	2,116	1,205	1,699	2,139	1,046	1,013	614	7,716
Roseville city	139,110	2,829	4,753	2,564	4,310	6,083	4,255	2,985	3,378	23,575
Sacramento city	508,517	11,326	16,009	10,366	12,252	17,634	10,510	7,791	9,057	67,610
Salinas city	156,275	2,492	2,876	2,738	3,064	3,153	1,367	1,865	2,235	14,422
San Bernardino city	215,929	3,838	4,795	2,610	4,568	5,438	2,521	2,314	2,081	19,532
San Buenaventura (Ventura) city	111,120	3,988	4,597	2,884	3,649	5,037	2,933	2,344	2,611	19,458
San Clemente city	64,850	2,820	2,528	1,674	1,626	3,173	2,523	1,385	1,363	11,744
San Diego city	1,425,999	30,494	47,210	28,509	35,783	48,489	30,584	23,373	22,311	189,049
San Francisco city	883,305	23,977	29,161	20,385	23,356	32,881	21,482	17,182	22,842	138,128
San Jose city	1,030,119	23,741	33,787	19,524	24,615	32,998	23,726	16,231	16,959	134,053
San Leandro city	89,683	2,987	3,829	1,308	2,623	3,171	2,342	1,446	2,522	13,412
San Marcos city	96,834	2,169	2,783	980	2,037	2,716	1,681	2,232	2,000	11,646
San Mateo city	105,016	2,474	3,967	2,053	2,514	3,888	3,578	2,431	3,331	17,795
San Ramon city	75,832	1,338	2,382	884	1,956	1,930	2,005	725	824	8,324
Santa Ana city	332,727	6,384	7,634	4,891	5,876	8,576	5,069	3,247	4,647	32,306
Santa Barbara city	91,330	3,010	3,183	2,730	2,601	4,681	2,764	1,184	2,680	16,640
Santa Clara city	129,489	2,673	4,034	3,327	2,330	4,257	2,394	2,201	1,910	16,419
Santa Clarita city	210,085	4,986	8,908	4,670	5,719	6,415	4,678	2,102	3,000	26,584
Santa Cruz city	64,729	1,219	1,607	1,131	2,033	2,714	1,603	369	578	8,428
Santa Maria city	107,424	1,341	2,515	901	2,100	2,235	1,932	1,182	1,228	9,578
Santa Monica city	91,417	2,256	3,094	1,711	2,944	4,093	1,623	1,630	3,694	15,695
Santa Rosa city	177,587	4,692	5,592	4,371	5,688	7,345	5,604	4,129	3,862	30,999
Simi Valley city	125,844	4,048	3,827	3,778	4,654	4,670	3,741	2,241	2,578	21,662
South Gate city	94,439	2,068	2,081	1,971	1,268	2,558	1,267	1,037	799	8,900
South San Francisco city	67,736	1,735	3,670	2,026	2,171	2,681	2,668	1,477	1,507	12,530
Stockton city	311,189	6,106	9,070	6,095	6,621	9,550	8,078	4,167	3,663	38,174
Sunnyvale city	153,175	3,024	4,894	2,439	3,221	3,706	3,301	2,516	3,260	18,443
Temecula city	114,749	2,650	3,842	1,636	2,585	3,186	1,715	1,097	1,437	11,656
Thousand Oaks city	127,720	2,705	5,368	2,864	3,666	5,914	3,642	2,967	4,450	23,503
Torrance city	145,181	6,158	5,467	2,467	5,211	6,426	4,630	2,241	4,978	25,953
Tracy city	91,803	2,111	2,888	1,399	1,578	2,613	1,082	732	838	8,242

Table B-3: Cities - Older Population by Age—*Continued*

	Total Population	60 to 61 Years	62 to 64 Years	65 to 66 Years	67 to 69 Years	70 to 74 Years	75 to 79 Years	80 to 84 Years	85 Years and Over	65 Years and Over
California—Cont.										
Turlock city	73,490	1,453	1,297	983	2,278	2,460	2,010	1,088	824	9,643
Tustin city	79,787	2,262	2,507	1,426	1,078	1,258	1,769	903	1,319	7,753
Union City city	74,568	1,474	3,513	2,027	2,182	2,641	1,648	1,318	1,875	11,691
Upland city	77,002	1,830	2,797	980	2,222	2,490	2,847	1,615	1,368	11,522
Vacaville city	100,147	3,212	2,456	1,907	2,675	4,316	2,843	1,025	2,065	14,831
Vallejo city	121,915	3,798	5,930	2,937	4,306	4,722	3,550	2,450	1,810	19,775
Victorville city	122,305	2,314	2,611	735	2,295	2,893	1,781	1,225	894	9,823
Visalia city	133,783	2,164	4,566	2,060	3,064	4,425	2,510	1,952	1,886	15,897
Vista city	101,227	2,456	3,380	1,368	1,928	2,384	1,482	1,534	1,248	9,944
Walnut Creek city	69,814	2,978	2,384	1,452	3,058	5,870	3,803	4,416	3,624	22,223
West Covina city	106,314	2,312	5,147	1,883	3,157	4,794	3,250	2,058	2,483	17,625
Westminster city	90,931	2,282	2,315	1,327	2,938	5,162	3,586	2,949	1,689	17,651
Whittier city	86,060	1,881	2,480	2,023	2,004	2,627	1,759	2,023	2,309	12,745
Yorba Linda city	67,804	2,261	2,497	2,716	2,050	4,405	2,020	1,338	1,621	14,150
Yuba City city	66,988	1,567	2,441	1,563	1,540	2,556	2,538	1,020	1,787	11,004
Colorado										
Arvada city	120,127	3,248	4,671	3,418	4,448	6,733	3,450	1,726	2,750	22,525
Aurora city	373,487	8,605	11,095	6,438	11,645	10,800	6,924	4,153	4,236	44,196
Boulder city	107,355	2,263	2,803	1,614	2,137	3,573	2,172	1,110	1,741	12,347
Broomfield city	69,267	1,051	2,080	1,958	1,574	2,192	1,722	1,363	809	9,618
Centennial city	110,822	2,332	4,504	2,756	3,333	4,597	2,727	1,169	1,384	15,966
Colorado Springs city	472,666	9,894	15,286	10,057	11,939	16,297	9,729	6,997	7,639	62,658
Denver city	716,492	14,356	19,981	11,334	18,315	22,196	13,959	8,759	9,433	83,996
Fort Collins city	167,823	3,502	4,791	3,412	4,086	4,261	3,111	1,271	1,870	18,011
Greeley city	107,345	2,936	4,577	1,837	2,286	2,591	1,701	1,320	1,873	11,608
Lakewood city	156,779	4,274	6,159	2,748	5,149	6,625	4,570	4,117	3,461	26,670
Longmont city	95,986	2,738	3,328	2,529	2,969	3,866	2,445	1,761	2,267	15,837
Loveland city	77,444	2,172	2,561	1,766	1,613	3,919	2,995	1,377	2,168	13,838
Pueblo city	111,751	2,720	4,863	2,578	4,009	5,179	3,553	2,969	2,691	20,979
Thornton city	139,430	1,706	3,719	2,018	2,272	3,965	2,341	1,367	859	12,822
Westminster city	113,473	3,495	4,490	1,936	3,359	4,302	2,039	2,059	1,653	15,348
Connecticut										
Bridgeport city	144,898	2,874	4,355	2,557	2,381	3,612	3,777	1,727	2,223	16,277
Danbury city	84,731	2,245	2,240	961	2,520	2,612	1,194	1,133	1,675	10,095
Hartford city	122,591	1,832	2,910	2,053	2,073	4,471	2,484	1,249	1,744	14,074
New Britain city	72,440	1,193	2,301	1,264	1,632	1,837	1,605	1,133	1,203	8,674
New Haven city	130,407	2,461	2,555	2,020	2,355	3,684	1,904	737	1,344	12,044
Norwalk city	89,049	2,600	4,395	2,068	3,177	4,165	2,379	2,318	1,867	15,974
Stamford city	129,770	3,050	4,408	2,219	3,644	5,878	3,476	2,640	3,267	21,124
Waterbury city	108,086	3,404	3,138	1,367	2,646	2,676	2,655	2,019	2,067	13,430
Delaware										
Wilmington city	70,653	1,988	2,404	985	2,121	1,895	1,885	695	765	8,346
District of Columbia										
Washington city	702,455	13,894	19,259	11,735	14,102	22,996	16,161	9,731	10,901	85,626
Florida										
Boca Raton city	99,241	2,260	4,902	3,461	4,266	7,900	6,018	4,408	3,712	29,765
Boynton Beach city	78,038	1,400	1,771	2,501	3,242	3,452	4,038	1,594	3,049	17,876
Cape Coral city	189,342	6,294	7,527	5,925	8,680	15,024	8,678	3,903	5,878	48,088
Clearwater city	116,484	3,161	4,751	3,249	3,631	6,948	4,219	3,388	5,030	26,465
Coral Springs city	133,493	3,013	5,890	3,243	3,772	4,813	1,866	1,305	1,431	16,430
Daytona Beach city	68,862	1,574	3,360	1,772	2,901	3,971	2,249	1,574	2,145	14,612
Deerfield Beach city	80,854	2,145	4,097	2,540	2,617	4,353	4,268	2,527	3,092	19,397
Delray Beach city	69,356	2,299	3,073	1,811	1,974	5,099	3,067	2,816	2,742	17,509
Deltona city	91,946	2,353	3,734	1,908	2,454	3,121	2,969	2,165	2,052	14,669
Fort Lauderdale city	182,611	7,699	7,305	3,300	8,018	8,598	5,888	4,117	3,378	33,299
Fort Myers city	82,260	2,718	3,261	2,096	4,392	4,795	2,904	2,943	2,790	19,920
Gainesville city	133,851	1,884	2,400	2,202	2,668	3,468	2,304	840	2,021	13,503
Hialeah city	238,950	6,381	8,340	5,374	7,504	9,428	7,572	6,078	9,602	45,558
Hollywood city	154,813	4,831	5,128	2,962	3,468	7,018	5,958	2,815	3,036	25,257
Homestead city	70,469	531	1,053	563	1,671	1,945	1,271	449	376	6,275
Jacksonville city	903,896	21,229	30,448	19,006	25,382	31,816	21,448	13,522	12,958	124,132
Kissimmee city	73,596	2,024	2,290	620	2,528	1,975	2,398	919	479	8,919
Lakeland city	110,494	2,817	3,753	2,827	3,135	5,357	4,095	3,360	2,804	21,578
Largo city	85,008	2,721	4,603	2,631	3,459	5,466	4,244	4,003	3,636	23,439
Lauderhill city	72,081	1,227	2,454	1,340	2,011	2,551	1,550	752	1,325	9,529
Melbourne city	82,823	2,932	4,345	2,633	2,676	3,922	1,682	2,122	3,149	16,184
Miami city	470,911	10,470	15,074	9,917	13,442	17,764	14,130	14,204	13,566	83,023
Miami Beach city	91,715	1,715	3,045	1,726	2,645	4,254	2,422	2,470	1,879	15,396
Miami Gardens city	113,085	3,222	4,294	1,977	3,075	4,288	3,453	1,679	1,984	16,456
Miramar city	140,827	4,205	3,288	1,990	2,072	3,922	2,521	2,341	1,323	14,169
North Port city	68,637	1,583	2,979	2,869	2,850	5,473	4,039	4,048	1,540	20,819
Orlando city	285,705	7,612	8,351	4,372	5,303	8,546	5,946	2,959	4,028	31,154
Palm Bay city	114,190	2,116	5,890	4,245	4,602	5,992	4,163	3,376	3,952	26,330
Palm Coast city	87,617	1,875	3,489	2,761	4,387	6,966	4,817	3,487	4,120	26,538
Pembroke Pines city	172,387	5,520	5,849	4,272	4,669	9,381	6,544	3,854	3,664	32,384
Plantation city	94,291	2,375	2,921	1,464	3,489	4,124	3,513	1,233	1,542	15,365
Pompano Beach city	111,930	3,278	4,612	1,278	3,452	4,525	5,446	3,564	4,222	22,487

Table B-3: Cities - Older Population by Age—*Continued*

	Total Population	60 to 61 Years	62 to 64 Years	65 to 66 Years	67 to 69 Years	70 to 74 Years	75 to 79 Years	80 to 84 Years	85 Years and Over	65 Years and Over
Florida—Cont.										
Port St. Lucie city	195,251	5,238	5,322	5,120	8,929	10,215	7,127	5,997	3,738	41,126
St. Petersburg city	265,100	6,993	10,170	7,126	8,267	10,972	7,804	6,694	6,131	46,994
Sunrise city	95,461	3,456	3,733	2,101	4,451	4,282	3,072	2,697	2,485	19,088
Tallahassee city	193,560	3,996	5,460	3,728	4,116	4,840	3,001	1,900	1,607	19,192
Tamarac city	66,043	2,730	3,222	1,923	3,404	3,749	2,426	2,261	3,652	17,415
Tampa city	392,905	8,578	9,323	5,969	8,957	12,491	7,438	7,091	7,349	49,295
Weston city	71,224	1,330	1,950	1,071	1,191	2,040	1,026	874	784	6,986
West Palm Beach city	111,389	3,654	2,794	1,826	2,665	5,745	4,199	3,019	4,463	21,917
Georgia										
Albany city	71,646	2,071	1,974	1,269	1,906	2,584	1,543	951	1,797	10,050
Alpharetta city	66,263	1,287	1,853	1,063	1,309	1,927	1,191	467	508	6,465
Athens-Clarke County unified govt (bal)	126,000	1,901	3,627	2,461	2,590	4,080	2,469	1,486	1,697	14,783
Atlanta city	498,073	9,690	13,087	6,437	10,941	13,983	10,199	6,923	6,820	55,303
Augusta-Richmond County consolidated govt (bal)	196,138	5,129	8,655	3,651	5,502	7,856	4,498	3,282	2,777	27,566
Columbus city	194,160	6,604	5,329	3,925	4,813	6,396	4,086	3,168	3,698	26,086
Johns Creek city	84,292	2,127	3,168	1,323	1,858	2,445	1,652	964	1,207	9,449
Macon-Bibb County	153,095	3,278	6,765	3,683	4,720	5,867	3,647	3,255	2,802	23,974
Roswell city	94,648	4,600	3,442	1,241	2,709	3,142	2,298	2,347	1,150	12,887
Sandy Springs city	108,798	2,459	3,157	1,924	2,170	3,760	3,473	1,673	2,300	15,300
Savannah city	145,852	2,897	4,098	2,971	3,259	5,707	3,044	2,838	2,683	20,502
South Fulton city	97,266	1,739	4,022	2,190	3,589	3,222	2,049	489	851	12,390
Warner Robins city	75,413	2,421	2,237	1,359	1,350	2,276	1,288	877	885	8,035
Hawaii										
Urban Honolulu CDP	347,403	9,906	12,254	9,772	11,680	17,671	9,770	8,713	12,809	70,415
Iowa										
Boise City city	228,807	5,464	8,746	4,897	7,250	8,527	6,212	3,319	4,968	35,173
Meridian city	106,794	1,879	2,789	1,324	2,108	2,736	2,424	930	818	10,340
Nampa city	96,245	2,287	3,081	2,402	2,288	3,634	3,379	1,294	1,793	14,790
Illinois										
Aurora city	206,389	3,453	4,425	1,926	4,319	4,709	2,869	2,269	2,391	18,483
Bloomington city	77,955	1,369	3,798	1,688	1,607	2,352	1,930	1,408	1,528	10,513
Champaign city	88,033	1,298	2,839	1,153	2,202	2,487	1,741	825	1,441	9,849
Chicago city	2,705,988	63,252	85,347	48,501	65,891	89,676	65,658	38,378	41,608	349,712
Decatur city	71,860	3,056	3,082	1,433	2,851	3,575	2,754	2,306	1,964	14,883
Elgin city	110,893	2,647	4,476	1,681	4,077	3,499	2,649	1,061	1,048	14,015
Evanston city	74,110	1,665	2,591	1,466	2,215	3,262	1,517	1,136	2,090	11,686
Joliet city	149,356	3,726	3,194	2,157	2,449	4,232	2,080	1,229	1,635	13,782
Naperville city	147,823	3,976	5,653	2,730	2,838	4,972	2,911	1,706	2,023	17,180
Peoria city	115,720	2,743	4,057	2,977	2,645	4,477	2,391	2,093	3,128	17,711
Rockford city	147,676	4,627	5,049	3,482	3,525	7,071	4,898	2,981	4,614	26,571
Springfield city	114,512	2,777	5,255	3,368	3,692	4,278	3,395	2,142	2,912	19,787
Waukegan city	82,934	1,954	1,835	1,446	2,072	1,412	1,485	572	677	7,664
Indiana										
Bloomington city	86,522	2,406	1,098	1,073	1,720	1,810	1,255	746	1,688	8,292
Carmel city	95,767	2,086	3,707	2,187	2,567	3,030	2,583	1,585	1,266	13,218
Evansville city	117,967	3,522	3,959	2,491	3,883	3,315	2,991	2,279	3,345	18,304
Fishers city	93,790	1,607	2,601	763	1,995	2,775	1,669	663	1,646	9,511
Fort Wayne city	264,170	5,843	8,688	5,366	7,164	9,503	6,081	4,191	4,131	36,436
Gary city	69,602	1,705	2,786	2,265	2,273	3,932	2,295	1,569	1,804	14,138
Hammond city	75,806	2,057	2,721	1,582	1,685	2,943	1,858	1,003	1,318	10,389
Indianapolis city (bal)	864,131	21,180	27,460	17,419	20,392	26,921	17,903	12,760	12,206	107,601
Lafayette city	72,393	1,711	2,496	1,538	1,755	2,434	1,946	715	1,574	9,962
Muncie city	70,178	1,064	2,065	1,814	1,428	2,002	1,695	1,544	1,668	10,151
Noblesville city	66,358	940	1,894	882	1,971	1,061	1,311	777	998	7,000
South Bend city	103,869	2,352	3,535	2,219	2,087	2,971	2,316	1,859	2,164	13,616
Iowa										
Ames city	67,155	748	1,141	1,230	1,237	1,292	1,188	699	943	6,589
Ankeny city	65,282	1,031	1,529	1,096	1,091	1,952	1,032	74	758	8,003
Cedar Rapids city	133,169	3,303	4,409	3,435	3,161	4,957	2,614	2,974	2,770	19,911
Davenport city	102,080	3,314	3,643	2,311	3,337	3,591	2,298	1,790	1,981	15,308
Des Moines city	216,990	3,825	6,937	3,355	5,469	5,372	4,313	3,216	3,711	25,436
Iowa City city	76,291	1,317	3,276	984	1,922	2,051	1,093	815	1,373	8,238
Sioux City city	82,762	1,921	3,139	1,418	2,608	2,706	1,221	2,290	1,380	11,623
Waterloo city	67,797	1,395	2,443	2,148	1,704	2,669	2,388	1,262	1,804	11,975
West Des Moines city	67,127	1,331	2,174	1,662	1,910	2,324	2,463	862	669	9,890
Kansas										
Kansas City city	154,361	3,474	4,890	3,903	3,149	4,092	3,542	2,543	1,375	18,604
Lawrence city	97,293	1,235	2,305	2,611	1,993	2,046	1,851	1,393	1,983	11,877
Olathe city	139,588	2,648	4,325	2,432	2,464	3,988	2,723	825	1,575	14,007
Overland Park city	192,525	5,679	7,429	4,233	7,163	7,211	4,431	3,459	4,455	30,952
Shawnee city	65,844	1,370	2,215	1,678	1,823	1,800	1,562	834	689	8,386
Topeka city	125,908	3,454	4,975	3,935	5,644	4,439	3,845	3,476	2,818	24,157
Wichita city	389,259	10,014	13,690	8,304	11,273	14,406	8,495	6,959	7,662	57,099
Kentucky										
Bowling Green city	68,393	1,756	2,137	1,787	1,274	1,752	1,624	778	1,015	8,230
Lexington-Fayette urban county	323,780	6,908	11,374	6,670	8,675	10,170	8,238	4,728	4,478	42,959
Louisville/Jefferson County metro govt (bal)	620,149	18,392	23,090	14,650	19,943	21,567	14,837	12,474	11,914	95,385

Table B-3: Cities - Older Population by Age—*Continued*

	Total Population	60 to 61 Years	62 to 64 Years	65 to 66 Years	67 to 69 Years	70 to 74 Years	75 to 79 Years	80 to 84 Years	85 Years and Over	65 Years and Over
Louisiana										
Baton Rouge city	221,606	4,477	7,681	5,414	6,292	7,864	5,410	4,398	4,597	33,975
Bossier City city	68,222	1,434	2,394	1,518	2,090	2,519	1,054	1,631	1,430	10,242
Kenner city	66,656	2,948	2,124	1,628	3,220	2,882	1,905	1,354	1,077	12,066
Lafayette city	126,149	2,800	4,402	2,909	4,503	3,788	2,644	1,747	2,221	17,812
Lake Charles city	77,999	2,448	3,652	1,322	1,591	3,408	1,999	1,781	1,313	11,414
New Orleans city	391,006	9,091	15,461	8,722	12,744	14,350	9,594	6,232	5,890	57,532
Shreveport city	189,149	5,145	6,482	4,488	8,039	6,200	5,225	4,444	3,787	32,183
Maine										
Portland city	66,420	1,742	3,481	1,025	1,577	1,845	1,397	1,069	1,649	8,562
Maryland										
Baltimore city	602,495	16,082	23,893	11,709	17,394	21,038	14,964	8,823	10,141	84,069
Frederick city	72,152	1,303	2,177	1,193	1,374	2,882	2,135	894	1,181	9,659
Gaithersburg city	68,294	2,219	2,717	1,372	1,622	2,197	1,442	1,179	1,147	8,959
Rockville city	68,252	1,669	2,043	1,361	2,357	2,393	2,396	1,619	1,353	11,479
Massachusetts										
Boston city	695,926	14,508	17,995	12,282	16,695	18,718	15,404	9,359	9,956	82,414
Brockton city	95,781	2,230	4,899	1,888	2,398	3,588	2,456	1,086	1,863	13,279
Cambridge city	118,967	1,833	2,990	1,916	2,046	3,731	2,408	1,097	1,021	12,219
Fall River city	89,662	3,147	3,402	1,610	3,207	3,396	2,279	2,235	2,277	15,004
Framingham city	73,123	1,602	2,571	1,767	2,378	3,446	2,311	1,204	1,595	12,701
Lawrence city	80,370	1,323	1,948	1,015	1,391	1,859	1,264	422	1,080	7,031
Lowell city	111,666	2,424	2,831	2,112	2,290	2,687	1,417	1,122	1,513	11,141
Lynn city	94,655	1,473	4,525	2,002	1,377	3,368	2,086	1,262	1,473	11,568
New Bedford city	95,323	1,610	3,197	1,356	2,327	3,294	1,809	1,498	2,541	12,825
Newton city	88,911	1,504	3,154	2,468	2,654	4,677	3,798	2,013	2,239	17,849
Quincy city	94,590	2,267	2,280	1,831	3,230	2,948	2,618	1,622	2,299	14,548
Somerville city	81,568	1,319	2,025	636	946	1,588	1,481	911	727	6,289
Springfield city	155,029	3,471	4,017	3,532	3,219	5,492	4,181	1,811	2,397	20,632
Worcester city	185,883	4,309	7,352	2,831	4,723	6,466	4,120	3,526	3,097	24,763
Michigan										
Ann Arbor city	121,885	1,962	3,341	1,518	2,326	3,581	2,331	1,326	2,028	13,110
Dearborn city	94,325	2,281	3,169	1,803	2,872	2,754	1,852	950	1,583	11,814
Detroit city	672,681	16,758	25,434	13,090	18,791	23,654	15,052	11,728	11,844	94,159
Farmington Hills city	81,103	2,583	4,038	1,944	2,603	4,298	3,307	2,468	2,243	16,863
Flint city	95,932	2,418	3,244	1,381	3,461	3,265	2,076	1,372	1,572	13,127
Grand Rapids city	200,230	3,935	5,746	3,786	4,268	6,934	3,665	2,824	3,365	24,842
Kalamazoo city	76,557	1,196	2,375	1,385	1,381	1,795	1,582	913	992	8,048
Lansing city	117,388	2,660	4,297	2,379	3,414	3,699	1,917	1,376	2,340	15,125
Livonia city	93,970	3,236	4,507	2,332	2,440	3,210	3,111	2,806	2,018	15,917
Rochester Hills city	74,700	2,065	2,498	1,944	1,864	3,441	2,005	1,170	2,226	12,650
Southfield city	73,141	1,538	4,502	2,797	2,924	4,169	3,105	1,353	2,443	16,791
Sterling Heights city	132,967	3,862	5,291	3,464	3,319	5,509	4,078	2,740	3,247	22,357
Troy city	84,259	2,910	3,057	1,695	3,107	3,832	2,820	1,242	1,178	13,874
Warren city	134,583	3,935	6,193	3,047	3,280	6,143	3,339	3,393	3,508	22,710
Westland city	81,714	2,857	3,730	1,924	2,360	3,592	2,434	1,788	1,598	13,696
Wyoming city	75,812	2,266	2,316	1,719	2,230	2,314	1,240	997	927	9,427
Minnesota										
Blaine city	65,215	1,643	2,816	1,192	1,241	2,877	1,278	620	372	7,580
Bloomington city	85,574	2,559	3,996	1,859	3,686	3,443	3,766	2,351	2,640	17,745
Brooklyn Park city	80,614	1,774	1,974	2,243	1,858	1,254	2,056	1,632	860	9,903
Duluth city	85,884	2,701	3,297	2,345	2,573	3,753	1,826	2,213	2,743	15,453
Eagan city	66,539	1,843	1,974	1,175	1,886	1,805	1,092	1,370	964	8,292
Lakeville city	65,871	1,143	1,927	1,012	1,835	1,251	1,427	583	354	6,462
Maple Grove city	71,812	2,725	3,272	2,507	1,638	3,780	1,554	742	916	11,137
Minneapolis city	425,395	8,152	10,917	8,376	10,060	10,742	7,634	4,174	5,044	46,030
Plymouth city	79,437	2,528	2,454	1,441	2,598	2,468	2,655	1,279	756	11,197
Rochester city	116,957	3,093	3,423	2,189	2,871	4,638	3,387	1,988	2,964	18,037
St. Cloud city	68,928	1,551	2,500	952	1,431	2,192	1,934	584	874	7,967
St. Paul city	307,701	6,999	8,044	5,504	7,005	8,176	5,072	3,174	4,328	33,259
Woodbury city	71,299	1,639	1,967	1,192	3,062	2,773	1,157	1,035	729	9,948
Mississippi										
Gulfport city	71,865	2,019	2,377	1,718	1,302	1,921	1,887	1,109	774	8,711
Jackson city	164,720	3,606	6,324	3,908	4,465	5,217	3,551	1,997	2,788	21,926
Missouri										
Columbia city	123,182	2,400	3,233	2,249	3,144	2,248	1,937	1,569	2,292	13,439
Independence city	116,939	4,298	4,278	3,157	3,732	5,047	3,131	1,284	3,301	19,652
Kansas City city	491,809	11,697	17,226	8,630	12,950	15,103	12,596	7,268	8,447	64,994
Lee's Summit city	98,919	3,255	3,447	2,227	2,549	4,711	2,649	2,658	2,328	17,122
O'Fallon city	88,464	2,449	3,308	1,319	1,505	1,998	1,797	1,662	1,261	9,542
St. Charles city	70,770	1,441	3,409	2,017	1,830	2,901	1,813	1,712	1,571	11,844
St. Joseph city	75,437	1,847	3,281	1,861	2,504	3,331	2,209	1,276	1,772	12,953
St. Louis city	302,838	9,270	12,532	5,206	8,540	11,460	6,720	4,324	5,489	41,739
Springfield city	168,113	4,275	5,890	2,949	5,877	6,564	6,980	3,128	4,055	29,553
Montana										
Billings city	109,544	3,284	3,947	2,210	4,058	4,833	2,479	2,429	3,198	19,207
Missoula city	74,427	1,923	2,188	841	2,311	2,685	1,803	837	1,053	9,530

Table B-3: Cities - Older Population by Age—*Continued*

	Total Population	60 to 61 Years	62 to 64 Years	65 to 66 Years	67 to 69 Years	70 to 74 Years	75 to 79 Years	80 to 84 Years	85 Years and Over	65 Years and Over
Nebraska										
Lincoln city	287,399	5,903	9,087	5,873	7,728	9,437	5,719	4,495	4,612	37,864
Omaha city	468,267	11,566	15,628	9,516	12,088	16,732	9,002	7,677	8,813	63,828
Nevada										
Henderson city	310,374	7,819	12,088	8,774	11,724	15,056	10,366	6,455	6,318	58,693
Las Vegas city	644,664	15,493	22,075	12,131	18,995	27,278	17,451	10,832	11,400	98,087
North Las Vegas city	245,949	5,491	7,520	3,123	6,182	8,460	4,525	2,537	1,350	26,177
Reno city	250,989	5,393	10,769	5,849	8,488	10,794	5,814	5,174	3,661	39,780
Sparks city	104,254	1,978	4,345	2,321	3,298	6,244	2,755	1,365	1,901	17,884
New Hampshire										
Manchester city	112,529	2,139	2,586	1,495	2,558	3,414	2,114	1,576	3,060	14,217
Nashua city	89,257	3,508	4,047	2,065	2,940	4,024	2,677	1,341	2,369	15,416
New Jersey										
Bayonne city	65,082	2,086	3,186	929	2,004	2,319	1,741	968	1,694	9,655
Camden city	73,968	1,785	2,599	989	1,552	2,020	1,553	388	749	7,251
Clifton city	85,272	2,468	2,932	2,116	2,787	2,774	2,361	1,111	2,596	13,745
East Orange city	64,469	1,617	2,001	1,408	1,549	1,517	1,325	1,201	1,455	8,455
Elizabeth city	128,882	2,694	3,625	2,144	2,120	3,731	2,104	1,486	1,141	12,726
Jersey City city	265,560	4,890	8,502	4,510	5,657	7,265	5,409	2,429	3,056	28,326
Newark city	282,102	5,365	9,924	4,255	4,828	7,881	4,348	3,202	3,490	28,004
Passaic city	69,945	1,148	1,687	938	1,781	1,675	1,284	437	754	6,869
Paterson city	145,626	4,134	4,817	2,046	2,953	4,556	2,355	2,590	1,488	15,988
Trenton city	83,973	1,839	2,739	1,876	1,931	1,459	1,040	1,839	1,445	9,590
Union City city	68,521	1,753	1,658	915	1,437	1,515	1,280	1,207	855	7,209
New Mexico										
Albuquerque city	560,234	14,491	18,891	12,037	16,181	24,743	14,101	9,888	11,461	88,411
Las Cruces city	102,929	1,191	3,465	2,945	2,644	5,107	2,700	2,522	1,800	17,718
Rio Rancho city	98,016	2,940	3,195	3,240	3,192	4,624	2,547	1,411	1,584	16,598
Santa Fe city	84,605	1,434	3,616	2,773	3,853	6,025	3,812	2,038	1,690	20,191
New York										
Albany city	97,273	1,539	3,912	2,298	1,942	3,027	1,715	2,123	2,262	13,367
Buffalo city	256,322	6,024	9,430	5,428	5,312	8,642	5,182	3,334	4,067	31,965
Mount Vernon city	67,606	1,990	2,094	884	1,707	1,753	1,609	1,135	2,366	9,454
New Rochelle city	78,747	2,493	2,486	1,829	1,360	1,836	3,236	1,730	2,339	12,330
New York city	8,398,748	204,633	278,183	165,265	224,246	310,425	227,074	158,103	160,367	1,245,480
Rochester city	206,290	4,912	5,828	3,346	5,245	6,031	3,233	3,009	2,559	23,423
Schenectady city	65,570	2,270	2,363	1,054	1,710	2,404	1,302	1,366	1,483	9,319
Syracuse city	142,740	3,104	4,397	2,881	2,800	3,519	2,937	1,697	2,449	16,283
Yonkers city	199,646	5,002	7,169	4,071	5,377	8,616	7,169	4,319	4,617	34,169
North Carolina										
Asheville city	92,460	1,677	3,042	1,552	3,242	5,649	3,527	1,520	2,600	18,090
Charlotte city	872,506	20,180	25,069	15,450	19,339	25,615	14,641	10,590	9,140	94,775
Concord city	94,134	1,495	2,819	841	2,045	4,719	2,268	1,529	1,618	13,020
Durham city	274,497	5,950	9,204	5,201	7,268	7,756	6,355	3,745	3,160	33,485
Fayetteville city	209,465	4,280	5,700	3,939	4,426	6,713	4,740	2,684	3,022	25,524
Gastonia city	77,021	2,150	3,169	2,056	1,867	2,942	1,873	1,582	1,294	11,614
Greensboro city	294,726	7,623	9,439	5,895	7,743	10,682	7,292	4,106	5,334	41,052
Greenville city	93,136	1,113	2,332	1,597	1,035	2,683	853	1,353	1,099	8,620
High Point city	114,322	2,497	4,142	1,998	3,514	4,019	2,316	2,554	2,245	16,646
Jacksonville city	72,895	1,396	870	946	1,017	507	731	550	417	4,168
Raleigh city	470,509	9,588	13,162	6,511	12,509	12,977	8,652	5,789	6,774	53,212
Wilmington city	122,610	2,465	5,210	2,803	3,871	5,645	3,101	2,202	3,362	20,984
Winston-Salem city	246,334	5,641	8,402	4,704	6,241	9,421	5,547	4,217	3,928	34,058
North Dakota										
Bismarck city	71,843	1,853	2,269	2,303	1,928	2,352	1,817	1,434	2,520	12,354
Fargo city	125,040	3,781	4,323	2,283	2,159	4,175	1,618	2,305	2,494	15,034
Ohio										
Akron city	198,025	5,683	9,055	4,536	5,705	7,387	4,990	2,553	4,592	29,763
Canton city	70,469	1,319	3,032	1,683	2,159	2,825	1,637	883	1,657	10,844
Cincinnati city	302,615	7,696	11,041	5,802	6,986	8,995	6,569	3,624	5,773	37,749
Cleveland city	383,781	11,043	14,806	8,375	10,777	13,503	9,450	5,862	6,768	54,735
Columbus city	895,877	20,726	26,947	15,698	20,137	24,553	15,365	11,532	8,860	96,145
Dayton city	140,638	2,827	5,086	3,117	3,897	5,019	3,070	1,849	2,482	19,434
Lorain city	64,031	1,729	2,835	1,092	2,353	2,132	1,721	1,584	1,534	10,416
Parma city	78,746	2,507	3,090	1,927	2,492	2,848	3,213	1,744	1,709	13,933
Toledo city	274,973	6,586	9,071	5,871	9,219	7,622	5,435	5,525	4,942	38,614
Youngstown city	64,958	1,932	3,378	1,885	2,354	1,971	2,245	972	2,122	11,549
Oklahoma										
Broken Arrow city	110,123	2,467	2,728	2,297	3,515	4,272	3,355	1,296	1,764	16,499
Edmond city	93,118	2,096	3,014	1,812	3,044	3,822	2,545	1,624	1,599	14,446
Lawton city	92,860	2,292	2,554	1,144	2,571	3,129	1,703	1,488	1,545	11,580
Norman city	123,469	1,993	2,914	2,235	2,376	4,340	2,635	1,405	1,309	14,300
Oklahoma City city	649,410	14,519	19,482	12,119	15,512	20,871	14,196	8,948	11,388	83,034
Tulsa city	401,112	10,238	13,514	8,087	12,048	14,114	9,677	7,354	7,695	58,975
Oregon										
Beaverton city	98,951	2,090	3,084	1,659	2,907	2,000	1,753	1,272	1,172	10,763
Bend city	97,590	896	3,949	2,328	3,423	4,764	2,283	1,005	2,596	16,399

Table B-3: Cities - Older Population by Age—*Continued*

	Total Population	60 to 61 Years	62 to 64 Years	65 to 66 Years	67 to 69 Years	70 to 74 Years	75 to 79 Years	80 to 84 Years	85 Years and Over	65 Years and Over
Oregon—Cont.										
Eugene city	171,259	4,646	5,828	4,048	5,672	6,520	4,672	2,513	2,702	26,127
Gresham city	110,165	2,408	3,374	2,125	2,947	3,632	2,164	2,290	1,742	14,900
Hillsboro city	108,382	1,790	2,728	1,453	3,945	2,723	1,842	772	1,776	12,511
Medford city	82,348	2,765	3,591	1,506	2,796	3,361	3,032	1,447	2,655	14,797
Portland city	652,573	12,901	21,350	15,344	17,304	22,975	14,254	8,500	8,752	87,129
Salem city	173,420	4,439	7,295	3,905	5,776	5,813	3,944	3,829	2,336	25,603
Pennsylvania										
Allentown city	121,429	2,608	3,556	2,157	2,543	4,523	1,725	1,535	2,573	15,056
Bethlehem city	75,979	2,464	2,673	1,395	1,399	3,310	2,941	1,913	2,295	13,253
Erie city	96,459	1,840	2,965	2,506	2,728	3,662	2,461	1,779	2,415	15,551
Philadelphia city	1,584,138	39,076	52,672	29,002	40,775	54,218	38,731	26,859	26,170	215,755
Pittsburgh city	301,038	8,321	10,972	7,305	8,582	9,815	8,846	6,078	6,448	47,074
Reading city	88,508	1,972	2,905	1,082	1,605	2,760	1,480	748	1,491	9,166
Scranton city	77,186	2,265	2,704	1,293	2,281	3,786	2,168	1,436	1,832	12,796
Rhode Island										
Cranston city	81,282	2,851	3,612	1,919	2,216	3,057	1,345	1,265	2,433	12,235
Pawtucket city	71,842	1,463	3,611	1,586	1,909	2,367	1,705	1,043	1,475	10,085
Providence city	179,335	4,205	3,759	2,689	3,603	5,085	3,718	2,796	3,101	20,992
Warwick city	80,842	2,725	3,532	2,586	2,792	4,114	2,661	1,998	1,999	16,150
South Carolina										
Charleston city	141,088	1,989	4,476	1,975	4,963	5,695	3,061	2,007	2,601	20,302
Columbia city	133,610	2,286	3,594	1,788	2,824	3,669	1,837	1,288	1,639	13,045
Greenville city	68,543	2,029	2,203	1,468	2,055	2,492	1,377	1,211	1,219	9,822
North Charleston city	119,214	2,256	3,372	1,840	2,058	3,755	2,062	1,393	1,237	12,345
Rock Hill city	74,308	1,657	2,021	1,748	1,768	2,968	1,431	1,584	932	10,431
South Dakota										
Rapid City city	75,448	2,118	3,124	1,837	1,846	3,761	1,948	1,837	2,197	13,426
Sioux Falls city	181,906	4,872	5,272	3,084	4,010	6,156	3,640	1,435	3,230	21,555
Tennessee										
Chattanooga city	180,551	4,199	7,986	4,529	4,318	7,803	6,051	3,743	4,049	30,493
Clarksville city	156,800	3,091	3,800	2,122	2,298	2,699	2,241	1,573	1,826	12,759
Franklin city	80,920	1,752	2,693	1,131	1,486	2,495	2,067	1,867	741	9,787
Jackson city	66,900	2,332	2,620	1,367	1,809	2,032	1,381	1,550	1,596	9,735
Johnson City city	68,245	1,934	2,898	1,346	2,241	2,939	1,678	1,382	1,464	11,050
Knoxville city	187,514	4,667	5,804	3,079	4,511	6,127	4,241	3,495	2,726	24,179
Memphis city	650,632	18,430	24,605	12,991	17,749	20,612	16,481	6,793	10,310	84,936
Murfreesboro city	141,336	2,495	3,053	1,942	3,207	3,934	2,566	1,379	938	13,966
Nashville-Davidson metropolitan govt (bal)	665,498	13,470	20,240	11,121	17,077	20,190	13,343	8,756	9,426	79,913
Texas										
Abilene city	125,456	2,456	4,039	1,678	2,538	3,252	3,512	2,278	2,481	15,739
Allen city	103,378	1,115	4,344	2,069	1,902	3,393	1,301	891	1,029	10,585
Amarillo city	200,880	4,402	6,332	3,260	5,528	6,113	4,108	3,659	3,745	26,413
Arlington city	398,122	8,709	11,735	6,166	9,138	12,042	6,935	4,764	4,413	43,458
Austin city	964,243	20,252	26,371	16,682	17,968	22,972	11,862	9,994	10,784	90,262
Baytown city	77,962	1,591	1,987	2,474	1,357	2,736	1,294	1,017	1,055	9,933
Beaumont city	118,425	3,658	4,467	2,244	2,941	4,315	3,615	2,344	2,342	17,801
Brownsville city	183,389	4,249	3,484	2,934	3,366	5,663	3,235	2,472	3,676	21,346
Bryan city	85,447	1,219	1,872	1,064	2,223	1,842	1,608	1,121	642	8,500
Carrollton city	136,869	4,189	4,660	2,964	3,418	4,240	2,896	1,600	2,013	17,131
Cedar Park city	75,553	2,090	1,762	660	1,145	1,713	662	1,011	1,139	6,330
College Station city	116,218	1,086	2,330	990	1,754	2,547	2,172	1,058	505	9,026
Conroe city	87,656	1,460	2,213	1,649	2,731	1,839	2,030	1,586	1,419	11,254
Corpus Christi city	326,566	8,065	10,188	7,077	10,221	11,222	8,077	5,139	5,129	46,865
Dallas city	1,345,076	29,267	39,484	21,862	26,555	36,458	26,177	14,653	18,090	143,795
Denton city	138,553	2,484	3,285	2,304	2,664	4,661	2,491	1,358	1,928	15,406
Edinburg city	98,671	1,472	2,695	1,279	1,824	1,743	1,419	1,891	731	8,887
El Paso city	682,686	14,580	21,096	11,455	16,531	20,913	16,760	11,125	11,564	88,348
Fort Worth city	898,919	21,274	24,101	13,753	17,168	23,054	14,137	8,190	11,248	87,550
Frisco city	188,153	2,678	3,807	1,949	3,848	4,421	3,341	1,260	1,489	16,308
Garland city	242,402	7,245	6,654	5,218	5,425	8,204	4,904	4,225	2,105	30,081
Georgetown city	74,176	1,241	3,390	2,614	4,085	5,280	3,106	3,132	2,949	21,166
Grand Prairie city	194,600	4,179	5,838	2,937	3,915	6,210	2,045	1,500	1,849	18,456
Harlingen city	65,434	1,018	1,569	1,111	1,474	2,802	1,997	1,756	1,590	10,730
Houston city	2,326,090	50,551	65,464	37,633	45,170	62,745	41,234	28,324	30,713	245,819
Irving city	242,228	4,568	5,423	2,425	2,713	3,964	3,077	1,481	1,809	15,469
Killeen city	149,102	1,937	3,651	1,194	2,377	2,710	1,973	1,091	254	9,599
Laredo city	259,512	3,288	5,276	2,586	5,009	6,290	5,441	2,848	2,572	24,746
League City city	106,188	3,821	3,903	2,066	3,976	2,187	960	1,229	1,457	11,875
Lewisville city	106,205	1,955	2,619	1,240	1,567	1,926	1,850	1,413	1,320	9,316
Longview city	81,424	2,114	2,261	1,851	1,790	3,070	1,312	2,080	2,392	12,495
Lubbock city	255,885	6,238	6,849	3,939	6,460	7,173	5,695	4,096	4,085	31,448
McAllen city	143,429	1,924	2,977	1,578	2,685	4,269	4,005	3,052	1,381	16,970
McKinney city	191,666	2,792	5,030	2,824	5,291	5,769	3,292	2,649	1,624	21,449
Mansfield city	74,786	964	1,579	1,159	1,362	1,492	1,337	382	795	6,527
Mesquite city	142,874	3,567	4,384	2,099	2,396	3,571	2,542	1,439	1,688	13,735
Midland city	142,339	3,749	4,099	1,694	3,502	2,715	2,128	2,361	1,860	14,260
Mission city	84,829	1,363	2,028	1,275	2,158	3,299	2,222	1,091	1,525	11,570
Missouri City city	72,978	2,453	3,153	1,818	2,326	2,181	2,645	697	720	10,387
New Braunfels city	85,566	1,647	3,278	1,815	2,579	3,975	924	1,133	2,042	12,468

Table B-3: Cities - Older Population by Age—*Continued*

	Total Population	60 to 61 Years	62 to 64 Years	65 to 66 Years	67 to 69 Years	70 to 74 Years	75 to 79 Years	80 to 84 Years	85 Years and Over	65 Years and Over
Texas—Cont.										
North Richland Hills city	70,839	2,169	2,636	2,039	2,168	2,717	1,011	1,594	1,608	11,137
Odessa city	122,440	2,971	3,560	597	1,989	4,186	1,606	2,209	1,020	11,607
Pasadena city	153,212	3,372	3,871	2,443	3,169	3,684	2,279	1,503	1,077	14,155
Pearland city	124,321	2,266	2,517	3,006	3,420	5,486	2,219	2,277	496	16,904
Pharr city	79,704	822	2,023	1,352	1,785	2,276	1,814	586	621	8,434
Plano city	287,765	7,227	9,758	4,841	8,579	10,595	5,898	3,118	4,995	38,026
Richardson city	120,954	2,992	3,578	2,456	2,432	5,714	2,724	1,818	1,374	16,518
Round Rock city	128,490	2,804	4,068	1,596	2,349	4,661	1,918	934	856	12,314
Rowlett city	66,686	1,271	3,869	889	1,678	1,689	1,173	399	253	6,081
San Angelo city	101,824	1,882	3,247	2,308	3,279	3,669	2,547	1,489	1,899	15,191
San Antonio city	1,532,212	35,033	44,029	25,154	37,619	48,324	33,742	22,528	22,324	189,691
Sugar Land city	118,614	3,361	5,121	3,656	4,554	5,363	3,284	1,784	2,000	20,641
Temple city	76,251	1,598	1,964	1,254	2,536	3,047	2,599	2,224	1,547	13,207
Tyler city	105,727	2,686	4,167	2,035	2,710	3,463	2,751	2,264	1,830	15,053
Victoria city	67,020	1,302	2,728	1,508	2,655	2,404	1,946	1,200	1,439	11,152
Waco city	138,180	1,787	4,912	2,449	2,458	4,136	2,787	1,292	2,167	15,289
Wichita Falls city	104,568	1,636	3,078	2,154	2,248	3,199	2,601	1,770	1,891	13,863
Utah										
Layton city	77,306	1,350	2,574	1,707	1,254	1,904	1,150	1,313	400	7,728
Lehi city	66,029	594	1,091	740	1,150	1,577	1,128	494	99	5,188
Ogden city	87,305	1,290	2,489	1,314	1,729	2,696	1,163	1,514	884	9,300
Orem city	97,512	1,532	2,738	1,156	1,414	2,208	1,879	1,494	1,073	9,224
Provo city	116,713	1,103	1,775	728	1,293	1,728	1,218	1,025	1,153	7,145
St. George city	87,178	2,189	3,093	2,385	4,416	4,229	3,855	3,028	3,132	21,045
Salt Lake City city	200,576	3,970	6,450	2,906	4,207	5,474	3,612	2,879	1,873	20,951
Sandy city	96,901	2,600	3,964	2,271	3,744	3,913	2,685	1,558	1,343	15,514
South Jordan city	74,155	831	1,314	608	1,361	1,523	1,617	988	496	6,593
West Jordan city	116,047	1,675	2,295	1,527	2,373	2,912	1,696	252	318	9,078
West Valley City city	136,420	2,510	2,620	1,650	1,845	4,199	2,064	1,607	1,102	12,467
Virginia										
Alexandria city	160,530	3,865	4,316	3,327	2,454	5,763	3,167	1,868	3,016	19,595
Chesapeake city	242,634	6,715	7,598	5,024	5,927	8,685	5,589	3,669	3,151	32,045
Hampton city	134,313	3,690	4,237	2,515	4,386	5,189	3,735	2,046	2,824	20,695
Lynchburg city	82,126	1,854	3,035	1,019	2,310	2,582	2,429	1,881	1,685	11,906
Newport News city	178,626	5,284	5,692	3,300	3,918	6,500	4,446	3,262	1,991	23,417
Norfolk city	244,076	5,494	7,792	4,645	5,289	6,637	3,781	2,998	3,921	27,271
Portsmouth city	94,632	2,641	2,750	2,280	2,465	3,455	2,224	1,967	1,543	13,934
Richmond city	228,783	5,477	7,798	3,787	7,456	7,039	4,469	2,529	4,933	30,213
Roanoke city	99,920	2,828	4,015	3,013	2,423	5,016	2,356	1,046	3,051	16,905
Suffolk city	91,185	2,733	3,605	2,205	2,154	3,463	2,804	1,230	1,289	13,145
Virginia Beach city	450,189	10,746	15,574	8,712	14,254	14,477	11,428	7,182	7,798	63,851
Washington										
Auburn city	82,782	2,575	2,387	1,253	2,564	3,269	2,206	1,161	1,035	11,488
Bellevue city	147,595	3,345	4,266	2,760	3,575	4,711	3,887	2,652	3,729	21,314
Bellingham city	90,660	1,443	2,526	1,531	2,950	3,337	2,544	1,519	1,365	13,246
Everett city	111,263	2,839	3,480	2,079	2,588	3,275	2,849	1,309	1,848	13,948
Federal Way city	97,037	2,141	4,011	1,849	1,804	4,356	2,102	908	1,221	12,240
Kennewick city	82,950	1,824	4,004	1,662	1,838	3,227	2,059	1,363	1,206	11,355
Kent city	129,613	2,572	4,851	2,437	3,008	4,422	2,595	1,479	2,424	16,365
Kirkland city	89,557	2,820	2,996	1,652	2,236	2,047	1,874	905	730	9,444
Marysville city	69,765	1,848	2,071	1,685	1,804	2,550	1,180	827	998	9,044
Pasco city	71,727	948	2,126	923	1,074	2,118	1,656	829	328	6,928
Redmond city	67,680	1,062	1,388	612	1,251	1,317	880	536	817	5,413
Renton city	102,152	2,583	4,148	2,314	2,558	2,142	1,606	1,902	2,185	12,707
Sammamish city	65,726	2,323	1,656	560	1,013	1,942	741	264	165	4,685
Seattle city	744,949	13,876	20,892	14,927	19,673	25,061	15,182	10,686	11,724	97,253
Spokane city	219,197	6,402	7,438	3,463	6,875	11,199	5,282	3,388	4,217	34,424
Spokane Valley city	99,703	1,803	3,181	2,219	2,571	4,018	2,522	2,303	1,413	15,046
Tacoma city	216,271	4,429	6,212	4,972	6,163	7,294	5,097	2,676	3,519	29,721
Vancouver city	183,017	4,127	6,413	4,168	5,588	9,146	5,018	3,076	3,275	30,271
Yakima city	93,874	1,481	3,077	2,161	2,950	3,122	2,999	2,586	2,163	15,981
Wisconsin										
Appleton city	74,345	2,102	2,686	1,240	2,327	2,730	1,818	1,453	1,593	11,161
Eau Claire city	68,256	905	1,967	1,866	1,783	2,181	1,681	1,596	1,294	10,401
Green Bay city	104,880	2,564	3,718	2,152	2,402	2,683	2,500	2,239	1,991	13,967
Kenosha city	100151	2,615	3,454	1,699	2,608	3,333	2,026	1,193	1,793	12,652
Madison city	258034	5,606	5,533	4,336	6,446	7,755	5,558	3,826	4,369	32,290
Milwaukee city	592002	13,509	19,662	9,491	14,307	16,183	9,417	6,449	8,414	64,261
Oshkosh city	66737	1,795	2,488	1,508	1,232	1,459	1,824	1,155	1,885	9,063
Racine city	77434	2,733	2,262	1,561	1,657	1,802	1,610	1,712	852	9,194
Waukesha city	72549	1,528	3,241	1,363	1,319	2,702	2,153	1,333	1,730	10,600

Table B-4: Metropolitan/Micropolitan Statistical Areas - Older Population by Age

	Total Population	60 to 61 Years	62 to 64 Years	65 to 66 Years	67 to 69 Years	70 to 74 Years	75 to 79 Years	80 to 84 Years	85 Years and Over	65 Years and Over
Aberdeen, WA Micro Area	73,901	2,785	3,074	2,191	3,543	4,356	3,466	1,207	1,549	16,312
Abilene, TX Metro Area	174,006	4,304	6,467	3,045	4,403	6,225	5,314	3,501	3,166	25,654
Adrian, MI Micro Area	98,266	3,148	4,324	3,097	3,905	3,877	3,323	1,760	2,130	18,092
Akron, OH Metro Area	704,845	20,216	30,705	16,135	25,712	31,188	23,425	12,365	15,827	124,652
Alamogordo, NM Micro Area	66,781	1,250	3,125	1,013	3,034	2,459	2,484	903	829	10,722
Albany, GA Metro Area	151,158	5,370	3,930	3,184	4,315	6,563	3,535	3,029	2,575	23,201
Albany, OR Metro Area	127,335	2,504	4,989	3,508	5,015	6,110	3,812	3,072	3,069	24,586
Albany-Schenectady-Troy, NY Metro Area	883,169	23,495	35,623	20,430	30,012	39,165	25,345	18,545	19,966	153,463
Albertville, AL Micro Area	96,109	2,842	3,442	2,563	2,556	4,225	3,470	1,917	1,756	16,487
Albuquerque, NM Metro Area	916,791	25,970	32,874	22,283	28,357	42,502	25,790	16,839	17,822	153,593
Alexandria, LA Metro Area	153,044	3,315	6,200	2,873	4,284	7,330	4,173	3,638	2,442	24,740
Allentown-Bethlehem-Easton, PA-NJ Metro Area	842,913	23,489	33,035	22,284	24,799	38,179	26,536	17,572	23,164	152,534
Altoona, PA Metro Area	122,492	3,739	4,465	3,446	4,437	6,277	4,903	3,285	3,145	25,493
Amarillo, TX Metro Area	268,356	7,219	8,524	4,712	7,604	8,724	5,691	5,035	4,851	36,617
Ames, IA Metro Area	98,105	1,842	2,036	2,214	1,930	2,387	2,399	1,227	1,405	11,562
Anchorage, AK Metro Area	399,148	11,377	11,493	8,541	9,774	12,256	6,036	4,906	4,347	45,860
Ann Arbor, MI Metro Area	370,963	8,595	11,824	7,277	10,152	14,221	9,179	5,011	5,935	51,775
Anniston-Oxford-Jacksonville, AL Metro Area	114,277	3,407	4,448	2,960	3,764	5,516	4,733	1,781	1,761	20,515
Appleton, WI Metro Area	237,524	6,661	8,703	4,671	7,095	8,492	6,155	4,735	3,829	34,977
Asheville, NC Metro Area	459,585	13,225	19,514	12,572	17,756	28,898	20,061	9,612	13,766	102,665
Ashtabula, OH Micro Area	97,493	3,118	4,814	2,990	3,311	4,539	3,478	1,970	2,281	18,569
Athens, OH Micro Area	65,818	1,155	2,353	1,689	1,776	1,806	1,465	798	1,103	8,637
Athens, TX Micro Area	82,299	2,860	4,060	2,454	3,452	4,343	4,141	2,168	1,561	18,119
Athens-Clarke County, GA Metro Area	211,802	4,183	5,916	4,435	5,374	6,972	5,464	3,203	2,930	28,378
Atlanta-Sandy Springs-Roswell, GA Metro Area	5,950,828	141,733	189,255	105,365	151,292	203,119	127,459	73,949	70,693	731,877
Atlantic City-Hammonton, NJ Metro Area	265,429	7,441	10,594	5,641	7,375	14,340	9,805	5,329	5,068	47,558
Auburn, NY Micro Area	77,145	2,224	3,153	2,052	2,611	3,575	1,870	2,538	1,676	14,322
Auburn-Opelika, AL Metro Area	163,941	4,017	5,258	3,591	3,963	5,781	2,302	2,474	1,776	19,887
Augusta-Richmond County, GA-SC Metro Area	605,903	15,665	23,732	13,597	17,284	28,266	15,504	10,890	10,304	95,845
Augusta-Waterville, ME Micro Area	122,083	3,703	6,262	3,402	4,271	6,954	4,444	2,221	3,578	24,870
Austin-Round Rock, TX Metro Area	2,168,316	45,651	61,907	39,769	46,315	64,885	35,061	24,837	24,255	235,122
Bakersfield, CA Metro Area	896,764	17,795	27,331	16,341	18,516	24,449	15,794	12,300	10,676	98,076
Baltimore-Columbia-Towson, MD Metro Area	2,802,789	74,904	111,540	58,257	78,683	117,521	80,313	47,997	52,193	434,964
Bangor, ME Metro Area	151,096	5,134	6,121	3,891	4,460	7,854	4,956	2,970	3,630	27,761
Barnstable Town, MA Metro Area	213,413	7,053	11,621	8,744	11,203	17,375	12,431	8,030	7,670	65,453
Baton Rouge, LA Metro Area	831,310	20,668	29,960	18,283	24,264	30,505	20,899	13,202	11,026	118,179
Battle Creek, MI Metro Area	134,487	5,030	4,898	3,756	3,799	5,977	4,008	2,784	3,723	24,047
Bay City, MI Metro Area	103,923	4,126	4,933	2,670	3,836	5,315	3,985	2,000	3,051	20,857
Beaumont-Port Arthur, TX Metro Area	410,233	10,979	15,144	7,596	10,083	17,295	11,842	7,099	8,262	62,177
Beaver Dam, WI Micro Area	87,847	3,438	3,297	2,267	3,128	3,237	2,619	1,699	2,621	15,571
Beckley, WV Metro Area	117,272	3,228	5,435	3,888	5,548	5,339	4,556	3,099	2,224	24,654
Bellingham, WA Metro Area	225,685	5,753	9,003	5,159	7,971	11,061	6,736	3,816	4,604	39,347
Bend-Redmond, OR Metro Area	191,996	4,622	10,310	5,615	8,487	10,154	6,011	3,727	4,754	38,748
Billings, MT Metro Area	171,894	5,594	6,215	3,802	6,862	6,910	4,837	3,395	4,381	30,187
Binghamton, NY Metro Area	240,219	8,596	8,978	5,741	7,628	11,694	8,290	5,813	7,461	46,627
Birmingham-Hoover, AL Metro Area	1,151,801	32,242	43,848	25,322	37,626	48,783	33,676	21,823	19,644	186,874
Bismarck, ND Metro Area	132,317	2,970	3,654	3,781	4,071	3,888	3,523	2,525	3,363	21,151
Blacksburg-Christiansburg-Radford, VA Metro Area	181,926	3,080	5,852	3,553	6,092	8,196	4,793	3,797	3,630	30,061
Bloomington, IL Metro Area	190,884	4,018	7,487	4,526	4,478	5,876	4,165	2,887	3,638	25,570
Bloomington, IN Metro Area	167,762	4,902	4,779	2,859	4,229	6,496	3,175	2,487	3,708	22,954
Bloomsburg-Berwick, PA Metro Area	83,696	2,556	3,825	2,239	3,503	3,544	2,263	2,186	2,821	16,556
Bluefield, WV-VA Micro Area	99,986	3,163	4,439	2,941	4,146	6,131	4,759	2,495	1,665	22,137
Boise City, ID Metro Area	732,257	14,666	26,214	15,696	21,644	28,683	20,835	10,427	11,133	108,418
Boston-Cambridge-Newton, MA-NH Metro Area	4,875,390	128,462	178,477	107,463	140,165	192,946	131,858	87,697	104,908	765,037
Boulder, CO Metro Area	326,078	9,273	12,610	7,384	9,213	12,149	7,100	4,321	5,866	46,033
Bowling Green, KY Metro Area	177,183	4,402	5,111	4,735	4,538	7,187	4,005	2,487	2,728	25,680
Bozeman, MT Micro Area	111,876	3,204	3,598	1,836	3,082	4,326	3,227	849	1,108	14,428
Brainerd, MN Micro Area	94,408	2,623	5,400	3,237	3,960	5,537	4,443	2,745	2,140	22,062
Branson, MO Micro Area	87,601	2,299	4,041	3,107	3,598	6,850	3,166	3,061	2,592	22,374
Bremerton-Silverdale, WA Metro Area	269,805	7,159	11,337	6,713	9,795	13,750	9,399	4,866	3,225	47,748
Bridgeport-Stamford-Norwalk, CT Metro Area	943,823	25,819	37,762	18,648	24,723	38,652	27,938	17,973	21,890	149,824
Brownsville-Harlingen, TX Metro Area	423,908	7,250	10,084	6,252	10,411	15,698	10,067	7,278	8,300	58,006
Brunswick, GA Metro Area	116,864	3,672	4,878	3,367	4,976	6,385	4,443	2,234	2,528	23,933
Buffalo-Cheektowaga-Niagara Falls, NY Metro Area	1,130,152	35,678	48,046	26,473	35,968	52,348	35,723	24,746	29,771	205,029
Burlington, NC Metro Area	166,436	4,544	5,997	4,339	5,630	6,118	4,441	4,492	3,361	28,381
Burlington-South Burlington, VT Metro Area	220,612	6,186	9,248	5,987	6,598	9,377	6,050	3,530	4,284	35,826
California-Lexington Park, MD Metro Area	112,664	3,076	3,696	2,138	2,442	4,116	3,321	1,857	1,132	15,006
Canton-Massillon, OH Metro Area	398,655	10,957	16,191	10,460	13,865	19,546	14,936	8,658	10,317	77,782
Cape Coral-Fort Myers, FL Metro Area	754,610	21,371	31,154	23,153	36,332	59,155	42,168	27,760	27,692	216,260
Cape Girardeau, MO-IL Metro Area	93,647	2,736	3,254	2,935	1,991	3,889	2,358	2,312	2,503	15,988
Carbondale-Marion, IL Metro Area	124,475	3,942	5,037	3,145	3,696	5,533	4,587	1,965	2,626	21,552
Carson City, NV Metro Area	55,414	1,348	2,011	1,495	1,677	3,062	1,702	1,275	1,987	11,198
Casper, WY Metro Area	79,115	1,741	3,319	1,434	3,201	2,546	1,551	1,481	1,687	11,900
Cedar Rapids, IA Metro Area	272,295	7,195	8,785	6,166	7,618	11,797	7,801	6,567	5,685	45,634
Centralia, WA Micro Area	79,604	2,757	3,966	1,431	3,763	4,698	3,118	1,928	1,642	16,580
Chambersburg-Waynesboro, PA Metro Area	154,835	4,643	5,786	3,643	6,233	6,637	6,262	3,232	3,936	29,943
Champaign-Urbana, IL Metro Area	237,356	5,298	8,779	4,269	5,502	8,973	5,145	3,636	4,572	32,097
Charleston, WV Metro Area	211,285	6,018	11,388	6,608	9,656	9,064	8,089	4,809	5,213	43,439
Charleston-North Charleston, SC Metro Area	787,643	19,492	26,300	16,293	23,315	35,526	20,361	11,064	12,787	119,346
Charlotte-Concord-Gastonia, NC-SC Metro Area	2,569,213	57,911	84,142	50,664	68,733	93,639	62,691	37,970	34,079	347,776

Table B-4: Metropolitan/Micropolitan Statistical Areas - Older Population by Age—*Continued*

	Total Population	60 to 61 Years	62 to 64 Years	65 to 66 Years	67 to 69 Years	70 to 74 Years	75 to 79 Years	80 to 84 Years	85 Years and Over	65 Years and Over
Charlottesville, VA Metro Area	231,565	6,619	7,738	5,557	7,770	11,164	8,382	4,853	5,044	42,770
Chattanooga, TN-GA Metro Area	558,703	15,126	23,987	13,462	16,519	27,776	18,825	12,359	11,287	100,228
Cheyenne, WY Metro Area	98,976	2,921	4,251	2,800	3,593	3,359	3,349	1,270	1,792	16,163
Chicago-Naperville-Elgin, IL-IN-WI Metro Area	9,497,790	249,768	339,377	195,427	259,141	351,437	243,815	157,202	176,383	1,383,405
Chico, CA Metro Area	231,256	6,272	9,528	6,963	7,986	10,320	8,903	4,207	4,441	42,820
Chillicothe, OH Micro Area	76,931	2,083	3,399	1,401	2,693	3,569	3,794	1,207	692	13,356
Cincinnati, OH-KY-IN Metro Area	2,189,442	57,132	80,752	47,622	63,263	85,676	57,217	37,858	39,799	331,435
Claremont-Lebanon, NH-VT Micro Area	217,215	7,124	9,463	7,203	8,474	12,720	8,466	5,118	5,114	47,095
Clarksburg, WV Micro Area	89,718	2,801	4,295	2,300	4,078	4,401	3,233	1,820	2,442	18,274
Clarksville, TN-KY Metro Area	290,745	6,192	8,391	4,211	6,053	6,527	5,664	3,879	3,609	29,943
Clearlake, CA Micro Area	64,382	2,233	3,090	2,904	3,531	3,345	2,856	1,059	1,161	14,856
Cleveland, TN Metro Area	124,748	2,639	4,532	3,418	3,649	5,273	4,126	2,800	2,434	21,700
Cleveland-Elyria, OH Metro Area	2,057,009	62,215	86,798	55,553	68,344	91,343	70,128	45,826	49,776	380,970
Coeur d'Alene, ID Metro Area	161,505	2,834	7,364	4,211	6,080	7,852	6,241	3,558	2,611	30,553
College Station-Bryan, TX Metro Area	265,024	3,404	5,968	3,742	5,495	7,847	5,638	3,414	2,009	28,145
Colorado Springs, CO Metro Area	738,939	17,881	24,515	15,850	18,665	26,690	14,950	10,237	11,241	97,633
Columbia, MO Metro Area	180,005	4,259	6,012	3,995	4,449	4,755	3,069	2,637	3,032	21,937
Columbia, SC Metro Area	833,165	20,599	30,710	17,391	25,084	33,947	19,614	14,108	13,307	123,451
Columbus, GA-AL Metro Area	307,149	10,836	8,898	6,055	7,399	12,463	7,054	5,164	5,229	43,364
Columbus, IN Metro Area	82,753	1,945	2,654	2,482	2,242	2,865	2,712	2,092	1,156	13,549
Columbus, OH Metro Area	2,106,541	53,571	70,864	40,813	54,876	72,291	47,446	32,741	30,795	278,962
Concord, NH Micro Area	151,132	5,731	5,757	4,772	5,266	6,964	4,757	2,789	3,875	28,423
Cookeville, TN Micro Area	111,825	3,417	4,323	2,311	3,556	5,276	4,139	1,994	2,257	19,533
Coos Bay, OR Micro Area	64,389	1,913	3,471	2,218	2,847	4,647	3,348	2,480	1,773	17,313
Corning, NY Micro Area	95,796	3,316	3,957	2,969	3,666	4,175	3,521	2,172	2,160	18,663
Corpus Christi, TX Metro Area	452,927	12,019	15,891	10,055	15,421	15,783	12,347	7,680	7,274	68,560
Corvallis, OR Metro Area	92,101	2,097	2,866	3,011	2,105	3,956	2,701	1,658	1,412	14,843
Crestview-Fort Walton Beach-Destin, FL Metro Area	278,644	7,578	10,017	7,121	9,088	13,682	9,002	6,599	3,130	48,622
Cullman, AL Micro Area	83,442	3,235	2,888	1,779	2,596	4,741	2,765	2,805	855	15,541
Cumberland, MD-WV Metro Area	97,915	2,264	3,988	2,609	3,921	4,829	4,053	2,814	2,022	20,248
Dallas-Fort Worth-Arlington, TX Metro Area	7,540,371	170,352	227,779	127,220	170,040	228,713	145,253	92,377	89,898	853,501
Dalton, GA Metro Area	143,983	2,731	4,442	2,386	4,504	5,454	3,377	2,248	2,297	20,266
Danville, IL Metro Area	76,806	1,893	2,646	2,354	2,682	3,244	2,783	1,896	2,197	15,156
Danville, VA Micro Area	101,642	3,968	4,930	3,224	3,920	5,763	4,167	2,832	2,496	22,402
Daphne-Fairhope-Foley, AL Metro Area	218,022	5,841	9,233	5,340	7,249	14,563	9,100	4,364	3,827	44,443
Davenport-Moline-Rock Island, IA-IL Metro Area	380,106	10,383	14,761	9,868	12,760	15,663	12,352	9,451	8,139	68,233
Dayton, OH Metro Area	806,548	22,371	30,998	18,851	26,604	36,975	27,840	17,215	17,754	145,239
Decatur, AL Metro Area	152,046	5,042	6,162	3,748	4,544	7,278	4,271	3,582	3,091	26,514
Decatur, IL Metro Area	104,712	3,984	4,703	2,151	4,395	5,135	3,983	3,062	2,441	21,167
Deltona-Daytona Beach-Ormond Beach, FL Metro Area	659,605	20,690	28,255	22,136	30,014	42,106	29,133	19,795	25,904	169,088
Denver-Aurora-Lakewood, CO Metro Area	2,932,415	73,103	95,957	56,135	77,753	103,080	59,407	40,460	40,874	377,709
Des Moines-West Des Moines, IA Metro Area	655,409	12,416	20,573	12,428	17,479	21,480	15,378	9,624	10,335	86,724
Detroit-Warren-Dearborn, MI Metro Area	4,326,442	126,680	175,900	101,995	133,616	180,805	123,553	83,606	86,377	709,952
Dothan, AL Metro Area	148,245	3,971	5,750	3,464	5,923	7,161	5,132	3,361	2,869	27,910
Dover, DE Metro Area	178,550	4,291	6,512	4,135	5,205	7,998	5,537	3,957	2,980	29,812
DuBois, PA Micro Area	79,388	2,422	3,030	2,743	2,522	3,689	3,285	1,911	2,117	16,267
Dubuque, IA Metro Area	96,854	2,384	4,035	2,171	3,282	4,065	3,139	2,113	2,671	17,441
Duluth, MN-WI Metro Area	278,799	8,889	12,500	8,237	10,020	12,243	8,304	6,568	7,332	52,704
Dunn, NC Micro Area	134,214	2,707	3,972	2,100	3,283	4,796	3,595	1,887	1,380	17,041
Durham-Chapel Hill, NC Metro Area	575,412	13,231	21,674	11,816	19,393	22,818	16,190	9,216	8,727	88,160
East Stroudsburg, PA Metro Area	169,507	6,307	8,859	4,437	5,671	6,886	5,008	3,555	2,571	28,128
Eau Claire, WI Metro Area	168,669	4,383	6,312	4,412	5,741	6,506	4,589	3,548	3,465	28,261
El Centro, CA Metro Area	181,827	4,268	4,128	3,923	4,169	5,267	4,116	3,392	2,645	23,512
Elizabeth City, NC Micro Area	66,815	1,800	3,539	1,703	2,304	4,072	2,437	1,012	1,497	13,025
Elizabethtown-Fort Knox, KY Metro Area	152,459	4,823	5,529	2,496	4,999	5,755	3,625	3,316	1,953	22,144
Elkhart-Goshen, IN Metro Area	205,560	4,862	6,901	4,454	5,348	6,962	5,014	3,814	4,138	29,730
Elmira, NY Metro Area	84,254	2,401	3,166	2,591	3,203	3,725	3,208	1,981	1,905	16,613
El Paso, TX Metro Area	844,723	17,157	26,060	13,919	19,771	25,010	19,382	12,716	12,670	103,468
Enid, OK Metro Area	60,913	1,419	1,987	1,556	1,361	2,515	1,848	959	1,600	9,839
Erie, PA Metro Area	272,061	6,707	11,444	6,796	8,501	12,718	7,871	5,972	7,068	48,926
Eugene, OR Metro Area	379,611	11,174	15,163	11,352	15,099	18,580	12,664	8,427	7,578	73,700
Eureka-Arcata-Fortuna, CA Micro Area	136,373	4,426	6,565	2,745	5,423	7,059	3,664	2,588	2,817	24,296
Evansville, IN-KY Metro Area	314,672	9,275	12,885	7,378	10,481	13,145	9,200	6,265	7,233	53,702
Fairbanks, AK Metro Area	98,971	2,224	3,191	1,994	3,356	1,996	1,133	868	866	10,213
Fargo, ND-MN Metro Area	245,471	5,880	7,496	4,322	4,549	8,129	3,869	4,517	4,694	30,080
Faribault-Northfield, MN Micro Area	66,523	1,273	2,775	1,641	1,805	2,424	1,791	922	1,714	10,297
Farmington, MO Micro Area	66,692	1,474	2,085	1,165	977	4,441	2,069	1,130	1,561	11,343
Farmington, NM Metro Area	125,043	3,425	4,098	2,754	4,236	4,240	3,592	2,056	2,223	19,101
Fayetteville, NC Metro Area	387,094	8,245	11,268	6,580	8,700	11,784	9,275	4,759	4,304	45,402
Fayetteville-Springdale-Rogers, AR-MO Metro Area	553,795	13,940	15,900	10,029	14,865	15,673	13,531	7,268	9,194	70,560
Findlay, OH Micro Area	75,930	1,995	2,703	1,647	2,380	3,193	1,736	1,896	1,977	12,829
Flagstaff, AZ Metro Area	142,854	2,742	5,143	2,453	3,757	4,951	3,627	1,585	1,440	17,813
Flint, MI Metro Area	406,892	13,555	15,648	10,260	14,276	16,601	12,941	9,577	7,505	71,160
Florence, SC Metro Area	204,961	5,515	8,972	5,506	8,174	8,415	6,380	4,526	3,037	36,038
Florence-Muscle Shoals, AL Metro Area	147,149	3,575	6,315	3,952	5,043	7,618	4,976	4,396	3,505	29,490
Fond du Lac, WI Metro Area	103,066	3,406	4,209	2,097	4,259	4,499	3,332	1,855	2,970	19,012
Forest City, NC Micro Area	66,826	2,997	3,252	1,979	2,996	3,216	2,679	1,907	1,281	14,058
Fort Collins, CO Metro Area	350,518	9,695	12,582	9,317	9,436	15,502	10,225	4,995	5,527	55,002
Fort Payne, AL Micro Area	71,385	1,978	2,943	1,042	2,927	3,408	1,907	1,435	1,542	12,261
Fort Smith, AR-OK Metro Area	282,318	6,342	9,153	5,679	9,780	12,850	9,519	5,835	4,169	47,832

Table B-4: Metropolitan/Micropolitan Statistical Areas - Older Population by Age—*Continued*

	Total Population	60 to 61 Years	62 to 64 Years	65 to 66 Years	67 to 69 Years	70 to 74 Years	75 to 79 Years	80 to 84 Years	85 Years and Over	65 Years and Over
Fort Wayne, IN Metro Area	437,631	11,371	14,235	9,401	12,672	17,249	11,459	7,146	7,914	65,841
Frankfort, KY Micro Area	73,478	2,205	2,021	1,083	2,649	3,797	2,111	1,922	1,079	12,641
Fresno, CA Metro Area	994,400	21,434	26,987	17,493	21,706	31,803	17,929	15,424	17,185	121,540
Gadsden, AL Metro Area	102,501	3,112	4,765	2,934	3,565	5,020	4,150	1,769	2,194	19,632
Gainesville, FL Metro Area	288,711	6,059	9,496	6,222	8,649	9,750	7,903	3,954	5,133	41,611
Gainesville, GA Metro Area	202,148	5,237	6,008	3,150	4,860	9,494	5,546	3,831	3,197	30,078
Gallup, NM Micro Area	72,290	2,843	2,552	1,140	1,185	2,668	1,290	1,484	1,514	9,281
Gettysburg, PA Metro Area	102,811	2,833	4,638	2,210	4,104	5,526	3,515	2,990	2,289	20,634
Glens Falls, NY Metro Area	125,462	4,234	6,472	4,138	4,368	6,772	3,580	3,333	3,888	26,079
Glenwood Springs, CO Micro Area	78,170	2,306	3,926	2,546	1,889	3,374	2,308	945	531	11,593
Goldsboro, NC Metro Area	123,248	4,921	5,065	2,343	3,507	6,328	3,457	2,884	1,988	20,507
Grand Forks, ND-MN Metro Area	102,299	2,749	3,280	1,941	2,786	3,634	2,710	1,671	2,139	14,881
Grand Island, NE Metro Area	85,104	1,364	3,856	2,490	2,648	2,797	2,873	1,132	2,284	14,224
Grand Junction, CO Metro Area	153,207	4,003	6,053	3,427	4,908	8,190	4,253	4,073	3,950	28,801
Grand Rapids-Wyoming, MI Metro Area	1,069,405	25,152	39,502	22,763	29,435	39,133	27,323	18,220	18,951	155,825
Grants Pass, OR Metro Area	87,393	3,204	3,925	3,215	3,589	6,498	4,232	3,405	1,924	22,863
Great Falls, MT Metro Area	81,643	2,108	4,256	1,917	2,881	3,603	2,789	1,875	1,940	15,005
Greeley, CO Metro Area	314,305	7,982	11,606	6,167	8,184	9,700	6,439	3,653	4,080	38,223
Green Bay, WI Metro Area	321,591	9,335	11,577	7,769	9,846	12,389	10,033	6,067	5,074	51,178
Greeneville, TN Micro Area	69,087	2,903	3,004	1,305	2,683	4,586	3,539	1,536	1,160	14,809
Greenfield Town, MA Micro Area	70,963	2,717	4,630	2,228	2,894	4,546	1,938	1,636	2,182	15,424
Greensboro-High Point, NC Metro Area	767,711	19,388	30,771	16,644	25,024	31,454	21,518	14,234	15,440	124,314
Greenville, NC Metro Area	179,914	4,043	6,763	4,186	3,625	6,564	3,510	3,346	2,309	23,540
Greenville-Anderson-Mauldin, SC Metro Area	906,626	24,272	32,201	21,517	30,503	37,494	27,574	19,076	14,068	150,232
Greenwood, SC Micro Area	95,654	2,941	3,142	1,463	3,378	4,802	3,291	2,491	2,162	17,587
Gulfport-Biloxi-Pascagoula, MS Metro Area	397,261	11,589	12,150	8,199	10,884	18,855	13,066	8,054	4,220	63,278
Hagerstown-Martinsburg, MD-WV Metro Area	268,049	8,462	10,669	5,974	8,357	11,981	7,409	5,722	4,184	43,627
Hammond, LA Metro Area	133,777	3,640	4,141	2,425	4,699	4,882	3,217	2,548	1,316	19,087
Hanford-Corcoran, CA Metro Area	151,366	1,902	3,636	2,361	2,124	4,266	2,466	2,784	1,412	15,413
Harrisburg-Carlisle, PA Metro Area	574,659	14,819	24,118	13,910	19,975	24,964	17,426	12,787	13,096	102,158
Harrisonburg, VA Metro Area	135,277	3,657	4,524	2,216	2,973	5,693	3,747	2,798	2,458	19,885
Hartford-West Hartford-East Hartford, CT Metro Area	1,206,300	33,890	49,118	26,716	37,202	53,256	37,960	24,243	30,020	209,397
Hattiesburg, MS Metro Area	149,119	3,871	4,382	2,622	4,290	5,522	3,796	2,041	2,590	20,861
Helena, MT Micro Area	78,791	2,672	3,655	2,200	3,362	4,191	2,489	1,184	2,058	15,484
Hermiston-Pendleton, OR Micro Area	88,920	3,280	2,208	1,659	2,771	3,101	2,750	1,366	1,415	13,062
Hickory-Lenoir-Morganton, NC Metro Area	368,416	11,278	15,688	9,208	12,364	19,259	13,081	7,995	7,594	69,501
Hilo, HI Micro Area	200,983	6,789	9,414	5,133	10,205	12,065	7,260	3,743	4,237	42,643
Hilton Head Island-Bluffton-Beaufort, SC Metro Area	217,686	4,592	9,899	6,664	9,243	17,914	11,897	6,203	4,386	56,307
Hinesville, GA Metro Area	80,008	1,398	2,692	1,007	2,086	1,089	1,026	1,021	461	6,690
Hobbs, NM Micro Area	69,611	2,509	1,263	1,749	1,443	1,578	1,542	620	924	7,856
Holland, MI Micro Area	117,327	2,084	4,822	2,785	3,851	5,388	3,772	2,018	1,994	19,808
Homosassa Springs, FL Metro Area	147,929	5,256	9,191	6,985	9,420	13,054	10,321	7,242	6,810	53,832
Hot Springs, AR Metro Area	99,154	3,688	5,072	2,145	5,404	5,138	3,709	3,639	2,956	22,991
Houma-Thibodaux, LA Metro Area	209,136	5,715	8,039	5,058	6,899	6,961	6,852	3,155	3,254	32,179
Houston-The Woodlands-Sugar Land, TX Metro Area	6,997,384	159,295	211,260	130,164	157,876	205,662	130,780	83,184	73,053	780,719
Huntington-Ashland, WV-KY-OH Metro Area	352,823	9,214	13,532	9,743	11,611	18,751	12,748	7,162	7,793	67,808
Huntsville, AL Metro Area	462,693	12,738	13,525	10,206	11,644	19,534	12,240	10,006	7,130	70,760
Huntsville, TX Micro Area	84,993	2,308	2,992	2,087	1,939	4,048	1,836	1,720	1,690	13,320
Hutchinson, KS Micro Area	62,342	2,075	2,740	1,592	1,872	3,020	2,307	1,860	1,781	12,432
Idaho Falls, ID Metro Area	149,051	2,987	4,388	2,935	3,495	4,850	3,497	1,378	2,877	19,032
Indiana, PA Micro Area	84,501	2,404	3,652	1,922	2,825	4,472	2,835	2,164	2,405	16,623
Indianapolis-Carmel-Anderson, IN Metro Area	2,048,428	50,776	68,382	41,797	54,392	71,357	49,919	32,192	31,421	281,078
Iowa City, IA Metro Area	173,401	3,411	6,176	2,755	4,691	5,443	3,308	2,709	2,920	21,826
Ithaca, NY Metro Area	102,793	2,308	4,931	2,097	2,046	4,443	2,144	1,440	2,039	14,209
Jackson, MI Metro Area	158,823	4,824	6,195	4,555	4,950	7,432	5,281	3,060	3,269	28,547
Jackson, MS Metro Area	583,080	14,814	20,357	13,039	16,281	21,806	14,705	9,206	9,044	84,081
Jackson, TN Metro Area	129,209	4,230	5,420	3,612	4,559	5,175	3,265	2,519	3,178	22,308
Jacksonville, FL Metro Area	1,534,701	36,755	57,425	38,158	46,155	65,547	43,531	26,668	22,734	242,793
Jacksonville, NC Metro Area	197,683	3,169	3,706	2,750	3,081	4,596	3,443	2,556	1,610	18,036
Jamestown-Dunkirk-Fredonia, NY Micro Area	127,939	4,056	5,424	3,768	4,380	6,120	4,837	2,574	3,908	25,587
Janesville-Beloit, WI Metro Area	163,129	4,553	5,876	3,766	5,469	6,581	3,745	4,366	3,224	27,151
Jefferson, GA Micro Area	70,422	1,480	2,255	1,515	1,876	2,588	2,168	896	1,201	10,244
Jefferson City, MO Metro Area	150,243	4,603	5,344	2,579	4,861	7,327	5,095	2,638	2,369	24,869
Johnson City, TN Metro Area	203,921	5,469	8,931	5,884	7,041	9,981	7,349	4,585	4,951	39,791
Johnstown, PA Metro Area	131,730	4,633	6,201	4,037	5,352	6,850	5,489	3,571	4,365	29,664
Jonesboro, AR Metro Area	132,532	3,452	3,939	2,430	3,499	5,684	4,027	2,332	1,827	19,799
Joplin, MO Metro Area	178,902	3,508	5,827	3,614	4,763	8,316	4,709	4,178	3,511	29,091
Kahului-Wailuku-Lahaina, HI Metro Area	167,295	4,208	7,553	4,998	5,761	7,914	4,959	2,914	3,957	30,503
Kalamazoo-Portage, MI Metro Area	340,318	7,931	13,020	7,504	10,080	14,587	10,090	5,858	5,798	53,917
Kalispell, MT Micro Area	102,106	3,376	5,264	3,055	4,057	5,500	3,771	2,172	1,403	19,958
Kankakee, IL Metro Area	110,024	2,622	4,660	2,696	2,872	4,752	3,009	2,252	2,763	18,344
Kansas City, MO-KS Metro Area	2,142,419	54,577	79,029	45,088	61,604	82,057	55,775	35,943	37,831	318,298
Kapaa, HI Micro Area	72,133	2,790	3,476	2,263	2,520	4,103	2,552	1,665	1,606	14,709
Keene, NH Micro Area	76,493	2,512	3,896	1,829	3,465	3,700	2,854	2,003	1,244	15,095
Kennewick-Richland, WA Metro Area	296,224	6,416	9,880	5,737	6,301	11,842	6,779	4,230	4,360	39,249
Key West, FL Micro Area	75,027	2,372	3,428	2,675	3,969	4,218	3,183	2,081	846	16,972
Killeen-Temple, TX Metro Area	451,681	8,626	11,661	6,615	9,861	14,437	9,871	5,829	4,089	50,702
Kingsport-Bristol-Bristol, TN-VA Metro Area	306,562	8,219	15,936	8,009	11,454	17,357	13,271	8,420	7,573	68,076
Kingston, NY Metro Area	178,599	7,267	7,028	4,761	6,472	9,173	6,732	3,589	4,398	35,125
Klamath Falls, OR Micro Area	67,653	2,826	2,693	1,990	2,924	4,060	2,157	1,898	1,581	14,610

Table B-4: Metropolitan/Micropolitan Statistical Areas - Older Population by Age—*Continued*

	Total Population	60 to 61 Years	62 to 64 Years	65 to 66 Years	67 to 69 Years	70 to 74 Years	75 to 79 Years	80 to 84 Years	85 Years and Over	65 Years and Over
Knoxville, TN Metro Area	882,598	23,811	36,103	21,255	31,318	43,149	30,318	19,905	16,006	161,951
Kokomo, IN Metro Area	82,366	2,202	3,044	1,681	2,792	4,541	3,117	1,423	2,363	15,917
La Crosse-Onalaska, WI-MN Metro Area	136,808	3,845	5,643	3,021	4,153	5,837	3,791	2,706	3,632	23,140
Lafayette, LA Metro Area	489,364	12,384	16,618	11,567	13,824	16,385	11,911	8,064	8,209	69,960
Lafayette-West Lafayette, IN Metro Area	222,676	4,434	6,751	4,164	5,063	7,221	5,101	2,192	3,774	27,515
LaGrange, GA Micro Area	70,034	1,175	3,532	1,952	1,722	2,335	2,007	993	1,056	10,065
Lake Charles, LA Metro Area	209,548	5,117	9,677	4,360	5,763	8,857	5,434	3,334	3,489	31,237
Lake City, FL Micro Area	70,503	1,903	3,228	1,250	2,464	3,719	2,610	1,307	1,628	12,978
Lake Havasu City-Kingman, AZ Metro Area	209,550	6,191	12,583	9,025	10,774	17,333	13,867	7,152	5,643	63,794
Lakeland-Winter Haven, FL Metro Area	708,009	18,239	24,036	16,988	23,866	40,292	30,432	16,855	14,993	143,426
Lancaster, PA Metro Area	543,557	13,348	20,945	11,007	19,426	22,835	18,873	14,477	12,133	98,751
Lansing-East Lansing, MI Metro Area	481,893	12,893	19,382	10,355	16,267	18,316	12,519	7,575	8,684	73,716
Laredo, TX Metro Area	275,910	3,625	6,010	2,801	5,207	6,810	5,592	2,997	2,596	26,003
Las Cruces, NM Metro Area	217,522	3,749	8,076	4,712	6,095	9,044	6,520	3,125	3,125	34,786
Las Vegas-Henderson-Paradise, NV Metro Area	2,231,647	50,888	76,232	42,811	65,694	92,964	60,877	35,327	31,017	328,690
Laurel, MS Micro Area	81,762	2,829	3,951	2,626	2,329	4,204	2,867	1,103	1,683	14,812
Lawrence, KS Metro Area	121,436	1,992	3,546	3,221	2,745	2,932	2,134	1,873	2,395	15,300
Lawton, OK Metro Area	125,696	3,919	3,535	1,863	3,336	4,234	2,677	2,186	1,942	16,238
Lebanon, PA Metro Area	141,314	3,995	6,070	3,042	5,583	6,541	4,445	3,949	4,149	27,709
Lewiston, ID-WA Metro Area	63,018	2,139	2,778	1,975	2,251	3,645	2,840	2,336	1,819	14,866
Lewiston-Auburn, ME Metro Area	107,679	3,310	4,085	3,605	3,697	4,071	3,842	2,022	2,055	19,292
Lexington-Fayette, KY Metro Area	516,697	12,554	17,608	11,782	13,258	18,373	13,557	8,176	7,530	72,676
Lima, OH Metro Area	102,663	3,241	4,156	2,073	3,010	4,988	3,095	2,833	1,931	17,930
Lincoln, NE Metro Area	333,964	7,283	11,551	7,470	9,267	11,472	7,533	5,604	5,421	46,767
Little Rock-North Little Rock-Conway, AR Metro Area	741,357	17,802	25,973	16,070	23,140	30,286	20,964	11,848	12,519	114,827
Logan, UT-ID Metro Area	141,476	2,214	3,429	2,455	2,727	2,843	2,382	2,027	1,248	13,682
London, KY Micro Area	128,214	2,358	5,489	2,431	4,747	5,004	3,235	2,858	2,254	20,529
Longview, TX Metro Area	219,417	6,745	7,119	5,108	6,124	9,561	5,107	5,645	4,134	35,679
Longview, WA Metro Area	108,987	2,956	5,284	3,146	4,389	5,114	3,345	2,368	2,494	20,856
Los Angeles-Long Beach-Anaheim, CA Metro Area	13,291,486	335,482	426,626	250,214	342,579	458,952	313,438	223,837	258,165	1,847,185
Louisville/Jefferson County, KY-IN Metro Area	1,296,815	37,507	50,505	29,636	41,449	53,493	34,709	25,379	23,396	208,062
Lubbock, TX Metro Area	319,995	8,402	9,361	5,733	8,340	8,598	7,316	5,344	4,573	39,904
Lufkin, TX Micro Area	87,092	1,752	3,544	2,176	2,203	3,445	2,575	1,525	1,972	13,896
Lumberton, NC Micro Area	131,831	3,309	5,846	2,630	4,048	5,689	3,687	1,477	2,330	19,861
Lynchburg, VA Metro Area	265,405	7,527	11,162	6,715	10,407	11,048	8,761	6,954	6,320	50,205
Macon-Bibb County, GA Metro Area	226,680	5,210	10,445	6,767	6,789	9,240	5,809	4,648	3,693	36,946
Madera, CA Metro Area	157,672	3,106	4,949	2,850	3,373	7,290	2,937	2,981	2,668	22,099
Madison, WI Metro Area	660,422	17,652	21,057	13,887	19,987	24,442	15,538	11,211	11,507	96,572
Manchester-Nashua, NH Metro Area	415,247	13,605	15,991	9,152	12,730	16,346	11,127	6,859	8,636	64,850
Manhattan, KS Metro Area	97,980	1,946	2,298	1,320	2,576	2,451	2,316	742	1,179	10,584
Manitowoc, WI Micro Area	79,074	2,619	3,818	2,028	3,499	3,360	2,814	1,907	2,333	15,941
Mankato-North Mankato, MN Metro Area	101,647	2,057	2,925	2,046	2,362	3,957	2,351	1,972	2,250	14,938
Mansfield, OH Metro Area	121,099	2,979	4,665	2,743	4,095	5,776	4,262	3,108	3,751	23,735
Marinette, WI-MI Micro Area	63,417	2,171	3,651	1,885	2,719	3,915	3,006	1,671	2,039	15,235
Marion, IN Micro Area	65,936	1,631	2,873	1,401	2,504	2,753	2,548	1,756	1,571	12,533
Marion, OH Micro Area	65,256	2,115	2,369	1,516	2,486	2,751	1,862	1,103	1,689	11,407
Marquette, MI Micro Area	66,516	1,932	2,990	1,813	2,454	3,250	2,459	1,348	1,500	12,824
Marshall, TX Micro Area	66,726	1,442	3,288	2,375	2,340	2,014	1,696	1,308	1,144	10,877
Martinsville, VA Micro Area	64,947	2,110	3,013	1,676	2,858	3,630	2,975	2,093	1,937	15,169
McAllen-Edinburg-Mission, TX Metro Area	865,939	13,681	21,022	12,013	18,865	22,625	17,757	14,213	10,542	96,015
Meadville, PA Micro Area	85,063	2,589	4,020	2,685	2,724	4,979	3,321	2,155	1,692	17,556
Medford, OR Metro Area	219,564	6,533	9,908	6,352	9,845	12,840	9,183	4,387	6,082	48,689
Memphis, TN-MS-AR Metro Area	1,350,064	37,517	53,766	28,819	37,739	49,560	33,405	18,647	20,369	188,539
Merced, CA Metro Area	274,765	5,396	7,463	3,454	5,555	8,507	6,579	3,178	3,475	30,748
Meridian, MS Micro Area	104,181	3,222	2,844	2,181	3,514	4,897	3,882	1,933	1,976	18,383
Miami-Fort Lauderdale-West Palm Beach, FL Metro Area	6,198,782	164,851	217,307	129,233	187,539	276,473	213,375	150,298	170,413	1,127,331
Michigan City-La Porte, IN Metro Area	110,007	2,782	4,302	2,655	3,878	5,409	3,931	1,860	1,943	19,676
Midland, MI Metro Area	83,209	2,652	3,521	2,209	2,845	3,616	3,024	1,576	2,269	15,539
Midland, TX Metro Area	177,218	3,946	5,332	2,616	4,202	3,796	3,165	3,048	2,333	19,160
Milwaukee-Waukesha-West Allis, WI Metro Area	1,576,113	46,271	64,178	34,925	46,218	60,157	41,637	29,737	33,384	246,058
Minneapolis-St. Paul-Bloomington, MN-WI Metro Area	3,629,190	90,376	124,821	75,487	102,516	123,412	87,132	57,605	61,141	507,293
Minot, ND Micro Area	75,668	1,556	2,531	1,743	1,597	2,543	2,044	1,126	1,515	10,568
Missoula, MT Metro Area	118,791	3,045	4,381	2,844	4,202	5,055	3,799	1,617	1,528	18,257
Mobile, AL Metro Area	413,757	12,203	13,855	10,357	11,798	17,218	12,798	7,415	6,972	66,558
Modesto, CA Metro Area	549,815	11,222	17,348	13,107	13,084	16,946	13,055	7,758	8,557	72,507
Monroe, LA Metro Area	176,805	5,975	6,874	3,358	4,680	8,258	6,042	2,884	2,395	27,617
Monroe, MI Metro Area	150,439	4,296	6,092	3,561	5,553	6,957	4,858	2,876	3,738	27,543
Montgomery, AL Metro Area	373,401	10,572	12,584	7,583	11,268	15,482	9,867	6,850	6,199	57,249
Morehead City, NC Micro Area	69,524	1,976	3,786	2,203	3,119	5,448	3,513	1,559	1,613	17,455
Morgantown, WV Metro Area	140,259	3,288	4,977	2,676	4,214	5,100	3,695	2,024	2,245	19,954
Morristown, TN Metro Area	118,581	3,751	5,428	2,804	3,971	6,269	3,551	3,952	1,698	22,245
Moses Lake, WA Micro Area	97,331	1,312	4,016	2,570	2,199	3,975	2,724	1,288	1,325	14,081
Mount Airy, NC Micro Area	71,948	2,207	3,071	2,535	2,566	3,243	3,032	1,726	1,964	15,066
Mount Pleasant, MI Micro Area	70,562	1,377	2,644	1,090	1,936	2,362	1,615	1,101	990	9,094
Mount Vernon-Anacortes, WA Metro Area	128,206	3,888	5,392	3,632	5,085	7,059	4,303	3,545	2,992	26,616
Muncie, IN Metro Area	114,772	2,229	4,352	2,941	2,615	5,449	3,220	2,521	3,185	19,931
Muskegon, MI Metro Area	173,588	4,990	7,194	4,455	5,276	7,858	5,118	3,471	3,263	29,441
Muskogee, OK Micro Area	68,362	1,653	2,336	1,214	2,280	2,762	1,936	1,650	1,478	11,320
Myrtle Beach-Conway-North Myrtle Beach, SC-NC Metro Area	480,891	15,522	26,944	17,216	28,335	39,186	23,636	9,867	8,654	126,894
Nacogdoches, TX Micro Area	65,711	1,979	1,269	1,272	1,473	2,959	2,042	937	867	9,550

Table B-4: Metropolitan/Micropolitan Statistical Areas - Older Population by Age—*Continued*

	Total Population	60 to 61 Years	62 to 64 Years	65 to 66 Years	67 to 69 Years	70 to 74 Years	75 to 79 Years	80 to 84 Years	85 Years and Over	65 Years and Over
Napa, CA Metro Area	139,417	4,062	5,221	3,160	5,438	7,258	5,005	3,236	2,708	26,805
Naples-Immokalee-Marco Island, FL Metro Area	378,488	9,879	16,905	13,380	17,410	29,421	26,458	17,526	18,268	122,463
Nashville-Davidson--Murfreesboro--Franklin, TN Metro Area	1,932,099	47,349	62,241	39,255	51,504	66,994	46,388	28,229	23,901	256,271
New Bern, NC Metro Area	123,433	3,839	5,372	2,717	4,093	7,446	5,065	4,055	2,149	25,525
New Castle, PA Micro Area	86,184	3,556	3,827	2,584	3,126	4,734	4,210	2,452	1,872	18,978
New Haven-Milford, CT Metro Area	857,620	26,473	34,295	17,779	28,172	37,199	27,022	16,007	22,610	148,789
New Orleans-Metairie, LA Metro Area	1,270,399	35,503	51,093	31,383	40,787	50,435	34,998	22,722	20,857	201,182
New Philadelphia-Dover, OH Micro Area	92,176	2,141	4,583	1,987	3,642	4,423	3,639	2,084	2,252	18,027
New York-Newark-Jersey City, NY-NJ-PA Metro Area	19,979,477	525,811	720,490	414,194	556,849	788,673	567,029	385,745	430,919	3,143,409
Niles-Benton Harbor, MI Metro Area	154,141	5,067	7,289	4,211	5,816	7,299	4,712	3,744	4,686	30,468
North Port-Sarasota-Bradenton, FL Metro Area	821,573	21,567	40,647	27,487	43,151	66,811	53,468	37,464	36,472	264,853
North Wilkesboro, NC Micro Area	68,557	1,387	4,527	2,020	2,955	3,415	2,682	2,326	1,297	14,695
Norwich-New London, CT Metro Area	266,784	8,362	11,577	7,250	7,733	12,368	9,005	5,843	6,115	48,314
Oak Harbor, WA Micro Area	84,460	2,650	3,998	2,879	2,932	6,862	3,585	2,711	1,834	20,803
Ocala, FL Metro Area	359,977	8,819	16,205	9,565	18,238	27,931	23,858	12,277	12,155	104,024
Ocean City, NJ Metro Area	92,560	3,499	4,706	2,621	4,529	6,435	4,966	2,882	2,635	24,068
Odessa, TX Metro Area	162,124	3,833	4,542	1,002	3,774	5,328	2,064	2,772	1,261	15,171
Ogden-Clearfield, UT Metro Area	676,948	12,683	19,901	12,550	15,528	17,557	11,077	10,090	7,439	74,241
Ogdensburg-Massena, NY Micro Area	108,047	3,285	3,942	2,277	3,189	5,265	2,806	2,381	2,550	18,468
Oklahoma City, OK Metro Area	1,396,445	31,605	45,537	26,840	36,799	52,469	34,238	21,072	22,571	193,989
Olean, NY Micro Area	76,840	2,066	3,833	1,800	2,796	3,853	3,302	1,366	1,524	14,641
Olympia-Tumwater, WA Metro Area	286,419	8,248	11,206	7,942	9,796	13,679	7,529	4,909	5,381	49,236
Omaha-Council Bluffs, NE-IA Metro Area	941,924	23,243	31,194	18,940	24,984	34,241	20,482	14,676	16,979	130,302
Opelousas, LA Micro Area	82,764	2,407	3,111	1,715	3,096	2,999	2,599	1,356	1,402	13,167
Orangeburg, SC Micro Area	86,934	2,667	3,271	1,966	4,166	3,931	4,191	1,059	1,553	16,866
Orlando-Kissimmee-Sanford, FL Metro Area	2,572,962	71,056	81,000	50,536	73,345	100,483	70,429	45,156	41,220	381,169
Oshkosh-Neenah, WI Metro Area	171,020	4,362	5,966	3,800	5,301	6,697	4,751	3,062	4,386	27,997
Ottawa-Peru, IL Micro Area	147,853	3,821	6,478	3,963	5,512	6,883	5,358	4,157	3,512	29,385
Owensboro, KY Metro Area	119,691	3,714	4,413	2,272	4,111	5,446	4,106	2,423	2,279	20,637
Owosso, MI Micro Area	68,192	2,150	2,887	1,789	2,450	3,277	2,151	1,511	1,419	12,597
Oxnard-Thousand Oaks-Ventura, CA Metro Area	850,967	22,436	28,401	20,144	24,575	31,341	21,965	15,666	18,528	132,219
Paducah, KY-IL Micro Area	98,658	2,610	4,919	1,995	2,987	5,454	3,399	2,771	3,337	19,943
Palatka, FL Micro Area	74,163	2,668	2,667	2,227	2,441	5,935	3,921	2,073	717	17,314
Palm Bay-Melbourne-Titusville, FL Metro Area	596,849	21,484	28,664	17,680	26,935	31,680	26,236	18,110	20,627	141,268
Panama City, FL Metro Area	202,977	6,260	8,620	4,042	6,836	9,709	6,406	4,004	3,737	34,734
Parkersburg-Vienna, WV Metro Area	92,499	2,631	3,337	1,917	3,513	5,360	4,031	1,998	1,749	18,568
Pensacola-Ferry Pass-Brent, FL Metro Area	494,883	15,742	20,164	9,762	16,530	21,898	14,848	10,158	8,216	81,412
Peoria, IL Metro Area	368,683	10,249	16,229	7,774	12,536	17,069	10,162	7,793	10,889	66,223
Philadelphia-Camden-Wilmington, PA-NJ-DE-MD Metro Area	6,096,372	165,437	233,192	136,533	176,561	244,231	174,787	116,434	125,171	973,717
Phoenix-Mesa-Scottsdale, AZ Metro Area	4,857,962	114,076	162,727	97,708	137,956	207,471	144,066	89,516	83,307	760,024
Pine Bluff, AR Metro Area	90,306	2,813	3,760	1,857	4,105	3,530	1,786	1,915	2,136	15,329
Pinehurst-Southern Pines, NC Micro Area	98,682	2,437	5,100	3,283	3,222	6,186	5,811	2,029	3,053	23,584
Pittsburgh, PA Metro Area	2,324,743	73,791	106,767	65,273	83,882	109,532	82,485	57,710	65,156	464,038
Pittsfield, MA Metro Area	126,348	3,004	7,615	3,935	5,234	7,449	5,491	3,301	3,829	29,239
Plattsburgh, NY Micro Area	80,695	3,459	2,897	1,983	2,556	3,326	2,212	1,948	1,498	13,523
Pocatello, ID Metro Area	87,138	2,372	2,214	2,091	2,733	2,536	1,957	1,411	1,616	12,344
Port Angeles, WA Micro Area	76,737	2,317	4,062	3,477	3,838	5,583	4,040	2,122	3,101	22,161
Portland-South Portland, ME Metro Area	535,420	15,908	24,457	16,483	19,458	26,102	16,842	12,932	12,472	104,289
Portland-Vancouver-Hillsboro, OR-WA Metro Area	2,478,996	60,332	89,417	56,055	75,673	96,281	62,259	38,797	39,815	368,880
Port St. Lucie, FL Metro Area	482,040	14,040	18,840	13,522	20,399	33,180	25,587	19,130	15,809	127,627
Portsmouth, OH Micro Area	75,502	2,323	2,799	2,034	2,689	2,879	2,759	1,494	1,671	13,526
Pottsville, PA Micro Area	142,067	3,978	6,357	3,476	5,858	6,909	4,563	3,925	4,148	28,879
Prescott, AZ Metro Area	231,993	8,026	13,459	10,573	14,342	18,916	13,981	8,473	7,371	73,656
Providence-Warwick, RI-MA Metro Area	1,621,337	49,234	65,936	37,390	48,574	72,556	46,961	32,320	39,700	277,501
Provo-Orem, UT Metro Area	632,705	7,252	13,182	6,224	9,003	14,110	8,899	6,366	4,791	49,393
Pueblo, CO Metro Area	167,529	4,435	7,511	3,934	5,503	8,475	5,066	3,954	3,900	30,832
Punta Gorda, FL Metro Area	184,998	6,692	10,865	8,139	13,307	17,892	13,351	10,720	10,912	74,321
Quincy, IL-MO Micro Area	76,007	2,127	2,838	1,637	2,222	3,676	3,547	1,594	2,212	14,888
Racine, WI Metro Area	196,584	6,975	7,395	4,724	6,152	8,049	5,638	4,137	3,701	32,401
Raleigh, NC Metro Area	1,362,540	28,855	42,968	22,067	35,090	47,688	28,572	15,796	16,656	165,869
Rapid City, SD Metro Area	147,316	3,889	7,903	3,919	4,598	7,798	3,620	2,843	3,476	26,254
Reading, PA Metro Area	420,152	11,167	15,374	10,129	12,347	18,387	12,000	8,592	10,860	72,315
Redding, CA Metro Area	180,040	5,361	8,430	4,575	6,453	10,453	6,499	5,095	3,952	37,027
Reno, NV Metro Area	471,265	12,086	21,293	11,125	16,398	21,285	12,609	8,799	7,232	77,448
Richmond, IN Micro Area	65,936	1,750	2,853	1,878	2,254	2,718	2,048	1,700	1,847	12,445
Richmond, VA Metro Area	1,303,621	31,870	51,262	30,203	40,282	51,632	34,121	22,671	24,290	203,199
Richmond-Berea, KY Micro Area	108,961	2,590	3,398	2,360	3,355	3,995	2,643	1,730	1,813	15,896
Riverside-San Bernardino-Ontario, CA Metro Area	4,622,361	104,268	140,398	83,028	117,923	153,082	112,244	69,273	68,643	604,193
Roanoke, VA Metro Area	314,515	9,533	13,214	8,345	11,977	17,261	12,417	6,365	8,073	64,438
Roanoke Rapids, NC Micro Area	70,250	2,388	3,217	2,927	2,356	3,396	2,929	1,797	1,214	14,619
Rochester, MN Metro Area	219,802	6,059	7,138	4,932	6,033	9,164	7,373	4,063	5,070	36,635
Rochester, NY Metro Area	1,071,082	33,402	46,266	24,869	34,507	49,739	34,735	21,873	24,713	190,436
Rockford, IL Metro Area	337,658	10,658	13,599	6,797	10,422	15,884	10,327	7,111	7,081	57,622
Rocky Mount, NC Metro Area	146,021	5,856	5,860	3,688	5,624	7,322	5,965	2,571	2,580	27,750
Rome, GA Metro Area	97,927	1,905	4,442	2,121	2,755	4,282	3,578	1,954	1,843	16,533
Roseburg, OR Micro Area	110,283	3,505	5,494	4,149	6,380	5,706	5,264	4,144	2,281	27,924
Roswell, NM Micro Area	64,689	2,222	2,265	813	2,494	2,598	1,706	1,660	1,559	10,830
Russellville, AR Micro Area	85,535	2,889	2,672	1,746	2,305	3,702	2,608	1,419	1,651	13,431
Sacramento--Roseville--Arden-Arcade, CA Metro Area	2,345,210	59,959	87,936	51,000	67,136	94,604	61,329	43,101	44,627	361,797
Saginaw, MI Metro Area	190,800	4,744	8,110	4,754	6,284	9,836	6,121	4,618	5,153	36,766

Table B-4: Metropolitan/Micropolitan Statistical Areas - Older Population by Age—*Continued*

	Total Population	60 to 61 Years	62 to 64 Years	65 to 66 Years	67 to 69 Years	70 to 74 Years	75 to 79 Years	80 to 84 Years	85 Years and Over	65 Years and Over
St. Cloud, MN Metro Area	199,801	4,666	7,082	3,536	5,429	7,518	5,598	3,353	4,276	29,710
St. George, UT Metro Area	171,700	3,765	5,359	4,369	6,901	9,582	6,903	5,015	4,525	37,295
St. Joseph, MO-KS Metro Area	126,991	3,487	5,422	3,213	3,847	5,430	3,992	1,949	2,930	21,361
St. Louis, MO-IL Metro Area	2,804,724	80,396	118,921	64,501	86,610	116,211	83,481	54,651	57,901	463,355
Salem, OH Micro Area	102,665	3,595	4,391	2,695	4,661	5,024	4,218	2,430	2,147	21,175
Salem, OR Metro Area	432,102	10,068	17,940	9,627	14,573	15,766	11,683	8,992	8,134	68,775
Salinas, CA Metro Area	435,594	8,547	15,325	9,989	9,666	14,738	8,903	7,832	8,363	59,491
Salisbury, MD-DE Metro Area	409,979	13,165	20,032	12,244	21,323	25,821	19,034	11,494	8,876	98,792
Salt Lake City, UT Metro Area	1,222,540	24,862	35,421	19,502	25,585	35,495	22,147	16,140	12,951	131,820
San Angelo, TX Metro Area	119,310	2,600	4,086	2,629	4,053	4,605	2,734	1,838	2,438	18,297
San Antonio-New Braunfels, TX Metro Area	2,518,036	59,329	77,471	42,739	66,989	87,759	58,193	36,789	36,204	328,673
San Diego-Carlsbad, CA Metro Area	3,343,364	78,949	112,534	66,686	87,669	117,946	80,677	57,763	59,080	469,821
Sandusky, OH Micro Area	74,615	2,586	2,587	1,865	2,639	4,648	2,730	1,557	2,718	16,157
San Francisco-Oakland-Hayward, CA Metro Area	4,729,484	122,269	167,711	100,456	139,378	183,478	125,228	87,901	95,715	732,156
San Jose-Sunnyvale-Santa Clara, CA Metro Area	1,999,107	46,330	65,852	39,023	47,414	64,101	47,140	33,186	38,328	269,192
San Luis Obispo-Paso Robles-Arroyo Grande, CA Metro Area	284,010	7,581	12,502	7,683	11,316	16,424	9,250	6,418	6,503	57,594
Santa Cruz-Watsonville, CA Metro Area	274,255	7,085	11,441	8,196	9,637	11,620	7,120	4,941	3,835	45,349
Santa Fe, NM Metro Area	150,056	4,211	7,769	5,176	7,463	10,798	6,858	3,543	2,730	36,568
Santa Maria-Santa Barbara, CA Metro Area	446,527	10,347	14,553	8,705	12,099	16,779	12,760	8,421	9,638	68,402
Santa Rosa, CA Metro Area	499,942	15,657	20,698	14,196	20,476	25,550	16,420	9,408	11,980	98,030
Savannah, GA Metro Area	389,494	10,081	12,278	9,647	8,878	15,237	9,457	6,392	5,596	55,207
Scranton--Wilkes-Barre--Hazleton, PA Metro Area	555,485	18,644	23,023	14,107	18,075	29,663	18,911	14,535	15,650	110,941
Searcy, AR Micro Area	78,727	2,254	2,083	1,317	2,412	3,326	1,901	2,044	1,307	12,307
Seattle-Tacoma-Bellevue, WA Metro Area	3,939,363	97,668	134,336	80,154	105,531	136,249	89,126	53,463	63,508	528,031
Sebastian-Vero Beach, FL Metro Area	157,413	6,173	9,941	6,448	7,438	13,374	10,603	6,403	7,118	51,384
Sebring, FL Metro Area	105,424	3,470	4,491	4,692	4,999	7,697	8,134	5,096	6,627	37,245
Seneca, SC Micro Area	78,374	2,575	3,583	2,163	4,100	5,099	3,617	2,172	1,482	18,633
Sevierville, TN Metro Area	97,892	2,938	3,451	3,129	3,059	5,644	3,342	1,995	1,991	19,160
Shawnee, OK Micro Area	72,679	2,482	2,667	1,466	2,165	3,512	1,618	1,255	1,805	11,821
Sheboygan, WI Metro Area	115,456	3,303	4,485	3,911	3,538	4,517	3,276	2,762	2,692	20,696
Shelby, NC Micro Area	97,645	3,740	4,344	2,897	4,010	3,677	2,816	2,623	2,074	18,097
Shelton, WA Micro Area	65,507	1,964	2,733	2,168	2,584	4,593	2,665	1,260	1,592	14,862
Sherman-Denison, TX Metro Area	133,991	3,234	4,525	2,334	4,313	7,378	4,323	2,737	2,521	23,606
Show Low, AZ Micro Area	110,445	4,037	3,401	2,380	4,097	5,649	3,918	1,934	2,184	20,162
Shreveport-Bossier City, LA Metro Area	436,341	11,360	16,326	9,743	16,111	16,361	12,221	9,086	8,532	72,054
Sierra Vista-Douglas, AZ Metro Area	126,770	4,462	5,808	3,639	4,969	7,522	6,003	3,095	3,174	28,402
Sioux City, IA-NE-SD Metro Area	169,354	4,735	6,832	3,491	5,045	6,128	4,230	3,745	3,727	26,366
Sioux Falls, SD Metro Area	266,100	6,421	8,457	4,942	6,928	9,904	5,339	2,895	5,617	35,625
Somerset, PA Micro Area	73,952	2,728	3,384	2,119	3,162	3,782	3,382	2,104	1,976	16,525
South Bend-Mishawaka, IN-MI Metro Area	322,424	9,493	12,859	9,323	9,089	12,881	9,084	5,775	7,468	53,620
Spartanburg, SC Metro Area	341,298	10,331	11,524	7,970	11,075	14,662	11,567	5,822	5,027	56,123
Spokane-Spokane Valley, WA Metro Area	573,527	14,587	21,653	12,105	17,880	29,449	17,409	10,600	9,664	97,107
Springfield, IL Metro Area	207,676	5,573	9,476	6,252	6,776	9,110	6,423	4,129	4,507	37,197
Springfield, MA Metro Area	631,761	16,862	24,094	14,500	20,785	26,888	18,662	10,755	15,143	106,733
Springfield, MO Metro Area	468,126	11,859	16,222	9,956	15,432	19,007	15,689	8,968	8,731	77,783
Springfield, OH Metro Area	134,585	3,533	5,748	3,067	5,165	6,653	4,466	2,757	3,849	25,957
State College, PA Metro Area	162,805	3,423	5,246	2,969	3,944	6,022	4,386	2,818	2,676	22,815
Statesboro, GA Micro Area	77,296	1,513	2,902	986	2,166	2,022	1,254	1,154	963	8,545
Staunton-Waynesboro, VA Metro Area	123,007	3,834	5,310	3,770	5,032	6,037	4,497	2,908	3,451	25,695
Stevens Point, WI Micro Area	70,942	1,625	2,794	1,569	2,321	2,936	2,093	1,319	1,428	11,666
Stillwater, OK Micro Area	82,040	2,360	1,481	1,794	1,716	3,044	1,489	1,596	1,341	10,980
Stockton-Lodi, CA Metro Area	752,660	16,613	25,856	14,654	17,730	24,340	18,037	10,152	10,931	95,844
Sumter, SC Metro Area	106,512	2,216	4,009	2,895	3,072	4,301	3,281	2,147	1,872	17,568
Sunbury, PA Micro Area	91,083	3,223	3,665	2,541	3,803	4,574	3,036	2,479	3,214	19,647
Syracuse, NY Metro Area	650,502	19,745	26,499	15,232	21,406	27,350	19,448	12,851	15,116	111,403
Talladega-Sylacauga, AL Micro Area	92,812	2,749	4,256	2,218	3,360	4,854	3,082	2,274	1,583	17,371
Tallahassee, FL Metro Area	387,455	10,742	14,435	8,694	11,664	15,109	9,655	4,825	5,527	55,474
Tampa-St. Petersburg-Clearwater, FL Metro Area	3,142,663	88,362	123,646	83,073	107,593	157,518	115,170	79,519	79,560	622,433
Terre Haute, IN Metro Area	168,679	4,585	6,222	3,372	5,755	7,338	4,792	3,683	3,442	28,382
Texarkana, TX-AR Metro Area	151,675	4,174	5,754	3,632	4,294	6,962	5,507	2,476	2,138	25,009
The Villages, FL Metro Area	128,754	3,574	8,130	6,172	14,892	21,081	17,945	8,216	4,848	73,154
Toledo, OH Metro Area	602,871	17,951	22,767	15,839	20,743	21,032	15,850	12,363	12,053	97,880
Topeka, KS Metro Area	232,594	6,715	10,852	6,339	10,348	8,851	7,514	5,427	5,015	43,494
Torrington, CT Micro Area	181,111	7,202	9,255	5,070	7,707	9,548	7,068	4,144	4,360	37,897
Traverse City, MI Micro Area	149,914	4,259	8,042	5,517	6,032	8,371	6,270	2,736	4,352	33,278
Trenton, NJ Metro Area	369,811	10,956	12,075	8,928	10,697	12,990	8,786	7,407	7,193	56,001
Truckee-Grass Valley, CA Micro Area	99,696	3,531	5,307	3,658	5,826	8,009	4,169	2,932	3,152	27,746
Tucson, AZ Metro Area	1,039,073	27,714	38,184	27,449	37,670	52,154	41,296	25,669	21,309	205,547
Tullahoma-Manchester, TN Micro Area	104,410	2,950	5,185	2,844	2,354	5,887	3,625	3,053	2,221	19,964
Tulsa, OK Metro Area	993,928	25,800	34,847	21,092	29,648	40,818	26,822	17,482	17,401	153,263
Tupelo, MS Micro Area	140,552	3,211	5,481	1,804	4,348	5,800	3,578	2,862	2,115	20,507
Tuscaloosa, AL Metro Area	244,895	5,970	8,368	4,735	7,487	9,144	6,102	3,688	3,236	34,392
Twin Falls, ID Micro Area	109,264	3,067	4,305	1,959	2,132	5,040	3,366	1,857	1,613	15,967
Tyler, TX Metro Area	230,221	6,473	8,043	4,981	7,232	9,483	8,194	4,527	3,171	37,588
Ukiah, CA Micro Area	87,606	2,270	4,626	3,524	3,052	5,744	2,860	2,417	1,475	19,072
Urban Honolulu, HI Metro Area	980,080	25,824	33,817	23,534	30,159	40,717	26,642	22,287	30,273	173,612
Utica-Rome, NY Metro Area	291,410	9,323	12,592	7,914	9,018	13,471	9,048	7,314	8,640	55,405
Valdosta, GA Metro Area	145,577	3,852	4,533	1,946	4,499	4,891	4,218	1,939	1,976	19,469
Vallejo-Fairfield, CA Metro Area	446,610	14,409	16,124	10,010	14,383	18,357	12,340	6,696	8,811	70,597
Victoria, TX Metro Area	99,047	2,096	4,094	2,087	3,496	3,352	3,300	2,224	1,999	16,458

Table B-4: Metropolitan/Micropolitan Statistical Areas - Older Population by Age—*Continued*

	Total Population	60 to 61 Years	62 to 64 Years	65 to 66 Years	67 to 69 Years	70 to 74 Years	75 to 79 Years	80 to 84 Years	85 Years and Over	65 Years and Over
Vineland-Bridgeton, NJ Metro Area	150,972	3,978	4,762	3,568	4,450	5,663	4,103	3,121	2,317	23,222
Virginia Beach-Norfolk-Newport News, VA-NC Metro Area	1,729,114	47,080	58,745	34,902	50,341	64,775	44,568	30,517	28,095	253,198
Visalia-Porterville, CA Metro Area	465,861	10,084	13,983	7,206	9,235	14,594	8,854	6,439	6,294	52,622
Waco, TX Metro Area	270,566	5,702	9,762	5,980	7,589	9,920	6,664	5,027	4,855	40,035
Walla Walla, WA Metro Area	65,611	2,375	2,358	2,085	2,373	2,380	2,470	1,214	2,054	12,576
Warner Robins, GA Metro Area	193,729	4,955	5,887	3,418	4,194	7,185	3,792	2,689	2,708	23,986
Warsaw, IN Micro Area	79,344	2,058	3,791	1,313	2,535	3,844	2,638	1,190	1,548	13,068
Washington-Arlington-Alexandria, DC-VA-MD-WV Metro Area	6,251,240	145,981	208,185	122,896	159,931	205,321	143,879	90,217	90,747	812,991
Waterloo-Cedar Falls, IA Metro Area	169,659	3,397	6,860	4,402	4,966	6,565	6,378	2,849	3,493	28,653
Watertown-Fort Atkinson, WI Micro Area	85,129	3,101	2,704	2,054	3,035	3,763	2,754	1,758	1,281	14,645
Watertown-Fort Drum, NY Metro Area	111,755	2,578	3,805	1,956	3,575	3,534	2,824	1,921	1,648	15,458
Wausau, WI Metro Area	135,428	3,719	5,302	3,316	4,097	6,033	3,772	3,526	3,026	23,770
Weirton-Steubenville, WV-OH Metro Area	120,228	2,910	6,645	3,974	5,007	6,729	4,805	3,889	3,025	27,429
Wenatchee, WA Metro Area	119,943	3,440	3,979	3,378	3,639	5,528	3,975	2,769	2,374	21,663
Wheeling, WV-OH Metro Area	140,045	4,688	6,508	3,908	6,402	7,334	4,435	3,837	4,514	30,430
Whitewater-Elkhorn, WI Micro Area	103,718	2,236	4,559	2,563	3,963	4,235	2,932	2,013	2,440	18,146
Wichita, KS Metro Area	645,031	17,717	23,534	13,785	18,721	23,308	16,166	11,840	13,150	96,970
Wichita Falls, TX Metro Area	151,306	3,561	5,471	3,580	3,992	5,522	4,504	2,916	2,750	23,264
Williamsport, PA Metro Area	113,664	3,541	5,097	3,492	3,654	5,066	4,325	3,063	2,301	21,901
Wilmington, NC Metro Area	294,436	7,137	12,533	6,700	9,988	14,985	9,262	5,308	6,253	52,496
Wilson, NC Micro Area	81,455	3,359	2,587	2,817	3,280	2,778	2,165	2,263	1,501	14,804
Winchester, VA-WV Metro Area	141,848	4,006	5,546	3,761	4,910	6,326	4,892	2,590	2,662	25,141
Winston-Salem, NC Metro Area	671,456	20,451	28,262	15,234	21,932	31,313	20,495	14,338	13,096	116,408
Wisconsin Rapids-Marshfield, WI Micro Area	73,055	1,905	3,375	2,648	2,182	3,345	3,134	1,740	1,891	14,940
Wooster, OH Micro Area	115,967	3,321	5,024	2,655	4,004	4,742	4,723	1,774	2,366	20,264
Worcester, MA-CT Metro Area	947,866	25,655	39,180	20,494	28,810	38,232	24,978	17,957	18,297	148,768
Yakima, WA Metro Area	251,446	5,327	8,249	4,884	6,801	8,723	5,582	4,613	3,726	34,329
York-Hanover, PA Metro Area	448,273	11,949	20,436	9,712	15,833	19,806	14,252	8,843	9,692	78,138
Youngstown-Warren-Boardman, OH-PA Metro Area	538,952	16,984	25,208	15,717	20,800	27,899	20,554	11,870	18,439	115,279
Yuba City, CA Metro Area	174,848	4,892	7,189	3,136	4,774	5,633	4,694	2,711	3,298	24,246
Yuma, AZ Metro Area	212,128	5,447	5,844	3,498	6,540	9,660	9,338	7,789	3,154	39,979
Zanesville, OH Micro Area	86183	3,369	3,361	2,391	2,998	3,278	3,255	1,843	1,424	15,189

Table B-5: 116th Congressional Districts - Older Population by Age

	Total Population	60 to 61 Years	62 to 64 Years	65 to 66 Years	67 to 69 Years	70 to 74 Years	75 to 79 Years	80 to 84 Years	85 Years and Over	65 Years and Over
Alabama										
Congressional District 1	715,346	20,568	26,405	17,650	22,410	35,745	24,406	14,245	12,627	127,083
Congressional District 2	678,122	18,690	24,281	15,776	21,007	30,710	20,756	14,390	12,723	115,362
Congressional District 3	708,409	19,235	27,145	16,013	23,160	35,141	22,735	12,289	10,181	119,519
Congressional District 4	686,297	20,934	26,866	15,111	24,038	35,782	25,942	13,938	13,332	128,143
Congressional District 5	725,634	19,201	25,140	17,182	20,672	31,705	20,948	16,551	12,667	119,725
Congressional District 6	713,595	20,253	26,053	16,992	22,655	31,547	20,251	15,071	12,536	119,052
Congressional District 7	660,468	18,966	25,735	15,195	21,984	22,921	17,504	11,999	11,176	100,779
Alaska										
Congressional District (at Large)	737,438	20,287	25,725	17,076	20,251	22,303	12,674	8,326	7,370	88,000
Arizona										
Congressional District 1	770,392	19,076	27,417	18,948	26,604	41,840	32,137	17,654	11,646	148,829
Congressional District 2	724,747	21,967	29,319	20,633	26,865	40,943	32,367	17,990	18,404	157,202
Congressional District 3	798,359	18,318	22,511	13,427	22,979	24,676	17,876	12,890	7,571	99,419
Congressional District 4	809,426	24,906	41,554	28,735	40,762	61,267	44,976	28,098	20,480	224,318
Congressional District 5	841,344	20,422	25,621	17,852	24,458	39,889	27,244	15,819	15,881	141,143
Congressional District 6	783,621	23,091	31,802	20,166	26,935	37,543	28,757	18,613	17,340	149,354
Congressional District 7	854,749	14,327	21,806	8,605	11,863	18,515	10,201	6,238	5,174	60,596
Congressional District 8	794,820	19,194	29,349	20,040	29,368	50,278	36,701	23,707	23,125	183,219
Congressional District 9	794,188	18,893	26,753	14,253	18,758	21,754	16,234	10,906	13,118	95,023
Arkansas										
Congressional District 1	724,622	20,011	26,930	17,180	22,799	36,191	26,920	14,354	13,711	131,155
Congressional District 2	765,124	18,272	26,984	16,332	24,033	32,268	21,547	13,374	14,284	121,838
Congressional District 3	819,235	20,723	24,280	15,615	23,233	29,808	23,571	12,441	13,378	118,046
Congressional District 4	704,844	22,405	28,291	16,307	26,857	36,185	25,173	17,319	14,796	136,637
California										
Congressional District 1	711,282	21,197	34,689	20,971	29,370	41,890	29,062	18,516	16,073	155,882
Congressional District 2	722,370	21,745	32,866	21,468	31,415	41,755	25,994	16,450	16,421	153,503
Congressional District 3	748,104	21,162	26,167	15,787	19,935	27,609	19,532	11,025	13,330	107,218
Congressional District 4	754,525	22,924	34,740	20,560	30,852	43,792	27,982	18,149	18,546	159,881
Congressional District 5	730,955	22,251	31,480	19,561	27,390	31,781	22,819	14,173	14,483	130,207
Congressional District 6	777,985	18,418	23,939	14,086	17,506	25,168	15,453	10,490	13,045	95,748
Congressional District 7	753,640	18,774	29,888	16,422	22,160	31,595	20,237	14,982	14,795	120,191
Congressional District 8	717,107	22,878	24,084	11,552	18,158	27,498	18,578	10,711	10,476	96,973
Congressional District 9	775,148	18,611	25,641	14,805	18,781	27,329	19,691	11,288	11,330	103,224
Congressional District 10	761,485	16,286	24,757	16,980	18,226	24,361	17,432	10,590	11,294	98,883
Congressional District 11	762,290	21,068	27,967	15,964	24,563	33,033	21,763	16,874	15,084	127,281
Congressional District 12	764,043	20,605	25,037	16,573	19,690	27,521	18,595	14,435	19,400	116,214
Congressional District 13	764,304	18,133	23,871	15,395	21,390	28,455	17,083	13,312	12,426	108,061
Congressional District 14	759,415	18,818	29,152	17,366	23,344	29,555	21,718	14,336	19,325	125,644
Congressional District 15	789,174	18,447	26,991	14,490	21,322	27,101	19,317	11,717	12,930	106,877
Congressional District 16	749,967	15,132	19,550	10,949	13,228	21,484	13,286	9,397	9,790	78,134
Congressional District 17	777,468	17,129	27,398	14,426	16,279	21,927	17,461	12,962	13,023	96,078
Congressional District 18	750,295	18,499	25,956	16,632	19,765	27,589	18,855	14,089	19,265	116,195
Congressional District 19	763,028	19,136	23,569	15,794	20,082	25,840	18,205	11,394	11,658	102,973
Congressional District 20	739,352	15,896	26,938	17,472	19,432	25,334	16,139	13,021	12,582	103,980
Congressional District 21	713,625	11,290	16,386	10,198	11,647	15,868	9,638	9,932	7,331	64,614
Congressional District 22	771,095	16,313	22,658	13,347	19,448	26,251	15,237	11,284	13,776	99,343
Congressional District 23	747,852	17,656	26,141	15,491	16,857	25,307	16,592	12,855	11,477	98,579
Congressional District 24	738,707	18,113	27,330	16,636	23,562	33,711	22,313	15,021	16,220	127,463
Congressional District 25	716,257	19,388	23,671	14,765	20,777	22,472	18,301	8,674	8,800	93,789
Congressional District 26	728,927	18,786	24,919	16,647	20,277	26,739	18,375	13,206	16,413	111,657
Congressional District 27	705,509	18,409	25,511	16,173	23,123	29,517	20,818	16,477	20,949	127,057
Congressional District 28	709,450	18,989	24,947	12,642	19,967	27,392	19,984	15,072	15,679	110,736
Congressional District 29	707,741	14,425	22,580	12,168	17,003	18,925	12,851	12,511	8,910	82,368
Congressional District 30	766,513	18,438	25,750	16,524	21,982	28,704	20,434	13,596	17,881	119,121
Congressional District 31	751,527	15,882	21,147	13,071	19,900	22,005	14,113	10,096	9,201	88,386
Congressional District 32	716,199	17,914	26,223	13,227	17,443	25,227	16,879	12,284	11,504	96,564
Congressional District 33	704,818	18,428	25,994	14,475	22,235	35,841	22,082	15,955	21,452	132,040
Congressional District 34	748,812	19,669	20,705	13,682	16,717	21,939	14,587	12,093	14,830	93,848
Congressional District 35	769,589	14,961	18,189	14,699	14,516	17,238	12,196	8,470	7,379	74,498
Congressional District 36	752,138	19,667	31,333	19,891	33,265	42,936	33,663	20,800	21,007	171,562
Congressional District 37	738,174	19,797	21,730	12,866	18,092	20,077	16,614	11,380	13,847	92,876
Congressional District 38	716,331	17,337	23,927	15,030	17,423	25,158	19,185	14,328	16,426	107,550
Congressional District 39	726,541	19,629	26,064	15,894	20,302	30,668	16,945	13,713	14,340	111,862
Congressional District 40	716,470	11,638	17,403	9,783	14,701	16,861	10,564	7,427	8,087	67,423
Congressional District 41	775,626	13,737	20,613	11,409	14,360	19,411	12,812	6,713	8,830	73,535
Congressional District 42	826,801	16,881	22,626	12,451	18,272	23,443	20,271	13,187	11,886	99,510
Congressional District 43	753,696	17,856	23,511	13,596	18,053	23,507	15,985	9,146	12,257	92,544
Congressional District 44	725,177	17,484	20,122	11,882	14,983	18,844	11,680	8,231	9,704	75,324
Congressional District 45	797,608	21,393	24,332	15,234	23,279	31,584	22,023	13,178	17,525	122,823
Congressional District 46	735,139	16,853	17,963	11,986	13,236	18,943	11,600	8,573	10,252	74,590
Congressional District 47	710,853	19,980	25,570	12,282	18,943	21,224	15,781	10,900	12,125	91,255
Congressional District 48	719,486	22,703	25,149	14,381	20,279	35,469	23,599	15,454	18,592	127,774
Congressional District 49	731,513	22,240	24,569	15,838	21,352	31,515	23,243	15,028	15,853	122,829
Congressional District 50	751,551	20,056	27,624	16,650	19,845	27,474	20,014	13,725	14,500	112,208
Congressional District 51	747,510	15,581	20,202	13,166	16,155	21,289	14,366	12,053	11,343	88,372
Congressional District 52	767,172	16,181	26,526	16,499	20,444	29,408	19,670	13,210	13,389	112,620
Congressional District 53	796,701	17,929	27,569	14,731	20,762	24,242	14,334	12,862	12,539	99,470

Table B-5: 116th Congressional Districts - Older Population by Age—*Continued*

	Total Population	60 to 61 Years	62 to 64 Years	65 to 66 Years	67 to 69 Years	70 to 74 Years	75 to 79 Years	80 to 84 Years	85 Years and Over	65 Years and Over
Colorado										
Congressional District 1	841,497	18,966	24,958	14,205	21,456	26,806	16,722	10,369	11,436	100,994
Congressional District 2	812,357	23,386	31,863	20,480	22,215	36,001	20,696	11,086	11,611	122,089
Congressional District 3	753,595	21,771	32,079	21,696	26,043	37,372	25,307	16,099	13,669	140,186
Congressional District 4	836,061	23,454	29,981	17,849	24,947	29,237	18,605	13,217	12,948	116,803
Congressional District 5	815,466	21,377	27,580	18,388	22,800	31,511	18,056	11,765	12,793	115,313
Congressional District 6	835,273	20,377	27,554	15,150	23,124	26,120	15,530	10,406	10,852	101,182
Congressional District 7	801,315	19,260	26,397	15,583	20,232	31,203	17,237	12,936	14,097	111,288
Connecticut										
Congressional District 1	715,049	19,181	29,121	15,030	22,236	31,476	23,687	14,007	18,416	124,852
Congressional District 2	699,657	21,770	31,977	18,392	21,926	32,782	21,677	14,074	17,204	126,055
Congressional District 3	712,272	22,741	26,935	15,775	23,362	31,576	23,265	13,412	17,490	124,880
Congressional District 4	739,090	20,248	29,073	14,961	18,295	29,561	21,306	13,609	17,460	115,192
Congressional District 5	706,597	21,740	29,837	13,981	23,099	30,608	22,513	14,841	17,126	122,168
Delaware										
Congressional District (at Large)	967,171	26,537	41,002	24,560	35,335	48,000	36,377	17,880	18,604	180,756
District of Columbia										
Delegate District (at Large)	702,455	13,894	19,259	11,735	14,102	22,996	16,161	9,731	10,901	85,626
Florida										
Congressional District 1	784,532	23,574	31,016	17,107	26,412	36,181	24,205	16,966	11,534	132,405
Congressional District 2	733,749	21,282	30,628	18,159	28,630	39,955	27,610	18,855	15,245	148,454
Congressional District 3	758,275	18,579	26,310	19,566	25,847	34,546	23,218	11,890	13,141	128,208
Congressional District 4	819,177	19,638	33,144	21,850	23,334	36,936	24,227	16,836	14,047	137,230
Congressional District 5	738,862	17,852	23,860	13,805	21,346	27,162	17,834	9,142	8,976	98,265
Congressional District 6	781,896	24,282	33,733	27,032	36,543	50,087	34,681	23,092	28,871	200,306
Congressional District 7	786,041	21,453	24,644	15,036	19,786	32,306	18,684	14,305	13,944	114,061
Congressional District 8	768,139	28,097	39,048	24,632	35,363	45,462	37,135	24,660	28,313	195,565
Congressional District 9	902,812	25,262	28,518	16,736	30,229	36,027	30,962	15,006	16,615	145,575
Congressional District 10	839,504	21,796	25,251	15,981	21,337	25,669	14,548	10,450	9,800	97,785
Congressional District 11	789,849	24,799	41,938	27,503	45,514	76,146	68,524	34,756	29,226	281,669
Congressional District 12	792,410	24,413	33,150	23,915	32,015	50,078	39,202	25,692	23,063	193,965
Congressional District 13	735,935	24,096	33,791	22,441	29,472	40,350	30,126	23,501	25,694	171,584
Congressional District 14	782,973	19,045	22,444	14,866	19,477	27,538	16,882	12,782	12,969	104,514
Congressional District 15	808,723	19,737	29,880	18,253	22,042	38,561	25,255	16,189	12,649	132,949
Congressional District 16	852,096	21,706	38,738	25,043	38,161	56,344	44,425	31,452	31,418	226,843
Congressional District 17	789,236	22,019	36,990	28,068	43,056	61,656	51,314	37,636	34,052	255,782
Congressional District 18	780,772	23,287	32,453	20,945	32,403	50,148	42,163	29,716	26,048	201,423
Congressional District 19	836,359	24,525	35,306	27,039	41,975	69,727	52,060	35,598	38,239	264,638
Congressional District 20	809,153	21,458	25,275	12,811	20,017	27,266	18,808	14,076	15,921	108,899
Congressional District 21	785,042	21,619	28,056	18,679	26,156	50,551	41,056	27,753	37,306	201,501
Congressional District 22	753,363	22,293	34,009	19,880	26,380	40,693	33,706	21,410	23,499	165,568
Congressional District 23	756,447	20,178	25,815	17,793	25,302	34,994	26,584	16,587	16,575	137,835
Congressional District 24	784,469	21,125	26,554	14,172	20,482	28,649	17,260	13,538	13,870	107,971
Congressional District 25	775,326	18,448	29,355	17,045	24,674	34,022	29,523	18,977	23,395	147,636
Congressional District 26	790,373	19,518	23,383	15,000	22,508	28,279	22,477	16,068	13,117	117,449
Congressional District 27	763,812	18,544	24,950	16,916	22,479	33,688	24,053	20,095	23,473	140,704
Georgia										
Congressional District 1	744,385	19,352	25,610	17,435	20,994	28,455	19,515	12,659	10,157	109,215
Congressional District 2	665,539	19,618	22,842	15,078	19,744	28,033	17,711	12,737	12,200	105,503
Congressional District 3	740,700	20,326	25,743	17,281	21,758	31,757	20,948	11,801	11,321	114,866
Congressional District 4	785,104	20,507	28,364	15,729	23,042	25,894	14,336	7,965	8,691	95,657
Congressional District 5	793,039	15,679	21,622	11,166	18,841	22,351	16,398	8,000	9,939	86,695
Congressional District 6	754,299	18,491	24,216	14,392	20,358	26,773	15,492	10,892	10,944	98,851
Congressional District 7	803,976	19,007	22,768	11,747	16,757	24,252	14,785	9,219	7,947	84,707
Congressional District 8	714,720	18,391	24,234	15,479	21,798	28,405	20,896	11,674	11,071	109,323
Congressional District 9	765,320	20,799	27,689	16,615	29,485	40,138	28,063	16,138	12,327	142,766
Congressional District 10	767,352	18,216	26,864	15,946	20,154	31,773	20,895	12,207	10,006	110,981
Congressional District 11	781,313	18,514	26,315	12,584	18,873	30,387	18,147	11,744	10,449	102,184
Congressional District 12	723,334	18,386	26,449	14,003	19,552	29,474	16,637	12,979	10,249	102,894
Congressional District 13	757,521	16,929	25,007	12,869	18,715	25,056	14,226	7,600	7,060	85,526
Congressional District 14	722,873	17,316	25,010	15,617	21,042	27,146	21,631	11,385	10,439	107,260
Hawaii										
Congressional District 1	709,286	18,134	25,078	17,483	22,407	31,713	20,618	16,466	24,283	132,970
Congressional District 2	711,205	21,477	29,182	18,445	26,238	33,086	20,795	14,143	15,790	128,497
Idaho										
Congressional District 1	912,950	18,934	35,540	23,112	30,067	41,480	30,869	15,714	14,256	155,498
Congressional District 2	841,258	19,670	29,241	19,036	24,309	30,393	21,855	12,903	15,447	123,943
Illinois										
Congressional District 1	706,550	21,043	28,177	16,526	20,517	24,919	22,518	13,556	14,825	112,861
Congressional District 2	694,459	18,572	25,225	14,664	19,871	27,854	18,808	14,456	15,506	111,159
Congressional District 3	704,050	17,940	27,942	13,846	18,287	28,663	19,327	13,533	14,512	108,168
Congressional District 4	702,062	15,238	20,959	11,024	14,612	19,686	12,795	6,536	7,138	71,791
Congressional District 5	743,699	17,376	24,674	13,337	18,825	22,825	15,488	11,618	13,653	95,746
Congressional District 6	730,345	20,991	30,894	17,842	23,012	28,754	22,829	13,570	13,197	119,204
Congressional District 7	707,513	17,221	21,386	13,124	20,185	26,326	17,762	10,150	8,967	96,514
Congressional District 8	707,268	20,351	24,894	14,735	18,770	25,736	15,728	11,222	11,427	97,618
Congressional District 9	721,481	17,204	27,082	14,524	23,044	31,994	21,044	14,455	21,276	126,337
Congressional District 10	711,265	19,579	25,677	16,203	18,843	27,529	18,198	12,335	16,786	109,894

Table B-5: 116th Congressional Districts - Older Population by Age—*Continued*

	Total Population	60 to 61 Years	62 to 64 Years	65 to 66 Years	67 to 69 Years	70 to 74 Years	75 to 79 Years	80 to 84 Years	85 Years and Over	65 Years and Over
Illinois—Cont.										
Congressional District 11	722,584	19,146	20,593	13,529	16,401	25,147	15,914	8,239	10,903	90,133
Congressional District 12	687,072	22,162	27,302	16,551	22,320	29,541	22,757	12,561	14,238	117,968
Congressional District 13	704,211	18,418	28,105	14,789	19,806	28,636	20,119	12,004	16,142	111,496
Congressional District 14	742,235	20,053	25,948	15,063	19,681	26,862	18,791	10,723	11,627	102,747
Congressional District 15	691,196	20,699	25,708	16,827	25,298	30,726	24,526	18,868	17,685	133,930
Congressional District 16	684,888	20,007	27,710	15,451	23,474	32,511	21,794	16,071	15,289	124,590
Congressional District 17	679,926	20,382	27,650	17,525	22,608	31,266	23,645	15,023	16,821	126,888
Congressional District 18	700,276	18,578	29,365	17,154	23,904	32,182	23,833	16,855	19,576	133,504
Indiana										
Congressional District 1	714,756	18,847	30,086	17,695	22,024	29,929	20,822	13,563	14,430	118,463
Congressional District 2	723,483	19,467	27,415	18,031	21,652	28,225	20,452	13,738	16,719	118,817
Congressional District 3	747,060	19,878	27,692	15,627	22,356	30,350	21,824	12,045	13,571	115,773
Congressional District 4	768,025	19,737	28,906	16,703	21,284	31,011	21,549	13,898	13,555	118,000
Congressional District 5	784,462	17,001	29,251	15,924	21,745	29,541	21,549	13,334	14,306	116,399
Congressional District 6	719,771	19,029	27,992	17,998	23,907	31,393	23,288	16,464	14,369	127,419
Congressional District 7	760,466	19,175	22,764	15,387	17,438	22,533	15,591	10,676	10,647	92,272
Congressional District 8	718,591	20,195	30,141	16,602	25,521	29,376	22,877	14,634	15,650	124,660
Congressional District 9	755,264	21,848	27,254	16,027	24,039	31,381	21,062	13,504	13,330	119,343
Iowa										
Congressional District 1	773,628	21,140	30,045	18,975	23,214	34,690	24,965	17,878	19,498	139,220
Congressional District 2	783,983	21,997	32,421	18,092	25,196	32,638	22,926	17,096	18,478	134,426
Congressional District 3	843,598	18,164	29,126	17,433	24,244	30,570	21,981	13,626	15,503	123,357
Congressional District 4	754,936	20,948	31,956	20,032	23,637	30,612	25,078	19,319	22,137	140,815
Kansas										
Congressional District 1	698,323	18,116	24,975	15,747	20,060	26,863	20,159	15,441	17,640	115,910
Congressional District 2	713,845	18,717	28,864	17,123	26,239	26,658	21,078	14,470	17,516	123,084
Congressional District 3	775,243	18,786	27,606	19,091	21,147	25,845	18,094	11,801	12,806	108,784
Congressional District 4	724,099	19,886	26,808	16,350	21,516	27,411	19,227	14,085	15,824	114,413
Kentucky										
Congressional District 1	721,124	21,530	29,682	17,188	24,042	34,948	24,781	17,181	15,093	133,233
Congressional District 2	769,850	20,929	29,776	15,787	23,981	33,973	21,977	15,710	12,640	124,068
Congressional District 3	749,110	20,368	27,812	17,495	24,553	28,311	19,178	15,395	15,541	120,473
Congressional District 4	754,387	22,192	27,846	16,864	23,042	31,978	20,285	12,744	11,993	116,906
Congressional District 5	695,105	17,862	30,425	18,817	23,659	31,471	20,647	15,249	12,116	121,959
Congressional District 6	778,826	19,339	27,550	17,236	21,846	30,274	20,504	13,628	11,265	114,753
Louisiana										
Congressional District 1	806,638	24,838	31,306	18,778	27,187	33,528	21,871	15,223	13,608	130,195
Congressional District 2	794,121	19,098	31,371	18,957	23,866	29,514	19,927	12,834	10,444	115,542
Congressional District 3	783,545	19,135	30,084	17,828	21,977	28,793	19,604	13,562	13,458	115,222
Congressional District 4	747,314	19,323	27,573	17,961	25,136	29,520	22,491	14,539	12,945	122,592
Congressional District 5	738,249	20,524	27,334	16,195	23,240	33,619	21,985	15,301	10,916	121,256
Congressional District 6	790,111	20,017	28,649	18,228	22,548	28,022	22,496	12,036	12,473	115,803
Maine										
Congressional District 1	685,535	21,471	31,835	21,283	25,264	34,911	23,254	16,631	17,583	138,926
Congressional District 2	652,869	22,720	32,227	20,976	24,875	36,644	22,595	14,787	17,266	137,143
Maryland										
Congressional District 1	741,621	22,863	32,145	17,547	24,628	38,721	25,726	17,245	15,117	138,984
Congressional District 2	768,511	19,835	29,769	16,168	22,416	27,526	18,604	12,600	12,292	109,606
Congressional District 3	754,636	18,239	27,616	14,705	19,128	30,736	21,480	12,411	17,034	115,494
Congressional District 4	760,398	18,146	27,606	16,076	20,768	27,133	17,659	11,268	10,289	103,193
Congressional District 5	757,621	20,433	28,977	15,352	20,130	28,971	19,626	11,169	10,486	105,734
Congressional District 6	758,943	19,420	28,629	17,287	21,095	29,827	21,823	15,451	13,265	118,748
Congressional District 7	716,136	19,444	28,365	15,217	20,946	29,409	20,940	12,516	13,973	113,001
Congressional District 8	784,852	21,036	31,356	18,285	23,358	31,013	23,301	14,265	16,059	126,281
Massachusetts										
Congressional District 1	736,481	19,753	31,731	17,872	24,497	33,478	24,527	13,501	18,278	132,153
Congressional District 2	745,347	19,289	31,607	16,847	24,421	32,482	18,990	13,958	15,002	121,700
Congressional District 3	771,096	23,969	27,267	14,828	21,403	24,971	16,772	13,030	14,523	105,527
Congressional District 4	766,019	19,606	30,676	18,434	21,843	33,988	20,827	16,057	16,587	127,736
Congressional District 5	775,135	19,955	27,926	19,325	19,512	32,303	21,623	15,749	16,865	125,377
Congressional District 6	780,524	19,882	34,381	18,419	26,785	38,089	22,901	17,075	22,927	146,196
Congressional District 7	820,086	15,922	21,452	12,826	18,317	19,885	17,311	10,342	10,668	89,349
Congressional District 8	764,891	21,511	29,442	16,298	22,872	30,625	23,041	13,289	18,546	124,671
Congressional District 9	742,570	22,660	33,546	21,455	29,806	44,965	30,156	18,117	20,333	164,832
Michigan										
Congressional District 1	699,220	24,589	35,053	23,201	31,079	40,591	31,863	18,204	18,537	163,475
Congressional District 2	743,361	19,115	27,670	17,335	23,506	29,121	20,976	14,544	14,105	119,587
Congressional District 3	749,975	20,230	28,984	16,391	19,595	29,949	19,908	12,928	14,020	112,791
Congressional District 4	704,592	20,710	31,896	19,395	24,194	36,026	25,461	17,434	14,967	137,477
Congressional District 5	671,115	22,331	28,296	16,861	23,745	31,278	22,961	15,089	14,616	124,550
Congressional District 6	721,736	18,473	29,956	17,506	23,976	32,758	22,257	14,269	14,089	124,855
Congressional District 7	706,811	21,397	29,927	18,773	26,384	32,537	24,371	13,747	14,811	130,623
Congressional District 8	749,011	20,088	28,724	16,574	24,461	28,406	18,525	11,568	13,102	112,636
Congressional District 9	715,259	22,598	28,667	16,336	20,681	29,456	20,830	15,161	16,889	119,353
Congressional District 10	722,722	22,207	31,215	19,531	24,966	34,453	25,380	14,663	13,560	132,553
Congressional District 11	733,920	23,076	30,566	19,022	22,584	32,689	21,428	13,344	14,436	123,503
Congressional District 12	709,832	18,870	25,061	13,162	20,643	27,041	18,013	12,058	13,059	103,976

Table B-5: 116th Congressional Districts - Older Population by Age—*Continued*

	Total Population	60 to 61 Years	62 to 64 Years	65 to 66 Years	67 to 69 Years	70 to 74 Years	75 to 79 Years	80 to 84 Years	85 Years and Over	65 Years and Over
Michigan—Cont.										
Congressional District 13	663,867	17,506	24,926	14,178	19,101	23,633	16,662	11,551	12,140	97,265
Congressional District 14	704,494	19,154	29,678	16,596	21,298	30,174	18,485	15,294	15,962	117,809
Minnesota										
Congressional District 1	678,418	17,047	26,862	16,151	19,768	27,588	20,968	14,780	18,318	117,573
Congressional District 2	714,141	18,144	23,053	14,479	20,088	23,502	18,245	11,454	11,325	99,093
Congressional District 3	723,994	20,273	28,034	17,410	22,174	27,695	21,705	13,223	12,476	114,683
Congressional District 4	717,766	19,082	24,905	15,078	21,401	25,637	16,342	12,427	13,752	104,637
Congressional District 5	718,802	14,662	21,642	14,389	18,498	19,734	14,484	9,723	14,244	91,072
Congressional District 6	722,715	16,208	26,060	13,437	18,722	25,714	16,932	9,966	9,306	94,077
Congressional District 7	663,069	19,300	27,892	16,782	21,710	31,269	23,473	17,677	19,328	130,239
Congressional District 8	672,274	21,230	30,933	19,017	26,934	33,309	23,913	17,463	16,624	137,260
Mississippi										
Congressional District 1	769,595	20,138	29,030	15,868	22,332	33,580	21,959	15,984	11,824	121,547
Congressional District 2	695,797	18,369	29,483	15,983	21,483	28,911	20,039	10,135	10,200	106,751
Congressional District 3	746,155	20,435	26,116	17,678	22,679	32,206	23,514	13,141	13,669	122,887
Congressional District 4	774,983	23,742	25,337	17,016	22,528	34,092	24,424	14,511	10,667	123,238
Missouri										
Congressional District 1	728,365	21,583	28,646	14,533	20,929	27,268	17,270	11,915	14,661	106,576
Congressional District 2	760,689	21,723	33,627	20,070	25,915	33,042	26,655	18,819	19,329	143,830
Congressional District 3	793,405	20,457	34,714	17,076	22,607	36,508	23,950	14,932	12,931	128,004
Congressional District 4	770,500	20,134	30,858	17,507	23,690	34,335	24,015	15,685	15,166	130,398
Congressional District 5	771,847	18,733	29,431	15,941	22,056	30,165	21,783	13,914	15,839	119,698
Congressional District 6	780,002	22,702	30,066	17,033	23,214	35,165	22,927	14,672	15,523	128,534
Congressional District 7	783,672	18,182	28,753	17,030	25,509	36,757	26,332	16,094	16,590	138,312
Congressional District 8	737,972	20,532	33,152	17,828	24,809	37,636	26,454	18,229	14,766	139,722
Montana										
Congressional District (at Large)	1,062,305	33,041	46,691	28,002	40,696	52,357	37,014	21,417	20,753	200,239
Nebraska										
Congressional District 1	653,684	16,149	22,582	14,177	18,562	24,284	15,674	12,827	13,573	99,097
Congressional District 2	673,005	15,720	21,479	13,109	16,650	22,300	12,699	10,124	11,159	86,041
Congressional District 3	602,579	16,763	26,418	17,026	21,988	24,757	22,560	15,309	17,220	118,860
Nevada										
Congressional District 1	685,427	14,470	22,451	12,825	18,373	29,530	19,270	11,125	8,538	99,661
Congressional District 2	729,771	19,097	32,532	18,820	24,711	34,804	21,247	14,516	11,982	126,080
Congressional District 3	846,761	19,439	30,134	17,495	27,113	36,201	24,996	13,678	14,256	133,739
Congressional District 4	772,433	19,450	28,814	15,134	23,958	33,032	20,504	13,508	9,504	115,640
New Hampshire										
Congressional District 1	686,820	22,070	27,019	16,120	24,048	32,442	19,760	11,756	16,237	120,363
Congressional District 2	669,638	23,256	29,161	18,993	23,243	31,753	22,289	13,928	14,587	124,793
New Jersey										
Congressional District 1	731,297	21,830	26,581	14,998	22,310	29,191	20,735	13,143	13,348	113,725
Congressional District 2	703,117	23,465	28,327	17,619	23,377	37,584	27,099	16,192	14,963	136,834
Congressional District 3	742,905	22,222	31,019	18,537	23,710	37,319	25,798	18,565	18,902	142,831
Congressional District 4	748,858	21,526	27,290	18,621	25,193	37,022	27,786	17,059	21,470	147,151
Congressional District 5	730,707	21,693	30,618	18,804	22,387	33,307	21,786	15,144	19,802	131,230
Congressional District 6	730,114	19,702	28,372	15,702	19,854	24,494	19,286	12,642	13,022	105,000
Congressional District 7	730,778	21,879	28,797	16,092	22,531	29,411	21,988	12,944	17,568	120,534
Congressional District 8	764,837	15,570	23,375	11,730	13,723	21,570	14,865	10,596	9,908	82,392
Congressional District 9	765,382	19,471	25,944	14,642	19,711	27,524	19,366	13,946	15,791	110,980
Congressional District 10	759,704	18,804	28,515	14,493	19,311	22,683	19,152	9,097	14,125	98,861
Congressional District 11	744,805	20,403	30,864	16,119	21,915	32,548	24,794	16,594	20,066	132,036
Congressional District 12	756,016	20,785	26,931	17,590	21,124	29,607	17,245	14,356	16,793	116,715
New Mexico										
Congressional District 1	697,064	20,065	26,104	16,092	22,114	33,498	18,584	12,975	14,195	117,458
Congressional District 2	700,113	18,105	26,326	16,320	23,816	30,971	21,842	15,332	14,129	122,410
Congressional District 3	698,251	20,058	25,515	18,778	25,283	34,337	23,522	14,281	12,411	128,612
New York										
Congressional District 1	718,726	20,183	27,859	14,133	21,765	37,347	25,950	14,518	15,291	129,004
Congressional District 2	709,605	21,122	26,622	14,935	19,416	27,729	17,853	13,241	15,811	108,985
Congressional District 3	707,576	21,975	31,657	16,309	23,290	37,550	26,055	19,977	23,439	146,620
Congressional District 4	729,582	22,068	25,394	17,187	22,327	30,529	21,127	15,179	19,043	125,392
Congressional District 5	757,972	24,551	25,856	15,616	18,578	29,672	21,002	13,497	12,282	110,647
Congressional District 6	734,183	24,532	29,296	18,704	22,912	32,650	23,054	15,930	17,036	130,286
Congressional District 7	720,811	16,184	20,849	11,295	15,587	22,425	14,207	11,666	9,801	84,981
Congressional District 8	791,211	17,673	27,706	16,024	21,410	28,158	20,927	15,573	16,737	118,829
Congressional District 9	730,957	18,165	25,494	14,404	21,153	28,701	20,920	11,375	13,506	110,059
Congressional District 10	711,678	15,915	20,739	15,417	20,803	27,673	20,029	13,380	16,857	114,159
Congressional District 11	732,886	18,886	29,748	16,628	23,229	31,025	22,096	15,561	15,038	123,577
Congressional District 12	698,928	15,749	20,417	12,896	19,580	25,845	21,964	13,206	16,717	110,208
Congressional District 13	795,633	16,779	24,619	14,422	17,955	24,564	18,526	13,581	12,590	101,638
Congressional District 14	706,440	14,995	20,626	12,691	16,335	22,483	19,058	12,097	11,791	94,455
Congressional District 15	743,959	15,463	19,173	10,156	14,927	22,084	15,875	9,701	7,598	80,341
Congressional District 16	732,981	19,113	28,439	15,187	20,326	29,444	23,504	18,506	20,835	127,802
Congressional District 17	741,445	19,411	28,097	15,317	23,006	30,561	19,316	16,617	19,321	124,138
Congressional District 18	722,226	20,053	30,379	16,408	21,572	28,053	19,020	12,671	13,092	110,816

Table B-5: 116th Congressional Districts - Older Population by Age—*Continued*

	Total Population	60 to 61 Years	62 to 64 Years	65 to 66 Years	67 to 69 Years	70 to 74 Years	75 to 79 Years	80 to 84 Years	85 Years and Over	65 Years and Over
New York—Cont.										
Congressional District 19	700,310	23,297	30,582	19,650	27,937	36,235	26,109	16,640	17,548	144,119
Congressional District 20	722,529	18,488	29,697	15,995	24,083	30,322	19,812	15,336	17,760	123,308
Congressional District 21	701,112	21,970	28,593	16,534	23,014	34,654	21,448	15,469	14,768	125,887
Congressional District 22	697,372	22,244	28,915	17,230	23,132	32,393	22,942	16,052	18,748	130,497
Congressional District 23	693,764	21,256	29,244	19,777	23,072	32,746	24,453	13,935	16,529	130,512
Congressional District 24	701,664	21,109	28,608	15,806	22,227	31,407	20,513	15,212	16,996	122,161
Congressional District 25	718,565	21,446	31,278	16,234	22,501	31,565	22,077	13,688	17,225	123,290
Congressional District 26	707,190	20,414	27,723	16,241	21,574	30,626	21,739	14,408	18,663	123,251
Congressional District 27	712,904	24,692	33,050	18,068	23,774	36,405	23,738	17,511	17,607	137,103
North Carolina										
Congressional District 1	761,087	20,863	28,403	19,283	25,861	31,033	22,839	14,569	12,496	126,081
Congressional District 2	858,938	20,840	29,542	15,559	24,397	35,186	21,573	11,076	9,813	117,604
Congressional District 3	756,375	20,610	30,241	18,148	20,957	39,026	25,880	16,226	11,897	132,134
Congressional District 4	871,589	18,189	26,351	13,561	23,019	26,520	18,222	10,436	10,351	102,109
Congressional District 5	762,960	22,304	32,827	18,886	26,022	36,113	24,045	17,338	16,560	138,964
Congressional District 6	772,716	19,553	33,183	17,299	27,970	34,173	23,203	17,146	16,340	136,131
Congressional District 7	809,820	24,274	37,982	21,614	31,303	46,828	28,580	16,327	16,005	160,657
Congressional District 8	797,935	16,789	27,642	15,686	23,256	32,021	23,607	12,533	12,484	119,587
Congressional District 9	792,434	19,044	29,280	17,417	24,057	32,477	23,638	12,400	12,566	122,555
Congressional District 10	762,919	21,454	33,646	20,814	26,661	36,194	25,588	16,193	15,453	140,903
Congressional District 11	768,166	23,782	32,413	21,607	30,072	48,517	33,190	19,565	20,981	173,932
Congressional District 12	880,550	18,414	25,010	14,373	17,936	23,060	14,260	8,661	8,849	87,139
Congressional District 13	788,131	21,383	30,906	18,203	23,880	35,007	23,085	15,331	15,272	130,778
North Dakota										
Congressional District (at Large)	760,077	20,382	25,405	17,786	19,942	26,319	18,784	15,163	18,439	116,433
Ohio										
Congressional District 1	740,979	17,804	27,387	15,381	21,838	29,493	18,263	12,682	14,260	111,917
Congressional District 2	734,712	20,985	27,370	16,939	21,506	29,738	22,182	15,208	13,954	119,527
Congressional District 3	812,264	20,482	23,709	13,144	17,248	21,009	13,888	10,132	8,584	84,005
Congressional District 4	707,219	22,568	30,308	18,219	23,350	31,251	21,839	14,667	14,126	123,452
Congressional District 5	717,088	22,708	28,891	19,702	23,281	31,369	22,947	16,015	17,198	130,512
Congressional District 6	694,694	22,031	31,993	19,038	26,026	35,350	26,059	15,631	16,928	139,032
Congressional District 7	734,091	20,237	29,928	17,633	25,766	33,625	26,363	14,753	16,926	135,066
Congressional District 8	731,637	18,790	29,405	17,972	21,845	31,579	24,052	13,656	14,326	123,430
Congressional District 9	716,235	21,046	27,312	15,612	24,060	25,943	19,018	13,758	13,958	112,349
Congressional District 10	725,301	20,808	26,703	16,939	23,835	32,733	23,330	15,737	16,397	128,971
Congressional District 11	678,001	20,812	28,829	17,229	22,450	27,868	21,510	13,155	17,666	119,878
Congressional District 12	789,634	20,632	28,264	17,634	23,711	30,182	21,452	15,345	15,152	123,476
Congressional District 13	707,603	21,513	30,402	18,470	24,848	31,386	25,017	14,206	18,563	132,490
Congressional District 14	720,551	23,483	32,395	21,406	26,422	36,947	25,298	17,421	18,054	145,548
Congressional District 15	759,569	19,542	29,259	16,840	22,865	32,070	22,445	13,177	13,376	120,773
Congressional District 16	719,864	20,658	30,262	20,593	26,178	33,838	30,170	16,141	18,817	145,737
Oklahoma										
Congressional District 1	803,029	20,567	28,086	17,125	23,401	30,573	20,790	14,400	13,713	120,002
Congressional District 2	747,632	19,164	29,006	17,555	26,590	36,706	26,861	18,679	15,150	141,541
Congressional District 3	778,026	20,594	28,156	16,584	22,521	33,798	22,323	14,898	15,780	125,904
Congressional District 4	791,927	19,002	26,448	15,669	22,062	32,541	20,452	14,725	12,812	118,261
Congressional District 5	822,465	20,193	26,782	15,813	22,073	28,828	19,098	12,953	15,128	113,893
Oregon										
Congressional District 1	858,910	21,278	32,379	17,763	27,995	31,920	24,106	11,487	14,543	127,814
Congressional District 2	831,343	25,685	36,743	23,218	35,269	45,930	30,263	18,502	20,256	173,438
Congressional District 3	841,456	19,485	28,051	20,259	23,235	29,142	18,014	11,787	11,814	114,251
Congressional District 4	814,998	23,151	34,363	25,855	33,535	43,765	31,627	21,660	16,917	173,359
Congressional District 5	844,006	21,200	34,234	20,661	31,822	37,227	24,823	18,364	17,852	150,749
Pennsylvania										
Congressional District 1	713,685	21,276	30,093	19,437	21,895	33,147	25,088	16,824	15,560	131,951
Congressional District 2	727,380	17,772	24,678	13,909	19,069	25,165	16,314	12,392	10,784	97,633
Congressional District 3	736,340	19,269	24,080	13,964	18,874	24,510	18,988	12,078	13,481	101,895
Congressional District 4	727,449	18,683	29,832	19,679	22,226	30,040	22,240	16,081	19,389	129,655
Congressional District 5	718,076	17,800	26,348	13,956	20,679	28,330	19,098	15,430	17,687	115,180
Congressional District 6	734,876	18,578	29,758	17,418	20,739	30,442	20,587	12,654	15,906	117,746
Congressional District 7	731,168	18,758	29,226	18,512	22,592	32,225	22,219	15,612	19,717	130,877
Congressional District 8	696,956	24,380	29,280	18,187	23,266	35,467	23,443	17,524	18,422	136,309
Congressional District 9	702,489	21,386	29,708	19,165	26,228	34,201	22,594	18,710	19,643	140,541
Congressional District 10	734,849	18,196	31,205	16,542	24,462	30,937	22,475	15,097	17,388	126,901
Congressional District 11	737,394	19,123	29,977	15,587	27,110	32,191	25,072	19,623	15,908	135,491
Congressional District 12	701,192	19,865	29,799	17,776	22,632	34,215	25,712	17,183	17,042	134,560
Congressional District 13	692,835	21,101	29,645	18,344	27,131	34,793	28,300	17,620	17,580	143,768
Congressional District 14	684,084	22,079	33,692	18,679	27,500	36,842	26,508	18,207	18,777	146,513
Congressional District 15	680,927	22,289	30,127	19,346	24,868	34,024	26,910	16,861	19,090	141,099
Congressional District 16	686,525	20,924	30,982	19,366	22,054	34,496	23,672	16,072	18,398	134,058
Congressional District 17	717,264	22,672	31,876	21,398	23,967	32,926	24,236	16,392	20,872	139,791
Congressional District 18	683,571	21,082	29,243	18,324	23,990	28,337	22,932	16,822	17,996	128,401
Rhode Island										
Congressional District 1	532,590	15,608	20,054	12,855	14,986	23,011	16,879	11,912	13,064	92,707
Congressional District 2	524,725	17,796	21,889	12,673	15,916	23,830	14,203	9,921	13,395	89,938

Table B-5: 116th Congressional Districts - Older Population by Age—*Continued*

	Total Population	60 to 61 Years	62 to 64 Years	65 to 66 Years	67 to 69 Years	70 to 74 Years	75 to 79 Years	80 to 84 Years	85 Years and Over	65 Years and Over
South Carolina										
Congressional District 1	809,610	18,916	30,071	18,583	27,980	44,277	27,250	14,462	14,812	147,364
Congressional District 2	717,231	18,596	26,648	16,238	22,680	32,341	20,492	11,686	12,653	116,090
Congressional District 3	697,467	18,804	26,196	18,105	25,802	32,814	24,936	17,344	11,585	130,586
Congressional District 4	736,750	21,476	25,398	16,171	24,196	30,451	21,363	13,275	12,169	117,625
Congressional District 5	731,341	19,127	25,191	17,435	25,170	32,720	22,172	14,495	11,088	123,080
Congressional District 6	659,483	17,720	23,527	14,122	20,255	29,517	18,342	11,679	10,454	104,369
Congressional District 7	732,245	22,225	34,626	22,043	34,027	48,135	28,907	15,517	12,011	160,640
South Dakota										
Congressional District (at Large)	882,235	22,722	36,227	22,888	26,029	36,105	23,706	15,869	21,761	146,358
Tennessee										
Congressional District 1	720,358	20,891	33,001	20,964	26,288	39,238	27,591	18,316	15,833	148,230
Congressional District 2	753,229	20,490	29,663	17,133	25,506	37,294	25,263	16,877	13,062	135,135
Congressional District 3	736,889	19,384	33,768	19,575	24,222	37,536	26,419	15,345	14,792	137,889
Congressional District 4	798,482	21,342	27,577	17,062	20,883	33,651	20,929	15,050	10,682	118,257
Congressional District 5	777,696	16,899	24,582	14,409	20,276	24,002	17,019	10,468	10,924	97,098
Congressional District 6	784,725	21,695	31,930	20,044	26,008	36,615	26,704	16,569	12,916	138,856
Congressional District 7	786,523	19,301	28,695	15,388	24,240	29,394	21,136	15,610	10,557	116,325
Congressional District 8	699,385	19,388	30,953	17,194	26,112	31,284	20,744	14,731	14,369	124,434
Congressional District 9	712,723	19,925	26,229	12,766	18,594	22,882	16,958	7,046	10,327	88,573
Texas										
Congressional District 1	725,555	19,232	25,507	16,594	22,122	31,129	22,046	15,176	13,206	120,273
Congressional District 2	803,041	18,580	25,707	16,418	17,466	26,550	17,721	9,001	8,613	95,769
Congressional District 3	899,784	17,570	27,595	13,378	22,728	27,769	17,672	9,680	10,181	101,408
Congressional District 4	759,648	19,844	27,699	16,782	24,306	34,939	23,632	15,308	11,951	126,918
Congressional District 5	749,808	17,781	27,182	14,975	18,974	25,904	19,065	12,581	12,340	103,839
Congressional District 6	804,816	18,008	23,897	14,088	19,595	24,145	15,547	10,527	9,843	93,745
Congressional District 7	775,198	17,676	25,661	13,944	17,170	20,956	12,853	7,988	11,714	84,625
Congressional District 8	871,420	22,879	27,884	18,335	26,836	29,374	20,693	14,839	10,437	120,514
Congressional District 9	786,925	17,647	20,867	12,683	18,028	18,558	14,117	8,024	8,947	80,357
Congressional District 10	896,798	24,618	26,916	20,485	18,487	31,306	20,061	12,182	12,912	115,433
Congressional District 11	782,337	19,577	27,856	14,366	24,492	32,403	22,151	16,452	13,223	123,087
Congressional District 12	812,102	19,136	26,568	15,990	18,797	27,665	17,377	11,329	13,987	105,145
Congressional District 13	711,672	17,349	25,300	14,639	19,929	26,902	20,357	14,007	12,974	108,808
Congressional District 14	763,380	19,562	26,355	15,295	20,630	29,146	17,931	11,492	11,692	106,186
Congressional District 15	795,511	13,748	20,301	11,227	17,099	21,372	14,506	13,624	8,113	85,941
Congressional District 16	733,764	14,748	22,496	12,302	17,091	21,542	17,802	11,095	11,872	91,704
Congressional District 17	793,513	13,742	23,344	14,637	20,102	25,659	17,167	11,376	9,395	98,336
Congressional District 18	801,885	18,015	22,367	13,265	14,205	21,072	13,645	8,067	6,268	76,522
Congressional District 19	731,759	17,002	22,599	14,963	17,959	21,870	19,378	13,732	12,454	100,356
Congressional District 20	846,337	18,220	20,453	12,688	19,650	23,147	17,704	10,480	10,309	93,978
Congressional District 21	818,281	22,993	29,797	16,580	26,569	35,550	22,695	14,108	15,849	131,351
Congressional District 22	935,386	19,124	31,472	17,334	21,040	29,042	16,116	11,917	8,944	104,393
Congressional District 23	794,879	18,246	24,070	14,403	20,313	30,224	16,934	14,095	9,894	105,863
Congressional District 24	817,147	20,855	26,135	13,102	17,662	23,496	16,390	11,531	9,516	91,697
Congressional District 25	786,976	17,573	24,547	16,557	23,022	31,810	20,064	13,611	10,595	115,659
Congressional District 26	894,192	18,808	25,642	12,321	18,036	27,134	15,106	9,338	8,275	90,210
Congressional District 27	739,719	18,400	27,404	17,997	24,827	27,589	21,186	13,724	13,632	118,955
Congressional District 28	768,719	12,520	21,031	10,383	17,732	23,797	16,828	10,041	11,026	89,807
Congressional District 29	765,435	14,094	20,186	12,413	14,141	16,004	9,396	7,865	4,622	64,441
Congressional District 30	804,679	18,793	24,225	15,143	18,758	23,140	12,599	7,281	9,766	86,687
Congressional District 31	883,347	16,438	26,276	14,451	20,446	30,936	17,784	12,388	10,376	106,381
Congressional District 32	769,852	20,093	24,338	14,768	17,221	24,868	17,041	11,534	10,419	95,901
Congressional District 33	777,745	15,507	18,495	11,705	14,589	18,422	11,614	6,265	6,045	68,640
Congressional District 34	727,688	13,829	20,337	10,873	18,809	26,043	18,500	14,177	13,582	101,984
Congressional District 35	818,369	17,495	23,355	13,530	18,161	21,137	13,765	7,545	9,166	83,304
Congressional District 36	754,178	19,112	26,748	16,039	19,571	32,428	20,041	12,506	10,797	111,382
Utah										
Congressional District 1	776,910	15,290	22,640	14,463	17,066	20,225	12,608	10,213	8,227	82,802
Congressional District 2	779,772	17,994	23,739	13,770	21,388	25,800	17,770	14,555	10,977	104,260
Congressional District 3	773,622	12,220	21,333	11,099	15,948	23,393	15,503	10,489	8,610	85,042
Congressional District 4	830,801	14,215	20,421	11,917	15,035	22,102	13,273	9,417	7,449	79,193
Vermont										
Congressional District (at Large)	626,299	19,275	29,759	18,940	24,188	32,627	21,829	13,142	13,149	123,875
Virginia										
Congressional District 1	813,878	19,264	30,016	16,260	26,179	32,178	22,890	15,350	11,055	123,912
Congressional District 2	743,410	19,736	24,835	15,196	24,364	27,264	18,590	12,494	14,337	112,245
Congressional District 3	744,804	19,843	24,074	14,915	18,246	25,425	18,277	12,003	11,560	100,426
Congressional District 4	747,291	20,917	30,404	17,216	23,524	29,531	18,834	12,937	13,086	115,128
Congressional District 5	739,410	22,237	30,350	19,885	28,518	38,560	27,017	19,180	17,180	150,340
Congressional District 6	755,437	21,452	30,172	19,176	26,354	34,209	26,231	17,672	17,516	141,158
Congressional District 7	812,385	17,545	33,837	19,541	24,390	33,422	22,656	14,633	13,592	128,234
Congressional District 8	795,467	18,103	23,552	14,323	17,843	24,424	16,295	11,421	12,418	96,724
Congressional District 9	704,831	20,369	29,449	18,378	27,960	37,568	27,923	17,090	16,901	145,820
Congressional District 10	862,308	21,692	26,398	16,327	22,167	27,375	20,581	11,149	10,804	108,403
Congressional District 11	798,464	19,001	25,779	14,814	19,569	24,401	16,683	10,631	9,737	95,835

Table B-5: 116th Congressional Districts - Older Population by Age—*Continued*

	Total Population	60 to 61 Years	62 to 64 Years	65 to 66 Years	67 to 69 Years	70 to 74 Years	75 to 79 Years	80 to 84 Years	85 Years and Over	65 Years and Over
Washington										
Congressional District 1	768,363	20,924	28,193	16,545	21,292	27,538	15,626	10,332	10,330	101,663
Congressional District 2	755,546	21,490	29,745	17,425	23,506	34,959	23,107	12,629	13,704	125,330
Congressional District 3	743,322	20,329	31,509	18,314	25,931	35,742	21,757	14,712	12,302	128,758
Congressional District 4	735,031	15,451	26,290	16,122	19,023	28,435	17,952	11,711	10,744	103,987
Congressional District 5	725,964	19,687	27,572	15,987	22,799	36,135	22,962	14,525	13,433	125,841
Congressional District 6	731,742	20,868	31,689	22,632	28,756	41,302	27,796	13,103	14,005	147,594
Congressional District 7	799,589	16,606	24,558	17,405	23,705	30,137	17,529	10,703	14,641	114,120
Congressional District 8	754,721	22,619	28,332	16,290	20,067	26,795	18,584	10,831	10,286	102,853
Congressional District 9	765,285	17,350	24,249	14,752	18,018	25,550	16,750	12,892	15,070	103,032
Congressional District 10	756,028	17,880	27,092	15,945	21,698	27,976	19,986	11,663	13,541	110,809
West Virginia										
Congressional District 1	606,136	16,452	25,008	14,522	25,452	29,716	21,911	14,498	14,120	120,219
Congressional District 2	624,120	17,512	27,929	19,396	25,868	27,663	20,548	13,895	12,985	120,355
Congressional District 3	575,576	19,185	25,116	17,145	25,291	30,237	22,197	12,658	13,114	120,642
Wisconsin										
Congressional District 1	717,716	22,449	27,959	17,751	23,421	28,722	19,410	15,144	14,128	118,576
Congressional District 2	768,067	20,579	25,935	16,406	23,708	28,685	18,497	13,628	14,792	115,716
Congressional District 3	724,568	19,906	30,619	18,704	23,747	32,279	23,484	15,368	16,324	129,906
Congressional District 4	710,573	17,836	24,096	13,520	18,134	21,221	13,201	8,651	12,267	86,994
Congressional District 5	731,341	23,064	32,442	17,539	22,765	33,118	23,305	17,737	18,038	132,502
Congressional District 6	714,886	23,513	29,197	17,939	26,453	30,710	23,212	15,455	18,362	132,131
Congressional District 7	710,420	23,020	33,063	19,874	26,587	37,233	25,955	18,001	16,961	144,611
Congressional District 8	735,997	22,031	29,546	17,529	24,626	31,001	23,416	15,592	13,883	126,047
Wyoming										
Congressional District (at Large)	577,737	17,661	23,770	13,385	22,474	23,608	17,470	10,362	9,258	96,557

PART C
RACE AND ETHNICITY

RACE AND ETHNICITY

While it is clear that the nation's population continues to grow more diverse, these tables show how diversity is not uniform across the country and how large differences occur at smaller geographic levels. Racial and ethnic identification in the Census is obtained in a number of different ways including direct questions on race and Hispanic Origin. Other questions obtain data on ancestry, language spoken at home, and place of birth.

The Census and American Community Survey also allow for respondents to identify with more than one racial group. The term race "Alone" means the respondent identifies with that single racial group. Those who identify with two or more racial groups are identified here as "Multi-race". Hispanic Origin is obtained in a separate question. The tables in this section present only selected major response categories which are not exhaustive – White, Non-Hispanic; Black Alone; Asian Alone; Multi-race; and Hispanic. A relatively small number of individuals identify themselves as "some other race" and are not included here. The American Indian and Alaskan Native population is also a relatively small population but very important in specific areas. Summary data for this population is included in a separate table.

Unlike many other tables in this volume, the ACS sample population counts by race and Hispanic Origin are often too small to be reported. As a result, the Census files do not report results for these categories and they are indicated here by "na". It is important to also note that the

Percent of Persons 65 Years and Over
Who are Minority (Not - White, Non-Hispanic)

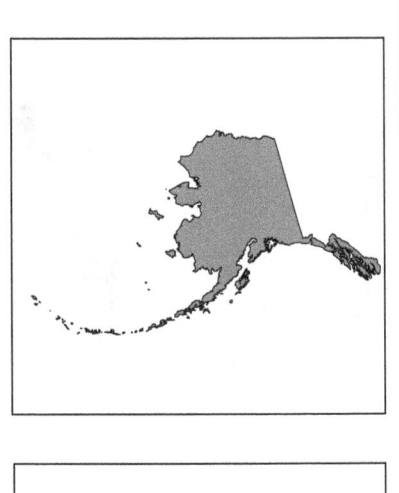
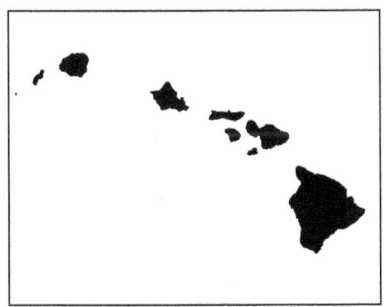
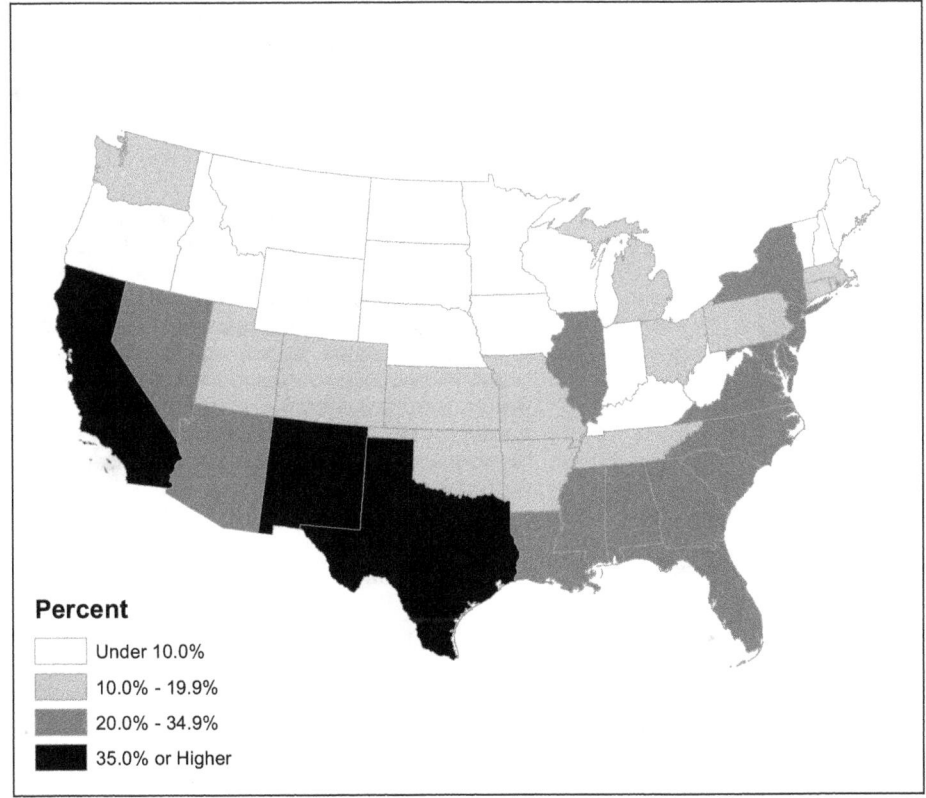

Percent

☐	Under 10.0%
☐	10.0% - 19.9%
☐	20.0% - 34.9%
☐	35.0% or Higher

age structure of many minority populations are younger than the White population due to historic immigration and fertility patterns. Part C – Race and Ethnicity presents data only for the population age 65 and over and therefore may exhibit different distributions of the racial and Hispanic Origin population than for the general population. For example, in the White Non-Hispanic population, 20.3 percent are age 65 and over but among the Hispanic population, only 7.4 percent are 65 and over. Those who identify as Multi-race are even lower at 5.3 percent which may result from a larger number of mixed race children.

In the nation as a whole, 76.5 percent of the population age 65 and over is White, Non-Hispanic which means that nearly one out of every four (23.5 percent) people over age 65 identifies with some minority group. Across states, the proportion of the 65 and over population that is White, Non-Hispanic population ranges from a low of 26.8 percent in the State of Hawaii to a high of 97.3 percent in the State of Maine. Thirty-four states have a higher proportion of White, Non-Hispanic population than the national average. Among the 65 year and over population, Hawaii and the District of Columbia are both "majority minority" which means their proportion of minority populations is actually greater than 50 percent. In Hawaii, 73.2 percent of the population identifies with a minority group (mostly Asian Alone and Multi-race) while in the District of Columbia, 65.9 percent of the 65 and over population is minority and mostly Black Alone.

Seven states have less than one percent of their 65 and over population that is Black Alone while in six states, more than one of every five people 65 and over is Black Alone. Not surprising, Hawaii has the largest percentage of 65 and over population that is Asian Alone at 53.7 percent with California a distant second at 16.0 percent. Every other state is less than ten percent Asian Alone and 13 states are less than 1 percent. Hawaii is also the state with the highest Multi-race population at 10.6 percent but Oklahoma has the second highest proportion at 3.5 percent. At 32.6 percent, New Mexico has the highest percentage of Hispanic population age 65 and over followed by Texas (23.1 percent) and California (20.3 percent). Six states are less than 1 percent Hispanic but nine states have more than the U.S. average of 8.4 percent.

Black Alone

For the age 65 and over population, the District of Columbia (57.1 percent), Mississippi (27.5 percent), Louisiana (25.2 percent), Maryland (24.6 percent), Georgia (23.5 percent) and South Carolina (20.5 percent) are the only states with proportions over 20 percent. Among the 427 counties with reported populations, 75 are greater than 20 percent Black Alone with Prince George's County, Maryland having the highest percentage at 66.5 percent. There are 111 counties with at least some Black Alone population over age 65 but less than 5.0 percent. South Fulton, Georgia, at 89.0 percent, is the city with the

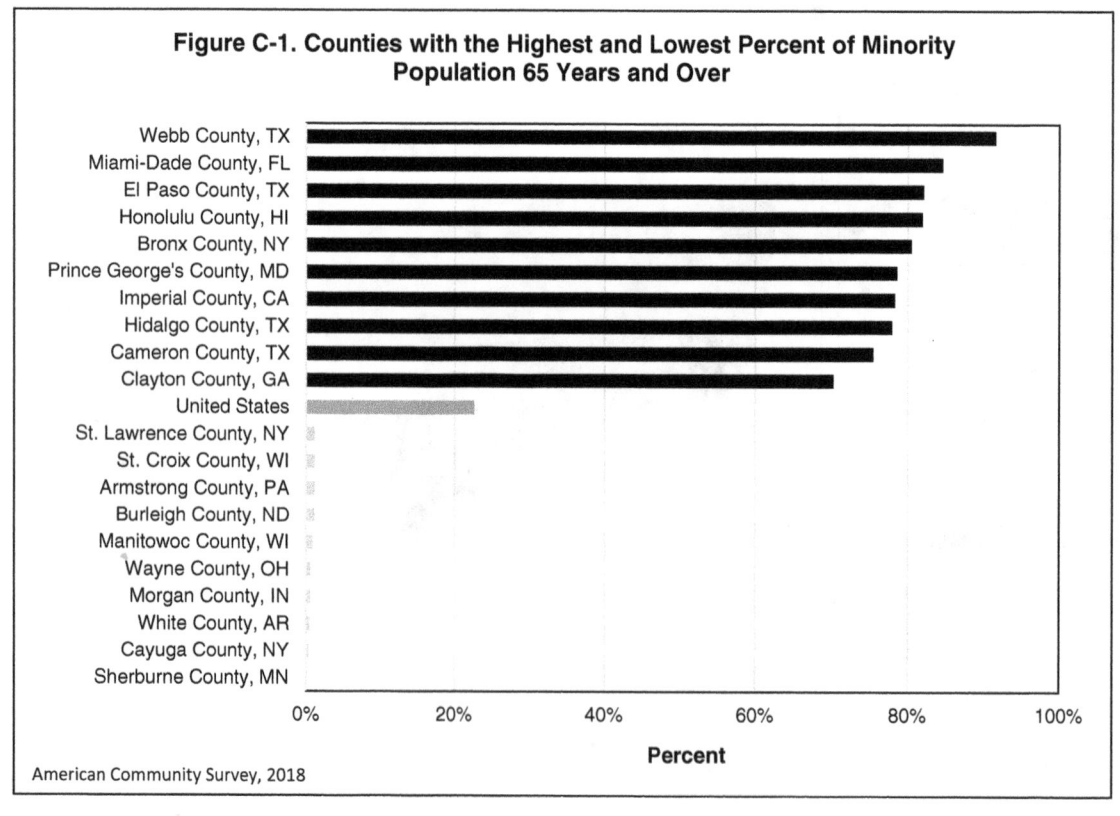

Figure C-1. Counties with the Highest and Lowest Percent of Minority Population 65 Years and Over

American Community Survey, 2018

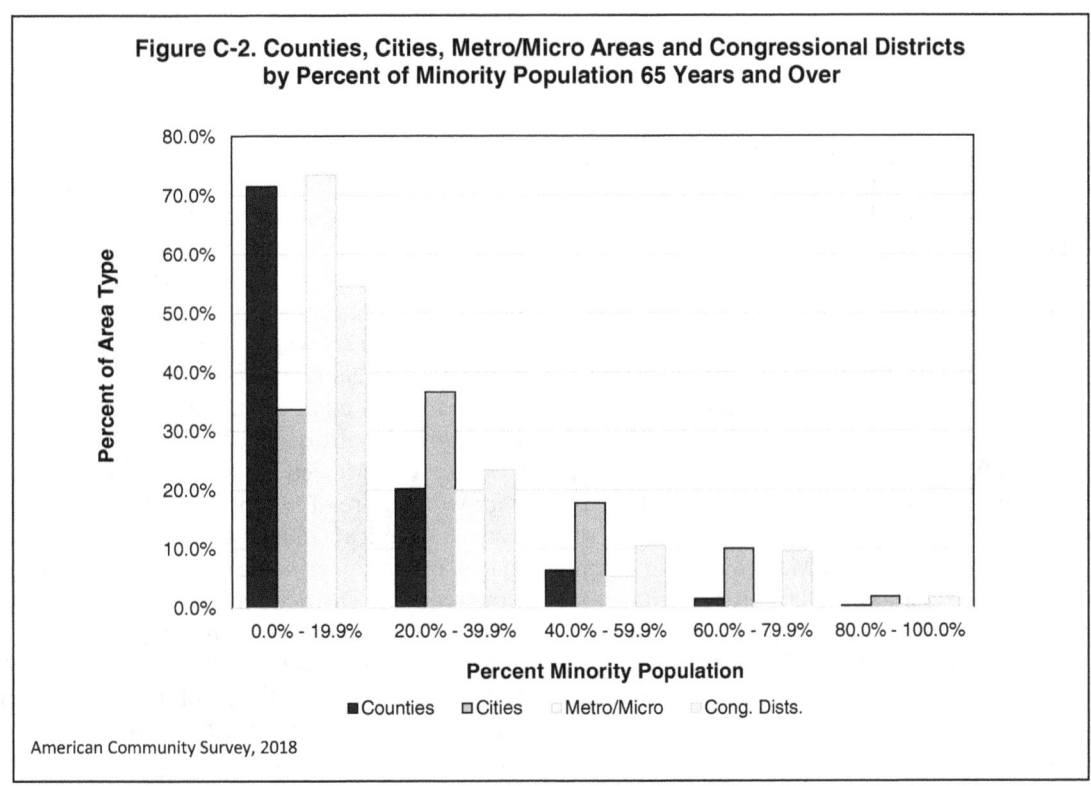

Figure C-2. Counties, Cities, Metro/Micro Areas and Congressional Districts by Percent of Minority Population 65 Years and Over

American Community Survey, 2018

highest proportion of Black Alone population. It is followed closely by East Orange, New Jersey (87.4 percent), Detroit, Michigan (83.2 percent) and Gary, Indiana at 81.3 percent. In 22 cities the Black Alone population is a majority of the total 65 and over population. The Orangeburg, South Carolina metropolitan area has the highest proportion of Black Alone population at 53.0 percent. More than one out of every five people age 65 and over are Black Alone in 52 metropolitan areas. Congressional District 5 in Georgia has the largest proportion of Black Alone at 65.4 percent followed by district 3 in Pennsylvania at 63.2 percent. Fifteen districts are a majority Black Alone.

Asian Alone

Nationally, 4.5 percent of the 65 and over population is Asian Alone. Of the 814 counties reported here, only 261 have large enough Asian Alone populations to be reported in the 2018 ACS. Ninety-two counties exceed that average with Honolulu, Hawaii having the highest proportion at 63.4 percent. Seven other counties have at least 25 percent Asian Alone including the California counties of Alameda (30.0 percent), San Francisco (44.8 percent), San Mateo (28.7 percent) and Santa Clara (34.3 percent) and the Hawaiian counties of Hawaii (29.8 percent), Kauai (41.7 percent) and Maui (38.4 percent). Urban Honolulu, Hawaii Census Designated Place has the highest percentage of 65 and over that is

Asian Alone at 71.9 percent followed closely by Milpitas City, California at 70.0 percent. Five other California cities have more than 50 percent Asian Alone population and 108 cities are well above the national average at over 10 percent. Only four metro/micropolitan areas have greater than 30 percent Asian Alone population. Three are in Hawaii – Urban Honolulu (63.4 percent), the Kapaa, Hawaii micropolitan area (41.7 percent), Kahului-Wailuku-Lahaina (38.4 percent) and one in California – San Jose-Sunnyvale-Santa Clara, CA metropolitan area at 33.5 percent. Congressional District 1 in Hawaii has the highest proportion at 69.0 followed by California's 17th and 12th Congressional Districts at 49.9 percent and 44.3 percent, respectively. Nineteen other districts have more than 20 percent Asian Alone: 13 of which are in California with two in New York and one each in Hawaii and Washington State.

Multi-race

The four Hawaiian counties also have the largest proportion of Multi-race 65 and over population: Hawaii at 11.6 percent, Kauai at 11.2 percent, Honolulu at 10.6 percent and Maui at 8.9 percent. Muskogee County, Oklahoma has 5.0 percent of Multi-race population over 65 greater, respectively. Nationally, about 1.1 percent of the 65 and over population identifies as Multi-race and 188 counties exceed that level.

Hispanic

The Hispanic population has grown to more than 59.7 million people in the United States or 18.3 percent of the total population. Among those 65 years and over, 8.4 percent are Hispanic. California has the largest Hispanic population over 65 at nearly 1,151,000 followed by Texas at 832,400 and Florida at 668,200. However, New Mexico has the largest percentage of Hispanic population over the age of 65 at 32.6 percent. North and South Dakota have the smallest absolute number of Hispanic population, both at less than 1,000 while West Virginia has the smallest percentage. Webb County, Texas has the largest percentage of its Hispanic population in the 65 and over age group at 91.3 percent followed by El Paso County, Texas at 78.2 percent. The 65 and over population is more than 25 percent Hispanic in 34 counties, most of which are in California (10), New Mexico (6) and Texas (10). Hialeah City, Florida has the largest percentage of Hispanic 65 and over at 96.6 percent. In 27 cities the 65 and over population is a majority Hispanic and 96 cities are more than 25 percent Hispanic 65 and over. At the metropolitan area level, Laredo, Texas is the largest percentage with 91.3 percent Hispanic 65 and over. El Paso, Texas is the next largest with 78.1 percent. Five metropolitan areas are over 70 percent. California's 40th Congressional District has the largest percentage at 77.3 percent. California has 13 districts where more than 30 percent of the 65 and over population is Hispanic while Texas has the second highest at 10 districts.

Native American

The American Indian and Alaska Native population is a small proportion of the nation's total and is not included in the data tables because most of the areas would have no data reported. However, the American Indian and Alaska Native population is also concentrated in specific areas and represents an important segment of those communities. Many of these areas are in states with federal or state reservations but not all. Included in the following table are areas where at least five percent of the total population is Native American. This includes 16 counties, 2 cities, 13 metropolitan and micropolitan areas and 13 congressional districts. Within these areas, McKinley County, New Mexico which is the Gallup, New Mexico micropolitan area (79.7 percent) has the largest proportion of American Indian and Alaska Native population that is 65 and over while Tulsa County, Oklahoma and Congressional District 3 in Arizona are lowest at just 5.0 percent. Apache County and Navajo County, Arizona, McKinley County and San Juan County, New Mexico and Robeson County, North Carolina, are all counties with more than 30 percent Native American. Additionally, the Farmington, New Mexico metropolitan area, the Gallup, New Mexico micropolitan area, the Lumberton, North Carolina micropolitan area and the Show Low, Arizona micropolitan area are also greater than 30 percent Native American.

Percent Native American/Alaskan Native for Areas with 5 Percent or More Native American/Alaskan Native Popoulation

	Percent of Total Population	Percent of Population 65 Years or Over		Percent of Total Population	Percent of Population 65 Years or Over
Counties					
Anchorage Municipality, Alaska	7.6%	9.7%	Pennington County, South Dakota	9.5%	6.2%
Apache County, Arizona	75.0%	11.9%	Pottawatomie County, Oklahoma	12.9%	9.2%
Coconino County, Arizona	26.7%	9.0%	Robeson County, North Carolina	40.5%	13.5%
Creek County, Oklahoma	10.5%	11.2%	Rogers County, Oklahoma	13.6%	11.2%
Matanuska-Susitna Borough, Alaska	7.7%	6.8%	San Juan County, New Mexico	40.0%	10.8%
McKinley County, New Mexico	79.7%	10.4%	Sandoval County, New Mexico	12.4%	9.6%
Muskogee County, Oklahoma	18.0%	8.9%	Tulsa County, Oklahoma	5.0%	9.1%
Navajo County, Arizona	45.2%	11.3%	Wagoner County, Oklahoma	9.1%	9.2%
Places					
Anchorage municipality, Alaska	7.6%	9.7%	Norman city, Oklahoma	5.3%	1.7%
Metropolitan Statistical Areas					
Albuquerque, New Mexico Metro Area	5.7%	9.7%	Lumberton, North Carolina Micro Area	40.5%	13.5%
Anchorage, Alaska Metro Area	7.6%	8.9%	Muskogee, Oklahoma Micro Area	18.0%	8.9%
Bismarck, North Dakota Metro Area	6.4%	3.9%	Rapid City, South Dakota Metro Area	8.3%	5.4%
Farmington, New Mexico Metro Area	40.0%	10.8%	Shawnee, Oklahoma Micro Area	12.9%	9.2%
Flagstaff, Arizona Metro Area	26.7%	9.0%	Show Low, Arizona Micro Area	45.2%	11.3%
Fort Smith, Arkansas-Oklahoma Metro Area	6.1%	11.1%	Tulsa, Oklahoma Metro Area	7.3%	10.3%
Gallup, New Mexico Micro Area	79.7%	10.4%			
116th Congressional Districts					
Congressional District (at Large) (116th Congress), Alaska	15.1%	9.7%	Congressional District (at Large) (116th Congress), North Dakota	6.1%	6.5%
Congressional District 1 (116th Congress), Arizona	23.5%	10.1%	Congressional District 1 (116th Congress), Oklahoma	9.8%	8.6%
Congressional District 3 (116th Congress), Arizona	5.0%	9.3%	Congressional District 2 (116th Congress), Oklahoma	10.9%	10.3%
Congressional District (at Large) (116th Congress), Montana	6.4%	9.1%	Congressional District 3 (116th Congress), Oklahoma	10.9%	8.4%
Congressional District 2 (116th Congress), New Mexico	5.6%	13.7%	Congressional District 4 (116th Congress), Oklahoma	7.0%	8.9%
Congressional District 3 (116th Congress), New Mexico	18.9%	10.8%	Congressional District (at Large) (116th Congress), South Dakota	6.3%	6.1%
Congressional District 9 (116th Congress), North Carolina	7.8%	13.5%			

Table C-1: States - Older Population by Race and Hispanic Origin

Name	Total Population		White, Non-Hispanic		Black, Alone		Asian, Alone		Multi-race, Alone		Hispanic	
	65 Years and Over	85 Years and Over	65 Years and Over	85 Years and Over	65 Years and Over	85 Years and Over	65 Years and Over	85 Years and Over	65 Years and Over	85 Years and Over	65 Years and Over	85 Years and Over
United States	52,423,114	6,303,848	40,077,660	5,048,663	4,853,097	473,494	2,368,901	253,405	599,134	51,524	4,405,949	468,207
Alabama.................................	829,663	85,242	639,098	66,633	163,513	15,995	7,026	465	7,459	693	10,307	1,202
Alaska...................................	88,000	7,370	64,478	5,484	2,413	393	5,614	544	2,336	232	2,613	0
Arizona..................................	1,259,103	132,739	1,001,865	110,448	30,381	2,331	28,798	2,745	17,347	1,049	160,071	13,658
Arkansas................................	507,676	56,169	438,155	49,531	51,632	4,976	3,236	52	5,257	471	7,546	1,031
California...............................	5,667,337	729,580	3,205,624	439,359	296,969	33,487	904,857	118,545	112,701	11,717	1,150,551	126,562
Colorado................................	807,855	87,406	672,119	75,565	21,132	1,798	18,970	1,574	9,111	280	85,120	7,687
Connecticut............................	613,147	87,696	515,600	79,933	41,938	3,638	14,614	997	4,362	374	37,639	2,913
Delaware................................	180,756	18,604	143,971	16,293	26,466	1,837	4,419	131	900	0	4,194	226
District of Columbia	85,626	10,901	29,184	3,372	48,883	7,062	2,297	83	1,578	218	4,636	256
Florida...................................	4,358,784	561,000	3,186,708	422,356	391,842	37,853	85,053	6,618	45,164	4,028	668,222	92,352
Georgia..................................	1,456,428	142,800	1,019,102	105,908	342,360	28,939	39,504	4,063	12,779	951	40,383	3,226
Hawaii...................................	261,467	40,073	70,089	7,537	1,451	0	140,530	27,691	27,651	2,819	8,160	524
Idaho....................................	279,441	29,703	258,687	28,034	975	69	3,965	672	3,098	56	9,518	490
Illinois..................................	1,990,548	259,568	1,518,523	214,060	230,409	24,377	90,426	7,197	15,312	1,226	137,496	12,783
Indiana..................................	1,051,146	126,577	947,062	114,984	66,074	7,244	11,586	1,045	5,812	539	19,998	2,765
Iowa.....................................	537,818	75,616	517,908	74,083	5,719	112	4,976	282	1,989	233	6,327	749
Kansas...................................	462,191	63,786	414,488	59,108	17,995	2,437	6,843	404	3,946	268	17,608	1,367
Kentucky................................	731,392	78,648	672,896	72,987	40,326	4,343	4,941	288	4,776	283	7,406	836
Louisiana...............................	720,610	73,844	504,109	57,138	181,566	14,294	7,834	313	5,747	519	19,042	1,502
Maine....................................	276,069	34,849	268,753	34,387	923	0	1,822	167	1,928	20	1,948	234
Maryland................................	931,041	108,515	609,781	78,788	228,662	21,177	49,097	4,770	12,754	927	31,651	2,746
Massachusetts.........................	1,137,541	153,729	979,189	140,164	52,044	4,783	43,494	3,701	10,656	507	52,423	3,167
Michigan................................	1,720,453	204,293	1,459,515	177,736	177,656	19,307	29,676	2,130	16,445	1,919	32,891	2,878
Minnesota..............................	888,634	115,373	831,764	110,933	19,556	1,431	17,161	1,765	5,358	456	10,583	652
Mississippi.............................	474,423	46,360	335,316	35,666	130,312	9,910	2,229	178	2,118	70	3,932	503
Missouri................................	1,035,074	124,805	914,512	112,073	81,059	10,016	11,580	434	9,969	1,011	15,499	1,047
Montana................................	200,239	20,753	187,264	19,879	na	na	1,283	207	2,766	113	2,436	166
Nebraska................................	303,998	41,952	281,560	39,756	7,198	913	3,266	273	2,486	21	8,843	965
Nevada..................................	475,120	44,280	336,074	32,956	31,286	2,091	45,404	2,838	6,844	758	52,968	5,521
New Hampshire........................	245,156	30,824	236,251	30,049	1,112	269	2,199	105	1,810	100	3,000	448
New Jersey	1,438,289	195,758	1,032,365	156,239	148,935	14,777	100,739	7,773	14,628	976	148,362	16,653
New Mexico	368,480	40,735	213,343	23,736	7,225	1,014	4,383	65	5,303	466	120,209	13,826
New York................................	3,212,065	432,629	2,211,876	326,586	409,461	45,842	217,006	19,978	46,347	3,237	363,849	39,569
North Carolina.........................	1,688,574	179,067	1,315,904	147,569	285,766	24,783	25,662	1,608	13,514	1,179	35,035	3,901
North Dakota...........................	116,433	18,439	111,517	17,992	302	0	549	0	535	97	898	120
Ohio.....................................	1,996,163	248,285	1,747,398	222,500	180,251	19,425	25,434	2,830	13,249	811	27,190	2,493
Oklahoma...............................	619,601	72,583	511,275	64,176	31,930	3,324	8,329	282	21,391	1,463	15,579	913
Oregon..................................	739,611	81,382	667,253	75,017	7,555	434	20,703	2,092	12,251	1,107	26,456	2,322
Pennsylvania...........................	2,332,369	313,640	2,054,641	285,626	168,586	19,661	45,919	3,382	12,806	1,119	52,222	4,166
Rhode Island...........................	182,645	26,459	161,166	24,238	5,932	349	2,987	399	1,912	205	9,723	995
South Carolina.........................	899,754	84,772	686,405	67,936	184,692	15,157	7,417	431	5,295	276	14,817	991
South Dakota...........................	146,358	21,761	138,504	21,219	925	149	667	0	408	0	961	25
Tennessee...............................	1,104,797	113,462	949,949	99,133	121,270	11,236	11,079	854	7,327	680	13,788	1,241
Texas....................................	3,599,599	382,935	2,252,675	260,087	332,771	28,253	144,380	8,911	37,484	4,103	832,421	82,480
Utah.....................................	351,297	35,263	315,582	32,720	1,806	119	7,137	499	2,574	162	21,615	1,529
Vermont.................................	123,875	13,149	117,695	12,799	1,397	0	1,526	34	1,672	198	1,015	0
Virginia..................................	1,318,225	148,186	993,080	116,045	207,046	21,579	63,050	5,168	14,820	1,650	40,043	3,673
Washington.............................	1,163,987	128,056	988,422	114,030	24,035	2,435	78,290	7,825	18,424	1,056	42,581	2,292
West Virginia...........................	361,216	40,219	343,831	38,730	10,999	1,001	1,638	141	1,824	174	2,318	304
Wisconsin...............................	986,483	124,755	917,267	118,442	30,361	2,874	9,306	856	6,296	707	18,604	1,666
Wyoming	96,557	9,258	87,867	8,643	na	na	na	na	615	0	5,252	592

Table C-2: Counties - Older Population by Race and Hispanic Origin

Name	Total Population 65 Years and Over	Total Population 85 Years and Over	White, Non-Hispanic 65 Years and Over	White, Non-Hispanic 85 Years and Over	Black, Alone 65 Years and Over	Black, Alone 85 Years and Over	Asian, Alone 65 Years and Over	Asian, Alone 85 Years and Over	Multi-race, Alone 65 Years and Over	Multi-race, Alone 85 Years and Over	Hispanic 65 Years and Over	Hispanic 85 Years and Over
Alabama												
Baldwin County	44,443	3,827	40,873	3,743	2,361	0	na	na	na	na	609	0
Calhoun County	20,515	1,761	16,721	1,262	3,066	499	na	na	na	na	na	na
Cullman County	15,541	855	14,820	855	na	na	na	na	na	na	na	na
DeKalb County	12,261	1,542	11,644	1,392	na	na	na	na	na	na	na	na
Elmore County	12,299	985	10,670	985	939	0	na	na	na	na	na	na
Etowah County	19,632	2,194	16,984	1,764	2,192	381	na	na	na	na	na	na
Houston County	18,790	1,854	14,828	1,469	3,439	317	na	na	na	na	282	52
Jefferson County	104,700	11,594	65,372	8,414	36,474	2,846	890	93	1,076	27	576	214
Lauderdale County	18,419	2,162	16,977	1,946	921	153	na	na	na	na	na	na
Lee County	19,887	1,776	15,053	1,446	3,602	277	na	na	na	na	na	na
Limestone County	15,095	1,796	12,709	1,718	1,394	0	na	na	na	na	na	na
Madison County	55,665	5,334	42,849	4,741	9,447	428	1,416	83	969	53	1,168	0
Marshall County	16,487	1,756	15,541	1,756	na	na	na	na	na	na	555	0
Mobile County	66,558	6,972	45,801	4,584	18,376	1,877	na	na	na	na	958	335
Montgomery County	34,276	3,875	18,533	1,896	14,635	1,947	465	0	na	na	191	0
Morgan County	20,464	2,547	18,553	2,547	1,382	0	na	na	na	na	na	na
St. Clair County	14,760	1,336	13,581	1,204	na	na	na	na	na	na	na	na
Shelby County	33,295	3,025	29,741	2,378	2,193	262	na	na	na	na	na	na
Talladega County	14,422	1,273	10,742	1,012	3,473	104	na	na	na	na	na	na
Tuscaloosa County	27,472	2,537	20,604	1,831	6,424	687	na	na	na	na	na	na
Walker County	12,061	1,159	11,549	1,055	na	na	na	na	na	na	na	na
Alaska												
Anchorage Municipality	32,809	3,056	23,241	2,225	1,555	70	3,575	395	638	143	1,461	0
Fairbanks North Star Borough	10,213	866	8,559	721	na	na	na	na	na	na	na	na
Matanuska-Susitna Borough	13,051	1,291	11,418	933	na	na	na	na	498	89	177	0
Arizona												
Apache County	10,932	1,303	3,688	164	na	na	na	na	na	na	na	na
Cochise County	28,402	3,174	21,121	2,640	na	na	na	na	na	na	5,443	223
Coconino County	17,813	1,440	12,480	694	na	na	na	na	na	na	1,318	158
Maricopa County	669,199	77,143	541,016	67,112	21,732	1,473	20,526	2,068	6,838	452	76,708	5,997
Mohave County	63,794	5,643	56,949	5,643	na	na	na	na	na	na	4,307	0
Navajo County	20,162	2,184	12,728	1,215	na	na	na	na	na	na	1,290	307
Pima County	205,547	21,309	157,411	16,291	4,331	671	4,484	404	4,210	172	35,414	3,773
Pinal County	90,825	6,164	75,033	5,236	2,133	0	na	na	1,834	35	10,439	706
Yavapai County	73,656	7,371	67,665	6,962	na	na	na	na	na	na	3,569	215
Yuma County	39,979	3,154	26,342	2,202	na	na	na	na	na	na	12,110	856
Arkansas												
Benton County	36,290	4,673	33,705	3,849	na	na	439	0	368	177	1,535	479
Craighead County	15,167	1,102	13,974	1,102	968	0	na	na	na	na	na	na
Faulkner County	15,720	1,549	14,262	1,541	925	8	na	na	na	na	na	na
Garland County	22,991	2,956	21,775	2,784	na	na	na	na	na	na	na	na
Jefferson County	11,671	1,715	6,449	1,291	5,106	424	na	na	na	na	na	na
Lonoke County	9,757	963	8,915	643	na	na	na	na	na	na	na	na
Pulaski County	61,104	7,487	44,138	6,063	14,758	1,291	410	0	196	0	1,460	133
Saline County	21,793	2,148	20,376	1,711	na	na	na	na	na	na	na	na
Sebastian County	20,168	2,045	17,748	1,968	1,201	0	na	na	na	na	829	77
Washington County	26,922	3,243	25,354	3,022	na	na	na	na	na	na	798	221
White County	12,307	1,307	12,254	1,307	na	na	na	na	na	na	na	na
California												
Alameda County	230,510	27,564	102,853	11,892	26,560	2,916	69,084	9,559	4,613	555	25,575	2,360
Butte County	42,820	4,441	37,651	4,273	na	na	1,224	128	950	0	2,706	40
Contra Costa County	181,267	20,195	113,592	13,520	13,814	1,069	30,202	3,180	5,423	205	20,517	2,224
El Dorado County	40,427	4,453	35,849	4,155	na	na	1,304	206	728	85	2,127	0
Fresno County	121,540	17,185	65,947	10,483	4,791	426	11,175	1,370	2,594	114	37,841	4,726
Humboldt County	24,296	2,817	21,473	2,541	na	na	na	na	778	176	809	167
Imperial County	23,512	2,645	5,103	643	na	na	na	na	na	na	17,325	2,002
Kern County	98,076	10,676	58,672	6,975	4,126	60	6,031	502	1,927	398	27,190	2,893
Kings County	15,413	1,412	8,391	955	na	na	na	na	na	na	5,374	300
Lake County	14,856	1,161	12,510	1,129	na	na	na	na	na	na	1,268	0
Los Angeles County	1,375,959	192,748	550,896	86,259	120,547	16,505	271,157	38,315	28,835	3,278	412,316	48,709
Madera County	22,099	2,668	13,950	2,083	na	na	na	na	na	na	6,026	585
Marin County	58,213	6,346	50,806	5,420	na	na	3,151	269	615	176	2,806	573
Mendocino County	19,072	1,475	16,815	1,415	na	na	na	na	na	na	1,336	0
Merced County	30,748	3,475	16,051	2,070	1,229	134	2,373	298	404	131	10,848	921
Monterey County	59,491	8,363	35,904	5,027	1,603	226	5,459	1,171	1,128	141	15,372	1,749
Napa County	26,805	2,708	20,762	2,393	na	na	1,989	130	534	0	3,181	99
Nevada County	27,746	3,152	25,467	3,152	na	na	na	na	na	na	na	na
Orange County	471,226	65,417	280,510	43,194	6,596	180	103,282	11,566	6,448	1,131	72,754	9,173
Placer County	76,749	9,123	65,212	8,039	na	na	4,638	427	650	100	5,123	557
Riverside County	353,025	42,890	220,996	32,140	19,393	1,435	24,664	1,719	5,289	693	82,150	6,921
Sacramento County	217,444	27,506	136,190	17,306	17,212	1,842	34,438	5,253	5,156	497	23,708	2,904
San Bernardino County	251,168	25,753	123,537	14,727	20,100	1,723	23,505	1,449	5,280	284	79,260	7,453
San Diego County	469,821	59,080	304,575	40,536	16,407	1,596	57,913	6,956	8,135	1,007	82,280	9,371
San Francisco County	138,128	22,842	53,430	7,344	7,532	1,748	61,869	11,213	2,558	445	12,672	2,198
San Joaquin County	95,844	10,931	51,612	6,699	6,095	957	15,669	1,725	3,780	30	20,634	1,581
San Luis Obispo County	57,594	6,503	49,535	5,859	na	na	na	na	1,176	199	4,786	207
San Mateo County	124,038	18,768	65,927	11,006	3,286	524	35,560	4,567	2,416	50	15,869	2,408
Santa Barbara County	68,402	9,638	49,482	7,103	1,072	146	3,098	708	1,080	142	13,784	1,500
Santa Clara County	261,252	37,517	125,113	20,891	5,529	377	89,735	11,074	4,954	825	35,874	4,051

Table C-2: Counties - Older Population by Race and Hispanic Origin—*Continued*

Name	Total Population		White, Non-Hispanic		Black, Alone		Asian, Alone		Multi-race, Alone		Hispanic	
	65 Years and Over	85 Years and Over	65 Years and Over	85 Years and Over	65 Years and Over	85 Years and Over	65 Years and Over	85 Years and Over	65 Years and Over	85 Years and Over	65 Years and Over	85 Years and Over
California—Cont.												
Santa Cruz County	45,349	3,835	35,991	3,152	na	na	2,024	311	1,671	142	6,291	293
Shasta County	37,027	3,952	34,065	3,579	na	na	na	na	650	0	1,542	286
Solano County	70,597	8,811	36,945	4,993	9,236	613	13,540	2,030	1,395	0	8,442	857
Sonoma County	98,030	11,980	84,141	10,706	na	na	3,266	245	1,848	0	8,455	1,018
Stanislaus County	72,507	8,557	47,597	5,937	1,921	176	4,085	652	1,465	121	16,896	1,596
Sutter County	14,863	2,269	9,543	1,403	na	na	2,246	447	na	na	2,055	305
Tulare County	52,622	6,294	29,500	4,070	na	na	1,608	257	1,163	5	19,761	1,671
Ventura County	132,219	18,528	89,603	13,540	2,102	235	11,218	1,676	1,839	130	27,995	2,978
Yolo County	27,177	3,545	19,009	2,574	na	na	2,481	468	268	51	4,886	420
Yuba County	9,383	1,029	7,350	825	na	na	na	na	na	na	1,195	110
Colorado												
Adams County	53,109	4,739	37,826	3,870	601	126	1,852	52	1,040	0	11,907	691
Arapahoe County	85,009	9,712	67,806	8,420	6,167	460	4,169	439	872	80	6,061	390
Boulder County	46,033	5,866	41,871	5,653	na	na	1,206	49	264	0	2,525	164
Broomfield County	9,618	809	8,498	761	na	na	na	na	na	na	na	na
Denver County	83,996	9,433	55,955	6,020	8,470	811	2,860	71	1,706	64	15,044	2,235
Douglas County	39,922	3,749	37,468	3,499	na	na	751	60	78	0	1,605	190
El Paso County	91,397	10,794	76,454	9,240	3,698	225	3,049	508	774	33	6,847	602
Jefferson County	95,519	11,847	85,052	10,963	na	na	2,141	241	549	0	7,092	418
Larimer County	55,002	5,527	50,924	5,407	na	na	708	55	385	0	2,434	65
Mesa County	28,801	3,950	26,848	3,725	na	na	na	na	na	na	1,645	225
Pueblo County	30,832	3,900	20,941	2,866	na	na	na	na	504	0	8,948	990
Weld County	38,223	4,080	31,520	3,439	na	na	na	na	724	0	5,698	558
Connecticut												
Fairfield County	149,824	21,890	119,026	19,724	12,357	861	5,196	389	778	104	12,685	916
Hartford County	152,674	22,534	122,250	20,077	13,965	1,591	4,065	0	1,322	62	11,787	804
Litchfield County	37,897	4,360	36,772	4,360	na	na	na	na	na	na	423	0
Middlesex County	32,442	4,339	30,727	4,339	850	0	na	na	na	na	651	0
New Haven County	148,789	22,610	122,963	20,298	12,377	763	3,071	502	946	153	9,649	894
New London County	48,314	6,115	43,176	5,419	1,819	423	1,253	29	362	0	1,522	244
Tolland County	24,281	3,147	22,609	3,070	na	na	na	na	na	na	375	0
Windham County	18,926	2,701	18,077	2,646	na	na	na	na	na	na	547	55
Delaware												
Kent County	29,812	2,980	22,420	2,499	6,206	475	na	na	na	na	382	0
New Castle County	87,093	10,165	64,031	8,726	16,295	1,012	3,230	131	654	0	2,823	226
Sussex County	63,851	5,459	57,520	5,068	3,965	350	na	na	na	na	989	0
Florida												
Alachua County	37,727	4,765	28,888	4,118	5,404	569	1,749	78	na	na	1,299	0
Bay County	30,927	3,293	27,637	2,934	1,772	211	na	na	na	na	803	16
Brevard County	141,268	20,627	119,841	17,580	9,590	1,567	2,390	455	970	95	7,922	1,010
Broward County	324,525	40,544	183,899	28,245	59,574	5,288	10,195	744	5,368	728	67,727	5,622
Charlotte County	74,321	10,912	69,039	9,677	na	na	na	na	na	na	2,061	555
Citrus County	53,832	6,810	49,928	6,601	na	na	na	na	na	na	na	na
Clay County	34,752	2,576	28,825	2,200	2,218	0	na	na	na	na	1,813	234
Collier County	122,463	18,268	108,487	16,302	3,000	263	na	na	na	na	8,703	1,444
Columbia County	12,978	1,628	10,963	1,581	1,284	0	na	na	na	na	na	na
Duval County	133,599	14,134	90,785	10,237	28,502	2,485	5,843	503	1,311	93	6,778	867
Escambia County	52,996	6,102	41,167	4,888	8,237	626	1,959	353	652	37	640	127
Flagler County	35,344	4,904	28,452	2,934	na	na	na	na	na	na	na	na
Hernando County	52,643	6,749	45,776	5,868	2,110	175	na	na	na	na	4,001	555
Highlands County	37,245	6,627	32,168	5,862	na	na	na	na	na	na	2,926	620
Hillsborough County	205,808	24,244	134,664	16,077	22,624	1,817	6,259	321	4,337	499	39,516	5,316
Indian River County	51,384	7,118	47,273	6,738	na	na	na	na	na	na	na	na
Lake County	95,124	9,082	82,336	8,022	5,184	62	na	na	na	na	5,625	763
Lee County	216,260	27,692	190,096	25,912	7,946	115	2,847	244	1,000	0	13,896	1,421
Leon County	38,914	3,694	29,209	2,844	7,792	744	679	0	500	0	756	106
Manatee County	107,787	13,799	97,933	12,941	3,929	484	1,477	138	na	na	4,375	236
Marion County	104,024	12,155	89,189	10,017	6,894	1,328	na	na	na	na	6,304	418
Martin County	50,419	8,115	46,244	7,694	na	na	na	na	na	na	1,648	201
Miami-Dade County	447,968	68,933	69,222	10,234	63,508	7,968	6,482	371	6,093	518	313,981	51,071
Monroe County	16,972	846	13,951	795	na	na	na	na	na	na	2,536	51
Nassau County	18,787	1,159	17,427	1,124	na	na	na	na	na	na	na	na
Okaloosa County	34,105	2,628	28,690	2,332	2,703	133	1,214	119	na	na	994	44
Orange County	164,884	18,844	86,713	11,882	26,842	2,237	9,759	167	2,940	259	40,346	4,840
Osceola County	48,427	4,802	22,053	2,431	5,103	141	1,381	0	1,354	110	20,193	2,230
Palm Beach County	354,838	60,936	281,672	52,040	30,200	3,049	5,949	479	2,721	185	35,219	5,215
Pasco County	122,134	13,520	108,011	12,751	3,282	385	1,911	0	857	35	8,147	417
Pinellas County	241,848	35,047	212,132	31,851	12,089	1,165	4,489	268	2,619	402	10,475	1,523
Polk County	143,426	14,993	114,352	12,441	12,724	1,201	2,521	265	832	0	12,877	1,086
Putnam County	17,314	717	14,637	565	na	na	na	na	na	na	na	na
St. Johns County	51,740	4,574	46,707	4,073	na	na	na	na	na	na	1,699	119
St. Lucie County	77,208	7,694	59,975	7,101	9,551	325	na	na	na	na	6,881	220
Santa Rosa County	28,416	2,114	26,068	2,114	na	na	na	na	na	na	na	na
Sarasota County	157,066	22,673	146,549	21,397	2,731	376	2,571	195	822	128	4,771	804
Seminole County	72,734	8,492	53,563	6,136	6,210	534	na	na	na	na	9,555	1,549
Sumter County	73,154	4,848	70,832	4,515	na	na	na	na	na	na	na	na
Volusia County	133,744	21,000	114,796	18,955	7,514	599	na	na	na	na	9,485	1,355
Walton County	14,517	502	13,616	388	na	na	na	na	na	na	na	na

Table C-2: Counties - Older Population by Race and Hispanic Origin—*Continued*

Name	Total Population 65 Years and Over	Total Population 85 Years and Over	White, Non-Hispanic 65 Years and Over	White, Non-Hispanic 85 Years and Over	Black, Alone 65 Years and Over	Black, Alone 85 Years and Over	Asian, Alone 65 Years and Over	Asian, Alone 85 Years and Over	Multi-race, Alone 65 Years and Over	Multi-race, Alone 85 Years and Over	Hispanic 65 Years and Over	Hispanic 85 Years and Over
Georgia												
Barrow County	10,243	1,006	8,436	904	814	71	na	na	na	na	674	0
Bartow County	14,651	1,569	13,207	1,518	na	na	na	na	na	na	na	na
Bibb County	23,974	2,802	13,202	2,193	9,885	609	na	na	na	na	na	na
Bulloch County	8,545	963	6,725	818	1,820	145	na	na	na	na	na	na
Carroll County	16,788	1,261	13,534	922	2,569	156	na	na	na	na	na	na
Catoosa County	12,069	799	11,387	707	na	na	na	na	na	na	na	na
Chatham County	44,131	4,738	28,899	3,511	13,602	1,227	na	na	na	na	283	0
Cherokee County	36,209	2,256	32,249	1,994	1,058	0	na	na	na	na	1,719	0
Clarke County	15,023	1,745	9,630	1,177	4,463	241	na	na	na	na	590	327
Clayton County	26,880	1,689	7,993	497	15,136	792	2,037	400	422	0	1,348	0
Cobb County	92,828	9,353	70,622	7,191	13,984	1,530	3,486	482	467	0	4,026	150
Columbia County	21,329	2,175	16,605	1,725	2,655	0	na	na	na	na	na	na
Coweta County	20,747	1,544	16,333	1,355	3,218	90	na	na	na	na	na	na
DeKalb County	93,989	11,708	38,499	6,746	46,915	4,302	4,378	245	1,230	72	2,834	343
Dougherty County	13,899	1,987	6,292	660	7,538	1,327	na	na	na	na	na	na
Douglas County	17,286	1,530	11,229	1,161	4,425	285	na	na	na	na	na	na
Fayette County	20,284	2,027	15,360	1,753	3,754	135	na	na	na	na	438	25
Floyd County	16,533	1,843	14,114	1,393	1,879	450	na	na	na	na	na	na
Forsyth County	28,398	1,598	24,656	1,487	677	0	1,758	58	na	na	1,151	53
Fulton County	122,675	13,278	61,425	7,889	52,101	4,577	4,722	431	992	29	3,053	352
Glynn County	16,955	2,011	14,072	1,926	2,594	85	na	na	na	na	na	na
Gwinnett County	93,705	9,315	57,642	6,376	15,292	789	12,561	1,204	538	80	7,075	866
Hall County	30,078	3,197	26,056	2,707	1,499	0	na	na	na	na	1,765	212
Henry County	26,256	3,449	16,402	1,759	8,569	1,690	na	na	na	na	na	na
Houston County	18,359	2,032	14,286	1,683	3,552	349	na	na	na	na	na	na
Jackson County	10,244	1,201	9,072	1,047	na	na	na	na	na	na	na	na
Lowndes County	14,530	1,583	9,534	1,170	4,033	228	na	na	na	na	na	na
Muscogee County	26,086	3,698	14,054	2,368	10,418	1,004	na	na	na	na	764	0
Newton County	14,379	1,294	9,146	1,038	4,516	256	na	na	na	na	na	na
Paulding County	16,871	1,305	14,407	1,305	796	0	na	na	na	na	na	na
Richmond County	28,148	2,777	13,533	1,617	13,089	1,086	na	na	na	na	493	0
Rockdale County	12,806	1,088	7,452	806	4,799	236	na	na	na	na	220	0
Spalding County	12,014	1,269	8,969	1,153	2,901	116	na	na	na	na	na	na
Troup County	10,065	1,056	7,573	1,000	2,388	56	na	na	na	na	na	na
Walker County	13,093	1,227	12,195	1,158	na	na	na	na	na	na	na	na
Walton County	14,070	1,388	12,020	1,209	1,410	179	na	na	na	na	na	na
Whitfield County	14,588	1,644	12,513	1,644	na	na	na	na	na	na	1,450	0
Hawaii												
Hawaii County	42,643	4,237	19,763	1,544	na	na	12,689	1,792	4,945	604	1,840	89
Honolulu County	173,612	30,273	31,376	4,499	1,157	0	110,004	22,690	18,361	1,730	4,312	311
Kauai County	14,709	1,606	5,840	428	na	na	6,127	981	1,645	0	630	0
Maui County	30,492	3,954	13,102	1,066	na	na	11,707	2,225	2,700	485	1,378	124
Idaho												
Ada County	67,476	6,646	63,546	6,519	na	na	1,560	127	na	na	1,537	0
Bannock County	12,344	1,616	11,446	1,491	na	na	na	na	na	na	371	65
Bonneville County	15,046	2,395	14,619	2,395	na	na	na	na	na	na	147	0
Canyon County	31,930	3,481	27,217	2,651	na	na	na	na	na	na	2,647	290
Kootenai County	30,553	2,611	29,354	2,602	na	na	na	na	na	na	na	na
Twin Falls County	12,925	1,207	12,186	1,207	na	na	na	na	na	na	367	0
Illinois												
Adams County	13,297	1,867	12,787	1,722	na	na	na	na	na	na	na	na
Champaign County	26,318	3,662	23,003	3,527	1,440	59	918	0	na	na	511	76
Cook County	757,941	100,113	428,415	66,645	176,028	19,026	53,740	5,361	7,501	604	93,955	8,563
DeKalb County	13,305	1,540	12,370	1,530	na	na	na	na	na	na	238	10
DuPage County	143,761	18,214	116,695	16,607	3,354	346	15,340	538	1,244	157	7,154	566
Kane County	73,081	7,571	58,377	6,263	3,009	263	2,909	244	588	0	8,758	801
Kankakee County	18,344	2,763	15,892	2,420	1,858	326	na	na	na	na	442	17
Kendall County	13,493	1,875	11,300	1,715	na	na	na	na	na	na	754	119
Lake County	99,801	12,788	81,258	11,399	4,442	241	6,227	559	522	123	7,257	466
LaSalle County	20,841	2,540	19,799	2,502	na	na	na	na	na	na	907	0
McHenry County	44,617	5,179	41,725	5,014	na	na	na	na	na	na	1,578	78
McLean County	22,728	3,397	21,269	3,218	753	179	370	0	na	na	336	0
Macon County	21,167	2,441	18,486	2,412	2,053	29	na	na	na	na	na	na
Madison County	45,758	5,227	42,220	5,227	2,168	164	na	na	na	na	425	0
Peoria County	30,201	4,560	26,477	4,181	3,173	379	na	na	na	na	320	0
Rock Island County	26,909	3,289	24,301	3,034	1,456	69	na	na	na	na	1,084	186
St. Clair County	40,953	4,693	30,148	3,986	9,525	696	na	na	na	na	528	0
Sangamon County	34,683	4,453	31,784	3,892	2,169	451	na	na	na	na	na	na
Tazewell County	25,258	4,480	24,291	4,480	na	na	na	na	na	na	na	na
Vermilion County	15,156	2,197	13,434	1,768	1,362	429	na	na	na	na	na	na
Will County	90,429	11,009	71,765	8,490	7,693	715	4,144	414	993	60	5,961	1,330
Williamson County	12,562	1,224	12,198	1,117	na	na	na	na	na	na	na	na
Winnebago County	49,568	6,226	43,007	5,751	3,696	426	870	0	206	0	1,843	49
Indiana												
Allen County	54,528	6,099	47,749	5,720	4,448	249	833	50	142	40	1,277	40
Bartholomew County	13,549	1,156	12,856	1,078	na	na	na	na	na	na	na	na

Table C-2: Counties - Older Population by Race and Hispanic Origin—*Continued*

Name	Total Population		White, Non-Hispanic		Black, Alone		Asian, Alone		Multi-race, Alone		Hispanic	
	65 Years and Over	85 Years and Over	65 Years and Over	85 Years and Over	65 Years and Over	85 Years and Over	65 Years and Over	85 Years and Over	65 Years and Over	85 Years and Over	65 Years and Over	85 Years and Over
Indiana—Cont.												
Boone County	8,752	1,472	8,616	1,415	na	na	na	na	na	na	na	na
Clark County	18,361	1,289	16,927	1,129	na	na	na	na	na	na	na	na
Delaware County	19,931	3,185	18,413	2,935	947	178	na	na	na	na	na	na
Elkhart County	29,730	4,138	27,791	3,929	707	59	na	na	na	na	774	150
Floyd County	12,434	1,684	11,878	1,636	na	na	na	na	na	na	na	na
Grant County	12,533	1,571	11,575	1,394	na	na	na	na	na	na	na	na
Hamilton County	41,308	4,946	37,807	4,482	1,247	178	1,379	178	na	na	321	72
Hancock County	12,948	1,174	11,959	1,174	na	na	na	na	na	na	na	na
Hendricks County	22,917	1,884	21,496	1,784	na	na	na	na	na	na	na	na
Howard County	15,917	2,363	14,894	2,192	na	na	na	na	na	na	na	na
Johnson County	22,720	2,029	21,984	2,029	na	na	na	na	na	na	na	na
Kosciusko County	13,068	1,548	12,438	1,368	na	na	na	na	na	na	na	na
Lake County	79,924	10,516	53,971	7,145	16,680	2,118	na	na	449	36	8,023	1,217
LaPorte County	19,676	1,943	18,031	1,853	1,195	90	na	na	na	na	240	0
Madison County	23,638	2,891	21,975	2,754	1,333	14	na	na	na	na	220	54
Marion County	120,092	14,097	88,028	10,158	27,132	3,059	2,279	524	567	0	2,665	534
Monroe County	19,046	3,224	18,279	3,210	na	na	na	na	na	na	na	na
Morgan County	11,732	1,462	11,670	1,462	na	na	na	na	na	na	na	na
Porter County	27,395	3,079	25,651	3,062	na	na	na	na	na	na	835	17
St. Joseph County	43,160	6,631	37,655	6,112	3,183	250	697	0	733	228	776	41
Tippecanoe County	22,392	3,177	20,907	3,005	139	0	607	0	na	na	681	172
Vanderburgh County	30,123	4,504	28,033	4,334	2,063	170	na	na	na	na	na	na
Vigo County	17,118	2,089	16,418	2,031	251	58	na	na	na	na	na	na
Wayne County	12,445	1,847	11,885	1,738	na	na	na	na	na	na	na	na
Iowa												
Black Hawk County	21,218	2,505	20,059	2,478	911	0	na	na	na	na	43	27
Dallas County	10,686	1,646	10,298	1,646	na	na	na	na	na	na	na	na
Dubuque County	17,441	2,671	17,053	2,646	na	na	na	na	na	na	na	na
Johnson County	17,571	2,093	16,632	1,866	124	0	na	na	na	na	356	227
Linn County	36,397	4,681	34,289	4,380	558	41	na	na	na	na	514	129
Polk County	63,048	7,258	58,851	7,122	1,929	0	1,181	60	323	76	774	0
Pottawattamie County	16,444	2,085	15,622	1,999	na	na	na	na	na	na	na	na
Scott County	27,591	3,144	25,823	2,962	962	0	na	na	na	na	684	138
Story County	11,562	1,405	11,281	1,405	na	na	226	0	na	na	na	na
Woodbury County	15,799	2,010	14,240	1,939	na	na	na	na	na	na	434	0
Kansas												
Butler County	10,133	1,161	9,679	1,076	na	na	na	na	na	na	na	na
Douglas County	15,300	2,395	13,658	1,758	na	na	na	na	na	na	na	na
Johnson County	86,524	11,116	80,090	10,892	1,782	0	2,230	98	312	0	2,080	126
Leavenworth County	12,165	1,671	10,653	1,413	na	na	na	na	na	na	na	na
Riley County	7,035	1,030	6,431	946	na	na	na	na	na	na	na	na
Sedgwick County	74,308	9,743	62,952	8,280	4,853	947	2,065	126	960	12	3,427	318
Shawnee County	32,776	3,615	28,278	3,244	2,155	159	na	na	525	74	1,560	124
Wyandotte County	20,344	1,605	11,956	1,080	5,194	292	390	12	170	0	2,243	221
Kentucky												
Boone County	17,363	1,398	17,003	1,398	na	na	na	na	na	na	na	na
Bullitt County	13,098	876	12,294	876	na	na	na	na	na	na	na	na
Campbell County	14,825	1,829	14,094	1,829	na	na	na	na	na	na	na	na
Christian County	8,870	1,220	7,073	1,034	1,492	186	na	na	na	na	na	na
Daviess County	17,052	1,861	16,259	1,861	na	na	na	na	na	na	na	na
Fayette County	42,959	4,478	36,330	3,310	4,795	1,108	554	0	580	0	539	60
Hardin County	15,845	1,620	13,327	1,423	1,516	197	na	na	na	na	na	na
Jefferson County	124,421	15,879	101,641	14,240	18,362	1,350	1,568	169	1,016	66	1,847	54
Kenton County	24,028	2,487	22,809	2,371	na	na	na	na	na	na	na	na
McCracken County	13,390	2,654	11,733	1,937	na	na	na	na	na	na	na	na
Madison County	12,719	1,463	11,846	1,227	na	na	na	na	na	na	na	na
Oldham County	8,651	648	8,273	565	na	na	na	na	na	na	na	na
Warren County	17,362	1,651	15,224	1,560	758	55	na	na	na	na	365	36
Louisiana												
Ascension Parish	14,179	1,529	11,420	1,366	2,502	163	na	na	na	na	na	na
Bossier Parish	17,634	2,125	14,362	1,937	2,961	188	na	na	na	na	na	na
Caddo Parish	41,620	5,211	24,855	3,344	15,493	1,743	na	na	na	na	601	65
Calcasieu Parish	30,465	3,451	23,176	2,908	5,922	543	na	na	na	na	na	na
East Baton Rouge Parish	62,577	6,571	38,161	4,594	21,469	1,514	1,655	218	na	na	893	245
Iberia Parish	10,381	826	7,606	777	2,472	0	na	na	na	na	na	na
Jefferson Parish	74,241	8,064	52,725	6,844	12,326	499	2,044	54	557	84	6,331	534
Lafayette Parish	31,864	3,394	25,133	3,179	5,648	215	na	na	na	na	330	0
Lafourche Parish	15,537	1,818	13,186	1,126	1,774	692	na	na	na	na	na	na
Livingston Parish	18,939	1,584	17,175	1,578	na	na	na	na	na	na	na	na
Orleans Parish	57,532	5,890	19,939	2,295	33,980	3,301	1,231	41	483	150	1,912	148
Ouachita Parish	22,852	2,196	16,782	1,926	5,498	270	na	na	na	na	na	na
Rapides Parish	21,274	2,054	15,451	1,801	4,901	153	na	na	na	na	na	na
St. Landry Parish	13,167	1,402	8,553	1,070	4,532	332	na	na	na	na	na	na
St. Tammany Parish	43,644	4,636	38,076	4,437	3,324	44	na	na	na	na	1,734	155
Tangipahoa Parish	19,087	1,316	14,858	950	3,674	366	na	na	na	na	na	na
Terrebonne Parish	16,642	1,436	12,423	1,216	2,319	103	na	na	na	na	na	na

Table C-2: Counties - Older Population by Race and Hispanic Origin—*Continued*

Name	Total Population		White, Non-Hispanic		Black, Alone		Asian, Alone		Multi-race, Alone		Hispanic	
	65 Years and Over	85 Years and Over	65 Years and Over	85 Years and Over	65 Years and Over	85 Years and Over	65 Years and Over	85 Years and Over	65 Years and Over	85 Years and Over	65 Years and Over	85 Years and Over
Maine												
Androscoggin County	19,292	2,055	18,495	2,055	na	na	na	na	342	0	na	na
Aroostook County	16,193	2,822	15,811	2,822	na	na	na	na	na	na	na	na
Cumberland County	53,973	6,638	52,361	6,574	na	na	840	0	na	na	236	64
Kennebec County	24,870	3,578	23,813	3,415	na	na	na	na	na	na	na	na
Penobscot County	27,761	3,630	27,404	3,630	na	na	na	na	na	na	na	na
York County	42,314	4,575	41,254	4,575	na	na	na	na	na	na	na	na
Maryland												
Allegany County	14,147	1,132	13,873	1,095	na	na	na	na	na	na	na	na
Anne Arundel County	84,811	9,261	69,724	8,116	9,648	651	2,869	418	1,004	0	1,729	76
Baltimore County	142,542	20,360	105,568	17,124	27,637	2,473	5,521	125	1,419	218	2,317	312
Calvert County	13,475	1,555	11,330	1,418	1,782	60	na	na	na	na	na	na
Carroll County	27,509	3,370	26,749	3,314	497	56	na	na	na	na	na	na
Cecil County	16,204	1,894	15,038	1,763	na	na	na	na	na	na	na	na
Charles County	19,917	2,322	12,055	1,595	6,730	703	na	na	na	na	na	na
Frederick County	36,820	4,629	32,360	4,293	2,146	173	1,024	0	20	0	1,233	163
Harford County	42,005	4,790	35,758	4,297	3,466	330	1,201	115	191	48	1,326	0
Howard County	44,739	3,608	30,422	2,724	6,582	509	5,962	375	830	0	1,096	0
Montgomery County	163,645	21,765	100,930	15,715	21,446	2,059	23,667	2,750	3,622	87	14,349	1,154
Prince George's County	120,625	11,940	25,807	3,821	80,164	6,891	5,838	501	2,613	84	6,448	601
St. Mary's County	15,006	1,132	12,004	783	na	na	na	na	na	na	na	na
Washington County	26,066	2,751	24,239	2,610	1,646	77	na	na	na	na	153	64
Wicomico County	16,246	1,751	12,543	1,476	3,179	148	na	na	na	na	na	na
Massachusetts												
Barnstable County	65,453	7,670	62,679	7,328	na	na	na	na	na	na	na	na
Berkshire County	29,239	3,829	28,321	3,778	na	na	na	na	na	na	na	na
Bristol County	94,856	13,241	88,026	12,111	1,325	110	944	143	1,414	128	2,394	138
Essex County	134,878	20,793	117,766	19,427	3,377	232	2,942	245	781	99	11,324	790
Franklin County	15,424	2,182	15,040	2,104	na	na	na	na	na	na	na	na
Hampden County	78,765	12,063	64,475	10,958	4,887	489	1,077	0	311	22	8,282	594
Hampshire County	27,968	3,080	26,341	3,027	na	na	947	0	na	na	398	41
Middlesex County	246,060	33,994	213,809	30,951	7,589	831	15,736	1,621	1,779	80	7,476	511
Norfolk County	118,958	18,516	103,141	17,486	4,976	320	8,210	205	406	62	1,978	256
Plymouth County	93,606	10,661	84,542	9,654	4,659	554	584	0	874	0	1,418	104
Suffolk County	96,952	11,683	52,501	7,917	21,668	2,057	8,548	1,092	3,697	0	12,533	617
Worcester County	129,842	15,596	117,097	15,002	2,391	0	3,744	395	683	116	5,760	83
Michigan												
Allegan County	19,808	1,994	18,438	1,791	na	na	na	na	na	na	819	148
Bay County	20,857	3,051	20,294	3,051	na	na	na	na	na	na	na	na
Berrien County	30,468	4,686	26,625	4,204	2,527	348	na	na	na	na	484	71
Calhoun County	24,047	3,723	20,981	3,370	2,079	276	na	na	na	na	411	0
Clinton County	13,620	1,015	12,888	1,015	na	na	na	na	na	na	na	na
Eaton County	20,280	1,910	18,611	1,845	na	na	na	na	na	na	342	0
Genesee County	71,160	7,505	57,609	6,239	11,088	1,082	na	na	749	41	1,293	184
Grand Traverse County	18,378	2,684	17,972	2,684	na	na	na	na	na	na	na	na
Ingham County	39,816	5,759	33,173	4,836	3,206	314	1,409	426	694	43	1,490	140
Isabella County	9,094	990	8,361	919	na	na	na	na	na	na	na	na
Jackson County	28,547	3,269	26,475	3,018	1,116	95	na	na	187	0	480	71
Kalamazoo County	39,828	4,425	35,537	4,130	2,644	128	na	na	482	140	667	0
Kent County	89,751	10,779	78,511	10,457	5,413	119	2,111	0	789	203	3,059	0
Lapeer County	15,967	1,369	15,468	1,369	na	na	na	na	na	na	na	na
Lenawee County	18,092	2,130	17,536	2,130	na	na	na	na	na	na	383	0
Livingston County	33,118	2,895	32,036	2,825	na	na	na	na	na	na	na	na
Macomb County	149,007	18,692	133,909	17,110	8,126	834	3,676	270	1,383	179	1,605	299
Marquette County	12,824	1,500	12,331	1,500	na	na	na	na	na	na	na	na
Midland County	15,539	2,269	14,600	2,093	na	na	na	na	na	na	na	na
Monroe County	27,543	3,738	26,183	3,289	na	na	na	na	na	na	na	na
Muskegon County	29,441	3,263	25,879	2,957	2,539	250	na	na	na	na	530	56
Oakland County	211,586	27,438	170,372	24,152	27,409	2,381	8,437	383	1,630	133	3,044	273
Ottawa County	43,416	5,329	41,086	5,149	na	na	na	na	na	na	1,361	66
Saginaw County	36,766	5,153	29,529	4,453	5,115	428	na	na	316	48	2,011	142
St. Clair County	30,013	2,807	28,733	2,607	na	na	na	na	na	na	na	na
Shiawassee County	12,597	1,419	12,146	1,403	na	na	na	na	na	na	na	na
Van Buren County	14,089	1,373	12,528	1,234	na	na	na	na	na	na	587	0
Washtenaw County	51,775	5,935	42,743	4,814	4,713	525	2,376	442	915	77	991	77
Wayne County	270,261	33,176	159,702	20,175	94,281	11,644	6,415	331	2,815	568	6,630	458
Minnesota												
Anoka County	49,826	4,354	46,506	4,282	961	0	1,150	72	397	0	555	0
Blue Earth County	9,447	1,589	9,074	1,589	na	na	na	na	na	na	na	na
Carver County	12,680	514	11,982	514	na	na	na	na	na	na	na	na
Dakota County	59,233	6,412	55,632	6,412	844	0	1,650	0	288	0	848	0
Hennepin County	176,860	23,877	156,246	21,737	10,191	1,047	5,901	743	1,297	127	2,633	297
Olmsted County	24,295	3,483	22,504	3,202	286	0	1,022	165	na	na	na	na
Ramsey County	79,420	11,530	68,416	10,546	4,029	370	4,228	614	703	0	1,880	0
Rice County	10,297	1,714	9,884	1,714	na	na	na	na	na	na	na	na
St. Louis County	38,593	5,692	37,662	5,465	na	na	na	na	258	0	na	na
Scott County	16,292	1,999	14,699	1,837	na	na	656	53	na	na	na	na

Table C-2: Counties - Older Population by Race and Hispanic Origin—*Continued*

Name	Total Population 65 Years and Over	Total Population 85 Years and Over	White, Non-Hispanic 65 Years and Over	White, Non-Hispanic 85 Years and Over	Black, Alone 65 Years and Over	Black, Alone 85 Years and Over	Asian, Alone 65 Years and Over	Asian, Alone 85 Years and Over	Multi-race, Alone 65 Years and Over	Multi-race, Alone 85 Years and Over	Hispanic 65 Years and Over	Hispanic 85 Years and Over
Minnesota—Cont.												
Sherburne County	10,593	1,360	10,593	1,360	na	na	na	na	na	na	na	na
Stearns County	23,995	3,498	23,262	3,498	316	0	na	na	na	na	na	na
Washington County	38,724	4,175	36,536	4,175	693	0	828	0	na	na	374	0
Wright County	17,122	1,400	16,799	1,339	na	na	na	na	na	na	na	na
Mississippi												
DeSoto County	22,973	2,171	19,089	1,902	3,632	269	na	na	na	na	0	0
Forrest County	10,366	1,195	7,465	898	2,901	297	na	na	na	na	na	na
Harrison County	30,988	2,845	24,347	2,190	4,892	96	na	na	na	na	815	393
Hinds County	33,279	3,850	14,011	1,860	18,951	1,990	na	na	na	na	na	na
Jackson County	22,736	815	18,155	702	3,606	68	na	na	na	na	na	na
Jones County	11,875	1,375	9,043	1,184	2,744	191	na	na	na	na	na	na
Lauderdale County	12,938	1,753	8,820	1,117	3,939	610	na	na	na	na	na	na
Lee County	12,097	1,115	10,185	1,071	1,742	16	na	na	na	na	na	na
Madison County	13,758	1,736	9,831	1,438	3,810	298	na	na	na	na	na	na
Rankin County	23,460	2,160	20,160	2,070	2,934	90	na	na	na	na	na	na
Missouri												
Boone County	21,937	3,032	19,959	2,984	1,044	48	na	na	na	na	na	na
Buchanan County	15,014	2,038	13,334	2,038	na	na	na	na	na	na	na	na
Cape Girardeau County	12,949	1,914	12,624	1,914	na	na	na	na	na	na	na	na
Cass County	17,994	1,949	16,739	1,949	na	na	na	na	na	na	na	na
Christian County	13,424	1,891	13,258	1,891	na	na	na	na	na	na	na	na
Clay County	34,841	3,298	32,011	3,154	1,016	11	na	na	75	0	1,015	51
Cole County	12,974	1,053	11,942	1,001	676	0	na	na	na	na	na	na
Franklin County	17,948	2,201	17,530	2,095	na	na	na	na	na	na	na	na
Greene County	48,313	5,816	45,868	5,541	na	na	na	na	443	0	741	0
Jackson County	104,740	13,748	78,478	10,548	20,084	2,704	1,428	57	879	0	3,618	439
Jasper County	18,699	2,312	17,759	2,182	na	na	na	na	na	na	na	na
Jefferson County	33,824	3,014	32,654	3,014	na	na	na	na	na	na	na	na
Platte County	15,028	1,337	13,730	1,337	na	na	na	na	na	na	382	0
St. Charles County	59,689	6,712	57,054	6,657	1,410	0	404	0	489	55	310	0
St. Francois County	11,343	1,561	10,664	1,561	na	na	na	na	na	na	na	na
St. Louis County	180,521	24,454	142,828	20,536	29,977	3,529	4,339	212	1,229	64	1,896	58
Montana												
Cascade County	15,005	1,940	14,274	1,940	na	na	na	na	na	na	na	na
Flathead County	19,958	1,403	19,275	1,403	na	na	na	na	na	na	na	na
Gallatin County	14,428	1,108	13,699	962	na	na	na	na	na	na	na	na
Lewis and Clark County	12,668	1,813	12,399	1,813	na	na	na	na	na	na	na	na
Missoula County	18,257	1,528	17,624	1,356	na	na	na	na	na	na	na	na
Yellowstone County	27,163	3,942	25,962	3,833	na	na	na	na	na	na	137	0
Nebraska												
Douglas County	73,861	9,740	63,843	8,493	5,628	671	1,036	173	844	0	2,563	379
Lancaster County	43,830	5,149	41,113	4,943	495	131	1,119	0	329	0	774	75
Sarpy County	22,169	2,881	19,740	2,681	905	111	na	na	229	21	889	68
Nevada												
Clark County	328,690	31,017	211,551	21,654	29,329	2,061	40,314	2,211	5,480	674	41,937	4,572
Washoe County	76,172	7,186	62,550	6,154	1,332	30	4,055	210	890	84	6,348	554
New Hampshire												
Cheshire County	15,095	1,244	14,838	1,223	na	na	na	na	na	na	na	na
Grafton County	18,635	2,226	18,015	2,226	na	na	na	na	na	na	na	na
Hillsborough County	64,850	8,636	61,097	8,193	743	269	1,479	105	276	69	1,342	147
Merrimack County	28,423	3,875	26,850	3,854	na	na	na	na	na	na	na	na
Rockingham County	55,401	6,797	53,767	6,619	na	na	na	na	na	na	547	178
Strafford County	19,182	2,464	18,803	2,362	na	na	na	na	na	na	na	na
New Jersey												
Atlantic County	47,558	5,068	35,565	4,328	5,413	618	2,907	0	656	0	3,332	122
Bergen County	160,999	26,056	115,606	21,442	7,134	918	19,622	2,161	2,592	109	16,110	1,446
Burlington County	75,275	9,730	59,306	8,324	10,341	1,057	3,067	112	478	51	2,273	186
Camden County	79,240	9,136	57,287	7,215	11,981	999	4,067	336	770	0	5,403	586
Cape May County	24,068	2,635	23,330	2,467	na	na	na	na	na	na	na	na
Cumberland County	23,222	2,317	16,322	2,030	2,841	132	na	na	na	na	3,178	132
Essex County	108,532	15,642	48,946	9,494	38,604	4,328	5,596	241	1,296	202	14,616	1,457
Gloucester County	46,579	6,059	39,693	5,503	4,003	343	1,190	76	na	na	1,583	137
Hudson County	79,918	10,725	28,143	4,415	9,292	1,053	10,164	1,280	2,307	222	33,672	4,622
Hunterdon County	23,280	2,922	21,505	2,744	na	na	na	na	na	na	na	na
Mercer County	56,001	7,193	39,038	5,789	9,045	1,159	4,051	103	na	na	3,632	142
Middlesex County	124,138	18,158	80,270	14,384	8,791	512	20,706	1,401	1,818	0	12,755	1,861
Monmouth County	109,200	14,565	92,688	13,035	6,697	506	4,995	298	694	122	4,486	585
Morris County	84,314	12,437	70,634	11,085	2,169	264	6,207	452	610	0	4,724	520
Ocean County	136,278	18,547	126,070	17,875	2,523	177	2,234	86	na	na	4,494	409
Passaic County	73,211	9,257	43,786	5,955	6,901	634	3,722	580	253	78	18,680	2,010
Salem County	11,735	1,431	9,836	1,212	1,538	219	na	na	na	na	na	na
Somerset County	51,619	7,227	38,200	6,117	3,963	263	6,483	396	288	30	2,917	421
Sussex County	23,676	1,947	22,597	1,803	na	na	na	na	na	na	437	86
Union County	80,253	11,851	45,819	8,339	16,429	1,348	3,888	39	461	125	14,293	1,844
Warren County	19,193	2,855	17,724	2,683	na	na	na	na	na	na	620	87

Table C-2: Counties - Older Population by Race and Hispanic Origin—*Continued*

Name	Total Population		White, Non-Hispanic		Black, Alone		Asian, Alone		Multi-race, Alone		Hispanic	
	65 Years and Over	85 Years and Over	65 Years and Over	85 Years and Over	65 Years and Over	85 Years and Over	65 Years and Over	85 Years and Over	65 Years and Over	85 Years and Over	65 Years and Over	85 Years and Over
New Mexico												
Bernalillo County	111,216	13,687	65,813	8,031	2,597	507	2,687	65	2,095	217	37,342	4,865
Chaves County	10,830	1,559	6,404	1,038	na	na	na	na	na	na	3,581	466
Doña Ana County	34,786	3,125	16,909	1,929	na	na	na	na	na	na	16,333	1,196
Lea County	7,856	924	4,988	694	na	na	na	na	na	na	2,484	160
McKinley County	9,281	1,514	0	0	na	na	na	na	na	na	na	na
Otero County	10,722	829	8,028	654	na	na	na	na	na	na	2,010	126
Sandoval County	25,763	2,094	16,897	1,448	na	na	na	na	na	na	6,012	421
San Juan County	19,101	2,223	10,829	1,237	na	na	na	na	na	na	2,257	177
Santa Fe County	36,568	2,730	24,547	1,248	na	na	na	na	na	na	10,658	1,462
Valencia County	13,675	1,754	6,875	812	na	na	na	na	na	na	5,984	942
New York												
Albany County	52,316	7,050	45,268	6,134	3,898	550	1,508	310	467	56	1,364	51
Bronx County	183,165	21,188	35,720	7,752	61,242	4,912	6,342	521	6,478	632	84,174	7,587
Broome County	36,793	6,334	34,413	6,270	871	28	1,030	36	na	na	na	na
Cattaraugus County	14,641	1,524	14,173	1,475	na	na	na	na	na	na	na	na
Cayuga County	14,322	1,676	14,275	1,676	na	na	na	na	na	na	na	na
Chautauqua County	25,587	3,908	24,642	3,743	na	na	na	na	na	na	630	165
Chemung County	16,613	1,905	15,038	1,780	na	na	na	na	na	na	na	na
Clinton County	13,523	1,498	13,261	1,453	na	na	na	na	na	na	na	na
Dutchess County	51,573	6,488	43,762	5,865	3,699	145	1,672	137	181	0	2,411	316
Erie County	165,216	23,971	143,513	20,955	14,649	2,338	2,205	107	1,101	198	3,323	336
Jefferson County	15,458	1,648	14,718	1,648	na	na	na	na	na	na	0	0
Kings County	358,797	45,796	146,673	23,170	124,816	14,191	37,368	3,908	6,369	541	53,023	4,414
Livingston County	11,117	1,016	10,941	1,001	na	na	na	na	na	na	na	na
Madison County	13,087	1,389	12,626	1,389	na	na	na	na	na	na	na	na
Monroe County	128,110	17,686	108,798	15,946	11,738	1,128	2,719	257	756	42	4,462	444
Nassau County	241,330	39,183	182,385	33,355	21,440	1,857	16,706	959	3,104	321	18,463	2,761
New York County	268,834	39,609	141,420	22,062	38,747	5,694	29,189	3,755	8,443	298	63,040	9,243
Niagara County	39,813	5,800	37,322	5,534	1,666	210	na	na	na	na	172	13
Oneida County	42,555	6,889	40,305	6,702	998	59	496	0	na	na	731	128
Onondaga County	78,867	12,018	70,401	10,851	4,957	686	1,526	191	557	23	1,322	267
Ontario County	21,645	2,645	20,992	2,428	na	na	na	na	na	na	115	0
Orange County	53,391	7,057	42,655	5,943	3,886	449	na	na	433	0	5,438	600
Oswego County	19,449	1,709	18,823	1,709	na	na	na	na	na	na	na	na
Putnam County	17,094	1,596	15,590	1,596	na	na	na	na	na	na	933	0
Queens County	357,630	45,173	134,045	23,458	64,400	6,976	84,007	7,266	8,407	267	67,947	7,283
Rensselaer County	26,557	3,732	25,348	3,695	652	37	na	na	222	0	255	0
Richmond County	77,054	8,601	58,491	7,245	4,803	633	6,989	229	363	51	6,537	443
Rockland County	51,109	7,876	37,646	6,471	5,426	561	3,784	492	612	0	4,023	501
St. Lawrence County	18,468	2,550	18,258	2,550	na	na	na	na	na	na	na	na
Saratoga County	40,850	4,076	40,159	4,076	na	na	na	na	na	na	na	na
Schenectady County	26,852	4,314	23,784	3,988	1,203	97	na	na	na	na	264	173
Steuben County	18,663	2,160	18,211	2,160	na	na	na	na	na	na	na	na
Suffolk County	250,082	31,103	210,163	26,675	12,534	1,774	6,666	251	2,228	266	18,954	2,077
Sullivan County	14,198	1,117	12,224	931	na	na	na	na	na	na	921	35
Tompkins County	14,209	2,039	13,705	1,878	na	na	na	na	na	na	na	na
Ulster County	35,125	4,398	31,902	3,677	1,234	0	na	na	220	112	1,618	643
Warren County	14,361	2,261	13,913	2,211	na	na	na	na	na	na	na	na
Wayne County	17,292	2,110	16,149	1,976	na	na	na	na	na	na	na	na
Westchester County	165,337	26,582	117,570	20,843	20,122	2,870	8,179	1,086	2,571	310	18,528	1,620
North Carolina												
Alamance County	28,381	3,361	22,346	2,964	4,683	397	na	na	na	na	866	0
Brunswick County	43,663	2,703	39,466	2,553	na	na	na	na	na	na	na	na
Buncombe County	51,821	7,511	47,847	6,816	2,353	255	na	na	na	na	491	182
Burke County	18,047	1,702	16,822	1,249	na	na	na	na	na	na	na	na
Cabarrus County	28,208	3,071	22,835	2,784	3,792	157	na	na	na	na	1,006	0
Caldwell County	16,043	2,011	15,293	1,873	na	na	na	na	na	na	na	na
Carteret County	17,455	1,613	16,253	1,515	na	na	na	na	na	na	na	na
Catawba County	28,020	3,006	25,368	2,963	1,617	43	na	na	na	na	412	0
Chatham County	17,876	2,840	15,095	2,342	na	na	na	na	na	na	553	72
Cleveland County	18,097	2,074	14,808	1,718	2,830	238	na	na	na	na	na	na
Craven County	19,588	1,630	15,682	1,329	3,399	301	na	na	na	na	na	na
Cumberland County	40,158	3,700	21,436	2,258	14,296	908	1,402	199	441	138	1,835	110
Davidson County	30,038	2,636	27,136	2,636	1,591	0	na	na	na	na	507	0
Durham County	41,915	4,202	25,005	2,727	13,358	1,405	1,369	0	495	0	1,441	70
Forsyth County	60,385	7,111	45,329	6,088	11,865	828	1,015	93	899	102	1,347	0
Franklin County	11,633	950	8,085	538	2,900	164	na	na	na	na	na	na
Gaston County	35,389	3,645	30,339	3,344	4,131	301	na	na	na	na	518	0
Guilford County	80,474	10,598	57,073	8,729	19,143	1,491	2,054	0	479	0	1,547	378
Harnett County	17,041	1,380	12,695	1,114	3,208	144	na	na	na	na	792	67
Henderson County	30,339	3,661	28,459	3,214	na	na	na	na	na	na	na	na
Iredell County	27,867	2,547	24,542	2,397	2,083	150	na	na	na	na	376	0
Johnston County	27,396	3,135	21,930	2,565	3,885	214	na	na	na	na	1,368	307
Lincoln County	14,281	1,364	13,568	1,350	na	na	na	na	na	na	na	na
Mecklenburg County	122,591	12,802	79,418	9,561	32,241	2,444	4,850	147	840	155	5,644	970
Moore County	23,584	3,053	20,803	2,834	na	na	na	na	na	na	na	na
Nash County	17,446	1,855	11,488	1,317	5,403	499	na	na	na	na	na	na
New Hanover County	41,479	4,952	35,367	4,356	4,697	530	na	na	na	na	671	0

Table C-2: Counties - Older Population by Race and Hispanic Origin—*Continued*

Name	Total Population 65 Years and Over	Total Population 85 Years and Over	White, Non-Hispanic 65 Years and Over	White, Non-Hispanic 85 Years and Over	Black, Alone 65 Years and Over	Black, Alone 85 Years and Over	Asian, Alone 65 Years and Over	Asian, Alone 85 Years and Over	Multi-race, Alone 65 Years and Over	Multi-race, Alone 85 Years and Over	Hispanic 65 Years and Over	Hispanic 85 Years and Over
North Carolina—Cont.												
Onslow County	18,036	1,610	14,170	1,238	2,733	315	na	na	na	na	558	0
Orange County	20,753	972	16,854	838	2,365	134	827	0	na	na	362	0
Pitt County	23,540	2,309	15,692	1,559	7,304	687	na	na	na	na	91	63
Randolph County	25,207	2,452	23,284	2,290	1,055	50	na	na	na	na	368	0
Robeson County	19,861	2,330	7,810	1,489	4,592	398	na	na	na	na	257	0
Rockingham County	18,633	2,390	14,961	1,994	3,051	396	na	na	na	na	na	na
Rowan County	24,596	2,601	20,966	2,360	2,864	241	na	na	na	na	na	na
Rutherford County	14,058	1,281	13,024	1,128	na	na	na	na	na	na	na	na
Surry County	15,066	1,964	13,806	1,903	na	na	na	na	na	na	na	na
Union County	29,790	2,920	24,807	2,246	3,242	573	475	52	na	na	1,117	49
Wake County	126,840	12,571	95,560	10,518	20,976	1,403	5,507	313	1,130	138	3,867	199
Wayne County	20,507	1,988	13,278	1,299	6,182	650	na	na	na	na	474	0
Wilkes County	14,695	1,297	13,844	1,044	na	na	na	na	na	na	na	na
Wilson County	14,804	1,501	9,345	933	5,182	500	na	na	na	na	189	68
North Dakota												
Burleigh County	15,157	2,661	14,994	2,661	na	na	na	na	na	na	na	na
Cass County	21,599	3,206	21,186	3,206	na	na	na	na	na	na	na	na
Grand Forks County	8,863	1,175	8,553	1,175	na	na	na	na	na	na	na	na
Ward County	8,462	1,424	8,331	1,424	na	na	na	na	na	na	na	na
Ohio												
Allen County	17,930	1,931	16,117	1,784	1,234	147	na	na	na	na	na	na
Ashtabula County	18,569	2,281	17,753	2,261	na	na	na	na	na	na	na	na
Athens County	8,637	1,103	8,288	955	na	na	na	na	na	na	na	na
Belmont County	14,350	2,069	13,665	1,948	na	na	na	na	na	na	na	na
Butler County	56,272	6,490	51,023	5,814	2,444	272	1,513	51	675	319	617	34
Clark County	25,957	3,849	23,691	3,473	1,782	283	na	na	na	na	na	na
Clermont County	32,976	3,187	32,400	3,101	na	na	na	na	na	na	na	na
Columbiana County	21,175	2,147	20,583	2,078	na	na	na	na	na	na	na	na
Cuyahoga County	226,137	31,808	160,093	24,224	53,913	6,054	4,535	614	2,365	44	5,208	872
Delaware County	27,578	2,905	26,014	2,905	na	na	236	0	na	na	na	na
Erie County	16,157	2,718	15,003	2,391	na	na	na	na	na	na	na	na
Fairfield County	24,675	2,170	23,320	2,170	na	na	na	na	na	na	na	na
Franklin County	157,541	18,180	121,416	14,455	26,989	2,754	4,878	412	1,950	115	2,405	362
Geauga County	19,507	2,027	18,512	1,975	na	na	na	na	na	na	na	na
Greene County	29,059	2,286	26,282	2,200	1,585	86	na	na	na	na	na	na
Hamilton County	125,017	16,897	95,746	14,478	25,716	2,307	1,794	68	826	44	860	0
Hancock County	12,829	1,977	12,542	1,977	na	na	na	na	na	na	na	na
Jefferson County	14,457	1,518	13,294	1,518	na	na	na	na	na	na	na	na
Lake County	46,347	5,847	43,897	5,754	1,598	19	na	na	na	na	189	74
Licking County	28,733	3,520	27,647	3,470	na	na	na	na	na	na	na	na
Lorain County	56,905	7,094	50,065	6,255	3,042	290	na	na	33	0	2,697	113
Lucas County	70,209	8,461	56,464	6,707	9,788	1,348	na	na	472	0	1,906	53
Mahoning County	48,140	8,163	41,350	7,410	5,221	709	na	na	79	6	1,151	38
Marion County	11,407	1,689	11,048	1,689	na	na	na	na	na	na	na	na
Medina County	32,074	3,000	31,009	2,838	na	na	na	na	na	na	na	na
Miami County	20,536	1,822	19,038	1,762	na	na	na	na	na	na	na	na
Montgomery County	95,644	13,646	76,195	11,793	15,741	1,630	1,253	186	980	37	1,226	37
Muskingum County	15,189	1,424	14,647	1,376	na	na	na	na	na	na	na	na
Portage County	27,185	2,762	25,581	2,762	na	na	na	na	na	na	na	na
Richland County	23,735	3,751	21,772	2,955	na	na	na	na	na	na	na	na
Ross County	13,356	692	12,040	661	na	na	na	na	na	na	na	na
Scioto County	13,526	1,671	13,288	1,588	na	na	na	na	na	na	na	na
Stark County	72,062	9,795	66,900	8,978	3,771	537	na	na	141	0	na	na
Summit County	97,467	13,065	83,811	11,860	10,538	1,074	1,833	80	523	0	436	51
Trumbull County	43,149	6,266	39,609	5,927	2,578	248	na	na	na	na	na	na
Tuscarawas County	18,027	2,252	17,681	2,193	na	na	na	na	na	na	na	na
Warren County	33,380	4,439	31,718	4,439	na	na	926	0	na	na	na	na
Wayne County	20,264	2,366	20,150	2,366	na	na	na	na	na	na	na	na
Wood County	20,051	2,790	19,024	2,655	na	na	na	na	na	na	366	0
Oklahoma												
Canadian County	18,831	2,714	16,760	2,472	na	na	na	na	218	0	359	164
Cleveland County	37,308	3,826	32,761	3,592	1,005	36	773	48	1,012	115	704	0
Comanche County	15,223	1,873	11,269	1,683	1,657	190	na	na	570	0	632	0
Creek County	12,424	1,760	11,111	1,688	na	na	na	na	259	27	55	0
Muskogee County	11,320	1,478	8,465	1,121	1,095	139	na	na	567	33	na	na
Oklahoma County	108,277	13,902	82,670	11,573	12,957	1,529	2,705	133	1,949	110	5,055	290
Payne County	10,980	1,341	9,387	1,233	na	na	na	na	312	0	na	na
Pottawatomie County	11,821	1,805	10,192	1,715	na	na	na	na	277	0	175	0
Rogers County	14,987	1,574	12,827	1,463	na	na	na	na	440	23	69	0
Tulsa County	93,319	10,975	76,758	10,250	5,961	320	1,384	47	3,377	122	2,877	98
Wagoner County	12,971	959	11,239	932	na	na	na	na	449	0	66	27
Oregon												
Benton County	14,843	1,412	13,855	1,185	na	na	318	52	na	na	133	75
Clackamas County	74,649	8,426	69,740	7,821	na	na	2,311	126	526	186	1,888	468
Deschutes County	38,748	4,754	36,702	4,047	na	na	na	na	na	na	na	na
Douglas County	27,924	2,281	26,587	2,183	na	na	na	na	na	na	na	na
Jackson County	48,689	6,082	44,953	5,867	na	na	na	na	na	na	1,675	23

Table C-2: Counties - Older Population by Race and Hispanic Origin—*Continued*

Name	Total Population 65 Years and Over	Total Population 85 Years and Over	White, Non-Hispanic 65 Years and Over	White, Non-Hispanic 85 Years and Over	Black, Alone 65 Years and Over	Black, Alone 85 Years and Over	Asian, Alone 65 Years and Over	Asian, Alone 85 Years and Over	Multi-race, Alone 65 Years and Over	Multi-race, Alone 85 Years and Over	Hispanic 65 Years and Over	Hispanic 85 Years and Over
Oregon—Cont.												
Josephine County	22,863	1,924	21,248	1,665	na	na	na	na	na	na	na	na
Klamath County	14,610	1,581	13,010	1,489	na	na	na	na	na	na	878	92
Lane County	73,700	7,578	68,185	7,473	na	na	na	na	1,386	38	1,859	22
Linn County	24,586	3,069	22,214	2,979	na	na	na	na	624	0	1,215	90
Marion County	53,475	6,568	48,360	6,281	na	na	254	0	805	0	3,579	287
Multnomah County	108,862	11,642	91,044	10,198	4,726	202	7,912	894	1,198	52	3,494	57
Polk County	15,300	1,566	14,109	1,566	na	na	na	na	na	na	904	0
Umatilla County	11,922	1,245	10,623	1,169	na	na	na	na	na	na	627	57
Washington County	80,377	9,604	68,135	8,838	753	0	5,572	395	1,544	0	4,002	326
Yamhill County	17,824	2,161	16,794	2,161	na	na	na	na	na	na	703	0
Pennsylvania												
Adams County	20,634	2,289	20,251	2,231	na	na	na	na	na	na	175	58
Allegheny County	229,919	33,833	202,101	30,612	21,309	2,885	3,571	156	1,305	139	1,432	41
Armstrong County	14,277	1,881	14,117	1,840	na	na	na	na	na	na	na	na
Beaver County	35,619	4,737	33,507	4,514	na	na	na	na	na	na	na	na
Berks County	72,315	10,860	64,868	10,337	1,724	139	na	na	685	0	4,665	216
Blair County	25,493	3,145	24,929	3,145	na	na	na	na	na	na	na	na
Bucks County	117,060	13,463	107,769	12,621	2,708	482	3,855	127	305	116	2,095	117
Butler County	34,949	5,618	34,539	5,588	na	na	na	na	na	na	na	na
Cambria County	29,664	4,365	28,862	4,287	na	na	na	na	na	na	na	na
Carbon County	13,384	1,781	13,151	1,781	na	na	na	na	na	na	na	na
Centre County	22,815	2,676	22,439	2,597	na	na	46	0	na	na	na	na
Chester County	85,168	10,541	77,216	10,128	3,747	367	2,141	46	280	0	1,784	0
Clearfield County	16,267	2,117	16,039	2,117	na	na	na	na	na	na	na	na
Columbia County	12,712	2,114	12,495	2,099	na	na	na	na	na	na	na	na
Crawford County	17,556	1,692	17,042	1,631	na	na	na	na	na	na	na	na
Cumberland County	46,768	6,140	44,187	5,857	na	na	1,027	0	na	na	323	0
Dauphin County	46,818	6,384	38,292	5,448	5,947	675	1,221	227	na	na	1,097	34
Delaware County	92,451	14,624	75,778	13,003	11,371	1,169	3,387	145	649	44	1,219	295
Erie County	48,926	7,068	45,841	6,907	1,704	81	na	na	na	na	766	80
Fayette County	27,692	3,922	26,409	3,891	na	na	na	na	na	na	na	na
Franklin County	29,943	3,936	29,078	3,790	na	na	na	na	na	na	na	na
Indiana County	16,623	2,405	16,135	2,194	na	na	na	na	na	na	na	na
Lackawanna County	41,876	6,370	40,216	6,289	na	na	539	23	208	10	478	0
Lancaster County	98,751	12,133	90,858	11,510	2,278	234	1,532	135	759	0	3,449	254
Lawrence County	18,978	1,872	18,284	1,872	na	na	na	na	na	na	na	na
Lebanon County	27,709	4,149	25,778	4,114	na	na	na	na	na	na	1,230	35
Lehigh County	62,294	10,260	53,345	9,307	1,722	397	2,124	0	148	0	4,924	556
Luzerne County	63,359	8,590	60,376	8,475	632	0	na	na	na	na	1,572	115
Lycoming County	21,901	2,301	21,281	2,167	na	na	na	na	na	na	na	na
Mercer County	23,990	4,010	22,874	3,847	na	na	na	na	na	na	na	na
Monroe County	28,128	2,571	23,737	2,178	2,981	393	na	na	na	na	1,125	0
Montgomery County	147,157	21,958	126,979	19,891	10,407	992	7,024	765	633	0	2,116	310
Northampton County	57,663	8,268	52,546	8,122	1,250	0	584	42	420	0	2,766	104
Northumberland County	19,647	3,214	19,064	3,087	na	na	na	na	na	na	na	na
Philadelphia County	215,755	26,170	99,214	13,230	87,807	10,452	12,373	1,189	2,848	188	14,975	1,382
Schuylkill County	28,879	4,148	28,436	4,148	na	na	na	na	na	na	138	0
Somerset County	16,525	1,976	16,276	1,976	na	na	na	na	na	na	na	na
Washington County	42,146	4,395	40,986	4,217	na	na	na	na	na	na	na	na
Westmoreland County	79,436	10,770	77,469	10,358	887	82	na	na	na	na	na	na
York County	78,138	9,692	73,461	9,424	1,929	113	572	116	639	39	1,555	0
Rhode Island												
Kent County	30,919	4,434	29,507	4,196	na	na	na	na	na	na	402	0
Newport County	18,639	1,798	17,257	1,759	na	na	na	na	na	na	na	na
Providence County	97,383	15,326	79,886	13,465	5,101	268	1,945	320	1,066	85	8,773	995
Washington County	26,155	3,220	25,255	3,179	na	na	na	na	na	na	na	na
South Carolina												
Aiken County	32,745	3,900	26,169	3,175	5,851	725	na	na	na	na	na	na
Anderson County	35,930	3,018	31,120	2,936	4,189	82	na	na	na	na	na	na
Beaufort County	51,535	4,276	45,125	3,452	4,890	727	na	na	na	na	885	0
Berkeley County	30,809	2,548	21,964	1,913	6,146	466	na	na	675	133	936	0
Charleston County	66,098	8,256	47,622	6,645	16,715	1,585	na	na	na	na	965	0
Darlington County	12,640	1,053	8,141	585	4,452	439	na	na	na	na	na	na
Dorchester County	22,439	1,983	17,079	1,531	4,443	195	na	na	na	na	na	na
Florence County	23,398	1,984	14,945	1,305	8,113	679	na	na	na	na	na	na
Greenville County	80,987	8,754	67,064	8,116	10,285	387	785	101	na	na	2,044	150
Greenwood County	12,995	1,704	9,902	1,476	3,047	228	na	na	na	na	na	na
Horry County	83,231	5,951	74,488	5,564	5,419	138	na	na	na	na	1,830	249
Kershaw County	11,928	1,393	9,036	1,223	2,668	170	na	na	na	na	na	na
Lancaster County	19,635	1,629	16,812	1,359	2,581	270	na	na	na	na	na	na
Laurens County	12,626	497	9,566	468	3,039	29	na	na	na	na	na	na
Lexington County	46,772	4,925	41,073	4,580	3,880	274	245	0	220	0	1,251	0
Oconee County	18,633	1,482	16,862	1,482	na	na	na	na	na	na	na	na
Orangeburg County	16,866	1,553	7,731	1,002	8,939	551	na	na	na	na	na	na
Pickens County	20,689	1,799	19,234	1,493	na	na	na	na	na	na	na	na
Richland County	52,878	5,606	29,710	3,567	19,993	1,834	998	58	880	0	1,472	147
Spartanburg County	50,178	4,542	41,173	3,887	7,423	551	na	na	na	na	411	0

Table C-2: Counties - Older Population by Race and Hispanic Origin—*Continued*

Name	Total Population		White, Non-Hispanic		Black, Alone		Asian, Alone		Multi-race, Alone		Hispanic	
	65 Years and Over	85 Years and Over	65 Years and Over	85 Years and Over	65 Years and Over	85 Years and Over	65 Years and Over	85 Years and Over	65 Years and Over	85 Years and Over	65 Years and Over	85 Years and Over
South Carolina—Cont.												
Sumter County	17,568	1,872	9,226	1,164	7,850	708	na	na	na	na	na	na
York County	39,364	2,894	32,120	2,227	5,489	446	na	na	na	na	1,143	221
South Dakota												
Minnehaha County	25,354	3,762	24,518	3,762	na	na	59	0	na	na	0	0
Pennington County	20,474	2,828	18,781	2,624	na	na	na	na	na	na	na	na
Tennessee												
Anderson County	15,305	1,490	14,532	1,479	na	na	na	na	na	na	na	na
Blount County	27,168	2,520	25,485	2,520	na	na	na	na	na	na	na	na
Bradley County	18,022	2,214	17,083	2,063	na	na	na	na	na	na	na	na
Davidson County	84,450	9,949	60,940	7,530	18,424	1,548	1,940	251	370	163	2,198	326
Greene County	14,809	1,160	14,410	963	na	na	na	na	na	na	na	na
Hamilton County	63,597	7,878	52,352	7,136	9,449	612	na	na	140	0	372	0
Knox County	73,277	7,891	66,873	7,168	4,413	599	1,058	57	354	67	579	0
Madison County	16,581	2,230	12,163	1,864	4,240	366	na	na	na	na	na	na
Maury County	14,739	1,344	13,221	1,250	1,414	94	na	na	na	na	na	na
Montgomery County	18,581	2,308	14,856	1,797	2,614	511	na	na	na	na	444	0
Putnam County	13,201	1,759	12,608	1,712	na	na	na	na	na	na	na	na
Robertson County	10,130	604	9,573	604	na	na	na	na	na	na	na	na
Rutherford County	33,545	2,634	29,223	2,236	2,259	132	788	0	na	na	1,001	266
Sevier County	19,160	1,991	18,870	1,991	na	na	na	na	na	na	na	na
Shelby County	127,036	14,963	67,741	9,952	54,418	4,834	2,329	47	794	81	1,845	49
Sullivan County	34,801	3,729	33,397	3,681	na	na	na	na	na	na	na	na
Sumner County	29,379	3,459	27,351	2,989	na	na	na	na	na	na	na	na
Washington County	23,505	2,967	22,395	2,925	na	na	na	na	na	na	na	na
Williamson County	30,783	1,986	27,978	1,833	1,187	0	923	0	na	na	na	na
Wilson County	22,498	1,761	20,165	1,560	1,740	107	na	na	na	na	na	na
Texas												
Angelina County	13,896	1,972	11,318	1,698	1,475	200	na	na	na	na	686	74
Bastrop County	12,308	596	10,137	596	na	na	na	na	na	na	1,697	0
Bell County	38,659	3,064	26,496	2,489	5,271	150	na	na	149	54	4,824	280
Bexar County	240,452	25,750	102,653	12,840	15,272	1,242	6,475	258	3,093	748	114,567	11,247
Bowie County	15,312	1,410	12,239	1,166	2,740	168	na	na	na	na	na	na
Brazoria County	43,656	3,623	29,054	2,790	4,469	35	3,232	0	na	na	7,032	798
Brazos County	20,996	1,309	15,675	1,109	2,196	0	322	0	na	na	2,533	81
Cameron County	58,006	8,300	14,231	2,126	na	na	na	na	na	na	42,387	6,174
Collin County	110,445	10,644	83,950	8,786	6,294	298	12,107	729	760	0	7,120	934
Comal County	26,442	3,363	22,179	3,076	na	na	na	na	na	na	3,721	227
Coryell County	7,299	550	5,975	391	645	57	na	na	na	na	291	0
Dallas County	283,182	31,424	153,163	20,691	59,237	6,578	16,086	381	2,782	226	51,282	3,513
Denton County	87,138	8,514	69,288	6,686	4,103	97	5,450	386	1,127	222	7,252	1,123
Ector County	15,171	1,261	8,872	1,101	na	na	na	na	na	na	5,938	160
Ellis County	22,760	2,147	18,173	1,443	1,492	351	na	na	na	na	2,493	307
El Paso County	103,054	12,670	18,450	2,444	2,248	204	1,150	0	1,049	0	80,588	10,022
Fort Bend County	87,280	7,629	39,905	4,373	15,406	471	18,004	1,290	1,350	95	12,789	1,495
Galveston County	48,735	4,419	34,461	3,749	5,865	304	1,384	0	901	0	6,349	366
Grayson County	23,606	2,521	21,163	2,347	na	na	na	na	na	na	544	0
Gregg County	18,974	2,827	14,969	2,590	2,719	177	na	na	na	na	663	60
Guadalupe County	22,092	1,829	15,034	1,189	463	0	na	na	na	na	5,569	496
Harris County	494,414	49,533	246,985	29,048	87,378	6,462	40,842	4,066	6,130	661	114,039	9,339
Harrison County	10,877	1,144	8,376	1,144	na	na	na	na	na	na	na	na
Hays County	24,844	1,943	18,167	1,535	na	na	na	na	na	na	5,080	61
Henderson County	18,119	1,561	16,332	1,538	na	na	na	na	na	na	na	na
Hidalgo County	96,015	10,542	21,210	2,474	na	na	na	na	299	49	73,495	8,068
Hunt County	14,784	1,003	13,382	991	na	na	na	na	na	na	388	0
Jefferson County	36,578	5,126	21,769	3,759	10,755	1,150	903	165	na	na	3,060	52
Johnson County	23,673	1,534	21,188	1,429	na	na	na	na	na	na	2,012	105
Kaufman County	15,025	1,622	12,525	1,436	1,427	123	na	na	na	na	1,003	63
Liberty County	10,882	603	8,946	501	859	102	na	na	na	na	903	0
Lubbock County	37,599	4,398	27,666	3,391	1,616	86	415	0	101	0	7,628	921
McLennan County	36,582	4,459	27,648	3,626	4,230	290	na	na	na	na	4,085	543
Midland County	18,200	2,333	12,299	1,832	na	na	na	na	na	na	4,008	466
Montgomery County	78,414	5,611	65,509	5,305	1,758	133	2,333	53	na	na	6,661	120
Nacogdoches County	9,550	867	7,714	588	na	na	na	na	na	na	410	148
Nueces County	52,731	5,881	22,312	3,278	1,729	0	910	0	na	na	26,683	2,498
Orange County	13,333	1,730	11,772	1,541	na	na	na	na	na	na	na	na
Parker County	21,356	1,950	19,794	1,771	na	na	na	na	na	na	1,096	179
Potter County	13,638	1,748	10,516	1,521	828	43	na	na	na	na	1,770	88
Randall County	20,619	2,606	18,559	2,356	na	na	na	na	na	na	1,159	250
Rockwall County	12,282	1,234	10,902	1,172	na	na	na	na	na	na	789	62
San Patricio County	10,035	843	5,462	324	na	na	na	na	na	na	4,250	470
Smith County	37,588	3,171	30,237	2,210	5,114	921	na	na	na	na	1,697	40
Tarrant County	235,476	27,000	165,116	20,318	25,740	2,461	11,568	377	2,754	521	29,526	3,290
Taylor County	19,400	2,620	15,704	1,869	760	360	na	na	na	na	2,453	391
Tom Green County	17,887	2,322	12,976	2,066	na	na	na	na	na	na	4,316	222
Travis County	123,434	13,640	84,528	10,492	9,518	999	6,235	513	1,315	130	21,905	1,552
Victoria County	14,935	1,811	9,258	1,151	na	na	na	na	na	na	4,524	626
Walker County	9,226	1,013	7,530	838	1,075	0	na	na	na	na	434	175

Table C-2: Counties - Older Population by Race and Hispanic Origin—*Continued*

Name	Total Population		White, Non-Hispanic		Black, Alone		Asian, Alone		Multi-race, Alone		Hispanic	
	65 Years and Over	85 Years and Over	65 Years and Over	85 Years and Over	65 Years and Over	85 Years and Over	65 Years and Over	85 Years and Over	65 Years and Over	85 Years and Over	65 Years and Over	85 Years and Over
Texas—Cont.												
Webb County	26,003	2,596	2,190	454	na	na	na	na	na	na	23,745	2,142
Wichita County	19,162	2,351	15,824	2,167	772	88	na	na	na	na	2,333	96
Williamson County	68,659	7,312	55,471	6,212	2,648	35	3,084	26	638	96	7,246	975
Wise County	10,070	1,096	9,274	1,029	na	na	na	na	na	na	625	67
Utah												
Cache County	11,531	1,174	11,281	1,174	na	na	na	na	na	na	133	0
Davis County	35,673	3,139	32,140	2,831	na	na	na	na	315	40	1,900	228
Salt Lake County	125,461	12,282	108,391	10,926	781	0	4,545	455	1,118	46	9,594	675
Tooele County	6,359	669	5,630	669	na	na	na	na	na	na	630	0
Utah County	48,066	4,479	44,023	4,134	na	na	598	44	109	0	2,889	301
Washington County	37,295	4,525	34,962	4,525	na	na	na	na	na	na	1,441	0
Weber County	29,562	3,266	26,422	3,035	na	na	na	na	303	0	2,309	206
Vermont												
Chittenden County	26,108	3,083	23,646	3,069	na	na	na	na	na	na	na	na
Virginia												
Albemarle County	20,964	2,866	18,126	2,528	na	na	746	87	na	na	na	na
Arlington County	24,837	3,274	17,866	1,968	2,199	653	2,318	404	270	53	2,286	196
Augusta County	16,099	1,927	15,234	1,658	na	na	na	na	na	na	na	na
Bedford County	16,691	1,760	15,509	1,615	na	na	na	na	na	na	na	na
Chesterfield County	52,026	4,358	40,459	3,978	8,254	252	1,609	0	360	0	1,347	151
Fairfax County	154,639	16,063	103,096	11,260	10,474	950	27,084	2,661	2,645	573	11,736	709
Fauquier County	11,933	896	10,092	602	na	na	na	na	na	na	na	na
Frederick County	15,161	1,733	14,340	1,733	na	na	na	na	na	na	435	0
Hanover County	18,887	2,297	16,758	2,163	na	na	na	na	na	na	na	na
Henrico County	51,563	7,576	35,038	5,917	12,273	1,078	2,630	172	691	306	1,042	198
James City County	19,525	2,065	17,069	1,992	na	na	na	na	na	na	na	na
Loudoun County	37,721	3,868	26,270	3,382	2,431	41	5,601	278	973	0	2,588	134
Montgomery County	12,143	1,606	11,665	1,606	na	na	na	na	na	na	na	na
Prince William County	46,514	3,331	29,478	2,352	6,724	127	4,399	276	1,186	112	4,270	352
Roanoke County	19,691	2,084	18,816	2,084	na	na	na	na	na	na	na	na
Rockingham County	15,209	1,955	14,954	1,955	na	na	na	na	na	na	34	0
Spotsylvania County	19,210	1,388	15,417	1,281	2,468	107	na	na	260	0	544	0
Stafford County	15,406	742	12,272	693	1,755	21	na	na	179	0	557	28
York County	11,536	1,571	8,832	1,307	1,482	232	na	na	na	na	na	na
Washington												
Benton County	30,082	3,690	26,791	3,385	na	na	na	na	na	na	1,639	0
Chelan County	14,418	1,582	13,466	1,514	na	na	na	na	na	na	765	68
Clallam County	22,161	3,101	21,239	3,101	na	na	na	na	na	na	na	na
Clark County	74,468	7,158	67,177	6,898	677	110	2,880	45	1,240	39	1,922	66
Cowlitz County	20,856	2,494	19,285	2,426	na	na	na	na	na	na	381	0
Franklin County	9,167	670	6,223	670	na	na	na	na	na	na	2,529	0
Grant County	14,081	1,325	11,109	987	na	na	na	na	na	na	2,165	68
Grays Harbor County	16,312	1,549	14,743	1,507	na	na	na	na	na	na	na	na
Island County	20,803	1,834	19,126	1,717	na	na	na	na	na	na	292	46
King County	294,891	38,126	221,809	30,878	12,421	1,406	43,854	4,992	5,087	330	9,005	494
Kitsap County	47,748	3,225	42,277	2,997	na	na	2,693	164	882	0	638	41
Lewis County	16,580	1,642	15,727	1,502	na	na	na	na	na	na	404	0
Mason County	14,862	1,592	13,897	1,415	na	na	na	na	na	na	na	na
Pierce County	123,257	13,351	101,196	11,608	5,345	530	9,132	830	2,136	144	3,670	292
Skagit County	26,616	2,992	24,537	2,926	na	na	na	na	556	11	829	0
Snohomish County	109,883	12,031	92,537	11,085	1,485	241	9,879	538	1,378	11	3,059	97
Spokane County	83,502	8,547	77,814	8,023	na	na	1,454	226	673	124	1,898	174
Thurston County	49,236	5,381	43,703	5,255	na	na	2,449	57	415	69	1,581	0
Whatcom County	39,347	4,604	35,624	4,182	na	na	na	na	776	0	795	0
Yakima County	34,329	3,726	26,300	3,417	na	na	na	na	240	0	6,335	269
West Virginia												
Berkeley County	17,561	1,433	15,663	1,295	na	na	na	na	na	na	na	na
Cabell County	16,984	1,698	16,532	1,678	na	na	na	na	na	na	na	na
Harrison County	13,272	1,854	12,676	1,854	na	na	na	na	na	na	na	na
Kanawha County	37,659	4,694	34,782	4,478	1,884	180	na	na	na	na	na	na
Monongalia County	13,176	1,697	12,720	1,697	na	na	na	na	na	na	na	na
Raleigh County	15,492	1,245	14,122	1,209	na	na	na	na	na	na	na	na
Wood County	17,190	1,597	16,811	1,597	na	na	na	na	na	na	na	na
Wisconsin												
Brown County	39,372	4,135	37,091	3,937	na	na	348	0	na	na	1,093	143
Dane County	74,937	9,041	70,044	8,395	1,356	158	1,536	294	394	54	1,500	140
Dodge County	15,571	2,621	15,141	2,560	na	na	na	na	na	na	na	na
Eau Claire County	16,689	1,830	15,909	1,784	na	na	na	na	na	na	na	na
Fond du Lac County	19,012	2,970	18,606	2,932	na	na	na	na	na	na	na	na
Jefferson County	14,645	1,281	14,060	1,202	na	na	na	na	na	na	206	42
Kenosha County	23,669	3,201	21,765	3,115	na	na	na	na	na	na	875	86
La Crosse County	19,122	2,817	18,863	2,817	na	na	na	na	na	na	na	na
Manitowoc County	15,941	2,333	15,810	2,333	na	na	na	na	na	na	na	na
Marathon County	23,770	3,026	23,365	2,923	na	na	82	0	na	na	na	na

Table C-2: Counties - Older Population by Race and Hispanic Origin—*Continued*

Name	Total Population		White, Non-Hispanic		Black, Alone		Asian, Alone		Multi-race, Alone		Hispanic	
	65 Years and Over	85 Years and Over	65 Years and Over	85 Years and Over	65 Years and Over	85 Years and Over	65 Years and Over	85 Years and Over	65 Years and Over	85 Years and Over	65 Years and Over	85 Years and Over
Wisconsin—Cont.												
Milwaukee County...............................	128,936	19,165	94,678	15,538	22,996	2,368	2,544	283	959	212	7,126	732
Outagamie County...............................	27,576	3,097	26,389	3,097	na	na	na	na	na	na	372	0
Ozaukee County..................................	17,689	1,834	17,010	1,733	na	na	na	na	na	na	na	na
Portage County...................................	11,666	1,428	11,507	1,428	na	na	na	na	na	na	na	na
Racine County....................................	32,401	3,701	28,523	3,452	2,134	183	na	na	na	na	1,237	50
Rock County......................................	27,151	3,224	25,344	3,100	na	na	na	na	na	na	377	18
St. Croix County.................................	12,492	1,280	12,350	1,280	na	na	na	na	na	na	na	na
Sheboygan County..............................	20,696	2,692	20,019	2,591	na	na	281	101	na	na	219	0
Walworth County................................	18,146	2,440	17,620	2,405	na	na	na	na	na	na	197	35
Washington County.............................	24,354	2,397	23,839	2,312	na	na	na	na	na	na	na	na
Waukesha County...............................	75,079	9,988	71,948	9,988	na	na	916	0	113	0	1,299	0
Winnebago County..............................	27,997	4,386	27,156	4,341	na	na	na	na	na	na	na	na
Wood County.....................................	14,940	1,891	14,652	1,891	na	na	na	na	na	na	na	na
Wyoming												
Laramie County..................................	16,163	1,792	13,975	1,498	na	na	na	na	na	na	1,338	294
Natrona County..................................	11,900	1,687	11,404	1,639	na	na	na	na	na	na	268	48

Table C-3: Cities - Older Population by Race and Hispanic Origin

Name	Total Population 65 Years and Over	Total Population 85 Years and Over	White, Non-Hispanic 65 Years and Over	White, Non-Hispanic 85 Years and Over	Black, Alone 65 Years and Over	Black, Alone 85 Years and Over	Asian, Alone 65 Years and Over	Asian, Alone 85 Years and Over	Multi-race, Alone 65 Years and Over	Multi-race, Alone 85 Years and Over	Hispanic 65 Years and Over	Hispanic 85 Years and Over
Alabama												
Auburn city	5,252	351	4,449	298	na	na	na	na	na	na	na	na
Birmingham city	32,361	3,618	8,169	1,583	23,320	1,965	na	na	na	na	70	70
Dothan city	13,304	1,609	10,148	1,252	2,649	289	na	na	na	na	na	na
Hoover city	15,152	1,651	13,500	1,441	577	0	na	na	na	na	na	na
Huntsville city	33,334	3,619	22,863	3,108	7,935	428	na	na	na	na	853	0
Mobile city	33,153	4,344	19,494	2,674	12,944	1,468	na	na	na	na	na	na
Montgomery city	27,928	3,437	13,941	1,738	12,979	1,667	465	0	na	na	142	0
Tuscaloosa city	12,475	1,333	7,945	1,056	4,134	258	na	na	na	na	na	na
Alaska												
Anchorage municipality	32,809	3,056	23,241	2,225	1,555	70	3,575	395	638	143	1,461	0
Arizona												
Avondale city	7,662	528	3,612	322	680	70	na	na	na	na	2,793	136
Buckeye city	12,006	343	7,703	299	na	na	na	na	na	na	1,422	44
Chandler city	30,221	2,192	22,792	1,906	1,026	83	2,620	118	47	0	3,678	85
Flagstaff city	6,692	306	5,606	147	na	na	na	na	na	na	769	96
Glendale city	32,779	2,903	23,222	2,308	1,107	0	1,064	108	687	0	6,800	487
Goodyear city	14,839	493	12,038	424	na	na	na	na	na	na	1,981	0
Mesa city	83,582	9,417	71,531	8,294	1,659	0	na	na	558	83	8,458	903
Peoria city	31,097	4,167	26,716	3,892	na	na	1,081	162	na	na	1,446	75
Phoenix city	178,699	19,934	126,191	15,516	10,348	836	6,679	678	2,054	114	32,894	2,628
Scottsdale city	58,368	8,821	54,586	8,134	na	na	1,431	200	na	na	1,596	0
Surprise city	30,777	2,215	28,091	2,176	na	na	na	na	na	na	1,154	39
Tempe city	20,178	2,395	15,632	2,070	1,032	0	1,032	271	157	0	2,285	54
Tucson city	80,806	9,359	50,788	5,853	3,797	635	2,289	56	2,449	54	21,797	2,723
Yuma city	15,465	1,308	9,388	897	na	na	na	na	na	na	4,960	315
Arkansas												
Conway city	8,099	1,085	7,269	1,085	571	0	na	na	na	na	na	na
Fayetteville city	6,564	1,175	6,331	1,175	na	na	na	na	na	na	na	na
Fort Smith city	12,359	1,517	10,073	1,517	1,201	0	na	na	na	na	742	0
Jonesboro city	8,745	865	8,256	865	425	0	na	na	na	na	na	na
Little Rock city	27,950	3,959	17,633	2,923	9,426	969	na	na	na	na	430	67
North Little Rock city	11,141	1,405	8,810	1,248	1,574	157	na	na	na	na	na	na
Rogers city	6,577	798	5,856	425	na	na	na	na	na	na	721	373
Springdale city	8,428	1,940	7,602	1,719	na	na	na	na	na	na	449	221
California												
Alameda city	13,565	1,425	8,332	870	na	na	3,376	469	na	na	725	32
Alhambra city	14,890	3,187	2,420	734	na	na	7,528	1,762	na	na	4,468	646
Anaheim city	41,460	4,796	18,755	2,719	1,274	0	10,064	1,244	570	109	10,789	724
Antioch city	14,372	1,452	6,146	825	2,462	41	2,297	292	na	na	3,236	294
Bakersfield city	40,509	5,503	23,479	3,759	3,292	60	2,713	250	166	0	10,344	1,347
Baldwin Park city	7,962	615	0	0	na	na	2,522	273	1,249	0	4,421	145
Bellflower city	7,840	841	2,053	377	na	na	1,446	179	na	na	3,346	244
Berkeley city	16,662	1,511	11,951	853	na	na	2,365	191	145	0	607	0
Buena Park city	9,949	1,121	3,273	484	na	na	4,066	195	na	na	2,163	351
Burbank city	15,541	2,557	11,360	2,070	na	na	1,234	8	na	na	1,966	94
Camarillo city	14,347	2,373	10,968	1,725	na	na	na	na	na	na	1,810	92
Carlsbad city	22,329	4,101	19,552	3,737	na	na	na	na	na	na	840	102
Carson city	13,747	1,684	0	0	3,638	211	3,901	535	na	na	4,501	839
Chico city	12,616	1,616	10,764	1,611	na	na	na	na	na	na	1,244	5
Chino city	12,106	1,020	4,359	495	na	na	1,126	0	na	na	4,708	261
Chino Hills city	7,838	821	2,313	485	na	na	3,474	243	na	na	1,589	93
Chula Vista city	31,145	4,246	9,743	1,682	na	na	6,549	622	1,001	213	13,920	1,942
Citrus Heights city	14,503	2,113	12,026	1,743	na	na	na	na	na	na	1,312	325
Clovis city	15,491	1,825	10,277	1,739	na	na	1,482	0	157	0	2,885	86
Compton city	9,116	1,670	0	0	5,549	1,459	na	na	na	na	3,264	209
Concord city	20,253	2,188	13,819	1,794	na	na	2,134	248	1,667	0	2,889	117
Corona city	16,276	1,342	8,025	1,101	609	0	2,435	127	586	79	4,819	35
Costa Mesa city	13,097	2,507	9,293	2,281	na	na	na	na	na	na	2,297	60
Daly City city	18,142	3,278	3,635	844	na	na	11,588	1,784	na	na	2,395	605
Davis city	7,506	954	6,308	704	na	na	1,015	250	na	na	na	na
Downey city	15,694	1,866	5,105	895	na	na	na	na	na	na	8,413	783
El Cajon city	12,503	2,138	10,448	1,615	na	na	na	na	na	na	1,050	411
Elk Grove city	23,605	3,032	13,117	1,683	1,481	79	6,165	1,107	451	0	1,931	163
El Monte city	15,384	2,034	0	0	na	na	7,000	1,022	731	0	7,030	711
Escondido city	21,512	3,109	13,675	2,091	na	na	2,634	577	na	na	3,537	238
Fairfield city	15,227	2,380	8,090	1,556	2,027	73	3,223	559	234	0	1,547	71
Folsom city	9,530	916	7,429	778	na	na	1,482	124	na	na	216	0
Fontana city	16,851	1,413	4,621	563	1,678	75	2,462	231	na	na	7,771	491
Fremont city	30,434	4,244	11,112	2,100	na	na	14,693	1,809	802	0	2,781	165
Fresno city	60,638	8,155	32,663	5,184	3,242	377	6,849	932	1,108	69	17,068	1,604
Fullerton city	18,229	2,894	10,100	1,703	na	na	4,729	499	na	na	3,107	692
Garden Grove city	21,707	3,310	7,111	1,347	na	na	10,035	1,730	na	na	4,318	197
Glendale city	35,731	5,373	25,145	4,022	na	na	4,839	405	682	0	4,700	946
Hawthorne city	8,587	1,121	1,409	259	2,235	161	na	na	na	na	3,663	497
Hayward city	20,792	2,537	6,281	944	1,411	24	7,925	1,329	711	49	4,136	240

Table C-3: Cities - Older Population by Race and Hispanic Origin—*Continued*

Name	Total Population		White, Non-Hispanic		Black, Alone		Asian, Alone		Multi-race, Alone		Hispanic	
	65 Years and Over	85 Years and Over	65 Years and Over	85 Years and Over	65 Years and Over	85 Years and Over	65 Years and Over	85 Years and Over	65 Years and Over	85 Years and Over	65 Years and Over	85 Years and Over
California—Cont.												
Hemet city	21,434	2,879	14,245	2,510	na	na	na	na	na	na	4,878	231
Hesperia city	11,938	1,059	6,801	677	na	na	na	na	na	na	4,142	310
Huntington Beach city	33,121	4,100	24,901	2,956	na	na	4,727	596	157	69	2,933	548
Indio city	19,395	909	12,046	628	na	na	na	na	na	na	6,639	281
Inglewood city	12,357	1,631	0	0	7,555	1,151	na	na	na	na	3,138	168
Irvine city	29,682	3,386	17,219	2,407	na	na	8,745	534	542	307	1,989	138
Jurupa Valley city	12,830	1,936	5,678	1,172	na	na	na	na	na	na	5,239	520
Laguna Niguel city	11,267	1,456	8,806	1,260	na	na	na	na	na	na	954	129
Lake Elsinore city	7,588	460	3,217	0	na	na	na	na	na	na	2,760	460
Lake Forest city	12,928	1,197	8,914	759	na	na	2,470	152	na	na	809	237
Lakewood city	9,585	1,232	5,865	985	na	na	1,725	100	na	na	861	62
Lancaster city	15,937	1,612	6,221	1,138	2,923	154	na	na	453	15	5,322	102
Livermore city	12,311	1,372	9,824	1,289	na	na	919	71	na	na	711	12
Lodi City	10,112	1,610	7,429	1,508	na	na	886	87	526	0	1,706	15
Long Beach city	52,953	7,063	26,146	3,522	6,497	728	8,976	1,342	1,506	323	10,456	1,340
Los Angeles city	512,427	69,755	216,997	32,305	50,915	7,010	90,778	13,069	8,540	907	147,509	16,613
Lynwood city	5,786	502	0	0	na	na	na	na	na	na	4,054	308
Madera city	6,546	1,042	2,699	899	na	na	na	na	na	na	3,375	143
Manteca city	11,318	1,067	7,626	767	na	na	na	na	na	na	1,909	201
Menifee city	16,906	2,446	11,780	1,570	na	na	na	na	na	na	2,624	137
Merced city	9,912	1,237	5,057	617	na	na	535	0	na	na	3,889	550
Milpitas city	9,268	1,279	0	0	na	na	6,486	980	na	na	na	na
Mission Viejo city	19,372	2,972	15,203	2,214	na	na	2,572	421	na	na	1,513	337
Modesto city	27,056	3,614	17,456	2,028	na	na	1,278	385	529	121	6,267	856
Moreno Valley city	17,054	1,507	3,779	573	4,078	101	2,469	214	125	0	6,747	619
Mountain View city	9,074	1,724	5,602	955	na	na	2,531	523	na	na	845	246
Murrieta city	13,702	3,025	10,014	2,798	na	na	na	na	na	na	2,261	115
Napa city	14,605	1,657	12,205	1,631	na	na	na	na	na	na	1,667	26
Newport Beach city	20,241	3,323	17,672	3,273	na	na	na	na	na	na	na	na
Norwalk city	14,543	1,763	3,070	771	na	na	3,194	246	na	na	7,652	746
Oakland city	58,105	6,015	19,624	1,718	16,595	1,338	13,828	2,001	1,008	160	6,259	676
Oceanside city	30,065	3,197	20,187	1,924	na	na	3,457	577	353	0	4,943	537
Ontario city	16,575	1,517	4,926	578	1,135	82	1,913	117	489	0	8,383	740
Orange city	16,644	2,084	10,019	1,231	na	na	3,782	453	na	na	2,382	400
Oxnard city	20,331	2,936	6,901	1,226	na	na	2,942	109	na	na	9,842	1,557
Palmdale city	17,379	1,567	7,425	1,051	2,557	58	na	na	na	na	5,986	394
Palo Alto city	13,105	2,138	9,328	1,744	na	na	3,024	290	na	na	na	na
Pasadena city	23,746	3,945	12,583	1,674	2,558	536	4,114	969	na	na	3,902	260
Perris city	4,609	195	0	0	na	na	na	na	na	na	2,751	195
Pittsburg city	7,026	469	2,778	52	na	na	1,755	125	na	na	1,866	210
Pleasanton city	12,434	1,226	8,476	849	na	na	2,918	268	na	na	784	71
Pomona city	16,981	2,303	4,059	714	1,763	230	2,337	259	169	0	8,256	1,100
Rancho Cordova city	11,997	1,182	6,890	814	na	na	1,482	139	na	na	2,068	103
Rancho Cucamonga city	22,373	1,906	11,312	731	1,163	0	2,461	293	613	0	6,726	761
Redding city	16,724	2,509	15,278	2,367	na	na	na	na	na	na	728	142
Redlands city	11,760	1,814	8,239	1,270	na	na	na	na	na	na	1,906	458
Redondo Beach city	9,059	823	6,171	735	na	na	na	na	na	na	na	na
Redwood City city	12,463	1,920	7,607	1,502	na	na	1,413	127	na	na	2,877	222
Rialto city	12,792	917	2,578	381	2,831	195	na	na	na	na	6,666	341
Richmond city	15,060	2,071	3,960	369	4,467	722	3,210	632	na	na	3,187	348
Riverside city	34,595	4,539	19,123	2,874	2,058	336	3,543	94	215	46	9,548	1,264
Rocklin city	7,716	614	6,082	536	na	na	na	na	na	na	505	0
Roseville city	23,575	3,378	19,358	2,794	na	na	1,643	281	72	44	2,240	259
Sacramento city	67,610	9,057	30,675	3,893	9,109	1,128	15,009	2,557	2,061	232	11,378	1,595
Salinas city	14,422	2,235	5,011	1,309	na	na	2,018	373	na	na	7,149	515
San Bernardino city	19,532	2,081	6,825	844	2,356	176	1,928	168	366	84	7,992	705
San Buenaventura (Ventura) city	19,458	2,611	14,064	2,056	na	na	na	na	na	na	3,811	348
San Clemente city	11,744	1,363	9,373	1,191	na	na	na	na	na	na	1,458	102
San Diego city	189,049	22,311	110,555	14,576	9,401	787	31,592	3,194	2,896	148	34,515	3,697
San Francisco city	138,128	22,842	53,430	7,344	7,532	1,748	61,869	11,213	2,558	445	12,672	2,198
San Jose city	134,053	16,959	52,603	7,433	4,025	251	49,211	5,276	2,935	667	24,598	3,033
San Leandro city	13,412	2,522	4,947	809	na	na	4,839	1,307	na	na	1,527	100
San Marcos city	11,646	2,000	8,390	1,120	na	na	na	na	na	na	1,942	343
San Mateo city	17,795	3,331	9,831	1,949	na	na	4,848	1,051	298	0	1,784	326
San Ramon city	8,324	824	4,583	582	na	na	2,968	4	na	na	na	na
Santa Ana city	32,306	4,647	7,208	1,505	na	na	7,992	1,331	288	37	16,100	1,665
Santa Barbara city	16,640	2,680	12,164	1,983	na	na	na	na	na	na	3,926	489
Santa Clara city	16,419	1,910	7,410	1,353	na	na	6,942	511	na	na	1,536	0
Santa Clarita city	26,584	3,000	17,787	1,900	na	na	3,638	275	863	49	3,618	590
Santa Cruz city	8,428	578	7,254	578	na	na	na	na	na	na	727	0
Santa Maria city	9,578	1,228	4,656	647	na	na	na	na	na	na	3,597	481
Santa Monica city	15,695	3,694	12,553	2,825	na	na	na	na	na	na	1,145	369
Santa Rosa city	30,999	3,862	25,122	3,462	na	na	1,894	103	na	na	3,564	297
Simi Valley city	21,662	2,578	15,495	1,658	na	na	2,272	534	127	0	3,442	386
South Gate city	8,900	799	0	0	na	na	na	na	na	na	7,982	640
South San Francisco city	12,530	1,507	4,798	991	na	na	4,572	93	na	na	2,261	417
Stockton city	38,174	3,663	14,727	1,541	3,755	403	9,781	1,178	1,890	30	8,962	511

Table C-3: Cities - Older Population by Race and Hispanic Origin—*Continued*

Name	Total Population		White, Non-Hispanic		Black, Alone		Asian, Alone		Multi-race, Alone		Hispanic	
	65 Years and Over	85 Years and Over	65 Years and Over	85 Years and Over	65 Years and Over	85 Years and Over	65 Years and Over	85 Years and Over	65 Years and Over	85 Years and Over	65 Years and Over	85 Years and Over
California—Cont.												
Sunnyvale city	18,443	3,260	9,083	1,304	na	na	7,570	1,625	na	na	1,568	277
Temecula city	11,656	1,437	7,616	1,060	na	na	1,595	218	na	na	1,595	47
Thousand Oaks city	23,503	4,450	20,112	4,263	na	na	1,700	89	na	na	1,452	98
Torrance city	25,953	4,978	12,601	2,542	na	na	10,375	2,032	na	na	2,194	420
Tracy city	8,242	838	3,273	437	na	na	1,870	0	na	na	2,235	200
Turlock city	9,643	824	6,233	509	na	na	na	na	na	na	1,668	209
Tustin city	7,753	1,319	4,739	672	na	na	1,554	253	na	na	1,311	386
Union City city	11,691	1,875	2,407	388	na	na	6,252	884	na	na	1,942	339
Upland city	11,522	1,368	6,498	824	na	na	1,744	64	na	na	2,048	333
Vacaville city	14,831	2,065	8,878	1,458	na	na	1,724	254	na	na	1,202	24
Vallejo city	19,775	1,810	6,780	664	3,965	33	6,205	816	na	na	2,828	329
Victorville city	9,823	894	3,759	394	1,934	202	na	na	na	na	2,765	169
Visalia city	15,897	1,886	10,558	1,378	na	na	na	na	na	na	4,109	447
Vista city	9,944	1,248	6,216	680	na	na	na	na	na	na	2,263	352
Walnut Creek city	22,223	3,624	17,252	2,977	na	na	3,913	627	na	na	na	na
West Covina city	17,625	2,483	3,715	217	na	na	5,810	1,104	499	33	6,623	1,006
Westminster city	17,651	1,689	4,500	660	na	na	11,785	897	na	na	1,062	132
Whittier city	12,745	2,309	4,733	826	na	na	na	na	na	na	6,573	1,101
Yorba Linda city	14,150	1,621	9,632	1,081	na	na	2,705	400	na	na	1,521	140
Yuba City city	11,004	1,787	6,700	1,084	na	na	2,164	447	na	na	1,230	142
Colorado												
Arvada city	22,525	2,750	20,621	2,579	na	na	na	na	na	na	1,492	78
Aurora city	44,196	4,236	30,265	3,058	5,772	531	2,614	301	500	80	5,193	343
Boulder city	12,347	1,741	11,256	1,692	na	na	na	na	na	na	330	0
Broomfield city	9,618	809	8,498	761	na	na	na	na	na	na	na	na
Centennial city	15,966	1,384	13,749	1,250	na	na	837	29	na	na	525	105
Colorado Springs city	62,658	7,639	52,199	6,465	2,324	177	2,502	469	603	33	5,053	387
Denver city	83,996	9,433	55,955	6,020	8,470	811	2,860	71	1,706	64	15,044	2,235
Fort Collins city	18,011	1,870	16,941	1,815	na	na	na	na	na	na	647	0
Greeley city	11,608	1,873	9,863	1,691	na	na	na	na	na	na	1,367	143
Lakewood city	26,670	3,461	21,865	2,989	na	na	na	na	na	na	3,114	340
Longmont city	15,837	2,267	13,513	2,176	na	na	na	na	na	na	1,764	91
Loveland city	13,838	2,168	13,314	2,103	na	na	na	na	na	na	na	na
Pueblo city	20,979	2,691	13,007	1,947	na	na	na	na	na	na	7,258	700
Thornton city	12,822	859	9,600	722	na	na	na	na	na	na	2,493	137
Westminster city	15,348	1,653	12,634	1,653	na	na	na	na	na	na	2,368	0
Connecticut												
Bridgeport city	16,277	2,223	5,945	1,670	5,157	319	na	na	na	na	4,120	234
Danbury city	10,095	1,675	7,969	1,569	na	na	na	na	na	na	690	16
Hartford city	14,074	1,744	3,644	812	5,196	604	na	na	401	0	5,072	328
New Britain city	8,674	1,203	6,085	1,123	na	na	na	na	na	na	1,695	80
New Haven city	12,044	1,344	4,637	761	4,393	373	na	na	na	na	2,277	210
Norwalk city	15,974	1,867	11,483	1,431	2,146	260	na	na	na	na	2,160	176
Stamford city	21,124	3,267	15,528	3,056	1,735	0	727	46	na	na	3,134	165
Waterbury city	13,430	2,067	8,385	1,809	2,284	81	na	na	na	na	2,394	50
Delaware												
Wilmington city	8,346	765	3,358	548	4,429	217	na	na	na	na	418	0
District of Columbia												
Washington city	85,626	10,901	29,184	3,372	48,883	7,062	2,297	83	1,578	218	4,636	256
Florida												
Boca Raton city	29,765	3,712	26,819	3,103	na	na	na	na	na	na	1,847	609
Boynton Beach city	17,876	3,049	12,408	2,588	3,816	0	na	na	na	na	1,059	461
Cape Coral city	48,088	5,878	39,975	5,415	na	na	na	na	na	na	5,037	463
Clearwater city	26,465	5,030	22,541	4,626	na	na	na	na	na	na	1,489	110
Coral Springs city	16,430	1,431	9,928	1,201	2,938	230	na	na	na	na	2,453	0
Daytona Beach city	14,612	2,145	10,989	1,791	2,866	249	na	na	na	na	na	na
Deerfield Beach city	19,397	3,092	14,087	2,624	3,149	468	na	na	na	na	2,287	0
Delray Beach city	17,509	2,742	13,829	2,579	2,685	154	na	na	na	na	na	na
Deltona city	14,669	2,052	7,979	1,519	na	na	na	na	na	na	4,901	373
Fort Lauderdale city	33,299	3,378	21,233	2,775	5,923	311	na	na	na	na	5,412	214
Fort Myers city	19,920	2,790	15,017	2,556	2,776	41	na	na	na	na	1,649	16
Gainesville city	13,503	2,021	8,703	1,491	3,226	530	na	na	na	na	1,040	0
Hialeah city	45,558	9,602	1,027	339	na	na	na	na	na	na	43,994	9,098
Hollywood city	25,257	3,036	15,358	2,477	2,190	119	na	na	na	na	6,819	440
Homestead city	6,275	376	0	0	na	na	na	na	na	na	4,234	367
Jacksonville city	124,132	12,958	82,325	9,182	27,943	2,364	5,468	503	1,255	93	6,722	867
Kissimmee city	8,919	479	0	0	na	na	na	na	na	na	5,520	262
Lakeland city	21,578	2,804	16,461	2,465	2,823	248	na	na	na	na	2,143	30
Largo city	23,439	3,636	22,114	3,564	na	na	na	na	na	na	na	na
Lauderhill city	9,529	1,325	0	0	6,045	737	na	na	na	na	na	na
Melbourne city	16,184	3,149	12,867	2,345	na	na	na	na	na	na	na	na
Miami city	83,023	13,566	5,869	815	12,053	1,280	na	na	na	na	66,659	11,549
Miami Beach city	15,396	1,879	5,663	604	na	na	na	na	na	na	9,211	1,275
Miami Gardens city	16,456	1,984	0	0	11,087	1,005	na	na	na	na	4,972	704
Miramar city	14,169	1,323	0	0	7,364	492	na	na	na	na	4,388	376

Table C-3: Cities - Older Population by Race and Hispanic Origin—*Continued*

Name	Total Population		White, Non-Hispanic		Black, Alone		Asian, Alone		Multi-race, Alone		Hispanic	
	65 Years and Over	85 Years and Over	65 Years and Over	85 Years and Over	65 Years and Over	85 Years and Over	65 Years and Over	85 Years and Over	65 Years and Over	85 Years and Over	65 Years and Over	85 Years and Over
Florida—Cont.												
North Port city	20,819	1,540	17,987	1,488	na	na	na	na	na	na	na	na
Orlando city	31,154	4,028	13,539	1,367	7,388	830	1,053	19	na	na	9,481	1,812
Palm Bay city	26,330	3,952	17,286	2,621	3,747	652	na	na	na	na	3,938	759
Palm Coast city	26,538	4,120	20,486	2,206	na	na	na	na	na	na	na	na
Pembroke Pines city	32,384	3,664	13,157	1,847	5,163	82	na	na	na	na	12,334	1,609
Plantation city	15,365	1,542	11,243	1,380	763	61	na	na	na	na	2,359	101
Pompano Beach city	22,487	4,222	15,978	3,045	4,047	604	na	na	na	na	2,209	411
Port St. Lucie city	41,126	3,738	31,119	3,349	5,898	275	na	na	na	na	3,870	114
St. Petersburg city	46,994	6,131	35,945	5,429	6,959	594	1,170	0	na	na	2,453	182
Sunrise city	19,088	2,485	7,331	1,557	3,745	507	na	na	na	na	6,973	147
Tallahassee city	19,192	1,607	13,351	1,076	4,580	425	549	0	na	na	520	106
Tamarac city	17,415	3,652	10,255	2,609	na	na	na	na	na	na	3,481	321
Tampa city	49,295	7,349	24,461	4,069	11,952	1,349	1,464	242	716	186	10,624	1,222
Weston city	6,986	784	3,816	645	na	na	na	na	na	na	2,478	84
West Palm Beach city	21,917	4,463	13,546	3,163	5,568	1,155	na	na	na	na	2,336	145
Georgia												
Albany city	10,050	1,797	4,088	528	5,893	1,269	na	na	na	na	na	na
Alpharetta city	6,465	508	4,737	429	na	na	735	0	na	na	na	na
Athens-Clarke County unified govt (bal)	14,783	1,697	9,460	1,129	4,417	241	na	na	na	na	552	327
Atlanta city	55,303	6,820	21,130	2,949	32,799	3,775	839	0	274	29	312	67
Augusta-Richmond County consolidated govt (bal)	27,566	2,777	13,044	1,617	12,996	1,086	na	na	na	na	493	0
Columbus city	26,086	3,698	14,054	2,368	10,418	1,004	na	na	na	na	764	0
Johns Creek city	9,449	1,207	6,320	663	na	na	1,978	378	na	na	na	na
Macon-Bibb County	23,974	2,802	13,202	2,193	9,885	609	na	na	na	na	na	na
Roswell city	12,887	1,150	11,340	1,150	na	na	na	na	na	na	na	na
Sandy Springs city	15,300	2,300	12,618	2,128	1,255	0	na	na	na	na	852	119
Savannah city	20,502	2,683	10,673	1,633	9,256	1,050	na	na	na	na	283	0
South Fulton city	12,390	851	0	0	11,023	437	na	na	na	na	na	na
Warner Robins city	8,035	885	5,509	629	2,526	256	na	na	na	na	na	na
Hawaii												
Urban Honolulu CDP	70,415	12,809	9,942	1,324	na	na	50,633	10,675	6,002	593	1,672	88
Iowa												
Boise City city	35,173	4,968	32,782	4,841	na	na	504	127	na	na	1,230	0
Meridian city	10,340	818	9,692	818	na	na	na	na	na	na	na	na
Nampa city	14,790	1,793	11,892	1,154	na	na	na	na	na	na	1,253	99
Illinois												
Aurora city	18,483	2,391	10,777	1,541	2,111	0	1,000	161	na	na	4,595	689
Bloomington city	10,513	1,528	9,396	1,358	576	170	na	na	na	na	na	na
Champaign city	9,849	1,441	8,112	1,441	742	0	592	0	na	na	na	na
Chicago city	349,712	41,608	134,573	19,981	120,953	13,309	24,902	2,595	3,390	260	67,332	5,508
Decatur city	14,883	1,964	12,401	1,935	2,029	29	na	na	na	na	na	na
Elgin city	14,015	1,048	10,267	786	na	na	na	na	na	na	1,619	70
Evanston city	11,686	2,090	8,915	1,417	1,841	424	na	na	na	na	727	249
Joliet city	13,782	1,635	8,569	1,101	2,555	302	na	na	na	na	2,417	232
Naperville city	17,180	2,023	14,183	1,896	na	na	2,357	117	na	na	62	0
Peoria city	17,711	3,128	14,387	2,767	2,994	361	na	na	na	na	160	0
Rockford city	26,571	4,614	21,396	4,139	3,185	426	na	na	na	na	1,377	49
Springfield city	19,787	2,912	17,063	2,351	2,083	451	na	na	na	na	na	na
Waukegan city	7,664	677	3,084	534	1,666	35	na	na	na	na	2,206	108
Indiana												
Bloomington city	8,292	1,688	7,753	1,674	na	na	na	na	na	na	na	na
Carmel city	13,218	1,266	12,011	1,177	na	na	na	na	na	na	na	na
Evansville city	18,304	3,345	16,359	3,175	1,918	170	na	na	na	na	na	na
Fishers city	9,511	1,646	8,662	1,615	na	na	na	na	na	na	na	na
Fort Wayne city	36,436	4,131	30,681	3,802	4,250	249	425	0	142	40	1,024	40
Gary city	14,138	1,804	0	0	11,500	1,475	na	na	na	na	na	na
Hammond city	10,389	1,318	7,042	978	1,316	92	na	na	na	na	1,981	248
Indianapolis city (bal)	107,601	12,206	77,763	8,426	25,159	3,019	2,052	405	567	0	2,653	534
Lafayette city	9,962	1,574	9,346	1,574	118	0	na	na	na	na	300	0
Muncie city	10,151	1,668	8,747	1,418	947	178	na	na	na	na	na	na
Noblesville city	7,000	998	6,306	941	na	na	na	na	na	na	na	na
South Bend city	13,616	2,164	10,326	1,925	2,390	198	na	na	na	na	628	41
Iowa												
Ames city	6,589	943	6,363	943	na	na	na	na	na	na	na	na
Ankeny city	8,003	758	7,711	758	na	na	na	na	na	na	na	na
Cedar Rapids city	19,911	2,770	18,121	2,469	544	41	na	na	na	na	na	na
Davenport city	15,308	1,981	13,958	1,799	707	0	na	na	na	na	521	138
Des Moines city	25,436	3,711	22,649	3,586	1,449	0	565	49	na	na	507	0
Iowa City city	8,238	1,373	7,940	1,304	na	na	na	na	na	na	na	na
Sioux City city	11,623	1,380	10,297	1,309	na	na	na	na	na	na	201	0
Waterloo city	11,975	1,804	11,025	1,777	911	0	na	na	na	na	27	27
West Des Moines city	9,890	669	8,858	669	na	na	na	na	na	na	na	na

Table C-3: Cities - Older Population by Race and Hispanic Origin—*Continued*

Name	Total Population		White, Non-Hispanic		Black, Alone		Asian, Alone		Multi-race, Alone		Hispanic	
	65 Years and Over	85 Years and Over	65 Years and Over	85 Years and Over	65 Years and Over	85 Years and Over	65 Years and Over	85 Years and Over	65 Years and Over	85 Years and Over	65 Years and Over	85 Years and Over
Kansas												
Kansas City city	18,604	1,375	10,394	900	5,016	242	na	na	na	na	2,243	221
Lawrence city	11,877	1,983	10,276	1,346	na	na	na	na	na	na	na	na
Olathe city	14,007	1,575	12,263	1,575	780	0	na	na	na	na	454	0
Overland Park city	30,952	4,455	28,063	4,273	674	0	1,070	56	na	na	950	126
Shawnee city	8,386	689	7,756	647	na	na	na	na	na	na	na	na
Topeka city	24,157	2,818	20,195	2,447	1,926	159	na	na	na	na	1,381	124
Wichita city	57,099	7,662	46,583	6,199	4,853	947	1,810	126	593	12	3,297	318
Kentucky												
Bowling Green city	8,230	1,015	6,762	924	na	na	na	na	na	na	na	na
Lexington-Fayette urban county	42,959	4,478	36,330	3,310	4,795	1,108	554	0	580	0	539	60
Louisville/Jefferson County metro govt (bal)	95,385	11,914	76,068	10,480	15,659	1,240	1,183	87	796	66	1,692	41
Louisiana												
Baton Rouge city	33,975	4,597	18,387	3,122	13,629	1,058	na	na	na	na	na	na
Bossier City city	10,242	1,430	7,776	1,242	2,155	188	na	na	na	na	na	na
Kenner city	12,066	1,077	7,402	806	3,071	103	na	na	na	na	1,166	168
Lafayette city	17,812	2,221	13,345	2,017	4,076	204	na	na	na	na	na	na
Lake Charles city	11,414	1,313	7,232	828	3,756	485	na	na	na	na	na	na
New Orleans city	57,532	5,890	19,939	2,295	33,980	3,301	1,231	41	483	150	1,912	148
Shreveport city	32,183	3,787	17,543	2,411	13,805	1,376	na	na	na	na	na	na
Maine												
Portland city	8,562	1,649	8,371	1,649	na	na	na	na	na	na	na	na
Maryland												
Baltimore city	84,069	10,141	26,619	3,334	53,486	6,139	1,374	165	1,729	422	1,200	141
Frederick city	9,659	1,181	6,864	1,015	1,674	166	na	na	na	na	672	0
Gaithersburg city	8,959	1,147	5,170	766	866	0	1,643	293	na	na	876	46
Rockville city	11,479	1,353	8,060	1,119	na	na	1,366	211	na	na	780	0
Massachusetts												
Boston city	82,414	9,956	41,415	6,293	20,660	2,057	8,107	989	3,466	0	10,367	617
Brockton city	13,279	1,863	7,103	1,298	4,316	554	na	na	na	na	934	11
Cambridge city	12,219	1,021	10,345	631	1,003	288	499	3	na	na	483	99
Fall River city	15,004	2,277	13,907	2,075	na	na	na	na	na	na	na	na
Framingham city	12,701	1,595	9,748	1,258	na	na	na	na	na	na	956	0
Lawrence city	7,031	1,080	2,367	642	na	na	na	na	na	na	4,265	438
Lowell city	11,141	1,513	7,301	1,365	471	0	1,913	17	na	na	1,461	131
Lynn city	11,568	1,473	7,655	1,242	1,646	176	na	na	na	na	2,716	55
New Bedford city	12,825	2,541	10,476	2,059	na	na	na	na	na	na	1,209	92
Newton city	17,849	2,239	15,941	2,239	na	na	1,260	0	na	na	na	na
Quincy city	14,548	2,299	10,082	2,145	na	na	4,064	0	na	na	na	na
Somerville city	6,289	727	5,104	727	na	na	na	na	na	na	na	na
Springfield city	20,632	2,397	9,738	1,600	4,527	418	na	na	na	na	5,815	357
Worcester city	24,763	3,097	19,407	3,097	1,065	0	1,395	0	na	na	2,720	0
Michigan												
Ann Arbor city	13,110	2,028	11,058	1,642	na	na	808	174	na	na	na	na
Dearborn city	11,814	1,583	11,223	1,583	na	na	na	na	na	na	na	na
Detroit city	94,159	11,844	10,752	1,192	78,350	10,196	na	na	1,083	150	2,627	306
Farmington Hills city	16,863	2,243	12,149	1,818	3,376	350	949	75	na	na	na	na
Flint city	13,127	1,572	5,863	798	6,599	774	na	na	na	na	na	na
Grand Rapids city	24,842	3,365	19,398	3,145	4,126	17	na	na	358	203	862	0
Kalamazoo city	8,048	992	6,855	992	1,084	0	na	na	na	na	na	na
Lansing city	15,125	2,340	10,168	1,631	2,812	195	na	na	na	na	1,143	140
Livonia city	15,917	2,018	14,777	1,922	na	na	na	na	na	na	na	na
Rochester Hills city	12,650	2,226	11,169	2,158	na	na	718	0	na	na	na	na
Southfield city	16,791	2,443	4,912	1,386	11,416	1,021	na	na	na	na	na	na
Sterling Heights city	22,357	3,247	20,772	3,083	na	na	798	52	na	na	na	na
Troy city	13,874	1,178	11,258	918	na	na	2,039	108	na	na	na	na
Warren city	22,710	3,508	18,603	3,183	1,739	0	1,553	97	na	na	na	na
Westland city	13,696	1,598	11,457	1,449	1,965	73	na	na	na	na	na	na
Wyoming city	9,427	927	7,346	848	na	na	na	na	na	na	994	0
Minnesota												
Blaine city	7,580	372	6,618	372	na	na	na	na	na	na	na	na
Bloomington city	17,745	2,640	16,742	2,528	na	na	na	na	na	na	na	na
Brooklyn Park city	9,903	860	7,408	612	1,028	112	1,152	136	na	na	na	na
Duluth city	15,453	2,743	15,018	2,526	na	na	na	na	na	na	na	na
Eagan city	8,292	964	7,281	964	na	na	na	na	na	na	na	na
Lakeville city	6,462	354	6,239	354	na	na	na	na	na	na	na	na
Maple Grove city	11,137	916	10,151	916	na	na	na	na	na	na	na	na
Minneapolis city	46,030	5,044	35,056	4,066	6,718	664	1,822	179	522	127	1,583	127
Plymouth city	11,197	756	10,209	711	na	na	na	na	na	na	na	na
Rochester city	18,037	2,964	16,477	2,701	275	0	853	165	na	na	na	na
St. Cloud city	7,967	874	7,485	874	na	na	na	na	na	na	na	na
St. Paul city	33,259	4,328	25,010	3,694	3,236	313	2,894	321	442	0	1,542	0
Woodbury city	9,948	729	9,251	729	na	na	na	na	na	na	na	na
Mississippi												
Gulfport city	8,711	774	5,866	615	2,291	57	na	na	na	na	na	na
Jackson city	21,926	2,788	6,654	1,283	15,002	1,505	na	na	na	na	na	na

Table C-3: Cities - Older Population by Race and Hispanic Origin—*Continued*

Name	Total Population		White, Non-Hispanic		Black, Alone		Asian, Alone		Multi-race, Alone		Hispanic	
	65 Years and Over	85 Years and Over	65 Years and Over	85 Years and Over	65 Years and Over	85 Years and Over	65 Years and Over	85 Years and Over	65 Years and Over	85 Years and Over	65 Years and Over	85 Years and Over
Missouri												
Columbia city	13,439	2,292	12,174	2,244	na	na	na	na	na	na	na	na
Independence city	19,652	3,301	18,026	3,301	na	na	na	na	na	na	na	na
Kansas City city	64,994	8,447	42,987	5,324	17,242	2,715	1,351	139	558	0	2,723	269
Lee's Summit city	17,122	2,328	15,093	2,158	na	na	na	na	na	na	na	na
O'Fallon city	9,542	1,261	8,983	1,206	na	na	na	na	na	na	na	na
St. Charles city	11,844	1,571	11,459	1,571	na	na	na	na	na	na	na	na
St. Joseph city	12,953	1,772	11,287	1,772	na	na	na	na	na	na	na	na
St. Louis city	41,739	5,489	20,454	2,505	18,994	2,764	1,258	0	na	na	433	36
Springfield city	29,553	4,055	27,584	3,791	na	na	na	na	na	na	na	na
Montana												
Billings city	19,207	3,198	18,310	3,089	na	na	na	na	na	na	na	na
Missoula city	9,530	1,053	9,162	942	na	na	na	na	na	na	na	na
Nebraska												
Lincoln city	37,864	4,612	35,219	4,406	471	131	1,119	0	329	0	726	75
Omaha city	63,828	8,813	54,212	7,646	5,628	671	953	173	790	0	2,298	299
Nevada												
Henderson city	58,693	6,318	44,406	5,011	3,578	59	6,318	446	562	192	4,186	682
Las Vegas city	98,087	11,400	61,952	7,012	10,578	1,153	8,957	949	1,473	99	14,525	2,196
North Las Vegas city	26,177	1,350	12,544	645	5,339	220	3,208	77	951	48	4,721	360
Reno city	39,780	3,661	32,619	3,093	605	10	2,658	160	534	54	2,998	251
Sparks city	17,884	1,901	14,000	1,749	na	na	na	na	na	na	2,093	44
New Hampshire												
Manchester city	14,217	3,060	12,965	3,034	474	0	356	26	na	na	372	0
Nashua city	15,416	2,369	13,945	2,190	na	na	991	32	na	na	423	147
New Jersey												
Bayonne city	9,655	1,694	6,363	1,107	na	na	692	389	na	na	2,514	571
Camden city	7,251	749	0	0	3,110	183	na	na	na	na	3,140	414
Clifton city	13,745	2,596	8,998	1,726	na	na	1,282	278	na	na	3,185	477
East Orange city	8,455	1,455	0	0	7,390	1,367	na	na	na	na	na	na
Elizabeth city	12,726	1,141	3,870	534	2,670	85	na	na	na	na	6,115	522
Jersey City city	28,326	3,056	7,065	554	6,453	751	6,697	556	613	37	8,143	1,195
Newark city	28,004	3,490	4,841	1,353	13,339	1,194	na	na	na	na	8,804	837
Passaic city	6,869	754	1,045	121	na	na	na	na	na	na	4,906	527
Paterson city	15,988	1,488	2,290	390	4,577	327	415	0	na	na	8,641	771
Trenton city	9,590	1,445	0	0	5,033	656	na	na	na	na	1,839	142
Union City city	7,209	855	997	185	na	na	na	na	na	na	5,934	670
New Mexico												
Albuquerque city	88,411	11,461	53,750	7,070	2,308	317	2,652	65	1,496	217	28,037	3,956
Las Cruces city	17,718	1,800	9,679	1,465	na	na	na	na	na	na	6,743	335
Rio Rancho city	16,598	1,584	12,179	1,271	na	na	na	na	na	na	3,345	313
Santa Fe city	20,191	1,690	12,385	762	na	na	na	na	na	na	6,961	928
New York												
Albany city	13,367	2,262	8,897	1,588	3,304	550	na	na	na	na	na	na
Buffalo city	31,965	4,067	18,321	2,164	10,977	1,596	389	107	173	0	1,921	200
Mount Vernon city	9,454	2,366	3,041	1,300	6,023	1,066	na	na	na	na	274	0
New Rochelle city	12,330	2,339	7,717	1,490	2,913	465	na	na	na	na	1,385	289
New York city	1,245,480	160,367	516,349	83,687	294,008	32,406	163,895	15,679	30,060	1,789	274,721	28,970
Rochester city	23,423	2,559	12,199	1,744	8,366	728	na	na	385	0	2,315	119
Schenectady city	9,319	1,483	7,027	1,157	893	97	na	na	na	na	na	na
Syracuse city	16,283	2,449	11,544	1,726	3,677	522	409	39	196	0	568	162
Yonkers city	34,169	4,617	20,357	3,492	3,531	281	1,997	226	na	na	8,399	652
North Carolina												
Asheville city	18,090	2,600	15,333	2,174	2,213	244	na	na	na	na	na	na
Charlotte city	94,775	9,140	55,161	6,287	30,258	2,333	4,282	0	647	88	4,645	824
Concord city	13,020	1,618	9,304	1,331	2,600	157	na	na	na	na	na	na
Durham city	33,485	3,160	18,520	1,997	11,458	1,093	1,324	0	na	na	1,441	70
Fayetteville city	25,524	3,022	11,620	1,580	10,343	908	959	199	393	138	1,682	110
Gastonia city	11,614	1,294	8,574	1,186	2,661	108	na	na	na	na	na	na
Greensboro city	41,052	5,334	26,964	4,172	11,574	784	1,137	0	na	na	1,140	378
Greenville city	8,620	1,099	5,954	935	2,555	101	na	na	na	na	na	na
High Point city	16,646	2,245	10,451	1,723	5,372	522	483	0	na	na	267	0
Jacksonville city	4,168	417	3,175	295	767	122	na	na	na	na	na	na
Raleigh city	53,212	6,774	37,350	5,573	12,283	978	1,285	47	608	57	1,930	119
Wilmington city	20,984	3,362	16,649	3,124	3,578	238	na	na	na	na	na	na
Winston-Salem city	34,058	3,928	21,672	3,328	10,199	498	na	na	na	na	917	0
North Dakota												
Bismarck city	12,354	2,520	12,257	2,520	na	na	na	na	na	na	na	na
Fargo city	15,034	2,494	14,627	2,494	na	na	na	na	na	na	na	na
Ohio												
Akron city	29,763	4,592	21,467	3,638	7,405	906	na	na	na	na	na	na
Canton city	10,844	1,657	8,079	1,246	2,394	326	na	na	na	na	na	na
Cincinnati city	37,749	5,773	21,946	4,262	14,670	1,467	na	na	462	44	126	0
Cleveland city	54,735	6,768	21,923	2,731	26,769	3,006	1,497	383	1,141	0	3,519	648
Columbus city	96,145	8,860	64,405	6,123	24,394	2,074	3,915	398	1,799	74	1,704	109
Dayton city	19,434	2,482	11,161	1,357	7,758	1,025	na	na	na	na	na	na

Table C-3: Cities - Older Population by Race and Hispanic Origin—*Continued*

Name	Total Population		White, Non-Hispanic		Black, Alone		Asian, Alone		Multi-race, Alone		Hispanic	
	65 Years and Over	85 Years and Over	65 Years and Over	85 Years and Over	65 Years and Over	85 Years and Over	65 Years and Over	85 Years and Over	65 Years and Over	85 Years and Over	65 Years and Over	85 Years and Over
Ohio—Cont.												
Lorain city	10,416	1,534	7,295	1,394	1,507	140	na	na	na	na	1,614	0
Parma city	13,933	1,709	13,084	1,709	na	na	na	na	na	na	na	na
Toledo city	38,614	4,942	27,898	3,884	8,377	863	na	na	221	0	1,537	10
Youngstown city	11,549	2,122	6,893	1,523	3,940	555	na	na	na	na	na	na
Oklahoma												
Broken Arrow city	16,499	1,764	14,490	1,621	na	na	554	0	574	0	167	46
Edmond city	14,446	1,599	12,929	1,355	na	na	na	na	156	28	na	na
Lawton city	11,580	1,545	8,053	1,371	1,545	174	na	na	490	0	503	0
Norman city	14,300	1,309	12,740	1,238	na	na	na	na	487	0	216	0
Oklahoma City city	83,034	11,388	62,212	9,871	9,617	1,025	3,426	104	1,576	19	4,035	160
Tulsa city	58,975	7,695	46,090	7,051	6,347	478	753	47	1,877	67	1,990	52
Oregon												
Beaverton city	10,763	1,172	8,238	992	na	na	1,387	180	na	na	697	0
Bend city	16,399	2,596	15,319	2,327	na	na	na	na	na	na	na	na
Eugene city	26,127	2,702	24,080	2,619	na	na	na	na	327	38	853	0
Gresham city	14,900	1,742	12,532	1,620	na	na	na	na	na	na	1,130	0
Hillsboro city	12,511	1,776	10,343	1,431	na	na	595	215	na	na	863	130
Medford city	14,797	2,655	12,576	2,463	na	na	na	na	na	na	989	0
Portland city	87,129	8,752	72,044	7,483	4,163	202	7,350	719	963	52	2,282	57
Salem city	25,603	2,336	22,882	2,203	na	na	na	na	517	0	1,516	133
Pennsylvania												
Allentown city	15,056	2,573	10,270	2,293	789	63	na	na	na	na	3,397	217
Bethlehem city	13,253	2,295	10,405	2,161	na	na	na	na	na	na	1,937	79
Erie city	15,551	2,415	13,337	2,334	1,221	81	na	na	na	na	na	na
Philadelphia city	215,755	26,170	99,214	13,230	87,807	10,452	12,373	1,189	2,848	188	14,975	1,382
Pittsburgh city	47,074	6,448	33,888	4,645	11,353	1,734	868	69	329	0	457	0
Reading city	9,166	1,491	4,644	1,201	923	0	na	na	na	na	3,241	216
Scranton city	12,796	1,832	11,550	1,793	na	na	na	na	na	na	319	0
Rhode Island												
Cranston city	12,235	2,433	11,535	2,433	na	na	na	na	na	na	405	0
Pawtucket city	10,085	1,475	7,516	1,099	769	43	na	na	na	na	1,162	100
Providence city	20,992	3,101	11,439	2,190	2,899	169	530	190	na	na	6,001	564
Warwick city	16,150	1,999	15,116	1,842	na	na	na	na	na	na	na	na
South Carolina												
Charleston city	20,302	2,601	13,606	1,726	6,153	875	na	na	na	na	na	na
Columbia city	13,045	1,639	8,081	663	4,255	886	na	na	na	na	na	na
Greenville city	9,822	1,219	7,907	1,034	1,721	185	na	na	na	na	na	na
North Charleston city	12,345	1,237	6,754	846	4,779	365	na	na	na	na	543	0
Rock Hill city	10,431	932	6,429	539	3,301	393	na	na	na	na	na	na
South Dakota												
Rapid City city	13,426	2,197	12,454	2,189	na	na	na	na	na	na	na	na
Sioux Falls city	21,555	3,230	20,823	3,230	na	na	59	0	na	na	0	0
Tennessee												
Chattanooga city	30,493	4,049	20,518	3,437	8,900	612	na	na	na	na	372	0
Clarksville city	12,759	1,826	9,534	1,371	2,558	455	na	na	na	na	0	0
Franklin city	9,787	741	8,689	741	na	na	na	na	na	na	na	na
Jackson city	9,735	1,596	6,168	1,230	3,448	366	na	na	na	na	na	na
Johnson City city	11,050	1,464	10,102	1,422	na	na	na	na	na	na	na	na
Knoxville city	24,179	2,726	20,003	2,134	3,602	468	na	na	na	na	172	0
Memphis city	84,936	10,310	36,807	5,893	45,784	4,290	684	47	na	na	1,222	49
Murfreesboro city	13,966	938	11,539	672	1,007	0	na	na	na	na	na	na
Nashville-Davidson metropolitan govt (bal).	79,913	9,426	57,373	7,106	17,564	1,449	1,940	251	328	163	2,130	326
Texas												
Abilene city	15,739	2,481	12,288	1,754	760	360	na	na	na	na	2,230	367
Allen city	10,585	1,029	7,881	688	na	na	1,408	134	na	na	na	na
Amarillo city	26,413	3,745	21,796	3,268	1,145	43	na	na	na	na	2,629	338
Arlington city	43,458	4,413	29,555	3,685	4,983	235	3,076	216	405	205	5,277	42
Austin city	90,262	10,784	59,555	7,973	7,536	816	4,712	513	799	130	17,736	1,398
Baytown city	9,933	1,055	3,990	350	2,012	180	na	na	na	na	3,222	185
Beaumont city	17,801	2,342	8,671	1,394	7,381	846	na	na	na	na	1,150	0
Brownsville city	21,346	3,676	0	0	na	na	na	na	na	na	18,086	3,347
Bryan city	8,500	642	5,184	561	1,426	0	na	na	na	na	1,890	81
Carrollton city	17,131	2,013	11,035	1,203	1,401	161	2,315	306	na	na	2,134	343
Cedar Park city	6,330	1,139	4,325	468	na	na	na	na	na	na	1,305	607
College Station city	9,026	505	7,826	505	na	na	na	na	na	na	524	0
Conroe city	11,254	1,419	8,660	1,242	na	na	na	na	na	na	1,828	120
Corpus Christi city	46,865	5,129	20,066	2,865	1,729	0	857	0	na	na	23,206	2,159
Dallas city	143,795	18,090	71,649	11,126	37,924	4,602	4,493	145	1,071	102	28,708	2,080
Denton city	15,406	1,928	13,115	1,741	407	0	na	na	na	na	973	106
Edinburg city	8,887	731	0	0	na	na	na	na	na	na	6,982	569
El Paso city	88,348	11,564	16,928	2,401	1,950	204	1,019	0	833	0	67,786	8,959
Fort Worth city	87,550	11,248	50,482	6,703	14,851	1,933	4,429	141	1,121	239	16,010	2,229
Frisco city	16,308	1,489	10,792	1,170	1,385	11	2,242	41	na	na	1,610	126
Garland city	30,081	2,105	18,512	1,356	3,081	191	3,324	161	477	53	4,416	344
Georgetown city	21,166	2,949	19,628	2,801	na	na	na	na	na	na	1,030	148

Table C-3: Cities - Older Population by Race and Hispanic Origin—*Continued*

Name	Total Population		White, Non-Hispanic		Black, Alone		Asian, Alone		Multi-race, Alone		Hispanic	
	65 Years and Over	85 Years and Over	65 Years and Over	85 Years and Over	65 Years and Over	85 Years and Over	65 Years and Over	85 Years and Over	65 Years and Over	85 Years and Over	65 Years and Over	85 Years and Over
Texas—Cont.												
Grand Prairie city	18,456	1,849	9,239	1,190	1,703	225	1,246	0	na	na	6,230	434
Harlingen city	10,730	1,590	3,402	916	na	na	na	na	na	na	7,036	674
Houston city	245,819	30,713	103,636	17,783	61,078	4,464	20,843	3,058	2,724	179	58,714	5,229
Irving city	15,469	1,809	8,900	1,629	590	99	2,182	0	na	na	3,617	10
Killeen city	9,599	254	3,589	254	3,268	0	na	na	61	0	1,325	0
Laredo city	24,746	2,572	2,091	454	na	na	na	na	na	na	22,587	2,118
League City city	11,875	1,457	7,909	1,457	na	na	na	na	na	na	698	0
Lewisville city	9,316	1,320	6,772	1,265	826	0	692	0	na	na	901	55
Longview city	12,495	2,392	9,577	2,155	2,030	177	na	na	na	na	565	60
Lubbock city	31,448	4,085	22,982	3,078	1,504	86	415	0	na	na	6,379	921
McAllen city	16,970	1,381	2,417	120	na	na	na	na	na	na	13,805	1,261
McKinney city	21,449	1,624	16,788	1,524	1,829	0	937	51	na	na	1,827	49
Mansfield city	6,527	795	5,702	787	220	0	na	na	na	na	406	8
Mesquite city	13,735	1,688	9,013	1,355	1,276	86	na	na	na	na	2,261	247
Midland city	14,260	1,860	9,373	1,599	na	na	na	na	na	na	3,037	226
Mission city	11,570	1,525	0	0	na	na	na	na	na	na	7,990	1,211
Missouri City city	10,387	720	3,855	210	3,816	203	1,544	174	na	na	na	na
New Braunfels city	12,468	2,042	10,215	1,778	na	na	na	na	na	na	2,082	204
North Richland Hills city	11,137	1,608	9,460	1,324	na	na	na	na	na	na	779	203
Odessa city	11,607	1,020	7,056	891	na	na	na	na	na	na	4,190	129
Pasadena city	14,155	1,077	7,841	582	na	na	na	na	na	na	5,555	457
Pearland city	16,904	496	9,148	334	3,208	35	2,755	0	na	na	1,781	127
Pharr city	8,434	621	0	0	na	na	na	na	na	na	6,327	312
Plano city	38,026	4,995	29,814	4,113	1,849	236	4,566	437	341	0	1,533	312
Richardson city	16,518	1,374	11,912	1,022	na	na	2,504	76	na	na	833	224
Round Rock city	12,314	856	9,027	807	606	0	na	na	na	na	1,353	49
Rowlett city	6,081	253	5,065	191	na	na	na	na	na	na	184	62
San Angelo city	15,191	1,899	10,936	1,762	na	na	na	na	na	na	3,660	103
San Antonio city	189,691	22,324	73,337	9,826	11,260	1,154	5,079	258	2,728	627	98,918	11,004
Sugar Land city	20,641	2,000	9,696	1,129	na	na	7,833	583	na	na	1,805	169
Temple city	13,207	1,547	9,790	1,209	na	na	na	na	na	na	1,523	43
Tyler city	15,053	1,830	11,175	1,179	3,026	611	na	na	na	na	749	40
Victoria city	11,152	1,439	6,155	779	na	na	na	na	na	na	3,844	626
Waco city	15,289	2,167	10,069	1,787	2,924	187	na	na	na	na	2,119	193
Wichita Falls city	13,863	1,891	10,920	1,707	772	88	na	na	na	na	2,018	96
Utah												
Layton city	7,728	400	6,834	242	na	na	na	na	na	na	538	118
Lehi city	5,188	99	4,843	99	na	na	na	na	na	na	na	na
Ogden city	9,300	884	7,674	805	na	na	na	na	na	na	1,256	54
Orem city	9,224	1,073	8,336	944	na	na	na	na	na	na	715	85
Provo city	7,145	1,153	5,982	1,032	na	na	na	na	na	na	617	121
St. George city	21,045	3,132	19,844	3,132	na	na	na	na	na	na	na	na
Salt Lake City city	20,951	1,873	18,338	1,669	na	na	963	94	222	46	759	64
Sandy city	15,514	1,343	13,574	1,057	na	na	na	na	na	na	na	na
South Jordan city	6,593	496	6,393	496	na	na	na	na	na	na	na	na
West Jordan city	9,078	318	7,876	318	na	na	na	na	na	na	488	0
West Valley City city	12,467	1,102	8,548	704	na	na	720	74	na	na	2,688	144
Virginia												
Alexandria city	19,595	3,016	12,634	1,906	3,821	615	1,110	495	364	0	2,391	0
Chesapeake city	32,045	3,151	21,114	1,801	9,117	1,214	na	na	na	na	447	136
Hampton city	20,695	2,824	9,681	1,600	9,903	1,161	na	na	na	na	na	na
Lynchburg city	11,906	1,685	8,663	1,388	2,349	297	na	na	na	na	na	na
Newport News city	23,417	1,991	13,867	1,458	7,714	441	883	36	na	na	876	56
Norfolk city	27,271	3,921	14,641	2,204	10,601	1,421	1,084	259	613	37	336	0
Portsmouth city	13,934	1,543	7,024	829	6,429	594	na	na	na	na	na	na
Richmond city	30,213	4,933	13,850	2,266	14,849	2,573	na	na	na	na	672	0
Roanoke city	16,905	3,051	12,009	2,422	3,920	552	na	na	na	na	na	na
Suffolk city	13,145	1,289	8,124	789	4,414	392	na	na	na	na	na	na
Virginia Beach city	63,851	7,798	47,525	6,965	8,755	376	5,516	177	573	129	1,527	151
Washington												
Auburn city	11,488	1,035	8,856	873	na	na	na	na	na	na	470	0
Bellevue city	21,314	3,729	15,187	2,860	na	na	4,991	747	na	na	421	0
Bellingham city	13,246	1,365	12,147	1,365	na	na	na	na	na	na	na	na
Everett city	13,948	1,848	11,214	1,596	na	na	na	na	na	na	647	0
Federal Way city	12,240	1,221	8,597	995	254	0	1,560	55	na	na	1,468	171
Kennewick city	11,355	1,206	9,531	970	na	na	na	na	na	na	813	0
Kent city	16,365	2,424	10,566	1,703	1,025	460	3,540	254	na	na	969	0
Kirkland city	9,444	730	8,412	609	na	na	883	121	na	na	na	na
Marysville city	9,044	998	7,952	895	na	na	na	na	na	na	na	na
Pasco city	6,928	328	4,301	328	na	na	na	na	na	na	2,529	0
Redmond city	5,413	817	4,017	804	na	na	1,182	13	na	na	na	na
Renton city	12,707	2,185	8,585	1,869	na	na	2,601	257	na	na	413	0
Sammamish city	4,685	165	3,975	165	na	na	666	0	na	na	na	na
Seattle city	97,253	11,724	69,175	8,695	6,086	692	16,417	2,052	2,253	208	2,461	58
Spokane city	34,424	4,217	31,161	3,981	na	na	na	na	172	0	1,428	139
Spokane Valley city	15,046	1,413	14,213	1,334	na	na	na	na	na	na	638	47
Tacoma city	29,721	3,519	22,473	3,079	2,276	189	3,359	157	591	47	638	47
Vancouver city	30,271	3,275	27,244	3,170	na	na	1,221	0	393	39	668	66
Yakima city	15,981	2,163	13,394	2,163	na	na	na	na	na	na	1,883	0

Table C-3: Cities - Older Population by Race and Hispanic Origin—*Continued*

Name	Total Population		White, Non-Hispanic		Black, Alone		Asian, Alone		Multi-race, Alone		Hispanic	
	65 Years and Over	85 Years and Over	65 Years and Over	85 Years and Over	65 Years and Over	85 Years and Over	65 Years and Over	85 Years and Over	65 Years and Over	85 Years and Over	65 Years and Over	85 Years and Over
Wisconsin												
Appleton city	11,161	1,593	10,503	1,593	na	na	na	na	na	na	na	na
Eau Claire city	10,401	1,294	9,851	1,248	na	na	na	na	na	na	na	na
Green Bay city	13,967	1,991	12,629	1,945	na	na	na	na	na	na	755	46
Kenosha city	12,652	1,793	11,123	1,707	na	na	na	na	na	na	762	86
Madison city	32,290	4,369	29,140	3,921	1,140	158	715	150	0	0	1,267	140
Milwaukee city	64,261	8,414	37,236	5,850	19,285	1,645	1,223	247	815	166	5,478	474
Oshkosh city	9,063	1,885	8,753	1,885	na	na	na	na	na	na	na	na
Racine city	9,194	852	6,984	792	1,496	51	na	na	na	na	664	9
Waukesha city	10,600	1,730	9,680	1,730	na	na	na	na	na	na	na	na

Table C-4: Metropolitan/Micropolitan Statistical Areas - Older Population by Race and Hispanic Origin

Name	Total Population		White, Non-Hispanic		Black, Alone		Asian, Alone		Multi-race, Alone		Hispanic	
	65 Years and Over	85 Years and Over	65 Years and Over	85 Years and Over	65 Years and Over	85 Years and Over	65 Years and Over	85 Years and Over	65 Years and Over	85 Years and Over	65 Years and Over	85 Years and Over
Aberdeen, WA Micro Area	16,312	1,549	14,743	1,507	na	na	na	na	na	na	na	na
Abilene, TX Metro Area	25,654	3,166	21,207	2,333	792	360	na	na	na	na	2,980	473
Adrian, MI Micro Area	18,092	2,130	17,536	2,130	na	na	na	na	na	na	383	0
Akron, OH Metro Area	124,652	15,827	109,392	14,622	11,723	1,074	2,069	80	523	0	619	51
Alamogordo, NM Micro Area	10,722	829	8,028	654	na	na	na	na	na	na	2,010	126
Albany, GA Metro Area	23,201	2,575	13,302	1,048	9,464	1,527	na	na	na	na	na	na
Albany, OR Metro Area	24,586	3,069	22,214	2,979	na	na	na	na	624	0	1,215	90
Albany-Schenectady-Troy, NY Metro Area	153,463	19,966	141,095	18,657	6,159	684	2,829	396	1,486	56	2,137	224
Albertville, AL Micro Area	16,487	1,756	15,541	1,756	na	na	na	na	na	na	555	0
Albuquerque, NM Metro Area	153,593	17,822	91,988	10,539	3,196	507	3,268	65	2,812	294	49,835	6,267
Alexandria, LA Metro Area	24,740	2,442	18,432	2,189	5,334	153	na	na	na	na	na	na
Allentown-Bethlehem-Easton, PA-NJ Metro Area	152,534	23,164	136,766	21,893	3,429	425	2,999	99	745	0	8,467	747
Altoona, PA Metro Area	25,493	3,145	24,929	3,145	na	na	na	na	na	na	na	na
Amarillo, TX Metro Area	36,617	4,851	31,193	4,296	1,245	96	na	na	na	na	3,094	359
Ames, IA Metro Area	11,562	1,405	11,281	1,405	na	na	226	0	na	na	na	na
Anchorage, AK Metro Area	45,860	4,347	34,659	3,158	1,783	248	3,769	466	1,136	232	1,638	0
Ann Arbor, MI Metro Area	51,775	5,935	42,743	4,814	4,713	525	2,376	442	915	77	991	77
Anniston-Oxford-Jacksonville, AL Metro Area	20,515	1,761	16,721	1,262	3,066	499	na	na	na	na	na	na
Appleton, WI Metro Area	34,977	3,829	33,736	3,829	na	na	na	na	na	na	372	0
Asheville, NC Metro Area	102,665	13,766	96,330	12,557	2,990	308	na	na	724	0	1,683	643
Ashtabula, OH Micro Area	18,569	2,281	17,753	2,261	na	na	na	na	na	na	na	na
Athens, OH Micro Area	8,637	1,103	8,288	955	na	na	na	na	na	na	na	na
Athens, TX Micro Area	18,119	1,561	16,332	1,538	na	na	na	na	na	na	na	na
Athens-Clarke County, GA Metro Area	28,378	2,930	21,601	2,189	5,450	414	na	na	na	na	629	327
Atlanta-Sandy Springs-Roswell, GA Metro Area	731,877	70,693	474,336	49,263	189,445	15,758	31,865	3,257	7,015	280	27,514	2,190
Atlantic City-Hammonton, NJ Metro Area	47,558	5,068	35,565	4,328	5,413	618	2,907	0	656	0	3,332	122
Auburn, NY Micro Area	14,322	1,676	14,275	1,676	na	na	na	na	na	na	na	na
Auburn-Opelika, AL Metro Area	19,887	1,776	15,053	1,446	3,602	277	na	na	na	na	na	na
Augusta-Richmond County, GA-SC Metro Area	95,845	10,304	65,495	7,158	26,004	2,622	2,145	458	754	0	1,527	66
Augusta-Waterville, ME Micro Area	24,870	3,578	23,813	3,415	na	na	na	na	na	na	na	na
Austin-Round Rock, TX Metro Area	235,122	24,255	171,820	19,420	13,327	1,261	9,678	539	2,611	346	37,945	2,767
Bakersfield, CA Metro Area	98,076	10,676	58,672	6,975	4,126	60	6,031	502	1,927	398	27,190	2,893
Baltimore-Columbia-Towson, MD Metro Area	434,964	52,193	303,325	39,572	101,866	10,158	17,106	1,198	5,233	688	7,895	529
Bangor, ME Metro Area	27,761	3,630	27,404	3,630	na	na	na	na	na	na	na	na
Barnstable Town, MA Metro Area	65,453	7,670	62,679	7,328	na	na	na	na	na	na	na	na
Baton Rouge, LA Metro Area	118,179	11,026	80,238	8,724	33,145	1,833	1,802	218	675	0	2,420	251
Battle Creek, MI Metro Area	24,047	3,723	20,981	3,370	2,079	276	na	na	na	na	411	0
Bay City, MI Metro Area	20,857	3,051	20,294	3,051	na	na	na	na	na	na	na	na
Beaumont-Port Arthur, TX Metro Area	62,177	8,262	44,472	6,579	12,914	1,411	920	165	na	na	3,669	107
Beaver Dam, WI Micro Area	15,571	2,621	15,141	2,560	na	na	na	na	na	na	na	na
Beckley, WV Metro Area	24,654	2,224	22,570	2,048	1,719	155	na	na	na	na	na	na
Bellingham, WA Metro Area	39,347	4,604	35,624	4,182	na	na	na	na	776	0	795	0
Bend-Redmond, OR Metro Area	38,748	4,754	36,702	4,047	na	na	na	na	na	na	137	0
Billings, MT Metro Area	30,187	4,381	28,863	4,272	na	na	na	na	na	na	na	na
Binghamton, NY Metro Area	46,627	7,461	44,026	7,397	929	28	1,030	36	na	na	467	0
Birmingham-Hoover, AL Metro Area	186,874	19,644	140,329	15,518	40,850	3,344	1,607	93	1,429	27	2,166	662
Bismarck, ND Metro Area	21,151	3,363	20,530	3,363	na	na	na	na	na	na	na	na
Blacksburg-Christiansburg-Radford, VA Metro Area	30,061	3,630	28,636	3,630	na	na	na	na	na	na	na	na
Bloomington, IL Metro Area	25,570	3,638	24,104	3,459	753	179	370	0	na	na	343	0
Bloomington, IN Metro Area	22,954	3,708	22,148	3,694	na	na	na	na	na	na	na	na
Bloomsburg-Berwick, PA Metro Area	16,556	2,821	16,209	2,806	na	na	na	na	na	na	na	na
Bluefield, WV-VA Micro Area	22,137	1,665	20,916	1,637	na	na	na	na	na	na	na	na
Boise City, ID Metro Area	108,418	11,133	99,118	10,021	na	na	2,838	667	1,531	0	4,333	290
Boston-Cambridge-Newton, MA-NH Metro Area	765,037	104,908	644,329	94,416	42,462	3,994	36,446	3,163	8,214	241	35,464	2,558
Boulder, CO Metro Area	46,033	5,866	41,871	5,653	na	na	1,206	49	264	0	2,525	164
Bowling Green, KY Metro Area	25,680	2,728	23,267	2,637	931	55	na	na	na	na	467	36
Bozeman, MT Micro Area	14,428	1,108	13,699	962	na	na	na	na	na	na	na	na
Brainerd, MN Micro Area	22,062	2,140	21,525	2,130	na	na	na	na	na	na	na	na
Branson, MO Micro Area	22,374	2,592	21,219	2,529	na	na	na	na	na	na	na	na
Bremerton-Silverdale, WA Metro Area	47,748	3,225	42,277	2,997	na	na	2,693	164	882	0	638	41
Bridgeport-Stamford-Norwalk, CT Metro Area	149,824	21,890	119,026	19,724	12,357	861	5,196	389	778	104	12,685	916
Brownsville-Harlingen, TX Metro Area	58,006	8,300	14,231	2,126	na	na	na	na	na	na	42,387	6,174
Brunswick, GA Metro Area	23,933	2,528	19,337	2,385	4,307	143	na	na	na	na	na	na
Buffalo-Cheektowaga-Niagara Falls, NY Metro Area	205,029	29,771	180,835	26,489	16,315	2,548	2,463	150	1,334	198	3,495	349
Burlington, NC Metro Area	28,381	3,361	22,346	2,964	4,683	397	na	na	na	na	866	0
Burlington-South Burlington, VT Metro Area	35,826	4,284	32,927	4,270	na	na	na	na	na	na	na	na
California-Lexington Park, MD Metro Area	15,006	1,132	12,004	783	na	na	na	na	na	na	na	na
Canton-Massillon, OH Metro Area	77,782	10,317	72,531	9,500	3,771	537	na	na	141	0	na	na
Cape Coral-Fort Myers, FL Metro Area	216,260	27,692	190,096	25,912	7,946	115	2,847	244	1,000	0	13,896	1,421
Cape Girardeau, MO-IL Metro Area	15,988	2,503	15,313	2,463	na	na	na	na	na	na	na	na
Carbondale-Marion, IL Metro Area	21,552	2,626	20,109	2,519	948	0	na	na	na	na	na	na
Carson City, NV Metro Area	11,198	1,987	9,775	1,493	na	na	na	na	na	na	1,000	395
Casper, WY Metro Area	11,900	1,687	11,404	1,639	na	na	na	na	na	na	268	48
Cedar Rapids, IA Metro Area	45,634	5,685	43,228	5,286	672	41	na	na	na	na	555	129
Centralia, WA Micro Area	16,580	1,642	15,727	1,502	na	na	na	na	na	na	404	0

Table C-4: Metropolitan/Micropolitan Statistical Areas - Older Population by Race and Hispanic Origin—*Continued*

Name	Total Population		White, Non-Hispanic		Black, Alone		Asian, Alone		Multi-race, Alone		Hispanic	
	65 Years and Over	85 Years and Over	65 Years and Over	85 Years and Over	65 Years and Over	85 Years and Over	65 Years and Over	85 Years and Over	65 Years and Over	85 Years and Over	65 Years and Over	85 Years and Over
Chambersburg-Waynesboro, PA Metro Area	29,943	3,936	29,078	3,790	na	na	na	na	na	na	na	na
Champaign-Urbana, IL Metro Area	32,097	4,572	28,655	4,437	1,481	59	918	0	na	na	560	76
Charleston, WV Metro Area	43,439	5,213	40,530	4,997	1,916	180	na	na	na	na	na	na
Charleston-North Charleston, SC Metro Area	119,346	12,787	86,665	10,089	27,304	2,246	1,536	69	1,252	159	2,185	224
Charlotte-Concord-Gastonia, NC-SC Metro Area	347,776	34,079	269,557	28,156	58,572	4,674	6,864	329	2,723	155	10,222	1,240
Charlottesville, VA Metro Area	42,770	5,044	36,279	4,676	4,898	175	1,006	87	134	0	548	106
Chattanooga, TN-GA Metro Area	100,228	11,287	86,927	10,302	10,581	821	1,283	130	578	0	662	34
Cheyenne, WY Metro Area	16,163	1,792	13,975	1,498	na	na	na	na	na	na	1,338	294
Chicago-Naperville-Elgin, IL-IN-WI Metro Area	1,383,405	176,383	938,868	132,283	213,321	22,837	86,568	7,116	12,124	1,066	135,591	13,253
Chico, CA Metro Area	42,820	4,441	37,651	4,273	na	na	1,224	128	950	0	2,706	40
Chillicothe, OH Micro Area	13,356	692	12,040	661	na	na	na	na	na	na	na	na
Cincinnati, OH-KY-IN Metro Area	331,435	39,799	291,999	36,502	29,767	2,579	5,026	205	1,874	363	2,580	150
Claremont-Lebanon, NH-VT Micro Area	47,095	5,114	45,649	5,083	na	na	na	na	na	na	252	0
Clarksburg, WV Micro Area	18,274	2,442	17,665	2,442	na	na	na	na	na	na	na	na
Clarksville, TN-KY Metro Area	29,943	3,609	24,059	2,912	4,468	697	na	na	na	na	574	0
Clearlake, CA Micro Area	14,856	1,161	12,510	1,129	na	na	na	na	na	na	1,268	0
Cleveland, TN Metro Area	21,700	2,434	20,720	2,273	na	na	na	na	na	na	na	na
Cleveland-Elyria, OH Metro Area	380,970	49,776	303,576	41,046	59,336	6,433	5,914	1,061	2,706	44	8,862	1,151
Coeur d'Alene, ID Metro Area	30,553	2,611	29,354	2,602	na	na	na	na	na	na	na	na
College Station-Bryan, TX Metro Area	28,145	2,009	20,766	1,756	2,940	8	322	0	na	na	3,729	126
Colorado Springs, CO Metro Area	97,633	11,241	81,938	9,687	3,813	225	3,049	508	1,114	33	7,144	602
Columbia, MO Metro Area	21,937	3,032	19,959	2,984	1,044	48	na	na	na	na	na	na
Columbia, SC Metro Area	123,451	13,307	87,173	10,574	30,951	2,457	1,243	58	1,100	0	2,971	147
Columbus, GA-AL Metro Area	43,364	5,229	25,930	3,496	15,146	1,407	na	na	427	102	1,269	0
Columbus, IN Metro Area	13,549	1,156	12,856	1,078	na	na	na	na	na	na	na	na
Columbus, OH Metro Area	278,962	30,795	237,846	26,987	29,343	2,754	5,603	412	3,091	165	3,106	395
Concord, NH Micro Area	28,423	3,875	26,850	3,854	na	na	na	na	na	na	na	na
Cookeville, TN Micro Area	19,533	2,257	18,656	2,210	na	na	na	na	na	na	na	na
Coos Bay, OR Micro Area	17,313	1,773	15,361	1,552	na	na	na	na	na	na	na	na
Corning, NY Micro Area	18,663	2,160	18,211	2,160	na	na	na	na	na	na	na	na
Corpus Christi, TX Metro Area	68,560	7,274	32,574	4,114	1,794	0	959	49	na	na	31,885	3,006
Corvallis, OR Metro Area	14,843	1,412	13,855	1,185	na	na	318	52	na	na	133	75
Crestview-Fort Walton Beach-Destin, FL Metro Area	48,622	3,130	42,306	2,720	2,971	133	1,316	119	570	114	1,015	44
Cullman, AL Micro Area	15,541	855	14,820	855	na	na	na	na	na	na	na	na
Cumberland, MD-WV Metro Area	20,248	2,022	19,477	1,985	na	na	na	na	na	na	na	na
Dallas-Fort Worth-Arlington, TX Metro Area	853,501	89,898	593,453	67,349	99,106	9,920	46,501	1,957	8,037	1,013	104,064	9,694
Dalton, GA Metro Area	20,266	2,297	18,084	2,297	na	na	na	na	na	na	1,461	0
Danville, IL Metro Area	15,156	2,197	13,434	1,768	1,362	429	na	na	na	na	na	na
Danville, VA Metro Area	22,402	2,496	15,917	1,909	5,938	587	na	na	na	na	na	na
Daphne-Fairhope-Foley, AL Metro Area	44,443	3,827	40,873	3,743	2,361	0	na	na	na	na	609	0
Davenport-Moline-Rock Island, IA-IL Metro Area	68,233	8,139	63,003	7,606	2,559	69	117	0	202	96	2,221	324
Dayton, OH Metro Area	145,239	17,754	121,515	15,755	17,334	1,716	2,599	186	1,356	37	1,947	97
Decatur, AL Metro Area	26,514	3,091	23,508	2,972	2,185	95	na	na	na	na	na	na
Decatur, IL Metro Area	21,167	2,441	18,486	2,412	2,053	29	na	na	na	na	na	na
Deltona-Daytona Beach-Ormond Beach, FL Metro Area	169,088	25,904	143,248	21,889	10,710	1,320	2,157	497	1,428	0	11,897	2,264
Denver-Aurora-Lakewood, CO Metro Area	377,709	40,874	302,646	34,118	15,861	1,490	12,146	911	4,354	144	42,842	3,924
Des Moines-West Des Moines, IA Metro Area	86,724	10,335	82,093	10,190	1,966	0	1,181	60	352	85	1,142	0
Detroit-Warren-Dearborn, MI Metro Area	709,952	86,377	540,220	68,238	130,671	14,987	19,204	984	6,313	880	12,106	1,172
Dothan, AL Metro Area	27,910	2,869	22,533	2,403	4,760	379	na	na	na	na	333	52
Dover, DE Metro Area	29,812	2,980	22,420	2,499	6,206	475	na	na	na	na	382	0
DuBois, PA Micro Area	16,267	2,117	16,039	2,117	na	na	na	na	na	na	na	na
Dubuque, IA Metro Area	17,441	2,671	17,053	2,646	na	na	na	na	na	na	na	na
Duluth, MN-WI Metro Area	52,704	7,332	51,272	7,058	na	na	na	na	311	0	197	109
Dunn, NC Micro Area	17,041	1,380	12,695	1,114	3,208	144	na	na	na	na	792	67
Durham-Chapel Hill, NC Metro Area	88,160	8,727	62,583	6,533	19,736	2,052	2,283	0	714	0	2,398	142
East Stroudsburg, PA Metro Area	28,128	2,571	23,737	2,178	2,981	393	na	na	na	na	1,125	0
Eau Claire, WI Metro Area	28,261	3,465	27,234	3,372	na	na	364	0	na	na	na	na
El Centro, CA Metro Area	23,512	2,645	5,103	643	na	na	na	na	na	na	17,325	2,002
Elizabeth City, NC Micro Area	13,025	1,497	8,212	1,192	4,269	173	na	na	na	na	na	na
Elizabethtown-Fort Knox, KY Metro Area	22,144	1,953	19,285	1,756	1,807	197	na	na	na	na	na	na
Elkhart-Goshen, IN Metro Area	29,730	4,138	27,791	3,929	707	59	na	na	na	na	774	150
Elmira, NY Metro Area	16,613	1,905	15,038	1,780	na	na	na	na	na	na	na	na
El Paso, TX Metro Area	103,468	12,670	18,636	2,444	2,248	204	1,150	0	1,096	0	80,769	10,022
Enid, OK Metro Area	9,839	1,600	9,181	1,600	na	na	na	na	na	na	na	na
Erie, PA Metro Area	48,926	7,068	45,841	6,907	1,704	81	na	na	na	na	766	80
Eugene, OR Metro Area	73,700	7,578	68,185	7,473	na	na	na	na	1,386	38	1,859	22
Eureka-Arcata-Fortuna, CA Micro Area	24,296	2,817	21,473	2,541	na	na	na	na	778	176	809	167
Evansville, IN-KY Metro Area	53,702	7,233	50,454	7,017	2,442	194	na	na	na	na	na	na
Fairbanks, AK Metro Area	10,213	866	8,559	721	na	na	na	na	na	na	na	na
Fargo, ND-MN Metro Area	30,080	4,694	29,305	4,694	137	0	na	na	na	na	398	0
Faribault-Northfield, MN Micro Area	10,297	1,714	9,884	1,714	na	na	na	na	na	na	na	na
Farmington, MO Micro Area	11,343	1,561	10,664	1,561	na	na	na	na	na	na	na	na
Farmington, NM Metro Area	19,101	2,223	10,829	1,237	na	na	na	na	na	na	2,257	177
Fayetteville, NC Metro Area	45,402	4,304	23,931	2,552	16,129	1,218	1,443	199	441	138	2,101	110
Fayetteville-Springdale-Rogers, AR-MO Metro Area	70,560	9,194	65,958	8,073	422	168	879	46	602	207	2,442	700

Table C-4: Metropolitan/Micropolitan Statistical Areas - Older Population by Race and Hispanic Origin—Continued

Name	Total Population 65 Years and Over	Total Population 85 Years and Over	White, Non-Hispanic 65 Years and Over	White, Non-Hispanic 85 Years and Over	Black, Alone 65 Years and Over	Black, Alone 85 Years and Over	Asian, Alone 65 Years and Over	Asian, Alone 85 Years and Over	Multi-race, Alone 65 Years and Over	Multi-race, Alone 85 Years and Over	Hispanic 65 Years and Over	Hispanic 85 Years and Over
Findlay, OH Micro Area	12,829	1,977	12,542	1,977	na	na	na	na	na	na	na	na
Flagstaff, AZ Metro Area	17,813	1,440	12,480	694	na	na	na	na	na	na	1,318	158
Flint, MI Metro Area	71,160	7,505	57,609	6,239	11,088	1,082	na	na	749	41	1,293	184
Florence, SC Metro Area	36,038	3,037	23,086	1,890	12,565	1,118	na	na	na	na	na	na
Florence-Muscle Shoals, AL Metro Area	29,490	3,505	26,031	3,199	2,774	243	na	na	na	na	na	na
Fond du Lac, WI Metro Area	19,012	2,970	18,606	2,932	na	na	na	na	na	na	na	na
Forest City, NC Micro Area	14,058	1,281	13,024	1,128	na	na	na	na	na	na	na	na
Fort Collins, CO Metro Area	55,002	5,527	50,924	5,407	na	na	708	55	385	0	2,434	65
Fort Payne, AL Micro Area	12,261	1,542	11,644	1,392	na	na	na	na	na	na	na	na
Fort Smith, AR-OK Metro Area	47,832	4,169	41,225	3,907	1,749	58	na	na	1,259	60	987	77
Fort Wayne, IN Metro Area	65,841	7,914	58,845	7,493	4,458	249	833	50	265	40	1,361	82
Frankfort, KY Micro Area	12,641	1,079	11,531	1,011	na	na	na	na	na	na	na	na
Fresno, CA Metro Area	121,540	17,185	65,947	10,483	4,791	426	11,175	1,370	2,594	114	37,841	4,726
Gadsden, AL Metro Area	19,632	2,194	16,984	1,764	2,192	381	na	na	na	na	na	na
Gainesville, FL Metro Area	41,611	5,133	32,466	4,478	5,467	577	1,766	78	na	na	1,456	0
Gainesville, GA Metro Area	30,078	3,197	26,056	2,707	1,499	0	na	na	na	na	1,765	212
Gallup, NM Micro Area	9,281	1,514	na	na	na	na	na	na	na	na	na	na
Gettysburg, PA Metro Area	20,634	2,289	20,251	2,231	na	na	na	na	na	na	175	58
Glens Falls, NY Metro Area	26,079	3,888	25,542	3,838	na	na	na	na	na	na	na	na
Glenwood Springs, CO Micro Area	11,593	531	10,879	531	na	na	na	na	na	na	12	0
Goldsboro, NC Metro Area	20,507	1,988	13,278	1,299	6,182	650	na	na	na	na	474	0
Grand Forks, ND-MN Metro Area	14,881	2,139	14,023	2,117	na	na	na	na	na	na	287	0
Grand Island, NE Metro Area	14,224	2,284	13,098	2,247	na	na	na	na	na	na	719	0
Grand Junction, CO Metro Area	28,801	3,950	26,848	3,725	na	na	na	na	na	na	1,645	225
Grand Rapids-Wyoming, MI Metro Area	155,825	18,951	141,397	18,406	5,700	155	2,693	0	1,091	281	4,787	109
Grants Pass, OR Metro Area	22,863	1,924	21,248	1,665	na	na	na	na	na	na	na	na
Great Falls, MT Metro Area	15,005	1,940	14,274	1,940	na	na	na	na	na	na	na	na
Greeley, CO Metro Area	38,223	4,080	31,520	3,439	na	na	na	na	724	0	5,698	558
Green Bay, WI Metro Area	51,178	5,074	48,804	4,852	na	na	348	0	398	16	1,101	151
Greeneville, TN Micro Area	14,809	1,160	14,410	963	na	na	na	na	na	na	na	na
Greenfield Town, MA Micro Area	15,424	2,182	15,040	2,104	na	na	na	na	na	na	na	na
Greensboro-High Point, NC Metro Area	124,314	15,440	95,318	13,013	23,249	1,937	2,352	48	912	64	2,187	378
Greenville, NC Metro Area	23,540	2,309	15,692	1,559	7,304	687	na	na	na	na	91	63
Greenville-Anderson-Mauldin, SC Metro Area	150,232	14,068	126,984	13,013	18,903	804	785	101	1,152	90	2,412	150
Greenwood, SC Micro Area	17,587	2,162	13,282	1,898	4,159	264	na	na	na	na	na	na
Gulfport-Biloxi-Pascagoula, MS Metro Area	63,278	4,220	50,956	3,452	9,114	164	na	na	na	na	1,522	438
Hagerstown-Martinsburg, MD-WV Metro Area	43,627	4,184	39,902	3,905	2,799	77	na	na	na	na	573	64
Hammond, LA Metro Area	19,087	1,316	14,858	950	3,674	366	na	na	na	na	na	na
Hanford-Corcoran, CA Metro Area	15,413	1,412	8,391	955	na	na	na	na	na	na	5,374	300
Harrisburg-Carlisle, PA Metro Area	102,158	13,096	90,870	11,863	6,668	738	2,262	241	867	220	1,546	34
Harrisonburg, VA Metro Area	19,885	2,458	19,360	2,458	na	na	na	na	na	na	250	0
Hartford-West Hartford-East Hartford, CT Metro Area	209,397	30,020	175,586	27,486	15,291	1,591	4,760	77	1,743	62	12,813	804
Hattiesburg, MS Metro Area	20,861	2,590	16,721	2,092	4,048	498	na	na	na	na	na	na
Helena, MT Micro Area	15,484	2,058	15,065	2,008	na	na	na	na	na	na	na	na
Hermiston-Pendleton, OR Micro Area	13,062	1,415	11,763	1,339	na	na	na	na	na	na	627	57
Hickory-Lenoir-Morganton, NC Metro Area	69,501	7,594	64,452	6,960	3,064	391	507	0	na	na	827	102
Hilo, HI Micro Area	42,643	4,237	19,763	1,544	na	na	12,689	1,792	4,945	604	1,840	89
Hilton Head Island-Bluffton-Beaufort, SC Metro Area	56,307	4,386	48,457	3,452	6,302	837	na	na	na	na	913	0
Hinesville, GA Metro Area	6,690	461	4,532	338	1,777	77	na	na	na	na	235	0
Hobbs, NM Micro Area	7,856	924	4,988	694	na	na	na	na	na	na	2,484	160
Holland, MI Micro Area	19,808	1,994	18,438	1,791	na	na	na	na	na	na	819	148
Homosassa Springs, FL Metro Area	53,832	6,810	49,928	6,601	na	na	na	na	na	na	na	na
Hot Springs, AR Metro Area	22,991	2,956	21,775	2,784	na	na	na	na	na	na	na	na
Houma-Thibodaux, LA Metro Area	32,179	3,254	25,609	2,342	4,093	795	na	na	na	na	na	na
Houston-The Woodlands-Sugar Land, TX Metro Area	780,719	73,053	438,351	47,002	117,508	7,899	65,919	5,409	10,862	756	149,520	12,140
Huntington-Ashland, WV-KY-OH Metro Area	67,808	7,793	65,795	7,528	1,054	88	na	na	na	na	na	na
Huntsville, AL Metro Area	70,760	7,130	55,558	6,459	10,841	428	1,514	83	1,008	53	1,756	78
Huntsville, TX Micro Area	13,320	1,690	11,093	1,473	1,355	42	na	na	na	na	527	175
Hutchinson, KS Micro Area	12,432	1,781	11,577	1,712	na	na	na	na	na	na	na	na
Idaho Falls, ID Metro Area	19,032	2,877	18,376	2,877	na	na	na	na	na	na	376	0
Indiana, PA Micro Area	16,623	2,405	16,135	2,194	na	na	na	na	na	na	na	na
Indianapolis-Carmel-Anderson, IN Metro Area	281,078	31,421	239,987	26,662	31,548	3,313	4,474	702	1,454	162	3,796	760
Iowa City, IA Metro Area	21,826	2,920	20,786	2,693	151	0	na	na	na	na	356	227
Ithaca, NY Metro Area	14,209	2,039	13,705	1,878	na	na	na	na	na	na	na	na
Jackson, MI Metro Area	28,547	3,269	26,475	3,018	1,116	95	na	na	187	0	480	71
Jackson, MS Metro Area	84,081	9,044	52,575	6,365	30,544	2,679	na	na	na	na	350	0
Jackson, TN Metro Area	22,308	3,178	17,146	2,812	4,919	366	na	na	na	na	na	na
Jacksonville, FL Metro Area	242,793	22,734	187,415	17,925	33,937	2,833	8,503	714	2,441	93	10,395	1,220
Jacksonville, NC Metro Area	18,036	1,610	14,170	1,238	2,733	315	na	na	na	na	558	0
Jamestown-Dunkirk-Fredonia, NY Micro Area	25,587	3,908	24,642	3,743	na	na	na	na	na	na	630	165
Janesville-Beloit, WI Metro Area	27,151	3,224	25,344	3,100	na	na	na	na	na	na	377	18
Jefferson, GA Micro Area	10,244	1,201	9,072	1,047	na	na	na	na	na	na	na	na
Jefferson City, MO Metro Area	24,869	2,369	23,724	2,317	676	0	na	na	na	na	na	na
Johnson City, TN Metro Area	39,791	4,951	37,993	4,868	na	na	na	na	na	na	623	41
Johnstown, PA Metro Area	29,664	4,365	28,862	4,287	na	na	na	na	na	na	na	na

Table C-4: Metropolitan/Micropolitan Statistical Areas - Older Population by Race and Hispanic Origin—Continued

Name	Total Population		White, Non-Hispanic		Black, Alone		Asian, Alone		Multi-race, Alone		Hispanic	
	65 Years and Over	85 Years and Over	65 Years and Over	85 Years and Over	65 Years and Over	85 Years and Over	65 Years and Over	85 Years and Over	65 Years and Over	85 Years and Over	65 Years and Over	85 Years and Over
Jonesboro, AR Metro Area	19,799	1,827	17,958	1,732	1,087	0	na	na	na	na	281	55
Joplin, MO Metro Area	29,091	3,511	27,692	3,381	na	na	na	na	na	na	627	0
Kahului-Wailuku-Lahaina, HI Metro Area	30,503	3,957	13,110	1,066	na	na	11,710	2,228	2,700	485	1,378	124
Kalamazoo-Portage, MI Metro Area	53,917	5,798	48,065	5,364	3,125	267	na	na	1,054	140	1,254	0
Kalispell, MT Micro Area	19,958	1,403	19,275	1,403	na	na	na	na	na	na	na	na
Kankakee, IL Metro Area	18,344	2,763	15,892	2,420	1,858	326	na	na	na	na	442	17
Kansas City, MO-KS Metro Area	318,298	37,831	269,432	33,463	29,962	3,170	5,227	320	2,234	0	10,215	837
Kapaa, HI Micro Area	14,709	1,606	5,840	428	na	na	6,127	981	1,645	0	630	0
Keene, NH Micro Area	15,095	1,244	14,838	1,223	na	na	na	na	na	na	na	na
Kennewick-Richland, WA Metro Area	39,249	4,360	33,014	4,055	na	na	na	na	413	0	4,168	0
Key West, FL Micro Area	16,972	846	13,951	795	na	na	na	na	na	na	2,536	51
Killeen-Temple, TX Metro Area	50,702	4,089	36,009	3,278	5,916	207	na	na	750	81	5,799	357
Kingsport-Bristol-Bristol, TN-VA Metro Area	68,076	7,573	65,514	7,227	na	na	na	na	na	na	na	na
Kingston, NY Metro Area	35,125	4,398	31,902	3,677	1,234	0	na	na	220	112	1,618	643
Klamath Falls, OR Micro Area	14,610	1,581	13,010	1,489	na	na	na	na	na	na	878	92
Knoxville, TN Metro Area	161,951	16,006	151,748	15,203	6,221	668	1,259	57	620	78	1,917	0
Kokomo, IN Metro Area	15,917	2,363	14,894	2,192	na	na	na	na	na	na	na	na
La Crosse-Onalaska, WI-MN Metro Area	23,140	3,632	22,818	3,632	na	na	na	na	na	na	na	na
Lafayette, LA Metro Area	69,960	8,209	54,518	6,911	13,446	1,237	701	0	na	na	823	0
Lafayette-West Lafayette, IN Metro Area	27,515	3,774	25,849	3,536	205	66	607	0	na	na	742	172
LaGrange, GA Micro Area	10,065	1,056	7,573	1,000	2,388	56	na	na	na	na	na	na
Lake Charles, LA Metro Area	31,237	3,489	23,847	2,946	5,922	543	na	na	na	na	na	na
Lake City, FL Micro Area	12,978	1,628	10,963	1,581	1,284	0	na	na	na	na	na	na
Lake Havasu City-Kingman, AZ Metro Area	63,794	5,643	56,949	5,643	na	na	na	na	na	na	4,307	0
Lakeland-Winter Haven, FL Metro Area	143,426	14,993	114,352	12,441	12,724	1,201	2,521	265	832	0	12,877	1,086
Lancaster, PA Metro Area	98,751	12,133	90,858	11,510	2,278	234	1,532	135	759	0	3,449	254
Lansing-East Lansing, MI Metro Area	73,716	8,684	64,672	7,696	4,737	379	1,434	426	776	43	2,157	140
Laredo, TX Metro Area	26,003	2,596	2,190	454	na	na	na	na	na	na	23,745	2,142
Las Cruces, NM Metro Area	34,786	3,125	16,909	1,929	na	na	na	na	na	na	16,333	1,196
Las Vegas-Henderson-Paradise, NV Metro Area	328,690	31,017	211,551	21,654	29,329	2,061	40,314	2,211	5,480	674	41,937	4,572
Laurel, MS Micro Area	14,812	1,683	10,491	1,420	4,233	263	na	na	na	na	na	na
Lawrence, KS Metro Area	15,300	2,395	13,658	1,758	na	na	na	na	na	na	na	na
Lawton, OK Metro Area	16,238	1,942	12,258	1,748	1,657	190	na	na	570	0	632	0
Lebanon, PA Metro Area	27,709	4,149	25,778	4,114	na	na	na	na	na	na	1,230	35
Lewiston, ID-WA Metro Area	14,866	1,819	13,758	1,819	na	na	na	na	na	na	na	na
Lewiston-Auburn, ME Metro Area	19,292	2,055	18,495	2,055	na	na	na	na	342	0	na	na
Lexington-Fayette, KY Metro Area	72,676	7,530	64,392	6,120	6,069	1,350	652	0	706	0	578	60
Lima, OH Metro Area	17,930	1,931	16,117	1,784	1,234	147	na	na	na	na	na	na
Lincoln, NE Metro Area	46,767	5,421	43,988	5,215	495	131	1,119	0	329	0	780	75
Little Rock-North Little Rock-Conway, AR Metro Area	114,827	12,519	94,069	10,330	17,024	1,917	1,110	52	240	0	1,892	199
Logan, UT-ID Metro Area	13,682	1,248	13,325	1,248	na	na	na	na	na	na	144	0
London, KY Micro Area	20,529	2,254	20,056	2,239	na	na	na	na	na	na	na	na
Longview, TX Metro Area	35,679	4,134	28,754	3,862	4,834	212	na	na	na	na	1,103	60
Longview, WA Metro Area	20,856	2,494	19,285	2,426	na	na	na	na	na	na	381	0
Los Angeles-Long Beach-Anaheim, CA Metro Area	1,847,185	258,165	831,406	129,453	127,143	16,685	374,439	49,881	35,283	4,409	485,070	57,882
Louisville/Jefferson County, KY-IN Metro Area	208,062	23,396	180,868	21,466	20,418	1,467	2,144	343	1,857	66	2,555	54
Lubbock, TX Metro Area	39,904	4,573	29,021	3,528	1,850	110	415	0	111	0	8,344	935
Lufkin, TX Micro Area	13,896	1,972	11,318	1,698	1,475	200	na	na	na	na	686	74
Lumberton, NC Micro Area	19,861	2,330	7,810	1,489	4,592	398	na	na	na	na	257	0
Lynchburg, VA Metro Area	50,205	6,320	41,574	5,633	6,806	597	na	na	490	0	382	90
Macon-Bibb County, GA Metro Area	36,946	3,693	22,927	2,928	13,132	765	na	na	na	na	na	na
Madera, CA Metro Area	22,099	2,668	13,950	2,083	na	na	na	na	na	na	6,026	585
Madison, WI Metro Area	96,572	11,507	91,223	10,837	1,446	166	1,706	310	538	54	1,500	140
Manchester-Nashua, NH Metro Area	64,850	8,636	61,097	8,193	743	269	1,479	105	276	69	1,342	147
Manhattan, KS Metro Area	10,584	1,179	9,749	1,095	na	na	na	na	na	na	na	na
Manitowoc, WI Micro Area	15,941	2,333	15,810	2,333	na	na	na	na	na	na	na	na
Mankato-North Mankato, MN Metro Area	14,938	2,250	14,492	2,250	na	na	na	na	na	na	na	na
Mansfield, OH Metro Area	23,735	3,751	21,772	2,955	na	na	na	na	na	na	na	na
Marinette, WI-MI Micro Area	15,235	2,039	14,942	2,034	na	na	na	na	na	na	na	na
Marion, IN Micro Area	12,533	1,571	11,575	1,394	na	na	na	na	na	na	na	na
Marion, OH Micro Area	11,407	1,689	11,048	1,689	na	na	na	na	na	na	na	na
Marquette, MI Micro Area	12,824	1,500	12,331	1,500	na	na	na	na	na	na	na	na
Marshall, TX Micro Area	10,877	1,144	8,376	1,144	na	na	na	na	na	na	na	na
Martinsville, VA Micro Area	15,169	1,937	11,560	1,590	3,275	294	na	na	na	na	na	na
McAllen-Edinburg-Mission, TX Metro Area	96,015	10,542	21,210	2,474	na	na	na	na	299	49	73,495	8,068
Meadville, PA Micro Area	17,556	1,692	17,042	1,631	na	na	na	na	na	na	na	na
Medford, OR Metro Area	48,689	6,082	44,953	5,867	na	na	na	na	na	na	1,675	23
Memphis, TN-MS-AR Metro Area	188,539	20,369	114,620	14,434	67,002	5,633	2,620	47	1,903	206	2,471	49
Merced, CA Metro Area	30,748	3,475	16,051	2,070	1,229	134	2,373	298	404	131	10,848	921
Meridian, MS Micro Area	18,383	1,976	11,913	1,243	6,291	707	na	na	na	na	na	na
Miami-Fort Lauderdale-West Palm Beach, FL Metro Area	1,127,331	170,413	534,793	90,519	153,282	16,305	22,626	1,594	14,182	1,431	416,927	61,908
Michigan City-La Porte, IN Metro Area	19,676	1,943	18,031	1,853	1,195	90	na	na	na	na	240	0
Midland, MI Metro Area	15,539	2,269	14,600	2,093	na	na	na	na	na	na	na	na
Midland, TX Metro Area	19,160	2,333	12,940	1,832	na	na	na	na	na	na	4,274	466
Milwaukee-Waukesha-West Allis, WI Metro Area	246,058	33,384	207,475	29,571	24,155	2,418	3,783	335	1,152	212	8,703	732

Table C-4: Metropolitan/Micropolitan Statistical Areas - Older Population by Race and Hispanic Origin—*Continued*

Name	Total Population		White, Non-Hispanic		Black, Alone		Asian, Alone		Multi-race, Alone		Hispanic	
	65 Years and Over	85 Years and Over	65 Years and Over	85 Years and Over	65 Years and Over	85 Years and Over	65 Years and Over	85 Years and Over	65 Years and Over	85 Years and Over	65 Years and Over	85 Years and Over
Minneapolis-St. Paul-Bloomington, MN-WI Metro Area........................	507,293	61,141	462,691	57,679	17,474	1,417	14,916	1,482	3,715	297	7,204	340
Minot, ND Micro Area	10,568	1,515	10,360	1,515	na	na	na	na	na	na	na	na
Missoula, MT Metro Area	18,257	1,528	17,624	1,356	na	na	na	na	na	na	na	na
Mobile, AL Metro Area	66,558	6,972	45,801	4,584	18,376	1,877	na	na	na	na	958	335
Modesto, CA Metro Area	72,507	8,557	47,597	5,937	1,921	176	4,085	652	1,465	121	16,896	1,596
Monroe, LA Metro Area	27,617	2,395	20,779	2,125	6,154	270	na	na	na	na	na	na
Monroe, MI Metro Area	27,543	3,738	26,183	3,289	na	na	na	na	na	na	na	na
Montgomery, AL Metro Area	57,249	6,199	37,217	3,662	18,094	2,505	1,041	0	na	na	191	0
Morehead City, NC Micro Area	17,455	1,613	16,253	1,515	na	na	na	na	na	na	na	na
Morgantown, WV Metro Area	19,954	2,245	19,346	2,245	na	na	na	na	na	na	na	na
Morristown, TN Metro Area	22,245	1,698	21,505	1,617	na	na	na	na	na	na	na	na
Moses Lake, WA Micro Area	14,081	1,325	11,109	987	na	na	na	na	na	na	2,165	68
Mount Airy, NC Micro Area	15,066	1,964	13,806	1,903	na	na	na	na	na	na	na	na
Mount Pleasant, MI Micro Area	9,094	990	8,361	919	na	na	na	na	na	na	na	na
Mount Vernon-Anacortes, WA Metro Area	26,616	2,992	24,537	2,926	na	na	na	na	556	11	829	0
Muncie, IN Metro Area	19,931	3,185	18,413	2,935	947	178	na	na	na	na	na	na
Muskegon, MI Metro Area	29,441	3,263	25,879	2,957	2,539	250	na	na	na	na	530	56
Muskogee, OK Micro Area	11,320	1,478	8,465	1,121	1,095	139	na	na	567	33	na	na
Myrtle Beach-Conway-North Myrtle Beach, SC-NC Metro Area	126,894	8,654	113,954	8,117	8,540	138	na	na	na	na	2,454	399
Nacogdoches, TX Micro Area	9,550	867	7,714	588	na	na	na	na	na	na	410	148
Napa, CA Metro Area	26,805	2,708	20,762	2,393	na	na	1,989	130	534	0	3,181	99
Naples-Immokalee-Marco Island, FL Metro Area	122,463	18,268	108,487	16,302	3,000	263	na	na	1,589	257	8,703	1,444
Nashville-Davidson--Murfreesboro--Franklin, TN Metro Area	256,271	23,901	217,751	20,102	27,126	2,320	4,087	285	1,589	257	5,098	745
New Bern, NC Metro Area	25,525	2,149	20,040	1,494	4,768	655	na	na	na	na	na	na
New Castle, PA Micro Area	18,978	1,872	18,284	1,872	na	na	na	na	na	na	na	na
New Haven-Milford, CT Metro Area	148,789	22,610	122,963	20,298	12,377	763	3,071	502	946	153	9,649	894
New Orleans-Metairie, LA Metro Area	201,182	20,857	127,722	15,130	56,749	4,364	3,689	95	1,521	234	12,031	1,030
New Philadelphia-Dover, OH Micro Area	18,027	2,252	17,681	2,193	na	na	na	na	na	na	na	na
New York-Newark-Jersey City, NY-NJ-PA Metro Area	3,143,409	430,919	1,911,707	302,404	464,586	50,116	287,718	25,758	50,494	3,604	471,842	52,106
Niles-Benton Harbor, MI Metro Area	30,468	4,686	26,625	4,204	2,527	348	na	na	na	na	484	71
North Port-Sarasota-Bradenton, FL Metro Area	264,853	36,472	244,482	34,338	6,660	860	3,006	138	1,194	0	9,146	1,040
North Wilkesboro, NC Micro Area	14,695	1,297	13,844	1,044	na	na	na	na	na	na	na	na
Norwich-New London, CT Metro Area	48,314	6,115	43,176	5,419	1,819	423	1,253	29	362	0	1,522	244
Oak Harbor, WA Micro Area	20,803	1,834	19,126	1,717	na	na	na	na	na	na	292	46
Ocala, FL Metro Area	104,024	12,155	89,189	10,017	6,894	1,328	na	na	na	na	6,304	418
Ocean City, NJ Metro Area	24,068	2,635	23,330	2,467	na	na	na	na	na	na	na	na
Odessa, TX Metro Area	15,171	1,261	8,872	1,101	na	na	na	na	na	na	5,938	160
Ogden-Clearfield, UT Metro Area	74,241	7,439	66,929	6,900	963	119	na	na	707	40	4,759	434
Ogdensburg-Massena, NY Micro Area	18,468	2,550	18,258	2,550	na	na	na	na	na	na	na	na
Oklahoma City, OK Metro Area	193,989	22,571	158,150	19,564	15,444	1,710	4,465	181	4,064	288	6,721	498
Olean, NY Micro Area	14,641	1,524	14,173	1,475	na	na	na	na	na	na	na	na
Olympia-Tumwater, WA Metro Area	49,236	5,381	43,703	5,255	na	na	2,449	57	415	69	1,581	0
Omaha-Council Bluffs, NE-IA Metro Area	130,302	16,979	116,893	15,446	6,577	782	1,755	173	1,275	107	3,822	447
Opelousas, LA Micro Area	13,167	1,402	8,553	1,070	4,532	332	na	na	na	na	na	na
Orangeburg, SC Micro Area	16,866	1,553	7,731	1,002	8,939	551	na	na	na	na	na	na
Orlando-Kissimmee-Sanford, FL Metro Area	381,169	41,220	244,665	28,471	43,339	2,974	14,700	478	6,430	722	75,719	9,382
Oshkosh-Neenah, WI Metro Area	27,997	4,386	27,156	4,341	na	na	na	na	na	na	na	na
Ottawa-Peru, IL Micro Area	29,385	3,512	27,970	3,474	na	na	na	na	na	na	1,041	0
Owensboro, KY Metro Area	20,637	2,279	19,732	2,279	na	na	na	na	na	na	na	na
Owosso, MI Micro Area	12,597	1,419	12,146	1,403	na	na	na	na	na	na	na	na
Oxnard-Thousand Oaks-Ventura, CA Metro Area	132,219	18,528	89,603	13,540	2,102	235	11,218	1,676	1,839	130	27,995	2,978
Paducah, KY-IL Micro Area	19,943	3,337	18,021	2,603	1,292	493	na	na	na	na	na	na
Palatka, FL Micro Area	17,314	na	14,637	565	na	na	na	na	na	na	na	na
Palm Bay-Melbourne-Titusville, FL Metro Area	141,268	20,627	119,841	17,580	9,590	1,567	2,390	455	970	95	7,922	1,010
Panama City, FL Metro Area	34,734	3,737	31,233	3,378	1,928	211	na	na	na	na	858	16
Parkersburg-Vienna, WV Metro Area	18,568	1,749	18,189	1,749	na	na	na	na	na	na	na	na
Pensacola-Ferry Pass-Brent, FL Metro Area	81,412	8,216	67,235	7,002	8,786	626	2,715	353	1,068	37	1,045	127
Peoria, IL Metro Area	66,223	10,889	61,399	10,505	3,245	379	162	0	445	5	805	0
Philadelphia-Camden-Wilmington, PA-NJ-DE-MD Metro Area	973,717	125,171	732,147	101,616	160,885	17,110	40,469	2,927	6,959	399	34,830	3,352
Phoenix-Mesa-Scottsdale, AZ Metro Area	760,024	83,307	616,049	72,348	23,865	1,473	21,412	2,197	8,672	487	87,147	6,703
Pine Bluff, AR Metro Area	15,329	2,136	9,460	1,637	5,718	499	na	na	na	na	na	na
Pinehurst-Southern Pines, NC Micro Area	23,584	3,053	20,803	2,834	na	na	na	na	na	na	na	na
Pittsburgh, PA Metro Area	464,038	65,156	429,128	61,020	25,272	3,358	4,812	248	2,164	386	2,584	130
Pittsfield, MA Metro Area	29,239	3,829	28,321	3,778	na	na	na	na	na	na	na	na
Plattsburgh, NY Micro Area	13,523	1,498	13,261	1,453	na	na	na	na	na	na	na	na
Pocatello, ID Metro Area	12,344	1,616	11,446	1,491	na	na	na	na	na	na	371	65
Port Angeles, WA Micro Area	22,161	3,101	21,239	3,101	na	na	na	na	na	na	na	na
Portland-South Portland, ME Metro Area	104,289	12,472	101,288	12,408	410	0	1,293	0	696	0	448	64
Portland-Vancouver-Hillsboro, OR-WA Metro Area	368,880	39,815	324,944	36,616	6,520	317	19,033	1,510	4,571	292	12,385	971
Port St. Lucie, FL Metro Area	127,627	15,809	106,219	14,795	11,136	545	na	na	na	na	8,529	421
Portsmouth, OH Micro Area	13,526	1,671	13,288	1,588	na	na	na	na	na	na	na	na
Pottsville, PA Micro Area	28,879	4,148	28,436	4,148	na	na	na	na	na	na	138	0
Prescott, AZ Metro Area	73,656	7,371	67,665	6,962	na	na	na	na	na	na	3,569	215
Providence-Warwick, RI-MA Metro Area	277,501	39,700	249,192	36,349	7,257	459	3,931	542	3,326	333	12,117	1,133
Provo-Orem, UT Metro Area	49,393	4,791	45,350	4,446	na	na	598	44	109	0	2,889	301

Table C-4: Metropolitan/Micropolitan Statistical Areas - Older Population by Race and Hispanic Origin—*Continued*

Name	Total Population		White, Non-Hispanic		Black, Alone		Asian, Alone		Multi-race, Alone		Hispanic	
	65 Years and Over	85 Years and Over	65 Years and Over	85 Years and Over	65 Years and Over	85 Years and Over	65 Years and Over	85 Years and Over	65 Years and Over	85 Years and Over	65 Years and Over	85 Years and Over
Pueblo, CO Metro Area	30,832	3,900	20,941	2,866	na	na	na	na	504	0	8,948	990
Punta Gorda, FL Metro Area	74,321	10,912	69,039	9,677	na	na	na	na	na	na	2,061	555
Quincy, IL-MO Micro Area	14,888	2,212	14,338	2,067	na	na	na	na	na	na	na	na
Racine, WI Metro Area	32,401	3,701	28,523	3,452	2,134	183	na	na	na	na	1,237	50
Raleigh, NC Metro Area	165,869	16,656	125,575	13,621	27,761	1,781	5,950	403	1,243	187	5,423	676
Rapid City, SD Metro Area	26,254	3,476	24,541	3,272	na	na	na	na	na	na	na	na
Reading, PA Metro Area	72,315	10,860	64,868	10,337	1,724	139	na	na	685	0	4,665	216
Redding, CA Metro Area	37,027	3,952	34,065	3,579	na	na	na	na	650	0	1,542	286
Reno, NV Metro Area	77,448	7,232	63,826	6,200	1,332	30	4,055	210	890	84	6,348	554
Richmond, IN Micro Area	12,445	1,847	11,885	1,738	na	na	na	na	na	na	na	na
Richmond, VA Metro Area	203,199	24,290	141,083	17,561	51,171	5,756	4,832	172	2,079	400	3,543	483
Richmond-Berea, KY Micro Area	15,896	1,813	14,961	1,577	na	na	na	na	na	na	na	na
Riverside-San Bernardino-Ontario, CA Metro Area	604,193	68,643	344,533	46,867	39,493	3,158	48,169	3,168	10,569	977	161,410	14,374
Roanoke, VA Metro Area	64,438	8,073	56,836	7,329	5,205	576	na	na	na	na	439	168
Roanoke Rapids, NC Micro Area	14,619	1,214	6,939	620	7,069	594	na	na	na	na	na	na
Rochester, MN Metro Area	36,635	5,070	34,519	4,775	346	0	1,022	165	na	na	496	18
Rochester, NY Metro Area	190,436	24,713	168,859	22,607	12,722	1,243	3,076	391	825	42	5,055	561
Rockford, IL Metro Area	57,622	7,081	50,758	6,606	3,696	426	870	0	286	0	2,066	49
Rocky Mount, NC Metro Area	27,750	2,580	16,337	1,760	10,696	781	na	na	na	na	298	13
Rome, GA Metro Area	16,533	1,843	14,114	1,393	1,879	450	na	na	na	na	na	na
Roseburg, OR Micro Area	27,924	2,281	26,587	2,183	na	na	na	na	na	na	na	na
Roswell, NM Micro Area	10,830	1,559	6,404	1,038	na	na	na	na	na	na	3,581	466
Russellville, AR Micro Area	13,431	1,651	12,817	1,612	na	na	na	na	na	na	272	0
Sacramento--Roseville--Arden-Arcade, CA Metro Area	361,797	44,627	256,260	32,074	18,359	1,874	42,861	6,354	6,802	733	35,844	3,881
Saginaw, MI Metro Area	36,766	5,153	29,529	4,453	5,115	428	na	na	316	48	2,011	142
St. Cloud, MN Metro Area	29,710	4,276	28,820	4,276	374	0	na	na	na	na	172	0
St. George, UT Metro Area	37,295	4,525	34,962	4,525	na	na	na	na	na	na	1,441	0
St. Joseph, MO-KS Metro Area	21,361	2,930	19,450	2,861	na	na	na	na	na	na	na	na
St. Louis, MO-IL Metro Area	463,355	57,901	384,941	49,722	62,415	7,398	7,471	212	3,047	384	4,645	200
Salem, OH Micro Area	21,175	2,147	20,583	2,078	na	na	na	na	na	na	na	na
Salem, OR Metro Area	68,775	8,134	62,469	7,847	na	na	254	0	805	0	4,483	287
Salinas, CA Metro Area	59,491	8,363	35,904	5,027	1,603	226	5,459	1,171	1,128	141	15,372	1,749
Salisbury, MD-DE Metro Area	98,792	8,876	85,923	8,044	9,397	664	934	127	na	na	1,245	0
Salt Lake City, UT Metro Area	131,820	12,951	114,021	11,595	781	0	4,545	455	1,217	46	10,224	675
San Angelo, TX Metro Area	18,297	2,438	13,237	2,104	na	na	na	na	na	na	4,465	300
San Antonio-New Braunfels, TX Metro Area	328,673	36,204	167,968	20,585	16,393	1,302	7,277	402	4,366	974	134,731	13,635
San Diego-Carlsbad, CA Metro Area	469,821	59,080	304,575	40,536	16,407	1,596	57,913	6,956	8,135	1,007	82,280	9,371
Sandusky, OH Micro Area	16,157	2,718	15,003	2,391	na	na	na	na	na	na	na	na
San Francisco-Oakland-Hayward, CA Metro Area	732,156	95,715	386,608	49,182	51,829	6,296	199,866	28,788	15,625	1,431	77,439	9,763
San Jose-Sunnyvale-Santa Clara, CA Metro Area	269,192	38,328	129,472	21,427	5,534	382	90,163	11,074	5,054	825	38,972	4,321
San Luis Obispo-Paso Robles-Arroyo Grande, CA Metro Area	57,594	6,503	49,535	5,859	na	na	na	na	1,176	199	4,786	207
Santa Cruz-Watsonville, CA Metro Area	45,349	3,835	35,991	3,152	na	na	2,024	311	1,671	142	6,291	293
Santa Fe, NM Metro Area	36,568	2,730	24,547	1,248	na	na	na	na	na	na	10,658	1,462
Santa Maria-Santa Barbara, CA Metro Area	68,402	9,638	49,482	7,103	1,072	146	3,098	708	1,080	142	13,784	1,500
Santa Rosa, CA Metro Area	98,030	11,980	84,141	10,706	na	na	3,266	245	1,848	0	8,455	1,018
Savannah, GA Metro Area	55,207	5,596	38,568	4,315	14,879	1,281	na	na	235	0	395	0
Scranton--Wilkes-Barre--Hazleton, PA Metro Area	110,941	15,650	106,213	15,454	1,094	39	1,211	23	566	10	2,074	115
Searcy, AR Micro Area	12,307	1,307	12,254	1,307	na	na	na	na	na	na	na	na
Seattle-Tacoma-Bellevue, WA Metro Area	528,031	63,508	415,542	53,571	19,251	2,177	62,865	6,360	8,601	485	15,734	883
Sebastian-Vero Beach, FL Metro Area	51,384	7,118	47,273	6,738	na	na	na	na	na	na	na	na
Sebring, FL Metro Area	37,245	6,627	32,168	5,862	na	na	na	na	na	na	2,926	620
Seneca, SC Micro Area	18,633	1,482	16,862	1,482	na	na	na	na	na	na	na	na
Sevierville, TN Micro Area	19,160	1,991	18,870	1,991	na	na	na	na	na	na	na	na
Shawnee, OK Micro Area	11,821	1,805	10,192	1,715	na	na	na	na	277	0	175	0
Sheboygan, WI Metro Area	20,696	2,692	20,019	2,591	na	na	281	101	na	na	219	0
Shelby, NC Micro Area	18,097	2,074	14,808	1,718	2,830	238	na	na	na	na	na	na
Shelton, WA Micro Area	14,862	1,592	13,897	1,415	na	na	na	na	na	na	na	na
Sherman-Denison, TX Metro Area	23,606	2,521	21,163	2,347	na	na	na	na	na	na	544	na
Show Low, AZ Micro Area	20,162	2,184	12,728	1,215	na	na	na	na	na	na	1,290	307
Shreveport-Bossier City, LA Metro Area	72,054	8,532	47,821	5,944	22,445	2,464	na	na	520	59	783	65
Sierra Vista-Douglas, AZ Metro Area	28,402	3,174	21,121	2,640	na	na	na	na	na	na	5,443	223
Sioux City, IA-NE-SD Metro Area	26,366	3,727	24,289	3,656	na	na	na	na	na	na	712	0
Sioux Falls, SD Metro Area	35,625	5,617	34,767	5,602	na	na	66	0	na	na	15	15
Somerset, PA Micro Area	16,525	1,976	16,276	1,976	na	na	na	na	na	na	na	na
South Bend-Mishawaka, IN-MI Metro Area	53,620	7,468	47,585	6,930	3,628	269	704	0	757	228	786	41
Spartanburg, SC Metro Area	56,123	5,027	45,182	4,313	9,152	610	na	na	490	27	448	0
Spokane-Spokane Valley, WA Metro Area	97,107	9,664	90,661	9,140	na	na	1,666	226	769	124	2,089	174
Springfield, IL Metro Area	37,197	4,507	34,219	3,946	2,169	451	na	na	na	na	na	na
Springfield, MA Metro Area	106,733	15,143	90,816	13,985	4,959	501	2,024	0	521	22	8,680	635
Springfield, MO Metro Area	77,783	8,731	74,093	8,409	na	na	na	na	1,122	0	973	47
Springfield, OH Metro Area	25,957	3,849	23,691	3,473	1,782	283	na	na	na	na	na	na
State College, PA Metro Area	22,815	2,676	22,439	2,597	na	na	46	0	na	na	na	na
Statesboro, GA Micro Area	8,545	963	6,725	818	1,820	145	na	na	na	na	na	na
Staunton-Waynesboro, VA Metro Area	25,695	3,451	23,346	2,834	1,878	379	na	na	na	na	na	na
Stevens Point, WI Micro Area	11,666	1,428	11,507	1,428	na	na	na	na	na	na	na	na

Table C-4: Metropolitan/Micropolitan Statistical Areas - Older Population by Race and Hispanic Origin—Continued

Name	Total Population		White, Non-Hispanic		Black, Alone		Asian, Alone		Multi-race, Alone		Hispanic	
	65 Years and Over	85 Years and Over	65 Years and Over	85 Years and Over	65 Years and Over	85 Years and Over	65 Years and Over	85 Years and Over	65 Years and Over	85 Years and Over	65 Years and Over	85 Years and Over
Stillwater, OK Micro Area	10,980	1,341	9,387	1,233	na	na	na	na	312	0	na	na
Stockton-Lodi, CA Metro Area	95,844	10,931	51,612	6,699	6,095	957	15,669	1,725	3,780	30	20,634	1,581
Sumter, SC Metro Area	17,568	1,872	9,226	1,164	7,850	708	na	na	na	na	na	na
Sunbury, PA Micro Area	19,647	3,214	19,064	3,087	na	na	na	na	na	na	na	na
Syracuse, NY Metro Area	111,403	15,116	101,850	13,949	5,136	686	1,798	191	935	23	1,770	267
Talladega-Sylacauga, AL Micro Area	17,371	1,583	12,839	1,214	4,325	212	na	na	na	na	na	na
Tallahassee, FL Metro Area	55,474	5,527	40,459	3,747	12,803	1,534	679	0	500	0	966	246
Tampa-St. Petersburg-Clearwater, FL Metro Area	622,433	79,560	500,583	66,547	40,105	3,542	13,080	676	8,030	936	62,139	7,811
Terre Haute, IN Metro Area	28,382	3,442	27,682	3,384	251	58	na	na	na	na	na	na
Texarkana, TX-AR Metro Area	25,009	2,138	20,210	1,762	4,255	239	na	na	na	na	na	na
The Villages, FL Metro Area	73,154	4,848	70,832	4,515	na	na	na	na	na	na	na	na
Toledo, OH Metro Area	97,880	12,053	82,629	10,164	10,123	1,483	1,299	298	703	0	2,720	53
Topeka, KS Metro Area	43,494	5,015	38,406	4,616	2,159	159	na	na	662	92	1,803	124
Torrington, CT Micro Area	37,897	4,360	36,772	4,360	na	na	na	na	na	na	423	0
Traverse City, MI Micro Area	33,278	4,352	32,538	4,304	na	na	na	na	na	na	na	na
Trenton, NJ Metro Area	56,001	7,193	39,038	5,789	9,045	1,159	4,051	103	na	na	3,632	142
Truckee-Grass Valley, CA Micro Area	27,746	3,152	25,467	3,152	na	na	na	na	na	na	na	na
Tucson, AZ Metro Area	205,547	21,309	157,411	16,291	4,331	671	4,484	404	4,210	172	35,414	3,773
Tullahoma-Manchester, TN Micro Area	19,964	2,201	18,595	1,962	na	na	na	na	na	na	na	na
Tulsa, OK Metro Area	153,263	17,401	127,151	16,025	8,223	601	1,752	47	5,558	255	3,222	132
Tupelo, MS Micro Area	20,507	2,115	17,658	1,964	2,530	53	na	na	na	na	na	na
Tuscaloosa, AL Metro Area	34,392	3,236	24,452	1,988	9,496	1,229	na	na	na	na	383	19
Twin Falls, ID Micro Area	15,967	1,613	15,159	1,613	na	na	na	na	na	na	436	0
Tyler, TX Metro Area	37,588	3,171	30,237	2,210	5,114	921	na	na	na	na	1,697	40
Ukiah, CA Micro Area	19,072	1,475	16,815	1,415	na	na	na	na	na	na	1,336	0
Urban Honolulu, HI Metro Area	173,612	30,273	31,376	4,499	1,157	0	110,004	22,690	18,361	1,730	4,312	311
Utica-Rome, NY Metro Area	55,405	8,640	52,828	8,453	1,060	59	511	0	na	na	818	128
Valdosta, GA Metro Area	19,469	1,976	13,411	1,436	5,056	355	na	na	na	na	na	na
Vallejo-Fairfield, CA Metro Area	70,597	8,811	36,945	4,993	9,236	613	13,540	2,030	1,395	0	8,442	857
Victoria, TX Metro Area	16,458	1,999	10,661	1,339	na	na	na	na	na	na	4,644	626
Vineland-Bridgeton, NJ Metro Area	23,222	2,317	16,322	2,030	2,841	132	na	na	na	na	3,178	132
Virginia Beach-Norfolk-Newport News, VA-NC Metro Area	253,198	28,095	171,179	20,713	63,668	6,010	10,301	572	2,321	274	5,409	406
Visalia-Porterville, CA Metro Area	52,622	6,294	29,500	4,070	na	na	1,608	257	1,163	5	19,761	1,671
Waco, TX Metro Area	40,035	4,855	29,968	3,743	4,973	500	na	na	na	na	4,452	612
Walla Walla, WA Metro Area	12,576	2,054	10,748	1,575	na	na	na	na	na	na	1,140	245
Warner Robins, GA Metro Area	23,986	2,708	17,779	1,841	5,318	836	na	na	na	na	na	na
Warsaw, IN Micro Area	13,068	1,548	12,438	1,368	na	na	na	na	na	na	na	na
Washington-Arlington-Alexandria, DC-VA-MD-WV Metro Area	812,991	90,747	473,566	57,496	196,264	20,248	77,343	7,695	14,516	1,127	53,467	4,258
Waterloo-Cedar Falls, IA Metro Area	28,653	3,493	27,422	3,466	911	0	na	na	na	na	115	27
Watertown-Fort Atkinson, WI Micro Area	14,645	1,281	14,060	1,202	na	na	na	na	na	na	206	42
Watertown-Fort Drum, NY Metro Area	15,458	1,648	14,718	1,648	na	na	na	na	na	na	0	0
Wausau, WI Metro Area	23,770	3,026	23,365	2,923	na	na	82	0	na	na	na	na
Weirton-Steubenville, WV-OH Metro Area	27,429	3,025	25,959	2,987	na	na	na	na	na	na	na	na
Wenatchee, WA Metro Area	21,663	2,374	20,300	2,173	na	na	na	na	na	na	1,144	201
Wheeling, WV-OH Metro Area	30,430	4,514	29,128	4,350	na	na	na	na	na	na	na	na
Whitewater-Elkhorn, WI Micro Area	18,146	2,440	17,620	2,405	na	na	na	na	na	na	197	35
Wichita, KS Metro Area	96,970	13,150	84,419	11,570	4,853	947	2,187	169	1,122	12	4,359	336
Wichita Falls, TX Metro Area	23,264	2,750	19,720	2,483	806	122	na	na	na	na	2,506	179
Williamsport, PA Metro Area	21,901	2,301	21,281	2,167	na	na	na	na	na	na	na	na
Wilmington, NC Metro Area	52,496	6,253	44,438	5,317	6,471	870	na	na	na	na	671	0
Wilson, NC Micro Area	14,804	1,501	9,345	933	5,182	500	na	na	na	na	189	68
Winchester, VA-WV Metro Area	25,141	2,662	23,580	2,628	na	na	na	na	na	na	870	34
Winston-Salem, NC Metro Area	116,408	13,096	97,039	12,014	14,602	887	1,490	93	1,025	102	1,854	0
Wisconsin Rapids-Marshfield, WI Micro Area	14,940	1,891	14,652	1,891	na	na	na	na	na	na	na	na
Wooster, OH Micro Area	20,264	2,366	20,150	2,366	na	na	na	na	na	na	na	na
Worcester, MA-CT Metro Area	148,768	18,297	135,174	17,648	2,391	0	3,819	395	912	171	6,307	138
Yakima, WA Metro Area	34,329	3,726	26,300	3,417	na	na	na	na	240	0	6,335	269
York-Hanover, PA Metro Area	78,138	9,692	73,461	9,424	1,929	113	572	116	639	39	1,555	0
Youngstown-Warren-Boardman, OH-PA Metro Area	115,279	18,439	103,833	17,184	8,508	1,066	na	na	295	28	1,529	124
Yuba City, CA Metro Area	24,246	3,298	16,893	2,228	na	na	2,692	541	601	63	3,250	415
Yuma, AZ Metro Area	39,979	3,154	26,342	2,202	na	na	na	na	na	na	12,110	856
Zanesville, OH Micro Area	15,189	1,424	14,647	1,376	na	na	na	na	na	na	na	na

Table C-5: 116th Congressional Districts - Older Population by Race and Hispanic Origin

Name	Total Population 65 Years and Over	Total Population 85 Years and Over	White, Non-Hispanic 65 Years and Over	White, Non-Hispanic 85 Years and Over	Black, Alone 65 Years and Over	Black, Alone 85 Years and Over	Asian, Alone 65 Years and Over	Asian, Alone 85 Years and Over	Multi-race, Alone 65 Years and Over	Multi-race, Alone 85 Years and Over	Hispanic 65 Years and Over	Hispanic 85 Years and Over
Alabama												
Congressional District 1	127,083	12,627	98,519	9,577	24,477	2,359	na	na	984	155	1,682	367
Congressional District 2	115,362	12,723	86,939	9,517	24,847	2,942	na	na	1,024	133	939	52
Congressional District 3	119,519	10,181	91,578	7,683	24,318	2,228	1,015	0	750	53	1,689	0
Congressional District 4	128,143	13,332	116,969	12,344	6,769	706	na	na	1,714	209	1,558	24
Congressional District 5	119,725	12,667	100,782	11,665	13,322	696	1,553	83	1,788	116	2,143	78
Congressional District 6	119,052	12,536	103,424	11,142	11,160	778	1,563	93	749	0	1,726	523
Congressional District 7	100,779	11,176	40,887	4,705	58,620	6,286	na	na	na	na	570	158
Alaska												
Congressional District (at Large)	88,000	7,370	64,478	5,484	2,413	393	5,614	544	2,336	232	2,613	0
Arizona												
Congressional District 1	148,829	11,646	109,478	7,501	1,773	0	1,690	261	2,538	122	16,306	1,478
Congressional District 2	157,202	18,404	128,558	15,706	2,812	410	3,832	395	3,185	291	19,156	1,602
Congressional District 3	99,419	7,571	46,518	2,915	4,390	473	2,606	21	2,401	0	42,709	4,023
Congressional District 4	224,318	20,480	202,186	19,356	2,163	45	na	na	3,353	184	13,468	851
Congressional District 5	141,143	15,881	122,488	14,158	2,565	0	3,996	442	870	117	10,411	1,209
Congressional District 6	149,354	17,340	133,085	15,520	2,195	256	4,635	467	1,086	138	7,669	906
Congressional District 7	60,596	5,174	26,125	2,867	6,432	513	1,992	138	912	0	25,441	1,656
Congressional District 8	183,219	23,125	160,045	21,323	4,245	133	4,784	477	2,255	138	12,397	1,183
Congressional District 9	95,023	13,118	73,382	11,102	3,806	501	3,475	544	747	59	12,514	750
Arkansas												
Congressional District 1	131,155	13,711	112,487	11,998	13,899	1,376	na	na	2,929	209	1,144	55
Congressional District 2	121,838	14,284	101,166	12,415	16,792	1,670	1,058	0	319	0	1,987	199
Congressional District 3	118,046	13,378	109,623	12,333	1,687	168	1,399	0	1,097	177	3,610	700
Congressional District 4	136,637	14,796	114,879	12,785	19,254	1,762	na	na	912	85	805	77
California												
Congressional District 1	155,882	16,073	140,319	15,206	796	0	2,393	235	2,910	0	8,004	486
Congressional District 2	153,503	16,421	135,143	14,514	900	39	4,311	365	2,771	368	8,860	1,307
Congressional District 3	107,218	13,330	71,680	9,071	6,251	608	12,088	2,133	1,917	63	13,713	1,223
Congressional District 4	159,881	18,546	137,508	15,875	na	na	6,366	708	3,606	383	10,513	1,532
Congressional District 5	130,207	14,483	92,223	11,161	6,388	285	15,097	1,637	3,041	0	14,188	1,288
Congressional District 6	95,748	13,045	49,174	6,560	11,529	1,546	18,208	2,759	2,641	377	14,320	2,151
Congressional District 7	120,191	14,795	85,273	11,070	5,713	255	16,144	2,357	2,444	121	9,655	940
Congressional District 8	96,973	10,476	66,132	7,568	6,016	736	3,729	248	1,761	104	18,962	1,826
Congressional District 9	103,224	11,330	57,099	6,574	7,844	783	15,873	1,905	3,154	80	20,799	1,947
Congressional District 10	98,883	11,294	63,235	7,770	3,085	445	7,447	785	2,651	121	22,317	2,200
Congressional District 11	127,281	15,084	81,093	10,641	9,260	821	20,424	2,597	4,591	133	13,827	892
Congressional District 12	116,214	19,400	46,447	6,232	6,657	1,389	51,501	9,957	2,089	445	9,671	1,483
Congressional District 13	108,061	12,426	49,207	4,775	20,914	2,271	25,669	4,064	2,095	275	9,335	840
Congressional District 14	125,644	19,325	57,290	9,793	4,068	883	44,225	5,582	2,575	50	16,184	2,804
Congressional District 15	106,877	12,930	49,832	6,309	5,579	709	35,145	4,064	1,913	352	13,487	1,480
Congressional District 16	78,134	9,790	37,165	5,724	4,620	483	5,989	929	1,210	159	29,435	2,602
Congressional District 17	96,078	13,023	35,528	5,504	1,693	85	47,987	6,489	1,615	54	9,510	826
Congressional District 18	116,195	19,265	83,604	14,295	882	59	21,844	3,158	2,012	673	7,735	1,080
Congressional District 19	102,973	11,658	40,421	5,328	3,402	255	32,764	3,073	2,279	98	23,772	2,605
Congressional District 20	103,980	12,582	66,821	8,279	1,909	231	7,992	1,512	2,934	283	25,469	2,291
Congressional District 21	64,614	7,331	23,561	2,935	2,545	105	4,280	398	1,690	45	32,893	3,848
Congressional District 22	99,343	13,776	62,169	10,131	2,380	101	7,929	823	1,708	46	25,531	2,498
Congressional District 23	98,579	11,477	66,331	8,208	4,391	515	4,828	508	2,297	413	20,825	2,000
Congressional District 24	127,463	16,220	100,198	13,004	1,184	146	5,028	905	2,328	341	18,784	1,744
Congressional District 25	93,789	8,800	54,869	5,367	6,268	233	10,465	1,227	1,492	84	20,689	1,789
Congressional District 26	111,657	16,413	75,828	12,371	1,647	241	8,653	1,142	1,708	130	24,309	2,560
Congressional District 27	127,057	20,949	47,259	7,802	6,479	1,241	50,672	8,779	2,129	788	20,797	2,289
Congressional District 28	110,736	15,679	72,931	11,097	1,885	193	16,031	1,806	1,963	0	18,055	2,364
Congressional District 29	82,368	8,910	30,399	4,126	3,192	723	11,587	1,354	1,363	107	36,354	2,686
Congressional District 30	119,121	17,881	81,209	13,243	3,219	402	17,672	1,811	1,345	142	15,473	2,210
Congressional District 31	88,386	9,201	39,128	4,691	8,520	336	10,205	700	1,804	153	28,531	3,165
Congressional District 32	96,564	11,504	24,665	3,207	3,229	369	23,191	2,976	4,667	217	44,121	4,807
Congressional District 33	132,040	21,452	104,846	18,325	2,819	188	12,846	1,220	2,514	279	9,662	1,452
Congressional District 34	93,848	14,830	10,419	1,346	3,380	175	34,444	6,204	1,146	334	45,518	6,941
Congressional District 35	74,498	7,379	21,157	2,604	6,487	743	7,538	510	1,768	53	37,780	3,469
Congressional District 36	171,562	21,007	124,283	18,256	5,401	66	6,465	456	2,484	218	32,350	1,880
Congressional District 37	92,876	13,847	28,803	4,842	30,820	5,053	10,254	1,492	2,515	232	21,020	2,182
Congressional District 38	107,550	16,426	30,096	6,146	2,936	179	23,754	3,094	2,006	322	49,209	6,772
Congressional District 39	111,862	14,340	44,920	6,624	2,681	292	41,229	4,463	1,923	152	21,511	2,809
Congressional District 40	67,423	8,087	7,325	1,254	4,121	636	3,319	342	1,221	0	52,140	5,843
Congressional District 41	73,535	8,830	30,964	4,979	8,750	915	6,954	367	727	83	26,379	2,598
Congressional District 42	99,510	11,886	60,336	8,115	4,863	415	10,005	678	1,902	319	22,149	2,396
Congressional District 43	92,544	12,257	22,255	3,568	24,976	2,773	21,732	3,311	2,891	182	21,090	2,448
Congressional District 44	75,324	9,704	11,656	1,737	17,424	2,904	7,335	931	1,275	348	37,732	4,038
Congressional District 45	122,823	17,525	83,166	12,863	1,620	8	23,612	2,222	1,909	529	11,059	1,850
Congressional District 46	74,590	10,252	28,056	4,658	1,530	52	16,164	2,730	895	146	27,888	2,666
Congressional District 47	91,255	12,125	46,524	6,260	6,406	732	23,026	2,985	1,509	317	13,962	1,928
Congressional District 48	127,774	18,592	84,703	13,561	na	na	28,966	3,188	1,461	126	11,169	1,609
Congressional District 49	122,829	15,853	96,449	12,702	1,583	198	10,179	1,159	1,773	146	12,410	1,516
Congressional District 50	112,208	14,500	86,129	10,833	2,180	285	6,763	1,451	2,728	530	13,919	1,483

Table C-5: 116th Congressional Districts - Older Population by Race and Hispanic Origin—*Continued*

Name	Total Population 65 Years and Over	Total Population 85 Years and Over	White, Non-Hispanic 65 Years and Over	White, Non-Hispanic 85 Years and Over	Black, Alone 65 Years and Over	Black, Alone 85 Years and Over	Asian, Alone 65 Years and Over	Asian, Alone 85 Years and Over	Multi-race, Alone 65 Years and Over	Multi-race, Alone 85 Years and Over	Hispanic 65 Years and Over	Hispanic 85 Years and Over
California—Cont.												
Congressional District 51	88,372	11,343	18,660	3,350	5,683	618	13,041	1,907	1,812	384	49,447	5,387
Congressional District 52	112,620	13,389	82,749	10,234	1,967	33	16,473	1,427	1,554	98	9,265	1,688
Congressional District 53	99,470	12,539	58,767	8,671	5,954	501	15,021	1,422	1,985	314	18,774	1,844
Colorado												
Congressional District 1	100,994	11,436	71,485	7,968	8,680	866	3,025	71	1,738	64	16,105	2,235
Congressional District 2	122,089	11,611	113,066	10,951	na	na	2,168	295	733	0	5,340	365
Congressional District 3	140,186	13,669	117,664	12,048	na	na	na	na	1,564	41	18,604	1,567
Congressional District 4	116,803	12,948	100,348	11,293	408	39	1,582	104	1,548	62	12,843	1,383
Congressional District 5	115,313	12,793	98,095	11,203	3,898	225	3,089	508	1,291	33	8,188	638
Congressional District 6	101,182	10,852	80,874	9,254	6,337	531	5,100	491	1,053	80	7,909	573
Congressional District 7	111,288	14,097	90,587	12,848	764	93	2,652	98	1,184	0	16,131	926
Connecticut												
Congressional District 1	124,852	18,416	99,079	16,259	12,707	1,516	3,433	0	1,051	39	9,118	602
Congressional District 2	126,055	17,204	116,745	16,323	2,947	476	1,972	106	1,046	55	3,246	299
Congressional District 3	124,880	17,490	103,758	15,608	11,374	561	2,745	414	492	0	6,337	907
Congressional District 4	115,192	17,460	88,792	15,463	10,289	809	4,348	351	696	104	11,353	837
Congressional District 5	122,168	17,126	107,226	16,280	4,621	276	2,116	126	1,077	176	7,585	268
Delaware												
Congressional District (at Large)	180,756	18,604	143,971	16,293	26,466	1,837	4,419	131	900	0	4,194	226
District of Columbia												
Delegate District (at Large)	85,626	10,901	29,184	3,372	48,883	7,062	2,297	83	1,578	218	4,636	256
Florida												
Congressional District 1	132,405	11,534	111,517	9,910	11,776	759	4,034	472	1,638	151	2,305	171
Congressional District 2	148,454	15,245	130,414	13,398	11,683	1,254	1,438	132	1,205	74	3,308	387
Congressional District 3	128,208	13,141	104,482	11,165	13,532	1,334	3,132	230	1,595	0	5,377	412
Congressional District 4	137,230	14,047	118,008	11,875	7,943	757	4,924	564	841	42	5,576	809
Congressional District 5	98,265	8,976	54,355	5,250	36,356	3,443	2,148	0	1,523	51	3,777	283
Congressional District 6	200,306	28,871	171,538	24,667	11,826	1,382	2,784	505	1,818	119	12,721	2,264
Congressional District 7	114,061	13,944	78,221	9,710	9,200	945	5,695	214	1,352	176	20,462	3,184
Congressional District 8	195,565	28,313	169,480	24,666	10,648	1,567	2,750	635	1,450	95	10,682	1,430
Congressional District 9	145,575	16,615	92,500	10,940	13,296	957	2,932	173	2,702	110	36,967	4,640
Congressional District 10	97,785	9,800	48,589	6,553	21,878	1,639	6,121	148	1,446	211	19,422	1,460
Congressional District 11	281,669	29,226	255,472	25,947	9,700	939	na	na	1,517	200	12,980	1,382
Congressional District 12	193,965	23,063	174,484	21,608	4,599	508	3,039	0	1,463	215	10,389	800
Congressional District 13	171,584	25,694	146,790	23,184	10,847	1,042	3,677	268	2,013	222	8,278	1,140
Congressional District 14	104,514	12,969	58,735	7,635	15,289	1,457	3,994	242	1,511	253	25,358	3,168
Congressional District 15	132,949	12,649	102,291	10,059	10,850	605	2,204	61	2,986	352	15,470	1,678
Congressional District 16	226,843	31,418	201,678	28,397	8,195	948	3,143	217	1,261	0	12,906	1,856
Congressional District 17	255,782	34,052	231,676	30,932	9,096	1,163	na	na	1,016	0	11,295	1,778
Congressional District 18	201,423	26,048	169,304	24,396	14,514	832	3,116	130	2,098	107	13,322	583
Congressional District 19	264,638	38,239	236,579	35,969	7,405	41	na	na	1,400	135	14,880	1,726
Congressional District 20	108,899	15,921	36,775	8,333	46,468	4,887	2,828	380	2,057	315	21,571	2,006
Congressional District 21	201,501	37,306	162,333	32,814	13,172	728	3,515	300	1,571	126	21,745	3,370
Congressional District 22	165,568	23,499	131,475	20,051	12,772	1,530	2,858	167	1,185	156	17,438	1,630
Congressional District 23	137,835	16,575	79,861	11,269	12,353	959	5,095	246	2,451	257	39,397	4,023
Congressional District 24	107,971	13,870	16,106	2,330	49,832	5,578	na	na	1,424	193	44,241	6,254
Congressional District 25	147,636	23,395	49,284	4,962	4,935	487	619	19	1,677	301	92,975	17,846
Congressional District 26	117,449	13,117	24,085	1,680	7,621	721	2,580	31	1,776	5	82,891	10,685
Congressional District 27	140,704	23,473	30,676	4,656	6,056	1,391	2,469	0	2,188	162	102,489	17,387
Georgia												
Congressional District 1	109,215	10,157	82,231	8,054	24,172	2,057	1,263	46	276	0	1,035	0
Congressional District 2	105,503	12,200	59,504	7,085	42,821	4,800	854	165	875	0	1,450	91
Congressional District 3	114,866	11,321	88,461	9,339	21,974	1,459	999	0	288	164	2,992	414
Congressional District 4	95,657	8,691	41,495	4,598	46,347	3,557	4,185	457	1,177	72	2,570	7
Congressional District 5	86,695	9,939	25,773	3,753	56,741	5,824	2,201	266	646	29	1,203	67
Congressional District 6	98,851	10,944	78,329	9,294	6,660	101	7,664	928	1,064	0	5,174	621
Congressional District 7	84,707	7,947	55,867	5,530	9,252	501	11,914	917	605	80	6,972	919
Congressional District 8	109,323	11,071	79,964	8,745	25,757	2,141	1,326	137	580	48	1,550	48
Congressional District 9	142,766	12,327	129,846	11,427	6,330	211	645	0	2,695	477	3,304	411
Congressional District 10	110,981	10,006	82,583	7,661	24,212	1,931	1,176	31	324	44	2,164	383
Congressional District 11	102,184	10,449	87,092	8,747	8,387	1,075	2,208	469	708	8	3,643	150
Congressional District 12	102,894	10,249	71,256	7,804	27,283	1,921	1,875	458	840	0	1,751	66
Congressional District 13	85,526	7,060	40,894	4,109	37,538	2,733	2,221	189	965	29	3,404	0
Congressional District 14	107,260	10,439	96,307	9,762	4,886	628	na	na	1,736	0	3,171	49
Hawaii												
Congressional District 1	132,970	24,283	20,490	2,882	883	0	91,769	19,090	12,763	1,365	3,351	218
Congressional District 2	128,497	15,790	49,599	4,655	568	0	48,761	8,601	14,888	1,454	4,809	306
Idaho												
Congressional District 1	155,498	14,256	143,146	13,036	na	na	2,696	540	1,850	4	4,823	346
Congressional District 2	123,943	15,447	115,541	14,998	na	na	1,269	132	1,248	52	4,695	144

Table C-5: 116th Congressional Districts - Older Population by Race and Hispanic Origin—*Continued*

Name	Total Population		White, Non-Hispanic		Black, Alone		Asian, Alone		Multi-race, Alone		Hispanic	
	65 Years and Over	85 Years and Over	65 Years and Over	85 Years and Over	65 Years and Over	85 Years and Over	65 Years and Over	85 Years and Over	65 Years and Over	85 Years and Over	65 Years and Over	85 Years and Over
Illinois												
Congressional District 1	112,861	14,825	46,810	6,836	59,716	7,205	1,800	271	798	63	3,732	449
Congressional District 2	111,159	15,506	47,896	8,881	54,630	5,488	na	na	983	137	6,539	1,086
Congressional District 3	108,168	14,512	83,352	11,153	4,270	850	4,858	731	875	104	15,108	1,778
Congressional District 4	71,791	7,138	25,178	3,702	2,173	174	3,212	39	1,392	274	40,816	2,925
Congressional District 5	95,746	13,653	71,840	11,313	2,008	370	10,801	763	795	0	10,447	1,162
Congressional District 6	119,204	13,197	101,929	11,434	2,313	373	9,984	849	1,122	125	3,892	416
Congressional District 7	96,514	8,967	31,708	3,442	50,350	4,490	5,568	783	589	0	8,717	252
Congressional District 8	97,618	11,427	69,835	9,841	2,940	532	14,985	497	1,067	32	8,774	525
Congressional District 9	126,337	21,276	100,628	18,099	5,881	708	13,133	1,534	1,108	26	5,664	875
Congressional District 10	109,894	16,786	87,336	15,058	4,668	231	9,456	984	901	123	7,503	390
Congressional District 11	90,133	10,903	65,032	8,360	6,784	420	6,773	268	929	60	10,773	1,795
Congressional District 12	117,968	14,238	102,092	13,164	13,055	956	699	0	547	0	1,339	129
Congressional District 13	111,496	16,142	101,435	15,323	5,954	500	2,153	45	850	88	1,016	186
Congressional District 14	102,747	11,627	94,115	10,729	1,688	204	2,888	397	510	0	3,876	297
Congressional District 15	133,930	17,685	129,342	17,047	2,002	638	na	na	927	0	1,207	0
Congressional District 16	124,590	15,289	118,208	15,129	1,214	57	1,101	0	505	54	3,496	49
Congressional District 17	126,888	16,821	113,996	15,377	8,189	859	486	0	653	135	3,463	428
Congressional District 18	133,504	19,576	127,791	19,172	2,574	322	1,041	36	761	5	1,134	41
Indiana												
Congressional District 1	118,463	14,430	89,393	10,952	18,343	2,208	1,432	0	634	36	8,925	1,234
Congressional District 2	118,817	16,719	109,684	15,811	4,388	309	1,031	0	1,098	228	2,095	191
Congressional District 3	115,773	13,571	107,586	13,000	4,501	249	1,247	50	421	89	1,827	183
Congressional District 4	118,000	13,555	112,458	12,766	1,751	279	943	61	939	81	1,445	392
Congressional District 5	116,399	14,306	104,550	12,932	7,576	778	2,539	242	484	105	1,319	249
Congressional District 6	127,419	14,369	122,337	13,792	2,906	396	849	109	298	0	997	72
Congressional District 7	92,272	10,647	65,484	7,304	23,000	2,650	1,533	460	531	0	2,240	411
Congressional District 8	124,660	15,650	120,864	15,400	2,508	228	na	na	273	0	565	0
Congressional District 9	119,343	13,330	114,706	13,027	1,101	147	1,584	123	1,134	0	585	33
Iowa												
Congressional District 1	139,220	19,498	134,098	18,980	1,737	41	1,528	172	282	11	1,169	181
Congressional District 2	134,426	18,478	129,003	17,898	1,829	0	931	8	445	0	2,152	528
Congressional District 3	123,357	15,503	117,618	15,221	1,966	0	1,488	60	666	222	1,569	0
Congressional District 4	140,815	22,137	137,189	21,984	187	71	1,029	42	596	0	1,437	40
Kansas												
Congressional District 1	115,910	17,640	107,483	16,946	1,626	190	874	71	852	164	4,800	269
Congressional District 2	123,084	17,516	112,274	15,964	4,342	1,008	873	54	1,393	92	3,682	312
Congressional District 3	108,784	12,806	93,825	12,057	7,007	292	2,620	110	534	0	4,377	347
Congressional District 4	114,413	15,824	100,906	14,141	5,020	947	2,476	169	1,167	12	4,749	439
Kentucky												
Congressional District 1	133,233	15,093	122,508	13,463	7,045	1,060	na	na	1,005	105	2,209	570
Congressional District 2	124,068	12,640	115,843	12,352	4,162	252	1,403	0	1,082	0	1,361	36
Congressional District 3	120,473	15,541	97,765	13,902	18,362	1,350	1,496	169	1,016	66	1,847	54
Congressional District 4	116,906	11,993	112,772	11,794	2,375	32	na	na	426	0	713	116
Congressional District 5	121,959	12,116	120,131	11,941	592	91	na	na	na	na	565	0
Congressional District 6	114,753	11,265	103,877	9,535	7,790	1,558	913	0	1,036	112	711	60
Louisiana												
Congressional District 1	130,195	13,608	109,401	12,477	10,481	411	1,379	19	938	135	6,490	511
Congressional District 2	115,542	10,444	41,500	4,613	65,629	5,140	2,644	76	870	150	5,467	485
Congressional District 3	115,222	13,458	88,567	10,971	22,685	2,387	701	0	1,468	49	1,667	0
Congressional District 4	122,592	12,945	86,296	9,661	32,660	3,021	na	na	923	99	1,394	83
Congressional District 5	121,256	10,916	86,872	9,199	30,589	1,617	na	na	745	86	1,678	0
Congressional District 6	115,803	12,473	91,473	10,217	19,522	1,718	1,723	218	803	0	2,346	423
Maine												
Congressional District 1	138,926	17,583	134,885	17,356	503	0	1,501	0	842	0	914	227
Congressional District 2	137,143	17,266	133,868	17,031	420	0	na	na	1,086	20	1,034	7
Maryland												
Congressional District 1	138,984	15,117	120,821	13,704	13,397	885	1,954	127	976	271	1,947	113
Congressional District 2	109,606	12,292	75,566	9,574	25,780	2,024	4,650	523	1,283	0	2,176	0
Congressional District 3	115,494	17,034	88,320	14,016	16,436	1,941	6,833	815	1,345	56	2,691	206
Congressional District 4	103,193	10,289	35,181	4,610	58,001	5,140	3,896	251	2,292	55	4,371	191
Congressional District 5	105,734	10,486	60,305	6,359	36,883	3,057	4,016	542	1,099	29	3,273	499
Congressional District 6	118,748	13,265	90,465	10,511	8,216	656	11,410	1,275	1,075	42	7,285	781
Congressional District 7	113,001	13,973	47,136	6,725	57,001	6,402	4,870	168	2,367	429	1,998	372
Congressional District 8	126,281	16,059	91,987	13,289	12,948	1,072	11,468	1,069	2,317	45	7,910	584
Massachusetts												
Congressional District 1	132,153	18,278	116,091	17,110	5,349	530	1,350	0	823	22	8,810	606
Congressional District 2	121,700	15,002	110,381	14,330	1,663	12	4,092	354	669	116	4,394	112
Congressional District 3	105,527	14,523	87,969	13,320	2,487	50	5,126	275	950	56	9,862	822
Congressional District 4	127,736	16,587	118,908	15,831	1,550	110	4,126	76	752	190	2,233	164
Congressional District 5	125,377	16,865	108,074	15,480	3,536	118	9,051	1,148	412	24	4,266	95
Congressional District 6	146,196	22,927	132,989	21,345	3,892	611	3,366	587	1,025	99	5,848	285
Congressional District 7	89,349	10,668	43,779	6,867	24,465	2,430	9,018	704	2,782	0	11,179	667
Congressional District 8	124,671	18,546	105,114	16,976	7,661	785	6,168	414	1,683	0	3,445	238
Congressional District 9	164,832	20,333	155,884	18,905	1,441	137	1,197	143	1,560	0	2,386	178

Table C-5: 116th Congressional Districts - Older Population by Race and Hispanic Origin—*Continued*

Name	Total Population		White, Non-Hispanic		Black, Alone		Asian, Alone		Multi-race, Alone		Hispanic	
	65 Years and Over	85 Years and Over	65 Years and Over	85 Years and Over	65 Years and Over	85 Years and Over	65 Years and Over	85 Years and Over	65 Years and Over	85 Years and Over	65 Years and Over	85 Years and Over
Michigan												
Congressional District 1	163,475	18,537	157,430	18,062	729	118	387	63	1,834	117	1,151	79
Congressional District 2	119,587	14,105	108,343	13,322	4,090	486	1,958	0	582	78	4,185	219
Congressional District 3	112,791	14,020	101,513	13,447	6,869	293	1,226	0	814	203	2,165	0
Congressional District 4	137,477	14,967	131,000	14,372	1,473	146	678	103	1,070	0	2,647	271
Congressional District 5	124,550	14,616	103,671	12,779	15,973	1,510	na	na	1,372	89	3,290	279
Congressional District 6	124,855	14,089	112,981	12,950	6,338	634	1,133	27	1,857	347	2,648	202
Congressional District 7	130,623	14,811	122,561	13,873	3,881	300	na	na	1,112	85	2,114	399
Congressional District 8	112,636	13,102	102,366	11,922	3,795	427	2,759	495	1,337	43	2,481	215
Congressional District 9	119,353	16,889	103,336	15,402	9,480	826	3,908	322	1,205	116	1,279	223
Congressional District 10	132,553	13,560	126,700	12,893	1,996	292	1,161	21	837	63	1,665	291
Congressional District 11	123,503	14,436	108,713	13,437	4,217	351	7,850	166	765	228	1,515	138
Congressional District 12	103,976	13,059	88,539	11,256	7,571	828	3,120	515	1,605	301	3,054	159
Congressional District 13	97,265	12,140	40,068	5,030	53,343	6,792	na	na	655	97	2,540	45
Congressional District 14	117,809	15,962	52,294	8,991	57,901	6,304	3,510	157	1,400	152	2,157	358
Minnesota												
Congressional District 1	117,573	18,318	113,707	17,957	482	14	1,422	165	317	98	1,594	70
Congressional District 2	99,093	11,325	92,937	11,163	1,529	0	2,488	53	834	109	1,130	0
Congressional District 3	114,683	12,476	106,222	11,888	3,342	112	3,888	431	624	0	478	0
Congressional District 4	104,637	13,752	91,927	12,768	4,673	370	4,874	614	831	0	2,186	0
Congressional District 5	91,072	14,244	77,076	12,620	7,983	935	2,458	384	847	127	2,215	297
Congressional District 6	94,077	9,306	90,560	9,245	639	0	1,298	0	445	61	903	0
Congressional District 7	130,239	19,328	125,821	19,045	482	0	305	10	561	53	1,485	176
Congressional District 8	137,260	16,624	133,514	16,247	426	0	428	108	899	8	592	109
Mississippi												
Congressional District 1	121,547	11,824	96,024	10,356	23,820	1,370	na	na	428	70	727	0
Congressional District 2	106,751	10,200	51,590	5,538	53,401	4,650	na	na	na	na	722	0
Congressional District 3	122,887	13,669	88,730	11,069	32,762	2,574	361	0	na	na	508	65
Congressional District 4	123,238	10,667	98,972	8,703	20,329	1,316	1,205	166	589	0	1,975	438
Missouri												
Congressional District 1	106,576	14,661	54,269	8,284	46,934	6,071	2,365	0	1,225	190	1,415	36
Congressional District 2	143,830	19,329	135,874	18,804	2,475	222	3,566	212	602	33	1,273	58
Congressional District 3	128,004	12,931	123,971	12,507	1,902	211	na	na	669	161	909	158
Congressional District 4	130,398	15,166	121,799	14,484	2,522	105	1,274	25	2,224	321	1,706	153
Congressional District 5	119,698	15,839	92,524	12,588	20,327	2,704	1,238	57	1,011	0	4,240	490
Congressional District 6	128,534	15,523	121,243	15,345	3,078	94	1,208	82	915	0	1,874	2
Congressional District 7	138,312	16,590	132,115	16,021	998	275	821	58	1,948	73	2,289	33
Congressional District 8	139,722	14,766	132,717	14,040	2,823	334	na	na	1,375	233	1,793	117
Montana												
Congressional District (at Large)	200,239	20,753	187,264	19,879	na	na	1,283	207	2,766	113	2,436	166
Nebraska												
Congressional District 1	99,097	13,573	93,175	13,224	1,183	180	1,691	5	492	21	2,170	143
Congressional District 2	86,041	11,159	75,376	9,850	5,944	733	1,036	173	1,018	0	2,692	379
Congressional District 3	118,860	17,220	113,009	16,682	71	0	539	95	976	0	3,981	443
Nevada												
Congressional District 1	99,661	8,538	57,640	5,465	8,817	811	10,653	370	2,295	248	20,329	1,653
Congressional District 2	126,080	11,982	105,760	10,119	1,392	30	5,033	627	1,351	84	10,437	949
Congressional District 3	133,739	14,256	93,965	10,803	7,949	456	20,187	1,358	1,455	280	10,266	1,542
Congressional District 4	115,640	9,504	78,709	6,569	13,128	794	9,531	483	1,743	146	11,936	1,377
New Hampshire												
Congressional District 1	120,363	16,237	116,826	16,062	667	0	686	73	912	0	1,159	102
Congressional District 2	124,793	14,587	119,425	13,987	445	269	1,513	32	898	100	1,841	346
New Jersey												
Congressional District 1	113,725	13,348	85,729	10,993	15,401	1,228	5,221	404	1,122	0	6,723	723
Congressional District 2	136,834	14,963	113,693	13,375	11,219	1,251	3,294	8	1,503	7	7,388	306
Congressional District 3	142,831	18,902	123,363	17,249	10,234	1,057	4,164	198	937	51	4,396	347
Congressional District 4	147,151	21,470	125,959	19,912	7,632	578	6,867	339	817	122	6,020	641
Congressional District 5	131,230	19,802	105,189	16,643	5,713	550	10,212	1,852	1,985	0	8,138	739
Congressional District 6	105,000	13,022	68,492	9,670	8,712	570	14,107	773	1,835	0	12,105	1,868
Congressional District 7	120,534	17,568	100,547	15,609	4,101	309	8,906	478	253	60	6,948	996
Congressional District 8	82,392	9,908	27,441	4,816	8,046	215	6,333	369	2,283	302	41,765	4,582
Congressional District 9	110,980	15,791	63,705	11,232	8,515	913	12,230	889	888	187	25,772	2,608
Congressional District 10	98,861	14,125	27,856	5,213	48,197	5,488	7,780	1,017	1,252	111	15,470	2,773
Congressional District 11	132,036	20,066	111,286	18,329	4,153	624	9,415	697	899	11	5,923	405
Congressional District 12	116,715	16,793	79,105	13,198	17,012	1,994	12,210	749	854	125	7,714	665
New Mexico												
Congressional District 1	117,458	14,195	71,218	8,437	2,550	507	2,785	65	2,428	217	38,273	4,935
Congressional District 2	122,410	14,129	69,474	8,956	3,387	228	na	na	1,232	84	43,267	4,850
Congressional District 3	128,612	12,411	72,651	6,343	1,288	279	1,179	0	1,643	165	38,669	4,041
New York												
Congressional District 1	129,004	15,291	113,304	13,453	3,915	634	2,767	100	460	0	8,445	1,076
Congressional District 2	108,985	15,811	86,632	13,892	7,051	436	3,086	151	1,746	176	10,788	1,124
Congressional District 3	146,620	23,439	114,079	19,061	4,783	1,282	18,335	809	1,268	106	8,309	2,181

Table C-5: 116th Congressional Districts - Older Population by Race and Hispanic Origin—*Continued*

Name	Total Population 65 Years and Over	85 Years and Over	White, Non-Hispanic 65 Years and Over	85 Years and Over	Black, Alone 65 Years and Over	85 Years and Over	Asian, Alone 65 Years and Over	85 Years and Over	Multi-race, Alone 65 Years and Over	85 Years and Over	Hispanic 65 Years and Over	85 Years and Over
New York—Cont.												
Congressional District 4	125,392	19,043	91,010	16,062	15,989	1,206	6,143	415	1,984	311	11,116	1,119
Congressional District 5	110,647	12,282	22,989	4,279	55,636	5,855	12,713	888	2,747	53	14,221	1,041
Congressional District 6	130,286	17,036	60,709	10,044	5,593	567	44,850	4,553	2,499	153	17,870	1,837
Congressional District 7	84,981	9,801	21,928	2,924	8,836	631	20,720	3,067	3,297	125	34,671	3,319
Congressional District 8	118,829	16,737	41,539	8,606	57,390	6,318	6,105	609	1,746	182	15,557	963
Congressional District 9	110,059	13,506	37,202	4,834	57,865	7,167	6,920	913	2,043	168	8,951	790
Congressional District 10	114,159	16,857	83,816	12,144	5,471	789	14,530	1,516	2,075	65	9,623	2,579
Congressional District 11	123,577	15,038	90,730	12,391	6,012	851	16,311	769	1,106	124	10,053	945
Congressional District 12	110,208	16,717	81,411	14,077	4,620	439	11,412	1,152	1,596	111	11,902	1,038
Congressional District 13	101,638	12,590	10,673	1,691	35,215	4,657	4,126	338	5,835	233	55,489	6,483
Congressional District 14	94,455	11,791	34,617	5,955	9,818	880	16,403	1,556	2,713	0	33,479	3,466
Congressional District 15	80,341	7,598	2,857	856	29,380	1,634	2,188	53	2,272	307	51,160	4,859
Congressional District 16	127,802	20,835	66,998	13,668	33,145	4,685	5,023	353	2,879	289	21,747	2,079
Congressional District 17	124,138	19,321	92,622	15,844	12,472	1,389	7,476	1,177	2,151	283	10,662	958
Congressional District 18	110,816	13,092	91,489	11,326	7,404	642	3,053	250	753	0	8,606	849
Congressional District 19	144,119	17,548	134,075	16,192	3,929	196	1,362	108	674	175	4,556	894
Congressional District 20	123,308	17,760	110,816	16,288	6,119	684	2,750	366	1,471	56	2,542	417
Congressional District 21	125,887	14,768	122,308	14,656	798	50	1,044	20	538	25	529	42
Congressional District 22	130,497	18,748	124,027	18,465	2,133	87	2,046	36	961	32	1,500	128
Congressional District 23	130,512	16,529	124,801	15,765	1,886	369	748	181	606	0	1,699	165
Congressional District 24	122,161	16,996	112,142	15,695	5,727	703	1,582	191	693	23	1,995	384
Congressional District 25	123,290	17,225	104,247	15,645	11,558	968	2,666	257	756	42	4,426	444
Congressional District 26	123,251	18,663	101,453	15,528	15,839	2,410	1,748	150	1,186	198	2,906	340
Congressional District 27	137,103	17,607	133,402	17,245	877	313	na	na	292	0	1,047	49
North Carolina												
Congressional District 1	126,081	12,496	69,527	7,317	51,052	4,873	1,408	55	1,251	50	2,305	221
Congressional District 2	117,604	9,813	91,915	8,072	19,557	1,200	1,982	90	1,047	190	2,871	273
Congressional District 3	132,134	11,897	102,864	9,353	24,740	2,301	na	na	850	132	1,840	54
Congressional District 4	102,109	10,351	73,883	8,487	19,107	1,295	5,119	313	912	57	3,013	199
Congressional District 5	138,964	16,560	120,167	15,137	14,208	1,220	1,108	93	1,332	102	1,737	27
Congressional District 6	136,131	16,340	108,725	13,679	22,247	2,310	1,141	48	1,254	117	2,910	186
Congressional District 7	160,657	16,005	126,990	12,510	27,106	2,875	1,559	105	1,028	34	3,306	458
Congressional District 8	119,587	12,484	90,949	10,277	21,245	1,522	1,835	329	838	88	3,562	227
Congressional District 9	122,555	12,566	87,372	9,858	21,884	1,927	2,333	60	560	113	2,226	119
Congressional District 10	140,903	15,453	125,287	14,274	12,276	1,019	950	0	992	0	1,496	160
Congressional District 11	173,932	20,981	164,612	19,130	2,496	578	na	na	1,625	141	2,781	813
Congressional District 12	87,139	8,849	48,066	5,855	30,725	2,275	3,294	139	758	155	4,985	900
Congressional District 13	130,778	15,272	105,547	13,620	19,123	1,388	2,384	0	1,067	0	2,003	264
North Dakota												
Congressional District (at Large)	116,433	18,439	111,517	17,992	302	0	549	0	535	97	898	120
Ohio												
Congressional District 1	111,917	14,260	89,110	12,461	18,932	1,725	2,226	30	481	44	1,071	0
Congressional District 2	119,527	13,954	109,730	13,104	7,596	681	805	124	799	0	547	45
Congressional District 3	84,005	8,584	54,438	5,325	24,800	2,657	1,899	398	1,137	0	1,722	122
Congressional District 4	123,452	14,126	115,812	13,151	3,889	515	767	0	151	4	2,673	415
Congressional District 5	130,512	17,198	122,785	16,405	2,904	617	833	113	799	25	2,785	38
Congressional District 6	139,032	16,928	133,510	16,547	2,737	289	na	na	911	23	na	na
Congressional District 7	135,066	16,926	127,938	16,129	4,453	511	na	na	401	0	897	105
Congressional District 8	123,430	14,326	114,210	13,214	4,234	555	2,562	51	976	319	1,107	187
Congressional District 9	112,349	13,958	91,368	11,222	12,288	1,429	2,273	917	520	19	5,892	316
Congressional District 10	128,971	16,397	106,523	14,458	17,396	1,716	1,735	186	1,383	37	1,670	37
Congressional District 11	119,878	17,666	58,995	10,400	55,360	6,384	1,541	157	1,479	25	2,480	700
Congressional District 12	123,476	15,152	115,714	14,490	3,194	436	2,321	0	1,431	194	753	32
Congressional District 13	132,490	18,563	117,962	17,262	11,307	1,166	1,495	91	156	6	1,432	38
Congressional District 14	145,548	18,054	135,702	17,532	5,206	243	2,330	205	1,027	0	905	74
Congressional District 15	120,773	13,376	113,789	12,761	3,488	97	1,478	162	1,230	115	855	241
Congressional District 16	145,737	18,817	139,812	18,039	2,467	404	1,628	231	368	0	1,358	143
Oklahoma												
Congressional District 1	120,002	13,713	99,531	12,733	6,812	428	1,684	47	4,138	122	3,075	125
Congressional District 2	141,541	15,150	112,770	12,641	4,548	480	637	54	7,771	580	1,280	119
Congressional District 3	125,904	15,780	109,998	14,514	3,536	564	1,420	0	2,886	149	3,353	238
Congressional District 4	118,261	12,812	100,234	11,356	5,929	596	1,868	68	4,377	497	2,911	103
Congressional District 5	113,893	15,128	88,742	12,932	11,105	1,256	2,720	113	2,219	115	4,960	328
Oregon												
Congressional District 1	127,814	14,543	112,231	13,209	934	5	6,926	665	1,669	0	5,242	380
Congressional District 2	173,438	20,256	158,928	18,589	na	na	1,745	310	4,258	340	6,805	733
Congressional District 3	114,251	11,814	96,353	10,376	4,643	202	8,253	894	1,166	52	3,587	290
Congressional District 4	173,359	16,917	160,592	16,171	na	na	1,915	97	3,260	242	4,066	227
Congressional District 5	150,749	17,852	139,149	16,672	na	na	1,864	126	1,898	473	6,756	692
Pennsylvania												
Congressional District 1	131,951	15,560	120,352	14,438	3,036	497	5,620	392	406	116	2,209	117
Congressional District 2	97,633	10,784	58,946	7,989	18,335	1,347	7,755	473	1,275	70	12,270	990
Congressional District 3	101,895	13,481	30,911	4,395	64,337	8,417	3,588	510	1,452	118	2,060	227
Congressional District 4	129,655	19,389	112,682	17,649	9,468	973	5,036	500	532	0	1,939	267

Table C-5: 116th Congressional Districts - Older Population by Race and Hispanic Origin—*Continued*

Name	Total Population		White, Non-Hispanic		Black, Alone		Asian, Alone		Multi-race, Alone		Hispanic	
	65 Years and Over	85 Years and Over	65 Years and Over	85 Years and Over	65 Years and Over	85 Years and Over	65 Years and Over	85 Years and Over	65 Years and Over	85 Years and Over	65 Years and Over	85 Years and Over
Pennsylvania—Cont.												
Congressional District 5	115,180	17,687	90,601	14,821	17,256	2,000	4,640	351	770	44	1,927	503
Congressional District 6	117,746	15,906	104,353	15,203	4,815	367	2,565	120	729	0	5,561	216
Congressional District 7	130,877	19,717	115,565	18,618	3,964	397	2,835	42	658	0	7,817	660
Congressional District 8	136,309	18,422	127,213	17,770	3,464	443	1,679	23	771	10	3,611	115
Congressional District 9	140,541	19,643	135,328	19,455	1,695	44	1,004	94	284	15	2,600	35
Congressional District 10	126,901	17,388	112,537	16,202	8,009	770	2,721	343	967	39	2,874	34
Congressional District 11	135,491	15,908	126,589	15,204	2,828	315	1,566	135	949	0	3,550	254
Congressional District 12	134,560	17,042	132,041	16,623	702	100	343	54	389	79	991	186
Congressional District 13	143,768	17,580	139,804	16,843	2,151	142	na	na	809	417	558	113
Congressional District 14	146,513	18,777	142,172	18,353	2,266	271	818	92	403	0	797	61
Congressional District 15	141,099	19,090	138,928	18,639	na	na	na	na	304	16	710	175
Congressional District 16	134,058	18,398	128,459	18,000	2,945	245	1,040	32	408	35	1,018	172
Congressional District 17	139,791	20,872	132,148	19,949	4,315	635	1,607	87	1,010	160	902	41
Congressional District 18	128,401	17,996	106,012	15,475	18,433	2,452	2,180	69	690	0	828	0
Rhode Island												
Congressional District 1	92,707	13,064	78,148	11,574	4,615	243	1,699	320	1,385	127	6,171	556
Congressional District 2	89,938	13,395	83,018	12,664	1,317	106	1,288	79	527	78	3,552	439
South Carolina												
Congressional District 1	147,364	14,812	121,628	12,537	20,129	1,752	1,896	166	1,149	133	2,467	224
Congressional District 2	116,090	12,653	92,182	10,464	19,527	1,962	1,470	58	436	0	2,298	98
Congressional District 3	130,586	11,585	108,541	10,108	19,379	1,477	na	na	436	0	1,696	0
Congressional District 4	117,625	12,169	97,573	11,074	15,519	740	1,365	178	1,163	117	1,912	150
Congressional District 5	123,080	11,088	93,204	8,496	26,740	2,371	779	0	507	0	1,603	221
Congressional District 6	104,369	10,454	47,182	5,465	53,568	4,914	296	0	1,225	26	2,092	49
Congressional District 7	160,640	12,011	126,095	9,792	29,830	1,941	1,081	29	379	0	2,749	249
South Dakota												
Congressional District (at Large)	146,358	21,761	138,504	21,219	925	149	667	0	408	0	961	25
Tennessee												
Congressional District 1	148,230	15,833	142,658	14,874	1,817	301	na	na	812	81	1,875	242
Congressional District 2	135,135	13,062	126,035	12,272	5,716	666	1,323	57	589	67	1,472	0
Congressional District 3	137,889	14,792	123,946	13,901	10,671	681	1,169	130	385	11	1,120	10
Congressional District 4	118,257	10,682	108,845	9,585	5,391	674	880	0	1,169	18	1,864	405
Congressional District 5	97,098	10,924	73,272	8,505	18,700	1,548	1,940	251	370	163	2,238	326
Congressional District 6	138,856	12,916	130,613	12,072	3,929	649	na	na	1,921	100	1,397	0
Congressional District 7	116,325	10,557	105,564	9,510	7,371	697	1,380	0	467	130	1,305	153
Congressional District 8	124,434	14,369	103,902	12,617	16,736	1,617	1,389	0	1,084	79	1,487	56
Congressional District 9	88,573	10,327	35,114	5,797	50,939	4,403	1,051	47	na	na	1,030	49
Texas												
Congressional District 1	120,273	13,206	96,683	10,917	16,531	1,874	1,178	0	970	0	4,551	415
Congressional District 2	95,769	8,613	70,209	7,901	5,408	179	6,926	111	1,156	49	12,281	373
Congressional District 3	101,408	10,181	76,886	8,339	6,294	298	11,269	729	537	0	6,187	918
Congressional District 4	126,918	11,951	108,553	10,703	11,202	744	1,024	7	1,344	274	4,090	213
Congressional District 5	103,839	12,340	84,102	10,267	8,193	1,039	1,102	95	437	6	9,233	897
Congressional District 6	93,745	9,843	69,684	7,350	11,036	1,164	3,261	112	935	205	8,611	911
Congressional District 7	84,625	11,714	56,183	8,666	6,491	549	9,651	1,107	754	86	11,823	1,349
Congressional District 8	120,514	10,437	97,933	9,223	6,676	641	3,356	172	3,018	0	9,313	401
Congressional District 9	80,357	8,947	17,298	2,546	32,355	1,920	14,787	1,958	230	0	16,265	2,523
Congressional District 10	115,433	12,912	87,411	10,970	8,960	875	5,675	422	1,436	86	11,918	574
Congressional District 11	123,087	13,223	96,740	11,750	3,476	78	966	72	1,308	44	20,986	1,279
Congressional District 12	105,145	13,987	86,570	11,616	4,383	360	3,687	161	975	112	8,911	1,738
Congressional District 13	108,808	12,974	91,773	11,482	2,759	479	1,685	0	603	13	11,933	938
Congressional District 14	106,186	11,692	71,839	9,202	17,896	1,454	2,780	165	1,185	0	12,818	871
Congressional District 15	85,941	8,113	27,190	2,628	445	0	na	na	680	0	56,557	5,485
Congressional District 16	91,704	11,872	18,063	2,401	1,950	204	1,019	0	767	0	70,050	9,267
Congressional District 17	98,336	9,395	73,400	8,002	11,183	536	2,342	0	808	119	10,383	738
Congressional District 18	76,522	6,268	19,358	1,908	35,739	3,008	2,862	0	792	0	17,887	1,352
Congressional District 19	100,356	12,454	73,966	9,814	3,242	519	1,176	0	500	43	21,045	2,086
Congressional District 20	93,978	10,309	29,452	4,285	3,925	12	2,614	91	1,034	251	57,620	5,771
Congressional District 21	131,351	15,849	107,320	12,917	2,388	223	1,622	149	2,213	607	18,383	2,043
Congressional District 22	104,393	8,944	56,029	5,618	11,543	292	19,412	1,416	1,402	182	16,493	1,531
Congressional District 23	105,863	9,894	41,079	4,169	2,963	48	2,506	55	931	249	58,641	5,622
Congressional District 24	91,697	9,516	68,465	7,945	3,910	311	10,081	356	1,173	71	7,888	833
Congressional District 25	115,659	10,595	96,723	8,930	5,869	804	2,847	136	1,012	27	9,406	698
Congressional District 26	90,210	8,275	73,081	6,632	4,282	178	3,915	30	1,092	278	8,061	1,157
Congressional District 27	118,955	13,632	67,818	8,478	5,296	679	1,546	9	1,921	158	42,134	4,203
Congressional District 28	89,807	11,026	28,107	3,512	3,418	476	na	na	774	284	57,658	7,033
Congressional District 29	64,441	4,622	15,492	1,391	7,421	528	1,152	0	1,150	46	39,065	2,657
Congressional District 30	86,687	9,766	25,815	3,739	42,581	4,765	2,001	49	1,176	96	15,287	1,117
Congressional District 31	106,381	10,376	81,710	8,701	7,332	185	4,735	117	787	150	12,070	1,255
Congressional District 32	95,901	10,419	73,088	8,613	6,117	791	7,089	237	927	53	8,417	690
Congressional District 33	68,640	6,045	18,966	2,681	15,964	1,582	2,982	150	658	148	29,460	1,552
Congressional District 34	101,984	13,582	31,046	4,407	na	na	na	na	na	na	68,598	8,945
Congressional District 35	83,304	9,166	28,911	3,809	6,751	861	1,947	559	1,083	32	44,860	4,028
Congressional District 36	111,382	10,797	85,732	8,575	8,139	597	2,125	223	1,415	378	13,538	1,017

Table C-5: 116th Congressional Districts - Older Population by Race and Hispanic Origin—*Continued*

Name	Total Population		White, Non-Hispanic		Black, Alone		Asian, Alone		Multi-race, Alone		Hispanic	
	65 Years and Over	85 Years and Over	65 Years and Over	85 Years and Over	65 Years and Over	85 Years and Over	65 Years and Over	85 Years and Over	65 Years and Over	85 Years and Over	65 Years and Over	85 Years and Over
Utah												
Congressional District 1	82,802	8,227	75,188	7,588	963	119	894	0	1,009	116	4,762	458
Congressional District 2	104,260	10,977	95,431	10,688	na	na	2,270	38	683	46	5,156	205
Congressional District 3	85,042	8,610	76,168	7,857	na	na	1,854	76	281	0	5,257	569
Congressional District 4	79,193	7,449	68,795	6,587	601	0	2,119	385	601	0	6,440	297
Vermont												
Congressional District (at Large)	123,875	13,149	117,695	12,799	1,397	0	1,526	34	1,672	198	1,015	0
Virginia												
Congressional District 1	123,912	11,055	98,589	8,684	17,402	1,772	3,509	81	702	152	3,678	366
Congressional District 2	112,245	14,337	83,968	12,580	17,893	1,054	7,130	423	1,030	129	2,308	151
Congressional District 3	100,426	11,560	53,028	5,854	41,680	5,117	2,616	81	940	133	1,638	255
Congressional District 4	115,128	13,086	67,561	7,751	42,790	5,065	1,110	0	1,122	106	2,257	128
Congressional District 5	150,340	17,180	118,459	14,028	27,217	2,787	1,330	87	1,831	53	1,533	225
Congressional District 6	141,158	17,516	125,318	15,645	11,553	1,420	2,613	0	467	0	1,383	535
Congressional District 7	128,234	13,592	100,916	11,659	19,219	1,352	4,378	172	1,646	306	2,140	221
Congressional District 8	96,724	12,418	64,253	8,696	12,325	2,140	10,307	1,193	1,567	125	9,602	264
Congressional District 9	145,820	16,901	138,265	16,295	4,605	346	na	na	1,454	145	941	53
Congressional District 10	108,403	10,804	81,796	8,125	4,657	442	13,624	1,395	2,319	76	5,888	621
Congressional District 11	95,835	9,737	60,927	6,728	7,705	84	16,346	1,736	1,742	425	8,675	854
Washington												
Congressional District 1	101,663	10,330	89,166	9,474	773	0	7,230	731	1,144	4	2,083	32
Congressional District 2	125,330	13,704	108,640	12,813	1,522	241	8,708	444	2,104	18	3,624	143
Congressional District 3	128,758	12,302	118,309	11,811	807	110	3,322	126	2,425	189	2,892	66
Congressional District 4	103,987	10,744	84,770	9,592	480	65	1,741	375	1,207	27	14,020	470
Congressional District 5	125,841	13,433	116,475	12,286	1,278	83	1,954	250	1,225	275	3,552	541
Congressional District 6	147,594	14,005	132,897	12,904	3,198	262	5,304	573	2,585	47	1,975	112
Congressional District 7	114,120	14,641	95,249	13,170	2,756	0	11,601	1,186	1,373	208	2,552	58
Congressional District 8	102,853	10,286	88,379	9,173	2,786	655	5,883	340	1,308	0	3,522	118
Congressional District 9	103,032	15,070	62,756	10,509	7,192	751	24,347	3,302	2,951	147	4,326	354
Congressional District 10	110,809	13,541	91,781	12,298	3,243	268	8,200	498	2,102	141	4,035	398
West Virginia												
Congressional District 1	120,219	14,120	116,466	13,934	2,120	70	na	na	632	0	556	38
Congressional District 2	120,355	12,985	112,145	12,332	4,426	302	na	na	695	174	1,473	245
Congressional District 3	120,642	13,114	115,220	12,464	4,453	629	na	na	497	0	na	na
Wisconsin												
Congressional District 1	118,576	14,128	110,144	13,497	2,971	320	1,279	16	1,051	192	2,705	189
Congressional District 2	115,716	14,792	109,126	14,080	1,979	166	1,560	294	663	54	1,899	198
Congressional District 3	129,906	16,324	126,136	16,205	585	27	825	6	846	0	1,394	67
Congressional District 4	86,994	12,267	55,949	9,267	21,869	2,063	1,919	265	850	166	6,119	474
Congressional District 5	132,502	18,038	126,283	17,323	1,799	218	1,307	53	497	46	2,652	361
Congressional District 6	132,131	18,362	128,690	18,058	702	0	1,147	134	432	0	764	66
Congressional District 7	144,611	16,961	140,319	16,480	219	50	493	88	1,038	181	1,171	160
Congressional District 8	126,047	13,883	120,620	13,532	237	30	776	0	919	68	1,900	151
Wyoming												
Congressional District (at Large)	96,557	9,258	87,867	8,643	na	na	na	na	615	0	5,252	592

PART D

HOUSEHOLD RELATIONSHIP

HOUSEHOLD RELATIONSHIP

Though people live in a multitude of different living arrangements, the Census classifies everyone as living in either households or group quarters facilities. Those living in households live in either family or non-family households. A family household is comprised of two or more individuals related by blood, marriage, or adoption to the householder. Non-family households are ones where all of the individuals are unrelated or it is occupied by a single person living alone. There are no other household types. All households have a single householder which is generally the person who owns or rents the unit and is "Person Number 1" on the questionnaire. Group quarters facilities can be either institutional or non-institutional. Examples of institutional facilities

include correctional facilities, nursing homes and other institutional health facilities. Non-institutional group quarters include college student housing, military and other group home situations. For the older population described here, the group quarters total will be predominantly nursing home facilities.

A slight majority (54.9 percent) of U.S. households, where the householder is age 65 or over, are family households – those that include related family members – leaving 45.1 percent who live in non-family households. Householders age 65 and over living alone make up 93.5 percent of all non-family householders age 65 and over. About 2.9 percent of the 65 and over population lives in group quarters, a total of 1.5 million people. The percent of householders 65 and over who are living alone ranges from a low of

Percent of Grandparents 60 Years and Over
Who are Responsible for Grandchildren

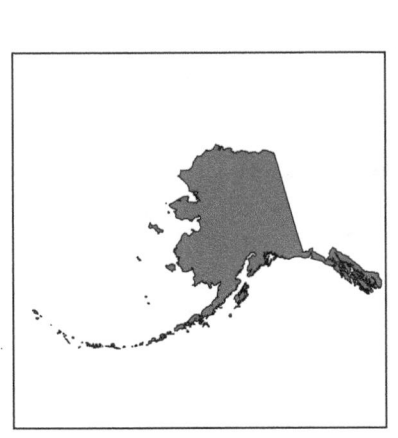

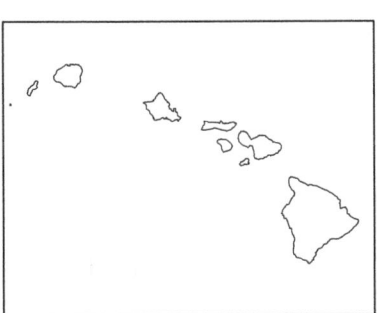

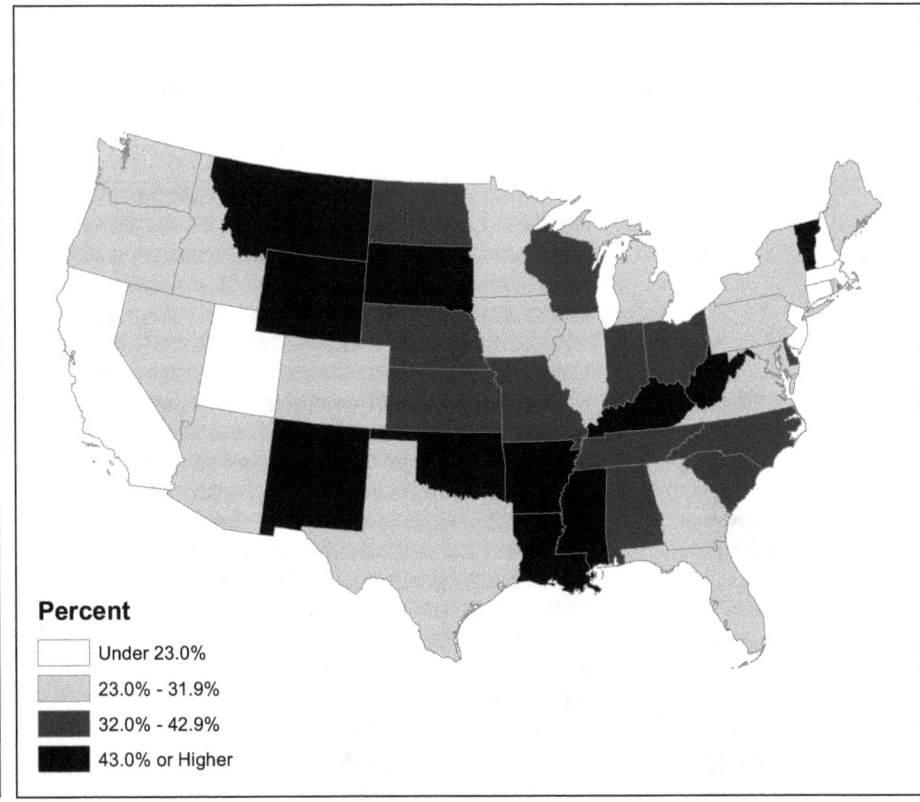

Percent

- ☐ Under 23.0%
- ☐ 23.0% - 31.9%
- ☐ 32.0% - 42.9%
- ■ 43.0% or Higher

34.2 percent in Hawaii to a high of 56.3 percent in the District of Columbia. Family householders 65 and over as a percentage of all householders shows the District of Columbia having the lowest percentage at 38.4 while Utah has the highest at 64.0 percent. Hawaii is a close second at 61.9 percent. North Dakota has the highest percent population 65 and over living in group quarters at 6.3 percent while at 1.3 percent, Nevada is the lowest.

The aging Baby Boom population is faced with care of older parents as well as care for younger grandchildren. Nationally, 3.9 million people over the age of 65 are grandparents living with their grandchildren. Not only are they living with their grandchildren but more than one quarter of them are responsible for care of their grandchildren. In the Census data, a "responsible grandparent" is defined as being financially responsible for such needs as food, shelter, clothing, day care, etc. More than a million grandparents (27.9 percent) 65 and over are responsible for their grandchildren. That percent varies from a low of 12.6 percent in the District of Columbia to 57.3 percent in West Virginia. Of those responsible, many have incomes below the poverty level. Nationwide, 16.4 percent of grandparents responsible for grandchildren are in poverty. Hawaii has the lowest percent at 2.5 while the South Dakota is the highest at 43.7 percent. Fourteen states have 20 percent or more of responsible grandparents below the poverty level. While mortality and divorce take a toll on older couple's relationships, more than half

(56.6 percent) of the population 60 and over are currently married. The District of Columbia has the lowest percent (34.1 percent) while Utah is highest at 65.9 percent.

More than half of the 814 counties have a higher percent of the 65 and over population that are family householders than the U.S. average. Newton County, Georgia has the highest percent (72.9 percent) while Lake County, California has the lowest at 37.0 percent. The percentage of householders who are 65 and over living alone varies from a low of 23.4 percent in Newton County, Georgia to a high of 60.0 percent in Wilson County, North Carolina with 351 counties above the national average. More than 58 percent of counties with reported responsible grandparents have a higher percentage of grandparents responsible for their grandchildren than the U.S. as a whole. Henderson County, Texas is the highest at 86.3 percent while the lowest (9.3 percent) is Contra Costa County, California. More than 83 percent of the grandparents responsible for grandchildren are in poverty in Calhoun County, Alabama which is the nation's highest rate and 146 counties are above the national rate. At 71.3 percent, Douglas County, Colorado has the highest percentage of those 65 and over who are now married. Thirty-three counties have less than 50 percent who are married and Bronx County, New York has the lowest percent at 36.7 percent. Denver County, Colorado has the highest percentage of 65 and over who are divorced at 26.8 percent.

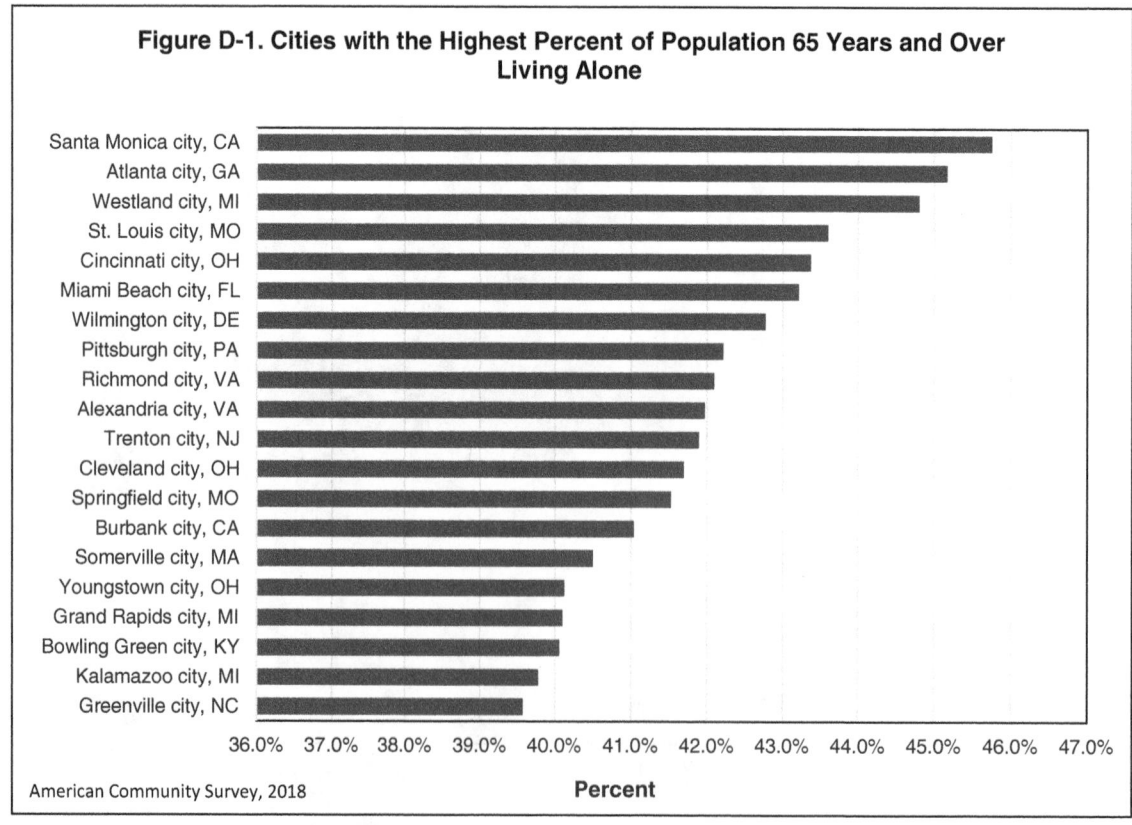

Figure D-1. Cities with the Highest Percent of Population 65 Years and Over Living Alone

American Community Survey, 2018

Goodyear city, Arizona has the highest percentage of family households among the 65 and over population at 79.6 percent. Bowling Green, Kentucky has the lowest percent of family households with only about one out of three (30.1 percent) households occupied by a family. That also makes Bowling Green the city with the highest percentage of householders 65 and over living alone at 65.5 percent while Goodyear city is lowest at 16.4 percent. There are 323 cities where the percent of householders living alone is above the national average of 42.1 percent. In Jackson city, Mississippi the percentage of grandparents responsible for grandchildren is highest at 70.1 percent while the national average is only 27.8 percent. 105 cities exceed the national rate while Hartford city, Connecticut (3.8 percent) is the lowest in the nation. The ACS reports that in Hartford, 100 percent of responsible grandparents are living in poverty. That is based on a very small number of sample cases and the next highest is Compton city, California at 62.2 percent. With 9.7 percent of the 65 and over population in group quarters, the city of Syracuse, New York has the highest proportion.

Householders over the age of 65 that head family households ranges from a low of 37.0 percent in the Clearlake, California micropolitan area to a high of 69.9 percent in the El Centro, California metro area. Other metropolitan areas with high percentages of family households include: the Sevierville, Tennessee micro (69.7 percent), Provo-Orem, Utah metro (69.7 percent), the Gallup, New Mexico micro (68.5 percent) and the Ogden-Clearfield, Utah metropolitan area (68.2 percent). As expected, those metros with high percentages of family households have low percentages of householders 65 and over living alone. More than 86 percent of grandparents in the Athens, Texas micropolitan area are responsible for their grandchildren. The Anniston-Oxford-Jacksonville, Alabama metropolitan area has the highest percent of poverty grandparents responsible for grandchildren at 83.6 percent, more than five times the national rate of 16.4 percent. It's one of 124 metro areas above the national average.

Congressional District 3 in Utah has the highest percentage of family households (70.2 percent) while Congressional District 10 in New York is lowest at 37.3 percent. The percentage of persons 65 and over living alone is highest in New York's District 10 (59.2 percent) compared to District 26 in Florida at 26.8 percent. The percent of grandparents responsible for grandchildren is highest in West Virginia's 3rd Congressional District at 69.2 percent and 36.5 percent are poverty households. The district with the highest poverty percentage is New York's 15th Congressional District at 51.7 percent. Congressional Districts with a higher percentage of responsible grandparents in poverty than the national average number 172. Almost 70 percent of persons 60 and older are married in Utah's 3rd Congressional District but only one in three are married in the District of Columbia's at Large Delegate District.

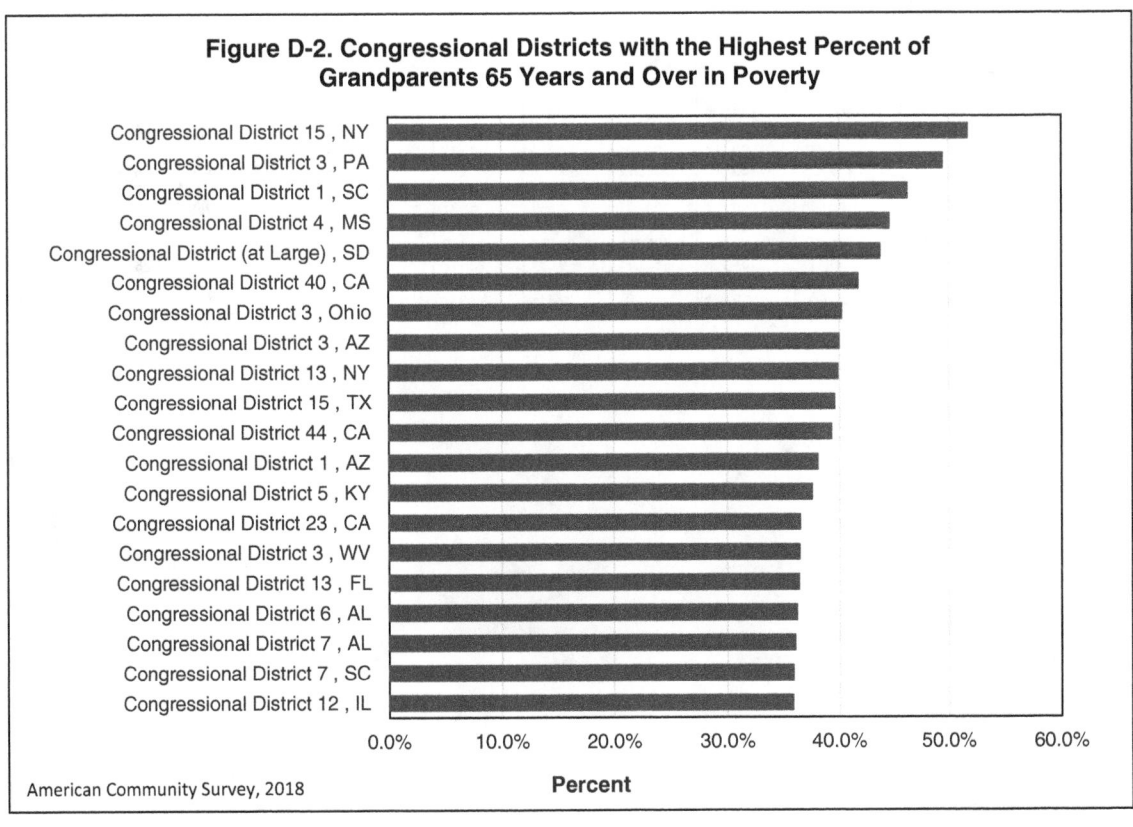

Figure D-2. Congressional Districts with the Highest Percent of Grandparents 65 Years and Over in Poverty

American Community Survey, 2018

Table D-1: States - Household Relationship, Grandparents, and Marital Status

	Total Householders 65 Years and Over	Family Householders 65 Years and Over	Non-Family Householders 65 Years and Over		Persons 65 Years and Over Living in Group Quarters	Grandparents 60 Years and Over Living with Grandchildren			Marital Status - Persons 60 Years and Over		
			Male Living Alone	Female Living Alone		Total	Responsible for Grandchildren	Responsible for Grandchildren and In Poverty	Now Married	Widowed	Divorced
United States	31,842,901	17,481,227	4,313,862	9,107,534	1,518,402	3,924,403	1,093,863	178,875	41,454,476	13,268,392	11,254,678
Alabama..............................	523,973	297,667	67,220	148,746	18,772	58,230	24,698	7,295	650,342	233,566	172,838
Alaska.................................	53,173	29,659	8,201	12,417	2,881	10,011	4,130	777	76,122	18,492	23,186
Arizona...............................	754,387	428,853	101,430	194,042	18,645	95,166	26,950	6,376	995,985	283,362	283,250
Arkansas............................	314,838	178,319	40,773	88,404	18,010	30,533	14,866	3,368	400,873	137,564	113,426
California............................	3,197,217	1,819,335	406,270	843,481	141,775	665,089	114,921	14,302	4,400,059	1,381,735	1,214,233
Colorado.............................	499,802	272,148	69,786	142,117	15,300	52,513	13,546	1,351	679,413	174,619	208,897
Connecticut........................	374,793	197,095	52,374	115,644	26,873	35,368	6,597	829	485,704	153,668	132,992
Delaware.............................	107,758	63,521	13,323	26,840	4,129	11,822	4,566	526	149,489	39,881	34,657
District of Columbia	58,898	22,637	11,337	21,829	3,072	5,869	737	215	40,456	19,852	22,449
Florida................................	2,522,233	1,400,894	343,615	683,267	85,610	298,893	76,917	11,404	3,150,747	1,080,738	994,898
Georgia...............................	886,919	502,350	110,896	253,737	32,306	135,553	41,120	6,092	1,164,584	382,694	330,816
Hawaii.................................	143,128	88,617	18,760	30,181	6,996	36,010	5,980	150	192,282	65,791	47,043
Idaho..................................	168,614	97,532	23,258	43,046	5,286	15,603	4,885	521	240,935	58,646	60,102
Illinois................................	1,242,040	656,665	175,741	382,630	71,383	129,419	32,808	5,003	1,571,485	529,141	400,393
Indiana................................	659,809	355,264	92,417	196,704	38,971	59,269	23,875	3,744	849,950	273,562	234,368
Iowa....................................	338,159	176,017	48,157	106,432	23,825	18,282	5,443	509	444,386	141,209	102,082
Kansas................................	287,156	151,742	38,394	89,888	20,048	21,349	8,843	1,106	384,594	116,880	94,439
Kentucky.............................	458,020	255,036	60,625	130,791	24,545	51,094	25,927	6,652	586,753	200,944	163,401
Louisiana............................	446,979	244,451	62,415	128,528	22,970	55,209	23,770	6,617	551,394	203,914	160,673
Maine..................................	175,923	88,387	25,847	52,755	9,578	10,660	2,889	302	217,181	65,389	68,889
Maryland.............................	558,175	304,000	73,261	162,554	27,381	79,402	19,525	1,485	734,090	231,775	205,353
Massachusetts....................	700,037	360,298	96,593	218,443	39,165	78,563	16,431	1,170	875,237	275,078	238,597
Michigan.............................	1,093,561	585,316	156,067	323,385	50,507	90,567	22,186	2,675	1,385,137	433,762	385,450
Minnesota...........................	552,433	292,977	80,386	163,710	35,422	37,638	11,054	1,050	746,809	199,312	181,800
Mississippi..........................	303,363	168,899	41,462	86,483	16,885	34,731	16,968	4,551	361,599	146,971	100,331
Missouri..............................	651,569	352,265	90,478	192,324	40,107	51,312	18,186	3,963	836,531	268,562	229,977
Montana..............................	123,306	67,356	20,148	31,911	5,064	10,276	5,445	932	171,557	45,400	42,551
Nebraska............................	194,541	99,320	28,979	61,688	11,933	11,373	3,902	276	253,877	79,258	55,658
Nevada................................	279,933	152,154	45,785	68,195	6,268	43,397	12,796	1,697	359,099	107,281	129,909
New Hampshire....................	145,788	79,401	20,526	40,210	9,485	12,122	2,781	125	206,288	58,326	54,355
New Jersey..........................	867,467	484,869	97,029	263,350	42,500	118,977	21,740	2,517	1,163,291	371,627	260,262
New Mexico.........................	228,095	122,623	35,152	62,619	7,386	26,425	12,825	2,966	276,275	84,980	90,110
New York.............................	1,972,352	1,023,680	270,888	620,416	117,080	256,507	59,277	10,713	2,397,519	836,815	614,027
North Carolina.....................	1,044,996	582,897	133,089	303,641	42,731	112,951	38,454	6,397	1,367,322	450,304	348,163
North Dakota.......................	73,062	36,403	12,097	22,931	7,298	2,937	1,239	348	96,971	31,240	19,488
Ohio....................................	1,261,472	666,942	183,082	380,052	75,005	110,581	39,019	6,015	1,568,122	519,958	451,543
Oklahoma............................	389,886	215,179	55,272	111,320	20,911	44,499	20,693	3,358	488,442	173,339	141,734
Oregon................................	461,267	244,545	61,898	132,927	18,390	41,841	11,510	1,076	587,892	157,851	188,696
Pennsylvania.......................	1,458,606	771,268	205,194	445,487	86,534	121,867	36,449	5,266	1,860,649	614,662	426,336
Rhode Island.......................	113,963	56,145	17,655	37,282	9,086	10,342	2,963	209	131,748	49,536	41,024
South Carolina	552,651	316,956	72,702	149,782	19,077	64,239	23,333	5,947	709,037	241,616	178,756
South Dakota.......................	91,545	49,903	12,659	26,250	8,325	5,413	2,493	1,089	122,917	34,871	30,254
Tennessee...........................	681,024	383,843	90,184	190,791	30,772	78,477	33,213	5,793	897,165	288,199	245,013
Texas..................................	2,107,858	1,240,229	265,875	552,522	91,126	389,631	106,698	17,936	2,955,464	950,920	796,772
Utah....................................	210,551	134,763	22,554	49,756	5,107	38,877	7,152	779	329,081	72,607	65,471
Vermont..............................	78,032	40,808	10,797	23,127	4,059	5,131	2,227	755	98,850	27,492	29,749
Virginia...............................	801,030	438,147	108,019	232,340	28,335	106,815	31,841	4,889	1,063,912	349,501	268,503
Washington..........................	713,855	391,137	99,509	196,785	28,290	78,166	22,433	2,536	971,275	248,482	282,054
West Virginia.......................	231,585	126,430	34,968	65,071	9,634	22,117	12,672	3,060	283,161	99,916	72,065
Wisconsin............................	625,177	331,719	90,744	185,908	31,120	38,910	12,536	1,394	837,032	234,912	195,534
Wyoming.............................	61,902	34,566	9,971	14,795	2,444	4,377	2,354	769	85,393	22,192	22,111

Table D-2: Counties - Household Relationship, Grandparents, and Marital Status

	Total Householders 65 Years and Over	Family Householders 65 Years and Over	Non-Family Householders 65 Years and Over		Persons 65 Years and Over Living in Group Quarters	Grandparents 60 Years and Over Living with Grandchildren			Marital Status - Persons 60 Years and Over		
			Male Living Alone	Female Living Alone		Total	Responsible for Grandchildren	Responsible for Grandchildren and In Poverty	Now Married	Widowed	Divorced
Alabama											
Baldwin County	27,136	16,288	3,291	6,321	977	3,250	1,150	160	na	na	na
Calhoun County	13,456	7,807	1,376	4,078	331	1,148	275	230	na	na	na
Cullman County	9,912	5,188	1,083	3,296	136	na	na	na	na	na	na
DeKalb County	8,140	4,765	912	2,439	268	1,021	410	na	na	na	na
Elmore County	7,794	4,697	1,014	2,083	395	na	na	na	na	na	na
Etowah County	12,152	6,797	1,464	3,690	539	1,535	1,134	172	na	na	na
Houston County	11,982	6,721	1,561	3,570	380	1,336	694	55	14,597	5,095	3,972
Jefferson County	67,575	37,386	7,100	21,135	2,379	8,830	3,703	1,417	79,320	27,507	27,124
Lauderdale County	11,532	7,306	1,188	2,804	355	689	310	na	na	na	na
Lee County	11,705	7,320	1,570	2,557	267	2,400	604	na	na	na	na
Limestone County	9,407	5,550	969	2,639	97	2,689	1,514	746	na	na	na
Madison County	36,105	20,587	4,376	10,671	622	2,775	1,348	286	46,027	12,893	12,403
Marshall County	10,016	5,848	1,308	2,789	509	1,019	428	253	na	na	na
Mobile County	43,522	24,258	6,428	12,102	1,331	3,893	1,524	510	48,018	19,265	16,244
Montgomery County	22,480	11,988	3,134	6,895	1,015	3,268	1,356	478	23,757	8,881	9,868
Morgan County	13,592	7,746	1,381	4,343	410	2,208	1,280	na	na	na	na
St. Clair County	8,954	4,971	1,417	2,224	425	na	na	na	na	na	na
Shelby County	20,757	12,107	2,165	5,994	427	1,788	493	na	na	na	na
Talladega County	9,142	5,338	1,345	2,279	416	na	na	na	na	na	na
Tuscaloosa County	16,785	10,384	2,097	4,256	608	1,914	860	135	na	na	na
Walker County	7,671	4,474	887	2,271	273	na	na	na	na	na	na
Alaska											
Anchorage Municipality	19,776	11,293	2,391	4,783	1,431	3,088	721	190	28,529	6,994	8,657
Fairbanks North Star Borough	6,987	na	na	na	na	na	na	na	na	na	na
Matanuska-Susitna Borough	7,032	4,087	1,268	1,327	194	1,993	635	126	10,810	3,648	3,614
Arizona											
Apache County	6,942	4,122	1,122	1,654	86	1,695	533	170	8,628	2,328	1,453
Cochise County	19,349	9,637	3,446	5,163	220	1,821	930	224	na	na	na
Coconino County	10,903	6,977	1,584	2,013	215	2,279	722	54	na	na	na
Maricopa County	391,504	220,018	50,602	106,240	11,139	56,720	13,330	1,665	527,315	152,158	158,499
Mohave County	39,594	24,329	5,797	7,900	580	2,339	805	136	51,557	14,237	13,130
Navajo County	12,780	7,223	2,199	2,948	216	3,307	1,670	482	15,235	5,347	4,284
Pima County	126,887	70,010	16,733	34,152	3,000	12,921	3,630	907	156,211	47,881	46,915
Pinal County	51,749	33,906	5,914	9,887	1,263	5,193	2,328	1,440	77,343	17,991	17,708
Yavapai County	47,659	23,693	8,113	13,773	1,142	2,318	570	154	na	na	na
Yuma County	22,994	15,078	2,636	4,215	288	3,393	962	502	35,079	8,592	4,553
Arkansas											
Benton County	22,134	13,163	2,122	6,245	760	2,135	1,144	0	32,109	10,089	5,873
Craighead County	9,754	5,413	1,048	2,996	610	na	na	na	na	na	na
Faulkner County	9,348	5,730	694	2,598	361	618	297	na	na	na	na
Garland County	14,925	8,966	1,518	4,044	555	na	na	na	na	na	na
Jefferson County	7,901	4,309	728	2,632	547	na	na	na	na	na	na
Lonoke County	5,827	3,626	691	1,510	384	na	na	na	na	na	na
Pulaski County	37,415	20,242	4,818	11,569	2,898	4,184	1,766	358	43,735	14,714	18,240
Saline County	12,627	8,438	1,502	2,503	489	na	na	na	na	na	na
Sebastian County	13,267	6,620	2,365	3,659	812	1,109	454	0	na	na	na
Washington County	16,807	10,784	1,353	4,212	1,004	1,579	781	9	na	na	na
White County	8,138	na	na	na	na	na	na	na	na	na	na
California											
Alameda County	129,181	68,967	16,438	37,713	6,474	32,223	7,777	585	173,836	56,277	48,621
Butte County	25,859	14,820	2,963	7,009	819	3,267	648	62	32,895	9,616	11,365
Contra Costa County	102,492	57,643	12,869	29,036	3,781	18,889	1,760	148	145,716	38,271	42,414
El Dorado County	24,149	14,378	2,662	5,888	243	na	na	na	na	na	na
Fresno County	72,341	39,867	9,938	20,582	3,551	14,787	3,247	431	94,553	34,928	23,017
Humboldt County	16,123	7,932	2,804	4,259	528	na	na	na	na	na	na
Imperial County	10,251	7,163	882	1,983	203	5,434	728	32	na	na	na
Kern County	57,042	33,149	8,502	14,034	2,579	14,414	2,947	592	80,788	28,531	20,129
Kings County	9,949	6,458	1,180	2,037	607	1,192	338	59	10,327	5,351	2,992
Lake County	9,808	3,630	2,442	3,259	270	na	na	na	na	na	na
Los Angeles County	750,779	426,486	97,027	197,510	39,988	189,035	28,759	4,646	1,020,512	349,175	272,063
Madera County	11,632	7,043	1,676	2,461	494	1,063	302	51	na	na	na
Marin County	37,113	19,333	3,587	12,084	2,039	na	na	na	45,892	10,517	12,612
Mendocino County	12,167	5,677	2,230	3,547	378	na	na	na	na	na	na
Merced County	18,366	10,238	2,384	5,211	254	4,755	545	25	23,988	8,329	6,440
Monterey County	34,561	20,662	5,109	7,967	1,247	9,135	1,366	0	47,758	14,680	11,745
Napa County	15,144	8,521	1,787	4,237	671	na	na	na	na	na	na
Nevada County	16,239	9,195	2,117	3,899	574	na	na	na	na	na	na
Orange County	259,739	148,567	30,802	69,300	13,843	51,408	9,022	1,289	367,488	114,801	103,220
Placer County	46,330	25,363	4,972	14,210	1,439	6,349	1,113	na	62,074	17,447	17,248
Riverside County	189,868	110,573	26,324	44,456	4,686	47,452	7,154	647	277,078	83,179	71,640
Sacramento County	127,146	67,876	16,974	38,106	5,805	23,488	3,398	166	163,892	55,410	56,953
San Bernardino County	136,143	82,805	14,951	33,409	5,600	40,667	8,298	1,093	205,502	71,081	54,987
San Diego County	268,419	153,732	34,568	68,549	10,072	45,584	9,073	991	366,840	107,902	115,502
San Francisco County	83,021	40,851	14,878	24,100	3,737	10,780	1,297	52	95,133	31,224	25,272
San Joaquin County	51,357	30,010	5,545	13,483	4,358	14,483	2,148	394	70,081	29,848	21,884
San Luis Obispo County	35,948	20,916	4,615	9,145	1,056	2,922	686	na	48,310	10,852	12,329

Table D-2: Counties - Household Relationship, Grandparents, and Marital Status—*Continued*

	Total Householders 65 Years and Over	Family Householders 65 Years and Over	Non-Family Householders 65 Years and Over		Persons 65 Years and Over Living in Group Quarters	Grandparents 60 Years and Over Living with Grandchildren			Marital Status - Persons 60 Years and Over		
			Male Living Alone	Female Living Alone		Total	Responsible for Grandchildren	Responsible for Grandchildren and In Poverty	Now Married	Widowed	Divorced
California—Cont.											
San Mateo County	68,731	39,948	8,431	17,992	3,908	15,266	1,730	93	97,020	29,547	23,256
Santa Barbara County	41,277	24,066	4,917	10,596	1,601	6,032	927	114	55,278	15,208	14,214
Santa Clara County	138,818	86,233	13,809	33,568	6,568	35,284	4,990	221	215,938	60,017	47,130
Santa Cruz County	27,799	15,542	3,167	7,341	607	na	na	na	37,938	8,270	10,181
Shasta County	22,428	12,951	3,409	5,169	971	3,222	1,151	0	28,086	10,009	8,641
Solano County	38,327	23,564	4,398	8,978	1,758	9,437	2,058	304	59,713	16,570	16,618
Sonoma County	62,227	31,420	7,895	19,283	1,891	4,107	597	na	72,218	21,020	26,615
Stanislaus County	41,197	25,302	3,389	11,082	1,733	8,104	1,806	338	56,989	19,945	16,515
Sutter County	8,546	4,773	1,068	2,301	363	na	na	na	na	na	na
Tulare County	29,774	17,143	3,277	8,721	1,852	7,923	2,594	1,004	43,840	13,563	11,911
Ventura County	76,222	44,974	7,872	20,278	2,662	13,276	2,282	258	107,978	31,538	26,903
Yolo County	15,948	9,614	2,272	3,768	587	na	na	na	23,626	5,654	6,230
Yuba County	6,622	na	na	na	na	na	na	na	na	na	na
Colorado											
Adams County	31,537	17,122	3,949	9,817	889	7,669	1,825	40	42,194	13,195	15,218
Arapahoe County	52,237	28,946	6,878	15,467	1,457	7,191	1,491	0	72,260	18,329	22,140
Boulder County	29,132	14,918	4,419	8,230	994	na	na	103	40,958	8,830	11,883
Broomfield County	5,908	na	na	na	na	na	na	na	na	na	na
Denver County	56,532	23,374	10,468	20,443	2,443	3,536	712	207	54,851	16,262	31,666
Douglas County	24,015	15,092	2,233	6,065	248	2,685	861	0	42,455	6,926	7,379
El Paso County	54,936	31,430	7,504	14,573	1,242	6,586	1,485	274	77,839	19,578	23,846
Jefferson County	60,542	33,646	7,878	17,260	1,965	4,906	1,291	0	82,158	21,241	22,509
Larimer County	33,694	20,026	3,675	8,838	1,097	na	na	na	na	na	na
Mesa County	18,280	8,518	3,461	5,743	382	1,114	327	na	na	na	na
Pueblo County	19,899	10,244	3,317	5,806	876	3,025	1,666	97	21,903	8,805	8,225
Weld County	22,416	14,075	1,917	5,791	247	5,061	967	123	34,288	9,412	9,385
Connecticut											
Fairfield County	92,257	50,512	10,921	28,839	5,123	10,180	1,598	177	125,150	36,188	29,285
Hartford County	93,454	46,758	12,982	31,352	8,888	7,876	1,383	28	111,838	38,821	34,523
Litchfield County	23,504	11,901	3,695	7,124	1,060	na	na	na	na	na	na
Middlesex County	19,247	9,579	3,211	5,837	1,392	na	na	na	na	na	na
New Haven County	90,805	48,155	12,734	27,683	6,425	9,320	2,196	502	111,642	41,065	31,491
New London County	29,852	15,924	5,178	8,040	1,943	1,255	246	na	39,012	10,432	12,770
Tolland County	14,669	7,544	2,457	3,946	1,135	na	na	na	na	na	na
Windham County	11,005	6,722	1,196	2,823	907	na	na	na	na	na	na
Delaware											
Kent County	17,737	10,355	2,496	4,158	789	1,782	1,177	130	na	na	na
New Castle County	52,290	29,126	6,903	14,000	2,180	7,160	2,459	269	69,556	20,490	19,238
Sussex County	37,731	24,040	3,924	8,682	1,160	2,880	930	127	56,483	11,180	9,946
Florida											
Alachua County	22,273	11,277	2,986	7,205	1,622	1,605	523	65	26,068	7,963	9,323
Bay County	19,306	10,728	2,802	5,335	862	2,240	874	na	24,560	9,261	8,249
Brevard County	84,167	45,342	13,561	22,168	2,158	7,258	1,853	151	104,714	35,376	36,414
Broward County	186,926	96,821	27,005	54,787	5,926	29,566	5,794	536	225,116	80,936	88,833
Charlotte County	42,134	24,960	6,557	9,367	1,055	1,600	954	62	57,205	16,767	11,226
Citrus County	33,165	17,305	5,445	9,299	706	na	na	na	na	na	na
Clay County	19,867	12,100	3,107	4,460	665	3,371	450	0	na	na	na
Collier County	68,705	41,679	7,733	16,590	676	6,793	969	0	96,802	22,040	18,391
Columbia County	7,568	4,100	972	2,323	698	na	na	na	na	na	na
Duval County	82,536	42,582	12,109	25,688	3,443	11,350	4,109	721	93,751	36,463	37,935
Escambia County	33,082	18,110	5,148	8,745	1,990	3,167	1,250	41	37,213	16,379	13,630
Flagler County	19,787	13,277	2,291	3,603	289	na	na	na	na	na	na
Hernando County	32,130	19,639	4,173	7,371	699	3,279	1,390	257	na	na	na
Highlands County	21,675	12,453	3,633	4,446	802	na	na	na	na	na	na
Hillsborough County	120,806	66,193	15,057	36,099	3,270	20,729	5,826	1,239	158,733	53,077	52,647
Indian River County	27,705	15,825	3,846	7,015	706	na	na	na	na	na	na
Lake County	55,463	34,882	5,192	13,706	1,145	5,989	2,416	229	73,873	20,284	17,343
Lee County	121,190	71,607	15,651	29,549	3,067	8,522	3,014	527	156,851	47,674	43,494
Leon County	24,514	13,839	3,378	6,955	968	1,657	366	na	31,397	8,034	10,748
Manatee County	64,211	36,667	7,023	18,632	1,397	3,700	582	83	82,112	21,929	23,446
Marion County	62,379	36,695	8,095	15,359	1,372	3,961	2,204	853	76,854	23,845	20,104
Martin County	30,294	15,194	3,802	9,518	879	na	na	na	na	na	na
Miami-Dade County	223,196	130,439	29,129	55,355	12,530	57,071	10,090	1,413	283,973	120,787	111,051
Monroe County	9,842	5,384	1,438	2,105	265	na	na	na	na	na	na
Nassau County	10,932	6,772	1,327	2,352	266	794	240	na	na	na	na
Okaloosa County	20,687	11,514	2,893	5,696	890	1,811	496	na	na	na	na
Orange County	86,430	49,422	10,252	23,451	3,532	20,696	3,853	948	130,077	39,833	43,349
Osceola County	22,387	14,275	3,230	4,037	623	9,827	1,045	106	34,083	11,242	14,998
Palm Beach County	213,876	105,305	31,690	68,787	4,781	19,424	4,615	1,150	238,754	89,954	75,110
Pasco County	72,140	36,757	11,594	19,742	2,223	8,243	2,226	0	83,780	34,367	26,749
Pinellas County	150,207	69,917	23,365	50,263	8,166	11,010	3,686	1,247	155,208	68,516	67,794
Polk County	84,267	50,260	10,641	20,690	1,655	7,629	1,997	576	105,597	38,226	27,043
Putnam County	10,815	5,988	2,079	2,226	312	na	na	na	na	na	na
St. Johns County	30,553	18,599	2,728	8,617	414	na	na	na	na	na	na

Table D-2: Counties - Household Relationship, Grandparents, and Marital Status—Continued

	Total Householders 65 Years and Over	Family Householders 65 Years and Over	Non-Family Householders 65 Years and Over		Persons 65 Years and Over Living in Group Quarters	Grandparents 60 Years and Over Living with Grandchildren			Marital Status - Persons 60 Years and Over		
			Male Living Alone	Female Living Alone		Total	Responsible for Grandchildren	Responsible for Grandchildren and In Poverty	Now Married	Widowed	Divorced
Florida—Cont.											
St. Lucie County	44,264	27,174	5,353	10,094	988	7,135	2,425	na	55,703	19,898	16,153
Santa Rosa County	15,555	11,051	1,591	2,086	538	2,594	913	0	na	na	na
Sarasota County	95,330	53,394	10,896	26,229	2,758	4,351	1,355	123	114,562	34,850	27,965
Seminole County	42,666	25,590	4,476	11,544	1,642	6,176	2,004	81	59,176	19,545	17,577
Sumter County	44,756	27,271	6,064	10,076	761	na	na	na	na	na	na
Volusia County	78,826	41,587	11,816	21,400	2,486	5,953	1,881	155	92,332	33,589	33,894
Walton County	8,972	4,348	1,740	2,438	297	na	na	na	na	na	na
Georgia											
Barrow County	6,000	3,798	609	1,541	122	957	188	50	na	na	na
Bartow County	7,726	4,874	912	1,335	211	na	na	na	na	na	na
Bibb County	15,152	7,632	2,100	5,194	964	3,130	1,589	342	na	na	na
Bulloch County	5,700	na	na	na	na	na	na	na	na	na	na
Carroll County	9,980	5,113	1,087	3,063	279	na	na	na	na	na	na
Catoosa County	7,493	na	na	na	na	na	na	na	na	na	na
Chatham County	27,712	15,323	4,019	7,836	1,279	4,147	885	106	31,341	13,698	9,794
Cherokee County	20,674	14,235	1,857	4,308	333	3,353	1,106	na	na	na	na
Clarke County	9,394	5,146	1,004	2,974	402	na	na	na	na	na	na
Clayton County	15,984	8,977	2,167	4,154	496	3,657	1,291	127	19,105	9,169	7,992
Cobb County	54,626	32,853	5,251	15,185	1,367	8,476	1,961	370	80,233	20,864	21,097
Columbia County	11,988	7,293	1,300	3,395	168	2,710	1,230	na	na	na	na
Coweta County	12,305	7,796	1,132	2,727	137	1,586	894	0	na	na	na
DeKalb County	57,625	29,015	7,703	19,429	2,030	9,764	3,125	446	66,712	23,471	25,917
Dougherty County	8,530	4,108	1,417	2,579	307	463	201	0	na	na	na
Douglas County	9,366	6,203	722	2,310	133	2,713	1,033	na	na	na	na
Fayette County	12,900	7,907	1,156	3,724	192	na	na	na	na	na	na
Floyd County	10,194	5,780	1,108	3,252	638	1,209	794	na	na	na	na
Forsyth County	15,347	10,544	1,383	3,032	226	2,987	361	na	na	na	na
Fulton County	80,507	38,484	11,674	28,217	2,381	10,518	2,910	558	86,252	30,752	34,691
Glynn County	10,819	6,921	1,145	2,753	445	na	na	na	na	na	na
Gwinnett County	48,689	31,995	4,626	10,892	1,436	15,880	1,669	0	89,062	20,508	20,454
Hall County	16,870	11,144	2,007	3,458	455	2,026	555	0	na	na	na
Henry County	14,756	9,356	1,460	3,818	180	na	na	na	na	na	na
Houston County	10,875	6,285	1,484	3,049	516	2,917	1,220	na	na	na	na
Jackson County	5,719	na	na	na	na	na	na	na	na	na	na
Lowndes County	9,605	5,163	875	3,423	311	na	na	na	na	na	na
Muscogee County	17,648	8,643	2,550	6,004	474	1,214	390	0	16,981	7,477	8,680
Newton County	8,151	5,944	360	1,546	265	2,291	1,116	na	na	na	na
Paulding County	9,480	na	na	na	na	na	na	na	na	na	na
Richmond County	19,335	9,227	3,523	6,456	1,537	2,509	741	153	17,588	8,592	9,928
Rockdale County	7,593	4,378	1,017	2,022	304	na	na	na	na	na	na
Spalding County	7,333	4,606	473	1,762	250	na	na	na	na	na	na
Troup County	6,585	na	na	na	na	1,556	835	430	na	na	na
Walker County	8,551	4,804	1,107	2,640	339	1,975	951	na	na	na	na
Walton County	8,386	5,476	563	2,212	368	1,235	292	45	na	na	na
Whitfield County	9,248	4,169	1,959	2,874	219	na	na	na	na	na	na
Hawaii											
Hawaii County	25,848	14,000	4,872	5,883	672	na	na	na	32,596	10,298	10,042
Honolulu County	91,320	58,146	11,165	18,717	5,569	26,879	3,561	106	123,217	46,317	28,346
Kauai County	9,017	5,463	1,063	2,223	352	2,510	473	na	na	na	na
Maui County	16,935	11,008	1,660	3,350	400	3,099	928	na	24,821	5,802	6,133
Idaho											
Ada County	40,387	22,419	4,595	12,173	1,276	3,162	668	102	57,912	13,645	15,110
Bannock County	7,726	4,242	1,315	1,895	207	na	na	na	na	na	na
Bonneville County	9,539	5,494	1,140	2,594	236	na	na	na	na	na	na
Canyon County	19,229	11,222	2,193	5,205	578	3,636	510	na	na	na	na
Kootenai County	19,738	11,076	2,811	5,339	649	1,013	582	na	na	na	na
Twin Falls County	7,820	4,725	743	2,109	258	na	na	na	na	na	na
Illinois											
Adams County	8,147	na	na	na	na	na	na	na	na	na	na
Champaign County	16,434	7,954	2,337	5,758	873	958	339	na	na	na	na
Cook County	480,363	240,533	72,557	155,437	24,908	61,134	13,021	2,736	527,676	216,937	155,698
DeKalb County	8,121	4,202	1,483	2,299	559	na	na	na	na	na	na
DuPage County	85,766	49,464	9,311	25,119	4,877	9,671	1,803	122	131,786	35,267	24,062
Kane County	43,059	24,440	4,385	13,686	1,581	6,359	755	0	61,941	16,786	16,903
Kankakee County	10,631	5,485	1,461	3,465	1,289	na	na	na	na	na	na
Kendall County	8,356	5,489	1,034	1,821	175	na	na	na	na	na	na
Lake County	60,453	33,938	7,922	17,343	3,177	7,634	1,526	135	89,499	23,141	20,240
LaSalle County	13,647	7,097	2,299	3,825	1,122	545	348	na	na	na	na
McHenry County	26,901	15,364	2,923	8,344	572	3,447	1,287	na	na	na	na
McLean County	14,126	7,760	1,877	4,267	761	na	na	na	na	na	na
Macon County	13,096	6,965	2,132	3,694	993	na	na	na	na	na	na
Madison County	29,762	16,419	4,541	7,944	1,502	1,999	590	399	37,206	12,007	10,269
Peoria County	17,416	8,805	2,895	5,274	1,368	1,029	316	105	na	na	na
Rock Island County	17,298	9,060	2,457	5,498	970	1,068	514	151	na	na	na
St. Clair County	26,546	13,216	4,538	8,338	1,289	2,181	464	52	na	na	na

Table D-2: Counties - Household Relationship, Grandparents, and Marital Status—*Continued*

	Total Householders 65 Years and Over	Family Householders 65 Years and Over	Non-Family Householders 65 Years and Over		Persons 65 Years and Over Living in Group Quarters	Grandparents 60 Years and Over Living with Grandchildren			Marital Status - Persons 60 Years and Over		
			Male Living Alone	Female Living Alone		Total	Responsible for Grandchildren	Responsible for Grandchildren and In Poverty	Now Married	Widowed	Divorced
Illinois—Cont.											
Sangamon County	22,318	11,103	3,431	7,427	942	1,451	483	0	na	na	na
Tazewell County	15,919	8,801	2,388	4,608	1,138	687	529	260	na	na	na
Vermilion County	9,996	4,534	2,170	3,079	478	773	202	30	na	na	na
Will County	51,204	32,335	5,913	11,682	1,936	9,609	1,871	51	84,955	20,110	16,011
Williamson County	8,284	na	na	na	na	na	na	na	na	na	na
Winnebago County	31,273	17,381	3,310	9,906	1,732	2,599	1,393	0	43,822	11,537	9,746
Indiana											
Allen County	35,683	18,258	5,346	11,568	1,713	3,331	1,595	143	44,153	13,379	11,667
Bartholomew County	8,957	4,583	1,645	2,678	586	na	na	na	na	na	na
Boone County	5,352	na	na	na	na	na	na	na	na	na	na
Clark County	11,810	6,693	1,259	3,807	75	na	na	na	na	na	na
Delaware County	12,849	7,138	1,527	4,114	1,147	570	307	na	na	na	na
Elkhart County	17,003	10,343	2,030	4,325	1,109	1,480	210	na	na	na	na
Floyd County	6,881	4,268	755	1,782	844	na	na	na	na	na	na
Grant County	8,420	na	na	na	na	na	na	111	na	na	na
Hamilton County	24,184	14,291	2,452	7,000	670	2,940	1,054	169	na	na	na
Hancock County	8,585	na	na	na	na	na	na	na	na	na	na
Hendricks County	12,843	7,755	1,639	3,206	545	1,430	838	na	na	na	na
Howard County	10,516	6,743	988	2,656	432	na	na	na	na	na	na
Johnson County	13,691	8,248	1,246	3,840	838	2,010	761	na	na	na	na
Kosciusko County	8,548	4,523	1,044	2,757	445	na	na	na	na	na	na
Lake County	52,044	25,724	7,431	17,148	2,290	5,178	1,530	259	56,713	24,017	19,514
LaPorte County	13,199	6,839	1,908	4,244	483	na	na	na	na	na	na
Madison County	14,595	8,454	1,572	4,247	872	1,450	523	184	na	na	na
Marion County	76,295	37,538	11,860	24,937	4,136	8,179	3,253	780	82,687	30,985	34,552
Monroe County	12,536	5,979	1,997	3,776	631	na	na	na	na	na	na
Morgan County	7,099	4,021	757	1,902	444	670	415	na	na	na	na
Porter County	16,756	9,706	1,766	4,899	1,063	2,196	649	na	na	na	na
St. Joseph County	27,801	13,175	4,763	9,295	1,939	2,003	441	244	33,205	11,540	9,982
Tippecanoe County	13,694	7,393	2,464	3,760	917	1,646	1,084	na	na	na	na
Vanderburgh County	18,773	9,840	2,915	5,333	1,598	2,116	1,259	na	na	na	na
Vigo County	9,677	5,420	1,271	2,545	1,015	685	360	na	na	na	na
Wayne County	8,133	3,921	1,335	2,346	682	na	na	na	na	na	na
Iowa											
Black Hawk County	13,831	7,379	1,960	4,155	563	na	na	na	na	na	na
Dallas County	6,967	na	na	na	na	na	na	na	na	na	na
Dubuque County	10,313	5,519	1,002	3,463	1,272	na	na	na	na	na	na
Johnson County	10,996	6,789	1,308	2,756	471	na	na	na	na	na	na
Linn County	23,528	11,890	3,258	7,784	817	na	na	na	na	na	na
Polk County	39,485	20,153	5,798	12,252	1,911	2,825	1,036	148	50,843	15,550	13,676
Pottawattamie County	10,494	5,669	1,670	3,015	348	na	na	na	na	na	na
Scott County	16,858	8,173	2,506	5,828	952	na	na	na	na	na	na
Story County	7,369	na	na	na	na	na	na	na	na	na	na
Woodbury County	10,023	5,258	1,338	3,237	421	na	na	na	na	na	na
Kansas											
Butler County	6,401	na	na	na	na	na	na	na	na	na	na
Douglas County	9,782	4,834	946	3,506	431	na	na	na	na	na	na
Johnson County	52,962	31,797	4,389	15,820	2,628	3,209	1,062	0	80,515	19,297	15,479
Leavenworth County	7,105	3,923	569	2,541	715	na	na	na	na	na	na
Riley County	4,379	na	na	na	na	na	na	na	na	na	na
Sedgwick County	47,194	22,925	7,612	15,389	2,038	4,367	1,228	32	59,429	18,770	17,506
Shawnee County	20,366	10,271	2,881	6,343	1,447	1,305	826	372	na	na	na
Wyandotte County	12,679	6,969	1,836	3,552	433	2,649	1,048	72	15,015	5,249	5,512
Kentucky											
Boone County	10,925	6,944	803	2,991	325	na	na	na	na	na	na
Bullitt County	7,742	5,070	1,281	1,326	77	na	na	na	na	na	na
Campbell County	9,207	4,146	1,609	3,291	566	738	272	39	na	na	na
Christian County	5,652	na	na	na	na	na	na	na	na	na	na
Daviess County	11,193	5,881	1,631	3,178	901	895	328	na	na	na	na
Fayette County	26,964	13,851	3,095	9,644	1,158	2,917	1,179	223	34,605	10,289	10,015
Hardin County	9,928	6,208	965	2,709	336	na	na	na	na	na	na
Jefferson County	79,978	42,306	11,222	23,937	3,894	6,933	3,083	604	92,844	32,569	31,653
Kenton County	14,963	7,855	2,849	3,788	798	1,556	922	78	na	na	na
McCracken County	8,624	3,983	1,245	3,011	459	na	na	na	na	na	na
Madison County	7,772	4,412	977	2,160	416	na	na	na	na	na	na
Oldham County	4,507	3,064	583	827	350	na	na	na	na	na	na
Warren County	10,751	5,356	1,472	3,355	619	na	na	na	na	na	na
Louisiana											
Ascension Parish	8,396	4,973	558	2,438	184	na	na	na	na	na	na
Bossier Parish	11,700	5,968	2,093	3,361	630	na	na	na	na	na	na
Caddo Parish	26,450	14,612	4,338	7,091	2,174	2,854	1,408	414	29,032	11,997	8,111
Calcasieu Parish	20,476	10,713	2,775	6,422	779	2,696	2,208	0	na	na	na
East Baton Rouge Parish	38,674	21,954	4,436	11,241	1,220	4,682	1,943	461	47,490	16,857	15,942
Iberia Parish	7,137	na	na	na	na	1,131	650	na	na	na	na

Table D-2: Counties - Household Relationship, Grandparents, and Marital Status—*Continued*

	Total Householders 65 Years and Over	Family Householders 65 Years and Over	Non-Family Householders 65 Years and Over		Persons 65 Years and Over Living in Group Quarters	Grandparents 60 Years and Over Living with Grandchildren			Marital Status - Persons 60 Years and Over		
			Male Living Alone	Female Living Alone		Total	Responsible for Grandchildren	Responsible for Grandchildren and In Poverty	Now Married	Widowed	Divorced
Louisiana—Cont.											
Jefferson Parish	45,851	25,363	6,136	13,185	1,582	7,906	2,152	577	55,860	18,905	19,627
Lafayette Parish	19,755	11,179	2,179	5,756	977	2,279	1,128	66	na	na	na
Lafourche Parish	9,583	5,360	825	3,196	392	na	na	na	na	na	na
Livingston Parish	9,735	5,301	1,155	2,628	328	1,576	691	na	na	na	na
Orleans Parish	35,584	14,352	7,054	12,826	1,600	3,341	669	294	33,427	16,381	15,415
Ouachita Parish	13,610	7,187	1,831	4,194	888	na	na	0	na	na	na
Rapides Parish	13,287	6,843	2,011	4,377	1,075	1,194	805	251	na	na	na
St. Landry Parish	8,223	4,186	1,216	2,731	628	na	na	na	na	na	na
St. Tammany Parish	26,871	15,929	3,670	6,726	629	2,698	908	583	35,532	11,978	8,904
Tangipahoa Parish	11,765	6,275	1,463	3,751	570	na	na	na	na	na	na
Terrebonne Parish	10,103	6,309	1,575	2,090	427	1,004	467	na	na	na	na
Maine											
Androscoggin County	12,277	5,575	2,028	4,263	949	na	na	na	na	na	na
Aroostook County	10,076	4,612	2,346	2,853	1,090	na	na	0	na	na	na
Cumberland County	34,701	16,731	4,895	10,750	1,652	2,667	870	na	na	na	na
Kennebec County	16,362	7,464	2,831	4,903	1,341	na	na	na	na	na	na
Penobscot County	17,420	8,418	3,414	4,774	1,034	na	na	na	na	na	na
York County	27,343	14,625	3,075	8,598	913	na	na	na	na	na	na
Maryland											
Allegany County	9,052	4,266	1,546	2,894	996	na	na	na	na	na	na
Anne Arundel County	51,838	30,512	6,460	12,723	2,015	8,068	3,048	0	73,108	20,177	17,835
Baltimore County	86,617	44,849	11,216	28,337	5,300	10,976	2,263	387	105,305	40,553	31,048
Calvert County	7,043	4,335	736	1,821	239	na	na	na	na	na	na
Carroll County	16,008	9,495	1,711	4,344	1,132	2,206	532	na	na	na	na
Cecil County	9,943	6,430	1,460	1,870	335	2,250	1,163	na	na	na	na
Charles County	10,869	7,304	1,434	1,828	358	2,449	653	154	na	na	na
Frederick County	22,623	12,263	3,239	6,517	831	2,601	464	0	32,485	9,133	7,794
Harford County	25,045	14,125	2,645	7,560	697	3,065	1,023	77	37,977	10,183	8,577
Howard County	25,500	15,442	2,398	7,121	724	na	na	na	41,314	9,556	7,974
Montgomery County	91,392	51,882	9,847	26,585	4,579	14,068	2,052	59	133,286	34,523	32,726
Prince George's County	70,471	39,014	10,073	19,229	2,794	15,002	3,888	292	87,323	28,759	29,651
St. Mary's County	9,007	4,485	1,185	2,880	689	na	na	na	na	na	na
Washington County	15,971	8,421	2,024	4,739	1,038	1,228	232	na	na	na	na
Wicomico County	10,517	5,775	1,354	3,091	458	na	na	na	na	na	na
Massachusetts											
Barnstable County	39,226	22,053	3,685	12,082	1,689	1,862	549	86	na	na	na
Berkshire County	18,271	9,247	2,299	6,001	1,146	1,196	629	86	na	na	na
Bristol County	59,402	30,750	7,740	18,704	3,449	7,335	1,662	407	75,563	26,889	19,339
Essex County	80,745	42,547	10,123	24,965	4,560	10,295	1,775	99	103,574	32,977	29,078
Franklin County	9,784	5,082	1,633	2,829	442	na	na	na	na	na	na
Hampden County	49,293	24,343	7,725	15,109	2,907	5,117	1,218	136	56,450	20,287	18,479
Hampshire County	17,362	9,043	2,368	5,500	623	na	na	na	na	na	na
Middlesex County	152,626	79,881	21,151	47,081	7,465	17,495	3,662	0	191,444	56,950	49,836
Norfolk County	73,338	39,060	10,175	22,203	4,000	8,900	1,573	0	93,671	28,020	24,348
Plymouth County	56,023	30,100	7,281	16,257	3,559	6,336	1,654	na	76,096	23,061	18,475
Suffolk County	62,805	26,942	10,888	22,362	3,785	8,955	1,499	276	59,172	21,913	22,783
Worcester County	77,110	39,318	10,909	24,091	5,478	9,008	1,847	44	103,919	34,870	26,896
Michigan											
Allegan County	11,325	7,031	1,479	2,288	798	1,539	616	na	na	na	na
Bay County	13,107	7,027	2,005	3,684	727	na	na	na	na	na	na
Berrien County	19,901	10,926	3,252	5,086	983	1,847	464	43	na	na	na
Calhoun County	15,477	8,042	2,646	4,211	1,103	880	350	40	na	na	na
Clinton County	8,604	4,849	1,356	2,123	209	na	na	na	na	na	na
Eaton County	12,391	7,103	1,809	3,085	528	na	na	na	na	na	na
Genesee County	47,441	25,288	6,789	14,045	1,478	3,383	959	228	54,518	17,468	19,195
Grand Traverse County	11,527	6,222	1,585	3,090	854	na	na	na	na	na	na
Ingham County	25,597	12,776	4,176	7,618	675	1,702	275	69	32,520	8,969	10,589
Isabella County	5,749	2,948	766	1,907	488	na	na	na	na	na	na
Jackson County	17,558	9,085	3,251	4,816	1,050	1,528	475	0	na	na	na
Kalamazoo County	25,026	12,121	3,992	8,183	886	1,297	227	0	31,909	9,150	10,155
Kent County	56,530	29,825	6,901	18,787	2,940	6,173	1,129	135	77,241	21,560	19,239
Lapeer County	10,168	5,931	1,406	2,722	577	1,152	257	na	na	na	na
Lenawee County	11,422	6,240	1,590	3,388	871	na	na	na	na	na	na
Livingston County	20,572	12,784	1,742	5,372	433	na	na	na	na	na	na
Macomb County	93,956	48,379	13,656	29,953	3,681	11,683	2,328	74	119,798	40,196	31,649
Marquette County	8,026	4,038	1,669	2,000	485	na	na	na	na	na	na
Midland County	9,892	5,256	1,194	3,193	320	na	na	na	na	na	na
Monroe County	18,137	10,302	2,441	5,164	830	1,284	563	na	na	na	na
Muskegon County	18,617	10,444	2,135	5,186	1,332	1,631	504	94	na	na	na
Oakland County	133,560	69,376	17,592	43,007	4,526	10,228	1,382	139	170,499	53,189	47,616
Ottawa County	26,813	16,296	3,171	7,030	920	2,186	222	na	na	na	na
Saginaw County	23,894	12,808	3,168	7,358	1,367	1,136	651	183	27,755	9,849	8,036
St. Clair County	18,670	10,626	2,274	5,143	696	999	336	na	na	na	na
Shiawassee County	7,895	4,296	1,187	2,157	309	na	na	na	na	na	na

Table D-2: Counties - Household Relationship, Grandparents, and Marital Status—*Continued*

	Total Householders 65 Years and Over	Family Householders 65 Years and Over	Non-Family Householders 65 Years and Over		Persons 65 Years and Over Living in Group Quarters	Grandparents 60 Years and Over Living with Grandchildren			Marital Status - Persons 60 Years and Over		
			Male Living Alone	Female Living Alone		Total	Responsible for Grandchildren	Responsible for Grandchildren and In Poverty	Now Married	Widowed	Divorced
Michigan—Cont.											
Van Buren County	8,273	4,984	840	2,228	405	897	244	na	na	na	na
Washtenaw County	32,797	18,522	3,980	9,410	1,892	2,010	408	na	42,232	10,948	10,644
Wayne County	179,772	87,076	27,254	61,175	8,227	21,116	4,270	368	175,668	78,728	77,216
Minnesota											
Anoka County	29,075	17,274	3,348	7,856	897	4,833	977	0	47,015	11,206	10,238
Blue Earth County	5,618	na	na	na	na	na	na	na	na	na	na
Carver County	7,658	4,314	963	2,190	166	na	na	na	na	na	na
Dakota County	36,874	20,026	4,627	11,488	1,421	3,431	1,428	87	53,301	11,778	12,422
Hennepin County	111,929	54,480	18,235	35,201	5,756	9,144	1,689	171	139,577	35,272	44,221
Olmsted County	14,876	8,001	1,751	4,813	1,152	na	na	na	na	na	na
Ramsey County	51,150	24,048	7,895	17,839	3,439	3,821	687	170	55,576	19,585	21,584
Rice County	6,671	3,381	694	2,485	449	na	na	na	na	na	na
St. Louis County	24,853	11,981	4,346	7,724	2,040	1,148	530	23	30,519	9,748	8,508
Scott County	8,759	5,767	800	1,870	766	1,242	532	na	na	na	na
Sherburne County	6,298	3,672	710	1,805	393	na	na	na	na	na	na
Stearns County	14,462	7,872	2,158	4,070	1,450	na	na	na	na	na	na
Washington County	23,743	13,362	2,927	6,821	694	na	na	na	na	na	na
Wright County	10,471	6,396	775	3,105	379	na	na	na	na	na	na
Mississippi											
DeSoto County	13,892	7,437	2,069	3,681	231	2,102	910	0	na	na	na
Forrest County	6,425	3,146	1,197	1,944	533	na	na	na	na	na	na
Harrison County	19,440	11,482	2,792	4,620	818	1,973	1,222	352	23,936	8,131	6,992
Hinds County	19,645	11,211	2,491	5,636	1,506	2,820	1,557	79	25,424	9,835	6,936
Jackson County	14,177	8,424	1,790	3,446	413	1,427	812	na	na	na	na
Jones County	7,485	4,512	662	2,073	585	na	na	na	na	na	na
Lauderdale County	8,416	na	na	na	na	na	na	na	na	na	na
Lee County	7,784	na	na	na	na	na	na	na	na	na	na
Madison County	8,409	na	na	na	na	na	na	na	na	na	na
Rankin County	14,879	7,765	1,690	4,870	1,452	na	na	na	na	na	na
Missouri											
Boone County	14,295	7,378	2,162	4,502	779	na	na	na	na	na	na
Buchanan County	9,946	5,383	1,383	2,449	578	929	592	na	na	na	na
Cape Girardeau County	7,618	4,356	791	2,471	805	na	na	na	na	na	na
Cass County	11,620	6,462	889	3,868	505	na	na	na	na	na	na
Christian County	8,121	na	na	na	na	na	na	na	na	na	na
Clay County	20,702	11,598	2,402	6,330	785	2,564	1,048	na	na	na	na
Cole County	8,385	na	na	na	na	na	na	na	na	na	na
Franklin County	11,011	6,306	1,245	3,321	320	na	na	na	na	na	na
Greene County	32,556	15,285	5,602	10,969	1,573	1,846	1,023	191	35,380	12,192	12,602
Jackson County	66,109	34,262	10,146	18,780	3,691	7,971	1,942	412	77,492	26,272	29,287
Jasper County	13,326	6,603	2,098	4,404	373	1,091	438	137	na	na	na
Jefferson County	20,859	11,904	3,171	5,253	1,153	1,885	383	na	na	na	na
Platte County	8,509	5,049	881	1,905	350	na	na	na	na	na	na
St. Charles County	37,374	21,895	4,065	10,861	1,291	3,264	854	na	55,681	15,828	11,459
St. Francois County	7,061	na	na	na	na	na	na	na	na	na	na
St. Louis County	115,361	64,383	12,840	35,860	7,076	7,732	2,787	729	146,692	47,058	36,309
Montana											
Cascade County	9,377	4,735	1,909	2,585	402	na	na	na	na	na	na
Flathead County	11,891	6,729	1,397	3,448	371	1,493	568	na	na	na	na
Gallatin County	8,441	5,061	1,274	1,731	203	na	na	na	na	na	na
Lewis and Clark County	7,748	3,492	1,790	1,768	254	na	na	na	na	na	na
Missoula County	11,491	6,060	1,683	3,209	238	na	na	na	na	na	na
Yellowstone County	17,535	9,356	2,364	5,444	849	1,545	793	546	na	na	na
Nebraska											
Douglas County	48,243	22,764	7,420	16,363	2,338	3,202	1,289	53	56,045	19,461	19,157
Lancaster County	28,792	14,855	4,028	9,163	335	2,097	460	na	36,872	10,463	8,889
Sarpy County	13,859	8,023	1,979	3,625	616	1,656	564	na	na	na	na
Nevada											
Clark County	187,797	103,390	29,992	44,906	3,912	33,966	9,237	1,229	242,221	75,829	89,883
Washoe County	47,863	24,922	8,174	12,336	958	4,870	1,872	239	61,447	15,599	22,298
New Hampshire											
Cheshire County	9,178	4,375	1,199	3,367	535	na	na	na	na	na	na
Grafton County	11,656	6,521	1,802	2,919	795	na	na	na	na	na	na
Hillsborough County	38,337	20,376	5,156	11,230	3,253	3,243	648	73	53,633	17,260	14,306
Merrimack County	16,924	8,430	2,506	5,343	1,181	1,620	313	na	na	na	na
Rockingham County	31,923	18,566	4,247	8,114	1,492	3,267	816	0	50,611	11,738	11,380
Strafford County	11,506	6,237	1,403	3,221	417	na	na	na	na	na	na
New Jersey											
Atlantic County	28,355	16,928	3,123	7,526	1,712	4,255	1,145	172	38,296	11,044	9,696
Bergen County	94,096	53,741	10,237	28,400	4,398	14,370	1,827	0	130,581	40,922	25,890
Burlington County	46,078	26,523	5,373	13,451	2,249	5,572	1,200	156	64,558	18,020	15,229
Camden County	50,199	26,222	6,077	15,967	2,918	6,611	966	28	58,998	20,822	18,360
Cape May County	14,880	8,398	2,112	3,969	1,043	na	na	na	na	na	na
Cumberland County	14,558	7,500	2,015	4,781	1,699	906	495	37	na	na	na

Table D-2: Counties - Household Relationship, Grandparents, and Marital Status—*Continued*

	Total Householders 65 Years and Over	Family Householders 65 Years and Over	Non-Family Householders 65 Years and Over		Persons 65 Years and Over Living in Group Quarters	Grandparents 60 Years and Over Living with Grandchildren			Marital Status - Persons 60 Years and Over		
			Male Living Alone	Female Living Alone		Total	Responsible for Grandchildren	Responsible for Grandchildren and In Poverty	Now Married	Widowed	Divorced
New Jersey—Cont.											
Essex County	64,811	34,509	7,173	21,006	4,412	9,928	2,027	576	76,572	28,380	21,689
Gloucester County	27,052	15,618	3,217	7,741	902	3,925	1,152	na	39,473	13,705	7,799
Hudson County	49,125	25,462	6,194	16,337	2,114	7,992	975	268	59,056	21,451	17,047
Hunterdon County	13,988	8,358	1,632	3,570	353	na	na	na	na	na	na
Mercer County	35,066	18,725	4,915	10,816	2,106	3,174	1,512	330	43,970	13,521	12,668
Middlesex County	70,241	41,612	6,880	20,487	2,639	18,041	2,560	496	103,383	34,503	19,094
Monmouth County	69,245	38,447	7,240	22,041	2,527	7,062	1,004	0	96,726	26,718	18,975
Morris County	48,046	28,442	4,361	13,406	2,889	5,337	670	na	72,478	20,307	14,512
Ocean County	90,433	47,480	10,198	30,090	2,871	5,385	1,857	49	107,192	35,699	21,425
Passaic County	41,317	24,645	4,204	11,058	2,124	7,958	1,094	194	57,534	19,094	12,988
Salem County	7,083	4,043	692	1,993	556	435	189	na	na	na	na
Somerset County	29,312	18,581	2,020	8,306	1,587	na	na	na	48,313	12,028	8,794
Sussex County	14,851	9,251	1,691	3,488	811	na	na	na	na	na	na
Union County	46,489	24,303	5,764	14,944	2,074	8,539	1,176	42	58,233	24,130	15,476
Warren County	12,242	6,081	1,911	3,973	516	842	408	na	na	na	na
New Mexico											
Bernalillo County	69,183	34,972	11,497	20,485	2,453	7,016	3,473	736	76,187	27,676	31,610
Chaves County	6,568	3,347	1,123	1,815	358	na	na	na	na	na	na
Doña Ana County	20,682	11,790	2,253	6,112	405	4,608	2,230	618	na	na	na
Lea County	4,873	2,392	869	1,403	237	na	na	na	na	na	na
McKinley County	5,709	3,913	459	1,323	202	1,309	642	169	na	na	na
Otero County	6,635	na	na	na	na	na	na	na	na	na	na
Sandoval County	15,111	10,148	1,336	3,040	505	2,167	1,297	227	na	na	na
San Juan County	12,097	7,730	1,720	2,483	419	2,549	1,050	437	na	na	na
Santa Fe County	22,869	12,132	3,217	6,149	437	1,687	606	na	27,422	5,049	10,622
Valencia County	8,607	4,869	1,401	2,121	108	na	na	na	na	na	na
New York											
Albany County	32,402	16,009	5,526	9,975	3,246	2,482	389	na	38,870	13,297	11,034
Bronx County	115,624	52,562	20,620	39,972	9,988	24,031	6,501	2,810	94,638	53,999	45,487
Broome County	23,184	12,010	2,389	8,247	1,496	na	na	0	27,952	9,670	7,793
Cattaraugus County	9,120	4,794	1,832	1,972	749	660	457	0	11,921	3,469	2,889
Cayuga County	8,949	4,436	1,334	2,862	592	na	na	na	na	na	na
Chautauqua County	15,814	8,021	2,407	4,907	1,659	1,196	433	na	na	na	na
Chemung County	10,247	5,458	1,459	3,256	1,096	na	na	na	na	na	na
Clinton County	8,126	4,110	1,357	2,244	499	573	445	190	na	na	na
Dutchess County	31,844	16,893	4,288	9,465	2,440	3,261	657	61	39,249	12,977	12,743
Erie County	108,411	52,753	14,831	38,337	6,171	7,352	3,279	511	122,890	45,431	34,738
Jefferson County	9,611	5,114	1,292	3,104	468	523	303	na	na	na	na
Kings County	222,026	114,617	27,565	73,420	10,730	43,383	11,109	2,707	250,435	97,244	63,694
Livingston County	6,572	3,691	875	1,778	345	na	na	na	na	na	na
Madison County	7,634	4,101	962	2,258	351	na	na	na	na	na	na
Monroe County	81,774	39,683	11,791	27,536	6,245	6,760	1,709	346	99,541	33,732	26,980
Nassau County	137,207	82,816	12,822	37,835	6,491	23,118	2,926	0	206,197	61,688	34,508
New York County	183,754	68,889	34,050	75,241	7,532	14,311	2,745	1,170	148,015	59,560	56,405
Niagara County	26,063	13,003	4,507	7,871	1,535	1,895	711	173	33,123	11,374	9,539
Oneida County	25,518	13,762	3,704	7,321	3,328	2,182	765	0	34,600	10,537	8,206
Onondaga County	50,806	25,797	7,476	16,078	2,779	3,749	1,119	246	63,783	21,208	15,979
Ontario County	13,724	6,669	2,148	4,266	649	na	na	na	na	na	na
Orange County	31,943	17,894	3,903	9,307	1,689	5,895	1,716	na	44,564	13,571	11,162
Oswego County	12,220	6,045	2,206	3,579	238	na	na	na	na	na	na
Putnam County	9,588	5,994	1,807	1,577	433	na	na	na	na	na	na
Queens County	199,825	112,955	23,754	57,391	11,800	43,971	9,614	667	262,727	97,679	55,131
Rensselaer County	17,102	9,912	2,554	4,235	1,173	na	na	na	21,858	6,954	5,190
Richmond County	45,957	26,033	5,147	13,539	2,538	9,191	1,332	99	62,871	21,846	13,070
Rockland County	29,598	18,075	2,251	8,490	2,075	3,714	930	na	43,173	11,591	8,497
St. Lawrence County	12,077	5,720	2,038	4,024	1,146	849	248	na	na	na	na
Saratoga County	25,959	14,515	2,923	8,101	667	1,521	254	na	na	na	na
Schenectady County	16,415	8,547	1,842	5,121	1,083	na	na	0	na	na	na
Steuben County	11,538	5,618	1,863	3,579	949	586	250	48	15,196	4,665	4,496
Suffolk County	144,184	86,361	15,226	38,651	6,796	23,354	4,149	724	206,912	63,816	45,797
Sullivan County	8,582	4,066	1,568	2,466	961	na	na	na	na	na	na
Tompkins County	9,079	4,936	1,267	2,372	505	na	na	na	na	na	na
Ulster County	21,616	11,556	3,309	6,051	1,329	2,317	816	99	27,219	8,634	9,077
Warren County	9,284	4,826	1,548	2,686	497	na	na	na	na	na	na
Wayne County	10,643	5,768	987	3,454	520	na	na	na	na	na	na
Westchester County	102,529	53,500	13,935	32,873	7,024	10,134	1,148	100	124,482	41,751	29,927
North Carolina											
Alamance County	17,636	8,485	2,540	6,335	999	2,699	582	0	na	na	na
Brunswick County	25,219	16,938	2,758	4,664	488	na	na	170	na	na	na
Buncombe County	32,253	16,454	4,215	10,441	2,216	2,229	629	na	40,934	11,980	11,345
Burke County	10,686	6,198	1,274	3,016	624	2,463	369	na	na	na	na
Cabarrus County	16,169	9,776	1,585	4,634	773	1,989	472	0	na	na	na
Caldwell County	9,499	5,752	1,452	2,128	280	na	na	26	na	na	na
Carteret County	11,038	6,263	1,249	3,220	293	na	na	na	na	na	na
Catawba County	18,289	10,679	2,156	5,005	497	2,513	1,079	0	na	na	na
Chatham County	10,611	6,101	1,077	2,810	334	na	na	na	na	na	na
Cleveland County	10,539	6,505	1,094	2,890	289	na	na	na	na	na	na

Table D-2: Counties - Household Relationship, Grandparents, and Marital Status—*Continued*

	Total Householders 65 Years and Over	Family Householders 65 Years and Over	Non-Family Householders 65 Years and Over		Persons 65 Years and Over Living in Group Quarters	Grandparents 60 Years and Over Living with Grandchildren			Marital Status - Persons 60 Years and Over		
			Male Living Alone	Female Living Alone		Total	Responsible for Grandchildren	Responsible for Grandchildren and In Poverty	Now Married	Widowed	Divorced
North Carolina—Cont.											
Craven County	12,794	6,802	1,671	4,000	530	na	na	na	na	na	na
Cumberland County	25,938	12,955	4,396	8,059	641	3,996	1,505	306	29,456	14,083	8,567
Davidson County	18,381	9,728	3,065	4,875	802	2,183	957	na	na	na	na
Durham County	25,415	15,479	2,782	6,962	1,371	na	na	na	33,289	8,868	9,681
Forsyth County	39,419	19,112	5,853	13,361	828	3,553	939	104	43,748	16,298	15,576
Franklin County	6,965	4,679	750	1,394	259	na	na	na	na	na	na
Gaston County	22,081	12,072	2,367	7,033	1,023	3,355	990	154	28,762	10,103	7,010
Guilford County	50,210	27,758	5,582	15,212	2,178	5,523	2,289	397	65,643	19,536	18,680
Harnett County	9,992	5,884	1,343	2,708	537	1,239	219	na	na	na	na
Henderson County	18,920	11,505	1,767	5,496	906	802	450	na	na	na	na
Iredell County	16,967	10,411	1,950	4,199	413	1,466	960	na	na	na	na
Johnston County	15,581	8,072	2,070	5,439	528	na	na	na	na	na	na
Lincoln County	8,680	5,758	703	1,911	299	na	na	na	na	na	na
Mecklenburg County	72,989	39,793	8,374	22,935	2,325	9,965	2,442	323	98,773	30,185	32,619
Moore County	14,474	8,216	1,734	4,014	948	na	na	na	na	na	na
Nash County	12,037	6,301	1,712	3,583	418	na	na	na	na	na	na
New Hanover County	26,105	12,990	3,606	8,524	982	na	na	na	na	na	na
Onslow County	10,186	6,133	1,556	2,219	212	1,924	528	0	na	na	na
Orange County	12,791	6,985	1,582	3,636	219	na	na	na	na	na	na
Pitt County	14,472	8,124	2,056	4,019	565	1,818	762	235	na	na	na
Randolph County	15,535	9,094	1,981	4,139	748	1,628	635	na	na	na	na
Robeson County	12,744	7,458	1,683	3,193	615	1,552	558	267	15,003	6,980	4,006
Rockingham County	12,727	6,895	1,687	3,985	664	1,797	1,224	182	na	na	na
Rowan County	15,670	8,857	2,268	4,200	1,191	1,810	1,035	87	na	na	na
Rutherford County	9,054	5,376	1,309	1,907	562	na	na	na	na	na	na
Surry County	9,879	5,369	1,205	3,143	585	na	na	na	na	na	na
Union County	16,342	10,561	1,384	4,178	680	2,766	514	88	na	na	na
Wake County	75,259	44,119	7,295	22,259	2,278	8,905	1,780	0	114,671	28,784	25,653
Wayne County	13,389	8,103	1,200	3,979	277	2,218	1,015	428	na	na	na
Wilkes County	10,532	5,314	1,799	3,300	286	na	na	na	na	na	na
Wilson County	9,989	3,829	2,118	3,875	522	na	na	na	na	na	na
North Dakota											
Burleigh County	9,661	na	na	na	na	na	na	na	na	na	na
Cass County	13,333	6,691	2,193	3,986	904	na	na	na	na	na	na
Grand Forks County	5,666	2,974	828	1,683	485	na	na	na	na	na	na
Ward County	5,402	na	na	na	na	na	na	na	na	na	na
Ohio											
Allen County	11,540	5,889	1,966	3,499	703	650	288	na	na	na	na
Ashtabula County	11,704	6,544	1,665	3,373	859	na	na	na	na	na	na
Athens County	5,581	2,514	912	2,078	242	na	na	0	na	na	na
Belmont County	8,880	na	na	na	na	na	na	na	na	na	na
Butler County	34,810	19,617	5,339	9,104	1,867	4,749	2,057	82	48,243	16,345	12,378
Clark County	17,429	8,945	2,191	5,971	996	1,664	846	144	na	na	na
Clermont County	20,408	11,452	3,073	5,674	749	1,759	914	na	na	na	na
Columbiana County	12,925	7,112	2,122	3,276	1,270	977	296	21	na	na	na
Cuyahoga County	150,843	69,133	25,967	51,176	8,502	10,742	3,999	368	149,318	60,520	56,844
Delaware County	16,459	9,840	1,558	4,698	370	na	na	na	na	na	na
Erie County	10,135	5,233	1,470	3,409	536	na	na	na	na	na	na
Fairfield County	15,127	8,684	1,646	4,481	931	1,104	276	na	na	na	na
Franklin County	100,883	55,141	12,873	30,125	3,491	12,939	3,657	1,393	121,579	38,974	43,949
Geauga County	11,976	8,059	1,418	2,462	657	na	na	na	na	na	na
Greene County	18,525	11,229	2,427	4,550	474	2,185	861	na	na	na	na
Hamilton County	81,102	39,177	12,736	27,749	6,744	6,310	2,451	560	93,560	31,546	31,331
Hancock County	8,173	4,160	1,300	2,495	519	na	na	na	na	na	na
Jefferson County	9,203	5,005	1,146	3,030	596	712	185	na	na	na	na
Lake County	28,890	16,905	3,278	7,894	1,385	2,882	778	24	na	na	na
Licking County	16,952	9,770	1,875	4,591	468	1,800	831	156	na	na	na
Lorain County	35,685	19,070	4,475	11,104	1,925	2,186	657	103	46,101	15,447	11,556
Lucas County	43,704	22,979	6,537	13,417	3,163	4,143	1,425	348	53,166	16,289	18,083
Mahoning County	30,605	14,493	5,294	10,066	2,472	1,464	553	54	35,405	13,569	11,116
Marion County	6,905	3,619	991	2,067	592	na	na	na	na	na	na
Medina County	19,624	12,193	1,689	5,391	1,044	1,008	171	na	na	na	na
Miami County	11,957	6,389	2,024	3,544	629	na	na	na	na	na	na
Montgomery County	62,017	31,319	9,114	20,136	4,609	4,284	1,412	188	65,930	25,630	23,969
Muskingum County	10,134	5,572	1,341	2,941	564	na	na	na	na	na	na
Portage County	16,186	8,087	3,161	4,125	856	1,936	299	na	na	na	na
Richland County	15,028	8,301	1,522	4,894	843	na	na	na	na	na	na
Ross County	8,430	5,034	1,128	2,183	541	na	na	na	na	na	na
Scioto County	8,572	4,712	1,492	2,279	755	1,190	546	na	na	na	na
Stark County	45,960	24,624	6,360	13,790	2,750	3,158	765	297	54,695	18,324	15,634
Summit County	61,595	32,376	9,293	18,125	2,692	5,342	1,369	78	72,511	24,025	25,977
Trumbull County	27,428	14,034	3,577	8,834	1,544	1,655	557	0	31,552	12,133	9,451
Tuscarawas County	11,470	5,226	1,973	4,037	646	na	na	na	na	na	na
Warren County	19,136	12,152	2,454	4,280	1,629	1,487	550	na	na	na	na
Wayne County	12,744	7,327	1,690	3,304	246	na	na	na	na	na	na
Wood County	12,245	6,927	1,347	3,280	867	1,350	485	na	na	na	na

Table D-2: Counties - Household Relationship, Grandparents, and Marital Status—*Continued*

	Total Householders 65 Years and Over	Family Householders 65 Years and Over	Non-Family Householders 65 Years and Over		Persons 65 Years and Over Living in Group Quarters	Grandparents 60 Years and Over Living with Grandchildren			Marital Status - Persons 60 Years and Over		
			Male Living Alone	Female Living Alone		Total	Responsible for Grandchildren	Responsible for Grandchildren and In Poverty	Now Married	Widowed	Divorced
Oklahoma											
Canadian County	10,317	6,305	1,430	2,549	395	2,269	981	228	na	na	na
Cleveland County	24,398	13,379	2,806	7,662	842	2,733	1,612	318	30,664	8,691	8,280
Comanche County	9,851	5,192	1,700	2,708	826	2,407	836	107	na	na	na
Creek County	8,005	4,827	1,021	2,073	304	1,134	546	18	na	na	na
Muskogee County	7,165	3,731	1,079	2,191	662	757	283	0	na	na	na
Oklahoma County	69,935	35,910	10,668	22,066	3,233	6,191	2,551	402	80,388	28,949	30,885
Payne County	7,462	na	na	na	na	na	na	na	na	na	na
Pottawatomie County	7,298	3,983	1,238	1,930	352	903	490	57	na	na	na
Rogers County	8,552	5,189	1,151	2,058	755	1,268	444	26	na	na	na
Tulsa County	59,066	31,349	8,272	18,136	2,460	7,253	2,903	319	72,629	24,200	24,120
Wagoner County	8,077	5,134	1,187	1,631	150	1,243	529	99	na	na	na
Oregon											
Benton County	8,774	5,333	916	2,160	264	na	na	na	na	na	na
Clackamas County	45,626	24,996	5,150	13,537	1,835	5,099	1,112	0	65,228	15,743	16,004
Deschutes County	25,139	14,402	2,966	6,605	699	na	na	na	na	na	na
Douglas County	17,844	10,455	2,659	3,807	339	na	na	na	na	na	na
Jackson County	29,411	15,504	3,130	9,403	1,420	2,410	867	na	na	na	na
Josephine County	14,454	7,894	1,961	3,912	344	na	na	na	na	na	na
Klamath County	8,846	4,146	1,973	2,325	253	na	na	na	na	na	na
Lane County	46,536	23,562	6,636	13,122	1,756	3,874	1,114	131	56,087	14,538	20,205
Linn County	15,144	8,127	2,069	4,099	572	1,790	652	na	na	na	na
Marion County	31,849	17,235	4,427	9,049	2,240	4,380	1,878	431	40,158	12,726	16,609
Multnomah County	70,367	31,824	10,971	24,909	2,620	6,653	1,290	0	77,788	22,214	33,632
Polk County	9,211	6,082	862	2,043	273	na	na	na	na	na	na
Umatilla County	7,442	4,000	948	2,334	544	na	na	na	na	na	na
Washington County	49,424	26,389	4,949	15,462	1,889	5,884	702	0	65,503	17,734	21,892
Yamhill County	11,361	5,904	1,686	3,241	474	1,676	561	na	na	na	na
Pennsylvania											
Adams County	12,529	6,608	2,283	3,191	968	773	285	na	na	na	na
Allegheny County	153,284	71,832	24,023	53,910	7,748	9,568	3,205	481	173,787	62,807	44,338
Armstrong County	9,246	5,038	1,212	2,795	268	845	242	na	na	na	na
Beaver County	23,418	12,155	3,695	7,175	525	923	469	0	28,421	8,756	5,549
Berks County	43,204	23,949	6,133	12,425	2,996	4,210	1,170	270	58,219	19,519	11,955
Blair County	16,090	8,217	1,992	5,242	1,328	na	na	0	na	na	na
Bucks County	69,401	40,341	8,805	18,530	3,138	9,124	1,874	171	105,953	27,384	17,775
Butler County	22,151	11,921	2,857	7,089	1,302	1,983	804	0	32,610	8,708	6,983
Cambria County	19,834	10,904	2,513	6,056	1,029	867	480	0	23,346	9,102	3,995
Carbon County	8,006	na	na	na	na	na	na	na	na	na	na
Centre County	13,802	7,722	1,808	3,931	930	na	na	na	na	na	na
Chester County	51,086	30,822	6,162	12,974	2,494	4,468	800	0	79,650	17,009	13,587
Clearfield County	10,186	5,221	1,489	3,281	668	na	na	na	na	na	na
Columbia County	7,962	3,546	1,474	2,844	597	na	na	na	na	na	na
Crawford County	11,241	6,513	1,839	2,523	160	1,257	706	55	na	na	na
Cumberland County	29,114	15,634	3,013	9,404	1,732	1,406	733	0	39,709	10,864	8,128
Dauphin County	29,930	15,301	4,167	9,423	2,309	3,743	1,200	165	36,076	13,273	10,237
Delaware County	55,867	28,372	8,268	17,813	3,855	6,272	2,081	26	70,790	26,805	17,130
Erie County	31,393	16,752	4,989	8,713	2,421	1,807	454	97	38,128	13,649	8,752
Fayette County	17,735	9,480	2,781	5,160	879	1,239	733	na	22,891	7,786	4,916
Franklin County	18,693	11,640	1,760	5,053	693	na	na	na	na	na	na
Indiana County	10,360	6,332	1,356	2,567	206	742	315	na	na	na	na
Lackawanna County	26,916	13,671	4,165	8,339	2,064	1,187	588	66	32,661	11,329	8,743
Lancaster County	57,454	34,906	6,077	15,204	4,510	3,939	732	99	84,704	22,435	14,608
Lawrence County	11,822	6,686	1,616	3,264	684	1,096	635	139	na	na	na
Lebanon County	17,563	10,079	2,029	5,162	1,160	1,100	341	na	na	na	na
Lehigh County	36,901	19,779	4,586	11,136	3,118	3,010	732	97	49,219	17,176	10,800
Luzerne County	39,885	19,404	5,232	13,898	3,083	3,043	1,120	25	46,169	18,579	11,120
Lycoming County	13,364	7,392	1,526	4,050	946	593	194	0	na	na	na
Mercer County	15,513	7,256	2,055	5,617	1,308	516	185	na	na	na	na
Monroe County	15,553	9,089	2,160	3,655	510	na	na	na	na	na	na
Montgomery County	87,931	48,789	10,854	26,713	6,646	9,642	1,745	142	124,616	36,123	24,688
Northampton County	35,162	19,352	4,476	10,255	1,896	2,686	779	0	44,860	16,266	9,244
Northumberland County	12,466	6,360	2,146	3,678	1,020	na	na	na	na	na	na
Philadelphia County	144,301	63,511	24,301	52,520	7,629	19,422	4,386	1,730	121,314	66,424	54,956
Schuylkill County	18,720	9,587	3,017	5,361	1,532	1,152	784	na	20,913	9,617	4,743
Somerset County	9,473	5,273	1,426	2,484	923	na	na	na	na	na	na
Washington County	26,622	14,123	4,052	7,869	1,151	1,259	468	na	34,337	10,607	8,077
Westmoreland County	50,820	27,478	6,311	16,068	2,069	2,646	689	90	66,832	19,592	14,327
York County	47,981	25,869	7,107	13,805	2,406	4,974	2,348	55	66,092	21,461	16,278
Rhode Island											
Kent County	20,449	9,190	2,921	7,937	1,074	1,981	711	na	na	na	na
Newport County	12,166	6,475	1,417	3,717	657	na	na	na	na	na	na
Providence County	60,005	27,426	10,607	20,512	5,435	6,351	1,711	209	61,427	29,233	24,104
Washington County	15,603	9,896	1,846	3,398	1,185	na	na	na	na	na	na

Table D-2: Counties - Household Relationship, Grandparents, and Marital Status—*Continued*

| | Total Householders 65 Years and Over | Family Householders 65 Years and Over | Non-Family Householders 65 Years and Over | | Persons 65 Years and Over Living in Group Quarters | Grandparents 60 Years and Over Living with Grandchildren | | | Marital Status - Persons 60 Years and Over | | |
			Male Living Alone	Female Living Alone		Total	Responsible for Grandchildren	Responsible for Grandchildren and In Poverty	Now Married	Widowed	Divorced
South Carolina											
Aiken County	20,602	11,496	2,840	5,892	772	1,352	635	0	na	na	na
Anderson County	23,011	11,980	3,758	6,831	968	2,086	613	201	na	na	na
Beaufort County	29,332	19,888	2,875	5,678	502	na	na	na	na	na	na
Berkeley County	17,710	10,579	2,226	4,606	450	3,710	720	302	24,532	8,177	7,302
Charleston County	42,527	23,625	6,200	11,639	978	4,813	3,082	1,471	50,139	16,424	14,936
Darlington County	8,433	4,140	1,232	2,926	397	na	na	na	na	na	na
Dorchester County	12,874	8,006	1,664	2,950	223	1,926	809	na	na	na	na
Florence County	13,974	8,414	1,496	3,863	757	1,786	477	na	na	na	na
Greenville County	49,062	29,078	5,393	13,528	1,388	5,756	2,370	318	67,588	21,764	16,198
Greenwood County	8,028	4,791	451	2,554	547	996	384	na	na	na	na
Horry County	48,521	28,245	7,128	11,222	620	4,546	1,454	401	66,937	20,608	15,869
Kershaw County	7,450	4,320	1,043	1,634	208	na	na	na	na	na	na
Lancaster County	11,175	6,380	1,501	2,680	394	na	na	122	na	na	na
Laurens County	7,397	na	na	na	na	na	na	na	na	na	na
Lexington County	30,215	16,565	3,844	8,981	1,014	4,544	2,097	219	38,904	12,228	12,211
Oconee County	11,515	na	na	na	na	na	na	na	na	na	na
Orangeburg County	11,251	5,680	1,159	3,922	533	na	na	na	na	na	na
Pickens County	13,758	7,138	2,138	4,333	294	na	na	na	na	na	na
Richland County	33,419	18,298	4,170	10,407	1,324	4,423	969	30	38,308	16,726	12,441
Spartanburg County	30,293	18,656	3,135	7,882	964	3,597	1,271	261	41,146	13,211	10,434
Sumter County	10,897	6,482	1,372	2,952	625	1,547	316	190	na	na	na
York County	22,448	12,415	3,512	5,713	640	3,286	1,214	127	31,398	12,323	7,533
South Dakota											
Minnehaha County	16,459	7,981	2,181	5,756	726	na	na	na	20,271	6,972	6,309
Pennington County	13,001	7,122	978	3,706	929	1,075	657	na	na	na	na
Tennessee											
Anderson County	8,995	5,386	1,535	1,952	524	na	na	na	na	na	na
Blount County	15,806	10,518	1,262	3,559	385	1,641	572	na	na	na	na
Bradley County	11,158	6,132	1,142	3,473	547	1,783	705	na	na	na	na
Davidson County	55,686	27,646	8,552	17,344	1,537	5,952	2,190	636	60,584	20,961	23,319
Greene County	8,422	5,503	1,013	1,765	599	na	na	na	na	na	na
Hamilton County	38,869	21,944	4,851	11,520	2,221	4,533	1,292	75	51,154	17,949	13,588
Knox County	46,281	25,763	5,907	13,140	1,734	3,814	1,751	477	58,483	19,477	15,576
Madison County	10,420	5,652	1,710	2,975	456	1,083	516	na	na	na	na
Maury County	9,199	4,991	1,264	2,537	528	1,345	331	na	na	na	na
Montgomery County	11,008	6,446	1,817	2,560	500	2,052	210	na	na	na	na
Putnam County	7,759	4,628	1,070	2,023	390	na	na	na	na	na	na
Robertson County	5,876	3,655	541	1,323	185	1,439	820	na	na	na	na
Rutherford County	19,666	11,622	2,148	5,554	623	2,981	960	273	na	na	na
Sevier County	11,040	7,696	1,144	1,802	270	na	na	na	na	na	na
Shelby County	81,716	42,381	12,249	25,791	3,108	10,599	4,425	652	101,032	31,857	32,278
Sullivan County	23,310	11,652	3,213	7,462	647	1,965	664	264	na	na	na
Sumner County	18,119	10,552	1,534	5,405	537	1,910	784	0	na	na	na
Washington County	14,279	7,873	2,205	3,998	1,123	1,603	1,275	na	na	na	na
Williamson County	17,284	11,815	1,460	3,924	367	na	na	na	na	na	na
Wilson County	13,424	8,626	1,627	3,018	532	1,218	291	na	na	na	na
Texas											
Angelina County	7,583	3,887	1,298	2,060	1,156	na	na	na	na	na	na
Bastrop County	6,748	4,525	487	1,400	554	na	na	na	na	na	na
Bell County	23,244	14,164	2,445	6,103	1,267	2,696	1,253	173	31,395	10,970	7,144
Bexar County	137,915	81,365	17,977	35,170	5,461	28,084	6,638	1,352	178,932	64,910	63,658
Bowie County	9,487	4,614	1,314	3,455	944	na	na	na	na	na	na
Brazoria County	24,397	14,435	3,633	5,894	1,464	6,437	1,589	17	36,941	11,181	9,840
Brazos County	13,213	7,876	1,434	3,695	388	na	na	na	na	na	na
Cameron County	33,403	21,900	3,753	7,012	928	9,199	1,266	298	43,747	17,807	8,567
Collin County	57,562	35,998	4,853	15,761	1,288	14,749	2,660	384	101,115	26,723	20,750
Comal County	14,429	9,987	1,262	2,844	328	1,543	626	na	na	na	na
Coryell County	4,773	2,553	469	1,631	492	na	na	na	na	na	na
Dallas County	166,769	93,107	22,144	46,867	6,247	35,036	9,333	1,433	225,598	75,658	73,762
Denton County	46,502	28,566	4,854	12,246	1,556	9,107	2,155	25	80,887	20,998	18,799
Ector County	9,917	5,249	946	3,572	482	940	418	na	na	na	na
Ellis County	13,075	8,263	1,927	2,730	503	1,943	554	55	na	na	na
El Paso County	61,672	35,742	8,588	16,019	1,844	14,655	4,843	993	77,690	29,669	23,433
Fort Bend County	43,524	29,230	4,003	9,032	1,004	13,173	1,987	233	87,074	18,659	15,015
Galveston County	30,752	16,126	5,226	8,428	1,519	3,670	822	na	37,740	12,272	13,112
Grayson County	14,802	9,080	1,818	3,771	748	1,483	872	213	na	na	na
Gregg County	11,452	6,490	1,337	3,382	1,233	1,058	254	na	na	na	na
Guadalupe County	12,067	7,647	1,492	2,805	526	2,010	1,255	na	na	na	na
Harris County	285,358	170,463	36,325	71,564	7,881	70,651	17,163	2,853	409,046	129,738	119,329
Harrison County	6,821	na	na	na	na	na	na	na	na	na	na
Hays County	13,714	8,952	967	3,341	268	2,603	484	na	na	na	na
Henderson County	10,841	6,325	1,306	2,970	382	915	790	na	na	na	na
Hidalgo County	56,271	36,294	5,568	13,461	1,782	14,414	3,298	1,580	74,825	32,018	14,656
Hunt County	9,007	4,936	1,493	2,446	440	na	na	na	na	na	na
Jefferson County	21,966	11,210	3,202	7,151	1,109	2,860	1,162	307	28,184	9,817	8,872

Table D-2: Counties - Household Relationship, Grandparents, and Marital Status—*Continued*

	Total Householders 65 Years and Over	Family Householders 65 Years and Over	Non-Family Householders 65 Years and Over		Persons 65 Years and Over Living in Group Quarters	Grandparents 60 Years and Over Living with Grandchildren			Marital Status - Persons 60 Years and Over		
			Male Living Alone	Female Living Alone		Total	Responsible for Grandchildren	Responsible for Grandchildren and In Poverty	Now Married	Widowed	Divorced
Texas—Cont.											
Johnson County	13,050	8,447	1,159	3,240	714	3,764	1,403	46	na	na	na
Kaufman County	8,730	5,444	1,127	1,841	567	2,612	715	0	na	na	na
Liberty County	7,206	3,693	882	2,385	261	na	na	na	na	na	na
Lubbock County	23,330	13,579	1,980	6,791	989	3,175	1,862	34	30,085	10,088	10,601
McLennan County	22,514	13,054	2,357	6,568	1,155	2,444	880	52	31,001	9,262	7,081
Midland County	12,129	5,620	1,879	4,333	277	2,374	951	0	na	na	na
Montgomery County	45,322	25,817	4,703	12,406	1,386	8,299	1,303	345	65,363	19,563	19,518
Nacogdoches County	6,068	na	na	na	na	na	na	na	na	na	na
Nueces County	31,260	18,041	4,218	7,848	1,733	5,614	2,472	484	40,918	15,183	13,370
Orange County	8,095	5,118	743	2,095	205	na	na	na	na	na	na
Parker County	11,869	7,080	1,634	2,947	649	na	na	na	na	na	na
Potter County	9,383	4,037	1,882	3,411	1,013	1,226	543	258	na	na	na
Randall County	12,575	7,506	1,608	3,389	181	na	na	na	na	na	na
Rockwall County	6,727	4,628	189	1,800	447	na	na	na	na	na	na
San Patricio County	5,873	3,541	666	1,615	221	1,571	162	na	na	na	na
Smith County	22,791	14,087	1,883	6,364	875	2,903	795	166	na	na	na
Tarrant County	141,809	83,661	16,647	38,290	5,326	27,797	7,953	1,228	198,529	60,911	60,220
Taylor County	11,722	6,615	1,260	3,701	697	1,219	497	na	na	na	na
Tom Green County	11,584	6,510	1,322	3,248	338	1,262	545	na	na	na	na
Travis County	73,603	42,361	11,131	18,222	2,589	10,187	2,288	598	103,489	26,668	32,572
Victoria County	9,159	4,915	1,058	2,995	545	na	na	na	na	na	na
Walker County	5,524	na	na	na	na	na	na	na	na	na	na
Webb County	15,185	8,711	1,459	4,377	351	5,620	742	259	17,415	7,919	4,787
Wichita County	12,421	6,859	1,354	3,870	1,299	1,252	872	0	na	na	na
Williamson County	35,790	21,401	4,704	8,879	894	8,217	1,169	66	60,402	15,025	14,697
Wise County	5,198	3,405	762	1,010	232	na	na	na	na	na	na
Utah											
Cache County	7,056	4,111	970	1,937	213	na	na	na	na	na	na
Davis County	20,403	14,837	1,147	4,155	381	5,741	570	0	na	na	na
Salt Lake County	76,120	46,031	8,553	20,119	2,203	14,376	2,700	493	110,164	27,009	29,218
Tooele County	3,537	na	na	na	na	na	na	na	na	na	na
Utah County	28,053	19,722	2,793	5,178	864	7,987	1,280	214	48,240	10,176	5,670
Washington County	22,266	14,899	2,394	4,376	194	na	na	na	na	na	na
Weber County	18,545	11,725	1,810	4,578	449	2,274	684	na	27,019	6,341	6,779
Vermont											
Chittenden County	16,604	8,771	2,187	4,795	759	na	na	na	na	na	na
Virginia											
Albemarle County	12,912	7,254	1,395	3,672	436	na	na	na	na	na	na
Arlington County	16,853	7,610	2,852	5,713	519	na	na	na	17,541	5,931	5,982
Augusta County	10,715	5,994	1,211	2,823	419	na	na	na	na	na	na
Bedford County	9,191	na	na	na	na	na	na	na	na	na	na
Chesterfield County	31,844	19,054	3,511	8,259	758	4,641	2,379	471	48,647	12,164	9,284
Fairfax County	85,588	52,368	9,286	21,590	1,613	15,542	1,659	426	140,826	32,276	26,419
Fauquier County	6,873	3,962	544	2,087	212	na	na	na	na	na	na
Frederick County	8,763	5,341	1,272	2,047	126	1,643	468	na	na	na	na
Hanover County	10,935	7,068	1,020	2,816	257	na	na	na	na	na	na
Henrico County	32,004	15,458	3,796	11,756	1,240	5,403	1,447	76	37,132	14,565	13,844
James City County	11,180	7,266	996	2,548	183	na	na	na	na	na	na
Loudoun County	19,719	11,801	2,136	5,210	486	6,766	1,210	197	36,311	9,803	6,767
Montgomery County	7,323	3,941	906	2,387	286	na	na	na	na	na	na
Prince William County	23,805	14,581	2,703	5,907	536	8,978	1,231	0	42,741	10,756	8,922
Roanoke County	12,225	6,717	1,456	3,588	435	na	na	na	na	na	na
Rockingham County	9,382	5,357	1,282	2,576	187	na	na	na	na	na	na
Spotsylvania County	10,491	7,440	750	2,222	247	2,608	542	na	na	na	na
Stafford County	7,863	5,276	811	1,427	214	2,882	873	na	na	na	na
York County	6,668	3,059	1,084	2,405	113	na	na	na	na	na	na
Washington											
Benton County	18,215	10,328	2,951	4,264	351	na	na	na	na	na	na
Chelan County	8,663	4,591	1,374	2,173	348	na	na	na	na	na	na
Clallam County	14,164	7,602	2,646	3,270	409	na	na	na	na	na	na
Clark County	45,341	26,016	5,034	13,260	1,393	4,653	1,560	343	65,310	16,087	17,499
Cowlitz County	13,407	7,871	1,459	3,759	563	2,299	1,706	na	na	na	na
Franklin County	4,766	3,042	539	1,089	217	na	na	na	na	na	na
Grant County	7,992	4,379	1,055	1,748	283	na	na	na	na	na	na
Grays Harbor County	8,920	5,067	1,661	1,930	386	na	na	na	na	na	na
Island County	12,750	7,351	1,692	3,168	154	na	na	na	na	na	na
King County	180,631	92,275	25,627	55,483	9,391	23,238	4,811	139	241,295	58,789	71,348
Kitsap County	30,033	16,523	4,505	7,665	1,015	2,341	504	na	41,524	10,495	11,467
Lewis County	10,886	5,599	1,918	3,253	295	1,161	486	na	na	na	na
Mason County	8,846	4,641	1,474	2,160	304	na	na	na	na	na	na
Pierce County	75,373	41,989	9,859	21,573	3,198	9,137	3,361	189	103,070	26,896	33,323
Skagit County	15,788	9,419	1,864	3,936	386	1,026	234	137	na	na	na
Snohomish County	65,481	37,287	8,912	16,692	2,888	10,425	1,925	115	95,356	26,284	27,704
Spokane County	52,471	26,597	7,770	16,614	2,303	5,103	2,097	321	63,238	20,871	21,250

Table D-2: Counties - Household Relationship, Grandparents, and Marital Status—*Continued*

	Total Householders 65 Years and Over	Family Householders 65 Years and Over	Non-Family Householders 65 Years and Over		Persons 65 Years and Over Living in Group Quarters	Grandparents 60 Years and Over Living with Grandchildren			Marital Status - Persons 60 Years and Over		
			Male Living Alone	Female Living Alone		Total	Responsible for Grandchildren	Responsible for Grandchildren and In Poverty	Now Married	Widowed	Divorced
Washington—Cont.											
Thurston County	29,900	16,511	3,436	8,918	1,133	2,511	838	0	41,680	10,727	11,881
Whatcom County	24,312	13,653	3,796	5,342	850	1,664	664	69	na	na	na
Yakima County	21,499	12,469	2,933	5,636	709	3,197	871	424	27,935	8,984	7,384
West Virginia											
Berkeley County	11,073	6,070	1,744	2,875	63	na	na	na	na	na	na
Cabell County	10,637	5,572	1,758	3,108	526	na	na	na	na	na	na
Harrison County	8,381	3,838	1,396	2,968	600	na	na	na	na	na	na
Kanawha County	24,807	12,744	4,059	7,639	708	1,704	853	96	28,651	11,269	7,782
Monongalia County	8,232	4,645	1,167	2,223	414	na	na	na	na	na	na
Raleigh County	10,449	na	na	na	na	na	na	na	na	na	na
Wood County	11,237	5,392	1,508	3,977	405	na	na	na	na	na	na
Wisconsin											
Brown County	24,964	12,621	3,793	8,025	880	1,036	325	0	33,554	9,035	8,124
Dane County	47,609	25,054	5,613	14,457	1,074	3,753	1,653	na	65,962	13,356	15,130
Dodge County	9,515	5,400	1,136	2,638	813	na	na	na	na	na	na
Eau Claire County	10,408	5,522	1,350	3,274	375	na	na	na	na	na	na
Fond du Lac County	11,716	6,614	1,233	3,518	593	na	na	na	na	na	na
Jefferson County	9,124	5,668	1,005	2,268	358	na	na	na	na	na	na
Kenosha County	14,984	7,893	2,013	4,920	763	1,729	894	na	na	na	na
La Crosse County	12,015	6,236	1,831	3,636	949	na	na	na	na	na	na
Manitowoc County	10,386	5,471	1,391	3,436	758	na	na	na	na	na	na
Marathon County	15,425	8,039	2,096	4,927	841	812	82	na	na	na	na
Milwaukee County	84,663	38,553	15,778	28,414	4,375	9,576	3,712	700	87,477	34,228	33,612
Outagamie County	17,486	9,990	2,189	4,968	812	na	na	na	na	na	na
Ozaukee County	11,685	6,347	888	4,201	301	na	na	na	na	na	na
Portage County	7,783	3,593	1,519	2,398	182	na	na	na	na	na	na
Racine County	20,635	10,598	3,478	6,303	1,628	1,399	392	64	na	na	na
Rock County	17,695	9,271	2,150	5,669	840	na	na	na	na	na	na
St. Croix County	7,760	4,476	805	2,274	501	128	21	na	na	na	na
Sheboygan County	13,487	6,753	2,122	4,329	518	na	na	na	na	na	na
Walworth County	11,193	6,011	1,506	3,409	476	691	297	na	na	na	na
Washington County	14,198	8,892	1,326	3,671	711	na	na	na	na	na	na
Waukesha County	46,371	26,521	5,015	13,889	1,177	2,786	516	na	69,623	18,879	12,027
Winnebago County	18,183	8,483	2,930	6,298	1,071	na	na	na	na	na	na
Wood County	9,953	5,107	1,379	3,258	584	na	na	na	na	na	na
Wyoming											
Laramie County	11,096	5,740	1,866	3,244	324	na	na	na	na	na	na
Natrona County	7,880	na	na	na	na	562	na	na	na	na	na

Table D-3: Cities - Household Relationship, Grandparents, and Marital Status

	Total Householders 65 Years and Over	Family Householders 65 Years and Over	Non-Family Householders 65 Years and Over		Persons 65 Years and Over Living in Group Quarters	Grandparents 60 Years and Over Living with Grandchildren			Marital Status - Persons 60 Years and Over		
			Male Living Alone	Female Living Alone		Total	Responsible for Grandchildren	Responsible for Grandchildren and In Poverty	Now Married	Widowed	Divorced
Alabama											
Auburn city	3,078	na	na	na	na	na	na	na	na	na	na
Birmingham city	22,749	10,719	3,306	7,631	887	2,077	973	427	18,166	9,443	11,336
Dothan city	8,443	4,532	1,244	2,632	370	896	618	55	9,917	3,630	2,809
Hoover city	8,841	6,079	268	2,459	189	na	na	na	na	na	na
Huntsville city	21,385	12,008	2,612	6,497	536	1,906	969	350	24,165	7,512	6,851
Mobile city	21,750	10,281	3,851	7,265	904	1,173	549	106	19,671	10,568	9,420
Montgomery city	18,587	9,562	2,873	5,689	1,015	3,028	1,356	478	18,246	7,605	8,765
Tuscaloosa city	7,840	4,346	1,353	2,141	98	na	na	na	na	na	na
Alaska											
Anchorage municipality	19,776	11,293	2,391	4,783	1,431	3,088	721	190	28,529	6,994	8,657
Arizona											
Avondale city	4,308	2,508	750	691	153	1,473	241	112	na	na	na
Buckeye city	5,705	na	na	na	na	na	na	na	na	na	na
Chandler city	16,709	10,047	1,525	4,621	522	3,700	683	0	25,692	6,222	7,968
Flagstaff city	4,178	na	na	na	na	na	na	na	na	na	na
Glendale city	18,642	9,547	2,879	5,551	1,021	4,197	1,173	162	23,237	8,548	10,755
Goodyear city	7,258	5,774	266	926	88	na	na	na	na	na	na
Mesa city	48,772	27,777	5,913	13,185	1,954	6,406	1,546	0	67,308	18,061	16,877
Peoria city	18,656	10,178	1,971	5,780	782	2,048	534	na	na	na	na
Phoenix city	107,117	54,707	19,075	29,989	3,853	22,514	6,084	1,152	128,755	47,086	55,687
Scottsdale city	36,272	19,453	3,787	11,725	882	na	na	na	47,205	11,259	12,488
Surprise city	18,125	11,339	1,951	4,220	201	1,830	420	na	na	na	na
Tempe city	13,034	6,937	2,069	3,166	275	1,331	365	na	na	na	na
Tucson city	52,276	25,119	8,376	16,826	1,959	6,061	2,050	679	50,275	23,014	24,819
Yuma city	9,186	5,829	746	1,998	248	na	na	na	na	na	na
Arkansas											
Conway city	4,447	na	na	na	na	na	na	na	na	na	na
Fayetteville city	4,201	na	na	na	na	na	na	na	na	na	na
Fort Smith city	8,043	na	na	na	na	na	na	na	na	na	na
Jonesboro city	5,818	na	na	na	na	na	na	na	na	na	na
Little Rock city	17,594	8,445	2,519	6,263	1,892	2,176	779	na	na	na	na
North Little Rock city	7,135	3,606	771	2,377	572	na	na	na	na	na	na
Rogers city	4,044	2,600	408	983	372	na	na	na	na	na	na
Springdale city	4,978	na	na	na	na	na	na	na	na	na	na
California											
Alameda city	8,447	3,714	1,076	3,311	579	na	na	na	na	na	na
Alhambra city	7,285	4,606	622	1,808	514	na	na	na	na	na	na
Anaheim city	20,945	11,515	2,286	6,466	2,406	6,468	655	0	31,406	11,274	8,933
Antioch city	6,874	4,152	811	1,606	418	2,501	678	110	na	na	na
Bakersfield city	22,204	13,010	2,532	6,155	1,935	5,143	1,026	300	33,889	11,753	8,457
Baldwin Park city	3,214	2,386	298	491	281	1,651	461	na	na	na	na
Bellflower city	3,817	1,896	544	1,239	263	na	na	na	na	na	na
Berkeley city	11,462	5,068	2,243	3,297	292	na	na	na	na	na	na
Buena Park city	4,904	3,236	367	836	569	na	na	na	na	na	na
Burbank city	10,096	3,641	2,213	4,163	399	na	na	na	na	na	na
Camarillo city	9,179	na	na	na	na	na	na	na	na	na	na
Carlsbad city	13,084	8,520	1,258	2,918	326	na	na	na	na	na	na
Carson city	6,971	4,745	266	1,873	99	3,153	418	0	na	na	na
Chico city	8,570	3,527	1,180	3,553	419	na	na	na	na	na	na
Chino city	5,716	3,564	696	1,089	697	na	na	na	na	na	na
Chino Hills city	3,550	2,227	140	1,138	0	na	na	na	na	na	na
Chula Vista city	14,910	9,027	1,653	3,604	915	6,680	880	na	24,024	8,438	8,072
Citrus Heights city	9,539	4,077	1,178	3,988	308	na	na	na	na	na	na
Clovis city	9,531	4,962	1,498	2,790	265	na	na	na	na	na	na
Compton city	4,758	2,724	417	1,513	106	2,641	802	499	na	na	na
Concord city	11,688	5,379	1,564	4,190	562	na	na	na	na	na	na
Corona city	7,160	4,612	749	1,509	279	3,306	353	na	na	na	na
Costa Mesa city	8,335	3,717	1,685	2,421	760	na	na	na	na	na	na
Daly City city	8,444	5,189	1,112	2,012	567	na	na	na	na	na	na
Davis city	4,645	2,633	796	1,035	110	na	na	na	na	na	na
Downey city	7,277	5,156	667	1,180	372	na	na	na	na	na	na
El Cajon city	5,999	3,249	864	1,403	1,140	na	na	na	na	na	na
Elk Grove city	12,035	7,617	781	3,184	410	4,154	435	0	na	na	na
El Monte city	6,620	4,375	624	1,484	580	3,807	396	0	na	na	na
Escondido city	12,019	6,392	1,389	3,851	876	1,596	244	0	na	na	na
Fairfield city	8,335	5,090	925	2,097	371	na	na	na	na	na	na
Folsom city	5,660	3,406	406	1,808	335	na	na	na	na	na	na
Fontana city	7,231	4,840	550	1,723	74	6,432	1,270	282	na	na	na
Fremont city	13,788	9,312	1,488	2,524	788	na	na	na	na	na	na
Fresno city	36,313	18,320	4,983	12,092	2,122	7,270	936	146	44,284	17,280	13,214
Fullerton city	10,226	5,597	965	2,822	1,046	1,557	459	na	na	na	na
Garden Grove city	9,679	6,315	821	1,987	948	5,636	1,039	222	16,871	7,975	4,352
Glendale city	18,215	9,636	2,105	6,035	1,286	na	na	na	na	na	na
Hawthorne city	4,888	2,737	753	1,339	304	1,992	175	na	na	na	na
Hayward city	10,293	6,158	775	2,878	964	4,815	1,805	na	14,398	5,549	4,789

Table D-3: Cities - Household Relationship, Grandparents, and Marital Status—*Continued*

	Total Householders 65 Years and Over	Family Householders 65 Years and Over	Non-Family Householders 65 Years and Over		Persons 65 Years and Over Living in Group Quarters	Grandparents 60 Years and Over Living with Grandchildren			Marital Status - Persons 60 Years and Over		
			Male Living Alone	Female Living Alone		Total	Responsible for Grandchildren	Responsible for Grandchildren and In Poverty	Now Married	Widowed	Divorced
California—Cont.											
Hemet city	12,375	6,345	2,280	3,103	459	na	na	na	na	na	na
Hesperia city	6,818	4,616	798	1,298	0	1,876	601	196	na	na	na
Huntington Beach city	20,467	11,172	3,293	5,407	613	na	na	na	23,733	6,938	9,067
Indio city	12,417	na	na	na	na	na	na	na	na	na	na
Inglewood city	7,918	3,699	1,662	2,316	758	1,965	275	na	na	na	na
Irvine city	17,345	9,588	2,126	4,466	232	na	na	na	na	na	na
Jurupa Valley city	5,476	3,528	378	1,467	483	2,463	423	na	na	na	na
Laguna Niguel city	6,905	3,849	1,044	1,922	161	na	na	na	na	na	na
Lake Elsinore city	2,749	1,869	300	544	0	na	na	na	na	na	na
Lake Forest city	7,709	4,766	622	2,050	154	na	na	na	na	na	na
Lakewood city	5,200	3,170	670	1,206	15	na	na	na	na	na	na
Lancaster city	8,875	5,140	1,144	2,258	603	2,387	513	175	na	na	na
Livermore city	7,192	4,200	934	1,865	234	na	na	na	na	na	na
Lodi City	6,230	3,160	720	2,196	429	na	na	na	na	na	na
Long Beach city	31,067	16,132	4,803	8,431	2,076	5,759	1,285	264	40,585	13,540	14,310
Los Angeles city	288,751	148,104	44,256	82,049	16,589	61,482	9,925	1,373	350,863	127,745	110,627
Lynwood city	2,608	1,991	403	214	478	na	na	na	na	na	na
Madera city	2,850	1,171	438	1,201	111	na	na	na	na	na	na
Manteca city	7,040	4,663	490	1,672	192	na	na	na	na	na	na
Menifee city	9,799	5,479	1,103	2,436	71	na	na	na	na	na	na
Merced city	6,613	3,180	504	2,608	154	na	na	na	na	na	na
Milpitas city	4,392	2,917	457	646	44	na	na	na	na	na	na
Mission Viejo city	10,393	6,688	582	2,865	1,221	na	na	na	na	na	na
Modesto city	15,223	9,153	1,379	4,268	837	2,721	880	211	19,830	7,423	7,487
Moreno Valley city	6,958	5,350	520	1,021	183	5,087	228	0	14,885	3,955	4,097
Mountain View city	5,756	na	na	na	na	na	na	na	na	na	na
Murrieta city	7,282	4,319	863	1,699	89	na	na	na	na	na	na
Napa city	8,742	3,930	1,227	3,198	314	na	na	na	na	na	na
Newport Beach city	11,992	6,014	1,426	3,848	262	na	na	na	na	na	na
Norwalk city	6,801	4,505	448	1,442	879	2,967	330	na	na	na	na
Oakland city	37,316	16,420	5,923	13,070	1,699	5,171	1,691	277	33,687	14,808	15,617
Oceanside city	18,880	10,322	1,749	5,855	170	2,891	340	98	na	na	na
Ontario city	8,310	5,563	354	2,095	340	3,319	244	na	na	na	na
Orange city	9,020	5,065	1,277	2,478	583	na	na	na	na	na	na
Oxnard city	9,102	6,724	778	1,446	632	4,200	1,023	0	na	na	na
Palmdale city	8,879	5,323	934	2,370	38	4,206	699	na	na	na	na
Palo Alto city	7,856	3,915	699	2,888	336	na	na	na	na	na	na
Pasadena city	14,655	7,274	2,154	4,746	1,394	na	na	na	na	na	na
Perris city	1,811	na	na	na	na	na	na	na	na	na	na
Pittsburg city	3,108	1,920	168	984	245	na	na	na	na	na	na
Pleasanton city	7,142	3,719	836	2,445	219	na	na	na	na	na	na
Pomona city	8,556	5,442	622	2,204	1,076	4,041	624	100	na	na	na
Rancho Cordova city	7,093	4,278	663	1,813	91	na	na	na	na	na	na
Rancho Cucamonga city	10,869	7,245	966	2,172	159	3,735	364	na	na	na	na
Redding city	10,065	5,537	1,049	3,148	888	na	na	na	na	na	na
Redlands city	7,484	4,496	617	2,204	609	na	na	na	na	na	na
Redondo Beach city	5,749	na	na	na	na	na	na	na	na	na	na
Redwood City city	7,272	3,689	1,081	2,216	263	na	na	na	na	na	na
Rialto city	5,957	3,887	453	1,403	143	2,942	737	na	na	na	na
Richmond city	8,175	5,105	707	2,175	374	na	na	na	na	na	na
Riverside city	17,387	10,719	1,607	3,949	1,217	6,776	624	124	26,633	10,270	7,738
Rocklin city	5,072	2,471	450	1,847	70	na	na	na	na	na	na
Roseville city	14,164	7,021	1,862	4,793	578	na	na	na	na	na	na
Sacramento city	40,628	19,771	5,769	13,934	1,841	7,849	1,348	38	44,472	18,202	18,348
Salinas city	8,116	4,949	1,022	2,069	666	3,332	148	0	na	na	na
San Bernardino city	10,266	5,185	1,285	3,384	1,109	3,485	1,334	263	13,525	6,449	4,896
San Buenaventura (Ventura) city	12,031	6,446	1,538	3,730	371	na	na	na	na	na	na
San Clemente city	6,396	3,713	863	1,636	285	na	na	na	na	na	na
San Diego city	110,754	63,109	15,649	27,528	3,148	15,667	3,204	385	142,701	42,860	46,488
San Francisco city	83,021	40,851	14,878	24,100	3,737	10,780	1,297	52	95,133	31,224	25,272
San Jose city	68,180	42,819	6,393	16,540	2,995	21,764	3,186	221	108,963	32,637	23,505
San Leandro city	7,415	3,846	612	2,660	310	2,070	300	na	na	na	na
San Marcos city	6,903	3,004	1,500	2,055	85	na	na	na	na	na	na
San Mateo city	10,492	5,402	1,675	3,106	609	na	na	na	na	na	na
San Ramon city	4,157	2,158	384	1,533	14	na	na	na	na	na	na
Santa Ana city	14,538	10,069	1,147	3,062	1,281	9,138	2,272	494	25,032	9,271	4,965
Santa Barbara city	10,865	5,975	1,471	3,093	456	na	na	na	na	na	na
Santa Clara city	8,261	5,081	1,001	1,727	463	na	na	na	na	na	na
Santa Clarita city	16,083	8,877	1,746	4,578	209	na	na	na	na	na	na
Santa Cruz city	5,094	2,799	772	1,068	6	na	na	na	na	na	na
Santa Maria city	5,010	3,228	516	996	333	2,079	425	na	na	na	na
Santa Monica city	11,136	3,516	2,767	4,412	635	na	na	na	na	na	na
Santa Rosa city	20,307	9,222	2,441	7,126	881	na	na	na	na	na	na
Simi Valley city	13,520	6,807	1,395	4,716	405	na	na	na	na	na	na
South Gate city	4,131	3,034	233	804	0	na	na	na	na	na	na

Table D-3: Cities - Household Relationship, Grandparents, and Marital Status—*Continued*

	Total Householders 65 Years and Over	Family Householders 65 Years and Over	Non-Family Householders 65 Years and Over		Persons 65 Years and Over Living in Group Quarters	Grandparents 60 Years and Over Living with Grandchildren			Marital Status - Persons 60 Years and Over		
			Male Living Alone	Female Living Alone		Total	Responsible for Grandchildren	Responsible for Grandchildren and In Poverty	Now Married	Widowed	Divorced
California—Cont.											
South San Francisco city	6,432	4,035	993	1,331	332	na	na	na	na	na	na
Stockton city	19,714	11,240	2,146	5,291	1,746	5,472	752	277	24,457	12,483	8,658
Sunnyvale city	9,604	5,529	827	2,454	600	na	na	na	na	na	na
Temecula city	6,337	3,937	437	1,591	11	na	na	na	na	na	na
Thousand Oaks city	13,526	8,542	1,207	3,232	485	na	na	na	na	na	na
Torrance city	15,257	8,347	2,327	4,410	719	na	na	na	na	na	na
Tracy city	4,163	2,768	336	904	131	na	na	na	na	na	na
Turlock city	5,417	3,141	412	1,770	333	na	na	na	na	na	na
Tustin city	4,036	2,378	350	1,190	269	3,133	170	na	na	na	na
Union City city	5,253	3,899	447	565	320	na	na	na	na	na	na
Upland city	6,867	4,148	870	1,624	318	na	na	na	na	na	na
Vacaville city	8,159	4,936	841	2,231	808	na	na	na	na	na	na
Vallejo city	10,423	6,551	1,220	2,094	541	3,957	807	na	16,607	5,295	4,345
Victorville city	6,064	3,924	659	1,370	368	na	na	na	na	na	na
Visalia city	9,818	4,958	888	3,742	502	na	na	na	na	na	na
Vista city	5,624	2,941	922	1,229	397	787	348	36	na	na	na
Walnut Creek city	14,353	6,781	1,672	5,794	671	na	na	na	na	na	na
West Covina city	7,546	5,470	451	1,273	498	3,665	693	na	na	na	na
Westminster city	7,501	5,445	440	1,444	216	na	na	na	na	na	na
Whittier city	6,420	3,308	748	2,047	370	2,171	264	na	na	na	na
Yorba Linda city	8,002	5,383	911	1,477	278	na	na	na	na	na	na
Yuba City city	6,382	3,334	683	2,054	275	na	na	na	na	na	na
Colorado											
Arvada city	14,039	7,867	1,504	4,371	295	na	na	na	na	na	na
Aurora city	26,953	14,358	3,386	8,661	719	5,638	1,284	0	34,023	11,487	11,200
Boulder city	7,982	3,610	1,304	2,762	508	na	na	na	na	na	na
Broomfield city	5,908	na	na	na	na	na	na	na	na	na	na
Centennial city	9,508	5,844	1,155	2,299	231	na	na	na	na	na	na
Colorado Springs city	37,885	20,219	5,857	10,809	1,215	4,435	709	229	50,269	13,175	16,513
Denver city	56,532	23,374	10,468	20,443	2,443	3,536	712	207	54,851	16,262	31,666
Fort Collins city	11,496	5,772	1,233	4,016	506	na	na	na	na	na	na
Greeley city	7,087	3,621	877	2,263	201	na	na	na	na	na	na
Lakewood city	16,911	7,720	2,964	5,634	870	na	na	na	na	na	na
Longmont city	9,656	5,177	1,219	2,910	392	na	na	na	na	na	na
Loveland city	8,409	5,049	1,099	2,118	428	na	na	na	na	na	na
Pueblo city	13,875	6,697	2,483	4,304	876	1,700	1,059	na	na	na	na
Thornton city	7,800	4,013	603	3,095	329	1,399	212	na	na	na	na
Westminster city	9,916	5,607	1,558	2,699	79	na	na	na	na	na	na
Connecticut											
Bridgeport city	10,346	4,080	2,442	3,720	705	2,003	99	45	na	na	na
Danbury city	6,133	3,566	533	1,907	719	na	na	na	na	na	na
Hartford city	8,831	3,941	1,567	2,980	1,054	733	28	28	na	na	na
New Britain city	5,621	2,119	1,291	2,119	664	na	na	na	na	na	na
New Haven city	7,968	3,945	1,245	2,592	710	na	na	na	na	na	na
Norwalk city	10,872	5,529	1,224	3,655	436	na	na	na	na	na	na
Stamford city	12,629	6,468	1,286	4,574	620	na	na	na	na	na	na
Waterbury city	9,041	3,813	1,321	3,506	730	na	na	na	na	na	na
Delaware											
Wilmington city	5,866	2,023	1,146	2,423	490	na	na	na	na	na	na
District of Columbia											
Washington city	58,898	22,637	11,337	21,829	3,072	5,869	737	215	40,456	19,852	22,449
Florida											
Boca Raton city	18,122	8,710	4,169	4,481	386	na	na	na	na	na	na
Boynton Beach city	10,430	4,655	1,310	4,218	472	na	na	na	na	na	na
Cape Coral city	27,070	18,564	2,993	4,746	283	3,271	1,034	na	na	na	na
Clearwater city	17,120	6,861	3,101	6,241	1,047	na	na	na	na	na	na
Coral Springs city	8,449	5,541	638	1,708	89	na	na	na	na	na	na
Daytona Beach city	8,605	4,272	1,335	2,503	898	na	na	na	na	na	na
Deerfield Beach city	12,200	5,366	2,230	3,953	813	na	na	na	na	na	na
Delray Beach city	11,705	5,501	2,308	3,370	278	na	na	na	na	na	na
Deltona city	7,276	4,832	893	1,027	137	na	na	na	na	na	na
Fort Lauderdale city	19,813	9,847	3,576	4,529	606	na	na	na	20,713	8,937	11,315
Fort Myers city	10,903	5,149	1,971	3,561	823	na	na	na	na	na	na
Gainesville city	8,012	3,892	1,014	2,985	1,272	na	na	na	na	na	na
Hialeah city	21,708	12,597	2,898	5,232	1,417	na	na	50	27,424	14,213	12,131
Hollywood city	14,285	7,856	2,127	3,764	1,034	na	na	na	19,080	4,906	7,132
Homestead city	2,122	na	na	na	na	1,440	0	na	na	na	na
Jacksonville city	76,032	39,363	11,376	23,290	3,247	11,050	4,061	721	86,073	33,720	36,203
Kissimmee city	4,052	na	na	na	na	na	na	na	na	na	na
Lakeland city	13,155	6,050	1,907	4,790	743	na	na	na	na	na	na
Largo city	14,786	6,099	2,369	5,583	631	na	na	na	na	na	na
Lauderhill city	6,441	3,116	767	2,467	307	na	na	na	na	na	na

Table D-3: Cities - Household Relationship, Grandparents, and Marital Status—*Continued*

	Total Householders 65 Years and Over	Family Householders 65 Years and Over	Non-Family Householders 65 Years and Over		Persons 65 Years and Over Living in Group Quarters	Grandparents 60 Years and Over Living with Grandchildren			Marital Status - Persons 60 Years and Over		
			Male Living Alone	Female Living Alone		Total	Responsible for Grandchildren	Responsible for Grandchildren and In Poverty	Now Married	Widowed	Divorced
Florida—Cont.											
Melbourne city	10,170	4,513	1,684	3,907	665	na	na	na	na	na	na
Miami city	45,095	21,815	9,234	12,494	3,228	6,666	1,777	133	42,200	22,858	22,194
Miami Beach city	10,710	3,579	2,420	4,232	398	na	na	na	na	na	na
Miami Gardens city	9,742	6,902	1,053	1,703	93	3,755	1,241	162	na	na	na
Miramar city	5,109	3,540	876	491	106	3,077	849	na	na	na	na
North Port city	11,014	7,440	963	1,711	104	na	na	na	na	na	na
Orlando city	18,900	7,442	3,564	7,377	795	3,597	875	140	20,786	8,099	10,969
Palm Bay city	15,364	8,388	3,573	2,592	409	1,151	537	na	na	na	na
Palm Coast city	14,828	10,103	1,632	2,794	151	na	na	na	na	na	na
Pembroke Pines city	18,567	9,651	2,050	6,367	274	na	na	na	na	na	na
Plantation city	8,418	4,809	961	2,376	268	na	na	na	na	na	na
Pompano Beach city	13,352	6,071	2,640	4,008	430	1,524	374	na	na	na	na
Port St. Lucie city	21,897	14,782	2,118	4,376	453	5,112	2,000	na	na	na	na
St. Petersburg city	28,351	13,377	4,418	9,489	2,272	2,471	669	76	28,735	13,882	14,404
Sunrise city	11,102	5,026	1,485	4,082	624	na	na	na	na	na	na
Tallahassee city	11,880	6,391	1,509	3,793	754	na	na	na	na	na	na
Tamarac city	11,743	5,444	1,217	4,683	208	na	na	na	na	na	na
Tampa city	31,364	14,721	4,623	11,042	982	3,706	939	0	30,750	14,977	14,665
Weston city	3,280	na	na	na	na	na	na	na	na	na	na
West Palm Beach city	12,879	5,397	1,785	5,188	805	na	na	na	na	na	na
Georgia											
Albany city	6,242	2,322	1,379	2,345	307	na	na	na	na	na	na
Alpharetta city	3,743	na	na	na	na	na	na	na	na	na	na
Athens-Clarke County unified govt (bal)	9,273	5,080	1,004	2,919	402	na	na	na	na	na	na
Atlanta city	40,686	14,308	8,017	16,958	1,385	4,103	1,483	192	29,103	14,951	16,797
Augusta-Richmond County consolidated govt (bal).	18,909	9,012	3,370	6,398	1,537	2,509	741	153	17,222	8,340	9,651
Columbus city	17,648	8,643	2,550	6,004	474	1,214	390	0	16,981	7,477	8,680
Johns Creek city	4,176	2,738	310	1,128	194	na	na	na	na	na	na
Macon-Bibb County	15,152	7,632	2,100	5,194	964	3,130	1,589	342	na	na	na
Roswell city	7,520	na	na	na	na	na	na	na	na	na	na
Sandy Springs city	9,541	4,502	1,504	3,047	283	na	na	na	na	na	na
Savannah city	13,243	6,293	2,344	4,187	641	1,255	530	106	na	na	na
South Fulton city	7,700	na	na	na	na	na	na	na	na	na	na
Warner Robins city	5,478	na	na	na	na	na	na	na	na	na	na
Hawaii											
Urban Honolulu CDP	40,268	22,188	6,672	10,041	2,387	7,849	1,271	51	43,683	18,826	12,117
Iowa											
Boise City city	22,584	10,222	3,502	8,114	767	na	na	na	na	na	na
Meridian city	5,859	na	na	na	na	na	na	na	na	na	na
Nampa city	9,508	4,700	1,237	3,314	464	na	na	na	na	na	na
Illinois											
Aurora city	11,020	6,000	1,339	3,483	438	1,556	118	na	na	na	na
Bloomington city	6,317	na	na	na	na	na	na	na	na	na	na
Champaign city	5,774	2,745	621	2,023	303	na	na	na	na	na	na
Chicago city	229,844	104,977	43,183	75,186	10,823	31,551	7,687	2,084	208,417	103,418	81,483
Decatur city	9,140	4,663	1,265	2,907	893	na	na	na	na	na	na
Elgin city	7,342	4,174	912	2,205	716	na	na	na	na	na	na
Evanston city	7,379	3,451	561	2,840	734	na	na	na	na	na	na
Joliet city	8,394	4,578	1,161	2,441	744	2,198	388	0	na	na	na
Naperville city	9,457	6,108	915	2,392	838	na	na	na	na	na	na
Peoria city	10,274	4,704	1,853	3,360	816	na	na	na	na	na	na
Rockford city	16,750	8,636	1,727	6,125	1,478	847	534	0	19,844	6,782	6,108
Springfield city	12,893	5,867	2,283	4,623	762	886	411	na	na	na	na
Waukegan city	4,818	2,574	1,067	1,067	583	1,220	452	na	na	na	na
Indiana											
Bloomington city	5,687	na	na	na	na	na	na	na	na	na	na
Carmel city	7,603	4,525	740	2,230	294	na	na	na	na	na	na
Evansville city	11,731	5,632	1,997	3,656	1,304	1,102	760	na	na	na	na
Fishers city	5,320	na	na	na	na	na	na	na	na	na	na
Fort Wayne city	24,810	12,010	4,205	8,314	1,298	2,275	1,090	106	27,691	9,189	9,069
Gary city	9,418	4,972	984	3,101	384	912	365	0	na	na	na
Hammond city	7,138	3,373	1,219	2,436	140	na	na	na	na	na	na
Indianapolis city (bal)	68,504	33,671	10,952	22,102	3,833	7,565	3,001	749	73,851	27,184	31,566
Lafayette city	6,077	2,809	1,130	2,113	469	na	na	na	na	na	na
Muncie city	6,857	na	na	na	na	na	na	na	na	na	na
Noblesville city	4,276	2,051	475	1,716	289	na	na	na	na	na	na
South Bend city	9,506	4,149	1,647	3,475	906	na	na	na	na	na	na
Iowa											
Ames city	4,147	na	na	na	na	na	na	na	na	na	na
Ankeny city	5,142	na	na	na	na	na	na	na	na	na	na
Cedar Rapids city	12,836	6,138	2,017	4,278	642	na	na	na	na	na	na
Davenport city	9,367	4,417	1,295	3,513	757	na	na	na	na	na	na

Table D-3: Cities - Household Relationship, Grandparents, and Marital Status—*Continued*

	Total Householders 65 Years and Over	Family Householders 65 Years and Over	Non-Family Householders 65 Years and Over		Persons 65 Years and Over Living in Group Quarters	Grandparents 60 Years and Over Living with Grandchildren			Marital Status - Persons 60 Years and Over		
			Male Living Alone	Female Living Alone		Total	Responsible for Grandchildren	Responsible for Grandchildren and In Poverty	Now Married	Widowed	Divorced
Iowa—Cont.											
Des Moines city	16,685	7,254	3,122	5,513	843	1,363	405	148	16,425	7,328	7,551
Iowa City city	5,255	na	na	na	na	na	na	na	na	na	na
Sioux City city	7,283	3,659	1,090	2,406	389	na	na	na	na	na	na
Waterloo city	8,154	3,937	1,032	2,944	283	na	na	na	na	na	na
West Des Moines city	6,358	na	na	na	na	na	na	na	na	na	na
Kansas											
Kansas City city	11,709	6,451	1,725	3,211	299	2,415	1,048	72	13,826	4,791	5,160
Lawrence city	7,647	3,535	751	2,986	304	na	na	na	na	na	na
Olathe city	8,432	5,539	472	2,260	653	na	na	na	na	na	na
Overland Park city	19,297	10,720	2,163	6,221	884	1,425	569	na	na	na	na
Shawnee city	4,535	na	na	na	na	na	na	na	na	na	na
Topeka city	15,459	6,822	2,234	5,646	1,229	1,077	728	na	na	na	na
Wichita city	36,646	17,142	6,059	12,504	1,824	2,844	803	32	43,245	14,032	15,010
Kentucky											
Bowling Green city	5,035	1,517	791	2,505	571	na	na	na	na	na	na
Lexington-Fayette urban county	26,964	13,851	3,095	9,644	1,158	2,917	1,179	223	34,605	10,289	10,015
Louisville/Jefferson County metro govt (bal)	61,682	33,329	8,471	18,157	3,082	5,979	2,701	492	70,464	25,726	24,683
Louisiana											
Baton Rouge city	21,311	12,105	3,036	5,596	788	2,416	1,419	461	na	na	na
Bossier City city	6,459	3,120	914	2,224	551	na	na	na	na	na	na
Kenner city	7,446	4,162	1,093	2,002	315	na	na	na	na	na	na
Lafayette city	11,790	6,430	1,566	3,230	685	na	na	na	na	na	na
Lake Charles city	8,012	na	na	na	na	na	na	na	na	na	na
New Orleans city	35,584	14,352	7,054	12,826	1,600	3,341	669	294	33,427	16,381	15,415
Shreveport city	19,851	10,953	3,196	5,447	2,174	2,116	886	180	na	na	na
Maine											
Portland city	5,449	2,220	912	2,126	569	na	na	na	na	na	na
Maryland											
Baltimore city	57,264	22,977	10,569	20,871	3,147	7,167	1,682	256	44,179	25,740	26,135
Frederick city	5,710	2,751	923	1,897	650	na	na	na	na	na	na
Gaithersburg city	4,865	2,687	621	1,399	186	na	na	na	na	na	na
Rockville city	7,175	3,244	968	2,588	594	na	na	na	na	na	na
Massachusetts											
Boston city	53,784	23,245	9,515	18,653	3,058	7,477	1,285	211	50,254	17,605	19,361
Brockton city	7,542	3,195	1,538	2,307	714	na	na	na	na	na	na
Cambridge city	8,519	3,304	1,495	3,193	339	na	na	na	na	na	na
Fall River city	9,771	4,218	1,753	3,570	722	na	na	na	na	na	na
Framingham city	6,830	4,113	776	1,671	791	na	na	na	na	na	na
Lawrence city	4,387	1,959	754	1,449	432	1,361	298	na	na	na	na
Lowell city	6,108	2,938	1,135	1,809	784	na	na	na	na	na	na
Lynn city	7,139	2,916	973	2,605	258	na	na	na	na	na	na
New Bedford city	8,184	3,325	1,021	3,716	1,011	442	236	na	na	na	na
Newton city	10,928	6,376	1,356	2,898	506	na	na	na	na	na	na
Quincy city	9,181	3,682	2,195	3,098	299	na	na	na	na	na	na
Somerville city	4,390	1,539	381	2,166	101	na	na	na	na	na	na
Springfield city	12,418	5,803	2,213	3,683	439	1,760	787	136	11,483	5,395	4,907
Worcester city	14,900	6,006	2,678	5,704	1,779	1,549	627	na	15,418	8,190	6,113
Michigan											
Ann Arbor city	8,275	4,573	894	2,534	638	na	na	na	na	na	na
Dearborn city	7,367	3,716	1,208	2,322	254	na	na	na	na	na	na
Detroit city	66,285	28,833	11,698	23,516	3,273	9,742	2,113	151	42,992	29,681	34,432
Farmington Hills city	10,120	5,124	1,678	3,067	356	na	na	na	na	na	na
Flint city	9,182	4,272	1,624	2,824	129	na	na	na	na	na	na
Grand Rapids city	16,875	6,673	2,305	7,655	1,702	1,400	299	135	15,043	7,281	7,034
Kalamazoo city	5,457	2,044	793	2,408	366	na	na	na	na	na	na
Lansing city	9,985	4,532	1,622	3,335	136	578	143	na	na	na	na
Livonia city	10,322	5,012	1,720	3,489	895	na	na	na	na	na	na
Rochester Hills city	8,254	4,322	632	3,094	428	na	na	na	na	na	na
Southfield city	11,169	4,696	1,730	4,362	532	na	na	na	na	na	na
Sterling Heights city	13,015	7,838	1,563	3,484	654	na	na	na	na	na	na
Troy city	7,644	4,779	763	1,941	232	na	na	na	na	na	na
Warren city	14,523	6,941	2,468	4,769	783	2,396	491	74	na	na	na
Westland city	10,074	3,712	1,456	4,679	560	na	na	na	na	na	na
Wyoming city	5,251	2,764	979	1,371	249	na	na	na	na	na	na
Minnesota											
Blaine city	4,267	na	na	na	na	na	na	na	na	na	na
Bloomington city	12,145	5,934	1,785	4,017	570	na	na	na	na	na	na
Brooklyn Park city	5,098	3,685	470	867	48	na	na	na	na	na	na
Duluth city	9,899	4,520	1,982	3,020	1,001	na	na	na	na	na	na
Eagan city	4,453	na	na	na	na	na	na	na	na	na	na
Lakeville city	3,787	na	na	na	na	na	na	na	na	na	na
Maple Grove city	6,625	na	na	na	na	na	na	na	na	na	na

Table D-3: Cities - Household Relationship, Grandparents, and Marital Status—*Continued*

	Total Householders 65 Years and Over	Family Householders 65 Years and Over	Non-Family Householders 65 Years and Over		Persons 65 Years and Over Living in Group Quarters	Grandparents 60 Years and Over Living with Grandchildren			Marital Status - Persons 60 Years and Over		
			Male Living Alone	Female Living Alone		Total	Responsible for Grandchildren	Responsible for Grandchildren and In Poverty	Now Married	Widowed	Divorced
Minnesota—Cont.											
Minneapolis city	29,348	12,221	6,581	8,835	2,176	3,199	853	171	30,775	7,463	14,968
Plymouth city	6,872	3,394	1,208	2,186	300	na	na	na	na	na	na
Rochester city	11,259	5,483	1,383	4,160	1,022	na	na	na	na	na	na
St. Cloud city	4,876	na	na	na	na	na	na	na	na	na	na
St. Paul city	21,422	8,585	3,927	8,203	1,710	2,445	218	112	19,399	7,405	11,700
Woodbury city	5,952	na	na	na	na	na	na	na	na	na	na
Mississippi											
Gulfport city	5,550	2,984	995	1,371	319	na	na	na	na	na	na
Jackson city	13,245	7,119	1,616	4,203	1,156	1,880	1,318	28	na	na	na
Missouri											
Columbia city	9,132	na	na	na	na	na	na	na	na	na	na
Independence city	12,015	6,669	1,725	3,105	828	1,310	531	na	na	na	na
Kansas City city	41,780	19,084	7,904	13,119	1,821	3,677	1,481	521	43,315	18,084	19,329
Lee's Summit city	10,450	6,260	794	3,182	507	na	na	na	na	na	na
O'Fallon city	5,962	na	na	na	na	na	na	na	na	na	na
St. Charles city	7,341	3,336	1,095	2,694	589	na	na	na	na	na	na
St. Joseph city	8,757	4,562	1,305	2,182	578	856	592	na	na	na	na
St. Louis city	29,792	10,413	7,390	10,805	2,056	na	na	na	22,078	11,482	14,977
Springfield city	21,055	8,145	4,321	7,947	1,204	1,257	617	na	na	na	na
Montana											
Billings city	12,848	6,173	1,633	4,776	739	605	151	na	na	na	na
Missoula city	6,564	2,712	1,019	2,430	238	na	na	na	na	na	na
Nebraska											
Lincoln city	25,353	12,572	3,382	8,769	297	2,018	460	na	30,157	9,945	7,722
Omaha city	41,787	19,198	6,898	14,158	2,153	3,103	1,289	53	46,616	16,822	17,572
Nevada											
Henderson city	34,479	19,253	4,358	9,511	532	4,347	941	77	45,548	12,732	14,327
Las Vegas city	57,088	30,846	10,007	13,624	2,046	9,638	3,243	477	69,183	23,992	25,854
North Las Vegas city	14,796	9,644	1,613	2,857	326	4,097	793	84	21,773	6,452	6,904
Reno city	26,259	10,854	5,987	7,946	697	2,072	1,330	na	26,559	8,405	14,623
Sparks city	10,698	6,380	995	2,814	207	na	na	na	na	na	na
New Hampshire											
Manchester city	8,273	3,903	1,586	2,211	1,013	na	na	na	na	na	na
Nashua city	9,562	4,628	1,352	3,379	541	na	na	na	na	na	na
New Jersey											
Bayonne city	6,109	2,720	1,120	2,184	11	na	na	na	na	na	na
Camden city	4,766	na	na	na	na	1,233	443	0	na	na	na
Clifton city	7,380	4,068	859	2,201	128	na	na	na	na	na	na
East Orange city	5,494	2,554	644	2,232	567	na	na	na	na	na	na
Elizabeth city	7,324	4,009	962	2,266	514	na	na	na	na	na	na
Jersey City city	17,688	9,311	2,578	5,067	901	3,346	510	149	20,681	7,030	6,477
Newark city	17,220	8,200	1,720	6,755	1,183	2,993	752	124	16,279	8,420	6,279
Passaic city	3,874	1,631	773	1,247	115	na	na	na	na	na	na
Paterson city	10,224	5,955	780	2,984	243	na	na	194	na	na	na
Trenton city	7,207	3,120	1,101	2,916	572	543	348	na	na	na	na
Union City city	4,774	2,223	848	1,703	180	na	na	na	na	na	na
New Mexico											
Albuquerque city	55,046	25,944	9,682	17,373	2,141	5,676	2,899	718	56,304	23,002	27,216
Las Cruces city	10,769	5,673	1,180	3,691	250	na	na	na	na	na	na
Rio Rancho city	9,930	6,494	936	2,107	485	1,400	791	na	na	na	na
Santa Fe city	13,618	6,434	1,985	4,260	327	na	na	na	na	na	na
New York											
Albany city	8,897	3,735	1,658	3,120	1,303	na	na	na	na	na	na
Buffalo city	21,624	10,172	3,658	7,129	1,286	1,564	937	379	19,256	8,709	10,354
Mount Vernon city	6,096	2,740	1,349	1,948	732	na	na	na	na	na	na
New Rochelle city	7,613	3,981	1,065	2,339	1,107	na	na	na	na	na	na
New York city	767,186	375,056	111,136	259,563	42,588	134,887	31,301	7,453	818,686	330,328	233,787
Rochester city	16,006	5,974	3,580	5,610	2,063	1,301	372	107	11,731	6,761	7,190
Schenectady city	6,127	2,513	962	2,204	452	na	na	na	na	na	na
Syracuse city	10,721	4,118	2,232	4,108	1,594	1,116	418	158	8,907	5,147	4,470
Yonkers city	21,929	9,984	3,923	7,587	786	na	na	na	21,576	8,625	7,514
North Carolina											
Asheville city	11,818	5,140	928	5,262	1,139	na	na	na	na	na	na
Charlotte city	56,551	30,555	7,096	17,182	1,856	8,332	2,260	323	74,153	23,459	26,772
Concord city	7,679	4,523	720	2,326	465	na	na	na	na	na	na
Durham city	20,298	12,297	2,190	5,651	911	na	na	na	26,623	7,206	7,959
Fayetteville city	16,511	8,033	2,697	5,322	500	1,554	510	218	17,853	8,771	5,247
Gastonia city	7,309	3,486	976	2,553	603	na	na	na	na	na	na
Greensboro city	26,459	12,857	3,677	9,185	1,501	3,669	1,495	397	30,892	10,079	11,178
Greenville city	5,662	2,227	891	2,520	452	na	na	na	na	na	na
High Point city	10,080	5,852	779	3,294	490	818	334	0	na	na	na
Jacksonville city	2,941	na	na	na	na	na	na	na	na	na	na

Table D-3: Cities - Household Relationship, Grandparents, and Marital Status—*Continued*

| | Total Householders 65 Years and Over | Family Householders 65 Years and Over | Non-Family Householders 65 Years and Over | | Persons 65 Years and Over Living in Group Quarters | Grandparents 60 Years and Over Living with Grandchildren | | | Marital Status - Persons 60 Years and Over | | |
			Male Living Alone	Female Living Alone		Total	Responsible for Grandchildren	Responsible for Grandchildren and In Poverty	Now Married	Widowed	Divorced
North Carolina—Cont.											
Raleigh city	33,431	16,605	3,708	12,495	1,331	2,277	459	0	42,811	13,126	12,572
Wilmington city	14,175	5,816	2,093	5,624	267	na	na	na	na	na	na
Winston-Salem city	23,621	10,420	4,150	8,391	673	1,969	716	104	22,379	10,169	9,955
North Dakota											
Bismarck city	7,969	na	na	na	na	na	na	na	na	na	na
Fargo city	9,594	4,246	1,853	3,140	876	na	na	na	na	na	na
Ohio											
Akron city	19,483	9,883	3,246	5,723	703	2,046	650	40	18,810	7,614	10,590
Canton city	7,625	3,292	1,417	2,663	592	na	na	na	na	na	na
Cincinnati city	26,344	9,342	6,092	10,278	2,856	1,800	1,020	297	21,284	10,784	14,587
Cleveland city	38,722	14,402	9,997	12,821	1,950	3,604	1,396	244	27,893	14,935	19,210
Columbus city	63,167	32,729	8,438	19,936	2,237	8,791	2,570	1,320	66,951	24,151	33,151
Dayton city	13,731	5,655	2,905	4,602	1,044	na	na	34	8,719	6,825	6,520
Lorain city	7,035	2,867	1,397	2,606	421	na	na	na	na	na	na
Parma city	8,792	4,490	1,524	2,651	860	na	na	na	na	na	na
Toledo city	25,440	11,658	4,386	9,046	1,330	3,304	1,215	348	24,965	10,030	11,830
Youngstown city	7,822	2,838	1,630	3,003	617	na	na	na	na	na	na
Oklahoma											
Broken Arrow city	9,346	6,167	551	2,442	443	1,859	639	49	na	na	na
Edmond city	8,679	5,571	850	2,129	354	na	na	na	na	na	na
Lawton city	7,754	3,924	1,480	2,195	826	na	na	na	na	na	na
Norman city	9,153	4,810	887	3,211	498	na	na	na	na	na	na
Oklahoma City city	54,178	27,057	8,377	17,756	2,256	5,817	2,267	243	59,688	23,151	24,360
Tulsa city	38,643	18,636	6,284	12,675	1,567	4,006	1,624	319	41,006	16,326	17,285
Oregon											
Beaverton city	7,603	na	na	na	na	na	na	na	na	na	na
Bend city	11,110	5,145	1,220	4,387	441	na	na	na	na	na	na
Eugene city	18,122	7,013	3,145	6,854	977	na	na	na	na	na	na
Gresham city	9,363	4,274	1,264	3,547	521	1,059	204	na	na	na	na
Hillsboro city	7,778	3,575	421	3,611	454	na	na	na	na	na	na
Medford city	9,036	4,581	1,087	3,021	800	na	na	na	na	na	na
Portland city	57,005	25,283	9,111	20,375	2,039	5,074	984	na	61,025	17,306	26,944
Salem city	15,873	7,789	2,993	4,538	1,429	1,631	927	na	18,741	6,207	8,455
Pennsylvania											
Allentown city	8,331	4,125	1,134	2,465	1,061	na	na	na	na	na	na
Bethlehem city	7,903	3,474	1,058	3,225	998	na	na	na	na	na	na
Erie city	10,444	4,336	2,548	3,222	954	na	na	na	na	na	na
Philadelphia city	144,301	63,511	24,301	52,520	7,629	19,422	4,386	1,730	121,314	66,424	54,956
Pittsburgh city	32,982	12,141	6,222	13,646	2,054	1,648	720	140	29,939	13,000	11,141
Reading city	5,978	2,700	1,114	2,061	266	1,472	714	na	na	na	na
Scranton city	7,941	3,851	1,089	2,871	1,022	na	na	na	na	na	na
Rhode Island											
Cranston city	7,654	3,536	1,268	2,700	512	na	na	na	na	na	na
Pawtucket city	6,774	3,346	1,114	2,054	259	na	na	na	na	na	na
Providence city	13,328	5,182	2,767	4,968	1,427	na	na	na	na	na	na
Warwick city	11,091	4,577	1,404	4,818	487	na	na	na	na	na	na
South Carolina											
Charleston city	13,963	6,197	2,035	5,362	338	na	na	na	na	na	na
Columbia city	8,917	na	na	na	na	920	427	30	na	na	na
Greenville city	6,599	na	na	na	na	na	na	na	na	na	na
North Charleston city	7,496	4,035	1,078	2,122	341	2,472	1,481	616	na	na	na
Rock Hill city	5,845	2,844	597	2,011	407	1,145	537	na	na	na	na
South Dakota											
Rapid City city	8,957	4,632	926	3,028	882	816	438	na	na	na	na
Sioux Falls city	14,186	6,591	2,013	5,041	621	na	na	na	na	na	na
Tennessee											
Chattanooga city	20,047	8,991	2,978	7,779	1,458	2,689	737	75	19,283	10,274	8,570
Clarksville city	7,492	4,475	1,116	1,813	493	1,427	210	na	na	na	na
Franklin city	6,006	na	na	na	na	na	na	na	na	na	na
Jackson city	6,510	2,680	1,344	2,446	456	na	na	na	na	na	na
Johnson City city	6,827	3,088	1,590	2,107	825	na	na	na	na	na	na
Knoxville city	16,442	7,167	2,817	5,829	1,069	1,177	708	257	14,487	8,128	8,643
Memphis city	56,780	25,868	9,454	20,552	2,314	6,595	2,709	652	58,014	22,902	25,331
Murfreesboro city	8,601	4,379	1,103	2,959	270	na	na	na	na	na	na
Nashville-Davidson metropolitan govt (bal)	52,740	26,107	8,186	16,376	1,438	5,598	2,133	636	56,672	20,086	22,405
Texas											
Abilene city	9,709	5,062	1,183	3,318	718	956	248	na	na	na	na
Allen city	5,183	na	na	na	na	na	na	na	na	na	na
Amarillo city	17,074	8,205	2,838	5,959	966	1,687	520	73	20,144	8,395	6,039
Arlington city	25,203	15,688	2,756	6,576	829	5,883	2,538	260	36,825	11,522	11,022
Austin city	53,957	29,111	8,851	14,555	2,004	7,749	1,668	598	73,405	21,138	25,112
Baytown city	5,868	3,991	749	1,102	479	1,240	526	na	na	na	na
Beaumont city	10,825	5,943	1,575	3,091	495	976	607	na	na	na	na

Table D-3: Cities - Household Relationship, Grandparents, and Marital Status—Continued

	Total Householders 65 Years and Over	Family Householders 65 Years and Over	Non-Family Householders 65 Years and Over		Persons 65 Years and Over Living in Group Quarters	Grandparents 60 Years and Over Living with Grandchildren			Marital Status - Persons 60 Years and Over		
			Male Living Alone	Female Living Alone		Total	Responsible for Grandchildren	Responsible for Grandchildren and In Poverty	Now Married	Widowed	Divorced
Texas—Cont.											
Brownsville city	11,430	7,576	1,010	2,502	478	3,082	493	98	16,963	6,223	3,889
Bryan city	5,852	2,874	957	1,813	245	na	na	na	na	na	na
Carrollton city	9,519	6,002	1,069	2,300	529	na	na	na	na	na	na
Cedar Park city	2,886	1,823	263	800	216	na	na	na	na	na	na
College Station city	5,365	na	na	na	na	na	na	na	na	na	na
Conroe city	7,856	4,013	675	3,071	386	na	na	na	na	na	na
Corpus Christi city	27,629	16,161	3,707	6,698	1,680	5,280	2,312	407	35,100	12,959	12,304
Dallas city	88,938	45,863	12,835	27,429	2,632	14,248	4,478	1,051	105,325	40,907	39,993
Denton city	8,968	4,817	1,022	2,931	396	na	na	na	na	na	na
Edinburg city	4,650	na	na	na	na	na	na	na	na	na	na
El Paso city	53,524	30,107	7,775	14,678	1,756	10,959	3,598	417	65,076	25,105	19,961
Fort Worth city	55,700	30,551	7,568	16,510	1,788	11,149	3,996	543	69,936	24,365	23,517
Frisco city	7,405	3,853	859	2,693	324	na	na	na	na	na	na
Garland city	16,237	10,060	1,117	4,761	545	5,674	1,237	0	na	na	na
Georgetown city	12,684	7,506	1,418	3,286	206	na	na	na	na	na	na
Grand Prairie city	10,128	6,348	1,561	1,841	185	2,639	1,173	82	na	na	na
Harlingen city	6,270	4,057	651	1,379	392	na	na	na	na	na	na
Houston city	151,420	80,883	22,879	43,591	4,824	28,419	7,540	1,014	179,290	69,723	61,416
Irving city	8,277	4,612	1,049	2,286	353	3,382	593	202	13,215	3,390	5,795
Killeen city	5,812	3,190	671	1,729	65	1,115	292	na	na	na	na
Laredo city	14,292	8,400	1,271	4,017	351	5,421	726	259	16,400	7,369	4,528
League City city	6,742	3,103	1,242	1,991	586	na	na	na	na	na	na
Lewisville city	4,946	2,484	415	1,871	299	na	na	na	na	na	na
Longview city	7,341	3,944	1,041	2,192	1,132	na	na	na	na	na	na
Lubbock city	19,833	11,280	1,674	6,069	917	2,095	1,294	34	23,593	8,679	8,779
McAllen city	10,160	6,567	1,120	2,180	894	na	na	na	na	na	na
McKinney city	10,076	6,741	410	2,886	372	na	na	na	na	na	na
Mansfield city	3,653	2,328	298	953	155	na	na	na	na	na	na
Mesquite city	8,820	4,393	966	3,030	524	1,695	640	0	na	na	na
Midland city	9,382	4,289	1,547	3,249	277	2,208	951	na	na	na	na
Mission city	6,720	4,257	397	2,066	109	na	na	na	na	na	na
Missouri City city	5,928	na	na	na	na	na	na	na	na	na	na
New Braunfels city	6,933	4,292	613	1,829	296	na	na	na	na	na	na
North Richland Hills city	7,090	4,475	388	2,063	278	na	na	na	na	na	na
Odessa city	8,100	na	na	na	na	na	na	na	na	na	na
Pasadena city	8,322	4,942	928	2,302	491	1,919	379	103	na	na	na
Pearland city	9,174	6,112	1,198	1,864	469	na	na	na	na	na	na
Pharr city	5,023	2,699	968	1,241	0	na	na	na	na	na	na
Plano city	22,495	13,233	2,064	6,671	476	2,718	386	na	na	na	na
Richardson city	9,703	5,443	2,045	2,058	408	na	na	na	na	na	na
Round Rock city	5,623	2,880	1,411	1,251	207	na	na	na	na	na	na
Rowlett city	na	na	na	na	na	na	na	na	na	na	na
San Angelo city	9,991	5,416	924	3,172	338	1,188	532	na	na	na	na
San Antonio city	112,450	63,768	15,073	30,818	5,026	21,054	5,151	1,249	135,118	53,497	51,723
Sugar Land city	10,314	6,516	1,093	2,464	114	na	na	na	na	na	na
Temple city	7,481	4,581	357	2,332	767	na	na	na	na	na	na
Tyler city	9,055	5,133	746	2,993	714	1,257	236	na	na	na	na
Victoria city	6,962	3,564	758	2,493	545	na	na	na	na	na	na
Waco city	9,383	5,110	1,001	2,959	852	1,076	329	na	na	na	na
Wichita Falls city	9,028	4,715	1,024	3,060	1,161	na	na	0	na	na	na
Utah											
Layton city	4,281	na	na	na	na	na	na	na	na	na	na
Lehi city	2,816	na	na	na	na	na	na	na	na	na	na
Ogden city	6,379	2,872	923	2,285	59	na	na	na	na	na	na
Orem city	4,933	3,555	397	964	162	na	na	na	na	na	na
Provo city	4,560	2,847	557	1,087	512	na	na	na	na	na	na
St. George city	12,957	8,618	1,266	2,675	194	na	na	na	na	na	na
Salt Lake City city	14,311	6,281	3,033	4,585	417	na	na	na	na	na	na
Sandy city	9,341	5,857	1,016	2,162	180	na	na	na	na	na	na
South Jordan city	4,058	na	na	na	na	na	na	na	na	na	na
West Jordan city	4,550	3,526	458	528	87	na	na	na	na	na	na
West Valley City city	6,852	4,548	919	1,289	166	2,099	402	0	na	na	na
Virginia											
Alexandria city	13,624	4,780	2,250	5,973	243	na	na	na	na	na	na
Chesapeake city	18,389	11,325	1,846	4,843	396	2,918	656	151	27,772	9,208	6,533
Hampton city	12,573	6,035	1,885	4,090	379	na	na	203	na	na	na
Lynchburg city	7,727	3,329	906	3,214	818	na	na	na	na	na	na
Newport News city	15,446	6,994	1,995	5,878	850	1,864	516	49	na	na	na
Norfolk city	18,377	8,895	3,208	5,730	644	2,297	779	231	17,160	8,312	9,157
Portsmouth city	9,668	4,091	1,731	3,624	322	447	161	na	na	na	na
Richmond city	21,348	7,950	4,397	8,319	481	1,409	540	na	14,790	9,463	11,784
Roanoke city	11,021	5,389	1,590	3,736	868	na	na	na	na	na	na
Suffolk city	8,257	4,009	1,516	2,664	305	na	na	na	na	na	na
Virginia Beach city	40,323	22,875	5,768	10,925	721	5,557	1,830	99	55,021	16,552	13,131

Table D-3: Cities - Household Relationship, Grandparents, and Marital Status—*Continued*

	Total Householders 65 Years and Over	Family Householders 65 Years and Over	Non-Family Householders 65 Years and Over		Persons 65 Years and Over Living in Group Quarters	Grandparents 60 Years and Over Living with Grandchildren			Marital Status - Persons 60 Years and Over		
			Male Living Alone	Female Living Alone		Total	Responsible for Grandchildren	Responsible for Grandchildren and In Poverty	Now Married	Widowed	Divorced
Washington											
Auburn city	7,522	3,641	1,404	1,857	297	na	na	na	na	na	na
Bellevue city	12,440	6,978	1,704	3,110	647	na	na	na	na	na	na
Bellingham city	8,672	4,112	1,405	2,403	528	na	na	na	na	na	na
Everett city	8,600	3,546	1,771	2,777	812	na	na	na	na	na	na
Federal Way city	7,679	4,134	1,238	2,227	444	na	na	na	na	na	na
Kennewick city	6,553	3,664	1,096	1,467	212	na	na	na	na	na	na
Kent city	9,298	4,914	604	3,380	338	1,530	364	na	na	na	na
Kirkland city	6,343	3,336	589	2,092	417	na	na	na	na	na	na
Marysville city	6,205	2,940	745	2,109	311	na	na	na	na	na	na
Pasco city	3,832	2,414	289	1,033	40	na	na	na	na	na	na
Redmond city	2,993	1,573	255	1,165	271	na	na	na	na	na	na
Renton city	7,514	3,947	623	2,434	303	na	na	na	na	na	na
Sammamish city	2,577	na	na	na	na	na	na	na	na	na	na
Seattle city	61,825	27,222	12,541	19,870	3,297	4,707	584	na	68,347	16,590	25,305
Spokane city	21,816	10,456	3,664	7,034	1,313	2,126	806	166	24,893	8,857	9,359
Spokane Valley city	10,574	4,551	1,399	4,391	476	na	na	na	na	na	na
Tacoma city	18,254	8,500	3,320	6,043	1,231	2,087	791	140	20,720	6,459	8,540
Vancouver city	19,345	8,859	2,219	7,717	798	1,129	263	na	na	na	na
Yakima city	10,440	4,653	1,769	3,929	487	na	na	na	na	na	na
Wisconsin											
Appleton city	6,963	3,941	690	2,210	533	na	na	na	na	na	na
Eau Claire city	6,794	na	na	na	na	na	na	na	na	na	na
Green Bay city	8,978	3,780	1,863	3,055	447	na	na	na	na	na	na
Kenosha city	8,044	3,909	951	3,050	617	na	na	na	na	na	na
Madison city	21,198	9,738	2,647	7,612	582	na	na	na	23,515	5,619	8,788
Milwaukee city	42,162	19,456	8,726	12,816	2,330	5,481	2,523	269	39,382	16,865	19,622
Oshkosh city	6,107	2,330	1,043	2,537	690	na	na	na	na	na	na
Racine city	6,171	na	na	na	na	na	na	na	na	na	na
Waukesha city	6,698	3,678	690	2,197	217	na	na	na	na	na	na

Table D-4: Metropolitan/Micropolitan Statistical Areas - Household Relationship, Grandparents, and Marital Status

	Total Householders 65 Years and Over	Family Householders 65 Years and Over	Non-Family Householders 65 Years and Over — Male Living Alone	Female Living Alone	Persons 65 Years and Over Living in Group Quarters	Grandparents 60 Years and Over Living with Grandchildren — Total	Responsible for Grandchildren	Responsible for Grandchildren and In Poverty	Marital Status - Persons 60 Years and Over — Now Married	Widowed	Divorced
Aberdeen, WA Micro Area	8,920	5,067	1,661	1,930	386	na	na	na	na	na	na
Abilene, TX Metro Area	15,770	9,137	1,753	4,666	973	1,845	1,067	124	22,128	6,961	5,456
Adrian, MI Micro Area	11,422	6,240	1,590	3,388	871	na	na	na	na	na	na
Akron, OH Metro Area	77,781	40,463	12,454	22,250	3,548	7,278	1,668	111	92,972	32,038	33,391
Alamogordo, NM Micro Area	6,635	na	na	na	na	na	na	na	na	na	na
Albany, GA Metro Area	14,219	7,450	2,068	4,164	560	1,187	370	27	na	na	na
Albany, OR Metro Area	15,144	8,127	2,069	4,099	572	1,790	652	na	na	na	na
Albany-Schenectady-Troy, NY Metro Area	95,951	51,417	13,324	28,540	6,247	6,682	1,491	195	122,305	38,426	31,108
Albertville, AL Micro Area	10,016	5,848	1,308	2,789	509	1,019	428	253	na	na	na
Albuquerque, NM Metro Area	94,579	50,693	14,623	26,042	3,066	9,833	5,229	1,135	113,042	36,235	40,908
Alexandria, LA Metro Area	15,380	8,236	2,242	4,777	1,213	1,704	1,123	251	na	na	na
Allentown-Bethlehem-Easton, PA-NJ Metro Area	92,311	49,747	12,118	27,430	6,036	7,316	2,405	221	121,251	43,381	25,667
Altoona, PA Metro Area	16,090	8,217	1,992	5,242	1,328	na	na	0	na	na	na
Amarillo, TX Metro Area	23,028	12,177	3,616	7,110	1,267	2,485	867	258	29,396	11,241	8,299
Ames, IA Metro Area	7,369	na	na	na	na	na	na	na	na	na	na
Anchorage, AK Metro Area	26,808	15,380	3,659	6,110	1,625	5,081	1,356	316	39,339	10,642	12,271
Ann Arbor, MI Metro Area	32,797	18,522	3,980	9,410	1,892	2,010	408	na	42,232	10,948	10,644
Anniston-Oxford-Jacksonville, AL Metro Area	13,456	7,807	1,376	4,078	331	1,148	275	230	na	na	na
Appleton, WI Metro Area	22,073	12,630	2,861	6,159	902	1,000	154	na	na	na	na
Asheville, NC Metro Area	64,037	34,488	8,418	19,494	3,747	4,210	1,443	na	80,731	24,241	19,713
Ashtabula, OH Micro Area	11,704	6,544	1,665	3,373	859	na	na	na	na	na	na
Athens, OH Micro Area	5,581	2,514	912	2,078	242	na	na	0	na	na	na
Athens, TX Micro Area	10,841	6,325	1,306	2,970	382	915	790	na	na	na	na
Athens-Clarke County, GA Metro Area	17,820	9,979	2,027	5,445	605	1,618	268	8	na	na	na
Atlanta-Sandy Springs-Roswell, GA Metro Area	432,497	251,423	49,073	119,803	11,622	79,529	19,559	1,978	608,373	175,418	172,885
Atlantic City-Hammonton, NJ Metro Area	28,355	16,928	3,123	7,526	1,712	4,255	1,145	172	38,296	11,044	9,696
Auburn, NY Micro Area	8,949	4,436	1,334	2,862	592	na	na	na	na	na	na
Auburn-Opelika, AL Metro Area	11,705	7,320	1,570	2,557	267	2,400	604	na	na	na	na
Augusta-Richmond County, GA-SC Metro Area	60,753	32,525	9,582	17,972	2,974	7,991	2,706	153	73,099	25,044	24,466
Augusta-Waterville, ME Micro Area	16,362	7,464	2,831	4,903	1,341	na	na	na	na	na	na
Austin-Round Rock, TX Metro Area	133,162	79,050	17,827	32,703	4,752	23,383	4,425	784	201,218	51,955	56,785
Bakersfield, CA Metro Area	57,042	33,149	8,502	14,034	2,579	14,414	2,947	592	80,788	28,531	20,129
Baltimore-Columbia-Towson, MD Metro Area	267,577	141,153	35,738	81,732	13,153	36,875	9,273	936	336,300	116,809	97,231
Bangor, ME Metro Area	17,420	8,418	3,414	4,774	1,034	na	na	na	na	na	na
Barnstable Town, MA Metro Area	39,226	22,053	3,685	12,082	1,689	1,862	549	na	na	na	na
Baton Rouge, LA Metro Area	70,045	40,391	8,526	18,779	2,976	9,766	3,458	758	93,813	29,768	31,072
Battle Creek, MI Metro Area	15,477	8,042	2,646	4,211	1,103	880	350	40	na	na	na
Bay City, MI Metro Area	13,107	7,027	2,005	3,684	727	na	na	na	na	na	na
Beaumont-Port Arthur, TX Metro Area	37,296	20,707	5,095	10,952	1,701	4,430	1,553	412	50,290	16,632	14,090
Beaver Dam, WI Micro Area	9,515	5,400	1,136	2,638	813	na	na	na	na	na	na
Beckley, WV Metro Area	16,440	8,591	3,057	4,575	511	1,962	1,167	302	na	na	na
Bellingham, WA Metro Area	24,312	13,653	3,796	5,342	850	1,664	664	69	na	na	na
Bend-Redmond, OR Metro Area	25,139	14,402	2,966	6,605	699	na	na	na	na	na	na
Billings, MT Metro Area	19,232	10,364	2,663	5,759	915	1,565	793	546	na	na	na
Binghamton, NY Metro Area	29,458	15,573	3,057	9,948	1,829	2,868	685	0	36,028	12,611	9,311
Birmingham-Hoover, AL Metro Area	118,093	66,972	13,893	34,347	4,017	12,549	4,998	1,606	145,854	49,904	43,983
Bismarck, ND Metro Area	13,014	6,898	1,478	4,465	1,355	na	na	na	na	na	na
Blacksburg-Christiansburg-Radford, VA Metro Area	18,506	9,715	3,083	5,344	854	1,308	568	na	na	na	na
Bloomington, IL Metro Area	16,015	8,822	2,077	4,894	947	na	na	na	na	na	na
Bloomington, IN Metro Area	14,936	6,973	2,405	4,718	764	na	na	na	na	na	na
Bloomsburg-Berwick, PA Metro Area	10,275	4,721	1,707	3,749	1,016	893	396	na	na	na	na
Bluefield, WV-VA Micro Area	14,834	8,347	2,374	3,940	583	1,778	903	138	na	na	na
Boise City, ID Metro Area	65,182	37,247	7,741	18,313	1,928	7,367	1,686	204	91,779	22,411	23,977
Boston-Cambridge-Newton, MA-NH Metro Area	468,966	243,333	65,268	144,203	25,278	55,847	11,118	460	589,951	179,885	160,811
Boulder, CO Metro Area	29,132	14,918	4,419	8,230	994	na	na	103	40,958	8,830	11,883
Bowling Green, KY Metro Area	15,939	7,909	2,850	4,523	794	2,067	664	548	na	na	na
Bozeman, MT Micro Area	8,441	5,061	1,274	1,731	203	na	na	na	na	na	na
Brainerd, MN Micro Area	13,607	7,946	1,974	3,210	754	479	207	17	19,815	4,074	3,567
Branson, MO Micro Area	14,109	8,532	1,647	3,672	443	na	na	na	na	na	na
Bremerton-Silverdale, WA Metro Area	30,033	16,523	4,505	7,665	1,015	2,341	504	na	41,524	10,495	11,467
Bridgeport-Stamford-Norwalk, CT Metro Area	92,257	50,512	10,921	28,839	5,123	10,180	1,598	177	125,150	36,188	29,285
Brownsville-Harlingen, TX Metro Area	33,403	21,900	3,753	7,012	928	9,199	1,266	298	43,747	17,807	8,567
Brunswick, GA Metro Area	15,458	9,679	1,777	3,954	499	na	na	na	na	na	na
Buffalo-Cheektowaga-Niagara Falls, NY Metro Area	134,474	65,756	19,338	46,208	7,706	9,247	3,990	684	156,013	56,805	44,277
Burlington, NC Metro Area	17,636	8,485	2,540	6,335	999	2,699	582	0	na	na	na
Burlington-South Burlington, VT Metro Area	22,055	11,664	2,851	6,553	1,065	2,389	1,240	508	na	na	na
California-Lexington Park, MD Metro Area	9,007	4,485	1,185	2,880	689	na	na	na	na	na	na
Canton-Massillon, OH Metro Area	49,338	26,530	6,861	14,645	3,030	3,204	765	297	59,376	19,317	16,634
Cape Coral-Fort Myers, FL Metro Area	121,190	71,607	15,651	29,549	3,067	8,522	3,014	527	156,851	47,674	43,494
Cape Girardeau, MO-IL Metro Area	9,720	5,453	1,080	3,187	891	na	na	na	na	na	na
Carbondale-Marion, IL Metro Area	14,043	7,160	2,327	4,315	662	na	na	na	na	na	na
Carson City, NV Metro Area	7,131	3,258	1,314	2,514	754	na	na	na	na	na	na

Table D-4: Metropolitan/Micropolitan Statistical Areas - Household Relationship, Grandparents, and Marital Status—*Continued*

	Total Householders 65 Years and Over	Family Householders 65 Years and Over	Non-Family Householders 65 Years and Over		Persons 65 Years and Over Living in Group Quarters	Grandparents 60 Years and Over Living with Grandchildren			Marital Status - Persons 60 Years and Over		
			Male Living Alone	Female Living Alone		Total	Responsible for Grandchildren	Responsible for Grandchildren and In Poverty	Now Married	Widowed	Divorced
Casper, WY Metro Area	7,880	na	na	na	na	562	363	na	na	na	na
Cedar Rapids, IA Metro Area	28,796	14,903	4,228	9,019	1,353	1,936	356	na	35,466	12,344	10,213
Centralia, WA Micro Area	10,886	5,599	1,918	3,253	295	1,161	486	na	na	na	na
Chambersburg-Waynesboro, PA Metro Area	18,693	11,640	1,760	5,053	693	na	na	na	na	na	na
Champaign-Urbana, IL Metro Area	20,067	9,859	2,913	6,857	1,241	1,105	434	na	26,505	9,280	7,018
Charleston, WV Metro Area	28,326	14,808	4,322	8,706	848	2,728	1,626	206	34,996	13,021	9,038
Charleston-North Charleston, SC Metro Area	73,111	42,210	10,090	19,195	1,651	10,449	4,611	1,916	94,097	30,628	26,329
Charlotte-Concord-Gastonia, NC-SC Metro Area	206,470	118,153	24,326	58,497	7,806	26,611	8,461	962	284,144	89,563	77,796
Charlottesville, VA Metro Area	25,656	14,493	2,960	7,078	913	1,660	1,172	190	34,213	11,489	6,251
Chattanooga, TN-GA Metro Area	62,125	35,221	8,063	17,804	3,016	8,118	3,554	324	80,276	28,451	22,000
Cheyenne, WY Metro Area	11,096	5,740	1,866	3,244	324	na	na	na	na	na	na
Chicago-Naperville-Elgin, IL-IN-WI Metro Area	858,556	455,236	118,452	265,246	42,502	109,625	24,182	3,888	1,078,047	371,531	279,496
Chico, CA Metro Area	25,859	14,820	2,963	7,009	819	3,267	648	62	32,895	9,616	11,365
Chillicothe, OH Micro Area	8,430	5,034	1,128	2,183	541	na	na	na	na	na	na
Cincinnati, OH-KY-IN Metro Area	208,494	111,658	31,119	61,957	13,551	19,624	8,496	1,129	269,102	88,351	75,098
Claremont-Lebanon, NH-VT Micro Area	29,867	16,703	4,432	7,670	1,551	2,327	531	na	38,700	10,618	9,967
Clarksburg, WV Metro Area	11,562	5,584	1,864	3,874	724	na	na	na	na	na	na
Clarksville, TN-KY Metro Area	18,117	10,672	2,931	4,180	1,092	2,844	375	na	25,435	7,083	9,502
Clearlake, CA Micro Area	9,808	3,630	2,442	3,259	270	na	na	na	na	na	na
Cleveland, TN Metro Area	13,167	7,370	1,451	3,910	637	1,938	813	0	na	na	na
Cleveland-Elyria, OH Metro Area	247,018	125,360	36,827	78,027	13,513	17,401	5,732	503	280,853	98,971	87,380
Coeur d'Alene, ID Metro Area	19,738	11,076	2,811	5,339	649	1,013	582	na	na	na	na
College Station-Bryan, TX Metro Area	17,983	10,559	2,203	5,013	642	1,945	798	na	21,581	6,757	5,522
Colorado Springs, CO Metro Area	58,991	33,509	8,229	15,666	1,298	6,953	1,517	306	82,960	21,140	25,613
Columbia, MO Metro Area	14,295	7,378	2,162	4,502	779	na	na	na	na	na	na
Columbia, SC Metro Area	78,101	43,347	10,508	22,329	2,911	11,215	3,291	380	93,904	34,709	29,652
Columbus, GA-AL Metro Area	28,711	15,348	3,598	9,314	690	2,421	840	190	32,680	12,021	11,021
Columbus, IN Metro Area	8,957	4,583	1,645	2,678	586	na	na	na	na	na	na
Columbus, OH Metro Area	173,268	96,295	21,045	50,335	6,774	20,793	5,675	1,782	225,731	70,847	70,121
Concord, NH Micro Area	16,924	8,430	2,506	5,343	1,181	1,620	313	na	na	na	na
Cookeville, TN Micro Area	11,946	6,748	1,669	3,341	568	na	na	na	na	na	na
Coos Bay, OR Micro Area	10,783	5,330	2,198	2,730	293	na	na	na	na	na	na
Corning, NY Micro Area	11,538	5,618	1,863	3,579	949	586	250	48	15,196	4,665	4,496
Corpus Christi, TX Metro Area	40,269	23,931	5,283	9,775	2,104	7,472	2,634	484	54,290	18,860	15,690
Corvallis, OR Metro Area	8,774	5,333	916	2,160	264	na	na	na	na	na	na
Crestview-Fort Walton Beach-Destin, FL Metro Area	29,659	15,862	4,633	8,134	1,187	2,420	715	44	39,188	10,417	13,421
Cullman, AL Micro Area	9,912	5,188	1,083	3,296	136	na	na	na	na	na	na
Cumberland, MD-WV Metro Area	12,799	6,443	2,143	3,867	1,126	na	na	na	na	na	na
Dallas-Fort Worth-Arlington, TX Metro Area	490,522	290,053	57,806	131,772	18,440	99,614	25,548	3,309	728,917	217,042	201,231
Dalton, GA Metro Area	12,910	5,859	2,428	4,377	304	2,093	378	47	na	na	na
Danville, IL Metro Area	9,996	4,534	2,170	3,079	478	773	202	30	na	na	na
Danville, VA Micro Area	14,421	8,348	1,569	4,202	842	1,906	891	370	na	na	na
Daphne-Fairhope-Foley, AL Metro Area	27,136	16,288	3,291	6,321	977	3,250	1,150	160	na	na	na
Davenport-Moline-Rock Island, IA-IL Metro Area	42,545	21,125	6,665	13,926	2,417	2,546	738	195	51,993	17,598	15,022
Dayton, OH Metro Area	92,499	48,937	13,565	28,230	5,712	8,476	2,686	448	108,638	37,767	33,398
Decatur, AL Metro Area	17,149	9,690	2,058	5,243	464	2,764	1,558	555	na	na	na
Decatur, IL Metro Area	13,096	6,965	2,132	3,694	993	na	na	na	na	na	na
Deltona-Daytona Beach-Ormond Beach, FL Metro Area	98,613	54,864	14,107	25,003	2,775	7,626	2,204	155	120,475	39,995	40,822
Denver-Aurora-Lakewood, CO Metro Area	237,112	125,670	33,249	71,535	7,200	27,017	6,326	281	314,793	79,259	103,545
Des Moines-West Des Moines, IA Metro Area	54,699	27,568	7,749	17,434	2,895	3,342	1,123	187	70,037	21,534	18,628
Detroit-Warren-Dearborn, MI Metro Area	456,698	234,172	63,924	147,372	18,140	46,595	8,909	717	540,179	190,728	171,370
Dothan, AL Metro Area	18,008	10,087	2,381	5,360	730	1,643	733	79	21,279	7,928	5,529
Dover, DE Metro Area	17,737	10,355	2,496	4,158	789	1,782	1,177	130	na	na	na
DuBois, PA Micro Area	10,186	5,221	1,489	3,281	668	na	na	na	na	na	na
Dubuque, IA Metro Area	10,313	5,519	1,002	3,463	1,272	na	na	na	na	na	na
Duluth, MN-WI Metro Area	33,939	16,918	5,792	10,139	2,658	1,736	709	23	42,484	13,638	11,228
Dunn, NC Micro Area	9,992	5,884	1,343	2,708	537	1,239	219	na	na	na	na
Durham-Chapel Hill, NC Metro Area	53,500	31,096	5,830	15,010	2,240	5,774	993	98	71,492	19,551	19,486
East Stroudsburg, PA Metro Area	15,553	9,089	2,160	3,655	510	na	na	na	na	na	na
Eau Claire, WI Metro Area	17,510	9,316	2,432	5,364	753	na	na	na	na	na	na
El Centro, CA Metro Area	10,251	7,163	882	1,983	203	5,434	728	32	na	na	na
Elizabeth City, NC Micro Area	8,400	5,039	1,041	2,021	265	na	na	na	na	na	na
Elizabethtown-Fort Knox, KY Metro Area	13,754	8,539	1,594	3,575	533	2,040	872	183	na	na	na
Elkhart-Goshen, IN Metro Area	17,003	10,343	2,030	4,325	1,109	1,480	210	na	na	na	na
Elmira, NY Metro Area	10,247	5,458	1,459	3,256	1,096	na	na	na	na	na	na
El Paso, TX Metro Area	61,959	35,847	8,619	16,170	1,844	14,655	4,843	993	78,001	29,885	23,485
Enid, OK Metro Area	6,272	na	na	na	na	na	na	na	na	na	na
Erie, PA Metro Area	31,393	16,752	4,989	8,713	2,421	1,807	454	97	38,128	13,649	8,752
Eugene, OR Metro Area	46,536	23,562	6,636	13,122	1,756	3,874	1,114	131	56,087	14,538	20,205
Eureka-Arcata-Fortuna, CA Micro Area	16,123	7,932	2,804	4,259	528	na	na	na	na	na	na
Evansville, IN-KY Metro Area	32,167	17,542	4,811	8,705	2,749	3,970	2,568	929	43,700	12,578	12,764
Fairbanks, AK Metro Area	6,987	na	na	na	na	na	na	na	na	na	na

Table D-4: Metropolitan/Micropolitan Statistical Areas - Household Relationship, Grandparents, and Marital Status—*Continued*

	Total Householders 65 Years and Over	Family Householders 65 Years and Over	Non-Family Householders 65 Years and Over		Persons 65 Years and Over Living in Group Quarters	Grandparents 60 Years and Over Living with Grandchildren			Marital Status - Persons 60 Years and Over		
			Male Living Alone	Female Living Alone		Total	Responsible for Grandchildren	Responsible for Grandchildren and In Poverty	Now Married	Widowed	Divorced
Fargo, ND-MN Metro Area	19,059	9,573	3,264	5,702	1,265	909	320	na	na	na	na
Faribault-Northfield, MN Micro Area	6,671	3,381	694	2,485	449	na	na	na	na	na	na
Farmington, MO Micro Area	7,061	na	na	na	na	na	na	na	na	na	na
Farmington, NM Metro Area	12,097	7,730	1,720	2,483	419	2,549	1,050	437	na	na	na
Fayetteville, NC Metro Area	29,362	14,767	4,952	9,115	965	4,505	1,907	375	32,978	16,321	9,942
Fayetteville-Springdale-Rogers, AR-MO Metro Area	42,779	26,102	4,042	11,388	1,896	3,846	1,953	9	63,167	18,193	13,661
Findlay, OH Micro Area	8,173	4,160	1,300	2,495	519	na	na	na	na	na	na
Flagstaff, AZ Metro Area	10,903	6,977	1,584	2,013	215	2,279	722	54	na	na	na
Flint, MI Metro Area	47,441	25,288	6,789	14,045	1,478	3,383	959	228	54,518	17,468	19,195
Florence, SC Metro Area	22,407	12,554	2,728	6,789	1,154	2,458	721	279	28,129	9,585	6,633
Florence-Muscle Shoals, AL Metro Area	18,903	11,351	1,933	5,030	637	1,251	557	245	na	na	na
Fond du Lac, WI Metro Area	11,716	6,614	1,233	3,518	593	na	na	na	na	na	na
Forest City, NC Micro Area	9,054	5,376	1,309	1,907	562	na	na	na	na	na	na
Fort Collins, CO Metro Area	33,694	20,026	3,675	8,838	1,097	na	na	na	na	na	na
Fort Payne, AL Micro Area	8,140	4,765	912	2,439	268	1,021	410	na	na	na	na
Fort Smith, AR-OK Metro Area	30,619	16,017	4,852	8,699	1,733	2,695	1,047	66	35,255	13,290	11,019
Fort Wayne, IN Metro Area	42,222	21,988	5,927	13,464	2,360	3,686	1,655	184	54,686	16,526	12,785
Frankfort, KY Micro Area	8,330	4,597	1,287	2,280	285	1,188	407	na	na	na	na
Fresno, CA Metro Area	72,341	39,867	9,938	20,582	3,551	14,787	3,247	431	94,553	34,928	23,017
Gadsden, AL Metro Area	12,152	6,797	1,464	3,690	539	1,535	1,134	172	na	na	na
Gainesville, FL Metro Area	24,269	12,637	3,178	7,633	1,729	2,132	585	81	29,753	8,541	10,252
Gainesville, GA Metro Area	16,870	11,144	2,007	3,458	455	2,026	555	0	na	na	na
Gallup, NM Micro Area	5,709	3,913	459	1,323	202	1,309	642	169	na	na	na
Gettysburg, PA Metro Area	12,529	6,608	2,283	3,191	968	773	285	na	na	na	na
Glens Falls, NY Metro Area	16,847	8,738	2,892	4,508	868	na	na	na	na	na	na
Glenwood Springs, CO Micro Area	5,314	2,263	1,072	1,524	281	na	na	na	na	na	na
Goldsboro, NC Metro Area	13,389	8,103	1,200	3,979	277	2,218	1,015	428	na	na	na
Grand Forks, ND-MN Metro Area	9,459	4,594	1,806	2,798	972	na	na	na	na	na	na
Grand Island, NE Metro Area	8,741	na	na	na	na	na	na	na	na	na	na
Grand Junction, CO Metro Area	18,280	8,518	3,461	5,743	382	1,114	327	na	na	na	na
Grand Rapids-Wyoming, MI Metro Area	97,417	54,104	12,061	29,219	4,476	9,175	1,698	299	137,869	36,200	30,116
Grants Pass, OR Metro Area	14,454	7,894	1,961	3,912	344	na	na	na	na	na	na
Great Falls, MT Metro Area	9,377	4,735	1,909	2,585	402	na	na	na	na	na	na
Greeley, CO Metro Area	22,416	14,075	1,917	5,791	247	5,061	967	123	34,288	9,412	9,385
Green Bay, WI Metro Area	32,733	16,694	5,384	9,894	1,098	1,351	399	0	43,878	11,758	10,144
Greeneville, TN Micro Area	8,422	5,503	1,013	1,765	599	na	na	na	na	na	na
Greenfield Town, MA Micro Area	9,784	5,082	1,633	2,829	442	na	na	na	na	na	na
Greensboro-High Point, NC Metro Area	78,472	43,747	9,250	23,336	3,590	8,948	4,148	796	100,713	32,163	27,746
Greenville, NC Metro Area	14,472	8,124	2,056	4,019	565	1,818	762	235	na	na	na
Greenville-Anderson-Mauldin, SC Metro Area	93,228	52,949	12,173	26,452	3,536	10,011	3,817	634	123,458	38,532	31,164
Greenwood, SC Micro Area	10,883	6,611	894	3,133	721	1,059	384	na	na	na	na
Gulfport-Biloxi-Pascagoula, MS Metro Area	39,804	23,616	5,436	9,528	1,323	4,401	2,509	1,265	50,776	16,550	13,591
Hagerstown-Martinsburg, MD-WV Metro Area	27,044	14,491	3,768	7,614	1,101	1,654	314	0	37,430	10,459	10,218
Hammond, LA Metro Area	11,765	6,275	1,463	3,751	570	na	na	na	na	na	na
Hanford-Corcoran, CA Metro Area	9,949	6,458	1,180	2,037	607	1,192	338	59	10,327	5,351	2,992
Harrisburg-Carlisle, PA Metro Area	64,145	34,101	7,804	20,075	4,285	5,703	2,166	207	83,809	26,086	19,757
Harrisonburg, VA Metro Area	12,547	6,571	2,023	3,738	482	na	na	na	na	na	na
Hartford-West Hartford-East Hartford, CT Metro Area	127,370	63,881	18,650	41,135	11,415	11,230	1,890	150	159,937	51,691	47,841
Hattiesburg, MS Metro Area	13,122	7,048	1,576	4,306	681	1,196	226	90	na	na	na
Helena, MT Micro Area	9,420	4,492	1,963	2,235	304	na	na	na	na	na	na
Hermiston-Pendleton, OR Micro Area	8,178	4,336	1,138	2,481	596	495	243	na	na	na	na
Hickory-Lenoir-Morganton, NC Metro Area	43,086	25,135	5,881	11,145	1,657	6,951	2,104	26	58,435	18,817	11,603
Hilo, HI Micro Area	25,848	14,000	4,872	5,883	672	na	na	na	32,596	10,298	10,042
Hilton Head Island-Bluffton-Beaufort, SC Metro Area	32,829	21,925	3,248	6,574	672	na	na	na	na	na	na
Hinesville, GA Metro Area	4,212	na	na	na	na	1,259	541	31	na	na	na
Hobbs, NM Micro Area	4,873	2,392	869	1,403	237	na	na	na	na	na	na
Holland, MI Micro Area	11,325	7,031	1,479	2,288	798	1,539	616	na	na	na	na
Homosassa Springs, FL Metro Area	33,165	17,305	5,445	9,299	706	na	na	na	na	na	na
Hot Springs, AR Metro Area	14,925	8,966	1,518	4,044	555	na	na	na	na	na	na
Houma-Thibodaux, LA Metro Area	19,686	11,669	2,400	5,286	819	2,198	1,035	25	na	na	na
Houston-The Woodlands-Sugar Land, TX Metro Area	446,713	266,267	56,428	111,513	13,923	103,820	23,335	3,635	661,975	198,827	181,389
Huntington-Ashland, WV-KY-OH Metro Area	41,113	23,123	5,860	11,705	2,163	4,796	2,440	687	51,506	20,120	12,736
Huntsville, AL Metro Area	45,512	26,137	5,345	13,310	719	5,464	2,862	1,032	58,071	17,075	15,514
Huntsville, TX Metro Area	7,993	na	na	na	na	na	na	na	na	na	na
Hutchinson, KS Micro Area	7,982	3,803	1,107	2,947	574	na	na	na	na	na	na
Idaho Falls, ID Metro Area	11,776	7,047	1,204	3,214	278	1,822	497	na	na	na	na
Indiana, PA Micro Area	10,360	6,332	1,356	2,567	206	742	315	na	na	na	na
Indianapolis-Carmel-Anderson, IN Metro Area	173,440	94,617	23,660	51,074	8,644	19,309	7,547	1,400	225,650	69,778	66,829
Iowa City, IA Metro Area	13,552	8,312	1,625	3,472	788	na	na	na	na	na	na
Ithaca, NY Metro Area	9,079	4,936	1,267	2,372	505	na	na	na	na	na	na
Jackson, MI Metro Area	17,558	9,085	3,251	4,816	1,050	1,528	475	0	na	na	na

Table D-4: Metropolitan/Micropolitan Statistical Areas - Household Relationship, Grandparents, and Marital Status—*Continued*

	Total Householders 65 Years and Over	Family Householders 65 Years and Over	Non-Family Householders 65 Years and Over		Persons 65 Years and Over Living in Group Quarters	Grandparents 60 Years and Over Living with Grandchildren			Marital Status - Persons 60 Years and Over		
			Male Living Alone	Female Living Alone		Total	Responsible for Grandchildren	Responsible for Grandchildren and In Poverty	Now Married	Widowed	Divorced
Jackson, MS Metro Area	52,662	29,177	6,949	15,609	4,534	6,727	3,352	252	63,600	25,169	19,534
Jackson, TN Metro Area	13,726	7,758	2,067	3,818	645	1,275	584	na	na	na	na
Jacksonville, FL Metro Area	146,371	81,168	19,809	41,896	5,296	19,189	5,129	747	185,489	61,377	60,009
Jacksonville, NC Metro Area	10,186	6,133	1,556	2,219	212	1,924	528	0	na	na	na
Jamestown-Dunkirk-Fredonia, NY Micro Area	15,814	8,021	2,407	4,907	1,659	1,196	433	na	na	na	na
Janesville-Beloit, WI Metro Area	17,695	9,271	2,150	5,669	840	na	na	na	na	na	na
Jefferson, GA Micro Area	5,719	na	na	na	na	na	na	na	na	na	na
Jefferson City, MO Metro Area	15,935	8,627	2,084	5,006	1,055	861	258	na	21,995	5,497	4,108
Johnson City, TN Metro Area	23,772	13,398	3,587	6,551	1,937	2,877	1,894	744	31,291	10,853	8,487
Johnstown, PA Metro Area	19,834	10,904	2,513	6,056	1,029	867	480	0	23,346	9,102	3,995
Jonesboro, AR Metro Area	12,583	7,390	1,307	3,504	838	1,515	1,097	174	na	na	na
Joplin, MO Metro Area	19,793	10,108	2,611	6,471	751	1,663	530	144	na	na	na
Kahului-Wailuku-Lahaina, HI Metro Area	16,943	11,008	1,660	3,358	403	3,099	928	na	24,821	5,805	6,142
Kalamazoo-Portage, MI Metro Area	33,299	17,105	4,832	10,411	1,291	2,194	471	65	44,418	12,729	12,647
Kalispell, MT Micro Area	11,891	6,729	1,397	3,448	371	1,493	568	na	na	na	na
Kankakee, IL Metro Area	10,631	5,485	1,461	3,465	1,289	na	na	na	na	na	na
Kansas City, MO-KS Metro Area	195,894	109,931	22,661	57,255	10,565	20,720	6,453	730	263,881	78,206	72,948
Kapaa, HI Micro Area	9,017	5,463	1,063	2,223	352	2,510	473	na	na	na	na
Keene, NH Micro Area	9,178	4,375	1,199	3,367	535	na	na	na	na	na	na
Kennewick-Richland, WA Metro Area	22,981	13,370	3,490	5,353	568	na	na	na	34,155	7,185	9,534
Key West, FL Micro Area	9,842	5,384	1,438	2,105	265	na	na	na	na	na	na
Killeen-Temple, TX Metro Area	30,645	18,096	3,126	8,771	1,928	3,480	1,476	258	40,141	14,333	10,344
Kingsport-Bristol-Bristol, TN-VA Metro Area	43,634	22,936	6,436	13,001	1,183	3,544	1,356	382	49,384	19,368	18,157
Kingston, NY Metro Area	21,616	11,556	3,309	6,051	1,329	2,317	816	99	27,219	8,634	9,077
Klamath Falls, OR Micro Area	8,846	4,146	1,973	2,325	253	na	na	na	na	na	na
Knoxville, TN Metro Area	99,845	58,065	13,014	26,130	4,202	9,317	4,198	766	130,764	43,500	33,675
Kokomo, IN Metro Area	10,516	6,743	988	2,656	432	na	na	na	na	na	na
La Crosse-Onalaska, WI-MN Metro Area	14,525	7,627	2,212	4,202	1,115	na	na	na	na	na	na
Lafayette, LA Metro Area	44,567	25,243	5,362	12,230	2,399	6,080	2,916	1,426	55,906	20,971	13,429
Lafayette-West Lafayette, IN Metro Area	17,007	9,013	3,240	4,650	1,020	1,910	1,127	80	22,340	6,835	7,139
LaGrange, GA Micro Area	6,585	na	na	na	na	1,556	835	430	na	na	na
Lake Charles, LA Metro Area	20,957	11,161	2,808	6,422	779	2,696	2,208	0	na	na	na
Lake City, FL Micro Area	7,568	4,100	972	2,323	698	na	na	na	na	na	na
Lake Havasu City-Kingman, AZ Metro Area	39,594	24,329	5,797	7,900	580	2,339	805	136	51,557	14,237	13,130
Lakeland-Winter Haven, FL Metro Area	84,267	50,260	10,641	20,690	1,655	7,629	1,997	576	105,597	38,226	27,043
Lancaster, PA Metro Area	57,454	34,906	6,077	15,204	4,510	3,939	732	99	84,704	22,435	14,608
Lansing-East Lansing, MI Metro Area	46,592	24,728	7,341	12,826	1,412	3,274	426	69	64,289	17,460	16,451
Laredo, TX Metro Area	15,185	8,711	1,459	4,377	351	5,620	742	259	17,415	7,919	4,787
Las Cruces, NM Metro Area	20,682	11,790	2,253	6,112	405	4,608	2,230	618	na	na	na
Las Vegas-Henderson-Paradise, NV Metro Area	187,797	103,390	29,992	44,906	3,912	33,966	9,237	1,229	242,221	75,829	89,883
Laurel, MS Micro Area	9,654	6,076	979	2,361	585	na	na	na	na	na	na
Lawrence, KS Metro Area	9,782	4,834	946	3,506	431	na	na	na	na	na	na
Lawton, OK Metro Area	10,434	5,570	1,787	2,826	876	2,445	858	107	na	na	na
Lebanon, PA Metro Area	17,563	10,079	2,029	5,162	1,160	1,100	341	na	na	na	na
Lewiston, ID-WA Metro Area	8,946	4,839	1,053	2,751	601	784	372	na	na	na	na
Lewiston-Auburn, ME Metro Area	12,277	5,575	2,028	4,263	949	na	na	na	na	na	na
Lexington-Fayette, KY Metro Area	44,993	24,867	5,082	14,476	1,922	4,678	1,932	449	58,511	18,219	17,334
Lima, OH Metro Area	11,540	5,889	1,966	3,499	703	650	288	na	na	na	na
Lincoln, NE Metro Area	30,654	15,931	4,371	9,599	509	2,121	460	na	39,477	11,176	9,228
Little Rock-North Little Rock-Conway, AR Metro Area	69,133	40,750	8,124	18,883	4,275	7,957	3,171	894	90,782	27,739	28,163
Logan, UT-ID Metro Area	8,243	5,066	1,002	2,124	245	na	na	na	na	na	na
London, KY Micro Area	12,308	7,445	1,022	3,534	963	2,277	1,217	492	na	na	na
Longview, TX Metro Area	21,507	12,788	2,677	5,737	2,250	2,798	1,386	337	29,962	8,736	7,908
Longview, WA Metro Area	13,407	7,871	1,459	3,759	563	2,299	1,706	na	na	na	na
Los Angeles-Long Beach-Anaheim, CA Metro Area	1,010,518	575,053	127,829	266,810	53,831	240,443	37,781	5,935	1,388,000	463,976	375,283
Louisville/Jefferson County, KY-IN Metro Area	129,880	72,550	17,471	36,847	5,988	13,030	4,993	688	169,074	51,867	49,501
Lubbock, TX Metro Area	24,925	14,393	2,216	7,336	1,049	3,240	1,906	34	31,787	10,998	10,842
Lufkin, TX Micro Area	7,583	3,887	1,298	2,060	1,156	na	na	na	na	na	na
Lumberton, NC Micro Area	12,744	7,458	1,683	3,193	615	1,552	558	267	15,003	6,980	4,006
Lynchburg, VA Metro Area	31,368	16,648	4,123	10,008	1,435	2,188	916	137	38,067	14,218	10,140
Macon-Bibb County, GA Metro Area	23,565	11,695	3,525	7,865	1,430	4,377	1,837	342	26,832	11,016	7,637
Madera, CA Metro Area	11,632	7,043	1,676	2,461	494	1,063	302	51	na	na	na
Madison, WI Metro Area	61,984	32,451	8,042	18,805	1,832	4,359	1,818	38	85,003	18,626	19,353
Manchester-Nashua, NH Metro Area	38,337	20,376	5,156	11,230	3,253	3,243	648	73	53,633	17,260	14,306
Manhattan, KS Metro Area	6,689	3,439	1,000	2,227	566	na	na	na	na	na	na
Manitowoc, WI Micro Area	10,386	5,471	1,391	3,436	758	na	na	na	na	na	na
Mankato-North Mankato, MN Metro Area	9,313	5,071	1,137	2,825	957	na	na	na	na	na	na
Mansfield, OH Metro Area	15,028	8,301	1,522	4,894	843	na	na	na	na	na	na
Marinette, WI-MI Micro Area	9,494	4,896	1,772	2,602	768	na	na	na	na	na	na
Marion, IN Micro Area	8,420	na	na	na	na	na	na	111	na	na	na
Marion, OH Micro Area	6,905	3,619	991	2,067	592	na	na	na	na	na	na

Table D-4: Metropolitan/Micropolitan Statistical Areas - Household Relationship, Grandparents, and Marital Status—Continued

	Total Householders 65 Years and Over	Family Householders 65 Years and Over	Non-Family Householders 65 Years and Over		Persons 65 Years and Over Living in Group Quarters	Grandparents 60 Years and Over Living with Grandchildren			Marital Status - Persons 60 Years and Over		
			Male Living Alone	Female Living Alone		Total	Responsible for Grandchildren	Responsible for Grandchildren and In Poverty	Now Married	Widowed	Divorced
Marquette, MI Micro Area	8,026	4,038	1,669	2,000	485	na	na	na	na	na	na
Marshall, TX Micro Area	6,821	na	na	na	na	na	na	na	na	na	na
Martinsville, VA Micro Area	9,267	4,989	1,334	2,802	622	893	696	38	na	na	na
McAllen-Edinburg-Mission, TX Metro Area	56,271	36,294	5,568	13,461	1,782	14,414	3,298	1,580	74,825	32,018	14,656
Meadville, PA Micro Area	11,241	6,513	1,839	2,523	160	1,257	706	55	na	na	na
Medford, OR Metro Area	29,411	15,504	3,130	9,403	1,420	2,410	867	na	na	na	na
Memphis, TN-MS-AR Metro Area	120,430	63,701	17,816	35,905	4,493	16,400	7,227	885	150,287	50,800	45,150
Merced, CA Metro Area	18,366	10,238	2,384	5,211	254	4,755	545	25	23,988	8,329	6,440
Meridian, MS Micro Area	12,145	6,727	1,827	3,170	420	1,247	857	375	na	na	na
Miami-Fort Lauderdale-West Palm Beach, FL Metro Area....	623,998	332,565	87,824	178,929	23,237	106,061	20,499	3,099	747,843	291,677	274,994
Michigan City-La Porte, IN Metro Area	13,199	6,839	1,908	4,244	483	na	na	na	na	na	na
Midland, MI Metro Area	9,892	5,256	1,194	3,193	320	na	na	na	na	na	na
Midland, TX Metro Area	12,836	5,852	2,039	4,648	330	2,402	979	28	na	na	na
Milwaukee-Waukesha-West Allis, WI Metro Area	156,917	80,313	23,007	50,175	6,564	13,337	4,627	700	196,454	62,817	51,981
Minneapolis-St. Paul-Bloomington, MN-WI Metro Area	313,964	165,992	43,886	95,109	15,856	27,892	6,568	524	427,120	107,212	116,743
Minot, ND Micro Area	6,758	na	na	na	na	na	na	na	na	na	na
Missoula, MT Metro Area	11,491	6,060	1,683	3,209	238	na	na	na	na	na	na
Mobile, AL Metro Area	43,522	24,258	6,428	12,102	1,331	3,893	1,524	510	48,018	19,265	16,244
Modesto, CA Metro Area	41,197	25,302	3,389	11,082	1,733	8,104	1,806	338	56,989	19,945	16,515
Monroe, LA Metro Area	16,717	8,806	2,514	4,999	1,030	2,330	442	0	na	na	na
Monroe, MI Metro Area	18,137	10,302	2,441	5,164	830	1,284	563	na	na	na	na
Montgomery, AL Metro Area	37,384	21,125	4,955	10,774	1,521	4,174	1,668	619	42,276	15,827	14,112
Morehead City, NC Micro Area	11,038	6,263	1,249	3,220	293	na	na	na	na	na	na
Morgantown, WV Metro Area	12,186	7,332	1,698	2,867	631	na	na	na	na	na	na
Morristown, TN Metro Area	13,095	7,783	1,263	3,431	663	1,923	1,075	na	na	na	na
Moses Lake, WA Micro Area	7,992	4,379	1,055	1,748	283	na	na	na	na	na	na
Mount Airy, NC Micro Area	9,879	5,369	1,205	3,143	585	na	na	na	na	na	na
Mount Pleasant, MI Micro Area	5,749	2,948	766	1,907	488	na	na	na	na	na	na
Mount Vernon-Anacortes, WA Metro Area	15,788	9,419	1,864	3,936	386	1,026	234	137	na	na	na
Muncie, IN Metro Area	12,849	7,138	1,527	4,114	1,147	570	307	na	na	na	na
Muskegon, MI Metro Area	18,617	10,444	2,135	5,186	1,332	1,631	504	94	na	na	na
Muskogee, OK Micro Area	7,165	3,731	1,079	2,191	662	757	283	0	na	na	na
Myrtle Beach-Conway-North Myrtle Beach, SC-NC Metro Area	73,740	45,183	9,886	15,886	1,108	5,912	2,243	571	107,079	27,593	23,764
Nacogdoches, TX Micro Area	6,068	na	na	na	na	na	na	na	na	na	na
Napa, CA Metro Area	15,144	8,521	1,787	4,237	671	na	na	na	na	na	na
Naples-Immokalee-Marco Island, FL Metro Area	68,705	41,679	7,733	16,590	676	6,793	969	0	96,802	22,040	18,391
Nashville-Davidson--Murfreesboro--Franklin, TN Metro Area	157,468	89,390	19,064	44,428	5,506	21,353	7,571	977	212,054	62,332	61,083
New Bern, NC Metro Area	16,581	8,909	2,404	4,810	653	1,552	715	na	na	na	na
New Castle, PA Micro Area	11,822	6,686	1,616	3,264	684	1,096	635	139	na	na	na
New Haven-Milford, CT Metro Area	90,805	48,155	12,734	27,683	6,425	9,320	2,196	502	111,642	41,065	31,491
New Orleans-Metairie, LA Metro Area	123,478	65,483	18,494	36,161	4,311	16,923	4,923	1,735	148,635	53,947	50,306
New Philadelphia-Dover, OH Micro Area	11,470	5,226	1,973	4,037	646	na	na	na	na	na	na
New York-Newark-Jersey City, NY-NJ-PA Metro Area	1,893,325	1,015,850	234,189	592,161	98,436	298,055	57,742	9,963	2,365,175	814,971	565,203
Niles-Benton Harbor, MI Metro Area	19,901	10,926	3,252	5,086	983	1,847	464	43	na	na	na
North Port-Sarasota-Bradenton, FL Metro Area	159,541	90,061	17,919	44,861	4,155	8,051	1,937	206	196,674	56,779	51,411
North Wilkesboro, NC Micro Area	10,532	5,314	1,799	3,300	286	na	na	na	na	na	na
Norwich-New London, CT Metro Area	29,852	15,924	5,178	8,040	1,943	1,255	246	na	39,012	10,432	12,770
Oak Harbor, WA Micro Area	12,750	7,351	1,692	3,168	154	na	na	na	na	na	na
Ocala, FL Metro Area	62,379	36,695	8,095	15,359	1,372	3,961	2,204	853	76,854	23,845	20,104
Ocean City, NJ Metro Area	14,880	8,398	2,112	3,969	1,043	na	na	na	na	na	na
Odessa, TX Metro Area	9,917	5,249	946	3,572	482	940	418	na	na	na	na
Ogden-Clearfield, UT Metro Area	44,316	30,208	3,384	10,028	889	8,908	1,287	0	74,129	15,018	12,994
Ogdensburg-Massena, NY Micro Area	12,077	5,720	2,038	4,024	1,146	849	248	na	na	na	na
Oklahoma City, OK Metro Area	123,243	66,521	17,351	37,258	5,363	12,506	5,572	1,003	152,450	50,906	48,594
Olean, NY Micro Area	9,120	4,794	1,832	1,972	749	660	457	0	11,921	3,469	2,889
Olympia-Tumwater, WA Metro Area	29,900	16,511	3,436	8,918	1,133	2,511	838	0	41,680	10,727	11,881
Omaha-Council Bluffs, NE-IA Metro Area	83,376	42,916	12,350	25,717	4,136	6,348	2,370	72	106,117	32,116	30,748
Opelousas, LA Micro Area	8,223	4,186	1,216	2,731	628	na	na	na	na	na	na
Orangeburg, SC Micro Area	11,251	5,680	1,159	3,922	533	na	na	na	na	na	na
Orlando-Kissimmee-Sanford, FL Metro Area	206,946	124,169	23,150	52,738	6,942	42,688	9,318	1,364	297,209	90,904	93,267
Oshkosh-Neenah, WI Metro Area	18,183	8,483	2,930	6,298	1,071	na	na	na	na	na	na
Ottawa-Peru, IL Micro Area	19,294	10,112	3,223	5,491	1,451	925	429	33	na	na	na
Owensboro, KY Metro Area	13,373	7,358	1,890	3,593	941	1,192	578	25	na	na	na
Owosso, MI Micro Area	7,895	4,296	1,187	2,157	309	na	na	na	na	na	na
Oxnard-Thousand Oaks-Ventura, CA Metro Area	76,222	44,974	7,872	20,278	2,662	13,276	2,282	258	107,978	31,538	26,903
Paducah, KY-IL Micro Area	12,805	6,312	1,639	4,245	768	1,841	1,134	245	na	na	na
Palatka, FL Micro Area	10,815	5,988	2,079	2,226	312	na	na	na	na	na	na
Palm Bay-Melbourne-Titusville, FL Metro Area	84,167	45,342	13,561	22,168	2,158	7,258	1,853	151	104,714	35,376	36,414
Panama City, FL Metro Area	21,480	12,113	3,141	5,732	1,020	2,381	1,015	na	27,991	9,958	8,853
Parkersburg-Vienna, WV Metro Area	12,125	6,028	1,672	4,065	405	na	na	na	na	na	na
Pensacola-Ferry Pass-Brent, FL Metro Area	48,637	29,161	6,739	10,831	2,528	5,761	2,163	41	65,009	22,244	20,605

Table D-4: Metropolitan/Micropolitan Statistical Areas - Household Relationship, Grandparents, and Marital Status—Continued

	Total Householders 65 Years and Over	Family Householders 65 Years and Over	Non-Family Householders 65 Years and Over		Persons 65 Years and Over Living in Group Quarters	Grandparents 60 Years and Over Living with Grandchildren			Marital Status - Persons 60 Years and Over		
			Male Living Alone	Female Living Alone		Total	Responsible for Grandchildren	Responsible for Grandchildren and In Poverty	Now Married	Widowed	Divorced
Peoria, IL Metro Area	40,156	21,341	6,113	12,098	3,284	2,116	922	365	55,216	16,930	13,237
Philadelphia-Camden-Wilmington, PA-NJ-DE-MD Metro Area	601,231	319,797	82,112	183,572	32,902	74,881	18,015	2,673	760,288	255,097	193,984
Phoenix-Mesa-Scottsdale, AZ Metro Area	443,253	253,924	56,516	116,127	12,402	61,913	15,658	3,105	604,658	170,149	176,207
Pine Bluff, AR Metro Area	9,953	5,561	862	3,298	905	488	183	20	na	na	na
Pinehurst-Southern Pines, NC Micro Area	14,474	8,216	1,734	4,014	948	na	na	na	na	na	na
Pittsburgh, PA Metro Area	303,276	152,027	44,931	100,066	13,942	18,463	6,610	857	371,160	122,306	86,133
Pittsfield, MA Metro Area	18,271	9,247	2,299	6,001	1,146	1,196	629	86	na	na	na
Plattsburgh, NY Micro Area	8,126	4,110	1,357	2,244	499	573	445	190	na	na	na
Pocatello, ID Metro Area	7,726	4,242	1,315	1,895	207	na	na	na	na	na	na
Port Angeles, WA Micro Area	14,164	7,602	2,646	3,270	409	na	na	na	na	na	na
Portland-South Portland, ME Metro Area	67,209	34,283	8,790	20,609	2,604	4,391	1,202	0	85,073	21,799	26,045
Portland-Vancouver-Hillsboro, OR-WA Metro Area	229,907	120,102	28,818	71,963	8,338	25,038	5,429	587	299,562	79,216	96,438
Port St. Lucie, FL Metro Area	74,558	42,368	9,155	19,612	1,867	8,947	3,470	0	90,815	32,268	26,432
Portsmouth, OH Micro Area	8,572	4,712	1,492	2,279	755	1,190	546	na	na	na	na
Pottsville, PA Micro Area	18,720	9,587	3,017	5,361	1,532	1,152	784	na	20,913	9,617	4,743
Prescott, AZ Metro Area	47,659	23,693	8,113	13,773	1,142	2,318	570	154	na	na	na
Providence-Warwick, RI-MA Metro Area	173,365	86,895	25,395	55,986	12,535	17,667	4,625	616	207,311	76,425	60,363
Provo-Orem, UT Metro Area	28,931	20,164	2,936	5,471	864	8,115	1,323	257	49,327	10,626	5,786
Pueblo, CO Metro Area	19,899	10,244	3,317	5,806	876	3,025	1,666	97	21,903	8,805	8,225
Punta Gorda, FL Metro Area	42,134	24,960	6,557	9,367	1,055	1,600	954	62	57,205	16,767	11,226
Quincy, IL-MO Micro Area	9,049	4,747	1,179	2,893	1,001	na	na	na	na	na	na
Racine, WI Metro Area	20,635	10,598	3,478	6,303	1,628	1,399	392	64	na	na	na
Raleigh, NC Metro Area	97,805	56,870	10,115	29,092	3,065	12,142	2,731	163	144,042	41,009	34,220
Rapid City, SD Metro Area	16,401	8,858	1,557	4,630	1,183	1,285	730	na	na	na	na
Reading, PA Metro Area	43,204	23,949	6,133	12,425	2,996	4,210	1,170	270	58,219	19,519	11,955
Redding, CA Metro Area	22,428	12,951	3,409	5,169	971	3,222	1,151	0	28,086	10,009	8,641
Reno, NV Metro Area	48,709	25,246	8,264	12,632	958	4,968	1,922	289	62,168	16,038	22,596
Richmond, IN Micro Area	8,133	3,921	1,335	2,346	682	na	na	na	na	na	na
Richmond, VA Metro Area	129,450	67,957	17,349	40,208	4,056	15,785	5,816	722	155,701	55,573	48,494
Richmond-Berea, KY Micro Area	9,739	5,645	1,128	2,682	672	901	308	na	na	na	na
Riverside-San Bernardino-Ontario, CA Metro Area	326,011	193,378	41,275	77,865	10,286	88,119	15,452	1,740	482,580	154,260	126,627
Roanoke, VA Metro Area	38,848	20,705	4,845	11,835	2,154	3,486	767	0	47,615	18,673	13,161
Roanoke Rapids, NC Micro Area	9,350	5,522	1,037	2,578	477	1,147	321	253	na	na	na
Rochester, MN Metro Area	22,103	12,533	2,523	6,625	1,749	1,298	217	na	31,666	8,228	6,070
Rochester, NY Metro Area	120,189	60,202	16,948	38,814	8,368	9,566	2,196	346	152,704	49,323	39,443
Rockford, IL Metro Area	36,083	20,429	3,913	10,945	1,973	3,430	1,948	0	51,367	13,642	11,144
Rocky Mount, NC Metro Area	19,318	10,343	2,602	5,846	562	1,925	741	179	na	na	na
Rome, GA Metro Area	10,194	5,780	1,108	3,252	638	1,209	794	na	na	na	na
Roseburg, OR Micro Area	17,844	10,455	2,659	3,807	339	na	na	na	na	na	na
Roswell, NM Micro Area	6,568	3,347	1,123	1,815	358	na	na	na	na	na	na
Russellville, AR Micro Area	7,873	4,615	1,029	2,142	625	na	na	na	na	na	na
Sacramento-Roseville-Arden-Arcade, CA Metro Area	213,573	117,231	26,880	61,972	8,074	35,492	5,536	388	285,913	85,845	90,196
Saginaw, MI Metro Area	23,894	12,808	3,168	7,358	1,367	1,136	651	183	27,755	9,849	8,036
St. Cloud, MN Metro Area	18,046	9,660	2,974	4,956	1,790	na	na	na	25,646	6,449	5,379
St. George, UT Metro Area	22,266	14,899	2,394	4,376	194	na	na	na	na	na	na
St. Joseph, MO-KS Metro Area	13,619	7,224	1,959	3,686	1,050	1,059	666	375	na	na	na
St. Louis, MO-IL Metro Area	297,140	160,859	41,288	88,545	16,585	22,528	6,973	1,800	378,447	122,852	101,516
Salem, OH Micro Area	12,925	7,112	2,122	3,276	1,270	977	296	21	na	na	na
Salem, OR Metro Area	41,060	23,317	5,289	11,092	2,513	5,020	1,950	431	53,442	15,802	18,833
Salinas, CA Metro Area	34,561	20,662	5,109	7,967	1,247	9,135	1,366	0	47,758	14,680	11,745
Salisbury, MD-DE Metro Area	59,544	35,913	7,010	14,843	2,270	4,361	1,672	160	82,685	19,448	18,193
Salt Lake City, UT Metro Area	79,657	48,146	9,073	21,021	2,203	14,977	3,127	493	117,779	28,760	30,210
San Angelo, TX Metro Area	11,834	6,682	1,400	3,248	338	1,262	545	na	na	na	na
San Antonio-New Braunfels, TX Metro Area	187,397	113,899	22,508	46,625	7,759	34,708	9,127	1,649	260,997	84,167	78,094
San Diego-Carlsbad, CA Metro Area	268,419	153,732	34,568	68,549	10,072	45,584	9,073	991	366,840	107,902	115,502
Sandusky, OH Micro Area	10,135	5,233	1,470	3,409	536	na	na	na	na	na	na
San Francisco-Oakland-Hayward, CA Metro Area	420,538	226,742	56,203	120,925	19,939	78,681	13,086	878	557,597	165,836	152,175
San Jose-Sunnyvale-Santa Clara, CA Metro Area	143,608	89,617	14,305	34,390	6,668	35,895	5,044	221	224,540	61,804	48,242
San Luis Obispo-Paso Robles-Arroyo Grande, CA Metro Area	35,948	20,916	4,615	9,145	1,056	2,922	686	na	48,310	10,852	12,329
Santa Cruz-Watsonville, CA Metro Area	27,799	15,542	3,167	7,341	607	na	na	na	37,938	8,270	10,181
Santa Fe, NM Metro Area	22,869	12,132	3,217	6,149	437	1,687	606	na	27,422	5,049	10,622
Santa Maria-Santa Barbara, CA Metro Area	41,277	24,066	4,917	10,596	1,601	6,032	927	114	55,278	15,208	14,214
Santa Rosa, CA Metro Area	62,227	31,420	7,895	19,283	1,891	4,107	597	na	72,218	21,020	26,615
Savannah, GA Metro Area	34,075	19,395	4,778	9,203	1,460	5,270	1,323	106	40,912	16,258	12,728
Scranton--Wilkes-Barre--Hazleton, PA Metro Area	70,268	34,962	9,976	23,143	5,295	4,739	1,953	147	84,012	31,336	20,555
Searcy, AR Micro Area	8,138	na	na	na	na	na	na	na	na	na	na
Seattle-Tacoma-Bellevue, WA Metro Area	321,485	171,551	44,398	93,748	15,477	42,800	10,097	443	439,721	111,969	132,375
Sebastian-Vero Beach, FL Metro Area	27,705	15,825	3,846	7,015	706	na	na	na	na	na	na
Sebring, FL Metro Area	21,675	12,453	3,633	4,446	802	na	na	na	na	na	na
Seneca, SC Micro Area	11,515	na	na	na	na	na	na	na	na	na	na
Sevierville, TN Micro Area	11,040	7,696	1,144	1,802	270	na	na	na	na	na	na

Table D-4: Metropolitan/Micropolitan Statistical Areas - Household Relationship, Grandparents, and Marital Status—*Continued*

	Total Householders 65 Years and Over	Family Householders 65 Years and Over	Non-Family Householders 65 Years and Over — Male Living Alone	Non-Family Householders 65 Years and Over — Female Living Alone	Persons 65 Years and Over Living in Group Quarters	Grandparents 60 Years and Over Living with Grandchildren — Total	Responsible for Grandchildren	Responsible for Grandchildren and In Poverty	Marital Status - Persons 60 Years and Over — Now Married	Widowed	Divorced
Shawnee, OK Micro Area	7,298	3,983	1,238	1,930	352	903	490	57	na	na	na
Sheboygan, WI Metro Area	13,487	6,753	2,122	4,329	518	na	na	na	na	na	na
Shelby, NC Micro Area	10,539	6,505	1,094	2,890	289	na	na	na	na	na	na
Shelton, WA Micro Area	8,846	4,641	1,474	2,160	304	na	na	na	na	na	na
Sherman-Denison, TX Metro Area	14,802	9,080	1,818	3,771	748	1,483	872	213	na	na	na
Show Low, AZ Micro Area	12,780	7,223	2,199	2,948	216	3,307	1,670	482	15,235	5,347	4,284
Shreveport-Bossier City, LA Metro Area	45,920	26,000	6,900	12,061	3,142	3,612	1,810	570	53,545	20,217	13,336
Sierra Vista-Douglas, AZ Metro Area	19,349	9,637	3,446	5,163	220	1,821	930	224	na	na	na
Sioux City, IA-NE-SD Metro Area	16,332	8,959	2,170	4,888	894	na	na	na	23,920	7,677	3,589
Sioux Falls, SD Metro Area	23,261	11,949	3,096	7,675	1,283	739	117	na	28,856	9,556	7,761
Somerset, PA Micro Area	9,473	5,273	1,426	2,484	923	na	na	na	na	na	na
South Bend-Mishawaka, IN-MI Metro Area	34,462	17,188	5,745	10,905	2,029	3,055	787	246	43,129	13,889	11,868
Spartanburg, SC Metro Area	33,815	20,869	3,587	8,613	1,182	4,374	1,706	373	46,168	14,460	11,255
Spokane-Spokane Valley, WA Metro Area	60,852	31,692	8,987	18,432	2,527	6,033	2,340	345	75,883	23,181	24,543
Springfield, IL Metro Area	24,003	12,242	3,524	7,844	942	1,589	589	0	29,990	9,597	8,317
Springfield, MA Metro Area	66,655	33,386	10,093	20,609	3,530	5,986	1,500	136	78,333	26,604	24,771
Springfield, MO Metro Area	50,083	25,939	7,431	15,593	2,484	2,982	1,418	252	61,989	18,285	19,383
Springfield, OH Metro Area	17,429	8,945	2,191	5,971	996	1,664	846	144	na	na	na
State College, PA Metro Area	13,802	7,722	1,808	3,931	930	na	na	na	na	na	na
Statesboro, GA Micro Area	5,700	na	na	na	na	na	na	na	na	na	na
Staunton-Waynesboro, VA Metro Area	17,316	8,538	2,630	5,284	856	na	na	na	na	na	na
Stevens Point, WI Micro Area	7,783	3,593	1,519	2,398	182	na	na	na	na	na	na
Stillwater, OK Micro Area	7,462	na	na	na	na	na	na	na	na	na	na
Stockton-Lodi, CA Metro Area	51,357	30,010	5,545	13,483	4,358	14,483	2,148	394	70,081	29,848	21,884
Sumter, SC Metro Area	10,897	6,482	1,372	2,952	625	1,547	316	190	na	na	na
Sunbury, PA Micro Area	12,466	6,360	2,146	3,678	1,020	na	na	na	na	na	na
Syracuse, NY Metro Area	70,660	35,943	10,644	21,915	3,368	4,913	1,435	257	90,405	29,392	23,036
Talladega-Sylacauga, AL Micro Area	10,347	6,242	1,369	2,556	416	na	na	0	na	na	na
Tallahassee, FL Metro Area	35,295	19,938	5,064	9,506	1,396	2,745	856	0	45,327	12,484	15,133
Tampa-St. Petersburg-Clearwater, FL Metro Area	375,283	192,506	54,189	113,475	14,358	43,261	13,128	2,743	439,161	167,551	157,472
Terre Haute, IN Metro Area	16,800	9,628	2,088	4,599	1,532	1,022	549	225	na	na	na
Texarkana, TX-AR Metro Area	15,677	7,471	2,467	5,414	1,298	2,411	933	21	na	na	na
The Villages, FL Metro Area	44,756	27,271	6,064	10,076	761	na	na	na	na	na	na
Toledo, OH Metro Area	60,641	32,314	8,725	18,059	4,380	5,900	1,989	403	78,952	22,364	24,266
Topeka, KS Metro Area	27,465	13,942	4,396	8,138	1,881	1,766	999	372	34,972	10,883	9,112
Torrington, CT Micro Area	23,504	11,901	3,695	7,124	1,060	na	na	na	na	na	na
Traverse City, MI Micro Area	19,878	11,272	2,649	5,048	1,170	1,069	513	na	na	na	na
Trenton, NJ Metro Area	35,066	18,725	4,915	10,816	2,106	3,174	1,512	330	43,970	13,521	12,668
Truckee-Grass Valley, CA Micro Area	16,239	9,195	2,117	3,899	574	na	na	na	na	na	na
Tucson, AZ Metro Area	126,887	70,010	16,733	34,152	3,000	12,921	3,630	907	156,211	47,881	46,915
Tullahoma-Manchester, TN Micro Area	12,013	6,133	1,425	3,946	443	1,648	880	137	na	na	na
Tulsa, OK Metro Area	96,079	53,670	13,247	27,200	4,060	11,731	4,929	479	123,699	40,776	36,032
Tupelo, MS Micro Area	12,167	7,800	976	3,204	973	1,475	632	65	na	na	na
Tuscaloosa, AL Metro Area	21,717	12,839	2,830	6,000	716	2,401	1,119	267	na	na	na
Twin Falls, ID Micro Area	9,741	5,798	1,128	2,504	298	na	na	na	na	na	na
Tyler, TX Metro Area	22,791	14,087	1,883	6,364	875	2,903	795	166	na	na	na
Ukiah, CA Micro Area	12,167	5,677	2,230	3,547	378	na	na	na	na	na	na
Urban Honolulu, HI Metro Area	91,320	58,146	11,165	18,717	5,569	26,879	3,561	106	123,217	46,317	28,346
Utica-Rome, NY Metro Area	33,811	17,731	4,836	10,002	3,780	2,654	889	0	45,338	14,095	10,451
Valdosta, GA Metro Area	13,374	6,753	1,691	4,738	365	na	na	na	na	na	na
Vallejo-Fairfield, CA Metro Area	38,327	23,564	4,398	8,978	1,758	9,437	2,058	304	59,713	16,570	16,618
Victoria, TX Metro Area	10,278	5,460	1,157	3,406	545	na	na	na	na	na	na
Vineland-Bridgeton, NJ Metro Area	14,558	7,500	2,015	4,781	1,699	906	495	37	na	na	na
Virginia Beach-Norfolk-Newport News, VA-NC Metro Area	157,793	85,316	22,337	45,976	4,468	18,572	5,846	1,061	204,895	68,523	57,122
Visalia-Porterville, CA Metro Area	29,774	17,143	3,277	8,721	1,852	7,923	2,594	1,004	43,840	13,563	11,911
Waco, TX Metro Area	24,632	14,105	2,814	7,178	1,314	2,638	880	52	33,142	9,929	8,087
Walla Walla, WA Metro Area	8,217	4,355	772	2,385	473	na	na	na	na	na	na
Warner Robins, GA Metro Area	14,460	8,250	2,127	4,026	765	3,312	1,220	0	na	na	na
Warsaw, IN Micro Area	8,548	4,523	1,044	2,757	445	na	na	na	na	na	na
Washington-Arlington-Alexandria, DC-VA-MD-WV Metro Area	470,638	259,386	62,013	133,585	17,322	85,311	15,592	1,540	654,726	182,846	169,221
Waterloo-Cedar Falls, IA Metro Area	18,517	10,090	2,563	5,527	839	na	na	na	na	na	na
Watertown-Fort Atkinson, WI Micro Area	9,124	5,668	1,005	2,268	358	na	na	na	na	na	na
Watertown-Fort Drum, NY Metro Area	9,611	5,114	1,292	3,104	468	523	303	na	na	na	na
Wausau, WI Metro Area	15,425	8,039	2,096	4,927	841	812	82	na	na	na	na
Weirton-Steubenville, WV-OH Metro Area	17,348	9,901	1,947	5,426	1,038	1,434	603	69	na	na	na
Wenatchee, WA Metro Area	13,101	7,159	1,813	3,487	466	na	na	na	na	na	na
Wheeling, WV-OH Metro Area	19,242	10,053	2,823	5,872	1,327	2,096	824	262	na	na	na
Whitewater-Elkhorn, WI Micro Area	11,193	6,011	1,506	3,409	476	691	297	na	na	na	na
Wichita, KS Metro Area	61,430	30,281	9,704	19,855	3,357	5,458	1,813	32	78,907	25,746	21,543
Wichita Falls, TX Metro Area	14,948	8,238	1,714	4,605	1,382	1,482	1,028	42	17,934	6,675	5,459

Table D-4: Metropolitan/Micropolitan Statistical Areas - Household Relationship, Grandparents, and Marital Status—Continued

| | Total Householders 65 Years and Over | Family Householders 65 Years and Over | Non-Family Householders 65 Years and Over | | Persons 65 Years and Over Living in Group Quarters | Grandparents 60 Years and Over Living with Grandchildren | | | Marital Status - Persons 60 Years and Over | | |
			Male Living Alone	Female Living Alone		Total	Responsible for Grandchildren	Responsible for Grandchildren and In Poverty	Now Married	Widowed	Divorced
Williamsport, PA Metro Area	13,364	7,392	1,526	4,050	946	593	194	0	na	na	na
Wilmington, NC Metro Area	32,231	16,843	4,205	10,198	1,186	2,598	984	275	41,131	14,870	12,131
Wilson, NC Micro Area	9,989	3,829	2,118	3,875	522	na	na	na	na	na	na
Winchester, VA-WV Metro Area	15,331	8,463	2,872	3,667	329	2,148	564	96	na	na	na
Winston-Salem, NC Metro Area	74,764	37,454	11,552	23,110	2,365	7,269	2,199	440	91,885	32,096	27,991
Wisconsin Rapids-Marshfield, WI Micro Area	9,953	5,107	1,379	3,258	584	na	na	na	na	na	na
Wooster, OH Micro Area	12,744	7,327	1,690	3,304	246	na	na	na	na	na	na
Worcester, MA-CT Metro Area	88,115	46,040	12,105	26,914	6,385	10,430	2,382	44	121,817	39,335	29,994
Yakima, WA Metro Area	21,499	12,469	2,933	5,636	709	3,197	871	424	27,935	8,984	7,384
York-Hanover, PA Metro Area	47,981	25,869	7,107	13,805	2,406	4,974	2,348	55	66,092	21,461	16,278
Youngstown-Warren-Boardman, OH-PA Metro Area	73,546	35,783	10,926	24,517	5,324	3,635	1,295	63	84,875	33,116	24,966
Yuba City, CA Metro Area	15,168	8,680	1,831	4,092	433	na	na	na	20,383	7,272	6,333
Yuma, AZ Metro Area	22,994	15,078	2,636	4,215	288	3,393	962	502	35,079	8,592	4,553
Zanesville, OH Micro Area	10,134	5,572	1,341	2,941	564	na	na	na	na	na	na

Table D-5: 116th Congressional Districts - Household Relationship, Grandparents, and Marital Status

	Total Householders 65 Years and Over	Family Householders 65 Years and Over	Non-Family Householders 65 Years and Over		Persons 65 Years and Over Living in Group Quarters	Grandparents 60 Years and Over Living with Grandchildren			Marital Status - Persons 60 Years and Over		
			Male Living Alone	Female Living Alone		Total	Responsible for Grandchildren	Responsible for Grandchildren and In Poverty	Now Married	Widowed	Divorced
Alabama											
Congressional District 1	81,162	46,118	11,305	21,505	2,728	8,236	2,981	747	97,124	34,574	28,737
Congressional District 2	71,219	39,680	9,707	20,714	3,599	6,618	2,803	659	85,435	35,690	23,724
Congressional District 3	73,987	43,105	9,421	19,939	2,870	8,288	2,320	312	97,794	33,170	21,895
Congressional District 4	80,677	45,890	10,292	23,139	2,857	9,688	5,034	1,732	104,242	39,905	23,409
Congressional District 5	76,457	45,129	8,394	21,684	1,684	9,301	4,968	1,462	100,806	29,935	23,387
Congressional District 6	71,378	43,393	7,232	19,546	2,262	7,509	2,544	922	101,501	29,392	23,539
Congressional District 7	69,093	34,352	10,869	22,219	2,772	8,590	4,048	1,461	63,440	30,900	28,147
Alaska											
Congressional District (at Large)	53,173	29,659	8,201	12,417	2,881	10,011	4,130	777	76,122	18,492	23,186
Arizona											
Congressional District 1	88,103	55,393	11,132	18,495	1,353	13,991	5,043	1,922	125,839	27,436	27,699
Congressional District 2	100,367	52,464	14,469	28,688	2,423	8,120	2,557	591	114,779	37,239	39,903
Congressional District 3	56,126	34,822	7,022	11,697	1,248	13,582	4,092	1,636	81,023	25,542	21,388
Congressional District 4	138,453	79,775	20,766	32,106	2,833	8,318	2,823	674	182,003	48,978	44,970
Congressional District 5	78,549	47,639	7,446	20,684	1,876	10,412	1,378	44	119,236	28,727	26,240
Congressional District 6	91,030	49,626	12,376	25,993	2,017	6,986	2,204	358	121,297	32,496	35,995
Congressional District 7	34,788	17,747	6,328	9,085	1,362	12,565	3,228	873	40,699	16,932	22,997
Congressional District 8	105,814	62,385	10,867	29,010	2,690	12,148	3,235	125	144,025	40,768	33,268
Congressional District 9	61,157	29,002	11,024	18,284	2,843	9,044	2,390	153	67,084	25,244	30,790
Arkansas											
Congressional District 1	82,565	46,046	12,163	22,535	4,874	9,011	5,192	1,696	99,159	38,811	29,123
Congressional District 2	74,690	42,785	8,925	21,477	4,309	7,531	2,866	654	94,339	31,207	29,447
Congressional District 3	72,354	41,953	8,206	19,998	3,948	7,037	3,320	151	99,876	28,939	25,242
Congressional District 4	85,229	47,535	11,479	24,394	4,879	6,954	3,488	867	107,499	38,607	29,614
California											
Congressional District 1	94,923	51,949	14,174	24,323	3,552	9,260	2,718	62	121,133	34,247	38,461
Congressional District 2	97,850	50,386	12,964	28,574	3,751	5,448	1,262	250	115,433	31,513	38,296
Congressional District 3	63,179	37,064	8,455	15,589	2,458	10,610	2,274	551	92,071	25,307	26,182
Congressional District 4	94,872	54,731	11,627	23,802	1,905	10,356	2,111	226	135,829	31,939	35,076
Congressional District 5	78,373	40,462	10,832	23,324	2,786	12,534	2,387	35	102,619	28,943	32,820
Congressional District 6	57,744	28,246	9,108	18,721	2,435	11,899	2,020	38	66,133	25,384	27,562
Congressional District 7	68,407	39,213	7,603	19,144	3,262	11,634	1,470	128	95,301	29,315	29,175
Congressional District 8	59,501	34,311	8,142	14,689	1,467	9,467	2,586	458	80,283	28,246	23,549
Congressional District 9	53,666	30,805	6,804	13,472	4,277	14,932	2,417	504	75,067	29,526	25,567
Congressional District 10	55,821	34,881	4,604	14,492	2,414	12,512	2,473	338	78,671	28,040	22,528
Congressional District 11	74,681	41,232	9,032	22,552	3,118	11,106	743	38	101,582	26,107	28,607
Congressional District 12	73,326	33,898	14,236	22,330	3,374	8,021	1,185	na	79,437	26,356	21,674
Congressional District 13	68,697	30,789	10,612	23,656	2,922	9,153	2,466	390	68,155	27,012	26,712
Congressional District 14	66,263	39,927	8,090	16,048	3,693	16,778	1,701	93	95,522	30,166	23,526
Congressional District 15	54,142	33,281	4,932	13,722	2,992	20,034	4,189	154	89,985	25,154	20,502
Congressional District 16	44,971	24,129	6,473	12,639	2,356	11,385	2,095	171	58,298	23,219	16,577
Congressional District 17	45,945	29,324	4,575	9,798	2,288	14,676	2,219	165	82,612	23,663	16,907
Congressional District 18	68,719	40,856	6,788	18,365	3,353	8,444	993	50	99,386	23,073	20,655
Congressional District 19	52,503	32,962	5,350	12,676	1,985	18,205	2,915	47	82,858	24,453	17,853
Congressional District 20	62,080	37,067	8,129	14,699	2,048	13,517	2,481	0	86,151	24,235	20,881
Congressional District 21	37,272	23,687	5,171	7,431	1,886	12,287	2,764	424	49,657	22,448	10,460
Congressional District 22	59,525	32,950	6,603	18,893	2,258	11,349	2,688	648	80,690	26,089	20,375
Congressional District 23	57,426	32,254	8,968	14,762	3,309	9,778	2,375	868	81,240	25,863	20,947
Congressional District 24	78,074	45,438	9,567	20,050	2,662	8,954	1,613	114	104,653	26,350	27,045
Congressional District 25	53,821	31,668	5,447	14,485	1,018	15,604	2,060	263	81,046	22,181	20,531
Congressional District 26	63,532	38,487	6,615	15,921	2,285	10,683	2,003	258	93,163	24,539	23,728
Congressional District 27	65,770	42,324	6,527	14,462	4,229	14,285	2,233	330	95,284	31,952	19,674
Congressional District 28	63,110	30,240	10,981	19,772	4,144	7,041	351	0	77,636	28,291	23,728
Congressional District 29	42,712	24,375	5,627	10,701	2,779	15,073	2,917	199	58,836	21,956	15,053
Congressional District 30	65,645	34,456	8,783	18,787	3,808	11,396	1,247	226	83,285	27,093	26,794
Congressional District 31	46,483	28,654	4,630	11,654	2,855	15,117	3,683	309	70,495	23,421	17,959
Congressional District 32	46,866	31,506	4,364	9,848	2,980	22,698	3,333	192	77,312	26,500	16,016
Congressional District 33	82,134	45,407	11,277	22,355	1,978	7,157	1,141	69	105,879	25,162	24,695
Congressional District 34	51,037	24,729	8,623	14,497	3,845	11,946	2,867	188	59,932	28,010	17,532
Congressional District 35	35,525	22,946	2,937	8,318	2,516	17,255	2,240	426	57,160	22,621	15,738
Congressional District 36	104,360	54,790	18,318	26,221	1,985	10,498	2,388	484	121,329	36,715	35,505
Congressional District 37	59,276	26,383	9,608	20,854	2,509	9,915	2,058	553	57,025	24,538	24,064
Congressional District 38	54,481	36,117	5,312	11,681	2,750	17,494	2,582	517	84,288	28,586	19,341
Congressional District 39	57,416	37,903	4,584	12,683	3,038	15,981	2,584	234	95,705	27,176	19,297
Congressional District 40	30,304	20,838	3,276	5,116	1,567	14,271	1,440	600	51,060	17,536	10,023
Congressional District 41	33,386	22,266	2,862	6,976	2,131	17,581	1,759	124	60,277	20,903	15,699
Congressional District 42	47,603	30,769	4,784	9,952	559	17,426	2,625	39	87,751	22,879	18,102
Congressional District 43	51,696	28,274	7,726	13,763	2,978	12,373	1,488	199	64,802	25,037	21,485
Congressional District 44	39,168	23,365	4,096	10,202	2,048	17,931	2,747	1,080	56,774	22,042	13,578
Congressional District 45	71,030	40,273	7,852	19,795	2,889	9,549	1,545	40	95,932	28,603	28,577
Congressional District 46	35,379	20,929	4,037	9,150	4,116	15,987	2,729	198	56,725	20,869	15,282
Congressional District 47	51,252	28,626	6,597	13,829	2,826	11,570	1,973	562	70,682	24,944	21,905
Congressional District 48	73,657	39,489	10,561	20,738	2,630	9,428	2,517	385	94,856	28,067	31,162
Congressional District 49	73,126	42,048	7,162	20,134	1,560	7,736	867	187	103,727	25,616	28,166
Congressional District 50	62,707	35,046	8,608	16,431	2,539	11,496	1,979	26	89,177	27,098	28,609

Table D-5: 116th Congressional Districts - Household Relationship, Grandparents, and Marital Status—*Continued*

	Total Householders 65 Years and Over	Family Householders 65 Years and Over	Non-Family Householders 65 Years and Over		Persons 65 Years and Over Living in Group Quarters	Grandparents 60 Years and Over Living with Grandchildren			Marital Status - Persons 60 Years and Over		
			Male Living Alone	Female Living Alone		Total	Responsible for Grandchildren	Responsible for Grandchildren and In Poverty	Now Married	Widowed	Divorced
California—Cont.											
Congressional District 51	45,161	28,656	4,272	10,702	1,734	15,951	3,219	631	61,918	25,243	18,709
Congressional District 52	65,678	37,496	9,221	16,502	1,771	6,243	1,213	179	90,417	21,059	27,096
Congressional District 53	56,942	31,433	8,744	14,201	3,157	13,065	2,988	0	74,820	26,450	24,248
Colorado											
Congressional District 1	66,607	29,520	11,738	22,928	2,769	4,030	931	207	72,194	19,223	36,038
Congressional District 2	75,019	44,075	9,781	18,187	2,117	5,112	725	0	116,614	20,558	28,383
Congressional District 3	85,549	45,710	13,340	23,156	2,587	7,810	3,215	391	112,071	33,333	34,423
Congressional District 4	70,674	41,463	8,262	18,598	2,013	9,181	2,919	356	105,756	26,070	25,817
Congressional District 5	69,981	40,367	9,466	18,347	2,018	7,226	1,568	357	98,571	25,149	29,102
Congressional District 6	62,030	34,827	7,756	18,334	1,401	9,786	1,869	0	89,632	22,056	25,552
Congressional District 7	69,942	36,186	9,443	22,567	2,395	9,368	2,319	40	84,575	28,230	29,582
Connecticut											
Congressional District 1	76,484	38,735	11,295	24,380	6,706	6,424	1,080	28	92,475	32,113	28,125
Congressional District 2	76,003	41,770	11,301	20,697	5,450	5,399	1,018	0	107,512	28,145	28,644
Congressional District 3	76,259	40,548	10,797	23,470	4,879	9,153	2,614	590	92,965	33,419	27,324
Congressional District 4	70,411	38,271	8,337	22,232	3,796	7,583	826	103	96,284	27,358	22,528
Congressional District 5	75,636	37,771	10,644	24,865	6,042	6,809	1,059	108	96,468	32,633	26,371
Delaware											
Congressional District (at Large)	107,758	63,521	13,323	26,840	4,129	11,822	4,566	526	149,489	39,881	34,657
District of Columbia											
Delegate District (at Large)	58,898	22,637	11,337	21,829	3,072	5,869	737	215	40,456	19,852	22,449
Florida											
Congressional District 1	79,682	45,984	11,529	19,195	3,715	8,322	2,913	85	106,164	33,173	34,972
Congressional District 2	91,997	53,952	12,816	23,210	4,122	8,277	3,530	737	117,255	37,756	33,280
Congressional District 3	75,812	41,277	11,456	20,473	4,958	8,474	2,828	764	94,188	29,971	31,770
Congressional District 4	82,281	45,479	10,670	24,017	2,461	9,226	1,925	142	109,472	32,816	32,307
Congressional District 5	62,413	32,696	9,589	18,622	3,685	9,007	3,678	605	64,043	29,193	29,466
Congressional District 6	116,759	65,812	16,140	29,467	3,460	9,271	2,308	186	146,613	46,998	45,786
Congressional District 7	67,126	36,676	8,269	20,325	2,937	9,198	2,312	81	85,673	31,822	29,897
Congressional District 8	113,656	62,581	17,494	29,466	2,864	8,520	2,139	262	148,145	48,235	44,311
Congressional District 9	75,299	46,077	10,038	16,394	1,537	17,136	2,746	788	106,366	37,484	36,096
Congressional District 10	50,722	31,279	5,568	11,951	2,035	14,298	3,066	697	81,796	22,012	24,014
Congressional District 11	172,181	102,310	22,124	42,469	2,648	9,033	4,888	572	216,579	64,661	47,252
Congressional District 12	117,538	58,082	17,363	36,119	3,589	11,455	2,952	152	132,374	55,408	43,074
Congressional District 13	105,500	49,067	17,596	34,102	6,800	8,021	3,005	1,095	108,203	47,847	51,547
Congressional District 14	61,564	31,290	8,728	19,627	2,327	9,452	2,710	585	72,887	29,035	29,889
Congressional District 15	76,150	47,031	7,692	18,905	1,617	11,114	2,460	511	107,377	30,483	29,899
Congressional District 16	137,379	75,386	15,940	41,254	3,850	9,283	2,351	454	168,402	51,935	46,592
Congressional District 17	147,229	87,615	19,853	33,787	3,585	7,961	3,371	141	193,237	57,708	41,914
Congressional District 18	119,666	65,741	14,768	33,974	2,495	13,455	4,807	41	144,343	48,433	44,058
Congressional District 19	149,957	86,935	20,405	37,127	3,624	9,376	2,511	448	193,730	57,361	46,097
Congressional District 20	59,499	30,160	8,385	18,246	2,927	15,294	4,636	927	64,609	33,131	33,342
Congressional District 21	121,552	58,872	18,112	40,085	2,402	9,515	963	231	132,837	52,731	42,189
Congressional District 22	101,164	49,199	16,654	30,448	2,788	8,017	1,159	na	114,220	39,713	38,934
Congressional District 23	80,170	42,522	11,526	23,121	1,362	11,248	2,314	446	102,527	31,216	33,523
Congressional District 24	58,706	32,937	8,942	14,485	4,788	15,152	4,735	695	63,359	27,429	32,409
Congressional District 25	70,493	44,706	6,295	16,372	3,037	19,003	2,029	88	100,396	37,601	37,165
Congressional District 26	53,165	36,359	4,682	9,557	2,474	19,159	2,693	375	86,447	31,648	23,801
Congressional District 27	74,573	40,869	10,981	20,469	3,523	10,626	1,888	255	89,505	34,938	31,314
Georgia											
Congressional District 1	68,406	40,286	8,738	18,228	3,038	10,343	3,299	486	86,003	31,100	24,373
Congressional District 2	67,752	35,249	9,187	21,783	3,454	6,487	2,916	745	74,048	34,593	23,549
Congressional District 3	70,993	40,675	8,427	19,438	2,119	10,715	4,591	727	91,343	32,496	25,522
Congressional District 4	54,297	32,532	5,655	14,681	1,549	15,819	3,736	199	79,112	21,961	25,008
Congressional District 5	61,350	26,114	11,142	22,107	2,266	8,748	3,605	965	47,548	25,831	26,812
Congressional District 6	56,858	33,673	5,551	16,414	1,401	7,609	1,102	0	88,541	20,012	18,821
Congressional District 7	44,166	28,689	4,138	10,206	1,427	11,361	1,287	0	79,142	17,859	18,708
Congressional District 8	68,232	36,290	9,154	21,460	3,673	9,096	3,934	717	81,547	32,155	23,550
Congressional District 9	85,846	52,436	10,952	20,784	2,210	7,426	2,006	92	125,282	29,606	24,531
Congressional District 10	66,509	40,052	8,224	16,681	2,768	9,435	1,765	371	92,764	28,198	23,340
Congressional District 11	60,558	36,350	6,269	16,137	1,363	8,074	2,123	196	89,117	21,914	26,368
Congressional District 12	65,340	34,675	8,572	21,595	3,635	9,471	3,720	379	78,824	30,270	24,796
Congressional District 13	49,732	29,721	5,077	13,905	1,152	10,191	3,053	191	69,994	22,203	20,972
Congressional District 14	66,880	35,576	9,810	20,318	2,251	10,778	3,983	1,024	81,319	34,496	24,466
Hawaii											
Congressional District 1	70,265	43,730	8,643	15,320	4,539	19,079	2,709	106	92,016	34,737	21,086
Congressional District 2	72,863	44,887	10,117	14,861	2,457	16,931	3,271	44	100,266	31,054	25,957
Idaho											
Congressional District 1	92,785	54,706	12,248	22,956	3,089	8,601	3,321	389	131,656	31,037	34,034
Congressional District 2	75,829	42,826	11,010	20,090	2,197	7,002	1,564	132	109,279	27,609	26,068

Table D-5: 116th Congressional Districts - Household Relationship, Grandparents, and Marital Status—*Continued*

	Total Householders 65 Years and Over	Family Householders 65 Years and Over	Non-Family Householders 65 Years and Over		Persons 65 Years and Over Living in Group Quarters	Grandparents 60 Years and Over Living with Grandchildren			Marital Status - Persons 60 Years and Over		
			Male Living Alone	Female Living Alone		Total	Responsible for Grandchildren	Responsible for Grandchildren and In Poverty	Now Married	Widowed	Divorced
Illinois											
Congressional District 1	75,535	38,100	12,215	23,303	2,767	11,729	3,586	1,255	66,935	35,634	30,292
Congressional District 2	70,616	34,904	10,068	23,608	4,112	8,865	1,569	210	70,644	34,774	26,096
Congressional District 3	65,535	36,522	9,404	18,435	3,300	9,290	915	132	87,794	31,175	16,686
Congressional District 4	41,750	22,747	6,549	11,315	1,567	9,735	1,489	147	54,734	19,133	13,606
Congressional District 5	59,359	29,262	8,859	19,372	2,855	4,743	1,127	280	70,693	25,473	18,734
Congressional District 6	69,318	42,438	6,175	19,494	3,684	8,921	2,361	122	115,822	26,880	18,160
Congressional District 7	68,489	29,107	13,002	24,920	2,415	7,303	2,215	229	56,398	29,151	21,188
Congressional District 8	56,235	32,380	6,485	16,706	3,372	10,034	959	0	86,785	24,232	19,470
Congressional District 9	79,138	38,070	11,278	27,790	6,369	5,650	1,160	344	90,325	31,675	23,112
Congressional District 10	66,510	36,977	8,438	19,858	4,560	7,727	2,115	190	91,921	27,371	20,055
Congressional District 11	52,546	30,402	5,756	14,726	2,420	7,353	1,498	0	76,231	22,071	19,976
Congressional District 12	76,976	39,448	13,172	22,858	4,615	5,650	2,037	731	89,974	32,796	27,588
Congressional District 13	70,188	35,980	10,719	22,116	4,868	4,238	1,728	63	90,354	30,456	24,975
Congressional District 14	62,076	35,824	7,596	17,767	1,165	7,986	1,342	197	98,025	24,267	19,496
Congressional District 15	85,584	45,319	11,877	26,129	5,910	4,692	1,990	387	106,802	35,366	26,914
Congressional District 16	78,940	43,551	10,348	23,450	5,762	5,770	2,931	91	106,245	33,161	21,643
Congressional District 17	80,793	40,678	13,514	24,862	5,470	5,009	2,279	345	97,529	32,476	28,738
Congressional District 18	82,452	44,956	10,286	25,921	6,172	4,724	1,507	280	114,274	33,050	23,664
Indiana											
Congressional District 1	76,616	39,227	10,334	24,721	3,648	7,714	2,300	591	87,966	34,289	27,544
Congressional District 2	73,760	39,521	10,906	21,881	4,105	5,242	1,372	266	98,439	30,075	23,199
Congressional District 3	73,190	39,048	10,481	22,087	4,648	6,456	2,749	184	98,905	29,293	23,884
Congressional District 4	73,454	42,121	10,649	19,062	4,343	6,587	3,388	364	98,857	32,157	26,817
Congressional District 5	70,733	39,714	7,919	21,515	3,578	6,632	2,748	542	99,217	27,932	23,651
Congressional District 6	82,018	43,780	12,116	24,359	5,202	6,606	3,090	98	100,855	35,176	27,009
Congressional District 7	59,136	29,195	9,740	18,799	2,935	6,734	2,603	702	61,494	23,629	27,960
Congressional District 8	76,786	41,625	10,578	22,627	6,257	5,939	3,122	734	101,973	31,443	28,090
Congressional District 9	74,116	41,033	9,694	21,653	4,255	7,359	2,503	263	102,244	29,568	26,214
Iowa											
Congressional District 1	86,615	45,574	11,663	27,276	7,278	4,438	763	0	113,346	36,597	26,999
Congressional District 2	85,169	42,986	13,220	27,379	5,231	5,192	2,024	217	110,894	35,268	27,887
Congressional District 3	77,565	40,161	10,986	24,068	4,395	4,709	1,610	218	99,434	30,873	26,533
Congressional District 4	88,810	47,296	12,288	27,709	6,921	3,943	1,046	74	120,712	38,471	20,663
Kansas											
Congressional District 1	71,833	36,116	10,856	23,323	6,680	4,448	2,182	293	95,183	30,209	21,529
Congressional District 2	76,380	40,353	9,771	24,029	5,903	5,005	2,361	646	99,634	31,881	26,267
Congressional District 3	66,710	39,666	6,225	19,541	3,147	5,978	2,230	72	97,427	24,842	21,607
Congressional District 4	72,233	35,607	11,542	22,995	4,318	5,918	2,070	95	92,350	29,948	25,036
Kentucky											
Congressional District 1	82,414	46,707	10,612	23,288	4,938	8,588	4,958	1,613	110,145	35,914	27,552
Congressional District 2	76,196	42,049	11,281	20,484	4,421	8,843	3,756	945	101,146	34,640	28,621
Congressional District 3	77,540	40,631	10,983	23,497	3,837	6,839	3,083	604	87,635	31,755	31,132
Congressional District 4	72,855	41,022	9,978	20,287	3,772	8,133	3,830	444	97,617	31,602	26,293
Congressional District 5	77,515	45,164	9,464	21,107	4,176	10,290	6,624	2,493	98,698	36,977	23,371
Congressional District 6	71,500	39,463	8,307	22,128	3,401	8,401	3,676	553	91,512	30,056	26,432
Louisiana											
Congressional District 1	80,976	45,034	10,378	23,633	2,753	10,170	3,631	926	106,010	35,208	30,147
Congressional District 2	71,183	35,155	11,884	22,171	3,141	12,289	4,368	1,469	72,530	34,595	31,911
Congressional District 3	74,293	41,381	9,278	21,255	3,748	9,665	5,534	1,508	93,001	35,775	22,387
Congressional District 4	78,294	41,905	12,629	22,153	5,363	6,354	3,311	952	90,739	35,143	22,673
Congressional District 5	74,058	40,490	10,964	21,184	5,962	8,919	4,575	1,432	90,664	34,316	26,782
Congressional District 6	68,175	40,486	7,282	18,132	2,003	7,812	2,351	330	98,450	28,877	26,773
Maine											
Congressional District 1	89,874	45,714	11,706	27,932	4,435	5,615	1,667	62	110,274	31,132	34,095
Congressional District 2	86,049	42,673	14,141	24,823	5,143	5,045	1,222	240	106,907	34,257	34,794
Maryland											
Congressional District 1	83,966	50,351	10,466	20,604	3,170	9,662	3,625	294	120,163	34,167	26,526
Congressional District 2	67,147	35,190	9,435	20,845	3,703	11,193	2,926	96	81,592	31,405	26,966
Congressional District 3	71,063	35,870	9,361	23,296	2,891	9,558	2,345	0	87,697	28,459	26,968
Congressional District 4	62,375	34,533	8,215	17,037	2,329	13,407	3,837	247	79,013	23,900	23,734
Congressional District 5	59,391	34,755	8,282	14,995	2,681	9,343	2,266	199	88,908	25,341	23,647
Congressional District 6	68,014	38,181	8,905	18,160	3,798	8,029	1,220	59	95,123	27,130	24,736
Congressional District 7	70,691	34,051	10,042	23,770	4,586	8,894	1,570	547	74,081	32,192	27,465
Congressional District 8	75,528	41,069	8,555	23,847	4,223	9,316	1,736	43	106,513	29,181	25,311
Massachusetts											
Congressional District 1	82,753	41,577	12,331	25,866	4,273	7,411	2,013	222	99,280	32,647	29,312
Congressional District 2	73,141	36,658	10,348	23,317	5,182	8,572	1,900	81	95,990	31,601	26,712
Congressional District 3	63,762	34,043	10,062	17,948	4,079	8,073	1,243	99	88,116	27,051	23,720
Congressional District 4	78,013	43,219	9,424	22,610	4,162	7,970	1,078	171	110,199	29,314	22,769
Congressional District 5	78,114	40,143	10,274	25,610	3,825	8,565	1,907	65	92,946	29,396	23,734
Congressional District 6	87,798	46,997	10,957	26,371	4,607	10,991	1,651	0	114,443	33,475	29,793
Congressional District 7	56,604	25,269	9,051	20,034	3,067	10,379	2,155	211	52,207	20,828	24,072
Congressional District 8	77,368	36,274	12,690	25,352	4,877	8,921	1,852	85	91,407	31,305	26,540
Congressional District 9	102,484	56,118	11,456	31,335	5,093	7,681	2,632	236	130,649	39,461	31,945

Table D-5: 116th Congressional Districts - Household Relationship, Grandparents, and Marital Status—*Continued*

	Total Householders 65 Years and Over	Family Householders 65 Years and Over	Non-Family Householders 65 Years and Over		Persons 65 Years and Over Living in Group Quarters	Grandparents 60 Years and Over Living with Grandchildren			Marital Status - Persons 60 Years and Over		
			Male Living Alone	Female Living Alone		Total	Responsible for Grandchildren	Responsible for Grandchildren and In Poverty	Now Married	Widowed	Divorced
Michigan											
Congressional District 1	101,550	57,608	15,802	25,330	5,826	4,414	1,883	202	141,899	37,185	28,628
Congressional District 2	74,092	41,985	9,907	20,559	3,935	7,860	1,324	100	101,864	29,231	23,349
Congressional District 3	71,288	39,285	9,040	20,965	3,962	5,103	1,488	254	97,455	26,849	25,190
Congressional District 4	85,844	47,908	12,296	23,046	4,029	5,207	2,028	272	116,079	33,962	28,007
Congressional District 5	82,413	43,232	12,678	24,292	3,207	4,804	1,714	411	95,216	32,847	31,595
Congressional District 6	77,966	42,677	11,545	21,281	3,227	7,084	2,225	511	104,574	28,875	27,832
Congressional District 7	81,726	45,315	11,651	22,826	5,097	5,726	1,862	8	110,089	31,450	27,306
Congressional District 8	70,961	40,079	8,417	20,157	1,794	4,958	730	69	100,720	25,400	23,863
Congressional District 9	77,949	38,497	11,470	25,970	3,157	7,721	1,602	126	91,063	32,669	29,031
Congressional District 10	82,431	46,038	11,447	23,231	3,587	8,019	1,610	175	116,536	33,134	23,753
Congressional District 11	74,520	40,464	9,367	23,104	2,939	7,393	1,634	263	108,071	30,743	24,470
Congressional District 12	68,141	35,510	9,646	21,879	2,997	5,703	992	133	79,571	27,076	25,413
Congressional District 13	66,480	29,365	10,274	24,703	2,877	8,266	1,745	51	49,828	30,847	33,685
Congressional District 14	78,200	37,353	12,527	26,042	3,873	8,309	1,349	100	72,172	33,494	33,328
Minnesota											
Congressional District 1	73,571	39,014	10,022	22,426	6,206	3,474	1,177	177	98,902	29,320	19,296
Congressional District 2	60,310	33,950	7,671	17,279	2,859	5,548	2,240	87	89,837	20,481	19,793
Congressional District 3	70,971	38,265	9,510	21,473	2,083	6,052	1,178	na	101,981	23,895	22,700
Congressional District 4	66,731	32,543	9,476	22,801	3,927	4,802	752	170	79,059	24,671	27,070
Congressional District 5	59,080	25,298	11,345	19,803	4,262	5,045	1,038	171	59,443	18,819	27,675
Congressional District 6	55,451	33,702	6,360	14,310	2,824	5,309	1,186	26	91,455	18,245	18,269
Congressional District 7	80,697	43,455	12,747	23,094	7,349	3,162	1,543	63	110,306	32,133	20,703
Congressional District 8	85,622	46,750	13,255	22,524	5,912	4,246	1,940	356	115,826	31,748	26,294
Mississippi											
Congressional District 1	76,815	41,439	10,022	23,043	4,024	8,091	3,433	327	95,722	38,638	24,497
Congressional District 2	70,855	39,398	9,987	20,375	3,801	8,993	4,068	857	77,572	36,510	23,346
Congressional District 3	76,840	43,534	9,955	21,993	5,513	9,129	5,303	1,513	94,407	35,896	24,978
Congressional District 4	78,853	44,528	11,498	21,072	3,547	8,518	4,164	1,854	93,898	35,927	27,510
Missouri											
Congressional District 1	73,344	32,500	13,317	25,124	4,162	5,753	2,199	683	67,155	30,628	32,018
Congressional District 2	89,159	52,848	9,065	25,820	5,778	6,574	1,717	na	126,664	36,529	24,318
Congressional District 3	78,130	46,099	9,724	20,806	3,759	6,580	1,850	524	118,551	31,059	23,538
Congressional District 4	80,682	45,322	10,834	22,686	5,273	4,840	1,865	316	111,074	34,000	24,689
Congressional District 5	75,846	38,472	11,437	22,674	4,250	8,109	2,660	598	84,665	31,049	34,319
Congressional District 6	77,515	42,858	10,918	21,348	5,912	8,148	2,587	522	107,186	34,194	27,966
Congressional District 7	89,835	46,739	12,783	28,263	3,960	5,482	2,429	432	107,580	34,972	32,147
Congressional District 8	87,058	47,427	12,400	25,603	7,013	5,826	2,879	713	113,656	36,131	30,982
Montana											
Congressional District (at Large)	123,306	67,356	20,148	31,911	5,064	10,276	5,445	932	171,557	45,400	42,551
Nebraska											
Congressional District 1	63,478	34,055	8,878	19,210	2,919	4,578	1,353	122	86,450	23,944	16,408
Congressional District 2	55,623	27,037	8,046	18,697	2,912	3,548	1,310	53	68,039	21,926	21,568
Congressional District 3	75,440	38,228	12,055	23,781	6,102	3,247	1,239	101	99,388	33,388	17,682
Nevada											
Congressional District 1	60,446	28,101	12,596	16,284	1,557	10,722	3,755	905	57,888	26,013	32,496
Congressional District 2	79,157	42,141	13,630	19,975	2,153	8,014	2,991	468	102,378	26,881	34,095
Congressional District 3	74,823	42,847	10,776	17,695	1,140	12,927	3,031	267	105,391	29,196	34,347
Congressional District 4	65,507	39,065	8,783	14,241	1,418	11,734	3,019	57	93,442	25,191	28,971
New Hampshire											
Congressional District 1	70,323	38,943	9,962	18,147	4,641	6,047	1,351	125	101,186	28,845	26,871
Congressional District 2	75,465	40,458	10,564	22,063	4,844	6,075	1,430	0	105,102	29,481	27,484
New Jersey											
Congressional District 1	71,071	37,688	8,489	22,367	3,826	9,176	1,643	28	86,359	31,561	25,370
Congressional District 2	82,565	47,664	9,856	22,972	5,538	8,119	2,443	349	112,557	33,113	22,745
Congressional District 3	91,189	50,710	11,270	27,196	3,633	8,967	2,225	205	119,844	36,640	24,619
Congressional District 4	94,196	49,521	9,522	32,829	3,249	7,464	2,159	232	118,452	37,256	25,319
Congressional District 5	77,517	46,049	9,019	20,932	5,199	10,246	1,501	na	111,998	32,882	22,194
Congressional District 6	59,850	36,364	6,269	16,159	2,459	14,479	2,002	496	90,287	27,412	16,784
Congressional District 7	69,109	40,202	6,718	20,127	2,966	8,509	602	29	107,051	30,134	18,856
Congressional District 8	49,058	25,397	6,012	16,692	2,215	8,944	1,195	42	60,882	21,988	16,296
Congressional District 9	65,187	35,405	7,093	20,998	1,384	12,116	1,434	194	84,517	28,854	20,667
Congressional District 10	59,944	30,345	7,209	20,190	2,908	11,250	2,479	844	65,259	27,492	24,638
Congressional District 11	75,106	45,263	6,740	20,750	5,679	8,991	1,099	0	111,960	33,047	20,257
Congressional District 12	72,675	40,261	8,832	22,138	3,444	10,716	2,958	98	94,125	31,248	22,517
New Mexico											
Congressional District 1	72,184	36,395	11,861	21,225	2,450	7,060	3,655	736	83,249	28,533	32,818
Congressional District 2	76,332	40,137	12,366	21,562	2,542	10,135	5,092	1,155	92,650	30,289	28,136
Congressional District 3	79,579	46,091	10,925	19,832	2,394	9,230	4,078	1,075	100,376	26,158	29,156
New York											
Congressional District 1	76,483	44,909	8,416	21,284	3,316	9,515	2,134	657	104,617	32,700	22,318
Congressional District 2	62,257	37,134	7,222	15,871	2,633	13,609	2,018	67	91,097	29,485	20,766
Congressional District 3	82,562	50,880	6,390	22,947	5,187	9,644	1,009	0	127,088	34,726	20,083

Table D-5: 116th Congressional Districts - Household Relationship, Grandparents, and Marital Status—*Continued*

	Total Householders 65 Years and Over	Family Householders 65 Years and Over	Non-Family Householders 65 Years and Over — Male Living Alone	Non-Family Householders 65 Years and Over — Female Living Alone	Persons 65 Years and Over Living in Group Quarters	Grandparents 60 Years and Over Living with Grandchildren — Total	Responsible for Grandchildren	Responsible for Grandchildren and In Poverty	Marital Status - Persons 60 Years and Over — Now Married	Widowed	Divorced
New York—Cont.											
Congressional District 4	72,166	42,289	7,169	20,968	3,167	13,591	1,811	0	102,619	32,706	19,124
Congressional District 5	58,232	35,789	6,855	13,977	5,281	21,080	4,108	160	81,153	32,140	18,692
Congressional District 6	72,457	41,017	7,559	21,627	3,526	11,799	2,077	260	100,681	34,929	19,787
Congressional District 7	52,238	26,546	6,123	18,011	1,728	10,522	3,548	1,192	62,092	21,642	14,509
Congressional District 8	75,998	38,815	8,689	26,494	4,459	14,801	2,336	276	75,560	35,925	22,543
Congressional District 9	68,265	36,501	8,804	21,088	2,838	12,325	3,158	531	76,083	28,404	20,355
Congressional District 10	78,025	29,077	14,274	31,955	2,110	6,459	1,724	565	68,622	24,212	22,735
Congressional District 11	73,411	38,966	9,538	22,811	3,627	14,331	2,797	640	97,050	34,620	20,093
Congressional District 12	75,496	28,709	13,727	30,912	2,994	2,569	450	0	68,680	23,382	19,892
Congressional District 13	63,218	28,186	9,860	23,475	5,063	13,272	2,483	990	49,616	27,280	24,900
Congressional District 14	53,283	27,724	8,354	15,969	4,267	9,281	3,170	303	63,023	24,125	15,665
Congressional District 15	54,658	24,949	10,560	17,971	1,498	12,999	3,363	1,738	39,273	24,578	20,667
Congressional District 16	80,291	37,548	13,930	27,178	7,543	10,805	2,946	847	80,283	36,065	27,536
Congressional District 17	74,563	42,922	7,124	22,485	5,198	8,064	1,267	51	101,057	28,959	20,978
Congressional District 18	66,493	37,072	9,282	18,225	4,031	9,381	2,287	0	91,611	27,716	23,768
Congressional District 19	87,516	47,503	12,656	24,444	5,638	7,052	1,950	310	113,324	35,655	28,613
Congressional District 20	77,086	39,503	11,769	23,384	6,276	5,402	1,445	195	94,067	31,307	27,251
Congressional District 21	79,962	41,382	12,140	23,834	4,297	4,851	1,795	343	104,398	32,728	23,748
Congressional District 22	80,325	42,258	10,546	24,512	6,387	6,648	2,005	87	104,737	33,077	26,686
Congressional District 23	81,195	42,033	13,012	22,981	6,505	4,273	1,508	212	104,693	34,392	26,954
Congressional District 24	78,035	39,697	10,965	25,000	4,129	6,508	1,691	259	98,725	32,769	24,937
Congressional District 25	78,730	37,896	11,397	26,858	6,194	6,712	1,709	346	94,993	32,954	26,019
Congressional District 26	82,533	38,226	13,566	28,648	4,300	5,358	2,512	408	85,832	33,773	29,053
Congressional District 27	86,874	46,149	10,961	27,507	4,888	5,656	1,976	276	116,545	36,566	26,355
North Carolina											
Congressional District 1	80,889	43,303	11,069	25,117	4,657	10,067	3,092	677	91,718	36,790	24,887
Congressional District 2	70,276	42,398	7,562	19,320	2,113	8,188	2,070	198	107,734	29,617	20,774
Congressional District 3	82,624	46,860	11,320	22,544	2,710	7,979	2,879	539	108,879	34,615	25,855
Congressional District 4	61,533	33,484	6,785	19,407	2,023	6,969	1,253	0	84,400	24,139	24,148
Congressional District 5	91,378	47,326	13,695	28,201	3,185	6,658	2,691	199	110,659	38,524	30,976
Congressional District 6	85,518	46,784	10,539	25,627	4,002	10,716	5,028	858	109,174	37,688	27,375
Congressional District 7	98,199	56,148	12,335	27,506	2,880	10,529	4,611	1,534	133,327	44,087	31,281
Congressional District 8	73,908	42,025	9,918	20,712	3,515	7,371	3,288	444	92,904	35,801	23,701
Congressional District 9	74,337	41,948	9,787	21,436	2,910	10,400	2,837	850	100,397	34,254	23,765
Congressional District 10	88,807	50,126	10,006	25,810	4,480	8,798	2,644	277	116,704	35,888	28,757
Congressional District 11	105,969	60,279	13,968	29,090	4,436	9,098	2,760	226	140,051	43,677	30,003
Congressional District 12	51,532	27,828	6,127	16,031	1,829	8,172	2,224	323	66,117	22,303	26,184
Congressional District 13	80,026	44,388	9,978	22,840	3,991	8,006	3,077	272	105,258	32,921	30,457
North Dakota											
Congressional District (at Large)	73,062	36,403	12,097	22,931	7,298	2,937	1,239	348	96,971	31,240	19,488
Ohio											
Congressional District 1	70,419	37,560	10,812	21,082	5,810	5,784	2,390	458	88,656	28,420	24,625
Congressional District 2	75,635	38,713	11,334	24,260	5,582	6,787	2,693	536	95,013	32,276	27,413
Congressional District 3	57,111	28,118	8,531	18,494	1,750	8,097	2,429	977	53,783	24,350	32,196
Congressional District 4	76,480	41,866	10,064	22,519	5,627	6,396	2,501	388	106,712	32,050	24,868
Congressional District 5	80,319	44,361	11,161	22,661	5,811	5,962	2,294	55	114,803	30,646	24,411
Congressional District 6	86,624	46,096	14,449	24,631	6,579	8,058	3,205	614	113,087	37,679	28,408
Congressional District 7	83,646	45,849	11,160	24,429	4,925	6,251	2,034	297	111,426	33,836	25,867
Congressional District 8	77,530	41,919	11,477	22,526	4,168	9,140	3,599	347	100,996	34,469	25,987
Congressional District 9	73,334	34,108	13,410	23,716	4,029	5,248	2,239	611	78,363	31,161	30,168
Congressional District 10	83,276	43,847	11,931	25,615	5,321	6,733	2,510	327	94,174	34,978	30,848
Congressional District 11	81,847	35,392	15,024	28,783	5,138	7,231	2,608	167	69,146	34,658	35,759
Congressional District 12	74,441	43,240	8,285	21,287	2,981	7,227	2,135	364	107,647	30,473	22,298
Congressional District 13	85,480	41,284	13,267	28,115	4,914	6,468	1,860	132	92,116	37,630	35,697
Congressional District 14	90,210	51,968	11,700	25,026	4,539	7,401	1,997	81	123,368	34,362	28,657
Congressional District 15	74,245	42,125	9,112	20,673	3,554	8,585	2,589	612	101,453	29,607	26,434
Congressional District 16	90,875	50,496	11,365	26,235	4,277	5,213	1,936	49	117,379	33,363	27,907
Oklahoma											
Congressional District 1	75,187	40,740	10,590	22,246	2,923	9,095	3,608	481	95,974	31,389	29,538
Congressional District 2	89,104	50,391	12,910	23,622	5,765	10,553	5,432	1,281	108,360	42,922	28,113
Congressional District 3	77,764	44,674	10,472	21,031	4,655	9,114	4,707	632	104,137	33,861	25,641
Congressional District 4	74,601	41,325	9,967	21,865	3,829	8,938	3,857	499	93,868	34,123	26,674
Congressional District 5	73,230	38,049	11,333	22,556	3,739	6,799	3,089	465	86,103	31,044	31,768
Oregon											
Congressional District 1	80,171	42,273	9,580	24,198	2,708	8,810	1,460	244	103,017	28,838	34,077
Congressional District 2	107,493	58,319	14,766	29,978	5,282	7,326	2,752	113	141,218	37,625	41,710
Congressional District 3	72,156	34,042	10,576	24,574	2,560	8,038	1,427	0	85,257	23,269	35,215
Congressional District 4	108,647	58,346	15,987	27,659	3,341	8,447	2,796	236	137,611	34,151	41,558
Congressional District 5	92,800	51,565	10,989	26,518	4,499	9,220	3,075	483	120,789	33,968	36,136
Pennsylvania											
Congressional District 1	77,257	45,198	9,608	20,549	3,886	10,365	1,972	171	118,740	31,173	20,564
Congressional District 2	60,881	29,015	9,672	20,499	3,150	10,964	1,644	461	58,668	28,269	26,114
Congressional District 3	73,242	29,372	12,944	28,696	4,000	7,443	2,567	1,269	52,456	33,265	26,231

Table D-5: 116th Congressional Districts - Household Relationship, Grandparents, and Marital Status—*Continued*

	Total Householders 65 Years and Over	Family Householders 65 Years and Over	Non-Family Householders 65 Years and Over		Persons 65 Years and Over Living in Group Quarters	Grandparents 60 Years and Over Living with Grandchildren			Marital Status - Persons 60 Years and Over		
			Male Living Alone	Female Living Alone		Total	Responsible for Grandchildren	Responsible for Grandchildren and In Poverty	Now Married	Widowed	Divorced
Pennsylvania—Cont.											
Congressional District 4	78,776	43,194	10,565	23,736	5,508	8,073	1,530	142	109,765	32,431	21,366
Congressional District 5	69,999	35,509	10,131	22,784	4,729	7,722	2,373	26	85,566	33,054	21,097
Congressional District 6	70,325	41,010	8,516	19,322	3,667	6,930	1,852	270	104,127	26,180	20,532
Congressional District 7	77,971	42,897	9,922	22,605	5,369	6,487	1,600	97	102,557	37,077	22,782
Congressional District 8	83,465	43,129	11,692	25,630	5,378	7,207	2,064	372	106,424	36,320	26,048
Congressional District 9	87,790	47,282	13,287	25,221	6,851	6,144	2,281	273	112,655	40,355	23,033
Congressional District 10	79,383	40,130	10,612	25,945	5,551	7,845	3,113	220	100,380	34,785	26,649
Congressional District 11	80,041	48,076	9,408	20,757	5,204	5,789	1,618	99	117,304	31,728	21,692
Congressional District 12	82,658	46,083	11,546	22,893	4,733	4,985	1,779	344	114,084	33,339	21,483
Congressional District 13	89,664	49,866	11,932	25,409	5,073	4,681	1,676	144	122,563	34,895	23,227
Congressional District 14	93,691	50,307	12,934	28,704	4,133	5,068	1,906	347	122,512	37,670	26,243
Congressional District 15	89,604	49,934	12,289	25,595	5,506	5,574	2,265	250	116,747	36,409	23,520
Congressional District 16	85,638	45,125	12,386	25,724	5,333	5,929	2,460	300	110,213	35,610	25,435
Congressional District 17	91,494	47,312	13,243	29,479	3,669	5,182	1,832	195	115,520	35,626	23,326
Congressional District 18	86,727	37,829	14,507	31,939	4,794	5,479	1,917	286	90,363	36,476	26,994
Rhode Island											
Congressional District 1	58,051	28,125	8,573	19,939	5,070	5,379	1,383	209	60,203	25,844	22,453
Congressional District 2	55,912	28,020	9,082	17,343	4,016	4,963	1,580	0	71,545	23,692	18,571
South Carolina											
Congressional District 1	88,046	54,240	10,783	20,887	1,712	8,680	3,155	1,460	121,744	33,082	28,376
Congressional District 2	74,110	41,524	9,056	21,998	2,243	8,734	3,600	322	93,536	31,630	26,860
Congressional District 3	81,613	45,582	11,822	22,978	3,830	8,268	3,086	513	104,054	33,422	25,930
Congressional District 4	71,349	42,334	7,724	19,678	2,256	7,517	2,445	446	96,339	31,818	24,436
Congressional District 5	74,188	42,822	10,464	18,568	2,555	10,691	3,871	855	94,672	34,836	21,842
Congressional District 6	65,991	34,479	9,871	19,725	3,714	10,174	4,096	1,245	72,773	34,770	21,213
Congressional District 7	97,354	55,975	12,982	25,948	2,767	10,175	3,080	1,106	125,919	42,058	30,099
South Dakota											
Congressional District (at Large)	91,545	49,903	12,659	26,250	8,325	5,413	2,493	1,089	122,917	34,871	30,254
Tennessee											
Congressional District 1	90,439	52,650	12,675	22,781	4,388	9,676	5,483	1,306	115,490	39,353	35,732
Congressional District 2	82,510	48,325	9,847	21,809	3,184	8,249	3,490	779	113,607	33,388	26,232
Congressional District 3	85,020	47,794	12,190	23,437	4,810	8,904	3,556	315	107,229	38,802	32,003
Congressional District 4	71,779	40,911	8,328	20,461	2,959	10,387	4,698	816	99,871	31,814	25,120
Congressional District 5	63,177	31,699	9,406	19,617	2,074	7,167	2,466	704	71,534	24,240	26,016
Congressional District 6	84,448	49,094	10,128	23,331	3,152	8,715	3,901	716	116,033	35,043	29,132
Congressional District 7	69,748	40,522	9,148	18,703	3,739	9,666	2,371	208	100,571	30,783	23,854
Congressional District 8	74,087	45,821	8,025	19,328	4,071	8,382	4,559	297	112,290	30,619	19,666
Congressional District 9	59,816	27,027	10,437	21,324	2,395	7,331	2,689	652	60,540	24,157	27,258
Texas											
Congressional District 1	72,798	41,760	9,301	19,942	5,367	8,915	3,090	324	93,781	34,589	23,987
Congressional District 2	54,196	33,936	6,285	12,752	2,114	12,385	3,148	470	87,528	20,115	19,767
Congressional District 3	53,124	32,398	4,555	15,246	1,096	13,137	1,840	384	92,482	25,040	18,412
Congressional District 4	78,259	45,369	10,013	21,909	4,786	9,753	4,396	1,245	103,520	33,760	27,230
Congressional District 5	62,596	35,267	8,361	16,714	3,856	10,642	3,738	152	83,578	30,973	22,250
Congressional District 6	53,825	32,730	6,215	13,857	2,133	10,333	3,325	436	79,247	24,871	21,899
Congressional District 7	48,644	26,526	6,378	14,293	659	10,100	1,221	0	73,776	20,970	21,050
Congressional District 8	69,143	40,178	8,360	17,822	2,875	12,650	2,892	412	102,292	29,741	28,024
Congressional District 9	44,663	26,269	5,928	11,449	1,233	11,802	2,927	717	58,184	23,971	18,565
Congressional District 10	65,686	40,001	7,118	17,363	3,020	11,488	3,450	439	101,076	27,559	25,515
Congressional District 11	78,507	42,864	10,138	23,537	3,636	8,208	3,714	109	99,189	33,009	28,229
Congressional District 12	64,573	35,022	8,197	19,756	2,993	7,384	1,806	494	84,414	27,964	25,891
Congressional District 13	66,844	37,667	9,268	18,999	4,420	6,373	3,132	597	90,204	30,923	21,401
Congressional District 14	64,687	34,455	10,118	18,455	3,570	8,823	2,679	395	84,422	28,056	26,795
Congressional District 15	49,383	31,433	5,728	11,336	2,170	12,841	4,464	1,767	68,732	27,609	13,928
Congressional District 16	54,922	31,077	7,796	14,993	1,844	11,950	3,677	524	67,685	26,241	21,250
Congressional District 17	60,429	34,992	7,752	16,698	3,312	6,854	2,438	74	77,926	24,617	20,777
Congressional District 18	48,394	26,654	7,697	12,397	1,348	10,478	2,666	734	54,363	22,092	23,496
Congressional District 19	61,282	34,780	6,574	18,579	3,727	7,731	3,602	362	81,113	28,264	21,967
Congressional District 20	54,396	32,485	6,904	13,709	2,162	13,723	3,325	601	67,213	25,230	25,431
Congressional District 21	78,403	48,546	8,561	19,908	2,882	8,651	1,276	0	113,139	30,038	26,079
Congressional District 22	53,978	35,555	5,923	11,570	1,511	16,139	2,260	233	103,500	22,035	18,586
Congressional District 23	61,757	38,169	8,891	13,404	1,252	13,443	4,380	956	88,185	27,508	21,600
Congressional District 24	53,834	31,409	6,620	14,308	1,949	8,584	1,308	69	84,930	20,701	22,333
Congressional District 25	67,419	40,640	8,407	16,776	3,374	9,015	3,119	414	96,880	26,427	23,892
Congressional District 26	47,608	30,594	4,345	11,880	1,708	9,717	2,267	98	85,864	20,846	19,495
Congressional District 27	72,287	43,002	10,477	17,139	4,449	11,087	3,821	840	92,742	32,883	25,706
Congressional District 28	51,475	31,875	4,899	13,222	2,000	12,982	1,798	639	67,640	26,054	18,045
Congressional District 29	34,966	22,457	4,322	7,081	717	13,991	3,579	747	51,590	20,240	13,287
Congressional District 30	51,624	29,404	7,230	13,519	2,273	11,692	4,232	839	60,958	26,829	25,425
Congressional District 31	58,418	35,042	7,149	14,889	2,161	10,594	2,249	239	90,891	25,902	21,415
Congressional District 32	54,836	31,628	6,865	14,998	1,556	9,839	2,159	0	84,604	21,029	22,723
Congressional District 33	41,573	23,479	6,581	10,429	1,150	14,584	4,724	895	51,817	20,643	17,253
Congressional District 34	58,605	36,286	6,338	14,654	2,456	14,049	2,673	578	79,949	31,462	14,265
Congressional District 35	47,397	26,333	7,009	12,277	2,103	9,151	2,070	715	61,635	21,429	25,164
Congressional District 36	67,327	39,947	9,572	16,662	3,264	10,543	3,253	438	90,415	31,300	25,640

Table D-5: 116th Congressional Districts - Household Relationship, Grandparents, and Marital Status—*Continued*

	Total Householders 65 Years and Over	Family Householders 65 Years and Over	Non-Family Householders 65 Years and Over		Persons 65 Years and Over Living in Group Quarters	Grandparents 60 Years and Over Living with Grandchildren			Marital Status - Persons 60 Years and Over		
			Male Living Alone	Female Living Alone		Total	Responsible for Grandchildren	Responsible for Grandchildren and In Poverty	Now Married	Widowed	Divorced
Utah											
Congressional District 1............	49,505	32,339	4,660	11,603	903	10,023	2,212	22	81,903	16,766	15,760
Congressional District 2............	63,114	38,234	8,115	15,598	1,469	7,291	1,356	279	94,894	21,543	18,957
Congressional District 3............	50,425	35,398	4,560	9,544	1,255	11,094	1,725	75	82,770	17,754	11,511
Congressional District 4............	47,507	28,792	5,219	13,011	1,480	10,469	1,859	403	69,514	16,544	19,243
Vermont											
Congressional District (at Large)	78,032	40,808	10,797	23,127	4,059	5,131	2,227	755	98,850	27,492	29,749
Virginia											
Congressional District 1............	71,096	44,534	7,651	16,392	1,695	11,163	3,355	0	111,953	29,443	19,828
Congressional District 2............	70,186	37,735	10,074	20,604	1,239	8,808	2,703	373	92,500	29,714	24,336
Congressional District 3............	65,980	30,907	10,081	23,334	2,893	6,403	2,107	618	69,838	30,556	28,603
Congressional District 4............	73,062	36,200	11,681	22,509	2,648	10,211	3,205	382	82,622	34,875	29,491
Congressional District 5............	92,839	51,720	11,782	27,058	3,960	8,475	4,079	671	116,932	44,997	26,105
Congressional District 6............	88,775	46,984	12,515	26,454	4,588	7,200	2,698	531	106,394	38,245	30,294
Congressional District 7............	77,751	45,751	8,922	21,377	2,621	12,423	5,276	944	111,584	30,884	25,129
Congressional District 8............	61,139	29,194	8,763	20,835	1,679	5,780	500	24	71,084	22,666	20,612
Congressional District 9............	91,160	47,966	14,058	26,706	4,457	8,255	3,820	747	110,963	42,564	27,873
Congressional District 10............	58,139	37,026	6,495	13,725	1,230	14,660	2,266	197	102,862	23,462	18,829
Congressional District 11............	50,903	30,130	5,997	13,346	1,325	13,437	1,832	402	87,180	22,095	17,403
Washington											
Congressional District 1............	59,798	36,004	7,268	14,486	2,108	8,810	2,013	212	95,255	19,658	25,057
Congressional District 2............	76,941	42,469	10,645	19,913	2,996	7,379	1,420	183	105,341	28,541	28,890
Congressional District 3............	80,415	46,306	10,076	22,290	2,398	8,776	3,887	602	111,051	28,473	30,122
Congressional District 4............	63,042	36,180	9,028	15,493	1,798	7,724	2,319	731	88,857	22,483	23,132
Congressional District 5............	79,411	41,711	11,072	23,744	3,369	7,837	2,659	345	100,170	29,369	31,544
Congressional District 6............	90,782	49,991	14,596	22,684	3,192	6,955	2,260	349	120,473	30,862	35,744
Congressional District 7............	71,815	34,484	12,226	22,957	3,824	4,910	1,117	na	86,856	17,072	29,792
Congressional District 8............	63,049	36,018	8,377	16,152	1,699	7,965	2,661	49	96,271	23,360	24,006
Congressional District 9............	60,457	30,791	7,959	18,661	3,892	11,570	2,055	65	78,875	23,401	23,296
Congressional District 10............	68,145	37,183	8,262	20,405	3,014	6,240	2,042	0	88,126	25,263	30,471
West Virginia											
Congressional District 1............	75,979	40,729	10,239	23,318	3,935	6,485	2,669	257	92,316	31,485	23,980
Congressional District 2............	76,898	42,734	12,475	19,544	2,663	7,629	4,464	782	97,405	32,191	24,281
Congressional District 3............	78,708	42,967	12,254	22,209	3,036	8,003	5,539	2,021	93,440	36,240	23,804
Wisconsin											
Congressional District 1............	74,558	39,690	11,007	22,551	3,578	6,270	1,806	235	101,686	28,055	25,153
Congressional District 2............	73,821	39,274	9,611	21,873	2,474	5,768	2,217	92	101,328	23,521	23,291
Congressional District 3............	82,297	43,674	12,629	23,753	5,127	3,999	984	75	110,782	32,989	24,470
Congressional District 4............	56,464	26,392	11,025	17,710	2,974	6,780	3,341	700	56,469	22,196	24,183
Congressional District 5............	83,076	45,276	9,439	26,535	3,666	4,936	957	0	114,017	34,242	24,862
Congressional District 6............	85,253	43,780	12,071	27,324	4,472	4,061	1,169	0	111,144	32,490	25,290
Congressional District 7............	91,109	50,194	13,697	24,246	4,892	3,688	1,037	138	128,626	31,659	26,361
Congressional District 8............	78,599	43,439	11,265	21,916	3,937	3,408	1,025	154	112,980	29,760	21,924
Wyoming											
Congressional District (at Large)	61,902	34,566	9,971	14,795	2,444	4,377	2,354	769	85,393	22,192	22,111

PART E

EDUCATIONAL ATTAINMENT AND VETERAN STATUS

EDUCATIONAL ATTAINMENT AND VETERANS STATUS

The population that in 2018 was age 65 and over was born before 1953. It includes generations born at a time when college, and even high school educations, weren't as universally accepted or expected as they are today. This factor is reflected in the educational attainment levels of the older population and also across geographic areas. In 1944 the Servicemen's Readjustment Act, known as the GI Bill was enacted giving a broad array of benefits to returning World War II veterans. Almost 8.9 million veterans are age 65 and over and almost 233,000 of them are women. Many of those veterans would have used education and training benefits from the GI Bill.

Education

Nationally, 30.8 percent of the population over 65 years has a no only school or equivalent education but more than one in four have a bachelor's degree or higher (28.2 percent). Among the states, California has the lowest percent of people with only a high school education at 20.3 percent while less than half of Pennsylvania's older population (42.3 percent) have not gone beyond high school. In the District of Columbia, 45.2 percent of residents 65 and over have a bachelor's degree or higher (the Nation's highest) compared to only 18.4 percent in West Virginia. In eight additional states, one-third or more of its older residents have a college education (Colorado, Connecticut, Maryland, Massachusetts, New Hampshire, Utah, Vermont and Washington). In 468 of the 814 counties, the percent of 65 and over with a high school education exceeds that of the nation and in 19 counties it's greater than 50 percent. Fayette County, Pennsylvania has the highest rate of persons with only a high school education at 61.2 percent while at 12.1 percent Marin County, California is lowest. More than 60 percent (62.7 percent) of Arlington County, Virginia residents 65 and over have bachelor's degrees which is more

Percent of the Population 65 Years and Over With a Bachelor's Degree or Higher

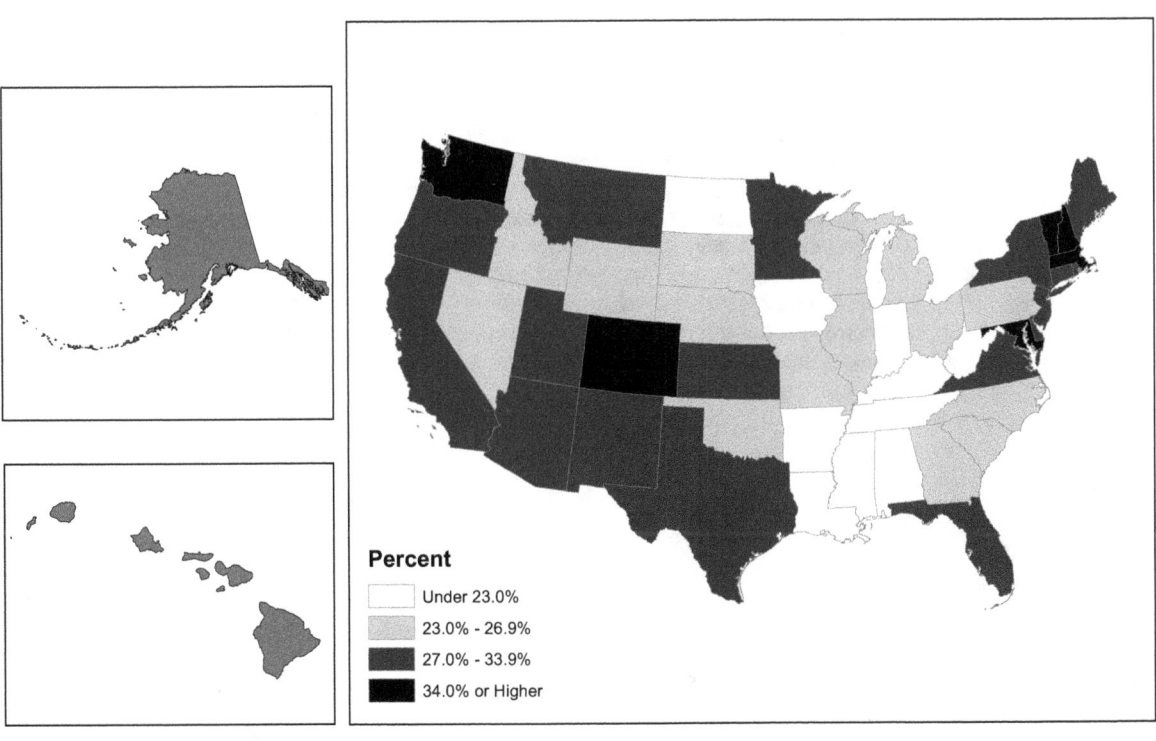

Percent

- Under 23.0%
- 23.0% - 26.9%
- 27.0% - 33.9%
- 34.0% or Higher

than twice the national rate of 28.2 percent. Almost 340 counties are above the national average but in 3 counties, less than 10 percent of the population has a college education. The lowest is Liberty County, Texas with 9.8 percent.

In 149 cities, the percent of older residents with only a high school education is above the national rate and Hammond city, Indiana, at 51.5 percent is the highest. Berkeley city, California is the city with the lowest percent of persons with only a high school education at 5.8 percent. The cities of Palo Alto and Davis, California have the highest percent of residents with a bachelor's degree or higher at 75 percent each. In 48 cities the percent of older residents with a bachelor's degree is over 50 percent. South Gate city, California is the lowest at 2.3 percent. In 19 cities the percent of persons 65 and over with a bachelor's degree is less than 10 percent. The Sunbury, Pennsylvania micropolitan area has the highest percent (60.6 percent) of persons with only a high school education and, while not the lowest, only 12.5 percent have a bachelor's degree or higher. The Santa Cruz-Watsonville, California metro area has the lowest percent of high school diploma holders at 13.6 percent. The Boulder, Colorado metro area has the highest percent of residents with a bachelor's degree or higher at 56.5 percent. The Martinsville, Virginia micropolitan area is lowest at 9.3 percent. In only three Congressional Districts do more than 50 percent of the residents 65 and over

have only a high school education. These are in District 6 in Ohio and Districts 14 and 15 in Pennsylvania. There are 10 Congressional Districts in the states of California (3), Colorado (1), Georgia (1), Maryland (1), New York (1), Virginia (2) and Washington (1) where more than 50 percent of the residents have a bachelor's degree or higher. Residents of Congressional District 33 in California have the highest percent of bachelor's degree holders at 58.5 percent while Texas' 29th district is lowest at 7.3 percent. In 278 Districts fewer than 30 percent of residents have bachelor's degrees or higher.

Veterans Status

As of 2018, all veterans currently 55 and over would have been born before 1963 which means that those who served in the Second World War would be among the oldest living veterans. Nationwide there are 12.1 million veterans age 55 and older and 8.9 million of them are age 65 and older. Not surprising, most older veterans are male (94.9 percent) but nearly 617,000 are females and 37.8 percent of them are age 65 and over.

Veterans by Age and Period of Service		
Age in 2018	Period of Birth	Primary Service Era
55 to 64	1954 to 1963	Gulf War
65 to 74	1944 to 1953	Vietnam Era
75 and Over	1943 or earlier	World War II

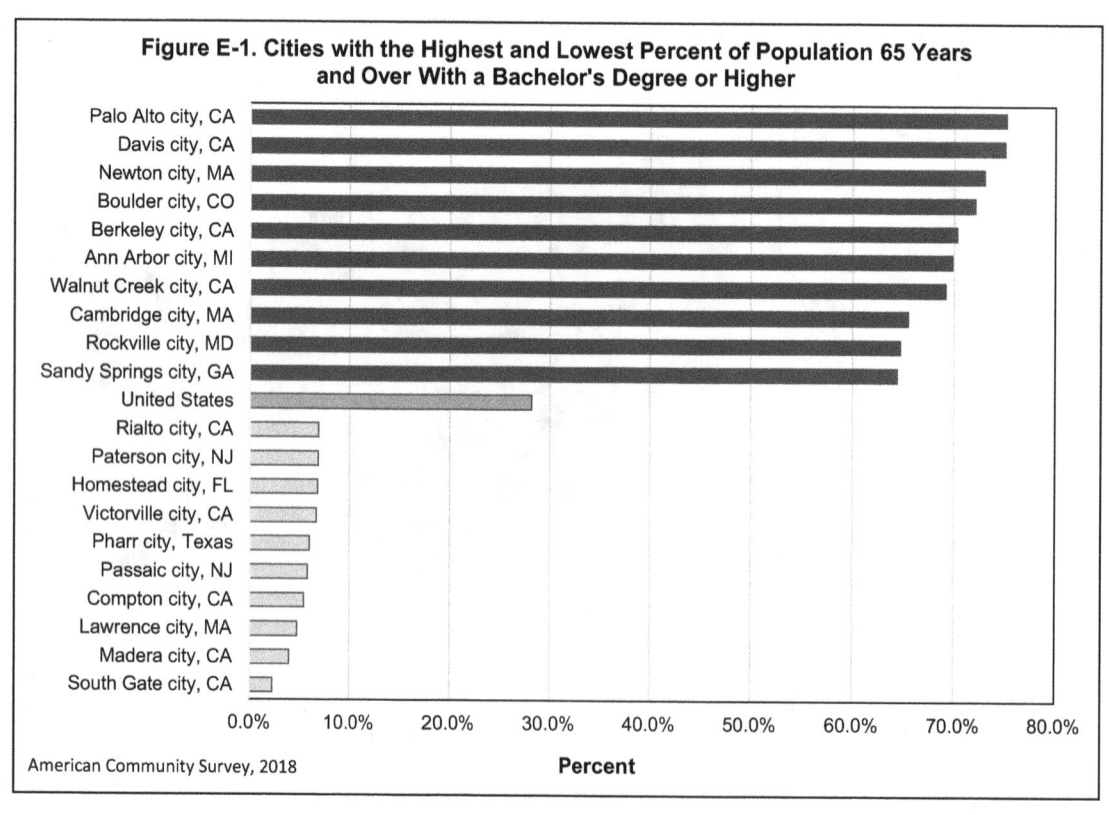

Figure E-1. Cities with the Highest and Lowest Percent of Population 65 Years and Over With a Bachelor's Degree or Higher

American Community Survey, 2018

Alaska has the highest percent of persons 65 and over who are veterans at 25.6 percent while the District of Columbia has the lowest percentage at 11.6 percent. In 38 states the percent of population 65 and over who are veterans is greater than the national average of 17.0 percent. Female veterans age 65 and over make up the largest percentage in Alaska at 5.5 percent while Connecticut is lowest at 1.8 percent. Los Angeles County, California has the largest number of veterans 65 and over with just over 131,000 and that is 9.5 percent of the total 65 and over population. Maricopa County, Arizona is the next closest with 125,600 veterans which makes up 18.8 percent of the total population age 65 and over. Montgomery County, Tennessee has the highest percentage of older population who are veterans at 34.3 percent while Kings County, New York is lowest at 4.8 percent. Female veterans age 65 and over make up the largest percentage in Lea County, New Mexico at 29.9 percent. In 83 counties the percentage of veterans who are female exceeds 10 percent but in 184 counties this group makes up less than 3 percent of veterans age 65 and over.

New York City is the city location for the most veterans age 65 and over with more than 78,400 and that's 6.3 percent of the total population that is at least 65 years old. It's the only city with more than 50,000 veterans and the next closest is Los Angeles with 41,400. Five other cities have over 30,000 vets including San Antonio, Texas (38,100), Philadelphia, Pennsylvania (32,400), San Diego, California (32,200), Chicago, Illinois (31,800),

and Phoenix, Arizona (31,700). In Homestead city, Florida nearly seven of ten (68.2 percent) veterans over the age of 65 is female. In 24 cities female veterans make up more than 25 percent of those over the age of 65.

With New York City having the highest number of veterans age 65 and over it's not surprising that the New York-Newark-Jersey City metropolitan area is largest with more than 313,000 older veterans. It's the largest but not in percentage terms. The percentage is only 10.0 compared to the highest area, the Cheyenne, Wyoming metropolitan area at 32.1 percent. In 29 metropolitan and micropolitan areas more than 25 percent of the 65 and over population are veterans. The Laredo, Texas metro area is lowest at 6.4 percent. Women make up 29.9 percent of older veterans in the Hobbs, New Mexico micro area but in 297 metropolitan and micropolitan areas the proportion of female vets is less than 5 percent. Ten Congressional Districts have greater than 40,000 veterans age 65 and over. Congressional District 11 in Florida is the largest at more than 62,500. California's 40th Congressional District is the smallest at just over 3,600. Florida's 1st Congressional District has the highest percentage of older population who are veterans at 28.5 percent while New York's 13th District is lowest at 4.4 percent. In 37 Congressional Districts the percentage of older female veterans is greater than 5 percent and Wisconsin's 7th district is highest at 10.2 percent. Seven districts have less than 1 percent female veterans with Wisconsin's 2nd District being the lowest at 0.5 percent.

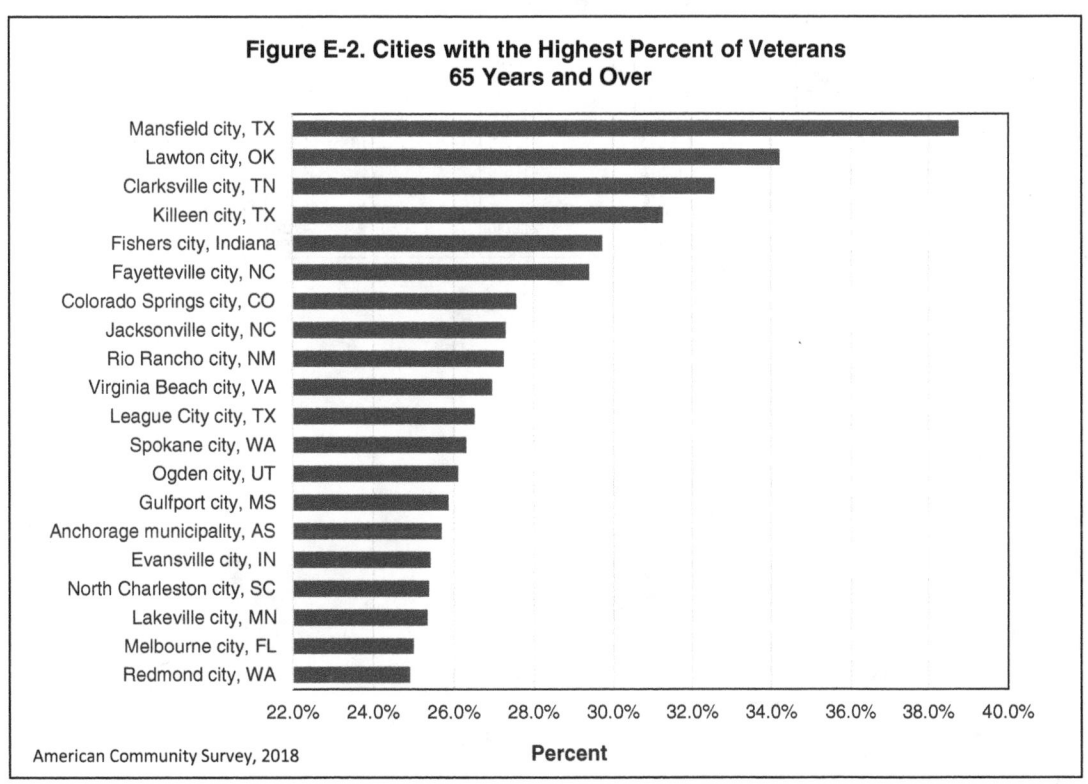

Figure E-2. Cities with the Highest Percent of Veterans 65 Years and Over

American Community Survey, 2018

Table E-1: States - Educational Attainment and Veterans Status, Persons 55 and Over

	High School or Equivalent	Some College or Associates Degree	Bachelor's Degree or Higher	Veterans by Age and Gender					
				Male			Female		
				55 to 64 Years	65 to 74 Years	75 Years and Over	55 to 64 Years	65 to 74 Years	75 Years and Over
United States	16,146,187	13,701,158	14,781,269	2,799,729	4,552,769	4,101,808	383,659	199,507	33,734
Alabama..............................	288,865	209,125	187,352	57,513	82,546	62,520	8,577	4,198	619
Alaska	21,855	27,953	28,693	11,175	13,837	7,470	1,934	968	283
Arizona...............................	314,104	415,064	372,926	70,724	129,160	118,977	11,969	6,152	1,502
Arkansas.............................	186,679	124,778	107,553	30,137	49,336	39,836	3,624	2,053	405
California............................	1,149,978	1,595,182	1,825,043	227,229	372,656	386,739	25,964	16,473	1,740
Colorado.............................	185,820	235,934	315,996	56,346	85,384	69,522	9,524	4,740	845
Connecticut.........................	194,387	134,739	206,383	24,142	44,772	48,938	3,119	854	408
Delaware.............................	60,989	42,852	55,314	11,883	18,364	16,475	1,903	401	261
District of Columbia	19,070	14,420	38,742	3,454	3,821	5,615	572	182	336
Florida................................	1,319,264	1,150,944	1,266,955	226,805	353,873	395,025	33,013	19,931	1,440
Georgia...............................	465,361	360,922	387,689	106,355	143,854	102,593	17,239	8,535	720
Hawaii................................	70,613	72,147	82,230	14,848	24,882	21,977	1,440	578	218
Idaho..................................	86,106	99,070	71,439	19,866	32,456	25,899	3,419	1,570	527
Illinois...............................	658,644	511,294	535,630	81,815	153,644	139,812	7,656	4,087	928
Indiana...............................	428,486	249,947	229,108	61,890	101,003	83,599	6,541	4,265	652
Iowa...................................	218,775	145,901	121,925	25,357	52,599	47,617	4,027	1,218	430
Kansas................................	152,781	132,052	133,729	27,104	43,857	39,682	4,073	1,765	405
Kentucky.............................	267,132	169,202	151,124	44,205	67,991	52,485	4,136	2,796	514
Louisiana............................	261,708	172,866	158,832	35,047	62,268	51,805	5,462	3,191	719
Maine.................................	92,354	71,578	83,544	20,328	28,998	24,540	2,503	1,029	621
Maryland.............................	266,306	209,582	331,232	59,946	76,744	74,099	11,345	5,313	1,247
Massachusetts......................	321,300	252,435	402,067	45,259	75,836	87,577	3,906	2,382	735
Michigan.............................	589,087	508,098	425,717	80,945	155,816	131,031	7,339	4,576	824
Minnesota...........................	299,220	251,847	263,333	44,762	82,503	78,308	5,223	2,672	532
Mississippi..........................	153,748	126,297	98,986	25,594	37,306	30,633	3,752	2,024	452
Missouri.............................	380,703	277,902	241,853	63,347	108,016	87,274	8,610	3,151	686
Montana..............................	62,803	60,305	60,539	11,275	23,768	17,861	1,679	1,331	318
Nebraska.............................	104,610	92,021	77,664	17,382	29,641	26,518	3,597	775	298
Nevada...............................	125,709	164,198	125,848	35,225	53,196	42,606	5,743	2,838	807
New Hampshire.....................	72,715	63,171	84,361	17,346	24,601	22,682	2,212	1,212	324
New Jersey...........................	484,136	285,892	451,081	40,273	81,958	98,841	4,739	2,694	853
New Mexico..........................	88,087	101,639	116,831	25,316	38,696	30,706	3,144	1,866	451
New York.............................	996,769	680,550	946,417	100,052	180,286	196,887	12,427	5,798	946
North Carolina......................	513,516	463,402	453,837	110,215	161,500	126,372	16,881	6,141	809
North Dakota........................	36,692	38,020	26,133	6,183	11,761	9,700	628	455	256
Ohio...................................	787,070	483,008	461,558	108,729	181,483	159,479	12,703	6,327	911
Oklahoma............................	204,914	182,663	152,353	39,988	69,590	54,647	4,560	3,718	501
Oregon................................	182,932	259,347	235,906	42,235	77,569	66,910	5,627	4,181	925
Pennsylvania........................	985,760	480,149	569,760	109,729	206,312	206,740	12,557	6,802	881
Rhode Island........................	57,826	38,059	55,509	6,708	16,099	14,325	1,082	373	218
South Carolina......................	283,110	241,171	237,261	58,989	98,138	72,076	9,543	5,091	752
South Dakota........................	54,023	40,342	37,505	8,904	14,707	12,840	818	592	317
Tennessee...........................	372,732	281,197	254,033	66,183	108,719	88,422	10,469	4,482	743
Texas.................................	933,996	960,027	986,108	216,345	324,925	257,109	31,682	16,901	1,571
Utah...................................	86,414	120,434	117,665	18,808	29,097	29,301	1,804	1,574	276
Vermont..............................	38,735	29,819	43,647	5,663	10,179	9,460	1,400	566	263
Virginia...............................	366,369	315,017	434,616	115,983	134,162	109,402	20,656	8,311	809
Washington..........................	280,507	391,661	396,100	84,672	130,886	98,242	13,199	6,382	1,005
West Virginia........................	154,474	76,968	66,425	19,410	36,383	29,476	2,079	2,309	512
Wisconsin............................	388,880	256,553	242,746	50,507	94,837	83,121	6,720	2,838	779
Wyoming	30,073	33,414	23,971	7,533	12,754	8,037	840	846	160

Table E-2: Counties - Educational Attainment and Veterans Status, Persons 55 and Over

	High School or Equivalent	Some College or Associates Degree	Bachelor's Degree or Higher	Veterans by Age and Gender					
				Male			Female		
				55 to 64 Years	65 to 74 Years	75 Years and Over	55 to 64 Years	65 to 74 Years	75 Years and Over
Alabama									
Baldwin County	12,184	14,200	13,767	4,211	5,547	4,467	618	45	71
Calhoun County	7,152	5,703	3,080	2,190	2,341	1,174	424	216	148
Cullman County	6,646	4,332	1,858	752	1,455	1,761	95	86	22
DeKalb County	4,298	2,739	1,707	1,046	766	833	282	0	26
Elmore County	4,014	3,037	3,481	1,034	1,265	846	92	211	201
Etowah County	6,578	5,348	4,636	678	1,155	1,954	310	170	87
Houston County	7,034	4,927	4,129	1,052	1,672	1,860	189	64	151
Jefferson County	32,258	30,169	29,440	5,697	9,948	7,144	1,074	525	389
Lauderdale County	7,531	3,761	4,417	902	1,700	1,169	0	0	201
Lee County	5,842	5,054	5,883	2,161	2,452	1,409	425	157	54
Limestone County	4,666	3,898	3,387	960	1,703	1,711	257	0	201
Madison County	13,336	14,774	20,475	7,141	7,235	4,356	1,213	366	144
Marshall County	6,069	3,584	3,718	1,612	929	1,341	94	67	37
Mobile County	25,903	15,772	14,147	4,336	6,201	5,200	674	560	35
Montgomery County	10,330	7,837	9,365	3,373	3,507	2,333	472	266	232
Morgan County	5,579	5,451	5,783	955	1,983	1,671	305	66	84
St. Clair County	6,839	2,852	1,520	871	1,622	1,763	0	0	201
Shelby County	8,528	10,384	11,449	1,833	3,567	2,997	25	49	202
Talladega County	5,612	3,236	2,243	1,292	1,329	623	78	0	145
Tuscaloosa County	10,230	6,517	8,017	1,663	2,343	1,966	167	120	85
Walker County	5,346	2,602	1,214	388	1,679	537	0	0	95
Alaska									
Anchorage Municipality	7,429	10,626	12,718	4,740	4,641	3,249	1,252	426	110
Fairbanks North Star Borough	2,356	2,913	3,315	1,903	2,221	238	261	344	224
Matanuska-Susitna Borough	3,431	5,185	3,219	2,015	2,104	1,097	168	72	83
Arizona									
Apache County	1,991	2,890	1,974	804	998	649	520	0	211
Cochise County	7,206	9,543	7,431	4,009	3,973	3,650	1,131	357	488
Coconino County	2,856	5,173	7,039	1,059	2,137	1,079	186	165	24
Maricopa County	166,850	218,557	211,296	38,438	61,310	60,747	5,453	2,773	859
Mohave County	21,757	25,099	9,587	3,432	8,522	6,573	466	411	619
Navajo County	4,904	7,413	3,814	1,128	2,606	1,640	117	0	146
Pima County	46,908	61,091	74,043	11,997	22,136	19,175	2,190	824	558
Pinal County	23,219	32,766	22,668	3,756	11,558	8,887	870	807	396
Yavapai County	16,506	27,537	23,416	2,400	8,881	8,611	496	485	475
Yuma County	11,454	10,986	5,328	2,166	2,947	4,602	317	153	114
Arkansas									
Benton County	12,432	9,920	9,218	1,861	3,326	3,925	572	48	85
Craighead County	5,074	3,542	3,118	733	969	1,183	108	0	201
Faulkner County	5,542	4,464	3,563	730	1,569	1,009	59	45	84
Garland County	7,745	6,259	6,197	1,322	2,153	2,446	583	102	201
Jefferson County	5,588	2,209	2,427	908	1,158	921	0	176	138
Lonoke County	4,059	2,541	1,009	601	1,165	827	88	86	201
Pulaski County	16,936	17,027	19,219	5,864	5,909	4,535	664	168	177
Saline County	9,375	5,071	5,278	815	2,967	2,367	16	0	149
Sebastian County	7,047	5,094	4,972	913	1,698	1,490	114	58	201
Washington County	9,678	5,156	8,875	1,788	2,380	2,540	151	0	88
White County	3,666	2,743	2,346	365	974	932	79	155	106
California									
Alameda County	53,146	55,566	86,871	6,938	10,243	12,622	966	451	377
Butte County	8,673	16,299	13,575	1,721	3,895	3,775	139	70	184
Contra Costa County	34,930	51,140	76,641	6,935	12,198	13,768	607	584	238
El Dorado County	8,793	15,761	14,273	2,205	5,106	3,167	87	93	211
Fresno County	26,123	36,231	28,466	6,046	8,553	8,552	474	274	331
Humboldt County	3,961	8,264	10,075	1,116	3,591	1,987	52	106	164
Imperial County	4,264	4,207	3,104	608	1,227	844	60	0	211
Kern County	22,051	30,211	19,922	5,554	9,109	6,934	553	398	527
Kings County	3,650	4,611	2,874	1,823	1,379	1,740	218	82	211
Lake County	4,302	5,151	3,361	754	1,337	1,506	104	124	80
Los Angeles County	271,933	324,192	401,630	38,399	57,129	70,510	2,865	3,001	573
Madera County	5,716	6,048	4,179	816	2,640	1,752	114	44	211
Marin County	7,042	14,175	35,010	1,995	2,678	3,950	160	264	201
Mendocino County	3,764	7,041	6,191	349	2,011	1,334	161	0	242
Merced County	6,310	8,063	4,362	1,952	1,744	1,985	387	72	105
Monterey County	9,909	16,416	19,880	2,358	4,808	4,539	351	23	142
Napa County	5,636	8,048	10,358	1,127	2,185	2,129	130	43	158
Nevada County	4,436	11,299	11,527	630	2,561	3,006	145	216	247
Orange County	87,328	133,965	178,361	12,363	28,144	32,643	1,437	680	499
Placer County	14,563	29,468	28,258	3,026	7,735	7,570	658	41	173
Riverside County	86,793	111,918	86,597	14,896	26,474	29,088	2,178	891	841
Sacramento County	48,255	71,892	66,653	12,830	19,137	17,874	1,775	1,365	378
San Bernardino County	61,974	75,283	51,733	15,601	21,877	17,576	1,011	733	362
San Diego County	84,677	135,379	171,826	31,145	41,586	36,604	4,585	2,156	812
San Francisco County	21,805	26,681	55,758	3,044	5,526	6,788	592	154	270
San Joaquin County	24,846	31,313	18,327	4,989	7,571	6,843	813	477	159

Table E-2: Counties - Educational Attainment and Veterans Status, Persons 55 and Over—*Continued*

	High School or Equivalent	Some College or Associates Degree	Bachelor's Degree or Higher	Veterans by Age and Gender					
				Male			Female		
				55 to 64 Years	65 to 74 Years	75 Years and Over	55 to 64 Years	65 to 74 Years	75 Years and Over
California—Cont.									
San Luis Obispo County	8,584	23,298	21,819	3,228	6,085	4,703	105	116	153
San Mateo County	20,876	32,090	54,770	4,042	5,569	8,093	422	336	229
Santa Barbara County	11,457	18,974	28,886	2,676	5,033	5,375	351	427	117
Santa Clara County	44,084	64,230	111,044	6,152	10,056	16,752	853	849	246
Santa Cruz County	6,170	13,014	20,715	1,468	2,801	2,949	79	0	163
Shasta County	9,066	16,050	8,067	1,793	3,953	3,565	312	124	111
Solano County	17,483	25,069	20,377	5,502	6,925	5,651	354	572	235
Sonoma County	15,830	34,246	40,109	3,705	7,153	7,416	346	302	183
Stanislaus County	21,199	18,262	12,849	3,659	4,878	4,209	208	420	204
Sutter County	2,715	4,320	3,766	1,001	935	1,208	183	134	211
Tulare County	12,730	15,095	8,488	2,566	3,357	3,210	337	158	102
Ventura County	28,674	40,232	44,490	5,030	10,639	10,622	939	524	171
Yolo County	4,493	6,200	11,975	803	2,023	1,897	41	0	156
Yuba County	1,803	3,110	2,239	1,139	731	1,002	322	104	166
Colorado									
Adams County	14,901	17,412	12,623	3,733	7,102	4,311	532	457	204
Arapahoe County	19,277	24,577	35,277	5,598	7,801	6,612	995	456	303
Boulder County	6,569	11,778	26,022	2,090	3,498	3,336	310	395	130
Broomfield County	2,480	2,445	4,160	325	799	791	0	87	204
Denver County	15,976	17,705	37,128	4,775	7,203	6,254	457	359	141
Douglas County	5,815	12,361	20,733	2,973	3,382	3,631	792	92	204
El Paso County	21,721	29,221	32,970	14,313	14,593	9,710	2,906	1,116	319
Jefferson County	21,692	27,704	39,755	4,972	9,535	8,627	904	497	199
Larimer County	11,698	15,831	25,500	2,664	4,880	5,069	793	61	289
Mesa County	7,753	9,800	8,611	2,269	3,088	2,774	250	14	156
Pueblo County	9,026	11,029	7,135	2,303	3,426	2,469	265	70	119
Weld County	12,206	12,570	9,257	2,292	4,515	2,782	96	168	205
Connecticut									
Fairfield County	38,903	29,705	61,637	4,158	8,620	11,831	262	103	230
Hartford County	49,923	32,222	47,351	6,178	9,869	11,230	750	191	256
Litchfield County	12,781	9,771	11,364	1,531	3,228	3,201	183	0	207
Middlesex County	8,982	8,687	12,589	1,075	2,485	2,237	203	0	207
New Haven County	52,791	32,358	43,805	5,340	11,125	11,526	1,037	180	166
New London County	16,852	11,087	15,163	3,140	5,737	5,123	434	211	135
Tolland County	8,639	5,108	9,431	1,304	2,048	1,714	207	169	207
Windham County	5,516	5,801	5,043	1,416	1,660	2,076	43	0	49
Delaware									
Kent County	10,441	7,221	5,973	2,706	3,430	3,561	346	139	110
New Castle County	29,434	19,106	29,278	6,432	8,366	7,167	857	225	47
Sussex County	21,114	16,525	20,063	2,745	6,568	5,747	700	37	229
Florida									
Alachua County	9,376	8,749	15,067	2,830	3,531	3,332	276	0	155
Bay County	10,923	9,063	7,766	4,866	3,781	3,195	981	197	227
Brevard County	43,159	43,261	39,875	11,138	15,177	16,644	1,434	1,570	481
Broward County	99,293	79,181	90,158	11,936	14,973	20,489	1,543	623	274
Charlotte County	24,459	20,657	21,146	2,312	5,950	9,723	219	240	293
Citrus County	20,112	18,486	9,994	2,770	7,369	7,141	137	23	256
Clay County	12,431	9,430	9,127	5,451	5,144	3,108	467	381	257
Collier County	24,947	28,833	58,748	2,376	6,943	14,044	381	296	85
Columbia County	4,409	4,247	2,049	1,179	1,706	1,584	105	69	127
Duval County	43,378	38,138	34,861	14,328	14,814	10,059	2,823	1,270	422
Escambia County	16,529	17,686	13,722	6,096	7,449	6,114	1,150	443	226
Flagler County	11,247	9,238	10,445	1,151	4,059	3,680	231	40	75
Hernando County	19,002	15,793	9,007	2,507	4,321	6,107	409	156	154
Highlands County	13,646	11,377	6,855	1,040	2,283	4,422	278	278	170
Hillsborough County	63,524	51,541	57,997	16,383	19,263	16,168	3,596	950	282
Indian River County	15,766	15,496	16,453	2,094	4,739	6,873	141	83	254
Lake County	33,033	28,755	23,218	4,799	8,497	9,018	601	718	132
Lee County	66,046	60,770	71,829	8,782	18,299	22,108	970	396	481
Leon County	10,063	9,103	16,407	3,082	3,669	2,962	51	41	288
Manatee County	34,565	28,470	35,769	4,420	9,239	13,062	537	206	309
Marion County	38,997	27,278	24,954	5,079	9,898	12,816	987	587	748
Martin County	13,928	14,010	17,797	953	4,616	5,166	0	40	164
Miami-Dade County	112,754	77,186	106,303	8,863	11,226	9,833	1,339	791	189
Monroe County	3,749	5,352	5,921	603	1,630	1,599	0	0	229
Nassau County	5,003	5,333	6,670	1,962	2,013	2,082	124	18	229
Okaloosa County	9,834	11,621	9,915	5,796	6,650	3,739	685	541	302
Orange County	47,518	37,878	43,689	12,727	13,862	10,530	2,154	1,701	393
Osceola County	15,885	11,385	9,819	5,329	4,075	2,507	445	122	129
Palm Beach County	89,774	88,955	140,918	8,975	18,115	33,434	844	633	227
Pasco County	46,638	35,533	25,689	7,001	13,092	14,710	1,279	851	304
Pinellas County	76,856	70,827	71,925	11,679	21,052	24,434	1,883	2,139	382
Polk County	53,947	40,795	28,430	7,539	14,238	13,046	1,018	757	197
Putnam County	7,394	4,741	2,486	1,313	2,383	1,692	10	108	229

Table E-2: Counties - Educational Attainment and Veterans Status, Persons 55 and Over—*Continued*

	High School or Equivalent	Some College or Associates Degree	Bachelor's Degree or Higher	Veterans by Age and Gender					
				Male			Female		
				55 to 64 Years	65 to 74 Years	75 Years and Over	55 to 64 Years	65 to 74 Years	75 Years and Over
Florida—Cont.									
St. Johns County	13,256	15,217	20,767	3,201	3,914	6,015	516	337	320
St. Lucie County	22,134	23,105	20,334	2,927	6,516	7,902	572	374	229
Santa Rosa County	10,154	8,792	7,090	4,632	4,231	3,362	1,094	388	100
Sarasota County	38,171	45,139	63,122	3,979	11,063	19,709	1,197	329	293
Seminole County	19,711	20,691	25,209	4,842	7,337	6,851	727	479	168
Sumter County	19,191	21,830	27,578	1,000	8,603	7,079	121	204	229
Volusia County	41,715	41,968	35,051	8,400	12,932	15,239	699	838	282
Walton County	4,519	4,157	4,558	1,504	2,371	1,360	79	170	187
Georgia									
Barrow County	3,462	2,649	2,392	865	528	635	67	0	226
Bartow County	5,782	3,334	2,540	858	1,422	486	0	27	226
Bibb County	7,488	6,453	5,486	1,620	2,641	1,608	459	322	136
Bulloch County	2,394	2,218	2,471	117	724	695	130	53	226
Carroll County	5,657	3,958	3,173	1,198	1,469	1,173	0	78	226
Catoosa County	5,285	3,045	1,791	959	1,380	664	0	169	226
Chatham County	12,823	11,729	14,495	2,939	4,242	3,976	958	229	77
Cherokee County	9,662	11,052	12,062	2,015	3,355	3,119	464	72	226
Clarke County	2,999	2,804	6,435	1,310	1,657	836	236	32	97
Clayton County	9,104	8,092	4,512	3,643	3,159	855	705	299	51
Cobb County	23,256	24,165	37,969	6,609	11,493	6,457	1,561	482	146
Columbia County	6,897	5,917	5,808	3,161	2,582	1,784	337	913	226
Coweta County	6,362	5,463	6,178	1,517	2,254	1,767	263	55	226
DeKalb County	25,290	21,039	36,158	7,142	7,726	5,047	1,672	325	120
Dougherty County	3,751	3,076	3,697	1,118	1,308	840	144	0	226
Douglas County	6,279	3,728	4,435	1,276	1,841	1,074	531	0	68
Fayette County	7,092	5,880	5,872	2,330	2,885	1,678	235	217	226
Floyd County	5,553	4,656	2,857	823	1,272	857	0	69	104
Forsyth County	7,732	8,583	9,579	1,151	2,394	2,456	0	60	226
Fulton County	27,255	29,653	53,636	6,139	7,311	7,728	760	390	278
Glynn County	3,296	4,511	7,166	765	1,617	1,631	138	186	143
Gwinnett County	25,175	26,207	28,362	7,382	7,977	5,943	874	498	103
Hall County	8,929	6,778	8,617	1,608	3,246	3,033	222	70	405
Henry County	11,119	6,593	6,016	3,591	3,495	2,495	587	535	70
Houston County	7,802	4,881	3,804	3,485	2,132	1,577	551	0	120
Jackson County	3,412	3,106	2,495	604	1,044	706	154	71	226
Lowndes County	4,615	3,373	2,962	1,194	2,036	823	242	139	66
Muscogee County	7,883	6,410	7,133	4,181	3,401	2,201	905	243	226
Newton County	3,842	5,273	2,969	938	1,212	1,244	62	62	226
Paulding County	5,372	3,791	3,978	1,390	1,211	764	344	0	226
Richmond County	10,339	6,425	4,825	2,703	3,908	2,559	576	181	110
Rockdale County	2,942	3,912	3,919	689	1,542	834	457	71	226
Spalding County	4,994	2,350	2,235	580	1,475	865	0	0	226
Troup County	4,790	2,244	2,082	518	1,145	477	98	0	226
Walker County	5,135	3,913	1,642	1,320	1,222	1,018	0	0	226
Walton County	4,918	3,113	3,753	547	1,647	1,166	29	41	89
Whitfield County	5,284	2,337	2,434	462	1,193	611	48	0	226
Hawaii									
Hawaii County	10,451	14,845	13,178	2,346	5,590	3,616	148	132	128
Honolulu County	47,101	45,493	53,584	9,804	14,896	14,833	1,277	406	180
Kauai County	3,107	4,224	5,306	623	1,470	1,041	0	0	189
Maui County	9,954	7,582	10,154	2,075	2,926	2,487	15	40	189
Idaho									
Ada County	18,254	24,533	22,307	5,369	7,960	5,223	1,321	123	222
Bannock County	3,799	4,571	3,121	524	1,183	1,308	102	105	186
Bonneville County	3,833	5,262	4,780	521	1,352	1,132	385	64	31
Canyon County	10,469	10,699	6,728	2,531	3,341	2,773	133	391	354
Kootenai County	8,510	10,837	8,963	2,608	4,242	3,315	98	50	10
Twin Falls County	3,509	5,700	2,145	910	1,097	1,360	116	442	204
Illinois									
Adams County	6,308	2,852	2,658	453	1,393	876	335	42	176
Champaign County	7,503	7,910	9,675	984	2,950	2,056	11	63	83
Cook County	220,658	175,407	221,921	21,423	38,489	42,517	1,982	1,142	716
DeKalb County	3,305	3,493	5,042	563	1,173	1,123	0	0	132
DuPage County	35,774	37,555	57,169	2,995	9,519	9,313	248	339	251
Kane County	22,918	19,951	19,192	3,315	6,104	5,636	487	89	18
Kankakee County	8,513	4,584	2,645	1,234	2,229	1,646	0	0	177
Kendall County	4,942	3,743	4,075	711	1,831	1,423	0	0	190
Lake County	25,462	24,759	38,238	6,220	6,366	7,032	942	400	195
LaSalle County	9,151	5,677	2,873	932	1,846	1,499	59	0	190
McHenry County	15,565	13,621	11,733	2,341	4,651	3,280	217	160	196
McLean County	7,607	5,557	8,293	1,103	1,980	1,536	131	60	65
Macon County	8,686	5,590	3,986	795	1,903	1,889	72	78	146
Madison County	16,946	13,320	10,877	3,611	5,376	3,710	135	247	78
Peoria County	9,810	9,974	7,806	1,292	2,580	2,528	332	84	65
Rock Island County	9,604	8,482	5,988	1,584	2,675	2,287	196	36	111

Table E-2: Counties - Educational Attainment and Veterans Status, Persons 55 and Over—*Continued*

				Veterans by Age and Gender					
				Male			Female		
	High School or Equivalent	Some College or Associates Degree	Bachelor's Degree or Higher	55 to 64 Years	65 to 74 Years	75 Years and Over	55 to 64 Years	65 to 74 Years	75 Years and Over
Illinois—Cont.									
St. Clair County	13,038	11,749	9,679	4,322	5,286	3,611	724	121	228
Sangamon County	11,598	8,787	11,576	2,122	3,588	2,854	87	125	20
Tazewell County	9,338	6,766	5,374	1,235	1,922	2,157	70	19	100
Vermilion County	6,824	4,284	2,140	615	1,644	1,460	58	54	30
Will County	32,420	24,576	22,283	4,214	7,735	6,988	216	0	73
Williamson County	4,717	3,619	2,759	316	1,763	1,061	177	35	190
Winnebago County	17,660	14,368	10,715	2,740	4,877	3,533	295	108	208
Indiana									
Allen County	20,698	15,309	12,087	3,095	5,747	3,288	368	408	95
Bartholomew County	5,834	3,455	2,454	793	676	729	112	0	124
Boone County	3,010	3,215	2,020	266	656	254	0	0	119
Clark County	7,900	4,605	3,418	1,027	2,540	1,126	73	123	140
Delaware County	7,950	4,659	4,389	1,059	1,482	1,987	279	46	198
Elkhart County	12,394	6,512	6,025	826	2,727	2,222	42	37	125
Floyd County	4,920	3,419	3,324	848	1,131	887	0	71	198
Grant County	5,221	3,256	1,360	667	1,353	1,198	83	47	198
Hamilton County	12,612	9,642	17,230	2,399	4,786	3,376	242	241	141
Hancock County	5,764	2,964	3,379	405	1,490	684	0	0	198
Hendricks County	7,663	5,969	7,130	2,077	1,770	1,741	52	63	198
Howard County	6,687	3,303	3,427	413	1,249	1,168	87	82	138
Johnson County	9,969	5,858	5,030	1,564	1,666	1,858	41	144	125
Kosciusko County	5,014	2,752	3,745	769	1,378	1,241	91	0	122
Lake County	36,702	16,190	13,065	4,675	6,851	6,025	463	164	303
LaPorte County	8,337	4,090	4,082	1,346	2,903	1,625	138	33	97
Madison County	10,194	6,003	4,389	1,508	3,069	2,095	288	99	77
Marion County	37,152	32,190	29,908	9,496	10,233	8,709	1,555	1,076	74
Monroe County	5,061	3,603	8,488	398	1,582	1,434	128	171	198
Morgan County	5,150	3,166	1,481	1,235	1,670	1,013	37	163	198
Porter County	12,641	5,309	6,786	1,578	2,624	2,649	162	0	198
St. Joseph County	17,358	9,121	11,480	1,960	3,034	3,584	358	258	102
Tippecanoe County	7,031	5,432	7,714	1,021	1,804	1,566	0	0	318
Vanderburgh County	10,739	8,014	7,216	1,713	2,980	2,907	85	86	275
Vigo County	6,439	4,055	4,998	1,563	1,554	995	149	0	198
Wayne County	5,232	2,860	2,440	578	1,006	1,110	86	0	198
Iowa									
Black Hawk County	8,930	5,469	4,574	1,594	2,111	1,743	306	95	110
Dallas County	3,628	3,863	2,771	410	1,091	761	221	0	24
Dubuque County	7,235	3,079	4,707	1,472	1,855	1,478	0	81	163
Johnson County	4,349	4,655	7,659	1,028	746	1,224	101	68	163
Linn County	14,705	9,229	8,868	1,887	4,491	3,332	345	65	128
Polk County	20,605	18,289	19,925	3,029	6,835	5,233	685	0	163
Pottawattamie County	7,347	4,392	2,727	892	2,243	1,503	260	0	163
Scott County	9,855	7,245	8,368	1,665	2,683	2,562	394	0	147
Story County	3,113	2,704	5,231	178	781	1,174	8	49	163
Woodbury County	5,646	4,607	3,630	1,302	1,453	1,517	18	30	163
Kansas									
Butler County	3,180	3,916	2,336	771	1,218	837	62	0	177
Douglas County	4,332	3,221	6,950	611	962	1,333	46	0	177
Johnson County	17,355	21,903	43,559	3,412	6,635	6,939	370	268	159
Leavenworth County	4,808	3,160	3,162	2,259	1,879	1,551	595	0	177
Riley County	1,994	1,896	2,771	412	855	523	83	125	177
Sedgwick County	23,414	23,035	19,851	6,239	6,514	5,873	859	391	181
Shawnee County	12,479	8,797	8,615	2,032	4,169	2,632	328	107	122
Wyandotte County	7,659	4,580	3,097	1,632	1,817	1,220	574	73	73
Kentucky									
Boone County	6,499	4,932	3,517	1,398	2,104	1,554	0	154	33
Bullitt County	6,270	2,871	1,299	929	1,743	1,184	0	50	270
Campbell County	4,879	3,249	4,350	1,065	1,515	822	165	0	147
Christian County	2,183	3,029	1,970	725	1,171	934	160	0	69
Daviess County	6,257	5,223	3,613	1,150	1,777	1,337	63	39	197
Fayette County	9,508	11,885	18,122	2,175	3,395	2,556	255	138	271
Hardin County	6,427	4,405	3,499	2,377	2,637	1,342	355	132	96
Jefferson County	38,211	33,823	35,855	8,630	10,894	9,615	1,053	593	164
Kenton County	8,783	6,434	6,451	1,829	2,374	2,083	384	49	197
McCracken County	5,014	4,142	2,875	1,077	906	685	0	272	197
Madison County	3,666	2,438	3,877	1,125	1,104	892	66	210	102
Oldham County	2,485	2,299	3,116	448	869	625	48	0	197
Warren County	4,692	4,477	4,665	773	2,096	1,501	128	0	197
Louisiana									
Ascension Parish	6,722	3,523	1,951	583	1,154	1,296	0	0	217
Bossier Parish	6,411	5,495	3,595	2,006	1,929	1,973	301	116	114
Caddo Parish	15,283	10,762	8,442	2,795	3,882	3,128	232	0	97
Calcasieu Parish	9,026	8,363	6,654	2,497	3,836	2,500	378	163	217
East Baton Rouge Parish	16,225	16,950	22,526	1,934	5,330	4,281	147	360	112

Table E-2: Counties - Educational Attainment and Veterans Status, Persons 55 and Over—*Continued*

	High School or Equivalent	Some College or Associates Degree	Bachelor's Degree or Higher	Veterans by Age and Gender					
				Male			Female		
				55 to 64 Years	65 to 74 Years	75 Years and Over	55 to 64 Years	65 to 74 Years	75 Years and Over
Louisiana—Cont.									
Iberia Parish	3,743	1,988	2,146	480	1,048	1,140	59	194	343
Jefferson Parish	27,109	17,035	18,909	3,073	4,410	4,749	767	69	274
Lafayette Parish	9,832	8,722	9,000	1,349	2,064	2,240	499	305	243
Lafourche Parish	5,392	2,248	3,234	319	1,227	1,011	0	89	217
Livingston Parish	7,582	4,814	2,907	1,366	1,659	1,199	0	166	217
Orleans Parish	15,361	13,130	18,564	2,696	4,020	3,023	631	348	116
Ouachita Parish	9,234	6,451	4,949	1,152	2,466	1,682	623	198	217
Rapides Parish	9,331	5,738	3,673	1,304	2,154	1,782	0	0	182
St. Landry Parish	4,132	2,565	2,440	429	1,252	529	151	0	217
St. Tammany Parish	14,360	10,856	13,378	1,275	4,248	3,453	158	221	79
Tangipahoa Parish	7,764	4,669	3,214	1,468	1,676	1,168	0	129	179
Terrebonne Parish	6,235	3,156	2,216	701	1,867	1,249	0	0	217
Maine									
Androscoggin County	8,475	4,870	2,528	1,186	2,518	1,476	164	183	336
Aroostook County	5,780	4,666	2,375	1,096	1,917	976	131	67	22
Cumberland County	13,709	13,429	23,194	3,204	4,679	5,219	302	170	144
Kennebec County	7,478	7,740	7,419	2,250	2,760	2,364	324	24	170
Penobscot County	10,814	6,557	7,412	2,347	2,469	2,112	212	167	231
York County	13,693	11,977	13,040	2,799	4,131	3,790	648	168	463
Maryland									
Allegany County	6,926	3,112	2,606	759	1,151	1,406	173	60	206
Anne Arundel County	26,777	21,913	26,438	8,138	10,185	8,015	1,906	650	475
Baltimore County	40,548	34,473	48,832	7,240	9,558	11,650	678	705	289
Calvert County	5,002	2,746	4,073	1,355	1,589	1,272	382	75	206
Carroll County	10,357	6,391	6,942	1,456	2,414	2,407	308	78	77
Cecil County	6,675	3,685	3,929	1,029	2,397	626	12	70	192
Charles County	7,938	4,965	4,408	3,579	2,177	2,392	724	35	269
Frederick County	12,101	7,905	12,381	2,743	3,306	3,317	710	127	153
Harford County	13,795	10,959	12,070	2,830	3,847	3,501	624	128	204
Howard County	9,415	8,122	24,148	1,907	4,571	3,142	208	214	137
Montgomery County	23,234	28,501	94,760	5,679	7,150	11,387	1,356	1,115	846
Prince George's County	33,270	31,446	38,258	10,742	9,539	9,064	1,893	1,090	183
St. Mary's County	6,235	2,740	3,992	2,102	1,393	1,582	361	42	227
Washington County	10,556	5,391	5,440	815	2,203	1,748	264	97	112
Wicomico County	5,932	3,766	3,801	837	1,755	1,131	46	96	206
Massachusetts									
Barnstable County	14,784	16,143	30,807	2,249	4,792	6,327	52	45	259
Berkshire County	10,102	6,000	10,722	1,406	2,012	2,083	113	52	99
Bristol County	31,673	21,733	18,833	4,116	7,536	6,947	293	384	245
Essex County	38,257	30,905	46,314	4,554	8,732	10,786	640	215	224
Franklin County	4,460	3,447	6,189	1,016	1,199	1,525	118	149	23
Hampden County	24,832	19,374	19,274	4,451	7,011	5,627	971	153	153
Hampshire County	7,147	6,035	12,928	852	1,978	2,062	133	60	211
Middlesex County	61,587	48,415	108,520	6,081	13,375	19,032	439	292	479
Norfolk County	31,493	26,692	48,333	4,460	6,061	9,347	169	160	105
Plymouth County	28,584	24,110	29,838	5,056	7,880	7,298	243	137	138
Suffolk County	25,641	16,581	29,207	2,538	4,047	5,223	187	240	251
Worcester County	41,883	31,639	37,919	8,446	10,889	10,824	548	390	37
Michigan									
Allegan County	8,640	4,756	3,750	615	1,644	1,397	62	26	107
Bay County	9,206	5,900	3,136	1,026	2,158	1,895	242	27	98
Berrien County	9,031	9,371	8,341	1,261	2,744	2,860	167	64	104
Calhoun County	9,335	7,052	4,948	1,281	2,841	1,825	300	6	105
Clinton County	4,849	4,790	2,867	601	1,134	921	0	106	172
Eaton County	6,034	8,013	4,702	785	1,896	1,688	68	0	88
Genesee County	26,041	21,716	13,504	4,259	5,723	5,424	234	100	171
Grand Traverse County	5,177	5,909	6,571	1,074	2,471	1,098	200	24	96
Ingham County	9,676	12,708	13,320	1,624	3,691	2,139	82	0	172
Isabella County	3,607	2,666	2,073	249	1,024	748	12	49	172
Jackson County	9,808	9,788	5,785	1,547	2,892	2,390	128	101	172
Kalamazoo County	12,302	10,950	13,228	2,205	3,579	3,359	215	253	189
Kent County	27,589	27,797	25,076	4,014	9,534	6,947	282	281	185
Lapeer County	6,803	4,672	2,748	624	1,682	951	15	152	32
Lenawee County	8,075	4,792	3,884	998	1,518	1,218	127	0	94
Livingston County	9,666	11,162	10,044	2,061	3,405	2,498	83	87	198
Macomb County	54,802	47,642	24,787	6,344	12,212	11,531	416	331	231
Marquette County	4,986	4,048	3,114	720	1,680	1,422	107	39	172
Midland County	6,422	4,324	3,692	315	1,759	1,565	0	45	172
Monroe County	11,606	7,770	5,413	1,489	2,834	1,802	61	136	179
Muskegon County	10,433	10,038	6,211	2,017	3,540	2,266	160	141	43
Oakland County	53,481	58,294	81,095	7,033	13,722	14,576	681	122	260
Ottawa County	14,156	12,582	12,372	1,641	3,055	3,513	147	214	130
Saginaw County	15,155	11,500	4,908	2,008	3,558	3,584	226	16	232

Table E-2: Counties - Educational Attainment and Veterans Status, Persons 55 and Over—*Continued*

	High School or Equivalent	Some College or Associates Degree	Bachelor's Degree or Higher	Veterans by Age and Gender					
				Male			Female		
				55 to 64 Years	65 to 74 Years	75 Years and Over	55 to 64 Years	65 to 74 Years	75 Years and Over
Michigan—Cont.									
St. Clair County	12,373	9,793	4,672	1,971	3,423	2,759	95	242	27
Shiawassee County	5,284	3,530	2,011	534	1,740	795	100	31	21
Van Buren County	4,094	4,355	3,831	468	1,071	742	15	80	51
Washtenaw County	11,548	13,616	23,662	1,683	3,928	3,610	84	180	255
Wayne County	92,198	75,566	58,997	13,766	20,353	17,804	1,413	753	361
Minnesota									
Anoka County	18,545	15,514	11,467	2,757	5,050	4,241	265	87	72
Blue Earth County	3,151	2,344	2,563	636	1,132	903	215	5	8
Carver County	4,179	3,138	4,699	367	1,148	1,052	56	78	27
Dakota County	17,047	20,138	19,265	3,934	5,940	5,910	627	12	144
Hennepin County	40,710	48,656	74,884	8,536	13,958	13,824	626	0	410
Olmsted County	6,040	6,927	9,740	1,327	2,500	1,987	134	170	125
Ramsey County	21,482	18,831	30,994	3,362	4,881	6,416	705	675	194
Rice County	3,359	2,303	3,601	437	701	1,056	199	0	80
St. Louis County	13,323	12,521	10,108	1,754	4,465	3,842	120	81	181
Scott County	5,277	4,455	5,141	1,005	1,242	1,166	75	0	147
Sherburne County	4,238	2,650	2,916	727	1,276	1,283	0	0	30
Stearns County	9,125	6,808	4,979	815	1,919	2,639	151	107	147
Washington County	11,871	11,407	13,264	1,965	4,040	3,296	53	0	147
Wright County	7,726	4,552	3,245	1,072	2,238	1,098	39	9	23
Mississippi									
DeSoto County	9,092	6,104	4,047	1,758	2,289	1,684	14	48	67
Forrest County	3,175	2,667	2,943	748	991	784	38	0	104
Harrison County	9,378	9,973	7,491	3,285	3,740	3,140	919	41	78
Hinds County	7,565	8,658	10,667	1,835	1,563	2,242	386	154	90
Jackson County	6,738	9,005	3,884	1,807	2,600	2,202	546	223	123
Jones County	4,970	2,337	1,843	322	709	698	0	35	177
Lauderdale County	3,584	4,242	2,061	1,179	1,378	985	69	0	218
Lee County	3,743	3,257	2,743	576	1,045	876	0	0	218
Madison County	2,291	3,971	6,478	488	1,096	604	71	45	218
Rankin County	8,670	7,145	5,822	819	1,238	1,171	68	57	138
Missouri									
Boone County	5,897	5,465	9,365	851	2,479	1,842	505	60	190
Buchanan County	5,660	3,601	4,161	1,114	1,880	1,114	31	29	190
Cape Girardeau County	5,320	2,551	2,889	617	976	1,179	71	0	146
Cass County	7,516	5,745	2,967	1,851	1,979	1,717	295	102	123
Christian County	4,992	5,207	2,198	1,246	1,741	952	59	50	190
Clay County	12,442	10,394	8,627	2,272	3,643	2,768	315	52	155
Cole County	4,565	3,192	4,262	420	1,083	720	200	0	190
Franklin County	6,895	4,687	3,228	1,276	1,786	2,203	108	0	80
Greene County	17,714	13,268	11,121	1,920	3,855	3,548	248	172	190
Jackson County	36,244	31,207	26,132	7,367	11,232	7,844	514	555	144
Jasper County	8,433	4,765	2,942	982	1,922	1,703	153	0	149
Jefferson County	13,701	10,666	5,325	2,307	3,995	3,340	439	152	173
Platte County	5,420	3,938	4,528	773	1,679	1,255	79	16	190
St. Charles County	21,302	18,381	14,807	3,765	6,259	5,259	302	38	136
St. Francois County	4,525	2,702	2,022	1,000	1,380	949	0	0	190
St. Louis County	47,017	48,670	66,500	7,824	13,132	15,390	739	400	257
Montana									
Cascade County	5,388	5,128	3,385	1,588	1,824	1,814	332	72	79
Flathead County	5,043	5,837	7,312	1,259	2,255	1,374	120	162	172
Gallatin County	3,130	3,745	6,717	572	1,345	1,062	0	223	108
Lewis and Clark County	3,311	4,208	4,234	959	1,896	884	225	66	159
Missoula County	4,779	5,731	6,410	844	2,685	1,878	154	111	172
Yellowstone County	9,477	8,587	7,428	1,312	2,955	2,605	188	29	160
Nebraska									
Douglas County	20,790	22,266	24,372	4,397	6,813	6,234	671	163	178
Lancaster County	12,878	14,214	13,677	1,954	5,295	2,741	459	0	161
Sarpy County	7,722	6,176	6,270	3,656	3,529	2,305	1,137	305	82
Nevada									
Clark County	90,663	105,842	86,939	24,242	34,560	27,898	4,393	2,340	686
Washoe County	16,369	29,786	23,610	5,502	9,151	6,762	691	293	139
New Hampshire									
Cheshire County	5,056	3,557	5,095	643	1,952	1,449	179	0	61
Grafton County	4,556	4,969	7,101	1,062	1,965	1,716	178	90	142
Hillsborough County	18,555	16,504	23,093	5,590	6,375	5,885	662	445	202
Merrimack County	9,056	7,271	9,641	1,533	2,333	2,564	419	77	182
Rockingham County	15,424	14,457	19,533	3,790	4,561	5,010	432	238	40
Strafford County	5,895	4,426	6,616	2,155	2,234	1,691	142	72	34
New Jersey									
Atlantic County	16,251	12,543	11,742	1,773	4,243	3,993	271	176	73
Bergen County	52,340	28,440	58,357	2,868	6,751	9,252	444	35	232
Burlington County	25,364	18,564	22,532	3,640	6,112	6,781	306	560	171

Table E-2: Counties - Educational Attainment and Veterans Status, Persons 55 and Over—*Continued*

| | | | | Veterans by Age and Gender | | | | | |
| | | | | Male | | | Female | | |
	High School or Equivalent	Some College or Associates Degree	Bachelor's Degree or Higher	55 to 64 Years	65 to 74 Years	75 Years and Over	55 to 64 Years	65 to 74 Years	75 Years and Over
New Jersey—Cont.									
Camden County	28,520	16,818	20,751	3,934	5,963	5,926	299	167	123
Cape May County	7,755	6,340	7,528	410	1,925	2,226	133	153	62
Cumberland County	8,154	4,907	3,801	954	1,791	1,619	39	50	206
Essex County	33,794	17,316	33,873	2,281	3,875	5,654	468	38	115
Gloucester County	19,928	9,299	11,052	2,552	4,172	3,790	262	0	392
Hudson County	25,675	10,751	19,227	1,340	2,453	2,571	451	195	131
Hunterdon County	7,118	5,915	8,782	747	1,640	2,437	56	0	210
Mercer County	18,239	10,664	20,217	1,642	2,261	3,081	0	99	71
Middlesex County	40,483	22,526	40,001	2,294	6,541	8,892	0	178	172
Monmouth County	33,236	23,933	43,830	3,730	6,134	7,255	671	310	197
Morris County	22,463	17,159	37,228	2,330	4,914	7,077	328	46	258
Ocean County	54,495	33,762	33,208	3,408	10,577	12,509	234	331	126
Passaic County	25,800	11,263	17,349	1,173	2,958	3,331	151	23	233
Salem County	5,592	3,191	1,551	678	741	910	54	27	210
Somerset County	14,995	9,930	22,542	717	2,912	2,844	72	92	69
Sussex County	8,768	5,228	7,521	1,371	1,713	2,055	304	57	210
Union County	28,615	12,640	24,510	1,581	2,706	4,758	196	131	261
Warren County	6,551	4,703	5,479	850	1,576	1,880	0	26	24
New Mexico									
Bernalillo County	24,670	28,745	44,258	8,460	11,676	9,524	1,133	473	243
Chaves County	2,066	2,957	2,753	963	629	732	47	63	84
Doña Ana County	6,807	8,119	9,714	2,107	4,184	2,201	582	182	141
Lea County	2,043	2,228	768	191	284	291	0	44	201
McKinley County	2,494	2,347	1,044	697	579	622	25	29	201
Otero County	3,386	3,343	2,484	2,041	1,577	1,532	186	71	201
Sandoval County	5,012	7,470	9,328	1,928	3,268	1,698	253	436	182
San Juan County	5,412	6,501	3,842	884	1,865	1,724	133	79	72
Santa Fe County	6,330	8,469	18,691	1,496	2,761	2,863	237	0	110
Valencia County	4,509	3,218	3,918	1,159	1,821	1,601	79	52	201
New York									
Albany County	15,189	13,571	18,403	2,784	3,885	3,746	475	202	176
Bronx County	50,100	28,169	32,956	5,749	6,597	5,470	206	97	192
Broome County	14,552	8,983	9,046	1,681	3,200	2,731	286	170	67
Cattaraugus County	6,193	3,427	2,880	546	1,606	1,279	211	69	201
Cayuga County	5,295	4,018	2,921	566	1,582	1,065	110	0	201
Chautauqua County	11,166	6,802	4,454	740	2,137	1,878	14	0	114
Chemung County	6,715	3,656	3,166	1,170	1,419	1,264	239	0	201
Clinton County	4,617	3,066	4,051	1,299	1,373	1,330	103	203	201
Dutchess County	13,731	14,450	16,927	2,415	4,784	4,672	84	42	247
Erie County	59,781	41,438	44,313	8,398	14,584	14,074	924	288	243
Jefferson County	6,416	3,787	3,218	1,348	1,224	1,489	141	53	36
Kings County	107,440	57,825	92,784	5,846	7,291	9,223	1,187	649	195
Livingston County	3,813	3,434	2,652	569	855	772	27	0	49
Madison County	5,112	4,184	2,573	1,229	1,212	1,264	94	18	201
Monroe County	37,132	31,523	42,335	4,531	8,887	9,027	1,130	164	347
Nassau County	77,587	49,280	86,748	3,982	10,808	16,956	835	158	461
New York County	46,365	38,800	121,785	4,297	6,765	13,004	220	64	250
Niagara County	15,782	10,187	7,810	2,133	4,247	3,556	100	142	165
Oneida County	15,110	11,334	10,445	2,703	3,045	4,053	132	149	121
Onondaga County	25,968	20,695	23,105	3,289	7,024	6,243	505	520	138
Ontario County	6,180	6,477	6,682	893	2,022	1,760	238	47	43
Orange County	17,676	15,153	12,794	2,930	3,521	3,986	348	230	164
Oswego County	7,504	5,290	4,020	1,164	2,378	1,584	85	210	130
Putnam County	4,615	5,414	5,899	474	1,780	1,430	86	149	56
Queens County	112,239	63,441	86,114	3,995	8,353	11,521	606	348	39
Rensselaer County	10,538	6,432	7,026	2,266	2,643	2,769	105	15	201
Richmond County	32,629	13,636	16,204	1,236	4,514	4,163	324	0	172
Rockland County	12,819	10,719	22,113	625	2,520	3,707	138	214	201
St. Lawrence County	8,476	4,428	2,870	952	2,351	1,721	278	44	22
Saratoga County	11,654	10,574	14,731	2,245	3,675	3,798	334	105	79
Schenectady County	9,002	5,829	9,292	1,581	1,681	2,126	188	0	133
Steuben County	7,513	4,298	4,203	1,109	1,556	1,438	185	66	79
Suffolk County	81,816	62,415	75,661	6,757	17,087	18,429	522	420	302
Sullivan County	4,415	3,284	3,872	678	1,459	1,103	0	0	105
Tompkins County	3,672	3,772	5,748	576	1,334	1,285	0	0	55
Ulster County	10,723	9,058	11,626	1,583	1,677	2,497	0	62	201
Warren County	4,572	3,807	4,544	943	1,040	1,142	129	0	201
Wayne County	6,507	4,369	4,016	1,338	1,832	1,392	172	26	201
Westchester County	39,596	29,943	71,379	2,453	6,438	11,078	300	19	437
North Carolina									
Alamance County	8,931	8,975	6,645	1,559	3,100	1,953	111	133	210
Brunswick County	13,321	12,610	15,514	1,527	5,579	2,735	175	128	210
Buncombe County	13,915	12,006	21,282	3,385	4,751	4,441	554	245	155
Burke County	5,908	4,951	3,196	820	1,979	1,429	0	44	42
Cabarrus County	10,106	7,696	6,490	1,563	2,596	2,164	258	90	15
Caldwell County	5,514	3,735	3,117	626	1,694	1,154	0	0	210

Table E-2: Counties - Educational Attainment and Veterans Status, Persons 55 and Over—*Continued*

	High School or Equivalent	Some College or Associates Degree	Bachelor's Degree or Higher	Veterans by Age and Gender					
				Male			Female		
				55 to 64 Years	65 to 74 Years	75 Years and Over	55 to 64 Years	65 to 74 Years	75 Years and Over
North Carolina—Cont.									
Carteret County	3,532	5,649	5,795	966	1,941	2,222	250	38	19
Catawba County	9,105	7,392	6,924	1,351	3,110	2,174	46	202	70
Chatham County	4,362	3,615	8,921	705	1,300	941	82	0	68
Cleveland County	6,998	4,778	3,431	2,038	1,427	1,291	200	0	210
Craven County	5,391	6,418	5,300	1,627	2,723	1,840	198	94	125
Cumberland County	13,247	12,372	8,958	7,181	6,432	3,752	1,973	482	93
Davidson County	10,521	8,821	3,658	1,710	2,459	1,489	229	146	96
Durham County	10,153	10,328	16,626	2,276	3,076	2,592	1,036	394	141
Forsyth County	20,811	16,445	16,580	3,604	5,898	5,321	588	101	213
Franklin County	3,954	4,046	1,782	906	909	504	62	179	210
Gaston County	11,731	11,040	4,527	2,454	3,225	2,852	277	46	108
Guilford County	22,999	21,631	25,138	6,046	6,829	6,221	411	221	86
Harnett County	5,844	5,030	2,942	2,468	1,551	1,147	419	0	116
Henderson County	7,720	8,878	10,761	1,310	2,552	3,198	172	0	140
Iredell County	8,913	8,647	6,901	1,076	2,734	1,845	134	59	210
Johnston County	9,186	7,496	5,207	1,424	3,227	1,582	76	77	210
Lincoln County	4,571	5,332	2,989	971	1,484	1,280	304	0	210
Mecklenburg County	29,681	36,096	42,954	7,131	9,683	8,447	994	120	186
Moore County	5,332	5,700	10,212	1,877	1,956	2,269	452	28	52
Nash County	6,167	4,579	3,746	1,070	1,522	686	73	83	210
New Hanover County	9,496	11,486	15,789	2,127	4,496	3,818	698	139	63
Onslow County	5,867	6,049	3,097	3,532	2,978	2,123	404	145	205
Orange County	2,820	4,372	11,298	912	1,135	1,173	326	0	210
Pitt County	7,317	6,131	5,952	2,168	2,894	2,212	494	68	212
Randolph County	9,310	6,269	4,033	1,697	2,749	1,829	0	0	63
Robeson County	6,794	5,017	2,401	1,141	1,658	1,010	32	22	210
Rockingham County	7,111	4,464	2,094	1,066	1,357	1,298	85	0	59
Rowan County	8,115	7,636	3,957	1,355	2,577	1,919	251	39	108
Rutherford County	5,478	3,519	1,774	636	1,322	832	0	18	210
Surry County	4,627	4,315	2,347	449	1,136	934	56	46	210
Union County	10,004	8,421	8,078	1,747	2,772	2,196	169	96	210
Wake County	28,472	33,023	54,156	9,104	10,417	8,411	871	1,012	239
Wayne County	7,558	6,634	2,838	2,637	2,913	1,571	251	163	210
Wilkes County	4,022	4,311	2,850	528	866	1,095	234	17	210
Wilson County	3,686	3,458	3,386	1,644	1,454	722	155	254	210
North Dakota									
Burleigh County	3,447	5,487	4,393	1,021	1,232	1,369	13	107	165
Cass County	5,101	8,046	6,690	1,161	2,585	1,248	139	44	161
Grand Forks County	2,933	3,725	1,829	393	942	1,008	120	0	44
Ward County	3,323	2,122	1,663	757	1,043	1,135	72	88	128
Ohio									
Allen County	9,242	3,148	2,971	577	1,459	1,765	69	0	195
Ashtabula County	8,071	4,535	3,441	1,373	1,460	1,202	141	0	58
Athens County	3,430	1,783	2,266	653	748	471	0	57	195
Belmont County	7,864	2,559	2,551	441	1,454	833	0	17	72
Butler County	21,693	15,230	12,076	3,624	4,352	4,166	739	140	122
Clark County	9,756	7,485	4,917	2,298	2,696	2,641	481	74	88
Clermont County	13,753	8,010	6,783	1,733	3,879	2,348	241	99	90
Columbiana County	11,085	4,044	3,289	1,449	2,004	2,139	66	11	38
Cuyahoga County	71,850	56,970	64,738	11,001	15,416	17,460	1,308	637	588
Delaware County	6,976	8,310	10,621	929	2,125	2,029	154	230	115
Erie County	5,920	5,504	2,768	575	1,569	1,032	0	14	195
Fairfield County	11,228	5,833	4,766	1,345	1,925	1,903	181	219	51
Franklin County	49,501	38,015	52,082	10,282	13,887	11,778	533	355	172
Geauga County	6,427	4,467	6,678	131	1,306	2,188	121	0	195
Greene County	10,217	6,014	10,181	2,295	3,401	1,596	532	247	151
Hamilton County	36,665	32,293	40,319	6,553	10,027	10,057	642	230	161
Hancock County	5,691	2,996	2,514	638	1,199	1,034	0	0	195
Jefferson County	8,193	2,778	1,480	1,015	1,347	1,485	14	124	195
Lake County	18,421	13,812	8,592	1,830	3,534	3,819	327	79	145
Licking County	12,987	6,303	6,195	2,269	3,423	2,766	268	0	123
Lorain County	20,246	15,243	13,631	2,314	5,383	4,194	182	590	111
Lucas County	21,393	19,897	18,472	4,100	5,446	5,296	395	143	174
Mahoning County	21,304	10,386	10,556	2,535	4,713	4,109	238	164	195
Marion County	5,937	2,675	1,714	556	1,063	1,013	115	0	53
Medina County	12,458	8,347	9,030	1,312	3,249	2,482	46	253	195
Miami County	8,783	4,381	3,529	2,010	1,274	1,263	209	75	195
Montgomery County	32,074	26,758	25,084	6,226	8,308	9,104	1,172	728	188
Muskingum County	8,167	2,877	1,737	728	1,703	1,108	106	0	195
Portage County	10,737	5,694	6,882	1,659	2,404	2,290	85	39	71
Richland County	9,660	6,432	3,421	996	2,322	2,118	114	117	195
Ross County	6,031	2,753	2,415	1,083	1,696	846	46	0	147
Scioto County	5,655	3,030	2,200	914	1,301	730	41	0	115
Stark County	33,852	18,281	11,215	4,466	6,797	5,760	483	154	216
Summit County	34,095	24,957	27,666	5,206	8,915	8,074	455	125	232

Table E-2: Counties - Educational Attainment and Veterans Status, Persons 55 and Over—*Continued*

	High School or Equivalent	Some College or Associates Degree	Bachelor's Degree or Higher	Veterans by Age and Gender					
				Male			Female		
				55 to 64 Years	65 to 74 Years	75 Years and Over	55 to 64 Years	65 to 74 Years	75 Years and Over
Ohio—Cont.									
Trumbull County	21,183	9,742	6,222	2,155	3,675	3,869	241	38	195
Tuscarawas County	9,794	2,950	2,258	844	1,919	1,496	99	109	195
Warren County	10,218	7,374	10,774	1,849	3,682	2,857	349	88	97
Wayne County	7,938	4,469	4,234	644	1,878	1,494	126	78	136
Wood County	8,159	4,960	5,093	788	2,244	1,725	46	14	104
Oklahoma									
Canadian County	5,973	5,436	5,749	1,249	1,787	1,198	225	198	59
Cleveland County	11,504	11,130	11,676	3,999	5,180	3,362	629	220	304
Comanche County	3,842	5,221	3,636	2,727	2,689	1,792	522	381	108
Creek County	4,179	4,248	2,430	895	1,577	1,105	82	32	90
Muskogee County	4,862	2,517	2,385	782	1,029	983	0	109	161
Oklahoma County	29,239	32,458	34,065	7,122	13,145	9,918	492	969	179
Payne County	3,049	3,112	4,265	565	1,344	1,094	48	31	161
Pottawatomie County	4,055	3,726	2,671	870	1,318	1,230	61	67	161
Rogers County	5,439	4,837	3,349	1,252	2,010	1,247	154	0	161
Tulsa County	26,957	29,000	28,656	5,620	8,936	8,301	685	714	211
Wagoner County	4,926	4,014	2,291	719	1,727	1,063	162	23	59
Oregon									
Benton County	2,860	4,470	6,971	697	1,253	1,286	99	79	160
Clackamas County	19,883	24,783	25,322	3,822	7,607	6,211	561	351	510
Deschutes County	6,713	15,792	14,833	2,262	4,645	3,547	91	75	191
Douglas County	9,301	9,706	5,165	1,705	3,837	2,485	61	287	31
Jackson County	10,369	16,968	16,523	2,350	4,925	4,563	450	238	373
Josephine County	8,383	8,468	4,296	1,491	2,647	3,084	329	0	207
Klamath County	3,808	5,316	3,635	1,154	1,489	1,513	218	335	298
Lane County	16,274	28,607	24,061	4,374	7,469	7,165	467	541	202
Linn County	7,427	8,990	5,331	1,339	3,293	2,515	374	57	207
Marion County	14,458	17,747	15,279	3,088	4,081	5,013	399	298	304
Multnomah County	22,543	33,069	43,842	5,051	9,106	7,157	694	1,264	259
Polk County	3,706	5,494	5,185	1,070	1,858	1,102	69	0	111
Umatilla County	3,862	3,884	2,693	1,033	1,170	1,309	75	87	207
Washington County	17,164	25,848	30,592	5,439	7,558	6,884	412	263	207
Yamhill County	3,699	6,925	6,242	671	1,488	1,682	123	60	207
Pennsylvania									
Adams County	8,128	4,225	4,635	872	2,030	1,963	448	103	177
Allegheny County	89,962	55,911	64,919	9,431	18,907	21,096	912	700	379
Armstrong County	7,645	2,589	1,762	640	1,685	1,609	143	8	177
Beaver County	16,479	9,774	5,784	2,223	3,245	3,780	321	68	21
Berks County	29,135	15,058	14,784	3,200	7,151	6,418	460	276	344
Blair County	12,960	5,019	4,860	1,475	2,609	2,260	132	0	70
Bucks County	41,294	25,651	40,705	4,215	9,738	10,789	318	69	179
Butler County	15,078	7,460	9,136	2,091	3,618	3,388	227	115	177
Cambria County	15,928	5,618	4,534	1,811	3,375	2,843	107	88	44
Carbon County	6,445	2,936	1,876	1,102	1,891	1,382	387	0	177
Centre County	9,019	3,543	8,743	1,160	2,004	1,281	172	0	177
Chester County	24,057	18,630	36,745	3,053	5,780	7,498	682	171	130
Clearfield County	8,561	2,317	2,188	1,004	1,191	1,414	126	22	49
Columbia County	6,460	1,804	2,476	475	976	877	90	73	358
Crawford County	9,324	3,249	3,464	869	1,638	1,715	78	36	29
Cumberland County	19,889	9,301	13,580	3,087	3,998	4,313	722	205	97
Dauphin County	20,551	9,821	9,525	3,141	3,461	3,747	435	147	177
Delaware County	32,565	19,796	30,105	4,568	7,020	7,445	837	102	180
Erie County	20,742	10,727	12,011	2,471	5,477	4,476	282	161	276
Fayette County	16,940	4,346	3,181	744	3,139	2,699	151	0	231
Franklin County	13,919	6,764	6,101	1,664	2,699	3,156	114	199	302
Indiana County	7,938	2,773	3,499	295	1,660	1,905	31	0	177
Lackawanna County	19,293	7,822	10,056	2,264	3,620	3,849	127	63	137
Lancaster County	37,850	18,415	24,116	4,675	7,799	7,863	146	421	275
Lawrence County	9,051	4,515	3,454	591	2,220	1,718	78	0	44
Lebanon County	12,667	5,381	5,225	892	3,028	2,463	106	29	116
Lehigh County	24,075	13,775	15,300	2,083	5,510	5,554	432	118	32
Luzerne County	30,579	11,826	13,130	2,889	5,567	6,003	305	56	119
Lycoming County	9,516	5,537	4,645	1,305	2,102	2,226	218	140	23
Mercer County	12,325	5,518	3,302	920	2,570	2,835	115	114	120
Monroe County	10,641	6,878	6,588	2,976	2,581	2,641	469	0	177
Montgomery County	48,327	30,560	53,717	4,681	10,794	13,026	232	559	169
Northampton County	25,735	10,949	13,191	1,840	4,412	4,890	303	104	177
Northumberland County	11,904	2,877	2,475	1,338	1,424	1,825	242	0	156
Philadelphia County	81,675	38,685	48,462	12,328	16,514	14,648	689	964	232
Schuylkill County	14,682	5,709	3,943	1,354	3,425	2,139	63	278	99
Somerset County	9,261	3,008	2,662	626	1,919	1,157	0	0	46
Washington County	21,053	8,062	9,144	1,284	5,128	3,873	149	160	203
Westmoreland County	36,680	19,653	17,087	2,900	7,011	7,416	522	513	188
York County	34,939	13,972	16,417	4,526	6,514	6,778	543	235	177

Table E-2: Counties - Educational Attainment and Veterans Status, Persons 55 and Over—*Continued*

	High School or Equivalent	Some College or Associates Degree	Bachelor's Degree or Higher	Veterans by Age and Gender					
				Male			Female		
				55 to 64 Years	65 to 74 Years	75 Years and Over	55 to 64 Years	65 to 74 Years	75 Years and Over
Rhode Island									
Kent County	9,696	8,770	8,464	1,893	3,741	2,395	357	246	109
Newport County	4,164	4,381	7,568	761	2,387	2,028	174	93	220
Providence County	35,309	18,072	23,185	2,480	6,785	6,851	429	34	166
Washington County	5,593	5,277	12,976	1,285	2,482	2,105	122	0	36
South Carolina									
Aiken County	11,073	7,483	9,157	3,126	2,604	2,655	138	7	214
Anderson County	11,484	9,820	6,457	2,202	3,730	2,523	384	112	132
Beaufort County	9,463	13,632	25,741	3,184	5,616	5,936	330	210	301
Berkeley County	10,926	9,911	6,333	3,101	4,693	2,643	1,062	833	105
Charleston County	18,163	14,433	27,582	5,953	7,527	6,369	616	307	97
Darlington County	4,821	3,114	1,816	1,236	1,026	868	125	99	214
Dorchester County	5,695	7,519	6,089	3,929	3,579	1,740	566	42	113
Florence County	8,752	5,437	4,714	951	2,414	2,051	251	139	214
Greenville County	25,725	20,165	23,740	4,066	6,822	6,326	610	485	433
Greenwood County	4,264	2,954	3,429	462	1,623	1,401	61	0	214
Horry County	26,316	27,230	21,916	3,471	10,961	5,770	342	323	366
Kershaw County	4,364	3,445	2,105	1,286	1,960	810	176	626	214
Lancaster County	6,888	4,813	5,159	938	2,196	1,250	0	72	214
Laurens County	3,813	3,198	2,589	483	1,134	699	41	0	214
Lexington County	13,541	12,954	13,569	2,708	5,414	4,536	559	427	118
Oconee County	4,348	5,423	4,829	1,054	1,756	2,040	0	89	214
Orangeburg County	5,124	5,587	3,211	1,078	1,208	486	35	138	214
Pickens County	6,594	5,696	4,337	699	1,732	1,628	390	51	80
Richland County	14,951	16,512	15,714	5,238	6,812	4,555	785	383	78
Spartanburg County	15,638	14,227	11,100	3,142	4,851	3,951	699	52	116
Sumter County	6,058	5,024	3,022	1,683	2,274	1,856	304	35	249
York County	11,712	11,098	11,097	2,833	4,509	2,980	627	439	130
South Dakota									
Minnehaha County	8,209	7,271	7,728	2,142	2,616	2,584	300	129	258
Pennington County	6,074	6,697	6,325	1,551	2,756	1,839	53	198	54
Tennessee									
Anderson County	3,560	5,229	4,104	735	2,181	1,309	97	0	172
Blount County	10,141	7,845	5,793	1,668	2,948	2,399	307	97	121
Bradley County	5,382	5,767	3,278	493	1,543	1,226	363	0	211
Davidson County	22,995	21,131	28,175	4,703	6,533	6,172	425	324	175
Greene County	6,066	3,601	1,543	569	1,702	1,190	62	0	114
Hamilton County	19,166	18,601	17,845	4,397	6,489	5,569	690	380	66
Knox County	22,269	20,206	22,547	4,181	6,147	6,590	377	376	345
Madison County	5,847	3,907	3,566	1,047	1,475	1,125	56	51	211
Maury County	5,313	4,086	2,740	676	1,988	1,036	168	0	211
Montgomery County	6,166	4,780	5,322	3,635	2,830	2,797	905	538	211
Putnam County	5,375	2,538	2,712	929	910	1,332	248	75	84
Robertson County	3,730	2,977	1,761	733	701	724	44	135	211
Rutherford County	10,849	10,560	7,521	2,124	4,070	1,875	337	94	170
Sevier County	6,122	5,870	3,599	1,536	2,071	1,408	152	192	211
Shelby County	37,658	31,275	38,608	8,467	13,025	7,294	1,623	406	229
Sullivan County	11,969	9,162	7,850	2,181	3,435	3,034	149	194	112
Sumner County	10,181	7,997	6,904	1,227	3,390	2,757	222	346	211
Washington County	7,410	7,000	5,593	1,326	2,369	2,408	301	312	273
Williamson County	5,668	7,744	14,820	998	2,429	2,464	102	53	211
Wilson County	8,994	6,078	4,581	897	2,121	1,994	201	28	211
Texas									
Angelina County	3,738	4,882	2,507	904	1,304	1,292	109	228	228
Bastrop County	3,735	4,088	3,026	1,286	1,685	840	473	0	62
Bell County	12,625	11,331	10,191	7,011	5,549	3,938	2,403	365	214
Bexar County	57,681	69,051	58,607	19,204	29,145	20,019	4,780	1,868	395
Bowie County	5,129	4,786	3,066	1,667	1,839	1,230	49	34	228
Brazoria County	13,559	12,908	9,947	2,202	3,827	3,199	69	202	104
Brazos County	4,169	5,963	8,912	658	2,179	1,311	44	114	228
Cameron County	13,233	11,022	7,531	1,574	4,304	2,899	155	220	120
Collin County	24,032	30,009	48,799	5,060	8,964	7,350	707	411	815
Comal County	6,887	7,427	10,216	2,369	2,872	2,017	616	122	175
Coryell County	2,022	3,038	979	1,315	1,147	735	447	132	228
Dallas County	60,708	74,193	87,604	15,499	22,265	16,627	1,278	1,361	430
Denton County	22,350	25,149	33,320	6,793	10,125	6,052	567	612	109
Ector County	4,394	4,166	2,272	377	1,230	966	125	0	228
Ellis County	6,947	6,908	6,124	1,134	2,198	1,816	141	142	228
El Paso County	21,980	19,546	15,485	5,539	6,889	5,821	561	294	195
Fort Bend County	18,423	24,032	31,465	3,838	5,265	4,731	503	463	260
Galveston County	13,384	15,916	14,881	4,549	6,655	3,808	450	291	49
Grayson County	7,812	7,686	5,190	1,248	2,858	1,936	149	595	195
Gregg County	5,685	6,350	4,540	1,478	1,757	1,848	187	39	170
Guadalupe County	7,480	5,944	5,830	3,310	2,679	1,993	1,014	283	71
Harris County	118,593	120,654	151,137	20,903	35,796	27,714	2,356	1,193	304

Table E-2: Counties - Educational Attainment and Veterans Status, Persons 55 and Over—*Continued*

	High School or Equivalent	Some College or Associates Degree	Bachelor's Degree or Higher	Veterans by Age and Gender					
				Male			Female		
				55 to 64 Years	65 to 74 Years	75 Years and Over	55 to 64 Years	65 to 74 Years	75 Years and Over
Texas—Cont.									
Harrison County	4,068	3,131	1,749	641	1,381	590	0	73	124
Hays County	5,016	6,176	11,758	1,519	2,504	1,589	217	85	134
Henderson County	5,840	5,673	3,922	1,230	1,985	1,390	208	0	133
Hidalgo County	18,717	14,099	11,736	1,979	4,567	3,807	190	277	99
Hunt County	5,373	4,596	2,599	1,441	1,844	1,424	426	0	228
Jefferson County	13,143	9,115	7,849	2,324	3,525	2,891	228	57	228
Johnson County	7,611	8,081	4,717	1,029	2,224	930	292	142	180
Kaufman County	4,295	4,253	2,915	1,004	1,487	1,319	439	120	228
Liberty County	3,999	3,193	1,061	1,166	1,375	729	0	0	228
Lubbock County	9,340	11,259	11,035	2,975	3,129	2,874	484	0	231
McLennan County	10,929	10,902	9,899	2,826	3,005	3,140	514	72	479
Midland County	3,718	4,384	6,036	1,167	1,082	1,558	71	0	228
Montgomery County	19,327	25,002	23,435	3,702	7,954	6,529	860	298	152
Nacogdoches County	3,472	2,782	2,323	553	1,279	518	42	0	77
Nueces County	13,014	12,166	12,421	4,134	5,309	4,081	577	171	161
Orange County	6,645	3,140	1,544	869	1,286	1,645	0	0	228
Parker County	6,896	6,388	6,090	997	2,300	1,623	193	92	351
Potter County	3,879	4,379	2,785	1,036	1,311	1,453	157	56	150
Randall County	3,669	5,535	8,174	1,582	2,071	1,761	367	71	228
Rockwall County	3,073	3,753	4,465	549	1,404	741	0	0	228
San Patricio County	2,551	2,990	1,440	404	753	883	93	13	53
Smith County	7,833	13,995	10,785	1,185	3,499	3,306	276	22	228
Tarrant County	58,912	68,565	69,008	21,492	22,682	19,743	2,645	1,649	550
Taylor County	6,510	5,438	4,723	1,294	2,250	1,910	118	105	287
Tom Green County	5,598	4,991	4,568	1,176	2,195	1,616	78	0	228
Travis County	23,641	24,601	60,882	8,714	9,152	8,321	636	602	369
Victoria County	4,380	4,676	2,363	856	1,016	1,508	9	0	228
Walker County	2,278	2,210	3,406	981	901	536	50	64	130
Webb County	4,751	3,993	3,145	619	671	720	183	56	228
Wichita County	6,203	5,719	3,935	1,884	2,113	1,452	359	25	100
Williamson County	14,898	19,803	27,359	6,098	6,536	5,034	795	719	256
Wise County	3,727	2,700	2,462	798	1,328	649	18	208	228
Utah									
Cache County	2,414	3,690	4,999	481	1,016	1,249	0	50	193
Davis County	8,740	11,795	12,482	2,979	3,459	2,845	349	53	111
Salt Lake County	29,638	41,535	43,552	5,857	9,359	8,923	636	618	82
Tooele County	2,360	1,784	1,764	1,009	940	370	192	281	193
Utah County	10,368	15,729	19,126	1,846	3,969	3,715	0	55	96
Washington County	9,363	13,756	12,230	1,101	2,552	4,219	81	237	193
Weber County	8,121	11,573	7,239	3,265	3,204	3,063	310	177	193
Vermont									
Chittenden County	6,282	6,494	11,468	1,209	1,363	2,457	373	0	193
Virginia									
Albemarle County	3,655	3,293	11,194	529	1,302	1,908	313	115	114
Arlington County	3,733	3,336	15,568	1,316	1,556	1,525	492	137	146
Augusta County	5,542	3,654	3,724	1,266	1,626	1,133	233	0	206
Bedford County	6,972	3,768	4,177	1,265	2,083	1,714	108	45	206
Chesterfield County	14,788	12,603	18,766	4,413	7,231	3,735	983	130	160
Fairfax County	24,220	28,919	89,384	13,329	13,178	11,932	2,631	1,280	326
Fauquier County	3,432	3,075	4,372	783	1,034	1,213	156	243	206
Frederick County	5,246	3,562	4,566	1,283	1,627	1,926	164	71	184
Hanover County	4,705	5,494	6,124	611	1,895	2,180	107	43	206
Henrico County	13,282	11,960	18,481	1,724	3,916	3,604	130	349	177
James City County	3,821	4,876	10,559	1,398	2,374	2,505	541	42	169
Loudoun County	6,694	9,195	18,234	3,598	2,845	2,978	498	354	206
Montgomery County	3,287	2,727	4,578	826	1,043	1,006	80	0	206
Prince William County	10,714	11,563	17,723	7,799	6,511	4,326	1,785	406	132
Roanoke County	6,176	6,327	5,224	654	2,209	1,832	195	44	118
Rockingham County	5,725	2,579	4,487	816	1,211	1,128	0	53	75
Spotsylvania County	6,186	5,310	5,277	3,003	1,896	1,761	287	105	109
Stafford County	4,065	4,152	5,724	3,996	2,845	1,609	488	170	178
York County	2,662	2,663	4,912	1,856	1,721	1,098	646	119	100
Washington									
Benton County	7,649	10,316	9,274	2,669	3,399	2,411	162	76	203
Chelan County	4,902	4,521	3,943	615	2,025	982	103	42	137
Clallam County	4,664	9,017	7,349	1,679	2,465	3,237	58	52	11
Clark County	18,341	27,830	23,954	5,932	7,927	5,911	362	649	272
Cowlitz County	5,811	8,375	4,454	1,019	2,675	1,768	54	139	204
Franklin County	1,874	2,053	2,842	694	975	341	0	30	276
Grant County	3,815	5,408	2,410	845	1,911	1,065	0	38	150
Grays Harbor County	4,727	6,768	2,940	1,130	2,382	1,139	166	114	204
Island County	3,393	7,233	9,475	1,707	2,511	2,449	359	87	147
King County	56,789	86,249	125,657	16,197	23,505	22,529	2,600	1,415	308
Kitsap County	9,079	18,366	18,655	6,511	7,768	4,512	529	424	173
Lewis County	5,449	6,275	3,393	1,052	2,278	1,843	218	0	148

Table E-2: Counties - Educational Attainment and Veterans Status, Persons 55 and Over—*Continued*

	High School or Equivalent	Some College or Associates Degree	Bachelor's Degree or Higher	Veterans by Age and Gender					
				Male			Female		
				55 to 64 Years	65 to 74 Years	75 Years and Over	55 to 64 Years	65 to 74 Years	75 Years and Over
Washington—Cont.									
Mason County	4,379	5,348	3,730	1,370	2,045	1,138	0	0	204
Pierce County	38,310	40,919	35,596	13,470	17,223	10,716	3,293	562	210
Skagit County	6,268	9,643	8,800	1,936	2,696	2,592	226	74	118
Snohomish County	27,004	38,109	33,476	8,959	12,084	8,801	927	471	115
Spokane County	23,280	30,536	25,296	6,494	11,134	7,906	1,462	584	531
Thurston County	11,162	15,245	19,951	4,841	6,292	4,665	1,128	734	124
Whatcom County	9,357	13,384	14,286	1,762	4,561	2,658	264	38	169
Yakima County	8,597	10,604	7,968	1,258	2,848	2,702	47	128	44
West Virginia									
Berkeley County	7,214	4,000	3,467	2,213	3,031	1,605	231	126	201
Cabell County	6,049	3,294	4,580	1,256	1,632	1,373	0	0	201
Harrison County	6,069	2,321	2,453	764	1,374	1,147	64	46	201
Kanawha County	14,756	7,759	9,218	1,125	3,458	2,712	139	146	197
Monongalia County	4,983	2,847	3,899	1,035	1,388	939	93	98	80
Raleigh County	5,761	3,419	2,563	760	1,138	968	0	0	274
Wood County	6,643	5,516	3,094	1,136	1,855	1,394	164	66	201
Wisconsin									
Brown County	17,115	11,036	8,903	2,048	3,734	3,285	240	384	263
Dane County	19,262	18,700	31,595	2,618	6,050	6,424	513	13	140
Dodge County	8,205	3,878	1,869	701	1,411	1,516	72	16	151
Eau Claire County	5,912	4,378	5,120	543	1,871	1,619	48	13	33
Fond du Lac County	8,045	5,447	3,287	899	1,711	2,020	52	13	102
Jefferson County	5,655	4,113	3,487	846	1,290	958	92	0	151
Kenosha County	8,591	7,155	5,053	1,376	2,501	2,007	433	120	151
La Crosse County	6,855	5,560	5,235	1,342	1,820	2,028	265	106	466
Manitowoc County	7,658	3,839	2,530	1,135	1,803	1,280	287	56	46
Marathon County	10,226	4,880	5,121	849	2,020	1,942	268	109	32
Milwaukee County	45,761	32,404	32,627	6,696	9,985	8,596	699	657	184
Outagamie County	11,915	5,893	6,281	1,519	2,478	2,213	100	0	45
Ozaukee County	5,370	5,289	6,354	409	1,455	1,198	60	0	151
Portage County	5,188	2,874	2,690	462	1,606	914	70	11	28
Racine County	11,726	8,611	8,767	1,824	3,337	2,304	84	353	196
Rock County	13,110	7,448	4,687	1,408	3,257	2,765	155	269	30
St. Croix County	5,105	3,135	2,785	551	1,246	601	33	38	80
Sheboygan County	9,196	5,532	4,019	1,241	2,185	2,109	84	0	79
Walworth County	7,063	4,891	4,638	827	1,640	1,130	34	14	151
Washington County	9,776	6,320	5,970	765	2,476	1,992	189	0	81
Waukesha County	24,918	20,742	25,555	2,838	5,959	7,157	271	72	268
Winnebago County	11,550	7,886	6,217	1,448	3,023	2,927	279	91	104
Wood County	6,273	4,008	3,147	974	1,945	1,353	62	0	151
Wyoming									
Laramie County	5,186	6,040	3,834	2,196	3,113	1,692	355	174	203
Natrona County	2,934	5,195	2,745	1,182	1,453	1,157	87	54	203

Table E-3: Cities - Educational Attainment and Veterans Status, Persons 55 and Over

| | High School or Equivalent | Some College or Associates Degree | Bachelor's Degree or Higher | Veterans by Age and Gender | | | | | |
| | | | | Male | | | Female | | |
				55 to 64 Years	65 to 74 Years	75 Years and Over	55 to 64 Years	65 to 74 Years	75 Years and Over
Alabama									
Auburn city	942	844	2,639	418	597	308	96	0	201
Birmingham city	10,224	9,577	6,847	2,107	3,514	2,033	482	188	89
Dothan city	4,431	3,953	3,340	710	1,038	1,594	156	54	150
Hoover city	2,419	4,576	7,724	341	1,294	1,286	0	141	91
Huntsville city	6,690	9,114	13,808	2,229	3,601	3,219	751	103	70
Mobile city	9,997	8,951	9,422	2,227	2,535	2,529	217	209	35
Montgomery city	8,379	6,043	7,638	2,963	3,025	2,036	436	237	232
Tuscaloosa city	3,546	2,767	4,927	934	1,133	1,087	80	0	85
Alaska									
Anchorage municipality	7,429	10,626	12,718	4,740	4,641	3,249	1,252	426	110
Arizona									
Avondale city	2,353	2,365	1,026	370	963	334	26	0	73
Buckeye city	3,270	3,429	2,801	769	1,778	580	0	0	211
Chandler city	7,988	9,116	9,900	2,277	2,617	1,952	289	67	282
Flagstaff city	1,030	1,856	3,565	400	825	439	160	44	211
Glendale city	9,282	11,453	6,782	2,368	3,208	2,554	356	213	113
Goodyear city	3,560	5,363	5,382	587	1,869	1,064	127	352	148
Mesa city	22,448	29,858	22,265	5,836	9,135	8,231	542	576	168
Peoria city	9,696	10,058	8,497	2,196	3,092	2,899	152	130	121
Phoenix city	41,949	57,735	50,070	9,805	15,518	14,875	1,969	992	388
Scottsdale city	9,881	16,791	30,215	1,831	3,414	5,693	382	42	501
Surprise city	7,730	11,131	9,865	1,986	2,723	2,955	200	174	289
Tempe city	3,181	5,618	9,761	1,296	1,713	1,757	162	0	211
Tucson city	18,698	23,428	25,310	6,370	8,308	7,094	1,403	339	177
Yuma city	4,723	3,796	2,454	1,024	801	1,631	165	78	114
Arkansas									
Conway city	2,761	2,270	2,254	252	599	422	0	45	201
Fayetteville city	1,193	1,230	3,785	693	198	642	67	0	78
Fort Smith city	3,692	3,070	3,612	706	781	778	102	58	201
Jonesboro city	2,456	2,282	2,188	481	691	964	108	0	201
Little Rock city	6,221	6,527	10,805	2,291	2,155	1,688	155	85	119
North Little Rock city	3,038	2,729	4,126	1,179	817	1,191	118	40	201
Rogers city	1,627	2,424	1,338	142	687	698	127	0	63
Springdale city	2,742	1,564	2,329	283	735	595	0	0	104
California									
Alameda city	1,877	4,660	5,329	498	569	775	50	70	110
Alhambra city	2,444	3,876	2,976	182	497	268	0	0	211
Anaheim city	9,643	11,035	10,363	803	2,500	3,170	300	202	85
Antioch city	4,098	5,253	3,167	814	1,021	1,143	61	0	132
Bakersfield city	8,927	13,609	8,330	2,567	4,007	2,730	234	213	204
Baldwin Park city	1,768	1,258	895	140	165	100	40	52	211
Bellflower city	2,061	1,480	1,301	242	612	4	95	0	211
Berkeley city	971	3,018	11,710	403	677	919	0	43	211
Buena Park city	2,312	3,675	2,700	40	746	739	0	0	211
Burbank city	3,984	5,739	4,225	342	708	1,316	0	0	211
Camarillo city	2,438	5,253	5,698	324	1,085	834	153	179	128
Carlsbad city	3,291	6,528	10,750	1,223	2,054	2,753	362	88	128
Carson city	3,218	4,420	2,784	816	890	643	0	137	55
Chico city	1,757	4,384	5,555	279	746	915	74	70	113
Chino city	2,945	3,422	2,229	451	753	998	64	0	84
Chino Hills city	1,559	1,221	3,910	653	376	159	37	0	211
Chula Vista city	6,189	7,646	7,890	2,958	2,394	1,689	619	256	343
Citrus Heights city	4,211	6,380	2,920	815	831	1,376	342	40	71
Clovis city	3,943	5,854	3,911	953	1,469	1,391	208	0	71
Compton city	2,535	2,448	493	100	566	320	57	0	114
Concord city	5,369	6,184	6,560	915	1,689	1,350	69	136	97
Corona city	4,070	5,184	3,903	674	815	811	42	0	70
Costa Mesa city	2,789	4,344	4,732	451	1,174	973	0	0	147
Daly City city	4,353	4,587	5,392	563	308	700	78	0	211
Davis city	517	1,303	5,632	69	315	583	41	0	211
Downey city	3,246	2,801	3,172	195	692	371	0	0	211
El Cajon city	3,381	4,454	2,122	842	906	1,008	84	19	211
Elk Grove city	4,141	9,286	6,686	1,501	1,852	1,465	212	328	78
El Monte city	3,644	1,952	1,750	443	328	473	0	0	211
Escondido city	4,915	6,648	6,345	1,525	1,971	1,248	367	47	243
Fairfield city	4,253	5,628	3,854	1,668	1,444	1,346	36	205	211
Folsom city	1,665	3,402	4,175	1,489	1,000	723	23	40	211
Fontana city	4,237	3,889	2,797	692	1,848	612	0	0	125
Fremont city	7,838	7,614	10,978	1,106	1,110	1,504	0	67	67
Fresno city	12,696	18,599	15,273	3,684	4,666	4,319	192	157	322
Fullerton city	2,786	6,695	6,898	729	644	1,193	227	0	53
Garden Grove city	5,993	4,816	3,698	658	1,043	780	179	0	70
Glendale city	8,908	7,134	9,939	275	877	1,492	0	61	211
Hawthorne city	2,006	2,053	1,171	246	300	738	0	45	211
Hayward city	7,313	5,347	3,974	285	1,228	941	51	0	211

Table E-3: Cities - Educational Attainment and Veterans Status, Persons 55 and Over—*Continued*

	High School or Equivalent	Some College or Associates Degree	Bachelor's Degree or Higher	Veterans by Age and Gender					
				Male			Female		
				55 to 64 Years	65 to 74 Years	75 Years and Over	55 to 64 Years	65 to 74 Years	75 Years and Over
California—Cont.									
Hemet city	5,308	7,645	3,288	469	1,880	1,625	0	149	344
Hesperia city	3,266	4,555	835	1,211	1,120	1,389	116	35	211
Huntington Beach city	4,940	10,967	14,908	1,729	3,219	2,988	80	66	100
Indio city	7,601	4,547	3,898	217	1,199	1,354	61	87	211
Inglewood city	2,436	4,112	2,729	1,182	835	675	39	152	52
Irvine city	3,797	6,605	16,944	834	1,505	1,039	0	0	211
Jurupa Valley city	2,979	3,313	1,579	322	893	769	0	0	104
Laguna Niguel city	1,827	3,372	5,556	419	744	982	0	0	139
Lake Elsinore city	1,906	2,925	828	282	459	260	0	0	211
Lake Forest city	2,186	4,826	4,900	722	1,146	737	0	0	211
Lakewood city	2,569	3,720	1,914	744	1,140	880	72	0	87
Lancaster city	4,224	3,690	3,068	1,316	1,306	1,284	435	0	66
Livermore city	2,517	3,618	5,082	834	968	946	55	0	298
Lodi City	2,552	3,881	2,225	616	811	1,316	0	38	107
Long Beach city	7,969	16,456	16,257	2,786	3,828	3,974	86	196	158
Los Angeles city	94,248	116,782	158,759	13,221	16,521	23,519	501	988	357
Lynwood city	1,488	505	401	26	174	221	0	0	211
Madera city	2,144	1,046	257	190	255	328	10	0	211
Manteca city	2,897	3,933	2,494	530	1,018	1,182	0	70	66
Menifee city	4,992	6,638	2,607	1,037	1,526	2,100	135	116	112
Merced city	1,922	3,229	1,679	661	633	764	45	72	211
Milpitas city	1,584	1,888	2,935	333	256	173	0	0	211
Mission Viejo city	4,122	5,531	8,549	292	1,427	1,700	149	40	72
Modesto city	8,034	7,376	6,355	1,554	2,097	1,749	187	375	181
Moreno Valley city	2,974	6,012	2,491	1,135	1,682	603	209	43	115
Mountain View city	730	1,577	5,697	210	407	466	0	0	211
Murrieta city	3,451	4,752	3,684	999	1,018	1,730	75	0	128
Napa city	3,295	4,490	5,362	567	1,042	1,179	0	43	152
Newport Beach city	2,710	4,493	11,974	160	1,313	1,765	0	0	66
Norwalk city	3,908	2,954	1,477	252	438	503	39	161	211
Oakland city	10,390	13,208	23,487	1,915	1,857	2,663	593	111	87
Oceanside city	5,952	8,370	10,546	2,642	3,038	2,208	583	424	173
Ontario city	4,669	4,166	1,643	728	901	570	0	0	211
Orange city	3,466	5,629	5,393	561	681	1,001	0	74	211
Oxnard city	4,563	5,243	3,612	1,112	1,124	1,705	185	113	59
Palmdale city	3,754	5,088	3,557	1,228	1,268	1,110	138	223	211
Palo Alto city	922	1,813	9,846	0	282	556	0	109	72
Pasadena city	4,074	6,102	10,042	666	690	1,453	94	0	92
Perris city	594	1,083	416	243	118	108	0	0	182
Pittsburg city	2,003	1,831	1,337	703	764	141	39	0	127
Pleasanton city	2,007	3,494	5,852	251	557	904	0	0	101
Pomona city	3,490	4,297	2,643	492	916	698	73	0	185
Rancho Cordova city	3,173	4,244	2,313	981	1,136	1,135	179	377	82
Rancho Cucamonga city	4,859	7,811	6,030	847	2,044	1,760	148	0	72
Redding city	4,178	6,601	4,584	818	1,457	1,296	0	78	111
Redlands city	2,180	2,638	5,344	1,115	531	1,211	212	0	211
Redondo Beach city	1,181	2,941	4,736	399	681	585	0	0	211
Redwood City city	2,478	3,492	4,787	762	1,145	648	0	130	211
Rialto city	3,895	2,690	873	734	1,005	556	40	40	70
Richmond city	2,974	4,782	4,323	281	948	814	0	68	211
Riverside city	7,334	9,422	9,963	1,754	1,740	2,769	331	47	227
Rocklin city	1,355	3,315	2,668	358	1,018	485	53	0	211
Roseville city	3,755	9,764	8,410	789	2,261	2,432	287	0	128
Sacramento city	13,313	19,232	21,729	3,019	5,824	4,474	322	303	73
Salinas city	3,076	3,391	1,951	328	1,178	629	136	0	211
San Bernardino city	5,014	4,706	2,865	1,625	1,221	1,173	127	0	211
San Buenaventura (Ventura) city	3,825	6,036	6,877	945	2,023	1,921	96	66	64
San Clemente city	1,548	3,472	5,488	496	710	818	95	0	211
San Diego city	28,366	51,480	75,478	10,880	16,975	13,755	1,468	723	701
San Francisco city	21,805	26,681	55,758	3,044	5,526	6,788	592	154	270
San Jose city	26,671	34,337	45,613	3,590	4,821	8,885	625	540	113
San Leandro city	4,709	3,249	2,491	363	546	1,270	143	0	211
San Marcos city	2,095	3,411	4,347	635	1,311	1,133	0	0	211
San Mateo city	3,493	5,144	7,222	392	931	1,329	71	206	147
San Ramon city	1,586	2,199	3,462	292	510	323	155	0	211
Santa Ana city	6,377	5,846	3,250	450	1,586	805	0	0	116
Santa Barbara city	2,432	4,041	7,961	75	918	943	36	0	211
Santa Clara city	3,551	4,125	6,958	336	547	894	25	0	211
Santa Clarita city	4,152	8,903	9,156	1,032	2,485	1,350	131	147	211
Santa Cruz city	816	2,793	3,917	77	687	377	79	0	211
Santa Maria city	1,938	3,442	1,873	331	944	554	44	0	117
Santa Monica city	2,131	3,494	8,949	274	867	884	0	0	211
Santa Rosa city	4,174	10,955	12,280	779	1,951	2,215	0	92	69
Simi Valley city	6,716	6,674	6,162	949	1,560	1,717	152	0	81
South Gate city	1,398	774	201	0	82	153	0	0	211
South San Francisco city	2,422	2,839	5,125	293	593	1,269	0	0	211

Table E-3: Cities - Educational Attainment and Veterans Status, Persons 55 and Over—*Continued*

	High School or Equivalent	Some College or Associates Degree	Bachelor's Degree or Higher	Veterans by Age and Gender					
				Male			Female		
				55 to 64 Years	65 to 74 Years	75 Years and Over	55 to 64 Years	65 to 74 Years	75 Years and Over
California—Cont.									
Stockton city	9,840	10,751	7,876	1,528	2,291	2,659	546	235	97
Sunnyvale city	3,043	5,597	7,317	532	403	1,623	0	0	165
Temecula city	2,712	4,276	3,594	1,497	1,448	973	0	76	317
Thousand Oaks city	3,879	7,272	10,099	444	2,042	2,382	0	38	211
Torrance city	6,589	7,096	10,228	555	1,526	1,813	0	0	211
Tracy city	2,186	2,988	1,259	753	927	473	119	50	211
Turlock city	2,377	2,397	1,362	268	399	613	0	14	211
Tustin city	1,540	1,934	3,238	491	472	165	0	0	211
Union City city	3,749	2,572	2,862	352	544	570	23	75	211
Upland city	2,136	4,024	4,228	505	609	1,242	0	0	211
Vacaville city	3,804	5,846	4,186	1,491	1,580	1,476	194	121	94
Vallejo city	4,629	6,501	6,075	914	1,548	1,359	80	47	211
Victorville city	3,406	3,363	652	620	1,498	445	0	41	211
Visalia city	4,031	5,854	3,296	650	1,163	625	56	40	45
Vista city	2,639	2,725	2,608	1,051	769	666	52	0	60
Walnut Creek city	2,015	4,325	15,371	405	885	1,718	143	0	211
West Covina city	4,835	3,976	4,085	504	641	706	0	0	211
Westminster city	3,295	4,335	3,347	38	873	759	0	0	95
Whittier city	3,371	3,665	2,484	303	467	707	0	19	211
Yorba Linda city	2,703	4,225	6,476	220	1,263	1,308	0	0	51
Yuba City city	2,075	3,024	2,883	796	748	896	183	134	211
Colorado									
Arvada city	6,044	6,729	8,474	1,026	2,058	1,861	145	86	64
Aurora city	12,680	13,902	12,629	3,309	4,541	2,870	830	149	290
Boulder city	1,141	2,023	8,898	232	378	739	47	116	83
Broomfield city	2,480	2,445	4,160	325	799	791	0	87	204
Centennial city	2,819	3,694	9,084	476	1,647	1,226	67	259	204
Colorado Springs city	13,933	20,608	23,084	9,519	9,292	6,932	1,682	713	319
Denver city	15,976	17,705	37,128	4,775	7,203	6,254	457	359	141
Fort Collins city	2,984	5,225	9,248	1,232	1,696	1,287	375	0	211
Greeley city	2,864	3,717	3,252	805	1,250	1,127	30	124	82
Lakewood city	6,352	7,510	9,975	1,429	2,579	3,418	298	133	60
Longmont city	3,412	4,629	6,509	948	1,675	1,361	131	144	99
Loveland city	4,036	3,913	5,432	254	1,044	1,825	149	0	204
Pueblo city	5,866	7,710	4,649	1,484	2,402	1,883	0	0	119
Thornton city	3,906	4,524	2,732	814	1,475	680	93	129	204
Westminster city	3,285	5,420	5,537	1,053	2,118	1,405	203	75	204
Connecticut									
Bridgeport city	4,528	2,199	3,327	597	766	954	138	0	207
Danbury city	2,740	1,931	3,907	1,099	1,057	723	0	0	207
Hartford city	4,889	2,153	1,456	418	811	340	54	0	207
New Britain city	2,950	1,674	1,831	242	512	723	0	0	207
New Haven city	3,933	1,363	3,515	405	1,036	212	0	62	207
Norwalk city	4,513	3,994	5,269	246	756	730	0	0	207
Stamford city	6,238	2,738	8,358	117	1,231	1,684	78	0	77
Waterbury city	5,959	2,795	1,156	274	584	865	401	0	207
Delaware									
Wilmington city	2,492	2,145	2,407	1,155	663	311	82	0	200
District of Columbia									
Washington city	19,070	14,420	38,742	3,454	3,821	5,615	572	182	336
Florida									
Boca Raton city	7,616	6,641	14,154	673	1,391	2,117	87	162	168
Boynton Beach city	5,162	4,361	4,671	940	676	1,339	0	48	229
Cape Coral city	18,888	13,542	12,438	3,690	5,468	3,586	177	109	229
Clearwater city	8,294	7,299	8,396	1,506	1,940	2,251	82	672	265
Coral Springs city	4,292	4,772	5,404	1,160	1,181	725	73	0	84
Daytona Beach city	4,798	4,044	4,070	440	1,773	1,117	29	196	238
Deerfield Beach city	6,017	4,356	5,643	605	667	2,078	0	70	229
Delray Beach city	4,633	3,768	7,346	347	891	1,137	86	48	76
Deltona city	5,221	3,769	2,562	2,410	1,598	1,268	117	0	76
Fort Lauderdale city	9,343	8,251	10,156	664	2,401	2,509	534	0	92
Fort Myers city	5,666	4,849	6,874	626	1,075	1,346	40	0	229
Gainesville city	2,830	2,604	5,919	1,119	1,545	870	152	0	229
Hialeah city	10,615	4,184	5,205	552	658	279	5	0	229
Hollywood city	7,286	5,530	7,154	682	1,592	1,448	222	262	229
Homestead city	1,918	995	424	471	8	124	5	54	229
Jacksonville city	40,591	35,686	31,085	13,663	13,780	9,310	2,823	1,229	181
Kissimmee city	3,796	1,499	2,192	1,288	375	187	281	90	229
Lakeland city	8,959	4,945	4,649	1,281	1,579	2,224	252	200	88
Largo city	8,324	7,615	4,910	1,499	2,541	1,802	61	416	229
Lauderhill city	4,142	1,182	2,644	102	303	163	0	0	229
Melbourne city	5,264	4,588	4,523	1,471	2,106	1,236	141	471	229
Miami city	19,559	13,713	16,506	1,337	1,881	982	132	0	229

Table E-3: Cities - Educational Attainment and Veterans Status, Persons 55 and Over—*Continued*

	High School or Equivalent	Some College or Associates Degree	Bachelor's Degree or Higher	Veterans by Age and Gender					
				Male			Female		
				55 to 64 Years	65 to 74 Years	75 Years and Over	55 to 64 Years	65 to 74 Years	75 Years and Over
Florida—Cont.									
Miami Beach city	2,868	2,793	6,769	265	269	499	51	0	229
Miami Gardens city	5,108	2,055	2,971	620	886	330	95	53	229
Miramar city	4,260	2,895	2,279	1,677	213	116	71	0	229
North Port city	5,657	6,054	5,699	1,247	2,203	2,290	61	0	229
Orlando city	10,503	6,184	9,465	3,146	2,364	1,283	489	80	138
Palm Bay city	9,908	6,514	4,394	1,860	3,681	2,276	0	70	216
Palm Coast city	9,205	6,873	7,036	979	3,545	2,821	0	40	75
Pembroke Pines city	13,453	8,358	7,180	809	624	1,369	0	0	229
Plantation city	2,251	4,143	6,743	251	676	846	0	0	120
Pompano Beach city	7,255	5,069	7,426	1,111	1,104	2,695	237	37	229
Port St. Lucie city	11,395	13,255	10,373	1,174	2,834	4,610	386	199	229
St. Petersburg city	14,567	11,109	16,099	2,858	3,927	5,003	640	323	268
Sunrise city	6,605	4,961	3,126	294	764	556	278	91	229
Tallahassee city	4,117	4,769	8,420	2,084	1,345	1,227	0	0	140
Tamarac city	5,926	4,317	4,162	746	764	1,261	82	0	229
Tampa city	14,113	10,534	13,769	3,780	4,070	3,253	1,167	72	229
Weston city	na	na	na	353	76	472	0	0	229
West Palm Beach city	5,070	6,272	7,289	534	731	2,253	27	38	84
Georgia									
Albany city	2,120	2,623	2,459	804	638	582	144	0	226
Alpharetta city	na	na	na	256	499	323	0	0	140
Athens-Clarke County unified govt (bal)	2,966	2,739	6,332	1,310	1,609	801	236	32	97
Atlanta city	12,998	11,453	22,980	3,124	3,212	3,393	314	75	53
Augusta-Richmond County consolidated govt (bal)	10,155	6,321	4,825	2,592	3,755	2,515	540	181	110
Columbus city	7,883	6,410	7,133	4,181	3,401	2,201	905	243	226
Johns Creek city	1,220	2,642	4,861	290	878	776	0	0	226
Macon-Bibb County	7,488	6,453	5,486	1,620	2,641	1,608	459	322	136
Roswell city	2,090	3,963	6,734	478	1,042	1,309	166	144	102
Sandy Springs city	2,012	3,048	9,849	182	679	1,106	0	70	189
Savannah city	5,919	5,531	6,152	1,166	2,059	1,810	264	0	32
South Fulton city	4,239	3,852	2,783	1,679	346	824	307	0	226
Warner Robins city	3,073	2,178	1,739	1,292	771	486	189	0	120
Hawaii									
Urban Honolulu CDP	18,852	15,216	23,972	2,091	4,552	5,426	509	107	94
Iowa									
Boise City city	9,557	13,006	12,055	2,782	4,154	3,515	768	82	106
Meridian city	2,658	3,150	3,635	1,160	1,554	258	257	0	107
Nampa city	4,939	5,488	2,790	1,178	1,345	1,402	0	330	202
Illinois									
Aurora city	4,580	4,808	3,893	1,014	1,326	1,602	37	91	190
Bloomington city	3,316	2,258	4,333	620	813	959	131	0	65
Champaign city	2,487	2,475	4,403	275	788	524	0	0	83
Chicago city	104,302	71,737	88,833	9,933	16,572	14,419	963	463	365
Decatur city	6,198	3,742	2,523	606	1,074	1,243	72	78	146
Elgin city	4,713	3,815	3,039	982	1,632	1,035	177	0	190
Evanston city	1,483	1,546	7,162	68	378	483	0	0	190
Joliet city	4,091	3,471	3,080	1,191	786	779	0	0	190
Naperville city	3,094	4,253	8,855	381	1,133	1,112	65	0	51
Peoria city	4,378	6,256	5,523	627	1,576	1,472	332	0	65
Rockford city	8,693	7,096	7,237	1,468	1,967	2,166	108	81	208
Springfield city	6,039	4,987	7,257	1,020	1,924	1,822	87	50	190
Waukegan city	2,724	1,728	860	711	680	400	35	0	190
Indiana									
Bloomington city	1,732	841	5,017	162	561	731	0	150	198
Carmel city	2,358	2,513	7,977	297	860	1,106	0	0	106
Evansville city	7,172	4,932	3,294	1,386	2,044	2,243	85	86	275
Fishers city	3,176	1,990	3,954	1,129	1,500	887	171	241	198
Fort Wayne city	14,079	10,655	7,839	2,415	4,069	2,199	308	355	95
Gary city	5,847	3,737	2,285	971	1,379	785	0	0	198
Hammond city	5,355	1,412	1,357	733	1,005	721	108	0	198
Indianapolis city (bal)	33,433	28,584	26,438	8,555	9,561	7,682	1,267	1,076	74
Lafayette city	3,887	1,861	2,656	665	894	863	0	0	221
Muncie city	3,781	2,407	2,157	765	639	1,165	188	46	198
Noblesville city	2,071	2,186	2,227	513	557	852	0	0	139
South Bend city	5,653	2,623	3,668	580	1,062	1,411	101	124	198
Iowa									
Ames city	1,442	1,199	3,789	44	325	600	0	0	163
Ankeny city	1,257	3,036	3,351	214	964	340	238	0	163
Cedar Rapids city	7,461	5,331	4,628	961	2,496	1,586	201	37	60
Davenport city	5,252	3,958	4,456	876	1,240	1,425	253	0	163
Des Moines city	9,081	7,277	6,275	1,420	2,304	2,131	263	0	163
Iowa City city	1,956	1,804	4,202	445	264	503	0	0	163
Sioux City city	4,152	3,495	2,600	1,024	1,135	1,135	0	30	163

Table E-3: Cities - Educational Attainment and Veterans Status, Persons 55 and Over—*Continued*

	High School or Equivalent	Some College or Associates Degree	Bachelor's Degree or Higher	Veterans by Age and Gender					
				Male			Female		
				55 to 64 Years	65 to 74 Years	75 Years and Over	55 to 64 Years	65 to 74 Years	75 Years and Over
Iowa—Cont.									
Waterloo city	5,566	2,846	2,079	852	1,158	997	38	95	110
West Des Moines city	2,454	2,859	4,307	774	1,162	732	154	0	163
Kansas									
Kansas City city	7,034	4,200	2,641	1,594	1,696	1,220	574	73	73
Lawrence city	3,110	2,352	6,003	563	545	1,212	0	0	177
Olathe city	3,516	3,487	5,996	717	1,338	951	52	0	89
Overland Park city	6,235	8,445	15,267	1,373	2,413	2,748	187	171	136
Shawnee city	1,955	2,837	3,223	309	1,025	421	0	0	177
Topeka city	9,151	6,468	6,077	1,356	2,954	2,196	279	0	122
Wichita city	17,117	17,350	16,199	4,994	4,613	4,014	701	259	115
Kentucky									
Bowling Green city	1,521	2,403	2,285	352	790	385	0	0	197
Lexington-Fayette urban county	9,508	11,885	18,122	2,175	3,395	2,556	255	138	271
Louisville/Jefferson County metro govt (bal)	32,007	25,349	23,531	7,175	8,367	7,462	977	579	149
Louisiana									
Baton Rouge city	8,765	7,901	12,525	1,245	2,569	2,525	90	360	112
Bossier City city	3,400	3,234	2,135	1,255	1,091	1,108	145	116	114
Kenner city	4,391	3,038	2,618	546	830	613	57	69	217
Lafayette city	4,186	5,592	6,148	732	995	1,437	421	118	232
Lake Charles city	3,073	2,924	3,324	825	1,271	705	57	0	217
New Orleans city	15,361	13,130	18,564	2,696	4,020	3,023	631	348	116
Shreveport city	11,122	8,318	7,298	2,197	2,520	2,344	232	0	217
Maine									
Portland city	1,766	1,566	4,748	705	374	1,124	0	0	170
Maryland									
Baltimore city	24,528	18,536	20,758	6,541	7,046	5,804	1,340	549	107
Frederick city	2,721	1,782	3,799	492	613	946	224	0	131
Gaithersburg city	870	2,443	4,778	403	573	565	131	39	206
Rockville city	1,358	2,131	7,425	172	336	908	126	0	206
Massachusetts									
Boston city	20,312	13,662	26,921	2,157	3,271	4,577	130	200	158
Brockton city	4,067	3,445	1,846	622	1,115	819	0	0	211
Cambridge city	1,512	1,567	7,997	94	513	483	0	77	91
Fall River city	4,299	2,644	1,656	520	775	1,407	21	307	211
Framingham city	2,588	3,117	5,719	151	126	780	46	0	82
Lawrence city	1,996	931	332	202	155	55	177	0	211
Lowell city	3,592	838	2,309	1,141	382	478	0	79	211
Lynn city	3,021	2,960	1,695	395	713	471	268	0	211
New Bedford city	4,103	1,798	2,018	295	715	613	0	0	97
Newton city	2,449	1,561	13,028	0	491	1,445	0	0	211
Quincy city	4,596	3,129	3,879	447	666	1,160	0	0	211
Somerville city	2,205	773	1,801	211	84	268	0	23	211
Springfield city	6,773	4,469	3,256	1,069	1,580	1,000	181	0	53
Worcester city	7,494	4,388	7,250	1,289	1,344	1,581	0	182	29
Michigan									
Ann Arbor city	1,528	2,223	9,154	94	473	1,261	37	71	253
Dearborn city	2,785	2,493	3,032	283	780	312	0	0	116
Detroit city	33,534	27,224	15,667	6,023	6,820	5,341	713	216	180
Farmington Hills city	3,755	4,870	6,550	357	909	1,948	44	0	118
Flint city	4,874	3,860	1,090	1,169	1,239	958	53	55	172
Grand Rapids city	7,674	6,440	8,191	766	2,765	1,174	134	48	130
Kalamazoo city	2,047	2,354	3,087	486	290	667	26	91	110
Lansing city	3,737	4,946	3,792	633	1,048	704	0	0	172
Livonia city	4,236	5,216	4,622	491	1,219	1,371	0	83	172
Rochester Hills city	3,305	3,648	4,793	285	466	738	0	0	87
Southfield city	3,254	5,474	6,180	941	1,501	923	144	0	172
Sterling Heights city	7,660	6,168	4,345	472	1,200	2,106	119	0	172
Troy city	3,234	2,919	6,262	345	692	955	64	0	63
Warren city	8,189	6,895	3,225	1,279	1,472	2,549	92	97	28
Westland city	4,953	3,933	2,397	925	1,102	936	144	104	190
Wyoming city	3,769	2,388	1,291	867	1,054	947	0	88	172
Minnesota									
Blaine city	2,622	2,470	1,189	463	777	307	0	0	147
Bloomington city	4,004	5,166	7,543	374	1,519	1,728	0	0	147
Brooklyn Park city	2,620	3,212	2,735	822	667	1,197	94	0	109
Duluth city	5,069	4,702	4,568	427	1,531	1,842	27	0	128
Eagan city	2,646	1,990	3,151	318	925	936	61	0	147
Lakeville city	1,783	1,995	2,310	667	754	735	67	0	147
Maple Grove city	3,308	3,396	3,879	599	1,206	694	0	0	147
Minneapolis city	9,299	10,550	20,073	2,569	4,231	2,875	215	0	155
Plymouth city	2,533	3,355	4,992	517	623	733	0	0	147
Rochester city	3,856	5,035	7,696	1,023	1,834	1,296	92	113	115

Table E-3: Cities - Educational Attainment and Veterans Status, Persons 55 and Over—*Continued*

	High School or Equivalent	Some College or Associates Degree	Bachelor's Degree or Higher	Veterans by Age and Gender					
				Male			Female		
				55 to 64 Years	65 to 74 Years	75 Years and Over	55 to 64 Years	65 to 74 Years	75 Years and Over
Minnesota—Cont.									
St. Cloud city	3,013	2,036	2,106	336	621	957	120	0	147
St. Paul city	8,109	7,034	12,863	1,676	1,613	2,581	305	395	136
Woodbury city	2,132	3,109	4,337	483	1,210	918	0	0	147
Mississippi									
Gulfport city	1,716	3,260	2,380	1,225	1,045	948	329	41	218
Jackson city	4,655	5,657	7,039	1,123	776	1,330	232	61	90
Missouri									
Columbia city	3,037	3,616	6,142	770	1,766	1,186	373	51	190
Independence city	8,410	5,904	3,435	1,675	2,345	1,470	49	10	190
Kansas City city	19,142	19,750	17,293	4,192	5,837	4,667	587	162	183
Lee's Summit city	4,908	4,840	6,308	845	1,710	1,588	160	36	190
O'Fallon city	3,536	3,254	2,200	864	813	987	0	0	85
St. Charles city	4,282	3,812	2,782	658	1,138	796	0	0	71
St. Joseph city	4,867	3,047	3,551	863	1,579	872	31	29	190
St. Louis city	11,832	11,771	11,016	3,629	3,813	2,521	525	317	114
Springfield city	11,356	7,512	6,127	1,142	2,088	2,128	52	40	190
Montana									
Billings city	6,738	5,846	5,915	784	2,114	1,719	188	29	160
Missoula city	2,069	3,259	3,841	197	1,170	609	154	111	172
Nebraska									
Lincoln city	10,670	12,666	12,135	1,586	4,279	2,055	439	0	161
Omaha city	18,692	18,844	20,882	3,747	6,006	5,384	543	122	175
Nevada									
Henderson city	15,271	19,508	19,458	3,825	6,127	4,982	346	368	627
Las Vegas city	27,509	31,264	25,124	6,673	9,413	9,467	1,356	561	152
North Las Vegas city	6,469	8,841	5,291	2,936	3,830	1,819	607	311	183
Reno city	7,961	15,885	12,835	2,495	4,736	3,254	465	220	96
Sparks city	4,134	8,026	3,672	1,044	2,420	1,652	58	42	80
New Hampshire									
Manchester city	4,052	3,158	4,209	1,241	1,055	1,397	393	178	192
Nashua city	4,322	3,858	5,100	1,366	1,209	1,236	0	0	192
New Jersey									
Bayonne city	3,743	811	2,165	121	800	589	39	0	210
Camden city	2,149	1,060	660	246	231	418	0	0	210
Clifton city	4,687	2,363	4,018	154	252	569	0	0	130
East Orange city	3,010	2,395	1,173	237	272	375	48	0	210
Elizabeth city	4,835	1,624	1,714	232	279	172	0	0	210
Jersey City city	8,934	3,888	7,950	725	403	835	61	0	126
Newark city	9,675	3,675	3,202	900	631	443	178	38	210
Passaic city	2,126	487	397	0	267	38	0	0	210
Paterson city	5,376	2,092	1,089	135	190	395	7	23	210
Trenton city	3,140	2,552	1,384	429	283	319	0	51	210
Union City city	1,958	758	996	158	215	61	0	0	210
New Mexico									
Albuquerque city	19,221	22,041	36,881	6,388	9,541	7,154	742	396	240
Las Cruces city	3,704	4,855	5,758	1,030	2,644	1,372	430	109	141
Rio Rancho city	3,953	5,242	6,060	1,629	2,552	1,365	237	423	179
Santa Fe city	3,606	4,488	10,505	577	1,491	1,600	53	0	110
New York									
Albany city	3,408	3,005	4,535	1,004	632	954	145	70	75
Buffalo city	10,650	6,614	7,771	2,135	3,154	2,115	196	0	201
Mount Vernon city	2,328	2,386	2,318	86	200	602	225	0	201
New Rochelle city	4,024	2,392	4,902	268	307	1,320	0	0	201
New York city	348,773	201,871	349,843	21,123	33,520	43,381	2,543	1,158	387
Rochester city	6,339	6,031	5,676	1,321	1,784	1,352	267	164	94
Schenectady city	3,363	1,503	2,501	640	419	585	78	0	93
Syracuse city	4,093	4,062	4,257	1,001	1,015	608	131	92	77
Yonkers city	9,025	6,382	9,239	843	1,117	1,754	25	0	56
North Carolina									
Asheville city	4,190	3,902	9,203	655	1,280	1,925	212	43	28
Charlotte city	22,319	28,651	31,812	5,917	7,657	6,423	821	120	126
Concord city	4,556	3,384	3,098	785	1,112	814	167	27	210
Durham city	7,758	8,065	13,707	1,979	2,138	2,269	1,036	344	141
Fayetteville city	7,582	8,097	6,432	4,476	4,880	2,438	1,335	89	93
Gastonia city	3,521	4,427	1,732	851	1,245	995	28	0	210
Greensboro city	9,466	11,716	15,192	2,288	3,202	2,674	221	120	51
Greenville city	2,195	2,491	3,078	775	832	594	61	68	212
High Point city	4,755	3,566	4,370	1,440	1,303	1,480	176	30	210
Jacksonville city	1,376	1,205	929	905	470	536	88	0	131
Raleigh city	11,130	13,097	22,946	2,783	3,257	4,146	297	725	220
Wilmington city	5,208	5,553	7,910	797	1,269	2,030	241	35	210
Winston-Salem city	11,011	8,386	10,630	2,267	3,495	2,927	119	46	40

Table E-3: Cities - Educational Attainment and Veterans Status, Persons 55 and Over—*Continued*

| | | | | Veterans by Age and Gender | | | | | |
| | High School or Equivalent | Some College or Associates Degree | Bachelor's Degree or Higher | Male | | | Female | | |
				55 to 64 Years	65 to 74 Years	75 Years and Over	55 to 64 Years	65 to 74 Years	75 Years and Over
North Dakota									
Bismarck city	2,868	4,222	3,647	743	895	1,046	0	101	165
Fargo city	3,251	5,364	5,013	958	1,951	1,161	108	44	161
Ohio									
Akron city	9,780	8,448	6,681	1,729	3,329	2,341	102	0	173
Canton city	4,666	3,279	1,468	1,219	762	626	157	80	89
Cincinnati city	9,403	9,061	12,413	3,003	2,775	2,769	183	0	75
Cleveland city	18,901	12,431	7,661	4,707	4,458	3,147	548	46	112
Columbus city	30,179	23,941	28,093	6,852	7,497	5,999	281	355	69
Dayton city	6,372	5,074	4,156	2,172	1,749	1,734	292	242	195
Lorain city	3,540	2,116	1,626	394	980	626	55	268	44
Parma city	5,539	4,241	2,374	554	1,040	853	114	0	124
Toledo city	12,815	11,760	7,185	2,649	2,881	2,905	212	70	174
Youngstown city	5,582	2,279	1,750	990	832	975	144	0	195
Oklahoma									
Broken Arrow city	4,571	6,503	4,307	1,012	1,753	1,545	186	48	161
Edmond city	2,457	4,216	7,301	458	1,426	1,506	45	123	161
Lawton city	2,355	4,268	2,867	2,144	2,156	1,348	417	349	108
Norman city	3,622	3,299	6,562	1,098	1,453	1,110	122	105	277
Oklahoma City city	22,988	25,419	24,160	5,011	9,020	7,218	720	591	129
Tulsa city	15,398	18,173	19,687	3,304	5,020	5,422	409	621	164
Oregon									
Beaverton city	2,062	2,836	5,469	463	1,210	923	180	0	207
Bend city	2,535	6,821	6,649	450	1,460	1,224	70	75	191
Eugene city	3,350	9,216	12,326	2,193	1,856	2,580	103	271	141
Gresham city	4,374	4,964	3,448	1,049	1,452	1,120	0	563	207
Hillsboro city	3,042	4,211	3,771	1,316	1,492	612	25	72	207
Medford city	3,594	4,454	4,930	689	1,592	1,860	0	0	96
Portland city	16,669	25,912	37,449	3,648	6,933	5,579	694	563	259
Salem city	6,371	8,058	9,329	1,518	1,944	2,612	287	83	256
Pennsylvania									
Allentown city	5,560	3,429	2,923	547	989	1,122	71	68	32
Bethlehem city	5,318	2,274	3,165	399	1,117	841	240	89	177
Erie city	6,861	3,205	2,936	1,012	1,409	1,436	57	109	276
Philadelphia city	81,675	38,685	48,462	12,328	16,514	14,648	689	964	232
Pittsburgh city	18,108	9,806	13,621	3,066	2,790	4,298	273	170	233
Reading city	2,127	1,496	1,555	243	776	425	68	0	65
Scranton city	6,542	1,777	2,389	825	953	936	0	40	106
Rhode Island									
Cranston city	4,399	2,548	3,437	648	755	823	32	0	99
Pawtucket city	3,164	1,840	2,030	270	458	730	0	0	220
Providence city	7,776	1,934	6,025	326	1,000	899	251	0	114
Warwick city	3,993	4,620	4,969	749	1,663	983	202	104	68
South Carolina									
Charleston city	5,596	4,694	9,384	1,640	2,191	1,989	28	388	97
Columbia city	3,522	3,464	4,698	1,420	1,961	805	199	59	78
Greenville city	1,560	2,153	5,009	428	684	526	0	42	214
North Charleston city	5,411	2,971	1,808	2,427	1,923	906	154	88	214
Rock Hill city	2,878	2,773	2,699	959	731	690	45	45	214
South Dakota									
Rapid City city	3,651	4,910	4,174	859	1,839	1,172	53	124	54
Sioux Falls city	6,429	6,020	7,299	1,995	2,322	2,331	426	95	258
Tennessee									
Chattanooga city	9,444	8,338	7,497	1,917	1,902	2,751	309	275	211
Clarksville city	3,916	3,305	3,638	2,277	1,690	1,714	585	538	211
Franklin city	2,061	2,244	4,628	471	530	905	102	53	211
Jackson city	2,866	2,012	2,226	274	695	535	0	0	211
Johnson City city	3,431	3,264	2,704	828	1,334	1,124	250	90	193
Knoxville city	8,367	6,036	6,223	1,297	1,498	2,177	214	0	335
Memphis city	25,632	20,797	22,432	5,650	7,379	3,941	1,171	274	110
Murfreesboro city	3,853	3,983	4,872	519	1,860	290	175	0	145
Nashville-Davidson metropolitan govt (bal)	21,657	20,539	25,742	4,654	6,069	5,977	425	240	175
Texas									
Abilene city	5,256	3,866	4,395	1,043	1,726	1,603	118	105	287
Allen city	2,228	3,153	4,328	744	788	766	275	73	228
Amarillo city	6,270	7,419	7,751	2,118	2,370	2,440	473	106	150
Arlington city	10,635	12,373	13,075	3,998	4,657	2,941	508	121	228
Austin city	17,534	17,490	43,712	6,803	6,440	6,033	471	669	193
Baytown city	1,970	2,465	1,880	301	530	241	0	0	228
Beaumont city	5,541	4,562	4,742	630	1,965	1,361	181	57	228
Brownsville city	3,837	2,998	2,365	326	751	535	0	0	228
Bryan city	2,281	1,768	3,132	169	838	453	0	114	228
Carrollton city	3,360	4,534	6,764	98	1,734	1,405	0	158	228
Cedar Park city	1,802	1,508	2,250	839	744	485	75	29	203
College Station city	1,334	2,800	4,653	419	977	781	0	0	228

Table E-3: Cities - Educational Attainment and Veterans Status, Persons 55 and Over—*Continued*

	High School or Equivalent	Some College or Associates Degree	Bachelor's Degree or Higher	Veterans by Age and Gender Male 55 to 64 Years	Male 65 to 74 Years	Male 75 Years and Over	Female 55 to 64 Years	Female 65 to 74 Years	Female 75 Years and Over
Texas—Cont.									
Conroe city	2,662	3,378	2,727	889	565	1,188	70	0	228
Corpus Christi city	11,425	11,023	11,370	3,696	4,700	3,687	505	171	161
Dallas city	28,074	33,393	48,074	6,532	10,107	8,125	313	807	345
Denton city	3,520	4,615	6,232	1,023	1,738	938	90	168	91
Edinburg city	1,498	1,775	1,596	413	432	399	12	0	99
El Paso city	19,053	17,745	14,624	5,041	6,177	5,525	561	294	187
Fort Worth city	19,193	22,599	26,316	9,932	7,045	6,320	1,289	497	529
Frisco city	4,260	3,328	7,697	676	882	822	35	0	228
Garland city	7,447	8,834	7,820	1,161	1,991	2,094	223	87	127
Georgetown city	2,850	6,933	11,074	917	2,332	2,097	180	372	228
Grand Prairie city	4,307	4,647	4,184	1,852	2,496	824	0	0	147
Harlingen city	3,640	2,704	1,624	507	1,475	737	0	71	228
Houston city	53,282	55,261	75,671	8,483	15,313	13,686	1,127	574	379
Irving city	4,498	3,833	3,873	1,416	761	916	133	0	139
Killeen city	2,957	2,934	2,475	2,919	1,538	1,138	1,231	96	228
Laredo city	4,534	3,943	3,037	583	566	691	77	56	228
League City city	2,893	4,463	4,478	2,520	2,002	900	233	18	228
Lewisville city	2,945	2,897	2,855	549	643	876	72	178	59
Longview city	3,347	4,256	2,901	1,127	1,150	1,393	45	0	170
Lubbock city	7,833	9,461	9,434	2,323	2,395	2,483	425	0	200
McAllen city	2,984	2,532	3,074	332	801	436	10	28	228
McKinney city	5,353	7,044	7,416	1,360	2,227	1,031	67	81	745
Mansfield city	1,720	2,586	1,664	279	1,483	780	21	38	228
Mesquite city	3,774	3,849	3,733	1,069	1,105	1,019	0	56	72
Midland city	3,065	3,680	4,477	1,167	576	1,212	0	0	228
Mission city	2,643	1,918	2,115	205	354	519	0	0	228
Missouri City city	1,418	3,358	4,817	488	629	484	82	78	228
New Braunfels city	3,575	4,050	4,093	644	1,329	995	186	76	157
North Richland Hills city	2,703	4,413	2,919	697	873	936	209	0	228
Odessa city	3,542	3,183	2,290	297	722	729	125	0	228
Pasadena city	3,774	3,726	2,449	719	1,432	876	161	0	228
Pearland city	5,424	6,018	3,845	249	1,739	650	0	202	228
Pharr city	1,817	1,621	500	147	427	465	0	146	228
Plano city	6,678	8,518	19,999	1,015	2,816	2,592	55	94	316
Richardson city	2,297	4,939	8,613	679	1,167	974	0	132	149
Round Rock city	2,430	4,670	3,942	1,128	1,084	869	258	0	105
Rowlett city	1,424	2,551	1,633	698	679	279	0	44	228
San Angelo city	4,426	4,430	4,155	1,128	1,762	1,411	78	0	228
San Antonio city	44,253	52,610	44,764	15,262	21,688	15,045	3,602	1,142	256
Sugar Land city	2,778	4,424	10,631	301	1,066	787	0	102	228
Temple city	4,252	3,482	3,626	1,124	952	1,526	328	219	212
Tyler city	2,393	5,185	5,224	586	1,197	1,269	0	22	228
Victoria city	3,167	3,491	1,984	541	812	887	0	0	228
Waco city	4,265	3,697	5,150	1,487	890	1,153	388	0	356
Wichita Falls city	4,420	4,037	2,854	1,261	1,066	1,092	195	0	100
Utah									
Layton city	1,520	2,623	2,761	905	739	588	111	0	193
Lehi city	1,528	1,548	1,841	27	357	220	0	0	193
Ogden city	2,392	3,106	2,361	802	1,394	719	112	121	193
Orem city	2,294	2,519	4,018	137	391	917	0	0	193
Provo city	944	2,139	3,767	134	775	715	0	0	60
St. George city	5,408	7,611	7,174	440	1,523	2,779	0	145	193
Salt Lake City city	4,135	5,692	9,946	1,423	1,735	1,910	186	62	193
Sandy city	3,653	5,173	5,833	436	954	1,037	181	0	193
South Jordan city	1,776	2,348	2,291	0	439	451	0	0	193
West Jordan city	2,475	3,475	2,470	413	646	815	0	48	193
West Valley City city	4,632	4,216	1,418	1,244	1,372	1,075	58	0	193
Virginia									
Alexandria city	2,339	4,399	10,344	1,888	1,470	1,697	234	77	206
Chesapeake city	9,028	9,569	9,118	5,388	4,314	2,973	638	254	206
Hampton city	6,543	6,610	5,262	3,423	2,484	2,000	1,392	428	42
Lynchburg city	3,173	3,140	4,241	1,180	1,214	610	307	0	206
Newport News city	8,186	6,412	5,341	4,351	2,116	1,859	789	208	206
Norfolk city	7,760	7,327	7,393	4,597	3,287	2,478	659	211	57
Portsmouth city	4,499	5,127	2,298	1,500	1,197	1,408	243	179	91
Richmond city	7,152	6,491	9,975	2,200	2,994	1,800	35	156	106
Roanoke city	6,423	3,824	3,951	1,449	2,013	1,102	155	202	54
Suffolk city	3,832	3,555	2,958	2,396	1,791	975	376	116	121
Virginia Beach city	16,512	19,379	22,727	10,439	9,795	6,445	1,844	779	183
Washington									
Auburn city	2,799	4,877	3,144	507	1,404	1,192	291	55	204
Bellevue city	2,443	5,741	12,011	566	1,123	1,746	176	81	135
Bellingham city	2,155	4,377	6,322	591	1,470	796	201	0	124
Everett city	3,204	4,853	3,655	1,060	911	1,335	60	35	204
Federal Way city	3,757	4,191	3,362	1,330	1,105	885	150	53	204
Kennewick city	3,527	3,975	2,321	1,384	1,294	705	0	0	91

Table E-3: Cities - Educational Attainment and Veterans Status, Persons 55 and Over—*Continued*

	High School or Equivalent	Some College or Associates Degree	Bachelor's Degree or Higher	Veterans by Age and Gender					
				Male			Female		
				55 to 64 Years	65 to 74 Years	75 Years and Over	55 to 64 Years	65 to 74 Years	75 Years and Over
Washington—Cont.									
Kent city	4,532	5,466	4,607	1,196	1,456	1,011	459	73	204
Kirkland city	1,555	3,419	3,899	349	891	528	43	39	204
Marysville city	2,581	3,550	1,918	1,129	1,398	578	138	0	204
Pasco city	1,425	1,589	1,988	694	738	153	0	30	138
Redmond city	594	1,334	3,029	361	734	353	83	131	129
Renton city	3,979	4,553	2,845	2,359	614	1,385	132	82	87
Sammamish city	738	1,409	2,313	241	642	247	0	0	67
Seattle city	14,115	22,717	48,439	2,972	6,091	6,935	794	539	136
Spokane city	8,385	11,599	12,217	3,003	5,421	3,184	545	294	150
Spokane Valley city	5,000	5,538	3,430	976	1,920	1,224	376	140	93
Tacoma city	8,952	9,145	8,546	2,719	4,338	2,427	482	181	84
Vancouver city	7,787	10,890	9,750	1,812	2,682	1,635	0	290	153
Yakima city	3,779	4,247	5,039	549	1,083	1,600	47	0	204
Wisconsin									
Appleton city	4,846	2,235	2,907	582	1,091	887	100	0	45
Eau Claire city	3,706	2,852	3,303	436	892	1,222	23	0	102
Green Bay city	7,013	3,068	2,858	975	1,470	1,536	156	56	161
Kenosha city	4,448	3,867	2,621	917	1,490	1,038	257	99	151
Madison city	7,019	6,909	16,245	562	2,133	2,755	171	0	136
Milwaukee city	21,890	15,441	13,883	3,486	5,634	3,217	341	374	85
Oshkosh city	3,827	2,792	1,759	351	445	1,255	0	0	101
Racine city	3,279	2,606	1,995	434	716	663	37	30	151
Waukesha city	3,685	3,054	2,977	469	855	1,309	0	0	151

Table E-4: Metropolitan/Micropolitan Statistical Areas - Educational Attainment and Veterans Status, Persons 55 and Over

	High School or Equivalent	Some College or Associates Degree	Bachelor's Degree or Higher	Veterans by Age and Gender					
				Male			Female		
				55 to 64 Years	65 to 74 Years	75 Years and Over	55 to 64 Years	65 to 74 Years	75 Years and Over
Aberdeen, WA Micro Area..	4,727	6,768	2,940	1,130	2,382	1,139	166	114	204
Abilene, TX Metro Area..	8,480	7,446	5,883	1,598	2,939	2,527	118	105	287
Adrian, MI Micro Area..	8,075	4,792	3,884	998	1,518	1,218	127	0	94
Akron, OH Metro Area..	44,832	30,651	34,548	6,865	11,319	10,364	540	164	241
Alamogordo, NM Micro Area...	3,386	3,343	2,484	2,041	1,577	1,532	186	71	201
Albany, GA Metro Area..	7,689	5,571	4,461	2,114	2,575	1,220	332	48	226
Albany, OR Metro Area..	7,427	8,990	5,331	1,339	3,293	2,515	374	57	207
Albany-Schenectady-Troy, NY Metro Area..	49,120	38,061	50,921	9,119	12,450	12,793	1,154	370	238
Albertville, AL Micro Area..	6,069	3,584	3,718	1,612	929	1,341	94	67	37
Albuquerque, NM Metro Area...	35,457	40,176	58,023	11,750	17,205	13,340	1,615	961	302
Alexandria, LA Metro Area...	11,414	6,347	4,078	1,802	2,472	2,318	0	0	182
Allentown-Bethlehem-Easton, PA-NJ Metro Area..............................	62,806	32,363	35,846	5,875	13,389	13,706	1,122	248	40
Altoona, PA Metro Area..	12,960	5,019	4,860	1,475	2,609	2,260	132	0	70
Amarillo, TX Metro Area...	8,604	10,537	11,294	2,643	3,618	3,437	524	127	150
Ames, IA Metro Area...	3,113	2,704	5,231	178	781	1,174	8	49	163
Anchorage, AK Metro Area...	10,860	15,811	15,937	6,755	6,745	4,346	1,420	498	135
Ann Arbor, MI Metro Area..	11,548	13,616	23,662	1,683	3,928	3,610	84	180	255
Anniston-Oxford-Jacksonville, AL Metro Area...................................	7,152	5,703	3,080	2,190	2,341	1,174	424	216	148
Appleton, WI Metro Area...	14,998	7,690	8,060	1,837	3,351	3,026	146	54	45
Asheville, NC Metro Area..	27,437	26,833	37,518	5,611	9,596	9,138	913	245	321
Ashtabula, OH Micro Area...	8,071	4,535	3,441	1,373	1,460	1,202	141	0	58
Athens, OH Micro Area..	3,430	1,783	2,266	653	748	471	0	57	195
Athens, TX Micro Area...	5,840	5,673	3,922	1,230	1,985	1,390	208	0	133
Athens-Clarke County, GA Metro Area...	7,703	5,529	9,874	2,213	2,845	1,711	448	32	97
Atlanta-Sandy Springs-Roswell, GA Metro Area...............................	208,469	189,945	237,409	51,348	69,532	49,426	8,773	3,222	406
Atlantic City-Hammonton, NJ Metro Area...	16,251	12,543	11,742	1,773	4,243	3,993	271	176	73
Auburn, NY Micro Area..	5,295	4,018	2,921	566	1,582	1,065	110	0	201
Auburn-Opelika, AL Metro Area..	5,842	5,054	5,883	2,161	2,452	1,409	425	157	54
Augusta-Richmond County, GA-SC Metro Area.................................	33,680	23,075	21,833	9,948	10,423	7,922	1,071	1,200	252
Augusta-Waterville, ME Micro Area...	7,478	7,740	7,419	2,250	2,760	2,364	324	24	170
Austin-Round Rock, TX Metro Area...	49,503	56,230	103,964	18,132	20,573	15,904	2,121	1,406	478
Bakersfield, CA Metro Area..	22,051	30,211	19,922	5,554	9,109	6,934	553	398	527
Baltimore-Columbia-Towson, MD Metro Area...................................	128,696	102,421	142,333	28,379	38,761	35,343	5,185	2,324	572
Bangor, ME Metro Area..	10,814	6,557	7,412	2,347	2,469	2,112	212	167	231
Barnstable Town, MA Metro Area..	14,784	16,143	30,807	2,249	4,792	6,327	52	45	259
Baton Rouge, LA Metro Area..	39,544	31,977	30,613	4,986	10,364	8,525	505	728	123
Battle Creek, MI Metro Area...	9,335	7,052	4,948	1,281	2,841	1,825	300	6	105
Bay City, MI Metro Area...	9,206	5,900	3,136	1,026	2,158	1,895	242	27	98
Beaumont-Port Arthur, TX Metro Area...	24,936	15,477	11,474	3,909	6,484	5,774	393	130	164
Beaver Dam, WI Micro Area...	8,205	3,878	1,869	701	1,411	1,516	72	16	151
Beckley, WV Metro Area...	9,749	4,937	3,793	970	2,390	1,372	0	69	274
Bellingham, WA Metro Area..	9,357	13,384	14,286	1,762	4,561	2,658	264	38	169
Bend-Redmond, OR Metro Area..	6,713	15,792	14,833	2,262	4,645	3,547	91	75	191
Billings, MT Metro Area...	10,314	9,144	8,755	1,450	3,218	2,882	188	175	163
Binghamton, NY Metro Area...	18,595	11,388	11,348	2,324	4,021	3,755	575	170	67
Birmingham-Hoover, AL Metro Area...	62,779	49,943	47,123	9,688	19,796	14,050	1,204	701	446
Bismarck, ND Metro Area..	5,691	7,060	5,498	1,376	1,623	1,684	13	113	165
Blacksburg-Christiansburg-Radford, VA Metro Area..........................	10,353	7,630	6,941	1,319	3,236	2,174	80	232	206
Bloomington, IL Metro Area..	8,933	6,193	8,836	1,158	2,284	1,666	131	60	85
Bloomington, IN Metro Area...	6,859	4,448	8,983	762	2,081	1,858	176	171	24
Bloomsburg-Berwick, PA Metro Area...	8,229	2,443	3,464	690	1,127	1,250	90	73	358
Bluefield, WV-VA Micro Area..	8,915	4,765	3,360	659	2,390	1,315	215	94	150
Boise City, ID Metro Area..	32,022	38,857	30,217	8,192	12,767	9,503	1,537	545	424
Boston-Cambridge-Newton, MA-NH Metro Area...............................	206,881	165,586	288,361	28,634	46,890	58,387	2,252	1,354	568
Boulder, CO Metro Area...	6,569	11,778	26,022	2,090	3,498	3,336	310	395	130
Bowling Green, KY Metro Area..	7,826	5,644	6,091	1,360	2,812	1,754	187	126	197
Bozeman, MT Micro Area...	3,130	3,745	6,717	572	1,345	1,062	0	223	108
Brainerd, MN Micro Area...	7,345	7,767	5,764	1,137	2,396	2,114	203	136	21
Branson, MO Micro Area..	7,713	7,636	4,476	1,290	3,232	1,533	308	19	190
Bremerton-Silverdale, WA Metro Area...	9,079	18,366	18,655	6,511	7,768	4,512	529	424	173
Bridgeport-Stamford-Norwalk, CT Metro Area..................................	38,903	29,705	61,637	4,158	8,620	11,831	262	103	230
Brownsville-Harlingen, TX Metro Area...	13,233	11,022	7,531	1,574	4,304	2,899	155	220	120
Brunswick, GA Metro Area...	6,014	6,227	8,114	1,014	2,832	2,148	138	186	180
Buffalo-Cheektowaga-Niagara Falls, NY Metro Area.........................	75,563	51,625	52,123	10,531	18,831	17,630	1,024	430	282
Burlington, NC Metro Area...	8,931	8,975	6,645	1,559	3,100	1,953	111	133	210
Burlington-South Burlington, VT Metro Area.....................................	10,248	8,579	13,568	1,618	2,262	2,851	465	49	193
California-Lexington Park, MD Metro Area..	6,235	2,740	3,992	2,102	1,393	1,582	361	42	227
Canton-Massillon, OH Metro Area...	36,510	19,652	11,636	4,608	7,545	6,095	651	154	216
Cape Coral-Fort Myers, FL Metro Area..	66,046	60,770	71,829	8,782	18,299	22,108	970	396	481
Cape Girardeau, MO-IL Metro Area..	6,916	3,177	3,055	747	1,245	1,325	131	0	172
Carbondale-Marion, IL Metro Area..	7,501	5,777	5,415	598	2,877	1,564	183	238	190
Carson City, NV Metro Area...	2,333	4,750	2,781	963	1,282	1,414	107	35	56
Casper, WY Metro Area..	2,934	5,195	2,745	1,182	1,453	1,157	87	54	203
Cedar Rapids, IA Metro Area..	19,071	11,161	10,779	2,326	5,562	4,039	472	65	128

Table E-4: Metropolitan/Micropolitan Statistical Areas - Educational Attainment and Veterans Status, Persons 55 and Over—*Continued*

	High School or Equivalent	Some College or Associates Degree	Bachelor's Degree or Higher	Veterans by Age and Gender					
				Male			Female		
				55 to 64 Years	65 to 74 Years	75 Years and Over	55 to 64 Years	65 to 74 Years	75 Years and Over
Centralia, WA Micro Area	5,449	6,275	3,393	1,052	2,278	1,843	218	0	148
Chambersburg-Waynesboro, PA Metro Area	13,919	6,764	6,101	1,664	2,699	3,156	114	199	302
Champaign-Urbana, IL Metro Area	9,769	9,511	10,895	1,136	3,451	2,418	48	63	90
Charleston, WV Metro Area	17,895	8,752	9,636	1,636	4,219	3,190	139	146	197
Charleston-North Charleston, SC Metro Area	34,784	31,863	40,004	12,983	15,799	10,752	2,244	1,182	215
Charlotte-Concord-Gastonia, NC-SC Metro Area	104,731	102,010	92,557	20,237	32,409	25,253	3,043	961	432
Charlottesville, VA Metro Area	9,550	7,519	19,738	1,998	3,134	3,302	506	160	153
Chattanooga, TN-GA Metro Area	33,434	28,250	22,841	7,305	9,998	8,195	723	590	66
Cheyenne, WY Metro Area	5,186	6,040	3,834	2,196	3,113	1,692	355	174	203
Chicago-Naperville-Elgin, IL-IN-WI Metro Area	424,257	337,260	407,837	51,087	89,950	89,303	5,150	2,414	808
Chico, CA Metro Area	8,673	16,299	13,575	1,721	3,895	3,775	139	70	184
Chillicothe, OH Micro Area	6,031	2,753	2,415	1,083	1,696	846	46	0	147
Cincinnati, OH-KY-IN Metro Area	114,337	85,001	88,096	20,111	31,524	26,660	2,631	760	282
Claremont-Lebanon, NH-VT Micro Area	14,105	11,657	16,660	2,090	4,544	3,754	616	294	146
Clarksburg, WV Micro Area	8,519	3,308	3,308	1,095	2,077	1,563	64	46	167
Clarksville, TN-KY Metro Area	9,385	8,439	7,777	4,519	4,273	3,977	1,065	538	69
Clearlake, CA Micro Area	4,302	5,151	3,361	754	1,337	1,506	104	124	80
Cleveland, TN Metro Area	6,616	7,076	3,560	686	1,906	1,435	363	0	211
Cleveland-Elyria, OH Metro Area	129,402	98,839	102,669	16,588	28,888	30,143	1,984	1,559	605
Coeur d'Alene, ID Metro Area	8,510	10,837	8,963	2,608	4,242	3,315	98	50	10
College Station-Bryan, TX Metro Area	6,736	7,685	10,310	1,008	2,709	1,762	44	114	82
Colorado Springs, CO Metro Area	22,908	31,748	35,232	15,066	15,338	10,083	3,070	1,116	353
Columbia, MO Metro Area	5,897	5,465	9,365	851	2,479	1,842	505	60	190
Columbia, SC Metro Area	37,480	35,838	32,997	9,624	15,196	10,803	1,652	1,436	141
Columbus, GA-AL Metro Area	14,592	10,371	10,863	6,122	5,617	3,944	1,052	812	81
Columbus, IN Metro Area	5,834	3,455	2,454	793	676	729	112	0	124
Columbus, OH Metro Area	101,611	66,285	79,903	17,152	26,171	20,903	1,677	866	287
Concord, NH Micro Area	9,056	7,271	9,641	1,533	2,333	2,564	419	77	182
Cookeville, TN Micro Area	7,183	3,567	3,821	1,252	1,360	1,570	248	106	84
Coos Bay, OR Micro Area	4,929	6,653	2,937	1,161	2,603	2,516	223	18	107
Corning, NY Micro Area	7,513	4,298	4,203	1,109	1,556	1,438	185	66	79
Corpus Christi, TX Metro Area	17,256	16,847	15,311	4,651	6,507	5,650	670	184	171
Corvallis, OR Metro Area	2,860	4,470	6,971	697	1,253	1,286	99	79	160
Crestview-Fort Walton Beach-Destin, FL Metro Area	14,353	15,778	14,473	7,300	9,021	5,099	764	711	375
Cullman, AL Micro Area	6,646	4,332	1,858	752	1,455	1,761	95	86	22
Cumberland, MD-WV Metro Area	9,798	4,417	3,797	1,218	1,870	2,244	173	60	102
Dallas-Fort Worth-Arlington, TX Metro Area	209,780	240,439	272,355	56,345	78,431	60,192	6,889	4,926	1,255
Dalton, GA Metro Area	7,212	3,431	2,818	494	1,621	1,016	215	0	226
Danville, IL Metro Area	6,824	4,284	2,140	615	1,644	1,460	58	54	30
Danville, VA Metro Area	9,001	4,509	2,978	1,372	2,247	1,573	391	0	129
Daphne-Fairhope-Foley, AL Metro Area	12,184	14,200	13,767	4,211	5,547	4,467	618	45	71
Davenport-Moline-Rock Island, IA-IL Metro Area	24,580	20,061	16,729	3,630	6,734	5,850	590	45	186
Dayton, OH Metro Area	51,074	37,153	38,794	10,531	12,983	11,963	1,913	1,050	234
Decatur, AL Metro Area	8,314	6,558	6,635	1,155	2,456	2,034	305	66	84
Decatur, IL Metro Area	8,686	5,590	3,986	795	1,903	1,889	72	78	146
Deltona-Daytona Beach-Ormond Beach, FL Metro Area	52,962	51,206	45,496	9,551	16,991	18,919	930	878	291
Denver-Aurora-Lakewood, CO Metro Area	82,271	106,308	153,917	23,689	37,356	30,993	4,077	1,948	430
Des Moines-West Des Moines, IA Metro Area	30,210	25,500	25,648	3,821	9,431	7,055	943	130	28
Detroit-Warren-Dearborn, MI Metro Area	229,323	207,129	182,343	31,799	54,797	50,119	2,703	1,687	563
Dothan, AL Metro Area	10,068	7,792	5,222	1,331	2,404	2,796	189	174	151
Dover, DE Metro Area	10,441	7,221	5,973	2,706	3,430	3,561	346	139	110
DuBois, PA Micro Area	8,561	2,317	2,188	1,004	1,191	1,414	126	22	49
Dubuque, IA Metro Area	7,235	3,079	4,707	1,472	1,855	1,478	0	81	163
Duluth, MN-WI Metro Area	18,942	16,364	13,355	2,520	6,197	4,994	234	206	181
Dunn, NC Micro Area	5,844	5,030	2,942	2,468	1,551	1,147	419	0	116
Durham-Chapel Hill, NC Metro Area	20,773	20,162	37,668	4,497	6,149	5,147	1,444	441	153
East Stroudsburg, PA Metro Area	10,641	6,878	6,588	2,976	2,581	2,641	469	0	177
Eau Claire, WI Metro Area	11,907	6,941	6,881	1,785	3,488	2,689	73	9	125
El Centro, CA Metro Area	4,264	4,207	3,104	608	1,227	844	60	0	211
Elizabeth City, NC Micro Area	4,320	2,970	2,463	965	1,763	1,130	231	0	210
Elizabethtown-Fort Knox, KY Metro Area	8,769	6,082	4,196	3,142	3,519	1,765	355	132	96
Elkhart-Goshen, IN Metro Area	12,394	6,512	6,025	826	2,727	2,222	42	37	125
Elmira, NY Metro Area	6,715	3,656	3,166	1,170	1,419	1,264	239	0	201
El Paso, TX Metro Area	21,980	19,660	15,532	5,577	6,929	5,821	561	294	195
Enid, OK Metro Area	3,872	2,674	2,448	500	788	498	117	0	161
Erie, PA Metro Area	20,742	10,727	12,011	2,471	5,477	4,476	282	161	276
Eugene, OR Metro Area	16,274	28,607	24,061	4,374	7,469	7,165	467	541	202
Eureka-Arcata-Fortuna, CA Micro Area	3,961	8,264	10,075	1,116	3,591	1,987	52	106	164
Evansville, IN-KY Metro Area	20,956	14,479	11,399	2,550	5,363	4,769	183	122	286
Fairbanks, AK Metro Area	2,356	2,913	3,315	1,903	2,221	238	261	344	224
Fargo, ND-MN Metro Area	8,274	10,600	8,667	1,705	3,357	1,918	187	44	198
Faribault-Northfield, MN Micro Area	3,359	2,303	3,601	437	701	1,056	199	0	80
Farmington, MO Micro Area	4,525	2,702	2,022	1,000	1,380	949	0	0	190
Farmington, NM Metro Area	5,412	6,501	3,842	884	1,865	1,724	133	79	72

Table E-4: Metropolitan/Micropolitan Statistical Areas - Educational Attainment and Veterans Status, Persons 55 and Over—*Continued*

| | High School or Equivalent | Some College or Associates Degree | Bachelor's Degree or Higher | Veterans by Age and Gender | | | | | |
| | | | | Male | | | Female | | |
				55 to 64 Years	65 to 74 Years	75 Years and Over	55 to 64 Years	65 to 74 Years	75 Years and Over
Fayetteville, NC Metro Area	14,723	14,046	9,883	8,318	6,827	4,044	2,079	627	93
Fayetteville-Springdale-Rogers, AR-MO Metro Area	24,746	16,533	19,669	4,230	6,666	6,868	830	205	123
Findlay, OH Micro Area	5,691	2,996	2,514	638	1,199	1,034	0	0	195
Flagstaff, AZ Metro Area	2,856	5,173	7,039	1,059	2,137	1,079	186	165	24
Flint, MI Metro Area	26,041	21,716	13,504	4,259	5,723	5,424	234	100	171
Florence, SC Metro Area	13,573	8,551	6,530	2,187	3,440	2,919	376	238	214
Florence-Muscle Shoals, AL Metro Area	12,568	6,416	5,817	1,255	2,467	2,059	0	0	201
Fond du Lac, WI Metro Area	8,045	5,447	3,287	899	1,711	2,020	52	13	102
Forest City, NC Micro Area	5,478	3,519	1,774	636	1,322	832	0	18	210
Fort Collins, CO Metro Area	11,698	15,831	25,500	2,664	4,880	5,069	793	61	289
Fort Payne, AL Micro Area	4,298	2,739	1,707	1,046	766	833	282	0	26
Fort Smith, AR-OK Metro Area	18,498	11,496	9,131	2,588	5,321	3,834	399	132	37
Fort Wayne, IN Metro Area	25,949	18,139	13,652	3,425	6,831	4,038	368	419	107
Frankfort, KY Micro Area	5,219	3,355	2,413	976	1,168	1,124	51	0	197
Fresno, CA Metro Area	26,123	36,231	28,466	6,046	8,553	8,552	474	274	331
Gadsden, AL Metro Area	6,578	5,348	4,636	678	1,155	1,954	310	170	87
Gainesville, FL Metro Area	11,134	9,906	15,561	3,194	3,976	3,640	298	42	155
Gainesville, GA Metro Area	8,929	6,778	8,617	1,608	3,246	3,033	222	70	405
Gallup, NM Micro Area	2,494	2,347	1,044	697	579	622	25	29	201
Gettysburg, PA Metro Area	8,128	4,225	4,635	872	2,030	1,963	448	103	177
Glens Falls, NY Metro Area	8,980	6,418	7,400	1,562	2,154	2,008	147	0	201
Glenwood Springs, CO Micro Area	2,098	2,658	5,864	1,133	665	897	158	250	204
Goldsboro, NC Metro Area	7,558	6,634	2,838	2,637	2,913	1,571	251	163	210
Grand Forks, ND-MN Metro Area	5,303	5,814	2,964	579	1,970	1,322	142	7	44
Grand Island, NE Metro Area	4,709	4,521	2,956	459	1,350	1,043	214	15	38
Grand Junction, CO Metro Area	7,753	9,800	8,611	2,269	3,088	2,774	250	14	156
Grand Rapids-Wyoming, MI Metro Area	51,024	46,628	42,224	6,961	15,240	12,430	534	588	222
Grants Pass, OR Metro Area	8,383	8,468	4,296	1,491	2,647	3,084	329	0	207
Great Falls, MT Metro Area	5,388	5,128	3,385	1,588	1,824	1,814	332	72	79
Greeley, CO Metro Area	12,206	12,570	9,257	2,292	4,515	2,782	96	168	205
Green Bay, WI Metro Area	22,974	14,367	10,250	3,054	5,095	4,217	337	396	267
Greeneville, TN Micro Area	6,066	3,601	1,543	569	1,702	1,190	62	0	114
Greenfield Town, MA Micro Area	4,460	3,447	6,189	1,016	1,199	1,525	118	149	23
Greensboro-High Point, NC Metro Area	39,420	32,364	31,265	8,809	10,935	9,348	496	221	120
Greenville, NC Metro Area	7,317	6,131	5,952	2,168	2,894	2,212	494	68	212
Greenville-Anderson-Mauldin, SC Metro Area	47,616	38,879	37,123	7,450	13,418	11,176	1,425	648	458
Greenwood, SC Micro Area	6,210	3,944	4,365	694	2,145	1,740	113	0	214
Gulfport-Biloxi-Pascagoula, MS Metro Area	18,935	21,737	14,153	5,331	7,886	5,798	1,515	320	197
Hagerstown-Martinsburg, MD-WV Metro Area	17,770	9,391	8,907	3,028	5,234	3,353	495	223	112
Hammond, LA Metro Area	7,764	4,669	3,214	1,468	1,676	1,168	0	129	179
Hanford-Corcoran, CA Metro Area	3,650	4,611	2,874	1,823	1,379	1,740	218	82	211
Harrisburg-Carlisle, PA Metro Area	44,388	20,908	24,514	6,807	8,330	8,572	1,216	352	197
Harrisonburg, VA Metro Area	7,351	3,479	5,838	1,208	1,541	1,160	0	177	75
Hartford-West Hartford-East Hartford, CT Metro Area	67,544	46,017	69,371	8,557	14,402	15,181	1,160	360	256
Hattiesburg, MS Metro Area	7,090	5,497	5,647	973	1,875	1,411	113	159	104
Helena, MT Micro Area	4,162	4,808	5,304	1,110	2,522	1,178	251	66	159
Hermiston-Pendleton, OR Micro Area	4,353	4,251	2,779	1,061	1,348	1,474	149	87	207
Hickory-Lenoir-Morganton, NC Metro Area	23,033	18,140	14,315	3,347	7,266	5,272	46	246	81
Hilo, HI Micro Area	10,451	14,845	13,178	2,346	5,590	3,616	148	132	128
Hilton Head Island-Bluffton-Beaufort, SC Metro Area	10,635	15,120	26,964	3,395	6,392	6,126	379	210	301
Hinesville, GA Metro Area	3,116	1,167	897	2,291	870	292	429	182	28
Hobbs, NM Micro Area	2,043	2,228	768	191	284	291	0	44	201
Holland, MI Micro Area	8,640	4,756	3,750	615	1,644	1,397	62	26	107
Homosassa Springs, FL Metro Area	20,112	18,486	9,994	2,770	7,369	7,141	137	23	256
Hot Springs, AR Metro Area	7,745	6,259	6,197	1,322	2,153	2,446	583	102	201
Houma-Thibodaux, LA Metro Area	11,627	5,404	5,450	1,020	3,094	2,260	0	89	217
Houston-The Woodlands-Sugar Land, TX Metro Area	191,504	207,831	236,592	37,256	62,471	47,345	4,279	2,559	454
Huntington-Ashland, WV-KY-OH Metro Area	29,392	14,116	12,764	3,733	5,457	5,849	170	459	166
Huntsville, AL Metro Area	18,002	18,672	23,862	8,101	8,938	6,067	1,470	366	144
Huntsville, TX Micro Area	3,847	3,350	4,225	1,153	1,538	1,055	50	64	130
Hutchinson, KS Micro Area	4,377	4,223	2,462	377	1,126	1,104	0	0	51
Idaho Falls, ID Metro Area	4,851	6,551	6,049	834	1,759	1,371	461	75	43
Indiana, PA Micro Area	7,938	2,773	3,499	295	1,660	1,905	31	0	177
Indianapolis-Carmel-Anderson, IN Metro Area	98,847	72,320	74,252	20,243	26,820	21,133	2,303	1,786	242
Iowa City, IA Metro Area	6,428	5,943	8,066	1,356	1,276	1,579	101	101	163
Ithaca, NY Metro Area	3,672	3,772	5,748	576	1,334	1,285	0	0	55
Jackson, MI Metro Area	9,808	9,788	5,785	1,547	2,892	2,390	128	101	172
Jackson, MS Metro Area	23,171	22,761	25,617	3,601	4,873	4,567	576	540	163
Jackson, TN Metro Area	8,323	5,890	4,112	1,400	1,970	1,303	56	51	211
Jacksonville, FL Metro Area	76,295	69,177	71,859	25,457	26,221	21,700	3,930	2,006	604
Jacksonville, NC Metro Area	5,867	6,049	3,097	3,532	2,978	2,123	404	145	205
Jamestown-Dunkirk-Fredonia, NY Micro Area	11,166	6,802	4,454	740	2,137	1,878	14	0	114
Janesville-Beloit, WI Metro Area	13,110	7,448	4,687	1,408	3,257	2,765	155	269	30
Jefferson, GA Micro Area	3,412	3,106	2,495	604	1,044	706	154	71	226
Jefferson City, MO Metro Area	10,115	5,132	6,554	1,209	2,656	1,860	311	0	190

Table E-4: Metropolitan/Micropolitan Statistical Areas - Educational Attainment and Veterans Status, Persons 55 and Over—*Continued*

| | High School or Equivalent | Some College or Associates Degree | Bachelor's Degree or Higher | Veterans by Age and Gender | | | | | |
| | | | | Male | | | Female | | |
				55 to 64 Years	65 to 74 Years	75 Years and Over	55 to 64 Years	65 to 74 Years	75 Years and Over
Johnson City, TN Metro Area	12,964	10,956	8,358	2,272	3,945	4,012	426	312	274
Johnstown, PA Metro Area	15,928	5,618	4,534	1,811	3,375	2,843	107	88	44
Jonesboro, AR Metro Area	7,251	4,240	3,495	1,066	1,240	1,471	108	0	201
Joplin, MO Metro Area	12,126	7,934	5,049	1,483	3,162	2,818	207	0	244
Kahului-Wailuku-Lahaina, HI Metro Area	9,954	7,585	10,162	2,075	2,926	2,487	15	40	189
Kalamazoo-Portage, MI Metro Area	16,396	15,305	17,059	2,673	4,650	4,101	230	333	197
Kalispell, MT Micro Area	5,043	5,837	7,312	1,259	2,255	1,374	120	162	172
Kankakee, IL Metro Area	8,513	4,584	2,645	1,234	2,229	1,646	0	0	177
Kansas City, MO-KS Metro Area	103,215	88,039	96,874	21,433	31,314	25,639	2,820	1,076	320
Kapaa, HI Micro Area	3,107	4,224	5,306	623	1,470	1,041	0	0	189
Keene, NH Micro Area	5,056	3,557	5,095	643	1,952	1,449	179	0	61
Kennewick-Richland, WA Metro Area	9,523	12,369	12,116	3,363	4,374	2,752	162	106	340
Key West, FL Micro Area	3,749	5,352	5,921	603	1,630	1,599	0	0	229
Killeen-Temple, TX Metro Area	16,024	16,179	12,064	9,089	7,218	5,105	3,111	713	214
Kingsport-Bristol-Bristol, TN-VA Metro Area	24,566	16,367	12,996	3,592	6,726	6,063	149	230	155
Kingston, NY Metro Area	10,723	9,058	11,626	1,583	1,677	2,497	0	62	201
Klamath Falls, OR Micro Area	3,808	5,316	3,635	1,154	1,489	1,513	218	335	298
Knoxville, TN Metro Area	52,659	43,153	41,898	9,579	15,925	14,153	1,057	552	519
Kokomo, IN Metro Area	6,687	3,303	3,427	413	1,249	1,168	87	82	138
La Crosse-Onalaska, WI-MN Metro Area	8,869	6,462	6,146	1,404	2,206	2,421	273	126	466
Lafayette, LA Metro Area	26,003	15,479	14,081	2,917	5,050	6,051	661	499	428
Lafayette-West Lafayette, IN Metro Area	8,995	6,982	8,497	1,347	2,261	1,889	0	0	318
LaGrange, GA Micro Area	4,790	2,244	2,082	518	1,145	477	98	0	226
Lake Charles, LA Metro Area	9,262	8,363	6,883	2,514	3,836	2,500	378	163	217
Lake City, FL Micro Area	4,409	4,247	2,049	1,179	1,706	1,584	105	69	127
Lake Havasu City-Kingman, AZ Metro Area	21,757	25,099	9,587	3,432	8,522	6,573	466	411	619
Lakeland-Winter Haven, FL Metro Area	53,947	40,795	28,430	7,539	14,238	13,046	1,018	757	197
Lancaster, PA Metro Area	37,850	18,415	24,116	4,675	7,799	7,863	146	421	275
Lansing-East Lansing, MI Metro Area	20,559	25,511	20,889	3,010	6,721	4,748	150	106	88
Laredo, TX Metro Area	4,751	3,993	3,145	619	671	720	183	56	228
Las Cruces, NM Metro Area	6,807	8,119	9,714	2,107	4,184	2,201	582	182	141
Las Vegas-Henderson-Paradise, NV Metro Area	90,663	105,842	86,939	24,242	34,560	27,898	4,393	2,340	686
Laurel, MS Micro Area	6,380	2,795	2,129	423	744	921	22	35	177
Lawrence, KS Metro Area	4,332	3,221	6,950	611	962	1,333	46	0	177
Lawton, OK Metro Area	4,309	5,625	3,677	2,782	2,813	1,880	522	381	108
Lebanon, PA Metro Area	12,667	5,381	5,225	892	3,028	2,463	106	29	116
Lewiston, ID-WA Metro Area	5,729	4,621	3,540	1,031	1,788	1,018	144	43	134
Lewiston-Auburn, ME Metro Area	8,475	4,870	2,528	1,186	2,518	1,476	164	183	336
Lexington-Fayette, KY Metro Area	19,889	18,793	25,519	4,012	6,088	5,196	349	251	274
Lima, OH Metro Area	9,242	3,148	2,971	577	1,459	1,765	69	0	195
Lincoln, NE Metro Area	13,622	15,141	14,571	2,135	5,828	2,817	466	0	123
Little Rock-North Little Rock-Conway, AR Metro Area	39,202	30,622	29,772	8,791	12,159	9,183	912	299	218
Logan, UT-ID Metro Area	3,288	4,365	5,547	642	1,093	1,386	0	50	198
London, KY Micro Area	7,836	4,391	2,220	754	1,707	1,441	0	68	76
Longview, TX Metro Area	12,651	11,099	7,090	2,401	3,315	3,444	273	51	228
Longview, WA Metro Area	5,811	8,375	4,454	1,019	2,675	1,768	54	139	204
Los Angeles-Long Beach-Anaheim, CA Metro Area	359,261	458,157	579,991	50,762	85,273	103,153	4,302	3,681	762
Louisville/Jefferson County, KY-IN Metro Area	72,683	54,036	52,579	13,491	20,436	15,666	1,237	1,009	351
Lubbock, TX Metro Area	9,733	11,541	11,607	3,018	3,361	2,874	484	0	231
Lufkin, TX Micro Area	3,738	4,882	2,507	904	1,304	1,292	109	228	228
Lumberton, NC Micro Area	6,794	5,017	2,401	1,141	1,658	1,010	32	22	210
Lynchburg, VA Metro Area	16,880	12,525	12,943	3,467	6,075	4,442	454	45	206
Macon-Bibb County, GA Metro Area	14,166	9,146	6,945	2,830	3,906	2,549	498	560	136
Madera, CA Metro Area	5,716	6,048	4,179	816	2,640	1,752	114	44	211
Madison, WI Metro Area	28,325	24,942	36,168	3,500	8,137	8,376	633	27	140
Manchester-Nashua, NH Metro Area	18,555	16,504	23,093	5,590	6,375	5,885	662	445	202
Manhattan, KS Metro Area	3,505	2,473	4,038	605	1,309	709	83	125	106
Manitowoc, WI Micro Area	7,658	3,839	2,530	1,135	1,803	1,280	287	56	46
Mankato-North Mankato, MN Metro Area	5,425	3,579	4,082	775	1,515	1,120	291	53	8
Mansfield, OH Metro Area	9,660	6,432	3,421	996	2,322	2,118	114	117	195
Marinette, WI-MI Micro Area	7,368	3,479	2,578	831	1,561	1,187	56	42	19
Marion, IN Micro Area	5,221	3,256	1,360	667	1,353	1,198	83	47	198
Marion, OH Micro Area	5,937	2,675	1,714	556	1,063	1,013	115	0	53
Marquette, MI Micro Area	4,986	4,048	3,114	720	1,680	1,422	107	39	172
Marshall, TX Micro Area	4,068	3,131	1,749	641	1,381	590	0	73	124
Martinsville, VA Micro Area	5,270	3,103	1,408	479	1,194	1,238	97	86	206
McAllen-Edinburg-Mission, TX Metro Area	18,717	14,099	11,736	1,979	4,567	3,807	190	277	99
Meadville, PA Micro Area	9,324	3,249	3,464	869	1,638	1,715	78	36	29
Medford, OR Metro Area	10,369	16,968	16,523	2,350	4,925	4,563	450	238	373
Memphis, TN-MS-AR Metro Area	60,837	46,303	48,605	12,673	19,347	11,403	2,552	650	344
Merced, CA Metro Area	6,310	8,063	4,362	1,952	1,744	1,985	387	72	105
Meridian, MS Micro Area	6,560	5,243	2,506	1,272	2,033	1,311	77	0	14
Miami-Fort Lauderdale-West Palm Beach, FL Metro Area	301,821	245,322	337,379	29,774	44,314	63,756	3,726	2,047	412
Michigan City-La Porte, IN Metro Area	8,337	4,090	4,082	1,346	2,903	1,625	138	33	97

Table E-4: Metropolitan/Micropolitan Statistical Areas - Educational Attainment and Veterans Status, Persons 55 and Over—*Continued*

	High School or Equivalent	Some College or Associates Degree	Bachelor's Degree or Higher	Veterans by Age and Gender					
				Male			Female		
				55 to 64 Years	65 to 74 Years	75 Years and Over	55 to 64 Years	65 to 74 Years	75 Years and Over
Midland, MI Metro Area	6,422	4,324	3,692	315	1,759	1,565	0	45	172
Midland, TX Metro Area	4,044	4,587	6,104	1,167	1,125	1,558	71	0	228
Milwaukee-Waukesha-West Allis, WI Metro Area	85,825	64,755	70,506	10,708	19,875	18,943	1,219	729	338
Minneapolis-St. Paul-Bloomington, MN-WI Metro Area	149,868	142,954	175,667	26,585	44,864	41,963	2,652	918	495
Minot, ND Micro Area	4,228	2,682	1,962	996	1,408	1,297	140	88	128
Missoula, MT Metro Area	4,779	5,731	6,410	844	2,685	1,878	154	111	172
Mobile, AL Metro Area	25,903	15,772	14,147	4,336	6,201	5,200	674	560	35
Modesto, CA Metro Area	21,199	18,262	12,849	3,659	4,878	4,209	208	420	204
Monroe, LA Metro Area	11,379	7,624	5,751	1,550	2,895	2,143	783	309	217
Monroe, MI Metro Area	11,606	7,770	5,413	1,489	2,834	1,802	61	136	179
Montgomery, AL Metro Area	19,123	13,145	14,631	5,262	5,699	4,161	698	477	232
Morehead City, NC Micro Area	3,532	5,649	5,795	966	1,941	2,222	250	38	19
Morgantown, WV Metro Area	8,240	3,862	5,492	1,255	2,069	1,393	93	98	94
Morristown, TN Metro Area	7,961	5,895	3,008	1,294	1,771	1,898	238	110	148
Moses Lake, WA Micro Area	3,815	5,408	2,410	845	1,911	1,065	0	38	150
Mount Airy, NC Micro Area	4,627	4,315	2,347	449	1,136	934	56	46	210
Mount Pleasant, MI Micro Area	3,607	2,666	2,073	249	1,024	748	12	49	172
Mount Vernon-Anacortes, WA Metro Area	6,268	9,643	8,800	1,936	2,696	2,592	226	74	118
Muncie, IN Metro Area	7,950	4,659	4,389	1,059	1,482	1,987	279	46	198
Muskegon, MI Metro Area	10,433	10,038	6,211	2,017	3,540	2,266	160	141	43
Muskogee, OK Micro Area	4,862	2,517	2,385	782	1,029	983	0	109	161
Myrtle Beach-Conway-North Myrtle Beach, SC-NC Metro Area	39,637	39,840	37,430	4,998	16,540	8,505	517	451	366
Nacogdoches, TX Micro Area	3,472	2,782	2,323	553	1,279	518	42	0	77
Napa, CA Metro Area	5,636	8,048	10,358	1,127	2,185	2,129	130	43	158
Naples-Immokalee-Marco Island, FL Metro Area	24,947	28,833	58,748	2,376	6,943	14,044	381	296	85
Nashville-Davidson--Murfreesboro--Franklin, TN Metro Area	80,103	67,405	70,947	12,831	24,011	18,958	1,972	1,106	254
New Bern, NC Metro Area	7,089	8,211	6,869	2,071	3,456	2,469	319	94	125
New Castle, PA Micro Area	9,051	4,515	3,454	591	2,220	1,718	78	0	44
New Haven-Milford, CT Metro Area	52,791	32,358	43,805	5,340	11,125	11,526	1,037	180	166
New Orleans-Metairie, LA Metro Area	67,146	47,592	55,401	8,397	14,786	12,799	1,584	662	309
New Philadelphia-Dover, OH Micro Area	9,794	2,950	2,258	844	1,919	1,496	99	109	195
New York-Newark-Jersey City, NY-NJ-PA Metro Area	948,843	592,038	990,871	65,008	135,332	173,410	8,231	3,878	923
Niles-Benton Harbor, MI Metro Area	9,031	9,371	8,341	1,261	2,744	2,860	167	64	104
North Port-Sarasota-Bradenton, FL Metro Area	72,736	73,609	98,891	8,399	20,302	32,771	1,734	535	450
North Wilkesboro, NC Micro Area	4,022	4,311	2,850	528	866	1,095	234	17	210
Norwich-New London, CT Metro Area	16,852	11,087	15,163	3,140	5,737	5,123	434	211	135
Oak Harbor, WA Micro Area	3,393	7,233	9,475	1,707	2,511	2,449	359	87	147
Ocala, FL Metro Area	38,997	27,278	24,954	5,079	9,898	12,816	987	587	748
Ocean City, NJ Metro Area	7,755	6,340	7,528	410	1,925	2,226	133	153	62
Odessa, TX Metro Area	4,394	4,166	2,272	377	1,230	966	125	0	228
Ogden-Clearfield, UT Metro Area	19,568	26,962	21,677	6,637	7,578	6,479	659	230	111
Ogdensburg-Massena, NY Micro Area	8,476	4,428	2,870	952	2,351	1,721	278	44	22
Oklahoma City, OK Metro Area	57,371	57,795	57,652	14,509	23,798	17,111	1,419	1,538	328
Olean, NY Micro Area	6,193	3,427	2,880	546	1,606	1,279	211	69	201
Olympia-Tumwater, WA Metro Area	11,162	15,245	19,951	4,841	6,292	4,665	1,128	734	124
Omaha-Council Bluffs, NE-IA Metro Area	42,996	37,957	37,503	10,343	14,402	11,539	2,148	468	287
Opelousas, LA Micro Area	4,132	2,565	2,440	429	1,252	529	151	0	217
Orangeburg, SC Micro Area	5,124	5,587	3,211	1,078	1,208	486	35	138	214
Orlando-Kissimmee-Sanford, FL Metro Area	116,147	98,709	101,935	27,697	33,771	28,906	3,927	3,020	458
Oshkosh-Neenah, WI Metro Area	11,550	7,886	6,217	1,448	3,023	2,927	279	91	104
Ottawa-Peru, IL Micro Area	13,077	7,943	4,029	1,232	2,628	2,273	59	11	15
Owensboro, KY Metro Area	8,247	5,842	3,937	1,297	2,206	1,773	63	39	54
Owosso, MI Micro Area	5,284	3,530	2,011	534	1,740	795	100	31	21
Oxnard-Thousand Oaks-Ventura, CA Metro Area	28,674	40,232	44,490	5,030	10,639	10,622	939	524	171
Paducah, KY-IL Micro Area	7,446	5,652	3,444	1,347	1,629	1,122	16	295	198
Palatka, FL Micro Area	7,394	4,741	2,486	1,313	2,383	1,692	10	108	229
Palm Bay-Melbourne-Titusville, FL Metro Area	43,159	43,261	39,875	11,138	15,177	16,644	1,434	1,570	481
Panama City, FL Metro Area	12,288	10,131	8,510	5,110	4,140	3,749	1,040	197	227
Parkersburg-Vienna, WV Metro Area	7,541	5,680	3,372	1,237	2,036	1,691	164	66	201
Pensacola-Ferry Pass-Brent, FL Metro Area	26,683	26,478	20,812	10,728	11,680	9,476	2,244	831	241
Peoria, IL Metro Area	23,963	19,316	15,112	2,919	5,675	5,384	475	191	118
Philadelphia-Camden-Wilmington, PA-NJ-DE-MD Metro Area	343,431	203,985	298,827	47,110	77,597	78,606	4,548	2,914	594
Phoenix-Mesa-Scottsdale, AZ Metro Area	190,069	251,323	233,964	42,194	72,868	69,634	6,323	3,580	967
Pine Bluff, AR Metro Area	7,596	2,742	2,976	1,236	1,534	1,146	22	176	138
Pinehurst-Southern Pines, NC Micro Area	5,332	5,700	10,212	1,877	1,956	2,269	452	28	52
Pittsburgh, PA Metro Area	203,837	107,795	111,013	19,313	42,733	43,861	2,425	1,564	505
Pittsfield, MA Metro Area	10,102	6,000	10,722	1,406	2,012	2,083	113	52	99
Plattsburgh, NY Micro Area	4,617	3,066	4,051	1,299	1,373	1,330	103	203	201
Pocatello, ID Metro Area	3,799	4,571	3,121	524	1,183	1,308	102	105	186
Port Angeles, WA Micro Area	4,664	9,017	7,349	1,679	2,465	3,237	58	52	11
Portland-South Portland, ME Metro Area	29,427	27,547	39,620	6,870	9,918	9,556	1,191	352	487
Portland-Vancouver-Hillsboro, OR-WA Metro Area	86,439	123,171	132,534	21,617	35,473	29,046	2,204	2,587	685
Port St. Lucie, FL Metro Area	36,062	37,115	38,131	3,880	11,132	13,068	572	414	164
Portsmouth, OH Micro Area	5,655	3,030	2,200	914	1,301	730	41	0	115
Pottsville, PA Micro Area	14,682	5,709	3,943	1,354	3,425	2,139	63	278	99

Table E-4: Metropolitan/Micropolitan Statistical Areas - Educational Attainment and Veterans Status, Persons 55 and Over—*Continued*

	High School or Equivalent	Some College or Associates Degree	Bachelor's Degree or Higher	Veterans by Age and Gender					
				Male			Female		
				55 to 64 Years	65 to 74 Years	75 Years and Over	55 to 64 Years	65 to 74 Years	75 Years and Over
Prescott, AZ Metro Area	16,506	27,537	23,416	2,400	8,881	8,611	496	485	475
Providence-Warwick, RI-MA Metro Area	89,499	59,792	74,342	10,824	23,635	21,272	1,375	757	327
Provo-Orem, UT Metro Area	10,569	16,448	19,444	1,926	4,060	3,866	0	96	96
Pueblo, CO Metro Area	9,026	11,029	7,135	2,303	3,426	2,469	265	70	119
Punta Gorda, FL Metro Area	24,459	20,657	21,146	2,312	5,950	9,723	219	240	293
Quincy, IL-MO Micro Area	7,153	3,136	2,761	578	1,507	1,171	335	42	176
Racine, WI Metro Area	11,726	8,611	8,767	1,824	3,337	2,304	84	353	196
Raleigh, NC Metro Area	41,612	44,565	61,145	11,434	14,553	10,497	1,009	1,268	239
Rapid City, SD Metro Area	8,010	7,801	8,060	2,088	3,732	2,070	73	207	54
Reading, PA Metro Area	29,135	15,058	14,784	3,200	7,151	6,418	460	276	344
Redding, CA Metro Area	9,066	16,050	8,067	1,793	3,953	3,565	312	124	111
Reno, NV Metro Area	16,844	29,910	24,191	5,746	9,327	6,852	691	293	139
Richmond, IN Micro Area	5,232	2,860	2,440	578	1,006	1,110	86	0	198
Richmond, VA Metro Area	56,795	49,779	64,445	12,863	21,506	14,884	2,029	903	297
Richmond-Berea, KY Micro Area	5,219	2,841	4,034	1,159	1,349	976	66	210	102
Riverside-San Bernardino-Ontario, CA Metro Area	148,767	187,201	138,330	30,497	48,351	46,664	3,189	1,624	865
Roanoke, VA Metro Area	21,772	17,151	16,114	3,326	6,493	5,758	902	415	177
Roanoke Rapids, NC Micro Area	4,950	2,524	2,219	1,032	489	846	161	55	210
Rochester, MN Metro Area	12,174	9,921	12,024	1,968	3,601	3,104	220	187	125
Rochester, NY Metro Area	57,783	49,456	58,269	8,958	14,728	13,991	1,567	293	352
Rockford, IL Metro Area	20,786	16,470	12,363	2,807	5,736	4,345	295	108	208
Rocky Mount, NC Metro Area	9,225	8,170	5,437	1,752	2,323	1,133	130	83	110
Rome, GA Metro Area	5,553	4,656	2,857	823	1,272	857	0	69	104
Roseburg, OR Micro Area	9,301	9,706	5,165	1,705	3,837	2,485	61	287	31
Roswell, NM Micro Area	2,066	2,957	2,753	963	629	732	47	63	84
Russellville, AR Micro Area	4,550	3,230	2,332	1,069	1,507	1,386	0	226	201
Sacramento--Roseville--Arden-Arcade, CA Metro Area	76,104	123,321	121,159	18,864	34,001	30,508	2,561	1,499	449
Saginaw, MI Metro Area	15,155	11,500	4,908	2,008	3,558	3,584	226	16	232
St. Cloud, MN Metro Area	11,828	8,232	5,904	938	2,418	3,250	151	132	66
St. George, UT Metro Area	9,363	13,756	12,230	1,101	2,552	4,219	81	237	193
St. Joseph, MO-KS Metro Area	9,273	4,956	5,238	1,414	2,211	1,620	57	29	198
St. Louis, MO-IL Metro Area	151,208	129,557	127,718	29,490	45,334	40,309	3,399	1,312	436
Salem, OH Micro Area	11,085	4,044	3,289	1,449	2,004	2,139	66	11	38
Salem, OR Metro Area	18,164	23,241	20,464	4,158	5,939	6,115	468	298	327
Salinas, CA Metro Area	9,909	16,416	19,880	2,358	4,808	4,539	351	23	142
Salisbury, MD-DE Metro Area	33,448	25,925	29,136	4,541	10,786	8,721	817	166	233
Salt Lake City, UT Metro Area	31,998	43,319	45,316	6,866	10,299	9,293	828	899	82
San Angelo, TX Metro Area	5,791	5,048	4,650	1,176	2,246	1,616	78	0	228
San Antonio-New Braunfels, TX Metro Area	82,984	93,254	85,780	27,727	39,374	27,636	7,003	2,599	425
San Diego-Carlsbad, CA Metro Area	84,677	135,379	171,826	31,145	41,586	36,604	4,585	2,156	812
Sandusky, OH Micro Area	5,920	5,504	2,768	575	1,569	1,032	0	14	195
San Francisco-Oakland-Hayward, CA Metro Area	137,799	179,652	309,050	22,954	36,214	45,221	2,747	1,789	635
San Jose-Sunnyvale-Santa Clara, CA Metro Area	45,783	67,211	112,930	6,330	10,924	17,438	893	849	246
San Luis Obispo-Paso Robles-Arroyo Grande, CA Metro Area	8,584	23,298	21,819	3,228	6,085	4,703	105	116	153
Santa Cruz-Watsonville, CA Metro Area	6,170	13,014	20,715	1,468	2,801	2,949	79	0	163
Santa Fe, NM Metro Area	6,330	8,469	18,691	1,496	2,761	2,863	237	0	110
Santa Maria-Santa Barbara, CA Metro Area	11,457	18,974	28,886	2,676	5,033	5,375	351	427	117
Santa Rosa, CA Metro Area	15,830	34,246	40,109	3,705	7,153	7,416	346	302	183
Savannah, GA Metro Area	16,786	14,330	16,828	4,345	5,420	4,494	1,203	373	104
Scranton--Wilkes-Barre--Hazleton, PA Metro Area	52,549	20,975	24,397	5,422	9,856	10,301	432	132	179
Searcy, AR Micro Area	3,666	2,743	2,346	365	974	932	79	155	106
Seattle-Tacoma-Bellevue, WA Metro Area	122,103	165,277	194,729	38,626	52,812	42,046	6,820	2,448	388
Sebastian-Vero Beach, FL Metro Area	15,766	15,496	16,453	2,094	4,739	6,873	141	83	254
Sebring, FL Metro Area	13,646	11,377	6,855	1,040	2,283	4,422	278	278	170
Seneca, SC Micro Area	4,348	5,423	4,829	1,054	1,756	2,040	0	89	214
Sevierville, TN Micro Area	6,122	5,870	3,599	1,536	2,071	1,408	152	192	211
Shawnee, OK Micro Area	4,055	3,726	2,671	870	1,318	1,230	61	67	161
Sheboygan, WI Metro Area	9,196	5,532	4,019	1,241	2,185	2,109	84	0	79
Shelby, NC Micro Area	6,998	4,778	3,431	2,038	1,427	1,291	200	0	210
Shelton, WA Micro Area	4,379	5,348	3,730	1,370	2,045	1,138	0	0	204
Sherman-Denison, TX Metro Area	7,812	7,686	5,190	1,248	2,858	1,936	149	595	195
Show Low, AZ Micro Area	4,904	7,413	3,814	1,128	2,606	1,640	117	0	146
Shreveport-Bossier City, LA Metro Area	28,070	18,816	14,111	5,244	6,951	6,012	680	247	150
Sierra Vista-Douglas, AZ Metro Area	7,206	9,543	7,431	4,009	3,973	3,650	1,131	357	488
Sioux City, IA-NE-SD Metro Area	9,761	7,600	5,222	1,785	2,680	2,745	26	59	198
Sioux Falls, SD Metro Area	12,795	9,551	10,197	2,736	3,738	3,150	582	200	258
Somerset, PA Micro Area	9,261	3,008	2,662	626	1,919	1,157	0	0	46
South Bend-Mishawaka, IN-MI Metro Area	21,184	12,445	13,792	2,479	4,242	4,636	376	258	129
Spartanburg, SC Metro Area	18,339	15,452	11,875	3,366	5,293	4,418	699	78	116
Spokane-Spokane Valley, WA Metro Area	27,435	36,250	28,258	7,240	13,168	8,999	1,647	768	531
Springfield, IL Metro Area	12,799	9,337	12,187	2,566	4,137	2,919	87	125	57
Springfield, MA Metro Area	31,979	25,409	32,202	5,303	8,989	7,689	1,104	213	153
Springfield, MO Metro Area	29,403	22,836	15,244	4,075	7,910	5,789	553	507	190
Springfield, OH Metro Area	9,756	7,485	4,917	2,298	2,696	2,641	481	74	88

Table E-4: Metropolitan/Micropolitan Statistical Areas - Educational Attainment and Veterans Status, Persons 55 and Over—*Continued*

	High School or Equivalent	Some College or Associates Degree	Bachelor's Degree or Higher	Veterans by Age and Gender					
				Male			Female		
				55 to 64 Years	65 to 74 Years	75 Years and Over	55 to 64 Years	65 to 74 Years	75 Years and Over
State College, PA Metro Area	9,019	3,543	8,743	1,160	2,004	1,281	172	0	177
Statesboro, GA Micro Area	2,394	2,218	2,471	117	724	695	130	53	226
Staunton-Waynesboro, VA Metro Area	8,590	6,202	5,962	2,075	2,424	1,625	297	0	206
Stevens Point, WI Micro Area	5,188	2,874	2,690	462	1,606	914	70	11	28
Stillwater, OK Micro Area	3,049	3,112	4,265	565	1,344	1,094	48	31	161
Stockton-Lodi, CA Metro Area	24,846	31,313	18,327	4,989	7,571	6,843	813	477	159
Sumter, SC Metro Area	6,058	5,024	3,022	1,683	2,274	1,856	304	35	249
Sunbury, PA Micro Area	11,904	2,877	2,475	1,338	1,424	1,825	242	0	156
Syracuse, NY Metro Area	38,584	30,169	29,698	5,682	10,614	9,091	684	748	198
Talladega-Sylacauga, AL Micro Area	6,956	3,690	2,805	1,576	1,644	695	78	0	145
Tallahassee, FL Metro Area	15,928	13,630	19,772	4,587	5,484	4,294	51	41	288
Tampa-St. Petersburg-Clearwater, FL Metro Area	206,020	173,694	164,618	37,570	57,728	61,419	7,167	4,096	649
Terre Haute, IN Metro Area	11,287	7,811	6,780	2,056	2,835	1,850	172	50	242
Texarkana, TX-AR Metro Area	8,372	7,658	4,597	1,786	2,256	1,679	102	96	198
The Villages, FL Metro Area	19,191	21,830	27,578	1,000	8,603	7,079	121	204	229
Toledo, OH Metro Area	33,146	26,778	24,446	5,393	8,402	7,570	506	157	201
Topeka, KS Metro Area	17,941	11,576	10,394	2,915	5,585	3,495	487	255	123
Torrington, CT Micro Area	12,781	9,771	11,364	1,531	3,228	3,201	183	0	207
Traverse City, MI Micro Area	9,325	9,545	12,189	1,486	4,039	2,310	247	62	105
Trenton, NJ Metro Area	18,239	10,664	20,217	1,642	2,261	3,081	0	99	71
Truckee-Grass Valley, CA Micro Area	4,436	11,299	11,527	630	2,561	3,006	145	216	247
Tucson, AZ Metro Area	46,908	61,091	74,043	11,997	22,136	19,175	2,190	824	558
Tullahoma-Manchester, TN Micro Area	8,087	4,187	3,465	1,679	1,796	1,951	17	0	73
Tulsa, OK Metro Area	49,640	47,762	39,801	9,237	16,095	13,563	1,134	860	250
Tupelo, MS Micro Area	6,389	5,884	3,694	874	1,938	1,315	188	84	218
Tuscaloosa, AL Metro Area	13,826	7,634	8,649	1,945	2,866	2,180	167	120	85
Twin Falls, ID Micro Area	4,388	6,888	2,642	1,096	1,193	1,731	116	542	204
Tyler, TX Metro Area	7,833	13,995	10,785	1,185	3,499	3,306	276	22	228
Ukiah, CA Micro Area	3,764	7,041	6,191	349	2,011	1,334	161	0	242
Urban Honolulu, HI Metro Area	47,101	45,493	53,584	9,804	14,896	14,833	1,277	406	180
Utica-Rome, NY Metro Area	20,010	14,996	13,249	3,319	4,074	4,964	160	251	145
Valdosta, GA Metro Area	6,874	4,290	3,422	1,565	2,360	1,353	242	156	66
Vallejo-Fairfield, CA Metro Area	17,483	25,069	20,377	5,502	6,925	5,651	354	572	235
Victoria, TX Metro Area	4,668	5,222	2,900	894	1,037	1,636	9	117	228
Vineland-Bridgeton, NJ Metro Area	8,154	4,907	3,801	954	1,791	1,619	39	50	206
Virginia Beach-Norfolk-Newport News, VA-NC Metro Area	70,360	72,371	79,574	37,848	32,165	24,861	7,519	2,661	342
Visalia-Porterville, CA Metro Area	12,730	15,095	8,488	2,566	3,357	3,210	337	158	102
Waco, TX Metro Area	12,496	11,583	9,986	2,867	3,689	3,279	514	259	479
Walla Walla, WA Metro Area	2,771	4,546	4,011	497	1,276	583	649	90	204
Warner Robins, GA Metro Area	9,730	5,991	4,773	4,318	3,033	2,007	776	0	120
Warsaw, IN Micro Area	5,014	2,752	3,745	769	1,378	1,241	91	0	122
Washington-Arlington-Alexandria, DC-VA-MD-WV Metro Area	175,442	168,829	373,150	67,368	62,852	64,550	12,854	5,620	988
Waterloo-Cedar Falls, IA Metro Area	12,948	6,849	6,138	1,746	3,138	2,425	329	95	131
Watertown-Fort Atkinson, WI Micro Area	5,655	4,113	3,487	846	1,290	958	92	0	151
Watertown-Fort Drum, NY Metro Area	6,416	3,787	3,218	1,348	1,224	1,489	141	53	36
Wausau, WI Metro Area	10,226	4,880	5,121	849	2,020	1,942	268	109	32
Weirton-Steubenville, WV-OH Metro Area	14,760	5,846	3,564	1,649	2,784	2,500	14	124	93
Wenatchee, WA Metro Area	6,341	7,205	5,943	1,028	2,693	1,169	103	42	137
Wheeling, WV-OH Metro Area	14,298	6,879	6,571	1,341	2,233	2,475	270	262	74
Whitewater-Elkhorn, WI Micro Area	7,063	4,891	4,638	827	1,640	1,130	34	14	151
Wichita, KS Metro Area	30,725	30,399	26,028	7,805	8,622	7,878	1,256	399	181
Wichita Falls, TX Metro Area	7,525	7,198	4,846	2,220	2,399	1,674	409	25	100
Williamsport, PA Metro Area	9,516	5,537	4,645	1,305	2,102	2,226	218	140	23
Wilmington, NC Metro Area	12,863	14,742	18,441	2,669	5,515	4,624	869	139	63
Wilson, NC Micro Area	3,686	3,458	3,386	1,644	1,454	722	155	254	210
Winchester, VA-WV Metro Area	8,710	5,475	7,051	1,740	3,113	2,835	164	129	184
Winston-Salem, NC Metro Area	41,355	32,768	23,898	7,005	10,688	9,235	917	359	234
Wisconsin Rapids-Marshfield, WI Micro Area	6,273	4,008	3,147	974	1,945	1,353	62	0	151
Wooster, OH Micro Area	7,938	4,469	4,234	644	1,878	1,494	126	78	136
Worcester, MA-CT Metro Area	47,399	37,440	42,962	9,862	12,549	12,900	591	390	61
Yakima, WA Metro Area	8,597	10,604	7,968	1,258	2,848	2,702	47	128	44
York-Hanover, PA Metro Area	34,939	13,972	16,417	4,526	6,514	6,778	543	235	177
Youngstown-Warren-Boardman, OH-PA Metro Area	54,812	25,646	20,080	5,610	10,958	10,813	594	316	120
Yuba City, CA Metro Area	4,518	7,430	6,005	2,140	1,666	2,210	505	238	166
Yuma, AZ Metro Area	11,454	10,986	5,328	2,166	2,947	4,602	317	153	114
Zanesville, OH Micro Area	8,167	2,877	1,737	728	1,703	1,108	106	0	195

Table E-5: 116th Congressional Districts - Educational Attainment and Veterans Status, Persons 55 and Over

	High School or Equivalent	Some College or Associates Degree	Bachelor's Degree or Higher	Veterans by Age and Gender					
				Male			Female		
				55 to 64 Years	65 to 74 Years	75 Years and Over	55 to 64 Years	65 to 74 Years	75 Years and Over
Alabama									
Congressional District 1	43,667	34,429	30,456	9,676	12,982	10,851	1,400	656	80
Congressional District 2	42,775	28,596	23,581	9,241	12,167	9,217	1,495	664	291
Congressional District 3	43,960	29,136	21,553	10,229	13,122	8,204	1,486	1,026	210
Congressional District 4	50,020	29,995	21,759	6,285	10,262	9,896	811	524	144
Congressional District 5	35,397	29,899	35,458	10,468	13,591	9,304	1,783	432	167
Congressional District 6	37,422	32,414	35,870	4,919	12,318	8,812	483	513	425
Congressional District 7	35,624	24,656	18,675	6,695	8,104	6,236	1,119	383	122
Alaska									
Congressional District (at Large)	21,855	27,953	28,693	11,175	13,837	7,470	1,934	968	283
Arizona									
Congressional District 1	31,365	49,516	44,620	7,418	16,375	12,432	1,355	701	281
Congressional District 2	36,642	47,438	59,773	12,822	17,870	16,386	2,862	810	503
Congressional District 3	22,948	28,013	15,984	5,337	8,954	6,395	624	426	386
Congressional District 4	67,585	83,623	48,861	9,150	29,401	25,275	1,896	1,474	839
Congressional District 5	41,103	47,638	41,567	8,956	14,104	13,970	1,158	780	332
Congressional District 6	31,584	47,350	62,438	6,738	11,452	14,104	1,462	430	570
Congressional District 7	16,323	16,467	9,415	3,772	5,125	4,041	425	500	22
Congressional District 8	50,201	65,316	53,819	9,944	17,441	18,692	1,349	795	538
Congressional District 9	16,353	29,703	36,449	6,587	8,438	7,682	838	236	316
Arkansas									
Congressional District 1	52,414	28,911	18,657	7,904	12,311	8,472	820	335	145
Congressional District 2	39,785	31,850	31,773	8,935	12,346	9,748	938	383	257
Congressional District 3	39,958	30,617	31,233	6,348	10,834	11,221	900	430	184
Congressional District 4	54,522	33,400	25,890	6,950	13,845	10,395	966	905	247
California									
Congressional District 1	35,545	62,372	44,983	7,332	15,547	15,195	840	424	341
Congressional District 2	24,628	47,153	72,177	5,414	12,262	11,443	545	458	482
Congressional District 3	25,208	33,179	31,905	8,063	10,259	9,432	921	911	321
Congressional District 4	34,802	62,762	52,022	6,370	18,836	15,545	901	134	203
Congressional District 5	24,683	45,649	46,466	5,373	10,375	10,033	638	398	195
Congressional District 6	21,391	28,052	27,771	5,177	8,651	6,388	517	372	205
Congressional District 7	25,368	43,163	39,558	7,489	10,156	11,004	1,101	969	314
Congressional District 8	26,796	34,888	17,636	7,418	11,495	8,503	328	514	366
Congressional District 9	28,439	33,973	20,424	5,167	7,680	8,500	759	591	214
Congressional District 10	28,480	26,963	18,265	5,639	7,722	6,159	378	540	215
Congressional District 11	20,679	32,421	61,063	4,060	7,581	8,611	312	307	172
Congressional District 12	18,078	22,455	46,850	2,769	4,571	5,413	592	154	236
Congressional District 13	18,996	25,080	47,131	3,484	3,769	6,036	786	224	201
Congressional District 14	22,313	31,139	51,908	3,886	5,384	8,259	295	336	236
Congressional District 15	29,843	27,089	34,148	2,852	6,009	6,113	284	160	308
Congressional District 16	17,180	19,692	11,639	5,322	4,992	4,799	520	144	337
Congressional District 17	18,331	24,179	39,370	2,341	3,197	5,338	342	135	177
Congressional District 18	13,926	27,252	67,748	2,784	5,182	8,147	344	427	169
Congressional District 19	20,899	27,171	30,331	2,809	4,406	6,043	298	354	113
Congressional District 20	16,979	29,534	37,078	3,547	7,863	7,584	517	23	214
Congressional District 21	14,830	13,010	7,561	3,710	3,534	4,254	292	143	272
Congressional District 22	22,360	32,295	25,542	4,685	7,115	6,890	698	361	124
Congressional District 23	22,097	34,510	23,003	5,473	10,081	8,312	983	420	445
Congressional District 24	20,327	42,861	51,117	5,930	11,188	10,324	552	543	189
Congressional District 25	21,687	27,458	26,242	4,547	7,588	5,360	572	429	99
Congressional District 26	21,706	34,075	39,202	4,079	9,191	8,985	785	524	152
Congressional District 27	23,347	28,472	43,781	2,396	4,347	5,584	137	88	146
Congressional District 28	24,113	26,979	38,145	1,268	3,511	5,420	94	139	211
Congressional District 29	17,713	20,570	13,460	1,640	1,685	3,996	205	365	80
Congressional District 30	20,440	31,554	49,463	2,667	4,554	6,941	128	84	245
Congressional District 31	20,323	24,891	22,024	4,873	7,044	6,085	582	179	99
Congressional District 32	23,966	22,584	17,209	3,337	4,342	3,985	232	97	193
Congressional District 33	17,485	30,425	77,199	2,236	6,143	11,828	230	197	209
Congressional District 34	18,079	13,140	18,928	3,976	2,147	2,094	122	186	179
Congressional District 35	17,480	18,171	9,991	3,079	4,189	3,099	137	40	189
Congressional District 36	42,934	51,796	49,151	3,970	13,065	15,727	936	542	483
Congressional District 37	17,181	23,168	30,626	3,283	2,843	4,977	0	39	131
Congressional District 38	28,046	25,051	20,673	2,600	4,962	6,206	195	226	107
Congressional District 39	23,201	30,405	43,001	3,543	5,050	6,273	379	114	128
Congressional District 40	10,876	8,524	6,299	1,003	1,798	1,560	177	207	64
Congressional District 41	14,863	21,157	14,922	3,454	4,696	4,547	629	90	339
Congressional District 42	27,039	35,769	20,159	6,206	7,752	8,013	613	259	583
Congressional District 43	20,094	26,902	23,609	3,130	4,510	5,402	185	457	52
Congressional District 44	16,016	17,140	9,207	2,962	3,685	2,656	57	137	151
Congressional District 45	21,532	33,545	58,149	2,832	7,646	7,402	194	79	164
Congressional District 46	16,031	19,375	12,672	1,544	4,123	4,112	255	237	57
Congressional District 47	16,856	27,864	27,416	3,794	6,054	6,509	433	295	313
Congressional District 48	21,369	35,729	54,669	3,862	8,639	10,482	204	164	382

Table E-5: 116th Congressional Districts - Educational Attainment and Veterans Status, Persons 55 and Over—*Continued*

	High School or Equivalent	Some College or Associates Degree	Bachelor's Degree or Higher	Veterans by Age and Gender					
				Male			Female		
				55 to 64 Years	65 to 74 Years	75 Years and Over	55 to 64 Years	65 to 74 Years	75 Years and Over
California—Cont.									
Congressional District 49	19,699	35,360	54,744	6,760	8,942	10,138	1,135	613	242
Congressional District 50	25,029	39,501	34,661	8,216	10,264	10,588	867	278	451
Congressional District 51	16,436	19,689	11,761	5,210	5,642	3,906	608	127	347
Congressional District 52	15,414	30,129	56,994	6,789	10,931	8,663	838	284	630
Congressional District 53	18,845	28,917	34,990	6,879	9,458	7,876	1,292	955	313
Colorado									
Congressional District 1	19,041	22,262	45,034	6,117	8,895	7,753	498	461	141
Congressional District 2	21,008	32,065	65,625	5,279	10,449	10,180	1,252	511	295
Congressional District 3	35,713	42,145	48,332	8,246	14,114	12,067	1,016	630	218
Congressional District 4	30,690	37,698	38,532	7,889	12,224	10,374	1,094	507	441
Congressional District 5	27,256	37,711	40,929	16,026	17,674	11,469	3,083	1,335	353
Congressional District 6	21,860	30,376	42,107	6,506	9,837	7,943	1,319	802	303
Congressional District 7	30,245	33,677	35,437	6,283	12,191	9,736	1,262	494	185
Connecticut									
Congressional District 1	43,825	25,065	36,721	4,981	9,050	9,333	599	49	208
Congressional District 2	40,259	32,034	42,704	7,498	11,975	11,444	940	380	144
Congressional District 3	43,286	28,219	38,233	3,885	9,660	9,223	782	204	111
Congressional District 4	28,228	22,109	48,881	2,420	6,066	8,600	216	79	265
Congressional District 5	38,789	27,312	39,844	5,358	8,021	10,338	582	142	170
Delaware									
Congressional District (at Large)	60,989	42,852	55,314	11,883	18,364	16,475	1,903	401	261
District of Columbia									
Delegate District (at Large)	19,070	14,420	38,742	3,454	3,821	5,615	572	182	336
Florida									
Congressional District 1	42,262	42,693	35,471	18,087	21,043	14,777	3,008	1,542	437
Congressional District 2	53,097	41,344	35,601	12,469	16,755	15,723	1,701	459	461
Congressional District 3	43,381	33,931	34,008	12,155	15,573	12,387	1,243	489	342
Congressional District 4	37,954	40,064	48,891	12,611	13,042	13,807	1,697	734	516
Congressional District 5	36,278	24,666	19,292	10,182	10,996	6,387	1,800	577	181
Congressional District 6	62,658	60,925	54,557	11,019	20,393	21,371	1,088	1,623	291
Congressional District 7	30,931	28,880	39,380	7,623	10,759	9,876	1,486	645	212
Congressional District 8	60,062	59,505	56,773	13,736	20,487	23,624	1,843	1,838	579
Congressional District 9	47,625	39,640	29,234	11,968	13,993	11,073	1,130	656	287
Congressional District 10	29,122	23,916	23,802	6,915	7,621	5,604	1,030	1,116	223
Congressional District 11	97,375	83,668	70,712	12,284	28,713	31,950	1,647	1,116	727
Congressional District 12	70,542	59,165	45,275	8,621	19,235	21,670	1,506	1,166	343
Congressional District 13	53,060	47,733	53,099	10,059	15,113	17,664	1,656	1,824	417
Congressional District 14	30,838	24,194	30,875	7,477	8,952	7,474	2,011	220	118
Congressional District 15	48,090	35,403	30,957	10,212	12,251	12,599	1,350	1,025	219
Congressional District 16	64,552	60,807	81,666	8,267	17,569	25,878	2,320	738	518
Congressional District 17	85,272	73,020	69,445	8,693	19,908	31,524	1,005	832	389
Congressional District 18	51,794	57,902	69,951	6,356	15,851	20,524	785	574	218
Congressional District 19	71,858	70,365	103,285	8,790	20,178	27,389	1,194	667	477
Congressional District 20	38,259	22,975	21,260	5,238	4,098	5,927	719	24	34
Congressional District 21	52,562	50,493	77,600	4,176	9,657	19,328	349	287	90
Congressional District 22	45,127	40,404	63,362	5,692	8,784	14,521	560	269	257
Congressional District 23	36,596	37,000	44,738	3,291	5,310	7,956	324	516	188
Congressional District 24	32,481	18,443	17,374	2,979	4,681	2,027	883	306	229
Congressional District 25	36,007	24,139	38,777	2,756	5,748	6,936	100	203	191
Congressional District 26	28,840	23,340	27,248	3,075	3,932	2,927	301	323	229
Congressional District 27	32,641	26,329	44,322	2,074	3,231	4,102	277	162	122
Georgia									
Congressional District 1	35,032	26,956	30,102	9,567	11,084	8,790	2,139	1,101	246
Congressional District 2	37,241	24,310	17,565	8,859	11,800	7,086	1,910	567	182
Congressional District 3	41,138	29,267	27,001	9,131	12,760	9,282	1,033	851	99
Congressional District 4	25,316	27,491	29,628	8,098	10,215	5,220	1,796	458	113
Congressional District 5	24,714	19,300	28,955	6,969	5,883	4,401	1,257	222	53
Congressional District 6	17,547	25,533	51,453	3,184	7,489	6,917	581	343	323
Congressional District 7	22,094	23,294	27,231	5,422	5,600	6,129	564	558	103
Congressional District 8	42,275	26,374	19,084	10,426	10,061	8,155	947	1,157	120
Congressional District 9	46,176	37,248	35,464	6,865	15,761	11,924	1,075	439	417
Congressional District 10	36,739	25,307	27,458	7,623	11,938	7,670	949	168	285
Congressional District 11	28,050	25,359	38,386	6,002	10,890	7,713	1,318	265	226
Congressional District 12	39,521	23,011	18,555	8,680	11,431	7,570	1,214	1,405	118
Congressional District 13	29,770	22,804	20,070	9,400	10,138	5,510	1,704	722	122
Congressional District 14	39,748	24,668	16,737	6,129	8,804	6,226	752	279	104
Hawaii									
Congressional District 1	35,475	33,499	42,419	6,475	10,293	11,393	806	276	119
Congressional District 2	35,138	38,648	39,811	8,373	14,589	10,584	634	302	187

Table E-5: 116th Congressional Districts - Educational Attainment and Veterans Status, Persons 55 and Over—*Continued*

	High School or Equivalent	Some College or Associates Degree	Bachelor's Degree or Higher	Veterans by Age and Gender					
				Male			Female		
				55 to 64 Years	65 to 74 Years	75 Years and Over	55 to 64 Years	65 to 74 Years	75 Years and Over
Idaho									
Congressional District 1	50,679	53,404	38,410	12,665	19,745	14,763	1,837	673	409
Congressional District 2	35,427	45,666	33,029	7,201	12,711	11,136	1,582	897	304
Illinois									
Congressional District 1	34,155	34,713	26,303	4,894	8,046	8,121	297	472	165
Congressional District 2	39,025	32,576	22,408	5,004	8,425	7,597	360	207	177
Congressional District 3	42,045	25,045	20,260	3,757	6,403	7,622	101	92	224
Congressional District 4	25,188	10,944	8,885	1,585	2,375	2,324	118	90	496
Congressional District 5	28,068	17,940	32,213	1,732	5,046	4,720	61	40	191
Congressional District 6	30,267	32,733	48,408	4,069	7,425	7,289	251	108	129
Congressional District 7	26,695	19,731	29,321	3,370	4,675	3,272	640	45	95
Congressional District 8	29,536	24,729	27,483	2,508	6,249	6,206	426	156	214
Congressional District 9	25,093	27,245	59,377	1,781	4,494	7,907	255	116	314
Congressional District 10	24,741	26,599	44,821	5,323	6,001	7,756	854	383	195
Congressional District 11	25,355	24,818	26,238	3,921	7,501	6,942	196	129	111
Congressional District 12	43,733	32,630	23,874	8,763	13,955	10,172	1,096	445	242
Congressional District 13	42,398	28,463	29,503	5,983	11,584	8,617	282	372	212
Congressional District 14	35,501	27,415	32,111	4,607	10,259	8,044	533	292	196
Congressional District 15	55,262	39,997	21,232	6,767	13,919	11,426	373	375	242
Congressional District 16	49,207	34,038	26,640	5,657	12,362	10,160	454	172	238
Congressional District 17	49,985	38,949	21,570	6,224	12,438	10,300	468	265	188
Congressional District 18	52,390	32,729	34,983	5,870	12,487	11,337	891	328	245
Indiana									
Congressional District 1	53,540	24,253	22,439	6,912	10,970	9,338	625	164	316
Congressional District 2	51,198	24,552	25,725	5,461	10,786	10,052	731	557	171
Congressional District 3	49,066	28,812	22,610	5,763	12,079	8,263	599	563	182
Congressional District 4	45,691	31,120	26,738	7,622	11,009	9,143	271	372	402
Congressional District 5	37,580	29,922	39,141	6,297	11,194	8,804	764	672	182
Congressional District 6	57,439	28,269	23,127	8,175	11,047	10,825	660	319	213
Congressional District 7	32,272	23,516	17,074	7,943	8,921	7,260	1,404	791	74
Congressional District 8	53,962	32,386	23,537	7,422	12,701	10,739	955	244	350
Congressional District 9	47,738	27,117	28,717	6,295	12,296	9,175	532	583	210
Iowa									
Congressional District 1	61,141	33,910	28,670	7,880	14,959	12,280	1,173	356	261
Congressional District 2	53,433	36,560	31,479	6,535	11,575	12,026	931	307	222
Congressional District 3	45,326	36,149	32,158	5,744	13,600	10,189	1,327	186	82
Congressional District 4	58,875	39,282	29,618	5,198	12,465	13,122	596	369	204
Kansas									
Congressional District 1	41,818	34,973	26,243	4,987	11,043	10,533	357	410	202
Congressional District 2	47,911	34,321	30,358	8,119	13,803	11,242	1,511	385	197
Congressional District 3	25,713	27,198	47,023	5,512	8,746	8,330	944	341	190
Congressional District 4	37,339	35,560	30,105	8,486	10,265	9,577	1,261	629	244
Kentucky									
Congressional District 1	56,677	29,817	22,051	6,793	11,979	9,155	617	497	217
Congressional District 2	45,822	29,243	23,992	10,208	14,516	9,990	1,233	396	301
Congressional District 3	37,371	32,647	34,002	8,491	10,536	9,418	1,053	550	164
Congressional District 4	44,644	28,897	26,198	7,559	11,817	8,218	686	447	156
Congressional District 5	45,909	21,343	13,046	4,150	9,842	7,610	81	400	240
Congressional District 6	36,709	27,255	31,835	7,004	9,301	8,094	466	506	290
Louisiana									
Congressional District 1	45,198	30,119	36,838	5,101	10,807	8,489	562	443	198
Congressional District 2	39,768	26,936	23,973	6,174	7,687	6,247	1,194	521	298
Congressional District 3	41,371	26,706	22,530	5,912	9,875	9,558	1,100	687	428
Congressional District 4	48,672	30,426	22,201	8,044	11,899	9,603	1,212	506	219
Congressional District 5	47,933	28,750	21,857	5,969	11,576	8,783	1,061	449	239
Congressional District 6	38,766	29,929	31,433	3,847	10,424	9,125	333	585	123
Maine									
Congressional District 1	39,494	36,879	52,339	9,572	13,077	13,097	1,481	371	488
Congressional District 2	52,860	34,699	31,205	10,756	15,921	11,443	1,022	658	405
Maryland									
Congressional District 1	49,649	33,267	39,233	6,667	14,807	10,936	727	405	299
Congressional District 2	35,099	27,682	29,032	7,902	9,931	8,644	1,464	560	166
Congressional District 3	30,341	25,640	46,023	6,355	9,196	9,857	1,193	1,126	519
Congressional District 4	30,004	27,379	31,019	9,932	8,617	8,896	1,601	448	219
Congressional District 5	33,578	24,744	34,546	11,476	10,414	9,540	2,412	834	379
Congressional District 6	33,299	23,649	47,059	5,811	7,593	8,646	1,575	609	774
Congressional District 7	29,297	25,592	38,255	6,909	8,980	7,771	1,280	741	295
Congressional District 8	25,039	21,629	66,065	4,894	7,206	9,809	1,093	590	371
Massachusetts									
Congressional District 1	43,166	31,583	37,968	7,493	11,948	9,632	1,206	279	185
Congressional District 2	35,779	29,026	41,766	7,048	9,163	10,194	488	525	37
Congressional District 3	30,245	22,561	34,394	5,308	5,772	9,020	515	181	114

Table E-5: 116th Congressional Districts - Educational Attainment and Veterans Status, Persons 55 and Over—*Continued*

| | | | | Veterans by Age and Gender | | | | | |
| | | | | Male | | | Female | | |
	High School or Equivalent	Some College or Associates Degree	Bachelor's Degree or Higher	55 to 64 Years	65 to 74 Years	75 Years and Over	55 to 64 Years	65 to 74 Years	75 Years and Over
Massachusetts—Cont.									
Congressional District 4	33,451	27,378	52,748	4,306	8,786	10,388	363	258	321
Congressional District 5	30,376	25,258	56,381	1,988	6,012	9,266	189	154	361
Congressional District 6	42,827	34,326	53,337	4,945	11,613	11,682	621	113	291
Congressional District 7	23,818	14,634	24,764	1,739	2,901	3,097	105	361	188
Congressional District 8	36,784	29,689	41,041	6,023	7,138	10,481	165	0	154
Congressional District 9	44,854	37,980	59,668	6,409	12,503	13,817	254	511	305
Michigan									
Congressional District 1	56,802	47,577	45,014	8,790	18,247	14,393	1,149	525	186
Congressional District 2	42,191	36,228	27,896	5,873	10,973	10,167	418	507	171
Congressional District 3	38,289	33,335	30,393	5,723	12,621	8,430	742	226	230
Congressional District 4	56,941	41,018	23,778	6,041	14,704	12,450	395	387	173
Congressional District 5	48,126	38,438	20,495	7,132	12,249	10,068	668	215	277
Congressional District 6	41,742	36,471	33,100	5,803	11,283	9,941	536	506	247
Congressional District 7	48,924	41,745	28,415	6,343	12,894	9,457	516	279	210
Congressional District 8	30,278	35,603	37,689	4,856	9,716	7,435	258	87	251
Congressional District 9	38,036	35,662	27,984	4,815	8,608	9,864	332	335	235
Congressional District 10	53,759	41,693	21,605	5,605	13,278	9,733	373	497	159
Congressional District 11	32,880	34,500	46,182	3,341	8,385	7,752	242	159	72
Congressional District 12	31,248	28,298	30,184	4,137	8,204	7,189	347	421	295
Congressional District 13	38,690	25,984	13,596	6,494	6,235	6,171	497	311	280
Congressional District 14	31,181	31,546	39,386	5,992	8,419	7,981	866	121	144
Minnesota									
Congressional District 1	46,669	30,620	28,381	5,463	10,833	9,585	999	279	134
Congressional District 2	30,983	30,900	31,383	6,619	8,941	9,766	825	62	156
Congressional District 3	28,024	32,909	47,858	4,464	9,265	10,013	368	61	368
Congressional District 4	28,108	26,469	40,599	4,408	7,506	7,843	758	675	194
Congressional District 5	22,752	23,941	35,456	4,839	6,729	6,798	344	40	211
Congressional District 6	37,292	27,093	21,409	5,361	10,524	8,303	425	188	88
Congressional District 7	54,536	37,360	25,483	6,104	12,876	12,534	703	817	165
Congressional District 8	50,856	42,555	32,764	7,504	15,829	13,466	801	550	290
Mississippi									
Congressional District 1	43,540	29,725	19,166	7,073	9,679	7,852	919	263	94
Congressional District 2	29,481	26,970	23,682	4,970	6,557	5,199	630	728	148
Congressional District 3	40,707	31,595	29,559	5,306	7,891	7,901	514	253	202
Congressional District 4	40,020	38,007	26,579	8,245	13,179	9,681	1,689	780	289
Missouri									
Congressional District 1	30,922	28,835	27,955	8,132	9,797	7,529	1,144	473	115
Congressional District 2	38,242	40,430	56,481	5,115	9,613	13,297	292	282	263
Congressional District 3	51,732	32,999	26,067	7,695	15,540	11,591	1,445	74	201
Congressional District 4	52,501	34,780	26,592	9,753	15,348	12,571	1,538	623	165
Congressional District 5	44,240	33,427	28,462	8,889	11,624	9,427	669	562	142
Congressional District 6	52,908	34,537	28,146	6,273	14,934	10,277	888	246	279
Congressional District 7	51,870	41,577	27,130	7,860	15,194	10,742	1,217	497	246
Congressional District 8	58,288	31,317	21,020	9,630	15,966	11,840	1,417	394	311
Montana									
Congressional District (at Large)	62,803	60,305	60,539	11,275	23,768	17,861	1,679	1,331	318
Nebraska									
Congressional District 1	33,919	29,934	26,341	6,763	11,764	7,935	1,209	185	248
Congressional District 2	25,068	25,871	27,959	5,875	8,317	7,267	1,295	341	178
Congressional District 3	45,623	36,216	23,364	4,744	9,560	11,316	1,093	249	96
Nevada									
Congressional District 1	28,759	31,494	19,109	7,299	9,476	7,898	1,189	973	75
Congressional District 2	28,834	49,990	35,926	9,944	15,786	12,386	1,082	379	384
Congressional District 3	35,894	42,305	43,344	8,932	13,288	11,771	1,018	567	640
Congressional District 4	32,222	40,409	27,469	9,050	14,646	10,551	2,454	919	231
New Hampshire									
Congressional District 1	35,910	31,074	40,931	9,590	12,659	12,241	1,237	613	214
Congressional District 2	36,805	32,097	43,430	7,756	11,942	10,441	975	599	285
New Jersey									
Congressional District 1	42,274	24,582	29,291	5,890	9,165	8,634	264	214	173
Congressional District 2	50,862	32,941	32,259	4,895	11,367	11,226	794	406	454
Congressional District 3	51,971	36,054	37,983	5,545	11,707	13,532	403	717	214
Congressional District 4	52,997	33,098	48,910	4,003	8,283	11,695	759	388	177
Congressional District 5	40,798	26,058	50,596	2,855	7,480	9,451	464	83	85
Congressional District 6	34,406	20,226	32,444	2,349	6,000	6,780	49	95	201
Congressional District 7	34,354	24,505	50,059	2,641	6,672	9,563	394	44	295
Congressional District 8	28,149	10,326	14,549	1,063	2,618	1,856	349	195	95
Congressional District 9	38,049	18,431	27,608	1,888	3,095	4,453	155	58	243
Congressional District 10	34,866	16,372	23,662	2,952	3,035	5,011	481	125	93
Congressional District 11	39,371	21,914	58,853	3,224	7,336	9,966	627	46	384
Congressional District 12	36,039	21,382	44,867	2,968	5,200	6,674	0	323	71

Table E-5: 116th Congressional Districts - Educational Attainment and Veterans Status, Persons 55 and Over—*Continued*

	High School or Equivalent	Some College or Associates Degree	Bachelor's Degree or Higher	Veterans by Age and Gender					
				Male			Female		
				55 to 64 Years	65 to 74 Years	75 Years and Over	55 to 64 Years	65 to 74 Years	75 Years and Over
New Mexico									
Congressional District 1	25,611	30,055	46,105	9,038	12,199	10,482	1,233	473	243
Congressional District 2	30,142	34,941	28,495	8,476	13,588	9,903	973	618	301
Congressional District 3	32,334	36,643	42,231	7,802	12,909	10,321	938	775	258
New York									
Congressional District 1	41,366	33,444	39,855	3,819	9,064	9,850	246	129	301
Congressional District 2	43,094	25,607	24,372	3,191	7,561	8,089	198	257	129
Congressional District 3	40,029	29,153	63,156	1,567	5,531	9,941	375	141	157
Congressional District 4	40,061	25,573	44,416	2,095	6,198	8,109	538	51	429
Congressional District 5	37,195	24,144	20,625	2,034	2,907	3,965	273	159	39
Congressional District 6	36,641	23,565	38,901	1,178	2,654	3,620	0	40	201
Congressional District 7	20,811	8,025	13,778	2,654	2,028	1,762	381	206	201
Congressional District 8	40,061	20,568	30,230	2,266	2,706	4,031	690	244	107
Congressional District 9	32,621	20,525	30,273	1,433	2,097	2,463	164	200	130
Congressional District 10	17,916	18,376	56,427	782	2,365	3,957	0	0	201
Congressional District 11	45,885	20,692	31,504	1,746	5,715	5,847	354	38	171
Congressional District 12	20,872	18,379	59,897	742	3,689	8,474	206	67	235
Congressional District 13	26,361	12,745	19,574	3,092	2,098	2,088	173	64	242
Congressional District 14	30,368	14,653	16,813	2,027	2,045	3,373	146	43	56
Congressional District 15	21,651	11,828	7,838	1,608	2,687	1,593	72	97	93
Congressional District 16	33,693	19,865	45,833	3,016	4,352	6,581	384	0	426
Congressional District 17	29,790	24,274	56,066	1,579	6,309	9,275	138	233	74
Congressional District 18	31,734	31,395	34,177	5,220	8,649	8,007	434	379	254
Congressional District 19	49,344	36,766	41,536	6,884	12,581	12,950	686	301	164
Congressional District 20	38,432	30,819	41,701	6,464	9,018	10,040	1,051	276	212
Congressional District 21	47,293	31,220	30,081	8,079	11,882	10,296	1,004	641	86
Congressional District 22	49,325	35,587	29,761	7,897	11,471	11,105	666	631	199
Congressional District 23	49,343	34,311	29,865	6,821	12,353	10,828	1,138	383	146
Congressional District 24	42,124	31,793	33,091	5,690	11,790	9,640	808	546	172
Congressional District 25	35,844	30,207	40,369	4,185	8,601	8,610	1,046	164	347
Congressional District 26	41,839	31,477	31,847	6,118	11,214	10,652	707	201	232
Congressional District 27	53,076	35,559	34,431	7,865	12,721	11,741	549	307	177
North Carolina									
Congressional District 1	38,115	31,614	29,886	7,872	10,374	7,173	1,360	745	175
Congressional District 2	35,425	34,196	32,635	10,681	11,755	6,893	1,198	588	116
Congressional District 3	39,297	38,541	33,501	12,277	16,704	13,529	2,265	470	358
Congressional District 4	19,789	24,773	46,855	5,908	6,301	6,694	892	974	239
Congressional District 5	46,837	37,535	31,599	6,672	12,782	11,305	1,079	303	237
Congressional District 6	45,910	36,185	31,475	9,015	12,542	9,100	388	251	158
Congressional District 7	51,998	44,779	42,587	8,384	18,675	11,889	2,080	535	63
Congressional District 8	36,920	34,404	29,265	11,702	13,204	9,229	2,458	622	118
Congressional District 9	36,369	33,006	33,880	6,236	11,180	9,481	1,025	359	209
Congressional District 10	46,527	39,491	32,719	9,540	13,066	11,614	1,065	400	168
Congressional District 11	52,456	46,477	50,349	8,501	16,885	14,710	1,262	380	326
Congressional District 12	23,599	25,407	25,515	6,543	6,927	4,895	923	120	12
Congressional District 13	40,274	36,994	33,571	6,884	11,105	9,860	886	394	234
North Dakota									
Congressional District (at Large)	36,692	38,020	26,133	6,183	11,761	9,700	628	455	256
Ohio									
Congressional District 1	35,619	27,271	32,451	6,354	10,405	8,817	712	302	120
Congressional District 2	42,484	28,606	32,213	6,836	11,600	9,746	693	115	245
Congressional District 3	30,508	22,222	18,777	6,779	6,462	5,143	348	194	63
Congressional District 4	61,189	27,336	19,519	5,950	12,656	9,157	668	467	303
Congressional District 5	53,490	30,869	29,539	6,088	11,506	10,868	570	173	255
Congressional District 6	69,994	28,856	19,648	6,546	14,941	12,167	686	432	258
Congressional District 7	62,944	30,641	21,794	7,252	13,578	10,994	631	916	286
Congressional District 8	52,029	30,667	22,499	9,509	10,382	9,765	1,486	440	150
Congressional District 9	37,865	31,912	23,340	6,789	10,643	7,512	491	533	176
Congressional District 10	43,976	33,945	35,923	8,706	12,046	11,127	1,761	975	234
Congressional District 11	38,073	29,088	31,555	5,746	8,102	8,120	761	306	159
Congressional District 12	44,291	29,404	38,087	5,979	12,239	10,603	795	366	191
Congressional District 13	56,445	32,569	25,623	7,770	12,179	10,606	600	123	187
Congressional District 14	51,922	36,098	42,139	4,975	10,815	12,599	688	201	295
Congressional District 15	50,253	26,155	28,964	6,973	12,189	9,500	806	354	212
Congressional District 16	55,988	37,369	39,487	6,477	11,740	12,755	1,007	430	583
Oklahoma									
Congressional District 1	35,886	37,550	34,890	7,239	12,226	10,340	918	737	218
Congressional District 2	53,805	38,148	24,377	7,739	15,652	13,592	675	482	130
Congressional District 3	43,376	37,405	29,494	7,155	12,504	9,960	894	552	167
Congressional District 4	39,816	35,376	29,195	10,600	16,176	10,069	1,610	1,077	393
Congressional District 5	32,031	34,184	34,397	7,255	13,032	10,686	463	870	100
Oregon									
Congressional District 1	28,970	42,456	47,449	7,576	12,690	10,896	749	323	75
Congressional District 2	44,141	63,765	49,952	10,268	18,659	17,174	1,414	918	558

Table E-5: 116th Congressional Districts - Educational Attainment and Veterans Status, Persons 55 and Over—*Continued*

	High School or Equivalent	Some College or Associates Degree	Bachelor's Degree or Higher	Veterans by Age and Gender					
				Male			Female		
				55 to 64 Years	65 to 74 Years	75 Years and Over	55 to 64 Years	65 to 74 Years	75 Years and Over
Oregon—Cont.									
Congressional District 3	27,102	35,777	41,281	6,124	10,151	7,702	639	1,264	259
Congressional District 4	45,101	65,274	47,973	10,146	21,381	17,739	1,523	903	304
Congressional District 5	37,618	52,075	49,251	8,121	14,688	13,399	1,302	773	573
Pennsylvania									
Congressional District 1	46,740	28,680	44,617	4,771	10,941	11,741	318	148	179
Congressional District 2	39,638	17,238	16,861	5,912	9,001	7,371	230	188	97
Congressional District 3	35,191	18,606	29,655	5,572	6,315	5,802	459	776	207
Congressional District 4	43,740	27,251	46,318	4,412	9,776	12,183	244	556	169
Congressional District 5	40,628	23,588	36,110	5,465	8,493	9,462	837	102	180
Congressional District 6	34,920	25,282	45,051	4,070	8,953	10,118	869	223	328
Congressional District 7	53,068	27,168	31,480	5,289	10,878	11,265	783	222	32
Congressional District 8	61,373	28,606	30,606	7,540	12,333	13,232	846	180	167
Congressional District 9	68,473	27,225	23,106	6,885	14,625	12,114	1,093	536	429
Congressional District 10	54,369	24,735	30,888	7,844	10,325	10,643	1,383	526	197
Congressional District 11	54,670	25,022	31,411	6,844	10,683	11,406	392	441	275
Congressional District 12	65,479	25,754	25,110	7,093	12,845	12,557	861	304	175
Congressional District 13	70,462	29,367	26,322	7,956	14,366	14,200	823	506	336
Congressional District 14	73,992	30,700	28,697	4,724	15,187	12,831	800	628	349
Congressional District 15	73,981	25,169	22,882	6,969	14,688	13,607	655	279	75
Congressional District 16	61,974	29,229	28,829	6,331	14,686	13,179	667	419	319
Congressional District 17	55,557	34,216	38,626	6,117	11,684	13,451	685	306	225
Congressional District 18	51,505	32,313	33,191	5,935	10,533	11,578	612	462	271
Rhode Island									
Congressional District 1	28,714	18,217	26,559	2,379	7,123	7,686	425	127	150
Congressional District 2	29,112	19,842	28,950	4,329	8,976	6,639	657	246	165
South Carolina									
Congressional District 1	36,692	39,157	61,387	13,566	19,330	15,237	2,164	1,078	301
Congressional District 2	34,286	31,893	34,612	9,399	12,343	10,231	1,157	625	141
Congressional District 3	41,753	34,933	26,856	6,002	12,273	10,992	1,169	338	154
Congressional District 4	35,928	30,941	32,743	6,715	10,788	9,049	1,068	537	437
Congressional District 5	44,591	31,378	26,304	8,425	13,828	8,988	1,414	1,198	368
Congressional District 6	35,119	27,487	18,539	7,340	10,750	6,830	1,243	644	132
Congressional District 7	54,741	45,382	36,820	7,542	18,826	10,749	1,328	671	366
South Dakota									
Congressional District (at Large)	54,023	40,342	37,505	8,904	14,707	12,840	818	592	317
Tennessee									
Congressional District 1	53,988	37,323	26,738	8,841	15,194	12,438	979	698	292
Congressional District 2	42,622	35,036	37,144	8,177	11,418	12,141	969	610	338
Congressional District 3	45,594	38,989	30,053	8,246	15,790	11,762	1,205	432	313
Congressional District 4	42,045	32,031	20,675	7,179	11,593	8,264	1,208	94	170
Congressional District 5	27,587	24,372	30,212	5,199	7,411	7,006	556	421	175
Congressional District 6	51,793	33,258	28,233	6,629	13,862	12,907	1,491	843	197
Congressional District 7	40,901	27,520	28,084	7,945	11,750	10,337	1,525	735	242
Congressional District 8	39,546	30,293	32,702	7,544	13,267	9,296	1,285	284	311
Congressional District 9	28,676	22,375	20,192	6,423	8,434	4,271	1,251	365	178
Texas									
Congressional District 1	36,139	39,678	26,635	5,791	12,506	10,155	629	397	258
Congressional District 2	23,454	25,827	36,809	4,930	7,832	7,846	322	336	149
Congressional District 3	20,409	26,986	47,005	4,534	7,349	6,611	497	278	815
Congressional District 4	43,925	36,861	28,586	8,283	13,715	10,537	1,005	929	243
Congressional District 5	31,150	29,737	25,082	5,350	10,205	8,141	1,137	467	235
Congressional District 6	25,380	29,033	26,748	7,822	11,381	6,351	983	558	481
Congressional District 7	12,350	21,708	41,225	3,618	5,437	4,352	489	56	202
Congressional District 8	33,649	35,830	34,348	7,800	12,199	10,239	1,024	362	171
Congressional District 9	20,287	19,012	21,346	2,516	3,976	3,476	546	215	228
Congressional District 10	29,817	32,776	40,415	5,944	9,500	8,262	819	289	229
Congressional District 11	35,779	35,340	30,309	6,152	11,550	11,170	898	275	206
Congressional District 12	28,408	30,684	32,685	10,718	9,707	9,627	1,368	726	351
Congressional District 13	31,530	30,959	26,582	6,443	10,453	8,842	984	484	181
Congressional District 14	32,419	31,088	27,657	8,582	12,091	8,321	747	348	116
Congressional District 15	18,535	16,345	13,614	4,462	5,673	4,428	756	413	99
Congressional District 16	19,782	18,403	15,320	5,212	6,474	5,678	561	294	195
Congressional District 17	28,094	27,309	29,077	5,618	8,475	6,896	615	509	498
Congressional District 18	22,644	17,034	16,326	3,983	5,003	3,075	447	330	65
Congressional District 19	29,655	27,230	22,091	6,360	7,816	8,149	781	151	380
Congressional District 20	21,910	25,534	19,613	8,363	11,247	7,566	1,867	328	64
Congressional District 21	25,533	40,100	57,327	8,602	13,477	11,981	1,709	1,445	322
Congressional District 22	23,397	30,012	35,491	4,405	8,008	6,302	473	693	260
Congressional District 23	24,154	24,276	20,790	5,300	9,889	6,810	1,207	520	358
Congressional District 24	18,994	27,740	36,357	4,208	7,445	7,434	517	587	306
Congressional District 25	27,105	32,059	44,565	6,659	10,467	8,025	1,735	844	368
Congressional District 26	23,648	26,527	32,857	8,017	10,137	6,489	750	846	109

Table E-5: 116th Congressional Districts - Educational Attainment and Veterans Status, Persons 55 and Over—*Continued*

| | High School or Equivalent | Some College or Associates Degree | Bachelor's Degree or Higher | Veterans by Age and Gender | | | | | |
| | | | | Male | | | Female | | |
				55 to 64 Years	65 to 74 Years	75 Years and Over	55 to 64 Years	65 to 74 Years	75 Years and Over
Texas—Cont.									
Congressional District 27	35,921	29,814	24,682	6,889	11,547	9,378	1,014	208	169
Congressional District 28	21,513	19,083	13,013	3,828	6,411	5,512	1,014	407	68
Congressional District 29	15,631	11,268	4,705	1,515	4,639	2,495	0	78	101
Congressional District 30	20,516	23,421	17,692	6,706	8,631	3,251	365	606	183
Congressional District 31	27,153	31,006	37,204	12,684	11,947	8,809	2,963	1,084	340
Congressional District 32	17,557	26,786	41,101	3,940	6,986	7,400	517	400	215
Congressional District 33	18,126	13,485	6,857	4,054	4,922	3,860	280	143	310
Congressional District 34	24,489	19,074	14,493	2,442	7,539	5,510	233	390	123
Congressional District 35	25,554	19,391	13,412	8,298	8,577	5,432	1,648	573	220
Congressional District 36	39,389	28,611	24,089	6,317	11,714	8,699	782	332	194
Utah									
Congressional District 1	21,692	28,392	26,099	7,490	8,712	7,480	685	296	118
Congressional District 2	26,754	35,515	34,990	4,921	8,225	9,638	620	641	220
Congressional District 3	16,895	28,259	34,264	2,751	6,246	6,752	317	209	141
Congressional District 4	21,073	28,268	22,312	3,646	5,914	5,431	182	428	82
Vermont									
Congressional District (at Large)	38,735	29,819	43,647	5,663	10,179	9,460	1,400	566	263
Virginia									
Congressional District 1	35,643	31,153	41,563	13,651	15,977	12,301	2,011	762	258
Congressional District 2	27,845	32,513	40,888	16,586	16,208	11,257	3,431	1,343	285
Congressional District 3	31,152	28,607	22,387	16,352	10,142	9,050	3,441	951	167
Congressional District 4	35,128	30,027	28,054	10,672	12,931	8,217	1,383	657	222
Congressional District 5	48,148	32,496	42,187	7,475	14,254	12,113	1,260	488	223
Congressional District 6	49,240	33,428	35,159	8,916	13,570	11,595	1,432	560	324
Congressional District 7	34,125	29,901	45,943	9,468	12,483	9,880	1,389	546	237
Congressional District 8	16,106	18,478	52,007	8,044	6,961	7,652	1,853	561	271
Congressional District 9	51,027	35,202	22,542	5,987	12,874	10,370	830	766	187
Congressional District 10	22,210	23,028	53,627	7,942	9,540	9,865	1,405	473	170
Congressional District 11	15,745	20,184	50,259	10,890	9,222	7,102	2,221	1,204	227
Washington									
Congressional District 1	24,450	36,210	33,576	6,117	12,034	7,250	544	510	136
Congressional District 2	25,538	42,365	47,324	9,704	12,752	11,453	1,358	406	300
Congressional District 3	34,080	50,057	35,455	9,106	15,216	11,080	1,132	939	306
Congressional District 4	26,891	33,372	26,337	6,176	11,019	7,622	209	272	425
Congressional District 5	34,613	46,752	37,130	8,655	16,199	11,104	2,460	1,028	543
Congressional District 6	33,304	53,834	52,238	13,668	21,299	14,311	1,546	771	284
Congressional District 7	15,317	30,996	58,785	3,974	7,768	8,878	742	602	139
Congressional District 8	29,301	35,382	31,207	8,058	13,299	8,052	1,367	615	173
Congressional District 9	24,589	27,564	38,326	7,049	7,164	7,654	957	289	156
Congressional District 10	32,424	35,129	35,722	12,165	14,136	10,838	2,884	950	213
West Virginia									
Congressional District 1	53,805	26,950	23,694	7,124	11,493	10,501	895	627	249
Congressional District 2	50,505	24,382	23,616	7,302	13,434	10,837	948	964	313
Congressional District 3	50,164	25,636	19,115	4,984	11,456	8,138	236	718	308
Wisconsin									
Congressional District 1	46,893	32,257	29,262	5,629	11,495	10,175	625	551	251
Congressional District 2	37,507	30,382	38,337	5,259	10,847	10,001	794	248	175
Congressional District 3	54,490	33,841	28,495	8,375	13,775	10,972	1,311	182	573
Congressional District 4	29,082	20,965	22,225	4,826	7,019	5,034	397	590	85
Congressional District 5	48,117	35,775	38,420	5,590	10,881	11,035	824	139	282
Congressional District 6	55,960	36,131	27,726	6,783	12,974	12,633	944	197	174
Congressional District 7	61,028	35,256	31,817	7,065	14,447	12,508	1,068	365	187
Congressional District 8	55,803	31,946	26,464	6,980	13,399	10,763	757	566	292
Wyoming									
Congressional District (at Large)	30,073	33,414	23,971	7,533	12,754	8,037	840	846	160

PART F

EMPLOYMENT AND LABOR FORCE STATUS

PART F. EMPLOYMENT AND LABOR FORCE STATUS

EMPLOYMENT AND LABOR FORCE STATUS

U.S. Bureau of Labor Statistics employment data show that between 1980 and 2018, the employment of people age 65 and over tripled (from 3.0 million to 9.7 million) while employment for the civilian non-institutional population 16 and over increased by more than 50 percent. The labor force participation rate for seniors was 12.5 in 1980 and increased to 19.6 in 2018.[1] These figures are beginning to be impacted by the Baby Boom generation as the oldest of that age cohort turned 72 in 2018. The older population has been working more and working longer in life and that trend can be expected to continue as those numbers swell as the youngest of the Baby Boomers age over 65.

The absolute number of employed persons is important but equally important is the rate at which the population participates in the labor force. Not everyone wants to work, so the older labor force is comprised of only those who are employed or unemployed and looking for work. Nationally, of the 73.1 million persons age 60 and over, 21.3 million or 29.2 percent are actively participating in the labor force. Even by age 70 more than 11 percent of the older population is participating in the labor force. Among the 60 and over population, Vermont has the highest participation rate at 37.5 percent while West Virginia (21.8 percent) has the lowest. There's a more narrow range between the highest (Vermont, 16.2 percent) and lowest (West Virginia, 9.1 percent) state for the labor force participation of the 70 and over population. In 10 states, more than one-third of the 60 and over labor force population is participating in the labor force (either employed or unemployed and looking for work). The unemployment rate for both the 60 and over and the 70 years and over is around 3.2 percent but varies from a low of 0.3 percent in North Dakota to a high of 6.2 percent in Delaware.

Los Angeles County, California has the largest 60 and over labor force with almost 613,000 people and the participation rate is 31.4 percent. Minnehaha County, South

Dakota has the highest participation rate at 42.1 percent and Citrus County, Florida the lowest at 12.2 percent. The 60 and over labor force participation rate is higher than the national average of 29.2 percent in 340 counties and greater than 35 percent in 87 counties. Unemployment is highest in Navajo County, Arizona where 15.2 percent of the 60 and over population are unemployed and looking for work. The unemployment rate for persons 70 and over is low with 784 of the 814 counties having rates below 10 percent. However, seven counties have unemployment rates greater than 20 percent for the 70 and over population with Jefferson County, Ohio having the highest rate of 24.3 percent. The unemployment rate for the 70 and over population is higher than the national average in 252 counties but among the 60 and over, 283 counties are above the national average.

Among cities, almost half (46.8 percent) of the Irving city, Texas population 60 and over participates in the labor force but at 25.1 percent, Berkeley city, California has the highest participation rate for the 70 and over population. In Pueblo city, Colorado, 17.6 percent of the 60 and over population participates in the labor force and is the lowest rate. Edinburg city, Texas has the lowest participation rate for the 70 and over population at 1.4 percent. Reading city, Pennsylvania has the highest unemployment rate for persons 60 and over at 13.8 percent and 29 cities have unemployment rates greater than 10 percent for the 70 and over population.

The New York-Northern New Jersey-Long Island metropolitan area has the largest 60 and over labor force with a population over 1.4 million and its participation rate at 32.3 percent is higher than the national rate of 29.2 percent. The Midland, Texas metropolitan area has the highest participation rate at 40.6 percent while the Homosassa Springs, Florida metro area is lowest at 12.2 percent. Labor force participation among the 60 and over population is above the national rate in 166 metropolitan and micropolitan areas. The highest labor force participation rate for the population 70 and over is 21.1 percent in the Claremont-Lebanon, New Hampshire-Vermont micropolitan area – well above the national average of 11.1 percent. The Show Low, Arizona micropolitan area has the highest unemployment rate among the 60 and over population at 15.2 percent the El Centro, California metro area is the only other area over 10 percent. 163

---

[1] U.S. Department of Labor, Bureau of Labor Statistics, Labor Force Statistics from the Current Population Survey, annual data obtained through, http://data.bls.gov.

Percent of the Population 60 Years and Over Participating in the Labor Force

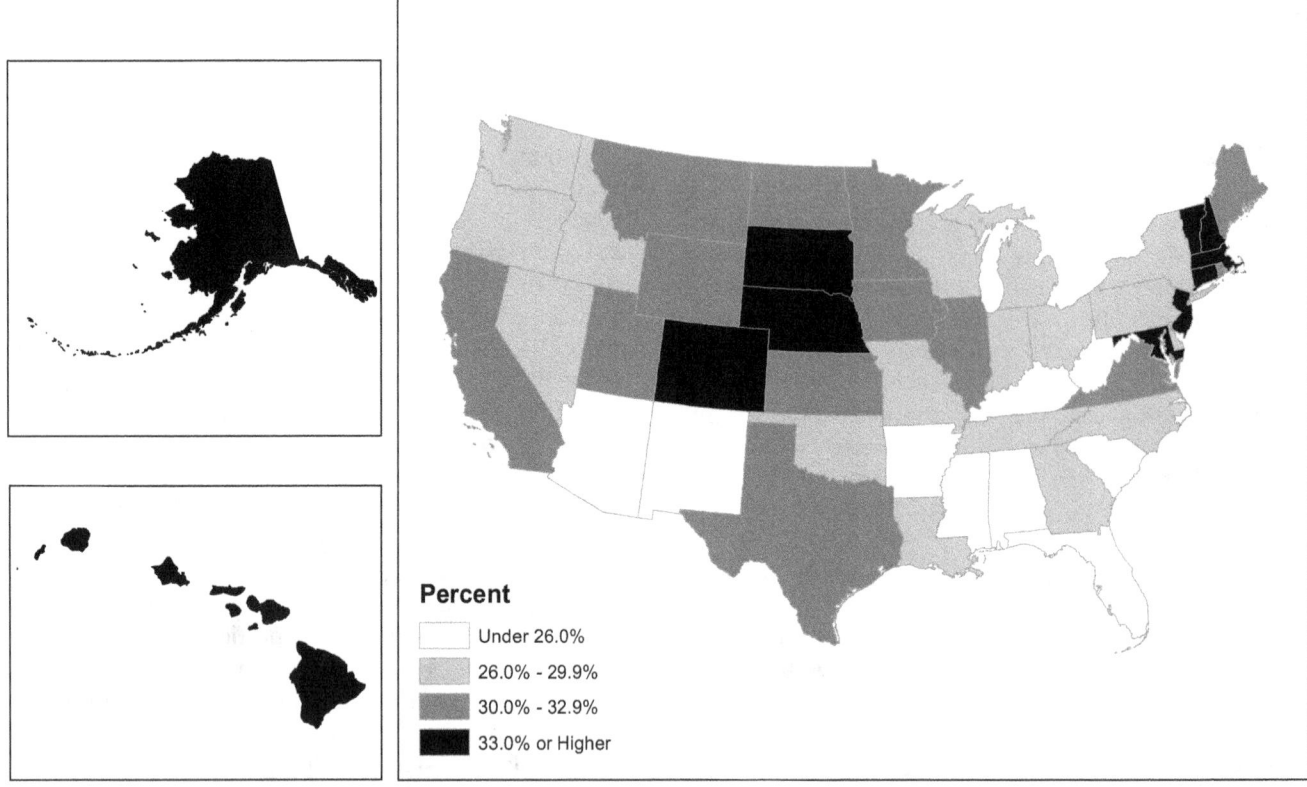

Percent

☐ Under 26.0%

▨ 26.0% - 29.9%

▨ 30.0% - 32.9%

■ 33.0% or Higher

Figure F-1. Cities with the Highest and Lowest Labor Force Participation of the Population 70 Years and Over

American Community Survey, 2018

metropolitan and micropolitan areas have unemployment rates higher than the nation for the 60 and over population and 145 are above the 70 and over rate.

Texas' 24th Congressional District has the highest labor force participation for the 60 and over population at 42.5 percent while Florida's 11th district has the lowest rate at 13.9 percent. More than half of all congressional districts (226) have participation rates above the national average for the 60 and over population and 196 districts have participation over 30 percent. In 204 districts the rate is above the national rate for the population 70 and over. At 8.5 percent Texas' 14th district has the highest unemployment among the 60 and over and California's 41st district is highest among the 70 and over population but still only 20.4 percent. In 73 districts the unemployment rate for the 70 and over population is less than two percent.

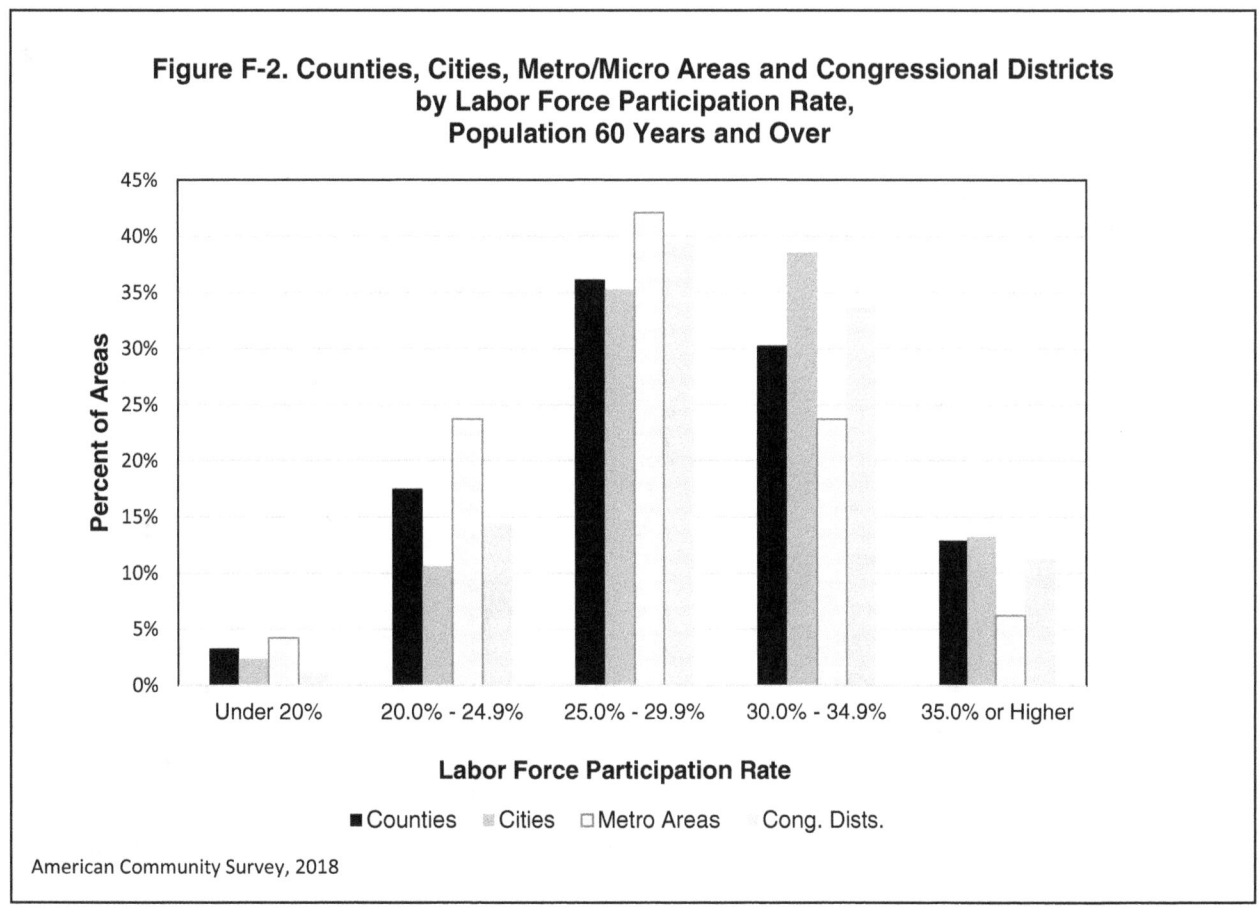

Figure F-2. Counties, Cities, Metro/Micro Areas and Congressional Districts by Labor Force Participation Rate, Population 60 Years and Over

American Community Survey, 2018

Table F-1: States - Employment and Labor Force Status, Civilian Labor Force

	60 to 61 Years		62 to 64 Years		65 to 69 Years		70 Years and Over		60 Years and Over Not in the Labor Force
	Employed	Unemployed	Employed	Unemployed	Employed	Unemployed	Employed	Unemployed	
United States	5,350,436	178,808	6,135,544	179,610	5,389,111	167,615	3,807,522	128,136	51,748,690
Alabama.................................	73,891	1,333	74,994	1,731	67,615	2,652	53,571	1,016	872,332
Alaska....................................	13,486	873	13,765	211	13,214	494	6,016	309	85,644
Arizona...................................	106,647	4,596	117,624	3,773	107,587	4,265	76,451	3,421	1,271,065
Arkansas................................	45,757	1,197	46,813	901	44,183	810	36,097	633	519,181
California................................	603,297	25,237	684,843	26,029	612,400	20,984	411,427	17,599	5,561,897
Colorado................................	99,414	3,685	108,395	2,882	101,520	2,390	65,824	2,956	769,792
Connecticut............................	72,930	2,439	90,502	2,490	75,243	3,043	56,978	2,118	560,027
Delaware................................	16,372	196	18,845	1,037	20,310	999	14,133	937	175,466
District of Columbia................	8,213	212	10,655	247	9,563	245	8,348	529	80,698
Florida...................................	348,297	13,900	382,319	13,752	361,089	14,133	282,277	12,591	4,337,290
Georgia.................................	156,217	4,843	170,674	3,598	142,950	5,109	102,276	2,465	1,482,560
Hawaii...................................	27,410	227	31,498	378	33,556	694	22,562	1,030	237,983
Idaho....................................	21,910	636	32,079	377	27,448	556	17,145	472	282,203
Illinois..................................	217,015	10,310	247,234	8,307	210,015	6,895	143,465	4,213	1,957,143
Indiana.................................	111,265	2,621	126,447	2,652	108,082	4,057	76,174	2,758	1,043,768
Iowa.....................................	58,812	1,324	73,514	771	60,118	1,038	42,312	632	505,041
Kansas..................................	49,195	1,611	61,916	1,069	54,472	878	34,146	937	441,725
Kentucky................................	64,114	1,459	68,909	2,053	64,988	1,859	49,878	1,455	771,988
Louisiana...............................	67,628	2,574	76,984	986	71,024	2,342	48,624	1,046	748,654
Maine....................................	28,638	506	35,191	641	31,235	613	19,569	630	267,299
Maryland................................	107,112	2,714	133,989	4,120	119,102	3,551	80,091	3,432	870,809
Massachusetts........................	127,260	4,278	156,157	5,406	144,119	4,816	101,238	2,987	1,041,855
Michigan................................	168,186	5,307	187,601	5,383	149,298	4,903	106,222	4,355	1,790,161
Minnesota..............................	100,699	3,699	117,724	3,688	98,314	2,109	64,575	974	852,179
Mississippi.............................	44,368	1,156	46,651	1,011	40,610	873	30,119	774	501,511
Missouri................................	96,681	2,271	121,761	2,782	97,804	3,327	71,459	1,877	1,050,405
Montana................................	22,029	457	24,921	491	21,893	1,151	17,389	411	191,229
Nebraska...............................	33,436	547	44,214	785	40,466	489	27,848	487	274,787
Nevada..................................	40,592	2,706	56,146	1,508	45,700	2,463	32,815	1,775	477,802
New Hampshire.......................	30,676	972	33,306	1,027	30,881	564	23,682	334	225,220
New Jersey.............................	170,937	5,812	200,296	6,644	172,567	5,544	125,240	6,384	1,328,848
New Mexico............................	32,063	1,147	33,020	1,194	31,770	1,201	22,006	795	381,457
New York................................	342,659	11,323	382,922	13,442	327,852	10,647	245,616	7,186	3,138,787
North Carolina........................	164,790	4,644	193,282	4,332	162,086	5,110	116,373	3,508	1,699,332
North Dakota..........................	14,001	328	14,896	120	12,906	436	10,343	34	109,156
Ohio......................................	206,410	5,495	236,648	5,868	203,266	6,089	131,563	4,486	1,992,854
Oklahoma...............................	58,888	1,513	66,701	922	60,870	947	51,101	699	615,958
Oregon..................................	64,967	1,845	78,484	2,132	69,901	2,638	45,131	1,647	749,435
Pennsylvania..........................	237,093	7,785	281,189	7,527	237,957	7,944	171,876	6,070	2,269,710
Rhode Island..........................	23,925	818	24,503	606	18,372	747	13,387	278	175,356
South Carolina........................	76,852	2,515	85,823	2,399	80,350	1,999	60,520	1,758	916,059
South Dakota..........................	15,773	60	21,347	263	20,583	454	14,718	117	131,992
Tennessee..............................	102,649	2,240	125,137	2,981	107,061	2,616	78,376	2,833	1,126,548
Texas....................................	406,407	16,734	453,786	17,240	410,714	14,075	293,202	8,882	3,517,985
Utah......................................	38,578	1,389	48,760	1,300	40,553	456	23,960	433	343,720
Vermont.................................	13,610	576	19,054	371	17,808	340	12,400	692	108,058
Virginia..................................	145,867	3,248	166,155	4,198	149,582	2,390	103,730	2,598	1,269,326
Washington............................	121,096	4,060	140,791	4,346	121,826	2,505	72,942	2,803	1,166,051
West Virginia..........................	24,201	1,017	30,475	948	29,066	657	20,914	290	384,850
Wisconsin..............................	115,220	2,139	125,419	2,316	97,408	2,133	62,950	1,314	982,839
Wyoming...............................	12,701	234	11,185	375	11,814	385	8,463	176	92,655

Table F-2: Counties - Employment and Labor Force Status, Civilian Labor Force

	60 to 61 Years		62 to 64 Years		65 to 69 Years		70 Years and Over		60 Years and Over Not in the Labor Force
	Employed	Unemployed	Employed	Unemployed	Employed	Unemployed	Employed	Unemployed	
Alabama									
Baldwin County	3,672	0	3,791	82	3,894	86	3,563	43	44,386
Calhoun County	1,642	59	2,800	0	1,368	0	1,465	38	20,998
Cullman County	na	na	na	na	na	na	na	na	na
DeKalb County	na	na	na	na	na	na	na	na	na
Elmore County	na	na	na	na	na	na	na	na	na
Etowah County	1,527	0	2,268	64	1,819	0	1,383	0	20,448
Houston County	1,661	11	1,471	34	1,866	41	1,410	22	19,294
Jefferson County	10,255	182	10,771	334	10,721	733	7,652	54	109,486
Lauderdale County	na	na	na	na	na	na	na	na	na
Lee County	2,627	0	2,874	176	2,147	157	1,434	0	19,747
Limestone County	na	na	na	na	na	na	na	na	na
Madison County	6,171	217	5,228	230	5,022	251	4,980	229	54,062
Marshall County	1,547	7	804	0	1,253	0	1,531	7	17,622
Mobile County	6,959	63	5,631	76	4,954	420	3,884	254	70,375
Montgomery County	3,272	0	3,064	169	3,943	193	2,216	63	34,897
Morgan County	1,437	62	2,246	0	1,678	137	1,117	0	22,308
St. Clair County	na	na	na	na	na	na	na	na	na
Shelby County	4,370	27	3,526	0	4,107	0	2,080	0	32,988
Talladega County	1,370	99	871	39	624	90	829	0	16,557
Tuscaloosa County	2,554	0	4,036	63	2,651	0	2,226	0	27,902
Walker County	na	na	na	na	na	na	na	na	na
Alaska									
Anchorage Municipality	6,111	312	4,592	0	5,257	322	2,289	0	29,809
Fairbanks North Star Borough	1,570	0	1,365	0	2,137	20	454	51	10,031
Matanuska-Susitna Borough	1,363	145	1,691	68	1,116	46	665	32	14,912
Arizona									
Apache County	795	0	676	0	721	0	265	20	12,793
Cochise County	2,910	46	1,889	63	2,454	33	1,537	36	29,704
Coconino County	1,716	6	2,447	0	1,603	46	1,660	50	18,170
Maricopa County	63,135	2,675	76,728	2,207	65,394	1,407	45,624	1,613	659,410
Mohave County	2,807	5	4,418	192	4,297	709	2,621	120	67,399
Navajo County	1,595	597	902	98	1,040	16	1,454	186	21,712
Pima County	17,385	633	15,324	620	17,807	655	10,362	517	208,142
Pinal County	5,659	285	5,602	157	5,098	653	3,878	242	97,060
Yavapai County	4,067	212	4,922	175	5,755	452	4,385	637	74,536
Yuma County	2,991	53	1,873	251	1,356	97	1,459	0	43,190
Arkansas									
Benton County	3,989	127	4,125	137	3,393	0	1,836	58	37,444
Craighead County	1,615	202	2,158	0	1,337	0	732	0	15,078
Faulkner County	1,380	104	1,968	43	1,582	0	917	0	16,805
Garland County	na	na	na	na	na	na	na	na	na
Jefferson County	na	na	na	na	na	na	na	na	na
Lonoke County	1,091	0	1,025	0	780	0	336	0	10,865
Pulaski County	5,454	185	7,522	261	6,636	69	4,855	101	59,795
Saline County	1,888	0	2,234	59	1,689	0	1,558	0	20,941
Sebastian County	2,094	0	1,631	0	1,459	292	1,909	58	19,616
Washington County	3,942	44	3,005	0	3,066	0	2,279	36	26,940
White County	na	na	na	na	na	na	na	na	na
California									
Alameda County	26,752	826	32,794	526	27,999	819	18,954	604	217,095
Butte County	2,442	186	3,860	115	3,034	46	2,566	109	46,262
Contra Costa County	20,007	953	22,830	434	23,772	663	13,607	623	171,013
El Dorado County	3,699	322	5,571	331	4,170	118	3,233	0	40,294
Fresno County	12,918	752	12,398	570	12,115	334	7,620	524	122,730
Humboldt County	1,968	121	3,988	0	2,663	59	2,035	156	24,297
Imperial County	2,520	187	1,626	261	1,640	313	1,082	312	23,967
Kern County	8,573	845	10,922	839	10,231	176	6,116	152	105,348
Kings County	1,141	0	1,256	261	1,002	98	1,137	0	16,056
Lake County	na	na	na	na	na	na	na	na	na
Los Angeles County	155,198	6,249	175,485	6,938	153,077	5,655	105,313	4,820	1,337,056
Madera County	1,236	206	1,607	85	2,144	0	2,170	56	22,650
Marin County	6,238	47	8,022	213	9,331	89	7,491	100	46,934
Mendocino County	1,195	106	2,717	116	2,474	57	2,235	0	17,068
Merced County	3,339	60	3,833	0	2,968	268	1,978	339	30,822
Monterey County	5,408	313	8,156	122	7,998	19	5,196	108	56,043
Napa County	2,361	76	3,276	73	2,875	61	2,035	44	25,287
Nevada County	na	na	na	na	na	na	na	na	na
Orange County	60,273	1,305	58,140	1,635	52,535	2,557	36,371	1,404	445,282
Placer County	7,367	88	7,223	387	6,001	506	4,084	351	77,115
Riverside County	29,723	1,059	35,988	1,327	28,241	829	19,339	2,035	364,323
Sacramento County	21,581	1,084	25,836	1,021	18,595	629	14,178	514	227,139
San Bernardino County	29,430	1,091	28,778	699	23,194	1,172	14,784	585	266,262
San Diego County	48,640	2,885	58,662	2,085	50,058	1,693	32,308	981	463,992
San Francisco County	16,708	494	15,485	811	15,127	568	10,142	482	131,449
San Joaquin County	9,326	447	11,240	344	8,756	0	5,955	72	102,173
San Luis Obispo County	4,557	67	5,858	0	5,763	120	3,258	91	57,963
San Mateo County	12,432	884	16,976	873	16,871	646	11,385	211	111,856
Santa Barbara County	7,321	484	7,239	450	7,712	88	6,411	355	63,242
Santa Clara County	30,687	1,203	36,817	1,613	30,422	673	18,906	770	248,499

Table F-2: Counties - Employment and Labor Force Status, Civilian Labor Force—*Continued*

	60 to 61 Years		62 to 64 Years		65 to 69 Years		70 Years and Over		60 Years and Over Not in the Labor Force
	Employed	Unemployed	Employed	Unemployed	Employed	Unemployed	Employed	Unemployed	
California—Cont.									
Santa Cruz County	4,642	158	5,866	660	8,308	374	4,149	46	39,672
Shasta County	2,055	40	3,373	90	3,340	59	2,021	144	39,696
Solano County	8,691	115	9,223	495	9,357	153	4,947	166	67,983
Sonoma County	10,275	656	11,086	463	12,451	486	10,073	217	88,678
Stanislaus County	6,108	345	6,534	347	6,824	38	3,810	202	76,869
Sutter County	1,834	0	1,896	84	1,288	0	1,276	0	14,959
Tulare County	5,301	317	6,652	429	4,270	61	2,816	169	56,674
Ventura County	15,076	536	14,274	561	16,610	1,109	9,832	383	124,675
Yolo County	3,128	193	3,307	0	2,582	67	1,609	127	27,242
Yuba County	1,183	0	1,651	0	1,260	0	526	0	10,370
Colorado									
Adams County	6,995	173	7,763	279	6,336	332	4,373	99	51,201
Arapahoe County	11,744	284	12,851	208	12,352	316	6,974	159	78,565
Boulder County	6,867	256	7,000	81	7,260	77	3,805	103	42,467
Broomfield County	na	na	na	na	na	na	na	na	na
Denver County	9,467	396	11,118	377	11,151	142	7,187	203	78,292
Douglas County	7,098	51	6,206	124	5,682	187	4,183	49	35,925
El Paso County	11,174	486	11,914	213	11,519	377	6,349	138	88,716
Jefferson County	13,183	622	13,584	546	12,239	161	8,324	312	88,155
Larimer County	6,019	268	6,872	183	7,654	69	3,813	159	52,242
Mesa County	2,805	136	2,893	42	2,570	149	2,337	0	27,925
Pueblo County	2,392	176	2,650	57	2,129	37	713	0	34,624
Weld County	4,991	331	5,893	403	4,984	218	3,292	78	37,621
Connecticut									
Fairfield County	18,405	679	24,707	730	20,949	1,174	16,498	1,024	129,239
Hartford County	17,007	330	21,703	785	17,201	904	12,557	397	140,996
Litchfield County	4,905	246	5,192	29	5,196	61	3,423	153	35,149
Middlesex County	4,103	139	5,521	206	3,901	40	3,142	180	29,014
New Haven County	17,644	409	20,421	260	17,624	453	13,893	201	138,652
New London County	5,840	331	5,933	317	5,844	179	4,546	60	45,203
Tolland County	2,523	152	3,806	54	2,579	102	1,729	103	23,231
Windham County	2,503	153	3,219	109	1,949	130	1,190	0	18,543
Delaware									
Kent County	2,343	0	2,602	142	2,505	445	1,939	180	30,459
New Castle County	9,918	86	10,760	723	10,731	437	6,323	544	83,539
Sussex County	4,111	110	5,483	172	7,074	117	5,871	213	61,468
Florida									
Alachua County	3,988	121	5,057	126	4,285	47	2,598	0	35,272
Bay County	3,395	543	3,598	240	2,317	84	1,928	49	32,604
Brevard County	12,016	773	13,383	50	11,218	190	7,610	209	145,967
Broward County	36,630	2,276	39,514	1,551	36,986	1,668	26,144	1,826	304,636
Charlotte County	3,591	211	5,281	120	4,459	0	3,261	170	74,785
Citrus County	1,173	0	2,163	34	2,044	172	2,390	335	59,968
Clay County	3,357	0	4,213	304	3,640	301	1,574	0	34,452
Collier County	5,098	635	8,207	61	8,692	348	9,326	95	116,785
Columbia County	1,097	0	1,250	0	520	162	540	47	14,493
Duval County	13,710	591	16,882	477	12,942	267	8,794	406	134,999
Escambia County	4,692	402	4,982	109	3,878	56	2,469	108	58,005
Flagler County	na	na	na	na	na	na	na	na	na
Hernando County	2,687	76	3,401	206	2,307	0	1,483	192	57,435
Highlands County	na	na	na	na	na	na	na	na	na
Hillsborough County	20,889	629	20,819	729	19,324	720	13,802	428	210,430
Indian River County	na	na	na	na	na	na	na	na	na
Lake County	4,884	168	7,208	92	5,027	621	5,468	109	97,271
Lee County	10,496	394	13,439	492	14,929	208	12,738	1,180	214,909
Leon County	4,218	133	4,935	239	4,246	156	3,428	130	38,254
Manatee County	5,914	214	8,612	618	6,980	451	6,908	502	106,969
Marion County	5,782	150	5,305	182	4,731	187	4,740	393	107,578
Martin County	2,573	244	3,788	0	2,704	194	3,453	151	49,722
Miami-Dade County	44,284	1,820	46,820	2,532	44,881	1,332	31,096	765	433,753
Monroe County	na	na	na	na	na	na	na	na	na
Nassau County	na	na	na	na	na	na	na	na	na
Okaloosa County	3,380	44	3,558	0	2,991	435	2,525	0	33,363
Orange County	21,629	349	19,776	751	18,853	1,327	11,791	273	165,506
Osceola County	6,068	0	5,046	380	3,752	32	2,827	25	50,910
Palm Beach County	25,126	999	29,240	1,186	28,853	1,038	29,692	1,560	333,281
Pasco County	8,082	344	7,894	673	8,393	292	6,029	225	125,624
Pinellas County	20,546	947	22,294	595	21,332	918	15,256	1,023	238,417
Polk County	11,339	256	9,148	144	9,257	188	9,237	478	145,654
Putnam County	na	na	na	na	na	na	na	na	na
St. Johns County	4,746	187	4,973	429	5,407	71	2,871	63	51,018
St. Lucie County	5,138	0	4,405	158	6,340	464	4,072	428	76,673
Santa Rosa County	3,809	42	3,433	0	2,398	0	1,244	76	31,615
Sarasota County	6,960	480	9,945	88	12,374	294	11,973	178	147,607
Seminole County	9,428	59	8,792	208	9,320	462	6,978	194	67,641
Sumter County	na	na	na	na	na	na	na	na	na
Volusia County	10,749	0	10,117	209	12,695	639	6,664	36	133,697
Walton County	na	na	na	na	na	na	na	na	na

Table F-2: Counties - Employment and Labor Force Status, Civilian Labor Force—*Continued*

	60 to 61 Years		62 to 64 Years		65 to 69 Years		70 Years and Over		60 Years and Over Not in the Labor Force
	Employed	Unemployed	Employed	Unemployed	Employed	Unemployed	Employed	Unemployed	
Georgia									
Barrow County	na	na	na	na	na	na	na	na	na
Bartow County	na	na	na	na	na	na	na	na	na
Bibb County	1,518	63	2,972	9	2,859	168	1,629	52	24,747
Bulloch County	751	69	1,427	0	882	0	733	0	9,098
Carroll County	na	na	na	na	na	na	na	na	na
Catoosa County	na	na	na	na	na	na	na	na	na
Chatham County	5,552	151	5,074	247	4,347	559	3,980	27	40,841
Cherokee County	3,686	83	5,338	88	3,838	345	2,979	0	34,234
Clarke County	1,311	0	1,357	12	1,588	58	1,538	34	14,736
Clayton County	3,449	226	3,276	363	3,657	161	1,639	188	28,156
Cobb County	11,652	396	14,932	205	12,338	692	9,999	370	83,878
Columbia County	3,035	0	2,738	0	2,503	0	1,243	0	20,678
Coweta County	na	na	na	na	na	na	na	na	na
DeKalb County	11,884	483	14,590	486	10,717	689	7,171	89	91,876
Dougherty County	1,851	29	1,602	0	1,008	242	795	0	13,609
Douglas County	na	na	na	na	na	na	na	na	na
Fayette County	2,014	0	2,987	102	1,759	63	1,855	145	19,012
Floyd County	na	na	na	na	na	na	na	na	na
Forsyth County	4,246	238	3,147	68	3,586	287	2,238	0	25,965
Fulton County	15,364	448	16,119	333	14,573	265	10,329	299	121,532
Glynn County	na	na	na	na	na	na	na	na	na
Gwinnett County	14,495	622	14,873	607	10,521	350	5,715	127	96,042
Hall County	2,940	109	2,503	0	2,097	0	2,077	189	31,408
Henry County	3,644	69	3,331	79	3,374	89	1,607	57	26,754
Houston County	2,617	0	1,692	0	1,453	28	1,385	0	19,938
Jackson County	na	na	na	na	na	na	na	na	na
Lowndes County	1,410	0	1,012	71	1,419	0	1,257	0	15,242
Muscogee County	3,282	60	2,376	27	2,250	114	1,146	41	28,723
Newton County	2,055	0	1,506	266	1,170	0	1,288	0	14,480
Paulding County	na	na	na	na	na	na	na	na	na
Richmond County	2,413	481	3,946	46	1,568	60	2,017	190	31,625
Rockdale County	na	na	na	na	na	na	na	na	na
Spalding County	na	na	na	na	na	na	na	na	na
Troup County	na	na	na	na	na	na	na	na	na
Walker County	na	na	na	na	na	na	na	na	na
Walton County	na	na	na	na	na	na	na	na	na
Whitfield County	na	na	na	na	na	na	na	na	na
Hawaii									
Hawaii County	3,567	0	5,272	47	4,968	49	3,900	492	40,551
Honolulu County	18,573	174	20,435	200	22,937	589	14,812	287	155,246
Kauai County	na	na	na	na	na	na	na	na	na
Maui County	3,018	30	3,631	131	3,251	0	2,836	164	29,183
Idaho									
Ada County	6,303	257	8,761	40	7,398	210	4,007	232	66,453
Bannock County	1,331	0	1,091	37	1,426	0	489	0	12,556
Bonneville County	1,703	33	1,729	0	1,265	0	491	51	15,709
Canyon County	2,096	0	3,351	182	3,119	268	1,240	0	33,318
Kootenai County	1,713	99	3,404	0	2,374	29	1,744	91	31,297
Twin Falls County	na	na	na	na	na	na	na	na	na
Illinois									
Adams County	na	na	na	na	na	na	na	na	na
Champaign County	3,215	231	3,332	8	3,061	41	2,365	0	26,403
Cook County	79,712	4,995	97,096	4,121	84,262	2,881	55,609	2,213	740,419
DeKalb County	1,215	0	1,827	10	1,482	62	1,237	0	13,117
DuPage County	21,684	343	22,465	730	19,785	748	12,800	183	129,020
Kane County	9,780	620	9,021	369	8,831	299	4,041	159	69,840
Kankakee County	1,818	8	2,213	0	1,409	113	967	18	19,080
Kendall County	na	na	na	na	na	na	na	na	na
Lake County	12,849	513	16,142	485	13,208	197	8,666	202	92,453
LaSalle County	1,878	78	1,562	296	1,981	47	1,545	0	20,848
McHenry County	6,265	490	7,325	269	5,155	143	3,190	221	42,035
McLean County	1,804	121	3,092	15	2,435	0	1,357	22	23,525
Macon County	2,286	130	2,028	0	1,907	46	1,074	0	22,383
Madison County	3,450	239	4,994	42	3,864	337	3,930	259	46,498
Peoria County	2,591	124	3,188	51	2,138	177	2,074	8	32,546
Rock Island County	1,349	123	2,449	54	2,607	196	1,876	0	27,498
St. Clair County	4,314	342	5,723	144	4,163	186	2,665	0	42,525
Sangamon County	3,388	16	4,173	311	3,870	64	2,532	7	34,324
Tazewell County	2,663	0	2,845	0	1,271	0	1,604	0	26,543
Vermilion County	1,361	54	1,383	0	1,518	75	710	41	14,553
Will County	13,378	487	11,925	211	10,951	356	4,882	223	89,982
Williamson County	na	na	na	na	na	na	na	na	na
Winnebago County	5,945	300	5,928	218	5,556	156	2,879	54	49,389
Indiana									
Allen County	5,914	292	6,374	388	6,502	80	3,476	38	52,586
Bartholomew County	na	na	na	na	na	na	na	na	na
Boone County	na	na	na	na	na	na	na	na	na

Table F-2: Counties - Employment and Labor Force Status, Civilian Labor Force—*Continued*

	60 to 61 Years		62 to 64 Years		65 to 69 Years		70 Years and Over		60 Years and Over Not in the Labor Force
	Employed	Unemployed	Employed	Unemployed	Employed	Unemployed	Employed	Unemployed	
Indiana—Cont.									
Clark County	2,723	58	2,239	62	2,251	0	1,877	75	17,540
Delaware County	1,226	52	2,846	0	1,284	119	1,860	0	19,125
Elkhart County	3,280	39	3,885	104	4,169	340	2,658	108	26,910
Floyd County	1,298	0	1,877	34	1,704	37	676	45	11,842
Grant County	699	0	1,429	162	1,201	0	985	0	12,561
Hamilton County	5,197	0	6,121	55	5,479	384	2,871	80	38,377
Hancock County	na	na	na	na	na	na	na	na	na
Hendricks County	4,026	0	3,197	52	1,760	0	1,832	98	22,946
Howard County	1,570	0	1,310	34	1,254	0	977	0	16,018
Johnson County	2,623	0	2,552	15	3,329	238	1,453	69	21,282
Kosciusko County	na	na	na	na	na	na	na	na	na
Lake County	7,784	235	9,658	301	7,680	244	4,165	109	83,373
LaPorte County	1,785	0	2,142	34	1,381	0	1,680	64	19,674
Madison County	1,135	0	2,551	0	1,722	150	1,619	0	25,251
Marion County	14,435	595	13,947	645	13,666	1,047	9,562	872	118,903
Monroe County	2,294	0	1,660	0	1,937	0	1,971	125	19,184
Morgan County	1,424	0	1,360	0	1,163	0	864	226	11,245
Porter County	2,790	0	3,536	146	2,147	0	1,833	110	28,643
St. Joseph County	5,671	135	5,800	0	5,162	42	3,290	220	40,739
Tippecanoe County	2,815	394	2,378	0	2,197	17	1,634	92	21,850
Vanderburgh County	3,396	32	3,649	50	2,881	61	2,584	0	30,540
Vigo County	1,464	26	1,807	0	1,938	70	1,207	0	17,142
Wayne County	na	na	na	na	na	na	na	na	na
Iowa									
Black Hawk County	1,675	46	2,849	37	2,286	0	1,284	39	21,149
Dallas County	na	na	na	na	na	na	na	na	na
Dubuque County	1,487	0	2,370	11	1,678	0	1,672	0	16,642
Johnson County	2,427	0	3,047	0	2,975	9	1,079	24	16,082
Linn County	4,365	133	4,201	72	4,478	168	2,533	45	32,991
Polk County	5,358	78	9,663	59	7,128	242	5,642	86	59,665
Pottawattamie County	1,758	0	2,312	0	1,391	0	1,751	0	15,932
Scott County	3,564	53	3,989	0	3,123	71	1,680	47	26,615
Story County	1,344	53	1,487	0	1,597	0	872	0	10,087
Woodbury County	2,314	38	2,685	62	1,616	74	1,060	6	14,762
Kansas									
Butler County	na	na	na	na	na	na	na	na	na
Douglas County	1,372	0	1,931	0	2,618	190	1,089	0	13,638
Johnson County	10,259	738	13,756	56	12,521	157	7,248	239	78,248
Leavenworth County	1,164	0	1,448	0	1,172	0	1,250	35	12,192
Riley County	1,422	0	682	0	762	0	940	97	6,287
Sedgwick County	8,105	353	9,639	466	8,072	208	4,533	100	74,534
Shawnee County	2,977	0	4,268	34	3,220	0	1,807	218	33,018
Wyandotte County	2,369	47	2,550	293	2,366	18	1,274	0	20,153
Kentucky									
Boone County	na	na	na	na	na	na	na	na	na
Bullitt County	na	na	na	na	na	na	na	na	na
Campbell County	2,310	81	1,877	79	1,450	53	1,230	31	14,229
Christian County	1,185	0	836	0	711	0	540	0	9,281
Daviess County	na	na	na	na	na	na	na	na	na
Fayette County	4,571	124	5,339	105	5,668	300	4,647	105	40,382
Hardin County	2,007	116	1,353	0	1,668	0	477	0	17,504
Jefferson County	13,736	226	14,116	544	13,913	293	9,198	157	123,454
Kenton County	2,294	350	3,287	153	2,720	26	2,340	0	23,134
McCracken County	na	na	na	na	na	na	na	na	na
Madison County	1,507	0	1,292	0	1,190	31	693	137	12,851
Oldham County	994	0	1,145	82	1,143	37	883	88	8,509
Warren County	1,624	0	1,219	0	2,186	206	1,809	0	16,855
Louisiana									
Ascension Parish	na	na	na	na	na	na	na	na	na
Bossier Parish	1,531	173	2,029	96	1,482	146	1,476	120	17,734
Caddo Parish	3,775	0	3,677	71	4,726	9	2,389	81	42,885
Calcasieu Parish	2,463	83	4,347	0	2,204	158	932	49	34,397
East Baton Rouge Parish	6,128	57	8,472	73	7,230	212	5,178	136	61,761
Iberia Parish	na	na	na	na	na	na	na	na	na
Jefferson Parish	9,045	363	8,258	28	8,774	402	6,750	129	70,893
Lafayette Parish	3,383	44	3,623	0	4,653	0	2,091	0	31,224
Lafourche Parish	1,668	0	1,459	63	1,636	0	726	0	17,345
Livingston Parish	na	na	na	na	na	na	na	na	na
Orleans Parish	5,431	50	6,237	153	5,880	279	3,911	177	59,966
Ouachita Parish	3,306	125	3,258	41	1,072	204	1,375	0	24,064
Rapides Parish	1,509	0	2,519	0	2,310	0	1,314	0	21,873
St. Landry Parish	1,104	66	1,179	0	1,359	97	1,331	0	13,549
St. Tammany Parish	3,669	522	4,873	148	4,949	0	3,686	0	43,221
Tangipahoa Parish	2,010	0	1,418	0	2,321	0	860	0	20,259
Terrebonne Parish	na	na	na	na	na	na	na	na	na
Maine									
Androscoggin County	2,304	41	2,198	98	2,638	176	920	0	18,312
Aroostook County	1,207	31	1,564	54	1,317	0	671	12	17,514

Table F-2: Counties - Employment and Labor Force Status, Civilian Labor Force—*Continued*

	60 to 61 Years		62 to 64 Years		65 to 69 Years		70 Years and Over		60 Years and Over Not in the Labor Force
	Employed	Unemployed	Employed	Unemployed	Employed	Unemployed	Employed	Unemployed	
Maine—Cont.									
Cumberland County	5,532	44	8,749	137	7,651	0	4,101	354	47,997
Kennebec County	2,307	30	3,214	27	2,150	72	2,191	0	24,844
Penobscot County	2,369	65	3,421	121	2,464	96	1,301	21	29,158
York County	5,486	0	5,763	0	5,041	15	2,710	63	40,611
Maryland									
Allegany County	1,099	108	969	64	1,077	68	903	0	14,096
Anne Arundel County	11,172	158	12,401	251	9,285	451	6,936	180	80,271
Baltimore County	14,592	153	19,558	463	17,760	491	13,140	287	133,114
Calvert County	na	na	na	na	na	na	na	na	na
Carroll County	3,257	0	4,244	0	2,717	0	1,857	0	27,548
Cecil County	1,714	74	2,393	44	1,813	76	1,805	0	17,068
Charles County	3,154	100	3,123	0	2,025	0	1,155	0	21,404
Frederick County	3,975	80	6,289	274	5,168	252	3,701	185	34,018
Harford County	5,023	76	6,159	71	3,768	187	2,912	180	41,625
Howard County	4,797	0	7,447	134	6,210	0	5,186	76	40,030
Montgomery County	20,408	200	25,992	1,339	29,184	695	16,766	1,306	133,126
Prince George's County	14,228	759	19,737	679	18,492	825	9,852	342	108,736
St. Mary's County	2,406	0	1,815	78	1,173	0	1,149	12	15,145
Washington County	3,475	0	3,184	49	2,831	75	1,193	79	26,321
Wicomico County	1,874	0	1,612	0	1,374	0	1,729	0	15,470
Massachusetts									
Barnstable County	5,259	183	7,101	105	7,600	646	6,018	85	57,130
Berkshire County	2,036	18	3,810	307	3,274	0	2,506	68	27,839
Bristol County	9,802	0	12,920	323	9,822	66	7,033	153	94,560
Essex County	14,536	861	18,734	1,070	17,325	484	13,455	145	120,365
Franklin County	2,098	0	2,354	46	2,163	98	1,630	12	14,370
Hampden County	7,987	151	9,298	230	8,146	79	4,383	163	79,146
Hampshire County	3,252	17	3,220	0	4,368	0	3,025	0	24,224
Middlesex County	29,931	1,442	36,859	1,172	34,650	1,203	26,670	920	211,954
Norfolk County	14,748	50	18,300	750	16,603	561	11,167	380	102,899
Plymouth County	10,384	396	12,986	237	11,370	405	8,291	164	86,920
Suffolk County	11,404	190	10,817	357	12,159	555	7,604	291	93,299
Worcester County	15,136	970	18,806	734	15,846	719	8,774	529	124,293
Michigan									
Allegan County	1,249	85	2,015	146	1,802	135	1,011	68	20,203
Bay County	2,087	48	2,134	0	986	0	1,262	0	23,399
Berrien County	3,673	0	3,797	1	3,515	0	2,498	25	29,315
Calhoun County	3,258	191	1,948	45	1,936	83	1,513	50	24,951
Clinton County	1,143	0	1,979	0	892	0	779	0	14,475
Eaton County	2,289	0	2,002	92	952	0	1,057	43	22,786
Genesee County	6,446	291	5,202	299	5,456	315	4,045	52	78,257
Grand Traverse County	na	na	na	na	na	na	na	na	na
Ingham County	4,762	66	4,748	0	4,189	232	2,842	52	40,611
Isabella County	952	29	1,057	71	716	0	594	0	9,696
Jackson County	2,621	48	3,230	73	2,090	52	1,708	0	29,744
Kalamazoo County	4,397	77	4,574	57	3,394	45	2,856	245	39,958
Kent County	10,949	444	12,197	63	10,305	319	7,509	166	87,225
Lapeer County	1,769	5	1,858	121	1,522	0	497	42	17,644
Lenawee County	1,732	0	2,115	63	1,894	209	888	63	18,600
Livingston County	4,260	0	4,675	219	3,969	80	2,228	104	32,711
Macomb County	16,041	419	16,630	803	14,226	309	8,053	493	153,443
Marquette County	790	14	1,099	0	714	105	743	0	14,281
Midland County	938	0	974	48	1,426	52	909	10	17,355
Monroe County	2,605	133	3,137	132	1,564	0	1,524	0	28,836
Muskegon County	2,833	12	3,301	0	2,255	0	1,424	128	31,672
Oakland County	24,408	560	27,719	677	24,061	546	17,112	886	204,835
Ottawa County	3,372	253	5,533	0	4,553	151	3,892	58	41,716
Saginaw County	2,286	25	3,837	0	3,414	54	1,837	135	38,032
St. Clair County	3,032	0	3,513	78	2,358	60	1,528	230	31,884
Shiawassee County	1,125	0	1,460	15	1,057	0	639	22	13,316
Van Buren County	1,023	21	1,838	16	1,107	82	1,034	0	14,144
Washtenaw County	5,177	247	6,498	792	5,805	101	4,253	77	49,244
Wayne County	25,255	1,061	28,655	965	19,960	1,248	12,560	817	296,403
Minnesota									
Anoka County	7,157	77	7,091	293	6,946	111	3,456	0	47,360
Blue Earth County	1,000	0	1,036	0	727	10	563	31	9,016
Carver County	1,405	78	1,807	60	1,532	0	845	39	12,434
Dakota County	8,686	331	7,543	50	6,133	82	3,465	38	58,378
Hennepin County	20,442	1,480	26,457	1,701	24,982	738	13,740	208	161,998
Olmsted County	3,128	129	2,296	0	2,347	130	2,061	89	22,673
Ramsey County	8,915	40	10,062	497	8,715	235	5,355	208	78,196
Rice County	952	16	1,711	14	934	0	284	0	10,434
St. Louis County	3,610	250	3,918	101	3,252	56	2,064	12	40,715
Scott County	1,992	46	3,276	0	1,706	50	1,470	0	15,135
Sherburne County	na	na	na	na	na	na	na	na	na
Stearns County	3,000	68	3,243	0	2,369	13	1,766	0	22,707
Washington County	4,254	200	5,513	86	4,166	9	2,763	0	37,334
Wright County	1,965	17	2,472	30	1,808	0	1,612	15	16,208

Table F-2: Counties - Employment and Labor Force Status, Civilian Labor Force—*Continued*

	60 to 61 Years		62 to 64 Years		65 to 69 Years		70 Years and Over		60 Years and Over Not in the Labor Force
	Employed	Unemployed	Employed	Unemployed	Employed	Unemployed	Employed	Unemployed	
Mississippi									
DeSoto County	3,544	105	3,888	237	2,380	64	2,254	0	22,138
Forrest County	na	na	na	na	na	na	na	na	na
Harrison County	2,197	266	2,307	59	2,183	39	2,416	19	32,891
Hinds County	3,488	46	3,906	335	3,586	47	2,236	0	34,448
Jackson County	2,536	71	1,728	0	1,322	0	692	0	26,261
Jones County	na	na	na	na	na	na	na	na	na
Lauderdale County	na	na	na	na	na	na	na	na	na
Lee County	na	na	na	na	na	na	na	na	na
Madison County	na	na	na	na	na	na	na	na	na
Rankin County	2,846	24	3,028	0	3,096	0	1,547	0	21,518
Missouri									
Boone County	2,532	33	3,041	222	2,795	0	1,619	0	21,966
Buchanan County	1,485	0	2,211	96	1,405	0	1,228	51	14,929
Cape Girardeau County	na	na	na	na	na	na	na	na	na
Cass County	1,358	111	2,699	36	1,848	54	1,006	5	18,198
Christian County	na	na	na	na	na	na	na	na	na
Clay County	4,059	39	4,913	43	3,348	72	3,264	128	34,011
Cole County	na	na	na	na	na	na	na	na	na
Franklin County	na	na	na	na	na	na	na	na	na
Greene County	3,929	0	5,149	86	3,093	32	2,477	134	50,199
Jackson County	10,922	92	13,718	326	10,217	548	9,034	250	104,172
Jasper County	1,294	0	1,227	226	1,963	7	1,735	0	18,005
Jefferson County	2,773	21	4,613	169	2,966	49	2,093	51	37,735
Platte County	na	na	na	na	na	na	na	na	na
St. Charles County	5,981	191	9,319	171	5,717	108	3,691	186	61,522
St. Francois County	na	na	na	na	na	na	na	na	na
St. Louis County	20,215	332	22,632	481	22,248	1,216	12,647	522	171,297
Montana									
Cascade County	1,409	0	2,622	79	1,154	0	1,285	0	14,820
Flathead County	2,063	46	2,511	84	2,147	116	1,494	0	20,137
Gallatin County	2,419	0	2,484	0	1,799	0	1,472	0	13,056
Lewis and Clark County	na	na	na	na	na	na	na	na	na
Missoula County	1,812	102	2,695	0	1,762	99	1,944	0	17,169
Yellowstone County	4,023	21	2,689	88	2,913	248	1,982	0	26,186
Nebraska									
Douglas County	8,624	170	11,203	442	9,277	271	6,897	122	68,418
Lancaster County	5,022	0	6,104	76	6,906	0	4,575	77	38,838
Sarpy County	2,775	0	2,766	14	2,408	44	1,345	0	22,215
Nevada									
Clark County	27,921	1,541	36,719	1,059	30,053	1,244	22,520	1,775	332,978
Washoe County	7,666	639	11,572	72	9,426	372	4,846	0	74,733
New Hampshire									
Cheshire County	1,412	29	2,234	0	2,144	67	1,658	0	13,959
Grafton County	2,135	20	1,836	0	2,306	43	2,664	29	16,149
Hillsborough County	9,907	82	9,648	408	9,157	13	5,384	121	59,726
Merrimack County	3,231	151	3,708	31	3,700	171	2,770	0	26,149
Rockingham County	7,148	281	8,921	137	6,907	270	4,776	97	50,655
Strafford County	3,065	68	2,817	290	1,992	0	1,849	66	17,574
New Jersey									
Atlantic County	4,152	174	6,863	35	4,711	171	3,765	466	45,256
Bergen County	19,640	421	21,830	812	21,308	372	17,548	596	139,313
Burlington County	9,214	177	10,924	549	8,541	286	6,004	161	70,608
Camden County	8,427	617	10,172	235	8,511	206	6,477	362	77,300
Cape May County	2,609	0	2,451	104	1,668	78	1,728	56	23,579
Cumberland County	2,380	20	2,091	0	1,773	0	1,305	7	24,386
Essex County	11,819	585	17,161	678	14,639	578	9,763	313	100,529
Gloucester County	7,390	133	5,193	326	6,490	118	3,310	72	44,003
Hudson County	9,987	303	14,360	220	8,733	189	6,503	45	76,221
Hunterdon County	3,205	40	2,652	52	3,233	107	1,576	0	21,245
Mercer County	8,536	254	6,869	166	7,531	220	4,796	97	50,563
Middlesex County	15,283	678	16,653	439	15,493	824	9,569	713	115,196
Monmouth County	13,827	518	16,023	516	12,860	309	10,725	366	100,168
Morris County	9,765	771	13,907	325	11,449	230	9,352	369	73,091
Ocean County	11,327	167	13,049	946	13,028	625	11,205	918	126,782
Passaic County	7,709	207	10,687	39	8,947	268	5,764	244	69,915
Salem County	1,200	0	1,238	42	1,074	12	1,001	64	12,030
Somerset County	7,261	217	9,103	974	7,120	256	4,102	522	46,493
Sussex County	4,182	189	4,134	110	3,267	179	1,631	200	21,709
Union County	10,032	255	12,182	34	10,314	420	7,737	813	71,987
Warren County	2,992	86	2,754	42	1,877	96	1,379	0	18,474
New Mexico									
Bernalillo County	11,781	190	9,526	431	9,552	427	6,579	455	114,160
Chaves County	1,088	189	956	84	1,001	0	954	0	11,045
Doña Ana County	1,996	235	3,248	45	3,402	0	1,522	0	36,163
Lea County	na	na	na	na	na	na	na	na	na
McKinley County	1,811	0	1,110	66	784	0	143	0	10,762
Otero County	na	na	na	na	na	na	na	na	na
Sandoval County	2,271	110	2,390	0	2,142	14	1,184	103	27,175

Table F-2: Counties - Employment and Labor Force Status, Civilian Labor Force—*Continued*

	60 to 61 Years		62 to 64 Years		65 to 69 Years		70 Years and Over		60 Years and Over Not in the Labor Force
	Employed	Unemployed	Employed	Unemployed	Employed	Unemployed	Employed	Unemployed	
New Mexico—Cont.									
San Juan County	1,716	68	1,873	105	1,329	105	1,172	80	20,176
Santa Fe County	2,818	153	4,555	44	4,715	240	3,472	96	32,455
Valencia County	na	na	na	na	na	na	na	na	na
New York									
Albany County	4,547	24	6,257	449	6,579	102	4,467	55	50,117
Bronx County	17,153	1,119	18,608	1,261	13,320	512	8,210	336	197,654
Broome County	4,279	142	3,917	228	3,122	124	2,645	106	36,353
Cattaraugus County	1,088	61	1,917	67	963	115	620	64	15,645
Cayuga County	1,093	22	1,544	13	1,428	0	1,171	0	14,428
Chautauqua County	2,300	76	2,783	0	2,277	58	1,582	0	25,991
Chemung County	1,348	0	1,381	56	1,145	35	758	23	17,434
Clinton County	1,311	62	1,067	0	1,028	52	604	0	15,755
Dutchess County	5,626	166	6,026	386	5,096	536	4,828	208	50,627
Erie County	17,812	437	19,536	533	14,248	317	12,026	0	164,935
Jefferson County	1,392	0	1,804	0	820	13	666	44	17,102
Kings County	35,634	928	42,189	2,225	35,936	782	22,699	403	359,022
Livingston County	1,143	27	1,519	24	1,048	0	916	0	11,311
Madison County	na	na	na	na	na	na	na	na	na
Monroe County	14,395	183	17,813	525	11,844	576	9,184	362	127,811
Nassau County	30,903	770	32,854	712	29,853	492	21,689	494	218,006
New York County	23,942	1,416	28,777	977	31,957	990	27,797	907	243,528
Niagara County	5,329	86	5,310	102	2,822	67	1,782	88	43,323
Oneida County	3,707	40	4,400	50	3,876	68	2,808	97	44,628
Onondaga County	8,288	108	9,983	362	8,516	227	5,762	314	78,297
Ontario County	2,566	163	2,977	27	1,938	0	1,197	0	21,300
Orange County	6,071	120	8,096	352	6,429	105	5,989	163	49,928
Oswego County	2,053	92	1,607	15	1,097	84	1,283	30	20,678
Putnam County	2,374	192	2,534	114	2,783	36	2,092	0	14,960
Queens County	40,524	1,984	42,568	1,362	33,863	1,331	21,185	1,053	355,433
Rensselaer County	2,607	58	3,164	0	2,342	58	1,656	0	27,775
Richmond County	7,344	121	9,249	65	8,873	379	4,978	52	79,650
Rockland County	5,143	166	7,108	324	6,723	505	5,124	59	45,615
St. Lawrence County	1,682	0	1,407	26	1,316	0	1,065	0	20,199
Saratoga County	4,620	64	4,000	185	4,398	199	3,292	122	38,204
Schenectady County	2,904	0	3,369	0	2,712	72	1,735	90	27,239
Steuben County	1,877	73	1,529	61	1,380	0	1,031	0	19,985
Suffolk County	29,765	882	31,064	581	26,893	602	22,223	471	238,398
Sullivan County	940	45	1,953	31	1,160	161	1,417	31	13,671
Tompkins County	1,476	0	3,012	162	1,561	0	1,559	0	13,678
Ulster County	5,335	297	4,420	258	4,085	109	2,898	258	31,760
Warren County	na	na	na	na	na	na	na	na	na
Wayne County	1,766	0	1,749	63	1,169	35	1,448	122	17,867
Westchester County	19,073	812	21,510	879	20,422	1,220	18,869	806	144,726
North Carolina									
Alamance County	2,912	119	3,407	0	2,871	84	1,760	45	27,724
Brunswick County	na	na	na	na	na	na	na	na	na
Buncombe County	4,857	48	6,481	141	5,060	149	3,869	0	50,040
Burke County	na	na	na	na	na	na	na	na	na
Cabarrus County	2,892	49	2,982	51	2,371	0	1,626	49	28,495
Caldwell County	1,327	15	1,276	0	1,245	216	951	0	16,826
Carteret County	974	42	2,092	79	1,317	72	1,110	46	17,485
Catawba County	2,750	52	3,322	138	2,476	110	2,867	206	27,066
Chatham County	na	na	na	na	na	na	na	na	na
Cleveland County	2,256	0	2,098	47	2,223	0	746	0	18,811
Craven County	1,364	0	2,139	0	1,047	0	1,297	224	20,735
Cumberland County	3,827	150	3,948	61	2,399	183	2,516	73	43,847
Davidson County	3,022	0	3,973	103	1,722	0	2,286	0	31,781
Durham County	4,989	56	6,076	303	5,814	72	3,650	67	38,857
Forsyth County	6,276	583	7,126	87	6,315	342	3,512	216	59,008
Franklin County	na	na	na	na	na	na	na	na	na
Gaston County	3,280	50	3,939	73	3,031	153	2,122	0	36,776
Guilford County	9,310	530	10,344	42	8,584	121	6,378	91	78,525
Harnett County	1,105	66	1,381	0	1,270	0	836	0	19,062
Henderson County	na	na	na	na	na	na	na	na	na
Iredell County	2,464	41	2,949	0	1,876	0	2,433	118	28,690
Johnston County	1,944	0	3,823	58	3,160	0	2,087	0	27,668
Lincoln County	na	na	na	na	na	na	na	na	na
Mecklenburg County	16,301	455	17,428	541	15,249	787	7,819	266	120,645
Moore County	1,525	0	2,499	77	2,504	0	1,995	85	22,436
Nash County	na	na	na	na	na	na	na	na	na
New Hanover County	2,989	169	4,562	387	3,222	48	2,204	0	42,188
Onslow County	1,795	0	1,942	0	1,669	32	863	0	18,610
Orange County	2,180	119	3,493	102	3,524	45	1,475	64	18,180
Pitt County	2,453	0	3,171	0	2,609	0	1,723	0	24,390
Randolph County	2,245	0	2,532	0	2,936	42	1,761	44	24,976
Robeson County	1,348	0	2,495	32	1,396	39	832	0	22,874
Rockingham County	1,228	156	2,058	0	1,074	0	902	105	20,489
Rowan County	1,516	0	2,221	42	2,118	368	1,768	0	24,911
Rutherford County	na	na	na	na	na	na	na	na	na

Table F-2: Counties - Employment and Labor Force Status, Civilian Labor Force—*Continued*

	60 to 61 Years		62 to 64 Years		65 to 69 Years		70 Years and Over		60 Years and Over Not in the Labor Force
	Employed	Unemployed	Employed	Unemployed	Employed	Unemployed	Employed	Unemployed	
North Carolina—Cont.									
Surry County	1,492	0	1,506	0	1,642	46	792	0	14,866
Union County	3,151	44	4,381	99	2,667	151	2,324	65	29,009
Wake County	15,839	656	17,341	838	15,270	558	10,777	325	121,259
Wayne County	2,531	97	2,764	96	1,900	53	2,113	94	20,845
Wilkes County	na	na	na	na	na	na	na	na	na
Wilson County	1,919	0	1,296	0	1,969	0	1,088	0	14,478
North Dakota									
Burleigh County	na	na	na	na	na	na	na	na	na
Cass County	3,481	0	4,141	0	2,373	0	2,172	0	20,300
Grand Forks County	1,423	115	1,465	0	902	33	626	0	8,267
Ward County	na	na	na	na	na	na	na	na	na
Ohio									
Allen County	2,301	181	1,928	97	1,403	50	1,034	0	18,333
Ashtabula County	1,429	23	2,958	0	1,643	22	1,660	0	18,766
Athens County	410	2	1,292	0	809	0	407	0	9,225
Belmont County	1,735	0	1,623	151	1,341	0	767	60	14,411
Butler County	6,782	162	7,947	111	6,997	210	3,526	25	55,193
Clark County	2,177	0	2,658	123	1,855	56	970	0	27,399
Clermont County	3,752	82	4,117	0	3,083	0	2,453	196	33,741
Columbiana County	2,164	174	1,962	0	2,118	125	890	59	21,669
Cuyahoga County	22,042	900	25,682	1,090	25,325	866	16,241	679	222,503
Delaware County	3,974	38	4,500	51	3,314	39	1,728	48	26,280
Erie County	na	na	na	na	na	na	na	na	na
Fairfield County	2,255	14	2,493	0	2,211	0	1,308	0	26,116
Franklin County	19,768	433	23,096	627	19,598	549	11,998	300	154,850
Geauga County	na	na	na	na	na	na	na	na	na
Greene County	3,146	38	3,283	0	3,130	0	1,298	139	29,299
Hamilton County	13,998	405	15,025	531	15,689	337	11,442	247	118,895
Hancock County	na	na	na	na	na	na	na	na	na
Jefferson County	872	9	1,309	45	723	29	418	134	16,286
Lake County	5,445	148	6,750	85	5,009	174	3,227	107	44,013
Licking County	3,468	125	3,165	104	2,367	41	1,602	107	29,298
Lorain County	5,043	232	7,116	129	6,381	229	4,459	0	55,996
Lucas County	7,284	49	7,803	113	6,145	219	4,521	411	72,079
Mahoning County	4,101	160	6,271	307	4,798	134	3,340	73	47,917
Marion County	na	na	na	na	na	na	na	na	na
Medina County	2,917	34	4,079	19	2,725	0	2,776	0	30,882
Miami County	na	na	na	na	na	na	na	na	na
Montgomery County	9,721	529	10,432	113	9,923	703	7,091	202	91,742
Muskingum County	2,269	40	1,426	0	1,129	0	602	0	16,453
Portage County	2,732	334	3,611	130	3,858	256	2,004	154	25,137
Richland County	2,160	0	1,927	141	1,454	48	1,011	47	24,591
Ross County	1,248	0	1,342	25	657	0	597	0	14,969
Scioto County	1,038	0	823	0	908	46	213	0	15,620
Stark County	7,262	114	7,250	195	6,221	304	3,739	69	72,526
Summit County	9,653	153	13,858	583	9,255	799	7,336	338	95,382
Trumbull County	4,038	119	3,607	92	3,617	192	2,014	41	44,243
Tuscarawas County	na	na	na	na	na	na	na	na	na
Warren County	3,346	26	4,261	0	3,740	0	2,468	0	31,832
Wayne County	1,976	0	2,682	0	2,010	0	1,392	135	20,414
Wood County	2,621	57	1,991	0	2,883	80	807	234	20,039
Oklahoma									
Canadian County	1,889	0	3,208	0	2,063	40	1,739	0	18,040
Cleveland County	3,470	140	3,984	0	4,231	0	4,200	0	34,899
Comanche County	2,031	18	1,199	52	1,487	58	863	0	16,682
Creek County	700	19	1,492	40	713	81	937	0	12,975
Muskogee County	961	14	948	0	760	0	779	41	11,806
Oklahoma County	11,279	197	13,804	136	12,124	145	11,324	231	102,588
Payne County	1,649	165	663	0	1,361	0	904	0	10,079
Pottawatomie County	1,422	30	1,454	0	740	18	783	0	12,523
Rogers County	1,261	31	1,797	0	1,352	11	953	42	15,192
Tulsa County	11,577	443	10,763	267	10,409	100	7,779	278	89,484
Wagoner County	1,279	37	1,625	59	1,050	59	859	0	13,325
Oregon									
Benton County	1,557	0	1,171	0	1,553	46	818	0	14,661
Clackamas County	8,230	354	8,610	0	7,486	225	4,272	140	74,346
Deschutes County	2,181	0	5,890	248	3,891	282	2,811	74	38,303
Douglas County	1,523	55	1,767	0	1,844	311	875	0	30,548
Jackson County	3,002	53	4,081	337	4,283	101	2,829	74	50,370
Josephine County	na	na	na	na	na	na	na	na	na
Klamath County	na	na	na	na	na	na	na	na	na
Lane County	6,632	232	7,067	507	6,832	425	3,782	258	74,302
Linn County	1,566	16	1,928	65	2,539	10	1,018	277	24,660
Marion County	5,757	36	6,872	59	4,287	52	2,929	0	56,692
Multnomah County	10,573	307	13,298	249	13,183	632	6,957	150	106,427
Polk County	1,149	0	1,616	0	849	0	641	0	15,844
Umatilla County	1,633	71	403	84	760	3	975	292	12,482
Washington County	9,269	134	11,908	393	8,982	347	6,281	47	77,508
Yamhill County	1,734	30	2,411	0	1,519	57	1,162	0	18,151

Table F-2: Counties - Employment and Labor Force Status, Civilian Labor Force—*Continued*

	60 to 61 Years		62 to 64 Years		65 to 69 Years		70 Years and Over		60 Years and Over Not in the Labor Force
	Employed	Unemployed	Employed	Unemployed	Employed	Unemployed	Employed	Unemployed	
Pennsylvania									
Adams County	2,428	38	2,643	0	1,415	55	1,254	43	20,229
Allegheny County	25,860	970	29,549	1,390	25,930	553	15,926	443	220,041
Armstrong County	1,553	25	1,412	43	848	0	655	57	15,035
Beaver County	3,223	99	3,988	64	4,974	140	1,655	12	33,483
Berks County	7,513	382	8,500	259	6,472	164	5,463	404	69,699
Blair County	2,444	46	2,086	22	2,693	0	1,214	0	25,192
Bucks County	13,355	473	17,899	793	14,875	737	10,664	586	102,719
Butler County	4,317	157	5,241	287	3,558	193	1,689	66	35,746
Cambria County	2,916	45	2,625	72	2,274	55	1,831	0	30,680
Carbon County	na	na	na	na	na	na	na	na	na
Centre County	2,062	32	3,549	63	2,186	0	1,500	25	22,067
Chester County	8,956	446	14,311	187	11,540	532	8,536	290	76,119
Clearfield County	1,370	0	1,250	0	1,570	13	680	12	16,824
Columbia County	1,395	0	1,729	34	1,560	34	597	0	12,128
Crawford County	1,567	119	2,105	24	1,673	32	1,426	112	17,107
Cumberland County	3,758	90	5,611	192	5,602	36	3,783	0	43,926
Dauphin County	4,345	291	6,750	161	4,821	246	4,156	133	45,121
Delaware County	9,405	438	12,294	289	11,521	361	7,564	286	86,772
Erie County	4,242	172	5,248	151	4,251	74	3,234	101	49,604
Fayette County	2,100	25	3,206	160	2,333	98	2,288	200	27,825
Franklin County	3,098	92	2,777	0	3,121	69	2,082	43	29,090
Indiana County	1,340	0	1,824	0	983	12	909	35	17,576
Lackawanna County	5,758	0	4,307	0	3,860	38	3,315	38	40,973
Lancaster County	10,289	0	11,513	490	10,464	101	8,766	109	91,312
Lawrence County	2,237	0	1,319	79	1,378	63	1,583	0	19,702
Lebanon County	1,861	0	3,601	0	2,822	0	2,214	67	27,209
Lehigh County	5,977	430	8,182	64	5,436	448	4,481	0	60,706
Luzerne County	5,883	215	7,248	156	6,711	118	5,530	218	60,180
Lycoming County	2,363	69	2,370	29	2,278	96	1,030	70	22,234
Mercer County	2,261	44	2,580	9	1,916	51	1,427	0	24,119
Monroe County	3,936	78	3,648	0	3,516	140	2,462	68	29,446
Montgomery County	16,794	608	21,770	593	19,055	447	14,593	842	127,678
Northampton County	5,389	76	5,232	222	5,721	43	3,791	0	56,397
Northumberland County	2,233	0	1,793	66	1,741	22	1,453	59	19,168
Philadelphia County	22,204	1,168	22,184	683	19,220	1,498	14,525	705	225,316
Schuylkill County	2,279	58	2,952	46	2,201	62	1,785	0	29,831
Somerset County	1,812	73	1,478	0	1,496	46	1,180	7	16,545
Washington County	4,185	117	4,737	75	3,749	26	2,945	74	42,376
Westmoreland County	7,484	149	8,880	72	8,386	358	6,084	323	77,159
York County	7,690	259	10,616	247	7,693	594	5,670	172	77,582
Rhode Island									
Kent County	4,412	0	4,258	258	2,709	181	2,180	44	30,590
Newport County	2,178	98	2,546	42	2,046	0	2,109	88	16,335
Providence County	13,715	603	12,962	182	9,036	223	5,828	0	96,717
Washington County	2,455	48	3,783	124	3,479	108	2,352	66	23,344
South Carolina									
Aiken County	2,131	71	2,512	340	2,360	61	1,691	140	34,642
Anderson County	3,107	94	3,370	76	3,220	47	1,874	0	36,629
Beaufort County	2,233	0	3,258	131	3,644	0	4,915	0	49,498
Berkeley County	3,737	87	3,515	0	3,129	77	2,254	82	31,525
Charleston County	4,942	0	7,528	82	6,724	144	4,904	168	64,804
Darlington County	na	na	na	na	na	na	na	na	na
Dorchester County	2,572	116	1,872	303	2,679	31	1,633	0	22,230
Florence County	2,070	0	2,163	0	2,055	43	2,364	0	23,461
Greenville County	9,091	356	8,619	226	8,910	286	5,919	48	79,927
Greenwood County	na	na	na	na	na	na	na	na	na
Horry County	5,963	443	6,032	286	7,135	170	4,230	82	87,178
Kershaw County	na	na	na	na	na	na	na	na	na
Lancaster County	na	na	na	na	na	na	na	na	na
Laurens County	807	0	1,636	71	1,316	36	1,098	0	12,147
Lexington County	5,674	52	5,745	90	4,070	52	2,773	95	48,190
Oconee County	na	na	na	na	na	na	na	na	na
Orangeburg County	916	76	1,015	71	1,340	0	1,501	12	17,873
Pickens County	2,257	0	1,399	143	1,533	49	971	0	21,443
Richland County	4,723	278	6,318	254	6,479	20	4,531	128	52,714
Spartanburg County	4,672	224	5,818	84	4,752	257	3,384	129	50,845
Sumter County	775	0	1,729	0	1,937	0	1,016	232	18,104
York County	5,394	0	4,623	0	3,451	184	2,590	201	38,546
South Dakota									
Minnehaha County	3,915	0	4,421	49	4,036	216	2,877	0	21,314
Pennington County	1,748	53	3,288	102	2,565	0	2,001	102	19,566
Tennessee									
Anderson County	na	na	na	na	na	na	na	na	na
Blount County	2,566	103	2,568	195	2,115	62	2,418	8	26,687
Bradley County	1,275	0	1,342	14	1,638	14	2,068	105	17,684
Davidson County	9,329	359	12,961	134	12,144	210	7,865	182	76,820
Greene County	1,325	0	1,156	0	951	0	1,017	0	16,267
Hamilton County	5,952	39	8,241	254	6,342	0	4,787	445	62,596

Table F-2: Counties - Employment and Labor Force Status, Civilian Labor Force—*Continued*

	60 to 61 Years		62 to 64 Years		65 to 69 Years		70 Years and Over		60 Years and Over Not in the Labor Force
	Employed	Unemployed	Employed	Unemployed	Employed	Unemployed	Employed	Unemployed	
Tennessee—Cont.									
Knox County	7,265	142	8,600	79	8,784	88	5,734	94	70,041
Madison County	1,750	0	2,255	185	1,906	0	1,335	26	16,425
Maury County	na	na	na	na	na	na	na	na	na
Montgomery County	1,909	205	2,259	160	1,495	0	548	0	21,564
Putnam County	na	na	na	na	na	na	na	na	na
Robertson County	na	na	na	na	na	na	na	na	na
Rutherford County	5,270	120	3,788	96	3,831	0	2,329	0	34,065
Sevier County	1,715	0	1,591	56	1,588	0	1,549	29	19,021
Shelby County	16,775	192	19,348	652	14,929	1,090	12,271	736	125,130
Sullivan County	2,337	119	2,601	56	2,570	25	1,715	0	38,358
Sumner County	2,767	0	3,099	167	4,035	0	2,437	0	28,618
Washington County	1,637	81	2,848	0	1,498	130	1,230	0	24,471
Williamson County	4,021	110	4,552	80	4,236	39	2,901	0	27,901
Wilson County	3,298	184	2,889	0	3,700	0	1,431	139	20,190
Texas									
Angelina County	870	61	1,108	0	750	0	506	0	15,897
Bastrop County	na	na	na	na	na	na	na	na	na
Bell County	2,891	227	3,833	403	4,306	279	4,255	0	37,967
Bexar County	25,467	579	26,587	766	26,407	620	17,829	349	242,365
Bowie County	na	na	na	na	na	na	na	na	na
Brazoria County	4,187	289	4,573	406	5,621	266	3,630	258	43,347
Brazos County	1,150	0	2,751	0	2,248	0	2,200	0	20,460
Cameron County	4,559	0	4,150	110	3,751	61	2,245	311	60,153
Collin County	13,919	652	16,825	674	16,861	291	10,353	263	99,909
Comal County	3,255	150	2,815	231	2,591	62	1,802	112	27,618
Coryell County	513	64	795	0	340	0	457	0	8,273
Dallas County	41,372	1,932	45,284	737	37,105	1,551	29,383	763	262,391
Denton County	13,289	860	13,756	114	10,274	403	8,901	430	80,803
Ector County	2,632	115	2,971	91	1,019	77	2,200	0	14,441
Ellis County	2,607	148	2,533	61	2,654	166	2,232	0	21,311
El Paso County	9,208	356	10,955	733	9,627	0	5,614	224	109,389
Fort Bend County	11,088	266	14,640	1,871	10,030	462	7,680	135	84,555
Galveston County	4,909	980	4,878	673	5,050	136	4,408	498	45,882
Grayson County	1,848	38	2,291	259	2,241	0	2,343	0	22,345
Gregg County	2,082	62	1,840	0	2,321	15	1,156	0	19,040
Guadalupe County	2,075	0	2,422	111	2,708	142	1,044	134	22,260
Harris County	67,712	2,648	78,213	3,154	64,098	2,813	42,174	1,951	477,559
Harrison County	na	na	na	na	na	na	na	na	na
Hays County	2,514	186	3,034	206	3,444	45	1,376	125	24,179
Henderson County	na	na	na	na	na	na	na	na	na
Hidalgo County	8,523	421	9,127	118	8,679	278	4,913	154	98,505
Hunt County	1,435	0	1,969	121	1,067	20	2,266	40	15,159
Jefferson County	3,085	134	3,787	0	2,837	278	2,683	94	39,884
Johnson County	2,528	130	2,315	58	2,722	69	1,811	0	22,833
Kaufman County	1,669	373	3,043	0	2,254	60	1,542	78	14,256
Liberty County	na	na	na	na	na	na	na	na	na
Lubbock County	5,723	159	5,388	119	4,415	35	3,374	154	35,376
McLennan County	3,771	267	4,451	219	4,140	0	3,074	80	34,909
Midland County	2,690	51	3,776	0	3,169	0	1,762	0	15,953
Montgomery County	7,927	656	8,798	208	10,242	575	4,510	223	76,288
Nacogdoches County	na	na	na	na	na	na	na	na	na
Nueces County	6,440	126	6,116	252	5,385	504	3,917	60	52,196
Orange County	na	na	na	na	na	na	na	na	na
Parker County	2,535	0	2,459	0	1,356	128	1,804	0	21,559
Potter County	1,755	41	1,387	84	1,913	26	1,364	0	13,264
Randall County	na	na	na	na	na	na	na	na	na
Rockwall County	na	na	na	na	na	na	na	na	na
San Patricio County	na	na	na	na	na	na	na	na	na
Smith County	4,382	86	3,904	224	3,409	151	3,104	106	36,738
Tarrant County	35,324	781	35,758	1,202	30,396	1,102	17,051	576	226,999
Taylor County	2,200	0	2,297	0	2,048	0	1,513	18	19,425
Tom Green County	1,662	0	1,676	0	2,424	0	1,867	0	16,899
Travis County	17,028	589	20,226	1,102	20,740	377	11,086	184	112,069
Victoria County	1,080	0	1,438	77	1,255	21	1,269	0	15,506
Walker County	na	na	na	na	na	na	na	na	na
Webb County	2,044	151	2,678	29	2,558	98	2,549	143	25,388
Wichita County	1,614	0	2,583	132	2,045	50	1,684	43	18,508
Williamson County	7,052	294	8,630	707	7,928	205	5,283	151	66,109
Wise County	na	na	na	na	na	na	na	na	na
Utah									
Cache County	1,440	0	1,919	12	1,801	49	340	0	10,884
Davis County	4,166	94	5,602	69	4,195	0	2,626	53	35,291
Salt Lake County	15,424	573	19,794	891	16,230	267	10,722	268	117,253
Tooele County	na	na	na	na	na	na	na	na	na
Utah County	4,170	172	8,021	41	5,417	41	3,001	56	47,108
Washington County	1,734	236	2,149	135	2,374	46	2,240	47	37,458
Weber County	3,616	0	3,124	24	3,673	0	890	0	31,264

Table F-2: Counties - Employment and Labor Force Status, Civilian Labor Force—*Continued*

	60 to 61 Years		62 to 64 Years		65 to 69 Years		70 Years and Over		60 Years and Over Not in the Labor Force
	Employed	Unemployed	Employed	Unemployed	Employed	Unemployed	Employed	Unemployed	
Vermont									
Chittenden County	3,073	180	4,794	0	3,637	170	2,200	195	22,721
Virginia									
Albemarle County	2,980	0	2,491	62	2,661	81	1,625	49	18,281
Arlington County	3,675	127	4,471	311	3,832	42	2,595	0	21,995
Augusta County	na	na	na	na	na	na	na	na	na
Bedford County	na	na	na	na	na	na	na	na	na
Chesterfield County	4,193	142	8,557	111	6,250	139	3,780	0	51,319
Fairfax County	22,201	448	25,506	169	25,093	623	15,574	605	132,392
Fauquier County	na	na	na	na	na	na	na	na	na
Frederick County	na	na	na	na	na	na	na	na	na
Hanover County	2,594	0	2,146	154	1,814	0	1,407	44	18,272
Henrico County	6,388	52	6,703	406	5,653	63	4,179	48	48,819
James City County	na	na	na	na	na	na	na	na	na
Loudoun County	6,352	35	6,708	93	6,834	149	3,405	159	33,002
Montgomery County	na	na	na	na	na	na	na	na	na
Prince William County	5,772	25	7,715	780	5,867	69	3,654	455	43,792
Roanoke County	2,420	0	1,638	0	1,517	0	1,783	0	18,551
Rockingham County	2,025	97	1,616	0	1,109	93	1,274	0	15,386
Spotsylvania County	1,505	0	2,670	63	2,332	0	1,120	33	19,345
Stafford County	2,480	61	2,401	178	2,335	0	1,480	0	13,931
York County	na	na	na	na	na	na	na	na	na
Washington									
Benton County	2,215	166	3,862	169	2,232	0	1,381	0	32,065
Chelan County	na	na	na	na	na	na	na	na	na
Clallam County	1,512	40	1,563	95	1,676	0	675	0	22,979
Clark County	8,295	243	9,612	263	6,411	101	4,841	300	74,470
Cowlitz County	na	na	na	na	na	na	na	na	na
Franklin County	na	na	na	na	na	na	na	na	na
Grant County	na	na	na	na	na	na	na	na	na
Grays Harbor County	na	na	na	na	na	na	na	na	na
Island County	1,085	61	1,895	73	1,453	41	1,107	0	21,736
King County	35,417	1,003	43,422	1,260	36,678	498	22,620	395	279,477
Kitsap County	4,177	317	5,726	101	5,242	97	3,093	0	47,491
Lewis County	1,348	0	1,948	0	612	0	1,196	13	18,186
Mason County	na	na	na	na	na	na	na	na	na
Pierce County	13,813	808	15,568	470	13,475	76	6,991	168	125,518
Skagit County	2,612	79	2,674	38	2,178	201	1,198	102	26,814
Snohomish County	15,141	243	14,396	518	14,345	149	6,248	529	110,809
Spokane County	7,343	252	8,013	331	7,402	246	3,500	129	86,718
Thurston County	5,125	168	5,786	83	4,462	114	2,448	67	50,437
Whatcom County	3,320	171	4,701	346	3,540	133	2,449	66	39,377
Yakima County	3,226	0	4,069	76	3,122	179	1,720	515	34,998
West Virginia									
Berkeley County	1,139	64	2,375	216	1,496	0	1,114	40	19,107
Cabell County	1,282	26	1,195	0	1,163	0	1,435	78	17,519
Harrison County	na	na	na	na	na	na	na	na	na
Kanawha County	1,502	39	4,156	0	3,667	99	2,518	27	38,938
Monongalia County	1,073	436	1,529	54	1,648	0	1,018	0	13,421
Raleigh County	923	0	952	137	1,418	0	967	0	16,910
Wood County	na	na	na	na	na	na	na	na	na
Wisconsin									
Brown County	5,111	173	4,227	14	4,121	63	1,922	0	40,177
Dane County	11,034	22	9,981	42	8,756	111	5,131	76	69,837
Dodge County	2,403	0	1,908	60	2,251	17	1,261	0	14,406
Eau Claire County	1,680	0	2,027	8	1,616	31	1,324	0	15,746
Fond du Lac County	na	na	na	na	na	na	na	na	na
Jefferson County	2,198	98	1,331	24	1,848	0	1,115	0	13,836
Kenosha County	3,623	45	3,709	76	2,437	41	1,168	159	23,167
La Crosse County	2,220	46	2,684	133	2,013	0	937	0	18,858
Manitowoc County	na	na	na	na	na	na	na	na	na
Marathon County	2,580	0	2,933	124	2,260	136	1,224	0	23,534
Milwaukee County	14,993	219	17,431	620	11,752	352	6,559	179	136,919
Outagamie County	3,777	55	3,347	12	2,600	152	894	0	28,235
Ozaukee County	na	na	na	na	na	na	na	na	na
Portage County	1,003	10	1,054	15	533	0	643	0	12,827
Racine County	4,341	14	4,059	93	2,807	60	2,377	0	33,020
Rock County	3,034	17	3,202	54	2,774	16	1,786	33	26,664
St. Croix County	1,656	0	1,985	0	1,526	0	577	63	11,819
Sheboygan County	2,472	77	2,203	30	1,928	40	1,072	94	20,568
Walworth County	1,730	0	2,651	0	2,143	45	1,348	39	16,985
Washington County	2,989	138	3,393	26	2,912	40	1,084	161	23,958
Waukesha County	8,923	174	11,538	193	7,583	40	5,401	76	73,477
Winnebago County	2,473	87	3,101	95	1,979	54	1,703	16	28,817
Wood County	na	na	na	na	na	na	na	na	na
Wyoming									
Laramie County	2,170	43	1,511	0	1,746	162	875	91	16,737
Natrona County	na	na	na	na	na	na	na	na	na

Table F-3: Cities - Employment and Labor Force Status, Civilian Labor Force

	60 to 61 Years		62 to 64 Years		65 to 69 Years		70 Years and Over		60 Years and Over Not in the Labor Force
	Employed	Unemployed	Employed	Unemployed	Employed	Unemployed	Employed	Unemployed	
Alabama									
Auburn city	na	na	na	na	na	na	na	na	na
Birmingham city	3,266	131	2,652	161	3,084	414	2,084	54	35,796
Dothan city	1,005	11	1,061	0	1,377	32	1,059	22	13,182
Hoover city	na	na	na	na	na	na	na	na	na
Huntsville city	2,395	22	2,276	230	2,784	238	3,396	229	30,626
Mobile city	2,979	31	2,555	76	2,692	348	2,003	94	33,741
Montgomery city	2,668	0	2,480	169	3,452	98	1,375	63	29,015
Tuscaloosa city	1,435	0	2,237	63	1,916	0	1,036	0	11,677
Alaska									
Anchorage municipality	6,111	312	4,592	0	5,257	322	2,289	0	29,809
Arizona									
Avondale city	1,093	0	840	49	783	0	484	0	8,315
Buckeye city	na	na	na	na	na	na	na	na	na
Chandler city	4,138	350	4,227	167	3,939	88	1,955	0	29,143
Flagstaff city	na	na	na	na	na	na	na	na	na
Glendale city	2,962	245	4,880	184	4,246	175	2,634	0	32,526
Goodyear city	na	na	na	na	na	na	na	na	na
Mesa city	7,616	151	6,929	189	7,113	162	5,994	199	82,945
Peoria city	3,389	142	4,377	54	2,434	0	1,246	85	31,694
Phoenix city	21,297	659	28,766	635	20,492	435	13,446	799	176,543
Scottsdale city	5,402	91	7,237	155	5,572	52	3,772	57	55,291
Surprise city	1,226	73	1,931	76	1,862	172	1,527	118	30,833
Tempe city	2,757	0	2,059	353	3,299	0	1,320	94	19,248
Tucson city	9,429	84	6,428	408	7,883	333	3,476	82	82,390
Yuma city	1,632	0	1,081	67	784	0	571	0	16,887
Arkansas									
Conway city	na	na	na	na	na	na	na	na	na
Fayetteville city	1,566	0	1,142	0	680	0	713	0	7,966
Fort Smith city	na	na	na	na	na	na	na	na	na
Jonesboro city	na	na	na	na	na	na	na	na	na
Little Rock city	2,503	140	3,986	218	3,576	35	2,057	101	27,417
North Little Rock city	na	na	na	na	na	na	na	na	na
Rogers city	na	na	na	na	na	na	na	na	na
Springdale city	na	na	na	na	na	na	na	na	na
California									
Alameda city	na	na	na	na	na	na	na	na	na
Alhambra city	497	27	1,846	48	1,094	42	487	86	14,965
Anaheim city	4,692	46	5,263	172	5,417	185	2,637	124	40,586
Antioch city	1,340	179	1,793	41	1,255	0	648	0	15,473
Bakersfield city	4,166	540	5,497	162	4,790	114	2,169	152	42,667
Baldwin Park city	1,005	63	1,062	137	496	48	387	0	9,530
Bellflower city	954	0	1,484	42	857	25	442	24	8,120
Berkeley city	1,819	39	1,957	55	2,532	0	2,665	29	13,606
Buena Park city	2,003	0	1,676	0	1,771	0	417	0	8,753
Burbank city	1,820	6	1,702	161	1,408	0	856	0	15,505
Camarillo city	1,069	0	1,095	0	1,124	46	1,438	0	12,994
Carlsbad city	na	na	na	na	na	na	na	na	na
Carson city	2,019	179	1,507	56	1,595	0	1,038	49	13,030
Chico city	1,133	44	1,281	115	1,309	0	718	109	12,497
Chino city	na	na	na	na	na	na	na	na	na
Chino Hills city	na	na	na	na	na	na	na	na	na
Chula Vista city	3,401	524	4,922	0	2,297	138	2,198	0	31,969
Citrus Heights city	1,124	403	2,878	124	1,794	0	1,247	66	13,043
Clovis city	na	na	na	na	na	na	na	na	na
Compton city	na	na	na	na	na	na	na	na	na
Concord city	3,421	44	3,175	0	2,644	0	1,207	0	19,250
Corona city	1,580	114	2,268	119	1,951	23	887	0	16,200
Costa Mesa city	1,753	108	1,639	44	1,146	177	1,364	263	12,254
Daly City city	na	na	na	na	na	na	na	na	na
Davis city	na	na	na	na	na	na	na	na	na
Downey city	1,355	0	2,494	54	1,500	108	884	0	14,990
El Cajon city	1,244	0	1,649	47	1,315	0	559	0	13,295
Elk Grove city	2,523	69	3,076	91	2,091	0	1,491	45	24,877
El Monte city	1,571	109	1,323	224	1,349	217	631	0	16,210
Escondido city	2,405	0	1,961	151	2,543	127	1,642	0	21,285
Fairfield city	1,733	51	1,631	0	2,303	0	1,125	0	14,600
Folsom city	na	na	na	na	na	na	na	na	na
Fontana city	1,430	53	2,517	57	981	120	893	0	18,384
Fremont city	3,668	327	4,907	46	3,028	190	2,380	26	29,168
Fresno city	6,006	525	6,391	170	6,306	205	3,613	268	61,179
Fullerton city	2,228	142	3,083	108	2,027	143	1,208	68	17,739
Garden Grove city	4,780	81	3,104	27	1,927	97	772	96	23,992
Glendale city	3,419	104	3,870	0	2,561	116	1,913	44	37,132
Hawthorne city	na	na	na	na	na	na	na	na	na
Hayward city	1,971	110	2,881	160	2,293	0	806	59	21,773
Hemet city	na	na	na	na	na	na	na	na	na
Hesperia city	na	na	na	na	na	na	na	na	na
Huntington Beach city	4,218	71	3,963	196	3,196	0	1,574	99	31,937

Table F-3: Cities - Employment and Labor Force Status, Civilian Labor Force—*Continued*

	60 to 61 Years		62 to 64 Years		65 to 69 Years		70 Years and Over		60 Years and Over Not in the Labor Force
	Employed	Unemployed	Employed	Unemployed	Employed	Unemployed	Employed	Unemployed	
California—Cont.									
Indio city	na	na	na	na	na	na	na	na	na
Inglewood city	1,731	132	1,068	0	1,663	152	901	0	12,172
Irvine city	4,045	42	3,489	192	3,880	477	3,479	80	26,343
Jurupa Valley city	1,749	74	2,243	0	1,455	71	655	346	12,159
Laguna Niguel city	na	na	na	na	na	na	na	na	na
Lake Elsinore city	na	na	na	na	na	na	na	na	na
Lake Forest city	na	na	na	na	na	na	na	na	na
Lakewood city	1,360	115	1,731	59	549	38	789	134	9,897
Lancaster city	2,188	128	1,461	162	1,894	0	824	193	17,015
Livermore city	na	na	na	na	na	na	na	na	na
Lodi City	1,010	110	1,325	0	1,135	0	1,001	0	10,140
Long Beach city	8,158	340	7,910	141	6,345	388	3,016	70	56,012
Los Angeles city	57,626	2,823	65,297	3,062	61,684	2,879	45,544	2,703	483,898
Lynwood city	na	na	na	na	na	na	na	na	na
Madera city	na	na	na	na	na	na	na	na	na
Manteca city	na	na	na	na	na	na	na	na	na
Menifee city	1,672	0	1,292	0	1,419	54	851	90	17,591
Merced city	961	60	569	0	1,112	127	966	65	9,467
Milpitas city	na	na	na	na	na	na	na	na	na
Mission Viejo city	2,734	0	1,960	96	1,837	198	1,830	25	17,762
Modesto city	1,884	78	2,753	32	2,572	38	2,001	73	28,874
Moreno Valley city	1,171	49	2,302	0	1,583	87	554	0	18,900
Mountain View city	na	na	na	na	na	na	na	na	na
Murrieta city	na	na	na	na	na	na	na	na	na
Napa city	na	na	na	na	na	na	na	na	na
Newport Beach city	na	na	na	na	na	na	na	na	na
Norwalk city	1,609	0	1,388	0	1,539	0	271	0	15,345
Oakland city	6,646	249	6,627	95	6,822	210	5,182	331	54,338
Oceanside city	2,876	313	2,360	0	2,820	269	2,498	45	28,850
Ontario city	2,009	43	1,960	0	1,721	38	764	0	17,537
Orange city	2,239	0	2,833	83	1,420	260	1,467	37	17,580
Oxnard city	2,851	237	2,988	100	2,050	231	553	111	21,720
Palmdale city	2,649	162	2,354	103	1,841	0	365	136	18,680
Palo Alto city	na	na	na	na	na	na	na	na	na
Pasadena city	2,431	27	2,319	122	2,987	130	2,424	110	20,859
Perris city	na	na	na	na	na	na	na	na	na
Pittsburg city	na	na	na	na	na	na	na	na	na
Pleasanton city	na	na	na	na	na	na	na	na	na
Pomona city	2,274	0	1,842	308	1,674	0	1,030	108	17,407
Rancho Cordova city	461	47	935	258	757	0	965	41	13,099
Rancho Cucamonga city	2,175	47	3,450	108	3,072	151	1,357	188	21,956
Redding city	1,211	0	1,652	0	1,190	0	1,191	94	17,101
Redlands city	na	na	na	na	na	na	na	na	na
Redondo Beach city	na	na	na	na	na	na	na	na	na
Redwood City city	na	na	na	na	na	na	na	na	na
Rialto city	1,528	106	1,483	48	1,026	0	987	150	13,227
Richmond city	1,986	62	2,207	99	2,552	271	1,181	127	13,097
Riverside city	3,642	187	3,863	221	3,669	53	1,758	503	36,091
Rocklin city	na	na	na	na	na	na	na	na	na
Roseville city	2,241	41	2,084	119	1,748	210	1,429	46	23,239
Sacramento city	6,818	265	7,104	229	5,431	335	3,555	105	71,103
Salinas city	1,657	49	1,445	0	2,592	0	837	0	13,210
San Bernardino city	1,576	251	2,048	44	1,963	199	635	42	21,407
San Buenaventura (Ventura) city	2,590	0	1,927	45	2,762	42	1,433	38	19,206
San Clemente city	na	na	na	na	na	na	na	na	na
San Diego city	17,828	913	25,586	1,273	22,005	467	12,419	676	185,586
San Francisco city	16,708	494	15,485	811	15,127	568	10,142	482	131,449
San Jose city	16,407	520	20,012	723	16,958	430	9,011	674	126,846
San Leandro city	na	na	na	na	na	na	na	na	na
San Marcos city	1,593	0	1,701	0	1,001	60	600	41	11,602
San Mateo city	1,793	91	2,245	361	1,856	0	1,762	44	16,084
San Ramon city	na	na	na	na	na	na	na	na	na
Santa Ana city	4,242	281	4,206	247	3,908	0	1,475	78	31,887
Santa Barbara city	na	na	na	na	na	na	na	na	na
Santa Clara city	na	na	na	na	na	na	na	na	na
Santa Clarita city	3,330	82	5,003	226	4,391	66	2,354	91	24,935
Santa Cruz city	870	54	754	0	1,391	70	911	46	7,158
Santa Maria city	1,123	0	1,220	41	927	0	658	0	9,465
Santa Monica city	na	na	na	na	na	na	na	na	na
Santa Rosa city	3,218	280	3,066	128	3,970	159	2,865	89	27,508
Simi Valley city	3,063	0	1,888	93	3,373	47	1,249	39	19,785
South Gate city	1,030	0	997	209	1,282	55	639	0	8,837
South San Francisco city	na	na	na	na	na	na	na	na	na
Stockton city	2,852	199	3,176	194	3,300	0	2,106	0	41,523
Sunnyvale city	2,027	148	2,889	396	1,553	45	1,128	0	18,175
Temecula city	1,149	42	2,219	0	783	35	744	0	13,176
Thousand Oaks city	1,881	174	2,775	177	2,314	265	1,819	78	22,093
Torrance city	3,705	81	4,176	0	1,755	34	2,564	102	25,161
Tracy city	na	na	na	na	na	na	na	na	na

Table F-3: Cities - Employment and Labor Force Status, Civilian Labor Force—*Continued*

	60 to 61 Years		62 to 64 Years		65 to 69 Years		70 Years and Over		60 Years and Over Not in the Labor Force
	Employed	Unemployed	Employed	Unemployed	Employed	Unemployed	Employed	Unemployed	
California—Cont.									
Turlock city	na	na	na	na	na	na	na	na	na
Tustin city	na	na	na	na	na	na	na	na	na
Union City city	na	na	na	na	na	na	na	na	na
Upland city	1,463	36	1,427	82	1,316	0	1,191	0	10,634
Vacaville city	1,631	39	1,196	50	1,193	0	669	25	15,696
Vallejo city	2,759	25	3,329	342	2,216	153	1,329	60	19,290
Victorville city	na	na	na	na	na	na	na	na	na
Visalia city	1,246	39	2,462	0	1,500	0	927	72	16,381
Vista city	na	na	na	na	na	na	na	na	na
Walnut Creek city	na	na	na	na	na	na	na	na	na
West Covina city	1,597	11	3,189	94	1,813	38	689	0	17,653
Westminster city	1,645	0	661	0	1,135	49	682	0	18,076
Whittier city	na	na	na	na	na	na	na	na	na
Yorba Linda city	na	na	na	na	na	na	na	na	na
Yuba City city	na	na	na	na	na	na	na	na	na
Colorado									
Arvada city	2,384	143	2,859	74	3,246	39	1,638	0	20,061
Aurora city	6,355	200	5,933	77	6,560	0	2,854	159	41,758
Boulder city	1,661	49	1,922	43	1,966	77	1,602	54	10,039
Broomfield city	na	na	na	na	na	na	na	na	na
Centennial city	1,904	0	2,646	50	2,664	145	1,636	0	13,757
Colorado Springs city	6,486	387	7,555	0	7,395	235	4,545	60	61,175
Denver city	9,467	396	11,118	377	11,151	142	7,187	203	78,292
Fort Collins city	2,575	224	2,606	44	2,652	69	999	159	16,976
Greeley city	1,821	96	1,894	309	1,462	40	767	0	12,732
Lakewood city	2,688	154	3,430	237	2,755	38	2,274	93	25,434
Longmont city	2,040	0	1,811	38	1,791	0	888	0	15,335
Loveland city	na	na	na	na	na	na	na	na	na
Pueblo city	1,294	138	1,672	31	1,307	37	557	0	23,526
Thornton city	na	na	na	na	na	na	na	na	na
Westminster city	na	na	na	na	na	na	na	na	na
Connecticut									
Bridgeport city	1,674	176	2,666	0	1,852	36	1,165	0	15,937
Danbury city	na	na	na	na	na	na	na	na	na
Hartford city	845	131	1,824	51	951	289	667	0	14,058
New Britain city	na	na	na	na	na	na	na	na	na
New Haven city	1,148	98	1,270	0	1,506	62	938	0	12,038
Norwalk city	2,000	45	3,072	97	2,365	128	1,468	149	13,645
Stamford city	2,433	0	3,159	80	2,702	39	2,323	354	17,492
Waterbury city	1,448	0	1,467	0	1,051	58	736	0	15,212
Delaware									
Wilmington city	1,463	25	997	116	1,166	21	452	50	8,448
District of Columbia									
Washington city	8,213	212	10,655	247	9,563	245	8,348	529	80,698
Florida									
Boca Raton city	1,457	0	2,835	0	3,274	64	4,025	300	24,972
Boynton Beach city	na	na	na	na	na	na	na	na	na
Cape Coral city	na	na	na	na	na	na	na	na	na
Clearwater city	2,241	38	2,572	119	2,364	73	1,865	0	25,105
Coral Springs city	2,008	170	2,751	94	3,854	0	1,490	0	14,966
Daytona Beach city	na	na	na	na	na	na	na	na	na
Deerfield Beach city	na	na	na	na	na	na	na	na	na
Delray Beach city	na	na	na	na	na	na	na	na	na
Deltona city	na	na	na	na	na	na	na	na	na
Fort Lauderdale city	4,697	284	3,255	615	3,602	147	2,807	322	32,574
Fort Myers city	na	na	na	na	na	na	na	na	na
Gainesville city	1,546	121	1,725	0	1,421	0	1,172	0	11,802
Hialeah city	3,774	161	4,865	0	3,705	0	1,706	0	46,068
Hollywood city	3,142	371	2,954	0	2,225	193	2,884	117	23,330
Homestead city	na	na	na	na	na	na	na	na	na
Jacksonville city	13,086	591	15,293	387	11,852	267	8,165	406	125,762
Kissimmee city	na	na	na	na	na	na	na	na	na
Lakeland city	2,090	93	1,636	40	1,222	0	1,128	120	21,819
Largo city	na	na	na	na	na	na	na	na	na
Lauderhill city	na	na	na	na	na	na	na	na	na
Melbourne city	2,147	133	1,747	0	1,375	0	1,017	0	17,042
Miami city	5,875	115	6,749	512	7,097	222	4,876	0	83,121
Miami Beach city	na	na	na	na	na	na	na	na	na
Miami Gardens city	1,468	0	2,248	59	1,642	0	961	174	17,420
Miramar city	na	na	na	na	na	na	na	na	na
North Port city	na	na	na	na	na	na	na	na	na
Orlando city	5,000	25	3,507	120	3,475	878	3,304	100	30,708
Palm Bay city	na	na	na	na	na	na	na	na	na
Palm Coast city	na	na	na	na	na	na	na	na	na
Pembroke Pines city	3,714	0	4,111	8	2,213	364	1,417	468	31,458
Plantation city	na	na	na	na	na	na	na	na	na
Pompano Beach city	2,012	0	2,830	31	1,225	170	955	70	23,084

Table F-3: Cities - Employment and Labor Force Status, Civilian Labor Force—*Continued*

	60 to 61 Years		62 to 64 Years		65 to 69 Years		70 Years and Over		60 Years and Over Not in the Labor Force
	Employed	Unemployed	Employed	Unemployed	Employed	Unemployed	Employed	Unemployed	
Florida—Cont.									
Port St. Lucie city....................................	na	na	na	na	na	na	na	na	na
St. Petersburg city..................................	3,930	241	5,176	0	5,082	209	2,405	90	47,024
Sunrise city...	na	na	na	na	na	na	na	na	na
Tallahassee city......................................	2,603	0	2,481	199	2,495	79	1,455	130	19,206
Tamarac city...	na	na	na	na	na	na	na	na	na
Tampa city..	5,153	83	3,647	0	4,058	242	3,358	121	50,534
Weston city...	na	na	na	na	na	na	na	na	na
West Palm Beach city..............................	2,526	0	1,028	0	1,295	214	1,280	0	22,022
Georgia									
Albany city..	1,339	0	1,230	0	595	242	551	0	10,138
Alpharetta city..	na	na	na	na	na	na	na	na	na
Athens-Clarke County unified govt (bal)........	1,311	0	1,324	12	1,588	58	1,511	34	14,473
Atlanta city...	5,160	159	5,003	186	5,834	56	4,658	206	56,818
Augusta-Richmond County consolidated govt (bal)........	2,363	481	3,896	46	1,568	60	1,897	190	30,849
Columbus city...	3,282	60	2,376	27	2,250	114	1,146	41	28,723
Johns Creek city.....................................	na	na	na	na	na	na	na	na	na
Macon-Bibb County................................	1,518	63	2,972	9	2,859	168	1,629	52	24,747
Roswell city..	na	na	na	na	na	na	na	na	na
Sandy Springs city..................................	na	na	na	na	na	na	na	na	na
Savannah city...	1,513	99	1,909	142	2,188	454	1,807	27	19,358
South Fulton city.....................................	na	na	na	na	na	na	na	na	na
Warner Robins city..................................	na	na	na	na	na	na	na	na	na
Hawaii									
Urban Honolulu CDP................................	7,589	125	7,494	92	9,506	253	6,545	213	60,758
Iowa									
Boise City city...	4,176	0	4,911	40	3,463	90	1,650	232	34,821
Meridian city...	na	na	na	na	na	na	na	na	na
Nampa city..	na	na	na	na	na	na	na	na	na
Illinois									
Aurora city..	2,656	0	2,419	195	2,032	253	1,347	49	17,410
Bloomington city.....................................	816	91	1,656	0	985	0	707	0	11,425
Champaign city.......................................	775	0	1,037	0	1,547	0	930	0	9,697
Chicago city..	35,180	3,382	41,899	2,051	34,403	1,955	22,137	1,088	356,216
Decatur city..	1,786	55	1,230	0	1,224	46	752	0	15,928
Elgin city..	na	na	na	na	na	na	na	na	na
Evanston city..	1,214	0	1,817	0	1,510	0	1,738	0	9,663
Joliet city..	1,969	44	1,677	0	1,749	25	729	104	14,405
Naperville city...	2,895	79	2,616	42	1,832	189	1,181	0	17,975
Peoria city..	1,709	47	1,834	31	1,300	100	1,303	0	18,187
Rockford city..	2,114	222	2,720	168	3,079	0	1,964	54	25,926
Springfield city.......................................	1,820	0	2,339	151	2,284	42	1,403	0	19,780
Waukegan city..	na	na	na	na	na	na	na	na	na
Indiana									
Bloomington city.....................................	na	na	na	na	na	na	na	na	na
Carmel city...	na	na	na	na	na	na	na	na	na
Evansville city..	2,211	32	1,629	50	2,103	61	1,052	0	18,647
Fishers city...	na	na	na	na	na	na	na	na	na
Fort Wayne city.......................................	3,910	138	4,441	388	4,351	80	2,182	38	35,439
Gary city...	865	0	857	60	1,275	0	561	0	15,011
Hammond city...	na	na	na	na	na	na	na	na	na
Indianapolis city (bal).............................	12,777	476	12,590	605	12,391	900	8,903	847	106,752
Lafayette city..	na	na	na	na	na	na	na	na	na
Muncie city...	na	na	na	na	na	na	na	na	na
Noblesville city.......................................	na	na	na	na	na	na	na	na	na
South Bend city......................................	1,404	74	1,704	0	1,154	0	1,142	0	14,025
Iowa									
Ames city...	na	na	na	na	na	na	na	na	na
Ankeny city...	na	na	na	na	na	na	na	na	na
Cedar Rapids city...................................	2,717	99	2,515	72	2,491	168	1,010	45	18,506
Davenport city..	2,527	45	1,873	0	1,639	71	599	37	15,474
Des Moines city......................................	2,333	30	3,662	59	2,354	170	2,128	0	25,462
Iowa City city..	na	na	na	na	na	na	na	na	na
Sioux City city..	na	na	na	na	na	na	na	na	na
Waterloo city..	833	46	1,155	37	1,304	0	398	39	12,001
West Des Moines city..............................	na	na	na	na	na	na	na	na	na
Kansas									
Kansas City city......................................	2,330	47	2,266	293	2,030	0	1,155	0	18,847
Lawrence city...	na	na	na	na	na	na	na	na	na
Olathe city..	na	na	na	na	na	na	na	na	na
Overland Park city...................................	4,054	409	4,832	56	4,121	157	2,573	54	27,804
Shawnee city..	na	na	na	na	na	na	na	na	na
Topeka city...	2,264	0	2,838	34	2,241	0	1,310	218	23,681
Wichita city...	5,551	328	7,171	466	6,628	208	3,547	100	56,804
Kentucky									
Bowling Green city..................................	na	na	na	na	na	na	na	na	na
Lexington-Fayette urban county.................	4,571	124	5,339	105	5,668	300	4,647	105	40,382
Louisville/Jefferson County metro govt (bal)........	10,785	199	10,820	521	9,982	171	6,499	91	97,799

Table F-3: Cities - Employment and Labor Force Status, Civilian Labor Force—*Continued*

	60 to 61 Years		62 to 64 Years		65 to 69 Years		70 Years and Over		60 Years and Over Not in the Labor Force
	Employed	Unemployed	Employed	Unemployed	Employed	Unemployed	Employed	Unemployed	
Louisiana									
Baton Rouge city	3,061	57	3,600	73	3,578	158	2,949	0	32,657
Bossier City city	na	na	na	na	na	na	na	na	na
Kenner city	na	na	na	na	na	na	na	na	na
Lafayette city	1,566	44	1,708	0	3,381	0	1,043	0	17,272
Lake Charles city	na	na	na	na	na	na	na	na	na
New Orleans city	5,431	50	6,237	153	5,880	279	3,911	177	59,966
Shreveport city	2,604	0	2,761	0	4,021	0	2,183	81	32,160
Maine									
Portland city	na	na	na	na	na	na	na	na	na
Maryland									
Baltimore city	8,665	509	10,080	484	8,463	299	5,795	261	89,488
Frederick city	na	na	na	na	na	na	na	na	na
Gaithersburg city	na	na	na	na	na	na	na	na	na
Rockville city	na	na	na	na	na	na	na	na	na
Massachusetts									
Boston city	8,524	190	9,592	260	10,575	555	6,404	291	78,526
Brockton city	na	na	na	na	na	na	na	na	na
Cambridge city	1,321	0	1,706	64	2,524	48	1,748	76	9,555
Fall River city	na	na	na	na	na	na	na	na	na
Framingham city	na	na	na	na	na	na	na	na	na
Lawrence city	429	82	915	147	450	138	618	0	7,523
Lowell city	2,185	55	1,704	37	1,315	0	436	37	10,627
Lynn city	na	na	na	na	na	na	na	na	na
New Bedford city	1,161	0	1,223	41	874	25	1,286	0	13,022
Newton city	na	na	na	na	na	na	na	na	na
Quincy city	1,357	0	1,107	0	1,797	52	835	0	13,947
Somerville city	na	na	na	na	na	na	na	na	na
Springfield city	1,691	151	1,650	211	1,890	79	1,059	0	21,389
Worcester city	2,716	71	3,376	195	2,453	53	1,311	0	26,249
Michigan									
Ann Arbor city	1,427	20	1,909	676	1,682	0	1,729	0	10,970
Dearborn city	1,543	43	1,656	77	1,460	56	787	0	11,642
Detroit city	6,771	568	7,378	427	4,999	687	3,429	596	111,496
Farmington Hills city	na	na	na	na	na	na	na	na	na
Flint city	645	47	1,155	261	594	0	871	30	15,186
Grand Rapids city	2,520	106	2,721	26	2,230	95	2,155	166	24,504
Kalamazoo city	553	0	879	43	952	0	521	81	8,590
Lansing city	1,369	66	1,773	0	1,486	148	1,149	36	16,055
Livonia city	2,078	59	2,331	115	1,673	167	1,167	0	16,070
Rochester Hills city	na	na	na	na	na	na	na	na	na
Southfield city	na	na	na	na	na	na	na	na	na
Sterling Heights city	2,664	24	2,558	82	2,698	0	919	59	22,506
Troy city	na	na	na	na	na	na	na	na	na
Warren city	2,481	77	2,676	205	1,483	38	1,036	134	24,708
Westland city	na	na	na	na	na	na	na	na	na
Wyoming city	na	na	na	na	na	na	na	na	na
Minnesota									
Blaine city	na	na	na	na	na	na	na	na	na
Bloomington city	na	na	na	na	na	na	na	na	na
Brooklyn Park city	na	na	na	na	na	na	na	na	na
Duluth city	1,637	37	1,777	0	1,258	0	946	0	15,796
Eagan city	na	na	na	na	na	na	na	na	na
Lakeville city	na	na	na	na	na	na	na	na	na
Maple Grove city	na	na	na	na	na	na	na	na	na
Minneapolis city	5,177	304	5,592	649	6,891	196	3,801	0	42,489
Plymouth city	na	na	na	na	na	na	na	na	na
Rochester city	2,324	129	1,676	0	1,600	130	1,605	89	17,000
St. Cloud city	na	na	na	na	na	na	na	na	na
St. Paul city	3,896	40	4,257	111	3,791	0	2,703	114	33,390
Woodbury city	na	na	na	na	na	na	na	na	na
Mississippi									
Gulfport city	na	na	na	na	na	na	na	na	na
Jackson city	1,836	27	2,922	335	2,779	0	1,235	0	22,722
Missouri									
Columbia city	1,319	33	1,740	222	2,393	0	1,112	0	12,253
Independence city	2,223	46	2,338	131	1,809	41	1,386	40	20,214
Kansas City city	7,538	107	9,523	111	7,355	286	6,068	185	62,744
Lee's Summit city	na	na	na	na	na	na	na	na	na
O'Fallon city	na	na	na	na	na	na	na	na	na
St. Charles city	na	na	na	na	na	na	na	na	na
St. Joseph city	1,178	0	1,993	96	1,156	0	1,092	51	12,515
St. Louis city	5,546	283	5,886	363	3,866	203	2,974	0	44,420
Springfield city	2,366	0	2,995	0	1,392	32	1,631	134	31,168
Montana									
Billings city	na	na	na	na	na	na	na	na	na
Missoula city	na	na	na	na	na	na	na	na	na

Table F-3: Cities - Employment and Labor Force Status, Civilian Labor Force—*Continued*

	60 to 61 Years		62 to 64 Years		65 to 69 Years		70 Years and Over		60 Years and Over Not in the Labor Force
	Employed	Unemployed	Employed	Unemployed	Employed	Unemployed	Employed	Unemployed	
Nebraska									
Lincoln city	4,390	0	5,037	76	5,515	0	3,853	77	33,906
Omaha city	7,374	170	9,486	442	7,951	271	6,010	68	59,250
Nevada									
Henderson city	4,775	225	5,656	113	5,562	176	2,984	629	58,480
Las Vegas city	8,701	766	9,336	281	9,243	521	6,649	143	100,015
North Las Vegas city	2,660	263	3,879	157	2,099	0	1,794	55	28,281
Reno city	3,462	349	6,130	0	4,800	226	2,494	0	38,481
Sparks city	na	na	na	na	na	na	na	na	na
New Hampshire									
Manchester city	1,514	0	1,714	68	1,274	0	867	106	13,399
Nashua city	na	na	na	na	na	na	na	na	na
New Jersey									
Bayonne city	na	na	na	na	na	na	na	na	na
Camden city	na	na	na	na	na	na	na	na	na
Clifton city	na	na	na	na	na	na	na	na	na
East Orange city	na	na	na	na	na	na	na	na	na
Elizabeth city	na	na	na	na	na	na	na	na	na
Jersey City city	2,830	181	5,429	0	3,068	121	2,852	0	27,237
Newark city	3,036	0	4,327	0	3,305	198	2,133	0	30,294
Passaic city	na	na	na	na	na	na	na	na	na
Paterson city	1,786	0	2,680	0	1,853	46	1,525	0	17,049
Trenton city	na	na	na	na	na	na	na	na	na
Union City city	na	na	na	na	na	na	na	na	na
New Mexico									
Albuquerque city	9,646	190	7,877	431	7,841	397	5,385	455	89,571
Las Cruces city	na	na	na	na	na	na	na	na	na
Rio Rancho city	na	na	na	na	na	na	na	na	na
Santa Fe city	na	na	na	na	na	na	na	na	na
New York									
Albany city	671	0	2,036	206	1,820	102	1,172	0	12,811
Buffalo city	3,196	160	4,325	265	2,741	100	1,883	0	34,749
Mount Vernon city	na	na	na	na	na	na	na	na	na
New Rochelle city	na	na	na	na	na	na	na	na	na
New York city	124,597	5,568	141,391	5,890	123,949	3,994	84,869	2,751	1,235,287
Rochester city	2,169	106	2,569	65	1,927	149	1,478	54	25,646
Schenectady city	na	na	na	na	na	na	na	na	na
Syracuse city	1,122	82	2,216	49	1,644	75	1,334	166	17,096
Yonkers city	3,133	244	3,582	171	3,311	282	3,130	253	32,234
North Carolina									
Asheville city	na	na	na	na	na	na	na	na	na
Charlotte city	13,839	426	13,331	376	12,100	738	5,758	266	93,190
Concord city	na	na	na	na	na	na	na	na	na
Durham city	4,054	56	5,562	221	4,942	72	2,443	0	31,289
Fayetteville city	2,305	150	2,615	61	1,499	140	1,564	73	27,055
Gastonia city	1,261	0	1,566	73	1,619	31	625	0	11,758
Greensboro city	4,948	489	4,921	42	4,056	98	3,105	91	40,364
Greenville city	745	0	1,203	0	959	0	788	0	8,370
High Point city	1,612	41	2,373	103	1,638	23	1,152	0	16,343
Jacksonville city	na	na	na	na	na	na	na	na	na
Raleigh city	6,665	209	7,214	648	6,705	123	4,619	0	49,779
Wilmington city	1,486	169	2,644	128	1,779	0	1,192	0	21,261
Winston-Salem city	3,558	541	4,734	87	3,660	160	2,282	0	33,079
North Dakota									
Bismarck city	na	na	na	na	na	na	na	na	na
Fargo city	2,573	0	2,989	0	1,841	0	1,577	0	14,158
Ohio									
Akron city	3,204	123	4,774	159	3,091	547	1,663	90	30,850
Canton city	na	na	na	na	na	na	na	na	na
Cincinnati city	4,640	240	4,542	305	4,564	211	3,244	121	38,619
Cleveland city	4,674	438	5,251	437	5,298	222	2,378	308	61,578
Columbus city	12,859	252	14,598	272	12,931	261	6,625	300	95,720
Dayton city	1,384	164	2,300	0	1,808	257	1,048	37	20,349
Lorain city	na	na	na	na	na	na	na	na	na
Parma city	1,687	0	1,700	188	1,364	0	986	197	13,408
Toledo city	3,303	49	3,909	113	3,466	178	1,923	113	41,217
Youngstown city	1,012	0	1,240	0	1,353	55	634	27	12,538
Oklahoma									
Broken Arrow city	1,762	0	1,692	0	1,493	0	1,710	39	14,998
Edmond city	1,113	0	1,550	0	1,792	81	1,659	0	13,361
Lawton city	1,493	0	991	38	1,024	58	595	0	12,227
Norman city	1,138	87	1,264	0	1,765	0	1,706	0	13,247
Oklahoma City city	9,454	197	11,042	136	9,646	35	8,672	141	77,712
Tulsa city	7,368	157	6,883	241	6,462	100	4,957	216	56,343
Oregon									
Beaverton city	1,272	81	1,411	143	1,971	242	813	0	10,004
Bend city	na	na	na	na	na	na	na	na	na

Table F-3: Cities - Employment and Labor Force Status, Civilian Labor Force—*Continued*

	60 to 61 Years		62 to 64 Years		65 to 69 Years		70 Years and Over		60 Years and Over Not in the Labor Force
	Employed	Unemployed	Employed	Unemployed	Employed	Unemployed	Employed	Unemployed	
Oregon—Cont.									
Eugene city	2,941	111	3,230	299	2,564	121	1,740	147	25,448
Gresham city	na	na	na	na	na	na	na	na	na
Hillsboro city	na	na	na	na	na	na	na	na	na
Medford city	na	na	na	na	na	na	na	na	na
Portland city	7,842	110	10,796	249	10,553	495	5,632	150	85,553
Salem city	2,652	36	3,994	59	2,097	41	1,378	0	27,080
Pennsylvania									
Allentown city	1,348	288	1,867	0	1,401	324	1,052	0	14,940
Bethlehem city	na	na	na	na	na	na	na	na	na
Erie city	890	43	1,356	0	1,585	0	1,006	53	15,423
Philadelphia city	22,204	1,168	22,184	683	19,220	1,498	14,525	705	225,316
Pittsburgh city	5,690	161	5,478	316	5,734	212	2,737	0	46,039
Reading city	893	183	699	24	567	30	684	220	10,743
Scranton city	1,522	0	1,502	0	1,022	0	953	0	12,766
Rhode Island									
Cranston city	na	na	na	na	na	na	na	na	na
Pawtucket city	na	na	na	na	na	na	na	na	na
Providence city	2,764	103	1,624	0	1,722	0	1,473	0	21,270
Warwick city	na	na	na	na	na	na	na	na	na
South Carolina									
Charleston city	1,197	0	2,379	0	2,333	120	1,515	152	19,071
Columbia city	1,158	50	1,492	100	2,179	20	958	71	12,897
Greenville city	na	na	na	na	na	na	na	na	na
North Charleston city	1,361	0	1,829	0	1,367	63	841	0	12,512
Rock Hill city	na	na	na	na	na	na	na	na	na
South Dakota									
Rapid City city	na	na	na	na	na	na	na	na	na
Sioux Falls city	3,410	0	3,338	0	3,038	216	2,290	0	19,407
Tennessee									
Chattanooga city	2,792	39	4,207	96	3,458	0	2,348	187	29,551
Clarksville city	1,385	205	1,493	86	1,024	0	548	0	14,909
Franklin city	na	na	na	na	na	na	na	na	na
Jackson city	1,323	0	1,389	185	980	0	959	0	9,851
Johnson City city	na	na	na	na	na	na	na	na	na
Knoxville city	3,178	0	2,868	79	2,266	26	1,819	0	24,414
Memphis city	11,543	148	11,223	374	9,285	947	7,726	416	86,309
Murfreesboro city	1,588	0	1,317	96	1,309	0	1,047	0	14,157
Nashville-Davidson metropolitan govt (bal)	8,782	359	12,389	134	11,524	179	7,006	182	73,068
Texas									
Abilene city	1,839	0	2,007	0	1,601	0	1,193	18	15,576
Allen city	na	na	na	na	na	na	na	na	na
Amarillo city	3,217	32	3,255	84	3,769	153	2,451	0	24,186
Arlington city	6,960	87	6,853	90	5,665	222	3,125	0	40,900
Austin city	12,558	589	16,890	1,093	15,093	377	7,845	184	82,256
Baytown city	na	na	na	na	na	na	na	na	na
Beaumont city	2,183	0	1,943	0	1,425	223	1,486	39	18,627
Brownsville city	2,397	0	1,404	110	1,556	44	1,198	104	22,266
Bryan city	na	na	na	na	na	na	na	na	na
Carrollton city	2,847	191	2,557	0	2,190	98	2,678	0	15,419
Cedar Park city	na	na	na	na	na	na	na	na	na
College Station city	604	0	1,543	0	846	0	1,245	0	8,204
Conroe city	na	na	na	na	na	na	na	na	na
Corpus Christi city	5,268	126	5,105	252	5,232	504	3,687	60	44,884
Dallas city	18,568	1,051	23,224	329	17,447	829	14,331	554	136,213
Denton city	1,843	185	1,589	0	2,539	38	2,345	70	12,566
Edinburg city	603	45	915	41	840	0	80	0	10,530
El Paso city	8,267	249	9,989	690	8,440	0	5,198	224	90,967
Fort Worth city	13,328	627	11,854	595	10,352	584	6,512	445	88,628
Frisco city	1,892	42	1,903	151	1,716	0	1,176	55	15,858
Garland city	5,863	93	3,677	82	4,302	165	3,085	36	26,677
Georgetown city	na	na	na	na	na	na	na	na	na
Grand Prairie city	2,473	225	3,497	0	2,498	0	1,454	108	18,218
Harlingen city	na	na	na	na	na	na	na	na	na
Houston city	31,789	1,473	35,932	1,510	31,396	1,354	22,037	1,120	235,223
Irving city	3,308	38	3,599	188	2,547	60	2,170	0	13,550
Killeen city	667	81	1,658	277	1,173	0	1,395	0	9,936
Laredo city	1,871	151	2,250	29	2,438	98	2,460	143	23,870
League City city	na	na	na	na	na	na	na	na	na
Lewisville city	na	na	na	na	na	na	na	na	na
Longview city	na	na	na	na	na	na	na	na	na
Lubbock city	4,513	0	4,386	0	3,092	35	3,098	35	29,376
McAllen city	na	na	na	na	na	na	na	na	na
McKinney city	1,860	0	2,963	53	2,955	128	1,657	0	19,655
Mansfield city	na	na	na	na	na	na	na	na	na
Mesquite city	2,374	149	2,661	0	1,663	150	1,232	0	13,457
Midland city	na	na	na	na	na	na	na	na	na
Mission city	na	na	na	na	na	na	na	na	na

Table F-3: Cities - Employment and Labor Force Status, Civilian Labor Force—*Continued*

	60 to 61 Years		62 to 64 Years		65 to 69 Years		70 Years and Over		60 Years and Over Not in the Labor Force
	Employed	Unemployed	Employed	Unemployed	Employed	Unemployed	Employed	Unemployed	
Texas—Cont.									
Missouri City city	na	na	na	na	na	na	na	na	na
New Braunfels city	na	na	na	na	na	na	na	na	na
North Richland Hills city	na	na	na	na	na	na	na	na	na
Odessa city	na	na	na	na	na	na	na	na	na
Pasadena city	1,875	229	2,598	185	1,897	0	907	85	13,622
Pearland city	na	na	na	na	na	na	na	na	na
Pharr city	na	na	na	na	na	na	na	na	na
Plano city	4,798	668	5,328	315	6,394	163	3,792	0	33,553
Richardson city	2,137	142	2,125	67	1,443	0	2,256	145	14,773
Round Rock city	na	na	na	na	na	na	na	na	na
Rowlett city	na	na	na	na	na	na	na	na	na
San Angelo city	1,120	0	1,334	0	2,166	0	1,753	0	13,947
San Antonio city	20,330	505	20,935	492	21,422	516	13,874	349	190,330
Sugar Land city	2,395	200	2,654	45	2,183	123	1,738	49	19,736
Temple city	na	na	na	na	na	na	na	na	na
Tyler city	na	na	na	na	na	na	na	na	na
Victoria city	na	na	na	na	na	na	na	na	na
Waco city	1,282	0	2,666	183	1,581	0	1,666	0	14,610
Wichita Falls city	1,152	0	1,935	132	1,738	50	1,340	43	12,187
Utah									
Layton city	na	na	na	na	na	na	na	na	na
Lehi city	na	na	na	na	na	na	na	na	na
Ogden city	893	0	1,288	0	903	0	265	0	9,730
Orem city	1,096	0	1,824	0	941	0	655	0	8,978
Provo city	804	120	968	41	560	0	351	0	7,179
St. George city	na	na	na	na	na	na	na	na	na
Salt Lake City city	2,523	260	3,428	112	2,659	0	2,241	54	20,094
Sandy city	na	na	na	na	na	na	na	na	na
South Jordan city	na	na	na	na	na	na	na	na	na
West Jordan city	na	na	na	na	na	na	na	na	na
West Valley City city	1,565	45	1,369	45	817	56	1,389	113	12,198
Virginia									
Alexandria city	2,249	67	2,889	67	3,336	0	2,739	29	16,400
Chesapeake city	3,930	139	3,509	172	3,902	48	2,805	0	31,853
Hampton city	2,683	45	2,035	0	1,423	31	908	0	21,497
Lynchburg city	1,309	0	1,379	0	638	74	948	96	12,351
Newport News city	3,706	0	3,090	56	2,752	0	1,377	48	23,364
Norfolk city	3,337	0	2,921	190	3,349	67	2,664	205	27,824
Portsmouth city	1,710	0	1,248	0	1,232	32	709	0	14,394
Richmond city	2,635	261	3,411	63	3,183	33	1,931	54	31,917
Roanoke city	1,585	197	2,298	168	1,301	59	1,314	17	16,809
Suffolk city	1,625	0	2,310	33	1,416	53	1,029	0	12,952
Virginia Beach city	7,536	100	9,402	101	8,330	68	5,111	144	59,379
Washington									
Auburn city	na	na	na	na	na	na	na	na	na
Bellevue city	1,871	0	2,364	0	2,666	0	1,694	0	20,330
Bellingham city	na	na	na	na	na	na	na	na	na
Everett city	1,599	44	1,533	306	1,793	0	810	169	14,013
Federal Way city	1,479	38	2,685	39	1,522	0	1,189	0	11,440
Kennewick city	na	na	na	na	na	na	na	na	na
Kent city	1,831	0	3,093	211	1,515	58	753	56	16,271
Kirkland city	1,713	0	1,495	0	1,771	0	1,345	0	8,936
Marysville city	na	na	na	na	na	na	na	na	na
Pasco city	na	na	na	na	na	na	na	na	na
Redmond city	na	na	na	na	na	na	na	na	na
Renton city	na	na	na	na	na	na	na	na	na
Sammamish city	na	na	na	na	na	na	na	na	na
Seattle city	7,995	454	12,436	345	12,484	266	7,143	80	90,818
Spokane city	3,576	150	3,420	208	3,155	112	2,166	96	35,381
Spokane Valley city	na	na	na	na	na	na	na	na	na
Tacoma city	2,950	97	3,140	213	3,481	0	2,473	125	27,883
Vancouver city	3,327	100	3,524	128	2,445	38	2,457	84	28,708
Yakima city	na	na	na	na	na	na	na	na	na
Wisconsin									
Appleton city	na	na	na	na	na	na	na	na	na
Eau Claire city	na	na	na	na	na	na	na	na	na
Green Bay city	1,736	64	1,504	0	1,487	49	447	0	14,962
Kenosha city	2,059	0	2,480	0	845	41	878	25	12,393
Madison city	4,415	0	3,561	0	3,593	111	2,329	0	29,420
Milwaukee city	6,916	164	9,159	369	5,643	133	3,544	132	71,372
Oshkosh city	1,080	71	1,548	0	724	0	382	0	9,541
Racine city	na	na	na	na	na	na	na	na	na
Waukesha city	na	na	na	na	na	na	na	na	na

Table F-4: Metropolitan/Micropolitan Statistical Areas - Employment and Labor Force Status, Civilian Labor Force

	60 to 61 Years		62 to 64 Years		65 to 69 Years		70 Years and Over		60 Years and Over Not in the Labor Force
	Employed	Unemployed	Employed	Unemployed	Employed	Unemployed	Employed	Unemployed	
Aberdeen, WA Micro Area	na	na	na	na	na	na	na	na	na
Abilene, TX Metro Area	2,730	0	3,189	0	2,754	0	2,040	18	25,694
Adrian, MI Micro Area	1,732	0	2,115	63	1,894	209	888	63	18,600
Akron, OH Metro Area	12,385	487	17,469	713	13,113	1,055	9,340	492	120,519
Alamogordo, NM Micro Area	na	na	na	na	na	na	na	na	na
Albany, GA Metro Area	3,517	29	2,299	53	1,820	275	1,431	0	23,077
Albany, OR Metro Area	1,566	16	1,928	65	2,539	10	1,018	277	24,660
Albany-Schenectady-Troy, NY Metro Area	15,372	146	17,402	634	16,826	455	11,772	267	149,707
Albertville, AL Micro Area	1,547	7	804	7	1,253	0	1,531	7	17,622
Albuquerque, NM Metro Area	15,493	412	13,328	464	12,372	698	8,653	558	160,459
Alexandria, LA Metro Area	1,619	60	2,713	0	2,619	0	1,543	0	25,701
Allentown-Bethlehem-Easton, PA-NJ Metro Area	16,297	696	17,568	328	14,127	587	10,190	46	149,219
Altoona, PA Metro Area	2,444	46	2,086	22	2,693	0	1,214	0	25,192
Amarillo, TX Metro Area	5,186	102	4,852	84	4,988	153	3,104	12	33,879
Ames, IA Metro Area	1,344	53	1,487	0	1,597	0	872	0	10,087
Anchorage, AK Metro Area	7,474	457	6,283	68	6,373	368	2,954	32	44,721
Ann Arbor, MI Metro Area	5,177	247	6,498	792	5,805	101	4,253	77	49,244
Anniston-Oxford-Jacksonville, AL Metro Area	1,642	59	2,800	0	1,368	0	1,465	38	20,998
Appleton, WI Metro Area	4,760	55	4,403	12	3,429	152	1,334	23	36,173
Asheville, NC Metro Area	9,088	48	10,943	141	9,647	276	7,450	0	97,811
Ashtabula, OH Micro Area	1,429	23	2,958	0	1,643	22	1,660	0	18,766
Athens, OH Micro Area	410	2	1,292	0	809	0	407	0	9,225
Athens, TX Micro Area	na	na	na	na	na	na	na	na	na
Athens-Clarke County, GA Metro Area	3,048	8	2,879	31	3,017	58	2,669	40	26,727
Atlanta-Sandy Springs-Roswell, GA Metro Area	89,958	3,056	98,690	2,711	81,487	3,199	54,546	1,555	727,663
Atlantic City-Hammonton, NJ Metro Area	4,152	174	6,863	35	4,711	171	3,765	466	45,256
Auburn, NY Micro Area	1,093	22	1,544	13	1,428	0	1,171	0	14,428
Auburn-Opelika, AL Metro Area	2,627	0	2,874	176	2,147	157	1,434	0	19,747
Augusta-Richmond County, GA-SC Metro Area	8,302	569	10,689	386	7,326	121	5,899	330	101,620
Augusta-Waterville, ME Micro Area	2,307	30	3,214	27	2,150	72	2,191	0	24,844
Austin-Round Rock, TX Metro Area	28,769	1,103	33,487	2,015	33,796	627	18,876	460	223,547
Bakersfield, CA Metro Area	8,573	845	10,922	839	10,231	176	6,116	152	105,348
Baltimore-Columbia-Towson, MD Metro Area	48,313	896	61,043	1,403	48,807	1,428	36,374	984	422,160
Bangor, ME Metro Area	2,369	65	3,421	121	2,464	96	1,301	21	29,158
Barnstable Town, MA Metro Area	5,259	183	7,101	105	7,600	646	6,018	85	57,130
Baton Rouge, LA Metro Area	11,790	316	14,322	142	11,510	391	8,264	265	121,807
Battle Creek, MI Metro Area	3,258	191	1,948	45	1,936	83	1,513	50	24,951
Bay City, MI Metro Area	2,087	48	2,134	0	986	0	1,262	0	23,399
Beaumont-Port Arthur, TX Metro Area	5,425	160	6,787	0	5,289	371	4,975	94	65,199
Beaver Dam, WI Micro Area	2,403	0	1,908	60	2,251	17	1,261	0	14,406
Beckley, WV Metro Area	1,146	0	1,844	137	2,102	0	1,214	0	26,874
Bellingham, WA Metro Area	3,320	171	4,701	346	3,540	133	2,449	66	39,377
Bend-Redmond, OR Metro Area	2,181	0	5,890	248	3,891	282	2,811	74	38,303
Billings, MT Metro Area	4,401	21	2,829	88	3,511	248	2,147	0	28,751
Binghamton, NY Metro Area	5,216	229	4,778	271	4,300	124	3,574	106	45,603
Birmingham-Hoover, AL Metro Area	18,124	209	17,432	424	17,440	802	13,173	54	195,306
Bismarck, ND Metro Area	1,869	109	2,278	0	2,313	0	1,931	0	19,275
Blacksburg-Christiansburg-Radford, VA Metro Area	1,616	0	2,356	0	2,772	0	1,508	92	30,649
Bloomington, IL Metro Area	2,595	121	3,583	15	2,666	0	1,705	22	26,368
Bloomington, IN Metro Area	2,607	0	2,077	0	2,502	0	2,324	125	23,000
Bloomsburg-Berwick, PA Metro Area	1,585	0	2,380	34	1,938	34	889	88	15,989
Bluefield, WV-VA Micro Area	1,664	34	1,399	0	1,081	90	833	0	24,638
Boise City, ID Metro Area	8,611	257	13,254	222	11,049	478	6,103	232	109,092
Boston-Cambridge-Newton, MA-NH Metro Area	91,216	3,288	109,434	4,013	101,006	3,478	73,812	2,063	683,666
Boulder, CO Metro Area	6,867	256	7,000	81	7,260	77	3,805	103	42,467
Bowling Green, KY Metro Area	2,197	34	1,766	0	3,167	206	2,374	0	25,449
Bozeman, MT Micro Area	2,419	0	2,484	0	1,799	0	1,472	0	13,056
Brainerd, MN Micro Area	1,485	27	2,448	38	2,358	16	1,347	7	22,359
Branson, MO Micro Area	na	na	na	na	na	na	na	na	na
Bremerton-Silverdale, WA Metro Area	4,177	317	5,726	101	5,242	97	3,093	0	47,491
Bridgeport-Stamford-Norwalk, CT Metro Area	18,405	679	24,707	730	20,949	1,174	16,498	1,024	129,239
Brownsville-Harlingen, TX Metro Area	4,559	0	4,150	110	3,751	61	2,245	311	60,153
Brunswick, GA Metro Area	na	na	na	na	na	na	na	na	na
Buffalo-Cheektowaga-Niagara Falls, NY Metro Area	23,141	523	24,846	635	17,070	384	13,808	88	208,258
Burlington, NC Metro Area	2,912	119	3,407	0	2,871	84	1,760	45	27,724
Burlington-South Burlington, VT Metro Area	4,563	180	6,137	0	4,654	170	2,746	195	32,615
California-Lexington Park, MD Metro Area	2,406	0	1,815	78	1,173	0	1,149	12	15,145
Canton-Massillon, OH Metro Area	7,435	114	7,694	195	6,677	304	4,183	69	78,259
Cape Coral-Fort Myers, FL Metro Area	10,496	394	13,439	492	14,929	208	12,738	1,180	214,909
Cape Girardeau, MO-IL Metro Area	na	na	na	na	na	na	na	na	na
Carbondale-Marion, IL Metro Area	1,736	88	2,666	44	1,259	93	1,026	195	23,424
Carson City, NV Metro Area	na	na	na	na	na	na	na	na	na
Casper, WY Metro Area	na	na	na	na	na	na	na	na	na
Cedar Rapids, IA Metro Area	5,737	145	5,057	109	5,265	168	3,411	45	41,677
Centralia, WA Micro Area	1,348	0	1,948	0	612	0	1,196	13	18,186
Chambersburg-Waynesboro, PA Metro Area	3,098	92	2,777	0	3,121	69	2,082	43	29,090
Champaign-Urbana, IL Metro Area	3,638	276	3,697	16	3,652	41	2,796	78	31,980

Table F-4: Metropolitan/Micropolitan Statistical Areas - Employment and Labor Force Status, Civilian Labor Force—*Continued*

	60 to 61 Years		62 to 64 Years		65 to 69 Years		70 Years and Over		60 Years and Over Not in the Labor Force
	Employed	Unemployed	Employed	Unemployed	Employed	Unemployed	Employed	Unemployed	
Charleston, WV Metro Area..	1,899	39	4,769	0	3,915	99	2,808	27	47,289
Charleston-North Charleston, SC Metro Area....................	11,251	203	12,915	385	12,532	252	8,791	250	118,559
Charlotte-Concord-Gastonia, NC-SC Metro Area...............	39,478	639	41,875	806	33,545	1,643	23,152	859	347,832
Charlottesville, VA Metro Area..	5,146	0	4,548	98	5,218	81	4,027	49	37,960
Chattanooga, TN-GA Metro Area..	9,522	54	11,935	254	9,964	31	7,032	596	99,953
Cheyenne, WY Metro Area..	2,170	43	1,511	0	1,746	162	875	91	16,737
Chicago-Naperville-Elgin, IL-IN-WI Metro Area................	162,162	7,728	186,999	6,774	158,918	4,971	99,219	3,585	1,342,194
Chico, CA Metro Area...	2,442	186	3,860	115	3,034	46	2,566	109	46,262
Chillicothe, OH Micro Area..	1,248	0	1,342	25	657	0	597	0	14,969
Cincinnati, OH-KY-IN Metro Area	37,004	1,183	42,307	874	37,887	702	26,877	670	321,815
Claremont-Lebanon, NH-VT Micro Area.............................	4,714	111	5,556	0	5,922	57	6,375	249	40,698
Clarksburg, WV Micro Area...	1,178	196	1,880	80	1,332	85	967	29	19,623
Clarksville, TN-KY Metro Area..	3,298	205	3,559	160	2,457	0	1,258	0	33,589
Clearlake, CA Micro Area..	na	na	na	na	na	na	na	na	na
Cleveland, TN Metro Area...	1,393	0	1,397	0	1,777	14	2,163	105	22,022
Cleveland-Elyria, OH Metro Area......................................	38,207	1,352	46,339	1,367	41,608	1,283	28,313	786	370,728
Coeur d'Alene, ID Metro Area...	1,713	99	3,404	0	2,374	29	1,744	91	31,297
College Station-Bryan, TX Metro Area..............................	1,644	0	3,226	0	2,767	99	2,728	0	27,053
Colorado Springs, CO Metro Area.....................................	12,249	486	12,830	281	12,072	377	6,945	138	94,651
Columbia, MO Metro Area..	2,532	33	3,041	222	2,795	0	1,619	0	21,966
Columbia, SC Metro Area...	11,983	425	13,809	344	13,107	153	8,304	255	126,380
Columbus, GA-AL Metro Area..	5,828	132	4,104	27	3,454	114	2,151	41	47,247
Columbus, IN Metro Area..	na	na	na	na	na	na	na	na	na
Columbus, OH Metro Area	33,303	670	38,193	835	31,531	706	19,066	502	278,591
Concord, NH Micro Area..	3,231	151	3,708	31	3,700	171	2,770	0	26,149
Cookeville, TN Micro Area...	1,708	0	2,065	0	1,504	0	1,112	111	20,773
Coos Bay, OR Micro Area...	na	na	na	na	na	na	na	na	na
Corning, NY Micro Area...	1,877	73	1,529	61	1,380	0	1,031	0	19,985
Corpus Christi, TX Metro Area..	7,664	126	7,270	252	6,992	847	4,943	60	68,316
Corvallis, OR Metro Area...	1,557	0	1,171	0	1,553	46	818	0	14,661
Crestview-Fort Walton Beach-Destin, FL Metro Area........	4,377	123	5,111	14	4,445	435	3,990	58	47,664
Cullman, AL Micro Area...	na	na	na	na	na	na	na	na	na
Cumberland, MD-WV Metro Area.......................................	1,612	108	1,681	64	1,756	68	1,084	0	20,127
Dallas-Fort Worth-Arlington, TX Metro Area....................	118,234	4,941	127,709	3,030	107,937	3,879	78,599	2,150	805,153
Dalton, GA Metro Area...	2,160	0	2,197	227	1,456	51	1,284	0	20,064
Danville, IL Metro Area...	1,361	54	1,383	0	1,518	75	710	41	14,553
Danville, VA Micro Area..	1,993	155	2,278	120	2,055	28	1,541	0	23,130
Daphne-Fairhope-Foley, AL Metro Area.............................	3,672	0	3,791	82	3,894	86	3,563	43	44,386
Davenport-Moline-Rock Island, IA-IL Metro Area.............	6,012	204	7,496	54	6,551	267	4,454	47	68,292
Dayton, OH Metro Area..	13,775	567	16,692	256	14,322	703	10,227	341	141,725
Decatur, AL Metro Area...	2,263	98	2,529	0	2,094	137	1,469	106	29,022
Decatur, IL Metro Area..	2,286	130	2,028	0	1,907	46	1,074	0	22,383
Deltona-Daytona Beach-Ormond Beach, FL Metro Area......	12,038	0	12,451	209	14,568	748	9,021	363	168,635
Denver-Aurora-Lakewood, CO Metro Area	51,410	1,526	55,047	1,534	50,431	1,175	32,807	861	351,978
Des Moines-West Des Moines, IA Metro Area	8,670	178	12,273	59	10,199	260	7,572	107	80,395
Detroit-Warren-Dearborn, MI Metro Area..........................	74,765	2,045	83,050	2,863	66,096	2,243	41,978	2,572	736,920
Dothan, AL Metro Area..	2,067	42	2,335	34	2,630	73	1,829	69	28,552
Dover, DE Metro Area..	2,343	0	2,602	142	2,505	445	1,939	180	30,459
DuBois, PA Micro Area..	1,370	0	1,250	0	1,570	13	680	12	16,824
Dubuque, IA Metro Area..	1,487	0	2,370	11	1,678	0	1,672	0	16,642
Duluth, MN-WI Metro Area..	4,839	286	5,433	101	4,382	143	2,784	12	56,113
Dunn, NC Micro Area...	1,105	66	1,381	0	1,270	0	836	0	19,062
Durham-Chapel Hill, NC Metro Area..................................	8,953	470	12,593	405	12,070	150	6,178	252	81,994
East Stroudsburg, PA Metro Area......................................	3,936	78	3,648	0	3,516	140	2,462	68	29,446
Eau Claire, WI Metro Area..	2,834	0	3,206	19	2,982	31	2,239	12	27,633
El Centro, CA Metro Area..	2,520	187	1,626	261	1,640	313	1,082	312	23,967
Elizabeth City, NC Micro Area..	na	na	na	na	na	na	na	na	na
Elizabethtown-Fort Knox, KY Metro Area..........................	2,449	150	1,809	0	1,831	67	797	0	25,393
Elkhart-Goshen, IN Metro Area	3,280	39	3,885	104	4,169	340	2,658	108	26,910
Elmira, NY Metro Area..	1,348	0	1,381	56	1,145	35	758	23	17,434
El Paso, TX Metro Area	9,246	356	10,955	733	9,627	0	5,653	224	109,891
Enid, OK Metro Area..	na	na	na	na	na	na	na	na	na
Erie, PA Metro Area	4,242	172	5,248	151	4,251	74	3,234	101	49,604
Eugene, OR Metro Area..	6,632	232	7,067	507	6,832	425	3,782	258	74,302
Eureka-Arcata-Fortuna, CA Micro Area.............................	1,968	121	3,988	0	2,663	59	2,035	156	24,297
Evansville, IN-KY Metro Area...	5,703	32	5,787	161	4,968	84	4,451	78	54,538
Fairbanks, AK Metro Area...	1,570	0	1,365	0	2,137	20	454	51	10,031
Fargo, ND-MN Metro Area..	4,341	22	5,060	0	3,529	65	3,047	11	27,381
Faribault-Northfield, MN Micro Area.................................	952	16	1,711	14	934	0	284	0	10,434
Farmington, MO Micro Area..	na	na	na	na	na	na	na	na	na
Farmington, NM Metro Area..	1,716	68	1,873	105	1,329	105	1,172	80	20,176
Fayetteville, NC Metro Area..	4,162	150	4,497	149	2,994	183	2,614	73	50,051
Fayetteville-Springdale-Rogers, AR-MO Metro Area	8,309	171	8,013	201	6,958	0	4,659	94	71,995
Findlay, OH Micro Area...	na	na	na	na	na	na	na	na	na
Flagstaff, AZ Metro Area...	1,716	6	2,447	0	1,603	46	1,660	50	18,170
Flint, MI Metro Area..	6,446	291	5,202	299	5,456	315	4,045	52	78,257

Table F-4: Metropolitan/Micropolitan Statistical Areas - Employment and Labor Force Status, Civilian Labor Force—*Continued*

	60 to 61 Years		62 to 64 Years		65 to 69 Years		70 Years and Over		60 Years and Over Not in the Labor Force
	Employed	Unemployed	Employed	Unemployed	Employed	Unemployed	Employed	Unemployed	
Florence, SC Metro Area	2,900	0	3,473	0	2,769	43	2,706	0	38,634
Florence-Muscle Shoals, AL Metro Area	1,731	48	2,386	84	1,035	70	1,265	0	32,761
Fond du Lac, WI Metro Area	na	na	na	na	na	na	na	na	na
Forest City, NC Micro Area	na	na	na	na	na	na	na	na	na
Fort Collins, CO Metro Area	6,019	268	6,872	183	7,654	69	3,813	159	52,242
Fort Payne, AL Micro Area	na	na	na	na	na	na	na	na	na
Fort Smith, AR-OK Metro Area	3,185	0	3,880	13	3,458	292	3,891	58	48,550
Fort Wayne, IN Metro Area	7,600	292	7,820	388	7,548	80	4,590	90	63,039
Frankfort, KY Micro Area	na	na	na	na	na	na	na	na	na
Fresno, CA Metro Area	12,918	752	12,398	570	12,115	334	7,620	524	122,730
Gadsden, AL Metro Area	1,527	0	2,268	64	1,819	0	1,383	0	20,448
Gainesville, FL Metro Area	4,349	121	5,253	126	4,368	47	2,674	0	40,228
Gainesville, GA Metro Area	2,940	109	2,503	0	2,097	0	2,077	189	31,408
Gallup, NM Micro Area	1,811	0	1,110	66	784	0	143	0	10,762
Gettysburg, PA Metro Area	2,428	38	2,643	0	1,415	55	1,254	43	20,229
Glens Falls, NY Metro Area	2,611	46	3,262	40	2,739	47	1,974	172	25,894
Glenwood Springs, CO Micro Area	na	na	na	na	na	na	na	na	na
Goldsboro, NC Metro Area	2,531	97	2,764	96	1,900	53	2,113	94	20,845
Grand Forks, ND-MN Metro Area	1,953	146	2,257	6	1,256	33	1,105	0	14,154
Grand Island, NE Metro Area	na	na	na	na	na	na	na	na	na
Grand Junction, CO Metro Area	2,805	136	2,893	42	2,570	149	2,337	0	27,925
Grand Rapids-Wyoming, MI Metro Area	15,919	868	20,307	78	15,947	470	12,990	355	153,545
Grants Pass, OR Metro Area	na	na	na	na	na	na	na	na	na
Great Falls, MT Metro Area	1,409	0	2,622	79	1,154	0	1,285	0	14,820
Greeley, CO Metro Area	4,991	331	5,893	403	4,984	218	3,292	78	37,621
Green Bay, WI Metro Area	6,417	183	5,143	36	5,337	132	2,515	62	52,265
Greeneville, TN Micro Area	1,325	0	1,156	0	951	0	1,017	0	16,267
Greenfield Town, MA Micro Area	2,098	0	2,354	46	2,163	98	1,630	12	14,370
Greensboro-High Point, NC Metro Area	12,783	686	14,934	42	12,594	163	9,041	240	123,990
Greenville, NC Metro Area	2,453	0	3,171	0	2,609	0	1,723	0	24,390
Greenville-Anderson-Mauldin, SC Metro Area	15,262	450	15,024	516	14,979	418	9,862	48	150,146
Greenwood, SC Micro Area	1,693	174	1,858	0	959	50	1,395	72	17,469
Gulfport-Biloxi-Pascagoula, MS Metro Area	5,438	337	4,990	59	3,668	109	3,282	19	69,115
Hagerstown-Martinsburg, MD-WV Metro Area	4,614	64	5,559	265	4,327	75	2,307	119	45,428
Hammond, LA Metro Area	2,010	0	1,418	0	2,321	0	860	0	20,259
Hanford-Corcoran, CA Metro Area	1,141	0	1,256	261	1,002	98	1,137	0	16,056
Harrisburg-Carlisle, PA Metro Area	8,911	381	13,317	387	11,133	297	8,564	190	97,915
Harrisonburg, VA Metro Area	2,310	237	2,228	0	1,545	93	1,647	0	20,006
Hartford-West Hartford-East Hartford, CT Metro Area	23,633	621	31,030	1,045	23,681	1,046	17,428	680	193,241
Hattiesburg, MS Metro Area	1,341	84	1,533	0	1,944	0	1,284	0	22,928
Helena, MT Micro Area	na	na	na	na	na	na	na	na	na
Hermiston-Pendleton, OR Micro Area	1,817	71	498	84	912	3	1,014	292	13,859
Hickory-Lenoir-Morganton, NC Metro Area	7,170	152	7,402	138	5,737	409	5,042	206	70,211
Hilo, HI Micro Area	3,567	0	5,272	47	4,968	49	3,900	492	40,551
Hilton Head Island-Bluffton-Beaufort, SC Metro Area	2,511	0	3,691	131	4,525	0	5,179	0	54,761
Hinesville, GA Metro Area	826	49	544	0	833	0	627	26	7,875
Hobbs, NM Micro Area	na	na	na	na	na	na	na	na	na
Holland, MI Micro Area	1,249	85	2,015	146	1,802	135	1,011	68	20,203
Homosassa Springs, FL Metro Area	1,173	0	2,163	34	2,044	172	2,390	335	59,968
Hot Springs, AR Metro Area	na	na	na	na	na	na	na	na	na
Houma-Thibodaux, LA Metro Area	2,605	0	3,582	63	2,617	0	2,144	0	34,922
Houston-The Woodlands-Sugar Land, TX Metro Area	99,623	4,839	114,498	6,465	98,040	4,340	64,980	3,065	755,424
Huntington-Ashland, WV-KY-OH Metro Area	3,573	86	4,955	118	4,759	48	4,952	104	71,959
Huntsville, AL Metro Area	7,716	217	6,040	230	6,188	251	6,156	305	69,920
Huntsville, TX Micro Area	na	na	na	na	na	na	na	na	na
Hutchinson, KS Micro Area	na	na	na	na	na	na	na	na	na
Idaho Falls, ID Metro Area	2,040	33	2,261	0	1,466	0	891	51	19,665
Indiana, PA Micro Area	1,340	0	1,824	0	983	12	909	35	17,576
Indianapolis-Carmel-Anderson, IN Metro Area	33,960	595	33,779	767	30,757	1,953	20,583	1,345	276,497
Iowa City, IA Metro Area	2,760	17	3,546	0	3,323	9	1,576	24	20,158
Ithaca, NY Metro Area	1,476	0	3,012	162	1,561	0	1,559	0	13,678
Jackson, MI Metro Area	2,621	48	3,230	73	2,090	52	1,708	0	29,744
Jackson, MS Metro Area	9,314	132	11,051	408	9,684	134	6,465	331	81,733
Jackson, TN Metro Area	2,158	0	2,809	185	2,498	0	1,545	26	22,737
Jacksonville, FL Metro Area	23,527	803	28,387	1,210	23,734	639	15,112	469	243,092
Jacksonville, NC Metro Area	1,795	0	1,942	0	1,669	32	863	0	18,610
Jamestown-Dunkirk-Fredonia, NY Micro Area	2,300	76	2,783	0	2,277	58	1,582	0	25,991
Janesville-Beloit, WI Metro Area	3,034	17	3,202	54	2,774	16	1,786	33	26,664
Jefferson, GA Micro Area	na	na	na	na	na	na	na	na	na
Jefferson City, MO Metro Area	2,729	0	2,494	0	2,112	198	1,595	37	25,651
Johnson City, TN Metro Area	2,586	81	4,127	66	2,754	190	2,567	0	41,820
Johnstown, PA Metro Area	2,916	45	2,625	72	2,274	55	1,831	0	30,680
Jonesboro, AR Metro Area	2,205	202	2,313	0	1,804	0	1,133	0	19,533
Joplin, MO Metro Area	2,143	0	2,597	226	2,878	13	2,528	0	28,041
Kahului-Wailuku-Lahaina, HI Metro Area	3,027	30	3,631	131	3,259	0	2,836	164	29,186
Kalamazoo-Portage, MI Metro Area	5,420	98	6,412	73	4,501	127	3,890	245	54,102
Kalispell, MT Micro Area	2,063	46	2,511	84	2,147	116	1,494	0	20,137

Table F-4: Metropolitan/Micropolitan Statistical Areas - Employment and Labor Force Status, Civilian Labor Force—*Continued*

	60 to 61 Years		62 to 64 Years		65 to 69 Years		70 Years and Over		60 Years and Over Not in the Labor Force
	Employed	Unemployed	Employed	Unemployed	Employed	Unemployed	Employed	Unemployed	
Kankakee, IL Metro Area	1,818	8	2,213	0	1,409	113	967	18	19,080
Kansas City, MO-KS Metro Area	34,510	1,229	43,153	768	35,403	913	26,196	668	309,064
Kapaa, HI Micro Area	na	na	na	na	na	na	na	na	na
Keene, NH Micro Area	1,412	29	2,234	0	2,144	67	1,658	0	13,959
Kennewick-Richland, WA Metro Area	3,139	166	5,235	251	3,287	171	1,845	0	41,451
Key West, FL Micro Area	na	na	na	na	na	na	na	na	na
Killeen-Temple, TX Metro Area	3,855	455	4,802	403	5,290	279	4,857	16	51,032
Kingsport-Bristol-Bristol, TN-VA Metro Area	4,284	119	5,500	109	4,490	25	4,124	0	73,580
Kingston, NY Metro Area	5,335	297	4,420	258	4,085	109	2,898	258	31,760
Klamath Falls, OR Micro Area	na	na	na	na	na	na	na	na	na
Knoxville, TN Metro Area	13,821	267	17,225	458	15,302	150	11,700	285	162,657
Kokomo, IN Metro Area	1,570	0	1,310	34	1,254	0	977	0	16,018
La Crosse-Onalaska, WI-MN Metro Area	2,818	73	3,447	133	2,444	0	1,217	7	22,489
Lafayette, LA Metro Area	7,480	365	7,179	71	8,071	158	3,756	0	71,882
Lafayette-West Lafayette, IN Metro Area	3,117	394	3,119	24	2,827	17	1,782	92	27,328
LaGrange, GA Micro Area	na	na	na	na	na	na	na	na	na
Lake Charles, LA Metro Area	2,505	83	4,759	0	2,283	158	1,013	49	35,181
Lake City, FL Micro Area	1,097	0	1,250	0	520	162	540	47	14,493
Lake Havasu City-Kingman, AZ Metro Area	2,807	5	4,418	192	4,297	709	2,621	120	67,399
Lakeland-Winter Haven, FL Metro Area	11,339	256	9,148	144	9,257	188	9,237	478	145,654
Lancaster, PA Metro Area	10,289	0	11,513	490	10,464	101	8,766	109	91,312
Lansing-East Lansing, MI Metro Area	8,194	66	8,729	92	6,033	232	4,678	95	77,872
Laredo, TX Metro Area	2,044	151	2,678	29	2,558	98	2,549	143	25,388
Las Cruces, NM Metro Area	1,996	235	3,248	45	3,402	0	1,522	0	36,163
Las Vegas-Henderson-Paradise, NV Metro Area	27,921	1,541	36,719	1,059	30,053	1,244	22,520	1,775	332,978
Laurel, MS Micro Area	na	na	na	na	na	na	na	na	na
Lawrence, KS Metro Area	1,372	0	1,931	0	2,618	190	1,089	0	13,638
Lawton, OK Metro Area	2,228	18	1,235	52	1,566	58	896	0	17,639
Lebanon, PA Metro Area	1,861	0	3,601	0	2,822	0	2,214	67	27,209
Lewiston, ID-WA Metro Area	na	na	na	na	na	na	na	na	na
Lewiston-Auburn, ME Metro Area	2,304	41	2,198	98	2,638	176	920	0	18,312
Lexington-Fayette, KY Metro Area	7,742	124	7,852	533	8,549	434	7,483	251	69,870
Lima, OH Metro Area	2,301	181	1,928	97	1,403	50	1,034	0	18,333
Lincoln, NE Metro Area	5,321	7	6,478	76	7,293	0	5,099	77	41,250
Little Rock-North Little Rock-Conway, AR Metro Area	10,353	289	13,019	363	11,024	69	8,019	116	115,350
Logan, UT-ID Metro Area	1,560	0	2,305	12	2,076	49	343	8	12,972
London, KY Micro Area	1,171	0	2,049	75	1,311	0	934	0	22,836
Longview, TX Metro Area	3,890	524	3,335	111	4,326	15	2,496	0	34,846
Longview, WA Metro Area	na	na	na	na	na	na	na	na	na
Los Angeles-Long Beach-Anaheim, CA Metro Area	215,471	7,554	233,625	8,573	205,612	8,212	141,684	6,224	1,782,338
Louisville/Jefferson County, KY-IN Metro Area	22,655	431	24,234	782	22,974	550	16,017	456	207,975
Lubbock, TX Metro Area	5,885	183	5,564	146	4,578	66	3,548	154	37,543
Lufkin, TX Micro Area	870	61	1,108	0	750	0	506	0	15,897
Lumberton, NC Micro Area	1,348	0	2,495	32	1,396	39	832	0	22,874
Lynchburg, VA Metro Area	4,665	101	5,802	0	4,060	74	3,296	160	50,736
Macon-Bibb County, GA Metro Area	2,261	103	4,147	9	4,018	168	2,190	52	39,653
Madera, CA Metro Area	1,236	206	1,607	85	2,144	0	2,170	56	22,650
Madison, WI Metro Area	14,149	124	12,907	92	11,508	123	7,322	87	88,969
Manchester-Nashua, NH Metro Area	9,907	82	9,648	408	9,157	13	5,384	121	59,726
Manhattan, KS Metro Area	1,474	0	1,176	0	1,036	0	1,173	97	9,872
Manitowoc, WI Micro Area	na	na	na	na	na	na	na	na	na
Mankato-North Mankato, MN Metro Area	1,738	7	2,071	16	1,250	10	1,063	31	13,734
Mansfield, OH Metro Area	2,160	0	1,927	141	1,454	48	1,011	47	24,591
Marinette, WI-MI Micro Area	1,036	0	1,803	11	1,154	0	597	12	16,444
Marion, IN Micro Area	699	0	1,429	162	1,201	0	985	0	12,561
Marion, OH Micro Area	na	na	na	na	na	na	na	na	na
Marquette, MI Micro Area	790	14	1,099	0	714	105	743	0	14,281
Marshall, TX Micro Area	na	na	na	na	na	na	na	na	na
Martinsville, VA Micro Area	na	na	na	na	na	na	na	na	na
McAllen-Edinburg-Mission, TX Metro Area	8,523	421	9,127	118	8,679	278	4,913	154	98,505
Meadville, PA Micro Area	1,567	119	2,105	24	1,673	32	1,426	112	17,107
Medford, OR Metro Area	3,002	53	4,081	337	4,283	101	2,829	74	50,370
Memphis, TN-MS-AR Metro Area	24,622	446	28,040	897	21,421	1,509	16,678	847	185,362
Merced, CA Metro Area	3,339	60	3,833	0	2,968	268	1,978	339	30,822
Meridian, MS Micro Area	1,977	75	1,169	0	1,017	67	1,269	0	18,875
Miami-Fort Lauderdale-West Palm Beach, FL Metro Area	106,040	5,095	115,574	5,269	110,720	4,038	86,932	4,151	1,071,670
Michigan City-La Porte, IN Metro Area	1,785	0	2,142	34	1,381	0	1,680	64	19,674
Midland, MI Metro Area	938	0	974	48	1,426	52	909	10	17,355
Midland, TX Metro Area	2,709	51	3,834	0	3,183	0	1,762	0	16,899
Milwaukee-Waukesha-West Allis, WI Metro Area	29,628	699	35,136	839	24,392	493	14,757	463	250,100
Minneapolis-St. Paul-Bloomington, MN-WI Metro Area	62,183	2,422	72,601	2,883	61,601	1,395	36,316	591	482,498
Minot, ND Micro Area	1,063	72	1,466	109	1,151	0	1,124	0	9,670
Missoula, MT Metro Area	1,812	102	2,695	0	1,762	99	1,944	0	17,169
Mobile, AL Metro Area	6,959	63	5,631	76	4,954	420	3,884	254	70,375
Modesto, CA Metro Area	6,108	345	6,534	347	6,824	38	3,810	202	76,869
Monroe, LA Metro Area	3,787	125	3,857	41	1,539	204	1,719	0	29,194
Monroe, MI Metro Area	2,605	133	3,137	132	1,564	0	1,524	0	28,836

Table F-4: Metropolitan/Micropolitan Statistical Areas - Employment and Labor Force Status, Civilian Labor Force—*Continued*

	60 to 61 Years		62 to 64 Years		65 to 69 Years		70 Years and Over		60 Years and Over Not in the Labor Force
	Employed	Unemployed	Employed	Unemployed	Employed	Unemployed	Employed	Unemployed	
Montgomery, AL Metro Area	5,634	22	5,862	306	5,011	279	3,856	125	59,310
Morehead City, NC Micro Area	974	42	2,092	79	1,317	72	1,110	46	17,485
Morgantown, WV Metro Area	1,649	436	2,094	54	2,339	0	1,421	0	20,226
Morristown, TN Metro Area	1,240	160	2,214	0	1,921	0	1,870	31	23,988
Moses Lake, WA Micro Area	na	na	na	na	na	na	na	na	na
Mount Airy, NC Micro Area	1,492	0	1,506	0	1,642	46	792	0	14,866
Mount Pleasant, MI Micro Area	952	29	1,057	71	716	0	594	0	9,696
Mount Vernon-Anacortes, WA Metro Area	2,612	79	2,674	38	2,178	201	1,198	102	26,814
Muncie, IN Metro Area	1,226	52	2,846	0	1,284	119	1,860	0	19,125
Muskegon, MI Metro Area	2,833	12	3,301	0	2,255	0	1,424	128	31,672
Muskogee, OK Micro Area	961	14	948	0	760	0	779	41	11,806
Myrtle Beach-Conway-North Myrtle Beach, SC-NC Metro Area	8,479	490	9,260	359	10,540	236	5,953	326	133,717
Nacogdoches, TX Micro Area	na	na	na	na	na	na	na	na	na
Napa, CA Metro Area	2,361	76	3,276	73	2,875	61	2,035	44	25,287
Naples-Immokalee-Marco Island, FL Metro Area	5,098	635	8,207	61	8,692	348	9,326	95	116,785
Nashville-Davidson--Murfreesboro--Franklin, TN Metro Area	30,711	820	33,959	681	33,656	262	20,051	693	245,028
New Bern, NC Metro Area	2,161	0	2,338	0	1,424	56	1,589	279	26,889
New Castle, PA Micro Area	2,237	0	1,319	79	1,378	63	1,583	0	19,702
New Haven-Milford, CT Metro Area	17,644	409	20,421	260	17,624	453	13,893	201	138,652
New Orleans-Metairie, LA Metro Area	20,960	935	22,763	329	22,917	740	16,679	306	202,149
New Philadelphia-Dover, OH Micro Area	na	na	na	na	na	na	na	na	na
New York-Newark-Jersey City, NY-NJ-PA Metro Area	348,597	13,027	403,473	14,383	353,252	11,990	261,648	10,051	2,973,265
Niles-Benton Harbor, MI Metro Area	3,673	0	3,797	1	3,515	0	2,498	25	29,315
North Port-Sarasota-Bradenton, FL Metro Area	12,874	694	18,557	706	19,354	745	18,881	680	254,576
North Wilkesboro, NC Micro Area	na	na	na	na	na	na	na	na	na
Norwich-New London, CT Metro Area	5,840	331	5,933	317	5,844	179	4,546	60	45,203
Oak Harbor, WA Micro Area	1,085	61	1,895	73	1,453	41	1,107	0	21,736
Ocala, FL Metro Area	5,782	150	5,305	182	4,731	187	4,740	393	107,578
Ocean City, NJ Metro Area	2,609	0	2,451	104	1,668	78	1,728	56	23,579
Odessa, TX Metro Area	2,632	115	2,971	91	1,019	77	2,200	0	14,441
Ogden-Clearfield, UT Metro Area	8,582	119	9,801	118	8,716	0	4,151	62	75,276
Ogdensburg-Massena, NY Micro Area	1,682	0	1,407	26	1,316	0	1,065	0	20,199
Oklahoma City, OK Metro Area	18,992	337	24,030	136	21,985	225	19,321	237	185,868
Olean, NY Micro Area	1,088	61	1,917	67	963	115	620	64	15,645
Olympia-Tumwater, WA Metro Area	5,125	168	5,786	83	4,462	114	2,448	67	50,437
Omaha-Council Bluffs, NE-IA Metro Area	14,726	183	18,414	616	15,123	358	11,173	170	123,926
Opelousas, LA Micro Area	1,104	66	1,179	0	1,359	97	1,331	0	13,549
Orangeburg, SC Micro Area	916	76	1,015	71	1,340	0	1,501	12	17,873
Orlando-Kissimmee-Sanford, FL Metro Area	42,009	576	40,822	1,431	36,952	2,442	27,064	601	381,328
Oshkosh-Neenah, WI Metro Area	2,473	87	3,101	95	1,979	54	1,703	16	28,817
Ottawa-Peru, IL Micro Area	2,682	89	2,478	296	2,659	47	2,013	7	29,413
Owensboro, KY Metro Area	2,189	0	1,555	176	2,057	0	1,387	93	21,307
Owosso, MI Micro Area	1,125	0	1,460	15	1,057	0	639	22	13,316
Oxnard-Thousand Oaks-Ventura, CA Metro Area	15,076	536	14,274	561	16,610	1,109	9,832	383	124,675
Paducah, KY-IL Micro Area	1,149	0	1,402	0	1,431	72	1,595	0	21,823
Palatka, FL Micro Area	na	na	na	na	na	na	na	na	na
Palm Bay-Melbourne-Titusville, FL Metro Area	12,016	773	13,383	50	11,218	190	7,610	209	145,967
Panama City, FL Metro Area	3,611	543	3,961	240	2,436	84	1,970	49	36,720
Parkersburg-Vienna, WV Metro Area	1,077	0	1,281	42	987	68	1,468	0	19,613
Pensacola-Ferry Pass-Brent, FL Metro Area	8,501	444	8,415	109	6,276	56	3,713	184	89,620
Peoria, IL Metro Area	6,098	143	7,064	51	4,351	177	4,576	8	70,233
Philadelphia-Camden-Wilmington, PA-NJ-DE-MD Metro Area	108,577	4,220	129,138	4,464	113,371	4,710	80,802	3,912	923,152
Phoenix-Mesa-Scottsdale, AZ Metro Area	68,794	2,960	82,330	2,364	70,492	2,060	49,502	1,855	756,470
Pine Bluff, AR Metro Area	na	na	na	na	na	na	na	na	na
Pinehurst-Southern Pines, NC Micro Area	1,525	0	2,499	77	2,504	0	1,995	85	22,436
Pittsburgh, PA Metro Area	48,722	1,542	57,013	2,091	49,778	1,368	31,242	1,175	451,665
Pittsfield, MA Metro Area	2,036	18	3,810	307	3,274	0	2,506	68	27,839
Plattsburgh, NY Micro Area	1,311	62	1,067	0	1,028	52	604	0	15,755
Pocatello, ID Metro Area	1,331	0	1,091	37	1,426	0	489	0	12,556
Port Angeles, WA Micro Area	1,512	40	1,563	95	1,676	0	675	0	22,979
Portland-South Portland, ME Metro Area	11,619	44	15,122	137	13,541	15	7,468	417	96,291
Portland-Vancouver-Hillsboro, OR-WA Metro Area	39,031	1,134	47,300	905	38,494	1,418	24,596	637	365,114
Port St. Lucie, FL Metro Area	7,711	244	8,193	158	9,044	658	7,525	579	126,395
Portsmouth, OH Micro Area	1,038	0	823	0	908	46	213	0	15,620
Pottsville, PA Micro Area	2,279	58	2,952	46	2,201	62	1,785	0	29,831
Prescott, AZ Metro Area	4,067	212	4,922	175	5,755	452	4,385	637	74,536
Providence-Warwick, RI-MA Metro Area	33,727	818	37,423	929	28,194	813	20,420	431	269,916
Provo-Orem, UT Metro Area	4,268	172	8,181	41	5,417	41	3,050	56	48,601
Pueblo, CO Metro Area	2,392	176	2,650	57	2,129	37	713	0	34,624
Punta Gorda, FL Metro Area	3,591	211	5,281	120	4,459	0	3,261	170	74,785
Quincy, IL-MO Micro Area	1,626	0	1,702	0	1,398	38	1,861	0	13,228
Racine, WI Metro Area	4,341	14	4,059	93	2,807	60	2,377	0	33,020
Raleigh, NC Metro Area	19,074	707	22,265	925	19,768	558	13,470	325	160,600
Rapid City, SD Metro Area	2,315	53	4,180	102	3,128	0	2,633	102	25,533
Reading, PA Metro Area	7,513	382	8,500	259	6,472	164	5,463	404	69,699
Redding, CA Metro Area	2,055	40	3,373	90	3,340	59	2,021	144	39,696
Reno, NV Metro Area	7,666	639	11,661	72	9,471	372	4,884	0	76,062

Table F-4: Metropolitan/Micropolitan Statistical Areas - Employment and Labor Force Status, Civilian Labor Force—*Continued*

	60 to 61 Years		62 to 64 Years		65 to 69 Years		70 Years and Over		60 Years and Over Not in the Labor Force
	Employed	Unemployed	Employed	Unemployed	Employed	Unemployed	Employed	Unemployed	
Richmond, IN Micro Area...............................	na	na	na	na	na	na	na	na	na
Richmond, VA Metro Area..............................	21,364	455	26,772	868	21,903	254	15,926	312	198,477
Richmond-Berea, KY Micro Area.....................	1,854	13	1,374	0	1,494	31	868	137	16,113
Riverside-San Bernardino-Ontario, CA Metro Area	59,153	2,150	64,766	2,026	51,435	2,001	34,123	2,620	630,585
Roanoke, VA Metro Area...............................	6,346	197	6,801	195	5,425	79	4,599	17	63,526
Roanoke Rapids, NC Micro Area.....................	1,051	42	1,848	8	1,474	14	876	0	14,911
Rochester, MN Metro Area.............................	4,740	154	3,876	63	3,746	139	3,079	89	33,946
Rochester, NY Metro Area.............................	21,105	373	24,882	726	16,754	611	13,404	522	191,727
Rockford, IL Metro Area...............................	6,665	300	6,768	295	6,422	156	3,968	54	57,251
Rocky Mount, NC Metro Area.........................	3,125	73	3,505	139	3,280	0	2,858	80	26,406
Rome, GA Metro Area..................................	na	na	na	na	na	na	na	na	na
Roseburg, OR Micro Area..............................	1,523	55	1,767	0	1,844	311	875	0	30,548
Roswell, NM Micro Area...............................	1,088	189	956	84	1,001	0	954	0	11,045
Russellville, AR Micro Area...........................	na	na	na	na	na	na	na	na	na
Sacramento--Roseville--Arden-Arcade, CA Metro Area	35,775	1,687	41,937	1,739	31,348	1,320	23,104	992	371,790
Saginaw, MI Metro Area...............................	2,286	25	3,837	0	3,414	54	1,837	135	38,032
St. Cloud, MN Metro Area.............................	3,734	79	4,120	67	2,831	13	2,162	58	28,394
St. George, UT Metro Area............................	1,734	236	2,149	135	2,374	46	2,240	47	37,458
St. Joseph, MO-KS Metro Area.......................	1,997	0	2,963	96	2,069	0	1,437	51	21,657
St. Louis, MO-IL Metro Area..........................	48,797	1,488	61,056	1,494	48,521	2,489	31,509	1,025	466,293
Salem, OH Micro Area..................................	2,164	174	1,962	0	2,118	125	890	59	21,669
Salem, OR Metro Area..................................	6,906	36	8,488	59	5,136	52	3,570	0	72,536
Salinas, CA Metro Area................................	5,408	313	8,156	122	7,998	19	5,196	108	56,043
Salisbury, MD-DE Metro Area........................	7,531	110	9,200	172	10,551	166	8,679	357	95,223
Salt Lake City, UT Metro Area.......................	16,856	672	20,946	891	16,785	267	10,892	268	124,526
San Angelo, TX Metro Area...........................	1,707	0	1,676	0	2,424	0	1,886	0	17,290
San Antonio-New Braunfels, TX Metro Area.......	34,609	862	35,331	1,322	35,016	1,044	24,075	670	332,544
San Diego-Carlsbad, CA Metro Area................	48,640	2,885	58,662	2,085	50,058	1,693	32,308	981	463,992
Sandusky, OH Micro Area.............................	na	na	na	na	na	na	na	na	na
San Francisco-Oakland-Hayward, CA Metro Area	82,137	3,204	96,107	2,857	93,100	2,785	61,579	2,020	678,347
San Jose-Sunnyvale-Santa Clara, CA Metro Area.	31,591	1,203	38,484	1,717	31,886	673	19,518	770	255,532
San Luis Obispo-Paso Robles-Arroyo Grande, CA Metro Area	4,557	67	5,858	0	5,763	120	3,258	91	57,963
Santa Cruz-Watsonville, CA Metro Area............	4,642	158	5,866	660	8,308	374	4,149	46	39,672
Santa Fe, NM Metro Area..............................	2,818	153	4,555	44	4,715	240	3,472	96	32,455
Santa Maria-Santa Barbara, CA Metro Area.......	7,321	484	7,239	450	7,712	88	6,411	355	63,242
Santa Rosa, CA Metro Area...........................	10,275	656	11,086	463	12,451	486	10,073	217	88,678
Savannah, GA Metro Area.............................	6,961	151	6,749	247	5,583	559	4,525	27	52,764
Scranton--Wilkes-Barre--Hazleton, PA Metro Area	12,121	215	12,198	167	10,958	173	9,174	277	107,325
Searcy, AR Micro Area.................................	na	na	na	na	na	na	na	na	na
Seattle-Tacoma-Bellevue, WA Metro Area..........	64,371	2,054	73,386	2,248	64,498	723	35,859	1,092	515,804
Sebastian-Vero Beach, FL Metro Area..............	na	na	na	na	na	na	na	na	na
Sebring, FL Metro Area................................	na	na	na	na	na	na	na	na	na
Seneca, SC Micro Area................................	na	na	na	na	na	na	na	na	na
Sevierville, TN Micro Area............................	1,715	0	1,591	56	1,588	0	1,549	29	19,021
Shawnee, OK Micro Area..............................	1,422	30	1,454	0	740	18	783	0	12,523
Sheboygan, WI Metro Area............................	2,472	77	2,203	30	1,928	40	1,072	94	20,568
Shelby, NC Micro Area................................	2,256	0	2,098	47	2,223	0	746	0	18,811
Shelton, WA Micro Area...............................	na	na	na	na	na	na	na	na	na
Sherman-Denison, TX Metro Area...................	1,848	38	2,291	259	2,241	0	2,343	0	22,345
Show Low, AZ Micro Area.............................	1,595	597	902	98	1,040	16	1,454	186	21,712
Shreveport-Bossier City, LA Metro Area............	6,357	173	6,210	167	7,387	155	4,642	213	74,436
Sierra Vista-Douglas, AZ Metro Area...............	2,910	46	1,889	63	2,454	33	1,537	36	29,704
Sioux City, IA-NE-SD Metro Area....................	3,461	38	4,303	62	2,786	143	1,980	123	25,037
Sioux Falls, SD Metro Area...........................	4,839	0	5,459	49	5,442	304	3,672	0	30,738
Somerset, PA Micro Area..............................	1,812	73	1,478	0	1,496	46	1,180	7	16,545
South Bend-Mishawaka, IN-MI Metro Area........	6,802	135	7,258	0	5,925	42	4,352	328	51,130
Spartanburg, SC Metro Area.........................	4,959	224	6,309	127	5,265	257	3,910	129	56,798
Spokane-Spokane Valley, WA Metro Area..........	8,731	267	9,063	358	8,863	289	4,155	129	101,492
Springfield, IL Metro Area............................	3,741	33	4,430	311	4,073	64	2,644	7	36,943
Springfield, MA Metro Area...........................	11,239	168	12,518	230	12,514	79	7,408	163	103,370
Springfield, MO Metro Area...........................	6,410	106	8,202	86	5,797	60	4,534	216	80,453
Springfield, OH Metro Area...........................	2,177	0	2,658	123	1,855	56	970	0	27,399
State College, PA Metro Area........................	2,062	32	3,549	63	2,186	0	1,500	25	22,067
Statesboro, GA Micro Area...........................	751	69	1,427	0	882	0	733	0	9,098
Staunton-Waynesboro, VA Metro Area.............	2,613	0	2,834	101	2,269	0	2,187	44	24,791
Stevens Point, WI Micro Area........................	1,003	10	1,054	15	533	0	643	0	12,827
Stillwater, OK Micro Area.............................	1,649	165	663	0	1,361	0	904	0	10,079
Stockton-Lodi, CA Metro Area.......................	9,326	447	11,240	344	8,756	0	5,955	72	102,173
Sumter, SC Metro Area................................	775	0	1,729	0	1,937	0	1,016	232	18,104
Sunbury, PA Micro Area...............................	2,233	0	1,793	66	1,741	22	1,453	59	19,168
Syracuse, NY Metro Area..............................	12,018	200	13,712	450	11,120	504	7,788	344	112,050
Talladega-Sylacauga, AL Micro Area...............	1,542	99	1,084	39	742	90	965	0	19,815
Tallahassee, FL Metro Area...........................	6,540	133	6,648	239	5,620	259	4,118	130	56,964
Tampa-St. Petersburg-Clearwater, FL Metro Area	52,204	1,996	54,408	2,203	51,356	1,930	36,570	1,868	631,906
Terre Haute, IN Metro Area...........................	2,761	138	2,919	0	2,749	93	2,163	0	28,366
Texarkana, TX-AR Metro Area........................	1,722	63	2,892	0	1,641	27	1,588	65	26,939

Table F-4: Metropolitan/Micropolitan Statistical Areas - Employment and Labor Force Status, Civilian Labor Force—*Continued*

	60 to 61 Years		62 to 64 Years		65 to 69 Years		70 Years and Over		60 Years and Over Not in the Labor Force
	Employed	Unemployed	Employed	Unemployed	Employed	Unemployed	Employed	Unemployed	
The Villages, FL Metro Area	na	na	na	na	na	na	na	na	na
Toledo, OH Metro Area	10,711	230	10,866	113	9,832	312	5,760	645	100,129
Topeka, KS Metro Area	4,284	0	6,011	39	4,171	0	2,568	218	43,770
Torrington, CT Micro Area	4,905	246	5,192	29	5,196	61	3,423	153	35,149
Traverse City, MI Micro Area	2,713	49	3,898	81	2,663	0	2,286	67	33,822
Trenton, NJ Metro Area	8,536	254	6,869	166	7,531	220	4,796	97	50,563
Truckee-Grass Valley, CA Micro Area	na	na	na	na	na	na	na	na	na
Tucson, AZ Metro Area	17,385	633	15,324	620	17,807	655	10,362	517	208,142
Tullahoma-Manchester, TN Micro Area	1,914	63	2,381	44	1,390	0	1,465	81	20,761
Tulsa, OK Metro Area	16,733	555	17,416	366	15,401	278	12,002	326	150,833
Tupelo, MS Micro Area	2,058	0	2,723	44	1,208	78	626	65	22,397
Tuscaloosa, AL Metro Area	3,049	0	4,578	63	2,985	0	2,561	0	35,494
Twin Falls, ID Micro Area	na	na	na	na	na	na	na	na	na
Tyler, TX Metro Area	4,382	86	3,904	224	3,409	151	3,104	106	36,738
Ukiah, CA Micro Area	1,195	106	2,717	116	2,474	57	2,235	0	17,068
Urban Honolulu, HI Metro Area	18,573	174	20,435	200	22,937	589	14,812	287	155,246
Utica-Rome, NY Metro Area	5,086	71	6,119	92	5,316	68	3,444	97	57,027
Valdosta, GA Metro Area	2,310	0	1,500	71	1,796	0	1,560	0	20,617
Vallejo-Fairfield, CA Metro Area	8,691	115	9,223	495	9,357	153	4,947	166	67,983
Victoria, TX Metro Area	1,351	0	1,528	77	1,489	21	1,341	0	16,841
Vineland-Bridgeton, NJ Metro Area	2,380	20	2,091	0	1,773	0	1,305	7	24,386
Virginia Beach-Norfolk-Newport News, VA-NC Metro Area	31,010	612	30,218	552	27,280	539	18,518	468	249,709
Visalia-Porterville, CA Metro Area	5,301	317	6,652	429	4,270	61	2,816	169	56,674
Waco, TX Metro Area	4,103	267	4,722	219	4,459	0	3,351	80	38,298
Walla Walla, WA Metro Area	1,835	0	899	0	1,407	200	816	60	12,092
Warner Robins, GA Metro Area	2,978	0	2,096	18	1,917	28	1,593	0	26,198
Warsaw, IN Micro Area	na	na	na	na	na	na	na	na	na
Washington-Arlington-Alexandria, DC-VA-MD-WV Metro Area	102,477	2,590	128,825	4,749	123,275	3,074	75,340	3,777	722,942
Waterloo-Cedar Falls, IA Metro Area	2,133	63	3,665	48	2,790	0	1,874	39	28,245
Watertown-Fort Atkinson, WI Micro Area	2,198	98	1,331	24	1,848	0	1,115	0	13,836
Watertown-Fort Drum, NY Metro Area	1,392	0	1,804	0	820	13	666	44	17,102
Wausau, WI Metro Area	2,580	0	2,933	124	2,260	136	1,224	0	23,534
Weirton-Steubenville, WV-OH Metro Area	1,765	92	2,458	79	1,737	29	1,244	134	29,446
Wenatchee, WA Metro Area	na	na	na	na	na	na	na	na	na
Wheeling, WV-OH Metro Area	2,981	37	3,324	151	3,263	36	1,584	60	30,190
Whitewater-Elkhorn, WI Micro Area	1,730	0	2,651	0	2,143	45	1,348	39	16,985
Wichita, KS Metro Area	10,522	453	12,675	466	10,120	208	5,711	100	97,966
Wichita Falls, TX Metro Area	2,163	13	2,931	132	2,536	50	2,129	43	22,299
Williamsport, PA Metro Area	2,363	69	2,370	29	2,278	96	1,030	70	22,234
Wilmington, NC Metro Area	4,570	169	6,029	387	3,713	124	3,200	0	53,974
Wilson, NC Micro Area	1,919	0	1,296	0	1,969	0	1,088	0	14,478
Winchester, VA-WV Metro Area	2,886	95	2,272	104	3,658	0	1,163	0	24,515
Winston-Salem, NC Metro Area	12,498	583	13,896	190	9,927	401	7,329	216	120,081
Wisconsin Rapids-Marshfield, WI Micro Area	na	na	na	na	na	na	na	na	na
Wooster, OH Micro Area	1,976	0	2,682	0	2,010	0	1,392	135	20,414
Worcester, MA-CT Metro Area	17,639	1,123	22,025	843	17,795	849	9,964	529	142,836
Yakima, WA Metro Area	3,226	0	4,069	76	3,122	179	1,720	515	34,998
York-Hanover, PA Metro Area	7,690	259	10,616	247	7,693	594	5,670	172	77,582
Youngstown-Warren-Boardman, OH-PA Metro Area	10,400	323	12,458	408	10,331	377	6,781	114	116,279
Yuba City, CA Metro Area	3,017	0	3,547	84	2,548	0	1,802	0	25,329
Yuma, AZ Metro Area	2,991	53	1,873	251	1,356	97	1,459	0	43,190
Zanesville, OH Micro Area	2,269	40	1,426	0	1,129	0	602	0	16,453

Table F-5: 116th Congressional Districts - Employment and Labor Force Status, Civilian Labor Force

	60 to 61 Years		62 to 64 Years		65 to 69 Years		70 Years and Over		60 Years and Over Not in the Labor Force
	Employed	Unemployed	Employed	Unemployed	Employed	Unemployed	Employed	Unemployed	
Alabama									
Congressional District 1	12,146	63	10,639	158	10,056	612	8,177	297	131,908
Congressional District 2	9,268	64	10,927	217	9,476	450	6,881	209	120,841
Congressional District 3	10,432	230	11,081	271	7,736	247	6,087	38	129,777
Congressional District 4	9,701	212	9,772	174	9,842	160	8,597	113	137,372
Congressional District 5	10,797	367	10,920	314	10,396	388	8,315	305	122,264
Congressional District 6	12,633	27	12,744	198	11,679	115	8,748	0	119,214
Congressional District 7	8,914	370	8,911	399	8,430	680	6,766	54	110,956
Alaska									
Congressional District (at Large)	13,486	873	13,765	211	13,214	494	6,016	309	85,644
Arizona									
Congressional District 1	9,811	962	10,219	98	10,796	743	9,262	541	152,890
Congressional District 2	14,454	453	11,381	505	13,751	517	7,895	431	159,101
Congressional District 3	10,726	266	8,601	591	7,626	442	5,131	117	106,748
Congressional District 4	12,237	363	15,313	708	13,766	1,156	10,864	757	235,614
Congressional District 5	12,751	518	11,365	306	12,269	346	10,398	150	139,083
Congressional District 6	14,592	522	20,371	256	16,991	207	11,976	358	138,974
Congressional District 7	7,247	353	10,938	155	5,764	271	3,692	295	68,014
Congressional District 8	11,936	729	14,537	523	14,509	360	10,521	269	178,378
Congressional District 9	12,893	430	14,899	631	12,115	223	6,712	503	92,263
Arkansas									
Congressional District 1	11,713	458	10,259	115	10,960	68	9,162	200	135,161
Congressional District 2	10,314	350	13,102	375	12,084	222	8,827	116	121,704
Congressional District 3	12,643	251	11,375	247	11,143	9	7,819	239	119,323
Congressional District 4	11,087	138	12,077	164	9,996	511	10,289	78	142,993
California									
Congressional District 1	9,090	341	15,007	469	13,596	538	10,405	358	161,964
Congressional District 2	13,631	352	19,794	528	21,563	392	17,221	356	134,277
Congressional District 3	12,333	241	13,372	350	12,360	67	7,531	233	108,060
Congressional District 4	14,367	545	15,860	958	13,366	613	10,566	557	160,713
Congressional District 5	14,715	767	17,206	838	16,333	580	10,049	325	123,125
Congressional District 6	10,520	564	10,611	229	7,468	455	5,131	201	102,926
Congressional District 7	10,193	665	14,272	750	10,769	174	8,701	313	123,016
Congressional District 8	12,531	479	9,011	260	6,356	454	6,966	119	107,759
Congressional District 9	10,536	598	10,738	385	9,675	0	7,109	32	108,403
Congressional District 10	9,133	483	10,576	347	9,306	38	4,669	242	105,132
Congressional District 11	14,312	505	15,571	393	17,659	596	10,303	487	116,490
Congressional District 12	13,980	446	13,306	811	12,372	568	8,332	437	111,604
Congressional District 13	12,169	332	13,285	196	13,085	315	10,534	519	99,630
Congressional District 14	12,618	621	16,835	873	15,464	646	11,095	154	115,308
Congressional District 15	12,286	478	16,141	213	12,765	314	7,498	140	102,480
Congressional District 16	8,409	664	8,939	195	7,205	357	4,526	465	82,056
Congressional District 17	12,162	632	15,478	948	10,997	444	5,859	65	94,020
Congressional District 18	12,427	681	16,212	589	16,090	106	10,951	234	103,360
Congressional District 19	12,635	480	13,797	193	12,791	337	6,738	599	98,108
Congressional District 20	10,188	367	14,147	886	15,437	369	9,124	154	96,142
Congressional District 21	5,937	21	6,360	1,032	6,197	277	3,387	164	68,915
Congressional District 22	10,372	373	11,170	172	10,734	227	6,866	409	97,991
Congressional District 23	8,565	1,089	10,559	776	8,735	35	6,185	152	106,280
Congressional District 24	11,998	551	13,372	450	13,629	250	10,014	484	122,158
Congressional District 25	11,893	506	12,020	561	12,644	113	5,789	513	92,809
Congressional District 26	12,452	536	12,613	468	13,401	1,020	8,656	306	105,910
Congressional District 27	11,435	125	14,660	272	14,048	242	9,439	283	120,473
Congressional District 28	12,485	565	14,356	302	10,688	417	9,115	320	106,424
Congressional District 29	8,208	483	12,725	611	10,068	613	4,647	265	81,753
Congressional District 30	11,955	332	15,252	1,126	15,384	966	13,615	940	103,739
Congressional District 31	9,379	298	10,362	200	10,001	566	4,693	230	89,686
Congressional District 32	11,373	336	13,177	736	9,778	445	5,025	266	99,565
Congressional District 33	12,067	512	17,297	407	16,443	591	21,184	623	107,338
Congressional District 34	12,004	311	10,719	311	10,224	367	4,998	74	95,214
Congressional District 35	8,375	363	8,977	458	7,645	123	3,314	298	78,095
Congressional District 36	10,509	202	13,308	742	11,013	151	10,406	956	175,275
Congressional District 37	12,494	779	11,494	604	12,302	620	6,995	681	88,434
Congressional District 38	10,930	763	12,134	255	9,147	208	4,371	134	110,872
Congressional District 39	13,912	255	16,124	410	13,066	306	8,123	317	105,042
Congressional District 40	7,646	356	8,530	312	5,794	191	3,546	62	70,027
Congressional District 41	7,952	310	9,433	466	7,257	211	3,315	849	78,092
Congressional District 42	10,422	505	11,687	119	9,473	432	5,195	230	100,954
Congressional District 43	12,123	279	11,621	519	10,155	326	7,137	383	91,368
Congressional District 44	9,012	606	8,841	514	7,439	259	4,472	207	81,580
Congressional District 45	15,120	323	14,744	386	14,935	1,076	12,437	354	109,173
Congressional District 46	10,053	327	9,674	459	8,390	322	4,154	138	75,889
Congressional District 47	13,739	383	13,249	206	9,972	558	5,002	36	93,660
Congressional District 48	15,400	393	13,956	320	13,478	565	9,365	531	121,618
Congressional District 49	16,045	604	13,027	314	12,369	633	10,286	319	116,041
Congressional District 50	12,691	627	14,808	267	11,722	510	7,444	97	111,722

Table F-5: 116th Congressional Districts - Employment and Labor Force Status, Civilian Labor Force—*Continued*

	60 to 61 Years		62 to 64 Years		65 to 69 Years		70 Years and Over		60 Years and Over Not in the Labor Force
	Employed	Unemployed	Employed	Unemployed	Employed	Unemployed	Employed	Unemployed	
California—Cont.									
Congressional District 51	7,517	853	9,716	424	8,422	521	3,312	473	92,917
Congressional District 52	10,696	118	13,802	963	12,353	95	9,874	265	107,161
Congressional District 53	10,303	912	14,918	456	10,837	385	5,758	250	101,149
Colorado									
Congressional District 1	12,862	487	14,602	385	13,382	216	8,516	273	94,195
Congressional District 2	15,714	574	18,181	226	18,148	183	11,087	450	112,775
Congressional District 3	12,669	648	15,306	370	13,425	411	9,581	1,201	140,425
Congressional District 4	15,809	498	16,657	595	14,863	432	10,661	459	110,264
Congressional District 5	13,874	540	13,726	281	13,474	413	8,441	173	113,348
Congressional District 6	15,146	284	15,241	208	15,568	362	8,161	208	93,935
Congressional District 7	13,340	654	14,682	817	12,660	373	9,377	192	104,850
Connecticut									
Congressional District 1	13,087	322	18,371	674	13,857	601	10,827	462	114,953
Congressional District 2	14,835	753	19,659	638	15,066	555	10,703	230	117,363
Congressional District 3	15,361	455	15,955	389	15,798	456	11,177	341	114,624
Congressional District 4	14,234	583	19,548	346	16,052	953	13,336	956	98,505
Congressional District 5	15,413	326	16,969	443	14,470	478	10,935	129	114,582
Delaware									
Congressional District (at Large)	16,372	196	18,845	1,037	20,310	999	14,133	937	175,466
District of Columbia									
Delegate District (at Large)	8,213	212	10,655	247	9,563	245	8,348	529	80,698
Florida									
Congressional District 1	12,907	612	13,845	269	11,006	491	7,771	279	139,815
Congressional District 2	11,312	620	12,148	513	9,429	839	7,283	187	158,033
Congressional District 3	12,128	323	12,223	430	12,132	438	7,093	0	128,330
Congressional District 4	12,628	578	16,727	729	13,197	137	9,813	202	136,001
Congressional District 5	10,406	318	10,950	297	8,697	235	5,628	332	103,114
Congressional District 6	14,163	37	15,175	301	17,852	941	10,525	399	198,928
Congressional District 7	14,240	104	13,897	265	14,142	605	10,863	296	105,746
Congressional District 8	15,555	834	17,330	50	14,989	190	10,479	209	203,074
Congressional District 9	13,649	84	12,032	401	10,247	389	8,804	166	153,583
Congressional District 10	14,397	279	11,803	694	11,686	989	7,196	171	97,617
Congressional District 11	9,444	290	12,757	422	10,309	768	13,290	1,197	299,929
Congressional District 12	14,562	826	13,752	906	13,436	491	10,968	704	195,883
Congressional District 13	14,152	465	16,638	362	16,289	719	10,567	544	169,735
Congressional District 14	11,998	413	9,115	584	10,468	292	7,148	203	105,782
Congressional District 15	12,029	234	15,408	180	10,006	309	8,692	309	135,399
Congressional District 16	13,097	612	18,026	757	16,857	814	16,269	813	220,042
Congressional District 17	11,557	830	14,193	416	15,547	131	12,473	404	259,240
Congressional District 18	14,306	378	15,305	412	15,230	807	13,107	810	196,808
Congressional District 19	12,536	394	15,751	433	17,784	335	16,829	1,206	259,201
Congressional District 20	15,057	518	12,389	693	11,804	863	7,222	225	106,861
Congressional District 21	13,000	865	14,753	482	15,450	565	16,248	903	188,910
Congressional District 22	13,051	628	18,916	1,011	17,738	249	14,749	784	154,744
Congressional District 23	13,310	1,327	15,463	598	14,277	880	13,630	1,396	122,947
Congressional District 24	12,441	318	11,739	868	11,822	282	7,558	311	110,311
Congressional District 25	11,885	796	15,837	259	11,767	627	9,216	282	144,770
Congressional District 26	11,428	826	11,837	804	13,679	336	7,498	207	113,735
Congressional District 27	13,059	391	14,310	616	15,249	411	11,358	52	128,752
Georgia									
Congressional District 1	11,660	321	11,416	247	11,258	601	7,505	53	111,116
Congressional District 2	10,040	146	10,454	77	8,541	548	6,683	20	111,454
Congressional District 3	10,949	0	13,526	58	11,211	306	6,342	296	118,247
Congressional District 4	12,893	231	13,640	968	10,402	385	6,239	178	99,592
Congressional District 5	8,783	364	9,918	314	9,559	219	6,082	136	88,621
Congressional District 6	14,694	340	14,627	262	14,240	480	11,172	331	85,412
Congressional District 7	12,604	407	13,208	263	10,155	425	5,468	127	83,825
Congressional District 8	9,573	174	9,357	151	9,484	124	6,876	85	116,124
Congressional District 9	11,744	622	12,632	108	12,780	205	9,135	320	143,708
Congressional District 10	11,303	196	11,124	31	9,118	383	10,249	133	113,524
Congressional District 11	11,914	688	14,634	205	10,626	687	9,333	277	98,649
Congressional District 12	9,406	604	12,757	46	7,359	101	6,487	236	110,733
Congressional District 13	10,150	616	12,627	641	10,388	476	5,224	172	87,168
Congressional District 14	10,504	134	10,754	227	7,829	169	5,481	101	114,387
Hawaii									
Congressional District 1	13,160	125	15,338	112	17,235	471	11,223	213	118,305
Congressional District 2	14,250	102	16,160	266	16,321	223	11,339	817	119,678
Idaho									
Congressional District 1	9,452	505	16,398	300	14,789	466	9,559	148	158,355
Congressional District 2	12,458	131	15,681	77	12,659	90	7,586	324	123,848
Illinois									
Congressional District 1	12,988	661	13,911	912	11,367	305	8,061	374	113,502
Congressional District 2	10,990	869	11,337	490	9,580	320	7,136	264	113,970
Congressional District 3	11,336	640	15,592	613	9,853	574	5,693	496	109,253

Table F-5: 116th Congressional Districts - Employment and Labor Force Status, Civilian Labor Force—*Continued*

	60 to 61 Years		62 to 64 Years		65 to 69 Years		70 Years and Over		60 Years and Over Not in the Labor Force
	Employed	Unemployed	Employed	Unemployed	Employed	Unemployed	Employed	Unemployed	
Illinois—Cont.									
Congressional District 4	9,281	428	10,616	24	8,107	328	3,283	169	75,752
Congressional District 5	10,669	650	15,021	257	12,335	510	7,004	107	91,243
Congressional District 6	15,397	376	18,869	696	16,734	289	10,105	244	108,379
Congressional District 7	9,240	803	9,471	494	10,124	267	7,229	339	97,154
Congressional District 8	15,140	1,218	14,877	725	13,449	544	7,434	348	89,128
Congressional District 9	11,863	655	16,098	518	15,988	516	11,328	273	113,384
Congressional District 10	13,117	460	16,169	758	15,053	195	9,594	270	99,534
Congressional District 11	13,291	237	11,377	470	10,378	399	7,160	153	86,407
Congressional District 12	11,149	564	13,423	278	9,913	537	6,968	408	124,192
Congressional District 13	11,458	497	12,261	314	11,157	348	8,231	61	113,692
Congressional District 14	13,741	459	14,977	201	11,651	535	7,503	182	99,499
Congressional District 15	11,703	540	12,355	183	10,076	523	10,447	243	134,267
Congressional District 16	13,054	393	13,770	798	12,938	244	8,035	114	122,961
Congressional District 17	11,181	330	12,375	328	9,571	340	8,549	131	132,115
Congressional District 18	11,619	530	14,735	248	11,741	121	9,705	37	132,711
Indiana									
Congressional District 1	11,373	235	14,165	447	10,860	244	6,822	219	123,031
Congressional District 2	12,965	283	15,156	158	12,718	382	9,508	400	114,129
Congressional District 3	13,553	445	16,149	388	11,767	329	8,007	90	112,615
Congressional District 4	13,714	445	14,312	333	11,517	126	8,067	365	117,764
Congressional District 5	10,748	100	15,406	596	13,167	818	9,101	247	112,468
Congressional District 6	11,457	341	13,782	121	11,906	413	8,590	59	127,771
Congressional District 7	11,907	495	9,870	295	9,908	763	7,127	705	93,141
Congressional District 8	11,580	219	14,235	203	12,995	417	9,914	188	125,245
Congressional District 9	13,968	58	13,372	111	13,244	565	9,038	485	117,604
Iowa									
Congressional District 1	15,143	312	17,641	168	15,056	330	11,193	144	130,365
Congressional District 2	15,257	326	18,723	136	15,100	168	9,401	161	129,572
Congressional District 3	12,703	199	16,837	237	13,877	260	10,545	107	115,882
Congressional District 4	15,709	487	20,313	230	16,085	280	11,173	220	129,222
Kansas									
Congressional District 1	12,540	221	15,346	169	13,498	178	9,443	325	107,281
Congressional District 2	12,009	44	15,279	85	13,893	306	8,856	253	119,940
Congressional District 3	12,891	785	16,520	349	15,088	175	8,920	239	100,209
Congressional District 4	11,755	561	14,771	466	11,993	219	6,927	120	114,295
Kentucky									
Congressional District 1	10,993	90	10,633	0	10,735	262	9,249	251	142,232
Congressional District 2	11,051	195	11,272	346	10,507	408	7,421	126	133,447
Congressional District 3	12,286	95	13,314	544	13,533	293	8,934	157	119,497
Congressional District 4	12,938	624	13,897	354	11,289	184	9,759	366	117,533
Congressional District 5	5,995	194	8,315	187	7,034	247	4,814	88	143,372
Congressional District 6	10,851	261	11,478	622	11,890	465	9,701	467	115,907
Louisiana									
Congressional District 1	14,575	522	14,838	176	14,858	79	10,062	101	131,128
Congressional District 2	10,675	465	12,170	153	11,524	756	7,776	205	122,287
Congressional District 3	10,869	602	13,345	71	11,491	399	6,079	115	121,470
Congressional District 4	9,456	294	10,330	295	10,941	349	8,509	213	129,101
Congressional District 5	10,546	370	11,726	86	10,245	463	6,808	147	128,723
Congressional District 6	11,507	321	14,575	205	11,965	296	9,390	265	115,945
Maine									
Congressional District 1	15,382	74	19,282	268	17,236	15	10,870	417	128,688
Congressional District 2	13,256	432	15,909	373	13,999	598	8,699	213	138,611
Maryland									
Congressional District 1	14,847	273	17,930	199	13,997	395	12,368	665	133,318
Congressional District 2	11,230	188	16,291	245	13,169	192	8,563	336	108,996
Congressional District 3	13,628	85	15,185	400	14,586	329	10,701	139	106,296
Congressional District 4	13,016	578	17,427	506	13,855	794	9,429	280	93,060
Congressional District 5	14,011	725	16,910	544	13,870	191	7,461	224	101,208
Congressional District 6	13,133	370	15,923	995	16,668	615	9,401	289	109,403
Congressional District 7	11,356	415	14,085	489	12,235	600	9,031	357	112,242
Congressional District 8	15,891	80	20,238	742	20,722	435	13,137	1,142	106,286
Massachusetts									
Congressional District 1	13,242	186	16,899	566	13,764	96	9,501	231	129,152
Congressional District 2	14,344	524	16,345	497	16,751	718	8,664	496	114,257
Congressional District 3	15,459	1,218	16,918	873	13,218	504	8,808	102	99,663
Congressional District 4	14,376	221	19,858	439	17,489	169	13,297	425	111,744
Congressional District 5	15,036	552	17,052	824	19,410	783	13,283	558	105,760
Congressional District 6	14,733	622	20,690	836	18,602	346	15,275	309	129,046
Congressional District 7	9,864	286	11,592	107	11,478	583	7,675	288	84,850
Congressional District 8	15,597	212	17,438	855	15,480	621	10,134	171	115,116
Congressional District 9	14,609	457	19,365	409	17,927	996	14,601	407	152,267
Michigan									
Congressional District 1	13,102	524	14,049	404	11,485	324	9,810	158	173,261
Congressional District 2	11,289	312	13,123	52	10,264	187	8,177	186	122,782
Congressional District 3	12,939	867	14,611	86	11,632	441	9,074	260	112,095
Congressional District 4	10,202	355	12,651	255	9,393	314	6,909	262	149,742

Table F-5: 116th Congressional Districts - Employment and Labor Force Status, Civilian Labor Force—*Continued*

	60 to 61 Years		62 to 64 Years		65 to 69 Years		70 Years and Over		60 Years and Over Not in the Labor Force
	Employed	Unemployed	Employed	Unemployed	Employed	Unemployed	Employed	Unemployed	
Michigan—Cont.									
Congressional District 5	10,554	388	10,547	328	8,899	397	7,414	210	136,440
Congressional District 6	12,722	284	14,531	220	11,669	277	8,845	472	124,264
Congressional District 7	12,566	231	14,091	456	9,820	330	7,180	183	137,090
Congressional District 8	13,800	130	14,402	395	12,368	312	7,987	455	111,599
Congressional District 9	13,670	533	14,091	708	13,026	309	7,853	525	119,903
Congressional District 10	13,037	186	14,284	380	12,327	161	5,889	413	139,298
Congressional District 11	15,474	333	17,199	589	13,439	457	9,744	37	119,873
Congressional District 12	10,349	346	11,713	970	8,345	308	6,281	106	109,489
Congressional District 13	8,198	265	9,006	312	5,637	588	3,849	88	111,754
Congressional District 14	10,284	553	13,303	228	10,994	498	7,210	1,000	122,571
Minnesota									
Congressional District 1	12,673	325	16,151	73	12,497	238	9,261	182	110,082
Congressional District 2	13,415	409	13,464	110	10,007	163	6,341	54	96,327
Congressional District 3	13,675	965	16,852	1,068	16,081	542	9,061	203	104,543
Congressional District 4	12,378	160	13,884	583	11,062	244	7,074	208	103,031
Congressional District 5	9,398	564	12,858	829	12,714	196	7,086	44	83,687
Congressional District 6	12,487	282	14,722	268	10,964	143	6,557	73	90,849
Congressional District 7	13,699	410	15,887	280	13,411	238	11,017	91	122,398
Congressional District 8	12,974	584	13,906	477	11,578	345	8,178	119	141,262
Mississippi									
Congressional District 1	12,119	339	13,785	305	10,264	381	7,500	191	125,831
Congressional District 2	10,397	235	10,801	503	9,710	140	8,360	159	114,298
Congressional District 3	11,886	161	13,546	128	11,739	243	7,363	405	123,967
Congressional District 4	9,966	421	8,519	75	8,897	109	6,896	19	137,415
Missouri									
Congressional District 1	13,562	283	13,195	524	11,899	606	6,608	55	110,073
Congressional District 2	14,876	410	19,285	355	17,002	860	10,730	555	135,107
Congressional District 3	11,879	224	17,821	373	12,095	509	8,282	149	131,843
Congressional District 4	10,474	290	14,610	399	11,649	318	8,034	223	135,393
Congressional District 5	11,539	137	15,051	326	11,646	472	10,360	269	118,062
Congressional District 6	13,466	199	15,756	183	11,303	197	9,518	300	130,380
Congressional District 7	10,446	40	13,367	336	10,649	250	9,579	222	140,358
Congressional District 8	10,439	688	12,676	286	11,561	115	8,348	104	149,189
Montana									
Congressional District (at Large)	22,029	457	24,921	491	21,893	1,151	17,389	411	191,229
Nebraska									
Congressional District 1	11,466	20	13,581	96	13,162	57	9,282	162	89,952
Congressional District 2	10,154	170	13,066	456	11,014	315	7,581	122	80,362
Congressional District 3	11,816	357	17,567	233	16,290	117	10,985	203	104,473
Nevada									
Congressional District 1	7,159	682	10,490	369	9,006	811	8,275	466	99,324
Congressional District 2	12,009	708	17,489	363	14,581	686	9,582	0	122,291
Congressional District 3	11,117	642	14,455	256	11,449	256	8,895	1,087	135,155
Congressional District 4	10,307	674	13,712	520	10,664	710	6,063	222	121,032
New Hampshire									
Congressional District 1	15,758	732	16,075	656	13,533	219	11,518	244	110,717
Congressional District 2	14,918	240	17,231	371	17,348	345	12,164	90	114,503
New Jersey									
Congressional District 1	13,235	764	15,058	446	13,601	320	9,200	492	109,020
Congressional District 2	14,895	234	14,950	413	13,205	364	9,901	967	133,697
Congressional District 3	15,176	241	17,432	975	14,878	631	11,776	374	134,589
Congressional District 4	15,684	229	16,809	645	16,547	497	11,284	438	133,834
Congressional District 5	16,783	769	19,851	689	19,447	286	12,871	647	112,198
Congressional District 6	13,912	418	15,982	546	12,866	623	9,369	511	98,847
Congressional District 7	16,725	469	18,755	712	15,999	468	10,516	379	107,187
Congressional District 8	10,824	185	13,639	208	9,974	194	5,938	57	80,318
Congressional District 9	12,678	0	14,605	233	12,340	355	10,833	281	105,070
Congressional District 10	12,404	544	16,366	498	11,345	380	8,539	780	95,324
Congressional District 11	14,161	1,054	21,703	471	17,348	596	13,532	661	113,777
Congressional District 12	14,460	905	15,146	808	15,017	830	11,481	797	104,987
New Mexico									
Congressional District 1	12,588	302	10,884	431	9,728	684	6,519	524	121,967
Congressional District 2	9,267	475	10,221	549	9,517	114	6,827	39	129,832
Congressional District 3	10,208	370	11,915	214	12,525	403	8,660	232	129,658
New York									
Congressional District 1	13,392	503	15,008	197	12,209	198	10,868	142	124,529
Congressional District 2	14,853	261	14,963	212	12,157	306	9,144	358	104,475
Congressional District 3	15,312	402	19,916	724	16,456	224	15,401	301	131,516
Congressional District 4	16,295	486	14,924	281	16,832	366	9,239	240	114,191
Congressional District 5	16,970	463	13,824	608	11,268	347	6,461	101	111,012
Congressional District 6	15,332	449	16,182	560	12,104	778	8,012	480	130,217
Congressional District 7	8,494	210	9,738	265	7,007	162	4,907	179	91,052
Congressional District 8	10,645	184	14,098	422	11,387	108	5,623	239	121,502
Congressional District 9	12,434	508	13,513	1,175	11,175	438	8,719	62	105,694
Congressional District 10	9,752	643	13,453	584	17,234	306	13,989	432	94,420

Table F-5: 116th Congressional Districts - Employment and Labor Force Status, Civilian Labor Force—*Continued*

	60 to 61 Years		62 to 64 Years		65 to 69 Years		70 Years and Over		60 Years and Over Not in the Labor Force
	Employed	Unemployed	Employed	Unemployed	Employed	Unemployed	Employed	Unemployed	
New York—Cont.									
Congressional District 11	11,613	216	13,456	257	13,803	490	7,803	74	124,499
Congressional District 12	9,938	693	12,179	0	14,582	320	13,507	328	94,827
Congressional District 13	9,080	584	10,396	1,041	7,992	435	4,272	72	109,164
Congressional District 14	8,399	930	11,243	166	8,054	238	5,954	404	94,688
Congressional District 15	8,398	688	7,273	181	4,911	127	2,976	256	90,167
Congressional District 16	13,070	480	15,453	916	12,506	956	10,007	398	121,568
Congressional District 17	13,500	439	16,030	797	16,617	910	14,226	401	108,726
Congressional District 18	13,825	537	16,631	646	13,826	528	12,088	400	102,743
Congressional District 19	16,742	531	16,208	670	15,390	819	12,106	463	135,069
Congressional District 20	11,475	173	14,158	647	13,495	297	9,028	184	122,036
Congressional District 21	12,425	228	13,120	272	10,518	295	8,233	368	130,991
Congressional District 22	13,057	229	13,883	427	11,920	529	8,914	242	132,455
Congressional District 23	12,258	363	14,674	389	11,278	216	8,690	146	132,998
Congressional District 24	12,253	222	14,188	453	11,721	278	9,062	466	123,235
Congressional District 25	13,942	183	17,397	525	11,412	460	8,741	362	122,992
Congressional District 26	13,028	396	13,985	415	10,779	188	8,229	35	124,333
Congressional District 27	16,177	322	17,029	612	11,219	328	9,417	53	139,688
North Carolina									
Congressional District 1	13,275	307	13,203	416	13,857	117	10,320	388	123,464
Congressional District 2	12,275	568	15,072	483	12,276	278	8,092	147	118,795
Congressional District 3	11,701	284	14,784	292	10,396	310	7,861	413	136,944
Congressional District 4	13,153	397	14,814	625	13,722	325	8,922	322	94,369
Congressional District 5	13,889	668	16,468	87	14,162	585	9,771	225	138,240
Congressional District 6	12,197	652	15,805	42	13,728	159	8,243	370	137,671
Congressional District 7	13,191	416	16,252	768	12,525	445	10,077	504	168,735
Congressional District 8	10,313	149	12,617	277	9,292	478	8,037	207	122,606
Congressional District 9	11,782	166	14,806	131	12,289	421	7,265	293	123,726
Congressional District 10	13,507	150	16,979	348	13,874	412	9,457	261	141,015
Congressional District 11	13,849	15	14,415	177	14,034	830	12,341	121	174,345
Congressional District 12	11,813	383	12,644	541	11,486	629	5,753	48	87,266
Congressional District 13	13,845	489	15,423	145	10,445	121	10,234	209	132,156
North Dakota									
Congressional District (at Large)	14,001	328	14,896	120	12,906	436	10,343	34	109,156
Ohio									
Congressional District 1	11,807	266	13,213	449	12,879	186	8,627	189	109,492
Congressional District 2	12,655	369	13,264	107	12,380	204	9,960	254	118,689
Congressional District 3	12,510	292	12,149	241	10,004	320	6,227	173	86,280
Congressional District 4	14,447	577	15,225	322	11,787	343	7,561	97	125,969
Congressional District 5	14,563	233	14,613	24	13,094	103	7,410	707	131,364
Congressional District 6	12,811	311	13,943	339	11,701	289	7,766	379	145,517
Congressional District 7	13,576	183	15,698	498	11,950	99	8,375	70	134,782
Congressional District 8	11,827	162	15,642	377	12,109	283	7,385	25	123,815
Congressional District 9	11,612	168	13,408	571	11,194	612	7,231	506	115,405
Congressional District 10	13,108	612	14,040	265	13,631	703	8,726	367	125,030
Congressional District 11	10,457	781	12,636	613	12,600	815	8,375	482	122,760
Congressional District 12	13,602	280	15,971	336	14,048	173	7,042	206	120,714
Congressional District 13	13,009	373	15,577	728	13,445	766	7,955	259	132,293
Congressional District 14	15,841	496	20,443	260	16,542	463	11,348	386	135,647
Congressional District 15	10,904	231	14,120	503	11,024	261	7,191	184	125,156
Congressional District 16	13,681	161	16,706	235	14,878	469	10,384	202	139,941
Oklahoma									
Congressional District 1	13,955	550	14,288	383	12,654	249	9,627	278	116,671
Congressional District 2	10,118	88	11,741	77	10,450	175	9,349	92	147,621
Congressional District 3	11,910	363	14,001	198	13,340	244	11,109	45	123,444
Congressional District 4	10,623	276	11,965	111	12,351	145	10,105	105	118,030
Congressional District 5	12,282	236	14,706	153	12,075	134	10,911	179	110,192
Oregon									
Congressional District 1	12,944	299	17,462	449	14,033	517	9,566	95	126,106
Congressional District 2	12,905	450	16,854	718	15,303	386	11,273	564	177,413
Congressional District 3	12,485	367	14,604	249	13,688	545	6,755	150	112,944
Congressional District 4	12,944	355	13,168	619	14,389	792	8,720	636	179,250
Congressional District 5	13,689	374	16,396	97	12,488	398	8,817	202	153,722
Pennsylvania									
Congressional District 1	15,813	473	19,787	995	16,359	840	11,996	697	116,360
Congressional District 2	9,167	176	11,215	458	8,807	548	5,571	91	104,050
Congressional District 3	11,503	992	9,621	225	9,725	950	7,899	614	103,715
Congressional District 4	14,383	554	19,298	391	17,203	344	12,488	731	112,778
Congressional District 5	11,301	492	14,511	289	12,852	361	9,674	286	109,562
Congressional District 6	12,327	683	17,823	343	14,124	618	11,008	510	108,646
Congressional District 7	13,028	506	14,581	286	12,007	576	9,169	68	128,640
Congressional District 8	14,377	318	14,978	195	14,015	332	10,461	296	134,997
Congressional District 9	13,210	364	16,873	224	13,407	217	9,696	385	137,259
Congressional District 10	11,289	640	17,063	414	12,728	662	10,002	182	123,322
Congressional District 11	14,081	0	16,339	588	14,590	315	11,613	232	126,833
Congressional District 12	12,588	183	15,466	374	9,884	228	8,515	244	136,742
Congressional District 13	13,706	383	13,884	209	13,376	258	8,837	216	143,645
Congressional District 14	13,976	291	16,988	332	14,432	491	10,701	540	144,533

Table F-5: 116th Congressional Districts - Employment and Labor Force Status, Civilian Labor Force—*Continued*

	60 to 61 Years		62 to 64 Years		65 to 69 Years		70 Years and Over		60 Years and Over
	Employed	Unemployed	Employed	Unemployed	Employed	Unemployed	Employed	Unemployed	Not in the Labor Force
Pennsylvania—Cont.									
Congressional District 15.............	13,422	218	13,475	200	11,296	168	7,580	244	146,912
Congressional District 16.............	13,215	443	14,795	550	11,763	305	9,085	279	135,529
Congressional District 17.............	15,145	792	19,138	708	17,708	411	9,288	198	130,951
Congressional District 18.............	14,562	277	15,354	746	13,681	320	8,293	257	125,236
Rhode Island									
Congressional District 1.............	11,633	550	11,894	148	8,354	410	6,532	168	88,680
Congressional District 2.............	12,292	268	12,609	458	10,018	337	6,855	110	86,676
South Carolina									
Congressional District 1.............	11,022	87	14,230	516	14,077	74	12,024	250	144,071
Congressional District 2.............	11,472	173	12,359	589	11,549	113	7,922	270	116,887
Congressional District 3.............	10,647	624	11,930	290	10,185	259	7,150	191	134,310
Congressional District 4.............	12,752	309	13,337	310	12,733	543	8,614	177	115,724
Congressional District 5.............	11,911	296	11,236	43	9,493	534	7,784	544	125,557
Congressional District 6.............	7,328	518	9,278	213	8,911	263	6,639	244	112,222
Congressional District 7.............	11,720	508	13,453	438	13,402	213	10,387	82	167,288
South Dakota									
Congressional District (at Large).............	15,773	60	21,347	263	20,583	454	14,718	117	131,992
Tennessee									
Congressional District 1.............	10,089	360	12,633	198	10,843	340	9,097	29	158,533
Congressional District 2.............	11,832	245	14,214	421	12,709	192	10,247	133	135,295
Congressional District 3.............	10,892	61	15,433	438	11,866	83	9,223	628	142,417
Congressional District 4.............	12,038	221	12,961	405	10,980	142	8,372	479	121,578
Congressional District 5.............	10,787	406	14,568	134	13,087	210	8,583	322	90,482
Congressional District 6.............	12,890	247	14,837	237	14,218	90	9,288	407	140,267
Congressional District 7.............	9,622	458	12,571	240	10,309	218	6,258	22	124,554
Congressional District 8.............	12,141	159	16,002	256	14,165	394	9,829	120	121,709
Congressional District 9.............	12,358	83	11,918	652	8,884	947	7,479	693	91,713
Texas									
Congressional District 1.............	11,898	647	10,524	345	11,638	208	8,227	195	121,330
Congressional District 2.............	12,034	76	16,186	643	12,223	839	9,879	423	87,753
Congressional District 3.............	12,494	652	15,467	674	16,034	291	9,578	263	91,120
Congressional District 4.............	10,212	617	13,062	620	11,325	95	11,848	266	126,416
Congressional District 5.............	10,839	612	13,838	186	11,959	503	7,214	269	103,382
Congressional District 6.............	13,335	390	13,778	151	11,723	476	6,956	229	88,612
Congressional District 7.............	11,041	444	15,309	980	12,888	174	9,623	309	77,194
Congressional District 8.............	13,147	734	14,494	260	14,032	642	6,982	223	120,763
Congressional District 9.............	12,510	531	10,796	411	11,950	298	6,460	240	75,675
Congressional District 10.............	15,214	427	14,252	796	14,373	501	9,793	209	111,402
Congressional District 11.............	13,078	249	14,863	225	13,060	439	11,830	64	116,712
Congressional District 12.............	13,764	364	13,878	692	11,334	474	7,959	422	101,962
Congressional District 13.............	11,302	268	12,864	216	12,529	336	10,866	194	102,882
Congressional District 14.............	9,422	1,393	11,061	883	9,872	618	8,406	692	109,756
Congressional District 15.............	9,072	302	9,577	152	8,717	116	4,918	190	86,946
Congressional District 16.............	8,692	308	9,572	733	8,732	0	5,231	224	95,456
Congressional District 17.............	8,594	408	12,186	219	10,864	269	7,621	147	95,114
Congressional District 18.............	10,163	543	12,422	396	8,318	320	6,051	628	78,063
Congressional District 19.............	11,142	488	11,684	146	10,823	107	8,755	206	96,606
Congressional District 20.............	11,460	445	11,113	160	10,558	0	7,265	241	91,409
Congressional District 21.............	13,899	457	16,293	710	16,398	482	13,339	144	122,419
Congressional District 22.............	13,083	210	16,209	2,135	12,386	603	8,858	293	101,212
Congressional District 23.............	9,858	236	10,652	264	11,815	546	8,316	0	106,492
Congressional District 24.............	15,320	380	17,333	468	13,771	536	11,086	113	79,680
Congressional District 25.............	10,915	950	11,392	533	13,678	282	9,229	61	110,739
Congressional District 26.............	13,621	683	14,186	169	11,065	308	8,432	430	85,766
Congressional District 27.............	11,717	126	11,902	338	12,485	1,027	8,466	60	118,638
Congressional District 28.............	6,420	380	8,854	337	7,774	453	5,436	218	93,486
Congressional District 29.............	8,863	590	11,056	127	8,008	245	3,222	199	66,411
Congressional District 30.............	10,698	703	12,289	173	9,887	280	5,690	215	89,770
Congressional District 31.............	9,770	521	12,326	1,110	12,234	484	9,538	151	102,961
Congressional District 32.............	15,606	357	15,550	203	12,898	581	12,333	152	82,652
Congressional District 33.............	8,975	695	8,732	188	8,056	634	5,050	396	69,916
Congressional District 34.............	8,615	118	8,264	198	7,504	61	5,435	311	105,644
Congressional District 35.............	8,195	278	9,585	739	9,453	204	4,221	378	91,101
Congressional District 36.............	11,439	152	12,237	660	10,350	643	9,089	127	112,545
Utah									
Congressional District 1.............	10,271	65	11,191	187	11,460	95	3,814	62	83,587
Congressional District 2.............	11,096	847	12,099	247	9,185	102	7,595	140	104,682
Congressional District 3.............	7,508	197	13,433	87	10,082	172	5,938	56	81,122
Congressional District 4.............	9,703	280	12,037	779	9,826	87	6,613	175	74,329
Vermont									
Congressional District (at Large).............	13,610	576	19,054	371	17,808	340	12,400	692	108,058
Virginia									
Congressional District 1.............	14,001	367	14,570	1,086	14,313	239	9,906	462	118,248
Congressional District 2.............	13,744	298	14,474	139	12,907	279	8,328	384	106,211
Congressional District 3.............	11,985	130	10,838	208	11,164	139	7,193	84	102,537

Table F-5: 116th Congressional Districts - Employment and Labor Force Status, Civilian Labor Force—*Continued*

	60 to 61 Years		62 to 64 Years		65 to 69 Years		70 Years and Over		60 Years and Over Not in the Labor Force
	Employed	Unemployed	Employed	Unemployed	Employed	Unemployed	Employed	Unemployed	
Virginia—Cont.									
Congressional District 4	12,358	532	15,137	508	11,413	124	8,977	153	117,247
Congressional District 5	14,458	226	16,458	514	14,598	180	12,207	113	144,173
Congressional District 6	13,797	600	16,122	328	11,820	246	10,638	199	139,032
Congressional District 7	12,461	253	18,885	474	15,290	159	9,563	81	122,450
Congressional District 8	12,091	379	15,784	417	14,744	222	10,747	95	83,900
Congressional District 9	9,973	101	11,431	82	10,541	172	8,111	173	155,054
Congressional District 10	16,588	116	15,656	244	17,354	505	10,440	315	95,275
Congressional District 11	14,411	246	16,800	198	15,438	125	7,620	539	85,199
Washington									
Congressional District 1	13,784	200	15,501	500	12,790	276	6,771	349	100,609
Congressional District 2	13,343	394	14,648	745	12,671	257	7,471	581	126,455
Congressional District 3	12,507	243	15,067	411	10,669	309	8,434	438	132,518
Congressional District 4	8,432	382	12,685	511	10,517	350	5,982	668	106,201
Congressional District 5	12,310	267	11,596	428	11,324	489	5,966	352	130,368
Congressional District 6	12,504	576	13,642	409	14,916	179	9,462	99	148,364
Congressional District 7	10,994	376	14,685	363	15,273	264	8,259	80	104,990
Congressional District 8	15,349	408	15,495	325	10,954	124	7,693	44	103,412
Congressional District 9	10,885	389	14,246	432	12,294	135	7,647	82	98,521
Congressional District 10	10,988	825	13,226	222	10,418	122	5,257	110	114,613
West Virginia									
Congressional District 1	8,770	798	10,523	245	10,194	264	7,455	29	123,401
Congressional District 2	7,029	159	12,128	566	10,985	303	7,477	183	126,966
Congressional District 3	8,402	60	7,824	137	7,887	90	5,982	78	134,483
Wisconsin									
Congressional District 1	14,818	139	16,671	358	12,146	146	7,530	233	116,943
Congressional District 2	16,144	50	15,715	144	13,043	189	8,495	139	108,311
Congressional District 3	12,980	148	16,407	341	12,067	346	9,611	198	128,333
Congressional District 4	10,157	219	11,226	415	7,753	133	4,586	132	94,305
Congressional District 5	16,087	330	18,243	271	13,876	299	8,276	249	130,377
Congressional District 6	15,431	512	16,622	135	12,804	347	9,040	157	129,793
Congressional District 7	15,105	286	16,397	433	13,614	374	8,911	121	145,453
Congressional District 8	14,498	455	14,138	219	12,105	299	6,501	85	129,324
Wyoming									
Congressional District (at Large)	12,701	234	11,185	375	11,814	385	8,463	176	92,655

PART G

INCOME AND POVERTY

INCOME AND POVERTY

The Census Bureau reports that the 2018 real median household income (adjusted for inflation) of $63,179 for all households was not a statistically different from the 2017 median[1]. At the same time, inflation pushes prices higher which disproportionately affects persons on fixed incomes, a group which includes many seniors. The Census definition of income includes sources of cash income: wages and salary, social security, retirement, interest, dividends and rent, for example. It does not include measures of assets and may not be a good measure of overall wealth. However, it still illustrates the wide variation across states and sub-state areas in income distributions and poverty. Most importantly poverty, because that population likely has very little in assets to offset their limited money income.

This historical data indicates that the median household income of householders age 65 and over is considerably below that of all householders. However, it also shows that the gap which had narrowed between 2010 and 2013 has widened in the last 5 years. This may be an indication of greater income growth among all households, as the impact of the recession fades, while seniors aren't seeing as large a benefit.

Median Household Income, Adjusted for Inflation

	Householder 65 Years and Over	All Households	Gap
2010	$34,381	$50,046	$15,665
2011	$35,107	$50,502	$15,395
2012	$36,743	$51,371	$14,628
2013	$37,847	$52,250	$14,403
2014	$39,186	$53,657	$14,471
2015	$40,971	$55,775	$14,804
2016	$42,113	$57,617	$15,504
2017	$43,735	$60,336	$16,601
2018	$44,992	$61,937	$16,945

U.S. Census Bureau, American Community Survey 1-year Estimates, Table B19049.

---

[1] U.S. Census Bureau, Current Population Reports, P60-266, *Income and Poverty in the United States: 2018*, U.S. Government Printing Office, Washington, DC, September 2019.

Median Income

There are 19 states above the national median income of householders age 65 and over. Hawaii has the highest median income at $65,078 followed closely by Maryland at $59,536. West Virginia has the lowest at $36,147 followed by Louisiana ($36,345), and Mississippi ($36,415).

The county with the highest median income, with more than $95,000, is Fairfax County, Virginia followed by Arlington County, Virginia at $93,449. In 392 counties, householders age 65 and over have median incomes greater than the national average and 82 counties have a median income over $60,000 while the median in 224 counties is below $40,000. Each of the counties in the states of Connecticut (8), Delaware (3), Hawaii (4), Nevada (2), New Hampshire (6) and Vermont (1) have median incomes above the national median. Among householders 65 and over, Sammamish city, Washington is the city with the highest median income at $115,756 and at $17,361, Madera city, California has the lowest median income, about 40 percent of the national figure. In 279 cities the median income is less than the national median and in 42 cities it is below $30,000. More than 200 cities (211) have median incomes above $50,000. New York City, the city with the largest number of householders 65 and over had a median income of $37,417, more than seven thousand dollars below the national figure.

The Washington-Arlington-Alexandria, DC-VA-MD metro area has the highest median for householders age 65 and over at $77,094 followed by the Santa Maria-Santa Barbara, CA metro with a median of $75,494. Twenty-six other areas have medians above $60,000. The Valdosta, Georgia metro area has the lowest median at $22,466 and 327 metropolitan and micropolitan areas have median incomes below the national median of $44,992. Congressional districts with median incomes above the national figure number 198. The highest median ($88,255) is in Virginia's 10th Congressional District while the lowest is New York's 15th Congressional District at only $18,411. Fifty congressional districts have median incomes that are less than $35,000 while 49 districts have medians above $50,000.

Poverty Status and Receipt of Food Stamps

Poverty status is determined by comparing total family or unrelated individual income to the established

Median Household Income of Householders 65 Years and Over

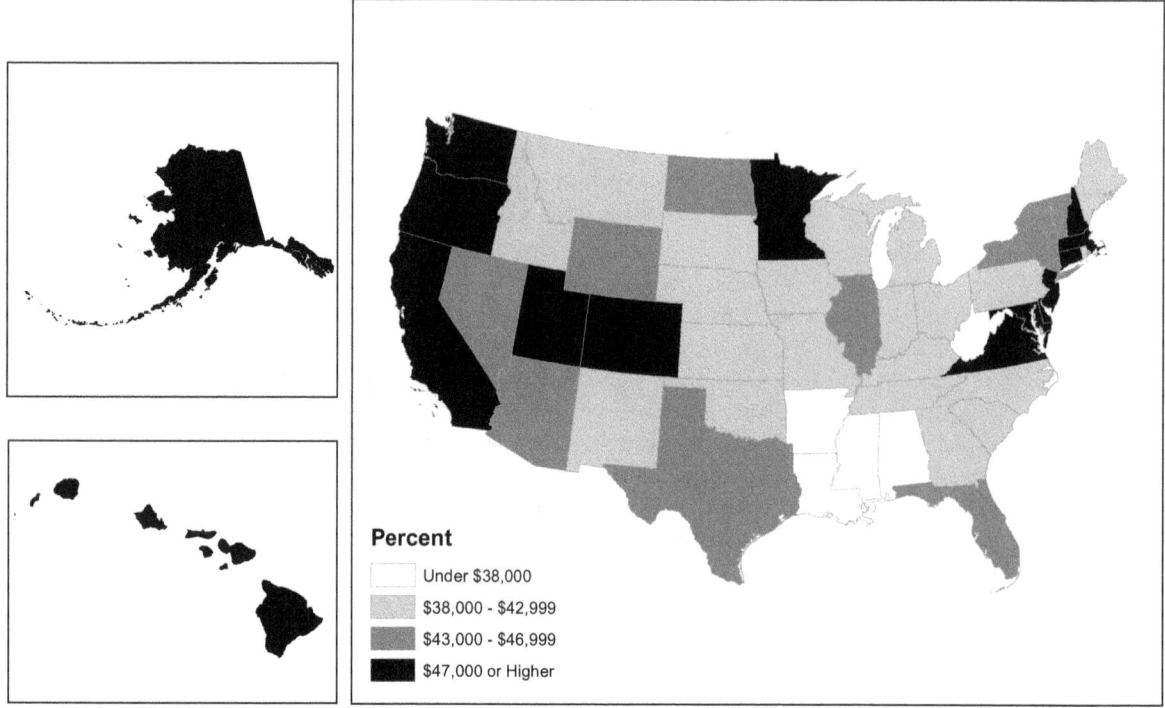

Percent
- Under $38,000
- $38,000 - $42,999
- $43,000 - $46,999
- $47,000 or Higher

national poverty thresholds which vary by size and type of household and number of children. When a family or single person household is determined to be in poverty, every member of the family is so defined. In 2018, the national poverty rate for persons age 55 to 64 years was 10.6 percent, for persons 65 to 74 years it declines to 8.8 percent then increases again to 10.4 percent for the 75 and over population. This pattern of decline to the 65 to 74 population followed by an increase in the 75 and over holds for every state except Arkansas and Hawaii. The poverty rate decreases across each age in both states. The pattern does not hold for other sub-state areas.

The poverty rate for the 55 to 64 population is higher than the national rate in 25 states and the highest rate (19.5 percent) is in the District of Columbia. The District of Columbia is also the highest for the 65 to 74 (12.3 percent) and for the 75 and over population at 20.7 percent. New Hampshire has the lowest rate among the 55 to 64 age category at 5.8 as well as the other ages at 4.4 percent for the 65 to 74 population and 5.8 percent for the 75 and over population. While the District of Columbia has the highest 75 and over rate, the next closest state is North Dakota at 16.1 percent. Seven states are above 13 percent and nineteen states are above the national rate for the 75 and over population. SNAP refers to the Supplemental Nutrition Assistance Program, what used

to be known as the food stamp program. SNAP recipient households are those containing one or more people age 60 and over. The District of Columbia (18.5 percent) and the State of New York (16.1 percent) have the highest percentages of food stamp recipient households. Wyoming has the lowest rate of food stamp recipients at 3.4 percent. Twenty-four states are above the national rate of 10.0 percent.

Apache County, Arizona has the highest rate of poverty among the 55 to 64 population at 32.1 percent and 28.7 percent of the 75 and over population is also in poverty. Both measures are more than two and a half times the national rates for their respective age groups. Apache County is not the highest rate among the 75 and over population however. That distinction belongs to Webb County, Texas at 30.3 percent. Fauquier County, Virginia has the lowest poverty rate for the 55 to 64 population at only 1.4 percent. Seven counties: Spalding County, Georgia, Rice County, Minnesota, Chatham County, North Carolina, Anoka County, Minnesota, Madison County, Tennessee, Montgomery County, Virginia and Cheshire County, New Hampshire all have less than 2 percent of their 75 and over population in poverty. There are 355 counties with poverty rates above the national figure for the 55 to 64 population and 267 are above the nation for the 75 and over population. Bronx County, New York

Percent of the Population 75 Years and Over
With Income Below the Poverty Level

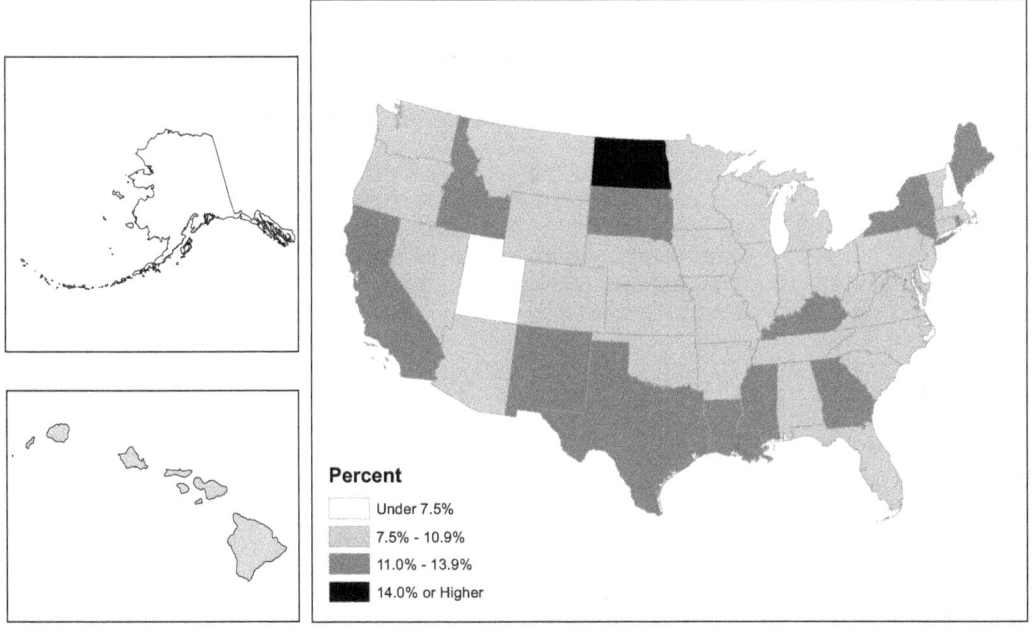

Percent

Under 7.5%

7.5% - 10.9%

11.0% - 13.9%

14.0% or Higher

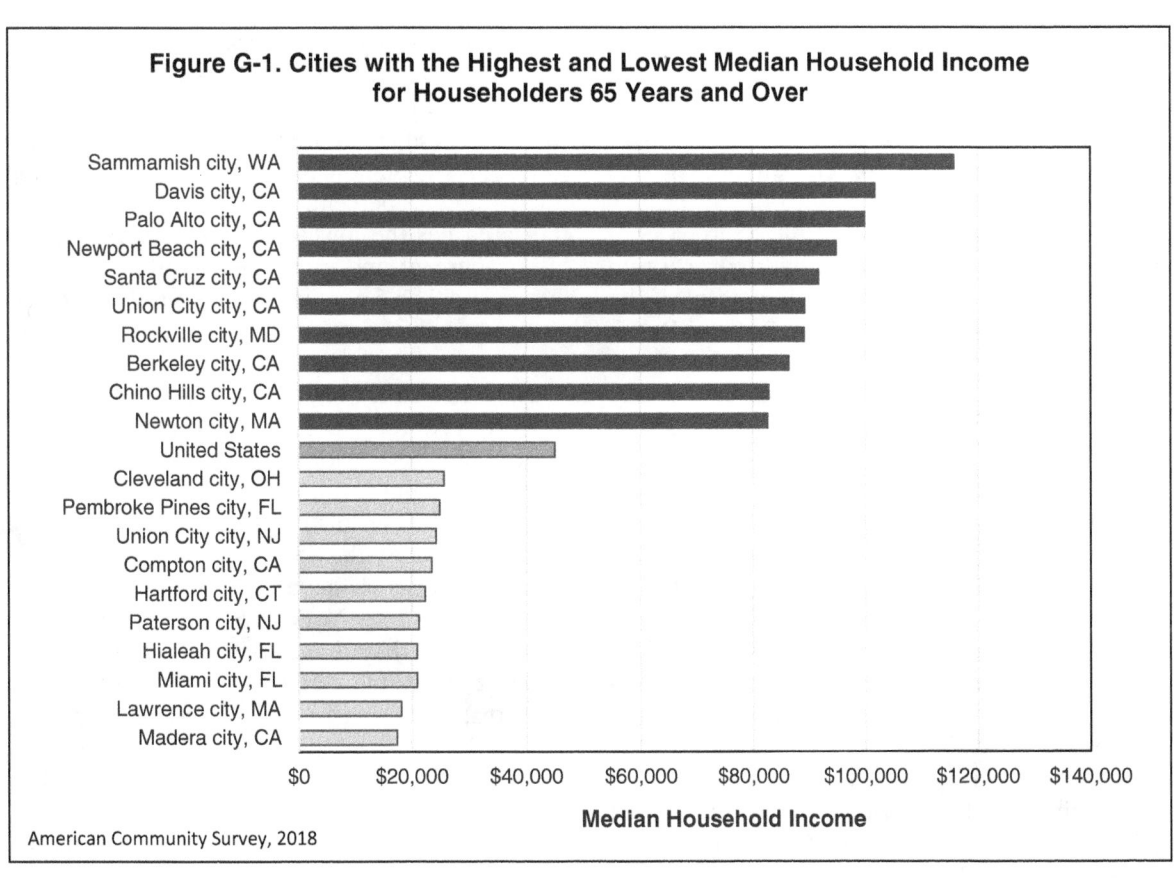

**Figure G-1. Cities with the Highest and Lowest Median Household Income
for Householders 65 Years and Over**

American Community Survey, 2018

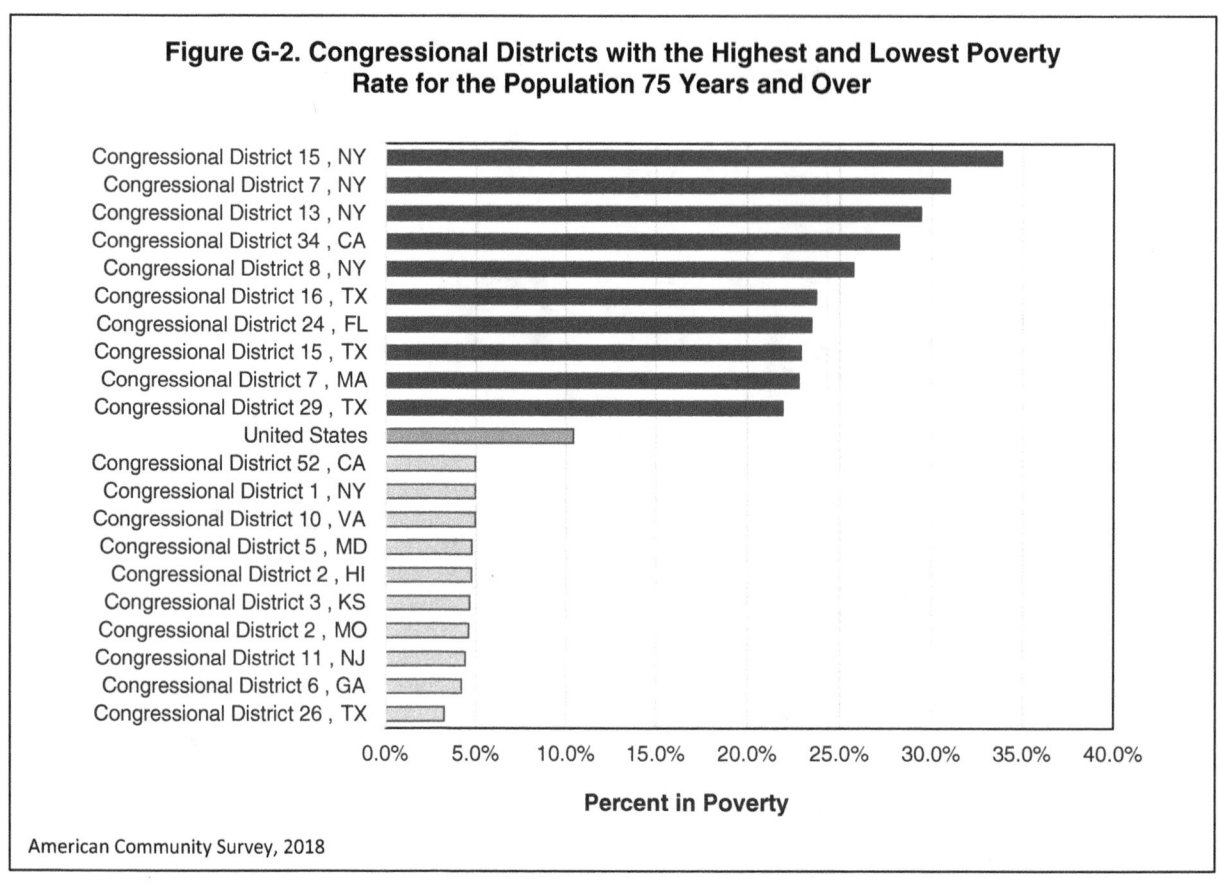

Figure G-2. Congressional Districts with the Highest and Lowest Poverty Rate for the Population 75 Years and Over

American Community Survey, 2018

has the highest food stamp recipient rate at 39.9 percent while Bedford County, Virginia is lowest at 1.3 percent. Ten percent or more households with a person 60 years or over receive food stamps in 298 counties and in 16 counties more than 20 percent are recipient households.

In 15 cities, more than 25 percent of the 55 to 64 population is in poverty and the 75 and over poverty rate is over 25 percent in 21 cities. Almost 40 percent of the 75 and over population (37.5 percent) of Miami Beach city, Florida is in poverty followed closely by Lawrence, Massachusetts at 36.6 percent. In 36 cities the poverty rate for persons 75 and over is less than 3 percent. The poverty rate for persons 55 to 64 is over 25 percent in 15 cities. Almost half (48.3 percent) of the households with a member 60 or over in Hialeah, Florida is receiving food stamps. In 35 cities, at least 25 percent of the households are receiving food stamps. Carlsbad, California has a reported rate at only 0.2 percent.

The Show Low, Arizona micropolitan area has the highest rate of poverty (30.1 percent) among the 55 to 64 population while the California-Lexington Park, Maryland metropolitan area is lowest at 3.1 percent. Fifteen other metropolitan areas are below 5 percent in the rate of poverty for 55 to 64 year olds. Among the 75 and over population, the Valdosta, Georgia metropolitan area has the highest rate (34.3 percent) and the Keene, New

Hampshire micro has the lowest rate which, along with the Faribault-Northfield, Minnesota miropolitan area are both below two percent. Only 11 areas have more than 20 percent of households receiving food stamps with the highest being the McAllen-Edinburg-Mission, Texas metro at 29.5 percent. The Villages, Florida metropolitan area has the lowest percent receiving food stamps at 1.7 percent and in 50 metropolitan or micropolitan areas, less than 5 percent of the households receive food stamps.

New York's 15th Congressional District has the highest poverty rate (30.1 percent) among the 55 to 64 population and New York's 13th is second highest at 29.4 percent. Virginia's 10th district is the lowest at 3.3 percent and 18 other districts have a poverty rate under 5 percent. Among the 75 and over population, five congressional districts have poverty rates over 25 percent, led again by New York's 15th district at 33.8 percent. New York's 7th and 13th districts have the next highest rates at 31.0 percent and 29.4 percent, respectively. The 26th district of Texas is the lowest at 3.3 percent. New York's 15th district also has the highest percent (51.8 percent) of households with members over 60 receiving food stamps. Four additional districts have more than 30 percent of the households receiving food stamps: Florida's 24th district and New York's 7th, 8th and 13th districts.

Table G-1: States - Income, Poverty Status and Receipt of Food Stamps (SNAP)

	Income of Households with Householder 65 Years and Over						Poverty Rate of Persons			Households with 1 or More Persons 60 Years and Over	
	Total Households	Less Than $25,000	$25,000 - $49,999	$50,000 - $99,999	$100,000 or More	Median Household Income	55 to 64 Years	65 to 74 Years	75 Years and Over	Receiving SNAP	Not Receiving SNAP
United States	31,842,901	8,908,748	8,434,430	8,665,585	5,834,138	$44,992	10.6%	8.8%	10.4%	4,911,453	44,078,046
Alabama	523,973	177,372	142,847	131,520	72,234	$37,977	14.3%	9.1%	10.5%	79,020	691,104
Alaska	53,173	11,482	11,929	17,077	12,685	$59,339	9.7%	5.3%	7.0%	9,038	80,831
Arizona	754,387	196,293	208,469	222,901	126,724	$46,152	11.3%	7.6%	9.2%	95,379	1,025,932
Arkansas	314,838	104,423	95,253	76,713	38,449	$37,762	14.1%	9.9%	9.3%	40,349	424,639
California....................................	3,197,217	806,111	693,706	845,612	851,788	$54,272	10.4%	8.2%	11.7%	336,819	4,886,186
Colorado....................................	499,802	121,589	121,671	145,925	110,617	$51,537	8.4%	5.7%	8.6%	52,969	730,690
Connecticut................................	374,793	89,237	86,241	102,170	97,145	$54,629	8.1%	6.1%	8.6%	59,887	525,169
Delaware	107,758	22,428	26,329	37,963	21,038	$54,744	12.1%	5.8%	5.9%	12,205	151,255
District of Columbia	58,898	18,137	10,931	13,243	16,587	$50,873	19.5%	12.3%	20.7%	15,847	69,673
Florida.......................................	2,522,233	725,039	674,610	681,047	441,537	$43,804	11.8%	9.7%	10.8%	475,117	3,218,340
Georgia	886,919	266,041	241,208	229,427	150,243	$42,781	11.6%	8.2%	11.2%	153,473	1,246,759
Hawaii	143,128	26,021	32,361	37,315	47,431	$65,078	8.2%	6.3%	6.1%	20,806	199,176
Idaho...	168,614	48,579	47,459	50,045	22,531	$42,678	8.6%	6.2%	11.1%	14,937	235,748
Illinois.......................................	1,242,040	347,744	324,257	343,344	226,695	$44,955	10.2%	7.1%	9.4%	218,741	1,689,866
Indiana	659,809	188,838	200,309	193,340	77,322	$41,342	10.0%	6.3%	8.6%	67,876	935,535
Iowa..	338,159	92,615	102,473	98,643	44,428	$42,995	8.1%	4.7%	9.3%	31,881	468,497
Kansas	287,156	79,764	85,160	80,087	42,145	$42,989	9.7%	6.4%	8.5%	24,461	409,801
Kentucky....................................	458,020	151,338	133,773	117,988	54,921	$38,254	14.4%	8.4%	11.3%	71,920	622,113
Louisiana	446,979	158,503	124,105	104,736	59,635	$36,345	15.2%	10.2%	13.5%	84,621	604,876
Maine	175,923	53,766	51,139	45,580	25,438	$40,435	10.8%	6.8%	11.3%	32,335	228,218
Maryland....................................	558,175	117,018	122,627	160,592	157,938	$59,536	7.5%	5.4%	8.3%	79,904	813,914
Massachusetts............................	700,037	187,580	163,662	186,696	162,099	$49,756	8.5%	6.6%	10.8%	128,425	950,954
Michigan....................................	1,093,561	299,222	330,944	314,240	149,155	$42,816	11.0%	7.6%	9.3%	172,535	1,480,115
Minnesota	552,433	143,816	148,669	167,196	92,752	$47,054	7.8%	5.5%	8.8%	53,888	779,027
Mississippi.................................	303,363	107,318	84,556	76,207	35,282	$36,415	16.0%	10.3%	13.5%	51,894	401,239
Missouri.....................................	651,569	193,177	195,414	174,960	88,018	$41,038	10.9%	6.6%	9.1%	78,403	895,284
Montana.....................................	123,306	34,330	35,958	35,839	17,179	$42,745	10.9%	7.9%	10.4%	11,980	175,720
Nebraska	194,541	55,148	56,264	53,728	29,401	$42,851	8.5%	5.1%	9.8%	17,369	271,425
Nevada	279,933	73,827	75,389	79,066	51,651	$46,406	12.5%	8.5%	10.5%	44,144	400,921
New Hampshire............................	145,788	35,163	37,403	43,595	29,627	$50,240	5.8%	4.4%	5.8%	12,057	219,110
New Jersey	867,467	206,280	204,540	232,610	224,037	$53,637	7.1%	6.1%	8.6%	111,625	1,264,434
New Mexico	228,095	74,120	61,060	58,919	33,996	$39,989	16.4%	12.1%	13.6%	44,135	297,159
New York....................................	1,972,352	599,505	459,009	490,622	423,216	$45,302	11.2%	9.2%	13.0%	499,993	2,597,283
North Carolina.............................	1,044,996	313,005	295,730	279,356	156,905	$41,169	11.3%	6.9%	10.1%	161,385	1,428,678
North Dakota...............................	73,062	21,765	19,231	19,960	12,106	$44,824	7.6%	5.0%	16.1%	6,519	101,504
Ohio..	1,261,472	363,334	379,456	347,721	170,961	$41,406	11.0%	7.0%	9.3%	191,217	1,707,548
Oklahoma...................................	389,886	116,616	114,828	102,864	55,578	$40,928	12.2%	7.5%	9.0%	54,564	525,419
Oregon.......................................	461,267	115,677	129,224	138,718	77,648	$47,314	11.4%	6.8%	8.8%	90,159	591,314
Pennsylvania...............................	1,458,606	424,359	422,713	391,993	219,541	$41,762	9.8%	6.2%	9.8%	253,514	1,938,408
Rhode Island	113,963	35,943	27,430	28,922	21,668	$42,424	9.1%	8.5%	12.4%	26,763	147,403
South Carolina	552,651	161,680	155,941	151,433	83,597	$42,161	13.4%	8.1%	10.6%	79,100	740,453
South Dakota	91,545	24,945	27,530	26,034	13,036	$42,361	9.2%	5.2%	13.4%	7,757	126,896
Tennessee	681,024	210,230	194,130	178,954	97,710	$39,933	12.6%	7.5%	10.2%	112,281	924,731
Texas...	2,107,858	614,146	546,723	567,769	379,220	$44,319	11.1%	8.7%	12.2%	362,718	3,050,745
Utah..	210,551	42,294	55,429	70,118	42,710	$53,670	6.8%	4.6%	7.2%	21,858	305,050
Vermont.....................................	78,032	20,448	22,252	21,391	13,941	$44,302	8.8%	7.8%	9.9%	10,559	105,648
Virginia......................................	801,030	207,446	184,523	221,093	187,968	$51,401	8.8%	6.3%	9.8%	89,043	1,159,569
Washington.................................	713,855	157,376	185,312	220,147	151,020	$52,150	8.8%	5.7%	8.5%	115,695	987,635
West Virginia..............................	231,585	77,637	72,001	57,622	24,325	$36,147	15.1%	9.2%	10.3%	44,926	289,568
Wisconsin	625,177	175,158	193,300	176,192	80,527	$41,362	8.1%	5.8%	9.2%	76,154	866,100
Wyoming	61,902	14,865	18,952	16,352	11,733	$44,870	7.7%	5.7%	8.3%	3,208	90,384

Table G-2: Counties - Income, Poverty Status and Receipt of Food Stamps (SNAP)

	Income of Households with Householder 65 Years and Over					Poverty Rate of Persons			Households with 1 or More Persons 60 Years and Over	
	Total Households	Less Than $25,000	$25,000 - $49,999	$50,000 - $99,999	$100,000 or More	Median Household Income	55 to 64 Years	65 to 74 Years	75 Years and Over	Receiving SNAP	Not Receiving SNAP
Alabama											
Baldwin County	27,136	6,706	7,540	8,310	4,580	$47,300	10.5%	7.6%	8.0%	2,244	35,982
Calhoun County	13,456	5,258	3,450	3,368	1,380	$33,567	11.2%	14.9%	5.7%	1,868	17,639
Cullman County	9,912	3,551	3,431	1,998	932	$30,681	13.6%	12.4%	9.3%	1,029	12,863
DeKalb County	8,140	3,512	2,906	1,241	481	$26,838	17.0%	11.5%	12.6%	1,785	10,405
Elmore County	7,794	2,296	2,048	2,159	1,291	$41,787	13.5%	3.5%	6.6%	1,124	11,127
Etowah County	12,152	2,810	4,553	2,864	1,925	$41,448	16.4%	4.8%	8.4%	1,243	16,400
Houston County	11,982	4,291	2,882	3,024	1,785	$37,734	14.2%	10.9%	16.5%	1,559	15,851
Jefferson County	67,575	20,408	16,239	18,255	12,673	$44,980	14.9%	9.0%	7.4%	11,491	91,092
Lauderdale County	11,532	2,749	3,938	3,177	1,668	$43,608	15.0%	4.3%	11.4%	689	15,067
Lee County	11,705	3,259	3,360	2,393	2,693	$42,058	15.9%	7.2%	7.5%	648	17,553
Limestone County	9,407	3,026	2,473	2,441	1,467	$43,727	10.7%	8.6%	10.9%	1,026	12,505
Madison County	36,105	8,966	7,651	12,297	7,191	$53,943	8.4%	5.7%	7.2%	4,761	48,243
Marshall County	10,016	3,475	2,651	2,514	1,376	$39,081	13.5%	9.3%	8.7%	1,374	13,896
Mobile County	43,522	15,646	13,012	10,119	4,745	$36,328	15.1%	8.9%	11.1%	8,292	54,684
Montgomery County	22,480	7,730	5,018	5,982	3,750	$43,866	12.5%	8.5%	18.4%	5,376	28,512
Morgan County	13,592	3,784	4,048	3,171	2,589	$42,992	11.7%	7.0%	8.2%	1,739	18,145
St. Clair County	8,954	3,259	3,390	1,661	644	$31,735	7.9%	19.8%	10.7%	1,307	12,108
Shelby County	20,757	4,846	5,563	5,624	4,724	$49,880	6.8%	5.4%	7.1%	1,655	29,491
Talladega County	9,142	3,694	2,190	2,283	975	$33,795	16.7%	13.0%	9.2%	1,554	12,099
Tuscaloosa County	16,785	4,795	4,337	4,823	2,830	$45,869	15.5%	8.0%	8.5%	1,766	25,136
Walker County	7,671	3,078	1,674	2,012	907	$32,382	22.1%	4.7%	9.5%	1,212	9,284
Alaska											
Anchorage Municipality	19,776	2,652	4,014	6,701	6,409	$72,750	6.9%	2.2%	7.4%	2,818	30,308
Fairbanks North Star Borough	6,987	1,710	987	2,673	1,617	$74,368	10.9%	7.5%	11.4%	521	10,563
Matanuska-Susitna Borough	7,032	2,194	1,658	1,882	1,298	$44,906	15.1%	7.3%	12.5%	1,151	11,406
Arizona											
Apache County	6,942	3,161	1,811	1,322	648	$29,064	32.1%	17.5%	28.7%	2,124	8,845
Cochise County	19,349	6,914	4,459	5,207	2,769	$39,478	11.4%	8.7%	8.2%	3,508	23,927
Coconino County	10,903	2,125	2,008	4,612	2,158	$61,858	8.9%	4.6%	11.3%	1,250	15,905
Maricopa County	391,504	93,777	106,070	117,457	74,200	$48,809	9.9%	6.1%	8.4%	45,440	561,758
Mohave County	39,594	10,586	13,224	12,134	3,650	$41,844	17.1%	8.9%	8.4%	4,992	49,481
Navajo County	12,780	4,526	3,675	3,626	953	$36,983	30.1%	10.6%	15.9%	2,602	15,666
Pima County	126,887	32,414	32,357	37,829	24,287	$48,961	12.1%	8.4%	9.0%	16,934	164,355
Pinal County	51,749	11,984	16,087	16,330	7,348	$46,508	9.3%	8.6%	8.9%	5,776	68,638
Yavapai County	47,659	14,075	14,880	12,542	6,162	$41,657	11.3%	8.7%	8.8%	3,973	58,713
Yuma County	22,994	8,125	7,225	5,271	2,373	$33,236	16.5%	16.9%	12.0%	4,426	29,203
Arkansas											
Benton County	22,134	5,731	7,126	5,718	3,559	$42,240	7.8%	4.2%	5.5%	1,608	32,182
Craighead County	9,754	3,396	2,453	2,737	1,168	$38,386	11.4%	5.6%	8.6%	1,841	12,597
Faulkner County	9,348	2,791	3,063	1,997	1,497	$40,140	17.4%	12.6%	12.6%	1,104	13,267
Garland County	14,925	3,943	3,584	5,734	1,664	$47,454	13.3%	9.8%	9.2%	1,587	19,198
Jefferson County	7,901	3,470	1,756	1,514	1,161	$29,648	15.2%	17.2%	19.4%	1,278	10,267
Lonoke County	5,827	1,750	1,612	1,680	785	$43,170	13.7%	1.5%	5.1%	1,113	8,641
Pulaski County	37,415	10,137	10,611	8,993	7,674	$44,832	11.4%	10.6%	9.1%	3,639	54,039
Saline County	12,627	2,674	4,286	3,916	1,751	$45,888	10.6%	7.5%	16.5%	676	17,146
Sebastian County	13,267	3,559	4,835	3,340	1,533	$36,444	13.7%	8.4%	3.0%	1,271	17,386
Washington County	16,807	4,280	5,196	4,839	2,492	$44,084	10.8%	7.8%	8.4%	1,210	24,747
White County	8,138	3,039	2,454	1,793	852	$35,995	19.9%	9.9%	9.9%	1,665	9,511
California											
Alameda County	129,181	29,237	26,327	31,555	42,062	$61,059	7.0%	7.8%	9.5%	13,095	200,600
Butte County	25,859	7,869	6,488	6,542	4,960	$41,708	17.9%	10.1%	9.5%	4,138	35,416
Contra Costa County	102,492	19,222	19,190	27,742	36,338	$70,271	7.1%	4.7%	7.6%	6,601	162,286
El Dorado County	24,149	4,616	5,187	6,737	7,609	$65,525	7.5%	6.1%	8.8%	1,994	35,393
Fresno County	72,341	22,322	17,976	18,752	13,291	$42,085	16.0%	10.4%	12.5%	11,325	102,070
Humboldt County	16,123	3,832	4,028	4,702	3,561	$52,090	15.0%	8.2%	6.6%	2,041	22,067
Imperial County	10,251	3,361	2,177	3,144	1,569	$43,996	19.1%	13.0%	19.8%	3,012	14,223
Kern County	57,042	17,852	14,878	14,045	10,267	$39,933	19.0%	11.5%	12.0%	10,136	87,533
Kings County	9,949	2,877	2,267	2,773	2,032	$49,177	11.5%	14.8%	14.2%	1,429	13,238
Lake County	9,808	2,487	3,304	2,498	1,519	$41,092	14.3%	14.3%	9.1%	1,517	13,493
Los Angeles County	750,779	228,632	159,152	177,898	185,097	$47,509	12.1%	9.9%	15.0%	86,626	1,194,796
Madera County	11,632	2,804	3,348	3,248	2,232	$46,088	16.1%	10.3%	11.6%	1,451	17,627
Marin County	37,113	5,134	5,381	9,971	16,627	$86,917	5.9%	5.0%	6.7%	724	51,884
Mendocino County	12,167	3,144	3,027	3,824	2,172	$48,551	17.1%	10.7%	12.2%	1,115	15,903
Merced County	18,366	5,102	5,329	4,287	3,648	$42,311	12.9%	9.8%	16.5%	2,451	28,045
Monterey County	34,561	5,922	7,618	10,619	10,402	$62,802	6.6%	5.4%	8.3%	2,895	50,613
Napa County	15,144	2,810	3,164	4,006	5,164	$66,096	6.2%	9.5%	5.1%	1,607	21,250
Nevada County	16,239	3,367	4,099	4,702	4,071	$55,269	14.2%	3.3%	4.4%	1,122	22,738
Orange County	259,739	56,054	50,649	72,147	80,889	$63,253	8.3%	7.6%	12.0%	20,967	403,707
Placer County	46,330	10,150	10,784	13,906	11,490	$56,777	7.2%	6.5%	9.2%	1,750	66,737
Riverside County	189,868	51,807	46,174	49,347	42,540	$47,839	10.8%	9.4%	10.6%	19,140	287,502
Sacramento County	127,146	32,671	28,749	36,039	29,687	$52,515	10.1%	7.7%	12.6%	15,709	196,093
San Bernardino County	136,143	39,348	33,938	38,402	24,455	$45,396	11.0%	7.6%	14.1%	25,258	216,777
San Diego County	268,419	59,293	57,411	74,628	77,087	$59,367	8.7%	7.4%	9.8%	26,157	404,545
San Francisco County	83,021	25,801	14,774	19,172	23,274	$51,999	11.7%	9.2%	17.0%	6,237	120,335
San Joaquin County	51,357	13,848	11,266	15,518	10,725	$51,137	11.0%	8.7%	11.2%	7,984	83,422

Table G-2: Counties - Income, Poverty Status and Receipt of Food Stamps (SNAP)—*Continued*

	Income of Households with Householder 65 Years and Over					Poverty Rate of Persons			Households with 1 or More Persons 60 Years and Over	
	Total Households	Less Than $25,000	$25,000 - $49,999	$50,000 - $99,999	$100,000 or More	Median Household Income	55 to 64 Years	65 to 74 Years	75 Years and Over	Receiving SNAP	Not Receiving SNAP
California—Cont.											
San Luis Obispo County	35,948	6,109	7,291	11,456	11,092	$65,113	8.4%	7.4%	9.6%	1,894	48,722
San Mateo County	68,731	12,947	10,613	18,127	27,044	$80,772	6.7%	6.3%	7.3%	3,203	105,500
Santa Barbara County	41,277	6,860	7,840	10,335	16,242	$75,494	8.3%	4.7%	7.2%	3,726	58,727
Santa Clara County	138,818	28,687	22,911	37,641	49,579	$69,974	6.8%	5.4%	10.3%	9,346	227,350
Santa Cruz County	27,799	5,638	5,450	7,563	9,148	$64,052	6.3%	6.7%	5.6%	3,561	39,905
Shasta County	22,428	5,341	7,037	6,586	3,464	$44,086	13.1%	8.5%	12.5%	2,981	30,835
Solano County	38,327	6,715	8,527	11,692	11,393	$68,900	8.8%	4.4%	8.2%	3,744	62,489
Sonoma County	62,227	13,482	13,856	18,084	16,805	$57,797	7.1%	6.2%	6.5%	3,251	87,555
Stanislaus County	41,197	12,963	10,060	11,020	7,154	$43,614	14.2%	9.4%	10.2%	6,044	60,736
Sutter County	8,546	2,241	2,676	1,942	1,687	$44,529	13.2%	9.5%	9.0%	739	13,385
Tulare County	29,774	9,480	8,410	7,666	4,218	$40,377	20.0%	12.6%	13.2%	6,782	43,120
Ventura County	76,222	14,640	16,954	20,510	24,118	$61,641	6.8%	5.7%	9.7%	6,017	112,567
Yolo County	15,948	2,523	3,882	4,881	4,662	$64,710	12.1%	6.6%	11.9%	2,109	23,120
Yuba County	6,622	1,550	2,513	1,433	1,126	$41,697	18.1%	3.0%	6.8%	708	10,050
Colorado											
Adams County	31,537	7,411	8,657	9,980	5,489	$49,110	9.5%	5.1%	2.8%	4,414	48,991
Arapahoe County	52,237	11,146	12,039	15,479	13,573	$56,507	5.1%	4.8%	7.0%	5,304	79,015
Boulder County	29,132	5,622	6,443	7,974	9,093	$63,254	6.9%	4.4%	7.1%	1,709	43,854
Broomfield County	5,908	749	1,490	1,978	1,691	$64,367	3.9%	3.3%	3.2%	112	8,414
Denver County	56,532	17,027	12,680	15,465	11,360	$45,728	12.2%	8.7%	12.0%	8,025	76,271
Douglas County	24,015	2,788	4,693	7,905	8,629	$77,274	3.8%	2.2%	2.7%	1,394	38,599
El Paso County	54,936	13,034	13,109	16,496	12,297	$52,601	9.6%	4.1%	9.3%	6,159	82,776
Jefferson County	60,542	12,515	13,381	17,441	17,205	$59,836	4.7%	4.1%	8.6%	3,797	89,575
Larimer County	33,694	6,991	9,480	9,655	7,568	$50,962	5.7%	6.6%	7.1%	3,094	48,552
Mesa County	18,280	5,884	5,971	4,180	2,245	$40,594	11.7%	5.0%	10.7%	2,549	24,246
Pueblo County	19,899	7,517	5,302	5,569	1,511	$35,054	13.6%	10.5%	17.1%	3,711	24,783
Weld County	22,416	5,818	6,044	6,165	4,389	$46,519	9.1%	6.9%	8.2%	2,790	36,309
Connecticut											
Fairfield County	92,257	20,234	17,931	24,499	29,593	$61,304	7.6%	6.3%	8.7%	12,986	132,407
Hartford County	93,454	24,708	22,182	23,619	22,945	$49,734	9.6%	6.4%	9.5%	18,418	126,187
Litchfield County	23,504	5,252	5,985	6,493	5,774	$53,134	3.9%	4.4%	6.8%	1,715	35,100
Middlesex County	19,247	3,497	5,336	5,617	4,797	$58,322	5.7%	5.9%	4.9%	2,190	28,568
New Haven County	90,805	22,656	22,278	24,919	20,952	$50,825	8.5%	6.5%	9.8%	16,637	123,681
New London County	29,852	7,527	6,534	9,337	6,454	$53,268	9.1%	5.2%	6.7%	4,553	41,964
Tolland County	14,669	2,509	3,583	4,246	4,331	$62,599	5.6%	4.8%	4.5%	1,021	21,504
Windham County	11,005	2,854	2,412	3,440	2,299	$55,450	8.8%	7.2%	9.4%	2,367	15,758
Delaware											
Kent County	17,737	4,548	4,216	6,628	2,345	$50,495	15.9%	7.7%	4.9%	3,361	24,576
New Castle County	52,290	10,337	12,686	18,412	10,855	$56,325	11.6%	4.7%	6.5%	5,628	76,772
Sussex County	37,731	7,543	9,427	12,923	7,838	$55,293	10.5%	6.6%	5.5%	3,216	49,907
Florida											
Alachua County	22,273	6,588	4,469	6,149	5,067	$50,442	9.4%	7.1%	11.8%	2,502	30,402
Bay County	19,306	5,376	5,855	5,643	2,432	$43,403	13.6%	7.0%	7.6%	3,813	27,590
Brevard County	84,167	22,188	23,762	25,336	12,881	$44,377	10.2%	6.3%	8.6%	9,906	112,095
Broward County	186,926	60,965	47,143	45,732	33,086	$40,980	10.8%	10.8%	14.7%	43,479	254,093
Charlotte County	42,134	11,020	10,822	13,572	6,720	$48,467	9.1%	6.1%	8.0%	3,030	50,260
Citrus County	33,165	11,001	10,985	8,772	2,407	$38,779	16.6%	13.2%	6.9%	3,712	39,386
Clay County	19,867	5,945	4,679	5,406	3,837	$46,923	6.5%	5.6%	10.1%	2,558	28,766
Collier County	68,705	11,373	14,843	18,026	24,463	$71,418	7.8%	4.4%	5.8%	4,499	85,012
Columbia County	7,568	2,979	1,826	1,913	850	$33,484	12.4%	5.1%	14.6%	2,282	9,258
Duval County	82,536	25,749	19,171	24,340	13,276	$45,289	11.1%	8.2%	10.7%	21,614	110,006
Escambia County	33,082	8,159	10,749	9,739	4,435	$42,471	9.4%	4.3%	7.8%	6,510	44,460
Flagler County	19,787	3,896	4,470	7,738	3,683	$56,133	8.1%	6.1%	5.4%	1,800	23,785
Hernando County	32,130	10,894	9,717	9,320	2,199	$34,568	18.4%	14.2%	10.1%	6,493	37,768
Highlands County	21,675	6,053	8,147	4,922	2,553	$35,723	16.3%	16.6%	6.4%	3,101	23,798
Hillsborough County	120,806	35,529	32,686	32,085	20,506	$42,103	13.1%	9.7%	10.0%	26,580	167,842
Indian River County	27,705	6,406	7,131	8,585	5,583	$52,635	23.0%	7.5%	4.9%	4,632	34,954
Lake County	55,463	13,559	17,623	16,747	7,534	$44,406	7.9%	10.1%	7.1%	5,195	69,043
Lee County	121,190	31,454	30,414	33,023	26,299	$48,650	11.7%	9.7%	8.9%	9,252	150,186
Leon County	24,514	6,482	5,209	6,555	6,268	$55,324	12.8%	8.7%	9.0%	3,552	34,055
Manatee County	64,211	14,130	19,350	16,576	14,155	$47,595	6.6%	5.6%	8.1%	5,586	78,982
Marion County	62,379	19,645	20,195	16,801	5,738	$36,821	11.6%	9.5%	9.3%	8,950	75,234
Martin County	30,294	7,932	6,921	8,683	6,758	$51,140	12.2%	9.9%	9.3%	2,265	37,018
Miami-Dade County	223,196	96,282	47,901	43,641	35,372	$31,109	13.3%	16.7%	21.1%	125,948	251,898
Monroe County	9,842	1,650	2,155	2,299	3,738	$73,185	10.0%	6.1%	9.3%	1,053	13,520
Nassau County	10,932	2,555	2,156	3,292	2,929	$59,725	13.0%	12.0%	9.8%	2,370	13,680
Okaloosa County	20,687	5,554	5,602	5,543	3,988	$46,319	14.5%	9.0%	2.9%	3,262	28,395
Orange County	86,430	27,617	22,798	22,562	13,453	$41,055	12.3%	8.8%	13.2%	25,177	127,651
Osceola County	22,387	6,505	6,940	5,280	3,662	$41,746	8.4%	9.5%	7.0%	9,111	31,157
Palm Beach County	213,876	56,526	51,009	55,539	50,802	$49,628	9.7%	10.5%	9.7%	24,909	267,376
Pasco County	72,140	22,562	22,069	19,369	8,140	$39,287	12.5%	10.8%	9.2%	10,958	92,236
Pinellas County	150,207	45,248	45,374	38,434	21,151	$39,443	11.8%	9.5%	10.5%	18,620	193,539
Polk County	84,267	25,331	25,359	23,902	9,675	$40,291	14.8%	13.1%	10.5%	15,307	102,774

Table G-2: Counties - Income, Poverty Status and Receipt of Food Stamps (SNAP)—*Continued*

		Income of Households with Householder 65 Years and Over					Poverty Rate of Persons			Households with 1 or More Persons 60 Years and Over	
	Total Households	Less Than $25,000	$25,000 - $49,999	$50,000 - $99,999	$100,000 or More	Median Household Income	55 to 64 Years	65 to 74 Years	75 Years and Over	Receiving SNAP	Not Receiving SNAP
Florida—Cont.											
Putnam County	10,815	3,669	3,536	2,824	786	$34,967	16.9%	12.7%	11.6%	1,907	13,447
St. Johns County	30,553	5,626	7,389	10,457	7,081	$55,809	7.3%	5.2%	3.6%	3,128	39,919
St. Lucie County	44,264	12,470	12,971	11,082	7,741	$41,290	10.6%	11.0%	7.8%	6,968	57,013
Santa Rosa County	15,555	1,769	5,100	5,745	2,941	$57,146	7.1%	1.8%	10.9%	2,715	24,263
Sarasota County	95,330	18,846	23,538	29,404	23,542	$55,150	11.4%	5.5%	8.0%	5,231	115,155
Seminole County	42,666	9,842	10,389	14,421	8,014	$52,315	9.1%	5.5%	5.3%	6,823	61,831
Sumter County	44,756	7,737	10,975	18,134	7,910	$54,324	10.5%	3.7%	3.9%	896	51,444
Volusia County	78,826	19,781	24,480	22,754	11,811	$44,182	14.6%	6.7%	13.1%	11,219	101,085
Walton County	8,972	2,053	2,912	2,614	1,393	$46,364	11.1%	6.9%	11.1%	870	12,540
Georgia											
Barrow County	6,000	1,664	1,801	1,729	806	$41,774	6.1%	3.3%	9.4%	672	9,157
Bartow County	7,726	2,717	2,401	1,830	778	$32,988	19.2%	8.7%	10.0%	1,252	11,818
Bibb County	15,152	4,953	4,582	3,790	1,827	$40,435	18.8%	8.5%	22.8%	3,755	18,999
Bulloch County	5,700	1,806	1,822	1,408	664	$45,150	18.7%	6.6%	7.5%	1,387	7,299
Carroll County	9,980	3,374	2,829	2,469	1,308	$39,000	12.8%	16.2%	9.1%	2,093	14,580
Catoosa County	na	na	na	na	na	$36,481	5.7%	4.7%	13.0%	578	10,516
Chatham County	27,712	6,315	7,722	9,033	4,642	$49,365	9.8%	5.9%	10.2%	4,058	36,617
Cherokee County	20,674	4,098	6,101	5,630	4,845	$50,913	6.1%	8.0%	9.9%	1,739	30,089
Clarke County	9,394	2,260	2,852	2,173	2,109	$43,825	14.7%	7.9%	9.7%	1,697	12,914
Clayton County	15,984	4,436	6,491	2,878	2,179	$38,723	15.5%	7.0%	16.7%	4,915	24,543
Cobb County	54,626	10,029	13,259	16,450	14,888	$57,919	5.2%	4.3%	4.4%	5,373	84,948
Columbia County	11,988	2,921	1,976	4,743	2,348	$57,555	4.1%	5.9%	10.5%	412	17,332
Coweta County	12,305	2,711	2,981	3,957	2,656	$57,001	12.5%	2.1%	6.6%	1,201	18,771
DeKalb County	57,625	13,328	14,643	16,533	13,121	$51,220	11.0%	6.8%	9.7%	11,829	82,458
Dougherty County	8,530	2,974	2,378	1,936	1,242	$42,619	23.4%	16.1%	19.2%	1,997	10,760
Douglas County	9,366	2,421	1,807	2,965	2,173	$55,038	6.9%	4.8%	7.5%	1,514	15,737
Fayette County	12,900	2,031	3,618	3,316	3,935	$61,769	2.2%	1.0%	3.2%	630	17,444
Floyd County	10,194	3,380	2,838	2,828	1,148	$32,760	9.9%	12.3%	8.2%	1,888	13,174
Forsyth County	15,347	2,462	4,263	3,835	4,787	$59,687	5.1%	3.4%	4.9%	1,179	25,756
Fulton County	80,507	24,809	17,339	19,066	19,293	$47,505	11.3%	8.0%	13.9%	17,114	108,716
Glynn County	10,819	2,342	2,930	3,430	2,117	$52,148	15.4%	6.1%	4.5%	1,050	14,422
Gwinnett County	48,689	12,893	12,717	14,314	8,765	$46,985	6.9%	6.1%	10.9%	7,671	85,871
Hall County	16,870	4,063	4,460	4,297	4,050	$49,653	9.6%	5.6%	11.3%	2,260	23,487
Henry County	14,756	3,151	4,062	3,976	3,567	$50,810	5.1%	3.7%	5.3%	2,706	23,525
Houston County	10,875	2,747	3,859	2,385	1,884	$46,302	14.5%	5.0%	6.5%	1,376	17,753
Jackson County	5,719	1,405	1,669	1,638	1,007	$47,192	4.3%	2.6%	2.9%	789	8,224
Lowndes County	9,605	4,566	1,769	2,087	1,183	$27,337	24.3%	11.4%	29.3%	1,775	12,388
Muscogee County	17,648	5,118	5,206	5,126	2,198	$40,542	19.9%	12.2%	9.3%	3,991	22,619
Newton County	8,151	1,696	2,693	2,708	1,054	$48,227	10.5%	8.8%	3.3%	2,145	11,518
Paulding County	9,480	2,575	2,603	2,735	1,567	$41,350	6.1%	6.1%	8.6%	1,421	14,912
Richmond County	19,335	6,957	5,846	4,373	2,159	$32,653	18.2%	12.5%	11.9%	3,469	25,012
Rockdale County	7,593	1,660	2,153	2,198	1,582	$49,464	5.5%	1.8%	5.4%	829	12,109
Spalding County	7,333	1,828	2,791	1,636	1,078	$43,231	19.4%	5.9%	1.9%	1,444	9,019
Troup County	6,585	2,672	1,327	1,707	879	$37,904	19.1%	13.1%	16.3%	1,127	9,478
Walker County	8,551	4,225	2,044	1,561	721	$25,584	8.8%	6.5%	5.7%	668	11,965
Walton County	8,386	2,283	2,480	2,368	1,255	$45,932	7.4%	7.7%	4.5%	1,162	11,659
Whitfield County	9,248	4,391	2,521	1,759	577	$26,077	6.2%	14.0%	15.4%	859	13,122
Hawaii											
Hawaii County	25,848	5,970	7,646	7,308	4,924	$47,733	11.7%	11.9%	4.3%	5,626	32,856
Honolulu County	91,320	15,613	17,951	23,938	33,818	$73,837	6.6%	5.3%	7.2%	11,992	130,338
Kauai County	9,017	1,593	2,051	1,887	3,486	$66,461	8.9%	2.1%	3.6%	828	11,995
Maui County	16,935	2,845	4,705	4,182	5,203	$59,979	11.7%	5.1%	2.6%	2,360	23,970
Idaho											
Ada County	40,387	11,332	9,861	12,774	6,420	$46,227	5.7%	5.5%	12.0%	2,208	59,086
Bannock County	7,726	2,675	1,889	2,547	615	$37,118	9.8%	4.7%	13.5%	995	10,496
Bonneville County	9,539	2,681	2,797	2,404	1,657	$45,137	8.5%	4.9%	16.5%	1,040	12,962
Canyon County	19,229	4,749	6,967	5,091	2,422	$42,249	8.8%	6.0%	6.7%	2,015	26,255
Kootenai County	19,738	5,582	5,005	5,970	3,181	$46,860	6.0%	6.3%	11.5%	1,962	26,414
Twin Falls County	7,820	1,928	2,900	1,790	1,202	$39,445	16.1%	4.1%	13.8%	741	11,615
Illinois											
Adams County	8,147	2,754	2,143	2,659	591	$36,825	6.1%	9.9%	18.8%	1,191	10,332
Champaign County	16,434	3,403	3,735	5,158	4,138	$60,019	7.3%	2.6%	6.6%	2,187	23,845
Cook County	480,363	154,058	116,708	117,394	92,203	$41,726	12.7%	9.5%	11.2%	114,684	628,960
DeKalb County	8,121	1,992	2,407	2,350	1,372	$47,219	3.8%	4.3%	6.4%	1,336	11,122
DuPage County	85,766	16,622	17,860	26,181	25,103	$62,068	4.6%	4.4%	10.3%	8,631	129,666
Kane County	43,059	9,640	11,183	14,100	8,136	$51,536	5.8%	5.3%	7.3%	5,126	64,131
Kankakee County	10,631	3,847	3,272	2,495	1,017	$32,112	13.4%	14.1%	17.2%	2,244	14,732
Kendall County	na	na	na	na	na	$58,960	4.9%	5.8%	3.4%	538	11,714
Lake County	60,453	12,611	13,713	17,258	16,871	$59,919	7.8%	4.9%	7.3%	7,824	89,553
LaSalle County	13,647	4,101	4,545	3,500	1,501	$36,282	14.3%	2.1%	9.2%	2,134	17,150
McHenry County	26,901	5,843	6,304	9,136	5,618	$53,225	4.1%	1.8%	8.0%	2,247	42,532
McLean County	14,126	3,260	3,402	4,076	3,388	$54,886	9.1%	6.5%	10.3%	1,612	19,937
Macon County	13,096	3,080	4,586	3,513	1,917	$42,393	11.4%	7.5%	7.6%	2,523	17,186
Madison County	29,762	6,968	9,271	9,155	4,368	$45,635	13.0%	9.9%	4.7%	4,847	38,764

Table G-2: Counties - Income, Poverty Status and Receipt of Food Stamps (SNAP)—*Continued*

		Income of Households with Householder 65 Years and Over					Poverty Rate of Persons			Households with 1 or More Persons 60 Years and Over	
	Total Households	Less Than $25,000	$25,000 - $49,999	$50,000 - $99,999	$100,000 or More	Median Household Income	55 to 64 Years	65 to 74 Years	75 Years and Over	Receiving SNAP	Not Receiving SNAP
Illinois—Cont.											
Peoria County	17,416	5,131	3,983	5,685	2,617	$45,497	16.9%	8.7%	9.6%	2,194	25,805
Rock Island County	17,298	4,826	5,164	5,146	2,162	$42,720	12.2%	5.6%	10.5%	2,619	22,430
St. Clair County	26,546	8,194	6,556	7,986	3,810	$41,865	15.9%	5.1%	10.0%	5,833	36,703
Sangamon County	22,318	4,792	5,565	6,972	4,989	$52,751	9.3%	6.7%	3.9%	3,534	29,428
Tazewell County	15,919	3,275	5,419	4,982	2,243	$47,892	9.1%	5.9%	6.8%	2,097	20,763
Vermilion County	9,996	3,329	3,115	2,640	912	$36,581	15.6%	7.9%	9.8%	1,058	12,597
Will County	51,204	8,851	12,898	18,838	10,617	$58,677	5.9%	3.5%	7.8%	7,020	80,681
Williamson County	8,284	2,985	3,311	1,639	349	$32,166	11.6%	6.7%	9.9%	1,344	11,191
Winnebago County	31,273	8,316	9,643	9,062	4,252	$41,250	10.2%	5.0%	5.2%	5,938	42,135
Indiana											
Allen County	35,683	10,866	10,675	9,363	4,779	$40,383	7.4%	5.0%	9.0%	4,347	48,063
Bartholomew County	8,957	2,669	2,713	2,753	822	$39,720	3.4%	8.2%	12.3%	686	11,694
Boone County	na	na	na	na	na	$49,917	3.9%	2.7%	7.2%	348	8,233
Clark County	11,810	3,012	4,100	3,190	1,508	$44,228	8.3%	6.1%	11.0%	1,442	16,410
Delaware County	12,849	3,909	3,888	4,425	627	$38,031	9.0%	2.9%	8.3%	1,638	16,640
Elkhart County	17,003	4,499	5,072	5,229	2,203	$43,503	9.1%	3.6%	9.4%	1,013	25,709
Floyd County	6,881	1,493	1,854	2,663	871	$51,155	9.6%	1.7%	6.3%	267	11,185
Grant County	8,420	2,704	2,852	2,332	532	$37,365	17.8%	5.9%	10.2%	1,402	10,599
Hamilton County	24,184	4,043	6,492	7,894	5,755	$56,254	4.3%	3.4%	7.3%	899	38,235
Hancock County	na	na	na	na	na	$37,546	2.5%	10.6%	10.1%	455	11,294
Hendricks County	12,843	1,405	4,264	4,889	2,285	$54,496	4.7%	2.5%	5.7%	1,456	20,779
Howard County	10,516	1,901	3,179	3,972	1,464	$51,294	6.9%	6.6%	2.4%	703	13,824
Johnson County	13,691	2,799	4,734	4,782	1,376	$47,235	7.6%	4.8%	5.7%	1,058	19,965
Kosciusko County	8,548	2,212	2,087	2,708	1,541	$49,604	5.5%	6.5%	7.3%	379	12,102
Lake County	52,044	16,263	15,356	14,755	5,670	$39,970	10.0%	8.3%	7.2%	5,584	73,313
LaPorte County	13,199	3,710	3,935	3,609	1,945	$38,730	7.0%	6.8%	7.0%	1,540	16,457
Madison County	14,595	3,582	5,419	4,368	1,226	$41,135	18.3%	7.8%	2.6%	1,975	19,817
Marion County	76,295	23,070	22,782	20,672	9,771	$40,266	13.3%	7.1%	11.1%	14,058	108,189
Monroe County	12,536	2,259	3,851	4,144	2,282	$52,015	15.8%	4.5%	2.5%	1,283	17,066
Morgan County	7,099	1,908	1,654	2,789	748	$49,803	9.6%	7.2%	9.8%	657	9,573
Porter County	16,756	3,231	5,286	5,507	2,732	$49,622	9.7%	3.6%	2.3%	953	25,401
St. Joseph County	27,801	9,898	8,552	6,392	2,959	$36,552	11.0%	9.7%	13.3%	2,217	40,387
Tippecanoe County	13,694	2,972	3,756	3,810	3,156	$52,843	13.1%	2.6%	7.0%	1,010	20,431
Vanderburgh County	18,773	6,017	5,830	5,339	1,587	$36,911	14.2%	7.3%	11.8%	2,020	27,052
Vigo County	9,677	2,244	2,729	3,109	1,595	$48,681	10.2%	5.7%	8.5%	921	14,358
Wayne County	8,133	2,908	2,430	2,321	474	$32,414	13.5%	7.6%	9.0%	1,357	10,605
Iowa											
Black Hawk County	13,831	3,636	3,834	4,412	1,949	$47,195	12.1%	4.2%	12.1%	1,743	18,322
Dallas County	6,967	1,681	1,708	2,391	1,187	$51,477	5.0%	0.3%	14.4%	476	9,168
Dubuque County	10,313	2,743	3,232	2,864	1,474	$44,943	7.6%	4.6%	12.9%	1,120	14,408
Johnson County	10,996	1,979	2,252	3,590	3,175	$66,966	7.7%	4.1%	8.3%	422	16,374
Linn County	23,528	5,350	7,275	7,027	3,876	$45,427	6.8%	4.2%	5.7%	1,903	31,561
Polk County	39,485	8,966	13,596	11,378	5,545	$44,365	8.8%	3.9%	7.2%	4,285	56,272
Pottawattamie County	10,494	2,821	3,577	3,035	1,061	$39,973	11.5%	6.0%	7.6%	1,128	14,713
Scott County	16,858	3,815	5,450	5,372	2,221	$45,275	9.0%	5.5%	8.4%	1,249	25,122
Story County	7,369	1,544	1,754	2,526	1,545	$53,876	4.0%	3.6%	7.0%	233	10,048
Woodbury County	10,023	2,554	2,803	3,045	1,621	$44,593	9.7%	6.3%	5.8%	1,420	14,404
Kansas											
Butler County	6,401	2,326	1,612	1,585	878	$35,738	5.3%	6.3%	8.9%	492	9,836
Douglas County	9,782	2,664	2,149	2,792	2,177	$50,354	8.2%	5.2%	12.0%	537	13,810
Johnson County	52,962	8,782	14,124	16,472	13,584	$58,086	5.2%	3.6%	4.5%	1,965	80,109
Leavenworth County	7,105	1,668	1,641	2,355	1,441	$55,975	20.0%	2.5%	3.2%	726	10,153
Riley County	4,379	686	1,036	1,349	1,308	$67,469	5.2%	0.9%	3.3%	199	6,574
Sedgwick County	47,194	13,259	14,300	13,925	5,710	$41,754	12.7%	6.0%	7.2%	5,991	67,463
Shawnee County	20,366	6,114	6,323	4,961	2,968	$42,669	12.7%	10.8%	11.7%	1,892	27,829
Wyandotte County	12,679	3,823	3,738	3,501	1,617	$39,849	15.2%	9.0%	4.4%	2,238	18,592
Kentucky											
Boone County	10,925	2,131	2,691	3,616	2,487	$58,170	2.2%	1.8%	2.9%	644	15,962
Bullitt County	7,742	1,966	2,509	2,483	784	$43,175	12.0%	6.3%	8.0%	763	11,532
Campbell County	9,207	3,040	2,826	2,025	1,316	$38,048	13.4%	11.2%	16.5%	472	14,240
Christian County	5,652	1,620	1,785	1,302	945	$40,975	16.2%	5.2%	12.5%	845	7,770
Daviess County	11,193	3,763	3,066	2,704	1,660	$38,405	13.2%	10.3%	9.8%	1,786	14,568
Fayette County	26,964	5,607	7,367	8,276	5,714	$51,536	9.7%	3.9%	5.5%	2,580	38,891
Hardin County	9,928	2,960	2,301	3,183	1,484	$46,009	15.0%	6.2%	6.7%	1,171	14,161
Jefferson County	79,978	21,768	21,373	24,041	12,796	$44,992	12.8%	7.5%	7.0%	10,336	110,214
Kenton County	14,963	3,835	3,747	4,920	2,461	$49,420	4.4%	4.1%	8.0%	1,421	21,849
McCracken County	8,624	3,425	2,305	1,738	1,156	$33,742	12.7%	4.3%	11.2%	811	11,265
Madison County	7,772	2,414	2,217	1,873	1,268	$40,919	8.2%	6.8%	14.1%	741	11,069
Oldham County	4,507	888	923	1,294	1,402	$63,750	7.4%	1.0%	9.5%	116	7,676
Warren County	10,751	3,505	2,450	3,290	1,506	$44,587	14.7%	1.3%	10.2%	1,410	15,356
Louisiana											
Ascension Parish	8,396	2,375	2,459	2,406	1,156	$41,449	3.0%	8.4%	11.0%	1,085	13,079
Bossier Parish	11,700	2,452	4,185	3,335	1,728	$48,416	10.9%	5.9%	5.5%	1,521	15,325

Table G-2: Counties - Income, Poverty Status and Receipt of Food Stamps (SNAP)—*Continued*

	Income of Households with Householder 65 Years and Over					Poverty Rate of Persons			Households with 1 or More Persons 60 Years and Over	
	Total Households	Less Than $25,000	$25,000 - $49,999	$50,000 - $99,999	$100,000 or More	Median Household Income	55 to 64 Years	65 to 74 Years	75 Years and Over	Receiving SNAP	Not Receiving SNAP
Louisiana—Cont.											
Caddo Parish	26,450	9,446	6,662	7,246	3,096	$38,313	14.6%	8.8%	10.6%	5,931	33,836
Calcasieu Parish	20,476	7,170	6,001	4,604	2,701	$38,353	8.0%	3.9%	13.9%	2,705	28,727
East Baton Rouge Parish	38,674	9,796	9,285	10,952	8,641	$51,068	14.2%	8.3%	9.5%	6,444	53,268
Iberia Parish	7,137	2,734	1,929	1,136	1,338	$33,213	10.2%	12.1%	18.7%	1,559	9,111
Jefferson Parish	45,851	14,235	12,636	11,574	7,406	$41,957	12.9%	7.5%	10.6%	8,597	62,890
Lafayette Parish	19,755	5,021	6,129	5,248	3,357	$42,056	12.0%	5.8%	4.7%	3,243	27,397
Lafourche Parish	9,583	3,655	3,385	1,344	1,199	$29,754	9.7%	7.2%	8.8%	1,182	13,637
Livingston Parish	9,735	3,580	2,592	2,028	1,535	$36,526	9.3%	6.0%	6.2%	3,059	15,265
Orleans Parish	35,584	16,232	7,521	6,609	5,222	$29,641	24.2%	15.9%	24.3%	9,253	45,515
Ouachita Parish	13,610	5,451	3,333	2,680	2,146	$32,506	13.1%	14.0%	25.7%	2,196	19,558
Rapides Parish	13,287	4,923	3,964	3,284	1,116	$34,434	16.1%	12.5%	11.3%	2,044	18,204
St. Landry Parish	8,223	3,827	2,490	1,418	488	$27,714	23.9%	18.5%	21.0%	1,436	11,102
St. Tammany Parish	26,871	7,618	6,965	7,655	4,633	$45,975	7.7%	7.3%	9.7%	2,430	38,208
Tangipahoa Parish	11,765	3,865	3,900	3,076	924	$36,689	18.8%	9.2%	18.2%	2,446	16,465
Terrebonne Parish	10,103	3,647	2,978	2,823	655	$37,372	15.6%	10.9%	15.3%	1,122	14,143
Maine											
Androscoggin County	12,277	4,991	4,031	2,394	861	$32,517	13.3%	7.2%	10.4%	2,904	15,555
Aroostook County	10,076	4,887	2,698	1,955	536	$26,091	13.3%	12.2%	14.8%	2,888	12,110
Cumberland County	34,701	7,798	9,062	11,123	6,718	$51,713	8.8%	4.5%	9.9%	3,520	47,168
Kennebec County	16,362	4,943	4,397	4,725	2,297	$41,368	8.5%	6.7%	13.6%	3,692	20,508
Penobscot County	17,420	6,255	5,317	3,412	2,436	$34,521	12.4%	7.3%	9.5%	4,085	21,744
York County	27,343	6,993	8,053	7,433	4,864	$44,620	7.8%	5.3%	10.8%	4,450	36,811
Maryland											
Allegany County	9,052	3,042	3,175	2,097	738	$33,272	10.9%	9.1%	12.7%	1,298	11,177
Anne Arundel County	51,838	6,871	10,310	18,214	16,443	$71,379	5.6%	3.1%	6.7%	3,488	78,552
Baltimore County	86,617	18,830	21,260	26,478	20,049	$54,651	7.5%	5.9%	7.0%	12,734	124,084
Calvert County	na	na	na	na	na	$84,541	3.9%	2.9%	2.5%	921	11,992
Carroll County	16,008	2,617	4,147	5,031	4,213	$57,145	6.5%	3.2%	6.3%	1,601	24,051
Cecil County	9,943	2,030	2,602	3,282	2,029	$56,362	5.9%	2.4%	7.2%	2,214	14,481
Charles County	10,869	1,905	2,091	3,974	2,899	$68,245	4.4%	5.4%	4.8%	1,279	18,810
Frederick County	22,623	4,402	5,011	5,815	7,395	$64,362	4.3%	3.1%	7.9%	1,739	35,702
Harford County	25,045	5,187	6,968	7,054	5,836	$51,451	4.9%	3.6%	7.0%	1,935	38,363
Howard County	25,500	2,968	4,635	7,539	10,358	$83,410	3.5%	3.6%	8.1%	2,666	39,833
Montgomery County	91,392	14,668	12,430	22,871	41,423	$90,160	5.1%	4.5%	7.8%	8,618	136,633
Prince George's County	70,471	12,177	13,148	22,430	22,716	$71,135	5.6%	5.2%	9.1%	8,896	110,353
St. Mary's County	9,007	2,424	2,007	2,626	1,950	$50,902	3.1%	8.5%	7.3%	1,733	13,564
Washington County	15,971	4,054	3,993	5,313	2,611	$49,541	11.3%	6.5%	10.6%	2,623	21,916
Wicomico County	10,517	3,420	2,584	2,939	1,574	$40,131	9.8%	7.4%	12.2%	2,549	13,143
Massachusetts											
Barnstable County	39,226	7,427	9,627	11,909	10,263	$57,059	6.9%	6.3%	9.0%	2,840	50,519
Berkshire County	18,271	5,082	5,470	4,122	3,597	$43,191	10.0%	6.3%	9.9%	2,289	24,288
Bristol County	59,402	16,798	15,885	17,518	9,201	$44,422	8.9%	7.7%	11.0%	14,053	77,517
Essex County	80,745	20,326	19,559	22,349	18,511	$50,803	10.2%	7.7%	10.8%	16,421	110,292
Franklin County	9,784	2,609	2,477	2,806	1,892	$47,292	10.0%	8.0%	2.8%	1,794	13,499
Hampden County	49,293	16,259	12,360	13,875	6,799	$41,090	14.8%	8.1%	10.5%	13,557	60,660
Hampshire County	17,362	3,638	3,606	4,882	5,236	$62,458	6.3%	4.8%	7.6%	2,202	23,948
Middlesex County	152,626	36,282	32,441	39,024	44,879	$58,160	5.4%	5.0%	9.4%	18,633	218,045
Norfolk County	73,338	15,968	17,245	18,910	21,215	$56,954	5.1%	4.8%	10.0%	8,280	104,413
Plymouth County	56,023	13,291	13,120	16,709	12,903	$54,355	7.4%	4.4%	9.8%	8,914	78,798
Suffolk County	62,805	25,587	12,222	11,750	13,246	$34,767	15.1%	11.7%	23.9%	23,891	74,786
Worcester County	77,110	23,561	18,505	21,895	13,149	$43,702	8.2%	6.8%	7.7%	15,534	108,598
Michigan											
Allegan County	11,325	3,052	3,664	3,467	1,142	$41,390	12.2%	8.5%	13.1%	836	16,416
Bay County	13,107	3,069	5,002	4,060	976	$42,623	8.9%	6.2%	6.3%	1,536	18,423
Berrien County	19,901	6,216	5,569	5,189	2,927	$40,021	9.9%	8.8%	14.2%	3,306	25,650
Calhoun County	15,477	3,566	5,808	4,111	1,992	$40,536	13.4%	5.3%	9.6%	2,187	20,909
Clinton County	8,604	1,546	2,981	2,763	1,314	$47,445	7.2%	2.4%	2.8%	979	11,628
Eaton County	12,391	2,172	2,926	5,010	2,283	$58,669	8.3%	3.2%	8.3%	1,177	17,888
Genesee County	47,441	12,245	15,159	14,071	5,966	$43,177	14.8%	9.5%	7.1%	10,171	61,052
Grand Traverse County	11,527	2,338	2,225	3,709	3,255	$59,911	10.9%	6.6%	7.7%	1,084	15,429
Ingham County	25,597	5,820	8,421	6,512	4,844	$45,961	12.7%	8.4%	10.0%	4,004	34,609
Isabella County	5,749	2,009	1,321	1,457	962	$38,059	11.7%	9.0%	11.9%	857	7,898
Jackson County	17,558	5,020	5,441	4,886	2,211	$40,598	10.4%	4.8%	7.7%	1,688	24,908
Kalamazoo County	25,026	7,046	8,176	6,771	3,033	$40,641	8.8%	5.4%	6.3%	2,758	35,135
Kent County	56,530	16,263	17,159	15,920	7,188	$42,680	9.2%	6.9%	8.7%	7,771	79,114
Lapeer County	10,168	2,501	3,031	3,371	1,265	$45,597	8.7%	6.6%	11.2%	1,394	14,468
Lenawee County	11,422	3,432	3,478	3,425	1,087	$37,496	9.5%	3.5%	2.8%	1,142	15,840
Livingston County	20,572	3,371	5,866	7,926	3,409	$55,791	3.1%	3.3%	9.7%	1,148	31,065
Macomb County	93,956	26,367	29,080	26,489	12,020	$41,915	7.9%	8.1%	10.3%	15,003	132,634
Marquette County	8,026	1,824	2,603	2,988	611	$44,684	8.9%	5.6%	5.8%	1,056	10,662
Midland County	9,892	2,412	3,150	3,081	1,249	$42,670	14.5%	4.2%	8.0%	1,366	13,191
Monroe County	18,137	4,923	6,008	5,749	1,457	$42,669	6.1%	4.3%	10.1%	3,026	23,136

Table G-2: Counties - Income, Poverty Status and Receipt of Food Stamps (SNAP)—*Continued*

	Income of Households with Householder 65 Years and Over					Poverty Rate of Persons			Households with 1 or More Persons 60 Years and Over	
Total Households	Less Than $25,000	$25,000 - $49,999	$50,000 - $99,999	$100,000 or More	Median Household Income	55 to 64 Years	65 to 74 Years	75 Years and Over	Receiving SNAP	Not Receiving SNAP
Michigan—Cont.										
Muskegon County	18,617	4,719	6,596	5,534	1,768	$40,414	12.5%	6.7%	10.4%	3,497	24,890
Oakland County	133,560	31,653	31,222	39,608	31,077	$54,006	7.7%	5.8%	8.4%	14,461	190,172
Ottawa County	26,813	6,195	8,670	8,474	3,474	$46,234	6.5%	2.9%	8.2%	1,343	37,751
Saginaw County	23,894	6,287	8,173	6,402	3,032	$40,637	13.7%	6.2%	9.9%	3,586	30,921
St. Clair County	18,670	5,009	6,062	5,334	2,265	$42,805	10.9%	7.5%	11.1%	3,161	25,662
Shiawassee County	7,895	1,809	3,208	2,336	542	$40,475	14.4%	5.2%	5.0%	1,229	10,739
Van Buren County	8,273	2,414	2,378	2,566	915	$40,028	8.8%	8.0%	9.5%	898	11,653
Washtenaw County	32,797	6,350	7,374	9,805	9,268	$60,875	5.2%	5.1%	7.3%	3,115	46,139
Wayne County	179,772	60,514	52,658	46,493	20,107	$37,563	17.4%	12.6%	12.1%	51,530	227,614
Minnesota										
Anoka County	29,075	5,456	8,427	10,244	4,948	$52,453	4.5%	4.6%	1.3%	2,826	44,500
Blue Earth County	5,618	1,350	1,475	1,673	1,120	$49,474	6.8%	3.8%	13.3%	355	7,423
Carver County	7,658	1,588	2,567	2,409	1,094	$48,313	2.5%	3.5%	6.7%	544	11,403
Dakota County	36,874	8,405	8,881	12,174	7,414	$53,539	5.4%	3.9%	5.8%	2,702	54,954
Hennepin County	111,929	27,874	26,027	32,902	25,126	$51,717	9.5%	6.0%	10.6%	14,040	158,240
Olmsted County	14,876	3,936	3,852	4,366	2,722	$47,576	5.9%	3.9%	7.6%	1,195	20,686
Ramsey County	51,150	11,112	13,363	15,545	11,130	$52,040	10.2%	6.3%	8.0%	8,548	69,526
Rice County	6,671	1,897	2,263	1,478	1,033	$39,992	5.7%	8.0%	1.7%	465	8,832
St. Louis County	24,853	7,120	7,858	7,191	2,684	$41,127	10.9%	5.0%	10.9%	2,568	33,991
Scott County	8,759	1,603	2,744	2,483	1,929	$50,589	6.4%	3.9%	4.7%	705	15,140
Sherburne County	6,298	1,736	1,502	2,002	1,058	$49,296	1.8%	8.9%	5.8%	160	9,778
Stearns County	14,462	4,081	4,989	3,637	1,755	$40,217	5.4%	5.0%	9.4%	1,244	20,092
Washington County	23,743	4,492	5,151	8,490	5,610	$60,874	3.5%	3.1%	5.4%	1,405	34,455
Wright County	10,471	2,601	3,016	3,449	1,405	$45,324	4.7%	6.2%	6.7%	494	15,399
Mississippi										
DeSoto County	13,892	2,710	5,324	4,347	1,511	$45,235	6.2%	6.0%	11.4%	1,604	20,682
Forrest County	6,425	2,178	2,143	1,047	1,057	$38,034	28.6%	11.3%	12.6%	1,312	8,010
Harrison County	19,440	5,293	5,537	5,566	3,044	$43,061	12.6%	8.7%	10.6%	4,020	25,572
Hinds County	19,645	5,977	5,029	5,612	3,027	$45,901	15.3%	5.6%	12.3%	3,611	27,786
Jackson County	14,177	4,166	3,992	4,501	1,518	$41,961	14.7%	8.1%	8.3%	1,356	20,506
Jones County	na	na	na	na	na	$32,192	12.7%	16.3%	17.9%	787	10,351
Lauderdale County	8,416	3,887	2,268	1,532	729	$26,543	19.2%	21.4%	23.3%	1,606	9,787
Lee County	7,784	2,555	1,864	2,476	889	$40,252	11.9%	4.6%	8.0%	669	10,942
Madison County	8,409	1,689	2,497	2,451	1,772	$50,241	2.5%	2.1%	21.4%	512	12,870
Rankin County	14,879	3,337	4,079	5,141	2,322	$50,145	13.6%	5.6%	7.4%	903	19,358
Missouri										
Boone County	14,295	2,883	4,287	4,041	3,084	$49,620	10.1%	5.7%	4.4%	1,480	20,731
Buchanan County	9,946	2,809	2,373	3,361	1,403	$47,264	16.0%	5.0%	11.4%	1,401	13,394
Cape Girardeau County	7,618	2,738	2,527	1,702	651	$36,354	14.2%	7.0%	10.9%	809	10,140
Cass County	11,620	2,997	3,480	3,767	1,376	$44,677	3.7%	9.0%	4.1%	601	16,939
Christian County	8,121	3,147	1,808	2,304	862	$41,016	7.9%	4.7%	11.9%	746	12,108
Clay County	20,702	3,853	6,724	6,587	3,538	$48,622	7.9%	3.8%	3.0%	1,104	31,488
Cole County	8,385	2,123	1,578	2,898	1,786	$57,029	5.4%	1.3%	10.3%	331	11,301
Franklin County	11,011	3,354	3,278	3,420	959	$38,368	6.2%	5.5%	4.7%	683	15,686
Greene County	32,556	12,042	11,518	6,250	2,746	$31,468	15.7%	7.8%	9.0%	7,109	39,597
Jackson County	66,109	19,752	18,047	19,341	8,969	$43,533	11.1%	5.1%	9.2%	9,632	94,060
Jasper County	13,326	5,263	3,733	3,275	1,055	$34,112	16.7%	6.0%	13.8%	1,966	15,894
Jefferson County	20,859	5,410	5,926	6,466	3,057	$46,369	8.5%	5.7%	6.2%	2,271	31,668
Platte County	8,509	1,587	2,053	2,561	2,308	$61,150	3.4%	2.1%	8.7%	430	12,807
St. Charles County	37,374	6,577	11,564	12,643	6,590	$51,593	5.3%	2.2%	5.8%	2,216	56,120
St. Francois County	7,061	2,679	1,804	1,966	612	$39,961	16.6%	9.1%	9.6%	472	9,566
St. Louis County	115,361	24,330	32,565	33,728	24,738	$50,736	7.2%	5.6%	7.7%	9,659	158,565
Montana										
Cascade County	9,377	2,645	3,283	2,533	916	$39,344	12.3%	11.8%	5.1%	1,439	12,535
Flathead County	11,891	3,108	3,172	3,392	2,219	$46,514	5.9%	6.4%	10.5%	574	18,313
Gallatin County	8,441	1,980	1,910	2,804	1,747	$59,375	6.0%	5.0%	9.6%	339	14,526
Lewis and Clark County	7,748	1,702	2,097	1,885	2,064	$51,645	10.5%	8.1%	13.3%	691	11,186
Missoula County	11,491	3,304	3,231	3,682	1,274	$43,706	10.0%	5.7%	14.0%	1,950	15,706
Yellowstone County	17,535	4,806	5,354	5,177	2,198	$39,613	11.4%	9.7%	10.3%	1,177	25,014
Nebraska										
Douglas County	48,243	12,719	13,820	13,486	8,218	$44,437	10.5%	5.3%	9.3%	7,103	68,210
Lancaster County	28,792	6,541	8,198	9,454	4,599	$49,126	8.6%	4.4%	6.3%	2,137	41,034
Sarpy County	13,859	3,301	3,515	4,178	2,865	$50,495	5.7%	5.7%	3.6%	955	19,970
Nevada										
Clark County	187,797	51,591	50,792	50,432	34,982	$44,806	13.3%	8.9%	10.6%	33,991	269,439
Washoe County	47,863	10,661	12,154	15,052	9,996	$52,743	10.0%	6.5%	9.8%	5,864	69,626
New Hampshire										
Cheshire County	9,178	2,896	2,373	2,113	1,796	$46,890	5.5%	5.4%	1.0%	661	14,005
Grafton County	11,656	2,397	2,726	3,760	2,773	$55,311	6.1%	2.4%	7.7%	418	16,056
Hillsborough County	38,337	9,569	9,309	10,585	8,874	$50,623	5.5%	4.0%	7.5%	4,152	59,522
Merrimack County	16,924	4,631	4,802	4,603	2,888	$45,560	4.9%	4.7%	3.9%	1,139	25,295
Rockingham County	31,923	6,861	7,318	10,525	7,219	$57,413	3.8%	4.3%	5.1%	1,777	50,677
Strafford County	11,506	2,498	3,188	4,052	1,768	$51,067	5.3%	5.0%	6.1%	1,711	17,048

Table G-2: Counties - Income, Poverty Status and Receipt of Food Stamps (SNAP)—*Continued*

		Income of Households with Householder 65 Years and Over					Poverty Rate of Persons			Households with 1 or More Persons 60 Years and Over	
	Total Households	Less Than $25,000	$25,000 - $49,999	$50,000 - $99,999	$100,000 or More	Median Household Income	55 to 64 Years	65 to 74 Years	75 Years and Over	Receiving SNAP	Not Receiving SNAP
New Jersey											
Atlantic County	28,355	5,764	7,314	9,413	5,864	$53,520	9.6%	6.9%	8.6%	4,227	39,211
Bergen County	94,096	21,773	19,941	20,605	31,777	$60,163	5.3%	4.8%	9.1%	8,908	139,253
Burlington County	46,078	7,901	12,234	14,944	10,999	$56,670	4.8%	2.8%	5.1%	3,132	69,509
Camden County	50,199	12,617	13,371	13,333	10,878	$48,470	10.8%	6.5%	7.7%	8,026	71,656
Cape May County	14,880	3,316	3,611	4,806	3,147	$54,050	12.4%	4.0%	5.2%	931	20,790
Cumberland County	14,558	5,347	2,877	4,448	1,886	$36,350	8.9%	13.5%	7.3%	2,022	19,561
Essex County	64,811	19,310	13,209	15,703	16,589	$49,746	13.0%	9.0%	10.8%	14,842	94,480
Gloucester County	27,052	5,833	7,886	7,537	5,796	$49,393	4.3%	4.0%	10.3%	2,679	40,654
Hudson County	49,125	18,634	11,943	10,304	8,244	$34,845	10.7%	11.2%	18.9%	15,231	70,146
Hunterdon County	13,988	1,627	3,346	4,395	4,620	$71,856	6.0%	2.6%	3.1%	712	20,204
Mercer County	35,066	8,548	7,560	8,842	10,116	$58,989	8.2%	7.1%	8.2%	3,829	51,044
Middlesex County	70,241	15,398	16,755	19,404	18,684	$57,013	5.2%	6.2%	9.5%	9,109	106,390
Monmouth County	69,245	15,142	12,585	19,918	21,600	$64,848	4.9%	3.7%	7.6%	7,063	101,248
Morris County	48,046	7,106	9,370	13,977	17,593	$73,007	4.3%	4.1%	4.5%	2,325	75,971
Ocean County	90,433	19,682	28,611	26,614	15,526	$46,380	6.6%	5.9%	5.3%	4,897	116,429
Passaic County	41,317	12,398	8,261	10,242	10,416	$49,998	9.6%	9.5%	11.0%	11,812	58,296
Salem County	7,083	1,885	1,360	2,326	1,512	$60,583	14.9%	5.2%	15.1%	1,011	9,864
Somerset County	29,312	5,542	6,508	6,972	10,290	$67,178	3.1%	3.6%	7.1%	1,863	46,625
Sussex County	14,851	2,289	3,355	4,651	4,556	$67,165	4.2%	3.8%	4.6%	597	23,572
Union County	46,489	12,475	11,103	11,380	11,531	$48,821	6.5%	6.8%	10.6%	7,397	70,782
Warren County	12,242	3,693	3,340	2,796	2,413	$39,408	3.6%	5.9%	10.5%	1,012	18,749
New Mexico											
Bernalillo County	69,183	20,639	17,319	18,461	12,764	$44,441	13.7%	9.7%	11.7%	12,850	93,024
Chaves County	6,568	2,298	1,870	1,632	768	$33,984	17.3%	18.7%	13.0%	1,854	8,180
Doña Ana County	20,682	7,553	5,121	4,804	3,204	$36,765	22.2%	11.7%	20.7%	6,260	25,054
Lea County	4,873	1,599	2,146	642	486	$31,787	13.9%	10.7%	12.0%	805	7,184
McKinley County	5,709	2,244	1,390	1,400	675	$34,031	26.4%	17.9%	11.7%	1,900	8,098
Otero County	6,635	2,129	1,788	2,057	661	$39,711	22.7%	15.7%	15.2%	1,350	8,865
Sandoval County	15,111	3,686	4,128	4,942	2,355	$47,922	7.4%	8.2%	10.0%	1,798	20,939
San Juan County	12,097	3,839	3,575	3,145	1,538	$38,127	23.2%	14.2%	16.3%	2,666	15,959
Santa Fe County	22,869	3,717	6,268	6,916	5,968	$57,495	8.2%	5.4%	8.4%	2,616	30,027
Valencia County	8,607	3,400	2,378	2,217	612	$33,879	14.8%	10.5%	13.5%	1,549	12,106
New York											
Albany County	32,402	7,984	7,351	9,461	7,606	$52,994	8.7%	4.9%	6.7%	5,315	44,380
Bronx County	115,624	55,920	23,142	23,481	13,081	$27,351	24.8%	19.3%	26.8%	76,988	115,749
Broome County	23,184	7,056	6,374	6,197	3,557	$42,493	13.4%	6.0%	12.2%	4,698	29,882
Cattaraugus County	9,120	2,835	2,743	2,948	594	$38,669	14.0%	10.8%	13.5%	2,077	11,661
Cayuga County	8,949	2,525	2,940	2,565	919	$39,176	11.3%	6.6%	7.7%	1,566	11,714
Chautauqua County	15,814	5,586	4,780	3,835	1,613	$34,639	14.2%	8.1%	10.6%	4,247	19,306
Chemung County	10,247	3,610	2,729	2,463	1,445	$40,295	8.9%	10.5%	11.5%	1,895	12,774
Clinton County	8,126	1,910	2,864	2,041	1,311	$41,069	10.8%	8.2%	3.5%	1,997	11,668
Dutchess County	31,844	7,336	7,127	8,847	8,534	$59,005	8.3%	3.6%	7.1%	4,862	45,947
Erie County	108,411	32,497	30,227	30,820	14,867	$41,643	10.4%	6.9%	8.4%	21,458	140,418
Jefferson County	9,611	3,072	2,818	2,723	998	$39,128	10.4%	5.9%	9.8%	1,765	12,992
Kings County	222,026	93,830	45,187	43,267	39,742	$32,386	15.4%	15.7%	25.4%	109,317	254,772
Livingston County	6,572	1,576	1,870	2,033	1,093	$48,765	4.2%	2.2%	5.0%	452	10,448
Madison County	7,634	2,279	2,216	2,588	551	$42,102	7.7%	9.3%	7.6%	837	11,735
Monroe County	81,774	24,061	22,312	22,221	13,180	$42,241	10.0%	7.3%	11.0%	14,861	110,303
Nassau County	137,207	24,772	27,548	35,321	49,566	$72,205	4.2%	3.9%	6.1%	10,984	208,118
New York County	183,754	66,639	33,976	33,988	49,151	$42,404	16.6%	16.8%	19.0%	56,930	209,863
Niagara County	26,063	8,290	8,522	5,943	3,308	$37,743	9.9%	10.9%	9.3%	4,210	37,001
Oneida County	25,518	8,235	6,414	6,991	3,878	$40,400	14.9%	6.1%	11.3%	4,546	34,849
Onondaga County	50,806	14,603	14,565	13,348	8,290	$43,021	8.6%	6.2%	10.8%	9,197	68,210
Ontario County	13,724	3,313	4,203	4,453	1,755	$46,449	8.6%	4.7%	6.5%	1,228	18,776
Orange County	31,943	8,368	7,708	7,842	8,025	$49,589	8.3%	5.8%	5.6%	4,500	48,525
Oswego County	12,220	4,061	3,393	3,002	1,764	$37,428	10.9%	10.8%	7.1%	2,868	16,328
Putnam County	9,588	1,467	2,176	2,874	3,071	$64,787	3.3%	5.4%	3.7%	964	15,132
Queens County	199,825	66,665	44,455	47,372	41,333	$42,468	9.9%	10.6%	15.9%	60,917	274,587
Rensselaer County	17,102	2,727	4,612	6,415	3,348	$59,098	7.2%	6.0%	2.1%	2,449	22,832
Richmond County	45,957	13,348	9,372	10,644	12,593	$50,738	9.7%	9.6%	12.4%	9,860	68,368
Rockland County	29,598	5,847	5,635	8,022	10,094	$71,840	7.1%	5.5%	9.2%	4,804	41,183
St. Lawrence County	12,077	4,513	4,139	2,561	864	$33,354	12.2%	7.8%	10.5%	2,768	14,954
Saratoga County	25,959	4,701	6,867	7,965	6,426	$57,710	6.1%	3.3%	3.5%	2,592	35,303
Schenectady County	16,415	4,540	4,478	4,452	2,945	$44,250	10.9%	6.5%	11.6%	2,485	21,358
Steuben County	11,538	3,765	2,759	3,332	1,682	$42,400	11.9%	5.0%	11.0%	1,603	16,237
Suffolk County	144,184	28,649	28,910	41,367	45,258	$63,326	6.7%	4.6%	6.2%	16,894	215,116
Sullivan County	8,582	2,377	2,639	2,284	1,282	$44,047	16.0%	7.4%	15.4%	1,949	11,271
Tompkins County	9,079	1,695	2,716	2,856	1,812	$51,306	6.1%	2.1%	5.4%	1,255	13,776
Ulster County	21,616	4,723	5,870	6,710	4,313	$50,562	10.4%	8.7%	8.5%	3,032	30,475
Warren County	9,284	2,222	2,431	2,776	1,855	$49,860	11.5%	6.0%	5.0%	1,488	12,311
Wayne County	10,643	3,219	2,740	3,161	1,523	$43,581	5.8%	5.6%	8.1%	2,047	14,335
Westchester County	102,529	21,142	21,102	26,120	34,165	$63,919	8.9%	5.1%	8.9%	15,727	140,213
North Carolina											
Alamance County	17,636	5,884	4,777	4,155	2,820	$38,522	10.1%	6.7%	8.9%	2,214	24,375
Brunswick County	25,219	5,576	5,940	8,742	4,961	$53,228	12.1%	6.7%	7.4%	1,393	33,186
Buncombe County	32,253	9,134	8,871	8,557	5,691	$43,866	8.1%	5.4%	14.7%	3,068	43,283

Table G-2: Counties - Income, Poverty Status and Receipt of Food Stamps (SNAP)—*Continued*

	Income of Households with Householder 65 Years and Over					Poverty Rate of Persons			Households with 1 or More Persons 60 Years and Over	
Total Households	Less Than $25,000	$25,000 - $49,999	$50,000 - $99,999	$100,000 or More	Median Household Income	55 to 64 Years	65 to 74 Years	75 Years and Over	Receiving SNAP	Not Receiving SNAP
North Carolina—Cont.										
Burke County	10,686	3,313	3,792	2,813	768	$37,438	9.1%	10.3%	7.3%	1,470	14,923
Cabarrus County	16,169	4,353	5,179	4,929	1,708	$41,506	8.1%	5.6%	3.6%	1,990	23,613
Caldwell County	9,499	3,908	2,981	2,178	432	$32,203	15.3%	5.6%	11.6%	1,653	12,419
Carteret County	11,038	2,230	3,420	4,049	1,339	$47,978	10.6%	5.0%	6.8%	620	14,650
Catawba County	18,289	5,622	5,331	4,695	2,641	$39,714	11.4%	4.5%	7.1%	1,320	25,570
Chatham County	10,611	2,103	2,124	3,310	3,074	$64,834	5.9%	6.8%	1.5%	963	14,025
Cleveland County	10,539	4,770	2,839	2,158	772	$29,942	16.0%	19.8%	9.1%	2,140	14,270
Craven County	12,794	4,380	3,747	3,135	1,532	$34,723	10.5%	6.2%	18.0%	2,299	16,584
Cumberland County	25,938	7,567	7,110	7,014	4,247	$40,785	10.4%	8.9%	9.4%	5,298	35,682
Davidson County	18,381	6,821	5,674	4,067	1,819	$34,303	13.0%	7.2%	11.1%	3,521	26,261
Durham County	25,415	5,889	6,983	6,968	5,575	$48,974	9.3%	5.4%	7.3%	4,229	37,036
Forsyth County	39,419	12,683	10,869	10,698	5,169	$39,644	12.2%	8.3%	8.0%	5,270	54,934
Franklin County	6,965	1,977	2,066	1,954	968	$44,270	9.8%	6.7%	12.2%	2,375	8,476
Gaston County	22,081	7,533	7,593	5,137	1,818	$33,894	9.9%	7.2%	11.9%	3,885	30,383
Guilford County	50,210	15,665	12,682	11,998	9,865	$42,272	10.2%	7.1%	9.6%	9,032	68,720
Harnett County	9,992	3,622	2,585	2,889	896	$37,090	14.1%	11.3%	8.7%	1,803	13,788
Henderson County	18,920	5,133	5,331	4,757	3,699	$41,580	7.8%	6.0%	7.5%	1,148	24,280
Iredell County	16,967	4,592	4,662	5,417	2,296	$46,513	8.7%	4.0%	8.2%	1,206	24,828
Johnston County	15,581	4,707	4,224	4,258	2,392	$41,188	13.2%	3.4%	8.8%	3,272	21,482
Lincoln County	8,680	2,340	2,322	2,483	1,535	$47,340	8.9%	6.0%	5.3%	961	12,603
Mecklenburg County	72,989	18,611	19,677	20,211	14,490	$47,101	9.0%	5.7%	10.2%	12,594	106,767
Moore County	14,474	3,509	3,430	4,226	3,309	$51,536	9.8%	9.1%	9.7%	667	19,834
Nash County	12,037	3,283	4,316	3,103	1,335	$38,871	10.5%	6.0%	13.6%	2,272	15,166
New Hanover County	26,105	6,256	7,397	7,601	4,851	$47,259	15.2%	6.9%	8.2%	3,323	34,457
Onslow County	10,186	2,522	3,382	3,517	765	$43,431	10.6%	6.6%	8.2%	1,405	16,038
Orange County	12,791	2,349	2,398	3,880	4,164	$71,164	9.4%	5.2%	3.8%	1,476	18,888
Pitt County	14,472	4,602	4,124	4,094	1,652	$36,786	19.0%	7.3%	6.9%	3,271	20,591
Randolph County	15,535	4,991	5,432	3,484	1,628	$36,237	13.3%	4.4%	17.3%	2,254	20,944
Robeson County	12,744	5,625	3,662	2,514	943	$26,869	19.9%	14.2%	24.3%	5,052	15,205
Rockingham County	12,727	4,485	3,942	3,127	1,173	$36,538	14.5%	8.2%	14.4%	2,402	16,474
Rowan County	15,670	5,054	5,384	3,560	1,672	$35,849	9.6%	6.3%	8.7%	2,212	20,542
Rutherford County	9,054	3,692	2,825	1,915	622	$32,969	16.0%	13.3%	10.6%	1,704	11,733
Surry County	9,879	3,976	2,894	2,079	930	$28,772	9.2%	8.5%	15.8%	1,397	12,493
Union County	16,342	2,944	4,738	4,905	3,755	$53,453	5.9%	2.8%	5.2%	2,189	24,930
Wake County	75,259	14,217	17,447	23,928	19,667	$61,338	6.0%	3.9%	7.7%	7,246	114,303
Wayne County	13,389	4,888	3,863	2,717	1,921	$32,024	14.7%	9.0%	21.6%	3,646	17,643
Wilkes County	10,532	4,013	3,651	2,337	531	$32,310	13.7%	4.6%	9.9%	1,500	13,199
Wilson County	9,989	4,128	1,599	2,916	1,346	$34,868	18.7%	8.6%	16.1%	2,253	13,296
North Dakota										
Burleigh County	9,661	2,550	2,286	3,174	1,651	$49,946	6.0%	2.5%	15.2%	309	13,147
Cass County	13,333	2,795	3,502	4,055	2,981	$52,304	4.9%	2.8%	13.2%	907	20,368
Grand Forks County	5,666	1,742	1,874	1,266	784	$36,000	6.0%	4.8%	21.0%	552	8,341
Ward County	5,402	1,929	1,055	1,420	998	$39,576	14.6%	7.1%	15.9%	822	7,352
Ohio										
Allen County	11,540	4,154	3,664	2,790	932	$34,450	9.1%	4.5%	13.6%	1,214	16,594
Ashtabula County	11,704	4,848	3,375	2,272	1,209	$31,814	12.9%	13.3%	16.1%	2,358	14,772
Athens County	5,581	2,086	1,234	1,443	818	$36,701	23.6%	8.3%	19.1%	1,205	7,369
Belmont County	8,880	3,147	3,177	1,939	617	$32,928	12.5%	6.7%	7.7%	1,474	11,492
Butler County	34,810	8,269	12,198	8,687	5,656	$42,814	9.2%	5.7%	4.8%	6,437	48,060
Clark County	17,429	4,347	5,798	5,308	1,976	$43,489	11.7%	5.7%	8.4%	2,484	22,170
Clermont County	20,408	5,966	5,040	6,611	2,791	$45,628	8.2%	7.7%	10.0%	2,564	29,506
Columbiana County	12,925	4,264	4,710	2,800	1,151	$35,028	10.8%	6.4%	7.8%	2,456	16,777
Cuyahoga County	150,843	50,249	42,802	36,005	21,787	$38,275	15.3%	10.7%	11.7%	32,304	193,237
Delaware County	16,459	2,277	3,983	6,374	3,825	$64,446	3.5%	3.3%	2.3%	497	24,715
Erie County	10,135	3,370	3,742	2,111	912	$33,304	9.5%	4.5%	7.6%	1,007	13,442
Fairfield County	15,127	4,042	4,244	5,271	1,570	$42,169	9.7%	6.4%	5.7%	2,121	20,890
Franklin County	100,883	24,105	26,616	31,199	18,963	$49,550	11.9%	6.0%	11.7%	18,178	143,239
Geauga County	11,976	2,344	2,744	3,783	3,105	$59,476	5.0%	3.9%	3.4%	659	16,708
Greene County	18,525	3,845	4,160	5,949	4,571	$56,529	11.6%	5.3%	7.9%	1,949	24,908
Hamilton County	81,102	23,506	20,473	21,363	15,760	$44,898	11.1%	7.0%	9.9%	11,805	112,633
Hancock County	8,173	2,260	2,405	2,234	1,274	$39,319	6.1%	6.5%	5.4%	675	11,161
Jefferson County	9,203	3,252	3,017	2,106	828	$31,658	12.7%	7.2%	11.9%	1,695	11,896
Lake County	28,890	6,853	10,160	8,448	3,429	$43,536	6.6%	5.9%	5.5%	2,787	40,947
Licking County	16,952	4,599	4,930	5,111	2,312	$44,946	8.5%	4.4%	6.4%	1,375	24,969
Lorain County	35,685	9,187	10,399	11,588	4,511	$44,923	9.8%	5.5%	9.5%	4,711	48,019
Lucas County	43,704	13,673	11,898	12,483	5,650	$40,180	15.6%	11.4%	9.4%	8,169	58,707
Mahoning County	30,605	9,204	10,798	8,184	2,419	$36,895	10.8%	9.7%	6.8%	5,256	40,963
Marion County	6,905	2,578	1,976	1,639	712	$34,044	18.3%	4.2%	7.1%	1,250	9,625
Medina County	19,624	3,609	6,370	5,841	3,804	$48,575	4.8%	5.5%	6.1%	1,182	27,759
Miami County	11,957	4,023	3,720	2,968	1,246	$35,891	5.0%	2.5%	5.7%	1,759	16,013
Montgomery County	62,017	17,099	19,025	16,864	9,029	$41,719	12.9%	7.6%	9.0%	8,045	83,318
Muskingum County	10,134	3,688	3,246	2,469	731	$33,676	13.0%	10.2%	7.3%	2,678	12,714
Portage County	16,186	4,793	4,680	4,550	2,163	$40,608	6.5%	4.9%	8.7%	2,265	23,253
Richland County	15,028	4,318	5,881	3,761	1,068	$38,049	15.5%	6.1%	8.4%	1,995	18,632

Table G-2: Counties - Income, Poverty Status and Receipt of Food Stamps (SNAP)—*Continued*

	Income of Households with Householder 65 Years and Over						Poverty Rate of Persons			Households with 1 or More Persons 60 Years and Over	
	Total Households	Less Than $25,000	$25,000 - $49,999	$50,000 - $99,999	$100,000 or More	Median Household Income	55 to 64 Years	65 to 74 Years	75 Years and Over	Receiving SNAP	Not Receiving SNAP
Ohio—Cont.											
Ross County	8,430	2,884	2,439	2,329	778	$34,007	13.0%	8.0%	9.3%	1,646	10,762
Scioto County	8,572	3,735	2,545	1,691	601	$28,464	20.4%	10.6%	21.5%	2,873	9,889
Stark County	45,960	13,957	15,643	11,861	4,499	$38,107	9.5%	5.9%	11.1%	6,020	59,837
Summit County	61,595	15,900	18,253	18,752	8,690	$44,196	11.2%	5.9%	7.1%	10,747	83,416
Trumbull County	27,428	9,029	7,607	7,949	2,843	$39,016	14.4%	11.3%	8.5%	3,724	36,044
Tuscarawas County	11,470	4,704	3,438	2,323	1,005	$33,348	3.9%	6.1%	8.9%	1,280	15,378
Warren County	19,136	2,929	5,420	6,145	4,642	$54,663	4.5%	3.2%	5.6%	939	28,336
Wayne County	12,744	3,859	3,450	4,149	1,286	$42,604	8.2%	3.2%	4.5%	1,855	17,270
Wood County	12,245	2,678	3,566	4,269	1,732	$48,765	9.8%	3.6%	13.7%	622	17,664
Oklahoma											
Canadian County	10,317	2,670	2,067	4,011	1,569	$53,768	11.0%	3.1%	4.5%	538	16,442
Cleveland County	24,398	5,443	6,452	7,558	4,945	$51,369	6.3%	5.5%	3.9%	2,905	32,223
Comanche County	9,851	2,761	2,737	2,654	1,699	$41,902	12.1%	8.0%	10.6%	2,015	13,433
Creek County	8,005	2,570	2,583	1,954	898	$36,822	8.5%	5.5%	6.6%	776	10,505
Muskogee County	7,165	2,586	2,431	1,487	661	$36,215	9.1%	9.6%	10.8%	1,220	9,575
Oklahoma County	69,935	18,508	19,374	19,428	12,625	$45,801	12.9%	7.9%	8.0%	10,469	95,214
Payne County	7,462	1,677	2,416	1,846	1,523	$43,135	17.2%	7.9%	12.3%	298	9,587
Pottawatomie County	7,298	2,304	2,371	2,183	440	$35,899	17.6%	6.6%	10.8%	1,505	10,054
Rogers County	8,552	2,124	2,633	2,588	1,207	$47,284	6.8%	4.8%	7.3%	929	12,628
Tulsa County	59,066	15,285	17,560	15,204	11,017	$44,404	10.7%	5.8%	7.6%	6,966	82,734
Wagoner County	8,077	1,923	2,364	2,594	1,196	$47,797	10.0%	5.2%	5.3%	1,043	11,442
Oregon											
Benton County	8,774	1,602	2,376	2,718	2,078	$54,289	8.9%	5.5%	3.1%	1,055	11,717
Clackamas County	45,626	9,279	12,108	14,832	9,407	$52,941	6.2%	6.5%	7.6%	5,901	62,541
Deschutes County	25,139	5,881	6,155	8,564	4,539	$53,448	8.5%	4.2%	16.4%	3,642	32,510
Douglas County	17,844	5,418	5,896	4,677	1,853	$36,598	20.7%	9.3%	8.3%	4,429	19,701
Jackson County	29,411	7,739	8,428	8,443	4,801	$46,127	14.4%	6.7%	11.0%	5,582	37,248
Josephine County	14,454	3,699	5,062	4,126	1,567	$42,213	15.5%	5.8%	4.8%	3,514	16,754
Klamath County	8,846	2,575	3,632	1,929	710	$35,648	17.1%	10.7%	12.2%	2,175	10,757
Lane County	46,536	11,659	12,205	15,195	7,477	$48,569	13.5%	9.1%	8.9%	11,308	56,295
Linn County	15,144	4,378	3,944	5,584	1,238	$46,979	12.5%	4.5%	13.2%	2,988	18,223
Marion County	31,849	9,123	8,703	9,270	4,753	$43,725	12.5%	8.3%	7.0%	7,779	42,276
Multnomah County	70,367	18,836	17,398	17,736	16,397	$48,439	12.0%	6.4%	11.3%	14,782	92,619
Polk County	9,211	1,911	2,621	2,652	2,027	$53,544	15.9%	8.8%	7.3%	1,740	10,942
Umatilla County	7,442	2,253	2,551	1,828	810	$37,210	9.2%	7.2%	6.6%	1,969	9,014
Washington County	49,424	10,500	13,847	15,893	9,184	$51,052	6.2%	7.1%	6.0%	5,947	71,691
Yamhill County	11,361	3,084	2,935	3,193	2,149	$48,433	13.5%	7.9%	7.1%	2,194	14,599
Pennsylvania											
Adams County	12,529	3,454	3,476	4,085	1,514	$42,944	4.1%	4.4%	13.3%	1,112	17,443
Allegheny County	153,284	49,410	41,613	38,797	23,464	$40,257	9.4%	6.3%	11.1%	26,708	200,058
Armstrong County	9,246	3,313	3,181	2,190	562	$35,020	9.2%	5.8%	14.6%	2,113	11,175
Beaver County	23,418	6,965	8,198	5,550	2,705	$34,808	8.0%	3.8%	8.2%	2,705	30,916
Berks County	43,204	10,858	14,096	11,603	6,647	$42,434	8.0%	6.2%	10.4%	8,042	57,802
Blair County	16,090	4,551	5,263	4,982	1,294	$40,804	11.6%	6.5%	9.8%	2,616	20,232
Bucks County	69,401	14,174	15,931	20,737	18,559	$57,781	4.7%	4.0%	5.6%	6,048	101,933
Butler County	22,151	5,857	7,882	5,626	2,786	$37,952	7.1%	4.8%	4.4%	2,265	32,736
Cambria County	19,834	6,703	6,403	5,139	1,589	$34,540	10.8%	6.9%	9.4%	3,713	24,461
Carbon County	8,006	2,559	2,714	1,819	914	$35,391	7.1%	6.9%	16.6%	1,182	11,177
Centre County	13,802	2,734	4,921	3,557	2,590	$44,422	5.4%	0.9%	4.2%	1,163	19,268
Chester County	51,086	7,475	11,183	17,068	15,360	$63,713	5.7%	3.0%	6.0%	3,078	75,782
Clearfield County	10,186	3,926	3,557	2,252	451	$34,871	12.1%	8.5%	7.8%	2,101	12,856
Columbia County	7,962	3,130	2,371	1,907	554	$29,724	5.8%	5.0%	8.1%	1,128	11,116
Crawford County	11,241	3,055	3,811	3,300	1,075	$38,724	12.6%	6.1%	8.8%	1,889	14,543
Cumberland County	29,114	5,730	8,885	8,525	5,974	$49,808	4.4%	4.3%	6.3%	3,134	38,353
Dauphin County	29,930	6,938	10,280	7,528	5,184	$44,820	9.6%	5.7%	8.9%	4,584	40,438
Delaware County	55,867	12,669	15,195	15,845	12,158	$50,115	7.6%	4.5%	9.1%	8,650	79,359
Erie County	31,393	9,232	10,489	8,101	3,571	$38,291	12.6%	4.9%	10.1%	6,361	39,425
Fayette County	17,735	6,793	4,708	4,663	1,571	$31,006	13.8%	8.9%	11.2%	4,722	22,227
Franklin County	18,693	5,186	4,941	5,832	2,734	$46,280	5.2%	5.0%	14.2%	1,723	24,488
Indiana County	10,360	2,961	3,762	2,516	1,121	$37,627	9.2%	6.4%	10.3%	2,029	12,943
Lackawanna County	26,916	8,142	7,328	7,956	3,490	$41,984	12.0%	6.9%	9.7%	5,508	34,700
Lancaster County	57,454	13,109	17,106	17,394	9,845	$48,434	6.8%	3.7%	9.8%	6,742	78,171
Lawrence County	11,822	3,550	3,954	3,297	1,021	$37,495	16.8%	6.5%	7.0%	1,873	15,830
Lebanon County	17,563	4,797	4,746	5,863	2,157	$45,034	6.9%	5.8%	6.2%	1,910	23,646
Lehigh County	36,901	9,875	13,188	8,234	5,604	$40,819	10.3%	5.8%	9.7%	5,794	50,925
Luzerne County	39,885	14,374	11,091	9,896	4,524	$36,035	10.3%	6.0%	11.3%	8,019	52,430
Lycoming County	13,364	4,147	3,811	3,547	1,859	$40,105	11.6%	6.0%	12.5%	2,634	17,352
Mercer County	15,513	5,066	5,310	4,079	1,058	$35,674	9.7%	7.1%	6.6%	1,875	20,201
Monroe County	15,553	4,161	4,409	5,072	1,911	$45,719	13.2%	8.7%	11.0%	2,712	24,479
Montgomery County	87,931	17,523	21,479	26,524	22,405	$56,113	4.0%	3.6%	7.4%	6,886	126,572
Northampton County	35,162	8,855	9,238	11,277	5,792	$48,693	7.1%	4.5%	6.1%	5,220	45,995
Northumberland County	12,466	5,503	3,942	2,260	761	$28,428	9.0%	9.2%	11.7%	2,171	16,143
Philadelphia County	144,301	60,062	34,992	32,551	16,696	$31,824	22.6%	14.1%	19.0%	63,597	161,597
Schuylkill County	18,720	8,284	5,338	3,781	1,317	$27,751	10.4%	9.5%	13.5%	3,104	23,629
Somerset County	9,473	2,841	3,453	2,579	600	$35,497	10.8%	6.8%	7.1%	1,753	12,370

Table G-2: Counties - Income, Poverty Status and Receipt of Food Stamps (SNAP)—*Continued*

	Income of Households with Householder 65 Years and Over					Poverty Rate of Persons			Households with 1 or More Persons 60 Years and Over	
	Total Households	Less Than $25,000	$25,000 - $49,999	$50,000 - $99,999	$100,000 or More	Median Household Income	55 to 64 Years	65 to 74 Years	75 Years and Over	Receiving SNAP	Not Receiving SNAP
Pennsylvania—Cont.											
Washington County	26,622	7,580	7,594	6,940	4,508	$42,354	9.8%	4.6%	8.5%	3,814	36,387
Westmoreland County	50,820	13,909	16,522	14,536	5,853	$40,344	7.7%	5.2%	8.1%	8,114	66,194
York County	47,981	12,701	15,392	14,313	5,575	$42,493	6.3%	3.2%	5.5%	5,808	68,213
Rhode Island											
Kent County	20,449	6,748	6,545	4,279	2,877	$37,717	6.5%	8.9%	11.2%	4,373	26,982
Newport County	12,166	3,045	2,944	2,708	3,469	$50,861	3.4%	7.0%	14.4%	1,811	14,928
Providence County	60,005	22,508	13,064	15,741	8,692	$37,304	12.7%	10.7%	13.9%	19,053	75,705
Washington County	15,603	2,117	3,753	4,999	4,734	$68,457	2.3%	2.6%	8.6%	1,011	22,017
South Carolina											
Aiken County	20,602	5,792	6,041	4,854	3,915	$44,533	13.6%	7.4%	6.2%	2,791	27,473
Anderson County	23,011	9,340	5,963	4,874	2,834	$31,773	12.4%	7.0%	14.6%	3,357	30,347
Beaufort County	29,332	3,790	7,632	9,294	8,616	$65,477	12.3%	5.8%	3.0%	1,420	37,003
Berkeley County	17,710	3,577	4,739	6,468	2,926	$52,814	15.4%	6.4%	8.4%	1,462	27,654
Charleston County	42,527	10,052	10,644	11,820	10,011	$52,038	13.0%	7.8%	7.1%	4,095	57,220
Darlington County	8,433	3,388	2,824	1,668	553	$28,112	19.6%	13.7%	22.8%	2,316	10,880
Dorchester County	12,874	3,546	3,361	3,574	2,393	$44,398	10.9%	4.8%	5.0%	2,096	17,301
Florence County	13,974	3,544	4,916	3,755	1,759	$42,463	20.1%	4.9%	14.2%	2,838	18,135
Greenville County	49,062	12,666	13,662	15,016	7,718	$44,163	12.3%	6.4%	8.3%	7,286	68,050
Greenwood County	8,028	2,933	2,377	2,177	541	$35,379	10.2%	9.3%	7.0%	1,419	10,023
Horry County	48,521	11,029	14,633	16,424	6,435	$47,208	12.2%	7.3%	5.9%	3,839	65,060
Kershaw County	7,450	2,135	2,571	2,071	673	$39,472	10.2%	5.8%	15.0%	1,028	9,682
Lancaster County	11,175	3,350	3,363	3,061	1,401	$41,497	7.6%	9.1%	9.6%	1,203	14,892
Laurens County	7,397	2,689	2,177	1,802	729	$37,077	13.1%	9.7%	14.0%	1,496	9,498
Lexington County	30,215	7,335	9,832	8,562	4,486	$45,066	8.2%	6.6%	11.9%	3,378	42,781
Oconee County	11,515	3,729	3,646	2,638	1,502	$35,825	11.9%	10.3%	7.3%	1,308	15,365
Orangeburg County	11,251	4,822	3,488	2,074	867	$30,565	25.8%	16.9%	28.4%	2,213	13,558
Pickens County	13,758	4,633	4,606	2,593	1,926	$35,382	12.2%	7.0%	11.2%	1,446	18,214
Richland County	33,419	9,580	8,822	9,128	5,889	$44,933	11.0%	9.1%	12.8%	6,189	46,551
Spartanburg County	30,293	8,828	8,672	8,860	3,933	$42,690	11.2%	5.7%	10.6%	3,318	43,725
Sumter County	10,897	3,341	3,231	2,802	1,523	$41,470	13.9%	9.3%	9.1%	2,776	14,154
York County	22,448	6,155	5,883	6,651	3,759	$45,748	7.7%	6.0%	12.0%	2,784	33,810
South Dakota											
Minnehaha County	16,459	5,026	4,486	4,471	2,476	$43,220	8.0%	6.9%	11.4%	1,909	23,371
Pennington County	13,001	2,739	4,538	3,708	2,016	$44,463	15.2%	4.8%	12.5%	1,137	17,321
Tennessee											
Anderson County	8,995	1,968	2,733	3,034	1,260	$46,973	11.6%	12.2%	8.8%	1,679	12,220
Blount County	15,806	3,905	4,822	4,564	2,515	$44,871	9.0%	8.7%	6.7%	1,343	22,258
Bradley County	11,158	3,456	3,816	2,310	1,576	$39,637	9.4%	5.4%	14.8%	1,457	13,869
Davidson County	55,686	14,809	13,310	16,078	11,489	$49,374	11.1%	7.9%	8.6%	8,245	77,458
Greene County	8,422	3,484	1,985	1,944	1,009	$33,269	9.8%	6.7%	6.9%	1,098	12,178
Hamilton County	38,869	11,019	10,297	11,028	6,525	$44,686	10.2%	5.1%	8.2%	5,340	53,460
Knox County	46,281	12,341	12,162	13,880	7,898	$47,145	10.8%	4.2%	8.3%	5,667	62,645
Madison County	10,420	3,346	2,593	2,739	1,742	$39,167	11.0%	4.7%	1.1%	1,425	14,591
Maury County	9,199	2,794	2,588	2,561	1,256	$37,343	10.2%	7.3%	9.9%	1,546	13,044
Montgomery County	11,008	2,388	4,426	2,752	1,442	$39,727	12.9%	3.3%	2.2%	1,299	18,078
Putnam County	7,759	2,769	2,323	1,502	1,165	$35,659	10.2%	2.1%	9.7%	558	11,926
Robertson County	5,876	1,215	2,032	1,454	1,175	$41,837	10.1%	5.0%	7.0%	468	10,273
Rutherford County	19,666	4,372	6,398	6,578	2,318	$45,941	7.0%	4.5%	6.8%	2,148	31,528
Sevier County	11,040	2,734	3,467	2,330	2,509	$40,843	9.2%	6.2%	6.9%	1,575	14,538
Shelby County	81,716	27,548	18,412	21,289	14,467	$40,742	15.7%	8.8%	14.9%	19,134	112,281
Sullivan County	23,310	8,017	7,073	5,636	2,584	$35,771	11.4%	10.1%	10.3%	3,831	28,458
Sumner County	18,119	4,366	5,431	5,094	3,228	$45,795	8.1%	6.3%	10.5%	3,176	24,671
Washington County	14,279	5,144	3,520	4,058	1,557	$38,284	10.6%	14.5%	6.4%	1,989	19,327
Williamson County	17,284	1,938	4,590	5,156	5,600	$69,919	2.0%	1.8%	6.6%	878	26,784
Wilson County	13,424	2,929	3,743	4,666	2,086	$50,433	7.9%	4.2%	8.3%	2,532	18,310
Texas											
Angelina County	7,583	2,840	2,658	1,557	528	$31,032	12.2%	9.1%	14.3%	1,523	10,521
Bastrop County	na	na	na	na	na	$41,606	19.4%	9.6%	11.2%	954	11,027
Bell County	23,244	6,246	6,126	7,276	3,596	$46,665	9.6%	8.2%	9.4%	3,577	31,724
Bexar County	137,915	41,649	32,911	39,747	23,608	$45,743	14.7%	9.1%	14.3%	26,964	192,117
Bowie County	9,487	3,312	2,401	2,546	1,228	$40,864	18.0%	10.4%	19.3%	1,827	13,001
Brazoria County	24,397	5,530	6,423	6,806	5,638	$52,066	6.4%	5.1%	12.4%	2,225	37,642
Brazos County	13,213	3,966	3,114	3,476	2,657	$48,007	11.8%	8.3%	9.6%	1,517	18,039
Cameron County	33,403	15,270	8,781	7,312	2,040	$29,663	18.2%	18.6%	20.7%	10,304	40,890
Collin County	57,562	10,692	13,380	17,760	15,730	$61,362	5.5%	5.6%	10.5%	3,054	98,191
Comal County	14,429	2,976	3,592	4,244	3,617	$59,871	7.2%	4.7%	2.2%	997	22,691
Coryell County	4,773	1,829	1,434	1,153	357	$31,994	10.2%	7.0%	22.4%	597	6,257
Dallas County	166,769	48,492	40,287	43,768	34,222	$45,984	11.0%	9.1%	12.7%	27,926	260,616
Denton County	46,502	7,297	12,456	15,485	11,264	$60,060	6.2%	2.6%	4.2%	3,049	81,741
Ector County	9,917	3,456	2,489	2,524	1,448	$39,185	7.1%	8.0%	17.0%	1,395	15,306
Ellis County	13,075	2,554	3,363	4,121	3,037	$55,527	5.9%	2.8%	2.8%	794	19,378
El Paso County	61,672	27,042	15,047	13,131	6,452	$30,966	15.0%	14.2%	23.7%	20,726	77,537
Fort Bend County	43,524	7,283	10,690	12,998	12,553	$60,966	4.8%	5.5%	8.9%	6,653	78,530

Table G-2: Counties - Income, Poverty Status and Receipt of Food Stamps (SNAP)—*Continued*

	Income of Households with Householder 65 Years and Over					Poverty Rate of Persons			Households with 1 or More Persons 60 Years and Over	
	Total Households	Less Than $25,000	$25,000 - $49,999	$50,000 - $99,999	$100,000 or More	Median Household Income	55 to 64 Years	65 to 74 Years	75 Years and Over	Receiving SNAP	Not Receiving SNAP
Texas—Cont.											
Galveston County	30,752	7,914	7,799	8,233	6,806	$48,018	13.5%	8.1%	7.1%	4,449	42,140
Grayson County	14,802	3,477	4,585	4,850	1,890	$46,428	9.5%	7.0%	8.5%	1,415	19,355
Gregg County	11,452	3,214	3,700	2,798	1,740	$45,314	12.9%	7.6%	11.1%	1,347	16,561
Guadalupe County	12,067	2,816	3,115	3,759	2,377	$53,375	7.3%	11.4%	6.5%	699	19,503
Harris County	285,358	80,114	71,250	76,226	57,768	$46,799	12.2%	9.4%	13.0%	63,546	441,099
Harrison County	na	na	na	na	na	$40,325	9.9%	4.9%	7.2%	1,837	8,363
Hays County	13,714	2,650	3,503	4,781	2,780	$57,079	6.1%	5.6%	7.0%	1,661	21,255
Henderson County	10,841	3,774	3,389	2,277	1,401	$34,003	13.2%	8.3%	7.6%	855	15,243
Hidalgo County	56,271	27,120	13,971	10,963	4,217	$26,392	22.6%	25.4%	27.3%	25,550	60,986
Hunt County	9,007	2,864	2,768	2,402	973	$35,195	14.7%	5.9%	4.2%	1,508	13,219
Jefferson County	21,966	7,768	6,241	4,954	3,003	$34,208	10.8%	8.5%	13.5%	5,928	28,998
Johnson County	13,050	3,035	3,224	4,984	1,807	$52,703	9.2%	2.7%	6.3%	1,958	20,342
Kaufman County	8,730	2,112	2,057	2,871	1,690	$53,500	11.5%	7.5%	14.3%	1,050	13,544
Liberty County	7,206	2,459	2,103	1,818	826	$41,655	6.1%	6.6%	6.7%	1,213	9,483
Lubbock County	23,330	5,311	5,533	7,961	4,525	$53,797	7.7%	6.5%	6.9%	4,073	33,367
McLennan County	22,514	6,726	6,651	5,969	3,168	$41,305	7.6%	7.1%	6.0%	2,155	32,262
Midland County	12,129	3,493	2,782	3,124	2,730	$46,334	8.0%	2.6%	17.3%	948	18,762
Montgomery County	45,322	10,285	12,444	12,644	9,949	$49,898	8.3%	7.5%	10.6%	4,616	68,338
Nacogdoches County	6,068	1,915	2,029	1,614	510	$37,518	11.8%	11.6%	5.9%	1,194	7,586
Nueces County	31,260	11,015	7,066	8,174	5,005	$38,365	12.7%	11.0%	11.6%	8,797	43,247
Orange County	8,095	1,540	3,437	2,351	767	$43,761	7.5%	2.3%	6.6%	1,660	11,094
Parker County	11,869	2,739	2,418	3,771	2,941	$57,142	6.2%	3.1%	14.4%	669	17,879
Potter County	9,383	3,712	2,723	2,114	834	$32,707	16.9%	9.9%	9.2%	1,421	13,258
Randall County	12,575	2,326	4,319	3,277	2,653	$48,223	3.8%	3.2%	2.2%	367	17,724
Rockwall County	na	na	na	na	na	$52,268	3.3%	1.9%	4.4%	422	11,207
San Patricio County	5,873	1,933	1,528	1,592	820	$42,865	12.9%	14.8%	11.5%	2,099	6,846
Smith County	22,791	6,782	5,728	5,750	4,531	$44,119	14.0%	12.2%	10.2%	3,268	30,140
Tarrant County	141,809	39,025	32,530	39,843	30,411	$49,391	9.1%	6.3%	10.1%	18,679	216,582
Taylor County	11,722	3,378	3,426	3,038	1,880	$43,605	9.8%	6.6%	8.6%	1,918	16,407
Tom Green County	11,584	3,420	2,869	3,175	2,120	$44,982	11.1%	6.8%	7.2%	1,125	15,413
Travis County	73,603	14,163	15,198	20,835	23,407	$61,206	8.8%	6.8%	7.1%	8,938	116,757
Victoria County	9,159	3,024	3,487	1,756	892	$33,779	12.4%	8.8%	18.1%	1,970	11,813
Walker County	na	na	na	na	na	$42,406	10.3%	6.2%	8.6%	1,011	7,040
Webb County	15,185	7,405	3,125	3,278	1,377	$27,601	17.1%	21.0%	30.3%	5,891	18,786
Wichita County	12,421	3,821	3,911	2,855	1,834	$37,131	16.3%	8.8%	6.7%	2,047	16,734
Williamson County	35,790	5,929	8,211	13,102	8,548	$61,118	5.3%	2.3%	5.4%	3,070	56,011
Wise County	5,198	1,349	1,381	1,659	809	$45,695	9.6%	4.1%	17.9%	713	8,372
Utah											
Cache County	7,056	1,316	2,021	2,559	1,160	$52,307	4.2%	4.1%	11.8%	423	10,531
Davis County	20,403	2,667	4,708	6,915	6,113	$66,250	2.4%	3.9%	2.7%	1,676	30,928
Salt Lake County	76,120	15,095	19,185	24,479	17,361	$56,846	6.7%	4.0%	7.5%	10,233	111,913
Tooele County	na	na	na	na	na	$42,192	7.5%	2.7%	12.6%	550	6,444
Utah County	28,053	4,702	6,732	10,085	6,534	$60,342	5.5%	4.6%	4.9%	2,839	40,913
Washington County	22,266	4,821	6,416	7,844	3,185	$49,585	12.9%	5.4%	7.5%	1,799	26,811
Weber County	18,545	3,999	4,796	6,205	3,545	$51,913	7.9%	5.3%	9.2%	1,620	27,102
Vermont											
Chittenden County	16,604	3,497	4,322	4,831	3,954	$52,228	4.9%	9.9%	13.1%	2,097	23,328
Virginia											
Albemarle County	12,912	1,984	3,513	3,337	4,078	$59,752	6.0%	6.0%	6.2%	669	18,536
Arlington County	16,853	3,477	1,873	3,374	8,129	$93,449	5.2%	5.0%	15.1%	1,350	26,122
Augusta County	10,715	3,531	2,665	2,887	1,632	$44,925	9.2%	10.3%	8.7%	1,254	13,972
Bedford County	9,191	2,106	3,293	2,436	1,356	$41,781	12.8%	1.4%	10.9%	185	14,447
Chesterfield County	31,844	5,981	7,369	10,104	8,390	$59,449	5.1%	5.1%	5.8%	2,414	48,189
Fairfax County	85,588	10,715	11,348	22,189	41,336	$95,777	4.1%	3.1%	8.0%	6,315	139,459
Fauquier County	6,873	1,724	1,159	1,872	2,118	$61,173	1.4%	6.3%	6.8%	693	9,821
Frederick County	8,763	1,653	2,006	2,726	2,378	$60,863	4.3%	3.4%	2.3%	812	13,846
Hanover County	10,935	2,580	1,819	3,354	3,182	$60,141	2.9%	3.2%	10.5%	949	16,574
Henrico County	32,004	8,547	8,281	7,671	7,505	$46,905	6.8%	6.7%	10.3%	3,721	46,399
James City County	na	na	na	na	na	$79,036	7.1%	6.9%	2.9%	744	15,077
Loudoun County	19,719	2,531	2,723	5,905	8,560	$84,778	2.9%	2.4%	7.1%	1,452	37,306
Montgomery County	7,323	1,850	1,532	2,360	1,581	$54,248	11.1%	5.0%	1.1%	682	10,140
Prince William County	23,805	3,020	3,593	7,605	9,587	$86,477	3.6%	3.3%	7.6%	2,227	42,581
Roanoke County	12,225	2,771	4,231	3,616	1,607	$46,688	6.5%	3.8%	4.9%	798	16,812
Rockingham County	9,382	2,380	2,913	2,588	1,501	$43,302	6.8%	6.5%	10.7%	652	14,265
Spotsylvania County	10,491	1,854	1,893	4,019	2,725	$62,885	7.2%	7.4%	4.6%	1,539	15,668
Stafford County	7,863	780	1,432	3,269	2,382	$75,654	4.8%	1.5%	2.6%	382	13,975
York County	na	na	na	na	na	$65,237	5.7%	2.8%	13.4%	143	10,055
Washington											
Benton County	18,215	3,309	4,847	6,477	3,582	$53,977	7.4%	3.6%	2.9%	2,015	25,476
Chelan County	8,663	2,085	2,291	2,699	1,588	$48,048	6.0%	4.6%	8.5%	1,769	12,416
Clallam County	14,164	4,095	3,473	4,715	1,881	$45,612	11.0%	10.3%	6.4%	2,026	16,857
Clark County	45,341	9,520	12,639	13,330	9,852	$51,008	8.0%	4.4%	9.8%	5,952	64,083
Cowlitz County	13,407	3,681	4,031	4,100	1,595	$40,021	13.5%	5.9%	4.5%	3,461	17,090

Table G-2: Counties - Income, Poverty Status and Receipt of Food Stamps (SNAP)—*Continued*

		Income of Households with Householder 65 Years and Over					Poverty Rate of Persons			Households with 1 or More Persons 60 Years and Over	
	Total Households	Less Than $25,000	$25,000 - $49,999	$50,000 - $99,999	$100,000 or More	Median Household Income	55 to 64 Years	65 to 74 Years	75 Years and Over	Receiving SNAP	Not Receiving SNAP
Washington—Cont.											
Franklin County	4,766	622	1,595	1,607	942	$53,025	11.2%	8.2%	27.7%	1,340	6,620
Grant County	7,992	2,748	2,098	1,770	1,376	$38,994	11.3%	7.0%	16.2%	1,366	10,373
Grays Harbor County	8,920	2,096	2,975	2,540	1,309	$40,270	13.7%	6.0%	10.3%	2,195	11,683
Island County	12,750	2,581	3,093	4,470	2,606	$53,861	8.4%	6.5%	4.3%	1,023	16,717
King County	180,631	36,697	42,200	49,883	51,851	$57,921	7.0%	5.3%	9.8%	28,157	257,893
Kitsap County	30,033	5,677	7,023	10,174	7,159	$61,929	9.4%	4.9%	7.4%	3,427	41,509
Lewis County	10,886	2,981	3,975	2,544	1,386	$38,184	10.9%	6.1%	7.4%	2,650	13,083
Mason County	8,846	2,124	2,235	3,663	824	$52,683	12.8%	7.5%	5.3%	1,418	11,544
Pierce County	75,373	15,125	18,932	26,335	14,981	$54,145	7.4%	4.5%	6.9%	12,325	107,913
Skagit County	15,788	3,673	4,158	4,490	3,467	$50,733	8.0%	9.6%	5.7%	2,225	20,932
Snohomish County	65,481	13,073	15,899	21,223	15,286	$54,757	7.2%	5.2%	7.7%	11,788	98,755
Spokane County	52,471	13,913	16,619	14,703	7,236	$41,503	13.5%	6.7%	8.4%	11,098	68,688
Thurston County	29,900	6,155	7,084	10,641	6,020	$56,913	8.3%	5.3%	8.9%	3,807	42,555
Whatcom County	24,312	5,009	6,073	8,690	4,540	$56,088	11.8%	6.0%	7.0%	2,827	32,970
Yakima County	21,499	6,420	5,421	5,982	3,676	$44,042	13.4%	8.4%	10.1%	5,412	26,627
West Virginia											
Berkeley County	11,073	1,654	4,150	4,105	1,164	$45,129	13.1%	6.6%	5.4%	1,327	16,108
Cabell County	10,637	3,102	3,774	2,453	1,308	$37,480	19.1%	5.1%	8.2%	1,686	13,365
Harrison County	8,381	2,751	2,955	2,018	657	$35,853	12.0%	10.2%	9.1%	1,780	10,963
Kanawha County	24,807	7,551	8,523	5,398	3,335	$36,360	13.1%	9.1%	8.7%	3,954	31,264
Monongalia County	8,232	1,780	2,688	2,205	1,559	$46,844	14.0%	5.4%	3.6%	1,150	11,275
Raleigh County	10,449	3,997	3,184	1,909	1,359	$29,881	27.8%	9.0%	13.4%	3,693	11,298
Wood County	11,237	4,055	2,887	3,043	1,252	$38,648	9.3%	8.2%	11.3%	2,249	13,355
Wisconsin											
Brown County	24,964	7,068	8,875	5,840	3,181	$37,211	6.6%	4.6%	10.1%	3,425	34,368
Dane County	47,609	7,749	13,083	15,083	11,694	$56,596	3.7%	4.0%	6.6%	3,878	67,232
Dodge County	9,515	2,606	3,329	2,862	718	$39,478	5.4%	4.1%	9.9%	713	13,851
Eau Claire County	10,408	2,887	3,197	3,094	1,230	$45,080	7.2%	6.9%	4.8%	616	14,313
Fond du Lac County	11,716	3,722	3,887	3,119	988	$36,061	6.7%	7.8%	12.4%	1,627	15,941
Jefferson County	9,124	1,938	2,698	3,102	1,386	$48,829	4.2%	3.9%	5.0%	1,063	12,205
Kenosha County	14,984	3,898	4,478	4,558	2,050	$44,894	9.5%	5.9%	5.1%	2,330	21,261
La Crosse County	12,015	2,970	4,181	3,359	1,505	$41,429	3.7%	3.2%	7.8%	653	17,068
Manitowoc County	10,386	3,533	3,758	2,442	653	$35,381	9.8%	4.9%	8.6%	777	14,411
Marathon County	15,425	4,149	5,001	4,672	1,603	$38,645	5.4%	4.2%	10.3%	1,511	20,855
Milwaukee County	84,663	28,524	24,677	21,515	9,947	$36,457	15.7%	10.1%	12.8%	21,559	113,770
Outagamie County	17,486	5,488	5,861	4,562	1,575	$38,799	5.6%	3.7%	11.8%	1,431	25,421
Ozaukee County	11,685	3,542	2,747	2,936	2,460	$45,719	4.5%	4.2%	3.7%	385	17,159
Portage County	7,783	2,520	2,067	2,628	568	$41,675	8.8%	4.7%	10.3%	1,078	9,979
Racine County	20,635	5,316	6,048	6,407	2,864	$45,036	9.6%	8.3%	8.6%	3,073	28,418
Rock County	17,695	4,946	6,382	4,912	1,455	$39,189	10.4%	5.5%	7.3%	2,713	23,764
St. Croix County	7,760	1,753	2,615	2,457	935	$43,938	5.2%	2.1%	5.3%	326	11,688
Sheboygan County	13,487	3,622	4,607	3,854	1,404	$40,382	4.7%	3.1%	7.5%	837	18,547
Walworth County	11,193	2,976	2,814	3,232	2,171	$47,179	4.3%	6.3%	8.0%	1,196	15,501
Washington County	14,198	2,844	5,156	4,511	1,687	$44,667	3.6%	2.9%	6.8%	1,135	21,769
Waukesha County	46,371	9,590	12,503	14,872	9,406	$52,299	3.9%	3.7%	6.0%	1,986	67,369
Winnebago County	18,183	5,339	6,234	4,690	1,920	$37,327	7.8%	5.3%	8.9%	1,053	25,749
Wood County	9,953	2,878	2,723	3,662	690	$45,981	8.0%	3.2%	17.6%	1,222	12,891
Wyoming											
Laramie County	11,096	2,664	3,087	3,259	2,086	$48,352	6.8%	2.9%	5.0%	680	15,954
Natrona County	7,880	1,935	2,737	1,796	1,412	$40,939	7.4%	9.2%	5.4%	439	11,114

Table G-3: Cities - Income, Poverty Status and Receipt of Food Stamps (SNAP)

	Income of Households with Householder 65 Years and Over					Poverty Rate of Persons			Households with 1 or More Persons 60 Years and Over	
	Total Households	Less Than $25,000	$25,000 - $49,999	$50,000 - $99,999	$100,000 or More	Median Household Income	55 to 64 Years	65 to 74 Years	75 Years and Over	Receiving SNAP	Not Receiving SNAP
Alabama											
Auburn city	na	na	na	na	na	$58,098	9.5%	1.0%	2.7%	172	5,395
Birmingham city	22,749	9,994	5,876	4,190	2,689	$28,941	25.6%	15.4%	11.8%	6,847	28,370
Dothan city	8,443	2,674	2,130	2,152	1,487	$40,858	14.0%	8.9%	15.3%	1,026	10,782
Hoover city	8,841	1,223	1,737	2,891	2,990	$78,328	4.2%	2.6%	2.0%	94	12,061
Huntsville city	21,385	4,998	4,712	7,301	4,374	$55,464	11.8%	8.4%	8.0%	3,115	25,789
Mobile city	21,750	8,219	5,794	5,324	2,413	$36,067	21.0%	8.7%	9.4%	4,217	26,211
Montgomery city	18,587	6,576	4,067	5,084	2,860	$41,503	11.7%	9.2%	17.1%	4,965	23,566
Tuscaloosa city	7,840	2,563	1,522	1,971	1,784	$48,761	26.5%	13.2%	11.5%	1,164	12,089
Alaska											
Anchorage municipality	19,776	2,652	4,014	6,701	6,409	$72,750	6.9%	2.2%	7.4%	2,818	30,308
Arizona											
Avondale city	4,308	1,100	1,512	1,107	589	$43,220	14.0%	9.5%	12.1%	1,051	6,820
Buckeye city	na	na	na	na	na	$53,527	7.7%	6.0%	8.8%	968	8,253
Chandler city	16,709	3,632	4,257	5,254	3,566	$54,195	8.7%	3.9%	6.7%	922	27,384
Flagstaff city	4,178	698	571	1,349	1,560	$77,725	6.7%	4.2%	12.4%	179	5,992
Glendale city	18,642	5,586	5,354	5,004	2,698	$41,356	15.7%	7.2%	8.6%	4,044	27,709
Goodyear city	na	na	na	na	na	$64,400	6.0%	2.1%	3.6%	942	10,585
Mesa city	48,772	11,639	14,348	15,363	7,422	$47,143	8.2%	7.9%	7.8%	4,795	67,938
Peoria city	18,656	4,881	5,392	5,282	3,101	$46,791	8.7%	7.5%	8.4%	1,827	26,783
Phoenix city	107,131	31,613	28,864	27,876	18,764	$42,520	12.6%	7.4%	11.3%	20,517	163,197
Scottsdale city	36,272	6,893	8,389	9,602	11,388	$61,815	4.9%	4.3%	6.0%	1,103	51,312
Surprise city	18,125	3,853	4,216	7,418	2,638	$55,679	9.0%	4.0%	7.3%	766	22,948
Tempe city	13,034	2,614	2,464	4,264	3,692	$64,087	11.3%	4.6%	10.9%	1,801	18,821
Tucson city	52,276	18,435	14,176	13,282	6,383	$37,404	17.6%	12.8%	13.9%	10,846	67,873
Yuma city	9,186	3,501	2,403	2,176	1,106	$36,296	14.9%	13.4%	18.0%	2,039	12,366
Arkansas											
Conway city	4,447	1,027	1,388	883	1,149	$43,928	22.0%	8.5%	1.3%	753	5,838
Fayetteville city	4,201	708	1,038	1,413	1,042	$52,679	16.5%	3.9%	0.0%	740	7,437
Fort Smith city	8,043	1,981	2,852	2,225	985	$41,011	13.4%	11.5%	4.5%	1,094	10,156
Jonesboro city	5,818	1,871	1,532	1,974	441	$38,750	12.4%	4.8%	9.4%	1,298	7,585
Little Rock city	17,594	5,567	4,204	3,817	4,006	$43,618	13.2%	10.8%	12.0%	1,716	26,050
North Little Rock city	7,135	2,145	2,039	1,884	1,067	$43,526	11.7%	16.2%	9.3%	715	8,955
Rogers city	4,044	1,403	880	1,253	508	$47,627	12.9%	4.4%	4.2%	974	5,796
Springdale city	4,978	1,452	1,700	1,260	566	$36,475	3.5%	8.9%	8.6%	197	7,694
California											
Alameda city	8,447	2,029	2,066	2,011	2,341	$54,971	7.1%	7.2%	12.4%	629	12,179
Alhambra city	7,285	3,251	1,491	1,697	846	$31,910	15.3%	12.1%	15.2%	677	11,260
Anaheim city	20,945	6,308	3,703	5,758	5,176	$52,094	8.9%	11.9%	14.5%	4,063	33,730
Antioch city	6,874	1,737	1,251	2,421	1,465	$53,878	10.9%	5.9%	5.6%	1,618	11,942
Bakersfield city	22,204	6,271	5,894	5,501	4,538	$43,467	16.2%	7.5%	11.2%	4,278	36,293
Baldwin Park city	3,214	910	652	1,142	510	$56,172	9.5%	6.0%	9.9%	784	6,972
Bellflower city	3,817	1,741	824	712	540	$27,033	19.8%	4.9%	9.7%	880	7,208
Berkeley city	11,462	2,423	1,738	2,442	4,859	$86,382	11.6%	9.2%	17.7%	791	15,260
Buena Park city	4,904	675	1,229	1,477	1,523	$66,958	3.4%	4.0%	4.7%	330	8,859
Burbank city	10,096	4,049	1,696	2,490	1,861	$41,366	6.5%	7.5%	22.0%	430	15,035
Camarillo city	9,179	2,127	1,585	2,730	2,737	$60,961	1.5%	6.9%	7.0%	158	11,702
Carlsbad city	13,084	1,275	2,618	4,017	5,174	$81,462	14.1%	1.2%	6.0%	41	19,592
Carson city	6,971	1,803	1,244	1,805	2,119	$57,662	8.4%	7.3%	17.8%	771	11,322
Chico city	8,570	3,460	1,130	1,811	2,169	$42,079	12.2%	11.5%	13.7%	1,392	10,876
Chino city	5,716	1,496	1,047	1,624	1,549	$55,523	6.5%	6.3%	16.4%	323	9,718
Chino Hills city	na	na	na	na	na	$82,845	4.5%	1.5%	11.9%	352	9,066
Chula Vista city	14,910	4,822	3,048	3,331	3,709	$46,569	6.8%	9.7%	18.8%	2,502	26,886
Citrus Heights city	9,539	2,631	1,761	3,539	1,608	$54,138	7.7%	7.3%	19.9%	1,493	13,299
Clovis city	9,531	1,501	2,781	2,892	2,357	$53,505	11.4%	8.1%	0.0%	666	12,963
Compton city	4,758	2,422	1,165	664	507	$23,486	19.1%	16.0%	36.0%	1,178	7,875
Concord city	11,688	2,897	2,221	3,265	3,305	$63,144	8.5%	7.5%	6.6%	1,043	19,293
Corona city	7,160	1,604	1,536	2,505	1,515	$59,299	9.1%	9.0%	12.3%	914	13,573
Costa Mesa city	8,335	2,790	1,730	2,051	1,764	$46,478	8.6%	12.3%	16.4%	811	12,000
Daly City city	na	na	na	na	na	$65,432	6.5%	6.3%	8.8%	565	13,926
Davis city	4,645	591	466	1,178	2,410	$101,778	8.4%	3.2%	12.3%	0	6,723
Downey city	7,277	1,634	1,648	1,822	2,173	$59,028	10.1%	7.5%	5.6%	452	13,581
El Cajon city	5,999	1,709	1,606	1,608	1,076	$42,993	14.8%	8.0%	18.8%	1,252	10,120
Elk Grove city	12,035	1,677	2,852	4,038	3,468	$71,260	5.4%	1.9%	11.6%	726	21,503
El Monte city	6,620	2,507	1,797	1,230	1,086	$35,689	15.1%	13.0%	20.0%	1,760	11,665
Escondido city	12,019	3,796	2,629	3,105	2,489	$45,423	14.0%	9.3%	17.4%	1,515	18,175
Fairfield city	8,335	1,432	1,944	2,596	2,363	$64,965	7.0%	4.8%	9.3%	721	13,647
Folsom city	na	na	na	na	na	$64,054	6.1%	2.3%	9.3%	465	9,221
Fontana city	7,231	2,420	1,852	2,070	889	$41,468	8.0%	6.5%	13.5%	1,644	14,116
Fremont city	13,788	2,248	2,879	3,453	5,208	$68,288	3.9%	5.0%	9.0%	786	25,535
Fresno city	36,313	12,426	7,851	9,961	6,075	$41,672	20.8%	10.5%	12.4%	6,629	51,302
Fullerton city	10,226	1,201	3,043	3,288	2,694	$59,695	6.5%	3.5%	8.1%	501	17,071
Garden Grove city	9,679	3,052	1,980	2,537	2,110	$48,911	12.7%	8.7%	25.7%	1,827	18,713
Glendale city	18,215	8,284	3,797	3,651	2,483	$27,386	12.6%	11.1%	21.3%	2,021	29,778
Hawthorne city	4,888	1,506	1,032	1,324	1,026	$41,740	6.4%	4.3%	15.2%	783	8,222
Hayward city	10,293	2,251	2,798	3,249	1,995	$51,593	5.9%	8.4%	3.6%	1,394	16,976

Table G-3: Cities - Income, Poverty Status and Receipt of Food Stamps (SNAP)—*Continued*

	Income of Households with Householder 65 Years and Over						Poverty Rate of Persons			Households with 1 or More Persons 60 Years and Over	
	Total Households	Less Than $25,000	$25,000 - $49,999	$50,000 - $99,999	$100,000 or More	Median Household Income	55 to 64 Years	65 to 74 Years	75 Years and Over	Receiving SNAP	Not Receiving SNAP
California—Cont.											
Hemet city	12,375	4,759	4,315	2,555	746	$30,255	16.1%	17.7%	12.2%	2,100	14,952
Hesperia city	6,818	2,304	978	2,739	797	$51,031	16.6%	12.3%	7.0%	1,585	10,290
Huntington Beach city	20,467	3,705	3,995	6,632	6,135	$70,344	9.3%	5.4%	7.6%	933	29,708
Indio city	12,417	4,720	2,319	3,342	2,036	$40,763	11.1%	15.8%	11.5%	531	16,122
Inglewood city	7,918	2,951	1,671	2,121	1,175	$40,712	15.5%	9.2%	14.4%	1,194	11,226
Irvine city	17,345	4,041	2,391	4,192	6,721	$73,756	10.7%	7.5%	9.3%	1,013	27,803
Jurupa Valley city	5,476	1,339	1,539	1,226	1,372	$47,619	6.4%	7.1%	8.7%	1,188	9,642
Laguna Niguel city	na	na	na	na	na	$77,086	9.4%	4.3%	14.0%	42	11,676
Lake Elsinore city	na	na	na	na	na	$33,277	8.4%	8.9%	9.2%	492	5,169
Lake Forest city	7,709	1,022	1,613	2,621	2,453	$72,672	4.4%	6.6%	9.3%	282	11,705
Lakewood city	5,200	1,060	1,480	1,690	970	$51,899	7.2%	6.5%	10.9%	274	9,292
Lancaster city	8,875	3,191	1,968	1,795	1,921	$39,599	18.2%	12.2%	14.3%	1,367	14,647
Livermore city	na	na	na	na	na	$79,507	0.6%	3.2%	1.7%	380	11,360
Lodi City	6,230	1,437	1,539	1,499	1,755	$51,538	9.9%	9.0%	18.1%	521	9,594
Long Beach city	31,067	8,974	7,619	7,758	6,716	$44,702	12.3%	8.0%	14.1%	3,416	52,570
Los Angeles city	288,751	98,678	58,309	63,420	68,344	$44,370	15.0%	12.5%	17.7%	38,148	449,039
Lynwood city	na	na	na	na	na	$45,500	8.1%	7.2%	19.2%	964	5,464
Madera city	na	na	na	na	na	$17,361	14.3%	19.7%	17.8%	906	5,307
Manteca city	7,040	1,568	1,888	2,281	1,303	$50,620	7.0%	5.0%	1.7%	1,122	10,080
Menifee city	9,799	2,719	2,559	2,919	1,602	$45,224	11.2%	5.6%	13.5%	685	14,260
Merced city	6,613	1,834	1,694	1,516	1,569	$42,334	17.3%	14.3%	11.5%	586	9,405
Milpitas city	na	na	na	na	na	$71,489	8.3%	6.0%	19.7%	358	8,587
Mission Viejo city	na	na	na	na	na	$77,366	5.0%	2.1%	15.7%	459	15,654
Modesto city	15,223	4,146	3,931	4,348	2,798	$47,865	16.6%	8.5%	7.1%	2,775	22,554
Moreno Valley city	6,958	1,595	1,537	2,284	1,542	$57,763	12.1%	4.8%	11.1%	1,818	13,225
Mountain View city	5,756	971	1,265	1,548	1,972	$69,200	11.0%	4.0%	10.7%	295	8,622
Murrieta city	7,282	914	1,772	2,776	1,820	$59,853	5.6%	4.9%	8.3%	247	11,071
Napa city	8,742	1,654	1,896	2,558	2,634	$58,545	4.9%	9.0%	2.6%	619	12,734
Newport Beach city	11,992	1,892	1,515	2,772	5,813	$95,000	11.9%	4.7%	14.2%	107	17,027
Norwalk city	6,801	2,768	1,059	1,762	1,212	$37,886	13.4%	11.5%	14.6%	1,459	11,225
Oakland city	37,316	12,566	7,118	7,545	10,087	$45,618	12.5%	15.3%	13.8%	4,822	52,395
Oceanside city	18,880	4,880	3,758	5,820	4,422	$54,336	5.8%	6.8%	6.7%	1,661	25,831
Ontario city	8,310	2,220	1,899	2,695	1,496	$50,457	11.0%	10.0%	21.6%	1,521	13,737
Orange city	9,020	2,183	1,321	2,711	2,805	$65,722	6.8%	6.9%	11.7%	683	15,577
Oxnard city	9,102	2,275	2,087	2,575	2,165	$53,114	6.9%	4.5%	10.7%	1,968	17,309
Palmdale city	8,879	2,510	3,071	1,733	1,565	$37,175	8.4%	5.8%	8.6%	2,071	15,857
Palo Alto city	na	na	na	na	na	$99,933	6.1%	5.3%	8.8%	304	11,364
Pasadena city	14,655	5,158	2,212	2,983	4,302	$49,598	10.2%	9.3%	21.0%	730	20,110
Perris city	na	na	na	na	na	$45,250	8.6%	8.1%	10.7%	908	3,772
Pittsburg city	na	na	na	na	na	$41,083	11.5%	5.0%	18.5%	897	6,815
Pleasanton city	na	na	na	na	na	$75,403	3.1%	5.4%	10.9%	508	10,495
Pomona city	8,556	2,112	2,251	1,959	2,234	$47,071	10.5%	10.2%	11.9%	1,480	14,167
Rancho Cordova city	7,093	2,009	2,432	1,818	834	$41,264	12.9%	9.6%	9.0%	1,096	10,375
Rancho Cucamonga city	10,869	2,070	2,435	2,435	3,929	$63,281	5.0%	4.0%	10.3%	2,219	19,272
Redding city	10,065	2,573	2,786	2,789	1,917	$44,400	9.5%	7.3%	16.5%	1,009	13,892
Redlands city	7,484	1,917	2,351	1,469	1,747	$42,041	5.5%	1.3%	13.1%	365	10,853
Redondo Beach city	na	na	na	na	na	$77,219	5.5%	4.9%	2.2%	83	9,275
Redwood City city	na	na	na	na	na	$64,801	7.7%	13.4%	2.8%	612	10,410
Rialto city	5,957	1,481	1,427	1,925	1,124	$51,335	10.8%	8.9%	14.1%	2,097	9,706
Richmond city	8,175	1,667	1,545	2,649	2,314	$67,781	8.5%	9.9%	12.1%	881	13,242
Riverside city	17,387	3,820	3,468	5,091	5,008	$59,607	8.6%	8.0%	11.1%	1,876	28,847
Rocklin city	na	na	na	na	na	$60,201	1.7%	3.7%	6.4%	162	7,804
Roseville city	14,164	4,246	2,954	3,402	3,562	$47,438	6.9%	8.6%	11.7%	501	20,582
Sacramento city	40,628	12,528	9,261	10,237	8,602	$44,972	11.8%	10.6%	13.3%	6,142	60,129
Salinas city	8,116	1,991	2,055	2,144	1,926	$50,091	7.9%	10.6%	15.4%	646	12,399
San Bernardino city	10,266	4,271	2,127	2,331	1,537	$35,581	19.8%	14.2%	16.7%	3,870	15,375
San Buenaventura (Ventura) city	12,031	2,672	2,592	2,654	4,113	$59,850	8.3%	8.4%	10.0%	830	18,038
San Clemente city	na	na	na	na	na	$79,219	8.5%	5.9%	7.1%	908	9,962
San Diego city	110,754	24,244	23,365	30,728	32,417	$60,924	9.2%	8.1%	9.7%	11,280	162,990
San Francisco city	83,021	25,801	14,774	19,172	23,274	$51,999	11.7%	9.2%	17.0%	6,237	120,335
San Jose city	68,180	15,773	11,571	17,646	23,190	$64,029	7.5%	7.2%	11.6%	6,531	116,499
San Leandro city	7,415	1,578	1,613	2,342	1,882	$58,391	6.9%	6.2%	10.3%	1,060	12,717
San Marcos city	6,903	1,851	2,143	1,996	913	$41,344	4.2%	14.2%	12.4%	285	10,887
San Mateo city	10,492	2,255	1,633	2,946	3,658	$78,298	8.3%	6.5%	5.2%	415	15,336
San Ramon city	na	na	na	na	na	$44,076	6.3%	6.7%	17.0%	55	8,152
Santa Ana city	14,538	5,053	2,998	3,717	2,770	$45,161	9.5%	13.2%	20.2%	2,374	25,306
Santa Barbara city	10,865	1,756	1,967	2,793	4,349	$77,182	12.8%	6.4%	5.9%	625	15,298
Santa Clara city	8,261	1,835	1,513	2,509	2,404	$65,164	6.1%	5.1%	10.1%	429	13,738
Santa Clarita city	16,083	3,423	3,018	5,135	4,507	$62,025	5.6%	4.8%	13.0%	1,772	24,911
Santa Cruz city	na	na	na	na	na	$91,839	6.9%	5.9%	9.4%	543	7,152
Santa Maria city	5,010	941	1,553	1,525	991	$50,688	9.2%	3.3%	8.5%	623	8,468
Santa Monica city	11,136	3,910	1,679	1,860	3,687	$49,447	16.8%	10.7%	18.1%	582	14,919
Santa Rosa city	20,307	4,638	5,107	6,121	4,441	$51,749	7.6%	9.8%	7.5%	683	28,139
Simi Valley city	13,520	1,928	4,576	4,060	2,956	$50,970	3.9%	3.9%	10.5%	775	19,469
South Gate city	4,131	1,208	1,229	1,084	610	$37,591	13.4%	13.6%	8.6%	1,283	7,020

Table G-3: Cities - Income, Poverty Status and Receipt of Food Stamps (SNAP)—*Continued*

	Income of Households with Householder 65 Years and Over					Poverty Rate of Persons			Households with 1 or More Persons 60 Years and Over	
	Total Households	Less Than $25,000	$25,000 - $49,999	$50,000 - $99,999	$100,000 or More	Median Household Income	55 to 64 Years	65 to 74 Years	75 Years and Over	Receiving SNAP	Not Receiving SNAP
California—Cont.											
South San Francisco city	na	na	na	na	na	$74,283	na	na	na	313	10,720
Stockton city	19,714	5,931	4,275	5,661	3,847	$47,763	13.5%	11.2%	11.2%	3,861	32,261
Sunnyvale city	9,604	1,708	1,714	3,487	2,695	$60,752	4.8%	1.6%	12.3%	416	16,803
Temecula city	6,337	1,275	817	2,252	1,993	$69,060	7.8%	3.2%	8.9%	447	11,069
Thousand Oaks city	13,526	1,985	2,584	3,538	5,419	$76,060	5.7%	5.6%	9.0%	383	19,137
Torrance city	15,257	1,957	3,972	4,337	4,991	$65,774	8.9%	4.0%	4.4%	410	24,090
Tracy city	na	na	na	na	na	$64,441	4.7%	4.2%	11.4%	636	8,174
Turlock city	5,417	2,016	1,188	1,474	739	$32,108	11.1%	8.6%	24.7%	675	7,860
Tustin city	4,036	737	637	1,127	1,535	$71,985	5.1%	6.4%	19.5%	1,177	6,692
Union City city	na	na	na	na	na	$89,290	6.0%	1.9%	10.8%	712	8,563
Upland city	6,867	1,766	1,624	1,624	1,853	$52,520	7.3%	7.0%	10.3%	378	10,362
Vacaville city	8,159	1,391	2,129	2,356	2,283	$61,310	8.2%	4.2%	7.1%	567	12,504
Vallejo city	10,423	2,277	2,106	3,307	2,733	$71,526	11.2%	5.6%	7.6%	1,682	17,504
Victorville city	6,064	1,583	1,920	2,293	268	$41,312	19.5%	4.1%	4.2%	1,408	8,792
Visalia city	9,818	2,361	2,940	2,684	1,833	$48,474	9.8%	10.0%	9.9%	1,678	13,170
Vista city	5,624	1,629	1,052	1,457	1,486	$52,582	5.9%	9.1%	13.1%	204	10,290
Walnut Creek city	na	na	na	na	na	$69,840	3.6%	4.5%	8.7%	229	18,547
West Covina city	7,546	2,037	1,354	2,734	1,421	$53,111	8.8%	10.4%	10.3%	809	13,882
Westminster city	7,501	2,636	1,637	1,760	1,468	$42,784	17.8%	18.9%	20.4%	1,195	11,564
Whittier city	6,420	1,913	1,100	1,967	1,440	$51,306	6.1%	7.2%	8.9%	210	11,499
Yorba Linda city	na	na	na	na	na	$75,428	1.6%	6.0%	5.8%	219	11,272
Yuba City city	6,382	1,631	2,149	1,322	1,280	$42,477	17.6%	11.6%	11.6%	408	9,580
Colorado											
Arvada city	14,039	2,873	3,181	3,717	4,268	$59,417	3.0%	4.8%	4.9%	847	19,579
Aurora city	26,953	6,391	6,728	9,055	4,779	$51,262	7.2%	6.3%	8.1%	3,479	40,756
Boulder city	7,982	1,370	1,894	1,757	2,961	$65,688	7.1%	4.2%	3.8%	229	11,919
Broomfield city	5,908	749	1,490	1,978	1,691	$64,367	3.9%	3.3%	3.2%	112	8,414
Centennial city	9,508	922	2,207	2,922	3,457	$77,116	2.7%	1.9%	2.9%	113	14,424
Colorado Springs city	37,885	10,238	9,283	10,362	8,002	$48,629	10.7%	4.7%	10.7%	4,686	54,861
Denver city	56,532	17,027	12,680	15,465	11,360	$45,728	12.2%	8.7%	12.0%	8,025	76,271
Fort Collins city	11,496	2,879	3,267	3,428	1,922	$45,405	6.4%	8.7%	11.3%	1,101	16,868
Greeley city	7,087	2,332	1,790	1,786	1,179	$40,550	13.4%	7.5%	14.0%	1,100	11,776
Lakewood city	16,911	4,639	3,926	5,080	3,266	$47,620	6.2%	6.0%	13.1%	876	25,521
Longmont city	9,656	1,951	2,710	2,677	2,318	$51,049	8.9%	5.8%	5.4%	983	13,544
Loveland city	8,409	1,985	2,539	2,130	1,755	$47,769	1.1%	8.5%	8.0%	907	11,694
Pueblo city	13,875	5,941	3,713	3,438	783	$29,630	18.9%	15.1%	19.6%	3,354	15,738
Thornton city	7,800	2,109	2,162	2,229	1,300	$42,323	4.5%	2.6%	3.3%	858	11,743
Westminster city	9,916	2,242	2,731	2,841	2,102	$49,897	4.9%	2.4%	4.8%	536	16,247
Connecticut											
Bridgeport city	10,346	5,066	1,826	2,317	1,137	$26,760	22.3%	18.9%	15.9%	5,867	12,347
Danbury city	6,133	1,023	1,693	1,851	1,566	$55,370	12.4%	3.0%	7.2%	578	9,023
Hartford city	8,831	4,907	1,621	1,228	1,075	$22,360	26.0%	21.8%	17.3%	5,738	8,402
New Britain city	5,621	2,174	1,655	950	842	$30,006	16.1%	13.3%	6.9%	2,389	6,916
New Haven city	7,968	3,514	1,327	1,668	1,459	$33,689	28.9%	15.8%	30.8%	3,789	8,596
Norwalk city	10,872	2,923	2,422	3,097	2,430	$50,689	10.0%	8.6%	10.2%	1,686	14,627
Stamford city	12,629	3,638	1,881	3,088	4,022	$57,847	8.0%	13.9%	12.7%	2,212	17,330
Waterbury city	9,041	3,711	3,254	1,573	503	$30,209	8.9%	11.4%	10.5%	4,658	9,949
Delaware											
Wilmington city	5,866	1,913	1,851	1,372	730	$36,250	25.8%	12.5%	7.5%	1,443	8,415
District of Columbia											
Washington city	58,898	18,137	10,931	13,243	16,587	$50,873	19.5%	12.3%	20.7%	15,847	69,673
Florida											
Boca Raton city	18,122	4,130	2,944	4,065	6,983	$77,395	7.9%	5.8%	8.4%	377	24,366
Boynton Beach city	10,430	3,638	2,921	2,723	1,148	$36,016	4.5%	22.1%	11.3%	1,731	11,754
Cape Coral city	27,070	7,525	7,131	7,837	4,577	$44,579	13.5%	9.0%	12.6%	2,093	34,686
Clearwater city	17,120	6,500	5,130	3,573	1,917	$34,222	10.4%	12.6%	14.1%	3,321	20,145
Coral Springs city	8,449	1,472	1,965	2,415	2,597	$64,424	8.2%	5.2%	3.6%	2,360	13,338
Daytona Beach city	8,605	2,140	2,911	2,476	1,078	$42,710	24.9%	8.7%	14.4%	2,041	10,618
Deerfield Beach city	12,200	4,859	3,032	2,830	1,479	$33,694	16.7%	17.5%	17.9%	2,178	15,000
Delray Beach city	11,705	2,423	3,056	3,942	2,284	$52,172	15.8%	6.4%	10.6%	546	14,993
Deltona city	7,276	1,852	2,953	1,788	683	$40,102	11.3%	7.3%	12.9%	2,296	10,694
Fort Lauderdale city	19,813	5,247	4,536	5,104	4,926	$50,913	14.8%	8.5%	8.6%	5,042	27,355
Fort Myers city	10,903	3,500	3,242	2,357	1,804	$40,374	13.8%	7.6%	15.3%	1,077	14,418
Gainesville city	8,012	2,588	1,733	2,185	1,506	$44,250	11.2%	11.7%	7.7%	1,149	10,089
Hialeah city	21,708	12,221	4,561	3,065	1,861	$20,925	12.8%	21.0%	25.6%	17,662	18,908
Hollywood city	14,285	4,393	3,821	3,641	2,430	$43,798	9.6%	8.7%	11.6%	2,873	19,558
Homestead city	na	na	na	na	na	$27,386	24.3%	7.8%	26.5%	2,168	2,589
Jacksonville city	76,032	24,154	17,881	22,085	11,912	$44,431	11.6%	8.6%	11.0%	21,107	101,077
Kissimmee city	na	na	na	na	na	$32,835	9.9%	14.1%	12.9%	2,188	6,646
Lakeland city	13,155	4,718	3,933	2,940	1,564	$32,285	19.7%	17.4%	13.3%	3,029	15,641
Largo city	14,786	4,184	5,502	3,635	1,465	$36,625	12.9%	7.9%	5.5%	2,039	18,237
Lauderhill city	na	na	na	na	na	$30,226	11.3%	18.6%	22.5%	2,892	6,582

Table G-3: Cities - Income, Poverty Status and Receipt of Food Stamps (SNAP)—*Continued*

	Income of Households with Householder 65 Years and Over					Poverty Rate of Persons			Households with 1 or More Persons 60 Years and Over	
	Total Households	Less Than $25,000	$25,000 - $49,999	$50,000 - $99,999	$100,000 or More	Median Household Income	55 to 64 Years	65 to 74 Years	75 Years and Over	Receiving SNAP	Not Receiving SNAP
Florida—Cont.											
Melbourne city	10,170	4,347	1,949	2,568	1,306	$29,888	10.8%	9.1%	16.3%	2,283	13,589
Miami city	45,095	25,712	7,520	7,142	4,721	$20,895	23.5%	27.9%	28.8%	31,220	37,905
Miami Beach city	10,710	4,590	1,762	1,878	2,480	$35,216	16.9%	18.3%	37.5%	3,946	11,429
Miami Gardens city	9,742	3,649	2,560	2,559	974	$37,396	15.2%	19.9%	19.7%	5,758	10,054
Miramar city	na	na	na	na	na	$47,728	5.8%	9.0%	11.4%	2,140	10,551
North Port city	na	na	na	na	na	$56,995	na	na	na	1,146	13,633
Orlando city	18,900	7,517	4,539	4,915	1,929	$35,377	11.8%	11.2%	13.1%	5,798	27,220
Palm Bay city	15,364	5,086	4,516	4,157	1,605	$37,413	11.2%	9.5%	11.3%	853	20,897
Palm Coast city	14,828	2,884	3,300	6,347	2,297	$55,763	6.1%	4.9%	6.6%	1,049	17,821
Pembroke Pines city	18,567	9,303	3,566	3,717	1,981	$24,910	11.6%	23.3%	34.2%	3,176	24,741
Plantation city	8,418	2,189	2,134	1,781	2,314	$47,857	6.3%	12.3%	4.4%	1,295	11,934
Pompano Beach city	13,352	3,668	3,240	4,246	2,198	$48,517	11.9%	10.2%	8.7%	3,177	17,297
Port St. Lucie city	21,897	5,277	6,598	6,722	3,300	$45,203	7.6%	7.7%	6.4%	2,465	31,038
St. Petersburg city	28,351	7,913	7,306	8,096	5,036	$44,421	10.4%	8.6%	11.9%	4,824	37,207
Sunrise city	11,102	4,661	3,808	1,798	835	$30,270	7.0%	9.1%	16.1%	3,743	13,509
Tallahassee city	11,880	3,247	2,814	2,737	3,082	$48,916	13.2%	8.6%	12.2%	2,957	16,674
Tamarac city	11,743	3,895	3,281	3,656	911	$34,460	14.1%	11.2%	8.7%	2,416	13,519
Tampa city	31,364	12,952	7,563	5,796	5,053	$33,529	14.5%	14.4%	12.5%	10,364	37,714
Weston city	na	na	na	na	na	$75,730	6.0%	6.2%	2.8%	278	5,670
West Palm Beach city	12,879	3,792	3,182	2,837	3,068	$46,371	10.1%	12.4%	5.8%	2,773	15,473
Georgia											
Albany city	6,242	2,831	1,505	1,190	716	$29,798	24.4%	21.7%	23.0%	1,790	7,737
Alpharetta city	na	na	na	na	na	$61,850	1.8%	2.7%	5.1%	0	6,556
Athens-Clarke County unified govt (bal)	9,273	2,243	2,814	2,131	2,085	$43,800	14.9%	8.0%	9.9%	1,697	12,707
Atlanta city	40,686	17,570	7,857	7,222	8,037	$32,812	20.2%	15.5%	22.2%	12,103	46,274
Augusta-Richmond County consolidated govt (bal)	18,909	6,870	5,636	4,244	2,159	$32,867	18.8%	12.8%	11.0%	3,308	24,447
Columbus city	17,648	5,118	5,206	5,126	2,198	$40,542	19.9%	12.2%	9.3%	3,991	22,619
Johns Creek city	na	na	na	na	na	$70,544	0.9%	0.0%	7.0%	260	8,784
Macon-Bibb County	15,152	4,953	4,582	3,790	1,827	$40,435	18.8%	8.5%	22.8%	3,755	18,999
Roswell city	7,520	1,040	1,839	1,576	3,065	$71,991	4.6%	0.0%	1.7%	1,035	12,610
Sandy Springs city	9,541	2,003	1,597	2,530	3,411	$65,884	4.8%	2.9%	12.9%	536	13,331
Savannah city	13,243	4,252	3,852	2,892	2,247	$42,790	17.1%	7.4%	14.4%	3,185	15,901
South Fulton city	na	na	na	na	na	$50,523	6.7%	4.4%	11.8%	1,657	10,682
Warner Robins city	na	na	na	na	na	$45,686	14.4%	10.7%	5.3%	632	8,920
Hawaii											
Urban Honolulu CDP	40,268	9,522	8,209	9,418	13,119	$58,572	9.0%	7.5%	9.9%	5,989	53,098
Iowa											
Boise City city	22,584	7,150	6,622	5,617	3,195	$37,472	5.0%	7.0%	18.0%	1,395	32,498
Meridian city	na	na	na	na	na	$52,259	6.9%	3.3%	9.3%	205	9,720
Nampa city	9,508	2,717	3,348	2,513	930	$40,175	8.6%	7.3%	6.0%	979	12,660
Illinois											
Aurora city	11,020	2,996	3,070	3,174	1,780	$41,750	6.7%	8.2%	4.4%	2,404	16,176
Bloomington city	6,317	1,438	1,279	1,567	2,033	$62,013	11.9%	6.7%	10.7%	880	9,574
Champaign city	5,774	816	1,195	1,874	1,889	$66,190	4.9%	1.0%	8.4%	707	8,216
Chicago city	229,844	92,826	54,232	47,472	35,314	$32,795	18.3%	13.6%	14.7%	77,849	280,726
Decatur city	9,140	2,643	3,060	2,171	1,266	$39,330	15.2%	10.3%	8.5%	2,296	11,640
Elgin city	7,342	2,247	2,178	1,745	1,172	$38,427	5.2%	6.4%	3.5%	1,152	12,418
Evanston city	7,379	1,563	1,271	1,568	2,977	$73,448	16.5%	1.1%	7.1%	1,014	9,543
Joliet city	8,394	1,821	2,137	2,880	1,556	$52,479	9.9%	7.0%	6.8%	2,127	12,488
Naperville city	9,457	1,186	1,856	3,185	3,230	$70,406	3.3%	2.4%	7.3%	481	16,731
Peoria city	10,274	3,445	1,670	3,248	1,911	$50,246	19.0%	11.5%	10.0%	1,861	14,665
Rockford city	16,750	4,739	5,177	4,259	2,575	$39,716	15.6%	7.6%	6.3%	3,516	21,222
Springfield city	12,893	3,019	3,171	3,993	2,710	$52,152	11.9%	8.2%	4.7%	2,537	16,846
Waukegan city	4,818	1,561	1,558	1,202	497	$36,708	10.6%	11.2%	14.1%	982	6,910
Indiana											
Bloomington city	5,687	1,116	1,829	1,561	1,181	$48,174	28.4%	5.8%	0.1%	679	7,410
Carmel city	na	na	na	na	na	$69,042	3.4%	0.0%	6.4%	177	12,288
Evansville city	11,731	4,211	3,743	3,212	565	$33,723	20.5%	9.4%	11.0%	1,786	16,346
Fishers city	na	na	na	na	na	$50,281	4.6%	1.8%	7.9%	0	9,376
Fort Wayne city	24,810	8,050	7,739	5,810	3,211	$37,822	8.7%	5.1%	6.8%	3,786	32,294
Gary city	9,418	3,090	3,459	2,433	436	$35,291	15.2%	16.3%	11.5%	2,604	10,655
Hammond city	7,138	2,525	1,805	2,043	765	$38,754	22.3%	8.5%	6.7%	918	10,122
Indianapolis city (bal)	68,504	20,839	20,490	18,053	9,122	$40,094	13.5%	7.3%	10.9%	13,154	96,834
Lafayette city	6,077	1,821	1,999	1,084	1,173	$40,493	16.7%	3.1%	5.7%	831	9,238
Muncie city	6,857	2,707	1,979	1,845	326	$32,692	13.1%	3.9%	9.3%	1,413	8,189
Noblesville city	na	na	na	na	na	$44,444	na	na	na	183	6,590
South Bend city	9,506	4,064	3,211	1,320	911	$29,776	19.2%	17.9%	14.3%	1,369	13,277
Iowa											
Ames city	na	na	na	na	na	$58,353	0.6%	4.7%	2.8%	46	5,588
Ankeny city	na	na	na	na	na	$44,933	3.6%	0.0%	10.5%	56	7,111
Cedar Rapids city	12,836	3,320	3,934	3,752	1,830	$44,569	7.2%	5.1%	6.3%	1,307	17,536
Davenport city	9,367	2,829	2,826	2,433	1,279	$39,713	10.2%	6.8%	10.6%	1,079	14,207

Table G-3: Cities - Income, Poverty Status and Receipt of Food Stamps (SNAP)—*Continued*

	Income of Households with Householder 65 Years and Over					Poverty Rate of Persons			Households with 1 or More Persons 60 Years and Over	
	Total Households	Less Than $25,000	$25,000 - $49,999	$50,000 - $99,999	$100,000 or More	Median Household Income	55 to 64 Years	65 to 74 Years	75 Years and Over	Receiving SNAP	Not Receiving SNAP
Iowa—Cont.											
Des Moines city	16,685	4,917	5,316	4,566	1,886	$41,391	15.9%	5.2%	9.9%	3,423	22,828
Iowa City city	5,255	943	1,206	1,883	1,223	$65,012	8.7%	3.7%	3.6%	205	8,334
Sioux City city	7,283	1,842	2,179	2,329	933	$41,782	11.7%	7.1%	3.7%	1,113	11,036
Waterloo city	8,154	2,649	2,161	2,314	1,030	$42,433	16.7%	5.8%	15.1%	1,504	9,846
West Des Moines city	6,358	1,020	2,395	1,526	1,417	$47,320	4.1%	6.2%	2.6%	616	8,844
Kansas											
Kansas City city	11,709	3,584	3,475	3,209	1,441	$39,072	16.1%	9.9%	4.7%	2,202	17,219
Lawrence city	7,647	2,223	1,557	2,212	1,655	$50,214	11.2%	6.6%	14.5%	537	10,305
Olathe city	8,432	1,499	2,119	3,173	1,641	$56,191	10.5%	6.7%	4.7%	857	13,105
Overland Park city	19,297	3,278	5,424	6,443	4,152	$54,648	3.5%	3.8%	1.5%	562	29,636
Shawnee city	na	na	na	na	na	$55,992	2.3%	2.1%	6.0%	147	7,111
Topeka city	15,459	5,448	5,030	2,774	2,207	$39,085	17.8%	13.4%	12.2%	1,771	20,201
Wichita city	36,646	10,670	11,438	10,307	4,231	$40,497	14.5%	6.1%	7.1%	5,480	50,903
Kentucky											
Bowling Green city	5,035	2,450	1,144	796	645	$26,082	21.6%	2.4%	10.8%	942	7,857
Lexington-Fayette urban county	26,964	5,607	7,367	8,276	5,714	$51,536	9.7%	3.9%	5.5%	2,580	38,891
Louisville/Jefferson County metro govt (bal)	61,682	18,430	17,051	17,732	8,469	$41,177	15.1%	8.9%	7.5%	9,645	84,753
Louisiana											
Baton Rouge city	21,311	6,066	5,484	5,235	4,526	$47,440	20.4%	10.5%	12.0%	4,830	26,108
Bossier City city	6,459	1,592	1,915	1,986	966	$49,167	12.1%	8.0%	9.8%	991	8,532
Kenner city	7,446	2,794	1,861	1,454	1,337	$34,178	15.7%	12.8%	14.7%	2,263	9,342
Lafayette city	11,790	2,417	3,735	3,358	2,280	$48,488	10.9%	6.0%	8.0%	1,468	15,713
Lake Charles city	8,012	3,771	1,334	2,044	863	$27,184	9.9%	8.9%	17.1%	1,491	11,340
New Orleans city	35,584	16,232	7,521	6,609	5,222	$29,641	24.2%	15.9%	24.3%	9,253	45,515
Shreveport city	19,851	6,778	5,175	5,657	2,241	$38,975	14.5%	9.6%	6.4%	4,498	25,150
Maine											
Portland city	5,449	1,738	1,422	1,351	938	$40,591	18.0%	6.5%	9.3%	1,242	8,130
Maryland											
Baltimore city	57,264	21,906	14,892	13,112	7,354	$35,242	21.7%	11.9%	15.2%	20,296	70,153
Frederick city	5,710	1,121	877	1,947	1,765	$74,054	10.9%	6.7%	2.8%	819	8,353
Gaithersburg city	4,865	1,347	556	1,307	1,655	$70,763	7.9%	8.5%	4.1%	609	8,223
Rockville city	na	na	na	na	na	$89,211	0.0%	2.6%	13.5%	1,235	8,877
Massachusetts											
Boston city	53,784	21,757	10,412	9,943	11,672	$35,671	15.5%	12.1%	23.4%	21,586	62,034
Brockton city	7,542	2,704	1,805	2,048	985	$41,821	11.3%	10.1%	23.3%	4,072	10,377
Cambridge city	8,519	1,984	1,117	2,203	3,215	$72,448	10.8%	6.0%	10.5%	1,162	11,420
Fall River city	9,771	3,635	3,689	2,056	391	$27,171	16.5%	10.7%	14.9%	4,700	10,553
Framingham city	6,830	1,067	1,821	2,513	1,429	$63,302	3.3%	7.9%	3.4%	680	10,303
Lawrence city	4,387	2,561	820	421	585	$18,110	28.1%	21.7%	36.6%	3,671	4,478
Lowell city	6,108	2,312	1,238	1,096	1,462	$36,233	11.4%	6.8%	13.7%	2,274	9,437
Lynn city	7,139	3,230	1,131	2,160	618	$36,753	15.8%	15.2%	25.6%	3,632	9,479
New Bedford city	8,184	3,689	2,145	1,744	606	$27,949	17.3%	22.1%	18.6%	3,235	9,468
Newton city	na	na	na	na	na	$82,593	6.3%	5.2%	11.7%	1,134	13,672
Quincy city	9,181	3,474	2,353	1,847	1,507	$39,131	7.8%	11.0%	16.0%	1,721	12,103
Somerville city	4,390	1,666	905	905	914	$37,135	5.3%	11.8%	22.0%	1,747	5,707
Springfield city	12,418	5,904	2,278	2,919	1,317	$28,269	25.3%	15.4%	19.5%	7,146	12,795
Worcester city	14,900	7,051	3,435	2,779	1,635	$26,599	14.4%	17.9%	10.1%	6,081	19,569
Michigan											
Ann Arbor city	8,275	1,410	1,513	2,395	2,957	$71,211	6.3%	3.8%	9.7%	659	11,543
Dearborn city	7,367	2,713	1,867	1,729	1,058	$38,638	12.7%	10.6%	12.1%	1,625	10,501
Detroit city	66,285	27,907	19,449	14,001	4,928	$30,428	29.0%	20.0%	19.7%	32,920	71,412
Farmington Hills city	10,120	1,954	2,356	2,951	2,859	$59,553	3.8%	8.7%	7.2%	954	14,558
Flint city	9,182	3,107	3,153	2,502	420	$37,752	32.8%	13.9%	8.3%	4,147	10,234
Grand Rapids city	16,875	5,743	4,986	4,335	1,811	$40,065	19.5%	11.4%	8.6%	4,121	20,536
Kalamazoo city	5,457	1,326	2,298	1,435	398	$40,122	20.2%	3.6%	6.1%	517	7,876
Lansing city	9,985	2,636	3,348	2,785	1,216	$40,603	22.6%	14.4%	12.9%	2,829	12,691
Livonia city	10,322	2,234	2,922	3,618	1,548	$50,118	4.2%	5.2%	7.4%	411	15,530
Rochester Hills city	8,254	1,708	1,662	2,660	2,224	$63,387	7.7%	4.6%	0.6%	318	11,245
Southfield city	11,169	3,693	2,515	3,419	1,542	$43,147	14.6%	12.1%	15.9%	2,908	13,545
Sterling Heights city	13,015	3,200	3,639	4,159	2,017	$46,680	7.0%	4.9%	8.2%	2,454	18,548
Troy city	7,644	1,089	1,684	2,863	2,008	$67,878	8.3%	4.2%	8.1%	245	12,596
Warren city	14,523	4,318	4,761	3,840	1,604	$39,376	9.2%	11.2%	12.0%	3,307	20,322
Westland city	10,074	3,705	3,240	2,711	418	$36,167	11.3%	9.2%	7.9%	2,191	13,351
Wyoming city	5,251	1,427	1,824	1,601	399	$43,854	9.7%	8.5%	12.1%	1,035	8,246
Minnesota											
Blaine city	na	na	na	na	na	$53,027	6.1%	7.3%	1.1%	344	7,516
Bloomington city	12,145	2,748	3,446	3,908	2,043	$48,626	6.6%	5.0%	10.1%	583	16,430
Brooklyn Park city	5,098	832	968	2,200	1,098	$56,913	8.9%	2.1%	4.9%	1,310	7,499
Duluth city	9,899	3,083	2,546	2,981	1,289	$43,327	19.7%	6.3%	12.5%	1,295	13,239
Eagan city	4,453	453	955	1,903	1,142	$65,110	5.2%	0.9%	1.1%	170	7,639
Lakeville city	na	na	na	na	na	$51,410	na	na	na	340	5,987
Maple Grove city	na	na	na	na	na	$59,344	1.3%	2.5%	8.7%	140	10,875

Table G-3: Cities - Income, Poverty Status and Receipt of Food Stamps (SNAP)—*Continued*

	Income of Households with Householder 65 Years and Over					Poverty Rate of Persons			Households with 1 or More Persons 60 Years and Over	
Total Households	Less Than $25,000	$25,000 - $49,999	$50,000 - $99,999	$100,000 or More	Median Household Income	55 to 64 Years	65 to 74 Years	75 Years and Over	Receiving SNAP	Not Receiving SNAP
Minnesota—Cont.										
Minneapolis city	29,348	9,814	5,698	7,711	6,125	$46,041	18.7%	12.4%	17.8%	7,461	38,974
Plymouth city	6,872	1,148	1,854	1,727	2,143	$71,351	3.3%	3.2%	3.7%	382	10,734
Rochester city	11,259	3,270	2,697	3,514	1,778	$46,659	7.6%	2.9%	8.6%	1,091	15,617
St. Cloud city	4,876	1,219	1,572	1,152	933	$45,225	8.2%	6.0%	8.3%	566	7,495
St. Paul city	21,422	5,906	4,462	6,335	4,719	$51,494	14.3%	9.2%	9.7%	6,288	29,373
Woodbury city	na	na	na	na	na	$75,674	0.9%	3.0%	0.0%	0	8,565
Mississippi										
Gulfport city	5,550	1,792	1,336	1,915	507	$44,196	19.6%	11.6%	20.2%	1,736	7,605
Jackson city	13,245	4,247	3,359	3,755	1,884	$45,778	17.3%	6.4%	11.7%	3,188	17,844
Missouri										
Columbia city	9,132	1,464	2,837	2,607	2,224	$52,014	10.9%	4.1%	3.1%	1,119	12,478
Independence city	12,015	2,852	3,691	4,030	1,442	$46,462	8.9%	4.4%	3.8%	1,422	18,025
Kansas City city	41,780	13,930	10,970	11,262	5,618	$39,622	12.7%	5.8%	10.9%	6,506	60,168
Lee's Summit city	10,450	2,333	2,980	2,956	2,181	$48,967	2.7%	2.7%	7.1%	583	15,298
O'Fallon city	5,962	1,158	1,974	1,826	1,004	$48,478	2.7%	1.3%	1.2%	234	10,378
St. Charles city	7,341	1,656	2,209	2,599	877	$45,082	8.7%	0.5%	10.4%	816	10,630
St. Joseph city	8,757	2,576	2,134	2,958	1,089	$43,646	17.4%	6.1%	12.1%	1,241	11,319
St. Louis city	29,792	12,522	7,908	6,093	3,269	$31,545	20.1%	12.3%	16.7%	8,931	38,321
Springfield city	21,055	9,270	7,253	3,308	1,224	$27,717	23.2%	11.8%	11.2%	5,829	23,511
Montana										
Billings city	12,848	3,510	4,198	3,673	1,467	$39,002	10.7%	10.0%	9.4%	923	17,712
Missoula city	6,564	1,947	1,904	1,952	761	$41,793	14.1%	7.5%	11.4%	1,187	8,555
Nebraska										
Lincoln city	25,353	5,987	7,259	8,140	3,967	$48,413	9.8%	5.1%	6.7%	2,096	35,403
Omaha city	41,787	11,617	12,055	11,329	6,786	$42,644	11.3%	5.9%	9.4%	6,898	58,672
Nevada										
Henderson city	34,479	6,978	9,517	10,376	7,608	$53,462	6.9%	5.4%	8.2%	3,472	48,357
Las Vegas city	57,088	18,115	14,119	14,759	10,095	$42,787	17.9%	10.5%	11.5%	12,433	78,799
North Las Vegas city	14,796	3,246	4,377	4,103	3,070	$48,112	12.9%	8.0%	8.7%	2,987	22,449
Reno city	26,259	7,652	6,761	7,547	4,299	$45,966	11.0%	8.8%	10.7%	3,525	36,708
Sparks city	10,698	1,849	3,164	3,537	2,148	$54,482	11.8%	4.6%	11.2%	1,388	14,969
New Hampshire										
Manchester city	8,273	2,855	1,941	2,268	1,209	$38,389	7.4%	6.4%	10.9%	2,045	11,199
Nashua city	9,562	2,807	2,368	2,252	2,135	$43,313	8.0%	4.0%	10.4%	1,383	14,957
New Jersey										
Bayonne city	6,109	2,101	1,596	1,657	755	$39,066	6.2%	5.2%	20.3%	1,332	9,873
Camden city	na	na	na	na	na	$27,239	41.6%	20.7%	10.0%	4,169	5,470
Clifton city	7,380	2,219	1,618	1,864	1,679	$48,115	3.1%	8.0%	7.4%	2,391	10,608
East Orange city	5,494	1,987	1,176	1,588	743	$32,377	20.9%	18.2%	10.6%	1,565	7,432
Elizabeth city	7,324	3,166	2,012	1,351	795	$31,434	6.5%	7.3%	23.4%	2,330	10,873
Jersey City city	17,688	7,012	3,827	3,785	3,064	$36,980	16.2%	15.2%	22.7%	6,455	24,548
Newark city	17,220	7,777	4,123	2,988	2,332	$28,785	23.9%	13.7%	15.6%	7,807	24,932
Passaic city	na	na	na	na	na	$30,238	14.5%	15.3%	21.1%	2,379	4,611
Paterson city	10,224	5,622	1,007	2,224	1,371	$21,202	22.6%	19.8%	26.5%	5,880	12,266
Trenton city	7,207	2,702	1,869	1,772	864	$33,904	29.3%	16.9%	18.7%	1,880	9,474
Union City city	4,774	2,523	960	737	554	$24,234	4.7%	13.9%	26.3%	1,588	6,517
New Mexico										
Albuquerque city	55,046	16,220	13,982	14,827	10,017	$44,479	14.6%	9.0%	10.5%	10,789	74,450
Las Cruces city	10,769	3,926	2,790	2,586	1,467	$33,256	22.4%	7.8%	12.3%	2,389	12,441
Rio Rancho city	9,930	2,241	2,906	3,381	1,402	$44,741	3.3%	7.0%	6.3%	943	13,411
Santa Fe city	13,618	2,195	3,870	4,544	3,009	$54,819	6.3%	7.4%	7.3%	1,614	15,991
New York										
Albany city	8,897	3,047	2,011	2,181	1,658	$38,361	19.6%	7.2%	13.7%	2,949	10,706
Buffalo city	21,624	8,304	5,350	5,024	2,946	$35,773	24.6%	12.2%	14.5%	10,997	25,370
Mount Vernon city	6,096	1,447	1,747	1,795	1,107	$48,557	15.3%	7.8%	14.4%	2,137	8,109
New Rochelle city	na	na	na	na	na	$51,475	10.5%	7.2%	10.4%	1,197	10,388
New York city	767,186	296,402	156,132	158,752	155,900	$37,417	15.1%	14.5%	20.7%	314,012	923,339
Rochester city	16,006	7,258	3,829	3,171	1,748	$29,320	27.3%	17.6%	17.1%	8,171	17,351
Schenectady city	6,127	2,560	1,505	1,318	744	$32,685	18.9%	14.8%	21.4%	1,420	7,732
Syracuse city	10,721	4,479	3,330	1,963	949	$30,961	22.0%	12.3%	18.0%	5,364	12,520
Yonkers city	21,929	7,091	5,637	4,649	4,552	$40,300	15.4%	4.9%	12.5%	6,705	27,041
North Carolina										
Asheville city	11,818	3,096	3,655	3,070	1,997	$43,036	8.4%	8.5%	6.5%	1,552	13,731
Charlotte city	56,551	15,232	14,820	15,183	11,316	$46,559	9.3%	6.2%	11.3%	11,597	81,949
Concord city	7,679	2,082	2,525	2,162	910	$40,956	12.3%	8.6%	2.7%	1,162	10,507
Durham city	20,298	4,999	5,435	5,665	4,199	$47,415	10.2%	6.4%	8.4%	3,704	30,186
Fayetteville city	16,511	4,856	4,363	4,311	2,981	$41,491	10.3%	8.8%	10.1%	3,418	22,071
Gastonia city	7,309	2,473	2,272	1,545	1,019	$35,988	16.3%	3.5%	14.9%	1,371	10,501
Greensboro city	26,459	10,013	6,086	5,717	4,643	$35,385	13.1%	8.8%	11.3%	5,239	36,539
Greenville city	5,662	1,804	1,858	1,211	789	$35,500	16.2%	4.7%	2.9%	1,511	7,216
High Point city	10,080	2,773	3,053	2,970	1,284	$39,719	13.0%	5.5%	7.9%	2,351	13,811
Jacksonville city	na	na	na	na	na	$33,688	10.0%	12.9%	21.4%	506	4,591

Table G-3: Cities - Income, Poverty Status and Receipt of Food Stamps (SNAP)—*Continued*

	Income of Households with Householder 65 Years and Over					Poverty Rate of Persons			Households with 1 or More Persons 60 Years and Over	
	Total Households	Less Than $25,000	$25,000 - $49,999	$50,000 - $99,999	$100,000 or More	Median Household Income	55 to 64 Years	65 to 74 Years	75 Years and Over	Receiving SNAP	Not Receiving SNAP
North Carolina—Cont.											
Raleigh city	33,431	7,468	7,768	9,302	8,893	$57,881	8.6%	5.2%	8.9%	4,754	48,167
Wilmington city	14,175	3,689	4,512	3,348	2,626	$41,663	21.2%	10.0%	9.2%	2,368	18,206
Winston-Salem city	23,621	8,145	6,678	6,106	2,692	$37,336	13.4%	7.5%	8.8%	3,635	33,031
North Dakota											
Bismarck city	7,969	2,376	1,599	2,608	1,386	$50,349	8.0%	3.4%	16.8%	309	10,643
Fargo city	9,594	2,253	2,682	2,801	1,858	$49,092	6.2%	2.6%	17.8%	736	14,543
Ohio											
Akron city	19,483	5,942	6,052	5,807	1,682	$37,015	19.6%	6.7%	14.9%	6,261	25,624
Canton city	7,625	2,933	2,489	1,620	583	$35,509	16.1%	8.6%	9.1%	2,160	8,800
Cincinnati city	26,344	10,846	5,001	6,018	4,479	$33,172	18.7%	13.5%	12.8%	7,226	36,180
Cleveland city	38,722	18,928	10,358	6,274	3,162	$25,631	30.6%	20.1%	20.0%	18,872	43,378
Columbus city	63,167	18,520	16,246	19,397	9,004	$44,530	15.9%	8.5%	16.4%	15,504	87,654
Dayton city	13,731	5,670	3,993	3,130	938	$30,326	28.0%	10.3%	16.8%	3,607	17,718
Lorain city	7,035	3,234	1,984	1,405	412	$27,091	19.0%	14.8%	27.1%	1,501	8,639
Parma city	8,792	2,303	2,623	3,095	771	$45,904	9.8%	6.3%	8.8%	1,053	12,373
Toledo city	25,440	10,426	6,578	6,532	1,904	$32,260	21.2%	14.4%	12.8%	7,030	32,259
Youngstown city	7,822	3,231	3,104	1,067	420	$26,712	24.4%	17.6%	5.9%	2,805	9,604
Oklahoma											
Broken Arrow city	9,346	1,823	2,499	2,901	2,123	$54,060	5.4%	5.0%	6.2%	535	13,105
Edmond city	8,679	1,349	2,119	2,874	2,337	$66,860	8.4%	2.6%	5.2%	483	11,743
Lawton city	7,754	2,015	2,289	2,236	1,214	$43,288	11.9%	8.8%	12.9%	1,703	9,979
Norman city	9,153	1,913	2,204	2,928	2,108	$55,919	12.1%	4.9%	0.0%	1,132	12,272
Oklahoma City city	54,178	14,722	14,426	15,655	9,375	$45,349	13.2%	7.7%	7.6%	8,532	73,965
Tulsa city	38,643	11,060	11,439	9,631	6,513	$42,075	13.2%	6.7%	7.6%	5,065	53,395
Oregon											
Beaverton city	7,603	2,005	2,245	1,958	1,395	$46,117	6.6%	4.3%	12.5%	1,917	9,461
Bend city	11,110	3,033	3,230	3,017	1,830	$44,846	7.9%	2.4%	19.0%	1,210	14,044
Eugene city	18,122	4,761	4,527	5,457	3,377	$48,030	12.4%	10.6%	6.7%	3,977	22,327
Gresham city	9,363	3,152	2,688	2,966	557	$40,811	7.9%	6.8%	13.3%	2,309	11,971
Hillsboro city	7,778	2,130	2,013	2,830	805	$43,097	9.0%	6.4%	2.9%	1,072	10,987
Medford city	9,036	2,764	2,469	2,617	1,186	$41,133	16.3%	5.0%	11.9%	3,083	11,100
Portland city	57,005	15,059	14,043	13,074	14,829	$48,949	13.7%	6.6%	11.5%	12,122	74,367
Salem city	15,873	4,971	3,703	4,156	3,043	$42,269	16.6%	10.0%	5.3%	4,277	21,108
Pennsylvania											
Allentown city	8,331	3,352	3,215	1,085	679	$29,507	22.9%	10.8%	18.3%	3,426	10,861
Bethlehem city	7,903	2,763	1,871	2,088	1,181	$37,290	11.6%	6.4%	9.1%	2,584	10,256
Erie city	10,444	4,477	3,477	2,074	416	$29,606	23.3%	11.7%	13.0%	3,568	11,207
Philadelphia city	144,301	60,062	34,992	32,551	16,696	$31,824	22.6%	14.1%	19.0%	63,597	161,597
Pittsburgh city	32,982	14,472	7,134	6,937	4,439	$29,712	18.4%	11.8%	16.8%	10,034	39,797
Reading city	5,978	2,761	1,624	1,019	574	$26,364	24.0%	21.8%	23.4%	4,381	6,137
Scranton city	7,941	3,041	2,203	2,080	617	$33,372	20.7%	10.9%	13.2%	2,843	9,523
Rhode Island											
Cranston city	7,654	2,139	2,168	2,060	1,287	$44,530	9.1%	3.8%	8.9%	1,680	11,135
Pawtucket city	6,774	2,255	1,760	1,744	1,015	$40,899	18.1%	6.6%	14.3%	2,174	8,729
Providence city	13,328	6,140	2,498	2,602	2,088	$33,203	23.0%	17.6%	24.6%	7,831	12,648
Warwick city	11,091	3,431	3,947	2,101	1,612	$37,891	6.1%	10.7%	9.1%	2,888	13,380
South Carolina											
Charleston city	13,963	3,796	2,934	4,440	2,793	$51,791	11.2%	10.0%	6.0%	863	18,403
Columbia city	8,917	3,087	1,913	2,414	1,503	$40,825	18.4%	9.1%	14.0%	2,054	11,675
Greenville city	6,599	1,737	1,097	2,419	1,346	$60,048	21.5%	3.5%	12.2%	1,286	8,773
North Charleston city	7,496	1,759	2,442	2,068	1,227	$43,619	16.0%	6.0%	7.0%	1,500	10,816
Rock Hill city	5,845	1,917	1,956	945	1,027	$35,325	8.6%	15.3%	5.7%	1,424	7,865
South Dakota											
Rapid City city	8,957	2,142	3,075	2,211	1,529	$40,417	20.8%	6.8%	14.1%	910	11,337
Sioux Falls city	14,186	4,192	4,211	3,721	2,062	$42,228	8.8%	7.7%	12.8%	1,786	19,923
Tennessee											
Chattanooga city	20,047	6,856	5,653	4,688	2,850	$37,651	11.4%	7.4%	11.3%	3,333	26,816
Clarksville city	7,492	1,758	2,813	1,957	964	$38,460	16.6%	2.2%	2.1%	993	12,536
Franklin city	6,006	915	1,813	1,496	1,782	$59,356	3.0%	1.6%	6.4%	565	8,902
Jackson city	6,510	2,385	1,843	1,303	979	$31,993	13.6%	6.1%	1.7%	1,062	9,076
Johnson City city	6,827	2,619	1,555	1,718	935	$34,339	16.1%	15.8%	10.3%	1,140	9,697
Knoxville city	16,442	5,881	4,847	4,063	1,651	$34,777	19.2%	6.1%	14.2%	3,609	21,886
Memphis city	56,780	22,522	13,348	13,255	7,655	$32,013	20.2%	12.2%	18.3%	17,271	74,272
Murfreesboro city	8,601	2,339	2,046	3,069	1,147	$49,172	9.5%	5.5%	9.5%	704	12,820
Nashville-Davidson metropolitan govt (bal)	52,740	14,413	12,835	14,935	10,557	$48,008	11.5%	8.1%	8.6%	7,825	73,654
Texas											
Abilene city	9,709	3,066	2,604	2,355	1,684	$39,868	10.2%	6.6%	9.3%	1,785	13,051
Allen city	na	na	na	na	na	$54,214	11.8%	12.4%	26.2%	188	9,818
Amarillo city	17,074	5,230	5,480	3,837	2,527	$37,652	11.8%	7.0%	5.4%	1,629	24,189
Arlington city	25,203	6,063	6,057	7,339	5,744	$51,684	7.0%	7.7%	9.8%	3,188	39,392
Austin city	53,957	11,097	11,421	15,066	16,373	$57,100	9.4%	7.4%	7.5%	7,439	86,685
Baytown city	5,868	1,399	1,768	1,725	976	$42,344	13.2%	4.4%	12.0%	1,122	8,334

Table G-3: Cities - Income, Poverty Status and Receipt of Food Stamps (SNAP)—*Continued*

	Income of Households with Householder 65 Years and Over					Poverty Rate of Persons			Households with 1 or More Persons 60 Years and Over	
	Total Households	Less Than $25,000	$25,000 - $49,999	$50,000 - $99,999	$100,000 or More	Median Household Income	55 to 64 Years	65 to 74 Years	75 Years and Over	Receiving SNAP	Not Receiving SNAP
Texas—Cont.											
Beaumont city	10,825	3,766	2,578	2,561	1,920	$34,203	10.7%	5.7%	14.2%	3,270	14,114
Brownsville city	11,430	5,526	3,399	1,705	800	$26,559	12.6%	18.7%	28.2%	5,256	14,241
Bryan city	5,852	2,051	1,815	1,225	761	$37,865	11.3%	9.9%	13.0%	1,048	7,328
Carrollton city	9,519	1,673	2,401	3,535	1,910	$56,628	11.0%	3.6%	4.7%	1,003	15,416
Cedar Park city	na	na	na	na	na	$55,921	1.0%	1.7%	2.3%	177	5,867
College Station city	5,365	1,457	884	1,492	1,532	$69,008	13.8%	5.2%	7.7%	156	7,807
Conroe city	7,856	2,635	1,465	2,805	951	$44,719	8.6%	12.6%	16.5%	843	10,003
Corpus Christi city	27,629	9,503	6,165	7,410	4,551	$39,693	13.3%	11.1%	12.0%	7,765	37,524
Dallas city	88,938	30,419	21,085	20,749	16,685	$40,457	15.5%	13.4%	15.2%	17,369	133,106
Denton city	8,968	1,209	2,935	2,566	2,258	$57,206	2.4%	1.9%	2.7%	579	13,523
Edinburg city	4,650	2,280	919	828	623	$26,585	12.9%	19.6%	29.7%	2,369	6,222
El Paso city	53,524	23,194	12,644	11,751	5,935	$31,715	13.5%	12.9%	23.2%	16,158	67,228
Fort Worth city	55,700	19,156	11,941	14,858	9,745	$39,839	12.7%	7.9%	14.7%	10,808	81,957
Frisco city	7,405	1,470	1,909	2,338	1,688	$57,624	3.3%	5.4%	3.5%	164	14,695
Garland city	16,237	4,326	4,389	4,226	3,296	$46,457	4.3%	6.5%	8.8%	2,881	25,900
Georgetown city	na	na	na	na	na	$62,997	5.1%	2.1%	6.9%	590	15,238
Grand Prairie city	10,128	2,541	2,739	3,007	1,841	$48,529	11.1%	5.8%	19.7%	960	18,186
Harlingen city	6,270	1,634	2,435	1,798	403	$40,684	15.5%	7.5%	8.8%	1,095	7,465
Houston city	151,420	49,577	38,934	36,395	26,514	$40,922	15.2%	10.9%	17.4%	40,288	215,773
Irving city	8,277	2,261	1,993	2,119	1,904	$46,399	9.1%	4.5%	11.6%	1,012	16,989
Killeen city	5,812	1,919	1,417	1,530	946	$44,299	8.8%	13.1%	6.6%	1,619	8,697
Laredo city	14,292	6,805	2,996	3,114	1,377	$28,490	16.5%	19.6%	30.5%	5,503	17,279
League City city	na	na	na	na	na	$66,301	19.7%	3.8%	10.8%	735	12,719
Lewisville city	4,946	1,065	1,405	1,817	659	$50,026	1.7%	3.4%	6.0%	523	8,661
Longview city	7,341	2,267	2,365	1,713	996	$44,880	11.2%	6.9%	16.0%	1,142	10,241
Lubbock city	19,833	4,474	4,706	6,894	3,759	$53,973	7.8%	7.4%	6.5%	3,375	27,489
McAllen city	10,160	4,735	1,744	2,432	1,249	$29,578	16.2%	24.3%	28.2%	4,121	10,405
McKinney city	10,076	2,312	3,049	2,834	1,881	$43,912	3.2%	2.5%	13.2%	624	17,613
Mansfield city	na	na	na	na	na	$64,358	2.1%	0.9%	3.0%	291	5,591
Mesquite city	8,820	2,268	2,561	2,551	1,440	$39,944	11.5%	3.9%	20.1%	840	14,322
Midland city	9,382	2,673	1,991	2,479	2,239	$50,169	8.4%	3.2%	20.3%	872	15,054
Mission city	na	na	na	na	na	$28,895	20.3%	24.0%	26.8%	2,224	7,540
Missouri City city	na	na	na	na	na	$63,989	na	na	na	1,221	9,943
New Braunfels city	na	na	na	na	na	$48,049	10.2%	9.4%	2.6%	326	10,401
North Richland Hills city	7,090	1,476	1,942	2,093	1,579	$55,035	6.5%	6.9%	7.9%	555	10,070
Odessa city	8,100	2,394	2,358	2,102	1,246	$39,634	6.6%	10.3%	14.0%	679	12,341
Pasadena city	8,322	2,327	2,181	2,714	1,100	$45,507	11.2%	13.7%	6.3%	2,298	12,229
Pearland city	na	na	na	na	na	$53,808	6.1%	4.1%	20.6%	576	13,009
Pharr city	na	na	na	na	na	$26,382	17.7%	29.1%	31.1%	2,573	5,074
Plano city	22,495	4,207	4,349	7,393	6,546	$65,380	5.0%	5.8%	10.5%	1,295	34,444
Richardson city	9,703	1,876	1,998	2,874	2,955	$60,027	5.8%	2.7%	3.0%	531	14,595
Round Rock city	5,623	1,105	1,412	1,713	1,393	$60,137	3.5%	0.6%	10.4%	656	11,054
Rowlett city	na	na	na	na	na	$67,481	4.2%	3.7%	0.0%	586	6,619
San Angelo city	9,991	2,993	2,454	2,550	1,994	$45,180	10.6%	4.6%	7.7%	1,064	12,654
San Antonio city	112,450	37,356	27,256	30,286	17,552	$41,521	16.2%	9.9%	16.1%	23,753	151,246
Sugar Land city	na	na	na	na	na	$69,534	2.6%	4.2%	5.2%	319	17,326
Temple city	7,481	2,032	2,378	1,910	1,161	$40,901	12.4%	8.5%	10.6%	927	9,495
Tyler city	9,055	2,513	2,415	1,666	2,461	$43,121	15.4%	10.6%	10.0%	1,413	12,665
Victoria city	6,962	2,403	2,621	1,156	782	$33,679	14.0%	9.2%	17.4%	1,831	8,525
Waco city	9,383	2,750	2,576	2,940	1,117	$41,434	10.8%	8.9%	8.3%	1,557	13,657
Wichita Falls city	9,028	2,863	2,703	2,286	1,176	$38,756	17.9%	10.4%	6.8%	1,463	12,069
Utah											
Layton city	na	na	na	na	na	$67,067	3.7%	6.5%	1.6%	679	6,462
Lehi city	na	na	na	na	na	$61,599	2.1%	7.3%	5.4%	214	3,914
Ogden city	6,379	2,482	1,550	1,782	565	$35,946	9.1%	8.0%	16.4%	871	8,345
Orem city	4,933	625	1,233	2,040	1,035	$59,968	3.8%	0.9%	6.2%	364	8,394
Provo city	4,560	1,042	832	1,514	1,172	$59,654	18.0%	11.1%	3.6%	646	5,425
St. George city	12,957	2,705	4,016	4,445	1,791	$48,258	14.2%	8.5%	9.6%	933	15,376
Salt Lake City city	14,311	3,704	3,545	3,464	3,598	$48,871	15.4%	8.7%	5.9%	2,720	20,476
Sandy city	9,341	1,620	2,490	3,056	2,175	$58,266	3.9%	0.8%	7.0%	441	13,752
South Jordan city	na	na	na	na	na	$65,252	1.1%	0.0%	6.8%	0	5,709
West Jordan city	4,550	372	1,184	2,114	880	$60,422	7.2%	2.6%	7.9%	1,470	7,048
West Valley City city	6,852	1,674	2,249	2,008	921	$38,956	6.9%	9.6%	14.9%	1,807	9,825
Virginia											
Alexandria city	13,624	2,885	2,251	2,932	5,556	$76,004	9.7%	7.8%	10.2%	954	19,285
Chesapeake city	18,389	3,692	3,169	6,487	5,041	$67,901	4.6%	4.5%	4.2%	1,707	29,170
Hampton city	12,573	4,334	2,616	3,955	1,668	$44,311	7.2%	8.9%	15.3%	1,332	17,966
Lynchburg city	7,727	2,064	2,507	2,468	688	$37,951	13.5%	2.3%	11.7%	1,333	9,913
Newport News city	15,446	6,027	2,911	4,842	1,666	$40,134	16.7%	9.2%	24.0%	2,291	23,011
Norfolk city	18,377	6,318	4,418	5,385	2,256	$40,469	18.8%	10.3%	12.6%	4,054	25,269
Portsmouth city	9,668	4,090	2,430	1,923	1,225	$31,054	22.0%	11.9%	20.5%	1,481	11,933
Richmond city	21,348	8,463	5,434	4,513	2,938	$31,551	15.9%	15.1%	11.5%	4,079	26,935
Roanoke city	11,021	4,137	3,242	2,294	1,348	$33,535	20.5%	10.1%	9.1%	1,908	14,949
Suffolk city	8,257	2,694	1,551	2,572	1,440	$48,297	6.9%	4.3%	5.7%	1,463	12,346
Virginia Beach city	40,323	6,425	9,121	13,583	11,194	$63,367	6.2%	2.3%	6.4%	2,367	59,739

Table G-3: Cities - Income, Poverty Status and Receipt of Food Stamps (SNAP)—*Continued*

	Income of Households with Householder 65 Years and Over					Poverty Rate of Persons			Households with 1 or More Persons 60 Years and Over	
	Total Households	Less Than $25,000	$25,000 - $49,999	$50,000 - $99,999	$100,000 or More	Median Household Income	55 to 64 Years	65 to 74 Years	75 Years and Over	Receiving SNAP	Not Receiving SNAP
Washington											
Auburn city	7,522	1,452	1,802	2,471	1,797	$57,511	14.1%	3.7%	10.0%	1,405	10,702
Bellevue city	12,440	2,060	3,003	2,911	4,466	$67,352	9.0%	7.2%	7.5%	1,330	17,503
Bellingham city	8,672	2,164	1,893	2,987	1,628	$55,214	12.8%	7.1%	7.1%	1,015	11,019
Everett city	8,600	2,621	1,964	2,571	1,444	$47,941	6.7%	10.8%	16.1%	2,393	12,651
Federal Way city	7,679	1,103	2,211	2,167	2,198	$62,646	7.4%	3.7%	3.3%	1,177	11,923
Kennewick city	6,553	1,086	2,079	2,329	1,059	$50,965	12.6%	3.6%	1.9%	1,078	9,997
Kent city	9,298	3,057	1,674	3,073	1,494	$49,167	6.9%	6.2%	12.5%	2,453	13,049
Kirkland city	6,343	744	1,256	2,173	2,170	$62,482	3.9%	2.9%	11.2%	265	9,860
Marysville city	6,205	1,254	1,887	1,983	1,081	$49,624	1.6%	5.9%	9.7%	951	8,447
Pasco city	na	na	na	na	na	$49,513	10.9%	11.3%	28.3%	1,106	5,150
Redmond city	na	na	na	na	na	$57,027	5.5%	0.0%	9.2%	361	5,115
Renton city	7,514	1,466	1,814	2,737	1,497	$60,141	6.2%	8.2%	7.8%	1,883	11,474
Sammamish city	na	na	na	na	na	$115,756	na	na	na	172	5,557
Seattle city	61,825	15,704	14,382	14,165	17,574	$52,599	10.6%	8.2%	14.4%	12,509	78,532
Spokane city	21,816	6,308	6,672	5,993	2,843	$39,392	19.3%	5.6%	12.7%	6,405	26,880
Spokane Valley city	10,574	3,254	3,469	2,547	1,304	$37,028	13.0%	8.8%	6.2%	2,126	13,024
Tacoma city	18,254	5,184	4,533	5,452	3,085	$47,350	11.4%	7.4%	7.7%	4,859	23,871
Vancouver city	19,345	5,222	6,006	5,272	2,845	$43,049	10.1%	4.5%	11.0%	3,146	25,502
Yakima city	10,440	3,917	2,195	2,474	1,854	$40,671	16.2%	12.8%	13.3%	2,970	11,280
Wisconsin											
Appleton city	6,963	2,306	2,106	1,774	777	$40,431	8.3%	2.0%	12.4%	1,058	9,855
Eau Claire city	6,794	1,999	2,058	1,943	794	$43,625	8.4%	6.8%	6.0%	343	8,788
Green Bay city	8,978	2,791	3,681	1,314	1,192	$35,135	9.5%	6.0%	12.2%	2,298	11,979
Kenosha city	8,044	2,299	2,630	2,068	1,047	$42,527	10.4%	6.5%	4.4%	1,676	11,061
Madison city	21,198	3,587	4,824	6,777	6,010	$59,926	6.0%	5.1%	8.2%	2,010	28,425
Milwaukee city	42,162	15,976	12,715	9,478	3,993	$33,547	21.1%	12.5%	15.0%	17,541	53,824
Oshkosh city	6,107	2,439	1,686	1,415	567	$33,988	11.3%	4.7%	8.4%	579	8,682
Racine city	6,171	1,906	1,901	1,615	749	$38,234	14.2%	11.1%	12.2%	1,711	8,523
Waukesha city	6,698	1,888	2,037	2,158	615	$42,951	6.6%	3.7%	10.9%	342	9,977

Table G-4: Metropolitan/Micropolitan Statistical Areas - Income, Poverty Status and Receipt of Food Stamps (SNAP)

	Income of Households with Householder 65 Years and Over					Poverty Rate of Persons			Households with 1 or More Persons 60 Years and Over	
	Total Households	Less Than $25,000	$25,000 - $49,999	$50,000 - $99,999	$100,000 or More	Median Household Income	55 to 64 Years	65 to 74 Years	75 Years and Over	Receiving SNAP	Not Receiving SNAP
Aberdeen, WA Micro Area	8,920	2,096	2,975	2,540	1,309	$40,270	13.7%	6.0%	10.3%	2,195	11,683
Abilene, TX Metro Area	15,770	4,158	5,286	4,070	2,256	$42,135	9.4%	5.9%	8.6%	2,138	22,020
Adrian, MI Micro Area	11,422	3,432	3,478	3,425	1,087	$37,496	9.5%	3.5%	2.8%	1,142	15,840
Akron, OH Metro Area	77,781	20,693	22,933	23,302	10,853	$43,529	10.1%	5.7%	7.4%	13,012	106,669
Alamogordo, NM Micro Area	6,635	2,129	1,788	2,057	661	$39,711	22.7%	15.7%	15.2%	1,350	8,865
Albany, GA Metro Area	14,219	4,434	4,060	3,752	1,973	$42,692	17.2%	12.0%	16.9%	3,064	18,930
Albany, OR Metro Area	15,144	4,378	3,944	5,584	1,238	$46,979	12.5%	4.5%	13.2%	2,988	18,223
Albany-Schenectady-Troy, NY Metro Area	95,951	21,138	24,647	29,257	20,909	$53,056	8.1%	5.2%	5.9%	13,891	129,093
Albertville, AL Micro Area	10,016	3,475	2,651	2,514	1,376	$39,081	13.5%	9.3%	8.7%	1,374	13,896
Albuquerque, NM Metro Area	94,579	28,513	24,333	25,942	15,791	$43,492	13.1%	9.7%	11.4%	16,325	128,616
Alexandria, LA Metro Area	15,380	5,343	5,222	3,534	1,281	$33,261	17.9%	11.9%	10.0%	2,480	20,878
Allentown-Bethlehem-Easton, PA-NJ Metro Area	92,311	24,982	28,480	24,126	14,723	$42,647	7.9%	5.4%	9.0%	13,208	126,846
Altoona, PA Metro Area	16,090	4,551	5,263	4,982	1,294	$40,804	11.6%	6.5%	9.8%	2,616	20,232
Amarillo, TX Metro Area	23,028	6,395	7,245	5,677	3,711	$40,113	9.4%	6.6%	5.1%	1,898	32,704
Ames, IA Metro Area	7,369	1,544	1,754	2,526	1,545	$53,876	4.0%	3.6%	7.0%	233	10,048
Anchorage, AK Metro Area	26,808	4,846	5,672	8,583	7,707	$66,468	9.3%	3.7%	8.9%	3,969	41,714
Ann Arbor, MI Metro Area	32,797	6,350	7,374	9,805	9,268	$60,875	5.2%	5.1%	7.3%	3,115	46,139
Anniston-Oxford-Jacksonville, AL Metro Area	13,456	5,258	3,450	3,368	1,380	$33,567	11.2%	14.9%	5.7%	1,868	17,639
Appleton, WI Metro Area	22,073	6,984	7,150	5,971	1,968	$38,202	6.2%	3.6%	11.7%	1,734	32,514
Asheville, NC Metro Area	64,037	18,911	17,433	16,199	11,494	$42,172	9.2%	5.5%	11.2%	5,558	83,087
Ashtabula, OH Micro Area	11,704	4,848	3,375	2,272	1,209	$31,814	12.9%	13.3%	16.1%	2,358	14,772
Athens, OH Micro Area	5,581	2,086	1,234	1,443	818	$36,701	23.6%	8.3%	19.1%	1,205	7,369
Athens, TX Micro Area	10,841	3,774	3,389	2,277	1,401	$34,003	13.2%	8.3%	7.6%	855	15,243
Athens-Clarke County, GA Metro Area	17,820	4,743	5,282	4,145	3,650	$43,088	10.2%	7.2%	8.3%	2,288	25,293
Atlanta-Sandy Springs-Roswell, GA Metro Area	432,497	107,067	116,251	116,410	92,769	$48,467	9.1%	6.3%	9.1%	72,107	644,694
Atlantic City-Hammonton, NJ Metro Area	28,355	5,764	7,314	9,413	5,864	$53,520	9.6%	6.9%	8.6%	4,227	39,211
Auburn, NY Micro Area	8,949	2,525	2,940	2,565	919	$39,176	11.3%	6.6%	7.7%	1,566	11,714
Auburn-Opelika, AL Metro Area	11,705	3,259	3,360	2,393	2,693	$42,058	15.9%	7.2%	7.5%	648	17,553
Augusta-Richmond County, GA-SC Metro Area	60,753	18,798	16,277	16,178	9,500	$42,105	13.9%	7.9%	9.2%	8,325	81,194
Augusta-Waterville, ME Micro Area	16,362	4,943	4,397	4,725	2,297	$41,368	8.5%	6.7%	13.6%	3,692	20,508
Austin-Round Rock, TX Metro Area	133,162	26,193	28,906	41,618	36,445	$59,175	8.3%	5.7%	6.9%	15,373	209,927
Bakersfield, CA Metro Area	57,042	17,852	14,878	14,045	10,267	$39,933	19.0%	11.5%	12.0%	10,136	87,533
Baltimore-Columbia-Towson, MD Metro Area	267,577	59,043	63,678	78,949	65,907	$54,750	9.2%	5.8%	8.5%	43,396	383,287
Bangor, ME Metro Area	17,420	6,255	5,317	3,412	2,436	$34,521	12.4%	7.3%	9.5%	4,085	21,744
Barnstable Town, MA Metro Area	39,226	7,427	9,627	11,909	10,263	$57,059	6.9%	6.3%	9.0%	2,840	50,519
Baton Rouge, LA Metro Area	70,045	19,916	16,878	20,145	13,106	$46,890	12.9%	8.3%	9.8%	12,834	99,207
Battle Creek, MI Metro Area	15,477	3,566	5,808	4,111	1,992	$40,536	13.4%	5.3%	9.6%	2,187	20,909
Bay City, MI Metro Area	13,107	3,069	5,002	4,060	976	$42,623	8.9%	6.2%	6.3%	1,536	18,423
Beaumont-Port Arthur, TX Metro Area	37,296	11,369	12,130	9,113	4,684	$38,147	10.0%	6.9%	11.6%	8,671	49,411
Beaver Dam, WI Micro Area	9,515	2,606	3,329	2,862	718	$39,478	5.4%	4.1%	9.9%	713	13,851
Beckley, WV Metro Area	16,440	6,305	4,506	3,873	1,756	$30,920	24.6%	11.3%	14.0%	5,380	17,861
Bellingham, WA Metro Area	24,312	5,009	6,073	8,690	4,540	$56,088	11.8%	6.0%	7.0%	2,827	32,970
Bend-Redmond, OR Metro Area	25,139	5,881	6,155	8,564	4,539	$53,448	8.5%	4.2%	16.4%	3,642	32,510
Billings, MT Metro Area	19,232	5,181	5,931	5,663	2,457	$40,354	10.9%	9.3%	10.7%	1,323	27,294
Binghamton, NY Metro Area	29,458	8,925	8,179	7,817	4,537	$42,300	12.1%	5.6%	13.5%	5,727	38,325
Birmingham-Hoover, AL Metro Area	118,093	36,936	30,848	30,355	19,954	$41,550	13.4%	8.9%	7.8%	17,034	159,269
Bismarck, ND Metro Area	13,014	3,353	3,098	4,468	2,095	$50,436	6.1%	2.8%	14.6%	667	17,306
Blacksburg-Christiansburg-Radford, VA Metro Area	18,506	5,770	4,871	5,649	2,216	$40,593	11.4%	7.8%	7.1%	1,728	23,540
Bloomington, IL Metro Area	16,015	3,791	4,059	4,579	3,586	$52,977	8.5%	6.0%	10.3%	1,843	22,734
Bloomington, IN Metro Area	14,936	3,111	4,400	4,835	2,590	$49,669	17.0%	4.1%	3.4%	1,627	20,620
Bloomsburg-Berwick, PA Metro Area	10,275	3,905	3,143	2,432	795	$30,503	8.4%	6.4%	8.9%	1,352	14,391
Bluefield, WV-VA Micro Area	14,834	4,885	5,514	3,848	587	$33,722	23.1%	4.8%	12.9%	3,449	17,281
Boise City, ID Metro Area	65,182	17,961	18,481	19,611	9,129	$43,566	6.5%	5.7%	10.2%	4,697	92,504
Boston-Cambridge-Newton, MA-NH Metro Area	468,966	120,813	105,093	123,319	119,741	$52,919	7.6%	6.2%	11.2%	79,627	654,059
Boulder, CO Metro Area	29,132	5,622	6,443	7,974	9,093	$63,254	6.9%	4.4%	7.1%	1,709	43,854
Bowling Green, KY Metro Area	15,939	5,967	3,854	4,456	1,662	$39,556	15.6%	4.1%	12.9%	1,919	22,766
Bozeman, MT Micro Area	8,441	1,980	1,910	2,804	1,747	$59,375	6.0%	5.0%	9.6%	339	14,526
Brainerd, MN Micro Area	13,607	3,511	4,301	4,152	1,643	$42,595	14.9%	4.7%	8.0%	1,080	18,522
Branson, MO Micro Area	14,109	4,292	4,509	3,770	1,538	$40,680	12.3%	10.7%	3.4%	1,550	17,472
Bremerton-Silverdale, WA Metro Area	30,033	5,677	7,023	10,174	7,159	$61,929	9.4%	4.9%	7.4%	3,427	41,509
Bridgeport-Stamford-Norwalk, CT Metro Area	92,257	20,234	17,931	24,499	29,593	$61,304	7.6%	6.3%	8.7%	12,986	132,407
Brownsville-Harlingen, TX Metro Area	33,403	15,270	8,781	7,312	2,040	$29,663	18.2%	18.6%	20.7%	10,304	40,890
Brunswick, GA Metro Area	15,458	4,470	3,659	4,361	2,968	$48,035	13.6%	8.8%	6.3%	1,987	20,055
Buffalo-Cheektowaga-Niagara Falls, NY Metro Area	134,474	40,787	38,749	36,763	18,175	$40,586	10.3%	7.7%	8.6%	25,668	177,419
Burlington, NC Metro Area	17,636	5,884	4,777	4,155	2,820	$38,522	10.1%	6.7%	8.9%	2,214	24,375
Burlington-South Burlington, VT Metro Area	22,055	5,159	6,182	5,992	4,722	$48,247	5.7%	9.7%	14.9%	3,016	31,154
California-Lexington Park, MD Metro Area	9,007	2,424	2,007	2,626	1,950	$50,902	3.1%	8.5%	7.3%	1,733	13,564
Canton-Massillon, OH Metro Area	49,338	14,981	16,636	13,075	4,646	$38,144	10.1%	5.6%	11.3%	6,173	64,476
Cape Coral-Fort Myers, FL Metro Area	121,190	31,454	30,414	33,023	26,299	$48,650	11.7%	9.7%	8.9%	9,252	150,186
Cape Girardeau, MO-IL Metro Area	9,720	3,835	3,052	2,039	794	$33,542	16.1%	9.6%	11.1%	1,210	12,381
Carbondale-Marion, IL Metro Area	14,043	4,558	4,584	3,297	1,604	$34,902	14.1%	8.4%	11.4%	2,399	18,346
Carson City, NV Metro Area	7,131	1,861	1,780	2,330	1,160	$49,146	9.5%	2.9%	18.9%	392	10,170
Casper, WY Metro Area	7,880	1,935	2,737	1,796	1,412	$40,939	7.4%	9.2%	5.4%	439	11,114

Table G-4: Metropolitan/Micropolitan Statistical Areas - Income, Poverty Status and Receipt of Food Stamps (SNAP)—*Continued*

	Income of Households with Householder 65 Years and Over					Poverty Rate of Persons			Households with 1 or More Persons 60 Years and Over	
	Total Households	Less Than $25,000	$25,000 - $49,999	$50,000 - $99,999	$100,000 or More	Median Household Income	55 to 64 Years	65 to 74 Years	75 Years and Over	Receiving SNAP	Not Receiving SNAP
Cedar Rapids, IA Metro Area	28,796	7,007	9,073	8,243	4,473	$44,286	6.8%	4.7%	6.1%	2,128	38,742
Centralia, WA Micro Area	10,886	2,981	3,975	2,544	1,386	$38,184	10.9%	6.1%	7.4%	2,650	13,083
Chambersburg-Waynesboro, PA Metro Area	18,693	5,186	4,941	5,832	2,734	$46,280	5.2%	5.0%	14.2%	1,723	24,488
Champaign-Urbana, IL Metro Area	20,067	4,247	4,702	6,216	4,902	$55,853	7.5%	2.5%	5.8%	2,349	28,817
Charleston, WV Metro Area	28,326	8,811	9,303	6,526	3,686	$36,561	15.3%	9.9%	10.3%	6,134	35,891
Charleston-North Charleston, SC Metro Area	73,111	17,175	18,744	21,862	15,330	$51,163	13.2%	6.9%	7.0%	7,653	102,175
Charlotte-Concord-Gastonia, NC-SC Metro Area	206,470	56,791	59,897	57,193	32,589	$43,169	8.7%	5.8%	9.1%	29,762	297,925
Charlottesville, VA Metro Area	25,656	4,988	5,703	7,818	7,147	$60,069	11.4%	5.7%	6.6%	1,639	35,754
Chattanooga, TN-GA Metro Area	62,125	20,098	16,479	16,161	9,387	$40,561	10.1%	5.3%	9.1%	7,636	85,533
Cheyenne, WY Metro Area	11,096	2,664	3,087	3,259	2,086	$48,352	6.8%	2.9%	5.0%	680	15,954
Chicago-Naperville-Elgin, IL-IN-WI Metro Area	858,556	237,125	211,391	236,425	173,615	$47,175	9.7%	7.2%	9.7%	157,051	1,193,405
Chico, CA Metro Area	25,859	7,869	6,488	6,542	4,960	$41,708	17.9%	10.1%	9.5%	4,138	35,416
Chillicothe, OH Micro Area	8,430	2,884	2,439	2,329	778	$34,007	13.0%	8.0%	9.3%	1,646	10,762
Cincinnati, OH-KY-IN Metro Area	208,494	56,039	57,503	58,295	36,657	$45,369	8.7%	6.1%	8.7%	26,060	294,927
Claremont-Lebanon, NH-VT Micro Area	29,867	6,887	7,962	9,380	5,638	$50,333	7.9%	5.2%	6.9%	2,346	39,824
Clarksburg, WV Micro Area	11,562	3,924	3,801	2,803	1,034	$35,850	11.4%	8.6%	8.3%	2,020	15,116
Clarksville, TN-KY Metro Area	18,117	4,163	6,738	4,702	2,514	$40,952	13.1%	3.8%	4.9%	2,426	28,362
Clearlake, CA Micro Area	9,808	2,487	3,304	2,498	1,519	$41,092	14.3%	14.3%	9.1%	1,517	13,493
Cleveland, TN Metro Area	13,167	3,923	4,779	2,743	1,722	$38,934	10.9%	5.7%	12.9%	1,990	16,565
Cleveland-Elyria, OH Metro Area	247,018	72,242	72,475	65,665	36,636	$41,780	12.0%	8.5%	9.7%	41,643	326,670
Coeur d'Alene, ID Metro Area	19,738	5,582	5,005	5,970	3,181	$46,860	6.0%	6.3%	11.5%	1,962	26,414
College Station-Bryan, TX Metro Area	17,983	5,418	4,462	4,684	3,419	$45,902	11.1%	8.1%	10.4%	1,910	23,509
Colorado Springs, CO Metro Area	58,991	13,767	14,230	17,926	13,068	$52,900	9.4%	4.3%	8.8%	6,402	88,758
Columbia, MO Metro Area	14,295	2,883	4,287	4,041	3,084	$49,620	10.1%	5.7%	4.4%	1,480	20,731
Columbia, SC Metro Area	78,101	21,669	23,210	21,464	11,758	$43,517	11.2%	8.2%	12.3%	13,141	107,161
Columbus, GA-AL Metro Area	28,711	8,349	7,578	9,043	3,741	$41,812	17.4%	10.1%	12.1%	5,790	37,949
Columbus, IN Metro Area	8,957	2,669	2,713	2,753	822	$39,720	3.4%	8.2%	12.3%	686	11,694
Columbus, OH Metro Area	173,268	40,969	47,614	55,749	28,936	$48,666	10.3%	5.6%	9.1%	25,093	249,521
Concord, NH Micro Area	16,924	4,631	4,802	4,603	2,888	$45,560	4.9%	4.7%	3.9%	1,139	25,295
Cookeville, TN Micro Area	11,946	4,486	3,671	2,274	1,515	$32,488	10.9%	5.5%	9.8%	1,206	16,940
Coos Bay, OR Micro Area	10,783	3,133	2,853	2,779	2,018	$46,959	12.4%	6.1%	5.2%	3,054	12,381
Corning, NY Micro Area	11,538	3,765	2,759	3,332	1,682	$42,400	11.9%	5.0%	11.0%	1,603	16,237
Corpus Christi, TX Metro Area	40,269	13,399	9,364	11,058	6,448	$41,216	14.2%	11.9%	10.9%	12,124	53,739
Corvallis, OR Metro Area	8,774	1,602	2,376	2,718	2,078	$54,289	8.9%	5.5%	3.1%	1,055	11,717
Crestview-Fort Walton Beach-Destin, FL Metro Area	29,659	7,607	8,514	8,157	5,381	$46,336	13.6%	8.4%	5.2%	4,132	40,935
Cullman, AL Micro Area	9,912	3,551	3,431	1,998	932	$30,681	13.6%	12.4%	9.3%	1,029	12,863
Cumberland, MD-WV Metro Area	12,799	4,622	3,765	3,352	1,060	$33,898	10.4%	9.8%	14.4%	1,893	15,838
Dallas-Fort Worth-Arlington, TX Metro Area	490,522	124,806	118,716	141,289	105,711	$50,378	8.8%	6.4%	10.3%	60,441	774,552
Dalton, GA Metro Area	12,910	6,232	3,587	2,289	802	$25,639	5.7%	12.5%	14.0%	1,689	18,055
Danville, IL Metro Area	9,996	3,329	3,115	2,640	912	$36,581	15.6%	7.9%	9.3%	1,058	12,597
Danville, VA Micro Area	14,421	5,072	4,493	3,567	1,289	$33,340	15.0%	10.9%	14.8%	2,667	19,465
Daphne-Fairhope-Foley, AL Metro Area	27,136	6,706	7,540	8,310	4,580	$47,300	10.5%	7.6%	8.0%	2,244	35,982
Davenport-Moline-Rock Island, IA-IL Metro Area	42,545	11,005	13,133	13,098	5,309	$43,275	10.8%	5.3%	9.6%	4,707	58,603
Dayton, OH Metro Area	92,499	24,967	26,905	25,781	14,846	$43,789	11.6%	6.4%	8.3%	11,753	124,239
Decatur, AL Metro Area	17,149	5,258	5,189	3,852	2,850	$40,484	12.4%	8.5%	6.8%	2,416	23,128
Decatur, IL Metro Area	13,096	3,080	4,586	3,513	1,917	$42,393	11.4%	7.5%	7.6%	2,523	17,186
Deltona-Daytona Beach-Ormond Beach, FL Metro Area	98,613	23,677	28,950	30,492	15,494	$46,472	13.5%	6.6%	11.4%	13,019	124,870
Denver-Aurora-Lakewood, CO Metro Area	237,112	52,839	53,760	71,138	59,375	$56,275	6.9%	5.1%	7.3%	23,354	352,401
Des Moines-West Des Moines, IA Metro Area	54,699	13,117	17,395	16,316	7,871	$44,524	7.9%	3.9%	8.4%	5,200	77,373
Detroit-Warren-Dearborn, MI Metro Area	456,698	129,415	127,919	129,221	70,143	$43,554	11.4%	8.8%	10.5%	86,697	621,615
Dothan, AL Metro Area	18,008	6,876	4,712	4,191	2,229	$34,716	15.9%	10.5%	14.7%	2,634	23,026
Dover, DE Metro Area	17,737	4,548	4,216	6,628	2,345	$50,495	15.9%	7.7%	4.9%	3,361	24,576
DuBois, PA Micro Area	10,186	3,926	3,557	2,252	451	$34,871	12.1%	8.5%	7.8%	2,101	12,856
Dubuque, IA Metro Area	10,313	2,743	3,232	2,864	1,474	$44,943	7.6%	4.6%	12.9%	1,120	14,408
Duluth, MN-WI Metro Area	33,939	9,459	10,912	10,151	3,417	$41,287	11.3%	5.4%	9.9%	3,266	46,940
Dunn, NC Micro Area	9,992	3,622	2,585	2,889	896	$37,090	14.1%	11.3%	8.7%	1,803	13,788
Durham-Chapel Hill, NC Metro Area	53,500	11,746	13,462	15,275	13,017	$54,517	8.3%	5.7%	6.0%	7,770	77,100
East Stroudsburg, PA Metro Area	15,553	4,161	4,409	5,072	1,911	$45,719	13.2%	8.7%	11.0%	2,712	24,479
Eau Claire, WI Metro Area	17,510	5,282	5,345	5,012	1,871	$40,139	8.0%	8.2%	6.9%	1,072	24,528
El Centro, CA Metro Area	10,251	3,361	2,177	3,144	1,569	$43,996	19.1%	13.0%	19.8%	3,012	14,223
Elizabeth City, NC Micro Area	8,400	3,073	2,587	1,925	815	$31,906	20.7%	6.5%	16.2%	1,324	11,627
Elizabethtown-Fort Knox, KY Metro Area	13,754	4,438	3,352	4,099	1,865	$41,976	13.8%	10.0%	7.1%	1,729	19,788
Elkhart-Goshen, IN Metro Area	17,003	4,499	5,072	5,229	2,203	$43,503	9.1%	3.6%	9.4%	1,013	25,709
Elmira, NY Metro Area	10,247	3,610	2,729	2,463	1,445	$40,295	8.9%	10.5%	11.5%	1,895	12,774
El Paso, TX Metro Area	61,959	27,192	15,184	13,131	6,452	$30,955	15.2%	14.2%	23.6%	20,882	77,792
Enid, OK Metro Area	6,272	1,882	2,145	1,339	906	$34,916	7.8%	6.8%	5.6%	603	8,062
Erie, PA Metro Area	31,393	9,232	10,489	8,101	3,571	$38,291	12.6%	4.9%	10.1%	6,361	39,425
Eugene, OR Metro Area	46,536	11,659	12,205	15,195	7,477	$48,569	13.5%	9.1%	8.9%	11,308	56,295
Eureka-Arcata-Fortuna, CA Micro Area	16,123	3,832	4,028	4,702	3,561	$52,090	15.0%	8.2%	6.6%	2,041	22,067
Evansville, IN-KY Metro Area	32,167	10,395	9,137	9,176	3,459	$38,000	13.1%	7.7%	10.3%	3,378	47,047
Fairbanks, AK Metro Area	6,987	1,710	987	2,673	1,617	$74,368	10.9%	7.5%	11.4%	521	10,563
Fargo, ND-MN Metro Area	19,059	4,249	5,108	5,828	3,874	$50,727	5.0%	2.2%	12.9%	1,272	27,493
Faribault-Northfield, MN Micro Area	6,671	1,897	2,263	1,478	1,033	$39,992	5.7%	8.0%	1.7%	465	8,832

Table G-4: Metropolitan/Micropolitan Statistical Areas - Income, Poverty Status and Receipt of Food Stamps (SNAP)—*Continued*

	Income of Households with Householder 65 Years and Over					Poverty Rate of Persons			Households with 1 or More Persons 60 Years and Over	
	Total Households	Less Than $25,000	$25,000 - $49,999	$50,000 - $99,999	$100,000 or More	Median Household Income	55 to 64 Years	65 to 74 Years	75 Years and Over	Receiving SNAP	Not Receiving SNAP
Farmington, MO Micro Area	7,061	2,679	1,804	1,966	612	$39,961	16.6%	9.1%	9.6%	472	9,566
Farmington, NM Metro Area	12,097	3,839	3,575	3,145	1,538	$38,127	23.2%	14.2%	16.3%	2,666	15,959
Fayetteville, NC Metro Area	29,362	8,866	8,229	7,726	4,541	$38,578	12.0%	9.2%	9.4%	6,171	40,464
Fayetteville-Springdale-Rogers, AR-MO Metro Area	42,779	11,448	13,709	11,318	6,304	$41,943	10.0%	6.4%	7.2%	3,234	62,577
Findlay, OH Micro Area	8,173	2,260	2,405	2,234	1,274	$39,319	6.1%	6.5%	5.4%	675	11,161
Flagstaff, AZ Metro Area	10,903	2,125	2,008	4,612	2,158	$61,858	8.9%	4.6%	11.3%	1,250	15,905
Flint, MI Metro Area	47,441	12,245	15,159	14,071	5,966	$43,177	14.8%	9.5%	7.1%	10,171	61,052
Florence, SC Metro Area	22,407	6,932	7,740	5,423	2,312	$36,614	19.9%	8.2%	17.2%	5,154	29,015
Florence-Muscle Shoals, AL Metro Area	18,903	6,149	5,669	4,783	2,302	$37,885	15.5%	7.7%	10.2%	1,633	24,260
Fond du Lac, WI Metro Area	11,716	3,722	3,887	3,119	988	$36,061	6.7%	7.8%	12.4%	1,627	15,941
Forest City, NC Micro Area	9,054	3,692	2,825	1,915	622	$32,969	16.0%	13.3%	10.6%	1,704	11,733
Fort Collins, CO Metro Area	33,694	6,991	9,480	9,655	7,568	$50,962	5.7%	6.6%	7.1%	3,094	48,552
Fort Payne, AL Micro Area	8,140	3,512	2,906	1,241	481	$26,838	17.0%	11.5%	12.6%	1,785	10,405
Fort Smith, AR-OK Metro Area	30,619	9,831	10,584	7,088	3,116	$33,380	14.0%	8.9%	9.2%	4,214	39,354
Fort Wayne, IN Metro Area	42,222	12,691	12,687	11,298	5,546	$41,206	6.9%	4.6%	8.3%	4,603	57,851
Frankfort, KY Micro Area	8,330	1,509	3,076	2,806	939	$47,340	12.6%	5.8%	6.8%	1,307	10,310
Fresno, CA Metro Area	72,341	22,322	17,976	18,752	13,291	$42,085	16.0%	10.4%	12.5%	11,325	102,070
Gadsden, AL Metro Area	12,152	2,810	4,553	2,864	1,925	$41,448	16.4%	4.8%	8.4%	1,243	16,400
Gainesville, FL Metro Area	24,269	7,234	5,149	6,763	5,123	$48,737	10.6%	7.1%	11.2%	3,157	33,758
Gainesville, GA Metro Area	16,870	4,063	4,460	4,297	4,050	$49,653	9.6%	5.6%	11.3%	2,260	23,487
Gallup, NM Micro Area	5,709	2,244	1,390	1,400	675	$34,031	26.4%	17.9%	11.7%	1,900	8,098
Gettysburg, PA Metro Area	12,529	3,454	3,476	4,085	1,514	$42,944	4.1%	4.4%	13.3%	1,112	17,443
Glens Falls, NY Metro Area	16,847	4,675	4,283	4,687	3,202	$46,150	12.8%	8.9%	5.8%	3,129	21,687
Glenwood Springs, CO Micro Area	na	na	na	na	na	$44,905	6.9%	13.3%	13.5%	630	10,194
Goldsboro, NC Metro Area	13,389	4,888	3,863	2,717	1,921	$32,024	14.7%	9.0%	21.6%	3,646	17,643
Grand Forks, ND-MN Metro Area	9,459	3,035	2,861	2,157	1,406	$36,973	9.1%	4.9%	17.7%	1,187	13,148
Grand Island, NE Metro Area	8,741	2,664	2,663	2,171	1,243	$37,688	6.2%	5.7%	5.3%	622	12,426
Grand Junction, CO Metro Area	18,280	5,884	5,971	4,180	2,245	$40,594	11.7%	5.0%	10.7%	2,549	24,246
Grand Rapids-Wyoming, MI Metro Area	97,417	26,490	30,880	28,227	11,820	$43,207	9.2%	6.3%	7.9%	11,023	136,308
Grants Pass, OR Metro Area	14,454	3,699	5,062	4,126	1,567	$42,213	15.5%	5.8%	4.8%	3,514	16,754
Great Falls, MT Metro Area	9,377	2,645	3,283	2,533	916	$39,344	12.3%	11.8%	5.1%	1,439	12,535
Greeley, CO Metro Area	22,416	5,818	6,044	6,165	4,389	$46,519	9.1%	6.9%	8.2%	2,790	36,309
Green Bay, WI Metro Area	32,733	9,542	11,498	7,912	3,781	$37,038	6.5%	4.7%	9.8%	3,975	44,843
Greeneville, TN Micro Area	8,422	3,484	1,985	1,944	1,009	$33,269	9.8%	6.7%	6.9%	1,098	12,178
Greenfield Town, MA Micro Area	9,784	2,609	2,477	2,806	1,892	$47,292	10.0%	8.0%	2.8%	1,794	13,499
Greensboro-High Point, NC Metro Area	78,472	25,141	22,056	18,609	12,666	$39,500	11.4%	6.8%	12.0%	13,688	106,138
Greenville, NC Metro Area	14,472	4,602	4,124	4,094	1,652	$36,786	19.0%	7.3%	6.9%	3,271	20,591
Greenville-Anderson-Mauldin, SC Metro Area	93,228	29,328	26,408	24,285	13,207	$39,539	12.4%	6.9%	10.6%	13,585	126,109
Greenwood, SC Micro Area	10,883	4,004	3,158	3,066	655	$35,729	10.4%	9.9%	9.4%	1,922	13,516
Gulfport-Biloxi-Pascagoula, MS Metro Area	39,804	10,574	11,488	11,992	5,750	$43,314	13.3%	8.7%	9.2%	6,137	54,061
Hagerstown-Martinsburg, MD-WV Metro Area	27,044	5,708	8,143	9,418	3,775	$47,545	12.1%	6.6%	8.8%	3,950	38,024
Hammond, LA Metro Area	11,765	3,865	3,900	3,076	924	$36,689	18.8%	9.2%	18.2%	2,446	16,465
Hanford-Corcoran, CA Metro Area	9,949	2,877	2,267	2,773	2,032	$49,177	11.5%	14.8%	14.2%	1,429	13,238
Harrisburg-Carlisle, PA Metro Area	64,145	13,829	20,662	17,783	11,871	$47,664	7.2%	5.1%	7.8%	8,213	86,396
Harrisonburg, VA Metro Area	12,547	3,224	4,213	3,128	1,982	$40,824	11.2%	5.4%	9.7%	1,039	18,518
Hartford-West Hartford-East Hartford, CT Metro Area	127,370	30,714	31,101	33,482	32,073	$52,078	8.6%	6.1%	8.2%	21,629	176,259
Hattiesburg, MS Metro Area	13,122	3,840	4,111	3,115	2,056	$41,757	25.0%	11.1%	10.7%	2,308	16,264
Helena, MT Micro Area	9,420	2,058	2,660	2,445	2,257	$49,902	9.2%	6.5%	10.9%	773	13,693
Hermiston-Pendleton, OR Micro Area	8,178	2,414	2,852	2,102	810	$37,355	9.7%	6.5%	6.4%	2,176	10,099
Hickory-Lenoir-Morganton, NC Metro Area	43,086	14,500	13,612	10,409	4,565	$37,323	11.3%	6.1%	8.8%	4,757	59,814
Hilo, HI Micro Area	25,848	5,970	7,646	7,308	4,924	$47,733	11.7%	11.9%	4.3%	5,626	32,856
Hilton Head Island-Bluffton-Beaufort, SC Metro Area	32,829	4,580	9,380	9,747	9,122	$61,596	14.1%	5.5%	3.3%	1,748	41,075
Hinesville, GA Metro Area	4,212	1,436	958	1,320	498	$37,621	10.5%	11.3%	17.8%	1,664	5,999
Hobbs, NM Micro Area	4,873	1,599	2,146	642	486	$31,787	13.9%	10.7%	12.0%	805	7,184
Holland, MI Micro Area	11,325	3,052	3,664	3,467	1,142	$41,390	12.2%	8.5%	13.1%	836	16,416
Homosassa Springs, FL Metro Area	33,165	11,001	10,985	8,772	2,407	$38,779	16.6%	13.2%	6.9%	3,712	39,386
Hot Springs, AR Metro Area	14,925	3,943	3,584	5,734	1,664	$47,454	13.3%	9.8%	9.2%	1,587	19,198
Houma-Thibodaux, LA Metro Area	19,686	7,302	6,363	4,167	1,854	$33,004	12.8%	9.2%	11.8%	2,304	27,780
Houston-The Woodlands-Sugar Land, TX Metro Area	446,731	116,511	112,743	121,937	95,522	$48,752	10.7%	8.4%	11.9%	83,512	691,684
Huntington-Ashland, WV-KY-OH Metro Area	41,113	13,506	13,459	10,068	4,080	$36,870	16.4%	10.9%	11.2%	7,250	51,408
Huntsville, AL Metro Area	45,512	11,992	10,124	14,738	8,658	$52,263	8.9%	6.3%	8.0%	5,787	60,748
Huntsville, TX Metro Area	7,993	1,878	2,668	1,897	1,550	$41,250	13.5%	5.3%	9.7%	1,130	10,103
Hutchinson, KS Micro Area	7,982	2,296	3,646	1,605	435	$35,266	10.1%	11.2%	4.0%	1,206	10,248
Idaho Falls, ID Metro Area	11,776	3,221	3,207	3,309	2,039	$46,644	8.8%	4.7%	15.1%	1,178	16,104
Indiana, PA Micro Area	10,360	2,961	3,762	2,516	1,121	$37,627	9.2%	6.4%	10.3%	2,029	12,943
Indianapolis-Carmel-Anderson, IN Metro Area	173,440	44,217	52,619	53,330	23,274	$44,268	10.0%	6.1%	8.6%	21,750	251,643
Iowa City, IA Metro Area	13,552	2,449	3,103	4,378	3,622	$64,872	7.0%	3.5%	8.6%	673	19,931
Ithaca, NY Metro Area	9,079	1,695	2,716	2,856	1,812	$51,306	6.1%	2.1%	5.4%	1,255	13,776
Jackson, MI Metro Area	17,558	5,020	5,441	4,886	2,211	$40,598	10.4%	4.8%	7.7%	1,688	24,908
Jackson, MS Metro Area	52,662	15,430	14,180	14,746	8,306	$44,350	11.7%	5.7%	13.8%	7,372	71,456
Jackson, TN Metro Area	13,726	4,469	3,684	3,569	2,004	$36,342	12.2%	4.5%	6.2%	1,677	19,170
Jacksonville, FL Metro Area	146,371	40,355	33,998	44,326	27,692	$49,221	9.9%	7.4%	9.1%	30,057	195,535
Jacksonville, NC Metro Area	10,186	2,522	3,382	3,517	765	$43,431	10.6%	6.6%	8.2%	1,405	16,038
Jamestown-Dunkirk-Fredonia, NY Micro Area	15,814	5,586	4,780	3,835	1,613	$34,639	14.2%	8.1%	10.6%	4,247	19,306

Table G-4: Metropolitan/Micropolitan Statistical Areas - Income, Poverty Status and Receipt of Food Stamps (SNAP)—*Continued*

	Income of Households with Householder 65 Years and Over					Poverty Rate of Persons			Households with 1 or More Persons 60 Years and Over	
	Total Households	Less Than $25,000	$25,000 - $49,999	$50,000 - $99,999	$100,000 or More	Median Household Income	55 to 64 Years	65 to 74 Years	75 Years and Over	Receiving SNAP	Not Receiving SNAP
Janesville-Beloit, WI Metro Area	17,695	4,946	6,382	4,912	1,455	$39,189	10.4%	5.5%	7.3%	2,713	23,764
Jefferson, GA Micro Area	5,719	1,405	1,669	1,638	1,007	$47,192	4.3%	2.6%	2.9%	789	8,224
Jefferson City, MO Metro Area	15,935	4,192	4,676	4,638	2,429	$44,823	6.2%	2.7%	12.5%	1,050	21,994
Johnson City, TN Metro Area	23,772	8,580	6,470	6,398	2,324	$36,943	14.0%	12.8%	9.0%	4,159	31,744
Johnstown, PA Metro Area	19,834	6,703	6,403	5,139	1,589	$34,540	10.8%	6.9%	9.4%	3,713	24,461
Jonesboro, AR Metro Area	12,583	4,198	3,512	3,344	1,529	$38,886	13.7%	6.0%	7.9%	2,175	16,247
Joplin, MO Metro Area	19,793	6,895	5,903	5,028	1,967	$35,791	14.3%	5.9%	10.2%	2,749	24,947
Kahului-Wailuku-Lahaina, HI Metro Area	16,943	2,845	4,713	4,182	5,203	$59,946	11.7%	5.1%	2.6%	2,360	23,987
Kalamazoo-Portage, MI Metro Area	33,299	9,460	10,554	9,337	3,948	$40,503	8.8%	6.2%	7.1%	3,656	46,788
Kalispell, MT Micro Area	11,891	3,108	3,172	3,392	2,219	$46,514	5.9%	6.4%	10.5%	574	18,313
Kankakee, IL Metro Area	10,631	3,847	3,272	2,495	1,017	$32,112	13.4%	14.1%	17.2%	2,244	14,732
Kansas City, MO-KS Metro Area	195,894	46,692	55,182	59,387	34,633	$48,074	9.1%	4.9%	6.6%	17,738	287,147
Kapaa, HI Micro Area	9,017	1,593	2,051	1,887	3,486	$66,461	8.9%	2.1%	3.6%	828	11,995
Keene, NH Micro Area	9,178	2,896	2,373	2,113	1,796	$46,890	5.5%	5.4%	1.0%	661	14,005
Kennewick-Richland, WA Metro Area	22,981	3,931	6,442	8,084	4,524	$53,810	8.3%	4.7%	8.4%	3,355	32,096
Key West, FL Micro Area	9,842	1,650	2,155	2,299	3,738	$73,185	10.0%	6.1%	9.3%	1,053	13,520
Killeen-Temple, TX Metro Area	30,645	8,758	8,485	9,262	4,140	$43,958	9.9%	8.0%	11.5%	4,509	41,636
Kingsport-Bristol-Bristol, TN-VA Metro Area	43,634	16,785	13,183	9,684	3,982	$34,187	11.7%	10.8%	12.3%	7,158	55,036
Kingston, NY Metro Area	21,616	4,723	5,870	6,710	4,313	$50,562	10.4%	8.7%	8.5%	3,032	30,475
Klamath Falls, OR Micro Area	8,846	2,575	3,632	1,929	710	$35,648	17.1%	10.7%	12.2%	2,175	10,757
Knoxville, TN Metro Area	99,845	28,166	27,308	29,265	15,106	$43,666	11.4%	6.6%	8.8%	13,501	132,115
Kokomo, IN Metro Area	10,516	1,901	3,179	3,972	1,464	$51,294	6.9%	6.6%	2.4%	703	13,824
La Crosse-Onalaska, WI-MN Metro Area	14,525	3,625	4,969	4,286	1,645	$41,799	5.1%	3.2%	8.5%	692	20,774
Lafayette, LA Metro Area	44,567	15,008	13,203	9,445	6,911	$35,331	14.8%	9.9%	10.7%	8,711	58,974
Lafayette-West Lafayette, IN Metro Area	17,007	3,909	4,968	4,726	3,404	$48,251	12.2%	3.0%	6.1%	1,281	25,376
LaGrange, GA Micro Area	6,585	2,672	1,327	1,707	879	$37,904	19.1%	13.1%	16.3%	1,127	9,478
Lake Charles, LA Metro Area	20,957	7,394	6,001	4,701	2,861	$38,421	7.7%	3.8%	13.7%	2,705	29,756
Lake City, FL Micro Area	7,568	2,979	1,826	1,913	850	$33,484	12.4%	5.1%	14.6%	2,282	9,258
Lake Havasu City-Kingman, AZ Metro Area	39,594	10,586	13,224	12,134	3,650	$41,844	17.1%	8.9%	8.4%	4,992	49,481
Lakeland-Winter Haven, FL Metro Area	84,267	25,331	25,359	23,902	9,675	$40,291	14.8%	13.1%	10.5%	15,307	102,774
Lancaster, PA Metro Area	57,454	13,109	17,106	17,394	9,845	$48,434	6.8%	3.7%	9.8%	6,742	78,171
Lansing-East Lansing, MI Metro Area	46,592	9,538	14,328	14,285	8,441	$49,012	10.5%	5.9%	8.2%	6,160	64,125
Laredo, TX Metro Area	15,185	7,405	3,125	3,278	1,377	$27,601	17.1%	21.0%	30.3%	5,891	18,786
Las Cruces, NM Metro Area	20,682	7,553	5,121	4,804	3,204	$36,765	22.2%	11.7%	20.7%	6,260	25,054
Las Vegas-Henderson-Paradise, NV Metro Area	187,791	51,591	50,792	50,432	34,982	$44,806	13.3%	8.9%	10.6%	33,991	269,439
Laurel, MS Micro Area	9,654	3,349	2,406	2,811	1,088	$32,476	12.7%	16.0%	17.5%	1,310	13,165
Lawrence, KS Metro Area	9,782	2,664	2,149	2,792	2,177	$50,354	8.2%	5.2%	12.0%	537	13,810
Lawton, OK Metro Area	10,434	2,903	2,944	2,876	1,711	$41,794	12.3%	7.7%	10.6%	2,102	14,191
Lebanon, PA Metro Area	17,563	4,797	4,746	5,863	2,157	$45,034	6.9%	5.8%	6.2%	1,910	23,646
Lewiston, ID-WA Metro Area	8,946	2,487	2,842	2,752	865	$43,457	12.5%	12.4%	9.4%	1,185	11,798
Lewiston-Auburn, ME Metro Area	12,277	4,991	4,031	2,394	861	$32,517	13.3%	7.2%	10.4%	2,904	15,555
Lexington-Fayette, KY Metro Area	44,993	10,745	11,965	13,695	8,588	$49,358	10.5%	5.2%	7.1%	4,700	64,734
Lima, OH Metro Area	11,540	4,154	3,664	2,790	932	$34,450	9.1%	4.5%	13.6%	1,214	16,594
Lincoln, NE Metro Area	30,654	6,951	8,700	9,884	5,119	$49,251	8.1%	4.2%	6.4%	2,170	43,704
Little Rock-North Little Rock-Conway, AR Metro Area	69,133	18,809	21,051	17,202	12,071	$43,496	12.6%	9.3%	10.7%	7,212	98,279
Logan, UT-ID Metro Area	8,243	1,535	2,336	2,958	1,414	$52,648	4.8%	3.6%	10.1%	585	12,212
London, KY Micro Area	12,308	5,339	3,773	2,524	672	$28,424	21.8%	11.4%	15.7%	3,740	14,861
Longview, TX Metro Area	21,507	6,841	7,209	4,809	2,648	$38,181	12.7%	11.3%	14.0%	3,518	29,081
Longview, WA Metro Area	13,407	3,681	4,031	4,100	1,595	$40,021	13.5%	5.9%	4.5%	3,461	17,090
Los Angeles-Long Beach-Anaheim, CA Metro Area	1,010,518	284,686	209,801	250,045	265,986	$51,529	11.2%	9.3%	14.2%	107,593	1,598,503
Louisville/Jefferson County, KY-IN Metro Area	129,880	34,511	36,875	39,570	18,924	$44,978	11.5%	6.6%	8.1%	14,846	185,180
Lubbock, TX Metro Area	24,925	6,043	5,966	8,239	4,677	$52,219	7.7%	6.8%	7.1%	4,381	35,152
Lufkin, TX Micro Area	7,583	2,840	2,658	1,557	528	$31,032	12.2%	9.1%	14.3%	1,523	10,521
Lumberton, NC Micro Area	12,744	5,625	3,662	2,514	943	$26,869	19.9%	14.2%	24.3%	5,052	15,205
Lynchburg, VA Metro Area	31,368	9,243	10,657	8,268	3,200	$36,321	10.8%	3.2%	13.1%	3,585	41,922
Macon-Bibb County, GA Metro Area	23,565	8,393	6,137	6,569	2,466	$40,466	18.8%	11.2%	20.8%	4,877	30,074
Madera, CA Metro Area	11,632	2,804	3,348	3,248	2,232	$46,088	16.1%	10.3%	11.6%	1,451	17,627
Madison, WI Metro Area	61,984	12,529	16,871	19,103	13,481	$52,559	4.2%	4.2%	7.3%	5,902	86,151
Manchester-Nashua, NH Metro Area	38,337	9,569	9,309	10,585	8,874	$50,623	5.5%	4.0%	7.5%	4,152	59,522
Manhattan, KS Metro Area	6,689	1,471	1,547	2,288	1,383	$58,750	4.0%	1.7%	6.0%	266	9,764
Manitowoc, WI Micro Area	10,386	3,533	3,758	2,442	653	$35,381	9.8%	4.9%	8.6%	777	14,411
Mankato-North Mankato, MN Metro Area	9,313	2,725	2,141	2,886	1,561	$46,494	6.0%	4.9%	15.8%	491	12,797
Mansfield, OH Metro Area	15,028	4,318	5,881	3,761	1,068	$38,049	15.5%	6.1%	8.4%	1,995	18,632
Marinette, WI-MI Micro Area	9,494	3,668	2,754	2,681	391	$32,390	12.4%	7.6%	9.4%	930	12,895
Marion, IN Micro Area	8,420	2,704	2,852	2,332	532	$37,365	17.8%	5.9%	10.2%	1,402	10,599
Marion, OH Micro Area	6,905	2,578	1,976	1,639	712	$34,044	18.3%	4.2%	7.1%	1,250	9,625
Marquette, MI Micro Area	8,026	1,824	2,603	2,988	611	$44,684	8.9%	5.6%	5.8%	1,056	10,662
Marshall, TX Micro Area	na	na	na	na	na	$40,325	9.9%	4.9%	7.2%	1,837	8,363
Martinsville, VA Micro Area	9,267	4,306	2,874	1,639	448	$26,202	26.3%	16.5%	19.6%	2,018	11,550
McAllen-Edinburg-Mission, TX Metro Area	56,271	27,120	13,971	10,963	4,217	$26,392	22.6%	25.4%	27.3%	25,550	60,986
Meadville, PA Micro Area	11,241	3,055	3,811	3,300	1,075	$38,724	12.6%	6.1%	8.8%	1,889	14,543
Medford, OR Metro Area	29,411	7,739	8,428	8,443	4,801	$46,127	14.4%	6.7%	11.0%	5,582	37,248
Memphis, TN-MS-AR Metro Area	120,430	38,306	30,768	31,766	19,590	$40,437	14.0%	8.8%	13.1%	25,307	165,736

Table G-4: Metropolitan/Micropolitan Statistical Areas - Income, Poverty Status and Receipt of Food Stamps (SNAP)—*Continued*

	Income of Households with Householder 65 Years and Over					Poverty Rate of Persons			Households with 1 or More Persons 60 Years and Over	
	Total Households	Less Than $25,000	$25,000 - $49,999	$50,000 - $99,999	$100,000 or More	Median Household Income	55 to 64 Years	65 to 74 Years	75 Years and Over	Receiving SNAP	Not Receiving SNAP
Merced, CA Metro Area	18,366	5,102	5,329	4,287	3,648	$42,311	12.9%	9.8%	16.5%	2,451	28,045
Meridian, MS Micro Area	12,145	5,851	2,986	2,231	1,077	$26,047	19.6%	20.1%	18.3%	2,410	13,931
Miami-Fort Lauderdale-West Palm Beach, FL Metro Area	623,998	213,773	146,053	144,912	119,260	$40,029	11.6%	13.2%	15.5%	194,336	773,367
Michigan City-La Porte, IN Metro Area	13,199	3,710	3,935	3,609	1,945	$38,730	7.0%	6.8%	7.0%	1,540	16,457
Midland, MI Metro Area	9,892	2,412	3,150	3,081	1,249	$42,670	14.5%	4.2%	8.0%	1,366	13,191
Midland, TX Metro Area	12,836	3,842	3,125	3,124	2,745	$42,946	7.9%	2.8%	16.5%	976	19,495
Milwaukee-Waukesha-West Allis, WI Metro Area	156,917	44,500	45,083	43,834	23,500	$42,494	10.3%	7.0%	9.4%	25,065	220,067
Minneapolis-St. Paul-Bloomington, MN-WI Metro Area	313,964	71,534	79,538	99,262	63,630	$51,961	7.0%	5.2%	7.5%	33,454	454,905
Minot, ND Micro Area	6,758	2,469	1,368	1,784	1,137	$38,583	13.8%	7.6%	16.6%	1,110	9,126
Missoula, MT Metro Area	11,491	3,304	3,231	3,682	1,274	$43,706	10.0%	5.7%	14.0%	1,950	15,706
Mobile, AL Metro Area	43,522	15,646	13,012	10,119	4,745	$36,328	15.1%	8.9%	11.1%	8,292	54,684
Modesto, CA Metro Area	41,197	12,963	10,060	11,020	7,154	$43,614	14.2%	9.4%	10.2%	6,044	60,736
Monroe, LA Metro Area	16,717	6,428	4,501	3,500	2,288	$32,687	16.4%	12.3%	22.9%	2,493	24,051
Monroe, MI Metro Area	18,137	4,923	6,008	5,749	1,457	$42,669	6.1%	4.3%	10.1%	3,026	23,136
Montgomery, AL Metro Area	37,384	13,161	8,694	9,624	5,905	$40,662	14.7%	8.7%	15.5%	7,772	48,391
Morehead City, NC Micro Area	11,038	2,230	3,420	4,049	1,339	$47,978	10.6%	5.0%	6.8%	620	14,650
Morgantown, WV Metro Area	12,186	2,690	4,315	3,054	2,127	$44,817	11.4%	5.7%	3.8%	1,637	16,847
Morristown, TN Metro Area	13,095	3,629	4,605	3,869	992	$39,024	12.2%	2.2%	6.1%	2,277	18,144
Moses Lake, WA Micro Area	7,992	2,748	2,098	1,770	1,376	$38,994	11.3%	7.0%	16.2%	1,366	10,373
Mount Airy, NC Micro Area	9,879	3,976	2,894	2,079	930	$28,772	9.2%	8.5%	15.8%	1,397	12,493
Mount Pleasant, MI Micro Area	5,749	2,009	1,321	1,457	962	$38,059	11.7%	9.0%	11.9%	857	7,898
Mount Vernon-Anacortes, WA Metro Area	15,788	3,673	4,158	4,490	3,467	$50,733	8.0%	9.6%	5.7%	2,225	20,932
Muncie, IN Metro Area	12,849	3,909	3,888	4,425	627	$38,031	9.0%	2.9%	8.3%	1,638	16,640
Muskegon, MI Metro Area	18,617	4,719	6,596	5,534	1,768	$40,414	12.5%	6.7%	10.4%	3,497	24,890
Muskogee, OK Micro Area	7,165	2,586	2,431	1,487	661	$36,215	9.1%	9.6%	10.8%	1,220	9,575
Myrtle Beach-Conway-North Myrtle Beach, SC-NC Metro Area	73,740	16,605	20,573	25,166	11,396	$49,548	12.2%	7.1%	6.4%	5,232	98,246
Nacogdoches, TX Micro Area	6,068	1,915	2,029	1,614	510	$37,518	11.8%	11.6%	5.9%	1,194	7,586
Napa, CA Metro Area	15,144	2,810	3,164	4,006	5,164	$66,096	6.2%	9.5%	5.1%	1,607	21,250
Naples-Immokalee-Marco Island, FL Metro Area	68,705	11,373	14,843	18,026	24,463	$71,418	7.8%	4.4%	5.8%	4,499	85,012
Nashville-Davidson--Murfreesboro--Franklin, TN Metro Area	157,468	38,640	43,319	45,859	29,650	$47,790	9.3%	6.1%	8.7%	22,103	227,416
New Bern, NC Metro Area	16,581	5,766	4,647	4,276	1,892	$35,447	11.1%	5.4%	18.8%	2,751	21,406
New Castle, PA Micro Area	11,822	3,550	3,954	3,297	1,021	$37,495	16.8%	6.5%	7.0%	1,873	15,830
New Haven-Milford, CT Metro Area	90,805	22,656	22,278	24,919	20,952	$50,825	8.5%	6.5%	9.8%	16,637	123,681
New Orleans-Metairie, LA Metro Area	123,478	42,910	31,892	29,129	19,547	$38,550	14.9%	10.0%	14.0%	23,969	168,952
New Philadelphia-Dover, OH Micro Area	11,470	4,704	3,438	2,323	1,005	$33,348	3.9%	6.1%	8.9%	1,280	15,378
New York-Newark-Jersey City, NY-NJ-PA Metro Area	1,893,325	547,677	403,409	454,774	487,465	$49,679	10.0%	9.0%	13.0%	458,012	2,571,199
Niles-Benton Harbor, MI Metro Area	19,901	6,216	5,569	5,189	2,927	$40,021	9.9%	8.8%	14.2%	3,306	25,650
North Port-Sarasota-Bradenton, FL Metro Area	159,541	32,976	42,888	45,980	37,697	$52,635	9.1%	5.6%	8.0%	10,817	194,137
North Wilkesboro, NC Micro Area	10,532	4,013	3,651	2,337	531	$32,310	13.7%	4.6%	9.9%	1,500	13,199
Norwich-New London, CT Metro Area	29,852	7,527	6,534	9,337	6,454	$53,268	9.1%	5.2%	6.7%	4,553	41,964
Oak Harbor, WA Micro Area	12,750	2,581	3,093	4,470	2,606	$53,861	8.4%	6.5%	4.3%	1,023	16,717
Ocala, FL Metro Area	62,379	19,645	20,195	16,801	5,738	$36,821	11.6%	9.5%	9.3%	8,950	75,234
Ocean City, NJ Metro Area	14,880	3,316	3,611	4,806	3,147	$54,050	12.4%	4.0%	5.2%	931	20,790
Odessa, TX Metro Area	9,917	3,456	2,489	2,524	1,448	$39,185	7.1%	8.0%	17.0%	1,395	15,306
Ogden-Clearfield, UT Metro Area	44,316	7,667	11,653	14,758	10,238	$55,357	4.6%	4.4%	6.0%	3,504	65,551
Ogdensburg-Massena, NY Micro Area	12,077	4,513	4,139	2,561	864	$33,354	12.2%	7.8%	10.5%	2,768	14,954
Oklahoma City, OK Metro Area	123,243	31,866	33,673	36,136	21,568	$46,376	11.0%	6.8%	6.6%	16,554	168,628
Olean, NY Micro Area	9,120	2,835	2,743	2,948	594	$38,669	14.0%	10.8%	13.5%	2,077	11,661
Olympia-Tumwater, WA Metro Area	29,900	6,155	7,084	10,641	6,020	$56,913	8.3%	5.3%	8.9%	3,807	42,555
Omaha-Council Bluffs, NE-IA Metro Area	83,376	21,591	24,255	24,001	13,529	$44,696	9.5%	5.0%	8.1%	10,061	118,232
Opelousas, LA Micro Area	8,223	3,827	2,490	1,418	488	$27,714	23.9%	18.5%	21.0%	1,436	11,102
Orangeburg, SC Micro Area	11,251	4,822	3,488	2,074	867	$30,565	25.8%	16.9%	28.4%	2,213	13,558
Orlando-Kissimmee-Sanford, FL Metro Area	206,946	57,523	57,750	59,010	32,663	$43,855	10.4%	8.5%	9.3%	46,306	289,682
Oshkosh-Neenah, WI Metro Area	18,183	5,339	6,234	4,690	1,920	$37,327	7.8%	5.3%	8.9%	1,053	25,749
Ottawa-Peru, IL Micro Area	19,294	5,720	6,212	5,516	1,846	$38,104	13.5%	3.3%	8.3%	3,166	23,736
Owensboro, KY Metro Area	13,373	4,352	3,724	3,355	1,942	$38,464	12.2%	9.5%	8.7%	2,062	17,542
Owosso, MI Micro Area	7,895	1,809	3,208	2,336	542	$40,475	14.4%	5.2%	5.0%	1,229	10,739
Oxnard-Thousand Oaks-Ventura, CA Metro Area	76,222	14,640	16,954	20,510	24,118	$61,641	6.8%	5.7%	9.7%	6,017	112,567
Paducah, KY-IL Micro Area	12,805	4,791	3,478	2,952	1,584	$36,004	10.3%	6.0%	9.1%	1,713	16,248
Palatka, FL Micro Area	10,815	3,669	3,536	2,824	786	$34,967	16.9%	12.7%	11.6%	1,907	13,447
Palm Bay-Melbourne-Titusville, FL Metro Area	84,167	22,188	23,762	25,336	12,881	$44,377	10.2%	6.3%	8.6%	9,906	112,095
Panama City, FL Metro Area	21,480	6,113	6,473	6,289	2,605	$42,654	13.4%	6.4%	6.9%	3,948	30,960
Parkersburg-Vienna, WV Metro Area	12,125	4,142	3,051	3,610	1,322	$40,086	10.4%	7.9%	10.6%	2,651	14,455
Pensacola-Ferry Pass-Brent, FL Metro Area	48,637	9,928	15,849	15,484	7,376	$47,172	8.6%	3.4%	8.9%	9,225	68,723
Peoria, IL Metro Area	40,156	10,191	11,072	12,884	6,009	$47,267	12.6%	7.4%	8.1%	4,663	55,768
Philadelphia-Camden-Wilmington, PA-NJ-DE-MD Metro Area	601,231	152,506	148,919	172,559	127,247	$49,838	10.2%	6.2%	9.8%	110,949	828,179
Phoenix-Mesa-Scottsdale, AZ Metro Area	443,253	105,761	122,157	133,787	81,548	$48,451	9.8%	6.4%	8.5%	51,216	630,396
Pine Bluff, AR Metro Area	9,953	4,469	2,168	1,970	1,346	$29,133	17.6%	14.8%	17.1%	1,662	13,039
Pinehurst-Southern Pines, NC Micro Area	14,474	3,509	3,430	4,226	3,309	$51,536	9.8%	9.1%	9.7%	667	19,834
Pittsburgh, PA Metro Area	303,276	93,827	89,698	78,302	41,449	$39,285	9.1%	5.8%	9.7%	50,441	399,603
Pittsfield, MA Metro Area	18,271	5,082	5,470	4,122	3,597	$43,191	10.0%	6.3%	9.9%	2,289	24,288
Plattsburgh, NY Micro Area	8,126	1,910	2,864	2,041	1,311	$41,069	10.8%	8.2%	3.5%	1,997	11,668
Pocatello, ID Metro Area	7,726	2,675	1,889	2,547	615	$37,118	9.8%	4.7%	13.5%	995	10,496

Table G-4: Metropolitan/Micropolitan Statistical Areas - Income, Poverty Status and Receipt of Food Stamps (SNAP)—Continued

	Income of Households with Householder 65 Years and Over					Poverty Rate of Persons			Households with 1 or More Persons 60 Years and Over	
	Total Households	Less Than $25,000	$25,000 - $49,999	$50,000 - $99,999	$100,000 or More	Median Household Income	55 to 64 Years	65 to 74 Years	75 Years and Over	Receiving SNAP	Not Receiving SNAP
Port Angeles, WA Micro Area	14,164	4,095	3,473	4,715	1,881	$45,612	11.0%	10.3%	6.4%	2,026	16,857
Portland-South Portland, ME Metro Area	67,209	15,622	19,002	19,995	12,590	$48,613	8.4%	4.9%	10.1%	8,629	90,836
Portland-Vancouver-Hillsboro, OR-WA Metro Area	229,907	53,067	60,895	67,293	48,652	$50,500	8.7%	6.2%	8.9%	36,262	315,763
Port St. Lucie, FL Metro Area	74,558	20,402	19,892	19,765	14,499	$44,078	11.2%	10.6%	8.4%	9,233	94,031
Portsmouth, OH Micro Area	8,572	3,735	2,545	1,691	601	$28,464	20.4%	10.6%	21.5%	2,873	9,889
Pottsville, PA Micro Area	18,720	8,284	5,338	3,781	1,317	$27,751	10.4%	9.5%	13.5%	3,104	23,629
Prescott, AZ Metro Area	47,659	14,075	14,880	12,542	6,162	$41,657	11.3%	8.7%	8.8%	3,973	58,713
Providence-Warwick, RI-MA Metro Area	173,365	52,741	43,315	46,440	30,869	$43,118	9.0%	8.2%	11.9%	40,816	224,920
Provo-Orem, UT Metro Area	28,931	5,110	6,822	10,352	6,647	$60,040	5.5%	4.7%	4.7%	2,885	42,115
Pueblo, CO Metro Area	19,899	7,517	5,302	5,569	1,511	$35,054	13.6%	10.5%	17.1%	3,711	24,783
Punta Gorda, FL Metro Area	42,134	11,020	10,822	13,572	6,720	$48,467	9.1%	6.1%	8.0%	3,030	50,260
Quincy, IL-MO Micro Area	9,049	3,044	2,667	2,734	604	$35,929	5.8%	8.7%	17.4%	1,304	12,005
Racine, WI Metro Area	20,635	5,316	6,048	6,407	2,864	$45,036	9.6%	8.3%	8.6%	3,073	28,418
Raleigh, NC Metro Area	97,805	20,901	23,737	30,140	23,027	$55,915	7.3%	4.0%	8.2%	12,893	144,261
Rapid City, SD Metro Area	16,401	3,495	5,449	4,980	2,477	$46,063	13.4%	3.6%	13.1%	1,397	22,905
Reading, PA Metro Area	43,204	10,858	14,096	11,603	6,647	$42,434	8.0%	6.2%	10.4%	8,042	57,802
Redding, CA Metro Area	22,428	5,341	7,037	6,586	3,464	$44,086	13.1%	8.5%	12.5%	2,981	30,835
Reno, NV Metro Area	48,709	10,894	12,401	15,154	10,260	$52,634	9.9%	6.5%	9.7%	6,007	70,649
Richmond, IN Micro Area	8,133	2,908	2,430	2,321	474	$32,414	13.5%	7.6%	9.0%	1,357	10,605
Richmond, VA Metro Area	129,450	35,578	31,369	35,062	27,441	$47,903	8.2%	7.5%	10.3%	15,936	182,535
Richmond-Berea, KY Micro Area	9,739	3,202	2,895	2,315	1,327	$38,286	11.3%	8.0%	11.5%	1,348	13,195
Riverside-San Bernardino-Ontario, CA Metro Area	326,011	91,155	80,112	87,749	66,995	$46,628	10.9%	8.6%	11.9%	44,398	504,279
Roanoke, VA Metro Area	38,848	11,436	11,643	10,281	5,488	$43,059	11.1%	5.9%	7.2%	4,074	54,631
Roanoke Rapids, NC Micro Area	9,350	3,563	3,037	2,064	686	$33,392	15.2%	12.6%	17.5%	2,824	10,858
Rochester, MN Metro Area	22,103	5,508	6,151	6,760	3,684	$47,740	5.3%	3.9%	7.4%	1,624	31,228
Rochester, NY Metro Area	120,189	34,068	33,998	33,636	18,487	$42,911	9.1%	6.2%	9.8%	19,703	164,106
Rockford, IL Metro Area	36,083	9,700	10,868	10,253	5,262	$42,072	10.0%	5.0%	5.6%	6,483	48,876
Rocky Mount, NC Metro Area	19,318	5,920	5,780	5,244	2,374	$39,031	13.3%	6.5%	14.8%	4,144	24,579
Rome, GA Metro Area	10,194	3,380	2,838	2,828	1,148	$32,760	9.9%	12.3%	8.2%	1,888	13,174
Roseburg, OR Micro Area	17,844	5,418	5,896	4,677	1,853	$36,598	20.7%	9.3%	8.3%	4,429	19,701
Roswell, NM Micro Area	6,568	2,298	1,870	1,632	768	$33,984	17.3%	18.7%	13.0%	1,854	8,180
Russellville, AR Micro Area	7,873	2,851	2,635	2,020	367	$36,266	18.2%	4.3%	6.4%	719	11,690
Sacramento--Roseville--Arden-Arcade, CA Metro Area	213,573	49,960	48,602	61,563	53,448	$55,485	9.4%	7.2%	11.4%	21,562	321,343
Saginaw, MI Metro Area	23,894	6,287	8,173	6,402	3,032	$40,637	13.7%	6.2%	9.9%	3,586	30,921
St. Cloud, MN Metro Area	18,046	5,502	5,695	4,711	2,138	$39,756	6.2%	6.0%	10.4%	1,453	25,406
St. George, UT Metro Area	22,266	4,821	6,416	7,844	3,185	$49,585	12.9%	5.4%	7.5%	1,799	26,811
St. Joseph, MO-KS Metro Area	13,619	4,253	4,069	3,320	1,977	$45,329	16.3%	6.0%	10.0%	1,748	18,674
St. Louis, MO-IL Metro Area	297,140	73,589	85,490	87,768	50,293	$46,272	9.7%	6.0%	7.8%	36,737	414,032
Salem, OH Micro Area	12,925	4,264	4,710	2,800	1,151	$35,028	10.8%	6.4%	7.8%	2,456	16,777
Salem, OR Metro Area	41,060	11,034	11,324	11,922	6,780	$45,886	13.2%	8.4%	7.0%	9,519	53,218
Salinas, CA Metro Area	34,561	5,922	7,618	10,619	10,402	$62,802	6.6%	5.4%	8.3%	2,895	50,613
Salisbury, MD-DE Metro Area	59,544	13,563	15,983	18,852	11,146	$50,470	10.2%	6.6%	6.2%	7,124	78,392
Salt Lake City, UT Metro Area	79,657	15,809	20,759	25,439	17,650	$55,905	6.7%	3.9%	7.8%	10,783	118,357
San Angelo, TX Metro Area	11,834	3,498	3,013	3,203	2,120	$44,544	11.0%	6.6%	8.2%	1,125	15,688
San Antonio-New Braunfels, TX Metro Area	187,397	53,009	45,840	55,015	33,533	$47,035	12.8%	8.5%	12.2%	31,885	265,258
San Diego-Carlsbad, CA Metro Area	268,419	59,293	57,411	74,628	77,087	$59,367	8.7%	7.4%	9.8%	26,157	404,545
Sandusky, OH Micro Area	10,135	3,370	3,742	2,111	912	$33,304	9.5%	4.5%	7.6%	1,007	13,442
San Francisco-Oakland-Hayward, CA Metro Area	420,538	92,341	76,285	106,567	145,345	$66,565	7.7%	6.8%	9.9%	29,680	640,605
San Jose-Sunnyvale-Santa Clara, CA Metro Area	143,608	29,420	23,900	39,193	51,095	$69,998	6.7%	5.3%	10.2%	9,617	234,607
San Luis Obispo-Paso Robles-Arroyo Grande, CA Metro Area	35,948	6,109	7,291	11,456	11,092	$65,113	8.4%	7.4%	9.6%	1,894	48,722
Santa Cruz-Watsonville, CA Metro Area	27,799	5,638	5,450	7,563	9,148	$64,052	6.3%	6.7%	5.6%	3,561	39,905
Santa Fe, NM Metro Area	22,869	3,717	6,268	6,916	5,968	$57,495	8.2%	5.4%	8.4%	2,616	30,027
Santa Maria-Santa Barbara, CA Metro Area	41,277	6,860	7,840	10,335	16,242	$75,494	8.3%	4.7%	7.2%	3,726	58,727
Santa Rosa, CA Metro Area	62,227	13,482	13,856	18,084	16,805	$57,797	7.1%	6.2%	6.5%	3,251	87,555
Savannah, GA Metro Area	34,075	7,844	9,674	10,855	5,702	$48,583	10.5%	5.8%	10.0%	4,789	47,250
Scranton--Wilkes-Barre--Hazleton, PA Metro Area	70,268	23,556	19,177	18,999	8,536	$39,173	10.9%	6.3%	10.6%	14,115	91,808
Searcy, AR Micro Area	8,138	3,039	2,454	1,793	852	$35,995	19.9%	9.9%	9.9%	1,665	9,511
Seattle-Tacoma-Bellevue, WA Metro Area	321,485	64,895	77,031	97,441	82,118	$56,154	7.1%	5.1%	8.7%	52,270	464,561
Sebastian-Vero Beach, FL Metro Area	27,705	6,406	7,131	8,585	5,583	$52,563	23.0%	7.5%	4.9%	4,632	34,954
Sebring, FL Metro Area	21,675	6,053	8,147	4,922	2,553	$35,723	16.3%	16.6%	6.4%	3,101	23,798
Seneca, SC Micro Area	11,515	3,729	3,646	2,638	1,502	$35,825	11.9%	10.3%	7.3%	1,308	15,365
Sevierville, TN Micro Area	11,040	2,734	3,467	2,330	2,509	$40,843	9.2%	6.2%	6.9%	1,575	14,538
Shawnee, OK Micro Area	7,298	2,304	2,371	2,183	440	$35,899	17.6%	6.6%	10.8%	1,505	10,054
Sheboygan, WI Metro Area	13,487	3,622	4,607	3,854	1,404	$40,382	4.7%	3.1%	7.5%	837	18,547
Shelby, NC Micro Area	10,539	4,770	2,839	2,158	772	$29,942	16.0%	19.8%	9.1%	2,140	14,270
Shelton, WA Micro Area	8,846	2,124	2,235	3,663	824	$52,683	12.8%	7.5%	5.3%	1,418	11,544
Sherman-Denison, TX Metro Area	14,802	3,477	4,585	4,850	1,890	$46,428	9.5%	7.0%	8.3%	1,415	19,355
Show Low, AZ Micro Area	12,780	4,526	3,675	3,626	953	$36,983	30.1%	10.6%	15.9%	2,602	15,666
Shreveport-Bossier City, LA Metro Area	45,920	14,892	13,278	12,213	5,537	$39,727	15.0%	8.9%	9.4%	8,861	58,981
Sierra Vista-Douglas, AZ Metro Area	19,349	6,914	4,459	5,207	2,769	$39,478	11.4%	8.7%	8.2%	3,508	23,927
Sioux City, IA-NE-SD Metro Area	16,332	4,305	4,497	5,164	2,366	$42,738	9.9%	4.7%	5.7%	1,954	23,760
Sioux Falls, SD Metro Area	23,261	6,747	6,872	6,527	3,115	$42,088	6.2%	5.3%	12.5%	2,028	32,215
Somerset, PA Micro Area	9,473	2,841	3,453	2,579	600	$35,497	10.8%	6.8%	7.1%	1,753	12,370
South Bend-Mishawaka, IN-MI Metro Area	34,462	11,216	10,559	8,895	3,792	$38,017	10.0%	8.3%	11.5%	2,892	49,733

Table G-4: Metropolitan/Micropolitan Statistical Areas - Income, Poverty Status and Receipt of Food Stamps (SNAP)—*Continued*

	Income of Households with Householder 65 Years and Over					Poverty Rate of Persons			Households with 1 or More Persons 60 Years and Over	
	Total Households	Less Than $25,000	$25,000 - $49,999	$50,000 - $99,999	$100,000 or More	Median Household Income	55 to 64 Years	65 to 74 Years	75 Years and Over	Receiving SNAP	Not Receiving SNAP
Spartanburg, SC Metro Area	33,815	10,076	9,704	9,954	4,081	$42,592	11.1%	6.2%	11.0%	3,776	48,474
Spokane-Spokane Valley, WA Metro Area	60,852	16,011	19,603	17,428	7,810	$41,838	13.3%	6.6%	9.6%	12,510	79,754
Springfield, IL Metro Area	24,003	4,977	5,935	7,609	5,482	$53,462	9.2%	6.3%	3.8%	3,704	31,619
Springfield, MA Metro Area	66,655	19,897	15,966	18,757	12,035	$44,828	12.6%	7.2%	9.8%	15,759	84,608
Springfield, MO Metro Area	50,083	17,917	16,915	10,859	4,392	$32,938	13.5%	6.8%	10.0%	9,469	63,622
Springfield, OH Metro Area	17,429	4,347	5,798	5,308	1,976	$43,489	11.7%	5.7%	8.4%	2,484	22,170
State College, PA Metro Area	13,802	2,734	4,921	3,557	2,590	$44,422	5.4%	0.9%	4.2%	1,163	19,268
Statesboro, GA Micro Area	5,700	1,806	1,822	1,408	664	$45,150	18.7%	6.6%	7.5%	1,387	7,299
Staunton-Waynesboro, VA Metro Area	17,316	6,334	4,541	4,341	2,100	$38,254	9.7%	11.5%	10.3%	2,380	22,084
Stevens Point, WI Micro Area	7,783	2,520	2,067	2,628	568	$41,675	8.8%	4.7%	10.3%	1,078	9,979
Stillwater, OK Micro Area	7,462	1,677	2,416	1,846	1,523	$43,135	17.2%	7.9%	12.3%	298	9,587
Stockton-Lodi, CA Metro Area	51,357	13,848	11,266	15,518	10,725	$51,137	11.0%	8.7%	11.2%	7,984	83,422
Sumter, SC Metro Area	10,897	3,341	3,231	2,802	1,523	$41,470	13.9%	9.3%	9.1%	2,776	14,154
Sunbury, PA Micro Area	12,466	5,503	3,942	2,260	761	$28,428	9.0%	9.2%	11.7%	2,171	16,143
Syracuse, NY Metro Area	70,660	20,943	20,174	18,938	10,605	$41,974	8.9%	7.4%	9.8%	12,902	96,273
Talladega-Sylacauga, AL Micro Area	10,347	4,064	2,449	2,633	1,201	$34,368	14.0%	11.1%	8.2%	1,661	14,092
Tallahassee, FL Metro Area	35,295	9,808	8,692	9,459	7,336	$47,787	13.3%	8.2%	9.6%	5,549	48,612
Tampa-St. Petersburg-Clearwater, FL Metro Area	375,283	114,233	109,846	99,208	51,996	$39,816	12.9%	10.1%	10.0%	62,651	491,385
Terre Haute, IN Metro Area	16,800	4,554	4,901	5,252	2,093	$43,211	11.0%	5.0%	9.0%	1,500	24,250
Texarkana, TX-AR Metro Area	15,677	5,569	3,908	4,287	1,913	$39,474	15.5%	11.3%	18.2%	2,781	20,884
The Villages, FL Metro Area	44,756	7,737	10,975	18,134	7,910	$54,324	10.5%	3.7%	3.9%	896	51,444
Toledo, OH Metro Area	60,641	17,395	17,390	17,645	8,211	$41,531	13.6%	9.4%	10.2%	9,071	83,601
Topeka, KS Metro Area	27,465	7,796	8,706	7,394	3,569	$42,951	10.8%	8.8%	10.9%	2,273	38,004
Torrington, CT Micro Area	23,504	5,252	5,985	6,493	5,774	$53,134	3.9%	4.4%	6.8%	1,715	35,100
Traverse City, MI Micro Area	19,878	4,531	4,781	5,901	4,665	$52,052	12.0%	5.0%	6.7%	1,613	27,281
Trenton, NJ Metro Area	35,066	8,548	7,560	8,842	10,116	$58,989	8.2%	7.1%	8.2%	3,829	51,044
Truckee-Grass Valley, CA Micro Area	16,239	3,367	4,099	4,702	4,071	$55,269	14.2%	3.3%	4.4%	1,122	22,738
Tucson, AZ Metro Area	126,887	32,414	32,357	37,829	24,287	$48,961	12.1%	8.4%	9.0%	16,934	164,355
Tullahoma-Manchester, TN Micro Area	12,013	3,287	4,305	3,233	1,188	$39,605	14.1%	7.3%	6.0%	2,089	16,739
Tulsa, OK Metro Area	96,079	25,927	29,367	25,279	15,506	$43,300	10.0%	5.7%	8.2%	11,345	133,931
Tupelo, MS Micro Area	12,167	4,257	2,851	3,804	1,255	$38,256	13.4%	5.8%	7.9%	1,707	16,711
Tuscaloosa, AL Metro Area	21,717	7,795	5,251	5,299	3,372	$36,568	15.2%	10.8%	11.6%	2,851	31,023
Twin Falls, ID Micro Area	9,741	2,376	3,523	2,436	1,406	$40,642	13.7%	3.6%	11.5%	1,000	14,910
Tyler, TX Metro Area	22,791	6,782	5,728	5,750	4,531	$44,119	14.0%	12.2%	10.2%	3,268	30,140
Ukiah, CA Micro Area	12,167	3,144	3,027	3,824	2,172	$48,551	17.1%	10.7%	12.2%	1,115	15,903
Urban Honolulu, HI Metro Area	91,320	15,613	17,951	23,938	33,818	$73,837	6.6%	5.3%	7.2%	11,992	130,338
Utica-Rome, NY Metro Area	33,811	10,561	9,045	9,327	4,878	$40,676	13.9%	6.1%	10.1%	5,752	45,591
Valdosta, GA Metro Area	13,374	7,014	2,557	2,435	1,368	$22,466	22.7%	14.9%	34.3%	2,294	17,852
Vallejo-Fairfield, CA Metro Area	38,327	6,715	8,527	11,692	11,393	$68,900	8.8%	4.4%	8.2%	3,744	62,489
Victoria, TX Metro Area	10,278	3,530	3,623	1,875	1,250	$33,755	11.8%	8.2%	20.9%	2,004	13,208
Vineland-Bridgeton, NJ Metro Area	14,558	5,347	2,877	4,448	1,886	$36,350	8.9%	13.5%	7.3%	2,022	19,561
Virginia Beach-Norfolk-Newport News, VA-NC Metro Area	157,793	40,653	33,155	49,625	34,360	$53,899	9.8%	5.8%	9.9%	17,481	228,257
Visalia-Porterville, CA Metro Area	29,774	9,480	8,410	7,666	4,218	$40,377	20.0%	12.6%	13.2%	6,782	43,120
Waco, TX Metro Area	24,632	7,752	7,288	6,337	3,255	$39,653	8.2%	7.4%	7.3%	2,798	34,555
Walla Walla, WA Metro Area	8,217	2,295	1,964	2,205	1,753	$46,734	12.0%	10.2%	8.8%	1,342	10,082
Warner Robins, GA Metro Area	14,460	3,757	5,075	3,090	2,538	$45,771	15.1%	7.2%	5.5%	2,516	22,465
Warsaw, IN Micro Area	8,548	2,212	2,087	2,708	1,541	$49,604	5.5%	6.5%	7.3%	379	12,102
Washington-Arlington-Alexandria, DC-VA-MD-WV Metro Area	470,638	84,365	76,417	128,776	181,080	$77,094	6.2%	4.9%	9.5%	55,494	725,204
Waterloo-Cedar Falls, IA Metro Area	18,517	4,717	5,193	6,004	2,603	$47,951	11.0%	4.0%	11.1%	1,958	24,322
Watertown-Fort Atkinson, WI Micro Area	9,124	1,938	2,698	3,102	1,386	$48,829	4.2%	3.9%	5.0%	1,063	12,205
Watertown-Fort Drum, NY Metro Area	9,611	3,072	2,818	2,723	998	$39,128	10.4%	5.9%	9.8%	1,765	12,992
Wausau, WI Metro Area	15,425	4,149	5,001	4,672	1,603	$38,645	5.4%	4.2%	10.3%	1,511	20,855
Weirton-Steubenville, WV-OH Metro Area	17,348	5,603	5,345	4,719	1,681	$35,283	12.2%	5.1%	9.8%	2,935	22,485
Wenatchee, WA Metro Area	13,101	3,115	3,229	4,450	2,307	$52,336	5.7%	4.3%	8.4%	2,358	18,752
Wheeling, WV-OH Metro Area	19,242	6,531	6,122	4,718	1,871	$34,612	12.2%	8.1%	11.7%	2,551	24,497
Whitewater-Elkhorn, WI Micro Area	11,193	2,976	2,814	3,232	2,171	$47,179	4.3%	6.3%	8.0%	1,196	15,501
Wichita, KS Metro Area	61,430	17,621	18,723	17,537	7,549	$41,018	11.4%	6.1%	7.6%	6,777	88,974
Wichita Falls, TX Metro Area	14,948	4,575	4,611	3,571	2,191	$38,484	14.2%	8.2%	7.4%	2,215	20,421
Williamsport, PA Metro Area	13,364	4,147	3,811	3,547	1,859	$40,105	11.6%	6.0%	12.5%	2,634	17,352
Wilmington, NC Metro Area	32,231	7,710	9,186	9,632	5,703	$46,935	16.1%	7.6%	8.9%	4,668	43,472
Wilson, NC Micro Area	9,989	4,128	1,599	2,916	1,346	$34,868	18.7%	8.6%	16.1%	2,253	13,296
Winchester, VA-WV Metro Area	15,331	4,032	3,696	4,479	3,124	$49,707	11.8%	5.7%	5.1%	2,059	22,312
Winston-Salem, NC Metro Area	74,764	24,459	22,597	19,413	8,295	$37,832	13.3%	7.6%	8.6%	11,386	104,334
Wisconsin Rapids-Marshfield, WI Micro Area	9,953	2,878	2,723	3,662	690	$45,981	8.0%	3.2%	17.6%	1,222	12,891
Wooster, OH Micro Area	12,744	3,859	3,450	4,149	1,286	$42,604	8.2%	3.2%	4.5%	1,855	17,270
Worcester, MA-CT Metro Area	88,115	26,415	20,917	25,335	15,448	$45,122	8.3%	6.9%	7.9%	17,901	124,356
Yakima, WA Metro Area	21,499	6,420	5,421	5,982	3,676	$44,042	13.4%	8.4%	10.1%	5,412	26,627
York-Hanover, PA Metro Area	47,981	12,701	15,392	14,313	5,575	$42,493	6.3%	3.2%	5.5%	5,808	68,213
Youngstown-Warren-Boardman, OH-PA Metro Area	73,546	23,299	23,715	20,212	6,320	$37,283	11.9%	9.7%	7.4%	10,855	97,208
Yuba City, CA Metro Area	15,168	3,791	5,189	3,375	2,813	$43,140	15.5%	6.7%	8.3%	1,447	23,435
Yuma, AZ Metro Area	22,994	8,125	7,225	5,271	2,373	$33,236	16.5%	16.9%	12.0%	4,426	29,203
Zanesville, OH Micro Area	10,134	3,688	3,246	2,469	731	$33,676	13.0%	10.2%	7.3%	2,678	12,714

Table G-5: 116th Congressional Districts - Income, Poverty Status and Receipt of Food Stamps (SNAP)

	Total Households	Income of Households with Householder 65 Years and Over					Poverty Rate of Persons			Households with 1 or More Persons 60 Years and Over	
		Less Than $25,000	$25,000 - $49,999	$50,000 - $99,999	$100,000 or More	Median Household Income	55 to 64 Years	65 to 74 Years	75 Years and Over	Receiving SNAP	Not Receiving SNAP
Alabama											
Congressional District 1	81,162	26,471	24,214	20,656	9,821	$38,175	13.9%	8.4%	10.2%	12,154	104,014
Congressional District 2	71,219	25,552	18,485	17,822	9,360	$37,519	15.0%	8.3%	12.1%	11,589	94,690
Congressional District 3	73,987	27,082	20,506	17,632	8,767	$34,596	14.9%	11.7%	10.9%	9,542	99,701
Congressional District 4	80,677	30,550	24,108	17,193	8,826	$32,322	15.8%	9.6%	9.5%	11,305	105,201
Congressional District 5	76,457	19,940	20,509	22,349	13,659	$46,329	10.5%	6.3%	9.1%	8,761	102,328
Congressional District 6	71,378	18,224	17,313	20,509	15,332	$50,203	8.8%	5.8%	6.2%	5,604	100,388
Congressional District 7	69,093	29,553	17,712	15,359	6,469	$29,622	21.6%	14.4%	16.6%	20,065	84,782
Alaska											
Congressional District (at Large)	53,173	11,482	11,929	17,077	12,685	$59,339	9.7%	5.3%	7.0%	9,038	80,831
Arizona											
Congressional District 1	88,103	21,538	22,713	27,904	15,948	$49,761	14.9%	8.7%	10.5%	12,594	113,129
Congressional District 2	100,367	27,963	25,266	28,850	18,288	$46,432	11.3%	8.2%	8.4%	11,532	130,228
Congressional District 3	56,126	19,044	14,933	16,120	6,029	$40,343	14.2%	12.3%	13.4%	17,651	75,807
Congressional District 4	138,453	39,014	44,376	39,308	15,755	$41,192	12.1%	9.0%	9.4%	12,219	177,464
Congressional District 5	78,549	16,702	21,895	26,452	13,500	$50,660	6.3%	6.8%	6.2%	5,940	113,102
Congressional District 6	91,030	18,879	23,743	26,133	22,275	$53,056	7.2%	4.3%	6.5%	5,312	132,452
Congressional District 7	34,788	13,652	8,899	7,747	4,490	$33,381	20.9%	11.9%	14.1%	14,797	53,646
Congressional District 8	105,814	23,957	31,087	34,319	16,451	$48,046	8.2%	4.9%	8.2%	7,598	139,405
Congressional District 9	61,157	15,544	15,557	16,068	13,988	$49,042	9.5%	4.5%	11.9%	7,736	90,699
Arkansas											
Congressional District 1	82,565	30,649	25,525	18,428	7,963	$34,120	17.6%	12.4%	8.3%	14,674	106,763
Congressional District 2	74,690	21,979	22,217	18,397	12,097	$41,906	13.2%	9.9%	11.6%	7,870	103,230
Congressional District 3	72,354	21,060	22,806	19,167	9,321	$40,711	10.7%	7.4%	6.5%	5,734	101,667
Congressional District 4	85,229	30,735	24,705	20,721	9,068	$34,826	14.8%	9.9%	10.8%	12,071	112,979
California											
Congressional District 1	94,923	24,845	26,416	27,115	16,547	$44,835	15.2%	8.3%	8.7%	10,630	131,704
Congressional District 2	97,850	19,119	18,863	28,537	31,331	$63,909	9.5%	6.3%	7.3%	5,627	133,240
Congressional District 3	63,179	13,269	16,778	16,965	16,167	$54,498	11.6%	7.4%	9.5%	7,458	95,307
Congressional District 4	94,872	19,298	24,031	27,829	23,714	$56,287	8.8%	6.0%	7.4%	5,837	135,345
Congressional District 5	78,373	15,928	18,942	22,105	21,398	$58,173	7.4%	6.7%	6.3%	6,486	117,506
Congressional District 6	57,744	18,969	13,021	14,727	11,027	$43,011	13.4%	10.7%	13.1%	9,773	87,977
Congressional District 7	68,407	13,382	15,112	21,458	18,455	$60,090	7.8%	4.9%	13.4%	5,624	106,722
Congressional District 8	59,501	18,224	14,511	19,173	7,593	$44,111	13.6%	8.1%	14.8%	10,491	87,605
Congressional District 9	53,666	13,212	11,457	15,727	13,270	$54,495	11.2%	8.7%	9.5%	8,051	88,541
Congressional District 10	55,821	16,465	13,436	16,160	9,760	$46,466	12.4%	7.9%	9.3%	8,012	84,231
Congressional District 11	74,681	14,731	13,007	19,119	27,824	$73,023	6.7%	5.1%	8.6%	4,194	114,177
Congressional District 12	73,326	24,500	12,868	16,470	19,488	$47,917	12.9%	9.2%	19.3%	5,528	104,175
Congressional District 13	68,697	19,321	13,107	15,747	20,522	$55,019	10.7%	11.7%	13.7%	7,390	97,915
Congressional District 14	66,263	12,045	11,156	18,834	24,228	$75,747	5.7%	6.4%	7.0%	3,111	104,535
Congressional District 15	54,142	8,903	12,375	14,615	18,249	$66,041	4.5%	5.0%	5.3%	5,376	89,657
Congressional District 16	44,971	15,600	11,357	10,531	7,483	$37,205	19.0%	12.2%	16.5%	8,946	68,283
Congressional District 17	45,945	9,649	7,902	12,401	15,993	$67,918	5.5%	4.2%	11.3%	2,280	84,404
Congressional District 18	68,719	12,049	10,514	16,705	29,451	$82,429	6.9%	5.4%	8.6%	3,182	100,716
Congressional District 19	52,503	12,439	9,120	13,849	17,095	$63,457	7.6%	6.7%	10.5%	5,419	88,930
Congressional District 20	62,080	11,421	12,757	18,730	19,172	$63,819	6.3%	5.5%	7.3%	6,464	90,092
Congressional District 21	37,272	13,560	10,599	8,250	4,863	$33,899	18.5%	15.7%	16.3%	8,061	54,775
Congressional District 22	59,525	15,212	15,347	17,379	11,587	$48,714	13.2%	8.9%	9.3%	8,062	82,814
Congressional District 23	57,426	17,631	13,951	14,500	11,344	$43,595	17.4%	10.0%	12.8%	8,643	86,865
Congressional District 24	78,074	13,147	15,237	21,993	27,697	$69,506	8.6%	6.0%	8.1%	5,704	108,604
Congressional District 25	53,821	12,099	13,461	14,972	13,289	$52,346	8.6%	6.8%	11.7%	6,390	84,924
Congressional District 26	63,532	12,658	12,830	16,595	21,449	$66,578	6.9%	5.7%	9.5%	5,283	94,286
Congressional District 27	65,770	16,884	15,027	16,715	17,144	$52,226	9.9%	8.7%	14.2%	3,753	103,224
Congressional District 28	63,110	26,082	11,375	11,567	14,086	$34,411	10.9%	12.4%	20.7%	4,906	99,295
Congressional District 29	42,712	15,570	9,933	10,071	7,138	$37,583	13.5%	12.1%	17.4%	7,342	70,858
Congressional District 30	65,645	14,435	12,729	18,446	20,035	$62,476	9.8%	6.8%	9.7%	5,028	101,485
Congressional District 31	46,483	12,669	12,129	11,545	10,140	$46,080	10.2%	7.4%	12.4%	9,809	72,489
Congressional District 32	46,866	12,682	9,405	14,799	9,980	$53,112	8.6%	7.6%	11.6%	6,943	80,783
Congressional District 33	82,134	14,968	12,441	17,243	37,482	$87,688	8.8%	4.9%	8.2%	1,835	115,825
Congressional District 34	51,037	26,028	10,367	8,879	5,763	$24,134	20.4%	21.1%	28.2%	10,264	78,856
Congressional District 35	35,525	10,212	9,173	9,309	6,831	$45,420	9.8%	8.5%	14.5%	6,446	62,198
Congressional District 36	104,360	33,035	26,658	23,559	21,108	$40,838	14.5%	13.7%	10.7%	7,717	139,059
Congressional District 37	59,276	20,616	12,341	13,816	12,503	$44,138	16.0%	11.3%	19.2%	7,883	88,988
Congressional District 38	54,481	15,816	13,410	13,828	11,427	$45,999	9.9%	8.8%	14.0%	7,472	85,841
Congressional District 39	57,416	9,597	13,499	15,429	18,891	$66,446	6.8%	5.9%	10.1%	3,225	95,966
Congressional District 40	30,304	10,733	8,239	6,859	4,473	$39,273	15.3%	11.9%	16.6%	5,412	57,712
Congressional District 41	33,386	7,584	7,821	9,356	8,625	$55,202	9.2%	7.3%	10.2%	6,371	59,058
Congressional District 42	47,603	10,180	10,918	14,742	11,763	$57,084	8.3%	5.6%	10.8%	4,657	81,354
Congressional District 43	51,696	14,489	12,280	12,323	12,604	$46,787	14.3%	8.0%	11.1%	5,770	83,840
Congressional District 44	39,168	13,957	9,654	9,137	6,420	$37,614	15.2%	12.4%	19.6%	8,699	66,239
Congressional District 45	71,030	13,646	12,632	19,363	25,389	$70,500	6.5%	6.5%	11.0%	3,964	106,762
Congressional District 46	35,379	11,809	6,710	9,835	7,025	$46,927	10.1%	11.5%	15.9%	6,671	60,405
Congressional District 47	51,252	14,311	10,950	13,347	12,644	$51,026	11.6%	8.1%	15.4%	5,418	84,973

Table G-5: 116th Congressional Districts - Income, Poverty Status and Receipt of Food Stamps (SNAP)—*Continued*

		Income of Households with Householder 65 Years and Over					Poverty Rate of Persons			Households with 1 or More Persons 60 Years and Over	
	Total Households	Less Than $25,000	$25,000 - $49,999	$50,000 - $99,999	$100,000 or More	Median Household Income	55 to 64 Years	65 to 74 Years	75 Years and Over	Receiving SNAP	Not Receiving SNAP
California—Cont.											
Congressional District 48	73,657	17,010	13,799	19,618	23,230	$62,028	8.6%	7.9%	12.3%	4,491	110,467
Congressional District 49	73,126	12,070	14,378	20,073	26,605	$73,918	7.6%	4.5%	6.1%	3,909	107,127
Congressional District 50	62,707	13,305	14,253	18,303	16,846	$56,261	8.7%	6.7%	9.1%	6,081	97,727
Congressional District 51	45,161	16,691	9,817	11,906	6,747	$37,221	15.5%	13.3%	20.8%	11,931	64,823
Congressional District 52	65,678	11,365	13,685	17,358	23,270	$70,699	7.0%	6.3%	5.0%	3,786	96,649
Congressional District 53	56,942	12,691	11,928	17,700	14,623	$58,646	7.3%	7.2%	11.4%	5,014	90,853
Colorado											
Congressional District 1	66,607	18,922	15,160	18,304	14,221	$47,940	10.4%	7.5%	11.3%	9,031	93,272
Congressional District 2	75,019	13,207	17,069	21,717	23,026	$63,719	5.1%	4.5%	6.1%	4,631	112,818
Congressional District 3	85,549	26,084	23,466	24,590	11,409	$41,781	11.9%	8.2%	11.4%	12,023	116,233
Congressional District 4	70,674	17,895	17,309	20,061	15,409	$50,191	8.6%	5.4%	8.8%	7,475	106,704
Congressional District 5	69,981	16,734	17,129	21,639	14,479	$51,968	10.4%	4.4%	9.1%	7,616	103,284
Congressional District 6	62,030	11,992	14,007	19,477	16,554	$61,109	5.1%	4.9%	5.3%	5,677	95,691
Congressional District 7	69,942	16,755	17,531	20,137	15,519	$51,198	7.6%	4.7%	7.4%	6,516	102,688
Connecticut											
Congressional District 1	76,484	20,229	17,727	19,620	18,908	$50,479	9.3%	6.5%	9.9%	15,018	102,535
Congressional District 2	76,003	16,070	18,240	23,367	18,326	$56,603	7.1%	4.9%	6.7%	10,126	109,250
Congressional District 3	76,259	17,728	19,726	21,163	17,642	$51,964	8.7%	6.9%	8.7%	11,614	106,004
Congressional District 4	70,411	16,951	12,359	17,748	23,353	$60,806	7.9%	7.1%	9.5%	12,080	100,151
Congressional District 5	75,636	18,259	18,189	20,272	18,916	$52,173	7.6%	5.1%	7.9%	11,049	107,229
Delaware											
Congressional District (at Large)	107,758	22,428	26,329	37,963	21,038	$54,744	12.1%	5.8%	5.9%	12,205	151,255
District of Columbia											
Delegate District (at Large)	58,898	18,137	10,931	13,243	16,587	$50,873	19.5%	12.3%	20.7%	15,847	69,673
Florida											
Congressional District 1	79,682	17,914	25,133	23,747	12,888	$46,481	11.0%	5.6%	7.7%	13,950	111,340
Congressional District 2	91,997	28,440	28,446	22,918	12,193	$38,685	15.0%	7.5%	7.3%	16,498	118,295
Congressional District 3	75,812	23,582	20,626	19,974	11,630	$41,283	11.5%	8.0%	12.3%	13,665	99,600
Congressional District 4	82,281	19,279	18,026	26,158	18,818	$54,455	7.9%	6.5%	8.0%	10,637	113,984
Congressional District 5	62,413	22,565	16,504	16,192	7,152	$36,917	16.5%	11.2%	12.8%	21,474	77,162
Congressional District 6	116,759	28,340	34,159	36,175	18,085	$46,159	12.4%	6.6%	11.2%	15,697	147,383
Congressional District 7	67,126	19,079	15,940	20,157	11,950	$47,364	9.8%	6.0%	7.5%	13,407	92,780
Congressional District 8	113,656	29,113	31,249	34,486	18,808	$45,873	12.7%	6.6%	7.6%	14,958	148,953
Congressional District 9	75,299	22,941	22,323	21,242	8,793	$41,667	9.4%	10.5%	10.6%	20,431	101,548
Congressional District 10	50,722	14,751	14,264	13,520	8,187	$42,030	14.0%	10.2%	12.4%	14,870	77,350
Congressional District 11	172,181	46,177	51,639	55,613	18,752	$43,120	12.2%	9.3%	7.1%	16,478	203,969
Congressional District 12	117,538	35,541	37,188	31,098	13,711	$39,759	12.3%	10.1%	10.1%	14,132	151,768
Congressional District 13	105,500	32,411	30,448	26,975	15,666	$39,043	11.7%	9.8%	9.8%	15,491	135,247
Congressional District 14	61,564	20,084	15,661	15,355	10,464	$39,372	13.4%	11.1%	10.4%	17,697	82,988
Congressional District 15	76,150	20,582	21,844	21,691	12,033	$44,056	12.8%	10.8%	9.2%	13,107	104,348
Congressional District 16	137,379	30,587	38,742	36,049	32,001	$49,337	9.9%	6.7%	9.1%	10,656	172,202
Congressional District 17	147,229	37,773	41,379	44,678	23,399	$46,373	13.4%	9.1%	7.8%	13,168	176,418
Congressional District 18	119,660	31,077	30,447	31,080	27,062	$48,077	9.9%	9.0%	9.7%	12,135	153,821
Congressional District 19	149,957	35,884	35,350	38,745	39,978	$53,203	10.3%	8.1%	8.5%	9,944	184,235
Congressional District 20	59,499	21,789	16,006	14,672	7,032	$35,764	14.0%	13.5%	16.9%	24,592	76,506
Congressional District 21	121,552	33,436	30,801	33,092	24,223	$46,182	9.3%	11.3%	8.9%	14,316	147,523
Congressional District 22	101,164	26,512	22,566	26,238	25,848	$52,513	9.8%	8.8%	9.5%	12,507	136,085
Congressional District 23	80,170	28,179	18,580	17,163	16,248	$38,494	9.9%	12.8%	17.2%	13,500	107,801
Congressional District 24	58,706	26,187	14,230	13,134	5,155	$29,005	17.9%	18.1%	23.5%	36,602	64,229
Congressional District 25	70,493	22,938	17,919	15,834	13,802	$43,127	10.4%	12.0%	16.7%	34,053	82,037
Congressional District 26	53,165	19,371	11,419	12,163	10,212	$40,418	10.9%	12.9%	15.9%	27,368	69,446
Congressional District 27	74,573	30,507	13,721	12,898	17,447	$34,752	12.0%	17.5%	21.8%	33,784	81,322
Georgia											
Congressional District 1	68,406	19,270	18,702	20,045	10,389	$44,647	13.7%	7.7%	9.0%	11,110	93,855
Congressional District 2	67,752	25,602	19,427	15,095	7,628	$33,366	20.9%	13.3%	17.4%	18,510	83,029
Congressional District 3	70,993	18,917	19,745	19,036	13,295	$44,988	12.8%	8.0%	9.1%	11,860	99,066
Congressional District 4	54,297	13,481	12,865	16,135	11,816	$51,644	9.2%	5.4%	7.1%	12,826	83,600
Congressional District 5	61,350	23,871	15,422	12,049	10,008	$35,945	19.1%	15.0%	19.3%	18,287	73,939
Congressional District 6	56,858	7,212	13,675	17,075	18,896	$66,224	4.4%	2.3%	4.2%	3,512	88,050
Congressional District 7	44,166	11,394	11,572	12,481	8,719	$47,659	6.1%	6.7%	11.9%	6,181	77,750
Congressional District 8	68,232	27,003	18,443	15,271	7,515	$33,199	16.8%	11.7%	17.0%	11,364	92,358
Congressional District 9	85,846	24,530	25,653	22,826	12,837	$41,250	9.4%	7.8%	9.4%	12,208	114,283
Congressional District 10	66,509	18,564	19,034	18,552	10,359	$42,971	10.9%	7.0%	9.6%	10,441	94,308
Congressional District 11	60,558	13,430	16,188	15,228	15,712	$51,260	7.8%	6.8%	9.5%	6,621	89,098
Congressional District 12	65,340	24,540	17,679	15,915	7,206	$34,698	17.4%	11.2%	14.3%	11,839	84,758
Congressional District 13	49,732	11,682	13,590	15,548	8,912	$49,391	7.8%	3.6%	7.2%	8,378	79,561
Congressional District 14	66,880	26,545	19,213	14,171	6,951	$31,672	9.2%	10.4%	11.8%	10,336	93,104

Table G-5: 116th Congressional Districts - Income, Poverty Status and Receipt of Food Stamps (SNAP)—*Continued*

	Income of Households with Householder 65 Years and Over					Poverty Rate of Persons			Households with 1 or More Persons 60 Years and Over	
	Total Households	Less Than $25,000	$25,000 - $49,999	$50,000 - $99,999	$100,000 or More	Median Household Income	55 to 64 Years	65 to 74 Years	75 Years and Over	Receiving SNAP	Not Receiving SNAP
Hawaii											
Congressional District 1	70,265	12,678	13,573	17,957	26,057	$72,537	6.6%	6.0%	7.2%	9,408	97,979
Congressional District 2	72,863	13,343	18,788	19,358	21,374	$59,763	9.8%	6.6%	4.7%	11,398	101,197
Idaho											
Congressional District 1	92,785	25,883	25,988	28,551	12,363	$43,638	9.0%	7.1%	8.9%	8,033	128,049
Congressional District 2	75,829	22,696	21,471	21,494	10,168	$40,833	8.2%	5.0%	13.8%	6,904	107,699
Illinois											
Congressional District 1	75,535	22,836	19,711	20,255	12,733	$43,751	16.5%	9.8%	9.2%	23,277	93,161
Congressional District 2	70,616	22,058	20,793	19,186	8,579	$39,543	15.8%	10.5%	11.5%	16,257	93,646
Congressional District 3	65,535	20,123	15,888	17,996	11,528	$43,945	8.2%	7.5%	11.0%	9,970	94,116
Congressional District 4	41,750	16,838	10,116	10,235	4,561	$31,513	10.4%	9.7%	10.2%	12,249	61,735
Congressional District 5	59,359	15,708	16,484	14,757	12,410	$45,516	8.0%	7.0%	10.2%	10,471	82,410
Congressional District 6	69,318	13,379	14,448	20,440	21,051	$63,169	3.9%	3.6%	9.0%	4,703	106,237
Congressional District 7	68,489	30,755	13,333	11,523	12,878	$29,666	21.2%	16.8%	18.6%	24,988	75,263
Congressional District 8	56,235	12,908	13,966	17,678	11,683	$52,929	5.5%	5.6%	9.4%	9,865	84,943
Congressional District 9	79,138	21,969	16,954	19,147	21,068	$51,077	11.4%	7.8%	9.2%	12,441	102,698
Congressional District 10	66,510	14,699	14,879	17,104	19,828	$58,832	8.0%	6.1%	9.8%	9,773	94,005
Congressional District 11	52,546	10,218	13,466	17,346	11,516	$56,393	6.7%	4.8%	6.0%	9,283	78,307
Congressional District 12	76,976	24,625	22,757	20,526	9,068	$38,609	15.5%	8.3%	9.2%	15,682	100,535
Congressional District 13	70,188	17,349	20,216	20,279	12,344	$45,791	10.9%	6.1%	7.1%	10,930	95,849
Congressional District 14	62,076	12,240	14,018	22,301	13,517	$55,942	5.4%	3.0%	9.5%	5,106	96,076
Congressional District 15	85,584	25,841	26,854	24,061	8,828	$39,705	11.5%	8.0%	7.5%	11,905	109,265
Congressional District 16	78,940	20,237	24,557	22,558	11,588	$42,221	7.4%	3.7%	7.8%	9,668	105,616
Congressional District 17	80,793	25,454	24,147	22,479	8,713	$39,046	13.4%	6.1%	8.4%	14,209	105,322
Congressional District 18	82,452	20,507	21,670	25,473	14,802	$48,394	7.1%	5.7%	8.6%	7,964	110,682
Indiana											
Congressional District 1	76,616	21,661	22,910	22,730	9,315	$42,318	9.9%	7.3%	6.1%	7,560	107,962
Congressional District 2	73,760	22,725	23,259	18,999	8,777	$38,600	9.4%	6.9%	11.8%	5,158	106,030
Congressional District 3	73,190	22,000	22,359	20,256	8,575	$40,532	6.3%	5.0%	7.5%	6,991	103,343
Congressional District 4	73,454	17,451	22,196	23,505	10,302	$46,935	9.1%	5.3%	6.9%	6,814	106,007
Congressional District 5	70,733	15,020	21,624	21,452	12,637	$47,481	9.8%	4.9%	6.8%	5,797	102,842
Congressional District 6	82,018	27,040	23,465	25,912	5,601	$37,166	9.9%	6.7%	9.9%	7,990	111,755
Congressional District 7	59,136	19,507	17,946	15,950	5,733	$37,409	14.2%	7.8%	11.9%	12,687	83,050
Congressional District 8	76,786	23,683	23,273	21,982	7,848	$38,813	12.1%	6.2%	9.1%	7,526	109,682
Congressional District 9	74,116	19,751	23,277	22,554	8,534	$43,357	9.8%	6.9%	7.9%	7,353	104,864
Iowa											
Congressional District 1	86,615	22,155	27,245	25,660	11,555	$43,876	7.7%	4.4%	8.4%	7,843	118,284
Congressional District 2	85,169	25,089	24,677	23,862	11,541	$40,785	8.1%	5.6%	10.5%	9,178	118,387
Congressional District 3	77,565	19,912	24,481	23,007	10,165	$43,587	8.8%	4.3%	9.2%	7,686	108,903
Congressional District 4	88,810	25,459	26,070	26,114	11,167	$42,766	7.7%	4.3%	9.3%	7,174	122,923
Kansas											
Congressional District 1	71,833	23,021	22,803	18,159	7,850	$37,033	7.5%	7.7%	10.9%	5,402	99,620
Congressional District 2	76,380	22,523	22,508	20,903	10,446	$42,241	12.6%	7.2%	9.6%	7,262	105,933
Congressional District 3	66,710	12,703	17,955	20,803	15,249	$55,683	7.2%	4.6%	4.6%	4,231	100,684
Congressional District 4	72,233	21,517	21,894	20,222	8,600	$39,665	11.5%	6.2%	8.3%	7,566	103,564
Kentucky											
Congressional District 1	82,414	30,488	24,655	19,858	7,413	$35,340	16.0%	10.2%	13.0%	12,457	111,176
Congressional District 2	76,196	26,358	21,300	19,783	8,755	$37,835	13.7%	7.5%	12.1%	11,041	106,120
Congressional District 3	77,540	21,558	21,056	22,983	11,943	$43,940	13.1%	7.6%	7.1%	10,336	106,047
Congressional District 4	72,855	20,756	20,406	20,524	11,169	$43,312	8.6%	5.8%	10.1%	6,951	104,919
Congressional District 5	77,515	32,722	25,415	14,689	4,689	$29,322	23.3%	13.4%	16.4%	21,297	93,832
Congressional District 6	71,500	19,456	20,941	20,151	10,952	$43,315	12.3%	6.2%	8.5%	9,838	100,019
Louisiana											
Congressional District 1	80,976	25,323	21,696	20,781	13,176	$41,745	11.0%	8.2%	12.0%	10,109	115,289
Congressional District 2	71,183	29,719	18,476	14,315	8,673	$30,929	21.7%	14.1%	20.8%	21,440	92,443
Congressional District 3	74,293	26,095	21,792	16,021	10,385	$35,035	13.1%	8.3%	12.2%	13,088	100,261
Congressional District 4	78,294	29,402	22,646	18,619	7,627	$35,093	18.0%	10.7%	13.5%	15,925	99,940
Congressional District 5	74,058	29,440	21,919	15,802	6,897	$31,226	18.3%	14.1%	16.9%	14,857	99,284
Congressional District 6	68,175	18,524	17,576	19,198	12,877	$47,269	9.0%	5.9%	6.4%	9,238	97,659
Maine											
Congressional District 1	89,874	22,003	24,547	26,451	16,873	$48,197	8.2%	5.6%	9.9%	12,977	118,750
Congressional District 2	86,049	31,763	26,592	19,129	8,565	$34,390	13.3%	7.9%	12.9%	19,358	109,468
Maryland											
Congressional District 1	83,966	17,779	23,664	23,794	18,729	$50,771	7.2%	4.8%	7.2%	11,188	117,255
Congressional District 2	67,147	15,617	18,010	19,718	13,802	$49,927	9.9%	5.1%	7.8%	11,650	99,318
Congressional District 3	71,063	14,426	15,633	19,208	21,796	$61,894	5.8%	5.1%	9.3%	9,814	101,772
Congressional District 4	62,375	10,663	10,897	21,546	19,269	$69,671	5.7%	4.8%	9.9%	6,808	95,382
Congressional District 5	59,391	10,141	11,333	18,508	19,409	$71,405	4.2%	4.7%	4.8%	6,994	96,705
Congressional District 6	68,014	14,731	14,447	18,655	20,181	$59,217	7.8%	5.7%	9.0%	9,090	99,577
Congressional District 7	70,691	20,946	15,787	19,956	14,002	$46,834	15.5%	10.0%	10.3%	18,387	93,518
Congressional District 8	75,528	12,715	12,856	19,207	30,750	$80,518	4.5%	3.7%	7.9%	5,973	110,387

Table G-5: 116th Congressional Districts - Income, Poverty Status and Receipt of Food Stamps (SNAP)—Continued

	Income of Households with Householder 65 Years and Over					Poverty Rate of Persons			Households with 1 or More Persons 60 Years and Over	
	Total Households	Less Than $25,000	$25,000 - $49,999	$50,000 - $99,999	$100,000 or More	Median Household Income	55 to 64 Years	65 to 74 Years	75 Years and Over	Receiving SNAP	Not Receiving SNAP
Massachusetts											
Congressional District 1	82,753	25,172	20,955	23,024	13,602	$43,917	12.3%	7.4%	9.3%	18,125	106,102
Congressional District 2	73,141	21,773	17,743	19,566	14,059	$44,143	8.6%	6.9%	7.9%	13,993	102,230
Congressional District 3	63,762	17,340	14,541	16,941	14,940	$50,000	8.2%	6.1%	9.4%	13,819	93,768
Congressional District 4	78,013	17,017	16,701	22,138	22,157	$61,320	5.1%	4.1%	10.7%	10,245	107,335
Congressional District 5	78,114	18,439	15,734	20,500	23,441	$60,239	4.9%	5.7%	10.4%	8,519	110,198
Congressional District 6	87,798	19,958	22,581	24,152	21,107	$52,014	7.7%	5.9%	9.3%	11,938	122,186
Congressional District 7	56,604	22,405	10,821	11,411	11,967	$37,279	15.7%	11.6%	22.8%	24,012	68,921
Congressional District 8	77,368	21,803	17,975	19,138	18,452	$48,551	7.1%	6.4%	11.2%	14,178	108,166
Congressional District 9	102,484	23,673	26,611	29,826	22,374	$51,085	9.0%	7.0%	9.2%	13,596	132,048
Michigan											
Congressional District 1	101,550	28,050	31,171	30,161	12,168	$41,866	11.6%	6.6%	8.0%	11,692	133,697
Congressional District 2	74,092	19,721	24,600	22,111	7,660	$42,020	9.5%	5.4%	11.0%	9,214	102,180
Congressional District 3	71,288	18,458	22,771	20,504	9,555	$43,659	10.0%	6.7%	7.4%	9,170	98,971
Congressional District 4	85,844	23,619	30,459	23,258	8,508	$39,956	12.0%	7.9%	7.2%	12,510	113,800
Congressional District 5	82,413	22,129	27,300	24,326	8,658	$41,642	14.9%	8.3%	7.8%	15,694	107,233
Congressional District 6	77,966	22,235	24,133	22,346	9,252	$40,431	9.4%	7.0%	10.1%	9,592	106,668
Congressional District 7	81,726	20,556	23,974	25,806	11,390	$45,631	8.1%	4.2%	6.8%	8,791	112,452
Congressional District 8	70,961	14,212	20,201	21,931	14,617	$51,895	6.6%	5.1%	7.5%	6,441	101,428
Congressional District 9	77,949	23,866	21,530	21,069	11,484	$40,889	9.5%	9.0%	10.3%	12,892	107,784
Congressional District 10	82,431	20,986	26,648	24,285	10,512	$43,293	8.8%	6.3%	10.5%	11,673	115,140
Congressional District 11	74,520	14,461	19,124	24,405	16,530	$55,111	6.2%	4.8%	7.2%	5,437	112,186
Congressional District 12	68,141	19,649	19,066	18,700	10,726	$42,230	9.2%	7.4%	7.3%	9,239	94,075
Congressional District 13	66,480	28,098	19,666	14,787	3,929	$31,380	24.9%	20.0%	18.9%	27,324	77,782
Congressional District 14	78,200	23,182	20,301	20,551	14,166	$43,451	17.3%	10.8%	12.2%	22,866	96,719
Minnesota											
Congressional District 1	73,571	21,284	20,834	21,327	10,126	$42,884	7.3%	5.5%	10.7%	5,367	100,871
Congressional District 2	60,310	13,895	15,488	19,358	11,569	$51,545	6.0%	4.5%	5.8%	4,043	90,549
Congressional District 3	70,971	13,820	18,273	22,189	16,689	$54,672	5.3%	2.7%	6.5%	5,037	103,987
Congressional District 4	66,731	14,067	16,752	20,666	15,246	$53,947	8.2%	5.5%	7.1%	9,662	92,499
Congressional District 5	59,080	17,980	14,201	16,123	10,776	$43,662	13.7%	10.0%	13.0%	10,746	79,099
Congressional District 6	55,451	12,652	15,269	18,589	8,941	$49,746	4.3%	5.5%	6.4%	3,682	84,344
Congressional District 7	80,697	25,525	22,200	22,862	10,110	$40,149	8.2%	5.2%	10.5%	7,220	109,899
Congressional District 8	85,622	24,593	25,652	26,082	9,295	$41,527	10.3%	6.1%	9.7%	8,131	117,779
Mississippi											
Congressional District 1	76,815	27,190	23,059	19,273	7,293	$34,888	13.2%	7.9%	12.3%	10,196	103,970
Congressional District 2	70,855	26,593	20,178	16,654	7,430	$34,689	17.9%	12.0%	15.1%	17,309	91,043
Congressional District 3	76,840	29,255	19,259	18,352	9,974	$35,439	15.9%	11.4%	14.6%	11,128	102,869
Congressional District 4	78,853	24,280	22,060	21,928	10,585	$40,049	16.9%	10.2%	12.3%	13,261	103,357
Missouri											
Congressional District 1	73,344	25,246	21,319	17,826	8,953	$37,992	14.8%	11.0%	14.9%	16,433	96,763
Congressional District 2	89,159	14,330	23,858	28,307	22,664	$57,429	4.9%	2.4%	4.6%	3,456	126,106
Congressional District 3	78,130	19,147	24,630	23,839	10,514	$45,202	7.2%	4.1%	7.5%	4,730	115,112
Congressional District 4	80,682	24,589	26,409	20,746	8,938	$38,278	10.5%	7.9%	10.4%	8,593	112,622
Congressional District 5	75,846	22,855	21,831	21,300	9,860	$41,732	12.4%	5.7%	8.3%	10,643	105,833
Congressional District 6	77,515	20,762	22,991	22,732	11,030	$43,082	9.4%	4.8%	8.3%	7,001	110,191
Congressional District 7	89,835	31,261	29,127	21,290	8,157	$35,771	14.0%	7.4%	8.9%	14,522	113,112
Congressional District 8	87,058	34,987	25,249	18,920	7,902	$33,099	15.1%	10.3%	11.6%	13,025	115,545
Montana											
Congressional District (at Large)	123,306	34,330	35,958	35,839	17,179	$42,745	10.9%	7.9%	10.4%	11,980	175,720
Nebraska											
Congressional District 1	63,478	15,869	18,365	18,953	10,291	$46,707	7.3%	4.2%	8.1%	4,228	89,415
Congressional District 2	55,623	14,259	15,686	15,629	10,049	$45,909	9.8%	5.0%	8.6%	7,365	79,679
Congressional District 3	75,440	25,020	22,213	19,146	9,061	$38,182	8.5%	6.1%	12.1%	5,776	102,331
Nevada											
Congressional District 1	60,446	23,974	16,859	12,713	6,900	$33,059	20.8%	15.3%	15.9%	17,339	77,349
Congressional District 2	79,157	17,886	20,541	25,149	15,581	$51,673	9.7%	6.5%	10.4%	8,587	114,486
Congressional District 3	74,823	15,459	19,484	22,881	16,999	$55,104	8.1%	5.9%	8.1%	7,880	112,215
Congressional District 4	65,507	16,508	18,505	18,323	12,171	$46,842	13.1%	8.1%	8.6%	10,338	96,871
New Hampshire											
Congressional District 1	70,323	16,553	17,709	22,057	14,004	$51,370	5.9%	4.0%	6.6%	6,925	106,034
Congressional District 2	75,465	18,610	19,694	21,538	15,623	$49,330	5.8%	4.7%	5.2%	5,132	113,076
New Jersey											
Congressional District 1	71,071	17,260	19,860	18,712	15,239	$48,204	8.7%	5.4%	8.2%	10,040	102,094
Congressional District 2	82,565	19,547	20,204	26,257	16,557	$52,062	9.8%	7.0%	8.2%	9,575	115,362
Congressional District 3	91,189	17,349	26,150	28,806	18,884	$52,317	5.1%	3.9%	5.4%	5,775	127,798
Congressional District 4	94,196	20,924	23,634	26,660	22,978	$52,823	4.5%	5.1%	6.4%	5,928	128,881
Congressional District 5	77,517	15,211	16,210	18,704	27,392	$68,862	3.9%	4.1%	7.2%	4,694	116,151
Congressional District 6	59,850	14,518	11,541	17,481	16,310	$59,112	6.9%	5.6%	9.3%	8,889	93,481
Congressional District 7	69,109	11,618	15,536	18,611	23,344	$68,360	3.8%	3.8%	6.6%	3,964	107,869
Congressional District 8	49,058	19,041	13,440	9,302	7,275	$32,390	10.1%	10.0%	16.6%	15,502	72,480

Table G-5: 116th Congressional Districts - Income, Poverty Status and Receipt of Food Stamps (SNAP)—Continued

		Income of Households with Householder 65 Years and Over					Poverty Rate of Persons			Households with 1 or More Persons 60 Years and Over	
	Total Households	Less Than $25,000	$25,000 - $49,999	$50,000 - $99,999	$100,000 or More	Median Household Income	55 to 64 Years	65 to 74 Years	75 Years and Over	Receiving SNAP	Not Receiving SNAP
New Jersey—Cont.											
Congressional District 9	65,187	21,070	13,722	14,602	15,793	$43,980	10.2%	9.1%	13.0%	16,276	93,265
Congressional District 10	59,944	22,110	11,669	15,530	10,635	$42,161	14.6%	10.7%	16.3%	18,989	87,338
Congressional District 11	75,106	11,033	14,855	20,458	28,760	$73,318	3.4%	3.3%	4.4%	3,172	115,453
Congressional District 12	72,675	16,599	17,719	17,487	20,870	$53,948	6.7%	7.3%	8.4%	8,821	104,262
New Mexico											
Congressional District 1	72,184	21,789	18,194	19,291	12,910	$43,986	13.9%	9.6%	11.7%	13,191	99,255
Congressional District 2	76,332	28,704	21,683	17,715	8,230	$32,328	19.5%	14.1%	16.8%	18,118	94,952
Congressional District 3	79,579	23,627	21,183	21,913	12,856	$43,886	16.3%	12.6%	12.1%	12,826	102,952
New York											
Congressional District 1	76,483	14,757	16,821	22,716	22,189	$60,994	7.9%	4.3%	5.0%	7,827	108,616
Congressional District 2	62,257	11,668	12,588	19,280	18,721	$66,924	5.8%	5.5%	6.8%	7,278	99,121
Congressional District 3	82,562	16,241	14,658	18,934	32,729	$75,202	4.0%	4.7%	7.8%	7,546	117,978
Congressional District 4	72,166	13,606	15,604	18,582	24,374	$66,708	4.9%	3.3%	7.0%	5,418	109,446
Congressional District 5	58,232	16,111	12,443	14,586	15,092	$51,089	8.4%	9.0%	13.8%	22,460	86,051
Congressional District 6	72,457	24,421	16,110	16,992	14,934	$41,185	10.5%	11.4%	16.9%	20,574	101,473
Congressional District 7	52,238	26,324	9,210	9,244	7,460	$24,731	18.8%	19.5%	31.0%	32,107	54,553
Congressional District 8	75,998	32,831	15,452	15,248	12,467	$30,720	16.2%	16.3%	25.7%	36,657	83,000
Congressional District 9	68,265	25,720	13,804	15,280	13,461	$39,723	11.4%	12.2%	21.9%	31,474	82,450
Congressional District 10	78,025	24,819	15,123	13,607	24,476	$48,226	12.5%	13.3%	18.1%	19,984	92,606
Congressional District 11	73,411	24,691	15,962	15,307	17,451	$43,569	11.8%	12.0%	17.3%	21,845	100,153
Congressional District 12	75,496	19,367	13,935	15,897	26,297	$62,353	11.6%	8.1%	12.2%	11,388	96,745
Congressional District 13	63,218	34,463	12,399	10,932	5,424	$21,349	25.1%	24.4%	29.4%	39,734	65,765
Congressional District 14	53,283	22,539	11,633	12,575	6,536	$31,985	12.4%	10.8%	19.1%	18,601	70,144
Congressional District 15	54,658	32,241	9,362	8,598	4,457	$18,411	30.8%	26.5%	33.9%	47,623	44,261
Congressional District 16	80,291	22,912	19,515	18,270	19,594	$46,401	12.5%	8.9%	11.8%	22,494	100,402
Congressional District 17	74,563	13,097	13,662	21,193	26,611	$73,749	7.3%	5.2%	7.6%	9,279	103,831
Congressional District 18	66,493	15,385	14,612	18,533	17,963	$56,768	6.4%	4.9%	6.3%	9,350	100,624
Congressional District 19	87,516	21,351	23,211	26,787	16,167	$49,111	11.2%	6.6%	7.5%	12,052	120,448
Congressional District 20	77,086	18,338	19,138	22,816	16,794	$51,838	8.7%	5.7%	7.0%	12,369	102,653
Congressional District 21	79,962	23,398	24,212	20,953	11,399	$41,057	11.1%	6.7%	7.2%	15,596	105,042
Congressional District 22	80,325	24,674	22,406	22,447	10,798	$40,487	12.7%	7.3%	10.2%	15,463	107,388
Congressional District 23	81,195	24,893	24,393	22,048	9,861	$40,572	11.3%	6.9%	10.6%	14,711	107,646
Congressional District 24	78,035	22,851	22,162	21,037	11,985	$42,194	8.8%	6.3%	10.0%	13,922	104,621
Congressional District 25	78,730	23,459	21,457	21,219	12,595	$42,083	10.1%	7.4%	11.5%	14,465	106,219
Congressional District 26	82,533	26,920	22,752	21,755	11,106	$39,400	13.3%	8.6%	9.4%	19,737	103,259
Congressional District 27	86,874	22,428	26,385	25,786	12,275	$44,051	6.6%	5.6%	6.4%	10,039	122,788
North Carolina											
Congressional District 1	80,889	28,505	21,051	20,355	10,978	$37,439	13.2%	9.1%	14.0%	18,807	103,893
Congressional District 2	70,276	16,942	19,677	21,684	11,973	$47,759	8.0%	4.9%	9.3%	9,474	100,496
Congressional District 3	82,624	24,512	24,782	24,291	9,039	$39,915	14.5%	7.0%	10.4%	11,981	113,519
Congressional District 4	61,533	12,322	13,257	18,428	17,526	$61,906	7.9%	4.8%	7.4%	7,343	93,005
Congressional District 5	91,378	31,235	27,078	23,093	9,972	$36,198	12.1%	6.7%	9.5%	11,124	123,795
Congressional District 6	85,518	26,089	25,022	21,545	12,862	$40,399	10.1%	6.4%	10.5%	12,951	116,494
Congressional District 7	98,199	28,861	26,706	27,667	14,965	$43,272	14.7%	7.5%	11.4%	17,703	127,852
Congressional District 8	73,908	20,972	22,170	20,006	10,760	$40,879	9.8%	7.7%	7.7%	9,740	102,217
Congressional District 9	74,337	21,516	20,639	18,982	13,200	$42,440	9.7%	6.2%	12.4%	14,776	99,460
Congressional District 10	88,807	29,831	26,757	21,287	10,932	$37,510	10.9%	9.0%	9.7%	11,626	119,973
Congressional District 11	105,969	32,826	31,451	27,497	14,195	$38,727	13.1%	7.1%	8.3%	12,210	138,930
Congressional District 12	51,532	14,721	14,250	13,895	8,666	$41,755	10.4%	7.1%	10.5%	11,698	75,952
Congressional District 13	80,026	24,673	22,890	20,626	11,837	$39,633	11.6%	6.6%	10.0%	11,952	113,092
North Dakota											
Congressional District (at Large)	73,062	21,765	19,231	19,960	12,106	$44,824	7.6%	5.0%	16.1%	6,519	101,504
Ohio											
Congressional District 1	70,419	18,865	18,635	19,835	13,084	$46,592	10.8%	7.1%	9.0%	10,397	97,708
Congressional District 2	75,635	23,317	20,237	19,896	12,185	$41,069	10.4%	7.1%	10.8%	10,790	103,769
Congressional District 3	57,111	17,420	15,075	16,743	7,873	$41,786	17.4%	7.7%	14.8%	15,367	79,697
Congressional District 4	76,480	22,937	23,887	21,484	8,172	$39,423	8.5%	5.0%	10.8%	8,651	108,279
Congressional District 5	80,319	19,364	26,471	23,243	11,241	$43,566	6.9%	6.2%	7.5%	6,496	112,066
Congressional District 6	86,624	29,405	27,896	22,345	6,978	$35,479	12.6%	7.2%	11.7%	15,864	113,276
Congressional District 7	83,646	24,198	27,660	22,634	9,154	$39,738	9.0%	5.3%	9.0%	9,637	112,628
Congressional District 8	77,530	20,956	25,923	20,504	10,147	$41,370	8.6%	5.3%	6.6%	12,152	103,624
Congressional District 9	73,334	26,448	21,722	18,422	6,742	$35,530	16.5%	10.5%	13.0%	17,088	97,224
Congressional District 10	83,276	21,761	24,235	23,332	13,948	$44,705	12.5%	7.1%	8.7%	10,484	111,724
Congressional District 11	81,847	30,914	21,805	18,388	10,740	$34,334	22.3%	13.4%	14.3%	24,921	98,966
Congressional District 12	74,441	16,720	21,572	23,010	13,139	$48,401	6.5%	5.1%	6.9%	6,505	105,499
Congressional District 13	85,480	28,176	25,606	23,132	8,566	$37,432	13.3%	9.5%	9.1%	16,465	112,210
Congressional District 14	90,210	21,416	28,255	25,182	15,357	$45,809	6.2%	6.2%	6.2%	8,183	124,761
Congressional District 15	74,245	18,990	22,604	22,338	10,313	$44,273	9.3%	6.5%	7.4%	10,689	102,595
Congressional District 16	90,875	22,447	27,873	27,233	13,322	$45,140	6.2%	4.7%	6.2%	7,528	123,522

Table G-5: 116th Congressional Districts - Income, Poverty Status and Receipt of Food Stamps (SNAP)—Continued

	Income of Households with Householder 65 Years and Over					Poverty Rate of Persons			Households with 1 or More Persons 60 Years and Over	
	Total Households	Less Than $25,000	$25,000 - $49,999	$50,000 - $99,999	$100,000 or More	Median Household Income	55 to 64 Years	65 to 74 Years	75 Years and Over	Receiving SNAP	Not Receiving SNAP
Oklahoma											
Congressional District 1	75,187	19,602	22,615	19,364	13,606	$44,008	11.0%	6.0%	6.9%	8,731	105,701
Congressional District 2	89,104	34,187	26,472	20,336	8,109	$34,047	15.1%	11.4%	12.8%	15,191	113,546
Congressional District 3	77,764	22,878	23,111	21,402	10,373	$40,807	11.1%	5.0%	8.7%	8,022	106,309
Congressional District 4	74,601	19,683	22,129	20,980	11,809	$43,937	9.7%	7.1%	7.2%	10,770	99,730
Congressional District 5	73,230	20,266	20,501	20,782	11,681	$43,833	13.9%	7.9%	8.3%	11,850	100,133
Oregon											
Congressional District 1	80,171	18,826	21,220	23,779	16,346	$50,072	7.6%	7.0%	6.9%	11,559	111,027
Congressional District 2	107,493	28,021	32,644	32,173	14,655	$43,390	12.2%	5.8%	10.8%	22,771	133,656
Congressional District 3	72,156	18,417	18,947	19,584	15,208	$48,159	11.4%	6.0%	10.9%	14,494	98,052
Congressional District 4	108,647	28,231	30,014	35,290	15,112	$46,907	14.6%	7.5%	8.3%	24,680	129,307
Congressional District 5	92,800	22,182	26,399	27,892	16,327	$48,133	10.8%	7.5%	7.1%	16,655	119,272
Pennsylvania											
Congressional District 1	77,257	16,565	17,694	22,849	20,149	$56,764	4.8%	3.8%	5.8%	7,130	114,788
Congressional District 2	60,881	24,793	15,734	14,242	6,112	$31,624	22.0%	12.9%	18.3%	29,991	70,287
Congressional District 3	73,242	31,076	16,277	16,063	9,826	$32,286	23.3%	15.5%	20.1%	29,813	78,800
Congressional District 4	78,776	15,354	19,817	24,388	19,217	$55,453	4.2%	3.8%	7.9%	6,066	112,036
Congressional District 5	69,999	17,290	19,197	18,873	14,639	$48,160	9.3%	5.2%	9.6%	12,470	97,156
Congressional District 6	70,325	12,920	16,817	22,123	18,465	$57,334	7.6%	4.5%	7.4%	8,940	100,658
Congressional District 7	77,971	20,519	23,712	21,619	12,121	$43,786	9.6%	5.4%	7.8%	12,153	106,350
Congressional District 8	83,465	26,567	23,885	22,179	10,834	$39,830	11.2%	7.1%	11.7%	15,920	111,727
Congressional District 9	87,790	29,386	26,600	22,209	9,595	$35,972	7.1%	6.4%	10.2%	11,264	117,605
Congressional District 10	79,383	19,587	25,759	20,997	13,040	$44,414	7.6%	5.0%	8.0%	11,603	107,370
Congressional District 11	80,041	18,307	24,216	25,079	12,439	$47,889	6.2%	3.3%	7.8%	8,358	110,830
Congressional District 12	82,658	26,530	26,640	20,434	9,054	$37,416	9.4%	6.6%	10.5%	11,902	110,247
Congressional District 13	89,664	26,483	28,049	25,973	9,159	$39,813	8.5%	5.4%	10.7%	12,609	115,619
Congressional District 14	93,691	27,939	28,387	25,383	11,982	$39,527	9.2%	5.9%	8.2%	16,091	123,428
Congressional District 15	89,604	29,292	30,557	22,096	7,659	$36,189	10.3%	6.7%	8.6%	15,989	114,418
Congressional District 16	85,638	25,233	29,365	22,279	8,761	$37,237	11.6%	5.6%	7.8%	13,802	113,039
Congressional District 17	91,494	26,151	27,244	23,484	14,615	$41,373	6.2%	4.2%	9.2%	10,105	124,638
Congressional District 18	86,727	30,367	22,763	21,723	11,874	$37,784	12.6%	7.8%	12.3%	19,308	109,412
Rhode Island											
Congressional District 1	58,051	20,293	12,643	14,355	10,760	$40,471	11.4%	10.2%	11.6%	15,009	71,336
Congressional District 2	55,912	15,650	14,787	14,567	10,908	$43,904	7.0%	7.0%	13.2%	11,754	76,067
South Carolina											
Congressional District 1	88,046	16,136	21,293	28,450	22,167	$59,422	11.9%	6.4%	5.4%	5,706	120,159
Congressional District 2	74,110	18,731	22,430	19,879	13,070	$45,584	9.3%	7.5%	10.4%	8,908	103,301
Congressional District 3	81,613	29,979	23,769	18,154	9,711	$34,669	11.9%	8.4%	10.7%	12,719	105,681
Congressional District 4	71,349	18,866	19,535	22,185	10,763	$44,904	11.9%	5.9%	8.5%	8,789	101,362
Congressional District 5	74,188	23,491	21,485	20,240	8,972	$40,183	11.0%	8.1%	12.3%	12,214	99,297
Congressional District 6	65,991	25,657	19,624	14,309	6,401	$33,391	22.0%	11.1%	16.0%	16,628	83,327
Congressional District 7	97,354	28,820	27,805	28,216	12,513	$40,601	16.7%	9.8%	12.5%	14,136	127,326
South Dakota											
Congressional District (at Large)	91,545	24,945	27,530	26,034	13,036	$42,361	9.2%	5.2%	13.4%	7,757	126,896
Tennessee											
Congressional District 1	90,439	32,002	26,636	21,728	10,073	$36,022	12.5%	9.2%	8.6%	15,073	118,830
Congressional District 2	82,510	22,642	23,916	22,936	13,016	$43,394	11.2%	5.6%	7.9%	9,972	111,859
Congressional District 3	85,020	26,490	24,017	23,392	11,121	$39,328	12.2%	7.5%	9.7%	13,789	112,439
Congressional District 4	71,779	21,164	23,171	19,078	8,366	$39,884	12.6%	6.1%	10.5%	11,162	99,824
Congressional District 5	63,177	17,017	15,324	18,226	12,610	$48,620	11.6%	8.0%	9.1%	9,221	88,560
Congressional District 6	84,448	24,662	25,182	22,967	11,637	$40,883	10.6%	7.3%	10.0%	13,765	115,082
Congressional District 7	69,748	21,422	21,757	16,338	10,231	$38,757	12.2%	5.7%	12.3%	9,026	98,341
Congressional District 8	74,087	20,003	20,436	20,133	13,515	$44,503	12.0%	7.3%	8.4%	12,556	100,921
Congressional District 9	59,816	24,828	13,691	14,156	7,141	$31,185	19.6%	11.8%	18.6%	17,717	78,875
Texas											
Congressional District 1	72,798	23,764	21,718	17,645	9,671	$37,872	13.1%	10.6%	11.5%	12,275	95,504
Congressional District 2	54,196	10,854	12,840	14,805	15,697	$57,726	8.6%	6.2%	6.9%	4,673	87,483
Congressional District 3	53,124	10,483	12,194	15,860	14,587	$60,614	5.5%	6.2%	11.1%	2,890	90,376
Congressional District 4	78,259	22,787	24,300	21,763	9,409	$41,248	12.4%	7.8%	9.8%	10,425	106,497
Congressional District 5	62,596	17,954	19,197	16,861	8,584	$39,274	11.7%	7.8%	10.3%	7,138	90,902
Congressional District 6	53,825	12,708	13,212	15,934	11,971	$51,433	6.7%	4.9%	6.3%	4,829	85,025
Congressional District 7	48,644	9,873	11,386	12,840	14,545	$60,582	8.8%	4.9%	11.7%	6,671	81,600
Congressional District 8	69,143	16,520	20,015	18,231	14,377	$47,638	9.0%	7.2%	10.1%	7,951	103,534
Congressional District 9	44,663	14,726	11,597	12,475	5,865	$39,740	11.8%	9.4%	19.5%	17,207	66,078
Congressional District 10	65,686	14,809	15,900	19,289	15,688	$54,337	9.0%	5.5%	5.8%	4,678	102,951
Congressional District 11	78,507	24,317	22,086	19,162	12,942	$40,508	8.9%	6.4%	13.1%	6,908	108,597
Congressional District 12	64,573	18,525	14,314	17,936	13,798	$48,401	8.0%	6.8%	13.7%	5,764	95,870
Congressional District 13	66,844	20,067	19,916	17,457	9,404	$40,000	11.3%	7.4%	8.2%	7,494	93,137
Congressional District 14	64,687	18,856	16,795	16,638	12,398	$43,572	11.0%	7.7%	9.7%	11,904	89,982
Congressional District 15	49,383	20,171	12,405	11,632	5,175	$31,495	18.0%	20.7%	22.9%	18,024	62,112
Congressional District 16	54,922	24,085	12,700	12,044	6,093	$31,615	14.8%	13.6%	23.7%	17,692	69,448

Table G-5: 116th Congressional Districts - Income, Poverty Status and Receipt of Food Stamps (SNAP)—*Continued*

	Income of Households with Householder 65 Years and Over					Poverty Rate of Persons			Households with 1 or More Persons 60 Years and Over	
	Total Households	Less Than $25,000	$25,000 - $49,999	$50,000 - $99,999	$100,000 or More	Median Household Income	55 to 64 Years	65 to 74 Years	75 Years and Over	Receiving SNAP	Not Receiving SNAP
Texas—Cont.											
Congressional District 17	60,429	18,717	16,161	16,099	9,452	$42,451	10.1%	7.8%	9.1%	7,247	84,731
Congressional District 18	48,394	18,563	12,640	11,739	5,452	$34,683	18.5%	15.1%	16.9%	16,319	68,027
Congressional District 19	61,282	18,530	17,093	16,960	8,699	$41,381	10.4%	7.8%	10.1%	9,246	83,464
Congressional District 20	54,396	17,732	14,509	14,527	7,628	$39,661	14.4%	10.6%	12.8%	12,000	72,845
Congressional District 21	78,403	14,573	18,307	24,086	21,437	$59,847	7.9%	4.7%	5.6%	6,117	112,257
Congressional District 22	53,978	9,685	13,937	15,116	15,240	$57,709	5.4%	5.4%	10.5%	7,443	91,978
Congressional District 23	61,757	22,183	15,310	14,492	9,772	$37,562	13.6%	12.9%	16.2%	16,033	79,886
Congressional District 24	53,834	10,645	12,942	15,154	15,093	$57,379	7.2%	3.5%	6.3%	4,368	87,931
Congressional District 25	67,419	14,021	17,604	21,053	14,741	$53,205	8.1%	4.8%	7.9%	6,016	99,050
Congressional District 26	47,608	7,361	12,293	15,361	12,593	$61,210	6.5%	2.5%	3.3%	3,255	85,041
Congressional District 27	72,287	23,822	18,637	19,430	10,398	$39,625	13.2%	9.7%	13.6%	17,537	93,869
Congressional District 28	51,475	20,035	13,223	12,973	5,244	$36,376	15.8%	16.5%	21.3%	17,595	63,959
Congressional District 29	34,966	14,625	8,200	8,452	3,689	$32,137	19.1%	17.1%	21.9%	13,331	53,589
Congressional District 30	51,624	19,069	12,043	13,443	7,069	$37,505	17.7%	14.1%	20.3%	14,115	74,903
Congressional District 31	58,418	12,175	13,849	20,250	12,144	$56,006	7.0%	4.5%	6.9%	6,501	86,777
Congressional District 32	54,836	11,202	12,082	15,076	16,476	$57,900	5.3%	4.9%	8.7%	5,292	89,328
Congressional District 33	41,573	17,748	10,520	10,031	3,274	$31,051	17.0%	13.4%	17.3%	12,729	58,273
Congressional District 34	58,605	27,189	15,119	11,679	4,618	$28,094	19.0%	17.4%	20.0%	18,981	71,269
Congressional District 35	47,397	18,397	11,415	12,003	5,582	$34,947	18.5%	13.0%	20.7%	12,705	69,460
Congressional District 36	67,327	17,375	20,264	19,273	10,415	$44,270	10.1%	7.9%	8.6%	9,365	95,012
Utah											
Congressional District 1	49,505	9,120	13,114	17,010	10,261	$54,525	6.2%	4.1%	8.8%	4,467	74,238
Congressional District 2	63,114	14,029	18,400	19,157	11,528	$48,228	10.2%	6.3%	6.5%	7,010	88,460
Congressional District 3	50,425	9,042	11,189	17,968	12,226	$60,140	6.0%	4.0%	6.9%	4,332	71,541
Congressional District 4	47,507	10,103	12,726	15,983	8,695	$53,114	4.5%	3.5%	6.9%	6,049	70,811
Vermont											
Congressional District (at Large)	78,032	20,448	22,252	21,391	13,941	$44,302	8.8%	7.8%	9.9%	10,559	105,648
Virginia											
Congressional District 1	71,096	14,099	13,613	23,413	19,971	$64,681	6.4%	4.4%	7.2%	7,069	104,993
Congressional District 2	70,186	14,815	15,381	22,178	17,812	$58,655	7.7%	3.8%	8.7%	5,439	101,120
Congressional District 3	65,980	23,525	14,580	18,413	9,462	$40,563	14.2%	8.8%	14.5%	10,451	92,788
Congressional District 4	73,062	23,288	18,293	19,996	11,485	$42,168	10.9%	10.0%	9.7%	11,958	101,972
Congressional District 5	92,839	26,411	25,736	25,280	15,412	$43,029	11.0%	6.5%	11.2%	9,689	126,483
Congressional District 6	88,775	26,099	27,255	24,132	11,289	$40,598	12.0%	6.4%	10.3%	10,698	119,492
Congressional District 7	77,751	17,601	18,072	22,239	19,839	$54,233	6.1%	5.7%	8.6%	8,236	112,881
Congressional District 8	61,139	10,709	9,062	14,470	26,898	$84,592	6.2%	5.4%	10.4%	5,010	92,369
Congressional District 9	91,160	36,055	27,029	20,591	7,485	$31,869	15.5%	12.0%	11.9%	12,355	119,180
Congressional District 10	58,139	7,746	8,378	16,034	25,981	$88,255	3.3%	2.0%	5.0%	4,253	99,215
Congressional District 11	50,903	7,098	7,124	14,347	22,334	$85,530	4.2%	3.6%	10.0%	3,885	89,076
Washington											
Congressional District 1	59,798	10,275	13,977	19,244	16,302	$59,401	7.1%	4.4%	6.7%	7,725	91,583
Congressional District 2	76,941	16,772	19,161	24,786	16,222	$53,203	7.8%	6.6%	7.6%	11,274	108,516
Congressional District 3	80,415	18,521	24,146	23,486	14,262	$46,823	9.5%	4.8%	8.3%	13,984	108,339
Congressional District 4	63,042	16,233	16,693	19,161	10,955	$48,138	10.6%	6.9%	9.6%	12,305	82,810
Congressional District 5	79,411	21,387	24,848	22,175	11,001	$41,904	13.4%	6.8%	9.0%	15,597	103,166
Congressional District 6	90,782	20,130	22,480	30,919	17,253	$53,436	9.9%	6.0%	7.6%	12,430	120,586
Congressional District 7	71,815	15,057	17,685	17,783	21,290	$55,973	7.5%	5.7%	9.5%	9,718	95,980
Congressional District 8	63,049	12,400	13,846	21,925	14,878	$60,637	5.4%	3.5%	8.5%	8,705	98,172
Congressional District 9	60,457	13,152	14,735	16,667	15,903	$54,991	8.7%	6.9%	10.5%	13,138	84,363
Congressional District 10	68,145	13,449	17,741	24,001	12,954	$53,885	9.2%	5.4%	7.5%	10,819	94,120
West Virginia											
Congressional District 1	75,979	25,718	21,927	19,491	8,843	$37,794	11.1%	8.6%	9.3%	11,650	96,457
Congressional District 2	76,898	21,610	25,897	20,091	9,300	$38,553	14.0%	8.4%	8.2%	13,360	99,216
Congressional District 3	78,708	30,309	24,177	18,040	6,182	$31,773	20.5%	10.8%	13.5%	19,916	93,895
Wisconsin											
Congressional District 1	74,558	18,618	21,368	23,148	11,424	$46,291	7.3%	6.4%	6.7%	8,380	105,666
Congressional District 2	73,821	15,991	21,689	22,039	14,102	$48,913	5.7%	4.4%	7.0%	8,276	102,537
Congressional District 3	82,297	25,037	24,920	23,854	8,486	$40,284	8.0%	6.2%	9.8%	9,466	111,328
Congressional District 4	56,464	20,329	16,901	12,950	6,284	$34,237	18.6%	11.7%	15.9%	19,153	73,990
Congressional District 5	83,076	19,531	24,666	26,136	12,743	$46,717	5.2%	4.0%	7.0%	5,963	118,588
Congressional District 6	85,253	25,850	27,858	22,220	9,325	$38,539	7.0%	5.1%	9.1%	7,164	118,301
Congressional District 7	91,109	26,357	29,710	25,526	9,516	$39,772	8.3%	5.6%	10.1%	9,490	125,079
Congressional District 8	78,599	23,445	26,188	20,319	8,647	$37,869	7.1%	4.7%	10.4%	8,262	110,611
Wyoming											
Congressional District (at Large)	61,902	14,865	18,952	16,352	11,733	$44,870	7.7%	5.7%	8.3%	3,208	90,384

PART H
DISABILITY STATUS AND TYPE

DISABILITY STATUS AND TYPE

Life expectancy at birth in the United States has steadily increased and the latest data from the National Center for Health Statistics says women's life expectancy has increased from 77.4 years in 1980 to 81.1 years in 2017, unchanged from a year earlier. Male life expectancy has also increased from 70.0 years in 1980 to 76.1 years in 2017 but that represents a 0.1 year decline from 2016[1]. Both have declined from 2014, though more quickly for males which also widened the gap between male and female life expectancy to 5.0 years even though it has declined from its peak in the 1970s. It is unclear whether

the increasing life span will bring increased incidence of disability or if medical advances will ease the process of aging. Part of the uncertainty lies in the data. While life expectancy can be calculated based on detailed mortality data, measuring basic functions of activity that are defined as disabilities is much more difficult.

The Census Bureau's American Community Survey asks a series of questions about activities of daily living to measure the extent of identified disabilities. These are not clinical measures but the respondent's identification of difficulties they experience. These include difficulties in: vision, hearing, cognitive ability, ambulatory ability, and self-care ability.

In the United States, just almost 25 percent of the population age 65 to 74 indicated that they experience some disability but that percentage nearly doubles for those age 75 and over where 47.5 percent have a disability. For the over

[1] U.S. Department of Health and Human Services, Centers for Disease Control and Prevention, National Center for Health Statistics, National Vital Statistics Reports, Vol. 68, No. 7, *United States Life Tables, 2017*.

Percent of the Population 75 Years and Over With a Disability

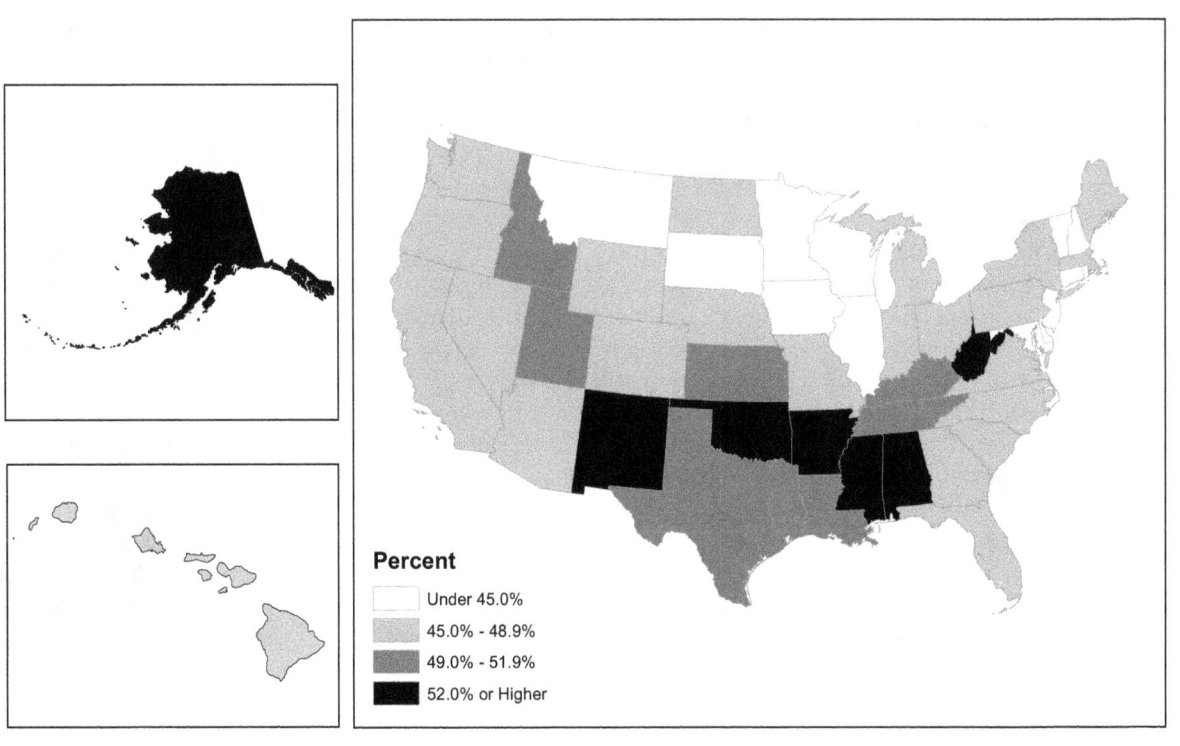

Percent

Under 45.0%

45.0% - 48.9%

49.0% - 51.9%

52.0% or Higher

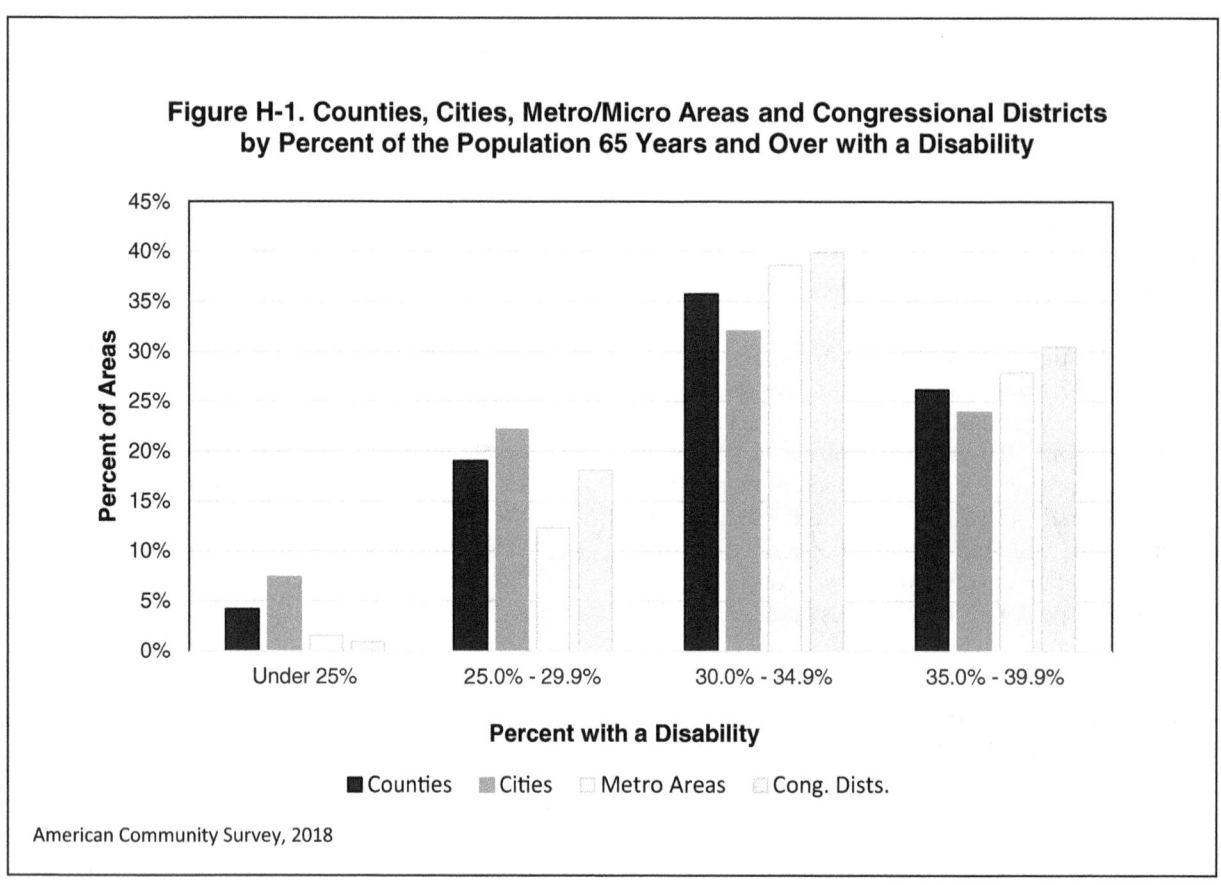

Figure H-1. Counties, Cities, Metro/Micro Areas and Congressional Districts by Percent of the Population 65 Years and Over with a Disability

American Community Survey, 2018

75 population, ambulatory difficulty is most prevalent at 31.0 percent followed by hearing difficulty (21.7 percent), cognitive difficulty (13.1 percent), self-care difficulty (12.8 percent) and vision difficult at 9.0 percent. Among the states, New Mexico has the highest percent of 75 and over population (56.4 percent) indicating that they have a disability. Alaska has the highest percentage of those with cognitive disabilities at 18.2 and is also highest for those with hearing (30.5 percent) and vision (14.3 percent) disabilities. Arkansas is highest for ambulatory (38.0 percent) disabilities while California is highest for self-care difficulties at 16.5 percent. Delaware has the lowest percent for disabilities overall at 42.6 percent. The states with the lowest percent of persons 75 and over experiencing difficulties are: Delaware for vision (5.9 percent) difficulty; the District of Columbia for hearing (14.7 percent), South Dakota for cognitive (7.7 percent); Wyoming for ambulatory difficulty (23.9 percent) and for self-care difficulty at 7.4 percent.

There is wide variation across the nation's counties in the percentage of 75 and over population with a disability or experiencing difficulty. The ACS even reports that Dallas County, Iowa how no one experiencing self-care difficulties though this is likely due to a small sample size. Beaufort County, South Carolina has the lowest experience of any county with only 0.6 percent of the population experiencing vision difficulties while Craighead County, Arkansas has the highest percentage of persons experiencing ambulatory difficulties at 61.2 percent. Overall, Craighead County also has the highest percent reporting any disability at 79.4 percent. In 269 counties, greater than 50 percent of the population 75 and over report some disability and only 18 counties have less than one-third of the population reporting any disability. In seven counties more than 50 percent of the 75 and over population report having ambulatory difficulties.

In Jonesboro city, Arkansas, 74.5 percent of the 75 and over population (the highest of all cities) reports some disability while Sammamish city, Washington is the lowest at 15.5 percent. In 182 cities, more than 50 percent of the over 75 population reports some disability. Among

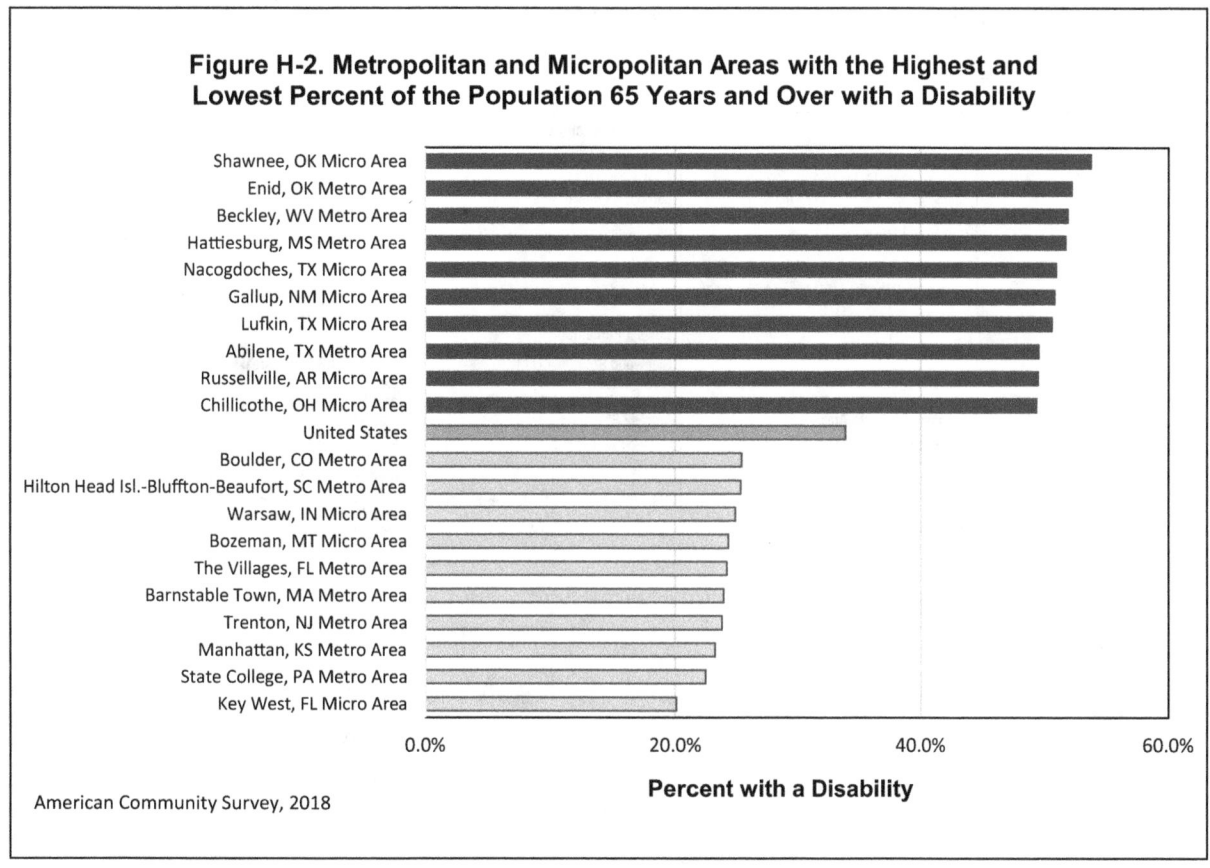

Figure H-2. Metropolitan and Micropolitan Areas with the Highest and Lowest Percent of the Population 65 Years and Over with a Disability

American Community Survey, 2018

all cities, ambulatory difficulty is most common and reported by 56.6 percent of the 75 and over population in Pasco city, Washington. Turlock, California has the highest percent reporting for vision (30.3 percent) and Jonesboro, Arkansas is highest for hearing difficulties. Forty percent of the over 75 population reports a cognitive disability in Clifton, New Jersey. Ambulatory disability is highest in Pasco, Washington at 56.6 percent and self-care disabilities are reported by 39.4 percent in Glendale, California. Cities reporting that at least one-third of the 75 and over population have ambulatory difficulty number 208.

Across all metropolitan and micropolitan areas, (186 of 512 areas) more than 50 percent of the 75 and over population report some form of disability. The Joneboro, Arkansas metropolitan area is highest where three of every four people 75 and over (76.0 percent) report a disability. Jonesboro's highest rank is also seen in the data for hearing (39.8 percent) and ambulatory (57.2 percent) difficulty. The Warsaw, Indiana micropolitan area is lowest in overall reporting of some disability at 28.1 percent. The Pocatello, Idaho metropolitan area has the highest reporting of vision difficulty (28.1 percent)

while self-care difficulties are reported the most in the Moses Lake, Washington micro area (29.6 percent). The 75 and over population report low levels of disability in a number of areas. Less than five percent of the population report vision difficulties in 55 metros; 13 areas report cognitive difficulty at less than five percent and 16 areas report self-care difficulty at less than five percent.

Almost two-thirds (65.0 percent) of the 75 and over population report some type of disability Texas' 15th Congressional District, the highest of all districts but 132 districts have more than 50 percent of residents reporting some disability. New York's 12th district is the lowest but even here, 35.6 percent report some type of disability. The highest percent of persons with a hearing difficulty (35.3 percent) is reported in Congressional District 5 in Kentucky. West Virginia's 3rd district is highest for persons with a vision difficulty (19.5 percent). Nearly a quarter (24.3 percent) of California's 34th district population 75 and over has cognitive difficulties. New York's 13th district is highest for ambulatory difficulties at 46.5 percent while Colorado's 2nd district is lowest at 19.6 percent. California's the 28th district is highest with 30.1 percent of older residents reporting self-care difficulties.

Metropolitan and Micropolitan Areas with the Highest and Lowest Percentage by Disability Type, Population 65 and Over

Vision Difficulty	Hearing Difficulty	Cognitive Difficulty	Ambulatory Difficulty	Self-Care Difficulty
Highest Percentage				
Beckley, WV Metro Area - 17.2% Laurel, MS Micro Area - 15.0% Gallup, NM Micro Area - 14.5% Hattiesburg, MS Metro Area - 14.0% Show Low, AZ Micro Area - 13.6%	Nacogdoches, TX Micro Area - 27.9% Hinesville, GA Metro Area - 27.5% Gallup, NM Micro Area -27.4% Russellville, AR Micro Area - 27.3% Hermiston-Pendleton, OR Micro Area - 25.7%	Cookeville, TN Micro Area - 20.5% Laredo, TX Metro Area - 20.4% Greeneville, TN Micro Area - 19.5% Seneca, SC Micro Area - 19.5% Lufkin, TX Micro Area - 17.4%	Beckley, WV Metro Area - 39.1% Enid, OK Metro Area - 38.8% Shawnee, OK Micro Area - 37.6% El Centro, CA Metro Area - 36.4% Cullman, AL Micro Area - 36.1%	Laredo, TX Metro Area - 21.0% Clearlake, CA Micro Area - 18.6% Roswell, NM Micro Area - 17.3% McAllen-Edinburg-Mission, TX Metro Area - 17.3% Martinsville, VA Micro Area 16.3%
Lowest Percentage				
State College, PA Metro Area - 2.6% Hilton Head Island-Bluffton-Beaufort, SC Metro Area - 2.4% Coeur d'Alene, ID Metro Area - 2.0% Daphne-Fairhope-Foley, AL Metro Area - 1.9% Glenwood Springs, CO Micro Area - 1.3%	Vineland-Bridgeton, NJ Metro Area - 9.3% Key West, FL Micro Area - 9.3% Santa Cruz-Watsonville, CA Metro Area - 9.2% Trenton, NJ Metro Area - 9.0% State College, PA Metro Area - 8.9%	Glenwood Springs, CO Micro Area - 2.9% Faribault-Northfield, MN Micro Area - 2.8% Dubuque, IA Metro Area - 2.6% Key West, FL Micro Area - 2.5% Manhattan, KS Metro Area - 2.3%	Manhattan, KS Metro Area 12.4% Corvallis, OR Metro Area - 12.3% Key West, FL Micro Area - 12.2% Bozeman, MT Micro Area - 11.3% The Villages, FL Metro Area - 11.3%	Ukiah, CA Micro Area - 2.5% The Villages, FL Metro Area - 2.5% Fargo, ND-MN Metro Area - 2.3% Faribault-Northfield, MN Micro Area - 2.0% Warsaw, IN Micro Area - 1.1%

Table H-1: States - Disability Status and Type of Disability

	Total Population		With a Disability		With a Hearing Disability		With a Vision Disability		With a Cognitive Disability		With an Ambulatory Disability		With a Self-Care Disability	
	65 to 74 Years	75 Years and Over	65 to 74 Years	75 Years and Over	65 to 74 Years	75 Years and Over	65 to 74 Years	75 Years and Over	65 to 74 Years	75 Years and Over	65 to 74 Years	75 Years and Over	65 to 74 Years	75 Years and Over
United States	30,571,313	21,851,801	7,388,678	9,941,082	2,696,862	4,534,931	1,261,467	1,889,936	1,536,107	2,731,526	4,450,622	6,478,109	1,258,570	2,674,919
Alabama..............	493,396	336,267	148,589	168,411	53,816	71,152	25,347	31,102	30,573	52,126	91,807	114,848	26,180	46,632
Alaska	59,630	28,370	17,701	14,644	9,123	8,368	4,056	3,920	3,201	4,986	9,020	9,703	2,697	3,970
Arizona..................	727,956	531,147	180,421	238,893	77,189	119,977	32,763	46,914	36,060	61,035	103,514	145,848	26,702	50,551
Arkansas	296,808	210,868	95,265	110,181	33,401	53,228	16,131	22,268	19,264	28,808	63,491	75,321	18,460	29,198
California..............	3,286,461	2,380,876	739,879	1,129,176	238,108	506,371	125,105	216,102	167,837	353,828	452,268	759,059	154,989	382,876
Colorado	502,418	305,437	107,023	139,690	48,392	70,502	15,848	26,651	18,785	33,019	57,115	83,659	12,379	29,750
Connecticut..........	343,060	270,087	64,864	109,347	21,500	49,521	9,728	19,323	13,411	30,847	38,276	69,645	9,541	31,415
Delaware..............	107,895	72,861	24,856	29,771	9,434	11,382	2,929	4,140	4,959	7,488	14,403	18,699	2,337	6,754
District of Columbia	48,833	36,793	12,240	17,825	2,146	5,210	2,621	3,484	3,732	5,644	7,809	12,896	2,533	4,751
Florida..................	2,404,234	1,954,550	536,343	869,115	183,006	387,836	93,908	169,767	109,203	241,465	320,015	573,676	79,604	230,206
Georgia	896,948	559,480	229,701	255,148	81,576	115,695	41,224	51,899	49,426	69,506	142,374	167,478	34,637	64,449
Hawaii	149,372	112,095	30,392	51,255	11,545	24,801	5,984	7,351	6,892	18,145	15,959	31,921	5,185	13,012
Idaho....................	168,397	111,044	42,386	54,577	21,690	29,682	5,986	11,066	8,201	15,644	20,317	31,687	5,970	12,939
Illinois..................	1,143,329	847,219	257,176	358,916	85,612	151,846	44,850	66,309	49,987	86,029	157,648	238,918	47,487	94,578
Indiana.................	613,699	437,447	157,023	197,793	63,205	90,661	25,168	37,083	30,291	48,807	93,689	130,820	22,456	48,205
Iowa.....................	299,333	238,485	62,819	97,607	26,895	50,056	8,427	17,052	11,528	20,061	34,394	56,557	9,219	20,434
Kansas	264,050	198,141	69,077	92,922	30,099	46,492	10,007	17,129	13,771	22,759	39,276	58,760	10,322	20,361
Kentucky...............	435,465	295,927	138,639	143,131	51,155	71,114	26,389	29,341	30,288	42,627	87,331	96,316	23,054	41,136
Louisiana..............	434,897	285,713	125,151	140,370	43,317	61,882	25,779	31,689	25,751	38,683	80,046	92,520	25,005	39,263
Maine....................	163,953	112,116	38,920	51,438	16,414	28,700	5,858	7,885	8,739	12,607	21,838	29,645	5,059	9,840
Maryland...............	546,442	384,599	115,145	164,015	36,767	70,120	17,533	29,122	24,039	47,675	71,097	105,350	17,988	46,127
Massachusetts..............	656,546	480,995	136,014	208,100	49,654	90,449	19,941	35,857	28,819	54,348	77,042	132,431	22,247	60,122
Michigan...............	1,009,186	711,267	252,134	320,443	96,673	149,808	38,126	53,342	49,797	86,570	153,467	200,666	43,953	83,185
Minnesota.............	510,486	378,148	106,712	158,096	44,747	76,667	14,082	25,948	20,856	31,784	55,677	95,053	17,502	32,666
Mississippi............	284,356	190,067	85,506	97,226	26,785	41,791	18,788	23,683	18,365	28,946	56,158	68,216	13,499	29,647
Missouri................	596,623	438,451	167,128	196,525	64,664	93,318	29,596	35,216	36,854	48,242	103,714	127,260	30,100	43,540
Montana................	121,055	79,184	28,424	33,891	13,185	18,094	4,156	5,618	5,086	8,795	14,848	18,579	3,432	6,978
Nebraska..............	172,853	131,145	39,214	59,399	16,871	29,400	6,294	10,693	6,245	13,107	21,737	36,791	5,212	12,734
Nevada.................	291,996	183,124	73,085	85,093	28,188	41,163	14,553	18,545	14,897	23,413	45,867	56,456	12,536	24,030
New Hampshire...............	146,599	98,557	30,760	41,553	13,133	22,246	4,347	6,656	5,509	9,239	16,260	22,927	4,315	8,838
New Jersey	812,353	625,936	158,339	261,697	47,459	106,254	27,046	45,482	31,618	69,194	104,125	178,490	31,125	75,899
New Mexico	221,209	147,271	63,869	81,274	26,800	43,844	9,911	18,649	12,470	24,709	38,481	50,301	10,161	19,617
New York...............	1,811,595	1,400,470	380,856	602,158	107,374	233,143	66,874	109,628	78,402	172,009	241,740	412,821	70,068	192,331
North Carolina..............	1,013,996	674,578	256,884	309,408	95,707	142,567	43,927	58,682	55,669	87,177	152,896	196,297	42,563	74,677
North Dakota..............	64,047	52,386	14,008	22,824	6,842	12,223	2,553	5,459	2,355	4,561	7,355	15,552	1,479	3,965
Ohio.....................	1,152,361	843,802	282,458	375,323	99,750	165,977	47,869	69,310	56,935	94,653	167,810	241,012	48,111	90,837
Oklahoma..............	361,839	257,762	121,686	134,015	51,645	67,847	23,654	29,457	25,850	35,501	78,381	90,340	19,492	31,180
Oregon.................	447,596	292,015	111,117	133,538	46,157	71,069	16,978	24,448	22,462	36,374	63,640	82,033	18,607	30,888
Pennsylvania..................	1,311,159	1,021,210	300,787	446,724	105,885	202,092	46,842	77,253	62,262	113,836	182,699	285,453	47,964	109,225
Rhode Island..................	103,271	79,374	23,923	32,996	9,776	14,986	3,316	6,435	5,619	8,184	14,124	21,303	4,997	9,095
South Carolina	553,062	346,692	144,078	158,711	48,550	71,249	25,501	30,760	30,441	47,604	85,872	102,909	23,770	45,021
South Dakota	85,022	61,336	19,203	24,475	8,203	10,805	2,333	4,224	2,917	4,308	10,906	14,854	1,889	4,535
Tennessee.............	658,560	446,237	188,885	213,653	75,781	97,962	34,005	44,824	41,789	63,016	115,464	144,182	31,158	55,604
Texas....................	2,174,294	1,425,305	578,872	700,861	214,297	318,848	114,096	148,196	126,109	212,569	359,716	477,436	108,782	201,521
Utah	212,206	139,091	47,194	66,823	20,146	34,164	7,386	12,048	8,904	15,397	24,478	38,699	6,412	13,679
Vermont................	75,755	48,120	18,245	20,213	8,490	10,970	2,929	3,665	4,922	5,094	9,047	11,245	2,666	4,493
Virginia..................	779,502	538,723	180,239	247,816	64,298	112,761	31,113	49,775	37,914	69,718	110,234	159,308	33,948	68,222
Washington............	710,781	453,206	178,713	210,176	75,877	102,126	26,481	37,386	36,864	57,918	99,554	136,209	27,150	57,076
West Virginia..............	215,290	145,926	69,144	75,714	28,803	37,573	13,925	17,077	15,141	21,385	42,233	49,627	11,732	18,981
Wisconsin.............	571,672	414,811	122,303	171,532	48,811	81,187	17,701	27,681	22,256	38,688	67,506	99,892	20,896	37,275
Wyoming	59,467	37,090	15,288	16,600	7,921	9,752	1,503	4,342	2,842	3,398	7,904	8,441	1,000	2,611

Table H-2: Counties - Disability Status and Type of Disability

	Total Population		With a Disability		With a Hearing Disability		With a Vision Disability		With a Cognitive Disability		With an Ambulatory Disability		With a Self-Care Disability	
	65 to 74 Years	75 Years and Over	65 to 74 Years	75 Years and Over	65 to 74 Years	75 Years and Over	65 to 74 Years	75 Years and Over	65 to 74 Years	75 Years and Over	65 to 74 Years	75 Years and Over	65 to 74 Years	75 Years and Over
Alabama														
Baldwin County	27,152	17,291	6,459	7,179	3,093	3,357	364	454	955	975	4,053	5,077	445	1,319
Calhoun County	12,240	8,275	3,684	4,664	2,213	2,101	972	1,039	606	1,401	2,282	3,551	445	1,769
Cullman County	9,116	6,425	3,488	3,725	1,201	1,246	499	344	345	721	2,547	3,018	380	741
DeKalb County	7,377	4,884	2,012	3,198	1,044	1,414	193	470	243	1,057	1,152	2,148	300	705
Elmore County	7,550	4,749	2,365	2,683	903	1,713	577	183	237	563	1,996	1,142	533	627
Etowah County	11,519	8,113	3,805	3,693	1,160	1,567	755	517	885	1,205	2,485	2,452	314	1,458
Houston County	11,027	7,763	3,227	3,815	931	1,730	342	558	943	1,164	2,457	2,588	539	983
Jefferson County	61,976	42,724	16,641	20,312	5,791	9,042	3,509	3,500	2,508	6,026	10,328	14,130	3,333	5,337
Lauderdale County	10,360	8,059	3,183	3,857	1,881	2,138	414	324	450	1,143	1,757	1,993	584	1,110
Lee County	13,335	6,552	4,343	4,572	1,408	1,669	641	654	1,319	1,405	2,332	3,421	1,155	1,755
Limestone County	9,066	6,029	2,398	3,010	1,058	1,640	501	698	237	454	1,354	1,921	71	846
Madison County	32,318	23,347	7,961	11,109	2,932	4,964	1,010	1,915	1,488	3,312	4,299	7,035	1,509	2,324
Marshall County	9,344	7,143	3,201	3,023	1,252	1,071	417	427	470	752	2,127	2,148	573	1,006
Mobile County	39,373	27,185	10,657	11,803	4,119	5,468	2,038	2,180	2,750	3,931	6,983	8,340	2,103	3,965
Montgomery County	20,454	13,822	6,516	7,677	1,861	2,992	1,360	1,939	1,161	2,497	3,691	5,350	691	2,743
Morgan County	12,050	8,414	3,580	4,588	1,288	1,728	491	1,615	1,284	1,674	2,068	2,954	798	1,280
St. Clair County	9,027	5,733	3,829	1,782	1,206	240	895	536	1,064	795	2,435	1,477	1,100	477
Shelby County	20,352	12,943	5,399	6,667	1,889	3,359	945	1,240	1,339	1,494	3,300	4,085	1,408	1,620
Talladega County	8,757	5,665	3,098	3,108	706	801	312	476	477	1,182	1,821	2,060	410	774
Tuscaloosa County	16,811	10,661	4,709	4,085	1,150	1,604	947	556	882	1,395	3,063	2,761	1,229	822
Walker County	7,142	4,919	3,186	3,050	697	1,261	713	516	740	965	2,310	2,184	842	1,082
Alaska														
Anchorage Municipality	21,792	11,017	5,140	5,202	2,409	2,373	967	1,253	934	2,078	2,850	3,623	1,218	1,358
Fairbanks North Star Borough	7,346	2,867	2,414	1,443	1,747	860	312	638	525	701	596	1,102	0	701
Matanuska-Susitna Borough	8,779	4,272	3,007	2,571	1,258	1,571	1,278	831	595	867	1,511	1,609	565	768
Arizona														
Apache County	6,466	4,466	3,055	3,069	1,644	1,686	992	832	1,091	779	1,748	1,690	643	705
Cochise County	16,130	12,272	3,907	5,910	1,985	3,053	411	1,337	806	1,556	2,404	4,017	460	2,039
Coconino County	11,161	6,652	2,908	2,959	1,581	1,239	435	816	340	1,007	1,307	2,206	77	1,006
Maricopa County	388,129	281,070	89,078	124,555	38,307	62,083	16,098	23,724	17,323	30,724	51,705	79,337	14,023	28,788
Mohave County	37,132	26,662	10,566	12,400	3,483	4,617	1,400	2,235	2,367	2,916	7,630	8,644	1,901	2,597
Navajo County	12,126	8,036	3,390	4,793	1,501	2,702	1,146	1,592	392	1,200	1,527	2,710	471	893
Pima County	117,273	88,274	27,988	41,056	11,782	20,748	6,174	6,147	5,686	12,411	15,141	24,128	3,450	7,808
Pinal County	55,006	35,819	17,687	15,647	8,188	8,738	1,586	3,970	3,883	3,519	9,861	7,831	2,418	2,196
Yavapai County	43,831	29,825	10,152	11,200	4,348	5,900	1,684	3,268	1,542	3,580	5,948	6,045	1,183	1,871
Yuma County	19,698	20,281	4,798	8,573	2,066	4,379	871	936	1,107	1,307	2,739	4,259	962	1,616
Arkansas														
Benton County	20,281	16,009	5,642	6,896	1,654	2,557	650	1,126	1,218	1,172	4,150	4,666	1,207	1,370
Craighead County	8,860	6,307	2,669	4,626	1,067	2,430	852	978	719	321	1,452	3,569	447	766
Faulkner County	9,915	5,805	3,432	3,739	1,324	2,117	260	1,202	862	865	2,568	2,168	515	863
Garland County	12,687	10,304	3,422	5,830	1,339	2,823	824	714	1,356	1,553	2,266	4,245	879	1,722
Jefferson County	6,982	4,689	1,964	2,231	516	1,314	195	510	522	747	1,350	1,697	383	547
Lonoke County	5,831	3,926	1,205	1,733	513	645	18	526	87	669	864	1,267	122	751
Pulaski County	37,165	23,939	11,098	10,772	3,299	4,621	1,414	1,689	2,744	2,715	7,381	6,844	2,453	2,410
Saline County	12,750	9,043	4,348	4,747	2,199	2,659	427	739	471	1,595	2,041	3,227	815	1,562
Sebastian County	11,997	8,171	3,029	4,069	1,238	1,963	421	718	182	1,453	1,958	2,868	525	1,380
Washington County	15,964	10,958	4,549	5,055	1,365	2,270	463	1,212	1,069	884	2,950	2,990	612	1,025
White County	7,055	5,252	2,141	2,928	761	1,594	449	831	422	698	1,662	2,192	354	588
California														
Alameda County	136,742	93,768	25,709	43,427	7,592	17,336	5,495	9,054	5,555	13,444	16,682	30,510	6,263	14,787
Butte County	25,269	17,551	6,431	7,928	2,506	3,333	1,258	1,586	1,571	2,818	2,665	5,361	1,160	2,517
Contra Costa County	106,358	74,990	20,851	33,623	5,494	15,441	2,975	5,029	4,037	10,196	12,844	22,671	3,028	9,351
El Dorado County	25,428	14,999	5,399	6,337	1,771	3,162	408	1,232	1,346	846	3,183	3,528	663	635
Fresno County	71,002	50,538	21,201	29,036	6,769	14,411	5,205	5,950	5,478	9,382	12,295	21,016	3,646	8,950
Humboldt County	15,227	9,069	4,398	4,241	2,133	1,920	610	903	922	1,090	2,570	2,685	323	1,122
Imperial County	13,359	10,153	4,465	6,795	1,174	1,496	1,017	1,314	969	2,081	3,268	5,235	1,177	2,436
Kern County	59,306	38,770	17,015	18,793	4,909	8,373	4,157	3,173	4,591	7,619	11,486	13,396	3,125	7,225
Kings County	8,751	6,662	2,981	3,285	1,135	1,932	331	412	637	340	1,785	2,101	634	320
Lake County	9,780	5,076	3,185	2,461	1,080	1,345	651	386	856	346	2,013	1,571	1,582	1,146
Los Angeles County	785,211	590,748	181,892	284,328	48,818	117,156	29,211	56,513	45,841	92,557	117,668	197,985	49,079	112,173
Madera County	13,513	8,586	4,332	3,448	2,389	2,044	403	737	426	1,182	1,973	2,022	351	668
Marin County	33,696	24,517	3,902	8,282	1,405	3,882	541	1,755	497	2,022	1,921	4,635	651	2,200
Mendocino County	12,320	6,752	3,137	2,249	1,436	1,355	722	450	600	230	1,445	961	237	240
Merced County	17,516	13,232	5,757	7,848	2,322	4,129	714	1,804	1,366	2,467	3,735	4,955	1,166	2,116
Monterey County	34,393	25,098	5,832	11,923	2,434	6,023	612	1,854	889	3,202	3,030	7,301	1,000	3,739
Napa County	15,856	10,949	3,322	4,352	1,508	2,046	313	1,159	319	1,115	1,883	2,689	482	1,239
Nevada County	17,493	10,253	3,698	4,416	1,567	2,854	988	726	391	954	2,124	2,592	350	846
Orange County	266,534	204,692	44,671	89,147	13,476	38,311	6,984	17,119	9,248	29,731	24,496	58,906	8,958	31,804
Placer County	43,316	33,433	7,263	15,132	2,743	6,865	906	1,439	1,116	3,464	4,428	8,358	1,235	3,669
Riverside County	200,679	152,346	50,956	72,239	16,600	35,202	8,202	13,199	11,783	18,626	33,252	47,406	9,260	22,287
Sacramento County	128,232	89,212	32,614	42,874	9,833	17,313	4,950	6,379	6,886	15,478	19,035	29,186	6,263	15,877
San Bernardino County	153,354	97,814	42,340	53,045	13,091	25,862	7,557	12,971	10,021	19,351	26,199	35,261	7,432	17,036
San Diego County	272,301	197,520	57,049	93,401	20,197	41,858	10,339	16,856	13,993	30,421	35,038	62,879	12,194	31,236
San Francisco County	76,622	61,506	15,235	31,918	5,283	14,609	2,050	6,064	4,233	12,801	8,429	21,817	3,579	14,265
San Joaquin County	56,724	39,120	15,733	20,252	5,836	9,623	2,765	4,160	4,275	5,668	10,246	13,385	3,502	6,522
San Luis Obispo County	35,423	22,171	7,185	10,298	3,181	5,405	1,877	2,249	1,469	2,447	4,239	6,522	1,392	2,427

Table H-2: Counties - Disability Status and Type of Disability—*Continued*

	Total Population		With a Disability		With a Hearing Disability		With a Vision Disability		With a Cognitive Disability		With an Ambulatory Disability		With a Self-Care Disability	
	65 to 74 Years	75 Years and Over	65 to 74 Years	75 Years and Over	65 to 74 Years	75 Years and Over	65 to 74 Years	75 Years and Over	65 to 74 Years	75 Years and Over	65 to 74 Years	75 Years and Over	65 to 74 Years	75 Years and Over
California—Cont.														
San Mateo County	69,894	54,144	11,222	23,750	3,797	10,411	879	5,076	2,378	6,776	6,403	15,742	1,596	8,321
Santa Barbara County	37,583	30,819	6,812	12,528	2,063	6,822	890	2,160	1,169	3,517	3,826	7,452	1,002	3,110
Santa Clara County	145,646	115,606	25,179	52,396	7,408	24,731	3,493	10,140	5,985	15,194	15,079	36,276	4,736	17,641
Santa Cruz County	29,453	15,896	5,183	6,963	1,911	2,204	1,565	976	678	2,504	2,538	4,575	869	1,713
Shasta County	21,481	15,546	7,590	8,197	3,173	3,826	1,664	1,023	1,898	1,823	4,187	4,599	1,481	1,759
Solano County	42,750	27,847	9,367	14,250	2,871	6,394	728	3,198	2,013	4,357	6,049	10,304	1,600	5,008
Sonoma County	60,222	37,808	12,102	17,374	5,092	8,238	1,287	2,769	2,044	4,699	6,372	12,142	1,947	5,127
Stanislaus County	43,137	29,370	13,155	14,847	4,757	7,479	3,129	4,637	3,295	4,850	8,903	10,540	3,984	4,917
Sutter County	7,747	7,116	2,093	3,281	1,025	1,550	109	496	337	1,029	1,278	2,516	217	809
Tulare County	31,035	21,587	9,798	11,173	3,321	5,474	2,793	1,789	2,216	3,440	6,462	6,390	1,959	2,665
Ventura County	76,060	56,159	16,898	26,756	6,426	13,029	3,741	5,286	2,378	8,421	9,054	16,836	3,103	8,053
Yolo County	15,764	11,413	3,406	5,054	1,050	2,185	817	518	173	1,531	1,811	3,136	565	1,451
Yuba County	5,796	3,587	1,725	1,792	767	957	123	492	343	295	973	1,223	35	137
Colorado														
Adams County	33,327	19,782	8,299	9,880	3,741	5,472	1,096	2,075	1,686	2,279	4,546	5,396	989	1,836
Arapahoe County	53,847	31,162	9,437	14,051	3,526	6,503	1,749	2,199	2,344	3,321	5,991	8,613	1,916	3,119
Boulder County	28,746	17,287	4,597	6,845	1,993	3,817	702	1,385	515	1,080	2,167	3,699	169	1,295
Broomfield County	5,724	3,894	1,185	1,194	746	878	223	207	53	53	811	435	53	106
Denver County	51,845	32,151	10,797	14,711	4,006	6,030	1,597	2,897	1,773	2,815	5,280	8,787	1,347	3,398
Douglas County	25,884	14,038	4,468	5,429	1,635	2,927	300	714	527	1,279	2,636	3,028	299	752
El Paso County	56,961	34,436	13,503	15,392	5,577	6,593	2,610	3,537	2,851	3,805	8,131	9,012	1,738	3,136
Jefferson County	58,442	37,077	12,405	16,610	5,932	9,017	1,968	3,186	1,451	4,675	5,832	9,696	1,104	4,351
Larimer County	34,255	20,747	6,045	9,325	3,293	5,376	802	1,918	999	2,253	2,453	4,927	394	1,621
Mesa County	16,525	12,276	4,182	6,511	2,120	2,657	732	767	842	2,371	2,331	4,770	346	2,252
Pueblo County	17,912	12,920	5,276	6,982	2,245	4,240	802	1,908	869	1,502	3,287	4,038	787	1,075
Weld County	24,051	14,172	6,109	7,869	2,518	3,527	527	1,262	1,042	1,730	3,438	5,118	652	1,404
Connecticut														
Fairfield County	82,023	67,801	12,800	25,463	3,528	11,486	2,580	4,454	2,586	7,008	7,445	16,448	2,093	7,116
Hartford County	84,582	68,092	16,052	29,324	3,923	12,736	2,583	5,413	4,431	9,256	10,398	18,974	2,108	9,616
Litchfield County	22,325	15,572	4,474	5,552	2,257	2,756	526	952	658	1,408	2,430	3,389	649	1,407
Middlesex County	18,512	13,930	2,870	5,464	1,393	2,264	357	967	515	1,528	1,264	2,808	567	613
New Haven County	83,150	65,639	17,077	27,185	5,823	11,325	2,210	4,449	3,684	7,128	10,027	18,978	2,216	8,712
New London County	27,351	20,963	6,405	7,937	2,409	4,826	323	1,607	918	1,616	3,940	3,882	1,195	1,080
Tolland County	14,080	10,201	2,620	4,188	1,024	2,057	767	717	279	1,273	1,180	2,637	121	1,291
Windham County	11,037	7,889	2,566	4,234	1,143	2,071	382	764	340	1,630	1,592	2,529	592	1,580
Delaware														
Kent County	17,338	12,474	4,194	4,700	1,135	1,751	570	396	1,013	1,107	2,870	2,710	616	1,303
New Castle County	51,061	36,032	11,452	15,666	3,977	5,429	1,416	2,536	2,104	3,897	6,980	10,227	1,014	2,931
Sussex County	39,496	24,355	9,210	9,405	4,322	4,202	943	1,208	1,842	2,484	4,553	5,762	707	2,520
Florida														
Alachua County	22,670	15,057	4,715	5,619	2,067	3,243	558	1,035	1,737	1,519	2,750	3,580	1,060	1,653
Bay County	18,171	12,756	6,559	7,417	2,175	3,426	1,431	1,420	1,236	2,118	3,571	5,771	643	1,590
Brevard County	76,295	64,973	17,419	30,515	6,886	13,172	2,614	5,488	2,521	8,470	9,273	21,267	2,176	7,854
Broward County	181,134	143,391	38,986	66,209	10,554	28,044	6,864	16,586	7,910	22,746	25,324	46,237	7,700	22,495
Charlotte County	39,338	34,983	8,710	16,721	2,915	8,373	975	2,688	781	4,798	5,492	10,008	1,429	3,632
Citrus County	29,459	24,373	7,460	10,748	3,561	5,321	1,167	3,014	686	1,965	4,533	7,089	694	1,586
Clay County	22,608	12,144	6,374	6,143	2,354	2,653	1,149	731	996	897	3,452	4,382	416	940
Collier County	60,211	62,252	10,084	22,990	3,594	13,089	645	4,141	2,907	4,996	4,547	12,687	1,514	4,995
Columbia County	7,433	5,545	2,399	2,955	914	1,110	375	732	685	1,125	1,186	1,869	123	651
Duval County	81,885	51,714	21,492	24,971	5,716	9,382	4,315	5,576	4,609	6,716	13,557	16,672	2,190	5,564
Escambia County	30,821	22,175	6,956	9,320	2,328	4,692	1,292	1,422	1,433	2,132	4,375	6,027	1,320	2,431
Flagler County	19,115	16,229	4,598	6,903	2,087	4,029	808	1,749	664	2,091	2,436	4,335	581	1,709
Hernando County	28,039	24,604	7,517	11,264	3,205	6,833	904	2,123	1,873	2,941	5,207	7,140	1,326	2,632
Highlands County	17,388	19,857	3,757	7,595	1,793	4,540	411	1,112	724	1,357	2,543	4,333	487	884
Hillsborough County	122,675	83,133	29,467	39,879	9,777	16,919	5,626	7,931	6,354	10,956	18,789	27,100	5,035	12,613
Indian River County	27,260	24,124	4,554	8,904	2,198	5,975	611	1,113	764	1,790	2,317	5,463	691	2,017
Lake County	51,370	43,754	13,473	19,383	4,559	9,418	2,465	2,745	1,904	4,595	8,057	11,736	2,247	5,046
Lee County	118,640	97,620	20,592	36,614	8,818	18,207	3,545	6,116	4,192	9,677	10,029	23,037	3,774	9,885
Leon County	24,218	14,696	5,489	6,990	2,234	2,390	1,266	1,452	1,504	2,334	3,066	4,707	675	2,588
Manatee County	58,114	49,673	11,031	21,124	4,640	9,629	1,244	3,232	1,868	4,164	6,110	13,613	1,491	3,320
Marion County	55,734	48,290	13,209	20,820	4,573	10,312	2,310	3,219	2,250	4,275	8,666	13,048	1,457	3,298
Martin County	24,414	26,005	3,406	10,570	1,151	4,223	481	2,754	363	3,208	2,320	5,278	596	650
Miami-Dade County	240,150	207,818	48,884	97,665	10,461	28,365	10,251	20,827	14,108	37,137	28,774	71,037	8,236	38,984
Monroe County	10,862	6,110	1,164	2,214	421	1,136	240	561	154	273	764	1,524	88	699
Nassau County	11,571	7,216	2,801	2,993	930	1,339	692	555	599	636	1,443	1,910	382	606
Okaloosa County	20,721	13,384	6,922	6,715	1,951	2,677	1,382	808	1,656	2,012	3,803	4,608	671	1,915
Orange County	100,096	64,788	25,433	34,782	8,696	12,725	4,717	6,172	4,844	10,477	15,589	24,031	3,438	9,432
Osceola County	30,076	18,351	8,393	10,883	2,441	5,500	2,668	1,864	2,711	3,692	4,736	7,969	1,262	2,440
Palm Beach County	171,961	182,877	31,813	72,421	10,269	31,504	4,866	12,567	6,481	18,619	17,943	48,572	4,139	18,532
Pasco County	67,383	54,751	16,732	25,018	5,635	11,641	2,669	3,836	2,525	6,273	10,130	15,398	2,493	4,963
Pinellas County	130,087	111,761	31,291	48,882	10,245	22,266	4,519	11,198	5,638	12,713	19,167	32,274	4,479	12,309
Polk County	81,146	62,280	20,981	29,537	7,558	13,824	4,359	6,473	4,399	7,187	13,407	17,314	4,211	5,761
Putnam County	10,603	6,711	2,233	2,638	921	744	169	298	699	419	1,097	1,744	151	473
St. Johns County	31,588	20,152	4,751	7,878	1,387	3,778	1,049	637	883	1,858	2,741	5,435	1,213	1,539

Table H-2: Counties - Disability Status and Type of Disability—*Continued*

	Total Population		With a Disability		With a Hearing Disability		With a Vision Disability		With a Cognitive Disability		With an Ambulatory Disability		With a Self-Care Disability	
	65 to 74 Years	75 Years and Over	65 to 74 Years	75 Years and Over	65 to 74 Years	75 Years and Over	65 to 74 Years	75 Years and Over	65 to 74 Years	75 Years and Over	65 to 74 Years	75 Years and Over	65 to 74 Years	75 Years and Over
Florida—Cont.														
St. Lucie County	42,687	34,521	8,553	16,486	2,364	7,297	981	4,226	1,363	4,083	6,490	12,128	838	4,549
Santa Rosa County	17,369	11,047	4,865	6,200	1,909	2,352	1,236	1,001	819	1,012	3,003	3,929	511	1,506
Sarasota County	79,335	77,731	11,716	29,859	4,695	14,815	1,310	3,517	1,054	6,583	5,821	18,029	805	7,153
Seminole County	42,822	29,912	9,568	12,174	4,147	5,420	1,586	2,923	2,377	3,686	6,604	8,415	1,918	3,834
Sumter County	42,145	31,009	7,577	9,930	3,983	6,101	1,818	1,914	1,195	1,461	2,853	5,302	468	1,349
Volusia County	75,141	58,603	18,268	30,251	6,730	16,499	3,566	7,766	3,057	9,380	11,313	19,953	2,508	9,194
Walton County	9,170	5,347	2,576	1,980	1,520	924	430	409	719	483	1,716	1,384	372	274
Georgia														
Barrow County	6,657	3,586	2,200	1,664	751	1,189	200	166	281	386	1,557	996	127	198
Bartow County	9,592	5,059	3,034	2,899	1,072	1,551	568	897	616	548	2,438	2,246	434	756
Bibb County	14,270	9,704	3,917	4,742	1,696	2,375	939	845	1,178	1,056	2,571	3,243	954	1,333
Bulloch County	5,174	3,371	1,615	1,181	504	397	461	83	309	275	850	770	246	296
Carroll County	10,265	6,523	3,606	2,293	721	1,025	777	526	659	378	2,896	1,541	171	577
Catoosa County	7,073	4,996	2,042	2,203	591	983	422	459	693	1,207	1,203	1,805	525	859
Chatham County	26,411	17,720	5,780	9,923	2,680	4,930	847	2,341	842	2,443	3,466	6,093	514	1,943
Cherokee County	23,411	12,798	4,950	5,242	1,804	2,736	895	1,332	1,103	1,162	3,227	3,398	650	2,046
Clarke County	9,267	5,756	1,993	2,009	605	1,096	256	210	415	426	1,531	1,436	330	595
Clayton County	18,120	8,760	4,859	4,318	1,566	1,174	880	544	1,025	1,173	2,992	3,218	965	1,069
Cobb County	58,731	34,097	10,799	14,170	3,335	6,430	1,699	3,612	1,446	4,544	7,374	9,904	1,794	3,798
Columbia County	14,134	7,195	3,464	3,493	1,041	1,612	551	502	1,071	1,172	1,668	1,664	468	239
Coweta County	13,281	7,466	3,699	3,530	1,675	1,483	576	246	902	747	1,795	2,488	465	312
DeKalb County	60,229	33,760	14,373	13,788	3,478	5,249	1,473	2,452	3,608	4,022	9,065	9,569	1,599	4,369
Dougherty County	8,281	5,618	3,579	2,933	822	1,295	709	595	1,183	990	2,954	1,664	951	687
Douglas County	11,146	6,140	2,409	3,090	730	1,623	647	393	250	1,159	1,059	1,851	204	1,064
Fayette County	12,685	7,599	2,468	3,040	1,235	1,203	48	609	34	1,152	1,372	1,805	222	164
Floyd County	9,158	7,375	2,770	3,345	1,117	1,513	929	526	393	955	2,227	2,061	521	1,107
Forsyth County	17,876	10,522	3,685	4,072	1,374	2,237	808	1,350	125	913	1,672	2,686	175	1,009
Fulton County	72,837	49,838	16,436	23,546	4,370	9,448	3,439	4,938	3,074	5,828	10,773	14,457	2,733	7,292
Glynn County	10,477	6,478	2,452	3,211	621	1,543	222	359	485	647	1,439	2,167	471	566
Gwinnett County	60,565	33,140	8,882	14,065	3,195	6,250	1,095	2,170	2,046	3,812	5,260	10,113	1,358	3,441
Hall County	17,504	12,574	3,418	5,816	1,600	3,332	1,021	1,242	922	1,496	1,425	3,336	648	1,449
Henry County	16,799	9,457	4,829	4,013	1,414	2,087	1,327	844	1,050	596	2,744	2,402	868	551
Houston County	11,255	7,104	5,052	3,283	2,282	1,828	1,263	876	700	841	2,970	2,150	1,061	872
Jackson County	5,979	4,265	1,310	2,191	544	984	64	432	241	1,448	652	1,779	223	472
Lowndes County	8,651	5,879	2,102	2,257	837	1,379	638	587	531	190	1,381	1,240	221	478
Muscogee County	15,134	10,952	5,071	5,561	1,305	2,658	1,160	799	1,822	2,252	3,176	3,119	364	1,304
Newton County	8,976	5,403	3,453	2,701	1,469	1,820	995	249	844	1,057	2,076	2,304	260	762
Paulding County	10,502	6,369	1,969	2,090	774	1,434	204	646	541	1,018	754	1,443	247	1,084
Richmond County	17,357	10,791	4,635	4,481	1,438	1,895	1,092	1,236	404	1,181	2,750	2,826	746	1,640
Rockdale County	8,048	4,758	2,438	1,368	551	713	623	350	788	184	1,403	1,187	519	132
Spalding County	7,150	4,864	2,010	1,532	895	504	44	517	344	214	1,673	1,065	181	372
Troup County	6,009	4,056	1,729	1,853	572	878	331	595	348	590	978	986	326	580
Walker County	7,325	5,768	1,853	3,167	1,070	1,698	217	455	485	1,249	920	1,959	0	312
Walton County	8,145	5,925	2,140	2,538	494	1,212	273	364	500	792	1,471	1,582	194	310
Whitfield County	8,814	5,774	2,202	3,339	1,021	622	278	506	350	746	1,274	2,731	522	973
Hawaii														
Hawaii County	27,403	15,240	7,989	7,257	2,524	4,055	1,889	718	2,098	2,824	4,401	4,407	1,871	1,460
Honolulu County	94,410	79,202	17,741	36,162	6,990	17,134	3,223	5,717	3,989	12,953	8,977	23,074	2,163	10,147
Kauai County	8,886	5,823	1,312	3,034	449	1,300	378	344	215	697	848	1,546	331	516
Maui County	18,665	11,827	3,350	4,802	1,582	2,312	494	572	590	1,671	1,733	2,894	820	889
Idaho														
Ada County	41,657	25,819	8,969	12,150	4,471	5,658	1,406	2,704	1,484	3,547	4,323	6,946	1,167	3,307
Bannock County	7,360	4,984	2,442	3,204	1,537	1,542	188	1,353	581	1,405	1,283	2,304	443	583
Bonneville County	8,907	6,139	1,817	3,247	722	2,021	285	591	447	671	1,055	2,242	596	1,163
Canyon County	19,122	12,808	6,193	5,413	3,473	2,987	1,061	973	1,152	2,068	2,375	2,967	652	1,192
Kootenai County	18,143	12,410	3,750	5,686	1,998	3,792	241	362	578	1,409	1,271	2,780	591	828
Twin Falls County	7,295	5,630	1,485	2,696	535	1,277	584	485	361	490	997	1,568	415	748
Illinois														
Adams County	6,908	6,389	2,114	2,495	621	1,243	284	1,204	334	890	1,487	1,343	246	437
Champaign County	15,669	10,649	3,046	5,201	1,039	2,303	242	427	350	759	2,001	3,201	344	1,184
Cook County	432,528	325,413	97,659	132,738	24,811	49,049	21,404	26,782	22,279	35,029	63,558	91,636	20,619	39,809
DeKalb County	7,777	5,528	1,678	2,181	525	1,090	98	380	789	501	710	1,369	234	665
DuPage County	85,229	58,532	12,527	23,862	4,101	10,815	1,423	4,340	2,004	5,249	7,339	14,470	2,545	7,538
Kane County	44,610	28,471	9,064	9,929	2,355	3,933	1,410	1,511	1,537	2,235	5,758	6,891	1,772	2,563
Kankakee County	10,320	8,024	3,322	3,548	992	1,200	723	600	723	915	1,936	2,228	1,013	1,126
Kendall County	7,857	5,636	1,431	2,134	839	1,019	185	400	221	478	814	1,550	307	775
Lake County	59,310	40,491	11,269	17,321	3,967	6,291	1,824	3,332	2,102	4,467	6,122	11,813	2,017	4,073
LaSalle County	11,642	9,199	3,724	3,819	1,509	2,030	604	450	741	738	2,156	2,265	679	611
McHenry County	27,717	16,900	4,149	7,700	1,894	4,156	834	1,259	801	1,110	2,278	4,484	574	1,561
McLean County	13,243	9,485	2,406	4,564	1,145	2,196	397	610	363	603	1,289	2,643	373	1,027
Macon County	11,681	9,486	2,544	4,257	1,068	2,395	381	532	443	196	1,864	3,164	228	623
Madison County	25,559	20,199	7,543	9,147	2,834	4,470	2,089	1,629	1,358	2,585	3,938	6,347	818	2,480
Peoria County	17,450	12,751	3,422	5,959	1,230	2,735	51	898	602	1,129	2,009	3,956	970	1,352
Rock Island County	14,839	12,070	3,879	4,804	1,549	1,821	461	361	342	756	2,037	3,219	327	534
St. Clair County	23,697	17,256	5,381	8,601	1,939	4,255	1,155	2,042	826	1,888	3,232	5,258	918	2,101

Table H-2: Counties - Disability Status and Type of Disability—*Continued*

	Total Population		With a Disability		With a Hearing Disability		With a Vision Disability		With a Cognitive Disability		With an Ambulatory Disability		With a Self-Care Disability	
	65 to 74 Years	75 Years and Over	65 to 74 Years	75 Years and Over	65 to 74 Years	75 Years and Over	65 to 74 Years	75 Years and Over	65 to 74 Years	75 Years and Over	65 to 74 Years	75 Years and Over	65 to 74 Years	75 Years and Over
Illinois—Cont.														
Sangamon County	20,374	14,309	3,942	5,990	1,267	3,067	349	1,355	527	1,297	2,471	4,485	572	1,169
Tazewell County	14,100	11,158	3,948	5,127	1,902	2,165	365	497	585	1,014	2,970	4,006	1,662	1,490
Vermilion County	8,280	6,876	2,296	2,924	898	1,332	307	522	310	488	1,335	2,015	175	620
Will County	55,014	35,415	10,902	15,419	3,324	6,023	1,205	3,178	1,520	4,012	6,935	10,268	1,804	5,227
Williamson County	7,234	5,328	2,042	2,831	731	1,006	285	633	584	860	1,202	2,211	191	995
Winnebago County	28,470	21,098	7,188	8,059	2,761	3,398	1,159	1,323	1,323	2,220	4,532	5,371	1,145	2,052
Indiana														
Allen County	32,465	22,063	7,887	9,903	2,631	3,586	1,161	1,696	2,358	2,367	5,474	6,485	1,882	2,069
Bartholomew County	7,589	5,960	1,820	1,960	1,308	668	219	228	399	299	643	1,609	324	200
Boone County	5,213	3,539	1,063	1,367	503	687	117	403	0	653	544	843	90	327
Clark County	11,434	6,927	3,817	3,162	1,599	1,506	283	439	980	1,080	2,566	2,118	421	763
Delaware County	11,005	8,926	2,974	3,759	1,262	1,773	371	921	501	1,093	1,576	2,744	405	765
Elkhart County	16,764	12,966	3,626	6,146	1,486	2,797	810	1,549	847	1,504	2,028	3,809	400	1,150
Floyd County	7,549	4,885	1,990	1,779	1,235	836	142	303	437	327	873	1,206	106	332
Grant County	6,658	5,875	2,534	2,586	856	1,619	214	103	273	476	1,726	1,644	195	498
Hamilton County	24,820	16,488	5,081	6,911	1,436	2,785	750	972	462	1,578	2,974	4,098	211	2,217
Hancock County	8,105	4,843	2,419	2,017	1,222	536	694	479	636	259	1,474	1,475	231	633
Hendricks County	13,788	9,129	3,075	4,676	1,373	1,756	877	991	495	1,366	1,755	3,050	170	869
Howard County	9,014	6,903	2,579	2,832	1,113	1,420	320	828	313	909	1,589	1,946	400	520
Johnson County	13,445	9,275	2,239	3,341	1,028	1,828	291	399	610	977	807	1,657	234	467
Kosciusko County	7,692	5,376	1,736	1,414	669	701	292	422	297	87	1,087	727	73	68
Lake County	46,107	33,817	12,786	15,688	4,146	7,793	2,165	1,908	2,066	5,046	8,415	10,394	2,124	4,613
LaPorte County	11,942	7,734	3,692	3,624	1,292	1,324	436	442	931	564	2,197	2,719	352	1,054
Madison County	13,697	9,941	3,672	5,004	1,684	2,351	410	673	603	1,369	2,598	3,360	566	1,179
Marion County	71,251	48,841	16,948	25,077	5,904	10,552	2,472	5,880	3,326	5,741	10,320	18,016	3,397	7,705
Monroe County	11,357	7,689	1,637	4,353	834	1,903	385	145	164	1,238	756	2,663	121	977
Morgan County	7,181	4,551	1,854	1,708	751	1,195	287	237	183	89	1,417	884	237	231
Porter County	16,416	10,979	3,142	4,948	1,223	2,281	422	769	538	1,158	1,536	2,462	398	1,284
St. Joseph County	24,807	18,353	4,847	9,083	1,585	3,924	969	2,475	1,063	2,373	2,984	6,051	561	2,301
Tippecanoe County	13,232	9,160	4,046	3,854	2,111	1,779	1,081	556	775	936	2,060	2,272	376	750
Vanderburgh County	17,208	12,915	4,763	5,232	2,039	2,385	1,424	820	644	900	2,535	3,840	781	1,039
Vigo County	9,772	7,346	2,766	3,145	1,142	1,739	694	314	362	710	1,831	1,977	450	327
Wayne County	6,850	5,595	2,643	2,215	914	1,016	201	525	521	606	1,728	1,645	315	819
Iowa														
Black Hawk County	12,031	9,187	2,966	4,021	1,079	2,277	290	677	1,113	1,127	1,230	2,312	424	908
Dallas County	6,306	4,380	1,487	1,948	1,000	957	137	387	91	316	393	1,016	99	0
Dubuque County	9,518	7,923	2,049	3,305	618	1,588	180	553	126	309	1,234	1,662	248	236
Johnson County	10,545	7,026	1,730	2,755	578	1,550	241	393	169	1,284	594	1,788	182	912
Linn County	20,663	15,734	4,272	6,410	1,861	3,883	514	1,428	688	1,367	2,320	3,763	607	1,327
Polk County	37,623	25,425	7,964	11,237	3,083	5,608	764	2,227	1,120	1,979	4,625	5,735	612	2,139
Pottawattamie County	9,537	6,907	2,180	3,180	718	1,283	318	671	298	718	1,621	2,194	397	620
Scott County	15,956	11,635	2,533	4,095	1,306	1,542	500	480	820	927	1,668	2,527	510	1,280
Story County	6,531	5,031	1,661	1,648	672	767	268	181	211	533	899	979	342	276
Woodbury County	9,056	6,743	1,970	3,396	726	1,729	505	703	606	1,143	1,104	1,739	535	1,124
Kansas														
Butler County	5,607	4,526	1,026	2,163	565	1,015	147	392	25	1,171	527	1,700	172	514
Douglas County	8,898	6,402	1,410	2,800	532	1,703	199	559	340	635	754	1,338	163	680
Johnson County	52,636	33,888	11,683	14,335	4,393	7,189	1,252	2,725	2,057	3,960	6,145	9,061	2,002	3,709
Leavenworth County	7,158	5,007	2,161	3,005	1,039	1,658	324	850	456	873	1,213	1,237	394	468
Riley County	4,131	2,904	612	930	275	371	168	129	149	28	258	529	101	147
Sedgwick County	43,922	30,386	11,837	14,607	4,195	7,300	1,268	2,908	2,883	4,287	7,187	10,379	2,191	3,854
Shawnee County	19,335	13,441	4,600	6,024	2,043	3,244	523	981	693	1,346	3,229	3,454	435	1,633
Wyandotte County	12,322	8,022	4,184	4,299	1,359	2,014	944	809	1,008	1,044	2,872	2,511	851	673
Kentucky														
Boone County	10,778	6,585	2,568	3,173	861	2,088	581	501	430	998	1,708	1,962	374	750
Bullitt County	8,216	4,882	2,290	2,700	849	1,640	423	851	123	588	1,372	2,175	224	591
Campbell County	8,677	6,148	2,426	2,708	942	1,333	808	371	693	851	1,377	1,867	661	668
Christian County	4,930	3,940	1,649	1,444	925	916	239	481	215	198	877	1,064	122	497
Daviess County	9,801	7,251	3,426	2,739	1,159	1,563	1,306	489	847	420	2,387	1,783	688	563
Fayette County	25,515	17,444	6,162	7,870	1,503	3,133	1,109	1,618	979	1,927	4,065	5,118	800	1,712
Hardin County	9,340	6,505	3,259	3,774	1,453	2,010	490	518	697	1,130	2,159	2,383	528	587
Jefferson County	73,082	51,339	19,210	24,055	5,516	9,814	2,677	4,159	4,157	7,384	13,105	16,620	3,663	5,981
Kenton County	14,905	9,123	3,331	3,685	1,434	1,707	565	789	787	881	1,970	2,025	675	1,303
McCracken County	7,005	6,385	1,646	2,680	352	762	429	176	253	733	1,151	1,906	816	696
Madison County	7,750	4,969	2,842	2,370	788	1,457	525	177	729	522	2,106	1,251	607	503
Oldham County	5,450	3,201	1,296	1,263	406	761	217	401	255	290	796	609	318	336
Warren County	10,748	6,614	3,480	3,493	965	1,617	395	380	111	1,183	2,094	2,215	977	1,147
Louisiana														
Ascension Parish	9,536	4,643	1,959	2,908	670	1,561	221	657	386	795	973	2,303	460	795
Bossier Parish	10,598	7,036	2,490	3,970	1,150	1,050	561	349	157	566	1,382	2,493	315	1,001
Caddo Parish	24,039	17,581	5,928	7,895	2,532	3,234	985	1,618	1,178	2,360	3,990	5,531	959	2,855
Calcasieu Parish	18,380	12,085	5,042	7,100	2,098	3,660	1,095	2,213	1,539	2,079	3,138	4,400	1,566	1,703
East Baton Rouge Parish	37,907	24,670	11,227	11,628	3,263	5,099	2,771	3,618	1,901	2,612	6,577	7,270	2,246	3,052
Iberia Parish	6,346	4,035	1,225	2,043	441	978	246	275	226	299	706	1,305	174	211

Table H-2: Counties - Disability Status and Type of Disability—Continued

	Total Population		With a Disability		With a Hearing Disability		With a Vision Disability		With a Cognitive Disability		With an Ambulatory Disability		With a Self-Care Disability	
	65 to 74 Years	75 Years and Over	65 to 74 Years	75 Years and Over	65 to 74 Years	75 Years and Over	65 to 74 Years	75 Years and Over	65 to 74 Years	75 Years and Over	65 to 74 Years	75 Years and Over	65 to 74 Years	75 Years and Over
Louisiana—Cont.														
Jefferson Parish	43,668	30,573	12,273	13,793	5,302	6,403	2,785	2,876	2,594	2,865	7,172	9,432	1,511	2,924
Lafayette Parish	19,487	12,377	4,960	5,305	1,298	2,024	414	966	563	1,145	3,605	3,339	1,268	1,520
Lafourche Parish	8,428	7,109	2,553	3,644	1,371	1,403	278	715	323	1,004	1,444	2,262	228	1,315
Livingston Parish	11,358	7,581	3,930	3,548	1,580	1,966	1,073	600	1,023	1,297	2,699	2,310	368	1,359
Orleans Parish	35,816	21,716	8,450	10,223	2,012	3,463	2,072	2,191	1,599	2,274	6,226	6,601	2,333	2,387
Ouachita Parish	13,420	9,432	3,342	3,933	727	2,251	488	760	682	963	2,217	2,206	413	808
Rapides Parish	12,525	8,749	4,405	3,926	1,610	2,148	569	1,022	999	932	3,641	2,720	1,234	848
St. Landry Parish	7,810	5,357	1,525	1,921	614	942	155	503	196	359	747	1,185	115	384
St. Tammany Parish	26,701	16,943	6,974	8,381	2,269	3,834	1,239	2,049	1,436	2,898	4,539	5,018	1,230	1,815
Tangipahoa Parish	12,006	7,081	3,736	3,858	866	1,642	893	674	1,297	1,424	2,361	2,335	1,115	1,309
Terrebonne Parish	10,490	6,152	3,040	3,891	1,119	1,474	160	441	551	1,663	2,355	2,698	633	1,546
Maine														
Androscoggin County	11,373	7,919	2,860	3,400	1,059	1,170	263	460	486	846	1,775	2,378	478	685
Aroostook County	9,245	6,948	3,136	3,903	1,247	2,094	673	563	810	652	1,823	2,214	439	995
Cumberland County	32,032	21,941	5,536	8,927	2,313	5,155	844	1,550	1,153	1,693	2,595	5,088	630	1,225
Kennebec County	14,627	10,243	3,302	4,800	1,284	3,520	112	688	972	1,058	1,804	2,808	257	1,405
Penobscot County	16,205	11,556	4,319	6,088	1,686	3,488	591	1,008	832	1,648	2,216	3,552	798	1,606
York County	25,145	17,169	6,060	7,484	1,931	3,813	1,407	1,295	1,402	2,095	3,625	3,829	616	1,046
Maryland														
Allegany County	7,659	6,488	1,802	2,877	666	1,413	212	810	213	980	1,098	1,938	263	747
Anne Arundel County	50,315	34,496	10,059	13,574	3,254	7,438	741	1,809	1,848	3,087	6,519	8,093	1,432	2,967
Baltimore County	79,614	62,928	15,645	26,369	5,123	11,446	2,613	5,237	3,365	8,007	9,328	17,520	1,937	8,162
Calvert County	8,347	5,128	1,822	2,038	779	1,201	89	185	631	497	970	868	500	468
Carroll County	15,914	11,595	3,803	4,565	1,155	2,181	919	1,101	710	814	1,433	2,784	537	945
Cecil County	10,255	5,949	2,423	2,935	761	1,423	271	535	278	912	1,599	2,025	310	1,103
Charles County	12,206	7,711	2,324	3,491	755	1,435	422	704	330	977	1,362	2,775	648	1,258
Frederick County	22,016	14,804	5,520	5,471	2,395	2,535	342	694	880	1,541	3,196	3,457	540	1,161
Harford County	24,914	17,091	4,845	7,882	2,073	3,887	1,204	1,126	536	1,839	3,051	4,368	426	1,777
Howard County	28,055	16,684	6,068	6,598	2,958	3,489	651	625	1,004	2,502	3,319	3,878	787	1,965
Montgomery County	92,931	70,714	13,123	30,330	4,583	12,590	1,988	5,311	2,774	9,613	6,781	18,916	1,446	10,079
Prince George's County	75,705	44,920	15,577	19,115	3,971	6,095	3,159	2,727	4,439	6,560	10,092	12,758	3,103	6,436
St. Mary's County	8,696	6,310	2,325	2,947	631	1,846	349	920	591	475	1,963	1,674	497	677
Washington County	14,612	11,454	4,088	5,622	1,404	2,543	434	1,194	958	1,484	2,805	3,527	636	1,064
Wicomico County	9,275	6,971	1,668	3,530	749	1,243	44	992	206	1,354	981	2,530	206	658
Massachusetts														
Barnstable County	37,322	28,131	5,884	9,420	2,055	5,014	913	1,939	1,718	1,873	2,811	5,542	932	2,109
Berkshire County	16,618	12,621	3,318	5,736	994	2,777	887	738	630	1,474	1,644	3,342	325	1,561
Bristol County	55,249	39,607	14,092	19,665	5,624	9,083	1,961	3,864	2,978	5,104	8,903	13,453	2,829	6,170
Essex County	77,602	57,276	14,971	26,105	4,781	10,475	1,911	4,729	2,949	7,080	9,212	15,801	2,465	7,868
Franklin County	9,668	5,756	1,699	2,366	1,102	1,161	301	317	141	592	820	1,464	267	860
Hampden County	44,824	33,941	11,852	16,806	3,363	7,330	1,730	2,593	2,893	4,221	6,918	11,325	2,507	4,847
Hampshire County	17,349	10,619	2,584	3,684	1,257	1,547	227	304	541	666	1,060	2,288	562	1,168
Middlesex County	139,129	106,931	25,979	43,918	10,738	20,121	3,912	7,004	4,265	10,661	14,326	25,333	3,329	11,362
Norfolk County	66,183	52,775	12,508	21,200	4,908	9,345	1,611	1,578	2,793	4,668	5,882	13,505	2,024	6,768
Plymouth County	56,045	37,561	10,998	15,030	5,179	6,664	1,661	2,282	1,837	4,489	4,979	9,538	1,558	4,134
Suffolk County	56,509	40,443	17,046	21,832	3,836	7,175	2,864	6,020	4,376	7,825	12,169	16,428	3,307	7,481
Worcester County	76,499	53,343	14,649	21,771	5,708	9,405	1,732	4,390	3,698	5,587	8,144	14,174	2,142	5,645
Michigan														
Allegan County	12,024	7,784	2,123	2,812	888	1,575	215	728	124	693	1,113	1,507	98	850
Bay County	11,821	9,036	2,245	3,324	892	1,680	348	884	319	917	1,356	1,962	310	733
Berrien County	17,326	13,142	4,113	6,354	1,357	2,940	430	670	816	1,968	2,594	3,547	466	1,952
Calhoun County	13,532	10,515	3,293	5,168	1,183	2,266	387	679	418	1,494	2,060	3,407	642	1,908
Clinton County	8,301	5,319	1,750	1,821	619	706	145	234	385	333	988	1,214	184	404
Eaton County	12,199	8,081	2,936	3,981	1,431	2,391	363	1,074	372	464	1,918	1,944	634	1,023
Genesee County	41,137	30,023	11,069	14,104	3,187	6,642	1,550	1,492	3,268	3,756	7,690	8,870	2,815	3,858
Grand Traverse County	11,168	7,210	2,292	3,100	1,035	1,811	364	388	510	1,115	981	1,480	246	880
Ingham County	24,438	15,378	6,319	7,715	2,323	3,543	1,502	1,446	1,146	2,281	4,174	5,424	858	2,005
Isabella County	5,388	3,706	1,576	1,455	384	786	108	220	540	402	886	879	385	358
Jackson County	16,937	11,610	4,591	5,123	1,187	2,671	307	1,641	1,185	1,649	3,251	2,423	677	1,012
Kalamazoo County	23,674	16,154	5,157	5,808	1,596	2,363	964	748	1,118	964	3,016	3,635	1,316	1,206
Kent County	53,249	36,502	11,144	16,119	5,105	7,080	1,621	2,221	2,026	3,865	5,636	9,441	1,678	3,972
Lapeer County	9,971	5,996	2,541	2,725	1,136	1,077	218	355	478	395	1,512	2,002	541	652
Lenawee County	10,879	7,213	2,434	3,403	1,013	1,654	399	880	290	870	1,541	2,284	255	855
Livingston County	20,546	12,572	3,514	4,815	1,761	2,678	303	652	341	1,219	1,727	2,769	432	1,218
Macomb County	85,055	63,952	23,659	29,099	7,553	13,336	4,208	4,783	4,667	8,129	15,621	18,725	4,379	7,565
Marquette County	7,517	5,307	1,767	1,884	706	1,224	350	313	472	359	924	914	600	402
Midland County	8,670	6,869	1,601	3,178	867	1,514	267	546	100	823	472	2,097	0	483
Monroe County	16,071	11,472	3,917	4,900	1,615	2,145	361	388	730	926	2,417	2,591	189	1,395
Muskegon County	17,589	11,852	4,645	5,765	1,668	2,251	654	876	784	1,673	3,042	3,219	749	1,565
Oakland County	124,807	86,779	25,939	40,316	10,101	18,876	3,940	6,633	5,057	11,170	14,868	27,324	4,562	11,978
Ottawa County	24,574	18,842	4,618	7,682	2,140	3,159	721	993	889	2,357	2,899	3,697	344	1,598
Saginaw County	20,874	15,892	5,240	7,555	1,926	2,855	498	1,226	1,144	2,309	3,391	4,621	826	1,568
St. Clair County	17,842	12,171	5,749	6,458	2,484	3,467	803	536	1,325	1,799	3,375	3,768	893	1,658
Shiawassee County	7,516	5,081	2,212	2,347	1,171	1,253	182	253	205	438	1,145	1,403	223	554

Table H-2: Counties - Disability Status and Type of Disability—*Continued*

	Total Population		With a Disability		With a Hearing Disability		With a Vision Disability		With a Cognitive Disability		With an Ambulatory Disability		With a Self-Care Disability	
	65 to 74 Years	75 Years and Over	65 to 74 Years	75 Years and Over	65 to 74 Years	75 Years and Over	65 to 74 Years	75 Years and Over	65 to 74 Years	75 Years and Over	65 to 74 Years	75 Years and Over	65 to 74 Years	75 Years and Over
Michigan—Cont.														
Van Buren County	8,497	5,592	2,602	2,535	1,486	1,070	722	483	265	715	1,683	1,636	326	844
Washtenaw County	31,650	20,125	6,745	8,409	2,574	4,356	577	1,135	1,079	2,328	4,146	5,247	1,434	2,075
Wayne County	158,195	112,066	46,285	53,886	14,337	20,820	9,788	11,305	10,796	16,678	31,272	38,392	10,010	16,584
Minnesota														
Anoka County	30,693	19,133	7,412	7,844	3,100	4,021	719	862	891	1,333	4,823	3,948	1,175	1,469
Blue Earth County	5,193	4,254	1,201	1,775	704	668	187	217	216	484	487	1,201	351	553
Carver County	7,705	4,975	1,703	1,267	1,004	654	59	209	336	273	641	759	366	269
Dakota County	35,378	23,855	6,722	11,115	3,030	5,215	1,100	1,947	1,303	2,315	3,506	7,052	1,171	2,102
Hennepin County	103,695	73,165	21,306	29,236	7,580	11,740	3,272	4,987	4,910	5,805	11,388	18,034	4,654	5,617
Olmsted County	13,199	11,096	2,292	4,565	894	2,132	214	814	618	1,282	1,141	2,986	121	1,214
Ramsey County	46,131	33,289	9,149	13,229	2,745	5,109	726	1,677	2,870	3,437	5,418	8,069	1,908	3,844
Rice County	5,870	4,427	952	1,634	424	897	92	246	183	93	525	878	82	119
St. Louis County	22,338	16,255	5,198	5,829	1,910	2,968	786	1,189	677	1,728	2,018	3,620	456	1,325
Scott County	9,855	6,437	1,602	2,823	314	1,216	379	350	203	525	893	1,700	301	735
Sherburne County	6,640	3,953	1,560	2,355	1,078	847	164	409	329	503	748	1,381	238	233
Stearns County	13,349	10,646	2,827	4,489	1,268	2,204	299	480	625	671	1,606	2,577	528	961
Washington County	23,389	15,335	4,020	6,545	1,887	3,250	411	1,656	435	1,586	1,999	3,388	269	1,357
Wright County	10,215	6,907	2,887	3,828	1,532	1,840	25	556	528	537	1,673	2,192	243	447
Mississippi														
DeSoto County	13,793	9,180	2,953	4,834	723	2,322	666	1,121	545	2,059	1,783	3,555	450	1,539
Forrest County	6,342	4,024	3,569	2,364	703	1,176	1,118	914	367	1,224	2,334	1,753	1,072	649
Harrison County	18,652	12,336	5,347	6,161	1,717	3,092	721	2,059	1,287	2,093	3,839	4,529	806	2,070
Hinds County	19,901	13,378	4,761	6,891	579	2,155	691	1,704	1,061	2,461	3,655	5,333	1,038	3,060
Jackson County	13,578	9,158	4,932	4,365	1,345	1,943	503	1,217	722	1,305	3,819	3,042	483	946
Jones County	7,153	4,722	2,232	2,015	399	868	845	550	1,410	518	1,435	1,487	626	928
Lauderdale County	7,326	5,612	2,101	3,069	439	1,329	687	796	525	492	1,840	1,980	370	206
Lee County	6,900	5,197	1,749	2,677	1,004	1,217	459	567	191	408	1,203	1,586	323	681
Madison County	8,831	4,927	742	2,480	119	927	257	536	176	1,028	441	1,875	148	1,231
Rankin County	14,472	8,988	3,464	4,127	1,816	1,168	508	1,152	885	985	1,779	3,093	805	1,542
Missouri														
Boone County	13,199	8,738	3,745	3,541	1,854	2,225	378	720	390	1,074	1,902	2,336	524	877
Buchanan County	9,068	5,946	2,350	2,686	804	1,599	466	596	264	624	1,537	1,997	669	804
Cape Girardeau County	7,054	5,895	1,500	2,612	800	1,489	80	685	233	487	620	1,783	114	948
Cass County	10,353	7,641	3,042	2,954	1,214	1,453	444	202	594	831	1,785	1,768	617	453
Christian County	7,994	5,430	2,746	3,385	953	1,207	366	670	747	1,299	1,805	1,476	607	757
Clay County	21,151	13,690	4,819	5,625	1,643	3,251	480	792	993	1,607	3,410	3,684	678	1,248
Cole County	7,917	5,057	1,352	1,714	541	835	157	219	143	769	655	1,064	144	474
Franklin County	10,318	7,630	3,005	3,952	953	1,853	767	329	361	476	2,144	2,692	389	865
Greene County	26,967	21,346	9,367	8,588	5,225	4,236	4,168	1,267	5,090	2,365	6,630	5,478	3,606	1,708
Jackson County	60,958	43,782	15,602	18,919	4,994	8,001	2,755	3,520	2,833	4,859	9,849	13,034	1,678	4,400
Jasper County	10,633	8,066	3,403	3,672	1,106	1,924	306	422	653	741	2,491	2,008	815	558
Jefferson County	20,819	13,005	7,753	5,904	3,478	3,412	1,180	761	1,359	1,034	4,513	3,496	1,554	1,510
Platte County	9,309	5,719	2,582	2,872	1,038	1,769	139	886	597	626	1,191	1,302	392	936
St. Charles County	35,112	24,577	8,133	10,144	3,276	4,310	1,067	1,539	1,308	2,433	4,573	7,156	1,070	1,751
St. Francois County	6,583	4,760	2,065	2,365	951	1,262	179	260	319	118	1,182	1,404	395	303
St. Louis County	101,719	78,802	20,145	33,116	6,712	13,329	2,822	6,023	3,967	7,807	12,183	23,131	2,720	9,061
Montana														
Cascade County	8,401	6,604	1,983	2,849	708	1,444	161	553	782	1,435	1,151	1,639	163	746
Flathead County	12,612	7,346	2,492	3,143	1,374	1,903	380	330	238	581	1,279	1,560	417	652
Gallatin County	9,244	5,184	1,631	1,822	699	1,135	219	168	260	523	649	965	208	373
Lewis and Clark County	7,994	4,674	1,438	2,088	1,030	1,496	250	478	212	538	595	1,011	31	407
Missoula County	11,313	6,944	3,443	3,025	1,268	1,852	621	389	738	562	1,525	1,636	363	752
Yellowstone County	15,657	11,506	3,498	4,838	1,488	1,909	281	1,060	497	1,666	2,182	2,647	259	1,222
Nebraska														
Douglas County	44,590	29,271	9,480	13,394	3,345	6,586	2,023	2,849	1,788	3,399	5,903	9,170	1,468	2,845
Lancaster County	26,715	17,115	6,059	8,493	2,713	4,242	502	1,379	1,062	2,684	3,721	4,827	875	1,919
Sarpy County	13,398	8,771	2,139	3,702	932	1,596	441	630	319	1,012	876	2,274	251	1,033
Nevada														
Clark County	201,469	127,221	51,478	59,413	18,656	28,841	10,999	13,341	11,448	16,768	33,176	39,892	9,216	17,418
Washoe County	48,330	27,842	10,222	12,622	4,337	5,734	1,825	1,806	1,883	3,709	6,287	8,744	1,945	3,309
New Hampshire														
Cheshire County	8,994	6,101	2,139	2,389	686	1,186	418	204	609	333	1,237	1,403	439	423
Grafton County	11,006	7,629	2,542	2,792	1,235	1,737	369	462	431	380	1,217	1,275	270	530
Hillsborough County	38,228	26,622	8,818	11,166	3,528	5,869	1,039	2,008	1,038	2,524	4,880	5,621	1,100	2,127
Merrimack County	17,002	11,421	3,181	4,656	1,067	2,530	317	549	630	1,196	1,732	2,591	724	1,070
Rockingham County	33,773	21,628	5,586	9,505	2,030	5,303	502	1,543	1,503	2,230	3,080	5,848	688	2,510
Strafford County	11,333	7,849	2,405	3,280	1,637	1,732	441	409	655	1,027	1,364	2,053	406	595
New Jersey														
Atlantic County	27,356	20,202	7,165	7,559	1,789	2,609	910	885	1,305	1,590	4,816	5,516	1,041	1,678
Bergen County	87,492	73,507	15,007	29,264	4,294	12,367	1,726	5,432	2,188	8,071	9,313	20,260	2,924	10,414
Burlington County	42,934	32,341	8,498	14,527	2,887	6,439	1,406	2,367	1,503	3,808	5,406	9,536	1,136	3,718
Camden County	46,138	33,102	12,468	15,018	5,009	6,726	2,353	2,909	2,693	4,794	8,206	10,334	3,190	3,256
Cape May County	13,585	10,483	2,781	4,670	1,206	1,660	434	540	633	911	1,842	2,999	366	744

Table H-2: Counties - Disability Status and Type of Disability—*Continued*

	Total Population		With a Disability		With a Hearing Disability		With a Vision Disability		With a Cognitive Disability		With an Ambulatory Disability		With a Self-Care Disability	
	65 to 74 Years	75 Years and Over	65 to 74 Years	75 Years and Over	65 to 74 Years	75 Years and Over	65 to 74 Years	75 Years and Over	65 to 74 Years	75 Years and Over	65 to 74 Years	75 Years and Over	65 to 74 Years	75 Years and Over
New Jersey—Cont.														
Cumberland County	13,681	9,541	4,271	3,649	897	1,167	991	366	1,035	955	3,534	2,583	1,193	970
Essex County	61,942	46,590	12,292	17,808	2,644	7,602	2,685	4,410	2,012	5,580	8,966	12,398	2,788	6,193
Gloucester County	27,623	18,956	7,153	8,806	2,449	4,135	1,018	1,551	1,438	1,759	5,081	5,927	1,274	2,445
Hudson County	45,607	34,311	9,615	15,624	2,198	4,311	1,883	2,572	2,357	4,384	6,204	11,879	2,848	5,936
Hunterdon County	14,129	9,151	2,167	2,948	521	1,403	219	326	497	740	1,239	1,646	412	616
Mercer County	32,615	23,386	5,014	7,828	1,363	3,483	816	1,125	820	1,597	2,858	5,204	563	2,332
Middlesex County	71,032	53,106	13,682	25,412	3,639	10,777	2,152	3,918	2,710	5,382	9,053	15,604	1,808	5,476
Monmouth County	62,724	46,476	10,935	18,769	3,493	7,546	2,691	3,155	1,944	4,228	6,989	12,949	2,052	5,156
Morris County	46,320	37,994	5,553	15,470	2,027	7,418	735	1,945	1,248	3,027	3,145	8,462	899	3,369
Ocean County	72,024	64,254	14,426	26,279	4,735	9,662	2,513	3,831	1,912	6,091	8,905	18,639	2,020	6,356
Passaic County	41,271	31,940	9,237	13,445	2,368	5,172	1,816	3,398	2,332	5,894	6,726	10,455	2,556	5,350
Salem County	6,759	4,976	1,708	1,608	581	771	216	184	456	344	1,163	1,078	428	350
Somerset County	28,538	23,081	2,822	9,529	1,070	3,492	548	1,447	613	2,969	1,421	6,367	597	3,271
Sussex County	14,613	9,063	2,847	4,047	852	1,891	207	926	1,045	1,018	1,828	2,527	831	1,084
Union County	45,176	35,077	8,286	15,332	2,276	5,526	1,367	3,625	2,598	4,576	5,699	11,871	2,035	6,245
Warren County	10,794	8,399	2,412	4,105	1,161	2,097	360	570	279	1,476	1,731	2,256	164	940
New Mexico														
Bernalillo County	66,685	44,531	16,642	23,960	6,325	11,566	2,127	4,605	3,102	7,592	9,318	15,727	1,982	6,861
Chaves County	5,905	4,925	2,443	2,665	645	1,758	330	718	679	1,055	1,392	2,054	655	1,175
Doña Ana County	19,851	14,935	5,343	7,914	2,371	4,262	1,071	2,296	481	2,081	3,426	4,855	617	2,535
Lea County	4,770	3,086	1,469	1,804	289	859	136	146	322	864	1,352	1,084	140	793
McKinley County	4,993	4,288	1,828	2,820	959	1,543	352	971	428	862	1,084	1,630	370	714
Otero County	6,506	4,216	1,693	2,015	782	1,209	158	216	240	1,045	736	1,542	292	480
Sandoval County	16,289	9,474	4,710	5,687	1,466	2,523	248	399	1,441	1,974	3,033	3,215	475	621
San Juan County	11,230	7,871	3,929	4,305	2,043	2,531	268	804	726	1,032	2,198	2,171	269	628
Santa Fe County	23,437	13,131	4,561	5,836	2,113	2,625	441	927	958	2,087	2,627	4,135	808	1,373
Valencia County	8,244	5,431	2,963	2,911	1,312	1,974	476	932	366	448	1,787	1,886	734	370
New York														
Albany County	30,005	22,311	5,591	7,403	1,655	2,700	1,012	1,104	996	1,461	2,864	4,434	965	1,171
Bronx County	101,971	81,194	32,693	39,766	4,984	9,941	9,266	11,402	7,779	13,922	23,344	31,076	6,691	14,885
Broome County	19,617	17,176	4,512	8,238	2,079	3,764	418	1,791	502	2,453	2,301	4,918	728	2,009
Cattaraugus County	8,449	6,192	2,436	2,445	737	1,191	247	318	1,034	568	1,001	1,300	204	391
Cayuga County	8,238	6,084	2,487	2,607	924	1,116	681	1,062	416	1,057	1,107	1,460	239	1,044
Chautauqua County	14,268	11,319	3,427	4,967	1,085	2,460	493	1,038	444	1,434	2,190	3,175	680	1,486
Chemung County	9,519	7,094	2,386	3,904	1,081	2,304	485	892	490	1,325	1,496	2,679	385	1,472
Clinton County	7,865	5,658	1,865	2,863	686	1,185	374	812	648	849	1,329	2,078	523	863
Dutchess County	29,217	22,356	7,107	10,235	3,045	5,249	1,361	1,279	985	2,622	3,671	6,667	835	3,214
Erie County	91,755	73,461	20,578	30,173	6,988	13,511	3,721	4,803	5,066	6,812	12,158	18,314	3,858	7,992
Jefferson County	9,065	6,393	2,428	2,826	1,143	1,319	541	572	457	499	1,347	1,736	306	425
Kings County	204,057	154,740	49,655	75,396	9,365	22,025	9,193	14,999	10,405	24,955	36,431	58,186	10,268	31,081
Livingston County	6,462	4,655	998	2,121	524	1,458	162	551	200	525	450	1,254	139	410
Madison County	7,724	5,363	1,637	2,205	412	1,260	26	330	426	344	1,172	1,098	219	404
Monroe County	72,844	55,266	14,587	23,040	4,030	9,483	1,777	3,222	3,043	4,881	8,477	15,844	1,969	5,478
Nassau County	132,963	108,367	17,725	40,558	5,196	15,585	1,931	4,948	2,458	11,603	11,029	28,425	3,068	13,328
New York County	146,350	122,484	29,330	53,746	4,993	17,197	5,661	11,378	6,941	18,439	21,549	40,056	7,824	19,183
Niagara County	23,034	16,779	6,583	7,681	1,493	3,582	646	1,863	838	2,304	5,048	4,534	712	2,149
Oneida County	23,065	19,490	5,270	7,445	2,051	3,320	593	647	1,285	1,791	3,267	4,472	1,608	2,291
Onondaga County	44,565	34,302	8,757	15,273	2,933	7,928	1,320	2,983	2,171	4,262	5,509	9,542	1,672	3,404
Ontario County	12,678	8,967	2,473	4,789	1,157	2,261	317	582	285	1,247	1,269	2,970	190	634
Orange County	31,913	21,478	5,613	8,738	1,870	4,187	1,198	939	1,061	2,752	3,642	5,433	1,143	2,483
Oswego County	11,699	7,750	2,875	3,724	1,431	2,135	915	368	523	751	1,375	2,312	435	632
Putnam County	10,434	6,660	1,650	2,532	776	973	105	641	301	497	780	1,925	420	470
Queens County	201,575	156,055	37,696	66,123	8,396	21,170	7,404	12,181	7,087	20,414	25,538	49,023	7,655	24,548
Rensselaer County	16,007	10,550	4,298	4,543	1,583	2,069	419	1,002	684	720	2,513	2,835	256	1,066
Richmond County	45,983	31,071	9,069	12,453	2,309	4,109	1,326	2,271	2,394	2,810	6,197	10,072	1,939	5,386
Rockland County	27,953	23,156	4,530	9,877	1,513	4,822	660	1,290	504	2,302	2,276	5,195	795	2,849
St. Lawrence County	10,731	7,737	3,246	3,920	1,101	2,245	372	795	597	1,233	1,983	2,450	599	982
Saratoga County	24,666	16,184	5,523	6,724	1,601	3,873	1,634	1,890	1,390	1,325	2,863	3,757	564	1,008
Schenectady County	14,836	12,016	2,662	5,567	1,037	2,127	196	732	609	1,508	1,241	3,771	450	1,678
Steuben County	10,810	7,853	1,876	2,848	853	1,392	375	454	262	768	928	1,717	446	722
Suffolk County	140,468	109,614	23,627	41,246	7,995	17,206	3,943	7,470	5,192	10,653	13,660	26,776	4,395	11,988
Sullivan County	8,370	5,828	2,562	2,937	808	1,284	587	588	373	783	1,523	1,805	327	797
Tompkins County	8,586	5,623	1,994	2,414	777	1,516	301	150	295	475	1,034	1,080	246	265
Ulster County	20,406	14,719	4,244	6,763	2,116	2,882	1,077	707	822	1,955	2,443	3,713	621	1,967
Warren County	8,507	5,854	1,227	2,617	431	1,279	225	414	151	359	742	1,828	17	860
Wayne County	9,930	7,362	2,582	3,349	1,096	1,576	76	431	407	742	1,569	2,423	496	868
Westchester County	88,333	77,004	15,136	30,548	3,723	11,059	2,269	4,241	3,360	8,944	9,214	20,208	2,088	11,788
North Carolina														
Alamance County	16,087	12,294	5,604	5,598	1,833	2,667	863	814	1,037	1,374	3,010	3,166	746	1,027
Brunswick County	29,382	14,281	5,022	6,190	2,655	3,671	985	683	1,002	1,817	2,555	3,349	647	860
Buncombe County	30,369	21,452	5,334	9,730	1,797	5,798	592	2,317	1,147	2,247	2,851	5,758	821	2,030
Burke County	10,041	8,006	3,936	4,219	1,845	2,363	782	1,448	1,340	719	1,741	1,807	855	745
Cabarrus County	16,885	11,323	4,022	5,385	1,960	2,077	456	990	999	2,198	2,506	3,317	454	1,455
Caldwell County	9,563	6,480	2,604	3,629	524	1,316	611	944	553	1,208	1,462	2,860	500	1,026
Carteret County	10,770	6,685	3,286	3,184	1,367	1,999	324	241	680	1,062	1,821	1,972	426	915
Catawba County	16,899	11,121	4,191	5,411	1,966	2,265	235	1,141	621	1,310	2,615	3,935	463	1,391

Table H-2: Counties - Disability Status and Type of Disability—*Continued*

	Total Population		With a Disability		With a Hearing Disability		With a Vision Disability		With a Cognitive Disability		With an Ambulatory Disability		With a Self-Care Disability	
	65 to 74 Years	75 Years and Over	65 to 74 Years	75 Years and Over	65 to 74 Years	75 Years and Over	65 to 74 Years	75 Years and Over	65 to 74 Years	75 Years and Over	65 to 74 Years	75 Years and Over	65 to 74 Years	75 Years and Over
North Carolina—Cont.														
Chatham County	10,282	7,594	1,506	4,447	791	2,624	672	1,382	405	2,098	198	2,858	59	1,010
Cleveland County	10,584	7,513	2,117	2,521	1,000	1,133	383	380	438	572	1,183	1,653	427	524
Craven County	11,039	8,549	1,881	4,219	838	1,725	397	391	294	961	1,134	2,972	502	1,017
Cumberland County	23,590	16,568	9,266	8,143	2,402	3,342	1,961	2,326	1,714	3,102	6,911	5,773	1,889	2,568
Davidson County	18,009	12,029	5,685	5,722	1,470	2,355	610	671	2,348	1,530	3,967	4,050	1,690	1,270
Durham County	25,580	16,335	5,678	6,677	1,668	2,709	1,074	1,096	1,210	1,702	2,916	4,649	776	2,147
Forsyth County	35,754	24,631	7,390	10,226	2,137	4,261	934	1,894	1,184	2,366	4,576	6,300	1,073	2,120
Franklin County	7,716	3,917	2,243	1,993	784	1,265	265	467	522	431	1,631	1,086	510	186
Gaston County	21,405	13,984	6,748	6,293	2,387	3,634	1,589	1,382	1,272	1,377	4,405	3,444	1,364	1,011
Guilford County	47,619	32,855	10,953	13,861	3,746	6,373	1,203	2,301	1,799	4,565	6,333	8,976	1,385	3,789
Harnett County	10,179	6,862	2,986	3,043	1,376	1,349	873	632	963	849	1,732	1,620	859	661
Henderson County	16,862	13,477	3,918	5,081	1,953	2,773	666	725	623	1,100	2,183	2,895	679	1,019
Iredell County	16,741	11,126	3,889	6,332	1,485	3,054	853	890	542	1,439	2,381	3,768	321	1,550
Johnston County	17,262	10,134	4,323	6,953	1,813	2,320	555	756	575	2,089	1,842	5,238	687	2,169
Lincoln County	8,903	5,378	1,977	2,102	828	978	126	209	345	727	1,086	852	279	278
Mecklenburg County	76,140	46,451	14,874	18,929	5,598	8,610	1,986	4,111	2,632	5,397	8,111	11,491	2,759	4,507
Moore County	12,691	10,893	3,276	4,477	1,507	2,425	960	1,128	442	1,354	1,699	2,141	418	1,298
Nash County	10,666	6,780	3,611	3,123	1,329	1,090	684	491	1,061	669	1,476	1,867	176	770
New Hanover County	25,026	16,453	4,608	6,834	1,493	4,567	721	1,572	967	2,179	2,961	3,884	1,195	1,239
Onslow County	10,427	7,609	3,828	4,320	2,007	2,300	233	1,144	866	1,050	2,422	2,471	365	553
Orange County	13,577	7,176	3,704	1,611	1,084	535	210	254	449	331	1,824	1,159	437	235
Pitt County	14,375	9,165	4,377	5,780	1,717	2,941	678	386	543	2,017	2,388	3,771	650	1,181
Randolph County	14,752	10,455	4,028	4,874	2,161	1,679	855	1,731	927	1,370	2,231	2,982	720	974
Robeson County	12,367	7,494	4,589	3,871	1,691	2,069	1,020	587	1,411	1,576	3,227	2,807	1,065	1,270
Rockingham County	10,751	7,882	2,101	3,068	445	1,573	385	600	785	376	1,497	2,199	502	1,427
Rowan County	14,426	10,170	4,624	4,622	1,769	2,641	641	1,284	856	1,376	3,164	3,107	395	1,140
Rutherford County	8,191	5,867	3,093	2,959	1,110	1,430	212	829	558	1,068	1,442	1,746	599	843
Surry County	8,344	6,722	2,986	3,112	1,163	1,460	729	692	624	728	1,802	2,338	342	844
Union County	18,134	11,656	3,922	5,372	1,587	1,626	589	770	563	1,534	1,688	3,304	926	1,406
Wake County	79,867	46,973	15,657	19,288	5,586	7,798	3,049	3,379	3,544	4,936	8,954	12,903	1,916	4,178
Wayne County	12,178	8,329	2,903	4,479	879	1,836	284	443	843	1,268	2,084	2,647	397	1,481
Wilkes County	8,390	6,305	3,397	3,420	1,091	1,057	632	432	1,186	1,088	1,772	2,437	147	1,119
Wilson County	8,875	5,929	2,615	2,379	900	1,510	456	378	622	350	2,019	1,150	375	332
North Dakota														
Burleigh County	8,440	6,717	1,511	3,450	596	2,082	248	865	318	707	716	2,335	117	562
Cass County	12,327	9,272	2,259	3,983	1,272	1,750	283	1,345	33	1,102	586	2,804	90	448
Grand Forks County	5,070	3,793	987	1,032	326	257	102	239	115	86	632	748	157	225
Ward County	4,562	3,900	1,033	1,901	333	1,393	202	804	141	496	945	1,277	188	571
Ohio														
Allen County	10,071	7,859	2,568	3,936	1,021	2,471	601	780	386	989	1,623	2,246	297	795
Ashtabula County	10,840	7,729	3,329	3,658	1,619	1,458	701	938	801	668	1,786	2,244	585	834
Athens County	5,271	3,366	1,360	1,868	715	846	106	422	463	610	696	1,073	307	575
Belmont County	8,320	6,030	2,012	2,902	870	1,004	354	198	120	606	995	2,089	314	411
Butler County	33,315	22,957	8,289	10,607	2,611	4,621	2,129	2,028	2,393	2,174	5,824	6,593	2,807	2,502
Clark County	14,885	11,072	4,814	5,252	1,752	3,004	682	810	943	1,609	2,830	2,754	732	911
Clermont County	20,034	12,942	5,249	5,186	2,637	2,910	585	1,344	582	1,129	2,704	2,672	960	1,303
Columbiana County	12,380	8,795	3,429	3,482	1,031	1,834	827	241	577	1,079	2,170	2,354	844	1,017
Cuyahoga County	125,549	100,588	30,926	45,364	9,052	16,933	5,426	9,052	5,949	11,021	19,271	29,940	5,724	11,364
Delaware County	16,937	10,641	3,210	4,907	1,384	2,168	731	685	827	1,393	1,495	3,418	495	1,659
Erie County	9,152	7,005	2,269	2,789	816	1,315	711	338	360	774	1,554	1,698	627	967
Fairfield County	14,690	9,985	3,505	4,463	975	1,648	432	452	739	448	1,959	3,140	503	1,373
Franklin County	95,467	62,074	21,220	27,867	6,772	11,659	3,611	4,135	4,193	7,407	13,147	17,862	3,236	6,417
Geauga County	11,093	8,414	2,022	2,425	708	1,383	205	635	180	396	1,119	1,383	211	557
Greene County	17,023	12,036	4,265	6,281	1,206	2,239	786	1,188	920	1,309	2,521	4,558	938	1,449
Hamilton County	71,904	53,113	15,240	20,246	4,942	8,451	2,785	3,618	3,345	6,809	8,892	13,326	2,773	5,531
Hancock County	7,220	5,609	1,602	2,597	845	1,661	282	554	154	819	786	1,204	195	906
Jefferson County	8,211	6,246	1,688	3,148	594	806	284	458	581	1,171	1,091	2,384	267	1,418
Lake County	26,430	19,917	7,535	9,049	2,129	4,632	1,442	1,898	1,320	2,235	4,309	5,709	1,082	2,014
Licking County	16,778	11,955	5,089	6,115	2,723	2,774	901	1,203	893	1,367	2,945	4,152	1,196	1,706
Lorain County	33,246	23,659	7,668	9,341	1,998	4,214	1,029	1,747	1,802	1,846	4,796	5,531	1,414	1,798
Lucas County	41,432	28,777	11,532	12,932	4,212	6,541	1,267	1,754	2,571	4,065	6,522	7,978	1,875	3,018
Mahoning County	26,506	21,634	5,359	9,566	2,228	4,016	954	1,496	970	2,284	2,604	5,713	893	2,274
Marion County	6,753	4,654	1,531	2,468	534	1,263	193	275	500	717	1,094	1,853	342	600
Medina County	18,922	13,152	4,193	4,670	1,976	2,321	442	1,079	1,045	655	2,169	2,518	553	1,062
Miami County	11,586	8,950	2,735	3,857	850	2,234	202	851	408	387	1,366	2,322	523	1,132
Montgomery County	53,821	41,823	14,015	18,510	3,747	7,051	2,418	2,892	2,855	4,829	8,769	12,793	1,925	4,280
Muskingum County	8,667	6,522	3,008	3,001	1,215	1,783	265	136	346	248	1,368	1,596	244	784
Portage County	16,502	10,683	3,612	4,071	1,394	2,041	719	1,143	1,388	869	2,482	2,281	552	835
Richland County	12,614	11,121	3,003	4,865	879	2,231	499	1,177	783	1,594	1,970	2,729	823	1,127
Ross County	7,663	5,693	2,803	3,519	1,153	1,313	451	821	557	658	1,908	2,001	407	771
Scioto County	7,602	5,924	2,605	3,059	1,134	1,279	548	952	648	974	1,623	1,930	133	898
Stark County	40,575	31,487	8,807	14,589	2,440	5,785	1,363	2,541	2,252	3,652	5,423	8,831	1,285	2,462
Summit County	56,533	40,934	11,803	17,477	3,361	6,361	2,652	2,987	2,070	3,263	7,386	12,094	2,116	3,819
Trumbull County	24,720	18,429	5,338	7,674	1,752	3,038	744	908	1,025	2,524	3,425	5,114	1,118	2,360
Tuscarawas County	10,052	7,975	2,841	3,189	1,464	1,740	320	839	471	834	1,427	2,246	365	491

Table H-2: Counties - Disability Status and Type of Disability—*Continued*

	Total Population		With a Disability		With a Hearing Disability		With a Vision Disability		With a Cognitive Disability		With an Ambulatory Disability		With a Self-Care Disability	
	65 to 74 Years	75 Years and Over	65 to 74 Years	75 Years and Over	65 to 74 Years	75 Years and Over	65 to 74 Years	75 Years and Over	65 to 74 Years	75 Years and Over	65 to 74 Years	75 Years and Over	65 to 74 Years	75 Years and Over
Ohio—Cont.														
Warren County	20,150	13,230	5,612	6,402	2,792	2,867	961	1,544	905	1,794	3,320	4,686	474	2,005
Wayne County	11,401	8,863	2,063	4,407	686	2,112	416	440	416	999	1,131	2,617	255	739
Wood County	11,728	8,323	2,665	2,990	1,043	1,349	240	469	394	693	1,281	1,972	376	643
Oklahoma														
Canadian County	11,559	7,272	3,403	3,872	1,670	2,389	770	448	691	1,330	1,911	2,450	662	745
Cleveland County	22,723	14,585	7,146	7,477	3,088	3,857	748	1,365	459	1,717	4,604	4,839	1,146	1,057
Comanche County	8,942	6,281	4,046	3,048	1,475	1,414	628	661	1,093	603	2,816	1,771	548	490
Creek County	7,295	5,129	1,669	2,754	719	1,741	552	933	378	879	981	1,712	229	628
Muskogee County	6,256	5,064	1,883	2,552	791	1,245	82	854	522	836	1,147	1,784	127	596
Oklahoma County	64,312	43,965	20,441	22,906	7,669	10,598	3,994	4,233	4,459	6,431	12,841	16,363	3,276	6,069
Payne County	6,554	4,426	1,477	2,108	987	1,106	127	504	314	604	599	1,524	217	565
Pottawatomie County	7,143	4,678	3,298	2,891	927	1,414	770	555	799	783	2,224	2,106	544	618
Rogers County	8,932	6,055	2,419	2,689	1,046	1,604	368	732	419	638	1,415	1,748	348	564
Tulsa County	55,676	37,643	14,584	17,321	6,013	7,287	2,787	3,365	3,132	4,080	9,538	11,701	2,068	4,109
Wagoner County	8,011	4,960	2,733	2,560	1,283	1,500	442	418	771	567	2,099	1,575	334	714
Oregon														
Benton County	9,072	5,771	1,711	2,148	691	1,285	351	925	591	587	886	931	189	444
Clackamas County	45,498	29,151	10,678	12,276	3,800	6,402	2,184	2,035	2,600	3,128	6,688	8,022	2,223	2,587
Deschutes County	24,256	14,492	5,064	5,928	2,764	3,406	1,266	1,756	1,422	1,651	1,928	3,486	390	1,392
Douglas County	16,235	11,689	4,139	5,860	1,628	3,677	607	1,639	552	1,149	2,317	3,054	225	545
Jackson County	29,037	19,652	5,715	8,729	2,020	5,092	453	1,449	1,065	2,532	3,754	4,796	962	2,295
Josephine County	13,302	9,561	3,664	3,690	1,662	2,323	618	910	774	826	2,146	2,166	938	733
Klamath County	8,974	5,636	2,731	2,526	1,416	1,442	527	284	700	441	1,347	1,682	696	821
Lane County	45,031	28,669	11,380	14,257	5,256	7,538	1,312	2,266	2,357	3,802	6,227	8,433	2,063	4,146
Linn County	14,633	9,953	4,376	5,061	2,130	2,345	562	1,029	392	2,277	1,995	3,163	203	1,100
Marion County	31,067	22,408	8,499	10,625	3,021	5,905	1,451	1,302	2,239	3,174	5,826	7,660	1,655	2,638
Multnomah County	68,421	40,441	15,180	18,561	5,673	8,923	2,573	2,492	2,752	4,839	9,045	10,925	2,347	3,230
Polk County	8,899	6,401	1,955	2,692	884	978	202	352	106	357	1,216	1,756	314	288
Umatilla County	7,002	4,920	2,921	2,389	1,567	1,236	636	664	353	453	1,437	1,204	257	537
Washington County	49,120	31,257	10,250	14,150	3,733	6,743	874	2,809	2,007	4,464	5,884	8,944	2,246	4,281
Yamhill County	10,561	7,263	2,844	3,518	1,531	1,959	31	566	487	478	1,387	2,134	402	633
Pennsylvania														
Adams County	11,840	8,794	2,326	3,557	1,205	1,404	242	682	293	978	1,033	2,544	40	937
Allegheny County	127,349	102,570	27,100	43,694	8,599	19,370	3,801	7,459	4,480	11,017	16,819	27,409	3,680	12,623
Armstrong County	7,953	6,324	1,729	2,972	995	1,084	144	423	564	683	885	2,159	324	563
Beaver County	19,774	15,845	4,112	7,669	1,812	4,109	560	973	1,019	1,747	2,899	4,753	621	1,352
Berks County	40,863	31,452	10,370	14,201	2,894	6,240	1,381	1,474	2,256	3,467	6,297	8,344	952	3,366
Blair County	14,160	11,333	3,372	4,214	1,452	2,166	505	886	544	960	2,104	2,428	546	936
Bucks County	66,697	50,363	11,300	19,584	4,349	8,421	1,317	2,805	1,996	3,671	6,526	12,848	1,546	4,708
Butler County	19,769	15,180	3,867	7,835	1,283	3,451	416	898	763	1,947	2,362	4,410	427	1,352
Cambria County	16,239	13,425	4,548	6,274	1,758	2,820	595	1,507	791	1,598	2,638	4,005	726	2,102
Carbon County	7,838	5,546	2,618	2,548	1,121	1,374	213	426	964	921	1,231	1,851	656	595
Centre County	12,935	9,880	1,948	2,955	828	1,115	324	238	120	844	794	1,969	300	804
Chester County	49,622	35,546	6,799	13,825	2,901	7,312	802	2,910	1,080	2,986	3,596	9,044	705	2,741
Clearfield County	8,954	7,313	2,170	3,439	1,076	1,420	273	827	246	849	1,211	2,035	513	811
Columbia County	7,264	5,448	1,449	2,778	336	972	455	292	160	790	863	1,951	287	1,149
Crawford County	10,388	7,168	3,072	3,439	1,230	1,875	303	1,013	483	676	1,909	2,135	475	752
Cumberland County	26,506	20,262	6,391	8,566	2,310	3,897	1,522	2,043	1,125	2,638	3,394	5,303	768	1,991
Dauphin County	26,977	19,841	5,963	8,448	2,129	3,317	1,351	1,473	1,351	2,403	3,810	5,865	1,225	2,367
Delaware County	51,559	40,892	9,480	17,084	2,932	7,190	1,247	3,019	1,874	5,334	6,111	11,476	1,344	5,408
Erie County	28,015	20,911	7,613	8,980	2,753	4,767	1,225	1,278	1,484	2,616	4,735	5,545	1,176	2,331
Fayette County	15,618	12,074	4,009	5,586	1,798	2,158	515	1,156	722	1,195	2,183	3,747	369	1,164
Franklin County	16,513	13,430	4,399	5,621	1,800	2,929	904	795	1,090	2,057	2,106	3,354	288	1,225
Indiana County	9,219	7,404	2,219	3,622	832	2,134	557	1,111	514	1,140	999	2,457	225	1,082
Lackawanna County	23,139	18,737	5,514	8,458	2,519	4,525	613	1,190	971	1,599	3,347	5,458	585	1,914
Lancaster County	53,268	45,483	11,493	17,154	4,735	8,322	2,055	2,887	2,751	4,303	5,792	11,077	1,382	3,855
Lawrence County	10,444	8,534	2,981	4,339	1,234	2,340	287	947	358	852	1,733	2,895	253	960
Lebanon County	15,166	12,543	2,813	4,808	1,048	1,935	764	668	186	1,466	1,593	3,658	261	1,478
Lehigh County	34,924	27,370	6,295	11,575	2,386	3,812	1,088	1,951	1,521	3,901	3,791	7,709	1,015	2,303
Luzerne County	35,297	28,062	8,834	11,355	3,631	6,292	1,205	2,850	1,310	2,952	5,642	7,606	1,733	3,324
Lycoming County	12,212	9,689	2,959	4,249	1,223	1,530	703	1,010	485	1,015	1,819	3,162	369	1,433
Mercer County	13,190	10,800	2,892	5,589	1,063	3,030	651	671	701	1,283	1,544	3,806	466	1,411
Monroe County	16,994	11,134	4,548	4,704	1,691	2,352	419	549	1,135	1,210	2,656	2,922	1,259	1,558
Montgomery County	80,682	66,475	14,547	26,596	4,421	12,267	2,522	4,105	2,583	6,564	7,924	15,679	2,242	7,498
Northampton County	31,706	25,957	6,572	10,842	2,052	5,103	1,158	2,513	1,085	2,698	4,587	6,473	1,382	2,259
Northumberland County	10,918	8,729	2,464	4,193	784	1,682	267	876	455	1,100	1,618	2,540	475	582
Philadelphia County	123,995	91,760	40,594	45,650	7,396	14,618	8,202	8,851	12,653	12,577	31,403	34,620	10,108	13,278
Schuylkill County	16,243	12,636	3,887	6,223	1,943	2,735	356	1,307	725	1,635	1,943	4,245	232	1,397
Somerset County	9,063	7,462	2,314	3,314	1,148	2,224	227	329	603	997	1,328	1,039	363	261
Washington County	24,150	17,996	5,326	8,293	1,454	3,776	1,000	1,292	643	2,670	3,261	5,073	760	2,304
Westmoreland County	44,074	35,362	9,927	15,467	3,904	6,317	955	2,435	1,625	2,835	5,534	10,062	1,512	3,003
York County	45,351	32,787	9,263	15,592	3,249	7,566	1,390	2,199	2,580	4,271	5,319	9,448	1,326	3,202
Rhode Island														
Kent County	17,708	13,211	3,657	5,835	1,520	2,867	410	650	695	1,388	2,141	3,165	429	1,022
Newport County	10,725	7,914	1,875	2,983	959	1,815	94	567	344	283	928	2,058	238	355
Providence County	54,020	43,363	15,010	19,044	5,516	7,777	2,205	3,935	3,967	5,103	10,158	13,150	3,953	6,475
Washington County	15,612	10,543	2,597	3,926	1,236	1,959	414	815	436	1,083	801	2,364	335	950

Table H-2: Counties - Disability Status and Type of Disability—*Continued*

	Total Population		With a Disability		With a Hearing Disability		With a Vision Disability		With a Cognitive Disability		With an Ambulatory Disability		With a Self-Care Disability	
	65 to 74 Years	75 Years and Over	65 to 74 Years	75 Years and Over	65 to 74 Years	75 Years and Over	65 to 74 Years	75 Years and Over	65 to 74 Years	75 Years and Over	65 to 74 Years	75 Years and Over	65 to 74 Years	75 Years and Over
South Carolina														
Aiken County	19,572	13,173	5,014	6,115	1,961	3,198	383	1,564	566	1,573	2,696	3,925	598	1,555
Anderson County	21,431	14,499	7,209	7,529	2,609	3,254	1,328	1,254	1,399	2,021	5,052	4,495	1,547	2,176
Beaufort County	30,321	21,214	5,265	7,106	2,293	2,839	854	126	1,208	963	2,431	5,467	424	2,094
Berkeley County	19,795	11,014	6,562	5,057	2,017	3,021	893	966	1,733	1,895	4,210	2,979	1,742	633
Charleston County	41,190	24,908	8,845	10,441	2,074	4,415	1,203	1,107	1,544	3,222	5,617	7,161	1,658	4,235
Darlington County	7,784	4,856	1,259	3,091	463	942	204	915	507	399	529	1,948	85	1,038
Dorchester County	14,149	8,290	3,877	4,273	1,247	1,774	715	1,566	728	1,360	2,230	2,740	459	713
Florence County	14,311	9,087	2,722	3,544	799	1,608	512	683	786	797	1,750	2,212	216	431
Greenville County	48,406	32,581	11,459	14,684	3,501	6,471	1,925	2,413	2,584	5,246	7,255	9,922	1,226	3,981
Greenwood County	6,891	6,104	1,628	3,024	408	1,753	536	137	378	658	882	1,719	523	1,042
Horry County	55,355	27,876	12,875	12,746	4,638	6,741	1,425	1,834	1,826	3,805	8,431	8,966	2,238	3,570
Kershaw County	7,416	4,512	2,929	2,274	985	573	922	487	854	630	1,693	1,561	806	1,024
Lancaster County	11,944	7,691	2,509	3,154	666	1,519	577	625	522	695	1,411	1,901	768	737
Laurens County	7,864	4,762	3,386	2,132	1,353	1,037	71	371	1,082	899	1,616	1,496	164	908
Lexington County	28,755	18,017	8,349	8,655	3,054	3,687	2,051	1,474	1,697	2,312	5,214	5,403	1,252	1,989
Oconee County	11,362	7,271	2,973	3,869	1,526	1,772	692	1,392	1,006	2,595	1,184	1,927	176	792
Orangeburg County	10,063	6,803	2,332	2,693	606	1,509	607	763	797	1,156	1,443	1,927	583	607
Pickens County	11,813	8,876	3,334	4,322	900	2,029	185	616	689	791	2,339	2,756	194	795
Richland County	33,194	19,684	10,051	9,614	3,123	3,562	2,314	2,591	1,555	1,956	7,064	6,336	2,489	2,440
Spartanburg County	29,925	20,253	8,075	10,069	2,868	5,191	1,419	2,436	1,739	3,715	4,281	6,452	996	2,757
Sumter County	10,268	7,300	3,098	3,482	976	1,253	1,072	585	392	1,293	1,834	2,454	335	1,461
York County	24,750	14,614	4,635	5,582	2,017	2,395	490	1,055	887	1,961	1,703	2,640	704	1,610
South Dakota														
Minnehaha County	15,728	9,626	3,106	3,658	1,085	1,376	514	873	605	1,178	1,678	2,325	367	850
Pennington County	12,496	7,978	3,053	4,353	1,128	2,390	266	631	644	666	2,083	2,473	494	710
Tennessee														
Anderson County	8,791	6,514	2,611	3,150	1,206	1,448	534	686	539	1,041	1,667	2,045	174	1,091
Blount County	15,985	11,183	3,403	5,032	1,135	2,853	351	602	734	804	1,882	3,178	630	885
Bradley County	10,508	7,514	3,606	3,230	1,290	1,453	478	715	1,184	819	2,726	2,098	494	1,072
Davidson County	51,192	33,258	13,200	16,077	4,858	6,770	2,371	3,881	2,658	5,027	8,499	11,509	2,151	5,236
Greene County	8,574	6,235	3,396	3,057	1,874	1,695	869	577	1,068	1,712	2,393	1,653	1,174	1,042
Hamilton County	37,068	26,529	9,976	12,719	3,881	5,822	1,335	1,808	2,383	3,538	6,914	9,732	2,114	3,661
Knox County	43,474	29,803	10,111	14,367	4,087	5,581	1,513	2,736	2,743	3,760	5,424	9,049	1,697	3,639
Madison County	9,864	6,717	2,452	2,572	828	1,094	818	790	504	854	1,091	1,810	287	306
Maury County	8,771	5,968	1,642	2,877	680	1,389	95	776	328	855	876	1,885	336	298
Montgomery County	10,473	8,108	3,834	4,145	1,866	2,748	477	1,226	870	976	2,215	1,722	759	429
Putnam County	7,324	5,877	2,293	3,508	1,032	2,070	289	494	1,029	1,470	1,322	2,502	319	800
Robertson County	6,282	3,848	1,727	1,790	460	588	418	531	447	341	1,054	1,034	290	458
Rutherford County	21,357	12,188	5,030	5,735	2,127	2,127	1,027	671	785	1,823	2,547	4,621	765	1,567
Sevier County	11,832	7,328	2,639	4,159	1,496	1,674	299	606	314	2,098	1,168	3,154	425	1,315
Shelby County	78,438	48,598	20,005	24,159	5,578	8,258	5,180	5,262	4,104	7,850	13,316	17,122	2,527	7,374
Sullivan County	19,684	15,117	6,921	7,993	2,863	3,707	1,179	2,878	1,525	1,859	4,666	4,876	1,862	2,138
Sumner County	17,579	11,800	5,174	5,994	2,185	2,727	1,067	1,308	1,219	1,589	3,441	4,521	619	2,022
Washington County	13,610	9,895	4,463	4,363	2,353	2,575	1,183	1,009	365	1,225	2,628	2,233	1,023	777
Williamson County	19,230	11,553	2,704	3,909	1,431	2,428	212	544	351	520	1,329	1,883	384	599
Wilson County	14,078	8,420	3,460	3,765	1,293	2,197	393	274	780	846	2,250	2,631	423	946
Texas														
Angelina County	7,824	6,072	2,534	4,011	1,076	2,144	326	1,152	472	1,782	1,658	2,059	411	1,292
Bastrop County	8,145	4,163	1,984	2,219	1,279	1,204	522	145	590	351	1,164	1,299	753	760
Bell County	23,177	15,482	6,273	7,011	2,178	3,130	1,002	716	1,574	1,892	3,587	4,678	568	2,045
Bexar County	144,102	96,350	42,926	48,901	15,956	23,275	10,375	12,984	9,189	16,012	28,545	34,591	8,044	14,584
Bowie County	8,901	6,411	1,628	1,756	591	646	521	125	396	430	632	931	150	333
Brazoria County	27,924	15,732	5,208	6,781	2,190	3,072	671	1,204	897	2,146	3,279	4,965	744	2,308
Brazos County	12,805	8,191	3,629	3,456	1,492	1,199	373	403	864	820	1,539	2,169	667	757
Cameron County	32,361	25,645	9,802	12,533	4,118	5,223	2,265	4,222	2,366	5,691	5,834	8,765	2,601	6,047
Collin County	70,111	40,334	13,904	18,050	5,966	6,602	1,197	4,066	3,134	4,855	7,865	13,003	2,243	5,474
Comal County	16,771	9,671	2,949	4,780	1,358	2,026	447	976	687	1,658	1,412	2,913	279	1,211
Coryell County	4,391	2,908	1,752	1,813	589	934	241	417	75	1,004	1,236	1,420	113	501
Dallas County	173,179	110,003	41,600	50,590	13,017	20,169	10,033	11,881	8,012	15,086	26,503	35,479	9,139	16,253
Denton County	56,137	31,001	11,209	13,863	3,908	7,366	2,150	1,498	2,484	4,351	6,839	9,309	2,133	4,205
Ector County	9,074	6,097	2,855	3,900	1,289	1,684	706	1,293	525	761	1,553	2,589	161	1,009
Ellis County	13,642	9,118	4,690	5,407	2,015	1,991	797	950	568	1,520	2,679	3,748	916	1,212
El Paso County	58,474	44,580	20,683	24,645	5,625	10,024	4,472	5,469	5,087	9,605	15,160	19,827	5,213	9,843
Fort Bend County	57,913	29,367	11,144	12,677	4,214	4,970	2,413	2,872	2,976	4,851	5,928	9,178	2,204	4,474
Galveston County	31,210	17,525	10,197	8,224	3,818	3,904	1,613	1,110	1,404	2,513	6,101	5,439	1,542	2,140
Grayson County	14,025	9,581	3,888	3,871	1,374	1,967	692	439	1,373	975	2,500	2,799	881	952
Gregg County	10,948	8,026	2,498	3,971	705	1,504	209	744	757	1,059	1,707	2,865	336	696
Guadalupe County	13,907	8,185	3,434	4,137	1,689	1,695	1,293	1,146	741	1,220	1,994	2,459	1,237	1,425
Harris County	309,174	185,240	75,172	88,014	22,446	37,041	15,010	17,397	18,619	24,685	48,466	58,956	15,876	25,325
Harrison County	6,729	4,148	2,014	2,289	893	1,241	693	110	403	592	1,434	1,803	273	335
Hays County	15,966	8,878	3,904	3,542	1,522	2,308	622	761	415	1,440	1,915	2,133	856	853
Henderson County	10,249	7,870	2,943	4,210	1,451	2,341	357	1,487	581	1,078	1,796	2,215	271	845
Hidalgo County	53,503	42,512	18,569	26,968	6,422	12,722	4,801	7,732	4,335	9,261	9,875	18,622	5,526	10,775
Hunt County	8,756	6,028	3,306	2,890	1,419	1,506	529	339	374	882	2,156	1,869	516	559
Jefferson County	20,168	16,410	6,537	9,266	2,270	4,100	1,644	2,390	1,391	2,615	3,978	6,169	779	2,543
Johnson County	14,267	9,406	2,792	3,147	1,131	1,684	472	668	364	883	1,291	1,437	257	321
Kaufman County	9,169	5,856	2,937	1,797	1,348	1,048	355	264	538	351	1,771	997	365	408

Table H-2: Counties - Disability Status and Type of Disability—*Continued*

	Total Population		With a Disability		With a Hearing Disability		With a Vision Disability		With a Cognitive Disability		With an Ambulatory Disability		With a Self-Care Disability	
	65 to 74 Years	75 Years and Over	65 to 74 Years	75 Years and Over	65 to 74 Years	75 Years and Over	65 to 74 Years	75 Years and Over	65 to 74 Years	75 Years and Over	65 to 74 Years	75 Years and Over	65 to 74 Years	75 Years and Over
Texas—Cont.														
Liberty County	7,064	3,818	3,576	2,179	1,387	803	683	449	403	870	1,560	1,563	562	767
Lubbock County	21,476	16,123	5,816	8,687	2,536	4,140	897	1,958	758	1,429	3,602	5,317	400	2,106
McLennan County	21,315	15,267	6,452	8,591	2,096	4,169	608	1,780	1,269	2,499	4,050	6,130	1,073	2,534
Midland County	10,396	7,804	2,654	4,970	1,006	2,251	779	1,258	831	1,717	2,055	2,985	302	891
Montgomery County	49,292	29,122	11,838	15,498	5,427	6,132	1,990	3,151	2,082	5,186	6,460	10,681	2,157	2,713
Nacogdoches County	5,704	3,846	2,433	2,186	1,173	1,359	748	191	768	791	1,641	1,170	440	355
Nueces County	31,740	20,991	8,122	11,017	2,080	4,522	893	2,171	2,210	3,905	5,464	7,545	1,464	3,526
Orange County	7,618	5,715	2,598	3,214	812	1,675	180	131	666	828	2,007	2,685	414	614
Parker County	13,043	8,313	3,327	3,395	2,012	1,596	576	229	728	1,402	1,616	1,727	569	912
Potter County	7,825	5,813	2,304	2,357	766	1,017	307	592	535	384	1,572	984	451	216
Randall County	11,961	8,658	2,028	3,654	800	2,048	663	427	206	1,256	1,341	2,355	321	1,149
Rockwall County	7,624	4,658	2,133	1,635	457	757	122	100	314	663	1,639	740	226	383
San Patricio County	6,051	3,984	2,356	2,833	1,171	1,222	357	614	698	694	1,517	2,109	597	751
Smith County	21,696	15,892	4,849	7,294	1,601	3,790	550	1,222	1,483	2,026	3,436	4,552	628	1,312
Tarrant County	144,190	91,286	34,998	41,768	12,373	19,379	6,133	8,122	7,402	12,735	23,739	29,034	4,830	13,285
Taylor County	9,952	9,448	3,798	5,119	1,308	2,418	714	429	486	2,001	2,357	3,263	334	1,623
Tom Green County	10,993	6,894	2,633	3,011	1,434	1,499	777	879	390	633	958	1,691	98	865
Travis County	79,943	43,491	14,049	18,880	6,007	7,216	2,440	2,903	3,442	5,434	8,150	14,154	2,672	5,418
Victoria County	8,370	6,565	3,002	3,512	1,043	1,634	1,027	500	247	1,022	1,563	2,589	423	954
Walker County	5,886	3,340	1,213	1,395	491	485	0	192	0	287	811	966	0	217
Webb County	14,818	11,185	5,756	5,882	1,940	2,522	1,801	1,359	2,810	2,414	4,014	4,524	2,638	2,737
Wichita County	10,811	8,351	3,832	3,856	1,933	1,750	712	1,164	712	1,155	2,449	2,490	382	1,471
Williamson County	43,077	25,582	9,962	13,855	3,571	7,136	1,353	3,105	1,777	2,915	4,132	8,637	1,154	2,652
Wise County	6,176	3,894	1,876	2,539	560	1,691	95	496	479	950	1,223	1,749	215	591
Utah														
Cache County	6,693	4,838	1,082	1,975	537	998	139	245	59	732	531	1,110	133	379
Davis County	21,801	13,872	4,649	6,568	2,697	3,762	439	1,120	938	1,502	2,012	3,962	581	1,255
Salt Lake County	76,748	48,713	15,422	23,057	5,924	11,350	2,263	4,452	3,811	5,352	7,956	13,238	2,333	4,529
Tooele County	3,834	2,525	849	1,220	211	758	32	197	0	117	601	543	56	293
Utah County	28,779	19,287	7,141	9,388	2,864	4,598	1,538	1,419	1,609	1,919	3,832	5,031	1,359	2,003
Washington County	20,852	16,443	4,932	7,965	2,679	3,974	543	1,125	593	1,780	2,154	4,608	158	1,400
Weber County	18,226	11,336	3,728	4,875	1,267	2,475	819	1,103	659	1,256	1,933	3,136	755	1,202
Vermont														
Chittenden County	15,828	10,280	3,410	3,276	1,447	1,740	792	554	713	945	2,413	1,975	529	599
Virginia														
Albemarle County	11,638	9,326	1,839	3,727	478	1,832	264	378	533	1,158	1,212	2,342	595	1,562
Arlington County	14,875	9,962	2,771	4,071	809	1,535	376	832	490	1,271	1,900	2,730	305	1,658
Augusta County	9,242	6,857	2,221	2,702	593	1,570	177	400	828	1,067	1,494	1,800	373	521
Bedford County	9,920	6,771	1,913	3,608	857	1,845	300	623	533	1,258	999	2,561	664	1,813
Chesterfield County	33,410	18,616	5,479	9,437	1,602	5,007	1,031	2,210	1,201	2,265	3,265	5,699	721	2,137
Fairfax County	94,081	60,558	13,355	23,697	4,773	9,894	2,650	3,571	2,161	5,954	6,868	15,901	1,715	6,808
Fauquier County	6,857	5,076	866	2,889	433	1,430	0	233	74	720	474	1,644	71	420
Frederick County	8,804	6,357	1,364	3,636	688	1,645	205	1,142	320	1,563	593	2,611	272	1,799
Hanover County	10,985	7,902	2,783	3,609	1,036	2,366	219	507	366	528	1,638	2,223	374	702
Henrico County	30,230	21,333	6,845	10,187	1,930	4,455	917	2,418	890	2,854	4,440	7,346	1,586	2,949
James City County	10,940	8,585	1,444	2,391	711	1,283	33	211	282	487	999	1,128	360	234
Loudoun County	22,929	14,792	4,424	6,484	1,702	2,774	256	1,012	574	1,671	2,555	3,974	559	1,636
Montgomery County	7,235	4,908	1,271	1,975	392	814	11	374	113	461	1,001	1,347	39	620
Prince William County	29,185	17,329	5,477	8,405	1,979	4,088	521	2,502	1,073	2,675	3,537	5,494	1,111	3,459
Roanoke County	10,884	8,807	1,501	2,641	780	894	81	520	173	1,052	897	1,689	305	397
Rockingham County	8,363	6,846	1,857	2,860	820	1,660	209	757	645	767	869	1,650	222	813
Spotsylvania County	12,022	7,188	3,391	3,630	1,099	1,311	833	194	999	883	2,450	1,822	960	845
Stafford County	10,389	5,017	2,079	2,168	887	1,080	492	384	58	666	1,014	1,176	204	423
York County	7,097	4,439	2,008	1,960	1,002	1,157	0	233	343	409	1,147	1,079	354	514
Washington														
Benton County	18,189	11,893	5,744	6,028	2,315	3,453	656	999	1,233	1,553	2,953	3,582	337	872
Chelan County	8,315	6,103	2,988	2,636	1,784	1,389	1,010	521	626	952	1,158	1,824	0	760
Clallam County	12,898	9,263	3,827	4,464	1,811	2,248	649	279	430	1,371	1,947	3,063	581	1,073
Clark County	46,501	27,967	10,307	12,298	3,943	6,656	2,082	2,008	1,528	4,217	5,101	7,643	1,300	3,688
Cowlitz County	12,649	8,207	3,861	3,815	1,906	2,012	273	364	897	979	2,125	3,013	781	791
Franklin County	5,691	3,476	1,685	1,820	1,040	437	101	82	714	153	830	1,598	375	619
Grant County	8,744	5,337	2,440	3,174	1,037	795	252	378	321	1,163	1,382	2,551	343	1,512
Grays Harbor County	10,090	6,222	3,033	2,915	1,458	1,463	468	551	919	535	2,064	1,768	678	599
Island County	12,673	8,130	3,806	2,847	1,637	1,478	713	343	1,177	775	2,117	1,675	1,442	541
King County	177,427	117,464	36,196	53,663	13,430	23,964	4,101	10,251	7,829	16,830	22,184	33,769	5,712	16,846
Kitsap County	30,258	17,490	8,048	7,311	3,477	3,474	624	1,089	1,450	1,826	4,318	4,464	849	1,150
Lewis County	9,892	6,688	3,388	3,496	1,402	2,088	429	723	1,103	671	1,804	1,946	336	488
Mason County	9,345	5,517	2,224	2,730	1,090	1,329	288	651	392	1,144	1,310	2,293	763	1,236
Pierce County	75,617	47,640	20,718	22,741	7,738	10,274	3,304	3,167	3,835	6,219	12,295	14,687	3,752	6,160
Skagit County	15,776	10,840	3,724	4,849	1,268	2,449	478	502	780	1,503	1,749	3,273	468	1,009
Snohomish County	68,890	40,993	16,997	18,080	6,942	9,296	2,999	3,413	4,080	4,605	10,165	11,645	3,196	5,416
Spokane County	50,548	32,954	14,235	16,208	6,346	7,812	2,205	4,115	3,014	4,226	7,332	11,441	1,947	3,660
Thurston County	31,417	17,819	7,656	8,652	2,966	3,978	1,250	1,603	1,450	2,202	3,670	6,124	846	2,470
Whatcom County	24,191	15,156	5,453	7,145	2,980	4,279	1,378	1,181	1,579	1,427	3,214	3,804	896	1,938
Yakima County	20,408	13,921	5,616	6,149	2,650	3,237	696	1,015	792	1,569	3,547	4,404	596	2,502

Table H-2: Counties - Disability Status and Type of Disability—*Continued*

	Total Population		With a Disability		With a Hearing Disability		With a Vision Disability		With a Cognitive Disability		With an Ambulatory Disability		With a Self-Care Disability	
	65 to 74 Years	75 Years and Over	65 to 74 Years	75 Years and Over	65 to 74 Years	75 Years and Over	65 to 74 Years	75 Years and Over	65 to 74 Years	75 Years and Over	65 to 74 Years	75 Years and Over	65 to 74 Years	75 Years and Over
West Virginia														
Berkeley County	11,700	5,861	4,107	2,360	1,265	1,215	131	376	728	942	2,501	1,350	154	213
Cabell County	9,817	7,167	2,067	3,390	593	1,307	185	1,520	538	973	1,435	1,925	345	919
Harrison County	7,572	5,700	1,911	2,613	876	1,567	259	569	290	675	1,213	1,624	155	509
Kanawha County	22,025	15,634	5,772	7,405	1,834	3,686	442	1,249	1,020	1,924	3,380	3,697	1,249	1,676
Monongalia County	7,893	5,283	2,714	3,292	1,097	1,456	446	231	798	1,413	1,632	2,161	431	878
Raleigh County	9,377	6,115	3,862	3,813	1,750	2,027	1,374	1,535	1,711	741	2,830	2,997	317	985
Wood County	9,881	7,309	2,681	3,590	919	1,043	410	559	250	951	1,795	2,430	651	814
Wisconsin														
Brown County	23,038	16,334	4,368	5,980	1,317	2,887	747	880	984	1,160	2,104	3,840	593	1,234
Dane County	45,480	29,457	7,833	10,296	3,432	5,059	917	1,684	1,383	1,985	4,158	5,918	1,150	2,496
Dodge County	8,632	6,939	1,830	2,662	830	1,262	300	223	268	730	1,055	1,426	314	487
Eau Claire County	9,766	6,923	1,872	4,230	1,075	1,527	167	559	363	840	990	3,135	296	952
Fond du Lac County	10,855	8,157	2,075	4,033	642	1,626	70	855	201	1,120	1,240	2,095	279	1,011
Jefferson County	8,852	5,793	1,721	2,145	613	1,064	227	318	335	144	977	1,171	255	407
Kenosha County	14,134	9,535	3,068	4,026	1,215	1,452	492	603	287	804	1,483	2,448	578	1,041
La Crosse County	10,745	8,377	2,704	4,083	1,042	1,496	699	402	771	943	1,055	2,614	202	721
Manitowoc County	8,887	7,054	1,545	2,772	807	953	168	430	222	690	827	1,734	156	1,007
Marathon County	13,446	10,324	2,916	3,838	946	1,586	330	466	362	979	1,957	2,629	518	982
Milwaukee County	74,510	54,426	19,726	24,773	5,649	10,224	3,054	4,492	5,109	6,470	12,725	15,458	4,733	6,961
Outagamie County	15,817	11,759	2,990	5,602	1,381	2,777	839	1,279	128	1,223	959	3,403	262	862
Ozaukee County	10,123	7,566	1,789	2,342	716	1,224	29	293	171	292	674	881	132	335
Portage County	6,826	4,840	1,501	2,308	641	1,007	398	488	341	693	947	1,125	520	417
Racine County	18,925	13,476	4,034	5,393	1,269	2,237	684	1,049	1,032	1,384	2,356	2,926	888	1,158
Rock County	15,816	11,335	4,116	5,361	1,269	2,298	320	429	929	813	2,455	3,592	678	800
St. Croix County	7,732	4,760	1,764	1,305	1,084	936	150	320	193	345	667	796	93	98
Sheboygan County	11,966	8,730	2,136	3,138	614	1,831	294	357	595	656	1,276	1,400	205	417
Walworth County	10761	7385	1,845	2,843	778	1,803	108	641	242	684	1,055	1,497	593	479
Washington County	13929	10425	1,874	3,981	654	1,434	273	367	205	1,293	1,119	2,181	257	796
Waukesha County	42738	32341	8,073	13,845	3,165	6,689	1,083	1,885	963	3,259	4,891	9,077	905	4,231
Winnebago County	15798	12199	3,319	4,970	1,340	2,278	310	694	683	1,113	2,056	2,805	907	1,021
Wood County	8175	6765	1,776	3,150	863	1,436	367	386	267	855	978	2,130	786	682
Wyoming														
Laramie County	9752	6411	2,209	3,086	1,221	1,958	262	865	447	817	1,165	1,638	70	350
Natrona County	7181	4719	1,900	2,767	959	1,519	199	968	802	854	1,089	1,544	258	355

Table H-3: Cities - Disability Status and Type of Disability

	Total Population		With a Disability		With a Hearing Disability		With a Vision Disability		With a Cognitive Disability		With an Ambulatory Disability		With a Self-Care Disability	
	65 to 74 Years	75 Years and Over	65 to 74 Years	75 Years and Over	65 to 74 Years	75 Years and Over	65 to 74 Years	75 Years and Over	65 to 74 Years	75 Years and Over	65 to 74 Years	75 Years and Over	65 to 74 Years	75 Years and Over
Alabama														
Auburn city	3,666	1,586	907	982	153	475	na	na	0	212	724	662	335	111
Birmingham city	19,421	12,940	6,132	5,650	1,634	1,697	1,002	941	1,089	1,277	3,858	3,808	1,058	1,163
Dothan city	7,568	5,736	2,080	2,639	506	1,346	194	287	513	785	1,504	1,802	389	621
Hoover city	9,533	5,619	1,666	2,867	566	1,596	246	236	38	806	1,038	1,839	421	695
Huntsville city	18,537	14,797	4,159	6,936	1,439	3,178	658	1,254	637	1,488	2,436	4,050	651	1,395
Mobile city	18,913	14,240	4,017	6,063	857	2,319	586	861	1,282	1,980	2,723	4,096	1,091	1,982
Montgomery city	16,691	11,237	5,309	6,333	1,295	2,704	1,290	1,609	1,086	2,167	3,075	4,565	449	2,182
Tuscaloosa city	7,250	5,225	1,580	2,024	488	717	271	316	315	407	771	1,120	554	320
Alaska														
Anchorage municipality	21,792	11,017	5,140	5,202	2,409	2,373	967	1,253	934	2,078	2,850	3,623	1,218	1,358
Arizona														
Avondale city	5,198	2,464	1,906	1,410	895	583	195	319	593	321	1,285	1,105	245	400
Buckeye city	9,783	2,223	1,911	1,231	767	911	43	398	272	530	1,149	758	212	141
Chandler city	19,499	10,722	4,659	5,483	2,542	2,294	731	1,359	908	1,684	2,104	4,056	592	1,894
Flagstaff city	4,526	2,166	1,040	765	711	483	100	165	66	153	370	406	62	210
Glendale city	21,544	11,235	6,112	5,993	2,566	2,863	1,224	1,170	825	1,658	3,681	3,823	1,113	1,537
Goodyear city	10,745	4,094	2,606	1,387	1,620	644	505	199	321	359	1,192	866	324	197
Mesa city	48,196	35,386	10,822	15,781	4,856	8,325	2,105	3,509	2,031	3,945	5,886	9,567	1,338	3,547
Peoria city	17,915	13,182	4,325	6,491	2,081	3,665	1,031	577	697	1,478	2,131	4,514	673	1,911
Phoenix city	107,571	71,128	26,824	33,065	10,281	14,851	4,779	6,075	5,162	9,033	16,538	24,018	4,785	9,344
Scottsdale city	30,005	28,363	3,602	10,944	1,310	4,896	704	2,048	744	2,810	2,064	5,909	738	2,292
Surprise city	16,847	13,930	3,426	5,097	1,746	2,795	491	1,267	599	717	1,841	2,920	262	808
Tempe city	12,347	7,831	2,757	3,889	1,093	2,198	421	1,057	611	1,208	1,906	2,209	721	759
Tucson city	48,363	32,443	11,637	15,973	4,248	7,963	2,315	2,197	3,122	5,454	7,253	10,417	1,795	4,120
Yuma city	6,373	9,092	2,156	3,465	712	1,345	550	429	515	602	1,354	2,309	464	1,133
Arkansas														
Conway city	5,431	2,668	1,720	1,750	792	1,158	0	583	494	278	1,210	752	124	361
Fayetteville city	3,565	2,999	903	1,546	70	635	0	234	481	347	704	987	0	482
Fort Smith city	7,690	4,669	1,724	1,980	692	1,043	290	504	39	772	1,143	1,345	453	516
Jonesboro city	4,646	4,099	903	3,052	256	1,843	393	446	174	52	356	2,205	46	224
Little Rock city	16,786	11,164	3,442	5,100	849	1,539	367	592	1,221	1,102	2,109	3,128	848	1,275
North Little Rock city	7,151	3,990	2,558	1,498	559	512	193	306	491	624	2,169	1,179	868	455
Rogers city	3,667	2,910	1,025	1,151	295	283	164	164	164	51	775	1,000	337	200
Springdale city	3,914	4,514	1,559	2,113	359	1,141	302	644	182	345	1,204	1,433	287	554
California														
Alameda city	8,388	5,177	1,236	2,210	392	710	116	163	71	736	844	1,577	192	904
Alhambra city	7,807	7,083	1,758	3,681	514	1,548	176	668	455	1,047	802	2,586	505	1,479
Anaheim city	24,919	16,541	5,214	7,610	1,472	3,284	887	1,637	843	2,139	2,808	5,855	880	3,146
Antioch city	7,723	6,649	2,632	3,623	379	1,623	465	498	794	967	2,232	2,468	730	1,122
Bakersfield city	23,461	17,048	7,413	7,824	2,257	3,317	1,563	1,363	2,652	3,035	4,934	6,035	1,513	3,385
Baldwin Park city	5,038	2,924	1,540	1,426	615	486	494	172	557	460	817	1,100	352	498
Bellflower city	4,839	3,001	1,024	1,482	210	509	0	279	46	448	987	1,157	141	552
Berkeley city	10,973	5,689	1,961	2,205	414	1,017	398	386	301	751	1,165	927	284	585
Buena Park city	6,020	3,929	897	2,313	233	642	216	346	306	764	492	1,482	206	663
Burbank city	7,169	8,372	2,264	4,725	955	2,079	590	1,274	915	2,226	1,417	3,294	1,225	2,562
Camarillo city	6,775	7,572	1,308	3,539	780	2,406	153	444	105	1,085	338	1,781	170	1,080
Carlsbad city	11,218	11,111	1,288	4,630	340	2,630	192	986	343	1,501	669	3,038	210	1,022
Carson city	8,358	5,389	2,345	2,274	832	1,039	86	304	626	634	1,528	1,425	647	698
Chico city	7,415	5,201	1,237	2,486	498	1,310	334	806	409	643	598	1,418	338	645
Chino city	7,735	4,371	1,412	2,517	310	1,148	311	473	390	1,315	960	1,254	407	904
Chino Hills city	4,646	3,192	1,139	1,407	204	726	109	368	481	1,074	601	1,188	212	993
Chula Vista city	18,063	13,082	5,081	7,089	1,911	2,553	1,439	1,915	1,757	1,057	3,595	4,704	1,802	2,547
Citrus Heights city	8,513	5,990	2,407	3,752	894	1,948	228	533	295	1,822	1,494	2,590	439	1,604
Clovis city	10,022	5,469	2,427	3,163	516	1,837	366	1,183	875	582	1,147	2,428	305	719
Compton city	5,117	3,999	1,448	2,063	264	368	416	374	358	299	958	1,864	424	1,067
Concord city	12,177	8,076	3,489	3,819	977	1,634	431	821	503	1,647	2,383	2,787	142	1,297
Corona city	9,310	6,966	1,872	2,479	672	924	422	293	350	661	1,065	1,699	320	622
Costa Mesa city	7,409	5,688	1,421	2,907	422	1,148	113	1,011	379	1,364	763	2,024	466	1,100
Daly City city	9,413	8,729	1,808	4,871	275	1,819	317	1,127	537	1,669	1,086	3,248	214	1,976
Davis city	3,973	3,533	525	1,415	283	626	76	153	120	406	318	922	108	500
Downey city	10,404	5,290	2,257	2,772	463	1,582	119	810	537	1,405	1,433	2,177	813	1,534
El Cajon city	6,768	5,735	2,346	3,303	853	1,429	573	799	273	1,526	1,261	2,473	552	1,909
Elk Grove city	14,260	9,345	3,047	5,238	1,132	1,795	944	787	787	2,703	1,177	3,978	558	2,933
El Monte city	8,524	6,860	2,104	3,625	687	1,722	449	1,023	396	1,055	1,188	3,047	557	1,539
Escondido city	12,431	9,081	1,604	4,849	360	2,277	206	857	463	1,887	1,123	3,132	119	1,835
Fairfield city	8,755	6,472	2,046	3,102	606	1,276	79	687	580	852	1,601	1,913	868	892
Folsom city	5,746	3,784	1,900	1,586	686	781	91	477	549	265	1,217	1,002	286	175
Fontana city	11,304	5,547	2,736	3,094	964	1,538	539	730	551	1,294	2,277	2,062	640	1,139
Fremont city	16,547	13,887	2,857	6,558	836	2,332	378	1,480	433	1,586	1,654	4,887	776	1,959
Fresno city	35,295	25,343	11,604	14,125	3,630	7,140	3,468	3,087	3,327	4,906	6,906	10,598	2,367	5,039
Fullerton city	10,231	7,998	1,367	3,332	240	1,437	343	702	233	672	922	2,265	169	1,172
Garden Grove city	11,846	9,861	2,181	4,491	599	2,441	576	854	676	2,081	1,105	3,396	382	1,531
Glendale city	18,235	17,496	6,182	10,031	730	3,692	516	1,882	1,662	3,240	4,616	7,757	3,768	6,890
Hawthorne city	4,990	3,597	1,182	2,135	570	486	200	352	295	326	670	1,720	217	695
Hayward city	12,593	8,199	2,048	3,615	619	988	236	737	494	1,160	1,578	2,785	476	1,860

Table H-3: Cities - Disability Status and Type of Disability—*Continued*

	Total Population		With a Disability		With a Hearing Disability		With a Vision Disability		With a Cognitive Disability		With an Ambulatory Disability		With a Self-Care Disability	
	65 to 74 Years	75 Years and Over	65 to 74 Years	75 Years and Over	65 to 74 Years	75 Years and Over	65 to 74 Years	75 Years and Over	65 to 74 Years	75 Years and Over	65 to 74 Years	75 Years and Over	65 to 74 Years	75 Years and Over
California—Cont.														
Hemet city	12,877	8,557	3,965	4,522	810	2,028	903	1,199	831	1,148	2,903	3,278	676	1,220
Hesperia city	6,633	5,305	1,708	2,353	640	1,297	55	759	49	601	1,268	1,369	217	540
Huntington Beach city	19,533	13,588	3,018	6,472	1,064	2,856	328	846	411	2,686	1,559	3,761	639	1,907
Indio city	12,672	6,723	3,253	3,210	586	1,582	106	502	217	813	2,717	1,737	308	467
Inglewood city	7,734	4,623	1,923	2,264	161	504	433	612	457	520	1,374	1,652	469	563
Irvine city	17,668	12,014	2,436	5,827	521	2,363	826	1,119	379	1,185	972	3,892	545	2,867
Jurupa Valley city	8,133	4,697	2,328	2,739	447	1,568	238	444	1,071	978	1,515	2,107	541	956
Laguna Niguel city	6,762	4,505	738	2,010	47	1,402	117	414	8	719	494	969	368	583
Lake Elsinore city	4,031	3,557	938	1,870	194	657	208	345	259	594	807	1,493	150	1,180
Lake Forest city	9,086	3,842	1,337	1,438	228	723	349	302	311	579	805	1,083	188	454
Lakewood city	5,305	4,280	1,204	2,828	320	1,184	222	654	218	1,312	763	1,793	116	999
Lancaster city	9,265	6,672	2,277	3,007	889	826	243	1,111	661	913	1,343	2,123	752	500
Livermore city	7,206	5,105	1,100	2,193	519	912	445	636	145	265	699	1,491	45	667
Lodi City	5,616	4,496	1,050	2,052	164	1,202	202	111	184	146	768	1,193	419	457
Long Beach city	32,423	20,530	6,629	10,032	1,967	3,547	1,321	1,787	1,417	2,686	4,232	6,685	1,511	3,444
Los Angeles city	295,610	216,817	74,405	110,338	19,462	44,559	12,669	22,130	21,192	39,185	49,963	76,534	21,009	44,038
Lynwood city	3,238	2,548	1,082	1,079	217	334	181	323	289	208	616	849	152	849
Madera city	3,650	2,896	1,017	620	543	317	50	370	0	396	464	314	142	91
Manteca city	6,397	4,921	1,150	3,020	364	1,318	145	638	119	908	718	2,261	169	895
Menifee city	8,410	8,496	2,208	5,359	838	2,270	437	799	510	1,173	1,354	3,550	190	1,130
Merced city	5,586	4,326	2,254	2,870	784	1,424	335	457	714	1,044	1,441	1,512	823	945
Milpitas city	5,291	3,977	645	2,635	180	1,124	121	653	83	650	358	1,763	112	812
Mission Viejo city	10,684	8,688	1,923	3,641	943	1,043	158	479	441	1,338	839	2,658	276	1,305
Modesto city	15,764	11,292	4,962	5,425	2,151	2,707	1,161	1,540	1,314	1,829	3,931	4,166	1,366	2,204
Moreno Valley city	11,199	5,855	2,474	2,897	901	1,243	331	642	805	767	1,484	1,910	813	1,309
Mountain View city	4,959	4,115	721	2,051	211	679	0	242	0	755	470	1,038	40	367
Murrieta city	6,061	7,641	1,713	3,988	437	2,071	213	279	519	1,174	1,033	2,672	316	1,638
Napa city	8,791	5,814	2,187	2,222	1,258	866	215	492	93	587	1,033	1,519	347	726
Newport Beach city	11,333	8,908	1,141	2,763	531	1,356	239	329	285	192	256	1,419	124	556
Norwalk city	7,952	6,591	2,324	3,601	621	1,654	139	514	620	1,440	1,470	2,729	505	930
Oakland city	35,131	22,974	8,457	12,466	2,622	5,609	2,796	2,915	3,038	4,172	5,524	9,127	2,166	3,832
Oceanside city	17,504	12,561	5,471	5,672	2,698	2,351	816	492	817	1,382	3,960	3,428	1,121	971
Ontario city	10,283	6,292	3,161	3,182	526	1,221	736	895	229	858	2,281	2,323	541	973
Orange city	9,746	6,898	1,516	3,474	528	1,123	166	132	185	736	898	2,292	220	1,493
Oxnard city	11,205	9,126	3,006	5,410	768	2,156	608	1,445	431	1,655	2,298	4,115	847	2,314
Palmdale city	10,828	6,551	3,487	2,892	947	1,412	442	802	907	1,135	2,569	2,548	577	1,326
Palo Alto city	5,670	7,435	871	2,816	470	1,401	58	432	197	697	324	1,753	79	981
Pasadena city	11,945	11,801	2,413	6,100	647	1,802	101	698	396	2,157	1,879	4,511	720	2,860
Perris city	3,478	1,131	1,384	625	542	219	273	38	617	186	928	370	770	105
Pittsburg city	4,098	2,928	746	1,991	112	758	160	504	259	867	594	1,454	196	488
Pleasanton city	7,209	5,225	1,097	2,135	516	729	297	835	18	463	490	943	46	242
Pomona city	9,367	7,614	3,535	4,414	1,308	1,661	507	1,120	784	1,609	2,179	3,586	482	1,802
Rancho Cordova city	6,801	5,196	1,912	3,047	812	1,381	453	1,025	191	962	1,056	1,931	363	1,294
Rancho Cucamonga city	14,115	8,258	3,212	5,531	601	3,047	223	1,395	888	2,134	1,955	4,177	424	1,900
Redding city	9,404	7,320	3,605	3,700	1,095	1,726	930	530	1,196	642	2,053	2,313	963	1,131
Redlands city	6,939	4,821	1,553	2,056	783	667	354	151	340	594	673	1,353	435	603
Redondo Beach city	5,861	3,198	800	1,219	403	312	0	208	254	296	582	937	0	165
Redwood City city	7,989	4,474	1,332	2,202	513	713	128	943	114	513	808	1,674	153	1,013
Rialto city	7,951	4,841	1,683	2,633	435	980	320	398	201	935	1,218	1,967	393	661
Richmond city	9,774	5,286	2,305	2,637	227	1,559	568	597	838	1,270	1,464	1,776	362	883
Riverside city	20,166	14,429	4,645	7,169	1,655	3,830	707	1,380	1,292	2,453	3,028	4,912	1,384	2,908
Rocklin city	5,043	2,673	864	1,296	187	665	46	133	241	430	651	844	207	461
Roseville city	12,957	10,618	2,180	4,995	592	1,864	209	553	320	1,239	1,314	2,722	278	1,442
Sacramento city	40,252	27,358	12,048	13,601	3,279	4,455	2,107	1,438	2,823	4,937	7,364	9,885	2,567	4,907
Salinas city	8,955	5,467	1,526	2,554	637	1,302	226	468	86	1,072	720	1,874	322	1,286
San Bernardino city	12,616	6,916	4,602	4,806	1,319	1,961	1,136	1,554	1,186	2,030	3,349	3,513	678	1,345
San Buenaventura (Ventura) city	11,570	7,888	2,416	4,156	874	2,237	564	862	401	1,212	1,394	2,158	316	652
San Clemente city	6,473	5,271	1,564	2,604	724	1,058	147	450	186	1,078	587	1,962	116	787
San Diego city	112,781	76,268	22,886	37,114	6,909	15,797	4,347	6,599	6,599	13,357	13,290	25,036	4,941	12,208
San Francisco city	76,622	61,506	15,235	31,918	5,283	14,609	2,050	6,064	4,233	12,801	8,429	21,817	3,579	14,265
San Jose city	77,137	56,916	14,537	25,978	3,891	12,162	2,186	4,875	3,546	8,294	9,229	19,134	3,186	9,393
San Leandro city	7,102	6,310	1,296	2,884	309	860	201	165	201	1,075	877	2,065	280	1,479
San Marcos city	5,733	5,913	1,310	2,667	699	1,701	434	659	378	1,259	604	1,890	302	1,090
San Mateo city	8,455	9,340	1,653	4,227	566	1,884	72	877	453	1,394	920	3,207	225	1,594
San Ramon city	4,770	3,554	389	1,114	138	460	190	46	0	260	0	1,022	0	272
Santa Ana city	19,343	12,963	3,901	6,381	1,063	2,996	698	1,468	1,563	2,329	2,300	4,723	1,289	2,642
Santa Barbara city	10,012	6,628	1,371	2,945	212	1,062	176	670	378	631	700	1,789	87	831
Santa Clara city	9,914	6,505	1,945	2,580	718	1,065	165	352	644	480	1,429	1,777	354	451
Santa Clarita city	16,804	9,780	5,040	5,068	1,225	2,912	1,310	1,339	748	1,684	3,527	3,810	855	1,771
Santa Cruz city	5,878	2,550	1,093	1,013	643	469	na	na	114	282	492	781	199	301
Santa Maria city	5,236	4,342	1,352	2,368	445	1,058	144	475	116	738	959	1,810	85	645
Santa Monica city	8,748	6,947	806	2,999	459	1,475	0	326	69	749	251	2,202	137	1,004
Santa Rosa city	17,404	13,595	2,746	6,242	737	2,945	137	727	522	2,026	1,854	3,879	585	1,862
Simi Valley city	13,102	8,560	3,565	3,844	1,472	1,704	778	895	755	1,141	2,155	2,540	949	1,253
South Gate city	5,797	3,103	1,332	1,429	427	352	394	75	232	193	948	947	588	500
South San Francisco city	6,878	5,652	1,090	2,040	341	805	123	589	367	466	621	1,285	33	764
Stockton city	22,266	15,908	6,280	8,418	2,099	4,066	1,377	2,347	2,312	3,153	4,389	5,879	1,349	2,927

Table H-3: Cities - Disability Status and Type of Disability—*Continued*

	Total Population		With a Disability		With a Hearing Disability		With a Vision Disability		With a Cognitive Disability		With an Ambulatory Disability		With a Self-Care Disability	
	65 to 74 Years	75 Years and Over	65 to 74 Years	75 Years and Over	65 to 74 Years	75 Years and Over	65 to 74 Years	75 Years and Over	65 to 74 Years	75 Years and Over	65 to 74 Years	75 Years and Over	65 to 74 Years	75 Years and Over
California—Cont.														
Sunnyvale city	9,366	9,077	1,524	4,788	424	2,491	27	1,120	481	1,685	705	3,489	413	1,976
Temecula city	7,407	4,249	1,575	2,337	954	1,381	76	415	187	507	860	1,262	238	727
Thousand Oaks city	12,444	11,059	2,738	5,092	1,106	2,221	837	1,011	348	1,796	856	3,222	232	1,257
Torrance city	14,104	11,849	2,028	4,094	638	1,733	315	247	304	1,216	1,068	2,419	674	1,110
Tracy city	5,590	2,652	1,197	1,610	554	499	135	344	306	309	669	920	178	541
Turlock city	5,721	3,922	1,901	2,712	591	1,537	283	1,189	601	921	1,200	1,878	699	1,007
Tustin city	3,762	3,991	258	1,467	0	797	34	370	0	628	206	882	0	664
Union City city	6,850	4,841	992	2,142	140	887	188	221	83	993	552	1,661	286	1,095
Upland city	5,692	5,830	1,924	2,231	664	888	165	649	200	416	1,040	1,609	196	401
Vacaville city	8,898	5,933	2,443	2,768	1,056	1,264	148	328	441	954	1,501	2,069	423	1,413
Vallejo city	11,965	7,810	2,518	4,025	480	1,699	419	1,260	456	1,470	1,618	3,065	309	1,452
Victorville city	5,923	3,900	1,836	1,949	351	842	470	408	486	615	828	1,320	330	568
Visalia city	9,549	6,348	2,929	3,502	741	2,000	794	719	562	851	2,427	1,331	384	376
Vista city	5,680	4,264	1,022	1,756	414	731	200	593	163	538	568	1,188	117	277
Walnut Creek city	10,380	11,843	1,090	5,224	652	2,896	0	626	282	1,008	289	3,165	0	1,135
West Covina city	9,834	7,791	2,176	3,794	1,101	1,601	436	623	548	1,592	1,210	3,190	435	1,816
Westminster city	9,427	8,224	2,396	3,201	752	1,435	387	1,049	279	870	1,396	2,059	516	950
Whittier city	6,654	6,091	1,416	2,718	506	1,247	179	421	220	832	661	1,807	248	1,034
Yorba Linda city	9,171	4,979	1,369	1,546	472	666	115	150	256	279	606	993	322	188
Yuba City city	5,659	5,345	1,538	2,496	733	1,238	109	380	284	969	1,000	1,883	153	619
Colorado														
Arvada city	14,599	7,926	2,861	3,623	1,230	2,000	519	796	151	1,170	1,735	2,122	532	1,103
Aurora city	28,883	15,313	5,649	7,898	1,815	3,455	1,316	1,373	1,403	2,082	3,833	5,209	1,485	1,771
Boulder city	7,324	5,023	1,011	1,352	313	521	283	287	147	165	467	456	93	43
Broomfield city	5,724	3,894	1,185	1,194	746	878	223	207	53	53	811	435	53	106
Centennial city	10,686	5,280	1,094	1,891	507	1,125	251	492	251	676	625	809	0	468
Colorado Springs city	38,293	24,365	9,099	11,369	4,289	4,976	2,039	2,715	1,838	2,578	5,165	6,436	1,259	2,067
Denver city	51,845	32,151	10,797	14,711	4,006	6,030	1,597	2,897	1,773	2,815	5,280	8,787	1,347	3,398
Fort Collins city	11,759	6,252	2,623	2,733	951	1,461	353	657	562	893	1,153	1,419	211	334
Greeley city	6,714	4,894	1,515	2,717	685	1,694	117	217	147	681	903	1,699	138	643
Lakewood city	14,522	12,148	3,621	4,874	1,922	2,434	523	1,088	492	1,685	1,768	3,322	323	1,927
Longmont city	9,364	6,473	1,583	3,089	430	1,818	342	785	165	534	953	2,002	0	943
Loveland city	7,298	6,540	1,108	2,930	542	1,631	138	670	309	682	704	1,630	183	759
Pueblo city	11,766	9,213	3,576	4,934	1,079	3,004	420	1,504	618	1,056	2,386	2,822	520	897
Thornton city	8,255	4,567	1,783	2,257	915	1,281	270	679	529	762	881	1,016	214	241
Westminster city	9,597	5,751	2,162	3,348	733	2,067	132	406	580	878	844	2,239	97	525
Connecticut														
Bridgeport city	8,550	7,727	2,858	3,435	807	847	660	546	618	1,303	1,925	2,697	346	1,029
Danbury city	6,093	4,002	796	1,603	280	787	87	531	105	791	385	1,224	117	679
Hartford city	8,597	5,477	1,955	3,287	307	647	371	854	619	1,579	1,300	2,038	201	1,119
New Britain city	4,733	3,941	1,346	1,180	298	110	407	145	426	323	1,261	840	386	143
New Haven city	8,059	3,985	2,324	1,778	625	549	130	278	791	542	1,731	1,475	157	1,030
Norwalk city	9,410	6,564	1,590	2,740	211	986	526	702	411	788	880	1,943	226	526
Stamford city	11,741	9,383	1,670	4,392	433	2,931	485	639	420	1,027	936	2,734	447	1,104
Waterbury city	6,689	6,741	2,502	3,473	267	1,398	483	1,008	522	1,148	1,804	2,941	305	785
Delaware														
Wilmington city	5,001	3,345	1,322	1,814	162	251	279	770	504	568	737	1,032	266	171
District of Columbia														
Washington city	48,833	36,793	12,240	17,825	2,146	5,210	2,621	3,484	3,732	5,644	7,809	12,896	2,533	4,751
Florida														
Boca Raton city	15,627	14,138	2,254	5,516	624	3,116	533	606	236	882	1,205	2,887	445	804
Boynton Beach city	9,195	8,681	2,302	3,535	306	1,590	159	881	606	1,141	1,054	2,076	407	760
Cape Coral city	29,629	18,459	5,521	7,890	2,357	4,524	960	1,362	1,260	2,327	2,956	4,223	1,165	1,698
Clearwater city	13,828	12,637	2,518	4,671	575	2,217	335	1,314	120	1,840	1,906	3,480	752	1,521
Coral Springs city	11,828	4,602	2,044	2,547	161	1,001	403	329	638	909	1,715	2,051	705	1,085
Daytona Beach city	8,644	5,968	2,213	2,841	771	1,384	257	704	274	666	1,362	1,864	45	837
Deerfield Beach city	9,510	9,887	1,764	4,540	572	2,275	81	386	287	1,246	1,364	2,550	216	1,267
Delray Beach city	8,884	8,625	1,176	2,389	495	1,075	292	369	144	380	447	1,676	117	714
Deltona city	7,483	7,186	2,701	4,355	548	2,385	1,053	2,037	267	2,044	1,718	2,542	414	932
Fort Lauderdale city	19,916	13,383	4,661	5,610	515	3,049	1,137	1,621	858	2,038	3,643	4,347	678	2,479
Fort Myers city	11,283	8,637	1,514	4,010	571	1,347	351	744	132	615	790	3,366	192	1,513
Gainesville city	8,338	5,165	1,948	1,821	758	987	378	456	707	595	1,393	1,083	639	644
Hialeah city	22,306	23,252	6,465	12,093	1,277	3,145	1,736	4,075	3,000	5,684	3,981	9,059	1,310	5,280
Hollywood city	13,448	11,809	2,300	4,291	993	2,211	336	883	873	1,723	958	2,601	442	1,381
Homestead city	4,179	2,096	1,578	1,179	601	555	170	153	415	457	958	876	109	199
Jacksonville city	76,204	47,928	20,869	23,075	5,538	8,577	4,268	5,055	4,448	6,336	13,111	15,635	2,190	5,344
Kissimmee city	5,123	3,796	1,627	2,047	202	807	374	605	596	884	1,261	1,499	70	684
Lakeland city	11,319	10,259	2,668	4,143	648	1,654	575	445	957	596	2,091	2,822	695	1,129
Largo city	11,556	11,883	3,200	4,974	1,072	2,047	339	1,619	207	776	1,748	3,411	340	1,097
Lauderhill city	5,902	3,627	1,980	2,388	415	373	372	759	441	818	1,513	1,809	350	921
Melbourne city	9,231	6,953	2,035	2,995	631	1,356	429	492	72	659	1,058	1,789	233	790
Miami city	41,123	41,900	9,100	21,647	1,405	4,611	2,111	4,781	2,143	6,961	5,376	16,775	1,924	8,736
Miami Beach city	8,625	6,771	1,839	2,806	498	956	349	760	264	876	1,039	1,704	0	840
Miami Gardens city	9,340	7,116	1,707	3,103	253	969	300	950	1,068	665	976	2,035	469	1,734

Table H-3: Cities - Disability Status and Type of Disability—*Continued*

	Total Population		With a Disability		With a Hearing Disability		With a Vision Disability		With a Cognitive Disability		With an Ambulatory Disability		With a Self-Care Disability	
	65 to 74 Years	75 Years and Over	65 to 74 Years	75 Years and Over	65 to 74 Years	75 Years and Over	65 to 74 Years	75 Years and Over	65 to 74 Years	75 Years and Over	65 to 74 Years	75 Years and Over	65 to 74 Years	75 Years and Over
Florida—Cont.														
Miramar city	7,984	6,185	1,503	1,741	193	1,037	480	753	143	660	835	1,321	318	625
North Port city	11,192	9,627	1,871	4,592	344	2,046	267	286	85	781	1,302	2,873	118	1,424
Orlando city	18,221	12,933	4,529	4,794	1,390	2,019	1,060	603	1,161	1,864	2,524	3,544	476	2,079
Palm Bay city	14,839	11,491	4,411	5,043	1,773	1,749	268	1,131	1,110	1,567	2,490	4,282	519	1,812
Palm Coast city	14,114	12,424	3,569	5,440	1,848	3,284	520	1,436	625	1,739	1,794	3,354	496	1,313
Pembroke Pines city	18,322	14,062	4,349	6,543	1,353	2,104	413	1,996	1,203	1,480	2,354	4,022	1,288	1,681
Plantation city	9,077	6,288	2,223	3,011	1,704	1,144	108	403	135	1,166	758	2,216	93	932
Pompano Beach city	9,255	13,232	2,019	6,618	699	2,315	511	1,367	477	1,205	1,287	5,058	234	1,864
Port St. Lucie city	24,264	16,862	4,425	7,956	984	3,684	693	2,250	787	2,790	3,109	5,885	321	3,058
St. Petersburg city	26,365	20,629	6,284	9,268	1,621	4,003	855	1,923	1,122	2,579	3,896	4,522	627	1,717
Sunrise city	10,834	8,254	3,272	4,105	797	1,399	915	1,200	943	2,137	2,614	3,231	994	2,110
Tallahassee city	12,684	6,508	2,556	2,974	998	876	453	726	761	1,116	1,420	1,759	329	1,284
Tamarac city	9,076	8,339	1,820	3,971	369	2,227	432	319	100	1,230	1,200	2,410	185	1,360
Tampa city	27,417	21,878	7,198	12,421	1,588	4,989	2,010	2,690	2,079	3,890	5,228	9,393	1,117	4,308
Weston city	4,302	2,684	575	801	285	290	0	84	166	119	290	455	48	272
West Palm Beach city	10,236	11,681	2,368	5,307	531	2,186	398	616	435	2,059	1,321	3,899	186	2,071
Georgia														
Albany city	5,759	4,291	2,356	2,341	536	925	709	537	1,107	839	2,017	1,319	924	613
Alpharetta city	4,299	2,166	1,220	494	270	367	473	221	150	301	858	414	211	46
Athens-Clarke County unified govt (bal)	9,131	5,652	1,932	1,946	558	1,062	243	190	415	363	1,483	1,398	330	577
Atlanta city	31,361	23,942	9,104	11,863	1,633	3,650	1,605	2,195	1,817	3,178	6,534	8,088	1,353	3,530
Augusta-Richmond County consolidated govt (bal)	17,009	10,557	4,502	4,325	1,305	1,895	959	1,236	395	1,181	2,750	2,670	746	1,596
Columbus city	15,134	10,952	5,071	5,561	1,305	2,658	1,160	799	1,822	2,252	3,176	3,119	364	1,304
Johns Creek city	5,626	3,823	814	1,552	553	1,251	189	108	0	234	72	689	0	592
Macon-Bibb County	14,270	9,704	3,917	4,742	1,696	2,375	939	845	1,178	1,056	2,571	3,243	954	1,333
Roswell city	7,092	5,795	1,014	2,245	506	925	159	657	0	339	549	1,259	0	434
Sandy Springs city	7,854	7,446	824	3,176	346	1,038	114	369	145	738	268	1,719	43	1,193
Savannah city	11,937	8,565	3,195	4,923	1,098	2,377	425	1,920	750	1,346	2,482	3,102	352	968
South Fulton city	9,001	3,389	1,639	1,587	529	469	213	654	535	525	1,490	1,214	675	644
Warner Robins city	4,985	3,050	2,423	1,272	574	421	841	145	259	518	1,999	1,000	640	453
Hawaii														
Urban Honolulu CDP	39,123	31,292	6,264	13,789	2,648	6,456	793	2,424	2,067	4,889	3,066	8,800	760	3,070
Iowa														
Boise City city	20,674	14,499	4,343	7,563	2,062	3,586	814	2,265	1,094	2,500	2,155	4,531	858	2,262
Meridian city	6,168	4,172	1,477	2,115	624	804	108	60	78	264	986	1,034	0	713
Nampa city	8,324	6,466	2,793	2,707	1,595	1,154	684	253	405	1,259	921	1,458	471	645
Illinois														
Aurora city	10,954	7,529	1,836	3,451	352	1,487	397	373	503	1,425	1,263	2,448	227	1,220
Bloomington city	5,647	4,866	862	2,110	232	832	174	412	33	362	546	1,080	87	655
Champaign city	5,842	4,007	607	2,136	208	1,262	100	222	87	260	471	995	87	379
Chicago city	204,068	145,644	54,214	59,628	11,756	19,682	13,913	14,460	13,046	17,509	36,810	42,868	11,688	19,224
Decatur city	7,859	7,024	2,098	3,337	965	1,609	247	280	280	159	1,547	2,833	169	538
Elgin city	9,257	4,758	2,429	2,276	685	1,644	219	372	764	297	1,244	857	474	206
Evanston city	6,943	4,743	804	1,848	313	837	78	496	232	417	470	1,086	265	478
Joliet city	8,838	4,944	1,933	1,959	316	679	89	268	297	520	1,113	1,402	508	533
Naperville city	10,540	6,640	1,421	2,499	384	981	81	464	120	255	870	1,363	64	553
Peoria city	10,099	7,612	2,211	3,306	655	1,427	0	623	253	855	1,457	2,221	737	539
Rockford city	14,078	12,493	3,642	5,099	1,429	2,161	968	941	626	1,576	2,145	3,445	384	1,209
Springfield city	11,338	8,449	2,309	3,425	807	1,823	310	525	321	987	1,326	2,819	360	751
Waukegan city	4,930	2,734	1,221	1,210	417	366	82	336	379	115	716	664	389	197
Indiana														
Bloomington city	4,603	3,689	529	2,013	261	1,027	157	0	20	618	242	1,190	20	649
Carmel city	7,784	5,434	1,107	2,120	328	1,008	369	186	0	395	635	1,110	82	414
Evansville city	9,689	8,615	3,036	3,730	1,043	1,597	1,003	504	452	817	1,721	2,798	703	884
Fishers city	5,533	3,978	729	1,910	97	563	89	256	70	581	488	1,335	63	1,285
Fort Wayne city	22,033	14,403	6,237	6,502	1,974	2,322	880	1,018	2,032	1,400	4,513	4,322	1,504	1,321
Gary city	8,470	5,668	2,608	2,275	683	754	145	167	508	531	1,936	1,804	636	800
Hammond city	6,210	4,179	2,236	2,437	808	1,035	1,010	58	473	812	1,414	1,561	610	639
Indianapolis city (bal)	64,732	42,869	16,125	21,488	5,628	9,181	2,241	4,883	3,226	4,764	9,775	15,219	3,388	6,404
Lafayette city	5,727	4,235	2,025	1,613	956	647	712	424	344	505	1,036	1,265	179	317
Muncie city	5,244	4,907	1,194	1,820	240	718	90	456	203	397	820	1,393	301	316
Noblesville city	3,914	3,086	930	944	439	427	70	274	139	197	311	667	44	232
South Bend city	7,277	6,339	1,888	2,959	376	1,233	179	228	422	733	1,276	2,183	295	466
Iowa														
Ames city	3,759	2,830	871	1,023	317	610	240	46	174	263	475	682	259	152
Ankeny city	6,139	1,864	880	754	489	563	43	203	101	146	333	436	0	146
Cedar Rapids city	11,553	8,358	2,251	3,546	635	1,875	355	749	454	1,205	1,465	2,300	568	1,053
Davenport city	9,239	6,069	2,015	2,069	953	641	493	185	765	584	1,405	1,285	510	567
Des Moines city	14,196	11,240	3,313	5,301	990	2,516	402	1,123	526	757	2,254	2,772	163	917
Iowa City city	4,957	3,281	1,234	1,559	443	779	85	101	169	840	314	959	173	621
Sioux City city	6,732	4,891	1,108	2,496	330	1,114	86	556	329	939	546	1,230	257	898
Waterloo city	6,521	5,454	1,921	2,739	480	1,588	269	551	858	716	892	1,568	251	607
West Des Moines city	5,896	3,994	1,807	1,384	934	431	145	0	167	330	634	854	171	284

Table H-3: Cities - Disability Status and Type of Disability—*Continued*

	Total Population		With a Disability		With a Hearing Disability		With a Vision Disability		With a Cognitive Disability		With an Ambulatory Disability		With a Self-Care Disability	
	65 to 74 Years	75 Years and Over	65 to 74 Years	75 Years and Over	65 to 74 Years	75 Years and Over	65 to 74 Years	75 Years and Over	65 to 74 Years	75 Years and Over	65 to 74 Years	75 Years and Over	65 to 74 Years	75 Years and Over
Kansas														
Kansas City city	11,144	7,460	3,956	4,071	1,312	1,843	870	809	1,008	1,037	2,765	2,414	851	666
Lawrence city	6,650	5,227	754	2,327	158	1,385	0	420	199	555	360	1,112	61	533
Olathe city	8,884	5,123	2,162	1,996	831	969	126	182	726	483	1,387	1,493	402	419
Overland Park city	18,607	12,345	4,021	5,676	1,715	2,501	680	1,222	819	1,839	2,003	3,219	529	1,373
Shawnee city	5,301	3,085	890	818	275	559	0	34	29	250	552	284	213	155
Topeka city	14,018	10,139	3,737	4,766	1,713	2,553	372	796	577	988	2,586	2,699	337	1,242
Wichita city	33,983	23,116	9,371	10,688	3,419	5,058	1,134	2,001	2,471	3,137	5,574	7,403	1,692	3,351
Kentucky														
Bowling Green city	4,813	3,417	1,753	1,960	700	832	70	292	0	600	1,053	1,155	206	567
Lexington-Fayette urban county	25,515	17,444	6,162	7,870	1,503	3,133	1,109	1,618	979	1,927	4,065	5,118	800	1,712
Louisville/Jefferson County metro govt (bal)	56,160	39,225	15,832	18,824	4,524	7,496	2,145	3,623	3,555	6,141	10,865	13,031	3,037	4,689
Louisiana														
Baton Rouge city	19,570	14,405	5,616	7,535	1,233	3,133	1,859	2,745	941	1,780	2,734	4,546	587	1,862
Bossier City city	6,127	4,115	1,204	2,505	354	620	242	324	157	422	964	1,357	315	815
Kenner city	7,730	4,336	1,896	1,620	1,035	589	75	237	510	252	972	1,141	293	298
Lafayette city	11,200	6,612	2,757	2,959	789	833	301	300	528	608	1,883	2,054	478	1,065
Lake Charles city	6,321	5,093	2,553	3,295	892	1,446	476	1,293	988	821	1,702	1,882	835	679
New Orleans city	35,816	21,716	8,450	10,223	2,012	3,463	2,072	2,191	1,599	2,274	6,226	6,601	2,333	2,387
Shreveport city	18,727	13,456	4,319	5,723	1,620	2,067	743	1,038	737	1,705	2,860	4,271	950	2,098
Maine														
Portland city	4,447	4,115	985	1,858	268	1,042	39	433	351	215	786	1,128	94	205
Maryland														
Baltimore city	50,141	33,928	16,574	15,269	2,941	4,273	3,115	3,324	3,758	4,536	12,247	10,753	3,949	4,167
Frederick city	5,449	4,210	1,702	1,605	651	812	166	244	296	539	991	1,068	216	537
Gaithersburg city	5,191	3,768	1,278	1,345	202	642	346	52	0	653	1,076	823	396	558
Rockville city	6,111	5,368	977	2,297	388	641	57	222	54	597	702	1,665	70	1,068
Massachusetts														
Boston city	47,695	34,719	14,105	18,925	3,352	6,115	2,464	5,124	3,799	6,726	9,905	14,404	2,771	7,012
Brockton city	7,874	5,405	1,875	2,595	638	274	933	320	180	481	615	1,461	118	852
Cambridge city	7,693	4,526	1,299	1,982	405	885	146	248	292	287	646	1,041	180	343
Fall River city	8,213	6,791	2,922	4,375	1,185	1,967	191	951	631	1,030	2,127	3,380	128	2,173
Framingham city	7,591	5,110	737	1,920	143	884	181	120	208	186	509	1,028	47	204
Lawrence city	4,265	2,766	1,856	1,443	542	392	809	72	869	835	1,495	988	1,162	747
Lowell city	7,089	4,052	2,556	1,754	730	590	542	530	599	510	1,594	1,268	870	409
Lynn city	6,747	4,821	2,110	2,841	487	630	251	416	305	1,152	1,500	1,936	157	760
New Bedford city	6,977	5,848	1,694	2,444	573	1,172	210	390	701	1,114	1,154	1,849	564	1,233
Newton city	9,799	8,050	1,155	3,226	665	1,591	331	1,036	76	993	238	1,781	78	599
Quincy city	8,009	6,539	1,496	2,866	537	1,083	201	141	278	590	810	2,076	242	807
Somerville city	3,170	3,119	978	1,219	438	407	217	112	25	93	554	888	25	213
Springfield city	12,243	8,389	3,648	4,308	441	1,435	161	770	1,229	1,975	2,454	2,682	862	2,018
Worcester city	14,020	10,743	2,960	4,850	1,252	2,238	399	1,070	768	1,315	1,640	3,196	522	1,277
Michigan														
Ann Arbor city	7,425	5,685	1,272	1,772	377	979	112	325	197	450	864	1,347	194	624
Dearborn city	7,429	4,385	1,149	2,228	441	1,073	380	479	376	576	552	1,622	417	573
Detroit city	55,535	38,624	20,445	19,921	5,247	6,174	4,684	4,366	5,879	6,613	14,324	15,154	5,357	7,489
Farmington Hills city	8,845	8,018	2,659	3,304	823	1,170	527	540	253	1,265	1,770	2,388	721	1,449
Flint city	8,107	5,020	3,879	2,444	542	828	504	191	1,473	907	3,015	1,773	894	817
Grand Rapids city	14,988	9,854	3,072	4,912	1,361	1,976	837	569	720	1,159	1,287	3,231	360	1,251
Kalamazoo city	4,561	3,487	898	1,181	391	491	32	198	82	62	583	687	179	167
Lansing city	9,492	5,633	3,020	3,395	962	1,390	1,042	502	503	1,007	1,957	2,393	516	659
Livonia city	7,982	7,935	1,627	3,569	705	1,341	108	485	120	477	955	2,547	41	656
Rochester Hills city	7,249	5,401	1,266	2,573	663	1,529	243	352	329	741	693	1,794	217	862
Southfield city	9,890	6,901	2,096	3,728	819	1,473	387	750	539	1,564	1,352	3,145	428	1,680
Sterling Heights city	12,292	10,065	2,591	4,763	770	2,742	446	625	617	1,622	1,423	3,401	393	1,736
Troy city	8,634	5,240	1,713	1,885	511	854	261	447	462	560	844	1,178	288	425
Warren city	12,470	10,240	4,130	4,561	1,407	2,398	1,122	766	973	996	2,855	2,544	992	1,241
Westland city	7,876	5,820	2,309	2,673	867	1,120	759	422	347	570	1,257	1,949	496	907
Wyoming city	6,263	3,164	1,413	1,637	346	587	175	7	294	712	703	993	328	478
Minnesota														
Blaine city	5,310	2,270	1,198	1,232	714	602	243	188	70	268	535	823	217	336
Bloomington city	8,988	8,757	1,800	2,913	817	1,414	194	614	457	392	527	1,596	56	525
Brooklyn Park city	5,355	4,548	842	2,329	196	495	58	650	234	694	572	1,446	479	537
Duluth city	8,671	6,782	2,085	2,506	716	1,326	184	576	372	537	716	1,787	108	690
Eagan city	4,866	3,426	717	1,507	283	823	232	393	352	541	498	1,098	387	500
Lakeville city	4,098	2,364	705	1,016	435	421	184	444	85	388	200	483	88	277
Maple Grove city	7,925	3,212	847	793	330	290	0	73	0	73	517	340	339	282
Minneapolis city	29,178	16,852	8,348	6,629	2,274	2,713	1,789	976	2,155	1,465	5,006	4,495	2,063	1,490
Plymouth city	6,507	4,690	1,218	1,403	531	569	60	37	163	0	534	850	351	66
Rochester city	9,698	8,339	1,842	3,778	666	1,790	155	689	557	1,141	913	2,526	83	1,125
St. Cloud city	4,575	3,392	1,293	1,710	686	432	241	64	661	316	736	1,057	327	475
St. Paul city	20,685	12,574	4,483	6,040	1,276	2,297	248	634	1,884	1,822	2,649	4,013	1,241	2,279
Woodbury city	7,027	2,921	1,278	1,213	424	940	73	304	64	313	754	615	37	375

Table H-3: Cities - Disability Status and Type of Disability—*Continued*

	Total Population		With a Disability		With a Hearing Disability		With a Vision Disability		With a Cognitive Disability		With an Ambulatory Disability		With a Self-Care Disability	
	65 to 74 Years	75 Years and Over	65 to 74 Years	75 Years and Over	65 to 74 Years	75 Years and Over	65 to 74 Years	75 Years and Over	65 to 74 Years	75 Years and Over	65 to 74 Years	75 Years and Over	65 to 74 Years	75 Years and Over
Mississippi														
Gulfport city	4,941	3,770	1,429	1,449	250	741	181	440	151	630	1,198	1,057	322	473
Jackson city	13,590	8,336	3,327	4,329	342	1,407	361	1,043	707	1,369	2,967	3,301	940	1,697
Missouri														
Columbia city	7,641	5,798	1,990	2,102	1,021	1,524	239	586	130	676	765	1,492	94	601
Independence city	11,936	7,716	3,729	3,312	1,339	1,527	916	517	628	635	2,370	1,969	616	637
Kansas City city	36,683	28,311	8,765	11,598	2,708	5,366	1,051	2,281	1,659	3,111	5,828	8,360	1,185	3,134
Lee's Summit city	9,487	7,635	1,828	3,641	645	1,371	158	519	295	1,324	1,073	2,605	64	598
O'Fallon city	4,822	4,720	729	2,335	245	1,191	0	551	0	480	551	1,541	60	298
St. Charles city	6,748	5,096	1,725	2,082	595	458	170	511	307	790	1,188	1,759	244	523
St. Joseph city	7,696	5,257	1,938	2,264	486	1,205	423	556	145	597	1,397	1,752	641	777
St. Louis city	25,206	16,533	7,811	7,192	1,572	2,305	1,988	1,451	1,260	1,729	5,972	4,932	1,901	1,365
Springfield city	15,390	14,163	6,618	5,865	4,184	2,632	3,031	1,061	4,005	1,620	4,683	3,890	2,849	1,326
Montana														
Billings city	11,101	8,106	2,452	3,179	1,043	1,285	252	727	260	1,061	1,393	1,669	244	941
Missoula city	5,837	3,693	1,863	1,276	754	600	118	147	394	226	1,047	934	174	355
Nebraska														
Lincoln city	23,038	14,826	5,175	7,541	2,306	3,588	444	1,290	835	2,591	3,324	4,397	734	1,711
Omaha city	38,336	25,492	8,375	11,295	2,811	5,439	1,912	2,565	1,701	2,982	5,197	7,723	1,243	2,691
Nevada														
Henderson city	35,554	23,139	7,063	9,149	2,920	5,102	1,212	2,552	1,022	1,598	4,497	5,750	1,238	2,692
Las Vegas city	58,404	39,683	15,780	20,329	5,754	10,088	3,622	4,149	4,501	7,101	10,190	13,800	2,616	5,384
North Las Vegas city	17,765	8,412	4,052	3,985	975	1,460	805	1,072	367	1,083	2,704	2,644	671	981
Reno city	25,131	14,649	6,041	7,213	2,388	3,131	1,111	1,287	1,089	2,401	4,136	4,970	1,536	2,184
Sparks city	11,863	6,021	2,828	2,787	1,269	1,283	503	279	466	907	1,545	1,960	300	560
New Hampshire														
Manchester city	7,467	6,750	1,910	3,736	419	1,753	190	631	164	1,072	1,358	2,629	409	1,255
Nashua city	9,029	6,387	2,070	2,841	897	1,467	201	609	147	466	1,204	1,055	417	310
New Jersey														
Bayonne city	5,252	4,403	1,415	2,338	562	250	222	322	669	1,091	750	1,878	571	1,148
Camden city	4,561	2,690	2,171	1,710	747	536	455	494	1,072	760	1,907	1,061	988	268
Clifton city	7,677	6,068	2,707	3,534	595	1,983	527	1,012	761	2,425	1,883	2,979	565	1,770
East Orange city	4,474	3,981	1,026	1,070	68	354	106	113	223	272	902	933	259	189
Elizabeth city	7,995	4,731	754	1,674	98	424	172	335	239	709	484	1,161	99	886
Jersey City city	17,432	10,894	4,005	4,772	703	1,326	952	394	757	1,011	2,547	4,051	951	1,538
Newark city	16,964	11,040	5,342	4,758	1,629	1,703	1,348	1,584	1,027	1,532	3,898	3,523	1,758	1,602
Passaic city	4,394	2,475	980	1,067	321	635	449	419	429	625	737	863	173	439
Paterson city	9,555	6,433	2,554	3,134	390	625	546	1,295	576	985	2,139	2,719	1,350	1,821
Trenton city	5,266	4,324	1,502	1,483	455	214	196	258	187	276	1,117	1,092	317	414
Union City city	3,867	3,342	765	1,202	275	477	254	258	238	226	577	814	484	331
New Mexico														
Albuquerque city	52,961	35,450	12,486	18,613	5,141	9,068	1,641	3,743	2,458	6,601	6,518	12,450	1,169	5,591
Las Cruces city	10,696	7,022	3,150	3,528	1,135	1,972	358	1,355	405	589	2,308	2,015	437	974
Rio Rancho city	11,056	5,542	3,038	3,333	1,021	1,568	172	245	1,138	787	1,983	1,740	410	445
Santa Fe city	12,651	7,540	2,377	3,591	820	1,304	151	518	711	1,140	1,446	2,681	474	806
New York														
Albany city	7,267	6,100	1,953	2,732	297	1,223	643	119	392	693	1,093	1,449	232	329
Buffalo city	19,382	12,583	6,214	5,597	1,305	1,889	1,560	1,687	1,760	2,041	3,574	3,589	1,175	1,641
Mount Vernon city	4,344	5,110	1,234	3,496	49	858	387	867	243	1,048	999	2,382	87	1,474
New Rochelle city	5,025	7,305	555	2,299	172	536	145	256	35	652	348	1,813	0	1,042
New York city	699,936	545,544	158,443	247,484	30,047	74,442	32,850	52,231	34,606	80,540	113,059	188,413	34,377	95,083
Rochester city	14,622	8,801	4,092	3,514	886	1,382	346	785	1,338	762	2,426	2,538	500	1,008
Schenectady city	5,168	4,151	904	1,877	209	370	131	419	250	701	327	1,331	105	606
Syracuse city	9,200	7,083	2,120	2,837	633	941	399	463	908	1,250	1,472	1,862	518	817
Yonkers city	18,064	16,105	3,864	7,987	805	2,597	458	1,556	1,054	2,586	2,605	5,594	727	2,993
North Carolina														
Asheville city	10,443	7,647	1,894	3,357	625	1,514	289	782	813	463	739	2,234	349	481
Charlotte city	60,404	34,371	12,049	14,532	4,367	6,220	1,512	3,381	2,177	4,196	6,596	9,073	2,759	2,918
Concord city	7,605	5,415	1,656	2,152	621	562	265	450	544	832	1,081	1,495	301	727
Durham city	20,225	13,260	4,631	5,198	1,147	2,007	1,074	834	1,052	1,231	2,426	3,788	776	1,554
Fayetteville city	15,078	10,446	6,090	5,279	1,817	2,562	1,420	1,800	1,503	2,058	4,521	3,321	1,128	1,443
Gastonia city	6,865	4,749	2,220	1,936	795	1,233	710	443	734	421	1,505	780	650	299
Greensboro city	24,320	16,732	5,597	7,331	1,489	3,054	673	1,251	1,147	2,716	3,400	4,785	244	1,756
Greenville city	5,315	3,305	1,772	1,995	418	1,223	262	23	199	566	1,158	1,316	446	362
High Point city	9,531	7,115	2,305	2,718	841	1,072	280	240	218	558	1,469	2,096	514	1,065
Jacksonville city	2,470	1,698	917	1,005	374	319	155	257	105	140	580	351	188	0
Raleigh city	31,997	21,215	5,876	8,964	2,088	3,316	802	1,955	1,220	2,496	3,165	6,205	715	2,496
Wilmington city	12,319	8,665	1,967	4,657	662	3,042	391	1,096	574	1,398	1,159	2,420	505	984
Winston-Salem city	20,366	13,692	4,037	5,147	900	1,821	509	1,009	782	1,241	2,627	3,619	527	1,379
North Dakota														
Bismarck city	6,583	5,771	1,072	3,061	260	1,800	248	791	228	707	606	2,265	117	555
Fargo city	8,617	6,417	1,645	3,433	794	1,542	234	1,288	27	1,030	415	2,452	64	417

Table H-3: Cities - Disability Status and Type of Disability—*Continued*

	Total Population		With a Disability		With a Hearing Disability		With a Vision Disability		With a Cognitive Disability		With an Ambulatory Disability		With a Self-Care Disability	
	65 to 74 Years	75 Years and Over	65 to 74 Years	75 Years and Over	65 to 74 Years	75 Years and Over	65 to 74 Years	75 Years and Over	65 to 74 Years	75 Years and Over	65 to 74 Years	75 Years and Over	65 to 74 Years	75 Years and Over
Ohio														
Akron city	17,628	12,135	4,219	5,813	932	2,030	1,262	923	623	1,228	2,628	4,015	904	1,331
Canton city	6,667	4,177	1,741	2,128	165	790	360	451	425	749	1,424	1,495	286	678
Cincinnati city	21,783	15,966	5,650	7,155	1,484	2,841	1,034	1,380	1,233	2,787	3,969	5,256	1,099	2,030
Cleveland city	32,655	22,080	12,062	11,537	2,516	3,154	1,989	2,913	2,467	3,145	8,203	8,006	2,430	3,150
Columbus city	60,388	35,757	14,695	16,184	4,439	6,062	2,845	2,130	3,261	5,070	9,358	10,741	2,183	4,573
Dayton city	12,033	7,401	4,203	3,733	797	1,477	1,072	570	1,296	1,106	3,111	2,308	625	936
Lorain city	5,577	4,839	1,816	1,182	561	537	326	203	772	290	1,193	816	714	340
Parma city	7,267	6,666	1,702	2,535	751	1,061	218	712	310	614	764	1,781	69	648
Toledo city	22,712	15,902	7,116	8,167	2,294	3,500	814	1,219	1,875	2,755	4,400	5,479	1,413	2,201
Youngstown city	6,210	5,339	1,781	2,655	478	933	334	720	350	574	1,172	1,851	306	792
Oklahoma														
Broken Arrow city	10,084	6,415	2,561	2,551	738	1,346	499	293	463	397	1,772	1,429	392	403
Edmond city	8,678	5,768	2,996	3,018	930	1,841	1,089	542	534	1,084	1,792	2,218	556	1,168
Lawton city	6,844	4,736	3,333	2,153	1,264	881	605	622	925	489	2,402	1,221	426	464
Norman city	8,951	5,349	2,990	2,477	1,057	1,411	241	190	86	566	2,362	1,363	510	516
Oklahoma City city	48,502	34,532	13,785	18,945	5,641	8,731	2,508	3,795	3,171	5,428	8,627	13,470	2,470	4,119
Tulsa city	34,249	24,726	8,616	11,554	3,620	4,307	1,679	2,576	1,857	2,999	5,489	8,228	952	3,119
Oregon														
Beaverton city	6,566	4,197	1,153	1,960	244	645	81	245	237	842	608	1,055	234	514
Bend city	10,515	5,884	2,613	2,714	1,511	1,723	431	819	760	771	1,104	1,870	285	896
Eugene city	16,240	9,887	3,562	5,022	1,718	2,656	91	1,023	873	1,441	1,676	3,108	339	1,979
Gresham city	8,704	6,196	2,437	3,498	651	1,312	277	839	537	879	1,456	1,518	200	571
Hillsboro city	8,121	4,390	1,734	1,999	907	794	93	513	146	500	804	1,764	148	897
Medford city	7,663	7,134	1,923	3,358	451	1,673	122	285	340	1,030	1,362	1,930	297	1,004
Portland city	55,623	31,506	12,060	13,951	4,740	7,014	2,239	1,561	2,102	3,875	7,259	8,604	2,088	2,373
Salem city	15,494	10,109	3,738	4,230	1,357	2,565	630	325	1,196	963	2,467	2,764	797	1,148
Pennsylvania														
Allentown city	9,223	5,833	2,562	2,379	1,090	1,007	648	627	669	808	1,329	1,567	581	643
Bethlehem city	6,104	7,149	1,420	3,502	400	1,362	383	507	427	962	1,151	2,293	514	857
Erie city	8,896	6,655	3,004	2,999	972	1,429	685	350	959	830	1,868	2,218	593	750
Philadelphia city	123,995	91,760	40,594	45,650	7,396	14,618	8,202	8,851	12,653	12,577	31,403	34,620	10,108	13,278
Pittsburgh city	25,702	21,372	6,914	9,695	1,175	3,723	731	1,600	1,879	2,034	5,011	6,975	1,158	3,008
Reading city	5,447	3,719	2,342	1,974	223	784	320	393	874	496	1,680	1,049	222	196
Scranton city	7,360	5,436	2,154	2,379	959	1,407	306	395	581	304	1,482	1,710	216	677
Rhode Island														
Cranston city	7,192	5,043	825	2,218	250	1,118	198	628	359	907	600	1,445	277	720
Pawtucket city	5,862	4,223	1,479	2,397	793	753	306	494	114	333	963	1,707	162	458
Providence city	11,377	9,615	3,795	4,113	714	1,186	407	1,014	2,212	1,412	2,854	3,483	1,927	2,209
Warwick city	9,492	6,658	1,733	2,803	796	1,368	176	417	377	741	1,041	1,844	247	697
South Carolina														
Charleston city	12,633	7,669	2,638	2,565	477	1,261	69	202	1,162	1,204	1,581	1,562	801	858
Columbia city	8,281	4,764	1,770	2,320	480	765	488	291	220	274	1,151	1,365	358	230
Greenville city	6,015	3,807	811	1,867	29	756	331	326	119	485	535	1,239	59	343
North Charleston city	7,653	4,692	2,132	2,615	328	622	418	412	202	441	1,434	2,006	261	1,181
Rock Hill city	6,484	3,947	1,079	1,828	245	318	113	175	180	507	601	951	193	391
South Dakota														
Rapid City city	7,444	5,982	1,691	3,128	395	1,771	198	473	260	494	1,080	1,648	177	675
Sioux Falls city	13,250	8,305	2,606	3,228	967	1,193	444	674	549	927	1,255	2,050	311	709
Tennessee														
Chattanooga city	16,650	13,843	5,366	6,962	1,417	2,791	771	1,311	1,003	2,104	3,899	5,228	1,160	1,661
Clarksville city	7,119	5,640	2,362	2,407	1,269	1,084	428	760	574	687	1,213	1,615	465	429
Franklin city	5,112	4,675	729	1,384	456	535	92	372	136	262	229	787	185	228
Jackson city	5,208	4,527	1,352	1,495	325	534	491	290	261	561	568	1,201	176	135
Johnson City city	6,526	4,524	2,042	2,056	713	1,004	600	512	328	807	1,079	1,344	206	533
Knoxville city	13,717	10,462	4,163	5,319	1,540	1,842	755	1,101	1,258	1,543	2,624	3,750	633	1,424
Memphis city	51,352	33,584	13,084	16,779	3,534	5,502	3,270	4,266	2,832	6,315	9,269	12,101	1,805	5,920
Murfreesboro city	9,083	4,883	1,629	1,910	678	792	88	173	243	741	932	1,651	108	477
Nashville-Davidson metropolitan govt (bal)	48,388	31,525	12,768	14,895	4,509	6,527	2,341	3,587	2,629	4,580	8,362	10,443	2,127	4,611
Texas														
Abilene city	7,468	8,271	2,775	4,845	897	2,220	527	429	313	2,001	1,910	3,138	291	1,623
Allen city	7,364	3,221	1,595	1,518	659	533	0	310	166	598	943	1,212	138	554
Amarillo city	14,901	11,512	3,341	5,346	1,357	2,831	736	864	741	1,539	2,053	2,904	578	1,135
Arlington city	27,346	16,112	6,698	7,154	2,514	3,424	1,442	1,180	1,921	1,991	4,629	4,096	802	2,155
Austin city	57,622	32,640	10,476	15,299	3,414	5,247	1,640	3,082	2,496	3,600	5,705	11,403	2,390	4,306
Baytown city	6,567	3,366	1,390	2,034	608	644	299	721	313	1,268	827	1,657	91	584
Beaumont city	9,500	8,301	3,018	5,085	1,320	2,300	783	1,264	597	1,104	1,570	3,247	196	1,615
Brownsville city	11,963	9,383	3,763	5,151	1,851	2,612	866	2,060	1,103	2,878	2,434	3,831	1,680	2,826
Bryan city	5,129	3,371	1,631	1,390	609	542	315	263	404	476	897	714	602	403
Carrollton city	10,622	6,509	1,574	2,796	476	1,275	37	297	582	1,025	818	1,833	148	632
Cedar Park city	3,518	2,812	799	1,881	321	978	0	421	296	329	150	865	41	272
College Station city	5,291	3,735	1,274	1,573	490	581	58	82	415	224	311	1,043	0	239
Conroe city	6,219	5,035	2,161	3,159	939	1,568	374	816	140	665	1,129	2,041	0	372
Corpus Christi city	28,520	18,345	7,073	9,410	1,800	3,840	598	1,635	1,762	3,008	4,817	6,635	1,209	3,147
Dallas city	84,875	58,920	20,761	27,850	5,861	10,887	6,463	6,669	3,399	6,505	12,457	19,333	4,746	8,927

Table H-3: Cities - Disability Status and Type of Disability—*Continued*

	Total Population		With a Disability		With a Hearing Disability		With a Vision Disability		With a Cognitive Disability		With an Ambulatory Disability		With a Self-Care Disability	
	65 to 74 Years	75 Years and Over	65 to 74 Years	75 Years and Over	65 to 74 Years	75 Years and Over	65 to 74 Years	75 Years and Over	65 to 74 Years	75 Years and Over	65 to 74 Years	75 Years and Over	65 to 74 Years	75 Years and Over
Texas—Cont.														
Denton city	9,629	5,777	1,840	2,517	923	1,444	64	387	384	807	1,045	1,322	254	746
Edinburg city	4,846	4,041	1,805	2,698	467	1,655	187	831	708	663	1,272	1,899	600	1,023
El Paso city	48,899	39,449	16,657	21,157	4,568	8,364	3,137	4,097	4,066	8,087	12,429	17,325	4,080	8,168
Fort Worth city	53,975	33,575	13,706	15,541	4,738	6,740	2,791	3,232	2,548	4,958	9,928	11,875	1,775	5,169
Frisco city	10,218	6,090	1,243	2,391	439	1,021	103	480	278	482	800	1,890	179	394
Garland city	18,847	11,234	4,080	5,010	1,256	1,680	914	1,290	677	1,903	2,830	3,806	1,240	2,118
Georgetown city	11,979	9,187	1,885	3,718	598	1,823	302	346	321	840	754	2,364	0	334
Grand Prairie city	13,062	5,394	2,959	2,838	1,056	1,507	262	211	941	1,061	1,963	1,961	778	839
Harlingen city	5,387	5,343	1,877	2,532	342	999	411	633	519	966	1,459	1,241	506	819
Houston city	145,548	100,271	39,441	46,943	11,189	19,562	9,202	9,469	11,390	14,837	24,982	31,988	10,025	13,514
Irving city	9,102	6,367	2,095	2,061	722	1,073	619	439	500	600	1,558	1,292	155	761
Killeen city	6,281	3,318	1,890	1,641	379	726	157	115	793	614	861	1,037	274	903
Laredo city	13,885	10,861	5,331	5,775	1,893	2,522	1,606	1,359	2,715	2,369	3,735	4,417	2,446	2,692
League City city	8,229	3,646	2,271	1,988	524	1,159	0	273	302	942	1,660	1,193	128	774
Lewisville city	4,733	4,583	762	2,526	166	1,124	202	383	99	830	598	1,790	303	710
Longview city	6,711	5,784	1,338	2,715	399	1,001	42	612	374	435	640	1,937	244	449
Lubbock city	17,572	13,876	4,670	7,481	1,910	3,651	679	1,812	574	1,326	2,839	4,425	228	1,855
McAllen city	8,532	8,438	2,220	4,699	960	1,698	91	1,035	207	1,233	1,453	2,429	759	1,535
McKinney city	13,884	7,565	2,404	3,183	855	1,477	180	1,038	693	955	1,155	2,323	140	1,228
Mansfield city	4,013	2,514	1,099	1,029	691	622	93	354	122	362	412	808	86	418
Mesquite city	8,066	5,669	1,957	2,013	702	802	309	361	740	556	1,396	1,336	526	493
Midland city	7,911	6,349	2,225	3,763	619	1,998	426	902	637	1,246	1,668	2,049	302	561
Mission city	6,732	4,838	2,100	3,102	1,201	1,704	887	755	100	763	845	2,253	143	712
Missouri City city	6,325	4,062	1,370	1,092	479	393	248	483	87	646	785	789	82	479
New Braunfels city	8,369	4,099	1,529	2,503	611	1,287	407	659	173	539	732	1,384	166	784
North Richland Hills city	6,924	4,213	1,814	1,864	404	797	316	447	395	430	1,208	1,173	108	435
Odessa city	6,772	4,835	2,044	2,996	801	1,232	387	923	446	761	1,263	2,087	64	760
Pasadena city	9,296	4,859	2,834	2,403	905	966	544	559	416	381	1,915	1,685	523	441
Pearland city	11,912	4,992	1,808	1,834	725	1,047	83	147	373	530	1,065	1,192	132	310
Pharr city	5,413	3,021	2,234	1,976	600	731	453	181	677	675	910	1,439	508	949
Plano city	24,015	14,011	3,835	6,446	1,612	2,158	469	1,159	654	2,296	2,103	4,815	1,029	2,225
Richardson city	10,602	5,916	2,477	1,545	1,061	690	212	242	377	318	1,389	869	527	404
Round Rock city	8,606	3,708	2,573	2,123	745	1,343	205	284	707	668	1,159	1,618	275	615
Rowlett city	4,256	1,825	1,191	814	500	168	257	66	256	248	947	382	0	208
San Angelo city	9,256	5,935	2,028	2,463	1,051	1,334	760	738	297	389	731	1,409	56	621
San Antonio city	111,097	78,594	33,116	39,791	11,882	18,508	8,269	11,022	7,370	13,348	22,312	27,817	6,511	11,674
Sugar Land city	13,573	7,068	1,845	3,372	789	938	247	617	301	923	736	2,470	153	656
Temple city	6,837	6,370	1,808	3,051	731	1,238	284	315	326	631	1,004	2,037	165	598
Tyler city	8,208	6,845	1,618	2,570	400	1,178	28	404	500	839	1,356	1,965	537	860
Victoria city	6,567	4,585	2,456	2,475	820	843	911	398	212	786	1,269	1,952	396	789
Waco city	9,043	6,246	2,727	3,203	480	1,664	353	722	753	834	1,838	2,308	709	769
Wichita Falls city	7,601	6,262	2,594	2,950	1,221	1,433	564	998	614	1,010	1,632	1,915	230	1,148
Utah														
Layton city	4,865	2,863	1,261	1,323	633	605	0	147	445	632	636	1,041	284	434
Lehi city	3,467	1,721	755	686	421	350	0	43	40	181	279	243	na	na
Ogden city	5,739	3,561	1,616	1,874	516	810	278	583	339	256	990	1,270	431	289
Orem city	4,778	4,446	1,243	1,740	333	846	214	315	201	382	802	756	204	242
Provo city	3,749	3,396	997	1,808	563	1,027	255	301	189	232	622	1,119	230	413
St. George city	11,030	10,015	2,846	5,268	1,467	2,901	193	619	247	1,129	1,205	3,182	0	1,011
Salt Lake City city	12,587	8,364	3,568	4,166	1,350	1,924	575	619	765	1,268	1,867	2,664	848	1,110
Sandy city	9,928	5,586	1,762	2,759	891	962	140	754	266	339	681	1,452	56	594
South Jordan city	3,492	3,101	258	1,541	122	674	0	164	0	432	136	917	46	251
West Jordan city	6,812	2,266	1,237	1,091	532	566	269	173	591	188	594	428	165	131
West Valley City city	7,694	4,773	2,048	2,410	717	977	182	445	291	380	1,154	1,527	379	294
Virginia														
Alexandria city	11,544	8,051	1,310	3,318	362	1,308	168	980	184	967	702	2,001	250	845
Chesapeake city	19,636	12,409	3,933	5,833	962	2,365	735	653	475	1,263	2,498	4,084	631	1,195
Hampton city	12,090	8,605	4,049	4,337	1,029	2,315	648	677	1,504	1,669	2,659	3,068	884	984
Lynchburg city	5,911	5,995	1,317	2,654	220	1,338	38	745	490	843	932	1,105	373	462
Newport News city	13,718	9,699	3,470	4,920	1,086	1,929	766	1,250	333	935	2,117	2,493	620	1,240
Norfolk city	16,571	10,700	4,386	6,351	1,244	2,198	371	1,706	1,202	2,191	3,131	4,627	1,092	2,116
Portsmouth city	8,200	5,734	2,002	2,949	425	788	96	624	336	936	1,641	2,293	480	984
Richmond city	18,282	11,931	5,058	6,232	882	2,630	1,242	1,033	932	2,304	3,595	3,476	1,100	1,108
Roanoke city	10,452	6,453	2,855	2,211	639	837	1,126	545	416	502	1,532	1,398	539	724
Suffolk city	7,822	5,323	2,175	2,219	781	882	273	306	87	870	974	1,492	217	554
Virginia Beach city	37,443	26,408	8,618	12,240	3,004	5,325	1,003	2,384	2,387	3,705	5,481	8,478	1,823	3,627
Washington														
Auburn city	7,086	4,402	2,542	1,893	757	685	400	305	71	375	1,482	1,359	461	275
Bellevue city	11,046	10,268	1,565	4,379	388	1,500	343	648	280	1,724	1,070	2,960	147	1,895
Bellingham city	7,818	5,428	1,911	2,174	989	1,283	344	311	708	532	1,191	872	263	395
Everett city	7,942	6,006	3,062	3,044	1,050	1,915	866	580	843	1,158	1,755	2,194	507	1,258
Federal Way city	8,009	4,231	2,523	1,510	919	849	369	367	566	347	1,844	771	404	320
Kennewick city	6,727	4,628	2,621	2,198	749	946	484	334	635	752	1,428	1,339	223	188
Kent city	9,867	6,498	1,458	3,779	659	1,595	105	454	537	1,027	751	2,816	375	1,456
Kirkland city	5,935	3,509	381	1,284	128	488	0	216	176	282	152	785	45	403
Marysville city	6,039	3,005	1,704	1,045	693	501	580	76	457	169	1,340	589	408	214
Pasco city	4,115	2,813	1,110	1,770	719	392	101	82	216	148	432	1,593	54	614

Table H-3: Cities - Disability Status and Type of Disability—*Continued*

	Total Population		With a Disability		With a Hearing Disability		With a Vision Disability		With a Cognitive Disability		With an Ambulatory Disability		With a Self-Care Disability	
	65 to 74 Years	75 Years and Over	65 to 74 Years	75 Years and Over	65 to 74 Years	75 Years and Over	65 to 74 Years	75 Years and Over	65 to 74 Years	75 Years and Over	65 to 74 Years	75 Years and Over	65 to 74 Years	75 Years and Over
Washington—Cont.														
Redmond city	3,180	2,233	449	1,091	271	370	129	212	0	138	243	579	83	224
Renton city	7,014	5,693	2,037	3,983	437	2,213	130	535	495	1,345	1,691	2,673	500	1,144
Sammamish city	3,515	1,170	821	181	464	54	220	0	72	24	318	95	65	31
Seattle city	59,661	37,592	11,824	15,901	4,294	7,074	936	3,488	3,297	5,080	7,521	9,722	1,960	5,470
Spokane city	21,537	12,887	5,998	5,789	2,588	2,942	1,095	1,540	1,432	1,110	3,851	4,017	1,337	1,167
Spokane Valley city	8,808	6,238	3,364	3,778	1,585	1,429	423	1,092	924	1,166	1,377	2,888	188	677
Tacoma city	18,429	11,292	5,808	5,187	1,886	1,929	602	763	989	1,423	3,526	3,260	1,043	1,763
Vancouver city	18,902	11,369	5,255	4,906	1,648	2,126	834	974	961	1,999	2,814	3,370	600	1,838
Yakima city	8,233	7,748	2,759	2,722	933	1,544	468	502	434	728	2,028	1,915	351	1,099
Wisconsin														
Appleton city	6,297	4,864	1,554	3,086	499	1,319	579	898	39	351	452	1,572	173	393
Eau Claire city	5,830	4,571	1,186	2,947	625	1,000	47	386	269	588	630	2,268	164	751
Green Bay city	7,237	6,730	1,391	2,803	436	1,395	79	166	443	246	819	1,750	303	402
Kenosha city	7,640	5,012	1,390	2,022	542	875	257	95	227	341	595	1,302	111	542
Madison city	18,537	13,753	2,582	4,752	1,260	2,685	450	872	443	1,287	1,074	2,240	348	1,196
Milwaukee city	39,981	24,280	12,531	11,237	2,848	4,190	1,885	2,503	3,549	3,371	8,612	7,806	3,584	4,068
Oshkosh city	4,199	4,864	1,215	1,650	363	918	141	309	152	679	763	856	250	392
Racine city	5,020	4,174	1,465	1,856	283	645	194	386	364	741	1,046	869	429	386
Waukesha city	5,384	5,216	1,456	2,945	422	1,292	77	555	349	550	1,158	1,764	222	836

Table H-4: Metropolitan/Micropolitan Statistical Areas - Disability Status and Type of Disability

	Total Population		With a Disability		With a Hearing Disability		With a Vision Disability		With a Cognitive Disability		With an Ambulatory Disability		With a Self-Care Disability	
	65 to 74 Years	75 Years and Over	65 to 74 Years	75 Years and Over	65 to 74 Years	75 Years and Over	65 to 74 Years	75 Years and Over	65 to 74 Years	75 Years and Over	65 to 74 Years	75 Years and Over	65 to 74 Years	75 Years and Over
Aberdeen, WA Micro Area	10,090	6,222	3,033	2,915	1,458	1,463	468	551	919	535	2,064	1,768	678	599
Abilene, TX Metro Area	13,673	11,981	5,781	6,488	2,238	3,134	1,125	911	908	2,190	3,510	4,168	824	1,901
Adrian, MI Micro Area	10,879	7,213	2,434	3,403	1,013	1,654	399	880	290	870	1,541	2,284	255	855
Akron, OH Metro Area	73,035	51,617	15,415	21,548	4,755	8,402	3,371	4,130	3,458	4,132	9,868	14,375	2,668	4,654
Alamogordo, NM Micro Area	6,506	4,216	1,693	2,015	782	1,209	158	216	240	1,045	736	1,542	292	480
Albany, GA Metro Area	14,062	9,139	5,208	4,150	1,477	1,744	851	831	1,549	1,353	4,008	2,314	1,167	1,031
Albany, OR Metro Area	14,633	9,953	4,376	5,061	2,130	2,345	562	1,029	392	2,277	1,995	3,163	203	1,100
Albany-Schenectady-Troy, NY Metro Area	89,607	63,856	19,271	25,723	6,289	11,606	3,508	5,129	3,946	5,574	10,235	15,631	2,530	5,249
Albertville, AL Micro Area	9,344	7,143	3,201	3,023	1,252	1,071	417	427	470	752	2,127	2,148	573	1,006
Albuquerque, NM Metro Area	93,142	60,451	24,937	33,027	9,378	16,422	2,898	6,159	4,935	10,140	14,459	21,136	3,191	7,967
Alexandria, LA Metro Area	14,487	10,253	5,487	4,772	2,123	2,584	595	1,115	1,406	1,415	3,945	3,410	1,490	1,099
Allentown-Bethlehem-Easton, PA-NJ Metro Area	85,262	67,272	17,897	29,070	6,720	12,386	2,819	5,460	3,849	8,996	11,340	18,289	3,217	6,097
Altoona, PA Metro Area	14,160	11,333	3,372	4,214	1,452	2,166	505	886	544	960	2,104	2,478	546	936
Amarillo, TX Metro Area	21,040	15,577	4,549	6,811	1,668	3,681	1,027	1,019	741	1,857	3,108	3,999	807	1,446
Ames, IA Metro Area	6,531	5,031	1,661	1,648	672	767	268	181	211	533	899	979	342	276
Anchorage, AK Metro Area	30,571	15,289	8,147	7,773	3,667	3,944	2,245	2,084	1,529	2,945	4,361	5,232	1,783	2,126
Ann Arbor, MI Metro Area	31,650	20,125	6,745	8,409	2,574	4,356	577	1,135	1,079	2,328	4,146	5,247	1,434	2,075
Anniston-Oxford-Jacksonville, AL Metro Area	12,240	8,275	3,684	4,664	2,213	2,101	972	1,039	606	1,401	2,282	3,551	445	1,769
Appleton, WI Metro Area	20,258	14,719	3,667	6,939	1,704	3,757	880	1,343	190	1,607	1,330	3,921	355	1,202
Asheville, NC Metro Area	59,226	43,439	12,030	18,365	4,693	10,485	1,627	4,049	2,391	4,026	6,521	11,130	1,718	3,476
Ashtabula, OH Micro Area	10,840	7,729	3,329	3,658	1,619	1,458	701	938	801	668	1,786	2,244	585	834
Athens, OH Micro Area	5,271	3,366	1,360	1,868	715	846	106	422	463	610	696	1,073	307	575
Athens, TX Micro Area	10,249	7,870	2,943	4,210	1,451	2,341	357	1,487	581	1,078	1,796	2,215	271	845
Athens-Clarke County, GA Metro Area	16,781	11,597	4,493	4,536	1,954	2,466	480	485	1,090	893	2,807	2,796	778	1,237
Atlanta-Sandy Springs-Roswell, GA Metro Area	459,776	272,101	105,660	118,095	34,139	51,875	17,436	23,305	20,975	31,330	65,777	79,226	13,736	30,848
Atlantic City-Hammonton, NJ Metro Area	27,356	20,202	7,165	7,559	1,789	2,609	910	885	1,305	1,590	4,816	5,516	1,041	1,678
Auburn, NY Metro Area	8,238	6,084	2,487	2,607	924	1,116	681	1,062	416	1,057	1,107	1,460	239	1,044
Auburn-Opelika, AL Metro Area	13,335	6,552	4,343	4,572	1,408	1,669	641	654	1,319	1,405	2,332	3,421	1,155	1,755
Augusta-Richmond County, GA-SC Metro Area	59,147	36,698	15,348	17,127	5,496	8,057	2,259	3,862	2,327	4,295	8,382	10,519	2,110	5,098
Augusta-Waterville, ME Micro Area	14,627	10,243	3,302	4,800	1,284	3,520	112	688	972	1,058	1,804	2,808	257	1,405
Austin-Round Rock, TX Metro Area	150,969	84,153	31,487	39,710	13,220	18,387	5,592	7,387	6,785	10,620	16,432	27,119	6,194	10,246
Bakersfield, CA Metro Area	59,306	38,770	17,015	18,793	4,909	8,373	4,157	3,173	4,591	7,619	11,486	13,396	3,125	7,225
Baltimore-Columbia-Towson, MD Metro Area	254,461	180,503	57,973	75,109	17,865	33,059	9,243	13,354	11,335	20,980	36,414	47,991	9,081	20,114
Bangor, ME Metro Area	16,205	11,556	4,319	6,088	1,686	3,488	591	1,008	832	1,648	2,216	3,552	798	1,606
Barnstable Town, MA Metro Area	37,322	28,131	5,884	9,420	2,055	5,014	913	1,939	1,718	1,873	2,811	5,542	932	2,109
Baton Rouge, LA Metro Area	73,052	45,127	20,863	22,601	6,950	9,850	5,314	6,094	4,456	5,727	12,555	14,715	3,896	6,801
Battle Creek, MI Metro Area	13,532	10,515	3,293	5,168	1,183	2,266	387	679	418	1,494	2,060	3,407	642	1,908
Bay City, MI Metro Area	11,821	9,036	2,245	3,324	892	1,680	348	884	319	917	1,356	1,962	310	733
Beaumont-Port Arthur, TX Metro Area	34,974	27,203	10,693	15,175	3,267	6,608	1,936	2,905	2,314	3,865	6,952	11,074	1,298	3,749
Beaver Dam, WI Micro Area	8,632	6,939	1,830	2,662	830	1,262	300	223	268	730	1,055	1,426	314	487
Beckley, WV Metro Area	14,775	9,879	6,617	6,004	2,920	3,013	2,049	2,130	2,315	1,055	4,675	4,824	866	1,234
Bellingham, WA Metro Area	24,191	15,156	5,453	7,145	2,980	4,279	1,378	1,181	1,579	1,427	3,214	3,804	896	1,938
Bend-Redmond, OR Metro Area	24,256	14,492	5,064	5,928	2,764	3,406	1,266	1,756	1,422	1,651	1,928	3,486	390	1,392
Billings, MT Metro Area	17,574	12,613	3,924	5,420	1,731	2,262	369	1,270	513	1,713	2,421	2,946	345	1,227
Binghamton, NY Metro Area	25,063	21,564	5,686	9,914	2,664	4,355	469	1,942	736	2,643	2,840	5,857	830	2,040
Birmingham-Hoover, AL Metro Area	111,731	75,143	32,648	36,221	11,520	15,454	6,995	6,763	6,415	10,396	20,465	24,257	6,959	9,067
Bismarck, ND Metro Area	11,740	9,411	1,999	4,614	996	2,914	261	1,135	326	925	818	3,079	132	803
Blacksburg-Christiansburg-Radford, VA Metro Area	17,841	12,220	4,401	5,749	1,518	1,854	677	903	1,203	1,090	3,442	4,310	529	1,414
Bloomington, IL Metro Area	14,880	10,690	2,810	5,091	1,325	2,461	397	780	432	726	1,574	2,909	421	1,089
Bloomington, IN Metro Area	13,584	9,370	2,311	5,220	1,302	2,333	660	402	228	1,395	1,225	3,262	121	1,190
Bloomsburg-Berwick, PA Metro Area	9,286	7,270	1,828	3,517	558	1,331	455	366	367	873	1,067	2,412	458	1,353
Bluefield, WV-VA Micro Area	13,218	8,919	5,869	4,653	2,935	2,525	1,232	941	1,409	1,022	3,678	2,945	1,267	1,090
Boise City, ID Metro Area	66,023	42,395	16,401	19,661	8,422	9,957	2,673	4,217	2,968	6,236	7,254	11,280	2,017	5,280
Boston-Cambridge-Newton, MA-NH Metro Area	440,574	324,463	89,493	140,870	33,109	60,815	12,902	23,565	18,378	37,980	51,012	88,506	13,777	40,718
Boulder, CO Metro Area	28,746	17,287	4,597	6,845	1,993	3,817	702	1,385	515	1,080	2,167	3,699	169	1,295
Bowling Green, KY Metro Area	16,460	9,220	5,559	5,029	1,958	2,315	449	750	733	1,628	3,294	3,175	1,292	1,635
Bozeman, MT Micro Area	9,244	5,184	1,631	1,822	699	1,135	219	168	260	523	649	965	208	373
Brainerd, MN Micro Area	12,734	9,328	2,419	3,768	1,181	1,853	253	549	461	602	1,120	1,966	231	817
Branson, MO Micro Area	13,555	8,819	3,888	4,194	1,270	1,993	1,127	242	805	663	2,286	2,189	623	965
Bremerton-Silverdale, WA Metro Area	30,258	17,490	8,048	7,311	3,477	3,474	624	1,089	1,450	1,826	4,318	4,464	849	1,150
Bridgeport-Stamford-Norwalk, CT Metro Area	82,023	67,801	12,800	25,463	3,528	11,486	2,580	4,454	2,586	7,008	7,445	16,448	2,093	7,116
Brownsville-Harlingen, TX Metro Area	32,361	25,645	9,802	12,533	4,118	5,223	2,265	4,222	2,366	5,691	5,834	8,765	2,601	6,047
Brunswick, GA Metro Area	14,728	9,205	3,447	4,809	1,402	2,305	266	554	518	913	1,829	3,244	674	797
Buffalo-Cheektowaga-Niagara Falls, NY Metro Area	114,789	90,240	27,161	37,854	8,481	17,093	4,367	6,666	5,904	9,116	17,206	22,848	4,570	10,141
Burlington, NC Metro Area	16,087	12,294	5,604	5,598	1,833	2,667	863	814	1,037	1,374	3,010	3,166	746	1,027
Burlington-South Burlington, VT Metro Area	21,962	13,864	4,726	4,959	2,087	2,350	823	996	1,143	1,470	2,954	2,883	754	984
California-Lexington Park, MD Metro Area	8,696	6,310	2,325	2,947	631	1,846	349	920	591	475	1,963	1,674	497	677
Canton-Massillon, OH Metro Area	43,871	33,911	9,542	15,966	3,099	6,651	1,589	2,868	2,587	3,990	5,793	9,598	1,302	2,779
Cape Coral-Fort Myers, FL Metro Area	118,640	97,620	20,592	36,614	8,818	18,207	3,545	6,116	4,192	9,677	10,029	23,037	3,774	9,885
Cape Girardeau, MO-IL Metro Area	8,815	7,173	2,020	3,527	977	1,934	267	934	257	702	1,064	2,352	296	1,059
Carbondale-Marion, IL Metro Area	12,374	9,178	3,904	4,891	1,468	1,999	721	852	1,323	1,530	2,786	3,844	455	1,688
Carson City, NV Metro Area	6,234	4,964	1,589	2,397	748	1,369	464	579	356	526	602	1,132	160	715
Casper, WY Metro Area	7,181	4,719	1,900	2,767	959	1,519	199	968	802	854	1,089	1,544	258	355
Cedar Rapids, IA Metro Area	25,581	20,053	5,103	8,353	2,198	5,300	589	1,707	1,037	1,557	2,582	4,587	670	1,526
Centralia, WA Micro Area	9,892	6,688	3,388	3,496	1,402	2,088	429	723	1,103	671	1,804	1,946	336	488
Chambersburg-Waynesboro, PA Metro Area	16,513	13,430	4,399	5,621	1,800	2,929	904	795	1,090	2,057	2,106	3,354	288	1,225
Champaign-Urbana, IL Metro Area	18,744	13,353	3,768	6,252	1,463	2,832	259	680	380	1,016	2,270	3,892	381	1,301

Table H-4: Metropolitan/Micropolitan Statistical Areas - Disability Status and Type of Disability—*Continued*

	Total Population		With a Disability		With a Hearing Disability		With a Vision Disability		With a Cognitive Disability		With an Ambulatory Disability		With a Self-Care Disability	
	65 to 74 Years	75 Years and Over	65 to 74 Years	75 Years and Over	65 to 74 Years	75 Years and Over	65 to 74 Years	75 Years and Over	65 to 74 Years	75 Years and Over	65 to 74 Years	75 Years and Over	65 to 74 Years	75 Years and Over
Charleston, WV Metro Area	25,328	18,111	6,953	8,604	2,284	4,228	890	1,662	1,505	2,289	4,352	4,652	1,634	2,195
Charleston-North Charleston, SC Metro Area	75,134	44,212	19,284	19,771	5,338	9,210	2,811	3,639	4,005	6,477	12,057	12,880	3,859	5,581
Charlotte-Concord-Gastonia, NC-SC Metro Area	213,036	134,740	48,594	58,945	18,596	27,115	7,599	11,642	9,047	17,073	27,383	34,598	8,246	13,916
Charlottesville, VA Metro Area	24,491	18,279	4,995	8,087	1,416	4,199	529	1,276	859	2,055	3,276	5,265	1,265	2,546
Chattanooga, TN-GA Metro Area	57,757	42,471	16,118	20,982	6,645	10,415	2,584	3,425	4,337	6,847	10,222	15,082	3,043	5,595
Cheyenne, WY Metro Area	9,752	6,411	2,209	3,086	1,221	1,958	262	865	447	817	1,165	1,638	70	350
Chicago-Naperville-Elgin, IL-IN-WI Metro Area	806,005	577,400	170,089	238,470	49,200	95,226	31,791	44,757	34,950	60,620	106,447	159,525	33,417	69,711
Chico, CA Metro Area	25,269	17,551	6,431	7,928	2,506	3,333	1,258	1,586	1,571	2,818	2,665	5,361	1,160	2,517
Chillicothe, OH Micro Area	7,663	5,693	2,803	3,519	1,153	1,313	451	821	557	658	1,908	2,001	407	771
Cincinnati, OH-KY-IN Metro Area	196,561	134,874	46,764	57,250	17,479	25,924	8,973	11,189	9,743	16,608	28,432	36,721	9,436	15,854
Claremont-Lebanon, NH-VT Micro Area	28,397	18,698	6,665	7,524	2,977	4,266	1,158	1,132	1,529	1,051	2,875	4,117	751	1,524
Clarksburg, WV Micro Area	10,779	7,495	3,033	3,509	1,276	1,997	670	634	526	990	1,717	2,383	209	724
Clarksville, TN-KY Metro Area	16,791	13,152	5,883	6,170	3,121	3,845	767	1,707	1,104	1,404	3,353	3,266	881	1,292
Clearlake, CA Micro Area	9,780	5,076	3,185	2,461	1,080	1,345	651	386	856	346	2,013	1,571	1,582	1,146
Cleveland, TN Metro Area	12,340	9,360	4,575	4,007	1,705	1,808	709	844	1,552	1,095	3,505	2,611	822	1,325
Cleveland-Elyria, OH Metro Area	215,240	165,730	52,344	70,849	15,863	29,483	8,544	14,411	10,296	16,153	31,664	45,081	8,984	16,795
Coeur d'Alene, ID Metro Area	18,143	12,410	3,750	5,686	1,998	3,792	241	362	578	1,409	1,271	2,780	591	828
College Station-Bryan, TX Metro Area	17,084	11,061	4,773	4,544	1,802	1,729	502	403	976	1,172	2,447	2,879	744	983
Colorado Springs, CO Metro Area	61,205	36,428	15,306	16,056	6,317	7,060	2,847	3,537	3,051	4,069	9,162	9,391	1,971	3,400
Columbia, MO Metro Area	13,199	8,738	3,745	3,541	1,854	2,225	378	720	390	1,074	1,902	2,336	524	877
Columbia, SC Metro Area	76,422	47,029	23,571	22,534	8,168	8,635	5,708	5,244	4,765	5,504	15,019	14,820	4,802	6,399
Columbus, GA-AL Metro Area	25,917	17,447	8,808	9,186	3,043	3,993	1,590	1,626	2,430	3,787	4,808	5,774	826	2,226
Columbus, IN Metro Area	7,589	5,960	1,820	1,960	1,308	668	219	228	399	299	643	1,609	324	200
Columbus, OH Metro Area	167,980	110,982	39,165	51,447	14,456	22,463	6,198	7,999	7,524	12,875	22,961	33,038	6,558	13,202
Concord, NH Micro Area	17,002	11,421	3,181	4,656	1,067	2,530	317	549	630	1,196	1,732	2,591	724	1,070
Cookeville, TN Micro Area	11,143	8,390	4,016	5,106	1,686	2,542	542	729	1,717	2,178	2,212	3,840	809	1,347
Coos Bay, OR Micro Area	9,712	7,601	3,133	3,931	1,166	2,253	456	1,119	914	1,352	1,655	2,724	592	880
Corning, NY Micro Area	10,810	7,853	1,876	2,848	853	1,392	375	454	262	768	928	1,717	446	722
Corpus Christi, TX Metro Area	41,259	27,301	11,436	14,687	3,836	6,305	1,385	2,892	2,996	4,812	7,152	10,359	2,061	4,367
Corvallis, OR Metro Area	9,072	5,771	1,711	2,148	691	1,285	351	925	591	587	886	931	189	444
Crestview-Fort Walton Beach-Destin, FL Metro Area	29,891	18,731	9,498	8,695	3,471	3,601	1,812	1,217	2,375	2,495	5,519	5,992	1,043	2,189
Cullman, AL Micro Area	9,116	6,425	3,488	3,725	1,201	1,246	499	344	345	721	2,547	3,018	380	741
Cumberland, MD-WV Metro Area	11,359	8,889	2,809	4,133	981	2,046	270	1,129	479	1,257	1,590	2,735	335	1,239
Dallas-Fort Worth-Arlington, TX Metro Area	525,973	327,528	124,400	148,014	45,060	65,228	23,071	28,915	24,597	44,935	77,848	101,146	21,624	44,146
Dalton, GA Metro Area	12,344	7,922	3,505	4,356	1,439	823	708	1,047	701	884	2,243	3,417	829	1,392
Danville, IL Metro Area	8,280	6,876	2,296	2,924	898	1,332	307	522	310	488	1,335	2,015	175	620
Danville, VA Micro Area	12,907	9,495	4,110	3,804	1,735	1,863	971	920	998	1,257	1,831	2,261	427	1,104
Daphne-Fairhope-Foley, AL Metro Area	27,152	17,291	6,459	7,179	3,093	3,357	364	454	955	975	4,053	5,077	445	1,319
Davenport-Moline-Rock Island, IA-IL Metro Area	38,291	29,942	8,653	11,946	3,596	5,292	1,379	1,514	2,010	2,615	4,730	8,055	992	2,128
Dayton, OH Metro Area	82,430	62,809	21,015	28,648	5,803	11,524	3,406	4,931	4,183	6,525	12,656	19,673	3,386	6,861
Decatur, AL Metro Area	15,570	10,944	5,277	5,875	1,822	2,068	785	1,804	1,602	2,226	3,154	4,078	1,340	1,961
Decatur, IL Metro Area	11,681	9,486	2,544	4,257	1,068	2,395	381	532	443	196	1,864	3,164	228	623
Deltona-Daytona Beach-Ormond Beach, FL Metro Area	94,256	74,832	22,866	37,154	8,817	20,528	4,374	9,515	3,721	11,471	13,749	24,288	3,089	10,903
Denver-Aurora-Lakewood, CO Metro Area	236,968	140,741	48,688	63,127	20,590	31,315	7,121	11,451	8,215	14,801	26,074	36,663	5,772	13,767
Des Moines-West Des Moines, IA Metro Area	51,387	35,337	10,487	15,254	4,587	7,651	1,042	2,916	1,508	2,625	5,580	7,522	908	2,540
Detroit-Warren-Dearborn, MI Metro Area	416,416	293,536	107,687	137,299	37,372	60,254	19,260	24,264	22,664	39,390	68,375	92,980	20,817	39,655
Dothan, AL Metro Area	16,548	11,362	4,410	5,584	1,292	2,476	688	1,252	1,240	1,605	3,083	3,544	799	1,604
Dover, DE Metro Area	17,338	12,474	4,194	4,700	1,135	1,751	570	396	1,013	1,107	2,870	2,710	616	1,303
DuBois, PA Micro Area	8,954	7,313	2,170	3,439	1,076	1,420	273	827	246	849	1,211	2,035	513	811
Dubuque, IA Metro Area	9,518	7,923	2,049	3,305	618	1,588	180	553	126	309	1,234	1,662	248	236
Duluth, MN-WI Metro Area	30,500	22,204	7,066	8,333	2,810	4,135	969	1,771	1,078	2,239	2,807	5,098	805	1,588
Dunn, NC Micro Area	10,179	6,862	2,986	3,043	1,376	1,349	873	632	963	849	1,732	1,620	859	661
Durham-Chapel Hill, NC Metro Area	54,027	34,133	12,116	13,871	4,166	6,194	2,265	2,869	2,315	4,630	5,524	9,473	1,314	3,866
East Stroudsburg, PA Metro Area	16,994	11,134	4,548	4,704	1,691	2,352	419	549	1,135	1,210	2,656	2,922	1,259	1,558
Eau Claire, WI Metro Area	16,659	11,602	3,675	6,298	1,839	2,818	541	759	629	1,247	2,064	3,996	551	1,145
El Centro, CA Metro Area	13,359	10,153	4,465	6,795	1,174	1,496	1,017	1,314	969	2,081	3,268	5,235	1,177	2,436
Elizabeth City, NC Micro Area	8,079	4,946	2,106	2,967	549	899	334	604	335	1,390	1,197	1,746	365	594
Elizabethtown-Fort Knox, KY Metro Area	13,250	8,894	4,534	5,233	2,130	2,933	678	904	928	1,849	2,785	3,582	761	1,095
Elkhart-Goshen, IN Metro Area	16,764	12,966	3,626	6,146	1,486	2,797	810	1,549	847	1,504	2,028	3,809	400	1,150
Elmira, NY Metro Area	9,519	7,094	2,386	3,904	1,081	2,304	485	892	490	1,325	1,496	2,679	385	1,472
El Paso, TX Metro Area	58,700	44,788	20,837	24,833	5,748	10,132	4,547	5,575	5,087	9,711	15,244	19,968	5,257	9,843
Enid, OK Metro Area	5,432	4,407	2,137	2,718	809	1,161	179	678	446	551	1,513	2,091	580	672
Erie, PA Metro Area	28,015	20,911	7,613	8,980	2,753	4,767	1,225	1,278	1,484	2,616	4,735	5,545	1,176	2,331
Eugene, OR Metro Area	45,031	28,669	11,380	14,257	5,256	7,538	1,312	2,266	2,357	3,802	6,227	8,433	2,063	4,146
Eureka-Arcata-Fortuna, CA Micro Area	15,227	9,069	4,398	4,241	2,133	1,920	610	903	922	1,090	2,570	2,685	323	1,122
Evansville, IN-KY Metro Area	31,004	22,698	8,497	9,767	3,399	4,760	2,085	1,521	1,129	2,041	4,802	6,868	1,383	2,066
Fairbanks, AK Metro Area	7,346	2,867	2,414	1,443	1,747	860	312	638	525	701	596	1,102	0	701
Fargo, ND-MN Metro Area	17,000	13,080	2,657	6,010	1,391	3,058	463	1,543	112	1,324	769	4,166	100	563
Faribault-Northfield, MN Micro Area	5,870	4,427	952	1,634	424	897	92	246	183	93	525	878	82	119
Farmington, MO Micro Area	6,583	4,760	2,065	2,365	951	1,262	179	260	319	118	1,182	1,404	395	303
Farmington, NM Metro Area	11,230	7,871	3,929	4,305	2,043	2,531	268	804	726	1,032	2,198	2,171	269	628
Fayetteville, NC Metro Area	27,064	18,338	10,793	8,866	2,977	3,548	2,143	2,655	2,022	3,294	8,161	6,372	1,996	2,962
Fayetteville-Springdale-Rogers, AR-MO Metro Area	40,567	29,993	11,777	13,604	3,870	5,752	1,399	2,922	2,845	2,664	7,786	8,650	1,870	2,694
Findlay, OH Micro Area	7,220	5,609	1,602	2,597	845	1,661	282	554	154	819	786	1,204	195	906
Flagstaff, AZ Metro Area	11,161	6,652	2,908	2,959	1,581	1,239	435	816	340	1,007	1,307	2,206	77	1,006
Flint, MI Metro Area	41,137	30,023	11,069	14,104	3,187	6,642	1,550	1,492	3,268	3,756	7,690	8,870	2,815	3,858

Table H-4: Metropolitan/Micropolitan Statistical Areas - Disability Status and Type of Disability—*Continued*

	Total Population		With a Disability		With a Hearing Disability		With a Vision Disability		With a Cognitive Disability		With an Ambulatory Disability		With a Self-Care Disability	
	65 to 74 Years	75 Years and Over	65 to 74 Years	75 Years and Over	65 to 74 Years	75 Years and Over	65 to 74 Years	75 Years and Over	65 to 74 Years	75 Years and Over	65 to 74 Years	75 Years and Over	65 to 74 Years	75 Years and Over
Florence, SC Metro Area	22,095	13,943	3,981	6,635	1,262	2,550	716	1,598	1,293	1,196	2,279	4,160	301	1,469
Florence-Muscle Shoals, AL Metro Area	16,613	12,877	5,070	5,875	2,243	2,889	755	633	854	2,124	2,879	3,683	958	2,109
Fond du Lac, WI Metro Area	10,855	8,157	2,075	4,033	642	1,626	70	855	201	1,120	1,240	2,095	279	1,011
Forest City, NC Micro Area	8,191	5,867	3,093	2,959	1,110	1,430	212	829	558	1,068	1,442	1,746	599	843
Fort Collins, CO Metro Area	34,255	20,747	6,045	9,325	3,293	5,376	802	1,918	999	2,253	2,453	4,927	394	1,621
Fort Payne, AL Micro Area	7,377	4,884	2,012	3,198	1,044	1,414	193	470	243	1,057	1,152	2,148	300	705
Fort Smith, AR-OK Metro Area	28,309	19,523	9,587	10,392	4,199	5,156	1,894	2,467	1,199	3,090	6,324	6,814	1,779	3,114
Fort Wayne, IN Metro Area	39,322	26,519	9,552	11,568	3,536	4,596	1,267	2,117	2,656	2,630	6,220	7,299	1,895	2,204
Frankfort, KY Micro Area	7,529	5,112	2,970	3,120	1,106	1,581	587	584	772	776	2,126	2,129	799	797
Fresno, CA Metro Area	71,002	50,538	21,201	29,036	6,769	14,411	5,205	5,950	5,478	9,382	12,295	21,016	3,646	8,950
Gadsden, AL Metro Area	11,519	8,113	3,805	3,693	1,160	1,567	755	517	885	1,205	2,485	2,452	314	1,458
Gainesville, FL Metro Area	24,621	16,990	5,485	6,891	2,560	4,024	634	1,171	2,018	1,979	3,043	4,319	1,252	1,968
Gainesville, GA Metro Area	17,504	12,574	3,418	5,816	1,600	3,332	1,021	1,242	922	1,496	1,425	3,336	648	1,449
Gallup, NM Micro Area	4,993	4,288	1,828	2,820	959	1,543	352	971	428	862	1,084	1,630	370	714
Gettysburg, PA Metro Area	11,840	8,794	2,326	3,557	1,205	1,404	242	682	293	978	1,033	2,544	40	937
Glens Falls, NY Metro Area	15,278	10,801	3,140	4,972	1,117	1,962	297	763	512	1,372	1,686	3,262	181	1,762
Glenwood Springs, CO Micro Area	7,809	3,784	1,179	1,857	504	969	56	90	119	208	638	1,103	292	0
Goldsboro, NC Metro Area	12,178	8,329	2,903	4,479	879	1,836	284	443	843	1,268	2,084	2,647	397	1,481
Grand Forks, ND-MN Metro Area	8,361	6,520	1,645	2,327	659	988	162	409	199	251	1,018	1,672	246	562
Grand Island, NE Metro Area	7,935	6,289	1,841	2,761	896	1,322	132	453	383	617	937	1,303	254	395
Grand Junction, CO Metro Area	16,525	12,276	4,182	6,511	2,120	2,657	732	767	842	2,371	2,331	4,770	346	2,252
Grand Rapids-Wyoming, MI Metro Area	91,331	64,494	19,621	27,766	9,155	12,682	2,707	3,794	3,583	7,008	10,663	15,124	2,582	6,048
Grants Pass, OR Metro Area	13,302	9,561	3,664	3,690	1,662	2,323	618	910	774	826	2,146	2,166	938	733
Great Falls, MT Metro Area	8,401	6,604	1,983	2,849	708	1,444	161	553	782	1,435	1,151	1,639	163	746
Greeley, CO Metro Area	24,051	14,172	6,109	7,869	2,518	3,527	527	1,262	1,042	1,730	3,438	5,118	652	1,404
Green Bay, WI Metro Area	30,004	21,174	5,873	7,646	2,115	3,751	890	1,219	1,176	1,470	2,936	4,771	770	1,493
Greeneville, TN Micro Area	8,574	6,235	3,396	3,057	1,874	1,695	869	577	1,068	1,712	2,393	1,653	1,174	1,042
Greenfield Town, MA Micro Area	9,668	5,756	1,699	2,366	1,102	1,161	301	317	141	592	820	1,464	267	860
Greensboro-High Point, NC Metro Area	73,122	51,192	17,082	21,803	6,352	9,625	2,443	4,632	3,511	6,311	10,061	14,157	2,607	6,190
Greenville, NC Metro Area	14,375	9,165	4,377	5,780	1,717	2,941	678	386	543	2,017	2,388	3,771	650	1,181
Greenville-Anderson-Mauldin, SC Metro Area	89,514	60,718	25,388	28,667	8,363	12,791	3,509	4,654	5,754	8,957	16,262	18,669	3,131	7,860
Greenwood, SC Micro Area	9,643	7,944	2,522	3,937	484	2,156	688	602	392	1,161	1,548	2,496	689	1,296
Gulfport-Biloxi-Pascagoula, MS Metro Area	37,938	25,340	11,636	12,612	3,660	5,893	1,645	3,464	2,142	3,582	8,562	8,967	1,289	3,464
Hagerstown-Martinsburg, MD-WV Metro Area	26,312	17,315	8,195	7,982	2,669	3,758	565	1,570	1,686	2,426	5,306	4,877	790	1,277
Hammond, LA Metro Area	12,006	7,081	3,736	3,858	866	1,642	893	674	1,297	1,424	2,361	2,335	1,115	1,309
Hanford-Corcoran, CA Metro Area	8,751	6,662	2,981	3,285	1,135	1,932	331	412	637	340	1,785	2,101	634	320
Harrisburg-Carlisle, PA Metro Area	58,849	43,309	13,859	18,441	5,274	7,775	3,059	3,649	2,690	5,434	7,959	12,089	2,258	4,559
Harrisonburg, VA Metro Area	10,882	9,003	2,796	4,056	1,234	2,355	225	956	828	1,246	1,329	2,469	257	1,247
Hartford-West Hartford-East Hartford, CT Metro Area	117,174	92,223	21,542	38,976	6,340	17,057	3,707	7,097	5,225	12,057	12,842	24,419	2,796	11,520
Hattiesburg, MS Metro Area	12,434	8,427	5,289	5,272	1,194	2,077	1,753	1,110	691	2,217	3,210	4,052	1,380	1,302
Helena, MT Micro Area	9,753	5,731	1,964	2,324	1,293	1,654	250	535	291	559	920	1,061	83	407
Hermiston-Pendleton, OR Micro Area	7,531	5,531	3,234	2,770	1,772	1,463	680	743	391	594	1,731	1,545	375	646
Hickory-Lenoir-Morganton, NC Metro Area	40,831	28,670	11,801	14,470	4,590	6,533	1,878	3,777	2,790	3,580	6,219	9,391	1,896	3,429
Hilo, HI Micro Area	27,403	15,240	7,989	7,257	2,524	4,055	1,889	718	2,098	2,824	4,401	4,407	1,871	1,460
Hilton Head Island-Bluffton-Beaufort, SC Metro Area	33,821	22,486	5,875	8,222	2,385	3,390	974	374	1,208	1,260	2,829	6,445	424	2,094
Hinesville, GA Metro Area	4,182	2,508	1,819	1,306	1,078	705	181	197	470	608	1,045	780	64	404
Hobbs, NM Micro Area	4,770	3,086	1,469	1,804	289	859	136	146	322	864	1,352	1,084	140	793
Holland, MI Micro Area	12,024	7,784	2,123	2,812	888	1,575	215	728	124	693	1,113	1,507	98	850
Homosassa Springs, FL Metro Area	29,459	24,373	7,460	10,748	3,561	5,321	1,167	3,014	686	1,965	4,533	7,089	694	1,586
Hot Springs, AR Metro Area	12,687	10,304	3,422	5,830	1,339	2,823	824	714	1,356	1,553	2,266	4,245	879	1,722
Houma-Thibodaux, LA Metro Area	18,918	13,261	5,593	7,535	2,490	2,877	438	1,156	874	2,667	3,799	4,960	861	2,861
Houston-The Woodlands-Sugar Land, TX Metro Area	493,702	287,017	119,525	136,256	40,623	57,283	22,663	27,127	26,581	41,265	73,080	92,534	23,197	38,154
Huntington-Ashland, WV-KY-OH Metro Area	40,105	27,703	10,796	14,540	4,388	7,064	1,411	3,664	2,382	4,509	6,353	9,954	1,719	3,761
Huntsville, AL Metro Area	41,384	29,376	10,359	14,119	3,990	6,604	1,511	2,613	1,725	3,766	5,653	8,956	1,580	3,170
Huntsville, TX Metro Area	8,074	5,246	1,891	2,509	701	1,357	127	665	62	806	1,250	1,715	178	580
Hutchinson, KS Micro Area	6,484	5,948	1,936	2,615	1,198	1,218	184	591	216	420	1,091	1,674	168	464
Idaho Falls, ID Metro Area	11,280	7,752	2,266	3,986	926	2,649	340	806	582	877	1,280	2,609	620	1,476
Indiana, PA Micro Area	9,219	7,404	2,219	3,622	832	2,134	557	1,111	514	1,140	999	2,457	225	1,082
Indianapolis-Carmel-Anderson, IN Metro Area	167,546	113,532	38,649	52,569	14,815	22,813	6,428	10,372	6,848	12,928	23,019	35,033	5,301	14,488
Iowa City, IA Metro Area	12,889	8,937	2,029	3,323	818	1,777	247	558	237	1,357	736	2,217	220	1,012
Ithaca, NY Metro Area	8,586	5,623	1,994	2,414	777	1,516	301	150	295	475	1,034	1,080	246	265
Jackson, MI Metro Area	16,937	11,610	4,591	5,123	1,187	2,671	307	1,641	1,185	1,649	3,251	2,423	677	1,012
Jackson, MS Metro Area	51,126	32,955	12,090	15,758	3,195	5,380	1,914	4,137	2,471	5,015	8,405	11,764	2,154	6,635
Jackson, TN Metro Area	13,346	8,962	3,083	3,241	914	1,370	922	880	657	968	1,638	2,419	632	520
Jacksonville, FL Metro Area	149,860	92,933	36,451	42,715	10,507	17,491	7,417	7,512	7,133	10,247	21,993	28,936	4,570	8,789
Jacksonville, NC Metro Area	10,427	7,609	3,828	4,320	2,007	2,300	233	1,144	866	1,050	2,422	2,471	365	553
Jamestown-Dunkirk-Fredonia, NY Micro Area	14,268	11,319	3,427	4,967	1,085	2,460	493	1,038	444	1,434	2,190	3,175	680	1,486
Janesville-Beloit, WI Metro Area	15,816	11,335	4,116	5,361	1,269	2,298	320	429	929	813	2,455	3,592	678	800
Jefferson, GA Micro Area	5,979	4,265	1,310	2,191	544	984	64	432	241	1,448	652	1,779	223	472
Jefferson City, MO Metro Area	14,767	10,102	3,034	3,572	1,335	1,813	480	361	456	1,334	1,465	2,531	381	971
Johnson City, TN Metro Area	22,906	16,885	7,881	7,937	3,668	4,366	1,966	1,902	1,010	2,138	4,385	5,062	1,458	1,521
Johnstown, PA Metro Area	16,239	13,425	4,548	6,274	1,758	2,820	595	1,507	791	1,598	2,638	4,005	726	2,102
Jonesboro, AR Metro Area	11,613	8,186	3,419	5,700	1,357	2,989	1,017	1,237	872	437	1,901	4,289	713	1,079
Joplin, MO Metro Area	16,693	12,398	5,423	5,951	1,923	2,567	704	986	1,101	1,038	3,630	3,663	1,166	1,030
Kahului-Wailuku-Lahaina, HI Metro Area	18,673	11,830	3,350	4,802	1,582	2,312	494	572	590	1,671	1,733	2,894	820	889
Kalamazoo-Portage, MI Metro Area	32,171	21,746	7,759	8,343	3,082	3,433	1,686	1,231	1,383	1,679	4,699	5,271	1,642	2,050
Kalispell, MT Micro Area	12,612	7,346	2,492	3,143	1,374	1,903	380	330	238	581	1,279	1,560	417	652

Table H-4: Metropolitan/Micropolitan Statistical Areas - Disability Status and Type of Disability—Continued

	Total Population		With a Disability		With a Hearing Disability		With a Vision Disability		With a Cognitive Disability		With an Ambulatory Disability		With a Self-Care Disability	
	65 to 74 Years	75 Years and Over	65 to 74 Years	75 Years and Over	65 to 74 Years	75 Years and Over	65 to 74 Years	75 Years and Over	65 to 74 Years	75 Years and Over	65 to 74 Years	75 Years and Over	65 to 74 Years	75 Years and Over
Kankakee, IL Metro Area	10,320	8,024	3,322	3,548	992	1,200	723	600	723	915	1,936	2,228	1,013	1,126
Kansas City, MO-KS Metro Area	188,749	129,549	48,499	57,115	17,679	28,226	7,008	10,530	9,550	14,454	28,915	35,320	7,083	12,905
Kapaa, HI Micro Area	8,886	5,823	1,312	3,034	449	1,300	378	344	215	697	848	1,546	331	516
Keene, NH Micro Area	8,994	6,101	2,139	2,389	686	1,186	418	204	609	333	1,237	1,403	439	423
Kennewick-Richland, WA Metro Area	23,880	15,369	7,429	7,848	3,355	3,890	757	1,081	1,947	1,706	3,783	5,180	712	1,491
Key West, FL Micro Area	10,862	6,110	1,164	2,214	421	1,136	240	561	154	273	530	1,524	88	699
Killeen-Temple, TX Metro Area	30,913	19,789	9,075	9,704	3,323	4,644	1,610	1,521	1,936	3,133	5,465	6,818	788	2,780
Kingsport-Bristol-Bristol, TN-VA Metro Area	38,812	29,264	14,447	16,348	5,627	6,852	2,753	4,394	3,665	4,193	9,653	10,432	3,223	4,255
Kingston, NY Metro Area	20,406	14,719	4,244	6,763	2,116	2,882	1,077	707	822	1,955	2,443	3,713	621	1,967
Klamath Falls, OR Micro Area	8,974	5,636	2,731	2,526	1,416	1,442	527	284	700	441	1,347	1,682	696	821
Knoxville, TN Metro Area	95,722	66,229	23,787	29,942	10,112	13,313	3,550	5,594	5,441	7,799	12,774	19,131	3,643	7,432
Kokomo, IN Metro Area	9,014	6,903	2,579	2,832	1,113	1,420	320	828	313	909	1,589	1,946	400	520
La Crosse-Onalaska, WI-MN Metro Area	13,011	10,129	3,233	4,960	1,230	1,987	747	599	937	1,174	1,299	3,049	319	751
Lafayette, LA Metro Area	41,776	28,184	11,405	14,152	2,821	5,107	2,275	2,994	1,556	3,905	7,944	9,616	2,498	4,565
Lafayette-West Lafayette, IN Metro Area	16,448	11,067	5,233	4,911	2,693	2,352	1,158	738	1,031	1,301	2,488	2,745	604	917
LaGrange, GA Micro Area	6,009	4,056	1,729	1,853	572	878	331	595	348	590	978	986	326	580
Lake Charles, LA Metro Area	18,980	12,257	5,492	7,171	2,274	3,660	1,095	2,213	1,539	2,117	3,412	4,471	1,566	1,703
Lake City, FL Micro Area	7,433	5,545	2,399	2,955	914	1,110	375	732	685	1,125	1,186	1,869	123	651
Lake Havasu City-Kingman, AZ Metro Area	37,132	26,662	10,566	12,400	3,483	4,617	1,400	2,235	2,367	2,916	7,630	8,644	1,901	2,597
Lakeland-Winter Haven, FL Metro Area	81,146	62,280	20,981	29,537	7,558	13,824	4,359	6,473	4,399	7,187	13,407	17,314	4,211	5,761
Lancaster, PA Metro Area	53,268	45,483	11,493	17,154	4,735	8,322	2,055	2,887	2,751	4,303	5,792	11,077	1,382	3,855
Lansing-East Lansing, MI Metro Area	44,938	28,778	11,005	13,517	4,373	6,640	2,010	2,754	1,903	3,078	7,080	8,582	1,676	3,432
Laredo, TX Metro Area	14,818	11,185	5,756	5,882	1,940	2,522	1,801	1,359	2,810	2,414	4,014	4,524	2,638	2,737
Las Cruces, NM Metro Area	19,851	14,935	5,343	7,914	2,371	4,262	1,071	2,296	481	2,081	3,426	4,855	617	2,535
Las Vegas-Henderson-Paradise, NV Metro Area	201,469	127,221	51,478	59,413	18,656	28,841	10,999	13,341	11,448	16,768	33,176	39,892	9,216	17,418
Laurel, MS Micro Area	9,159	5,653	3,161	2,619	492	1,271	1,277	893	1,592	748	2,087	1,875	638	1,248
Lawrence, KS Metro Area	8,898	6,402	1,410	2,800	532	1,703	199	559	340	635	754	1,338	163	680
Lawton, OK Metro Area	9,433	6,805	4,240	3,225	1,580	1,584	689	766	1,126	603	2,919	1,793	609	495
Lebanon, PA Metro Area	15,166	12,543	2,813	4,808	1,048	1,935	764	668	186	1,466	1,593	3,658	261	1,478
Lewiston, ID-WA Metro Area	7,871	6,995	1,360	3,532	891	1,510	14	543	297	781	520	2,478	112	970
Lewiston-Auburn, ME Metro Area	11,373	7,919	2,860	3,400	1,059	1,170	263	460	486	846	1,775	2,378	478	685
Lexington-Fayette, KY Metro Area	43,413	29,263	10,788	13,551	3,066	6,502	1,516	2,989	2,057	3,913	6,797	8,837	1,326	3,448
Lima, OH Metro Area	10,071	7,859	2,568	3,936	1,021	2,471	601	780	386	989	1,623	2,246	297	795
Lincoln, NE Metro Area	28,209	18,558	6,250	9,043	2,735	4,376	623	1,393	1,062	2,828	3,775	5,256	916	2,016
Little Rock-North Little Rock-Conway, AR Metro Area	69,496	45,331	21,724	22,591	7,854	10,896	2,361	4,689	4,561	6,567	13,812	14,648	4,336	6,066
Logan, UT-ID Metro Area	8,025	5,657	1,236	2,269	674	1,170	156	245	59	743	548	1,232	150	400
London, KY Micro Area	12,182	8,347	4,553	4,277	1,408	2,822	517	1,378	979	1,243	3,060	3,011	441	1,441
Longview, TX Metro Area	20,793	14,886	6,123	7,577	2,440	3,280	719	1,814	1,268	2,020	3,414	5,156	1,059	1,376
Longview, WA Metro Area	12,649	8,207	3,861	3,815	1,906	2,012	273	364	897	979	2,125	3,013	781	791
Los Angeles-Long Beach-Anaheim, CA Metro Area	1,051,745	795,440	226,563	373,475	62,294	155,467	36,195	73,632	55,089	122,288	142,164	256,891	58,037	143,977
Louisville/Jefferson County, KY-IN Metro Area	124,578	83,484	34,612	39,209	12,145	18,035	4,556	7,861	6,561	11,236	22,520	26,590	5,951	9,403
Lubbock, TX Metro Area	22,671	17,233	6,377	9,359	2,952	4,429	915	2,174	776	1,622	3,827	5,774	400	2,434
Lufkin, TX Micro Area	7,824	6,072	2,534	4,011	1,076	2,144	326	1,152	472	1,782	1,658	2,059	411	1,292
Lumberton, NC Micro Area	12,367	7,494	4,589	3,871	1,691	2,069	1,020	587	1,411	1,576	3,227	2,807	1,065	1,270
Lynchburg, VA Metro Area	28,170	22,035	6,243	10,845	2,241	5,474	614	2,371	1,913	2,731	3,816	6,094	1,775	3,087
Macon-Bibb County, GA Metro Area	22,796	14,150	5,888	6,692	2,071	2,941	1,170	1,524	1,849	1,590	3,843	4,747	1,581	1,954
Madera, CA Metro Area	13,513	8,586	4,332	3,448	2,389	2,044	403	737	426	1,182	1,973	2,022	351	668
Madison, WI Metro Area	58,316	38,256	10,750	13,647	5,153	6,867	1,363	2,159	2,148	2,881	5,818	7,556	1,564	3,320
Manchester-Nashua, NH Metro Area	38,228	26,622	8,818	11,166	3,528	5,869	1,039	2,008	1,038	2,524	4,880	5,621	1,100	2,127
Manhattan, KS Metro Area	6,347	4,237	967	1,364	422	628	185	176	168	67	536	714	110	186
Manitowoc, WI Micro Area	8,887	7,054	1,545	2,772	807	953	168	430	222	690	827	1,734	156	1,007
Mankato-North Mankato, MN Metro Area	8,365	6,573	2,180	2,938	1,049	1,407	576	323	312	522	829	2,043	365	1,024
Mansfield, OH Metro Area	12,614	11,121	3,003	4,865	879	2,231	499	1,177	783	1,594	1,970	2,729	823	1,127
Marinette, WI-MI Micro Area	8,519	6,716	2,248	2,914	864	1,455	363	845	178	601	1,336	1,434	263	631
Marion, IN Micro Area	6,658	5,875	2,534	2,586	856	1,619	214	103	273	476	1,726	1,644	195	498
Marion, OH Micro Area	6,753	4,654	1,531	2,468	534	1,263	193	275	500	717	1,094	1,853	342	600
Marquette, MI Micro Area	7,517	5,307	1,767	1,884	706	1,224	350	313	472	359	924	914	600	402
Marshall, TX Micro Area	6,729	4,148	2,014	2,289	893	1,241	693	110	403	592	1,434	1,803	273	335
Martinsville, VA Micro Area	8,164	7,005	2,382	4,006	989	1,390	663	953	397	1,366	1,658	2,860	766	1,620
McAllen-Edinburg-Mission, TX Metro Area	53,503	42,512	18,569	26,968	6,422	12,722	4,801	7,732	4,335	9,261	9,875	18,622	5,526	10,775
Meadville, PA Micro Area	10,388	7,168	3,072	3,439	1,230	1,875	303	1,013	483	676	1,909	2,135	475	752
Medford, OR Metro Area	29,037	19,652	5,715	8,729	2,020	5,092	453	1,449	1,065	2,532	3,754	4,796	962	2,295
Memphis, TN-MS-AR Metro Area	116,118	72,421	30,421	37,046	9,205	13,833	7,044	8,027	6,164	11,531	19,732	26,381	4,402	11,564
Merced, CA Metro Area	17,516	13,232	5,757	7,848	2,322	4,129	714	1,804	1,366	2,467	3,735	4,955	1,166	2,116
Meridian, MS Micro Area	10,592	7,791	3,990	4,303	1,260	1,750	1,009	1,173	880	824	2,792	2,649	370	339
Miami-Fort Lauderdale-West Palm Beach, FL Metro Area	593,245	534,086	119,683	236,295	31,284	87,913	21,981	49,980	28,499	78,502	72,041	165,846	20,075	80,011
Michigan City-La Porte, IN Metro Area	11,942	7,734	3,692	3,624	1,292	1,324	436	442	931	564	2,197	2,719	352	1,054
Midland, MI Metro Area	8,670	6,869	1,601	3,178	867	1,514	267	546	100	823	472	2,097	0	483
Midland, TX Metro Area	10,614	8,546	2,709	5,578	1,006	2,490	779	1,418	831	1,877	2,110	3,514	302	891
Milwaukee-Waukesha-West Allis, WI Metro Area	141,300	104,758	31,462	44,941	10,184	19,571	4,439	7,037	6,448	11,314	19,409	27,597	6,027	12,323
Minneapolis-St. Paul-Bloomington, MN-WI Metro Area	301,415	205,878	62,376	85,990	25,529	38,415	7,981	14,004	12,740	18,286	33,956	51,226	10,800	17,612
Minot, ND Micro Area	5,883	4,685	1,555	2,372	667	1,670	348	928	193	716	1,171	1,605	200	702
Missoula, MT Micro Area	11,313	6,944	3,443	3,025	1,268	1,852	621	389	738	562	1,525	1,636	363	752
Mobile, AL Metro Area	39,373	27,185	10,657	11,803	4,119	5,468	2,038	2,180	2,750	3,931	6,983	8,340	2,103	3,965
Modesto, CA Metro Area	43,137	29,370	13,155	14,847	4,757	7,479	3,129	4,637	3,295	4,850	8,903	10,540	3,984	4,917
Monroe, LA Metro Area	16,296	11,321	4,022	4,522	1,106	2,616	559	775	753	1,084	2,573	2,486	646	821

Table H-4: Metropolitan/Micropolitan Statistical Areas - Disability Status and Type of Disability—*Continued*

	Total Population		With a Disability		With a Hearing Disability		With a Vision Disability		With a Cognitive Disability		With an Ambulatory Disability		With a Self-Care Disability	
	65 to 74 Years	75 Years and Over	65 to 74 Years	75 Years and Over	65 to 74 Years	75 Years and Over	65 to 74 Years	75 Years and Over	65 to 74 Years	75 Years and Over	65 to 74 Years	75 Years and Over	65 to 74 Years	75 Years and Over
Monroe, MI Metro Area	16,071	11,472	3,917	4,900	1,615	2,145	361	388	730	926	2,417	2,591	189	1,395
Montgomery, AL Metro Area	34,333	22,916	11,121	13,357	3,464	5,722	2,337	2,496	1,704	4,333	7,230	8,756	1,582	4,473
Morehead City, NC Micro Area	10,770	6,685	3,286	3,184	1,367	1,999	324	241	680	1,062	1,821	1,972	426	915
Morgantown, WV Metro Area	11,990	7,964	3,707	4,469	1,496	2,119	800	363	921	1,730	2,185	2,916	516	1,076
Morristown, TN Metro Area	13,044	9,201	5,398	4,466	1,894	2,264	332	791	1,287	929	3,665	3,047	1,019	1,245
Moses Lake, WA Micro Area	8,744	5,337	2,440	3,174	1,037	795	252	378	321	1,163	1,382	2,551	343	1,512
Mount Airy, NC Micro Area	8,344	6,722	2,986	3,112	1,163	1,460	729	692	624	728	1,802	2,338	342	844
Mount Pleasant, MI Micro Area	5,388	3,706	1,576	1,455	384	786	108	220	540	402	886	879	385	358
Mount Vernon-Anacortes, WA Metro Area	15,776	10,840	3,724	4,849	1,268	2,449	478	502	780	1,503	1,749	3,273	468	1,009
Muncie, IN Metro Area	11,005	8,926	2,974	3,759	1,262	1,773	371	921	501	1,093	1,576	2,744	405	765
Muskegon, MI Metro Area	17,589	11,852	4,645	5,765	1,668	2,251	654	876	784	1,673	3,042	3,219	749	1,565
Muskogee, OK Micro Area	6,256	5,064	1,883	2,552	791	1,245	82	854	522	836	1,147	1,784	127	596
Myrtle Beach-Conway-North Myrtle Beach, SC-NC Metro Area	84,737	42,157	17,897	18,936	7,293	10,412	2,410	2,517	2,828	5,622	10,986	12,315	2,885	4,430
Nacogdoches, TX Micro Area	5,704	3,846	2,433	2,186	1,173	1,359	748	191	768	791	1,641	1,170	440	355
Napa, CA Metro Area	15,856	10,949	3,322	4,352	1,508	2,046	313	1,159	319	1,115	1,883	2,689	482	1,239
Naples-Immokalee-Marco Island, FL Metro Area	60,211	62,252	10,084	22,990	3,594	13,089	645	4,141	2,907	4,996	4,547	12,687	1,514	4,995
Nashville-Davidson--Murfreesboro--Franklin, TN Metro Area	157,753	98,518	38,672	45,322	15,350	21,466	6,085	8,919	7,498	12,516	23,079	31,168	5,795	12,207
New Bern, NC Metro Area	14,256	11,269	2,532	5,721	1,303	2,561	555	728	404	1,359	1,312	4,050	550	1,351
New Castle, PA Micro Area	10,444	8,534	2,981	4,339	1,234	2,340	287	947	358	852	1,733	2,895	253	960
New Haven-Milford, CT Metro Area	83,150	65,639	17,077	27,185	5,823	11,325	2,210	4,449	3,684	7,128	10,027	18,978	2,216	8,712
New Orleans-Metairie, LA Metro Area	122,605	78,577	32,642	36,915	11,220	15,994	7,185	7,794	7,018	10,259	20,756	24,316	5,905	8,364
New Philadelphia-Dover, OH Micro Area	10,052	7,975	2,841	3,189	1,464	1,740	320	839	471	834	1,427	2,246	365	491
New York-Newark-Jersey City, NY-NJ-PA Metro Area	1,759,716	1,383,693	342,642	587,645	85,235	211,849	63,235	108,843	70,201	172,298	227,799	417,345	69,066	201,089
Niles-Benton Harbor, MI Metro Area	17,326	13,142	4,113	6,354	1,357	2,940	430	670	816	1,968	2,594	3,547	466	1,952
North Port-Sarasota-Bradenton, FL Metro Area	137,449	127,404	22,747	50,983	9,335	24,444	2,554	6,749	2,922	10,747	11,931	31,642	2,296	10,473
North Wilkesboro, NC Micro Area	8,390	6,305	3,397	3,420	1,091	1,057	632	432	1,186	1,088	1,772	2,437	147	1,119
Norwich-New London, CT Metro Area	27,351	20,963	6,405	7,937	2,409	4,826	323	1,607	918	1,616	3,940	3,882	1,195	1,080
Oak Harbor, WA Micro Area	12,673	8,130	3,806	2,847	1,637	1,478	713	343	1,177	775	2,117	1,675	1,442	541
Ocala, FL Metro Area	55,734	48,290	13,209	20,820	4,573	10,312	2,310	3,219	2,250	4,275	8,666	13,048	1,457	3,298
Ocean City, NJ Metro Area	13,585	10,483	2,781	4,670	1,206	1,660	434	540	633	911	1,842	2,999	366	744
Odessa, TX Metro Area	9,074	6,097	2,855	3,900	1,289	1,684	706	1,293	525	761	1,553	2,589	161	1,009
Ogden-Clearfield, UT Metro Area	45,635	28,606	9,786	13,106	4,483	7,447	1,540	2,420	1,905	3,014	4,557	7,760	1,384	2,536
Ogdensburg-Massena, NY Micro Area	10,731	7,737	3,246	3,920	1,101	2,245	372	795	597	1,233	1,983	2,450	599	982
Oklahoma City, OK Metro Area	116,108	77,881	37,354	40,867	14,995	21,186	6,936	7,056	7,090	10,818	23,431	27,589	6,097	8,982
Olean, NY Micro Area	8,449	6,192	2,436	2,445	737	1,191	247	318	1,034	568	1,001	1,300	204	391
Olympia-Tumwater, WA Metro Area	31,417	17,819	7,656	8,652	2,966	3,978	1,250	1,603	1,450	2,202	3,670	6,124	846	2,470
Omaha-Council Bluffs, NE-IA Metro Area	78,165	52,137	16,653	23,440	6,154	10,891	3,091	4,706	2,714	5,737	10,446	15,592	2,342	5,100
Opelousas, LA Micro Area	7,810	5,357	1,525	1,921	614	942	155	503	196	359	747	1,185	115	384
Orangeburg, SC Micro Area	10,063	6,803	2,332	2,693	606	1,509	607	763	797	1,156	1,443	1,927	583	607
Orlando-Kissimmee-Sanford, FL Metro Area	224,364	156,805	56,867	77,222	19,843	33,063	11,436	13,704	11,836	22,450	34,986	52,151	8,865	20,752
Oshkosh-Neenah, WI Metro Area	15,798	12,199	3,319	4,970	1,340	2,278	310	694	683	1,113	2,056	2,805	907	1,021
Ottawa-Peru, IL Micro Area	16,358	13,027	4,749	5,171	2,077	2,689	704	547	922	856	2,701	3,047	811	709
Owensboro, KY Metro Area	11,829	8,808	3,789	3,548	1,241	2,080	1,397	692	944	662	2,531	2,185	702	771
Owosso, MI Micro Area	7,516	5,081	2,212	2,347	1,171	1,253	182	253	205	438	1,145	1,403	223	554
Oxnard-Thousand Oaks-Ventura, CA Metro Area	76,060	56,159	16,898	26,756	6,426	13,029	3,741	5,286	2,378	8,421	9,054	16,836	3,103	8,053
Paducah, KY-IL Micro Area	10,436	9,507	2,732	4,224	756	1,445	638	374	464	974	1,626	2,944	890	1,014
Palatka, FL Micro Area	10,603	6,711	2,233	2,638	921	744	169	298	699	419	1,097	1,744	151	473
Palm Bay-Melbourne-Titusville, FL Metro Area	76,295	64,973	17,419	30,515	6,886	13,172	2,614	5,488	2,521	8,470	9,273	21,267	2,176	7,854
Panama City, FL Metro Area	20,587	14,147	7,341	8,225	2,630	3,911	1,489	1,502	1,279	2,578	4,015	6,100	861	1,993
Parkersburg-Vienna, WV Metro Area	10,790	7,778	3,234	4,000	1,203	1,453	675	559	374	951	2,205	2,582	775	849
Pensacola-Ferry Pass-Brent, FL Metro Area	48,190	33,222	11,821	15,520	4,237	7,044	2,528	2,423	2,252	3,144	7,378	9,956	1,831	3,937
Peoria, IL Metro Area	37,379	28,844	8,603	12,949	3,627	6,124	464	1,515	1,328	2,340	5,719	8,956	2,792	3,215
Philadelphia-Camden-Wilmington, PA-NJ-DE-MD Metro Area	557,325	416,392	126,422	181,299	37,663	74,731	20,770	31,772	28,658	46,646	83,995	122,794	23,297	47,436
Phoenix-Mesa-Scottsdale, AZ Metro Area	443,135	316,889	106,765	140,202	46,495	70,821	17,684	27,694	21,206	34,243	61,566	87,168	16,441	30,984
Pine Bluff, AR Metro Area	9,492	5,837	3,012	2,791	1,123	1,583	391	614	638	855	2,005	2,085	557	664
Pinehurst-Southern Pines, NC Micro Area	12,691	10,893	3,276	4,477	1,507	2,425	960	1,128	442	1,354	1,699	2,141	418	1,298
Pittsburgh, PA Metro Area	258,687	205,351	56,070	91,516	19,845	40,265	7,391	14,636	9,816	22,094	33,943	57,613	7,693	22,361
Pittsfield, MA Metro Area	16,618	12,621	3,318	5,736	994	2,777	887	738	630	1,474	1,644	3,342	325	1,561
Plattsburgh, NY Micro Area	7,865	5,658	1,865	2,863	686	1,185	374	812	648	849	1,329	2,078	523	863
Pocatello, ID Metro Area	7,360	4,984	2,442	3,204	1,537	1,542	188	1,353	581	1,405	1,283	2,304	443	583
Port Angeles, WA Micro Area	12,898	9,263	3,827	4,464	1,811	2,248	649	279	430	1,371	1,947	3,063	581	1,073
Portland-South Portland, ME Metro Area	62,043	42,246	12,262	17,836	4,586	9,863	2,251	3,035	2,814	4,371	6,687	9,401	1,424	2,625
Portland-Vancouver-Hillsboro, OR-WA Metro Area	228,009	140,871	51,326	62,830	19,554	32,041	7,889	10,041	9,531	17,453	29,348	38,448	8,780	14,906
Port St. Lucie, FL Metro Area	67,101	60,526	11,959	27,056	3,515	11,520	1,462	6,980	1,726	7,291	8,810	17,406	1,434	5,199
Portsmouth, OH Micro Area	7,602	5,924	2,605	3,059	1,134	1,279	548	952	648	974	1,623	1,930	133	898
Pottsville, PA Micro Area	16,243	12,636	3,887	6,223	1,943	2,735	356	1,307	725	1,635	1,943	4,245	232	1,397
Prescott, AZ Metro Area	43,831	29,825	10,152	11,200	4,348	5,900	1,684	3,268	1,542	3,580	5,948	6,045	1,183	1,871
Providence-Warwick, RI-MA Metro Area	158,520	118,981	38,015	52,661	15,400	24,069	5,277	10,299	8,597	13,288	23,027	34,756	7,826	15,265
Provo-Orem, UT Metro Area	29,337	20,056	7,413	9,897	2,953	4,822	1,538	1,713	1,654	2,044	4,058	5,352	1,454	2,156
Pueblo, CO Metro Area	17,912	12,920	5,276	6,982	2,245	4,240	802	1,908	869	1,502	3,287	4,038	787	1,075
Punta Gorda, FL Metro Area	39,338	34,983	8,710	16,721	2,915	8,373	975	2,688	781	4,798	5,492	10,008	1,429	3,632
Quincy, IL-MO Micro Area	7,535	7,353	2,270	2,822	675	1,367	284	1,221	354	972	1,569	1,531	268	530
Racine, WI Metro Area	18,925	13,476	4,034	5,393	1,269	2,237	684	1,049	1,032	1,384	2,356	2,926	888	1,158
Raleigh, NC Metro Area	104,845	61,024	22,223	28,234	8,183	11,383	3,869	4,602	4,641	7,456	12,427	19,227	3,113	6,533

Table H-4: Metropolitan/Micropolitan Statistical Areas - Disability Status and Type of Disability—*Continued*

	Total Population		With a Disability		With a Hearing Disability		With a Vision Disability		With a Cognitive Disability		With an Ambulatory Disability		With a Self-Care Disability	
	65 to 74 Years	75 Years and Over	65 to 74 Years	75 Years and Over	65 to 74 Years	75 Years and Over	65 to 74 Years	75 Years and Over	65 to 74 Years	75 Years and Over	65 to 74 Years	75 Years and Over	65 to 74 Years	75 Years and Over
Rapid City, SD Metro Area	16,315	9,939	4,235	4,970	1,389	2,645	628	728	856	893	2,507	2,678	494	793
Reading, PA Metro Area	40,863	31,452	10,370	14,201	2,894	6,240	1,381	1,474	2,256	3,467	6,297	8,344	952	3,366
Redding, CA Metro Area	21,481	15,546	7,590	8,197	3,173	3,826	1,664	1,023	1,898	1,823	4,187	4,599	1,481	1,759
Reno, NV Metro Area	48,808	28,640	10,339	13,079	4,420	5,870	1,825	1,851	1,883	3,755	6,321	9,110	1,979	3,625
Richmond, IN Micro Area	6,850	5,595	2,643	2,215	914	1,016	201	525	521	606	1,728	1,645	315	819
Richmond, VA Metro Area	122,117	81,082	27,353	40,325	8,451	19,575	4,946	9,165	4,983	10,941	16,798	26,086	5,158	10,227
Richmond-Berea, KY Micro Area	9,710	6,186	3,653	3,186	1,013	1,921	731	733	1,109	937	2,602	1,918	935	760
Riverside-San Bernardino-Ontario, CA Metro Area	354,033	250,160	93,296	125,284	29,691	61,064	15,759	26,170	21,804	37,977	59,451	82,667	16,692	39,323
Roanoke, VA Metro Area	37,583	26,855	8,036	8,697	2,891	3,142	1,983	1,911	1,042	2,909	4,523	6,049	1,402	2,376
Roanoke Rapids, NC Micro Area	8,679	5,940	1,642	2,491	627	1,081	574	133	550	422	1,100	1,765	483	335
Rochester, MN Metro Area	20,129	16,506	3,744	6,563	1,544	3,185	519	1,319	797	1,668	1,733	4,215	270	1,616
Rochester, NY Metro Area	109,115	81,321	22,590	35,145	7,721	16,005	2,459	5,106	4,169	7,769	13,097	23,560	2,945	7,733
Rockford, IL Metro Area	33,103	24,519	7,975	9,781	3,299	3,940	1,224	1,323	1,410	2,570	4,943	6,213	1,232	2,316
Rocky Mount, NC Metro Area	16,634	11,116	4,579	4,857	1,548	1,713	953	708	1,363	1,269	2,213	2,799	305	1,161
Rome, GA Metro Area	9,158	7,375	2,770	3,345	1,117	1,513	929	526	393	955	2,227	2,061	521	1,107
Roseburg, OR Micro Area	16,235	11,689	4,139	5,860	1,628	3,677	607	1,639	552	1,149	2,317	3,054	225	545
Roswell, NM Micro Area	5,905	4,925	2,443	2,665	645	1,758	330	718	679	1,055	1,392	2,054	655	1,175
Russellville, AR Micro Area	7,753	5,678	2,984	3,356	1,536	1,966	523	669	289	1,005	1,795	2,230	362	1,087
Sacramento--Roseville--Arden-Arcade, CA Metro Area..	212,740	149,057	48,682	69,397	15,397	29,525	7,081	9,568	9,521	21,319	28,457	44,208	8,726	21,632
Saginaw, MI Metro Area	20,874	15,892	5,240	7,555	1,926	2,855	498	1,226	1,144	2,309	3,391	4,621	826	1,568
St. Cloud, MN Metro Area	16,483	13,227	3,461	5,834	1,541	3,004	357	553	886	1,116	1,866	3,279	592	1,036
St. George, UT Metro Area	20,852	16,443	4,932	7,965	2,679	3,974	543	1,125	593	1,780	2,154	4,608	158	1,400
St. Joseph, MO-KS Metro Area	12,490	8,871	3,187	4,046	1,097	1,826	753	800	322	953	2,044	3,144	717	1,159
St. Louis, MO-IL Metro Area	267,322	196,033	66,064	85,099	22,884	37,452	12,194	14,697	11,288	19,980	40,217	57,883	10,395	21,138
Salem, OH Micro Area	12,380	8,795	3,429	3,482	1,031	1,834	827	241	577	1,079	2,170	2,354	844	1,017
Salem, OR Metro Area	39,966	28,809	10,454	13,317	3,905	6,883	1,653	1,654	2,345	3,531	7,042	9,416	1,969	2,926
Salinas, CA Metro Area	34,393	25,098	5,832	11,923	2,434	6,023	612	1,854	889	3,202	3,030	7,301	1,000	3,739
Salisbury, MD-DE Metro Area	59,388	39,404	12,965	16,912	5,886	7,063	1,316	2,769	2,564	4,837	6,719	10,629	1,080	4,243
Salt Lake City, UT Metro Area	80,582	51,238	16,271	24,277	6,135	12,108	2,295	4,649	3,811	5,469	8,557	13,781	2,389	4,822
San Angelo, TX Metro Area	11,287	7,010	2,633	3,089	1,434	1,577	777	879	390	633	958	1,691	98	865
San Antonio-New Braunfels, TX Metro Area	197,487	131,186	55,858	66,178	21,326	30,645	13,272	16,753	12,542	21,280	36,021	45,414	10,985	18,566
San Diego-Carlsbad, CA Metro Area	272,301	197,520	57,049	93,401	20,197	41,858	10,339	16,856	13,993	30,421	35,038	62,879	12,194	31,236
Sandusky, OH Micro Area	9,152	7,005	2,269	2,789	816	1,315	711	338	360	774	1,554	1,698	627	967
San Francisco-Oakland-Hayward, CA Metro Area	423,312	308,844	76,919	141,000	23,571	61,679	11,940	26,978	16,700	45,239	46,279	95,375	15,117	48,924
San Jose-Sunnyvale-Santa Clara, CA Metro Area	150,538	118,654	26,262	53,203	8,075	24,927	3,880	10,256	6,101	15,381	15,398	36,668	4,775	17,786
San Luis Obispo-Paso Robles-Arroyo Grande, CA Metro Area	35,423	22,171	7,185	10,298	3,181	5,405	1,877	2,249	1,469	2,447	4,239	6,522	1,392	2,427
Santa Cruz-Watsonville, CA Metro Area	29,453	15,896	5,183	6,963	1,911	2,204	1,565	976	678	2,504	2,538	4,575	869	1,713
Santa Fe, NM Metro Area	23,437	13,131	4,561	5,836	2,113	2,625	441	927	958	2,087	2,627	4,135	808	1,373
Santa Maria-Santa Barbara, CA Metro Area	37,583	30,819	6,812	12,528	2,063	6,822	890	2,160	1,169	3,517	3,826	7,452	1,002	3,110
Santa Rosa, CA Metro Area	60,222	37,808	12,102	17,374	5,092	8,238	1,287	2,769	2,044	4,699	6,372	12,142	1,947	5,127
Savannah, GA Metro Area	33,762	21,445	7,323	11,727	3,199	6,056	1,032	2,871	1,472	2,904	4,149	7,284	619	2,316
Scranton--Wilkes-Barre--Hazleton, PA Metro Area	61,845	49,096	14,880	20,818	6,475	11,401	1,874	4,256	2,388	4,646	9,211	13,355	2,389	5,319
Searcy, AR Micro Area	7,055	5,252	2,214	2,928	761	1,594	449	831	422	698	1,662	2,192	354	588
Seattle-Tacoma-Bellevue, WA Metro Area	321,934	206,097	73,911	94,484	28,110	43,534	10,404	16,831	15,744	27,654	44,644	60,101	12,660	28,422
Sebastian-Vero Beach, FL Metro Area	27,260	24,124	4,554	8,904	2,198	5,975	611	1,113	764	1,790	2,317	5,463	691	2,017
Sebring, FL Metro Area	17,388	19,857	3,757	7,595	1,793	4,540	411	1,112	724	1,357	2,543	4,333	487	884
Seneca, SC Micro Area	11,362	7,271	2,973	3,869	1,526	1,772	692	1,392	1,006	2,595	1,184	1,927	176	792
Sevierville, TN Micro Area	11,832	7,328	2,639	4,159	1,496	1,674	299	606	314	2,098	1,168	3,154	425	1,315
Shawnee, OK Micro Area	7,143	4,678	3,298	2,891	927	1,414	770	555	799	783	2,224	2,106	544	618
Sheboygan, WI Metro Area	11,966	8,730	2,136	3,138	614	1,831	294	357	595	656	1,276	1,400	205	417
Shelby, NC Micro Area	10,584	7,513	2,117	2,521	1,000	1,133	383	380	438	572	1,183	1,653	427	524
Shelton, WA Micro Area	9,345	5,517	2,224	2,730	1,090	1,329	288	651	392	1,144	1,310	2,293	763	1,236
Sherman-Denison, TX Metro Area	14,025	9,581	3,888	3,871	1,374	1,967	692	439	1,373	975	2,500	2,799	881	952
Show Low, AZ Micro Area	12,126	8,036	3,390	4,793	1,501	2,702	1,146	1,592	392	1,200	1,527	2,710	471	893
Shreveport-Bossier City, LA Metro Area	42,215	29,839	10,776	14,247	4,583	5,579	1,710	2,332	1,783	3,240	6,774	9,432	1,604	4,569
Sierra Vista-Douglas, AZ Metro Area	16,130	12,272	3,907	5,910	1,985	3,053	411	1,337	806	1,556	2,404	4,017	460	2,039
Sioux City, IA-NE-SD Metro Area	14,664	11,702	2,969	5,288	1,280	2,714	614	1,022	807	1,814	1,672	3,010	761	1,743
Sioux Falls, SD Metro Area	21,774	13,851	4,191	5,326	1,630	1,877	522	1,058	633	1,285	2,287	3,527	414	1,378
Somerset, PA Micro Area	9,063	7,462	2,314	3,314	1,148	2,224	227	329	603	997	1,328	1,039	363	261
South Bend-Mishawaka, IN-MI Metro Area	31,293	22,327	6,358	10,875	2,413	4,884	1,145	2,759	1,352	2,781	3,676	7,046	860	2,646
Spartanburg, SC Metro Area	33,707	22,416	9,670	10,990	3,443	5,506	1,567	2,476	2,187	4,048	5,093	7,196	1,461	2,841
Spokane-Spokane Valley, WA Metro Area	59,434	37,673	17,156	18,818	8,028	9,455	2,585	4,419	3,650	4,715	8,496	12,976	2,427	4,302
Springfield, IL Metro Area	22,138	15,059	4,098	6,471	1,367	3,455	356	1,425	527	1,388	2,527	4,686	572	1,271
Springfield, MA Metro Area	62,173	44,560	14,436	20,490	4,620	8,877	1,957	2,897	3,434	4,887	7,978	13,613	3,069	6,015
Springfield, MO Metro Area	44,395	33,388	14,689	14,845	7,183	7,310	4,764	2,403	6,533	4,414	10,132	8,641	4,661	2,859
Springfield, OH Metro Area	14,885	11,072	4,814	5,252	1,752	3,004	682	810	943	1,609	2,830	2,754	732	911
State College, PA Metro Area	12,935	9,880	1,948	2,955	828	1,115	324	238	120	844	794	1,969	300	804
Statesboro, GA Micro Area	5,174	3,371	1,615	1,181	504	397	461	83	309	275	850	770	246	296
Staunton-Waynesboro, VA Metro Area	14,839	10,856	4,296	3,953	1,013	1,985	489	942	1,209	1,416	2,986	2,775	840	851
Stevens Point, WI Micro Area	6,826	4,840	1,501	2,308	641	1,007	398	488	341	693	947	1,125	520	417
Stillwater, OK Micro Area	6,554	4,426	1,477	2,108	987	1,106	127	504	314	604	599	1,524	217	565
Stockton-Lodi, CA Metro Area	56,724	39,120	15,733	20,252	5,836	9,623	2,765	4,160	4,275	5,668	10,246	13,385	3,502	6,522
Sumter, SC Metro Area	10,268	7,300	3,098	3,482	976	1,253	1,072	585	392	1,293	1,834	2,454	335	1,461
Sunbury, PA Micro Area	10,918	8,729	2,464	4,193	784	1,682	267	876	455	1,100	1,618	2,540	475	582
Syracuse, NY Metro Area	63,988	47,415	13,269	21,202	4,776	11,323	2,261	3,681	3,120	5,357	8,056	12,952	2,326	4,440
Talladega-Sylacauga, AL Micro Area	10,432	6,939	3,537	3,859	1,034	910	452	634	668	1,396	1,943	2,640	410	1,030

Table H-4: Metropolitan/Micropolitan Statistical Areas - Disability Status and Type of Disability—*Continued*

	Total Population		With a Disability		With a Hearing Disability		With a Vision Disability		With a Cognitive Disability		With an Ambulatory Disability		With a Self-Care Disability	
	65 to 74 Years	75 Years and Over	65 to 74 Years	75 Years and Over	65 to 74 Years	75 Years and Over	65 to 74 Years	75 Years and Over	65 to 74 Years	75 Years and Over	65 to 74 Years	75 Years and Over	65 to 74 Years	75 Years and Over
Tallahassee, FL Metro Area	35,467	20,007	8,965	10,211	3,306	4,247	2,095	2,175	2,302	3,219	5,139	6,757	1,031	3,526
Tampa-St. Petersburg-Clearwater, FL Metro Area	348,184	274,249	85,007	125,043	28,862	57,659	13,718	25,088	16,390	32,883	53,293	81,912	13,333	32,517
Terre Haute, IN Metro Area	16,465	11,917	4,988	5,009	1,995	2,734	987	582	975	1,081	3,060	3,268	681	520
Texarkana, TX-AR Metro Area	14,888	10,121	4,228	3,647	935	1,559	1,077	665	542	926	2,783	2,226	332	763
The Villages, FL Metro Area	42,145	31,009	7,577	9,930	3,983	6,101	1,818	1,914	1,195	1,461	2,853	5,302	468	1,349
Toledo, OH Metro Area	57,614	40,266	15,096	17,350	5,477	8,203	1,931	2,316	3,175	5,097	8,618	10,930	2,521	4,022
Topeka, KS Metro Area	25,538	17,956	6,094	8,175	2,762	4,753	651	1,356	849	1,925	3,937	4,809	502	2,206
Torrington, CT Micro Area	22,325	15,572	4,474	5,552	2,257	2,756	526	952	658	1,408	2,430	3,389	649	1,407
Traverse City, MI Micro Area	19,920	13,358	4,177	5,977	1,889	3,383	527	1,102	718	1,649	1,926	2,966	669	1,320
Trenton, NJ Metro Area	32,615	23,386	5,014	7,828	1,363	3,483	816	1,125	820	1,597	2,858	5,204	563	2,332
Truckee-Grass Valley, CA Micro Area	17,493	10,253	3,698	4,416	1,567	2,854	988	726	391	954	2,124	2,592	350	846
Tucson, AZ Metro Area	117,273	88,274	27,988	41,056	11,782	20,748	6,174	6,147	5,686	12,411	15,141	24,128	3,450	7,808
Tullahoma-Manchester, TN Micro Area	11,085	8,879	3,420	4,262	1,493	2,246	961	1,142	893	1,926	1,916	2,961	374	772
Tulsa, OK Metro Area	91,558	61,705	25,148	29,318	10,311	13,754	4,870	6,258	5,459	7,292	16,590	19,481	3,667	6,983
Tupelo, MS Micro Area	11,952	8,555	3,496	4,295	1,628	2,206	1,123	923	991	971	2,342	2,455	878	1,036
Tuscaloosa, AL Metro Area	21,366	13,026	6,540	5,769	1,656	2,268	1,289	816	1,249	1,934	4,193	3,693	1,332	1,294
Twin Falls, ID Micro Area	9,131	6,836	2,026	3,162	727	1,517	584	512	381	624	1,326	1,988	676	760
Tyler, TX Metro Area	21,696	15,892	4,849	7,294	1,601	3,790	550	1,222	1,483	2,026	3,436	4,552	628	1,312
Ukiah, CA Micro Area	12,320	6,752	3,137	2,249	1,436	1,355	722	450	600	230	1,445	961	237	240
Urban Honolulu, HI Metro Area	94,410	79,202	17,741	36,162	6,990	17,134	3,223	5,717	3,989	12,953	8,977	23,074	2,163	10,147
Utica-Rome, NY Metro Area	30,403	25,002	6,852	9,862	2,530	4,601	878	894	1,695	2,372	3,926	5,757	1,935	2,821
Valdosta, GA Metro Area	11,336	8,133	2,980	3,427	1,063	1,896	867	670	648	374	1,962	1,951	250	688
Vallejo-Fairfield, CA Metro Area	42,750	27,847	9,367	14,250	2,871	6,394	728	3,198	2,013	4,357	6,049	10,304	1,600	5,008
Victoria, TX Metro Area	8,935	7,523	3,189	4,000	1,230	1,902	1,027	580	247	1,142	1,584	2,819	423	1,069
Vineland-Bridgeton, NJ Metro Area	13,681	9,541	4,271	3,649	897	1,167	991	366	1,035	955	3,534	2,583	1,193	970
Virginia Beach-Norfolk-Newport News, VA-NC Metro Area	150,018	103,180	36,370	48,168	12,035	20,441	4,494	8,923	7,863	13,597	23,068	31,886	6,982	12,719
Visalia-Porterville, CA Metro Area	31,035	21,587	9,798	11,173	3,321	5,474	2,793	1,789	2,216	3,440	6,462	6,390	1,959	2,665
Waco, TX Metro Area	23,489	16,546	6,999	9,164	2,323	4,306	760	1,935	1,456	2,616	4,581	6,619	1,468	2,856
Walla Walla, WA Metro Area	6,838	5,738	1,569	2,881	542	1,601	446	1,022	152	723	954	1,685	346	815
Warner Robins, GA Metro Area	14,797	9,189	6,451	4,545	3,040	2,531	1,414	1,019	1,104	1,205	3,718	2,833	1,109	1,059
Warsaw, IN Micro Area	7,692	5,376	1,736	1,414	669	701	292	422	297	87	1,087	727	73	68
Washington-Arlington-Alexandria, DC-VA-MD-WV Metro Area	488,148	324,843	91,182	141,098	29,558	55,886	15,070	24,592	19,682	41,879	53,708	90,541	14,824	41,861
Waterloo-Cedar Falls, IA Metro Area	15,933	12,720	3,546	5,073	1,350	3,002	345	759	1,190	1,245	1,511	2,751	531	1,034
Watertown-Fort Atkinson, WI Micro Area	8,852	5,793	1,721	2,145	613	1,064	227	318	335	144	977	1,171	255	407
Watertown-Fort Drum, NY Metro Area	9,065	6,393	2,428	2,826	1,143	1,319	541	572	457	499	1,347	1,736	306	425
Wausau, WI Metro Area	13,446	10,324	2,916	3,838	946	1,586	330	466	362	979	1,957	2,629	518	982
Weirton-Steubenville, WV-OH Metro Area	15,710	11,719	3,614	5,950	1,360	1,839	622	556	1,038	2,075	2,141	3,857	616	2,073
Wenatchee, WA Metro Area	12,545	9,118	4,647	4,382	2,640	2,035	1,215	1,034	833	1,358	1,822	3,257	87	864
Wheeling, WV-OH Metro Area	17,644	12,786	4,472	6,193	1,857	3,250	831	680	382	1,579	2,221	4,269	654	1,891
Whitewater-Elkhorn, WI Micro Area	10,761	7,385	1,845	2,843	778	1,803	108	641	242	684	1,055	1,497	593	479
Wichita, KS Metro Area	55,814	41,156	14,532	19,780	5,352	9,841	1,726	3,978	3,280	6,296	8,445	13,744	2,614	5,139
Wichita Falls, TX Metro Area	13,094	10,170	4,527	4,732	2,063	2,246	758	1,391	772	1,250	3,045	3,192	438	1,800
Williamsport, PA Metro Area	12,212	9,689	2,959	4,249	1,223	1,530	703	1,010	485	1,015	1,819	3,162	369	1,433
Wilmington, NC Metro Area	31,673	20,823	6,427	8,719	2,373	5,304	1,290	2,105	1,504	2,642	4,008	5,208	1,246	1,916
Wilson, NC Micro Area	8,875	5,929	2,615	2,379	900	1,510	456	378	622	350	2,019	1,150	375	332
Winchester, VA-WV Metro Area	14,997	10,144	3,376	5,610	1,693	2,542	746	1,473	722	2,205	1,468	3,751	385	2,172
Winston-Salem, NC Metro Area	68,479	47,929	17,236	21,441	5,603	9,168	1,982	3,233	4,340	5,755	11,087	13,647	3,302	5,192
Wisconsin Rapids-Marshfield, WI Micro Area	8,175	6,765	1,776	3,150	863	1,436	367	386	267	855	978	2,130	786	682
Wooster, OH Micro Area	11,401	8,863	2,063	4,407	686	2,112	416	440	416	999	1,131	2,617	255	739
Worcester, MA-CT Metro Area	87,536	61,232	17,215	26,005	6,851	11,476	2,114	5,154	4,038	7,217	9,736	16,703	2,734	7,225
Yakima, WA Metro Area	20,408	13,921	5,616	6,149	2,650	3,237	696	1,015	792	1,569	3,547	4,404	596	2,502
York-Hanover, PA Metro Area	45,351	32,787	9,263	15,592	3,249	7,566	1,390	2,199	2,580	4,271	5,319	9,448	1,326	3,202
Youngstown-Warren-Boardman, OH-PA Metro Area	64,416	50,863	13,589	22,829	5,043	10,084	2,349	3,075	2,696	6,091	7,573	14,633	2,477	6,045
Yuba City, CA Metro Area	13,543	10,703	3,818	5,073	1,792	2,507	232	988	680	1,324	2,251	3,739	252	946
Yuma, AZ Metro Area	19,698	20,281	4,798	8,573	2,066	4,379	871	936	1,107	1,307	2,739	4,259	962	1,616
Zanesville, OH Micro Area	8,667	6,522	3008	3001	1,215	1,783	265	136	346	248	1,368	1,596	244	784

Table H-5: 116th Congressional Districts - Disability Status and Type of Disability

	Total Population		With a Disability		With a Hearing Disability		With a Vision Disability		With a Cognitive Disability		With an Ambulatory Disability		With a Self-Care Disability	
	65 to 74 Years	75 Years and Over	65 to 74 Years	75 Years and Over	65 to 74 Years	75 Years and Over	65 to 74 Years	75 Years and Over	65 to 74 Years	75 Years and Over	65 to 74 Years	75 Years and Over	65 to 74 Years	75 Years and Over
Alabama														
Congressional District 1	75,805	51,278	19,750	22,050	8,194	10,165	2,686	2,999	3,902	5,903	12,693	15,527	2,808	6,312
Congressional District 2	67,493	47,869	20,438	26,645	6,271	11,547	3,693	5,000	4,167	8,233	13,917	17,983	3,618	7,437
Congressional District 3	74,314	45,205	25,510	23,419	9,219	8,565	4,495	4,752	6,498	8,155	14,753	16,933	4,991	7,174
Congressional District 4	74,931	53,212	26,927	26,404	9,344	10,533	5,021	4,267	4,783	8,933	17,059	19,466	4,289	7,722
Congressional District 5	69,559	50,166	18,914	24,807	7,957	11,208	2,619	5,321	4,083	7,890	10,498	15,430	3,476	6,323
Congressional District 6	71,194	47,858	16,642	23,746	6,866	10,938	3,221	4,144	3,200	6,969	9,730	15,117	3,493	6,149
Congressional District 7	60,100	40,679	20,408	21,340	5,965	8,196	3,612	4,619	3,940	6,043	13,157	14,392	3,505	5,515
Alaska														
Congressional District (at Large)	59,630	28,370	17,701	14,644	9,123	8,368	4,056	3,920	3,201	4,986	9,020	9,703	2,697	3,970
Arizona														
Congressional District 1	87,392	61,437	24,200	28,787	11,525	15,615	5,761	7,234	5,071	6,857	13,206	15,777	3,091	4,787
Congressional District 2	88,441	68,761	20,090	29,935	8,617	15,354	4,244	5,253	3,989	7,671	11,214	17,904	2,372	6,126
Congressional District 3	61,082	38,337	18,477	22,503	7,246	10,984	3,018	3,411	3,993	8,095	11,113	14,883	2,852	5,301
Congressional District 4	130,764	93,554	36,729	40,747	14,922	20,005	4,527	9,155	7,910	9,977	21,273	22,641	5,740	7,020
Congressional District 5	82,199	58,944	16,948	25,466	7,939	12,705	3,387	5,532	3,255	6,072	8,933	15,380	2,264	6,464
Congressional District 6	84,644	64,710	15,153	25,050	5,516	12,058	2,450	4,301	2,524	5,875	8,912	14,789	2,275	5,347
Congressional District 7	38,983	21,613	11,919	10,573	4,254	4,672	2,882	2,285	2,927	3,238	8,276	7,795	2,396	3,569
Congressional District 8	99,686	83,533	23,705	35,941	11,703	19,524	4,375	5,508	3,589	7,109	12,842	22,029	3,704	7,061
Congressional District 9	54,765	40,258	13,200	19,891	5,467	9,060	2,119	4,235	2,802	6,141	7,745	14,650	2,008	4,876
Arkansas														
Congressional District 1	76,170	54,985	25,256	30,913	8,824	14,295	4,928	6,156	4,794	7,129	16,471	21,965	4,836	8,279
Congressional District 2	72,633	49,205	23,844	25,537	8,500	12,873	3,344	5,264	5,171	7,702	15,539	17,015	4,706	6,562
Congressional District 3	68,656	49,390	19,515	23,040	6,561	10,285	2,336	4,403	3,571	4,967	13,533	14,450	3,503	5,325
Congressional District 4	79,349	57,288	26,650	30,691	9,516	15,775	5,523	6,445	5,728	9,010	17,948	21,891	5,415	9,032
California														
Congressional District 1	92,231	63,651	25,133	29,874	10,623	14,617	4,544	4,528	4,953	7,370	13,571	18,252	4,342	7,069
Congressional District 2	94,638	58,865	18,446	23,339	8,165	11,144	2,802	4,514	3,299	5,045	9,293	14,456	2,411	5,851
Congressional District 3	63,331	43,887	16,368	20,520	6,565	10,167	1,778	3,453	3,053	5,698	9,279	13,768	2,622	5,885
Congressional District 4	95,204	64,677	20,860	28,537	7,995	14,063	2,748	4,272	4,208	6,716	12,232	16,091	3,528	6,623
Congressional District 5	78,732	51,475	16,550	24,242	5,777	11,559	2,126	5,140	2,613	7,058	9,836	16,720	3,051	7,994
Congressional District 6	56,760	38,988	16,268	19,527	4,450	6,430	2,425	1,955	3,234	6,500	10,349	13,407	3,353	6,882
Congressional District 7	70,177	50,014	15,750	23,349	5,273	10,408	2,472	4,342	3,459	8,680	8,364	15,711	3,083	8,733
Congressional District 8	57,208	39,765	17,286	20,542	6,467	11,566	3,213	5,411	4,252	6,673	9,558	12,378	2,241	6,455
Congressional District 9	60,915	42,309	18,342	21,514	5,660	10,710	3,096	3,839	4,589	6,786	12,263	14,011	3,906	7,460
Congressional District 10	59,567	39,316	16,713	20,513	6,283	9,763	3,444	5,735	3,897	6,095	11,125	14,420	4,453	6,329
Congressional District 11	73,560	53,721	13,128	23,049	3,133	10,047	1,714	3,480	2,947	7,357	8,456	15,498	1,921	6,188
Congressional District 12	63,784	52,430	12,727	26,872	4,462	12,000	1,543	4,593	3,683	10,517	7,342	18,351	3,137	12,240
Congressional District 13	65,240	42,821	13,416	21,285	3,975	9,065	3,511	3,906	3,736	7,092	8,676	14,533	3,047	7,144
Congressional District 14	70,265	55,379	12,136	25,525	4,214	11,489	1,252	5,954	2,777	8,309	6,354	17,425	1,925	9,115
Congressional District 15	62,913	43,964	10,253	18,395	2,924	7,300	1,659	4,398	1,632	5,665	6,769	13,148	2,546	6,437
Congressional District 16	45,661	32,473	16,274	18,567	6,284	10,056	3,515	4,809	4,057	6,407	9,712	12,726	2,745	5,773
Congressional District 17	52,632	43,446	9,227	20,906	2,612	8,657	1,281	3,644	2,127	6,028	5,422	15,275	2,065	7,475
Congressional District 18	63,986	52,209	9,377	22,311	2,949	10,842	1,318	4,074	2,090	5,503	5,030	13,910	1,340	6,151
Congressional District 19	61,716	41,257	11,950	18,333	3,502	8,623	1,837	4,052	2,170	5,586	7,735	13,268	2,337	7,055
Congressional District 20	62,238	41,742	10,746	18,853	4,592	8,090	2,270	2,801	1,619	5,668	5,152	11,811	1,685	5,352
Congressional District 21	37,713	26,901	11,347	15,380	3,063	6,729	1,635	1,893	2,554	5,325	7,435	10,816	1,777	4,343
Congressional District 22	59,046	40,297	15,128	21,106	4,693	10,505	3,896	3,931	3,765	6,063	9,772	13,437	2,876	5,025
Congressional District 23	57,655	40,924	18,035	19,640	6,266	8,968	4,591	4,096	4,520	7,270	10,891	14,059	3,822	6,929
Congressional District 24	73,909	53,554	14,096	23,145	5,300	12,490	2,767	4,433	2,638	6,087	8,108	14,179	2,394	5,574
Congressional District 25	58,014	35,775	15,431	16,080	4,485	7,710	2,853	4,409	3,596	5,052	10,247	11,560	3,208	5,221
Congressional District 26	63,663	47,994	13,678	22,961	5,070	11,229	3,002	4,409	1,664	7,197	7,167	14,416	2,374	6,845
Congressional District 27	68,813	58,244	12,375	25,105	3,432	9,466	1,114	4,051	2,375	7,759	7,829	18,148	2,876	10,899
Congressional District 28	60,001	50,735	17,216	25,929	4,019	10,542	2,441	5,773	5,049	9,568	12,472	17,788	7,457	14,681
Congressional District 29	48,096	34,272	15,853	19,472	5,138	7,930	3,722	4,902	5,819	7,640	9,990	13,772	4,309	7,472
Congressional District 30	67,210	51,911	13,189	25,183	3,154	11,172	1,998	3,755	2,900	6,165	9,167	17,447	4,653	10,538
Congressional District 31	54,976	33,410	14,252	19,553	3,888	9,176	2,202	4,217	3,960	7,176	9,494	13,774	2,761	5,781
Congressional District 32	55,897	40,667	13,532	20,993	4,219	8,826	2,694	3,985	3,449	5,981	8,425	15,763	3,267	8,654
Congressional District 33	72,551	59,489	9,568	23,761	3,745	12,337	1,192	3,587	2,265	6,423	4,348	15,361	1,962	7,586
Congressional District 34	52,338	41,510	13,896	22,957	3,415	9,091	2,315	5,443	4,154	9,618	9,142	16,509	3,171	9,170
Congressional District 35	46,453	28,045	13,214	15,924	3,691	6,306	2,534	3,885	2,390	6,467	9,153	11,767	2,683	5,938
Congressional District 36	96,092	75,470	24,890	31,608	7,247	15,485	4,270	6,310	5,061	6,518	17,285	20,001	3,462	7,614
Congressional District 37	51,035	41,841	12,962	19,557	2,945	7,688	1,998	3,083	3,749	7,256	9,318	13,284	4,300	7,734
Congressional District 38	57,611	49,939	12,533	23,559	3,427	10,609	1,585	3,973	2,906	7,058	7,088	16,107	2,292	7,518
Congressional District 39	66,864	44,998	9,409	18,489	2,207	7,942	1,334	3,561	1,968	6,228	6,006	12,534	1,519	7,272
Congressional District 40	41,345	26,078	10,800	13,305	2,397	5,186	1,414	3,112	2,352	4,980	6,693	8,803	3,003	5,782
Congressional District 41	45,180	28,355	11,464	14,678	3,785	7,408	1,549	2,945	3,785	4,587	7,348	10,012	3,612	5,526
Congressional District 42	54,166	45,344	13,315	24,203	4,858	11,179	2,307	3,769	2,794	7,203	7,877	16,607	1,992	8,664
Congressional District 43	55,156	37,388	13,322	17,883	3,195	6,464	2,628	4,282	2,158	5,329	8,445	11,991	3,128	5,055
Congressional District 44	45,709	29,615	12,189	14,408	2,771	4,834	2,174	2,115	3,025	3,946	8,253	9,743	3,752	5,805
Congressional District 45	70,097	52,726	9,915	22,222	2,994	9,266	1,888	4,035	1,885	7,038	4,953	14,339	1,686	8,550
Congressional District 46	44,165	30,425	9,303	14,328	2,677	6,275	1,654	2,483	2,215	4,495	5,428	10,376	2,003	6,389
Congressional District 47	52,449	38,806	10,439	17,506	3,263	7,143	1,570	3,351	2,044	5,976	6,730	11,928	1,586	5,139
Congressional District 48	70,129	57,645	11,031	25,044	2,895	10,766	1,418	5,245	2,183	9,338	5,682	15,720	2,942	8,732
Congressional District 49	68,705	54,124	14,314	23,710	6,834	10,086	1,995	4,458	2,971	7,845	8,978	15,341	3,002	6,360
Congressional District 50	63,969	48,239	12,716	23,000	5,050	11,991	1,843	3,918	2,515	6,913	7,806	14,979	2,637	7,266

Table H-5: 116th Congressional Districts - Disability Status and Type of Disability—*Continued*

	Total Population		With a Disability		With a Hearing Disability		With a Vision Disability		With a Cognitive Disability		With an Ambulatory Disability		With a Self-Care Disability	
	65 to 74 Years	75 Years and Over	65 to 74 Years	75 Years and Over	65 to 74 Years	75 Years and Over	65 to 74 Years	75 Years and Over	65 to 74 Years	75 Years and Over	65 to 74 Years	75 Years and Over	65 to 74 Years	75 Years and Over
California—Cont.														
Congressional District 51	50,610	37,762	14,395	22,406	4,064	8,002	4,244	4,885	4,471	7,594	9,789	15,938	4,264	8,021
Congressional District 52	66,351	46,269	12,028	20,350	3,699	9,502	1,551	3,715	3,415	6,501	6,556	13,934	2,075	6,675
Congressional District 53	59,735	39,735	13,094	19,676	4,317	7,472	2,179	3,193	2,847	6,479	7,875	13,467	2,406	7,907
Colorado														
Congressional District 1	62,467	38,527	12,903	17,407	4,913	7,535	2,068	3,096	2,143	3,425	6,358	9,979	1,433	3,844
Congressional District 2	78,696	43,393	12,945	17,075	7,142	9,995	1,761	3,004	1,967	3,545	5,407	8,125	715	2,451
Congressional District 3	85,111	55,075	20,031	26,773	10,369	13,908	3,138	5,438	3,466	7,162	10,095	17,698	2,476	6,868
Congressional District 4	72,033	44,770	16,389	21,422	6,597	10,901	1,710	3,463	2,953	4,475	9,429	14,045	1,642	3,813
Congressional District 5	72,699	42,614	17,145	19,156	7,437	8,985	3,057	4,491	3,448	4,777	10,244	11,126	2,126	4,058
Congressional District 6	64,394	36,788	11,741	17,075	4,988	7,951	1,989	2,971	2,298	4,015	6,908	10,317	2,139	3,677
Congressional District 7	67,018	44,270	15,869	20,782	6,946	11,227	2,125	4,188	2,510	5,620	8,674	12,369	1,848	5,039
Connecticut														
Congressional District 1	68,742	56,110	13,533	24,209	3,440	11,075	1,861	4,249	3,287	7,551	8,424	15,706	1,617	7,921
Congressional District 2	73,100	52,955	14,957	22,320	5,948	11,280	1,934	4,184	2,431	6,387	8,285	12,501	2,509	5,101
Congressional District 3	70,713	54,167	14,808	22,435	5,176	8,963	1,720	4,348	3,446	5,916	8,671	14,788	1,895	7,201
Congressional District 4	62,817	52,375	9,628	20,375	2,503	8,982	2,274	2,969	2,096	5,371	5,691	13,965	1,703	5,665
Congressional District 5	67,688	54,480	11,938	20,008	4,433	9,221	1,939	3,573	2,151	5,622	7,205	12,685	1,817	5,527
Delaware														
Congressional District (at Large)	107,895	72,861	24,856	29,771	9,434	11,382	2,929	4,140	4,959	7,488	14,403	18,699	2,337	6,754
District of Columbia														
Delegate District (at Large)	48,833	36,793	12,240	17,825	2,146	5,210	2,621	3,484	3,732	5,644	7,809	12,896	2,533	4,751
Florida														
Congressional District 1	79,700	52,705	22,154	24,620	8,177	10,707	4,479	3,691	4,785	5,792	13,422	16,130	3,013	6,271
Congressional District 2	86,744	61,710	26,189	33,037	9,021	15,780	5,182	6,688	5,630	9,617	15,904	21,381	4,352	7,666
Congressional District 3	79,959	48,249	19,598	21,955	7,323	10,474	2,550	3,751	4,674	4,730	12,017	14,446	2,088	4,582
Congressional District 4	82,120	55,110	15,354	24,926	4,465	11,061	3,561	4,255	2,620	6,009	9,566	16,367	2,412	5,568
Congressional District 5	62,313	35,952	21,259	17,250	6,115	6,186	4,458	4,369	5,403	5,629	13,114	11,700	2,150	4,202
Congressional District 6	113,662	86,644	26,891	42,403	10,278	23,366	5,205	9,948	4,573	13,116	16,067	27,292	3,628	12,425
Congressional District 7	67,128	46,933	14,434	20,922	5,272	8,336	1,986	4,603	3,116	6,404	9,735	14,711	2,374	5,771
Congressional District 8	105,457	90,108	22,875	40,030	9,271	19,490	3,225	6,687	3,564	10,421	12,026	27,258	2,954	10,032
Congressional District 9	82,992	62,583	22,105	33,880	6,783	15,173	5,146	6,922	5,974	10,716	12,824	21,601	3,513	8,234
Congressional District 10	62,987	34,798	16,566	17,469	6,343	6,617	3,489	3,185	3,068	5,064	10,549	12,249	2,474	4,510
Congressional District 11	149,163	132,506	35,369	54,405	15,877	28,848	6,049	9,816	5,742	10,548	19,688	33,880	3,881	9,634
Congressional District 12	106,008	87,957	25,746	38,717	9,179	18,127	4,337	6,714	4,345	8,837	15,213	25,596	3,409	8,973
Congressional District 13	92,263	79,321	22,277	35,331	6,701	15,780	2,851	8,364	3,818	10,253	14,084	22,224	3,563	8,403
Congressional District 14	61,881	42,633	15,562	22,165	4,054	8,731	2,675	4,253	4,163	6,131	10,620	15,867	2,927	7,141
Congressional District 15	78,856	54,093	20,144	24,481	7,809	10,939	4,707	4,947	3,206	5,807	12,882	15,952	4,626	7,118
Congressional District 16	119,548	107,295	21,342	43,569	8,756	20,400	3,180	7,052	3,373	10,268	11,067	27,535	2,259	9,129
Congressional District 17	132,780	123,002	26,719	51,061	10,991	26,732	3,259	7,395	3,839	10,771	15,790	30,283	3,500	10,036
Congressional District 18	103,496	97,927	18,598	39,803	5,734	16,710	2,455	9,692	2,684	10,065	12,505	25,696	1,927	7,743
Congressional District 19	138,741	125,897	22,890	46,916	9,471	24,494	3,448	7,265	4,326	12,660	11,814	28,400	4,483	12,385
Congressional District 20	60,094	48,805	15,174	25,651	2,562	10,515	3,914	6,471	3,591	10,217	10,289	17,484	2,948	9,293
Congressional District 21	95,386	106,115	18,214	42,957	6,232	19,153	2,348	7,820	4,006	10,720	10,649	29,515	2,508	11,166
Congressional District 22	86,953	78,615	15,158	33,172	3,844	15,252	2,666	6,700	2,523	9,100	10,140	22,938	2,808	9,675
Congressional District 23	78,089	59,746	15,133	24,887	5,551	9,665	1,719	4,938	3,325	8,315	7,958	17,505	2,682	8,670
Congressional District 24	63,303	44,668	15,935	20,978	3,241	4,767	3,924	4,928	3,968	7,481	9,804	15,863	3,444	8,197
Congressional District 25	75,741	71,895	16,254	33,359	3,926	13,841	2,864	8,671	6,662	12,261	8,501	22,503	2,253	11,441
Congressional District 26	65,787	51,662	11,895	21,865	3,457	7,660	2,571	4,681	3,168	8,446	6,222	15,397	1,609	8,805
Congressional District 27	73,083	67,621	12,508	33,306	2,573	9,032	1,660	5,961	3,057	12,087	7,565	23,903	1,819	13,136
Georgia														
Congressional District 1	66,884	42,331	16,022	21,961	6,634	11,090	1,764	3,946	3,022	5,884	9,031	13,703	1,985	4,942
Congressional District 2	62,855	42,648	19,733	20,388	6,805	8,763	4,280	3,806	6,060	6,310	13,333	12,318	4,408	4,423
Congressional District 3	70,796	44,070	20,326	19,186	7,890	8,395	3,185	3,225	4,499	5,099	12,354	12,389	2,296	3,102
Congressional District 4	64,665	30,992	14,988	12,618	4,789	5,928	2,443	1,853	3,954	4,057	9,122	9,198	1,986	3,922
Congressional District 5	52,358	34,337	14,074	16,400	2,109	4,625	2,705	3,041	2,900	4,095	9,537	11,591	2,374	5,045
Congressional District 6	61,523	37,328	10,326	13,754	3,943	7,345	1,830	2,859	1,508	2,683	5,544	8,650	1,078	3,937
Congressional District 7	52,756	31,951	8,320	13,358	2,621	5,779	1,589	2,556	2,048	3,668	4,740	9,091	1,334	3,075
Congressional District 8	65,682	43,641	19,322	20,169	7,196	9,640	4,065	4,593	3,230	4,343	11,636	12,959	3,324	5,501
Congressional District 9	86,238	56,528	24,663	27,526	10,099	12,461	4,837	6,011	5,556	7,782	14,530	18,172	3,717	5,381
Congressional District 10	67,873	43,108	18,295	17,809	6,229	9,453	2,516	2,752	3,650	4,046	11,905	11,053	1,446	4,003
Congressional District 11	61,844	40,340	13,325	17,835	4,913	8,315	2,358	4,494	2,691	4,629	9,204	11,921	1,624	5,071
Congressional District 12	63,029	39,865	18,506	18,424	7,040	8,238	4,348	4,818	3,860	5,214	10,501	12,102	2,994	5,064
Congressional District 13	56,640	28,886	14,850	15,294	4,131	6,599	2,195	3,641	2,100	4,975	10,203	9,893	2,899	4,430
Congressional District 14	63,805	43,455	16,951	20,426	7,177	9,064	3,109	4,304	4,348	6,721	10,734	14,438	3,172	6,553
Hawaii														
Congressional District 1	71,603	61,367	13,265	27,997	5,271	13,131	2,514	4,482	3,344	10,416	6,704	17,804	1,451	7,895
Congressional District 2	77,769	50,728	17,127	23,258	6,274	11,670	3,470	2,869	3,548	7,729	9,255	14,117	3,734	5,117
Idaho														
Congressional District 1	94,659	60,839	24,028	27,468	12,586	15,260	2,975	4,370	3,891	7,578	10,770	15,257	2,695	6,031
Congressional District 2	73,738	50,205	18,358	27,109	9,104	14,422	3,011	6,696	4,310	8,066	9,547	16,430	3,275	6,908
Illinois														
Congressional District 1	61,962	50,899	18,603	22,042	3,547	6,743	5,776	5,366	3,437	5,273	12,428	16,483	3,888	6,947
Congressional District 2	62,389	48,770	14,828	21,519	3,260	6,356	3,150	3,234	2,781	5,880	10,054	14,657	2,905	6,291

Table H-5: 116th Congressional Districts - Disability Status and Type of Disability—*Continued*

	Total Population		With a Disability		With a Hearing Disability		With a Vision Disability		With a Cognitive Disability		With an Ambulatory Disability		With a Self-Care Disability	
	65 to 74 Years	75 Years and Over	65 to 74 Years	75 Years and Over	65 to 74 Years	75 Years and Over	65 to 74 Years	75 Years and Over	65 to 74 Years	75 Years and Over	65 to 74 Years	75 Years and Over	65 to 74 Years	75 Years and Over
Illinois—Cont.														
Congressional District 3	60,796	47,372	13,716	19,151	5,094	7,492	2,341	3,421	2,866	4,874	7,956	12,793	3,005	6,211
Congressional District 4	45,322	26,469	9,399	10,133	2,817	3,801	1,944	1,866	2,374	2,754	5,998	6,808	2,045	2,800
Congressional District 5	54,987	40,759	9,682	15,604	2,932	7,229	1,923	3,676	1,810	4,994	6,028	11,068	1,625	4,741
Congressional District 6	69,608	49,596	10,672	19,881	3,528	9,028	1,189	4,036	920	4,044	6,143	12,402	1,766	5,563
Congressional District 7	59,635	36,879	17,955	15,677	2,856	4,564	4,763	3,664	5,834	4,959	12,928	11,635	4,735	4,874
Congressional District 8	59,241	38,377	11,968	16,199	3,234	7,615	1,454	2,271	2,507	4,249	7,220	9,293	2,397	5,081
Congressional District 9	69,562	56,775	12,536	22,995	3,792	10,255	1,878	5,233	2,430	5,381	7,725	15,712	2,727	7,369
Congressional District 10	62,575	47,319	11,371	19,591	3,526	7,046	1,486	3,377	2,821	4,580	6,908	13,399	2,128	4,553
Congressional District 11	55,077	35,056	10,320	13,528	2,810	5,438	1,055	2,250	1,942	3,003	6,564	9,014	1,822	4,305
Congressional District 12	68,412	49,556	20,039	25,754	7,324	12,414	4,040	5,053	3,750	6,614	12,657	17,325	3,094	6,103
Congressional District 13	63,231	48,265	13,525	20,531	5,233	9,928	2,714	3,077	2,198	3,341	8,492	13,633	1,964	4,323
Congressional District 14	61,606	41,141	9,347	16,840	4,986	7,160	2,094	3,214	1,667	3,610	4,598	10,520	1,609	4,113
Congressional District 15	72,851	61,079	20,675	28,543	8,810	13,323	2,735	5,302	3,577	7,146	11,912	18,999	2,950	7,129
Congressional District 16	71,436	53,154	17,179	20,863	6,934	9,497	1,795	3,099	3,165	4,370	10,118	12,528	2,934	4,569
Congressional District 17	71,399	55,489	19,044	24,306	7,798	11,435	2,592	3,479	3,320	5,478	10,648	16,341	2,750	3,869
Congressional District 18	73,240	60,264	16,317	25,759	7,131	12,522	1,921	4,691	2,588	5,479	9,271	16,308	3,143	5,737
Indiana														
Congressional District 1	69,648	48,815	17,535	22,454	5,799	10,642	2,911	3,004	2,934	6,499	11,012	14,358	2,606	6,298
Congressional District 2	67,908	50,909	16,540	23,578	6,666	10,643	2,957	5,501	3,319	5,486	9,471	15,112	2,047	5,460
Congressional District 3	68,333	47,440	15,544	19,886	6,466	8,494	1,910	3,610	4,066	4,064	9,833	13,120	2,636	3,822
Congressional District 4	68,998	49,002	18,914	22,343	8,259	10,553	3,643	4,524	3,949	5,884	11,179	14,619	2,576	4,698
Congressional District 5	67,210	49,189	14,175	22,047	5,257	10,015	1,632	3,085	1,828	4,824	8,563	13,836	1,129	5,660
Congressional District 6	73,298	54,121	20,457	23,179	8,589	10,915	3,201	4,976	4,777	5,646	11,853	16,157	3,131	6,481
Congressional District 7	55,358	36,914	15,274	19,095	4,965	7,982	2,397	4,758	2,946	4,892	9,737	14,113	3,339	6,117
Congressional District 8	71,499	53,161	19,901	23,497	8,808	10,888	4,310	4,072	3,242	5,813	11,770	15,650	2,667	4,391
Congressional District 9	71,447	47,896	18,683	21,714	8,396	10,529	2,207	3,553	3,230	5,699	10,271	13,855	2,325	5,278
Iowa														
Congressional District 1	76,879	62,341	15,890	26,248	6,285	14,844	1,544	4,677	3,203	5,091	8,371	13,990	2,412	4,864
Congressional District 2	75,926	58,500	15,983	23,161	7,395	10,833	2,676	4,027	3,305	4,697	8,954	15,070	2,520	6,089
Congressional District 3	72,247	51,110	15,309	21,790	6,646	10,317	1,651	4,310	2,100	4,046	8,766	11,731	1,715	3,728
Congressional District 4	74,281	66,534	15,637	26,408	6,569	14,062	2,556	4,038	2,920	6,227	8,303	15,766	2,572	5,753
Kansas														
Congressional District 1	62,670	53,240	17,572	24,896	8,617	11,596	2,889	4,203	3,376	4,748	9,278	16,871	1,907	4,455
Congressional District 2	70,020	53,064	18,364	25,529	9,308	14,061	2,778	4,759	3,517	6,112	10,616	13,802	2,457	5,831
Congressional District 3	66,083	42,701	16,096	18,948	5,931	9,462	2,196	3,571	3,102	5,004	9,104	11,709	2,853	4,382
Congressional District 4	65,277	49,136	17,045	23,549	6,243	11,373	2,144	4,596	3,776	6,895	10,278	16,378	3,105	5,693
Kentucky														
Congressional District 1	76,178	57,055	24,218	24,374	10,093	11,694	4,913	4,563	4,054	5,894	13,980	15,273	3,702	6,262
Congressional District 2	73,741	50,327	23,276	24,614	8,689	12,586	4,425	4,611	4,271	7,445	14,783	16,477	3,842	6,932
Congressional District 3	70,359	50,114	18,639	23,664	5,147	9,535	2,636	4,159	4,117	7,186	12,866	16,310	3,545	5,869
Congressional District 4	71,884	45,022	18,819	20,597	7,265	10,238	3,796	3,999	3,620	6,033	11,544	12,994	3,544	5,745
Congressional District 5	73,947	48,012	32,220	27,494	13,195	15,999	6,727	7,686	9,244	9,406	19,879	20,494	4,839	10,905
Congressional District 6	69,356	45,397	21,467	22,388	6,766	11,062	3,892	4,323	4,982	6,663	14,279	14,768	3,582	5,423
Louisiana														
Congressional District 1	79,493	50,702	20,995	24,367	8,668	10,892	3,847	4,601	4,853	7,112	12,863	15,767	3,686	5,486
Congressional District 2	72,337	43,205	21,854	22,318	5,574	8,139	6,137	6,307	5,050	5,490	14,524	14,878	4,687	5,471
Congressional District 3	68,598	46,624	19,195	24,774	5,603	10,570	4,259	6,450	3,515	7,228	12,856	15,974	4,578	7,058
Congressional District 4	72,617	49,975	21,942	24,916	8,655	11,145	3,441	5,010	4,039	6,018	14,227	16,503	4,274	7,479
Congressional District 5	73,054	48,202	22,327	21,206	7,183	10,259	4,696	4,383	4,979	6,047	14,229	14,960	4,753	6,041
Congressional District 6	68,798	47,005	18,838	22,789	7,634	10,877	3,399	4,938	3,315	6,788	11,347	14,438	3,027	7,728
Maine														
Congressional District 1	81,458	57,468	16,016	24,383	5,903	14,002	2,567	4,208	3,951	5,851	8,887	13,254	1,876	4,244
Congressional District 2	82,495	54,648	22,904	27,055	10,511	14,698	3,291	3,677	4,788	6,756	12,951	16,391	3,183	5,596
Maryland														
Congressional District 1	80,896	58,088	15,962	25,373	5,822	11,843	2,277	4,325	2,555	6,842	9,427	16,333	1,968	5,898
Congressional District 2	66,110	43,496	15,112	19,284	4,748	7,161	2,418	3,924	2,277	6,628	9,906	12,887	2,158	5,532
Congressional District 3	64,569	50,925	14,460	20,429	5,371	9,579	2,196	3,136	3,094	5,882	8,830	12,750	2,143	5,762
Congressional District 4	63,977	39,216	13,398	14,825	3,335	5,855	2,314	2,049	3,362	4,325	8,649	8,981	2,537	4,791
Congressional District 5	64,453	41,281	12,526	18,504	4,107	8,065	2,091	3,288	3,364	5,326	8,102	12,533	2,685	5,535
Congressional District 6	68,209	50,539	14,483	23,313	4,900	10,521	1,821	3,846	3,050	7,317	8,825	14,194	2,001	5,863
Congressional District 7	65,572	47,429	17,260	21,050	3,854	8,617	2,796	4,230	4,040	5,837	11,335	14,011	3,491	5,798
Congressional District 8	72,656	53,625	11,944	21,237	4,630	8,479	1,620	4,324	2,297	5,518	6,023	13,661	1,005	6,948
Massachusetts														
Congressional District 1	75,847	56,306	18,035	25,467	5,457	11,540	3,106	3,565	4,507	6,232	9,737	16,285	3,040	7,146
Congressional District 2	73,750	47,950	13,502	20,794	5,946	8,591	1,377	3,655	2,579	5,694	7,248	13,810	2,292	5,778
Congressional District 3	61,202	44,325	12,723	19,117	4,307	8,952	2,765	3,985	2,746	4,895	7,598	10,982	3,188	6,095
Congressional District 4	74,265	53,471	14,440	24,516	6,570	11,544	2,731	4,079	2,076	5,321	7,800	15,677	2,691	6,226
Congressional District 5	71,140	54,237	12,913	20,771	5,113	8,644	1,568	2,744	2,759	4,945	7,359	11,653	1,500	4,267
Congressional District 6	83,293	62,903	15,417	27,840	5,342	12,049	1,245	4,789	2,059	7,126	9,187	17,432	1,471	8,491
Congressional District 7	51,028	38,321	16,188	19,945	4,518	7,035	2,506	5,421	4,276	6,306	11,128	14,224	2,348	7,401
Congressional District 8	69,795	54,876	14,668	23,288	4,856	8,757	2,605	2,922	3,174	5,966	7,700	15,871	2,665	6,815
Congressional District 9	96,226	68,606	18,128	26,362	7,545	13,337	2,038	4,697	4,643	7,863	9,285	16,497	3,052	7,903

Table H-5: 116th Congressional Districts - Disability Status and Type of Disability—Continued

	Total Population		With a Disability		With a Hearing Disability		With a Vision Disability		With a Cognitive Disability		With an Ambulatory Disability		With a Self-Care Disability	
	65 to 74 Years	75 Years and Over	65 to 74 Years	75 Years and Over	65 to 74 Years	75 Years and Over	65 to 74 Years	75 Years and Over	65 to 74 Years	75 Years and Over	65 to 74 Years	75 Years and Over	65 to 74 Years	75 Years and Over
Michigan														
Congressional District 1	94,871	68,604	22,752	28,192	10,687	16,328	2,836	5,409	3,672	7,105	12,033	15,861	3,327	5,801
Congressional District 2	69,962	49,625	15,178	21,494	5,760	9,187	1,998	2,916	2,968	6,012	9,211	11,889	2,139	5,309
Congressional District 3	65,935	46,856	14,846	20,589	7,302	9,635	1,969	2,708	2,338	4,874	7,621	11,912	2,032	5,052
Congressional District 4	79,615	57,862	21,012	26,457	8,742	12,703	2,124	3,696	4,384	6,721	11,409	16,457	3,188	5,359
Congressional District 5	71,884	52,666	18,902	23,933	6,581	11,224	2,638	3,655	4,712	6,530	12,795	14,319	4,189	6,211
Congressional District 6	74,240	50,615	17,520	21,455	7,313	10,167	2,709	3,112	2,942	5,234	9,989	12,501	2,742	5,466
Congressional District 7	77,694	52,929	18,520	23,553	7,318	11,932	1,967	4,815	3,261	5,947	11,898	12,681	2,592	5,678
Congressional District 8	69,441	43,195	13,866	19,458	6,083	9,450	2,443	2,767	2,331	4,809	8,151	12,774	1,669	4,908
Congressional District 9	66,473	52,880	16,397	23,343	5,295	10,500	3,140	4,169	3,345	5,195	10,567	15,491	3,746	5,900
Congressional District 10	78,950	53,603	23,707	25,024	8,791	11,722	3,351	3,100	4,297	7,479	14,922	16,028	3,822	6,522
Congressional District 11	74,295	49,208	16,109	22,236	6,972	11,026	2,177	3,600	3,215	5,302	8,697	14,330	2,203	5,466
Congressional District 12	60,846	43,130	14,018	19,882	4,690	9,304	2,138	3,349	2,333	5,482	9,010	13,099	2,929	5,049
Congressional District 13	56,912	40,353	20,249	21,158	5,512	7,487	4,742	5,449	5,452	6,803	14,285	15,643	5,110	7,925
Congressional District 14	68,068	49,741	19,058	23,669	5,627	9,143	3,894	4,597	4,547	9,077	12,879	17,681	4,265	8,539
Minnesota														
Congressional District 1	63,507	54,066	12,916	21,549	5,598	11,201	1,902	3,356	2,287	3,966	6,336	13,597	1,697	4,816
Congressional District 2	58,069	41,024	10,932	18,331	4,533	8,346	1,746	3,295	1,834	3,582	5,581	11,313	1,736	3,508
Congressional District 3	67,279	47,404	11,447	17,832	4,988	6,786	941	3,324	1,787	3,688	5,460	10,136	2,275	3,436
Congressional District 4	62,116	42,521	11,897	17,093	3,834	7,269	975	2,513	3,187	4,266	6,885	10,103	2,007	4,998
Congressional District 5	52,621	38,451	14,336	16,305	4,564	7,437	2,718	2,058	3,571	3,202	9,075	10,561	2,931	3,127
Congressional District 6	57,873	36,204	12,920	16,879	6,694	8,186	1,034	2,512	2,432	3,233	6,683	8,903	2,054	2,570
Congressional District 7	69,761	60,478	14,428	25,679	6,517	14,451	2,091	4,649	3,139	4,440	7,826	15,689	2,711	4,817
Congressional District 8	79,260	58,000	17,836	24,428	8,019	12,991	2,675	4,241	2,619	5,407	7,831	14,751	2,091	5,394
Mississippi														
Congressional District 1	71,780	49,767	21,402	24,741	7,454	11,587	5,480	5,544	4,283	7,444	13,359	16,865	3,590	8,321
Congressional District 2	66,377	40,374	20,267	20,756	4,832	8,330	4,705	5,354	4,359	7,001	14,381	14,704	2,966	7,390
Congressional District 3	72,563	50,324	19,313	25,016	7,186	9,879	3,519	6,340	4,461	6,351	12,300	17,027	3,147	6,905
Congressional District 4	73,636	49,602	24,524	26,713	7,313	11,995	5,084	6,445	5,262	8,150	16,118	19,620	3,796	7,031
Missouri														
Congressional District 1	62,730	43,846	17,825	19,239	4,289	6,927	3,307	4,523	3,434	5,187	13,250	14,520	3,528	5,924
Congressional District 2	79,027	64,803	14,359	26,770	5,644	11,480	2,097	3,536	2,377	5,432	7,285	17,146	1,597	5,728
Congressional District 3	76,191	51,813	19,718	21,776	8,455	10,717	3,124	3,930	2,820	6,323	11,331	15,126	2,953	4,732
Congressional District 4	75,532	54,866	22,455	25,561	8,542	13,974	3,287	3,587	4,733	6,361	14,497	15,471	4,376	4,339
Congressional District 5	68,162	51,536	17,925	21,993	5,871	9,689	3,351	3,828	3,459	5,062	11,634	14,964	2,029	4,966
Congressional District 6	75,412	53,122	19,365	23,865	7,606	12,397	2,465	5,288	3,352	6,210	11,259	15,760	3,419	6,230
Congressional District 7	79,296	59,016	25,015	26,738	10,721	12,955	6,688	4,571	8,432	6,004	16,441	14,955	6,419	5,143
Congressional District 8	80,273	59,449	30,466	30,583	13,536	15,179	5,277	5,953	8,247	7,663	18,017	19,318	5,779	6,478
Montana														
Congressional District (at Large)	121,055	79,184	28,424	33,891	13,185	18,094	4,156	5,618	5,086	8,795	14,848	18,579	3,432	6,978
Nebraska														
Congressional District 1	57,023	42,074	12,552	19,878	5,292	8,985	1,505	2,858	1,980	4,622	7,444	11,857	1,455	4,548
Congressional District 2	52,059	33,982	10,367	15,018	3,850	7,404	2,151	3,235	1,852	3,896	6,285	10,006	1,615	3,220
Congressional District 3	63,771	55,089	16,295	24,503	7,729	13,011	2,638	4,600	2,413	4,589	8,008	14,928	2,142	4,966
Nevada														
Congressional District 1	60,728	38,933	18,263	19,631	5,712	9,907	4,795	4,067	5,163	5,861	12,823	14,794	3,753	6,109
Congressional District 2	78,335	47,745	17,615	22,294	7,616	10,791	3,436	4,383	3,065	5,969	10,410	14,308	2,776	5,430
Congressional District 3	80,809	52,930	17,287	22,006	7,678	11,485	3,234	4,970	2,851	5,371	10,494	13,617	2,963	6,593
Congressional District 4	72,124	43,516	19,920	21,162	7,182	8,980	3,088	5,125	3,818	6,212	12,140	13,737	3,044	5,898
New Hampshire														
Congressional District 1	72,610	47,753	14,743	22,051	6,081	11,553	1,949	3,378	2,582	5,450	8,206	12,946	1,789	4,845
Congressional District 2	73,989	50,804	16,017	19,502	7,052	10,693	2,398	3,278	2,927	3,789	8,054	9,981	2,526	3,993
New Jersey														
Congressional District 1	66,499	47,226	17,770	21,485	6,822	9,511	2,945	3,643	3,762	6,387	12,052	14,782	4,211	4,985
Congressional District 2	78,580	58,254	19,615	22,559	5,917	8,079	3,149	3,033	4,276	4,418	13,560	15,774	3,632	5,043
Congressional District 3	79,566	63,265	15,872	28,240	5,364	11,746	2,621	4,178	2,217	7,444	9,523	19,380	2,238	7,526
Congressional District 4	80,836	66,315	14,283	26,477	4,418	10,448	2,576	4,300	2,246	5,630	9,468	18,389	2,212	6,148
Congressional District 5	74,498	56,732	11,032	20,964	3,160	9,647	1,345	3,840	2,521	5,080	7,037	13,105	1,833	6,111
Congressional District 6	60,050	44,950	12,270	19,650	3,140	8,495	2,552	3,055	2,981	4,428	8,385	12,364	1,782	4,757
Congressional District 7	68,034	52,500	10,003	20,475	3,566	9,339	1,336	3,445	1,954	6,036	5,597	13,412	1,751	6,771
Congressional District 8	47,023	35,369	9,186	15,203	2,451	5,592	1,666	3,505	2,003	4,493	5,720	10,240	2,548	5,771
Congressional District 9	61,877	49,103	14,675	22,561	3,751	8,639	2,315	5,470	2,784	9,061	10,413	17,878	4,072	9,560
Congressional District 10	56,487	42,374	13,054	19,436	3,163	5,882	2,685	3,249	2,759	5,715	9,854	15,579	3,647	7,247
Congressional District 11	70,582	61,454	9,348	23,376	2,616	10,605	1,433	3,694	2,104	5,594	5,916	13,960	1,623	6,517
Congressional District 12	68,321	48,394	11,231	21,251	3,091	8,271	2,423	4,070	2,011	4,908	6,600	13,627	1,576	5,463
New Mexico														
Congressional District 1	71,704	45,754	18,437	24,442	7,104	11,891	2,382	4,263	3,555	7,665	10,892	15,884	2,206	6,830
Congressional District 2	71,107	51,303	24,144	28,561	10,195	17,092	5,527	7,300	4,621	9,059	15,199	17,299	4,229	7,510
Congressional District 3	78,398	50,214	21,288	28,271	9,501	14,861	2,002	7,086	4,294	7,985	12,390	17,118	3,726	5,277
New York														
Congressional District 1	73,245	55,759	10,500	21,364	3,186	8,869	1,437	3,450	2,635	5,038	5,955	13,618	2,076	5,780
Congressional District 2	62,080	46,905	12,621	18,501	4,334	7,899	2,142	2,848	2,285	5,471	7,891	12,394	2,322	6,168

Table H-5: 116th Congressional Districts - Disability Status and Type of Disability—*Continued*

	Total Population		With a Disability		With a Hearing Disability		With a Vision Disability		With a Cognitive Disability		With an Ambulatory Disability		With a Self-Care Disability	
	65 to 74 Years	75 Years and Over	65 to 74 Years	75 Years and Over	65 to 74 Years	75 Years and Over	65 to 74 Years	75 Years and Over	65 to 74 Years	75 Years and Over	65 to 74 Years	75 Years and Over	65 to 74 Years	75 Years and Over
New York—Cont.														
Congressional District 3	77,149	69,471	9,812	24,908	3,495	10,027	2,039	4,588	1,631	5,701	5,181	17,913	1,893	7,778
Congressional District 4	70,043	55,349	9,721	20,870	2,342	7,804	802	2,519	1,484	6,674	6,289	14,401	1,624	6,697
Congressional District 5	63,866	46,781	13,716	20,444	2,709	4,922	2,772	3,797	2,172	7,271	10,350	15,281	2,749	8,846
Congressional District 6	74,266	56,020	12,040	23,761	2,715	8,034	2,066	4,294	2,452	7,505	7,427	17,625	2,957	9,256
Congressional District 7	49,307	35,674	10,283	16,417	1,878	4,731	2,001	3,045	2,042	6,457	7,228	12,623	2,168	5,371
Congressional District 8	65,592	53,237	16,325	27,191	2,892	7,198	2,945	4,361	2,753	8,202	12,757	19,615	3,011	11,019
Congressional District 9	64,258	45,801	16,003	19,281	2,998	5,875	3,752	4,982	4,524	7,099	11,260	16,131	3,366	8,213
Congressional District 10	63,893	50,266	12,366	23,753	2,693	9,424	1,678	4,389	2,207	6,737	8,209	17,172	2,332	9,175
Congressional District 11	70,882	52,695	14,990	24,027	3,714	8,007	2,222	4,361	3,738	6,509	10,383	19,032	3,384	10,327
Congressional District 12	58,321	51,887	8,443	17,900	2,238	6,960	1,923	4,252	1,170	5,779	5,648	13,307	1,517	5,098
Congressional District 13	56,941	44,697	18,254	25,287	1,540	5,101	3,439	5,052	4,677	8,780	15,055	19,584	5,757	9,310
Congressional District 14	51,509	42,946	12,085	17,218	3,359	5,611	2,768	3,858	2,548	5,348	8,333	12,517	1,823	6,941
Congressional District 15	47,167	33,174	15,803	17,296	2,184	3,549	4,613	4,687	4,443	7,019	11,109	12,841	3,461	7,573
Congressional District 16	64,957	62,845	14,580	29,788	2,832	9,251	3,405	7,334	2,955	9,105	9,660	22,546	2,433	10,545
Congressional District 17	68,884	55,254	10,499	20,048	3,185	8,928	1,596	2,063	2,098	5,037	5,311	11,564	1,673	6,654
Congressional District 18	66,033	44,783	13,014	17,995	4,631	8,696	2,174	2,636	2,240	4,904	8,103	11,758	2,163	4,869
Congressional District 19	83,822	60,297	19,020	28,746	8,229	13,461	3,587	4,120	2,896	7,494	10,256	16,889	2,667	7,849
Congressional District 20	70,400	52,908	14,728	20,517	4,783	8,001	2,552	3,674	3,227	4,758	7,553	12,908	1,951	4,094
Congressional District 21	74,202	51,685	17,711	23,761	6,253	11,985	3,036	4,846	3,650	5,902	10,566	14,985	2,747	5,756
Congressional District 22	72,755	57,742	16,867	24,451	6,765	11,706	2,216	3,906	3,540	5,851	9,119	14,519	3,388	6,352
Congressional District 23	75,595	54,917	17,764	23,708	6,983	12,690	2,379	3,876	3,429	6,073	9,730	13,911	2,400	5,684
Congressional District 24	69,440	52,721	15,424	23,517	5,682	12,018	2,423	4,656	3,314	6,564	9,225	14,720	2,779	5,632
Congressional District 25	70,300	52,990	14,205	21,995	3,851	8,773	1,654	3,155	2,985	4,755	8,235	15,187	1,918	5,308
Congressional District 26	68,441	54,810	16,851	23,633	4,853	10,535	3,040	3,794	3,957	5,967	10,586	14,375	3,077	5,854
Congressional District 27	78,247	58,856	17,231	25,781	7,050	13,088	2,213	5,085	3,350	6,009	10,321	15,405	2,432	6,182
North Carolina														
Congressional District 1	76,177	49,904	20,734	23,361	5,939	9,666	4,081	3,373	4,866	6,696	13,743	15,458	4,721	7,042
Congressional District 2	75,142	42,462	18,293	19,048	7,356	8,728	3,240	2,747	4,055	4,764	10,142	11,805	3,354	4,430
Congressional District 3	78,131	54,003	19,776	28,155	8,311	13,215	2,691	4,424	3,810	7,655	10,938	18,289	3,089	6,019
Congressional District 4	63,100	39,009	13,945	15,376	4,914	5,773	2,190	3,010	2,796	4,291	7,422	10,892	1,328	3,613
Congressional District 5	81,021	57,943	21,220	25,771	7,686	11,942	3,849	4,293	4,749	6,803	12,724	16,036	2,453	6,270
Congressional District 6	79,442	56,689	19,592	25,914	7,654	11,744	3,797	6,431	4,674	8,461	10,251	15,720	2,632	5,786
Congressional District 7	99,745	60,912	22,948	29,585	8,378	13,887	4,539	4,928	5,261	8,197	15,017	18,876	4,434	6,969
Congressional District 8	70,963	48,624	21,550	21,779	7,922	9,819	4,256	5,393	4,716	7,747	14,396	13,301	2,856	6,212
Congressional District 9	73,951	48,604	19,709	23,064	7,176	9,720	2,893	4,048	4,316	7,485	12,717	15,926	4,242	5,476
Congressional District 10	83,669	57,234	21,724	24,497	8,525	12,054	3,265	4,949	4,294	5,771	12,381	14,685	3,428	5,354
Congressional District 11	100,196	73,736	26,354	33,832	11,122	18,334	4,737	8,126	5,745	8,137	14,213	20,009	4,589	6,772
Congressional District 12	55,369	31,770	11,473	13,681	3,877	6,049	1,848	3,333	1,932	4,370	6,440	8,372	2,102	3,346
Congressional District 13	77,090	53,688	19,566	25,345	6,847	11,636	2,541	3,627	4,455	6,800	12,512	16,928	3,335	7,388
North Dakota														
Congressional District (at Large)	64,047	52,386	14,008	22,824	6,842	12,223	2,553	5,459	2,355	4,561	7,355	15,552	1,479	3,965
Ohio														
Congressional District 1	66,712	45,205	16,466	19,241	6,302	8,365	2,702	3,363	3,155	5,847	9,967	12,825	2,517	5,099
Congressional District 2	68,183	51,344	16,099	22,408	6,753	10,102	2,390	5,652	3,372	6,502	9,189	13,948	2,614	7,226
Congressional District 3	51,401	32,604	15,140	15,080	4,596	6,103	2,897	2,645	3,354	4,457	10,289	9,654	2,746	4,149
Congressional District 4	72,820	50,632	17,102	22,690	5,708	11,655	2,418	3,767	3,330	4,564	9,469	14,215	2,855	4,401
Congressional District 5	74,352	56,160	17,619	23,851	6,249	12,682	2,831	4,246	3,331	5,733	9,727	14,451	2,690	5,060
Congressional District 6	80,414	58,618	23,056	27,346	9,900	12,556	4,369	5,185	4,239	8,558	13,310	18,520	3,361	7,492
Congressional District 7	77,024	58,042	17,270	25,815	6,396	11,055	2,058	5,555	3,852	7,167	9,846	17,058	2,749	5,228
Congressional District 8	71,396	52,034	18,799	23,540	6,940	11,771	3,832	4,603	3,977	5,058	11,710	14,161	4,327	5,138
Congressional District 9	65,615	46,734	19,303	20,481	6,618	7,794	3,422	3,621	4,377	5,294	11,820	13,509	3,698	5,674
Congressional District 10	73,507	55,464	19,180	25,719	5,331	9,694	3,358	4,113	3,927	6,398	11,807	17,760	3,002	5,825
Congressional District 11	67,547	52,331	18,276	23,468	4,175	7,998	3,359	5,565	3,249	6,084	11,767	15,617	3,711	6,038
Congressional District 12	71,527	51,949	15,570	24,837	6,932	11,986	2,550	3,664	3,053	6,775	7,743	15,303	2,528	6,346
Congressional District 13	74,704	57,786	17,283	24,730	5,356	10,025	3,502	4,244	3,509	6,178	10,897	15,641	3,630	5,829
Congressional District 14	84,775	60,773	19,194	25,219	6,610	11,974	3,593	4,993	3,916	5,240	10,847	15,880	2,632	5,602
Congressional District 15	71,775	48,998	17,446	23,048	6,160	10,504	2,513	3,961	3,405	5,135	10,540	15,085	3,075	5,795
Congressional District 16	80,609	65,128	14,655	27,850	5,724	11,713	2,075	4,133	2,889	5,663	8,882	17,385	1,976	5,935
Oklahoma														
Congressional District 1	71,099	48,903	19,269	21,901	8,067	9,813	3,611	4,371	4,300	5,154	12,890	14,553	2,639	5,228
Congressional District 2	80,851	60,690	30,779	33,361	14,914	17,903	6,500	9,319	6,871	9,659	19,247	22,880	4,501	8,406
Congressional District 3	72,903	53,001	23,566	27,723	10,046	14,781	4,464	6,181	4,922	7,038	14,658	17,650	4,739	6,021
Congressional District 4	70,272	47,989	26,135	25,517	10,865	13,222	4,465	4,600	4,566	6,380	17,480	17,033	3,973	4,878
Congressional District 5	66,714	47,179	21,937	25,513	7,753	12,128	4,614	4,986	5,191	7,270	14,106	18,224	3,640	6,647
Oregon														
Congressional District 1	77,678	50,136	17,547	23,100	7,239	11,849	1,598	3,621	3,159	6,684	10,017	14,245	3,398	6,113
Congressional District 2	104,417	69,021	27,161	31,050	12,739	17,572	4,973	6,702	5,246	8,213	14,585	19,190	4,353	8,076
Congressional District 3	72,636	41,615	16,804	19,105	6,029	8,923	3,062	2,659	3,151	4,589	9,757	11,403	2,047	3,559
Congressional District 4	103,155	70,204	26,865	33,285	11,841	18,142	3,668	7,360	5,595	9,489	14,093	19,104	3,789	7,486
Congressional District 5	89,710	61,039	22,740	26,998	8,309	14,583	3,677	4,106	5,311	7,399	15,188	18,091	5,020	5,654
Pennsylvania														
Congressional District 1	74,479	57,472	13,285	22,723	4,787	10,190	1,716	3,101	2,390	4,551	7,745	14,699	2,003	5,692
Congressional District 2	58,143	39,490	21,120	20,077	4,572	7,149	5,073	4,692	7,112	6,279	16,160	16,421	5,682	7,411
Congressional District 3	57,348	44,547	16,891	22,105	2,017	6,203	2,781	3,385	5,028	5,147	13,358	15,534	3,980	5,221

Table H-5: 116th Congressional Districts - Disability Status and Type of Disability—*Continued*

	Total Population		With a Disability		With a Hearing Disability		With a Vision Disability		With a Cognitive Disability		With an Ambulatory Disability		With a Self-Care Disability	
	65 to 74 Years	75 Years and Over	65 to 74 Years	75 Years and Over	65 to 74 Years	75 Years and Over	65 to 74 Years	75 Years and Over	65 to 74 Years	75 Years and Over	65 to 74 Years	75 Years and Over	65 to 74 Years	75 Years and Over
Pennsylvania—Cont.														
Congressional District 4	71,945	57,710	12,460	24,091	3,844	10,635	2,123	3,815	2,189	6,165	6,792	14,195	1,785	6,748
Congressional District 5	62,965	52,215	12,283	21,266	3,909	8,858	1,595	3,842	2,387	6,668	7,996	14,574	1,790	6,231
Congressional District 6	68,599	49,147	12,242	19,999	4,296	10,191	1,626	3,760	2,718	4,363	6,912	12,689	1,297	4,246
Congressional District 7	73,329	57,548	14,876	23,739	4,972	9,438	2,327	4,791	3,200	7,411	9,758	15,178	2,944	5,397
Congressional District 8	76,920	59,389	19,100	26,170	8,080	13,724	2,467	4,797	3,104	5,841	11,316	16,241	3,347	6,503
Congressional District 9	79,594	60,947	18,824	26,717	7,213	11,723	2,749	4,087	3,517	6,872	10,550	17,508	2,582	6,807
Congressional District 10	71,941	54,960	16,562	23,767	5,742	10,134	3,620	4,249	3,772	6,717	9,680	15,558	2,478	5,872
Congressional District 11	74,888	60,603	15,368	24,704	5,855	12,430	2,661	4,152	3,950	6,568	8,030	15,504	2,112	5,461
Congressional District 12	74,623	59,937	17,384	26,652	7,879	13,234	2,466	4,487	2,808	6,682	9,667	16,203	2,591	5,385
Congressional District 13	80,268	63,500	19,369	26,598	8,679	13,997	2,878	4,488	3,785	6,900	10,402	14,971	2,134	4,802
Congressional District 14	83,021	63,492	19,513	29,275	7,324	11,881	2,573	4,981	2,940	7,176	11,173	18,675	2,738	6,560
Congressional District 15	78,238	62,861	20,417	28,818	8,846	14,027	2,998	5,595	4,216	6,859	11,442	17,590	3,419	6,552
Congressional District 16	75,916	58,142	19,718	28,217	7,421	14,565	2,828	4,495	3,647	6,838	11,875	17,567	2,781	6,253
Congressional District 17	78,291	61,500	15,368	26,074	6,072	13,781	2,101	4,376	2,211	6,453	9,351	15,083	1,898	6,479
Congressional District 18	70,651	57,750	16,007	25,732	4,377	9,932	2,260	4,160	3,288	6,346	10,492	17,263	2,403	7,605
Rhode Island														
Congressional District 1	50,852	41,855	13,604	17,401	5,680	7,634	1,754	3,261	2,957	3,904	8,708	11,645	2,695	4,838
Congressional District 2	52,419	37,519	10,319	15,595	4,096	7,352	1,562	3,174	2,662	4,280	5,416	9,658	2,302	4,257
South Carolina														
Congressional District 1	90,840	56,524	19,791	21,973	6,782	10,135	3,271	2,851	4,287	5,833	11,541	15,519	3,805	6,354
Congressional District 2	71,259	44,831	20,014	20,376	7,359	9,501	4,110	4,170	3,634	4,882	11,849	13,150	3,394	4,848
Congressional District 3	76,721	53,865	23,735	27,037	8,306	13,016	3,692	5,191	5,639	8,589	14,545	16,947	2,983	8,354
Congressional District 4	70,818	46,807	16,922	21,686	5,330	9,470	3,233	3,925	3,930	7,973	9,931	14,016	2,222	5,581
Congressional District 5	75,325	47,755	19,973	21,045	7,866	9,270	4,060	4,420	4,899	7,241	10,346	13,283	4,194	6,816
Congressional District 6	63,894	40,475	19,361	20,145	4,676	7,721	3,877	5,127	3,668	5,815	12,123	13,424	3,375	5,750
Congressional District 7	104,205	56,435	24,282	26,449	8,231	12,136	3,258	5,076	4,384	7,271	15,537	16,570	3,797	7,318
South Dakota														
Congressional District (at Large)	85,022	61,336	19,203	24,475	8,203	10,805	2,333	4,224	2,917	4,308	10,906	14,854	1,889	4,535
Tennessee														
Congressional District 1	86,490	61,740	30,126	31,910	13,562	14,442	5,509	7,903	5,409	10,090	18,948	21,676	6,173	8,439
Congressional District 2	79,933	55,202	19,534	24,690	7,889	11,120	2,796	4,083	5,003	5,761	10,650	15,193	3,450	5,545
Congressional District 3	81,333	56,556	24,540	27,487	10,191	12,889	4,052	5,210	5,292	8,273	16,087	19,537	3,787	7,860
Congressional District 4	71,596	46,661	21,562	21,727	8,687	10,408	4,887	4,795	5,278	6,569	12,448	14,641	3,339	5,027
Congressional District 5	58,687	38,411	15,774	18,247	6,179	8,237	2,474	4,418	2,925	5,708	9,853	12,803	2,425	5,602
Congressional District 6	82,667	56,189	23,853	27,967	9,425	13,722	3,499	5,430	6,737	8,684	14,714	19,754	3,488	7,648
Congressional District 7	69,022	47,303	17,775	20,120	7,560	11,305	2,658	4,455	3,248	4,480	10,557	11,056	3,389	3,569
Congressional District 8	74,590	49,844	21,137	24,321	8,484	10,377	4,177	4,310	4,777	7,184	11,957	17,007	2,981	5,920
Congressional District 9	54,242	34,331	14,584	17,184	3,804	5,462	3,953	4,220	3,120	6,267	10,250	12,515	2,126	5,994
Texas														
Congressional District 1	69,845	50,428	20,037	26,209	7,851	13,436	3,025	4,878	4,754	7,405	13,351	16,593	3,000	5,175
Congressional District 2	60,434	35,335	12,125	16,299	4,666	7,886	1,688	3,118	3,001	3,245	6,792	10,362	3,387	3,891
Congressional District 3	63,875	37,533	11,086	16,269	4,195	6,396	1,121	3,817	2,613	4,584	6,065	11,693	2,061	4,895
Congressional District 4	76,027	50,891	21,845	22,734	8,900	10,737	3,559	3,202	4,694	6,427	13,785	14,096	3,538	5,791
Congressional District 5	59,853	43,986	16,598	20,364	6,848	9,830	2,408	5,246	2,857	4,913	10,167	13,007	2,693	4,549
Congressional District 6	57,828	35,917	15,163	17,785	5,846	8,544	2,622	3,631	2,700	5,559	9,722	12,671	2,374	5,758
Congressional District 7	52,070	32,555	8,295	14,529	3,126	5,638	1,558	2,780	1,994	4,923	5,039	10,495	1,375	5,159
Congressional District 8	74,545	45,969	17,617	24,231	7,754	10,739	2,751	4,788	2,871	7,369	10,435	16,617	3,303	4,706
Congressional District 9	49,269	31,088	13,731	14,884	3,417	5,758	3,461	3,424	2,837	5,383	8,587	10,037	2,171	5,583
Congressional District 10	70,278	45,155	14,387	21,407	5,308	9,311	2,949	3,644	4,133	5,058	9,946	14,385	3,120	5,485
Congressional District 11	71,261	51,826	19,147	26,979	9,031	13,059	4,113	5,458	3,766	7,374	10,650	17,006	2,955	6,029
Congressional District 12	62,452	42,693	15,139	19,250	6,348	9,325	2,512	3,198	2,955	6,003	9,518	12,494	1,777	4,674
Congressional District 13	61,470	47,338	17,930	22,240	7,284	11,640	3,450	4,778	3,366	6,064	11,929	14,414	2,305	5,485
Congressional District 14	65,071	41,115	20,072	20,807	7,555	9,629	3,782	4,358	3,273	6,073	12,270	13,915	2,823	6,051
Congressional District 15	49,698	36,243	15,351	22,526	5,477	10,541	4,159	6,476	4,159	7,574	8,631	15,032	5,391	9,383
Congressional District 16	50,935	40,769	17,079	22,128	4,506	8,807	3,156	4,706	4,438	8,510	12,618	17,821	4,363	8,624
Congressional District 17	60,398	37,938	17,242	18,424	6,450	8,181	2,245	2,737	4,048	5,163	11,006	12,777	2,880	5,413
Congressional District 18	48,542	27,980	15,071	13,411	3,839	6,060	3,577	3,090	4,338	4,723	11,025	9,064	4,365	3,667
Congressional District 19	54,792	45,564	18,089	23,952	7,692	11,589	3,216	4,572	2,920	6,466	11,637	15,491	2,579	6,420
Congressional District 20	55,485	38,493	14,691	18,255	5,144	7,735	2,655	5,320	3,276	5,852	10,025	13,752	3,205	5,429
Congressional District 21	78,699	52,652	17,916	24,255	6,980	11,724	3,892	3,994	3,104	7,044	9,798	15,704	2,309	4,973
Congressional District 22	67,416	36,977	12,575	15,657	4,487	6,335	2,253	2,473	3,012	4,949	7,302	10,872	2,427	5,006
Congressional District 23	64,940	40,923	22,537	22,921	7,416	11,366	6,266	7,380	5,376	8,127	14,972	16,266	3,803	7,804
Congressional District 24	54,260	37,437	10,740	15,076	3,348	6,892	1,669	2,523	2,226	4,289	6,567	10,435	2,103	4,474
Congressional District 25	71,389	44,270	14,675	19,369	6,336	9,593	2,893	3,534	2,749	6,434	7,245	13,378	1,475	4,252
Congressional District 26	57,491	32,719	12,073	14,321	4,402	7,213	2,262	1,867	2,550	4,319	7,159	9,779	2,146	4,571
Congressional District 27	70,413	48,542	20,991	25,487	7,914	11,482	3,896	5,381	3,808	7,865	12,970	17,361	3,710	7,289
Congressional District 28	51,912	37,895	19,912	21,767	8,188	11,398	6,483	6,326	5,299	7,476	12,217	15,862	5,447	8,290
Congressional District 29	42,538	21,883	12,085	11,180	3,573	4,095	2,145	2,521	4,025	3,193	7,332	8,245	2,265	3,319
Congressional District 30	57,041	29,646	17,108	16,936	4,244	5,830	5,073	4,727	3,105	5,877	10,920	12,678	4,268	7,201
Congressional District 31	65,833	40,548	16,106	20,627	5,687	10,173	2,355	3,821	3,284	4,807	7,652	13,076	1,655	4,551
Congressional District 32	56,907	38,994	11,310	17,143	4,254	7,168	2,365	3,284	1,795	4,605	7,101	11,578	2,160	5,097
Congressional District 33	44,716	23,924	13,056	11,154	4,819	4,374	2,788	1,718	3,308	3,452	9,461	7,960	2,420	3,384
Congressional District 34	55,725	46,259	18,152	23,321	8,332	9,262	3,565	6,311	5,588	9,013	11,082	16,613	5,094	9,503
Congressional District 35	52,828	30,476	17,457	16,331	5,808	7,284	4,845	4,557	4,532	6,115	11,985	10,741	4,572	4,596
Congressional District 36	68,038	43,344	21,484	22,633	7,272	9,818	3,807	4,558	3,355	6,336	12,755	15,166	3,263	5,044

Table H-5: 116th Congressional Districts - Disability Status and Type of Disability—*Continued*

	Total Population		With a Disability		With a Hearing Disability		With a Vision Disability		With a Cognitive Disability		With an Ambulatory Disability		With a Self-Care Disability	
	65 to 74 Years	75 Years and Over	65 to 74 Years	75 Years and Over	65 to 74 Years	75 Years and Over	65 to 74 Years	75 Years and Over	65 to 74 Years	75 Years and Over	65 to 74 Years	75 Years and Over	65 to 74 Years	75 Years and Over
Utah														
Congressional District 1	51,754	31,048	11,525	14,299	5,254	7,408	2,218	2,335	2,114	3,647	5,424	8,731	1,764	3,079
Congressional District 2	60,958	43,302	14,743	21,301	6,487	10,923	2,038	3,429	1,818	4,990	7,810	12,766	1,454	4,399
Congressional District 3	50,440	34,602	10,966	16,495	4,615	8,749	1,614	3,996	2,047	3,411	6,063	9,098	1,428	3,420
Congressional District 4	49,054	30,139	9,960	14,728	3,790	7,084	1,516	2,288	2,925	3,349	5,181	8,104	1,766	2,781
Vermont														
Congressional District (at Large)	75,755	48,120	18,245	20,213	8,490	10,970	2,929	3,665	4,922	5,094	9,047	11,245	2,666	4,493
Virginia														
Congressional District 1	74,617	49,295	15,508	20,040	5,960	10,845	2,233	3,217	2,270	4,400	8,917	12,328	2,587	4,635
Congressional District 2	66,824	45,421	16,129	22,170	6,245	10,394	1,838	4,553	4,686	6,767	9,416	13,677	2,667	6,294
Congressional District 3	58,586	41,840	15,382	21,076	3,838	8,066	2,164	4,202	2,479	5,739	11,041	14,780	4,050	5,853
Congressional District 4	70,271	44,857	17,429	22,600	4,938	10,219	3,383	4,410	3,355	6,664	11,132	13,670	3,197	5,440
Congressional District 5	86,963	63,377	20,330	29,843	7,693	13,952	2,683	5,034	4,624	7,840	11,927	18,939	4,012	8,864
Congressional District 6	79,739	61,419	20,363	25,751	7,099	12,522	3,586	6,076	5,168	7,616	12,082	16,046	3,510	6,717
Congressional District 7	77,353	50,881	17,889	26,114	6,705	11,686	3,884	5,870	4,592	7,279	10,995	17,297	4,056	6,886
Congressional District 8	56,590	40,134	9,911	16,060	2,717	6,483	1,762	2,704	1,716	4,142	6,062	9,980	1,533	4,073
Congressional District 9	83,906	61,914	28,103	29,537	11,369	14,163	6,595	6,107	6,012	8,453	18,683	19,100	5,839	7,254
Congressional District 10	65,869	42,534	10,664	19,257	4,256	7,922	1,558	4,120	1,479	6,260	5,496	12,353	1,346	6,751
Congressional District 11	58,784	37,051	8,531	15,368	3,478	6,509	1,427	3,482	1,533	4,558	4,483	11,138	1,151	5,455
Washington														
Congressional District 1	65,375	36,288	13,754	15,756	6,202	7,600	2,361	3,057	2,981	4,908	7,028	9,887	2,003	4,316
Congressional District 2	75,890	49,440	18,595	20,472	7,506	11,071	3,780	3,038	5,348	4,511	11,312	12,527	4,317	5,653
Congressional District 3	79,987	48,771	20,449	22,652	8,537	12,618	3,082	3,916	4,000	6,560	10,689	14,291	2,735	5,625
Congressional District 4	63,580	40,407	18,946	20,009	8,929	8,812	2,264	2,870	3,430	5,085	10,376	14,001	1,890	5,833
Congressional District 5	74,921	50,920	20,988	25,925	9,861	13,264	3,356	6,051	4,156	6,366	10,703	17,326	2,980	6,051
Congressional District 6	92,690	54,904	25,145	22,981	11,371	10,935	2,975	3,612	4,679	6,640	13,700	14,960	4,210	5,607
Congressional District 7	71,247	42,873	14,087	18,512	5,542	8,453	1,118	4,536	3,190	4,863	8,993	10,792	2,083	5,357
Congressional District 8	63,152	39,701	17,555	19,332	7,677	9,219	3,521	2,977	2,639	5,200	9,445	13,085	2,279	4,008
Congressional District 9	58,320	44,712	12,643	21,809	4,017	9,872	1,528	3,857	3,053	8,373	8,204	14,038	1,964	8,220
Congressional District 10	65,619	45,190	16,551	22,728	6,235	10,282	2,496	3,472	3,388	5,412	9,104	15,302	2,689	6,406
West Virginia														
Congressional District 1	69,690	50,529	20,776	25,991	8,263	12,160	3,796	3,995	3,623	7,521	11,783	16,825	3,532	6,628
Congressional District 2	72,927	47,428	20,311	23,156	7,672	11,167	2,747	4,107	4,001	6,657	12,199	13,939	3,262	5,360
Congressional District 3	72,673	47,969	28,057	26,567	12,868	14,246	7,382	8,975	7,517	7,207	18,251	18,863	4,938	6,993
Wisconsin														
Congressional District 1	69,894	48,682	14,007	19,377	5,262	8,443	1,625	3,142	2,119	4,699	7,427	11,276	2,549	4,525
Congressional District 2	68,799	46,917	13,519	17,703	6,095	8,711	1,538	2,836	2,698	3,116	7,587	10,184	2,155	3,372
Congressional District 3	74,730	55,176	17,153	24,383	7,763	11,037	3,058	3,651	3,111	6,117	8,881	14,931	2,985	4,680
Congressional District 4	52,875	34,119	14,798	14,798	3,892	6,529	2,360	2,972	4,160	5,060	10,017	10,974	3,961	5,146
Congressional District 5	73,422	59,080	14,474	24,533	5,071	11,431	2,183	3,458	2,340	5,128	8,764	14,913	1,992	6,072
Congressional District 6	75,102	57,029	14,985	23,068	6,256	10,664	1,894	3,552	2,964	5,518	8,264	12,495	2,580	5,519
Congressional District 7	83,694	60,917	19,461	24,288	8,838	13,326	2,684	3,993	2,814	4,918	9,852	13,379	2,888	4,069
Congressional District 8	73,156	52,891	13,906	21,272	5,634	11,046	2,359	4,077	2,050	4,132	6,714	11,740	1,786	3,892
Wyoming														
Congressional District (at Large)	59,467	37,090	15,288	16,600	7,921	9,752	1,503	4,342	2,842	3,398	7,904	8,441	1,000	2,611

PART I

HEALTH INSURANCE

HEALTH INSURANCE COVERAGE AND TYPE OF INSURANCE

At age 65, most Americans become eligible and obtain health insurance coverage through the national Medicare program. Of the 52.4 million population age 65 and over, 93.5 percent are insured by Medicare. Some have earlier eligibility and 9.6 percent of the population age 55 to 64 have coverage through Medicare. Among the 65 and over population, the District of Columbia has the lowest Medicare coverage rate at 88.6 percent while Idaho has the highest coverage level at 96.1. Ten other states are above 95 percent, including Arizona, Connecticut, Idaho, Michigan, Mississippi, Montana, Oregon, South Carolina, West Virginia and Wisconsin. Among the 55 to 64 population, Medicare coverage is highest in West Virginia at 17.8 percent and lowest in Hawaii at 5.8 percent.

However, the categories reported in the ACS are not mutually exclusive. People can obtain coverage through multiple plans depending on their individual and family situations and the benefits offered by different plans. This is seen in the ACS data on insurance coverage where the percentage by coverage type far exceeds 100 percent. For example, while 93.5 percent of the 65 and over population is covered by Medicare, 31.1 percent hold employer based coverage, 30.6 percent are in direct pay plans, and 13.5 percent obtain Medicaid.

Private employer based coverage is most important for the 55 to 64 population as 60.9 percent are covered by such plans. Coverage is highest in New Hampshire at 70.7 percent but even the lowest level of coverage (New Mexico) is over 50 percent. Employer based plans cover only 31.1 percent of the 65 and over population where the Hawaii is highest at 50.3 percent and South Dakota is lowest at 18.6 percent.

North Dakota has highest percentage of the 55 to 64 population covered by direct purchase plans with 20.4

Percent of the Population 65 Years and Over
With Direct Pay Health Insurance Coverage

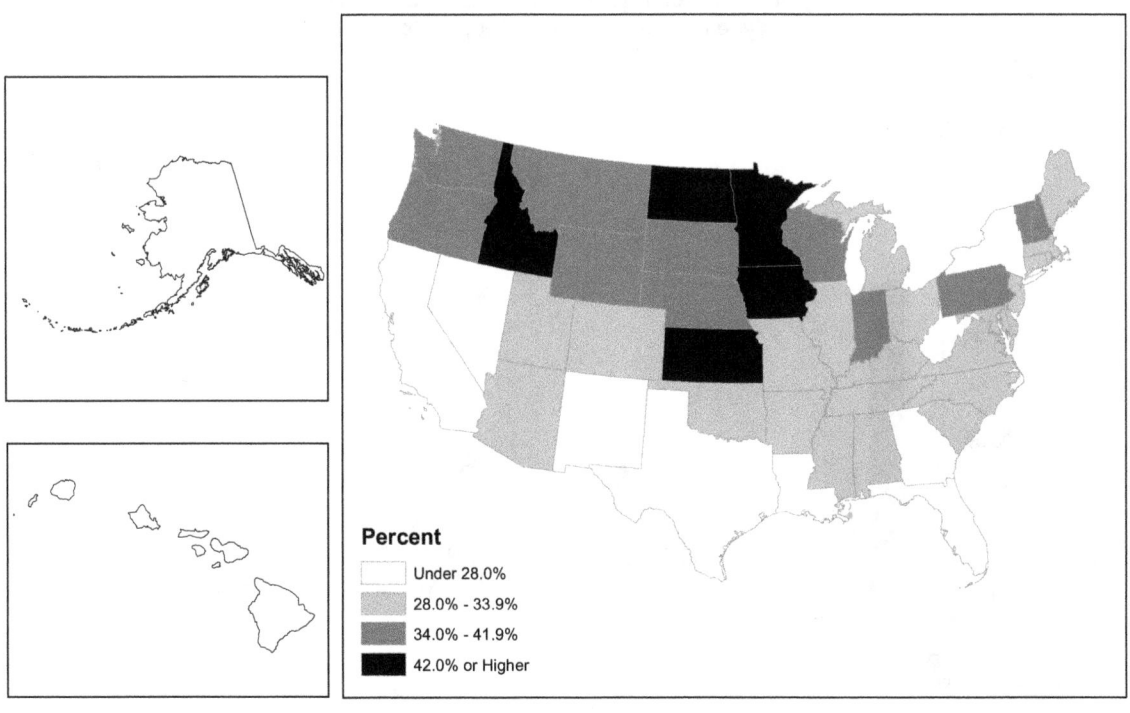

Percent

	Under 28.0%
	28.0% - 33.9%
	34.0% - 41.9%
	42.0% or Higher

percent. Among the 65 and over group, 49.7 percent of Minnesota's population has direct purchase plans. Alaska is lowest at 13.3 percent. Thirty-seven states have at least 30 percent of the 65 and over population covered by direct purchase plans. For the 55 to 64 population, in all but two states, direct purchase covers between 10 and 20 percent of the population.

The national Medicare program covers only 9.6 percent of the 55 to 64 population and this is mainly for persons with eligible disabilities. By contrast, 93.5 percent of the 65 and over population has Medicare coverage and even in the District of Columbia (the lowest), 88.6 percent have Medicare. Medicaid coverage is more evenly distributed between the 55 to 64 and 65 and over populations. Nationwide, 14.3 percent of the 55 to 64 population has Medicaid compared to 13.5 percent of the 65 and over. The District of Columbia has the highest Medicaid coverage rate for both age categories at 31.6 percent (55 to 64) and 24.9 percent for the 65 and over. North Dakota has the lowest Medicaid coverage among the 55 to 64 group at 6.3 but Virginia and Wyoming are close at 6.4 and 6.5 percent, respectively, but New Hampshire is lowest for the 65 and over population at 6.9 percent.

County coverage of the 55 to 64 population through employer based plans varied from a low of 25.5 percent in McKinley County, New Mexico to a high of 81.8 percent in Washington County, Rhode Island. There is an equally wide range among the 65 and over population starting at the low of 10.1 percent Miami-Dade County, Florida to the highest coverage of 67.2 percent in Clinton County, Michigan. Direct purchase plans are more prevalent among the 65 and over than then the 55 to 64 population. The county with the highest percent of direct purchase for the 55 to 64 is Sumter County, Florida at 35.3 percent while Stearns County, Minnesota is highest among the 65 and over population at 58.4 percent.

Coverage through Medicare shows a narrow range for the 65 and over population where 99.1 percent of the population in Clark County, Indiana is the highest, while the lowest coverage is 84.7 percent in Arlington County, Virginia. Among the 55 to 64 population only a little more than one-quarter of the population (27.7 percent) is covered in Raleigh County, West Virginia, the highest coverage level. Medicaid covers 41.5 percent of the 65 and over population in Imperial County, California but Bronx County, New York is highest for the 55 to 64 population at 42.8 percent.

Employer based plans cover 68.5 percent of the 65 and over population in Davis city, California but only 4.3 percent in Hialeah, Florida. Among the 55 to 64 population. Davis city is also the highest for the 55 to 64 population at 90.7 percent coverage while the lowest (25.4 percent) is Homestead, Florida. For direct pay coverage, Ankeny city, Iowa has the highest rate for the 65 and over population at 66.8

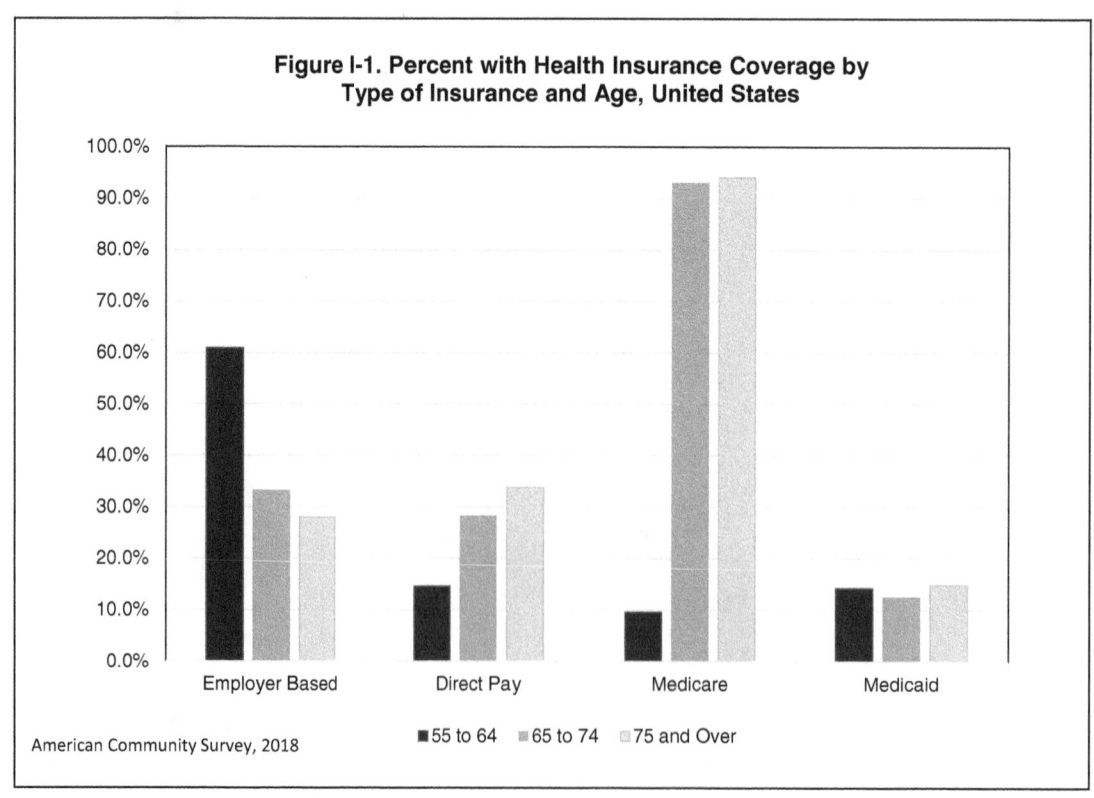

Figure I-1. Percent with Health Insurance Coverage by Type of Insurance and Age, United States

American Community Survey, 2018

■ 55 to 64   ■ 65 to 74   ▢ 75 and Over

percent. More than 95 percent of the 65 and over is covered by Medicare in 101 counties with Fishers city, Indiana being the highest at a reported 99.7 percent. The Medicaid program covers 59.0 percent of the 65 and over population in Lawrence, Massachusetts but only 1.3 percent in Fishers, Indiana because most are covered by Medicare.

Employer based plans for the 55 to 64 population cover at least 50 percent in 430 of the 512 metropolitan and micropolitan areas. In comparison to the 65 and over population, only 18 metro and micro areas have coverage rates over 50 percent. The California-Lexington Park, Maryland metropolitan area has the highest coverage for the 55 to 64 population (78.9 percent) while the Lansing-East Lansing, Michigan metro is highest among the 65 and over population at 62.8 percent. Direct purchase plans are more prevalent among the 65 and over than the 55 to 64 population. The coverage range for the 65 and over population is from a low of 10.6 percent in the Gallup, New Mexico micropolitan area to a high of 55.2 percent in the St. Cloud, Minnesota metropolitan area. For the 55 to 64 population, the The Villages, Florida metro area is the highest at 35.3 percent and the lowest is 2.7 percent in the Alamogordo, New Mexico micropolitan area. Nearly 100 percent (98.8 percent) of the 65 and over population in the Cullman, Alabama micropolitan area is covered by Medicare and 190 areas have over 95 percent coverage. The Enid, Oklahoma metro area has the lowest percent of Medicare coverage at 87.9 percent. The El Centro, California metropolitan area has the highest Medicaid coverage of the 65 and over population at 41.5 percent.

Among congressional districts, only 27 districts have Medicare coverage rates under 90 percent for the 65 and over population with the 29th district of Texas lowest at 87.5 percent. Medicaid coverage for the 65 and over population is highest in New York's 15th Congressional District at 54.7 percent. In 152 congressional districts more than one-third of the 65 and over population carries direct pay coverage as do 145 districts for employer based coverage. Maryland's 5th Congressional District has the highest coverage rate for employer based plans at 58.1 percent. Minnesota's 7th district is highest at 54.0 percent for direct pay coverage.

COVERAGE OPTIONS DEFINED

Health insurance coverage in the ACS defines coverage to include plans and programs that provide comprehensive health coverage. Plans that provide insurance for specific conditions or situations such as cancer and long-term care policies are not considered comprehensive coverage. The types of coverage are derived from a series of questions asked of all respondents by their "yes" or "no" response for each type. The types of coverage are further identified as either private or public insurance coverage. While the question is asked of all respondents, the data is reported for only the civilian non-institutional population.

Private Insurance Coverage

Employer Based – Insurance through a current or former employer or union (of this person or another family member)

Direct Purchase – Insurance purchased directly from an insurance company (by this person or another family member)

Public Insurance Coverage

Medicare – Insurance coverage by Medicare for people 65 and over, or people with certain disabilities

Medicaid – Insurance coverage by Medicaid, Medical Assistance, or any kind of government-assistance plan for those with low incomes or a disability

Highest and Lowest Metropolitan and Micropolitan Area Percent of Coverage for the Population 65 Years and Over by Health Insurance Type

Employer Based	Direct Pay	Medicare	Medicaid
Highest Percentage			
Congressional District 5, MD - 58.1%	Congressional District 7, MN - 54.0%	Congressional District 11, FL - 97.6%	Congressional District 15, NY - 54.7%
Congressional District 5, MI - 56.9%	Congressional District 3, MN - 53.7%	Congressional District 9, GA - 96.9%	Congressional District 34, CA - 51.5%
Congressional District 4, MD - 55.3%	Congressional District 2, MN - 52.1%	Congressional District 3, AL - 96.6%	Congressional District 13, NY - 45.9%
Congressional District 8, MI - 54.5%	Congressional District 6, MN - 50.5%	Congressional District 1, CA - 96.5%	Congressional District 7, NY - 42.5%
Congressional District 20, NY - 54.1%	Congressional District 1, MN - 50.5%	Congressional District 5, MI - 96.4%	Congressional District 29, CA - 39.7%
Lowest Percentage			
Congressional District 34, CA - 14.0%	Congressional District 15, NY - 10.0%	Congressional District 5, NY - 88.3%	Congressional District 16, OH - 6.1%
Congressional District 25, FL - 12.7%	Congressional District 13, NY - 7.7%	Congressional District 9, TX - 88.2%	Congressional District 3, MO - 6.0%
Congressional District 26, FL - 12.5%	Congressional District 44, CA - 7.2%	Congressional District 35, CA - 87.9%	Congressional District 6, GA - 5.7%
Congressional District 27, FL - 12.1%	Congressional District 34, CA - 5.8%	Congressional District 8, VA - 87.5%	Congressional District 14, IL - 5.3%
Congressional District 24, FL - 11.0%	Congressional District 40, CA - 4.3%	Congressional District 29, TX - 87.5%	Congressional District 2, MO - 4.4%

Table I-1: States - Persons With Health Insurance by Source of Insurance

	Private Health Insurance Coverage						Public Health Insurance Coverage					
	Employer Based			Direct Purchase			Medicare			Medicaid/CHIP		
	55 to 64 Years	65 to 74 Years	75 Years and Over	55 to 64 Years	65 to 74 Years	75 Years and Over	55 to 64 Years	65 to 74 Years	75 Years and Over	55 to 64 Years	65 to 74 Years	75 Years and Over
United States	25,747,143	10,182,658	6,134,232	6,156,583	8,660,172	7,399,991	4,071,407	28,463,695	20,554,217	6,047,552	3,853,447	3,249,462
Alabama..............................	376,662	170,782	92,731	96,097	141,293	113,867	103,391	472,861	320,431	90,138	63,168	47,164
Alaska.................................	56,324	28,191	11,537	8,223	7,980	3,716	6,384	54,510	27,051	14,471	9,657	4,905
Arizona...............................	479,605	190,107	135,297	129,099	207,391	176,556	78,359	686,435	514,533	142,369	90,923	69,759
Arkansas.............................	200,635	74,554	44,038	59,326	91,857	78,323	59,755	283,047	197,177	76,913	37,429	32,827
California............................	2,730,561	1,074,175	637,554	743,700	683,254	593,266	352,156	2,993,261	2,261,536	960,920	595,735	557,700
Colorado.............................	435,998	148,015	82,764	109,166	141,978	110,752	55,601	468,790	290,495	94,406	47,063	38,880
Connecticut.........................	355,074	134,426	85,290	64,720	90,486	94,664	35,620	311,130	251,702	66,780	40,425	39,020
Delaware..............................	91,277	48,726	29,311	15,246	34,090	26,834	13,150	102,634	69,111	21,614	10,601	7,821
District of Columbia	38,453	22,644	18,035	8,289	10,158	7,397	6,726	42,296	33,527	22,124	12,117	9,222
Florida................................	1,486,578	611,166	440,628	562,629	598,519	580,097	290,643	2,242,657	1,863,131	316,048	328,346	321,642
Georgia...............................	761,401	293,194	163,323	180,441	230,533	172,240	138,010	840,175	529,832	139,393	123,060	88,899
Hawaii.................................	124,814	78,648	52,782	24,311	33,095	32,486	10,379	136,853	105,965	22,959	16,340	14,555
Idaho..................................	121,594	40,535	24,170	42,447	67,902	50,179	22,624	162,120	106,432	19,929	18,643	13,284
Illinois................................	1,091,741	383,952	231,275	218,426	345,358	318,192	133,940	1,050,021	784,079	221,414	119,243	92,831
Indiana................................	567,970	185,225	118,191	110,574	206,155	171,270	96,861	579,563	405,812	109,336	57,209	41,639
Iowa...................................	285,268	82,723	47,749	68,180	135,417	123,217	34,015	282,043	219,586	55,910	26,239	23,520
Kansas................................	244,789	68,575	37,054	58,343	105,638	91,205	33,546	245,339	182,329	33,395	23,641	18,380
Kentucky.............................	341,772	147,742	86,000	74,340	131,463	107,194	94,015	414,259	276,228	125,680	58,680	41,433
Louisiana	321,239	139,760	79,361	84,882	106,198	80,201	83,380	402,649	265,997	122,242	62,545	43,639
Maine..................................	126,626	47,723	29,841	32,154	48,859	40,026	21,949	156,390	103,512	29,886	23,986	21,718
Maryland.............................	557,288	284,172	170,663	103,775	143,784	126,124	59,503	491,758	359,231	104,117	60,783	54,268
Massachusetts.....................	634,790	285,236	157,847	116,002	189,636	176,841	73,364	596,054	446,042	183,334	102,095	84,288
Michigan.............................	899,141	468,513	314,018	190,403	300,926	266,170	168,357	960,563	676,989	233,086	121,065	86,575
Minnesota...........................	515,475	141,717	75,025	111,706	238,063	203,309	52,209	482,001	349,063	96,837	41,781	36,594
Mississippi..........................	200,304	66,311	34,166	48,886	84,784	64,624	63,771	271,636	179,336	68,994	44,209	36,369
Missouri..............................	505,931	161,726	107,894	118,871	182,519	156,460	102,955	563,733	406,138	81,795	50,512	41,094
Montana..............................	83,656	27,410	16,452	29,473	46,448	35,191	14,626	116,081	74,580	21,332	10,944	7,358
Nebraska.............................	160,449	43,959	21,165	41,468	65,054	59,750	18,579	162,178	120,624	19,216	14,823	15,277
Nevada...............................	223,161	86,557	42,036	46,918	66,307	49,584	36,115	271,076	175,858	59,535	31,564	24,111
New Hampshire....................	150,610	51,318	28,200	23,585	49,265	41,206	19,453	135,850	91,254	17,874	8,610	8,238
New Jersey	847,917	347,201	208,042	152,309	197,838	206,866	92,606	738,907	588,695	139,906	91,483	87,792
New Mexico	138,298	70,120	40,514	34,356	48,310	38,676	32,309	206,953	141,358	63,738	32,203	26,133
New York.............................	1,642,258	773,807	462,426	329,133	390,876	372,246	234,004	1,667,852	1,303,933	544,097	317,853	293,445
North Carolina......................	799,624	323,350	186,985	218,191	329,032	244,432	153,565	962,999	638,887	140,689	115,163	86,561
North Dakota........................	63,678	17,593	10,043	19,429	28,620	26,523	6,904	60,123	46,749	6,041	4,412	5,724
Ohio...................................	1,035,889	398,162	270,908	196,029	349,926	289,687	163,032	1,078,589	782,116	238,834	111,516	81,042
Oklahoma............................	280,820	110,740	67,956	70,130	113,439	96,761	57,972	339,950	241,339	43,126	36,777	26,159
Oregon................................	312,291	118,008	79,431	88,300	161,048	123,004	51,933	423,545	280,008	98,139	48,881	37,899
Pennsylvania........................	1,203,759	453,862	284,820	260,742	459,593	438,999	171,503	1,230,151	950,554	259,780	143,958	127,586
Rhode Island........................	99,989	30,327	17,997	19,546	34,889	27,174	14,054	96,693	73,230	26,323	17,345	13,747
South Carolina	375,380	179,058	97,052	108,914	167,665	122,854	86,190	530,178	332,197	83,812	63,809	44,226
South Dakota	69,599	19,044	8,141	23,076	32,144	24,347	9,791	79,920	55,360	8,803	6,640	6,345
Tennessee	517,215	188,433	106,243	123,639	207,849	164,234	116,533	625,474	421,152	115,719	80,095	57,539
Texas..................................	1,867,422	679,026	358,412	465,902	504,803	396,503	272,191	1,982,523	1,325,988	306,566	280,860	221,386
Utah...................................	196,727	74,488	41,725	52,620	62,890	53,011	20,211	194,215	133,520	22,441	18,126	14,404
Vermont..............................	58,591	25,773	11,539	13,569	26,485	18,473	9,087	70,808	45,336	18,054	9,264	6,878
Virginia...............................	701,812	298,839	179,903	162,599	238,077	187,850	96,781	722,948	508,204	70,935	60,968	51,762
Washington..........................	614,072	233,163	128,619	132,038	232,262	171,976	84,012	665,225	432,666	133,685	71,970	62,976
West Virginia........................	142,940	86,282	54,290	27,968	51,061	45,156	46,131	206,796	137,899	53,858	27,228	18,277
Wisconsin............................	558,536	152,846	95,790	123,482	217,636	182,798	67,474	545,579	392,630	95,764	58,911	52,972
Wyoming	51,140	14,754	8,999	12,931	21,319	17,480	5,688	56,304	34,815	5,195	4,549	3,599

Table I-2: Counties - Persons With Health Insurance by Source of Insurance

	Private Health Insurance Coverage						Public Health Insurance Coverage					
	Employer Based			Direct Purchase			Medicare			Medicaid/CHIP		
	55 to 64 Years	65 to 74 Years	75 Years and Over	55 to 64 Years	65 to 74 Years	75 Years and Over	55 to 64 Years	65 to 74 Years	75 Years and Over	55 to 64 Years	65 to 74 Years	75 Years and Over
Alabama												
Baldwin County	19,275	9,912	4,602	6,253	7,351	6,636	3,886	26,497	16,388	2,659	2,592	1,712
Calhoun County	8,658	3,910	1,706	2,702	3,028	3,042	2,799	11,892	8,014	2,200	1,525	1,098
Cullman County	6,499	2,531	2,331	1,659	2,882	1,996	1,915	9,096	6,260	1,961	1,357	755
DeKalb County	5,029	2,164	965	1,474	2,206	1,706	1,897	7,279	4,679	1,735	597	937
Elmore County	6,734	3,876	1,570	1,403	1,385	1,167	1,378	7,335	4,497	1,233	503	223
Etowah County	7,544	4,066	1,987	2,234	4,441	3,264	2,638	11,085	7,631	2,823	1,427	1,609
Houston County	8,155	3,999	2,088	2,161	3,715	2,629	2,706	10,722	7,350	1,672	1,537	1,676
Jefferson County	52,613	21,804	10,273	10,150	18,651	15,968	13,810	57,901	41,013	12,344	8,367	6,545
Lauderdale County	7,868	4,175	3,505	2,185	3,543	3,443	1,685	10,136	7,820	1,256	964	1,180
Lee County	9,532	6,217	1,990	2,100	4,037	2,704	2,496	12,909	6,462	2,043	1,161	724
Limestone County	8,044	3,427	2,971	2,197	3,282	2,927	1,133	8,482	5,898	1,660	490	810
Madison County	33,617	14,199	9,090	7,994	9,880	9,749	4,901	30,873	22,375	3,945	3,077	2,108
Marshall County	6,477	3,836	1,834	2,085	2,845	2,750	2,693	8,374	6,580	1,729	1,212	848
Mobile County	30,667	10,915	5,547	6,397	9,882	7,512	8,790	38,055	26,009	7,591	5,433	3,199
Montgomery County	16,488	8,531	6,006	3,820	3,459	3,350	4,602	18,989	12,665	4,817	3,335	2,371
Morgan County	9,917	4,919	3,029	3,033	3,770	2,802	2,148	11,790	8,054	2,356	995	974
St. Clair County	7,495	2,787	1,376	1,450	2,248	1,633	1,166	8,764	5,621	1,206	1,352	447
Shelby County	20,757	8,434	3,589	4,264	6,593	5,397	2,830	19,603	12,469	1,463	1,916	1,897
Talladega County	6,388	3,155	1,684	1,668	2,702	1,861	1,814	8,578	5,453	1,853	1,182	1,113
Tuscaloosa County	14,771	7,235	2,854	2,523	4,462	2,570	3,659	15,951	10,022	2,749	2,515	1,564
Walker County	5,649	2,903	2,144	1,170	2,114	1,325	1,541	6,854	4,814	1,134	743	719
Alaska												
Anchorage Municipality	23,034	10,236	4,905	3,933	2,960	1,149	1,626	19,904	10,259	3,899	3,822	1,965
Fairbanks North Star Borough	6,314	3,471	1,037	689	845	402	1,429	6,600	2,688	1,707	891	165
Matanuska-Susitna Borough	7,896	3,784	1,482	879	1,447	574	1,122	8,220	4,200	3,558	1,522	952
Arizona												
Apache County	2,671	1,642	358	118	1,104	914	1,184	5,616	4,405	1,949	1,729	1,299
Cochise County	6,534	3,605	1,967	2,156	5,091	4,043	1,817	15,352	12,037	3,469	1,987	1,515
Coconino County	9,892	3,553	1,768	3,629	3,139	1,769	1,449	10,471	6,337	2,562	1,377	1,490
Maricopa County	303,925	103,422	70,663	76,830	106,244	88,891	41,233	363,392	271,218	70,665	45,770	34,753
Mohave County	15,095	9,198	6,456	3,900	12,449	11,384	4,474	35,494	26,217	8,707	4,625	2,612
Navajo County	4,456	3,164	1,109	1,814	3,599	2,470	2,166	11,562	7,801	5,762	1,832	1,661
Pima County	70,028	31,267	25,934	17,973	29,264	26,087	12,255	111,414	86,444	24,392	16,235	14,816
Pinal County	28,684	13,237	9,546	7,474	15,001	12,144	5,485	52,268	34,912	7,940	4,570	3,701
Yavapai County	18,558	11,161	8,610	9,145	17,277	13,321	3,541	42,981	29,304	7,026	6,094	1,517
Yuma County	8,887	4,920	5,264	2,955	7,142	9,025	2,567	18,373	18,762	5,111	4,009	4,064
Arkansas												
Benton County	19,193	5,382	2,799	5,229	5,557	5,671	2,048	19,363	15,332	3,114	2,713	2,071
Craighead County	6,355	2,491	704	2,045	3,283	2,320	1,488	8,733	5,827	1,780	1,193	1,260
Faulkner County	7,821	3,637	878	1,848	3,041	2,589	2,697	8,633	5,555	2,110	1,011	813
Garland County	7,238	3,343	3,074	2,720	3,774	4,607	3,401	12,102	10,110	2,245	1,528	1,395
Jefferson County	4,126	2,018	1,087	1,821	2,682	1,756	1,482	6,524	4,142	1,741	533	1,168
Lonoke County	5,109	1,556	687	1,081	2,145	1,675	1,169	5,597	3,666	1,524	260	447
Pulaski County	29,196	11,800	6,485	8,158	12,071	8,049	5,633	35,673	21,743	8,861	3,345	2,942
Saline County	9,334	4,365	3,968	2,759	4,865	3,121	1,466	12,342	8,666	1,879	761	911
Sebastian County	9,509	1,852	1,328	2,050	3,242	3,186	2,690	11,291	7,557	3,061	1,326	1,088
Washington County	14,910	4,405	3,079	4,145	4,967	4,401	3,038	15,271	9,777	2,585	1,013	1,082
White County	3,450	2,318	1,158	2,384	2,898	2,155	1,626	6,885	5,056	2,947	1,049	1,165
California												
Alameda County	129,376	52,123	32,532	26,779	26,729	23,621	12,121	121,326	88,027	39,382	24,005	18,652
Butte County	13,458	7,725	6,291	4,951	7,601	6,912	3,114	24,400	17,063	9,145	3,598	3,756
Contra Costa County	106,890	48,506	28,342	22,162	28,611	24,616	7,825	95,438	70,282	19,384	10,827	10,348
El Dorado County	21,577	11,627	5,801	6,565	8,134	5,709	2,305	24,166	14,511	4,702	1,795	1,933
Fresno County	51,192	24,122	11,416	12,114	15,560	12,062	9,771	66,293	47,706	33,063	15,635	13,803
Humboldt County	8,150	4,587	2,232	3,474	5,358	3,264	2,744	14,684	8,749	4,678	2,395	1,061
Imperial County	7,858	4,082	1,779	1,466	2,722	1,725	2,481	12,013	9,999	6,910	4,509	5,240
Kern County	45,838	17,670	9,978	10,651	13,068	9,287	10,458	54,265	36,704	27,590	14,550	9,733
Kings County	6,702	1,711	1,438	1,567	2,428	2,119	1,626	8,014	6,358	2,993	2,289	1,936
Lake County	3,427	1,795	1,726	2,247	3,005	2,358	1,529	8,674	4,951	3,196	1,899	727
Los Angeles County	627,469	226,593	127,625	191,403	104,688	91,535	83,872	701,795	555,869	294,681	191,076	192,586
Madera County	6,949	3,982	1,996	2,379	3,695	2,306	1,561	12,566	8,266	5,508	1,249	2,013
Marin County	24,826	13,514	9,916	10,728	10,655	9,756	1,953	31,150	23,637	3,041	2,099	2,113
Mendocino County	6,549	3,280	1,353	2,320	3,544	2,461	991	11,895	6,553	3,067	1,491	930
Merced County	12,496	4,541	1,664	3,310	5,377	3,921	3,021	16,498	12,914	7,936	5,436	4,480
Monterey County	25,381	11,120	5,266	8,444	7,402	7,380	3,973	31,103	23,975	8,702	5,386	6,759
Napa County	12,298	5,440	4,180	2,923	3,820	3,921	769	14,921	10,107	2,077	2,544	1,165
Nevada County	8,916	5,104	3,667	4,010	6,747	4,813	1,484	16,579	9,877	2,980	1,814	1,098
Orange County	248,850	73,844	49,952	77,618	53,754	46,140	19,833	242,952	196,543	56,931	38,505	40,943
Placer County	37,133	19,027	12,733	7,572	15,247	12,664	4,890	40,253	31,581	6,575	3,544	3,903
Riverside County	152,662	52,588	35,890	39,638	36,567	37,538	24,382	185,611	146,166	61,592	34,829	29,748
Sacramento County	115,708	59,503	34,164	25,241	26,357	23,702	16,128	119,700	84,628	41,037	25,998	19,713
San Bernardino County	138,605	42,308	20,990	26,692	22,875	17,059	19,187	138,421	93,368	53,244	27,551	25,704
San Diego County	229,581	84,710	51,640	62,140	52,770	51,215	24,936	249,031	189,005	64,211	39,645	38,550
San Francisco County	60,325	28,794	15,574	16,526	14,758	14,305	7,654	67,262	58,696	21,047	18,936	23,025
San Joaquin County	45,806	18,399	11,977	11,870	14,316	11,890	10,080	52,003	36,181	20,018	12,690	9,392
San Luis Obispo County	25,085	13,457	7,015	6,787	10,984	7,308	2,575	33,024	21,512	4,088	3,240	2,331

Table I-2: Counties - Persons With Health Insurance by Source of Insurance—*Continued*

| | Private Health Insurance Coverage | | | | | | Public Health Insurance Coverage | | | | | |
| | Employer Based | | | Direct Purchase | | | Medicare | | | Medicaid/CHIP | | |
	55 to 64 Years	65 to 74 Years	75 Years and Over	55 to 64 Years	65 to 74 Years	75 Years and Over	55 to 64 Years	65 to 74 Years	75 Years and Over	55 to 64 Years	65 to 74 Years	75 Years and Over
California—Cont.												
San Mateo County	68,331	31,555	20,687	20,273	18,570	18,660	4,587	61,681	50,970	10,401	9,204	8,366
Santa Barbara County	27,908	11,430	9,497	9,314	13,452	12,820	3,520	34,642	29,389	9,332	4,373	3,252
Santa Clara County	151,700	50,802	32,364	36,618	35,002	30,972	12,862	130,669	108,862	32,051	26,147	31,015
Santa Cruz County	22,519	12,619	5,268	7,074	7,949	5,969	2,172	27,041	15,050	4,401	4,546	2,549
Shasta County	15,355	7,219	4,699	3,769	8,395	6,226	3,099	20,786	14,731	5,752	2,552	1,756
Solano County	40,076	21,174	10,603	8,004	10,183	8,337	4,433	38,716	26,592	8,005	5,037	4,251
Sonoma County	43,418	22,113	14,203	13,873	17,394	13,884	5,377	55,451	36,240	10,742	6,618	4,541
Stanislaus County	29,451	12,093	4,833	9,604	12,873	10,301	8,809	40,242	27,755	17,331	9,295	6,839
Sutter County	5,066	1,863	1,480	1,977	1,527	1,672	1,403	7,499	6,558	3,192	1,958	1,868
Tulare County	21,312	6,334	3,576	4,722	7,652	5,666	5,267	29,475	20,415	14,974	7,231	5,105
Ventura County	72,059	26,363	15,172	21,011	20,333	19,386	6,194	70,318	54,534	14,104	8,970	8,745
Yolo County	15,755	8,715	4,350	1,711	3,553	2,533	1,082	14,511	10,426	4,631	2,560	2,238
Yuba County	3,539	1,223	478	1,248	1,038	1,278	2,290	5,512	3,481	2,230	839	379
Colorado												
Adams County	35,478	11,317	5,879	5,727	9,812	8,017	3,573	30,467	18,654	8,527	3,455	2,831
Arapahoe County	52,307	17,445	8,595	11,573	12,373	10,077	4,708	49,168	29,672	9,070	5,008	4,145
Boulder County	27,969	10,516	4,884	7,520	8,272	7,369	1,765	26,576	16,184	3,809	1,618	1,670
Broomfield County	5,794	2,456	1,598	1,640	1,911	1,427	70	5,204	3,725	343	280	271
Denver County	39,832	14,455	9,121	10,652	12,619	10,477	8,268	47,672	30,193	13,126	7,482	6,982
Douglas County	34,121	9,780	4,892	6,180	6,859	4,686	1,982	23,547	13,825	1,966	1,453	793
El Paso County	43,878	14,631	7,516	12,769	16,412	11,311	6,544	53,763	32,678	13,342	4,664	4,270
Jefferson County	59,753	19,521	12,057	12,016	15,374	13,157	5,609	54,309	35,529	7,175	3,963	3,594
Larimer County	30,428	10,523	5,600	6,749	10,799	7,880	1,956	31,923	19,347	4,148	2,955	2,046
Mesa County	10,463	3,571	2,513	3,439	6,156	5,724	2,090	15,878	11,942	4,000	1,431	973
Pueblo County	11,458	4,925	4,529	1,769	6,016	4,212	5,013	16,783	12,235	5,978	2,454	2,558
Weld County	21,220	5,960	3,948	5,758	8,061	4,901	3,727	23,072	13,716	4,867	2,856	1,951
Connecticut												
Fairfield County	90,109	31,603	18,171	21,310	24,525	23,598	5,670	72,301	63,112	13,886	7,652	9,702
Hartford County	88,992	34,134	23,621	11,912	18,954	21,751	10,607	76,427	63,929	18,484	10,948	11,761
Litchfield County	22,916	8,263	5,075	4,721	7,113	6,695	2,611	20,317	14,573	3,475	2,977	2,064
Middlesex County	20,259	7,734	4,612	2,161	4,430	5,571	1,879	17,289	12,813	2,747	1,903	1,265
New Haven County	79,132	31,114	19,503	15,413	20,801	23,520	8,190	75,902	61,280	18,880	10,339	9,376
New London County	25,190	11,082	8,124	5,712	7,765	7,132	3,310	25,203	19,580	5,316	3,650	2,282
Tolland County	16,147	6,051	3,707	2,146	3,808	3,815	1,470	13,207	9,238	1,447	1,504	866
Windham County	12,329	4,445	2,477	1,345	3,090	2,582	1,883	10,484	7,177	2,545	1,452	1,704
Delaware												
Kent County	14,096	8,757	5,036	2,286	5,441	3,816	4,462	16,606	11,848	5,630	2,074	1,322
New Castle County	53,441	22,888	13,452	6,612	16,382	13,392	4,891	47,718	33,847	11,078	4,720	4,079
Sussex County	23,740	17,081	10,823	6,348	12,267	9,626	3,797	38,310	23,416	4,906	3,807	2,420
Florida												
Alachua County	19,133	7,855	3,954	5,476	6,715	4,852	2,983	21,255	14,359	2,971	4,289	3,239
Bay County	14,162	5,601	3,287	4,409	5,479	3,750	3,832	16,907	11,944	3,625	2,873	1,997
Brevard County	53,194	20,233	18,479	19,202	20,546	20,714	10,587	73,134	62,574	9,990	8,005	8,432
Broward County	133,315	40,021	23,831	63,660	29,849	29,461	19,812	158,739	132,301	22,375	27,423	26,300
Charlotte County	17,919	9,809	9,325	6,054	17,096	15,023	4,886	38,227	33,774	1,802	2,685	3,598
Citrus County	10,298	6,547	7,461	5,471	7,847	8,834	3,516	28,544	24,083	2,808	3,294	2,538
Clay County	17,723	5,289	3,050	4,294	5,161	3,173	3,080	21,835	11,762	2,076	3,302	1,192
Collier County	27,861	16,483	15,087	13,404	20,623	31,541	3,677	57,215	60,542	2,973	4,739	3,612
Columbia County	4,462	1,267	1,248	2,195	2,211	1,769	1,461	7,014	5,276	938	1,607	1,066
Duval County	67,382	19,235	12,133	15,314	16,077	14,609	12,191	77,479	48,233	14,727	12,112	9,135
Escambia County	19,690	7,008	4,831	8,053	11,187	7,811	6,093	29,693	20,231	5,349	3,475	2,132
Flagler County	9,945	6,505	5,832	2,798	4,587	5,225	1,740	18,131	15,784	1,571	2,390	4,169
Hernando County	12,253	7,703	7,354	4,985	5,092	6,614	5,431	27,326	23,666	6,195	3,128	4,175
Highlands County	6,726	3,403	5,209	1,888	5,240	8,460	1,522	15,980	18,694	1,747	2,492	1,963
Hillsborough County	92,431	32,098	14,422	27,644	23,445	19,785	17,648	113,370	79,260	20,477	16,959	16,386
Indian River County	10,977	7,296	7,575	5,600	9,764	8,390	3,572	26,457	23,562	3,838	2,004	1,667
Lake County	24,859	16,860	11,168	9,720	13,602	13,208	5,762	48,023	42,151	5,106	4,790	3,562
Lee County	57,607	39,370	27,277	22,203	36,948	36,820	11,333	112,993	93,092	11,262	9,582	11,067
Leon County	20,799	9,745	5,630	4,202	7,154	4,518	2,797	22,927	14,194	4,284	3,098	1,768
Manatee County	34,820	17,883	15,123	11,237	16,329	15,515	6,406	53,890	47,210	4,721	5,493	3,953
Marion County	24,577	14,320	14,369	9,325	12,961	12,318	5,405	53,879	46,833	6,200	5,192	5,526
Martin County	14,800	9,503	6,796	5,358	8,046	11,045	2,366	23,304	25,078	2,436	2,281	2,238
Miami-Dade County	153,888	31,306	14,068	78,147	25,937	19,337	26,258	213,395	195,209	39,152	76,251	87,706
Monroe County	6,173	3,526	1,363	2,497	3,335	2,026	744	10,298	5,923	666	1,293	915
Nassau County	6,277	2,755	2,460	2,945	4,755	2,357	1,437	11,105	6,946	1,802	1,369	1,257
Okaloosa County	12,965	5,919	2,989	3,443	4,591	3,540	2,551	19,981	13,056	2,784	2,007	1,341
Orange County	88,559	25,787	12,430	25,302	21,433	15,892	15,035	88,948	61,530	18,571	14,509	13,507
Osceola County	20,275	4,392	2,345	6,972	5,098	3,481	5,999	28,830	17,676	6,538	8,105	4,365
Palm Beach County	108,947	49,064	43,502	42,873	46,758	62,022	13,749	159,641	175,064	20,810	17,146	23,087
Pasco County	36,186	16,029	13,021	10,626	14,449	15,532	10,189	64,809	52,641	10,819	10,828	7,348
Pinellas County	84,793	31,617	23,941	31,649	31,228	33,326	16,242	121,571	105,621	16,919	13,675	11,987
Polk County	44,420	23,676	17,723	15,550	22,471	19,602	13,306	76,643	60,461	13,853	11,993	11,406
Putnam County	4,526	1,729	2,018	1,239	3,408	2,157	2,366	10,107	6,568	1,349	1,331	475
St. Johns County	24,291	10,886	6,218	7,227	11,435	8,250	1,946	29,351	19,499	2,427	3,980	1,283

Table I-2: Counties - Persons With Health Insurance by Source of Insurance—*Continued*

| | Private Health Insurance Coverage | | | | | | Public Health Insurance Coverage | | | | | |
| | Employer Based | | | Direct Purchase | | | Medicare | | | Medicaid/CHIP | | |
	55 to 64 Years	65 to 74 Years	75 Years and Over	55 to 64 Years	65 to 74 Years	75 Years and Over	55 to 64 Years	65 to 74 Years	75 Years and Over	55 to 64 Years	65 to 74 Years	75 Years and Over
Florida—Cont.												
St. Lucie County	22,704	10,025	8,060	10,338	12,529	10,677	5,502	40,432	33,557	4,616	5,177	5,763
Santa Rosa County	13,639	6,540	3,981	4,226	2,949	3,413	2,524	16,574	10,739	2,342	808	972
Sarasota County	34,364	21,160	22,334	16,112	33,427	35,510	6,204	76,169	74,591	5,873	4,183	7,482
Seminole County	38,791	10,633	5,008	10,705	9,949	9,000	5,011	40,797	27,856	4,331	4,098	3,255
Sumter County	7,588	15,110	10,045	6,469	14,348	14,352	1,481	40,399	30,842	1,378	1,903	3,478
Volusia County	40,800	17,799	14,961	16,885	19,923	18,689	10,003	71,056	56,178	9,793	6,406	7,104
Walton County	5,103	1,988	1,226	2,586	3,367	1,494	1,187	8,883	5,101	727	531	461
Georgia												
Barrow County	4,511	2,392	1,105	1,768	1,642	918	1,394	6,436	3,416	779	553	272
Bartow County	7,436	3,639	978	2,287	1,617	1,846	2,279	9,423	4,886	1,955	1,844	817
Bibb County	9,782	5,227	3,167	3,326	4,178	3,907	2,618	13,082	9,164	2,821	3,237	1,852
Bulloch County	4,049	1,606	1,251	819	1,101	853	939	5,056	3,244	1,140	853	342
Carroll County	7,482	3,550	2,178	3,251	2,560	2,219	2,310	9,928	6,315	1,837	1,693	1,331
Catoosa County	5,453	2,454	1,103	864	2,266	1,870	869	6,944	4,793	531	1,126	314
Chatham County	22,132	9,205	4,923	4,640	5,525	5,227	3,312	24,978	16,978	3,575	3,852	2,337
Cherokee County	22,646	6,546	2,890	3,845	7,536	3,725	1,761	22,473	12,244	1,694	1,823	1,085
Clarke County	6,106	5,109	1,737	1,240	2,489	1,580	1,341	8,774	5,301	1,517	1,597	1,485
Clayton County	17,542	5,307	2,865	3,994	3,589	1,764	4,152	16,520	7,978	4,366	2,898	1,943
Cobb County	64,717	21,315	9,052	12,838	17,275	12,863	5,152	52,591	32,233	4,634	3,585	3,540
Columbia County	12,972	4,749	3,554	1,657	3,042	2,170	1,877	13,773	6,906	642	1,362	494
Coweta County	10,592	5,222	2,045	2,174	3,978	2,058	2,125	12,818	7,235	1,427	1,438	808
DeKalb County	52,784	19,726	8,401	12,492	14,390	9,053	7,820	54,397	32,125	10,084	8,582	6,168
Dougherty County	5,700	2,402	1,503	1,223	2,187	1,955	1,258	7,844	5,429	1,795	1,874	1,530
Douglas County	11,448	4,167	1,624	1,705	3,510	1,761	1,542	10,530	5,447	1,417	1,126	835
Fayette County	12,554	5,467	2,988	3,501	3,539	1,875	439	12,183	7,501	1,043	1,727	1,082
Floyd County	7,563	2,736	2,352	1,853	3,133	2,598	2,300	8,905	6,658	1,285	800	963
Forsyth County	18,379	5,397	3,246	4,921	4,536	5,034	421	16,586	10,283	798	1,097	1,483
Fulton County	70,056	26,295	17,362	18,429	18,212	15,846	11,355	66,496	47,126	15,910	12,623	7,740
Glynn County	6,846	2,957	2,129	2,112	2,569	2,050	1,601	10,002	6,089	1,429	745	434
Gwinnett County	67,746	18,184	9,341	17,546	13,060	8,869	7,613	55,690	31,106	9,567	5,191	4,303
Hall County	15,025	5,033	4,349	2,883	6,113	6,306	1,728	17,032	12,139	2,431	2,270	2,454
Henry County	18,823	7,293	3,625	4,181	3,594	2,630	2,060	16,156	8,914	2,534	1,546	608
Houston County	10,688	4,619	3,903	2,869	2,179	1,686	3,216	10,813	6,748	2,083	1,684	860
Jackson County	5,133	1,966	1,386	834	1,422	1,130	332	5,804	4,104	531	658	1,115
Lowndes County	6,111	3,335	3,203	2,108	2,026	1,277	1,039	7,880	5,724	1,677	1,400	838
Muscogee County	8,970	3,752	2,415	2,942	4,815	3,517	4,238	14,088	10,664	3,924	3,102	2,704
Newton County	6,474	2,251	1,839	2,359	2,036	2,173	992	8,613	5,260	1,473	1,396	596
Paulding County	13,256	4,353	1,748	2,769	2,125	1,094	1,723	10,284	6,233	600	1,261	537
Richmond County	13,399	5,190	3,060	2,604	3,027	2,106	2,750	16,349	9,675	3,383	3,320	1,740
Rockdale County	8,242	3,998	1,882	2,010	1,604	1,283	729	7,396	4,508	541	1,560	295
Spalding County	4,219	2,415	1,395	681	1,979	1,383	1,272	6,936	4,718	1,122	664	1,248
Troup County	5,192	2,011	1,169	1,286	1,350	986	1,751	5,538	3,912	1,257	1,000	785
Walker County	6,059	1,378	1,208	1,285	1,656	1,895	736	7,012	5,369	840	889	1,178
Walton County	7,799	2,489	2,436	1,589	2,547	2,682	1,172	7,853	5,573	1,190	1,425	375
Whitfield County	7,045	1,731	714	1,066	2,353	2,500	1,344	7,993	5,532	1,258	1,061	578
Hawaii												
Hawaii County	15,345	10,875	6,116	4,865	8,262	5,499	2,460	25,653	14,312	6,020	3,499	2,973
Honolulu County	87,738	56,128	38,721	13,386	19,319	21,813	5,244	86,107	74,813	13,082	10,818	9,975
Kauai County	6,886	3,956	2,777	819	1,548	773	759	7,971	5,438	1,268	501	419
Maui County	14,817	7,689	5,168	5,241	3,966	4,401	1,916	17,114	11,402	2,589	1,522	1,188
Idaho												
Ada County	35,726	11,218	7,399	10,896	16,386	11,887	4,943	39,737	24,699	3,858	4,845	4,092
Bannock County	6,064	1,470	730	1,833	3,888	2,470	998	7,009	4,815	869	562	734
Bonneville County	8,158	2,756	1,484	1,661	2,782	2,478	1,255	8,731	5,953	1,424	1,761	596
Canyon County	13,393	4,051	1,679	4,600	8,178	6,834	3,045	18,657	12,496	2,903	2,296	1,360
Kootenai County	11,651	4,625	2,929	4,781	6,731	4,889	1,525	17,531	11,849	1,445	1,470	1,203
Twin Falls County	5,807	1,275	1,218	2,179	4,000	2,525	1,145	7,230	5,403	1,284	692	877
Illinois												
Adams County	6,424	2,317	1,481	1,125	2,271	2,880	635	6,433	5,579	929	1,030	835
Champaign County	15,814	7,989	5,035	2,371	4,582	3,440	1,672	14,362	9,830	3,288	716	1,062
Cook County	386,124	134,041	74,743	76,406	107,267	103,341	51,824	385,833	301,745	107,669	61,340	47,772
DeKalb County	8,480	3,598	1,873	1,879	2,231	2,391	927	7,450	4,862	833	453	328
DuPage County	99,922	30,374	15,795	19,179	30,199	23,904	4,978	78,656	53,385	7,803	4,749	6,073
Kane County	48,190	13,682	8,793	8,362	19,355	13,405	4,010	41,342	26,956	5,346	2,476	2,122
Kankakee County	8,366	3,242	1,866	1,508	3,116	3,004	2,316	9,159	7,643	2,109	1,414	1,047
Kendall County	8,691	3,862	1,455	2,068	2,764	3,026	907	7,611	5,388	594	179	227
Lake County	69,358	18,885	10,141	14,131	17,499	13,880	4,908	54,276	37,803	6,672	3,527	3,444
LaSalle County	9,780	4,236	2,251	2,898	4,766	4,007	1,277	10,908	8,239	1,904	321	682
McHenry County	33,373	10,058	4,577	7,165	9,388	8,042	1,633	26,036	16,283	2,103	1,498	776
McLean County	15,267	5,786	3,075	2,854	4,614	3,562	1,209	12,138	8,328	1,400	607	612
Macon County	9,973	4,449	3,413	1,794	4,530	2,968	1,611	10,938	8,813	1,790	1,245	1,286
Madison County	24,994	8,008	6,524	4,321	7,365	8,964	5,953	23,978	18,824	5,689	2,337	1,955
Peoria County	16,282	5,320	5,565	2,414	5,843	4,897	1,957	16,887	11,608	3,249	1,331	424
Rock Island County	13,404	5,602	5,785	2,117	5,514	3,802	2,117	14,036	11,249	3,170	1,257	1,112
St. Clair County	22,204	7,581	4,260	3,948	6,212	4,368	4,815	21,992	16,462	6,623	2,793	2,566

Table I-2: Counties - Persons With Health Insurance by Source of Insurance—*Continued*

	Private Health Insurance Coverage						Public Health Insurance Coverage					
	Employer Based			Direct Purchase			Medicare			Medicaid/CHIP		
	55 to 64 Years	65 to 74 Years	75 Years and Over	55 to 64 Years	65 to 74 Years	75 Years and Over	55 to 64 Years	65 to 74 Years	75 Years and Over	55 to 64 Years	65 to 74 Years	75 Years and Over
Illinois—Cont.												
Sangamon County	20,062	11,340	7,979	3,055	4,884	4,912	2,127	19,103	13,723	3,747	2,241	971
Tazewell County	13,381	5,733	5,048	2,217	5,672	4,615	1,496	13,514	10,329	1,966	1,208	861
Vermilion County	6,041	2,493	1,933	1,385	2,886	3,134	1,349	7,880	6,363	1,793	1,038	662
Will County	65,474	21,096	10,638	11,446	17,160	15,388	4,690	49,837	33,952	7,221	4,544	3,334
Williamson County	5,173	2,368	2,153	637	1,834	1,227	1,600	6,848	5,137	1,546	889	255
Winnebago County	24,178	9,894	6,329	7,266	9,223	9,128	4,306	26,709	19,675	6,338	3,237	1,919
Indiana												
Allen County	30,862	9,271	5,185	5,762	10,756	7,917	4,789	30,788	20,444	5,217	3,670	1,895
Bartholomew County	6,957	2,471	1,202	830	3,022	2,765	1,008	6,760	5,612	617	488	310
Boone County	6,358	1,214	373	1,038	1,675	1,193	695	5,153	3,229	965	41	301
Clark County	10,652	3,744	2,782	1,795	4,234	2,556	1,921	11,314	6,875	1,384	764	880
Delaware County	9,035	4,413	2,333	1,522	4,074	3,177	1,774	10,723	7,760	1,149	1,168	516
Elkhart County	15,627	4,299	1,739	4,249	5,096	5,927	2,014	14,767	12,417	2,317	550	1,659
Floyd County	8,622	3,099	1,559	1,063	2,862	2,219	1,324	7,397	4,091	920	894	422
Grant County	5,597	2,835	2,846	858	2,271	2,564	1,159	6,423	5,531	2,264	1,096	685
Hamilton County	29,247	7,342	4,941	5,368	8,684	7,201	1,594	23,871	15,898	1,940	986	605
Hancock County	5,962	2,292	1,245	2,079	2,328	2,068	1,070	7,939	4,461	579	1,120	249
Hendricks County	16,348	4,766	2,991	2,860	4,284	3,523	1,917	12,581	8,797	824	269	1,076
Howard County	7,724	5,440	2,980	1,053	1,961	2,199	1,156	8,694	6,625	1,332	572	400
Johnson County	13,549	4,249	2,678	2,364	5,391	3,815	1,526	12,613	8,575	1,404	1,393	1,384
Kosciusko County	6,906	1,312	1,029	1,498	2,453	2,293	468	7,352	4,838	697	347	408
Lake County	44,685	17,058	11,919	7,356	12,924	11,384	6,629	43,966	32,026	10,143	5,740	3,407
LaPorte County	9,862	3,365	1,905	2,375	6,172	3,862	1,820	11,428	7,554	1,944	779	550
Madison County	9,099	5,125	4,282	3,278	3,022	3,576	2,753	12,788	9,577	3,554	1,594	604
Marion County	70,863	24,064	12,449	13,334	19,524	16,004	12,773	65,241	45,605	19,667	7,957	7,267
Monroe County	10,038	2,358	2,133	843	4,337	3,583	1,566	10,514	7,122	3,018	1,132	397
Morgan County	7,741	3,081	1,921	1,043	1,875	1,698	856	6,816	4,115	1,392	542	365
Porter County	16,606	6,447	3,062	3,304	5,763	5,047	1,979	15,379	10,252	1,669	908	393
St. Joseph County	23,795	6,470	4,356	4,682	8,342	6,981	3,952	23,442	17,281	3,014	2,959	2,222
Tippecanoe County	11,706	3,138	2,762	1,925	5,351	3,633	2,197	12,538	8,398	2,570	817	695
Vanderburgh County	16,552	4,120	4,104	2,828	5,675	4,739	2,278	16,616	11,586	4,115	2,064	1,083
Vigo County	7,177	2,772	1,742	1,685	4,045	3,322	2,624	9,417	6,607	1,987	798	1,166
Wayne County	5,179	1,299	1,396	606	1,877	2,334	1,946	6,284	4,976	1,580	881	490
Iowa												
Black Hawk County	10,653	4,312	3,039	1,981	4,457	4,613	1,854	11,312	8,810	3,216	1,201	1,208
Dallas County	6,539	2,801	1,217	1,027	3,020	2,628	320	5,937	4,099	536	398	487
Dubuque County	9,047	2,613	1,783	2,673	4,594	4,177	1,176	8,770	7,566	1,598	655	680
Johnson County	10,944	3,978	2,756	2,016	5,468	2,814	1,302	9,999	6,608	1,248	468	663
Linn County	21,730	6,001	3,941	2,884	8,341	6,978	2,077	19,612	15,323	3,089	1,880	1,528
Polk County	41,572	11,821	7,013	6,699	18,763	12,061	5,324	35,612	23,792	9,293	3,135	2,402
Pottawattamie County	9,392	2,385	1,194	1,365	4,469	3,415	1,355	8,978	6,617	2,653	1,000	424
Scott County	16,724	6,670	3,169	2,801	6,925	5,324	2,066	15,036	10,881	2,975	1,662	1,344
Story County	5,819	3,440	2,054	2,143	2,820	2,567	752	5,718	4,611	698	426	370
Woodbury County	8,494	2,222	951	1,973	2,814	2,746	871	8,381	6,476	2,726	843	807
Kansas												
Butler County	6,723	870	510	1,658	2,143	2,003	819	5,429	4,198	609	442	399
Douglas County	7,722	3,763	1,463	2,390	3,163	2,673	452	8,285	5,937	1,222	571	503
Johnson County	56,048	16,398	7,952	9,295	19,484	15,988	4,481	46,666	31,677	3,362	2,323	1,835
Leavenworth County	6,898	2,275	1,148	1,731	2,589	2,315	1,148	6,706	4,750	1,637	235	335
Riley County	3,973	2,151	852	1,143	1,632	1,215	361	4,005	2,599	517	201	171
Sedgwick County	41,875	8,877	4,694	8,526	17,130	12,884	5,077	41,852	28,678	7,756	6,306	3,198
Shawnee County	14,505	6,155	4,482	4,179	6,982	5,985	3,162	17,634	12,864	2,566	2,300	1,574
Wyandotte County	11,400	3,471	1,683	1,711	3,434	2,542	2,689	10,811	7,657	3,237	1,693	677
Kentucky												
Boone County	12,680	4,339	1,811	2,282	3,021	2,525	655	10,155	6,375	877	690	317
Bullitt County	7,373	2,898	1,065	1,259	3,156	1,619	1,051	7,710	4,760	2,108	602	879
Campbell County	9,233	2,630	1,537	1,644	2,897	1,914	912	8,123	5,762	1,586	947	739
Christian County	3,438	2,034	1,368	470	837	1,304	839	4,532	3,440	1,502	615	369
Daviess County	7,901	3,271	2,395	1,809	3,697	3,100	1,706	9,480	6,644	3,094	1,464	1,197
Fayette County	23,073	9,652	7,923	4,806	9,039	6,645	4,372	24,602	16,516	6,331	2,143	1,363
Hardin County	7,028	3,774	2,351	1,386	2,730	2,316	1,488	8,729	6,083	3,305	1,960	2,041
Jefferson County	66,678	29,025	15,538	12,924	24,201	23,196	12,414	68,092	48,202	18,694	8,423	4,832
Kenton County	14,483	5,295	2,167	3,019	3,857	3,124	2,583	14,102	8,599	2,736	1,342	677
McCracken County	5,808	2,513	1,981	1,061	3,219	2,419	1,480	6,674	5,647	1,767	357	837
Madison County	6,845	2,375	1,292	1,593	1,762	1,393	1,091	7,547	4,521	1,989	887	350
Oldham County	6,443	2,111	1,262	1,118	2,611	1,432	617	5,078	2,847	1,016	1,021	446
Warren County	8,480	3,853	2,015	1,997	3,905	2,580	2,351	10,452	6,131	2,640	920	680
Louisiana												
Ascension Parish	10,992	2,841	1,295	1,871	1,873	668	1,232	8,831	4,506	1,332	1,219	1,086
Bossier Parish	7,628	4,358	2,192	1,874	2,548	1,598	2,124	9,707	6,634	1,822	1,685	1,209
Caddo Parish	16,362	8,241	5,172	5,160	6,018	6,134	5,131	21,493	15,717	7,249	3,236	3,177
Calcasieu Parish	14,669	5,619	3,693	4,027	5,053	4,303	4,496	17,838	11,196	4,958	1,995	1,870
East Baton Rouge Parish	29,808	15,828	9,565	8,212	8,975	6,417	5,813	35,924	23,076	10,636	6,771	4,373
Iberia Parish	5,353	2,770	855	1,620	2,218	1,721	1,755	5,726	3,916	1,864	641	652
Jefferson Parish	35,229	13,135	6,626	7,739	8,288	7,288	6,459	39,524	28,933	10,114	5,384	4,185

Table I-2: Counties - Persons With Health Insurance by Source of Insurance—*Continued*

| | Private Health Insurance Coverage | | | | | | Public Health Insurance Coverage | | | | | |
| | Employer Based | | | Direct Purchase | | | Medicare | | | Medicaid/CHIP | | |
	55 to 64 Years	65 to 74 Years	75 Years and Over	55 to 64 Years	65 to 74 Years	75 Years and Over	55 to 64 Years	65 to 74 Years	75 Years and Over	55 to 64 Years	65 to 74 Years	75 Years and Over
Louisiana—Cont.												
Lafayette Parish	15,249	6,570	3,587	6,450	7,040	5,679	3,754	18,213	11,599	5,891	2,248	859
Lafourche Parish	7,336	3,017	1,405	1,456	2,134	1,867	2,237	7,748	6,814	2,058	1,287	2,261
Livingston Parish	8,492	4,090	2,418	2,927	1,670	637	1,602	10,738	7,090	2,530	937	364
Orleans Parish	21,149	9,190	4,300	7,898	5,951	5,093	7,296	33,241	20,160	16,500	7,422	4,593
Ouachita Parish	11,685	4,292	3,278	2,462	3,292	2,707	1,445	12,966	8,514	3,157	2,969	1,386
Rapides Parish	9,345	4,160	2,656	2,082	2,973	2,290	2,628	11,758	7,979	3,821	1,771	825
St. Landry Parish	6,412	3,423	1,209	718	1,763	1,347	2,041	6,887	4,596	1,740	1,255	581
St. Tammany Parish	23,004	10,034	5,483	5,581	5,246	4,860	3,288	25,312	15,855	4,845	2,474	1,578
Tangipahoa Parish	8,704	3,554	2,080	1,951	2,689	2,177	1,982	11,014	6,446	2,232	1,003	564
Terrebonne Parish	8,384	3,178	1,151	1,769	1,973	1,713	2,521	9,597	5,890	2,716	1,260	1,483
Maine												
Androscoggin County	9,939	2,171	1,491	1,082	3,777	2,961	1,924	10,927	7,076	2,240	2,372	2,027
Aroostook County	5,333	1,897	1,013	1,947	2,802	2,868	1,506	8,854	6,119	1,961	2,011	2,081
Cumberland County	29,611	9,673	5,256	6,768	8,228	6,758	2,118	30,297	20,172	3,422	3,153	2,380
Kennebec County	10,634	5,631	2,528	2,748	4,311	3,299	2,717	13,591	9,156	3,090	2,014	2,439
Penobscot County	13,506	4,506	3,451	2,491	4,443	4,320	3,792	15,672	10,362	5,061	3,296	1,899
York County	23,051	7,504	6,588	5,189	7,312	5,669	2,752	23,857	16,750	3,435	2,782	3,021
Maryland												
Allegany County	4,968	3,195	2,363	1,186	2,140	2,762	1,094	6,938	6,165	2,028	1,174	973
Anne Arundel County	55,313	26,103	18,319	8,779	14,015	11,447	4,673	45,971	33,151	7,415	4,415	2,758
Baltimore County	79,508	40,555	25,749	17,116	25,382	24,748	9,562	71,823	58,740	13,538	8,391	9,298
Calvert County	10,262	5,099	2,281	1,021	2,533	1,937	1,063	7,527	4,904	1,405	630	386
Carroll County	19,780	8,118	5,012	3,055	5,595	4,649	2,010	15,039	11,019	2,946	1,399	1,392
Cecil County	10,290	4,602	2,191	2,111	2,955	2,230	1,772	9,769	5,574	2,413	695	264
Charles County	16,583	8,084	4,154	2,313	3,007	1,590	735	11,140	7,312	1,982	2,044	704
Frederick County	27,012	10,676	6,409	4,226	6,836	5,840	1,792	19,955	13,912	2,729	1,103	1,137
Harford County	26,693	10,624	8,764	3,566	6,505	5,812	2,986	23,766	16,579	3,532	3,541	2,362
Howard County	32,219	17,298	8,363	4,643	6,751	5,890	2,286	25,118	15,779	2,906	2,272	2,640
Montgomery County	97,154	52,823	31,984	21,916	19,837	20,968	4,867	78,891	64,814	11,782	9,511	11,892
Prince George's County	81,993	43,920	24,167	14,358	16,010	11,592	6,115	66,653	40,542	13,798	8,668	6,872
St. Mary's County	10,955	5,793	3,343	1,204	2,121	1,625	1,331	7,774	5,280	1,099	529	687
Washington County	12,916	6,352	3,909	1,988	4,893	4,632	2,024	13,903	10,841	2,805	1,396	1,521
Wicomico County	8,448	4,146	2,337	1,167	3,025	2,112	1,555	8,742	6,683	2,238	1,247	1,114
Massachusetts												
Barnstable County	24,468	16,107	10,925	7,565	13,739	11,528	1,778	35,488	26,575	6,259	3,919	2,178
Berkshire County	12,880	6,656	4,918	1,644	5,038	5,150	2,259	15,315	11,786	4,967	1,991	1,953
Bristol County	52,549	22,191	10,004	8,607	16,250	16,996	8,652	51,815	36,631	16,563	10,120	7,016
Essex County	74,478	34,331	17,949	14,614	23,446	23,461	8,862	71,500	52,991	22,342	12,739	10,734
Franklin County	7,183	4,938	2,382	2,111	3,113	2,277	2,061	8,758	5,331	3,453	1,577	1,094
Hampden County	38,551	18,370	10,358	5,660	11,930	12,744	6,759	41,887	30,888	16,052	9,117	6,901
Hampshire County	15,702	9,528	4,132	2,896	3,822	4,088	2,193	15,881	9,812	3,621	1,508	1,403
Middlesex County	150,368	68,001	36,879	27,258	39,096	37,964	12,978	120,856	99,760	32,413	17,317	15,744
Norfolk County	72,970	30,174	18,088	13,113	20,674	18,926	4,363	60,061	46,092	13,244	8,684	8,091
Plymouth County	55,623	25,116	13,351	9,864	16,867	14,209	5,386	51,584	34,619	12,667	7,578	5,918
Suffolk County	47,412	19,418	10,052	8,085	10,534	8,917	7,870	51,007	37,084	28,049	15,522	13,242
Worcester County	80,236	29,181	18,034	13,723	23,790	19,758	10,203	68,512	49,465	22,963	11,805	9,761
Michigan												
Allegan County	11,217	4,009	1,962	2,569	4,991	2,573	1,516	11,439	7,122	2,719	862	662
Bay County	10,567	6,505	4,815	2,144	3,338	2,363	2,853	11,626	8,429	2,841	854	430
Berrien County	14,093	7,746	4,351	3,002	6,158	6,296	1,997	16,674	12,552	3,661	1,457	1,242
Calhoun County	10,508	6,549	5,041	1,807	3,491	3,626	3,269	12,594	9,708	3,737	1,696	1,426
Clinton County	8,617	5,479	3,673	1,234	1,838	1,411	1,431	7,630	5,202	1,294	433	484
Eaton County	12,126	8,334	5,200	1,865	2,754	2,197	1,618	12,114	7,734	1,933	807	1,325
Genesee County	35,222	22,671	19,251	6,134	9,434	8,562	10,370	39,667	29,381	14,290	5,540	3,117
Grand Traverse County	8,367	4,250	2,422	2,641	3,711	4,177	990	10,785	6,863	1,716	1,166	644
Ingham County	22,279	15,676	7,897	2,519	6,259	5,155	4,223	23,564	14,627	5,248	3,284	1,641
Isabella County	4,895	2,493	1,876	913	1,433	1,411	949	5,186	3,497	1,039	643	584
Jackson County	14,994	7,438	4,745	2,645	5,063	4,871	3,105	15,817	11,091	3,563	1,733	885
Kalamazoo County	21,799	9,515	6,721	3,779	8,298	7,908	2,765	22,688	15,364	3,360	2,774	1,066
Kent County	53,721	18,056	11,025	12,499	16,866	15,413	7,700	50,072	34,754	11,506	5,675	3,665
Lapeer County	8,688	5,752	3,413	2,686	3,118	2,439	1,297	9,498	5,875	1,734	924	598
Lenawee County	9,490	4,621	2,883	1,846	3,222	2,972	1,941	10,368	6,867	2,274	1,028	442
Livingston County	22,945	11,346	6,394	4,373	7,433	5,445	2,363	19,766	12,173	1,998	850	846
Macomb County	85,048	40,778	28,225	14,893	27,973	25,686	13,888	81,755	60,934	18,814	11,941	8,488
Marquette County	6,186	3,951	2,681	1,017	1,893	2,071	1,033	7,372	4,939	1,357	784	406
Midland County	7,395	5,107	4,258	1,127	2,419	2,104	1,609	8,390	6,681	2,285	387	709
Monroe County	17,066	8,222	5,924	2,399	4,276	3,548	2,129	15,886	10,949	2,610	1,423	1,196
Muskegon County	15,406	6,640	3,958	3,215	5,904	4,822	3,746	16,771	11,277	4,293	1,968	1,663
Oakland County	124,888	60,236	34,680	28,520	40,541	33,800	15,234	116,367	82,683	18,648	10,085	10,398
Ottawa County	26,166	8,927	6,526	5,098	8,359	7,560	1,723	23,708	18,181	2,881	1,924	2,109
Saginaw County	16,755	12,136	7,973	3,891	5,526	6,267	4,132	19,770	14,959	5,798	2,451	1,849
St. Clair County	16,421	8,969	5,599	3,699	4,872	4,679	3,230	17,031	11,451	4,036	2,663	1,505
Shiawassee County	7,156	4,867	2,987	1,109	2,220	2,264	1,202	7,346	4,785	1,612	961	972

Table I-2: Counties - Persons With Health Insurance by Source of Insurance—*Continued*

	Private Health Insurance Coverage						Public Health Insurance Coverage					
	Employer Based			Direct Purchase			Medicare			Medicaid/CHIP		
	55 to 64 Years	65 to 74 Years	75 Years and Over	55 to 64 Years	65 to 74 Years	75 Years and Over	55 to 64 Years	65 to 74 Years	75 Years and Over	55 to 64 Years	65 to 74 Years	75 Years and Over
Michigan—Cont.												
Van Buren County	6,254	3,076	1,469	2,186	2,527	1,721	1,271	8,185	5,139	2,279	1,080	630
Washtenaw County	30,617	18,127	11,048	5,329	7,737	6,907	4,148	29,315	19,178	4,235	3,186	2,364
Wayne County	136,623	72,549	51,139	26,059	36,372	34,716	33,141	147,274	106,944	57,817	30,831	20,378
Minnesota												
Anoka County	37,933	9,402	4,205	4,770	14,221	10,628	1,601	28,121	17,685	5,760	1,815	1,285
Blue Earth County	4,613	994	375	717	2,847	2,425	479	5,061	3,786	875	390	673
Carver County	10,979	2,270	1,035	1,719	3,319	3,225	412	7,339	4,834	503	309	117
Dakota County	44,899	11,699	5,465	7,252	17,773	13,303	3,741	32,883	22,906	6,077	1,858	1,505
Hennepin County	107,330	28,841	13,214	24,495	45,131	39,200	9,428	95,517	67,996	20,838	10,845	9,467
Olmsted County	15,713	6,060	3,582	2,345	5,590	5,084	957	12,592	10,255	2,074	941	1,304
Ramsey County	43,418	15,506	8,972	9,277	19,958	15,639	4,795	43,519	30,657	11,577	5,100	3,436
Rice County	5,254	1,052	1,025	1,736	2,666	2,359	486	5,576	4,026	949	408	555
St. Louis County	19,768	8,202	5,107	4,320	9,965	7,394	3,301	21,551	14,737	4,880	1,420	1,727
Scott County	12,844	2,217	1,340	3,220	5,086	3,550	818	9,609	5,671	1,640	606	144
Sherburne County	9,395	1,585	582	1,069	3,344	2,276	875	6,470	3,565	839	752	342
Stearns County	12,973	3,702	1,788	2,896	7,578	6,427	1,553	13,090	9,720	1,962	488	936
Washington County	28,083	7,751	3,946	4,286	10,751	7,926	1,223	22,191	14,862	2,802	1,095	1,430
Wright County	11,599	3,438	885	2,834	4,743	3,821	1,190	9,728	6,660	2,043	942	464
Mississippi												
DeSoto County	14,927	3,333	1,558	2,783	5,385	3,829	1,276	13,361	8,977	1,620	721	1,241
Forrest County	2,998	922	696	773	2,009	1,180	1,261	6,010	3,815	2,167	1,374	937
Harrison County	13,013	6,454	2,758	2,995	6,131	5,128	4,015	18,255	11,572	3,556	2,404	1,613
Hinds County	16,648	5,631	3,480	3,960	4,205	4,301	3,738	18,588	12,996	5,496	3,379	2,647
Jackson County	10,400	2,659	1,724	1,580	3,015	1,811	2,411	13,337	8,785	2,747	887	505
Jones County	4,251	1,558	857	1,193	1,492	2,478	1,920	6,639	4,381	2,047	1,746	647
Lauderdale County	5,162	1,633	956	620	1,439	1,316	1,794	6,713	5,415	1,431	1,490	1,873
Lee County	6,585	1,748	570	1,317	2,187	2,271	1,731	6,624	4,768	1,370	486	403
Madison County	10,747	2,901	772	1,691	2,837	1,116	548	8,771	4,736	670	1,167	278
Rankin County	12,548	4,233	1,537	1,729	3,668	3,420	1,361	13,693	8,279	1,321	1,175	1,331
Missouri												
Boone County	13,965	5,510	3,580	1,923	3,611	2,216	2,036	12,775	7,967	1,605	860	520
Buchanan County	6,122	2,444	1,204	1,665	5,151	2,674	2,186	8,753	5,338	1,585	740	730
Cape Girardeau County	5,853	2,193	1,377	1,372	3,196	2,595	1,430	6,814	5,381	1,350	578	335
Cass County	10,584	2,965	1,759	1,942	3,614	3,213	1,732	9,927	7,379	393	468	216
Christian County	7,364	2,380	878	1,619	3,211	2,160	1,092	7,646	5,248	403	996	921
Clay County	21,394	6,892	4,428	3,069	6,952	6,595	3,350	19,769	13,308	2,230	843	533
Cole County	6,950	3,859	1,800	1,612	2,081	1,689	394	7,126	4,784	240	293	224
Franklin County	9,310	2,857	2,279	2,101	2,480	2,153	1,850	9,718	7,379	1,029	826	373
Greene County	18,932	4,012	3,253	5,382	7,528	8,918	5,224	25,744	20,084	3,153	3,810	2,116
Jackson County	56,718	17,995	13,170	11,767	18,770	15,435	12,004	56,951	40,822	8,673	4,852	3,742
Jasper County	8,207	1,850	1,347	1,459	3,253	3,569	1,134	10,442	7,620	1,859	839	759
Jefferson County	21,610	7,791	3,745	4,029	4,396	3,965	3,077	19,778	12,018	3,654	1,034	522
Platte County	9,537	3,183	1,356	2,465	3,792	2,294	1,084	8,887	5,635	607	205	518
St. Charles County	42,406	10,286	7,303	6,094	11,548	8,688	3,745	33,578	23,381	2,064	1,505	2,062
St. Francois County	5,236	2,118	1,364	792	2,079	1,373	830	6,167	3,853	1,342	554	630
St. Louis County	97,523	33,729	23,530	21,690	26,129	24,445	11,573	93,202	72,486	10,220	5,776	6,263
Montana												
Cascade County	6,268	1,467	1,021	1,512	2,655	2,813	1,421	8,359	6,244	1,951	1,096	369
Flathead County	7,954	2,804	1,522	3,845	5,394	3,118	1,101	11,960	7,081	2,052	1,199	794
Gallatin County	8,418	2,939	1,064	2,681	3,577	2,636	825	8,744	4,986	817	717	281
Lewis and Clark County	6,006	2,520	1,598	1,682	2,070	1,647	835	7,887	4,396	1,001	690	502
Missoula County	8,913	3,036	2,424	3,404	3,457	2,889	1,358	10,778	6,715	1,054	1,527	827
Yellowstone County	14,121	3,767	2,604	2,893	6,427	4,804	1,735	15,242	10,690	2,893	1,250	1,318
Nebraska												
Douglas County	43,349	12,658	6,429	8,559	14,718	9,626	5,618	41,797	27,115	6,205	3,736	3,760
Lancaster County	25,485	7,419	2,830	5,781	10,331	8,400	2,154	24,727	16,755	3,114	2,671	2,383
Sarpy County	13,363	4,213	2,099	2,989	4,239	3,216	1,002	12,812	8,244	1,272	942	903
Nevada												
Clark County	154,293	56,357	27,267	31,933	40,335	28,821	25,958	186,744	121,618	44,014	24,554	18,124
Washoe County	38,612	15,954	6,834	8,898	14,210	10,223	4,494	45,487	27,091	7,106	3,801	3,048
New Hampshire												
Cheshire County	7,471	2,706	1,409	1,834	2,186	2,402	1,620	8,433	5,667	540	532	404
Grafton County	9,299	4,549	2,807	1,866	2,693	3,096	1,540	10,463	6,945	1,778	805	650
Hillsborough County	46,772	12,987	5,980	5,767	13,557	11,465	5,688	33,906	23,587	4,799	2,233	2,670
Merrimack County	15,660	5,136	3,939	2,526	4,934	3,700	2,205	15,764	10,983	1,633	1,407	756
Rockingham County	39,895	15,261	7,095	5,349	11,354	8,762	3,133	31,109	20,682	2,402	1,924	1,878
Strafford County	12,242	3,651	2,863	1,203	3,708	3,817	1,579	10,978	7,548	2,303	456	1,053
New Jersey												
Atlantic County	26,943	10,942	7,416	4,615	7,646	6,602	3,495	25,487	18,548	6,318	4,020	2,808
Bergen County	96,080	33,992	21,139	17,635	22,014	23,635	5,692	79,671	68,715	9,977	7,784	7,835
Burlington County	47,759	21,957	12,308	8,270	10,863	11,191	5,460	39,669	30,108	5,625	2,199	2,579
Camden County	44,322	19,867	10,747	9,443	11,734	12,177	8,072	42,203	31,416	11,158	7,955	3,585
Cape May County	10,567	5,177	3,846	2,564	4,565	3,494	1,949	13,092	9,635	1,765	1,006	694

Table I-2: Counties - Persons With Health Insurance by Source of Insurance—*Continued*

| | Private Health Insurance Coverage | | | | | | Public Health Insurance Coverage | | | | | |
| | Employer Based | | | Direct Purchase | | | Medicare | | | Medicaid/CHIP | | |
	55 to 64 Years	65 to 74 Years	75 Years and Over	55 to 64 Years	65 to 74 Years	75 Years and Over	55 to 64 Years	65 to 74 Years	75 Years and Over	55 to 64 Years	65 to 74 Years	75 Years and Over
New Jersey—Cont.												
Cumberland County	10,848	4,740	3,393	2,732	3,831	2,691	3,053	12,964	8,780	3,273	2,356	2,155
Essex County	56,980	24,030	13,184	10,214	10,469	9,870	9,025	55,543	43,084	18,200	8,765	9,519
Gloucester County	29,864	14,566	6,817	6,877	8,254	8,001	3,398	25,772	18,199	5,108	2,242	2,052
Hudson County	39,230	13,232	7,593	9,497	6,762	5,840	5,181	40,074	32,008	14,984	10,490	9,755
Hunterdon County	16,816	7,411	2,699	3,046	3,865	3,261	631	13,178	8,793	798	661	527
Mercer County	35,503	17,351	9,462	4,413	6,595	6,707	3,818	29,460	21,542	5,195	3,283	3,248
Middlesex County	76,764	31,064	17,824	15,859	15,729	17,565	7,745	63,036	50,002	8,545	8,814	10,118
Monmouth County	74,427	31,310	17,860	11,920	16,179	18,740	7,039	58,987	44,313	6,961	4,823	4,694
Morris County	57,431	20,836	15,542	8,881	14,222	14,938	4,360	41,504	35,348	5,181	2,858	4,179
Ocean County	57,665	32,209	25,018	11,211	20,992	25,269	6,593	67,773	62,660	8,870	4,849	4,893
Passaic County	38,857	13,979	7,197	5,650	7,397	8,645	5,081	36,355	30,160	12,897	6,824	5,496
Salem County	6,550	3,728	1,987	992	2,519	1,781	1,534	6,618	4,511	1,419	1,285	791
Somerset County	39,724	12,850	7,372	5,638	7,338	8,783	1,814	25,189	21,108	2,683	1,332	2,394
Sussex County	18,818	7,239	3,459	3,646	3,557	3,816	1,220	13,270	8,778	1,038	1,655	1,056
Union County	50,229	16,830	10,708	7,296	9,769	10,422	5,929	38,908	33,045	8,763	7,145	7,961
Warren County	12,540	3,891	2,471	1,910	3,538	3,438	1,517	10,154	7,942	1,148	1,137	1,453
New Mexico												
Bernalillo County	49,319	21,699	14,407	10,485	14,121	10,262	9,023	62,046	42,508	18,592	8,050	6,784
Chaves County	3,164	1,737	1,501	1,050	1,204	1,039	1,295	5,627	4,650	2,218	1,258	1,134
Doña Ana County	10,700	6,134	2,948	2,736	3,942	3,576	2,610	19,021	14,287	8,475	2,986	3,752
Lea County	3,834	1,454	515	608	881	1,224	684	4,306	2,984	1,011	266	750
McKinley County	2,049	1,134	603	738	307	675	883	4,622	4,202	3,321	1,805	1,598
Otero County	3,452	2,132	1,008	239	1,492	1,230	1,146	5,526	4,114	2,301	848	788
Sandoval County	11,665	5,215	2,323	2,878	2,303	2,346	2,277	15,397	9,213	2,608	2,979	1,928
San Juan County	7,981	2,882	1,749	1,396	2,375	1,905	2,564	10,630	7,293	3,972	2,650	1,246
Santa Fe County	13,481	8,741	4,885	4,853	7,555	4,917	1,690	21,948	12,920	3,555	1,828	824
Valencia County	5,446	3,686	1,783	1,434	1,886	1,051	1,187	8,090	5,140	2,162	806	549
New York												
Albany County	30,655	18,639	11,370	2,857	4,871	5,124	3,975	27,613	19,864	6,350	2,523	2,440
Bronx County	66,679	29,723	19,899	17,787	13,427	9,892	20,956	91,892	71,951	68,611	40,919	34,732
Broome County	18,330	9,711	7,171	3,279	4,259	5,592	3,275	18,860	15,792	5,086	2,057	2,561
Cattaraugus County	7,077	2,863	1,695	1,481	3,147	2,510	1,091	8,207	5,944	2,480	1,780	1,166
Cayuga County	7,294	3,316	2,732	1,940	1,950	2,404	1,331	7,896	5,759	2,587	1,206	695
Chautauqua County	12,418	4,560	3,024	3,151	4,977	4,624	3,260	13,275	10,826	3,639	1,490	1,954
Chemung County	8,456	3,216	2,855	1,531	2,136	1,654	1,910	9,283	6,509	2,193	1,548	950
Clinton County	7,715	3,962	2,155	1,717	1,832	1,709	1,387	7,780	5,144	2,053	852	1,064
Dutchess County	31,731	13,332	9,177	5,185	7,216	6,379	4,727	27,513	20,912	6,114	2,738	3,289
Erie County	86,786	39,802	23,543	16,238	27,730	30,179	14,617	87,481	68,177	23,971	10,688	8,102
Jefferson County	8,307	3,884	2,327	1,421	2,955	2,210	1,562	8,813	6,132	2,376	980	1,078
Kings County	151,525	71,013	33,659	36,332	29,029	21,052	23,860	185,220	145,073	87,421	60,554	59,606
Livingston County	6,463	2,582	1,214	1,441	1,798	1,896	1,242	6,282	4,356	1,426	387	517
Madison County	7,980	3,271	2,021	1,250	1,905	1,592	1,286	7,360	5,032	1,456	461	911
Monroe County	68,137	28,789	17,231	16,238	23,522	22,734	10,560	69,214	50,897	18,255	9,792	6,853
Nassau County	145,662	69,477	39,577	27,663	31,798	37,456	9,854	119,557	101,527	18,984	12,139	13,666
New York County	103,041	55,687	37,737	28,796	24,334	23,009	14,633	125,243	116,166	51,158	38,063	39,072
Niagara County	24,300	10,497	6,773	3,888	5,979	5,967	4,416	22,104	15,545	6,321	3,963	3,219
Oneida County	19,983	10,360	6,327	2,501	6,152	5,813	3,538	22,237	17,157	7,916	3,137	3,032
Onondaga County	47,515	21,888	14,925	7,925	10,870	11,246	7,938	41,553	32,407	9,282	5,729	4,908
Ontario County	11,318	4,707	2,303	2,880	4,730	4,138	1,274	12,263	8,490	1,990	1,588	1,111
Orange County	32,310	14,515	7,828	6,003	7,253	6,586	4,919	29,568	19,780	8,111	2,902	2,192
Oswego County	11,784	3,844	3,298	1,198	2,287	2,742	2,810	11,038	7,563	3,211	2,328	1,083
Putnam County	11,059	4,794	3,469	2,483	2,058	1,365	1,322	9,224	6,468	1,641	1,091	660
Queens County	165,323	68,196	36,650	38,402	27,076	24,532	19,545	179,235	144,110	80,823	45,840	43,248
Rensselaer County	17,348	10,066	5,433	1,715	4,072	3,581	2,485	15,653	9,603	2,918	1,747	950
Richmond County	46,559	20,184	10,086	6,868	7,971	4,793	6,824	42,678	28,370	9,265	6,528	4,552
Rockland County	28,404	13,960	9,918	3,102	5,405	6,140	4,300	26,460	21,708	5,829	3,563	3,445
St. Lawrence County	9,463	5,230	2,926	3,088	2,729	2,250	1,987	10,370	6,847	2,919	1,740	977
Saratoga County	25,356	15,535	8,232	2,951	5,392	6,470	2,188	23,555	15,705	3,858	1,332	1,214
Schenectady County	15,598	7,475	4,695	2,837	4,540	4,641	2,460	14,257	11,112	4,134	1,683	1,436
Steuben County	8,924	4,997	3,321	1,479	2,775	2,440	1,867	10,248	7,159	3,008	1,466	1,269
Suffolk County	161,138	73,981	44,031	27,065	35,640	35,034	14,444	130,481	103,901	26,424	12,638	12,834
Sullivan County	5,788	3,590	1,663	1,778	1,824	1,519	1,353	7,987	5,428	2,725	2,025	1,090
Tompkins County	8,652	4,743	2,930	1,676	2,104	1,981	501	7,856	5,278	1,312	1,228	191
Ulster County	17,718	8,462	6,097	3,386	5,186	3,978	1,873	18,966	14,073	4,979	2,223	2,585
Warren County	7,179	4,620	2,334	1,521	2,502	2,539	1,556	8,162	5,623	1,547	893	393
Wayne County	9,689	4,155	2,946	2,837	3,241	2,618	1,334	9,654	6,963	1,454	1,274	1,113
Westchester County	91,909	45,324	29,245	16,249	20,781	24,190	8,503	81,000	71,501	21,024	11,310	12,102
North Carolina												
Alamance County	14,844	4,804	3,550	3,694	4,932	4,580	2,141	14,988	11,682	1,426	1,387	1,879
Brunswick County	14,840	13,428	5,896	4,156	10,010	5,046	2,317	28,574	13,536	1,544	2,087	1,323
Buncombe County	21,159	8,462	4,693	6,571	9,615	7,428	2,943	28,864	19,182	3,433	3,781	2,551
Burke County	8,414	3,438	2,854	2,349	2,809	2,322	2,364	9,581	7,746	1,147	1,517	795
Cabarrus County	17,156	5,634	2,544	3,813	5,536	4,574	2,479	16,462	10,543	2,018	1,815	1,430
Caldwell County	7,095	1,852	875	1,600	3,302	2,025	1,713	9,382	6,062	1,702	1,391	870
Carteret County	6,133	4,769	2,806	2,434	3,682	1,952	1,032	10,510	6,396	1,015	775	746
Catawba County	13,836	4,588	2,361	3,859	6,297	5,063	1,878	16,259	10,772	2,398	762	818

Table I-2: Counties - Persons With Health Insurance by Source of Insurance—*Continued*

| | Private Health Insurance Coverage | | | | | | Public Health Insurance Coverage | | | | | |
| | Employer Based | | | Direct Purchase | | | Medicare | | | Medicaid/CHIP | | |
	55 to 64 Years	65 to 74 Years	75 Years and Over	55 to 64 Years	65 to 74 Years	75 Years and Over	55 to 64 Years	65 to 74 Years	75 Years and Over	55 to 64 Years	65 to 74 Years	75 Years and Over
North Carolina—Cont.												
Chatham County	7,811	5,107	2,857	2,263	3,316	2,651	505	9,531	7,301	470	769	566
Cleveland County	7,682	2,998	1,870	2,449	3,980	2,933	2,279	10,197	7,205	1,590	2,080	1,025
Craven County	7,339	3,886	2,087	1,980	3,573	2,732	1,013	10,166	8,156	1,659	1,292	1,233
Cumberland County	15,767	6,639	4,669	3,661	5,639	5,105	5,861	22,753	15,826	5,119	4,087	2,192
Davidson County	14,994	4,692	1,887	4,128	5,406	3,023	3,747	16,985	11,341	2,009	2,393	1,659
Durham County	22,958	10,661	5,661	4,802	6,585	3,540	2,975	23,216	14,996	2,763	2,098	1,903
Forsyth County	31,936	9,319	6,900	7,831	12,632	8,896	5,445	33,617	23,518	4,399	4,875	3,425
Franklin County	5,703	1,680	1,042	1,298	2,273	1,342	1,546	7,494	3,698	1,301	883	753
Gaston County	18,444	6,154	2,981	3,975	6,283	5,110	3,890	20,059	13,127	3,818	2,299	1,215
Guilford County	40,532	13,466	8,159	10,911	14,864	10,410	5,859	44,989	30,837	6,311	4,604	3,315
Harnett County	7,061	2,584	1,892	2,279	2,842	2,630	2,623	9,731	6,456	1,998	1,354	1,001
Henderson County	10,326	5,099	3,812	3,065	6,525	5,700	2,117	16,414	12,707	1,072	622	952
Iredell County	14,669	4,446	2,934	3,745	6,516	5,131	3,115	16,000	10,819	2,393	2,325	1,184
Johnston County	16,015	8,866	3,161	3,074	4,568	3,449	2,250	16,817	9,799	3,408	1,650	1,699
Lincoln County	8,124	3,144	1,622	3,344	3,268	1,493	1,094	8,391	5,151	1,009	998	811
Mecklenburg County	73,553	18,586	11,137	20,132	24,455	20,422	7,965	71,343	44,768	11,718	9,062	6,897
Moore County	7,185	4,162	3,353	2,370	4,905	4,410	1,859	12,135	9,982	1,164	1,329	1,276
Nash County	8,126	2,791	1,968	2,143	4,613	2,767	2,548	10,246	6,713	1,804	1,966	636
New Hanover County	18,361	9,486	5,334	6,267	9,640	7,306	3,157	24,215	15,560	2,346	1,737	1,648
Onslow County	7,736	4,044	3,146	3,050	1,527	1,322	1,806	10,288	7,437	1,542	1,541	1,632
Orange County	12,686	6,452	3,766	1,885	3,788	2,715	932	11,963	7,001	1,122	1,007	549
Pitt County	11,525	6,201	3,719	3,508	3,361	1,646	3,943	12,712	8,132	2,572	1,823	743
Randolph County	11,259	4,195	2,256	2,856	3,725	3,986	2,527	13,319	10,018	2,431	1,203	1,383
Robeson County	8,025	3,553	1,430	2,245	3,448	1,666	3,656	12,014	6,806	4,498	2,356	1,308
Rockingham County	7,931	2,429	1,661	2,360	3,190	2,483	2,173	10,087	7,616	1,706	1,411	1,152
Rowan County	11,162	4,172	2,317	2,996	4,631	3,979	3,208	13,545	9,306	1,914	1,759	1,322
Rutherford County	5,589	1,923	1,407	2,335	2,702	2,873	1,186	8,107	5,392	1,026	1,269	454
Surry County	5,625	2,129	2,078	1,838	2,336	2,374	1,516	7,939	6,427	768	960	580
Union County	17,879	5,957	2,377	5,189	6,760	5,204	1,977	16,726	11,177	1,478	891	904
Wake County	87,489	32,207	15,704	20,119	24,809	17,205	6,431	74,605	45,112	7,416	7,873	6,035
Wayne County	5,925	4,360	2,277	3,097	2,804	2,917	1,961	11,437	7,913	2,320	1,299	1,757
Wilkes County	5,135	1,363	1,740	2,131	2,556	2,553	1,754	8,060	6,064	1,292	879	823
Wilson County	6,314	2,565	1,651	1,145	2,754	2,188	1,397	8,169	5,599	2,023	643	925
North Dakota												
Burleigh County	8,878	3,191	1,357	2,064	3,199	3,080	1,000	7,916	6,143	573	437	210
Cass County	14,415	3,434	2,400	2,946	6,747	5,560	1,145	11,864	8,555	816	499	914
Grand Forks County	5,572	1,743	950	834	2,133	1,680	414	4,801	3,341	530	141	254
Ward County	4,995	1,530	960	1,010	2,162	2,572	273	4,290	3,508	761	529	438
Ohio												
Allen County	9,598	3,645	2,335	2,190	4,145	3,245	1,293	9,459	7,231	1,525	1,019	993
Ashtabula County	9,288	2,590	2,370	2,098	4,365	3,074	1,677	10,230	7,020	3,095	1,283	388
Athens County	4,672	1,711	1,326	600	1,448	885	894	4,807	3,243	1,883	703	244
Belmont County	6,928	3,812	1,961	1,923	2,080	1,299	1,077	7,281	5,217	1,620	1,050	509
Butler County	32,959	11,155	7,702	6,120	10,667	8,245	3,882	31,316	20,642	6,553	3,782	1,930
Clark County	11,407	6,320	4,448	2,033	3,775	3,611	2,828	13,806	10,524	2,535	1,745	1,097
Clermont County	19,793	8,085	3,909	4,399	5,585	3,573	2,720	19,125	12,327	3,849	2,062	1,151
Columbiana County	9,332	3,857	2,251	2,096	2,708	1,925	1,827	11,705	7,652	2,924	1,271	442
Cuyahoga County	109,085	43,718	32,004	21,017	33,882	29,969	17,186	116,856	93,601	34,505	17,922	13,051
Delaware County	17,413	6,996	4,441	4,454	5,745	4,161	955	15,656	10,391	1,458	627	668
Erie County	8,422	3,943	3,727	1,417	2,986	2,586	1,047	8,502	6,827	1,437	434	522
Fairfield County	13,161	4,738	2,435	2,678	4,001	3,592	2,768	14,192	9,271	2,814	690	485
Franklin County	92,290	34,128	18,311	16,611	26,613	21,291	14,295	85,593	59,596	25,657	8,879	6,567
Geauga County	11,332	3,724	3,390	1,997	4,352	3,825	1,193	10,540	7,754	1,025	268	190
Greene County	15,002	7,012	5,567	2,179	4,524	2,567	1,714	16,014	11,494	2,652	1,087	524
Hamilton County	70,479	24,799	16,664	13,614	20,292	16,360	9,469	66,336	47,702	16,858	8,202	4,563
Hancock County	8,026	2,037	2,064	1,115	2,668	2,410	658	7,025	5,055	916	737	286
Jefferson County	6,485	1,948	1,572	923	2,187	2,236	1,415	8,182	5,619	1,715	1,073	747
Lake County	24,294	9,494	7,232	5,193	8,585	7,691	3,067	24,493	19,000	2,761	2,034	1,339
Licking County	17,247	5,603	4,285	2,196	5,437	4,471	2,639	16,073	11,284	3,027	1,110	1,154
Lorain County	30,422	12,699	8,445	4,873	10,507	8,601	3,833	30,405	22,060	5,049	1,613	2,077
Lucas County	34,910	15,021	10,183	6,417	14,010	11,030	7,184	38,998	26,668	11,452	6,180	3,687
Mahoning County	22,226	8,534	5,332	4,634	6,836	6,370	4,295	25,118	19,675	5,013	2,532	1,838
Marion County	4,894	2,014	1,249	644	2,124	1,598	1,239	6,035	4,472	1,816	434	575
Medina County	20,246	7,001	5,289	3,139	4,468	4,980	1,181	17,296	12,302	1,743	658	694
Miami County	9,666	3,336	1,787	1,967	3,942	3,677	1,905	11,049	8,338	1,697	500	1,076
Montgomery County	45,844	17,302	14,109	8,282	14,783	12,320	6,692	50,803	37,180	12,958	4,865	3,360
Muskingum County	7,221	2,472	1,484	1,772	1,859	2,938	1,506	8,256	5,927	2,155	1,520	387
Portage County	14,283	7,370	2,912	2,469	4,775	3,099	2,731	15,168	9,843	3,028	1,551	1,248
Richland County	9,563	4,206	2,931	2,822	4,921	4,094	2,059	12,075	10,168	2,585	963	1,350
Ross County	5,280	2,445	1,809	1,501	2,706	2,063	1,795	7,243	5,403	2,395	888	449
Scioto County	5,650	1,796	2,128	1,261	2,366	2,432	1,715	7,442	5,345	2,716	1,633	982
Stark County	36,229	14,380	8,931	5,722	11,638	10,938	5,661	38,778	29,454	5,561	2,976	3,276
Summit County	49,832	19,698	13,977	10,202	17,706	13,681	8,363	53,760	38,736	12,821	4,649	3,845

Table I-2: Counties - Persons With Health Insurance by Source of Insurance—*Continued*

	Private Health Insurance Coverage						Public Health Insurance Coverage					
	Employer Based			Direct Purchase			Medicare			Medicaid/CHIP		
	55 to 64 Years	65 to 74 Years	75 Years and Over	55 to 64 Years	65 to 74 Years	75 Years and Over	55 to 64 Years	65 to 74 Years	75 Years and Over	55 to 64 Years	65 to 74 Years	75 Years and Over
Ohio—Cont.												
Trumbull County	18,158	7,516	4,247	3,416	8,232	6,293	2,976	23,305	17,021	5,853	1,676	1,568
Tuscarawas County	8,497	2,943	2,040	1,339	3,242	2,746	1,643	9,523	7,395	1,436	1,051	1,209
Warren County	23,097	6,612	4,504	4,019	6,340	3,677	2,373	19,008	12,380	1,687	813	762
Wayne County	10,477	4,500	2,199	2,215	4,754	3,539	1,173	11,024	8,520	1,863	868	1,000
Wood County	11,290	4,949	3,676	3,003	4,377	3,336	1,114	11,484	7,453	1,269	424	807
Oklahoma												
Canadian County	10,933	4,056	1,894	2,527	3,787	2,889	1,602	10,540	7,131	1,411	430	215
Cleveland County	22,325	9,541	4,453	4,202	6,816	5,669	3,538	21,017	14,011	1,414	1,109	1,032
Comanche County	6,201	3,042	1,691	1,158	1,966	2,149	2,175	8,227	5,321	1,022	1,317	814
Creek County	5,839	1,162	598	1,425	2,571	2,383	967	6,896	4,954	621	668	195
Muskogee County	4,715	1,918	978	1,040	1,689	1,570	1,186	6,050	4,599	993	608	525
Oklahoma County	54,925	25,737	14,392	14,345	17,737	15,072	9,188	60,120	41,432	7,423	7,315	4,382
Payne County	4,712	2,158	1,636	1,308	2,990	1,896	1,031	6,293	4,232	609	280	99
Pottawatomie County	4,847	2,685	1,683	1,071	1,692	1,607	1,058	6,967	4,340	1,679	915	488
Rogers County	7,919	2,525	1,743	1,880	3,576	2,471	1,196	8,185	5,588	821	553	580
Tulsa County	48,171	16,538	8,530	11,588	19,064	16,040	7,745	51,749	35,513	5,844	5,090	3,630
Wagoner County	6,622	2,620	1,236	1,446	3,072	2,298	767	7,804	4,810	719	413	483
Oregon												
Benton County	7,027	2,938	2,116	2,142	3,358	2,813	630	8,472	5,662	1,207	817	591
Clackamas County	39,254	12,764	9,018	12,042	15,900	12,465	3,045	42,871	27,759	6,431	4,805	2,631
Deschutes County	12,468	4,994	3,950	7,364	9,243	6,104	2,685	23,396	13,690	4,585	2,059	2,897
Douglas County	7,593	4,915	3,006	2,212	5,365	4,795	2,216	15,640	11,458	4,098	1,175	1,250
Jackson County	17,994	6,356	4,957	5,284	9,971	7,109	2,706	27,410	19,129	5,303	2,447	2,657
Josephine County	4,972	2,850	2,730	2,097	5,270	4,050	1,676	12,408	9,375	3,364	1,188	1,244
Klamath County	3,397	1,935	1,284	1,063	2,625	2,327	1,731	8,855	5,491	2,904	1,301	1,018
Lane County	26,377	10,726	6,679	7,828	14,773	11,895	5,558	43,253	28,057	9,692	4,622	3,462
Linn County	9,572	3,219	1,707	2,106	5,441	3,847	2,776	14,014	9,113	3,045	1,360	1,273
Marion County	24,175	7,492	6,593	4,829	11,030	9,926	3,275	29,775	21,689	9,254	4,582	3,324
Multnomah County	55,627	20,382	12,515	15,748	22,179	15,901	8,295	62,946	37,873	16,859	8,949	6,685
Polk County	6,236	3,313	2,452	778	3,346	2,505	1,110	8,467	6,208	1,671	874	908
Umatilla County	5,404	2,508	1,190	949	2,442	2,312	1,318	6,588	4,658	2,006	1,177	342
Washington County	46,895	14,297	7,954	9,173	20,315	14,440	3,917	45,636	29,416	8,233	4,934	2,848
Yamhill County	8,410	2,695	2,135	1,585	4,618	3,196	1,400	10,147	7,106	3,104	894	475
Pennsylvania												
Adams County	10,657	5,102	2,275	1,972	4,121	2,412	1,315	11,534	8,083	1,308	1,400	976
Allegheny County	121,843	46,143	28,249	28,860	45,661	45,562	13,477	118,860	96,012	22,911	13,841	14,193
Armstrong County	6,652	2,834	2,097	1,491	3,475	3,025	1,215	7,618	5,962	1,925	1,218	692
Beaver County	17,412	6,280	4,383	4,889	8,241	8,274	3,116	18,419	15,206	4,242	2,093	1,920
Berks County	40,602	11,402	7,351	7,058	14,849	15,483	5,749	38,472	29,424	7,180	4,254	3,734
Blair County	11,537	4,663	3,018	2,333	4,883	5,035	2,555	13,188	10,195	1,981	1,472	1,413
Bucks County	76,319	26,180	14,801	13,614	25,576	24,219	6,409	61,586	47,606	7,291	4,248	4,590
Butler County	21,139	6,492	4,702	4,279	8,194	5,791	1,836	19,050	14,128	2,869	1,453	1,870
Cambria County	12,254	5,584	4,622	3,158	5,992	5,884	3,105	15,507	12,739	4,075	2,265	2,540
Carbon County	7,151	1,912	966	1,458	3,400	2,002	1,192	7,379	5,090	1,245	545	980
Centre County	13,114	6,333	4,547	2,102	4,787	3,405	956	12,282	8,978	1,487	652	1,214
Chester County	54,195	18,488	10,806	12,825	17,696	16,828	3,696	45,669	33,891	4,234	3,203	2,971
Clearfield County	7,024	2,049	2,008	1,919	3,124	2,921	902	8,252	6,966	2,247	815	863
Columbia County	6,095	2,203	1,032	1,223	3,088	2,604	440	6,832	4,851	1,398	496	637
Crawford County	7,302	3,300	2,076	1,612	4,315	3,633	1,831	9,982	7,026	2,690	1,273	713
Cumberland County	24,692	10,032	6,704	4,614	9,063	7,301	2,150	24,854	18,807	2,568	1,922	1,598
Dauphin County	27,865	13,316	7,966	4,383	8,897	7,771	2,552	25,618	18,677	5,361	3,080	2,901
Delaware County	54,859	23,125	11,919	11,400	15,576	16,354	7,168	47,169	36,785	9,572	5,967	4,844
Erie County	24,678	7,823	5,745	5,339	10,698	8,678	4,703	26,857	19,023	7,369	4,029	2,396
Fayette County	12,035	4,370	3,445	3,445	5,444	4,658	2,330	14,911	11,672	4,152	1,279	2,256
Franklin County	14,575	7,331	5,961	3,263	6,491	5,708	1,581	16,235	12,704	1,695	1,864	1,614
Indiana County	8,308	3,308	2,203	1,519	3,362	2,984	1,435	9,017	7,137	2,159	1,050	1,360
Lackawanna County	20,759	8,393	5,431	3,728	8,763	9,324	3,238	21,970	17,200	4,540	2,032	2,245
Lancaster County	46,945	17,115	12,994	10,323	16,687	17,679	5,406	49,439	40,974	6,791	4,254	3,980
Lawrence County	8,082	2,240	2,158	2,535	4,716	4,486	1,500	9,997	7,816	2,348	851	760
Lebanon County	12,958	6,362	4,457	2,680	5,128	4,610	1,443	14,656	11,533	2,947	1,431	842
Lehigh County	30,581	9,088	7,428	6,073	13,081	9,737	3,848	33,227	24,587	7,682	3,699	2,559
Luzerne County	29,261	11,999	5,888	6,573	12,936	12,293	6,089	32,867	25,437	6,627	4,472	3,399
Lycoming County	11,194	4,327	2,344	1,850	4,488	3,553	1,721	11,408	8,776	2,727	796	1,362
Mercer County	10,923	2,940	1,760	2,404	4,728	5,043	1,964	12,297	9,949	2,109	1,830	1,563
Monroe County	16,786	5,070	3,233	2,834	6,006	4,548	3,260	16,054	10,684	4,864	1,846	1,337
Montgomery County	88,208	32,299	18,369	17,729	27,447	31,776	7,216	72,370	61,817	8,061	4,991	6,474
Northampton County	30,215	12,083	7,388	6,170	11,543	11,568	4,365	30,128	24,545	5,339	2,787	3,143
Northumberland County	8,476	2,084	2,214	2,122	4,015	3,805	1,459	10,471	7,857	2,406	1,917	1,028
Philadelphia County	91,460	38,663	21,254	21,848	28,483	29,175	25,995	115,535	85,405	57,688	29,253	20,749
Schuylkill County	12,881	4,848	3,560	3,570	5,922	5,981	3,090	15,297	11,587	3,164	1,746	1,685
Somerset County	7,583	2,719	1,251	1,483	3,235	3,802	1,063	8,546	6,908	1,847	1,284	594
Washington County	21,547	8,430	5,701	5,126	9,556	9,270	3,027	23,043	17,287	4,860	2,103	1,689
Westmoreland County	39,863	15,201	10,788	8,724	17,405	15,735	5,919	41,407	33,758	7,279	4,187	3,466
York County	44,313	15,121	9,789	9,442	15,782	14,986	6,054	42,909	30,775	7,410	3,944	4,111

Table I-2: Counties - Persons With Health Insurance by Source of Insurance—*Continued*

	Private Health Insurance Coverage						Public Health Insurance Coverage					
	Employer Based			Direct Purchase			Medicare			Medicaid/CHIP		
	55 to 64 Years	65 to 74 Years	75 Years and Over	55 to 64 Years	65 to 74 Years	75 Years and Over	55 to 64 Years	65 to 74 Years	75 Years and Over	55 to 64 Years	65 to 74 Years	75 Years and Over
Rhode Island												
Kent County	19,164	5,487	3,488	2,572	6,827	5,119	1,699	17,090	12,409	2,639	2,165	1,804
Newport County	8,976	4,474	2,729	2,256	4,877	3,574	515	10,146	7,432	786	1,213	1,025
Providence County	49,628	13,254	7,205	9,910	15,381	13,381	10,454	49,894	39,587	20,727	12,351	9,560
Washington County	16,699	5,632	3,573	3,231	6,126	3,198	955	14,800	9,936	1,077	1,511	1,094
South Carolina												
Aiken County	15,796	6,218	3,291	3,592	7,592	6,064	1,794	18,903	12,644	2,069	1,943	1,110
Anderson County	16,507	5,177	2,632	4,145	6,165	5,422	4,449	20,925	13,489	3,236	2,731	1,358
Beaufort County	12,624	9,887	6,783	6,767	11,306	9,978	2,488	28,662	20,455	2,099	2,516	484
Berkeley County	14,810	7,071	4,401	4,543	4,281	3,316	3,420	19,212	10,857	2,900	2,768	1,378
Charleston County	29,855	15,639	7,972	8,633	9,956	7,274	4,006	39,099	23,981	7,888	3,500	2,554
Darlington County	4,181	1,477	880	1,680	2,573	1,071	2,079	7,634	4,546	920	1,497	1,162
Dorchester County	11,399	4,711	2,365	2,393	3,400	2,818	2,651	13,685	8,153	2,279	1,624	922
Florence County	10,322	4,282	2,487	1,867	4,226	3,220	2,459	13,375	8,243	2,142	2,047	1,025
Greenville County	36,484	12,755	9,519	11,974	13,317	11,911	7,102	46,681	31,520	6,353	4,795	3,763
Greenwood County	5,044	1,807	2,272	1,254	2,365	1,936	1,276	6,527	5,759	857	1,390	1,582
Horry County	24,709	20,353	8,771	11,121	19,652	11,066	7,608	53,707	27,294	7,684	3,271	3,123
Kershaw County	5,834	2,593	1,551	1,030	1,910	1,738	1,238	7,170	4,421	1,123	848	1,030
Lancaster County	7,538	3,193	1,008	1,878	3,128	2,560	1,478	11,699	7,357	1,675	1,442	825
Laurens County	4,927	2,708	1,321	1,087	2,761	2,266	1,570	7,459	4,171	1,260	933	342
Lexington County	25,978	10,947	6,376	6,480	8,290	7,205	3,133	27,678	17,540	3,471	3,066	2,100
Oconee County	6,855	4,231	2,131	2,388	4,203	2,937	1,243	11,161	7,190	1,622	1,544	693
Orangeburg County	5,604	1,785	1,037	1,525	2,134	1,808	2,285	9,730	6,423	2,053	3,409	3,189
Pickens County	8,247	3,898	2,400	2,415	2,735	3,675	2,395	11,539	8,630	2,068	1,114	1,207
Richland County	27,316	14,335	7,192	7,408	9,779	4,798	4,234	31,178	18,763	4,248	4,328	3,022
Spartanburg County	22,552	8,646	2,998	5,928	9,146	7,426	6,041	28,127	19,519	4,311	3,102	2,201
Sumter County	5,607	2,863	1,822	2,731	3,584	1,940	2,354	9,797	6,665	2,653	2,364	1,120
York County	23,204	9,622	5,945	3,918	8,905	5,268	3,939	23,264	14,153	3,090	1,766	1,050
South Dakota												
Minnehaha County	15,889	3,530	1,405	3,270	6,237	4,812	1,436	14,642	9,043	2,176	710	992
Pennington County	8,480	3,049	1,296	1,993	3,572	3,204	1,596	12,186	7,409	1,289	1,409	427
Tennessee												
Anderson County	6,677	2,912	1,757	1,251	3,397	3,521	1,644	8,504	6,189	1,496	1,255	1,184
Blount County	11,424	4,305	3,861	2,247	6,253	4,542	1,916	15,535	10,563	2,957	1,858	615
Bradley County	8,700	2,552	1,224	1,391	4,532	3,230	1,706	10,150	6,932	1,745	1,231	1,335
Davidson County	49,858	21,197	8,278	10,723	14,299	9,237	7,774	46,826	31,558	7,396	4,596	3,427
Greene County	5,030	1,590	1,400	1,616	2,558	2,507	1,305	8,415	5,744	1,340	1,849	856
Hamilton County	30,332	7,978	6,482	5,923	13,620	12,248	5,317	35,157	25,161	4,214	5,009	3,485
Knox County	36,370	11,992	6,816	8,004	14,520	11,901	5,340	40,963	28,524	6,710	3,741	2,193
Madison County	8,731	1,601	1,670	2,161	2,585	2,278	835	9,565	6,366	1,675	1,301	878
Maury County	7,681	3,172	1,002	1,393	2,230	2,614	2,578	8,542	5,426	2,412	1,217	648
Montgomery County	9,397	2,234	2,505	2,691	3,497	2,532	3,437	10,095	7,803	2,638	1,228	321
Putnam County	4,305	1,998	1,352	2,762	3,160	2,748	1,882	7,279	5,532	1,267	963	512
Robertson County	6,434	2,207	1,015	568	1,508	1,750	803	5,705	3,735	1,379	770	580
Rutherford County	24,200	6,593	2,714	4,796	5,304	4,460	2,732	20,179	11,782	2,992	1,276	1,075
Sevier County	7,080	2,289	1,313	2,526	4,585	2,519	1,830	11,517	6,956	2,230	793	1,135
Shelby County	71,653	30,373	16,752	14,197	19,152	14,387	12,269	72,524	45,330	14,780	12,286	8,500
Sullivan County	11,789	3,981	2,852	4,498	8,231	6,727	4,256	19,036	14,659	2,343	2,786	2,531
Sumner County	14,753	5,447	2,135	4,555	4,535	3,900	3,832	17,013	11,263	3,053	1,372	1,713
Washington County	9,854	4,418	2,651	3,236	3,225	4,383	1,934	12,786	9,021	1,654	1,765	1,486
Williamson County	23,105	7,142	3,517	4,903	7,121	2,998	525	17,555	11,067	1,530	1,151	1,216
Wilson County	11,635	5,665	2,111	2,505	4,030	2,445	2,231	13,111	8,031	1,893	431	576
Texas												
Angelina County	5,023	2,907	1,716	1,423	2,680	2,156	1,748	7,287	5,340	1,879	1,183	819
Bastrop County	7,314	3,409	812	1,614	2,042	757	934	7,752	3,813	811	1,097	803
Bell County	15,378	8,559	4,364	4,433	5,724	4,994	3,563	21,892	14,118	3,665	2,470	1,317
Bexar County	112,285	44,722	23,702	27,263	28,243	22,904	24,043	130,614	89,512	29,993	20,842	17,681
Bowie County	6,934	4,111	1,433	1,007	1,280	1,272	1,514	8,025	5,793	1,057	612	322
Brazoria County	25,436	9,450	4,648	6,245	7,306	4,211	3,324	25,282	14,609	2,051	4,427	1,834
Brazos County	11,907	7,079	3,705	4,054	3,987	2,934	1,408	11,628	7,460	1,769	1,922	551
Cameron County	16,638	4,455	3,034	4,472	4,182	4,112	3,733	29,394	24,028	4,136	7,994	8,493
Collin County	80,984	24,768	9,633	17,413	18,690	12,417	3,776	62,485	37,693	4,197	6,415	3,747
Comal County	13,080	6,129	2,380	2,559	4,257	3,929	1,616	16,041	9,431	2,174	1,039	797
Coryell County	2,789	1,593	1,246	553	1,259	1,096	766	4,073	2,681	625	362	647
Dallas County	163,309	48,926	26,003	42,709	37,630	29,740	20,996	150,905	102,435	24,997	22,440	19,896
Denton County	70,374	20,703	9,916	14,936	16,361	8,858	4,613	52,367	28,428	3,184	4,100	2,617
Ector County	8,737	3,423	2,057	3,046	1,727	1,958	1,127	8,582	5,254	1,003	1,794	1,270
Ellis County	15,663	5,190	2,610	2,227	2,868	2,541	1,529	13,138	8,652	1,567	1,094	980
El Paso County	36,201	13,025	7,288	14,326	7,799	6,381	9,481	54,293	41,654	8,317	14,556	15,351
Fort Bend County	61,216	15,716	4,468	19,037	11,897	6,893	4,071	52,350	27,236	4,481	6,160	3,519
Galveston County	26,108	12,742	6,487	7,592	9,499	5,346	4,489	29,344	16,736	3,917	3,643	1,789
Grayson County	10,839	3,864	3,847	1,959	3,815	2,432	2,215	13,574	8,911	2,221	1,311	1,008
Gregg County	9,078	3,152	1,280	1,688	3,672	3,104	1,278	10,509	7,336	1,266	1,143	293
Guadalupe County	10,590	3,574	2,133	1,969	2,212	1,534	2,352	13,023	7,735	2,112	1,530	532
Harris County	288,227	88,670	40,842	73,049	59,419	48,276	36,089	273,917	172,157	59,124	43,716	32,026
Harrison County	4,912	1,858	1,033	1,542	2,153	1,342	1,411	6,335	3,863	1,557	555	127

Table I-2: Counties - Persons With Health Insurance by Source of Insurance—*Continued*

| | Private Health Insurance Coverage | | | | | | Public Health Insurance Coverage | | | | | |
| | Employer Based | | | Direct Purchase | | | Medicare | | | Medicaid/CHIP | | |
	55 to 64 Years	65 to 74 Years	75 Years and Over	55 to 64 Years	65 to 74 Years	75 Years and Over	55 to 64 Years	65 to 74 Years	75 Years and Over	55 to 64 Years	65 to 74 Years	75 Years and Over
Texas—Cont.												
Hays County	15,447	7,259	3,173	3,656	4,183	2,547	1,165	15,128	8,346	1,247	1,062	570
Henderson County	4,925	3,371	1,657	2,800	2,807	2,934	1,925	9,221	7,709	1,655	816	584
Hidalgo County	28,166	9,661	5,157	11,555	8,923	7,426	8,018	47,946	39,419	10,089	18,038	18,542
Hunt County	7,236	2,055	1,752	1,797	2,480	1,876	1,477	8,541	5,674	2,008	1,064	783
Jefferson County	18,631	6,886	4,866	3,774	4,337	3,922	3,761	18,354	15,934	3,764	2,930	1,988
Johnson County	14,216	5,504	1,374	1,201	2,235	2,216	1,788	12,879	8,754	1,841	784	1,379
Kaufman County	8,439	3,209	1,602	1,677	2,148	1,528	939	8,359	5,376	1,762	840	298
Liberty County	6,049	2,516	1,054	554	1,480	445	1,397	6,480	3,632	788	1,458	404
Lubbock County	20,341	8,035	5,389	3,987	5,471	5,414	3,435	19,909	15,297	3,490	2,467	2,192
McLennan County	18,012	6,555	4,620	2,838	6,253	5,874	3,888	19,354	14,442	3,631	2,586	1,929
Midland County	12,257	5,145	2,315	2,825	2,578	2,993	1,365	9,307	7,508	1,089	640	1,169
Montgomery County	49,166	15,495	5,870	11,194	10,578	8,500	4,413	44,212	28,136	2,680	3,252	3,055
Nacogdoches County	4,132	1,580	1,217	937	1,076	1,375	1,098	5,364	3,580	908	674	690
Nueces County	25,647	7,817	4,580	4,399	8,702	4,867	4,813	30,031	19,950	7,394	5,650	4,518
Orange County	6,906	1,869	1,636	1,543	2,056	2,364	1,245	7,382	5,614	1,282	1,191	533
Parker County	10,576	4,785	2,965	2,293	3,241	2,176	1,318	12,123	7,671	1,190	817	1,977
Potter County	7,167	2,429	1,440	972	1,431	1,734	1,432	7,128	4,853	1,546	1,101	532
Randall County	11,478	3,748	3,338	2,871	3,911	3,468	959	11,394	8,608	616	793	1,340
Rockwall County	8,043	2,249	1,217	1,446	2,675	2,036	553	6,888	4,457	348	642	415
San Patricio County	4,239	1,284	530	876	1,281	1,100	1,053	5,539	3,830	1,210	1,112	335
Smith County	13,755	5,690	3,826	5,771	9,123	8,459	3,055	20,550	15,222	3,425	2,424	1,011
Tarrant County	147,271	45,852	22,608	32,090	31,467	21,756	16,796	130,073	85,645	18,227	14,748	12,308
Taylor County	9,813	2,746	1,632	1,161	3,272	2,670	1,134	9,651	8,765	1,037	1,463	672
Tom Green County	8,228	5,514	3,060	1,635	1,792	2,150	726	10,071	6,547	1,826	879	934
Travis County	87,265	36,629	16,797	21,471	19,449	14,284	8,757	70,733	40,376	11,321	5,825	4,317
Victoria County	6,296	2,420	2,043	1,671	1,782	1,051	1,098	7,602	6,228	1,628	1,664	1,110
Walker County	4,059	3,880	1,967	619	1,252	640	890	5,258	3,111	645	533	198
Webb County	10,651	3,786	2,155	2,980	1,673	1,451	2,471	13,810	10,246	2,405	5,970	3,893
Wichita County	8,930	3,827	2,413	1,744	1,946	2,286	2,723	10,328	7,226	2,430	1,273	702
Williamson County	40,712	17,486	8,541	7,910	11,653	9,605	3,951	39,315	23,271	3,725	3,189	2,425
Wise County	6,137	2,006	1,235	1,582	1,829	1,446	1,005	5,996	3,636	563	431	213
Utah												
Cache County	7,449	1,648	752	1,707	1,960	1,595	805	6,367	4,625	306	660	180
Davis County	21,818	7,912	5,133	6,769	6,772	6,771	2,014	20,011	13,339	1,690	1,997	1,628
Salt Lake County	76,416	25,093	12,247	18,143	20,690	16,111	7,011	68,263	46,450	8,807	7,063	5,287
Tooele County	4,314	1,315	862	743	881	1,120	746	3,557	2,498	670	151	523
Utah County	28,090	11,296	7,807	7,943	8,533	7,373	1,847	26,873	18,539	2,739	2,027	1,973
Washington County	9,722	7,482	6,222	4,336	8,960	7,005	1,519	19,924	16,066	1,526	1,648	1,373
Weber County	19,515	8,284	4,214	3,233	4,074	3,954	3,088	16,417	10,727	2,848	1,958	1,240
Vermont												
Chittenden County	14,106	6,389	2,722	3,349	5,095	4,290	1,466	14,423	9,760	2,367	2,237	1,290
Virginia												
Albemarle County	10,210	5,079	2,304	2,225	4,106	4,880	607	10,902	8,798	425	330	375
Arlington County	18,713	9,443	5,562	5,389	2,896	2,122	1,236	11,676	9,351	654	1,033	1,271
Augusta County	7,344	2,112	1,203	958	3,625	4,152	1,173	8,696	6,714	514	394	273
Bedford County	7,957	2,648	1,811	2,494	3,965	3,403	1,591	9,840	6,469	748	711	822
Chesterfield County	32,927	13,629	7,705	6,527	11,775	7,987	2,957	31,968	18,181	2,897	2,052	1,504
Fairfax County	104,352	51,394	26,695	24,988	19,734	17,316	5,951	81,801	56,892	4,943	4,413	7,366
Fauquier County	7,853	2,610	2,093	1,536	2,061	1,474	246	6,630	4,767	27	341	397
Frederick County	8,044	3,242	2,114	2,060	2,931	2,706	526	8,318	6,063	734	155	898
Hanover County	12,475	4,382	2,795	2,085	4,193	3,783	721	10,604	7,489	477	777	566
Henrico County	29,573	10,912	5,486	6,587	9,961	9,027	2,953	27,818	20,036	2,412	2,887	2,217
James City County	7,416	4,777	4,652	1,970	4,776	3,669	383	10,634	8,407	360	531	372
Loudoun County	32,298	11,966	8,200	6,410	6,949	3,871	491	19,374	13,416	690	1,535	1,366
Montgomery County	6,853	2,421	1,469	1,485	1,763	1,974	1,088	6,924	4,665	820	301	551
Prince William County	35,128	14,503	6,426	7,285	7,382	5,038	2,124	25,355	15,608	988	2,330	1,833
Roanoke County	9,470	4,387	3,453	1,417	3,479	3,001	1,961	10,587	8,397	535	383	170
Rockingham County	7,453	2,076	1,253	1,717	3,175	3,211	1,118	8,040	6,499	776	748	800
Spotsylvania County	11,880	5,741	3,453	2,580	3,343	2,578	1,040	11,369	6,871	413	1,695	596
Stafford County	11,144	6,424	2,297	2,479	2,221	1,972	1,135	9,605	4,810	426	359	276
York County	5,841	2,146	1,813	1,299	2,720	2,021	417	6,321	3,987	315	439	170
Washington												
Benton County	15,204	5,954	4,927	2,576	5,687	5,276	3,156	17,554	11,526	3,890	1,456	1,140
Chelan County	5,807	2,531	2,533	910	3,118	3,090	1,097	7,916	5,731	2,840	674	1,094
Clallam County	6,081	3,057	2,467	2,595	4,907	3,314	951	12,549	8,720	1,618	1,749	1,240
Clark County	42,768	16,818	6,548	8,018	14,807	11,149	4,921	43,368	27,186	7,581	3,977	3,265
Cowlitz County	8,846	4,182	2,210	2,514	4,166	3,295	2,700	12,093	7,865	2,597	1,852	1,708
Franklin County	5,032	1,742	869	726	2,100	798	343	5,390	3,211	1,196	625	685
Grant County	5,777	2,235	786	1,360	2,013	821	1,024	7,473	4,925	1,358	713	1,276
Grays Harbor County	4,874	2,898	1,822	2,146	3,285	2,851	1,609	9,481	6,108	2,153	1,551	566
Island County	6,624	3,417	2,463	2,075	4,113	3,667	885	12,171	7,806	1,391	1,154	1,088
King County	187,474	63,265	32,316	38,100	55,824	43,175	15,429	161,599	111,534	28,708	17,008	18,487
Kitsap County	23,113	12,722	7,327	5,279	8,664	5,579	2,206	28,790	16,581	5,263	1,822	1,448
Lewis County	6,905	2,206	1,686	1,219	4,012	3,542	1,988	9,479	6,400	3,059	1,079	576

Table I-2: Counties - Persons With Health Insurance by Source of Insurance—*Continued*

| | Private Health Insurance Coverage | | | | | | Public Health Insurance Coverage | | | | | |
| | Employer Based | | | Direct Purchase | | | Medicare | | | Medicaid/CHIP | | |
	55 to 64 Years	65 to 74 Years	75 Years and Over	55 to 64 Years	65 to 74 Years	75 Years and Over	55 to 64 Years	65 to 74 Years	75 Years and Over	55 to 64 Years	65 to 74 Years	75 Years and Over
Washington—Cont.												
Mason County	5,296	3,414	1,598	1,650	3,549	1,859	2,274	9,071	5,307	2,757	1,181	857
Pierce County	73,026	23,891	13,450	11,472	24,318	17,841	11,235	70,788	45,269	14,171	8,824	6,821
Skagit County	11,411	5,157	3,122	2,828	6,883	4,795	1,666	14,930	10,506	1,947	1,875	1,304
Snohomish County	74,402	24,116	11,165	15,216	22,691	15,262	8,142	63,082	38,583	12,368	7,115	6,036
Spokane County	39,943	13,371	8,563	8,272	12,176	11,025	7,279	48,793	31,379	13,228	5,964	4,028
Thurston County	24,124	12,787	6,851	4,844	9,177	6,925	3,559	29,806	17,355	5,038	3,257	2,944
Whatcom County	14,244	8,592	3,893	4,846	8,785	4,679	3,187	23,227	14,525	5,956	1,990	1,990
Yakima County	15,786	4,895	3,544	2,575	7,295	5,292	2,830	19,215	13,324	5,647	2,626	2,056
West Virginia												
Berkeley County	9,659	4,700	2,326	1,683	3,816	2,557	1,952	11,292	5,861	2,619	2,214	800
Cabell County	5,791	4,397	3,054	1,190	2,903	3,052	2,540	9,453	6,922	3,278	752	1,019
Harrison County	5,590	2,663	1,535	772	2,175	1,917	1,206	7,000	5,030	1,930	973	356
Kanawha County	15,736	8,927	6,494	2,624	3,619	4,679	4,928	20,778	15,017	5,519	3,162	1,745
Monongalia County	7,186	4,067	2,028	1,571	1,551	1,715	1,290	7,312	4,901	1,871	1,010	294
Raleigh County	4,726	5,319	3,677	1,245	1,163	2,082	2,779	9,199	6,040	3,124	1,326	1,141
Wood County	6,418	4,102	2,610	1,978	2,912	2,727	2,470	9,411	6,958	2,322	1,751	1,257
Wisconsin												
Brown County	23,755	4,389	2,496	5,463	7,311	5,616	2,689	21,741	15,700	3,246	1,804	2,578
Dane County	48,691	21,317	10,642	8,617	17,402	12,194	3,027	42,528	28,612	3,756	3,790	2,688
Dodge County	10,056	2,179	1,175	2,297	3,829	3,536	687	8,262	6,122	1,016	627	426
Eau Claire County	9,369	3,010	1,849	1,481	4,789	3,661	1,339	9,670	6,635	1,544	1,296	816
Fond du Lac County	10,108	1,559	1,377	1,896	3,526	3,693	1,163	10,541	7,765	2,174	1,396	1,518
Jefferson County	8,808	2,563	1,420	2,430	4,021	3,063	617	8,686	5,581	1,058	552	797
Kenosha County	16,674	4,647	3,945	3,178	4,740	3,730	1,819	13,216	9,077	2,561	2,146	823
La Crosse County	11,083	1,763	1,525	1,755	4,719	2,852	1,491	10,427	7,883	1,487	1,636	662
Manitowoc County	9,023	1,720	779	1,846	4,101	4,443	1,369	8,705	6,671	1,836	702	662
Marathon County	13,747	2,684	1,269	3,464	6,398	4,923	958	13,019	9,759	1,675	1,505	1,710
Milwaukee County	67,549	25,369	14,805	12,395	18,542	15,763	13,007	69,522	51,598	25,568	12,350	10,761
Outagamie County	17,388	2,703	1,492	4,207	6,811	5,422	1,727	15,195	11,316	2,352	973	1,840
Ozaukee County	11,314	3,605	2,686	2,003	3,495	2,120	575	9,113	7,305	703	517	847
Portage County	5,930	852	1,312	1,918	3,325	2,389	1,028	6,748	4,683	1,216	358	371
Racine County	19,859	5,443	3,867	3,249	5,600	4,505	3,613	18,146	12,513	3,634	2,122	1,196
Rock County	15,545	5,503	3,791	2,391	5,479	5,822	1,281	14,972	10,782	3,334	1,775	1,655
St. Croix County	9,620	2,686	930	1,769	3,998	2,849	582	7,457	4,317	741	531	526
Sheboygan County	12,873	2,551	1,294	2,262	5,355	4,826	1,030	11,237	8,396	2,012	1,145	579
Walworth County	10,355	2,589	1,790	2,759	4,914	3,838	1,884	10,262	6,827	2,166	778	671
Washington County	15,729	2,898	2,193	2,976	5,328	4,973	1,356	13,399	10,053	1,500	1,197	834
Waukesha County	50,269	12,397	8,721	9,010	14,649	14,307	3,630	40,881	31,305	2,922	2,433	3,250
Winnebago County	16,793	3,395	1,737	2,591	5,525	6,193	1,581	15,309	11,623	2,355	1,144	1,662
Wood County	6,419	1,527	1,049	2,563	3,538	3,957	884	7,901	6,332	1,257	516	972
Wyoming												
Laramie County	9,732	3,871	2,272	1,679	2,196	2,558	629	9,449	5,890	643	482	975
Natrona County	7,045	1,884	1,068	1,707	3,036	2,947	1,017	6,602	4,511	552	800	383

Table I-3: Cities - Persons With Health Insurance by Source of Insurance

	Private Health Insurance Coverage						Public Health Insurance Coverage					
	Employer Based			Direct Purchase			Medicare			Medicaid/CHIP		
	55 to 64 Years	65 to 74 Years	75 Years and Over	55 to 64 Years	65 to 74 Years	75 Years and Over	55 to 64 Years	65 to 74 Years	75 Years and Over	55 to 64 Years	65 to 74 Years	75 Years and Over
Alabama												
Auburn city	4,331	1,960	622	940	987	815	445	3,520	1,586	304	379	43
Birmingham city	13,274	5,853	2,755	3,462	4,756	3,610	5,830	18,011	12,188	5,682	4,182	2,778
Dothan city	5,012	2,776	1,747	1,321	2,470	1,935	1,653	7,294	5,334	1,066	907	1,203
Hoover city	7,914	4,374	1,613	848	3,704	1,762	755	8,982	5,453	343	857	543
Huntsville city	14,000	8,635	5,683	3,526	5,167	5,994	2,337	17,497	14,101	2,687	2,135	1,067
Mobile city	12,378	5,440	2,693	3,199	3,707	3,409	4,511	18,115	13,492	4,449	2,339	1,532
Montgomery city	13,727	6,694	4,535	3,234	2,783	2,917	4,039	15,493	10,080	4,506	3,105	2,109
Tuscaloosa city	6,806	3,055	1,297	1,286	1,674	1,231	1,324	6,728	5,065	1,344	1,174	642
Alaska												
Anchorage municipality	23,034	10,236	4,905	3,933	2,960	1,149	1,626	19,904	10,259	3,899	3,822	1,965
Arizona												
Avondale city	3,864	1,564	449	765	1,098	442	779	4,438	2,371	1,570	847	548
Buckeye city	3,604	3,079	389	966	2,580	255	366	9,360	2,223	508	1,761	162
Chandler city	20,699	4,814	2,998	4,223	5,569	2,467	1,511	18,069	10,501	2,380	1,686	1,802
Flagstaff city	4,208	2,036	924	818	1,563	757	478	4,307	1,990	532	327	183
Glendale city	14,960	4,956	2,670	3,738	5,132	3,157	3,045	20,357	10,883	7,502	3,765	2,464
Goodyear city	5,965	3,074	1,136	1,009	2,422	1,914	639	10,399	4,046	1,045	627	474
Mesa city	35,283	13,733	8,227	9,655	14,351	12,830	5,477	44,086	33,573	5,648	5,855	3,837
Peoria city	15,553	5,157	4,324	3,207	5,309	3,748	2,030	16,842	12,403	3,014	1,419	979
Phoenix city	97,755	24,966	15,671	21,647	23,421	17,755	17,010	100,609	68,727	32,836	17,074	14,506
Scottsdale city	25,541	7,494	5,614	9,547	10,233	11,285	548	27,885	27,253	1,789	1,800	1,246
Surprise city	8,067	4,944	3,378	2,593	5,218	5,589	1,309	16,565	13,661	1,048	1,059	1,018
Tempe city	12,843	4,118	2,137	2,947	3,640	1,772	1,805	11,440	7,457	3,442	1,613	929
Tucson city	29,352	10,729	7,352	6,885	11,360	8,229	6,646	45,607	31,781	14,417	9,322	7,888
Yuma city	4,826	2,110	2,815	1,405	2,312	3,446	1,263	6,061	8,456	2,556	1,249	2,428
Arkansas												
Conway city	3,098	2,501	477	446	1,408	1,303	1,212	4,248	2,418	871	440	202
Fayetteville city	4,366	1,602	1,503	1,843	1,752	1,184	1,272	3,347	2,574	1,413	97	244
Fort Smith city	5,720	1,300	571	1,516	2,461	1,913	1,737	7,190	4,144	2,474	650	401
Jonesboro city	3,535	1,311	80	1,467	1,799	1,629	641	4,519	3,750	1,135	652	919
Little Rock city	15,510	5,597	3,165	3,909	5,105	3,627	2,820	15,440	9,804	4,453	2,114	1,081
North Little Rock city	3,602	2,152	1,134	701	3,190	1,055	1,264	7,141	3,590	1,707	535	337
Rogers city	5,016	763	967	691	750	872	213	3,300	2,696	799	552	457
Springdale city	6,285	1,008	397	1,248	1,107	1,680	589	3,813	3,797	491	487	365
California												
Alameda city	6,658	3,320	1,853	1,540	2,308	1,282	699	7,486	4,627	1,101	1,171	1,003
Alhambra city	3,725	1,712	1,162	2,478	1,004	880	455	7,204	6,643	2,589	2,245	2,893
Anaheim city	24,075	5,272	3,997	4,433	3,503	3,320	2,079	22,285	15,229	6,550	4,437	5,009
Antioch city	9,092	2,674	2,588	2,292	1,575	1,938	1,398	6,905	6,336	2,425	817	916
Bakersfield city	22,875	6,762	3,709	4,877	6,904	4,168	3,156	21,355	15,950	9,364	4,826	4,326
Baldwin Park city	3,437	956	259	1,010	486	138	885	4,431	2,653	2,586	811	929
Bellflower city	4,106	2,137	289	1,332	136	46	629	4,078	2,867	2,588	1,118	1,572
Berkeley city	7,520	5,057	2,676	2,707	3,041	1,793	927	9,820	5,471	2,351	1,454	695
Buena Park city	6,229	1,402	908	2,290	798	632	271	5,567	3,746	1,268	1,061	768
Burbank city	7,204	2,403	2,007	2,568	964	1,003	658	6,676	8,052	3,955	1,808	2,838
Camarillo city	5,835	3,485	1,778	773	1,567	2,724	426	6,477	7,398	589	430	651
Carlsbad city	10,590	3,407	2,254	5,020	3,797	3,897	741	10,768	10,656	1,494	425	873
Carson city	6,993	2,905	1,801	1,209	563	450	995	7,660	4,956	1,988	2,181	1,264
Chico city	4,789	2,416	2,041	1,112	1,932	1,760	675	7,024	4,825	2,033	1,380	706
Chino city	7,103	2,421	615	896	937	1,233	608	6,019	4,092	1,329	763	857
Chino Hills city	8,965	1,204	530	1,201	625	448	173	3,828	2,956	1,477	418	747
Chula Vista city	17,874	4,330	1,899	2,860	2,554	1,360	1,973	16,651	12,363	3,840	5,414	4,829
Citrus Heights city	6,778	3,735	2,385	1,525	2,350	1,726	729	7,971	5,216	2,810	824	486
Clovis city	6,743	4,683	2,114	1,322	2,873	1,300	1,065	9,347	5,101	2,009	1,195	839
Compton city	3,998	1,409	875	434	155	324	931	4,098	3,703	3,502	1,249	1,324
Concord city	13,331	6,507	2,211	2,937	2,445	2,208	1,012	11,056	7,369	2,237	1,564	1,060
Corona city	8,830	2,425	987	3,404	1,337	950	883	8,553	6,617	3,224	1,138	1,555
Costa Mesa city	6,486	1,209	965	2,105	1,904	962	727	6,979	5,514	998	965	960
Daly City city	10,994	3,803	3,045	1,539	2,567	2,120	591	8,371	8,097	1,861	1,841	1,845
Davis city	5,631	3,037	2,103	654	707	895	259	3,456	3,281	434	366	326
Downey city	6,619	2,056	1,150	1,899	339	519	585	9,750	4,632	2,535	2,480	1,748
El Cajon city	5,263	3,245	1,609	1,115	1,167	1,356	1,017	5,898	5,245	2,316	1,822	1,647
Elk Grove city	17,605	7,862	3,752	3,435	3,308	2,242	1,574	13,508	9,154	2,110	1,387	1,790
El Monte city	4,317	1,599	615	1,333	226	157	666	7,568	6,458	5,166	3,238	3,630
Escondido city	11,589	2,698	992	2,680	2,052	1,965	1,119	10,855	8,623	3,117	998	1,859
Fairfield city	8,822	4,532	2,330	1,468	1,861	2,109	1,044	7,983	6,268	1,812	999	939
Folsom city	6,367	2,806	1,528	1,614	1,475	1,177	552	5,629	3,512	1,347	1,084	421
Fontana city	12,426	3,684	985	1,399	1,478	656	1,025	9,827	5,346	3,100	1,796	2,387
Fremont city	21,565	5,908	4,793	3,901	2,767	2,265	832	14,085	12,553	3,874	2,494	2,569
Fresno city	22,852	13,068	6,073	5,485	6,672	6,085	5,547	32,724	23,681	20,384	9,192	7,160
Fullerton city	11,491	3,079	1,308	2,830	2,300	1,553	974	9,125	7,269	3,355	986	2,174
Garden Grove city	13,508	3,325	1,700	4,211	1,001	1,135	1,442	10,434	9,213	7,416	3,556	3,881
Glendale city	12,253	3,697	2,545	4,464	1,818	1,375	3,444	16,906	16,654	7,715	6,440	7,959
Hawthorne city	6,069	1,872	503	882	223	305	833	4,493	3,133	2,645	1,413	1,633
Hayward city	9,939	4,050	1,744	1,994	1,686	1,663	791	11,494	7,474	6,510	2,377	1,566

Table I-3: Cities - Persons With Health Insurance by Source of Insurance—*Continued*

| | Private Health Insurance Coverage | | | | | | Public Health Insurance Coverage | | | | | |
| | Employer Based | | | Direct Purchase | | | Medicare | | | Medicaid/CHIP | | |
	55 to 64 Years	65 to 74 Years	75 Years and Over	55 to 64 Years	65 to 74 Years	75 Years and Over	55 to 64 Years	65 to 74 Years	75 Years and Over	55 to 64 Years	65 to 74 Years	75 Years and Over
California—Cont.												
Hemet city	3,870	2,781	1,249	590	1,332	1,471	899	11,954	8,120	3,845	2,692	1,675
Hesperia city	5,460	1,644	1,646	1,382	658	696	1,273	6,040	5,262	3,360	1,753	1,449
Huntington Beach city	17,408	5,360	4,550	5,543	4,157	3,785	1,763	18,554	13,190	3,096	2,485	1,575
Indio city	6,759	1,977	1,467	1,157	2,910	3,034	2,220	12,287	6,300	4,402	3,692	1,194
Inglewood city	8,086	2,767	1,569	1,672	1,111	755	694	6,278	4,217	2,739	1,482	1,567
Irvine city	19,165	6,240	3,627	5,293	2,554	2,431	1,881	15,336	11,712	3,390	2,306	2,250
Jurupa Valley city	6,151	2,422	1,476	1,424	933	829	513	6,807	4,202	3,063	1,667	1,037
Laguna Niguel city	7,148	2,234	861	3,667	1,786	1,465	54	6,230	4,419	545	887	580
Lake Elsinore city	4,209	801	1,097	425	381	42	468	3,714	3,141	1,174	754	1,981
Lake Forest city	7,297	2,217	1,177	1,017	1,756	1,092	289	8,652	3,716	783	874	532
Lakewood city	8,839	2,004	1,787	3,333	1,053	660	405	5,158	4,114	1,009	1,099	923
Lancaster city	9,320	3,658	1,925	1,351	917	1,076	2,791	8,682	6,265	4,031	1,761	1,353
Livermore city	11,333	3,313	2,213	1,857	1,508	2,155	644	6,094	4,835	1,417	542	631
Lodi City	5,713	1,834	1,299	1,236	1,871	1,709	1,068	5,261	3,972	1,831	578	334
Long Beach city	35,821	10,389	5,086	8,467	5,925	3,543	3,975	28,972	19,031	13,921	7,530	4,982
Los Angeles city	208,844	81,155	44,913	67,415	39,201	35,440	33,094	266,699	203,552	127,067	87,703	84,199
Lynwood city	2,594	848	267	514	42	8	627	2,675	2,237	3,078	533	706
Madera city	1,455	457	356	616	997	474	456	3,589	2,778	2,374	805	902
Manteca city	5,567	2,140	1,700	1,919	2,232	1,580	1,023	6,104	4,775	2,327	666	995
Menifee city	6,492	2,745	2,412	1,566	1,343	1,993	617	8,010	8,346	2,053	1,471	1,563
Merced city	3,235	1,450	1,024	1,056	1,600	1,124	1,140	5,283	4,219	2,501	1,746	1,161
Milpitas city	5,925	2,079	723	1,608	879	575	221	4,830	3,699	1,544	1,341	1,788
Mission Viejo city	10,911	3,788	3,111	3,685	2,616	2,108	613	9,549	8,395	960	797	1,160
Modesto city	11,726	4,089	2,186	4,231	4,661	3,836	3,994	14,840	10,587	7,252	2,403	2,413
Moreno Valley city	10,712	2,428	945	1,763	1,133	401	1,037	9,432	5,610	4,458	1,604	1,624
Mountain View city	4,992	1,545	946	1,121	1,591	748	319	4,746	3,849	1,229	491	585
Murrieta city	7,503	1,664	2,739	1,314	1,472	1,349	1,207	5,731	7,564	1,378	823	1,281
Napa city	7,115	3,380	2,670	1,801	1,710	2,354	328	8,163	5,430	941	1,580	613
Newport Beach city	6,537	2,981	1,872	4,886	2,751	2,969	691	10,371	8,770	387	803	842
Norwalk city	6,603	1,904	1,139	1,608	571	559	1,122	6,473	6,209	3,352	2,003	1,771
Oakland city	25,310	12,736	7,778	6,091	5,587	6,037	4,646	31,579	22,122	10,968	9,399	6,333
Oceanside city	12,954	4,522	3,216	3,221	3,674	3,030	1,311	16,164	12,243	3,484	1,904	1,696
Ontario city	9,043	2,870	1,244	2,241	1,072	332	1,273	8,834	6,021	4,526	2,343	2,355
Orange city	12,814	2,651	1,096	3,076	2,476	1,951	1,492	8,920	6,695	1,876	1,410	921
Oxnard city	13,880	3,297	2,517	3,369	1,834	2,012	918	10,412	8,678	4,650	2,049	2,991
Palmdale city	10,794	4,063	2,530	2,857	1,194	959	1,626	9,639	6,551	5,063	2,603	1,600
Palo Alto city	6,495	2,755	2,962	1,471	1,883	2,612	330	5,084	6,703	839	501	1,508
Pasadena city	9,373	4,153	2,560	2,423	1,572	2,081	981	10,434	11,040	3,263	2,211	3,711
Perris city	3,631	703	293	565	543	180	821	3,048	1,086	2,575	1,630	504
Pittsburg city	4,839	1,687	780	1,376	1,004	848	412	3,383	2,880	1,955	638	1,229
Pleasanton city	7,991	3,242	2,433	1,652	2,286	1,271	377	6,897	5,146	444	581	501
Pomona city	6,100	2,423	1,035	1,579	853	840	1,589	8,171	6,956	4,211	2,666	3,406
Rancho Cordova city	5,991	3,369	1,581	1,012	1,385	1,157	1,113	6,379	5,009	2,590	897	1,399
Rancho Cucamonga city	16,676	4,724	1,907	2,925	1,162	1,270	951	12,866	8,131	2,257	1,983	2,645
Redding city	6,601	2,754	2,014	2,217	3,197	3,325	1,035	9,214	6,689	2,563	1,632	1,063
Redlands city	6,919	1,727	1,221	509	1,594	1,057	800	6,431	4,438	1,288	722	1,045
Redondo Beach city	6,692	2,326	1,364	2,030	1,428	742	306	5,471	2,845	579	739	605
Redwood City city	6,602	3,658	1,700	1,408	2,048	1,224	380	6,619	4,285	1,250	492	420
Rialto city	5,314	1,742	1,088	946	1,176	1,184	1,359	7,497	4,655	3,369	2,350	2,019
Richmond city	7,720	4,406	2,150	660	2,254	971	1,306	8,786	4,718	2,305	1,162	958
Riverside city	18,988	6,539	3,783	3,527	1,783	2,473	3,045	18,449	13,416	7,006	2,428	2,977
Rocklin city	5,669	2,214	961	1,313	1,438	1,288	183	4,947	2,624	553	821	277
Roseville city	11,552	6,263	3,529	2,267	3,476	2,874	1,406	11,716	9,884	1,516	1,036	1,750
Sacramento city	27,245	17,501	10,100	6,592	7,090	5,551	4,975	37,910	25,816	14,332	11,145	7,365
Salinas city	6,670	2,785	976	1,661	1,131	1,383	1,170	7,725	4,995	2,614	2,258	2,046
San Bernardino city	9,149	3,045	986	1,652	1,421	835	1,484	11,230	6,207	6,675	4,198	2,268
San Buenaventura (Ventura) city	10,547	4,851	2,317	3,038	2,685	3,552	1,045	10,295	7,704	2,550	1,182	883
San Clemente city	6,281	1,430	1,414	2,808	1,891	1,670	638	6,283	5,244	1,098	250	583
San Diego city	89,156	36,105	21,735	25,615	19,948	17,548	10,053	103,974	73,398	28,867	18,222	16,718
San Francisco city	60,325	28,794	15,574	16,526	14,758	14,305	7,654	67,262	58,696	21,047	18,936	23,025
San Jose city	79,173	27,799	15,842	16,292	16,233	13,534	8,344	68,818	54,410	20,104	18,128	17,743
San Leandro city	9,263	2,629	2,607	1,348	730	1,298	1,427	6,691	5,462	3,720	1,682	1,325
San Marcos city	6,950	1,850	1,941	1,403	933	1,808	953	5,122	5,775	1,350	560	1,483
San Mateo city	8,399	3,464	3,548	2,669	2,537	4,452	535	7,895	9,071	1,232	1,276	1,998
San Ramon city	6,747	1,734	921	940	1,277	879	182	4,393	3,554	890	995	1,063
Santa Ana city	14,760	3,308	2,015	4,506	1,502	1,639	1,828	16,744	12,078	7,715	5,520	4,908
Santa Barbara city	5,853	4,070	2,619	2,837	3,882	3,041	1,161	9,186	6,093	3,031	699	325
Santa Clara city	8,727	2,668	1,999	2,512	2,781	1,484	1,425	8,502	6,218	2,096	1,547	1,845
Santa Clarita city	19,608	6,495	2,677	4,857	3,431	3,071	1,915	15,428	9,333	3,820	2,111	1,833
Santa Cruz city	3,203	2,730	800	1,312	1,063	962	169	5,457	2,293	648	788	124
Santa Maria city	3,962	687	858	855	2,018	1,516	888	4,623	4,173	2,201	615	1,204
Santa Monica city	5,091	2,588	1,003	2,762	1,762	2,043	401	7,766	6,377	2,087	868	1,846
Santa Rosa city	11,514	5,673	4,719	4,152	4,421	5,338	2,528	15,556	12,956	4,397	2,251	1,727
Simi Valley city	12,114	4,027	2,192	4,060	3,520	2,723	892	12,461	8,387	1,472	1,632	928
South Gate city	2,971	1,056	121	833	85	31	856	4,981	3,012	3,308	1,708	1,155
South San Francisco city	7,072	3,679	2,464	1,610	1,150	1,211	622	5,966	5,465	726	1,634	979

Table I-3: Cities - Persons With Health Insurance by Source of Insurance—*Continued*

| | Private Health Insurance Coverage | | | | | | Public Health Insurance Coverage | | | | | |
| | Employer Based | | | Direct Purchase | | | Medicare | | | Medicaid/CHIP | | |
	55 to 64 Years	65 to 74 Years	75 Years and Over	55 to 64 Years	65 to 74 Years	75 Years and Over	55 to 64 Years	65 to 74 Years	75 Years and Over	55 to 64 Years	65 to 74 Years	75 Years and Over
California—Cont.												
Stockton city	14,014	6,014	4,705	3,311	4,739	3,999	4,605	20,457	14,823	9,934	6,246	4,966
Sunnyvale city	11,980	3,007	1,980	2,922	1,707	2,316	605	8,482	8,612	1,578	1,091	2,715
Temecula city	9,634	2,449	960	1,437	1,981	1,128	849	7,044	4,082	1,644	649	516
Thousand Oaks city	13,669	3,832	3,237	3,214	4,096	4,869	1,279	11,918	10,786	1,798	1,529	1,233
Torrance city	14,539	4,958	2,740	5,108	2,681	2,635	1,928	13,014	11,060	3,084	1,343	2,069
Tracy city	6,888	2,246	1,025	1,894	1,518	728	597	5,196	2,552	815	868	837
Turlock city	1,987	1,188	332	844	2,068	593	1,549	5,434	3,494	2,092	1,447	1,759
Tustin city	8,096	1,574	1,149	1,291	1,170	855	344	3,035	3,596	1,505	359	870
Union City city	6,213	2,094	887	619	1,028	1,234	195	5,889	4,771	3,097	954	994
Upland city	6,075	1,672	2,105	1,930	1,282	1,001	401	5,164	5,561	665	962	878
Vacaville city	6,804	4,157	1,829	972	2,521	1,792	806	7,950	5,647	1,075	1,115	366
Vallejo city	12,487	5,400	2,545	2,583	2,034	2,102	1,248	10,672	7,103	3,351	1,645	1,773
Victorville city	4,904	1,909	431	503	715	661	1,240	5,718	3,688	3,298	884	1,088
Visalia city	7,046	2,009	1,154	1,445	3,155	2,166	1,846	9,085	6,044	2,563	2,020	1,552
Vista city	7,796	1,396	785	1,699	935	1,091	682	5,288	3,894	1,510	834	807
Walnut Creek city	7,599	4,398	4,442	1,250	3,468	5,541	209	9,024	11,465	444	432	1,030
West Covina city	8,501	2,666	1,415	2,168	1,050	641	691	8,528	7,373	2,230	1,979	3,277
Westminster city	4,801	1,700	1,873	2,874	1,697	1,155	464	8,720	7,804	3,334	3,244	3,281
Whittier city	7,779	2,088	1,270	1,213	590	974	356	5,174	5,436	1,684	858	517
Yorba Linda city	6,573	3,925	1,498	1,979	1,771	763	313	8,301	4,768	301	971	336
Yuba City city	3,236	1,316	1,117	898	912	1,522	924	5,498	4,933	2,176	1,549	1,265
Colorado												
Arvada city	11,708	4,768	2,134	2,533	4,351	2,875	1,080	13,513	7,549	999	865	901
Aurora city	24,868	9,038	3,830	4,585	7,495	3,736	3,377	25,695	14,520	6,515	3,662	3,672
Boulder city	6,231	2,738	1,812	2,170	2,457	2,223	537	6,635	4,527	755	524	343
Broomfield city	5,794	2,456	1,598	1,640	1,911	1,427	70	5,204	3,725	343	280	271
Centennial city	10,709	3,428	1,516	2,494	2,738	2,242	455	9,822	5,109	1,087	360	183
Colorado Springs city	26,740	9,166	5,427	8,182	11,090	7,781	4,317	36,635	22,706	9,420	2,993	3,061
Denver city	39,832	14,455	9,121	10,652	12,619	10,477	8,268	47,672	30,193	13,126	7,482	6,982
Fort Collins city	10,477	3,243	1,691	2,358	3,739	2,308	734	11,442	5,710	1,982	877	600
Greeley city	6,845	1,531	1,292	2,091	1,632	1,453	2,252	6,439	4,666	2,081	794	871
Lakewood city	13,301	4,864	3,902	3,357	3,802	3,913	2,784	13,602	11,345	2,686	1,249	1,395
Longmont city	8,723	3,125	1,712	1,673	2,624	3,208	702	8,903	6,019	1,456	576	637
Loveland city	6,984	1,955	1,649	1,545	3,105	2,697	439	6,921	5,766	758	721	650
Pueblo city	5,643	3,195	3,011	1,103	3,811	2,906	3,500	10,766	8,621	4,732	1,743	2,226
Thornton city	9,358	2,797	1,557	1,383	2,421	2,005	942	7,463	4,233	1,618	430	377
Westminster city	11,947	3,809	2,201	2,154	2,358	2,756	419	8,740	5,628	1,130	669	656
Connecticut												
Bridgeport city	7,461	2,262	931	1,000	1,204	2,019	1,091	7,224	7,195	4,784	2,348	2,641
Danbury city	6,578	2,189	794	1,549	1,106	1,398	851	5,345	3,737	1,360	448	496
Hartford city	5,544	3,377	960	720	670	724	1,584	7,450	5,153	4,210	2,479	2,126
New Britain city	5,139	1,094	1,374	515	842	635	1,473	4,075	3,480	1,678	1,061	607
New Haven city	5,168	2,956	925	916	1,240	1,104	889	7,075	3,684	5,181	1,036	1,454
Norwalk city	7,915	3,864	1,256	2,567	2,357	2,003	959	7,864	6,101	1,461	928	1,369
Stamford city	10,427	4,587	2,615	3,093	3,601	3,931	584	10,363	8,661	1,538	1,780	1,626
Waterbury city	7,285	1,507	1,180	668	1,189	1,236	1,690	6,060	6,342	3,689	2,041	2,185
Delaware												
Wilmington city	5,766	1,908	552	566	1,573	1,315	1,139	4,660	2,834	2,791	806	426
District of Columbia												
Washington city	38,453	22,644	18,035	8,289	10,158	7,397	6,726	42,296	33,527	22,124	12,117	9,222
Florida												
Boca Raton city	9,874	4,789	3,850	3,000	3,589	4,503	551	14,410	13,005	264	385	1,472
Boynton Beach city	4,789	2,668	1,549	1,385	2,095	2,481	501	8,500	8,152	445	1,021	589
Cape Coral city	16,254	8,922	4,914	6,208	7,933	6,120	3,446	28,740	17,949	2,208	3,001	2,108
Clearwater city	9,631	3,227	3,337	2,152	2,561	3,885	1,189	12,745	11,902	2,119	2,429	1,964
Coral Springs city	10,586	3,328	898	3,355	2,105	1,555	1,978	10,616	4,235	1,289	1,611	1,242
Daytona Beach city	4,148	1,679	1,158	1,777	1,444	1,594	1,385	8,105	5,226	2,291	991	881
Deerfield Beach city	5,139	2,448	3,005	3,449	1,315	2,780	1,785	7,959	7,833	1,109	1,095	778
Delray Beach city	5,572	2,664	2,569	2,193	2,009	2,853	1,068	8,522	7,556	1,344	828	739
Deltona city	6,034	1,084	1,441	2,129	2,572	1,919	2,371	7,108	7,073	2,258	1,338	1,369
Fort Lauderdale city	14,129	4,262	3,284	7,389	3,905	2,374	2,802	18,118	12,624	3,748	3,650	2,693
Fort Myers city	6,068	3,951	1,698	1,151	3,499	2,615	1,088	10,240	8,034	1,702	1,019	1,619
Gainesville city	6,299	2,765	1,672	1,369	1,961	1,494	853	7,595	4,726	854	2,565	1,106
Hialeah city	10,676	1,518	447	7,666	1,008	717	2,159	20,615	22,221	4,271	11,364	13,705
Hollywood city	9,675	2,051	458	4,718	1,843	2,349	770	11,919	10,374	1,540	2,192	1,713
Homestead city	1,237	357	91	1,105	310	0	798	3,375	2,050	1,182	1,539	1,313
Jacksonville city	62,125	17,828	11,317	14,451	14,540	13,335	11,946	72,104	44,604	14,467	11,925	8,449
Kissimmee city	5,262	1,209	360	1,259	635	560	1,463	5,099	3,744	1,875	1,753	1,093
Lakeland city	6,234	3,243	2,927	2,249	2,796	3,493	3,212	10,495	9,665	3,035	2,441	1,195
Largo city	7,180	3,004	2,074	2,930	2,878	3,681	1,572	10,804	11,178	2,351	1,628	1,155
Lauderhill city	3,098	1,089	555	2,085	1,915	452	134	4,775	3,369	347	1,112	911
Melbourne city	5,974	2,180	1,720	3,356	1,500	2,148	1,989	8,752	6,428	841	1,491	1,018
Miami city	18,604	3,711	2,066	11,827	3,118	2,121	4,955	36,961	39,692	8,266	17,906	20,517

Table I-3: Cities - Persons With Health Insurance by Source of Insurance—*Continued*

	Private Health Insurance Coverage						Public Health Insurance Coverage					
	Employer Based			Direct Purchase			Medicare			Medicaid/CHIP		
	55 to 64 Years	65 to 74 Years	75 Years and Over	55 to 64 Years	65 to 74 Years	75 Years and Over	55 to 64 Years	65 to 74 Years	75 Years and Over	55 to 64 Years	65 to 74 Years	75 Years and Over
Florida—Cont.												
Miami Beach city	4,888	1,975	777	2,890	1,592	1,092	745	7,330	6,014	1,480	1,567	2,014
Miami Gardens city	5,786	1,663	776	1,150	935	769	1,514	8,126	6,763	2,504	2,772	2,238
Miramar city	9,236	2,137	192	2,180	432	343	1,871	6,945	6,008	371	1,577	2,509
North Port city	3,972	1,536	2,183	1,968	4,749	3,506	1,401	11,192	9,523	1,617	794	2,229
Orlando city	18,274	4,549	2,888	4,853	4,196	3,265	2,852	16,481	12,298	3,795	3,043	3,025
Palm Bay city	9,270	3,618	2,110	1,390	3,710	2,050	2,494	13,553	11,166	2,816	901	2,668
Palm Coast city	7,418	5,369	4,669	1,797	3,696	4,125	1,338	13,366	12,261	1,129	1,687	3,314
Pembroke Pines city	12,222	3,316	1,924	4,435	2,283	1,805	1,779	16,453	13,431	894	1,521	959
Plantation city	7,696	1,839	679	1,977	1,110	1,482	374	8,235	5,965	559	1,063	1,093
Pompano Beach city	6,819	2,202	2,495	3,582	1,681	3,173	1,558	8,630	11,992	2,377	1,818	1,602
Port St. Lucie city	14,719	6,665	3,182	6,071	7,863	4,908	3,378	22,428	16,491	1,317	2,208	3,375
St. Petersburg city	21,307	7,214	4,257	6,737	6,857	5,330	4,254	24,152	19,031	3,911	3,731	2,406
Sunrise city	6,784	1,605	976	3,404	1,760	1,731	767	8,965	7,468	1,503	2,071	2,833
Tallahassee city	10,438	4,975	2,196	2,215	4,009	1,868	1,542	11,801	6,136	1,763	2,080	1,120
Tamarac city	4,692	2,228	1,676	2,579	1,652	2,002	379	7,704	7,963	1,720	1,779	1,663
Tampa city	23,398	6,792	2,675	6,220	3,720	3,456	4,832	26,102	21,154	7,469	7,542	6,859
Weston city	4,616	883	655	3,925	733	480	205	3,381	2,684	402	342	453
West Palm Beach city	7,313	2,418	1,772	2,678	4,024	4,995	1,312	9,047	10,991	1,911	1,783	1,494
Georgia												
Albany city	4,208	1,439	1,112	764	1,321	1,416	1,124	5,486	4,102	1,687	1,874	1,108
Alpharetta city	6,741	2,022	718	1,250	724	1,070	289	4,094	2,017	149	165	102
Athens-Clarke County unified govt (bal)	6,001	5,059	1,701	1,207	2,460	1,532	1,341	8,638	5,197	1,502	1,565	1,485
Atlanta city	25,283	10,098	7,646	6,717	6,868	6,466	6,859	28,607	23,033	9,931	6,799	5,209
Augusta-Richmond County consolidated govt (bal)	12,932	5,172	2,973	2,543	2,820	2,019	2,689	16,001	9,441	3,282	3,271	1,696
Columbus city	8,970	3,752	2,415	2,942	4,815	3,517	4,238	14,088	10,664	3,924	3,102	2,704
Johns Creek city	7,843	1,469	1,572	1,929	1,977	1,417	426	5,082	3,292	436	222	508
Macon-Bibb County	9,782	5,227	3,167	3,326	4,178	3,907	2,618	13,082	9,164	2,821	3,237	1,852
Roswell city	9,153	2,496	2,210	2,745	2,419	2,522	798	6,151	5,377	826	306	638
Sandy Springs city	8,698	2,819	1,951	2,209	1,764	2,542	0	6,656	7,057	685	291	499
Savannah city	6,859	4,264	2,727	1,851	1,715	2,059	2,034	11,192	8,233	2,191	1,520	1,818
South Fulton city	5,725	4,488	1,694	1,599	1,569	299	1,644	8,776	3,166	1,610	3,006	409
Warner Robins city	4,294	1,772	1,940	952	645	397	2,235	4,914	2,936	1,391	1,269	414
Hawaii												
Urban Honolulu CDP	30,992	20,537	15,168	4,857	8,341	9,431	2,144	35,383	29,522	6,863	6,167	4,691
Iowa												
Boise City city	18,987	4,924	2,960	5,120	7,403	6,420	1,960	19,842	13,903	1,518	2,443	2,872
Meridian city	5,726	2,873	1,903	2,679	2,845	1,887	1,490	5,912	3,866	1,081	442	477
Nampa city	6,029	2,559	1,087	2,051	4,044	3,928	1,479	8,144	6,196	1,405	1,102	844
Illinois												
Aurora city	12,428	2,842	1,756	1,387	4,415	3,599	1,292	10,143	6,796	2,517	386	854
Bloomington city	7,291	2,880	1,920	1,238	1,959	1,663	782	5,014	4,211	752	301	297
Champaign city	4,643	3,179	1,738	685	1,318	954	387	5,527	3,745	493	45	528
Chicago city	164,237	55,652	30,964	31,143	41,440	33,381	28,676	182,295	135,234	69,902	37,418	25,694
Decatur city	6,533	3,056	2,307	951	2,784	2,039	1,354	7,181	6,428	1,371	1,020	1,200
Elgin city	8,921	2,968	1,335	1,792	3,408	1,584	1,897	8,136	4,429	1,919	701	278
Evanston city	5,469	2,953	1,331	1,791	3,043	2,664	1,031	6,104	4,423	1,302	473	567
Joliet city	10,315	3,176	1,117	1,591	2,446	1,809	1,360	8,019	4,344	2,117	912	391
Naperville city	17,107	4,075	1,988	3,627	3,352	2,652	1,027	9,443	5,836	648	530	799
Peoria city	8,223	2,675	3,304	1,105	3,215	3,201	986	9,959	6,877	2,671	1,164	392
Rockford city	8,958	4,985	3,863	3,057	4,449	5,084	2,337	12,867	11,262	4,349	2,097	1,196
Springfield city	10,928	6,543	4,934	1,358	2,421	1,892	1,688	10,651	8,002	2,855	1,596	747
Waukegan city	5,374	1,580	232	1,230	972	752	603	4,501	2,388	1,636	382	148
Indiana												
Bloomington city	2,946	1,151	1,285	426	1,500	1,984	663	4,053	3,399	1,635	533	201
Carmel city	9,807	2,589	1,707	1,395	2,356	2,282	461	7,045	5,159	614	74	315
Evansville city	8,754	2,290	2,624	1,700	2,804	3,066	1,935	9,216	7,420	3,729	1,646	813
Fishers city	8,561	1,549	1,207	1,523	2,559	1,862	379	5,533	3,947	0	123	0
Fort Wayne city	19,260	5,849	3,455	4,289	6,756	5,454	3,899	21,202	13,648	4,795	3,411	1,344
Gary city	4,184	2,639	1,816	1,279	1,747	1,997	1,280	8,171	5,391	2,863	2,076	550
Hammond city	6,143	2,888	1,456	781	1,355	1,392	1,211	5,832	4,140	1,711	808	166
Indianapolis city (bal)	63,635	21,484	10,583	12,512	18,214	14,650	12,031	59,000	39,745	17,785	7,335	6,097
Lafayette city	5,193	1,537	1,000	1,126	2,118	1,392	1,524	5,366	3,846	1,445	420	324
Muncie city	3,183	2,257	1,143	618	1,874	1,773	896	5,060	4,071	796	803	299
Noblesville city	3,960	1,265	545	635	1,236	1,472	359	3,779	2,858	500	378	194
South Bend city	6,226	1,581	1,490	1,230	2,198	2,484	1,842	6,923	5,902	1,314	1,219	1,204
Iowa												
Ames city	3,432	2,224	1,673	901	1,119	1,220	483	2,989	2,689	251	147	262
Ankeny city	5,729	2,345	270	436	4,286	1,057	341	6,046	1,654	518	134	74
Cedar Rapids city	12,454	3,184	2,058	1,342	4,202	4,312	1,221	10,764	8,066	1,624	1,359	981
Davenport city	9,365	3,125	1,423	1,551	4,059	2,721	1,507	8,829	5,466	2,418	1,411	1,063
Des Moines city	15,529	3,277	2,983	2,833	5,964	5,045	3,536	13,472	10,625	6,896	2,064	1,808
Iowa City city	4,905	1,992	1,593	1,354	2,585	1,364	1,003	4,650	3,106	614	130	250
Sioux City city	6,267	1,852	524	1,304	1,835	1,858	715	6,105	4,656	2,141	702	514
Waterloo city	4,690	2,001	1,565	917	2,154	2,721	1,431	6,183	5,258	2,204	799	597
West Des Moines city	6,902	2,746	698	649	2,384	2,267	511	5,460	3,793	352	850	741

Table I-3: Cities - Persons With Health Insurance by Source of Insurance—*Continued*

| | Private Health Insurance Coverage | | | | | | Public Health Insurance Coverage | | | | | |
| | Employer Based | | | Direct Purchase | | | Medicare | | | Medicaid/CHIP | | |
	55 to 64 Years	65 to 74 Years	75 Years and Over	55 to 64 Years	65 to 74 Years	75 Years and Over	55 to 64 Years	65 to 74 Years	75 Years and Over	55 to 64 Years	65 to 74 Years	75 Years and Over
Kansas												
Kansas City city	10,192	2,843	1,542	1,555	3,033	2,282	2,650	9,785	7,177	3,123	1,569	670
Lawrence city	4,555	2,880	1,224	1,604	2,639	2,099	258	6,087	4,889	991	279	503
Olathe city	10,373	2,060	1,190	2,017	3,806	2,795	1,116	8,346	4,611	626	764	371
Overland Park city	19,021	5,938	2,221	3,069	7,338	5,385	1,377	16,900	11,580	1,511	563	950
Shawnee city	6,560	1,357	487	579	1,599	1,178	523	4,960	2,814	87	157	110
Topeka city	8,833	3,995	3,246	2,306	4,903	4,315	2,600	12,666	9,694	2,470	1,919	1,064
Wichita city	29,900	6,835	3,582	6,847	12,716	9,996	4,046	32,629	21,702	6,327	4,887	2,856
Kentucky												
Bowling Green city	3,771	1,503	1,207	611	933	1,529	891	4,540	3,049	1,375	387	540
Lexington-Fayette urban county	23,073	9,652	7,923	4,806	9,039	6,645	4,372	24,602	16,516	6,331	2,143	1,363
Louisville/Jefferson County metro govt (bal)	50,177	21,120	11,397	9,386	18,319	17,037	10,894	52,269	36,867	16,928	7,642	3,690
Louisiana												
Baton Rouge city	11,376	7,300	4,892	3,597	4,577	3,731	3,523	18,436	13,437	6,534	3,981	3,013
Bossier City city	3,614	2,239	995	742	1,165	767	1,380	5,583	3,775	1,128	1,073	940
Kenner city	5,457	2,671	872	583	1,158	936	1,005	6,659	4,143	1,944	729	1,048
Lafayette city	8,716	4,368	1,512	3,626	5,022	2,892	2,844	10,122	6,032	3,661	1,355	516
Lake Charles city	3,983	1,721	1,208	1,659	1,856	1,206	2,429	6,162	4,567	2,124	1,100	830
New Orleans city	21,149	9,190	4,300	7,898	5,951	5,093	7,296	33,241	20,160	16,500	7,422	4,593
Shreveport city	11,163	5,911	3,903	4,026	4,792	4,867	4,255	16,554	11,592	6,330	2,728	2,274
Maine												
Portland city	6,094	1,516	669	1,745	1,018	1,133	827	4,107	3,542	1,707	633	438
Maryland												
Baltimore city	37,523	20,223	10,423	6,689	10,619	9,827	11,794	45,261	31,758	24,651	10,536	7,258
Frederick city	5,039	3,206	1,441	913	1,420	1,677	940	4,762	3,625	1,158	497	417
Gaithersburg city	6,163	2,207	2,107	1,248	969	1,193	558	4,886	3,463	690	1,123	934
Rockville city	5,970	4,527	2,135	1,277	622	2,034	106	4,952	4,907	637	745	1,408
Massachusetts												
Boston city	39,963	16,625	8,523	7,084	8,774	7,286	6,971	42,710	31,948	23,324	13,233	11,571
Brockton city	7,223	2,756	871	834	1,228	1,180	898	7,054	4,572	3,845	2,488	1,934
Cambridge city	5,674	4,292	1,820	2,015	2,490	1,204	153	6,690	4,275	1,480	1,085	698
Fall River city	5,336	2,376	1,373	1,348	2,550	2,539	2,303	7,608	6,326	5,230	2,567	2,304
Framingham city	5,229	3,579	1,351	962	1,970	1,962	734	6,325	4,420	668	771	1,186
Lawrence city	2,688	801	474	449	697	485	1,548	4,078	2,277	5,381	2,605	1,544
Lowell city	7,156	2,796	765	657	1,054	1,023	1,212	6,036	3,254	4,409	2,492	1,083
Lynn city	5,807	2,534	963	1,527	2,175	1,773	1,097	5,784	4,638	3,695	1,931	2,241
New Bedford city	4,794	1,629	1,056	547	1,385	1,584	981	6,707	5,067	3,419	2,079	1,681
Newton city	7,653	5,523	2,784	2,416	2,670	3,369	290	8,157	7,469	1,042	645	1,391
Quincy city	7,066	4,117	1,622	1,755	1,570	2,316	639	7,515	6,214	2,852	1,104	1,208
Somerville city	3,789	1,339	1,145	527	793	1,050	654	2,607	3,031	1,739	560	360
Springfield city	7,810	4,060	2,096	896	2,098	1,820	2,771	11,802	7,912	7,839	5,085	3,753
Worcester city	12,237	4,564	3,539	2,387	2,809	3,285	2,927	12,400	9,389	7,774	4,324	2,071
Michigan												
Ann Arbor city	6,741	4,621	3,140	1,424	1,385	1,971	1,216	6,868	5,378	1,218	327	466
Dearborn city	6,250	3,211	1,672	1,673	1,831	1,212	586	6,796	4,203	1,933	1,548	1,174
Detroit city	34,580	25,217	18,463	6,058	7,623	7,213	16,383	51,422	36,617	33,372	14,464	9,621
Farmington Hills city	8,235	3,842	2,939	1,958	3,357	4,013	405	8,557	7,606	1,321	817	887
Flint city	4,923	3,263	3,369	495	1,294	869	3,023	7,975	5,020	5,341	2,172	1,085
Grand Rapids city	11,256	4,540	2,945	2,639	4,566	4,097	2,396	14,179	8,818	5,753	2,184	1,273
Kalamazoo city	4,103	2,197	1,891	665	1,876	1,448	1,022	4,399	3,307	1,564	677	113
Lansing city	7,123	5,005	2,650	991	2,486	2,089	2,616	9,244	5,596	3,776	1,660	952
Livonia city	12,641	4,521	3,804	2,091	1,993	2,982	840	7,094	7,467	1,088	782	727
Rochester Hills city	6,853	4,093	2,339	1,526	2,646	1,829	755	6,603	5,057	584	649	445
Southfield city	5,999	5,357	2,916	1,673	1,336	1,557	1,579	9,432	6,511	2,317	1,349	1,548
Sterling Heights city	12,510	5,745	3,245	2,095	4,299	3,942	1,546	11,725	9,499	2,857	1,829	1,470
Troy city	8,713	3,933	2,276	2,454	2,864	1,909	964	7,819	5,011	900	743	957
Warren city	13,524	5,661	4,786	1,970	4,106	4,596	2,904	11,712	9,662	2,616	2,945	1,837
Westland city	7,881	2,906	2,335	1,940	2,205	2,480	2,000	7,427	5,495	2,233	1,724	955
Wyoming city	6,211	1,061	964	773	1,535	1,223	1,420	5,909	3,104	1,355	1,354	576
Minnesota												
Blaine city	6,287	1,854	104	1,136	1,935	1,143	482	5,034	1,974	572	226	208
Bloomington city	9,182	2,003	1,461	2,230	4,142	5,113	381	8,755	8,276	1,572	575	646
Brooklyn Park city	5,634	1,420	506	1,235	1,719	2,949	1,011	4,362	4,320	1,751	569	1,072
Duluth city	6,036	3,159	1,940	1,525	3,793	2,639	1,389	8,359	5,974	2,656	744	1,046
Eagan city	7,091	1,667	794	917	2,258	1,969	441	4,264	3,262	256	345	115
Lakeville city	6,370	699	563	900	2,191	1,362	548	3,862	2,347	317	75	93
Maple Grove city	9,445	1,803	442	1,440	4,073	1,655	318	7,511	3,056	573	630	58
Minneapolis city	22,888	6,537	2,944	6,266	11,302	6,637	3,451	26,699	15,105	9,543	5,773	3,676
Plymouth city	8,593	2,681	880	1,743	3,357	3,197	589	5,948	4,303	687	526	495
Rochester city	11,004	4,457	2,579	1,736	3,780	3,442	832	9,174	7,603	1,865	828	1,229
St. Cloud city	5,311	988	683	1,051	2,099	1,366	632	4,495	2,828	1,134	276	375
St. Paul city	19,285	7,316	3,461	4,314	7,837	4,764	2,657	19,089	11,499	7,479	3,663	1,850
Woodbury city	6,668	2,095	1,070	1,206	3,570	1,092	147	6,901	2,770	415	232	94

Table I-3: Cities - Persons With Health Insurance by Source of Insurance—*Continued*

| | Private Health Insurance Coverage | | | | | | Public Health Insurance Coverage | | | | | |
| | Employer Based | | | Direct Purchase | | | Medicare | | | Medicaid/CHIP | | |
	55 to 64 Years	65 to 74 Years	75 Years and Over	55 to 64 Years	65 to 74 Years	75 Years and Over	55 to 64 Years	65 to 74 Years	75 Years and Over	55 to 64 Years	65 to 74 Years	75 Years and Over
Mississippi												
Gulfport city	4,270	1,713	795	1,035	1,805	1,433	1,486	4,740	3,508	1,368	1,011	750
Jackson city	9,443	3,639	1,904	2,642	2,700	2,508	2,781	13,009	8,015	3,967	2,856	1,746
Missouri												
Columbia city	7,689	3,234	2,709	1,353	2,163	1,601	1,422	7,365	5,172	1,254	427	425
Independence city	10,887	3,338	2,300	2,039	4,025	2,929	1,937	11,042	7,100	1,531	1,077	419
Kansas City city	36,517	10,707	8,275	7,350	10,506	10,711	8,349	33,667	26,877	6,634	3,174	3,114
Lee's Summit city	10,366	3,801	2,515	1,429	3,475	2,111	1,012	9,163	7,228	529	318	234
O'Fallon city	9,561	1,777	1,564	772	1,747	1,622	666	4,649	4,462	91	177	336
St. Charles city	8,286	1,771	742	1,099	2,319	1,512	825	6,545	4,476	519	293	403
St. Joseph city	4,875	1,932	1,041	1,207	4,217	2,299	2,060	7,409	4,649	1,512	698	724
St. Louis city	19,834	6,633	3,368	4,333	4,891	2,796	5,343	23,504	15,140	8,500	4,554	3,593
Springfield city	9,021	1,580	1,437	2,371	4,069	5,493	4,153	14,471	13,225	2,781	2,781	1,370
Montana												
Billings city	9,619	2,399	1,904	2,089	4,859	3,091	1,147	10,712	7,374	1,870	868	1,157
Missoula city	4,374	1,706	1,206	1,579	1,789	1,534	775	5,433	3,464	533	1,142	251
Nebraska												
Lincoln city	21,612	6,599	2,394	4,481	8,838	7,489	1,988	21,481	14,486	2,639	2,559	2,186
Omaha city	35,738	11,118	5,682	7,243	12,290	7,917	5,011	35,821	23,521	5,860	3,263	3,434
Nevada												
Henderson city	25,842	11,947	5,715	6,484	8,822	6,529	2,761	33,912	22,381	3,947	1,803	3,168
Las Vegas city	41,432	15,526	8,866	9,132	10,997	7,618	7,302	54,756	38,125	15,317	8,204	5,446
North Las Vegas city	16,831	4,723	1,824	2,162	3,728	1,910	2,872	16,398	8,110	3,987	1,803	1,455
Reno city	18,963	7,346	3,004	4,668	7,512	5,396	2,527	23,779	14,171	3,524	2,315	2,214
Sparks city	7,555	4,533	1,149	1,617	3,065	2,236	1,008	11,041	5,846	1,999	851	442
New Hampshire												
Manchester city	8,249	2,585	1,293	877	1,859	2,460	1,071	6,891	5,971	1,514	1,033	1,224
Nashua city	10,392	2,857	1,525	1,215	3,624	2,201	1,805	7,916	5,712	1,543	490	328
New Jersey												
Bayonne city	4,111	1,441	1,303	1,217	643	568	764	5,178	4,369	1,711	1,097	1,536
Camden city	2,560	935	587	546	508	392	3,040	4,287	2,614	4,688	1,954	437
Clifton city	8,394	2,774	848	992	995	1,380	815	6,790	5,894	1,792	1,276	985
East Orange city	3,917	1,309	1,248	878	701	755	1,388	3,930	3,619	1,948	802	810
Elizabeth city	5,340	2,134	994	944	1,442	733	1,247	6,789	4,386	2,968	2,477	1,747
Jersey City city	13,852	5,290	2,322	2,761	2,664	1,291	2,317	15,066	9,572	6,161	3,977	3,392
Newark city	11,941	4,663	2,394	2,460	2,159	1,683	3,822	14,951	10,352	10,334	4,312	3,042
Passaic city	2,667	866	343	512	324	299	935	3,761	2,420	2,170	1,026	972
Paterson city	7,461	2,132	499	1,083	279	517	2,214	7,852	6,214	5,882	3,071	1,840
Trenton city	4,051	1,887	900	815	714	531	2,088	5,025	3,939	3,208	1,660	1,235
Union City city	2,279	1,153	482	522	344	646	227	3,205	3,054	1,259	1,298	1,038
New Mexico												
Albuquerque city	40,073	17,225	11,733	8,542	10,989	7,616	8,028	49,012	33,479	16,220	6,695	4,931
Las Cruces city	5,171	3,188	1,246	1,406	1,813	1,684	1,180	10,119	6,665	3,236	970	1,090
Rio Rancho city	7,957	3,963	1,629	1,609	1,308	1,243	1,120	10,458	5,408	975	1,886	849
Santa Fe city	5,876	4,434	2,558	2,515	3,915	2,931	414	11,663	7,363	1,493	1,441	490
New York												
Albany city	6,577	4,703	2,905	395	673	879	750	6,271	5,232	2,907	826	1,001
Buffalo city	14,714	7,580	4,157	2,810	3,147	2,668	5,363	18,525	11,602	10,614	4,231	2,802
Mount Vernon city	5,345	2,031	2,246	1,080	768	672	636	3,473	4,552	3,012	1,096	1,213
New Rochelle city	7,083	2,776	2,399	1,739	1,311	2,312	996	4,522	6,176	1,942	924	1,399
New York city	533,127	244,803	138,031	128,185	101,837	83,278	85,818	624,268	505,670	297,278	191,904	181,210
Rochester city	10,441	4,872	2,629	3,317	2,514	2,264	4,519	13,715	7,305	9,511	4,158	1,608
Schenectady city	5,416	2,351	1,046	706	1,085	917	1,187	4,881	3,820	2,068	956	663
Syracuse city	9,578	3,541	1,912	1,664	1,885	1,236	2,543	8,210	6,106	4,786	2,269	1,469
Yonkers city	16,021	7,236	5,338	3,225	3,343	4,887	2,725	16,729	15,718	7,456	3,750	3,682
North Carolina												
Asheville city	5,912	2,797	2,046	1,838	3,370	3,052	696	9,946	6,799	1,509	1,775	914
Charlotte city	56,648	13,717	7,710	15,724	19,117	14,522	6,398	56,632	33,237	10,157	7,633	5,376
Concord city	7,337	2,339	1,194	2,084	2,764	2,093	1,081	7,424	5,008	904	1,156	831
Durham city	18,679	8,143	4,816	3,865	5,466	2,872	2,301	18,297	12,034	2,261	1,914	1,584
Fayetteville city	9,249	4,640	2,289	2,252	3,622	2,816	3,039	14,241	9,878	2,743	2,538	1,639
Gastonia city	6,565	1,972	791	1,424	2,640	2,186	1,435	6,016	4,233	1,485	862	354
Greensboro city	18,923	6,811	4,248	5,187	7,407	5,651	3,488	22,994	15,499	4,109	2,814	1,718
Greenville city	3,009	2,020	1,535	1,522	1,246	479	1,192	4,367	3,020	835	548	195
High Point city	7,563	2,893	1,476	2,044	2,456	1,904	1,646	8,951	6,450	1,353	806	1,209
Jacksonville city	2,293	729	902	880	412	287	588	2,430	1,526	466	352	465
Raleigh city	33,331	13,158	6,507	7,137	10,317	7,967	3,599	30,269	20,290	4,155	4,630	2,541
Wilmington city	9,184	4,192	2,615	2,416	4,703	3,550	2,032	12,044	8,398	1,461	1,182	837
Winston-Salem city	18,753	5,279	4,157	4,577	7,023	3,993	3,186	18,839	12,853	3,351	3,512	2,273
North Dakota												
Bismarck city	6,618	2,349	979	1,098	2,653	2,639	642	6,112	5,197	543	248	210
Fargo city	9,722	2,230	1,146	2,173	4,747	3,984	717	8,332	5,728	631	391	825

Table I-3: Cities - Persons With Health Insurance by Source of Insurance—*Continued*

| | Private Health Insurance Coverage | | | | | | Public Health Insurance Coverage | | | | | |
| | Employer Based | | | Direct Purchase | | | Medicare | | | Medicaid/CHIP | | |
	55 to 64 Years	65 to 74 Years	75 Years and Over	55 to 64 Years	65 to 74 Years	75 Years and Over	55 to 64 Years	65 to 74 Years	75 Years and Over	55 to 64 Years	65 to 74 Years	75 Years and Over
Ohio												
Akron city	13,954	5,551	3,485	2,244	4,461	3,850	4,796	16,882	11,394	8,650	2,262	2,100
Canton city	4,097	2,417	1,084	574	2,063	1,467	1,633	6,125	3,899	1,704	747	672
Cincinnati city	19,634	7,041	4,834	4,174	5,196	4,089	5,213	20,234	13,775	10,368	4,745	2,047
Cleveland city	22,782	7,962	5,633	3,204	6,079	4,999	9,158	30,494	20,820	22,152	9,358	5,334
Columbus city	53,564	19,794	9,368	9,687	14,368	12,264	10,029	53,943	34,503	19,317	6,695	4,944
Dayton city	7,644	2,983	1,960	1,356	2,264	1,460	2,222	11,215	6,540	6,460	1,823	1,070
Lorain city	4,234	2,073	1,596	819	1,284	1,170	1,258	5,239	4,332	1,794	645	625
Parma city	7,782	2,868	2,247	1,178	2,530	1,731	1,165	6,970	5,911	947	587	363
Toledo city	18,280	8,269	6,261	2,631	7,499	5,455	5,307	21,204	15,108	10,078	4,846	3,166
Youngstown city	3,479	1,640	1,295	1,016	1,485	1,231	1,914	5,924	4,846	2,763	1,370	568
Oklahoma												
Broken Arrow city	8,338	2,750	1,598	1,616	3,525	2,953	824	9,544	5,920	381	787	475
Edmond city	7,344	2,943	2,150	2,291	3,485	2,198	849	8,217	5,404	333	847	799
Lawton city	4,056	2,054	1,416	647	1,704	1,318	1,214	6,482	3,841	774	1,140	724
Norman city	7,391	3,483	2,047	1,018	2,286	1,623	1,253	8,144	4,903	622	643	439
Oklahoma City city	44,720	17,964	10,202	11,678	14,072	12,523	6,859	45,227	32,773	5,416	5,266	2,890
Tulsa city	27,462	9,228	5,196	6,454	11,773	10,663	5,807	32,073	23,431	4,850	3,374	2,383
Oregon												
Beaverton city	6,026	1,979	1,103	1,599	1,823	1,115	907	6,078	3,836	1,905	794	546
Bend city	4,633	1,540	2,159	2,885	3,735	2,329	563	10,085	5,766	1,241	747	1,477
Eugene city	11,339	3,692	3,184	3,622	5,998	4,118	2,632	15,450	9,630	3,138	1,699	1,400
Gresham city	8,269	2,555	1,564	1,554	3,642	2,337	1,545	8,187	5,103	2,502	1,784	859
Hillsboro city	7,339	2,285	783	799	4,427	2,347	616	7,510	4,021	1,226	690	455
Medford city	6,018	1,469	2,120	2,390	2,602	2,202	706	7,493	6,654	2,283	1,034	740
Portland city	42,512	16,663	9,843	13,137	17,517	12,472	6,479	50,776	30,064	13,608	6,820	5,593
Salem city	12,551	4,931	3,825	2,512	5,603	4,399	1,448	14,469	9,626	4,784	2,178	1,374
Pennsylvania												
Allentown city	5,691	2,428	993	1,381	3,016	2,095	2,227	8,409	4,875	4,430	1,674	774
Bethlehem city	5,960	1,375	1,659	1,187	2,029	2,983	974	5,665	6,392	1,910	1,231	1,027
Erie city	5,702	2,037	1,683	1,331	3,328	2,968	2,133	8,650	6,013	3,659	2,009	1,212
Philadelphia city	91,460	38,663	21,254	21,848	28,483	29,175	25,995	115,535	85,405	57,688	29,253	20,749
Pittsburgh city	22,373	8,929	5,365	5,526	7,667	8,882	3,628	23,578	19,782	8,773	3,901	4,540
Reading city	3,732	1,190	560	431	1,963	1,191	2,346	5,026	3,653	3,467	1,731	955
Scranton city	6,033	2,468	1,544	966	2,382	2,473	1,388	7,033	4,601	2,833	1,174	572
Rhode Island												
Cranston city	7,820	2,134	1,020	1,875	1,620	1,859	812	6,386	4,734	2,465	994	566
Pawtucket city	5,578	1,239	686	1,319	2,276	1,092	2,247	5,577	4,139	3,603	1,147	1,441
Providence city	7,075	2,686	1,120	1,919	2,249	1,429	2,939	10,506	8,647	6,501	4,799	3,868
Warwick city	8,272	2,682	1,808	1,345	3,509	2,418	847	9,212	6,357	1,380	1,236	1,234
South Carolina												
Charleston city	11,152	5,560	2,617	2,594	3,332	1,780	1,091	12,078	7,366	1,292	634	233
Columbia city	6,392	3,730	1,239	2,100	1,498	1,274	1,618	7,438	4,267	1,646	1,072	564
Greenville city	4,180	1,864	1,128	1,397	2,392	1,566	875	5,794	3,760	1,705	579	840
North Charleston city	5,905	2,218	1,117	1,670	1,546	999	1,455	7,196	4,246	1,972	1,060	1,189
Rock Hill city	4,673	2,506	1,648	763	2,200	1,269	1,205	6,119	3,624	1,043	609	162
South Dakota												
Rapid City city	4,717	1,799	825	951	1,962	2,915	589	7,320	5,460	702	865	287
Sioux Falls city	14,176	3,352	1,554	2,574	5,510	4,190	1,684	12,160	7,827	2,093	618	1,320
Tennessee												
Chattanooga city	13,613	3,321	2,763	3,495	5,859	5,874	2,397	15,422	13,041	2,171	3,191	2,311
Clarksville city	5,414	1,521	1,818	1,692	2,067	1,435	2,444	6,777	5,335	2,185	907	240
Franklin city	8,111	2,643	1,300	1,693	1,554	1,267	254	4,795	4,422	657	245	457
Jackson city	5,407	877	1,165	1,206	898	1,445	473	4,920	4,176	966	809	768
Johnson City city	4,669	2,380	984	2,048	1,536	2,056	956	6,137	3,812	929	734	724
Knoxville city	11,743	3,669	1,561	2,044	4,444	3,608	2,428	12,570	9,870	3,814	1,582	1,032
Memphis city	42,054	19,567	12,499	8,969	10,829	8,891	9,543	47,664	31,343	12,556	10,214	7,328
Murfreesboro city	6,860	2,955	1,098	1,658	2,752	1,596	797	8,337	4,803	1,362	540	153
Nashville-Davidson metropolitan govt (bal)	47,230	20,030	8,169	9,861	13,386	8,991	7,695	44,295	29,924	7,359	4,454	3,325
Texas												
Abilene city	7,679	2,160	1,295	887	2,354	2,419	973	7,195	7,588	734	1,211	613
Allen city	11,446	2,997	908	2,239	2,108	1,250	93	6,881	2,438	250	1,046	81
Amarillo city	13,640	4,417	3,686	2,223	3,700	3,944	2,199	14,113	10,502	2,090	1,727	1,748
Arlington city	25,801	9,265	4,129	6,370	5,116	3,270	2,916	24,108	15,302	2,972	2,078	1,821
Austin city	67,089	26,699	12,822	15,843	12,843	10,815	7,725	49,367	29,728	10,213	3,899	3,453
Baytown city	3,377	2,101	469	875	1,129	672	1,130	5,646	2,936	1,427	1,178	802
Beaumont city	8,583	3,315	2,696	2,087	1,991	2,011	2,341	8,677	8,249	1,825	1,295	986
Brownsville city	6,669	1,262	815	2,120	856	866	2,029	10,532	8,275	1,968	4,145	3,598
Bryan city	4,249	2,016	1,358	2,055	1,660	990	723	4,820	2,689	1,125	981	254
Carrollton city	12,493	2,932	1,648	2,867	2,472	1,641	1,012	9,297	5,844	614	950	442
Cedar Park city	6,083	1,248	577	1,744	1,330	1,708	428	2,927	2,453	439	567	752
College Station city	5,358	3,483	1,802	1,454	1,529	1,547	384	4,746	3,686	561	682	177
Conroe city	4,472	2,204	806	1,480	1,214	1,270	668	5,046	4,864	324	570	823
Corpus Christi city	21,580	7,465	4,151	3,464	7,994	3,771	3,767	26,864	17,304	6,358	4,957	3,876

Table I-3: Cities - Persons With Health Insurance by Source of Insurance—*Continued*

	Private Health Insurance Coverage						Public Health Insurance Coverage					
	Employer Based			Direct Purchase			Medicare			Medicaid/CHIP		
	55 to 64 Years	65 to 74 Years	75 Years and Over	55 to 64 Years	65 to 74 Years	75 Years and Over	55 to 64 Years	65 to 74 Years	75 Years and Over	55 to 64 Years	65 to 74 Years	75 Years and Over
Texas—Cont.												
Dallas city	70,456	19,691	12,422	20,300	17,172	16,264	12,080	72,191	56,234	15,189	12,390	11,670
Denton city	7,947	4,813	2,450	2,181	2,737	2,040	1,428	9,025	5,277	805	461	232
Edinburg city	4,614	1,422	713	1,564	708	422	503	4,240	3,637	857	1,559	1,674
El Paso city	32,531	12,000	6,972	12,303	6,688	5,912	7,402	45,362	36,842	6,618	11,318	13,117
Fort Worth city	51,569	16,011	7,450	13,500	11,003	7,573	9,739	48,669	31,520	10,482	7,816	6,059
Frisco city	11,025	3,786	1,776	3,703	3,370	1,553	320	8,578	5,549	445	1,300	313
Garland city	17,676	6,345	2,598	5,963	5,852	3,267	1,971	16,871	10,211	1,827	1,601	2,564
Georgetown city	6,211	5,450	3,352	1,204	3,933	3,661	259	11,633	8,956	544	509	261
Grand Prairie city	11,144	5,358	1,043	3,332	2,632	919	2,277	11,950	5,009	1,915	1,856	993
Harlingen city	2,603	608	1,062	750	739	1,410	266	5,104	4,953	236	1,142	1,390
Houston city	123,068	38,284	21,066	31,358	26,913	26,517	19,319	127,250	91,923	34,482	24,437	19,232
Irving city	15,508	3,090	1,574	2,428	2,011	1,869	862	7,113	5,629	1,805	980	721
Killeen city	4,548	1,949	1,266	1,985	710	551	1,730	6,035	2,919	1,455	861	359
Laredo city	9,939	3,663	2,098	2,821	1,600	1,379	2,265	12,877	9,922	2,192	5,488	3,804
League City city	9,882	4,120	1,180	2,732	2,500	655	817	7,483	3,413	736	571	558
Lewisville city	6,972	1,539	819	1,721	1,030	1,574	261	4,338	4,274	80	42	372
Longview city	5,986	2,415	1,253	973	2,185	1,962	835	6,311	5,167	962	1,006	201
Lubbock city	15,534	6,660	4,556	3,056	4,347	4,511	2,258	16,404	13,073	2,844	2,095	1,566
McAllen city	4,554	1,601	857	2,641	1,076	1,784	742	7,991	7,052	457	2,642	3,310
McKinney city	12,331	5,113	1,708	1,796	3,783	2,532	947	12,557	7,191	993	908	675
Mansfield city	6,178	1,664	590	752	594	687	252	3,551	2,299	400	95	177
Mesquite city	8,625	1,963	1,529	1,860	1,615	1,561	1,115	7,345	5,255	1,237	418	904
Midland city	10,644	3,589	1,932	2,225	2,265	2,109	1,257	7,227	6,053	981	297	1,169
Mission city	3,957	1,492	1,030	930	2,315	1,314	895	5,275	4,729	940	1,552	1,644
Missouri City city	7,881	2,604	880	1,750	1,121	1,097	859	5,802	3,979	955	812	596
New Braunfels city	5,234	2,867	1,225	1,791	1,798	1,529	626	8,031	3,948	949	504	451
North Richland Hills city	7,373	2,683	1,354	1,061	1,659	1,493	215	6,310	4,039	179	596	246
Odessa city	7,019	2,631	1,936	2,699	1,241	1,437	757	6,280	4,354	787	1,161	919
Pasadena city	8,954	2,334	1,105	1,758	1,448	967	942	8,584	4,531	976	1,895	755
Pearland city	8,499	4,235	1,233	1,979	4,109	1,755	497	11,067	4,180	1,017	2,246	265
Pharr city	1,928	449	480	1,435	885	881	879	4,436	2,859	1,298	2,092	1,239
Plano city	26,290	8,432	2,636	5,694	6,748	3,435	1,042	21,801	13,273	1,701	2,384	2,096
Richardson city	10,415	2,668	1,892	1,727	3,268	1,794	581	10,029	5,358	628	554	438
Round Rock city	8,983	3,394	1,110	955	1,399	1,139	771	8,153	3,115	385	604	327
Rowlett city	8,375	1,070	435	1,930	769	653	425	3,834	1,668	308	256	411
San Angelo city	6,346	4,947	2,883	1,265	1,476	1,935	622	8,383	5,588	1,759	879	795
San Antonio city	86,893	34,291	18,768	20,689	21,238	18,913	19,894	99,292	72,455	26,091	15,932	15,419
Sugar Land city	13,179	3,584	2,282	3,941	4,041	2,349	320	12,752	6,245	1,027	480	353
Temple city	3,760	2,921	1,870	1,164	1,869	2,086	553	6,547	5,883	1,130	905	661
Tyler city	5,071	2,037	1,594	1,875	3,028	3,608	1,786	7,708	6,258	2,063	907	446
Victoria city	3,971	1,933	1,497	1,095	1,456	911	839	5,984	4,346	1,354	1,536	820
Waco city	8,335	3,039	2,058	1,076	2,711	2,629	1,948	7,812	5,676	2,221	955	1,023
Wichita Falls city	6,352	2,915	1,863	867	1,376	1,452	1,769	7,150	5,251	2,087	906	511
Utah												
Layton city	4,370	2,152	785	1,136	1,548	1,706	488	4,535	2,863	320	699	469
Lehi city	2,759	1,184	561	847	899	945	88	3,240	1,711	261	185	0
Ogden city	4,574	1,700	704	470	1,634	1,083	1,465	5,519	3,508	1,599	820	869
Orem city	5,609	1,612	1,611	1,718	1,911	1,721	353	4,525	4,169	341	455	555
Provo city	2,952	1,729	1,661	771	930	1,495	545	3,444	3,228	760	489	518
St. George city	5,473	3,807	4,274	2,076	4,904	3,773	1,173	10,420	9,731	823	799	959
Salt Lake City city	11,957	3,775	2,456	2,720	4,129	2,755	1,780	11,567	7,916	2,855	1,829	1,434
Sandy city	7,598	2,539	1,160	2,174	2,575	1,290	686	8,656	5,425	672	818	492
South Jordan city	4,841	1,392	1,298	715	1,001	1,183	50	3,099	3,101	0	274	167
West Jordan city	5,813	2,375	471	671	1,575	659	278	6,187	2,222	832	629	292
West Valley City city	7,643	1,731	892	1,831	1,414	1,121	1,071	6,058	4,419	1,259	865	583
Virginia												
Alexandria city	11,322	5,753	4,147	2,945	2,322	2,060	752	9,263	7,777	1,048	465	1,230
Chesapeake city	19,141	8,364	5,184	4,334	6,527	4,119	3,120	18,727	12,071	1,349	1,555	1,269
Hampton city	10,847	4,268	3,525	1,241	2,937	3,001	2,090	11,316	8,120	1,694	2,059	1,456
Lynchburg city	4,115	1,076	1,624	1,324	2,502	2,331	1,894	5,630	5,174	1,213	623	403
Newport News city	12,734	4,267	3,478	1,765	3,893	2,449	1,857	12,154	8,866	2,242	1,334	914
Norfolk city	12,512	5,365	2,419	3,675	4,628	2,349	3,374	15,402	10,063	3,742	2,112	1,574
Portsmouth city	5,883	2,962	1,967	1,509	1,939	1,494	866	7,911	5,322	1,512	545	603
Richmond city	13,349	4,977	2,821	3,762	5,217	3,791	3,752	17,228	11,221	4,615	2,752	1,602
Roanoke city	6,727	3,718	2,023	923	2,797	2,083	2,315	9,848	5,625	1,825	841	295
Suffolk city	8,996	3,623	1,161	1,282	2,872	1,854	945	7,301	5,019	720	696	515
Virginia Beach city	34,550	12,899	8,271	7,103	10,400	8,078	2,707	35,918	25,718	1,196	1,673	1,687
Washington												
Auburn city	6,335	1,987	1,385	695	2,123	1,627	1,315	6,654	4,021	2,794	978	944
Bellevue city	11,251	3,382	2,503	2,771	3,629	4,290	770	10,129	9,834	1,933	1,206	1,780
Bellingham city	4,129	2,368	1,423	1,480	2,443	1,459	1,724	7,331	5,084	1,927	531	859
Everett city	9,400	2,604	1,519	2,139	1,752	1,635	1,247	7,577	5,456	2,426	1,086	1,031
Federal Way city	8,785	2,105	826	1,238	2,261	1,342	845	7,346	3,896	1,529	756	434
Kennewick city	5,895	2,209	1,205	878	1,605	2,101	2,174	6,346	4,373	2,202	1,167	621
Kent city	10,821	3,053	1,270	1,113	2,484	1,603	1,599	9,556	6,367	2,431	963	1,462

Table I-3: Cities - Persons With Health Insurance by Source of Insurance—*Continued*

| | Private Health Insurance Coverage | | | | | | Public Health Insurance Coverage | | | | | |
| | Employer Based | | | Direct Purchase | | | Medicare | | | Medicaid/CHIP | | |
	55 to 64 Years	65 to 74 Years	75 Years and Over	55 to 64 Years	65 to 74 Years	75 Years and Over	55 to 64 Years	65 to 74 Years	75 Years and Over	55 to 64 Years	65 to 74 Years	75 Years and Over
Washington—Cont.												
Kirkland city	8,203	2,596	996	2,493	1,117	1,178	129	5,055	3,247	386	276	570
Marysville city	5,895	1,535	756	715	2,364	1,247	1,659	5,651	2,731	1,085	500	164
Pasco city	3,624	1,424	813	343	1,199	650	194	3,891	2,773	918	625	685
Redmond city	4,086	760	431	709	1,665	496	85	2,625	2,036	429	341	296
Renton city	8,426	2,501	1,749	1,463	2,263	2,594	938	6,418	5,571	1,528	437	744
Sammamish city	6,974	1,249	533	1,462	1,871	679	57	3,258	1,047	115	143	318
Seattle city	50,019	22,283	9,651	10,078	18,289	13,701	5,151	54,731	35,698	10,327	7,360	6,912
Spokane city	14,412	5,692	3,192	3,216	4,087	4,067	2,806	20,811	11,930	7,519	3,095	1,915
Spokane Valley city	7,626	2,262	1,637	1,213	2,158	2,356	1,317	8,667	5,833	2,398	1,020	737
Tacoma city	14,614	5,999	2,903	2,325	6,072	3,009	2,779	17,296	10,357	4,222	3,038	2,726
Vancouver city	14,439	7,271	2,868	2,417	5,892	4,648	2,277	17,617	10,878	2,928	2,179	1,633
Yakima city	5,641	2,632	2,013	1,313	3,357	2,560	1,579	7,791	7,380	1,815	1,529	1,333
Wisconsin												
Appleton city	5,745	1,194	600	1,250	2,648	2,294	816	5,960	4,586	1,444	523	1,238
Eau Claire city	4,791	2,100	1,569	595	2,858	2,324	647	5,730	4,450	938	869	615
Green Bay city	7,701	1,547	749	1,309	1,986	2,095	1,309	6,760	6,457	1,763	1,144	1,516
Kenosha city	9,218	2,464	2,537	1,217	2,892	1,800	1,332	7,404	4,643	1,703	1,088	657
Madison city	17,599	10,076	5,350	3,239	6,500	4,724	1,199	17,169	13,282	1,960	1,653	1,387
Milwaukee city	32,794	12,820	6,548	6,153	8,000	5,617	8,566	37,318	22,836	18,900	8,408	7,008
Oshkosh city	4,881	994	726	928	1,949	2,433	332	3,998	4,557	969	455	845
Racine city	5,540	1,517	1,196	741	1,084	979	1,414	4,866	3,974	2,232	861	449
Waukesha city	6,580	1,154	1,061	1,281	2,443	2,645	1,039	5,014	5,053	900	336	861

Table I-4: Metropolitan/Micropolitan Statistical Areas - Persons With Health Insurance by Source of Insurance

| | Private Health Insurance Coverage | | | | | | Public Health Insurance Coverage | | | | | |
| | Employer Based | | | Direct Purchase | | | Medicare | | | Medicaid/CHIP | | |
	55 to 64 Years	65 to 74 Years	75 Years and Over	55 to 64 Years	65 to 74 Years	75 Years and Over	55 to 64 Years	65 to 74 Years	75 Years and Over	55 to 64 Years	65 to 74 Years	75 Years and Over
Aberdeen, WA Micro Area	4,874	2,898	1,822	2,146	3,285	2,851	1,609	9,481	6,108	2,153	1,551	566
Abilene, TX Metro Area	12,083	3,615	2,385	2,012	4,629	3,259	2,039	13,231	11,115	1,557	1,657	801
Adrian, MI Micro Area	9,490	4,621	2,883	1,846	3,222	2,972	1,941	10,368	6,867	2,274	1,028	442
Akron, OH Metro Area	64,115	27,068	16,889	12,671	22,481	16,780	11,094	68,928	48,579	15,849	6,200	5,093
Alamogordo, NM Micro Area	3,452	2,132	1,008	239	1,492	1,230	1,146	5,526	4,114	2,301	848	788
Albany, GA Metro Area	9,326	4,176	2,546	2,167	3,750	2,677	1,902	13,527	8,528	2,464	2,956	2,228
Albany, OR Metro Area	9,572	3,219	1,707	2,106	5,441	3,847	2,776	14,014	9,113	3,045	1,360	1,273
Albany-Schenectady-Troy, NY Metro Area	92,645	53,478	31,029	10,837	20,048	20,605	11,543	85,051	59,065	17,704	7,730	6,538
Albertville, AL Micro Area	6,477	3,836	1,834	2,085	2,845	2,750	2,693	8,374	6,580	1,729	1,212	848
Albuquerque, NM Metro Area	67,577	31,123	18,857	14,973	18,581	13,769	12,839	87,457	57,876	24,247	11,877	9,354
Alexandria, LA Metro Area	10,712	4,451	2,922	2,169	3,409	2,501	2,995	13,670	9,352	4,257	2,156	951
Allentown-Bethlehem-Easton, PA-NJ Metro Area	80,487	26,974	18,253	15,611	31,562	26,745	10,922	80,888	62,164	15,414	8,168	8,135
Altoona, PA Metro Area	11,537	4,663	3,018	2,333	4,883	5,035	2,555	13,188	10,195	1,981	1,472	1,413
Amarillo, TX Metro Area	19,861	6,725	5,375	4,065	5,631	5,399	2,569	19,575	14,508	2,264	1,926	2,008
Ames, IA Metro Area	5,819	3,440	2,054	2,143	2,820	2,567	752	5,718	4,611	698	426	370
Anchorage, AK Metro Area	30,930	14,020	6,387	4,812	4,407	1,723	2,748	28,124	14,459	7,457	5,344	2,917
Ann Arbor, MI Metro Area	30,617	18,127	11,048	5,329	7,737	6,907	4,148	29,315	19,178	4,235	3,186	2,364
Anniston-Oxford-Jacksonville, AL Metro Area	8,658	3,910	1,706	2,702	3,028	3,042	2,799	11,892	8,014	2,200	1,525	1,098
Appleton, WI Metro Area	22,891	3,563	1,880	5,027	8,411	6,641	2,402	19,454	14,187	3,354	1,313	2,369
Asheville, NC Metro Area	38,316	16,999	10,725	11,669	20,871	16,216	7,442	57,151	39,642	7,032	5,054	4,465
Ashtabula, OH Micro Area	9,288	2,590	2,370	2,098	4,365	3,074	1,677	10,230	7,020	3,095	1,283	388
Athens, OH Micro Area	4,672	1,711	1,326	600	1,448	885	894	4,807	3,243	1,883	703	244
Athens, TX Micro Area	4,925	3,371	1,657	2,800	2,807	2,934	1,925	9,221	7,709	1,655	816	584
Athens-Clarke County, GA Metro Area	13,855	8,005	3,032	2,545	4,043	3,680	2,492	15,954	10,699	2,171	2,529	2,735
Atlanta-Sandy Springs-Roswell, GA Metro Area	443,188	158,268	81,208	105,845	117,468	84,192	59,870	427,281	258,425	66,595	55,312	37,594
Atlantic City-Hammonton, NJ Metro Area	26,943	10,942	7,416	4,615	7,646	6,602	3,495	25,487	18,548	6,318	4,020	2,808
Auburn, NY Micro Area	7,294	3,316	2,732	1,940	1,950	2,404	1,331	7,896	5,759	2,587	1,206	695
Auburn-Opelika, AL Metro Area	9,532	6,217	1,990	2,100	4,037	2,704	2,496	12,909	6,462	2,043	1,161	724
Augusta-Richmond County, GA-SC Metro Area	47,615	18,745	11,177	8,911	16,166	11,624	7,787	56,661	34,589	8,035	7,122	4,459
Augusta-Waterville, ME Micro Area	10,634	5,631	2,528	2,748	4,311	3,299	2,717	13,591	9,156	3,090	2,014	2,439
Austin-Round Rock, TX Metro Area	153,871	66,178	29,727	35,209	38,085	27,408	15,779	136,444	77,541	17,484	11,593	8,442
Bakersfield, CA Metro Area	45,838	17,670	9,978	10,651	13,068	9,287	10,458	54,265	36,704	27,590	14,550	9,733
Baltimore-Columbia-Towson, MD Metro Area	256,877	126,574	78,879	45,228	70,859	63,284	33,846	232,147	170,696	56,205	30,797	26,116
Bangor, ME Metro Area	13,506	4,506	3,451	2,491	4,443	4,320	3,792	15,672	10,362	5,061	3,296	1,899
Barnstable Town, MA Metro Area	24,468	16,107	10,925	7,565	13,739	11,528	1,778	35,488	26,575	6,259	3,919	2,178
Baton Rouge, LA Metro Area	57,470	27,910	15,942	14,971	16,051	10,649	11,410	68,450	42,473	18,553	11,185	7,015
Battle Creek, MI Metro Area	10,508	6,549	5,041	1,807	3,491	3,626	3,269	12,594	9,708	3,737	1,696	1,426
Bay City, MI Metro Area	10,567	6,505	4,815	2,144	3,338	2,363	2,853	11,626	8,429	2,841	854	430
Beaumont-Port Arthur, TX Metro Area	31,645	10,522	7,962	7,230	8,454	7,899	5,952	32,764	26,100	5,815	5,177	2,860
Beaver Dam, WI Micro Area	10,056	2,179	1,175	2,297	3,829	3,536	687	8,262	6,122	1,016	627	426
Beckley, WV Metro Area	8,010	7,651	4,788	2,347	2,304	3,080	3,792	14,427	9,615	4,081	1,998	1,813
Bellingham, WA Metro Area	14,244	8,592	3,893	4,846	8,785	4,679	3,187	23,227	14,525	5,956	1,990	1,990
Bend-Redmond, OR Metro Area	12,468	4,994	3,950	7,364	9,243	6,104	2,685	23,396	13,690	4,585	2,059	2,897
Billings, MT Metro Area	15,272	4,173	2,779	3,320	7,559	5,541	1,813	17,140	11,741	2,996	1,356	1,349
Binghamton, NY Metro Area	24,123	12,233	9,026	4,393	5,722	7,229	3,964	23,917	19,963	6,443	2,613	3,231
Birmingham-Hoover, AL Metro Area	93,993	39,338	18,973	20,069	33,520	27,252	22,113	105,739	72,547	19,127	13,482	10,742
Bismarck, ND Metro Area	12,686	4,074	2,332	3,001	4,225	4,166	1,301	10,939	8,554	1,017	754	376
Blacksburg-Christiansburg-Radford, VA Metro Area	13,380	5,172	2,830	3,111	4,974	4,097	2,489	17,114	11,525	1,631	1,321	879
Bloomington, IL Metro Area	17,292	6,528	3,571	3,067	5,237	3,893	1,478	13,734	9,379	1,604	785	767
Bloomington, IN Metro Area	11,451	3,149	2,526	1,688	5,293	4,216	1,962	12,658	8,525	3,897	1,248	422
Bloomsburg-Berwick, PA Metro Area	7,822	2,760	1,572	1,463	3,607	3,145	586	8,616	6,482	1,866	678	1,009
Bluefield, WV-VA Micro Area	6,272	3,726	2,799	1,197	3,371	2,608	3,676	12,741	8,437	3,441	1,690	1,543
Boise City, ID Metro Area	52,373	16,460	10,019	16,804	26,313	20,679	8,221	63,570	40,830	7,230	7,876	5,825
Boston-Cambridge-Newton, MA-NH Metro Area	452,988	195,952	106,277	79,486	125,679	116,056	44,171	397,095	301,826	113,420	64,220	56,660
Boulder, CO Metro Area	27,969	10,516	4,884	7,520	8,272	7,369	1,765	26,576	16,184	3,809	1,618	1,670
Bowling Green, KY Metro Area	11,223	5,331	2,518	2,750	5,824	3,520	4,074	16,119	8,607	4,010	1,293	1,127
Bozeman, MT Micro Area	8,418	2,939	1,064	2,681	3,577	2,636	825	8,744	4,986	817	717	281
Brainerd, MN Micro Area	8,325	3,065	2,233	2,663	5,957	5,118	1,708	12,209	8,648	2,642	1,141	557
Branson, MO Micro Area	6,527	2,660	3,026	2,519	4,323	4,181	1,729	13,294	8,582	1,528	1,596	781
Bremerton-Silverdale, WA Metro Area	23,113	12,722	7,327	5,279	8,664	5,579	2,206	28,790	16,581	5,263	1,822	1,448
Bridgeport-Stamford-Norwalk, CT Metro Area	90,109	31,603	18,171	21,310	24,525	23,598	5,670	72,301	63,112	13,886	7,652	9,702
Brownsville-Harlingen, TX Metro Area	16,638	4,455	3,034	4,472	4,182	4,112	3,733	29,394	24,028	4,136	7,994	8,493
Brunswick, GA Metro Area	9,955	4,780	3,087	3,189	3,140	2,517	2,757	13,440	8,816	1,810	1,365	572
Buffalo-Cheektowaga-Niagara Falls, NY Metro Area	111,086	50,299	30,316	20,126	33,709	36,146	19,033	109,585	83,722	30,292	14,651	11,321
Burlington, NC Metro Area	14,844	4,804	3,550	3,694	4,932	4,580	2,141	14,988	11,682	1,426	1,387	1,879
Burlington-South Burlington, VT Metro Area	19,910	8,227	3,220	4,266	7,524	5,966	2,088	20,434	13,123	3,848	2,836	2,001
California-Lexington Park, MD Metro Area	10,955	5,793	3,343	1,204	2,121	1,625	1,331	7,774	5,280	1,099	529	687
Canton-Massillon, OH Metro Area	39,211	16,211	9,620	6,414	12,599	11,870	5,966	41,672	31,645	6,026	3,053	3,462
Cape Coral-Fort Myers, FL Metro Area	57,607	39,370	27,277	22,203	36,948	36,820	11,333	112,993	93,092	11,262	9,582	11,067
Cape Girardeau, MO-IL Metro Area	7,078	2,439	1,702	1,637	3,805	3,129	2,184	8,462	6,619	1,928	856	585
Carbondale-Marion, IL Metro Area	8,737	4,676	3,605	1,533	3,248	2,733	2,485	11,647	8,763	2,642	1,331	1,018
Carson City, NV Metro Area	5,378	2,493	1,632	693	2,107	1,827	359	5,582	4,669	570	533	960
Casper, WY Metro Area	7,045	1,884	1,068	1,707	3,036	2,947	1,017	6,602	4,511	552	800	383
Cedar Rapids, IA Metro Area	26,632	6,972	4,959	4,139	10,592	9,300	2,361	24,104	19,387	3,750	2,389	1,754

Table I-4: Metropolitan/Micropolitan Statistical Areas - Persons With Health Insurance by Source of Insurance—*Continued*

| | Private Health Insurance Coverage | | | | | | Public Health Insurance Coverage | | | | | |
| | Employer Based | | | Direct Purchase | | | Medicare | | | Medicaid/CHIP | | |
	55 to 64 Years	65 to 74 Years	75 Years and Over	55 to 64 Years	65 to 74 Years	75 Years and Over	55 to 64 Years	65 to 74 Years	75 Years and Over	55 to 64 Years	65 to 74 Years	75 Years and Over
Centralia, WA Micro Area	6,905	2,206	1,686	1,219	4,012	3,542	1,988	9,479	6,400	3,059	1,079	576
Chambersburg-Waynesboro, PA Metro Area	14,575	7,331	5,961	3,263	6,491	5,708	1,581	16,235	12,704	1,695	1,864	1,614
Champaign-Urbana, IL Metro Area	18,603	9,368	5,890	3,167	5,784	4,805	1,894	17,195	12,217	3,731	980	1,190
Charleston, WV Metro Area	18,621	10,386	7,336	3,002	4,164	5,396	7,013	23,968	17,363	7,454	3,693	2,322
Charleston-North Charleston, SC Metro Area	56,064	27,421	14,738	15,569	17,637	13,408	10,077	71,996	42,991	13,067	7,892	4,854
Charlotte-Concord-Gastonia, NC-SC Metro Area	194,574	61,658	33,101	49,198	70,725	54,660	30,242	201,110	128,748	29,935	22,843	16,243
Charlottesville, VA Metro Area	20,034	10,075	5,410	3,449	8,945	7,746	1,641	22,736	17,285	2,362	1,255	597
Chattanooga, TN-GA Metro Area	46,623	13,175	9,410	9,187	19,949	18,447	9,194	55,055	40,380	7,287	7,526	5,732
Cheyenne, WY Metro Area	9,732	3,871	2,272	1,679	2,196	2,558	629	9,449	5,890	643	482	975
Chicago-Naperville-Elgin, IL-IN-WI Metro Area	808,500	266,290	148,659	156,321	232,579	207,095	84,968	732,091	537,928	153,306	88,017	69,020
Chico, CA Metro Area	13,458	7,725	6,291	4,951	7,601	6,912	3,114	24,400	17,063	9,145	3,598	3,756
Chillicothe, OH Micro Area	5,280	2,445	1,809	1,501	2,706	2,063	1,795	7,243	5,403	2,395	888	449
Cincinnati, OH-KY-IN Metro Area	198,302	68,213	41,073	37,411	58,210	43,216	25,469	184,190	123,997	37,410	19,673	11,417
Claremont-Lebanon, NH-VT Micro Area	22,559	10,522	5,727	4,817	8,467	6,830	4,099	26,839	17,417	4,914	2,534	1,641
Clarksburg, WV Micro Area	7,698	3,764	1,914	1,050	2,788	2,430	1,597	10,162	6,701	2,316	1,327	514
Clarksville, TN-KY Metro Area	14,187	4,814	3,954	3,625	4,513	3,991	4,508	16,015	12,311	4,444	2,114	690
Clearlake, CA Micro Area	3,427	1,795	1,726	2,247	3,005	2,358	1,529	8,674	4,951	3,196	1,899	727
Cleveland, TN Metro Area	9,285	2,703	1,535	1,794	5,065	3,946	2,120	11,982	8,688	1,894	1,367	1,461
Cleveland-Elyria, OH Metro Area	195,379	76,636	56,360	36,219	61,794	55,066	26,460	199,590	154,717	45,083	22,495	17,351
Coeur d'Alene, ID Metro Area	11,651	4,625	2,929	4,781	6,731	4,889	1,525	17,531	11,849	1,445	1,470	1,203
College Station-Bryan, TX Metro Area	13,533	8,560	4,603	4,742	4,945	4,148	1,785	15,585	10,127	1,921	2,672	1,079
Colorado Springs, CO Metro Area	46,180	15,611	7,928	13,085	17,707	12,157	6,772	57,956	34,618	13,862	5,123	4,368
Columbia, MO Metro Area	13,965	5,510	3,580	1,923	3,611	2,216	2,036	12,775	7,967	1,605	860	520
Columbia, SC Metro Area	62,778	29,754	15,837	16,731	22,180	15,339	9,693	72,754	45,182	10,581	9,343	7,183
Columbus, GA-AL Metro Area	17,402	8,248	3,785	5,496	7,919	5,250	6,274	24,758	17,017	5,736	4,368	3,087
Columbus, IN Metro Area	6,957	2,471	1,202	830	3,022	2,765	1,008	6,760	5,612	617	488	310
Columbus, OH Metro Area	161,990	59,776	34,331	29,897	50,164	40,792	24,470	154,103	105,561	38,457	12,824	10,130
Concord, NH Micro Area	15,660	5,136	3,939	2,526	4,934	3,700	2,205	15,764	10,983	1,633	1,407	756
Cookeville, TN Micro Area	6,461	3,085	1,917	3,711	4,368	3,549	2,381	10,987	7,900	1,832	1,493	1,226
Coos Bay, OR Micro Area	4,861	1,991	2,093	1,184	4,521	2,252	1,775	9,236	7,521	2,410	1,579	1,893
Corning, NY Micro Area	8,924	4,997	3,321	1,479	2,775	2,440	1,867	10,248	7,159	3,008	1,466	1,269
Corpus Christi, TX Metro Area	31,260	10,451	5,562	6,926	10,929	7,119	6,357	38,821	25,914	9,032	7,193	4,951
Corvallis, OR Metro Area	7,027	2,938	2,116	2,142	3,358	2,813	630	8,472	5,662	1,207	817	591
Crestview-Fort Walton Beach-Destin, FL Metro Area	18,068	7,907	4,215	6,029	7,958	5,034	3,738	28,864	18,157	3,511	2,538	1,802
Cullman, AL Micro Area	6,499	2,531	2,331	1,659	2,882	1,996	1,915	9,096	6,260	1,961	1,357	755
Cumberland, MD-WV Metro Area	7,591	4,330	2,931	1,625	3,328	3,938	1,426	10,511	8,436	2,348	1,534	1,293
Dallas-Fort Worth-Arlington, TX Metro Area	538,536	167,490	82,720	121,180	123,416	88,741	55,523	473,220	305,265	60,372	53,863	45,506
Dalton, GA Metro Area	10,725	2,264	1,090	1,232	3,261	2,969	1,827	11,396	7,616	1,629	1,569	824
Danville, IL Metro Area	6,041	2,493	1,933	1,385	2,886	3,134	1,349	7,880	6,363	1,793	1,038	662
Danville, VA Metro Area	8,798	3,722	2,668	3,191	4,528	4,044	2,876	12,706	8,668	1,632	1,165	1,250
Daphne-Fairhope-Foley, AL Metro Area	19,275	9,912	4,602	6,253	7,351	6,636	3,886	26,497	16,388	2,659	2,592	1,712
Davenport-Moline-Rock Island, IA-IL Metro Area	36,602	15,428	10,847	6,461	15,351	12,440	4,897	36,452	27,946	6,861	3,508	3,185
Dayton, OH Metro Area	70,512	27,650	21,463	12,428	23,249	18,564	10,311	77,866	57,012	17,307	6,452	4,960
Decatur, AL Metro Area	12,410	5,702	3,535	4,047	5,182	3,271	3,081	15,183	10,491	2,725	1,558	1,140
Decatur, IL Metro Area	9,973	4,449	3,413	1,794	4,530	2,968	1,611	10,938	8,813	1,790	1,245	1,286
Deltona-Daytona Beach-Ormond Beach, FL Metro Area	50,745	24,304	20,793	19,683	24,510	23,914	11,743	89,187	71,962	11,364	8,796	11,273
Denver-Aurora-Lakewood, CO Metro Area	235,368	76,738	42,667	50,282	61,799	49,232	25,637	217,983	134,175	41,958	22,396	19,029
Des Moines-West Des Moines, IA Metro Area	56,403	16,324	9,987	9,157	25,605	17,461	6,077	48,602	32,742	10,582	3,955	3,342
Detroit-Warren-Dearborn, MI Metro Area	394,613	199,630	129,450	80,230	120,309	106,765	69,153	391,691	280,060	103,047	57,294	42,213
Dothan, AL Metro Area	10,220	5,274	2,941	3,539	6,019	3,702	4,264	16,156	10,627	3,281	2,586	1,993
Dover, DE Metro Area	14,096	8,757	5,036	2,286	5,441	3,816	4,462	16,606	11,848	5,630	2,074	1,322
DuBois, PA Micro Area	7,024	2,049	2,008	1,919	3,124	2,921	902	8,252	6,966	2,247	815	863
Dubuque, IA Metro Area	9,047	2,613	1,783	2,673	4,594	4,177	1,176	8,770	7,566	1,598	655	680
Duluth, MN-WI Metro Area	27,465	10,301	6,616	5,881	14,036	10,872	4,491	29,456	20,276	6,556	2,227	2,126
Dunn, NC Micro Area	7,061	2,584	1,892	2,279	2,842	2,630	2,623	9,731	6,456	1,998	1,354	1,001
Durham-Chapel Hill, NC Metro Area	47,749	24,185	13,537	9,841	14,929	10,414	5,357	49,217	32,060	4,550	4,883	3,198
East Stroudsburg, PA Metro Area	16,786	5,070	3,233	2,834	6,006	4,548	3,260	16,054	10,684	4,864	1,846	1,337
Eau Claire, WI Metro Area	14,635	4,016	3,221	4,135	8,469	6,380	2,032	16,224	11,069	2,612	2,210	1,312
El Centro, CA Metro Area	7,858	4,082	1,779	1,466	2,722	1,725	2,481	12,013	9,999	6,910	4,509	5,240
Elizabeth City, NC Micro Area	5,058	2,891	2,216	1,959	1,982	1,684	1,451	8,020	4,662	1,185	700	631
Elizabethtown-Fort Knox, KY Metro Area	9,378	5,163	2,913	1,859	3,930	3,276	2,967	12,480	8,405	5,159	2,793	2,721
Elkhart-Goshen, IN Metro Area	15,627	4,299	1,739	4,249	5,096	5,927	2,014	14,767	12,417	2,317	550	1,659
Elmira, NY Metro Area	8,456	3,216	2,855	1,531	2,136	1,654	1,910	9,283	6,509	2,193	1,548	950
El Paso, TX Metro Area	36,515	13,064	7,323	14,326	7,871	6,381	9,632	54,519	41,842	8,424	14,556	15,433
Enid, OK Metro Area	4,313	1,379	1,560	1,289	1,712	1,351	489	4,819	3,832	605	783	472
Erie, PA Metro Area	24,678	7,823	5,745	5,339	10,698	8,678	4,703	26,857	19,023	7,369	4,029	2,396
Eugene, OR Metro Area	26,377	10,726	6,679	7,828	14,773	11,895	5,558	43,253	28,057	9,692	4,622	3,462
Eureka-Arcata-Fortuna, CA Micro Area	8,150	4,587	2,232	3,474	5,358	3,264	2,744	14,684	8,749	4,678	2,395	1,061
Evansville, IN-KY Metro Area	30,117	8,254	6,793	5,399	9,716	8,156	5,416	29,881	20,268	6,436	3,537	2,249
Fairbanks, AK Metro Area	6,314	3,471	1,037	689	845	402	1,429	6,600	2,688	1,707	891	165
Fargo, ND-MN Metro Area	19,699	4,791	2,890	3,594	8,036	7,941	1,600	16,258	12,045	1,762	796	1,290
Faribault-Northfield, MN Micro Area	5,254	1,052	1,025	1,736	2,666	2,359	486	5,576	4,026	949	408	555
Farmington, MO Micro Area	5,236	2,118	1,364	792	2,079	1,373	830	6,167	3,853	1,342	554	630
Farmington, NM Metro Area	7,981	2,882	1,749	1,396	2,375	1,905	2,564	10,630	7,293	3,972	2,650	1,246

Table I-4: Metropolitan/Micropolitan Statistical Areas - Persons With Health Insurance by Source of Insurance—*Continued*

	Private Health Insurance Coverage						Public Health Insurance Coverage					
	Employer Based			Direct Purchase			Medicare			Medicaid/CHIP		
	55 to 64 Years	65 to 74 Years	75 Years and Over	55 to 64 Years	65 to 74 Years	75 Years and Over	55 to 64 Years	65 to 74 Years	75 Years and Over	55 to 64 Years	65 to 74 Years	75 Years and Over
Fayetteville, NC Metro Area	18,308	7,478	5,014	4,240	6,895	6,143	6,929	26,075	17,424	5,946	4,814	2,289
Fayetteville-Springdale-Rogers, AR-MO Metro Area	36,140	10,540	6,462	10,357	12,014	11,019	6,280	38,815	28,031	6,749	4,118	3,777
Findlay, OH Micro Area	8,026	2,037	2,064	1,115	2,668	2,410	658	7,025	5,055	916	737	286
Flagstaff, AZ Metro Area	9,892	3,553	1,768	3,629	3,139	1,769	1,449	10,471	6,337	2,562	1,377	1,490
Flint, MI Metro Area	35,222	22,671	19,251	6,134	9,434	8,562	10,370	39,667	29,381	14,290	5,540	3,117
Florence, SC Metro Area	14,503	5,759	3,367	3,547	6,799	4,291	4,538	21,009	12,789	3,062	3,544	2,187
Florence-Muscle Shoals, AL Metro Area	11,989	5,559	4,751	3,819	5,133	4,814	3,256	16,102	12,412	2,281	1,932	1,742
Fond du Lac, WI Metro Area	10,108	1,559	1,377	1,896	3,526	3,693	1,163	10,541	7,765	2,174	1,396	1,518
Forest City, NC Micro Area	5,589	1,923	1,407	2,335	2,702	2,873	1,186	8,107	5,392	1,026	1,269	454
Fort Collins, CO Metro Area	30,428	10,523	5,600	6,749	10,799	7,880	1,956	31,923	19,347	4,148	2,955	2,046
Fort Payne, AL Micro Area	5,029	2,164	965	1,474	2,206	1,706	1,897	7,279	4,679	1,735	597	937
Fort Smith, AR-OK Metro Area	16,974	5,117	3,341	5,060	7,322	6,779	7,309	26,810	18,121	8,316	3,746	3,281
Fort Wayne, IN Metro Area	38,003	11,287	6,410	6,951	12,353	9,574	5,411	37,356	24,378	5,664	4,110	1,907
Frankfort, KY Micro Area	6,002	4,017	1,939	1,381	2,444	2,025	1,068	7,267	4,880	1,756	994	432
Fresno, CA Metro Area	51,192	24,122	11,416	12,114	15,560	12,062	9,771	66,293	47,706	33,063	15,635	13,803
Gadsden, AL Metro Area	7,544	4,066	1,987	2,234	4,441	3,264	2,638	11,085	7,631	2,823	1,427	1,609
Gainesville, FL Metro Area	19,875	8,137	4,300	6,218	7,208	5,518	3,374	23,170	16,152	3,399	4,381	3,406
Gainesville, GA Metro Area	15,025	5,033	4,349	2,883	6,113	6,306	1,728	17,032	12,139	2,431	2,270	2,454
Gallup, NM Micro Area	2,049	1,134	603	738	307	675	883	4,622	4,202	3,321	1,805	1,598
Gettysburg, PA Metro Area	10,657	5,102	2,275	1,972	4,121	2,412	1,315	11,534	8,083	1,308	1,400	976
Glens Falls, NY Metro Area	12,772	7,525	4,774	2,584	4,045	3,635	3,152	14,673	10,258	3,202	1,642	1,529
Glenwood Springs, CO Micro Area	6,011	1,892	901	2,845	1,410	1,195	604	7,428	3,580	1,328	848	703
Goldsboro, NC Metro Area	5,925	4,360	2,277	3,097	2,804	2,917	1,961	11,437	7,913	2,320	1,299	1,757
Grand Forks, ND-MN Metro Area	8,346	2,263	1,483	1,561	3,561	3,041	904	8,038	5,622	1,192	353	562
Grand Island, NE Metro Area	7,563	2,233	641	1,697	3,547	3,502	728	7,675	5,637	802	461	549
Grand Junction, CO Metro Area	10,463	3,571	2,513	3,439	6,156	5,724	2,090	15,878	11,942	4,000	1,431	973
Grand Rapids-Wyoming, MI Metro Area	90,663	32,381	22,160	20,268	29,424	25,925	11,661	86,993	61,466	17,411	9,560	6,598
Grants Pass, OR Metro Area	4,972	2,850	2,730	2,097	5,270	4,050	1,676	12,408	9,375	3,364	1,188	1,244
Great Falls, MT Metro Area	6,268	1,467	1,021	1,512	2,655	2,813	1,421	8,359	6,244	1,951	1,096	369
Greeley, CO Metro Area	21,220	5,960	3,948	5,758	8,061	4,901	3,727	23,072	13,716	4,867	2,856	1,951
Green Bay, WI Metro Area	30,696	5,499	3,083	6,944	9,850	7,581	3,264	28,375	20,296	4,116	2,252	3,197
Greeneville, TN Micro Area	5,030	1,590	1,400	1,616	2,558	2,507	1,305	8,415	5,744	1,340	1,849	856
Greenfield Town, MA Micro Area	7,183	4,938	2,382	2,111	3,113	2,277	2,061	8,758	5,331	3,453	1,577	1,094
Greensboro-High Point, NC Metro Area	59,722	20,090	12,076	16,127	21,779	16,879	10,559	68,395	48,471	10,448	7,218	5,850
Greenville, NC Metro Area	11,525	6,201	3,719	3,508	3,361	1,646	3,943	12,712	8,132	2,572	1,823	743
Greenville-Anderson-Mauldin, SC Metro Area	66,165	24,538	15,872	19,621	24,978	23,274	15,516	86,604	57,810	12,917	9,573	6,670
Greenwood, SC Micro Area	7,128	2,715	2,730	2,158	3,250	2,554	1,627	9,279	7,421	987	1,668	1,728
Gulfport-Biloxi-Pascagoula, MS Metro Area	27,441	10,674	5,378	6,024	11,179	9,115	7,682	37,300	24,167	7,151	3,866	2,168
Hagerstown-Martinsburg, MD-WV Metro Area	22,575	11,052	6,235	3,671	8,709	7,189	3,976	25,195	16,702	5,424	3,610	2,321
Hammond, LA Metro Area	8,704	3,554	2,080	1,951	2,689	2,177	1,982	11,014	6,446	2,232	1,003	564
Hanford-Corcoran, CA Metro Area	6,702	1,711	1,438	1,567	2,428	2,119	1,626	8,014	6,358	2,993	2,289	1,936
Harrisburg-Carlisle, PA Metro Area	57,545	25,538	15,823	10,015	19,759	16,633	5,054	55,648	40,532	8,897	5,457	4,942
Harrisonburg, VA Metro Area	10,531	2,528	1,672	2,109	3,756	3,841	1,224	10,385	8,445	1,207	1,118	910
Hartford-West Hartford-East Hartford, CT Metro Area	125,398	47,919	31,940	16,219	27,192	31,137	13,956	106,923	85,980	22,678	14,355	13,892
Hattiesburg, MS Metro Area	6,649	2,940	1,259	2,100	3,985	2,998	3,090	11,296	7,937	4,652	2,247	1,369
Helena, MT Micro Area	7,349	2,814	1,841	1,829	2,734	2,113	984	9,587	5,359	1,261	840	502
Hermiston-Pendleton, OR Micro Area	6,234	2,664	1,409	1,169	2,604	2,679	1,501	7,101	5,263	2,733	1,298	421
Hickory-Lenoir-Morganton, NC Metro Area	33,386	10,640	6,747	8,166	14,005	10,853	6,424	39,387	27,488	5,678	4,215	2,750
Hilo, HI Micro Area	15,345	10,875	6,116	4,865	8,262	5,499	2,460	25,653	14,312	6,020	3,499	2,973
Hilton Head Island-Bluffton-Beaufort, SC Metro Area	14,289	10,615	7,187	7,180	12,856	10,088	3,283	31,923	21,727	2,493	3,060	817
Hinesville, GA Metro Area	3,334	1,156	448	1,368	1,383	792	1,777	3,943	2,351	630	589	755
Hobbs, NM Micro Area	3,834	1,454	515	608	881	1,224	684	4,306	2,984	1,011	266	750
Holland, MI Micro Area	11,217	4,009	1,962	2,569	4,991	2,573	1,516	11,439	7,122	2,719	862	662
Homosassa Springs, FL Metro Area	10,298	6,547	7,461	5,471	7,847	8,834	3,516	28,544	24,083	2,808	3,294	2,538
Hot Springs, AR Metro Area	7,238	3,343	3,074	2,720	3,774	4,607	3,401	12,102	10,110	2,245	1,528	1,395
Houma-Thibodaux, LA Metro Area	15,720	6,195	2,556	3,225	4,107	3,580	4,758	17,345	12,704	4,774	2,547	3,744
Houston-The Woodlands-Sugar Land, TX Metro Area	465,902	148,776	67,535	119,775	103,135	74,799	55,372	441,560	268,289	74,481	63,109	43,197
Huntington-Ashland, WV-KY-OH Metro Area	24,524	15,089	10,399	5,186	10,110	8,469	10,130	38,361	25,796	12,423	4,292	3,429
Huntsville, AL Metro Area	41,661	17,626	12,061	10,191	13,162	12,676	6,034	39,355	28,273	5,605	3,567	2,918
Huntsville, TX Micro Area	5,276	4,407	2,394	787	1,606	1,003	1,530	7,350	4,975	1,028	545	408
Hutchinson, KS Micro Area	4,979	1,230	1,046	1,473	3,304	3,481	710	6,283	5,416	644	834	431
Idaho Falls, ID Metro Area	10,218	3,430	1,720	2,318	3,475	2,998	1,659	10,921	7,524	1,561	1,941	773
Indiana, PA Micro Area	8,308	3,308	2,203	1,519	3,362	2,984	1,435	9,017	7,137	2,159	1,050	1,360
Indianapolis-Carmel-Anderson, IN Metro Area	167,637	54,687	33,053	34,148	49,789	42,245	23,943	156,812	106,807	31,905	14,776	12,354
Iowa City, IA Metro Area	12,735	4,612	3,009	2,838	6,315	3,889	1,535	12,272	8,229	1,602	635	872
Ithaca, NY Metro Area	8,652	4,743	2,930	1,676	2,104	1,981	501	7,856	5,278	1,312	1,228	191
Jackson, MI Metro Area	14,994	7,438	4,745	2,645	5,063	4,871	3,105	15,817	11,091	3,563	1,733	885
Jackson, MS Metro Area	45,737	15,169	7,267	8,518	12,740	10,632	7,129	48,464	31,455	9,305	7,118	6,168
Jackson, TN Metro Area	11,156	2,649	2,062	2,331	4,268	3,287	1,418	12,913	8,473	2,438	1,584	1,018
Jacksonville, FL Metro Area	117,300	39,206	24,278	30,147	38,032	28,879	19,369	141,846	87,771	21,742	20,978	12,982
Jacksonville, NC Metro Area	7,736	4,044	3,146	3,050	1,527	1,322	1,806	10,288	7,437	1,542	1,541	1,632
Jamestown-Dunkirk-Fredonia, NY Micro Area	12,418	4,560	3,024	3,151	4,977	4,624	3,260	13,275	10,826	3,639	1,490	1,954

Table I-4: Metropolitan/Micropolitan Statistical Areas - Persons With Health Insurance by Source of Insurance—*Continued*

| | Private Health Insurance Coverage | | | | | | Public Health Insurance Coverage | | | | | |
| | Employer Based | | | Direct Purchase | | | Medicare | | | Medicaid/CHIP | | |
	55 to 64 Years	65 to 74 Years	75 Years and Over	55 to 64 Years	65 to 74 Years	75 Years and Over	55 to 64 Years	65 to 74 Years	75 Years and Over	55 to 64 Years	65 to 74 Years	75 Years and Over
Janesville-Beloit, WI Metro Area	15,545	5,503	3,791	2,391	5,479	5,822	1,281	14,972	10,782	3,334	1,775	1,655
Jefferson, GA Micro Area	5,133	1,966	1,386	834	1,422	1,130	332	5,804	4,104	531	658	1,115
Jefferson City, MO Metro Area	13,814	6,233	3,056	2,490	4,141	3,047	1,582	13,663	9,450	911	502	466
Johnson City, TN Metro Area	15,277	6,437	3,508	5,004	6,035	6,425	4,662	21,418	15,367	4,242	2,447	2,273
Johnstown, PA Metro Area	12,254	5,584	4,622	3,158	5,992	5,884	3,105	15,507	12,739	4,075	2,265	2,540
Jonesboro, AR Metro Area	7,774	2,832	995	2,739	3,659	2,884	1,937	11,412	7,501	2,597	1,602	1,656
Joplin, MO Metro Area	12,780	3,295	1,659	2,904	5,455	4,895	2,149	16,196	11,672	2,561	1,758	1,054
Kahului-Wailuku-Lahaina, HI Metro Area	14,845	7,689	5,168	5,241	3,966	4,401	1,916	17,122	11,402	2,589	1,522	1,188
Kalamazoo-Portage, MI Metro Area	28,053	12,591	8,190	5,965	10,825	9,629	4,036	30,873	20,503	5,639	3,854	1,696
Kalispell, MT Micro Area	7,954	2,804	1,522	3,845	5,394	3,118	1,101	11,960	7,081	2,052	1,199	794
Kankakee, IL Metro Area	8,366	3,242	1,866	1,508	3,116	3,004	2,316	9,159	7,643	2,109	1,414	1,047
Kansas City, MO-KS Metro Area	185,935	56,573	35,337	36,240	65,237	53,432	28,759	173,753	121,780	21,291	11,537	8,617
Kapaa, HI Micro Area	6,886	3,956	2,777	819	1,548	773	759	7,971	5,438	1,268	501	419
Keene, NH Micro Area	7,471	2,706	1,409	1,834	2,186	2,402	1,620	8,433	5,667	540	532	404
Kennewick-Richland, WA Metro Area	20,236	7,696	5,796	3,302	7,787	6,074	3,499	22,944	14,737	5,086	2,081	1,825
Key West, FL Micro Area	6,173	3,526	1,363	2,497	3,335	2,026	744	10,298	5,923	666	1,293	915
Killeen-Temple, TX Metro Area	19,110	11,148	5,963	5,137	8,436	6,746	4,469	28,808	18,036	4,605	3,045	2,029
Kingsport-Bristol-Bristol, TN-VA Metro Area	21,395	8,483	5,152	9,070	13,682	11,453	9,208	37,398	28,349	6,014	5,095	4,191
Kingston, NY Metro Area	17,718	8,462	6,097	3,386	5,186	3,978	1,873	18,966	14,073	4,979	2,223	2,585
Klamath Falls, OR Micro Area	3,397	1,935	1,284	1,063	2,625	2,327	1,731	8,855	5,491	2,904	1,301	1,018
Knoxville, TN Metro Area	70,852	25,847	15,887	17,037	34,859	29,189	14,860	91,889	62,855	15,282	10,413	6,062
Kokomo, IN Metro Area	7,724	5,440	2,980	1,053	1,961	2,199	1,156	8,694	6,625	1,332	572	400
La Crosse-Onalaska, WI-MN Metro Area	13,305	2,275	1,850	2,085	5,597	3,683	1,697	12,646	9,469	1,796	1,780	764
Lafayette, LA Metro Area	31,724	12,806	7,306	10,964	14,503	11,173	9,666	38,412	26,624	12,995	5,325	3,021
Lafayette-West Lafayette, IN Metro Area	14,630	3,755	3,064	2,447	6,699	4,565	2,833	15,724	10,207	3,065	967	788
LaGrange, GA Micro Area	5,192	2,011	1,169	1,286	1,350	986	1,751	5,538	3,912	1,257	1,000	785
Lake Charles, LA Metro Area	15,243	5,848	3,794	4,213	5,381	4,341	4,496	18,290	11,368	4,958	1,995	1,903
Lake City, FL Micro Area	4,462	1,267	1,248	2,195	2,211	1,769	1,461	7,014	5,276	938	1,607	1,066
Lake Havasu City-Kingman, AZ Metro Area	15,095	9,198	6,456	3,900	12,449	11,384	4,474	35,494	26,217	8,707	4,625	2,612
Lakeland-Winter Haven, FL Metro Area	44,420	23,676	17,723	15,550	22,471	19,602	13,306	76,643	60,461	13,853	11,993	11,406
Lancaster, PA Metro Area	46,945	17,115	12,994	10,323	16,687	17,679	5,406	49,439	40,974	6,791	4,254	3,980
Lansing-East Lansing, MI Metro Area	43,022	29,489	16,770	5,618	10,851	8,763	7,272	43,308	27,563	8,475	4,524	3,450
Laredo, TX Metro Area	10,651	3,786	2,155	2,980	1,673	1,451	2,471	13,810	10,246	2,405	5,970	3,893
Las Cruces, NM Metro Area	10,700	6,134	2,948	2,736	3,942	3,576	2,610	19,021	14,287	8,475	2,986	3,752
Las Vegas-Henderson-Paradise, NV Metro Area	154,293	56,357	27,267	31,933	40,335	28,821	25,958	186,744	121,618	44,014	24,554	18,124
Laurel, MS Micro Area	5,537	1,873	949	1,456	1,862	2,645	2,127	8,645	5,312	2,363	2,351	706
Lawrence, KS Metro Area	7,722	3,763	1,463	2,390	3,163	2,673	452	8,285	5,937	1,222	571	503
Lawton, OK Metro Area	6,788	3,204	1,947	1,158	2,152	2,168	2,181	8,706	5,807	1,053	1,317	821
Lebanon, PA Metro Area	12,958	6,362	4,457	2,680	5,128	4,610	1,443	14,656	11,533	2,947	1,431	842
Lewiston, ID-WA Metro Area	4,515	1,858	1,043	1,340	4,157	3,054	1,556	7,602	6,520	1,217	498	1,302
Lewiston-Auburn, ME Metro Area	9,939	2,171	1,491	1,082	3,777	2,961	1,924	10,927	7,076	2,240	2,372	2,027
Lexington-Fayette, KY Metro Area	38,869	15,817	12,092	7,756	15,267	11,293	7,612	41,851	27,736	10,675	3,771	3,032
Lima, OH Metro Area	9,598	3,645	2,335	2,190	4,145	3,245	1,293	9,459	7,231	1,525	1,019	993
Lincoln, NE Metro Area	27,093	7,933	2,957	6,062	10,845	9,235	2,391	26,143	18,059	3,207	2,748	2,656
Little Rock-North Little Rock-Conway, AR Metro Area	53,461	22,201	12,539	14,359	24,100	16,394	11,782	65,899	42,167	15,133	5,735	5,725
Logan, UT-ID Metro Area	8,285	1,911	1,021	2,105	2,576	1,887	989	7,688	5,412	550	660	207
London, KY Micro Area	8,401	2,277	1,531	1,184	3,946	1,907	3,742	11,533	7,635	3,807	1,679	1,220
Longview, TX Metro Area	16,436	5,741	1,918	2,814	6,112	5,207	2,022	19,470	13,481	2,154	2,626	1,405
Longview, WA Metro Area	8,846	4,182	2,210	2,514	4,166	3,295	2,700	12,093	7,865	2,597	1,852	1,708
Los Angeles-Long Beach-Anaheim, CA Metro Area	876,319	300,437	177,577	269,021	158,442	137,675	103,705	944,747	752,412	351,612	229,581	233,529
Louisville/Jefferson County, KY-IN Metro Area	118,003	46,368	25,043	21,445	42,066	35,348	21,944	117,647	78,061	28,645	13,726	8,627
Lubbock, TX Metro Area	20,931	8,367	5,640	4,289	5,831	5,796	3,650	21,104	16,347	3,651	2,626	2,335
Lufkin, TX Micro Area	5,023	2,907	1,716	1,423	2,680	2,156	1,748	7,287	5,340	1,879	1,183	819
Lumberton, NC Micro Area	8,025	3,553	1,430	2,245	3,448	1,666	3,656	12,014	6,806	4,498	2,356	1,308
Lynchburg, VA Metro Area	21,721	6,066	4,844	5,787	11,746	10,721	5,155	27,434	20,611	3,064	2,414	2,045
Macon-Bibb County, GA Metro Area	15,850	7,048	4,793	4,613	6,528	4,744	4,585	21,194	13,365	3,957	4,483	2,316
Madera, CA Metro Area	6,949	3,982	1,996	2,379	3,695	2,306	1,561	12,566	8,266	5,508	1,249	2,013
Madison, WI Metro Area	61,985	24,707	12,533	11,755	23,143	16,415	3,884	54,570	36,858	5,257	4,980	3,714
Manchester-Nashua, NH Metro Area	46,772	12,987	5,980	5,767	13,557	11,465	5,688	33,906	23,587	4,799	2,233	2,670
Manhattan, KS Metro Area	6,236	2,852	1,127	1,424	2,248	1,815	523	6,032	3,894	560	332	393
Manitowoc, WI Micro Area	9,023	1,720	779	1,846	4,101	4,443	1,369	8,705	6,671	1,836	702	662
Mankato-North Mankato, MN Metro Area	7,627	1,977	798	1,191	4,592	3,633	700	8,203	5,925	1,441	444	1,138
Mansfield, OH Metro Area	9,563	4,206	2,931	2,822	4,921	4,094	2,059	12,075	10,168	2,585	963	1,350
Marinette, WI-MI Micro Area	6,405	1,501	1,161	1,908	3,379	2,865	1,469	8,170	6,322	1,955	743	672
Marion, IN Micro Area	5,597	2,835	2,846	858	2,271	2,564	1,159	6,423	5,531	2,264	1,096	685
Marion, OH Micro Area	4,894	2,014	1,249	644	2,124	1,598	1,239	6,035	4,472	1,816	434	575
Marquette, MI Micro Area	6,186	3,951	2,681	1,017	1,893	2,071	1,033	7,372	4,939	1,357	784	406
Marshall, TX Micro Area	4,912	1,858	1,033	1,542	2,153	1,342	1,411	6,335	3,863	1,557	555	127
Martinsville, VA Micro Area	3,615	1,594	848	1,340	2,091	2,328	1,499	7,696	6,515	1,353	985	796
McAllen-Edinburg-Mission, TX Metro Area	28,166	9,661	5,157	11,555	8,923	7,426	8,018	47,946	39,419	10,089	18,038	18,542
Meadville, PA Micro Area	7,302	3,300	2,076	1,612	4,315	3,633	1,831	9,982	7,026	2,690	1,273	713
Medford, OR Metro Area	17,994	6,356	4,957	5,284	9,971	7,109	2,706	27,410	19,129	5,303	2,447	2,657

Table I-4: Metropolitan/Micropolitan Statistical Areas - Persons With Health Insurance by Source of Insurance—*Continued*

	Private Health Insurance Coverage						Public Health Insurance Coverage					
	Employer Based			Direct Purchase			Medicare			Medicaid/CHIP		
	55 to 64 Years	65 to 74 Years	75 Years and Over	55 to 64 Years	65 to 74 Years	75 Years and Over	55 to 64 Years	65 to 74 Years	75 Years and Over	55 to 64 Years	65 to 74 Years	75 Years and Over
Memphis, TN-MS-AR Metro Area	106,620	40,358	20,253	21,606	30,045	24,090	17,812	108,344	68,221	21,386	15,994	12,326
Merced, CA Metro Area	12,496	4,541	1,664	3,310	5,377	3,921	3,021	16,498	12,914	7,936	5,436	4,480
Meridian, MS Micro Area	6,869	2,019	1,257	1,316	3,010	2,289	2,548	9,701	7,594	1,862	1,986	2,089
Miami-Fort Lauderdale-West Palm Beach, FL Metro Area	396,150	120,391	81,401	184,680	102,544	110,820	59,819	531,775	502,574	82,337	120,820	137,093
Michigan City-La Porte, IN Metro Area	9,862	3,365	1,905	2,375	6,172	3,862	1,820	11,428	7,554	1,944	779	550
Midland, MI Metro Area	7,395	5,107	4,258	1,127	2,419	2,104	1,609	8,390	6,681	2,285	387	709
Midland, TX Metro Area	12,423	5,241	2,539	2,865	2,659	3,090	1,365	9,472	8,250	1,107	640	1,169
Milwaukee-Waukesha-West Allis, WI Metro Area	144,861	44,269	28,405	26,384	42,014	37,163	18,568	132,915	100,261	30,693	16,497	15,692
Minneapolis-St. Paul-Bloomington, MN-WI Metro Area	336,852	91,060	43,544	65,618	136,676	109,198	27,165	282,022	192,111	55,617	25,763	19,525
Minot, ND Micro Area	5,779	1,739	1,020	1,455	2,569	3,151	481	5,479	4,264	883	687	632
Missoula, MT Metro Area	8,913	3,036	2,424	3,404	3,457	2,889	1,358	10,778	6,715	1,054	1,527	827
Mobile, AL Metro Area	30,667	10,915	5,547	6,397	9,882	7,512	8,790	38,055	26,009	7,591	5,433	3,199
Modesto, CA Metro Area	29,451	12,093	4,833	9,604	12,873	10,301	8,809	40,242	27,755	17,331	9,295	6,839
Monroe, LA Metro Area	13,743	5,626	3,708	2,696	4,738	3,507	2,038	15,842	10,130	3,808	3,216	1,499
Monroe, MI Metro Area	17,066	8,222	5,924	2,399	4,276	3,548	2,129	15,886	10,949	2,610	1,423	1,196
Montgomery, AL Metro Area	28,510	14,384	8,641	6,164	6,445	6,101	7,518	32,507	21,407	6,844	4,808	3,594
Morehead City, NC Micro Area	6,133	4,769	2,806	2,434	3,682	1,952	1,032	10,510	6,396	1,015	775	746
Morgantown, WV Metro Area	9,953	5,963	2,916	1,894	2,282	2,823	1,979	11,182	7,369	2,509	1,354	333
Morristown, TN Metro Area	8,080	3,635	2,016	1,950	4,520	2,998	3,935	12,163	8,743	3,734	877	782
Moses Lake, WA Micro Area	5,777	2,235	786	1,360	2,013	821	1,024	7,473	4,925	1,358	713	1,276
Mount Airy, NC Micro Area	5,625	2,129	2,078	1,838	2,336	2,374	1,516	7,939	6,427	768	960	580
Mount Pleasant, MI Micro Area	4,895	2,493	1,876	913	1,433	1,411	949	5,186	3,497	1,039	643	584
Mount Vernon-Anacortes, WA Metro Area	11,411	5,157	3,122	2,828	6,883	4,795	1,666	14,930	10,506	1,947	1,875	1,304
Muncie, IN Metro Area	9,035	4,413	2,333	1,522	4,074	3,177	1,774	10,723	7,760	1,149	1,168	516
Muskegon, MI Metro Area	15,406	6,640	3,958	3,215	5,904	4,822	3,746	16,771	11,277	4,293	1,968	1,663
Muskogee, OK Micro Area	4,715	1,918	978	1,040	1,689	1,570	1,186	6,050	4,599	993	608	525
Myrtle Beach-Conway-North Myrtle Beach, SC-NC Metro Area	39,549	33,781	14,667	15,277	29,662	16,112	9,925	82,281	40,830	9,228	5,358	4,446
Nacogdoches, TX Micro Area	4,132	1,580	1,217	937	1,076	1,375	1,098	5,364	3,580	908	674	690
Napa, CA Metro Area	12,298	5,440	4,180	2,923	3,820	3,921	769	14,921	10,107	2,077	2,544	1,165
Naples-Immokalee-Marco Island, FL Metro Area	27,861	16,483	15,087	13,404	20,623	31,541	3,677	57,215	60,542	2,973	4,739	3,612
Nashville-Davidson--Murfreesboro--Franklin, TN Metro Area	153,088	56,665	23,557	33,194	44,745	30,811	23,819	147,371	93,632	24,034	14,546	11,294
New Bern, NC Metro Area	9,258	5,127	2,593	2,595	4,744	3,572	1,724	13,239	10,876	1,984	1,432	1,715
New Castle, PA Micro Area	8,082	2,240	2,158	2,535	4,716	4,486	1,500	9,997	7,816	2,348	851	760
New Haven-Milford, CT Metro Area	79,132	31,114	19,503	15,413	20,801	23,520	8,190	75,902	61,280	18,880	10,339	9,376
New Orleans-Metairie, LA Metro Area	94,136	37,811	19,435	23,709	23,673	18,786	20,901	113,514	73,876	36,787	17,704	11,573
New Philadelphia-Dover, OH Micro Area	8,497	2,943	2,040	1,339	3,242	2,746	1,643	9,523	7,395	1,436	1,051	1,209
New York-Newark-Jersey City, NY-NJ-PA Metro Area	1,665,220	727,781	432,445	327,612	352,780	354,215	195,329	1,588,997	1,294,378	485,179	304,673	298,169
Niles-Benton Harbor, MI Metro Area	14,093	7,746	4,351	3,002	6,158	6,296	1,997	16,674	12,552	3,661	1,457	1,242
North Port-Sarasota-Bradenton, FL Metro Area	69,184	39,043	37,457	27,349	49,756	51,025	12,610	130,059	121,801	10,594	9,676	11,435
North Wilkesboro, NC Micro Area	5,135	1,363	1,740	2,131	2,556	2,553	1,754	8,060	6,064	1,292	879	823
Norwich-New London, CT Metro Area	25,190	11,082	8,124	5,712	7,765	7,132	3,310	25,203	19,580	5,316	3,650	2,282
Oak Harbor, WA Micro Area	6,624	3,417	2,463	2,075	4,113	3,667	885	12,171	7,806	1,391	1,154	1,088
Ocala, FL Metro Area	24,577	14,320	14,369	9,325	12,961	12,318	5,405	53,879	46,833	6,200	5,192	5,526
Ocean City, NJ Metro Area	10,567	5,177	3,846	2,564	4,565	3,494	1,949	13,092	9,635	1,765	1,006	694
Odessa, TX Metro Area	8,737	3,423	2,057	3,046	1,727	1,958	1,127	8,582	5,254	1,003	1,794	1,270
Ogden-Clearfield, UT Metro Area	46,051	18,293	10,066	11,067	12,010	11,506	5,526	41,690	27,445	4,771	4,593	3,247
Ogdensburg-Massena, NY Micro Area	9,463	5,230	2,926	3,088	2,729	2,250	1,987	10,370	6,847	2,919	1,740	977
Oklahoma City, OK Metro Area	103,006	44,952	24,370	23,311	33,003	27,963	17,662	108,212	73,831	12,995	11,457	7,266
Olean, NY Micro Area	7,077	2,863	1,695	1,481	3,147	2,510	1,091	8,207	5,944	2,480	1,780	1,166
Olympia-Tumwater, WA Metro Area	24,124	12,787	6,851	4,844	9,177	6,925	3,559	29,806	17,355	5,038	3,257	2,944
Omaha-Council Bluffs, NE-IA Metro Area	75,591	21,794	11,385	15,342	27,562	19,286	9,223	73,769	48,564	11,716	6,388	6,075
Opelousas, LA Micro Area	6,412	3,423	1,209	718	1,763	1,347	2,041	6,887	4,596	1,740	1,255	581
Orangeburg, SC Micro Area	5,604	1,785	1,037	1,525	2,134	1,808	2,285	9,730	6,423	2,053	3,409	3,189
Orlando-Kissimmee-Sanford, FL Metro Area	172,484	57,672	30,951	52,699	50,082	41,581	31,807	206,598	149,213	34,546	31,502	24,689
Oshkosh-Neenah, WI Metro Area	16,793	3,395	1,737	2,591	5,525	6,193	1,581	15,309	11,623	2,355	1,144	1,662
Ottawa-Peru, IL Micro Area	13,431	5,353	3,167	3,612	6,891	5,580	1,629	15,485	11,685	2,679	718	875
Owensboro, KY Metro Area	9,178	4,021	2,652	2,129	4,018	3,541	2,256	11,508	8,161	3,661	1,649	1,589
Owosso, MI Micro Area	7,156	4,867	2,987	1,109	2,220	2,264	1,202	7,346	4,785	1,612	961	972
Oxnard-Thousand Oaks-Ventura, CA Metro Area	72,059	26,363	15,172	21,011	20,333	19,386	6,194	70,318	54,534	14,104	8,970	8,745
Paducah, KY-IL Micro Area	7,720	3,021	2,821	1,553	4,065	3,396	2,873	9,906	8,428	3,120	765	1,068
Palatka, FL Micro Area	4,526	1,729	2,018	1,239	3,408	2,157	2,366	10,107	6,568	1,349	1,331	475
Palm Bay-Melbourne-Titusville, FL Metro Area	53,194	20,233	18,479	19,202	20,546	20,714	10,587	73,134	62,574	9,990	7,375	8,432
Panama City, FL Metro Area	14,958	6,076	3,583	4,866	6,629	4,136	4,141	19,210	13,290	4,023	3,202	2,213
Parkersburg-Vienna, WV Metro Area	7,530	4,305	2,669	2,118	3,341	3,020	2,768	10,320	7,427	2,645	1,996	1,257
Pensacola-Ferry Pass-Brent, FL Metro Area	33,329	13,548	8,812	12,279	14,136	11,224	8,617	46,267	30,970	7,691	4,283	3,104
Peoria, IL Metro Area	35,691	12,792	11,708	5,822	13,448	11,531	4,204	36,012	26,192	6,035	2,973	1,633
Philadelphia-Camden-Wilmington, PA-NJ-DE-MD Metro Area	557,267	226,363	124,651	111,721	167,485	167,124	75,611	514,078	389,159	123,647	66,758	52,978
Phoenix-Mesa-Scottsdale, AZ Metro Area	332,609	116,659	80,209	84,304	121,245	101,035	46,718	415,660	306,130	78,605	50,340	38,454
Pine Bluff, AR Metro Area	5,459	2,386	1,133	2,086	3,098	2,075	1,809	8,647	5,134	2,505	794	1,346
Pinehurst-Southern Pines, NC Micro Area	7,185	4,162	3,353	2,370	4,475	4,410	1,859	12,135	9,982	1,164	1,329	1,276
Pittsburgh, PA Metro Area	240,491	89,750	59,365	56,814	97,976	92,315	30,920	243,308	194,025	48,238	26,174	26,086
Pittsfield, MA Metro Area	12,880	6,656	4,918	1,644	5,038	5,150	2,259	15,315	11,786	4,967	1,991	1,953
Plattsburgh, NY Micro Area	7,715	3,962	2,155	1,717	1,832	1,709	1,387	7,780	5,144	2,053	852	1,064
Pocatello, ID Metro Area	6,064	1,470	730	1,833	3,888	2,470	998	7,009	4,815	869	562	734

Table I-4: Metropolitan/Micropolitan Statistical Areas - Persons With Health Insurance by Source of Insurance—Continued

| | Private Health Insurance Coverage | | | | | | Public Health Insurance Coverage | | | | | |
| | Employer Based | | | Direct Purchase | | | Medicare | | | Medicaid/CHIP | | |
	55 to 64 Years	65 to 74 Years	75 Years and Over	55 to 64 Years	65 to 74 Years	75 Years and Over	55 to 64 Years	65 to 74 Years	75 Years and Over	55 to 64 Years	65 to 74 Years	75 Years and Over
Port Angeles, WA Micro Area	6,081	3,057	2,467	2,595	4,907	3,314	951	12,549	8,720	1,618	1,749	1,240
Portland-South Portland, ME Metro Area	56,087	18,749	12,677	12,860	17,491	13,982	5,024	58,889	39,759	7,457	6,233	5,678
Portland-Vancouver-Hillsboro, OR-WA Metro Area	199,328	68,939	39,439	48,774	81,394	59,482	23,434	212,454	134,117	44,082	24,121	16,409
Port St. Lucie, FL Metro Area	37,504	19,528	14,856	15,696	20,575	21,722	7,868	63,736	58,635	7,052	7,458	8,001
Portsmouth, OH Micro Area	5,650	1,796	2,128	1,261	2,366	2,432	1,715	7,442	5,345	2,716	1,633	982
Pottsville, PA Micro Area	12,881	4,848	3,560	3,570	5,922	5,981	3,090	15,297	11,587	3,164	1,746	1,685
Prescott, AZ Metro Area	18,558	11,161	8,610	9,145	17,277	13,321	3,541	42,981	29,304	7,026	6,094	1,517
Providence-Warwick, RI-MA Metro Area	152,538	52,518	28,001	28,153	51,139	44,170	22,706	148,508	109,861	42,886	27,465	20,763
Provo-Orem, UT Metro Area	28,908	11,359	7,896	8,073	8,621	7,930	1,929	27,431	19,308	2,898	2,073	2,045
Pueblo, CO Metro Area	11,458	4,925	4,529	1,769	6,016	4,212	5,013	16,783	12,235	5,978	2,454	2,558
Punta Gorda, FL Metro Area	17,919	9,809	9,325	6,054	17,096	15,023	4,886	38,227	33,774	1,802	2,685	3,598
Quincy, IL-MO Micro Area	7,396	2,476	1,714	1,274	2,685	3,355	947	6,972	6,498	1,192	1,030	949
Racine, WI Metro Area	19,859	5,443	3,867	3,249	5,600	4,505	3,613	18,146	12,513	3,634	2,122	1,196
Raleigh, NC Metro Area	109,207	42,753	19,907	24,491	31,650	21,996	10,227	98,916	58,609	12,125	10,406	8,487
Rapid City, SD Metro Area	12,042	4,030	1,642	3,362	5,151	4,129	1,939	15,933	9,116	1,515	1,655	779
Reading, PA Metro Area	40,602	11,402	7,351	7,058	14,849	15,483	5,749	38,472	29,424	7,180	4,254	3,734
Redding, CA Metro Area	15,355	7,219	4,699	3,769	8,395	6,226	3,099	20,786	14,731	5,752	2,552	1,756
Reno, NV Metro Area	38,830	16,083	7,104	8,983	14,283	10,611	4,537	45,965	27,889	7,182	3,863	3,093
Richmond, IN Micro Area	5,179	1,299	1,396	606	1,877	2,334	1,946	6,284	4,976	1,580	881	490
Richmond, VA Metro Area	115,362	44,890	26,185	24,678	41,016	31,328	15,616	114,639	77,270	12,619	11,425	7,629
Richmond-Berea, KY Micro Area	7,819	2,943	1,396	1,634	2,444	1,669	1,514	9,466	5,553	2,879	1,605	702
Riverside-San Bernardino-Ontario, CA Metro Area	291,267	94,896	56,880	66,330	59,442	54,597	43,569	324,032	239,534	114,836	62,380	55,452
Roanoke, VA Metro Area	29,483	13,360	9,449	4,742	11,709	7,744	6,584	36,134	25,075	3,568	2,416	1,445
Roanoke Rapids, NC Micro Area	5,983	2,105	896	1,237	2,120	2,393	2,035	8,169	5,586	1,614	1,490	669
Rochester, MN Metro Area	21,909	7,747	4,601	3,809	9,152	7,849	1,802	19,042	15,201	3,204	1,279	1,644
Rochester, NY Metro Area	101,008	42,458	25,313	8,170	35,840	33,521	15,997	104,276	75,265	25,149	13,669	10,236
Rockford, IL Metro Area	28,729	11,377	7,804	7,896	10,558	10,857	4,595	31,018	22,694	7,468	3,921	1,978
Rocky Mount, NC Metro Area	12,021	4,602	2,935	2,689	6,547	3,945	4,024	15,733	10,950	3,329	2,714	1,165
Rome, GA Metro Area	7,563	2,736	2,352	1,853	3,133	2,598	2,300	8,905	6,658	1,285	800	963
Roseburg, OR Micro Area	7,593	4,915	3,006	2,212	5,365	4,795	2,216	15,640	11,458	4,098	1,175	1,250
Roswell, NM Micro Area	3,164	1,737	1,501	1,050	1,204	1,039	1,295	5,627	4,650	2,218	1,258	1,134
Russellville, AR Micro Area	4,564	1,548	1,260	1,170	2,476	2,367	2,214	7,465	5,115	2,801	947	1,207
Sacramento--Roseville--Arden-Arcade, CA Metro Area	190,173	98,872	57,048	41,089	53,291	44,608	24,405	198,630	141,146	56,945	33,897	27,787
Saginaw, MI Metro Area	16,755	12,136	7,973	3,891	5,526	6,267	4,132	19,770	14,959	5,798	2,451	1,849
St. Cloud, MN Metro Area	15,950	4,343	2,437	3,761	8,984	7,404	2,081	16,120	11,981	2,633	657	1,331
St. George, UT Metro Area	9,722	7,482	6,222	4,336	8,960	7,005	1,519	19,924	16,066	1,526	1,648	1,373
St. Joseph, MO-KS Metro Area	8,999	3,312	1,983	2,479	6,475	3,879	2,846	11,699	8,028	2,097	950	999
St. Louis, MO-IL Metro Area	264,008	84,807	55,491	51,746	70,201	63,325	40,790	249,319	182,008	42,293	19,803	18,398
Salem, OH Micro Area	9,332	3,857	2,251	2,096	2,708	1,925	1,827	11,705	7,652	2,924	1,271	442
Salem, OR Metro Area	30,411	10,805	9,045	5,607	14,376	12,431	4,385	38,242	27,897	10,925	5,456	4,232
Salinas, CA Metro Area	25,381	11,120	5,266	8,444	7,402	7,380	3,973	31,103	23,975	8,702	5,386	6,759
Salisbury, MD-DE Metro Area	39,400	26,525	16,688	9,787	18,234	13,903	6,089	56,989	37,736	8,974	6,267	4,311
Salt Lake City, UT Metro Area	80,730	26,408	13,109	18,886	21,571	17,231	7,757	71,820	48,948	9,477	7,214	5,810
San Angelo, TX Metro Area	8,341	5,514	3,060	1,635	1,895	2,150	726	10,365	6,663	1,826	879	934
San Antonio-New Braunfels, TX Metro Area	152,364	62,472	33,763	37,255	40,213	33,533	30,230	181,649	122,101	36,720	25,518	20,637
San Diego-Carlsbad, CA Metro Area	229,586	84,710	51,640	62,140	52,770	51,215	24,936	249,031	189,005	64,211	39,645	38,550
Sandusky, OH Micro Area	8,422	3,943	3,727	1,417	2,986	2,586	1,047	8,502	6,827	1,437	434	522
San Francisco-Oakland-Hayward, CA Metro Area	389,748	174,492	107,051	96,468	99,323	90,958	34,140	376,857	291,612	93,255	65,071	62,504
San Jose-Sunnyvale-Santa Clara, CA Metro Area	156,640	52,427	33,343	37,455	37,000	31,981	13,271	135,177	111,801	33,678	26,437	31,421
San Luis Obispo-Paso Robles-Arroyo Grande, CA Metro Area	25,085	13,457	7,015	6,787	10,984	7,308	2,575	33,024	21,512	4,088	3,240	2,331
Santa Cruz-Watsonville, CA Metro Area	22,519	12,619	5,268	7,074	7,949	5,969	2,172	27,041	15,050	4,401	4,546	2,549
Santa Fe, NM Metro Area	13,481	8,741	4,885	4,853	7,555	4,917	1,690	21,948	12,920	3,555	1,828	824
Santa Maria-Santa Barbara, CA Metro Area	27,908	11,430	9,497	9,314	13,452	12,820	3,520	34,642	29,389	9,332	4,373	3,252
Santa Rosa, CA Metro Area	43,418	22,113	14,203	13,873	17,394	13,884	5,377	55,451	36,240	10,742	6,618	4,541
Savannah, GA Metro Area	30,440	12,928	6,441	6,455	7,153	6,335	4,625	32,004	20,401	4,614	4,982	2,914
Scranton--Wilkes-Barre--Hazleton, PA Metro Area	52,750	21,321	12,210	11,181	23,175	22,855	9,833	58,142	44,820	11,795	6,816	5,803
Searcy, AR Micro Area	3,450	2,318	1,158	2,384	2,898	2,155	1,626	6,885	5,056	2,947	1,049	1,165
Seattle-Tacoma-Bellevue, WA Metro Area	334,902	111,272	56,931	64,788	102,833	76,278	34,806	295,469	195,386	55,247	32,947	31,344
Sebastian-Vero Beach, FL Metro Area	10,977	7,296	7,575	5,600	9,764	8,390	3,572	26,457	23,562	3,838	2,004	1,667
Sebring, FL Metro Area	6,726	3,403	5,209	1,888	5,240	8,460	1,522	15,980	18,694	1,747	2,492	1,963
Seneca, SC Micro Area	6,855	4,231	2,131	2,388	4,203	2,937	1,243	11,161	7,190	1,622	1,544	693
Sevierville, TN Micro Area	7,080	2,289	1,313	2,526	4,585	2,519	1,830	11,517	6,956	2,230	793	1,135
Shawnee, OK Micro Area	4,847	2,685	1,683	1,071	1,692	1,607	1,058	6,967	4,340	1,679	915	488
Sheboygan, WI Metro Area	12,873	2,551	1,294	2,262	5,355	4,826	1,030	11,237	8,396	2,012	1,145	579
Shelby, NC Micro Area	7,682	2,998	1,870	2,449	3,980	2,933	2,279	10,197	7,205	1,590	2,080	1,025
Shelton, WA Micro Area	5,296	3,414	1,598	1,650	3,549	1,859	2,274	9,071	5,307	2,757	1,181	857
Sherman-Denison, TX Metro Area	10,839	3,864	3,847	1,959	3,815	2,432	2,215	13,574	8,911	2,221	1,311	1,008
Show Low, AZ Micro Area	4,456	3,164	1,109	1,814	3,599	2,470	2,166	11,562	7,801	5,762	1,832	1,661
Shreveport-Bossier City, LA Metro Area	27,820	14,781	8,653	7,904	10,731	9,866	8,846	38,182	27,327	12,323	6,251	5,158
Sierra Vista-Douglas, AZ Metro Area	6,534	3,605	1,967	2,156	5,091	4,043	1,817	15,352	12,037	3,469	1,987	1,515
Sioux City, IA-NE-SD Metro Area	14,575	3,043	1,321	4,417	5,222	4,891	1,538	13,782	11,040	3,852	1,404	1,723
Sioux Falls, SD Metro Area	21,452	5,069	1,946	4,350	8,185	6,349	2,108	20,231	12,928	2,418	1,191	1,686
Somerset, PA Micro Area	7,583	2,719	1,251	1,483	3,235	3,802	1,063	8,546	6,908	1,847	1,284	594
South Bend-Mishawaka, IN-MI Metro Area	29,180	8,501	5,579	6,284	10,782	8,510	5,091	29,790	21,208	4,226	3,510	2,659

Table I-4: Metropolitan/Micropolitan Statistical Areas - Persons With Health Insurance by Source of Insurance—*Continued*

	Private Health Insurance Coverage						Public Health Insurance Coverage					
	Employer Based			Direct Purchase			Medicare			Medicaid/CHIP		
	55 to 64 Years	65 to 74 Years	75 Years and Over	55 to 64 Years	65 to 74 Years	75 Years and Over	55 to 64 Years	65 to 74 Years	75 Years and Over	55 to 64 Years	65 to 74 Years	75 Years and Over
Spartanburg, SC Metro Area	24,255	9,832	3,488	6,566	9,919	8,466	7,257	31,840	21,510	5,124	3,327	2,473
Spokane-Spokane Valley, WA Metro Area	44,782	15,715	9,931	9,699	14,493	12,788	9,060	57,479	35,983	15,469	7,545	4,723
Springfield, IL Metro Area	21,587	12,332	8,333	3,407	5,283	5,255	2,296	20,833	14,463	3,969	2,353	996
Springfield, MA Metro Area	54,253	27,898	14,490	8,556	15,752	16,832	8,952	57,768	40,700	19,673	10,625	8,304
Springfield, MO Metro Area	31,900	7,941	5,036	9,171	14,022	13,525	8,307	42,500	31,389	5,237	5,722	3,890
Springfield, OH Metro Area	11,407	6,320	4,448	2,033	3,775	3,611	2,828	13,806	10,524	2,535	1,745	1,097
State College, PA Metro Area	13,114	6,333	4,547	2,102	4,787	3,405	956	12,282	8,978	1,487	652	1,214
Statesboro, GA Micro Area	4,049	1,606	1,251	819	1,101	853	939	5,056	3,244	1,140	853	342
Staunton-Waynesboro, VA Metro Area	10,805	3,688	2,070	1,673	5,016	5,606	1,883	13,902	10,468	1,247	1,106	620
Stevens Point, WI Micro Area	5,930	852	1,312	1,918	3,325	2,389	1,028	6,748	4,683	1,216	358	371
Stillwater, OK Micro Area	4,712	2,158	1,636	1,308	2,990	1,896	1,031	6,293	4,232	609	280	99
Stockton-Lodi, CA Metro Area	45,806	18,399	11,977	11,870	14,316	11,890	10,080	52,003	36,181	20,018	12,690	9,392
Sumter, SC Metro Area	5,607	2,863	1,822	2,731	3,584	1,940	2,354	9,797	6,665	2,653	2,364	1,120
Sunbury, PA Micro Area	8,476	2,084	2,214	2,122	4,015	3,805	1,459	10,471	7,857	2,406	1,917	1,028
Syracuse, NY Metro Area	67,279	29,003	20,244	10,373	15,062	15,580	12,034	59,951	45,002	13,949	8,518	6,902
Talladega-Sylacauga, AL Micro Area	7,692	3,474	1,684	2,378	3,163	2,395	2,441	10,253	6,727	2,367	1,437	1,368
Tallahassee, FL Metro Area	29,311	14,287	6,971	6,430	10,349	5,419	4,097	33,674	19,098	5,353	4,109	2,544
Tampa-St. Petersburg-Clearwater, FL Metro Area	225,663	87,447	58,738	74,904	74,214	75,257	49,510	327,076	261,188	54,410	44,590	39,896
Terre Haute, IN Metro Area	12,280	4,399	2,886	3,167	6,372	5,050	3,210	15,876	10,662	2,591	1,581	1,439
Texarkana, TX-AR Metro Area	10,586	5,516	1,917	1,843	3,497	2,576	2,830	13,860	9,216	2,597	1,547	983
The Villages, FL Metro Area	7,588	15,110	10,045	6,469	14,348	14,352	1,481	40,399	30,842	1,378	1,903	3,478
Toledo, OH Metro Area	50,645	21,412	14,784	10,358	19,934	15,905	8,929	54,600	36,958	13,137	6,845	4,675
Topeka, KS Metro Area	20,063	8,497	5,632	5,880	9,636	8,182	3,785	23,588	17,026	3,141	2,531	1,946
Torrington, CT Micro Area	22,916	8,263	5,075	4,721	7,113	6,695	2,611	20,317	14,573	3,475	2,977	2,064
Traverse City, MI Micro Area	13,363	7,715	4,946	5,211	7,768	7,058	2,410	19,433	12,745	3,290	1,919	1,248
Trenton, NJ Metro Area	35,503	17,351	9,462	4,413	6,595	6,707	3,818	29,460	21,542	5,195	3,283	3,248
Truckee-Grass Valley, CA Micro Area	8,916	5,104	3,667	4,010	6,747	4,813	1,484	16,579	9,877	2,980	1,814	1,098
Tucson, AZ Metro Area	70,028	31,267	25,934	17,973	29,264	26,087	12,255	111,414	86,444	24,392	16,235	14,816
Tullahoma-Manchester, TN Micro Area	7,866	2,569	2,342	1,280	4,582	4,342	1,877	10,708	8,524	3,164	1,275	1,266
Tulsa, OK Metro Area	76,817	25,124	13,840	18,396	32,889	26,348	12,967	85,506	58,631	8,975	7,851	5,726
Tupelo, MS Micro Area	8,985	2,360	735	2,253	3,847	3,096	3,204	11,597	7,784	2,971	1,726	1,765
Tuscaloosa, AL Metro Area	17,325	8,485	3,248	3,478	5,709	3,292	5,145	20,260	12,344	3,293	3,550	2,210
Twin Falls, ID Micro Area	7,360	1,646	1,537	2,900	5,227	3,317	1,583	8,984	6,569	1,537	885	955
Tyler, TX Metro Area	13,755	5,690	3,826	5,771	9,123	8,459	3,055	20,550	15,222	3,425	2,424	1,011
Ukiah, CA Micro Area	6,549	3,280	1,353	2,320	3,544	2,461	991	11,895	6,553	3,067	1,491	930
Urban Honolulu, HI Metro Area	87,738	56,128	38,721	13,386	19,319	21,813	5,244	86,107	74,813	13,082	10,818	9,975
Utica-Rome, NY Metro Area	26,441	13,263	8,521	3,634	8,128	7,684	4,047	29,237	22,348	9,542	3,947	3,498
Valdosta, GA Metro Area	8,713	4,259	4,027	2,279	2,656	1,825	1,468	10,326	7,929	2,061	1,994	916
Vallejo-Fairfield, CA Metro Area	40,076	21,174	10,603	8,004	10,183	8,337	4,433	38,716	26,592	8,005	5,037	4,251
Victoria, TX Metro Area	7,206	2,657	2,435	1,788	1,984	1,300	1,149	8,167	7,186	1,646	1,664	1,110
Vineland-Bridgeton, NJ Metro Area	10,848	4,740	3,393	2,732	3,831	2,691	3,053	12,964	8,780	3,273	2,356	2,155
Virginia Beach-Norfolk-Newport News, VA-NC Metro Area	133,044	55,136	36,887	27,409	47,520	33,447	17,731	141,653	98,265	13,929	12,027	9,351
Visalia-Porterville, CA Metro Area	21,312	6,334	3,576	4,722	7,652	5,666	5,267	29,475	20,415	14,974	7,231	5,105
Waco, TX Metro Area	18,966	6,996	4,877	3,689	6,908	6,232	4,076	21,329	15,562	3,905	2,945	2,068
Walla Walla, WA Metro Area	4,944	1,305	2,083	1,032	2,772	2,158	669	6,072	5,518	1,261	689	733
Warner Robins, GA Metro Area	12,623	5,670	4,565	3,640	3,106	2,276	3,848	14,181	8,744	2,956	2,043	1,279
Warsaw, IN Micro Area	6,906	1,312	1,029	1,498	2,453	2,293	468	7,352	4,838	697	347	408
Washington-Arlington-Alexandria, DC-VA-MD-WV Metro Area	532,652	261,644	151,740	110,480	111,145	91,844	37,008	425,992	300,270	66,013	47,883	46,376
Waterloo-Cedar Falls, IA Metro Area	14,068	5,299	3,635	3,066	6,599	6,764	2,154	15,211	12,070	3,542	1,326	1,509
Watertown-Fort Atkinson, WI Micro Area	8,808	2,563	1,420	2,430	4,021	3,063	617	8,686	5,581	1,058	552	797
Watertown-Fort Drum, NY Metro Area	8,307	3,884	2,327	1,421	2,955	2,210	1,562	8,813	6,132	2,376	980	1,078
Wausau, WI Metro Area	13,747	2,684	1,269	3,464	6,398	4,923	958	13,019	9,759	1,675	1,505	1,710
Weirton-Steubenville, WV-OH Metro Area	11,834	5,096	2,979	2,066	4,827	4,198	2,628	15,370	10,872	2,917	1,540	1,130
Wenatchee, WA Metro Area	9,352	3,197	3,289	1,630	5,074	4,261	1,254	12,030	8,700	3,313	1,122	1,674
Wheeling, WV-OH Metro Area	13,658	7,368	4,151	3,531	4,517	3,532	2,429	16,334	11,542	3,433	1,825	1,685
Whitewater-Elkhorn, WI Micro Area	10,355	2,589	1,790	2,759	4,914	3,838	1,884	10,262	6,827	2,166	778	671
Wichita, KS Metro Area	54,835	11,186	6,067	12,016	22,203	17,774	6,843	53,001	38,573	9,108	6,957	4,284
Wichita Falls, TX Metro Area	10,933	4,668	2,762	1,995	2,583	3,216	3,277	12,552	8,962	2,957	1,336	818
Williamsport, PA Metro Area	11,194	4,327	2,344	1,850	4,488	3,553	1,721	11,408	8,776	2,727	796	1,362
Wilmington, NC Metro Area	23,415	11,906	7,202	8,176	12,306	8,980	4,694	30,748	19,679	3,437	2,276	2,085
Wilson, NC Micro Area	6,314	2,565	1,651	1,145	2,754	2,188	1,397	8,169	5,599	2,023	643	925
Winchester, VA-WV Metro Area	10,860	5,312	3,212	2,610	4,786	4,181	1,805	14,189	9,821	2,219	437	1,248
Winston-Salem, NC Metro Area	58,131	18,206	12,179	14,469	23,627	16,715	13,099	64,828	45,603	8,830	9,576	7,142
Wisconsin Rapids-Marshfield, WI Micro Area	6,419	1,527	1,049	2,563	3,538	3,957	884	7,901	6,332	1,257	516	972
Wooster, OH Micro Area	10,477	4,042	2,199	2,215	4,754	3,539	1,173	11,024	8,520	1,863	868	1,000
Worcester, MA-CT Metro Area	92,565	33,626	20,511	15,068	26,880	22,340	12,086	78,996	56,642	25,508	13,257	11,465
Yakima, WA Metro Area	15,786	4,895	3,544	2,575	7,295	5,292	2,830	19,215	13,324	5,647	2,626	2,056
York-Hanover, PA Metro Area	44,313	15,121	9,789	9,442	15,782	14,986	6,054	42,909	30,775	7,410	3,944	4,111
Youngstown-Warren-Boardman, OH-PA Metro Area	51,307	18,990	11,339	10,454	19,796	17,706	9,235	60,720	46,645	12,975	6,038	4,969
Yuba City, CA Metro Area	8,605	3,086	1,958	3,225	2,565	2,950	3,693	13,011	10,039	5,422	2,797	2,247
Yuma, AZ Metro Area	8,887	4,920	5,264	2,955	7,142	9,025	2,567	18,373	18,762	5,111	4,009	4,064
Zanesville, OH Micro Area	7,221	2,472	1,484	1,772	1,859	2,938	1,506	8,256	5,927	2,155	1,520	387

Table I-5: 116th Congressional Districts - Persons With Health Insurance by Source of Insurance

| | Private Health Insurance Coverage | | | | | | Public Health Insurance Coverage | | | | | |
| | Employer Based | | | Direct Purchase | | | Medicare | | | Medicaid/CHIP | | |
	55 to 64 Years	65 to 74 Years	75 Years and Over	55 to 64 Years	65 to 74 Years	75 Years and Over	55 to 64 Years	65 to 74 Years	75 Years and Over	55 to 64 Years	65 to 74 Years	75 Years and Over
Alabama												
Congressional District 1	56,186	23,925	11,895	13,762	19,126	15,880	14,380	73,152	48,854	11,920	9,281	5,944
Congressional District 2	49,642	23,114	14,798	12,633	19,244	13,847	15,746	64,738	44,713	13,156	9,703	7,182
Congressional District 3	51,044	26,741	11,984	14,917	20,334	15,438	14,390	72,113	43,400	13,016	9,625	6,274
Congressional District 4	51,821	24,922	13,932	14,866	23,645	17,495	17,900	71,974	50,545	14,576	9,278	7,705
Congressional District 5	63,065	28,407	19,041	16,831	22,383	21,186	11,206	66,837	48,253	10,309	6,546	5,748
Congressional District 6	62,094	26,102	12,131	12,967	22,580	19,092	11,479	67,266	46,225	8,679	6,599	6,231
Congressional District 7	42,810	17,571	8,950	10,121	13,981	10,929	18,290	56,781	38,441	18,482	12,136	8,080
Alaska												
Congressional District (at Large)	56,324	28,191	11,537	8,223	7,980	3,716	6,384	54,510	27,051	14,471	9,657	4,905
Arizona												
Congressional District 1	44,574	23,244	15,226	14,464	24,417	18,881	10,391	82,540	60,054	18,171	10,372	9,829
Congressional District 2	50,284	24,111	19,556	12,866	26,131	22,451	8,514	84,042	67,132	16,384	9,739	8,724
Congressional District 3	37,319	13,577	7,672	9,524	12,782	6,957	9,586	57,170	37,007	20,813	15,352	10,593
Congressional District 4	62,330	33,811	24,661	20,338	44,428	42,199	12,082	124,862	90,668	22,214	14,136	7,987
Congressional District 5	63,408	23,778	15,054	15,716	26,121	19,761	6,325	76,530	56,693	7,081	8,699	4,884
Congressional District 6	71,613	21,204	14,855	21,247	24,676	22,719	5,809	79,684	63,106	9,648	7,207	5,072
Congressional District 7	30,434	7,340	3,355	6,158	5,437	3,990	9,942	35,830	20,599	24,084	10,482	7,170
Congressional District 8	62,367	27,053	24,919	14,134	29,588	29,109	7,439	95,471	80,687	11,969	8,439	8,443
Congressional District 9	57,276	15,989	9,999	14,652	13,811	10,489	8,271	50,306	38,587	12,005	6,497	7,057
Arkansas												
Congressional District 1	43,835	17,438	10,486	13,248	20,584	19,577	17,586	72,171	51,687	23,671	12,455	8,935
Congressional District 2	52,761	22,631	13,114	16,066	25,176	18,027	13,012	69,218	46,049	17,592	7,016	7,063
Congressional District 3	54,452	15,393	10,600	13,928	21,853	20,024	12,128	66,011	45,611	14,455	7,405	6,621
Congressional District 4	49,587	19,092	9,838	16,084	24,244	20,695	17,029	75,647	53,830	21,195	10,553	10,208
California												
Congressional District 1	55,849	29,022	20,811	17,004	31,164	25,857	12,358	89,164	61,265	25,021	10,888	8,457
Congressional District 2	60,517	34,226	20,306	23,600	30,227	21,724	8,448	88,838	56,841	16,033	9,816	6,574
Congressional District 3	51,958	26,935	13,830	12,555	14,733	12,936	9,983	58,657	41,765	16,360	9,689	6,589
Congressional District 4	72,107	39,613	24,046	19,352	30,253	23,803	10,465	89,265	62,077	16,476	8,743	7,549
Congressional District 5	65,511	29,957	20,216	16,904	18,603	18,026	7,498	71,629	48,664	16,866	10,185	7,050
Congressional District 6	43,264	23,453	14,288	10,954	10,142	7,716	8,647	53,155	36,747	24,637	16,122	11,620
Congressional District 7	69,561	35,878	19,512	13,137	16,160	15,285	7,021	65,315	47,488	16,957	10,000	8,812
Congressional District 8	44,737	15,800	9,502	12,229	10,101	7,912	10,306	53,840	38,590	24,530	7,893	8,093
Congressional District 9	52,683	20,508	13,527	11,931	15,376	12,615	9,901	56,122	39,275	20,298	13,154	8,412
Congressional District 10	44,361	18,584	8,468	14,519	17,697	13,328	10,898	55,469	37,228	21,183	11,453	9,026
Congressional District 11	71,120	33,556	19,891	15,525	19,898	19,040	4,661	65,321	49,778	12,139	7,044	7,438
Congressional District 12	51,391	22,869	12,799	13,046	13,092	12,283	7,077	56,098	49,801	18,362	15,755	19,788
Congressional District 13	51,039	25,467	16,193	11,895	12,902	10,911	7,699	58,509	40,320	18,465	14,007	9,811
Congressional District 14	68,411	32,278	20,398	19,393	16,646	17,696	4,706	62,158	52,382	11,363	11,727	11,169
Congressional District 15	65,073	22,960	13,817	12,377	13,103	11,968	3,739	56,067	41,522	18,087	9,203	7,482
Congressional District 16	29,924	11,506	4,583	6,934	10,953	7,779	9,099	42,520	30,819	27,405	14,002	11,785
Congressional District 17	64,676	19,640	11,191	14,390	10,340	8,869	3,681	45,896	41,151	12,441	8,027	12,732
Congressional District 18	63,686	25,221	17,612	19,166	20,049	17,624	3,795	57,774	48,102	9,201	5,491	8,414
Congressional District 19	57,579	19,930	11,322	12,103	12,478	10,483	6,713	55,187	39,928	15,978	16,011	12,951
Congressional District 20	47,559	22,007	10,349	15,121	15,250	13,221	6,550	56,656	39,495	14,691	9,288	9,488
Congressional District 21	25,200	6,433	4,158	5,900	6,876	5,950	7,345	34,920	25,626	22,097	12,442	10,331
Congressional District 22	43,125	20,692	9,848	10,483	15,542	11,860	6,896	55,398	38,452	20,458	10,445	8,254
Congressional District 23	49,195	19,645	11,829	10,885	13,536	9,286	8,617	53,096	38,290	22,593	10,454	7,088
Congressional District 24	53,554	25,243	16,797	16,320	24,731	20,325	6,191	68,424	51,465	13,744	7,711	5,626
Congressional District 25	60,114	20,919	10,873	15,233	10,745	8,475	7,205	53,190	34,890	16,345	8,387	6,941
Congressional District 26	60,576	22,198	12,945	17,268	17,118	16,889	5,206	58,733	46,526	12,383	7,614	7,833
Congressional District 27	48,134	19,040	12,517	19,191	12,132	8,619	4,824	61,525	54,465	20,412	14,025	18,132
Congressional District 28	45,632	15,484	9,406	18,308	8,105	6,225	7,874	54,983	48,249	24,092	19,018	19,938
Congressional District 29	37,378	12,928	6,140	8,962	4,606	3,699	7,242	42,910	31,937	27,307	16,281	16,433
Congressional District 30	54,664	21,322	13,890	21,213	13,915	14,236	4,700	62,035	48,380	18,460	12,239	11,567
Congressional District 31	50,901	14,872	6,590	8,181	7,545	6,252	5,513	50,316	31,480	15,072	11,051	9,435
Congressional District 32	48,342	15,382	7,305	11,912	5,821	3,972	5,743	48,385	38,489	20,523	12,393	13,859
Congressional District 33	56,239	27,313	16,700	24,747	17,323	18,700	2,699	66,155	57,336	8,390	4,657	9,167
Congressional District 34	28,797	9,155	3,974	7,575	3,146	2,274	5,591	47,083	38,430	30,479	23,922	24,399
Congressional District 35	39,309	12,689	4,324	7,297	5,242	3,548	5,165	39,220	26,276	16,798	10,635	10,933
Congressional District 36	47,632	22,368	17,012	17,361	21,180	24,123	11,966	90,001	72,671	26,769	18,982	12,061
Congressional District 37	40,374	16,379	11,062	12,756	6,287	6,988	6,946	44,692	39,563	21,338	13,956	14,336
Congressional District 38	53,587	16,997	10,671	13,162	6,166	6,744	5,472	50,232	46,863	17,225	12,701	11,977
Congressional District 39	61,217	19,589	9,033	16,498	10,284	7,849	4,025	59,697	42,813	12,807	9,837	11,475
Congressional District 40	26,414	7,051	2,794	6,824	1,648	1,232	4,432	36,086	24,311	22,794	13,985	11,744
Congressional District 41	41,937	12,420	6,805	7,974	4,791	4,227	6,109	39,807	26,447	17,866	7,677	7,079
Congressional District 42	55,573	16,508	11,555	13,258	9,347	8,452	5,626	50,817	44,038	15,488	7,713	10,166
Congressional District 43	45,421	17,121	8,705	12,330	6,570	4,504	7,773	48,835	34,870	23,275	13,606	12,261
Congressional District 44	35,555	11,550	6,596	7,352	3,147	2,281	7,704	39,981	27,283	24,658	13,356	10,195
Congressional District 45	71,225	22,256	14,796	19,375	16,919	13,531	3,932	63,546	51,148	9,651	6,540	7,236
Congressional District 46	43,178	8,400	4,646	8,188	4,816	5,409	5,395	38,804	28,091	15,627	9,713	9,368
Congressional District 47	54,628	17,423	9,779	15,301	8,545	6,449	5,305	47,559	36,699	20,763	11,714	10,211
Congressional District 48	59,413	18,319	16,185	25,590	16,078	14,574	4,541	65,559	56,076	12,414	10,392	10,463
Congressional District 49	59,203	18,685	13,528	20,799	17,952	16,634	4,341	64,750	51,989	10,061	6,377	6,752
Congressional District 50	60,522	21,441	12,501	14,862	12,778	13,247	6,148	56,867	46,546	14,582	5,797	7,998

Table I-5: 116th Congressional Districts - Persons With Health Insurance by Source of Insurance—*Continued*

	Private Health Insurance Coverage						Public Health Insurance Coverage					
	Employer Based			Direct Purchase			Medicare			Medicaid/CHIP		
	55 to 64 Years	65 to 74 Years	75 Years and Over	55 to 64 Years	65 to 74 Years	75 Years and Over	55 to 64 Years	65 to 74 Years	75 Years and Over	55 to 64 Years	65 to 74 Years	75 Years and Over
California—Cont.												
Congressional District 51	33,686	11,958	5,697	6,380	5,268	3,862	7,150	45,250	36,086	25,339	15,445	16,078
Congressional District 52	58,651	22,289	13,977	16,849	14,811	15,116	4,277	61,852	44,670	10,320	7,808	7,049
Congressional District 53	50,179	20,696	12,255	13,231	11,117	8,658	6,958	54,913	37,843	14,297	10,364	8,075
Colorado												
Congressional District 1	54,429	18,006	10,954	13,229	15,387	13,030	8,980	57,789	36,367	14,401	8,251	7,558
Congressional District 2	74,721	25,736	12,303	18,841	23,612	16,865	4,814	73,160	41,043	8,509	5,604	3,934
Congressional District 3	54,757	20,711	13,315	19,460	24,728	19,662	11,711	80,915	52,749	19,971	8,714	7,619
Congressional District 4	68,955	20,628	12,101	15,849	22,714	16,840	8,514	67,541	42,654	11,660	6,895	4,752
Congressional District 5	52,357	18,495	9,522	15,131	21,836	15,050	8,162	68,770	40,472	16,353	6,138	4,978
Congressional District 6	67,828	21,847	10,862	13,901	15,810	12,681	6,296	58,709	35,367	11,110	5,965	4,847
Congressional District 7	62,951	22,592	13,707	12,755	17,891	16,624	7,124	61,906	41,843	12,402	5,496	5,192
Connecticut												
Congressional District 1	70,459	28,159	19,270	8,898	15,612	18,133	8,149	62,458	52,727	14,796	9,285	10,136
Congressional District 2	77,207	29,480	18,734	12,216	19,785	18,881	8,604	67,924	48,996	12,492	8,444	5,999
Congressional District 3	66,739	27,378	17,713	12,115	18,427	18,723	6,851	64,956	50,530	14,135	7,506	7,081
Congressional District 4	69,212	23,056	13,363	16,995	19,606	19,305	3,740	54,682	48,497	11,400	6,503	8,072
Congressional District 5	71,457	26,353	16,210	14,496	17,056	19,622	8,276	61,110	50,952	13,957	8,687	7,732
Delaware												
Congressional District (at Large)	91,277	48,726	29,311	15,246	34,090	26,834	13,150	102,634	69,111	21,614	10,601	7,821
District of Columbia												
Delegate District (at Large)	38,453	22,644	18,035	8,289	10,158	7,397	6,726	42,296	33,527	22,124	12,117	9,222
Florida												
Congressional District 1	51,862	21,649	13,131	18,736	22,761	16,536	12,632	76,603	49,879	11,747	7,113	5,113
Congressional District 2	49,039	24,902	15,062	17,924	26,632	20,695	13,817	82,189	59,003	14,350	12,760	9,220
Congressional District 3	51,794	19,203	11,940	15,969	20,691	12,956	11,629	75,088	45,855	11,032	12,157	6,821
Congressional District 4	67,311	23,273	15,704	18,216	24,892	20,012	7,242	76,445	52,186	7,999	8,153	6,610
Congressional District 5	45,533	16,476	8,617	11,220	12,604	7,772	12,130	59,351	33,312	15,551	11,927	7,174
Congressional District 6	59,383	29,920	23,147	22,667	30,100	27,141	13,907	107,297	82,842	13,451	11,254	12,102
Congressional District 7	58,184	17,497	7,404	14,962	14,449	13,237	8,030	62,612	44,092	8,114	7,275	7,294
Congressional District 8	65,736	27,959	26,570	24,963	30,752	29,806	14,236	101,323	87,147	13,905	9,464	10,319
Congressional District 9	55,903	20,285	14,176	19,764	19,405	15,407	14,560	79,101	60,524	16,093	15,587	14,078
Congressional District 10	52,766	15,328	6,915	16,899	14,597	9,836	9,322	55,227	32,744	11,079	9,688	6,576
Congressional District 11	55,134	45,137	40,800	26,132	39,326	45,758	15,389	144,583	130,459	14,989	11,720	14,877
Congressional District 12	57,685	25,343	21,450	20,530	25,047	26,177	13,680	101,726	84,351	13,718	12,822	9,969
Congressional District 13	64,074	22,549	15,707	22,323	20,919	23,167	12,804	85,455	74,677	14,020	11,814	9,366
Congressional District 14	48,349	16,077	5,852	14,984	9,561	7,891	9,009	56,977	40,886	13,448	11,380	10,224
Congressional District 15	57,972	21,651	12,240	15,313	17,827	15,632	12,130	73,316	51,457	11,380	10,492	7,974
Congressional District 16	68,214	35,761	31,839	24,860	38,978	38,041	12,177	111,093	102,205	9,584	9,289	10,300
Congressional District 17	56,413	33,984	33,184	20,336	49,303	50,085	15,342	127,385	118,545	12,837	12,141	13,496
Congressional District 18	67,552	30,035	23,247	25,225	30,671	35,825	9,708	97,721	95,049	10,360	9,502	10,143
Congressional District 19	66,574	43,182	33,142	26,779	45,125	53,746	12,171	132,318	120,611	10,880	9,601	12,335
Congressional District 20	41,275	12,251	7,085	19,830	12,564	9,557	9,694	51,570	44,892	15,085	13,983	13,208
Congressional District 21	54,042	27,559	26,226	23,343	26,053	35,484	7,848	89,300	102,173	10,327	10,854	13,921
Congressional District 22	60,896	22,816	19,400	29,634	17,326	21,724	8,711	78,042	72,938	8,222	8,689	10,629
Congressional District 23	56,457	16,033	7,716	24,322	11,857	12,217	5,104	69,729	56,034	5,366	9,169	9,173
Congressional District 24	36,790	9,413	2,454	18,955	6,952	4,010	9,209	54,847	40,718	15,681	20,199	17,950
Congressional District 25	42,307	11,398	7,374	25,740	12,094	14,231	6,354	69,616	68,781	7,982	23,586	26,265
Congressional District 26	47,222	10,531	4,206	22,387	8,798	5,287	7,568	58,250	48,675	9,359	16,216	22,465
Congressional District 27	48,111	10,954	6,040	20,616	9,235	7,867	6,240	65,493	63,096	9,489	21,511	24,040
Georgia												
Congressional District 1	52,354	22,160	11,521	12,657	14,503	12,538	12,137	61,886	40,241	9,020	8,804	6,010
Congressional District 2	38,530	15,739	10,580	12,423	17,821	12,493	12,232	59,158	40,164	13,690	13,565	9,486
Congressional District 3	55,253	25,552	13,167	13,610	19,278	12,123	12,293	67,294	42,123	10,987	9,073	7,277
Congressional District 4	55,496	23,063	9,971	13,240	12,261	7,927	9,437	59,219	29,862	11,566	9,907	5,219
Congressional District 5	40,680	17,055	10,854	10,361	11,680	7,426	10,705	47,589	32,583	13,829	11,499	7,621
Congressional District 6	66,334	20,796	11,039	16,447	22,533	15,503	3,474	56,019	35,096	4,091	2,845	2,795
Congressional District 7	61,113	15,368	8,929	17,490	12,504	9,789	4,410	48,050	29,996	6,122	4,193	4,939
Congressional District 8	48,792	23,124	15,635	11,163	15,112	11,499	13,565	61,368	41,208	12,462	11,101	8,382
Congressional District 9	60,586	23,996	15,199	14,061	29,399	22,814	9,009	83,586	54,721	8,473	9,128	9,365
Congressional District 10	56,276	25,563	13,188	13,438	16,304	14,559	11,676	64,767	40,239	10,887	9,180	6,818
Congressional District 11	63,050	20,911	10,217	12,686	15,575	14,306	7,063	57,326	38,607	6,768	5,428	4,009
Congressional District 12	50,078	19,113	13,067	10,540	13,582	9,535	12,696	60,444	37,241	12,881	11,262	6,832
Congressional District 13	58,208	22,035	9,657	11,557	13,264	7,784	8,318	52,830	26,742	9,536	8,502	4,067
Congressional District 14	54,651	18,719	10,299	10,768	16,717	13,944	10,995	60,639	41,009	9,081	8,573	6,079
Hawaii												
Congressional District 1	64,347	42,137	29,698	10,235	14,452	16,870	3,909	65,440	57,631	9,995	8,719	8,177
Congressional District 2	60,467	36,511	23,084	14,076	18,643	15,616	6,470	71,413	48,334	12,964	7,621	6,378
Idaho												
Congressional District 1	62,133	24,035	14,076	23,754	37,400	28,161	12,752	91,567	58,136	11,031	10,319	6,516
Congressional District 2	59,461	16,500	10,094	18,693	30,502	22,018	9,872	70,553	48,296	8,898	8,324	6,768

Table I-5: 116th Congressional Districts - Persons With Health Insurance by Source of Insurance—*Continued*

	Private Health Insurance Coverage						Public Health Insurance Coverage					
	Employer Based			Direct Purchase			Medicare			Medicaid/CHIP		
	55 to 64 Years	65 to 74 Years	75 Years and Over	55 to 64 Years	65 to 74 Years	75 Years and Over	55 to 64 Years	65 to 74 Years	75 Years and Over	55 to 64 Years	65 to 74 Years	75 Years and Over
Illinois												
Congressional District 1	60,007	20,396	15,607	9,952	16,710	16,500	10,063	56,523	47,434	19,937	8,458	6,620
Congressional District 2	46,446	20,036	13,905	9,030	15,090	15,014	10,930	57,091	45,299	18,198	9,355	7,261
Congressional District 3	65,381	19,454	12,205	10,471	16,702	16,027	4,741	54,872	44,452	11,735	6,858	5,091
Congressional District 4	40,953	10,565	3,504	6,182	7,209	5,381	7,062	39,479	25,184	15,157	8,499	6,305
Congressional District 5	55,898	17,809	8,305	11,592	13,298	15,067	5,120	48,661	37,879	9,823	5,494	6,033
Congressional District 6	85,051	27,244	13,374	16,818	24,875	21,652	3,377	63,726	45,793	3,602	2,791	4,642
Congressional District 7	41,741	17,194	7,790	8,241	11,993	7,801	7,903	53,358	35,064	20,281	11,938	6,447
Congressional District 8	61,844	19,179	8,412	13,437	17,294	15,155	5,062	51,706	34,908	9,189	7,129	5,593
Congressional District 9	61,667	23,054	12,524	14,074	22,303	22,021	6,656	61,407	52,047	11,415	7,409	5,872
Congressional District 10	64,348	19,305	10,397	15,347	18,353	16,178	4,628	56,855	43,315	6,898	4,373	4,489
Congressional District 11	61,675	19,942	9,064	9,642	19,603	15,515	5,635	51,086	32,394	8,098	4,481	3,921
Congressional District 12	55,737	23,247	14,583	10,863	18,654	16,457	14,951	64,277	46,123	18,122	7,738	6,220
Congressional District 13	59,782	26,157	17,754	10,715	18,837	17,629	9,794	58,986	43,829	12,886	5,405	4,570
Congressional District 14	74,138	21,505	12,770	15,469	22,714	17,863	4,251	58,316	39,797	5,300	2,968	2,491
Congressional District 15	60,493	22,244	16,288	13,585	26,068	27,811	11,310	69,764	55,708	15,911	8,196	4,602
Congressional District 16	66,824	23,159	15,051	15,443	26,256	24,488	6,859	67,334	48,344	9,759	4,787	3,700
Congressional District 17	58,753	23,825	17,055	13,412	25,520	23,833	8,963	67,548	51,764	16,555	7,431	4,969
Congressional District 18	71,003	29,637	22,687	14,153	23,879	23,800	6,635	69,032	54,745	8,548	5,933	4,005
Indiana												
Congressional District 1	65,978	25,521	16,326	12,153	22,130	18,557	9,862	66,167	46,139	13,338	7,225	3,982
Congressional District 2	60,835	17,564	9,700	14,090	24,547	21,338	10,617	63,197	48,301	9,272	5,750	5,321
Congressional District 3	65,888	17,177	10,210	12,613	22,222	18,575	8,562	64,238	43,484	8,821	6,383	3,560
Congressional District 4	65,654	22,228	14,431	12,234	24,215	19,979	11,213	65,205	45,351	11,069	4,149	4,300
Congressional District 5	68,700	23,077	17,288	14,275	21,715	19,432	8,341	63,835	46,154	10,332	4,758	2,701
Congressional District 6	59,805	20,932	13,638	11,925	25,267	20,328	14,134	69,931	49,977	12,293	8,252	4,632
Congressional District 7	52,183	18,614	8,550	9,538	14,154	11,907	10,760	50,174	34,959	18,100	7,054	6,639
Congressional District 8	62,454	17,943	13,969	13,014	25,855	21,381	12,566	68,775	47,918	13,567	7,049	5,296
Congressional District 9	66,473	22,169	14,079	10,732	26,050	19,773	10,806	68,041	43,529	12,544	6,589	5,208
Iowa												
Congressional District 1	73,573	20,602	13,552	16,549	32,771	32,299	8,352	71,926	57,656	12,941	6,585	5,712
Congressional District 2	69,634	24,081	12,376	15,700	35,116	30,451	9,255	71,518	54,207	14,189	7,586	6,687
Congressional District 3	74,514	20,624	12,382	13,199	35,981	25,856	9,097	68,505	47,169	15,577	6,053	4,647
Congressional District 4	67,547	17,416	9,439	22,732	31,549	34,611	7,311	70,094	60,554	13,203	6,015	6,474
Kansas												
Congressional District 1	56,591	14,123	7,041	16,834	25,617	26,342	6,769	59,176	47,555	5,901	5,609	5,825
Congressional District 2	57,231	21,337	12,914	15,609	29,494	23,804	11,341	65,619	49,050	10,640	6,096	4,904
Congressional District 3	69,521	20,144	10,010	11,653	23,419	18,685	7,384	58,546	40,000	6,637	4,067	2,548
Congressional District 4	61,446	12,971	7,089	14,247	27,108	22,374	8,052	61,998	45,724	10,217	7,869	5,103
Kentucky												
Congressional District 1	52,834	24,870	15,941	14,619	21,763	19,347	16,484	72,803	52,564	23,076	10,913	6,504
Congressional District 2	57,820	24,546	13,882	10,772	24,085	19,678	15,122	70,458	46,649	21,769	10,561	9,436
Congressional District 3	64,305	27,545	14,894	11,740	23,297	22,673	12,317	65,542	47,034	18,694	8,338	4,832
Congressional District 4	67,645	26,021	13,463	14,282	20,178	16,021	11,028	67,723	42,308	14,497	7,793	4,450
Congressional District 5	41,026	19,086	11,752	10,547	19,216	12,655	25,892	70,973	44,941	27,745	13,550	11,430
Congressional District 6	58,142	25,674	16,068	12,380	22,924	16,820	13,172	66,760	42,732	19,899	7,525	4,781
Louisiana												
Congressional District 1	67,124	26,505	13,656	15,813	17,081	14,082	12,496	73,571	47,538	15,648	8,335	5,559
Congressional District 2	48,328	19,205	9,806	13,062	13,398	8,433	15,597	67,309	40,323	31,391	15,366	11,036
Congressional District 3	52,091	20,514	12,999	16,647	22,630	16,592	16,630	64,007	43,708	21,202	8,623	6,484
Congressional District 4	45,694	23,889	14,096	13,461	19,000	15,626	15,264	65,672	45,799	19,868	9,866	8,500
Congressional District 5	50,532	21,863	12,958	11,343	18,479	13,864	13,651	67,925	43,869	20,487	12,307	6,089
Congressional District 6	57,470	27,784	15,846	14,556	15,530	11,604	9,742	64,165	44,760	13,646	8,048	5,971
Maine												
Congressional District 1	68,295	25,685	16,649	16,707	23,248	18,863	7,836	77,315	53,418	10,672	8,686	8,821
Congressional District 2	58,331	22,038	13,192	15,447	25,611	21,163	14,113	79,075	50,094	19,214	15,300	12,897
Maryland												
Congressional District 1	77,114	36,921	24,642	15,272	24,922	20,131	9,490	76,219	55,788	14,487	7,164	5,953
Congressional District 2	61,414	33,497	17,300	12,798	18,951	14,473	11,149	59,743	40,654	15,857	8,417	6,460
Congressional District 3	64,790	31,841	22,914	13,627	19,106	19,090	5,845	58,579	48,012	10,939	6,420	6,020
Congressional District 4	71,994	34,662	22,411	10,334	13,553	10,968	4,833	57,063	57,063	12,611	7,855	4,750
Congressional District 5	78,514	40,915	20,535	12,259	15,172	11,169	5,864	57,231	38,121	9,044	5,951	5,220
Congressional District 6	66,825	32,704	19,450	15,007	18,734	17,158	6,669	60,658	47,019	11,404	7,722	8,014
Congressional District 7	58,679	32,326	18,391	9,967	16,113	15,317	11,135	59,114	44,163	20,832	11,117	9,867
Congressional District 8	77,958	41,306	25,020	14,511	17,233	17,818	4,518	63,151	49,899	8,943	6,137	7,984
Massachusetts												
Congressional District 1	65,798	32,179	19,261	10,049	21,232	21,758	10,914	70,219	52,024	24,302	12,312	10,389
Congressional District 2	70,708	30,833	16,213	13,327	21,822	18,781	10,198	66,472	43,950	21,828	11,390	8,419
Congressional District 3	74,814	26,259	13,541	10,314	16,616	13,480	9,478	54,870	45,498	24,948	10,843	8,934
Congressional District 4	81,381	35,060	18,376	14,907	21,672	21,425	7,094	67,698	49,456	13,105	9,146	8,363
Congressional District 5	70,480	35,174	18,741	12,814	18,682	20,838	5,597	62,313	50,706	15,490	8,316	7,249
Congressional District 6	81,776	38,048	21,195	17,169	27,144	26,173	7,444	75,535	58,455	15,938	10,549	10,268
Congressional District 7	42,927	16,906	8,782	8,378	11,080	7,769	7,582	45,189	35,465	26,896	15,245	12,463
Congressional District 8	74,827	31,143	17,773	10,659	18,594	18,983	6,884	63,522	50,564	20,131	11,816	9,030
Congressional District 9	72,079	39,634	23,965	18,385	32,794	27,634	8,173	90,236	64,474	20,696	12,478	9,173

Table I-5: 116th Congressional Districts - Persons With Health Insurance by Source of Insurance—*Continued*

| | Private Health Insurance Coverage | | | | | | Public Health Insurance Coverage | | | | | |
| | Employer Based | | | Direct Purchase | | | Medicare | | | Medicaid/CHIP | | |
	55 to 64 Years	65 to 74 Years	75 Years and Over	55 to 64 Years	65 to 74 Years	75 Years and Over	55 to 64 Years	65 to 74 Years	75 Years and Over	55 to 64 Years	65 to 74 Years	75 Years and Over
Michigan												
Congressional District 1	63,308	38,295	27,732	20,711	32,602	28,638	15,584	92,582	64,328	19,363	9,350	7,040
Congressional District 2	66,286	24,409	17,082	13,645	22,394	20,682	10,595	67,101	47,389	14,245	7,862	5,878
Congressional District 3	62,122	26,406	17,300	14,533	20,408	18,172	10,567	62,269	44,281	14,134	6,667	5,006
Congressional District 4	64,441	39,416	29,486	13,300	24,200	21,224	14,076	76,437	55,189	17,995	10,084	6,824
Congressional District 5	59,680	39,552	31,351	11,489	17,809	15,749	17,174	69,343	50,724	23,902	8,696	5,365
Congressional District 6	63,995	28,222	17,473	14,491	26,368	21,805	9,510	71,242	48,079	14,476	7,232	4,425
Congressional District 7	73,287	38,778	25,036	13,088	21,410	19,517	11,493	74,536	50,597	13,454	6,921	5,308
Congressional District 8	73,886	40,107	21,290	11,406	22,034	15,921	8,812	66,529	41,358	9,362	5,937	3,863
Congressional District 9	66,532	30,301	22,235	13,198	22,287	21,668	11,534	62,559	50,291	15,437	10,084	7,512
Congressional District 10	73,746	40,445	24,581	16,162	23,977	21,013	12,127	76,093	51,099	15,952	8,562	5,534
Congressional District 11	80,471	36,156	20,445	17,320	25,230	20,809	7,280	68,019	46,774	8,030	5,747	5,803
Congressional District 12	58,918	30,866	20,464	11,986	17,485	15,535	10,874	56,973	41,330	13,194	8,168	6,087
Congressional District 13	41,468	23,849	18,060	7,944	9,907	10,533	16,717	53,265	38,492	27,613	14,773	9,890
Congressional District 14	51,001	31,711	21,483	11,130	14,815	14,904	12,014	63,615	47,058	25,929	10,982	8,040
Minnesota												
Congressional District 1	62,586	16,365	10,234	13,757	30,736	28,614	6,838	60,742	49,208	11,532	5,136	5,191
Congressional District 2	71,569	16,617	8,551	12,925	29,304	22,334	5,546	54,354	38,856	9,521	3,498	2,824
Congressional District 3	77,354	20,492	8,935	14,736	32,336	29,192	3,927	61,583	44,927	9,187	4,089	3,856
Congressional District 4	62,303	21,209	11,537	12,095	27,250	20,831	5,760	58,790	39,559	13,459	5,706	4,114
Congressional District 5	47,067	13,627	7,556	11,561	20,755	17,312	6,001	48,645	34,940	14,835	7,572	6,219
Congressional District 6	71,136	16,673	6,384	12,657	27,581	19,926	5,228	55,147	33,739	8,566	3,688	2,807
Congressional District 7	58,730	13,495	7,068	17,481	34,121	36,220	7,854	66,634	54,607	12,811	5,366	5,562
Congressional District 8	64,730	23,239	14,760	16,494	35,980	28,880	11,055	76,106	53,227	16,926	6,726	6,021
Mississippi												
Congressional District 1	55,033	13,286	7,015	13,200	24,163	18,614	15,284	68,958	46,805	15,268	9,002	8,612
Congressional District 2	45,473	13,834	7,879	11,885	18,061	11,596	18,012	63,509	38,362	21,505	13,117	9,217
Congressional District 3	53,454	19,281	8,809	11,715	21,273	17,217	13,581	68,588	47,553	13,632	11,665	11,163
Congressional District 4	46,344	19,910	10,463	12,086	21,287	17,197	16,894	70,581	46,616	18,589	10,425	7,377
Missouri												
Congressional District 1	54,781	19,105	13,802	11,089	12,053	8,743	12,668	58,044	40,549	16,628	8,640	6,847
Congressional District 2	83,302	25,756	16,723	17,965	23,708	23,375	6,182	73,017	59,580	3,741	2,392	3,991
Congressional District 3	76,258	24,609	15,251	14,789	21,975	16,921	10,600	72,161	49,018	7,906	3,623	4,009
Congressional District 4	59,148	19,838	13,361	14,378	23,824	18,854	14,073	72,501	49,852	8,606	6,126	3,819
Congressional District 5	58,755	19,795	15,489	13,364	20,924	19,800	13,124	63,483	48,227	9,884	5,423	4,461
Congressional District 6	66,248	19,913	11,155	16,567	30,820	23,129	13,059	71,297	49,268	8,898	4,850	4,564
Congressional District 7	55,271	14,633	10,166	14,936	25,260	23,839	13,246	76,205	55,924	10,323	9,434	6,333
Congressional District 8	52,168	18,077	11,947	15,783	23,955	21,799	20,003	77,025	53,720	15,809	10,024	7,070
Montana												
Congressional District (at Large)	83,656	27,410	16,452	29,473	46,448	35,191	14,626	116,081	74,580	21,332	10,944	7,358
Nebraska												
Congressional District 1	54,931	15,279	6,547	13,145	21,163	20,221	5,140	53,701	39,362	5,517	4,976	5,166
Congressional District 2	52,987	14,892	7,761	10,112	16,781	11,037	6,460	48,850	31,341	6,963	3,816	4,166
Congressional District 3	52,531	13,788	6,857	18,211	27,110	28,492	6,979	59,627	49,921	6,736	6,031	5,945
Nevada												
Congressional District 1	39,585	13,900	5,357	6,771	9,313	7,296	11,692	55,613	36,489	21,005	13,018	7,700
Congressional District 2	61,556	26,190	13,027	13,997	23,944	17,985	9,003	73,155	46,283	11,973	6,328	5,418
Congressional District 3	65,304	24,581	12,921	16,290	18,700	14,149	6,972	74,871	50,591	11,225	6,027	5,950
Congressional District 4	56,716	21,886	10,731	9,860	14,350	10,154	8,448	67,437	42,495	15,332	6,191	5,043
New Hampshire												
Congressional District 1	74,682	26,942	13,279	11,089	25,702	21,291	7,819	68,390	44,402	9,285	3,881	4,758
Congressional District 2	75,928	24,376	14,921	12,496	23,563	19,915	11,634	67,460	46,852	8,589	4,729	3,480
New Jersey												
Congressional District 1	67,129	30,110	15,525	14,008	17,841	18,439	10,775	60,689	44,662	14,619	9,653	5,224
Congressional District 2	69,925	33,006	21,134	15,802	24,550	19,495	11,579	74,843	54,272	15,424	9,985	7,864
Congressional District 3	79,485	38,996	25,537	14,512	20,835	22,783	9,419	73,847	60,364	10,730	4,527	4,855
Congressional District 4	78,109	39,006	26,364	12,191	21,964	26,980	6,737	76,127	63,785	6,570	5,071	5,280
Congressional District 5	84,123	29,823	17,253	14,313	20,877	20,068	4,828	68,539	52,715	6,348	5,509	5,120
Congressional District 6	67,010	24,570	14,276	13,586	13,551	14,573	8,414	54,481	41,987	9,772	8,453	7,639
Congressional District 7	89,058	31,535	17,680	13,548	19,200	20,354	5,122	61,644	49,284	5,636	4,133	5,983
Congressional District 8	38,576	11,814	7,179	9,784	7,282	6,310	6,910	41,055	33,211	17,940	10,741	10,294
Congressional District 9	60,152	22,179	11,543	12,415	10,340	13,009	6,889	54,337	47,029	15,706	10,056	8,135
Congressional District 10	53,063	20,225	11,240	8,032	8,738	7,237	10,125	49,910	39,348	21,016	11,201	12,756
Congressional District 11	83,899	32,243	22,550	13,635	18,776	21,869	4,935	64,115	56,436	6,762	5,254	6,577
Congressional District 12	77,388	33,694	17,761	10,483	13,884	15,749	6,873	59,320	45,602	9,383	6,900	8,065
New Mexico												
Congressional District 1	52,783	23,344	14,701	10,937	15,245	10,503	10,316	67,014	43,731	20,330	8,597	7,311
Congressional District 2	38,382	23,317	11,894	9,698	15,447	13,457	10,992	66,652	49,144	24,027	11,634	11,704
Congressional District 3	47,133	23,459	13,919	13,721	17,618	14,716	11,001	73,287	48,483	19,381	11,972	7,118
New York												
Congressional District 1	78,384	38,620	21,908	12,182	17,025	18,737	7,516	68,602	53,321	11,067	6,398	6,466
Congressional District 2	76,326	34,615	19,686	11,734	15,320	15,736	6,513	57,110	44,402	14,401	5,392	5,801
Congressional District 3	81,859	39,855	26,011	17,637	21,336	20,278	4,529	70,057	64,064	9,771	5,322	8,618

Table I-5: 116th Congressional Districts - Persons With Health Insurance by Source of Insurance—*Continued*

| | Private Health Insurance Coverage | | | | | | Public Health Insurance Coverage | | | | | |
| | Employer Based | | | Direct Purchase | | | Medicare | | | Medicaid/CHIP | | |
	55 to 64 Years	65 to 74 Years	75 Years and Over	55 to 64 Years	65 to 74 Years	75 Years and Over	55 to 64 Years	65 to 74 Years	75 Years and Over	55 to 64 Years	65 to 74 Years	75 Years and Over
New York—Cont.												
Congressional District 4	70,574	35,551	18,540	13,163	16,549	20,028	5,966	62,329	52,401	10,514	7,568	6,677
Congressional District 5	62,709	22,592	13,656	11,444	5,703	6,052	7,100	54,958	42,702	26,988	14,022	12,269
Congressional District 6	60,918	25,174	12,447	15,617	10,627	8,929	6,354	67,744	51,395	27,143	17,273	16,994
Congressional District 7	35,167	11,928	5,021	8,547	6,863	4,100	6,080	44,067	33,840	31,104	18,642	17,471
Congressional District 8	49,627	24,448	10,185	11,506	9,705	7,833	8,800	58,670	49,038	25,489	20,191	18,004
Congressional District 9	50,292	22,766	11,975	11,656	8,729	6,178	6,725	58,196	43,290	21,464	16,321	16,859
Congressional District 10	44,881	27,240	14,184	10,814	12,462	10,737	4,164	55,694	48,437	17,578	12,879	13,596
Congressional District 11	64,360	29,026	15,931	11,000	11,655	8,088	9,921	65,511	49,061	19,051	13,572	13,276
Congressional District 12	42,669	23,876	20,395	16,410	12,836	12,634	4,502	48,712	49,884	12,974	8,332	10,690
Congressional District 13	39,678	16,966	8,766	8,710	4,498	3,363	11,882	50,384	40,083	39,903	25,328	21,333
Congressional District 14	38,433	15,723	10,110	11,704	7,137	6,657	6,649	46,424	38,825	24,767	14,295	13,107
Congressional District 15	24,334	9,261	5,211	7,204	5,508	2,493	10,549	44,550	31,368	42,716	24,792	19,135
Congressional District 16	62,485	29,013	21,803	12,326	12,235	16,821	8,039	57,813	56,308	20,995	13,266	14,435
Congressional District 17	68,586	37,315	22,773	8,724	15,318	16,005	7,338	64,305	51,288	13,254	7,549	7,977
Congressional District 18	71,702	30,696	18,006	12,923	14,629	12,389	9,457	60,748	41,644	13,247	5,748	5,430
Congressional District 19	72,120	38,024	23,129	13,494	21,972	18,256	9,519	79,927	57,151	18,045	9,825	7,862
Congressional District 20	70,692	41,414	25,351	8,727	14,788	16,021	10,249	66,174	48,049	16,171	6,837	5,501
Congressional District 21	67,028	36,477	19,756	12,938	20,156	17,352	12,453	71,905	48,480	18,473	8,044	7,185
Congressional District 22	66,086	32,181	21,646	10,326	17,624	18,043	11,499	69,843	52,777	20,782	8,826	8,438
Congressional District 23	65,939	29,416	19,511	14,090	22,894	19,944	12,274	71,669	51,399	18,699	10,678	7,848
Congressional District 24	71,951	31,903	22,723	13,546	17,797	17,959	12,214	65,534	49,915	14,956	9,635	7,533
Congressional District 25	65,044	27,631	16,439	15,266	22,830	21,498	10,291	66,741	48,621	17,875	9,498	6,826
Congressional District 26	60,573	29,555	19,455	10,529	19,885	22,144	10,537	65,470	50,993	21,851	9,495	7,536
Congressional District 27	79,841	32,541	17,808	16,916	24,795	23,971	12,884	74,715	55,197	14,819	8,125	6,578
North Carolina												
Congressional District 1	57,522	25,637	13,973	13,331	21,527	13,836	13,859	70,605	46,267	12,483	8,971	6,264
Congressional District 2	72,205	26,893	12,351	16,492	24,105	17,036	10,181	71,770	41,076	9,862	7,582	4,786
Congressional District 3	53,381	29,607	18,826	17,310	23,162	16,998	11,680	74,745	51,628	12,125	8,788	7,863
Congressional District 4	65,370	27,142	14,766	14,665	18,792	12,896	5,454	57,722	37,429	6,917	7,154	5,654
Congressional District 5	64,028	20,600	15,312	16,416	29,185	22,427	13,635	77,270	55,101	10,691	10,229	7,919
Congressional District 6	69,246	25,625	16,291	17,792	24,609	20,902	11,713	74,333	53,899	9,374	7,661	7,322
Congressional District 7	61,776	37,797	20,019	20,344	34,321	22,624	13,314	96,878	57,892	12,027	10,065	8,753
Congressional District 8	53,737	20,970	12,194	14,228	23,545	17,874	12,638	68,388	45,473	9,941	9,342	6,120
Congressional District 9	60,225	22,464	11,461	15,882	25,897	20,337	12,344	70,153	46,138	11,420	8,327	6,640
Congressional District 10	64,713	22,944	13,193	20,278	27,966	22,101	12,051	80,010	53,544	12,274	9,913	5,912
Congressional District 11	62,552	28,739	19,353	19,479	36,707	27,677	17,543	96,880	69,445	13,166	9,983	7,962
Congressional District 12	53,362	13,034	6,668	15,082	15,269	11,743	6,998	51,548	30,557	11,052	7,710	5,299
Congressional District 13	61,507	21,898	12,578	16,892	23,947	17,981	12,155	72,697	50,438	9,357	9,438	6,067
North Dakota												
Congressional District (at Large)	63,678	17,593	10,043	19,429	28,620	26,523	6,904	60,123	46,749	6,041	4,412	5,724
Ohio												
Congressional District 1	65,426	22,684	14,879	12,430	19,009	13,729	8,761	62,498	40,941	14,533	7,020	4,060
Congressional District 2	65,106	22,832	15,867	13,949	19,535	16,083	11,089	63,497	46,797	15,229	7,303	4,619
Congressional District 3	47,920	16,085	9,125	8,147	12,720	9,682	10,174	46,994	34,480	21,432	6,331	5,286
Congressional District 4	68,398	24,305	16,572	12,296	27,365	19,485	9,199	67,843	46,714	11,497	5,788	4,685
Congressional District 5	71,665	28,330	20,486	14,112	27,256	23,403	8,593	70,907	51,809	9,356	6,469	4,384
Congressional District 6	67,322	26,449	17,430	13,248	21,361	17,956	13,462	75,602	52,927	17,658	9,576	6,139
Congressional District 7	65,889	27,909	17,399	11,859	23,612	20,468	11,301	72,285	53,774	12,074	5,260	5,653
Congressional District 8	65,127	23,256	15,672	11,243	22,396	19,953	10,100	67,243	48,177	12,694	7,164	5,557
Congressional District 9	58,556	22,642	16,073	9,084	18,541	15,496	12,079	60,788	43,436	21,237	9,241	5,433
Congressional District 10	63,088	25,416	20,118	10,911	19,921	15,313	8,733	69,396	50,111	15,879	6,211	4,022
Congressional District 11	49,226	21,460	15,510	11,871	15,364	13,929	11,452	62,804	48,275	27,481	13,041	9,553
Congressional District 12	68,466	25,907	16,174	14,694	23,209	21,224	7,557	66,125	49,277	9,458	5,492	3,607
Congressional District 13	60,755	25,031	16,800	11,375	22,156	18,283	12,758	70,847	53,530	19,263	7,583	6,015
Congressional District 14	77,733	30,329	20,088	17,007	29,639	23,730	8,499	78,889	57,139	8,946	5,378	4,012
Congressional District 15	63,279	25,520	15,354	11,402	20,099	17,547	12,401	65,915	46,228	14,104	5,564	3,286
Congressional District 16	77,933	30,007	23,361	12,401	27,743	23,406	6,874	76,956	61,501	7,993	4,095	4,731
Oklahoma												
Congressional District 1	61,992	21,324	11,695	14,699	24,301	20,995	9,236	66,647	46,300	7,141	5,656	4,454
Congressional District 2	47,443	19,296	13,569	14,399	24,961	18,997	15,035	76,959	56,459	12,028	9,922	7,061
Congressional District 3	56,966	19,736	13,090	14,870	26,538	24,008	10,816	68,221	49,231	8,117	7,166	5,589
Congressional District 4	58,678	25,131	14,549	11,474	19,201	16,314	12,765	65,479	45,094	6,708	6,359	4,065
Congressional District 5	55,741	25,253	15,053	14,688	18,438	16,447	10,120	62,644	44,255	9,132	7,674	4,990
Oregon												
Congressional District 1	68,308	21,758	13,807	16,564	31,413	22,959	8,655	72,400	47,719	14,702	7,503	4,361
Congressional District 2	58,461	24,563	17,620	20,457	39,468	29,560	12,600	99,583	66,166	24,210	10,721	9,824
Congressional District 3	60,213	21,218	12,178	17,265	24,137	16,343	8,225	67,386	39,322	17,605	9,968	7,073
Congressional District 4	57,303	25,201	17,186	17,376	35,793	28,245	14,536	98,751	68,100	23,118	10,363	9,362
Congressional District 5	68,006	25,268	18,640	16,638	30,237	25,897	7,917	85,425	58,701	18,504	10,326	7,279
Pennsylvania												
Congressional District 1	86,696	29,028	16,005	15,151	28,052	27,627	7,195	68,548	54,154	8,034	4,793	5,267
Congressional District 2	41,167	16,868	9,271	9,599	12,015	12,373	13,700	53,493	36,516	29,040	15,317	8,729
Congressional District 3	43,591	19,935	10,469	10,633	13,319	13,606	10,442	54,131	41,630	25,269	11,794	10,636

Table I-5: 116th Congressional Districts - Persons With Health Insurance by Source of Insurance—*Continued*

	Private Health Insurance Coverage						Public Health Insurance Coverage					
	Employer Based			Direct Purchase			Medicare			Medicaid/CHIP		
	55 to 64 Years	65 to 74 Years	75 Years and Over	55 to 64 Years	65 to 74 Years	75 Years and Over	55 to 64 Years	65 to 74 Years	75 Years and Over	55 to 64 Years	65 to 74 Years	75 Years and Over
Pennsylvania—Cont.												
Congressional District 4	77,853	28,895	16,781	15,448	24,679	27,562	6,544	64,952	53,776	7,829	4,452	5,970
Congressional District 5	63,888	26,000	14,567	14,026	19,479	21,324	9,360	57,469	47,481	13,050	8,189	6,404
Congressional District 6	70,162	22,815	13,675	15,647	25,248	23,357	7,161	63,545	46,801	8,985	6,130	4,910
Congressional District 7	67,080	22,657	16,039	13,517	26,604	22,775	9,425	70,033	52,998	14,534	7,528	6,564
Congressional District 8	66,722	27,720	15,068	13,084	28,056	27,965	12,395	72,346	55,007	15,741	7,694	6,611
Congressional District 9	71,663	24,816	15,942	14,704	29,408	26,795	9,568	75,325	55,682	12,938	7,495	7,038
Congressional District 10	70,673	28,927	19,044	12,650	23,070	21,627	7,357	68,249	51,102	11,620	7,378	7,323
Congressional District 11	68,426	24,791	17,767	14,919	25,263	24,734	8,101	69,714	55,463	9,800	5,467	5,112
Congressional District 12	62,644	24,524	17,197	14,883	29,073	26,249	9,096	71,114	55,310	13,150	7,259	7,773
Congressional District 13	65,644	29,744	18,000	15,084	30,051	28,042	10,741	76,817	59,446	13,146	8,911	7,622
Congressional District 14	72,656	28,012	18,998	17,537	31,836	28,703	11,013	78,482	60,818	15,501	7,573	7,216
Congressional District 15	67,748	25,290	18,031	14,618	28,652	26,087	11,359	74,518	58,498	17,091	8,847	7,304
Congressional District 16	65,527	20,628	14,849	14,954	30,046	25,928	11,358	72,366	53,999	16,423	9,120	6,792
Congressional District 17	77,663	29,065	16,662	19,213	31,493	30,202	8,261	73,175	58,069	11,707	6,738	6,391
Congressional District 18	63,956	24,147	16,455	15,075	23,249	24,043	8,427	65,874	53,804	15,922	9,273	9,924
Rhode Island												
Congressional District 1	45,605	13,519	8,231	10,039	17,711	15,494	7,803	47,571	38,181	14,358	9,865	8,450
Congressional District 2	54,384	16,808	9,766	9,507	17,178	11,680	6,251	49,122	35,049	11,965	7,480	5,297
South Carolina												
Congressional District 1	58,815	33,314	18,871	19,417	26,411	21,624	10,448	86,751	55,049	11,995	7,922	3,632
Congressional District 2	61,352	27,797	14,848	14,237	22,839	16,429	7,132	68,272	43,476	7,964	7,531	6,007
Congressional District 3	53,934	22,953	13,547	14,423	23,828	19,918	13,912	73,749	51,165	11,798	9,338	7,026
Congressional District 4	53,165	19,823	11,072	16,748	20,069	17,610	11,195	67,782	45,067	9,021	7,358	4,884
Congressional District 5	56,169	24,535	13,705	13,126	24,870	16,733	13,270	72,580	45,849	13,302	8,243	5,951
Congressional District 6	39,226	16,968	10,016	13,016	14,400	8,802	12,970	60,736	37,675	14,184	13,166	9,536
Congressional District 7	52,719	33,668	14,993	17,947	35,248	21,738	17,263	100,308	53,916	15,548	10,251	7,190
South Dakota												
Congressional District (at Large)	69,599	19,044	8,141	23,076	32,144	24,347	9,791	79,920	55,360	8,803	6,640	6,345
Tennessee												
Congressional District 1	51,776	20,236	12,032	16,746	27,393	23,296	18,161	82,587	58,132	15,733	10,933	8,643
Congressional District 2	59,453	20,256	13,824	14,709	28,381	22,922	12,151	76,474	52,458	12,675	8,049	3,922
Congressional District 3	60,299	19,150	13,117	12,551	30,115	25,865	16,714	78,581	53,139	11,920	11,336	7,706
Congressional District 4	61,064	18,441	9,543	12,988	24,087	19,674	13,151	68,842	44,272	13,299	7,818	5,768
Congressional District 5	57,560	23,273	9,500	12,375	17,028	10,580	8,946	53,943	36,573	8,623	6,175	4,799
Congressional District 6	60,322	25,038	13,320	16,682	25,752	20,963	15,515	79,366	53,665	15,216	8,406	7,341
Congressional District 7	56,783	19,071	10,589	14,103	22,164	14,702	11,949	65,427	44,559	12,551	8,322	5,556
Congressional District 8	63,437	23,580	12,175	14,612	21,922	17,825	9,510	69,777	46,457	12,261	8,059	6,278
Congressional District 9	46,521	19,388	12,143	8,873	11,007	8,407	10,436	50,477	31,897	13,421	10,997	7,526
Texas												
Congressional District 1	47,101	19,082	11,393	13,790	24,728	20,605	9,747	65,406	46,931	11,151	7,645	4,435
Congressional District 2	61,062	20,863	8,727	13,489	13,059	10,126	5,160	54,321	33,328	5,315	5,656	2,789
Congressional District 3	73,011	22,752	8,802	16,138	17,914	11,628	2,707	56,669	35,101	3,427	5,808	3,414
Congressional District 4	56,710	22,277	12,887	12,549	20,073	16,578	11,257	71,352	47,422	10,497	8,553	4,523
Congressional District 5	43,688	18,968	12,166	13,822	14,066	13,924	8,965	54,313	40,993	8,900	5,831	5,580
Congressional District 6	63,521	20,069	8,794	10,561	11,168	7,969	6,812	53,211	33,954	7,874	5,199	4,235
Congressional District 7	55,972	17,868	7,966	15,605	11,465	10,832	5,100	44,806	30,552	7,577	5,457	5,629
Congressional District 8	68,410	24,306	11,296	17,310	16,922	12,652	7,814	68,131	43,845	5,414	4,958	4,392
Congressional District 9	41,654	13,785	5,673	11,690	7,934	5,594	5,696	42,760	28,123	10,664	8,597	8,495
Congressional District 10	66,543	23,866	14,614	17,104	17,848	13,339	6,686	63,846	41,757	6,711	4,840	4,661
Congressional District 11	54,402	25,481	16,494	17,320	18,394	15,747	7,250	66,583	47,455	7,503	7,536	5,665
Congressional District 12	58,413	20,314	11,400	12,442	13,818	10,992	7,110	56,845	39,760	5,997	5,288	5,764
Congressional District 13	52,736	19,388	13,681	12,106	18,170	17,872	9,334	57,922	43,317	8,658	5,991	5,419
Congressional District 14	57,363	24,091	13,985	14,972	16,762	10,597	10,536	59,976	39,651	9,085	8,057	4,841
Congressional District 15	33,386	11,190	5,270	11,646	8,425	6,497	7,275	45,899	33,265	9,351	12,885	12,999
Congressional District 16	32,582	12,592	7,059	12,278	6,742	6,023	7,446	47,142	37,909	6,500	11,887	13,464
Congressional District 17	50,958	21,817	12,635	12,826	17,588	14,332	7,704	54,597	34,601	7,592	9,245	4,932
Congressional District 18	41,346	11,199	5,681	9,783	7,601	6,327	9,006	44,367	26,308	14,324	9,159	5,942
Congressional District 19	46,805	17,730	12,434	9,911	15,421	15,453	7,292	51,549	42,438	8,133	7,032	5,119
Congressional District 20	42,952	17,643	10,644	9,394	10,110	8,625	8,750	50,409	36,295	12,109	7,812	8,229
Congressional District 21	69,396	31,553	17,626	14,728	19,803	19,062	7,927	72,828	49,301	6,609	5,029	4,365
Congressional District 22	69,741	19,483	8,124	21,439	15,077	10,137	5,049	61,329	33,787	6,317	8,244	3,917
Congressional District 23	41,867	20,087	7,877	11,940	12,165	8,853	9,629	59,663	38,036	9,549	11,763	9,035
Congressional District 24	70,189	16,668	11,058	12,395	14,282	10,776	3,333	47,927	34,302	3,383	3,746	2,700
Congressional District 25	56,691	29,352	12,887	12,501	19,588	14,812	5,974	65,957	41,330	6,350	3,936	4,454
Congressional District 26	71,736	22,331	10,636	16,375	17,143	9,319	4,531	53,356	30,134	3,535	3,920	3,089
Congressional District 27	52,954	20,891	12,365	12,323	18,263	12,614	10,000	65,807	44,956	11,891	10,957	7,700
Congressional District 28	34,380	12,237	6,414	9,779	9,447	6,894	8,775	47,558	35,155	9,588	15,714	11,729
Congressional District 29	32,967	7,089	3,480	7,163	5,059	3,554	5,681	36,258	20,107	13,453	9,829	4,567
Congressional District 30	43,185	15,325	5,324	13,032	8,357	4,992	9,986	49,768	27,924	12,030	10,608	8,273
Congressional District 31	55,771	25,959	12,649	12,098	17,237	14,453	7,336	60,786	37,019	7,207	5,659	3,742
Congressional District 32	64,412	17,561	10,831	16,161	17,381	14,356	4,842	50,973	36,886	4,551	4,432	4,262
Congressional District 33	28,498	10,351	2,753	9,816	6,913	3,928	7,797	38,988	22,000	9,981	8,449	6,942
Congressional District 34	30,608	9,281	6,903	8,786	9,871	8,018	7,843	50,956	42,938	8,599	12,973	14,480
Congressional District 35	39,161	14,148	6,220	11,238	9,637	6,373	11,899	47,309	27,888	16,718	9,158	6,347
Congressional District 36	57,251	21,429	11,664	11,392	16,372	12,650	9,942	62,956	41,220	10,023	9,007	5,257

Table I-5: 116th Congressional Districts - Persons With Health Insurance by Source of Insurance—*Continued*

	Private Health Insurance Coverage						Public Health Insurance Coverage					
	Employer Based			Direct Purchase			Medicare			Medicaid/CHIP		
	55 to 64 Years	65 to 74 Years	75 Years and Over	55 to 64 Years	65 to 74 Years	75 Years and Over	55 to 64 Years	65 to 74 Years	75 Years and Over	55 to 64 Years	65 to 74 Years	75 Years and Over
Utah												
Congressional District 1	54,013	20,223	9,649	13,250	12,988	11,434	6,207	47,218	29,724	4,991	5,387	3,098
Congressional District 2	46,614	19,941	13,022	15,140	21,915	17,520	5,796	56,756	41,748	8,511	5,218	4,713
Congressional District 3	47,324	17,761	11,308	12,755	14,631	13,265	3,699	46,521	33,434	4,388	3,038	3,638
Congressional District 4	48,776	16,563	7,746	11,475	13,356	10,792	4,509	43,720	28,614	4,551	4,483	2,955
Vermont												
Congressional District (at Large)	58,591	25,773	11,539	13,569	26,485	18,473	9,087	70,808	45,336	18,054	9,264	6,878
Virginia												
Congressional District 1	74,744	32,336	20,925	15,190	24,912	18,551	6,526	70,406	46,954	4,590	5,128	3,984
Congressional District 2	55,751	25,021	15,300	13,257	19,870	15,972	5,048	63,682	43,745	3,263	4,733	3,415
Congressional District 3	52,962	20,039	13,671	10,679	17,703	12,305	11,014	54,465	38,900	9,894	5,581	5,141
Congressional District 4	61,167	23,666	13,248	12,370	23,524	15,790	11,402	66,473	42,561	9,879	8,568	4,865
Congressional District 5	65,605	27,642	17,783	16,614	33,626	26,344	11,763	83,571	59,642	8,089	6,495	5,541
Congressional District 6	63,006	23,042	16,608	12,445	27,456	24,907	12,490	75,588	57,252	8,578	6,364	3,898
Congressional District 7	72,642	31,377	16,836	15,883	25,678	19,764	7,446	72,256	48,966	4,943	6,644	4,452
Congressional District 8	61,388	30,183	20,009	16,842	12,660	11,442	5,131	46,754	37,882	4,010	3,885	4,840
Congressional District 9	49,799	19,546	12,580	17,488	23,462	19,596	19,874	80,636	58,578	12,352	7,905	6,184
Congressional District 10	78,670	32,696	18,093	14,839	16,875	13,310	2,630	57,976	39,907	2,569	3,113	4,846
Congressional District 11	66,078	33,291	14,850	16,992	12,311	9,869	3,457	51,141	33,817	2,768	2,552	4,596
Washington												
Congressional District 1	68,854	23,116	9,007	17,404	21,157	13,173	4,214	59,544	34,738	9,829	5,250	5,308
Congressional District 2	63,193	24,431	13,777	15,590	26,756	19,541	9,585	71,425	46,719	12,988	8,343	6,457
Congressional District 3	65,244	26,050	11,865	13,696	27,631	21,087	11,381	75,544	47,296	15,855	7,943	5,951
Congressional District 4	48,251	16,950	11,521	9,283	21,864	14,436	8,661	59,409	38,445	13,771	6,208	5,982
Congressional District 5	55,991	20,064	13,295	12,615	20,091	17,628	11,082	72,060	48,685	18,185	8,877	6,269
Congressional District 6	60,737	31,529	18,008	17,267	31,963	20,967	9,272	88,295	52,313	14,999	8,686	6,656
Congressional District 7	58,850	27,648	13,803	12,233	23,823	16,125	5,480	64,757	40,607	9,354	6,326	5,523
Congressional District 8	76,032	21,073	13,475	13,324	22,532	16,218	8,120	58,734	37,951	12,572	6,379	5,219
Congressional District 9	60,115	18,120	9,138	10,672	16,980	16,165	6,788	53,709	42,420	12,912	6,590	8,582
Congressional District 10	56,805	24,182	14,730	9,954	19,465	16,636	9,429	61,748	43,492	13,220	7,368	7,029
West Virginia												
Congressional District 1	49,504	28,618	16,750	10,614	17,579	17,308	12,092	66,393	47,035	14,246	7,990	5,503
Congressional District 2	51,222	26,794	17,703	8,959	17,526	15,295	15,243	69,754	45,221	17,389	11,056	4,904
Congressional District 3	42,214	30,870	19,837	8,395	15,956	12,553	18,796	70,649	45,643	22,223	8,182	7,870
Wisconsin												
Congressional District 1	75,564	22,560	15,296	13,167	24,577	19,582	9,251	66,465	46,195	11,430	6,539	4,779
Congressional District 2	72,687	27,891	14,778	13,927	26,943	21,706	5,654	64,596	45,113	7,709	6,899	4,745
Congressional District 3	65,303	16,857	12,498	17,362	33,231	26,284	10,127	72,472	51,596	11,317	8,800	5,837
Congressional District 4	44,762	16,213	9,044	8,183	11,401	8,546	9,879	49,257	32,382	21,234	10,080	8,786
Congressional District 5	79,476	20,879	15,108	16,521	26,682	26,402	7,630	70,047	56,289	8,538	5,843	5,980
Congressional District 6	77,211	16,841	10,373	14,681	29,236	27,084	7,286	71,759	54,078	11,564	6,437	6,776
Congressional District 7	71,081	18,129	11,283	22,234	38,258	31,150	9,022	81,027	56,919	12,979	8,667	8,926
Congressional District 8	72,452	13,476	7,410	17,407	27,308	22,044	8,625	69,956	50,058	10,993	5,646	7,143
Wyoming												
Congressional District (at Large)	51,140	14,754	8,999	12,931	21,319	17,480	5,688	56,304	34,815	5,195	4,549	3,599

PART J
HOUSING SUMMARY

HOUSING SUMMARY

As the Baby Boom entered its household formation years in the late 1960s and 1970s, housing development grew to accommodate the growing adult population and their children. The Baby Boomers are now between the ages of 56 and 74 and their housing needs are changing. Senior residences take a number of forms from independent living apartments to full nursing care, often right within the same residential complex. Virtually every community has seen the development of some type of senior living arrangement. This generation grew up in an era of homeownership and many have the resources for seasonal and second homes. As they age, there will be changes in the market forces affecting housing markets both for primary residences and second homes. A challenge in the market will be location. Will the growing inventory of homes for sale be in the same locations as the demand from younger generations?

Nationwide, 78.2 percent of householders 65 and over are home owners while 21.8 percent are renters. Of home owners, 37.3 percent are still paying on a mortgage. Home ownership is highest in West Virginia where 86.3 percent are owners and 25.6 percent are still paying on a mortgage. In 45 states the percentage of home owners among householders 65 and over is greater than 75 percent. The District of Columbia has the lowest ownership rate at 58.0 percent and therefore the highest rental rate at 42.0 percent. They also have the highest percent of owners with a mortgage (49.4 percent). North Dakota has the lowest percentage of mortgage holders at 20.9 percent.

The American Community Survey also obtains data on whether meals are included in the rent for rental occupied units. This is often used as a measurement of congregate housing within the housing inventory. Renters in continuing care or life facilities are included here if their

Percent of Owner Householders 65 Years and Over Paying 35 Percent or Moreof Income on Owner Costs

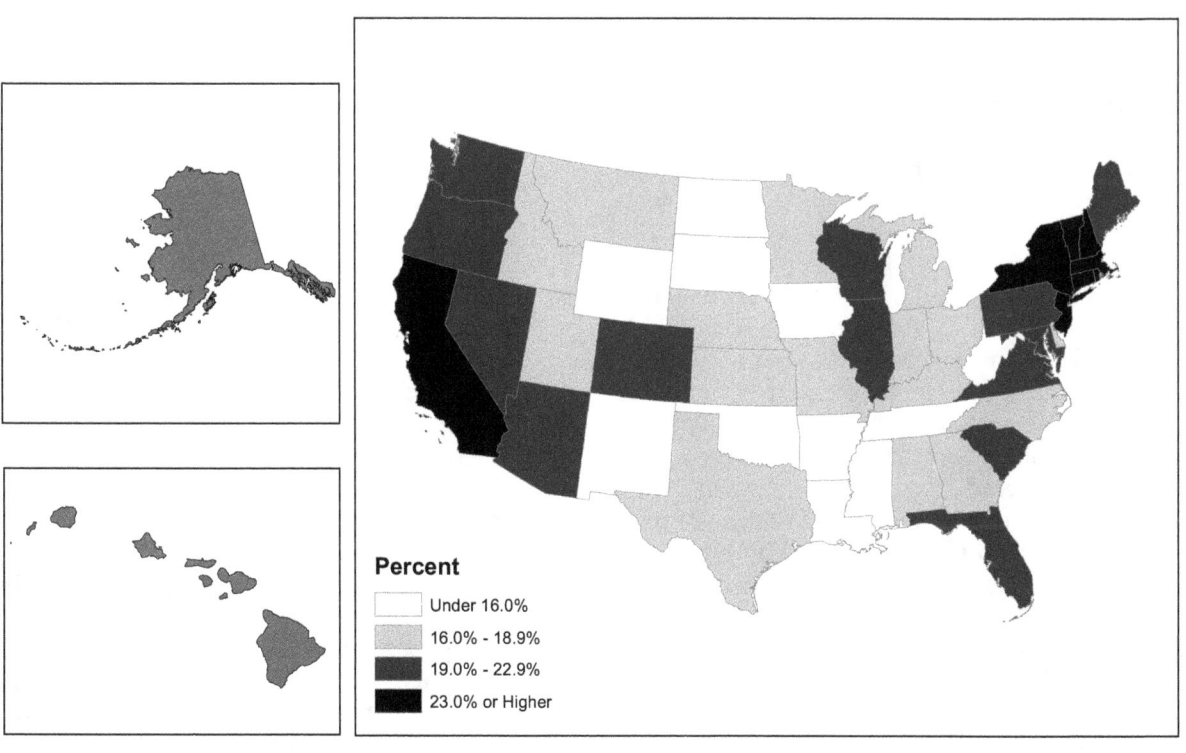

Percent

- Under 16.0%
- 16.0% - 18.9%
- 19.0% - 22.9%
- 23.0% or Higher

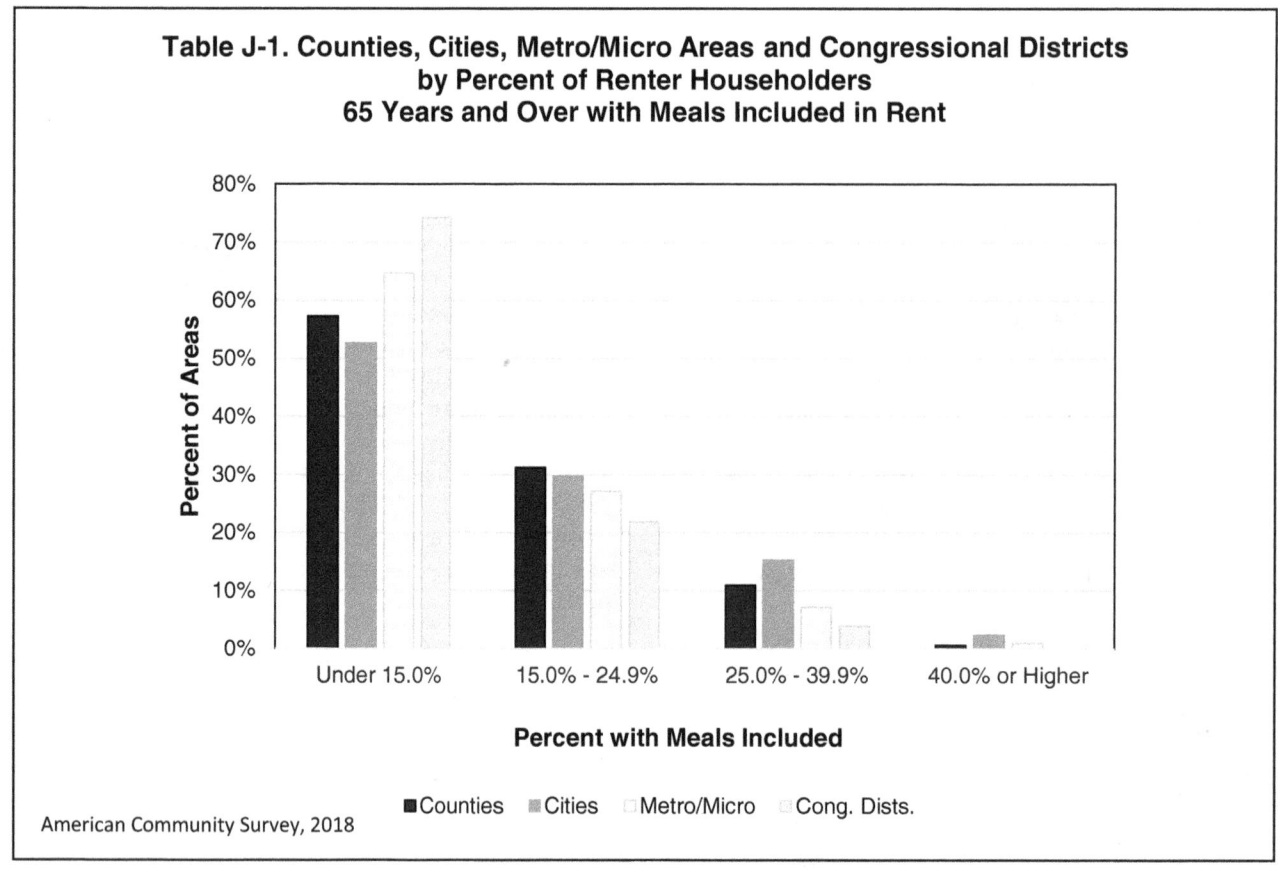

Table J-1. Counties, Cities, Metro/Micro Areas and Congressional Districts by Percent of Renter Householders 65 Years and Over with Meals Included in Rent

American Community Survey, 2018

contracts cover meal services. Nationwide, 10.7 percent of renter households have meals included in their rent. This varies from a low of 2.5 percent in Alaska to a high of 23.5 percent in Nebraska.

The nation's 2018 Consumer Expenditure Survey shows that, on average, housing accounts for about 32.8 percent of consumer units (roughly households) total expenditures and only slightly higher (33.3 percent) for households age 65 and over. Housing becomes a larger share of expenditures for the 75 and over who spend 35.7 percent[1]. The Census obtains data on owner and renter affordability of housing based on a measure of owner or renter costs as a percentage of income. When a household spends more than 35 percent of its income on housing costs it is considered a housing cost burden. Using this basis, 20.9 percent of owner householders 65 and over pay more than 35 percent on housing costs and would be considered to have a cost burden. For renters, 45.6 percent pay more than 35 percent of their income for rental costs nationwide. New Jersey has the highest

owner cost burden at 31.4 percent while California has the highest percentage of householders with renter cost burden at 51.9 percent. West Virginia ranks lowest on both owner and renter costs at 12.6 percent and 30.5 percent, respectively.

McKinley County, New Mexico shows the highest percentage of owner occupied units at 94.9 percent. At 28.6 percent, Bronx County, New York has the lowest percent of home owners among the 65 and over population. More than 85 percent of counties represented here have home ownership rates over 75 percent. Prince George's County, Maryland has the highest percentage of home owners who still have a mortgage at 63.8 percent. St. Landry Parish, Louisiana is lowest at 9.1 percent. Collier County, Florida has the highest percentage of householders 65 and over with meals included in their rent at 46.1 percent. This is often an indicator of large senior community residences. In 212 counties the percent of renters with meals included is less than 1 percent. More than 42 percent of owners in Warren County, New Jersey pay 35 percent or more of income on housing costs while Apache County, Arizona is lowest at 7.8 percent. For renters, Hunt County, Texas has the highest percentage of cost burden households

---

[1] U.S. Bureau of Labor Statistics, Consumer Expenditures, 2018, www.bls.gov/cex/2018/combined/age.xlsx

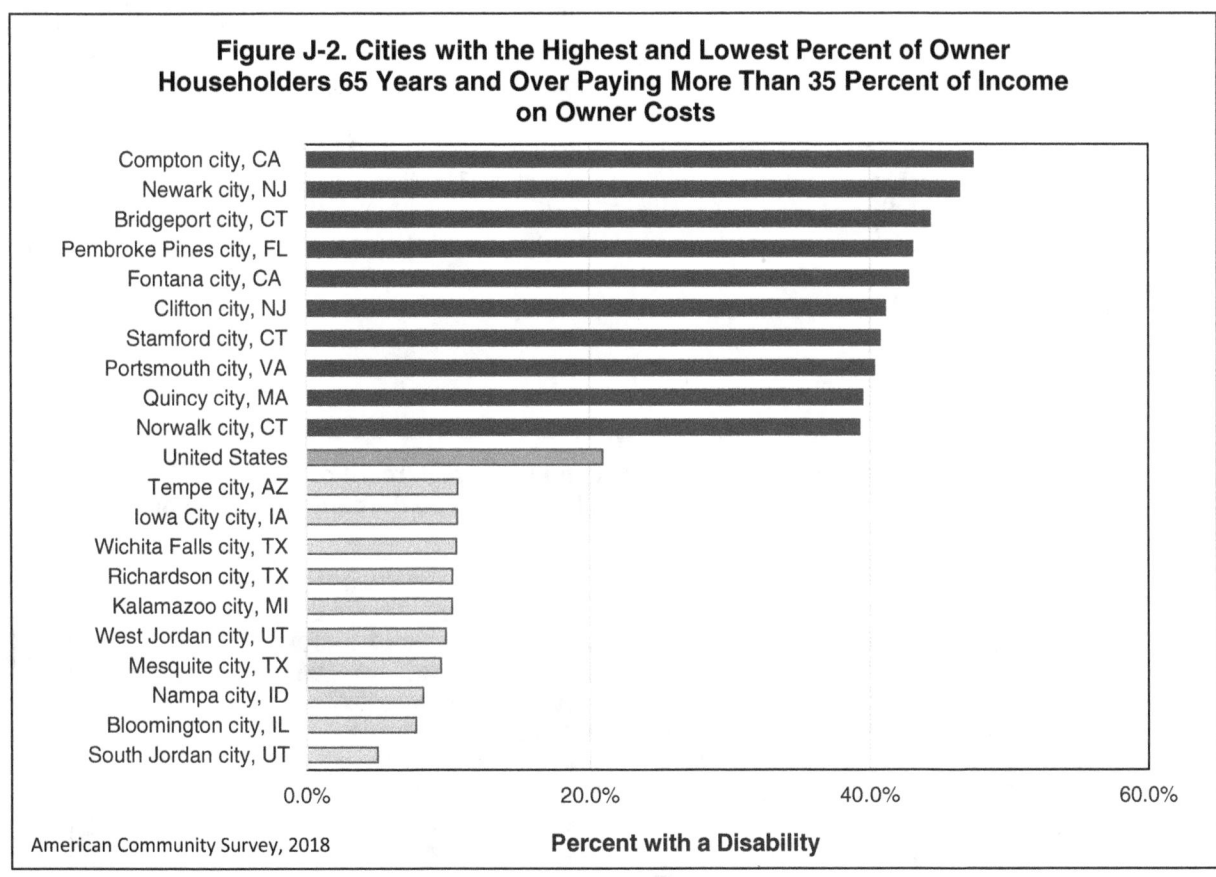

Figure J-2. Cities with the Highest and Lowest Percent of Owner Householders 65 Years and Over Paying More Than 35 Percent of Income on Owner Costs

American Community Survey, 2018

at 78.7 percent while Lauderdale County, Alabama is lowest at 9.9 percent.

Lehi, Utah is the city with the highest percentage (98.2 percent) of householders 65 and over who are home owners. At 70.3 percent, Lawrence, Massachusetts has the highest percentage of renter householders. New York City by far has the largest absolute number of renter householders with 339,858 and nearly three times the next largest (Los Angeles) at 124,631. Only 25 cities have fewer than 50 percent owner occupied householders over 65. In Lawrence, Massachusetts 73.7 percent of owner occupied households have a mortgage and in 129 cities, more than 50 percent of homeowners still pay on a mortgage. Iowa City, Iowa is the city with the highest percentage (66.8 percent) of rental households with meals included in the rent. Compton, California is the city with the highest percent (47.5 percent) of homeowners paying more than 35 percent of their incomes for housing costs. In Conroe, Texas more than 81.8 percent of rental householders pay more than 35 percent of their income on rental costs. In 61 other cities, more than 60 percent of renters fall in that rent burden category.

The range between the highest and lowest homeownership rate at the metropolitan level is less than that for counties and cities. The lowest rate is 63.2 percent found in the New York-Newark-Jersey City metropolitan area while the highest, at 94.9 percent, is in the Gallup, New Mexico micropolitan area. Seventy-seven metropolitan and micropolitan areas have ownership rates over 85 percent. In the Vallejo-Fairfield, California metropolitan area, 59.7 percent of owner householders still pay on their mortgage while only 9.1 percent still hold mortgages in the Opelousas, Louisiana micropolitan area. In the California-Lexington Park, Maryland metropolitan area, 36.9 percent of owner householders pay more than 35 percent of their incomes on housing costs. In the Tupelo, Mississippi micropolitan area only 6.9 percent have that cost burden. For renters, the Midland, Texas metro is highest at 69.3 percent and in 93 metro and micro areas, more than 50 percent of renters are burdened by rental costs.

Florida's 11th Congressional District has the highest home ownership rate at 90.4 percent among householders 65 and over though one-third (33.0 percent) are currently paying on a mortgage. In New York's 13th Congressional District renters are dominant with only 10.7 percent of older householders owning their home. Of those that do own, 30.9 percent still hold a mortgage. The homeownership rate for householders over 65 exceeds 75 percent in 330 congressional districts. In 27 districts more than 50 percent of the owner householders have a mortgage to pay and 16 of them are in California. In 42 congressional districts, more than 20 percent of all renter householders have meals included in their rent

payment. More than one quarter of all congressional districts (114) have more than 25 percent of older householders experiencing an owner cost burden in relation to their income. It's highest in New Jersey's 8th Congressional District at 44.9 and lowest in Louisiana's 3rd district at 11.7 percent. The rental cost burden is highest in the 4th Congressional District of New Jersey where nearly two-thirds (62.5 percent) of rental householders pay more than 35 percent of their income in rental costs.

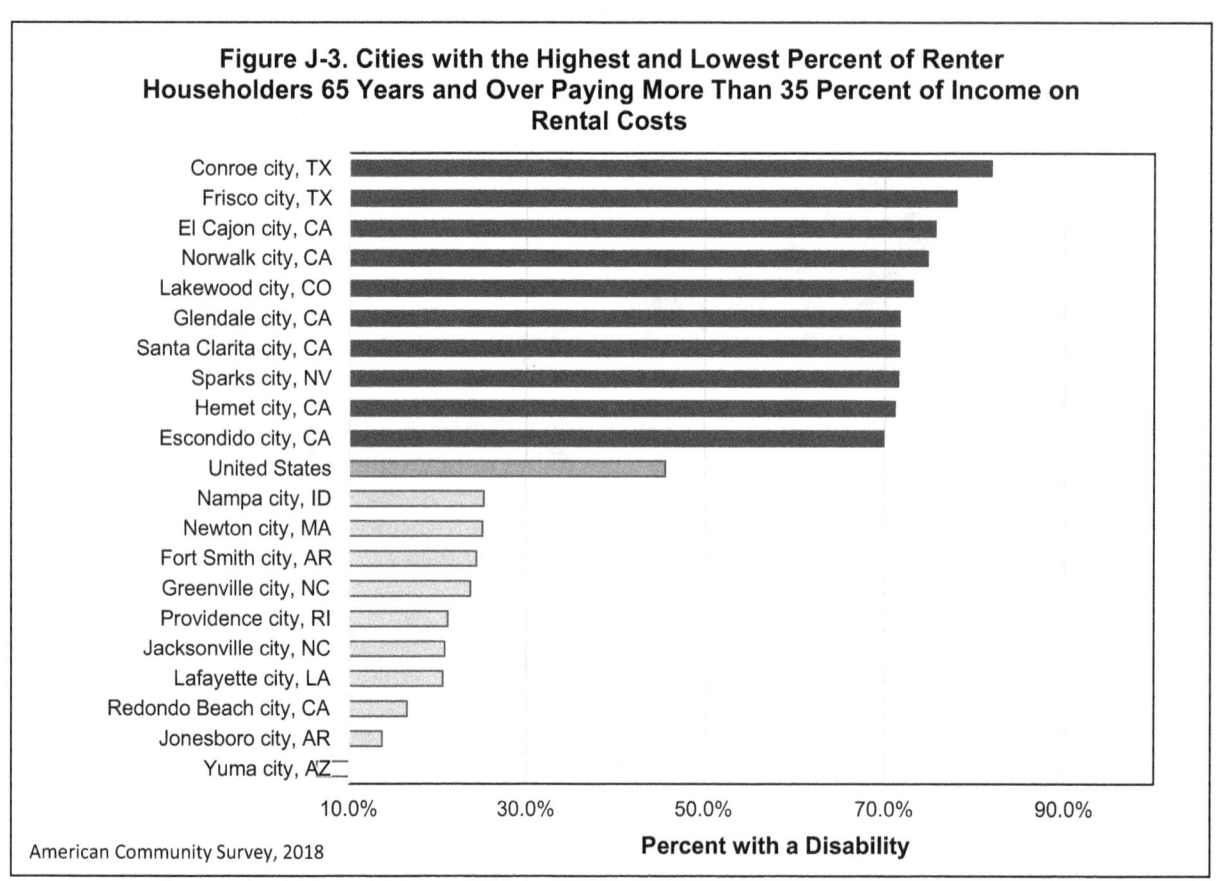

Figure J-3. Cities with the Highest and Lowest Percent of Renter Householders 65 Years and Over Paying More Than 35 Percent of Income on Rental Costs

American Community Survey, 2018

Table J-1: States - Summary of Housing and Householder Characteristics

	Total Housing Units	Total Households	Householders 65 Years and Over						
			Owner Occupied	Renter Occupied	Owner Householders		Renter Households With Meals Included in Rent	Percent of Owner Householders Who Pay 35% or More of income for Housing Costs	Percent of Renter Households Who Pay 35% or More of Income for Rental Costs
					With a Mortgage	Without a Mortgage			
United States	138,539,906	31,842,901	24,908,950	6,933,951	9,295,565	15,613,385	745,326	20.5%	44.8%
Alabama	2,274,711	523,973	433,427	90,546	142,735	290,692	6,234	71,447	31,456
Alaska	318,352	53,173	44,662	8,511	17,016	27,646	213	8,730	3,190
Arizona	3,035,902	754,387	614,755	139,632	259,593	355,162	20,332	117,381	66,165
Arkansas	1,380,521	314,838	257,980	56,858	75,160	182,820	4,814	38,406	17,582
California	14,277,867	3,197,217	2,325,138	872,079	1,124,367	1,200,771	72,278	631,536	452,201
Colorado	2,424,128	499,802	400,949	98,853	178,750	222,199	16,898	83,713	49,585
Connecticut	1,521,123	374,793	285,286	89,507	115,671	169,615	9,969	84,885	39,970
Delaware	438,659	107,758	91,333	16,425	38,917	52,416	1,532	17,114	5,945
District of Columbia	319,579	58,898	34,173	24,725	16,887	17,286	1,466	8,689	10,596
Florida	9,547,762	2,522,233	2,075,101	447,132	732,733	1,342,368	58,853	467,728	231,261
Georgia	4,326,266	886,919	713,877	173,042	292,233	421,644	15,081	135,518	76,698
Hawaii	546,261	143,128	108,774	34,354	49,412	59,362	1,875	23,506	13,206
Idaho	735,703	168,614	140,968	27,646	55,435	85,533	6,127	23,835	11,537
Illinois	5,376,176	1,242,040	977,391	264,649	347,059	630,332	33,640	224,460	119,456
Indiana	2,903,576	659,809	534,472	125,337	216,803	317,669	15,007	88,797	52,668
Iowa	1,409,568	338,159	272,492	65,667	79,272	193,220	12,792	41,710	26,407
Kansas	1,280,553	287,156	226,547	60,609	72,862	153,685	9,706	41,396	25,683
Kentucky	1,995,187	458,020	374,963	83,057	120,108	254,855	6,996	61,193	29,359
Louisiana	2,076,136	446,979	364,661	82,318	99,551	265,110	4,760	57,588	34,252
Maine	746,592	175,923	136,965	38,958	49,892	87,073	3,745	29,181	14,204
Maryland	2,458,779	558,175	440,956	117,219	207,057	233,899	14,664	96,792	51,542
Massachusetts	2,915,043	700,037	504,316	195,721	206,403	297,913	18,529	141,814	80,804
Michigan	4,614,552	1,093,561	897,905	195,656	323,531	574,374	24,870	170,074	85,817
Minnesota	2,455,637	552,433	432,298	120,135	150,676	281,622	24,158	81,328	57,977
Mississippi	1,332,631	303,363	258,693	44,670	65,172	193,521	2,830	39,069	15,532
Missouri	2,806,296	651,569	517,775	133,794	178,846	338,929	13,560	87,578	59,388
Montana	515,161	123,306	99,708	23,598	32,058	67,650	3,493	18,770	8,948
Nebraska	845,011	194,541	151,101	43,440	45,313	105,788	10,198	25,556	17,114
Nevada	1,268,717	279,933	205,623	74,310	101,244	104,379	4,863	46,795	38,339
New Hampshire............................	638,112	145,788	116,248	29,540	43,365	72,883	2,860	30,200	12,405
New Jersey	3,628,198	867,467	651,290	216,177	257,581	393,709	15,045	204,316	100,852
New Mexico	943,232	228,095	184,651	43,444	63,493	121,158	2,730	28,414	15,699
New York.....................................	8,363,847	1,972,352	1,283,046	689,306	444,219	838,827	28,453	341,365	331,779
North Carolina	4,684,962	1,044,996	850,055	194,941	332,594	517,461	20,399	158,143	82,647
North Dakota	377,661	73,062	55,235	17,827	11,530	43,705	3,049	8,344	8,316
Ohio	5,217,617	1,261,472	991,513	269,959	381,831	609,682	30,554	179,107	108,301
Oklahoma	1,743,073	389,886	316,907	72,979	90,878	226,029	8,222	46,908	27,536
Oregon	1,788,743	461,267	358,142	103,125	155,251	202,891	20,342	82,141	52,610
Pennsylvania...............................	5,713,136	1,458,606	1,132,246	326,360	371,666	760,580	41,429	234,601	140,794
Rhode Island...............................	469,153	113,963	78,721	35,242	32,632	46,089	2,947	21,093	12,547
South Carolina	2,318,291	552,651	470,185	82,466	183,406	286,779	9,715	91,829	32,942
South Dakota	397,506	91,545	71,166	20,379	17,304	53,862	3,433	9,313	7,730
Tennessee	2,992,412	681,024	559,507	121,517	182,785	376,722	12,368	85,015	47,459
Texas...	11,101,498	2,107,858	1,683,859	423,999	497,078	1,186,781	45,701	299,995	203,285
Utah	1,108,739	210,551	179,778	30,773	69,709	110,069	6,785	29,938	13,392
Vermont......................................	337,133	78,032	63,525	14,507	23,242	40,283	1,546	15,844	6,261
Virginia......................................	3,538,985	801,030	647,506	153,524	273,480	374,026	19,762	127,383	72,824
Washington.................................	3,148,084	713,855	556,154	157,701	235,442	320,712	30,151	123,981	75,221
West Virginia	893,742	231,585	199,823	31,762	51,113	148,710	1,597	25,230	9,696
Wisconsin	2,710,718	625,177	485,653	139,524	165,952	319,701	18,002	97,709	66,493
Wyoming	278,615	61,902	51,451	10,451	16,258	35,193	753	7,101	3,773

Table J-2: Counties - Summary of Housing and Householder Characteristics

					Householders 65 Years and Over				
					Owner Householders			Percent of Owner Householders Who Pay 35% or More of income for Housing Costs	Percent of Renter Households Who Pay 35% or More of Income for Rental Costs
	Total Housing Units	Total Households	Owner Occupied	Renter Occupied	With a Mortgage	Without a Mortgage	Renter Households With Meals Included in Rent		
Alabama									
Baldwin County	116,632	27,136	24,656	2,480	9,651	15,005	230	4,959	989
Calhoun County	53,888	13,456	11,525	1,931	4,481	7,044	99	2,366	893
Cullman County	38,029	9,912	8,617	1,295	2,134	6,483	na	na	na
DeKalb County	31,656	8,140	6,529	1,611	1,853	4,676	na	1,194	na
Elmore County	34,416	7,794	6,192	1,602	2,279	3,913	na	1,121	na
Etowah County	47,847	12,152	10,236	1,916	2,306	7,930	147	883	486
Houston County	47,805	11,982	9,824	2,158	3,683	6,141	34	1,679	789
Jefferson County	309,579	67,575	54,575	13,000	20,808	33,767	2,039	9,374	5,416
Lauderdale County	45,468	11,532	9,654	1,878	2,610	7,044	na	1,297	185
Lee County	70,372	11,705	9,271	2,434	4,248	5,023	na	1,513	468
Limestone County	36,535	9,407	8,512	895	3,487	5,025	na	1,427	na
Madison County	164,263	36,105	29,245	6,860	12,100	17,145	1,003	4,627	2,486
Marshall County	40,812	10,016	8,477	1,539	2,542	5,935	na	1,653	430
Mobile County	184,687	43,522	33,719	9,803	12,362	21,357	628	6,053	4,561
Montgomery County	105,170	22,480	16,772	5,708	6,244	10,528	105	2,920	2,740
Morgan County	52,284	13,592	10,807	2,785	3,618	7,189	363	1,046	1,089
St. Clair County	37,190	8,954	6,882	2,072	2,955	3,927	na	na	na
Shelby County	88,393	20,757	18,483	2,274	8,125	10,358	540	2,988	990
Talladega County	37,906	9,142	7,324	1,818	2,215	5,109	na	na	na
Tuscaloosa County	93,002	16,785	13,879	2,906	5,599	8,280	478	2,304	1,491
Walker County	31,249	7,671	6,342	1,329	1,369	4,973	na	na	na
Alaska									
Anchorage Municipality	118,233	19,776	16,708	3,068	7,279	9,429	na	3,113	1,114
Fairbanks North Star Borough	44,307	6,987	6,117	870	2,162	3,955	na	na	161
Matanuska-Susitna Borough	41,986	7,032	5,938	1,094	2,618	3,320	na	1,464	596
Arizona									
Apache County	32,942	6,942	6,219	723	718	5,501	na	481	na
Cochise County	61,318	19,349	16,205	3,144	6,251	9,954	402	2,755	1,377
Coconino County	66,838	10,903	9,217	1,686	3,312	5,905	na	1,428	592
Maricopa County	1,762,981	391,504	314,626	76,878	144,744	169,882	13,882	64,174	40,067
Mohave County	115,269	39,594	31,713	7,881	13,667	18,046	664	5,911	2,895
Navajo County	58,164	12,780	10,722	2,058	3,205	7,517	na	na	493
Pima County	462,778	126,887	99,230	27,657	39,304	59,926	4,264	16,550	12,009
Pinal County	177,186	51,749	46,752	4,997	19,966	26,786	na	8,922	2,284
Yavapai County	118,410	47,659	39,643	8,016	15,527	24,116	901	8,608	4,753
Yuma County	93,571	22,994	19,472	3,522	5,796	13,676	na	2,934	860
Arkansas									
Benton County	108,481	22,134	17,724	4,410	5,701	12,023	301	2,513	1,368
Craighead County	46,254	9,754	7,347	2,407	2,254	5,093	94	na	337
Faulkner County	50,520	9,348	7,474	1,874	2,681	4,793	156	1,310	772
Garland County	51,025	14,925	12,806	2,119	4,986	7,820	356	1,688	762
Jefferson County	33,382	7,901	6,186	1,715	1,337	4,849	na	na	na
Lonoke County	29,747	5,827	4,789	1,038	1,955	2,834	na	783	na
Pulaski County	185,967	37,415	29,739	7,676	10,816	18,923	854	4,945	2,753
Saline County	49,326	12,627	11,253	1,374	3,946	7,307	375	1,688	na
Sebastian County	57,229	13,267	10,511	2,756	2,169	8,342	133	1,309	829
Washington County	95,013	16,807	13,620	3,187	4,210	9,410	846	2,125	1,317
White County	33,954	8,138	6,401	1,737	2,328	4,073	211	na	701
California									
Alameda County	615,129	129,181	89,782	39,399	42,509	47,273	3,071	21,732	18,792
Butte County	100,038	25,859	21,044	4,815	9,311	11,733	505	5,843	2,723
Contra Costa County	415,955	102,492	82,201	20,291	42,971	39,230	3,362	20,442	11,075
El Dorado County	91,094	24,149	21,200	2,949	10,865	10,335	707	6,191	1,775
Fresno County	333,809	72,341	49,754	22,587	23,167	26,587	1,972	10,290	11,214
Humboldt County	63,308	16,123	12,213	3,910	4,784	7,429	629	2,040	2,009
Imperial County	57,893	10,251	7,230	3,021	3,151	4,079	0	1,689	1,575
Kern County	300,423	57,042	44,062	12,980	21,006	23,056	1,231	10,558	6,801
Kings County	46,649	9,949	7,594	2,355	3,065	4,529	na	1,423	983
Lake County	34,751	9,808	7,940	1,868	3,763	4,177	na	na	na
Los Angeles County	3,561,342	750,779	479,979	270,800	240,527	239,452	12,785	151,775	144,805
Madera County	50,971	11,632	10,477	1,155	4,910	5,567	0	3,510	747
Marin County	113,175	37,113	28,138	8,975	14,003	14,135	1,534	7,295	4,453
Mendocino County	40,934	12,167	9,538	2,629	3,536	6,002	103	na	1,052
Merced County	85,766	18,366	13,240	5,126	6,169	7,071	0	2,480	2,450
Monterey County	142,414	34,561	26,935	7,626	12,604	14,331	492	6,968	3,255
Napa County	55,465	15,144	11,686	3,458	5,400	6,286	518	3,092	1,812
Nevada County	54,264	16,239	13,361	2,878	5,887	7,474	246	na	864
Orange County	1,111,321	259,739	193,531	66,208	91,661	101,870	7,290	52,601	34,171
Placer County	167,122	46,330	38,196	8,134	17,974	20,222	1,436	12,264	4,604
Riverside County	848,646	189,868	152,292	37,576	74,624	77,668	2,918	45,253	21,880
Sacramento County	574,471	127,146	92,715	34,431	47,870	44,845	3,538	22,789	18,763
San Bernardino County	725,921	136,143	104,670	31,473	53,491	51,179	2,472	28,701	16,914
San Diego County	1,224,390	268,419	199,134	69,285	99,725	99,409	6,794	53,748	38,933
San Francisco County	401,478	83,021	44,329	38,692	17,814	26,515	2,545	11,372	15,403
San Joaquin County	245,561	51,357	37,218	14,139	17,528	19,690	1,475	10,272	6,743

Table J-2: Counties - Summary of Housing and Householder Characteristics—*Continued*

| | | | | Householders 65 Years and Over | | | | |
| | | | | Owner Householders | | | Percent of Owner Householders Who Pay 35% or More of income for Housing Costs | Percent of Renter Households Who Pay 35% or More of Income for Rental Costs |
	Total Housing Units	Total Households	Owner Occupied	Renter Occupied	With a Mortgage	Without a Mortgage	Renter Households With Meals Included in Rent		
California—Cont.									
San Luis Obispo County	122,971	35,948	28,866	7,082	14,478	14,388	303	7,640	2,533
San Mateo County	279,468	68,731	52,765	15,966	25,058	27,707	2,152	13,739	8,758
Santa Barbara County	158,315	41,277	31,958	9,319	13,758	18,200	1,868	6,619	4,410
Santa Clara County	678,530	138,818	102,184	36,634	45,152	57,032	4,799	25,846	18,366
Santa Cruz County	106,718	27,799	21,393	6,406	10,769	10,624	678	5,166	3,471
Shasta County	79,187	22,428	18,490	3,938	9,265	9,225	329	3,924	1,794
Solano County	158,815	38,327	29,649	8,678	17,698	11,951	1,090	7,278	4,370
Sonoma County	205,247	62,227	46,757	15,470	21,964	24,793	1,361	12,412	9,173
Stanislaus County	182,305	41,197	31,490	9,707	14,617	16,873	678	7,885	4,525
Sutter County	34,475	8,546	6,523	2,023	2,355	4,168	89	1,366	806
Tulare County	150,217	29,774	22,877	6,897	9,525	13,352	507	5,725	2,900
Ventura County	290,984	76,222	60,244	15,978	31,187	29,057	1,829	16,187	8,655
Yolo County	78,527	15,948	11,152	4,796	4,345	6,807	640	1,794	2,054
Yuba County	28,688	6,622	5,416	1,206	2,242	3,174	na	1,237	na
Colorado									
Adams County	175,623	31,537	25,286	6,251	11,605	13,681	935	5,751	3,328
Arapahoe County	254,250	52,237	39,203	13,034	19,510	19,693	2,069	8,995	6,449
Boulder County	137,465	29,132	23,622	5,510	10,853	12,769	1,385	4,591	3,163
Broomfield County	28,935	5,908	5,033	875	2,469	2,564	245	na	408
Denver County	330,884	56,532	39,247	17,285	17,072	22,175	2,319	8,750	8,471
Douglas County	128,744	24,015	20,843	3,172	11,458	9,385	1,134	4,868	1,401
El Paso County	275,393	54,936	44,701	10,235	21,046	23,655	1,553	8,547	5,687
Jefferson County	243,016	60,542	48,744	11,798	22,572	26,172	2,645	8,158	7,004
Larimer County	151,840	33,694	27,202	6,492	11,312	15,890	1,940	5,534	3,800
Mesa County	67,215	18,280	14,960	3,320	6,840	8,120	441	3,705	1,771
Pueblo County	71,451	19,899	15,707	4,192	5,809	9,898	638	3,316	1,990
Weld County	112,472	22,416	18,579	3,837	8,806	9,773	220	4,454	1,349
Connecticut									
Fairfield County	374,480	92,257	69,936	22,321	30,997	38,939	3,264	24,285	10,908
Hartford County	380,441	93,454	69,364	24,090	27,584	41,780	2,643	19,372	10,765
Litchfield County	88,402	23,504	20,025	3,479	6,842	13,183	174	5,104	1,323
Middlesex County	76,547	19,247	15,451	3,796	6,656	8,795	599	3,841	1,973
New Haven County	367,766	90,805	66,949	23,856	26,639	40,310	2,497	21,525	10,168
New London County	123,618	29,852	22,885	6,967	9,121	13,764	488	5,543	2,557
Tolland County	60,041	14,669	12,242	2,427	4,383	7,859	na	3,231	1,160
Windham County	49,828	11,005	8,434	2,571	3,449	4,985	304	1,984	1,116
Delaware									
Kent County	73,086	17,737	14,732	3,005	6,205	8,527	na	2,307	576
New Castle County	224,481	52,290	42,815	9,475	18,598	24,217	1,229	7,758	4,017
Sussex County	141,092	37,731	33,786	3,945	14,114	19,672	117	7,049	1,352
Florida									
Alachua County	118,966	22,273	18,184	4,089	5,260	12,924	1,089	2,995	2,191
Bay County	104,325	19,306	16,700	2,606	5,804	10,896	na	3,675	1,238
Brevard County	280,390	84,167	71,016	13,151	26,752	44,264	1,567	14,885	6,863
Broward County	826,949	186,926	149,264	37,662	54,480	94,784	5,147	47,095	21,309
Charlotte County	105,164	42,134	38,501	3,633	10,381	28,120	700	7,222	na
Citrus County	79,988	33,165	30,551	2,614	9,115	21,436	401	4,695	na
Clay County	81,807	19,867	16,872	2,995	7,956	8,916	245	2,211	1,845
Collier County	218,279	68,705	59,071	9,634	19,536	39,535	4,439	13,260	5,370
Columbia County	29,082	7,568	6,833	735	2,598	4,235	na	na	na
Duval County	412,591	82,536	61,348	21,188	27,248	34,100	2,199	12,332	10,340
Escambia County	142,454	33,082	25,925	7,157	8,574	17,351	601	4,225	2,656
Flagler County	52,534	19,787	17,742	2,045	7,818	9,924	111	3,068	na
Hernando County	87,534	32,130	27,071	5,059	9,575	17,496	805	4,809	2,175
Highlands County	55,760	21,675	19,579	2,096	5,184	14,395	na	2,581	na
Hillsborough County	590,847	120,806	93,212	27,594	36,603	56,609	4,466	20,328	14,915
Indian River County	81,037	27,705	24,332	3,373	7,546	16,786	247	na	na
Lake County	160,472	55,463	48,484	6,979	16,639	31,845	897	8,768	2,654
Lee County	399,741	121,190	102,843	18,347	35,043	67,800	3,836	23,589	9,818
Leon County	131,203	24,514	20,116	4,398	8,404	11,712	345	4,221	1,838
Manatee County	194,567	64,211	54,948	9,263	19,056	35,892	1,694	10,817	4,364
Marion County	170,513	62,379	55,809	6,570	19,604	36,205	483	9,686	3,264
Martin County	80,394	30,294	26,103	4,191	7,343	18,760	877	5,890	2,433
Miami-Dade County	1,032,000	223,196	149,423	73,773	55,949	93,474	1,520	48,843	38,584
Monroe County	53,457	9,842	8,546	1,296	2,767	5,779	na	na	na
Nassau County	39,981	10,932	9,654	1,278	3,501	6,153	148	na	462
Okaloosa County	97,971	20,687	16,085	4,602	6,121	9,964	276	2,818	2,132
Orange County	544,460	86,430	65,299	21,131	30,078	35,221	1,376	18,942	10,818
Osceola County	153,495	22,387	18,074	4,313	7,466	10,608	183	4,401	2,237
Palm Beach County	689,961	213,876	180,496	33,380	62,073	118,423	7,246	49,893	19,138
Pasco County	246,946	72,140	62,065	10,075	19,349	42,716	624	11,018	4,498
Pinellas County	510,120	150,207	119,004	31,203	37,541	81,463	6,339	28,530	15,849
Polk County	299,432	84,267	71,116	13,151	22,840	48,276	1,335	14,585	6,815

Table J-2: Counties - Summary of Housing and Householder Characteristics—*Continued*

				Householders 65 Years and Over					
					Owner Householders		Renter Households With Meals Included in Rent	Percent of Owner Householders Who Pay 35% or More of income for Housing Costs	Percent of Renter Households Who Pay 35% or More of Income for Rental Costs
	Total Housing Units	Total Households	Owner Occupied	Renter Occupied	With a Mortgage	Without a Mortgage			
Florida—Cont.									
Putnam County	37,374	10,815	9,396	1,419	2,758	6,638	na	na	na
St. Johns County	110,837	30,553	27,305	3,248	12,571	14,734	748	6,165	1,972
St. Lucie County	142,774	44,264	38,948	5,316	14,304	24,644	1,404	9,579	3,309
Santa Rosa County	73,056	15,555	13,852	1,703	5,113	8,739	na	2,080	na
Sarasota County	244,020	95,330	81,039	14,291	25,082	55,957	3,515	15,914	7,795
Seminole County	192,255	42,666	34,787	7,879	16,507	18,280	1,194	7,382	4,057
Sumter County	72,372	44,756	40,865	3,891	13,254	27,611	759	na	na
Volusia County	262,107	78,826	67,583	11,243	25,211	42,372	1,694	13,280	6,886
Walton County	53,376	8,972	8,163	809	3,105	5,058	na	1,255	na
Georgia									
Barrow County	28,952	6,000	5,048	952	2,717	2,331	na	na	na
Bartow County	41,529	7,726	5,814	1,912	2,089	3,725	na	na	na
Bibb County	70,058	15,152	10,695	4,457	4,160	6,535	930	2,191	1,948
Bulloch County	31,413	5,700	4,684	1,016	1,380	3,304	na	na	478
Carroll County	45,537	9,980	7,908	2,072	2,572	5,336	na	1,626	na
Catoosa County	27,528	7,493	6,932	561	2,794	4,138	na	na	na
Chatham County	125,687	27,712	22,604	5,108	9,286	13,318	372	3,829	2,104
Cherokee County	94,241	20,674	16,901	3,773	8,620	8,281	718	2,949	2,000
Clarke County	53,144	9,394	7,304	2,090	2,579	4,725	226	1,017	778
Clayton County	105,874	15,984	11,533	4,451	6,844	4,689	333	2,475	2,205
Cobb County	302,644	54,626	45,799	8,827	21,626	24,173	1,244	6,570	4,603
Columbia County	58,740	11,988	11,103	885	4,817	6,286	na	1,876	na
Coweta County	55,387	12,305	9,931	2,374	5,176	4,755	na	1,952	na
DeKalb County	314,314	57,625	44,313	13,312	23,161	21,152	1,115	8,768	6,522
Dougherty County	40,590	8,530	5,663	2,867	2,501	3,162	0	na	1,405
Douglas County	53,044	9,366	8,108	1,258	4,266	3,842	na	na	702
Fayette County	43,032	12,900	11,404	1,496	5,465	5,939	167	2,347	na
Floyd County	40,639	10,194	7,772	2,422	2,932	4,840	261	na	663
Forsyth County	84,113	15,347	13,292	2,055	7,226	6,066	227	2,334	1,043
Fulton County	480,354	80,507	53,065	27,442	28,311	24,754	4,278	12,742	12,741
Glynn County	43,518	10,819	8,837	1,982	3,698	5,139	225	na	na
Gwinnett County	312,905	48,689	41,356	7,333	20,160	21,196	1,024	9,489	3,526
Hall County	74,431	16,870	14,647	2,223	6,319	8,328	243	3,276	801
Henry County	82,826	14,756	12,257	2,499	5,875	6,382	na	1,890	1,454
Houston County	63,959	10,875	7,865	3,010	2,970	4,895	na	1,093	875
Jackson County	26,070	5,719	4,705	1,014	2,039	2,666	na	737	na
Lowndes County	48,525	9,605	8,010	1,595	3,665	4,345	na	2,534	435
Muscogee County	85,041	17,648	13,164	4,484	5,389	7,775	491	2,431	1,672
Newton County	39,691	8,151	6,775	1,376	3,547	3,228	na	1,269	na
Paulding County	58,043	9,480	7,691	1,789	4,201	3,490	na	1,702	na
Richmond County	89,098	19,335	14,534	4,801	6,341	8,193	102	3,917	2,595
Rockdale County	33,852	7,593	6,331	1,262	2,405	3,926	na	na	na
Spalding County	27,580	7,333	5,875	1,458	2,742	3,133	na	na	na
Troup County	28,636	6,585	5,165	1,420	1,945	3,220	162	na	na
Walker County	30,460	8,551	6,980	1,571	2,036	4,944	na	na	na
Walton County	34,263	8,386	6,865	1,521	2,553	4,312	na	na	na
Whitfield County	40,145	9,248	7,285	1,963	1,476	5,809	na	na	na
Hawaii									
Hawaii County	88,548	25,848	21,257	4,591	8,434	12,823	139	5,181	1,491
Honolulu County	352,582	91,320	67,675	23,645	31,534	36,141	1,512	13,134	9,727
Kauai County	31,242	9,017	6,589	2,428	2,791	3,798	na	na	886
Maui County	73,786	16,935	13,253	3,682	6,653	6,600	na	3,437	1,094
Idaho									
Ada County	186,486	40,387	32,827	7,560	14,703	18,124	1,864	6,425	3,049
Bannock County	34,441	7,726	6,529	1,197	1,849	4,680	493	823	722
Bonneville County	43,773	9,539	7,477	2,062	2,984	4,493	777	1,585	1,106
Canyon County	77,888	19,229	16,250	2,979	7,310	8,940	379	2,161	818
Kootenai County	72,500	19,738	15,983	3,755	6,734	9,249	885	3,481	2,230
Twin Falls County	33,711	7,820	6,652	1,168	2,783	3,869	351	964	na
Illinois									
Adams County	30,269	8,147	5,978	2,169	1,732	4,246	274	999	984
Champaign County	93,407	16,434	13,137	3,297	4,611	8,526	720	1,945	1,399
Cook County	2,200,296	480,363	349,251	131,112	135,918	213,333	11,271	105,365	66,634
DeKalb County	41,250	8,121	6,441	1,680	2,199	4,242	279	1,272	746
DuPage County	361,414	85,766	71,785	13,981	28,384	43,401	3,364	17,743	6,380
Kane County	189,475	43,059	36,243	6,816	15,075	21,168	953	10,434	3,483
Kankakee County	45,644	10,631	8,418	2,213	2,924	5,494	485	2,545	930
Kendall County	42,209	8,356	7,484	872	3,384	4,100	na	2,429	na
Lake County	265,149	60,453	50,392	10,061	20,969	29,423	2,518	14,022	4,646
LaSalle County	50,149	13,647	11,060	2,587	3,509	7,551	305	1,756	810
McHenry County	118,810	26,901	22,983	3,918	9,680	13,303	775	5,796	2,188
McLean County	72,676	14,126	11,766	2,360	4,284	7,482	244	1,393	844
Macon County	50,405	13,096	10,437	2,659	3,092	7,345	456	1,276	1,084
Madison County	119,625	29,762	24,147	5,615	8,484	15,663	738	3,748	1,727

Table J-2: Counties - Summary of Housing and Householder Characteristics—*Continued*

				Householders 65 Years and Over				
				Owner Householders			Percent of Owner Householders Who Pay 35% or More of income for Housing Costs	Percent of Renter Households Who Pay 35% or More of Income for Rental Costs
	Total Housing Units	Total Households	Owner Occupied	Renter Occupied	With a Mortgage	Without a Mortgage	Renter Households With Meals Included in Rent		
Illinois—Cont.									
Peoria County	83,650	17,416	13,857	3,559	4,493	9,364	517	2,124	1,349
Rock Island County	66,180	17,298	14,249	3,049	4,584	9,665	436	2,273	761
St. Clair County	120,612	26,546	20,159	6,387	6,996	13,163	833	3,308	2,385
Sangamon County	91,928	22,318	18,650	3,668	5,900	12,750	550	2,231	1,725
Tazewell County	59,053	15,919	13,020	2,899	4,253	8,767	874	1,864	1,150
Vermilion County	36,125	9,996	8,082	1,914	2,123	5,959	na	1,085	678
Will County	245,197	51,204	44,713	6,491	18,573	26,140	1,103	10,628	2,305
Williamson County	31,375	8,284	6,199	2,085	1,821	4,378	197	1,346	897
Winnebago County	125,731	31,273	24,653	6,620	10,189	14,464	1,339	5,053	2,600
Indiana									
Allen County	159,269	35,683	29,142	6,541	12,013	17,129	770	4,966	3,201
Bartholomew County	34,532	8,957	7,194	1,763	2,858	4,336	na	na	na
Boone County	27,548	5,352	3,868	1,484	1,546	2,322	na	na	na
Clark County	51,096	11,810	9,035	2,775	3,778	5,257	661	1,589	1,396
Delaware County	52,731	12,849	10,730	2,119	4,353	6,377	459	1,662	864
Elkhart County	79,495	17,003	14,021	2,982	6,178	7,843	460	2,442	1,251
Floyd County	33,022	6,881	6,087	794	2,783	3,304	na	748	294
Grant County	30,494	8,420	6,998	1,422	2,312	4,686	na	na	na
Hamilton County	129,530	24,184	19,021	5,163	10,370	8,651	1,307	3,898	2,644
Hancock County	30,586	8,585	6,679	1,906	2,798	3,881	383	1,331	na
Hendricks County	63,172	12,843	10,572	2,271	5,363	5,209	692	1,328	1,106
Howard County	39,559	10,516	8,778	1,738	3,862	4,916	351	na	718
Johnson County	61,792	13,691	10,979	2,712	5,453	5,526	293	2,032	1,185
Kosciusko County	38,744	8,548	7,625	923	2,277	5,348	na	934	402
Lake County	213,773	52,044	42,324	9,720	15,176	27,148	845	7,146	4,487
LaPorte County	49,209	13,199	11,096	2,103	4,435	6,661	490	1,782	665
Madison County	59,141	14,595	11,895	2,700	4,985	6,910	359	1,741	1,043
Marion County	424,396	76,295	56,145	20,150	29,021	27,124	1,917	12,238	8,707
Monroe County	62,067	12,536	10,171	2,365	4,540	5,631	518	1,528	963
Morgan County	28,476	7,099	6,226	873	3,530	2,696	na	na	na
Porter County	69,387	16,756	14,515	2,241	5,737	8,778	214	2,220	1,206
St. Joseph County	117,089	27,801	21,940	5,861	8,643	13,297	802	4,417	2,382
Tippecanoe County	76,740	13,694	10,424	3,270	4,173	6,251	491	1,256	1,018
Vanderburgh County	84,494	18,773	14,970	3,803	5,332	9,638	524	2,764	1,811
Vigo County	47,525	9,677	7,770	1,907	3,198	4,572	na	972	783
Wayne County	31,442	8,133	5,889	2,244	2,551	3,338	na	na	592
Iowa									
Black Hawk County	58,321	13,831	11,518	2,313	3,423	8,095	823	1,489	1,216
Dallas County	38,276	6,967	5,456	1,511	2,079	3,377	151	1,062	883
Dubuque County	41,514	10,313	7,937	2,376	2,323	5,614	881	1,513	739
Johnson County	65,024	10,996	8,941	2,055	3,544	5,397	677	1,185	841
Linn County	98,067	23,528	19,301	4,227	6,666	12,635	777	3,303	1,750
Polk County	204,626	39,485	30,586	8,899	12,822	17,764	1,467	5,516	3,687
Pottawattamie County	40,007	10,494	7,859	2,635	2,597	5,262	549	1,164	1,278
Scott County	74,655	16,858	13,292	3,566	4,645	8,647	892	1,932	2,022
Story County	40,766	7,369	6,255	1,114	1,304	4,951	289	815	356
Woodbury County	42,434	10,023	7,409	2,614	1,483	5,926	861	628	1,343
Kansas									
Butler County	27,082	6,401	5,122	1,279	1,483	3,639	360	1,017	na
Douglas County	51,068	9,782	8,062	1,720	3,617	4,445	526	2,036	1,126
Johnson County	244,476	52,962	41,289	11,673	19,066	22,223	2,986	8,844	5,319
Leavenworth County	29,998	7,105	5,147	1,958	2,225	2,922	233	824	na
Riley County	31,340	4,379	3,562	817	1,482	2,080	na	na	151
Sedgwick County	220,923	47,194	35,968	11,226	13,077	22,891	1,908	6,246	5,559
Shawnee County	80,187	20,366	15,343	5,023	5,733	9,610	969	2,992	2,752
Wyandotte County	68,301	12,679	9,710	2,969	3,629	6,081	71	2,019	1,404
Kentucky									
Boone County	50,035	10,925	8,628	2,297	4,262	4,366	382	1,182	na
Bullitt County	31,948	7,742	7,137	605	2,562	4,575	na	1,512	na
Campbell County	40,545	9,207	7,322	1,885	2,428	4,894	na	1,587	870
Christian County	30,004	5,652	4,313	1,339	1,631	2,682	na	na	333
Daviess County	43,375	11,193	8,483	2,710	3,273	5,210	134	1,055	1,142
Fayette County	142,688	26,964	21,157	5,807	8,758	12,399	817	3,532	1,941
Hardin County	47,058	9,928	8,989	939	3,198	5,791	na	na	276
Jefferson County	347,119	79,978	62,127	17,851	24,547	37,580	2,637	11,243	7,998
Kenton County	69,858	14,963	11,910	3,053	5,362	6,548	831	1,914	1,445
McCracken County	32,270	8,624	6,666	1,958	1,608	5,058	279	na	1,097
Madison County	37,060	7,772	5,611	2,161	1,955	3,656	na	na	811
Oldham County	22,293	4,507	4,234	273	1,750	2,484	na	943	na
Warren County	53,976	10,751	8,331	2,420	3,414	4,917	na	na	923
Louisiana									
Ascension Parish	48,685	8,396	7,246	1,150	2,287	4,959	na	957	na
Bossier Parish	57,836	11,700	9,877	1,823	3,561	6,316	na	1,070	736

Table J-2: Counties - Summary of Housing and Householder Characteristics—*Continued*

	Total Housing Units	Householders 65 Years and Over							
		Total Households	Owner Occupied	Renter Occupied	Owner Householders		Renter Households With Meals Included in Rent	Percent of Owner Householders Who Pay 35% or More of income for Housing Costs	Percent of Renter Households Who Pay 35% or More of Income for Rental Costs
					With a Mortgage	Without a Mortgage			
Louisiana—Cont.									
Caddo Parish	113,387	26,450	20,476	5,974	6,514	13,962	883	3,358	3,422
Calcasieu Parish	92,041	20,476	17,818	2,658	4,807	13,011	595	1,633	1,420
East Baton Rouge Parish	195,199	38,674	32,197	6,477	11,490	20,707	780	4,586	3,367
Iberia Parish	30,735	7,137	5,541	1,596	843	4,698	na	na	na
Jefferson Parish	188,663	45,851	36,789	9,062	10,451	26,338	299	5,895	4,998
Lafayette Parish	104,041	19,755	16,739	3,016	5,094	11,645	na	2,803	682
Lafourche Parish	41,623	9,583	7,776	1,807	1,527	6,249	175	936	na
Livingston Parish	58,285	9,735	8,080	1,655	2,442	5,638	na	964	na
Orleans Parish	191,620	35,584	24,414	11,170	7,365	17,049	757	8,741	4,849
Ouachita Parish	69,035	13,610	11,021	2,589	3,290	7,731	na	1,806	1,298
Rapides Parish	58,400	13,287	10,291	2,996	2,724	7,567	128	1,455	1,337
St. Landry Parish	36,932	8,223	6,838	1,385	623	6,215	na	993	332
St. Tammany Parish	104,838	26,871	23,006	3,865	8,315	14,691	306	4,490	1,898
Tangipahoa Parish	56,367	11,765	10,098	1,667	3,752	6,346	na	2,037	811
Terrebonne Parish	45,709	10,103	8,612	1,491	2,422	6,190	na	1,597	na
Maine									
Androscoggin County	50,052	12,277	8,865	3,412	2,915	5,950	343	2,207	1,461
Aroostook County	39,986	10,076	6,910	3,166	1,791	5,119	22	1,488	1,105
Cumberland County	145,725	34,701	25,892	8,809	11,060	14,832	1,127	5,678	2,494
Kennebec County	62,913	16,362	12,563	3,799	4,486	8,077	135	2,046	1,468
Penobscot County	76,144	17,420	13,279	4,141	4,032	9,247	481	2,449	1,439
York County	111,043	27,343	21,137	6,206	8,274	12,863	758	5,226	2,906
Maryland									
Allegany County	32,830	9,052	7,474	1,578	2,450	5,024	na	na	559
Anne Arundel County	226,432	51,838	45,341	6,497	22,614	22,727	729	9,529	2,623
Baltimore County	337,245	86,617	64,900	21,717	27,104	37,796	4,812	13,302	11,048
Calvert County	35,420	7,043	6,186	857	2,877	3,309	251	1,232	na
Carroll County	63,725	16,008	13,604	2,404	5,645	7,959	799	2,693	1,223
Cecil County	42,674	9,943	8,486	1,457	3,667	4,819	na	1,436	na
Charles County	61,244	10,869	9,034	1,835	4,791	4,243	298	1,576	991
Frederick County	99,032	22,623	17,784	4,839	8,260	9,524	826	3,559	2,172
Harford County	100,963	25,045	21,361	3,684	8,667	12,694	470	4,413	1,331
Howard County	120,822	25,500	20,436	5,064	8,455	11,981	1,148	3,778	2,388
Montgomery County	390,673	91,392	71,948	19,444	33,485	38,463	3,434	15,141	8,805
Prince George's County	333,858	70,471	57,756	12,715	36,828	20,928	686	15,043	5,929
St. Mary's County	45,998	9,007	7,196	1,811	3,810	3,386	na	2,654	na
Washington County	61,621	15,971	12,524	3,447	5,662	6,862	143	1,985	1,034
Wicomico County	42,469	10,517	7,208	3,309	2,337	4,871	295	na	1,158
Massachusetts									
Barnstable County	164,329	39,226	34,820	4,406	15,375	19,445	556	10,193	1,933
Berkshire County	69,393	18,271	14,706	3,565	5,178	9,528	593	3,841	1,091
Bristol County	236,308	59,402	41,508	17,894	15,148	26,360	784	9,406	7,776
Essex County	313,969	80,745	58,031	22,714	25,913	32,118	2,671	16,851	10,765
Franklin County	34,164	9,784	7,892	1,892	3,102	4,790	122	1,759	690
Hampden County	193,880	49,293	35,565	13,728	12,808	22,757	1,389	8,113	5,440
Hampshire County	64,058	17,362	13,714	3,648	4,876	8,838	514	2,421	1,661
Middlesex County	641,484	152,626	111,813	40,813	45,251	66,562	4,781	33,915	17,703
Norfolk County	280,289	73,338	52,160	21,178	20,126	32,034	2,949	14,669	8,037
Plymouth County	208,087	56,023	45,779	10,244	20,467	25,312	1,004	13,394	4,240
Suffolk County	342,069	62,805	29,597	33,208	15,125	14,472	1,276	9,849	12,495
Worcester County	336,474	77,110	55,014	22,096	21,718	33,296	1,789	16,053	8,876
Michigan									
Allegan County	51,517	11,325	10,104	1,221	3,812	6,292	na	2,392	372
Bay County	48,345	13,107	11,279	1,828	3,304	7,975	228	1,858	695
Berrien County	77,645	19,901	16,857	3,044	6,334	10,523	na	3,485	1,204
Calhoun County	60,879	15,477	12,391	3,086	4,503	7,888	428	2,272	921
Clinton County	31,967	8,604	7,751	853	2,768	4,983	na	1,201	142
Eaton County	47,669	12,391	10,931	1,460	4,563	6,368	148	1,271	470
Genesee County	192,614	47,441	38,514	8,927	14,451	24,063	973	7,476	3,921
Grand Traverse County	44,513	11,527	9,342	2,185	3,608	5,734	614	1,395	na
Ingham County	124,135	25,597	19,075	6,522	7,713	11,362	1,052	3,239	3,319
Isabella County	29,272	5,749	4,961	788	1,538	3,423	57	767	230
Jackson County	69,696	17,558	14,140	3,418	4,582	9,558	848	1,991	1,513
Kalamazoo County	112,806	25,026	19,357	5,669	6,814	12,543	648	3,486	2,307
Kent County	257,399	56,530	44,280	12,250	16,318	27,962	2,386	8,248	5,516
Lapeer County	36,804	10,168	9,244	924	3,304	5,940	49	1,716	na
Lenawee County	43,877	11,422	9,708	1,714	4,151	5,557	314	1,997	854
Livingston County	77,018	20,572	17,932	2,640	8,129	9,803	774	3,628	1,391
Macomb County	367,934	93,956	76,530	17,426	28,487	48,043	2,239	16,150	7,817
Marquette County	34,937	8,026	6,084	1,942	1,626	4,458	193	na	803
Midland County	37,115	9,892	8,184	1,708	2,516	5,668	202	1,433	498
Monroe County	64,803	18,137	14,694	3,443	5,761	8,933	na	2,403	2,251

Table J-2: Counties - Summary of Housing and Householder Characteristics—*Continued*

					Householders 65 Years and Over				
					Owner Householders				
	Total Housing Units	Total Households	Owner Occupied	Renter Occupied	With a Mortgage	Without a Mortgage	Renter Households With Meals Included in Rent	Percent of Owner Householders Who Pay 35% or More of income for Housing Costs	Percent of Renter Households Who Pay 35% or More of Income for Rental Costs
Michigan—Cont.									
Muskegon County	74,301	18,617	15,648	2,969	5,262	10,386	386	1,958	1,332
Oakland County	542,836	133,560	105,934	27,626	47,110	58,824	5,321	23,241	14,031
Ottawa County	110,839	26,813	24,118	2,695	8,638	15,480	758	4,868	1,545
Saginaw County	87,810	23,894	19,822	4,072	5,768	14,054	805	2,968	2,347
St. Clair County	72,380	18,670	16,053	2,617	5,414	10,639	445	2,566	1,221
Shiawassee County	30,272	7,895	6,415	1,480	1,944	4,471	na	960	572
Van Buren County	37,379	8,273	6,829	1,444	2,577	4,252	na	na	na
Washtenaw County	151,576	32,797	27,779	5,018	11,711	16,068	947	5,657	2,262
Wayne County	815,884	179,772	138,339	41,433	44,685	93,654	3,233	31,147	17,519
Minnesota									
Anoka County	133,184	29,075	24,399	4,676	10,587	13,812	656	4,067	2,663
Blue Earth County	28,815	5,618	4,848	770	1,133	3,715	214	664	427
Carver County	38,848	7,658	6,399	1,259	2,175	4,224	na	1,931	505
Dakota County	168,122	36,874	29,324	7,550	12,608	16,716	2,093	6,255	4,073
Hennepin County	537,773	111,929	82,569	29,360	34,329	48,240	4,386	18,160	13,803
Olmsted County	66,669	14,876	10,927	3,949	3,166	7,761	1,234	1,897	1,995
Ramsey County	220,680	51,150	36,208	14,942	13,592	22,616	3,118	6,447	7,769
Rice County	25,131	6,671	4,870	1,801	1,490	3,380	185	841	na
St. Louis County	105,006	24,853	19,110	5,743	6,162	12,948	950	2,653	2,178
Scott County	51,942	8,759	7,389	1,370	3,093	4,296	366	1,826	na
Sherburne County	34,301	6,298	5,176	1,122	2,196	2,980	429	1,014	na
Stearns County	65,280	14,462	10,922	3,540	3,442	7,480	142	2,260	1,733
Washington County	99,481	23,743	19,521	4,222	8,601	10,920	1,924	3,345	3,253
Wright County	52,464	10,471	8,890	1,581	2,908	5,982	516	1,702	759
Mississippi									
DeSoto County	68,524	13,892	12,841	1,051	4,697	8,144	na	2,112	336
Forrest County	33,218	6,425	5,224	1,201	1,431	3,793	na	na	264
Harrison County	93,896	19,440	15,332	4,108	4,218	11,114	423	2,004	1,625
Hinds County	104,339	19,645	16,005	3,640	5,037	10,968	0	2,344	1,443
Jackson County	62,727	14,177	12,069	2,108	3,092	8,977	na	1,523	706
Jones County	29,143	7,485	6,687	798	1,161	5,526	na	na	na
Lauderdale County	35,349	8,416	7,009	1,407	1,722	5,287	na	na	na
Lee County	37,051	7,784	6,217	1,567	1,772	4,445	na	na	na
Madison County	44,040	8,409	7,564	845	3,538	4,026	na	1,376	na
Rankin County	61,489	14,879	12,708	2,171	4,384	8,324	na	1,487	465
Missouri									
Boone County	78,945	14,295	11,349	2,946	4,773	6,576	658	1,956	1,278
Buchanan County	38,800	9,946	8,227	1,719	2,909	5,318	199	1,130	1,074
Cape Girardeau County	34,210	7,618	6,309	1,309	1,783	4,526	na	na	655
Cass County	42,442	11,620	9,718	1,902	3,362	6,356	111	2,356	na
Christian County	34,792	8,121	6,461	1,660	2,753	3,708	627	1,085	na
Clay County	98,914	20,702	16,081	4,621	6,800	9,281	287	2,955	1,529
Cole County	33,502	8,385	6,206	2,179	1,601	4,605	263	na	na
Franklin County	45,538	11,011	8,959	2,052	2,524	6,435	na	1,083	923
Greene County	134,555	32,556	23,286	9,270	7,831	15,455	401	3,968	5,897
Jackson County	325,973	66,109	50,213	15,896	19,215	30,998	1,313	10,350	7,407
Jasper County	51,798	13,326	10,430	2,896	4,312	6,118	270	1,732	1,107
Jefferson County	91,634	20,859	18,143	2,716	6,213	11,930	174	2,246	1,520
Platte County	42,374	8,509	6,568	1,941	2,409	4,159	401	1,007	1,231
St. Charles County	156,335	37,374	31,524	5,850	13,191	18,333	1,561	4,901	3,195
St. Francois County	30,242	7,061	5,675	1,386	1,848	3,827	276	na	na
St. Louis County	441,936	115,361	90,979	24,382	37,669	53,310	5,303	16,836	11,963
Montana									
Cascade County	39,037	9,377	7,639	1,738	3,175	4,464	268	1,347	678
Flathead County	49,088	11,891	9,624	2,267	4,252	5,372	151	1,714	686
Gallatin County	51,000	8,441	6,986	1,455	2,063	4,923	337	1,670	726
Lewis and Clark County	31,784	7,748	6,047	1,701	2,787	3,260	434	na	na
Missoula County	54,922	11,491	8,383	3,108	2,441	5,942	592	1,328	1,436
Yellowstone County	72,400	17,535	13,761	3,774	4,352	9,409	890	2,893	1,647
Nebraska									
Douglas County	237,325	48,243	34,603	13,640	13,979	20,624	3,307	7,227	6,319
Lancaster County	133,465	28,792	21,988	6,804	8,588	13,400	2,249	3,456	2,789
Sarpy County	69,957	13,859	10,597	3,262	4,738	5,859	1,030	1,969	1,514
Nevada									
Clark County	913,385	187,797	132,800	54,997	67,067	65,733	2,075	31,925	29,017
Washoe County	201,065	47,863	35,263	12,600	18,709	16,554	1,936	7,973	6,733
New Hampshire									
Cheshire County	35,724	9,178	7,257	1,921	2,744	4,513	na	2,224	926
Grafton County	53,071	11,656	9,491	2,165	3,788	5,703	257	2,107	871
Hillsborough County	172,044	38,337	28,773	9,564	11,618	17,155	809	7,433	4,328
Merrimack County	65,246	16,924	13,419	3,505	4,335	9,084	226	3,891	1,101
Rockingham County	133,207	31,923	25,392	6,531	10,032	15,360	1,042	6,638	2,441
Strafford County	54,311	11,506	9,019	2,487	2,132	6,887	182	1,782	1,168

Table J-2: Counties - Summary of Housing and Householder Characteristics—*Continued*

				Householders 65 Years and Over				
				Owner Householders			Percent of Owner Householders Who Pay 35% or More of income for Housing Costs	Percent of Renter Households Who Pay 35% or More of Income for Rental Costs
	Total Housing Units	Total Households	Owner Occupied	Renter Occupied	With a Mortgage	Without a Mortgage	Renter Households With Meals Included in Rent		
New Jersey									
Atlantic County	128,408	28,355	22,436	5,919	10,110	12,326	109	6,321	2,379
Bergen County	359,241	94,096	70,559	23,537	25,533	45,026	1,720	24,856	12,546
Burlington County	179,900	46,078	38,362	7,716	17,165	21,197	815	10,556	3,334
Camden County	206,109	50,199	37,333	12,866	14,764	22,569	978	12,053	5,792
Cape May County	99,427	14,880	12,793	2,087	4,883	7,910	215	3,000	1,050
Cumberland County	56,497	14,558	11,946	2,612	4,153	7,793	na	3,464	1,634
Essex County	318,814	64,811	37,474	27,337	16,014	21,460	637	14,663	10,985
Gloucester County	113,907	27,052	23,547	3,505	9,733	13,814	678	7,064	1,690
Hudson County	284,124	49,125	22,622	26,503	8,940	13,682	735	8,269	10,803
Hunterdon County	50,454	13,988	12,023	1,965	4,656	7,367	na	2,620	1,193
Mercer County	145,132	35,066	26,999	8,067	9,765	17,234	177	6,974	4,197
Middlesex County	302,255	70,241	54,861	15,380	21,172	33,689	877	17,038	6,815
Monmouth County	262,157	69,245	54,130	15,115	21,745	32,385	2,537	15,547	8,193
Morris County	194,256	48,046	37,808	10,238	15,299	22,509	1,554	11,670	3,971
Ocean County	284,918	90,433	79,871	10,562	29,113	50,758	1,337	22,231	5,727
Passaic County	177,277	41,317	26,255	15,062	10,163	16,092	353	9,858	7,064
Salem County	27,608	7,083	5,755	1,328	1,919	3,836	na	1,449	na
Somerset County	127,016	29,312	24,830	4,482	9,922	14,908	703	7,853	2,319
Sussex County	62,472	14,851	12,826	2,025	6,385	6,441	213	3,894	na
Union County	202,668	46,489	29,311	17,178	12,054	17,257	1,132	10,915	8,050
Warren County	45,558	12,242	9,549	2,693	4,093	5,456	na	4,021	1,387
New Mexico									
Bernalillo County	295,208	69,183	52,730	16,453	21,725	31,005	1,320	10,386	7,729
Chaves County	27,428	6,568	4,610	1,958	1,052	3,558	480	na	na
Doña Ana County	89,060	20,682	16,730	3,952	5,959	10,771	328	2,191	1,008
Lea County	26,765	4,873	3,725	1,148	515	3,210	na	na	na
McKinley County	26,344	5,709	5,419	290	1,380	4,039	na	na	na
Otero County	31,843	6,635	5,832	803	2,411	3,421	na	na	202
Sandoval County	57,318	15,111	12,499	2,612	5,521	6,978	309	1,937	557
San Juan County	51,273	12,097	10,611	1,486	2,371	8,240	76	1,195	451
Santa Fe County	73,463	22,869	19,291	3,578	8,080	11,211	217	3,109	1,307
Valencia County	31,409	8,607	7,601	1,006	2,556	5,045	na	1,671	na
New York									
Albany County	142,306	32,402	23,159	9,243	8,339	14,820	381	4,059	4,091
Bronx County	532,509	115,624	33,013	82,611	12,360	20,653	1,637	11,083	39,118
Broome County	91,258	23,184	17,964	5,220	5,736	12,228	306	3,248	2,406
Cattaraugus County	41,648	9,120	7,720	1,400	1,881	5,839	na	1,137	514
Cayuga County	37,162	8,949	7,039	1,910	2,354	4,685	310	1,587	572
Chautauqua County	67,661	15,814	12,177	3,637	3,646	8,531	46	1,902	1,265
Chemung County	38,924	10,247	7,706	2,541	2,195	5,511	64	na	1,215
Clinton County	36,732	8,126	6,299	1,827	2,164	4,135	na	1,362	524
Dutchess County	121,187	31,844	24,423	7,421	7,969	16,454	377	6,155	3,972
Erie County	429,704	108,411	79,426	28,985	27,330	52,096	3,004	14,848	14,263
Jefferson County	60,041	9,611	7,701	1,910	2,670	5,031	95	1,137	606
Kings County	1,053,667	222,026	94,932	127,094	34,534	60,398	641	33,968	66,809
Livingston County	27,616	6,572	5,278	1,294	1,488	3,790	na	980	na
Madison County	32,391	7,634	6,657	977	2,227	4,430	na	1,755	na
Monroe County	329,236	81,774	60,624	21,150	25,708	34,916	2,849	12,295	12,134
Nassau County	473,454	137,207	115,220	21,987	40,426	74,794	2,284	39,616	10,387
New York County	886,282	183,754	59,409	124,345	14,280	45,129	2,812	14,111	57,480
Niagara County	100,617	26,063	20,321	5,742	6,397	13,924	251	3,747	2,206
Oneida County	105,447	25,518	19,122	6,396	5,584	13,538	664	3,194	2,554
Onondaga County	209,344	50,806	38,858	11,948	14,444	24,414	1,198	6,672	4,784
Ontario County	51,224	13,724	10,627	3,097	4,235	6,392	620	2,009	1,326
Orange County	144,234	31,943	23,535	8,408	10,073	13,462	232	7,253	4,361
Oswego County	54,624	12,220	9,821	2,399	2,698	7,123	84	1,796	1,197
Putnam County	38,679	9,588	8,012	1,576	3,534	4,478	na	2,380	na
Queens County	865,809	199,825	116,533	83,292	36,040	80,493	883	38,634	43,181
Rensselaer County	73,266	17,102	13,799	3,303	5,307	8,492	368	1,492	1,817
Richmond County	181,186	45,957	35,971	9,986	14,080	21,891	174	11,350	5,182
Rockland County	106,723	29,598	22,676	6,922	7,792	14,884	312	8,241	3,239
St. Lawrence County	53,374	12,077	8,763	3,314	2,753	6,010	101	2,090	977
Saratoga County	107,379	25,959	20,103	5,856	8,650	11,453	1,118	3,353	3,082
Schenectady County	69,948	16,415	11,345	5,070	4,277	7,068	932	1,919	2,760
Steuben County	49,684	11,538	9,509	2,029	2,020	7,489	na	1,299	364
Suffolk County	576,845	144,184	122,059	22,125	47,951	74,108	1,491	42,382	12,364
Sullivan County	50,941	8,582	6,910	1,672	1,573	5,337	na	na	427
Tompkins County	43,883	9,079	7,147	1,932	2,812	4,335	443	na	881
Ulster County	85,431	21,616	17,956	3,660	6,142	11,814	na	4,451	1,562
Warren County	40,207	9,284	7,341	1,943	2,624	4,717	379	1,362	695
Wayne County	41,788	10,643	8,675	1,968	3,296	5,379	na	1,718	321
Westchester County	375,864	102,529	71,523	31,006	26,965	44,558	3,144	24,608	14,798
North Carolina									
Alamance County	71,655	17,636	13,903	3,733	5,176	8,727	523	2,204	1,610
Brunswick County	92,284	25,219	23,456	1,763	10,988	12,468	na	5,763	na
Buncombe County	126,577	32,253	25,769	6,484	8,504	17,265	1,182	3,741	3,536

Table J-2: Counties - Summary of Housing and Householder Characteristics—*Continued*

				Householders 65 Years and Over					
				Owner Householders				Percent of Owner Householders Who Pay 35% or More of income for Housing Costs	Percent of Renter Households Who Pay 35% or More of Income for Rental Costs
	Total Housing Units	Total Households	Owner Occupied	Renter Occupied	With a Mortgage	Without a Mortgage	Renter Households With Meals Included in Rent		
North Carolina—Cont.									
Burke County	41,316	10,686	9,049	1,637	3,666	5,383	na	1,130	na
Cabarrus County	80,867	16,169	13,196	2,973	6,079	7,117	381	2,482	1,635
Caldwell County	38,062	9,499	8,166	1,333	1,794	6,372	na	964	na
Carteret County	50,719	11,038	9,719	1,319	3,523	6,196	na	1,336	na
Catawba County	69,249	18,289	16,254	2,035	5,705	10,549	135	2,915	818
Chatham County	33,007	10,611	8,896	1,715	3,873	5,023	543	1,627	na
Cleveland County	43,673	10,539	8,957	1,582	2,353	6,604	na	1,408	652
Craven County	47,453	12,794	10,177	2,617	3,797	6,380	136	1,978	896
Cumberland County	147,123	25,938	19,892	6,046	8,031	11,861	317	4,383	2,414
Davidson County	75,593	18,381	15,120	3,261	5,730	9,390	na	3,057	1,193
Durham County	138,960	25,415	19,351	6,064	9,961	9,390	733	3,628	2,237
Forsyth County	166,941	39,419	29,426	9,993	12,583	16,843	1,471	6,073	4,359
Franklin County	29,018	6,965	6,060	905	2,124	3,936	na	na	na
Gaston County	93,885	22,081	18,022	4,059	7,857	10,165	373	2,609	1,715
Guilford County	230,468	50,210	37,992	12,218	17,946	20,046	2,226	8,294	6,792
Harnett County	52,561	9,992	8,240	1,752	3,382	4,858	na	1,954	593
Henderson County	58,099	18,920	15,807	3,113	6,294	9,513	632	3,057	855
Iredell County	75,611	16,967	14,304	2,663	6,361	7,943	na	2,247	1,312
Johnston County	77,354	15,581	12,867	2,714	5,556	7,311	na	2,616	830
Lincoln County	36,768	8,680	7,669	1,011	3,613	4,056	na	na	na
Mecklenburg County	454,104	72,989	54,517	18,472	26,889	27,628	2,567	11,790	10,572
Moore County	47,931	14,474	12,626	1,848	5,449	7,177	505	2,168	407
Nash County	43,152	12,037	10,189	1,848	3,794	6,395	na	na	na
New Hanover County	113,231	26,105	18,612	7,493	7,923	10,689	743	4,132	3,931
Onslow County	80,259	10,186	8,664	1,522	3,968	4,696	na	2,037	436
Orange County	59,198	12,791	10,664	2,127	3,992	6,672	218	1,740	820
Pitt County	80,244	14,472	11,228	3,244	5,561	5,667	212	2,271	1,086
Randolph County	62,628	15,535	13,172	2,363	4,813	8,359	544	1,924	1,140
Robeson County	53,186	12,744	10,197	2,547	2,546	7,651	na	2,435	999
Rockingham County	44,290	12,727	10,668	2,059	3,754	6,914	na	1,953	767
Rowan County	61,973	15,670	12,697	2,973	4,534	8,163	208	2,094	1,139
Rutherford County	34,473	9,054	7,361	1,693	1,517	5,844	na	na	na
Surry County	34,263	9,879	8,244	1,635	2,237	6,007	na	804	409
Union County	82,559	16,342	14,689	1,653	7,092	7,597	221	2,481	767
Wake County	441,828	75,259	57,576	17,683	28,101	29,475	2,674	8,890	7,779
Wayne County	54,467	13,389	10,505	2,884	3,865	6,640	397	2,040	975
Wilkes County	33,642	10,532	9,725	807	2,533	7,192	na	na	na
Wilson County	36,316	9,989	7,934	2,055	2,699	5,235	na	na	na
North Dakota									
Burleigh County	43,159	9,661	7,785	1,876	2,353	5,432	579	1,158	1,010
Cass County	83,903	13,333	8,264	5,069	2,265	5,999	1,091	1,160	2,801
Grand Forks County	33,393	5,666	4,032	1,634	1,078	2,954	132	na	1,049
Ward County	33,203	5,402	3,760	1,642	935	2,825	427	910	1,008
Ohio									
Allen County	45,192	11,540	9,286	2,254	3,578	5,708	290	1,483	947
Ashtabula County	46,198	11,704	9,576	2,128	3,296	6,280	443	2,803	918
Athens County	26,681	5,581	4,469	1,112	1,039	3,430	na	na	571
Belmont County	32,159	8,880	7,619	1,261	1,396	6,223	na	749	254
Butler County	152,725	34,810	26,761	8,049	12,459	14,302	511	5,318	3,045
Clark County	61,307	17,429	14,395	3,034	4,710	9,685	299	1,908	1,225
Clermont County	83,786	20,408	17,133	3,275	6,819	10,314	619	3,372	1,983
Columbiana County	46,848	12,925	11,250	1,675	3,729	7,521	250	1,064	841
Cuyahoga County	617,923	150,843	106,232	44,611	41,371	64,861	5,316	23,193	18,989
Delaware County	74,534	16,459	14,185	2,274	6,510	7,675	510	3,278	744
Erie County	37,907	10,135	7,844	2,291	2,998	4,846	440	na	na
Fairfield County	61,550	15,127	12,639	2,488	4,287	8,352	na	2,005	1,667
Franklin County	559,933	100,883	75,975	24,908	36,332	39,643	2,873	16,313	10,041
Geauga County	37,335	11,976	10,736	1,240	5,095	5,641	236	2,717	na
Greene County	70,856	18,525	15,266	3,259	6,886	8,380	777	1,682	1,246
Hamilton County	380,048	81,102	58,686	22,416	24,893	33,793	3,328	11,861	9,933
Hancock County	34,372	8,173	6,491	1,682	2,423	4,068	375	na	604
Jefferson County	32,470	9,203	7,293	1,910	2,254	5,039	0	1,112	654
Lake County	103,306	28,890	23,011	5,879	9,130	13,881	1,020	3,561	2,401
Licking County	71,052	16,952	13,587	3,365	4,881	8,706	285	1,522	1,332
Lorain County	131,931	35,685	29,236	6,449	12,106	17,130	790	5,442	2,967
Lucas County	203,491	43,704	33,817	9,887	14,555	19,262	1,308	7,194	4,012
Mahoning County	111,318	30,605	23,902	6,703	8,158	15,744	1,190	3,828	2,230
Marion County	27,907	6,905	5,484	1,421	2,382	3,102	437	na	na
Medina County	73,043	19,624	16,550	3,074	6,737	9,813	577	2,954	961
Miami County	44,352	11,957	9,631	2,326	4,493	5,138	278	2,248	722
Montgomery County	254,821	62,017	48,161	13,856	18,624	29,537	1,669	8,888	5,117
Muskingum County	37,948	10,134	7,884	2,250	2,986	4,898	na	1,380	817
Portage County	69,335	16,186	13,513	2,673	6,272	7,241	126	3,161	1,393
Richland County	54,173	15,028	11,703	3,325	3,559	8,144	346	1,767	1,375

Table J-2: Counties - Summary of Housing and Householder Characteristics—*Continued*

| | | | | Householders 65 Years and Over | | | | |
| | | | | Owner Householders | | | Percent of Owner Householders Who Pay 35% or More of income for Housing Costs | Percent of Renter Households Who Pay 35% or More of Income for Rental Costs |
	Total Housing Units	Total Households	Owner Occupied	Renter Occupied	With a Mortgage	Without a Mortgage	Renter Households With Meals Included in Rent		
Ohio—Cont.									
Ross County	32,070	8,430	7,043	1,387	2,122	4,921	na	na	na
Scioto County	34,514	8,572	6,989	1,583	1,574	5,415	na	na	na
Stark County	166,991	45,960	35,182	10,778	14,145	21,037	807	6,212	4,048
Summit County	246,191	61,595	47,740	13,855	20,002	27,738	1,408	7,594	5,077
Trumbull County	95,669	27,428	23,424	4,004	7,666	15,758	414	3,945	1,816
Tuscarawas County	40,234	11,470	8,369	3,101	2,466	5,903	315	1,778	1,351
Warren County	88,444	19,136	16,046	3,090	6,875	9,171	96	2,550	1,190
Wayne County	46,732	12,744	10,057	2,687	2,871	7,186	349	1,026	861
Wood County	54,092	12,245	9,788	2,457	4,143	5,645	80	1,705	651
Oklahoma									
Canadian County	48,974	10,317	8,490	1,827	2,984	5,506	313	1,399	703
Cleveland County	116,901	24,398	18,801	5,597	7,037	11,764	1,129	3,165	2,555
Comanche County	51,688	9,851	7,435	2,416	3,038	4,397	116	1,206	957
Creek County	30,778	8,005	7,136	869	2,158	4,978	na	953	331
Muskogee County	30,967	7,165	5,702	1,463	1,971	3,731	78	868	358
Oklahoma County	341,548	69,935	54,406	15,529	18,749	35,657	2,547	9,039	6,667
Payne County	36,824	7,462	6,243	1,219	1,880	4,363	138	na	231
Pottawatomie County	29,998	7,298	5,825	1,473	1,375	4,450	84	703	496
Rogers County	38,545	8,552	7,514	1,038	2,362	5,152	111	1,369	358
Tulsa County	284,556	59,066	44,493	14,573	14,543	29,950	2,408	7,032	6,338
Wagoner County	32,881	8,077	7,441	636	2,640	4,801	na	780	227
Oregon									
Benton County	38,442	8,774	7,287	1,487	2,665	4,622	520	1,130	668
Clackamas County	169,238	45,626	35,444	10,182	16,747	18,697	3,060	11,067	5,827
Deschutes County	91,040	25,139	19,170	5,969	9,590	9,580	1,105	4,009	3,309
Douglas County	50,564	17,844	14,548	3,296	4,413	10,135	309	2,586	1,239
Jackson County	96,251	29,411	22,712	6,699	9,109	13,603	1,281	5,371	2,923
Josephine County	39,354	14,454	11,623	2,831	4,593	7,030	365	1,822	na
Klamath County	33,682	8,846	7,394	1,452	2,649	4,745	na	na	na
Lane County	163,490	46,536	37,327	9,209	17,351	19,976	1,829	8,968	4,528
Linn County	50,891	15,144	11,899	3,245	4,856	7,043	785	2,799	1,497
Marion County	127,325	31,849	23,735	8,114	10,934	12,801	1,561	4,496	4,914
Multnomah County	353,878	70,367	49,762	20,605	21,403	28,359	3,340	13,930	10,499
Polk County	32,511	9,211	7,556	1,655	3,770	3,786	631	1,183	na
Umatilla County	30,681	7,442	5,623	1,819	2,250	3,373	110	na	927
Washington County	232,449	49,424	37,445	11,979	18,027	19,418	3,045	10,379	7,014
Yamhill County	39,394	11,361	8,567	2,794	4,118	4,449	825	2,745	na
Pennsylvania									
Adams County	42,572	12,529	10,101	2,428	3,738	6,363	309	2,999	812
Allegheny County	602,410	153,284	115,294	37,990	38,588	76,706	3,938	22,783	16,680
Armstrong County	32,785	9,246	7,319	1,927	1,638	5,681	101	1,405	852
Beaver County	79,662	23,418	17,761	5,657	4,939	12,822	312	2,817	1,255
Berks County	167,383	43,204	32,404	10,800	11,381	21,023	1,404	7,502	4,748
Blair County	56,957	16,090	12,910	3,180	3,778	9,132	216	1,801	961
Bucks County	251,507	69,401	56,355	13,046	21,605	34,750	2,931	14,005	6,772
Butler County	84,242	22,151	16,681	5,470	5,186	11,495	1,351	3,450	1,933
Cambria County	66,035	19,834	15,972	3,862	2,827	13,145	439	2,059	856
Carbon County	34,820	8,006	6,576	1,430	2,076	4,500	na	1,651	na
Centre County	67,155	13,802	10,964	2,838	3,018	7,946	135	1,675	1,197
Chester County	201,344	51,086	41,946	9,140	16,835	25,111	2,030	9,139	4,537
Clearfield County	39,267	10,186	8,209	1,977	1,692	6,517	na	1,393	na
Columbia County	30,320	7,962	6,429	1,533	1,690	4,739	226	1,814	544
Crawford County	44,946	11,241	9,404	1,837	3,332	6,072	72	1,444	265
Cumberland County	106,887	29,114	23,029	6,085	8,840	14,189	998	3,521	2,880
Dauphin County	124,803	29,930	21,726	8,204	7,803	13,923	1,096	4,407	3,051
Delaware County	224,876	55,867	41,047	14,820	16,121	24,926	3,675	10,558	8,199
Erie County	121,651	31,393	23,958	7,435	7,411	16,547	1,250	3,843	3,100
Fayette County	63,950	17,735	14,777	2,958	3,863	10,914	na	2,385	1,360
Franklin County	65,799	18,693	15,427	3,266	4,539	10,888	715	2,879	1,312
Indiana County	39,008	10,360	8,522	1,838	2,017	6,505	281	747	316
Lackawanna County	100,707	26,916	20,991	5,925	5,242	15,749	264	3,928	1,768
Lancaster County	212,243	57,454	42,445	15,009	13,815	28,630	3,753	6,987	8,049
Lawrence County	41,321	11,822	9,797	2,025	3,040	6,757	291	1,944	693
Lebanon County	58,010	17,563	13,949	3,614	4,856	9,093	356	2,668	1,752
Lehigh County	146,732	36,901	28,532	8,369	10,361	18,171	724	7,003	4,542
Luzerne County	150,280	39,885	30,759	9,126	8,010	22,749	1,127	6,257	2,424
Lycoming County	53,530	13,364	10,892	2,472	3,753	7,139	222	1,774	1,105
Mercer County	52,310	15,513	12,399	3,114	3,401	8,998	139	1,991	990
Monroe County	81,664	15,553	13,118	2,435	6,136	6,982	na	3,916	na
Montgomery County	336,194	87,931	66,387	21,544	26,029	40,358	4,968	17,440	12,470
Northampton County	123,428	35,162	27,290	7,872	10,254	17,036	1,439	6,462	3,547
Northumberland County	45,471	12,466	9,095	3,371	2,257	6,838	na	1,809	717
Philadelphia County	688,640	144,301	100,850	43,451	36,541	64,309	1,128	26,995	20,114
Schuylkill County	69,918	18,720	15,579	3,141	3,987	11,592	562	4,164	1,225
Somerset County	38,500	9,473	7,888	1,585	1,642	6,246	na	1,037	364

Table J-2: Counties - Summary of Housing and Householder Characteristics—*Continued*

| | | | | Householders 65 Years and Over | | | | |
| | | | | Owner Householders | | | | |
	Total Housing Units	Total Households	Owner Occupied	Renter Occupied	With a Mortgage	Without a Mortgage	Renter Households With Meals Included in Rent	Percent of Owner Householders Who Pay 35% or More of income for Housing Costs	Percent of Renter Households Who Pay 35% or More of Income for Rental Costs
Pennsylvania—Cont.									
Washington County	96,225	26,622	21,499	5,123	6,173	15,326	888	3,234	1,716
Westmoreland County	170,772	50,820	42,340	8,480	13,419	28,921	908	6,900	3,421
York County	184,880	47,981	38,551	9,430	13,985	24,566	1,174	8,025	4,880
Rhode Island									
Kent County	74,510	20,449	15,034	5,415	5,864	9,170	421	4,818	1,667
Newport County	42,682	12,166	9,112	3,054	3,815	5,297	111	na	630
Providence County	266,575	60,005	36,136	23,869	14,431	21,705	1,949	9,087	8,905
Washington County	64,332	15,603	13,995	1,608	6,662	7,333	329	3,060	na
South Carolina									
Aiken County	77,687	20,602	18,280	2,322	5,928	12,352	308	3,226	815
Anderson County	88,997	23,011	19,311	3,700	6,772	12,539	164	2,543	1,299
Beaufort County	101,255	29,332	26,485	2,847	12,977	13,508	596	6,431	1,605
Berkeley County	85,972	17,710	16,150	1,560	6,921	9,229	na	2,702	625
Charleston County	191,893	42,527	33,241	9,286	14,862	18,379	2,288	9,118	3,066
Darlington County	30,875	8,433	6,344	2,089	2,320	4,024	na	na	na
Dorchester County	61,654	12,874	10,964	1,910	4,282	6,682	na	2,550	925
Florence County	61,109	13,974	12,182	1,792	3,921	8,261	92	1,473	707
Greenville County	214,115	49,062	40,289	8,773	15,976	24,313	1,182	6,222	3,553
Greenwood County	31,550	8,028	6,261	1,767	2,128	4,133	338	na	na
Horry County	210,700	48,521	43,144	5,377	19,382	23,762	398	9,163	2,586
Kershaw County	29,375	7,450	6,954	496	2,389	4,565	na	na	na
Lancaster County	38,541	11,175	10,049	1,126	4,422	5,627	na	na	na
Laurens County	31,494	7,397	5,872	1,525	2,366	3,506	na	na	na
Lexington County	126,223	30,215	25,860	4,355	10,463	15,397	949	4,203	1,860
Oconee County	40,812	11,515	9,846	1,669	3,387	6,459	na	na	na
Orangeburg County	42,794	11,251	9,351	1,900	2,595	6,756	na	na	na
Pickens County	55,067	13,758	11,278	2,480	3,570	7,708	448	1,754	1,225
Richland County	175,056	33,419	28,386	5,033	14,296	14,090	366	7,196	2,803
Spartanburg County	131,448	30,293	25,580	4,713	8,788	16,792	403	3,186	1,653
Sumter County	48,282	10,897	8,982	1,915	3,526	5,456	403	na	686
York County	110,226	22,448	19,199	3,249	8,786	10,413	292	4,100	1,261
South Dakota									
Minnehaha County	84,009	16,459	11,374	5,085	3,339	8,035	1,247	1,352	2,379
Pennington County	49,249	13,001	10,256	2,745	3,512	6,744	456	1,916	1,608
Tennessee									
Anderson County	35,020	8,995	7,849	1,146	1,812	6,037	na	na	579
Blount County	58,673	15,806	14,141	1,665	4,403	9,738	208	1,786	661
Bradley County	44,157	11,158	10,039	1,119	3,476	6,563	na	2,113	234
Davidson County	319,508	55,686	40,548	15,138	15,575	24,973	2,834	6,622	5,450
Greene County	32,690	8,422	7,023	1,399	2,282	4,741	na	na	na
Hamilton County	160,807	38,869	31,080	7,789	11,901	19,179	1,499	4,164	3,760
Knox County	206,056	46,281	39,205	7,076	12,174	27,031	1,234	4,964	2,715
Madison County	43,382	10,420	8,675	1,745	2,454	6,221	157	1,263	794
Maury County	38,352	9,199	7,131	2,068	2,338	4,793	na	1,236	na
Montgomery County	82,596	11,008	9,247	1,761	2,559	6,688	133	1,020	952
Putnam County	34,977	7,759	5,801	1,958	1,462	4,339	na	na	1,164
Robertson County	27,765	5,876	5,350	526	1,950	3,400	na	647	na
Rutherford County	121,829	19,666	15,888	3,778	6,240	9,648	na	2,567	1,276
Sevier County	58,279	11,040	9,595	1,445	2,700	6,895	na	na	na
Shelby County	406,236	81,716	59,662	22,054	28,110	31,552	1,980	13,343	11,957
Sullivan County	75,724	23,310	19,091	4,219	6,783	12,308	276	3,041	1,114
Sumner County	73,709	18,119	15,418	2,701	6,540	8,878	781	3,215	914
Washington County	60,856	14,279	10,934	3,345	3,690	7,244	515	1,633	1,857
Williamson County	85,031	17,284	15,981	1,303	6,538	9,443	na	2,231	619
Wilson County	55,159	13,424	11,652	1,772	4,421	7,231	na	1,976	na
Texas									
Angelina County	36,995	7,583	6,133	1,450	1,480	4,653	na	na	na
Bastrop County	30,175	6,748	5,809	939	1,896	3,913	na	na	na
Bell County	142,436	23,244	18,490	4,754	5,357	13,133	337	2,469	2,044
Bexar County	700,241	137,915	106,742	31,173	35,917	70,825	3,829	17,587	14,273
Bowie County	40,038	9,487	8,163	1,324	2,030	6,133	389	1,319	730
Brazoria County	139,484	24,397	20,046	4,351	6,575	13,471	221	4,175	2,397
Brazos County	92,697	13,213	10,325	2,888	2,633	7,692	581	2,107	1,525
Cameron County	152,374	33,403	26,864	6,539	4,768	22,096	183	4,021	2,231
Collin County	377,384	57,562	42,985	14,577	19,817	23,168	2,025	8,898	7,520
Comal County	60,949	14,429	12,016	2,413	4,138	7,878	498	2,125	1,185
Coryell County	26,850	4,773	3,837	936	1,191	2,646	na	na	na
Dallas County	1,027,930	166,769	120,522	46,247	40,332	80,190	5,273	24,451	24,191
Denton County	319,979	46,502	36,659	9,843	16,632	20,027	1,345	7,353	5,361
Ector County	58,685	9,917	8,377	1,540	1,944	6,433	na	2,194	375
Ellis County	63,506	13,075	11,903	1,172	4,940	6,963	133	2,615	na
El Paso County	299,672	61,672	48,426	13,246	13,338	35,088	237	9,153	5,462
Fort Bend County	260,764	43,524	38,322	5,202	14,261	24,061	635	8,057	1,803

Table J-2: Counties - Summary of Housing and Householder Characteristics—*Continued*

				Householders 65 Years and Over				
				Owner Householders			Percent of Owner Householders Who Pay 35% or More of income for Housing Costs	Percent of Renter Households Who Pay 35% or More of Income for Rental Costs
	Total Housing Units	Total Households	Owner Occupied	Renter Occupied	With a Mortgage	Without a Mortgage	Renter Households With Meals Included in Rent		
Texas—Cont.									
Galveston County	148,293	30,752	24,568	6,184	7,160	17,408	806	4,278	3,068
Grayson County	56,735	14,802	12,216	2,586	2,985	9,231	290	1,800	1,361
Gregg County	52,093	11,452	8,130	3,322	2,554	5,576	663	na	1,574
Guadalupe County	60,138	12,067	10,797	1,270	2,441	8,356	na	1,831	777
Harris County	1,788,357	285,358	215,353	70,005	71,537	143,816	7,076	42,850	35,945
Harrison County	28,731	6,821	6,057	764	1,264	4,793	na	na	na
Hays County	81,999	13,714	11,608	2,106	4,663	6,945	179	2,304	992
Henderson County	41,483	10,841	9,700	1,141	2,558	7,142	na	na	na
Hidalgo County	281,655	56,271	47,414	8,857	9,423	37,991	349	9,234	3,237
Hunt County	38,087	9,007	6,947	2,060	1,878	5,069	na	1,041	1,622
Jefferson County	108,771	21,966	17,256	4,710	3,428	13,828	73	2,314	1,957
Johnson County	62,798	13,050	11,182	1,868	4,209	6,973	na	2,028	961
Kaufman County	42,483	8,730	6,993	1,737	2,638	4,355	0	1,112	na
Liberty County	31,734	7,206	6,456	750	896	5,560	na	1,168	na
Lubbock County	129,669	23,330	18,985	4,345	6,386	12,599	1,263	3,090	2,489
McLennan County	102,458	22,514	17,295	5,219	4,337	12,958	603	3,793	2,581
Midland County	61,872	12,129	9,706	2,423	2,735	6,971	678	1,777	1,679
Montgomery County	222,600	45,322	36,947	8,375	13,960	22,987	716	7,002	5,023
Nacogdoches County	28,482	6,068	5,121	947	982	4,139	na	na	na
Nueces County	149,961	31,260	24,713	6,547	7,131	17,582	777	3,758	3,650
Orange County	37,740	8,095	7,004	1,091	793	6,211	na	na	na
Parker County	50,820	11,869	10,631	1,238	3,662	6,969	na	2,029	682
Potter County	50,176	9,383	6,167	3,216	1,966	4,201	601	1,033	1,821
Randall County	55,241	12,575	11,612	963	3,972	7,640	na	1,975	229
Rockwall County	35,832	6,727	5,891	836	2,189	3,702	na	1,085	na
San Patricio County	28,478	5,873	4,741	1,132	1,220	3,521	262	789	na
Smith County	91,101	22,791	19,715	3,076	5,341	14,374	213	3,951	960
Tarrant County	779,037	141,809	107,309	34,500	34,998	72,311	5,359	18,051	19,246
Taylor County	57,793	11,722	9,133	2,589	1,875	7,258	530	1,278	1,241
Tom Green County	48,619	11,584	8,780	2,804	1,394	7,386	311	1,400	870
Travis County	527,786	73,603	56,744	16,859	20,782	35,962	2,396	12,777	7,939
Victoria County	37,079	9,159	7,047	2,112	1,736	5,311	na	na	1,243
Walker County	26,408	5,524	4,659	865	1,354	3,305	250	na	na
Webb County	84,466	15,185	11,013	4,172	2,959	8,054	na	2,039	2,079
Wichita County	56,007	12,421	9,458	2,963	2,538	6,920	241	1,296	1,879
Williamson County	198,636	35,790	29,233	6,557	12,854	16,379	871	5,428	3,390
Wise County	24,925	5,198	4,678	520	1,148	3,530	na	504	na
Utah									
Cache County	42,242	7,056	6,156	900	1,694	4,462	na	745	378
Davis County	110,428	20,403	18,591	1,812	7,043	11,548	489	1,913	909
Salt Lake County	403,687	76,120	61,542	14,578	24,752	36,790	3,108	11,583	6,548
Tooele County	22,463	3,537	3,235	302	1,739	1,496	na	na	na
Utah County	180,020	28,053	25,205	2,848	9,774	15,431	940	3,850	1,476
Washington County	71,349	22,266	19,435	2,831	9,042	10,393	1,006	3,744	1,379
Weber County	93,205	18,545	15,547	2,998	6,377	9,170	716	2,410	1,494
Vermont									
Chittenden County	70,359	16,604	12,437	4,167	5,229	7,208	485	3,019	2,103
Virginia									
Albemarle County	46,081	12,912	9,457	3,455	3,733	5,724	931	1,599	1,565
Arlington County	116,543	16,853	11,680	5,173	4,903	6,777	416	2,114	2,037
Augusta County	32,723	10,715	9,497	1,218	3,750	5,747	na	1,767	na
Bedford County	37,001	9,191	8,591	600	3,402	5,189	na	1,353	na
Chesterfield County	132,362	31,844	28,204	3,640	14,105	14,099	637	4,894	2,118
Fairfax County	415,485	85,588	72,976	12,612	37,238	35,738	2,769	14,529	6,842
Fauquier County	27,150	6,873	6,021	852	2,732	3,289	na	1,971	na
Frederick County	34,842	8,763	7,479	1,284	3,016	4,463	411	1,637	na
Hanover County	41,865	10,935	9,174	1,761	3,733	5,441	389	933	445
Henrico County	138,176	32,004	24,034	7,970	11,824	12,210	2,349	5,149	4,974
James City County	33,765	11,180	9,322	1,858	5,222	4,100	619	na	na
Loudoun County	136,509	19,719	15,319	4,400	8,530	6,789	1,089	3,286	1,569
Montgomery County	40,710	7,323	6,057	1,266	1,462	4,595	178	na	421
Prince William County	150,475	23,805	21,037	2,768	12,142	8,895	472	3,641	1,670
Roanoke County	41,020	12,225	10,033	2,192	3,806	6,227	174	1,268	na
Rockingham County	35,844	9,382	7,905	1,477	2,880	5,025	336	1,325	na
Spotsylvania County	48,147	10,491	9,093	1,398	4,734	4,359	na	1,697	350
Stafford County	50,458	7,863	7,073	790	4,108	2,965	na	1,328	na
York County	27,908	6,668	5,974	694	2,643	3,331	na	1,395	na
Washington									
Benton County	77,373	18,215	15,581	2,634	5,925	9,656	1,078	2,438	1,813
Chelan County	38,075	8,663	7,239	1,424	2,275	4,964	328	834	877
Clallam County	37,331	14,164	11,736	2,428	5,129	6,607	258	2,782	na
Clark County	186,159	45,341	36,409	8,932	16,231	20,178	1,611	8,877	3,927
Cowlitz County	44,959	13,407	10,767	2,640	5,008	5,759	591	2,044	1,115

Table J-2: Counties - Summary of Housing and Householder Characteristics—*Continued*

| | | | | Householders 65 Years and Over | | | | |
| | | | | Owner Householders | | | | |
	Total Housing Units	Total Households	Owner Occupied	Renter Occupied	With a Mortgage	Without a Mortgage	Renter Households With Meals Included in Rent	Percent of Owner Householders Who Pay 35% or More of income for Housing Costs	Percent of Renter Households Who Pay 35% or More of Income for Rental Costs
Washington—Cont.									
Franklin County	28,659	4,766	4,056	710	1,838	2,218	na	na	na
Grant County	37,969	7,992	6,326	1,666	2,242	4,084	566	1,265	433
Grays Harbor County	36,434	8,920	7,386	1,534	3,114	4,272	317	1,659	na
Island County	42,274	12,750	11,383	1,367	4,612	6,771	84	2,461	429
King County	952,597	180,631	128,050	52,581	54,595	73,455	10,749	33,963	26,820
Kitsap County	113,732	30,033	25,482	4,551	11,775	13,707	761	5,628	1,938
Lewis County	35,335	10,886	8,559	2,327	3,219	5,340	470	1,370	833
Mason County	33,685	8,846	8,059	787	3,850	4,209	223	na	na
Pierce County	351,009	75,373	57,110	18,263	26,718	30,392	3,269	14,911	8,988
Skagit County	54,451	15,788	12,665	3,123	4,865	7,800	798	3,186	1,652
Snohomish County	313,822	65,481	51,790	13,691	23,548	28,242	2,875	12,223	7,351
Spokane County	219,873	52,471	39,935	12,536	15,348	24,587	2,016	6,447	5,839
Thurston County	117,860	29,900	23,168	6,732	10,653	12,515	990	4,610	3,162
Whatcom County	97,867	24,312	19,486	4,826	9,326	10,160	703	4,215	2,242
Yakima County	89,129	21,499	17,215	4,284	5,862	11,353	736	3,618	1,491
West Virginia									
Berkeley County	49,425	11,073	10,143	930	3,806	6,337	na	1,160	101
Cabell County	46,324	10,637	9,140	1,497	2,064	7,076	244	948	501
Harrison County	31,765	8,381	6,747	1,634	1,608	5,139	388	696	712
Kanawha County	92,334	24,807	20,749	4,058	4,861	15,888	na	2,722	1,672
Monongalia County	45,069	8,232	6,950	1,282	2,061	4,889	na	na	529
Raleigh County	36,167	10,449	8,366	2,083	3,344	5,022	na	na	na
Wood County	40,294	11,237	9,481	1,756	3,277	6,204	na	1,339	696
Wisconsin									
Brown County	110,382	24,964	18,475	6,489	5,685	12,790	739	3,207	2,635
Dane County	236,932	47,609	37,574	10,035	15,277	22,297	1,620	7,276	4,535
Dodge County	37,912	9,515	6,646	2,869	2,316	4,330	549	1,401	1,179
Eau Claire County	44,400	10,408	7,988	2,420	3,110	4,878	364	1,897	1,085
Fond du Lac County	45,361	11,716	9,033	2,683	2,509	6,524	380	1,949	1,112
Jefferson County	36,004	9,124	7,534	1,590	2,744	4,790	143	1,299	558
Kenosha County	70,646	14,984	11,531	3,453	4,844	6,687	254	2,929	1,845
La Crosse County	50,573	12,015	8,347	3,668	2,567	5,780	458	1,345	1,350
Manitowoc County	37,578	10,386	8,575	1,811	2,072	6,503	322	1,104	700
Marathon County	59,706	15,425	11,846	3,579	3,135	8,711	506	1,728	1,497
Milwaukee County	419,585	84,663	55,219	29,444	22,092	33,127	3,261	13,503	15,941
Outagamie County	77,597	17,486	14,574	2,912	4,693	9,881	254	3,065	1,321
Ozaukee County	37,783	11,685	8,986	2,699	4,174	4,812	593	3,000	na
Portage County	31,129	7,783	5,982	1,801	1,776	4,206	444	972	1,128
Racine County	82,908	20,635	16,835	3,800	6,320	10,515	580	3,864	2,049
Rock County	69,235	17,695	12,889	4,806	4,938	7,951	140	2,421	1,898
St. Croix County	36,308	7,760	6,267	1,493	3,068	3,199	154	1,234	na
Sheboygan County	51,352	13,487	10,515	2,972	2,923	7,592	507	1,795	1,341
Walworth County	52,653	11,193	9,131	2,062	3,238	5,893	239	1,749	1,031
Washington County	57,201	14,198	11,908	2,290	4,170	7,738	118	2,514	1,182
Waukesha County	166,662	46,371	36,397	9,974	14,487	21,910	1,896	7,904	6,479
Winnebago County	76,015	18,183	13,700	4,483	3,756	9,944	1,100	2,717	2,042
Wood County	35,186	9,953	7,767	2,186	1,878	5,889	518	628	999
Wyoming									
Laramie County	43,892	11,096	8,948	2,148	4,403	4,545	340	1,713	na
Natrona County	37,181	7,880	6,545	1,335	2,425	4,120	na	904	623

Table J-3: Cities - Summary of Housing and Householder Characteristics

| | | | | Householders 65 Years and Over | | | | |
| | | | | Owner Householders | | Renter Households With Meals Included in Rent | Percent of Owner Householders Who Pay 35% or More of income for Housing Costs | Percent of Renter Households Who Pay 35% or More of Income for Rental Costs |
	Total Housing Units	Total Households	Owner Occupied	Renter Occupied	With a Mortgage	Without a Mortgage			
Alabama									
Auburn city	29,936	3,078	2,529	549	1,363	1,166	na	na	na
Birmingham city	116,157	22,749	16,334	6,415	5,711	10,623	296	3,917	2,960
Dothan city	32,058	8,443	6,725	1,718	2,633	4,092	34	1,126	703
Hoover city	34,261	8,841	7,855	986	3,421	4,434	na	na	na
Huntsville city	93,084	21,385	16,554	4,831	6,681	9,873	632	2,218	1,908
Mobile city	93,286	21,750	15,415	6,335	6,496	8,919	628	2,698	3,408
Montgomery city	92,595	18,587	12,998	5,589	4,997	8,001	105	1,905	2,692
Tuscaloosa city	51,811	7,840	5,687	2,153	2,360	3,327	448	na	1,145
Alaska									
Anchorage municipality	118,233	19,776	16,708	3,068	7,279	9,429	na	3,113	1,114
Arizona									
Avondale city	29,274	4,308	3,102	1,206	1,568	1,534	na	654	na
Buckeye city	24,329	5,705	5,051	654	2,585	2,466	na	na	na
Chandler city	97,701	16,709	13,325	3,384	6,912	6,413	591	2,173	2,152
Flagstaff city	29,541	4,178	3,380	798	1,473	1,907	na	na	351
Glendale city	90,048	18,642	13,290	5,352	6,218	7,072	537	2,718	2,610
Goodyear city	30,238	7,258	6,040	1,218	3,490	2,550	na	1,239	na
Mesa city	217,400	48,772	39,684	9,088	15,713	23,971	1,752	7,680	4,485
Peoria city	68,716	18,656	14,842	3,814	6,582	8,260	1,977	3,541	2,550
Phoenix city	627,844	107,117	78,284	28,833	38,647	39,637	4,032	17,302	15,724
Scottsdale city	141,329	36,272	30,043	6,229	13,427	16,616	1,662	7,744	3,253
Surprise city	56,633	18,125	16,043	2,082	8,244	7,799	588	2,860	1,399
Tempe city	80,754	13,034	10,069	2,965	3,875	6,194	402	1,076	1,108
Tucson city	239,420	52,276	36,138	16,138	14,273	21,865	1,895	7,353	7,561
Yuma city	43,071	9,186	7,459	1,727	2,159	5,300	na	1,392	110
Arkansas									
Conway city	26,828	4,447	3,088	1,359	1,421	1,667	156	na	na
Fayetteville city	39,407	4,201	3,274	927	743	2,531	264	na	350
Fort Smith city	39,380	8,043	5,953	2,090	1,149	4,804	133	na	509
Jonesboro city	31,736	5,818	3,951	1,867	1,507	2,444	94	na	256
Little Rock city	98,026	17,594	13,714	3,880	4,371	9,343	564	2,494	1,463
North Little Rock city	33,904	7,135	4,988	2,147	1,831	3,157	290	na	1,032
Rogers city	25,486	4,044	2,667	1,377	878	1,789	118	na	928
Springdale city	28,508	4,978	3,592	1,386	1,115	2,477	582	na	904
California									
Alameda city	32,496	8,447	5,656	2,791	2,354	3,302	204	na	1,506
Alhambra city	32,791	7,285	4,054	3,231	2,024	2,030	310	na	2,209
Anaheim city	108,802	20,945	13,765	7,180	6,835	6,930	713	4,086	4,075
Antioch city	36,364	6,874	4,873	2,001	2,006	2,867	na	769	na
Bakersfield city	130,103	22,204	16,355	5,849	8,355	8,000	1,231	3,450	3,810
Baldwin Park city	19,135	3,214	2,262	952	1,456	806	na	na	na
Bellflower city	25,806	3,817	1,846	1,971	857	989	na	na	1,045
Berkeley city	47,359	11,462	8,055	3,407	4,241	3,814	0	na	1,651
Buena Park city	23,801	4,904	3,767	1,137	1,785	1,982	na	na	na
Burbank city	46,530	10,096	5,480	4,616	2,622	2,858	285	na	2,410
Camarillo city	25,727	9,179	7,667	1,512	4,641	3,026	353	2,239	847
Carlsbad city	49,086	13,084	10,757	2,327	6,282	4,475	664	na	1,390
Carson city	24,083	6,971	5,553	1,418	3,050	2,503	na	na	na
Chico city	41,847	8,570	5,711	2,859	2,813	2,898	152	1,617	1,898
Chino city	27,870	5,716	4,383	1,333	2,151	2,232	339	1,022	na
Chino Hills city	25,151	3,550	3,132	418	1,729	1,403	na	na	na
Chula Vista city	85,108	14,910	11,180	3,730	4,893	6,287	37	2,715	2,129
Citrus Heights city	35,173	9,539	6,675	2,864	3,986	2,689	738	1,859	1,591
Clovis city	38,847	9,531	6,601	2,930	4,161	2,440	285	1,977	1,239
Compton city	25,249	4,758	3,188	1,570	1,971	1,217	na	1,514	898
Concord city	50,857	11,688	8,568	3,120	4,381	4,187	489	2,026	2,047
Corona city	46,097	7,160	5,659	1,501	3,359	2,300	216	2,199	676
Costa Mesa city	42,780	8,335	4,871	3,464	2,494	2,377	418	1,655	2,046
Daly City city	34,551	8,444	6,725	1,719	3,304	3,421	na	na	1,082
Davis city	26,158	4,645	3,549	1,096	1,512	2,037	413	na	722
Downey city	35,940	7,277	4,978	2,299	2,516	2,462	76	na	1,447
El Cajon city	35,371	5,999	3,987	2,012	2,419	1,568	259	na	1,521
Elk Grove city	55,038	12,035	10,178	1,857	5,854	4,324	282	2,538	na
El Monte city	32,043	6,620	3,627	2,993	1,347	2,280	0	na	1,633
Escondido city	53,516	12,019	8,477	3,542	4,201	4,276	690	2,422	2,475
Fairfield city	40,325	8,335	6,505	1,830	4,227	2,278	828	1,521	972
Folsom city	27,587	5,660	4,499	1,161	2,993	1,506	237	na	na
Fontana city	56,400	7,231	5,758	1,473	3,703	2,055	na	2,462	733
Fremont city	82,518	13,788	11,069	2,719	4,462	6,607	84	2,474	1,582
Fresno city	183,030	36,313	23,412	12,901	11,160	12,252	1,247	4,942	7,283
Fullerton city	46,936	10,226	8,114	2,112	3,438	4,676	427	1,959	835
Garden Grove city	45,601	9,679	6,081	3,598	2,743	3,338	0	1,636	1,507
Glendale city	78,195	18,215	6,418	11,797	2,839	3,579	423	na	8,450
Hawthorne city	30,843	4,888	2,468	2,420	1,730	738	na	na	1,559
Hayward city	51,898	10,293	7,040	3,253	3,356	3,684	269	2,093	2,107

Table J-3: Cities - Summary of Housing and Householder Characteristics—*Continued*

| | | | | | Householders 65 Years and Over | | | | |
| | | | | | Owner Householders | | | Percent of Owner Households Who Pay 35% or More of income for Housing Costs | Percent of Renter Households Who Pay 35% or More of income for Rental Costs |
	Total Housing Units	Total Households	Owner Occupied	Renter Occupied	With a Mortgage	Without a Mortgage	Renter Households With Meals Included in Rent		
California—Cont.									
Hemet city	31,313	12,375	9,353	3,022	3,070	6,283	644	na	2,149
Hesperia city	29,170	6,818	4,997	1,821	2,309	2,688	na	na	na
Huntington Beach city	81,215	20,467	15,606	4,861	7,128	8,478	na	3,836	2,632
Indio city	47,720	12,417	10,967	1,450	5,748	5,219	na	na	na
Inglewood city	37,753	7,918	3,920	3,998	2,506	1,414	na	1,342	2,007
Irvine city	108,463	17,345	12,034	5,311	6,279	5,755	987	3,245	1,953
Jurupa Valley city	25,025	5,476	3,794	1,682	2,406	1,388	na	1,137	na
Laguna Niguel city	28,245	6,905	5,277	1,628	2,929	2,348	na	na	na
Lake Elsinore city	19,044	2,749	1,752	997	1,200	552	na	na	na
Lake Forest city	32,687	7,709	6,734	975	3,298	3,436	na	1,821	na
Lakewood city	27,024	5,200	4,461	739	2,177	2,284	na	1,700	na
Lancaster city	49,466	8,875	6,067	2,808	3,133	2,934	na	1,920	1,431
Livermore city	32,124	7,192	5,525	1,667	2,325	3,200	na	964	na
Lodi City	25,298	6,230	4,835	1,395	2,163	2,672	354	na	851
Long Beach city	183,570	31,067	19,381	11,686	10,333	9,048	529	6,614	6,212
Los Angeles city	1,502,686	288,751	164,120	124,631	83,338	80,782	5,644	57,448	66,333
Lynwood city	16,385	2,608	1,923	685	938	985	na	na	na
Madera city	19,951	2,850	2,366	484	940	1,426	na	na	na
Manteca city	28,090	7,040	5,453	1,587	2,892	2,561	266	1,668	na
Menifee city	31,362	9,799	8,505	1,294	5,114	3,391	275	2,300	na
Merced city	28,221	6,613	3,975	2,638	2,112	1,863	na	na	1,178
Milpitas city	23,878	4,392	3,093	1,299	1,569	1,524	na	na	na
Mission Viejo city	34,916	10,393	9,048	1,345	5,189	3,859	na	2,572	na
Modesto city	73,101	15,223	11,289	3,934	5,675	5,614	377	3,253	1,921
Moreno Valley city	50,956	6,958	5,227	1,731	3,572	1,655	0	1,628	829
Mountain View city	36,445	5,756	3,910	1,846	1,544	2,366	166	632	1,111
Murrieta city	35,726	7,282	5,570	1,712	3,814	1,756	na	1,827	na
Napa city	30,601	8,742	6,268	2,474	2,949	3,319	493	1,588	1,284
Newport Beach city	45,591	11,992	8,166	3,826	3,617	4,549	551	na	2,024
Norwalk city	27,932	6,801	5,192	1,609	2,575	2,617	na	1,627	1,202
Oakland city	181,161	37,316	21,175	16,141	10,753	10,422	985	6,159	6,714
Oceanside city	64,155	18,880	14,105	4,775	7,801	6,304	na	3,772	2,672
Ontario city	52,032	8,310	6,224	2,086	4,008	2,216	na	1,747	745
Orange city	44,690	9,020	6,789	2,231	3,272	3,517	178	2,145	930
Oxnard city	56,467	9,102	6,972	2,130	2,881	4,091	0	1,459	1,259
Palmdale city	48,975	8,879	6,930	1,949	3,774	3,156	na	2,051	1,010
Palo Alto city	29,072	7,856	5,111	2,745	2,108	3,003	909	na	880
Pasadena city	60,805	14,655	8,634	6,021	3,992	4,642	295	na	3,069
Perris city	17,921	1,811	1,149	662	706	443	na	na	na
Pittsburg city	21,624	3,108	2,314	794	1,630	684	na	660	na
Pleasanton city	29,043	7,142	5,510	1,632	2,708	2,802	329	na	na
Pomona city	40,906	8,556	5,483	3,073	3,077	2,406	319	1,428	1,622
Rancho Cordova city	29,024	7,093	5,292	1,801	2,257	3,035	na	1,420	na
Rancho Cucamonga city	59,325	10,869	8,280	2,589	4,597	3,683	262	2,343	1,065
Redding city	38,451	10,065	7,236	2,829	4,045	3,191	187	1,395	906
Redlands city	28,300	7,484	6,056	1,428	2,278	3,778	na	na	na
Redondo Beach city	29,921	5,749	4,338	1,411	2,215	2,123	na	na	235
Redwood City city	31,960	7,272	5,080	2,192	2,344	2,736	292	1,680	1,375
Rialto city	26,155	5,957	4,950	1,007	2,470	2,480	na	1,187	na
Richmond city	38,607	8,175	6,298	1,877	3,894	2,404	na	1,687	730
Riverside city	92,992	17,387	13,020	4,367	6,198	6,822	542	2,501	2,555
Rocklin city	22,057	5,072	3,554	1,518	1,502	2,052	290	888	na
Roseville city	54,653	14,164	10,738	3,426	5,404	5,334	996	3,388	1,825
Sacramento city	194,998	40,628	25,151	15,477	12,477	12,674	851	5,498	8,130
Salinas city	41,655	8,116	5,652	2,464	2,542	3,110	na	983	987
San Bernardino city	62,694	10,266	6,606	3,660	2,489	4,117	270	1,025	1,706
San Buenaventura (Ventura) city	45,701	12,031	8,595	3,436	4,326	4,269	550	na	1,853
San Clemente city	27,083	6,396	5,164	1,232	2,770	2,394	na	na	na
San Diego city	554,896	110,754	78,405	32,349	37,799	40,606	1,527	20,682	17,282
San Francisco city	401,478	83,021	44,329	38,692	17,814	26,515	2,545	11,372	15,403
San Jose city	341,806	68,180	48,413	19,767	21,899	26,514	1,484	12,423	10,549
San Leandro city	32,654	7,415	5,140	2,275	1,965	3,175	281	888	914
San Marcos city	31,932	6,903	5,181	1,722	2,557	2,624	288	na	na
San Mateo city	43,415	10,492	7,695	2,797	3,100	4,595	359	2,191	1,529
San Ramon city	27,538	4,157	2,899	1,258	1,377	1,522	na	na	na
Santa Ana city	81,153	14,538	10,153	4,385	5,103	5,050	0	2,810	2,106
Santa Barbara city	38,577	10,865	7,043	3,822	3,164	3,879	841	na	2,102
Santa Clara city	48,630	8,261	5,795	2,466	2,448	3,347	167	na	992
Santa Clarita city	69,485	16,083	12,975	3,108	7,480	5,495	487	3,568	2,225
Santa Cruz city	23,962	5,094	4,290	804	2,459	1,831	na	na	na
Santa Maria city	27,722	5,010	4,058	952	2,344	1,714	160	na	na
Santa Monica city	51,046	11,136	4,169	6,967	1,939	2,230	712	na	4,138
Santa Rosa city	68,744	20,307	13,761	6,546	5,922	7,839	978	3,566	4,328
Simi Valley city	44,782	13,520	10,207	3,313	5,193	5,014	279	3,312	2,000
South Gate city	23,776	4,131	2,507	1,624	1,753	754	na	na	1,037
South San Francisco city	21,117	6,432	4,255	2,177	1,850	2,405	na	na	na

Table J-3: Cities - Summary of Housing and Householder Characteristics—*Continued*

| | | | | | Householders 65 Years and Over | | | | |
| | | | | | Owner Householders | | | | |
	Total Housing Units	Total Households	Owner Occupied	Renter Occupied	With a Mortgage	Without a Mortgage	Renter Households With Meals Included in Rent	Percent of Owner Householders Who Pay 35% or More of income for Housing Costs	Percent of Renter Households Who Pay 35% or More of Income for Rental Costs
California—Cont.									
Stockton city	101,928	19,714	12,479	7,235	6,256	6,223	542	3,136	3,405
Sunnyvale city	59,668	9,604	6,864	2,740	2,394	4,470	516	1,324	1,743
Temecula city	34,848	6,337	5,200	1,137	3,174	2,026	na	1,549	na
Thousand Oaks city	46,003	13,526	11,229	2,297	6,378	4,851	482	na	839
Torrance city	60,758	15,257	11,438	3,819	5,028	6,410	na	2,907	1,648
Tracy city	26,287	4,163	3,223	940	1,578	1,645	na	1,108	na
Turlock city	25,207	5,417	3,240	2,177	1,272	1,968	na	na	768
Tustin city	26,430	4,036	3,062	974	1,373	1,689	na	na	594
Union City city	20,836	5,253	3,955	1,298	2,026	1,929	268	na	na
Upland city	27,211	6,867	5,278	1,589	2,801	2,477	na	1,574	649
Vacaville city	33,789	8,159	6,494	1,665	3,658	2,836	126	2,003	na
Vallejo city	43,378	10,423	7,095	3,328	4,697	2,398	136	1,347	1,450
Victorville city	34,879	6,064	4,242	1,822	2,010	2,232	na	na	na
Visalia city	44,177	9,818	7,232	2,586	2,661	4,571	477	na	1,254
Vista city	31,822	5,624	4,289	1,335	2,370	1,919	na	927	723
Walnut Creek city	32,826	14,353	11,600	2,753	4,171	7,429	769	na	1,399
West Covina city	33,051	7,546	6,047	1,499	2,695	3,352	na	1,634	855
Westminster city	27,834	7,501	4,194	3,307	1,673	2,521	na	na	1,785
Whittier city	28,376	6,420	4,315	2,105	2,294	2,021	288	1,535	995
Yorba Linda city	23,595	8,002	7,166	836	4,347	2,819	na	2,344	na
Yuba City city	24,071	6,382	4,824	1,558	1,820	3,004	89	na	564
Colorado									
Arvada city	51,391	14,039	11,217	2,822	4,995	6,222	702	1,858	1,502
Aurora city	138,118	26,953	19,294	7,659	11,078	8,216	641	4,825	4,300
Boulder city	45,778	7,982	6,238	1,744	2,807	3,431	289	na	943
Broomfield city	28,935	5,908	5,033	875	2,469	2,564	245	na	408
Centennial city	39,982	9,508	8,628	880	4,026	4,602	na	1,608	na
Colorado Springs city	191,810	37,885	29,185	8,700	12,684	16,501	1,475	5,509	4,818
Denver city	330,884	56,532	39,247	17,285	17,072	22,175	2,319	8,750	8,471
Fort Collins city	70,450	11,496	8,408	3,088	3,202	5,206	941	1,770	1,889
Greeley city	40,558	7,087	5,454	1,633	2,422	3,032	116	1,274	665
Lakewood city	68,711	16,911	13,014	3,897	5,613	7,401	1,154	2,234	2,848
Longmont city	39,959	9,656	7,148	2,508	3,708	3,440	720	1,220	1,633
Loveland city	31,606	8,409	6,107	2,302	2,594	3,513	870	1,147	1,460
Pueblo city	49,245	13,875	10,258	3,617	3,819	6,439	466	2,520	1,799
Thornton city	47,781	7,800	6,426	1,374	3,181	3,245	na	1,630	na
Westminster city	47,325	9,916	7,481	2,435	3,985	3,496	1,030	1,920	1,618
Connecticut									
Bridgeport city	58,216	10,346	5,037	5,309	2,907	2,130	366	2,236	2,342
Danbury city	31,422	6,133	4,525	1,608	1,688	2,837	327	na	545
Hartford city	53,890	8,831	3,422	5,409	1,604	1,818	76	na	2,752
New Britain city	31,276	5,621	3,166	2,455	1,459	1,707	na	na	937
New Haven city	56,036	7,968	3,517	4,451	1,842	1,675	92	na	1,685
Norwalk city	37,380	10,872	7,088	3,784	3,443	3,645	176	2,786	1,730
Stamford city	54,513	12,629	8,445	4,184	4,485	3,960	440	3,438	2,193
Waterbury city	48,703	9,041	4,398	4,643	1,751	2,647	567	1,613	2,160
Delaware									
Wilmington city	35,460	5,866	3,753	2,113	1,826	1,927	281	na	1,002
District of Columbia									
Washington city	319,579	58,898	34,173	24,725	16,887	17,286	1,466	8,689	10,596
Florida									
Boca Raton city	56,586	18,122	14,803	3,319	4,962	9,841	513	4,564	na
Boynton Beach city	36,637	10,430	8,275	2,155	3,420	4,855	290	2,774	na
Cape Coral city	89,132	27,070	23,472	3,598	11,311	12,161	696	6,960	na
Clearwater city	58,662	17,120	12,566	4,554	4,032	8,534	468	3,008	2,148
Coral Springs city	46,005	8,449	7,110	1,339	4,593	2,517	na	na	na
Daytona Beach city	36,987	8,605	6,698	1,907	2,103	4,595	119	na	1,036
Deerfield Beach city	43,648	12,200	9,268	2,932	2,308	6,960	1,025	2,965	na
Delray Beach city	36,507	11,705	9,429	2,276	3,344	6,085	820	na	1,366
Deltona city	32,236	7,276	6,263	1,013	3,300	2,963	na	1,415	na
Fort Lauderdale city	96,063	19,813	14,633	5,180	5,270	9,363	162	4,798	2,538
Fort Myers city	42,413	10,903	7,012	3,891	2,314	4,698	1,373	na	2,028
Gainesville city	57,363	8,012	6,021	1,991	1,674	4,347	498	719	1,263
Hialeah city	75,182	21,708	12,817	8,891	4,112	8,705	378	3,747	5,176
Hollywood city	70,315	14,285	10,627	3,658	4,297	6,330	367	3,429	2,190
Homestead city	19,913	2,122	690	1,432	144	546	na	na	na
Jacksonville city	388,788	76,032	56,708	19,324	25,256	31,452	1,788	10,917	9,763
Kissimmee city	28,995	4,052	3,100	952	1,183	1,917	na	na	na
Lakeland city	49,574	13,155	9,719	3,436	2,474	7,245	564	na	2,093
Largo city	46,370	14,786	10,444	4,342	2,733	7,711	1,697	2,768	1,992
Lauderhill city	26,483	6,441	4,766	1,675	2,235	2,531	na	1,696	na

Table J-3: Cities - Summary of Housing and Householder Characteristics—*Continued*

| | | | | | Householders 65 Years and Over | | | | |
| | | | | | Owner Householders | | | | |
	Total Housing Units	Total Households	Owner Occupied	Renter Occupied	With a Mortgage	Without a Mortgage	Renter Households With Meals Included in Rent	Percent of Owner Householders Who Pay 35% or More of income for Housing Costs	Percent of Renter Households Who Pay 35% or More of Income for Rental Costs
Florida—Cont.									
Melbourne city	35,955	10,170	5,645	4,525	1,753	3,892	1,043	na	2,513
Miami city	211,030	45,095	20,039	25,056	5,100	14,939	499	6,764	13,091
Miami Beach city	70,516	10,710	5,680	5,030	1,996	3,684	0	na	1,878
Miami Gardens city	32,593	9,742	6,827	2,915	3,229	3,598	na	1,689	na
Miramar city	41,166	5,109	4,103	1,006	1,754	2,349	na	na	na
North Port city	29,630	11,014	8,843	2,171	3,734	5,109	na	na	na
Orlando city	137,280	18,900	11,090	7,810	5,059	6,031	530	3,129	4,674
Palm Bay city	45,285	15,364	13,854	1,510	6,538	7,316	na	3,024	na
Palm Coast city	36,832	14,828	13,351	1,477	6,409	6,942	na	na	na
Pembroke Pines city	61,951	18,567	14,738	3,829	4,881	9,857	na	6,350	na
Plantation city	37,333	8,418	7,478	940	3,745	3,733	na	1,873	na
Pompano Beach city	54,845	13,352	10,041	3,311	2,540	7,501	1,211	1,894	1,945
Port St. Lucie city	74,378	21,897	19,559	2,338	8,843	10,716	1,276	5,564	na
St. Petersburg city	134,583	28,351	21,653	6,698	7,956	13,697	705	5,215	3,662
Sunrise city	39,917	11,102	9,541	1,561	2,756	6,785	na	3,413	na
Tallahassee city	89,491	11,880	9,010	2,870	4,076	4,934	129	1,828	1,469
Tamarac city	32,458	11,743	10,478	1,265	4,090	6,388	na	3,106	na
Tampa city	171,855	31,364	21,051	10,313	8,110	12,941	778	5,491	4,632
Weston city	23,820	3,280	3,013	267	1,761	1,252	na	na	na
West Palm Beach city	50,593	12,879	9,940	2,939	3,138	6,802	881	na	1,617
Georgia									
Albany city	33,212	6,242	3,578	2,664	1,588	1,990	0	na	1,405
Alpharetta city	25,982	3,743	2,768	975	1,351	1,417	na	na	na
Athens-Clarke County unified govt (bal)	52,565	9,273	7,238	2,035	2,538	4,700	188	1,017	723
Atlanta city	255,433	40,686	23,492	17,194	11,785	11,707	2,114	5,998	7,780
Augusta-Richmond County consolidated govt (bal)	87,271	18,909	14,269	4,640	6,331	7,938	102	3,917	2,595
Columbus city	85,018	17,648	13,164	4,484	5,389	7,775	491	2,431	1,672
Johns Creek city	28,720	4,176	3,174	1,002	1,904	1,270	na	na	na
Macon-Bibb County	70,058	15,152	10,695	4,457	4,160	6,535	930	2,191	1,948
Roswell city	39,285	7,520	6,286	1,234	3,167	3,119	439	na	389
Sandy Springs city	53,194	9,541	6,985	2,556	3,449	3,536	1,086	1,664	1,158
Savannah city	60,460	13,243	9,398	3,845	3,795	5,603	214	1,778	1,573
South Fulton city	35,568	7,700	5,196	2,504	3,572	1,624	na	na	na
Warner Robins city	32,885	5,478	2,984	2,494	1,282	1,702	na	na	na
Hawaii									
Urban Honolulu CDP	153,191	40,268	24,666	15,602	9,209	15,457	947	4,626	6,344
Iowa									
Boise City city	102,201	22,584	16,683	5,901	6,985	9,698	1,817	2,931	2,694
Meridian city	37,525	5,859	5,392	467	2,392	3,000	na	na	na
Nampa city	35,911	9,508	7,572	1,936	3,310	4,262	349	623	487
Illinois									
Aurora city	68,669	11,020	8,630	2,390	3,513	5,117	178	2,262	973
Bloomington city	34,533	6,317	5,136	1,181	1,803	3,333	na	398	416
Champaign city	38,169	5,774	4,963	811	1,739	3,224	137	na	302
Chicago city	1,227,166	229,844	142,544	87,300	57,262	85,282	3,964	46,793	44,423
Decatur city	35,625	9,140	6,949	2,191	1,983	4,966	367	933	818
Elgin city	40,194	7,342	5,258	2,084	2,294	2,964	na	1,438	1,154
Evanston city	30,166	7,379	5,463	1,916	2,134	3,329	301	na	1,012
Joliet city	50,383	8,394	6,694	1,700	2,919	3,775	na	1,189	614
Naperville city	55,278	9,457	8,299	1,158	3,735	4,564	210	1,654	596
Peoria city	54,318	10,274	7,761	2,513	2,627	5,134	517	1,393	1,113
Rockford city	68,661	16,750	12,062	4,688	4,561	7,501	1,140	2,081	1,660
Springfield city	54,742	12,893	10,634	2,259	3,618	7,016	534	1,654	1,075
Waukegan city	30,756	4,818	3,185	1,633	1,478	1,707	na	na	714
Indiana									
Bloomington city	35,016	5,687	3,776	1,911	1,887	1,889	518	na	662
Carmel city	38,256	7,603	6,172	1,431	3,505	2,667	444	1,108	na
Evansville city	58,819	11,731	8,432	3,299	3,070	5,362	444	1,649	1,466
Fishers city	35,454	5,320	3,973	1,347	2,645	1,328	na	na	na
Fort Wayne city	115,386	24,810	19,105	5,705	7,784	11,321	685	2,925	2,843
Gary city	40,792	9,418	6,923	2,495	2,892	4,031	97	na	873
Hammond city	31,625	7,138	5,468	1,670	1,958	3,510	na	na	na
Indianapolis city (bal)	387,102	68,504	50,671	17,833	26,105	24,566	1,714	11,039	7,965
Lafayette city	33,492	6,077	4,070	2,007	1,614	2,456	na	na	834
Muncie city	32,336	6,857	5,300	1,557	2,018	3,282	200	na	717
Noblesville city	25,593	4,276	3,192	1,084	1,654	1,538	na	na	na
South Bend city	45,882	9,506	7,176	2,330	2,515	4,661	346	1,249	1,395
Iowa									
Ames city	27,578	4,147	3,604	543	831	2,773	na	na	301
Ankeny city	27,636	5,142	4,648	494	2,554	2,094	na	na	na

Table J-3: Cities - Summary of Housing and Householder Characteristics—*Continued*

					Householders 65 Years and Over			
				Owner Householders		Renter Households With Meals Included in Rent	Percent of Owner Householders Who Pay 35% or More of income for Housing Costs	Percent of Renter Households Who Pay 35% or More of Income for Rental Costs
	Total Housing Units	Total Households	Owner Occupied	Renter Occupied	With a Mortgage	Without a Mortgage			
Iowa—Cont.									
Cedar Rapids city	58,472	12,836	9,945	2,891	3,649	6,296	671	1,680	1,120
Davenport city	44,545	9,367	6,841	2,526	2,650	4,191	447	1,048	1,689
Des Moines city	92,061	16,685	12,963	3,722	5,482	7,481	400	2,736	1,162
Iowa City city	34,227	5,255	4,327	928	1,687	2,640	620	462	378
Sioux City city	33,920	7,283	5,216	2,067	1,135	4,081	716	na	1,067
Waterloo city	32,117	8,154	6,389	1,765	1,895	4,494	823	868	1,108
West Des Moines city	32,869	6,358	4,959	1,399	1,351	3,608	na	802	548
Kansas									
Kansas City city	64,067	11,709	8,845	2,864	3,328	5,517	71	1,858	1,404
Lawrence city	42,168	7,647	5,927	1,720	2,831	3,096	526	1,579	1,126
Olathe city	49,819	8,432	6,673	1,759	3,313	3,360	526	1,382	701
Overland Park city	84,469	19,297	13,606	5,691	6,394	7,212	1,623	3,111	2,686
Shawnee city	25,115	4,535	3,679	856	1,652	2,027	na	na	na
Topeka city	61,592	15,459	10,932	4,527	4,325	6,607	858	2,342	2,588
Wichita city	174,473	36,646	26,819	9,827	9,783	17,036	1,886	4,482	4,722
Kentucky									
Bowling Green city	27,910	5,035	2,904	2,131	1,090	1,814	na	na	863
Lexington-Fayette urban county	142,688	26,964	21,157	5,807	8,758	12,399	817	3,532	1,941
Louisville/Jefferson County metro govt (bal)	279,075	61,682	47,061	14,621	18,808	28,253	1,602	9,146	6,799
Louisiana									
Baton Rouge city	105,782	21,311	16,608	4,703	5,896	10,712	649	2,263	2,393
Bossier City city	31,909	6,459	5,119	1,340	2,352	2,767	na	na	na
Kenner city	29,159	7,446	5,487	1,959	2,156	3,331	135	na	na
Lafayette city	58,772	11,790	9,602	2,188	3,173	6,429	na	1,851	453
Lake Charles city	38,378	8,012	6,224	1,788	1,719	4,505	534	na	930
New Orleans city	191,620	35,584	24,414	11,170	7,365	17,049	757	8,741	4,849
Shreveport city	89,262	19,851	14,924	4,927	4,992	9,932	680	2,467	2,918
Maine									
Portland city	34,499	5,449	2,964	2,485	1,206	1,758	447	679	1,123
Maryland									
Baltimore city	293,633	57,264	36,891	20,373	16,005	20,886	373	9,849	7,919
Frederick city	29,641	5,710	3,910	1,800	2,006	1,904	251	714	989
Gaithersburg city	27,394	4,865	2,881	1,984	1,466	1,415	374	na	na
Rockville city	27,835	7,175	4,861	2,314	2,206	2,655	422	na	1,012
Massachusetts									
Boston city	299,472	53,784	24,888	28,896	12,945	11,943	655	8,017	10,487
Brockton city	33,884	7,542	4,819	2,723	2,525	2,294	na	1,062	1,086
Cambridge city	50,190	8,519	5,528	2,991	1,796	3,732	na	931	927
Fall River city	42,170	9,771	4,540	5,231	2,109	2,431	131	na	2,836
Framingham city	29,986	6,830	5,086	1,744	2,608	2,478	372	1,269	605
Lawrence city	27,549	4,387	1,301	3,086	959	342	338	na	1,271
Lowell city	39,691	6,108	3,807	2,301	1,881	1,926	na	na	780
Lynn city	33,242	7,139	3,368	3,771	1,950	1,418	na	1,022	1,690
New Bedford city	42,153	8,184	4,559	3,625	1,446	3,113	na	1,282	1,278
Newton city	32,758	10,928	8,143	2,785	3,381	4,762	747	2,565	697
Quincy city	42,366	9,181	4,860	4,321	1,896	2,964	724	1,920	2,072
Somerville city	34,753	4,390	2,167	2,223	781	1,386	na	424	895
Springfield city	63,618	12,418	7,058	5,360	3,088	3,970	248	2,005	2,493
Worcester city	78,085	14,900	8,134	6,766	3,452	4,682	343	3,122	3,253
Michigan									
Ann Arbor city	49,278	8,275	6,856	1,419	2,382	4,474	346	1,361	544
Dearborn city	34,129	7,367	6,207	1,160	1,993	4,214	350	1,889	na
Detroit city	362,863	66,285	46,199	20,086	12,812	33,387	301	11,908	7,401
Farmington Hills city	35,701	10,120	6,929	3,191	2,796	4,133	706	1,272	1,580
Flint city	54,300	9,182	7,104	2,078	2,354	4,750	na	na	1,201
Grand Rapids city	81,362	16,875	10,955	5,920	3,763	7,192	1,250	1,756	2,366
Kalamazoo city	30,215	5,457	3,744	1,713	1,366	2,378	317	385	729
Lansing city	56,085	9,985	6,758	3,227	3,148	3,610	265	953	1,317
Livonia city	38,131	10,322	9,222	1,100	3,047	6,175	na	1,378	na
Rochester Hills city	30,833	8,254	6,575	1,679	3,090	3,485	536	na	na
Southfield city	34,105	11,169	6,416	4,753	3,473	2,943	867	1,960	2,570
Sterling Heights city	50,580	13,015	10,586	2,429	3,742	6,844	785	1,653	1,448
Troy city	32,839	7,644	6,418	1,226	2,115	4,303	164	876	602
Warren city	60,123	14,523	12,015	2,508	3,502	8,513	334	2,003	1,164
Westland city	39,488	10,074	6,584	3,490	2,206	4,378	634	1,074	1,944
Wyoming city	28,817	5,251	3,696	1,555	1,962	1,734	na	na	na
Minnesota									
Blaine city	23,651	4,267	3,825	442	1,613	2,212	na	750	na
Bloomington city	37,381	12,145	9,040	3,105	3,404	5,636	588	2,236	1,620
Brooklyn Park city	28,982	5,098	4,078	1,020	1,957	2,121	na	772	na
Duluth city	39,092	9,899	7,348	2,551	2,414	4,934	330	1,206	963
Eagan city	25,751	4,453	3,598	855	1,685	1,913	85	na	309

Table J-3: Cities - Summary of Housing and Householder Characteristics—*Continued*

					Householders 65 Years and Over				
					Owner Households		Renter Households With Meals Included in Rent	Percent of Owner Householders Who Pay 35% or More of income for Housing Costs	Percent of Renter Households Who Pay 35% or More of Income for Rental Costs
	Total Housing Units	Total Households	Owner Occupied	Renter Occupied	With a Mortgage	Without a Mortgage			
Minnesota—Cont.									
Lakeville city	22,763	3,787	3,437	350	1,166	2,271	na	na	na
Maple Grove city	30,141	6,625	6,123	502	2,980	3,143	na	na	na
Minneapolis city	187,553	29,348	19,754	9,594	8,335	11,419	755	3,714	3,796
Plymouth city	33,739	6,872	5,703	1,169	2,383	3,320	na	1,328	597
Rochester city	51,953	11,259	7,583	3,676	2,229	5,354	1,234	1,414	1,914
St. Cloud city	27,300	4,876	3,717	1,159	1,523	2,194	na	628	527
St. Paul city	124,176	21,422	12,863	8,559	5,153	7,710	1,360	2,260	3,555
Woodbury city	27,098	5,952	5,347	605	2,886	2,461	na	1,158	na
Mississippi									
Gulfport city	34,954	5,550	3,918	1,632	1,058	2,860	215	na	784
Jackson city	74,640	13,245	10,418	2,827	3,229	7,189	0	1,788	1,321
Missouri									
Columbia city	53,066	9,132	6,950	2,182	3,672	3,278	395	1,235	966
Independence city	54,743	12,015	9,354	2,661	3,135	6,219	330	1,360	1,423
Kansas City city	236,054	41,780	30,174	11,606	12,035	18,139	719	7,327	5,108
Lee's Summit city	38,717	10,450	8,565	1,885	3,663	4,902	752	2,216	na
O'Fallon city	30,435	5,962	4,451	1,511	2,250	2,201	510	793	na
St. Charles city	31,133	7,341	5,500	1,841	1,983	3,517	694	925	1,137
St. Joseph city	33,008	8,757	7,038	1,719	2,593	4,445	199	1,038	1,074
St. Louis city	177,169	29,792	17,376	12,416	6,018	11,358	0	4,027	5,976
Springfield city	83,532	21,055	13,095	7,960	4,034	9,061	401	2,613	4,886
Montana									
Billings city	51,584	12,848	9,709	3,139	2,914	6,795	812	2,210	1,535
Missoula city	33,868	6,564	3,994	2,570	1,236	2,758	592	na	1,222
Nebraska									
Lincoln city	122,305	25,353	19,018	6,335	7,454	11,564	2,233	2,861	2,625
Omaha city	200,238	41,787	29,495	12,292	11,857	17,638	2,382	6,221	5,722
Nevada									
Henderson city	133,080	34,479	26,374	8,105	15,039	11,335	0	6,460	3,583
Las Vegas city	258,568	57,088	39,235	17,853	18,612	20,623	618	10,257	9,907
North Las Vegas city	84,248	14,796	12,242	2,554	7,094	5,148	na	3,027	1,566
Reno city	114,217	26,259	16,362	9,897	8,162	8,200	1,368	3,814	5,080
Sparks city	41,901	10,698	8,655	2,043	4,897	3,758	568	1,944	1,461
New Hampshire									
Manchester city	47,203	8,273	4,705	3,568	2,138	2,567	239	995	1,549
Nashua city	40,335	9,562	6,808	2,754	2,216	4,592	335	1,516	1,596
New Jersey									
Bayonne city	25,933	6,109	3,353	2,756	1,324	2,029	na	na	1,707
Camden city	28,233	4,766	3,086	1,680	903	2,183	na	na	544
Clifton city	32,088	7,380	4,865	2,515	1,515	3,350	198	1,999	na
East Orange city	25,968	5,494	2,447	3,047	1,184	1,263	84	na	896
Elizabeth city	43,813	7,324	2,699	4,625	870	1,829	na	na	2,539
Jersey City city	110,801	17,688	7,013	10,675	3,436	3,577	605	2,125	4,302
Newark city	114,061	17,220	6,274	10,946	2,788	3,486	0	2,919	4,227
Passaic city	20,631	3,874	1,292	2,582	487	805	na	na	na
Paterson city	52,014	10,224	3,382	6,842	1,735	1,647	155	na	2,821
Trenton city	33,672	7,207	4,886	2,321	1,718	3,168	na	na	na
Union City city	25,987	4,774	1,431	3,343	547	884	na	na	1,685
New Mexico									
Albuquerque city	248,681	55,046	39,756	15,290	16,720	23,036	1,320	7,116	7,023
Las Cruces city	46,113	10,769	7,843	2,926	3,580	4,263	328	na	757
Rio Rancho city	38,020	9,930	8,230	1,700	4,253	3,977	309	1,282	na
Santa Fe city	41,943	13,618	10,764	2,854	4,357	6,407	217	1,837	1,142
New York									
Albany city	51,457	8,897	5,507	3,390	2,326	3,181	316	na	2,124
Buffalo city	130,767	21,624	13,938	7,686	4,657	9,281	253	1,864	3,688
Mount Vernon city	27,752	6,096	2,738	3,358	1,163	1,575	463	na	1,694
New Rochelle city	28,215	7,613	4,328	3,285	1,204	3,124	na	na	na
New York city	3,519,453	767,186	339,858	427,328	111,294	228,564	6,147	109,146	211,770
Rochester city	98,552	16,006	9,146	6,860	3,538	5,608	329	1,752	3,714
Schenectady city	33,842	6,127	3,329	2,798	1,587	1,742	503	na	1,582
Syracuse city	67,589	10,721	6,747	3,974	2,349	4,398	0	1,057	1,375
Yonkers city	85,955	21,929	12,531	9,398	4,066	8,465	383	4,622	3,697
North Carolina									
Asheville city	47,889	11,818	8,064	3,754	2,548	5,516	891	1,317	2,115
Charlotte city	367,444	56,551	41,416	15,135	20,290	21,126	1,553	8,914	8,327
Concord city	36,854	7,679	5,920	1,759	2,488	3,432	277	1,183	na
Durham city	122,814	20,298	14,903	5,395	8,449	6,454	733	3,251	2,036
Fayetteville city	93,626	16,511	11,964	4,547	5,562	6,402	79	2,751	1,833
Gastonia city	34,204	7,309	5,308	2,001	2,913	2,395	352	1,048	886
Greensboro city	132,721	26,459	17,989	8,470	9,223	8,766	1,718	4,513	5,493

Table J-3: Cities - Summary of Housing and Householder Characteristics—*Continued*

				Householders 65 Years and Over				
				Owner Householders		Renter Households With Meals Included in Rent	Percent of Owner Householders Who Pay 35% or More of income for Housing Costs	Percent of Renter Households Who Pay 35% or More of Income for Rental Costs
	Total Housing Units	Total Households	Owner Occupied	Renter Occupied	With a Mortgage	Without a Mortgage			
North Carolina—Cont.									
Greenville city	43,813	5,662	3,949	1,713	2,293	1,656	na	na	406
High Point city	47,241	10,080	7,346	2,734	3,565	3,781	508	1,443	1,039
Jacksonville city	24,517	2,941	2,066	875	883	1,183	na	na	183
Raleigh city	209,792	33,431	22,331	11,100	11,639	10,692	1,485	3,259	5,684
Wilmington city	59,715	14,175	8,129	6,046	3,195	4,934	607	na	3,017
Winston-Salem city	110,472	23,621	16,137	7,484	7,523	8,614	1,300	3,449	3,445
North Dakota									
Bismarck city	34,606	7,969	6,158	1,811	1,832	4,326	579	1,034	1,010
Fargo city	61,895	9,594	5,141	4,453	1,469	3,672	1,026	na	2,518
Ohio									
Akron city	96,601	19,483	13,577	5,906	5,229	8,348	266	2,363	2,094
Canton city	33,994	7,625	5,188	2,437	2,752	2,436	156	na	662
Cincinnati city	161,429	26,344	14,573	11,771	6,349	8,224	1,414	3,448	5,062
Cleveland city	213,942	38,722	23,533	15,189	9,495	14,038	913	5,230	5,540
Columbus city	397,308	63,167	43,596	19,571	21,638	21,958	1,624	9,613	8,193
Dayton city	74,669	13,731	10,288	3,443	3,183	7,105	0	na	1,556
Lorain city	29,383	7,035	5,112	1,923	2,199	2,913	na	na	967
Parma city	35,636	8,792	6,977	1,815	2,180	4,797	124	886	558
Toledo city	138,915	25,440	18,325	7,115	6,844	11,481	954	3,853	3,001
Youngstown city	34,586	7,822	5,635	2,187	1,740	3,895	270	na	940
Oklahoma									
Broken Arrow city	41,432	9,346	7,932	1,414	3,374	4,558	420	1,317	733
Edmond city	35,574	8,679	6,640	2,039	2,762	3,878	493	975	1,148
Lawton city	40,339	7,754	5,485	2,269	2,393	3,092	116	997	933
Norman city	53,233	9,153	6,705	2,448	2,160	4,545	228	789	1,050
Oklahoma City city	277,140	54,178	41,042	13,136	14,578	26,464	2,722	7,062	5,788
Tulsa city	189,664	38,643	27,611	11,032	8,761	18,850	1,605	4,801	4,978
Oregon									
Beaverton city	39,469	7,603	5,011	2,592	2,288	2,723	690	1,662	1,667
Bend city	43,513	11,110	7,466	3,644	3,202	4,264	906	1,753	2,057
Eugene city	76,479	18,122	12,826	5,296	6,214	6,612	1,539	3,192	2,924
Gresham city	42,273	9,363	6,014	3,349	2,470	3,544	792	1,728	1,969
Hillsboro city	41,436	7,778	5,553	2,225	2,793	2,760	802	1,813	1,000
Medford city	34,954	9,036	5,746	3,290	2,141	3,605	908	1,045	1,561
Portland city	294,678	57,005	40,069	16,936	17,335	22,734	2,548	11,365	8,261
Salem city	67,833	15,873	11,068	4,805	5,472	5,596	1,100	1,910	3,172
Pennsylvania									
Allentown city	46,614	8,331	5,328	3,003	2,310	3,018	161	na	1,658
Bethlehem city	31,487	7,903	4,827	3,076	1,090	3,737	82	1,186	1,162
Erie city	45,782	10,444	7,146	3,298	2,121	5,025	391	1,478	1,328
Philadelphia city	688,846	144,301	100,850	43,451	36,541	64,309	1,128	26,995	20,114
Pittsburgh city	160,248	32,982	22,103	10,879	7,297	14,806	536	4,256	4,427
Reading city	32,796	5,978	3,003	2,975	1,130	1,873	na	na	1,015
Scranton city	34,681	7,941	5,621	2,320	1,550	4,071	na	na	807
Rhode Island									
Cranston city	34,701	7,654	5,689	1,965	2,191	3,498	na	1,165	na
Pawtucket city	31,960	6,774	4,233	2,541	1,686	2,547	na	1,359	1,213
Providence city	74,036	13,328	5,405	7,923	2,408	2,997	524	1,289	1,684
Warwick city	37,815	11,091	7,436	3,655	3,099	4,337	146	2,370	1,286
South Carolina									
Charleston city	67,006	13,963	10,264	3,699	4,715	5,549	493	3,544	1,133
Columbia city	55,672	8,917	6,692	2,225	3,099	3,593	47	1,385	1,277
Greenville city	34,603	6,599	4,295	2,304	1,485	2,810	373	587	999
North Charleston city	49,665	7,496	5,497	1,999	1,965	3,532	99	778	923
Rock Hill city	29,390	5,845	4,282	1,563	1,888	2,394	215	na	786
South Dakota									
Rapid City city	32,684	8,957	6,330	2,627	2,216	4,114	456	1,162	1,555
Sioux Falls city	77,447	14,186	9,556	4,630	3,285	6,271	1,276	1,286	2,201
Tennessee									
Chattanooga city	85,059	20,047	14,732	5,315	6,063	8,669	707	2,501	2,329
Clarksville city	62,705	7,492	5,800	1,692	1,901	3,899	133	721	952
Franklin city	32,092	6,006	5,270	736	2,398	2,872	na	na	na
Jackson city	29,256	6,510	4,899	1,611	1,380	3,519	na	na	769
Johnson City city	33,657	6,827	4,774	2,053	1,577	3,197	436	na	1,147
Knoxville city	93,937	16,442	12,482	3,960	4,015	8,467	833	2,093	1,118
Memphis city	300,305	56,780	38,847	17,933	16,560	22,287	1,012	8,944	8,979
Murfreesboro city	57,751	8,601	6,592	2,009	2,594	3,998	na	1,212	540
Nashville-Davidson metropolitan govt (bal)	307,785	52,740	38,188	14,552	14,703	23,485	2,564	6,257	5,194
Texas									
Abilene city	49,732	9,709	7,113	2,596	1,644	5,469	530	na	1,241
Allen city	38,445	5,183	3,860	1,323	2,050	1,810	na	na	na
Amarillo city	85,163	17,074	13,104	3,970	4,334	8,770	919	2,352	1,931

Table J-3: Cities - Summary of Housing and Householder Characteristics—*Continued*

| | | | | Householders 65 Years and Over | | | | |
| | | | | Owner Householders | | Renter Households With Meals Included in Rent | Percent of Owner Householders Who Pay 35% or More of income for Housing Costs | Percent of Renter Households Who Pay 35% or More of Income for Rental Costs |
	Total Housing Units	Total Households	Owner Occupied	Renter Occupied	With a Mortgage	Without a Mortgage			
Texas—Cont.									
Arlington city	145,021	25,203	20,110	5,093	6,916	13,194	831	3,261	3,101
Austin city	425,076	53,957	40,715	13,242	13,904	26,811	1,446	9,525	5,441
Baytown city	31,056	5,868	3,962	1,906	770	3,192	246	na	na
Beaumont city	50,621	10,825	8,057	2,768	2,023	6,034	73	966	1,038
Brownsville city	56,654	11,430	8,158	3,272	1,203	6,955	na	1,433	871
Bryan city	32,709	5,852	4,046	1,806	1,000	3,046	581	na	975
Carrollton city	50,756	9,519	6,873	2,646	2,504	4,369	531	1,005	1,784
Cedar Park city	25,880	2,886	2,024	862	878	1,146	na	428	na
College Station city	49,779	5,365	4,538	827	1,301	3,237	na	973	340
Conroe city	37,418	7,856	5,082	2,774	1,971	3,111	389	na	2,269
Corpus Christi city	132,153	27,629	21,481	6,148	6,841	14,640	777	3,422	3,438
Dallas city	590,607	88,938	61,012	27,926	18,657	42,355	3,309	15,106	15,852
Denton city	55,701	8,968	6,648	2,320	2,630	4,018	229	1,205	871
Edinburg city	31,590	4,650	3,965	685	1,326	2,639	na	na	na
El Paso city	252,256	53,524	40,803	12,721	11,594	29,209	237	7,646	5,197
Fort Worth city	337,072	55,700	39,492	16,208	10,905	28,587	2,435	7,163	8,253
Frisco city	68,947	7,405	5,320	2,085	3,000	2,320	242	1,518	1,624
Garland city	77,626	16,237	13,021	3,216	4,641	8,380	585	2,813	1,830
Georgetown city	29,347	12,684	10,838	1,846	4,559	6,279	441	2,001	na
Grand Prairie city	66,350	10,128	7,783	2,345	3,178	4,605	na	1,220	1,141
Harlingen city	25,591	6,270	5,455	815	864	4,591	183	na	na
Houston city	976,745	151,420	100,811	50,609	30,212	70,599	5,405	21,111	25,430
Irving city	92,427	8,277	5,233	3,044	1,550	3,683	383	1,001	948
Killeen city	59,877	5,812	4,258	1,554	948	3,310	na	na	748
Laredo city	78,601	14,292	10,212	4,080	2,890	7,322	na	1,868	2,079
League City city	40,046	6,742	5,260	1,482	2,716	2,544	425	na	na
Lewisville city	43,121	4,946	3,026	1,920	1,695	1,331	291	715	864
Longview city	35,037	7,341	4,450	2,891	1,085	3,365	663	na	1,365
Lubbock city	109,673	19,833	15,726	4,107	5,360	10,366	1,263	2,578	2,374
McAllen city	50,698	10,160	8,378	1,782	2,223	6,155	na	2,030	844
McKinney city	68,525	10,076	7,388	2,688	3,907	3,481	na	2,360	1,870
Mansfield city	23,203	3,653	3,303	350	1,236	2,067	na	na	na
Mesquite city	50,279	8,820	6,573	2,247	2,277	4,296	245	625	1,247
Midland city	51,373	9,382	7,276	2,106	2,207	5,069	534	na	na
Mission city	29,643	6,720	5,352	1,368	1,012	4,340	na	na	na
Missouri City city	26,023	5,928	5,537	391	2,255	3,282	na	na	na
New Braunfels city	33,688	6,933	4,760	2,173	1,707	3,053	424	990	na
North Richland Hills city	27,548	7,090	5,273	1,817	2,119	3,154	561	na	na
Odessa city	45,632	8,100	6,553	1,547	1,728	4,825	144	1,420	447
Pasadena city	52,392	8,322	6,585	1,737	1,983	4,602	na	1,046	867
Pearland city	45,490	9,174	7,467	1,707	4,139	3,328	na	2,399	na
Pharr city	24,899	5,023	3,987	1,036	644	3,343	na	na	na
Plano city	110,239	22,495	15,228	7,267	7,013	8,215	1,291	2,989	2,831
Richardson city	47,700	9,703	7,541	2,162	2,132	5,409	na	778	935
Round Rock city	44,961	5,623	4,105	1,518	2,073	2,032	na	759	859
Rowlett city	22,329	0	0	0	1,325	1,209	na	na	na
San Angelo city	41,981	9,991	7,448	2,543	1,296	6,152	311	na	817
San Antonio city	556,760	112,450	84,087	28,363	27,082	57,005	3,434	13,890	13,324
Sugar Land city	40,684	10,314	9,628	686	3,412	6,216	na	na	na
Temple city	31,729	7,481	5,301	2,180	1,400	3,901	232	na	1,017
Tyler city	41,820	9,055	6,912	2,143	1,983	4,929	213	na	782
Victoria city	27,425	6,962	4,971	1,991	1,633	3,338	na	na	1,243
Waco city	53,946	9,383	6,162	3,221	1,716	4,446	603	1,226	1,490
Wichita Falls city	41,977	9,028	6,269	2,759	1,853	4,416	241	665	1,675
Utah									
Layton city	25,870	4,281	3,690	591	1,345	2,345	na	400	na
Lehi city	18,681	2,816	2,764	52	932	1,832	na	na	na
Ogden city	33,395	6,379	4,657	1,722	1,994	2,663	276	983	763
Orem city	31,786	4,933	4,472	461	1,750	2,722	na	539	192
Provo city	34,695	4,560	3,887	673	1,484	2,403	na	454	468
St. George city	38,368	12,957	10,732	2,225	4,797	5,935	942	1,697	1,325
Salt Lake City city	86,597	14,311	9,745	4,566	4,287	5,458	633	2,098	1,814
Sandy city	35,004	9,341	7,562	1,779	3,143	4,419	614	na	na
South Jordan city	22,604	4,058	3,159	899	989	2,170	na	159	na
West Jordan city	33,794	4,550	4,281	269	1,628	2,653	na	422	na
West Valley City city	39,676	6,852	5,126	1,726	2,272	2,854	na	970	na
Virginia									
Alexandria city	76,527	13,624	9,021	4,603	4,309	4,712	559	1,810	2,214
Chesapeake city	91,783	18,389	14,926	3,463	6,948	7,978	na	2,806	1,215
Hampton city	60,096	12,573	8,613	3,960	3,643	4,970	401	1,809	2,270
Lynchburg city	32,521	7,727	5,206	2,521	1,840	3,366	267	605	1,683
Newport News city	78,028	15,446	9,363	6,083	4,477	4,886	557	2,252	3,339
Norfolk city	98,218	18,377	11,277	7,100	5,908	5,369	320	2,994	3,410
Portsmouth city	40,887	9,668	7,254	2,414	3,921	3,333	na	2,924	1,068
Richmond city	101,081	21,348	13,187	8,161	5,745	7,442	306	4,086	4,449
Roanoke city	47,009	11,021	8,252	2,769	3,041	5,211	445	na	1,341

Table J-3: Cities - Summary of Housing and Householder Characteristics—*Continued*

				Householders 65 Years and Over				
				Owner Householders		Renter Households With Meals Included in Rent	Percent of Owner Householders Who Pay 35% or More of income for Housing Costs	Percent of Renter Households Who Pay 35% or More of Income for Rental Costs
	Total Housing Units	Total Households	Owner Occupied	Renter Occupied	With a Mortgage	Without a Mortgage			
Virginia—Cont.									
Suffolk city	37,333	8,257	6,821	1,436	3,423	3,398	na	1,789	na
Virginia Beach city	186,134	40,323	32,631	7,692	16,420	16,211	1,793	6,804	4,717
Washington									
Auburn city	33,914	7,522	5,631	1,891	2,616	3,015	469	1,412	810
Bellevue city	62,580	12,440	9,248	3,192	4,264	4,984	772	3,032	1,559
Bellingham city	38,348	8,672	6,075	2,597	3,100	2,975	602	na	1,322
Everett city	45,146	8,600	5,230	3,370	2,375	2,855	821	1,701	1,739
Federal Way city	37,359	7,679	5,437	2,242	2,491	2,946	417	1,278	1,425
Kennewick city	31,914	6,553	5,374	1,179	2,167	3,207	na	na	na
Kent city	47,082	9,298	6,695	2,603	3,309	3,386	943	1,884	1,172
Kirkland city	38,202	6,343	4,053	2,290	2,095	1,958	129	967	1,449
Marysville city	26,748	6,205	4,927	1,278	2,148	2,779	na	1,038	na
Pasco city	22,053	3,832	3,132	700	1,444	1,688	na	na	na
Redmond city	28,169	2,993	2,193	800	784	1,409	na	na	na
Renton city	42,178	7,514	4,479	3,035	1,703	2,776	591	1,135	1,203
Sammamish city	23,125	2,577	2,349	228	1,166	1,183	na	273	na
Seattle city	360,579	61,825	37,797	24,028	14,544	23,253	4,280	9,713	11,382
Spokane city	99,331	21,816	15,313	6,503	6,821	8,492	544	2,985	2,287
Spokane Valley city	41,647	10,574	7,512	3,062	2,794	4,718	674	1,230	1,930
Tacoma city	92,579	18,254	11,275	6,979	5,869	5,406	1,314	3,524	2,998
Vancouver city	76,844	19,345	13,601	5,744	6,255	7,346	1,299	3,393	2,572
Yakima city	36,684	10,440	7,488	2,952	2,599	4,889	709	1,753	1,316
Wisconsin									
Appleton city	31,093	6,963	5,574	1,389	1,977	3,597	364	976	na
Eau Claire city	29,621	6,794	4,830	1,964	2,100	2,730	303	na	906
Green Bay city	43,533	8,978	6,189	2,789	1,857	4,332	na	1,051	722
Kenosha city	40,884	8,044	5,639	2,405	2,009	3,630	na	1,184	1,236
Madison city	116,616	21,198	15,386	5,812	6,166	9,220	988	2,784	2,588
Milwaukee city	259,687	42,162	27,827	14,335	11,400	16,427	758	7,430	6,613
Oshkosh city	29,137	6,107	4,041	2,066	857	3,184	213	na	871
Racine city	33,170	6,171	4,508	1,663	1,841	2,667	0	na	na
Waukesha city	30,734	6,698	4,385	2,313	1,863	2,522	444	1,077	1,439

Table J-4: Metropolitan/Micropolitan Statistical Areas - Summary of Housing and Householder Characteristics

| | | Householders 65 Years and Over | | | | | | | |
| | | | | | Owner Householders | | Renter Households With Meals Included in Rent | Percent of Owner Householders Who Pay 35% or More of income for Housing Costs | Percent of Renter Households Who Pay 35% or More of Income for Rental Costs |
	Total Housing Units	Total Households	Owner Occupied	Renter Occupied	With a Mortgage	Without a Mortgage			
Aberdeen, WA Micro Area...	36,434	8,920	7,386	1,534	3,114	4,272	317	1,659	na
Abilene, TX Metro Area...	72,105	15,770	12,790	2,980	2,642	10,148	530	1,596	1,313
Adrian, MI Micro Area..	43,877	11,422	9,708	1,714	4,151	5,557	314	1,997	854
Akron, OH Metro Area..	315,526	77,781	61,253	16,528	26,274	34,979	1,534	10,755	6,470
Alamogordo, NM Micro Area.......................................	31,843	6,635	5,832	803	2,411	3,421	na	na	202
Albany, GA Metro Area...	66,724	14,219	10,845	3,374	4,269	6,576	86	1,810	1,711
Albany, OR Metro Area...	50,891	15,144	11,899	3,245	4,856	7,043	785	2,799	1,497
Albany-Schenectady-Troy, NY Metro Area....................	410,484	95,951	71,713	24,238	27,549	44,164	2,799	11,326	12,059
Albertville, AL Micro Area..	40,812	10,016	8,477	1,539	2,542	5,935	na	1,653	430
Albuquerque, NM Metro Area......................................	391,088	94,579	74,292	20,287	29,929	44,363	1,629	14,029	8,505
Alexandria, LA Metro Area..	67,823	15,380	11,950	3,430	3,098	8,852	128	1,615	1,337
Allentown-Bethlehem-Easton, PA-NJ Metro Area..........	350,538	92,311	71,947	20,364	26,784	45,163	2,428	19,137	9,787
Altoona, PA Metro Area..	56,957	16,090	12,910	3,180	3,778	9,132	216	1,801	961
Amarillo, TX Metro Area...	110,049	23,028	18,826	4,202	6,123	12,703	919	3,172	2,050
Ames, IA Metro Area..	40,766	7,369	6,255	1,114	1,304	4,951	289	815	356
Anchorage, AK Metro Area...	160,219	26,808	22,646	4,162	9,897	12,749	95	4,577	1,710
Ann Arbor, MI Metro Area..	151,576	32,797	27,779	5,018	11,711	16,068	947	5,657	2,262
Anniston-Oxford-Jacksonville, AL Metro Area	53,888	13,456	11,525	1,931	4,481	7,044	99	2,366	893
Appleton, WI Metro Area..	98,531	22,073	18,503	3,570	5,763	12,740	555	4,195	1,723
Asheville, NC Metro Area...	230,920	64,037	52,115	11,922	18,266	33,849	1,852	8,711	5,158
Ashtabula, OH Micro Area..	46,198	11,704	9,576	2,128	3,296	6,280	443	2,803	918
Athens, OH Micro Area..	26,681	5,581	4,469	1,112	1,039	3,430	na	na	571
Athens, TX Micro Area...	41,483	10,841	9,700	1,141	2,558	7,142	na	na	na
Athens-Clarke County, GA Metro Area.........................	85,776	17,820	14,168	3,652	4,902	9,266	539	1,688	1,468
Atlanta-Sandy Springs-Roswell, GA Metro Area...........	2,331,002	432,497	341,358	91,139	167,028	174,330	9,648	65,737	45,445
Atlantic City-Hammonton, NJ Metro Area....................	128,408	28,355	22,436	5,919	10,110	12,326	109	6,321	2,379
Auburn, NY Micro Area..	37,162	8,949	7,039	1,910	2,354	4,685	310	1,587	572
Auburn-Opelika, AL Metro Area..................................	70,372	11,705	9,271	2,434	4,248	5,023	na	1,513	468
Augusta-Richmond County, GA-SC Metro Area	259,295	60,753	51,224	9,529	19,197	32,027	777	10,216	4,053
Augusta-Waterville, ME Micro Area.............................	62,913	16,362	12,563	3,799	4,486	8,077	135	2,046	1,468
Austin-Round Rock, TX Metro Area.............................	853,697	133,162	106,203	26,959	41,319	64,884	3,624	22,367	12,995
Bakersfield, CA Metro Area..	300,423	57,042	44,062	12,980	21,006	23,056	1,231	10,558	6,801
Baltimore-Columbia-Towson, MD Metro Area................	1,164,143	267,577	207,359	60,218	91,293	116,066	8,331	44,968	26,734
Bangor, ME Metro Area..	76,144	17,420	13,279	4,141	4,032	9,247	481	2,449	1,439
Barnstable Town, MA Metro Area...............................	164,329	39,226	34,820	4,406	15,375	19,445	556	10,193	1,933
Baton Rouge, LA Metro Area......................................	358,048	70,045	59,072	10,973	18,856	40,216	780	8,170	4,933
Battle Creek, MI Metro Area.......................................	60,879	15,477	12,391	3,086	4,503	7,888	428	2,272	921
Bay City, MI Metro Area...	48,345	13,107	11,279	1,828	3,304	7,975	228	1,858	695
Beaumont-Port Arthur, TX Metro Area.........................	178,050	37,296	30,692	6,604	5,288	25,404	270	3,663	2,676
Beaver Dam, WI Micro Area.......................................	37,912	9,515	6,646	2,869	2,316	4,330	549	1,401	1,179
Beckley, WV Metro Area..	57,683	16,440	13,966	2,474	4,600	9,366	na	1,787	641
Bellingham, WA Metro Area..	97,867	24,312	19,486	4,826	9,326	10,160	703	4,215	2,242
Bend-Redmond, OR Metro Area..................................	91,040	25,139	19,170	5,969	9,590	9,580	1,105	4,009	3,309
Billings, MT Metro Area...	79,628	19,232	15,244	3,988	4,725	10,519	890	3,234	1,717
Binghamton, NY Metro Area.......................................	113,860	29,458	23,099	6,359	6,722	16,377	372	4,093	2,846
Birmingham-Hoover, AL Metro Area............................	520,740	118,093	97,758	20,335	35,253	62,505	2,695	17,424	8,145
Bismarck, ND Metro Area..	60,824	13,014	10,775	2,239	2,927	7,848	615	1,661	1,234
Blacksburg-Christiansburg-Radford, VA Metro Area......	81,873	18,506	16,078	2,428	4,421	11,657	178	3,136	742
Bloomington, IL Metro Area..	80,721	16,015	13,246	2,769	4,785	8,461	244	1,547	860
Bloomington, IN Metro Area.......................................	72,324	14,936	12,226	2,710	5,543	6,683	518	1,902	1,144
Bloomsburg-Berwick, PA Metro Area...........................	38,559	10,275	8,136	2,139	2,032	6,104	354	2,196	700
Bluefield, WV-VA Micro Area......................................	50,750	14,834	12,548	2,286	2,767	9,781	na	1,445	275
Boise City, ID Metro Area...	283,285	65,182	53,780	11,402	23,734	30,046	2,423	8,988	4,302
Boston-Cambridge-Newton, MA-NH Metro Area...........	1,973,416	468,966	331,791	137,175	139,046	192,745	13,905	97,098	56,849
Boulder, CO Metro Area...	137,465	29,132	23,622	5,510	10,853	12,769	1,385	4,591	3,163
Bowling Green, KY Metro Area....................................	77,072	15,939	13,041	2,898	4,495	8,546	na	2,763	954
Bozeman, MT Micro Area...	51,000	8,441	6,986	1,455	2,063	4,923	337	1,670	726
Brainerd, MN Micro Area...	68,293	13,607	11,314	2,293	3,924	7,390	135	1,985	928
Branson, MO Micro Area..	52,251	14,109	12,060	2,049	4,263	7,797	na	2,040	1,006
Bremerton-Silverdale, WA Metro Area.........................	113,732	30,033	25,482	4,551	11,775	13,707	761	5,628	1,938
Bridgeport-Stamford-Norwalk, CT Metro Area..............	374,480	92,257	69,936	22,321	30,997	38,939	3,264	24,285	10,908
Brownsville-Harlingen, TX Metro Area.........................	152,374	33,403	26,864	6,539	4,768	22,096	183	4,021	2,231
Brunswick, GA Metro Area...	61,215	15,458	13,262	2,196	4,524	8,738	225	na	1,027
Buffalo-Cheektowaga-Niagara Falls, NY Metro Area......	530,321	134,474	99,747	34,727	33,727	66,020	3,255	18,595	16,469
Burlington, NC Metro Area...	71,655	17,636	13,903	3,733	5,176	8,727	523	2,204	1,610
Burlington-South Burlington, VT Metro Area.................	98,586	22,055	16,873	5,182	7,108	9,765	654	4,208	2,428
California-Lexington Park, MD Metro Area....................	45,998	9,007	7,196	1,811	3,810	3,386	na	2,654	na
Canton-Massillon, OH Metro Area...............................	180,625	49,338	37,931	11,407	15,175	22,756	807	6,605	4,129
Cape Coral-Fort Myers, FL Metro Area........................	399,741	121,190	102,843	18,347	35,043	67,800	3,836	23,589	9,818
Cape Girardeau, MO-IL Metro Area.............................	43,877	9,720	7,972	1,748	2,229	5,743	na	1,572	698
Carbondale-Marion, IL Metro Area..............................	60,406	14,043	10,219	3,824	2,695	7,524	661	1,636	1,771
Carson City, NV Metro Area.......................................	24,022	7,131	5,291	1,840	2,150	3,141	260	na	na
Casper, WY Metro Area...	37,181	7,880	6,545	1,335	2,425	4,120	na	904	623

Table J-4: Metropolitan/Micropolitan Statistical Areas - Summary of Housing and Householder Characteristics—*Continued*

	Total Housing Units	Householders 65 Years and Over							
		Total Households	Owner Householders	Renter Occupied	With a Mortgage	Without a Mortgage	Renter Households With Meals Included in Rent	Percent of Owner Householders Who Pay 35% or More of income for Housing Costs	Percent of Renter Households Who Pay 35% or More of Income for Rental Costs
			Owner Occupied						
Cedar Rapids, IA Metro Area	118,216	28,796	23,427	5,369	7,656	15,771	899	4,148	2,120
Centralia, WA Micro Area	35,335	10,886	8,559	2,327	3,219	5,340	470	1,370	833
Chambersburg-Waynesboro, PA Metro Area	65,799	18,693	15,427	3,266	4,539	10,888	715	2,879	1,312
Champaign-Urbana, IL Metro Area	106,732	20,067	16,103	3,964	5,337	10,766	858	2,053	1,637
Charleston, WV Metro Area	108,280	28,326	23,616	4,710	5,361	18,255	na	3,037	1,903
Charleston-North Charleston, SC Metro Area	339,519	73,111	60,355	12,756	26,065	34,290	2,490	14,370	4,616
Charlotte-Concord-Gastonia, NC-SC Metro Area	1,049,329	206,470	167,733	38,737	76,510	91,223	4,128	31,653	19,022
Charlottesville, VA Metro Area	103,303	25,656	19,952	5,704	8,423	11,529	939	2,771	2,226
Chattanooga, TN-GA Metro Area	245,558	62,125	51,972	10,153	18,317	33,655	1,499	7,376	4,675
Cheyenne, WY Metro Area	43,892	11,096	8,948	2,148	4,403	4,545	340	1,713	na
Chicago-Naperville-Elgin, IL-IN-WI Metro Area	3,858,653	858,556	667,114	191,442	263,088	404,026	21,816	181,373	95,095
Chico, CA Metro Area	100,038	25,859	21,044	4,815	9,311	11,733	505	5,843	2,723
Chillicothe, OH Micro Area	32,070	8,430	7,043	1,387	2,122	4,921	na	na	na
Cincinnati, OH-KY-IN Metro Area	938,179	208,494	161,128	47,366	68,351	92,777	5,832	30,639	20,430
Claremont-Lebanon, NH-VT Micro Area	126,341	29,867	24,974	4,893	8,723	16,251	556	5,921	2,489
Clarksburg, WV Micro Area	42,452	11,562	9,674	1,888	2,139	7,535	388	913	770
Clarksville, TN-KY Metro Area	120,476	18,117	15,017	3,100	4,615	10,402	133	2,352	1,285
Clearlake, CA Micro Area	34,751	9,808	7,940	1,868	3,763	4,177	na	na	na
Cleveland, TN Metro Area	53,586	13,167	11,783	1,384	3,861	7,922	na	2,288	265
Cleveland-Elyria, OH Metro Area	963,538	247,018	185,765	61,253	74,439	111,326	7,939	37,867	25,628
Coeur d'Alene, ID Metro Area	72,500	19,738	15,983	3,755	6,734	9,249	885	3,481	2,230
College Station-Bryan, TX Metro Area	110,533	17,983	14,647	3,336	3,701	10,946	581	3,277	1,602
Colorado Springs, CO Metro Area	288,688	58,991	48,431	10,560	22,858	25,573	1,553	9,090	5,845
Columbia, MO Metro Area	78,945	14,295	11,349	2,946	4,773	6,576	658	1,956	1,278
Columbia, SC Metro Area	359,090	78,101	67,322	10,779	29,149	38,173	1,591	14,065	5,484
Columbus, GA-AL Metro Area	135,253	28,711	22,858	5,853	8,980	13,878	491	4,329	2,150
Columbus, IN Metro Area	34,532	8,957	7,194	1,763	2,858	4,336	na	na	na
Columbus, OH Metro Area	869,414	173,268	136,866	36,402	59,295	77,571	3,975	26,995	14,918
Concord, NH Micro Area	65,246	16,924	13,419	3,505	4,335	9,084	226	3,891	1,101
Cookeville, TN Micro Area	50,971	11,946	9,576	2,370	2,075	7,501	na	1,094	1,218
Coos Bay, OR Micro Area	31,178	10,783	8,633	2,150	3,661	4,972	242	na	na
Corning, NY Micro Area	49,684	11,538	9,509	2,029	2,020	7,489	na	1,299	364
Corpus Christi, TX Metro Area	193,862	40,269	32,295	7,974	9,126	23,169	1,039	4,928	4,358
Corvallis, OR Metro Area	38,442	8,774	7,287	1,487	2,665	4,622	520	1,130	668
Crestview-Fort Walton Beach-Destin, FL Metro Area	151,347	29,659	24,248	5,411	9,226	15,022	276	4,073	2,444
Cullman, AL Micro Area	38,029	9,912	8,617	1,295	2,134	6,483	na	na	na
Cumberland, MD-WV Metro Area	45,984	12,799	10,929	1,870	3,349	7,580	na	2,277	597
Dallas-Fort Worth-Arlington, TX Metro Area	2,853,246	490,522	374,564	115,958	135,021	239,543	15,490	70,714	62,441
Dalton, GA Metro Area	56,306	12,910	10,265	2,645	1,880	8,385	407	1,380	1,472
Danville, IL Metro Area	36,125	9,996	8,082	1,914	2,123	5,959	na	1,085	678
Danville, VA Micro Area	53,669	14,421	12,199	2,222	3,474	8,725	59	1,939	985
Daphne-Fairhope-Foley, AL Metro Area	116,632	27,136	24,656	2,480	9,651	15,005	230	4,959	989
Davenport-Moline-Rock Island, IA-IL Metro Area	170,244	42,545	34,532	8,013	10,862	23,670	1,364	4,824	3,224
Dayton, OH Metro Area	370,029	92,499	73,058	19,441	30,003	43,055	2,724	12,818	7,085
Decatur, AL Metro Area	67,766	17,149	13,813	3,336	4,379	9,434	363	1,599	1,120
Decatur, IL Metro Area	50,405	13,096	10,437	2,659	3,092	7,345	456	1,276	1,084
Deltona-Daytona Beach-Ormond Beach, FL Metro Area	314,641	98,613	85,325	13,288	33,029	52,296	1,805	16,348	7,658
Denver-Aurora-Lakewood, CO Metro Area	1,195,543	237,112	184,225	52,887	87,704	96,521	9,347	38,936	27,328
Des Moines-West Des Moines, IA Metro Area	276,147	54,699	42,974	11,725	16,885	26,089	1,650	7,935	5,175
Detroit-Warren-Dearborn, MI Metro Area	1,912,856	456,698	364,032	92,666	137,129	226,903	12,061	78,448	42,208
Dothan, AL Metro Area	69,836	18,008	15,104	2,904	4,984	10,120	34	2,257	904
Dover, DE Metro Area	73,086	17,737	14,732	3,005	6,205	8,527	na	2,307	576
DuBois, PA Micro Area	39,267	10,186	8,209	1,977	1,692	6,517	na	1,393	na
Dubuque, IA Metro Area	41,514	10,313	7,937	2,376	2,323	5,614	881	1,513	739
Duluth, MN-WI Metro Area	144,323	33,939	26,102	7,837	8,019	18,083	1,070	3,927	2,764
Dunn, NC Micro Area	52,561	9,992	8,240	1,752	3,382	4,858	na	1,954	593
Durham-Chapel Hill, NC Metro Area	249,694	53,500	42,699	10,801	19,113	23,586	1,494	7,694	4,316
East Stroudsburg, PA Metro Area	81,664	15,553	13,118	2,435	6,136	6,982	na	3,916	na
Eau Claire, WI Metro Area	73,016	17,510	13,454	4,056	5,052	8,402	624	3,212	1,822
El Centro, CA Metro Area	57,893	10,251	7,230	3,021	3,151	4,079	0	1,689	1,575
Elizabeth City, NC Micro Area	29,979	8,400	6,959	1,441	2,799	4,160	na	na	na
Elizabethtown-Fort Knox, KY Metro Area	65,323	13,754	12,306	1,448	4,346	7,960	240	2,359	446
Elkhart-Goshen, IN Metro Area	79,495	17,003	14,021	2,982	6,178	7,843	460	2,442	1,251
Elmira, NY Metro Area	38,924	10,247	7,706	2,541	2,195	5,511	64	na	1,215
El Paso, TX Metro Area	300,964	61,959	48,713	13,246	13,408	35,305	237	9,228	5,462
Enid, OK Metro Area	26,802	6,272	5,243	1,029	1,655	3,588	na	na	na
Erie, PA Metro Area	121,615	31,393	23,958	7,435	7,411	16,547	1,250	3,843	3,100
Eugene, OR Metro Area	163,490	46,536	37,327	9,209	17,351	19,976	1,829	8,968	4,528
Eureka-Arcata-Fortuna, CA Micro Area	63,308	16,123	12,213	3,910	4,784	7,429	629	2,040	2,009
Evansville, IN-KY Metro Area	143,082	32,167	24,875	7,292	8,460	16,415	662	4,155	3,515
Fairbanks, AK Metro Area	44,307	6,987	6,117	870	2,162	3,955	na	na	161
Fargo, ND-MN Metro Area	110,709	19,059	12,476	6,583	3,132	9,344	1,255	1,859	3,470

Table J-4: Metropolitan/Micropolitan Statistical Areas - Summary of Housing and Householder Characteristics—*Continued*

						Householders 65 Years and Over			
					Owner Householders		Renter Households With Meals Included in Rent	Percent of Owner Households Who Pay 35% or More of income for Housing Costs	Percent of Renter Households Who Pay 35% or More of Income for Rental Costs
	Total Housing Units	Total Households	Owner Occupied	Renter Occupied	With a Mortgage	Without a Mortgage			
Faribault-Northfield, MN Micro Area	25,131	6,671	4,870	1,801	1,490	3,380	185	841	na
Farmington, MO Micro Area	30,242	7,061	5,675	1,386	1,848	3,827	276	na	na
Farmington, NM Metro Area	51,273	12,097	10,611	1,486	2,371	8,240	76	1,195	451
Fayetteville, NC Metro Area	168,287	29,362	22,838	6,524	9,372	13,466	317	5,388	2,604
Fayetteville-Springdale-Rogers, AR-MO Metro Area	221,914	42,779	34,651	8,128	10,500	24,151	1,147	5,055	2,875
Findlay, OH Micro Area	34,372	8,173	6,491	1,682	2,423	4,068	375	na	604
Flagstaff, AZ Metro Area	66,838	10,903	9,217	1,686	3,312	5,905	na	1,428	592
Flint, MI Metro Area	192,614	47,441	38,514	8,927	14,451	24,063	973	7,476	3,921
Florence, SC Metro Area	91,984	22,407	18,526	3,881	6,241	12,285	135	3,114	1,459
Florence-Muscle Shoals, AL Metro Area	72,198	18,903	15,580	3,323	4,290	11,290	na	2,419	702
Fond du Lac, WI Metro Area	45,361	11,716	9,033	2,683	2,509	6,524	380	1,949	1,112
Forest City, NC Micro Area	34,473	9,054	7,361	1,693	1,517	5,844	na	na	na
Fort Collins, CO Metro Area	151,840	33,694	27,202	6,492	11,312	15,890	1,940	5,534	3,800
Fort Payne, AL Micro Area	31,656	8,140	6,529	1,611	1,853	4,676	na	1,194	na
Fort Smith, AR-OK Metro Area	125,732	30,619	25,345	5,274	6,378	18,967	387	3,677	1,471
Fort Wayne, IN Metro Area	186,072	42,222	34,983	7,239	14,189	20,794	801	5,788	3,467
Frankfort, KY Micro Area	32,681	8,330	7,153	1,177	2,306	4,847	na	na	447
Fresno, CA Metro Area	333,809	72,341	49,754	22,587	23,167	26,587	1,972	10,290	11,214
Gadsden, AL Metro Area	47,847	12,152	10,236	1,916	2,306	7,930	147	883	486
Gainesville, FL Metro Area	126,992	24,269	20,088	4,181	5,816	14,272	1,089	3,328	2,209
Gainesville, GA Metro Area	74,431	16,870	14,647	2,223	6,319	8,328	243	3,276	801
Gallup, NM Micro Area	26,344	5,709	5,419	290	1,380	4,039	na	na	na
Gettysburg, PA Metro Area	42,572	12,529	10,101	2,428	3,738	6,363	309	2,999	812
Glens Falls, NY Metro Area	69,804	16,847	13,854	2,993	4,766	9,088	405	2,809	1,092
Glenwood Springs, CO Micro Area	39,213	5,314	4,471	843	1,775	2,696	na	1,562	na
Goldsboro, NC Metro Area	54,467	13,389	10,505	2,884	3,865	6,640	397	2,040	975
Grand Forks, ND-MN Metro Area	48,421	9,459	6,558	2,901	1,586	4,972	431	1,117	1,827
Grand Island, NE Metro Area	36,167	8,741	7,074	1,667	1,951	5,123	328	1,360	569
Grand Junction, CO Metro Area	67,215	18,280	14,960	3,320	6,840	8,120	441	3,705	1,771
Grand Rapids-Wyoming, MI Metro Area	424,695	97,417	80,324	17,093	28,763	51,561	3,239	14,660	8,011
Grants Pass, OR Metro Area	39,354	14,454	11,623	2,831	4,593	7,030	365	1,822	na
Great Falls, MT Metro Area	39,037	9,377	7,639	1,738	3,175	4,464	268	1,347	678
Greeley, CO Metro Area	112,472	22,416	18,579	3,837	8,806	9,773	220	4,454	1,349
Green Bay, WI Metro Area	144,173	32,733	25,054	7,679	7,460	17,594	924	4,386	3,397
Greeneville, TN Micro Area	32,690	8,422	7,023	1,399	2,282	4,741	na	na	na
Greenfield Town, MA Micro Area	34,164	9,784	7,892	1,892	3,102	4,790	122	1,759	690
Greensboro-High Point, NC Metro Area	337,386	78,472	61,832	16,640	26,513	35,319	2,770	12,171	8,699
Greenville, NC Metro Area	80,244	14,472	11,228	3,244	5,561	5,667	212	2,271	1,086
Greenville-Anderson-Mauldin, SC Metro Area	389,673	93,228	76,750	16,478	28,684	48,066	1,880	12,026	6,856
Greenwood, SC Micro Area	43,341	10,883	8,757	2,126	2,845	5,912	338	1,825	813
Gulfport-Biloxi-Pascagoula, MS Metro Area	182,544	39,804	32,972	6,832	8,665	24,307	466	4,027	2,379
Hagerstown-Martinsburg, MD-WV Metro Area	111,046	27,044	22,667	4,377	9,468	13,199	143	3,145	1,135
Hammond, LA Metro Area	56,367	11,765	10,098	1,667	3,752	6,346	na	2,037	811
Hanford-Corcoran, CA Metro Area	46,649	9,949	7,594	2,355	3,065	4,529	na	1,423	983
Harrisburg-Carlisle, PA Metro Area	252,622	64,145	49,309	14,836	18,306	31,003	2,094	8,843	6,120
Harrisonburg, VA Metro Area	54,152	12,547	9,673	2,874	3,678	5,995	664	1,652	1,403
Hartford-West Hartford-East Hartford, CT Metro Area	517,029	127,370	97,057	30,313	38,623	58,434	3,242	26,444	13,898
Hattiesburg, MS Metro Area	64,042	13,122	10,774	2,348	2,573	8,201	na	1,200	528
Helena, MT Micro Area	37,106	9,420	7,640	1,780	3,379	4,261	434	1,599	na
Hermiston-Pendleton, OR Micro Area	35,025	8,178	6,020	2,158	2,389	3,631	110	1,499	927
Hickory-Lenoir-Morganton, NC Metro Area	165,129	43,086	37,803	5,283	12,208	25,595	279	5,809	2,102
Hilo, HI Micro Area	88,548	25,848	21,257	4,591	8,434	12,823	139	5,181	1,491
Hilton Head Island-Bluffton-Beaufort, SC Metro Area	112,376	32,829	29,588	3,241	14,559	15,029	596	6,792	1,817
Hinesville, GA Metro Area	36,355	4,212	3,498	714	912	2,586	na	na	318
Hobbs, NM Micro Area	26,765	4,873	3,725	1,148	515	3,210	na	na	na
Holland, MI Micro Area	51,517	11,325	10,104	1,221	3,812	6,292	na	2,392	372
Homosassa Springs, FL Metro Area	79,988	33,165	30,551	2,614	9,115	21,436	401	4,695	na
Hot Springs, AR Metro Area	51,025	14,925	12,806	2,119	4,986	7,820	356	1,688	762
Houma-Thibodaux, LA Metro Area	87,332	19,686	16,388	3,298	3,949	12,439	354	2,533	1,166
Houston-The Woodlands-Sugar Land, TX Metro Area	2,637,669	446,713	350,418	96,295	116,657	233,761	9,454	69,236	48,954
Huntington-Ashland, WV-KY-OH Metro Area	165,837	41,113	35,126	5,987	10,177	24,949	244	5,141	1,940
Huntsville, AL Metro Area	200,798	45,512	37,757	7,755	15,587	22,170	1,003	6,054	2,598
Huntsville, TX Micro Area	34,507	7,993	7,098	895	1,789	5,309	250	na	na
Hutchinson, KS Micro Area	28,509	7,982	5,973	2,009	1,749	4,224	370	892	623
Idaho Falls, ID Metro Area	54,807	11,776	9,451	2,325	3,654	5,797	930	1,861	1,259
Indiana, PA Micro Area	39,008	10,360	8,522	1,838	2,017	6,505	281	747	316
Indianapolis-Carmel-Anderson, IN Metro Area	867,509	173,440	134,366	39,074	66,108	68,258	5,193	25,901	18,245
Iowa City, IA Metro Area	74,788	13,552	10,891	2,661	3,894	6,997	677	1,463	975
Ithaca, NY Metro Area	43,883	9,079	7,147	1,932	2,812	4,335	443	na	881
Jackson, MI Metro Area	69,696	17,558	14,140	3,418	4,582	9,558	848	1,991	1,513
Jackson, MS Metro Area	245,769	52,662	44,799	7,863	14,571	30,228	221	6,528	2,744
Jackson, TN Metro Area	56,960	13,726	11,693	2,033	2,832	8,861	192	1,508	837

Table J-4: Metropolitan/Micropolitan Statistical Areas - Summary of Housing and Householder Characteristics—*Continued*

			Householders 65 Years and Over						
				Owner Householders					
	Total Housing Units	Total Households	Owner Occupied	Renter Occupied	With a Mortgage	Without a Mortgage	Renter Households With Meals Included in Rent	Percent of Owner Householders Who Pay 35% or More of income for Housing Costs	Percent of Renter Households Who Pay 35% or More of Income for Rental Costs
Jacksonville, FL Metro Area	655,462	146,371	117,463	28,908	51,849	65,614	3,340	22,568	14,619
Jacksonville, NC Metro Area	80,259	10,186	8,664	1,522	3,968	4,696	na	2,037	436
Jamestown-Dunkirk-Fredonia, NY Micro Area	67,661	15,814	12,177	3,637	3,646	8,531	46	1,902	1,265
Janesville-Beloit, WI Metro Area	69,235	17,695	12,889	4,806	4,938	7,951	140	2,421	1,898
Jefferson, GA Micro Area	26,070	5,719	4,705	1,014	2,039	2,666	na	737	na
Jefferson City, MO Metro Area	65,775	15,935	12,628	3,307	2,819	9,809	278	950	1,289
Johnson City, TN Metro Area	98,498	23,772	18,644	5,128	5,540	13,104	570	2,463	2,692
Johnstown, PA Metro Area	66,035	19,834	15,972	3,862	2,827	13,145	439	2,059	856
Jonesboro, AR Metro Area	57,268	12,583	9,816	2,767	2,608	7,208	107	1,242	444
Joplin, MO Metro Area	76,587	19,793	15,773	4,020	6,189	9,584	341	2,300	1,653
Kahului-Wailuku-Lahaina, HI Metro Area	73,889	16,943	13,253	3,690	6,653	6,600	na	3,437	1,102
Kalamazoo-Portage, MI Metro Area	150,185	33,299	26,186	7,113	9,391	16,795	720	4,709	3,112
Kalispell, MT Micro Area	49,088	11,891	9,624	2,267	4,252	5,372	151	1,714	686
Kankakee, IL Metro Area	45,644	10,631	8,418	2,213	2,924	5,494	485	2,545	930
Kansas City, MO-KS Metro Area	917,911	195,894	152,534	43,360	60,691	91,843	5,677	30,836	19,529
Kapaa, HI Micro Area	31,242	9,017	6,589	2,428	2,791	3,798	na	na	886
Keene, NH Micro Area	35,724	9,178	7,257	1,921	2,744	4,513	na	2,224	926
Kennewick-Richland, WA Metro Area	106,032	22,981	19,637	3,344	7,763	11,874	1,128	3,148	2,097
Key West, FL Micro Area	53,457	9,842	8,546	1,296	2,767	5,779	na	na	na
Killeen-Temple, TX Metro Area	178,904	30,645	24,478	6,167	7,563	16,915	395	3,391	2,660
Kingsport-Bristol-Bristol, TN-VA Metro Area	149,268	43,634	37,023	6,611	11,734	25,289	640	6,483	2,036
Kingston, NY Metro Area	85,431	21,616	17,956	3,660	6,142	11,814	na	4,451	1,562
Klamath Falls, OR Micro Area	33,682	8,846	7,394	1,452	2,649	4,745	na	na	na
Knoxville, TN Metro Area	399,186	99,845	86,398	13,447	25,038	61,360	1,666	10,452	5,217
Kokomo, IN Metro Area	39,559	10,516	8,778	1,738	3,862	4,916	351	na	718
La Crosse-Onalaska, WI-MN Metro Area	59,352	14,525	10,437	4,088	2,841	7,596	545	1,727	1,377
Lafayette, LA Metro Area	211,681	44,567	37,065	7,502	8,106	28,959	na	4,739	2,484
Lafayette-West Lafayette, IN Metro Area	90,200	17,007	13,329	3,678	5,134	8,195	491	1,765	1,134
LaGrange, GA Micro Area	28,636	6,585	5,165	1,420	1,945	3,220	162	na	na
Lake Charles, LA Metro Area	95,671	20,957	18,299	2,658	4,807	13,492	595	1,633	1,420
Lake City, FL Micro Area	29,082	7,568	6,833	735	2,598	4,235	na	na	na
Lake Havasu City-Kingman, AZ Metro Area	115,269	39,594	31,713	7,881	13,667	18,046	664	5,911	2,895
Lakeland-Winter Haven, FL Metro Area	299,432	84,267	71,116	13,151	22,840	48,276	1,335	14,585	6,815
Lancaster, PA Metro Area	212,243	57,454	42,445	15,009	13,815	28,630	3,753	6,987	8,049
Lansing-East Lansing, MI Metro Area	203,771	46,592	37,757	8,835	15,044	22,713	1,256	5,711	3,931
Laredo, TX Metro Area	84,466	15,185	11,013	4,172	2,959	8,054	na	2,039	2,079
Las Cruces, NM Metro Area	89,060	20,682	16,730	3,952	5,959	10,771	328	2,191	1,008
Las Vegas-Henderson-Paradise, NV Metro Area	913,385	187,797	132,800	54,997	67,067	65,733	2,075	31,925	29,017
Laurel, MS Micro Area	37,293	9,654	8,309	1,345	1,525	6,784	na	na	na
Lawrence, KS Metro Area	51,068	9,782	8,062	1,720	3,617	4,445	526	2,036	1,126
Lawton, OK Metro Area	54,668	10,434	7,958	2,476	3,102	4,856	116	1,276	957
Lebanon, PA Metro Area	58,010	17,563	13,949	3,614	4,856	9,093	356	2,668	1,752
Lewiston, ID-WA Metro Area	28,344	8,946	6,986	1,960	2,411	4,575	566	939	na
Lewiston-Auburn, ME Metro Area	50,052	12,277	8,865	3,412	2,915	5,950	343	2,207	1,461
Lexington-Fayette, KY Metro Area	222,288	44,993	36,635	8,358	15,205	21,430	1,330	6,146	3,103
Lima, OH Metro Area	45,192	11,540	9,286	2,254	3,578	5,708	290	1,483	947
Lincoln, NE Metro Area	140,696	30,654	23,496	7,158	8,915	14,581	2,322	3,722	2,828
Little Rock-North Little Rock-Conway, AR Metro Area	328,929	69,133	56,448	12,685	20,382	36,066	1,493	9,263	5,000
Logan, UT-ID Metro Area	47,047	8,243	7,340	903	1,885	5,455	na	764	378
London, KY Micro Area	56,205	12,308	9,631	2,677	2,526	7,105	na	1,323	384
Longview, TX Metro Area	90,808	21,507	16,101	5,406	4,804	11,297	737	2,773	2,728
Longview, WA Metro Area	44,959	13,407	10,767	2,640	5,008	5,759	591	2,044	1,115
Los Angeles-Long Beach-Anaheim, CA Metro Area	4,672,663	1,010,518	673,510	337,008	332,188	341,322	20,075	204,376	178,976
Louisville/Jefferson County, KY-IN Metro Area	562,814	129,880	104,627	25,253	41,375	63,252	3,453	18,685	10,751
Lubbock, TX Metro Area	135,468	24,925	20,164	4,761	6,557	13,607	1,397	3,224	2,714
Lufkin, TX Micro Area	36,995	7,583	6,133	1,450	1,480	4,653	na	na	na
Lumberton, NC Micro Area	53,186	12,744	10,197	2,547	2,546	7,651	na	2,435	999
Lynchburg, VA Metro Area	117,697	31,368	25,887	5,481	8,769	17,118	267	3,584	2,595
Macon-Bibb County, GA Metro Area	101,899	23,565	18,132	5,433	6,757	11,375	930	3,864	2,560
Madera, CA Metro Area	50,971	11,632	10,477	1,155	4,910	5,567	0	3,510	747
Madison, WI Metro Area	290,894	61,984	48,851	13,133	18,995	29,856	1,899	9,169	5,988
Manchester-Nashua, NH Metro Area	172,044	38,337	28,773	9,564	11,618	17,155	809	7,433	4,328
Manhattan, KS Metro Area	41,175	6,689	5,349	1,340	1,908	3,441	na	na	477
Manitowoc, WI Micro Area	37,578	10,386	8,575	1,811	2,072	6,503	322	1,104	700
Mankato-North Mankato, MN Metro Area	42,424	9,313	7,656	1,657	2,031	5,625	685	1,207	851
Mansfield, OH Metro Area	54,173	15,028	11,703	3,325	3,559	8,144	346	1,767	1,375
Marinette, WI-MI Micro Area	45,232	9,494	8,096	1,398	1,906	6,190	na	1,154	454
Marion, IN Micro Area	30,494	8,420	6,998	1,422	2,312	4,686	na	na	na
Marion, OH Micro Area	27,907	6,905	5,484	1,421	2,382	3,102	437	na	na
Marquette, MI Micro Area	34,937	8,026	6,084	1,942	1,626	4,458	193	na	803
Marshall, TX Micro Area	28,731	6,821	6,057	764	1,264	4,793	na	na	na
Martinsville, VA Micro Area	33,589	9,267	7,561	1,706	1,502	6,059	na	na	na
McAllen-Edinburg-Mission, TX Metro Area	281,655	56,271	47,414	8,857	9,423	37,991	349	9,234	3,237

Table J-4: Metropolitan/Micropolitan Statistical Areas - Summary of Housing and Householder Characteristics—Continued

| | | | | | Householders 65 Years and Over | | | | |
| | | | | | Owner Householders | | | | |
	Total Housing Units	Total Households	Owner Occupied	Renter Occupied	With a Mortgage	Without a Mortgage	Renter Households With Meals Included in Rent	Percent of Owner Householders Who Pay 35% or More of income for Housing Costs	Percent of Renter Households Who Pay 35% or More of Income for Rental Costs
Meadville, PA Micro Area	44,946	11,241	9,404	1,837	3,332	6,072	72	1,444	265
Medford, OR Metro Area	96,251	29,411	22,712	6,699	9,109	13,603	1,281	5,371	2,923
Memphis, TN-MS-AR Metro Area	574,982	120,430	93,895	26,535	39,975	53,920	2,280	18,810	13,444
Merced, CA Metro Area	85,766	18,366	13,240	5,126	6,169	7,071	0	2,480	2,450
Meridian, MS Micro Area	48,290	12,145	10,439	1,706	2,125	8,314	na	na	661
Miami-Fort Lauderdale-West Palm Beach, FL Metro Area	2,548,910	623,998	479,183	144,815	172,502	306,681	13,913	145,831	79,031
Michigan City-La Porte, IN Metro Area	49,209	13,199	11,096	2,103	4,435	6,661	490	1,782	665
Midland, MI Metro Area	37,115	9,892	8,184	1,708	2,516	5,668	202	1,433	498
Midland, TX Metro Area	63,685	12,836	10,413	2,423	2,895	7,518	678	2,001	1,679
Milwaukee-Waukesha-West Allis, WI Metro Area	681,231	156,917	112,510	44,407	44,923	67,587	5,868	26,921	25,552
Minneapolis-St. Paul-Bloomington, MN-WI Metro Area	1,460,569	313,964	242,797	71,167	99,796	143,001	14,714	48,899	36,353
Minot, ND Micro Area	37,809	6,758	4,934	1,824	1,111	3,823	427	1,189	1,050
Missoula, MT Metro Area	54,922	11,491	8,383	3,108	2,441	5,942	592	1,328	1,436
Mobile, AL Metro Area	184,687	43,522	33,719	9,803	12,362	21,357	628	6,053	4,561
Modesto, CA Metro Area	182,305	41,197	31,490	9,707	14,617	16,873	678	7,885	4,525
Monroe, LA Metro Area	82,278	16,717	13,773	2,944	4,135	9,638	na	2,166	1,298
Monroe, MI Metro Area	64,803	18,137	14,694	3,443	5,761	8,933	na	2,403	2,251
Montgomery, AL Metro Area	168,054	37,384	29,442	7,942	10,503	18,939	105	5,485	3,182
Morehead City, NC Micro Area	50,719	11,038	9,719	1,319	3,523	6,196	na	1,336	na
Morgantown, WV Metro Area	60,241	12,186	10,715	1,471	2,643	8,072	200	1,244	573
Morristown, TN Metro Area	51,551	13,095	11,642	1,453	3,495	8,147	129	1,485	384
Moses Lake, WA Micro Area	37,969	7,992	6,326	1,666	2,242	4,084	566	1,265	433
Mount Airy, NC Micro Area	34,263	9,879	8,244	1,635	2,237	6,007	na	804	409
Mount Pleasant, MI Micro Area	29,272	5,749	4,961	788	1,538	3,423	57	767	230
Mount Vernon-Anacortes, WA Metro Area	54,451	15,788	12,665	3,123	4,865	7,800	798	3,186	1,652
Muncie, IN Metro Area	52,731	12,849	10,730	2,119	4,353	6,377	459	1,662	864
Muskegon, MI Metro Area	74,301	18,617	15,648	2,969	5,262	10,386	386	1,958	1,332
Muskogee, OK Micro Area	30,967	7,165	5,702	1,463	1,971	3,731	78	868	358
Myrtle Beach-Conway-North Myrtle Beach, SC-NC Metro Area	302,984	73,740	66,600	7,140	30,370	36,230	398	14,926	3,035
Nacogdoches, TX Micro Area	28,482	6,068	5,121	947	982	4,139	na	na	na
Napa, CA Metro Area	55,465	15,144	11,686	3,458	5,400	6,286	518	3,092	1,812
Naples-Immokalee-Marco Island, FL Metro Area	218,279	68,705	59,071	9,634	19,536	39,535	4,439	13,260	5,370
Nashville-Davidson--Murfreesboro--Franklin, TN Metro Area	801,341	157,468	127,567	29,901	47,912	79,655	4,217	20,609	10,348
New Bern, NC Metro Area	60,397	16,581	13,698	2,883	4,967	8,731	136	2,706	1,031
New Castle, PA Micro Area	41,321	11,822	9,797	2,025	3,040	6,757	291	1,944	693
New Haven-Milford, CT Metro Area	367,766	90,805	66,949	23,856	26,639	40,310	2,497	21,525	10,168
New Orleans-Metairie, LA Metro Area	559,529	123,478	97,812	25,666	29,741	68,071	1,400	20,717	12,243
New Philadelphia-Dover, OH Micro Area	40,234	11,470	8,369	3,101	2,466	5,903	315	1,778	1,351
New York-Newark-Jersey City, NY-NJ-PA Metro Area	8,021,225	1,893,325	1,196,404	696,921	439,269	757,135	25,947	391,066	340,662
Niles-Benton Harbor, MI Metro Area	77,645	19,901	16,857	3,044	6,334	10,523	na	3,485	1,204
North Port-Sarasota-Bradenton, FL Metro Area	438,587	159,541	135,987	23,554	44,138	91,849	5,209	26,731	12,159
North Wilkesboro, NC Micro Area	33,642	10,532	9,725	807	2,533	7,192	na	na	na
Norwich-New London, CT Metro Area	123,618	29,852	22,885	6,967	9,121	13,764	488	5,543	2,557
Oak Harbor, WA Micro Area	42,274	12,750	11,383	1,367	4,612	6,771	84	2,461	429
Ocala, FL Metro Area	170,513	62,379	55,809	6,570	19,604	36,205	483	9,686	3,264
Ocean City, NJ Metro Area	99,427	14,880	12,793	2,087	4,883	7,910	215	3,000	1,050
Odessa, TX Metro Area	58,685	9,917	8,377	1,540	1,944	6,433	na	2,194	375
Ogden-Clearfield, UT Metro Area	226,478	44,316	38,686	5,630	15,154	23,532	1,300	4,943	2,753
Ogdensburg-Massena, NY Micro Area	53,374	12,077	8,763	3,314	2,753	6,010	101	2,090	977
Oklahoma City, OK Metro Area	579,416	123,243	98,202	25,041	33,601	64,601	3,989	15,730	10,583
Olean, NY Micro Area	41,648	9,120	7,720	1,400	1,881	5,839	na	1,137	514
Olympia-Tumwater, WA Metro Area	117,860	29,900	23,168	6,732	10,653	12,515	990	4,610	3,162
Omaha-Council Bluffs, NE-IA Metro Area	390,387	83,376	62,006	21,370	24,184	37,822	5,154	11,816	9,422
Opelousas, LA Micro Area	36,932	8,223	6,838	1,385	623	6,215	na	993	332
Orangeburg, SC Micro Area	42,794	11,251	9,351	1,900	2,595	6,756	na	na	na
Orlando-Kissimmee-Sanford, FL Metro Area	1,050,682	206,946	166,644	40,302	70,690	95,954	3,650	39,493	19,766
Oshkosh-Neenah, WI Metro Area	76,015	18,183	13,700	4,483	3,756	9,944	1,100	2,717	2,042
Ottawa-Peru, IL Micro Area	69,133	19,294	15,759	3,535	4,791	10,968	305	2,594	1,019
Owensboro, KY Metro Area	51,605	13,373	10,388	2,985	3,724	6,664	134	1,269	1,288
Owosso, MI Micro Area	30,272	7,895	6,415	1,480	1,944	4,471	na	960	572
Oxnard-Thousand Oaks-Ventura, CA Metro Area	290,984	76,222	60,244	15,978	31,187	29,057	1,829	16,187	8,655
Paducah, KY-IL Micro Area	48,849	12,805	10,433	2,372	2,677	7,756	279	na	1,233
Palatka, FL Micro Area	37,374	10,815	9,396	1,419	2,758	6,638	na	na	na
Palm Bay-Melbourne-Titusville, FL Metro Area	280,390	84,167	71,016	13,151	26,752	44,264	1,567	14,885	6,863
Panama City, FL Metro Area	114,504	21,480	18,776	2,704	6,196	12,580	na	3,792	1,238
Parkersburg-Vienna, WV Metro Area	43,680	12,125	10,369	1,756	3,471	6,898	na	1,412	696
Pensacola-Ferry Pass-Brent, FL Metro Area	215,510	48,637	39,777	8,860	13,687	26,090	601	6,305	3,951
Peoria, IL Metro Area	166,773	40,156	32,962	7,194	10,336	22,626	1,439	4,959	2,849
Philadelphia-Camden-Wilmington, PA-NJ-DE-MD Metro Area	2,497,446	601,231	462,883	138,348	182,977	279,906	18,432	118,453	68,095
Phoenix-Mesa-Scottsdale, AZ Metro Area	1,940,167	443,253	361,378	81,875	164,710	196,668	13,972	73,096	42,351
Pine Bluff, AR Metro Area	42,308	9,953	7,821	2,132	1,723	6,098	na	na	na
Pinehurst-Southern Pines, NC Micro Area	47,931	14,474	12,626	1,848	5,449	7,177	505	2,168	407

Table J-4: Metropolitan/Micropolitan Statistical Areas - Summary of Housing and Householder Characteristics—*Continued*

				Householders 65 Years and Over				
				Owner Householders		Renter Households With Meals Included in Rent	Percent of Owner Householders Who Pay 35% or More of Income for Housing Costs	Percent of Renter Households Who Pay 35% or More of Income for Rental Costs
	Total Housing Units	Total Households	Owner Occupied	Renter Occupied	With a Mortgage	Without a Mortgage			
Pittsburgh, PA Metro Area	1,130,046	303,276	235,671	67,605	73,806	161,865	7,498	42,974	27,217
Pittsfield, MA Metro Area	69,393	18,271	14,706	3,565	5,178	9,528	593	3,841	1,091
Plattsburgh, NY Micro Area	36,732	8,126	6,299	1,827	2,164	4,135	na	1,362	524
Pocatello, ID Metro Area	34,441	7,726	6,529	1,197	1,849	4,680	493	823	722
Port Angeles, WA Micro Area	37,331	14,164	11,736	2,428	5,129	6,607	258	2,782	na
Portland-South Portland, ME Metro Area	275,704	67,209	51,142	16,067	21,033	30,109	2,274	11,540	5,680
Portland-Vancouver-Hillsboro, OR-WA Metro Area	1,008,538	229,907	174,468	55,439	79,148	95,320	11,899	47,912	29,520
Port St. Lucie, FL Metro Area	223,168	74,558	65,051	9,507	21,647	43,404	2,281	15,469	5,742
Portsmouth, OH Micro Area	34,514	8,572	6,989	1,583	1,574	5,415	na	na	na
Pottsville, PA Micro Area	69,918	18,720	15,579	3,141	3,987	11,592	562	4,164	1,225
Prescott, AZ Metro Area	118,410	47,659	39,643	8,016	15,527	24,116	901	8,608	4,753
Providence-Warwick, RI-MA Metro Area	705,461	173,365	120,229	53,136	47,780	72,449	3,731	30,499	20,323
Provo-Orem, UT Metro Area	183,774	28,931	26,018	2,913	10,021	15,997	959	3,954	1,495
Pueblo, CO Metro Area	71,451	19,899	15,707	4,192	5,809	9,898	638	3,316	1,990
Punta Gorda, FL Metro Area	105,164	42,134	38,501	3,633	10,381	28,120	700	7,222	na
Quincy, IL-MO Micro Area	34,940	9,049	6,672	2,377	1,773	4,899	274	1,038	1,033
Racine, WI Metro Area	82,908	20,635	16,835	3,800	6,320	10,515	580	3,864	2,049
Raleigh, NC Metro Area	548,200	97,805	76,503	21,302	35,781	40,722	2,710	12,652	8,644
Rapid City, SD Metro Area	65,885	16,401	13,376	3,025	4,424	8,952	456	2,308	1,777
Reading, PA Metro Area	167,383	43,204	32,404	10,800	11,381	21,023	1,404	7,502	4,748
Redding, CA Metro Area	79,187	22,428	18,490	3,938	9,265	9,225	329	3,924	1,794
Reno, NV Metro Area	203,338	48,709	36,109	12,600	19,416	16,693	1,936	8,206	6,733
Richmond, IN Micro Area	31,442	8,133	5,889	2,244	2,551	3,338	na	na	592
Richmond, VA Metro Area	535,243	129,450	102,761	26,689	46,636	56,125	3,916	22,090	14,000
Richmond-Berea, KY Micro Area	44,665	9,739	7,435	2,304	2,394	5,041	273	1,028	840
Riverside-San Bernardino-Ontario, CA Metro Area	1,574,567	326,011	256,962	69,049	128,115	128,847	5,390	73,954	38,794
Roanoke, VA Metro Area	147,101	38,848	31,910	6,938	11,016	20,894	950	4,936	3,723
Roanoke Rapids, NC Micro Area	35,928	9,350	6,938	2,412	1,894	5,044	na	na	879
Rochester, MN Metro Area	95,278	22,103	17,052	5,051	4,986	12,066	1,398	2,974	2,494
Rochester, NY Metro Area	482,352	120,189	91,892	28,297	36,704	55,188	3,700	18,387	14,455
Rockford, IL Metro Area	145,829	36,083	28,868	7,215	11,787	17,081	1,339	6,006	2,758
Rocky Mount, NC Metro Area	68,181	19,318	15,391	3,927	5,626	9,765	385	3,133	1,710
Rome, GA Metro Area	40,639	10,194	7,772	2,422	2,932	4,840	261	na	663
Roseburg, OR Micro Area	50,564	17,844	14,548	3,296	4,413	10,135	309	2,586	1,239
Roswell, NM Micro Area	27,428	6,568	4,610	1,958	1,052	3,558	480	na	na
Russellville, AR Micro Area	36,369	7,873	6,833	1,040	1,944	4,889	na	875	488
Sacramento--Roseville--Arden-Arcade, CA Metro Area	911,214	213,573	163,263	50,310	81,054	82,209	6,321	43,038	27,196
Saginaw, MI Metro Area	87,810	23,894	19,822	4,072	5,768	14,054	805	2,968	2,347
St. Cloud, MN Metro Area	82,549	18,046	13,391	4,655	4,061	9,330	276	2,699	2,383
St. George, UT Metro Area	71,349	22,266	19,435	2,831	9,042	10,393	1,006	3,744	1,379
St. Joseph, MO-KS Metro Area	54,038	13,619	11,178	2,441	3,656	7,522	199	1,484	1,115
St. Louis, MO-IL Metro Area	1,262,336	297,140	233,943	63,197	88,145	145,798	9,018	39,313	28,961
Salem, OH Micro Area	46,848	12,925	11,250	1,675	3,729	7,521	250	1,064	841
Salem, OR Metro Area	159,836	41,060	31,291	9,769	14,704	16,587	2,192	5,679	5,924
Salinas, CA Metro Area	142,414	34,561	26,935	7,626	12,604	14,331	492	6,968	3,255
Salisbury, MD-DE Metro Area	251,638	59,544	50,611	8,933	20,490	30,121	412	10,457	2,939
Salt Lake City, UT Metro Area	426,150	79,657	64,777	14,880	26,491	38,286	3,108	12,763	6,593
San Angelo, TX Metro Area	49,393	11,834	9,030	2,804	1,422	7,608	311	1,559	870
San Antonio-New Braunfels, TX Metro Area	905,875	187,397	149,237	38,160	47,729	101,508	4,665	24,471	18,152
San Diego-Carlsbad, CA Metro Area	1,224,390	268,419	199,134	69,285	99,725	99,409	6,794	53,748	38,933
Sandusky, OH Micro Area	37,907	10,135	7,844	2,291	2,998	4,846	440	na	na
San Francisco-Oakland-Hayward, CA Metro Area	1,825,205	420,538	297,215	123,323	142,355	154,860	12,664	74,580	58,481
San Jose-Sunnyvale-Santa Clara, CA Metro Area	697,955	143,608	106,091	37,517	47,727	58,364	4,799	27,230	18,923
San Luis Obispo-Paso Robles-Arroyo Grande, CA Metro Area	122,971	35,948	28,866	7,082	14,478	14,388	303	7,640	2,533
Santa Cruz-Watsonville, CA Metro Area	106,718	27,799	21,393	6,406	10,769	10,624	678	5,166	3,471
Santa Fe, NM Metro Area	73,463	22,869	19,291	3,578	8,080	11,211	217	3,109	1,307
Santa Maria-Santa Barbara, CA Metro Area	158,315	41,277	31,958	9,319	13,758	18,200	1,868	6,619	4,410
Santa Rosa, CA Metro Area	205,247	62,227	46,757	15,470	21,964	24,793	1,361	12,412	9,173
Savannah, GA Metro Area	163,292	34,075	28,267	5,808	11,519	16,748	421	4,719	2,281
Scranton--Wilkes-Barre--Hazleton, PA Metro Area	264,517	70,268	54,843	15,425	14,139	40,704	1,391	10,763	4,323
Searcy, AR Micro Area	33,954	8,138	6,401	1,737	2,328	4,073	211	na	701
Seattle-Tacoma-Bellevue, WA Metro Area	1,617,428	321,485	236,950	84,535	104,861	132,089	16,893	61,097	43,159
Sebastian-Vero Beach, FL Metro Area	81,037	27,705	24,332	3,373	7,546	16,786	247	na	na
Sebring, FL Metro Area	55,760	21,675	19,579	2,096	5,184	14,395	na	2,581	na
Seneca, SC Micro Area	40,812	11,515	9,846	1,669	3,387	6,459	na	na	na
Sevierville, TN Micro Area	58,279	11,040	9,595	1,445	2,700	6,895	na	na	na
Shawnee, OK Micro Area	29,998	7,298	5,825	1,473	1,375	4,450	84	703	496
Sheboygan, WI Metro Area	51,352	13,487	10,515	2,972	2,923	7,592	507	1,795	1,341
Shelby, NC Micro Area	43,673	10,539	8,957	1,582	2,353	6,604	na	1,408	652
Shelton, WA Micro Area	33,685	8,846	8,059	787	3,850	4,209	223	na	na

Table J-4: Metropolitan/Micropolitan Statistical Areas - Summary of Housing and Householder Characteristics—*Continued*

				Householders 65 Years and Over				
				Owner Householders				
	Total Housing Units	Total Households	Owner Occupied	Renter Occupied	With a Mortgage	Without a Mortgage	Renter Households With Meals Included in Rent	Percent of Owner Householders Who Pay 35% or More of income for Housing Costs	Percent of Renter Households Who Pay 35% or More of Income for Rental Costs
Sherman-Denison, TX Metro Area	56,735	14,802	12,216	2,586	2,985	9,231	290	1,800	1,361
Show Low, AZ Micro Area	58,164	12,780	10,722	2,058	3,205	7,517	na	na	493
Shreveport-Bossier City, LA Metro Area	204,144	45,920	37,004	8,916	11,741	25,263	981	5,421	4,395
Sierra Vista-Douglas, AZ Metro Area	61,318	19,349	16,205	3,144	6,251	9,954	402	2,755	1,377
Sioux City, IA-NE-SD Metro Area	71,056	16,332	13,170	3,162	2,455	10,715	888	1,253	1,514
Sioux Falls, SD Metro Area	111,652	23,261	16,899	6,362	4,674	12,225	1,648	2,340	2,875
Somerset, PA Micro Area	38,500	9,473	7,888	1,585	1,642	6,246	na	1,037	364
South Bend-Mishawaka, IN-MI Metro Area	143,517	34,462	28,153	6,309	10,674	17,479	802	5,091	2,461
Spartanburg, SC Metro Area	145,544	33,815	28,809	5,006	9,586	19,223	403	3,660	1,738
Spokane-Spokane Valley, WA Metro Area	249,137	60,852	47,346	13,506	18,780	28,566	2,100	8,196	6,170
Springfield, IL Metro Area	97,663	24,003	20,000	4,003	6,194	13,806	550	2,311	1,828
Springfield, MA Metro Area	257,938	66,655	49,279	17,376	17,684	31,595	1,903	10,534	7,101
Springfield, MO Metro Area	205,574	50,083	37,409	12,674	13,487	23,922	1,108	6,193	7,621
Springfield, OH Metro Area	61,307	17,429	14,395	3,034	4,710	9,685	299	1,908	1,225
State College, PA Metro Area	67,155	13,802	10,964	2,838	3,018	7,946	135	1,675	1,197
Statesboro, GA Micro Area	31,413	5,700	4,684	1,016	1,380	3,304	na	na	478
Staunton-Waynesboro, VA Metro Area	55,170	17,316	13,595	3,721	5,391	8,204	462	2,648	2,094
Stevens Point, WI Micro Area	31,129	7,783	5,982	1,801	1,776	4,206	444	972	1,128
Stillwater, OK Micro Area	36,824	7,462	6,243	1,219	1,880	4,363	138	na	231
Stockton-Lodi, CA Metro Area	245,561	51,357	37,218	14,139	17,528	19,690	1,475	10,272	6,743
Sumter, SC Metro Area	48,282	10,897	8,982	1,915	3,526	5,456	403	na	686
Sunbury, PA Micro Area	45,471	12,466	9,095	3,371	2,257	6,838	na	1,809	717
Syracuse, NY Metro Area	296,359	70,660	55,336	15,324	19,369	35,967	1,282	10,223	6,191
Talladega-Sylacauga, AL Micro Area	44,885	10,347	8,415	1,932	2,445	5,970	na	na	na
Tallahassee, FL Metro Area	171,457	35,295	29,524	5,771	11,405	18,119	345	5,590	2,051
Tampa-St. Petersburg-Clearwater, FL Metro Area	1,435,447	375,283	301,352	73,931	103,068	198,284	12,234	64,685	37,437
Terre Haute, IN Metro Area	75,293	16,800	13,562	3,238	5,063	8,499	413	1,855	1,214
Texarkana, TX-AR Metro Area	66,700	15,677	13,333	2,344	2,895	10,438	389	2,053	933
The Villages, FL Metro Area	72,372	44,756	40,865	3,891	13,254	27,611	759	na	na
Toledo, OH Metro Area	275,164	60,641	47,975	12,666	19,664	28,311	1,388	9,457	4,769
Topeka, KS Metro Area	105,397	27,465	21,435	6,030	8,175	13,260	992	4,234	3,080
Torrington, CT Micro Area	88,402	23,504	20,025	3,479	6,842	13,183	174	5,104	1,323
Traverse City, MI Micro Area	85,293	19,878	17,043	2,835	6,252	10,791	623	2,697	1,360
Trenton, NJ Metro Area	145,132	35,066	26,999	8,067	9,765	17,234	177	6,974	4,197
Truckee-Grass Valley, CA Micro Area	54,264	16,239	13,361	2,878	5,887	7,474	246	na	864
Tucson, AZ Metro Area	462,778	126,887	99,230	27,657	39,304	59,926	4,264	16,550	12,009
Tullahoma-Manchester, TN Micro Area	46,866	12,013	10,313	1,700	2,692	7,621	na	1,644	618
Tulsa, OK Metro Area	434,806	96,079	77,017	19,062	24,156	52,861	2,678	11,535	8,087
Tupelo, MS Micro Area	60,195	12,167	9,885	2,282	2,533	7,352	353	683	636
Tuscaloosa, AL Metro Area	110,843	21,717	17,719	3,998	6,474	11,245	558	3,079	1,702
Twin Falls, ID Micro Area	42,170	9,741	8,251	1,490	3,366	4,885	351	1,043	532
Tyler, TX Metro Area	91,101	22,791	19,715	3,076	5,341	14,374	213	3,951	960
Ukiah, CA Micro Area	40,934	12,167	9,538	2,629	3,536	6,002	103	na	1,052
Urban Honolulu, HI Metro Area	352,582	91,320	67,675	23,645	31,534	36,141	1,512	13,134	9,727
Utica-Rome, NY Metro Area	139,326	33,811	25,552	8,259	7,267	18,285	768	4,253	2,958
Valdosta, GA Metro Area	62,704	13,374	11,061	2,313	4,762	6,299	na	3,434	697
Vallejo-Fairfield, CA Metro Area	158,815	38,327	29,649	8,678	17,698	11,951	1,090	7,278	4,370
Victoria, TX Metro Area	41,067	10,278	8,086	2,192	2,084	6,002	na	1,145	1,243
Vineland-Bridgeton, NJ Metro Area	56,497	14,558	11,946	2,612	4,153	7,793	na	3,464	1,634
Virginia Beach-Norfolk-Newport News, VA-NC Metro Area	721,597	157,793	121,415	36,378	58,519	62,896	4,444	26,811	18,184
Visalia-Porterville, CA Metro Area	150,217	29,774	22,877	6,897	9,525	13,352	507	5,725	2,900
Waco, TX Metro Area	110,987	24,632	18,789	5,843	4,711	14,078	603	4,235	2,695
Walla Walla, WA Metro Area	27,382	8,217	6,311	1,906	1,876	4,435	642	na	769
Warner Robins, GA Metro Area	79,525	14,460	10,324	4,136	3,325	6,999	na	1,271	1,223
Warsaw, IN Micro Area	38,744	8,548	7,625	923	2,277	5,348	na	934	402
Washington-Arlington-Alexandria, DC-VA-MD-WV Metro Area	2,374,883	470,638	368,105	102,533	190,589	177,516	13,052	79,884	48,269
Waterloo-Cedar Falls, IA Metro Area	74,416	18,517	15,734	2,783	4,676	11,058	881	2,059	1,313
Watertown-Fort Atkinson, WI Micro Area	36,004	9,124	7,534	1,590	2,744	4,790	143	1,299	558
Watertown-Fort Drum, NY Metro Area	60,041	9,611	7,701	1,910	2,670	5,031	95	1,137	606
Wausau, WI Metro Area	59,706	15,425	11,846	3,579	3,135	8,711	506	1,728	1,497
Weirton-Steubenville, WV-OH Metro Area	58,798	17,348	14,190	3,158	3,898	10,292	282	1,560	930
Wenatchee, WA Metro Area	55,248	13,101	10,520	2,581	3,506	7,014	677	1,330	1,209
Wheeling, WV-OH Metro Area	68,798	19,242	16,220	3,022	3,524	12,696	na	2,186	1,018
Whitewater-Elkhorn, WI Micro Area	52,653	11,193	9,131	2,062	3,238	5,893	239	1,749	1,031
Wichita, KS Metro Area	277,530	61,430	47,633	13,797	15,862	31,771	2,350	8,138	6,591
Wichita Falls, TX Metro Area	65,446	14,948	11,795	3,153	2,850	8,945	241	1,617	1,908
Williamsport, PA Metro Area	53,530	13,364	10,892	2,472	3,753	7,139	222	1,774	1,105
Wilmington, NC Metro Area	142,860	32,231	24,124	8,107	9,523	14,601	832	4,956	4,154
Wilson, NC Micro Area	36,316	9,989	7,934	2,055	2,699	5,235	na	na	na
Winchester, VA-WV Metro Area	61,985	15,331	12,527	2,804	4,473	8,054	411	2,542	898

Table J-4: Metropolitan/Micropolitan Statistical Areas - Summary of Housing and Householder Characteristics—*Continued*

	Total Housing Units	Householders 65 Years and Over							
					Owner Householders		Renter Households With Meals Included in Rent	Percent of Owner Householders Who Pay 35% or More of income for Housing Costs	Percent of Renter Households Who Pay 35% or More of Income for Rental Costs
		Total Households	Owner Occupied	Renter Occupied	With a Mortgage	Without a Mortgage			
Winston-Salem, NC Metro Area	301,150	74,764	58,989	15,775	22,904	36,085	1,984	11,255	6,177
Wisconsin Rapids-Marshfield, WI Micro Area............................	35,186	9,953	7,767	2,186	1,878	5,889	518	628	999
Wooster, OH Micro Area..	46,732	12,744	10,057	2,687	2,871	7,186	349	1,026	861
Worcester, MA-CT Metro Area	386,302	88,115	63,448	24,667	25,167	38,281	2,093	18,037	9,992
Yakima, WA Metro Area	89,129	21,499	17,215	4,284	5,862	11,353	736	3,618	1,491
York-Hanover, PA Metro Area..	184,880	47,981	38,551	9,430	13,985	24,566	1,174	8,025	4,880
Youngstown-Warren-Boardman, OH-PA Metro Area....................	259,297	73,546	59,725	13,821	19,225	40,500	1,743	9,764	5,036
Yuba City, CA Metro Area..	63,163	15,168	11,939	3,229	4,597	7,342	183	2,603	1,541
Yuma, AZ Metro Area	93,571	22,994	19,472	3,522	5,796	13,676	na	2,934	860
Zanesville, OH Micro Area...	37,948	10,134	7,884	2,250	2,986	4,898	na	1,380	817

Table J-5: 116th Congressional Districts - Summary of Housing and Householder Characteristics

	Total Housing Units	Total Households	Owner Occupied	Renter Occupied	Householders 65 Years and Over			Percent of Owner Householders Who Pay 35% or More of income for Housing Costs	Percent of Renter Households Who Pay 35% or More of Income for Rental Costs
					Owner Householders		Renter Households With Meals Included in Rent		
					With a Mortgage	Without a Mortgage			
Alabama									
Congressional District 1	342,612	81,162	67,183	13,979	23,822	43,361	858	12,234	5,905
Congressional District 2	319,106	71,219	58,965	12,254	18,470	40,495	65	8,720	4,144
Congressional District 3	332,603	73,987	60,495	13,492	21,579	38,916	360	11,581	3,654
Congressional District 4	317,421	80,677	67,700	12,977	16,659	51,041	577	10,406	3,615
Congressional District 5	323,745	76,457	63,592	12,865	23,506	40,086	1,449	8,827	3,995
Congressional District 6	306,242	71,378	61,651	9,727	22,678	38,973	2,229	9,212	3,668
Congressional District 7	332,982	69,093	53,841	15,252	16,021	37,820	696	10,467	6,475
Alaska									
Congressional District (at Large)	318,352	53,173	44,662	8,511	17,016	27,646	213	8,730	3,190
Arizona									
Congressional District 1	348,097	88,103	76,621	11,482	26,129	50,492	305	11,443	3,783
Congressional District 2	350,105	100,367	78,460	21,907	30,994	47,466	4,163	14,793	10,529
Congressional District 3	280,554	56,126	44,901	11,225	18,711	26,190	244	8,121	4,062
Congressional District 4	406,015	138,453	117,133	21,320	47,457	69,676	1,738	22,256	9,211
Congressional District 5	335,108	78,549	67,611	10,938	29,671	37,940	1,537	12,876	5,045
Congressional District 6	370,737	91,030	73,866	17,164	34,685	39,181	3,605	17,434	9,700
Congressional District 7	271,997	34,788	23,883	10,905	11,001	12,882	180	5,242	5,803
Congressional District 8	326,339	105,814	89,362	16,452	40,971	48,391	4,583	17,388	8,986
Congressional District 9	346,950	61,157	42,918	18,239	19,974	22,944	3,977	7,828	9,046
Arkansas									
Congressional District 1	345,807	82,565	66,089	16,476	17,788	48,301	453	9,517	3,942
Congressional District 2	344,585	74,690	60,422	14,268	21,533	38,889	1,781	9,911	5,316
Congressional District 3	341,835	72,354	58,668	13,686	17,314	41,354	1,768	8,703	4,869
Congressional District 4	348,294	85,229	72,801	12,428	18,525	54,276	812	10,275	3,455
California									
Congressional District 1	330,882	94,923	78,764	16,159	34,689	44,075	1,164	19,704	7,518
Congressional District 2	321,744	97,850	76,013	21,837	33,586	42,427	2,392	18,053	10,707
Congressional District 3	270,628	63,179	49,535	13,644	23,073	26,462	1,777	11,413	6,536
Congressional District 4	364,607	94,872	81,260	13,612	38,881	42,379	2,254	24,426	7,327
Congressional District 5	286,652	78,373	57,708	20,665	28,711	28,997	1,932	14,296	10,902
Congressional District 6	292,709	57,744	36,129	21,615	18,217	17,912	1,551	8,412	11,478
Congressional District 7	279,623	68,407	55,134	13,273	29,563	25,571	1,987	14,195	7,573
Congressional District 8	305,372	59,501	47,358	12,143	23,446	23,912	374	13,474	5,869
Congressional District 9	255,332	53,666	40,395	13,271	19,748	20,647	1,317	9,802	6,625
Congressional District 10	249,754	55,821	42,730	13,091	20,265	22,465	991	11,524	6,027
Congressional District 11	283,153	74,681	58,920	15,761	30,216	28,704	3,029	14,705	8,969
Congressional District 12	363,935	73,326	36,401	36,925	14,630	21,771	2,256	9,547	14,636
Congressional District 13	312,782	68,697	43,187	25,510	21,007	22,180	1,715	11,304	11,328
Congressional District 14	269,449	66,263	50,943	15,320	23,183	27,760	1,921	12,906	8,499
Congressional District 15	264,147	54,142	41,239	12,903	19,383	21,856	1,450	9,380	6,955
Congressional District 16	232,761	44,971	31,206	13,765	14,905	16,301	195	7,709	7,143
Congressional District 17	275,227	45,945	34,693	11,252	14,626	20,067	1,234	8,139	5,269
Congressional District 18	290,127	68,719	53,715	15,004	23,765	29,950	3,307	12,982	7,860
Congressional District 19	244,280	52,503	36,659	15,844	17,961	18,698	1,038	10,584	8,037
Congressional District 20	251,904	62,080	47,974	14,106	23,734	24,240	994	12,421	6,701
Congressional District 21	203,575	37,272	26,104	11,168	10,896	15,208	140	6,074	4,514
Congressional District 22	257,742	59,525	44,314	15,211	19,923	24,391	2,114	9,341	7,637
Congressional District 23	277,136	57,426	44,493	12,933	21,762	22,731	1,372	10,982	6,882
Congressional District 24	286,337	78,074	61,524	16,550	28,673	32,851	2,171	14,406	7,057
Congressional District 25	235,065	53,821	42,409	11,412	23,128	19,281	911	12,609	6,896
Congressional District 26	246,029	63,532	50,882	12,650	26,392	24,490	1,550	13,382	6,587
Congressional District 27	262,422	65,770	44,449	21,321	19,934	24,515	1,989	13,211	11,237
Congressional District 28	329,887	63,110	32,138	30,972	15,757	16,381	923	11,495	19,321
Congressional District 29	220,112	42,712	27,152	15,560	13,418	13,734	597	10,024	8,759
Congressional District 30	294,061	65,645	45,408	20,237	23,393	22,015	2,349	14,108	12,359
Congressional District 31	239,462	46,483	33,862	12,621	16,482	17,380	1,444	8,335	6,922
Congressional District 32	206,019	46,866	35,049	11,817	16,114	18,935	222	9,509	5,530
Congressional District 33	327,602	82,134	60,124	22,010	30,483	29,641	1,217	18,904	12,428
Congressional District 34	285,916	51,037	15,773	35,264	6,727	9,046	1,286	4,654	17,077
Congressional District 35	209,556	35,525	25,739	9,786	14,425	11,314	658	.7,421	5,712
Congressional District 36	382,465	104,360	84,264	20,096	34,912	49,352	1,477	23,962	12,038
Congressional District 37	297,234	59,276	33,403	25,873	17,831	15,572	599	13,721	13,027
Congressional District 38	212,118	54,481	40,721	13,760	19,584	21,137	626	11,446	6,667
Congressional District 39	233,057	57,416	47,389	10,027	23,437	23,952	1,040	11,722	5,038
Congressional District 40	191,011	30,304	16,968	13,336	8,391	8,577	114	4,465	7,185
Congressional District 41	199,185	33,386	24,579	8,807	13,526	11,053	802	6,113	5,243
Congressional District 42	238,636	47,603	39,854	7,749	24,181	15,673	639	14,098	3,915
Congressional District 43	259,917	51,696	31,597	20,099	16,951	14,646	879	10,098	9,311
Congressional District 44	197,749	39,168	25,311	13,857	12,736	12,575	380	8,838	6,779
Congressional District 45	298,836	71,030	55,592	15,438	27,473	28,119	3,080	16,002	7,508
Congressional District 46	201,897	35,379	22,333	13,046	11,290	11,043	847	6,463	6,302
Congressional District 47	261,537	51,252	33,579	17,673	15,972	17,607	778	8,960	9,277
Congressional District 48	292,907	73,657	53,835	19,822	24,082	29,753	2,075	14,952	11,820
Congressional District 49	280,011	73,126	57,067	16,059	29,660	27,407	2,216	14,830	8,801
Congressional District 50	264,605	62,707	50,895	11,812	25,623	25,272	1,868	14,842	7,208

Table J-5: 116th Congressional Districts - Summary of Housing and Householder Characteristics—*Continued*

					Householders 65 Years and Over				
					Owner Householders			Percent of Owner Householders Who Pay 35% or More of income for Housing Costs	Percent of Renter Households Who Pay 35% or More of Income for Rental Costs
	Total Housing Units	Total Households	Owner Occupied	Renter Occupied	With a Mortgage	Without a Mortgage	Renter Households With Meals Included in Rent		
California—Cont.									
Congressional District 51	229,698	45,161	28,086	17,075	13,195	14,891	394	8,029	9,456
Congressional District 52	314,052	65,678	50,316	15,362	25,143	25,173	1,220	13,643	8,872
Congressional District 53	296,963	56,942	39,966	16,976	19,284	20,682	1,423	9,921	8,877
Colorado									
Congressional District 1	383,206	66,607	47,100	19,507	20,482	26,618	2,473	9,737	9,556
Congressional District 2	384,260	75,019	63,675	11,344	29,298	34,377	2,896	13,133	6,361
Congressional District 3	375,217	85,549	71,270	14,279	27,484	43,786	1,577	15,776	6,373
Congressional District 4	326,860	70,674	58,685	11,989	26,688	31,997	2,187	12,747	5,203
Congressional District 5	331,065	69,981	57,952	12,029	26,429	31,523	1,553	11,045	6,250
Congressional District 6	312,057	62,030	47,796	14,234	24,467	23,329	2,729	10,469	7,039
Congressional District 7	311,463	69,942	54,471	15,471	23,902	30,569	3,483	10,806	8,803
Connecticut									
Congressional District 1	305,611	76,484	56,833	19,651	20,969	35,864	2,043	15,752	8,826
Congressional District 2	309,743	76,003	60,640	15,363	24,915	35,725	1,337	15,014	6,523
Congressional District 3	307,058	76,259	58,156	18,103	25,261	32,895	1,658	18,537	7,959
Congressional District 4	291,150	70,411	51,568	18,843	23,180	28,388	2,307	19,166	9,085
Congressional District 5	307,561	75,636	58,089	17,547	21,346	36,743	2,624	16,416	7,577
Delaware									
Congressional District (at Large)	438,659	107,758	91,333	16,425	38,917	52,416	1,532	17,114	5,945
District of Columbia									
Delegate District (at Large)	319,579	58,898	34,173	24,725	16,887	17,286	1,466	8,689	10,596
Florida									
Congressional District 1	372,491	79,682	65,103	14,579	23,115	41,988	877	10,657	6,497
Congressional District 2	356,326	91,997	83,091	8,906	25,431	57,660	376	14,928	2,730
Congressional District 3	322,618	75,812	62,891	12,921	22,170	40,721	1,827	9,024	6,407
Congressional District 4	359,000	82,281	66,858	15,423	29,558	37,300	2,928	14,212	7,081
Congressional District 5	319,251	62,413	47,941	14,472	18,983	28,958	167	9,270	6,986
Congressional District 6	374,029	116,759	100,604	16,155	38,758	61,846	2,187	19,389	9,034
Congressional District 7	323,337	67,126	51,121	16,005	23,677	27,444	2,029	12,296	8,121
Congressional District 8	366,840	113,656	97,045	16,611	35,338	61,707	1,814	19,194	8,552
Congressional District 9	377,483	75,299	62,006	13,293	23,400	38,606	938	14,225	7,247
Congressional District 10	326,741	50,722	39,935	10,787	17,869	22,066	475	11,205	5,144
Congressional District 11	395,023	172,181	155,659	16,522	51,315	104,344	2,230	24,862	7,208
Congressional District 12	370,274	117,538	99,264	18,274	31,920	67,344	3,112	20,227	8,298
Congressional District 13	391,150	105,500	82,450	23,050	25,321	57,129	3,851	19,578	12,049
Congressional District 14	338,165	61,564	44,413	17,151	17,696	26,717	2,444	10,609	8,637
Congressional District 15	322,734	76,150	63,016	13,134	23,911	39,105	1,489	12,155	7,280
Congressional District 16	419,899	137,379	116,080	21,299	39,676	76,404	5,230	24,586	10,939
Congressional District 17	394,897	147,229	131,266	15,963	35,265	96,001	2,401	22,571	8,867
Congressional District 18	373,987	119,666	104,194	15,472	34,843	69,351	3,675	27,249	9,028
Congressional District 19	486,776	149,957	125,823	24,134	41,818	84,005	7,927	30,169	13,601
Congressional District 20	284,084	59,499	44,086	15,413	18,072	26,014	1,573	13,056	8,341
Congressional District 21	365,075	121,552	104,266	17,286	35,963	68,303	3,734	27,280	9,944
Congressional District 22	392,776	101,164	82,345	18,819	27,334	55,011	4,819	25,701	10,986
Congressional District 23	348,959	80,170	65,090	15,080	22,071	43,019	1,180	22,312	9,414
Congressional District 24	278,812	58,706	36,461	22,245	15,746	20,715	233	11,083	10,266
Congressional District 25	280,261	70,493	54,574	15,919	20,577	33,997	735	14,093	8,182
Congressional District 26	261,243	53,165	43,082	10,083	18,364	24,718	53	13,662	5,879
Congressional District 27	345,531	74,573	46,437	28,136	14,542	31,895	549	14,135	14,543
Georgia									
Congressional District 1	327,534	68,406	57,575	10,831	20,892	36,683	665	9,885	4,507
Congressional District 2	304,619	67,752	52,999	14,753	19,963	33,036	466	10,626	5,964
Congressional District 3	295,413	70,993	58,016	12,977	23,902	34,114	775	11,016	6,502
Congressional District 4	290,175	54,297	44,607	9,690	24,828	19,779	890	8,991	4,698
Congressional District 5	375,111	61,350	37,286	24,064	19,580	17,706	2,241	9,677	11,439
Congressional District 6	310,367	56,858	46,753	10,105	21,670	25,083	2,442	7,705	4,894
Congressional District 7	279,179	44,166	36,368	7,798	17,521	18,847	1,100	8,157	3,800
Congressional District 8	307,861	68,232	54,797	13,435	18,047	36,750	1,236	11,865	5,121
Congressional District 9	338,355	85,846	74,108	11,738	26,943	47,165	681	13,323	3,449
Congressional District 10	306,160	66,509	55,395	11,114	20,336	35,059	620	8,676	3,989
Congressional District 11	315,833	60,558	47,784	12,774	21,812	25,972	2,152	7,039	6,480
Congressional District 12	306,313	65,340	53,345	11,995	16,514	36,831	636	10,404	4,999
Congressional District 13	281,560	49,732	40,706	9,026	22,780	17,926	417	8,554	4,661
Congressional District 14	287,786	66,880	54,138	12,742	17,445	36,693	760	9,600	6,195
Hawaii									
Congressional District 1	266,405	70,265	50,833	19,432	23,219	27,614	1,295	9,964	8,179
Congressional District 2	279,856	72,863	57,941	14,922	26,193	31,748	580	13,542	5,027
Idaho									
Congressional District 1	379,737	92,785	78,930	13,855	33,425	45,505	2,381	13,993	5,504
Congressional District 2	355,966	75,829	62,038	13,791	22,010	40,028	3,746	9,842	6,033

Table J-5: 116th Congressional Districts - Summary of Housing and Householder Characteristics—*Continued*

| | | | | Householders 65 Years and Over | | | | |
| | | | | Owner Householders | | | | |
	Total Housing Units	Total Households	Owner Occupied	Renter Occupied	With a Mortgage	Without a Mortgage	Renter Households With Meals Included in Rent	Percent of Owner Householders Who Pay 35% or More of income for Housing Costs	Percent of Renter Households Who Pay 35% or More of Income for Rental Costs
Illinois									
Congressional District 1	305,477	75,535	53,809	21,726	23,176	30,633	973	14,804	10,480
Congressional District 2	295,933	70,616	53,972	16,644	23,208	30,764	2,206	16,047	8,229
Congressional District 3	262,309	65,535	54,238	11,297	16,124	38,114	737	14,544	6,516
Congressional District 4	255,850	41,750	29,297	12,453	10,681	18,616	406	9,752	7,108
Congressional District 5	332,067	59,359	45,077	14,282	16,779	28,298	1,241	14,395	6,433
Congressional District 6	282,616	69,318	58,128	11,190	24,833	33,295	3,399	16,403	5,639
Congressional District 7	353,542	68,489	37,269	31,220	16,646	20,623	1,078	13,823	16,626
Congressional District 8	261,437	56,235	46,009	10,226	19,749	26,260	1,998	11,426	4,528
Congressional District 9	314,126	79,138	59,749	19,389	21,173	38,576	3,480	17,681	8,659
Congressional District 10	269,795	66,510	54,346	12,164	21,051	33,295	2,886	15,327	5,886
Congressional District 11	263,185	52,546	44,650	7,896	18,631	26,019	946	10,011	3,351
Congressional District 12	324,841	76,976	59,811	17,165	17,924	41,887	1,809	8,727	6,674
Congressional District 13	323,873	70,188	56,955	13,233	18,376	38,579	2,449	7,398	4,393
Congressional District 14	274,264	62,076	54,799	7,277	22,681	32,118	1,270	14,673	4,059
Congressional District 15	319,303	85,584	70,856	14,728	15,845	55,011	1,170	9,781	4,783
Congressional District 16	299,875	78,940	64,484	14,456	22,046	42,438	3,091	11,827	5,559
Congressional District 17	324,006	80,793	65,118	15,675	19,809	45,309	2,004	8,989	5,096
Congressional District 18	313,677	82,452	68,824	13,628	18,327	50,497	2,497	8,852	5,437
Indiana									
Congressional District 1	311,047	76,616	63,321	13,295	23,516	39,805	1,209	10,541	5,984
Congressional District 2	309,712	73,760	61,205	12,555	22,793	38,412	1,957	10,445	5,109
Congressional District 3	323,808	73,190	60,678	12,512	22,727	37,951	1,319	9,470	5,389
Congressional District 4	321,823	73,454	59,967	13,487	25,661	34,306	1,958	7,558	5,801
Congressional District 5	333,524	70,733	56,175	14,558	27,126	29,049	2,516	10,499	6,842
Congressional District 6	317,609	82,018	66,654	15,364	26,012	40,642	1,617	11,532	6,423
Congressional District 7	337,244	59,136	43,208	15,928	21,707	21,501	1,174	8,893	6,471
Congressional District 8	325,176	76,786	62,338	14,448	21,673	40,665	1,418	9,349	5,533
Congressional District 9	323,633	74,116	60,926	13,190	25,588	35,338	1,839	10,510	5,116
Iowa									
Congressional District 1	345,013	86,615	70,820	15,795	20,731	50,089	3,607	11,142	6,031
Congressional District 2	348,994	85,169	67,636	17,533	20,535	47,101	2,729	10,784	6,779
Congressional District 3	362,175	77,565	61,309	16,256	21,695	39,614	2,371	10,801	7,086
Congressional District 4	353,386	88,810	72,727	16,083	16,311	56,416	4,085	8,983	6,511
Kansas									
Congressional District 1	322,461	71,833	57,357	14,476	12,698	44,659	2,031	9,482	5,213
Congressional District 2	321,371	76,380	60,934	15,446	19,585	41,349	2,219	11,380	6,815
Congressional District 3	317,624	66,710	52,040	14,670	23,195	28,845	3,057	11,041	6,723
Congressional District 4	319,097	72,233	56,216	16,017	17,384	38,832	2,399	9,493	6,932
Kentucky									
Congressional District 1	339,323	82,414	68,238	14,176	17,087	51,151	441	10,938	4,793
Congressional District 2	334,272	76,196	64,404	11,792	21,390	43,014	1,091	10,982	4,355
Congressional District 3	337,997	77,540	59,689	17,851	23,461	36,228	2,637	10,949	7,998
Congressional District 4	315,219	72,855	59,548	13,307	22,530	37,018	1,278	10,287	4,617
Congressional District 5	329,875	77,515	64,758	12,757	14,269	50,489	143	8,611	2,935
Congressional District 6	338,501	71,500	58,326	13,174	21,371	36,955	1,406	9,426	4,661
Louisiana									
Congressional District 1	343,004	80,976	67,021	13,955	21,182	45,839	772	13,251	7,139
Congressional District 2	354,621	71,183	53,466	17,717	14,466	39,000	728	11,727	8,142
Congressional District 3	346,380	74,293	62,662	11,631	14,132	48,530	741	7,342	4,537
Congressional District 4	354,195	78,294	63,484	14,810	16,977	46,507	981	8,704	5,850
Congressional District 5	335,292	74,058	59,258	14,800	13,863	45,395	504	8,898	4,796
Congressional District 6	342,644	68,175	58,770	9,405	18,931	39,839	1,034	7,666	3,788
Maine									
Congressional District 1	362,490	89,874	68,979	20,895	27,857	41,122	2,509	14,515	7,409
Congressional District 2	384,102	86,049	67,986	18,063	22,035	45,951	1,236	14,666	6,795
Maryland									
Congressional District 1	344,749	83,966	71,261	12,705	30,381	40,880	1,326	15,446	4,895
Congressional District 2	311,407	67,147	51,114	16,033	23,627	27,487	1,602	11,691	7,127
Congressional District 3	310,351	71,063	52,443	18,620	21,976	30,467	3,338	10,712	8,064
Congressional District 4	288,555	62,375	50,764	11,611	31,247	19,517	964	12,853	5,946
Congressional District 5	282,596	59,391	51,647	7,744	28,293	23,354	834	12,441	3,447
Congressional District 6	299,140	68,014	53,082	14,932	23,894	29,188	1,555	9,893	6,015
Congressional District 7	320,350	70,691	49,697	20,994	21,158	28,539	2,773	11,562	9,551
Congressional District 8	301,631	75,528	60,948	14,580	26,481	34,467	2,272	12,194	6,497
Massachusetts									
Congressional District 1	322,376	82,753	62,437	20,316	22,913	39,524	2,261	15,090	7,396
Congressional District 2	306,991	73,141	52,563	20,578	19,747	32,816	2,102	13,052	8,721
Congressional District 3	294,086	63,762	46,123	17,639	20,768	25,355	1,348	13,648	7,010
Congressional District 4	299,759	78,013	58,237	19,776	21,917	36,320	2,369	15,469	7,568
Congressional District 5	314,917	78,114	56,564	21,550	21,612	34,952	1,984	16,424	9,938
Congressional District 6	313,077	87,798	66,015	21,783	28,345	37,670	3,382	21,035	11,404
Congressional District 7	332,133	56,604	26,839	29,765	14,122	12,717	706	8,123	10,625
Congressional District 8	321,743	77,368	50,554	26,814	21,046	29,508	2,705	14,083	10,119
Congressional District 9	409,961	102,484	84,984	17,500	35,933	49,051	1,672	24,890	8,023

Table J-5: 116th Congressional Districts - Summary of Housing and Householder Characteristics—*Continued*

| | | | | | Householders 65 Years and Over | | | | |
| | | | | | Owner Householders | | | | |
	Total Housing Units	Total Households	Owner Occupied	Renter Occupied	With a Mortgage	Without a Mortgage	Renter Households With Meals Included in Rent	Percent of Owner Householders Who Pay 35% or More of income for Housing Costs	Percent of Renter Households Who Pay 35% or More of Income for Rental Costs
Michigan									
Congressional District 1	452,063	101,550	87,527	14,023	27,653	59,874	1,303	13,239	4,953
Congressional District 2	322,190	74,092	63,010	11,082	23,234	39,776	1,686	11,823	5,720
Congressional District 3	306,024	71,288	57,853	13,435	20,228	37,625	2,542	9,807	4,996
Congressional District 4	353,510	85,844	73,670	12,174	23,378	50,292	1,049	12,221	4,590
Congressional District 5	329,476	82,413	67,678	14,735	22,739	44,939	1,854	11,962	6,688
Congressional District 6	332,481	77,966	65,151	12,815	23,821	41,330	893	12,482	5,085
Congressional District 7	309,679	81,726	69,052	12,674	26,338	42,714	1,898	11,010	6,092
Congressional District 8	303,687	70,961	59,073	11,888	26,452	32,621	2,347	11,489	6,034
Congressional District 9	321,065	77,949	62,205	15,744	22,633	39,572	1,444	12,648	6,719
Congressional District 10	317,137	82,431	71,774	10,657	26,569	45,205	1,653	14,034	4,737
Congressional District 11	305,288	74,520	61,907	12,613	24,959	36,948	3,016	12,713	5,737
Congressional District 12	294,864	68,141	56,243	11,898	20,271	35,972	1,740	12,593	5,700
Congressional District 13	334,231	66,480	47,617	18,863	14,210	33,407	847	11,409	8,313
Congressional District 14	332,857	78,200	55,145	23,055	21,046	34,099	2,598	12,644	10,453
Minnesota									
Congressional District 1	294,916	73,571	59,044	14,527	15,630	43,414	4,128	9,604	6,398
Congressional District 2	276,721	60,310	48,300	12,010	19,584	28,716	3,265	9,991	6,856
Congressional District 3	297,695	70,971	55,515	15,456	23,542	31,973	2,484	12,573	7,918
Congressional District 4	284,901	66,731	49,304	17,427	19,786	29,518	4,237	9,034	9,630
Congressional District 5	314,415	59,080	40,929	18,151	15,959	24,970	2,454	8,258	8,175
Congressional District 6	273,868	55,451	45,899	9,552	17,726	28,173	1,827	8,784	5,058
Congressional District 7	332,937	80,697	64,439	16,258	15,467	48,972	3,205	10,544	6,831
Congressional District 8	380,184	85,622	68,868	16,754	22,982	45,886	2,558	12,540	7,111
Mississippi									
Congressional District 1	336,136	76,815	66,584	10,231	17,945	48,639	1,427	9,271	3,876
Congressional District 2	314,384	70,855	58,332	12,523	13,266	45,066	44	8,599	4,513
Congressional District 3	335,966	76,840	66,820	10,020	17,590	49,230	361	11,617	3,356
Congressional District 4	346,145	78,853	66,957	11,896	16,371	50,586	998	9,582	3,787
Missouri									
Congressional District 1	375,492	73,344	47,841	25,503	19,671	28,170	1,035	10,063	12,292
Congressional District 2	316,467	89,159	75,080	14,079	29,442	45,638	5,165	12,877	7,236
Congressional District 3	351,164	78,130	66,046	12,084	24,101	41,945	1,118	9,350	5,195
Congressional District 4	355,783	80,682	67,539	13,143	21,446	46,093	1,158	11,644	5,608
Congressional District 5	364,471	75,846	56,379	19,467	20,463	35,916	1,517	11,054	8,387
Congressional District 6	337,234	77,515	64,291	13,224	18,982	45,309	904	9,968	4,620
Congressional District 7	359,682	89,835	69,969	19,866	25,791	44,178	1,533	11,405	10,597
Congressional District 8	346,003	87,058	70,630	16,428	18,950	51,680	1,130	11,217	5,453
Montana									
Congressional District (at Large)	515,161	123,306	99,708	23,598	32,058	67,650	3,493	18,770	8,948
Nebraska									
Congressional District 1	277,762	63,478	49,879	13,599	16,293	33,586	3,860	7,738	4,985
Congressional District 2	277,601	55,623	40,362	15,261	16,658	23,704	3,928	8,078	7,010
Congressional District 3	289,648	75,440	60,860	14,580	12,362	48,498	2,410	9,740	5,119
Nevada									
Congressional District 1	303,535	60,446	36,054	24,392	16,764	19,290	1,254	9,797	14,045
Congressional District 2	318,043	79,157	61,808	17,349	30,827	30,981	2,549	13,076	8,614
Congressional District 3	353,018	74,823	55,373	19,450	27,630	27,743	645	12,324	9,341
Congressional District 4	294,121	65,507	52,388	13,119	26,023	26,365	415	11,598	6,339
New Hampshire									
Congressional District 1	323,177	70,323	55,807	14,516	21,722	34,085	1,229	14,541	5,823
Congressional District 2	314,935	75,465	60,441	15,024	21,643	38,798	1,631	15,659	6,582
New Jersey									
Congressional District 1	296,136	71,071	54,972	16,099	22,555	32,417	1,436	17,746	7,362
Congressional District 2	389,640	82,565	68,633	13,932	27,089	41,544	544	18,808	6,490
Congressional District 3	319,321	91,189	78,988	12,201	33,288	45,700	1,322	21,090	5,591
Congressional District 4	305,011	94,196	77,267	16,929	28,140	49,127	3,310	21,967	10,576
Congressional District 5	281,340	77,517	63,033	14,484	24,446	38,587	1,848	20,692	8,136
Congressional District 6	269,877	59,850	46,263	13,587	17,556	28,707	641	13,489	6,178
Congressional District 7	279,396	69,109	55,446	13,663	22,153	33,293	1,602	16,461	6,662
Congressional District 8	309,333	49,058	20,850	28,208	7,796	13,054	320	9,364	12,424
Congressional District 9	291,610	65,187	40,320	24,867	14,541	25,779	702	16,385	11,417
Congressional District 10	306,523	59,944	28,929	31,015	14,231	14,698	823	10,914	12,812
Congressional District 11	286,145	75,106	60,956	14,150	24,260	36,696	1,683	19,751	6,181
Congressional District 12	293,866	72,675	55,633	17,042	21,526	34,107	814	17,649	7,023
New Mexico									
Congressional District 1	305,436	72,184	55,417	16,767	21,836	33,581	1,320	10,753	7,594
Congressional District 2	317,171	76,332	60,878	15,454	18,385	42,493	808	8,919	4,793
Congressional District 3	320,625	79,579	68,356	11,223	23,272	45,084	602	8,742	3,312
New York									
Congressional District 1	313,707	76,483	65,690	10,793	25,219	40,471	684	21,741	6,185
Congressional District 2	241,558	62,257	51,962	10,295	19,702	32,260	519	18,192	5,585

Table J-5: 116th Congressional Districts - Summary of Housing and Householder Characteristics—*Continued*

| | | | | Householders 65 Years and Over | | | | | |
| | | | | Owner Householders | | | | | |
	Total Housing Units	Total Households	Owner Occupied	Renter Occupied	With a Mortgage	Without a Mortgage	Renter Households With Meals Included in Rent	Percent of Owner Householders Who Pay 35% or More of income for Housing Costs	Percent of Renter Households Who Pay 35% or More of income for Rental Costs
New York—Cont.									
Congressional District 3	263,898	82,562	71,358	11,204	24,248	47,110	1,362	24,132	5,642
Congressional District 4	251,171	72,166	58,359	13,807	21,013	37,346	1,312	21,125	6,200
Congressional District 5	245,943	58,232	38,054	20,178	17,239	20,815	236	12,494	8,605
Congressional District 6	291,793	72,457	40,196	32,261	9,042	31,154	498	11,975	18,047
Congressional District 7	279,981	52,238	15,597	36,641	5,449	10,148	80	4,944	18,638
Congressional District 8	327,386	75,998	36,232	39,766	14,273	21,959	214	13,365	19,590
Congressional District 9	308,907	68,265	27,297	40,968	11,328	15,969	237	8,793	21,828
Congressional District 10	356,873	78,025	34,550	43,475	10,278	24,272	1,143	10,057	20,480
Congressional District 11	286,957	73,411	49,940	23,471	17,030	32,910	218	17,140	12,401
Congressional District 12	447,343	75,496	34,333	41,163	6,526	27,807	966	8,690	17,167
Congressional District 13	317,822	63,218	6,736	56,482	2,084	4,652	1,019	na	30,224
Congressional District 14	267,609	53,283	24,728	28,555	8,203	16,525	168	10,093	15,031
Congressional District 15	271,880	54,658	8,274	46,384	3,716	4,558	962	3,525	20,634
Congressional District 16	289,690	80,291	45,176	35,115	14,578	30,598	1,943	14,281	17,256
Congressional District 17	263,296	74,563	56,990	17,573	21,726	35,264	1,698	19,964	8,363
Congressional District 18	279,979	66,493	50,036	16,457	21,071	28,965	351	14,427	8,648
Congressional District 19	368,804	87,516	72,757	14,759	22,532	50,225	989	15,627	5,596
Congressional District 20	335,473	77,086	55,241	21,845	21,279	33,962	2,018	8,807	11,026
Congressional District 21	379,958	79,962	63,430	16,532	20,772	42,658	1,416	11,666	5,084
Congressional District 22	327,130	80,325	63,534	16,791	18,835	44,699	1,100	11,897	6,675
Congressional District 23	344,294	81,195	65,889	15,306	17,910	47,979	799	10,308	5,728
Congressional District 24	319,924	78,035	60,608	17,427	21,781	38,827	1,722	11,086	6,351
Congressional District 25	318,631	78,730	57,932	20,798	24,505	33,427	2,754	11,924	11,945
Congressional District 26	346,239	82,533	59,363	23,170	19,694	39,669	2,355	9,663	10,931
Congressional District 27	317,601	86,874	68,784	18,090	24,186	44,598	1,690	13,870	7,919
North Carolina									
Congressional District 1	347,743	80,889	62,789	18,100	24,197	38,592	1,304	13,246	6,474
Congressional District 2	332,596	70,276	59,400	10,876	25,947	33,453	821	11,466	3,691
Congressional District 3	386,670	82,624	68,153	14,471	27,408	40,745	424	14,198	5,275
Congressional District 4	373,434	61,533	45,605	15,928	21,587	24,018	2,455	7,336	7,189
Congressional District 5	369,586	91,378	75,118	16,260	24,939	50,179	2,281	12,297	6,349
Congressional District 6	340,225	85,518	70,538	14,980	27,465	43,073	1,890	12,235	6,243
Congressional District 7	401,064	98,199	80,898	17,301	32,051	48,847	1,563	18,581	7,308
Congressional District 8	345,666	73,908	62,057	11,851	24,653	37,404	1,022	11,813	4,633
Congressional District 9	319,889	74,337	60,465	13,872	22,962	37,503	2,143	11,281	6,567
Congressional District 10	349,731	88,807	73,959	14,848	26,415	47,544	1,424	12,298	7,304
Congressional District 11	405,135	105,969	89,692	16,277	27,909	61,783	1,702	12,265	5,379
Congressional District 12	368,331	51,532	38,061	13,471	20,002	18,059	934	8,765	7,478
Congressional District 13	344,892	80,026	63,320	16,706	27,059	36,261	2,436	12,362	8,757
North Dakota									
Congressional District (at Large)	377,661	73,062	55,235	17,827	11,530	43,705	3,049	8,344	8,316
Ohio									
Congressional District 1	325,907	70,419	53,695	16,724	22,479	31,216	1,674	10,289	7,257
Congressional District 2	329,846	75,635	58,101	17,534	23,346	34,755	2,446	11,236	7,876
Congressional District 3	346,335	57,111	40,228	16,883	20,062	20,166	862	9,051	7,017
Congressional District 4	308,297	76,480	61,892	14,588	21,795	40,097	2,592	9,565	5,813
Congressional District 5	313,442	80,319	66,637	13,682	23,247	43,390	2,006	10,216	4,835
Congressional District 6	324,038	86,624	71,532	15,092	22,214	49,318	1,160	10,651	5,161
Congressional District 7	309,763	83,646	66,922	16,724	24,319	42,603	1,401	11,653	6,238
Congressional District 8	305,679	77,530	62,249	15,281	25,083	37,166	1,195	11,046	5,549
Congressional District 9	355,693	73,334	56,438	16,896	22,393	34,045	1,343	11,802	7,384
Congressional District 10	336,812	83,276	65,605	17,671	26,469	39,136	2,446	10,889	6,749
Congressional District 11	365,353	81,847	53,456	28,391	20,976	32,480	2,337	11,384	11,408
Congressional District 12	322,347	74,441	59,515	14,926	23,425	36,090	2,262	10,276	5,576
Congressional District 13	337,529	85,480	67,336	18,144	25,050	42,286	1,009	11,037	7,039
Congressional District 14	313,876	90,210	73,660	16,550	29,686	43,974	3,149	14,886	7,219
Congressional District 15	315,796	74,245	61,622	12,623	23,559	38,063	1,458	11,767	5,597
Congressional District 16	306,904	90,875	72,625	18,250	27,728	44,897	3,214	13,359	7,583
Oklahoma									
Congressional District 1	351,010	75,187	59,095	16,092	19,321	39,774	2,695	8,888	7,093
Congressional District 2	358,489	89,104	73,499	15,605	17,625	55,874	741	11,250	4,500
Congressional District 3	339,689	77,764	66,934	10,830	16,112	50,822	681	8,629	3,427
Congressional District 4	338,179	74,601	60,460	14,141	18,943	41,517	1,537	8,778	5,155
Congressional District 5	355,706	73,230	56,919	16,311	18,877	38,042	2,568	9,363	7,361
Oregon									
Congressional District 1	350,718	80,171	61,443	18,728	27,760	33,683	4,392	16,527	10,642
Congressional District 2	379,232	107,493	85,032	22,461	35,177	49,855	3,820	16,522	10,345
Congressional District 3	357,075	72,156	52,267	19,889	23,370	28,897	3,042	14,797	10,031
Congressional District 4	355,549	108,647	87,741	20,906	36,319	51,422	3,758	18,112	9,446
Congressional District 5	346,169	92,800	71,659	21,141	32,625	39,034	5,330	16,183	12,146
Pennsylvania									
Congressional District 1	284,309	77,257	62,682	14,575	23,932	38,750	3,066	16,307	7,695
Congressional District 2	281,169	60,881	42,976	17,905	15,243	27,733	615	10,591	9,098

Table J-5: 116th Congressional Districts - Summary of Housing and Householder Characteristics—*Continued*

| | | | | | Householders 65 Years and Over | | | | |
| | | | | | Owner Householders | | | | |
	Total Housing Units	Total Households	Owner Occupied	Renter Occupied	With a Mortgage	Without a Mortgage	Renter Households With Meals Included in Rent	Percent of Owner Householders Who Pay 35% or More of income for Housing Costs	Percent of Renter Households Who Pay 35% or More of Income for Rental Costs
Pennsylvania—Cont.									
Congressional District 3	356,890	73,242	50,464	22,778	19,804	30,660	513	14,534	9,744
Congressional District 4	298,536	78,776	59,166	19,610	22,981	36,185	5,282	14,861	11,686
Congressional District 5	288,899	69,999	51,048	18,951	18,627	32,421	3,721	13,206	10,000
Congressional District 6	284,624	70,325	54,975	15,350	21,810	33,165	2,401	11,967	7,072
Congressional District 7	295,135	77,971	60,507	17,464	22,344	38,163	2,210	14,735	8,714
Congressional District 8	353,958	83,465	66,428	17,037	19,822	46,606	1,672	14,836	5,074
Congressional District 9	319,959	87,790	72,019	15,771	21,782	50,237	1,865	16,927	5,789
Congressional District 10	314,051	79,383	59,506	19,877	22,134	37,372	2,796	11,740	8,866
Congressional District 11	295,042	80,041	61,726	18,315	20,734	40,992	4,135	10,845	9,727
Congressional District 12	334,117	82,658	65,807	16,851	17,531	48,276	858	11,886	5,748
Congressional District 13	324,575	89,664	73,447	16,217	20,327	53,120	1,515	12,295	5,402
Congressional District 14	326,328	93,691	77,542	16,149	23,291	54,251	1,796	12,198	6,333
Congressional District 15	345,360	89,604	72,618	16,986	16,072	56,546	1,936	9,921	5,390
Congressional District 16	320,962	85,638	67,264	18,374	21,155	46,109	2,651	12,012	6,490
Congressional District 17	335,368	91,494	71,435	20,059	23,681	47,754	2,591	14,670	7,652
Congressional District 18	353,854	86,727	62,636	24,091	20,396	42,240	1,806	11,070	10,314
Rhode Island									
Congressional District 1	231,833	58,051	37,097	20,954	15,341	21,756	1,739	10,580	8,248
Congressional District 2	237,320	55,912	41,624	14,288	17,291	24,333	1,208	10,513	4,299
South Carolina									
Congressional District 1	368,783	88,046	75,063	12,983	35,358	39,705	3,086	18,505	5,092
Congressional District 2	312,137	74,110	64,587	9,523	25,937	38,650	1,506	11,820	3,765
Congressional District 3	315,460	81,613	68,588	13,025	23,959	44,629	1,493	11,539	5,926
Congressional District 4	309,953	71,349	58,747	12,602	22,193	36,554	1,585	8,202	4,705
Congressional District 5	313,035	74,188	64,448	9,740	25,177	39,271	960	12,915	3,311
Congressional District 6	303,456	65,991	55,474	10,517	18,204	37,270	253	11,478	4,263
Congressional District 7	395,467	97,354	83,278	14,076	32,578	50,700	832	17,370	5,880
South Dakota									
Congressional District (at Large)	397,506	91,545	71,166	20,379	17,304	53,862	3,433	9,313	7,730
Tennessee									
Congressional District 1	355,315	90,439	75,559	14,880	22,719	52,840	1,011	10,712	5,124
Congressional District 2	336,989	82,510	70,884	11,626	21,585	49,299	1,495	8,663	4,192
Congressional District 3	333,867	85,020	70,727	14,293	22,417	48,310	1,670	9,489	5,728
Congressional District 4	325,787	71,779	60,233	11,546	18,504	41,729	631	9,901	3,558
Congressional District 5	354,215	63,177	46,974	16,203	17,528	29,446	2,913	7,366	5,530
Congressional District 6	333,581	84,448	71,522	12,926	24,057	47,465	1,801	10,810	5,273
Congressional District 7	332,235	69,748	61,172	8,576	16,771	44,401	448	8,542	2,873
Congressional District 8	297,297	74,087	62,001	12,086	21,105	40,896	1,387	9,994	5,147
Congressional District 9	323,126	59,816	40,435	19,381	18,099	22,336	1,012	9,538	10,034
Texas									
Congressional District 1	308,993	72,798	60,718	12,080	15,538	45,180	1,019	10,309	4,860
Congressional District 2	314,356	54,196	43,920	10,276	16,656	27,264	1,500	8,150	5,983
Congressional District 3	344,182	53,124	38,987	14,137	18,112	20,875	2,025	8,532	7,217
Congressional District 4	314,277	78,259	66,013	12,246	16,214	49,799	1,625	10,124	6,606
Congressional District 5	298,447	62,596	50,120	12,476	14,285	35,835	1,485	7,605	6,783
Congressional District 6	293,457	53,825	44,773	9,052	16,690	28,083	1,301	9,088	5,173
Congressional District 7	330,149	48,644	37,369	11,275	12,446	24,923	3,464	8,463	5,307
Congressional District 8	336,636	69,143	58,399	10,744	19,023	39,376	966	10,688	5,878
Congressional District 9	295,967	44,663	31,434	13,229	10,667	20,767	722	5,583	5,825
Congressional District 10	348,010	65,686	54,292	11,394	16,780	37,512	1,577	10,257	6,816
Congressional District 11	336,822	78,507	65,799	12,708	14,449	51,350	1,628	11,903	4,865
Congressional District 12	320,574	64,573	48,995	15,578	14,140	34,855	3,295	7,896	8,717
Congressional District 13	308,692	66,844	55,481	11,363	13,850	41,631	1,254	7,924	4,526
Congressional District 14	322,301	64,687	52,074	12,613	12,794	39,280	941	8,523	5,832
Congressional District 15	266,704	49,383	43,159	6,224	8,636	34,523	165	8,545	2,339
Congressional District 16	268,328	54,922	42,081	12,841	11,915	30,166	237	8,038	5,316
Congressional District 17	331,818	60,429	47,366	13,063	13,126	34,240	1,636	10,253	5,944
Congressional District 18	310,991	48,384	34,104	14,290	11,468	22,636	107	8,537	6,817
Congressional District 19	305,214	61,282	50,227	11,055	10,920	39,307	2,165	7,099	4,696
Congressional District 20	276,745	54,396	42,164	12,232	13,557	28,607	1,285	6,265	5,283
Congressional District 21	366,044	78,403	61,956	16,447	19,978	41,978	2,586	10,166	7,561
Congressional District 22	324,670	53,978	45,693	8,285	18,106	27,587	999	9,869	4,126
Congressional District 23	278,489	61,757	52,069	9,688	12,681	39,388	349	8,575	3,900
Congressional District 24	345,531	53,834	39,086	14,748	14,363	24,723	2,104	7,172	8,046
Congressional District 25	321,224	67,419	57,137	10,282	17,981	39,156	1,711	11,102	4,502
Congressional District 26	319,691	47,608	39,065	8,543	17,546	21,519	1,186	7,829	4,499
Congressional District 27	318,596	72,287	57,858	14,429	13,565	44,293	1,754	8,521	7,000
Congressional District 28	252,377	51,475	41,967	9,508	10,157	31,810	320	5,880	4,543
Congressional District 29	250,803	34,966	25,441	9,525	6,453	18,988	214	4,737	5,602
Congressional District 30	294,486	51,624	36,974	14,650	13,943	23,031	688	7,773	7,580
Congressional District 31	326,770	58,418	47,570	10,848	18,151	29,419	1,208	7,897	5,202
Congressional District 32	323,380	54,836	42,266	12,570	14,095	28,171	2,482	8,197	6,435
Congressional District 33	254,476	41,573	29,366	12,207	7,593	21,773	298	5,576	6,184

Table J-5: 116th Congressional Districts - Summary of Housing and Householder Characteristics—*Continued*

	Total Housing Units	Total Households	Owner Occupied	Renter Occupied	Householders 65 Years and Over		Renter Households With Meals Included in Rent	Percent of Owner Householders Who Pay 35% or More of income for Housing Costs	Percent of Renter Households Who Pay 35% or More of Income for Rental Costs
					Owner Householders				
					With a Mortgage	Without a Mortgage			
Texas—Cont.									
Congressional District 34	270,080	58,605	47,224	11,381	7,857	39,367	254	6,951	3,916
Congressional District 35	309,787	47,397	35,068	12,329	12,615	22,453	627	7,581	5,623
Congressional District 36	312,431	67,327	57,644	9,683	10,728	46,916	524	8,387	3,783
Utah									
Congressional District 1	283,194	49,505	42,627	6,878	15,832	26,795	1,254	5,580	3,042
Congressional District 2	300,123	63,114	53,079	10,035	22,010	31,069	1,682	9,526	3,714
Congressional District 3	255,835	50,425	44,598	5,827	15,119	29,479	1,762	7,577	2,731
Congressional District 4	269,587	47,507	39,474	8,033	16,748	22,726	2,087	7,255	3,905
Vermont									
Congressional District (at Large)	337,133	78,032	63,525	14,507	23,242	40,283	1,546	15,844	6,261
Virginia									
Congressional District 1	316,325	71,096	62,037	9,059	29,294	32,743	1,518	11,185	3,584
Congressional District 2	312,712	70,186	55,999	14,187	27,262	28,737	2,399	11,701	7,741
Congressional District 3	320,042	65,980	45,090	20,890	21,340	23,750	1,219	11,593	9,889
Congressional District 4	313,086	73,062	56,478	16,584	24,900	31,578	1,044	13,924	9,231
Congressional District 5	355,663	92,839	78,680	14,159	26,712	51,968	1,151	13,034	5,589
Congressional District 6	332,873	88,775	70,385	18,390	27,294	43,091	2,786	12,752	9,624
Congressional District 7	317,596	77,751	64,468	13,283	30,584	33,884	3,035	12,706	6,359
Congressional District 8	343,653	61,139	46,344	14,795	21,765	24,579	2,079	9,470	7,172
Congressional District 9	347,365	91,160	76,729	14,431	17,346	59,383	938	13,320	4,412
Congressional District 10	297,507	58,139	48,286	9,853	25,063	23,223	1,949	9,210	4,972
Congressional District 11	282,163	50,903	43,010	7,893	21,920	21,090	1,644	8,488	4,251
Washington									
Congressional District 1	305,187	59,798	47,901	11,897	21,737	26,164	1,688	11,488	6,358
Congressional District 2	322,817	76,941	61,253	15,688	27,366	33,887	3,506	14,495	7,962
Congressional District 3	307,432	80,415	65,641	14,774	27,426	38,215	2,690	13,649	6,171
Congressional District 4	274,077	63,042	51,488	11,554	18,167	33,321	2,444	9,308	4,322
Congressional District 5	317,951	79,411	61,997	17,414	23,959	38,038	3,227	10,707	8,065
Congressional District 6	335,421	90,782	74,074	16,708	34,754	39,320	2,653	17,180	7,550
Congressional District 7	381,782	71,815	48,812	23,003	19,206	29,606	4,804	12,687	12,400
Congressional District 8	303,858	63,049	52,414	10,635	22,915	29,499	2,650	12,121	5,443
Congressional District 9	305,552	60,457	41,509	18,948	17,689	23,820	3,584	11,358	8,627
Congressional District 10	294,007	68,145	51,065	17,080	22,223	28,842	2,905	10,988	8,323
West Virginia									
Congressional District 1	290,313	75,979	65,674	10,305	16,340	49,334	1,046	8,086	3,487
Congressional District 2	301,762	76,898	66,230	10,668	19,154	47,076	226	9,147	3,268
Congressional District 3	301,667	78,708	67,919	10,789	15,619	52,300	325	7,997	2,941
Wisconsin									
Congressional District 1	308,845	74,558	58,724	15,834	23,147	35,577	1,636	12,313	8,469
Congressional District 2	339,061	73,821	58,222	15,599	21,512	36,710	1,991	11,446	7,490
Congressional District 3	330,033	82,297	64,673	17,624	20,068	44,605	2,708	11,597	7,691
Congressional District 4	312,592	56,464	36,626	19,838	15,126	21,500	1,992	9,556	9,620
Congressional District 5	312,849	83,076	62,557	20,519	22,789	39,768	3,165	13,578	12,073
Congressional District 6	328,794	85,253	66,223	19,030	21,344	44,879	3,760	13,746	8,938
Congressional District 7	425,348	91,109	74,202	16,907	22,923	51,279	1,178	13,108	5,983
Congressional District 8	353,196	78,599	64,426	14,173	19,043	45,383	1,572	12,365	6,229
Wyoming									
Congressional District (at Large)	278,615	61,902	51,451	10,451	16,258	35,193	753	7,101	3,773

APPENDIXES

APPENDIX A. CORE BASED STATISTICAL AREAS (METROPOLITAN AND MICROPOLITAN), METROPOLITAN DIVISIONS, AND COMPONENTS (AS DEFINED AUGUST 2017)

Core based statistical area	State/County FIPS code	Title and Geographic Components	2010 Census Population	2018 Estimated Population
10100		Aberdeen, SD Micro area	40,602	43,191
	46013	Brown County, SD	36,531	39,316
	46045	Edmunds County, SD	4,071	3,875
10140		Aberdeen, WA Micro area	72,797	73,901
	53027	Grays Harbor County, WA	72,797	73,901
10180		Abilene, TX Metro area	165,252	171,451
	48059	Callahan County, TX	13,544	13,994
	48253	Jones County, TX	20,202	19,817
	48441	Taylor County, TX	131,506	137,640
10220		Ada, OK Micro area	37,492	38,247
	40123	Pontotoc County, OK	37,492	38,247
10300		Adrian, MI Micro area	99,892	98,266
	26091	Lenawee County, MI	99,892	98,266
10420		Akron, OH Metro area	703,200	704,845
	39133	Portage County, OH	161,419	162,927
	39153	Summit County, OH	541,781	541,918
10460		Alamogordo, NM Micro area	63,797	66,781
	35035	Otero County, NM	63,797	66,781
10500		Albany, GA Metro area	157,308	153,009
	13007	Baker County, GA	3,451	3,092
	13095	Dougherty County, GA	94,565	91,243
	13177	Lee County, GA	28,298	29,764
	13273	Terrell County, GA	9,315	8,611
	13321	Worth County, GA	21,679	20,299
10540		Albany, OR Metro area	116,672	127,335
	41043	Linn County, OR	116,672	127,335
10580		Albany-Schenectady-Troy, NY Metro area	870,716	883,169
	36001	Albany County, NY	304,204	307,117
	36083	Rensselaer County, NY	159,429	159,442
	36091	Saratoga County, NY	219,607	230,163
	36093	Schenectady County, NY	154,727	155,350
	36095	Schoharie County, NY	32,749	31,097
10620		Albemarle, NC Micro area	60,585	62,075
	37167	Stanly County, NC	60,585	62,075
10660		Albert Lea, MN Micro area	31,255	30,444
	27047	Freeborn County, MN	31,255	30,444
10700		Albertville, AL Micro area	93,019	96,109
	01095	Marshall County, AL	93,019	96,109
10740		Albuquerque, NM Metro area	887,077	915,927
	35001	Bernalillo County, NM	662,564	678,701
	35043	Sandoval County, NM	131,561	145,179
	35057	Torrance County, NM	16,383	15,591
	35061	Valencia County, NM	76,569	76,456
10760		Alexander City, AL Micro Area	41,616	40,497
	01123	Tallapoosa County, AL	41,616	40,497
10780		Alexandria, LA Metro area	153,922	153,044
	22043	Grant Parish, LA	22,309	22,482
	22079	Rapides Parish, LA	131,613	130,562
10820		Alexandria, MN Micro area	36,009	37,964
	27041	Douglas County, MN	36,009	37,964
10860		Alice, TX Micro area	40,838	40,822
	48249	Jim Wells County, TX	40,838	40,822
10900		Allentown-Bethlehem-Easton, PA-NJ Metro area	821,173	842,913
	34041	Warren County, NJ	108,692	105,779
	42025	Carbon County, PA	65,249	64,227
	42077	Lehigh County, PA	349,497	368,100
	42095	Northampton County, PA	297,735	304,807
10940		Alma, MI Micro area	42,476	40,599
	26057	Gratiot County, MI	42,476	40,599
10980		Alpena, MI Micro area	29,598	28,360
	26007	Alpena County, MI	29,598	28,360
11020		Altoona, PA Metro area	127,089	122,492
	42013	Blair County, PA	127,089	122,492
11060		Altus, OK Micro area	26,446	24,949
	40065	Jackson County, OK	26,446	24,949
11100		Amarillo, TX Metro area	251,933	265,947
	48011	Armstrong County, TX	1,901	1,892
	48065	Carson County, TX	6,182	6,005
	48359	Oldham County, TX	2,052	2,131
	48375	Potter County, TX	121,073	119,648
	48381	Randall County, TX	120,725	136,271
11140		Americus, GA Micro area	37,829	34,969
	13249	Schley County, GA	5,010	5,236
	13261	Sumter County, GA	32,819	29,733
11180		Ames, IA Metro area	89,542	98,105
	19169	Story County, IA	89,542	98,105
11220		Amsterdam, NY Micro area	50,219	49,455
	36057	Montgomery County, NY	50,219	49,455
11260		Anchorage, AK Metro area	380,821	399,148
	02020	Anchorage Municipality, AK	291,826	291,538
	02170	Matanuska-Susitna Borough, AK	88,995	107,610
11380		Andrews, TX Micro area	14,786	18,128
	48003	Andrews County, TX	14,786	18,128
11420		Angola, IN Micro area	34,185	34,586
	18151	Steuben County, IN	34,185	34,586
11460		Ann Arbor, MI Metro area	344,791	370,963
	26161	Washtenaw County, MI	344,791	370,963
11500		Anniston-Oxford-Jacksonville, AL Metro area	118,572	114,277
	01015	Calhoun County, AL	118,572	114,277
11540		Appleton, WI Metro area	225,666	237,524
	55015	Calumet County, WI	48,971	50,159
	55087	Outagamie County, WI	176,695	187,365
11580		Arcadia, FL Micro area	34,862	37,489
	12027	DeSoto County, FL	34,862	37,489
11620		Ardmore, OK Micro area	47,557	48,177
	40019	Carter County, OK	47,557	48,177
11660		Arkadelphia, AR Micro area	22,995	22,061
	05019	Clark County, AR	22,995	22,061
11680		Arkansas City-Winfield, KS Micro area	36,311	35,218
	20035	Cowley County, KS	36,311	35,218
11700		Asheville, NC Metro area	424,858	459,585
	37021	Buncombe County, NC	238,318	259,103
	37087	Haywood County, NC	59,036	61,971
	37089	Henderson County, NC	106,740	116,748
	37115	Madison County, NC	20,764	21,763
11740		Ashland, OH Micro area	53,139	53,745
	39005	Ashland County, OH	53,139	53,745
11780		Ashtabula, OH Micro area	101,497	97,493
	39007	Ashtabula County, OH	101,497	97,493
11820		Astoria, OR Micro area	37,039	39,764
	41007	Clatsop County, OR	37,039	39,764
11860		Atchison, KS Micro area	16,924	16,193
	20005	Atchison County, KS	16,924	16,193
11900		Athens, OH Micro area	64,757	65,818
	39009	Athens County, OH	64,757	65,818
11940		Athens, TN Micro area	52,266	53,285
	47107	McMinn County, TN	52,266	53,285
11980		Athens, TX Micro area	78,532	82,299
	48213	Henderson County, TX	78,532	82,299
12020		Athens-Clarke County, GA Metro area	192,541	211,306
	13059	Clarke County, GA	116,714	127,330
	13195	Madison County, GA	28,120	29,650
	13219	Oconee County, GA	32,808	39,272
	13221	Oglethorpe County, GA	14,899	15,054
12060		Atlanta-Sandy Springs-Roswell, GA Metro area	5,286,728	5,949,951
	13013	Barrow County, GA	69,367	80,809
	13015	Bartow County, GA	100,157	106,408
	13035	Butts County, GA	23,655	24,193
	13045	Carroll County, GA	110,527	118,121
	13057	Cherokee County, GA	214,346	254,149
	13063	Clayton County, GA	259,424	289,615
	13067	Cobb County, GA	688,078	756,865
	13077	Coweta County, GA	127,317	145,864
	13085	Dawson County, GA	22,330	25,083
	13089	DeKalb County, GA	691,893	756,558
	13097	Douglas County, GA	132,403	145,331
	13113	Fayette County, GA	106,567	113,459
	13117	Forsyth County, GA	175,511	236,612
	13121	Fulton County, GA	920,581	1,050,114
	13135	Gwinnett County, GA	805,321	927,781
	13143	Haralson County, GA	28,780	29,533
	13149	Heard County, GA	11,834	11,879
	13151	Henry County, GA	203,922	230,220
	13159	Jasper County, GA	13,900	14,040
	13171	Lamar County, GA	18,317	19,000
	13199	Meriwether County, GA	21,992	21,068
	13211	Morgan County, GA	17,868	18,853

Core based statistical area	State/County FIPS code	Title and Geographic Components	2010 Census Population	2018 Estimated Population
	13217	Newton County, GA	99,958	109,541
	13223	Paulding County, GA	142,324	164,044
	13227	Pickens County, GA	29,431	31,980
	13231	Pike County, GA	17,869	18,634
	13247	Rockdale County, GA	85,215	90,594
	13255	Spalding County, GA	64,073	66,100
	13297	Walton County, GA	83,768	93,503
12100		Atlantic City-Hammonton, NJ Metro area	274,549	265,429
	34001	Atlantic County, NJ	274,549	265,429
12120		Atmore, AL Micro Area	38,319	36,748
	01053	Escambia County, AL	38,319	36,748
12140		Auburn, IN Micro area	42,223	43,226
	18033	DeKalb County, IN	42,223	43,226
12180		Auburn, NY Micro area	80,026	77,145
	36011	Cayuga County, NY	80,026	77,145
12220		Auburn-Opelika, AL Metro area	140,247	163,941
	01081	Lee County, AL	140,247	163,941
12260		Augusta-Richmond County, GA-SC Metro area	564,873	604,167
	13033	Burke County, GA	23,316	22,423
	13073	Columbia County, GA	124,053	154,291
	13181	Lincoln County, GA	7,996	7,915
	13189	McDuffie County, GA	21,875	21,531
	13245	Richmond County, GA	200,549	201,554
	45003	Aiken County, SC	160,099	169,401
	45037	Edgefield County, SC	26,985	27,052
12300		Augusta-Waterville, ME Micro area	122,151	122,083
	23011	Kennebec County, ME	122,151	122,083
12380		Austin, MN Micro area	39,163	40,011
	27099	Mower County, MN	39,163	40,011
12420		Austin-Round Rock, TX Metro area	1,716,289	2,168,316
	48021	Bastrop County, TX	74,171	86,976
	48055	Caldwell County, TX	38,066	43,247
	48209	Hays County, TX	157,107	222,631
	48453	Travis County, TX	1,024,266	1,248,743
	48491	Williamson County, TX	422,679	566,719
12460		Bainbridge, GA Micro area	27,842	26,575
	13087	Decatur County, GA	27,842	26,575
12540		Bakersfield, CA Metro area	839,631	896,764
	06029	Kern County, CA	839,631	896,764
12580		Baltimore-Columbia-Towson, MD Metro area	2,710,489	2,802,789
	24003	Anne Arundel County, MD	537,656	576,031
	24005	Baltimore County, MD	805,029	828,431
	24013	Carroll County, MD	167,134	168,429
	24025	Harford County, MD	244,826	253,956
	24027	Howard County, MD	287,085	323,196
	24035	Queen Anne's County, MD	47,798	50,251
	24510	Baltimore city, MD	620,961	602,495
12620		Bangor, ME Metro area	153,923	151,096
	23019	Penobscot County, ME	153,923	151,096
12660		Baraboo, WI Micro area	61,976	64,249
	55111	Sauk County, WI Micro area	61,976	64,249
12680		Bardstown, KY Micro area	43,437	45,851
	21179	Nelson County, KY	43,437	45,851
12700		Barnstable Town, MA Metro area	215,888	213,413
	25001	Barnstable County, MA	215,888	213,413
12740		Barre, VT Micro area	59,534	58,140
	50023	Washington County, VT	59,534	58,140
12780		Bartlesville, OK Micro area	50,976	51,843
	40147	Washington County, OK	50,976	51,843
12820		Bastrop, LA Micro area	27,979	25,398
	22067	Morehouse Parish, LA	27,979	25,398
12860		Batavia, NY Micro area	60,079	57,511
	36037	Genesee County, NY	60,079	57,511
12900		Batesville, AR Micro area	36,647	37,678
	05063	Independence County, AR	36,647	37,678
12940		Baton Rouge, LA Metro area	802,484	831,310
	22005	Ascension Parish, LA	107,215	124,672
	22033	East Baton Rouge Parish, LA	440,171	440,956
	22037	East Feliciana Parish, LA	20,267	19,305
	22047	Iberville Parish, LA	33,387	32,721
	22063	Livingston Parish, LA	128,026	139,567
	22077	Pointe Coupee Parish, LA	22,802	21,940
	22091	St. Helena Parish, LA	11,203	10,262
	22121	West Baton Rouge Parish, LA	23,788	26,427
	22125	West Feliciana Parish, LA	15,625	15,460
12980		Battle Creek, MI Metro area	136,146	134,487
	26025	Calhoun County, MI	136,146	134,487
13020		Bay City, MI Metro area	107,771	103,923
	26017	Bay County, MI	107,771	103,923
13060		Bay City, TX Micro area	36,702	36,552
	48321	Matagorda County, TX	36,702	36,552
13100		Beatrice, NE Micro area	22,311	21,493
	31067	Gage County, NE Micro area	22,311	21,493
13140		Beaumont-Port Arthur, TX Metro area	403,190	409,526
	48199	Hardin County, TX	54,635	57,207
	48245	Jefferson County, TX	252,273	255,001
	48351	Newton County, TX	14,445	13,746
	48361	Orange County, TX	81,837	83,572
13180		Beaver Dam, WI Micro area	88,759	87,847
	55027	Dodge County, WI	88,759	87,847
13220		Beckley, WV Metro area	124,898	117,272
	54019	Fayette County, WV	46,039	43,018
	54081	Raleigh County, WV	78,859	74,254
13260		Bedford, IN Micro area	46,134	45,668
	18093	Lawrence County, IN	46,134	45,668
13300		Beeville, TX Micro area	31,861	32,587
	48025	Bee County, TX	31,861	32,587
13340		Bellefontaine, OH Micro area	45,858	45,358
	39091	Logan County, OH	45,858	45,358
13380		Bellingham, WA Metro area	201,140	225,685
	53073	Whatcom County, WA	201,140	225,685
13420		Bemidji, MN Micro area	44,442	46,847
	27007	Beltrami County, MN	44,442	46,847
13460		Bend-Redmond, OR Metro area	157,733	191,996
	41017	Deschutes County, OR	157,733	191,996
13500		Bennettsville, SC Micro area	28,933	26,398
	45069	Marlboro County, SC	28,933	26,398
13540		Bennington, VT Micro area	37,125	35,631
	50003	Bennington County, VT	37,125	35,631
13620		Berlin, NH-VT Micro area	39,361	37,839
	33007	Coos County, NH	33,055	31,589
	50009	Essex County, VT	6,306	6,250
13660		Big Rapids, MI Micro area	42,798	43,545
	26107	Mecosta County, MI	42,798	43,545
13700		Big Spring, TX Micro area	36,238	37,847
	48173	Glasscock County, TX	1,226	1,388
	48227	Howard County, TX	35,012	36,459
13720		Big Stone Gap, VA Micro area	61,313	56,503
	51051	Dickenson County, VA	15,903	14,523
	51195	Wise County, VA	41,452	38,012
	51720	Norton city, VA	3,958	3,968
13740		Billings, MT Metro area	158,934	171,677
	30009	Carbon County, MT	10,078	10,714
	30037	Golden Valley County, MT	884	826
	30111	Yellowstone County, MT	147,972	160,137
13780		Binghamton, NY Metro area	251,725	240,219
	36007	Broome County, NY	200,600	191,659
	36107	Tioga County, NY	51,125	48,560
13820		Birmingham-Hoover, AL Metro area	1,128,047	1,151,801
	01007	Bibb County, AL	22,915	22,400
	01009	Blount County, AL	57,322	57,840
	01021	Chilton County, AL	43,643	44,153
	01073	Jefferson County, AL	658,466	659,300
	01115	St. Clair County, AL	83,593	88,690
	01117	Shelby County, AL	195,085	215,707
	01127	Walker County, AL	67,023	63,711
13900		Bismarck, ND Metro area	114,778	132,678
	38015	Burleigh County, ND	81,308	95,273
	38059	Morton County, ND	27,471	31,095
	38065	Oliver County, ND	1,846	1,952
	38085	Sioux County, ND	4,153	4,358
13940		Blackfoot, ID Micro area	45,607	46,236
	16011	Bingham County, ID	45,607	46,236
13980		Blacksburg-Christiansburg-Radford, VA Metro area	178,237	184,029
	51063	Floyd County, VA	15,279	15,795
	51071	Giles County, VA	17,286	16,844
	51121	Montgomery County, VA	94,392	98,985
	51155	Pulaski County, VA	34,872	34,066
	51750	Radford city, VA	16,408	18,339
14010		Bloomington, IL Metro area	186,133	188,597
	17039	De Witt County, IL	16,561	15,769
	17113	McLean County, IL	169,572	172,828
14020		Bloomington, IN Metro area	159,549	167,762
	18105	Monroe County, IN	137,974	146,917
	18119	Owen County, IN	21,575	20,845
14100		Bloomsburg-Berwick, PA Metro area	85,562	83,696
	42037	Columbia County, PA	67,295	65,456
	42093	Montour County, PA	18,267	18,240
14140		Bluefield, WV-VA Micro area	107,342	99,986
	51185	Tazewell County, VA	45,078	40,855
	54055	Mercer County, WV	62,264	59,131
14180		Blytheville, AR Micro area	46,480	41,239
	05093	Mississippi County, AR	46,480	41,239
14220		Bogalusa, LA Micro area	47,168	46,582
	22117	Washington Parish, LA	47,168	46,582
14260		Boise City, ID Metro area	616,561	730,426
	16001	Ada County, ID	392,365	469,966
	16015	Boise County, ID	7,028	7,634
	16027	Canyon County, ID	188,923	223,499
	16045	Gem County, ID	16,719	17,634
	16073	Owyhee County, ID	11,526	11,693
14300		Bonham, TX Micro Area	33,915	35,286
	48147	Fannin County, TX	33,915	35,286

Core based statistical area	State/County FIPS code	Title and Geographic Components	2010 Census Population	2018 Estimated Population
14340		Boone, IA Micro area	26,306	26,346
	19015	Boone County, IA	26,306	26,346
14380		Boone, NC Micro area	51,079	55,945
	37189	Watauga County, NC	51,079	55,945
14420		Borger, TX Micro area	22,150	21,198
	48233	Hutchinson County, TX	22,150	21,198
14460		Boston-Cambridge Newton, MA-NH Metro area	4,552,402	4,875,390
14460		Boston, MA Metro Div 14454	1,887,792	2,030,772
	25021	Norfolk County, MA	670,850	705,388
	25023	Plymouth County, MA	494,919	518,132
	25025	Suffolk County, MA	722,023	807,252
14460		Cambridge-Newton-Framingham, MA Metro Div 15764	2,246,244	2,405,352
	25009	Essex County, MA	743,159	790,638
	25017	Middlesex County, MA	1,503,085	1,614,714
14460		Rockingham County-Strafford County-NH Metro Div 40484	418,366	439,266
	33015	Rockingham County, NH	295,223	309,176
	33017	Strafford County, NH	123,143	130,090
14500		Boulder, CO Metro area	294,567	326,078
	08013	Boulder County, CO	294,567	326,078
14540		Bowling Green, KY Metro area	158,599	177,432
	21003	Allen County, KY	19,956	21,122
	21031	Butler County, KY	12,690	12,772
	21061	Edmonson County, KY	12,161	12,274
	21227	Warren County, KY	113,792	131,264
14580		Bozeman, MT Micro area	89,513	111,876
	30031	Gallatin County, MT	89,513	111,876
14620		Bradford, PA Micro area	43,450	40,968
	42083	McKean County, PA	43,450	40,968
14660		Brainerd, MN Micro area	91,067	94,408
	27021	Cass County, MN	28,567	29,519
	27035	Crow Wing County, MN	62,500	64,889
14700		Branson, MO Micro area	83,877	87,601
	29209	Stone County, MO Micro area	32,202	31,749
	29213	Taney County, MO Micro area	51,675	55,852
14720		Breckenridge, CO Micro area	27,994	31,007
	08117	Summit County, CO	27,994	31,007
14740		Bremerton-Silverdale, WA Metro area	251,133	269,805
	53035	Kitsap County, WA	251,133	269,805
14780		Brenham, TX Micro area	33,718	35,108
	48477	Washington County, TX	33,718	35,108
14820		Brevard, NC Micro area	33,090	34,215
	37175	Transylvania County, NC	33,090	34,215
14860		Bridgeport-Stamford-Norwalk, CT Metro area	916,829	943,823
	09001	Fairfield County, CT	916,829	943,823
15020		Brookhaven, MS Micro area	34,869	34,205
	28085	Lincoln County, MS	34,869	34,205
15060		Brookings, OR Micro area	22,364	22,813
	41015	Curry County, OR	22,364	22,813
15100		Brookings, SD Micro area	31,965	35,232
	46011	Brookings County, SD	31,965	35,232
15140		Brownsville, TN Micro Area	18,787	17,335
	47075	Haywood County, TN	18,787	17,335
15180		Brownsville-Harlingen, TX Metro area	406,220	423,908
	48061	Cameron County, TX	406,220	423,908
15220		Brownwood, TX Micro area	38,106	37,924
	48049	Brown County, TX	38,106	37,924
15260		Brunswick, GA Metro area	112,370	118,456
	13025	Brantley County, GA	18,411	18,897
	13127	Glynn County, GA	79,626	85,219
	13191	McIntosh County, GA	14,333	14,340
15340		Bucyrus, OH Micro area	43,784	41,550
	39033	Crawford County, OH	43,784	41,550
15380		Buffalo-Cheektowaga-Niagara Falls, NY Metro area	1,135,509	1,130,152
	36029	Erie County, NY	919,040	919,719
	36063	Niagara County, NY	216,469	210,433
15420		Burley, ID Micro area	43,021	44,689
	16031	Cassia County, ID	22,952	23,864
	16067	Minidoka County, ID	20,069	20,825
15460		Burlington, IA-IL Micro area	47,656	45,847
	17071	Henderson County, IL	7,331	6,709
	19057	Des Moines County, IA	40,325	39,138
15500		Burlington, NC Metro area	151,131	166,436
	37001	Alamance County, NC	151,131	166,436
15540		Burlington-South Burlington, VT Metro area	211,261	221,083
	50007	Chittenden County, VT	156,545	164,572
	50011	Franklin County, VT	47,746	49,421
	50013	Grand Isle County, VT	6,970	7,090
15580		Butte-Silver Bow, MT Micro area	34,200	34,993
	30093	Silver Bow County, MT	34,200	34,993
15620		Cadillac, MI Micro area	47,584	48,579
	26113	Missaukee County, MI	14,849	15,113
	26165	Wexford County, MI	32,735	33,466
15660		Calhoun, GA Micro area	55,186	57,685

Core based statistical area	State/County FIPS code	Title and Geographic Components	2010 Census Population	2018 Estimated Population
	13129	Gordon County, GA	55,186	57,685
15680		California-Lexington Park, MD Metro area	105,151	112,664
	24037	St. Mary's County, MD	105,151	112,664
15700		Cambridge, MD Micro area	32,618	31,998
	24019	Dorchester County, MD	32,618	31,998
15740		Cambridge, OH Micro area	40,087	39,022
	39059	Guernsey County, OH	40,087	39,022
15780		Camden, AR Micro area	31,488	28,883
	05013	Calhoun County, AR	5,368	5,277
	05103	Ouachita County, AR	26,120	23,606
15820		Campbellsville, KY Micro area	24,512	25,549
	21217	Taylor County, KY	24,512	25,549
15860		Cañon City, CO Micro area	46,824	48,021
	08043	Fremont County, CO	46,824	48,021
15900		Canton, IL Micro area	37,069	34,844
	17057	Fulton County, IL	37,069	34,844
15940		Canton-Massillon, OH Metro area	404,422	398,655
	39019	Carroll County, OH	28,836	27,081
	39151	Stark County, OH	375,586	371,574
15980		Cape Coral-Fort Myers, FL Metro area	618,754	754,610
	12071	Lee County, FL	618,754	754,610
16020		Cape Girardeau, MO-IL Metro area	96,275	96,982
	17003	Alexander County, IL	8,238	6,060
	29017	Bollinger County, MO	12,363	12,169
	29031	Cape Girardeau County, MO	75,674	78,753
16060		Carbondale-Marion, IL Metro area	126,575	124,475
	17077	Jackson County, IL	60,218	57,419
	17199	Williamson County, IL	66,357	67,056
16100		Carlsbad-Artesia, NM Micro area	53,829	57,900
	35015	Eddy County, NM	53,829	57,900
16140		Carroll, IA Micro Area	20,816	20,154
	19027	Carroll County, IA	20,816	20,154
16180		Carson City, NV Metro area	55,274	55,414
	32510	Carson City, NV Metro area	55,274	55,414
16220		Casper, WY Metro area	75,450	79,115
	56025	Natrona County, WY	75,450	79,115
16260		Cedar City, UT Micro area	46,163	52,775
	49021	Iron County, UT	46,163	52,775
16300		Cedar Rapids, IA Metro area	257,940	272,295
	19011	Benton County, IA	26,076	25,642
	19105	Jones County, IA	20,638	20,744
	19113	Linn County, IA	211,226	225,909
16340		Cedartown, GA Micro area	41,475	42,470
	13233	Polk County, GA	41,475	42,470
16380		Celina, OH Micro area	40,814	40,959
	39107	Mercer County, OH	40,814	40,959
16420		Central City, KY Micro Area	31,499	30,774
	21177	Muhlenberg County, KY	31,499	30,774
16460		Centralia, IL Micro area	39,437	37,620
	17121	Marion County, IL	39,437	37,620
16500		Centralia, WA Micro area	75,455	79,604
	53041	Lewis County, WA	75,455	79,604
16540		Chambersburg-Waynesboro, PA Metro area	149,618	154,835
	42055	Franklin County, PA	149,618	154,835
16580		Champaign-Urbana, IL Metro area	231,891	239,643
	17019	Champaign County, IL	201,081	209,983
	17053	Ford County, IL	14,081	13,264
	17147	Piatt County, IL	16,729	16,396
16620		Charleston, WV Metro area	227,078	211,037
	54005	Boone County, WV	24,629	21,951
	54015	Clay County, WV	9,386	8,632
	54039	Kanawha County, WV	193,063	180,454
16660		Charleston-Mattoon, IL Micro area	64,921	61,693
	17029	Coles County, IL	53,873	50,885
	17035	Cumberland County, IL	11,048	10,808
16700		Charleston-North Charleston, SC Metro area	664,607	787,643
	45015	Berkeley County, SC	177,843	221,091
	45019	Charleston County, SC	350,209	405,905
	45035	Dorchester County, SC	136,555	160,647
16740		Charlotte-Concord-Gastonia, NC-SC Metro area	2,217,012	2,569,213
	37025	Cabarrus County, NC	178,011	211,342
	37071	Gaston County, NC	206,086	222,846
	37097	Iredell County, NC	159,437	178,435
	37109	Lincoln County, NC	78,265	83,770
	37119	Mecklenburg County, NC	919,628	1,093,901
	37159	Rowan County, NC	138,428	141,262
	37179	Union County, NC	201,292	235,908
	45023	Chester County, SC	33,140	32,251
	45057	Lancaster County, SC	76,652	95,380
	45091	York County, SC	226,073	274,118
16820		Charlottesville, VA Metro area	218,705	235,232
	51003	Albemarle County, VA	98,970	108,718
	51029	Buckingham County, VA	17,146	16,999
	51065	Fluvanna County, VA	25,691	26,783
	51079	Greene County, VA	18,403	19,779
	51125	Nelson County, VA	15,020	14,836
	51540	Charlottesville city, VA	43,475	48,117

Core based statistical area	State/County FIPS code	Title and Geographic Components	2010 Census Population	2018 Estimated Population
16860		Chattanooga, TN-GA Metro area	528,143	560,793
	13047	Catoosa County, GA	63,942	67,420
	13083	Dade County, GA	16,633	16,226
	13295	Walker County, GA	68,756	69,410
	47065	Hamilton County, TN	336,463	364,286
	47115	Marion County, TN	28,237	28,575
	47153	Sequatchie County, TN	14,112	14,876
16940		Cheyenne, WY Metro area	91,738	98,976
	56021	Laramie County, WY	91,738	98,976
16980		Chicago-Naperville-Elgin, IL-IN-WI Metro area	9,461,105	9,498,716
16980		Chicago-Naperville-Arlington Heights, IL Metro Div 16974	7,262,718	7,288,849
	17031	Cook County, IL	5,194,675	5,180,493
	17043	DuPage County, IL	916,924	928,589
	17063	Grundy County, IL	50,063	50,972
	17093	Kendall County, IL	114,736	127,915
	17111	McHenry County, IL	308,760	308,570
	17197	Will County, IL	677,560	692,310
16980		Elgin, IL Metro Div 20994	620,429	638,359
	17037	DeKalb County, IL	105,160	104,143
	17089	Kane County, IL	515,269	534,216
16980		Gary, IN Metro Div 23844	708,071	701,386
	18073	Jasper County, IN	33,478	33,370
	18089	Lake County, IN	496,005	484,411
	18111	Newton County, IN	14,244	14,011
	18127	Porter County, IN	164,343	169,594
16980		Lake County-Kenosha County, IL-WI Metro Div 29404	869,888	870,122
	17097	Lake County, IL	703,462	700,832
	55059	Kenosha County, WI	166,426	169,290
17020		Chico, CA Metro area	220,000	231,256
	06007	Butte County, CA	220,000	231,256
17060		Chillicothe, OH Micro area	78,064	76,931
	39141	Ross County, OH	78,064	76,931
17140		Cincinnati, OH-KY-IN Metro area	2,114,580	2,190,209
	18029	Dearborn County, IN	50,047	49,568
	18115	Ohio County, IN	6,128	5,844
	18161	Union County, IN	7,516	7,037
	21015	Boone County, KY	118,811	131,533
	21023	Bracken County, KY	8,488	8,239
	21037	Campbell County, KY	90,336	93,152
	21077	Gallatin County, KY	8,589	8,832
	21081	Grant County, KY	24,662	25,121
	21117	Kenton County, KY	159,720	166,051
	21191	Pendleton County, KY	14,877	14,529
	39015	Brown County, OH	44,846	43,602
	39017	Butler County, OH	368,130	382,378
	39025	Clermont County, OH	197,363	205,466
	39061	Hamilton County, OH	802,374	816,684
	39165	Warren County, OH	212,693	232,173
17200		Claremont-Lebanon, NH-VT Micro area	218,466	217,215
	33009	Grafton County, NH	89,118	89,786
	33019	Sullivan County, NH	43,742	43,144
	50017	Orange County, VT	28,936	28,999
	50027	Windsor County, VT	56,670	55,286
17220		Clarksburg, WV Micro area	94,196	92,822
	54017	Doddridge County, WV	8,202	8,406
	54033	Harrison County, WV	69,099	67,554
	54091	Taylor County, WV	16,895	16,862
17260		Clarksdale, MS Micro area	26,151	22,628
	28027	Coahoma County, MS	26,151	22,628
17300		Clarksville, TN-KY Metro area	260,625	292,264
	21047	Christian County, KY	73,955	71,671
	21221	Trigg County, KY	14,339	14,643
	47125	Montgomery County, TN	172,331	205,950
17340		Clearlake, CA Micro area	64,665	64,382
	06033	Lake County, CA	64,665	64,382
17380		Cleveland, MS Micro area	34,145	31,333
	28011	Bolivar County, MS	34,145	31,333
17420		Cleveland, TN Metro area	115,788	123,625
	47011	Bradley County, TN	98,963	106,727
	47139	Polk County, TN	16,825	16,898
17460		Cleveland-Elyria, OH Metro area	2,077,240	2,057,009
	39035	Cuyahoga County, OH	1,280,122	1,243,857
	39055	Geauga County, OH	93,389	94,031
	39085	Lake County, OH	230,041	230,514
	39093	Lorain County, OH	301,356	309,461
	39103	Medina County, OH	172,332	179,146
17500		Clewiston, FL Micro area	39,140	41,556
	12051	Hendry County, FL	39,140	41,556
17540		Clinton, IA Micro area	49,116	46,518
	19045	Clinton County, IA	49,116	46,518
17580		Clovis, NM Micro area	48,376	49,437
	35009	Curry County, NM	48,376	49,437
17660		Coeur d'Alene, ID Metro area	138,494	161,505
	16055	Kootenai County, ID	138,494	161,505
17700		Coffeyville, KS Micro area	35,471	32,120
	20125	Montgomery County, KS	35,471	32,120
17740		Coldwater, MI Micro area	45,248	43,622
	26023	Branch County, MI	45,248	43,622
17780		College Station-Bryan, TX Metro area	228,660	262,431
	48041	Brazos County, TX	194,851	226,758
	48051	Burleson County, TX	17,187	18,389
	48395	Robertson County, TX	16,622	17,284
17820		Colorado Springs, CO Metro area	645,613	738,939
	08041	El Paso County, CO	622,263	713,856
	08119	Teller County, CO	23,350	25,083
17860		Columbia, MO Metro area	162,642	180,005
	29019	Boone County, MO	162,642	180,005
17900		Columbia, SC Metro area	767,598	832,666
	45017	Calhoun County, SC	15,175	14,520
	45039	Fairfield County, SC	23,956	22,402
	45055	Kershaw County, SC	61,697	65,592
	45063	Lexington County, SC	262,391	295,032
	45079	Richland County, SC	384,504	414,576
	45081	Saluda County, SC	19,875	20,544
17980		Columbus, GA-AL Metro area	294,865	305,451
	01113	Russell County, AL	52,947	57,781
	13053	Chattahoochee County, GA	11,267	10,684
	13145	Harris County, GA	32,024	34,475
	13197	Marion County, GA	8,742	8,351
	13215	Muscogee County, GA	189,885	194,160
18020		Columbus, IN Metro area	76,794	82,753
	18005	Bartholomew County, IN	76,794	82,753
18060		Columbus, MS Micro area	59,779	58,930
	28087	Lowndes County, MS	59,779	58,930
18100		Columbus, NE Micro area	32,237	33,363
	31141	Platte County, NE	32,237	33,363
18140		Columbus, OH Metro area	1,901,974	2,106,541
	39041	Delaware County, OH	174,214	204,826
	39045	Fairfield County, OH	146,156	155,782
	39049	Franklin County, OH	1,163,414	1,310,300
	39073	Hocking County, OH	29,380	28,385
	39089	Licking County, OH	166,492	175,769
	39097	Madison County, OH	43,435	44,413
	39117	Morrow County, OH	34,827	35,112
	39127	Perry County, OH	36,058	36,033
	39129	Pickaway County, OH	55,698	58,086
	39159	Union County, OH	52,300	57,835
18180		Concord, NH Micro area	146,445	151,132
	33013	Merrimack County, NH	146,445	151,132
18220		Connersville, IN Micro area	24,277	23,047
	18041	Fayette County, IN	24,277	23,047
18260		Cookeville, TN Micro area	106,042	112,669
	47087	Jackson County, TN	11,638	11,758
	47133	Overton County, TN	22,083	22,068
	47141	Putnam County, TN	72,321	78,843
18300		Coos Bay, OR Micro area	63,043	64,389
	41011	Coos County, OR	63,043	64,389
18380		Cordele, GA Micro area	23,439	22,601
	13081	Crisp County, GA	23,439	22,601
18420		Corinth, MS Micro area	37,057	36,925
	28003	Alcorn County, MS	37,057	36,925
18460		Cornelia, GA Micro area	43,041	45,388
	13137	Habersham County, GA	43,041	45,388
18500		Corning, NY Micro area	98,990	95,796
	36101	Steuben County, NY	98,990	95,796
18580		Corpus Christi, TX Metro area	428,185	452,950
	48007	Aransas County, TX	23,158	23,792
	48355	Nueces County, TX	340,223	362,265
	48409	San Patricio County, TX	64,804	66,893
18620		Corsicana, TX Micro area	47,735	49,565
	48349	Navarro County, TX	47,735	49,565
18660		Cortland, NY Micro area	49,336	47,823
	36023	Cortland County, NY	49,336	47,823
18700		Corvallis, OR Metro area	85,579	92,101
	41003	Benton County, OR	85,579	92,101
18740		Coshocton, OH Micro area	36,901	36,629
	39031	Coshocton County, OH	36,901	36,629
18780		Craig, CO Micro area	13,795	13,188
	08081	Moffat County, CO	13,795	13,188
18820		Crawfordsville, IN Micro area	38,124	38,346
	18107	Montgomery County, IN	38,124	38,346
18860		Crescent City, CA Micro area	28,610	27,828
	06015	Del Norte County, CA	28,610	27,828
18880		Crestview-Fort Walton Beach-Destin, FL Metro area	235,865	278,644
	12091	Okaloosa County, FL	180,822	207,269
	12131	Walton County, FL	55,043	71,375
18900		Crossville, TN Micro area	56,053	59,673
	47035	Cumberland County, TN	56,053	59,673
18980		Cullman, AL Micro area	80,406	83,442
	01043	Cullman County, AL	80,406	83,442
19000		Cullowhee, NC Micro area	40,271	43,327
	37099	Jackson County, NC	40,271	43,327

Core based statistical area	State/County FIPS code	Title and Geographic Components	2010 Census Population	2018 Estimated Population
19060		Cumberland, MD-WV Metro area	103,299	97,915
	24001	Allegany County, MD	75,087	70,975
	54057	Mineral County, WV	28,212	26,940
19100		Dallas-Fort Worth-Arlington, TX Metro area	6,426,214	7,539,711
19100		Dallas-Plano-Irving, TX Metro Div 19124	4,230,520	5,007,190
	48085	Collin County, TX	782,341	1,005,146
	48113	Dallas County, TX	2,368,139	2,637,772
	48121	Denton County, TX	662,614	859,064
	48139	Ellis County, TX	149,610	179,436
	48231	Hunt County, TX	86,129	96,493
	48257	Kaufman County, TX	103,350	128,622
	48397	Rockwall County, TX	78,337	100,657
19100		Fort Worth-Arlington, TX Metro Div 23104	2,195,694	2,532,521
	48221	Hood County, TX	51,182	60,537
	48251	Johnson County, TX	150,934	171,361
	48367	Parker County, TX	116,927	138,371
	48425	Somervell County, TX	8,490	9,016
	48439	Tarrant County, TX	1,809,034	2,084,931
	48497	Wise County, TX	59,127	68,305
19140		Dalton, GA Metro area	142,227	143,983
	13213	Murray County, GA	39,628	39,921
	13313	Whitfield County, GA	102,599	104,062
19180		Danville, IL Metro area	81,625	76,806
	17183	Vermilion County, IL	81,625	76,806
19220		Danville, KY Micro area	53,174	54,744
	21021	Boyle County, KY	28,432	30,100
	21137	Lincoln County, KY	24,742	24,644
19260		Danville, VA Micro area	106,561	101,642
	51143	Pittsylvania County, VA	63,506	60,949
	51590	Danville city, VA	43,055	40,693
19300		Daphne-Fairhope-Foley, AL Metro area	182,265	218,022
	01003	Baldwin County, AL	182,265	218,022
19340		Davenport-Moline-Rock Island, IA-IL Metro area	379,690	381,451
	17073	Henry County, IL	50,486	49,090
	17131	Mercer County, IL	16,434	15,601
	17161	Rock Island County, IL	147,546	143,477
	19163	Scott County, IA	165,224	173,283
19380		Dayton, OH Metro area	799,232	806,548
	39057	Greene County, OH	161,573	167,995
	39109	Miami County, OH	102,506	106,222
	39113	Montgomery County, OH	535,153	532,331
19420		Dayton, TN Micro area	31,809	33,044
	47143	Rhea County, TN	31,809	33,044
19460		Decatur, AL Metro area	153,829	152,046
	01079	Lawrence County, AL	34,339	32,957
	01103	Morgan County, AL	119,490	119,089
19500		Decatur, IL Metro area	110,768	104,712
	17115	Macon County, IL	110,768	104,712
19540		Decatur, IN Micro area	34,387	35,636
	18001	Adams County, IN	34,387	35,636
19580		Defiance, OH Micro area	39,037	38,165
	39039	Defiance County, OH	39,037	38,165
19620		Del Rio, TX Micro area	48,879	49,208
	48465	Val Verde County, TX	48,879	49,208
19660		Deltona-Daytona Beach-Ormond Beach, FL Metro area	590,289	659,605
	12035	Flagler County, FL	95,696	112,067
	12127	Volusia County, FL	494,593	547,538
19700		Deming, NM Micro area	25,095	23,963
	35029	Luna County, NM	25,095	23,963
19740		Denver-Aurora-Lakewood, CO Metro area	2,543,482	2,932,415
	08001	Adams County, CO	441,603	511,868
	08005	Arapahoe County, CO	572,003	651,215
	08014	Broomfield County, CO	55,889	69,267
	08019	Clear Creek County, CO	9,088	9,605
	08031	Denver County, CO	600,158	716,492
	08035	Douglas County, CO	285,465	342,776
	08039	Elbert County, CO	23,086	26,282
	08047	Gilpin County, CO	5,441	6,121
	08059	Jefferson County, CO	534,543	580,233
	08093	Park County, CO	16,206	18,556
19760		DeRidder, LA Micro area	35,654	37,253
	22011	Beauregard Parish, LA	35,654	37,253
19780		Des Moines-West Des Moines, IA Metro area	569,633	655,409
	19049	Dallas County, IA	66,135	90,180
	19077	Guthrie County, IA	10,954	10,720
	19121	Madison County, IA	15,679	16,249
	19153	Polk County, IA	430,640	487,204
	19181	Warren County, IA	46,225	51,056
19820		Detroit-Warren-Dearborn, MI Metro area	4,296,250	4,326,442
19820		Detroit-Dearborn-Livonia, MI Metro Div 19804	1,820,584	1,753,893
	26163	Wayne County, MI	1,820,584	1,753,893
19820		Warren-Troy-Farmington Hills, MI Metro Div 47664	2,475,666	2,572,549
	26087	Lapeer County, MI	88,319	88,028

Core based statistical area	State/County FIPS code	Title and Geographic Components	2010 Census Population	2018 Estimated Population
	26093	Livingston County, MI	180,967	191,224
	26099	Macomb County, MI	840,978	874,759
	26125	Oakland County, MI	1,202,362	1,259,201
	26147	St. Clair County, MI	163,040	159,337
19860		Dickinson, ND Micro area	24,199	30,997
	38089	Stark County, ND	24,199	30,997
19940		Dixon, IL Micro area	36,031	34,223
	17103	Lee County, IL	36,031	34,223
19980		Dodge City, KS Micro area	33,848	33,888
	20057	Ford County, KS	33,848	33,888
20020		Dothan, AL Metro area	145,639	148,245
	01061	Geneva County, AL	26,790	26,314
	01067	Henry County, AL	17,302	17,209
	01069	Houston County, AL	101,547	104,722
20060		Douglas, GA Micro area	42,356	43,093
	13069	Coffee County, GA	42,356	43,093
20100		Dover, DE Metro area	162,310	178,550
	10001	Kent County, Delaware	162,310	178,550
20140		Dublin, GA Micro area	58,414	57,033
	13167	Johnson County, GA	9,980	9,708
	13175	Laurens County, GA	48,434	47,325
20180		DuBois, PA Micro area	81,642	79,388
	42033	Clearfield County, PA	81,642	79,388
20220		Dubuque, IA Metro area	93,653	96,854
	19061	Dubuque County, IA	93,653	96,854
20260		Duluth, MN-WI Metro area	279,771	278,799
	27017	Carlton County, MN	35,386	35,837
	27137	St. Louis County, MN	200,226	199,754
	55031	Douglas County, WI	44,159	43,208
20300		Dumas, TX Micro area	21,904	21,485
	48341	Moore County, TX	21,904	21,485
20340		Duncan, OK Micro area	45,048	43,265
	40137	Stephens County, OK	45,048	43,265
20380		Dunn, NC Micro area	114,678	134,214
	37085	Harnett County, NC	114,678	134,214
20420		Durango, CO Micro area	51,334	56,310
	08067	La Plata County, CO	51,334	56,310
20460		Durant, OK Micro area	42,416	47,192
	40013	Bryan County, OK	42,416	47,192
20500		Durham-Chapel Hill, NC Metro area	504,357	575,412
	37037	Chatham County, NC	63,505	73,139
	37063	Durham County, NC	267,587	316,739
	37135	Orange County, NC	133,801	146,027
	37145	Person County, NC	39,464	39,507
20540		Dyersburg, TN Micro area	38,335	37,320
	47045	Dyer County, TN	38,335	37,320
20580		Eagle Pass, TX Micro area	54,258	58,485
	48323	Maverick County, TX	54,258	58,485
20660		Easton, MD Micro area	37,782	36,968
	24041	Talbot County, MD	37,782	36,968
20700		East Stroudsburg, PA Metro area	169,842	169,507
	42089	Monroe County, PA	169,842	169,507
20740		Eau Claire, WI Metro area	161,151	168,669
	55017	Chippewa County, WI	62,415	64,135
	55035	Eau Claire County, WI	98,736	104,534
20780		Edwards, CO Micro area	52,197	54,993
	08037	Eagle County, CO	52,197	54,993
20820		Effingham, IL Micro area	34,242	34,208
	17049	Effingham County, IL	34,242	34,208
20900		El Campo, TX Micro area	41,280	41,619
	48481	Wharton County, TX	41,280	41,619
20940		El Centro, CA Metro area	174,528	181,827
	06025	Imperial County, CA	174,528	181,827
20980		El Dorado, AR Micro area	41,639	39,126
	05139	Union County, AR	41,639	39,126
21020		Elizabeth City, NC Micro area	64,094	63,771
	37029	Camden County, NC	9,980	10,710
	37139	Pasquotank County, NC	40,661	39,639
	37143	Perquimans County, NC	13,453	13,422
21060		Elizabethtown-Fort Knox, KY Metro area	148,338	153,378
	21093	Hardin County, KY	105,543	110,356
	21123	Larue County, KY	14,193	14,307
	21163	Meade County, KY	28,602	28,715
21120		Elk City, OK Micro area	22,119	21,709
	40009	Beckham County, OK	22,119	21,709
21140		Elkhart-Goshen, IN Metro area	197,559	205,560
	18039	Elkhart County, IN	197,559	205,560
21180		Elkins, WV Micro area	29,405	28,823
	54083	Randolph County, WV	29,405	28,823
21220		Elko, NV Micro area	50,805	54,463
	32007	Elko County, NV	48,818	52,460
	32011	Eureka County, NV	1,987	2,003
21260		Ellensburg, WA Micro area	40,915	47,364
	53037	Kittitas County, WA	40,915	47,364
21300		Elmira, NY Metro area	88,830	84,254
	36015	Chemung County, NY	88,830	84,254
21340		El Paso, TX Metro area	804,123	845,553
	48141	El Paso County, TX	800,647	840,758

Core based statistical area	State/ County FIPS code	Title and Geographic Components	2010 Census Population	2018 Estimated Population
	48229	Hudspeth County, TX	3,476	4,795
21380		Emporia, KS Micro area	33,690	33,406
	20111	Lyon County, KS	33,690	33,406
21420		Enid, OK Metro area	60,580	60,913
	40047	Garfield County, OK	60,580	60,913
21460		Enterprise, AL Micro area	49,948	51,909
	01031	Coffee County, AL	49,948	51,909
21500		Erie, PA Metro area	280,566	272,061
	42049	Erie County, PA	280,566	272,061
21540		Escanaba, MI Micro area	37,069	35,857
	26041	Delta County, MI	37,069	35,857
21580		Española, NM Micro area	40,246	39,006
	35039	Rio Arriba County, NM	40,246	39,006
21640		Eufaula, AL-GA Micro Area	29,970	27,160
	01005	Barbour County, AL	27,457	24,881
	13239	Quitman County, GA	2,513	2,279
21660		Eugene, OR Metro area	351,715	379,611
	41039	Lane County, OR	351,715	379,611
21700		Eureka-Arcata-Fortuna, CA Micro area	134,623	136,373
	06023	Humboldt County, CA	134,623	136,373
21740		Evanston, WY Micro area	21,118	20,299
	56041	Uinta County, WY	21,118	20,299
21780		Evansville, IN-KY Metro area	311,552	314,672
	18129	Posey County, IN	25,910	25,540
	18163	Vanderburgh County, IN	179,703	180,974
	18173	Warrick County, IN	59,689	62,567
	21101	Henderson County, KY	46,250	45,591
21820		Fairbanks, AK Metro area	97,581	98,971
	02090	Fairbanks North Star Borough, AK	97,581	98,971
21840		Fairfield, IA Micro area	16,843	18,381
	19101	Jefferson County, IA	16,843	18,381
21860		Fairmont, MN Micro Area	20,840	19,785
	27091	Martin County, MN	20,840	19,785
21900		Fairmont, WV Micro area	56,418	56,097
	54049	Marion County, WV	56,418	56,097
21980		Fallon, NV Micro area	24,877	24,440
	32001	Churchill County, NV	24,877	24,440
22020		Fargo, ND-MN Metro area	208,737	245,471
	27027	Clay County, MN	58,999	63,955
	38017	Cass County, ND	149,778	181,516
22060		Faribault-Northfield, MN Micro area	64,142	66,523
	27131	Rice County, MN	64,142	66,523
22100		Farmington, MO Micro area	65,359	66,692
	29187	St. Francois County, MO	65,359	66,692
22140		Farmington, NM Metro area	130,044	125,043
	35045	San Juan County, NM	130,044	125,043
22180		Fayetteville, NC Metro area	366,383	387,094
	37051	Cumberland County, NC	319,431	332,330
	37093	Hoke County, NC	46,952	54,764
22220		Fayetteville-Springdale-Rogers, AR-MO Metro area	463,204	549,128
	05007	Benton County, AR	221,339	272,608
	05087	Madison County, AR	15,717	16,481
	05143	Washington County, AR	203,065	236,961
	29119	McDonald County, MO	23,083	23,078
22260		Fergus Falls, MN Micro area	57,303	58,812
	27111	Otter Tail County, MN	57,303	58,812
22280		Fernley, NV Micro area	51,980	55,808
	32019	Lyon County, NV	51,980	55,808
22300		Findlay, OH Micro area	74,782	75,930
	39063	Hancock County, OH	74,782	75,930
22340		Fitzgerald, GA Micro area	17,634	16,787
	13017	Ben Hill County, GA	17,634	16,787
22380		Flagstaff, AZ Metro area	134,421	142,854
	04005	Coconino County, AZ	134,421	142,854
22420		Flint, MI Metro area	425,790	406,892
	26049	Genesee County, MI	425,790	406,892
22500		Florence, SC Metro area	205,566	204,961
	45031	Darlington County, SC	68,681	66,802
	45041	Florence County, SC	136,885	138,159
22520		Florence-Muscle Shoals, AL Metro area	147,137	147,149
	01033	Colbert County, AL	54,428	54,762
	01077	Lauderdale County, AL	92,709	92,387
22540		Fond du Lac, WI Metro area	101,633	103,066
	55039	Fond du Lac County, WI	101,633	103,066
22580		Forest City, NC Micro area	67,810	66,826
	37161	Rutherford County, NC	67,810	66,826
22620		Forrest City, AR Micro area	28,258	25,439
	05123	St. Francis County, AR	28,258	25,439
22660		Fort Collins, CO Metro area	299,630	350,518
	08069	Larimer County, CO	299,630	350,518
22700		Fort Dodge, IA Micro area	38,013	36,277
	19187	Webster County, IA	38,013	36,277
22780		Fort Leonard Wood, MO Micro area	52,274	52,014
	29169	Pulaski County, MO	52,274	52,014
22800		Fort Madison-Keokuk, IA-IL-MO Micro area	62,105	58,741
	17067	Hancock County, IL	19,104	17,844
	19111	Lee County, IA	35,862	34,055
	29045	Clark County, MO	7,139	6,842
22820		Fort Morgan, CO Micro area	28,159	28,558
	08087	Morgan County, CO	28,159	28,558
22840		Fort Payne, AL Micro Area	71,109	71,385
	01049	DeKalb County, AL	71,109	71,385
22860		Fort Polk South, LA Micro area	52,334	48,860
	22115	Vernon Parish, LA	52,334	48,860
22900		Fort Smith, AR-OK Metro area	280,467	282,318
	05033	Crawford County, AR	61,948	63,406
	05131	Sebastian County, AR	125,744	127,753
	40079	Le Flore County, OK	50,384	49,980
	40135	Sequoyah County, OK	42,391	41,179
23060		Fort Wayne, IN Metro area	416,257	437,631
	18003	Allen County, IN	355,329	375,351
	18179	Wells County, IN	27,636	28,206
	18183	Whitley County, IN	33,292	34,074
23140		Frankfort, IN Micro area	33,224	32,250
	18023	Clinton County, IN	33,224	32,250
23180		Frankfort, KY Micro area	70,706	73,478
	21005	Anderson County, KY	21,421	22,663
	21073	Franklin County, KY	49,285	50,815
23240		Fredericksburg, TX Micro area	24,837	26,804
	48171	Gillespie County, TX	24,837	26,804
23300		Freeport, IL Micro area	47,711	44,753
	17177	Stephenson County, IL	47,711	44,753
23340		Fremont, NE Micro area	36,691	36,791
	31053	Dodge County, NE	36,691	36,791
23380		Fremont, OH Micro area	60,944	58,799
	39143	Sandusky County, OH	60,944	58,799
23420		Fresno, CA Metro area	930,450	994,400
	06019	Fresno County, CA	930,450	994,400
23460		Gadsden, AL Metro area	104,430	102,501
	01055	Etowah County, AL	104,430	102,501
23500		Gaffney, SC Micro area	55,342	57,078
	45021	Cherokee County, SC	55,342	57,078
23540		Gainesville, FL Metro area	264,275	288,212
	12001	Alachua County, FL	247,336	269,956
	12041	Gilchrist County, FL	16,939	18,256
23580		Gainesville, GA Metro area	179,684	202,148
	13139	Hall County, GA	179,684	202,148
23620		Gainesville, TX Micro area	38,437	40,574
	48097	Cooke County, TX	38,437	40,574
23660		Galesburg, IL Micro area	52,919	50,112
	17095	Knox County, IL	52,919	50,112
23700		Gallup, NM Micro area	71,492	72,290
	35031	McKinley County, NM	71,492	72,290
23780		Garden City, KS Micro area	40,753	40,554
	20055	Finney County, KS	36,776	36,611
	20093	Kearny County, KS	3,977	3,943
23820		Gardnerville Ranchos, NV Micro area	46,997	48,467
	32005	Douglas County, NV	46,997	48,467
23860		Georgetown, SC Micro area	60,158	62,249
	45043	Georgetown County, SC	60,158	62,249
23900		Gettysburg, PA Metro area	101,407	102,811
	42001	Adams County, PA	101,407	102,811
23940		Gillette, WY Micro area	46,133	46,140
	56005	Campbell County, WY	46,133	46,140
23980		Glasgow, KY Micro area	52,272	54,206
	21009	Barren County, KY	42,173	44,176
	21169	Metcalfe County, KY	10,099	10,030
24020		Glens Falls, NY Metro area	128,923	125,462
	36113	Warren County, NY	65,707	64,265
	36115	Washington County, NY	63,216	61,197
24060		Glenwood Springs, CO Micro area	73,537	77,720
	08045	Garfield County, CO	56,389	59,770
	08097	Pitkin County, CO	17,148	17,950
24100		Gloversville, NY Micro area	55,531	53,591
	36035	Fulton County, NY	55,531	53,591
24140		Goldsboro, NC Metro area	122,623	123,248
	37191	Wayne County, NC	122,623	123,248
24220		Grand Forks, ND-MN Metro area	98,461	102,299
	27119	Polk County, MN	31,600	31,529
	38035	Grand Forks County, ND	66,861	70,770
24260		Grand Island, NE Metro area	81,850	85,088
	31079	Hall County, NE	58,607	61,607
	31081	Hamilton County, NE	9,124	9,280
	31093	Howard County, NE	6,274	6,468
	31121	Merrick County, NE	7,845	7,733
24300		Grand Junction, CO Metro area	146,723	153,207
	08077	Mesa County, CO	146,723	153,207
24330		Grand Rapids, MN Micro Area	45,058	45,108
	27061	Itasca County, MN	45,058	45,108
24340		Grand Rapids-Wyoming, MI Metro area	988,938	1,069,405
	26015	Barry County, MI	59,173	61,157
	26081	Kent County, MI	602,622	653,786
	26117	Montcalm County, MI	63,342	63,968
	26139	Ottawa County, MI	263,801	290,494
24380		Grants, NM Micro area	27,213	26,746

Core based statistical area	State/ County FIPS code	Title and Geographic Components	2010 Census Population	2018 Estimated Population
	35006	Cibola County, NM	27,213	26,746
24420		Grants Pass, OR Metro area	82,713	87,393
	41033	Josephine County, OR	82,713	87,393
24460		Great Bend, KS Micro area	27,674	26,111
	20009	Barton County, KS	27,674	26,111
24500		Great Falls, MT Metro area	81,327	81,643
	30013	Cascade County, MT	81,327	81,643
24540		Greeley, CO Metro area	252,825	314,305
	08123	Weld County, CO	252,825	314,305
24580		Green Bay, WI Metro area	306,241	321,591
	55009	Brown County, WI	248,007	263,378
	55061	Kewaunee County, WI	20,574	20,383
	55083	Oconto County, WI	37,660	37,830
24620		Greeneville, TN Micro area	68,831	69,087
	47059	Greene County, TN	68,831	69,087
24640		Greenfield Town, MA Micro area	71,372	70,963
	25011	Franklin County, MA	71,372	70,963
24660		Greensboro-High Point, NC Metro area	723,801	767,711
	37081	Guilford County, NC	488,406	533,670
	37151	Randolph County, NC	141,752	143,351
	37157	Rockingham County, NC	93,643	90,690
24700		Greensburg, IN Micro area	25,740	26,794
	18031	Decatur County, IN	25,740	26,794
24740		Greenville, MS Micro area	51,137	45,063
	28151	Washington County, MS	51,137	45,063
24780		Greenville, NC Metro area	168,148	179,914
	37147	Pitt County, NC	168,148	179,914
24820		Greenville, OH Micro area	52,959	51,323
	39037	Darke County, OH	52,959	51,323
24860		Greenville-Anderson-Mauldin, SC Metro area	824,112	906,626
	45007	Anderson County, SC	187,126	200,482
	45045	Greenville County, SC	451,225	514,213
	45059	Laurens County, SC	66,537	66,994
	45077	Pickens County, SC	119,224	124,937
24900		Greenwood, MS Micro area	42,914	38,830
	28015	Carroll County, MS	10,597	9,911
	28083	Leflore County, MS	32,317	28,919
24940		Greenwood, SC Micro area	95,078	95,282
	45001	Abbeville County, SC	25,417	24,541
	45047	Greenwood County, SC	69,661	70,741
24980		Grenada, MS Micro area	21,906	21,055
	28043	Grenada County, MS	21,906	21,055
25060		Gulfport-Biloxi-Pascagoula, MS Metro area	370,702	397,261
	28045	Hancock County, MS	43,929	47,334
	28047	Harrison County, MS	187,105	206,650
	28059	Jackson County, MS	139,668	143,277
25100		Guymon, OK Micro area	20,640	20,455
	40139	Texas County, OK	20,640	20,455
25180		Hagerstown-Martinsburg, MD-WV Metro area	251,599	268,049
	24043	Washington County, MD	147,430	150,926
	54003	Berkeley County, WV	104,169	117,123
25200		Hailey, ID Micro area	27,701	29,088
	16013	Blaine County, ID	21,376	22,601
	16025	Camas County, ID	1,117	1,127
	16063	Lincoln County, ID	5,208	5,360
25220		Hammond, LA Metro area	121,097	133,777
	22105	Tangipahoa Parish, LA	121,097	133,777
25260		Hanford-Corcoran, CA Metro area	152,982	151,366
	06031	Kings County, CA	152,982	151,366
25300		Hannibal, MO Micro area	38,948	38,804
	29127	Marion County, MO	28,781	28,592
	29173	Ralls County, MO	10,167	10,212
25420		Harrisburg-Carlisle, PA Metro area	549,475	574,659
	42041	Cumberland County, PA	235,406	251,423
	42043	Dauphin County, PA	268,100	277,097
	42099	Perry County, PA	45,969	46,139
25460		Harrison, AR Micro area	45,233	45,285
	05009	Boone County, AR	36,903	37,480
	05101	Newton County, AR	8,330	7,805
25500		Harrisonburg, VA Metro area	125,228	135,277
	51165	Rockingham County, VA	76,314	81,244
	51660	Harrisonburg city, VA	48,914	54,033
25540		Hartford-West Hartford-East Hartford, CT Metro area	1,212,381	1,206,300
	09003	Hartford County, CT	894,014	892,697
	09007	Middlesex County, CT	165,676	162,682
	09013	Tolland County, CT	152,691	150,921
25580		Hastings, NE Micro area	31,364	31,511
	31001	Adams County, NE	31,364	31,511
25620		Hattiesburg, MS Metro area	142,842	149,414
	28035	Forrest County, MS	74,934	75,036
	28073	Lamar County, MS	55,658	62,447
	28111	Perry County, MS	12,250	11,931
25700		Hays, KS Micro area	28,452	28,710
	20051	Ellis County, KS	28,452	28,710
25720		Heber, UT Micro area	23,530	33,240

Core based statistical area	State/ County FIPS code	Title and Geographic Components	2010 Census Population	2018 Estimated Population
	49051	Wasatch County, UT	23,530	33,240
25740		Helena, MT Micro area	74,801	80,797
	30043	Jefferson County, MT	11,406	12,097
	30049	Lewis and Clark County, MT	63,395	68,700
25760		Helena-West Helena, AR Micro area	21,757	18,029
	05107	Phillips County, AR	21,757	18,029
25780		Henderson, NC Micro area	45,422	44,582
	37181	Vance County, NC	45,422	44,582
25820		Hereford, TX Micro area	19,372	18,760
	48117	Deaf Smith County, TX	19,372	18,760
25840		Hermiston-Pendleton, OR Micro area	87,062	88,888
	41049	Morrow County, OR	11,173	11,372
	41059	Umatilla County, OR	75,889	77,516
25860		Hickory-Lenoir-Morganton, NC Metro area	365,497	368,416
	37003	Alexander County, NC	37,198	37,353
	37023	Burke County, NC	90,912	90,382
	37027	Caldwell County, NC	83,029	82,029
	37035	Catawba County, NC	154,358	158,652
25880		Hillsdale, MI Micro area	46,688	45,749
	26059	Hillsdale County, MI	46,688	45,749
25900		Hilo, HI Micro area	185,079	200,983
	15001	Hawaii County, HI	185,079	200,983
25940		Hilton Head Island-Bluffton-Beaufort, SC Metro area	187,010	217,686
	45013	Beaufort County, SC	162,233	188,715
	45053	Jasper County, SC	24,777	28,971
25980		Hinesville, GA Metro area	77,917	80,495
	13179	Liberty County, GA	63,453	61,497
	13183	Long County, GA	14,464	18,998
26020		Hobbs, NM Micro area	64,727	69,611
	35025	Lea County, NM	64,727	69,611
26090		Holland, MI Micro area	111,408	117,327
	26005	Allegan County, MI	111,408	117,327
26140		Homosassa Springs, FL Metro area	141,236	147,929
	12017	Citrus County, FL	141,236	147,929
26220		Hood River, OR Micro area	22,346	23,428
	41027	Hood River County, OR	22,346	23,428
26260		Hope, AR Micro Area	31,606	30,067
	05057	Hempstead County, AR	22,609	21,741
	05099	Nevada County, AR	8,997	8,326
26300		Hot Springs, AR Metro area	96,024	99,154
	05051	Garland County, AR	96,024	99,154
26340		Houghton, MI Micro area	38,784	38,332
	26061	Houghton County, MI	36,628	36,219
	26083	Keweenaw County, MI	2,156	2,113
26380		Houma-Thibodaux, LA Metro area	208,178	209,136
	22057	Lafourche Parish, LA	96,318	98,115
	22109	Terrebonne Parish, LA	111,860	111,021
26420		Houston-The Woodlands-Sugar Land, TX Metro area	5,920,416	6,997,384
	48015	Austin County, TX	28,417	29,989
	48039	Brazoria County, TX	313,166	370,200
	48071	Chambers County, TX	35,096	42,454
	48157	Fort Bend County, TX	585,375	787,858
	48167	Galveston County, TX	291,309	337,890
	48201	Harris County, TX	4,092,459	4,698,619
	48291	Liberty County, TX	75,643	86,323
	48339	Montgomery County, TX	455,746	590,925
	48473	Waller County, TX	43,205	53,126
26460		Hudson, NY Micro area	63,096	59,916
	36021	Columbia County, NY	63,096	59,916
26500		Huntingdon, PA Micro area	45,913	45,168
	42061	Huntingdon County, PA	45,913	45,168
26540		Huntington, IN Micro area	37,124	36,240
	18069	Huntington County, IN	37,124	36,240
26580		Huntington-Ashland, WV-KY-OH Metro area	364,908	352,823
	21019	Boyd County, KY	49,542	47,240
	21089	Greenup County, KY	36,910	35,268
	39087	Lawrence County, OH	62,450	59,866
	54011	Cabell County, WV	96,319	93,224
	54043	Lincoln County, WV	21,720	20,599
	54079	Putnam County, WV	55,486	56,682
	54099	Wayne County, WV	42,481	39,944
26620		Huntsville, AL Metro area	417,593	462,693
	01083	Limestone County, AL	82,782	96,174
	01089	Madison County, AL	334,811	366,519
26660		Huntsville, TX Micro area	82,446	87,220
	48455	Trinity County, TX	14,585	14,740
	48471	Walker County, TX	67,861	72,480
26700		Huron, SD Micro area	17,398	18,883
	46005	Beadle County, SD	17,398	18,883
26740		Hutchinson, KS Micro area	64,511	62,342
	20155	Reno County, KS	64,511	62,342
26780		Hutchinson, MN Micro area	36,651	35,873
	27085	McLeod County, MN	36,651	35,873
26820		Idaho Falls, ID Metro area	133,265	148,904
	16019	Bonneville County, ID	104,234	116,854
	16023	Butte County, ID	2,891	2,611

Core based statistical area	State/County FIPS code	Title and Geographic Components	2010 Census Population	2018 Estimated Population
	16051	Jefferson County, ID	26,140	29,439
26860		Indiana, PA Micro area	88,880	84,501
	42063	Indiana County, PA	88,880	84,501
26900		Indianapolis-Carmel-Anderson, IN Metro area	1,887,877	2,048,703
	18011	Boone County, IN	56,640	66,999
	18013	Brown County, IN	15,242	15,234
	18057	Hamilton County, IN	274,569	330,086
	18059	Hancock County, IN	70,002	76,351
	18063	Hendricks County, IN	145,448	167,009
	18081	Johnson County, IN	139,654	156,225
	18095	Madison County, IN	131,636	129,641
	18097	Marion County, IN	903,393	954,670
	18109	Morgan County, IN	68,894	70,116
	18133	Putnam County, IN	37,963	37,779
	18145	Shelby County, IN	44,436	44,593
26940		Indianola, MS Micro area	29,450	25,735
	28133	Sunflower County, MS	29,450	25,735
26960		Ionia, MI Micro area	63,905	64,210
	26067	Ionia County, MI	63,905	64,210
26980		Iowa City, IA Metro area	152,586	173,401
	19103	Johnson County, IA	130,882	151,260
	19183	Washington County, IA	21,704	22,141
27020		Iron Mountain, MI-WI Micro area	30,591	29,704
	26043	Dickinson County, MI	26,168	25,383
	55037	Florence County, WI	4,423	4,321
27060		Ithaca, NY Metro area	101,564	102,793
	36109	Tompkins County, NY	101,564	102,793
27100		Jackson, MI Metro area	160,248	158,823
	26075	Jackson County, MI	160,248	158,823
27140		Jackson, MS Metro area	567,122	580,166
	28029	Copiah County, MS	29,449	28,543
	28049	Hinds County, MS	245,285	237,085
	28089	Madison County, MS	95,203	105,630
	28121	Rankin County, MS	141,617	153,902
	28127	Simpson County, MS	27,503	26,758
	28163	Yazoo County, MS	28,065	28,248
27160		Jackson, OH Micro area	33,225	32,384
	39079	Jackson County, OH	33,225	32,384
27180		Jackson, TN Metro area	130,011	129,209
	47023	Chester County, TN	17,131	17,276
	47033	Crockett County, TN	14,586	14,328
	47113	Madison County, TN	98,294	97,605
27220		Jackson, WY-ID Micro area	31,464	34,721
	16081	Teton County, ID	10,170	11,640
	56039	Teton County, WY	21,294	23,081
27260		Jacksonville, FL Metro area	1,345,596	1,534,701
	12003	Baker County, FL	27,115	28,355
	12019	Clay County, FL	190,865	216,072
	12031	Duval County, FL	864,263	950,181
	12089	Nassau County, FL	73,314	85,832
	12109	St. Johns County, FL	190,039	254,261
27300		Jacksonville, IL Micro area	40,902	38,902
	17137	Morgan County, IL	35,547	33,976
	17171	Scott County, IL	5,355	4,926
27340		Jacksonville, NC Metro area	177,772	197,683
	37133	Onslow County, NC	177,772	197,683
27380		Jacksonville, TX Micro area	50,845	52,592
	48073	Cherokee County, TX	50,845	52,592
27420		Jamestown, ND Micro area	21,100	20,917
	38093	Stutsman County, ND	21,100	20,917
27460		Jamestown-Dunkirk-Fredonia, NY Micro area	134,905	127,939
	36013	Chautauqua County, NY	134,905	127,939
27500		Janesville-Beloit, WI Metro area	160,331	163,129
	55105	Rock County, WI	160,331	163,129
27540		Jasper, IN Micro area	54,734	54,975
	18037	Dubois County, IN	41,889	42,565
	18125	Pike County, IN	12,845	12,410
27600		Jefferson, GA Micro area	60,485	70,422
	13157	Jackson County, GA	60,485	70,422
27620		Jefferson City, MO Metro area	149,807	151,520
	29027	Callaway County, MO	44,332	44,889
	29051	Cole County, MO	75,990	76,796
	29135	Moniteau County, MO	15,607	16,121
	29151	Osage County, MO	13,878	13,714
27660		Jennings, LA Micro Area	31,594	31,582
	22053	Jefferson Davis Parish, LA	31,594	31,582
27700		Jesup, GA Micro area	30,099	29,808
	13305	Wayne County, GA	30,099	29,808
27740		Johnson City, TN Metro area	198,716	202,719
	47019	Carter County, TN	57,424	56,351
	47171	Unicoi County, TN	18,313	17,761
	47179	Washington County, TN	122,979	128,607
27780		Johnstown, PA Metro area	143,679	131,730
	42021	Cambria County, PA	143,679	131,730
27860		Jonesboro, AR Metro area	121,026	132,532
	05031	Craighead County, AR	96,443	108,558

Core based statistical area	State/County FIPS code	Title and Geographic Components	2010 Census Population	2018 Estimated Population
	05111	Poinsett County, AR	24,583	23,974
27900		Joplin, MO Metro area	175,518	178,902
	29097	Jasper County, MO	117,404	120,636
	29145	Newton County, MO	58,114	58,266
27920		Junction City, KS Micro area	34,362	32,594
	20061	Geary County, KS	34,362	32,594
27940		Juneau, AK Micro area	31,275	32,113
	02110	Juneau City and Borough, AK	31,275	32,113
27980		Kahului-Wailuku-Lahaina, HI Metro area	154,924	167,295
	15005	Kalawao County, HI	90	88
	15009	Maui County, HI	154,834	167,207
28020		Kalamazoo-Portage, MI Metro area	326,589	340,318
	26077	Kalamazoo County, MI	250,331	264,870
	26159	Van Buren County, MI	76,258	75,448
28060		Kalispell, MT Micro area	90,928	102,106
	30029	Flathead County, MT	90,928	102,106
28100		Kankakee, IL Metro area	113,449	110,024
	17091	Kankakee County, IL	113,449	110,024
28140		Kansas City, MO-KS Metro area	2,009,342	2,143,651
	20091	Johnson County, KS	544,179	597,555
	20103	Leavenworth County, KS	76,227	81,352
	20107	Linn County, KS	9,656	9,750
	20121	Miami County, KS	32,787	33,680
	20209	Wyandotte County, KS	157,505	165,324
	29013	Bates County, MO	17,049	16,320
	29025	Caldwell County, MO	9,424	9,108
	29037	Cass County, MO	99,478	104,954
	29047	Clay County, MO	221,939	246,365
	29049	Clinton County, MO	20,743	20,470
	29095	Jackson County, MO	674,158	700,307
	29107	Lafayette County, MO	33,381	32,598
	29165	Platte County, MO	89,322	102,985
	29177	Ray County, MO	23,494	22,883
28180		Kapaa, HI Micro area	67,091	72,133
	15007	Kauai County, HI	67,091	72,133
28260		Kearney, NE Micro area	52,591	56,159
	31019	Buffalo County, NE	46,102	49,615
	31099	Kearney County, NE	6,489	6,544
28300		Keene, NH Micro area	77,117	76,493
	33005	Cheshire County, NH	77,117	76,493
28340		Kendallville, IN Micro area	47,536	47,532
	18113	Noble County, IN	47,536	47,532
28380		Kennett, MO Micro area	31,953	29,423
	29069	Dunklin County, MO	31,953	29,423
28420		Kennewick-Richland, WA Metro area	253,340	296,224
	53005	Benton County, WA	175,177	201,877
	53021	Franklin County, WA	78,163	94,347
28500		Kerrville, TX Micro area	49,625	52,405
	48265	Kerr County, TX	49,625	52,405
28540		Ketchikan, AK Micro area	13,477	13,918
	02130	Ketchikan Gateway Borough, AK	13,477	13,918
28580		Key West, FL Micro area	73,090	75,027
	12087	Monroe County, FL	73,090	75,027
28620		Kill Devil Hills, NC Micro area	38,327	40,632
	37055	Dare County, NC	33,920	36,501
	37177	Tyrrell County, NC	4,407	4,131
28660		Killeen-Temple, TX Metro area	405,300	451,679
	48027	Bell County, TX	310,235	355,642
	48099	Coryell County, TX	75,388	74,808
	48281	Lampasas County, TX	19,677	21,229
28700		Kingsport-Bristol-Bristol, TN-VA Metro area	309,544	306,616
	47073	Hawkins County, TN	56,833	56,530
	47163	Sullivan County, TN	156,823	157,668
	51169	Scott County, VA	23,177	21,534
	51191	Washington County, VA	54,876	54,402
	51520	Bristol city, VA	17,835	16,482
28740		Kingston, NY Metro area	182,493	178,599
	36111	Ulster County, NY	182,493	178,599
28780		Kingsville, TX Micro area	32,477	31,571
	48261	Kenedy County, TX	416	442
	48273	Kleberg County, TX	32,061	31,129
28820		Kinston, NC Micro area	59,495	55,976
	37107	Lenoir County, NC	59,495	55,976
28860		Kirksville, MO Micro area	30,038	29,938
	29001	Adair County, MO	25,607	25,339
	29197	Schuyler County, MO	4,431	4,599
28900		Klamath Falls, OR Micro area	66,380	67,653
	41035	Klamath County, OR	66,380	67,653
28940		Knoxville, TN Metro area	837,571	883,309
	47001	Anderson County, TN	75,129	76,482
	47009	Blount County, TN	123,010	131,349
	47013	Campbell County, TN	40,716	39,583
	47057	Grainger County, TN	22,657	23,145
	47093	Knox County, TN	432,226	465,289
	47105	Loudon County, TN	48,556	53,054
	47129	Morgan County, TN	21,987	21,579
	47145	Roane County, TN	54,181	53,140
	47173	Union County, TN	19,109	19,688

Core based statistical area	State/County FIPS code	Title and Geographic Components	2010 Census Population	2018 Estimated Population
29020		Kokomo, IN Metro area	82,752	82,366
	18067	Howard County, IN	82,752	82,366
29060		Laconia, NH Micro area	60,088	61,022
	33001	Belknap County, NH	60,088	61,022
29100		La Crosse-Onalaska, WI-MN Metro area	133,665	136,808
	27055	Houston County, MN	19,027	18,578
	55063	La Crosse County, WI	114,638	118,230
29180		Lafayette, LA Metro area	466,750	489,364
	22001	Acadia Parish, LA	61,773	62,190
	22045	Iberia Parish, LA	73,240	70,941
	22055	Lafayette Parish, LA	221,578	242,782
	22099	St. Martin Parish, LA	52,160	53,621
	22113	Vermilion Parish, LA	57,999	59,830
29200		Lafayette-West Lafayette, IN Metro area	201,789	221,828
	18007	Benton County, IN	8,854	8,653
	18015	Carroll County, IN	20,155	20,127
	18157	Tippecanoe County, IN	172,780	193,048
29260		La Grande, OR Micro area	25,748	26,461
	41061	Union County, OR	25,748	26,461
29300		LaGrange, GA Micro area	67,044	70,034
	13285	Troup County, GA	67,044	70,034
29340		Lake Charles, LA Metro area	199,607	210,080
	22019	Calcasieu Parish, LA	192,768	203,112
	22023	Cameron Parish, LA	6,839	6,968
29380		Lake City, FL Micro area	67,531	70,503
	12023	Columbia County, FL	67,531	70,503
29420		Lake Havasu City-Kingman, AZ Metro area	200,186	209,550
	04015	Mohave County, AZ	200,186	209,550
29460		Lakeland-Winter Haven, FL Metro area	602,095	708,009
	12105	Polk County, FL	602,095	708,009
29500		Lamesa, TX Micro area	13,833	12,619
	48115	Dawson County, TX	13,833	12,619
29540		Lancaster, PA Metro area	519,445	543,557
	42071	Lancaster County, PA	519,445	543,557
29620		Lansing-East Lansing, MI Metro area	464,036	481,893
	26037	Clinton County, MI	75,382	79,332
	26045	Eaton County, MI	107,759	109,826
	26065	Ingham County, MI	280,895	292,735
29660		Laramie, WY Micro area	36,299	38,601
	56001	Albany County, WY	36,299	38,601
29700		Laredo, TX Metro area	250,304	275,910
	48479	Webb County, TX	250,304	275,910
29740		Las Cruces, NM Metro area	209,233	217,522
	35013	Doña Ana County, NM	209,233	217,522
29780		Las Vegas, NM Micro area	29,393	27,591
	35047	San Miguel County, NM	29,393	27,591
29820		Las Vegas-Henderson-Paradise, NV Metro area	1,951,269	2,231,647
	32003	Clark County, NV	1,951,269	2,231,647
29860		Laurel, MS Micro area	84,823	84,889
	28061	Jasper County, MS	17,062	16,428
	28067	Jones County, MS	67,761	68,461
29900		Laurinburg, NC Micro area	36,157	34,810
	37165	Scotland County, NC	36,157	34,810
29940		Lawrence, KS Metro area	110,826	121,436
	20045	Douglas County, KS	110,826	121,436
29980		Lawrenceburg, TN Micro area	41,869	43,734
	47099	Lawrence County, TN	41,869	43,734
30020		Lawton, OK Metro area	130,291	126,198
	40031	Comanche County, OK	124,098	120,422
	40033	Cotton County, OK	6,193	5,776
30060		Lebanon, MO Micro area	35,571	35,713
	29105	Laclede County, MO	35,571	35,713
30140		Lebanon, PA Metro area	133,568	141,314
	42075	Lebanon County, PA	133,568	141,314
30220		Levelland, TX Micro area	22,935	22,980
	48219	Hockley County, TX	22,935	22,980
30260		Lewisburg, PA Micro area	44,947	44,785
	42119	Union County, PA	44,947	44,785
30280		Lewisburg, TN Micro area	30,617	33,683
	47117	Marshall County, TN	30,617	33,683
30300		Lewiston, ID-WA Metro area	60,888	63,018
	16069	Nez Perce County, ID	39,265	40,408
	53003	Asotin County, WA	21,623	22,610
30340		Lewiston-Auburn, ME Metro area	107,702	107,679
	23001	Androscoggin County, ME	107,702	107,679
30380		Lewistown, PA Micro area	46,682	46,222
	42087	Mifflin County, PA	46,682	46,222
30420		Lexington, NE Micro area	26,370	25,705
	31047	Dawson County, NE	24,326	23,709
	31073	Gosper County, NE	2,044	1,996
30460		Lexington-Fayette, KY Metro area	472,099	516,697
	21017	Bourbon County, KY	19,985	20,184
	21049	Clark County, KY	35,613	36,249
	21067	Fayette County, KY	295,803	323,780
	21113	Jessamine County, KY	48,586	53,920
	21209	Scott County, KY	47,173	56,031
	21239	Woodford County, KY	24,939	26,533
30580		Liberal, KS Micro area	22,952	21,780
	20175	Seward County, KS	22,952	21,780
30620		Lima, OH Metro area	106,331	102,663
	39003	Allen County, OH	106,331	102,663
30660		Lincoln, IL Micro area	30,305	28,925
	17107	Logan County, IL	30,305	28,925
30700		Lincoln, NE Metro area	302,157	334,590
	31109	Lancaster County, NE	285,407	317,272
	31159	Seward County, NE	16,750	17,318
30780		Little Rock-North Little Rock-Conway, AR Metro area	699,757	741,104
	05045	Faulkner County, AR	113,237	124,806
	05053	Grant County, AR	17,853	18,188
	05085	Lonoke County, AR	68,356	73,657
	05105	Perry County, AR	10,445	10,352
	05119	Pulaski County, AR	382,748	392,680
	05125	Saline County, AR	107,118	121,421
30820		Lock Haven, PA Micro area	39,238	38,684
	42035	Clinton County, PA	39,238	38,684
30860		Logan, UT-ID Metro area	125,442	140,794
	16041	Franklin County, ID	12,786	13,726
	49005	Cache County, UT	112,656	127,068
30880		Logan, WV Micro area	36,743	32,607
	54045	Logan County, WV	36,743	32,607
30900		Logansport, IN Micro area	38,966	37,955
	18017	Cass County, IN	38,966	37,955
30940		London, KY Micro area	126,369	128,215
	21121	Knox County, KY	31,883	31,304
	21125	Laurel County, KY	58,849	60,669
	21235	Whitley County, KY	35,637	36,242
30980		Longview, TX Metro area	214,369	219,417
	48183	Gregg County, TX	121,730	123,707
	48401	Rusk County, TX	53,330	54,450
	48459	Upshur County, TX	39,309	41,260
31020		Longview, WA Metro area	102,410	108,987
	53015	Cowlitz County, WA	102,410	108,987
31060		Los Alamos, NM Micro area	17,950	19,101
	35028	Los Alamos County, NM	17,950	19,101
31080		Los Angeles-Long Beach-Anaheim, CA Metro area	12,828,837	13,291,486
31080		Anaheim-Santa Ana-Irvine, CA Metro Div 11244	3,010,232	3,185,968
	06059	Orange County, CA	3,010,232	3,185,968
31080		Los Angeles-Long Beach-Glendale, CA Metro Div 31084	9,818,605	10,105,518
	06037	Los Angeles County, CA	9,818,605	10,105,518
31140		Louisville/Jefferson County, KY-IN Metro area	1,235,708	1,297,301
	18019	Clark County, IN	110,232	117,360
	18043	Floyd County, IN	74,578	77,781
	18061	Harrison County, IN	39,364	40,350
	18143	Scott County, IN	24,181	23,878
	18175	Washington County, IN	28,262	27,943
	21029	Bullitt County, KY	74,319	81,069
	21103	Henry County, KY	15,416	16,106
	21111	Jefferson County, KY	741,096	770,517
	21185	Oldham County, KY	60,316	66,470
	21211	Shelby County, KY	42,074	48,518
	21215	Spencer County, KY	17,061	18,794
	21223	Trimble County, KY	8,809	8,515
31180		Lubbock, TX Metro area	290,805	319,068
	48107	Crosby County, TX	6,059	5,779
	48303	Lubbock County, TX	278,831	307,412
	48305	Lynn County, TX	5,915	5,877
31220		Ludington, MI Micro area	28,705	29,100
	26105	Mason County, MI	28,705	29,100
31260		Lufkin, TX Micro area	86,771	87,092
	48005	Angelina County, TX	86,771	87,092
31300		Lumberton, NC Micro area	134,168	131,831
	37155	Robeson County, NC	134,168	131,831
31340		Lynchburg, VA Metro area	252,634	263,353
	51009	Amherst County, VA	32,353	31,666
	51011	Appomattox County, VA	14,973	15,841
	51019	Bedford County, VA	68,676	78,747
	51031	Campbell County, VA	54,842	54,973
	51680	Lynchburg city, VA	75,568	82,126
31380		Macomb, IL Micro area	32,612	29,955
	17109	McDonough County, IL	32,612	29,955
31420		Macon, GA Metro area	232,293	229,737
	13021	Bibb County, GA	155,547	153,095
	13079	Crawford County, GA	12,630	12,318
	13169	Jones County, GA	28,669	28,616
	13207	Monroe County, GA	26,424	27,520
	13289	Twiggs County, GA	9,023	8,188
31460		Madera, CA Metro area	150,865	157,672
	06039	Madera County, CA	150,865	157,672
31500		Madison, IN Micro area	32,428	32,208
	18077	Jefferson County, IN	32,428	32,208

Core based statistical area	State/ County FIPS code	Title and Geographic Components	2010 Census Population	2018 Estimated Population
31540		Madison, WI Metro area	605,435	660,422
	55021	Columbia County, WI	56,833	57,358
	55025	Dane County, WI	488,073	542,364
	55045	Green County, WI	36,842	36,929
	55049	Iowa County, WI	23,687	23,771
31580		Madisonville, KY Micro area	46,920	45,068
	21107	Hopkins County, KY	46,920	45,068
31620		Magnolia, AR Micro area	24,552	23,537
	05027	Columbia County, AR	24,552	23,537
31660		Malone, NY Micro area	51,599	50,293
	36033	Franklin County, NY	51,599	50,293
31680		Malvern, AR Micro area	32,923	33,701
	05059	Hot Spring County, AR	32,923	33,701
31700		Manchester-Nashua, NH Metro area	400,721	415,247
	33011	Hillsborough County, NH	400,721	415,247
31740		Manhattan, KS Metro area	92,719	97,980
	20149	Pottawatomie County, KS	21,604	24,277
	20161	Riley County, KS	71,115	73,703
31820		Manitowoc, WI Micro area	81,442	79,074
	55071	Manitowoc County, WI	81,442	79,074
31860		Mankato-North Mankato, MN Metro area	96,740	101,647
	27013	Blue Earth County, MN	64,013	67,427
	27103	Nicollet County, MN	32,727	34,220
31900		Mansfield, OH Metro area	124,475	121,099
	39139	Richland County, OH	124,475	121,099
31930		Marietta, OH Micro area	61,778	60,155
	39167	Washington County, OH	61,778	60,155
31940		Marinette, WI-MI Micro area	65,778	63,417
	26109	Menominee County, MI	24,029	22,983
	55075	Marinette County, WI	41,749	40,434
31980		Marion, IN Micro area	70,061	65,936
	18053	Grant County, IN	70,061	65,936
32000		Marion, NC Micro area	44,996	45,507
	37111	McDowell County, NC	44,996	45,507
32020		Marion, OH Micro area	66,501	65,256
	39101	Marion County, OH	66,501	65,256
32100		Marquette, MI Micro area	67,077	66,516
	26103	Marquette County, MI	67,077	66,516
32140		Marshall, MN Micro area	25,857	25,629
	27083	Lyon County, MN	25,857	25,629
32180		Marshall, MO Micro area	23,370	22,895
	29195	Saline County, MO	23,370	22,895
32220		Marshall, TX Micro area	65,631	66,726
	48203	Harrison County, TX	65,631	66,726
32260		Marshalltown, IA Micro area	40,648	39,981
	19127	Marshall County, IA	40,648	39,981
32280		Martin, TN Micro area	35,021	33,415
	47183	Weakley County, TN	35,021	33,415
32300		Martinsville, VA Micro area	67,972	63,855
	51089	Henry County, VA	54,151	50,953
	51690	Martinsville city, VA	13,821	12,902
32340		Maryville, MO Micro area	23,370	22,304
	29147	Nodaway County, MO	23,370	22,304
32380		Mason City, IA Micro area	51,749	50,100
	19033	Cerro Gordo County, IA	44,151	42,647
	19195	Worth County, IA	7,598	7,453
32460		Mayfield, KY Micro area	37,121	37,317
	21083	Graves County, KY	37,121	37,317
32500		Maysville, KY Micro area	17,490	17,150
	21161	Mason County, KY	17,490	17,150
32540		McAlester, OK Micro area	45,837	43,877
	40121	Pittsburg County, OK	45,837	43,877
32580		McAllen-Edinburg-Mission, TX Metro area	774,769	865,939
	48215	Hidalgo County, TX	774,769	865,939
32620		McComb, MS Micro area	53,535	51,889
	28005	Amite County, MS	13,131	12,326
	28113	Pike County, MS	40,404	39,563
32660		McMinnville, TN Micro area	39,839	40,878
	47177	Warren County, TN	39,839	40,878
32700		McPherson, KS Micro area	29,180	28,537
	20113	McPherson County, KS	29,180	28,537
32740		Meadville, PA Micro area	88,765	85,063
	42039	Crawford County, PA	88,765	85,063
32780		Medford, OR Metro area	203,206	219,564
	41029	Jackson County, OR	203,206	219,564
32820		Memphis, TN-MS-AR Metro area	1,324,829	1,350,620
	05035	Crittenden County, AR	50,902	48,342
	28009	Benton County, MS	8,729	8,271
	28033	DeSoto County, MS	161,252	182,001
	28093	Marshall County, MS	37,144	35,451
	28137	Tate County, MS	28,886	28,759
	28143	Tunica County, MS	10,778	9,944
	47047	Fayette County, TN	38,413	40,507
	47157	Shelby County, TN	927,644	935,764
	47167	Tipton County, TN	61,081	61,581
32860		Menomonie, WI Micro area	43,857	45,131
	55033	Dunn County, WI	43,857	45,131
32900		Merced, CA Metro area	255,793	274,765

Core based statistical area	State/ County FIPS code	Title and Geographic Components	2010 Census Population	2018 Estimated Population
	06047	Merced County, CA	255,793	274,765
32940		Meridian, MS Micro area	107,449	100,948
	28023	Clarke County, MS	16,732	15,604
	28069	Kemper County, MS	10,456	10,027
	28075	Lauderdale County, MS	80,261	75,317
32980		Merrill, WI Micro area	28,743	27,689
	55069	Lincoln County, WI	28,743	27,689
33020		Mexico, MO Micro area	25,529	25,473
	29007	Audrain County, MO	25,529	25,473
33060		Miami, OK Micro area	31,848	31,175
	40115	Ottawa County, OK	31,848	31,175
33100		Miami-Fort Lauderdale-West Palm Beach, FL Metro area	5,564,635	6,198,782
33100		Fort Lauderdale-Pompano Beach-Deerfield Beach, FL Metro Div 22744	1,748,066	1,951,260
	12011	Broward County, FL	1,748,066	1,951,260
33100		Miami-Miami Beach-Kendall, FL Metro Div 33124	2,496,435	2,761,581
	12086	Miami-Dade County, FL	2,496,435	2,761,581
33100		West Palm Beach-Boca Raton-Delray Beach, FL Metro Div 48424	1,320,134	1,485,941
	12099	Palm Beach County, FL	1,320,134	1,485,941
33140		Michigan City-La Porte, IN Metro area	111,467	110,007
	18091	LaPorte County, IN	111,467	110,007
33180		Middlesborough, KY Micro area	28,691	26,569
	21013	Bell County, KY	28,691	26,569
33220		Midland, MI Metro area	83,629	83,209
	26111	Midland County, MI	83,629	83,209
33260		Midland, TX Metro area	141,671	178,331
	48317	Martin County, TX	4,799	5,753
	48329	Midland County, TX	136,872	172,578
33300		Milledgeville, GA Micro area	55,149	53,171
	13009	Baldwin County, GA	45,720	44,823
	13141	Hancock County, GA	9,429	8,348
33340		Milwaukee-Waukesha-West Allis, WI Metro area	1,555,908	1,576,113
	55079	Milwaukee County, WI	947,735	948,201
	55089	Ozaukee County, WI	86,395	89,147
	55131	Washington County, WI	131,887	135,693
	55133	Waukesha County, WI	389,891	403,072
33420		Mineral Wells, TX Micro area	28,111	28,875
	48363	Palo Pinto County, TX	28,111	28,875
33460		Minneapolis-St. Paul-Bloomington, MN Metro area	3,348,859	3,629,190
	27003	Anoka County, MN	330,844	353,813
	27019	Carver County, MN	91,042	103,551
	27025	Chisago County, MN	53,887	55,922
	27037	Dakota County, MN	398,552	425,423
	27053	Hennepin County, MN	1,152,425	1,259,428
	27059	Isanti County, MN	37,816	39,966
	27079	Le Sueur County, MN	27,703	28,494
	27095	Mille Lacs County, MN	26,097	26,139
	27123	Ramsey County, MN	508,640	550,210
	27139	Scott County, MN	129,928	147,381
	27141	Sherburne County, MN	88,499	96,036
	27143	Sibley County, MN	15,226	15,028
	27163	Washington County, MN	238,136	259,201
	27171	Wright County, MN	124,700	136,349
	55093	Pierce County, WI	41,019	42,555
	55109	St. Croix County, WI	84,345	89,694
33500		Minot, ND Micro area	69,540	75,934
	38049	McHenry County, ND	5,395	5,816
	38075	Renville County, ND	2,470	2,374
	38101	Ward County, ND	61,675	67,744
33540		Missoula, MT Metro area	109,299	118,791
	30063	Missoula County, MT	109,299	118,791
33580		Mitchell, SD Micro area	22,835	23,166
	46035	Davison County, SD	19,504	19,790
	46061	Hanson County, SD	3,331	3,376
33620		Moberly, MO Micro area	25,414	24,763
	29175	Randolph County, MO	25,414	24,763
33660		Mobile, AL Metro area	412,992	413,757
	01097	Mobile County, AL	412,992	413,757
33700		Modesto, CA Metro area	514,453	549,815
	06099	Stanislaus County, CA	514,453	549,815
33740		Monroe, LA Metro area	176,441	176,805
	22073	Ouachita Parish, LA	153,720	154,475
	22111	Union Parish, LA	22,721	22,330
33780		Monroe, MI Metro area	152,021	150,439
	26115	Monroe County, MI	152,021	150,439
33860		Montgomery, AL Metro area	374,536	373,225
	01001	Autauga County, AL	54,571	55,601
	01051	Elmore County, AL	79,303	81,887
	01085	Lowndes County, AL	11,299	9,974
	01101	Montgomery County, AL	229,363	225,763
33940		Montrose, CO Micro area	41,276	42,214
	08085	Montrose County, CO	41,276	42,214
33980		Morehead City, NC Micro area	66,469	69,524

Core based statistical area	State/County FIPS code	Title and Geographic Components	2010 Census Population	2018 Estimated Population
	37031	Carteret County, NC	66,469	69,524
34020		Morgan City, LA Micro area	54,650	49,774
	22101	St. Mary Parish, LA	54,650	49,774
34060		Morgantown, WV Metro area	129,709	140,259
	54061	Monongalia County, WV	96,189	106,420
	54077	Preston County, WV	33,520	33,839
34100		Morristown, TN Metro area	113,951	118,581
	47063	Hamblen County, TN	62,544	64,569
	47089	Jefferson County, TN	51,407	54,012
34140		Moscow, ID Micro area	37,244	40,134
	16057	Latah County, ID	37,244	40,134
34180		Moses Lake, WA Micro area	89,120	97,331
	53025	Grant County, WA	89,120	97,331
34220		Moultrie, GA Micro area	45,498	45,592
	13071	Colquitt County, GA	45,498	45,592
34260		Mountain Home, AR Micro area	41,513	41,619
	05005	Baxter County, AR	41,513	41,619
34300		Mountain Home, ID Micro area	27,038	27,259
	16039	Elmore County, ID	27,038	27,259
34340		Mount Airy, NC Micro area	73,673	71,948
	37171	Surry County, NC	73,673	71,948
34380		Mount Pleasant, MI Micro area	70,311	70,562
	26073	Isabella County, MI	70,311	70,562
34420		Mount Pleasant, TX Micro area	32,334	33,033
	48449	Titus County, TX	32,334	33,033
34460		Mount Sterling, KY Micro area	44,396	47,037
	21011	Bath County, KY	11,591	12,383
	21165	Menifee County, KY	6,306	6,451
	21173	Montgomery County, KY	26,499	28,203
34500		Mount Vernon, IL Micro area	38,827	37,820
	17081	Jefferson County, IL	38,827	37,820
34540		Mount Vernon, OH Micro area	60,921	61,893
	39083	Knox County, OH	60,921	61,893
34580		Mount Vernon-Anacortes, WA Metro area	116,901	128,206
	53057	Skagit County, WA	116,901	128,206
34620		Muncie, IN Metro area	117,671	114,772
	18035	Delaware County, IN	117,671	114,772
34660		Murray, KY Micro area	37,191	39,135
	21035	Calloway County, KY	37,191	39,135
34700		Muscatine, IA Micro area	42,745	42,929
	19139	Muscatine County, IA	42,745	42,929
34740		Muskegon, MI Metro area	172,188	173,588
	26121	Muskegon County, MI	172,188	173,588
34780		Muskogee, OK Micro area	70,990	68,362
	40101	Muskogee County, OK	70,990	68,362
34820		Myrtle Beach-Conway-North Myrtle Beach, NC-SC Metro area	376,722	480,891
	37019	Brunswick County, NC	107,431	136,744
	45051	Horry County, SC	269,291	344,147
34860		Nacogdoches, TX Micro area	64,524	65,711
	48347	Nacogdoches County, TX	64,524	65,711
34900		Napa, CA Metro area	136,484	139,417
	06055	Napa County, CA	136,484	139,417
34940		Naples-Immokalee-Marco Island, FL Metro area	321,520	378,488
	12021	Collier County, FL	321,520	378,488
34980		Nashville-Davidson--Murfreesboro--Franklin, TN Metro area	1,670,890	1,930,961
	47015	Cannon County, TN	13,801	14,462
	47021	Cheatham County, TN	39,105	40,439
	47037	Davidson County, TN	626,681	692,587
	47043	Dickson County, TN	49,666	53,446
	47081	Hickman County, TN	24,690	25,063
	47111	Macon County, TN	22,248	24,265
	47119	Maury County, TN	80,956	94,340
	47147	Robertson County, TN	66,283	71,012
	47149	Rutherford County, TN	262,604	324,890
	47159	Smith County, TN	19,166	19,942
	47165	Sumner County, TN	160,645	187,149
	47169	Trousdale County, TN	7,870	11,012
	47187	Williamson County, TN	183,182	231,729
	47189	Wilson County, TN	113,993	140,625
35020		Natchez, MS-LA Micro area	53,119	50,764
	22029	Concordia Parish, LA	20,822	19,572
	28001	Adams County, MS	32,297	31,192
35060		Natchitoches, LA Micro area	39,566	38,659
	22069	Natchitoches Parish, LA	39,566	38,659
35100		New Bern, NC Metro area	126,802	125,219
	37049	Craven County, NC	103,505	102,912
	37103	Jones County, NC	10,153	9,637
	37137	Pamlico County, NC	13,144	12,670
35140		Newberry, SC Micro area	37,508	38,520
	45071	Newberry County, SC	37,508	38,520
35220		New Castle, IN Micro area	49,462	48,271
	18065	Henry County, IN	49,462	48,271
35260		New Castle, PA Micro area	91,108	86,184
	42073	Lawrence County, PA	91,108	86,184
35300		New Haven-Milford, CT Metro area	862,477	857,620
	09009	New Haven County, CT	862,477	857,620
35380		New Orleans-Metairie, LA Metro area	1,189,866	1,270,399
	22051	Jefferson Parish, LA	432,552	434,051
	22071	Orleans Parish, LA	343,829	391,006
	22075	Plaquemines Parish, LA	23,042	23,410
	22087	St. Bernard Parish, LA	35,897	46,721
	22089	St. Charles Parish, LA	52,780	52,879
	22093	St. James Parish, LA	22,102	21,037
	22095	St. John the Baptist Parish, LA	45,924	43,184
	22103	St. Tammany Parish, LA	233,740	258,111
35420		New Philadelphia-Dover, OH Micro area	92,582	92,176
	39157	Tuscarawas County, OH	92,582	92,176
35440		Newport, OR Micro area	46,034	49,388
	41041	Lincoln County, OR	46,034	49,388
35460		Newport, TN Micro area	35,662	35,774
	47029	Cocke County, TN	35,662	35,774
35500		Newton, IA Micro area	36,842	37,147
	19099	Jasper County, IA	36,842	37,147
35580		New Ulm, MN Micro area	25,893	25,111
	27015	Brown County, MN	25,893	25,111
35620		New York-Newark-Jersey City, NY-NJ-PA Metro area	19,567,410	19,979,477
35620		Dutchess County-Putnam County, NY Metro Div 20524	397,198	392,610
	36027	Dutchess County, NY	297,488	293,718
	36079	Putnam County, NY	99,710	98,892
35620		Nassau County-Suffolk County, NY Metro Div 35004	2,832,882	2,839,436
	36059	Nassau County, NY	1,339,532	1,358,343
	36103	Suffolk County, NY	1,493,350	1,481,093
35620		Newark, NJ-PA Metro Div 35084	2,471,171	2,504,672
	34013	Essex County, NJ	783,969	799,767
	34019	Hunterdon County, NJ	128,349	124,714
	34027	Morris County, NJ	492,276	494,228
	34035	Somerset County, NJ	323,444	331,164
	34037	Sussex County, NJ	149,265	140,799
	34039	Union County, NJ	536,499	558,067
	42103	Pike County, PA	57,369	55,933
35620		New York-Jersey City-White Plains, NY-NJ Metro Div 35614	13,866,159	14,242,759
	34003	Bergen County, NJ	905,116	936,692
	34017	Hudson County, NJ	634,266	676,061
	34023	Middlesex County, NJ	809,858	829,685
	34025	Monmouth County, NJ	630,380	621,354
	34029	Ocean County, NJ	576,567	601,651
	34031	Passaic County, NJ	501,226	503,310
	36005	Bronx County, NY	1,385,108	1,432,132
	36047	Kings County, NY	2,504,700	2,582,830
	36061	New York County, NY	1,585,873	1,628,701
	36071	Orange County, NY	372,813	381,951
	36081	Queens County, NY	2,230,722	2,278,906
	36085	Richmond County, NY	468,730	476,179
	36087	Rockland County, NY	311,687	325,695
	36119	Westchester County, NY	949,113	967,612
35660		Niles-Benton Harbor, MI Metro area	156,813	154,141
	26021	Berrien County, MI	156,813	154,141
35700		Nogales, AZ Micro area	47,420	46,511
	04023	Santa Cruz County, AZ	47,420	46,511
35740		Norfolk, NE Micro area	48,271	48,504
	31119	Madison County, NE	34,876	35,392
	31139	Pierce County, NE	7,266	7,142
	31167	Stanton County, NE	6,129	5,970
35820		North Platte, NE Micro area	37,590	36,426
	31111	Lincoln County, NE	36,288	35,185
	31113	Logan County, NE	763	749
	31117	McPherson County, NE	539	492
35840		North Port-Sarasota-Bradenton, FL Metro area	702,281	821,573
	12081	Manatee County, FL	322,833	394,855
	12115	Sarasota County, FL	379,448	426,718
35860		North Vernon, IN Micro area	28,525	27,611
	18079	Jennings County, IN	28,525	27,611
35900		North Wilkesboro, NC Micro area	69,340	68,557
	37193	Wilkes County, NC	69,340	68,557
35940		Norwalk, OH Micro area	59,626	58,504
	39077	Huron County, OH	59,626	58,504
35980		Norwich-New London, CT Metro area	274,055	266,784
	09011	New London County, CT	274,055	266,784
36020		Oak Harbor, WA Micro area	78,506	84,460
	53029	Island County, WA	78,506	84,460
36100		Ocala, FL Metro area	331,298	359,977
	12083	Marion County, FL	331,298	359,977
36140		Ocean City, NJ Metro area	97,265	92,560
	34009	Cape May County, NJ	97,265	92,560
36220		Odessa, TX Metro area	137,130	162,124
	48135	Ector County, TX	137,130	162,124
36260		Ogden-Clearfield, UT Metro area	597,159	675,067
	49003	Box Elder County, UT	49,975	54,950

Core based statistical area	State/ County FIPS code	Title and Geographic Components	2010 Census Population	2018 Estimated Population
	49011	Davis County, UT	306,479	351,713
	49029	Morgan County, UT	9,469	12,045
	49057	Weber County, UT	231,236	256,359
36300		Ogdensburg-Massena, NY Micro area	111,944	108,047
	36089	St. Lawrence County, NY	111,944	108,047
36340		Oil City, PA Micro area	54,984	51,266
	42121	Venango County, PA	54,984	51,266
36380		Okeechobee, FL Micro area	39,996	41,537
	12093	Okeechobee County, FL	39,996	41,537
36420		Oklahoma City, OK Metro area	1,252,987	1,396,445
	40017	Canadian County, OK	115,541	144,447
	40027	Cleveland County, OK	255,755	281,669
	40051	Grady County, OK	52,431	55,551
	40081	Lincoln County, OK	34,273	34,920
	40083	Logan County, OK	41,848	47,291
	40087	McClain County, OK	34,506	39,985
	40109	Oklahoma County, OK	718,633	792,582
36460		Olean, NY Micro area	80,317	76,840
	36009	Cattaraugus County, NY	80,317	76,840
36500		Olympia-Tumwater, WA Metro area	252,264	286,419
	53067	Thurston County, WA	252,264	286,419
36540		Omaha-Council Bluffs, NE-IA Metro area	865,350	942,198
	19085	Harrison County, IA	14,928	14,134
	19129	Mills County, IA	15,059	15,063
	19155	Pottawattamie County, IA	93,158	93,533
	31025	Cass County, NE	25,241	26,159
	31055	Douglas County, NE	517,110	566,880
	31153	Sarpy County, NE	158,840	184,459
	31155	Saunders County, NE	20,780	21,303
	31177	Washington County, NE	20,234	20,667
36580		Oneonta, NY Micro area	62,259	59,749
	36077	Otsego County, NY	62,259	59,749
36620		Ontario, OR-ID Micro area	53,936	54,276
	16075	Payette County, ID	22,623	23,551
	41045	Malheur County, OR	31,313	30,725
36660		Opelousas, LA Micro area	83,384	82,764
	22097	St. Landry Parish, LA	83,384	82,764
36700		Orangeburg, SC Micro area	92,501	86,934
	45075	Orangeburg County, SC	92,501	86,934
36740		Orlando-Kissimmee-Sanford, FL Metro	2,134,411	2,572,962
	12069	Lake County, FL	297,052	356,495
	12095	Orange County, FL	1,145,956	1,380,645
	12097	Osceola County, FL	268,685	367,990
	12117	Seminole County, FL	422,718	467,832
36780		Oshkosh-Neenah, WI Metro area	166,994	171,020
	55139	Winnebago County, WI	166,994	171,020
36820		Oskaloosa, IA Micro area	22,381	22,000
	19123	Mahaska County, IA	22,381	22,000
36830		Othello, WA Micro area	18,728	19,759
	53001	Adams County, WA	18,728	19,759
36840		Ottawa, KS Micro area	25,992	25,631
	20059	Franklin County, KS	25,992	25,631
36860		Ottawa-Peru, IL Micro area	154,908	148,163
	17011	Bureau County, IL	34,978	32,993
	17099	LaSalle County, IL	113,924	109,430
	17155	Putnam County, IL	6,006	5,740
36900		Ottumwa, IA Micro area	44,378	44,222
	19051	Davis County, IA	8,753	9,017
	19179	Wapello County, IA	35,625	35,205
36940		Owatonna, MN Micro area	36,576	36,803
	27147	Steele County, MN	36,576	36,803
36980		Owensboro, KY Metro area	114,752	119,114
	21059	Daviess County, KY	96,656	101,104
	21091	Hancock County, KY	8,565	8,758
	21149	McLean County, KY	9,531	9,252
37020		Owosso, MI Micro area	70,648	68,192
	26155	Shiawassee County, MI	70,648	68,192
37060		Oxford, MS Micro area	47,351	54,793
	28071	Lafayette County, MS	47,351	54,793
37080		Oxford, NC Micro area	59,916	60,115
	37077	Granville County, NC	59,916	60,115
37100		Oxnard-Thousand Oaks-Ventura, CA Metro area	823,318	850,967
	06111	Ventura County, CA	823,318	850,967
37120		Ozark, AL Micro area	50,251	48,956
	01045	Dale County, AL	50,251	48,956
37140		Paducah, KY-IL Micro area	98,762	96,647
	17127	Massac County, IL	15,429	14,080
	21007	Ballard County, KY	8,249	7,979
	21139	Livingston County, KY	9,519	9,242
	21145	McCracken County, KY	65,565	65,346
37220		Pahrump, NV Micro area	43,946	45,346
	32023	Nye County, NV	43,946	45,346
37260		Palatka, FL Micro area	74,364	74,163
	12107	Putnam County, FL	74,364	74,163
37300		Palestine, TX Micro area	58,458	58,057
	48001	Anderson County, TX	58,458	58,057
37340		Palm Bay-Melbourne-Titusville, FL Metro area	543,376	596,849
	12009	Brevard County, FL	543,376	596,849
37420		Pampa, TX Micro area	22,535	21,895
	48179	Gray County, TX	22,535	21,895
37460		Panama City, FL Metro area	184,715	201,451
	12005	Bay County, FL	168,852	185,287
	12045	Gulf County, FL	15,863	16,164
37500		Paragould, AR Micro area	42,090	45,325
	05055	Greene County, AR	42,090	45,325
37540		Paris, TN Micro area	32,330	32,358
	47079	Henry County, TN	32,330	32,358
37580		Paris, TX Micro area	49,793	49,728
	48277	Lamar County, TX	49,793	49,728
37620		Parkersburg-Vienna, WV Metro area	92,673	90,033
	54105	Wirt County, WV	5,717	5,830
	54107	Wood County, WV	86,956	84,203
37660		Parsons, KS Micro area	21,607	19,964
	20099	Labette County, KS	21,607	19,964
37740		Payson, AZ Micro area	53,597	53,889
	04007	Gila County, AZ	53,597	53,889
37780		Pecos, TX Micro area	13,783	15,695
	48389	Reeves County, TX	13,783	15,695
37800		Pella, IA Micro Area	33,309	33,407
	19125	Marion County, IA	33,309	33,407
37860		Pensacola-Ferry Pass-Brent, FL Metro area	448,991	494,883
	12033	Escambia County, FL	297,619	315,534
	12113	Santa Rosa County, FL	151,372	179,349
37900		Peoria, IL Metro area	379,186	368,373
	17123	Marshall County, IL	12,640	11,534
	17143	Peoria County, IL	186,494	180,621
	17175	Stark County, IL	5,994	5,427
	17179	Tazewell County, IL	135,394	132,328
	17203	Woodford County, IL	38,664	38,463
37940		Peru, IN Micro area	36,903	35,567
	18103	Miami County, IN	36,903	35,567
37980		Philadelphia-Camden-Wilmington, PA-NJ-DE-MD Metro area	5,965,343	6,096,372
37980		Camden, NJ Metro Div 15804	1,250,679	1,243,870
	34005	Burlington County, NJ	448,734	445,384
	34007	Camden County, NJ	513,657	507,078
	34015	Gloucester County, NJ	288,288	291,408
37980		Montgomery County-Bucks County-Chester County, PA Metro Div 33874	1,924,009	1,978,845
	42017	Bucks County, PA	625,249	628,195
	42029	Chester County, PA	498,886	522,046
	42091	Montgomery County, PA	799,874	828,604
37980		Philadelphia, PA Metro Div 37964	2,084,985	2,148,889
	42045	Delaware County, PA	558,979	564,751
	42101	Philadelphia County, PA	1,526,006	1,584,138
37980		Wilmington, DE-MD-NJ Metro Div 48864	705,670	724,768
	10003	New Castle County, Delaware	538,479	559,335
	24015	Cecil County, MD	101,108	102,826
	34033	Salem County, NJ	66,083	62,607
38060		Phoenix-Mesa-Scottsdale, AZ Metro area	4,192,887	4,857,962
	04013	Maricopa County, AZ	3,817,117	4,410,824
	04021	Pinal County, AZ	375,770	447,138
38100		Picayune, MS Micro area	55,834	55,387
	28109	Pearl River County, MS	55,834	55,387
38180		Pierre, SD Micro area	21,361	22,064
	46065	Hughes County, SD	17,022	17,650
	46117	Stanley County, SD	2,966	3,022
	46119	Sully County, SD	1,373	1,392
38220		Pine Bluff, AR Metro area	100,258	89,515
	05025	Cleveland County, AR	8,689	8,018
	05069	Jefferson County, AR	77,435	68,114
	05079	Lincoln County, AR	14,134	13,383
38240		Pinehurst-Southern Pines, NC Micro area	88,247	98,682
	37125	Moore County, NC	88,247	98,682
38260		Pittsburg, KS Micro area	39,134	39,019
	20037	Crawford County, KS	39,134	39,019
38300		Pittsburgh, PA Metro area	2,356,285	2,324,743
	42003	Allegheny County, PA	1,223,348	1,218,452
	42005	Armstrong County, PA	68,941	65,263
	42007	Beaver County, PA	170,539	164,742
	42019	Butler County, PA	183,862	187,888
	42051	Fayette County, PA	136,606	130,441
	42125	Washington County, PA	207,820	207,346
	42129	Westmoreland County, PA	365,169	350,611
38340		Pittsfield, MA Metro area	131,219	126,348
	25003	Berkshire County, MA	131,219	126,348
38380		Plainview, TX Micro area	36,273	33,830
	48189	Hale County, TX	36,273	33,830
38420		Platteville, WI Micro area	51,208	51,554
	55043	Grant County, WI	51,208	51,554
38460		Plattsburgh, NY Micro area	82,128	80,695
	36019	Clinton County, NY	82,128	80,695

Core based statistical area	State/County FIPS code	Title and Geographic Components	2010 Census Population	2018 Estimated Population
38500		Plymouth, IN Micro area	47,051	46,248
	18099	Marshall County, IN	47,051	46,248
38540		Pocatello, ID Metro area	82,839	87,138
	16005	Bannock County, ID	82,839	87,138
38580		Point Pleasant, WV-OH Micro area	58,258	56,697
	39053	Gallia County, OH	30,934	29,979
	54053	Mason County, WV	27,324	26,718
38620		Ponca City, OK Micro area	46,562	44,161
	40071	Kay County, OK	46,562	44,161
38700		Pontiac, IL Micro area	38,950	35,761
	17105	Livingston County, IL	38,950	35,761
38740		Poplar Bluff, MO Micro area	42,794	42,639
	29023	Butler County, MO	42,794	42,639
38780		Portales, NM Micro area	19,846	18,743
	35041	Roosevelt County, NM	19,846	18,743
38820		Port Angeles, WA Micro area	71,404	76,737
	53009	Clallam County, WA	71,404	76,737
38840		Port Clinton, OH Micro area	41,428	40,769
	39123	Ottawa County, OH	41,428	40,769
38860		Portland-South Portland, ME Metro area	514,098	535,420
	23005	Cumberland County, ME	281,674	293,557
	23023	Sagadahoc County, ME	35,293	35,634
	23031	York County, ME	197,131	206,229
38900		Portland-Vancouver-Hillsboro, OR-WA Metro area	2,226,009	2,478,810
	41005	Clackamas County, OR	375,992	416,075
	41009	Columbia County, OR	49,351	52,377
	41051	Multnomah County, OR	735,334	811,880
	41067	Washington County, OR	529,710	597,695
	41071	Yamhill County, OR	99,193	107,002
	53011	Clark County, WA	425,363	481,857
	53059	Skamania County, WA	11,066	11,924
38920		Port Lavaca, TX Micro area	21,381	21,561
	48057	Calhoun County, TX	21,381	21,561
38940		Port St. Lucie, FL Metro area	424,107	482,040
	12085	Martin County, FL	146,318	160,912
	12111	St. Lucie County, FL	277,789	321,128
39020		Portsmouth, OH Micro area	79,499	75,502
	39145	Scioto County, OH	79,499	75,502
39060		Pottsville, PA Micro area	148,289	142,067
	42107	Schuylkill County, PA	148,289	142,067
39140		Prescott, AZ Metro area	211,033	231,993
	04025	Yavapai County, AZ	211,033	231,993
39220		Price, UT Micro area	21,403	20,269
	49007	Carbon County, UT	21,403	20,269
39260		Prineville, OR Micro area	20,978	23,867
	41013	Crook County, OR	20,978	23,867
39300		Providence-Warwick, RI-MA Metro area	1,600,852	1,621,337
	25005	Bristol County, MA	548,285	564,022
	44001	Bristol County, RI	49,875	48,649
	44003	Kent County, RI	166,158	163,861
	44005	Newport County, RI	82,888	82,542
	44007	Providence County, RI	626,667	636,084
	44009	Washington County, RI	126,979	126,179
39340		Provo-Orem, UT Metro area	526,810	633,768
	49023	Juab County, UT	10,246	11,555
	49049	Utah County, UT	516,564	622,213
39380		Pueblo, CO Metro area	159,063	167,529
	08101	Pueblo County, CO	159,063	167,529
39420		Pullman, WA Micro area	44,776	49,791
	53075	Whitman County, WA	44,776	49,791
39460		Punta Gorda, FL Metro area	159,978	184,998
	12015	Charlotte County, FL	159,978	184,998
39500		Quincy, IL-MO Micro area	77,314	75,546
	17001	Adams County, IL	67,103	65,691
	29111	Lewis County, MO	10,211	9,855
39540		Racine, WI Metro area	195,408	196,584
	55101	Racine County, WI	195,408	196,584
39580		Raleigh, NC Metro area	1,130,490	1,362,540
	37069	Franklin County, NC	60,619	67,560
	37101	Johnston County, NC	168,878	202,675
	37183	Wake County, NC	900,993	1,092,305
39660		Rapid City, SD Metro area	134,598	148,749
	46033	Custer County, SD	8,216	8,726
	46093	Meade County, SD	25,434	28,294
	46103	Pennington County, SD	100,948	111,729
39700		Raymondville, TX Micro area	22,134	21,515
	48489	Willacy County, TX	22,134	21,515
39740		Reading, PA Metro area	411,442	420,152
	42011	Berks County, PA	411,442	420,152
39780		Red Bluff, CA Micro area	63,463	63,916
	06103	Tehama County, CA	63,463	63,916
39820		Redding, CA Metro area	177,223	180,040
	06089	Shasta County, CA	177,223	180,040
39860		Red Wing, MN Micro area	46,183	46,403
	27049	Goodhue County, MN	46,183	46,403
39900		Reno, NV Metro area	425,417	469,764
	32029	Storey County, NV	4,010	4,029
	32031	Washoe County, NV	421,407	465,735
39940		Rexburg, ID Micro area	50,778	52,472
	16043	Fremont County, ID	13,242	13,168
	16065	Madison County, ID	37,536	39,304
39980		Richmond, IN Micro area	68,917	65,936
	18177	Wayne County, IN	68,917	65,936
40060		Richmond, VA Metro area	1,208,101	1,306,172
	51007	Amelia County, VA	12,690	13,013
	51033	Caroline County, VA	28,545	30,772
	51036	Charles City County, VA	7,256	6,941
	51041	Chesterfield County, VA	316,236	348,556
	51053	Dinwiddie County, VA	28,001	28,529
	51075	Goochland County, VA	21,717	23,244
	51085	Hanover County, VA	99,863	107,239
	51087	Henrico County, VA	306,935	329,261
	51101	King William County, VA	15,935	16,939
	51127	New Kent County, VA	18,429	22,391
	51145	Powhatan County, VA	28,046	29,189
	51149	Prince George County, VA	35,725	38,082
	51183	Sussex County, VA	12,087	11,237
	51570	Colonial Heights city, VA	17,411	17,833
	51670	Hopewell city, VA	22,591	22,596
	51730	Petersburg city, VA	32,420	31,567
	51760	Richmond city, VA	204,214	228,783
40080		Richmond-Berea, KY Micro area	99,972	109,118
	21151	Madison County, KY	82,916	92,368
	21203	Rockcastle County, KY	17,056	16,750
40100		Rio Grande City, TX Micro area	60,968	64,525
	48427	Starr County, TX	60,968	64,525
40140		Riverside-San Bernardino-Ontario, CA	4,224,851	4,622,361
	06065	Riverside County, CA	2,189,641	2,450,758
	06071	San Bernardino County, CA	2,035,210	2,171,603
40180		Riverton, WY Micro area	40,123	39,531
	56013	Fremont County, WY	40,123	39,531
40220		Roanoke, VA Metro area	308,707	314,172
	51023	Botetourt County, VA	33,148	33,277
	51045	Craig County, VA	5,190	5,064
	51067	Franklin County, VA	56,159	56,195
	51161	Roanoke County, VA	92,376	94,073
	51770	Roanoke city, VA	97,032	99,920
	51775	Salem city, VA	24,802	25,643
40260		Roanoke Rapids, NC Micro area	76,790	70,250
	37083	Halifax County, NC	54,691	50,574
	37131	Northampton County, NC	22,099	19,676
40300		Rochelle, IL Micro area	53,497	50,923
	17141	Ogle County, IL	53,497	50,923
40340		Rochester, MN Metro area	206,877	219,802
	27039	Dodge County, MN	20,087	20,822
	27045	Fillmore County, MN	20,866	21,058
	27109	Olmsted County, MN	144,248	156,277
	27157	Wabasha County, MN	21,676	21,645
40380		Rochester, NY Metro area	1,079,671	1,071,082
	36051	Livingston County, NY	65,393	63,227
	36055	Monroe County, NY	744,344	742,474
	36069	Ontario County, NY	107,931	109,864
	36073	Orleans County, NY	42,883	40,612
	36117	Wayne County, NY	93,772	90,064
	36123	Yates County, NY	25,348	24,841
40420		Rockford, IL Metro area	349,431	337,658
	17007	Boone County, IL	54,165	53,577
	17201	Winnebago County, IL	295,266	284,081
40460		Rockingham, NC Micro area	46,639	44,887
	37153	Richmond County, NC	46,639	44,887
40540		Rock Springs, WY Micro area	43,806	43,051
	56037	Sweetwater County, WY	43,806	43,051
40580		Rocky Mount, NC Metro area	152,392	146,021
	37065	Edgecombe County, NC	56,552	52,005
	37127	Nash County, NC	95,840	94,016
40620		Rolla, MO Micro area	45,156	44,732
	29161	Phelps County, MO	45,156	44,732
40660		Rome, GA Metro area	96,317	97,927
	13115	Floyd County, GA	96,317	97,927
40700		Roseburg, OR Micro area	107,667	110,283
	41019	Douglas County, OR	107,667	110,283
40740		Roswell, NM Micro area	65,645	64,689
	35005	Chaves County, NM	65,645	64,689
40760		Ruidoso, NM Micro Area	20,497	19,556
	35027	Lincoln County, NM	20,497	19,556
40780		Russellville, AR Micro area	83,939	85,535
	05115	Pope County, AR	61,754	64,000
	05149	Yell County, AR	22,185	21,535
40820		Ruston, LA Micro area	46,735	47,196
	22061	Lincoln Parish, LA	46,735	47,196
40860		Rutland, VT Micro area	61,642	58,672
	50021	Rutland County, VT	61,642	58,672
40900		Sacramento--Roseville--Arden-Arcade, CA Metro area	2,149,127	2,345,210
	06017	El Dorado County, CA	181,058	190,678

Core based statistical area	State/County FIPS code	Title and Geographic Components	2010 Census Population	2018 Estimated Population
	06061	Placer County, CA	348,432	393,149
	06067	Sacramento County, CA	1,418,788	1,540,975
	06113	Yolo County, CA	200,849	220,408
40940		Safford, AZ Micro area	37,220	38,072
	04009	Graham County, AZ	37,220	38,072
40980		Saginaw, MI Metro area	200,169	190,800
	26145	Saginaw County, MI	200,169	190,800
41060		St. Cloud, MN Metro area	189,093	199,801
	27009	Benton County, MN	38,451	40,545
	27145	Stearns County, MN	150,642	159,256
41100		St. George, UT Metro area	138,115	171,700
	49053	Washington County, UT	138,115	171,700
41140		St. Joseph, MO-KS Metro area	127,329	126,490
	20043	Doniphan County, KS	7,945	7,682
	29003	Andrew County, MO	17,291	17,607
	29021	Buchanan County, MO	89,201	88,571
	29063	DeKalb County, MO	12,892	12,630
41180		St. Louis, MO-IL Metro area	2,787,701	2,805,465
	17005	Bond County, IL	17,768	16,630
	17013	Calhoun County, IL	5,089	4,802
	17027	Clinton County, IL	37,762	37,639
	17083	Jersey County, IL	22,985	21,847
	17117	Macoupin County, IL	47,765	45,313
	17119	Madison County, IL	269,282	264,461
	17133	Monroe County, IL	32,957	34,335
	17163	St. Clair County, IL	270,056	261,059
	29071	Franklin County, MO	101,492	103,670
	29099	Jefferson County, MO	218,733	224,347
	29113	Lincoln County, MO	52,566	57,686
	29183	St. Charles County, MO	360,485	399,182
	29189	St. Louis County, MO	998,954	996,945
	29219	Warren County, MO	32,513	34,711
	29510	St. Louis city, MO	319,294	302,838
41220		St. Marys, GA Micro area	50,513	53,677
	13039	Camden County, GA	50,513	53,677
41260		St. Marys, PA Micro Area	31,946	30,169
	42047	Elk County, PA	31,946	30,169
41400		Salem, OH Micro area	107,841	102,665
	39029	Columbiana County, OH	107,841	102,665
41420		Salem, OR Metro area	390,738	432,102
	41047	Marion County, OR	315,335	346,868
	41053	Polk County, OR	75,403	85,234
41460		Salina, KS Micro area	61,697	60,203
	20143	Ottawa County, KS	6,091	5,802
	20169	Saline County, KS	55,606	54,401
41500		Salinas, CA Metro area	415,057	435,594
	06053	Monterey County, CA	415,057	435,594
41540		Salisbury, MD-DE Metro area	373,802	409,979
	10005	Sussex County, DE	197,145	229,286
	24039	Somerset County, MD	26,470	25,675
	24045	Wicomico County, MD	98,733	103,195
	24047	Worcester County, MD	51,454	51,823
41620		Salt Lake City, UT Metro area	1,087,873	1,222,540
	49035	Salt Lake County, UT	1,029,655	1,152,633
	49045	Tooele County, UT	58,218	69,907
41660		San Angelo, TX Metro area	111,823	119,711
	48235	Irion County, TX	1,599	1,522
	48451	Tom Green County, TX	110,224	118,189
41700		San Antonio-New Braunfels, TX Metro	2,142,508	2,518,036
	48013	Atascosa County, TX	44,911	50,310
	48019	Bandera County, TX	20,485	22,824
	48029	Bexar County, TX	1,714,773	1,986,049
	48091	Comal County, TX	108,472	148,373
	48187	Guadalupe County, TX	131,533	163,694
	48259	Kendall County, TX	33,410	45,641
	48325	Medina County, TX	46,006	50,921
	48493	Wilson County, TX	42,918	50,224
41740		San Diego-Carlsbad, CA Metro area	3,095,313	3,343,364
	06073	San Diego County, CA	3,095,313	3,343,364
41760		Sandpoint, ID Micro area	40,877	44,727
	16017	Bonner County, ID	40,877	44,727
41780		Sandusky, OH Micro area	77,079	74,615
	39043	Erie County, OH	77,079	74,615
41820		Sanford, NC Micro area	57,866	61,452
	37105	Lee County, NC	57,866	61,452
41860		San Francisco-Oakland-Hayward, CA Metro area	4,335,391	4,729,484
41860		Oakland-Hayward-Berkeley, CA Metro Div 36084	2,559,296	2,816,968
	06001	Alameda County, CA	1,510,271	1,666,753
	06013	Contra Costa County, CA	1,049,025	1,150,215
41860		San Francisco-Redwood City-South San Francisco, CA Metro Div 41884	1,523,686	1,652,850
	06075	San Francisco County, CA	805,235	883,305
	06081	San Mateo County, CA	718,451	769,545
41860		San Rafael, CA Metropolitan Div 42034	252,409	259,666
	06041	Marin County, CA	252,409	259,666
41940		San Jose-Sunnyvale-Santa Clara, CA Metro area	1,836,911	1,999,107
	06069	San Benito County, CA	55,269	61,537
	06085	Santa Clara County, CA	1,781,642	1,937,570
42020		San Luis Obispo-Paso Robles-Arroyo Grande, CA Metro area	269,637	284,010
	06079	San Luis Obispo County, CA	269,637	284,010
42100		Santa Cruz-Watsonville, CA Metro area	262,382	274,255
	06087	Santa Cruz County, CA	262,382	274,255
42140		Santa Fe, NM Metro area	144,170	150,056
	35049	Santa Fe County, NM	144,170	150,056
42200		Santa Maria-Santa Barbara, CA Metro	423,895	446,527
	06083	Santa Barbara County, CA	423,895	446,527
42220		Santa Rosa, CA Metro area	483,878	499,942
	06097	Sonoma County, CA	483,878	499,942
42300		Sault Ste. Marie, MI Micro area	38,520	37,517
	26033	Chippewa County, MI	38,520	37,517
42340		Savannah, GA Metro area	347,611	389,494
	13029	Bryan County, GA	30,233	38,109
	13051	Chatham County, GA	265,128	289,195
	13103	Effingham County, GA	52,250	62,190
42380		Sayre, PA Micro area	62,622	60,833
	42015	Bradford County, PA	62,622	60,833
42420		Scottsbluff, NE Micro area	38,971	37,906
	31007	Banner County, NE	690	730
	31157	Scotts Bluff County, NE	36,970	35,989
	31165	Sioux County, NE	1,311	1,187
42460		Scottsboro, AL Micro area	53,227	51,736
	01071	Jackson County, AL	53,227	51,736
42540		Scranton--Wilkes-Barre--Hazleton, PA Metro area	563,631	555,485
	42069	Lackawanna County, PA	214,437	210,793
	42079	Luzerne County, PA	320,918	317,646
	42131	Wyoming County, PA	28,276	27,046
42620		Searcy, AR Micro area	77,076	78,727
	05145	White County, AR	77,076	78,727
42660		Seattle-Tacoma-Bellevue, WA Metro area	3,439,809	3,939,363
42660		Seattle-Bellevue-Everett, WA Metro Div 42644	2,644,584	3,048,064
	53033	King County, WA	1,931,249	2,233,163
	53061	Snohomish County, WA	713,335	814,901
42660		Tacoma-Lakewood, WA Metro Div 45104	795,225	891,299
	53053	Pierce County, WA	795,225	891,299
42680		Sebastian-Vero Beach, FL Metro area	138,028	157,413
	12061	Indian River County, FL	138,028	157,413
42700		Sebring, FL Metro area	98,786	105,424
	12055	Highlands County, FL	98,786	105,424
42740		Sedalia, MO Micro area	42,201	42,542
	29159	Pettis County, MO	42,201	42,542
42780		Selinsgrove, PA Micro area	39,702	40,540
	42109	Snyder County, PA	39,702	40,540
42820		Selma, AL Micro area	43,820	38,310
	01047	Dallas County, AL	43,820	38,310
42860		Seneca, SC Micro area	74,273	78,374
	45073	Oconee County, SC	74,273	78,374
42900		Seneca Falls, NY Micro area	35,251	34,300
	36099	Seneca County, NY	35,251	34,300
42940		Sevierville, TN Micro area	89,889	97,892
	47155	Sevier County, TN	89,889	97,892
42980		Seymour, IN Micro area	42,376	44,111
	18071	Jackson County, IN	42,376	44,111
43020		Shawano, WI Micro area	46,181	45,454
	55078	Menominee County, WI	4,232	4,658
	55115	Shawano County, WI	41,949	40,796
43060		Shawnee, OK Micro area	69,442	72,679
	40125	Pottawatomie County, OK	69,442	72,679
43100		Sheboygan, WI Metro area	115,507	115,456
	55117	Sheboygan County, WI	115,507	115,456
43140		Shelby, NC Micro area	98,078	97,645
	37045	Cleveland County, NC	98,078	97,645
43180		Shelbyville, TN Micro area	45,058	49,038
	47003	Bedford County, TN	45,058	49,038
43220		Shelton, WA Micro area	60,699	65,507
	53045	Mason County, WA	60,699	65,507
43260		Sheridan, WY Micro area	29,116	30,233
	56033	Sheridan County, WY	29,116	30,233
43300		Sherman-Denison, TX Metro area	120,877	133,991
	48181	Grayson County, TX	120,877	133,991
43320		Show Low, AZ Micro area	107,449	110,445
	04017	Navajo County, AZ	107,449	110,445
43340		Shreveport-Bossier City, LA Metro area	439,811	436,341
	22015	Bossier Parish, LA	116,979	127,185
	22017	Caddo Parish, LA	254,969	242,922
	22031	De Soto Parish, LA	26,656	27,436
	22119	Webster Parish, LA	41,207	38,798
43380		Sidney, OH Micro area	49,423	48,627
	39149	Shelby County, OH	49,423	48,627
43420		Sierra Vista-Douglas, AZ Metro area	131,346	126,770

Core based statistical area	State/County FIPS code	Title and Geographic Components	2010 Census Population	2018 Estimated Population
	04003	Cochise County, AZ	131,346	126,770
43460		Sikeston, MO Micro area	39,191	38,458
	29201	Scott County, MO	39,191	38,458
43500		Silver City, NM Micro area	29,514	27,346
	35017	Grant County, NM	29,514	27,346
43580		Sioux City, IA-NE-SD Metro area	168,563	169,045
	19149	Plymouth County, IA	24,986	25,095
	19193	Woodbury County, IA	102,172	102,539
	31043	Dakota County, NE	21,006	20,083
	31051	Dixon County, NE	6,000	5,709
	46127	Union County, SD	14,399	15,619
43620		Sioux Falls, SD Metro area	228,261	265,653
	46083	Lincoln County, SD	44,828	58,807
	46087	McCook County, SD	5,618	5,546
	46099	Minnehaha County, SD	169,468	192,876
	46125	Turner County, SD	8,347	8,424
43660		Snyder, TX Micro area	16,921	16,866
	48415	Scurry County, TX	16,921	16,866
43700		Somerset, KY Micro area	63,063	64,623
	21199	Pulaski County, KY	63,063	64,623
43740		Somerset, PA Micro area	77,742	73,952
	42111	Somerset County, PA	77,742	73,952
43760		Sonora, CA Micro area	55,365	54,539
	06109	Tuolumne County, CA	55,365	54,539
43780		South Bend-Mishawaka, IN-MI Metro area	319,224	322,424
	18141	St. Joseph County, IN	266,931	270,771
	26027	Cass County, MI	52,293	51,653
43900		Spartanburg, SC Metro area	313,268	341,298
	45083	Spartanburg County, SC	284,307	313,888
	45087	Union County, SC	28,961	27,410
43940		Spearfish, SD Micro area	24,097	25,741
	46081	Lawrence County, SD	24,097	25,741
43980		Spencer, IA Micro area	16,667	16,134
	19041	Clay County, IA	16,667	16,134
44020		Spirit Lake, IA Micro area	16,667	17,153
	19059	Dickinson County, IA	16,667	17,153
44060		Spokane-Spokane Valley, WA Metro area	527,753	573,493
	53051	Pend Oreille County, WA	13,001	13,602
	53063	Spokane County, WA	471,221	514,631
	53065	Stevens County, WA	43,531	45,260
44100		Springfield, IL Metro area	210,170	207,636
	17129	Menard County, IL	12,705	12,288
	17167	Sangamon County, IL	197,465	195,348
44140		Springfield, MA Metro area	621,570	631,761
	25013	Hampden County, MA	463,490	470,406
	25015	Hampshire County, MA	158,080	161,355
44180		Springfield, MO Metro area	436,712	466,978
	29043	Christian County, MO	77,422	86,983
	29059	Dallas County, MO	16,777	16,762
	29077	Greene County, MO	275,174	291,923
	29167	Polk County, MO	31,137	32,201
	29225	Webster County, MO	36,202	39,109
44220		Springfield, OH Metro area	138,333	134,585
	39023	Clark County, OH	138,333	134,585
44260		Starkville, MS Micro area	47,671	49,599
	28105	Oktibbeha County, MS	47,671	49,599
44300		State College, PA Metro area	153,990	162,805
	42027	Centre County, PA	153,990	162,805
44340		Statesboro, GA Micro area	70,217	77,296
	13031	Bulloch County, GA	70,217	77,296
44420		Staunton-Waynesboro, VA Metro area	118,502	123,007
	51015	Augusta County, VA	73,750	75,457
	51790	Staunton city, VA	23,746	24,922
	51820	Waynesboro city, VA	21,006	22,628
44460		Steamboat Springs, CO Micro area	23,509	25,733
	08107	Routt County, CO	23,509	25,733
44500		Stephenville, TX Micro area	37,890	42,446
	48143	Erath County, TX	37,890	42,446
44540		Sterling, CO Micro area	22,709	21,528
	08075	Logan County, CO	22,709	21,528
44580		Sterling, IL Micro area	58,498	55,626
	17195	Whiteside County, IL	58,498	55,626
44620		Stevens Point, WI Micro area	70,019	70,942
	55097	Portage County, WI	70,019	70,942
44660		Stillwater, OK Micro area	77,350	82,040
	40119	Payne County, OK	77,350	82,040
44700		Stockton-Lodi, CA Metro area	685,306	752,660
	06077	San Joaquin County, CA	685,306	752,660
44740		Storm Lake, IA Micro area	20,260	19,874
	19021	Buena Vista County, IA	20,260	19,874
44780		Sturgis, MI Micro area	61,295	61,043
	26149	St. Joseph County, MI	61,295	61,043
44860		Sulphur Springs, TX Micro area	35,161	36,810
	48223	Hopkins County, TX	35,161	36,810
44900		Summerville, GA Micro area	26,015	24,790
	13055	Chattooga County, GA	26,015	24,790
44920		Summit Park, UT Micro area	36,324	41,933
	49043	Summit County, UT	36,324	41,933

Core based statistical area	State/County FIPS code	Title and Geographic Components	2010 Census Population	2018 Estimated Population
44940		Sumter, SC Metro area	107,456	106,512
	45085	Sumter County, SC	107,456	106,512
44980		Sunbury, PA Micro area	94,528	91,083
	42097	Northumberland County, PA	94,528	91,083
45000		Susanville, CA Micro area	34,895	30,802
	06035	Lassen County, CA	34,895	30,802
45020		Sweetwater, TX Micro area	15,216	14,751
	48353	Nolan County, TX	15,216	14,751
45060		Syracuse, NY Metro area	662,577	650,502
	36053	Madison County, NY	73,442	70,795
	36067	Onondaga County, NY	467,026	461,809
	36075	Oswego County, NY	122,109	117,898
45140		Tahlequah, OK Micro area	46,987	48,675
	40021	Cherokee County, OK	46,987	48,675
45180		Talladega-Sylacauga, AL Micro area	93,830	90,543
	01037	Coosa County, AL	11,539	10,715
	01121	Talladega County, AL	82,291	79,828
45220		Tallahassee, FL Metro area	367,413	385,145
	12039	Gadsden County, FL	46,389	45,894
	12065	Jefferson County, FL	14,761	14,288
	12073	Leon County, FL	275,487	292,502
	12129	Wakulla County, FL	30,776	32,461
45300		Tampa-St. Petersburg-Clearwater, FL Metro area	2,783,243	3,142,663
	12053	Hernando County, FL	172,778	190,865
	12057	Hillsborough County, FL	1,229,226	1,436,888
	12101	Pasco County, FL	464,697	539,630
	12103	Pinellas County, FL	916,542	975,280
45340		Taos, NM Micro area	32,937	32,835
	35055	Taos County, NM	32,937	32,835
45380		Taylorville, IL Micro area	34,800	32,661
	17021	Christian County, IL	34,800	32,661
45460		Terre Haute, IN Metro area	172,425	169,725
	18021	Clay County, IN	26,890	26,170
	18153	Sullivan County, IN	21,475	20,690
	18165	Vermillion County, IN	16,212	15,479
	18167	Vigo County, IN	107,848	107,386
45500		Texarkana, TX-AR Metro area	149,198	150,242
	05081	Little River County, AR	13,171	12,326
	05091	Miller County, AR	43,462	43,592
	48037	Bowie County, TX	92,565	94,324
45520		The Dalles, OR Micro area	25,213	26,505
	41065	Wasco County, OR	25,213	26,505
45540		The Villages, FL Metro area	93,420	128,754
	12119	Sumter County, FL	93,420	128,754
45580		Thomaston, GA Micro area	27,153	26,215
	13293	Upson County, GA	27,153	26,215
45620		Thomasville, GA Micro area	44,720	44,448
	13275	Thomas County, GA	44,720	44,448
45660		Tiffin, OH Micro area	56,745	55,207
	39147	Seneca County, OH	56,745	55,207
45700		Tifton, GA Micro area	40,118	40,571
	13277	Tift County, GA	40,118	40,571
45740		Toccoa, GA Micro area	26,175	26,035
	13257	Stephens County, GA	26,175	26,035
45780		Toledo, OH Metro area	610,001	602,871
	39051	Fulton County, OH	42,698	42,276
	39095	Lucas County, OH	441,815	429,899
	39173	Wood County, OH	125,488	130,696
45820		Topeka, KS Metro area	233,870	232,594
	20085	Jackson County, KS	13,462	13,280
	20087	Jefferson County, KS	19,126	18,975
	20139	Osage County, KS	16,295	15,941
	20177	Shawnee County, KS	177,934	177,499
	20197	Wabaunsee County, KS	7,053	6,899
45860		Torrington, CT Micro area	189,927	181,111
	09005	Litchfield County, CT	189,927	181,111
45900		Traverse City, MI Micro area	143,372	149,914
	26019	Benzie County, MI	17,525	17,753
	26055	Grand Traverse County, MI	86,986	92,573
	26079	Kalkaska County, MI	17,153	17,824
	26089	Leelanau County, MI	21,708	21,764
45940		Trenton, NJ Metro area	366,513	369,811
	34021	Mercer County, NJ	366,513	369,811
45980		Troy, AL Micro area	32,899	33,338
	01109	Pike County, AL	32,899	33,338
46020		Truckee-Grass Valley, CA Micro area	98,764	99,696
	06057	Nevada County, CA	98,764	99,696
46060		Tucson, AZ Metro area	980,263	1,039,073
	04019	Pima County, AZ	980,263	1,039,073
46100		Tullahoma-Manchester, TN Micro area	100,210	104,001
	47031	Coffee County, TN	52,796	55,700
	47051	Franklin County, TN	41,052	41,890
	47127	Moore County, TN	6,362	6,411
46140		Tulsa, OK Metro area	937,478	993,797
	40037	Creek County, OK	69,967	71,604
	40111	Okmulgee County, OK	40,069	38,335
	40113	Osage County, OK	47,472	47,014

Core based statistical area	State/County FIPS code	Title and Geographic Components	2010 Census Population	2018 Estimated Population
	40117	Pawnee County, OK	16,577	16,390
	40131	Rogers County, OK	86,905	91,984
	40143	Tulsa County, OK	603,403	648,360
	40145	Wagoner County, OK	73,085	80,110
46180		Tupelo, MS Micro area	136,268	140,552
	28057	Itawamba County, MS	23,401	23,517
	28081	Lee County, MS	82,910	85,202
	28115	Pontotoc County, MS	29,957	31,833
46220		Tuscaloosa, AL Metro area	230,162	243,575
	01065	Hale County, AL	15,760	14,726
	01107	Pickens County, AL	19,746	19,938
	01125	Tuscaloosa County, AL	194,656	208,911
46300		Twin Falls, ID Metro area	99,604	110,096
	16053	Jerome County, ID	22,374	24,015
	16083	Twin Falls County, ID	77,230	86,081
46340		Tyler, TX Metro area	209,714	230,221
	48423	Smith County, TX	209,714	230,221
46380		Ukiah, CA Micro area	87,841	87,606
	06045	Mendocino County, CA	87,841	87,606
46460		Union City, TN-KY Micro area	38,620	36,387
	21075	Fulton County, KY	6,813	6,120
	47131	Obion County, TN	31,807	30,267
46500		Urbana, OH Micro area	40,097	38,754
	39021	Champaign County, OH	40,097	38,754
46520		Urban Honolulu, HI Metro area	953,207	980,080
	15003	Honolulu County, HI	953,207	980,080
46540		Utica-Rome, NY Metro area	299,397	291,410
	36043	Herkimer County, NY	64,519	61,833
	36065	Oneida County, NY	234,878	229,577
46620		Uvalde, TX Micro area	26,405	26,846
	48463	Uvalde County, TX	26,405	26,846
46660		Valdosta, GA Metro area	139,588	146,174
	13027	Brooks County, GA	16,243	15,513
	13101	Echols County, GA	4,034	4,000
	13173	Lanier County, GA	10,078	10,340
	13185	Lowndes County, GA	109,233	116,321
46700		Vallejo-Fairfield, CA Metro area	413,344	446,610
	06095	Solano County, CA	413,344	446,610
46740		Valley, AL Micro area	34,215	33,615
	01017	Chambers County, AL	34,215	33,615
46780		Van Wert, OH Micro area	28,744	28,281
	39161	Van Wert County, OH	28,744	28,281
46820		Vermillion, SD Micro area	13,864	14,041
	46027	Clay County, SD	13,864	14,041
46860		Vernal, UT Micro area	32,588	35,438
	49047	Uintah County, UT	32,588	35,438
46900		Vernon, TX Micro area	13,535	12,820
	48487	Wilbarger County, TX	13,535	12,820
46980		Vicksburg, MS Micro area	58,377	55,178
	28021	Claiborne County, MS	9,604	9,002
	28149	Warren County, MS	48,773	46,176
47020		Victoria, TX Metro area	94,003	99,619
	48175	Goliad County, TX	7,210	7,584
	48469	Victoria County, TX	86,793	92,035
47080		Vidalia, GA Micro area	36,346	36,080
	13209	Montgomery County, GA	9,123	9,193
	13279	Toombs County, GA	27,223	26,887
47180		Vincennes, IN Micro area	38,440	36,895
	18083	Knox County, IN	38,440	36,895
47220		Vineland-Bridgeton, NJ Metro area	156,898	150,972
	34011	Cumberland County, NJ	156,898	150,972
47240		Vineyard Haven, MA Micro area	16,535	17,352
	25007	Dukes County, MA	16,535	17,352
47260		Virginia Beach-Norfolk-Newport News, VA-NC Metro area	1,676,822	1,728,733
	37053	Currituck County, NC	23,547	27,072
	37073	Gates County, NC	12,197	11,573
	51073	Gloucester County, VA	36,858	37,349
	51093	Isle of Wight County, VA	35,270	36,953
	51095	James City County, VA	67,009	76,397
	51115	Mathews County, VA	8,978	8,802
	51199	York County, VA	65,464	67,846
	51550	Chesapeake city, VA	222,209	242,634
	51650	Hampton city, VA	137,436	134,313
	51700	Newport News city, VA	180,719	178,626
	51710	Norfolk city, VA	242,803	244,076
	51735	Poquoson city, VA	12,150	12,190
	51740	Portsmouth city, VA	95,535	94,632
	51800	Suffolk city, VA	84,585	91,185
	51810	Virginia Beach city, VA	437,994	450,189
	51830	Williamsburg city, VA	14,068	14,896
47300		Visalia-Porterville, CA Metro area	442,179	465,861
	06107	Tulare County, CA	442,179	465,861
47340		Wabash, IN Micro area	32,888	31,280
	18169	Wabash County, IN	32,888	31,280
47380		Waco, TX Metro area	252,772	271,942
	48145	Falls County, TX	17,866	17,335
	48309	McLennan County, TX	234,906	254,607

Core based statistical area	State/County FIPS code	Title and Geographic Components	2010 Census Population	2018 Estimated Population
47420		Wahpeton, ND-MN Micro area	22,897	22,493
	27167	Wilkin County, MN	6,576	6,254
	38077	Richland County, ND	16,321	16,239
47460		Walla Walla, WA Metro area	62,859	64,981
	53013	Columbia County, WA	4,078	4,059
	53071	Walla Walla County, WA	58,781	60,922
47540		Wapakoneta, OH Micro area	45,949	45,804
	39011	Auglaize County, OH	45,949	45,804
47580		Warner Robins, GA Metro area	179,605	193,835
	13153	Houston County, GA	139,900	155,469
	13225	Peach County, GA	27,695	27,297
	13235	Pulaski County, GA	12,010	11,069
47620		Warren, PA Micro area	41,815	39,498
	42123	Warren County, PA	41,815	39,498
47660		Warrensburg, MO Micro area	52,595	53,652
	29101	Johnson County, MO	52,595	53,652
47700		Warsaw, IN Micro area	77,358	79,344
	18085	Kosciusko County, IN	77,358	79,344
47780		Washington, IN Micro area	31,648	33,147
	18027	Daviess County, IN	31,648	33,147
47820		Washington, NC Micro area	47,759	47,079
	37013	Beaufort County, NC	47,759	47,079
47900		Washington-Arlington-Alexandria, DC-VA-MD-WV Metro area	5,636,232	6,249,950
47900		Silver Spring-Frederick-Rockville, MD Metro Div 43524	1,205,162	1,308,215
	24021	Frederick County, MD	233,385	255,648
	24031	Montgomery County, MD	971,777	1,052,567
47900		Washington-Arlington-Alexandria, DC-VA-MD-WV Metro Div 47894	4,431,070	4,941,735
	11001	District of Columbia, DC	601,723	702,455
	24009	Calvert County, MD	88,737	92,003
	24017	Charles County, MD	146,551	161,503
	24033	Prince George's County, MD	863,420	909,308
	51013	Arlington County, VA	207,627	237,521
	51043	Clarke County, VA	14,034	14,523
	51047	Culpeper County, VA	46,689	51,859
	51059	Fairfax County, VA	1,081,726	1,150,795
	51061	Fauquier County, VA	65,203	70,675
	51107	Loudoun County, VA	312,311	406,850
	51153	Prince William County, VA	402,002	468,011
	51157	Rappahannock County, VA	7,373	7,252
	51177	Spotsylvania County, VA	122,397	134,238
	51179	Stafford County, VA	128,961	149,960
	51187	Warren County, VA	37,575	40,003
	51510	Alexandria city, VA	139,966	160,530
	51600	Fairfax city, VA	22,565	24,574
	51610	Falls Church city, VA	12,332	14,772
	51630	Fredericksburg city, VA	24,286	29,144
	51683	Manassas city, VA	37,821	41,641
	51685	Manassas Park city, VA	14,273	17,307
	54037	Jefferson County, WV	53,498	56,811
47920		Washington Court House, OH Micro area	29,030	28,666
	39047	Fayette County, OH	29,030	28,666
47940		Waterloo-Cedar Falls, IA Metro area	167,819	169,659
	19013	Black Hawk County, IA	131,090	132,408
	19017	Bremer County, IA	24,276	24,947
	19075	Grundy County, IA	12,453	12,304
47980		Watertown, SD Micro area	27,227	28,015
	46029	Codington County, SD	27,227	28,015
48020		Watertown-Fort Atkinson, WI Micro area	83,686	85,129
	55055	Jefferson County, WI	83,686	85,129
48060		Watertown-Fort Drum, NY Metro area	116,229	111,755
	36045	Jefferson County, NY	116,229	111,755
48100		Wauchula, FL Micro area	27,731	27,245
	12049	Hardee County, FL	27,731	27,245
48140		Wausau, WI Metro area	134,063	135,428
	55073	Marathon County, WI	134,063	135,428
48180		Waycross, GA Micro area	55,070	55,069
	13229	Pierce County, GA	18,758	19,389
	13299	Ware County, GA	36,312	35,680
48220		Weatherford, OK Micro area	27,469	29,036
	40039	Custer County, OK	27,469	29,036
48260		Weirton-Steubenville, WV-OH Metro area	124,454	117,064
	39081	Jefferson County, OH	69,709	65,767
	54009	Brooke County, WV	24,069	22,203
	54029	Hancock County, WV	30,676	29,094
48300		Wenatchee, WA Metro area	110,884	119,943
	53007	Chelan County, WA	72,453	77,036
	53017	Douglas County, WA	38,431	42,907
48460		West Plains, MO Micro area	40,400	40,076
	29091	Howell County, MO	40,400	40,076
48500		West Point, MS Micro Area	20,634	19,386
	28025	Clay County, MS	20,634	19,386
48540		Wheeling, WV-OH Metro area	147,950	140,045
	39013	Belmont County, OH	70,040	67,505
	54051	Marshall County, WV	33,107	30,785
	54069	Ohio County, WV	44,443	41,755

Core based statistical area	State/ County FIPS code	Title and Geographic Components	2010 Census Population	2018 Estimated Population
48580		Whitewater-Elkhorn, WI Micro area	102,228	103,718
	55127	Walworth County, WI	102,228	103,718
48620		Wichita, KS Metro area	630,919	644,888
	20015	Butler County, KS	65,880	66,765
	20079	Harvey County, KS	34,684	34,210
	20095	Kingman County, KS	7,858	7,310
	20173	Sedgwick County, KS	498,365	513,607
	20191	Sumner County, KS	24,132	22,996
48660		Wichita Falls, TX Metro area	151,306	151,306
	48009	Archer County, TX	9,054	8,786
	48077	Clay County, TX	10,752	10,456
	48485	Wichita County, TX	131,500	132,064
48700		Williamsport, PA Metro area	116,111	113,664
	42081	Lycoming County, PA	116,111	113,664
48780		Williston, ND Micro area	22,398	35,350
	38105	Williams County, ND	22,398	35,350
48820		Willmar, MN Micro area	42,239	42,855
	27067	Kandiyohi County, MN	42,239	42,855
48900		Wilmington, NC Metro area	254,884	294,436
	37129	New Hanover County, NC	202,667	232,274
	37141	Pender County, NC	52,217	62,162
48940		Wilmington, OH Micro area	42,040	42,057
	39027	Clinton County, OH	42,040	42,057
48980		Wilson, NC Micro area	81,234	81,455
	37195	Wilson County, NC	81,234	81,455
49020		Winchester, VA-WV Metro area	128,472	139,810
	51069	Frederick County, VA	78,305	88,355
	51840	Winchester city, VA	26,203	28,108
	54027	Hampshire County, WV	23,964	23,347
49080		Winnemucca, NV Micro area	16,528	16,786
	32013	Humboldt County, NV	16,528	16,786
49100		Winona, MN Micro area	51,461	50,825
	27169	Winona County, MN	51,461	50,825
49180		Winston-Salem, NC Metro area	640,595	671,456
	37057	Davidson County, NC	162,878	166,614
	37059	Davie County, NC	41,240	42,733

Core based statistical area	State/ County FIPS code	Title and Geographic Components	2010 Census Population	2018 Estimated Population
	37067	Forsyth County, NC	350,670	379,099
	37169	Stokes County, NC	47,401	45,467
	37197	Yadkin County, NC	38,406	37,543
49220		Wisconsin Rapids-Marshfield, WI Micro area	74,749	73,055
	55141	Wood County, WI	74,749	73,055
49260		Woodward, OK Micro area	20,081	20,222
	40153	Woodward County, OK	20,081	20,222
49300		Wooster, OH Micro area	114,520	115,967
	39169	Wayne County, OH	114,520	115,967
49340		Worcester, MA-CT Metro area	916,980	947,866
	09015	Windham County, CT	118,428	117,027
	25027	Worcester County, MA	798,552	830,839
49380		Worthington, MN Micro area	21,378	21,924
	27105	Nobles County, MN	21,378	21,924
49420		Yakima, WA Metro area	243,231	251,446
	53077	Yakima County, WA	243,231	251,446
49460		Yankton, SD Micro area	22,438	22,869
	46135	Yankton County, SD	22,438	22,869
49620		York-Hanover, PA Metro area	434,972	448,273
	42133	York County, PA	434,972	448,273
49660		Youngstown-Warren-Boardman, OH-PA Metro area	565,773	538,952
	39099	Mahoning County, OH	238,823	229,642
	39155	Trumbull County, OH	210,312	198,627
	42085	Mercer County, PA	116,638	110,683
49700		Yuba City, CA Metro area	166,892	174,848
	06101	Sutter County, CA	94,737	96,807
	06115	Yuba County, CA	72,155	78,041
49740		Yuma, AZ Metro area	195,751	212,128
	04027	Yuma County, AZ	195,751	212,128
49780		Zanesville, OH Micro area	86,074	86,183
	39119	Muskingum County, OH	86,074	86,183
49820		Zapata, TX Micro area	14,018	14,190
	48505	Zapata County, TX	14,018	14,190

APPENDIX B. CITIES BY COUNTY

The following table is arranged alphabetically by state. Under each state heading are listed all cities with a 2010 census population of 25,000 or more, along with their component counties and the population in each component.

State code	Place code	County code	Geographic Area Name	2010 census population
01			**ALABAMA**	4,779,736
01		00820	Alabaster city	30,352
01	117	00820	Shelby County	30,352
01		03076	Auburn city	53,380
01	081	03076	Lee County	53,380
01		05980	Bessemer city	27,456
01	073	05980	Jefferson County	27,456
01		07000	Birmingham city	212,237
01	073	07000	Jefferson County	210,609
01	117	07000	Shelby County	1,628
01		20104	Decatur city	55,683
01	083	20104	Limestone County	84
01	103	20104	Morgan County	55,599
01		21184	Dothan city	65,496
01	045	21184	Dale County	887
01	067	21184	Henry County	5
01	069	21184	Houston County	64,604
01		24184	Enterprise city	26,562
01	031	24184	Coffee County	26,139
01	045	24184	Dale County	423
01		26896	Florence city	39,319
01	077	26896	Lauderdale County	39,319
01		28696	Gadsden city	36,856
01	055	28696	Etowah County	36,856
01		35800	Homewood city	25,167
01	073	35800	Jefferson County	25,167
01		35896	Hoover city	81,619
01	073	35896	Jefferson County	58,582
01	117	35896	Shelby County	23,037
01		37000	Huntsville city	180,105
01	083	37000	Limestone County	1,521
01	089	37000	Madison County	178,584
01		45784	Madison city	42,938
01	083	45784	Limestone County	3,453
01	089	45784	Madison County	39,485
01		50000	Mobile city	195,111
01	097	50000	Mobile County	195,111
01		51000	Montgomery city	205,764
01	101	51000	Montgomery County	205,764
01		57048	Opelika city	26,477
01	081	57048	Lee County	26,477
01		59472	Phenix City city	32,822
01	081	59472	Lee County	4,153
01	113	59472	Russell County	28,669
01		62328	Prattville city	33,960
01	001	62328	Autauga County	32,168
01	051	62328	Elmore County	1,792
01		77256	Tuscaloosa city	90,468
01	125	77256	Tuscaloosa County	90,468
01		78552	Vestavia Hills city	34,033
01	073	78552	Jefferson County	34,019
01	117	78552	Shelby County	14

State code	Place code	County code	Geographic Area Name	2010 census population
02			**ALASKA**	710,231
02		03000	Anchorage municipality	291,826
02	020	03000	Anchorage Municipality	291,826
02		24230	Fairbanks city	31,535
02	090	24230	Fairbanks North Star Borough	31,535
02		36400	Juneau city and borough	31,275
02	110	36400	Juneau City and Borough	31,275
04			**ARIZONA**	6,392,017
04		02830	Apache Junction city	35,840
04	013	02830	Maricopa County	294
04	021	02830	Pinal County	35,546
04		04720	Avondale city	76,238
04	013	04720	Maricopa County	76,238
04		07940	Buckeye town	50,876
04	013	07940	Maricopa County	50,876
04		08220	Bullhead City city	39,540
04	015	08220	Mohave County	39,540
04		10530	Casa Grande city	48,571
04	021	10530	Pinal County	48,571
04		12000	Chandler city	236,123
04	013	12000	Maricopa County	236,123
04		22220	El Mirage city	31,797
04	013	22220	Maricopa County	31,797
04		23620	Flagstaff city	65,870
04	005	23620	Coconino County	65,870
04		23760	Florence town	25,536
04	021	23760	Pinal County	25,536
04		27400	Gilbert town	208,453
04	013	27400	Maricopa County	208,453
04		27820	Glendale city	226,721
04	013	27820	Maricopa County	226,721
04		28380	Goodyear city	65,275
04	013	28380	Maricopa County	65,275
04		37620	Kingman city	28,068
04	015	37620	Mohave County	28,068
04		39370	Lake Havasu City city	52,527
04	015	39370	Mohave County	52,527
04		44270	Marana town	34,961
04	019	44270	Pima County	34,961
04	021	44270	Pinal County	0
04		44410	Maricopa city	43,482
04	021	44410	Pinal County	43,482
04		46000	Mesa city	439,041
04	013	46000	Maricopa County	439,041
04		51600	Oro Valley town	41,011
04	019	51600	Pima County	41,011
04		54050	Peoria city	154,065
04	013	54050	Maricopa County	154,058
04	025	54050	Yavapai County	7

State code	Place code	County code	Geographic Area Name	2010 census population
04		55000	Phoenix city	1,445,632
04	013	55000	Maricopa County	1,445,632
04		57380	Prescott city	39,843
04	025	57380	Yavapai County	39,843
04		57450	Prescott Valley town	38,822
04	025	57450	Yavapai County	38,822
04		58150	Queen Creek town	26,361
04	013	58150	Maricopa County	25,912
04	021	58150	Pinal County	449
04		62140	Sahuarita town	25,259
04	019	62140	Pima County	25,259
04		63470	San Luis city	25,505
04	027	63470	Yuma County	25,505
04		65000	Scottsdale city	217,385
04	013	65000	Maricopa County	217,385
04		66820	Sierra Vista city	43,888
04	003	66820	Cochise County	43,888
04		71510	Surprise city	117,517
04	013	71510	Maricopa County	117,517
04		73000	Tempe city	161,719
04	013	73000	Maricopa County	161,719
04		77000	Tucson city	520,116
04	019	77000	Pima County	520,116
04		85540	Yuma city	93,064
04	027	85540	Yuma County	93,064
05			**ARKANSAS**	2,915,918
05		04840	Bella Vista town	26,461
05	007	04840	Benton County	26,461
05		05290	Benton city	30,681
05	125	05290	Saline County	30,681
05		05320	Bentonville city	35,301
05	007	05320	Benton County	35,301
05		15190	Conway city	58,908
05	045	15190	Faulkner County	58,908
05		23290	Fayetteville city	73,580
05	143	23290	Washington County	73,580
05		24550	Fort Smith city	86,209
05	131	24550	Sebastian County	86,209
05		33400	Hot Springs city	35,193
05	051	33400	Garland County	35,193
05		34750	Jacksonville city	28,364
05	119	34750	Pulaski County	28,364
05		35710	Jonesboro city	67,263
05	031	35710	Craighead County	67,263
05		41000	Little Rock city	193,524
05	119	41000	Pulaski County	193,524
05		50450	North Little Rock city	62,304
05	119	50450	Pulaski County	62,304
05		53390	Paragould city	26,113
05	055	53390	Greene County	26,113
05		55310	Pine Bluff city	49,083
05	069	55310	Jefferson County	49,083
05		60410	Rogers city	55,964
05	007	60410	Benton County	55,964
05		61670	Russellville city	27,920
05	115	61670	Pope County	27,920
05		63800	Sherwood city	29,523
05	119	63800	Pulaski County	29,523

State code	Place code	County code	Geographic Area Name	2010 census population
05		66080	Springdale city	69,797
05	007	66080	Benton County	6,054
05	143	66080	Washington County	63,743
05		68810	Texarkana city	29,919
05	091	68810	Miller County	29,919
05		74540	West Memphis city	26,245
05	035	74540	Crittenden County	26,245
06			**CALIFORNIA**	37,253,956
06		00296	Adelanto city	31,765
06	071	00296	San Bernardino County	31,765
06		00562	Alameda city	73,812
06	001	00562	Alameda County	73,812
06		00884	Alhambra city	83,089
06	037	00884	Los Angeles County	83,089
06		00947	Aliso Viejo city	47,823
06	059	00947	Orange County	47,823
06		02000	Anaheim city	336,265
06	059	02000	Orange County	336,265
06		02252	Antioch city	102,372
06	013	02252	Contra Costa County	102,372
06		02364	Apple Valley town	69,135
06	071	02364	San Bernardino County	69,135
06		02462	Arcadia city	56,364
06	037	02462	Los Angeles County	56,364
06		03064	Atascadero city	28,310
06	079	03064	San Luis Obispo County	28,310
06		03162	Atwater city	28,168
06	047	03162	Merced County	28,168
06		03386	Azusa city	46,361
06	037	03386	Los Angeles County	46,361
06		03526	Bakersfield city	347,483
06	029	03526	Kern County	347,483
06		03666	Baldwin Park city	75,390
06	037	03666	Los Angeles County	75,390
06		03820	Banning city	29,603
06	065	03820	Riverside County	29,603
06		04758	Beaumont city	36,877
06	065	04758	Riverside County	36,877
06		04870	Bell city	35,477
06	037	04870	Los Angeles County	35,477
06		04982	Bellflower city	76,616
06	037	04982	Los Angeles County	76,616
06		04996	Bell Gardens city	42,072
06	037	04996	Los Angeles County	42,072
06		05108	Belmont city	25,835
06	081	05108	San Mateo County	25,835
06		05290	Benicia city	26,997
06	095	05290	Solano County	26,997
06		06000	Berkeley city	112,580
06	001	06000	Alameda County	112,580
06		06308	Beverly Hills city	34,109
06	037	06308	Los Angeles County	34,109
06		08100	Brea city	39,282
06	059	08100	Orange County	39,282
06		08142	Brentwood city	51,481
06	013	08142	Contra Costa County	51,481
06		08786	Buena Park city	80,530
06	059	08786	Orange County	80,530

State code	Place code	County code	Geographic Area Name	2010 census population	State code	Place code	County code	Geographic Area Name	2010 census population
06		08954	Burbank city	103,340	06		18100	Davis city	65,622
06	037	08954	Los Angeles County	103,340	06	113	18100	Yolo County	65,622
06		09066	Burlingame city	28,806	06		18394	Delano city	53,041
06	081	09066	San Mateo County	28,806	06	029	18394	Kern County	53,041
06		09710	Calexico city	38,572	06		18996	Desert Hot Springs city	25,938
06	025	09710	Imperial County	38,572	06	065	18996	Riverside County	25,938
06		10046	Camarillo city	65,201	06		19192	Diamond Bar city	55,544
06	111	10046	Ventura County	65,201	06	037	19192	Los Angeles County	55,544
06		10345	Campbell city	39,349	06		19766	Downey city	111,772
06	085	10345	Santa Clara County	39,349	06	037	19766	Los Angeles County	111,772
06		11194	Carlsbad city	105,328	06		20018	Dublin city	46,036
06	073	11194	San Diego County	105,328	06	001	20018	Alameda County	46,036
06		11530	Carson city	91,714	06		20956	East Palo Alto city	28,155
06	037	11530	Los Angeles County	91,714	06	081	20956	San Mateo County	28,155
06		12048	Cathedral City city	51,200	06		21712	El Cajon city	99,478
06	065	12048	Riverside County	51,200	06	073	21712	San Diego County	99,478
06		12524	Ceres city	45,417	06		21782	El Centro city	42,598
06	099	12524	Stanislaus County	45,417	06	025	21782	Imperial County	42,598
06		12552	Cerritos city	49,041	06		22020	Elk Grove city	153,015
06	037	12552	Los Angeles County	49,041	06	067	22020	Sacramento County	153,015
06		13014	Chico city	86,187	06		22230	El Monte city	113,475
06	007	13014	Butte County	86,187	06	037	22230	Los Angeles County	113,475
06		13210	Chino city	77,983	06		22300	El Paso de Robles (Paso Robles)	29,793
06	071	13210	San Bernardino County	77,983	06	079	22300	San Luis Obispo County	29,793
06		13214	Chino Hills city	74,799	06		22678	Encinitas city	59,518
06	071	13214	San Bernardino County	74,799	06	073	22678	San Diego County	59,518
06		13392	Chula Vista city	243,916	06		22804	Escondido city	143,911
06	073	13392	San Diego County	243,916	06	073	22804	San Diego County	143,911
06		13588	Citrus Heights city	83,301	06		23042	Eureka city	27,191
06	067	13588	Sacramento County	83,301	06	023	23042	Humboldt County	27,191
06		13756	Claremont city	34,926	06		23182	Fairfield city	105,321
06	037	13756	Los Angeles County	34,926	06	095	23182	Solano County	105,321
06		14218	Clovis city	95,631	06		24638	Folsom city	72,203
06	019	14218	Fresno County	95,631	06	067	24638	Sacramento County	72,203
06		14260	Coachella city	40,704	06		24680	Fontana city	196,069
06	065	14260	Riverside County	40,704	06	071	24680	San Bernardino County	196,069
06		14890	Colton city	52,154	06		25338	Foster City city	30,567
06	071	14890	San Bernardino County	52,154	06	081	25338	San Mateo County	30,567
06		15044	Compton city	96,455	06		25380	Fountain Valley city	55,313
06	037	15044	Los Angeles County	96,455	06	059	25380	Orange County	55,313
06		16000	Concord city	122,067	06		26000	Fremont city	214,089
06	013	16000	Contra Costa County	122,067	06	001	26000	Alameda County	214,089
06		16350	Corona city	152,374	06		27000	Fresno city	494,665
06	065	16350	Riverside County	152,374	06	019	27000	Fresno County	494,665
06		16532	Costa Mesa city	109,960	06		28000	Fullerton city	135,161
06	059	16532	Orange County	109,960	06	059	28000	Orange County	135,161
06		16742	Covina city	47,796	06		28168	Gardena city	58,829
06	037	16742	Los Angeles County	47,796	06	037	28168	Los Angeles County	58,829
06		17568	Culver City city	38,883	06		29000	Garden Grove city	170,883
06	037	17568	Los Angeles County	38,883	06	059	29000	Orange County	170,883
06		17610	Cupertino city	58,302	06		29504	Gilroy city	48,821
06	085	17610	Santa Clara County	58,302	06	085	29504	Santa Clara County	48,821
06		17750	Cypress city	47,802	06		30000	Glendale city	191,719
06	059	17750	Orange County	47,802	06	037	30000	Los Angeles County	191,719
06		17918	Daly City city	101,123	06		30014	Glendora city	50,073
06	081	17918	San Mateo County	101,123	06	037	30014	Los Angeles County	50,073
06		17946	Dana Point city	33,351	06		30378	Goleta city	29,888
06	059	17946	Orange County	33,351	06	083	30378	Santa Barbara County	29,888
06		17988	Danville town	42,039	06		31960	Hanford city	53,967
06	013	17988	Contra Costa County	42,039	06	031	31960	Kings County	53,967

State code	Place code	County code	Geographic Area Name	2010 census population	State code	Place code	County code	Geographic Area Name	2010 census population
06		32548	Hawthorne city	84,293	06		43000	Long Beach city	462,257
06	037	32548	Los Angeles County	84,293	06	037	43000	Los Angeles County	462,257
06		33000	Hayward city	144,186	06		43280	Los Altos city	28,976
06	001	33000	Alameda County	144,186	06	085	43280	Santa Clara County	28,976
06		33182	Hemet city	78,657	06		44000	Los Angeles city	3,792,621
06	065	33182	Riverside County	78,657	06	037	44000	Los Angeles County	3,792,621
06		33434	Hesperia city	90,173	06		44028	Los Banos city	35,972
06	071	33434	San Bernardino County	90,173	06	047	44028	Merced County	35,972
06		33588	Highland city	53,104	06		44112	Los Gatos town	29,413
06	071	33588	San Bernardino County	53,104	06	085	44112	Santa Clara County	29,413
06		34120	Hollister city	34,928	06		44574	Lynwood city	69,772
06	069	34120	San Benito County	34,928	06	037	44574	Los Angeles County	69,772
06		36000	Huntington Beach city	189,992	06		45022	Madera city	61,416
06	059	36000	Orange County	189,992	06	039	45022	Madera County	61,416
06		36056	Huntington Park city	58,114	06		45400	Manhattan Beach city	35,135
06	037	36056	Los Angeles County	58,114	06	037	45400	Los Angeles County	35,135
06		36294	Imperial Beach city	26,324	06		45484	Manteca city	67,096
06	073	36294	San Diego County	26,324	06	077	45484	San Joaquin County	67,096
06		36448	Indio city	76,036	06		46114	Martinez city	35,824
06	065	36448	Riverside County	76,036	06	013	46114	Contra Costa County	35,824
06		36546	Inglewood city	109,673	06		46492	Maywood city	27,395
06	037	36546	Los Angeles County	109,673	06	037	46492	Los Angeles County	27,395
06		36770	Irvine city	212,375	06		46842	Menifee city	77,519
06	059	36770	Orange County	212,375	06	065	46842	Riverside County	77,519
06		39220	Laguna Hills city	30,344	06		46870	Menlo Park city	32,026
06	059	39220	Orange County	30,344	06	081	46870	San Mateo County	32,026
06		39248	Laguna Niguel city	62,979	06		46898	Merced city	78,958
06	059	39248	Orange County	62,979	06	047	46898	Merced County	78,958
06		39290	La Habra city	60,239	06		47766	Milpitas city	66,790
06	059	39290	Orange County	60,239	06	085	47766	Santa Clara County	66,790
06		39486	Lake Elsinore city	51,821	06		48256	Mission Viejo city	93,305
06	065	39486	Riverside County	51,821	06	059	48256	Orange County	93,305
06		39496	Lake Forest city	77,264	06		48354	Modesto city	201,165
06	059	39496	Orange County	77,264	06	099	48354	Stanislaus County	201,165
06		39892	Lakewood city	80,048	06		48648	Monrovia city	36,590
06	037	39892	Los Angeles County	80,048	06	037	48648	Los Angeles County	36,590
06		40004	La Mesa city	57,065	06		48788	Montclair city	36,664
06	073	40004	San Diego County	57,065	06	071	48788	San Bernardino County	36,664
06		40032	La Mirada city	48,527	06		48816	Montebello city	62,500
06	037	40032	Los Angeles County	48,527	06	037	48816	Los Angeles County	62,500
06		40130	Lancaster city	156,633	06		48872	Monterey city	27,810
06	037	40130	Los Angeles County	156,633	06	053	48872	Monterey County	27,810
06		40340	La Puente city	39,816	06		48914	Monterey Park city	60,269
06	037	40340	Los Angeles County	39,816	06	037	48914	Los Angeles County	60,269
06		40354	La Quinta city	37,467	06		49138	Moorpark city	34,421
06	065	40354	Riverside County	37,467	06	111	49138	Ventura County	34,421
06		40830	La Verne city	31,063	06		49270	Moreno Valley city	193,365
06	037	40830	Los Angeles County	31,063	06	065	49270	Riverside County	193,365
06		40886	Lawndale city	32,769	06		49278	Morgan Hill city	37,882
06	037	40886	Los Angeles County	32,769	06	085	49278	Santa Clara County	37,882
06		41124	Lemon Grove city	25,320	06		49670	Mountain View city	74,066
06	073	41124	San Diego County	25,320	06	085	49670	Santa Clara County	74,066
06		41474	Lincoln city	42,819	06		50076	Murrieta city	103,466
06	061	41474	Placer County	42,819	06	065	50076	Riverside County	103,466
06		41992	Livermore city	80,968	06		50258	Napa city	76,915
06	001	41992	Alameda County	80,968	06	055	50258	Napa County	76,915
06		42202	Lodi city	62,134	06		50398	National City city	58,582
06	077	42202	San Joaquin County	62,134	06	073	50398	San Diego County	58,582
06		42524	Lompoc city	42,434	06		50916	Newark city	42,573
06	083	42524	Santa Barbara County	42,434	06	001	50916	Alameda County	42,573

State code	Place code	County code	Geographic Area Name	2010 census population	State code	Place code	County code	Geographic Area Name	2010 census population
06		51182	Newport Beach city	85,186	06		59514	Rancho Palos Verdes city	41,643
06	059	51182	Orange County	85,186	06	037	59514	Los Angeles County	41,643
06		51560	Norco city	27,063	06		59587	Rancho Santa Margarita city	47,853
06	065	51560	Riverside County	27,063	06	059	59587	Orange County	47,853
06		52526	Norwalk city	105,549	06		59920	Redding city	89,861
06	037	52526	Los Angeles County	105,549	06	089	59920	Shasta County	89,861
06		52582	Novato city	51,904	06		59962	Redlands city	68,747
06	041	52582	Marin County	51,904	06	071	59962	San Bernardino County	68,747
06		53000	Oakland city	390,724	06		60018	Redondo Beach city	66,748
06	001	53000	Alameda County	390,724	06	037	60018	Los Angeles County	66,748
06		53070	Oakley city	35,432	06		60102	Redwood City city	76,815
06	013	53070	Contra Costa County	35,432	06	081	60102	San Mateo County	76,815
06		53322	Oceanside city	167,086	06		60466	Rialto city	99,171
06	073	53322	San Diego County	167,086	06	071	60466	San Bernardino County	99,171
06		53896	Ontario city	163,924	06		60620	Richmond city	103,701
06	071	53896	San Bernardino County	163,924	06	013	60620	Contra Costa County	103,701
06		53980	Orange city	136,416	06		60704	Ridgecrest city	27,616
06	059	53980	Orange County	136,416	06	029	60704	Kern County	27,616
06		54652	Oxnard city	197,899	06		62000	Riverside city	303,871
06	111	54652	Ventura County	197,899	06	065	62000	Riverside County	303,871
06		54806	Pacifica city	37,234	06		62364	Rocklin city	56,974
06	081	54806	San Mateo County	37,234	06	061	62364	Placer County	56,974
06		55156	Palmdale city	152,750	06		62546	Rohnert Park city	40,971
06	037	55156	Los Angeles County	152,750	06	097	62546	Sonoma County	40,971
06		55184	Palm Desert city	48,445	06		62896	Rosemead city	53,764
06	065	55184	Riverside County	48,445	06	037	62896	Los Angeles County	53,764
06		55254	Palm Springs city	44,552	06		62938	Roseville city	118,788
06	065	55254	Riverside County	44,552	06	061	62938	Placer County	118,788
06		55282	Palo Alto city	64,403	06		64000	Sacramento city	466,488
06	085	55282	Santa Clara County	64,403	06	067	64000	Sacramento County	466,488
06		55520	Paradise town	26,218	06		64224	Salinas city	150,441
06	007	55520	Butte County	26,218	06	053	64224	Monterey County	150,441
06		55618	Paramount city	54,098	06		65000	San Bernardino city	209,924
06	037	55618	Los Angeles County	54,098	06	071	65000	San Bernardino County	209,924
06		56000	Pasadena city	137,122	06		65028	San Bruno city	41,114
06	037	56000	Los Angeles County	137,122	06	081	65028	San Mateo County	41,114
06		56700	Perris city	68,386	06		65042	San Buenaventura (Ventura)	106,433
06	065	56700	Riverside County	68,386	06	111	65042	Ventura County	106,433
06		56784	Petaluma city	57,941	06		65070	San Carlos city	28,406
06	097	56784	Sonoma County	57,941	06	081	65070	San Mateo County	28,406
06		56924	Pico Rivera city	62,942	06		65084	San Clemente city	63,522
06	037	56924	Los Angeles County	62,942	06	059	65084	Orange County	63,522
06		57456	Pittsburg city	63,264	06		66000	San Diego city	1,307,402
06	013	57456	Contra Costa County	63,264	06	073	66000	San Diego County	1,307,402
06		57526	Placentia city	50,533	06		66070	San Dimas city	33,371
06	059	57526	Orange County	50,533	06	037	66070	Los Angeles County	33,371
06		57764	Pleasant Hill city	33,152	06		67000	San Francisco city	805,235
06	013	57764	Contra Costa County	33,152	06	075	67000	San Francisco County	805,235
06		57792	Pleasanton city	70,285	06		67042	San Gabriel city	39,718
06	001	57792	Alameda County	70,285	06	037	67042	Los Angeles County	39,718
06		58072	Pomona city	149,058	06		67112	San Jacinto city	44,199
06	037	58072	Los Angeles County	149,058	06	065	67112	Riverside County	44,199
06		58240	Porterville city	54,165	06		68000	San Jose city	945,942
06	107	58240	Tulare County	54,165	06	085	68000	Santa Clara County	945,942
06		58520	Poway city	47,811	06		68028	San Juan Capistrano city	34,593
06	073	58520	San Diego County	47,811	06	059	68028	Orange County	34,593
06		59444	Rancho Cordova city	64,776	06		68084	San Leandro city	84,950
06	067	59444	Sacramento County	64,776	06	001	68084	Alameda County	84,950
06		59451	Rancho Cucamonga city	165,269	06		68154	San Luis Obispo city	45,119
06	071	59451	San Bernardino County	165,269	06	079	68154	San Luis Obispo County	45,119

State code	Place code	County code	Geographic Area Name	2010 census population	State code	Place code	County code	Geographic Area Name	2010 census population
06		68196	San Marcos city	83,781	06		80238	Tracy city	82,922
06	073	68196	San Diego County	83,781	06	077	80238	San Joaquin County	82,922
06		68252	San Mateo city	97,207	06		80644	Tulare city	59,278
06	081	68252	San Mateo County	97,207	06	107	80644	Tulare County	59,278
06		68294	San Pablo city	29,139	06		80812	Turlock city	68,549
06	013	68294	Contra Costa County	29,139	06	099	80812	Stanislaus County	68,549
06		68364	San Rafael city	57,713	06		80854	Tustin city	75,540
06	041	68364	Marin County	57,713	06	059	80854	Orange County	75,540
06		68378	San Ramon city	72,148	06		80994	Twentynine Palms city	25,048
06	013	68378	Contra Costa County	72,148	06	071	80994	San Bernardino County	25,048
06		69000	Santa Ana city	324,528	06		81204	Union City city	69,516
06	059	69000	Orange County	324,528	06	001	81204	Alameda County	69,516
06		69070	Santa Barbara city	88,410	06		81344	Upland city	73,732
06	083	69070	Santa Barbara County	88,410	06	071	81344	San Bernardino County	73,732
06		69084	Santa Clara city	116,468	06		81554	Vacaville city	92,428
06	085	69084	Santa Clara County	116,468	06	095	81554	Solano County	92,428
06		69088	Santa Clarita city	176,320	06		81666	Vallejo city	115,942
06	037	69088	Los Angeles County	176,320	06	095	81666	Solano County	115,942
06		69112	Santa Cruz city	59,946	06		82590	Victorville city	115,903
06	087	69112	Santa Cruz County	59,946	06	071	82590	San Bernardino County	115,903
06		69196	Santa Maria city	99,553	06		82954	Visalia city	124,442
06	083	69196	Santa Barbara County	99,553	06	107	82954	Tulare County	124,442
06		70000	Santa Monica city	89,736	06		82996	Vista city	93,834
06	037	70000	Los Angeles County	89,736	06	073	82996	San Diego County	93,834
06		70042	Santa Paula city	29,321	06		83332	Walnut city	29,172
06	111	70042	Ventura County	29,321	06	037	83332	Los Angeles County	29,172
06		70098	Santa Rosa city	167,815	06		83346	Walnut Creek city	64,173
06	097	70098	Sonoma County	167,815	06	013	83346	Contra Costa County	64,173
06		70224	Santee city	53,413	06		83542	Wasco city	25,545
06	073	70224	San Diego County	53,413	06	029	83542	Kern County	25,545
06		70280	Saratoga city	29,926	06		83668	Watsonville city	51,199
06	085	70280	Santa Clara County	29,926	06	087	83668	Santa Cruz County	51,199
06		70742	Seaside city	33,025	06		84200	West Covina city	106,098
06	053	70742	Monterey County	33,025	06	037	84200	Los Angeles County	106,098
06		72016	Simi Valley city	124,237	06		84410	West Hollywood city	34,399
06	111	72016	Ventura County	124,237	06	037	84410	Los Angeles County	34,399
06		72520	Soledad city	25,738	06		84550	Westminster city	89,701
06	053	72520	Monterey County	25,738	06	059	84550	Orange County	89,701
06		73080	South Gate city	94,396	06		84816	West Sacramento city	48,744
06	037	73080	Los Angeles County	94,396	06	113	84816	Yolo County	48,744
06		73220	South Pasadena city	25,619	06		85292	Whittier city	85,331
06	037	73220	Los Angeles County	25,619	06	037	85292	Los Angeles County	85,331
06		73262	South San Francisco city	63,632	06		85446	Wildomar city	32,176
06	081	73262	San Mateo County	63,632	06	065	85446	Riverside County	32,176
06		73962	Stanton city	38,186	06		85922	Windsor town	26,801
06	059	73962	Orange County	38,186	06	097	85922	Sonoma County	26,801
06		75000	Stockton city	291,707	06		86328	Woodland city	55,468
06	077	75000	San Joaquin County	291,707	06	113	86328	Yolo County	55,468
06		75630	Suisun City city	28,111	06		86832	Yorba Linda city	64,234
06	095	75630	Solano County	28,111	06	059	86832	Orange County	64,234
06		77000	Sunnyvale city	140,081	06		86972	Yuba City city	64,925
06	085	77000	Santa Clara County	140,081	06	101	86972	Sutter County	64,925
06		78120	Temecula city	100,097	06		87042	Yucaipa city	51,367
06	065	78120	Riverside County	100,097	06	071	87042	San Bernardino County	51,367
06		78148	Temple City city	35,558	08			**COLORADO**	5,029,196
06	037	78148	Los Angeles County	35,558	08		03455	Arvada city	106,433
					08	001	03455	Adams County	2,849
06		78582	Thousand Oaks city	126,683	08	059	03455	Jefferson County	103,584
06	111	78582	Ventura County	126,683					
06		80000	Torrance city	145,438	08		04000	Aurora city	325,078
06	037	80000	Los Angeles County	145,438	08	001	04000	Adams County	39,871

State code	Place code	County code	Geographic Area Name	2010 census population
08	005	04000	Arapahoe County	285,090
08	035	04000	Douglas County	117
08		07850	Boulder city	97,385
08	013	07850	Boulder County	97,385
08		08675	Brighton city	33,352
08	001	08675	Adams County	33,009
08	123	08675	Weld County	343
08		09280	Broomfield city	55,889
08	014	09280	Broomfield County	55,889
08		12415	Castle Rock town	48,231
08	035	12415	Douglas County	48,231
08		12815	Centennial city	100,377
08	005	12815	Arapahoe County	100,377
08		16000	Colorado Springs city	416,427
08	041	16000	El Paso County	416,427
08		16495	Commerce City city	45,913
08	001	16495	Adams County	45,913
08		20000	Denver city	600,158
08	031	20000	Denver County	600,158
08		24785	Englewood city	30,255
08	005	24785	Arapahoe County	30,255
08		27425	Fort Collins city	143,986
08	069	27425	Larimer County	143,986
08		27865	Fountain city	25,846
08	041	27865	El Paso County	25,846
08		31660	Grand Junction city	58,566
08	077	31660	Mesa County	58,566
08		32155	Greeley city	92,889
08	123	32155	Weld County	92,889
08		43000	Lakewood city	142,980
08	059	43000	Jefferson County	142,980
08		45255	Littleton city	41,737
08	005	45255	Arapahoe County	39,328
08	035	45255	Douglas County	28
08	059	45255	Jefferson County	2,381
08		45970	Longmont city	86,270
08	013	45970	Boulder County	86,240
08	123	45970	Weld County	30
08		46465	Loveland city	66,859
08	069	46465	Larimer County	66,859
08		54330	Northglenn city	35,789
08	001	54330	Adams County	35,777
08	123	54330	Weld County	12
08		57630	Parker town	45,297
08	035	57630	Douglas County	45,297
08		62000	Pueblo city	106,595
08	101	62000	Pueblo County	106,595
08		77290	Thornton city	118,772
08	001	77290	Adams County	118,772
08	123	77290	Weld County	0
08		83835	Westminster city	106,114
08	001	83835	Adams County	63,696
08	059	83835	Jefferson County	42,418
08		84440	Wheat Ridge city	30,166
08	059	84440	Jefferson County	30,166
09			**CONNECTICUT**	3,574,097
09		08000	Bridgeport city	144,229
09	001	08000	Fairfield County	144,229
09		08420	Bristol city	60,477
09	003	08420	Hartford County	60,477
09		18430	Danbury city	80,893
09	001	18430	Fairfield County	80,893

State code	Place code	County code	Geographic Area Name	2010 census population
09		37000	Hartford city	124,775
09	003	37000	Hartford County	124,775
09		46450	Meriden city	60,868
09	009	46450	New Haven County	60,868
09		47290	Middletown city	47,648
09	007	47290	Middlesex County	47,648
09		49880	Naugatuck borough	31,862
09	009	49880	New Haven County	31,862
09		50370	New Britain city	73,206
09	003	50370	Hartford County	73,206
09		52000	New Haven city	129,779
09	009	52000	New Haven County	129,779
09		52280	New London city	27,620
09	011	52280	New London County	27,620
09		55990	Norwalk city	85,603
09	001	55990	Fairfield County	85,603
09		56200	Norwich city	40,493
09	011	56200	New London County	40,493
09		68100	Shelton city	39,559
09	001	68100	Fairfield County	39,559
09		73000	Stamford city	122,643
09	001	73000	Fairfield County	122,643
09		76500	Torrington city	36,383
09	005	76500	Litchfield County	36,383
09		80000	Waterbury city	110,366
09	009	80000	New Haven County	110,366
09		82800	West Haven city	55,564
09	009	82800	New Haven County	55,564
10			**DELAWARE**	897,934
10		21200	Dover city	36,047
10	001	21200	Kent County	36,047
10		50670	Newark city	31,454
10	003	50670	New Castle County	31,454
10		77580	Wilmington city	70,851
10	003	77580	New Castle County	70,851
11			**DISTRICT OF COLUMBIA**	601,723
11		50000	Washington city	601,723
11	001	50000	District of Columbia	601,723
12			**FLORIDA**	18,801,310
12		00950	Altamonte Springs city	41,496
12	117	00950	Seminole County	41,496
12		01700	Apopka city	41,542
12	095	01700	Orange County	41,542
12		02681	Aventura city	35,762
12	086	02681	Miami-Dade County	35,762
12		07300	Boca Raton city	84,392
12	099	07300	Palm Beach County	84,392
12		07525	Bonita Springs city	43,914
12	071	07525	Lee County	43,914
12		07875	Boynton Beach city	68,217
12	099	07875	Palm Beach County	68,217
12		07950	Bradenton city	49,546
12	081	07950	Manatee County	49,546
12		10275	Cape Coral city	154,305
12	071	10275	Lee County	154,305
12		11050	Casselberry city	26,241
12	117	11050	Seminole County	26,241
12		12875	Clearwater city	107,685
12	103	12875	Pinellas County	107,685

State code	Place code	County code	Geographic Area Name	2010 census population
12		12925	Clermont city	28,742
12	069	12925	Lake County	28,742
12		13275	Coconut Creek city	52,909
12	011	13275	Broward County	52,909
12		14125	Cooper City city	28,547
12	011	14125	Broward County	28,547
12		14250	Coral Gables city	46,780
12	086	14250	Miami-Dade County	46,780
12		14400	Coral Springs city	121,096
12	011	14400	Broward County	121,096
12		15968	Cutler Bay town	40,286
12	086	15968	Miami-Dade County	40,286
12		16335	Dania Beach city	29,639
12	011	16335	Broward County	29,639
12		16475	Davie town	91,992
12	011	16475	Broward County	91,992
12		16525	Daytona Beach city	61,005
12	127	16525	Volusia County	61,005
12		16725	Deerfield Beach city	75,018
12	011	16725	Broward County	75,018
12		16875	DeLand city	27,031
12	127	16875	Volusia County	27,031
12		17100	Delray Beach city	60,522
12	099	17100	Palm Beach County	60,522
12		17200	Deltona city	85,182
12	127	17200	Volusia County	85,182
12		17935	Doral city	45,704
12	086	17935	Miami-Dade County	45,704
12		18575	Dunedin city	35,321
12	103	18575	Pinellas County	35,321
12		24000	Fort Lauderdale city	165,521
12	011	24000	Broward County	165,521
12		24125	Fort Myers city	62,298
12	071	24125	Lee County	62,298
12		24300	Fort Pierce city	41,590
12	111	24300	St. Lucie County	41,590
12		25175	Gainesville city	124,354
12	001	25175	Alachua County	124,354
12		27322	Greenacres city	37,573
12	099	27322	Palm Beach County	37,573
12		28452	Hallandale Beach city	37,113
12	011	28452	Broward County	37,113
12		30000	Hialeah city	224,669
12	086	30000	Miami-Dade County	224,669
12		32000	Hollywood city	140,768
12	011	32000	Broward County	140,768
12		32275	Homestead city	60,512
12	086	32275	Miami-Dade County	60,512
12		35000	Jacksonville city	821,784
12	031	35000	Duval County	821,784
12		35875	Jupiter town	55,156
12	099	35875	Palm Beach County	55,156
12		36950	Kissimmee city	59,682
12	097	36950	Osceola County	59,682
12		38250	Lakeland city	97,422
12	105	38250	Polk County	97,422
12		39075	Lake Worth city	34,910
12	099	39075	Palm Beach County	34,910
12		39425	Largo city	77,648
12	103	39425	Pinellas County	77,648

State code	Place code	County code	Geographic Area Name	2010 census population
12		39525	Lauderdale Lakes city	32,593
12	011	39525	Broward County	32,593
12		39550	Lauderhill city	66,887
12	011	39550	Broward County	66,887
12		43125	Margate city	53,284
12	011	43125	Broward County	53,284
12		43975	Melbourne city	76,068
12	009	43975	Brevard County	76,068
12		45000	Miami city	399,457
12	086	45000	Miami-Dade County	399,457
12		45025	Miami Beach city	87,779
12	086	45025	Miami-Dade County	87,779
12		45060	Miami Gardens city	107,167
12	086	45060	Miami-Dade County	107,167
12		45100	Miami Lakes town	29,361
12	086	45100	Miami-Dade County	29,361
12		45975	Miramar city	122,041
12	011	45975	Broward County	122,041
12		49425	North Lauderdale city	41,023
12	011	49425	Broward County	41,023
12		49450	North Miami city	58,786
12	086	49450	Miami-Dade County	58,786
12		49475	North Miami Beach city	41,523
12	086	49475	Miami-Dade County	41,523
12		49675	North Port city	57,357
12	115	49675	Sarasota County	57,357
12		50575	Oakland Park city	41,363
12	011	50575	Broward County	41,363
12		50750	Ocala city	56,315
12	083	50750	Marion County	56,315
12		51075	Ocoee city	35,579
12	095	51075	Orange County	35,579
12		53000	Orlando city	238,300
12	095	53000	Orange County	238,300
12		53150	Ormond Beach city	38,137
12	127	53150	Volusia County	38,137
12		53575	Oviedo city	33,342
12	117	53575	Seminole County	33,342
12		54000	Palm Bay city	103,190
12	009	54000	Brevard County	103,190
12		54075	Palm Beach Gardens city	48,452
12	099	54075	Palm Beach County	48,452
12		54200	Palm Coast city	75,180
12	035	54200	Flagler County	75,180
12		54700	Panama City city	36,484
12	005	54700	Bay County	36,484
12		55775	Pembroke Pines city	154,750
12	011	55775	Broward County	154,750
12		55925	Pensacola city	51,923
12	033	55925	Escambia County	51,923
12		56975	Pinellas Park city	49,079
12	103	56975	Pinellas County	49,079
12		57425	Plantation city	84,955
12	011	57425	Broward County	84,955
12		57550	Plant City city	34,721
12	057	57550	Hillsborough County	34,721
12		58050	Pompano Beach city	99,845
12	011	58050	Broward County	99,845
12		58575	Port Orange city	56,048
12	127	58575	Volusia County	56,048

State code	Place code	County code	Geographic Area Name	2010 census population
12		58715	Port St. Lucie city	164,603
12	111	58715	St. Lucie County	164,603
12		60975	Riviera Beach city	32,488
12	099	60975	Palm Beach County	32,488
12		62100	Royal Palm Beach village	34,140
12	099	62100	Palm Beach County	34,140
12		62625	St. Cloud city	35,183
12	097	62625	Osceola County	35,183
12		63000	St. Petersburg city	244,769
12	103	63000	Pinellas County	244,769
12		63650	Sanford city	53,570
12	117	63650	Seminole County	53,570
12		64175	Sarasota city	51,917
12	115	64175	Sarasota County	51,917
12		69700	Sunrise city	84,439
12	011	69700	Broward County	84,439
12		70600	Tallahassee city	181,376
12	073	70600	Leon County	181,376
12		70675	Tamarac city	60,427
12	011	70675	Broward County	60,427
12		71000	Tampa city	335,709
12	057	71000	Hillsborough County	335,709
12		71900	Titusville city	43,761
12	009	71900	Brevard County	43,761
12		75812	Wellington village	56,508
12	099	75812	Palm Beach County	56,508
12		76582	Weston city	65,333
12	011	76582	Broward County	65,333
12		76600	West Palm Beach city	99,919
12	099	76600	Palm Beach County	99,919
12		78250	Winter Garden city	34,568
12	095	78250	Orange County	34,568
12		78275	Winter Haven city	33,874
12	105	78275	Polk County	33,874
12		78300	Winter Park city	27,852
12	095	78300	Orange County	27,852
12		78325	Winter Springs city	33,282
12	117	78325	Seminole County	33,282
13			**GEORGIA**	9,687,653
13		01052	Albany city	77,434
13	095	01052	Dougherty County	77,434
13		01696	Alpharetta city	57,551
13	121	01696	Fulton County	57,551
13		04000	Atlanta city	420,003
13	089	04000	DeKalb County	28,292
13	121	04000	Fulton County	391,711
13		19000	Columbus city	189,885
13	215	19000	Muscogee County	189,885
13		21380	Dalton city	33,128
13	313	21380	Whitfield County	33,128
13		23900	Douglasville city	30,961
13	097	23900	Douglas County	30,961
13		24600	Duluth city	26,600
13	135	24600	Gwinnett County	26,600
13		24768	Dunwoody city	46,267
13	089	24768	DeKalb County	46,267
13		25720	East Point city	33,712
13	121	25720	Fulton County	33,712
13		31908	Gainesville city	33,804
13	139	31908	Hall County	33,804
13		38964	Hinesville city	33,437
13	179	38964	Liberty County	33,437
13		42425	Johns Creek city	76,728
13	121	42425	Fulton County	76,728
13		43192	Kennesaw city	29,783
13	067	43192	Cobb County	29,783
13		44340	LaGrange city	29,588
13	285	44340	Troup County	29,588
13		45488	Lawrenceville city	28,546
13	135	45488	Gwinnett County	28,546
13		49000	Macon city	91,351
13	021	49000	Bibb County	90,885
13	169	49000	Jones County	466
13		49756	Marietta city	56,579
13	067	49756	Cobb County	56,579
13		51670	Milton city	32,661
13	121	51670	Fulton County	32,661
13		55020	Newnan city	33,039
13	077	55020	Coweta County	33,039
13		59724	Peachtree City city	34,364
13	113	59724	Fayette County	34,364
13		66668	Rome city	36,303
13	115	66668	Floyd County	36,303
13		67284	Roswell city	88,346
13	121	67284	Fulton County	88,346
13		68516	Sandy Springs city	93,853
13	121	68516	Fulton County	93,853
13		69000	Savannah city	136,286
13	051	69000	Chatham County	136,286
13		71492	Smyrna city	51,271
13	067	71492	Cobb County	51,271
13		73256	Statesboro city	28,422
13	031	73256	Bulloch County	28,422
13		73704	Stockbridge city	25,636
13	151	73704	Henry County	25,636
13		78800	Valdosta city	54,518
13	185	78800	Lowndes County	54,518
13		80508	Warner Robins city	66,588
13	153	80508	Houston County	66,224
13	225	80508	Peach County	364
15			**HAWAII**	1,360,301
15		06290	East Honolulu CDP	49,914
15	003	06290	Honolulu County	49,914
15		14650	Hilo CDP	43,263
15	001	14650	Hawaii County	43,263
15		22700	Kahului CDP	26,337
15	009	22700	Maui County	26,337
15		23150	Kailua CDP	38,635
15	003	23150	Honolulu County	38,635
15		28250	Kaneohe CDP	34,597
15	003	28250	Honolulu County	34,597
15		51050	Mililani Town CDP	27,629
15	003	51050	Honolulu County	27,629
15		62600	Pearl City CDP	47,698
15	003	62600	Honolulu County	47,698
15		71550	Urban Honolulu CDP	337,256
15	003	71550	Honolulu County	337,256
15		79700	Waipahu CDP	38,216
15	003	79700	Honolulu County	38,216

State code	Place code	County code	Geographic Area Name	2010 census population
16			**IDAHO**	1,567,582
16		08830	Boise City city	205,671
16	001	08830	Ada County	205,671
16		12250	Caldwell city	46,237
16	027	12250	Canyon County	46,237
16		16750	Coeur d'Alene city	44,137
16	055	16750	Kootenai County	44,137
16		39700	Idaho Falls city	56,813
16	019	39700	Bonneville County	56,813
16		46540	Lewiston city	31,894
16	069	46540	Nez Perce County	31,894
16		52120	Meridian city	75,092
16	001	52120	Ada County	75,092
16		56260	Nampa city	81,557
16	027	56260	Canyon County	81,557
16		64090	Pocatello city	54,255
16	005	64090	Bannock County	54,239
16	077	64090	Power County	16
16		64810	Post Falls city	27,574
16	055	64810	Kootenai County	27,574
16		67420	Rexburg city	25,484
16	065	67420	Madison County	25,484
16		82810	Twin Falls city	44,125
16	083	82810	Twin Falls County	44,125
17			**ILLINOIS**	12,830,632
17		00243	Addison village	36,942
17	043	00243	DuPage County	36,942
17		00685	Algonquin village	30,046
17	089	00685	Kane County	8,433
17	111	00685	McHenry County	21,613
17		01114	Alton city	27,865
17	119	01114	Madison County	27,865
17		02154	Arlington Heights village	75,101
17	031	02154	Cook County	75,101
17	097	02154	Lake County	0
17		03012	Aurora city	197,899
17	043	03012	DuPage County	49,433
17	089	03012	Kane County	130,976
17	093	03012	Kendall County	6,019
17	197	03012	Will County	11,471
17		04013	Bartlett village	41,208
17	031	04013	Cook County	16,797
17	043	04013	DuPage County	24,411
17	089	04013	Kane County	0
17		04078	Batavia city	26,045
17	043	04078	DuPage County	0
17	089	04078	Kane County	26,045
17		04845	Belleville city	44,478
17	163	04845	St. Clair County	44,478
17		05092	Belvidere city	25,585
17	007	05092	Boone County	25,585
17		05573	Berwyn city	56,657
17	031	05573	Cook County	56,657
17		06613	Bloomington city	76,610
17	113	06613	McLean County	76,610
17		07133	Bolingbrook village	73,366
17	043	07133	DuPage County	1,571
17	197	07133	Will County	71,795
17		09447	Buffalo Grove village	41,496
17	031	09447	Cook County	13,644
17	097	09447	Lake County	27,852
17		09642	Burbank city	28,925
17	031	09642	Cook County	28,925
17		10487	Calumet City city	37,042
17	031	10487	Cook County	37,042
17		11163	Carbondale city	25,902
17	077	11163	Jackson County	25,902
17	199	11163	Williamson County	0
17		11332	Carol Stream village	39,711
17	043	11332	DuPage County	39,711
17		11358	Carpentersville village	37,691
17	089	11358	Kane County	37,691
17		12385	Champaign city	81,055
17	019	12385	Champaign County	81,055
17		14000	Chicago city	2,695,598
17	031	14000	Cook County	2,695,598
17	043	14000	DuPage County	0
17		14026	Chicago Heights city	30,276
17	031	14026	Cook County	30,276
17		14351	Cicero town	83,891
17	031	14351	Cook County	83,891
17		15599	Collinsville city	25,579
17	119	15599	Madison County	22,573
17	163	15599	St. Clair County	3,006
17		17887	Crystal Lake city	40,743
17	111	17887	McHenry County	40,743
17		18563	Danville city	33,027
17	183	18563	Vermilion County	33,027
17		18823	Decatur city	76,122
17	115	18823	Macon County	76,122
17		19161	DeKalb city	43,862
17	037	19161	DeKalb County	43,862
17		19642	Des Plaines city	58,364
17	031	19642	Cook County	58,364
17		20591	Downers Grove village	47,833
17	043	20591	DuPage County	47,833
17		22255	East St. Louis city	27,006
17	163	22255	St. Clair County	27,006
17		23074	Elgin city	108,188
17	031	23074	Cook County	24,032
17	089	23074	Kane County	84,156
17		23256	Elk Grove Village village	33,127
17	031	23256	Cook County	33,127
17	043	23256	DuPage County	0
17		23620	Elmhurst city	44,121
17	031	23620	Cook County	0
17	043	23620	DuPage County	44,121
17		24582	Evanston city	74,486
17	031	24582	Cook County	74,486
17		27884	Freeport city	25,638
17	177	27884	Stephenson County	25,638
17		28326	Galesburg city	32,195
17	095	28326	Knox County	32,195
17		29730	Glendale Heights village	34,208
17	043	29730	DuPage County	34,208
17		29756	Glen Ellyn village	27,450
17	043	29756	DuPage County	27,450
17		29938	Glenview village	44,692
17	031	29938	Cook County	44,692
17		30926	Granite City city	29,849
17	119	30926	Madison County	29,849
17		32018	Gurnee village	31,295
17	097	32018	Lake County	31,295
17		32746	Hanover Park village	37,973
17	031	32746	Cook County	20,636
17	043	32746	DuPage County	17,337

State code	Place code	County code	Geographic Area Name	2010 census population
17		33383	Harvey city	25,282
17	031	33383	Cook County	25,282
17		34722	Highland Park city	29,763
17	097	34722	Lake County	29,763
17		35411	Hoffman Estates village	51,895
17	031	35411	Cook County	51,895
17	089	35411	Kane County	0
17		38570	Joliet city	147,433
17	093	38570	Kendall County	9,749
17	197	38570	Will County	137,684
17		38934	Kankakee city	27,537
17	091	38934	Kankakee County	27,537
17		41183	Lake in the Hills village	28,965
17	111	41183	McHenry County	28,965
17		42028	Lansing village	28,331
17	031	42028	Cook County	28,331
17		44407	Lombard village	43,165
17	043	44407	DuPage County	43,165
17		45694	McHenry city	26,992
17	111	45694	McHenry County	26,992
17		48242	Melrose Park village	25,411
17	031	48242	Cook County	25,411
17		49867	Moline city	43,483
17	161	49867	Rock Island County	43,483
17		51089	Mount Prospect village	54,167
17	031	51089	Cook County	54,167
17		51349	Mundelein village	31,064
17	097	51349	Lake County	31,064
17		51622	Naperville city	141,853
17	043	51622	DuPage County	94,533
17	197	51622	Will County	47,320
17		53000	Niles village	29,803
17	031	53000	Cook County	29,803
17		53234	Normal town	52,497
17	113	53234	McLean County	52,497
17		53481	Northbrook village	33,170
17	031	53481	Cook County	33,170
17		53559	North Chicago city	32,574
17	097	53559	Lake County	32,574
17		54638	Oak Forest city	27,962
17	031	54638	Cook County	27,962
17		54820	Oak Lawn village	56,690
17	031	54820	Cook County	56,690
17		54885	Oak Park village	51,878
17	031	54885	Cook County	51,878
17		55249	O'Fallon city	28,281
17	163	55249	St. Clair County	28,281
17		56640	Orland Park village	56,767
17	031	56640	Cook County	56,583
17	197	56640	Will County	184
17		56887	Oswego village	30,355
17	093	56887	Kendall County	30,355
17		57225	Palatine village	68,557
17	031	57225	Cook County	68,557
17	097	57225	Lake County	0
17		57875	Park Ridge city	37,480
17	031	57875	Cook County	37,480
17		58447	Pekin city	34,094
17	143	58447	Peoria County	0
17	179	58447	Tazewell County	34,094

State code	Place code	County code	Geographic Area Name	2010 census population
17		59000	Peoria city	115,007
17	143	59000	Peoria County	115,007
17		60287	Plainfield village	39,581
17	093	60287	Kendall County	2,079
17	197	60287	Will County	37,502
17		62367	Quincy city	40,633
17	001	62367	Adams County	40,633
17		65000	Rockford city	152,871
17	201	65000	Winnebago County	152,871
17		65078	Rock Island city	39,018
17	161	65078	Rock Island County	39,018
17		65442	Romeoville village	39,680
17	197	65442	Will County	39,680
17		66040	Round Lake Beach village	28,175
17	097	66040	Lake County	28,175
17		66703	St. Charles city	32,974
17	043	66703	DuPage County	543
17	089	66703	Kane County	32,431
17		68003	Schaumburg village	74,227
17	031	68003	Cook County	74,227
17	043	68003	DuPage County	0
17		70122	Skokie village	64,784
17	031	70122	Cook County	64,784
17		72000	Springfield city	116,250
17	167	72000	Sangamon County	116,250
17		73157	Streamwood village	39,858
17	031	73157	Cook County	39,858
17		75484	Tinley Park village	56,703
17	031	75484	Cook County	49,236
17	197	75484	Will County	7,467
17		77005	Urbana city	41,250
17	019	77005	Champaign County	41,250
17		77694	Vernon Hills village	25,113
17	097	77694	Lake County	25,113
17		79293	Waukegan city	89,078
17	097	79293	Lake County	89,078
17		80060	West Chicago city	27,086
17	043	80060	DuPage County	27,086
17		81048	Wheaton city	52,894
17	043	81048	DuPage County	52,894
17		81087	Wheeling village	37,648
17	031	81087	Cook County	37,642
17	097	81087	Lake County	6
17		82075	Wilmette village	27,087
17	031	82075	Cook County	27,087
17		83245	Woodridge village	32,971
17	031	83245	Cook County	0
17	043	83245	DuPage County	32,949
17	197	83245	Will County	22
18			**INDIANA**	6,483,802
18		01468	Anderson city	56,129
18	095	01468	Madison County	56,129
18		05860	Bloomington city	80,405
18	105	05860	Monroe County	80,405
18		10342	Carmel city	79,191
18	057	10342	Hamilton County	79,191
18		14734	Columbus city	44,061
18	005	14734	Bartholomew County	44,061
18		16138	Crown Point city	27,317
18	089	16138	Lake County	27,317

State code	Place code	County code	Geographic Area Name	2010 census population		State code	Place code	County code	Geographic Area Name	2010 census population
18		19486	East Chicago city	29,698		19			**IOWA**	3,046,355
18	089	19486	Lake County	29,698						
						19		01855	Ames city	58,965
18		20728	Elkhart city	50,949		19	169	01855	Story County	58,965
18	039	20728	Elkhart County	50,949						
						19		02305	Ankeny city	45,582
18		22000	Evansville city	117,429		19	153	02305	Polk County	45,582
18	163	22000	Vanderburgh County	117,429						
						19		06355	Bettendorf city	33,217
18		23278	Fishers town	76,794		19	163	06355	Scott County	33,217
18	057	23278	Hamilton County	76,794						
						19		09550	Burlington city	25,663
18		25000	Fort Wayne city	253,691		19	057	09550	Des Moines County	25,663
18	003	25000	Allen County	253,691						
						19		11755	Cedar Falls city	39,260
18		27000	Gary city	80,294		19	013	11755	Black Hawk County	39,260
18	089	27000	Lake County	80,294						
						19		12000	Cedar Rapids city	126,326
18		28386	Goshen city	31,719		19	113	12000	Linn County	126,326
18	039	28386	Elkhart County	31,719						
						19		14430	Clinton city	26,885
18		29898	Greenwood city	49,791		19	045	14430	Clinton County	26,885
18	081	29898	Johnson County	49,791						
						19		16860	Council Bluffs city	62,230
18		31000	Hammond city	80,830		19	155	16860	Pottawattamie County	62,230
18	089	31000	Lake County	80,830						
						19		19000	Davenport city	99,685
18		34114	Hobart city	29,059		19	163	19000	Scott County	99,685
18	089	34114	Lake County	29,059						
						19		21000	Des Moines city	203,433
18		38358	Jeffersonville city	44,953		19	153	21000	Polk County	203,419
18	019	38358	Clark County	44,953		19	181	21000	Warren County	14
						19		22395	Dubuque city	57,637
18		40392	Kokomo city	45,468		19	061	22395	Dubuque County	57,637
18	067	40392	Howard County	45,468						
						19		28515	Fort Dodge city	25,206
18		40788	Lafayette city	67,140		19	187	28515	Webster County	25,206
18	157	40788	Tippecanoe County	67,140						
						19		38595	Iowa City city	67,862
18		42426	Lawrence city	46,001		19	103	38595	Johnson County	67,862
18	097	42426	Marion County	46,001						
						19		49485	Marion city	34,768
18		46908	Marion city	29,948		19	113	49485	Linn County	34,768
18	053	46908	Grant County	29,948						
						19		49755	Marshalltown city	27,552
18		48528	Merrillville town	35,246		19	127	49755	Marshall County	27,552
18	089	48528	Lake County	35,246						
						19		50160	Mason City city	28,079
18		48798	Michigan City city	31,479		19	033	50160	Cerro Gordo County	28,079
18	091	48798	LaPorte County	31,479						
						19		60465	Ottumwa city	25,023
18		49932	Mishawaka city	48,252		19	179	60465	Wapello County	25,023
18	141	49932	St. Joseph County	48,252						
						19		73335	Sioux City city	82,684
18		51876	Muncie city	70,085		19	149	73335	Plymouth County	6
18	035	51876	Delaware County	70,085		19	193	73335	Woodbury County	82,678
						19		79950	Urbandale city	39,463
18		52326	New Albany city	36,372		19	049	79950	Dallas County	6,337
18	043	52326	Floyd County	36,372		19	153	79950	Polk County	33,126
						19		82425	Waterloo city	68,406
18		54180	Noblesville city	51,969		19	013	82425	Black Hawk County	68,406
18	057	54180	Hamilton County	51,969						
						19		83910	West Des Moines city	56,609
18		60246	Plainfield town	27,631		19	049	83910	Dallas County	11,569
18	063	60246	Hendricks County	27,631		19	153	83910	Polk County	44,999
						19	181	83910	Warren County	41
18		61092	Portage city	36,828						
18	127	61092	Porter County	36,828		20			**KANSAS**	2,853,118
18		64260	Richmond city	36,812						
18	177	64260	Wayne County	36,812		20		18250	Dodge City city	27,340
						20	057	18250	Ford County	27,340
18		68220	Schererville town	29,243						
18	089	68220	Lake County	29,243		20		25325	Garden City city	26,658
						20	055	25325	Finney County	26,658
18		71000	South Bend city	101,168						
18	141	71000	St. Joseph County	101,168		20		33625	Hutchinson city	42,080
						20	155	33625	Reno County	42,080
18		75428	Terre Haute city	60,785						
18	167	75428	Vigo County	60,785		20		36000	Kansas City city	145,786
						20	209	36000	Wyandotte County	145,786
18		78326	Valparaiso city	31,730						
18	127	78326	Porter County	31,730		20		38900	Lawrence city	87,643
						20	045	38900	Douglas County	87,643
18		82700	Westfield town	30,068						
18	057	82700	Hamilton County	30,068		20		39000	Leavenworth city	35,251
						20	103	39000	Leavenworth County	35,251
18		82862	West Lafayette city	29,596						
18	157	82862	Tippecanoe County	29,596						

State code	Place code	County code	Geographic Area Name	2010 census population
20		39075	Leawood city	31,867
20	091	39075	Johnson County	31,867
20		39350	Lenexa city	48,190
20	091	39350	Johnson County	48,190
20		44250	Manhattan city	52,281
20	149	44250	Pottawatomie County	146
20	161	44250	Riley County	52,135
20		52575	Olathe city	125,872
20	091	52575	Johnson County	125,872
20		53775	Overland Park city	173,372
20	091	53775	Johnson County	173,372
20		62700	Salina city	47,707
20	169	62700	Saline County	47,707
20		64500	Shawnee city	62,209
20	091	64500	Johnson County	62,209
20		71000	Topeka city	127,473
20	177	71000	Shawnee County	127,473
20		79000	Wichita city	382,368
20	173	79000	Sedgwick County	382,368
21			**KENTUCKY**	4,339,367
21		08902	Bowling Green city	58,067
21	227	08902	Warren County	58,067
21		17848	Covington city	40,640
21	117	17848	Kenton County	40,640
21		24274	Elizabethtown city	28,531
21	093	24274	Hardin County	28,531
21		27982	Florence city	29,951
21	015	27982	Boone County	29,951
21		28900	Frankfort city	25,527
21	073	28900	Franklin County	25,527
21		30700	Georgetown city	29,098
21	209	30700	Scott County	29,098
21		35866	Henderson city	28,757
21	101	35866	Henderson County	28,757
21		37918	Hopkinsville city	31,577
21	047	37918	Christian County	31,577
21		40222	Jeffersontown city	26,595
21	111	40222	Jefferson County	26,595
21		46027	Lexington-Fayette urban county	295,803
21	067	46027	Fayette County	295,803
21		56136	Nicholasville city	28,015
21	113	56136	Jessamine County	28,015
21		58620	Owensboro city	57,265
21	059	58620	Daviess County	57,265
21		58836	Paducah city	25,024
21	145	58836	McCracken County	25,024
21		65226	Richmond city	31,364
21	151	65226	Madison County	31,364
22			**LOUISIANA**	4,533,372
22		00975	Alexandria city	47,723
22	079	00975	Rapides Parish	47,723
22		05000	Baton Rouge city	229,493
22	033	05000	East Baton Rouge Parish	229,493
22		08920	Bossier City city	61,315
22	015	08920	Bossier Parish	61,315
22		13960	Central city	26,864
22	033	13960	East Baton Rouge Parish	26,864
22		36255	Houma city	33,727
22	109	36255	Terrebonne Parish	33,727
22		39475	Kenner city	66,702
22	051	39475	Jefferson Parish	66,702
22		40735	Lafayette city	120,623
22	055	40735	Lafayette Parish	120,623
22		41155	Lake Charles city	71,993
22	019	41155	Calcasieu Parish	71,993
22		51410	Monroe city	48,815
22	073	51410	Ouachita Parish	48,815
22		54035	New Iberia city	30,617
22	045	54035	Iberia Parish	30,617
22		55000	New Orleans city	343,829
22	071	55000	Orleans Parish	343,829
22		70000	Shreveport city	199,311
22	015	70000	Bossier Parish	2,702
22	017	70000	Caddo Parish	196,609
22		70805	Slidell city	27,068
22	103	70805	St. Tammany Parish	27,068
23			**MAINE**	1,328,361
23		02795	Bangor city	33,039
23	019	02795	Penobscot County	33,039
23		38740	Lewiston city	36,592
23	001	38740	Androscoggin County	36,592
23		60545	Portland city	66,194
23	005	60545	Cumberland County	66,194
23		71990	South Portland city	25,002
23	005	71990	Cumberland County	25,002
24			**MARYLAND**	5,773,552
24		01600	Annapolis city	38,394
24	003	01600	Anne Arundel County	38,394
24		04000	Baltimore city	620,961
24	510	04000	Baltimore city	620,961
24		08775	Bowie city	54,727
24	033	08775	Prince George's County	54,727
24		18750	College Park city	30,413
24	033	18750	Prince George's County	30,413
24		30325	Frederick city	65,239
24	021	30325	Frederick County	65,239
24		31175	Gaithersburg city	59,933
24	031	31175	Montgomery County	59,933
24		36075	Hagerstown city	39,662
24	043	36075	Washington County	39,662
24		45900	Laurel city	25,115
24	033	45900	Prince George's County	25,115
24		67675	Rockville city	61,209
24	031	67675	Montgomery County	61,209
24		69925	Salisbury city	30,343
24	045	69925	Wicomico County	30,343
25			**MASSACHUSETTS**	6,547,629
25		00840	Agawam Town city	28,438
25	013	00840	Hampden County	28,438
25		02690	Attleboro city	43,593
25	005	02690	Bristol County	43,593
25		03690	Barnstable Town city	45,193
25	001	03690	Barnstable County	45,193
25		05595	Beverly city	39,502
25	009	05595	Essex County	39,502
25		07000	Boston city	617,594
25	025	07000	Suffolk County	617,594
25		07740	Braintree Town city	35,744
25	021	07740	Norfolk County	35,744

State code	Place code	County code	Geographic Area Name	2010 census population
25		09000	Brockton city	93,810
25	023	09000	Plymouth County	93,810
25		11000	Cambridge city	105,162
25	017	11000	Middlesex County	105,162
25		13205	Chelsea city	35,177
25	025	13205	Suffolk County	35,177
25		13660	Chicopee city	55,298
25	013	13660	Hampden County	55,298
25		21990	Everett city	41,667
25	017	21990	Middlesex County	41,667
25		23000	Fall River city	88,857
25	005	23000	Bristol County	88,857
25		23875	Fitchburg city	40,318
25	027	23875	Worcester County	40,318
25		25172	Franklin Town city	31,635
25	021	25172	Norfolk County	31,635
25		26150	Gloucester city	28,789
25	009	26150	Essex County	28,789
25		29405	Haverhill city	60,879
25	009	29405	Essex County	60,879
25		30840	Holyoke city	39,880
25	013	30840	Hampden County	39,880
25		34550	Lawrence city	76,377
25	009	34550	Essex County	76,377
25		35075	Leominster city	40,759
25	027	35075	Worcester County	40,759
25		37000	Lowell city	106,519
25	017	37000	Middlesex County	106,519
25		37490	Lynn city	90,329
25	009	37490	Essex County	90,329
25		37875	Malden city	59,450
25	017	37875	Middlesex County	59,450
25		38715	Marlborough city	38,499
25	017	38715	Middlesex County	38,499
25		39835	Medford city	56,173
25	017	39835	Middlesex County	56,173
25		40115	Melrose city	26,983
25	017	40115	Middlesex County	26,983
25		40710	Methuen Town city	47,255
25	009	40710	Essex County	47,255
25		45000	New Bedford city	95,072
25	005	45000	Bristol County	95,072
25		45560	Newton city	85,146
25	017	45560	Middlesex County	85,146
25		46330	Northampton city	28,549
25	015	46330	Hampshire County	28,549
25		52490	Peabody city	51,251
25	009	52490	Essex County	51,251
25		53960	Pittsfield city	44,737
25	003	53960	Berkshire County	44,737
25		55745	Quincy city	92,271
25	021	55745	Norfolk County	92,271
25		56585	Revere city	51,755
25	025	56585	Suffolk County	51,755
25		59105	Salem city	41,340
25	009	59105	Essex County	41,340
25		62535	Somerville city	75,754
25	017	62535	Middlesex County	75,754
25		67000	Springfield city	153,060
25	013	67000	Hampden County	153,060
25		69170	Taunton city	55,874
25	005	69170	Bristol County	55,874
25		72600	Waltham city	60,632
25	017	72600	Middlesex County	60,632
25		73440	Watertown Town city	31,915
25	017	73440	Middlesex County	31,915
25		76030	Westfield city	41,094
25	013	76030	Hampden County	41,094
25		77890	West Springfield Town city	28,391
25	013	77890	Hampden County	28,391
25		78972	Weymouth Town city	53,743
25	021	78972	Norfolk County	53,743
25		81035	Woburn city	38,120
25	017	81035	Middlesex County	38,120
25		82000	Worcester city	181,045
25	027	82000	Worcester County	181,045
26			**MICHIGAN**	9,883,640
26		01380	Allen Park city	28,210
26	163	01380	Wayne County	28,210
26		03000	Ann Arbor city	113,934
26	161	03000	Washtenaw County	113,934
26		05920	Battle Creek city	52,347
26	025	05920	Calhoun County	52,347
26		06020	Bay City city	34,932
26	017	06020	Bay County	34,932
26		12060	Burton city	29,999
26	049	12060	Genesee County	29,999
26		21000	Dearborn city	98,153
26	163	21000	Wayne County	98,153
26		21020	Dearborn Heights city	57,774
26	163	21020	Wayne County	57,774
26		22000	Detroit city	713,777
26	163	22000	Wayne County	713,777
26		24120	East Lansing city	48,579
26	037	24120	Clinton County	1,969
26	065	24120	Ingham County	46,610
26		24290	Eastpointe city	32,442
26	099	24290	Macomb County	32,442
26		27440	Farmington Hills city	79,740
26	125	27440	Oakland County	79,740
26		29000	Flint city	102,434
26	049	29000	Genesee County	102,434
26		31420	Garden City city	27,692
26	163	31420	Wayne County	27,692
26		34000	Grand Rapids city	188,040
26	081	34000	Kent County	188,040
26		38640	Holland city	33,051
26	005	38640	Allegan County	7,016
26	139	38640	Ottawa County	26,035
26		40680	Inkster city	25,369
26	163	40680	Wayne County	25,369
26		41420	Jackson city	33,534
26	075	41420	Jackson County	33,534
26		42160	Kalamazoo city	74,262
26	077	42160	Kalamazoo County	74,262
26		42820	Kentwood city	48,707
26	081	42820	Kent County	48,707
26		46000	Lansing city	114,297
26	045	46000	Eaton County	4,734
26	065	46000	Ingham County	109,563

State code	Place code	County code	Geographic Area Name	2010 census population
26		47800	Lincoln Park city	38,144
26	163	47800	Wayne County	38,144
26		49000	Livonia city	96,942
26	163	49000	Wayne County	96,942
26		50560	Madison Heights city	29,694
26	125	50560	Oakland County	29,694
26		53780	Midland city	41,863
26	017	53780	Bay County	157
26	111	53780	Midland County	41,706
26		56020	Mount Pleasant city	26,016
26	073	56020	Isabella County	26,016
26		56320	Muskegon city	38,401
26	121	56320	Muskegon County	38,401
26		59440	Novi city	55,224
26	125	59440	Oakland County	55,224
26		59920	Oak Park city	29,319
26	125	59920	Oakland County	29,319
26		65440	Pontiac city	59,515
26	125	65440	Oakland County	59,515
26		65560	Portage city	46,292
26	077	65560	Kalamazoo County	46,292
26		65820	Port Huron city	30,184
26	147	65820	St. Clair County	30,184
26		69035	Rochester Hills city	70,995
26	125	69035	Oakland County	70,995
26		69800	Roseville city	47,299
26	099	69800	Macomb County	47,299
26		70040	Royal Oak city	57,236
26	125	70040	Oakland County	57,236
26		70520	Saginaw city	51,508
26	145	70520	Saginaw County	51,508
26		70760	St. Clair Shores city	59,715
26	099	70760	Macomb County	59,715
26		74900	Southfield city	71,739
26	125	74900	Oakland County	71,739
26		74960	Southgate city	30,047
26	163	74960	Wayne County	30,047
26		76460	Sterling Heights city	129,699
26	099	76460	Macomb County	129,699
26		79000	Taylor city	63,131
26	163	79000	Wayne County	63,131
26		80700	Troy city	80,980
26	125	80700	Oakland County	80,980
26		84000	Warren city	134,056
26	099	84000	Macomb County	134,056
26		86000	Westland city	84,094
26	163	86000	Wayne County	84,094
26		88900	Wyandotte city	25,883
26	163	88900	Wayne County	25,883
26		88940	Wyoming city	72,125
26	081	88940	Kent County	72,125
27			**MINNESOTA**	5,303,925
27		01486	Andover city	30,598
27	003	01486	Anoka County	30,598
27		01900	Apple Valley city	49,084
27	037	01900	Dakota County	49,084
27		06382	Blaine city	57,186
27	003	06382	Anoka County	57,186
27	123	06382	Ramsey County	0
27		06616	Bloomington city	82,893
27	053	06616	Hennepin County	82,893

State code	Place code	County code	Geographic Area Name	2010 census population
27		07948	Brooklyn Center city	30,104
27	053	07948	Hennepin County	30,104
27		07966	Brooklyn Park city	75,781
27	053	07966	Hennepin County	75,781
27		08794	Burnsville city	60,306
27	037	08794	Dakota County	60,306
27		13114	Coon Rapids city	61,476
27	003	13114	Anoka County	61,476
27		13456	Cottage Grove city	34,589
27	163	13456	Washington County	34,589
27		17000	Duluth city	86,265
27	137	17000	St. Louis County	86,265
27		17288	Eagan city	64,206
27	037	17288	Dakota County	64,206
27		18116	Eden Prairie city	60,797
27	053	18116	Hennepin County	60,797
27		18188	Edina city	47,941
27	053	18188	Hennepin County	47,941
27		22814	Fridley city	27,208
27	003	22814	Anoka County	27,208
27		31076	Inver Grove Heights city	33,880
27	037	31076	Dakota County	33,880
27		35180	Lakeville city	55,954
27	037	35180	Dakota County	55,954
27		39878	Mankato city	39,309
27	013	39878	Blue Earth County	39,305
27	079	39878	Le Sueur County	4
27	103	39878	Nicollet County	0
27		40166	Maple Grove city	61,567
27	053	40166	Hennepin County	61,567
27		40382	Maplewood city	38,018
27	123	40382	Ramsey County	38,018
27		43000	Minneapolis city	382,578
27	053	43000	Hennepin County	382,578
27		43252	Minnetonka city	49,734
27	053	43252	Hennepin County	49,734
27		43864	Moorhead city	38,065
27	027	43864	Clay County	38,065
27		47680	Oakdale city	27,378
27	163	47680	Washington County	27,378
27		49300	Owatonna city	25,599
27	147	49300	Steele County	25,599
27		51730	Plymouth city	70,576
27	053	51730	Hennepin County	70,576
27		54214	Richfield city	35,228
27	053	54214	Hennepin County	35,228
27		54880	Rochester city	106,769
27	109	54880	Olmsted County	106,769
27		55852	Roseville city	33,660
27	123	55852	Ramsey County	33,660
27		56896	St. Cloud city	65,842
27	009	56896	Benton County	6,396
27	141	56896	Sherburne County	6,785
27	145	56896	Stearns County	52,661
27		57220	St. Louis Park city	45,250
27	053	57220	Hennepin County	45,250
27		58000	St. Paul city	285,068
27	123	58000	Ramsey County	285,068
27		58738	Savage city	26,911
27	139	58738	Scott County	26,911
27		59350	Shakopee city	37,076
27	139	59350	Scott County	37,076

State code	Place code	County code	Geographic Area Name	2010 census population
27		59998	Shoreview city	25,043
27	123	59998	Ramsey County	25,043
27		71032	Winona city	27,592
27	169	71032	Winona County	27,592
27		71428	Woodbury city	61,961
27	163	71428	Washington County	61,961
28			**MISSISSIPPI**	2,967,297
28		06220	Biloxi city	44,054
28	047	06220	Harrison County	44,054
28		14420	Clinton city	25,216
28	049	14420	Hinds County	25,216
28		29180	Greenville city	34,400
28	151	29180	Washington County	34,400
28		29700	Gulfport city	67,793
28	047	29700	Harrison County	67,793
28		31020	Hattiesburg city	45,989
28	035	31020	Forrest County	41,000
28	073	31020	Lamar County	4,989
28		33700	Horn Lake city	26,066
28	033	33700	DeSoto County	26,066
28		36000	Jackson city	173,514
28	049	36000	Hinds County	172,891
28	089	36000	Madison County	622
28	121	36000	Rankin County	1
28		46640	Meridian city	41,148
28	075	46640	Lauderdale County	41,148
28		54040	Olive Branch city	33,484
28	033	54040	DeSoto County	33,484
28		55760	Pearl city	25,092
28	121	55760	Rankin County	25,092
28		69280	Southaven city	48,982
28	033	69280	DeSoto County	48,982
28		74840	Tupelo city	34,546
28	081	74840	Lee County	34,546
29			**MISSOURI**	5,988,927
29		03160	Ballwin city	30,404
29	189	03160	St. Louis County	30,404
29		06652	Blue Springs city	52,575
29	095	06652	Jackson County	52,575
29		11242	Cape Girardeau city	37,941
29	031	11242	Cape Girardeau County	37,941
29	201	11242	Scott County	0
29		13600	Chesterfield city	47,484
29	189	13600	St. Louis County	47,484
29		15670	Columbia city	108,500
29	019	15670	Boone County	108,500
29		24778	Florissant city	52,158
29	189	24778	St. Louis County	52,158
29		27190	Gladstone city	25,410
29	047	27190	Clay County	25,410
29		31276	Hazelwood city	25,703
29	189	31276	St. Louis County	25,703
29		35000	Independence city	116,830
29	047	35000	Clay County	0
29	095	35000	Jackson County	116,830
29		37000	Jefferson City city	43,079
29	027	37000	Callaway County	22
29	051	37000	Cole County	43,057
29		37592	Joplin city	50,150
29	097	37592	Jasper County	43,955
29	145	37592	Newton County	6,195
29		38000	Kansas City city	459,787
29	037	38000	Cass County	197
29	047	38000	Clay County	113,415
29	095	38000	Jackson County	302,499
29	165	38000	Platte County	43,676
29		39044	Kirkwood city	27,540
29	189	39044	St. Louis County	27,540
29		41348	Lee's Summit city	91,364
29	037	41348	Cass County	1,917
29	095	41348	Jackson County	89,447
29		42032	Liberty city	29,149
29	047	42032	Clay County	29,149
29		46586	Maryland Heights city	27,472
29	189	46586	St. Louis County	27,472
29		54074	O'Fallon city	79,329
29	183	54074	St. Charles County	79,329
29		60788	Raytown city	29,526
29	095	60788	Jackson County	29,526
29		64082	St. Charles city	65,794
29	183	64082	St. Charles County	65,794
29		64550	St. Joseph city	76,780
29	021	64550	Buchanan County	76,780
29		65000	St. Louis city	319,294
29	510	65000	St. Louis city	319,294
29		65126	St. Peters city	52,575
29	183	65126	St. Charles County	52,575
29		70000	Springfield city	159,498
29	043	70000	Christian County	2
29	077	70000	Greene County	159,496
29		75220	University City city	35,371
29	189	75220	St. Louis County	35,371
29		78442	Wentzville city	29,070
29	183	78442	St. Charles County	29,070
29		79820	Wildwood city	35,517
29	189	79820	St. Louis County	35,517
30			**MONTANA**	989,415
30		06550	Billings city	104,170
30	111	06550	Yellowstone County	104,170
30		08950	Bozeman city	37,280
30	031	08950	Gallatin County	37,280
30		32800	Great Falls city	58,505
30	013	32800	Cascade County	58,505
30		35600	Helena city	28,190
30	049	35600	Lewis and Clark County	28,190
30		50200	Missoula city	66,788
30	063	50200	Missoula County	66,788
31			**NEBRASKA**	1,826,341
31		03950	Bellevue city	50,137
31	153	03950	Sarpy County	50,137
31		17670	Fremont city	26,397
31	053	17670	Dodge County	26,397
31		19595	Grand Island city	48,520
31	079	19595	Hall County	48,520
31		25055	Kearney city	30,787
31	019	25055	Buffalo County	30,787
31		28000	Lincoln city	258,379
31	109	28000	Lancaster County	258,379
31		37000	Omaha city	408,958
31	055	37000	Douglas County	408,958

State code	Place code	County code	Geographic Area Name	2010 census population
32			**NEVADA**	2,700,551
32		09700	Carson City	55,274
32	510	09700	Carson City	55,274
32		31900	Henderson city	257,729
32	003	31900	Clark County	257,729
32		40000	Las Vegas city	583,756
32	003	40000	Clark County	583,756
32		51800	North Las Vegas city	216,961
32	003	51800	Clark County	216,961
32		60600	Reno city	225,221
32	031	60600	Washoe County	225,221
32		68400	Sparks city	90,264
32	031	68400	Washoe County	90,264
33			**NEW HAMPSHIRE**	1,316,470
33		14200	Concord city	42,695
33	013	14200	Merrimack County	42,695
33		18820	Dover city	29,987
33	017	18820	Strafford County	29,987
33		45140	Manchester city	109,565
33	011	45140	Hillsborough County	109,565
33		50260	Nashua city	86,494
33	011	50260	Hillsborough County	86,494
33		65140	Rochester city	29,752
33	017	65140	Strafford County	29,752
34			**NEW JERSEY**	8,791,894
34		02080	Atlantic City city	39,558
34	001	02080	Atlantic County	39,558
34		03580	Bayonne city	63,024
34	017	03580	Hudson County	63,024
34		05170	Bergenfield borough	26,764
34	003	05170	Bergen County	26,764
34		07600	Bridgeton city	25,349
34	011	07600	Cumberland County	25,349
34		10000	Camden city	77,344
34	007	10000	Camden County	77,344
34		13690	Clifton city	84,136
34	031	13690	Passaic County	84,136
34		19390	East Orange city	64,270
34	013	19390	Essex County	64,270
34		21000	Elizabeth city	124,969
34	039	21000	Union County	124,969
34		21480	Englewood city	27,147
34	003	21480	Bergen County	27,147
34		22470	Fair Lawn borough	32,457
34	003	22470	Bergen County	32,457
34		24420	Fort Lee borough	35,345
34	003	24420	Bergen County	35,345
34		25770	Garfield city	30,487
34	003	25770	Bergen County	30,487
34		28680	Hackensack city	43,010
34	003	28680	Bergen County	43,010
34		32250	Hoboken city	50,005
34	017	32250	Hudson County	50,005
34		36000	Jersey City city	247,597
34	017	36000	Hudson County	247,597
34		36510	Kearny town	40,684
34	017	36510	Hudson County	40,684

State code	Place code	County code	Geographic Area Name	2010 census population
34		40350	Linden city	40,499
34	039	40350	Union County	40,499
34		41310	Long Branch city	30,719
34	025	41310	Monmouth County	30,719
34		46680	Millville city	28,400
34	011	46680	Cumberland County	28,400
34		51000	Newark city	277,140
34	013	51000	Essex County	277,140
34		51210	New Brunswick city	55,181
34	023	51210	Middlesex County	55,181
34		55950	Paramus borough	26,342
34	003	55950	Bergen County	26,342
34		56550	Passaic city	69,781
34	031	56550	Passaic County	69,781
34		57000	Paterson city	146,199
34	031	57000	Passaic County	146,199
34		58200	Perth Amboy city	50,814
34	023	58200	Middlesex County	50,814
34		59190	Plainfield city	49,808
34	039	59190	Union County	49,808
34		61530	Rahway city	27,346
34	039	61530	Union County	27,346
34		65790	Sayreville borough	42,704
34	023	65790	Middlesex County	42,704
34		74000	Trenton city	84,913
34	021	74000	Mercer County	84,913
34		74630	Union City city	66,455
34	017	74630	Hudson County	66,455
34		76070	Vineland city	60,724
34	011	76070	Cumberland County	60,724
34		79040	Westfield town	30,316
34	039	79040	Union County	30,316
34		79610	West New York town	49,708
34	017	79610	Hudson County	49,708
35			**NEW MEXICO**	2,059,179
35		01780	Alamogordo city	30,403
35	035	01780	Otero County	30,403
35		02000	Albuquerque city	545,852
35	001	02000	Bernalillo County	545,852
35		12150	Carlsbad city	26,138
35	015	12150	Eddy County	26,138
35		16420	Clovis city	37,775
35	009	16420	Curry County	37,775
35		25800	Farmington city	45,877
35	045	25800	San Juan County	45,877
35		32520	Hobbs city	34,122
35	025	32520	Lea County	34,122
35		39380	Las Cruces city	97,618
35	013	39380	Doña Ana County	97,618
35		63460	Rio Rancho city	87,521
35	001	63460	Bernalillo County	130
35	043	63460	Sandoval County	87,391
35		64930	Roswell city	48,366
35	005	64930	Chaves County	48,366
35		70500	Santa Fe city	67,947
35	049	70500	Santa Fe County	67,947
36			**NEW YORK**	19,378,102
36		01000	Albany city	97,856
36	001	01000	Albany County	97,856

State code	Place code	County code	Geographic Area Name	2010 census population
36		03078	Auburn city	27,687
36	011	03078	Cayuga County	27,687
36		06607	Binghamton city	47,376
36	007	06607	Broome County	47,376
36		11000	Buffalo city	261,310
36	029	11000	Erie County	261,310
36		24229	Elmira city	29,200
36	015	24229	Chemung County	29,200
36		27485	Freeport village	42,860
36	059	27485	Nassau County	42,860
36		29113	Glen Cove city	26,964
36	059	29113	Nassau County	26,964
36		32402	Harrison village	27,472
36	119	32402	Westchester County	27,472
36		33139	Hempstead village	53,891
36	059	33139	Nassau County	53,891
36		38077	Ithaca city	30,014
36	109	38077	Tompkins County	30,014
36		38264	Jamestown city	31,146
36	013	38264	Chautauqua County	31,146
36		42554	Lindenhurst village	27,253
36	103	42554	Suffolk County	27,253
36		43335	Long Beach city	33,275
36	059	43335	Nassau County	33,275
36		47042	Middletown city	28,086
36	071	47042	Orange County	28,086
36		49121	Mount Vernon city	67,292
36	119	49121	Westchester County	67,292
36		50034	Newburgh city	28,866
36	071	50034	Orange County	28,866
36		50617	New Rochelle city	77,062
36	119	50617	Westchester County	77,062
36		51000	New York city	8,175,133
36	005	51000	Bronx County	1,385,108
36	047	51000	Kings County	2,504,700
36	061	51000	New York County	1,585,873
36	081	51000	Queens County	2,230,722
36	085	51000	Richmond County	468,730
36		51055	Niagara Falls city	50,193
36	063	51055	Niagara County	50,193
36		53682	North Tonawanda city	31,568
36	063	53682	Niagara County	31,568
36		55530	Ossining village	25,060
36	119	55530	Westchester County	25,060
36		59223	Port Chester village	28,967
36	119	59223	Westchester County	28,967
36		59641	Poughkeepsie city	32,736
36	027	59641	Dutchess County	32,736
36		63000	Rochester city	210,565
36	055	63000	Monroe County	210,565
36		63418	Rome city	33,725
36	065	63418	Oneida County	33,725
36		65255	Saratoga Springs city	26,586
36	091	65255	Saratoga County	26,586
36		65508	Schenectady city	66,135
36	093	65508	Schenectady County	66,135
36		70420	Spring Valley village	31,347
36	087	70420	Rockland County	31,347
36		73000	Syracuse city	145,170
36	067	73000	Onondaga County	145,170
36		75484	Troy city	50,129
36	083	75484	Rensselaer County	50,129
36		76540	Utica city	62,235
36	065	76540	Oneida County	62,235
36		76705	Valley Stream village	37,511
36	059	76705	Nassau County	37,511
36		78608	Watertown city	27,023
36	045	78608	Jefferson County	27,023
36		81677	White Plains city	56,853
36	119	81677	Westchester County	56,853
37			**NORTH CAROLINA**	9,535,483
37		01520	Apex town	37,476
37	183	01520	Wake County	37,476
37		02080	Asheboro city	25,012
37	151	02080	Randolph County	25,012
37		02140	Asheville city	83,393
37	021	02140	Buncombe County	83,393
37		09060	Burlington city	49,963
37	001	09060	Alamance County	49,308
37	081	09060	Guilford County	655
37		10740	Cary town	135,234
37	037	10740	Chatham County	1,422
37	183	10740	Wake County	133,812
37		11800	Chapel Hill town	57,233
37	063	11800	Durham County	2,836
37	135	11800	Orange County	54,397
37		12000	Charlotte city	731,424
37	119	12000	Mecklenburg County	731,424
37		14100	Concord city	79,066
37	025	14100	Cabarrus County	79,066
37		19000	Durham city	228,330
37	063	19000	Durham County	228,300
37	135	19000	Orange County	30
37	183	19000	Wake County	0
37		22920	Fayetteville city	200,564
37	051	22920	Cumberland County	200,564
37		25480	Garner town	25,745
37	183	25480	Wake County	25,745
37		25580	Gastonia city	71,741
37	071	25580	Gaston County	71,741
37		26880	Goldsboro city	36,437
37	191	26880	Wayne County	36,437
37		28000	Greensboro city	269,666
37	081	28000	Guilford County	269,666
37		28080	Greenville city	84,554
37	147	28080	Pitt County	84,554
37		31060	Hickory city	40,010
37	023	31060	Burke County	66
37	027	31060	Caldwell County	18
37	035	31060	Catawba County	39,926
37		31400	High Point city	104,371
37	057	31400	Davidson County	5,310
37	067	31400	Forsyth County	8
37	081	31400	Guilford County	99,042
37	151	31400	Randolph County	11
37		33120	Huntersville town	46,773
37	119	33120	Mecklenburg County	46,773
37		33560	Indian Trail town	33,518
37	179	33560	Union County	33,518
37		34200	Jacksonville city	70,145
37	133	34200	Onslow County	70,145

State code	Place code	County code	Geographic Area Name	2010 census population
37		35200	Kannapolis city	42,625
37	025	35200	Cabarrus County	33,194
37	159	35200	Rowan County	9,431
37		41960	Matthews town	27,198
37	119	41960	Mecklenburg County	27,198
37		43920	Monroe city	32,797
37	179	43920	Union County	32,797
37		44220	Mooresville town	32,711
37	097	44220	Iredell County	32,711
37		46340	New Bern city	29,524
37	049	46340	Craven County	29,524
37		55000	Raleigh city	403,892
37	063	55000	Durham County	1,067
37	183	55000	Wake County	402,825
37		57500	Rocky Mount city	57,477
37	065	57500	Edgecombe County	17,524
37	127	57500	Nash County	39,953
37		58860	Salisbury city	33,662
37	159	58860	Rowan County	33,662
37		59280	Sanford city	28,094
37	105	59280	Lee County	28,094
37		67420	Thomasville city	26,757
37	057	67420	Davidson County	26,493
37	151	67420	Randolph County	264
37		70540	Wake Forest town	30,117
37	069	70540	Franklin County	899
37	183	70540	Wake County	29,218
37		74440	Wilmington city	106,476
37	129	74440	New Hanover County	106,476
37		74540	Wilson city	49,167
37	195	74540	Wilson County	49,167
37		75000	Winston-Salem city	229,617
37	067	75000	Forsyth County	229,617
38			**NORTH DAKOTA**	672,591
38		07200	Bismarck city	61,272
38	015	07200	Burleigh County	61,272
38		25700	Fargo city	105,549
38	017	25700	Cass County	105,549
38		32060	Grand Forks city	52,838
38	035	32060	Grand Forks County	52,838
38		53380	Minot city	40,888
38	101	53380	Ward County	40,888
38		84780	West Fargo city	25,830
38	017	84780	Cass County	25,830
39			**OHIO**	11,536,504
39		01000	Akron city	199,110
39	153	01000	Summit County	199,110
39		03828	Barberton city	26,550
39	153	03828	Summit County	26,550
39		04720	Beavercreek city	45,193
39	057	04720	Greene County	45,193
39		07972	Bowling Green city	30,028
39	173	07972	Wood County	30,028
39		09680	Brunswick city	34,255
39	103	09680	Medina County	34,255
39		12000	Canton city	73,007
39	151	12000	Stark County	73,007
39		15000	Cincinnati city	296,943
39	061	15000	Hamilton County	296,943
39		16000	Cleveland city	396,815
39	035	16000	Cuyahoga County	396,815
39		16014	Cleveland Heights city	46,121
39	035	16014	Cuyahoga County	46,121
39		18000	Columbus city	787,033
39	041	18000	Delaware County	7,245
39	045	18000	Fairfield County	9,666
39	049	18000	Franklin County	770,122
39		19778	Cuyahoga Falls city	49,652
39	153	19778	Summit County	49,652
39		21000	Dayton city	141,527
39	113	21000	Montgomery County	141,527
39		21434	Delaware city	34,753
39	041	21434	Delaware County	34,753
39		22694	Dublin city	41,751
39	041	22694	Delaware County	4,018
39	049	22694	Franklin County	35,367
39	159	22694	Union County	2,366
39		25256	Elyria city	54,533
39	093	25256	Lorain County	54,533
39		25704	Euclid city	48,920
39	035	25704	Cuyahoga County	48,920
39		25914	Fairborn city	32,352
39	057	25914	Greene County	32,352
39		25970	Fairfield city	42,510
39	017	25970	Butler County	42,510
39	061	25970	Hamilton County	0
39		27048	Findlay city	41,202
39	063	27048	Hancock County	41,202
39		29106	Gahanna city	33,248
39	049	29106	Franklin County	33,248
39		29428	Garfield Heights city	28,849
39	035	29428	Cuyahoga County	28,849
39		31860	Green city	25,699
39	153	31860	Summit County	25,699
39		32592	Grove City city	35,575
39	049	32592	Franklin County	35,575
39		33012	Hamilton city	62,477
39	017	33012	Butler County	62,477
39		35476	Hilliard city	28,435
39	049	35476	Franklin County	28,435
39		36610	Huber Heights city	38,101
39	057	36610	Greene County	0
39	109	36610	Miami County	959
39	113	36610	Montgomery County	37,142
39		39872	Kent city	28,904
39	133	39872	Portage County	28,904
39		40040	Kettering city	56,163
39	057	40040	Greene County	467
39	113	40040	Montgomery County	55,696
39		41664	Lakewood city	52,131
39	035	41664	Cuyahoga County	52,131
39		41720	Lancaster city	38,780
39	045	41720	Fairfield County	38,780
39		43554	Lima city	38,771
39	003	43554	Allen County	38,771
39		44856	Lorain city	64,097
39	093	44856	Lorain County	64,097
39		47138	Mansfield city	47,821
39	139	47138	Richland County	47,821
39		47754	Marion city	36,837
39	101	47754	Marion County	36,837
39		48188	Mason city	30,712
39	165	48188	Warren County	30,712

State code	Place code	County code	Geographic Area Name	2010 census population
39		48244	Massillon city	32,149
39	151	48244	Stark County	32,149
39		48790	Medina city	26,678
39	103	48790	Medina County	26,678
39		49056	Mentor city	47,159
39	085	49056	Lake County	47,159
39		49840	Middletown city	48,694
39	017	49840	Butler County	45,994
39	165	49840	Warren County	2,700
39		54040	Newark city	47,573
39	089	54040	Licking County	47,573
39		56882	North Olmsted city	32,718
39	035	56882	Cuyahoga County	32,718
39		56966	North Ridgeville city	29,465
39	093	56966	Lorain County	29,465
39		57008	North Royalton city	30,444
39	035	57008	Cuyahoga County	30,444
39		61000	Parma city	81,601
39	035	61000	Cuyahoga County	81,601
39		66390	Reynoldsburg city	35,893
39	045	66390	Fairfield County	910
39	049	66390	Franklin County	26,157
39	089	66390	Licking County	8,826
39		67468	Riverside city	25,201
39	113	67468	Montgomery County	25,201
39		70380	Sandusky city	25,793
39	043	70380	Erie County	25,793
39		71682	Shaker Heights city	28,448
39	035	71682	Cuyahoga County	28,448
39		74118	Springfield city	60,608
39	023	74118	Clark County	60,608
39		74944	Stow city	34,837
39	153	74944	Summit County	34,837
39		75098	Strongsville city	44,750
39	035	75098	Cuyahoga County	44,750
39		77000	Toledo city	287,208
39	095	77000	Lucas County	287,208
39		77588	Troy city	25,058
39	109	77588	Miami County	25,058
39		79002	Upper Arlington city	33,771
39	049	79002	Franklin County	33,771
39		80892	Warren city	41,557
39	155	80892	Trumbull County	41,557
39		83342	Westerville city	36,120
39	041	83342	Delaware County	7,792
39	049	83342	Franklin County	28,328
39		83622	Westlake city	32,729
39	035	83622	Cuyahoga County	32,729
39		86548	Wooster city	26,119
39	169	86548	Wayne County	26,119
39		86772	Xenia city	25,719
39	057	86772	Greene County	25,719
39		88000	Youngstown city	66,982
39	099	88000	Mahoning County	66,971
39	155	88000	Trumbull County	11
39		88084	Zanesville city	25,487
39	119	88084	Muskingum County	25,487
40			**OKLAHOMA**	3,751,351
40		04450	Bartlesville city	35,750
40	113	04450	Osage County	3
40	147	04450	Washington County	35,747
40		09050	Broken Arrow city	98,850
40	143	09050	Tulsa County	80,634
40	145	09050	Wagoner County	18,216
40		23200	Edmond city	81,405
40	109	23200	Oklahoma County	81,405
40		23950	Enid city	49,379
40	047	23950	Garfield County	49,379
40		41850	Lawton city	96,867
40	031	41850	Comanche County	96,867
40		48350	Midwest City city	54,371
40	109	48350	Oklahoma County	54,371
40		49200	Moore city	55,081
40	027	49200	Cleveland County	55,081
40		50050	Muskogee city	39,223
40	101	50050	Muskogee County	39,223
40		52500	Norman city	110,925
40	027	52500	Cleveland County	110,925
40		55000	Oklahoma City city	579,999
40	017	55000	Canadian County	44,541
40	027	55000	Cleveland County	63,723
40	109	55000	Oklahoma County	471,671
40	125	55000	Pottawatomie County	64
40		56650	Owasso city	28,915
40	131	56650	Rogers County	2,614
40	143	56650	Tulsa County	26,301
40		59850	Ponca City city	25,387
40	071	59850	Kay County	25,387
40		66800	Shawnee city	29,857
40	125	66800	Pottawatomie County	29,857
40		70300	Stillwater city	45,688
40	119	70300	Payne County	45,688
40		75000	Tulsa city	391,906
40	113	75000	Osage County	6,136
40	131	75000	Rogers County	0
40	143	75000	Tulsa County	385,613
40	145	75000	Wagoner County	157
41			**OREGON**	3,831,074
41		01000	Albany city	50,158
41	003	01000	Benton County	6,463
41	043	01000	Linn County	43,695
41		05350	Beaverton city	89,803
41	067	05350	Washington County	89,803
41		05800	Bend city	76,639
41	017	05800	Deschutes County	76,639
41		15800	Corvallis city	54,462
41	003	15800	Benton County	54,462
41		23850	Eugene city	156,185
41	039	23850	Lane County	156,185
41		30550	Grants Pass city	34,533
41	033	30550	Josephine County	34,533
41		31250	Gresham city	105,594
41	051	31250	Multnomah County	105,594
41		34100	Hillsboro city	91,611
41	067	34100	Washington County	91,611
41		38500	Keizer city	36,478
41	047	38500	Marion County	36,478
41		40550	Lake Oswego city	36,619
41	005	40550	Clackamas County	34,066
41	051	40550	Multnomah County	2,544
41	067	40550	Washington County	9
41		45000	McMinnville city	32,187
41	071	45000	Yamhill County	32,187

State code	Place code	County code	Geographic Area Name	2010 census population	State code	Place code	County code	Geographic Area Name	2010 census population
41		47000	Medford city	74,907					
41	029	47000	Jackson County	74,907	42		73808	State College borough	42,034
					42	027	73808	Centre County	42,034
41		55200	Oregon City city	31,859					
41	005	55200	Clackamas County	31,859	42		85152	Wilkes-Barre city	41,498
					42	079	85152	Luzerne County	41,498
41		59000	Portland city	583,776					
41	005	59000	Clackamas County	744	42		85312	Williamsport city	29,381
41	051	59000	Multnomah County	581,485	42	081	85312	Lycoming County	29,381
41	067	59000	Washington County	1,547					
					42		87048	York city	43,718
41		61200	Redmond city	26,215	42	133	87048	York County	43,718
41	017	61200	Deschutes County	26,215					
					44			**RHODE ISLAND**	1,052,567
41		64900	Salem city	154,637					
41	047	64900	Marion County	130,398	44		19180	Cranston city	80,387
41	053	64900	Polk County	24,239	44	007	19180	Providence County	80,387
41		69600	Springfield city	59,403	44		22960	East Providence city	47,037
41	039	69600	Lane County	59,403	44	007	22960	Providence County	47,037
41		73650	Tigard city	48,035	44		54640	Pawtucket city	71,148
41	067	73650	Washington County	48,035	44	007	54640	Providence County	71,148
41		74950	Tualatin city	26,054	44		59000	Providence city	178,042
41	005	74950	Clackamas County	2,862	44	007	59000	Providence County	178,042
41	067	74950	Washington County	23,192					
					44		74300	Warwick city	82,672
41		80150	West Linn city	25,109	44	003	74300	Kent County	82,672
41	005	80150	Clackamas County	25,109					
					44		80780	Woonsocket city	41,186
42			**PENNSYLVANIA**	12,702,379	44	007	80780	Providence County	41,186
42		02000	Allentown city	118,032	45			**SOUTH CAROLINA**	4,625,364
42	077	02000	Lehigh County	118,032					
					45		00550	Aiken city	29,524
42		02184	Altoona city	46,320	45	003	00550	Aiken County	29,524
42	013	02184	Blair County	46,320					
					45		01360	Anderson city	26,686
42		06064	Bethel Park municipality	32,313	45	007	01360	Anderson County	26,686
42	003	06064	Allegheny County	32,313					
					45		13330	Charleston city	120,083
42		06088	Bethlehem city	74,982	45	015	13330	Berkeley County	8,095
42	077	06088	Lehigh County	19,343	45	019	13330	Charleston County	111,988
42	095	06088	Northampton County	55,639					
					45		16000	Columbia city	129,272
42		13208	Chester city	33,972	45	063	16000	Lexington County	559
42	045	13208	Delaware County	33,972	45	079	16000	Richland County	128,713
42		21648	Easton city	26,800	45		25810	Florence city	37,056
42	095	21648	Northampton County	26,800	45	041	25810	Florence County	37,056
42		24000	Erie city	101,786	45		29815	Goose Creek city	35,938
42	049	24000	Erie County	101,786	45	015	29815	Berkeley County	35,933
					45	019	29815	Charleston County	5
42		32800	Harrisburg city	49,528					
42	043	32800	Dauphin County	49,528	45		30850	Greenville city	58,409
					45	045	30850	Greenville County	58,409
42		33408	Hazleton city	25,340					
42	079	33408	Luzerne County	25,340	45		30985	Greer city	25,515
					45	045	30985	Greenville County	18,635
42		41216	Lancaster city	59,322	45	083	30985	Spartanburg County	6,880
42	071	41216	Lancaster County	59,322					
					45		34045	Hilton Head Island town	37,099
42		42168	Lebanon city	25,477	45	013	34045	Beaufort County	37,099
42	075	42168	Lebanon County	25,477					
					45		48535	Mount Pleasant town	67,843
42		50528	Monroeville municipality	28,386	45	019	48535	Charleston County	67,843
42	003	50528	Allegheny County	28,386					
					45		49075	Myrtle Beach city	27,109
42		54656	Norristown borough	34,324	45	051	49075	Horry County	27,109
42	091	54656	Montgomery County	34,324					
					45		50875	North Charleston city	97,471
42		60000	Philadelphia city	1,526,006	45	015	50875	Berkeley County	0
42	101	60000	Philadelphia County	1,526,006	45	019	50875	Charleston County	78,393
					45	035	50875	Dorchester County	19,078
42		61000	Pittsburgh city	305,704					
42	003	61000	Allegheny County	305,704	45		61405	Rock Hill city	66,154
					45	091	61405	York County	66,154
42		61536	Plum borough	27,126					
42	003	61536	Allegheny County	27,126	45		68290	Spartanburg city	37,013
					45	083	68290	Spartanburg County	37,013
42		63624	Reading city	88,082					
42	011	63624	Berks County	88,082	45		70270	Summerville town	43,392
					45	015	70270	Berkeley County	3,643
42		69000	Scranton city	76,089	45	019	70270	Charleston County	1,010
42	069	69000	Lackawanna County	76,089	45	035	70270	Dorchester County	38,739

State code	Place code	County code	Geographic Area Name	2010 census population
45		70405	Sumter city	40,524
45	085	70405	Sumter County	40,524
46			**SOUTH DAKOTA**	814,180
46		00100	Aberdeen city	26,091
46	013	00100	Brown County	26,091
46		52980	Rapid City city	67,956
46	103	52980	Pennington County	67,956
46		59020	Sioux Falls city	153,888
46	083	59020	Lincoln County	21,095
46	099	59020	Minnehaha County	132,793
47			**TENNESSEE**	6,346,105
47		03440	Bartlett city	54,613
47	157	03440	Shelby County	54,613
47		08280	Brentwood city	37,060
47	187	08280	Williamson County	37,060
47		08540	Bristol city	26,702
47	163	08540	Sullivan County	26,702
47		14000	Chattanooga city	167,674
47	065	14000	Hamilton County	167,674
47		15160	Clarksville city	132,929
47	125	15160	Montgomery County	132,929
47		15400	Cleveland city	41,285
47	011	15400	Bradley County	41,285
47		16420	Collierville town	43,965
47	047	16420	Fayette County	0
47	157	16420	Shelby County	43,965
47		16540	Columbia city	34,681
47	119	16540	Maury County	34,681
47		16920	Cookeville city	30,435
47	141	16920	Putnam County	30,435
47		27740	Franklin city	62,487
47	187	27740	Williamson County	62,487
47		28540	Gallatin city	30,278
47	165	28540	Sumner County	30,278
47		28960	Germantown city	38,844
47	157	28960	Shelby County	38,844
47		33280	Hendersonville city	51,372
47	165	33280	Sumner County	51,372
47		37640	Jackson city	65,211
47	113	37640	Madison County	65,211
47		38320	Johnson City city	63,152
47	019	38320	Carter County	1,252
47	163	38320	Sullivan County	367
47	179	38320	Washington County	61,533
47		39560	Kingsport city	48,205
47	073	39560	Hawkins County	2,854
47	163	39560	Sullivan County	45,351
47		40000	Knoxville city	178,874
47	093	40000	Knox County	178,874
47		41200	La Vergne city	32,588
47	149	41200	Rutherford County	32,588
47		41520	Lebanon city	26,190
47	189	41520	Wilson County	26,190
47		46380	Maryville city	27,465
47	009	46380	Blount County	27,465
47		48000	Memphis city	646,889
47	157	48000	Shelby County	646,889
47		50280	Morristown city	29,137
47	063	50280	Hamblen County	29,131
47	089	50280	Jefferson County	6
47		51560	Murfreesboro city	108,755
47	149	51560	Rutherford County	108,755
47		55120	Oak Ridge city	29,330
47	001	55120	Anderson County	26,271
47	145	55120	Roane County	3,059
47		69420	Smyrna town	39,974
47	149	69420	Rutherford County	39,974
47		70580	Spring Hill city	29,036
47	119	70580	Maury County	7,023
47	187	70580	Williamson County	22,013
48			**TEXAS**	25,145,561
48		01000	Abilene city	117,063
48	253	01000	Jones County	5,145
48	441	01000	Taylor County	111,918
48		01924	Allen city	84,246
48	085	01924	Collin County	84,246
48		03000	Amarillo city	190,695
48	375	03000	Potter County	105,486
48	381	03000	Randall County	85,209
48		04000	Arlington city	365,438
48	439	04000	Tarrant County	365,438
48		05000	Austin city	790,390
48	209	05000	Hays County	2
48	453	05000	Travis County	754,691
48	491	05000	Williamson County	35,697
48		06128	Baytown city	71,802
48	071	06128	Chambers County	4,116
48	201	06128	Harris County	67,686
48		07000	Beaumont city	118,296
48	245	07000	Jefferson County	118,296
48		07132	Bedford city	46,979
48	439	07132	Tarrant County	46,979
48		08236	Big Spring city	27,282
48	227	08236	Howard County	27,282
48		10768	Brownsville city	175,023
48	061	10768	Cameron County	175,023
48		10912	Bryan city	76,201
48	041	10912	Brazos County	76,201
48		11428	Burleson city	36,690
48	251	11428	Johnson County	29,111
48	439	11428	Tarrant County	7,579
48		13024	Carrollton city	119,097
48	085	13024	Collin County	2
48	113	13024	Dallas County	49,352
48	121	13024	Denton County	69,743
48		13492	Cedar Hill city	45,028
48	113	13492	Dallas County	44,477
48	139	13492	Ellis County	551
48		13552	Cedar Park city	48,937
48	453	13552	Travis County	489
48	491	13552	Williamson County	48,448
48		15364	Cleburne city	29,337
48	251	15364	Johnson County	29,337
48		15976	College Station city	93,857
48	041	15976	Brazos County	93,857
48		16432	Conroe city	56,207
48	339	16432	Montgomery County	56,207
48		16612	Coppell city	38,659
48	113	16612	Dallas County	37,905
48	121	16612	Denton County	754
48		16624	Copperas Cove city	32,032
48	027	16624	Bell County	0
48	099	16624	Coryell County	31,457
48	281	16624	Lampasas County	575

State code	Place code	County code	Geographic Area Name	2010 census population
48		17000	Corpus Christi city	305,215
48	007	17000	Aransas County	0
48	273	17000	Kleberg County	0
48	355	17000	Nueces County	305,215
48	409	17000	San Patricio County	0
48		19000	Dallas city	1,197,816
48	085	19000	Collin County	46,885
48	113	19000	Dallas County	1,124,296
48	121	19000	Denton County	26,579
48	257	19000	Kaufman County	0
48	397	19000	Rockwall County	56
48		19624	Deer Park city	32,010
48	201	19624	Harris County	32,010
48		19792	Del Rio city	35,591
48	465	19792	Val Verde County	35,591
48		19972	Denton city	113,383
48	121	19972	Denton County	113,383
48		20092	DeSoto city	49,047
48	113	20092	Dallas County	49,047
48		21628	Duncanville city	38,524
48	113	21628	Dallas County	38,524
48		21892	Eagle Pass city	26,248
48	323	21892	Maverick County	26,248
48		22660	Edinburg city	77,100
48	215	22660	Hidalgo County	77,100
48		24000	El Paso city	649,121
48	141	24000	El Paso County	649,121
48		24768	Euless city	51,277
48	439	24768	Tarrant County	51,277
48		25452	Farmers Branch city	28,616
48	113	25452	Dallas County	28,616
48		26232	Flower Mound town	64,669
48	121	26232	Denton County	64,457
48	439	26232	Tarrant County	212
48		27000	Fort Worth city	741,206
48	121	27000	Denton County	7,813
48	367	27000	Parker County	7
48	439	27000	Tarrant County	733,386
48	497	27000	Wise County	0
48		27648	Friendswood city	35,805
48	167	27648	Galveston County	25,510
48	201	27648	Harris County	10,295
48		27684	Frisco city	116,989
48	085	27684	Collin County	72,489
48	121	27684	Denton County	44,500
48		28068	Galveston city	47,743
48	167	28068	Galveston County	47,743
48		29000	Garland city	226,876
48	085	29000	Collin County	266
48	113	29000	Dallas County	226,608
48	397	29000	Rockwall County	2
48		29336	Georgetown city	47,400
48	491	29336	Williamson County	47,400
48		30464	Grand Prairie city	175,396
48	113	30464	Dallas County	123,487
48	139	30464	Ellis County	45
48	439	30464	Tarrant County	51,864
48		30644	Grapevine city	46,334
48	113	30644	Dallas County	0
48	121	30644	Denton County	0
48	439	30644	Tarrant County	46,334
48		30920	Greenville city	25,557
48	231	30920	Hunt County	25,557
48		31928	Haltom City city	42,409
48	439	31928	Tarrant County	42,409
48		32312	Harker Heights city	26,700
48	027	32312	Bell County	26,700
48		32372	Harlingen city	64,849
48	061	32372	Cameron County	64,849
48		35000	Houston city	2,099,451
48	157	35000	Fort Bend County	38,124
48	201	35000	Harris County	2,057,280
48	339	35000	Montgomery County	4,047
48		35528	Huntsville city	38,548
48	471	35528	Walker County	38,548
48		35576	Hurst city	37,337
48	439	35576	Tarrant County	37,337
48		37000	Irving city	216,290
48	113	37000	Dallas County	216,290
48		38632	Keller city	39,627
48	439	38632	Tarrant County	39,627
48		39148	Killeen city	127,921
48	027	39148	Bell County	127,921
48		39352	Kingsville city	26,213
48	273	39352	Kleberg County	26,213
48		39952	Kyle city	28,016
48	209	39952	Hays County	28,016
48		40588	Lake Jackson city	26,849
48	039	40588	Brazoria County	26,849
48		41212	Lancaster city	36,361
48	113	41212	Dallas County	36,361
48		41440	La Porte city	33,800
48	201	41440	Harris County	33,800
48		41464	Laredo city	236,091
48	479	41464	Webb County	236,091
48		41980	League City city	83,560
48	167	41980	Galveston County	81,998
48	201	41980	Harris County	1,562
48		42016	Leander city	26,521
48	453	42016	Travis County	1,077
48	491	42016	Williamson County	25,444
48		42508	Lewisville city	95,290
48	113	42508	Dallas County	841
48	121	42508	Denton County	94,449
48		43012	Little Elm city	25,898
48	121	43012	Denton County	25,898
48		43888	Longview city	80,455
48	183	43888	Gregg County	78,585
48	203	43888	Harrison County	1,870
48		45000	Lubbock city	229,573
48	303	45000	Lubbock County	229,573
48		45072	Lufkin city	35,067
48	005	45072	Angelina County	35,067
48		45384	McAllen city	129,877
48	215	45384	Hidalgo County	129,877
48		45744	McKinney city	131,117
48	085	45744	Collin County	131,117
48		46452	Mansfield city	56,368
48	139	46452	Ellis County	95
48	251	46452	Johnson County	1,652
48	439	46452	Tarrant County	54,621
48		47892	Mesquite city	139,824
48	113	47892	Dallas County	139,731
48	257	47892	Kaufman County	93
48		48072	Midland city	111,147
48	317	48072	Martin County	0
48	329	48072	Midland County	111,147

State code	Place code	County code	Geographic Area Name	2010 census population
48		48768	Mission city	77,058
48	215	48768	Hidalgo County	77,058
48		48804	Missouri City city	67,358
48	157	48804	Fort Bend County	61,755
48	201	48804	Harris County	5,603
48		50256	Nacogdoches city	32,996
48	347	50256	Nacogdoches County	32,996
48		50820	New Braunfels city	57,740
48	091	50820	Comal County	47,586
48	187	50820	Guadalupe County	10,154
48		52356	North Richland Hills city	63,343
48	439	52356	Tarrant County	63,343
48		53388	Odessa city	99,940
48	135	53388	Ector County	98,270
48	329	53388	Midland County	1,670
48		55080	Paris city	25,171
48	277	55080	Lamar County	25,171
48		56000	Pasadena city	149,043
48	201	56000	Harris County	149,043
48		56348	Pearland city	91,252
48	039	56348	Brazoria County	86,706
48	157	56348	Fort Bend County	721
48	201	56348	Harris County	3,825
48		57176	Pflugerville city	46,936
48	453	57176	Travis County	46,636
48	491	57176	Williamson County	300
48		57200	Pharr city	70,400
48	215	57200	Hidalgo County	70,400
48		58016	Plano city	259,841
48	085	58016	Collin County	254,525
48	121	58016	Denton County	5,316
48		58820	Port Arthur city	53,818
48	245	58820	Jefferson County	53,814
48	361	58820	Orange County	4
48		61796	Richardson city	99,223
48	085	61796	Collin County	28,569
48	113	61796	Dallas County	70,654
48		62828	Rockwall city	37,490
48	397	62828	Rockwall County	37,490
48		63284	Rosenberg city	30,618
48	157	63284	Fort Bend County	30,618
48		63500	Round Rock city	99,887
48	453	63500	Travis County	1,362
48	491	63500	Williamson County	98,525
48		63572	Rowlett city	56,199
48	113	63572	Dallas County	49,188
48	397	63572	Rockwall County	7,011
48		64472	San Angelo city	93,200
48	451	64472	Tom Green County	93,200
48		65000	San Antonio city	1,327,407
48	029	65000	Bexar County	1,327,381
48	091	65000	Comal County	0
48	325	65000	Medina County	26
48		65516	San Juan city	33,856
48	215	65516	Hidalgo County	33,856
48		65600	San Marcos city	44,894
48	055	65600	Caldwell County	3
48	187	65600	Guadalupe County	0
48	209	65600	Hays County	44,891
48		66128	Schertz city	31,465
48	029	66128	Bexar County	1,157
48	091	66128	Comal County	845
48	187	66128	Guadalupe County	29,463
48		66644	Seguin city	25,175
48	187	66644	Guadalupe County	25,175
48		67496	Sherman city	38,521
48	181	67496	Grayson County	38,521
48		68636	Socorro city	32,013
48	141	68636	El Paso County	32,013
48		69032	Southlake city	26,575
48	121	69032	Denton County	773
48	439	69032	Tarrant County	25,802
48		70808	Sugar Land city	78,817
48	157	70808	Fort Bend County	78,817
48		72176	Temple city	66,102
48	027	72176	Bell County	66,102
48		72368	Texarkana city	36,411
48	037	72368	Bowie County	36,411
48		72392	Texas City city	45,099
48	071	72392	Chambers County	0
48	167	72392	Galveston County	45,099
48		72530	The Colony city	36,328
48	121	72530	Denton County	36,328
48		74144	Tyler city	96,900
48	423	74144	Smith County	96,900
48		75428	Victoria city	62,592
48	469	75428	Victoria County	62,592
48		76000	Waco city	124,805
48	309	76000	McLennan County	124,805
48		76816	Waxahachie city	29,621
48	139	76816	Ellis County	29,621
48		76864	Weatherford city	25,250
48	367	76864	Parker County	25,250
48		77272	Weslaco city	35,670
48	215	77272	Hidalgo County	35,670
48		79000	Wichita Falls city	104,553
48	485	79000	Wichita County	104,553
48		80356	Wylie city	41,427
48	085	80356	Collin County	39,957
48	113	80356	Dallas County	415
48	397	80356	Rockwall County	1,055
49			**UTAH**	2,763,885
49		01310	American Fork city	26,263
49	049	01310	Utah County	26,263
49		07690	Bountiful city	42,552
49	011	07690	Davis County	42,552
49		11320	Cedar City city	28,857
49	021	11320	Iron County	28,857
49		13850	Clearfield city	30,112
49	011	13850	Davis County	30,112
49		16270	Cottonwood Heights city	33,433
49	035	16270	Salt Lake County	33,433
49		20120	Draper city	42,274
49	035	20120	Salt Lake County	40,532
49	049	20120	Utah County	1,742
49		36070	Holladay city	26,472
49	035	36070	Salt Lake County	26,472
49		40360	Kaysville city	27,300
49	011	40360	Davis County	27,300
49		43660	Layton city	67,311
49	011	43660	Davis County	67,311
49		44320	Lehi city	47,407
49	049	44320	Utah County	47,407
49		45860	Logan city	48,174
49	005	45860	Cache County	48,174

State code	Place code	County code	Geographic Area Name	2010 census population	State code	Place code	County code	Geographic Area Name	2010 census population
49		49710	Midvale city	27,964	51		48952	Manassas city	37,821
49	035	49710	Salt Lake County	27,964	51	683	48952	Manassas city	37,821
49		53230	Murray city	46,746	51		56000	Newport News city	180,719
49	035	53230	Salt Lake County	46,746	51	700	56000	Newport News city	180,719
49		55980	Ogden city	82,825	51		57000	Norfolk city	242,803
49	057	55980	Weber County	82,825	51	710	57000	Norfolk city	242,803
49		57300	Orem city	88,328	51		61832	Petersburg city	32,420
49	049	57300	Utah County	88,328	51	730	61832	Petersburg city	32,420
49		60930	Pleasant Grove city	33,509	51		64000	Portsmouth city	95,535
49	049	60930	Utah County	33,509	51	740	64000	Portsmouth city	95,535
49		62470	Provo city	112,488	51		67000	Richmond city	204,214
49	049	62470	Utah County	112,488	51	760	67000	Richmond city	204,214
49		64340	Riverton city	38,753	51		68000	Roanoke city	97,032
49	035	64340	Salt Lake County	38,753	51	770	68000	Roanoke city	97,032
49		65110	Roy city	36,884	51		76432	Suffolk city	84,585
49	057	65110	Weber County	36,884	51	800	76432	Suffolk city	84,585
49		65330	St. George city	72,897	51		82000	Virginia Beach city	437,994
49	053	65330	Washington County	72,897	51	810	82000	Virginia Beach city	437,994
49		67000	Salt Lake City city	186,440	51		86720	Winchester city	26,203
49	035	67000	Salt Lake County	186,440	51	840	86720	Winchester city	26,203
49		67440	Sandy city	87,461	53			**WASHINGTON**	6,724,540
49	035	67440	Salt Lake County	87,461	53		03180	Auburn city	70,180
49		70850	South Jordan city	50,418	53	033	03180	King County	62,761
49	035	70850	Salt Lake County	50,418	53	053	03180	Pierce County	7,419
49		71290	Spanish Fork city	34,691	53		05210	Bellevue city	122,363
49	049	71290	Utah County	34,691	53	033	05210	King County	122,363
49		72280	Springville city	29,466	53		05280	Bellingham city	80,885
49	049	72280	Utah County	29,466	53	073	05280	Whatcom County	80,885
49		75360	Taylorsville city	58,652	53		07380	Bothell city	33,505
49	035	75360	Salt Lake County	58,652	53	033	07380	King County	17,090
49		76680	Tooele city	31,605	53	061	07380	Snohomish County	16,415
49	045	76680	Tooele County	31,605	53		07695	Bremerton city	37,729
49		82950	West Jordan city	103,712	53	035	07695	Kitsap County	37,729
49	035	82950	Salt Lake County	103,712	53		08850	Burien city	33,313
49		83470	West Valley City city	129,480	53	033	08850	King County	33,313
49	035	83470	Salt Lake County	129,480	53		17635	Des Moines city	29,673
50			**VERMONT**	625,741	53	033	17635	King County	29,673
50		10675	Burlington city	42,417	53		20750	Edmonds city	39,709
50	007	10675	Chittenden County	42,417	53	061	20750	Snohomish County	39,709
51			**VIRGINIA**	8,001,024	53		22640	Everett city	103,019
51		01000	Alexandria city	139,966	53	061	22640	Snohomish County	103,019
51	510	01000	Alexandria city	139,966	53		23515	Federal Way city	89,306
51		07784	Blacksburg town	42,620	53	033	23515	King County	89,306
51	121	07784	Montgomery County	42,620	53		33805	Issaquah city	30,434
51		14968	Charlottesville city	43,475	53	033	33805	King County	30,434
51	540	14968	Charlottesville city	43,475	53		35275	Kennewick city	73,917
51		16000	Chesapeake city	222,209	53	005	35275	Benton County	73,917
51	550	16000	Chesapeake city	222,209	53		35415	Kent city	92,411
51		21344	Danville city	43,055	53	033	35415	King County	92,411
51	590	21344	Danville city	43,055	53		35940	Kirkland city	48,787
51		35000	Hampton city	137,436	53	033	35940	King County	48,787
51	650	35000	Hampton city	137,436	53		36745	Lacey city	42,393
51		35624	Harrisonburg city	48,914	53	067	36745	Thurston County	42,393
51	660	35624	Harrisonburg city	48,914	53		37900	Lake Stevens city	28,069
51		44984	Leesburg town	42,616	53	061	37900	Snohomish County	28,069
51	107	44984	Loudoun County	42,616	53		38038	Lakewood city	58,163
51		47672	Lynchburg city	75,568	53	053	38038	Pierce County	58,163
51	680	47672	Lynchburg city	75,568	53		40245	Longview city	36,648
					53	015	40245	Cowlitz County	36,648

State code	Place code	County code	Geographic Area Name	2010 census population
53		40840	Lynnwood city	35,836
53	061	40840	Snohomish County	35,836
53		43955	Marysville city	60,020
53	061	43955	Snohomish County	60,020
53		47560	Mount Vernon city	31,743
53	057	47560	Skagit County	31,743
53		51300	Olympia city	46,478
53	067	51300	Thurston County	46,478
53		53545	Pasco city	59,781
53	021	53545	Franklin County	59,781
53		56625	Pullman city	29,799
53	075	56625	Whitman County	29,799
53		56695	Puyallup city	37,022
53	053	56695	Pierce County	37,022
53		57535	Redmond city	54,144
53	033	57535	King County	54,144
53		57745	Renton city	90,927
53	033	57745	King County	90,927
53		58235	Richland city	48,058
53	005	58235	Benton County	48,058
53		61115	Sammamish city	45,780
53	033	61115	King County	45,780
53		62288	SeaTac city	26,909
53	033	62288	King County	26,909
53		63000	Seattle city	608,660
53	033	63000	King County	608,660
53		63960	Shoreline city	53,007
53	033	63960	King County	53,007
53		67000	Spokane city	208,916
53	063	67000	Spokane County	208,916
53		67167	Spokane Valley city	89,755
53	063	67167	Spokane County	89,755
53		70000	Tacoma city	198,397
53	053	70000	Pierce County	198,397
53		73465	University Place city	31,144
53	053	73465	Pierce County	31,144
53		74060	Vancouver city	161,791
53	011	74060	Clark County	161,791
53		75775	Walla Walla city	31,731
53	071	75775	Walla Walla County	31,731
53		77105	Wenatchee city	31,925
53	007	77105	Chelan County	31,925
53		80010	Yakima city	91,067
53	077	80010	Yakima County	91,067
54			**WEST VIRGINIA**	1,852,994
54		14600	Charleston city	51,400
54	039	14600	Kanawha County	51,400
54		39460	Huntington city	49,138
54	011	39460	Cabell County	45,214
54	099	39460	Wayne County	3,924
54		55756	Morgantown city	29,660
54	061	55756	Monongalia County	29,660
54		62140	Parkersburg city	31,492
54	107	62140	Wood County	31,492
54		86452	Wheeling city	28,486
54	051	86452	Marshall County	276
54	069	86452	Ohio County	28,210

State code	Place code	County code	Geographic Area Name	2010 census population
55			**WISCONSIN**	5,686,986
55		02375	Appleton city	72,623
55	015	02375	Calumet County	11,088
55	087	02375	Outagamie County	60,045
55	139	02375	Winnebago County	1,490
55		06500	Beloit city	36,966
55	105	06500	Rock County	36,966
55		10025	Brookfield city	37,920
55	133	10025	Waukesha County	37,920
55		22300	Eau Claire city	65,883
55	017	22300	Chippewa County	1,981
55	035	22300	Eau Claire County	63,902
55		25950	Fitchburg city	25,260
55	025	25950	Dane County	25,260
55		26275	Fond du Lac city	43,021
55	039	26275	Fond du Lac County	43,021
55		27300	Franklin city	35,451
55	079	27300	Milwaukee County	35,451
55		31000	Green Bay city	104,057
55	009	31000	Brown County	104,057
55		31175	Greenfield city	36,720
55	079	31175	Milwaukee County	36,720
55		37825	Janesville city	63,575
55	105	37825	Rock County	63,575
55		39225	Kenosha city	99,218
55	059	39225	Kenosha County	99,218
55		40775	La Crosse city	51,320
55	063	40775	La Crosse County	51,320
55		48000	Madison city	233,209
55	025	48000	Dane County	233,209
55		48500	Manitowoc city	33,736
55	071	48500	Manitowoc County	33,736
55		51000	Menomonee Falls village	35,626
55	133	51000	Waukesha County	35,626
55		53000	Milwaukee city	594,833
55	079	53000	Milwaukee County	594,833
55	131	53000	Washington County	0
55	133	53000	Waukesha County	0
55		54875	Mount Pleasant village	26,197
55	101	54875	Racine County	26,197
55		55750	Neenah city	25,501
55	139	55750	Winnebago County	25,501
55		56375	New Berlin city	39,584
55	133	56375	Waukesha County	39,584
55		58800	Oak Creek city	34,451
55	079	58800	Milwaukee County	34,451
55		60500	Oshkosh city	66,083
55	139	60500	Winnebago County	66,083
55		66000	Racine city	78,860
55	101	66000	Racine County	78,860
55		72975	Sheboygan city	49,288
55	117	72975	Sheboygan County	49,288
55		77200	Stevens Point city	26,717
55	097	77200	Portage County	26,717
55		78600	Sun Prairie city	29,364
55	025	78600	Dane County	29,364
55		78650	Superior city	27,244
55	031	78650	Douglas County	27,244

State code	Place code	County code	Geographic Area Name	2010 census population
55		84250	Waukesha city	70,718
55	133	84250	Waukesha County	70,718
55		84475	Wausau city	39,106
55	073	84475	Marathon County	39,106
55		84675	Wauwatosa city	46,396
55	079	84675	Milwaukee County	46,396
55		85300	West Allis city	60,411
55	079	85300	Milwaukee County	60,411
55		85350	West Bend city	31,078
55	131	85350	Washington County	31,078

State code	Place code	County code	Geographic Area Name	2010 census population
56			**WYOMING**	563,626
56	025	13150	Casper city	55,316
56	025	13150	Natrona County	55,316
56		13900	Cheyenne city	59,466
56	021	13900	Laramie County	59,466
56		31855	Gillette city	29,087
56	005	31855	Campbell County	29,087
56		45050	Laramie city	30,816
56	001	45050	Albany County	30,816

INDEX

INDEX

ACS. *See* American Community Survey

activities of daily living, *293*

AFF. *See* American FactFinder, xxiv

age structure: in ACS, xvii; in cities, 46, *46, 47, 60–67*; in congressional districts, *46,* 47, *47, 75–81*; in counties, *46,* 47, *49–59*; in Metropolitan and Micropolitan Statistical Areas, *46,* 46–47, *47, 68–74*; in states, *45,* 45–46, *46, 48*

Alabama: cities by county in, *438*; city populations of, *20, 60, 102, 143, 185, 226, 268, 310, 351, 394*; congressional district populations of, *36, 75, 118, 160, 201, 241, 284, 326, 367, 411*; county populations of, *8, 49, 90, 131, 173, 215, 256, 298, 339, 382*; disability status and type in, *297, 298, 310, 326*; educational attainment in, *172, 173, 185, 201*; employment and labor force status in, *214, 215, 226, 241*; health insurance in, *338, 339, 351, 367*; household relationships in, 128, *130, 131, 143, 160*; housing summary for, 378–79, *381, 382, 394, 411*; income in, *255, 256, 268, 284*; older population of, *48, 49, 60, 75*; population of, *6, 7*; poverty status in, *255, 256, 268, 284*; race and ethnicity in, *89, 90, 102, 118*; veterans status in, *172, 173, 185, 201*

Alaska: cities by county in, *438*; city populations of, *20, 60, 102, 143, 185, 226, 268, 310, 351, 394*; congressional district populations of, *36, 75, 118, 160, 201, 241, 284, 326, 367, 411*; county populations of, *8, 49, 90, 131, 173, 215, 256, 298, 339, 382*; disability status and type in, 294, *297, 298, 310, 326*; educational attainment in, *172, 173, 185, 201*; employment and labor force status in, *214, 215, 226, 241*; health insurance in, 336, *338, 339, 351, 367*; household relationships in, *130, 131, 143, 160*; housing summary for, 378, *381, 382, 394, 411*; income in, *255, 256, 268, 284*; older population of, 45–46, *46, 48, 49, 60, 75*; population of, *3, 6, 7*; poverty status in, *255, 256, 268, 284*; race and ethnicity in, 88, *89, 90, 102, 118*; veterans status in, 171, *172, 173, 185, 201*

Alaska Native population, 88, *88*

ambulatory difficulty, 294

American Community Survey (ACS): access to, xxvii–xxviii; accuracy of data of, xxix; background and overview information for, xxix–xxx; benefits of, ix, xiii–xiv; challenges of, xiv–xv; data collection versus data reporting, xv; data comparability in, xvi–xvii; decennial census compared with, xix; development of, ix, xi, xiii; estimate availability of, xvii–xviii; estimate decision with, xxiii–xxv; facts about, xiii; geographic areas in, xv–xvi; guidance on data products in, xxx; information in, xi; margin of error in, xxv; period estimates in, xxi–xxii; quality measures of, xxix–xxx; reference periods for, xx–xxi; residence rules in, xix–xx; sample of, xv; sample size of, xxix; subjects covered by, xvii; trade-offs with, ix–x; use of data of, xxx

American FactFinder (AFF), xxiv, xxvii

American Housing Survey, xiv–xv

American Indian population, 88, *88*

Arizona: cities by county in, *438–39*; city populations of, *20,*

60, 102, 143, 185, 226, 268, 310, 351, 394; congressional district populations of, *36, 75, 118, 160, 201, 241, 284, 326, 367, 411*; county populations of, *8, 49, 90, 131, 173, 215, 256, 298, 339, 382*; disability status and type in, *297, 298, 310, 326*; educational attainment in, *172, 173, 185, 201*; employment and labor force status in, 211, *214, 215, 226, 241*; health insurance in, 335, *338, 339, 351, 367*; household relationships in, *130, 131, 143, 160*; housing summary for, 378, *381, 382, 394, 411*; income in, *255, 256, 268, 284*; older population of, *48, 49, 60, 75*; population of, *6, 7*; poverty status in, 252, *255, 256, 268, 284*; race and ethnicity in, 88, *89, 90, 102, 118*; veterans status in, 171, *172, 173, 185, 201*

Arkansas: cities by county in, *439*; city populations of, *20, 60, 102, 143, 185, 226, 268, 310, 351, 394*; congressional district populations of, *36, 75, 160, 201, 241, 284, 326, 367, 411*; county populations of, *8, 49, 90, 131, 173, 215, 256, 298, 339, 382*; disability status and type in, 294–95, *297, 298, 310, 326*; educational attainment in, *172, 173, 185, 201*; employment and labor force status in, *214, 215, 226, 241*; health insurance in, *338, 339, 351, 367*; household relationships in, *130, 131, 143, 160*; housing summary for, *381, 382, 394, 411*; income in, *255, 256, 268, 284*; older population of, *48, 49, 60, 75*; population of, *6, 7*; poverty status in, 252, *255, 256, 268, 284*; race and ethnicity in, *89, 90, 102*; veterans status in, *172, 173, 185, 201*

Asian Alone, 87

Baby Boom generation: aging of, 3; employment of, 211; household relationships of, *127*, 128; housing needs of, 377

Baby Bust generation, aging of, 3

Black Alone, 86–87

California: cities by county in, *439–43*; city populations of, *20–22, 60–62, 102–4, 143–45, 185–87, 226–28, 268–70, 310–12, 351–53, 394–96*; congressional district populations of, *36–37, 75, 118–19, 160–61, 201–202, 241–42, 284–85, 326–27, 367–68, 411–12*; county populations of, *8–9, 49–50, 90–91, 131–32, 173–74, 215–16, 256–57, 298–99, 339–40, 382–83*; disability status and type in, 294–95, *297, 298–99, 310–12, 326–27*; educational attainment in, 169–70, *172, 173–74, 185–87, 201–202*; employment and labor force status in, 211, 213, *214, 215–16, 226–28, 241–42*; health insurance in, 336, *338, 339–40, 351–53, 367–68*; household relationships in, 128, *130, 131–32, 143–45, 160–61*; housing summary for, 378–80, *381, 382–83, 394–96, 411–12*; income in, 251, *255, 256–57, 268–70, 284–85*; older population of, *46, 48, 49–50, 60–62, 75*; population of, *3, 6, 7*; poverty status in, 254, *255, 256–57, 268–70, 284–85*; race and ethnicity in, 86–88, *89, 90–91, 102–4, 118–19*; veterans status in, 171, *172, 173–74, 185–87, 201–202*

Chicago: older population of, 46; population of, 3; veterans status in, 171 cities: by county, *438–64*; disability status and type in, *293*, 294–95, *310–18*; educational attainment in, 169–70, *185–93*; employment and labor force status in, 211, *212*, *213*, *226–33*; health insurance in, 336–37, *351–59*; household relationships of, *128*, 129, *143–51*; housing summary for, *378*, 379, *379*, *394–402*; income in, 251, *253*, *268–76*; older population in, *4*, *5*, *20–28*, 46, *46*, *47*, *60–67*; population of, 3, 5, *20–28*; poverty status in, 254, *268–76*; race and ethnicity in, *86*, 86–88, *87*, *102–10*; veterans status in, 171, *171*, *185–93*

coefficient of variation (CV), xxiii–xxiv

cognitive difficulty, 294

Colorado: cities by county in, *443–44*; city populations of, *22*, *62*, *104*, *145*, *187*, *228*, *270*, *312*, *353*, *396*; congressional district populations of, *37*, *76*, *119*, *161*, *202*, *242*, *285*, *327*, *368*, *412*; county populations of, *9*, *50*, *91*, *132*, *174*, *216*, *257*, *299*, *340*, *383*; disability status and type in, 295, *297*, *299*, *312*, *327*; educational attainment in, 169–70, *172*, *174*, *187*, *202*; employment and labor force status in, 211, *214*, *216*, *228*, *242*; health insurance in, *338*, *340*, *353*, *368*; household relationships in, 128, *130*, *132*, *145*, *161*; housing summary for, *381*, *383*, *396*, *412*; income in, *255*, *257*, *270*, *285*; older population of, 46, *48*, *50*, *62*, *76*; population of, 3, *6*, *7*; poverty status in, *255*, *257*, *270*, *285*; race and ethnicity in, *89*, *91*, *104*, *119*; veterans status in, *172*, *174*, *187*, *202*

congressional districts: disability status and type in, *293*, 295, *326–32*; educational attainment in, 170, *201–207*; employment and labor force status in, 213, *213*, *241–47*; health insurance in, 337, *367–73*; household relationships of, 129, *129*, *160–66*; housing summary for, *378*, 379–80, *411–17*; income in, 251, *284–90*; older population in, *5*, *36–42*, 46, *47*, *47*, *75–81*; population of, 5, *36–42*; poverty status in, 254, *254*, *284–90*; race and ethnicity in, *86*, 86–88, *87*, *118–24*; veterans status in, 171, *201–207*

Connecticut: cities by county in, *444*; city populations of, *22*, *62*, *104*, *145*, *187*, *228*, *270*, *312*, *353*, *396*; congressional district populations of, *37*, *76*, *119*, *161*, *202*, *242*, *285*, *327*, *368*, *412*; county populations of, *9*, *50*, *91*, *132*, *174*, *216*, *257*, *299*, *340*, *383*; disability status and type in, *297*, *299*, *312*, *327*; educational attainment in, 169, *172*, *174*, *187*, *202*; employment and labor force status in, *214*, *216*, *228*, *242*; health insurance in, 335, *338*, *340*, *353*, *368*; household relationships in, *130*, *132*, *145*, *161*; housing summary for, *381*, *383*, *396*, *412*; income in, 251, *255*, *257*, *270*, *285*; older population of, *48*, *50*, *62*, *76*; population of, 3, *6*, *7*; poverty status in, *255*, *257*, *270*, *285*; race and ethnicity in, *89*, *91*, *104*, *119*; veterans status in, 171, *172*, *174*, *187*, *202*

counties: cities by, *438–64*; disability status and type in, *293*, 294, *298–309*; educational attainment in, 169–70, *173–84*; employment and labor force status in, 211, *213*, *215–25*; health insurance in, 336, *339–50*; household relationships of, 128, *131–42*; housing summary for, *378*, 378–79, *382–93*; income in, 251, *256–67*; older population in, *5*, *8–19*, 46, *47*, *49–59*; populations of, *8–19*; poverty status in, 252, 254, *256–67*; race and ethnicity in, *86*, 86–88, *87*, *88*, *90–101*; veterans status in, *173–84*

CPS. *See* Current Population Survey

currency, of ACS estimate, xxiii–xxiv

Current Population Survey (CPS), xiv–xv, xxii, xxx

current residence, xx

CV. *See* coefficient of variation

data collection versus data reporting, xv

data profiles, xxvii

decennial census: ACS compared with, xvi–xvii, xix; data release with, xv; long form replacement of, xiii

Delaware: cities by county in, *444*; city populations of, *22*, *62*, *104*, *145*, *187*, *228*, *270*, *312*, *353*, *396*; congressional district populations of, *37*, *76*, *119*, *161*, *202*, *242*, *285*, *327*, *368*, *412*; county populations of, *9*, *50*, *91*, *132*, *174*, *216*, *257*, *299*, *340*, *383*; disability status and type in, 294, *297*, *299*, *312*, *327*; educational attainment in, *172*, *174*, *187*, *202*; employment and labor force status in, 211, *214*, *216*, *228*, *242*; health insurance in, *338*, *340*, *353*, *368*; household relationships in, *130*, *132*, *145*, *161*; housing summary for, *381*, *383*, *396*, *412*; income in, 251, *255*, *257*, *270*, *285*; older population of, 46, *48*, *50*, *62*, *76*; population of, 6, 7; poverty status in, *255*, *257*, *270*, *285*; race and ethnicity in, *89*, *91*, *104*, *119*; veterans status in, *172*, *174*, *187*, *202*

demographic characteristics, xvii

detailed tables, xxvii

direct purchase insurance coverage, 336, 337

disability status and type, 293–95; in cities, *293*, *310–18*; in congressional districts, *293*, *326–32*; in counties, *293*, *298–309*; in Metropolitan and Micropolitan Statistical Areas, *293*, *296*, *319–25*; in states, *293*, *297*

District of Columbia: cities by county in, *444*; city populations of, *22*, *62*, *104*, *145*, *187*, *228*, *270*, *312*, *353*, *396*; congressional district populations of, *37*, *76*, *119*, *161*, *202*, *242*, *285*, *327*, *368*, *412*; disability status and type in, 294, *297*, *312*, *327*; educational attainment in, 169, *172*, *187*, *202*; employment and labor force status in, *214*, *228*, *242*; health insurance in, 335–36, *338*, *353*, *368*; household relationships in, 128, *130*, *145*, *161*; housing summary for, 377, *381*, *396*, *412*; income in, *255*, *270*, *285*; older population of, 45–46, *46*, *48*, *62*, *76*; population of, 3, *6*, *7*; poverty status in, 252, *255*, *270*, *285*; race and ethnicity in, *86*, *89*, *104*, *119*; veterans status in, 171, *172*, *187*, *202*

economic characteristics, xvii

educational attainment, *169*, 169–70; in cities, *170*, *185–93*; in congressional districts, *201–207*; in counties, *173–84*; in Metropolitan and Micropolitan Statistical Areas, *194–200*; in states, 169, *172*

85 years and over: city populations of, *20–28*, 46, *46*, *60–67*, *102–10*; congressional district populations of, *36–42*, 46, *118–24*; county populations of, *8–19*, 46, *49–59*, *90–101*; Metro/Micro area populations of, *29–35*, 46, *47*, *68–74*, *111–17*; race and ethnicity in, 86–88, *87*, *89–124*; state populations of, 7, 45, 45–46, *46*, *48*, 89

employer based insurance coverage, 336, 337

employment and labor force status, 211, 213; in cities, *212*, *213*, *226–33*; in congressional districts, *213*, *241–47*; in counties, *213*, *215–25*; in Metropolitan and Micropolitan Statistical Areas, *213*, *234–40*; in states, *212*, 214

ethnicity. *See* race and ethnicity

Florida: cities by county in, *444–46*; city populations of, *22–23, 62–63, 104–5, 145–46, 187–88, 228–29, 270–71, 312–13, 353–54, 396–97*; congressional district populations of, *37, 76, 119, 161, 202, 242, 285, 327, 368, 412*; county populations of, *9–10, 50, 91, 132–33, 174–75, 216, 257–58, 299–300, 340–41, 383–84*; disability status and type in, *297, 299–300, 312–13, 327*; educational attainment in, *172, 174–75, 187–88, 202*; employment and labor force status in, 211, 213, *214, 216, 228–29, 242*; health insurance in, *336, 338, 340–41, 353–54, 368*; household relationships in, *130, 132–33, 145–46, 161*; housing summary for, *378–80, 381, 383–84, 396–97, 412*; income in, *255, 257–58, 270–71, 285*; older population of, 45–46, *46, 48, 50, 62–63, 76*; population of, 3, *6, 7*; poverty status in, 254, *255, 257–58, 270–71, 285*; race and ethnicity in, 88, *89, 91, 104–5, 119*; veterans status in, *172, 174–75, 187–88, 202*

food stamp receipt, 251–52, 254. *See also* poverty status

geographic areas, in ACS, xv–xvi
geographic comparison tables, xxvii
Georgia: cities by county in, *446*; city populations of, *23, 63, 105, 146, 188, 229, 271, 313, 354, 397*; congressional district populations of, *37, 76, 119, 161, 202, 242, 285, 327, 368, 412*; county populations of, *10, 51, 92, 133, 175, 217, 258, 300, 341, 384*; disability status and type in, *297, 300, 313, 327*; educational attainment in, *172, 175, 188, 202*; employment and labor force status in, *214, 217, 229, 242*; health insurance in, *338, 341, 354, 368*; household relationships in, 128, *130, 133, 146, 161*; housing summary of, *381, 384, 397, 412*; income in, *255, 258, 271, 285*; older population of, *46, 48, 51, 63, 76*; population of, *6, 7*; poverty status in, 252, *255, 258, 271, 285*; race and ethnicity in, 86–87, *89, 92, 105, 119*; veterans status in, *172, 175, 188, 202*

GI Bill, 169
grandparent: responsible, 128. *See also* household relationships

Hawaii: cities by county in, *446*; city populations of, *23, 63, 105, 146, 188, 229, 271, 313, 354, 397*; congressional district populations of, *37, 76, 119, 161, 202, 242, 286, 327, 368, 412*; county populations of, *10, 51, 92, 133, 175, 217, 258, 300, 341, 384*; disability status and type in, *297, 300, 313, 327*; educational attainment in, *172, 175, 188, 202*; employment and labor force status in, *214, 217, 229, 242*; health insurance in, 335, *338, 341, 354, 368*; household relationships in, 128, *130, 133, 146, 161*; housing summary for, *381, 384, 397, 412*; income in, 251, *255, 258, 271, 286*; older population of, 45–46, *46, 48, 51, 63, 76*; population of, *6, 7*; poverty status in, 252, *255, 258, 271, 286*; race and ethnicity in, 86–87, *89, 92, 105, 119*; veterans status in, *172, 175, 188, 202*

health insurance, 335–37, *336*; in ACS, xvii; in cities, *351–59*; in congressional districts, *367–73*; in counties, *339–50*; coverage options for, 337; in Metropolitan and Micropolitan Statistical Areas, 337, *360–66*; in states, *338*
hearing difficulty, 294
Hispanic, 88
householders 65 years and over, 127–28; city populations of, *4, 5, 20–28, 394–402*; congressional district populations of, *5,*

36–42, 411–17; county populations of, *5, 8–19, 382–93*; with meals included in rent, 377–80, *378*; Metro/Micro area populations of, *5, 29–35, 403–10*; owner costs of, 377, *377, 379*; rental costs, 379–80, *380*; state populations of, *4, 7, 381*
household relationships, 127–29; in ACS, xvii; in cities, *128, 143–51*; in congressional districts, *129, 160–66*; in counties, *131–42*; in Metropolitan and Micropolitan Statistical Areas, *152–59*; in states, *127, 130*
housing summary, 377–80; for cities, *378, 379, 394–402*; for congressional districts, *378, 411–17*; for counties, *378, 382–93*; for Metropolitan and Micropolitan Statistical Areas, *378, 403–10*; for states, *377*

Idaho: cities by county in, *447*; city populations of, *23, 63, 105, 146, 188, 229, 271, 313, 354, 397*; congressional district populations of, *37, 76, 119, 161, 203, 242, 286, 327, 368, 412*; county populations of, *10, 51, 92, 133, 175, 217, 258, 300, 341, 384*; disability status and type in, *297, 300, 313, 327*; educational attainment in, *172, 175, 188, 203*; employment and labor force status in, *214, 217, 229, 242*; health insurance in, 335, *338, 341, 354, 368*; household relationships in, *130, 133, 146, 161*; housing summary for, *381, 384, 397, 412*; income in, *255, 258, 271, 286*; older population of, *48, 51, 63, 76*; population of, *6, 7*; poverty status in, *255, 258, 271, 286*; race and ethnicity in, *89, 92, 105, 119*; veterans status in, *172, 175, 188, 203*
Illinois: cities by county in, *447–48*; city populations of, *23, 63, 105, 146, 188, 229, 271, 313, 354, 397*; congressional district populations of, *38, 76–77, 120, 162, 203, 242–43, 286, 327–28, 369, 413*; county populations of, 10–*11, 51, 92, 133–34, 175–76, 217, 258–59, 300–301, 341–42, 384–85*; disability status and type in, *297, 300–301, 313, 327–28*; educational attainment in, *172, 175–76, 188, 203*; employment and labor force status in, *214, 217, 229, 242–43*; health insurance in, *338, 341–42, 354, 369*; household relationships in, *130, 133–34, 146, 162*; housing summary for, *381, 384–85, 397, 413*; income in, *255, 258–59, 271, 286*; older population of, *48, 51, 63, 76–77*; population of, 3, *6, 7*; poverty status in, *255, 258–59, 271, 286*; race and ethnicity in, *89, 92, 105, 120*; veterans status in, *172, 175–76, 188, 203*
income, 251, *251*; in ACS, xvii; in cities, *253, 268–76*; in congressional districts, *284–90*; in counties, *256–67*; estimation of, xxi; in Metropolitan and Micropolitan Statistical Areas, *277–83*; in states, *252, 255*
Indiana: cities by county in, *448–49*; city populations of, *23, 63, 105, 146, 188, 229, 271, 313, 354, 397*; congressional district populations of, *38, 77, 120, 162, 203, 243, 286, 328, 369, 413*; county populations of, *11, 51–52, 92–93, 134, 176, 217–18, 259, 301, 342, 385*; disability status and type in, *297, 301, 313, 328*; educational attainment in, 170, *172, 176, 188, 203*; employment and labor force status in, *214, 217–18, 229, 243*; health insurance in, 336–37, *338, 342, 354, 369*; household relationships in, *130, 134, 146, 162*; housing summary for, *381, 385, 397, 413*; income in, *255, 259, 271, 286*; older population of, *48, 51–52, 63, 77*; population of, *6, 7*; poverty status in, *255, 259, 271, 286*; race and ethnicity in, 87, *89, 92–93, 105, 120*; veterans status in, *172, 176, 188, 203*

Iowa: cities by county in, *449*; city populations of, *23, 63, 105, 146–47, 188–89, 229, 271–72, 313, 354, 397–98*; congressional district populations of, *38, 77, 120, 162, 203, 243, 286, 328, 369, 413*; county populations of, *11, 52, 93, 134, 176, 218, 259, 301, 342, 385*; disability status and type in, *294, 297, 301, 313, 328*; educational attainment in, *172, 176, 188–89, 203*; employment and labor force status in, *214, 218, 229, 243*; health insurance in, *338, 342, 354, 369*; household relationships in, *130, 134, 146–47, 162*; housing summary for, *379, 381, 385, 397–98, 413*; income in, *255, 259, 271–72, 286*; older population of, *48, 52, 63, 77*; population of, *6, 7*; poverty status in, *255, 259, 271–72, 286*; race and ethnicity in, *89, 93, 105, 120*; veterans status in, *172, 176, 188–89, 203*

Kansas: cities by county in, *449–50*; city populations of, *24, 63, 106, 147, 189, 229, 272, 314, 355, 398*; congressional district populations of, *38, 77, 120, 162, 203, 243, 286, 328, 369, 413*; county populations of, *11, 52, 93, 134, 176, 218, 259, 301, 342, 385*; disability status and type in, *297, 301, 314, 328*; educational attainment in, *172, 176, 189, 203*; employment and labor force status in, *214, 218, 229, 243*; health insurance in, *338, 342, 355, 369*; household relationships in, *130, 134, 147, 162*; housing summary for, *381, 385, 398, 413*; income in, *255, 259, 272, 286*; older population of, *48, 52, 63, 77*; population of, *6, 7*; poverty status in, *255, 259, 272, 286*; race and ethnicity in, *89, 93, 106, 120*; veterans status in, *172, 176, 189, 203*

Kentucky: cities by county in, *450*; city populations of, *24, 63, 106, 147, 189, 229, 272, 314, 355, 398*; congressional district populations of, *38, 77, 120, 162, 203, 243, 286, 328, 369, 413*; county populations of, *11, 52, 93, 134, 176, 218, 259, 301, 342, 385*; disability status and type in, *295, 297, 301, 314, 328*; educational attainment in, *172, 176, 189, 203*; employment and labor force status in, *214, 218, 229, 243*; health insurance in, *338, 342, 355, 369*; household relationships in, *130, 134, 147, 162*; housing summary for, *381, 385, 398, 413*; income in, *255, 259, 272, 286*; older population of, *48, 52, 63, 77*; population of, *6, 7*; poverty status in, *255, 259, 272, 286*; race and ethnicity in, *89, 93, 106, 120*; veterans status in, *172, 176, 189, 203*

labor force status. *See* employment and labor force status
life expectancy, 293
long form, ix, xi, xiii, xix
Los Angeles: employment and labor force status in, 211; older population of, 46; population of, 3; veterans status in, 171
Louisiana: cities by county in, *450*; city populations of, *24, 64, 106, 147, 189, 230, 272, 314, 355, 398*; congressional district populations of, *38, 77, 120, 162, 203, 243, 286, 328, 369, 413*; county populations of, *11–12, 52, 93, 134–35, 176–77, 218, 259–60, 301–302, 342–43, 385–86*; disability status and type in, *297, 301–302, 314, 328*; educational attainment in, *172, 176–77, 189, 203*; employment and labor force status in, *214, 218, 230, 243*; health insurance in, *338, 342–43, 355, 369*; household relationships in, *130, 134–35, 147, 162*; housing summary for, 378, 380, *381, 385–86, 398, 413*; income in, 251, *255, 259–60, 272, 286*; older population of, *48, 52, 64, 77*; population of,

6, 7; poverty status in, *255, 259–60, 272, 286*; race and ethnicity in, *86, 89, 93, 106, 120*; veterans status in, *172, 176–77, 189, 203*

MAF. *See* Master Address File
Maine: cities by county in, *450*; city populations of, *24, 64, 106, 147, 189, 230, 272, 314, 355, 398*; congressional district populations of, *38, 77, 120, 162, 203, 243, 286, 328, 369, 413*; county populations of, *12, 52–53, 94, 135, 177, 218–19, 260, 302, 343, 386*; disability status and type in, *297, 302, 314, 328*; educational attainment in, *172, 177, 189, 203*; employment and labor force status in, *214, 218–19, 230, 243*; health insurance in, *338, 343, 355, 369*; household relationships in, *130, 135, 147, 162*; housing summary for, *381, 386, 398, 413*; income in, *255, 260, 272, 286*; older population of, *45–46, 46, 48, 52–53, 64, 77*; population of, *3, 6, 7*; poverty status in, *255, 260, 272, 286*; race and ethnicity in, *86, 89, 94, 106, 120*; veterans status in, *172, 177, 189, 203*
margins of error (MOE), xxv
marital status. *See* household relationships
Maryland: cities by county in, *450*; city populations of, *24, 64, 106, 147, 189, 230, 272, 314, 355, 398*; congressional district populations of, *38, 77, 120, 162, 203, 243, 286, 328, 369, 413*; county populations of, *12, 53, 94, 135, 177, 219, 260, 302, 343, 386*; disability status and type in, *297, 302, 314, 328*; educational attainment in, 169, *172, 177, 189, 203*; employment and labor force status in, *214, 219, 230, 243*; health insurance in, 337, *338, 343, 355, 369*; household relationships in, *130, 135, 147, 162*; housing summary for, 378, *381, 386, 398, 413*; income in, 251, *255, 260, 272, 286*; older population of, *46, 48, 53, 64, 77*; population of, *6, 7*; poverty status in, *255, 260, 272, 286*; race and ethnicity in, *86, 89, 94, 106, 120*; veterans status in, *172, 177, 189, 203*
Massachusetts: cities by county in, *450–51*; city populations of, *24, 64, 106, 147, 189, 230, 272, 314, 355, 398*; congressional district populations of, *38, 77, 120, 162, 203–4, 243, 287, 328, 369, 413*; county populations of, *12, 53, 94, 135, 177, 219, 260, 302, 343, 386*; disability status and type in, *297, 302, 314, 328*; educational attainment in, 169, *172, 177, 189, 203–4*; employment and labor force status in, *214, 219, 230, 243*; health insurance in, 337, *338, 343, 355, 369*; household relationships in, *130, 135, 147, 162*; housing summary for, 379, *381, 386, 398, 413*; income in, *255, 260, 272, 287*; older population of, *48, 53, 64, 77*; population of, *6, 7*; poverty status in, 254, *255, 260, 272, 287*; race and ethnicity in, *89, 94, 106, 120*; veterans status in, *172, 177, 189, 203–4*
Master Address File (MAF), xv
median income, 251, *251*. *See also* income
Medicaid, 335–37, *336*
Medicare, 335–37, *336*
Metropolitan and Micropolitan Statistical Areas: codes and populations for, *421–37*; disability status and type in, *293, 295, 296, 319–25*; educational attainment in, *194–200*; employment and labor force status in, 211, 213, *213, 234–40*; health insurance in, 337, *337, 360–66*; household relationships of, 129, *152–59*; housing summary for, *378,*

379, *403–10*; income in, 251, *277–83*; older population in, *5, 29–35, 46, 46–47, 47, 68–74*; population of, *5, 29–35*; poverty status in, 254, *277–83*; race and ethnicity in, *86, 86–88, 87, 111–17*; veterans status in, 171, *194–200*

Michigan: cities by county in, *451–52*; city populations of, *24, 64, 106, 147, 189, 230, 272, 314, 355, 398*; congressional district populations of, *39, 77–78, 121, 163, 204, 243–44, 287, 329, 370, 414*; county populations of, *12, 53, 94, 135–36, 177–78, 219, 260–61, 302–303, 343–44, 386–87*; disability status and type in, *297, 302–303, 314, 329*; educational attainment in, *172, 177–78, 189, 204*; employment and labor force status in, *214, 219, 230, 243–44*; health insurance in, *335, 338, 343–44, 355, 370*; household relationships in, *130, 135–36, 147, 163*; housing summary for, *381, 386–87, 398, 414*; income in, *255, 260–61, 272, 287*; older population of, *48, 53, 64, 77–78*; population of, *6, 7*; poverty status in, *255, 260–61, 272, 287*; race and ethnicity in, *87, 89, 94, 106, 121*; veterans status in, *172, 177–78, 189, 204*

Millennial generation, aging of, 3

Minnesota: cities by county in, *452–53*; city populations of, *24, 64, 106, 147–48, 189–90, 230, 272–73, 314, 355, 398–99*; congressional district populations of, *39, 78, 121, 163, 204, 244, 287, 329, 370, 414*; county populations of, *13, 53, 94–95, 178, 219, 261, 303, 344, 387*; disability status and type in, *297, 303, 314, 329*; educational attainment in, *172, 178, 189–90, 204*; employment and labor force status in, *214, 219, 230, 244*; health insurance in, *336–37, 338, 344, 355, 370*; household relationships in, *130, 147–48, 163*; housing summary for, *381, 387, 398–99, 414*; income in, *255, 261, 272–73, 287*; older population of, *48, 53, 64, 78*; population of, *6, 7*; poverty status in, *252, 255, 261, 272–73, 287*; race and ethnicity in, *89, 94–95, 106, 121*; veterans status in, *172, 178, 189–90, 204*

minorities. *See* race and ethnicity

Mississippi: cities by county in, *453*; city populations of, *25, 64, 106, 148, 190, 230, 273, 315, 356, 399*; congressional district populations of, *39, 78, 121, 163, 204, 244, 287, 329, 370, 414*; county populations of, *13, 54, 95, 136, 178, 220, 261, 303, 344, 387*; disability status and type in, *297, 303, 315, 329*; educational attainment in, *172, 178, 190, 204*; employment and labor force status in, *214, 220, 230, 244*; health insurance in, *335, 338, 344, 356, 370*; household relationships in, *130, 136, 148, 163*; housing summary for, *381, 387, 399, 414*; income in, 251, *255, 261, 273, 287*; older population of, *48, 54, 64, 78*; population of, 3, *6, 7*; poverty status in, *255, 261, 273, 287*; race and ethnicity in, *86, 89, 95, 106, 121*; veterans status in, *172, 178, 190, 204*

Missouri: cities by county in, *453*; city populations of, *25, 64, 107, 148, 190, 230, 273, 315, 356, 399*; congressional district populations of, *39, 78, 121, 163, 204, 244, 287, 329, 370, 414*; county populations of, *13, 54, 95, 136, 178, 220, 261, 303, 344, 387*; disability status and type in, *297, 303, 315, 329*; educational attainment in, *172, 178, 190, 204*; employment and labor force status in, *214, 220, 230, 244*; health insurance in, *338, 344, 356, 370*; household relationships in, *130, 136, 148, 163*; housing summary for, *381, 387, 399, 414*; income in, *255, 261, 273, 287*; older

population of, *48, 54, 64, 78*; population of, *6, 7*; poverty status in, *255, 261, 273, 287*; race and ethnicity in, *89, 95, 107, 121*; veterans status in, *172, 178, 190, 204*

MOE. *See* margins of error

Montana: cities by county in, *453*; city populations of, *25, 64, 107, 148, 190, 230–31, 273, 315, 356, 399*; congressional district populations of, *39, 78, 121, 163, 204, 244, 287, 329, 370, 414*; county populations of, *13, 54, 95, 136, 178, 220, 261, 303, 344, 387*; disability status and type in, *297, 303, 315, 329*; educational attainment in, *172, 178, 190, 204*; employment and labor force status in, *214, 220, 230–31, 244*; health insurance in, *335, 338, 344, 356, 370*; household relationships in, *130, 136, 148, 163*; housing summary for, *381, 387, 399, 414*; income in, *255, 261, 273, 287*; older population of, *48, 54, 64, 78*; population of, *6, 7*; poverty status in, *255, 261, 273, 287*; race and ethnicity in, *89, 95, 107, 121*; veterans status in, *172, 178, 190, 204*

Multi-race, 87

multiyear estimates in ACS, xxi–xxii, xxiv

narrative profiles, xxvii

national census, xiii

Native American, 88

Nebraska: cities by county in, *453*; city populations of, *25, 65, 107, 148, 190, 273, 315, 356, 399*; congressional district populations of, *39, 78, 121, 163, 204, 244, 287, 329, 370, 414*; county populations of, *13, 54, 95, 136, 178, 220, 261, 303, 344, 387*; disability status and type in, *297, 303, 315, 329*; educational attainment in, *172, 178, 190, 204*; employment and labor force status in, *214, 220, 244*; health insurance in, *338, 344, 356, 370*; household relationships in, *130, 136, 148, 163*; housing summary for, 378, *381, 387, 399, 414*; income in, *255, 261, 273, 287*; older population of, *48, 54, 65, 78*; population of, *6, 7*; poverty status in, *255, 261, 273, 287*; race and ethnicity in, *89, 95, 107, 121*; veterans status in, *172, 178, 190, 204*

Nevada: cities by county in, *454*; city populations of, *25, 65, 107, 148, 190, 231, 273, 315, 356, 399*; congressional district populations of, *39, 78, 121, 163, 204, 244, 287, 329, 370, 414*; county populations of, *13, 54, 136, 178, 220, 261, 303, 344, 387*; disability status and type in, *297, 303, 315, 329*; educational attainment in, *172, 178, 190, 204*; employment and labor force status in, *214, 220, 231, 244*; health insurance in, *338, 344, 356, 370*; household relationships in, *130, 136, 148, 163*; housing summary for, *381, 387, 399, 414*; income in, 251, *255, 261, 273, 287*; older population of, *48, 54, 65, 78*; population of, *6, 7*; poverty status in, *255, 261, 273, 287*; race and ethnicity in, *89, 107, 121*; veterans status in, *172, 178, 190, 204*

New Hampshire: cities by county in, *454*; city populations of, *25, 65, 107, 148, 190, 231, 273, 315, 356, 399*; congressional district populations of, *39, 78, 121, 163, 204, 244, 287, 329, 370, 414*; county populations of, *13, 54, 95, 136, 178, 220, 261, 303, 344, 387*; disability status and type in, *297, 303, 315, 329*; educational attainment in, 169, *172, 178, 190, 204*; employment and labor force status in, *214, 220, 231, 244*; health insurance in, *335, 338, 344, 356, 370*; household relationships in, *130, 136, 148, 163*; housing summary for, *381, 387, 399, 414*; income in, 251,

255, 261, 273, 287; older population of, 46, 46, 48, 54, 65, 78; population of, 6, 7; poverty status in, 252, 255, 261, 273, 287; race and ethnicity in, 89, 95, 107, 121; veterans status in, 172, 178, 190, 204

New Jersey: cities by county in, 454; city populations of, 25, 65, 107, 148, 190, 231, 273, 315, 356, 399; congressional district populations of, 39, 78, 121, 163, 204, 244, 287–88, 329, 370, 414; county populations of, 13–14, 54, 95, 136–37, 178–79, 220, 262, 303–4, 344–45, 388; disability status and type in, 295, 297, 303–4, 315, 329; educational attainment in, 172, 178–79, 190, 204; employment and labor force status in, 214, 220, 231, 244; health insurance in, 338, 344–45, 356, 370; household relationships in, 130, 136–37, 148, 163; housing summary for, 378, 380, 381, 388, 399, 414; income in, 255, 262, 273, 287–88; older population of, 48, 54, 65, 78; population of, 6, 7; poverty status in, 255, 262, 273, 287–88; race and ethnicity in, 87, 89, 95, 107, 121; veterans status in, 172, 178–79, 190, 204

New Mexico: cities by county in, 454; city populations of, 25, 65, 107, 148, 190, 231, 273, 315, 356, 399; congressional district populations of, 39, 78, 121, 163, 205, 244, 288, 329, 370, 414; county populations of, 14, 54–55, 96, 137, 179, 220–21, 262, 304, 345, 388; disability status and type in, 294, 297, 304, 315, 329; educational attainment in, 172, 179, 190, 205; employment and labor force status in, 214, 220–21, 231, 244; health insurance in, 335–36, 338, 345, 356, 370; household relationships in, 130, 137, 148, 163; housing summary for, 378, 381, 388, 399, 414; income in, 255, 262, 273, 288; older population of, 48, 54–55, 65, 78; population of, 6, 7; poverty status in, 255, 262, 273, 288; race and ethnicity in, 86, 88, 89, 96, 107, 121; veterans status in, 171, 172, 179, 190, 205

New York: cities by county in, 454–55; city populations of, 25, 65, 107, 148, 190, 231, 273, 315, 356, 399; congressional district populations of, 39–40, 78–79, 121–22, 163–64, 205, 244–45, 288, 329–30, 370–71, 414–15; county populations of, 14, 55, 96, 137, 179, 221, 262, 304, 345, 388; disability status and type in, 295, 297, 304, 315, 329–30; educational attainment in, 172, 179, 190, 205; employment and labor force status in, 214, 221, 231, 244–45; health insurance in, 336–37, 338, 345, 356, 370–71; household relationships in, 128, 130, 137, 148, 163–64; housing summary for, 378–80, 381, 388, 399, 414–15; income in, 251, 255, 262, 273, 288; older population of, 48, 55, 65, 78–81; population of, 3, 6, 7; poverty status in, 252, 254, 255, 262, 273, 288; race and ethnicity in, 89, 96, 107, 121–22; veterans status in, 171, 172, 179, 190, 205

New York City: housing summary for, 379; income in, 251; older population of, 46; population of, 3; veterans status in, 171

North Carolina: cities by county in, 455–56; city populations of, 25, 65, 107, 148–49, 190, 231, 273–74, 315, 356, 399–400; congressional district populations of, 40, 79, 122, 164, 205, 245, 288, 330, 371, 415; county populations of, 14–15, 55–56, 96–97, 137–38, 179–80, 221–22, 262–63, 304–5, 345–46, 388–89; disability status and type in, 297, 304–5, 315, 330; educational attainment in, 172, 179–80, 190, 205; employment and labor force status in, 214, 221–22, 231, 245; health insurance in, 338, 345–46, 356, 371;

household relationships in, 128, 130, 137–38, 148–49, 164; housing summary for, 381, 388–89, 399–400, 415; income in, 255, 262–63, 273–74, 288; older population of, 48, 55–56, 65, 79; population of, 6, 7; poverty status in, 252, 255, 262–63, 273–74, 288; race and ethnicity in, 88, 89, 96–97, 107, 122; veterans status in, 172, 179–80, 190, 205

North Dakota: cities by county in, 456; city populations of, 25, 65, 107, 149, 191, 231, 274, 315, 356, 400; congressional district populations of, 40, 79, 122, 164, 205, 245, 288, 330, 371, 415; county populations of, 15, 56, 97, 138, 180, 222, 263, 305, 346, 389; disability status and type in, 297, 305, 315, 330; educational attainment in, 172, 180, 191, 205; employment and labor force status in, 211, 214, 222, 231, 245; health insurance in, 336, 338, 346, 356, 371; household relationships in, 130, 138, 149, 164; housing summary for, 377, 381, 389, 400, 415; income in, 255, 263, 274, 288; older population of, 46, 48, 56, 65, 79; population of, 3, 6, 7; poverty status in, 252, 255, 263, 274, 288; race and ethnicity in, 89, 97, 107, 122; veterans status in, 172, 180, 191, 205

Ohio: cities by county in, 456–57; city populations of, 26, 65, 107–8, 149, 191, 231, 274, 316, 357, 400; congressional district populations of, 40, 79, 122, 164, 205, 245, 288, 330, 371, 415; county populations of, 15, 56, 97, 138, 180–81, 222, 263–64, 305–6, 346–47, 389–90; disability status and type in, 297, 305–6, 316, 330; educational attainment in, 172, 180–81, 191, 205; employment and labor force status in, 211, 214, 222, 231, 245; health insurance in, 338, 346–47, 357, 371; household relationships in, 130, 138, 149, 164; housing summary for, 381, 389–90, 400, 415; income in, 255, 263–64, 274, 288; older population of, 48, 56, 65, 79; population of, 6, 7; poverty status in, 255, 263–64, 274, 288; race and ethnicity in, 89, 97, 107–8, 122; veterans status in, 172, 180–81, 191, 205

Oklahoma: cities by county in, 457; city populations of, 26, 65, 108, 149, 191, 231, 274, 316, 357, 400; congressional district populations of, 40, 79, 122, 164, 205, 245, 289, 330, 371, 415; county populations of, 15–16, 56, 97, 139, 181, 222, 264, 306, 347, 390; disability status and type in, 297, 306, 316, 330; educational attainment in, 172, 181, 191, 205; employment and labor force status in, 214, 222, 231, 245; health insurance in, 338, 347, 357, 371; household relationships in, 130, 139, 149, 164; housing summary for, 381, 390, 400, 415; income in, 255, 264, 274, 289; older population of, 48, 56, 65, 79; population of, 6, 7; poverty status in, 255, 264, 274, 289; race and ethnicity in, 86–87, 89, 97, 108, 122; veterans status in, 172, 181, 191, 205

older population. See 85 years and over; householders 65 years and over; 75 years and over; 65 years and over

Oregon: cities by county in, 457–58; city populations of, 26, 65–66, 108, 149, 191, 231–32, 274, 316, 357, 400; congressional district populations of, 40, 79, 122, 164, 205–6, 245, 289, 330, 371, 415; county populations of, 16, 56, 97–98, 139, 181, 222, 264, 306, 347, 390; disability status and type in, 297, 306, 316, 330; educational attainment in, 172, 181, 191, 205–6; employment and labor force status in, 214, 222, 231–32, 245; health insurance in, 335, 338, 347, 357, 371; household relationships in, 130, 139, 149, 164;

housing summary for, *381, 390, 400, 415*; income in, *255, 264, 274, 289*; older population of, *48, 56, 65–66, 79*; population of, *6, 7*; poverty status in, *255, 264, 274, 289*; race and ethnicity in, *89, 97–98, 108, 122*; veterans status in, *172, 181, 191, 205–6*

Pennsylvania: cities by county in, *458*; city populations of, *26, 66, 108, 149, 191, 232, 274, 316, 357, 400*; congressional district populations of, *40–41, 79, 122–23, 164–65, 206, 245–46, 289, 330–31, 371–72, 415–16*; county populations of, *16, 57, 98, 139, 181, 223, 264–65, 306, 347, 390–91*; disability status and type in, *297, 306, 316, 330–31*; educational attainment in, 169–70, *172, 181, 191, 206*; employment and labor force status in, 211, *214*, 223, *232, 245–46*; health insurance in, *338, 347, 357, 371–72*; household relationships in, *130, 139, 149, 164–65*; housing summary for, *381, 390–91, 400, 415–16*; income in, *255, 264–65, 274, 289*; older population of, 45–46, *46, 48, 57, 66, 79*; population of, *3, 6, 7*; poverty status in, *255, 264–65, 274, 289*; race and ethnicity in, 87, *89, 98, 108, 122–23*; veterans status in, *172, 181, 191, 206*

period estimates, xxiv

point-in-time estimates, xxii, xxiv

Population Estimates Program, ix, xix

population summary and change, 3, 5, *6*; in cities, *20–28*; in congressional districts, *36–42*; in counties, *8–19*; in Metropolitan and Micropolitan Statistical Areas, *29–35*; in states, 7

poverty status, 251–52, 254; in ACS, xvii; in cities, *268–76*; in congressional districts, *254, 284–90*; in counties, *256–67*; in Metropolitan and Micropolitan Statistical Areas, *277–83*; in states, *253, 255*

private insurance coverage, 337

public insurance coverage, 337

Public Use Microdata Sample (PUMS), xiv, xviii, xxv, xxviii, xxx

race and ethnicity, 85–88; in ACS, xvii; in cities, *87, 102–10*; in congressional districts, *87, 88, 118–24*; in counties, *86, 87, 88, 90–101*; in Metropolitan and Micropolitan Statistical Areas, *87, 88, 111–17*; in states, *85, 86, 87, 89*

ranking tables, xxvii

reliability, of ACS estimate, xxiii–xxiv

residency rules, xvii, xix–xx

responsible grandparent, 128

Rhode Island: cities by county in, *458*; city populations of, *26, 66, 108, 149, 191, 232, 274, 316, 357, 400*; congressional district populations of, *41, 79, 123, 165, 206, 246, 289, 331, 372, 416*; county populations of, *16, 57, 98, 139, 182, 223, 265, 306, 348, 391*; disability status and type in, *297, 306, 316, 331*; educational attainment in, *172, 182, 191, 206*; employment and labor force status in, *214, 223, 232, 246*; health insurance in, 336, *338, 348, 357, 372*; household relationships in, *130, 139, 149, 165*; housing summary for, *381, 391, 400, 416*; income in, *255, 265, 274, 289*; older population of, *48, 57, 66, 79*; population of, *3, 6, 7*; poverty status in, *255, 265, 274, 289*; race and ethnicity in, *89, 98, 108, 123*; veterans status in, *172, 182, 191, 206*

RLS Demographics, Inc., xi–xii

sampling error, xxv

Scardamalia, Robert, xi–xii

school enrollment, xxi

selected population tables, xxvii

self-care difficulty, 294

Servicemen's Readjustment Act, 169

75 years and over: city populations of, *185–93, 268–76, 310–18, 351–59*; congressional district populations of, *201–207, 284–90, 326–32, 367–73*; county populations of, *173–84, 256–67, 298–309, 339–50*; disability status and type of, 293–95, *293–332*; educational attainment by, 169–70, *172–207*; health insurance in, 335–37, *335–73*; Metro/Micro area populations of, *194–200, 277–83, 319–25, 360–66*; poverty status of, 251–52, *253–54, 254, 255–90*; state populations of, *172, 255, 297, 338*; veterans status of, *170*, 170–71, *172–207*

short form, xiii

single-year estimates in ACS, xxi–xxii, xxiv

65 years and over: city populations of, *20–28*, 46, *47, 60–67*, 86, *102–10*, 129, *143–51, 185–93, 226–33, 268–76, 310–18, 351–59*; congressional district populations of, *36–42*, 47, *47*, 86, *118–24*, 129, *160–66, 201–207, 241–47, 284–90, 326–32, 367–73*; county populations of, *8–19*, 46, *47, 49–59*, 86, *90–101*, 128, *131–42, 173–84, 215–25, 256–67, 298–309, 339–50*; disability status and type of, 293–95, *293–332*; educational attainment by, 169–70, *172–207*; employment and labor force status of, 211, *212–47*, 213, *226–33*; health insurance in, 335–37, *335–73*; household relationships of, 127–29, *128, 129, 130–66*; income of, 251, *252–53, 255–90*; Medicare and, 335–37; Metro/Micro area populations of, *29–35, 46–47, 47, 68–74*, 86, *111–17*, 129, *152–59, 194–200, 234–40, 277–83, 319–25, 360–66*; poverty status of, 251–52, *253–54, 254, 255–90*; race and ethnicity in, *85, 86, 86–88, 87, 89–124*; state populations of, *6, 7, 45, 45–46, 46, 48, 85, 89*, 128, *172*, 211, *212, 214, 255, 297, 338*; veterans status of, *170*, 170–71, *172–207*. *See also* householders 65 years and over

SNAP. *See* Supplemental Nutrition Assistance Program

social characteristics, xvii

South Carolina: cities by county in, *458–59*; city populations of, *26, 66, 108, 149, 191, 232, 274, 316, 357, 400*; congressional district populations of, *41, 80, 123, 165, 206, 246, 289, 331, 372, 416*; county populations of, *16–17, 57, 98–99, 140, 182, 223, 265, 307, 348, 391*; disability status and type in, 294, *297, 307, 316, 331*; educational attainment in, *172, 182, 191, 206*; employment and labor force status in, *214, 223, 232, 246*; health insurance in, 335, *338, 348, 357, 372*; household relationships in, *130, 140, 149, 165*; housing summary for, *381, 391, 400, 416*; income in, *255, 265, 274, 289*; older population of, *46, 48, 57, 66, 80*; population of, *6, 7*; poverty status in, *255, 265, 274, 289*; race and ethnicity in, 86–87, *89, 98–99, 108, 123*; veterans status in, *172, 182, 191, 206*

South Dakota: cities by county in, *459*; city populations of, *26, 66, 108, 149, 191, 232, 274, 316, 357, 400*; congressional district populations of, *41, 80, 123, 165, 206, 246, 289, 331, 372, 416*; county populations of, *17, 57, 99, 140, 182, 223, 265, 307, 348, 391*; disability status and type in, 294, *297, 307, 316, 331*; educational attainment in, *172, 182,*

191, 206; employment and labor force status in, *211, 214, 223, 232, 246*; health insurance in, *335, 338, 348, 357, 372*; household relationships in, *128, 130, 140, 149, 165*; housing summary for, *381, 391, 400, 416*; income in, *255, 265, 274, 289*; older population of, *48, 57, 66, 80*; population of, *6, 7*; poverty status in, *255, 265, 274, 289*; race and ethnicity in, *89, 99, 108, 123*; veterans status in, *172, 182, 191, 206*

states: disability status and type in, *293*, 294, *297*; educational attainment in, 169, *169, 172*; employment and labor force status in, 211, *212, 214*; health insurance in, *335*, 335–36, *338*; household relationships of, *127*, 128, *130*; housing summary for, *377*, 377–78, *381*; income in, *251, 252, 255*; older population in, *4, 45*, 45–46, *46, 48*; population in, *3, 6, 7*; poverty status in, 252, *253, 255*; race and ethnicity in, *85*, 86–88, *87, 89*; veterans status in, 171, *172*

subject tables, xxvii
summary file data, xxvii–xxviii
Supplemental Nutrition Assistance Program (SNAP), 252
Survey of Income and Program Participation, xiv–xv

Tennessee: cities by county in, *459*; city populations of, *26, 66, 108, 149, 191, 232, 274, 316, 357, 400*; congressional district populations of, *41, 80, 123, 165, 206, 246, 289, 331, 372, 416*; county populations of, *17, 57–58, 99, 140, 182, 223–24, 265, 307, 348, 391*; disability status and type in, *297, 307, 316, 331*; educational attainment in, *172, 182, 191, 206*; employment and labor force status in, *214, 223–24, 232, 246*; health insurance in, *338, 348, 357, 372*; household relationships in, *130, 140, 149, 165*; housing summary for, *381, 391, 400, 416*; income in, *255, 265, 274, 289*; older population of, *48, 57–58, 66, 80*; population of, *6, 7*; poverty status in, 252, *255, 265, 274, 289*; race and ethnicity in, *89, 99, 108, 123*; veterans status in, 171, *172, 182, 191, 206*

Texas: cities by county in, *459–61*; city populations of, *26–27, 66–67, 108–9, 149–50, 191–92, 232–33, 274–75, 316–17, 357–58, 400–401*; congressional district populations of, *41, 80, 123, 165, 206–7, 246, 289–90, 331, 372, 416–17*; county populations of, *17–18, 58, 99–100, 140–41, 182–83, 224, 265–66, 307–8, 348–49, 391–92*; disability status and type in, 295, *297, 307–8, 316–17, 331*; educational attainment in, 170, *172, 182–83, 191–92, 206–7*; employment and labor force status in, 211, 213, *214, 224, 232–33, 246*; health insurance in, 337, *338, 348–49, 357–58, 372*; household relationships in, 128, *130, 140–41, 149–50, 165*; housing summary for, 378–79, *381, 391–92, 400–401, 416–17*; income in, *255, 265–66, 274–75, 289–90*; older population of, *45–46, 46, 48, 58, 66–67, 80*; population of, *3, 6, 7*; poverty status in, 252, 254, *255, 265–66, 274–75, 289–90*; race and ethnicity in, 86, 88, *89, 99–100, 108–9, 123*; veterans status in, *172, 182–83, 191–92, 206–7*

thematic maps, xxvii

Understanding and Using American Community Survey Data, xvi–xvii, xxiii, xxv
usual residence, xx
Utah: cities by county in, *461–62*; city populations of, *27, 67,*

109, 150, 192, 233, 275, 317, 358, 401; congressional district populations of, *42, 80, 123, 166, 207, 246, 290, 332, 373, 417*; county populations of, *18, 58, 100, 141, 183, 224, 266, 308, 349, 392*; disability status and type in, *297, 308, 317, 332*; educational attainment in, 169, *172, 183, 192, 207*; employment and labor force status in, *214, 224, 233, 246*; health insurance in, *338, 349, 358, 373*; household relationships in, 128, *130, 141, 150, 166*; housing summary for, *381, 392, 401, 417*; income in, *255, 266, 275, 290*; older population of, 45–46, *46, 48, 58, 67, 80*; population of, *3, 6, 7*; poverty status in, *255, 266, 275, 290*; race and ethnicity in, *89, 100, 109, 123*; veterans status in, *172, 183, 192, 207*

utility costs, xxi

Vermont: cities by county in, *462*; congressional district populations of, *42, 80, 123, 166, 207, 246, 290, 332, 373, 417*; county populations of, *18, 58, 100, 141, 183, 225, 266, 308, 349, 392*; disability status and type in, *297, 308, 332*; educational attainment in, 169, *172, 183, 207*; employment and labor force status in, 211, *214, 225, 246*; health insurance in, *338, 349, 373*; household relationships in, *130, 141, 166*; housing summary for, *381, 392, 417*; income in, 251, *255, 266, 290*; older population of, 45–46, *46, 48, 58, 80*; population of, *3, 6, 7*; poverty status in, *255, 266, 290*; race and ethnicity in, *89, 100, 123*; veterans status in, *172, 183, 207*

veterans status, 170, 170–71; in cities, *171*, 185–93; in congressional districts, *201–207*; in counties, 173–84; in Metropolitan and Micropolitan Statistical Areas, 194–200; in states, *172*

Virginia: cities by county in, *462*; city populations of, *27, 67, 109, 150, 192, 233, 275, 317, 358, 401–402*; congressional district populations of, *42, 80, 123, 166, 207, 246–47, 290, 332, 373, 417*; county populations of, *18, 59, 141, 183, 225, 266, 308, 349, 392*; disability status and type in, *297, 308, 317, 332*; educational attainment in, 169–70, *183, 192, 207*; employment and labor force status in, *214, 225, 233, 246–47*; health insurance in, 336, *338, 349, 358, 373*; household relationships in, *130, 141, 150, 166*; housing summary for, *381, 392, 401–402, 417*; income in, 251, *255, 266, 275, 290*; older population of, *48, 59, 67, 80*; population of, *6, 7*; poverty status in, 252, 254, *255, 266, 275, 290*; race and ethnicity in, *89, 109, 123*; veterans status in, *172, 183, 192, 207*

vision difficulty, 294
volume organization, xi–xii

Washington: cities by county in, *462–63*; city populations of, *27–28, 67, 109, 151, 192–93, 233, 276, 317–18, 358–59, 402*; congressional district populations of, *42, 81, 123, 166, 207, 247, 290, 332, 373, 417*; county populations of, *18, 59, 100, 141–42, 183–84, 225, 266–67, 308, 349–50, 392–93*; disability status and type in, 294–95, *297, 308, 317–18, 332*; educational attainment in, 169, *172, 183–84, 192–93, 207*; employment and labor force status in, *214, 225, 233, 247*; health insurance in, *338, 349–50, 358–59, 373*; household relationships in, *130, 141–42, 151, 166*; housing summary for, *381, 392–93, 402, 417*; income in,

251, *255*, *266–67*, *276*, *290*; older population of, *46*, *48*, *59*, *67*, *81*; population of, *6*, *7*; poverty status in, *255*, *266–67*, *276*, *290*; race and ethnicity in, *89*, *100*, *109*, *123*; veterans status in, *172*, *183–84*, *192–93*, *207*

West Virginia: cities by county in, *463*; congressional district populations of, *42*, *81*, *123*, *166*, *207*, *247*, *290*, *332*, *373*, *417*; county populations of, *19*, *59*, *100*, *142*, *184*, *225*, *267*, *309*, *350*, *393*; disability status and type in, 295, *297*, *309*, *332*; educational attainment in, 169, *172*, *184*, *207*; employment and labor force status in, 211, *214*, *225*, *247*; health insurance in, 335–36, *338*, *350*, *373*; household relationships in, 128, *130*, *142*, *166*; housing summary for, 377–78, *381*, *393*, *417*; income in, 251, *255*, *267*, *290*; older population of, 45–46, *46*, *48*, *59*, *81*; population of, *3*, *6*, *7*; poverty status in, *255*, *267*, *290*; race and ethnicity in, 88, *89*, *100*, *123*; veterans status in, *172*, *184*, *207*

Wisconsin: cities by county in, *463–64*; city populations of, *28*, *67*, *110*, *151*, *193*, *233*, *276*, *318*, *359*, *402*; congressional district populations of, *42*, *81*, *123*, *166*, *207*, *247*, *290*, *332*, *373*, *417*; county populations of, *19*, *59*, *100–101*, *142*, *184*, *225*, *267*, *309*, *350*, *393*; disability status and type in, *297*, *309*, *318*, *332*; educational attainment in, *172*, *184*, *193*, *207*; employment and labor force status in, *214*, *225*, *233*, *247*; health insurance in, 335, *338*, *350*, *359*, *373*; household relationships in, *130*, *142*, *151*, *166*; housing summary of, *381*, *393*, *402*, *417*; income in, *255*, *267*, *276*, *290*; older population of, *48*, *59*, *67*, *81*; population of, *6*, *7*; poverty status in, *255*, *267*, *276*, *290*; race and ethnicity in, *89*, *100–101*, *110*, *123*; veterans status in, *172*, *184*, *193*, *207*

Wyoming: cities by county in, *464*; congressional district populations of, *42*, *81*, *123*, *166*, *207*, *247*, *290*, *332*, *373*, *417*; county populations of, *19*, *59*, *101*, *142*, *184*, *225*, *267*, *309*, *350*, *393*; disability status and type in, 294, *297*, *309*, *332*; educational attainment in, *172*, *184*, *207*; employment and labor force status in, *214*, *225*, *247*; health insurance in, 336, *338*, *350*, *373*; household relationships in, *130*, *142*, *166*; housing summary of, *381*, *393*, *417*; income in, *255*, *267*, *290*; older population of, *48*, *59*, *81*; population of, *3*, *6*, *7*; poverty status in, 252, *255*, *267*, *290*; race and ethnicity in, *89*, *101*, *123*; veterans status in, *172*, *184*, *207*